Revelation

A True Translation of the Bible

Published by Hawaa Ayoub
ISBN 978-1-9996261-2-9

Cover Design: Lieu Pham, Covertopia.com

To Yemenis, wherever you may be in the world,

Contents

PREFACE

For almost eight years I lived in a remote region of Yemen then after two years abroad, I returned to live for another eleven years in its cities. The cities' residents come from all over Yemen and speak a number of different dialects. It was the life of complete immersion among the people of my origins for the first eight years as soon as I arrived in Yemen from UK which gave me access to a region and community inaccessible to most people. The region I lived in was isolated, or rather, kept itself isolated, assisted by the harshness of the routes which led to it and its remoteness from urban civilisation. It managed to keep outsiders away (locals from nearby Yemeni cities) due to the harsh terrain making it inaccessible. My people also rejected anything from the outside world; even Islam seemed to have either only arrived several decades before I arrived in the mountains or had only ever been accepted nominally. When I would learn proper Islam from books, I discovered the locals did not really know Islamic practice, except superficially (fasting in Ramadan and some prayer). But their way of life was interwoven with a strong and alive pagan culture which had never ceased to exist since antiquity, and they had added to it what little they knew about Islam. Many would recall with longing and pride, and some with shame, some of the things they used to do; while many still stubbornly held onto and practised the most ancient pagan rituals and beliefs well into the 2000s.

I learnt Arabic from this remote region with which I became one with from the age of fourteen. The only language they spoke was Arabic. You can imagine my surprise when I would live in the city to find friends and work colleagues could not understand many words and phrases I used; I could understand the city-people perfectly, and what I found amusing was even their modern and colloquial Arabic, many words were based on the original meanings of words in my village. I was pleasantly surprised to find the Saudi Arabian vocabulary contained and understood my people's vocabulary more than the urbanised Yemenis. The more Yemeni colleagues, friends, neighbours had lived city-life, or villages with direct access to cities, the less their familiarity with my vocabulary of Old Arabic. It was easy for me to switch to Classical Arabic, Modern Standard Arabic and words the local dialect used. There were many who did understand me, especially older people and those who came from other remote Yemeni regions where language is still in its purest and oldest form of Arabic. In the whole nineteen years of living in Yemen I would encounter many different dialects—all Arabic specific to Yemen (which experts call South Arabian language); some are difficult to understand even by the Yemeni Arabic speaker, until your ear becomes familiar to it. What I discovered was Arabic spoken by my people was Arabic in its earliest form, and many modern Arabic words have evolved from it, even if the speakers of the more modern dialects seem to no longer know the purer and earlier forms of vocabulary.

During late 2016 I was feeling extremely distressed by the notable rise and increase in open antisemitism and Islamophobia in Europe and America. I was also distressed by the events happening in Mosul and Raqqa, where in the name of fighting terrorism hundreds of thousands of innocent civilians were being killed, their ancient cities and buildings which they lived in levelled with them inside, those staying at home or trying to flee massacred by a coalition of western and local forces, and also local soldiers and militias who brutally tortured their victims. No one seemed to care they were causing such intolerable and unimaginable suffering to such a high density of civilian population in order to beat a small number of terrorists (namely 'Islamic State'). One can understand the need to defeat terrorism, and I myself want to see the extinction of all terrorists, but one cannot justify killing hundreds of thousands of innocent people, displacing and injuring hundreds of thousands more. Anyhow, the war in Yemen had also been raging for a couple of years, and once again there was a deliberate targeting of innocent civilians.

Like many who in times of distress turn to what their religion tells them, I did too, but I found no comfort, no answer, no calming of my distress over the suffering of humankind which was being featured daily on the news. My faith wobbled. As a reader of Quran, and someone who knows the complex and long history, not only of Islam, but Arab history, I recalled how the Quran mentions the Torah and Christian Bible still containing some truth; I recalled how many times I would hear interfaith dialogue speaking about the three religions being in essence the same, but differing only in specific points. So I decided to read the Torah and Christian Bible to find the mentioned similarities, the small grains of truth the Quran tells of. I was looking to reinforce my religion, as Islam, Judaism and Christianity, as well as religious dialogue, all seem to reinforce each other as divine Abrahamic religions—I wanted them to reassure me that the world and mankind would be alright, that things would become less horrific.

Immediately upon starting to read the Torah and New Testament, in English, the 'Hebraic' names struck me as Arabic words; and not only Arabic which most Arabs speak, but also the Arabic my people speak.

When I read the Bible, I was taken aback—it was as if the authors of the Bible (who existed millennia ago) were describing the culture and way of life my village people live and I had lived and experienced in the mountains of Yemen. It was not just the language, but the way of life, customs, superstitions described, the way of expression in the Bible—they were all distinctly Yemeni. What I found left me in more doubt, even of my own religion.

ACKNOWLDEGEMENTS

I would like to thank my children who have put up with me spending over a year in writing this book, where most of my days and nights were poured into putting it together. I am grateful for their support, and for the fact they took care of me, providing me with all my needs, and loving me. My daughters, thank you for taking care of me.

INTRODUCTION

'Tampering with history in the interests of the present is just as reprehensible as any other kind of misrepresentation. Honest mistakes can be expected anywhere and at any time, but the tendentious falsification of the past is another matter.' (Bowersock, 2001) [1]

I publish this book and hope it reaches the general public, but also linguists, Biblical scholars, archaeologists, historians, any and all persons interested in Biblical stories whether the interest is of an academic or personal nature. I did not embark on translating the text (the main body of this book) with anybody in mind, as I had only read the Torah and Bible to reinforce my faith, but upon discovering I could understand it as Arabic, I put pen to paper. In fact, when I read the Torah and Bible it was for my own personal wish to reinforce my belief in Islam through finding support for it in the Biblical texts—what I ended up with was more doubt about Quranic text authenticity. But this was surpassed by a delight and wonder that I could read, understand, and explain and share with the world the true meanings of the Bible and show with proof where it originated from, who its authors were, and why it was written.

I begin to write this introduction almost a year and a half after completing the translation of the Bible. It is important that facts are established as to why, up until this day, the truth of the Bible and its mysteries have evaded Biblical Studies and religious scholars alike, both the expert and the layman. Without addressing these issues which have stood between the truth coming to the light, would make it impossible to comprehend why something so obvious, so indisputable, remained in the dark for such a long period of time. It baffled me greatly because as soon as I read the first pages of the Torah, I knew what I was looking at, moving onto the KJV only proved it further.

For some time, I attributed it to the normal way ancient things are forgotten, I compared it to my people's remoteness and how they kept themselves isolated for such a long time. But still, it did not explain why, as most people of Arab countries (even speakers of colloquial Arabic and more modern Arabic dialects) would still be able to recognise the many words used as names in the Bible. Nor did it explain why the Bible, which has circulated and fascinated the modern world for centuries, could remain such a mystery with so many departments of the best academic institutions in the world researching it. Therefore, it is necessary to look into some of the significant reasons that have stood between the true revelation of the Bible.

Language

It is believed the Bible (OT) was written in Hebrew, a Hebrew which no longer existed by the time the Biblical stories would become the basis of a religion across the world; nor had anyone found an original Bible, the oldest texts found are from a much later date than since the stories were first created. Nor does anyone know how original Hebrew is actually pronounced—how it sounds. Yet all insist that it is Hebrew when all available proof shows it is not Hebrew, but Arabic. An ancient form of Arabic that still exists and has never stopped being spoken since times pre-historic and is in use today in remote areas where speakers of this Arabic (of the Bible) still speak this language and have never known any other language than Arabic. I describe the language as 'prehistoric' because it is the language of the Bible and there is no date that records when the Biblical stories were created, only for when the oldest existing Biblical texts are estimated at, and the stories and language existed long before they would be recorded as texts.

All the names in the Bible believed by scholars to be Hebraic names are indisputably Arabic words. The only reason one can attribute as to why scholars and non-scholars believe this Bible is written in Hebrew: a) no scholars have ever witnessed Hebrew written/pronounced in its original form as a living language; b) confusion has been created by the modern 'Hebrew' which is spoken by modern-Israel today—which is not Hebrew at all, but a modern language created in the 19th Century by Zionists for Europeans coming from a multitude of European countries (all who spoke different European languages and were/are natives of differing European countries), from the 1950s onwards this would include natives and speakers of languages from a multitude of Arab countries (other than Palestine) and Ethiopians, to have one language to unify them all while they created the new Jewish State on Palestine. But the creation of modern-Hebrew does give insight as to how scholars use different ancient languages, such as Arabic (among others), to try to give understanding in 'Hebrew'.

It is a well-known fact that modern-Hebrew was created out of Arabic by Eli Ezer Ben Yehouda (originally Perlman) along with other Europeans. Even the creator of this new-Hebrew language admitted to having no Hebrew to go on, but that he and others took Arabic words, grammar, syntax, etc. to create the new Hebrew. Of course, the modern-Hebrew creators liked to imagine they were just 'borrowing back' these words, a polite term for what is essentially appropriation, but the statements they make prove otherwise: they created a modern Hebrew by using Arabic words altered for European pronunciation and preference, and added Yiddish and Slavic words. Modern Hebrew was created from Arabic, as there was no route to an assumed Biblical Hebrew language which may or may not have existed, which is why some things make sense from the Bible through modern Hebrew; how modern Hebrew was created has been detailed in Yonatan Mendel and Ronald Ranta's *From the Arab Other to the Israeli Self*[2] and the quotes below are from their work.

'Ben-Yehouda noted that Arabic had a rich and ancient vocabulary, unlike Hebrew, which was "dead" as a spoken vernacular, and did not have the same continuity.'[3]

'As Ben-Yehouda (1912:9) states: 'Only those who, like me, compare words between these two languages [Arabic and Hebrew] can feel how little difference there is between them. You can actually decide that every root in Arabic also exists in Hebrew...We are allowed to rule that most of the words found in the Arabic vocabulary also existed in the Hebrew vocabulary, and that therefore these are not foreign roots.'[4]

Martin Plessner: '...as I wish the study of Arabic grammar to bring the [Jewish] students to even deeper understanding of Hebrew...through focusing on the systematic grammatical structures of Arabic...and through highlighting how the language of the Bible can be better understood through the study of Arabic. (1935: 1)'[5]

'According to Ben-Yehouda (1980: 10): 'I tended to conceptualise the Hebrew verbs in relation to the Arabic verbs, first as the Arabic serves as a witness for a language that has ceased to exist...and, second, as these similarities will help the speakers of Hebrew to realise how close these two languages are, in their spirit and characteristics, so close they are actually one language.'[6]

These are a few examples of how Zionism unintentionally led away from Biblical truth. Even when it is an undisputable fact that Hebrew did not exist, the European insists Arabic and Hebrew are sister languages: '...Ben-Yehouda wrote: 'when we tried to create a noun out of a verb that was known to us, I used to look at the noun's name in Arabic, which is Hebrew's sister language...and used it as my example for the creation of the new Hebrew noun. (1980: 13)'[7] that is as true as saying American English and British English are sister languages when they are one language. In confirming they are essentially one language, the early Zionists were aware of Arabic being the language of the Bible, but may have been confused by the words they could not recognise as they could not find them in the Arabic dialects available to them to 'borrow' from such as Classical (Quranic) Arabic, modern and colloquial Arabic.

It could be that later scholars of the Hebrew Bible, linguists, archaeologists, historians, etc. may not know what they believe is Hebrew is actually an ancient form of Arabic, but using the modern Hebrew based on later forms of Arabic have attempted to make sense of the Bible by attributing meanings to what supports a non-existent language (Biblical Hebrew) and have convinced themselves of its 'correctness', but have still failed to make sense of it.

What is assumed to be the original Hebrew language of the Old Testament is actually Arabic; I speak this ancient Arabic language and come from a people whose only language is Arabic and who had never been corrupted in their way of life, traditions, language by the outside world—including the nearest cities to their remote regions (at least up until early 2000s).

All the names in the Bible have a meaning; whereas Biblical scholars seek to find and give it meaning based on complicated and unsubstantiated speculations (based on Biblical stories with no physical proof, and no etymological proof) and seek to give deep, intellectual answers that only uncomfortably fit in with the theorising but never fit together and do not provide any solid answers about the Bible. I can prove without leaving a shadow of a doubt that the language of the Bible is Arabic, spoken and understood by millions of people, and especially by those whose lives and language has never been overdiluted or corrupted by progress, modernisation, linguistic corruption or external influences.

Westerners find it peculiar that all Jewish intelligentsia of medieval times spoke and wrote in Arabic, scholars try to explain it away as 'Arabisation' of Jews; that Arabs and Islam ruled the region so Arabic became the preferred language. This unsatisfactory explanation is based on a wrong theory that Jew (and Hebrew) is a race instead of being just a religion. If Hebrew had been a language it would have continued as did Arabic, and just as did the Jewish religion. Western theories also ignore these Jewish scholars were Arabs and Persians—so it is not a far cry for an Arab to speak and write Arabic regardless of religion, or that a Persian Jew living in Arab countries and/or following an Arabic religion, studying at Arab institutions would speak and write in Arabic. It makes perfect sense why all people of the Jewish faith, including philosophers and other intellectuals, in the Middle East all spoke and/or wrote in Arabic—it was the only full language they had known. History shows Jewish people used Arabic as the daily language; scholars wrote purely in Arabic, or wrote Arabic using Hebrew scripture or Hebrew using Arabic scripture (this also shows Hebrew was never a complete nor independent language). All Jewish intellectuals wrote their philosophical, theological, religious and scientific literature and books mostly in Arabic. This indicates those of the Jewish faith were all native speakers of the Arabic language; it also proves Hebrew was never a language in itself, it wasn't even a dialect of Arabic, but something else which I will prove in the body of this book.

What this also proves is people known as Jewish (for their religion) of medieval times either did not understand the meanings of the word-names in the Bible, too, as it was a language which was no longer remembered because these people were not familiar with the Old Arabic I speak of, this would be especially true if these Jewish intelligentsia originated from Iraq, Syria, Lebanon, or Iran i.e. people who did not speak Arabic in its purest forms to begin with. Another possibility is they knew exactly what the meanings of the Bible were, but did not want people to lose faith if the words were explained in their true meanings; and possibly up until medieval times the general population of the Arabic Middle East (regardless of religion) still knew these meanings, but simply did not care about what this meant as it made no difference to them. What proof there is from history and archaeology shows that even during times where it is believed 'Hebrew' emerged as a 'language' Hebrew was never a dominant language, it was never widespread and was not a much-used language (my translation will prove it was never a language which is why it was never widespread).

This translation of the Bible will also prove there is no such thing as a Jewish/Hebrew ethnicity (or 'race'). The people who first practised Judaism were of the same ethnicities of followers of pagan/polytheist, Christian, and Muslim religions; people of the Jewish faith did not come from somewhere else, nor were they a separate people from the people of the region (Arabs), they were one and the same. Unlike today, where converts or believers in Judaism are subject to a long and demanding process where specific Judaic 'authorities' determine whether one becomes a 'certified' Jew or not, Judaism in its original form was never, and could never have been, solely for those 'born Jewish', but like most religions was open to everyone to convert to if he/she wished to do so.

Just like all religions began in one area and spread to others through word, travel, conquest, and other cross-cultural influence, people went from paganism to Judaism to Christianity to Islam and so forth. And throughout these spans of time and across the Middle East (ME) region specifically, there had always been paganism practised before Judaism emerged and paganism would continue to be observed by many while others converted to Judaism, Christianity, Islam—and all the ME peoples went through the natural ebb and flow of these religions with masses converting to the newest religion, while masses stuck with their old religion, and in many cases the Arab countries' (with their individual ethnicities such as Saudi, Yemeni, Syria, Iraq, etc. (I am not using the ancient names of civilisations here but the modern definitions)) populations had its Christian, Jewish, Muslim and pagan followers; eventually becoming majorly Muslim towards modern times with minorities of Christian and Jewish followers. But all went through these religious trends with paganism, Judaism, Christianity and Islam being practised by the same people of their respective countries. The people did not all uproot and travel somewhere else with religion as an ethnicity, but people converted to the new or maintained their old religions. This can be seen in the survival of pagan rituals becoming part of Christian, Jewish and Muslim religious rituals—even if the people no longer know these are ancient paganistic rites/beliefs interwoven and accepted as part of their current monotheistic religions be it Judaism, Christianity or Islam.

If Jewish was a race or ethnicity restricted within a group of people that could only be passed down through birth, then Judaism would have remained within only one country of all the ancient Middle East peoples it emerged from (and it is not Palestine or modern-Israel), and other Arab countries would never have had their own native inhabitants who became Jewish, and, farther afield, no native Europeans would have become Jews. If you look at images of Jewish people in recent history prior World War II, the darker-skinned, dark-haired people in paintings, photographed or written about in works of literature (the fictional Daniel Deronda by George Eliot; the author Marcel Proust and his brother Robert Proust, for example) are obviously Arabs. When I see images of people from that period, I immediately recognise Arabs.

Of course, there are indigenous white Europeans who converted (whose parents/grandparents converted (and are distinctly different in physical features to the Arab-looking Jews)) to Judaism, but they have no biological ties (in the popular sense of 'race') to the Middle Eastern Jews who ended up in Europe whether by travel or displacement from conflict. Then there are the offspring of intermarriage between the European people of 'Jewish' (Arab) descent and the native white Europeans (regardless whether one converted to Judaism or the other to Christianity) and this is an example of how 'race' or ethnicities mix and do not hold 'pure' genes or DNA from a single race/ethnicity, but it remains a fact that the first Jews to arrive in Europe, centuries before their presence among the Europeans would cause the consternation of the native white Christian counterparts, were Arabs who had arrived in Europe so long ago to have forgotten their Arab roots and had lived among the European population until racism would rear its ugly head. The only ties between Jews from Ethiopia, Eritrea, Libya, Yemen, Egypt, Iraq, Russia, Poland, Ukraine, America, Britain, to name just a few of the different natives of their respective countries who converted to Judaism, is the Jewish faith and not a patriarchal or maternal bloodline or 'race'. In fact, the emergence of Judaism itself among the people long after they had practised different sorts of paganism dispels any claims of Judaism by birth or DNA, as even its very first adherents would had to have converted to this new religion when it emerged.

The fact remains none of the people from all over the world, including European Jews, and also closer to Yemen, Arab Jews who recite the Torah/Bible in Hebrew and those who believe Hebrew is a language—none have ever been able to translate the names in the Bible, or they suggest incorrect meanings, and the names have baffled them all alike. Because they do not speak the purest form of Arabic of ancestral times. My language, my people's language, proves Arabic was a spoken oral language long before it was written.

One can argue that Arabic came out of a mother language and is sibling to Hebrew. If that were the case Hebrew would have survived as did Arabic. If Hebrew were a language it would have survived just as did the Jewish religion. It makes no sense that a religion continued, was carried from one side of the world to the other, all its old and new worshippers all over the world pronouncing the Hebrew text in their prayers, and the first people to practise Judaism (Arabs) continued to practise the religion to this day from its emergence, that the language died—but not the Bible, not the religion. Hebrew was never a language, and in the main text of this book I will prove exactly what Hebrew is, where it came from, and what the word 'Hebrew' means.

One could also argue: if it is true the Bible is not Hebrew but Arabic, why did Arabs not explain the meanings of the Bible? There is more than one answer, and it is complicated:

- During early days of the Biblical stories—the stories had no religious meaning long before Judaism or any monotheist religion existed, but were part of a pagan culture (more about this in main text); after Judaism spread and had incorporated these stories as part of the religion—what was once understood (the language of the Bible) would lose its meanings the longer and wider it spread through time and geographical space.
- As generations progress, civilisations expand, contract, and evolve as cultures; the language itself (Arabic) evolves and old words are forgotten as can be seen in South Arabian language, Classical Arabic, Modern Standard Arabic and all the nuances between Arabic of different countries and within each of these different countries the different dialects or even different meanings of the same word within the same country. Through this evolvement the oldest form of Arabic is forgotten, the oldest Arabic they understand is Classical Arabic. Yemen is unique in this as it retained many Old Arabic dialects spoken uncorrupted by modernisation and modern Arabic dialects. The Arab people who are the intelligentsia in modern times in Arab countries no longer pronounce like the old Arabic even though many of its words still exist in the modern language (they are not aware of its roots and pure meanings). I believe that even until at least the first translation of the Old Testament from 'Hebrew' into a western language that there were Arabic people who fully understood the Old Arabic meanings of the Bible as can be seen in the word chosen to translate and name 'Eve' in the English version; I will explain further in the main text why 'Eve' proves that it is Arabic language. What would be interesting is that if anyone were to compare if 'Eve' was ever written as 'Hawwa' in early English, Latin or Greek translations (I have not, but it would be interesting to find out) and compare it to when the first time 'Eve' was given as the name for the English/non-Arabic translation—that would give a better indication of when at least the last people who both understood its Arabic meanings and interacted with the rest of the world, still lived.

- In these modern times people admit they know the Biblical stories are fictional, but still believe in the religion nonetheless—because it is their faith; another set of people are adamant the Biblical stories actually happened and are affronted by suggestions of otherwise. You can imagine in Medieval Middle East where there is a culture of co-existence between peoples of different faiths (nothing to do with race/ethnicity), where pagans, Jews, Christians, Muslims and other religions have lived with each other in harmony (despite western depictions of the region being nothing but religious wars)—like in modern times where people know these stories are fictional but it does not worry their absolute faith in the said religion, so it was in times when people still fully understood the meanings of the stories to their fullest.
- The same Arabic countries maintained their religious co-existence into modernity with the exception of some Arabic countries, especially those created by British Empire then upkept by American imperialism, such as Saudi Arabia. Some countries do not allow the Bible to be distributed, a direct consequence when the government is a vassal to Saudi Arabia such as Yemen's government; if Yemenis had easy or inconsequential access to the Bible, what I reveal in this book may have been found out decades ago. The greatest religious intolerance is from Saudi Arabia where a strict version of Islam was invented so religion could be used to police the people (among other forms of repression and distraction) lest the people rise and remove a corrupt government and replace it with one that serves the interests of the general population as opposed to enriching only the royal family and western imperialism. An example of this religious and cultural oppression: although it is a fact that natives of ancient Arabia were pagans, polytheists, Jews and Christians before Muslims would be added to the mix of religions of the same and one ancestral 'Saudi' people, KSA remains one of the most intolerant countries with regards to practising one's religious beliefs. The cosmetic changes which began in 2016 are just that: cosmetical, just another Saudi dictator's manoeuvres to appease western criticism—they do not reflect any true tolerance, human rights, or freedoms of any kind for the Saudi people and those who work/live in Saudi Arabia. In a similar way to how western experts have detached the Bible and its related studies from Arabs, Arab leaders in the Arabian Peninsula have detached the general population from access to Biblical texts through religious discourse and physical intervention, and it is these peoples who would still understand the words of the Bible as Arabic. Add that to the fact most modern Arabs no longer speak the ancient Old Arabic, with the exception of some parts of Yemen. It is also possible that if modern Arabs ever read the Bible, it is read in English and/or they read the names contained in the Bible as it would be pronounced in English or how modern and popular opinions pronounce the words as 'Hebraic', and do not read and pronounce it as Arabic.

The speculations of when Arabic as a language emerged is also a wrong conclusion as it is much older than what has been estimated by theorists. Arabic can also assist and explain the namings and meanings of ancient civilisations of the Middle East region, as the Arabic language has a direct and organic relation to these ancient civilisations.

Causes of Failure in Finding Biblical Truths

Reasons Bible Not Understood

The meaning of the Bible has evaded scholars due to misidentifying the language of the Bible as Hebrew instead of Arabic. This has resulted not only in misinterpreting the words, but also not understanding what the stories are really about.

Distortion of History

Historians theorise South Arabian Jews converted to Judaism with the flow of Jewish immigration coming from the time of the First Temple which is believed to have been built in Palestine, when in reality the Jewish religion did not originate from Palestine/Canaan—as the Biblical text shows.

Western Experts Exclusion of Arabs and Arabic

The West insists on telling eastern civilisations and populations what they are now, and what they were in the past. Only part of it is because the West has advanced in education, sciences, military might and political power, and since the Islamic Golden Age, Arab civilisations have fallen behind. But even if it is the West that does have the credible academic institutions which sort out 'what's what', it does not mean Arab culture, Arab history have no bearing on what has emerged from Arab culture and history. Arabs have a much longer history than any European or western civilisations; they have a recorded history; a trove of cultures which extend for millennia, from ancient civilisations of which the Arabs are the uncut continuing descendants.

'Through the efforts of western travellers and archaeologists, Biblical archaeology acquired a stranglehold on the study of the ancient Middle East'[8] rings true with regards to Biblical research. Western experts overlook Arabs' part and their direct relation to the creation/emergence of Judaism and Christianity. The way western scholars approach the Biblical stories and anything related to the Bible is as if these religions emerged and were carried in a bubble irrespective of the people (Arabs) they emerged from. Western experts have sought and failed to explain the origins, meanings and authors of the Bible by diligently attempting to find and confirm the adherents of the Jewish religion as a separate race among and surrounded by Arabs. Academia and science have been rearranged to accommodate this theory, while archaeology and science has proved there is no such thing i.e. a) not one piece of archaeological evidence has been found of an 'Israeli' people nor of an 'Israeli' culture, whereas all artefacts found show only Canaanites ever existed on the landmass now known as Palestine; b) there is no genetic marker to prove Jewish people are an individual or separate race or ethnicity; c) there can be no DNA to prove Jewish-ness especially that being Jewish means adopting the Jewish faith or being brought up practising the Jewish faith, and is not something you are born with or inherit in your genes. If experts did not disregard the only people ever to have existed on the land where the Abrahamic religions emerged, they would see that peoples' history, culture, language, literature (historical and modern) and even the religions Judaism, Christianity and Islam all tell the world the people of the Biblical stories are Arabs and their ancestors are Arabs. Modern Arabs are the only descendants of all the ancient civilisations that existed on Arab lands of the Levant and Arabian Peninsula.

But what stands out in academic work regarding the Bible is that western experts, be they Americans or Europeans, have excluded the indigenous people (Arabs) and the indigenous culture and history and only follow the line which claims 'Hebrew' or Jewish as a race, and therefore it becomes a quest for the truth or knowledge by ignoring the very truth, 'race' and people who are its subject matter. The result: all this academic expertise has never been able to find the truth about the Bible.

Although Judaism and Christianity were born in Arab lands, were borne and lived in their first forms by Arab peoples as a culture, a religion, a history—it is the West telling the Arab what it believes the Arabs' own religions are, and who and what its authors were. The Arabs are the ancestors and the descendants of the people who created these stories, but western experts, universities, even political figures and institutions, would prefer to tell Arabs that David and Jesus are a people (or characters) separate and unique from the Arabs (although these two figures are part of Arab culture); western scholars would like to separate the Arabs who believe in (or created) and carried these religions to the rest of the world, from these very religions. Nothing has prevented the true meanings of the Bible from being understood as much as a western insistence that the Jewish religion is a race with a separate culture, separate language.

Experts insist that being Jewish means being a separate race/ethnicity from Arabs, while archaeology and its findings have shown this is not the case at all. The Bible itself in its original language or translated into English (which, incidentally, still carries within it the original language) is still further proof Biblical stories are told and written with the Arabic language and the stories created by Arabs. One example of this distortion which takes experts away from the truth is some European Jews, especially Zionists, who are undeniably wholly indigenous European and are the varying natives of a multitude of distinct European countries insisting they are descendants of the Biblical characters of the OT. The problem with this is the Biblical characters never existed and its authors (Bible) were not even ancestral civilisations from Palestine. Not only is it impossible to descend from a fictional character, but even if we were to believe the Biblical stories to be true, if the Jewish religion were a race passed down through heredity—no white European would be a Jew, no African would be a Jew, nor non-Arab Asians. In fact, even Arabs of different Arab countries would not qualify as Jews as the religion would have been restricted within the one single people/area who would have been the very first Jews. But because Judaism is a religion, like all other religions, it was and still is open to all to convert to.

Another example is how erroneous western beliefs have attempted to use science to suit present political positions. Using pseudoscience, Nazis tried to determine European people of the Jewish faith as a different race so they could cast the latter as an 'inferior race'—a pretext to make it eligible (to Nazis) to eradicate European Jews in one of the worst genocides in modern history (the Holocaust). Zionists, insisting on a similar pseudoscience, either claim a genetic Jewish marker (which does not exist) or just a verbal claim of heredity, to give them a claim to the land originally called Palestine. For decades Zionists have claimed a biological ancestry gave them the right to commit a horrific genocide in modern times: the ethnic cleansing of Palestinians (the Nakba which occurred in 1948 and continues to this day). When in reality the people who call themselves Israeli in modern-Israel are European and are races and ethnicities from a multitude of different European countries, and from multiple Arab and African countries who arrived later on in the 1950s, who all claim to have biologically descended from the one single patriarchal individual.

These modern-day Israelis (Europeans) have had seven decades of digging up Palestine, and not one piece of evidence has been found to prove an Israeli culture, land or history; not one piece of evidence has been found to prove the Biblical characters or its stories. However, they have found many Arabic and pre-Islamic artefacts and much older Canaanite artefacts; the Israelis discard or demolish the Arabic pre-Islamic/Islamic finds as they prove Arab existence on the land and long before the time academic institutions have recognised Arabs at; but they claim the Canaanite artefacts as 'Israelite', when in fact they are Canaanite. The many Islamic buildings and artefacts discovered are demolished almost immediately (you can find an abundance of Israeli and Palestinian experts who testify to this). Modern-Israel expelled Palestinians from their homes and land and brought in Biblical experts to rename the areas (they had Arabic names) with Hebraic names from the Bible[9], and the work these experts conducted was nothing more than conjecture; they have for decades claimed to be natives specifically from Palestine and the peripheral parts of Syria, Iraq, Jordan, Egypt and Lebanon; they have claimed to have Jewish DNA, all based on Biblical stories; biased academic investigators have propelled this myth.

But what will Zionists and people who have named themselves Israeli claim when the truth is shown that the Biblical stories did not take place in Palestine, nor were the stories written/created by Jews? What will they say when it turns out the Torah and NT were fictional accounts? Since occupation of Palestine, European Jews in modern-Israel have imitated and appropriated Palestinian culture from clothes, music, dance, and food and claimed it as Israeli to give modern-Israel a culture to unify the newly-minted Israelis who in reality have nothing in common with each other except the belief in the Jewish religion[10], whereas the stories of the Bible tell of a non-Palestinian, non-Canaanite culture and are based on a different peoples' culture. This book is not about the Israeli-Palestinian conflict, but I have to point to the above facts as they are partially why the true meanings of the Bible and the truth of who wrote/created the Bible has eluded such a vast, branching and well-funded academic research and its many institutions. I am establishing here, in the introduction, the believed theories about the Bible, its stories, its creators, its ancestors, its descendants. I am also establishing why these beliefs, theories are incorrect so the body of the book will concentrate on the translation of the Bible and what its text and language actually tells us, not only about these stories but also about its creators.

'…neither the term Orient nor the concept of the West has any ontological stability…that these two supreme fictions lend themselves easily to manipulation and the organization of collective passion has never been more evident than in our time, when the mobilizations of fear, hatred, disgust and resurgent self-pride and arrogance—much of it having to do with Islam and the Arabs on one side, "we" westerners on the other—are very large-scale enterprises.'[11]

E. Said's observations on orientalism can be seen in how it affects the truth about the Bible and everything related to the Bible: western institutions ignore the people whose history and culture is interwoven with the Bible (Arabs) and chooses to take it solely from, and in collaboration with, modern-Israelis. It has been this way since the creation of modern-Israel in 1948 and on many different levels, what people like to call a Judaeo-Christian collaboration which is in fact a purely European-European collaboration excluding the native Arabs and preferring to deal with Europeans who call themselves Israeli (in relation to the Bible which is the only thing that I am concerned with here).

Biblical scholars, as well as politically and religiously motivated movements such as Zionism and Evangelism have created a certain direction for dialogue over the Bible, its stories, and what are believed to be the Biblical lands (Arab countries in the real world), the anthropological, racial, linguistic and historical theses revolving around the characters and assumed authors of the Biblical stories. The discourse could be better termed as tunnel-vision. The objective scholars, and the less objective scholars who are influenced by Zionism or Evangelism, have figuratively surgically removed the Bible and its authors, as well as adherents of early Judaism, from its natural heart and fabric: the region, history and people of Arabs. The scholars search for its meaning, its authors, its characters, its authenticity or lack thereof, among the ruins of Arabs' early ancestry, but peculiarly ignore the living Arabs who have preserved ancient history and culture.

There is a real and tangible disdain towards Arabs, who in their hundreds of millions are living time-capsules of the Bible, its stories, its authors. Since 2003, beginning with the American invasion of Iraq, the West and especially the US, UK and Russia (the latter being part of the west from an Arab perspective) have managed to brutally murder millions of innocent civilians of what is believed to be the Biblical lands, through direct acts of war or by enabling wars. These superpowers have also destroyed ancient artefacts, buildings, the very people and archaeology witness to what the Bible is and what it was all about: Iraq, Syria, Yemen. Not only do American and European countries supply weapons of mass murder to brutal authoritarian ME dictatorships who use them against civilians, but western superpowers have actively participated in these wars, where the needless deaths and unbearable suffering of millions of civilians is accompanied by the needless and deliberate destruction of ancient pre-Biblical sites and preserved artefacts which Iraqis and Yemenis have upkept for millennia. In Yemen, many such sites and relics were intentionally targeted and completely destroyed, and the same goes for Iraq and Syria.

Biases Preventing Truth Surfacing

Political, racial and religious positions of leading experts and institutions in the West have diverted from studying the Bible objectively; some leading scholars are aware of what they do. Objective scholars may not be aware, but the framework from which they base their own studies and research from, and on, is already misdirecting them and this is just another reason as to why no one has ever been able to interpret the Bible properly, and have not been able to identify its creators, its authenticity.

Western Influence on Bible and its Truths

There is an abundance of literature where the West and specifically American Evangelicals attempt to rewrite the meanings of the Biblical stories. They attempt to infuse it with spirituality, religiosity, modernism, historicity—which simply does not exist in the Bible written millennia ago by people who did not think with 20th and 21st Century Man ideas; nor do they share the western culture or modernity and its ways of thinking. Scholars also attribute to the Bible text complex contextual and literary features and tools, which again, the simple ancient creators of the Biblical stories did not possess nor did they use. But the simplicity of the Biblical stories, if read objectively, has not prevented scholarly institutions and its intellectuals who have devoted their entire academic careers studying the Bible from developing it into a field of studies, which instead of being objective and leading to the truth have, rather, gone off in the wrong direction and made the Bible seem it is something it is not: a historical document.

I am not saying the Bible is not a big and important document, of course it is, with people across the world interested in it as an ancient text and also for billions of worshippers of Jewish and Christian faith. But what I am saying is with all the time and research put into it, the studies are off-course; as a study, the scholars (academic and religious) have gone in the wrong direction, driven by misunderstandings, errors, honest misinterpretations; and some by religious-political-cultural biases. For all the resources and centuries spent on studying the Bible and all the branches of study which have sprung out of it, and especially over the last several decades, scholars have failed to understand what the Bible is, although it tells whoever reads it exactly what it is.

If you listen to (or read works of) Biblical scholars, you will find they base their important research on a wrong starting point. The wrong starting point is trying to read the Bible in Biblical Hebrew, a language believed to be dead long before any Biblical text was discovered as it had no continuance, not one individual knew the sounds or pronunciations of it, let alone could understand the meanings of its words; it was also determined that the characters and authors were 'Hebrew'. What this meant was effectively excising the Bible and everything directly related to it, from its natural language, culture, therefore removing the people who created it and upkept it—Arabs.

The starting point of Biblical research is an incorrect one, this explains why with all the linguistic, historical, religious studies put into it over a great span of time, has still come up with nothing in understanding it. It is because of this error many 'historical' conclusions about civilisations which existed, and were mentioned in the Bible, are wrong conclusions due to the Bible being used as a historical document when it is not. Only if you read it in Arabic or with its Arabic meanings translated into English can you understand how the Bible cannot be used to measure or estimate any ancient civilisation or actual historic event. Many scholars do state that the Bible is not a historical document, nonetheless many scholars continue to use the mentioned names of rulers, civilisations and the estimated dates of the Biblical texts and the estimations of when Biblical stories occurred to gauge actual historical events in the Middle East and any other cross-cultural/civilisation occurrence.

It is western scholars telling the world what Arabs and the Middle East were, regardless of the region and peoples' reality. This holds true with regards to the Bible, its meanings, origins, historicity/authenticity or lack thereof. Although these scholars display it as a result of findings of research, as truths reached from the conclusions of their studies, it is actually 'not "truths" but representations.'[12] as E. Said puts it in *Orientalism*. This fact is supported by my translation of the Bible in its true language (Arabic) and how it disproves all the wrong and erroneous 'findings' 'conclusions' of many (not all) scholars who have specialised in branches of Biblical Studies.

Effect of Religious & Political Bias of the Present on History & Truth

Distorting the Past

Archaeology has proven that all the characters and stories of the Bible did not exist, and that the stories were fictional accounts; what I have discovered, upon reading the Bible, further proves this. But this does not mean Judaism did not exist, of course it did and does to this day, but it did not exist during the creation and spreading of the Biblical stories, but at some point in time the people who would become the first Jews would adopt and adapt these stories and base Judaism on these stories.

Most Arabs (especially who have lived and grown up in Arab countries) know Islamic and Arabic history: the first Jews were Arabic, as were the first Christians and Muslims. The Jews mentioned in the Quran are Arabs; Muslims and Islam do not differentiate between the sons of Jacob, Ismael and Isaac, and their progeny—they are believed to be Arab ancestors beginning from Adam. Islam and Arabs maintain through religious texts and history Abraham, Jacob, Ismael, Isaac, Jesus, were neither Jewish nor Christian, but that they were all believers in God (as you can read throughout the Quran); whether the Quran be divine or myth is irrelevant, religion was never considered a cause to be from a different race/ethnicity. Almost every Arab country in the past had its native Jews, Christians—people who converted from paganism to the new religions as they emerged, but they were one and the same race/ethnicity with and within their respective countries.

Unfortunately, through spans of ancient and contemporary history tyrants and political interference has wiped out or displaced native Christians and Jews from the Arabian Peninsula. A pre-Islamic historic example: a Yemeni Jewish king attempted to force Yemeni Christians into Judaism, they refused and the historical and cultural narrative tells of the Christians being boarded-up in their churches and places of worship and set on fire (Yemenis believe this to be the account referred to in Chapter al-Buroog in the Quran); people of the Jewish faith within their respective native countries fared much better, and until this day minorities still live in their native lands, which brings us to a contemporary example: native Arab Jews in their different native Arab countries have been much reduced in numbers since modern-Israel persuaded them to leave for Palestine in the 1950s.

Saudi Arabia Archaeological Destruction

The ancient land of what is now called Saudi Arabia was once a melting-pot of different religions before it would become a less tolerant place, not just between religious factions, but even between tribes (long before the West would make it into the country known as KSA with its current borders and monarchs). But unlike other Arabic Islamic countries, the modern Saudi Arabia (government) does not allow pre-Islamic archaeological sites to be excavated and explored[13]; it has intentionally ruined Islamic-era structures, altering them at the cost of all their cultural and historical value so they can decorate with epitaphs praising current kings and princes (such as the modifications made to some of the doors of the Great Mosque surrounding the Ka'ba). They have also completely demolished pre-Islamic and Islamic-era sites (such as in the holy cities Mecca and Medina[14]). What is the reason behind this? Egypt, Iraq, Syria, Yemen all allow archaeological exploration and are proud of their ancestry from ancient civilisations.

Returning to the question as to why Saudi does not allow archaeological exploration of what are probably pre-Islamic sites; they are probably afraid, or certain, of what the archaeological findings may prove. They are not afraid archaeological sites may uncover pagan, or Jewish, or Christian civilisations, it would be superficial and misleading to state this is their fear, as Islam, the Quran, Islamic hadeeth and all neighbouring countries/civilisations' histories document this as a fact on the ancient lands of Arabia.

One might conclude they are afraid the Biblical Israel or its people originated in ancient Saudi Arabia, and fear Zionists and Zionism will relocate from Palestine to Saudi Arabia. I do not believe this to be the case, not only because European Zionists have already built a claim on Palestine and it would be even more difficult for white Europeans to pretend they originated from the ancient landmass of current Saudi Arabia, but let us say that even if it turned out that the authors or characters of the Biblical stories lived in Saudi Arabia that would only mean modern Saudi Arabians are the descendants of peoples they already know they are the descendants of: pagans, Jews, Christians and the earliest Muslims. Even if Saudi Arabia were to uncover proof of a Biblical past—it would never give European peoples who converted to Judaism the right or claim to KSA; it would not even give native Arabs of the Jewish faith in neighbouring countries such as Yemen, Libya, Iraq, or Jewish people from Iran the right or claim to Saudi Arabia. Saudi Arabia belongs to native modern Saudi Arabians—the only people descended of all and any ancient civilisations to have lived on its land.

Although recently Saudi Arabia has allowed some archaeological exploration, findings still have to go through government filters to see what is allowed (or not) to be publicised[15].

Distorting History—Arab Governments

This brings us to the real fear of Saudi monarchs/government: they are concerned if proof will be uncovered which shows the Biblical and Quranic stories to be completely fictional. If the Biblical stories of the Torah and NT are proven fictional, they believe, as would many believe, the Quranic stories to be fictional, too; they are similar to each other and believed by some to be the same. Saudi Arabia founded its monarchy and rule on the evidence of the Quran and pillars of faith; if proven false and people lose faith, Saudi Arabia would not crumble as a country because Saudis are a people and nation regardless of their faith, but the monarchy ruling people through religious oppression would fall.

As mentioned earlier in the introduction, some Arab countries do not allow the Bible to be distributed, due to Saudi Arabia's political and economic influence (using its version of an invented and strict Islam) upon neighbouring countries in the region, such as Yemen. Had the Yemeni governments not complied, Yemenis would most definitely have helped the world understand the Bible to its fullest much sooner than this date.

The problem with Saudi rulers, is no matter their wealth gives them access to the best educational institutions in the western world, they seem to remain ignorant (I am referring to the rulers of Saudi, and not the Saudi people). But they cannot be ignorant, and are fully aware the Quranic stories differ from the Biblical stories, but for political reasons do not want to uncover the truth about the Torah/Bible. They know the Quran and Islam makes it clear that the Torah and Christian Bible have been doctored and corrupted over time, and no longer exist in their true original form—this is what the Quran and hadeeth claim and what Arab history shows, and Saudis have been preaching for centuries even before they were called Saudis and before that in times pre-Islamic.

The point above requires further explanation. The Quran, hadeeth, history and a continuous Arab culture all state the original Torah, original Christian Bible and all related religious texts no longer exist because the people (in ancient history) in charge of upkeeping and teaching these texts (priests, scribes, etc.) changed them to gain profit and power by controlling religious knowledge. Whether this actually happened in history or not does not disprove my point, as it is what is believed by modern-day Arabs and has been a belief since pre-Islamic times and during Islamic emergence, and has continued to be documented throughout as part of history, and the belief survives to this present day. Even the Bible itself claims this: Jesus is quoted in the NT saying that the OT is a doctrine created by man and claims the priests have corrupted it to serve their worldly wants.

The Quranic and Biblical stories tell the same or similar stories; the characters in both books are the same or similar; the prophets and tyrants of the Biblical and Quranic stories are the same or similar. You would come to the conclusion that they are the same stories and characters if you were to read them superficially; or read one e.g. Muslim Arabs reading Quran, but hear second-hand the stories of the Bible; the same if an American or European Christian or Jew reads the Bible and only hears second-hand the stories of the Quran. Even the same individual reading the Bible in English and the Quran in Arabic may come to the same conclusion. The truth is, these stories are similar in that they describe Adam and Eve similarly; Abraham; Moses; David and Goliath; Virgin Mary and Jesus; the wanderings of the Children of Israel for forty years. Why wouldn't these stories be similar when they originate from the same one people, same one region in their origins, the same cultural pool. Anyone who superficially reads the Quran in Arabic and reads the Bible (Torah and NT) would come to this conclusion, because they will be reading the Bible in its incomplete translation, as all Bibles are read due to the fact they cannot understand all the words translated through 'Hebrew'. The Biblical stories cannot be understood and cannot be fully read without understanding the true meanings of the word-names of characters and places included in these stories so any reading of the Bible without knowing the meanings of the word-names is an incomplete reading.

It is only when you read the Bible (both OT and NT) in its correct language can you fully understand the Bible, and what becomes glaringly obvious is: the stories of the Quran are different than the stories of the Bible; the characters of the Quranic stories are different than the characters of the OT/NT, even if they are based on the same figure (be he/she real or fictional). The characters in the Quran are depicted as real people, special because they are prophets/messengers of God, some performing miracles, whereas the characters of the OT and NT are depicted as caricature—they are mocked by the text of the OT/NT itself. The proof of this is in the language, preserved by the Bible as a document, a work of literature (of many literatures to be precise). The Ibrahim of the Quran is not the Abraham of the OT; the same for the David of the OT and Dawood of the Quran; Moses of the OT (correct 'Hebrew' transliteration of Moses as in OT in body of this book) and Moosa of the Quran; The Jesus of the NT (correct Hebrew/Greek transliteration in body of this book) is not the 'Eesa of the Quran. The difference is not from a corruption of the names, or transliteration mistakes or differences in pronunciation of these names between the Bible and Quran, it is what the words mean in what is believed to be 'Hebrew' which I will prove is Arabic.

It could be that the difference between the Quran and Bible will allow the world (or at least religious people) to believe that even if the Bible is not a historical document, and a completely fictionalised work, that the Quran 'proves', or at least its claims testify, to there being an Abraham, Moses, Jacob, Jesus and other characters from the stories (but not as in the Bible) and that there once was a Torah and a Christian Bible which had long ceased to exist and was replaced by the corrupted texts which the current Bible that has been circulating the world for millennia seems to be.

What is probably the truth is that the Quran was also a fictionalised account based on the original fictional stories circulating in the culture (which are the basis of the Biblical stories). Although the Quran and Islamic history never hesitate to point out that the texts which make up today's Bible are not the real divine books as they have been corrupted, it could be these claims were made because it was still obvious back then that the OT/NT were fictionalised but the people who wanted to believe in monotheistic religions could not accept that these accounts were fictionalised from the beginning, and wanted to believe in prophets, God, miracles, and all the folklore so instead they accused the religious people of corrupting the texts, so in wanting to use the stories the Quran did, but in a non-caricature way. There is no avoiding a harsh truth: when the names of places and characters of the Bible are translated correctly and its authors identified and their reasons for creating these stories understood, it would still prove these texts (Quran, Torah, Christian Bible) were based on stories created by pagans in pre-historic times.

The only reason for writing this book and proving what I have found in the Bible, is solely because it is knowledge the rest of the world should know, and what many people, scholarly or otherwise, want to know: the true meanings and origins of the Bible. I do not want people to lose their Jewish, Christian or Islamic faith (I believe many know these stories are fictional anyway, even without them knowing the true meanings of the words). This is not about Islam versus Judaism and Christianity, nor is it the Bible versus the Quran, as the truth of what I have found and will present in this book also brings the Quranic stories authenticity into question; and it is not about sneering at people who believe in religions whether Judaism, Christianity or Islam, as I myself am a Muslim. I decided it is better and only fair that the world and interested individuals do know the indisputable truth and proof about the Bible. As mentioned earlier, the translations and meanings in the Bible are based solely on the language used in the Bible and as transliterated as Hebrew. I have not looked at the Quran to derive meanings for the words and language used in the Bible while I was translating them, and as mentioned before, the character and place names are actually different between the Quran and the Bible.

Modern-Israel Archaeological Destruction

'Any historian knows that the past can be exploited politically in contemporary conflicts. But nowhere is this so obvious than in the Middle East.'[16] said G.W. Bowersock from his experience working in the region, his essay shows one of the many reasons and ways prejudice, political and religious movements' biases manipulate and get in the way of the truth, especially with regards to the Middle East and Biblical Studies, in order to support a present political reality. It is interesting in that it supports what Palestinians and some Israelis have all been claiming and testifying to: modern-Israel destroys ancient ruins and artefacts where they prove pre-Islamic, Islamic and/or Arabic presence on the land once known as Canaan.

'A decade ago an Israeli scholar reminded me of the basic truth that archaeology is politics in that country...'[17] Bowersock's *Palestine: Ancient History and Modern Politics* evidences, and gives insight, how politics and Zionism is used to distort the truth of the past. He mentions how Israeli archaeologists disregard proof such as shows Arab culture in ancient Palestine. One example is the archaeological find of twenty-five documents related to a Jewish woman '...She and her family not only observed the transition from Arab kingdom to Roman province in the territory known as Arabia...It is clear that the relation between Jews and Arabs was a harmonious one.'[18]

He goes on to explain how politics has interfered with archaeological findings and proof, and contrasts how in modern-Israel all archaeological findings are greatly broadcast, except when it proves something which does not fit into the present state of modern-Israel's claims, in this instance archaeological findings are suppressed.

Bowersock points out how politics and western bias has interfered with the truth about history and distorted it 'If archaeology is politics, so inevitably is history...'[19] and he continues to show this in an example of how abundant proof that the original Phoenicians originated from the Arabian Gulf (i.e. Phoenicians were originally Arabs) has been ignored and later on experts have altered and made it seem that Phoenicians are colonisers of the Arabian Gulf '...we are confronted once again with manipulation of the past.'[20].

Another example which supports my point where I believe Arabic and Arabs existed earlier than officially recognised is in an artefact which was also intentionally suppressed, and true history distorted and manipulated, to serve present political interests by modern-Israel. An archaeological find in the Negev desert containing both Nabatean and Arabic writing on one stone was discarded by Israelis 'The finder of this inscription is inclined to date it to the middle of the second century AD, and it would therefore constitute by far the earliest example of the Arabic language.'[21]

All these archaeological discoveries which are discarded because they do not fit a political narrative and present created by the West, all prove civilisations which lived on Arab lands are the indigenous natives who live on as the indigenous Arabs in modern Arab countries.

The same biases, political, religious and racial, are what has led the Biblical Studies astray and further away from the truth.

Racial Biases Preventing Truth Surfacing

Early Zionists and What They Knew

It is possible that leading Zionists of 1948 and '50s were made aware of the meanings of the Bible. Ben Gurion (first modern-Israel Prime Minister) hated Arab Jews in general, but had a particular vehemence towards Yemeni Jews although modern-Israel had spent great effort and time in convincing them to emigrate; modern-Israel deceived them into leaving their native countries to live in the newly occupied Palestine (to be named Israel). The 'de-Arabisation' process[22], abusing Arab Jews and brainwashing them to forget their Arabic customs, roots, culture, may have been in part to avoid exposing the Torah/Bible's true meanings and origins.

1948 Zionists seem to be aware of the Yemeni civilisation being the originator of the Biblical stories. They also seem to be aware that the Yemenis are the first ethnicity to become Jews. What can be gleaned from the 'Yemenite Children Affair' (the kidnapping of thousands of Yemeni babies and children, sending them to white European Jews in modern-Israel, US and Europe who pretend to be their real parents[23]) is that there was an organised operation with the full knowledge of all those involved in the child-trafficking (hospital staff, government, adopting parents) to give Middle Eastern children to white European Jews, i.e. to manipulate ethnicity to serve Zionism and the state of modern-Israel.

Kidnapping babies and children is a barbaric and horrendous crime, but there is a greater malicious intent underlying modern-Israel's kidnapping of Yemeni new-borns and toddlers and giving them not only to European Jews in Israel but also to those living in Europe and America to bring up as their own 'biological' offspring. Decades later when the crime was exposed, some of the 'justifications' that were given as to why there was a methodical and widespread abduction of Yemeni and Arab babies in 1950s Israel have been: they were trying to give childless European Jews children; and the more racist and false claims by some that Yemeni parents were bad parents and the child was better off with European parents; that Yemeni parents had more children than they wanted or cared for, and did not care about losing some children. All these tendentious statements made by past and current modern-Israelis are just to cover-up the real reasons behind what has been documented as systemic and systematic operations of abducting Yemeni babies and children from their Jewish parents, with the knowledge of hospital staff, care home staff, judges and other government officials and also the 'receiving/adopting' parents who were all involved and/or aware these children were being taken without their parents' consent.

The true objective beneath this grave human rights abuse was these babies with their distinct Yemeni Arab features (just like many of the European Jews of Arab origins whose darker and distinct features are called 'Jewish' in popular European culture of the 18th and 19th Century) would give (and have given) white American and white European Jews 'offspring' with physical 'Jewish' features whereas in reality they are the abducted children or grandchildren and great grandchildren of Yemeni parents whose children were abducted from hospitals and elsewhere in 1950s Israel. The camps modern-Israeli Europeans had initially placed the arriving Yemenis in was one place the kidnappings occurred; Yemeni babies, toddlers and infants were snatched from their Jewish mothers' arms, never to be seen again. In hospitals, after giving birth to perfectly healthy Yemeni Jewish babies, the parents were told their new-borns had died but upon insisting to see their new-born child as most parents refused to believe he/she had died, and upon requesting to see the body for burial and farewell, the hospital staff would deny the distressed Yemeni parents the right to see and bury their allegedly deceased child—because there was no body, but the babies had been sent to various storage places in order to be given to white European parents.

The Israeli hospital staff and Israeli government were all involved in this (there have been official inquiries in modern-Israel over the past several decades since this was exposed, but the Israeli government has already 'lost' many files and has probably destroyed all other documented proof witness to the extent and scope of the abduction of Yemeni babies and their distribution to white European Jews across the western world; but the Israeli government and courts have already admitted to this happening (then ordered the documents regarding this case to be sealed for seventy years)), and although other Arab Jews were also targeted, their babies kidnapped and were told had died, it was mainly Yemeni babies who were kidnapped (for their physical features).

It is probable that Ben Gurion and other Zionist Europeans did this to Yemeni babies and parents because the Yemeni people, out of all Arabs, look exactly like the darker-skinned and olive-skinned European Jews who were most definitely descendants of Arab countries who had emigrated to the west and who stood out as physically and ethnically different from the white European Jews (the latter being white European converts to Judaism) pre-World War II and the Jewish Holocaust; and the white European Zionists of 1948 chose Yemenis to kidnap babies from as it would lend authenticity to what was and is an essentially white European invasion and colonisation of Palestine, when white European parents have darker-skinned, dark/brown-haired (more 'Jewish looking') offspring both in modern-Israel and the West. Anyone who looks at paintings or images of European Jews, or reads their descriptions in European literature, from pre-World War II and of the 18th and 19th Century, what you see is an Arab and distinctly Yemeni. I recognise Yemenis in these old images; even images from modern times when I recognise those who are obviously Yemeni or Arab even before I know their names, and when I learn they are Jewish I can see that my people travelled so far into the world and so early on as to have forgotten their Yemeni or Arab roots, or where they could be the more recently Israel-abducted Yemeni and Arab babies and their offspring who have never known, and will never know, their original roots and true parents; and this recognition was long before I ever learned of modern-Israel's 1950s child-trafficking operations.

Long before European Zionists would take over Palestine, European Zionists in the 19th Century travelled far and wide all-over Arab countries. Some were amazed to find large communities of Yemeni Jews in Yemen (e.g. Hermann Burchardt), and some of these European Zionists wondered in their writings if this is what original Jews looked like (they are no different than the dark-skinned European Jews of 18th/19th Century Europe except for the clothing and those exposed to harsh elements seem a little more sunburnt than the urban Yemeni Jews). It is difficult to believe with the arrival of Yemeni Jews in modern-Israel in the 1950s and European Zionists delegations constantly in Yemen to contact Yemeni Jews prior to that, that these Yemenis who naturally spoke fluent Arabic did not tell their white European 'compatriots' the true meanings of the Bible. Were the early European Zionist leaders aware of this? Was it the real reason behind the brutal 'de-Arabisation' process of all Arabs immediately upon arriving in Palestine/Israel and the brutal and methodical way European Zionists tore up the arriving Arab families and communities and worked hard to keep them in squalor and under a biased system where they were forced into less favourable conditions, and forced to forget their culture? Was the de-Arabisation process a way to make sure the truth about the Bible never got out? Or is it that these Yemeni Jews (who spoke Arabic and read the Torah all their lives) simply were not familiar with the Arabic my people speak, and therefore this is why the true translation was never revealed? These same Yemeni Jews, most of whom were convinced to emigrate to Palestine/modern-Israel by European Zionists, all had Jewish practise, cultural and religious traditions which differed in contrast against the different natives from all around the world who practised Judaism, it led many to describe Yemeni Jews as being more 'Jewish' than any other Jews. What these Yemeni Jews also possessed at home and brought with them to Palestine/modern-Israel were the oldest Torah scrolls, which may have contained alternative Biblical stories, possibly the closest to the original stories, which may have also explained and shown the Torah as perfectly Arabic. All the Yemeni Jews who owned these Torah scrolls and who arrived in Palestine/modern-Israel in the 1950s accused the modern-Israeli government of stealing these Torah scrolls which they had kept in the family for centuries—only to systemically and systematically disappear a few hours or days after arriving in modern-Israel. These old Yemeni Torah scrolls may have also brought the truth about the OT to light decades ago had their Yemeni owners not been dispossessed of them.

Archaeology and Distortion

Since 1948 European Zionists/Israelis have conducted extensive archaeological exploration, modern-Israel excavates about 300 sites a year - none have uncovered Biblical Israel, Israelite culture, or anything from the Bible. They have come across many Canaanite, Arabic and Islamic buildings, whole villages built and identified from different Islamic periods, unfortunately for archaeology, history and culture, modern-Israel's response has been to either destroy it completely (this is the action in most cases of Islamic finds), or to fallaciously present these ruins as a Biblical finding/site such as the one misleadingly named 'City of David' although there is no proof of it being from Biblical times, and what proof there is shows it from a different era[24]. Why do I mention this? Ignoring/distorting facts, finds, and evidence not only perverts history, but takes us further away from the true understanding of the Bible and everything related to it.

Archaeologists in Israel have split—some objectively arguing there is no evidence of any Biblical descriptions because it is fictional (minimalists), while other Israeli archaeologists (maximalists who excavate with the Bible as the literal guide) try to fabricate a past that never was, based on findings of Arabic and even more recent Islamic structures, or older Canaanite pottery, which they falsely claim to be 'Israelite' despite Western experts ascertain them as Canaanite and there being nothing Israelite found. Both sides of modern-Israel archaeologists argue about the dating/era attributed to the finds. Both sides tend to ignore the era of the Israelite stories never existed, not when they try to date it based on the lives or times of the Biblical characters[25].

With regards to minimalists, they too attempt to establish alternate theories still based on the Bible—as they claim Israel existed, but not like the Bible described; words to the effect that Jerusalem existed but as a small insignificant village. These minimalists, like their peers who dig with the trowel in one hand and the Bible in the other, seek to establish a history that never happened; they do this because they are faced with what archaeology has already proven: there was never such a thing as Israel, an Israeli people or any place, person mentioned in the Bible.

So although they argue about specific findings, both maximalists and minimalists still attempt to establish a non-existent history, a civilisation and people that never existed—except as a fictional story.

Even the theories Israeli archaeologists promulgate are invented to fit a political present: archaeologists knowing for certain Israel and its characters never existed, recreate another fabricated or erroneous theory that Israel collapsed, and under this circumstance Judah under Josiah created the Biblical stories '...so Josiah woke up one morning, looked to his left and to his right, and there was neither an Assyrian nor an Israelite to be seen. And then his officials decided to put into practice their religion and territorial ideas...Because they wanted to seize control of the territories of the kingdom of Israel and annex them...'[26]

The problem with Finklestein's Josiah theory, is Josiah and his rule were fictional accounts too. They have totally missed what the Biblical stories are really about, although the stories not only indicate but spell-out clearly what major topics were to its creators, and they tell us why they were created.

This translation of the Bible proves with indisputable evidence: Israel, Judah, David, Solomon did not exist. The fact is, the Biblical stories tell of an undated and prehistoric past; the stories carry a dramatized and fictional account of pagan cultural practises, which later on would become the basis of monotheistic religions. But it is modern-Israel's constant drive to establish a past that never was (although they have already forcefully taken most of Palestine and will remain as part of the Middle East, regardless of what the Bible proves) which has not allowed the truth of the Bible to come forward.

This Translation of the Bible

Biblical Studies' many branches and scholars have all vastly explored the Bible, searched for its meanings, its origins, its characters, its authors; they have searched for the reasons it was written. I can answer all their questions in this book, and the answers to all the mysteries of the Bible was never hidden, but in plain sight: its language—Arabic. I have translated exactly what the text says, and what is hidden to the non-local (the local is a remote and rural Yemeni) of the culture being described in the text.

In the main text, I will prove how the Torah/Old Testament are actually created in Old Arabic. It will become clear through the translation of what are considered 'Hebrew' names which I will translate into English based on their meanings in Arabic. In due course, it will become clear to the reader, every name is an Arabic word/compound word related to that story where the name is introduced in the Old Testament. The same will apply to the New Testament (Christian Bible) although the oldest NT text is in Koine Greek, it was based on original stories told or written in Arabic (which scholars erroneously call Hebrew).

In the Bible, people and place names are related to the story being told. All names are compound words, nouns, adjectives, adverbs which denote their roles in the story; and a characteristic of the story-telling was to allow some names to have more than one meaning which makes clear what Hebrew really is, and will be clarified in the main text of this book.

Where names are only listed in the OT without being given roles in the story, the names with multiple meanings cannot be definitely determined, i.e. although all possible translations can and have been translated, we cannot tell which were meant by the Biblical author; some listed names do make sense in relation to each other and there is an obvious pattern followed. Wordplay is a big part of the Biblical stories, it allowed the creators (early and later 'editors') to elaborate on the stories. But in the OT where the names are just lists and have more than one meaning, it cannot be determined which meaning or meanings were intended; they probably featured in other stories told that were not included or did not make it into the written Biblical texts, or maybe were not included in translations. But all the major names in the Bible, and that is most names in the Bible, can be understood because they are written in a language that still exists today.

Context

Many people claim that the Bible can be read in many different ways and mean different things to different people. This simply is not true. The Bible has specific stories with very direct and specific meanings. Songs and poetry with specific meanings by its writers may have different meanings to its listeners/readers where connotation plays a role along with denotation, and in that sense, anything could hold different meanings or even be misconstrued. Works of modern authors, fiction and non-fiction, are also written with specific meanings, but their stories can be understood differently by readers; that has more to do with the reader and not the author's intended meanings. It is slightly different with the Bible, the modern meanings given to them have been introduced by religious, western, and modern outlooks, from theories of religious people and Biblical scholars who have misunderstood (or never really known) the true meanings of the stories; all have imputed onto the Biblical stories representations that do not really exist in its text. With regards to the Bible, the names of people and places are meant as denotation at its most basic level.

Intertextuality

There is intertextuality in the Bible, but it was not planned as some modern literary feature, but can be detected because of the creators of these stories beliefs and customs, and because what was important to them are what is being described and repeated in different ways; and mostly, intertextuality is due to what were separate oral stories in early times eventually being gathered together in written form into one text by individuals in later times. As to who created these intertextualities and why, this can be determined only after the Bible is understood with its pure and basic meanings as intended by its creators, and also by the editors who would add and change the text much later on (in ancient history). Myself, I was able to immediately identify as I read along the Bible, not only because I speak the Biblical language, but as I have come from a people whose customs and beliefs are the same (without the smiting and warring), but for the sake of clarity the explanations of cultural background and other important aspects as to who created the Bible has been mentioned towards the end of this book.

Translating, Interpreting and Determining Meaning

When people translate texts, especially foreign and ancient texts, they take into consideration the literal meanings and the allusions. In the Bible there is the literal translation and what it means in the story—the words I have translated are exactly what was meant by its creators. Since the translation and interpretation of Biblical stories has been subject to many different interferences, this has left the Bible misunderstood and a mystery; and the more modern/recent the re-writing and re-interpreting, the more it has taken the meanings and intentions away from its original creators' intentions. Upon translating the names, the stories should become much clearer to the reader.

I have chosen to quote the verses where they elucidate the meaning of the name so readers can understand it fully in its context as meant by the creators of the stories. Where large chunks of Biblical verses have been quoted, I have placed them between quotation marks instead of following standards to make it easier to discern from my written explanations.

I suggest the KJV be read with this book so as to refer to the KJV to see the verses along with the translated meanings of this book. The translation follows the order of stories as they feature in the KJV.

I have explained the meanings of the words and what they mean in the language of the people who still actually speak the language of the Bible, and it will become evident they are the same and exact meanings intended by the creators of the Biblical stories. I will detail cultural background in a later chapter to make it clear in one section where these stories originated from and why.

Recognising the names in the Bible was straightforward, I immediately recognised most of them upon reading the Torah and KJV in English, which I began to read in December 2016 and reached 1 Chronicles before discontinuing it so I could read other literature I was more interested in (non-Bible related). When I resumed reading the Bible, I knew I had to translate it because it was obvious the whole world had no idea that it was in Arabic. Deciphering the word-names with all their possibilities to make sure the end-result was correct, then deciphering them again to check several times while typing this book was more time-consuming, as I had to be meticulous to arrive at the definite meanings.

I came to the conclusion that I had to know exactly what experts believed the 'Hebrew' meanings to be, and I believed that maybe they already had alternative meanings which could have deterred them from reaching the true meanings, so I referred to Eerdmans Dictionary of the Bible. What I discovered was most names in the Bible were not understood at all, Eerdmans Dictionary translated/explained them wrong, and in the few instances where Eerdmans got it right, it was when it was the exact same meaning in modern Arabic as the old Arabic, but the Dictionary would strangely ignore that it was the meaning of the word in Arabic and attribute the meaning to Aramaic, Akkadian or Hebrew (even when they give a wrong translation of the meaning of a word, it is based on its modern meaning in Arabic, but for whatever reasons (racial, political, discriminatory, (it could not be ignorance)) there is a bias to claim it as Hebrew, Aramaic or Akkadian—when it is right there in front of them in Arabic; Eerdmans Dictionary does mention 'Study of similar roots in related languages (e.g., Arabic, Ugarit) have enabled scholars to come to more informed opinions about the meaning of earlier unknown words…')[27].

It took approximately four months to finish translating the names in the Bible (KJV) in its entirety (long before I typed up this book), from the final days of March 2017 to 19th July 2017. It has taken from January 13th 2019 to March 2020 to complete putting together this book which included going over all the names and translating them and deciphering them from scratch again. This is the method I followed to make sure the words I translated were precise:

1. I took the 'Hebraic' name as written in English in the KJV; jotted its pronunciation/meaning in Arabic;

2. Referred to Eerdmans Dictionary of the Bible (EDB) to check for its 'Hebrew/Greek' transliteration and if a true or alternative meaning presented in the EDB were correct (I found most in EDB are incorrect meanings or stated as unknown in origin), I also referred to Eerdmans Dictionary to ascertain all possible meanings were accounted for;

3. Using the Hebrew/Aramaic/Greek transliteration from EDB and the key for transliteration, I wrote out the word using Arabic, giving each Hebrew/Aramaic/Greek consonant and vowel all the possible letters/phonemes (a separate line for each word with different but relevant letters/phonemes—but I did not add nor decrease the number of letters/phonemes but kept them the same as in the Hebrew/Aramaic/Greek transliteration although the Arabic words can be read without any vowels and still be complete Arabic words);

4. From the multiple words produced, I eliminated the ones which were just random letters and not words, and this left only the proper words: the words corresponded to exactly what is written and relayed in the Biblical story regarding the character/place name as Arabic words and Arabic meanings, exactly as written and kept in the KJV and other Bibles.

5. I double-checked the EDB transliterations with transliterations from other databases. Also, any name I could not find the transliteration of in EDB, I searched for using KJV Online to locate the names and also Messie2Vie website to find transliterations in Hebrew and Greek;

6. I also used Messie2Vie where the English words (not names) in both the KJV and Eerdmans Dictionary struck me as odd (to be explained in body of book) and did not fit in with the text of the Bible; these words which I found jarred against the text and story (even in English) I found had been completely mistranslated and misinterpreted by the original/historic and modern translations of the Bible.

The sources I used in ascertaining the translation of the Bible and why:

- Though I read the Torah[28] in English (produced by a Jewish author/publisher) before reading the KJV, I did not use it when translating as it was almost exactly the same as the KJV and added nothing.
- The King James Version Bible[29]—it was best to use an old translation not affected by modern political biases; and also, because the older it is, the closer it kept to a literal translation of the original authors of the Bible.
- Eerdmans Dictionary of the Bible[30]—it boasts 'Approximately 5000 entries identify all persons and places named in the Bible, as well as cultural, natural, geographical, and literary phenomena…To this end they have enlisted nearly 600 leading scholars and matched them with topics related to their areas of specialization.' So such an authority was a must in determining how experts believe the names are pronounced (from transliteration of the texts) and it also proved how the Biblical experts have no idea of what the true meanings of these words are (with the coincidental exception of a few names).
- Messie2Vie website[31]—it provided transliteration of words not transliterated or insufficiently transliterated by EDB.
- KJV Online[32] when I needed to locate all the times a specific name was mentioned or a specific name, and to attempt to make sure I had not missed any from the KJV (book).
- The Arabic my people and I speak and still use daily—my language holds the exact same meanings as that of the language of the original authors of the Bible.

From reading the Bible there were already large indicators jumping out of the text about who wrote it and why, but to be thorough, after I finished translating the Bible, I investigated its text to draw all the proof as to who created the Bible. The Bible holds abundant proof in its text as to who its authors were and why they created it. This can be identified not only from its original and true language, but also from its style of expression (how the descendants of its authors still speak today); its proverbs; its described customs; superstitions; terms of description used; the 'wanderings' of Moses and his people; the clothing and use of substances in adornment; food ingredients mentioned; the importance put on specific matters; the rituals and customs which in the Biblical stories were dramatized as festivals or significant events but to the creators of these stories and their modern-day descendants are still performed in their original form as routine in everyday life—all this tells us who the authors are, not the names of individuals, that is impossible, but where these stories came from and which people they were created by.

If we genuinely want to understand the Bible and its mysteries there are matters we have to establish and steps to take:

- It is believed to have been written in Biblical Hebrew although no copy or proof of the original Bible exists. What is available are texts written long after the original is believed to have been created; what archaeologists have discovered, although it is the earliest document found—it is not the earliest form of the Biblical stories.
- Only the true language of the Bible can translate it and make perfect sense of it (Arabic), this actuality has evaded all Biblical Studies research so far because it has attempted to understand it in a non-existent language (Hebrew).
- If the Biblical names can be translated with a language that has existed uncut through time, we should be able to translate many of the names and the translation would have to make sense to the story.

- Political and religious desires and biases, racism and other discriminations must be set aside so we can look at the words and text with no objective other than solely wanting to understand the meanings of these names and words—if they have meaning. Whether a person is pro-Israel or pro-Palestine, Zionist or Evangelist, Muslim, Jew, Christian or atheist, any and all possible biases need to be set aside when reading this ancient text as it is. Wanting to understand the meanings without any predetermined political, religious or racial 'shaping' will allow us to understand these words and why they were used. Only being objective will allow us to unlock the mysteries of the Bible.

The structure of the translation will be as follows:

Name as in KJV; Hebrew/Aramaic/Greek transliteration; word as in Arabic followed by meaning in English between quotation marks; the correct pronunciation (CP) in Arabic and as it is in the Bible; Bible quote or reference. Explanations will be included as and where needed. A slash (/) separates the different meanings of the same word/compound word; a dash (-) connects the different parts of the same compound word-name. Where it may be mistaken as separate letters: underlined letters or letters in italics in CP means they are one letter.

Pronunciation Key: for 'Correct Pronunciation':

ḥ pronounced as how the last part of 'ahh' if you felt pain;

p pronounced b;

ss as in pronouncing the 's' heavy in 'sausage';

kh as in last two letters of 'Gogh' in Dutch or 'loch' in Scottish;

ṭ as in last letter pronounced in German saying 'My Gott';

g as in 'golf';

k as in 'c' for 'crown'

ee as in 'see';

Names which end 's' in Greek are pronounced 'h' instead of 's'

Long or short 'a' as in 'father' or 'faather' as shown under CP.

h pronounced as 'wh' in who or 'h' in 'hope';

ph as in 'Philip';

sh as in 'hush';

f as in 'frog';

dh pronounced with a heavy 'th';

gh as in how 'r' in 'orange' pronounced in French;

q as in heavy 'caw'(sounds heavier than 'k', lighter 'g')

ei, ey, ai as in 'seal' 'hey' 'hay' 'hail'

oi pronounced 'woy' or as in 'Lois'

' as in pronouncing underlined Sana'a

x is pronounced combining two letters: kz (ك ، ز); and also can be pronounced: qss (ق ، ص)

Endnotes to Introduction

---

[1] Bowersock, G. W., 2001. Palestine: Ancient History and Modern Politics. In: E. Said & C. Hitchens, eds. Blaming the Victims: Spurious Scholarship and the Palestinian Question, London: Verso, p. 189.
[2] Mendel, Yonatan and Ranta, Ronald. From the Arab Other to the Israeli Self. Surrey: Ashgate Publishing Limited, 2016.
[3] Quoted in Mendel, Yonatan and Ranta, Ronald. From the Arab Other to the Israeli Self. Surrey: Ashgate Publishing Limited, 2016. p. 35.
[4] Ibid., p. 35.
[5] Ibid., p. 41.
[6] Ibid., p. 42.
[7] Ibid.
[8] Bowersock, G. W., 2001. Palestine: Ancient History and Modern Politics. In: E. Said & C. Hitchens, eds. Blaming the Victims: Spurious Scholarship and the Palestinian Question. London: Verso, p. 184.
[9] See Pappe, Ilan. The Ethnic Cleansing of Palestine. London: Oneworld Publications Limited, 2007. pp. 163, 226, 233.
[10] See Mendel, Yonatan and Ranta, Ronald. From the Arab Other to the Israeli Self. Surrey: Ashgate Publishing Limited, 2016.
[11] Said, Edward W. Orientalism. London: Penguin Books, 2003. pp. xii - xiii.
[12] Said, Edward W. Orientalism. London: Penguin Books, 2003. p. 21.
[13] Young, M., 2017. Hundreds of Mysterious Ancient Structures Discovered in Saudi Arabia. [Online] Available at: <https://.news.com.au////of-mysterious-ancient-structures-discovered-in-saudi-arabia/story/f0f4823511af5ac6f4c351963e85
[Accessed 05 January 2019].
[14] Swami, P., 2011. Analysis: Saudi Arabia's War Between God and Archaeology. [Online]
Available at: <https://.telegraph.co.uk//////Saudi-Arabias-war-between-god-and-archaeology.html>
[Accessed 05 January 2019].
[15] Shakespeare, N., 2018. Discovering Saudia Arabia's hidden archaeological treasures. [Online]
Available at: <https://.independent.co.uk//_reads/arabia-hidden-archaeology-alhijir-petra-charles-doughty-a8373686.html>
[Accessed 05 January 2019].
[16] Bowersock, G. W., 2001. Palestine: Ancient History and Modern Politics. In: E. Said & C. Hitchens, eds. Blaming the Victims: Spurious Scholarship and the Palestinian Question. London: Verso, p. 182.
[17] Ibid., p. 184.
[18] Ibid., pp. 185 -186.
[19] Ibid., p. 186.
[20] Ibid., p. 186.
[21] Ibid., pp. 190 - 191.
[22] For further reading on the 'de-Arabisation' process see Mendel, Yonatan and Ranta, Ronald. From the Arab Other to the Israeli Self. Surrey: Ashgate Publishing Limited, 2016; and Pappe, Ilan. The Ethnic Cleansing of Palestine. London: Oneworld Publications Limited, 2007. p. 254; and Shavit, Ari. My Promised Land. New York: Spiegel & Grau, 2013.
[23] Knell, Y., 2017. Missing babies: Israel's Yemenite children affair. [Online]
Available at: https://.bbc.co.uk//[Accessed 06 January 2019]; and Cook, J., 2016. The shocking story of Israel's disappeared babies: New information has come to light about thousands of mostly Yemeni children believed to have been abducted in the 1950s. [Online]

Available at: <https://.aljazeera.com////story-israel-disappeared-babies-160803081117881.html>
[Accessed 06 January 2019].
[24] Draper, R., 2010. Kings of Controversy. [Online]
Available at: <https://.nationalgeographic.com////and-solomon/>
[Accessed 06 January 2019].
[25] Hasson, N., 2017. Is the Bible a true story. [Online]
Available at: <https://.haaretz.com//is-the-bible-a-true-story-latest-archaeological-finds-yield-surprises-1.5626647>
[Accessed 06 January 2019].
[26] Lori, A., 2003. Grounds for Disbelief. [Online]
Available at: <https://.haaretz.com/.4777188>
[Accessed 06 January 2019].
[27] Wm. B. Eerdmans Publishing Co. Eerdmans Dictionary of the Bible. [ed.] D. Freedman, A. Myers and A. Beck. Michigan: Wm. B. Eerdmans Publishing Co., 2000. p. 181.
[28] The Jewish Publication Society of America. The Torah. London: Kuperard, 2004.
[29] The Holy Bible: King James Version. Glasgow: Harper Collins Publishers Limited, 1991.
[30] Wm. B. Eerdmans Publishing Co. Eerdmans Dictionary of the Bible. [ed.] D. Freedman, A. Myers and A. Beck. Michigan: Wm. B. Eerdmans Publishing Co., 2000.
[31] Messie2Vie, 2013. [Online]
Available at: https://.messie2vie.fr/
[Accessed 2017].
[32] King James Bible Online, 2019. King James Bible Online. [Online]
Available at: <https://.kingjamesbibleonline.org/>
[Accessed 2017].

REVELATION

A TRUE TRANSLATION OF THE BIBLE

Eden; ʿēden; نَيدِن 'he will guilt' 'he will bow/bend/face ground/lower/lower head'; عيدَن 'return/returned' 'listen and understand-guilted/bowed/bent' 'remember/be warned-guilted/bowed/bent' 'sticks'. All these meanings are present where 'Eden' is used:

'return/returned' because God will place 'the man whom he had formed' in this garden called Eden, and when he is punished he is still in the same place but it becomes a worse place with hard work, danger, pain and sorrow and eventually there will be death, and 'return/returned' is emphasised as a punishment for just as he was made from the ground/dust, at the end of a long, hard life he will return to be just dust in the ground.

A note on what is obviously the work of two different authors or an early author then someone who edited it later on: Gen.2:17 has Adam remain in Eden but it becomes a place where toil, suffering, pain and death can be experienced. Whereas Gen.2:22 has Adam and Eve pushed out of the borders of Eden and returned to work in 'the ground from whence he was taken.'. But this contradiction in the same story/chapter does not change the meanings of the word 'Eden' but a later editor felt he had to emphasise more the meaning of 'returned'.

'will bow/bend/face ground/lower/lower head' as God creates man to tend to this garden which includes these actions.

'will guilt' 'will bow/bend/face ground/lower head' 'listen and understand-guilted/bowed/bent' 'remember/be warned-guilted/bowed/bent' as God teaches Adam what he can eat and use, and what he cannot, with a warning that if he trespasses, he will be punished—which when he eventually does eat from the tree it causes Adam and Eve to be 'bowed' with shame as they can recognise nakedness, and they are also guilty for eating the fruit and are to be removed from Eden to live a lower and more difficult life as punishment. Cp: eyden, 'eyden. (Gen.2-3)

Pison; pîšôn; بيشُن 'water filtering out of/water running out from' 'will pour or flow out of/into' 'he/it will filter/filter impurities' 'he it will filter out' 'is filtering/filtering impurities' 'will be ready for copulation/ready to conceive(goats and similar animals)/is on heat' 'will copulate/will be sexually excited' 'fertile/verdant land'; from word (bsh/بش) 'water flowing heavily out of', the sound running water makes/to flow out of; (shn/شن) 'filter/filter impurities/flow(ed) out of/into' 'fertile animals/sexually excited/ready to conceive/copulated/ready to copulate' and the latter is based on the word (shn/nsh/شن/نش) and refers to goats, sheep and other such animals on heat, or copulated as well as the time following copulation expecting the animal to conceive from it; (b/ب) 'will' 'by/with'; (ee/î/ي) 'he/it'. Cp: beeshon.

Havilah; ḥăwîlâ; حَوِله'surrounding it' 'encompassing around'; from the word (ḥwl/حول) (same meaning). Cp: ḥawilah

'And a river went out of Eden to water the garden; and from thence it was parted, and became into four heads. The name of the first *is* Pison; that *is* it which compasseth the whole land of Havilah…' (Gen.2:10-11)

Gihon; gîḥôn, giḥôn; جيهُن، جِهُن 'came here'; and جيحُن ، جِحُن 'went through a long rough experience/time' (from the same word to create 'flour' (between rough surfaces)). As there is no indication from the verse itself, you can see from the names of the other rivers it is most likely to be 'came here'. Cp: geehun, gihun, geeḥun, giḥun. (Gen.2:13)

Hiddekel; ḥiddeqel; هَدَّخَل 'will-enter/interfere' or 'I will enter/interfere'. From (dkhl/دخل) 'went in' 'entered' and (daakhil/داخِل) 'inside'. Cp: hiddekhel.

'And the name of the third river is Hiddekel; that *is* it which goeth toward the east of Assyria.' (Gen.2.14)

Euphrates; Euphrátēs; يُفر آطيه 'he/they cross it' 'he/they passes it', it can also mean to 'he/they/it split it' (as tear or divide) and 'he/they separate it' 'he/they lose/lose chance/be deceived out of opportunity or wealth/money/possessions' (as people or features parting and going in different directions); from word (phrṭ/فرط) all have meanings 'tear/rip/split' 'to cross', 'to pass', 'is crossing', 'is passing', 'has crossed/passed', 'they/it/is/are passing/crossing it', or they 'have crossed/passed it' 'separated/been separated' 'lost chance' or 'deceived out of possessions/money/chance'; could also be يُفر آتيه 'he/they sweetens it' from word (phrt/phuraat/

فرت/فرات) 'sweet' 'sweet water'. The word given to name the river is used in the same way as the other rivers mentioned. Cp: yuphraaṭeyh, yuphraateyh. (Gen.2:14)

Adam; 'ādām; ئادَام 'is from blood' 'made bleed', 'is to last long' (he was initially immortal). Although Biblical scholars claim it means human/humankind (which has become a noun for human/mankind in Arabic based on religious stories), that is not the meaning of the word. It is a compound word the (') or (ء) means 'is' and is also a phoneme to bring attention to what is being spoken about, (dm/دم) 'blood/last long', (ādām) means 'from blood' 'to last long'; it is also ئعدام 'is from nothing/became nothing', (from the word 'dm/عدم 'nothing/non-existence/scarce'). It means he was made from blood, was supposed to last for a very long time and will last long for the duration of his life, was created from nothing and when he dies will be nothing again. All to fit in the role of the story. Cp: aadaam, a-'daam. (Gen.2:7-17)

Eve; although all transliterations present 'ḥawwâ'—the EDB attributes an incorrect meaning of the word and does not give a transliteration nor a meaning for 'Eve'. In the Bible, the verse which attributes Eve's name to the 'mother of all the living' is not the meaning of the name. All names/words in the Bible prove they are Arabic words, but the interesting thing about 'Eve' is that it highlights further that the early translators of the Bible knew their exact Arabic meanings. The 'v' in 'Eve', like the 'v' in 'Havilah' and 'David', is actually pronounced 'w'. 'Eve' is آوي/ئوي the correct pronunciation is 'aa-wee/a-wee' and means 'stay' 'stay overnight'; the original name as in what is believed to be Hebrew is ḥawwâ حوّا/حوّه also means 'staying/stayed' 'made him/it stay' 'still/stilled' 'made him/it still'; Cp: ḥawwa/ḥawwah. The word 'aa-wee/Eve' is in the form of telling or asking someone to stay, whereas the word 'ḥawwa' is in the form of giving the spoken about the characteristic of staying, being made to stay/still or saying they are not moving but staying/still.

There are two ways to understand the reason 'Eve' was given as a substitute word for 'Hawaa': the less likely is that in the original language as both 'Eve' and 'Hawaa' hold the same meaning it was interchangeable and used as preferred. What is most probable: there are several letters which are difficult for English speakers or non-Arabic speakers learning Arabic to pronounce correctly and cause physical difficulty (in throat) and frustration. One of these letters is 'ḥ' 'ح'; it is probable when the first non-Arab speakers would work on translations of the Bible in collaboration with people who spoke the original language, that the letter 'ḥ' caused great frustration and took much time that the local translator chose a word which was easier for a non-Middle Easterner to pronounce, but one that had the exact same meaning: Eve/Hawaa—'stay'.

'Therefore shall a man leave his father and his mother, and shall cleave unto his wife…' Gen.2:24)

Cain; qayin; كَين 'to gather/eat the berries called 'cain/كَين' and كَيْن is the fruit of the tree called 'arg/عَرْج or 'ilb/عِلب, when the fruit falls off it carpets the ground below and around the trees; the cain fruit is collected from the ground; the act of collecting (and eating) the cain fruit is (yitkayyan/yitkayyannu/ يِتْكَيَّن/يِتْكَيَّنُوْا). I'm not a botanist, but it could be the jojobe fruit or very similar (I have only ever eaten cain fruit in Yemen), but the fruit is abundant and is eaten fresh or dried. Cain's character is named after this fruit as he presents it to God as an offering. Cp: cayin.

'…that Cain brought of the fruit of the ground an offering unto the Lord.' (Gen.4:3)

Abel; hebel or 'ābēl; هعبَل 'will shake fat of sheep' 'will shake fat', عابِيل 'moving/shaking sheep fat' 'moving/shaking fat'; when sheep are fat, when they move you can see the fat roll or shake under the fur and it is called ('aabil, 'abl, ya'bul/يَعْبُل /عَبْل/عَابِل), it is also used to describe a plump/fat person whose body shakes when they move (it is a positive description as it is not negative to be fat) likened to how fat sheep shake. Abel's character offers God the fat of sheep. Cp: h'bel, 'aabeyl.

'And Abel, he also brought of the firstlings of his flock and of the fat thereof.' (Gen.4:4)

Nod; nôḏ; نود ، نُد 'rock/sway back and forth' (with upper body or just head) which is usually the gestures made when one is in sorrow, despair or moaning about what is happening to them, 'wiggle/loosen' e.g. to move a milk tooth back and forth (or that it is wriggling) before removing it from gum; نوذ ، نُذ 'harmed/were harmed/we harmed'. The place where Cain is sent as punishment for harm he has caused, and his and others' harm is mentioned; Cain is upset and bemoans his punishment. Cp: nood, nod, noov, nov. (Gen.4:11-16)

Enoch; ḥănôḵ; حَنوق ، حنُق 'upset and not eating or talking' when a person is upset and goes away, or stops eating and/or talking with others, or turns his back towards others because he/she is upset with them over something; it is also wordplay on هَنوح 'I will cry out in distress (or loudly)'; هَنوه 'I will warn/bring to attention/remind' 'I will seed/stone(of fruit)/plant' 'I will intend/decide within me' and all meanings refer to Cain being upset and made to leave his home, the child he has with his wife bears the names of this mood; when God becomes aware of Cain's crime he warns him of the curse and the curse is he will not be able to grow anything (his name 'Cain' the fruit are berries of which even the seed is cracked and collected for eating and also these seeds sow the ground with more trees; the meanings are shown in the curse and distress 'When thou tillest the ground, it shall not henceforth yield unto thee her strength…And Cain said unto the Lord, My punishment *is* greater than I can bear.'), so he is being warned he will no longer be able to 'Enoch' seed/sow the ground. But he does continue to progenate children and grandchildren and the first child he 'seeds' and the first city he builds/plants carry the one and same name of which both 'warning' but also 'seed/stone(of fruit)' (and by extension 'seed' of man) can continue to come to life and grow. If without the (ḥ) in transliteration, انوح would still have the same meaning as (hanooḥ) but in the first person 'I cry out in distress/loudly'. Cp: ḥanooq, ḥanoq, hanooḥ, hanooh. (Gen.4:10-17)

Irad; 'îrād̠; عِرآض ، عيرآض 'objected' 'strongly argued against or blocked an action/obstructed' 'wide/they are broad' 'laid broadways'. Cp: 'eeraadh, 'iraadh. The names of Cain's progeny are all negative words as fits with the theme of the story being told: Mehujael; mĕḥûyā'ēl; مَهوحآئَل / ميهوحآئَل 'is not-staying/still-the' 'he is not staying/still-the' 'not sitting/calming/letting it go', 'his water is rotten/deceived/deceitful'. Cp: mehu-ḥaa-el/ill, meihu-ḥaa-el/ill. Methusael; mĕṯûšā'ēl; مَذوسآئَل / ميذوسآئَل 'what did he ask' 'what flowed/leaked' 'what offended-the' 'what happened/what did he do-the'. Cp: mevu/meivu-saa-el/ill. What can be clearly seen is the creators of these stories used names with similar denotations of negativity and will continue in Lamech and his wives. (Gen.4:18)

Lamech; lemeḵ; wordplay on both لَمَك 'gathered-you' 'blamed-you' and لَمَح 'hinted' 'stealing glances/looking secretly/looking quickly' 'blinked' and means giving an indirect warning by telling it to someone else, it can also mean when a couple are attracted to each other or in love and one or both are stealing glances at each other. In this instance Lamech is blaming the people he has 'killed' or 'wounded' for insulting him, and he is at the same time issuing the warning for others to be cautious. Cp: lamak and lamaḥ.

'And Lamech said unto his wives…Hear my voice; ye wives of Lamech, hearken unto my speech: for I have slain a man to my wounding, and a young man to my hurt. If Cain shall be avenged sevenfold, truly Lamech seventy and sevenfold.' (Gen.4: 23-24)

Adah and Zilla, are also negative words as used in the theme of the story: Adah; Heb. 'āḏâ; عادَه ، عادا 'as usual' 'returns' 'not yet' and also a play on 'made enmity' 'counted'. Cp: 'aadah, 'aada. (Gen.4:19-23)

Zillah; ṣillâ; زِلّه ، زِلّا 'a mistake or sin' 'remove(d) him/it' (to permanently remove) 'wipe()d away him/it' 'went away/went out of sight' and usually has a mischievous connotation to it, e.g. when someone says 'where did he/they go?' using the word zl/زل it means the person(s) has mischievous intent behind the disappearing or going somewhere out of sight and has an even more specific meaning if one of the people that 'went/go' is a female: ('where did he go with her?'/وين زل ابها) means he has taken her somewhere to take sexual advantage of her. Cp: zillah, zilla. Both wife-characters have been given word-names to suit the speech of Lamech who speaks of killing others and how many he will kill. (Gen.4:19-23)

Jabal; yāḇāl; يآظَل 'he/it covers/shades' 'he/it stays in/under shade' 'he it misleads'; حآبَل 'impregnated' 'used ropes/tied with ropes' and is shown in that he has fathered many people, reinforced by raising cattle and living in tents, as raising cattle refers to fertility, and tents need rope and rope fibres '…he was the father as such as dwell in tents…'. Cp: yaadhaal, ḥaabaal. (Gen.4:20)

Jubal; yûḇāl; حوبآل 'pregnant/they are pregnant' 'ropes/twine' and this too refers fathering many offspring and refers to strings used in musical instruments '…he was the father of all such that handle the harp and organ.'. Cp: ḥubaal. (Gen.4:21)

Tubal-cain; tûḇal qayin, طُب الكَين 'good/fortune of cain(berries)' and it reflects how something good has come out of 'bad' Cain (the grandfather) and also reinforced by the sister's name (below). Cp: ṭub al-cayin. (Gen.4:22)

Naamah; na'ămâ; نَعيما ، نَعيمه ، نَعَما ، نَعمَه 'a blessing' 'gave blessings/fortunes' 'soft/smooth' 'lived good life'; something received, e.g. money, food supply, health anything which is received from another and has the same connotations as a 'blessing' whether seen as a gift or the action of blessing the recipient; the person who receives the physical gift whether an external receipt of something or even health in his/her own body—that person is 'blessed' the person or God who has giving it has 'blessed' the recipient, and the thing given is 'a blessing'; it also means 'smooth' and the meaning of 'blessing' is still connected as a blessing makes things/life smoother and easier; it supports the character name of her brother. Cp: na'amah, na'ama, na'<u>ai</u>mah, na'<u>ai</u>ma. (Gen.4.22)

Seth; šēṯ; سَف ، سيف 'carried gently' 'was carried gently' 'poured gently/pouring gentle spurts of water' 'became numb'; and refers to Eve conceiving from Adam and 'water' is the same word for 'semen'; this word also begins a new grouping of words for his son and those in the following chapter. Cp: se<u>ph</u>, sey<u>ph</u>. (Gen.4:25)

Enos; 'ĕnôš; عَنُص/عيْنُص ، عَنوص/عيْنوص 'wriggled/wriggled around'; نَنُش/نيْنُش ، نَنوش ، نيْنوش 'filtered/filter impurities/flow(ed) out of/into' 'fertile animals/sexually excited/ready to conceive/copulating/copulated/ready to copulate' and refers to the readiness and copulation of sheep, goats and similar animals and the following period expecting the animal to conceive from the copulation. The more the Biblical character names are read, the more there is a pattern to which words are chosen as names in the story: he is son of the replacement of 'Abel' whose word-name means 'shake fat of sheep/shake fat', 'Seth' has been given as a father as his water-related name, and 'Enos' is connected both to goat/sheep copulation and 'water' ('water' is the word for 'semen'). Cp: 'eno<u>ss</u>, 'eino<u>ss</u>, 'enw<u>ss</u>, 'einw<u>ss</u>, eno<u>sh</u>, eino<u>sh</u>, enw<u>sh</u>, einw<u>sh</u>. (Gen.4:26)

Cainan; qênān; could be كَينان which is a verb related to doing something with the cain fruit, such as gathering or eating it 'gathering cain/eating cain' 'sheltered from rain'; it could also be قَينان 'sat up straight/positioned standing up or straight up' 'made perky' 'topped up (with water/drink)' 'estimated measurements/eyeballed measurements'. Cp: keynaan, qeynaan. (Gen.5:9)

Mahaleel; mahălal'ēl; مَحيلَل نيل 'fidgets-the/moves around-the' 'fidgets/slightly moves or wiggles something (to make it fit/or right)-the' 'instead of-the/in the place of-the' from the word محلل 'fidgets/wiggles/slightly moves something (to make it fit/or right)' or 'instead/place'; آل/أل/نيل 'the'. Cp: maḥailal-al/ill/eyl. It could also have meanings related to 'circumcise/purify/sweeten/shed/shed blood' but it seems the names are from related group words in the authors' mind: Enos 'wriggle/squirm', his grandchild Mahaleel 'fidgets-the' and the word given to name the son in the story 'Jared' will also follow suit. (Gen.5:12)

Jared; yere<u>d</u>; yāred; عَرَد ، عارَد 'wobbles/wobbled head' 'neck bent to one side' 'stubborn' 'bruise/bruised/lump/lumpy', it is used to describe a person who wobbles his/her head too much and also if someone's neck is bent to one side (whether out of habit, deformed or meaning stubborn); يَرَد ، يارَد 'he comes home' 'he returns/responds'; جَرَد ، جارَد 'stripped leaves off completely' leaving only stem/stalk. Cp: 'ered, 'aared, yered, yaared, gered, gaared. (Gen.5:15)

In Gen.5:21-24, **Enoch** still holds the meanings above from (Gen.4:17): ḥănô<u>k</u>; هَنوح 'will cry out in distress (or loudly)'; هَنوه 'I will warn/bring to attention/remind' 'I will seed/stone(of fruit)/plant' 'I will intend/decide within me'; Cp: hanooḥ, hanooh. Across the Bible, even upon cursory reading, you can identify where the words, writing style changes or where even bigger 'edits' made to the stories by later 'editors' and the story jars within the text. Enoch was a precursor to Noah, Enoch was supposed to have Noah's role, but was edited out later on as can be seen 'And Enoch walked with God: and he was not; for God took him.' (Gen.5:24), his role was removed because someone preferred to use the version of the same word 'Noah' instead.

But because the stories were already well known they could not simply erase him, or maybe someone did and another author reintroduced him with a brief and vague explanation—he suddenly disappears; the word-name given to Enoch's son is also a pun by an author who kept it based on a different character of a similar name (Methusael): Methuselah; mĕ<u>t</u>ûšellaḥ; مَذصَلَح 'what did he do?' or 'what happened?'—the explanation/remedy, is: Methusaleh is given a son who fathers Lamech who in turn fathers Noah. It is also wordplay on مَذسَلَه 'what distracted/entertained him?' 'what comforted him?' 'what leaked/flowed him?/what made him leak/flow?' and the 'flow' refers to semen which is called 'water' and he has fathered many daughters and children keeping him entertained and distracted, as well as a very generous lifespan (on behalf of the author) of nine hundred-sixty-nine years. Cp: mevu-sellaḥ, mevu-sellah. (Gen.5:24-27)

It is obvious how words are used for their exact meaning(s) (even when there is wordplay it is still with specific intent for the story). See earlier Lamech (son of Methusael) whose name means both 'hints, threats and warnings' and 'blames'; and when the word Lamech is reintroduced as a different person (son of Methusaleh) the meaning is still about warning, hinting and blaming, and when he has a son the narration states: 'And he called his name Noah, saying, This *same* shall comfort us concerning our work and toil of our hands, because of the ground which the Lord hath cursed' (Gen.5:29)

Noah; nōaḥ; نَوَح 'cried out in distress/loudly'; it is the same word as Enoch, but in the past tense. Cp: <u>kn</u>*ow*aḥ. Also, نَوَه 'warned/brought to attention/reminded' 'seeded/the stone/seed(of fruit)' 'the/his intentions/unspoken thoughts'; Cp: <u>kn</u>*ow*ah. The word (nooḥ/نوح) describes an animal such as a cow when it bellows for a long time (especially when its calf is taken away) and as a simile when a person is making loud and long cries; (nhy/نهي) has meanings such as 'warning/end/noted/understood', and depending on how it is used in the sentence e.g. out of frustration is the equivalent (but not the literal meaning) of 'For God's sake!'. In the Biblical story Noah does what his name and wordplay implies, he cries out to the people in warning, but more importantly, as his name clearly shows, he and his wife, his children and their wives and the animals he has to gather in pairs (which it makes clear have to be male and female) are the 'seed/stone(of fruit)' which will plant and repopulate the earth after all animals and humans have been wiped out; and this further explains the verse mentioned earlier 'And he called his name Noah, saying, This same shall comfort us concerning our work and toil of our hands, because of the ground which the Lord hath cursed.'. (Gen.5:29-32;6)

The names given to the characters of Noah's sons also follow the method in the story:

Shem; šēm; شَم ، شيم 'a smell' 'smelled' because the story has them on an ark filled with animals for a long period of time; سَم ، سيم 'named' 'told samaaya story/naming story' 'poisoned' 'eye of needle' 'will thread needle' 'will be led through/followed' because getting the animals of large and irregular dimensions through a door/gate and into the ark would incur the same difficulty or precision needed to get a thread through the eye of a needle. Cp: <u>sh</u>em, <u>sh</u>eym, sem, seym. (Gen.5:32)

Japheth; yepeṯ, yāpeṯ; جَفَث ، جِفِث ، جآفَث ، جآفِث 'dry/dried' 'dried it' 'has dried', the story is about a flood and this son along with his family will remain dry. Cp: ge<u>ph</u>ef, gi<u>ph</u>if gaa<u>ph</u>af, gaa<u>ph</u>ef. (Gen.5:32)

Ham; ḥām; هآم 'worried'; حآم 'extremely heated/angry' 'hovered over/lingered over/circled around'; the word given as a name for the story based on Noah cursing Ham (through Canaan), the placement of the curse on Canaan allows the wordplay to come into effect that 'Ham/worried' is worried about his son's future; the curse is placed on Ham because instead of avoiding his father's nakedness, it indicates he may have lingered and watched his father in his drunk nakedness and informed his brothers about it—he does the opposite of his brothers who both cover Noah up without looking at him. Cp: haam, ḥaam. (Gen.9:22-27).

Canaan; kĕn'an; قَنعان/قَنعَن ، قينعان/قينعَن 'given up on' 'given up any hope' 'resolved to fate or what will happen' 'he/they gave up hope/resolved to fate' 'he/they were convinced/satisfied with answer/situation' 'he/they looked up/craned necks'; When Noah curses Ham, the father of Canaan who is already named for the purpose of the story, to be the servant of Shem and Japheth both Ham 'worried' and Canaan 'without hope/resolved to his fate' are aptly named. From the word (qn'/قنع) and means 'give up hope/be satisfied with what has happened or an answer/be resolved to the fate' it also means to look up (crane neck and lift head) from a lower position to who or what you are looking at. Cp: qan'aan, qan'an, qain'aan, qain'an. (Gen.9:22-27)

Ararat; 'ărārāṭ; عير آرآت 'stuck/abandoned in the wilderness' 'stuck/stranded in a difficult location(such as precipice)' 'abandoned' and is from the word ('r/عر) 'wilderness/naked/abandoned'. It is used to describe a person or animal getting lost in the wilderness, or getting marooned on a difficult precipice unable to move forwards or return back; it also describes taking unwanted cats to a distant area so they cannot return home. In the story it describes the place where Noah's ark is stuck while the waters have not fully receded, the passengers cannot sail, nor can they get off the ark. This meaning is emphasised by the doves Noah sends out who cannot find a place to rest and have to return to him as they too are stuck on the precipice in the ark; but also, in the last dove which does not return, it abandons the ark as it can now live elsewhere and indicates the people and animals can now leave the ark. Cp: 'airaaraat. (Gen.8:4-14)

The generations of the sons of Noah uses simple words and compound words. Some are obvious in their meaning, while others not so much because of wordplay used and not enough story to support determining one meaning over another; except where the names appear later in the Bible and its meaning determined. It should already be obvious by now that these stories are completely fictional and were not real people/events. It is astounding that scholars have been attempting and attributing these 'genealogies' as actual genealogy and claiming these fictional characters are the ancestors and therefore their descendants who lived/live in ancient Syria, Palestine, Iraq, Egypt, Arabian Peninsula and other such claims.

Biblical scholars, historians, archaeologists go out of their way to use the Bible and Biblical stories to figure out the geography of the area and its early and current inhabitants—which is an impossible task due to the fictionality of the stories. It would be easier, and logical, for scholars to see the names of people and places in the Bible for what they are, instead of corrupting them in an attempt to tailor them to suit 'proving' the Bible and its characters for the individual's personal, political or organisational objectives. It is evident from the Biblical text, names were created in these Biblical stories based on the language of the era and area (Arabic); the mention of civilisations which indisputably existed (along with names of fictional civilisations that did not exist) is not because the early 'progenitor' was named as per the Biblical stories and the nations came out of that character, but either some civilisations/cities/towns/villages already existed and based on meanings of the words the creators of the Biblical stories made up stories around them and gave the characters the names, or what is more likely: the popularity of these stories influenced the naming of areas once these stories spread out of their area of origin. The names given are simple, many are crude; the majority of the word-names can be explained as to why that certain word was used as a name in the story, and the more influential and significant the character in the Bible, the more obvious and clear the name assigned to him/her in relation to the role in the narrative.

Gomer; gōmer; غومَر 'submerged (in water or dirt)' 'covered with face or headveil' 'head/face/mouth covered' 'head/face veils' 'muffled/were muffled' 'speaks with face or mouth covered'; قومَر 'upset/envious/spiteful'; جومَر 'hot coals/hot'. Cp: ghoomar, qoomar, goomar. (Gen.10)

Magog; māgôg; ماجوج ، مآجُج 'moves like a wave' and refers to an area or land filled with people or crop, that its movement looks fluid like a current or wave. Cp: maagoog, magog. (Gen.10:2)

Madai; māday; ماضَي 'passed/past/passing' 'marked', مادَي 'touch/reach into' 'pus/turned into pus' 'reach for/pass to/extend' 'crossed the line/limits/took too many liberties/did too much'. Cp: maadhay, maaday. (Gen.10:2)

Javan; yāwān; عاوآن 'assisted/helped' 'howled'; غاوآن 'misled/misled to downfall' 'are on a folly/deceiving/in deceit'. Cp: 'aawaan, ghaawaan. (Gen.10:2)

Tubal; tubal; طُبَل 'a drum/drummed' 'drummed to mislead/and misled' 'encouraged to do bad/evil' 'good of', تَبَل 'gets soaked/wet', تذَل 'gets humiliated/denigrated', تدَل 'is shown' 'is pedalled'. Cp: ṭubal, tubal, tuval, tudal. (Gen.10:2)

Meshech; mešek; مَسَك 'held/caught', مَشَق and مَشَح both mean to 'pull at something until it gives or snaps' 'cut loose' 'pulled out of/pulled off'; مَشَق 'scared silly/frightened extremely' 'straw' 'fibres left after cow eats crop'. Cp: mesek, mesheq, mesheḥ. (Gen.10:2)

Tiras; tîrās; تِرآس ، تيرآس 'first/head first'; تِرآش ، تيرآش 'be sprayed' 'was sprayed' (with water); طِرآش ، طيرآش 'vomit/vomited' or intentionally splashed liquid over someone/something 'in stupor/scared unable to respond' 'deaf'. Cp: tiraas, teeraas, tiraash, teeraash, ṭiraash, ṭeeraash. (Gen.10:2)

Ashkenaz; 'aškĕnaz; نَسقينَس/نَسقي نس 'give people to drink' (water), عَش كعنز 'lived like female goats'; عَش قينعز 'lived perched on a rock'. Cp: asqeinas, 'ashk'naz, 'ashqein'z. (Gen.10:3)

Riphath; rîpat; could be: رِفَة ، ريفَة 'twitched/fluttered' 'eye-twitch', رِفَث ، ريفَث 'sexual intercourse'. Cp: riphat, riphaf. (Gen.10:3)

Togarmah; tōgarmâ, tôgarmâ; تُجَرمح ، توجَرمح 'scraped/bruised/battered' 'made loud thumping or knocking sound/noise', تُقَرمح ، توقَرمح 'corners or edges have been battered/broken off' 'made hollow or sharp knocking/tapping noise'. Cp: toogarmaḥ, togarmaḥ, tooqarmaḥ, toqarmaḥ. (Gen.10:3)

Elishah; 'ĕlîšâ; ئلي/ئيلي شا 'the one who wants' 'whatever he wants'. Cp: illeesha, eileesha. (Gen.10:4)

Tarshish; taršîš; تَرشِش ، تَرشيش 'light spraying' or 'a lot of light spray', طَرشِش ، طَرشيش 'a lot of vomiting' or intentionally splashing a little liquid over someone/something, 'deaf' 'scared into stupor/unable to respond, hear, speak' 'pretending not to hear/pretending to be deaf'. Cp: tarshish, tarsheesh, ṭarshish, ṭarsheesh. (Gen.10:4)

Kittim; kittîm; this word either is a single word or could be a compound word: it has meaning as single word كَتِم 'stifled', قِطِم 'snipped'; or a compound word where im/îm is 'them' هم or 'the' ام; when taking into consideration the many other words in the list it is most probably a compound word and is 'the' or 'them': قِطهم 'cut off-them/cut them off'; قِط ام 'cut off-the'. Cp: kittim, qiṭṭim, qiṭṭ-hum, qiṭṭ-um. (Gen.10:4)

Dodanim; dōdānîm; تودآن هم 'make bow-them' (make them bow or bend down), 'guilt-them/find them guilty'; تودآن ام 'made bow-the' 'made guilty/found guilty-the'. Cp: toodaan-hum, toodaan-um. (Gen.10:4)

Cush; kûš; قوش ، قُش 'to blow away litter/fibres/burnt remnants' 'remove completely in one swipe or scrape' 'litter/fibres/burnt remnants'; the word is used to describe tiny pieces of litter, left over burnt pieces and also the straw fibres left over after eaten by cattle which the wind blows away. It is also used as a curse (said in humour or seriousness) 'may God cush you' الله يقُشك meaning may God blow/scrape you away like litter. It makes up the word of tiny piece of litter or fibre (qishwash/قشواش); part of the word for 'crispy' bread (with black toasted parts) and the same to scrape something away or to drag it, as well as someone or an animal paralysed/immobilised with fear or shock is (qisht, qaashiṭ/قشط/قاشط/قشِط); قص ، قوص 'tell a story' 'cut' 'harden' 'be cruel/cruel'. Cp: qush, qoosh, quss, qooss. (Gen.10:6)

Mizraim; miṣrayim; مِصرَيهم 'put scarf on-them' 'their scarves', مِصرَي ام 'put scarf on-the', or 'knot/bundle-them/the' as people bundle things into scarfs or knot small things/small amounts into scarf or fabric for storage and/or travel; or مِزرَيهم 'insulted-them' 'their disgrace/embarrassment', مِزرَي ام 'offend-the'; from the words (mssr/مصر) the small square head scarf folded into a triangle worn by women; (mzr/مزر) which means an embarrassment/disgrace, to fill a person with insults/offense and embarrassment. Cp: missray-hum, missray-um, mizray-hum, mizray-um. (Gen.10:6)

Phut; pûṭ; فُت 'crush' (whether a person, food or object). Cp: phut. (Gen.10:6)

Seba; sĕḇā'; سَبآء ، سيبآء 'captured' 'left/left alone' which is more likely with the group of words it has been placed in (see following sons of Cush name meanings); شَبآء ، شيبآء 'swollen/rigid(from water/cold/etc)' 'young woman/girl' 'old person'. Cp: sebaa, seibaa, shebaa, sheibaa. (Gen.10:7)

Sabtah; saḇtâ; صَبَطه ، صَبطا 'a stuck or sticky situation' 'injured or hit (a target)' 'stuck it/stuck to it' 'injured/struck it/him/target'; سَبته ، سَبتا 'a belt' 'wore/tied belt' 'stopped doing/let it go' 'left it/him/her'. Cp: ssabtah, ssabtaa, sabtah, sabtaa. (Gen.10:7)

Raamah; ra'mâ; رَعمه ، رَعما 'caused to burst inside' (internal injuries) 'saw-blinded him' 'saw-blindness' 'saw-drank him/it'; رَئمه ، رَئما 'saw water' 'threw around' 'at a long distance apart/covering a great distance' 'killed/injured him/it'. Cp: ra'mah, ra'maa, ra-a mah, ra-a maa. (Gen.10:7)

Sabtecha; saḇtĕḵā'; شَبطيحاء 'will lie prone' 'will throw him onto his stomach' a move where someone is thrown to the ground and forced to lay prone (in wrestling and fighting); (sha/شَ/شا) 'will', (bṭḥ/بطح) 'exposed belly/lay on stomach'; شَبتيكآء 'will snap/cut it' like quickly snapping/cutting a piece of thread from word (btk/بتك) 'to snap/cut abruptly' 'a short piece of something'. Cp: shabṭeiḥaa, shabteikaa. (Gen.10:7)

Sheba; sĕḇā'; (same as Seba above(Gen.10:7)) 'captured' 'left/left alone/let go'; 'swollen/rigid(from water/cold/etc)' 'young woman/girl' 'old person'. As both 'Seba/Sheba' are mentioned in verse 7, it may have been the author's intention that one name had one set of meanings of 'seibaa' while the other had the meanings of 'sheibaa'. (Gen.10:7)

Dedan; dĕḏān; تَدآن ، تيدآن 'made to bow/bend' 'you are made to bow/bend' 'made/found guilty' 'you are found guilty'. Cp: tedaan, teidaan. (Gen.10:7)

Nimrod; nimrôḏ; نِمرود ، نِمرُد 'we turn/rebel against' 'of rebelling/turning against' 'respond with hostility' 'of responding with hostility' 'got out of control'; from (mrd/مرد) 'rebel/turn against/respond with hostility/go out of control'; نِم رود/رُد 'nag-respond/reply/return' 'gossip-respond/reply/return' from word (nm/نم) 'gossip/nag' and (rd/رد) 'respond' 'return/come back'. Cp: nimrood, nimrod, nim-rood, nim-rod. (Gen.10:8)

Babel; bāḇel; بآدَل 'swapped/mixed/messed up' 'changed'. Cp: baadel. (Gen.10:10)

Erech; 'ereḵ; ئَرَك 'I see you' 'showed you' 'penised you' 'your penis'; ئَرَخ 'he loosened'; ئَرَح 'he eased/rested' 'blew/made/fanned wind'. Cp: erek, erekh, ereḥ. (Gen.10:10)

Accad; 'akkaḏ; عَقَّد 'knotted'; ئَكَّد 'confirmed/reassured'; ئَخَّض 'took'. Cp: 'aqqad, akkad, akhadh. (Gen.10:10)

Calneh; kalnēh; كَلنيه 'all of us' 'we ate it/we fed it/him'; قَلنيه 'we said it' '(he)told us'. Cp: kalneyh, qalneyh. (Gen.10:10)

Shinar; šin'ār; شِنعآر 'we will be disgraced'; شِنئآر 'to go to a place aside/or cast aside' 'to change direction' (on a journey). Cp: shin'aar, shin-aar. (Gen.10:10)

Asshur; 'aššûr; ئَشّور ، ئَشُّر 'gestured/to signal'; ئَزّور ، ئَزُّر 'visit/the visit' 'the pilgrimage' 'squeeze' 'the tight/tightened/squeezed' 'the false oath'. Cp: a-shoor, a-shur, a-zzoor, a-zzur. (Gen.10:11)

Nineveh; nînĕwēh; نينويه ، نينَويه 'we bring to your attention/point out'; نينبيه ، نينَبيه 'we warn you/wake you up/point out'. Cp: neeneweyh, neeneiweyh, neenebeyh, neeneibeyh. (Gen.10:11)

Rehoboth; rĕḥōḇōṯ; ريحوبوت ، رَحوبوت 'she welcomed' 'she made space' 'was wide/spacious'. Cp: reḥoo-boot, reiḥooboot. (Gen.10:11)

Calah; kālaḥ; قالَه 'he said it'; قالَح 'eyes rolled upwards'; كالَه 'weighed it' 'measured out for him' 'ate it/him' 'cursed him/responded angrily to him' 'all of it'. Cp: qaalah, qaalaḥ, kaalah. (Gen.10:11)

Resen; resen; رَسَن 'went down at'; رَزَن 'became heavy' as in weight or potency (latter as in tea, e.g.); رَصَن 'stacked/packed' 'in a row'. Cp: resen, rezen, ressen. (Gen.10:12)

Ludim; lûḏîm; لُضهم ، لُض ام 'fold and press-them/the' 'crush them together' 'crush together-the'; لُتهم ، لُت ام 'crumple/press and crumple-them/the' 'crumpled-them/the' 'pressed and crumpled-them/the'—the action performed when washing clothes by pressing and crumpling a garment or garments against each other to cause the soap substance (natural substances used in the past) and the garments to rub against each other, or when mixing substances/ingredients together. Cp: ludhhum, ludh-um. luthum, lut-hum/um. (Gen.10:13)

Anamim; ʿănāmîm; نَانَامهم ، نَانَام ام 'put to sleep-them/the' also euphemism for 'sex' 'had sex with-them/the'; غانَامهم ، غانَام ام 'made great profit/made lots-them/the' 'their goats' 'goats-the'. Cp: aanaamhum, aanaam-um, ghaanaamhum, ghaanaam-um (Gen.10:13).

Lehabim; lĕhābîm; لَهابهم ، لَهاب ام ، ليهاب هم ، ليهاب ام 'it burnt-them/the' (as in burning sensation not flame) 'their flames' 'flames-the' 'to/will give-them/the' 'he will give them/the away' 'what if he gives them away/what if he gives away the'. Cp: lehaabhum, lehaab-um, leihaab-hum, leihaab-um. (Gen.10:13)

Naphtuhim; naptuḥîm; نَفتُحهم ، نَفتُح ام 'we open-them' 'we open-the'. Cp: naphtuḥ-hum, naphtuḥ-um. (Gen.10:13)

Pathrusim; paṯrusîm; بَفرُصهم ، بفرُص ام 'I will separate-them' 'I will separate-the' 'I will split open-them/the'. Cp: baphruss-hum, baphruss-um. (Gen.10:14)

Casluhim; kasluḥîm; كَصلُح هم ، كَصلُح ام 'try make amends between-them' 'try/go ahead fix-them' 'try/go ahead make amends between-the' 'try fix-the'. Cp: kassluḥhum, kassluḥ-um. (Gen.10:14)

Philistim; pĕlištîm; فَلِسط هم ، فَلِسط ام ، فِلِسطام ، فيلِسط هم ، فيلِسط ام ، فيلِسطام 'squash/flatten-them/the' 'two (or more) squashed/flattened'; فَلِشط هم ، فَلِشط ام ، فَلِشطام ، فيلِشط هم ، فيلِشط ام ، فيلِشطام 'in their coast' 'in the coast-them/the' 'in coasts/in two (or more) coasts' 'between coasts/between two (or more) coasts' 'then tear-them/the' 'in two (or more) torn' 'between two (or more) torn'; فَلِزت هم ، فَلِزت ام ، فَلِزتام ، فيلِزت هم ، فيلِزت ام ، فيلِزتام 'so cut/slice/kill-them/the' 'so throw/flit/flick into narrow space/hole-them/the' 'in the sliced/cut open/killed' 'between two (or more) sliced/cut open/killed'; فَلِزط هم ، فَلِزط ام ، فَلِزطام ، فيلِزط هم ، فيلِزط ام ، فيلِزطام 'so slide/poke/squeeze through-them/the' 'so run/dash quickly-them/the' 'in the dashing/sliding/poking/squeezing' 'between two (or more) slides/pokes/squeezes/dashes/'. Cp: phelisṭ-hum, phelisṭ-um, phelisṭam, pheilisṭ-hum, pheilisṭ-um, pheilisṭam, phelishṭ-hum, phelishṭ-um, phelishṭam, pheilishṭ-hum, pheilishṭ-um, pheilishṭam, phelizt-hum, phelizt-um, pheliztam, pheilizt-hum, pheilizt-um, pheiliztam, phelizṭ-hum, phelizṭ-um, phelizṭam, pheilizṭ-hum, pheilizṭ-um, pheilizṭam. (Gen.10:14)

Caphtorim; kaptôrîm; قَفطُرهم ، قفطُرام 'fold-them/the'; كَفطُرهم ، كَفطُرام 'go ahead/try-break fast-them/the' (give food to break the fast); كَبتُرهم ، كَبتُرام 'go ahead/try-cut short/snap/shorten-them/the'. qaphtor-hum, qaphṭor-um, kaphṭor-hum, kaphṭor-um, kabtor-hum, kabtor-um. (Gen.10:14)

Sidon; ṣîḏôn; صيدُن ، صيدون 'fish' 'to fish' 'block/to block' 'of blocking'; زيدُن ، زيدون 'give(s) extra' 'leaves extra/remains' 'deceives'. Cp: sseedon, sseedoon, zeedon, zeedoon. (Gen.10:15)

Heth; ḥeṯ; حَط 'to land/place/set down' 'left some' 'left behind/left it' 'let it be/left it alone'; حَث 'to border/fringe/keep within border/encourage'. Cp: ḥaṭ, ḥaf. (Gen.10:15)

Jebusite; yĕḇûs; يَبُس ، ييبُس 'dry/dried' 'stiff/stiffened'; جَبُس ، جيبُس 'stiffen/stiffens when dry/thick and cloying'; خَبُص ، خيبُص 'poked finger into' 'poked into' 'poked finger into anus' (usually has sexual and/or offensive meaning as it is when a man pokes his finger into another man's anus (above clothing) as a joke/prank; and to anything non-sexually poked; can also mean to unhygienically stick fingers into food or something which needs to remain clean or not be fingered) 'make a mess'. Cp: yebus, yeibus, gebus, geibus, khebuss, kheibuss. (Gen.10:16)

Amorite; 'ĕmōrî; نيموري ، نُموري 'a tiny sign/signal/hint/tiny piece or indication of something' 'tiny trace(of something)/barely visible' 'being/it' 'an order' 'my business/my things/my matters/concerns me'; عيموري ، عُموري 'a builder' 'my age/long life/long time'; both words are in the meaning 'my' as in possession or 'of' as in characteristic/adjective. Cp: amooree, eimooree, 'amooree, 'eimooree. (Gen.10:16)

Girgasite; girgāšî; جِرجآشي 'with/of/my frills' (grgsh/grgaash/جرجش/جِرجاش as in frills or folds sewed on garments); 'coarse flour/powder'. Cp: girgaashee. (Gen.10:16)

Hivite; ḥiwwî; حِوّي 'of stay/staying' (it is in form which gives the word the characteristic of the main word) 'contained/contained it'. Cp: ḥiwwee. (Gen.10:17)

Arkite; ʿarqî; عَرقي 'my vein' 'of vein' 'my sweat' 'of sweat' 'my root' 'of root'. Cp: 'arqee. (Gen.10:17)

Sinite; sînî; سيني ، سِني 'to be straight' 'in straight direction' 'in my direction' 'opposite me/facing me' 'direct' 'let go/left it' 'left it for while/long time'. Cp: sinee, seenee. (Gen.10:17)

Arvadite; 'arwad; عَروَض 'stood widthways/obstructed' 'objected against'; عَروَد 'wobbled' (head or object carried on head). Cp: 'arwadh, 'arwad. (Gen.10:18)

Zemarite; ṣĕmārî; زيمآري ، زَمآري 'of playing pipe' 'my playing pipe'; سيمآري ، سَمآري 'staying up/awake' 'fictional night/late night time stories' 'telling late/night time stories' (called samaara). Cp: zemaaree, zeimaaree; semaaree, seimaaree. (Gen.10:18)

Hamathite; ḥămāṯ; حيمآض ، حَمآض 'soured'; حيمآط ، حَمآط 'flakes that come off grain' 'tickling/scratching feeling in throat'. Cp: hamaadh, haimaadh, hamaaṭ, haimaaṭ. (Gen.10:18)

Gaza; ʿazzâ, Gáza; غآزّا/ه ، غَزّا/ه 'a blunt or deep pain/squeezing pain' 'it gave him deep/blunt pain' 'a deep resonating sound' (if made by person as if coming deep from the belly) ; جآزّا/ه ، جَزّا/ه 'to cut crop/grass' 'he cut it' 'cut to pieces' 'pieces' 'rewarded' 'he rewarded him' 'his retribution' 'allowed' 'he allowed it'; عآزّا/ه ، عَزّ/ه 'cherished/pride/proud' 'cherished him/his pride' 'lifted/raised (in status)' 'raised him' 'gave his condolences/respects/consoled bereaved'. Cp: ghazza(h), ghaazza(h); gazza(h), gaazza(h), 'azza(h), 'aazza(h). (Gen.10:19)

Sodom; sĕḏōm; سيدوم ، سَدوم 'black soot' the powdery soot that accumulates above a primitive oven, and cooking fireplace. Cp: sedoom, seidoom. (Gen.10:19)

Gomorrah; ʿămōrâ; غيمورا/ه ، غَمورا/ه 'to be buried/submerged under' 'buried/submerged it/him/them' 'were covered with face or headveil' 'their head/face/mouth covered' 'head/face veils' 'were muffled' 'spoke with face/mouth covered' 'stifled/were stifled-saw/water/dreamt'; جيمورا/ه ، جَمورا/ه 'hot coal' 'his hot coals'. Cp: ghamoora(h), ghaimoora(h), gamoora(h), gaimoora(h). (Gen.10:19)

Admah; 'aḏmâ; عَدمه ، عَدما 'scarce/became scarce' 'his paucity' 'non-existence' 'his nothingness'; عَظما ، عَظمه 'a bone' 'bony' 'his/its bone'. Cp: 'adma, 'admah, 'adhma, 'adhmah. (Gen.10:19)

Zeboim; ṣĕḇō'îm; سيبؤام ، سَبؤام ، سيبؤهم ، سَبؤهم 'they swore at them' 'they swore at the' 'they captured-them/the' 'they left/let go-them/the'; صيبؤام ، صَبؤام ، صيبؤهم ، صَبؤهم 'they injured/struck-them/the' 'they afflicted-them/the' 'they poured into/poured onto-them/the'; زَبؤهم ، زيبؤهم ، زَبؤام ، زيبؤام 'they penetrated them with penis' 'they penised-the'. Cp: seboo-hum, seiboo-hum, seboo-um, seiboo-um, sseboo-hum, sseiboo-hum, sseboo-um, sseiboo-um zeboo-hum, zeiboo-hum, zeboo-um, zeiboo-um. (Gen.10:19)

Lasha; lešaʿ; لَسَع 'stung/to sting'; لَشَئ 'fall apart/fell apart' 'why?/for what'. Cp: lasa', lasha (Gen.10:19)

To suit the narrative of the story where Ham means 'worried', Noah curses Canaan which means 'without hope', when the borders of Canaan are mentioned they too are given names with dark meanings: Sidon (fish/hunted), Sodom (soot), Gomorrah (hot coals, submerged, stifled), Gaza (a pain, to be cut down), Admah (a bone, scarcity), Lasha (stung, fall apart). In the Biblical stories most of these cities are destroyed or its inhabitants punished either by God or attacked and uprooted by others—the creators of these stories gave purposefully created names to relay the meanings with the narrative.

Elam; ʿêlām; عيلآم 'made marks/signals' 'taught' 'will blame' 'knew/found out'; نيلآم 'in pain' 'blamed'. Cp: 'eylaam, eylaam. (Gen.10:22)

Asshur; 'aššûr; نَشّر ، نَشّور 'gestured/to signal'; نَزّر ، نَزّور 'visit/the visit' 'the pilgrimage' 'squeeze' 'the tight/tightened/squeezed' 'the false oath'. Cp: a-shoor, a-shur, a-zzoor, a-zzur. (Gen.10:22)

Arphaxad; 'arpaḵšāḏ; عَربَك زآد 'your fucking/copulation has increased' 'he fucked you more'; عَرَفك زآد 'your smell/scent has increased/become stronger' 'your reputation/fame/knowledge of you has increased' 'your understanding knowledge has increased'. Cp: 'arbak-zaad, 'arphak-zaad. (Gen.10:22)

Lud; lûḏ; لوض ، لُض 'to fold or press together hard' 'burning sensation'; لوت ، لُت 'crumple/press and crumple' 'crumpled' 'pressed and crumpled'—e.g. the action performed when washing clothes by pressing and crumpling a garment or garments against each other to cause the soap substance and the garments to rub against each other, or when mixing substances/ingredients together. Cp: loodh, ludh, loot, lut. (Gen.10:22)

Aram; 'ărām; عَرآم ، عيرآم 'wilderness/uninhabited place (where it's easy to get lost)' 'to abandon something or someone in the wild' 'a tree called 'aram/fetched wood of 'aram tree'; نَرآم ، نيرآم 'see-the/I see the' 'penis-the/insult with 'penis-the'' 'to throw/to do with throwing' 'killed/the killed/the killer' 'thrown, strewn or located over a vast distance/over different areas' 'vast/distant/covering wide or many different areas'. Cp: 'araam, 'airaam, a-raam, air-aam, airaam. (Gen.10:22)

Uz; 'ûṣ; عوز 'to need' (help or something material) 'to need support' 'to support(with help, money, food, clothing(i.e. take care of material needs); عُز 'cherish/pride' 'raise(in status)'; نوز ، نُز 'push out/ooze'; عوص ، عُص 'twisted/bent/crooked' 'twist/bend' 'cruel/stuck' 'disobeyed/disobedient'. Cp: 'ooz, 'oz, ooz, oz, 'ooss, 'oss. (Gen.10:23)

Hul; ḥûl; حُل 'to remove clothes/undress' 'shed (leaves/hair/skin)' 'circumcise' 'shed blood' 'purify/cleanse' 'declare purified/permissible' 'make edible/touchable' 'beaten severely/beaten until skin peeled off' 'replace/replaced' 'sweet/sweetened'; حول 'to go around in circles' 'cock-eyed/cross-eyed' 'around/surround'. Cp: ḥol, ḥool. (Gen.10:23)

Gether; Heb. geṯer; جَثَر 'to dust off or shake something out of garment/fabric'. Cp: gefer. (Gen.10:23)

Mash; maš; ماش ، مَش 'to walk/walked' 'leave/left' or a response in the negative (no/not). Cp: mash, maash. (Gen.10:23)

Salah; šelaḥ; šĕlâ; صَلَح ، صيلح 'happened' 'fixed/was fixed' 'mediated/reconciliated'; صيلا ، صيله 'rock/stone' 'his rock/stone' 'reached/connected' 'arrived' 'arrived him/it' 'reached him/it' 'connected it' 'reached him/publicly apologised'; سَلَح ، سيلح 'had diarrhoea/defecated'; سيلا ، سيله 'a river from rain' 'leaked/flowed' 'asked/questioned' 'comforted/entertained/distracted'. Cp: sselaḥ, sseylaḥ, sseyla, sseylah, selaḥ, seylaḥ, seyla, seylah. (Gen.10:24)

Eber; 'ēḇer; عيذَر 'shadowed over' 'excused'; عيبَر 'extremely disfigured (for a reason)' 'against nature' 'nature in reverse/nature reversed'; غيبَر 'became dusty' 'became cloudy (with dust)'. Cp: 'eyver, 'eyber, gheyber. (Gen.10:24)

Peleg; peleg; بَلَغ 'passed on message' 'first ejaculation/menstruation' 'reached puberty'; فَلَق 'split/divided'. The story tells us it is 'split/divided' out of the possibilities because in this part of the Bible the authors return to adding the stories where they want it to have the exact meaning of the word/name 'the name of one *was* Peleg; for in his day was the earth divided;' (Gen.10:25); before finishing the lists and gradually going back to the method of providing the background stories as according to how they were told. Cp: belegh, pheleq. (Gen.10:25)

Joktan; yoqṭān; يُقطآن 'to come and live (somewhere in particular)' 'to gather/cook/eat lentils'. Cp: yoqṭaan. (Gen.10:25)

Almodad; 'almôḏāḏ; ئَلموضآض ، ئَلمُضآض a specific type of tree/plant 'mouthwash/washing mouth'; ئَلمودآد ، ئَلمُدآد 'the lying down/stretching out' 'the pus' 'the touching' 'the handing/extending'. Cp: almoodhaadh, almodhaadh, almoodaad, almodaad. (Gen.10:26)

Sheleph; šelep; سَلَف 'a loan'; شَلَف 'will gather up' 'will wrap'. Cp: seleph, sheleph. (Gen.10:26)

Hazarmaveth; ḥăṣarmāwṯ; هَزَرماوط ، هيزَرماوط 'I will swallow a lot' 'look, swallows a lot' 'he will swallow a lot'; from word (zrmṭ/زرمط) which means to swallow and eat food quickly, or make sounds while eating/chewing; حَصَرماوت 'sorrow/regret/great sorrow and despair-death'; حَضَرماوت ، حيضَرماوت 'ripened-almost dead/a lot/intensely' 'arrived-almost dead' 'prepared-almost dead' which is similar to Yemen's Hadhramout which means 'arrived-death'. Cp: hazarmaawṭ, ḥassarmaawt, ḥadharmaawt. (Gen.10:26)

Jerah; yeraḥ; يَرَح 'he left/he leaves' 'he fanned/winded' 'he rests'; جَرَح 'came and left' 'wounded' 'came-rested'; يَرَخ 'he loosens' 'he is too lenient(allows to become immoral)'; جَرَخ 'came-loosened' 'came-loose/immoral/too lenient'. Cp: yeraḥ, geraḥ, yerakh, gerakh. (Gen.10:26)

Hadoram; hădōrām; هيبورآم ، هَبورآم 'here is pots/rolls/folds/rolled up' 'he will roll/fold'. To break it down so it can be understood how some compound names are made: (h/هـ) means 'here/will'; (ă/َ/يـ/ا) means 'is/he'; (dōrām/بُرآم) means 'pots/folds/rolls'; هيضورآم ، هَضورآم 'I will harm-the' 'he will harm-the' 'here/see, harmed-the' (h/هـ) 'will/here/look/pay attention', (dōr/ضور) 'harm/create habit', (ām/آم) 'the'. Cp: habooraam, haibooraam, ha<u>dh</u>ooraam, hai<u>dh</u>ooraam. (Gen.10:27)

Uzal; 'ûzāl; نُزآل 'to be removed' 'was removed' 'is gone' (permanently removed or gone), 'went' 'disappeared'; نُذآل 'to be humiliated' 'is/was humiliated'; عُزآل 'are faraway'. Cp: uzaal, uvaal, 'uzaal. (Gen.10:27)

Diklah; diqlâ; دِخله ، دِخلا 'coming in/entering' 'they entered' 'his entrance/entering' 'his business/concerns him' 'brought him in'. Cp: di<u>kh</u>la, di<u>kh</u>lah. (Gen.10:27)

Obal; 'ôbāl; عُبآل 'fat sheep' 'rolling/shaking like fat sheep'; عُضآل 'sore/strained muscles' 'mouse/mice'; عُذآل 'disabled (physically)'. Cp: 'obaal, 'o<u>dh</u>aal, 'ovaal. (Gen.10:28)

Abimael; 'ăbîmā'ēl; نَبي/نُيبي ما نِل/ايل/آل 'father/my father-did not/what-the' 'refused-did not/what-the'; from words (abi/أبي) 'father/my father' 'refused', (ma/ما) 'what/did not', ('el/نِل/نيل/آل/ايل/آل) 'the'; عَبي/عيبي ما نَيل 'fill-what-the' 'pack-did not-the' 'shame-what-the' 'shame-did not-the' from words: (abi/عَبي/عيبي) 'pack/fill' 'shame/embarrass', (ma/ما) 'what/did not', ('el/نِل/نيل/آل/ايل/آل) 'the'. It may not make sense to read it as a sentence without the story, but when the Biblical stories begin to flesh out into more than just listing names it becomes very clear how these compound words were used to make the characters relevant to the story being told, and the character names were formed this way to entertain the audience and to allow the names to have more than one meaning where needed Cp: abee/aibee-maa-ill, 'abee/'aibee-maa-ill.(Gen.10:28)

Sheba; šĕbā'; šĕbā'; شَبآء 'young woman' 'swollen/rigid'; شيبآء 'old/is old' 'swollen/rigid' (with water, cold, blood, etc.); شيذآء ، شَذآء 'will harm'; شيبآع ، شَبآع 'have full stomach(plural)' 'satisfied(plural)' 'well-off' as in having plenty of food, money or other resources to satisfy basic needs. Cp: <u>sh</u>ebaa, <u>sh</u>eibaa, <u>sh</u>evaa, <u>sh</u>eivaa, <u>sh</u>ebaa', <u>sh</u>eibaa'. (Gen.10:28)

Ophir; 'ôpîr; أفير ، نُفير 'boiled' 'increased/multiplied'; نُوبير 'of/from beyond' 'I go beyond/pass' 'of good/piety' 'I am good towards'; عُثير ، عَثِر 'found' 'unable to walk(physical disability)' 'fell/tripped'. Cp: o-<u>ph</u>eer, o-beer, 'ofir, 'ofeer. (Gen.10:29)

Jobab; yôbāb; حُبآب 'kisses' 'love each other', units of fruit e.g., four tomatoes or peanuts would be 'four hoboob', 'spots/acne'; عُبآب 'overflowing water' 'water rushing like a river' 'floating in water', something swollen or risen with water, 'rotten and stinking'. Cp: ḥobaab, 'obaab. (Gen.10:29)

Mesha; mēšā'; ميشآء ، مي شآء 'walked' 'left/departed' 'take care of sheep/goats' 'shepherd' 'went along with/did not dispute' 'whatever he wanted/whatever he wants' 'water-wanted/water-he wanted'. Cp: mey<u>sh</u>aa, mey-<u>sh</u>aa. (Gen.10:30)

Sephar; sĕpār; سيفآر ، سَفآر '(a) journey/travel' 'he travelled' 'public immorality'. Cp: se<u>ph</u>aar, sey<u>ph</u>aar. (Gen.10:30)

The latter two names also show how compound words were used to create the Biblical stories: 'And their dwelling was far from Mesha, as though goes unto Sephar a mount of the east' (Gen.10:30). Mesha 'to walk' or 'leave'; Sephar 'a/to journey', both words are related and describe what is happening in the story.

Shinar as at (Gen.10:10); šin'ār; شِنئآر 'to go to a place aside/or cast aside' 'to change direction' (on a journey): 'as they journeyed from the east, that they found a place in the land of Shinar; and they dwelt there.'—the place name is the exact word used to describe what is happening in the story; شِنعآر 'will be disgraced'. Cp: <u>sh</u>in-aar, <u>sh</u>in'aar. (Gen.11:2)

Babel as at (Gen.10:10); bābel; بآدَل 'swapped/mixed/messed up' 'changed'. Change and mix up is what God did to the people who in the story were one in language and one as a people but he changed them to different languages and different peoples, so the city is named (by the author) according to what will happen: 'And the Lord said, Behold, the people *is* one, and they have all one language…let us go down and there confound their language, that they may not understand one another's speech. So the Lord scattered them abroad from thence upon the face of all the earth…Therefore is the name of it called Babel; because the Lord did there confound the language of all the earth: and from thence did the Lord scatter them abroad upon all the face of the earth.'. (Gen.11:1-9)

Peleg; as before means 'divided', the names of his sons are all related:

Reu; rĕʿû; رَئو ، رِيئ 'they saw' 'they dreamt' 'they narrated' 'they watered'; رَعو 'they shepherded'; ريعُ 'they watered/soaked/flooded'. Cp: ra-o, rei-o, r'o, rei'o. (Gen.11:19-21)

Serug; śĕrûg; سَروج ، سيرُج 'a light' 'shone a light' 'will shake' 'will wait'; شَروق ، شيرُق 'sunrise' 'sun rose/brightened/sun came through' 'mid-morning' 'day brightened'; سَروك ، سيرُك 'navel/belly button' 'your secret' 'pleased you' 'pleased' 'made you leave in early dark morning'; صَروك ، صيرُك 'knotted you/bundled you' 'ached you' 'blocked inside you/held within you' 'insisted on you' 'your bundle' 'your secret' 'your ache/aching'. Cp: seroog, seirug, <u>sh</u>erooq, <u>sh</u>eiroq, serook, seirok, <u>ss</u>erook, <u>ss</u>eirok. (Gen.11:21)

Nahor; nāḥôr; ناَهور ، ناَهُر 'daylight' 'flowed/ran like a river/rivered' 'of speaking cruelly/belittling'; ناَخور ، ناَخُر 'bored a hole through/hollow' 'snored' 'nostril'. Cp: naahoor, naahor, naa<u>kh</u>oor, naa<u>kh</u>or. (Gen.11:22)

So you have Peleg's three sons whose names read as: They saw Light/Sunrise Daylight. (Gen.11:19-22)

Terah; teraḥ; طَرَح 'set/place down' or 'lay down from tiredness/collapsed' 'sheet(linen)'; تَرَه 'see him/it' 'do you see him/it' 'she sees him/it'. Cp: ṭeraḥ, terah. (Gen.11:24)

Abram; 'abrām; نَبرآم 'pots' 'rolled up' 'rolls and folds/rolls/folds'. Cp: abraam. (Gen.11:27)

Haran; hārān; هآرآن '(two) wooden batons' (usually handles of tools); حآرآن 'feeling overheated' 'made fire'. Cp: haaraan, ḥaaraan. (Gen.11:27)

Lot; lôṭ; لُط ، لوط 'squeeze together' 'pressed and sagged' it means to squeeze something together or press against something firm, or become sagged from too much squeezing where it becomes (mulaṭlaṭ/مُلَطلَط). Cp: loṭ, looṭ. (Gen.11:27)

Ur of Chaldees; 'ûr; عُر 'wilderness/harsh faraway uninhabited place' 'abandoned/lost in harsh wilderness' 'naked'; Chaldees; Gk. Chaldaí; خَلدي means the 'sun/heat roasted' 'severely beat up' 'mole(s)/a mole' 'remembered forever' 'lived forever' (e.g. 'chalad my skin' خَلد جلدي means 'roasted/peeled my skin off', 'the sun has chaladatni' الشمش خلدتني means 'the sun has killed/roasted me'). (Gen.11:28) tells Haran died in Ur of Chaldees, therefore: Haran ('overheated') died in Ur ('the wilderness') of the Chaldees ('sun/heat roasted'). So he died from the unbearable heat/sun. Cp: 'ur, <u>kh</u>aldee. Heb.: kaśdîm; قَشط هم ، قَشط ام 'make/made crispy-them/the' 'scraped/dragged-them/the' from word قَشط to make bread crispy/toasty; it is also wordplay on: قَشدهم/ام 'boiled-them/the' 'beat/killed-them/the' (literally or figuratively), which also means to boil on intense heat for a long period of time when clarifying butter. Cp: qa<u>sh</u>ṭ-hum, qa<u>sh</u>ṭ-um, qa<u>sh</u>d-hum, qa<u>sh</u>d-um. Both the 'Hebrew' and 'Greek' (which are both Arabic) words have the exact same meaning: 'cooked on heat' and the 'Chaldee' in the same language means suffering/cooking from overheating under the sun. (Gen.11:28)

Daughters of Haran: Both daughters of Haran (Milcah, Iscah) are related to fertile land and fertility: Milcah; milkâ; مِلقَح 'pollen' or 'pollinated'. Cp: milqaḥ.

Iscah; yiskâ; is wordplay on both: يِسقا 'watered/be watered' (as in plants), and: يِزقح 'shoots of crop' 'sharp strike with stone' 'sharp strike/striking or shooting motion(e.g. dog urinating against object)'; it is the noun describing crops bursting out of the soil and while it is still young shoots, from the word زقح which this adverb is used in a number of ways in Arabic to describe different things which include a fast, sharp strike or shooting nature and also noun of young shoots of crop shooting up from the soil. Cp: yisqa, yizqaḥ.

These word-names are used in the story to contrast against Sarai's barrenness. Milcah and Iscah's fertile names are followed immediately by mentioning Sarai's infertility: 'And Abram and Nahor took them wives…and the name of Nahor's wife, Milcah, the daughter of Haran, the father of Milcah, and the father of Iscah. But Sarai was barren; she *had* no child.' (Gen.11:29-30)

Modern-day people may not find the Bible-names funny, not only because it has been misinterpreted into a religious narrative, but modern people will not find humour in what people millennia ago found hilarious. Even in this day, city people may not find the same amusement in what country/village people find entertaining. The Biblical stories made these words into names as a form of entertainment for the people telling and listening to these stories. To this day, in remote Yemen regions, wordplay, ditties made on people's names still elicit laughter out of rural people.

Sichem; šĕkem; شِكَم ، شيكَم 'pointy peaks' 'threaded/skewered' (on something sharp or thread(needle/stick) e.g. how flowers are made into garlands; fabrics sewn, kebabs skewered) 'complained about-the/them'; شِقَم

شيقَم ، 'pointy corners/a corner, tip or piece of something'; شيغم ، شِغَم 'an abdominal ache' 'shouted/screamed loud' (out of pain/fear). Cp: shekem, sheikem, sheqem, sheiqem, sheghem, sheighem. (Gen.12: 6)

Moreh; môreh; مُرَه 'bitter' 'passed' 'a dream/his dream' 'saw him/it'; 'bitter' relates to passing through Sichem 'abdominal aches' as myrrh (bitter) would be given to treat aches and 'passed' as they are passing through; 'a dream' 'saw him/it' as God appears to Abram (usually in a dream in the Bible) and so Abram saw him. Cp: moreh. (Gen.12:6)

Bethel; bêṯ-'ēl; بَت/بيت نَيل/نِل 'stay over-the': بَت/بات means to stay overnight, which Abram and family stay at Bethel; بَت/بيت can also mean 'daughter/girl' 'house' it could also mean 'you/he/she/it will(be)' when used as prefix to a verb meaning something could happen, or is happening (according to the verb, but in this case it is definitely about 'staying'. Cp bet-eyl/ill, beyt-eyl/ill. (Gen.12:8)

Hai; hāʿay, h'y; حاَئي ، حَي/حئي 'is alive' 'alive' 'healed' (from illness or wound)' 'still/staying' (stationary) 'is still/staying' 'is not moving' 'contained/containing'. It is 'still/staying' as Abram stays there for a while and it is connected to Bethel 'stay over-the'. Cp: ḥaa-ay, ḥay, ḥ-y. (Gen.12:8)

Jordan; yardēn; يَردين 'they come/are coming home', it implies when Lot and Abram decide to part ways and choose different lands to make home on. Cp: yardeyn. (Gen.13: 8-11)

Mamre; mamrē'; معمريى 'builder': Abram builds an altar there. Cp: m'mrey. (Gen.13:18)

Hebron; ḥeḇrôn; هَبرون ، هَبرُن 'they are doing good' 'will do good/piety towards' 'they/he will pass/go beyond' 'he/they will be innocent of' 'he/they do what is right'. From word (br/بر) which is usually used to describe someone doing good/piety towards God or parents, and means to pass as in physically pass by or get ahead of and also go beyond; in this instance it refers to them building an altar for the Lord (good/piety); خَبرون ، خَبرُن 'told them news/information' 'they told/informed/brought news' 'of news/information/of telling'. From word (khbr/خبر) 'news/told/spoke to/informed'; it refers to God informing Abraham that he will give him all the land he sees, and is the first place Abraham goes to after God tells him to walk through the land. Cp: habroon, habron, khabroon, khabron. (Gen.13:18)

The kings who do Abram wrong, by attacking Lot, are given names of which the compound words are negative or insulting and, as always, fit the role of the characters they serve:

Amraphel; 'amrāpel; نَمرعف ال ، نَمرع فَل 'the one with the nosebleed-the' 'the big nose-the' 'the evileyed-in the/said bad omen' (the latter means to be caused harm by an eye/envy) and as he is king of **Shinar** 'will be disgraced'—it fits the story as he will be defeated by Abram; it could also mean 'the one with the beautiful nose-the' but this has not been used in the story. Cp: amr'ph-el, amr'-phel. (Gen.14:1)

Arioch; 'aryōḵ; نَريوك 'I'll/they will show(ed) you' 'they watered you/will water you' 'your dream' and he is king of Ellasar; 'ellāsār; نَلّاسار 'he will not walk' 'may he not walk' which means 'may he be unsuccessful' (e.g. people say 'Allah la qaal' 'God did not say' means 'may it not happen'; 'laa satarak' 'may you not be covered' meaning may you be exposed in a lewd situation). Cp: aryook, ellaasaar. (Gen.14:1)

Chedorlaomer; kěḏôr-lāʿōmer; قيضُر لآعومَر 'disgusting-may he not rise/build' (also a curse for downfall) and he is king of **Elam** 'in pain'. Cp: qeidhor-laa-'oomer. (Gen.14:1)

Tidal; tiḏʿāl; تِضئال 'will be led astray' 'will be withered/shrunk'; تِذئال 'you will be humiliated' 'you will be diminished'. Cp: tidh-aal, tiv-aal. (Gen.14:1)

Bera; beraʿ; بَرَع 'outside' 'run like a gallop' used to describe four-legged animals galloping and also people when they make a lot of noise and movement while running in panic or a rush. And in the story, he ends up fleeing in defeat. He is king of **Sodom** 'black soot', The story mimics the meaning of the word-names: soot and ash are often scraped and taken away from the house to be dumped in a special pit. Bera of Sodom ends up: 'And the vale of Siddim was full of slimepits; and the kings of Sodom and Gomorrah fled, and fell there; and they that remained fled to the mountains.' Cp: bera' (Gen.14:2-10)

Birsha; biršaʿ; بِرصَع 'will pack crammed' 'will cram full' and is linked to: king of **Gomorrah** 'hot coals'—hot coals are usually piled in an oven, or crammed in a vessel from where they can be picked for various purposes. Cp: birssa'. (Gen.14:2-10)

Shinab; šin'āḇ; شِنئاَذ 'we will be harmed'; شِنعاَب 'we will be disgraced', and the rebelling kings are disgraced and harmed as they are not only defeat but also fall into slime pits. This name is connected to **Admah** 'scarcity/bone'. Cp: shin'aav, shin'aab. (Gen.14:2-10)

Shemeber; šem'ēḇer; شَم عيذَر/غيبَر 'smelled-dust cloud/shadowed'; سَم نَيبَر 'threaded needle(s)' 'threaded/named/told story/poisoned-he will go beyond/surpass/be good towards'; سَم عيبَر 'threaded/will lead/

follow-extremely disfigured (for a reason)' 'will lead/will follow-against nature' 'will lead/will follow-nature in reverse/nature reversed'. Cp: shem 'eyver/gheyber, sem-eyber, sem-'eyber. And he is king of Zeboiim; ṣĕḇō'îm; ṣĕḇōyîm; سيبؤهم ، سيبؤام ، سيبوي هم/ام 'they swore at them' 'they swore at the' 'they captured-them/the' 'they left/let go-them/the'; صيبؤهم ، صيبؤام ، صيبوي هم/ام 'they struck/wounded-them/the'; زيبؤهم ، زيبؤام ، زيبوي هم/ام 'they penetrated them with penis' 'they penetrated with penis-the' 'penis-them/the'. Cp: seiboo-hum, seiboo-um, seibooy-hum/um, sseiboo-hum, sseiboo-um, sseibooy-hum/um, zeiboo-hum, zeiboo-um, zeibooy-hum/um. (Gen.14:2-8)

Bela; bela'; بَلَع 'swallowed', بَلاً/بَلَى 'afflicted/an ailment/illness/suffering' 'soaked' and he is the fifth king out of five who will be defeated. Cp: bela', bela. (Gen.14:2-8)

Zoar; ṣō'ar; صُغَر/زُغَر ، صوغر/زوغر 'small' and also 'small' as in humiliated; شُعَر/سُعَر ، شوعَر/سوعَر 'will be disgraced' 'will become naked'; سُعَر ، سوعَر 'will be priced/price estimated' 'rabies/rabid'; زُعَر ، زوعَر 'roar/groan' 'roared/groaned' like an animal. Cp: ssoghar/zoghar, ssooghar/zooghar, sho'ar, so'ar, shoo'ar, soo'ar, so'ar, soo'ar, zo'ar, zoo'ar. (Gen.14:2-8)

Siddim; śiddîm; سِدّهم ، سِدّام 'the/their-truce/agreement/peace pact' from the word (sd/سد) which means to 'make peace with/get over a problem you have with someone'; it can also mean 'their dam/underground water dam', but in accordance with the story it is where the two sides met (five kings against four) and made an agreement to serve Chedorlaomer. Cp: sidd-hum, sidd-um. (Gen.14:3-4)

Rephaim; rĕpā'îm; رَبآئهم ، ريبآئهم 'he disciplined them/taught them a lesson' 'their god/master/parent/teacher/discipliner/grower/raiser' 'diluted and mixed them with water'. From the word (rb/رب) 'god/parent/teacher, etc.', to bring up children, whether by parents or a teacher, as 'disciplining' whether children or adults when they are behaving waywardly or 'to raise/grow', 'dilute and mix with water'. The word was chosen appropriately to suit the story as the Rephaim are being 'smote' and all the other 'peoples' have similar names describing their demise. Cp: rebaa-hum, reibaa-hum. (Gen.14:5)

Ashteroth Karnaim; 'aštĕrōṯ qarnayim; نَشطَرُط/نَشتيرُط قَرنَيهم ، قَرنَي ام 'their horns have been split' (the horns could be two or more) 'has been split-horns of the'. (shrṭ/شرط) is a tear that is split open lengthways or a 'condition/term', شَرَط (sharaṭ) is someone/something splitting something open by tearing, اشطرط (ishṭaraṭ) is when something splits (a tear appears) of its own accord or places conditions. It is where Rephaim were smote. عَشتَرُت/عَشتيرُت قَرنَيهم ، قَرنَي ام 'raised its/her tail-their horns/horns of the' 'made their horns lift/rise' ('ashteroth/raised its/her tail' describes a cow lifting her tail to be copulated or to excrete). Cp. ashṭaroṭ/ashteiroṭ qarnayhum, ashṭaroṭ/ashteiroṭ qarnay-um,'ashtarot/'ashteirot qarnayhum, 'ashtarot/'ashteirot qarnay-um. (Gen.14:5)

Zuzim; zûzim; زوزهم ، زوزام 'drive and squeeze-them/the' (into specific place/direction) and to suit the story the name place has been given 'Ham' worried—it reads as 'drive and squeeze them in worried'. Cp: zooz-hum, zooz-im. (Gen.14:5)

Emim; 'êmîm; ئيم هم/ام '(make)river-them' 'thread the (needles)' 'thread them' 'lead them through'; from (ym/im/iyim/يم) can mean 'river, sea or natural body of water' 'lead/lead through/lead ahead/follow through/thread needle'; and it is used the same as in this story to mean make them like a river (suggests something causing a flood). Cp: eym-hum/um. So they smote 'Emims in' Shaveh Kiriathaim; šāwēh qiryāṯayim; سآبيح قِرياتَيهم 'swam their villages', (sbh/سبح) 'swam/swimming/flooded/pool of water' (qrya/قرية) 'village'. This is the pattern of the whole Bible: words/compound words are made up to give the people and place names the exact role/activity in the story. Cp: saabeyḥ qiryaatay-hum (Gen.14:5)

Horite; ḥōrî; حوري ، حُري 'ploughed' from word حُر which means to plough the soil, 'was puzzled/in predicament/indecisive/did not know what to do'; it gives the form of the word makes the 'ploughing' being done to or by the people. It could also be wordplay on هوري ، هُري 'chase away with words/cruelty'; خوري ، خُري 'chased away with violence/made flee' 'run away or fall in haste/fear' 'lowed(like cow)' 'collapsed'. Cp: ḥooree, ḥoree, hooree, horee, khooree, khoree. (Gen.14:6)

They were in Seir; śē'îr; سيعير 'will be gloated over/at' or 'will be borrowed'; سيئير 'walked/left/sent off' 'went along(physically or agreed with/in talk)' 'will be penised'. 'gloated' fits the story. Cp: sey'eer, sey-eer. (Gen.14:6)

El-paran; 'êl pā'rān; ئِل/ئيل فآئرآن 'the fugitives/runaways' 'they did flee' and it refers to a pair fleeing, and ئِل/ئيل بآئرآن 'those who passed by/went beyond' 'the good/pious' 'they did go beyond' 'they were good/pious towards' and both meanings is in the form of speaking about two doing this action. Both meanings fit as they refer to people being displaced by conflict. Cp: ill/eyl-phaa-raan, ill/eyl-baa-raan. (Gen.14:6)

En-misphat; 'ên mišpāṭ; عين مِشباط 'look, a strap/switch/a belting' 'look, thrown/swiped'; ('ên/عين) the word for 'eye' also means 'look/pay attention', it could also be 'spring' so it could be 'spring of strap/belting or throwing'; (shbṭ/شَبَط) is to 'whip/strike with switch' 'lattice(with rope)' and also to throw something with a quick, short whipping motion. The negative 'look, a belting/throwing' fits the story and other names in the same line and those preceding it. Cp: 'eyn-mishbaaṭ. (Gen.14:7)

Kadesh; qādēš; كَادِش ، كَآديش 'falls like a heap' 'falls is thrown to the ground with a loud sound' 'pile/piles' (things on the ground) 'piled'; قَادِش ، قَآديش 'led/of being led' 'led/pimped' and the latter can mean leading an animal by a rope (usually to get somewhere specific or being led to slaughter) or a person led around like an animal, it is the same word used to describe a 'middle person/pimp' usually a female who mediates between two lovers and is called such because she is misleading the female lover to ruination of reputation and her life. This word fits too with the kings being led into battle, and with the smiting and people being destroyed, falling into pits, driven out of their land. Cp: kaadeysh, kaadesh, qaadeysh, qaadesh. (Gen.14:7)

Amalekites; 'ămālēqî, 'ămālēq; عَمَآليقي/ عيمآليقي ، عَمَآليق/ عيمآليق 'is/will/over/what—thrown(down)(which can also mean killed or died)/found' from (mlq/ملق) 'thrown down/away/to a specific place' 'found'; and can be broken down further: ('ă/'/عـ) 'will/over' (maa/مـ/ما) 'what' 'did not' 'water' (lq/لق) 'throw/thrown/find/found'; نَمَآليقي/ نيمآليقي ، نَمَآليق/ نيمآليق 'led/was led/was followed-thrown down/found' 'what did he find' 'river-found/thrown down' 'river-found/down'. Cp: 'amaaleyqee, 'aimaaleyqee,'amaaleyq, 'aimaaleyq, amaaleyqee, aimaaleyqee, amaaleyq, aimaaleyq. (Gen.14:7)

Amorites take on a nuance here: 'a builder' represents something high like a building so it can be thrown down as in the meaning of Kadesh and Amalekites and more specifically: Hazezon-tamar; ḥaṣāṣōn tāmār; is wordplay on: حَصيصون طامار 'buried with stones'; حَزيزون دامار 'corner/drive-destruction'; from words (Hazez/ḥṣṣ/حصحص) 'stones/pebbles', (ṭmr/طمر) means to rain over/cover/bury with stones or soil; the second meaning: حَزَزون دامار 'corner/drive-destruction' from words (Hazez/ḥṣ/حز) 'corner/cram/drive', (dmr/دمر) 'destroy'. Cp: hassaissoon-ṭaamaar, hazaizoon-daamaar. All the names in this line are to describe cornering, throwing down and destroying, the word-names chosen to enhance the story being told. (Gen.14:7)

'Mamre the Amorite' reinforces Amorite has been used as builder as it reads 'builder the builder' (see Mamre (Gen.13:18)). Eshcol; 'eškōl; نَشقُل ، نَشقول 'hang up (from a ring or rope attached to ceiling/wall)' it is how people in rural areas (without refrigerators) store various foods out of the way of insects, animals and also to allow it to be cooled/dried by the air. The same word is used to describe the 'twine/belts(used to hang anything up)', to 'raise a leg', to 'hang something from rope/straps'. Cp: eshqol, eshqool. In building, various kinds of rope is used to hang things from and to raise materials while working (the name is given to the brother whose name is 'builder from the builder'. (Gen.14:13)

Aner; 'ānēr; عآنير ، ئآنير 'will lighten/brighten/show' 'light/shine/brighten/show' made up of ('ā/ئا/عا) 'will/is' and (nēr/نير) 'brighten/lighten/show' ('nēr' can also mean 'fire' and other words not used here) from word (nr/noor/نر/نور) 'see/show/light/shine/brighten'; both (nwwr/nyyr/نوِّر ، نيِّر) can mean to apply the substance called 'noora' (whitewash) to the walls of the house to paint it white to brighten the rooms. It is the last step in finishing a house, he is the last of three brothers mentioned who all have names regarding building activities, but he also takes part in defeating the aggressors and saving Lot which contains the meaning 'will show' (as in a threat). Cp: 'aaneyr, a-aaneyr. (Gen.14:13)

Dan; dān; دآن 'bowed/bent/facing the ground/with face on ground/lowered/low/guilted/made guilty/found guilty', it is used here as where the kings are first defeated so they are lowered in might and reputation, and these kings are guilty of wrong-doing. Cp: daan. (Gen.14:14)

Hobah; ḥôḇâ; هوبا/هوبه ، هُبا/هُبه 'to come down on/swoop down on' whether in fighting or just arriving suddenly and/or in large numbers, also when a toddler, child or an object is playfully thrown upwards and caught; حوبا/حوبه ، حُبا/حُبه 'stayed it/him/them' 'stayed with it/him/them' 'made them stay/still' 'contained it/him/it-with' 'crawled/are crawling'. It is what is described happening as Abram and his men attack the kings, they also return the kidnapped Lot, people and goods stay with the correct people. Cp. hooba, hoobah, hoba, hobah, ḥooba, ḥoobah, ḥoba, ḥobah. (Gen.14:15)

Damascus; dammeśeq; is wordplay on: تَمَّزَق which means 'tore/ripped up' and also 'spat/spat a lot'; تَمَّصَق 'sucked/sucked a lot' 'sucked at his teeth'. In this line it means tore them up and spat them out (in defeating the kings). Cp, tammezeq, tammesseq. (Gen.14:15)

Melchizedek has a lot of wordplay, not all the combinations I present will have been used by the authors in the narration, but many have been used: malkî-ṣeḏeq; مَلكي صَدَق 'what is wrong/what is the matter-believed/honest/friend' 'my possession/belongs to me/I own-believed/honest/friend'. Being the 'priest of the most high God' he would be considered an honest.

مَلكي زَدَك 'what is wrong/what is the matter-gave you extra' 'what is wrong/what is the matter-your extra/your remains/leftovers' 'what is wrong/what is the matter-deceived you' 'my possession/belongs to me/I own-gave you extra' 'my possession/belongs to me/I own-your extra/your remains/leftovers' 'my possession/belongs to me/I own-deceived you'. Abram seems to be offended and shows he is an honest person, not only by stating he will keep nothing that is not his, but also by handing over everything which belongs to king of Sodom while keeping what is his and his three companions'. It is portrayed in Melchizedek giving Abram and the people bread and wine, and blessing them gives them even more.

مَلكي صَدَك 'what is wrong/what is the matter-blocked you/prevented you' 'what is wrong/what is the matter-fished you/your fish' 'my possession/belongs to me/I own-blocked you/prevented you' 'my possession/belongs to me/I own-fished you/your fish'. It shows the topic is about who owns what; as the king/high priest meet Abram on the way they have prevented him from continuing on his way home, but not in a hostile way, only to speak and offer food and drink.

مَلقي صَدَق 'throw(n)/cast-believed/honest/friend' 'met/connected-believed/honest/friend' 'did not meet/did not find/did not connect-believed/honest/friend'. As they are meeting Abram after he has killed ('thrown down' means to kill or slaughter) the kings and both he and the priest and Abram are described as being of the most-high God, it makes them both honest.

مَلقي زَدَك 'throw(n)/cast-gave you extra' 'met/connected-gave you extra' 'did not meet/did not find/did not connect-gave you extra' 'thrown(n)/cast-your extra/your remains/leftovers' 'met/connected-your extra/your remains/leftovers' 'did not meet/did not find/did not connect-your extra/your remains/leftovers' 'throw(n)/cast-deceived you' 'met/connected-deceived you' 'did not meet/did not find/did not connect-deceived you'. It is speaking about the spoils, most of which were originally taken away in battle either from other kings or from Abram and his people, and that these things are being discussed between the men.

مَلقي صَدَك 'throw(n) down-blocked you/prevented you' 'met/connected-blocked you/prevented you' 'did not meet/did not find/did not connect-blocked you/prevented you' 'throw(n) down-fished you/your fish' 'met/connected-fished you/your fish' 'did not meet/did not find/did not connect-fished you/your fish'. This is also a possible meaning for the word-name Melchizedek and still portrays that Abram has been met on the way and the king is trying to get something out of Abram.

مَلحي صَدَق 'is good-believed/honest/friend' 'nice/pretty-believed/honest/friend' 'has a beard-believed/honest/friend' 'is salted/salt-believed/honest/friend'; مَلحي زَدَك 'is good-gave you extra' 'nice/pretty-gave you extra' 'has a beard-gave you extra' 'is salted/salt-gave you extra' 'is good-your extra/your remains/leftovers' 'nice/pretty-your extra/your remains/leftovers' 'has a beard-your extra/your remains/leftovers' 'is salted/salt-your extra/your remains/leftovers' 'is good-deceived you' 'nice/pretty-deceived you' 'has a beard-deceived you' 'is salted/salt-deceived you'; مَلحي صَدَك 'is good-blocked you/prevented you' 'nice/pretty-blocked you/prevented you' 'has a beard-blocked you/prevented you' 'is salted/salt-blocked you/prevented you' 'is good-fished you/your fish' 'nice/pretty-fished you/your fish' 'has a beard-fished you/your fish' 'is salted/salt-fished you/your fish'.

These three possible word-name combinations which are from the word Melchizedek still portray that there is goodwill between the characters; the beard is the sign of honesty and the salt is exchanged by eating/sharing from another's food and drink which Melchizedek presents to Abram and this too creates a bond/pact of good/piety/honesty between its sharers; as explained in the other word-name meanings the conversation is about the spoils (goods and people) which a victorious Abram returns with after defeating the kings who initially stole them from others; it is also in Abram being honest and not keeping anything that was not originally or rightfully his and handing everything else back to king of Sodom.

مَلخع صَدَق 'roll it/him in slimy substance-believed/honest/friend'; مَلخع زَدَك 'roll it/him in slimy substance-gave you extra' 'roll it/him in slimy substance-your extra/your remains/leftovers' 'roll it/him in slimy substance-deceived you'; مَلخع صَدَك 'roll it/him in slimy substance-blocked you/prevented you' 'roll it/him in slimy substance-fished you/your fish'; and:

مَلخي صَدَق 'cover with slimy substance-believed/honest/friend'; مَلخي زَدَك 'cover with slimy substance-gave you extra' 'cover with slimy substance-your extra/your remains/leftovers' 'cover with slimy substance-deceived you'; مَلخي صَدَك 'cover with slimy substance-blocked you/prevented you' 'cover with slimy substance-fished you/your fish'.

These meanings are a direct reference to the kings who were killed and fell into the slime pits, and as they fell into it, they are covered by its slime and these kings and their people (the kings are killed) are prevented from returning home as they are taken away as spoils of battle. It portrays also the honest conduct of Abram in that he returns everything owned by king of Sodom although Abram has gained these extra resources (people and goods) through winning the battle, emphasising he is not deceiving anybody by refusing to take even a thread if it does not belong to him.

There is a lot of wordplay in the compound word 'Melchizedek', most are similar or repeated meanings but the nuances can be detected in the story being told in Gen.14.

Cp: malkee-ssedeq, malkee-zedek, malkee-ssedek, malqee-ssedeq, malqee-zedek, malqee-ssedek, malḥee-ssedeq, malḥee-zedek, malḥee-ssedek, malkh'-ssedeq, malkh'-zedek, malkh'-ssedek, malkhee-ssedeq, malkhee-zedek, malkhee-ssedek.

He is king of: Salem; šālēm; the word could be: سآليم 'greet/greeting' 'in peace/intact (unhurt/alive)' 'of mild/peaceful nature' 'delivered/received/handed over' 'ask the' 'flow/leak-the' 'flowed/leaked-river/sea' 'entertain/distract-the' 'comfort-the' 'survived/intact/whole-the' and again it is used to describe exactly what is happening in the story: Melchizedek meets Abram and his people in a peaceful way and comforts them with food and drink, he also gives Abram 'tithes of all' or Abram gives these tithes to Melchizedek; although the king of Sodom has been killed earlier in the chapter with the other four kings fighting against Chedorlaomer, he is mentioned alongside Melchizedek and/or there seems to be confusion maybe due to the work of an editor that Meclhizedek is the king of Salem and of Sodom due to additions of, or made to, verses 17-24; King of Sodom asks Abram for the people in exchange for giving Abram goods, Abram replies that he will return everything that is the king of Sodom's whole/intact to him; the king of Sodom has been mentioned alongside the king of Salem for a reason, so that the word-name 'Salem' given to Melchizedek can reflect its meanings of 'flow/leak-the' 'flowed/leaked-river/sea' as the king of Sodom character's climatic involvement is in a peace/subjugation agreement 'in the vale of Siddim, which is the salt sea' (one meaning of Siddim 'their dam/underground water dam') and where the battle between nine kings takes place—linking 'Melchizedek king of Salem' to 'flowing/leaking water'. The passage is about offering goods and asking for something in return, surviving, wholeness. Cp: saaleym. (Gen.14:18-24)

Shaveh; šāweh; شآوَه ، شآوِه 'chatted/had conversation' 'ewes'; سآوَه ، سآوِه 'did it' 'levelled it(to ground)/made it even' 'settled it(account or matter)/made it right/made it even'. All meanings (except 'ewes') are reflected: this king meets Abram at the valley of Shaveh and chats with him, they chat about what Abram did and what he will end up doing. The conversation is about Abram's victory over the kings then turns to the request made by King of Sodom that Abram give him all the people and everything; Abram makes clear he does not even want the most insignificant object such as a thread that does not belong to him so he will return everything to king of Sodom (and this includes Lot and the people going back to Sodom) and will only keep those he named as his companions. Therefore, Abram settles accounts and dealings with king of Sodom. Cp: shaaweh, saaweh. (Gen.14:17-24)

Eliezer; 'ĕlîʿezer; ئِلي/ئيلي عَزَر 'he who/the one who-is ugly/makes things ugly'; it could be word play also on ئِلي/ئيلي نَزَر 'he who/the one who-squeezes/tightens' 'he who/the one who-visits/pilgrimages', but it is not 'he who-helps' just because he is a servant as the word 'to help' is (waazar/wzr/وازَر/وزر). In this part of the story, it means 'he who/the one who is ugly/makes things ugly' as to point how unpleasant he is, he has been attributed to Damascus 'spitting a lot/sucking at his teeth' which is considered disgusting behaviour. Abram's words are in despair: 'And Abram said, Lord God, what wilt thou give me, seeing I go childless, and the steward of my house *is* this Eliezer of Damscus?' Not only is Abram worried he has no biological heir, but he is in disbelief and disgust when he says to God 'is this all I have, Eliezer of Damascus (he who is ugly-of spitting and sucking his teeth)?'—Abram's character cannot believe it and the choice of words indicate something unpleasant about Eliezer: 'and, lo, one born in my house is mine heir' indicating Abram's great distress that he will be succeeded by such an unpleasant heir. Cp: illee/eilee 'ezer, illee/eilee ezer. (Gen.15:1-4)

Kennites; qênî; قيني ، قِني 'sitting up straight/hold head up properly' 'sitting or standing up, perky' 'estimating/measuring liquid/topping up water(any liquid)' from word قن (same meaning), but qênî (the 'î'gives the described the attribute of the meaning as a characteristic or as an order. Cp: qeinee, qenee. (Gen.15:19)

Kenizzites; qĕnizzî; قَنِزّي ، قينِزّي 'to sit or stand perched on a rock/high place' 'to place something on a higher place or a rock'; كعنِزّي 'like female goats' 'try/go ahead-breed female goats'. Cp: qenizee, qeinizzee, k'nizee. (Gen.15:19)

Kadmonites; qadmōnî; قَدموني 'to come/appear first' 'to be ahead' 'presented'; or: كَظموني 'to suffocate' 'to stifle/make stuffy (the air/room)/to be humid'. Cp: qadmoonee, kadhmoonee. (Gen.15:19)

Perizzites; pĕrizzî; بَرزّي ، بيرِزّي 'bring forward/press on and push out' 'of bringing forward/pressing on and pushing out'; فِرصَّي ، فيرِصَّي 'split open/push out/emerge by pushing up or out/ divide by breaking or splitting' 'of splitting open/pushing out/emerging by pushing up or out/dividing by breaking or splitting'; فِرسّي ، فيرِسّي 'divide something into separate units' of dividing into small units' 'explain/explain in detail/make clear' 'of explaining/in detail/making clear'. Cp: barizee, beirizee, pharissee, pheirissee, pharissee, pheirissee. (Gen.15:20)

Hagar; hāgār; هاجَار 'abandoned/he abandoned' from words: (hg/هج) 'to leave (to somewhere else) in anger or for good' and the same meaning is (hgr/هجر) 'to leave for good (whether a place or relationship)/ abandonment'. So this character is given a compound word as a name which denotes her constant role in the story: when she is abused by Sarai, Hagar leaves; when Sarah insists—Abraham abandons Hagar in the wilderness; Hagar abandons Ishmael to die in the wilderness. Cp: haagaar. (Gen.16;21:10-21)

Shur; šûr; شور ، شَر 'discuss' it means talking and also listening, taking into consideration what others have to say before making a decision. It is the place name mentioned where Hagar discusses her situation with an angel and she takes God's advice; it is also mentioned again where Abraham tells the king of Gerar that Sarah is his sister: in the dream, Abimelech discusses Sarah's topic with God, he then discusses the same with his people. Although in both cases Hagar, Abraham, Abimelech are not in Shur, but the place name is brought up to reflect what is happening in the story: discussions. Cp: shoor, shur. (Gen.16:7-16;20)

Ishmael; yišmāʿē'l; يِسماعي ئل/ال 'He/She listens to-the', although all other 'el' ('the') ending names are transliterated: 'ēl, but here the word has been spelled to allow it to be understood as both 'he' and 'she' are hearing: the (y) means masculine is hearing by making it (yišmāʿ) 'he hears' يِسماع and the (ē) allows it to be (išmāʿē) 'listen to' اسماعي ordering a female to listen. Even with only ('l) it still reads as 'the' (whether ('l), ('ēl) ئل/ال/ئيل/ايل it all still reads and means 'the'). This has allowed Ishmael to mean 'hears/listen to-the' as God hears Hagar and Hagar listens to God: Not only '...and shalt call his name Ishmael; because the Lord hath heard thy affliction' but she is also being told to listen to God through the angel telling her what God wants her to do. Cp: yismaa'ey-el. (Gen.16:9-12)

Beer lahai-roi; bĕ'ēr laḥay rō'î; بَئير لَهي روي 'good (treatment) towards/to who saw her' 'good treatment towards who looked at her' meaning she worshipped/thanked/behaved piously towards God who saw her (he looked upon her situation and promised her 'multiplication of seed'). Cp: be-eyr lahay roo-ee. 'beer/ bĕ'ēr' does not mean 'a well' in this instance, as judging by all the words of place/person names in the entirety of the Bible, a water well would be the word used by people who speak this exact same language and that is: 'ḥisee' حِسي. The word can be broken down: (bĕ'ēr/beer) 'good to/piety' from بر; (la) 'towards/to' لَ ; (ḥay/hai) 'her' هي; (rō'î/roi) 'saw' روي . Exactly as said in the Bible: 'And she called the name of the Lord that spake unto her, Thou God seest me: for she said, Have I also here looked after him that seeth me? Wherefore the well was called Beer-lahai-roi...' (Gen.16:13-14)

Bered; bered; بَرَد 'I'll return'. It could also mean 'cold' or 'hailstones' but in this line it is 'I'll return' which is what Hagar does: she returns to Abram and Sarai after running away. In remote rural Yemen when a wife is upset with her husband, she packs her things and leaves to her family home and stays there until the issue is sorted, it is called 'she has run away'; the process of her husband going to his in-laws to solve the issue and convincing her to return, and her going back to her marital home, is called (rd/رد) 'return' in all its proper tenses according to the sentence. The same is being described in Hagar's story and why the name of 'Bered' has been given. It is worth mentioning the reason every place where Abram and family stop is between 'Kadesh' and somewhere else (Kadesh and Bered, Kadesh and Shur), because they are travelling from place to place, they get tired: when a person throws him/herself onto the bed/floor from tiredness, it is said he/she kadesh, kadeshu, kadasht etc. (See meaning of Kadesh under Kadesh (above)), as well as the story leading the characters from place to place (qadesh). Cp: bered. (Gen:16:14)

Relationship between Sarah and Hagar

It is worth looking at the Biblical story of Sarah and Hagar and what it says about the relationship between them. Biblical scholars explain it as a result of 'ethnical' conflict, Sarah and Hagar's relationship strained as they try to fulfil God's promises. They see the stories a result of historical, legal, religious theories. The answer is much simpler and more realistic. The creators of these stories are describing the stressful relationship between real (ancient and modern) women who share a husband.

Once a husband decides to marry, whether with his first wife's consent or not, even where the 'first-wife' allows him or agrees to his second marriage (encourages it in rare cases), the serenity, or good-will, seldom lasts long. If you have lived in communities where polygamy is not illegal, you will find most men do not take on more than one wife; you will find it rare that men take second wives (unless widowed or divorced). In these same societies the overwhelming majority of women oppose her husband's wish to marry over her. But it will happen once a husband is intent on marrying another.

Like any woman across the world, the first-wife feels insulted, embarrassed socially, angered and ashamed, frustrated—more so if she is in a loving relationship with her husband—imagine when the husband brings home the bride how the first-wife would feel. Most first-wives embark on all-out hostility towards the other wife, long before the wedding, this only increases when the new-wife arrives in the home. Even those who encourage their husbands to marry, live to regret it 'And Sarai said to Abram, My wrong be upon thee: I have given my maid into thy bosom…' (Gen.16:15), whether the second-wife is cordial, rude or hostile towards the first-wife.

Some stepwives do get along when both are extremely good-natured and docile, although even good-natured and highly moral people become hostile towards one another when under such a stressing situation: seeing the husband in love with another woman. The hostilities arise/increase when, e.g., one becomes pregnant and not the other; or one provides a male heir but not the other; when one feels her husband's love for her has decreased or he has shown favouritism towards the other; these are some of the reasons how relationships become strained between step-wives.

Although some 'new' wives purposely provoke their stepwife, in cases where both get along like 'honey and butter', all it takes is one of the examples above to happen to sour the relationship. Then even innocent actions can be misunderstood, e.g., in Gen.16 when Hagar becomes pregnant then scorns Sarai '…her mistress was despised in her eyes…' which Sarai reiterates to Abram in complaint. Maybe the authors wanted to show Hagar did give Sarai reason to complain, or maybe (as in modern days) what was a benign action seemed scornful to Sarai because of psychological, emotional torment she would have felt (if they were real women) when Hagar became pregnant, leaving Sarai feeling more bitter over her barrenness, more threatened by Hagar's pregnancy.

A number of things threaten step-wives: loss or lessening of a husband's love for her; jealousy, distress, hurt which any woman would feel if the man she loves engages in love and physical relationship with another woman; women who want children but cannot conceive (in old and current times) do feel distress over this problem (even without a step-wife in the picture), it makes her feel abnormal/incomplete—these feelings increase when a step-wife conceives. Also, wives in polygamous marriages are always threatened by each other (the old and new wives) as they could be the reason the other is divorced; and a pregnancy, any offspring, or one with a male heir has more control over the husband and could determine the other's fate: whether she (and her children) get more or less money/food/goods or is divorced.

This puts them into a constant struggle, which differs only if one wife is hostile while the other is docile, or if both are hostile. When only one is hostile, e.g. causing the other wife problems through stubbornness, tricks, deceit (usually behind the husband's back) which includes complaining/lying to the husband about the other wife; in this case, the docile wife suffers from her peer's torment, but could also suffer further when the husband falls for the hostile wife's tricks or succumbs to her complaints. The docile wife can suffer from arguments with her husband, she is often 'sent away' (turned out of the marital house to live with her parents) until issues are resolved. The worst case is when the hostile wife convinces the husband to divorce the docile one.

When both (or more when applicable) step-wives are hostile or strong-willed, they can make life very difficult for each other, and for the husband, too, when things get out of hand. But what you usually see where this happens, is one wife dominates the husband more than the other. Having offspring or a male heir usually (but not necessarily) strengthens the mother/wife's position in the family. And although the husband may be infatuated or more loyal towards the 'new' wife, it is usually the wife's character which determines who dominates the marriage and family life, it is not always the new wife getting her way. There are many 'new' and 'first' wives either being in control or suffering in the marriage.

When Sarai complains to Abram, and abuses Hagar, it is just the bad side of human nature getting the better of her (or at least what the authors of this story have portrayed), and wanting to be rid of Hagar although Hagar conceiving should have made Sarai's wish that Abram to have offspring treat her kindly as it the purpose behind Sarai's idea of Abram marrying Hagar; but it is a story depicting exactly how women behave in such marriage circumstances—always one, or both, trying to get rid of the other. Even when Sarah has a male heir she still feels threatened by Hagar and will not rest until she convinces Abraham to abandon both Hagar and Ishmael in the wilderness.

In the story of Sarah and Hagar, Sarah is the dominant step-wife, Hagar is the docile suffering wife because Sarah has Abraham's ear. One step-wife's hostility/hatred towards another usually extends to the step-wife's children: the children of the docile step-wife are usually maltreated by the bullish step-wife, and, unfortunately, in some cases where the husband is weak or completely under the dominating wife's whims, he also gives preferential treatment to her children at the expense of being unfair towards the docile wife's children (although both are his offspring). When Sarah is upset with Ishmael laughing with Isaac, she gives Abraham orders to get rid of both Ishmael and Hagar, and he complies. (Gen.21:9-10) It can be seen again in the relationship between Leah and Rachel and their children. When Jacob is certain Esau will kill his wives and children, he divides them into four groups so the latter groups have more chance of escaping and surviving and especially the last group. He forwards Bilhah and Zilbah and their children first (the least who matter to him), followed by Leah (whom he does not love) and her children, and he keeps Rachel (the one he loves) and Joseph until last. This not only shows the relationships of step wives and their children were understood by the authors of these stories, but it also shows although later editors would rewrite and make the twelve sons of Jacob into a leading role in the Bible, in the original stories they were insignificant with the exception of Joseph who they had Jacob love. (Gen.31;32:1-7)

Abram, Abraham, like all names in the Bible stand for something in the story being told. The character begins as Abram, but is renamed Abraham (by God according to the story).

Abram; 'ab̲rām; نَبرآم 'pots' 'rolled up/rolled and folded' 'rolls/folds/rolls and folds'. Cp: abraam. 'rolled up' i.e. has been rolled up or is rolled up; from word (brm/برم); it is also in the word 'pot' بُرما/بُرمَه for the sides are thick and high to contain the contents of the pot. The word 'abrum' أبرُم means to roll-up something: ابرُمه ، ابرُميه (abrumoh, abrumeeh) 'roll it up', and is also used when one has a deed/title, the contract is always rolled up and folded after being written, or read and is stored rolled-up. In modern use ابرَم ، ابرموا (abram, abramoo) is used to say an agreement was signed or written, agreed to, concluded: ابرم الإتفاق ; this modern use of the word 'abram (signed/reached) the contract' stems from the ancient and continued practise of rolling up deeds and other documents (which people in remote villages still do), all from the old word برم 'rolled/folded'.

Before going on to explain why this would be the word chosen for Ab̲ram in the Bible, first we must understand the meaning of his second/new name: Abraḥam; 'ab̲rāhām; نَبرآح آم 'pull up/draw up-the' 'clear-the'. Cp: abraaḥ-aam; from the word (brḥ/abraḥ/برح/أبرح) which means to pull up water from a well and 'clear(ed)/spacious/level/tidied'. It specifically refers to the action of letting down the bailing pouch on a rope, and pulling it back up, using both hands. The same word also means to clear/remove something (barriḥ/بَرِّح) whether a room or land to clear it, make it clean, look nice and tidy, or make it more spacious.

Abram in the Bible is the word chosen as a name for this specific character in the story because it refers to the uncircumcised penis, the foreskin is rolled around the glans: Abram نَبرام—the character is named for the role he is given in the story; and when he is ordered to circumcise himself and others, his name is changed to Abraham نَبرآح آم . Think of the motion Abraham carries out with his hands when he is circumcising his son and the men; he is performing the same motion carried out to this very day where circumcision is still done by people without medical training or medical utensils. To circumcise, the foreskin has to be stretched and kept taut: he is stimulating an erection, then pulling at the foreskin, by pulling in his direction at it, using one hand after the other to stretch the foreskin, the same motion as pulling up the rope and bailing pouch out of the well, from which his character name has been made out of.

Also, there is the word 'to clear' 'make tidy', so Abraham is pulling at their foreskin 'abrḥ-um' نُبرح ام and is clearing/making clean the penis 'brrḥ-hm' برّحهم . There is a reason why the name was given and why it was changed specifically when circumcision was ordered—because both are related to the word/names and action given by the author to the character: Abram—rolled/rolls/folds/pots, Abraham—pulled and cleared of the rolls/folds (foreskin). (Gen.17:5) 'Neither shall thy name anymore be called Abram, but thy name shall be Abraham;' Abram = uncircumcised, Abraham = circumcised.

There is the verse where God says '...walk before me, and be thou perfect.' just before telling him he needs to be circumcised. (Gen.17:1). In remote villages where the people know nothing of the Torah/Bible, when they talk about a new-born baby to be circumcised on the seventh or eighth day, or after he is circumcised, they say he is to be (ḥallil/حلِّل) purified/shed or stripped off/sweetened (and the word also means to shed: skin, leaves, hair, etc.), his (the baby's) penis will look 'maleeḥ' مَلِيح 'nice/pretty/good', it matters more to them that it looks aesthetically pleasing than it is religious ritual; the word (mlḥ/ملح) 'pretty/good' is also connected to the word (ḥl/حل) also used to mean 'circumcise/circumcised' and the request from God to Abraham is to make something 'not clean', clean—in real life it means to make something already pure 'sweeter/nicer/better'; something 'not pure' into 'pure' and that is the basis of the word (ḥll/حلل) and the act and word 'circumcise' just as it is to slaughter meat makes it pure enough to be eaten (ḥalaal/حلال), but it also makes the meat sweeter, better tasting. Both the ḥl/حل (i.e. the purifying and sweetening) of circumcision, and the slaughtering of meat for food come from removing excess blood, the excess skin/tissue from the penis is erectile tissue, i.e. would be filled with blood when erect—this excess is removed from the circumcised penis just as excess blood is removed from the slaughtered animal (whether you call it 'kosher/peeled/shed' or 'ḥalaal'). All these meanings and words (which do not differ in the meaning and idea behind circumcision) are reflected in Gen.17, where circumcision is mandatory and whoever is not circumcised is 'impure' in body and soul and cannot be part of God (in the story).

(Gen.17:10) 'This is my covenant, which ye shall keep, between me and you and thy seed after thee; Every man child among you shall be circumcised. And ye shall circumcise the flesh of your foreskin; and it shall be a token of the covenant betwixt me and you.' Which puts the importance of the meanings of the name Abram (rolled up (foreskin)) and Abraham (pull at the foreskin, clear them, make them perfect) at the heart of the covenant (contract) between God Abraham and his people.

Abram's wife is introduced as Sarai, before being changed to Sarah. Sarai; śārāy; صارآي is word play on: 'continue to insist' and also 'knot (it)' 'tie bundle' from the word (śr/صر) 'knot' and also means 'hold within' as the word is used to describe knots, a constipated stomach or knotted feeling in abdomen, to keep a secret or information, it is also used to describe tying a bundle in a small scarf or any fabric—the word (m<u>ss</u>r/ma<u>ss</u>ar/مصر) means small scarf and is what women usually tie things into a bundle in, be it personal affects, grain, papers, any kind of goods/objects; small objects or small amounts of grain, powder are tied into a corner of the scarf like a knot. In the story, she is first introduced as being infertile. In rural regions of Yemen, when women pray for other women who are infertile or have not become pregnant for a long time, they ask God to 'untie her knot'. Her name denotes her infertility, being 'knotted' on the inside and unable to conceive; how she and Abram withhold that she is his wife when he presents her as his sister (twice); it also implies her character role as an insistent person: she convinces Abram to marry Hagar in order to have offspring, she also insists Hagar is scorning her. Cp: <u>ss</u>aaraay.

When her name is changed to Sarah; śārâ; صارا ، صاره 'she is insistent/insisting' 'she is withholding' 'she is knotted/knotting' 'she has tied into a bundle/knot', it still means 'insistent' but in the absolute, and 'withholding', but the 'knotted' infertile meanings now extend to others such as the wife and maidservants of Abimelech when he takes Sarah and they are unable to have children until the truth is exposed and Abraham prays for them '...and God healed Abimelech, and his wife, and his maidservants; and they bare *children*. For the Lord had fast closed up all the wombs of the house of Abimelech, because of Sarah Abraham's wife.'; it makes her name and character more powerful as both her character and the word go from Sarai (continue to insist/repeat/nag) to Sarah (insistent): what she says—goes: when God exposes that she laughed at his news that she would have a child, she insists that she did not; she insists Abram gets rid of Ishmael and Hagar and that she does not want Ishmael to be heir with Isaac—and she gets her way. Cp: <u>ss</u>aara, <u>ss</u>aarah. (Gen.11:29-30; 12:11-19; 16:1-6; 17:15-16; 18:10-15; 20; 21:9-12)

Isaac; yiṣḥāq; يزحآق 'he pulls up water little by little' (during drought) 'swipes/drags water'. It is similar to Abraham's word meaning. 'Isaac' means to pull or swipe/drag water in small amounts. During normal times the action of pulling up water from a well is 'abrah' أبرَح, when there is drought and the wells dry up, water only comes up in small amounts in the bailing pouch, the process of bailing up water during drought is called (izḥaq/إزحَق) from word (zḥq/زحق). The word applies not only to pulling up little water during drought, but also in everyday use: moving something liquid from a solid surface to a bowl is 'zhq', a male actioner would be said 'yizḥaq' a female 'tizḥaq'. If tomatoes or cheese have been made into a dip on a stone grinder (or even water from cleaning the grinder), the liquid is moved from the stone slab to the bowl by using the side of the hand/palm to swipe/drag it into the bowl and that is called 'zhq/yizhaq/tizhaq', the same applies to moving/removing any liquid from one surface to another. In modern Arabic and in cities, although they use blenders, the Yemeni dips made from vegetables and spices is called 'zaḥaaweeq/zḥwq' زَحاويق even if the city-folk do not know the etymology of the word (in rural areas where the word 'yizḥaq' is used for the motion/action/process in making it, the dip itself actually has a different noun). An example of exactly what the motion 'Isaac' means is how window squeegees swiping/dragging away all the liquid no matter how small an amount. Cp: yizḥaaq.

Isaac is the product of Sarah who is old and barren and Abraham who is very old, as the story points out repeatedly. When Sarah is said to no longer menstruate, it alludes she is dried up like a well in drought and confirmed by the name given to her son who comes out of this dry well: 'Now Abraham and Sarah were old and well stricken in age; and it ceased to be with Sarah after the manner of women.' 'Then Abraham fell upon his face, and laughed, and said in his heart, Shall a *child* be born unto him that is an hundred years old? and shall Sarah, that is ninety years old bear…And God said, Sarah thy wife shall bear thee a son indeed; and thou shalt call his name Isaac…' (Gen.17:15-19; 18:9-14; 21:1-7)

Lot, as earlier in Genesis, still means: lôṭ; لُطّ ، لوط 'squeeze together'; it means to squeeze something together, or press against something firm, or become sagged from too much squeezing. In the Biblical story Lot lived among people where men have sex with men (a sin in the Bible). In the story, it precisely means men pressing against buttocks during anal sexual intercourse, and is what Sodom and Gomorrah are punished for. Lot, when he tries to persuade his compatriots to leave the angel-men alone and to have sex with his daughters instead, and in an attempt to physically block them from entering, Lot himself is raped as in 'lot': 'And they called unto Lot, and said unto him, *Where are* the men which came into thee this night? bring them out unto us that we may know them. And Lot went out at the door unto them, and shut the door after him. And said, I pray you, brethren, do not so wickedly. Behold now, I have two daughters which have not known man; let me, I pray you, bring them out unto you and do ye to them as *is* good in your eyes…And they said stand back. And they said *again*, This one *fellow* came in to sojourn, and he will needs be a judge: now will we deal worse with thee, than with them. And they pressed sore upon the man, *even* Lot, and came near to break the door.' (Gen. 19:1-10)

Zoar the same as at (Gen.14:2-8); has been used for specific meanings from earlier in Genesis: 'small' as in size. Lot says 'Behold now, this city *is* near to flee unto, and it *is* a little one: Oh, let me escape thither, (*is* it not a little one?) and my soul shall live'; but also for 'will disgrace/become naked' as when the place-name 'Zoar' is repeated it is narrated that Lot fears to stay there and leaves it to live in a cave, and the narration immediately has his daughters cause him great disgrace by intoxicating him to have sex with them. (Gen.14:2; 19:20)

Sodom 'black soot' and **Gomorrah** 'hot coals' as earlier in Genesis (see Sodom, Gomorrah (Gen.10:19). The story tells of the inhabitants being punished (for homosexuality) with exactly the meaning of the words given as their names: 'Then the Lord rained upon Sodom and Gomorrah brimstone and fire…' (Gen.19:24)

Moab; mô'āḇ; مُعآب 'of shame/rude/in obscenity' as he is a result of incest (and Moabites; 'of shame/rudeness/obscenity'). Cp: mo'aab. (Gen.19:31-38)

Ben-ammi; ben-'ammî; بَن عمّي 'son/child of-blinded/drank' 'we will make/give drink' 'we will make blind' 'my cousin' 'son/child of my uncle' as they gave him so much to drink, he was intoxicated and did not realise/see what he and they did (have sex): '…and he perceived not when she lay down, nor when she arose.'. (ben) 'son/child of/we will make/we will', (ammi) (drank/drink/blinded/uncle). It is also wordplay on 'we will make/give drink' which is how they intoxicate him: (b) 'will' (en) 'do/make/is' ('ammi) give/make drink/etc. Cp: ben-'ammee. It is also wordplay on the word 'cousin' 'ben-'ammi' as if read together 'moab, ben-ammi/ ben-'ammi, moab' they make a sentence which sums up the story: 'Of shame, my cousin' 'My cousin, of shame' so all their children would be the product of this incest and fit the names' meaning, but also it plays on the theme that Lot is both father and uncle of his daughters' children. (Ammon; 'ammôn; عمّون 'blinded/to blind' 'drank'. Cp: 'ammoon. (Gen.19:33-38)

Abimelech; 'ăḇîmeleḵ; is word play on: عَبي مَلَح 'pack/fill it nicely/well' as he does end up giving Sarah and Abraham a lot '…sheep, and oxen, and menservants, and womenservants…'; it is also نَبي مَلَك 'father/refused-what is wrong with you/what is with you' as he is unable to impregnate his wife and maids because it is not only said that God healed the women, but begins with '…and God healed Abimelech…' before that God says to him '…for I also withheld thee from sinning against me: therefore suffered I thee not to touch her' so Abimelech was made impotent and unable to have sex with a married woman (without knowing she was married) or his own women. 'melech' مَلَك ، مالك 'what?' 'what is wrong/what is with you?' is what one person says to the other, when the other has done something wrong, strange or confusing and it is meant to get an explanation as to what caused the offending person to do so. It is what his wife's/maids' reaction would be when he is unable to have sex with them. It is exactly the conversation between Abimelech and Abraham with the former reproaching the latter with many versions of the same phrase of 'melech/what is with you?': 'Then Abimelech called Abraham, and said unto him, What hast thou done unto us? and what have I offended thee, that thou hast brought on me and on my kingdom a great sin?' 'What sawest thou, that thou hast done this thing?'. Cp: 'abee meleḥ, abee melek. (Gen.20)

Abimelech is the king of Gerar; gĕrār; جَرآر ، جيرآر 'a pulling/drawing' 'pulled/drew a lot' from word (ger/جر) 'pull/draw' and it applies to physically pulling something, but can also be used figuratively, such as 'pulling/drawing' a person into wrongdoing (deceiving/encouraging), or coaxing/knowing how to make a person speak (whether the person is reluctant or just needs prompting), it is also used to describe wayward personalities and their behaviour (as well as 'dying' as the soul is believed to be struggling as it is pulling out of the body). The way the conversation goes between Abimelech and Abraham fulfils the word 'Gerar' for the story, as Abimelech needs to ask many times before Abraham opens up. Cp: geraar, geiraar. (Gen.20)

Paran; pā'rān; بآئرآن 'good/pious/they are good/pious' 'passed by/went beyond', combining 'pious/good' بر with 'passing/going beyond' بر, it is in the plural of two people and refers to both Hagar and Ishmael being good and passing out of sight because Sarah and Abraham have banished them. Cp: baa-raan. (Gen.21:12-21)

Phichol; pîḵōl; فيحول 'so he/it will solve/resolve' 'clever/he is clever' and denotes the issue between Abimelech and Abraham will be solved. From words (phḥl/فحل) 'clever' 'a stud/a sexually virile animal'; and (ph/ف) 'so/will', (ee/ي) 'he/it', (ḥl/حل) 'solve/resolve'. Cp: pheeḥool. (Gen.21:22-32)

Beer-sheba; bĕ'ēr šeḇa'; it could be بَئير سَبَع 'good/piety-seven': the 'good/piety' is a pact 'but according to the kindness that I have done unto thee, thou shalt do unto me, and to the land wherein thou hast sojourned.' (Gen.21:23). It could be a misinterpretation of šeḇa'/sheba as 'seven' because although Abraham does make a point of handing seven ewes directly into the hand of Abimelech although he has already handed over sheep and oxen to Abimelech, the author makes a point about them being ewes and about a discussion between Abraham and Abimelech: Abraham 'set seven ewe lambs of the flock by themselves' and 'What mean these seven ewe lambs which thou hast set by themselves?' 'And he said, For these seven ewe lambs shalt though take of my hand, that they may be a witness unto me, that I have digged this well. Wherefore he called that place Beer-sheba; because they sware both of them.' The name is more likely 'good/piety-ewes' 'Beer shewha' بَئير شوها/شوهَئ as 'shewha' means 'ewe' and also means 'chat/talk/conversation' and the emphasis is not on 'seven' in the story because seven as a number has appeared repeatedly in other stories but has not been added to the name where the number is directly mentioned. It could be wordplay on both 'seven' and 'ewe/conversation', but the emphasis in the story was put on naming the pact (agreement to be good to each other) after the ewes: shewha. Cp: be-eyr seba', be-eyr-shewha. (Gen.21:30-31)

Moriah; mōrîyâ; موريبا ، موريبه 'to show-him' 'to see-him' 'a dream/his dream/dreamt of him/it'; they all stem from the same/related word: (r/ر) 'see', (wr/ور) 'show/teach/explain', (ry/raayey/rayey/ري/رايْي/رَيي) 'dream' and all these different meanings and forms of the word are covered by the root word (r/ر) 'see/show/teach/dream' and they are all about 'seeing and showing'. In an earlier story God speaks to Abram through a vision, he speaks to Abimelech through a dream, later in Genesis, God will speak to Jacob in a dream; as the story begins, verse 3 tells us 'Abraham rose up early in the morning' it could be the initial story said he spoke to him in a dream. 'God did tempt Abraham' is God testing Abraham to show his belief/loyalty to God; God tells him i.e. shows him exactly where he has to go and what to do; Abraham shows God (him) he is willing to do as ordered no matter how difficult the request; God sees him willing to sacrifice his son; God shows him a ram to sacrifice instead of Isaac; Abraham sees the ram. And all this is to happen in the place name of a word which means 'show-him/see-him' Moriah. Cp: mooreeya, mooreeyah.

'...God did tempt Abraham...get thee into the land of Moriah...and Abraham lifted up his eyes, and saw the place afar off...seeing thou hast not withheld thy son, thine only son from me...And Abraham lifted up his eyes, and looked, and behold behind him a ram...' (Gen.22:1-14)

Jehovah-jireh; Biblical scholars theorise the name 'Jehovah' to have been created in the 16th century by combining the consonant letters of 'YHWH' and the vowel letters of the name 'Adonai' as a substitute to create: Jehovah. This is utter nonsense. Whether spelled Jehova/yĕhōwāh or YHWH it is a word with a meaning in daily use in the original language: Jehova; yĕhōwāh, YHWH; يَحُوآه/ ييحُوآه ، يحوه/يحوا it all means 'he/it-stays/stayed/contains/contained' and 'he/it-stayed/stilled it/contained it' from the word (ḥai/ḥo/حي/حو) both mean 'stay/still' and are used in all their different forms of plural, masculine, feminine, past, present etc in daily language (it can also mean 'heal/cured' but has not been used this way in this story), and it is equivalent to 'Hawaa' (see Eve). Even in the repeated sounds people make towards animals such as cattle, to give orders while shepherding or driving them into somewhere specific or getting them to stand still, either of these two words (ḥai/ḥo/حو/حي) are repeated as sounds to get them to stop. Cp: yeḥoowaah, yeiḥoowaah, yḥwh, yḥwa.

Jehovah-jireh is a name made out of two compound words combined: Jehovah/YHWH 'he-stayed/stilled it' يحوه—and jireh; yir'eh; يرئه ، يراه 'he sees it': يحوه يرئه 'he stayed/stilled it-he sees it' and it describes the ram being stilled by God in the bush and Abraham seeing it. Cp: yḥwh-yirah. 'And Abraham lifted up his eyes, and looked, and behold behind him a ram caught in a thicket by his horns…And Abraham called the name of that place Jehovah-yireh: as it is said to this day, In the mount of the Lord it shall be seen.' This is another prime example how these place/people names in the Bible are not actual places nor people, but creations of storytellers and an early people's imagination. (Gen.22:13-14)

Huz; hûz, ḥûz; could be: حز/حوز '(to) hold in/gather/corner/cram' or هُز 'to shake/swing back and forth/rock' (such as baby in its cradle or a hanging container etc.). Cp: ḥuz, huz. (Gen.22:21)

Buz; bûz; بُز 'take/pick up/carry' and also 'breastfeed'. Cp: buz. There is a reason why they are pointing out Huz and Buz are brothers: an often-used phrase when talking about someone who takes things in a flurry, and maybe not necessarily that person's to take, is ('yahuz wayabuz' يهُز ويبُز 'he rocks and takes') and ('he ḥuz and he buz' يحُز ويبُز 'he corners and takes'). In the story, both words are related to actions/activities around babies, rocking and breastfeeding. (Gen.22:21)

Kemuel; qĕmû'ēl; قَمُ/قيمُ ئِل 'they awakened-the' 'they suffocated with bad smell-the' 'they stood-the' 'had an erection-the', they are still baby related words when a noise awakens a baby which has just been breast-fed (buz) then rocked to sleep (huz); the second meaning describes a bad odour that the person(s) who can smell it feels suffocation(figuratively). The word describes a stimulated, erect penis to make babies. All three meanings are in the form that the 'actioner' of the (kemu) part of the word are plural (û/و). Cp: qemu-ill, qeimu-ill. (Gen.22:21)

Chesed; keśed; حَسَد 'envy/envying'; قَشَد 'clarify butter' 'boil on heat for a long time' 'mow people down' as in kill them or leave them collapsed on the ground, can mean to react angrily and leave people in shock or humiliated, or how a contagious disease has left lots of people dead or unwell; قَصَد to intentionally do something or approach someone (in modern Arabic it now means to intend as the words meant). Cp: ḥesed, qe<u>sh</u>ed, qe<u>ss</u>ed. (Gen.22:22)

Hazo; ḥăzô; حَزُ ، حيزو 'they crammed/crowded/cornered'; هَزُ ، هيزو 'they shook/swung/rocked'. Cp: ḥazo, ḥaizo, hazo, haizo. (Gen.22:22)

Pildash; pildāš; بِلدعس 'by/with stepping on' 'by/with feet' 'by/with force/physical oppression'; بِلدآس 'with/by secretly bringing in and placing/planting' 'by/with planting/whispering bad ideas into another's head/causing enmity by planting bad ideas'. From words (bl/بل) 'with/by'; (d's/دعس) 'stepping on/walking over' which is from (md's/مدعس) 'foot'; (ds/دس) 'secretly bringing in/planting/creeping in/ physical things or planting bad ideas in others minds by whispering or deceiving'. Cp: bild's, bildaas. (Gen22:22)

Jidlaph; yid̲lap̄; يِدلَف 'hand-scooped/gathered'; جِدلف 'to tatter the edges' (usually of plants) or 'swear at a lot'. Cp: yidla<u>ph</u>, gidla<u>ph</u>. (Gen.22:22)

Bethuel; bĕt̲û'ēl; بتُ ئِل ، بيتُ ئِل 'they stayed over-the' 'girl/daughter of-the'; بَضُ ئِل ، بيضُ ئِل 'laid eggs-the' 'white/whitened-the' 'shine light-the' 'abluted-the'. Cp: betu-ill, beitu-ill, be<u>dh</u>u-ill, bei<u>dh</u>u-ill. (Gen.22:22)

Rebekah; rib̲qâ; رِبخا ، رِبخه 'a rest' 'a relief (from work/travel/problem)'; رِبكا ، رِبكه 'a confusion/misunderstanding/panic/fluster'; Cp: rib<u>kh</u>a, rib<u>kh</u>ah, ribka, ribkah. (Gen.22:23)

Reumah; rĕûmâ; رَوما ، رَومه ، ريُما ، ريُمه 'threw' saw water' 'threw around' 'at a long distance apart/covering a great distance' 'killed/injured him/it/were killed/injured' 'spoilt (rotted/stinking/bad taste)'. Cp: reuma, reumah, reiuma, reiumah. (Gen.22:24)

Tebah; teb̲aḥ; طَبَح 'lay prone' 'naked belly exposed from clothes' 'to smack bald/exposed skin with palm of hand'. Cp: ṭabaḥ. (Gen.22:24)

Gaham; gaḥam; جَحَم 'hot coals'; جَهَم 'bit (without breaking skin), 'came, worried'. Cp: gaḥam, gaham. (Gen.22:24)

Thahash; taḥaš; تَحَش 'she is cutting grass' 'sleeves/clothes pulled up/rolled up'; طَهَش a predatory animal called 'tahash', and 'lost his mind/insane (caused by fear)'; تَحَس 'she felt' Cp: taḥa<u>sh</u>, ṭaha<u>sh</u>, taḥas. (Gen.22:24)

Maachah; ma'ăḵâ; مَعي خه ، مَعي خا ، مَعَ خه ، مَعَ خا 'with his brother' 'I have a brother/with a brother' 'with his brother/I have his brother'; مَعيكه ، مَعيكا ، معكه ،مَعَكا 'with you' 'it is with you'. Cp: ma' akha, ma' akhah, ma'ai kha, ma'ai khah, ma'aka, ma'akah, ma'aika, ma'aikah. (Gen.22:24)

Kirjath-arba; qiryaṯ 'arba'; قِريَة نَربَع 'village-four/locked/secured'; there is nothing to support this being the name. It is more likely خِرجَة نَربَع 'came out/took out-four/locked/secured' as Abraham pays four hundred shekels for the burying place, and emphasis is made that the environment and land he has purchased as a burying place is made secure. Cp: qiryat arba', khirgat arba'. (Gen.23) '...the land is worth four hundred shekels of silver...and Abraham weighed...four hundred shekels of silver...and the field...and the cave...and all the trees...were made sure...'

Heth is used in the same meanings as earlier in Genesis: ḥeṯ; حَط 'to land/place/set down/left behind'; حَث 'to border/fringe/keep within border/encourage', the authors use the word 'heth' to mean 'set down' and 'encourage' as Abraham is looking to place his dead somewhere and he also encourages 'the children of Heth' to encourage Ephron to sell him a specific piece of land. (Gen.23).

Ephron; 'eprôn; عَثرون ، عثرُن 'to find' as Abraham is trying to find a burying place for Sarah and will find it with the character suitably-named Ephron; نَفرون ، نَفرُن 'to increase/multiply' as in profit as Ephron will make four hundred shekels of silver out of the deal. Cp: 'efroon, 'efron, ephroon, ephron. Efron (the seller) is the son of Zohar; ṣōḥar; صوخر 'he put under his command/service' 'made pliant' and like his paternal name indicates, Ephron first offers to give the land for Abraham to use as he pleases. Cp: ssookhar. (Gen.23)

Machpelah; maḵpēlâ; مَخبي له ، مَخبيلا ، مَخب يلا ، مَخب يله 'hidden for him' 'hiding place for him' 'is hidden for/is hidden for him' 'hiding place for her' and it is exactly as the story wants it to be and mean: 'And Sarah died...give me a possession of a burying place with you, that I may bury my dead out of my sight...If it be your mind that I should bury my dead out of my sight; hear me, and intreat for me to Ephron the son of Zohar, That he may give me the cave of Machpelah...for a possession of a burying place amongst you.' Even the mention of a cave instead of just burying is meant to be a hiding place, just as it is a hiding place for real people during conflict. Cp: makhbey lah, makhbey la, makhb eyla, makhb eylah (Gen.23)

Rebekah (Gen.22:23); the wordplay is on all meanings riḇqâ; ربخا/ربخه 'a rest' 'a relief from work/travel/problem'; ربكا/ربكه 'a confusion/misunderstanding/panic/fluster' can be seen in this character's role in the major stories she stars in. In real life when people or animals rest from work or travel, it is said رَبخا 'rebekhah' (from the word ربخ (rbkh)) and the same word is exclaimed when something is achieved/done quicker than usual or not needed to be done at all, and simultaneously means 'a relief' 'well, good it's done' 'I can rest' (as almost everything done in rural village life is hard (manual) work and involves crossing long distances and/or harsh terrain). When Abraham's servant 'rests' the first meaning is introduced, she gives him and his camels to drink bringing in the meaning of 'relief', she offers to allow him to lodge/rest in her father's house and her family agree also to accommodate him; both rest and relief (from travel) is emphasised as the story focuses on camels and people being fed and watered, washed and given a place to rest; it is the 'relief' and 'rest' that the servant feels because he has immediately found the perfect wife for Isaac and so he is relieved to have quickly accomplished his master's mission and he expresses this in the retelling of the whole story to Laban.

The 'confusion/fluster' meaning is introduced when Rebekah sees Isaac approaching and she comes down from the camel then covers herself with a veil, it will be further emphasised later in the story where her involvement is confusing her blind husband Isaac to bless Jacob instead of Esau. Cp: ribkha, ribka. (Gen.24) (**Lahai-roi** 'who saw her' from earlier compound word 'Beer lahai-roi; بَئير لَهي روي 'good (treatment) towards/to who saw her' and is used here as earlier but without 'Beer/good/piety', to denote Isaac sees her (Rebekah) Gen.24:62-63)

Ketura; qěṭûrâ; could be قَطره ، قَطرا ، قيطره، قيطرا 'a drop' 'drips' 'molten metal/or tar-like substance used to seal', but is more likely to be قَضُره ، قَضُرا ، قيضُره ، قيضُرا 'disgusting/she is disgusting' 'she/they felt disgusted/repulsed' 'disgusts' as the story has Abraham send her and her sons away as they do not mean as much to him as Isaac. Cp: qeṭurah, qeṭura, qedhurah, qedhura. (Gen.25:1)

Zimran; zimrān; ذِمرآن 'guilty' 'being insulted/blamed/humiliated/ostracised' زِمرآن 'pipe player'; سِمرآن 'dark-skinned' 'stays up all night' 'of telling night (or) staying up stories'. Cp: vimraan, zimraan, simraan. (Gen.25:2)

Jokshan; yoqšān; يوقشآن 'he has fits/seizures' 'he/it becomes stiff/toasty' 'he/it scrapes away/removes in one go' 'littered/covered in fibres/litter'; يوقصآن 'he/it/they become hard/cruel' 'he/they/it cut' 'he/they tell story'. Cp: yooqshaan, yooqssaan. (Gen:25:2)

Medan; mĕdān; مَدآن ، ميدآن 'guilty' 'lowered/bent/bowed' 'put hands into' 'reached out to/extended hands' 'handed/passed/stashed/hid/planted with no one noticing' 'put hands on something not his/theirs' 'went over/overstepped/'took liberties'' 'did underhanded behaviour(done secretly)' 'secreted in/planted' 'hid underneath something hastily' 'in debt'; مَضآن ، ميضآن 'passed by' 'completed' 'signed/made mark' and the actions are by two or more people. Cp: medaan, meidaan, medhaan, meidhaan. (Gen.25:2)

Midian; midyān; مِديآن 'loans to others/is debtor to others' 'of guilt/found guilty/bowed/lowered/bent' 'reaches out with hand/stretches hand' 'extends/offers something to another (with hand)' 'reaches into' 'reach for/stretch arm to reach for' 'hands/passes/stashes/hides/plants with no one noticing' 'of underhanded behaviour(done secretly)' 'of stowing or stashing in/planted' 'hides (something) underneath something hastily' 'puts hands on something not his/theirs' 'went over/overstepped/'took liberties''; مِضيآن 'passing by/is passing/moving on' 'completed' 'signing/making mark'. Cp: midyaan, midhyaan. (Gen.25:2)

Ishbak; yišbāq; يِسبآق 'he/it beats(faster)/gets ahead'; يِشبآق 'he/it raises/places leg over' 'places rag between legs'. Cp: yisbaaq, yishbaaq. (Gen.25:2)

Shuah; šûaḥ; شوَح 'cried out like a goat'; صوَه 'squealed/sqeeked' (like bird). Cp: shuaḥ, ssuah. (Gen.25:2)

Asshurim; 'ăššûrîm; نَآشُّر هم ، نَآشُّر ام 'is-gesturing/signalling-them' 'is-gesturing/signalling-the'; نآزُّر هم ، نآزُّر ام 'is visiting/will visit-them/the' 'their/the pilgrimage' 'is-squeezing-them/the' 'tightened/squeezed-them/the' 'make false oath-them/the'; عآشِّر هم ، عآشِّر ام 'live(d) among/with-them/the' 'the tenth of them/the' 'a lot of people/tribe-them/the'; عآسِّر هم ، عآسِّر ام 'make/made difficult for them/'. Cp: a-aashur-hum, a-aashur-um, a-aazzur-hum, a-aazzur-um, 'aashur-hum, 'aashur-um. 'aasur-hum, 'aasur-um. (Gen.25:3)

Letushim; lĕṭûšîm; لَطُس/ليطُس هم/ام 'stick/stuck to bottom/side-them/the'; لَطُش/ليطُش هم/ام 'snatched/rapped-them/the'. Cp: leṭus/leiṭus-hum, leṭus/leiṭus-um, leṭush/leiṭush-hum, leṭush/leiṭush-um. (Gen.25:3)

Leummim; lĕ'ummîm; لَئومّهم/لَئومّ ام ، ليئومّ هم/ام 'for their mother' 'to the mother of-the' 'gathered-them/the' 'blamed-them/the' 'their/the blame' combined with 'mother' as her name is derogatory so the story blames the mother for their being sent away. Cp: le-umm-hum, le-umm-um, lei-umm-hum, lei-umm-um. (Gen.25:3)

Ephah; 'êpâ; عيفا ، عيفه 'gone off food' 'gone off it' (usually describes a sick animal refusing to eat), 'boil/boiled' 'boil/boiled it'; نَيفا ، نَيفه 'an abomination(physically mutated or a demon)' 'his abomination'; نَيفا/نَفّا the sound made to express something smells bad or being disgusted or fed up with something/someone. Cp: 'eypha, 'eyphah, eypha, eyphah, eypha, epha. (Gen.25:4)

Epher; 'ēper; عيثَر 'found' 'disabled/unable to move'; نَيفَر 'it will increase' 'it will boil'. Cp: 'eyfar, eyphar. (Gen.25:4)

Hanoch; ḥănôk; حَنُق ، حينُق Exact same meanings as Enoch: 'upset and not eating or talking' when a person is upset and goes away, or stops eating and/or talking with others, or turns his back towards others because he/she is upset with them over something; it is also wordplay on هَنَح ، هينَح 'will cry out in distress (or loudly)'. Cp: ḥanoq, ḥainoq, hanoḥ, hainoḥ. (Gen.25:4)

Abida; 'ăbîdā'; نَبي/نَيبي ضآع 'my father is lost' 'refused/rejected-lost/is lost; نَبي/نَيبي دآع 'my father-called' 'refused/rejected-called/cursed/claimed'; عَبيداء ، عيبيداء 'worshipper/of worshipping' 'worshipped' 'servant' 'served'. Cp: abee/aibee-dhaa', abee/aibee-daa', 'abeedaa, 'aibeedaa. (Gen.25:4)

Eldaah; 'eldā'â; نَلدآعا/نَلدآعه 'the-peeping game' (a game played with toddlers, like peekaboo), 'the-peeking/glimpsing' 'the-curse' 'the-call' 'the claim' 'the one who called/cursed/made claim'; نَلضآعا/نَلضآعه 'the-lost' 'the one who lost it'. Cp: el-daa'a, el-daa'ah, el-dhaa'a, el-dhaa'ah. (Gen.25:4)

Nebajoth; nĕbāyōt, nĕbāyôt; نَبآجوث ، نَبآجُث ، نيبآجوث ، نيبآجُث 'we will/pierce and burst out' 'pierced and burst out' (suitable name for a firstborn in the way the stories name their characters) ; نَبآجوت ، نَبآجُت ، نيبآجوت ، نيبآجُت ''struck by throwing something (at the target)' 'we threw and struck it' 'she struck it'; نَبآغوت ، نَبآغُت ، نيبآغوت ، نيبآغُت 'we/she startled/scared/feared' 'we/she wanted' 'we/she became immoral' 'we/she sexually immoral' 'we/she prostituted'; نَبآعوت ، نَبآعُت ، نيبآعوت ، نيبآعُت 'leapt' 'she/it leapt'. Cp: nebaagoof, nebaagof, neibaagoof, neibaagof, nebaagoot, nebaagot, neibaagoot, neibaagot, nebaaghoot, nebaaghot, neibaaghoot, neibaaghot, nebaa'oot, nebaa'ot, neibaa'oot, neibaa'ot. (Gen.25:13)

Kedar; qēdār; قيدآر 'are able' 'pots used on fire'; قيضآر 'are disgusting'. Cp: qeydaar, qeydhaar. (Gen.25:13)

Adbeel; 'ădbĕ'ēl; عيضبي ئِل ، عَضب ئِل 'muscles deformed-the' 'caused the muscles to be deformed'; عيذبي ئِل ، عَذب ئِل 'shrivelled and withered' 'shrivelled/withered-the' 'caused to shrivel/with' 'tortured-the' 'sweet-the'. Cp: 'adhbe-ill, 'aidhbei-ill, 'avbe-ill, 'aivbei-ill (Gen.25:13)

Mibsam; mibśām; مِبصآم 'has/is closed lips' 'does not close his/its lips'. Cp: mibssaam. (Gen.25:13)

Mishma; mišmā'; مِسمآع 'listening' or 'does not hear'. Cp: mismaa'. (Gen.25:14)

Dumah; dûmâ; دوما/دومه 'last(s) long' 'shadowy figure(or something you can see but not tell what it is' 'spins/dizzy' 'bloody/bleeds' 'small hut/dome structure' but is probably 'spinning/dizziness' as many names in this list express physical ailments. Cp: duma, dumah. (Gen.25:14)

Massa; maśśā'; مَسّآء 'causes problems/provokes' 'fought/argued' 'possessed or causes possessions (demonic)' 'arrived at night'; مَصّآء 'sucked'; مَزّآء 'wrang/squeezed water out of'; مَسّآع 'skin peels off/causes skin to peel off' 'of walking/wandering/seeking', مَصّآع 'partially deaf/pretends not to hear'. Cp: massaa, massaa, mazzaa, massaa', massaa'. (Gen.25:14)

Hadar; if KJV transliteration correct: حَدَر 'came down/slopes down'; هَذَر 'talked' 'wasted'; ḥădad; حَدَد ، حيدَد 'determined borders' 'sharpened'; هَدَد ، هيدَد 'threatened' 'demolished'. Cp: ḥadar, hadar, ḥadad, ḥaidad, hadad, haidad. (Gen.25:15)

Tema; têmā'; ذيمآء 'extremities or skin falls/fell off'; ضيمآء 'quenching/quenched thirst/dryness' 'giving/gave to drink/watering' 'thirsty/shrivelling/dying for water'. Cp: vaymaa-a, dhayma-a. (Gen.25:15)

Jetur; yĕṭûr; ييطر ، يَطر 'flies away (as in runs away)/chases away)' 'he/it flies/flees' 'he/it causes to flee/banishes' 'spills liquid in a stream (body or other liquid)' 'spills liquid in a stream'; عيطر ، عَطر 'twisted/wrang/mangled/pressed oils out of' 'twists/mangles' 'perfume(d)'. Cp: yeṭur, yeiṭur, 'eṭur, 'eiṭur. (Gen.25:15)

Naphish; nāpîš; نآفيش 'to spray/scatter all over (a place/person)'; نآفيس 'plenty of room' 'to make bigger/wider/baggier/more spacious' 'releasing air/puncturing/wind passing' 'the same'; نآبيش 'dug up'; نآبيص 'fell of cliff/high place' 'pushed of cliff/high place' 'broke bits off/pinched bits off'; نآبهص 'rubbed/scraped off, hair or skin colour'. Cp: naapheesh, naaphees, naabeesh, naabeess, naabhss. (Gen.25:15)

Kedemah; qēdĕmâ; قيضَما/ قيضيما ، قيضَمه/ قيضيمه 'closed mouth on pretending to bite' 'closed mouth on it/him'; كيضَما ، كيضيما ، كيضَمه ، كيضيمه 'suffocated/stifled' 'suffocated/stifled him/it'; جيذيما ، جيذيمه'gecko' (believed to cause leprosy) 'leper' 'gave him leprosy' 'extremities/sides fell/falling off' 'caused extremities/sides to be tattered/fall off'; جيديما ، جيديمه'bit/took light bites' 'bit him/it' 'bitten'; قيديما ، قيديمه '(he/it/they)came forward/went forward/presented' 'served it' 'presented him/it'. Cp: qeydhema, qeydheima, qeydhemah, qeydheimah, keydhema, keydheima, keydhemah, keydheimah, geyveiyma, geyveiymah, geydeima, geydeimah, qeydeima, qeydeimah. (Gen.25:15)

Esau and Jacob

Padan-aram; paddan-'ărām; بَدّن عرآم/عيرآم 'went out/took out-wilderness/uninhabited place' 'went out/took out-abandoned something or someone in the wild' 'went out/took out-tree called 'aram/fetched wood of 'aram tree'; بَدّن نُرآم/نُيرآم 'went out/took out-to throw/to do with throwing/kill' 'went out-thrown/spread/covering vast area' 'went out-penis-the/insult with 'penis-the'' 'went-see-the/I see the' 'went out-thrown, strewn or located over a vast distance/over different areas' 'went out-vast/distant/covering wide or many different areas'. Cp: baddan-'araam/'airaam, baddan-a-raam, airaam, air-aam. (Gen.25:20)

The authors of the story have repeat information already recently supplied that Rebekah is the sister of Laban, daughter of Bethuel. Gen.25:20 they repeat it as: 'And Isaac was forty years old when he took Rebekah to wife, the daughter of Bethuel the Syrian of Padan-aram, the sister to Laban the Syrian.' They are setting the stage for what will happen with Isaac, Rebekah and their children: Bethuel here means to 'they stayed over-the' 'lay eggs-the' Rebekah will have twins; Padan-aram 'after/went out-into the wilderness': Isaac, Rebekah and Jacob will end up living in the wilderness in their following stories.

Esau; 'ēśāw; wordplay on: عيشآو; 'they fed supper' 'supper' and عيصآو 'they disobeyed/did wrong'. The latter is because Esau, Jacob and Rebekah all do wrong and disobey by selling his birth right and deceiving Isaac to get the blessing, note how the word-name is composed in the form of plural people feeding someone else supper, plural people disobeying. 'supper' because that is his main role in the story: he is the hunter who brings home the meat, Isaac loves him more because he loves eating Esau's catch and cooking. The whole story revolves around eating supper: Esau sells his birth right during hunger and wanting to eat food cooked by Jacob; Isaac is deceived by eating a meal he expects from Esau and unknowingly giving the blessing to Jacob. Both words (name) of 'supper' and 'disobedience' are the centre of the stories regarding Jacob and Esau. Cp: 'eyshaaw, 'eyssaaw. (Gen.25:25-34; 27:1-33).

If we can concentrate on when and why 'Esau' becomes 'Edom', the meaning of the word is clearly emphasised: Edom; 'ĕḏôm; نَيدُم ، نَدُم ، نَيدوم ، نَدوم here it means 'I am spinning/dizzy', and not 'bleeding/bloody/of blood' or 'lasts/lasts long' (which are meanings of the word 'edom' too), exactly as the story tells us: 'And Esau said to Jacob, Feed me, I pray thee, with that same red *pottage*; for I *am* faint: therefore was his name called Edom.' as people feeling faint or dizzy whether from hunger or not do feel a head spinning dizziness, and also linked to people believing the person who feels dizzy does not have enough blood in his/her body from lack of food. Cp: edoom, eidoom, edom, eidom. (Gen.25:30)

Jacob; ya'ăqōḇ; wordplay on: يَعيقوب ، يَعقوب 'he follows/comes after' 'he looks after/takes care of' it means babysitting a child or a house or taking care of household chores or to watch over/take care of anything left in your care while another person usually goes outside the house to fetch wood, water, crops, etc. The person staying at home is said to (a'qob/اعقب), a male (ya'qob/يعقب), a female (ta'qob/تعقب). Biblical scholars have become confused with the verse 'and his hand took hold on Esau's heel…' and the similar sounding but completely different word ('arqoob/عرقوب) which means 'ankle' while 'Jacob' is a different word with different spelling and pronunciation and actually means he came after his brother (in sequence); this also shows that if early local translators i.e. local Arabs of the Levant also gave the meaning related to 'heel' that they did not speak the original language of the Bible which is the Old Arabic of the Arabian Peninsula. Cp: ya'aqoob, ya'aiqoob. In addition to it being 'he came after' his brother and 'he looks after' the house and household chores 'And the boys grew: and Esau was a cunning hunter, a man of the field; and Jacob was a plain man, dwelling in tents.' (Gen.25:27), there is a second word which the authors of the Biblical story play on: يَعيكوب ، يَعكوب 'he forces open' 'he dislocates' 'he forces open and takes/usurps' it describes opening something in a fashion similar to using a crowbar to break a lock/chain and is usually done for theft or when a key is lost, or something is jammed; and this word-name is enacted by making Jacob's character take by force and deceit Esau's birth right and his father's blessing: Jacob forces Esau under duress of hunger and dizziness to give away his birth right, then more forcefully takes Esau's blessing by tricking Isaac that he is Esau and taking away what was not his (in the story) to take. i.e. usurp and the story has Esau say '…Is not he rightly named Jacob? for he hath supplanted me these two times: he took away my birthright, and, behold, now he hath taken away my blessing.'. Cp: ya'akoob, ya'aikoob (Gen.25:26-34; 27)

Esek; 'ēśeq; عيسَج 'they tugged/pulled/a struggle' from word ('sg/عسج) and it describes that Isaac's men and Gerar's men were shoving and tugging, pulling at each other (note: 'Gerar' means 'a pulling'), an altercation over the well which has been suitably named with the same action 'And the herdmen of Gerar did strive with Isaac's herdmen, saying, The water is ours: and he called the name of the well Esek; because they strove with him. Cp: 'eyseg. (Gen.26:20)

Sitnah; śiṭnâ; صِطنه ، صِطنا 'we clung/stuck to it' 'we swooped down on' from word (ssṭee/صطي) 'to stick to something quickly/swoop down/fall sharply'. It also describes how they fought to keep hold (stick to) onto this well 'And they digged another well, and strove for that also: and he called the name of it Sitnah.' In modern Arabic use, the old word of 'stick to/cling to' is now used in the form 'sṭw' سطو to describe robbing a bank or shop, but is based on the old meaning to stick to quickly/swoop down on. Cp: ssiṭna, ssiṭnah. (Gen.26:21)

Rehoboth the same as at (Gen.10:11); rĕḥōḇôṯ; رَحوبَة ، ريحوبُت 'she welcomed/made space' 'was wide/spacious' from word (rḥb/رحب) 'spacious/welcoming'. The story tells there was no fighting (the opposite of welcoming) over this well and '…the Lord hath made room for us…'. Cp: reḥoobot, reiḥoobot. (Gen.26:22)

In addition to **Phichol** whose name means 'clever' 'he/it will solve/resolve' and appears whenever there is a problem to resolve and make peace between major characters in the stories, there is also Ahuzzath; 'ăḥuzzaṯ; نَهو/نَيهو زّعط 'he-sent away/told to leave' from words: (ahu/أهو) 'he/he who', (z't/زعط) means to turn someone away or throw them out in an unfriendly way to make them feel unwelcome in a very clear manner. 'Ahuzzath' word-name reflects it is this character who is behind Isaac being sent away, for it is mentioned he is a friend of Abimelech—and a friend can advise, prompt or incite another friend to do something, or he can do it on their behalf. The meaning of this compound word is reflected in the story, Isaac says 'Wherefore come ye to me, seeing ye hate me, and have sent me away from you?' and in the line where Isaac gets to (z't) send them away '…and Isaac sent them away…'. **Abimelech** is first to allow the 'what is wrong with you' line of questioning just as before with Abraham, and then to mention the plenty, the feast (just as where this compound word is used). Cp: a-hu-zz'ṭ, aihu-zz'ṭ. (Gen.26:26-31)

Shebah; šib'â; سِبئَح 'swam/flooded/filled with water'; شِوئه 'ewes' 'chatted/had conversation' it is more wordplay on Beer-sheba (good/piety-seven/ewes) now meaning 'good/piety-swam/filled with water' 'good/piety-chatted/had conversation' as this part of the story shows us after Abimelech makes a pact of peace with Isaac 'And it came to pass the same day, that Isaac's servants came, and told him concerning the well which they had digged, and said unto him, We have found water. And he called it Shebah: therefore the name of the city is Beer-sheba unto this day.' Cp: sibaḥ, shiwah. (Gen.26:32-33)

The naming of Esau's wive's and family follows the same pattern of giving adversary kings/strangers insulting names. The authors of the stories emphasise what has been stated that these women 'Which were a grief of mind unto Isaac and to Rebekah.', by giving them derogatory compound word-names and derogatory patronyms so that the names read as an insult.

Judith; yĕhûḏîṯ, Ioudíth; يَجُديث/ييجوديث ، جودِث/جُديث 'he hacked/severed by hacking at' 'hacked/sever(ed) by hacking at' (with stone or any object, or biting with teeth) and usually describes how animals/insects eat and ruin the tops of plants, and also means to 'swear at someone until they are tattered' (to insult them with a foul rant'; and جودِث/جُديث 'a string/a thread' and the string is usually cut by biting at with teeth or hacking at it with the thread placed on a hard place and a small stone used to hammer it which is the first meaning of 'Judith'.

In this story 'Judith' is meant to show all the negative attributes of the name given to her supported by Rebekah and Isaac disliking her; when Esau brings a third wife in, although she is added to the first two wives, her name and 'Judith' imply Esau severed his relations with the first two wives whom his parents dislike. She is the daughter of Beeri; bĕ'ērî; بَئيرِي/بيئيري 'by my prick/penis' which is an oft-used insult denoting how little respect for the person or thing being spoken about. Her name reads 'insulted/tattered-by my prick'. This is how 'bad' or undesirable characters are given insulting names in the Biblical stories, and according to the stories they are invoked by discrimination; in this particular part it is Rebekah and Isaac's dislike of 'Hittites'. Cp: yegudeef, yegoodeef, goodiff, goodeef, be-eyree/bei-eyree, goodit/goodeet be-eyree/bei-eyree. (Gen.26:34)

Bashemath; bāšĕmaṯ; بآشَمَت ، بآشيمَت 'I will cause a scene/cause people to gloat' 'a disgrace (status/being)/with disgrace' 'an awful mess'; and she is daughter of Elon; 'ēlôn, 'êlôn; نَيلَن ، نَيلَن 'until'; عيلَن 'in the open/public' 'upon them/above them' so her name reads 'I will cause people to gloat-until' or 'a disgrace-in the open/upon them'. Cp: baashemat, baasheimat, eylon, eilon, 'eylon, 'eilon. (Gen.26:34)

Hittite; ḥittî; حِطّي 'leave some' 'left (it/him/her)/left behind' 'put it down' 'put load down' 'land it (on ground)' 'lowly' 'hit/struck/landed(where the target or anything hits/lands on a person/object' (it can also be all the given meanings with 'of' in front to give them attribute of given meaning). It is portrayed in these women being unwanted and undesirable by Isaac and Rebekah, they are deemed not suitable as wives for Esau, and it indicates they want Esau to leave them. Cp: ḥiṭṭee. (Gen.26:34)

When Esau takes note of his parent's displeasure of his current wives, he goes to find a wife who will please them in place of their resentment for his Hittite wives. The name given to this character is Mahalath; maḥălaṯ; مَحَلّة ، مَحيلة 'in place of/instead of'. Cp: maḥalat, maḥailat. (Gen.28:8-9)

Bethel; bêṯ-'ēl; it is not the same as 'Bethel' in Abraham's story (Gen.12:8) which meant 'stay over'. In Jacob's story it is بَطئيل ، بَطِئل ، بيطِئل ، بيطئيل 'bad/wrong' 'evil' 'dreadful' 'cease/stop' 'droop/become useless/immobile/hang uselessly/can't move/go dead/numb' e.g. when a limb becomes temporarily or permanently disabled. The story tells us it was originally named Luz; lûz; لَذ ، لوذ 'run for your life' 'escape' 'take flight (from trouble or danger); and is aptly named as Jacob is running from Esau in fear for his life. Cp: lov, loov. Giving names to people and places to make the audience laugh is why the Biblical authors keep making up names of words in daily use: 'Luz/run for your life' becomes 'Bethel/bad/dreadful/cease' after Jacob has a bad dream. He was spooked and superstition plays a large part in rural areas today as it did in antiquity, and the superstition can be seen in the narration of taking the stone(s) he had used as pillows and performing a ritual because he had experienced the uneasy dream about God while sleeping on them, and he names the place Bethel (bad/evil/dreadful/cease) 'And he was afraid, and said, How dreadful is this place!' 'And Jacob rose up early in the morning and took the stone that he had put for his pillows and set it up for a pillar, and poured oil upon the top of it. And he called the name of that place Bethel: but the name of that city *was called* Luz at the first.' This signifies how the stones used as pillows are connected to his scary dream. Cp: beṭeyl, beṭill, beyṭill, beyṭeyl. (Gen.28:10-19)

Rachel; rāḥēl; راكيل ، راك يل 'leaning against-the' 'propped against-the' 'make lean/prop against-the' and her name is connected to the stone on the mouth of the well. It is from the word (rk/رك) which means to lean, relax or prop against something, used to tell people to sit comfortably against cushions, or to set an object leaning against something. Rachel is made up of a compound word depicting what the stone is doing and what Jacob does with the stone so that Rachel's flock can be watered. He asks the people to water Rachel's sheep, but they tell him they cannot until all flocks are gathered so everyone can help in rolling the stone which leans against the mouth of the well. When dealing with large rocks is part of daily life, you do not just lay a large stone flat on the ground, and if possible to avoid laying it directly on the ground, you lean it against a surface so it does not slip and is easier to pick it up/move it again—which in this story's case they have to do, but because it is a hard effort they do it communally and at certain times. But Jacob does this himself for Rachel's sake—hence the name Rachel perfectly named for the story introducing Rachel to Jacob. The story emphasises on '...a great stone was upon the well's mouth.' 'and they rolled the stone from the well's mouth, and watered the sheep, and put the stone again upon the well's mouth in his place', when Jacob sees Rachel he asks them to water the sheep which would include rolling the stone which is leaning agaist the well 'And they said, We cannot, until all the flocks be gathered together, and till they roll the stone from the well's mouth...' '...when Jacob saw Rachel...that Jacob went near, and rolled the stone from the well's mouth, and watered the flock...'. Cp: raakeyl, raak-eyl. (Gen.29:2-11)

Leah; lē'â; is wordplay on: ليئا ، لي ئه 'no' 'why her/him/it' 'mine/for me' and 'why?!' 'why did you do this–you?' as in 'why did you do this' which, in a nutshell, is what Jacob is saying in length directed at Laban '...and he said to Laban, What is this thou hast done unto me? did not I serve with thee for Rachel? Wherefore then hast thou beguiled me?'. Cp: ley-a, ley-ah, leyah. (Gen.29:23-25)

Zilpah; zilpâ; زِلبه/زل به ، زِلبا/زل با 'went/gone off with her' 'take her' and is from word (zl/زل) 'went off/gone off/disappeared' 'remove/leave forever' 'wiped out/removed permanently'; (b/ب) 'with'; (ah/ا/ـه) 'her'. It means the person(s) has mischievous intent behind the disappearing or going somewhere out of sight and when used about a male and female means went to have illicit sex. It is exactly as is meant by giving her this name that in the story Leah will give her as a wife to Jacob (they have sex and make children). Cp: zilbah zil-bah, zilba, zil-ba. (Gen.29:24; 30:9-10)

Bilhah; bilhâ; بِلهه/بِل هه ، بِلها/بِل ها 'with (the)-her' 'with (the)-take her' from words: (bl/بل) 'with the': (b/ب) 'with/by', (l/il/ل) 'the'; (h/ـه) 'take' also (hah)ها/هه 'take/here, take/will'; (a/aa/ـه/ا) 'her'; also (ha/hah/ها/هه) can mean 'here/here, take/take this/look(attention)/will). 'with (the)-take her' is exactly what is meant as Rachel gives Bilhah for Jacob to have sex with and make children. Cp: bilhah, bil-hah, bilha, bil-ha. (Gen.29:29; 30:3-7)

Reuben; rĕ'ûḇēn; رَئوبين ، ريئو بين 'saw into/between' 'saw-made clear/apparent' from words (reu/رئو) 'saw' and (beyn/بين) 'into/between/made clear'. And is emphasised by God seeing Leah's problem and Reuben seeing/finding mandrakes among the wheat in the field: '...and she called his name Reuben: for she said, Surely the Lord hath looked upon my affliction...' also 'And Reuben went in the days of wheat harvest into the field, and found mandrakes in the field.' Cp: re-u-beyn, rei-u-beyn. (Gen.29:31-32; 30:14)

Simeon; šim'ôn; سِمعُن ، سِمعون 'have heard/to hear/heard' (also means 'obeyed'); سِمئُن ، سِمئون 'ill/sick of/disgusted by'. Leah says '...Because the Lord hath heard that I *was* hated, he hath therefore given me this *son* also: and she called his name Simeon.' Cp: sim'on, sim'oon, simon, simoon. (Gen.29:33)

Levi; lēwî; ليوي ، ليوه 'twisted around/entwined' 'twisted it/twirled/entwined-it' as in something twisting around or on something, 'twisting words/going around/not being forthright/dishonest'; ليبي ، ليبه 'answered/answer/answer him(or it)' 'served/serve/serve him(or it)' 'my core/pulp/insides' 'core/pulp it' and serve means as in 'answer/respond and assist'. Leah says 'Now this time will my husband be joined unto me, because I have born him three sons: therefore, was his name called Levi.' Hoping her husband will not only be twisted around her physically when he needs, but will be emotionally attached to her seeing she has given him three sons; it is about physically twisting around/entwining and being responsive and loving which Leah hopes Jacob will become. Cp: leywee, leywh, leybee, leybh. (Gen.29:34)

Judah; yûd'ā, yûd'â, yûḏâ; يُدعا ، يُدعى ، يُدعه ، يُدع 'he is called/calls' from word (d'/دع) which can mean to 'call, or curse' 'to make a claim' 'make a false claim or an unproven claim' and not only to call on God, but to shout out or call for anyone like calling out to your mother or friend in another room, e.g., and is exactly explained in the story just like all the other names of children born in this part are self-explanatory as words and further explained by the text: 'Now will I praise the Lord: therefore she called his name Judah...'.

The question must be asked why scholars (both past and modern) would transliterate it as: yĕhûḏâ which would be يَهُدا ، ييهُده 'destroys/demolishes' 'gifts/sings wedding song' and would necessitate rearranging the letters of the word-name 'Judah' into a different word which these scholars would like to mean 'yehuda/Jews'. Judah is definitely not 'Yehuda' nor is it related to the word Jew/Jewish, but in desperation or desire, scholars have wanted Judah to mean Jew/Jewish, but 'Judah' and 'Jew/Jewish' are two separate words with unrelated meanings and different spelling and pronunciations. Scholars have used the Arabic word (Yehood/Yehoodee يهود/يهودي) which means 'Jews/Jewish', but because they do not understand the meaning of the word have tried to force 'Judah' onto 'Yehood'.

I will give the meaning of the word 'jew' and its meaning and how it came to be applied to the religion (misnomered in western culture as 'Judaism') later in this book, but trying to force 'yehuda' onto the word 'Judah' is forcing a large square peg into a small circular hole—it does not fit unless you destroy the circular hole and cut out a large square hole i.e. corrupt it, change it completely into something that it was not and is not. It could be overlooked if additional letters were added which still keep the word in its original pronunciation such as adding phonemes or letters that serve as phonemes such as in the two examples I gave above, another two examples of possible transliterations: yûdā', yûdaʿ, and they would still give a similar and understandable pronunciation and meaning to 'Judah' which is 'he is called'. But when words are intentionally given added letters to make them into a completely different word, and the sequence of the letters in the word are purposely rearranged to achieve a different and desired word—which we can see in 'Judah' and its transliteration, where 'Judah' is being corrupted to forcibly mean and be related to 'yehuda' when it is not and has completely separate meanings and are unrelated to each other (Yehuda, Judah). This is a deception (whether ill-intended or out of benign desire for it to have these meanings) that distorts history, language and more importantly it corrupts the Bible, its stories and its true meanings. Cp: yud'aa, yud'ah, yud'. (Gen.29:35)

Dan; dān; دآن as earlier where the word/name appeared in Genesis still means: 'bowed/bent/facing the ground/with face on ground/lowered/low/guilted/made guilty/found guilty', its meaning is reflected in the verses given to Rachel but not only in the verse 'God hath judged me, and hath also heard my voice, and hath given me a son: therefore called she his name Dan.' When Rachel's dialogue states she has been judged by God, she means punished and found 'guilty' by making her barren and it begins with her argument with Jacob where he angrily retorts that it is God who has made her barren but 'dan' does not mean 'judged'. Jacob's anger that it is not his fault but that it is God that has made Rachel barren when he snaps back at Rachel would suggest Jacob blames her for being unable to get pregnant, and when the text states 'hath judged me' it shows although he has punished Rachel, God has still responded favourably to her by allowing her handmaid to provide her with children. Cp: daan. (Gen.30:6)

Naphtali; naptālî; نَفتآلي 'we crush for me'. To understand we need to break-down the compound word: (n/ن) 'we'; (pht/فت) 'crush' to crush something like breaking and crushing bread with milk to make a dish called (phta/pht*h*/فتا/فته); (a/ا) 'for'; (lee/لي) 'me'. When someone asks another to prepare this dish they say (phtali) فت الي 'crush for me'; when a person is preparing this dish with other people or waiting for them to prepare it one would say 'naphutali' نَفُت الي . It is the same word used to describe two or more people wrestling/fighting: the victorious one is said to have 'crushed' (pht/فت) the other, the one who lost is said to have been 'crushed' or 'crushed him' (phtuh/فَتّه). The creator of the story has used it in both senses that it was a wrestling as Rachel describes it, and in the same way, it is others who helped her make this dish as Bilhah and Jacob have to bed each other to make the baby for her which is why it is in the 'we' plural form: 'With great wrestlings have I wrestled with my sister, and I have prevailed: and she called his name Naphtali.' Cp: naphtaalee (Gen.30:8)

Gad and Asher do not make sense as presented in the Biblical text. What is interesting is it does seem the names 'Gad' and 'Asher' have been swapped when the stories were put into text, and here is how we can see they have been swapped: Gad '...A troop cometh: and she called his name Gad.'; regarding Asher '...Happy am I, for the daughters will call me blessed: and she called his name Asher.' Gad; gāḏ; جاد 'new or renewed' 'found'; it could also be قعد 'seated/relaxed/waited (while crouching or sitting low)'. I believe it is in the first meaning as 'new' or 'renewed' the word has many forms and uses, but is used when applying new henna in events of celebration when women will visit so they can give their well-wishes and prayers to the new mother/bride/woman with happy occasion. It is used as (gad) جَد 'again/renew' such as in a fresh layer of henna on hands or feet, or a fresh coating of whitewash for the walls (always related to a happy occasion and in advance of receiving girls and women visitors who come to share the happiness; and the word has various uses with the same or similar meanings such as (gadeed/جديد) 'brand new'; (gad-did/gaddidee/جَدِّد/جَدِّدِي) 'renew (it)' (masculine and feminine). So the meaning of 'newness' or 'repeated' (she has had children before) and the happiness and women calling her blessed fits with the name Gad.

As for Asher; 'āšēr; نآشير 'I signal/gesture' but more likely in this case عآشير ، عَشير 'a lot of people' 'a group of people/tribe' 'lived with people(for a long time)' (and the latter means when a person not originally from the area lives a long time or life with these people), and is similar to tribe as it means a group of people who come from the same family, or village or area; and this meaning fits into 'a troop cometh…'; Asher also means to live among people as one of them. There has definitely been a mix up in the names of Gad and Asher either when the stories were first recorded as text or by later editors of these texts. Cp: gaad, g'd; aasheyr, 'aasheyr. (Gen.30:10-13).

Issachar; yiśśāḵār; يِصّآخار 'he becomes compliant/obedient' 'he is at your disposal' and what it means is a person does as told, is useful, is compliant/obedient, helpful; the word is in the form of speaking about a 'he/it' in the singular with the (yi/يِ) but the action adverb part of (ssaakhaar/صّآخار) denotes double (two people or two actions). This can be explained: (yi/he) refers to Jacob; the being compliant and doing as bidden (ssachar) is because in the story/Leah is referring to two actions for which she is rewarded the latest child: allowing Jacob to bed Zilbah, and Zilbah too is doing as requested by Leah and Jacob, and for 'hiring' Jacob to sleep with her and Jacob complying. The child born in the story is named after the action which brought him to life. (**sskhr**/صَخَّر) is used to describe when a person gets help from someone else, when a task is made easier through help or an obedient person, animal or luck, it is used in wishing good luck for someone to receive assistance, obedience or ease from another person/task. It is what is being described of how Jacob reacts in the story: as soon as he leaves work in the field Leah tells him he must sleep with her and he silently does as told, the epitome of obedience (Issachar). 'And Rachel said, Therefore he shall lie with thee to night for thy son's mandrakes. And Jacob came out of the field in the evening, and Leah went out to meet him, and said, Thou must come in unto me, for surely I have hired thee with my son's mandrakes. And he lay with her that night. And God hearkened unto Leah and she conceived, and bare Jacob the fifth son. And Leah said, God hath given me my hire, because I have given my maiden to my husband: and she called his name Issachar.' Cp: yissaakhaar. (Gen.30:18)

Zebulun; zĕḇûlûn; شي ضُلُن ، شَضُلُن ، شيضُلُن 'want to stay' 'I/they will stay' from the words: (zĕ/شي) 'want' or (zĕ/شي/شا،شَ) 'they/I will' and (ḇûl(ûn)/(ضُل(ُن) 'stayed/lingered' 'shaded' 'misguided/misled' in the plural. The story mentions six sons and the 'stay/dwell' is meant as in the plural, Leah believes all of them will live together, that Jacob will now want to stay with her '…now will my husband dwell with me, because I hath born him six sons: and she called his name Zebulun.' There are other possibilities for meaning of the word Zebulun as wordplay was intended by the original authors, but here in this instance it is about staying. Cp: shei-dhulun, shedhulun, sheidhulun. (Gen.30:20).

Dinah; dînâ; دينه ، دينا ، دِنا ، دِنه all mean 'to lower' 'to bow' 'to be lowered/bowed' and is also word play on دينح ، دِنح and all mean to 'bring shame upon', resulting or expressed by a head bowed in shame, or 'bowing down', 'bent neck' in the sense they cannot lift their heads from shame, such as in 'dinah/dinaḥ his head' دنّح راسه 'he made his head bow low' or 'dinat/dinaḥat their heads' دنّحت رؤوسهم 'she bowed their heads' (by a man or woman (from the family) doing something shameful, including when a female is caught having a romantic/physical relationship outside of marriage).

The word reflects her role in the story, she has sex (and is maybe in love) with a man without marriage—although some scholars write that she was raped by Shechem, there is no rape suggested in the Biblical story, the text narrates a romantic relationship, the word 'defiled' does not mean he raped her, but dishonoured her (and her family) by having sex while she is not his wife, and she took part in the act willingly (having a physical relationship without marriage was shameful back then, as it still is now in many societies). 'And Dinah…went out to see the daughters of the land. And when Shechem…saw her, he took her, and lay with her, and defiled her. And his soul clave unto Dinah…and he loved the damsel, and spake kindly unto the damsel.' The story shows that there is love between Shechem and Dinah; her father Jacob does not mind and agrees to the marriage, but it is her brothers who cannot get over the sexual activity between the lovers and in the story commit an honour-genocide before removing her from Shechem's house, which means she was living with her lover.

The whole Dinah story revolves around the meaning of her name that she lowered her relatives' heads in shame: '…and the men were grieved, and they were very wroth, because he had wrought folly in Israel in lying with Jacob's daughter, which thing ought not to be done…And the sons of Jacob answered Shechem and Hamor deceitfully, and said, because he had defiled Dinah their sister…that two of the sons of Jacob, Simeon and Levi, Dinah's brethren, took each man his sword, and came upon the city boldly, and slew all the males. And they slew Hamor and Shechem, and took Dinah out of Shechem's house, and went out...The sons of Jacob came upon the slain, and spoiled the city, because they had defiled their sister...And they said, Should he deal with our sister as with an harlot?' Cp: deenah, deena, dina, dinah, deenaḥ, dinaḥ. (Gen.30:21; 34)

Joseph; yôsēp̱; يوسيف ، يُسيف 'of sorrow/feels sorrow/regret' 'pours water gently over/rinses/cleanses' as in pouring water gently with pauses between to rinse/clean something. It is God washing away Rachel's 'reproach' allowing her to have a baby after barrenness. It is also the sorrow and regret Jacob and Joseph will feel when Joseph's brothers get rid of the latter. 'And God remembered Rachel, and God hearkened to her, and opened her womb. And she conceived, and bare a son; and said, God hath taken away my reproach: And she called his name Joseph...' Cp: yoseyp̲h̲, yooseyp̲h̲. (Gen.30:22-24;37)

When Jacob tells his wives of the dream he has, he mentions 'I am the God of Bethel, where thou anointedst the pillar.' (Gen.31:13), it is still the same place where Jacob had a bad dream and called the place '**Bethel**' 'bad'—although he is explaining he has been ordered to keep a vow made to God to return to the land of his kindred, the story is mentioning 'Bethel' 'bad' because the actions in the current story are of ill-intent, if not evil, at least bad. Laban; lāḇān; لعبان 'plays/a player' 'deceitful/trickster' and also: لآذان 'they escaping/fleeing' 'they escaped/fled' and it is what Jacob and his whole family do, and when Laban catches up with them, he expresses how cruel it is of Jacob to flee with his two daughters and all their children. In the story although Laban has already fulfilled his name-role when he deceives Jacob to work for seven years and marries him to Leah before getting him to work another seven years for Rachel, the story now projects Laban has turned against Jacob and intends to deceive him further, although it is only in Jacob's speech in the story narrative that expresses this—so Laban is being 'bad' and why 'Bethel' is mentioned. The same can be said of Jacob's actions as per the story and Jacob's actions of trickery also reflect 'Laban' and 'Bethel' meanings, both characters are behaving badly. Cp: l'baan, laavaan. (Gen.29;30;31)

Gilead; gilʿāḏ; is wordplay on: جِل عآب ، قِل عآب 'coming/saying/came/said-to shame/shame'; قِلعآذ 'say(ing)/said protection'; قِل عآض ، جِل عآض 'said recompense/replenish' 'came/coming the-recompense/replenish' 'said-teaching lesson/lecturing' 'came/coming the-teaching lesson/lecturing'; قِلآد ، قِلئآد 'placing responsibility' 'garlanding/placing on or around neck' 'copying/mimicking'; قِلعآد 'tumbled rock' 'large sliding/tumbling/tumbled rock'; قِلعآب 'tumbling/rolling stone(s)' 'tumbling/rolling/tumbled/rolled' (latter can be sound heard or action). The 'coming/saying the shame' because Laban has caught up with Jacob and is telling Jacob how shameful it is of him to run off with his daughters as if they were captives, for not allowing him to say goodbye to them and his grandchildren as per custom, for stealing his idols; Jacob is telling Laban how shameful his deceit and exploiting his labour for decades. 'said/came recompense/replenish' 'said/came the-teaching lesson/lecturing' is Laban and Jacob speaking about being not recompensed properly, and Jacob stating he did what he did to get his recompense for all the work done for Laban; Laban is teaching/lecturing Jacob that because Jacob's wives and children are his daughters and grandchildren that the land is for them to live on and replenish from. 'say(ing)-give protection' when God comes to Laban in a dream and warns him not to harm Jacob 'not to speak good or bad' is what is said to a person as advice to avoid conflict or provocation; Laban tells Jacob that if he wished to, he could harm him, but because God has told him not to and because Jacob's family are his children that he is protected. 'placing responsibility' Jacob and Laban are blaming each other for the bad behaviour (see Gilead/Galeed where the meaning of the word also involves stones), the responsibility is said to be carried or placed on the neck and the word means to carry the responsibility around the neck (figuratively) and this portrays the 'garlanded/placed on or around neck' meaning. 'rolling stones', they are in the mountain named after 'rolling stones'; 'Gilead' is the verb of a stone falling/rolling, and the stone itself is called (qal'oob/قَلعوب) and an extremely large rock that has slid or tumbled is called (qal'ood/قَلعود); stones are also involved in the custom/belief of 'gilead/galeed' قِلآد ، قِلئآد meanings, when topics of contention are being discussed. Cp: gil'aab, qil'aab, qil'aav, gil'aa<u>dh</u>, qil'aa<u>dh</u>, qil-aad, qilaad, qil'aad, qil'aab. (Gen.31)

Jegar-sahadutha; yĕgar śāhăḏûṯā'; حَجَر/حيجَر شآهَدوذآء/شآهيدُذآء 'stones have witnessed this' 'stones-witness this'. When Laban and Jacob are reproaching each other over their actions, Laban points out they are all family and wish no harm to each other, he requests a covenant and stones are piled to bear witness to what they say. Previously in Genesis Abraham did the same thing with ewes when he struck a covenant with Abimelech. Here, the stones as witnesses are the literal name given. Cp: ḥegar/ḥeigar <u>sh</u>aahadoo-vaa/shaahaidu-vaa. (Gen.31:44-47)

Galeed; galʿēd; similar to Gilead in word and meanings but in past tense: جَل عيب ، قَل عيب 'came/said-shame'; جَل عيض ، قَل عيض'came the recompense/replenish' 'said-recompense/replenish' 'came the-teaching lesson/lecturing' 'said-teaching lesson/lecturing' ; قَل عيذ 'said-protect/protection'; قَلئيد 'placed responsibilities' 'garlanded/placed around or on neck' and also noun of responsibilities which means something hanging from your neck, the closest thing would be 'garland of responsibility(ies)' 'copied/mimicked'; قَلعيد ، قَل عيد 'tumbled rock(s)' 'large sliding/tumbling/tumbled rock(s)' 'said-return' 'said/ordered festival'; جَل عيد 'came the festival/came to the festival/came return'; قَلعيب 'rolled stones'. For all the same reasons above of narrative between Jacob and Laban regarding 'Gilead', Laban wants it to be in the past, but wants stones to bear witness, Galeed also plays on جَل عيد 'came-festival' as part of the covenant included eating on the heaped stones (Galeed) and was followed by 'sacrifice upon the mount, and called his brethren to eat bread: and they did eat bread and tarried all night in the mount.' as is done in all festivals.

Regarding 'Galeed' 'placed responsibility' and 'rolled stones', this custom has a real practise in everyday life of people: 'Galeed/Gilead' needs to be explained in detail, it means: will be a witness against you if you are lying, and you will bear the responsibility of your actions (whether in this world or in front of God). In the story, it is the stones used between Laban and Jacob and there is a real life reason why stones were used in the story but this will be addressed later in the book; in rural Yemen when people are hashing it out, they still place a small stone between them, one person will reach out, pick up a stone and set it between them, and the term 'God gilead/galeed you' قَلدَك الله is said asking the person to prove what he is saying or urging him/her to re-examine what he has said or done, or in submitting to what that person has said so the matter can be put to rest. The phrase alone قَلدَك الله is still also used by urban Yemenis when having it out, discussing an issue, or letting go of the issue by saying 'God has placed responsibility around your neck'. Cp: gal 'eyb, qal 'eyb, gal 'eydh, qal 'eydh, qal'eyv, qal-eyd, qal'eyd, qal 'eyd, gal 'eyd, qal'eyb. (Gen.31)

Mizpah; miṣpâ, miṣpeh; is wordplay on مِذبَح/مِذبَح 'slaughter' and مِصبه/مِصبَه 'pouring place/pouring/pouring vessel' as Jacob offers sacrifice there, and blood is also poured from the slaughter of animals then collected blood from slaughtered animals and other liquid offerings—which is why it is also the word for 'altar' (both 'slaughter/مِذبَح' and 'pouring/مِصبه'): the use of these two meanings can be seen where 'Mizpah' and its variants in spelling are used as in killing of people or animals, as well as spilling/pouring of blood or water-related themes which imply something liquid; مِصبح/مِصبَح 'arose in the morning/from the morning' 'problems/ill-intent from morning' 'watching with ill-intent' as God has been invoked to watch over who transgresses, Laban warns Jacob not to marry-over his daughters and there is a warning in this sentence. When a person is (miṣpeḥ/مصبح) it is when they are in a foul mood or staring with a sour-face, brooding, angry facial expression and is believed to want to cause problems; it is said 'why are you/is your face mispeḥ?' and (subaaḥa/صُباحا) watching and wanting to cause problems or ill-will, 'do not saabiḥni' لاتصابحني 'do not cause me problems with your watching, ill-intent' and this is said in the morning and daytime (it has an equivalent word for the evening); and the words between Laban and Jacob are to the effect 'do not cause me problems, or else…'; and نِصبا/نِصبه/نِصبَه 'marker' 'portion/share' and is a stone set on a piece of land to demark whose land starts/ends and where, when more than one person owns parts of the same piece of land: 'And Laban said to Jacob, behold this heap, and behold this pillar, which I have cast betwixt me and thee; This heap be witness, and this pillar be witness, that I will not pass over this heap to thee, and that thou shalt not pass over this heap and this pillar unto me, for harm.' And it is followed by the slaughter/sacrifice of an animal. Cp: mivbḥ, mivbeḥ, mis͟sbh, mis͟sbeh, mis͟sbḥ, mis͟sbeḥ, nis͟sba, nis͟sbh, nis͟sbeh. (Gen.31:44-55)

Mahanaim; maḥănayim; مَحَنّي/مَحيني ام/هم 'put them through a lot/bothered-the/them'; مَهَنّي/مَهيني ام/هم 'gave enough/gave a lot/satisfied-the/them' and the word is used to mean satisfaction in food and other resources/wealth (or even content with lots of family, rest, etc.) but is mostly used referring to plenty of food or plenty of eating; and both words are being used in the story: when 'God's host' meets Jacob and family, it is a form of gratification. The quantity and types of gifts Jacob sends ahead to appease Esau is also to satisfy and gratify Esau; both Esau and Jacob repeat that they have 'enough' flock, etc. and so both are expressing God 'mahanaim' has given them more than enough. The second meaning 'bothered/troubled' describes a literal meaning to have caused bother or used to express gratitude towards a host in saying 'maḥannaa/we troubled you (the host)/مَحنّاكم' as it shows the host has gone to a lot of trouble to accommodate, entertain, feed, etc. his/her guests; this meaning of 'bothered/troubled' is shown in Jacob going through mental torment from fear of Esau, he also uses his children and flocks' 'trouble/suffering' as a way to have Esau go ahead in front of them, justifying they are tired from travel and need to move at their own pace; the wrestling with God is also a test/bother for Jacob. Cp: maḥanay/ maḥainay-um/hum, mahanay/mahainay-um/hum. (Gen.32;33)

Seir; śē'îr; takes on additional meanings as well as the one used earlier at Gen.14:6: as earlier it used for سيئير 'send off/go/walk/travel' 'go along with (as in agree with speech or actions)' 'will be penised', سيعير 'will be gloated over/at' or 'will be borrowed'; but also شيغير 'he will save' and means God will save them as Jacob begs him to. When Jacob is saying how much God has given him, and Esau doing the same, it is considered a form of gloating by boasting how much you have in comparison to the person you are speaking to (who may have less). There is a lot of walking and travelling mentioned in the verses of Gen.32 and 33; Jacob sends messengers to Esau, then he sends his servants to deliver cattle to Esau all sent in different groups; the message to Esau is also that Jacob is coming; and the word 'sent' is repeated often to emphasise why Esau has been placed in the story in 'the land of Seir'. Cp: sey-eer, sey'eer, sheyגheer. (Gen.32;33)

Jabbok; yabbōq; wordplay on: يبوق ، يبُّق the sound water makes flowing out of a narrow place or container e.g. 'glugs/he/it glugs' and also 'tore a slit in' 'made a tear in' from word (bq/بق); يبوخ ، يبُّخ 'inflates/pumps' 'swells/makes swell' 'inflates from heat' 'puffs up/blows' 'fucks' 'says he fucks' 'fuck your sister/with your sister' and is a vulgar insult claiming to have/had sex with a female relative (specifically the sister) of the male spoken about and making a show of it/spreading news about it (causes serious offense when said in hostility or said between adults, but is used as a joke which makes male and female relatives laugh when a male adult relative says it to a young boy to tease him), from word (bkh/بخ); يبوك ، يبُّك 'he goes/leaves' from word (bk/بك) 'go/leave' and all words and meanings describe Jacob and family going over the river and going towards Esau, but it also describes Jacob's strange wrestling match after which one muscle in his body is left withered, i.e. deflated and also could be a torn/strained muscle; the same word can be seen in when he meets his brother again, Jacob's family and wealth has swollen in size and numbers (both beasts and people swell in numbers from the act of copulation, procreate). '…and passed over the ford Jabbok. And he took them, and sent them over the brook, and sent over that he had.' Cp: yabboq, yabbooq, yabokh, yabookh, yabbok, yabbook. (Gen.32:22-23)

Jacob's name as earlier in Genesis: يعكوب ، يعكُب 'forces open' 'dislocates' 'forces open and takes/usurps' it describes opening something in a fashion similar to using a crowbar to break a lock/chain and is usually done for theft or when a key is lost, or something is jammed, where earlier it is used to enhance Jacob displacing Esau from his birth right and blessing, now it is used against Jacob in this part of the story when God dislocates Jacob's thigh/joint 'And when he saw that he prevailed not against him, he touched the hollow of his thigh; and the hollow of Jacob's thigh was out of joint, as he wrestled with him.' (Gen.32:24-25,32)

Israel; yiśrā'ēl; عِصرآ يِل/ئيل 'twisted muscle-the' 'twisted-the' from word ('ssr/عصر) 'twisted' which is always used to describe pulling/twisting a muscle and the painful condition of a twisted muscle; the word itself is created from (صر 'knot') and is also the feeling when a muscle is strained. In everyday language, which has remained unchanged since ancestral times, a person says ('assrt my neck (or arm, back, etc.)') and means 'I twisted a muscle in my neck/arm etc.'. The same word also means 'twist around-the' e.g. if someone (or an object) is facing you and you or they turn them round, or partially turn around, so that his/her back is facing you, or vice-versa is 'twisted-the' as it means turning something by twisting/twisting around him/her/it into a different position; it also means to squeeze all the liquid out of something, e.g. pressing/twisting clothes with your hands to get all the water out, getting juice out of any fruit is the action 'twisted-the'.

It refers to when God hurt Jacob's muscle and still Jacob would not let go although he had twisted his muscle. There is also a sexual nature implied in how God 'touched the hollow of his thigh' and in that Jacob does not let go especially that the narrators made sure they are alone: 'And when he saw that he prevailed not against him, he touched the hollow of his thigh; and the hollow of Jacob's thigh was out of joint, as he wrestled with him.' And although God's character is asking to be released, Jacob still won't let go and the story purposely brings to attention the connection between 'Jacob (dislocated/forced out of place)' and 'he touched the hollow of his thigh…was out of joint…' and '…What is thy name? And he said Jacob. And he said, Thy name shall be called no more Jacob, but Israel: for as a prince has thou power with God and with men, and hast prevailed' the latter part of the sentence meaning: 'even with a twisted muscle, you still won' and confirms 'twisted muscle-the' is what Israel means (and was straightforward when these stories were made for entertainment) 'Therefore the children of Israel eat not of the sinew which shrank, which is upon the hollow of the thigh, unto this day: because he touched the hollow of Jacob's thigh in the sinew that shrank.' Cp: 'issraa-ill/eyl. (Gen:32:24-32).

The misinterpretation of 'Israel' as 'God wrestles/fights' or 'He who fights with God' is because old and contemporary translators/interpreters are basing it on the word 'wrestle' from the old and current Arabic meaning of 'wrestle': صارع/مصارعه but this word is not what is spelled in the transliteration nor in the context and meaning of the Biblical text; although by nature of the Biblical authors' wordplay the transliteration could possibly be made into يِصراع/يِصرع يِل/نئيل/ئِل 'he threw down-the' 'he threw to the ground-the' but the transliteration would have to be rearranged and letters swapped around to make yiśrā'ēl into the form of the root word (ssr'/صرع) which can include, among other words, the meaning 'wrestle' if written in the form to mean 'wrestle', but as it is in the Biblical text the desired word yiśrā'ēl يِصراع/يِصرع يل/نئيل/ال does not read as 'fought with God' nor 'wrestled with God' but would read 'he threw down-the' 'he threw to the ground-the' as the root word which could mean 'wrestle' is not in the form to mean 'wrestle' but in the form which means to throw a person or thing violently onto the ground; nowhere in the story does it say this happens between Jacob and man-God, but there is plenty of proof (as well as the actual correct word) that it means 'twisted muscle-the' and any muscle which remains twisted or out of place for a long time eventually withers/dies and is what is being described in the story.

Peniel, Penuel; pĕnî'ēl; بَني/بيني نئيل/ئِل 'children of-the' 'in-the' 'in me-the' 'show/become apparent-the' and the latter meaning (show/become apparent-the) is in the form of speaking to a female; pĕnû'ēl; بَنو/بنُ/بينو/بينُ نئيل/ئِل 'children of-the' in-the' 'in them-the' 'show/become apparent-the' and the latter is speaking to/about plural subject/object. In the context of the story it seems to be 'show/become apparent' as it becomes apparent to Jacob when God refuses to tell his name '…I have seen God face to face…' and then when Peniel becomes Penuel, the sun rises i.e. shows itself/becomes apparent.

There is definitely a link between the etymology of the word (bn/bnee/بني/بن) 'child/children' 'birth/gave birth/procreated/offspring' from the same root word 'in-the' 'in me' as the creation of a child comes from inside a man (his semen/sperm called 'water') and a woman who receives the man's water inside her and the child is carried inside the female until it is born and once birthed it becomes apparent to the world outside its mother's womb. This is the meaning of the word 'child/children/ben/benee' in Arabic, and more importantly the story being told at Gen.32:24-32 is of Jacob being sexually touched by God which gives Jacob's offspring and their future progeny (children of Israel) a special status to God, which is repeated and confirmed by naming a place Peniel/Penuel in the narration, and linking it to what happened to Jacob's thigh ('thigh' being euphemism) and the 'children of Israel' which is the muscle which was twisted and shrivelled by God. Note also that after this sexual encounter with God how Jacob's character changes completely: he goes from a bold and eager to deceive trouble-maker to a meek and friendly, even fearful, character which even an illicit public relationship by a man with his daughter does not bother and goes further to be mild and do good in his reaction to the situation and requests of marriage (his sons now show the hot-blooded, deceptive and violent temperament which Jacob has lost), but this change in character only comes after he is euphemistically copulated by God, where his 'twisted muscle-the' withers as do his brash characteristics along with it i.e. he has been emasculated by the strange encounter with God. Cp. benee-eyl/ill, beinee- eyl/ill, benoo/benu-ill, beinoo/beinu-eyl/ill. (Gen.32:30-32)

Succoth; sukkôt; سوقُّف ، سُقُّف 'roofed/built a roof(s)' and as its meaning indicates it means to build a roof(s), whether it is houses, stables or any structure for people or animals it includes roofing and the roofing process is called (sqqph/سقّف) based on the word (sqf/سقف) 'roof', and is exactly what happens in the story: 'And Jacob journeyed to Succoth, and built him an house, and made booths for the cattle: therefore the name of the place is called Succoth.'; سوقّت ، سُقّت 'she/it watered/was watered'; سوقّط ، سُقّط 'fell/fallen/made fall' 'debauchery/sexual immorality/slut/became immoral' and both the meanings of 'watered' and 'fallen/sexual immorality/illicit sex' is also in the story that preceded with the wrestling match between God and Jacob (which was also implied by having all the other characters cross over the ford called Jabbok (which one meaning means to have illicit sex with someone's sister) while Jacob stayed) and in the story that follows which is of Dinah having sex without marriage with Shechem, and the story is about Dinah being 'defiled' the defilement is in reputation but also physically with the semen which is called 'water' in the same language of the people who created the Biblical stories. When living and marriage are mentioned the author makes a point to narrate 'make ye marriages with us, and give your daughters unto us, and take our daughters unto you.' is because in sexual intercourse it is the female who is 'watered' i.e. receives the semen/sperm; even how her brothers exact revenge, it begins with circumcising the male appendage that causes 'defilement' and this is used to render the men 'impotent' both against Dinah and against being able to defend themselves from her brothers; the 'fallen' meanings are reflected in the reputation of Dinah and her brothers and then in the physical fall of prince Shechem and all the city falling at the hands of Dinah's vengeful brothers. Cp: sooqoph, suqqoph, sooqot, suqqot, sooqqoṭ, suqqoṭ. (Gen.33:17; 34)

Shalem; as in Gen.14 it is still šālēm; سآليم ، سـآل يم 'ask the' 'flow/leak-the' 'flowed/leaked-river' 'entertain/distract-the' 'comfort-the' 'survived/intact/whole-the' and again it is used to describe exactly what is happening in the story: to buy land, it has to be asked for, and the country is called Shalem in this part of the story too (as was Melchizedek's country earlier). The naming allows the story to show the meanings: Dinah and Shechem find love and sexual comfort in each other; the requests 'ask-the' and granting them allows people to be happy and comforted, and the marriages and Dinah/Shechem's affair shows 'flow/leak-the' as in ejaculation of 'water'/semen; as Shechem will ask his father to ask for Dinah's marriage, Hamor asks Jacob for Dinah's marriage to his son, Hamor asks Jacob that he and his people live and marry among the people in Shalem (this links to Succoth 'she watered/she was watered' because marrying from each other allows them to procreate children), Shechem asks Jacob and sons to ask whatever dowry they please; when Jacob's sons ask that Shichem and all men of Shalem be circumcised they are both reflecting the 'ask' and 'distract' meanings because the circumcision is a ploy so they can massacre them all; and the whole chapter is ended with a question too; all to make the story suit the words chosen as a name for it. Cp: saaleym, saal-eym. (Gen.33:18-19;34)

Shechem; as earlier **Sichem** in Gen.12: 6; šěkem ; شِكَم ، شيكَم 'pointy peaks' 'threaded/skewered' (on something sharp or thread(needle/stick) e.g. how flowers are made into garlands; fabrics sewn, kebabs skewered) 'complained about-the/them'; شِقَم ، شيقَم 'pointy corners/a corner, tip or piece of something'; شَغَم ، شيغَم 'an abdominal ache' 'shouted/screamed loud' (out of pain). And the word-name plays a role in enhancing what will happen in the story and it plays on all meanings of the word: the offense is caused by Shechem making love to Dinah which her brothers complain about; Shechem is asked to circumcise and this plays on 'pointy/peaks' 'tip' meanings and also 'abdominal ache'; all the men have been circumcised and the story focuses '...and every male was circumcised...on the third day when they were sore...'; The story revolves around the cutting of penises, the pain and aches it causes, then the pain and screaming of being murdered. It makes a point to highlight that Levi and Simeon spoiled even the dead. Cp: <u>sh</u>ekem, <u>sh</u>eikem, <u>sh</u>eqem, <u>sh</u>eiqem, <u>shegh</u>em, <u>sh</u>ei<u>gh</u>em. (Gen.33:18-19;34)

Hamor; ḥămôr; is wordplay on: هعمُر 'will build/I will build' as his name is first mentioned in connection to Jacob buying land from him then Jacob erecting a structure for an altar; and هَمُر ، هيمُر 'I will order/command' 'he will order/command' 'I will pass' 'he will pass' 'here is bitterness/this is bitter' 'he will become bitter' and when he suggests they all live to together as one people, Jacob agrees and so do the people of Shalem whom he asks to also consent to circumcision and they obey 'And unto Hamor and unto Shechem his son hearkened all that went out to the gate of the city; and every male was circumcised...' but it becomes bitter as Jacob's sons massacre the people and destroy the city. Cp: ha'mor, hamor, haimor. (Gen.33:19-20;34)

El-elohe-Israel; 'ēl 'ĕlōhê yiśrā'ēl; (ايل/نئيل/ال) نِل نِلوهي عِصرا نِل/نئيل ، نِل نيلوهي عِصرآ نِل 'the-yes it is her/yes she did-twisted muscle the' and this needs to be broken down: (el/ 'ēl/ايل/نئيل/ال/نِل) 'the'; (elo/ 'ĕlō/إلو/نئيل) and means 'yes it is' or even 'it is' (confirming 'yes', the truth of the action/event/fact etc.); (he/hê/هي) 'her/she'; Israel as before is still 'twisted muscle-the'. This is a very specific reference to two things in the story: it elucidates the previous encounter between Jacob and God at Jabbok that the God who withered Jacob's muscle and renamed him 'Israel/Twisted muscle-the' is a female God; and a direct reference to Dinah and her role in the story: her name 'Dinah', as explained before, means to bring shame upon, resulting or expressed by a head bowed in shame, or bowing down, bent neck in the sense they cannot lift their heads from shame and is specifically meant when a daughter/sister/wife is caught having a romantic/physical relationship outside of marriage. In all the stories the word/compound word denotes what will happen in the story, and here it is no different with El-elohe-Israel, it sets the stage that Dinah will shame her father and brothers 'twisted muscle-the(Israel)' 'bent neck(Dinah)' and 'El-elohe-Israel' reinforcing that she (her) has shamed/twisted muscle of Jacob and this explains the sexual nature of God and Jacob's wrestling story, i.e. it refers to the penis (muscle) being squeezed/twisted with the vagina (muscle) and because it was an illicit relationship it caused shame/withering of the male 'Israel/Jacob' both physically and psychologically (his personality in the story). 'And he erected there an altar, and called it El-elohe-Israel.'. And from this point forward not only will the individual character 'Jacob' show weakness, vulnerability in his stories due to this encounter with God causing something to go wrong in Jacob, but also from this point onwards most of his twelve children and their progeny (in later stories) 'the children of Israel' will also show something has become intrinsically wrong in them, and the authors have this negative effect in them be intrinsic disobedience towards God and everyone God sends as prophets/messengers. Cp: ill-eloohey-'i<u>ss</u>raa-ill, eyl-eiloohey-'i<u>ss</u>raa-eyl (Gen.33:18-20)

Whenever **Bethel** along with Jacob are focused on by the story/authors, it is to emphasise 'bad, evil, dreadful' as well as 'cease' 'cease/stop' 'droop/become useless/immobile/hang uselessly/can't move/go dead/numb' and it sets for bad things to happen: Jacob is reminded of fleeing for his life from Esau, 'And they journeyed and the terror of God was upon the cities that were around about them…' and the name Luz/'flee' is mentioned again both as a name and reflected in the narration that they were not pursued. According to Gen.28 the name of the place was already called Bethel 'bad' 'evil' 'dreadful' by Jacob earlier but the authors want to emphasise this beyond doubt and name the pillar 'El-beth-el'; 'ēl bêṯ-'ēl; ئِل بَطئِل ، ئِل بَطئيل/ بيطئِل ، ئِل/ئيل بيطئيل 'the-bad' 'the-evil' 'the-dreadful' 'the-ceased/stopped' 'the-drooped/become useless/immobile/gone dead/numb'. Cp: ill-beṭill, ill-beṭeyl/beyṭill, ill/eyl-beyṭeyl.

If that was not atmospheric enough, they further enhance it with the death of Deborah to show the meanings of 'ceases/become dead/become numb': not only is death a bad/dreadful thing, but the word 'Deborah' has a specific negative meaning: Deborah; dĕḇôrâ; دَبُرا ، دَبُره ، دبيُرا، دَيبُره 'evil intended/fated' and is in the form of feminine adjective; it also has a similar meaning to 'unlucky' but with a stronger and more malicious meaning as in 'evil intent' 'evil fate' and the person described as being 'deboor/mdbir' brings evil upon those he/she is around, it has more meanings (negative and neutral) but these will be shown where the word 'Deborah' will be used again as a name with these other meanings in the Biblical stories. They have a woman suitably named 'Deborah/evil-fated' die at El-beth-el/'the-bad/evil-the' and because of the meaning of the word 'deborah' it extends to Rachel and she dies after leaving Bethel/el-Beth-el. Cp: debora, deborah, deibora, deiborah. (Gen.35)

Allon-bachuth; 'allôn bāḵûṯ; is wordplay on: ئَلُّن بآكُت 'until she left' 'now she left'; ئَلُّن بآحُط 'until/now-I place/set/leave' 'until/now-got sore throat/lost voice' both refer to the death and burial of Deborah. It could be bāḵûṯ/باكُت 'cried/pretended to cry' but it does not fit in with the context in that spelling, if it is a transliteration mistake/corruption it could be 'until she cried/pretended to cry' 'now she cried/pretended to cry'. allon-baakut, allon-baaḥuṭ. (Gen.35:8)

Ephrath; 'ep̱rāṯ; نَفرآط 'tears(as in rips)/tore' 'partings' 'parted from/deceived out of money/fortune/possessions' 'parted/deceived out of opportunity/chance' 'crossings/cross(ed)' and is from the same word used for **Euphrates** earlier in Genesis and with the same meanings 'but a little way to come to Ephrath…' meaning there was only a little distance to cross; 'tore' as Rachel dies from child labour ('tears') at this place; through death she and Jacob are 'parted/separated'; could also be نَفرآت 'the sweet/the sweet water'; نُفرآث 'cleansed guts/cleanser of guts' noun of occupation of man who cleans slaughtered animals intestines from faeces and other 'dirt' in preparation to be cooked (but not applied to men/women who clean their own slaughtered food) he often collects the unwanted skins and cleans them too, it is also the verb of pushing/squeezing these impurities out of the intestines (in preparation for cooking the cleaned intestines). Cp: e-phraaṭ, e-phraat, e-phraaf. (Gen.35:16-20)

Ben-oni; ben-'ônî; بَنئُني ، بَنئوني 'bring me up' 'nurture me' as in 'adopt me' asking another to bring up a child not biologically his/hers/theirs, 'by/with the baby/babies' 'my child/children'. The story has the mother thinking of her new-born baby as well as Joseph as she dies and naming the new-born with a plea 'bring me up' and the request is to multiple people, not in the singular (not to a single person to bring him up). Cp: ben-onee, ben-oonee. (Gen.35:18)

Benjamin; binyāmîn; بِن يآمهن 'children/child-calls them mother/makes them mother' 'children/child-their river/rivered them' and it refers to a child calling multiple women 'mother' as a motherless child would desperately seek maternal comfort/care from other women and fits with Rachel's request 'Ben-oni' is to multiple people to care for him as their own, but Benjamin also because she dies as they are near to Ephrath which is the same as Euphrates (a river in the earlier chapter), but also because Rachel dies due to birthing difficulties her condition conjures up to the audience haemorrhaging blood which would be described as 'rivering/flowing like a river' in real life, the Arabic use of the word (yamhin and other river-related words): 'And it came to pass, as her soul was in departing, (for she died), that she called his name Ben-oni: but his father called him Benjamin.' It could also be wordplay on بِن يآمين 'son/child-whose?' 'son/child-counts/lists/reminds' 'son/child-from where/from who'; in rural Yemen even if only one parent dies, the child is considered orphaned and especially if the deceased is the mother. There is nothing in this part of the story to suggest 'son of right' or 'good fortune' or 'south' but the context is that Rachel was reminding Jacob to take care of the new-born who will be left without a mother, she is reminding Jacob that he loves her the most and should love the two biological children she gave him more than his other sons from other wives. Cp: bin-yaam-hn, bin-yaa-meen, bin-yaameen. (Gen.35:18)

Bethlehem; bêṯ leḥem, bêṯ halaḥmî; بيت لَحَم 'house-chewed out/tore off strips of meat/ate plenty of meat' 'he will be-chewed out/tear off strips of meat/eat plenty of meat' 'girl/daughter-chewed out' as in shouted at/told off angrily; it may not be 'house' at all but 'he will be' or even 'girl/daughter'; بيت لَهَم ، بيت هَلَهمي 'he will be well fed/pampered' 'house-well fed/pampered/plumpened' 'daughter/girl-well fed/pampered/plumpened' and is from word (lhm/لهم) 'well fed/plumpened' when a person or animal is pampered with food to make them stronger/fatter for health and growth and in an animal's case for slaughter; it can also mean 'lehem/for them' but the meanings of 'for them' and 'well fed/plumpened' are not in the context of the current Biblical story. bêṯ halaḥmî; بيت هَلَحمي/هَلَحمه 'house/he will be-I will chew out/tears off strips of meat/eat plenty of meat' 'girl/daughter-I will chew out/tear off strips of meat off/eat plenty of meat', 'house/he will be-I will chew him out/tear off strips of meat/eat plenty of meat' 'girl/daughter-I will chew out/tear off strips of meat/eat plenty of meat'. When a person speaks angrily or shouts, it is said 'yilaaḥim/يلاحِم' (masculine) 'tilaaḥim/تلاحِم' (feminine) and has the same meaning as 'he/she is chewing out/biting heads off'—(leḥim/leḥimat/لَحِم/لِحمَت 'he/she chewed out.../bit the head off...' and the word is from (leḥem/liḥim/لَحَم/لِحِم/لحم) of how a predator tears off meat from its prey and also a human when pulling strips of meat off to eat or eating with gusto or greed, which are all from the root word (lḥm/لحم) 'meat/eat meat/butcher(meat)'. I cannot find anything in this part of the story that would suggest why it has been mentioned here other than its connection to one meaning of Ephrath: 'cleanses animal intestines' which is part of processing slaughtered meat and we are told Rachel died and was buried '...in the way to Ephrath, which is Bethlehem', it could be because later authors wanted to add something, but never got around to it, but it may still be related to conjuring up the terrible death of Rachel being torn apart by the birth of Benjamin because the author(s) has coupled it with Ephrath and Bethlehem to create word-imagery of how bloody and painful her death was. Cp: beyt-leḥem, beyt-lehem, beyt-ha-lahmee, beyt-ha-laḥmee, beyt-ha-laḥmh. (Gen.35:19)

Edar; ʿēḏer; wordplay on: عيذَر 'cast a shadow' as it is mentioned '...and spread his tent beyond the tower of Edar.' A tower would cast a shadow. غيدَر 'betrayed' as Reuben has committed adultery with his father's wife/concubine and also 'darkened' as this would darken the atmosphere between them (just as in casting a shadow) from the word غدرا 'darkness/dark'. نَيضَر 'he harmed' as Reuben has harmed Jacob by sleeping with Bilhah. 'Reuben' also takes on an additional meaning: رَئوبين ، ريئو بين 'water(ed)-into/between' 'water(ed)-made clear/apparent' as Rueben has sex with Jacob's wife ('water' and 'semen' are both 'water' in this Arabic) and this illicit affair and defilement of Jacob's wife with Reuben's water has not only become apparent/been seen by Jacob, but has become known to everyone. Cp: 'eyver, gheyder, eydher. (Gen.35:21-22)

Arbah; hʿaurbʿy; is wordplay on: عربا/عربه which is slang for sex: هعَوربئي 'they shagged/fucked' 'he fucked her' 'here, they fucked' 'I will fuck' and refers to Reuben and Bilhah. It is also ئربا/ئربه ، هئَوربئي 'is god/parent' 'I will/here is-my god/parent' 'mix and dilute with water' 'grow/raise/discipline/grow well' (e.g. raise children or cattle) 'I will raise/grow/bring up well' and it refers to Jacob returning to Isaac with a large family, wealth, cattle, etc. The name of the city where Isaac dwells when Jacob returns is Arbah 'god/parent/raise/grow/bring up/grow well' and this meaning is supported by the narrative naming all of Jacob's sons and specifying from which wives; this is to point out that God's promise to Abraham and Isaac has already begun with the multiplication of Jacob's seed—they are a gain/profit to his father and this allows Isaac to be satisfied before he dies '...old and full of days.' Cp: 'arbaa/'arbah, h'aurb-y, arbaa, arbah, h-aurb-y. (Gen.35:22-29)

In lists, I will not repeat names that have already been translated, especially if they do not have additional meanings in the Biblical stories.

Aholibamah; 'ohŏlîḇāmâ; ئُهولي ذآمه/ذآما 'he's the one-insulted/has disease' 'he's the one-ostracised/guilted'; ئوخُلي بآسه 'throw it off/undress' (it is literally 'throw off its mother' which means 'completely/utterly/violently' with 'absolute meanings of the action when 'mother' is used in the word). Cp: o-hoolee-vaamah/vaama, o-ḥoolee-baamah/baama (Gen.36:2)

Anah; ʿănâ; عَنه/عَنا ، عينه/عينا 'look/see' 'look there he is/look it's him' 'his eyes' 'his care/with care' 'suffered' 'meant him' 'helped him', also a sound made to get animals such as cow, goats or sheep back on track or back in correct land; غَنه/غَنا ، غينه/غينا 'sang' 'hummed' 'made muffled sound in throat(used in singing and reading)/made 'ghn' sounds' 'became rich' 'became independent of/no longer needed'. Cp: 'anah(na), 'ainah(na), ghanah(na), ghainah(na) (Gen.36:2)

Zibeon; ṣiḇʿôn; زِبئُن/زِبوُن 'lower belly(between naval and crotch)' 'penetrated with penis'. Cp: ziboon, zib-oon. (Gen.36:2)

Eliphaz; 'ĕlîpaz; ئِلي/ئيلي فز 'the one who/he who-provoke(d)/wins(won)' 'the one who/he who won'. Cp: illee/eilee-phaz. (Gen.36:4)

Reuel; rĕʿûʾēl; رَئوئِل ، ريئوئِل 'saw-the' 'dreamt-the' 'watered-the'; رَعوئِل 'shepherded-the'; ريعُ ئِل 'they watered/soaked/flooded-the'. Cp: reu-ill, reiu-ill, re'u-ill, rei'u-ill. (Gen.36:4)

Jeush; yĕʿûš; يَعُش ، ييعُش 'grazes/shepherds (in afternoon)' 'feeds cattle in evening' 'partially blind' 'he lives/survives'; جَعُش ، جيعُش '(of)furry/long hair'; جَئُش ، جيئُش 'took lots/picked many/took by the handfuls' 'took too much/many'. Cp: ye'ush, yei'ush, ge'ush, gei'ush, ge-ush, gei-ush. (Gen.36:5)

Jaalam; yaʿlām; يَعلآم 'he knows' 'he shows/teaches' 'he knows the way/route' 'makes a mark'. Cp: ya'laam. (Gen.36:5)

Korah; qōraḥ; كورَه 'a lot/loads/a heap/heap it' 'hated/hateful' 'in one go'; كورَح 'striking sound' (from striking one object with another); قورَه 'they read/read it/are educated' 'they teach/read to' 'they stopped moving/ceased what they were doing' 'they admitted'; قورَح 'sores/ulcers' 'burst/exploded' 'bursting sound'. Cp: koorah, koorah, qoorah, qoorah. (Gen.36:5)

Teman; têmān; طيمآن 'reassured (another person)' 'felt reassured'; ظيمآن 'guaranteed (another person)' 'felt guaranteed'. Cp: ṭeymaan, dheymaan. (Gen.36:11)

Omar; 'ômār; ئُمآر 'order/command' or 'being ordered/commanded' 'hint/trace of something' 'clue/sign'; عُمآر 'build/built' 'builder' 'lived long'. Cp: o-maar, 'omaar. (Gen.36:11)

Zepho; ṣĕpô; زَفُ ، زيفُ 'they followed with entourage (like a wedding procession e.g.)'; سَفُ ، سيفُ 'they carried gently' 'they poured gently/poured gentle spurts of water' 'became numb'; صَفُ ، صيفُ 'they cleaned' 'stacked stones/column of stones' 'they stacked in column' 'column/rows'. Cp: zepho, zeipho, sepho, seipho, ssepho, sseipho. (Gen.36:11)

Gatam; gaʿtām; جَعتآم 'to snip tips, limbs or edges off something' 'to nibble edges and corners off'; جَئذآم 'came-guilted/insulted/blamed/humiliated/ostracised/diseased' or a leprosy-like disease. كَعتآم 'hunch over/crouch'. Cp: ga'taam, ga-vaam, ka'taam. (Gen.36:11)

Kenaz; qĕnāz; قَنآز ، قينآز 'sitting/standing perched on a rock/high place' 'placed something on a higher place or a rock' someone who does these meanings. كَعنآز 'like female goats'. Cp: qenaaz, qeinaaz, k'naaz. (Gen.36:11)

Timna; timnaʿ, timnāʿ; تِمنَع ، تِمنآع 'she/it stops/prevents/doesn't allow'. Cp: timna', timnaa'. (Gen.36:12)

Nahath; naḥat; نَحَت 'he filed/sawed'; نَهَت 'she warned against' 'she barred/prohibited'; نَحَط 'we set down' (when removing load off head/shoulder and placing it on ground), 'we leave behind' 'we leave some'. Cp: naḥat, nahat, naḥaṭ. (Gen.36:13)

Zerah; zeraḥ; زَرَه 'squeezed it/tightened it/him' 'squeezed him/it' 'insulted a lot/disgraced him'; صَرَخ 'shouted/he shouted'; سَرَح 'went/he went'; ذَرَه 'sowed it/seeded it/procreated' 'had offspring' 'filled him with insults'. Cp: zerah, sserakh, seraḥ, verah. (Gen.36:13)

Shammah; šammâ; شَمَّه ، شَمَّا 'smelled him/it' 'powdered tobacco(similar to snuff)'; سَمَّه ، سَمَّا 'named him/it' 'told naming story/riddle' (called samaaya), 'poisoned him/it'; صَمَّه ، صَمَّا 'blocked him/it'. Cp: shammah, shamma, sammah, samma, ssammah, ssamma. (Gen.36:13)

Mizzah; mizzâ; مِزَّه ، مِزّا 'squeezed/squeeze' 'squeeze/squeezed him/it' 'a squeeze'; مِصَّه ، مِصّا 'sucked/suck' 'suck/sucked it' 'a suck'; مِسَّه ، مسّا 'touch/touched/possess/possessed' 'touched/possessed him/it' 'a touch' 'a possession'. Cp: mizzah, mizza, missah, missa, missah, missa. (Gen.36:13)

Lotan; lôṭān; لُطآن ، لوطآن 'squeezed together/against each other' 'sides stuck/pressed against each other' 'crushed against each other'. Cp: loṭaan, looṭaan. (Gen.36:20)

Shobal; šôḇāl; سُبآل ، سوبآل 'tails of sheep' prized because it contains fat for food; anything that is hanging or flopping down behind/beside something 'flopping/hanging/drooping/flapping'. Cp: sobaal, soobaal. (Gen.36:20)

Dishon; dîšôn; دِسون/ديسون ، دِسُن/ديسُن 'to stash/sneak and place something without anyone noticing/to plant something(discreetly)' (to be found by someone else), 'to plant/whisper bad ideas into another's head/cause enmity by planting bad ideas'; دِشون/ديشون ، دِشُن/ديشُن 'to make large tassels/bundles of anything (vegetable, clothes, hair)' 'pours heavily' 'sound of heavy water flowing'; تِزون/تيزون ، تِزُن/تيزُن 'to poke with red-hot bar (or any form of fire)'; تِشون/تيشون ، تِشُن/تيشُن 'is filtering impurities/is filtering out'; تِصون/تيصون ، تِصُن/تيصُن 'to sweep/sweep away' (with specific brush) 'sweep away dirt/litter'. Cp:

disoon, deesoon, dison, deeson, dishoon, deeshoon, dishon, deeshon, tishoon, teeshoon, tishon, teeshon, tizoon, teezoon, tizon, teezon, tissoon, teessoon, tisson, teesson. (Gen.36:21)

Ezer; 'ēzer, 'ēzer; نَيزَر 'it's too tight' 'it will squeeze/be too tight'; عيزر 'ugly/made ugly'. Cp: eyzer, 'eyz-er. (Gen.36:21)

Dishan; it is the same as 'Dishon' but in the form of two people doing the action or the action done twice; dîšān; دِسآن/ديسآن 'discreetly placed something/stashed/planted something(discreetly)' (to be found by someone else), 'planted/whispered bad ideas into another's head/caused enmity by planting bad ideas' ; دِشآن/ديشآن 'made large tassels/bundles of anything (vegetable, clothes, hair)' 'poured heavily' 'sound of heavy water flowing'; تِشآن/تيشآن 'is being filtered of impurities/is filtering out'; تِزآن/تيزآن 'to poke with red-hot bar (or any form of fire)'; تِصآن/تيصآن 'to sweep/sweep away' (with specific brush) 'sweep away dirt/litter'. Cp: disaan, deesaan, dishaan, deeshaan, tishaan, teeshaan, tizaan, teezaan, tissaan, teessaan. (Gen.36:21)

Hori; ḥōrî, ḥôri; حوري ، حُري 'ploughed' 'was/became perplexed/in predicament' 'checking/looking into' 'of ploughing' 'of perplexing/predicament'; خُري 'run away/ran away/fled/flee in haste/fear' 'collapse(d)' 'of fleeing/chasing away' 'of collapsing'. Cp: ḥooree, ḥoree, khooree, khoree. (Gen.36:22)

Hemam; hêmān; هيمآن 'worried/anxious' 'to have worries/two worries' 'to forcefully control/be bossy and unkind' 'hegemonize'. Cp: heymaan. (Gen.36:22)

Alvan; 'alwān; ئَلوآن 'colours' 'twirled around/entwined'; عَلوآن 'higher/made higher'; عَلفآن 'of leaves' 'should have…'. Cp: alwaan, 'alwaan, 'alphaan. (Gen.36:23)

Manahath; mānaḥat; مآنَحَت 'did not saw/file' 'granted'; مآنَهَت 'she did not prevent/prohibit/warn'; مآنَحَط 'we do not rest/put down our loads' 'we do not become lowly' 'we do not leave behind' 'we do not leave some'. maanahat, maanahat, maanaḥaṭ. (Gen.36:23)

Ebal; 'êbāl; عيبآل 'fat sheep' or fat animals 'shaking fat/shaking fat of sheep' 'rolling/shaking like fat sheep'; عيضآل 'muscles/strong' 'mice'. Cp: 'eybaal, 'eydhaal. (Gen.36:23)

Shepho; šēpô; شَفُ ، شيفُ 'they are healed' 'they saw' 'they gloated over/at'; سَفُ ، سيفُ 'carried gently' 'pour(ed) gently/pour(ed) gentle spurts of water' 'went numb' 'sipped/sip'; صِفُ ، صيفُ 'stacked stones' 'column of stones' 'made row/column' 'describe(d)' 'insult(ed)' 'summer' 'fish oil'; صِبُ ، صيبُ 'strike/hit/afflict' 'pour/poured'; سِبُ ، سيبُ 'swear at/insult' 'leave it/him/her alone/stop it' 'leave behind'. Cp: shepho, sheipho, sepho, seipho, ssepho, sseipho, ssebo, sseibo, sebo, seibo. (Gen.36:23)

Onam; 'ônām; نُن آم ، نُنآم 'moans/groans-the' 'sleeping'. Cp: on-aam, onaam. (Gen.36:23)

Ajah; 'ayyâ; عَجّه ، عَجّا 'overcrowded' 'over spilling(with fortune/good)/field filled with crops whose panicles seem packed and over spilling' 'stirred/shook' 'suffered/tortured/prolonged his suffering and torture' 'crying and gasping' 'is crooked/twisted/not forthright' 'made crooked/twisted'; نَجّه ، نَجّا 'he came/he's arriving'; نَيّه ، نَيّا an exclamation of displeasure, 'is-he/he is' 'is he?' 'which(e.g. one)'; عَيّا/عَيّه 'will-he/he will' 'will he?' 'warned/taught and remembered', a sound made to stop animals running off and bring them back to the right land/path; this last word fits in with the verse '…the children of Zibeon; both Ajah, and Anah: this was that Anah that found the mules in the wilderness, as he fed the assess of his father.' It seems they were a precursor to Saul and his story which begins with Saul and his brother searching for his father's donkeys. Cp: 'aggah, 'agga, aggah, agga, ayyah, ayya, 'ayyah, 'ayya. (Gen.36:24)

Hemdan; ḥemdān; حَمدآن 'grateful'; خَمدآن 'cooked/done'; هَمدآن 'dormant' 'tired and lying down not moving'. ḥemdaan, khemdaan, hemdaan. (Gen.36:26)

Eshban; 'ešbān; نَشبآن 'they have grown' (into teenagers/young men/women), 'swollen/rigid' (from water, cold, etc.); نَسبآن 'were let go/left' 'leave it'; نَصبآن 'demonic/of demons' 'hit/struck/landed on or in'; عصبآن 'angry, upset and fidgety'. Cp: eshbaan, esbaan, essbaan, 'essbaan. (Gen.36:26)

Ithran; yitrān; يِذرآن 'they sow/seed' 'they leave/leave behind' 'they insult greatly/fill with insults'; حِذرآن 'they are cautious/they warned/they were warned'; يِضرآن 'they develop a habit/become vicious'; عِذرآن 'shadows/two shadows/shadowed' 'excused'. Cp: yivraan, ḥivraan, yidhraan, 'ivraan. (Gen.36:26)

Cheran; kĕrān; قَرآن ، قيرآن 'read' 'connected' 'connected by horns/matching/connected by piece of wood' 'rope around horns/necks/yoke on necks' 'stopped moving/settled down/ceased what they were doing' 'admitted'; كَرآن ، كيرآن 'leased/rented' 'forced to move/flee/chased away'; حَرآن ، حيرآن 'ploughed' 'heated' 'inspected' 'puzzled/in predicament'; خَرآن ، خيرآن 'bolted away/fled/made people flee' 'collapsed' 'good fortune/good' 'shat/shitty'. Cp: qeraan, qeiraan, keraan, keiraan, ḥeraan, ḥeiraan, kheraan, kheiraan. (Gen.36:26)

Bilhan; bilhān; بِلهان 'with humiliation/insults' 'with provocation/spite' 'with what is here' 'stupid/slow/in a trance'; بِلحان 'of dates(fruit)' 'full of dates(fruit)' 'with the hennaed (person/thing)/richly coloured'. Cp: bilhaan, bilḥaan. (Gen.36:27)

Zavaan; za'ăwān; زَعوآن ، زَعيوآن 'fat' 'were fat' 'could/was able/succeeded' 'were able/could do it'; ضَعَوآن ، ضَعيوآن 'twisted/crumpled/floppy/can't sit or stand up' 'crumpled/squashed it' 'lost/of being lost/ confused' 'lost it'; ذَعوآن ، ذَعيوآن 'this/he is helpful'. Cp: za'awaan, za'aiwaan, dha'awaan, dha'aiwaan, va'awaan, va'aiwaan. (Gen.36:27)

Akan; 'ăqān; عَقآن ، عيقآن 'too salty' 'cruel to parents/disobedient' 'crippled/disabled' 'late' 'are obstacles' 'make/made late'. The three sons of Ezer 'made ugly' all state physical disabilities in the meanings of the words. Cp: 'aqaan, 'aiqaan. (Gen.36:27)

Aran; 'ărān; عَرآن ، عيرآن 'borrowed/of borrowing/lending' 'gloat(ing)' 'naked' singular and plural, 'made naked' 'running in the wild' 'pushing forward blindly' 'brash' 'lost in the wild'. (Sibling to Uz; 'to need' (help or something material) 'twisted/bent/not straight' and children of Dishan—all negative attributes/ meanings). Cp: 'araan, 'airaan. (Gen.36:28)

Beor; bĕ'ôr; بَعُر ، بيعُر 'with disgrace' 'will be disgraced' 'will push forward blindly/behave brashly' 'will be/become naked', animals such as donkeys, camels, 'scream/shout/sob for long time'; بيئر 'lose reputation/ bad reputation/ruin the reputation' 'spoiled/stale/expired' 'untrustworthy'. Cp: be'or, bei'or, bei-or/beior. (Gen.36:32)

Dinhabah; dinhāḇâ; دِن هاذه/هاذا 'bend over/bow-this one' 'guilty/guilt-this one'; دِنحآبه 'a disgrace' 'moving along while bent over/crouching to avoid being seen'. **Bela** 'swallowed/illness/ailment' is given a patronym (Beor) and city name (Dinhabah) of negative words similar to it. Cp: din haavah, din haava, dinḥaabah. (Gen.36:32)

Bozrah; boṣrâ; بُصره/بوصره ، بُصرا/بوصرا 'unripe/still green (fruit, vegetables, grain); بُزره/بوزره ، بوزرا/بوزرا 'a litter' of young animals, also used as simile for man/woman with many children, 'caused body to break' (from too much work or heavy load). Cp: bossrah, boossrah, bossra, boossra, bozrah, boozrah, bozra, boozra. (Gen.36:33)

Temani; têmānî; طيمآني 'my reassurance/reassured me' 'of reassuring'; طيمآنه 'reassured him/his reassurance'; ظيمآني 'my guarantee/guaranteed me' 'my quenching/of quenching' 'my thirst/of thirsting'; ظيمآنه 'guaranteed him/his guarantee' 'quenched him'. Cp: ṭeymaanee, ṭeymaanh, dheymaanee, dheymaanh. (Gen.36:34)

Husham; ḥušām, ḥûšām; خُشام ، خوشام 'big bites out of' 'ruin by crumbling/tattering/biting' 'chunks'; حُشام ، حوشام 'modest/they are modest/chaste'; حُسام ، حوسام 'sad and lonely' 'pitiful' 'heart-breaking' 'feel the/feeling the' 'touch/feel-the'. Cp: khooshaam, khushaam, ḥooshaam, ḥushaam, ḥoosaam, ḥusaam. (Gen.36:34)

Hadad; ḥăḏaḏ; حَدَد ، حيدَد 'determined borders' 'sharpened'; هَدَد ، هيدَد 'threatened' 'demolished'. Cp: ḥadad, ḥaidad, hadad, haidad. (Gen.36:35)

Bedad; bĕḏaḏ; بَدَد ، بيدَد 'to throw things around, break things' and without a reason—just tyranny, 'to waste things' through waste or breaking them, throwing them out. What is interesting is in rural Yemen there is a saying (yi-hadid wa yi-badid يِهَدِد ويِبَدِد) meaning 'he threatens and throws things around' which is exactly 'Hadad and Bedad' and these two word-names are given in the Bible in one verse: '...and Hadad the son of Bedad, who smote Midian in the field of Moab, reigned in his stead.'. Cp: bedad, beidad. (Gen.36:35)

Avith; 'ăwîṯ; عَويت ، عيويت 'howled'; غَويت ، غيويت 'misled' 'misled to downfall' 'deceived'; عَبيط ، عيبيط 'brash/foolish' 'armpit(s)'; عَبيث ، عيبيث 'ruined with flippancy' 'mess/making a mess'. The name of the land which Hadad son of Bedad takes over. Cp: 'aweet, 'aiweet, ghaweet, ghaiweet, 'abeeṭ, 'aibeeṭ, 'abeef, 'aibeef. (Gen.36:35)

Samlah; śamlâ; سَمله/سَملا 'dribble' 'poisoned him/for him' 'named him/for him' 'told naming story for him'; صَمله/صَملا 'by force/against will'; شَمله/شملا 'to fill or cover (with a substance or insults)' 'covered/ filled him' 'smelled him/for him'. Cp: samlah, samla, ssamlah, ssamla, shamlah, shamla. (Gen.36:36)

Masrekah; maśrēqâ; مصريقه/مَصريقا 'a theft' 'moving stealthily/quietly/unnoticed'; مشريقه/مَشريقا 'sunny/sun bursting through clouds', time of day between morning and noon, 'sunbathing'; مشريغه/مَشريغا 'choking on saliva, food or drink' (fits in with '...and Samlah [dribble] of Masrekah reigned in his stead.'). Cp: massreyqah, massreyqa, mashreyqah, mashreyqa, mashreyghah, mashreygha. (Gen.36:36)

Baal-hanan; ba'al ḥānān; بَعَل حآنآن 'from high-time is now' 'from high-felt affection'; بَعَل خآنآن 'from high-betrayed' 'from high-soaked/left to soak'; بَعَل هآنآن 'from high-insulted/disgraced' 'from high-gave satisfaction/gave plenty to satisfaction'. Cp: ba'al ḥaanaan, ba'al khaanaan, ba'al haanaan. (Gen.36:38)

Achbor; 'akbôr; نَخبُر 'tell/told' told/tell the news'. Cp: akhbor. (Gen.36:38)

Pau; pā'û; بآعو/بآعُ 'sold', or a specific unit of measuring length; more likely بائو/باوُ 'stayed instead/in place of' and fits in with '...Hadar reigned in his stead: and the name of his city was Pau...'. Cp: baa'oo, baa'u, baa-oo, baa-u. (Gen.36:39)

Mehetabel; mĕhêṭab'ēl; it could be مَحيطَب ئِل ، ميحيطَب ئِل 'woodpile/storage-the' but because of the other names surrounding it in the same verse it is probably: مَهيطَبئِل ، ميهيطَبئيل ، ميهيط بئِل/بئيل which is what the rain is called when the drops are light, few and far between (equivalent to 'spitting' in English when referring to light rain), 'slouched/hands flapping while walking' 'moving slowly' 'depressed/behaving depressed' 'scalded with-the'. Cp: meḥeytab ill/meiḥeytab ill, meheyṭabill/meiheyṭabeyl, meiheyṭa-bill/meiheyṭa-beyl. (Gen.36:39)

Matred; maṭrēd; مَطريت/مَطرَت 'it/she rained'; مَطريد ، مَطرَد 'thrown out/presence unwanted/told to leave/told not welcome' 'chase/chased'. Cp: maṭreyt, maṭret, maṭreyd, maṭred. (Gen.36:39)

Mezahab; mê zāhāḇ; مي ذآهآب 'water is being wasted/gone' from word 'zahab' (vhb/ذهب) 'to waste/finish quickly and needlessly' 'go(ne)/left' and although the same word means 'gold' it does not when referring to water and other substances/actions which means 'wasting/wasteful'. Cp: mey vaahaab. (Gen.36:39)

Jetheth; yĕṯēṯ; جَثيث ، جيثيث 'dry(as an order/request to dry something)' 'it/he dried/is dry' 'drought'. Cp: gefeyf, geifeyf. (Gen.36:40)

Elah; 'ēlâ; عيلاه/عيلَه 'above it/him' 'against it/him' 'about it/him' 'above/against/on' 'on it/him' 'he is responsible(for)/his responsibility/accountability' 'raised him/it(in status or physically). Cp: 'eylah. (Gen.36:41)

Pinon; pînōn; بينون 'children' 'bringing up children/babying' 'still a baby' 'have children' 'fingers'. Cp: beenoon. (Gen.36:41)

Mibzar; mibṣār; مِبصآر 'picked unripe' 'still unripe'; مِبزآر 'has a litter' (of young), 'too heavy load-breaks body' (weight or type of work). Cp: mibssaar, mibzaar. (Gen.36:42)

Magdiel; magdî'ēl; مَجديئيل ، مَجديئِل 'throw onto ground/throw about on ground' 'has fits/epileptic/possessed by demons' 'thrown down/sacrificed' 'place a block of wood beneath' (as platform or wedge); مَغدي ئيل/ئِل 'feed(ing)lunch-the' 'frustrating/swelling glands-the'. Cp: magdee-eyl, magdee-ill, maghdee-eyl/ill. (Gen.36:43)

Iram; 'îrām; عيرآم 'wilderness' 'abandoned in wilderness' 'gloat-the', a type of tree called iram; ئيرآم 'see-the/I see the' 'penis-the/insult with 'penis-the'' 'to throw/to do with throwing/killing/killed' 'thrown, strewn or located over a vast distance/over different areas' 'vast/distant/covering wide or many different areas'. Cp: 'eeraam, eeraam. (Gen.36:43)

Joseph's Story

Joseph; yôsēp; is word play on: يُسيف ، يوسيف 'of sorrow/feels sorrow/regret' 'rinses/cleanses' as in pouring water gently in bursts/pauses to rinse/clean something.

The story mentions **Shechem** as where his brothers are shepherding to emphasise 'screaming in pain, physical pain' is to happen in the story. For the same reason it has Joseph leave **Hebron** 'told them news/information' 'they told/informed/brought news' 'of news/information/of telling' as Jacob informs Joseph of his brothers' whereabouts and asks him to go to them specifically to find out if they are well and to return to Jacob with their news 'and bring me word again'; 'they are doing good' where Joseph is safe because his brothers cannot harm him in the presence of his father, and 'they/he will pass/go beyond' to go to Shechem where he will be harmed. (Gen.37:1-14)

Dothan; dōṯān; is wordplay on: دوفآن 'buried' 'they pushed' 'twice/two times'. The story has Joseph being cast into a well and is similar to being buried; from words (dphn/دفن) 'burial/buried'; 'they pushed' from word (dph/دف) 'pushed/shoved' and it is what we are told they did to Joseph 'And they took him, and cast him into a pit.'; 'twice/two times' from the word (d**owph/**دوف) 'happened' or 'number of times it happen(s/ed)': دوفا once, and 'دوفت/دوفات' preceded by a number means that number of times it happened, whether an action or incident or anything: Joseph was sold by his brothers, then sold again by Midianites. Cp: doophaan. (Gen.37:12-36)

Potiphar; the word in the Bible may not be what the words may mean in the ancient Egyptian language of Pharaonic times, but their meaning in Arabic as used by the authors of the Biblical stories. These authors created names and also used real names of existing civilisations/titles such as Pharaoh, Ramses, etc. but only as could be used to make up a fictionalised story where the word in Arabic pronunciation as a word/compound word would enhance the story and are not real people as already explained. pôṭîpar; wordplay on بوتي/ بُتي فَر 'my girl/daughter-boiled/lustful/flee/fled' as Potiphar's wife (poti/بُتي) becomes (boiled/lustful/فَر) with Joseph and attempts to seduce him; بوتي فَر 'I will bring-increase/prosper' as Potiphar 'brings' (Poti/بوتي) Joseph and Joseph 'brings' God's blessing into Potiphar's house and fields so 'prosper' is (phr/increase/فَر), even the jail prospers when Potiphar brings Joseph in; it is also on 'tears-flees' بُتي فَر as Potiphar's wife tears/pulls off (poti/بُتي) Joseph's clothes and Joseph flees (phar/فَر). Cp: bootee-phar, bo-tee-phar. (Gen.37:36;39)

Adullamite; 'ădullām; نَظولّام/نيظولّام'do/did injustice to' 'injustice' 'became dark/darkness' from word (dhlm/ظَلم) 'injustice' 'dark/darkness'; نَظَل/نيظَلّ آم 'mislead/misled-the' 'deceived-the' 'shaded/created shade-the' from word (dhl/ظل) 'deceit/to mislead' 'shade'. When Judah visits this person from Adullam, he does something which in the Bible is terrible: marries, or at least makes love to, and has a baby from a Canaanite woman. Cp: adhullaam, aidhullaam, adhull-aam, aidhull-aam. (Gen.38:1, 12,20-26)

Hirah; ḥîrâ; حيره ، حيرا 'a predicament' 'a puzzle' 'an open and infected wound' 'put him in a predicament'. It is the name given to the person who is from Adullam 'injustice/mislead-the' who Judah goes to before having sex with a Canaanite woman. 'hira' is meant as both a predicament and an open sore which effect the rest of the story. Both words 'Hira' and 'Adullamite' set the stage for the story and he is mentioned three times: before Judah marrying a Canaanite, before Judah visits a prostitute (which turns out to be his daughter-in-law) and before Judah finds out the prostitute he had sex with is his daughter-in-law—all are wrong, cause injustice and create predicaments. Cp: ḥeerah, ḥeera. (Gen.38:1, 12,20-26)

Shuah; šûa', šû'ā'; شوَع 'are mutated/freakishly ugly (they)' 'bleated like a kid', شوعاء 'is mutated/freakishly ugly (singular, person or animal)'. And is the name given to the Canaanite woman who Judah marries/beds, her name predicts she will give children with ugly meanings. Cp: shoa', shoo'aa. (Gen.38:2)

Er; 'ēr; عير 'a disgrace' 'disgraced/taunted and humiliated'; نير 'penis' 'penetrated with penis' 'insulted with penis(saying it to someone is a slur)'; and the whole Tamar story revolves over the loss of, and need of, a male from the line of Judah to impregnate her; the story revolves around her need to have a penis which can deliver the 'seed' of Judah because Er who was supposed to provide this for her was 'wicked' and killed by God, and he was 'disgraced'. Cp: 'eyr, eyr/e-yr. (Gen.38:3,6-7)

Onan; 'ônān; نُنآن 'groans/moans/groaning/moaning' and is the word said to express pain, the equivalent of 'ouch/ow', it is also عُنآن 'sufferance' from word ('n/'n'n/عن/عنعن) which means to cause distress (not severe pain, but something frustrating and bearable). The character fulfils the role created for its name: he is not happy to marry Tamar, he sexually and mentally frustrates Tamar by ejaculating on the ground instead of inside her, which also 'displeased the Lord'. He too is killed by God. Cp: onaan, 'onaan. (Gen.38:4,8-10)

Shelah; šelaḥ; صَلَح 'happened' 'he was right (as in perfect, ripe, mature, etc.)' 'fixed/works'; all are meant as he is left to reach the perfect age but Judah keeps him away from Tamar in fear he may die like his brothers who wed her, also when he is mentioned another part of the story 'happens': Judah impregnates Tamar. His name indicates he had grown and was ready for marriage. Cp: sselaḥ. (Gen.38:5,10-14,26)

Chezib; kĕzîḇ; كيذيب ، كَذيب 'lies/lied' 'told many lies' 'of telling lies'. No specific place of birth was mentioned for his brothers Er ad Onan, but for Shelah it is mentioned because his role in the story is where Judah lies to Tamar about wanting him to mature before marrying her, while Judah is keeping Shelah away from her 'lest…he die'; he is also connected by being born in 'chezib/lies' as Tamar has to lie and deceive Judah that she is a prostitute so she can be impregnated by him when she becomes aware that Judah is lying about marrying her to Shelah. Cp: keveeb, keiveeb. (Gen.38:5, 11-19,26)

Tamar; tāmār; دامآر 'destruction/destroyed'; ضامآر 'kept inside/in heart' 'hid thoughts/intentions' 'hid in soul/head/heart' and means to know, think or feel something but not say it out loud, to hide the true intentions, meanings or feelings from others, and her word-name and character role in the story is to bring the destruction of almost everyone in connection to her as well as keeping her intentions hidden from Judah until unable to hide her pregnancy, Judah also hides his true intentions about keeping Shelah away from her: as soon as Er marries her he is killed for being wicked; Onan is killed for intentionally avoiding impregnating her; Judah's reputation and honour are destroyed when she seduces him as a prostitute then as the father of her illegitimately conceived children. Cp: daamaar, dhaamaar. (Gen.38:6-26)

Timnath; is word play on: timnaṯ; طِمنَت 'she was reassured'; ظِمنَت 'she guaranteed/was guaranteed' as she now knows for certain Judah will not give her Shelah as husband, but this is also the turning point where she takes action to assure that she carries Judah's seed. timnaʿ, timnāʿ; تِمناع ، تِمنَع 'she/it stops/prevents/doesn't allow' as she is prevented from marrying Shelah therefore carrying Judah's seed. 'Timnath' is mentioned three times where it is made clear 'reassured' and 'prevented' are explicitly meant in the story. Cp: ṭimnat, dhimnat, timna', timnaa'. (Gen.38:12-14)

Pharez; pereṣ; is word play on: بَرَز 'bring forward/press on and push out'; فَرَص 'split open/push out/ emerge by pushing up or out/ divide by breaking or splitting'. Both meanings are meant '...his brother came out: and she said, How hast thou broken forth? *this* breach *be* upon thee: therefore his name was called Pharez'. Cp: berez, pheress. (Gen.38:29)

Zarah; zeraḥ; سَرَح 'went' 'he/it went/left' and refers to Zarah who was supposed to have come out of his mother first, disappearing back into her. '...that *the one* put out *his* hand...saying, This came out first. And it came to pass, as he drew back his hand, that behold his brother came out...And afterword came out his brother...and his name was called Zarah.'. Cp: serah. (Gen.38:28-30)

Zaphnath-paaneah; ṣāpĕnaṯ-paʿnēaḥ; wordplay on: زآفينَة/سآفينَة بَعنيه 'they escorted him/carried him gently-with care/in our eyes' from words (zph/زف) 'a procession/entourage' and (sph/سف) 'carry gently' and ('neah/عنيه) 'eyes/with care'. This is further directly stated in the text in Pharaoh's reaction to Joseph's interpretation/advice of the dream, praising him in front of the servants, he gives him gifts of clothes and even his own ring from off his hand 'carry gently/سف' ; he has Joseph ride in the second chariot beside him (a prominent position), i.e. in a procession: 'zph/زف' ; these meanings are made clearly in Gen.41:37-45. The second part of the name/title (paaneah/بَعنيَه) (with care/in our (my)eyes) is emphasising how fond Pharaoh has become of Joseph 'I'll carry you in my eyes' 'I'll put you in my eye and close it' is a form of expression used between couples, married or lovers, or even between family and friends when expressing to what degree they love/care for the spoken about; all mean they love/care about the person so much they will put him/her in the eye to protect him, carry him gently with as much preciousness, care and protection for the eye/eyesight. The Biblical story narrates how pampered and loved by Pharaoh Joseph is in Genesis 41, and mention of the eye is made 'And the thing was good in the eyes of Pharaoh, and in the eyes of all his servants.' and Pharaoh's special treatment of Joseph follows until verse 45 where Pharaoh nicknames him 'Zaphnath-paaneah' 'they escorted him/carried him gently-with care/in our eyes'. Cp: zaapheinat-ba-'neyah, saapheinat-ba-'neyah. (Gen.41:37-45)

Asenath; 'āsĕnaṯ; ئآسينَت ، ئآسَنَت 'became straight' 'straightened out' 'followed the correct path(morally)' 'she-faced right direction(positionally)'. It could mean his wife became a better person by marrying him, or was good to him by 'facing him' or God. Cp: aasenat, aaseinat. (Gen.41:45).

Poti-phera; pôṭî pera'; بُتي فَرَع 'girl/daughter-separated/prevented/separated or prevented fighting' 'girl/daughter-strong tall growing crops/stalks'. She is given to Joseph as wife at the same time Pharaoh strengthens and raises Joseph to a position of the highest status, also mentioned again when she bares him two sons—all mentions show a strengthening and growth like a tall stalk of crop. It is interesting although Pharaoh in English has a different pronunciation to the same word in Arabic that the Biblical verses which mention Asenath, the authors always add 'the daughter of Poti-phera the priest of On': On; 'ôn; ئون ، عون 'groan/moan', 'help/support/cooperation' the latter which is happening between Jospeh, Pharaoh and the rest of the country. So, if you place her father's name and follow it with his place of priesthood as it is set in the story you get: poti-phera-on: بُتي فرعون which reads 'daughter of Pharaoh' and Pharaoh is exactly as it is pronounced in Arabic (phr'on) and also the sentence reads as 'Asenath, daughter of Pharaoh'. Cp: botee-phera'; and: oon, 'on. (Gen.41:45,50)

Manasseh; mĕnaššeh; مَنَسِّه ، مينَسَّه 'made him forget' as in distracted him to forget and is exactly what is written in the story 'And Joseph called the name of the firstborn Manasseh: For God, *said he*, hath made me forget all my toil, and all my father's house.' Cp: menasseh, meinasseh. (Gen.41:51)

Ephraim; 'eprayim; نَفري هم/ام 'increase/multiply-them/the'; نَفرَيم ، نَفريم 'with gap between teeth/gap' usually describes a person with a gap between front teeth and also when a front tooth is missing such as removed milk tooth or lost adult tooth, also describes a gap where one should not be. When something is described as (yiphree/يِفري) which can be anything that starts as a small amount and has the quality to increase itself in size, quantity, strength, flavour, scent, etc. and is further explained as being the exact meaning of the word-name: 'And the name of the second called he Ephraim: For God hath caused me to be fruitful in the land of my affliction.' Cp: ephray-hum/um, ephrayim, ephrayum. (Gen.41:52)

Jacob's Family to Egypt

Goshen; gōšen; جوشَن 'take handfuls' 'they took handfuls/too much' 'many people' and is from word (gsh/جش) which means 'picked a lot (with hand(s))' and is against etiquette when offered something (e.g. sweets, biscuits). It also denotes plenty, excess, that you can fill your hands and take a lot. Joseph knows his family are suffering from famine and so is Egypt, but he offers them to come and live in an area called 'Goshen' denoting plenty '...come down unto me...And thou shalt dwell in the land of Goshen...And there I will nourish thee; for yet there are five years of famine; lest thou, and thy household, and all that thou hast, come to poverty.' Pharaoh is given dialogue which confirms the same, that they and their families and animals will have plenty to eat from 'I will give you the good of the land of Egypt, and ye shall eat the fat of the land.' Cp: gooshen. (Gen.45:9-18)

Hanoch; same as earlier.

Phallu; pallû'; فَلّى 'removed lice', 'picked through/went through thoroughly' 'said something (negative) and it happened/bad omen'; بَلّى 'soaked/wetted' 'became worn/faded' 'afflicted'. Cp: phallu, ballu. (Gen.46:9)

Hezron; ḥeṣrôn, ḥeṣrōn; حَسرون 'they are thinned/skinny'; حَصرون 'surrounded' 'they are surrounded/they surrounded' 'sorrow and regret/great despair, sorrow, regret'; حَذرون 'they are wary' 'they were warned/they warned'. Cp: ḥesroon, ḥessroon, ḥevroon. (Gen.46:9)

Carmi; karmî; قَرمي ، قَرمه 'a crumb/eating crumbs' 'a crumbling/crumbling something from its corners' 'broke off crumbs/corners' 'a person who admits (to something)' 'admit to me' 'a rejoinder/answering back' 'he cut him short/shut him up with a retort'; كَرمي ، كَرمه 'try to(or: go ahead) throw/threw like this' 'of generosity/generous' 'his generosity'. Cp: qarmee, qarmh, karmee, karmh. (Gen.46:9)

Jemuel; yĕmû'ēl; يَمُ/يِيمُ يَل 'rivered-the' 'mothered/called mother-the'; عَمُ/عيمُ يَل 'drank-the' 'blinded-the'; هَمُ/هيمُ يَل 'abandoned-the(in faraway area)' 'they worried-the' (can mean they caused another to worry or themselves were worried). Cp: yemu-ill, yeimu-ill, 'emu-ill, 'eimu-ill, hemu-ill, heimu-ill. (Gen.46:10)

Jamin; yāmîn; يآمهن 'made them mothers' 'their river' 'rivered-them'; يآمين 'he-who/who is he?' 'right (hand/side)' 'whose?' 'from where/who' 'he counts/lists/reminds' 'who are you'. Cp: yaamhn, yaameen. (Gen.46:10)

Ohad; 'ōhad; ئوحَد 'one (person)' 'lonely' 'sharpening'; ئوهَذ 'or this one'. Cp: ooḥad, oo-hav. (Gen.46:10)

Jachin; yākîn; يآقين 'certainty' 'perky' 'sitting/standing with head held high/proper posture' 'estimates liquid measures/tops up water'; يآخين 'he soaks' 'he betrays' 'he becomes brotherly'; يآخهن 'made them brothers' 'said 'akh' to them (disgusted/fed up)'. Cp: yaaqeen, yaakheen, yaakhhn. (Gen.46:10)

Shaul; šā'ûl; صآوُل 'stone/rock' (ssala is a large stone) 'made layer with stones' (ssalal are flattish stones approximately five-inch, used as a layer in the building process of the roof, they fully cover the roof and laid so as to connect each other and fill up gaps), 'reached/reaching' 'arrived/arriving' 'finding' 'public apology 'arriving'' 'connect/connecting/connected'; سآوُل 'asked/asking/questioned' 'leaked/leaking/flow/flowing' 'distracted/comforted/entertained'. Cp: ssaa-ul, saa-ul. (Gen.46:10)

Gershon; gēršôn; جيرصُن 'bells' 'rang/wore bells' 'made ringing sound'; غيرزُن 'a plait' 'plaited' 'stuck in mud'; غيرصُن 'young plants/small shoots' 'planted'. Cp: geyrsson, gheyrzon, gheyrsson. (Gen.46:11)

Kohath; qĕhāṯ; قَحآث ، قيحآث 'struck sharply with a throw' 'a sharp striking sound'; قَحآط ، قيحآط 'brushed hair' 'made a scratchy sound' 'scraped/scraping sound' 'unleavened bread'. Cp: qeḥaaf, qeiḥaaf, qeḥaaṭ, qeiḥaaṭ. (Gen.46:11)

Merari; mĕrārî; مَرآري ، ميرآري 'mirrors' 'made reflections/lots of glinting' 'passing along/of passing along' 'bitter/of bitterness'. Cp: meraaree, meiraaree. (Gen.46:11)

Hezron; as before.

Hamul; ḥāmûl; حاَمُل 'carrying' (anything physical, but also emotion such as hatred of another); خاَمُل 'lethargic' 'velvet/velvety fabric'. Cp: ḥaamul, khaamul. (Gen.46:12)

Tola; tôlā'; طُلاّع 'longest/longer' 'took long/longer' 'tall/tallest' 'painted' 'coated/completey covered (with liquid/semi-liquid substance)' 'beat severely'; تَلاّع 'she/it bends/twists'; طَلاّع 'went up/got on'; دُلاّع 'heavy/generous pouring' 'they are spoiled/brattish'. Cp: ṭolaa, tolaa', ṭolaa', dolaa'. (Gen.46:13)

Phuvah; puwwâ; فوّه 'yawned/yawning' 'aired/fanned'; بوّه 'milk breast/mother's breast' noun used to describe human breast with milk. Cp: phuwwah, buwwah. (Gen.46:13)

Job; wĕyôb; yôb; ويِيُب ، وييوب ، يُب ، يوب 'and he returns/and he returns/and he is going to and fro, or up and down' 'and he is being jerked up and down' 'and he is coming-going and coming-going'; (وي)جُب ، (وي)جوب '(and he)go(es) around all over the place' '(and he)answer/reply/respond' 'letter'; (وي)هُب ، (وي)هوب '(and he)swoop down on' 'give' 'he, with' 'with him'; (وي)عُب ،(وي)عوب '(and he) fill/filled/pack/packed' '(and he)float/overflow/leak water' '(and he)swollen with water' 'type of cheese(swollen and leaks water)' 'stank/rotted and stank' 'shame/disgrace' '(and he)shamed/disgraced'. Cp: weiyob, weiyoob, yob, yoob, (wei)gob, (wei)goob, (wei)hob, (wei)hoob, (wei)'ob, (wei)'oob. (Gen.46:13)

Shimron; šimrôn; شِمرُن ، شِمرون 'sleeves/clothes pulled up/unkempt'; سِمرُن ، سِمرون 'they stayed up late night or all night' 'fictional night time stories' 'told night time stories'. Cp: shimron, shimroon, simron simroon. (Gen.46:13)

Sered; sereḏ; زَرَط 'swallowed'; سَرَد 'I will come back' 'I will return(it)' 'I will respond' 'told story/account' 'narrated what happened'; صَرَد 'burnt black logs' 'burning and burying logs for charcoal' 'pretended to be deaf' 'moved stiffly avoiding answering'. Cp: zereṭ, sered, ssered. (Gen.46:14)

Jahleel; yaḥlĕ'ēl; جَهلي نيل 'children of-the' 'ignorance of-the' 'came for me-the'; يَحلي ئِل 'he sweetens-the' 'he circumcises/purifies/makes edible-the'. Cp: gahlei-ill, yaḥlei-ill. (Gen.46:14)

Ziphion; ṣipyôn; زِفيُن ، زفيون 'escorted them/they escorted' 'entourage/wedding procession'; سِفيُن ، سِفيون 'went/became numb' 'they poured gently/poured gentle spurts of water' 'they carried gently/carried them gently'; صِفيُن ، صِفيون 'became clear/clean/pure' 'became/stacked stone columns/rows'. Cp: ziphyon, ziphyoon, siphyon, siphyoon, ssiphyon, ssiphyoon. (Gen.46:14)

Haggi; ḥaggî; حَجّي 'hide/cover it'; هَجّي 'pronounce/teach to pronounce' 'abandoned/left'. Cp: ḥaggee, haggee. (Gen.46:16)

Shuni; šûnî; شُني 'filter (it)' (in the form said to female); سُني 'begin it/with' 'the first(time)' 'make it a habit/custom' 'teethed' 'my teeth' 'left for a long time/a while' 'became straight'. Cp: shunee, sunee. (Gen.46:16)

Ezbon; 'eṣbôn; نَصبُن 'washing clothes'; نَزبُن 'lower belly' between navel and groin, 'penetrate/touch with penis'. Cp: essbon, ezbon. (Gen.46:16)

Eri; 'ērî; عيري 'borrow' 'make naked' 'gloat at/over' 'my disgrace/shame'; ئيري 'show him/teach him' 'see/show' 'understand' 'my penis' 'insult with 'penis'' 'penetrate with penis'. Cp: 'eyree, eyree. (Gen.46:16)

Arodi; 'ărôḏî; عَرُضي ، عيرُضي 'came around me/came from behind me' 'obstructs (physically)' 'objects' 'causes trouble/confronts' 'my width'; عَرُدي ، عيرُدي 'wobbles' 'wobbles head'. Cp: 'arodhee, 'airodhee, 'arodee, 'airodee. (Gen.46:16)

Areli; 'ar'ēlî; نَرئِلي ، نَرئيلي 'I see-the one who' 'show me' 'see for me' 'water-the one who' 'water for me'; نَرعيلي 'see/I see-rose above/rose in status' 'shepherd for me/take care for me' 'be considerate with/for me'; عَرئِلي ، عَر ئيلي 'became naked/strip naked for me' 'abandoned in the wilderness for me' 'shame for me'; عَر عيلي 'became brash-rose above' 'stripped naked-rose above. Cp: ar-illee, ar-eylee, ar 'eylee, 'ar-illee, 'ar-'eylee. (Gen.46:16)

Jimnah; yimnâ; هِمنه ، همنا 'our worry/he worries us'; جِمنه ،جِمنا 'small clay jug for storing clarified butter'; يِمنه ، يِمنا 'to his right/to the right' 'he counts and lists/says he gave and gave' 'grants' 'from him' 'who, from him'; عِمنه ، عِمنا 'drank/gave to drink/drank it' 'our uncle'. Cp: himnah, himna, gimnah, gimna, yimnah, yimna, 'imnah, 'imna. (Gen.46:17)

Ishuah; yišwâ; يِشوه ، يِشوا 'is chatting' 'is being roasted/grilled'; يِصوا 'making squealing animal sounds (like chicks or any other squeaky sound)'; يِشوح 'bleating or making long sounds like animal'. Possibly: عِسوه ، عِسوا 'cold bread' 'broke/ate bread' and is the precursor to 'Jesus'. Cp: yishwah, yishwa, yisswa, yishwaḥ, 'iswah, 'iswa. (Gen.46:17)

Isui; yišwî; يِشوي 'he is roasting/grilling'; يِصوي 'he/it is making squealing animal sounds (like birds or any other squeaky sound'. Possibly: عِسوي 'my cold bread/of cold bread' 'breaking/eating cold bread' and is the original name for 'Jesse'. Cp: yishwee, yisswee, 'iswee. (Gen.46:17)

Beriah; běrî'â; بيريعه/ا ، بَريعه/ا 'galloped/ran like animals' 'with lots of water/irrigation/flooded' 'with lots of watering/flooding'; بيريئه/ا ، بَريئه/ا 'pious/good/innocent' 'she is pious/good/innocent' 'declare/ prove him innocent' 'pass by/get ahead of/surpass him/it' 'pass beyond him/it'. Cp: beree'ah(a), beiree'ah(a), beree-ah(a), beiree-ah(a). (Gen.46:17)

Serah; śeraḥ; صَرَخ 'shouted'; صَرَح 'spoke honestly/openly'; سَرَح 'went/left'. Cp: sserakh, sserah, serah. (Gen.46:17)

Heber; ḥeḇer; خَبَر 'news/information' 'told/spoke'; حَبَر 'chapped skin/chilblains'; خَضَر 'vegetables/fruit' 'became green (as in wet)' 'spoiled' 'unripe'; حَضَر 'ripe'. Cp: kheber, heber, khedher, hedher. (Gen.46:17)

Malchiel; malkî'ēl; مَلكي ئِل/ئيل 'what's with the(fem.)/what's wrong-the' 'my fortune-the'; مَلخيئيل 'what is the hallucination/why is he hallucinating/what about the hallucination' 'what is the imagination(s)'. Cp: malkee-ill/eyl, malkhee-ill, malkhee-eyl. (Gen.46:17)

Belah; bela'; بَلَع 'swallowed'; بَلَأ ، بَلَى 'an affliction/ailment/illness/suffering' 'afflicted/ailed' 'soaked/ wetted' 'worn/faded/has become old(object)'. Cp: bela', bela, bel-a. (Gen.46:21)

Becher; beḵer; بَكَر 'came early' 'early morning' 'firstborn' 'female calf' 'heifer'; بَحَر 'good riddance' 'sea/ ocean'; بَقَر 'cows' 'tore/a rip' 'ripped apart'; بَخَر 'burnt incense' 'good' 'fortune' 'in good health' 'will collapse/chase away/flee'. Cp: beker, beher, beqer, bekher. (Gen.46:21)

Ashbel; 'ašbēl; نَسبيل 'let it down/smooth it' (like hair or rope) 'let it hang down' 'sheep/lamb with large tail'; عَشبيل 'an entanglement(of rope/hair/branches—anything long or stringy)'. Cp: asbeel, 'ashbeel. (Gen.46:21)

Gera; gērā'; جيراء 'ran' 'neighbours/neighbourly' 'insurmountable suffering/pain' 'brutal/are brutal/unjust/ tyrants' 'injustice'; جيراع 'burped/burps' 'gave sips/fed in small sips/sipped/forced to sip'. Cp: geyraa, geyraa'. (Gen.46:21)

Naaman; na'ămān; نعيمآن ، نَعَمَآن 'blessings' 'two blessings' 'of/has blessings' 'soft/smooth' 'receiving something physical e.g. money, food, clothes, etc. any kind of gift/necessity, even health' 'received blessings' 'gave blessings/two blessings' 'made smooth/easy(ier)' 'lived in good life/blessings'; نَغيمآن ، نَغَمَآن 'we stifle/feel stifled' 'we suffocate/feel suffocated' 'we cover/we are covered' 'we muffle/are muffled' 'we depress/feel depressed'. Cp: na'amaan, na'aimaan, naghamaan, naghaimaan. (Gen.46:21)

Ehi; 'ēḥî; ئيهي 'her' 'she is' 'here she is'; ئيحي 'it stayed/it stayed still' 'stay' 'stay still'. Cp: eeyhee, eeyhee. (Gen.46:21)

Rosh; rō'š; روئش 'spray' 'wash'; روئس 'set aside/leave some' (e.g. food for someone absent) 'save' 'has headache'; روعش 'shook'. Cp: roosh/roo-sh, roos/roo-s, roo'sh. (Gen.46:21)

Muppim; muppîm; موبّهم ، مُبّهم 'what is with them?', but is said rhetorically when used in a phrase and actually means they don't care about the people spoken about as the word is used to mean 'scatter them/ disperse them/scare them away' and is always used with the word 'huppim' which follows it in the list Gen.46:21. Cp: mubbhum, moobbhum. (Gen.46:21)

Huppim; ḥuppîm; هوبّهم ، هُبّهم 'swoop down on them' 'he did with/to them' 'he-with them'. this word is always used in the phrase 'hubbhum wa mubbhum/ هوبّهم وموبّهم' 'swoop down on them and scatter them'. Cp: hubbhum, hoobbhum. (Gen.46:21)

Ard; 'ard; عَرض 'behind to one side' 'around (behind)' 'width' 'obstructed'; عَرد 'became stiff-necked' 'became stubborn/dug his heels in' 'wobbled his head/bent his neck' 'went off in a wrong direction'. Cp: 'ardh, 'ard. (Gen.46:21)

Hushim; ḥušîm; حوس ام ، حوسهم 'feel them/the'; حوسيم 'pitiful' (in plural); هوش هم/ام 'shoo-them/the'; خوشهم/ام 'hollow(ed) out/crumble(d)-them/the' 'bites/chunks'; حوشام 'they are modest/chaste'. Cp: hushum/um, huseem, hush-hum/um, khush-hum/um, hushum, hush-um. (Gen.46:23)

Jahzeel; yaḥṣě'ēl; يَحزي ئِل 'corrals/blocks-the' (term used in shepherding animals); يَخزي ئِل 'he swears at/ insults-the'; يَخذي ئِل ، يَخذيئِل 'he takes-the' 'he causes mind to fail/go insane/become mentally unstable'. Cp: yahzei-ill, yakhzei-ill, yakhvei-ill. (Gen.46:24)

Guni; gûnî; جُني/جوني ، جُنه/جونه 'a sack/sacks' 'his sack(s)' (usually made of beige fibres/burlap fabric, but also same word used for sacks made of modern polyester materials) 'sackcloth/his sackcloth', 'a bird of prey' (a specific bird of prey but I do not know its name in English) 'caused/what he caused/reaped'. Cp: gunee, goonee, gunh, goonh. (Gen.46:24)

Jezer; yēṣer; ييزر 'he/it squeezes too tight' 'tightening/squeezing' 'he visits' 'visiting'; جيزَر 'green pastures' 'harvest' 'cut crops of grass' 'to slaughter or beat up people as if mowing down crops' 'he slaughtered' 'graze animals/let animals graze freely'; عيصَر 'twisted' 'twisted(pulled) muscle'. Cp: yeyzer, geyzer, 'eysser. (Gen.46:24)

Shillem; şillēm; شلِّيم 'take/took them' 'took-river/sea'; سلِّيم 'ask/asked them/the' 'of questions/asking' 'greet/ greeted' 'of mild/peaceful manner/nature' 'intact/whole/survived' 'leaked/flowed-river/sea' 'leaked/flowed-the' 'delivered-the/received-the' 'distracted/entertained/comforted-the'. Cp: shilleym, silleym. (Gen.46:24)

Ramses; ram'amsēs; wordplay on: رَم نَمزيز ، رَم عَمزيز 'threw/thrown, strewn or located over a vast distance/areas-is squeezed' 'threw/thrown, strewn or located over a vast distance/areas-will squeeze' 'threw/ killed-is squeezed/will squeeze' 'saw the/watered the-is squeezed' 'saw the/watered the-will squeeze'; رَم نُمصيص ، رَم عَمصيص 'threw/thrown, strewn or located over a vast distance/areas-is sucked' 'threw/ thrown, strewn or located over a vast distance/areas-will suck' 'threw/killed-is sucked/will suck' 'saw the/ watered the-is sucked' 'saw the/watered the-will suck'. From words: (ram/رَم) 'throw/kill/strewn, etc.' and 'saw(r)-the(am حَم)'; ('a/ا/ا) 'is' and ('a/عَ) 'will'; (msēs/مزيز) 'squeeze(ed)' from word (mz/مز) 'squeeze(d)/ wring' (water out of or any liquid), and also (msēs /مصيص) 'suck(ed)' from word (mss/مص) 'suck(ed)'. Whether it was written by original authors or later editors of these stories what you see is the setting for the introduction of Moses' character and role which will begin in Egypt. The compound words for 'Ramses' the land where Jacob and family arrive and the word/meaning of 'Moses' are linked. Cp: ram-amzeyz; ram- 'amzeyz, ram-amsseyss; ram- 'amsseyss. (Gen.47.11)

Shiloh; šilōh; شِلوه 'take it/took it/carry it' and describes how Shiloh will take the sceptre from Judah; سيلوه 'ask/question him/asked/questioned him' 'of questioning/asking' 'flow(ed)/leak(ed)/of flowing' 'distract(ed)/ entertain(ed)/comfort(ed)'; صلوه 'reach(ed) it/him' 'arrive(d) it/him' 'connect(ed) it/him' 'publicly apologise(d)-him/to him' 'his rock'. Cp: shilooh, silooh, ssilooh. (Gen.49:10)

Atad; 'ātād; wordplay on عَاتَاد 'heavy' 'heavy equipment' 'equipment' and refers to the chariots, horsemen and 'very great company' arriving at the threshing floor for Jacob's mourning; عَاتَاب 'spoke about an issue/gently reproached' (in order to clear the air) and 'will forgive/repent on'; عَاتَاد 'will be harmed' which is what Joseph's brothers do and fear when they bring up all the evil they did to Joseph and fear his revenge and how Joseph forgives them. Cp: 'aataad, 'aataab, 'aataav. (Gen.50:6-21)

Abel-mizraim; 'ābēl-miṣrayim; عَابيل مِصرَي ام 'shook fat-bundle-the' and refers to the shaking of the bundled/wrapped corpse of Jacob and the movement of all their equipment on horse and chariots; it is also likening Jacob to 'fat of sheep/shaking fat of sheep' which is a prized substance and considered the best part of sheep meat—this is confirmed in the narrative by God accepting fat of sheep and other sacrifices. Cp: 'aabeyl-missray-um. (Gen.50:6-14)

Machir; mākîr; مآخير 'of good fortune' 'not of good fortune/not good' 'last/late' 'deferred/made late(r)' and refers to Jacob setting Ephraim before Manasseh in the blessing, but still blessing Manasseh and his children, but maintains he will be behind and lesser than Ephraim although he is the firstborn. Cp: maakheer. (Gen.48:12-20;50:23)

Exodus

Two fictional cities are created to give the story its setting; the narration and place names are exactly the meanings of the words given as names.

Pithom; pitōm; بِذوم 'with/do to the humiliated/guilted/blamed/ostracised' 'with humiliation/guilt/blame/ostracization'. As the story narrates: the children of Israel are accused of being disloyal and are abused and exploited in labour, the city appropriately named with the action taking place in the story. Cp: bi-voom. (Exod.1:7-22)

Raamses; ra'amsēs; رَئمزيز ، رَعَ مزيز 'saw/watered-squeezed(ed)' 'shepherded/brought up-squeeze(ed)'; رَئمصيص ، رَعَ مصيص 'saw/watered-suck(ed)' 'shepherded/brought up-suck' and again it refers to Moses' part in the story. There is only a slight difference between Ramses (Gen.47.11) and this Raamses at Exod.1:11, they are based on the same words and wordplay but both reflect what is happening in the respective stories and the word-names' slight difference is also reflected within its respective story. 'Ramses' tells of Jacob and sons living in vast areas and on the best of land in Egypt where they will shepherd livestock and live in plenty, it also indicates the story of Moses to come who will be thrown into the river and Moses to be breastfed; 'Raamses' denotes Moses will be spotted in the river and brought up/shepherded i.e. taken care of by the people who save him from the river and the people who find women to give him 'suck' (breastmilk/feed). Cp: ra-a-mzeyz, ra'a-mzeyz, ra-a-msseyss, ra'a-msseyss. (Exod.1:11)

Shiphrah; šiprâ; شِفره ، شِفرا 'labia minor/vaginal flaps' an appropriate name for a fictional midwife. Cp: shiphrah, shiphra. (Exod.1:15-21)

Puah; puwwâ; بُوّه ، بُوّا 'lactating breast/breast with milk'. It is what a lactating mother's breast is called, and again, very appropriate for naming a midwife in a story who deals with new mothers and babies who need to be breastfed; فوّه ، فوّا 'yawn/yawned' 'aired/fanned' but these latter meanings are not supported in the text. Cp: buwwah, buwwa, phuwwah, phuwwa. (Exod.1:15-21)

Miriam; miryām; مِريآم 'pass along-river' from words: (mr/مر) 'pass/cross/pass by/pass along' and (ym/يم) 'river/sea'. Although she is not named in Exodus 1 where her role is introduced, she is named 'Miriam' as Moses' sister later in the story. Her name denotes the role given to her in the story: she watches her mother throw Moses into the river and as she appears at the other end where Moses is picked up by Pharaoh's daughter she has followed the river and Moses; she is possibly one of the 'maidens' among Pharaoh's daughter's maids who are described 'and her maidens walked along by the river's side' and she suggests to Pharaoh's daughter that she can bring a wet nurse and it is Miriam/Moses' sister sent to fetch her: Miriam walked/followed the river—reflecting the choice of character name. When her name is first mentioned at Exodus 15, the story places her beside the sea while singing the song about Pharaoh dying in the Red Sea. Cp: mir-yaam. (Exod.1:3-7; 15:20-21).

Moses; mōšeh; wordplay on: موزِه 'squeeze him/it' (as in squeeze/wring water out of him) because Pharaoh's daughter takes him out of the danger of the river where he is wet and would end up drowning; and موصه 'suck him/it' and means to breastfeed him (give him to suck); موسه 'touched/possessed/was possessed/touched him/it' 'entangled/caused problems/provoked problems or fighting-him/it'. The word is in the form of a woman doing the action or told to do the action just as it is a woman character doing two of the three word-name actions: Pharaoh's daughter squeezing the water out; Pharaoh's daughter ordering a wet nurse for him: '...and when she saw the ark among the flags, she sent her maid to fetch it...And Pharaoh's daughter said unto her, Take this child away, and nurse it for me, and I will give thee thy wages. And the woman took the child and nursed it. And the child grew, and she brought him unto Pharaoh's daughter, and he became her son. And she called his name Moses: and she said, Because I drew him out of the water'. The meaning of 'entangled/caused problems/provoked problems or fighting' is relayed immediately after his name is introduced as he witnesses a physical assault and then gets involved which leads to a fight and Moses murdering a man, followed by witnessing another fight which causes Moses a serious problem. Cp: moozeh, moosseh, mooseh. (Exod.2:1-10)

Midian (Gen.25:2); midyān; مِديآن 'loans to others/is debtor to others' 'of guilt/found guilty/bowed/lowered/bent' 'reaches out with hand/stretches hand' 'extends/offers something to another (with hand)' 'reaches into' 'reach for/stretch arm to reach for' 'hands/passes/stashes/hides/plants with no one noticing' 'of underhanded behaviour(done secretly)' 'of stowing or stashing in/planted' 'hides (something) underneath something hastily' 'puts hands on something not his/theirs' 'went over/overstepped/'took liberties''; مِضيآن 'passing by/moving on' 'completed' 'signing/making mark' because Moses is guilty of murdering a man he has to leave Egypt and live in the appropriately named area; his spontaneous good deed towards the priest of Midian's daughters is considered like a debt which the priest repays with hospitality, kindness and giving his daughter to Moses as a wife. Cp: midyaan, midhyaan. (Exod.2:15-16; 3:1; 4:18-20; 18)

Zipporah; ṣippōrâ; wordplay on: زِبّورح 'his penis has gone', زِبّوره/زِبّورا 'of-penis (related to it in activity)'. The first and second meaning because she circumcises her son with a rock to save him, and so his penis as it was, is no longer and she is linked by name to being involved with doing something to it. سِبّوره/سِبّورا 'fixer' as she fixes/finds a solution to the problem of God wanting to kill her son. صِبّوره/صِبّورا 'of-patience' taking into account she has to leave her family, travel to foreign lands, face-off with God trying to kill her son where she has to use a sharp stone to circumcise her son to defend him—would make her a patient person. It is obvious the Bible as it exists today does not tell much of the story which includes Zipporah, Moses and God, and it has been left out or forgotten over the ages, but Zipporah's words and name still express she is suffering with Moses, whether having to travel to Egypt, of having to put up with Moses' wanderings and his obeisance to what God requests of him, even if it is to kill his firstborn, she says and does what depicts a person who is fed up and at the end of her tether—for not only does she circumcise her son in a brutal and rushed manner out of necessity, but she throws the foreskin at Moses' feet before telling him he is a 'bloody' husband (difficult? violent? uncaring?) because of endangering her son and causing his pain. Cp: zibboo-raḥ, zibboorah, zibboora, sibboorah, sibboora, ssibboorah, ssibboorah. (Exod.2:21; 4:25-26)

If read objectively, many parts of the stories in the Bible, some within the same chapter, jar against each other even when read in English, not only the obvious contradictions, but a difference in the style of narrating/writing can be detected, you can see at least some places where editing by different authors has occurred. Zipporah's story is one of them. It may be argued that it was God who attempted to slay Moses' firstborn, but from the Biblical story itself, it was obviously Moses: Zipporah's actions and words are directed at Moses. God, in the same chapter, tells Moses that he (God) will be in Moses' actions—so Moses will behave/be like God when implementing his actions. It could be that the later editors of the Bible understood Moses being possessed by God or misunderstood because Exod.4:22-26 go from God instructing Moses to tell Pharaoh to let the people go or else he will slay Pharaoh's firstborn to God finding Moses' firstborn in the inn and attempting to kill him, to Moses being the one attempting to kill his own son, whom Zibbora saves and then tells Moses 'Surely a bloody husband thou art to me.'. It is possible that more stories in their original form show 'prophets/heroes' being possessed by God but were edited, one such story which exists in unadulterated form is Samson. Characters from stories which were told as folklore, and popular in those times, were edited by later editors in writing, one such example is Enoch being replaced by Noah, but different editors of the Biblical texts restored Enoch even if not as a full story, but as a mention in a few lines. The same seems to have happened with Moses, one editor at least wanted further wordplay on his name to be emphasised: موسِه 'touched/possessed/was possessed/touched him/it' 'entangled/caused problems/provoked problems or fighting-him/it' Cp: mooseh, but other editors removed it, but not completely: God says to Moses 'Now therefore go, and I will be with thy mouth...and thou shalt be to him instead of God...And it came to pass by the way in the inn, that the Lord met him, and sought to kill him.' which results in Zipporah performing a quick circumcision and throwing the foreskin at Moses' feet, so Moses was both God and Moses as he was possessed/touched by God. (Exod.4)

Gershom; gēršōm; جيرشوم 'tattered' 'sides and tips nibbled at/bitten all around or torn' from word (grshm/جرشم) 'tattered all around/chunks missing from sides and tips' and reflects his penis will be in tatters when his mother 'took a sharp stone, and cut off the foreskin of her son. If you ever see people who use stones to cut things by pounding it, it is not a clean cut that is made, but a rugged and tattered removal. Also, جيرسوم 'neighbour-fainted/poison/poisoned' 'insufferable pain-fainted' from word (gr/geyr/goor/جر/جير/جور) 'neighbour/pull/draw' 'insufferable pain/suffering/injustice/tyranny/ruthless' and (soom/سوم) 'fainting/to faint/dizzy/dizziness' 'poison' and the meanings show how Moses feels about his life that he has 'been a stranger in a strange land'. Cp: geyrshoom, geyr-soom (Exod.2:22; 4:24-26)

Horeb; ḥōrēb, ḥôrēb; هوريب ، هُريب 'stand back' 'do not come nearer' 'move away', said to someone to stand at a safe distance, or to move out of the way; said for the safety of the person being told or so they do not get in the way of people working, or ruin what is being done. Usually said to curious children getting nearer to the spectacle of what is being done. And in the story, God is saying exactly that to Moses at mount Horeb 'stay away/stand back'. 'And Moses said, I will turn aside, and see this great sight, why the bush is not burnt. And when the Lord saw that he turned aside to see, God called unto him out of the midst of the bush, and said, Moses, Moses…And he said, Draw not nigh hither: put off thy shoes from off thy feet, for the place whereon thou standest is holy ground.' So God tells Moses 'stand back, don't come nearer,' possibly for his own safety, but also not to pollute holy ground. Cp: hooreyb, horeyb. (Exod.3:1-5)

Although in Exod.2:18 Moses' father-in-law, the priest of Midian, is named as 'Reuel' (Gen.36:4) because it fit to name him as 'saw-the' 'shepherded-the' 'watered-the' as his daughters see Moses and he sees them while they are shepherding and Moses helps them out by watering the flocks, his name is changed by an author to, Jethro; yiṯrô; عِذر 'shadow/in the shadow'; يِذر 'sows/seeds' 'fills' 'leaves/leaves behind' 'swears a lot at'; حِذر 'warned/were wary/were warned'; 'warned' because Moses, herding Jethro's flocks, has gone to 'the back side of the desert, and came to the mountain of God, even to Horeb.' and God warns him not to come near. Cp: 'ivro, yivro, ḥivro. (Exod.2:16-21;3:1;4:18-20)

I Am That I Am; 'ehyeh 'ăšer 'ehyeh; نِهيَه عيشَر نِهيَه 'she is-with child/calf-she is' 'she is-pregnant-she is' and the ('ăšer/عيشَر) does not mean a pregnant woman, but a pregnant cow or similar animal (there is a different word for pregnant human). The word ('ehyeh/إهيَه) 'she is' is repeat because it is important to the author of the Biblical story that the audience understands that this is the protagonist God of the story so it is used twice as confirmation that the God is a 'she is'. It says that God is called 'ai<u>sh</u>er and this is the word used for gestation of cows, 'aa<u>sh</u>uur, 'aa<u>sh</u>ira mean when a cow is 'in heat/ready to be copulated' and also 'gestating/pregnant/with calf'. It clearly states that the original God of the Biblical stories is a pregnant cow, i.e. a fertility goddess (see El-elohe-Israel). Interestingly, the burning bush described in this part of the story is how a pagan celebration which has survived into modernity is connected to 'ai<u>sh</u>er/'ăšer where the houses are decorated with dry bushes and set alight at night, and large bonfires are lit on mountain peaks: the point of the festival is to pray for girls and women who make wishes (girls wish to be married; married women wish to become pregnant; women with only daughters wish to have sons; grandmothers and mothers-in-law wishing for their daughters and daughters-in-law to have pregnancies, children and sons—all related to fertility); and the names chanted during this ritual/festival are Tassu'/تاسوع and 'Aa<u>sh</u>uur/عاشور (both are related to fertility of animals and humans, and to a human pregnancy which lasts for nine months, and to a bovine pregnancy and specifically cows which are believed to last for ten months (the word for pregnant cow ('aasher/'aashera) and names of the fertility deities are the same noun for numbers 9 and 10). The name of the festival is Eid Wuzoo 'Festival Light a Fire'. Cp: ehyah-'ai<u>sh</u>er-ehyah. (Exod.3)

Aaron; 'ahărōn; نَهَرون/نَهيرون 'drives away with cruel/harsh words' 'will drive away/speak angrily to' 'is-here-see/look' 'of wooden sticks/rods/batons/handles/use wooden handles/rods/batons'. From words ('a) أ/آ 'is' 'will'; (hrn/هرن) 'drive them away(with words)/direct angry speech at': (hr/هر) is 'drive away' (ōn/ون) makes it done to or by 'them/ plural'; (hrn/هرن) 'wooden handles(of tools or just sticks)/rod/use wooden stick against'; (h/هـ) 'here/look/see/pay attention/I will/will'; (ărōn) نَرون/نَيرون 'see/look/show/teach'. The character is named to serve the story narrative: God is angered at a reluctant Moses and speaks to him in the meaning of the word 'aaron' (to speak angrily to) after God has shown Moses what he can do with the rod, and the changing of the appearance of his hand to show the people as signs as God's dialogue, it is also emphasised by having Aaron appear and the narrative emphasise this: 'And the anger of the Lord was kindled against Moses, and he said, Is not Aaron the Levite thy brother? I know that he can speak well. And also, behold, he cometh forth to meet thee: and when he seeth thee, he will be glad in his heart' and in the same vein, Aaron is to show the people God's signs so they are seeing him yaroon/ărōn' while he is showing/teaching them, as well as his character's role in the story being related to all the word-name meanings including the use of 'rod(s)': 'And Aaron spake all the words which the Lord had spoken unto Moses, and did the signs in the sight of the people.'. Cp: aharoon; ahairoon. (Exod.4:10-14, 30)

Jehovah; yahwēh; يَحويه 'he/it makes him/it stay/still' 'he/it contains him/it' as before at (Gen.22:13-14) yĕhōwāh, YHWH; يَحُوآه/ يِيحُواه ، يحوه/يحوا it all means 'he/it-stays/stayed/contains/contained' and 'he/it-stayed/stilled it/contained it'. Cp: yaḥweyh, yeḥoowaah, yeiḥoowaah, yḥwh, yḥwa (Gen.6:3)

Libni; libnî; لِبني 'for my son' 'for building' 'my core/pulp/cored me' 'answer me/assist me'; لِفني 'wrap me up' 'of wrapping' 'of going around in circles/dishonest/deceitful'. Cp: libnee, li<u>ph</u>nee. (Exod.6:17)

Shimi; šimʻî; سِمعي 'my hearing' 'hears'; شِمئي 'smell(it)' 'smell' 'my smell'; سِمئي 'named/my name' 'poisoned' 'my illness/frustration/loss of interest'. Cp: sim'ee, <u>sh</u>im-ee, sim-ee. (Exod.6:17)

Amram; ʻamrām; نَمرام 'the thrower/thrown' 'the thrown/killed/killer' 'thrown/strewn over distance/various locations'; عَمرام 'built-the' 'lived/long age-the' 'will be thrown' 'drank/blinded-strewn over vast distance/various locations'. Cp: a-mraam, 'amraam, 'am-raam. (Exod.6:18)

Izhar; yiṣhar; يزهر 'flowers/blossoms'; يسهر 'stays up all night'; يصهر 'melts metals'; يظهر 'carries on back'; يزحر 'pushes with growl' (like pushing for bowel movement or baby); يسحر 'wakes up pre-dawn' 'has breakfast pre-dawn' 'casts spells'; يصحر 'becomes dry and barren'. Cp: yizhar, yisha̲r, yissha̲r, yidh̲har, yizḥar, yisḥar, yissḥar. (Exod.6:18)

Mahali; maḥlî; مَهلي 'at my own pace' 'take your time' 'she is not here'; مَحلي 'circumcised' 'purified' 'shed off' 'my place' 'where I take off my clothes' 'sweetened'. Cp: mahlee, maḥlee. (Exod.6:19)

Mushi; mûšî; موشي ، مُشي 'walked away/left' 'not so/it' 'no' 'drive/shepherd animals'. Cp: mush̲ee, moosh̲ee. (Exod.6:19)

Jochebed; yôḵeḇeḏ; يُخَبَط 'he/it strikes' 'he/it strikes here and there' (as in strike or searching randomly), 'threshes grain'; يُكَبَد 'it/he stifles/chokes/chocks/frustrates' 'it/he stifled/choked/was frustrated.'. Cp: yokh̲ebeṭ, yokebed. (Exod.6:20)

Nepheg; nep̄eg; نَفَج 'to dust(something heavy)' 'pound (as in dusting)' 'rushed out'; نَبَج 'strike with a throw' 'a thump'. Cp: nep̲h̲eg, nebeg. (Exod.6:21)

Zichri; ziḵrî; ذِكري 'mention/my mention' 'remember'; سِكري 'drunk/my drunkenness'; سِحري 'pre-dawn/predawn meal' 'magic'; زِحري 'push (for baby/bowel movement), or making similar sounds'. Cp: vikree, sikree, siḥree, ziḥree. (Exod.6:21)

Uzziel; ʿuzzîʾēl; عوزّي ئيل ، عُزّي ئيل 'honour/cherish-the' 'want/need-the' 'support/provide for-the'; عوصّي ئيل ، عُصّي ئيل 'disobeyed-the' 'became askew/crooked-the' 'fiddle it/shift it/move it in all directions(to make it right or fit)-the' 'became wooden/stiff-the'; عوضّي ئيل ، عُضّي ئيل 'got stiffened/sore muscles -the' 'recompense-the'; عوذي ئيل ، عُذي ئيل 'say a protection for/protect-the'; اوزّيئيل ، ئوزّيئيل 'removed/be removed/wiped out/be wiped out' 'left forever/disappeared'; اوذي ئيل ، ئوذي ئيل 'harmed/ was harmed-the'. Cp: 'oozzee-ill, 'uzzee-ill, 'oos̲s̲ee-ill, 'us̲s̲ee-ill, 'oodh̲ee-ill, 'udh̲ee-ill, 'oozzee-ill, oovvee-ill. (Exod.6:22)

Mishael; mîšaʾēl; ميش ئِل 'walked-the' 'not-the'; ميشَئِل 'what is he carrying?' 'what did he take?'; ميسَئِل 'what is he asking?' 'what did he ask?' 'lots of questions' 'matters/topics' 'not asking' 'doesn't care' 'water is leaking/flowing' 'flowing/leaking' 'what is leaking/flowing?'. Cp: meesh̲a-ill, meesh̲aill, meesaill. (Exod.6:22)

Elzaphan; 'elṣāp̄ān; ئَلزآفآن 'the escorted/the procession' (in form of two or plural); ئَلزآبآن 'the loins/below navel to above crotch'; ئَلسآفآن 'the carried gently' 'the/those who pour gently/pouring gentle spurts of water' 'the numbed' 'the ships'; ئَلصآفآن 'the stones/the two stones' 'the stacked stones/the columns' 'the reconciliation/they cleared the air between them' 'the cleaning/clearing/purifying'. Cp: elzaap̲h̲aan, elzaabaan, elsaap̲h̲aan, els̲s̲aap̲h̲aan. (Exod.6:22)

Zithri; siṯrî; سِتري 'cover/conceal' 'my cover/my concealment'; سِطري 'pour into/pour stream/line into' 'drain' 'line/my line(s)' 'make soft/fresh'. Cp: sitree, siṭree. (Exod.6:22)

Elisheba; 'ĕlîšeḇaʿ; ئيلي/ئِلي شَبَء 'the one who-young woman' 'the one who-swells/rigid' and the swelling means the same as when water makes wood swell, a penis from blood/erection, a head from cold weather; ئيلي/ئِلي شَبَع 'the one who/he who-sufficed/fed full/has plenty'; ئيلي/ئِلي شَوَع 'the one who-bleats (like a baby goat)' 'the one who-mutated/freakishly ugly' and the words were chosen as wordplay: Aaron marries Elisheba so she would be a young woman; her father and brother have names of physical deformities, ugliness or negativity, and so do the words given as names of her sons. Cp: eilee/illee-sh̲eba, eilee/illee-sh̲eba', eilee/illee-sh̲ewa'. (Exod.6.23)

Amminadab; ʿammînāḏāḇ; عَمّي نآضآب ، ئَمّيناضآب 'my uncle has protruding jaw and teeth' 'the one who has protruding jaw/teeth'; عَمّي نآدآب ، ئَمّينآدآب 'my uncle has scars' 'the one who has scars' 'my uncle is wailing/mourning loudly' 'the one who is wailing/mourning loudly'. Cp: 'ammeenaadh̲aab, ammeenaadh̲aab, 'ammeenaadaab, ammeenaadaab. (Exod.6:23)

Naashon; naḥšôn; نَخشُن ، نَخشون 'crumble/crumbled' 'poked at and crumbled' 'riddle(d) with holes'; نَهشُن ، نَهشون 'maul(ed)' 'chunks missing from'; نَحسُن ، نحسون 'bad luck' 'bringers of bad luck'. Cp: nak̲h̲*sh*on, nak̲h̲shoon, nahsh̲on, nahsh̲oon, naḥson, naḥsoon. (Exod.6:23)

Nadab; nāḏāḇ; نآضآب 'protruding jaw/teeth' 'pulled face made jaw/teeth protrude'; نآدآب 'a wailing' 'scars/ scarred'. Cp: naadh̲aab, naadaab. (Exod.6:23)

Abihu; 'ăḇîhû'; نَبيهُئ/ئبيبهُئ ، نَبي/ئبيبي هُئ 'refused/rejected him' 'my father-him/my father is him' 'his father'; نَبي/ئبيبي هُع 'rejected-gagged(with vomit, expression of disgust towards); عَبيهُئ/عيبيهُئ ،

عبي/عيبي هُئ 'fill/pack it/him' 'my shame/disgrace-is him/it'; عَبي/عيبي هُع 'my shame/disgrace-gagged/ repulsive' 'pack/fill-gagged/repulsive'. Cp: abeewho, aibeewho, abee-who, aibee-who, abee-ho', aibee-ho', 'abeewho, 'aibeewho, 'abee-who, 'aibee-who, 'abee-ho', 'aibee-ho'. (Exod.6:23)

Eleazar; 'el'azār; ئَل عَزآر 'the ugliness'; ئَل نَزآر 'the tightening(ed)/squeezed(ing)' 'the visiting/visited/ pilgrimaging/pilgrimmed'. Cp: el-'azaar, el-azaar. (Exod.6:23)

Ithamar; 'îṯāmār; ئي دآمآر 'is destruction/did destroy'; ئي ذآمآر 'is-complaining/moaning' 'is withering/ did wither'; ئي ضآمآر 'is withering/shrivelling' 'is keeping intentions hidden'. Cp: ee-daamaar, ee-vaamaar, ee-dhaamaar. (Exod.6:23)

Assir; 'assîr; ئَسّير 'the walking' 'am walking' 'the path/way' 'the prisoner' 'imprisoned'; عَسّير 'difficult/ make difficult'. Cp: a-sseer, 'asseer. (Exod.6:24)

Elkanah; 'elqānâ; ئَلكآنه/ا 'they were'; ئَلخآنه/ا 'the soaked' 'they betrayed him/the'; ئَلقآنه 'the channel(water channel)' 'the bottle/flask/any transportable drink vessel/also small water vessel' 'the topping up with water' 'the estimating measure of something liquid' (when mixing ingredients) 'the one carrying a bottle/small pot/small drink vessel' 'the one with head held high/body straight posture/erect' 'the person or object sitting/place/set upright' 'were perky' 'meet us' 'find us' 'the thrown'. Cp: el-kaanah(na), elkhaanah(na), el-qaanah(na). (Exod.6:24)

Abiasaph; 'ăḇî'āsāp; ئَبي/ئيبي عآزآف 'refused-turned away/went off food or drink' 'refused-play music' 'refused-twisted/turned things with hands/fingers to make sound' 'father-turned away/went off food or drink' 'father-played music/twisted and turned things with hands/fingers(to make sound)' 'refused-turned away(head or body)/avoided'; عبي/عيبي عآزآف 'fill/pack-turned away/went off food/drink' 'fill/pack-play music/twist and turn things with hands/fingers(to make sound)' 'fill/pack- turned away(head or body)/ avoided'; ئَبي/ئيبي ئآسآف 'refused-sorrow' 'father is sorry/remorseful'; ئَبي/ئيبي عآصآف 'father-twisted' (such as twist an ankle or twist something until it breaks off); عَبي/عيبي عآصآف 'fill/pack twisted crop' (asaph/'ssph/عصف) is crop which has been broken by wind or anything else. Cp: abee/aibee-'aazaaph, 'abee/'aibee-'aazaaph, abee/aibee-aasaaph, abee/aibee-'aassaaph, 'abee/'aibee-'aassaaph. (Exod.6:24).

Putiel; pûṭî'ēl; بُتي ئِل 'tear/rip-the' 'decide-the' 'I will bring/I am coming-the' 'daughter/girl-the/of' and is exactly as meant '…took him one of the daughter's of Putiel to wife…'. Cp: botee-ill. (Exod.6:25)

Phinehas; pînĕḥās; بينَحآس ، بينيحآس 'will bring bad luck' as in to bring bad luck to himself and/or others; بينَهآس ، بينيهآس 'will breathe/is breathing'; بينَخآش ، بينيخآش 'will create holes/crumble' 'will poke at and crumble/make holes'; بينَهآش ، بينيهآش 'will maul/take chunks out of'. Cp: beenehaas, beeneihaas, beenehaas, beeneihaas, beenekhaash, beeneikhaash, beenehaash, beeneihaash. (Exod.6:25)

Pesah; which has been described as '…the Lord's passover' is: pesaḥ; فَسَح 'gave permission' (to leave/go somewhere), 'made space/moved over' (the latter meaning to move over so someone can sit or pass through), 'spacious/wide/baggy/enough room'. The word is used as follows (phesah-lee, phesahat-lee/ فَسَح لي/فَسَحَت لي) when a male or female 'gave me permission'; (phsh, phsht/فسح/فسحت) a male or female 'gave permission', usually when someone takes permission from a mother or father to go somewhere and that is exactly what the whole story and the ritual named the 'passover' is about: asking for permission to leave, being declined permission to leave, then getting permission to leave 'Let my people go, let the people go, he refuseth to let the people go, he would not let them go'. This is further emphasised by the authors that God is giving the people 'permission/pesah' to leave as he instructs them to eat in a rush and dictates they eat while dressed for travel as he has given them permission to leave 'And thus shall ye eat it: with your loins girded, your shoes on your feet, and your staff in your hand; and ye shall eat it in haste: it is the Lord's passover.'. The creators of the story decided to add its second meaning which they used as God passing over, but the meaning is when you ask someone to 'move over/make space/excuse me' the person moves aside so another person can sit next to them or pass through the space they have made. It is this context that 'For I will pass through the land of Egypt this night, and will smite all the firstborn in the land of Egypt…And the blood shall be to you for a token upon the houses where ye are: and when I see the blood, I will pass over you, and the plague shall not be upon you to destroy you, when I smite the land of Egypt.' So, by seeing the marking with blood, God passes by the protected houses/people towards the unprotected houses, the same way a person moving aside to allow someone else to pass through. Cp: phesaḥ. (Exod.3-12)

Abib; 'āḇîḇ; عآبيب 'flowing' 'overflowing' 'swollen with water' 'bubbling or roaring water' 'floating/ floating in' 'lots of' 'stank/rotted and stank'. The overflowing/roaring water indicates the many people who came out of Egypt in the story and the 'land flowing with milk and honey...'. Cp: 'aabeeb. (Exod.13:4)

Etham; 'ēṯām; عيضآم 'bones' named directly because Joseph's bones were mentioned 'And Moses took the bones of Joseph with him: for he had straitly sworn the children of Israel, saying, God will surely visit you; and ye shall carry up my bones away hence with you. And they took their journey from Succoth, and encamped in Etham...'. Cp: 'eydhaam. (Exod.13:19-20)

Piha-hiroth; pî-haḥîrôṯ; بي هَحيرُث 'with/at-will scowl' 'at me/with me-I will scowl' from word (ḥrf/حرث) 'scowl'. When a person sees someone scowling or feels someone intends to harm them or has ill intentions towards them, one would say 'he/she scowls at me' (yḥrf/tḥrf/يحرث/تحرث). It means Pharaoh is scowling at the people who have left and intends to harm them which the story narrates. Cp: beehaheerof. (Exod.14:2-5)

Migdol; migdōl; مِجدول 'thrown/been thrown' 'of fits/suffers epilepsy/possessed by demons' 'wooden block/wedge'. It is meant as a 'wedge' as the story narrates God orders the children of Israel to camp between Migdol and the sea and it states Pharaoh believes 'They are entangled in the land, the wilderness hath shut them in.' so the story narrates Pharaoh believes he can catch up and kill them as they are wedged between him and the wilderness. Cp: migdool. (Exod.14:2-3)

Baal-zephon; ba'al ṣĕpōn; بَعَل زَفون/زيفون 'higher/above-procession/entourage'. The (zephon) describes both the procession of children of Israel as they are moving away, and Pharaoh and his army. The (baal) 'high/above' is Moses raising his hand over the sea so that first the procession of the children of Israel can pass through, and second when he raises his hand above so that the sea comes crashing down on Pharaoh's army. The compound word was made so 'baal/above' comes before the 'zephon/procession' as the raising of Moses hand comes before what happens to both caravans. Cp: ba'al zephoon/zeiphoon. (Exod.14)

Pharaoh; par'ō, par'ōh; is wordplay on فَرعو ، فَرعوه '(to) separate' as between people arguing or fighting; '(to)branch', '(to)divide' 'to separate' as in splitting/separating things/objects; it also means crops stalks growing high in length—a good, strong crop. فَرئو ، فَرئوه 'they fled/they fled him/fled from him'. The story narrates God saying to Pharaoh that he has made him high, mighty just to cut him down to make him an example to the world; even strong, high individuals will be 'smote' by God if they disobey 'And in very deed for this cause have I raised thee up.' (Exod.9:16) i.e. Pharaoh has risen high in power like a strong stalk (from phr'/فرع) the shooting stalk, the 'oh/وه' (ō/و/they/them-h/ه/he/him) he was raised in this instance by God). '...and thou shalt be cut off from the earth.' Cut off as a tall stalk of crop is cut from the soil (Exod.9:15). Cp: phar'oo, phar'ooh, phar-oo, phar-ooh.

Pharaoh 'fled him' 'fled from him' فَرئوه: (phr/phr'/فر/فرء) 'fled him' the children of Israel are fleeing from Pharaoh, 'And it was told the king of Egypt that the people fled.' 'And the children of Israel went into the midst of the sea...' 'And the Egyptians pursued and went in after them...'. The Egyptians and Pharaoh will also flee from God's punishment, 'Let us flee from the face of Israel...' 'And the Egyptians fled against it...' (Exod.14:5,22-23,25,27).

Pharaoh فَرعو ، فَرعوه as to separate between people arguing/fighting and also creating a physical divide of something: God is separating between Pharaoh's military might striking the children of Israel's vulnerability in all the miracles mentioned in the story, created to separate the children of Israel from the tyranny of Pharaoh; also 'And the angel of God, which went before the camp of Israel, removed and went behind them; and the pillar of the cloud went from before their face and stood behind them: And it came between the camp of the Egyptians and the camp of Israel; and it was a cloud of darkness to them, but it gave light by night to these; so that the one not came near the other all the night.' (Exod.14:19-20) فَرعوه 'separated between them' 'kept them away from each other'.

Pharaoh 'to divide' physically divide an object: 'But lift thou up thy rod, and stretch out thine hand over the sea, and divide it.' 'I will harden the heart of the Egyptians and they shall follow them: and I will get me honour upon Pharaoh, and upon all his host, upon his chariots and upon his horsemen.' '...and the waters were divided' 'And the waters returned, and covered the chariots, and the horsemen, and all the host of Pharaoh.' (Exod.14:16-17,21,28)

Pharaoh with all its meanings of separating from fighting and physically dividing can be seen as the sea is separated to allow the safe passage of the children of Israel (separating them from Pharaoh's attack), but at the same time this 'divide' is the death-trap and punishment for Pharaoh.

Palestina; pĕlāšet; فيلاَشط ، فلاَشِط 'between/in shores/coasts', and is mentioned as the inhabitants of the land Palestina who will fear the arrival of Moses' people, but it follows and is followed by repeated mention of Pharaoh and his army being drowned in the sea, i.e. drowning between two shores. Cp: phelaashet, pheilaashet. (Exod.15:14)

Shur is still 'discussion' as people speak amongst themselves against Moses and Moses discusses the problem with God. Marah; mārâ; مارا ، مارِه 'bitter' 'passing along/they are passing along'. Cp: maarah, maara (Exod.15:23-25)

Elim; 'êlim; عيلِم 'understood' 'knew/found out' 'was shown' 'was shown and understood' 'show' and all these meanings are used in the story: God teaches/shows the people what they have to do to avoid being punished, he knows and sees their 'murmurings'—the people should 'know/understand' what is requested of them. It is also ئيلِم 'in pain' 'caused pain'—the people are in pain from hunger and tiredness, exposed to the elements and they vociferate this suffering, God warns them he will punish them. Cp: 'eylim, eylim. (Exod.15:26-27; 16:1-12)

Sin; sîn; سين ، سِن 'set in right direction/face right direction' 'make straight' 'set straight' 'opposite/facing' 'direct/throughout'. Named to show how the people feel they are wandering without direction, and also because God will test them to see if they are on the right path (obeying him), also they will face him/look in his direction when his glory appears in the cloud. Cp: seen, sin. (Exod.16:1-10)

Sinai; sînay; سيني ، سِنَي 'in my direction' 'facing me' 'became straight' 'on right direction/path' 'opposite me/facing me' 'direct/straight'. With same use in narration as 'Sin' above. It is in God calling Moses to come to the mountain to speak to him, in telling the Children of Israel that 'I bare you on eagles' wings and brought you unto myself.', he asks them to do right towards him by obeying his commandments, '…the Lord will come down in the sight of all the people upon mount Sinai.'. Cp: seenay, sinay. (Exod.16:1)

Manna; mān; مآن ، مانّه ، مآنّا 'who/who is it' 'what is it' 'where is it from' and is named because '…they said one to another, It *is* manna: for they wist not what it *was*.'. It also means 'to grant/give/bless' and also has a negative meaning as it can also mean to say to a person 'I gave you…' and mention or list what you gave someone in the past or present (whether as charity or gifts) and is against etiquette: God gave/granted/blessed the people with 'manna' to eat 'This is the bread which the Lord hath given you to eat', and the story also narrates God doing the negative meaning of manna when some disobey and search for manna on the sabbath 'And the Lord said unto Moses, How long refuse ye to keep my commandments and my laws? See, for that the Lord hath given you the sabbath, therefore he giveth you on the sixth day the bread of two days…'. What 'manna' is based on is explained later in this book. Cp: maan, maannah, maanna. (Exod.16:15-35)

Sabbath; šabbāṯ; wordplay on: سَبّآت 'a person who leaves things' 'a person who leaves things unfinished' 'left it/let it go' and means to stop doing something in particular. It is also: سَبّعت 'doing weeks' 'resting/taking break' and means stayed somewhere other than the normal residence such as a married daughter staying at her parents' house for a while visiting, it is based on the word 'weeks' and can even be broken down to the word 'week' in Arabic literally meaning seven days. In real life, the visiting person may stay only days, or even several weeks and the word (sabbath سَبّعت is always used, but it basically means 'holiday' 'rest' from normal chores. Cp: sabbaat, sabb't. (Gen.2:2-3; Exod.16)

Massah; massâ; مَسّه ، مَسّا 'provoked/caused problems/argued intensely' and watching and wanting to cause problems or ill-will; it is used as 'do not maaseeni/لاتماسيني' 'do not cause me problems/do not entangle with me(in evening)' and also means 'do not tempt/aggravate me' but the word is out of (ms/مس) 'evening/reached evening' and 'touch' and is used as 'don't tangle with me/touch me (so as not to enflame me against you' and further means if any more tension is added, patience will dissolve and anger/violence will take over; and this is said in the afternoon/evening (it has an equivalent 'ssubaaḥa/صُباحا' for the morning/daytime). It can also mean 'possessed', but there is no 'possessed' action in this part of the story. The people are arguing with Moses because of thirst and anger at their situation. Cp: massah, massa. (Exod.17:1-7).

Meribah; mĕrîbâ; ميريبح ، مَريبح 'monkeyed' which means to cause a great scene of argument, quarrel, reproach heavily, without backing down or calming, may include physically flipping/throwing things around. The word is usually used in a pair phrase: in the story it has been chosen to pair it with 'Massa', but it is usually used with the word (shammat/شَمّت) which means to 'cause a scene/scandal and disgrace/mess' so when used as 'shammat and meribah' means 'caused a great scene of argument where people gloated at our disgrace' and 'turned everything over' and the person/party being argued with/shouted at are blamed for something(s). In the story, it is emphasised from the beginning of the chapter how the people 'chide' with Moses out of thirst and tiredness, they blame him for leaving Egypt and accuse him of sending them into the wilderness to die. The dialogue given to Moses '...they be almost ready to stone me.' reflects the intensity and continuance of the people's arguments and blame, exactly what the word 'meribah/monkeyed' means. Cp: mereebḥ, meireebḥ. (Exod.17:1-7)

Rephidim; rĕp̄îḏîm; رَفيدهم/ام ، ريفيدهم/ام 'prop up-them/the' used to refer to anyone or anything which needs support in being propped-up to stay in an upright position. From word (rphd/رفد) to 'prop up' someone or something by placing cushions, rocks, clothes, etc. at their sides to keep them in an upright position. In the Biblical story the victory against Amalek depended on Moses keeping his hands held up, and when he tires, his side loses the battle so Aaron and Hur prop him up with a stone beneath him and from either side with their bodies and so the name in the story of the location is given which means what is to happen in the story: 'And all the congregation...journeyed from the wilderness of Sin...and pitched in Rephidim...Then came Amalek and fought with Israel in Rephidim...And it came to pass when Moses held up his hand, that Israel prevailed: and when he let down his hand, Amalek prevailed. But Moses hands *were* heavy; and they took a stone, and put *it* under him, and he sat thereon; and Aaron and Hur stayed up his hands, the one on the one side, and the other on the other side; and his hands were steady until the going of the sun.' Cp: repheed-hum/um, reipheed-hum/um. (Exod.17:1,8,11-12)

Joshua; yĕhôšua'; is another name which has been forcibly corrupted to fit in a narrative whether by ancient interpretations or modern. Letters/phonemes have been added and the interpretation which experts like to believe is 'Yahweh saves' still cannot be made out of the word Joshua. The 'ĕh' in the yĕhôšua' transliteration has been added, and with it included the word would read: جَهُشوَع ،جيهُشوَع 'came he-freakishly mutated/ugly' and still could not be 'Yahweh saves'. Joshua; yôšua'; is wordplay on: جُشوَء ، جُشوَا 'picked a lot' 'took handfuls' 'many people' and is the meaning of 'army' as in many people, e.g. if you tell someone to take more you say 'gosh' جُش, if you ask how many people do you see coming, if the answer means many people they say 'gaysh/goshua' جيش/جُشوا (even in modern Arabic (جيش army)). The character is named 'Joshua/picked many' because in the story Moses tells Joshua to pick men and go fight. From word (gsh/جش) 'took a lot' and is when people offer something, instead of taking one or two (or a reasonable amount) a person takes handful(s), which is rude and a sign of greed. The second word and meaning is جُشوَع 'burped' 'greed/greedy' 'pull(ed) out/pluck by the handfuls' and is linked to the first meaning where a person takes more than he/she should; it could also be wordplay on its meanings: 'came-freakishly ugly/mutated' 'came-pulled/plucked out/ruined' 'came-bleating like a kid(goat)'. In this part of the story Joshua is meant to be 'picked a lot' as he picks men who will fight with him against Amalek 'And Moses said unto Joshua, Choose us out men, and go out, fight with Amalek...' Cp: goshua, goshua'. (Exod.17:9-14)

Hur; ḥûr; هُر 'fall apart' 'drive away/chase away(verbally)' and means to gesture and speak aggressively/unkindly to drive the recipient(s) of this language/behaviour away. خُر 'flee/make them flee' 'collapse' and has the same meanings to chase people away but by physical action. The first word is attached to the action of the person doing the 'hur' (the person driving others away), and the meaning and second word is attached to the action of the person(s) fleeing 'hur'. In this part of the story the character and name has been chosen because it is Moses standing with his hands raised causing the Amaleks to lose i.e. he is driving them away; Moses tells Joshua to go fight '...to morrow I will stand on the top of the hill with the rod of God in mine hand...when Moses held up his hand, that Israel prevailed: and when he let down his hand, Amalek prevailed.' So Hur and Aaron are used to keep Moses' hand/the gesture of driving people away going, in the story. Even **Aaron** whose pronunciation 'aha-roon' includes the word 'hur' has been used in wordplay to emphasise the meaning 'drive them away' so that both people propping him up (Rephidim) enact the meaning of word 'drive away'; how 'Aaron' has been used is a prime example how earlier authors created this character name with a specific meaning for the earlier stories, and how later authors/editors used further wordplay to give it new meanings to keep the stories being told in the same method where character names denote what will happen in the story. هُر can also mean 'fall apart' ; خُر 'fall down/collapse' but these latter meanings have not been used in the story. Cp: hur, khur. (Exod.17:9-12)

Jehovah-nissi; YHWH nissî, yĕhōwāh nissî; ييحوواه/يحوه/يحوا نِسّي 'he/it-stays/stayed/contained-forgot/made forget' 'he/it-made them stay/still/contained-forgot/made forget' referring to the Amaleks which God says will be forgotten '...for I will utterly put out the remembrance of Amalek from under heaven. And Moses built an altar, and called the name of it Jehova-nissi.' Cp: yeiḥoowaah/yḥwh/yḥwa-nisee. (Exod.17:14-15)

Eliezer appears as the name given to Moses second son with the explanation for the name '...for the God of my father, said he, was mine help.' But the word still actually means; 'ĕlîʿezer; ئِلي/ئيلي عَزَر 'he who/the one who-is ugly/makes things ugly'; it could be word play also on ئِلي/ئيلي نَزَر 'he who/the one who-squeezes/tightens'. It is meant as the first meaning as when people or life is spoiled/destroyed/killed it is also being 'made ugly', this is why Moses has suddenly been given a second son with the name Eliezer. It relays with the mention of all the ugliness Pharaoh did to the people, and the destruction and spoiling God did to Pharaoh and his people with the plagues and eventually total destruction which is repeated in the verses that follow, as the method of the Bible is to make words into a name with the exact events to follow. But 'Eliezer' is not 'he who-helps' as the word 'to help' is (waazar/wzr/وازَر/وزر); the later editors of these stories may have been unfamiliar with the original language meanings and gave it the meaning they understood or wanted so as to make 'ezer/نَزَر ، آزر' 'to help/assist' which is a word from a much later and modern Arabic such as Classical Arabic and Modern Arabic. This shows the great difference between spans of time, but also a difference of geographical location between the original creation and authors of the stories and when later translators/interpreters changed these stories with wrong interpretations based on not having a complete understanding of the Arabic of the Bible. (Exod.18:4-10)

Tabernacle Making

Bezaleel; bĕṣal'ēl; بيزَل ئِل 'bolts/makes bolts/joints-the'; بيصَل ئِل 'joins/connects-the' 'will use stones/make layer of stones' the latter describes a phase of laying a layer of five-inch long stones which are called '<u>ss</u>alal' as part of the building process and/or when these small, flattish stones are used in something. The word-name is created as he will be making the tabernacle and the words mean he is a 'joiner/carpenter' and his patronym is suitably Uri; 'ûrî; ئُري 'was shown/shown/taught' as to be 'shown' is to be taught how to do something (in this regards the making of Tabernacle) 'See, I have called by name Bezaleel the son of Uri...And I have filled him with the spirit of God in understanding, and in knowledge, and in all manner of workmanship, To devise cunning works, to work in gold, and in silver, and in brass, And in cutting of stones, to set them, and in carving of timber, to work in all manner of workmanship.' Cp: beizal-ill, bei<u>ss</u>al-ill; oo-ree. (Exod.31;35;36;38)

Aholiab; 'ohŏlî'āḇ; ئوهولي ئآب/عآب 'he's the one who-returns/rejects/refuses' 'he's the one who-shamed/shames/disgraced' 'he's the one who-packed/filled' as the things they make will fill the tabernacle and the people will over-fill with supply of materials for its making; ئوحولي ئآب/عآب 'undress/shed-returns/refuses' 'undress/shed/my undressing-shame/packed/filled' and refers to a place where a person can undress in privacy, and there is a link in the narration as God does not want to be seen by the people which is why he requires a tabernacle for his privacy, but also the materials are being supplied in excess for its making. Cp: oohoolee-aab, oohoolee-'aab, ooḥoolee-aab, ooḥoolee-'aab. His father's name is suitably: Ahisamach; 'ăḥîsāmāḵ; نَهي/ئيهي صاماآغ 'he will glue' 'she is/here is the glue' and نَحيز آماآك 'I tie you together/bind you/bundle you' which there will be a lot of binding together different materials to make the tabernacle and its objects and as he will be engraving metals and tailoring/embroidering fabrics. Cp: ahee/aihee-<u>ss</u>aamaa<u>gh</u>, aḥeezaamaak. (Exod.31:2-5; 35:30-34; 36; 38:22)

Urim/Thummim; 'urîm tûmmîm; ئورهم/ام 'show-them/the'; and عورهم/ام 'genitals/private parts-them/the' 'ḥurt-them/the' (literally 'their disgraceful parts/vulnerable/hurtful parts' and refers to genitals); and ذمّهم/ام 'find guilty/shame/ostracise-them/the'; and ضمّهم/ام 'hold together/squeeze-them/the'. 'show-them/the' because the 'breastplate' will show all the tribe names before God, but because the ritual of using it is in presence of people i.e. showing them. The 'find guilty/shame/blame them' not only because Aaron 'shall bear judgement of the children of Israel upon his heart before the Lord...' but also because the people are being judged and found innocent or guilty through this ritual. Cp: oor-hum, oor-um, 'oor-hum, 'oor-um; vumm-hum, vumm-um, <u>dh</u>umm-hum, <u>dh</u>umm-um. (More on Urim and Thummim later in the book). (Exod.28)

Levi (Gen.29:34) in this part of the story is not used as 'twisted around/entwined', but only the meaning of 'answered/answer/answer him(or it)' 'served/serve/serve him(or it)' and serve means as in 'answer/respond and assist' which the story has Levis answer and respond to Moses call of 'who is on God's side' and they unquestioningly obey his commands and kill thousands of their own people. Cp: leybee, leybh. (Exod.32:26-28)

Nun; nûn; نون ، نُن 'very young' from the word (noonoo/nunu/نونو/نُنُ) 'baby' 'extremely young'. In the story it signifies Joshua the son of Nun is still very young in age and either does not get the message out of innocence, like small children who hang around and stay even when adults make it clear they need to talk in private; or he is young and simply does not do as told such as teenagers out of wilfulness or independent thinking. Whether out of innocence or teenage rebellion, it is obvious the story has God and Moses wanting a private conversation, but because of his young age Joshua stayed put 'And the Lord spake to Moses face to face, as a man speaketh unto his friend. And he turned again into the camp: but his servant Joshua, the son of Nun, a young man, departed not out of the tabernacle.' Cp: noon, nun. (Exod.33:11)

Leviticus

At Lev.10, how names mentioned in earlier lists are used can be seen: **Nadab**; meaning of 'a wailing' (as in mourning) and **Abihu**'s meaning of 'refused/rejected him' has been used here to narrate how 'strange fire' should not be offered to God and these two characters are killed by God and their name/role fulfilled. Also, in the same manner the following characters have been created for their roles: **Elzaphan** 'the escorted with procession' (in form of two or plural), 'the carried gently' 'they cleared the air between them' 'the cleaning/clearing/purifying', and **Mishael** 'what is he carrying?' 'what did he take?', are asked to carry and do carry the bodies of Abihu and Nadab out of the camp; even the father name is mentioned because **Uzziel** means 'removed/be removed/wiped out/be wiped out' 'harmed/was harmed-the'; Uzziel 'disobeyed-the' 'removed/be removed/wiped out/be wiped out' 'harmed/was harmed-the' so all the names and characters created have a direct role and action as the literal meaning of the word chosen to name them. Also, **Ithamar**; 'is-destruction' 'is-complaining/moaning'; **Eleazar** 'the ugliness'. Aaron's sons' names are given to emphasise the death and destruction caused to their brothers and that they are not allowed to grieve. All the meanings of the names: the ugliness of destruction, destruction, complaining and the act of rending ones' clothes and pulling out hair (which is what has been done since ancient times and continued into modern times) in grief over the death of a loved one is also 'ugliness' as they are doing things to make themselves ugly. Complaining is focused on in Moses being upset they have not eaten the particular meat, and in Aaron's response over the events of the day.

Molech; mōleḵ; موْلَق 'thrown/cast' as in thrown into or away. It is depicted as the person who sacrifices or offers his children to Molech will be 'cut off' as in cast away from the people (through death). Cp: mooleq. (Lev.18:21; 20)

Shelomith; šĕlōmîṯ; شيلوميت ، شَلوميت 'they took-death' 'took/carried him dead' and is the name of the man who was taken by the people for blasphemy, and put to death; سيلوميت ، سَلوميت 'survived/was intact' 'greeted' 'asked to death(asked a lot/intensely)' 'received/delivered'. Before he is put to death he is taken from stage to stage: 'put him in ward...Bring forth him that curseth...that they should bring forth him that had cursed out of the camp, and stone him with stones. And the children of Israel did as Moses commanded.' so the word-name is reflected in the story. Although he is not named, they give his mother a name which reflects his demise Shelomith 'they took-death' and she is the daughter of Dibri; diḇrî; دِبري 'evil intended/fated' and is in the form of male or object adjective; it also has a similar meaning to 'unlucky' but with a stronger and more malicious meaning as in 'evil intent' 'evil fate' and the person described as being 'deboor/mdbir' brings evil upon those he/she is around, and just like the character named Deborah before him, he dies, but in a brutal fashion. What can also be seen in this part of the story is a culture where when a male, be he adult or child, does something wrong, or odd or strange whether in action or just how he is, the mother is often blamed in the words said to or about him (most of the time it is said in humour, and many times figuratively, but there is a tendency to mention the mother when something about a son is not favourable). Cp: sheloo-meet, sheiloomeet, seloomeet, seiloomeet, dibree. (Lev.24)

Numbers

Elizur; 'ĕlîṣûr; نِلي/نئيلي زُر/زوور 'he who/the one who-visits' 'he who/the one who-swears false oath' 'he who/the one who-tightens'. Cp: illee/eilee-zur, illee/eilee-zoor. (Num.1:5)

Shedeur; šĕḏê'ûr; شَديعُر 'will prostitute(be involved in prostitution or with prostitutes)' from word (sh/ش) 'will', and (d'r/دعر) involving acts of prostitution; شَدي/شيدي عُر 'leave/emigrate-in disgrace/to wilderness/naked' from word (shd/شد) 'emigrate/leave area(as in home)/leave forever' can also mean 'wrap around and tighten' (and 'šĕḏê' is 'shd' in the feminine 'she emigrates/leaves' 'emigrate(fem.)/leave(fem.)'), and (ur/عور، عُر) 'disgrace' 'wilderness' and can also mean 'made to leave in haste/head down and carrying on/pushing forward/behaving brashly'. Cp: shedey'ur, shedey/sheidey-'ur. (Num.1:5)

Shelumiel; šĕlumî'ēl; شَلومي/شيلومي ئِل 'they took-water-the' 'they took-what-the' 'they took-undergarment (shorter frock/robe warn beneath longer dress or at night time); سَلومي/سيلومي ئِل 'they asked/questioned-water-the' 'they leaked-water-the' 'they asked/questioned-what-the' 'they asked/questioned-undergarment/frock' 'of mild/peaceful nature-the' 'delivered/received-the' 'survived/intact-the' '(is or of)comfort(ed)/entertainment/distraction-water-the' 'is comfort/entertainment(as in distraction)-the' '(is or of)many questions-the). Cp: shelumee-ill, sheilumee-ill, selumee-ill, seilumee-ill. (Num.1:6)

Zurishaddai; ṣûrîšadday; زُري شَدَّي 'tighten-strengthen/wrap/bind tightly' 'tighten-emigrate/leave' 'tighten-she emigrates' and both words are in the feminine. Zuri may also mean 'visit/pilgrimage'. Shadday meanings: 'emigrate' 'leave/leave forever' 'wrap around and tighten or strengthen' 'strengthen (wrapping something around)' and is often the word used when packing things or dressing for travel: the person needs to pack things tightly, his/her body wrapped and strengthened for travel and against the elements. E.g. the word for a man's head turban is 'mashadda' a long shawl which is wrapped round and round the head, especially the longer the travel, the larger the turban to protect against the elements (as well as look nice); the action of putting on/wearing a turban is called 'mashddad', women's head turban has a different noun, but the act of putting it on, especially when getting ready to leave the current house they are in is 'mashddadi'. All the words are from the word (shd/شد) 'wrap around/strengthen/emigrate/leave' and even its meaning 'severe' is from the wrapping around and reinforcing associated with packing and binding things properly to withhold travel. Cp: zuree-shadday. (Num.1:6)

Nethaneel; nĕṯan'ēl; نَثَن/نيثَن نئيل 'we double/fold-the' 'we female-the'; نَدَن/نيدَن نئيل 'we guilt-the' 'we bow/bend/lower-the'; نَظَن/نيظَن نئيل 'we think/suspect-the'; نَطَن/نيطَن نئيل 'we clang-the' make a tinning or clanging noise'. Cp: nefan/neifan-ill, nedan/neidan-ill, nedhan/neidhan-ill, neṭan/neiṭan-ill. (Num.1:8)

Zuar; ṣû'ār; زُعار 'roaring like animals';شُعار 'were disgraced' 'will be disgraced'; سُعار 'priced/price estimated' 'will be disgraced'; صُعار 'have rabies'; زُغار/صُغار 'small (plural)' 'belittled'. Cp: zu'aar, shu'aar, su'aar, ssu'aar, zughaar/ssughaar. (Num.1:8)

Eliab; 'ĕlî'āḇ; نِلي/نئيلي نآب 'he who/the one who-rejects/refuses/returns' 'he is-father'; نِلي/نئيلي نآذ 'he who/the one who-harms/is harmed'; نِلي/نئيلي عاب 'he who/the one who-disgraced' (could mean caused others to feel shame or he himself was disgraced.' 'he who/the one who-has flaws/fault' 'he who/the one who-packed/filled'. Cp: illee/eilee-aab, illee/eilee-aav, illee/eilee-'aab. (Num.1:9)

Helon; ḥēlōn; حيلون 'purified/cleansed/circumcised/made edible/made touchable' 'declared permissible/purified' 'shed/undressed' 'beaten until skin peeled off/severely' 'trickster/deceivers' 'sweet/sweeteners' 'replaced/they replaced/took place of'; خيلون 'imagined' 'imaginer(s)' 'they allowed'; غيلون 'river' 'intense hatred' 'dug/stabbed deep'. Cp: heyloon, kheyloon, gheyloon. (Num.1:9)

Elishama; 'ĕlîšāmā'; نِلي/نئيلي سآماع 'he who/the one who-heard/listens' 'he who/the one who-made others hear' and what it means in this form is he exposed or insulted another person and allowed other people to hear (so the recipient of the accusations/insults feels more ashamed). Cp: illee/eilee-saamaa'. (Num.1:10)

Ammihud; 'ammîhuḏ; عَمّي هوذ 'my uncle-this/him' 'drink-this' 'blind(ed)-this/him'; عَمّي هود 'my uncle-'jew'' 'drink-'jew'' the meanings of the word 'jew' will be explained later in this book; ; عَمّي خوض 'my uncle-shake to stir/churn' 'drink-shake to stir/churn'; عَمّي خوذ 'my uncle-take/takes' 'drink- take/takes' 'blind(ed)- take/takes'. Cp: 'ammee-huv, 'ammee-hud,'ammee-khudh, 'ammee-khuv. (Num.1:10)

Gamaliel; gamlî'ēl; جَملي ئِل 'came-fetch water-the' came-instructed-the' 'came-told them what to say-the' 'came wearing frock' 'was grateful towards-the' 'ingratiate-the'. Cp: ga-mlee/gamlee-ill. (Num.1:10)

Pedahzur; pĕḏâṣûr; بَدَه/بيدَ زُر 'made him leave/took it out-under false oath(lies)' 'made him leave/took it out-tighten/visit/pilgrimage'; بَتهزُر ، بيتهزُر 'she/it tugged/tugging' 'you will tug'; بَتحضُر ، بيتحضُر 'she/it is ripening'. Cp: bedah/beida-zur, betahzur, beitahzur, betḥdhur, beitḥdhur. (Num.1:10)

Abidan; 'ăḇîḏān; نَبيدآن ، نئبيدآن 'never' 'kill everyone/everything' 'refused-guilt/to guilt/bend/bow'; عَبيدآن ، عيبيدآن 'they worshipped/served' 'worshippers/servants'; عَبي/عيبي دآن 'packed/filled-guilt/guilted' 'packed/filled-lowered/bow/bent' 'disgrace/shame-guilt/guilted' 'disgrace/shame-lowered/bow/bent'; نَبيضآن ، نئيبي ضآن 'lay eggs' 'whiten/brighten' 'father-thought/suspected'. Cp: abeedaan, aibeedaan, 'abeedaan, 'aibeedaan, 'abee-daan, 'aibee-daan, abeedhaan, aibeedhaan. (Num.1:11)

Gideoni; giḏ'ōnî; جدعوني 'they uprooted me' 'of uprooting' to remove something by pulling it up/out, 'snapped (top or piece off)' 'find-my help/support'; جِذعوني 'they broke me' 'of breaking' it is to break something by folding it or breaking it into two or more pieces without it separating from the main body (whether object or plant). Cp: gid'ooni, giv'ooni. (Num.1:11)

Ahiezer; 'ăḥî'ezer; نَهي/نئيهي عَزَر ، نَخي/نئيخي عَزَر 'she is/here she is-ugly/made ugly' 'my brother/brother of-ugly/made ugly'; نَهي/نئيهي نَزَر ، نَخي/نئيخي نَزَر 'she is/here she is-tightened' 'she is/here she is-visited/pilgrimage to' 'my brother/brother of-tightened' 'my brother/brother of-visited/pilgrimage to'. Cp: ahee/aihee-'ezer, akhee/aikhee-'ezer, ahee/aihee-ezer, akhee/aikhee-ezer. (Num.1:12)

Ammishiddai; 'ammîšaddāy; عَمّيشَدّآي/نَمّيشَدّآي ، عَمّي شَدّآي ، نَمّي شَدّآي the words ('am: uncle, drink, blind) can replace 'the/will' in the following meanings: 'the turbaned' 'the emigrated' 'the-she emigrated/left' 'will emigrate/wrap around/strengthen with wrapping' the word is still in the feminine and also in giving the attribute to who/what is being spoken about; 'mother/my mother-emigrated/leave/left'. Cp: 'ammeeshaddaay, ammeeshaddaay, 'ammee-shaddaay, ammee-shaddaay. (Num.1:12)

Pagiel; pag'î'ēl; بَغني ئِل ، بَغنيئِل 'wanted-the' 'immoral/prostitution/immoral sexual activities-the' 'will mislead to downfall-the' 'despise-the' 'dug deep/stabbed deep-the' 'exploited/took advantage of-the' 'chained-the' 'rivers/streams/will make flow like river' 'made up harsh rules/laws'; فَجعي ئِل 'scare-the'. Cp: baghee-ill, bagheeill, phag'ee-ill, (Num.1:13)

Ocran; 'okrān; عوكرآن 'difficult'; عوقرآن 'were petrified' 'laps (two)' 'ruined'. Cp: 'ookraan, 'ooqraan. (Num.1:13)

Deuel; dĕ'û'ēl; دَعْ ئِل ، ديعُ ئِل 'call/called/they called-the' 'they claimed/falsely claimed-the' 'curse/cursed/they cursed-the'. Cp: de'u-ill, dei'u-ill. (Num.1:14)

Ahira; 'ăḥîra'; نئيحيرَء 'a big problem/predicament/puzzle' 'an open inflamed sore/wound'; نئيخيرَء 'is good/good fortune' 'the last/last' 'make last/delay' 'defecate'; نئيخيرَع 'to make burst from bottom' (such as breaking or bursting from overload/too much packing or from beating) 'beat to a pulp'. Cp: aiḥeera, aikheera, aikheera'. (Num.1:15)

Enan; 'ênān; عينآن 'two eyes' 'clouds/became cloudy' 'means/meant/hinting/hinted' 'suffered/prolonged suffering'; ئينآن 'Ouch!/Ow!' 'moaning in pain'. Cp: 'eynaan, eynaan. (Num.1:15)

Lael; lā'ēl; لآ ئِل 'to/until-the' 'no-the/no to the'; لآئِل ، لآئيل 'night/nights' 'of the night' 'on the night of' 'lullaby' 'lull with song/repeat sound of word 'lal/lail''. Cp: laa-ill, laaill, laaeyl. (Num.3:24)

Zuriel; ṣûrî'ēl; زُري ئِل 'tighten-the' 'visit/pilgrimage-the'. Cp: zuree-ill. (Num.3:35)

Abihail; 'ăḇîḥayil; نَبي/نئيبي/عَبي/عيبي هَيِل 'father-shed' (like shedding hair, leaves, skin) 'father-here's the' 'father-cardamom' 'father-she is the' 'rejected-here's the/she is the' 'rejected-cardamom' 'packed-here's the' 'packed-she is the' 'packed-cardamom' 'shamed/disgrace-shed' 'shamed/disgraced-here's the/cardamom'; نَبي/نئيبي/عَبي/عيبي حَيِل 'father-purified/cleansed/circumcised' 'father-made edible/made touchable' 'father-declared purified/permissible' 'father/shed/undressed' (as in shed clothes, leaves, hair, skin, etc.), 'father-beat until skin peeled off/severely' 'father-stay/stayed/stilled-the' 'father-stuck in one place/indecisive' 'father-deceit/trickster' 'rejected-stuck in one place/indecisive/tricks/trickster' to mean stuck to one side or in certain place, 'packed-stuck in one place/tricks/trickster'. Cp: abee/aibee-hayil, 'abee/'aibee-hayil, 'abee/'aibee-ḥayil, 'abee/'aibee-ḥayil. (Num.3:35)

The Bitter Water Test; the bitter water test (Num.5:12-31) where a jealous husband can accuse, without proof, his wife of adultery, the priest makes her sip/drink from bitter water (dirt in water) to test her innocence/guilt. In the remote rural areas of Yemen, when talking about a wife who suffers/suffered from her husband's mistreatment, they say 'he made her sip bitter/myrrh' or 'he made her sip from the bitter cup'.

Nazarite; nāzîr; نَآذير 'warned/a warning/is warning' 'a vow' 'been set aside' 'of vows' 'of setting aside' and is made by a man or woman asking God to do something (either for the person themselves or a loved one) and if it comes true, they will do something pious such as fast a specific number of days, as well as give a specific amount of money, grain or slaughter an animal and feed the hungry. The 'vow' (nvr/نذر) is always kept and made to God and also other deities/special beings/idols. Cp: naaveer. (Num.6:1-27)

Hobab; ḥōḇāḇ; حوبآب 'spots/units/kisses/loved' 'friends/loved ones'; حوظآظ 'refuses/rejects a good thing', the latter meaning is definitely what is intended in this part of the story as Moses offers to give Hobab a worthy reward in the land which they are journeying towards, if he will stay, but he refuses i.e. 'refuses a good thing'. 'And Moses said unto Hobab, the son of Raguel the Midianite, Moses' father in law, We are journeying unto the place which the Lord said, I will give it to you: come thou with us, and we will do thee good: for the Lord hath spoken good concerning Israel.' And Hobab refuses and says he is leaving, 'And it shall be, if thou go with us, yea, it shall be, that what goodness the Lord shall do unto us, the same we will do unto thee.' Cp: ḥobaab, hodhaadh. (Num.10:29-33)

Raguel; Rhagouēl; رَجو يْل 'waited-the' 'made wait-the' 'implore-the' 'shook-the'; رَعويْل 'shepherded-the' 'took care of-the', رَئويْل ، ريئويْل 'saw-the' (can also mean 'they watered-the' 'they watered/soaked/flooded-the' but has not been used in the narration) and it is one of the explicitly changed names which the authors of the Bible keep changing for Moses' father-in-law. The western translations being provided a different name although it appears as 'Reuel' in the Hebrew texts also shows the local translators understanding of Arabic as he provides the western translators 'Raguel' which still suits the storyline (see Eve). He is now 'waited-the' 'implored-the' along with the former Reuel at Exod.2:18 (Gen.36:4) 'shepherded-the' 'saw-the' as he is being asked to shepherd them in the wilderness and be their 'eyes'. Also, his 'Midianite' is always mentioned everywhere he pops up in the stories because it means 'passing/moving on' i.e. 'leaving': it features in his dealings with Moses when he gives Moses permission to leave and return to Egypt; it is shown again in 'And Moses let his father in law depart; and he went his way into his own land.'; and later in the story where he appears again in Exodus he is again wanting to 'move on' and return to his land and refuses to stay/wait. 'And he said unto him, I will not go; but I will depart to mine own land, and to my kindred. And he said, Leave us not, I pray thee; forasmuch as thou knowest how we are to encamp in the wilderness, and thou mayest be to us instead of eyes. And they departed from the mount...' Cp: ragoo-ill, ra'oo-ill, raoo-ill, raioo-ill. (Exod.2:15-21; 3:1; 4:18-20; 18:27; Num.10:29-33)

Taberah; taḇ'ērâ; تَذعيره ، تَذ عيرا 'a great panic/violence and panic' 'harm(ed)-gloating'. The people are harmed by the fire caused, the fire is caused as punishment because they are complaining in a manner which means gloating in Arabic, also God will gloat at them. The people recount how well they were living in Egypt and blame Moses/God for no longer having a varied and rich diet; Moses is complaining with a very Arabic adage 'Did I father you' meaning 'I am not responsible for you': 'Have I conceived all this people? Have I begotten them, that thou shouldest say unto me, Carry them in thy bosom...'; God is gloating as he counts and lists how he will give them meat day after day and so much 'until it come out of your nostrils' so in return for their complaining he is gloating over them and over what he will do to harm them. Cp: tav'eyrah, tav-'eyra. (Num.11)

Eldad and Medad; 'eldāḏ mêḏāḏ; عِلدآد ميدآد 'talking nonsense-lying down' 'talking nonsense-spreading/extending/touching/possessing', but I believe the second word (Medad) is wordplay on another word 'Meldad' because the saying which is used a lot in Yemen is 'Eldad and Meldad' so it should be: عِلدآد مِلدآد 'lies and tricks/nonsense' 'he goes back and forth with words/speaks nonsense/talks confusingly and incoherently'. When someone comments a person is (ye-'eldad wa ye-meldad) it means he is 'going back and forth, straying from the subject in order to deceive/lie' or speaking nonsense. But we cannot change what the Biblical text shows, and the meanings of the presented word 'Medad' is relayed within the related story: Moses complains of the burden of prophesy, which again returns to a narrative where prophesying means being possessed by God's spirit, God's spirit enters the men around the tabernacle, but because the aptly named Eldad and Medad are in the camp, when the spirit comes upon them and they prophesy, it is noticed by the people who find it wrong/strange and run to inform Moses—of course, it could have been intentionally changed from 'Meldad' to 'Medad' by later authors who want the 'touch/touched' meaning of God laying his spirit onto the seventy elders and Eldad and Medad as they are prophesying because God has possessed them with his spirit. Cp: 'eldaad, meydaad, (or meldaad). (Num.11:16-29)

Kibroth-hattavah; qiḇrôṯ hatta'ăwâ; the first part is wordplay on: قِبرُت 'buried' and قِضرُت 'disgusted by' 'went off(food, etc.)' and both words are used because people were buried and because God found them disgusting, the story narrates repeatedly how God will give them so much meat, they will eat so long until they are repulsed/disgusted by it 'until it come out at your nostrils, and it be loathsome unto you'. Also, God is disgusted by the people as he chooses to smite them with plague while the meat is still between their teeth being chewed. (hattavah) حَتّى عَفه/عيفه 'until they went off it' as go off food and unable to eat it (hatta) 'until' (avah) 'they went off it'. Cp: qibrot hatta 'aphah/'aiphah, qidhrot hatta 'aphah/'aiphah. (Num.11:18-23,31-35)

Hazeroth; ḥăṣērôṯ; wordplay on: هَزيرُط ، هيزيرُط 'will swallow' 'he will swallow' (as in swallowing a lot) and it refers both to God killing the people as 'eating/swallowing' is used to describe God killing people, and refers to the people killed by the plague even before they could swallow 'And while the flesh was yet between their teeth, ere it was chewed, the wrath of the Lord was kindled against the people, and the Lord smote the people with a very great plague.' From word (zrt/زرط) 'swallow'. Also حَذيرُت ، حيذيرُت 'she warned' (in multiple warnings' which in the chapter that follows is the location where Miriam warns Moses against his marriage to an Ethiopian woman (the word is definitely not 'Ethiopian' but one of many mistranslations and misinterpretations which will be addressed later in this book), and where God punishes her, which in itself is a warning to her from God but also the punishment relays the correct meaning translation of 'Ethiopian' (see Cush). The word 'Hazeroth/warning' is in the feminine form and in the story although it is both Miriam and Aaron warning/speaking against Moses, only Miriam is punished with leprosy and temporarily being put outside the camp while she recovers. Cp: hazeyroṭ, haizeyroṭ, ḥaveyrot, ḥaiveyrot. (Num.11:35;12)

Shammua; šammûaʿ; سَمّوَع 'made other people hear' 'listened (without people's knowledge)' 'eavesdropped' and is one of the twelve sent to 'spy out the land'. Cp: sammua'. Zaccur; zakkûr; ذَكّر 'remember/mention'; زَقّر 'topped up with liquid/filled to brim with liquid'; شَقّر 'peep between gaps' 'take quick glances (between hiding behind cover)'. Cp: vakkur, shaqqur. (Num.13:4)

Shaphat; šāpāṭ; شافات 'seeings/saw' 'cured/healed' 'cured or satisfied at another's bad luck/revenge/gloating/recompense out of hatred or wrong' (and this kind of gloating/revenge is when a person who has been done wrong by another takes satisfaction in the offending person's harm or bad luck); Cp: shaaphaat. His father **Hori** 'investigate'. (Num.13:5)

Caleb; kālēḇ; قآليب 'flips/turns-over'; غآليب 'to overcome/be victor' 'causes despair/frustration'. He will be victorious in fighting against the inhabitants of the land 'Let us go up at once and possess it, for we are well able to overcome it.' Cp: qaaleyb, ghaaleyb. His father has the matching name of Jephunneh; yĕpunneh; جَفونّه ، جيفونّه 'turned it over' and means to turn a vessel over to allow everything to trickle out of it so that it empties/dries properly, 'swipe or remove something leaving nothing behind'. Cp: gephunneh, geyphunneh. (Num.13:6,30)

Igal; yig'āl; يِجعال '(he) creates/creating' 'lays eggs/bait' (usually used to describe a chicken laying an egg; also, the name of the egg placed where a chicken usually lays her eggs so it does not go off and lay its eggs somewhere else.). Cp: yig'aal. (Num.13:7)

Palti; palṭî; بَلطي 'sticks to/stick to'; فَلتي 'falls/fallen' (both physically to fall or figuratively as become immoral especially sexually). Cp: baltee, phaltee. His father Raphu; rāpû'; رافُئ 'eyes twitch' 'sexual intercourse/had sex'; رافع 'puts away' 'lifts up'. Cp: raaph-u, raaphu'. (Num.13:9)

Gaddiel; gaddî'ēl; جَدّي ئِل 'grandfather-the' 'find-the' 'new/again/renew-the'. Cp: gaddee-ill. Sodi; sôḏî; شُدي 'was tightened/wrapped around' 'emigrate/leave/was made to emigrate'; سُدي 'reconcile/sort it out' 'my dam'. Cp: shodee, sodee. (Num.13:10)

Gaddi; gaddi; جَدّ 'grandfather' 'find' 'new/again/renew'. Cp: gaddi. Susi; sûsî; زُزي 'drive' as in drive into a specific direction against their will; شُشي 'many things, important things/wondrous things' 'puzzling matters/chaos and confusion' 'wanted something'; شُسي 'matter-bad/evil/offense/offensive' 'wanted-evil/bad' 'wanted something done'; سُسي 'did evil' 'bad-bad/bad-evil/evil-evil/offense-offended'; سُشي 'do/did something' 'offend/evil/bad-matter/thing'. Cp: zuzee, shushee, shusee, susee, sushee. (Num.13:11)

Ammiel; 'ammî'ēl; عَمّي ئِل 'drink-the' blind-the' 'my uncle-the'; Cp: 'ammee-ill. Son of: Gemalli; gĕmallî; جَمَلّي ، جيمَلّي 'came-fetch(ed) water' (as in the chore of fetching water from a well), 'came-frock/wearing frock' the latter is a shirt, 'was grateful/ingratiate'. Cp: gemallee, geimallee. (Num.13:12)

Sethur; sēṯûr; سيتُر 'covers/hides/conceals' 'curtain/large fabric/fabric cover'. Cp: seytur. Michael; mîḵā'ēl; ميكا ئِل 'what is there-the' 'what is-the' 'what is the matter-the' 'weighs out/weighed out'; ميقائِل 'what is said?' 'what is said-the' 'who said' 'who said-the'; ميقائيل 'spending time at/spending time with' 'stay(ing)/

wait(ing)'; ميخآئيل 'imagining' 'hallucinating' 'is hallucinating/has hallucinated/imagined' 'hallucination/imagination'. Cp: meekaa-ill, meeqaa-ill, meeqaaeyl, mee<u>kh</u>aaeyl. (Num.13:13)

Nahbi; naḥbî; نَحبي 'crawls/we crawl' 'our slaughter/peril'. Cp: naḥbee. Vophsi; wopsî; ووفصي 'and separate' 'remove stone of fruit' 'disentangle'; بوفصي 'will/am separating' 'will/am removing stone of fruit' 'am disentangling'; ووفسي 'and pass wind' 'and copulates hen/(cockerel)passes wind into her'; بوفسي 'will/am passing wind' '(cockerel)will copulate hen'. Cp: woo<u>ph</u>ssee, boo<u>ph</u>ssee, woo<u>ph</u>see, boo<u>ph</u>see. (Num.13:14)

Geuel; gĕ'û'ēl; جَئو ئِل ، جيئو ئِل 'came-the' 'they came-the';جَئوئِل ، جيئوئِل 'wandered' 'made side' 'eats from another person's side' (from the same dish of food). Cp: ge-u-ill gei-u-ill, geuill, geiuill. Machi; mākî; ماحي 'rubbed out/rubbed away' 'of egg yolk/runny/coward'; ماخي 'my brain' 'my intelligence' 'of intelligence/brainy' 'what brother?' 'not my brother' 'limp/floppy'; ماكي 'what is there/what is wrong' 'what is it'; معكي 'with you' (said to female); ماقي 'what is it now/what is the problem' 'what did he say/what was said'. Cp: maaḥee, maa<u>kh</u>ee, m'kee, maakee, maaqee. (Num.13:15)

Oshea; ôšēa'; وسيَع 'wandered aimlessly' 'wandered seeking promiscuity'; وشيَع 'pulls strand of threads/fibres/hair out' 'became ugly/made ugly' and the latter word meaning seems to be intended as Oshea son of Nun/(very young) is renamed by Moses to: Jehoshua; yĕhôšua'; جَهُسوَع ، يَهُسوَع 'he who-wandering aimlessly' 'came he/came to him-wandering aimlessly' 'he is debauched/promiscuous' 'wandered committing immoral acts'; جَهُشوَع ، جيهُشوَع 'came he/came to him-freakishly mutated/ugly' 'came he/came to him-bleating like goat'; جَخُشوَع ، جيخُشوَع 'came-breaking/broke to pieces' it means pounding at something with another hard object until it breaks to pieces or splits open. Cp: oseya', o<u>sh</u>eya'; yehosua', gehosua', geho<u>sh</u>ua', geiho<u>sh</u>ua', ge<u>kh</u>o<u>sh</u>ua', gei<u>kh</u>o<u>sh</u>ua'. (Num.13:8,16)

Ahiman; 'aḥîman; نَهيمَن 'I rule over' 'I rule with brutality' 'who/what is she/where is she from'; نَخيمَن 'my brother is who' 'whose brother' 'I estimate'. Sheshai; šēšay; شيشَي 'things and lots of things/wondrous things' 'many matters, important matters' 'puzzling/serious matters' usually used to imply grandeur and opulence, 'wanted something'; شيسَي 'matter-bad/evil/offense/offensive' 'did something' 'wanted something done'; سيسَي 'did evil' 'bad-bad/bad-evil/evil-evil/offense-offended'; سيشَي 'do/did something' 'offend/evil/bad-matter/thing'; زيزَي 'drive out/away'; Talmai; talmay; تَلمَي 'carried water by hand' which would be unusual and more strenuous to carry it as a basket, people usually carry it on the head or shoulder because of its weight, could also mean 'tilled(ploughed)/my lines of land'. They all have negative names which are infused with an attribute of superiority, and in the story the spies that come back tell fantastical stories about the size and numbers of the people, the fruit of the land etc. The name of their country/father also has a negative word: Anak; 'ănāq; عيناَق 'throated' 'of necks/did something to neck' and implies something will/is being done to his throat. Cp: aheeman, a<u>kh</u>eeman; <u>sh</u>ey<u>sh</u>ay, <u>sh</u>eysay, seysay, sey<u>sh</u>ay, zeyzay; talmay, 'ainaaq. (Num.13:22)

Zoan; ṣō'an; زوعَن 'they are able/can do it' 'strong' 'fat' means to be strong and beautiful ('fat' not negative like in the west). It comes directly after naming the children of Anak, which the story describes in later verses as giants and able to defend against/defeat Moses' people. It is also followed by mentioning the milk, honey and fruit of the land which also implies there will be strength and fatness (plenty/good fortune) which is why **Hebron** 'told them news/information' 'they told/informed/brought news' 'of news/information/of telling' 'good/piety' is mentioned in the verses as well as meaning 'they/he will pass/go beyond' as they are travelling through the different areas in their mission, and refers to the news brought back of a fertile land with plentiful fruit 'and brought back word unto them...' and they also bring back news that it is inhabited by a strong people and the 'evil report of the land' causes the people to fear entering it; Zin; ṣin; زِن 'nag/incessantly complain'; سِن 'direct/straight line/made straight/on right path'; and relays the path they took to spy out the land, and is also mentioned because the people do not want to fight against the inhabitants of the land they have arrived at; and each name of city mentioned also implies something mentioned in the direct chapter whether Rehob 'space/spaciousness' 'plenty' etc. Cp: zoo'an; zin, sin. (Num.13:22-33)

Eshcol; same as before: 'eškōl; نَشقول 'hang up (from a ring or rope attached to ceiling/wall)' it is how people in rural areas (without refrigerators) store various foods out of the way of insects, animals and also to allow it to be cooled/dried by the air. The same word is used to describe the twine/belts used to hang anything up, to raise a leg, to hang something from rope/straps. In this story it is because the fruit is hung from a staff and carried by two people so it is hanging and carried in the way the word 'eshcol' means. Cp: e<u>sh</u>qool.

Hormah; ḥormâ; حورمه ، حورما 'deprived(of)/deprived him/her/them' 'forbidden' 'forbade it' 'forbade them him/them' 'woman' 'sacred'. Refers to God forbidding the people from entering the land because they would not do so when told so it was forbidden against them for forty years; furthermore, the people change their attitude and decide to immediately occupy the land, but Moses tells them they are forbidden from entering the land and the story narrates how they were prevented by defeat, and the story gives the place name the fitting 'hormah/forbidden' and in the story that follows in Chapter 15 a man does something forbidden (gathering sticks on sabbath) and is stoned to death for it. Cp: ḥormah, ḥorma. (Num.14; 15:32-36)

In Chapter 16, all the names describe the punishment, verbs, adjectives which apply in the story; those receiving punishment are aptly named.

Korah; qōraḥ; كورَه 'a lot' 'hated/hateful' 'in one go' 'loads/heaps/plenty'; كورَح 'striking sound' (from striking one object with another); قورَح 'sores/ulcers' 'burst/exploded' 'bursting sound'; and he is son of Lewi 'twirls around' and in language can also mean 'dishonest/not forthright', to deceive with words or talk too much nonsense to get to an objective and in this part of the story, the patronym describes Korah's behaviour. Cp: koorah, kooraḥ, qooraḥ. (Num.16:1)

Dathan; dāṯān; دآفآن 'buried' (in multiple actions). Cp: daaphaan. Abiram; 'ăḇîrām; نَبي/ئبيي رآم 'father/ refused-(was)thrown/killed'. Cp: abee-raam. Both are the sons of: **Eliab**; 'he who/the one who-rejects/ refuses/returns'; 'he who/the one who-harms/is harmed'; 'he who/the one who-disgraced' (could mean caused others to feel shame or he himself was disgraced.' And the paternal name also describes the behaviour of the 'sons' and also what happens to them in the story. (Num.16:1)

On; 'ôn; ئُن 'moans/groans' (from pain); عُن 'suffer' (physical sufferance) 'help/cooperate'. Cp: on, 'on. He is the son of: Peleth; peleṯ; فَلَث 'fell' (both physically to fall or figuratively as become immoral, especially sexually/morally). Cp: phelet. And the grandfather is **Reuben** 'saw into/between' 'saw-made clear/ apparent' and they will be seen opposing Moses and Aaron (**Aaron** meaning 'is-here-see/look'; 'drive them away') and their punishment will be witnessed by all, they will see God's Glory filling the tabernacle. (Num.16:1)

'**Korah**' there is hatred towards Moses and Aaron, and hatred towards the rebelling men; there is striking and bursting sounds '...that the ground clave asunder that was under them...'; '**Dathan**' the men, their wives, children and possessions are buried alive 'And the earth opened her mouth and swallowed them up, and all their houses, and all the men that appertained unto Korah, and all their goods.'; '**Peleth**' '**Abiram**' there is rejection of the men's incense offerings and they are thrown down into the opening in the earth, they fall morally and are disgraced with physical punishment, the other rebelling men offering incense also fall dead by fire and plague 'They, and all that appertained to them, went down alive into the pit, and the earth closed upon them: and they perished from among the congregation' ; '**On**' there is moaning and groaning or at least screaming while these people are being killed by God and the terror it creates among those watching 'And all Israel that were round about them fled at the cry of them...' (Num.16)

Zin; ṣin; زِن 'nag/incessantly complain' and is the same **Sin** mentioned earlier which has been changed into Zin in wordplay beginning from Num.13:21 to allow the narration that the people 'murmur' and they complain, nag and gripe about why they have been made to leave Egypt to suffer from travel and its travails, from hunger and thirst. Just as in Num.13, Zin is used here to show how people will complain and nag Moses because the story narrates they see him as deceiving them to leave Egypt where they were better off. Cp: zin. (Num.20)

Meribah; same as earlier.

Kadesh; qāḏēš; كآديش ، كآدَش 'falls like a heap' 'falls is thrown to the ground with a loud sound' 'pile/piles' (things on the ground) 'piled'; قآديش ، قآدِش 'led/of being led' 'led/pimped' and the latter can mean leading an animal by a rope (usually to get somewhere specific or being led to slaughter) or a person led around like an animal, it is the same word used to describe a 'middle person/pimp' usually a female who mediates between two lovers and is called such because she is misleading the female lover to ruination of reputation and her life. 'Kadesh' is still being used as explained earlier why it is used as the 'between place' between travels. Here it was used with the same meaning of the sound or action of falling like a heap and also for Miriam to die, a body would be like a heap on the ground. It also shows how the people are being led by Moses, but that they also feel they are being led on/misled which is expressed in the narration of the chapter. (Num.20:1)

Hor; hōr; هور 'drive away/chase away(verbally)' and means to gesture and speak aggressively/unkindly to drive away the recipient(s) of this language/behaviour which is exactly what Edom does to Moses and the people. It can be clearly seen that 'Hor' which is described here also as a mountain, the character name

'Hur' who along with Aaron assisted Moses when they were driving Amaleks away with a hand gesture and 'Horeb' (in the story also the name given to a mountain) where Moses was told to stand back—are all from the same word which means 'drive away/chase away(verbally)'. The word has no meaning nor relation as 'mountain' other than the story creators wanted to use the word to describe this specific action in the story. In addition to Edom driving them away with unkind words, it is the place they find most suitable to kill-off Aaron's character—remember his name also means 'drive them away' and is used again in the story where the action of being driven away is used as a place and character name. It is also خور 'make them flee/collapse' and has the same meanings to chase people away but by physical action as Edom says '...lest I come out against thee with the sword'. Cp: hoor, khoor. (Num.20:14-29)

Arad; ʽarād; عَرآض 'objected' 'made obstacles' 'blocked the way with his body' 'of obstructing' and the story has this king obstructing and capturing some of the children of Israel. Cp: 'araadh. The city is renamed 'Hormah' because they have deprived the inhabitants of their lives and cities i.e., they have made it 'forbidden' to them. (Num.21:1-3)

Hor as خور 'make them flee' (to chase people away by physical action) and 'collapse' are used again here when the people complain again about being deceived to leave Egypt 'And the Lord sent fiery serpents among the people, and they bit the people; and much people of Israel died.' so the people are being made to move along by physical force and is why the name of Hor has been mentioned again (it is the method of the Bible storytelling). Cp: khoor. (Num.21:4-10)

Oboth; ʽōḇōṯ; عوبوث 'messed around with' 'pointlessly/flippantly messed around with' 'messed about'; ئوذوت 'harmed'. The serpents come to harm the people when they mess about and do not want to obey orders. Cp: 'ooboof, oovoot. (Num.21:10)

Ije-abarim; ʽîyêʽăḇārîm, ʽîyê hāʽăḇārîm; ئيجي عَذآر/عيذآرهم/ام ، ئيجي هآعَذآر/عيذآرهم/ام 'came-shadows/shadowed-them/the', 'came-here is-shadows/shadowed-them/the' and is supported by '...and pitched at Ije-abarim, in the wilderness which is before Moab, toward the sunrising.' The shadow can be seen pulling away as the sun rises and the higher it gets. ئيجي ئَبآر/ئيبآرهم/ام ، ئيجي هآئَبآر/ئيبآرهم/ام 'came-went beyond-them/the' 'came-good/pious towards-them/the' although consecutive verses state they move on from that location, it does not seem to be implied by the word-name. It cannot be 'came-through-them/the' because the word to make that work is عبر 'through' and in the form it is in in the Bible ʽăḇārîm عَبآرهم/ام 'riding on-them/the' it would mean 'riding on' not 'passing through' and the word عبر is a modern word not used with the meaning 'through/ride on' as the Old Arabic word does not mean this at all—unless the editing was done during a much later date than believed it cannot be 'passing through'. Cp: eegey-'avaar/'aivaar-hum/um, eegey-haa-'avaar/'aivaar-hum-um, eegey-abaar/aibaar-hum/um, eegey-haa-abaar/aibaar-hum-um. (Num.21:11)

Zared; zāred; زآرَت 'visited' as they do not stay long before moving to the other side. Or شآرَد 'homeless/made homeless' 'displaced/dispersed' as the protagonists are still made to move on from place to place. Cp: zaaret, shaared. (Num.21:12)

Arnon; ʽarnôn; عَرنُن 'naked/nakedness' 'disgraced' 'abandoned in wilderness' and is linked by the story to 'Moab' ('of disgrace') and to wilderness. Cp: 'arnon. (Num.21:13)

Ar; ʽār; عآر 'a disgrace' 'naked' and is still linked to 'Moab' ('of disgrace') by being on its border. Cp: 'aar. (Num.21:15)

Beer still means 'good/piety to/towards' as God is giving them water. (Num.21:16)

Mattanah; mattānâ; مَطّآنه ، مَطّآنا 'a tinning/clanging' and means there was a metallic or hollow object being struck to produce the tinning/clanging sound—to accompany the song the story narrates being sang while the well is being excavated; مَثّآنه ، مثّآنا 'doubled/doubled us' 'folded/folded it' 'wiped away urine/sperm(without water) for me/us'; مَدّآنه ، مَدّآنا 'guilted/made guilty' 'bowed/lowered/bent' 'extended/reached for/reached into/put hands into' 'singing 'daana'' (the latter is popular in Arabic songs and is repeated in lines of song) which also fits with the verse narration of a song being sang while they worked; مَضّآنه ، مضّآنا 'we completed it/him' 'he completed/finished us' 'he entertained/distracted/passed time for us' 'what did he think/suspect' 'he/they did not suspect/think' 'it passed us along/allowed us to pass'. Cp: maṭṭaanah, maṭṭaana, maffaanah, maffaana, maddaanah, maddaana, madhaanah, madhaana. (Num.21:17-18)

Nahaliel; naḥălî'ēl; نَخَلي/نخيلي ئِل 'we leave-the' 'we let alone-the' 'we allow-the' 'we poke-the' 'we empty-the' 'we hollow-the' 'we allow-the'; نَحَلي/نحيلي ئِل 'we purify/cleanse/circumcise/make edible-the' 'we shed-the' 'we sweeten-the'. Cp: nakhalee-ill, nakhailee-ill, naḥalee-ill, naḥailee-ill. (Num.21:19)

Bamoth; bāmôṯ; بآمُت 'I'll die'; بآمُط 'I'll stretch'; بآمُث 'I will wipe away urine/sperm(without water)'; بآمُد 'I will hand/extend/reach out/reach into'. Cp: baamut, baamuṭ, baamuf, baamud. (Num.21:19-20)

Pisgah; pisgâ; بِزقه ، بزقا 'passed by' 'passed by just now/quickly passed by' 'divided into tiny pieces, scattered or spread it over various places'; بِسقه ، بسقا 'water/irrigate'; بِسغه ، بسغا 'they will tilt (tilt it)/swivel (swivel it)' 'tilt/move head to see or hear better'. Cp: bizqah, bizqa, bisqah, bisqa, bisghah, bisgha. (Num.21:20)

Jeshimon; yĕšîmôn; هَزيمُن ، هيزيمُن 'they defeated/they were defeated/to defeat' 'for a long time/it has been a long time' 'I will time'; جَزيمُن ، جيزيمُن 'they dare/to dare'; جَشيمُن ، جيشيمُن 'bit clean off/bitten clean off' 'picked many-who/whose/what/from where'. Cp: hezeemon, heizeemon, gezeemon, geizeemon, gesheemon, geisheemon. (Num.21:20)

Sihon; sihōn, sihôn; سِهون ، سِهُن 'hoped for' 'longed/hankered for' 'forgot/lapsed in thought'; سِحون ، سِحُن 'drag on buttocks' 'move forward in sitting position' (how babies drag forward in sitting position instead of crawling). Cp: sihoon, sihon, siḥoon, siḥon. (Num.21:23)

Jahaz; yahaṣ; يَحَز ، جَحَز 'he-crams/corners' 'came-cornered/crammed'; جَهَز 'made ready/prepared' 'finished off'; يَهَز ، جَهَز 'he shakes/swings' 'came-shook/swung'; يَخَذ 'takes/he takes'; يَخَز 'swears/insults'. Cp: yaḥaz, gaḥaz, gahaz, yahaz, gahaz, yakhav, yakhaz. (Num.21:23)

Heshbon; ḥešbôn; حَشبُن 'cut down/a cutting down' 'to carry on waist/hip' (like carrying child on waist or hip). Cp: ḥeshbon. (Num.21:25-26)

Chemosh; kĕmôš; خَمُش ، خيمُش 'to crumple (with squeezing motion) and mix up'; هَمُش ، هيمُش 'diminished and humiliated' 'mistreated'. Cp: khemosh, kheimosh, hemosh, heimosh. (Num.21:29)

Dibon; dîḇôn; تيذُن 'harmed/harm'. Cp: teevon. (Num.21:30)

Nophah; nōpah; نوفَه 'ceased to exist/died/wiped out' 'felt relief/breathed air/aired/could breathe'; نوفَح 'wafting odour'; نوبَح 'barking' 'spread out/relax over large space'. Cp: noophah, noophaḥ, noobaḥ.

Medeba; mêḏĕḇā'; ميذَبآء ، ميديباء 'wailing in mourning'; ميذَبآع ، ميديباع 'hair cut short or shaved off completely'. Cp: meydebaa, meydeibaa, meydebaa', meydeibaa'. (Num.21:30)

Jaazer; ya'ăzêr, ya'ăzēr; جَعَزير ، جَعيزير 'came-make/made ugly' and refers to how he and his sons will be put to death and also جَنَزير ، جَنَيزير 'slaughter(ed)' and also means 'green pastures' 'grazing animals'. Cp: ga-'azeyr, ga-'aizeyr, ga-azeyr, ga-aizeyr. (Num.21:32)

Bashan; bāšān; بآشآن 'filter(ed) impurities out of liquid/will filter impurities from liquid' 'will flow(ed) out of/into' 'ready for copulation/ready to conceive(goats and similar animals)/on heat' 'will copulate/will be sexually excited/will be ready to copulate/copulated' 'fertile/verdant land'. Cp: baashaan. (Num.21:33)

Og; 'ôg; عُج 'many/overcrowded/great crowd(s)' 'over spilling(with fortune/good)/field filled with crops whose panicles seem packed and over spilling' 'panting/gasping/out of breath from crying' 'suffered/tortured' 'prolonged suffering/torture' '(made/were/is)crooked' '(made/were/is)not forthright/dishonest'. Cp: 'og. (Num.21:33)

Edrei; 'eḏre'î; نَذرَعي ، نَذرِعي 'my forearm' 'measure length (by the forearm)'; نَدرَعي ، نَدرِعي 'defend' 'shield' 'ward away' usually said to protect someone like a child, a plant or other food sources. The story tells Moses not to worry as God has guaranteed Moses victory over his enemy. Cp: evra'ee, evre'ee, edra'ee, edre'ee. (Num.21:33)

Jericho; yĕrîḥô; يَريحُ ، ييريحُ ، جَريحُ ، جيريحُ 'he/they made wind/fanned' 'he/they rested/relaxed' 'came-wind' 'came-rested/relaxation/take a break' 'wounded'; يَريخُ ، ييريخُ ، جَريخُ ، جيريخُ 'he/they loosened' 'came-loosened'. Cp: yereeḥo, yeireeḥo, gereeḥo, geireeḥo, yereikho, yeireekho gereekho, geireekho. (Num.22:1)

Balak; bālāq; بآلآغ 'pass/send on greetings or information through messengers' and is what the king named Balak does throughout the first chapter where he is introduced. بآلآك 'ailed you' as with illness, problems, bad luck, etc. Cp: baalaagh, baalaak. (Num.22)

Zippor; ṣippôr, ṣippōr; زِبُّر ، زِبّور 'of-penis(related to activity involving)' as he is an enemy king an insulting name is given; سِبُّر ، سِبّور 'fixer' as in fixes problems or things and he is trying to fix the problem of fearing Moses' people; صِبِّر ، صِبّور 'patient/of patience' as his character is patient with Balaam's meanderings. Cp: zibbor, zibboor, sibbor, sibboor, ssibbor, ssibboor. (Num.22;23;24)

Balaam; bil'ām; بِلعان 'with/of curses' 'will curse' 'on purpose' as he is needed to curse Moses' people, 'on purpose' he purposely does not do this as God has told him not to; بِلغان 'has received message' as he has received Balak's messages; بِلئام 'with/of blame' as he blames the donkey for hurting him, then both Balaam and donkey blame/reproach each other; the angel blames Balaam for hitting the donkey; Balak will blame Balaam for blessing instead of cursing Moses' people. Cp: bil'aan, bilghaan, bil-aam. (Num.22;23;24)

Beor as at (Gen.36:32); bĕ'ôr; بَعُر ، بيعُر 'with disgrace' 'will be disgraced', animals such as donkeys, camels, 'scream/shout/sob for long time'; بيعُر 'will push forward blindly' and is used to describe a stubborn person (likened to an animal) who goes ahead with something or walks fast and with difficulty with head down even if he/she is wrong and goes ahead with it anyway; بيئر 'lose reputation, bad reputation, will ruin reputation' 'spoiled/stale/expired' 'spoiled/stale/expired' 'untrustworthy' and all words with all their meanings are shown in the narration: he deals with a donkey; the donkey talks; Balaam forces it to go forward when the path is blocked; he is supposed to say or shout out curses against Moses, but instead shouts out blessings; he loses his reputation and is seen as untrustworthy by Balak who hired him. Cp: be'or, bei'or, bei-or/beior. (Num.22;23;24)

Pethor; pĕṯôr; بَثّر ، بيثور 'with/by bulls' 'scatter/will scatter soil(or any powdery substance such as ash, flour, etc.)' 'expired/stale' and Balaam's use to Balak expires as he cannot use him for the said purpose; بَطر ، بيطر 'I/he will make fly/flee/expel/chase away/banish' 'he is turning/turned down a good thing' 'not knowing he has it good' it is the equivalent of 'turning one's nose up at' something good, it can also mean wasting limited resources, not knowing how good the situation is or turning down a good offer/situation; it is also when forcing people to leave in a hurry or in an unkind or even threatening way. It is exactly what the story narrates Balaam doing; the meanings are portrayed with many bulls being sacrificed along with rams on the altars, also the meanings of 'will expel/send away/make fly off/banish' which Balak does to Balaam at end of their stories. Cp: befor, beifor, beṭor, beiṭor. (Gen.22-24)

Kirjath-huzoth; qiryaṯ ḥuṣôṯ; قِريَة حوزَة ، خِرجَة حوزُت 'village/came out-squeezed/crammed/cornered' it refers to how the angel cornered Balaam and his donkey on their way to Balak, and also to how the curses are meant to corner and squeeze Moses's people so that they leave. Cp: qiryat ḥuzot, khirgat ḥuzot. (Num.22:39)

Baal; ba'al; بَعَل 'high/higher/high place/above' and is mentioned as exactly that in this story and also where the word appears before in the Biblical stories. '...and brought him up into the high places of Baal'; 'upon (them)' 'with upon (them)' 'spouse(s)'. Cp: ba'al. (Num.22:41)

Aram; as before

Zophim; ṣōpîm; زوفهم/ام 'escort away/lead in a procession-them/the' and is what Balaam is being asked to do with his curses. The same word has appeared in its different tenses/forms before in the Biblical stories with the exact same meaning of a procession made up of an entourage/many people. Cp: zooph-hum, zooph-um. **Pisgah** is meant here as 'tilt/move head to see better', as every time Balak moves Balaam it is to enable him to get a better view at the people and also 'to divide and scatter' as his curse is required to cause them to disperse. (Num.23:14)

Peor; pĕ'ôr; فَعُر ، فيعُر 'so he will gloat' 'so he will drive away' 'so he will-abandon/send out into wilderness' 'so he will disgrace'; بَعُر ، بيعُر 'with disgrace' 'will be disgraced' 'will push forward blindly/behave brashly' 'will be/become naked', animals such as donkeys, camels, 'scream/shout/sob for long time'; بيئر 'lose reputation/bad reputation/ruin the reputation' 'spoiled/stale/expired' 'untrustworthy' and is narrated in all its meanings: Balaam faces the wilderness instead of towards Jeshimon; Balak gloats at Balaam telling him 'I thought to promote thee unto great honour; but, lo, the Lord hath kept thee back from honour.'; Balaam gloats back that he would not have accepted from Balak a houseful of silver and gold and gloats further by telling him he will spread news of how Moses' people will defeat Balak's people in the future—'peor' does not differ from 'beor' meanings (except for animal meaning) and could also be wordplay on exactly 'beor' in spelling and meaning. The reason **Jeshimon** was mentioned beside Peor is to allow its meanings of 'defeat' 'humiliation' 'many people' to enhance the narration of the story where all these meanings are mentioned. Cp: phe'or, phei'or, be'or, bei'or, bei-or/beior. (Gen.23:28)

Sheth; šēṯ; شيف wordplay on 'saw/seeing' as Balaam is speaking about a vision, and 'gloating' unlike the earlier meaning from ('ar and 'or) where gloating is over giving or counting how much has or would be given, the type of gloating meant from word (shph/شف) is more malicious as it means gloating over another's misfortune or bad situation—which is exactly what Balaam is doing when he mentions Sheth as he is saying he will spread the news of the people's destruction/death as if he is happy about it. Cp: sheyph. (Num.24:13-24)

Chittim; šiṭṭîm; شِطّهم/ام ، شِطّام 'coast/shore-them/the' 'their coast/the coast' 'coasts/two or more coasts' 'split-them/the' 'split/torn' and the story says 'And ships shall come from the coast of Chittim…'. Cp: shiṭṭ-hum, shiṭṭ-um, shiṭṭum. (Num.24:24)

Baal-peor; baʿal pĕʿôr; بَعَل فيعَر/بيعَر 'high/higher/above/spouse-so he will disgrace/will be disgraced/will push forward blindly/behave brashly' 'high/higher/above/spouse-will be/become naked'; بَعَل بيئَر 'high/higher/above/spouse-lose reputation/bad reputation/ruin the reputation/spoiled/stale/expired' 'high/higher/above/spouse-untrustworthy'. And is what happens to Israel when they 'commit whoredom' i.e. take partners from the local women and worship other gods. 'baal/high/higher/above' refers to the heads of the transgressing men of Israel that God instructs to be slaughtered then hung up to the sun. Cp: ba'al phei'or/bei'or, ba'al-beior. (Num.25)

Phinehas; as before: 'will bring bad luck' and is in the form to bring bad luck to himself and/or others; 'will breathe'; 'will create holes/crumble' 'will poke holes and/or crumble'; 'will maul/take chunks out of' as he kills an Israeli man and Midianitish woman (the story never explains why it was acceptable that Moses married a Midianitish woman, but becomes a racist prohibition for everyone else because it is just a story based on wordplay and not meant to be taken as truth) using a javelin, so he creates holes/chunks in their bodies and also brings them bad fortune; his meaning 'bad fortune' is related to the plague affecting the people and because he helps stop it, in a way he breathes life back into the situation. Note: wherever Eleazar or Eliezer which both mean 'ugliness/makes ugly' are mentioned, it is to describe the wrong, death, destruction, i.e. the ugliness of the situation depicted in the stories. (Num.25)

Zimri; zimrî; ذِمري 'of guilt/of insult/of blame/humiliated/ostracised/diseased' it can have other meanings such as 'زِمري/pipe player' and سِمري 'stays up all night' 'tells night time stories', but it definitely holds the first meanings as he is doing what other Israelites have done which have caused shame and plague amongst the people and has been introduced into the story to add drama. Cp: vimree, zimree, simree. His father name Salu; sālû'; صالّئ ، صالّو 'grilled' 'arriving/public apology', and the apology includes a gift offered and the act of arriving symbolises the apologising person(s) has done wrong towards whom he/they are apologising to, and in the story refers to his (Zimri's) head to be hung in the sun as mentioned '…Take all the heads of the people, and hang them up before the Lord against the sun, that the fierce anger of the Lord may be turned away from Israel.' and it is implied that this has happened when Phinehas kills Zimri and the woman 'So the plague was stayed from the children of Israel…Phinehas, the son of Eleazer, the son of Aaron the priest, hath turned my wrath away from the children of Israel…'. Cp: ssaalu. (Num.25)

Cozbi; kozbî; كوذبي 'lies/liar' and she is the daughter of: Zur; ṣûr; زُر ، زور 'false oath' (saying something untrue under oath), and follows the insulting names given to men and women portrayed as enemies or bad in reputation in the stories being told. Cp: koovbee, zur, zoor. (Num.25:15-18)

Ozni; 'oznî; ئوزني 'commit adultery/fornicate'; عوزني 'want/want me' 'in need/support me' (as in with food or money etc.) 'cherish me'; عوذني 'protect/protect me' 'say protection for me'. Cp: ooznee, 'ooznee, 'oovnee. (Num.26:16)

Eri; ʿērî; ايري/ئيري 'my penis' 'he saw/sees' 'he waters' 'he dreams' 'he shows' 'he teaches'; عيري 'lend' 'disgrace/shame'. Cp: eyree, 'eyree. (Num.26:16)

Jashub; yāšûḇ; يآشُب ، ياشوب 'goes around in circles' (goes back and forth) (often said in pair with 'yalub' (yashoob wa yaloob 'goes in circles and cries for assistance' and describes a person in a state of anxiety or distress going back and forth or in circles, wringing his/her hands, asking for assistance with the matter (from God or other people)), 'swells and stiffens/grows bigger' e.g. wood swells from water, penis swells with blood, a head with cold, 'grows adolescent' '(fire)ignites fast or large/blazes'; عآشُب، عاشوب 'plants/herbs' 'gathering plants/herbs'; خآشُب ، خاشوب 'wooden' 'lumber' 'gathering timber' 'setting wooden beams in ceiling'; حآشُب ، حاشوب 'carrying on waist' 'clothes uplifted and tucked into waist'. Cp: yaashub, yaashoob, 'aashub, 'aashoob, khaashub, khaashoob, ḥaashub, ḥaashoob. (Num.26:24)

Jeezer; 'îʿezer; ئيئَذَر 'yes(or he will), he sows seeds/has children' 'yes(or he will), he scatters on ground' 'yes (or he will), he scatters soil/powdery substance'; ئيئَزَر 'yes(or he will), he tightens' 'yes(or he will), he visits/pilgrimages'; ئيعذَر 'yes(or he will), he excuses' 'yes(or he will), he shadows'; ئيعَزَر 'yes(or he will), he made ugly/became ugly'. Cp: ey-ever, ey-ezer, ey'ever, ey'ezer. (Num.26:30)

Helek; ḥēleq; حيلَق 'hugged/put arms around' 'surrounded' 'circle'; هيلَق 'he will find' 'he will throw down'; هيلَك 'he will perish/die'. Cp: ḥeyleq, heyleq, heylek. (Num.26:30)

Asriel; 'aśrî'ēl; نَصري يِل 'bundle/knot-the' 'keep in-the' 'insist-the'; عَصري يِل 'twist-the/twist muscle-the' (note the name 'Asriel' here as a person and family name is followed by 'Shechem' as a person and family name, just as in the renaming of Jacob to Israel (twisted muscle-the) in Genesis where his muscle is twisted/pulled, the story is followed by introducing Shechem and Shechem's story and both are linked to El-elohe-Israel 'the-yes it is her/yes she did-twisted muscle the' (Gen.32;33;34)). Cp: assree-ill, 'assree-ill. (Num.26:31)

Shemida; šĕmîdā'; شيميتاع ، شَميتاَع 'I have time to do it/get it done' 'I will take my time'. Cp: shemeetaa', sheimeetaa'. (Num.26:32)

Hepher; ḥēper; حيفَر 'dug holes/dug'; خيفَر 'became musty'. Cp: ḥeypher, kheypher. (Num.26:32)

Zelophehad; ṣĕlopĕḥād; زيلو/زَلوفي هآذ 'they disappeared/went-into-this/it/this one' 'was removed forever/wiped out-in-this one' and when used this way it means 'this was their demise/disappearance' 'this (or he/she) made them perish' and also 'they got used to this bad habit'. It is the first two meanings as the daughters whose father died without a male heir were to be left without an inheritance according to the custom and so were meant to disappear as a family name/die from hunger. Cp: zeiloo-phei-haav, zeloo-phei-haav. (Num.26:16;27)

Mahlah; maḥlâ; مَحله 'his place/replacing him/it' 'undressing place'; not only because they are asking their father's name should be given its place among his brethren through giving the daughters land, but also because they are standing at the door of the 'tabernacle'—there is a link between 'place/place to undress' and the tabernacle (which can be seen in the word chosen to name the character of one of the people who is assigned to create it: Aholiab 'my undressing-shame' and refers to a place where a person can undress in privacy); 'Mahlah' can also have other (ḥl/حل) meanings but they have not been used here. Cp: maḥlah. (Num.26:33; 27)

Noah; as before but specifically نَوه 'warned/brought to attention/reminded' 'the stone/seed(of fruit)' 'the/his intentions/unspoken thoughts' as she and her sisters are bringing attention to Moses and the whole congregation that the custom does not allow them to inherit as they have no brother and that they do deserve to receive land; that even if their father had no male heir to carry his seed into future generations, they should be allowed to receive land and plant it for their own offspring—it plays a lot on the meaning of 'seed/stone'. Cp: knowah. (Num.26:33; 27)

Hoglah; ḥoglâ; حوجله 'line or patterns made as borders on women's clothes' 'valid argument for him' as she and her sisters make an acceptable argument for their and their father's case and it is accepted by God 'The daughters of Zelophehad speak right'. Cp: ḥooglah. (Num.26:33; 27)

Milcah; milkâ; As before مِلقح to be 'pollen' or 'pollinated'; also, additional meaning for this story: مِلكه 'his possession' as they are asking to be afforded the same rights as if their father had had male offspring (pollinated); and they are asking 'Give unto us therefore a possession among the brethren of our father.'. Cp: milqaḥ, milkah. (Num.26:33; 27)

Tirzah; tirṣâ; تِرثه 'his inheritance/heritage/legacy' 'she inherits him/it' as they inherit him, and becomes law that daughters can inherit and more details about inheritance of people with no male heir is detailed. Cp: tirfah. (Num.26:33;27)

The rest of the chapter sticks to the pattern the daughters' names imply: inheritance is detailed (Tirzah), not only from individual to relatives (Milcah) but the land given to Israel (Tirzah), Joshua inheriting Moses leadership and also his part of 'spirit' and 'honour' (Tirzah). It is brought to Moses' attention where and when he will die (Noah). The new inheritance law becomes 'a statute of judgement' (Hoglah) as is judging Joshua through the Urim ritual. Setting Joshua over the congregation as leader is also putting him in a place, setting the stage for Israel to enter and live in the land is also setting the place (Mahlah). (Num.27)

Shuthelah; šûtelaḥ; شُذْلَح 'I will winnow'. Cp: shuvelaḥ. (Num.26:35)

Tahan; taḥan; طَحَن 'ground (grains)'. Cp: ṭaḥan. (Num.26:35)

Ahiram; 'ăḥîrām; نَخي رآم 'my brother-throws/thrown'; نَخيرآم 'pierce metal/make hole in metal' 'tear a hole/slit/piercing right to the end' 'the fortune-the' 'the last-the'; نَحيرآم 'they are sacred' 'it rotted/they are rotten/stinking' 'I forbid/they are forbidden'; نَهي رآم 'she is/here she is/her-throws/thrown'. Cp: akhee-raam, akheeraam, aḥeeraam, ahee-raam. (Num.26:35)

Shupham; šûp̄ām; شُف آم 'see-the' 'healed-the' 'gloated at-the'. Cp: shuph-aam. (Num.26:39)

Shuphamites; šûp̄āmîm; شُف آم هم/ام 'see-the-them/the' 'healed/cured the-them/the' 'gloat at the-them/ the'. Cp: shuph-aam-hum/um. (Num.26:39)

Hupham; ḥûp̄ām; هُف آم 'huff/puff-the' 'drive away/scatter away-the'. Cp: huph-aam. Usually the phrase is a duo of the words which have been combined in Num.26:39: 'shaapha-hum wa haapha-hum' 'he saw them and drove them away/scattered them away/took them away' and 'huph' means to huff while expressing anger much like a bull that charges at people or other animals. (Num.26:39)

Jesui; yišwî; يشوي 'he is roasting/grilling'; يصوي 'he/it is making squealing animal sounds (like birds or any other squeaky sound'; عِسوي 'my cold bread/of cold bread' 'breaking/eating bread' and is a combination of the earlier 'Ishuah' and 'Ishui' being made into one which is why, although they are usually mentioned as separate names together in the same verse or consecutive verses, only either Ishui or Ishuah appears here as 'Jesui' because the authors are formulating the story which in the end becomes 'Jesse' and 'Jesus' as separate stories. Cp: yishwee, yisswee, 'iswee. (Num.26:44)

Evi; 'ĕwî; عيوي 'howl' 'of howling' likened to an animal and showing a brutal death as most enemy kings in the story are depicted as being and their demise; ئيوي 'stay'. Cp: 'eiwee, eiwee. (Num.31)

Rekem; reqem; رَقَم 'pissed' 'spilled like piss' 'tattoed(with dots patterns)' 'spotted/dotted' 'marked'; رَكَم 'piled on top of each other'; رَجَم 'thrown away' (as unwanted litter) 'buried under stones'. Cp: reqem, rekem, regem. (Num.31)

Zur; ṣûr; زُر 'tighten' 'false oath'. Cp: zur. (Num.31)

Hur; ḥûr; as before, to be driven away by verbal cruelty and also physical violence. (Num.31)

Reba; reb̲a'; رَبَع 'galloped away/fled in terror'. Cp: reba'. (Num.31)

Jazer; As before, means slaughter, green pastures and grazing animals as the children of Reuben and Gad want to live there as they have many cattle and mention 'Even the country that God smote before the congregation of Israel, is a land for cattle, and thy servants have cattle'—it was important to the authors to make the land named for the slaughter of people. (Num.32:1-4)

Also, **Reuben** and **Gad** 'see/saw-between' and 'sat/relaxed' have been chosen as they saw land they liked and want to stay there and not journey on. The son's names also denote the narration of the story: (Num.32)

Ataroth; 'ăṭārôṯ; عَطآرُت ، عيطآرُت 'curled/twirled around'. As they are becoming fond of the land of Jazer; نَطآرُف ، نيطآرُف 'sides/ends/edges of' 'keep at hand/make ready/prepare' as in getting something to be easily picked up. Cp: 'aṭaarot, 'aiṭaarot, a-ṭaaruph, aiṭaaruph. (Num.32:3)

Nimrah; nimrâ; نِمره 'speak with hostility' 'bully' 'nag him/nag'. As they are reminded of predecessors actions whose hostile speech made the people fear entering the land. Cp: nimrah. (Num.32:3)

Elealeh; 'el 'ālēh; ئَل/ئِل عآليه 'what is on him' and means what is his responsibility/accountability, 'the/is/ what is-above him/above' 'what is about him/over or about him/it'. As Moses is saying words to the effect 'are you not going perform your responsibility' (helping the others cross over to the other side) and they respond they will carry out this responsibility. **Heshbon** is mentioned 'to carry on waist/hip' (like carrying child on waist or hip) because one of the reasons they want to stay is because they have little children who need safety so they do not have to carry their children over to the other side of Jordan. Cp: el- 'aaleyh. (Num.32:3)

Shebam; śĕb̄ām; شَبآم ، شيبآم 'I will ask with what/what for/why'; شَذآم ، شيذآم 'I will guilt/ostracise'; صَبآم ، صيبآم 'pour into/onto-the' 'afflict/strike/injure-the'. A reminder they will be punished if they disobey just like their predecessors were harmed for disobeying God. Cp: shebaam, sheibaam, shevaam, sheivaam, ssebaam, sseibaam. (Num.32:3)

Nebo; nĕb̲ô; نيبُ 'prophesied/predicted news or event' 'news/told' 'canine tooth'; نيذُ 'we will harm/ ostracise'. They are reminded of punishment. Cp: neibo, neivu. (Num.32:3)

Beon; bĕ'ôn; بيعُن 'they/I will help/support' 'they/I will sell'. Moses is asking for their help and they are explaining they will support the others. Cp: bei'on. (Num.32:3)

Most of the word-names given to the cities are the same as the character names—some with slight variations, so they can still imply the narrative.

Atroth; 'aṭrôṯ, 'aṭrōṯ; عَطرُت ، عَطروت 'curled/twirled around'. Cp: 'aṭrot, 'aṭroot. (Num.32:34)

Aroer; 'ărô'ēr; عيرُعير 'rabbits' 'disgrace/shame-gloated/were shamed' 'wilderness-shame' 'are a disgrace-were shamed'. It is a doubling of the same word to emphasise the disgrace that was felt and also the story allows that it was wilderness and they built it into cities. Cp: 'airo'eyr. (Num.32:34)

Shophan; šôpān; شُفَان 'they see/saw' 'they healed/were healed' and is in the form of two people or more doing the action or two of the same action. Cp: shophaan. (Num.32:35)

Jogbehah; yogbĕhâ; يوجبيها ، يوجبيهه ، يوجَبَها ، يوجبَهه 'fetches her/he fetches her' 'fetches many' 'brings gang/he brings gang' 'gathers people around/gangs around'. Cp: yogbehah, yogbeha, yogbeihah, yogbei-ha. (Num.32:35)

Beth-nimrah; bêt nimrâ; بيتنِمره/ا 'he will be bullied/spoken to hostilely' 'he will bully/speak with hostility' 'he will nag him' (Beth/bêt does not mean 'house' here, but 'you/it will' when used as suffix to a verb meaning something could happen, or is'). Cp: beytnimrah, beytnimra. (Num.32:36)

Beth-haran; bêt hārām; بيتحارآن 'they will plough' as in plough the land and the word is in the form of double, 'they will build a fire'; بيتحارام 'he/they will be prohibited/forbidden' 'he/they will become sacred' 'he/they will accompany women' 'he/they will rot and stink'. Cp: beythaaraan, beythaaraam. (Num.32:36)

Kirjathaim; qiryātayim; قِرياتَي ام 'village of/villages of-the'; قِرياتَ يم 'village of river/water/sea' 'village of floated/rivered'; خِرجاتي ام 'coming out of/took out of-the' 'took out-the'; خِرجاتَ يم 'came out of/took out of-water/river/sea'. Cp: qiryaatay-im, qiryaata-yim, khirgaatay-im, khirgaata-yim. (Num.32:37)

Baal-meon; ba'al mĕ'ôn; بَعَل ميعُن 'high/above-assisted/he should help' 'high/above-assistance/water of help' 'high/above-floppy/cowardly/immoral'. Cp: ba'al mei'on. (Num.32:38)

Shibmah; śibmâ; شِبما ، شِبمه 'will ask why/what for' 'what with'; شِذما ، شِذمه 'I will guilt/ostracise' 'I will harm-what with/why'; صِبما ، صِبمه 'pour onto/into' 'injured/struck/afflicted'. Cp: shibmah, shibma, shivmah, shivma, ssibmah, ssibma. (Num.32:38)

Jair; jā'îr, jā'îr; جائير 'ruthless' 'intolerable sufferance' 'tyrant'; يائير 'you penis' 'he penises' (as in penetrates with penis or uses word to insult); جاعير 'came-shame/disgrace' 'shouting loud' 'came-gloated' 'goat/sheep dung'; ياعير 'you-disgrace' 'he shames/gloats over' 'he lends'. Cp: gaa-eer, yaa-eer, gaa-'eer, yaa-'eer. (Num.32:41)

Havoth-jair; ḥawwōt jā'îr; حَوّوت جائير / يائير / جاعير / ياعير 'stayed/(OR) for nothing-intolerable sufferance/you penis/he penises/came-shame/shouting loud/came-gloated/you-disgrace/he shames/gloats over/he lends' or 'just enough (followed by all the meanings of 'jair'). حَوّوط 'surrounded' followed by the meanings of 'Jair'. Cp: ḥawwoot gaa-eer/gaa-'eer/yaa-'eer; ḥawwooṭ gaa-eer/yaa-eer/gaa-'eer/yaa-'eer. (Num.32:41)

Nobah; nōbah; نوبَح 'barked'; نوبَه 'a bee' 'we keep aware/notice'; نوذه 'harmed'. Cp: noobaḥ, noobah, noovah. (Num.32:42)

Kenath; qĕnāt; قَنات ، قينات 'perky posture' 'gives up'; قَناط ، قيناط 'wins others stone/tokens' (in game); كِناث ، كيناث 'like females'; كِناف ، كيناف 'a fold' (a specific sewed fold which makes clothes shorter); كِعناث 'folded over' (folded over and over); كِعناد 'for spitefulness/provocation'. Cp: qenaat, qeinaat, qenaaṭ, qeinaaṭ, kenaaf, keinaaf, kenaaph, keinaaph, k'naaf, k'naad. (Num.32:42)

Dophkah; dopqâ; توفقه ، توفقا 'understands' 'makes understands' 'parts (as in hair parting)'. توفكه ، توفكا 'is lovely/perfect'. Cp: toophqah, toophqa, toophkah, toophka. (Num.33.12)

Alush; 'ālûš; نألُز 'I squeeze against'; نألص 'I set alight' 'I have burning sensation'. Cp: aaluz, aaluss. (Num.33:13)

Rithmah; ritmâ; رِضمه/ا 'pile of stones/rocks'; رِدمه/ا 'packed with rocks'. Cp: ridhmah(ma), ridmah(ma). (Num.33:18)

Rimmon-parez; rimmōn pereṣ; رِمّون بَرَز/فَرَص 'threw-pressed/came forward/pushed out'; 'threw-split open/push out/emerge by pushing up or out/ divide by breaking or splitting'. Cp: rimmoon- barez, rimmoon-pharess. (Num.33:19)

Libnah; libnâ; لِبنه ، لبنا 'for his son' 'answered/assisted him' 'for building'; لِفنه ، لفنا 'wrapped him/it up' 'picked/gathered him/it'. Cp: libnah, libna, liphnah, liphna. (Num.33:20)

Rissah; rissâ; رِصّه ، رِصّا 'a stack' 'stacked it'. Cp: rissah, rissa. (Num.33:21)

Kehelatha; qĕhēlātâ; قَحيلاّثه/ا ، قيحيلاّثه/ا 'he has already sworn' (by God); قَهيلاّفه/ا ، قيهيلاّفه/ا 'he has already gathered up' قَحيلاّته/ا ، قيحيلاّته/ا 'has darkened' (such as the sky or a facial expression), 'has taken off/undressed' 'has declared permissible/purified' 'has purified/cleansed it/him' 'has circumcised him' 'has taken his/its place' 'has severely beaten/beaten until skin peeled off'; قَهيلآته/ا ، قيهيلآته/ا 'has already shed' (such as leaves, skin, hair), 'is already its time' 'it (he/she) has come/here'; كَحيلآته/ا ، كيحيلآته/ا 'darkened(face/sky/sun/etc.)' 'eyelined him with kohl'; كَهيلآته/ا ، كيهيلآته/ا 'darkened(face/sky/sun/etc.)'. Cp: qeḥeylaafah(fa), qeiḥeylaafah(fa), qeheylaap͟hah(fa), qeiheylaap͟hah(p͟ha), qeḥeylaatah(ta), qeiḥeylaatah(ta), qeheylaatah(ta), qeiheylaatah(ta), keḥeylaatah(ta), keiḥeylaatah(ta), keheylaatah(ta), keiheylaatah(ta). (Num.33:22)

Shapher; šap̱er; شَفَر 'vaginal flaps/labia minor'; سَفَر 'travel(ed)/journey(ed)' 'immorality' 'doing sins/immoral acts in public'; صَفَر 'whistled' 'yellow/became yellow' 'bile' 'yellow disease (such as malaria or similar). Cp: s͟hapher, sap͟her, ss͟ap͟her. (Num.33:23)

Haradah; ḥărāḏâ; حَرآده/ا ، حيرآده/ا 'with bent necks' 'stubbornness/stubborn people' 'went to one side (while moving)' 'became stubborn' 'incited/incited against' 'focused on with malicious intent'; حَرآضه/ا ، حيرآضه/ا 'incited/incited against' 'gets worked up/works up' 'folds/coils into itself ready to strike' such as a snake when preparing to defend itself or bite and figuratively used as person getting worked up. Cp: haraadah(da), hairaadah(da), haraad͟hah(d͟ha), hairaad͟hah(d͟ha). (Num.33:24)

Makheloth; maqhēlōṯ; مَقحيلوث 'well, he's already sworn' 'what has he sworn about?'; مَقحيلوت 'it/she's already darkened' 'well, she/it has already taken off/undressed/shed' 'what has she already taken off/undressed/shed?' 'well, she has already circumcised/purified/cleansed' 'well, she has already beaten until skin peeled off' 'well, she has already declared purified/permissible' 'well, she has already replaced'; مَقهيلوت 'well, she/it has already shed' 'what has she/it already shed?' 'well, what is there already?'; مَكحيلوت 'kohl pot of'. Cp: maqḥeyloof, maqḥeyloot, maqheyloot, makḥeyloot. (Num.33:25)

Tahath; taḥaṯ; تَحَت 'under/below' 'creating a border' (a decorative border such as with mud for lower wall (separates white wall from brown band all around bottom, or on hand and feet with henna); تَحَط 'is landing load/placing' 'is leaving behind'; تَحَث 'fringe' 'pushing/sweeping something upwards'. Cp: taḥat, taḥaṭ; taḥaf.

Tarah; tāraḥ; طآرَح 'set/placed down' or 'laid down/collapsed from tiredness/illness' 'sheets/bed linen' 'laid up in bed' and the word is in multiple actions, it is also the verb of feeding fodder to cattle in their stables; تآرَه 'she sees him/it' 'has dreams'. Cp: ṭaaraḥ, taarah. (Num.33:27)

Mithcah; miṯqâ; مِثقح 'a hatching/hatched', a tool used to pollinate or separate folds. Cp: mifqaḥ. (Num.33:28)

Hashmona; ḥašmōnâ; هَشمونه/ا 'belittled us'; هَزمونه/ا 'defeated us'; حَسمونه/ا 'our pity/of pity'; حَزمونه/ا 'bind it (into bundle)' 'our bundles' (as in large bundle of wood); خَشمونه/ا 'bit/tattered-us'. Cp: has͟hmoonah(na), hazmoonah(na), ḥasmoonah(na), ḥazmoonah(na), k͟has͟hmoonah(na). (Num.33:29)

Moseroth; mōsērôṯ; موزيرُط 'makes lots of swallowing sounds/swallows a lot' 'has been swallowed'; موشيرُط 'been torn/split'; موصيرُت 'wearing scarf' 'insisted/insisting on' 'knotted' 'the fate of'. Cp: moozeyroṭ, moos͟heyroṭ, mooss͟eyroṭ. (Num.33:30)

Bene-jaakan; bĕnê ya'ăqān; بني/بيني يَعَقآن/يَعيقآن 'children of disobedience' 'children of hardened hearts' 'children of too salty' 'children of braying(like donkeys)' children of delaying' 'inside/inside me-disobedience/hardened hearts/too salty/braying/delaying' 'became apparent-disobedience/hardened hearts/too salty/braying/delaying'. Cp: beney/beiney-ya'aqaan, beney/beiney-ya'aiqaan. (Num.33.31)

Hor-hagidgad; ḥōr-haggidgāḏ; هور هَجِّدجآد 'drive away-pounding' 'drive away-ants' (gdgd is a large type of ant which comes where there is spilt sugar, sweet or sticky substances); هور هَغِدغآد 'drive away-will inflame your glands(means will frustrate severely)' a simile as when a person gets so upset their glands swell just like from illness; هور هَقِطقآط 'drive away-pecking or pounding with fast, light, sharp movements/ (OR) snipping off'. (hor) can also be حور 'plough/perplex/look into' followed by same meanings of hagidgad above; (hor) can also be خور 'drive away/collapse' followed by all meanings of hagidgad above. Cp: hoor/ḥoor/k͟hoor-haggidgaad, hoor/ḥoor/khoor-hag͟hidg͟haad, hoor/ḥoor/k͟hoor-haqqiṭqaaṭ. (Num.33:32)

Jotbatha; yōṭḇāṯâ; يوطبآذه/ا 'not disgusted by this' 'can eat/palate/touch this' (implies something disgusting or distaste for subject); عوطبآذه/ا 'this is cotton' (as in plant or its fruit). Cp: yooṭbaavah(va), 'ootbaavah(va). (Num.33:33)

Ebronah; 'aḇrōnâ; عَذرونه/ا 'shadowed over us/our shadows' 'excused us/our excuse(s)'; غَبرونه/ا 'covered us with dust/cleaning away dust(by beating at object with stick, cloth or hand)'. Cp: avroonah(na), gha-broonah(na). (Num.33:34)

Ezion-gaber; 'eṣyôn geḇer; نَصيُن غَبَر 'sweep dust' as in sweep/brush dust away using a brush called 'mṣwanâ مصونا. Cp: assyon-gheber. (Num.33:35)

Zalmonah; ṣalmōnâ; ظَلمونه/ا 'caused us injustice' 'our injustice' the latter meaning they could have been caused injustice or they caused the injustice to others. Note that when they want to explain explicitly what is meant by the name, they give it an explanation (such as verses 37-38 where Hor and Aaron are linked) whereas other names are just listed. In this instance it is reminding of King Arad who would not allow them to use his highway which is followed by the Moses' people slaughtering many cities. Cp: dhal-moonah(na). (Num.33:41)

Punon; pûnōn; بُنون 'children' 'very young' 'fingers'. Cp: bunoon. (Num.33:42)

Iim; 'îyîm; عيي هم/ام 'will-he-them/the' 'he will-them/the' 'will he-them/the?' 'warn/beware of-them/the' 'teach-them/the' 'learn and remember-them/the'. Cp: 'eey-hum/um. (Num.33:45)

Almon-diblathaim; 'almōn diḇlāṯayim; عَلمون طِبلاَتَيهم/ام 'they knew/marked-their/the drumming(place)': a (miṭbaala/مِطبالا) is a high place where drums are beat, it was used as a lookout to spot danger approaching far-off, and warn the people; عَلمون ذِبلاَتَيهم/ام 'they knew/marked-their/the withering' 'they knew/marked-their wicks': (vbl/vibla(h)/ذبل/ذِبلا/ذِبله) means 'wither/withered' and also a 'wick' of a lamp/torch because it is withered and dries up and runs out through use. Cp: 'almoon ṭiblaatay-hum/um, 'almoon viblaatay-hum/um. (Num.33:46)

Beth-jesimoth; bêṯ hayĕšîmôṯ; بيت هَعَزيمُت/هَعيزيمُت 'girl/daughter-here/look/see invited'; بيت هَجَزيمُت/جيزيمُت 'girl/daughter-here/look/see dared'. (Beth/bêṯ/بيت) 'girl/daughter'; (ha/هـ) 'look/here/see/yes/here I am/will(be)'; (jesimoth/yĕšîmôṯ/عَزيمُت / جَزيمُت) 'invited/dared'. Cp: beyt-ha'ezeemot, beyt-ha'eizeemot, beyt-hagezeemot, beytt-hageizeemot. (Num.33:49) Note: this is a reminder or precursor to the Rahab story in Jericho which comes later in the Bible, even the mention of camping 'in the plains of Moab by Jordan *near* Jericho. And they pitched by Jordan, from Beth-jesimoth…' 'girl here invited' 'girl here dared' as Rahab both invites into her home two spies sent by Joshua and dares to help them by hiding them in her house and sending away the people who come searching for them.

Abel-shittim; 'āḇēl haššiṭṭîm; عآبيل هَشِطّهم/ام 'shaking fat-here/look-their/the coast' meaning it looks like good land/plenteous fortune likening it to the shaking fat of sheep; could also mean 'shaking sheep fat-will tear apart/split-them/the'. Cp: 'aabeyl hashiṭṭ-hum/um. (Num.33:49)

Akrabbim; 'aqrabbîm; نَغرَبّ هم/ام 'made them/the go over' 'ascent-them/the' from the word (mghrbba/مغربه/ا) which means a topographical area where there is a rise/swell which eventually goes down and once people pass over it they dip out of sight, the word itself from word (ghrb/غرب) 'go over/flow or boil over/set(like the sun)/west'. This is another example where Biblical experts use what they believe is the meaning of the word based on its modern Arabic meaning when they explain it as 'Scorpion pass' because the modern Arab word for scorpion is ('aqrab عقرب) but in the Arabic of the Bible 'scorpion' would be ('arqab/'rqb/عرقب)—the word itself (Akrabbim; 'aqrabbîm) is not related in any way to 'scorpion' in spelling, pronunciation or meaning as well as its true meaning ('ascent/goes over') is anchored by the context and text of the narration in the Biblical story and its literal description and name for an ascent in the mount which eventually takes people who go that route out of sight. Cp: aghrabb-hum/um. (Num.34:4)

Kadesh-barnea; qāḏēš barnēa'; كَآديش بَرنيَ 'falls like a heap-good/pious intention' 'falls/is thrown to the ground with a loud sound-good/pious intention' 'pile/piles(things on the ground)-good/pious intention' 'falls like a heap-passed by me/got ahead of me-is' 'falls/is thrown to the ground with a loud sound-passed by me/got ahead of me-is' 'pile/piles(things on the ground)-passed by me/got ahead of me-is'; 'kadesh' can also be قاديش 'led/led you' followed by all the possible meanings of 'barnea' above. Cp: kaadeysh bar-ney-a, qaadeysh bar-ney-a. (Num.34:4)

Hazar-addar; ḥăṣar-'addār; حَذَر/حيذَر نَدّآر 'warned-the potter/spinner'; حَذَر/حيذَر نَضّآر 'warned-the harmed/harmer'; حَصَر/حيصَر نَضّآر 'surrounded/blocked-the harmed/harmer/the vicious' 'great sorrow/despair/regret-the harmed/harmer/the vicious'; حَسَر/حيسَر نَضّآر 'became thinner-the harmed/harmer/the vicious'. Cp: ḥavar/ḥaivar addaar, ḥavar/ḥaivar adhaar, ḥassar/ḥaissar adhaar, ḥasar/ḥaisar adhaar. (Num.34:4)

Azmon; ʿaṣmôn; نَزمُن 'long ago/ancient times' 'timing/time/timed'; نَسمُن 'clarified butter/make clarified butter'; عَزمُن 'invitation'. Cp: azmon, asmon, 'azmon. (Num.34:4)

Zedad; ṣēḏāḏâ; صِدآده/ا ، صيدآده/ا 'blocked/they are blocking/preventing' 'fishing'; سِدآده/ا ، سيدآده/ا 'they have resolved their issues/made peace' 'dams/their dams/underground water cisterns'; زِدآده/ا ، زيدآده/ا 'deceived/deceit/deceivers' 'extra/they give extra'. Cp: sseddaadah(da), sseidaadah(da), seddaadah(da), seiddaadah(da), zeddaadah(da), zeiddaadah(da). (Num.34:8)

Ziphron; ziprôn; زِفرُن 'escorted away/led away in entourage'; سِفرُن 'travel' 'openly immoral/sinful'; صِفرُن 'whistling' 'yellowed' 'bile' 'disease like malaria'. Cp: ziphron, siphron, ssiphron. (Num.34:9)

Hazar-enan; ḥăṣar ʿênān; حَذَر/حيذَر عينآن 'warned-'; حَصَر/حيصَر عينآن 'surrounded/blocked-' 'great sorrow/despair/regret-'; حَسَر/حيسَر عينآن 'became thinner-' followed by meaning of 'Enan': 'two eyes' 'clouds' 'became cloudy' 'means/hinting' 'suffered'; حَذَر/حيذَر ئينآن 'warned-'; حَصَر/حيصَر ئينآن 'surrounded/blocked-'; حَسَر/حيسَر ئينآن 'became thinner-' followed by meanings of 'Enan': 'ouch!/ow!' 'moaning in pain' 'where/where to'. Cp: havar/haivar-'eynaan/eynaan, hassar/haissar-'eynaan/eynaan, hasar/haisar-'eynaan/eynaan. (Num.34:9)

Shepham; šĕpām; شِف/شيف آم 'cured-the' 'saw-the' this is supported with 'And ye shall point out your east border from Hazar-enan to Shepham'; 'cured the' 'gloated over misfortune-the'; سِف/سيف آم 'sip/sipped-the' 'poured gently/pouring gentle spurts of water-the' 'went numb-the' 'carried gently-the'; صِف/صيف آم 'stacked stones/column of stones-the' 'they stacked in column-the' 'column/rows-the' 'describe/insult-the'; صِب/صيب آم 'pour onto/into-the' 'eggs of the' 'strike/struck/hit target-the' 'afflict-the'. Cp: sheph-aam, sheiph-aam, seph-aam, seiph-aam, sseph-aam, sseiph-aam, sseb-aam, sseib-aam. (Num.34:10)

Riblah; riḇlâ; رِبله/ا 'god/parent/teacher/master-for him' 'raise/discipline/bring up-for him' 'mix and dilute with water for him/it'; رِدله/ا 'respond to him' 'return to it/him' and can have a negative meaning as in a bad a person has done will be returned on him by someone else (the same as 'comeuppance') 'come home to it/him'. Cp: riblah, ridlah. (Num.34:11)

Ain; ʿayin; عَيِن 'look at/inspect/look here' 'became cloudy'. Cp: 'ayin. (Num.34:11)

Chinnereth; kinnereṯ; كِنَّرِث 'as if we inherit' 'we try and inherit/we might inherit'. Cp: kinneref. (Num.34:11)

Elidad; 'ĕlîḏāḏ; ئِلي/ئيلي دآد 'he who/the one who-reached out/helped walk by holding hand(s)'; ئِلي/ئيلي ذآد 'he who/the one who-returns/recoils/repeats'. All the names of the men picked out to divide the land between the people have names that are involved in taking, dividing, spreading (all related to the same actions of dividing the land'. Cp: illee/eilee-daad, illee/eilee-vaad. (Num.34:21)

Chislon; kislộn; غِسلُن 'washed' 'ghsl tree/ghsl powder/leaves' (from ghsl tree, used to make natural shampoo/soap); كِسلُن 'new clothes/fabric for them' 'dressed with new fabric/clothes' 'wrapped in fabric for them'; حِصلُن 'they get/got' 'they find/found'. Cp: ghislon, kislon, ḥisslon. (Num.34:21)

Bukki; buqqî; بوقّي 'leave some' 'tear open/burst open' 'make a gash in it'; بوكّي 'was made to cry' 'cried' 'go/go there/leave'. Cp: buqqee, bukkee. (Num.34:22)

Jogli; yoglî; يوجلي 'he clears/purifies' 'he makes clear'; حوجلي 'my lines/borders (usually on clothes)' 'my argument/point'. Cp: yooglee, ḥooglee. (Num.34:22)

Hanniel; ḥannîʾēl; هَنّي ئِل 'satisfy-the' 'give a lot to-the' and is usually said concerning food or other forms of satisfaction and gratification. It is by giving a lot, or a fair portion, or the best of something to create this satisfaction meant by the word 'hanni'. Cp: hannee-ill. (Num.34:23)

Ephod; 'ēpōḏ; ايفوط ، ئيفوط 'wrap-around skirt' (similar to kilt, but longer) 'place skirt around/dress with skirt' 'put on a skirt' and it is a male garment. What can be seen from the name 'Hanniel son of Ephod' is the original idea of a story before it was developed later into Hannah and Samuel which the story keeps pointing out the latter was dressed in an 'ephod'. Cp: eyphooṭ, e-yphooṭ. (Num.34:23)

Shiphtan; šipṭān; شِفتآن 'saw them/of seeing' 'cured' 'gloated'; سِفتآن 'carried gently' 'they poured gently/poured gentle spurts of water' 'sips/sipping/two sips' 'numb' 'both went numb/stiff'; صِفطآن 'joking/teasing' 'got used to' 'cleaned'. Cp: shiphtaan, siphtaan, ssiphṭaan. (Num.34:24)

Parnach; parnāḵ; بَرنآق 'good/pious-picked/chose/picked through/made pure' 'went beyond/passed-picked/chose/picked through/made pure'. Cp: barnaaq. (Num.34:25)

Paltiel; palṭî'ēl; فَلتي يَل 'falls/fallen-the' (both physically to fall or figuratively as become immoral especially sexually); بَلطي يَل 'sticks to/stick to-the'. Cp: phaltee-ill, balṭee-ill. (Num.34:26)

Azzan; 'azzān; عَذّآن 'said a protection'; نَذّآن 'announced' 'gave permission' 'called to assemble' 'gave ear/ created handles for'; غَشّآن 'deceived' 'covering/mucous membrane or layer'; عَصّآن 'disobeyed' 'sticks'. All meanings are in the form referring to double actioners or two of the same action. Cp: 'avvaan, a-vvaan, ghashaan, 'assaan. (Num.34:26)

Ahihud; 'ăḥîhûḏ, 'ăḥîhuḏ; نَخي/نَيخي هُد 'brother- demolish/demolished' 'brother-guidance/was guided' 'brother-given gifts'; نَهي/نَيهي هُد 'her/she is/here she is-demolish/demolished' 'her/she is/here she is-guidance/was guided' 'her/she is/here she is-given gifts'; نَخي/نَهي حُد could be 'my brother/she is/here she is' followed by meaning of (ḥud) 'sharpen(ed)' 'made border' 'made line'. نَخي/نَهي meanings remain the same but the spelling of the last half of 'ăḥîhuḏ; هود is the meaning of the word 'Jew' which will be explained later in the book where there is more Biblical evidence/text to support the meanings of the word. Cp: akhee/aikhee-hud, ahee/aihee-hud, akhee/aikhee-ḥud, ahee/aihee-ḥud, akhee/aikhee-hood, ahee/ aihee-hood. (Num.34:27)

Shelomi; šĕlômî; شيلُمي ، شَلُمي 'took/take water' 'will gather/collect'; سيلُمي ، سَلُمي 'greet' 'mild/peaceful (person)' 'deliver/receive' 'water leaked/flowed' 'asked/of asking' 'distracted/entertained/comforted' 'of intactness/whole/survived'. Cp: shelomee, sheilomee, selomee, seilomee. (Num.34:27)

Pedahel; pĕḏah'ēl; فِدَه/فَدَه/فيدَه يَل 'his sacrifice-the' 'sacrificed for-the'; بِدَه/بَدَه/بيدَه يَل 'took it out/came out/showed-the'. Cp: phedah-ill, pheidah-ill, bedah-ill, beidah-ill. (Num.34:28)

Deuteronomy

Tophel; tōp̱el; طوف ال 'circulate around-the' 'wander around-the'; توفَل 'spat/spit(saliva)'; توف ال 'complete/repay-the' 'jumped-the'. Cp: ṭooph-el, toophel, tooph-el. (Deut.1:1)

Dizahab; dîzāhāḇ; تيذآهاب 'wastes' (such as water or other resources), 'purchased gold jewellery(for wedding)' 'was gifted gold jewellery(part of dowry given to female fiancé)'. Cp: teevaahaab. (Deut.1:1)

Elath; 'êlaṯ; نيلَط 'will get stuck together' 'will be squeezed against'; نيلَف 'will get used to it/habit' 'will gather'; عيلَت 'got above'; غيلَط 'deceived/shortchanged/conned/lied' 'made mistake/did wrong'; عيلَف 'leafy/ate leaves/gathered leaves/fodder'. Cp: eylaṭ, g͟heylaṭ eylap͟h, 'eylat, 'eylap͟h. (Deut.2:8)

Zamzummims; zamzummîm; زَمزومّ هم/ام 'grumble-the' 'drive away-the'; ذَمذومّ هم/ام 'guilt/ostracise-them/the'. Cp: zamzoomm-hum/um, vamvoom-hum/um. (Deut.2:20)

Avim; 'awwîm; عَوّيم 'float' 'teach/learn and remember/warn/be wary of-river/sea'; عَوّ هم/ام 'will-they-them/the' 'they will-them/the' 'will they-them/the?' 'howled/made howl-them/the' 'teach/learn and remember/warned-them/the'; عَبّ هم/ام 'float-them/the' 'rushing water-them/the' 'packed/filled-them/the' 'rotted and stank-them/the'. Cp: 'awweem, 'aww-hum/um, 'abb-hum/um. (Deut.2:23)

Hazerim; ḥăṣērîm; حَذير/حيذير هم/ام 'warn-them/the' 'beware of-them/the'; حَصير/حيصير هم/ام 'surround-them/the' 'great sorrow/despair-them/the'; حَضير/حيضير هم/ام 'prepare-them/the' 'ripen/ripened-them/the'. Cp: ḥaveyr-hum/um, ḥaiveyr-hum/um, ḥas͟seyr-hum/um, ḥais͟seyr-hum/um, ḥad͟heyr-hum/um, ḥaid͟heyr-hum/um. (Deut.2:23)

Kedemoth; qĕḏēmôṯ; قَضيمُت ، قيضيمُت 'bit tip off' 'pretended to bite by closing teeth on without biting'; كَضيمُت ، كيضيمُت 'caused to suffocate/suffocated'; جَذيمُت ، جيذيمُت 'caught/caused leprosy' 'made tips fall off' 'gecko of'; جَديمُت ، جيديمُت 'bit' 'bit all over with light bites' 'took small or light bites'; قَديمُت ، قيديمُت 'came forward/got ahead/presented'. Cp: qed͟heymot, qeid͟heymot, ked͟heymot, keid͟heymot, geveymot, geiveymot, gedeymot, geideymot, qedeymot, qeideymot. (Deut.2:26)

Argob; 'argōḇ; تَرقوب 'observe/keep eye on' 'pour water from one vessel to another' 'flow stream of liquid' and has a very specific meaning used when pouring water from one vessel to another as it means keeping eye on the stream of water leaving the vessel being poured from and on the mouth of receiving vessel so that not one drop is spilt. Cp: arqoob. (Deut.3:4)

Hermon; ḥermôn; حَرمُن 'deprived(of)' 'forbidden' 'a group of women' 'sacred' 'rotten/stinking'; هَرمُن 'will throw/kill' 'drove/chased away from'; خَرمُن 'fled/chased away from' 'collapsed from' 'pierced'. Cp: ḥermon, hermon, k͟hermon. (Deut.3:9)

Sirion; śiryōn; صِريون 'knotted/make knots' 'insistent/wayward' 'aching/throbbing pain' 'loud whistling/tinnitus noise'; سِريون 'left pre-dawn' 'walking' 'they will see/dream' 'they will water'; شِريون 'I will show/see them' ('show' as in let them see or as a threat) 'I will dream' 'I will water' 'buyers/bought' 'they are evil'. Cp: s͟siryoon, siryoon, s͟hiryoon. (Deut.3:9)

Shenir; śĕnîr; صَنير ، صينير 'stakes/dowels'; سَنير ، سينير 'we will light' (as in brighten) 'he will light' 'we will make fire' 'he will make fire'; شَنير ، شينير 'I will make fire' 'he will make fire' 'I will light' 'he will light' 'I will/he will change direction/go to one side (on journey)'. Cp: s͟seneer, s͟seineer, seneer, seineer, s͟heneer, s͟heineer. (Deut.3:9)

Salchah; salkâ; سَلكَه ، سلكا 'asked you' 'made fine(in texture)' 'went down that way(as in habit/behaviour)' 'made use of/made-do with' 'flowed/leaked-you/to you' 'entertained/comforted/distracted-you'; سَلحَه ، سلحا 'diarrhoea/faeces' 'scared the shit out of him'; سَلقَه/ا 'boiled/burned clean' used to say 'stomach has been 'salchah'' as in severe diarrhoea and pain from it; سَلخَه/ا 'torn from/torn' (such as a stem from a tree e.g.) 'he tore it/stripped it'; شَلقَه/ا 'I will find it/him' 'I will throw it/him down'; صَلحَه/ا 'made/fixed' 'reconciled/made peace'; صَلكَه/ا 'he reached/arrived you' literally as in arrived or reached, but also means to arrive with apology and show of respect. Cp: salkah(ka), salḥah(ḥa), salqah(qa), salk͟hah(k͟ha), s͟halqah(qa), s͟salḥah(ḥa), s͟salkah(ka). (Deut.3:10)

Rabbath; rabbîṯ; رَبّيت 'brought up/brought up properly' 'grew' 'disciplined' 'mixed and diluted with water'; رَبّيط 'tied' 'tyings' 'ropes' and this is what the authors intended by creating this name. The creators of these stories do not give the names for no reason at all, but for the specific purpose of making it entertaining and they (and later editors) make a point of pointing out exactly what they meant by the word-name.

In this instance, they are focusing on the size of the people and even their beds '…the remnant of giants; behold his bedstead was a bedstead of iron; is it not in Rabbath of the children of Ammon?' and goes on to describe the size of the bed. An important part of the beds is the latticing of the beds with rope which keeps the bed taut to hold up the bedding and people sitting/lying on it. Cp: rabbeet, rabbeeṭ. (Deut.3:11)

Geshuri; gĕšûr; جَشِر ، جيشِر 'bares his teeh/bore his teeth' 'takes/takes a lot/takes everything' and is in the form of a characteristic. حَشُر ، حيشُر 'greedy' 'made hungry/greedy'. Cp: geshur, geishur, ḥeshur, ḥeishur. (Deut.3:14)

Maachathi; ma'ăkâ; مَعَكه/ا ، مَعيكه/ا 'with you' 'with me-like' 'I have one like'; مَعَخه/ا ، مَعيخه/ا 'with his brother' 'I have a brother/with a brother' 'with his brother/I have his brother', but it seems the difference between the KJV transliteration and the modern transliteration as Hebrew in the latter has dropped some letters/phonemes. The KJV reads: ma'ăkātî; مَعَكآ ذي ، مَعي كآذي 'with you is her/she is with you' 'I have one like her/it' and they are speaking about a female person or feminine noun/object; مَعَخآ ذي ، مَعي خآ ذي 'with her brother/with this one's brother' 'with me is her brother/with me the brother of this one'. Cp: ma'akah(ka), ma'aikah(ka), ma'akhah(ka), ma'aikhah(ka), ma'akaa-vee, ma'aikaa-vee, ma'ai-kaa-vee, ma'akhaa-vee, ma'aikhaa-vee, ma'ai-kha-vee. (Deut.3:14)

Ashdoth-pisgah; 'ašdôt happisgâ; نَشدُت هَبِّسغه ، بِسغا 'emigrate/leave/pull yourself together/brace yourself/severe-look/pay attention-tilt/move head to see better' 'she became severe-look/pay attention-tilt/move head to see better' as Moses is being told to go to war and eventually told to go and look in different directions from (Pisgah) so he is turning his head and viewing the land in different directions from far up; it also relays with Moses being told he was supposed to emigrate into these areas, and Moses is begging to be allowed to leave towards the areas (beyond Jordan/Lebanon) but is told he has been forbidden from travelling there as a severe punishment. Cp: ashdot-ha-bbisghah(gha) (Deut.3:17-27)

Bezer; beṣer; بَصَر 'unripe' 'ripened'; بَزَر 'produce a litter' of young animals or children, 'broke body' from too much work or too heavy a load. It refers to accidentally killing a person i.e. the person was killed before his time (unripe) and his body has been broken (broke body). Cp: besser, bezer. (Deut.4:43)

Ramoth; rā'môṯ, rāmōṯ, rā'mōṯ; رآءمُت 'he saw-died/I died'; رآموت 'saw death' 'threw/killed' (plural action) 'thrown/strewn over vast distance/different locations'; راء موت 'he saw death'. Implies the killing or witnessing death. Cp: raa-mot, raamoot, raa-moot. (Deut.4:43)

Golan; gôlān; جُلآن 'two sides' (e.g. my side, your side, her side when speaking about the same portion of something whether a bowl of food or area of land, path etc.), 'wandered/they wandered (both)' 'they ate from someone else's side(in dish)' 'clear(ing)/purify(ing)/they are clear/purified' 'they made clear'; غُلآن 'intense hatreds' 'despised' 'dug deep/stabbed deep' 'exploited/took advantage of' 'made more expensive' 'made up laws/rules/made up severe laws/rules' in double or plural form. Refers to the hatred/revenge that can happen when a person is killed, and also the cities (sides) the murderer can escape to for safety. Cp: golaan, gholaan. (Deut.4:43)

Sion; śî'ōn; سيئون 'bad/they are bad' 'they will supply/allow to stay' 'they will moan/groan(in pain); صيئون 'brushed/swept/they brushed/swept away'. Cp: see-oon, ssee-oon. (Deut.4:48)

Beeroth; bĕ'ērôṯ; بَئيرُث ، بيئيرُث 'he gives inheritance to' 'he/I will inherit'; بَئيرُض ، بيئيرُض 'he buries in ground/soil' 'he creates soil/does with soil' the word itself does not mean 'land' but soil and the form of the word that something is to be done involving soil and it is immediately followed by 'there Aaron died, and there he was buried…'. Cp: be-eyrof, bei-eyrof, be-eyrodh, bei-eyrodh. (Deut.10:6)

Mosera; môsērâ; مُصيره 'his fate/end of fate-his' 'his death'. The reason the name Moseroth (Num.33:30) has been changed here is the same reason why the sequence of travel has been changed: in Num.33 they go from Moseroth-Bene jaakan-Hor hagidgad-Jotbathah-Ebronah-Ezion geber-Zin/Kadesh-mount Hor and Aaron goes up mount Hor and dies there. The author of this specific story in Deuteronomy wanted to create wordplay to fit the story better, so he changes the route/travel and alters the names slightly so it can be: 'And the children of Israel took their journey from Beeroth' (so it's more fitting to mention a place and narrate Aaron is to be buried in soil) 'of the children of Jaakan to Moserah: there Aaron died, and there he was buried…' so Aaron arrives at a place called 'his fate/end of fate-his/his death' suitably named for the death of his character. Cp: mosseyrah. (Deut.10:6)

Gudgodah; gudgōdâ; جودجوده/ا 'a large ant'(single); غودغوده/ا 'a frustration to degree of illness' 'swelling of glands' (illness); قوطقوطه/ا 'a tiny piece of something' 'a pecking/repeated light pounding of something' 'a snipping off of something'. Cp: gudgoodah(da), ghudghoodah(gha), quṭqooṭah(ta). (Deut.10:7)

Jotbath; yoṭbâ; يوطبه/ا 'he touches/can palate/eats it/him' 'he can touch/eat it' implying there is something distasteful about what is being spoken about. Cp: yooṭbah(ba). (Deut.10:7)

Lebanon; lĕḇānôn; لَبآنُن ، ليبآنُن 'for children/sons' 'for building/builders' 'milk/lots of milk' and it is pure milk, not churned nor what modern Arabic now calls 'laban', but pure milk freshly milked from cows/goats. It is mentioned as one of the areas for Moses' people to inherit, immediately followed by mention of the rive Euphrates—which now shows the meaning of: Euphrátēs; يُفرآتيه 'sweetens it' from word فرت/فرات 'sweet/sweet water'. It comes in the chapter where the sweetness of water and abundance of rain which will feed cattle and people (the feeding of cattle ensures plenty of milk and other food sources for people) is emphasised (Deut.11). The mention of Lebanon followed by river Euphrates denotes 'a land that floweth with milk and honey...' '...from the wilderness and Lebanon, from the river the river Euphrates...'. To the wandering thirsty, sweet water will be especially sweet. 'tastes like honey' is an expression used by the people whose language is the Arabic of the Bible to express hunger has made something, not especially tasty, taste as sweet as honey. The authors and later editors/authors were using descriptions of land surrounding them or lands they had travelled through as well as some names of actual places and rulers to fuel their creativity while they were revising/editing the Bible. Most of what they named were fictional and did not exist nor happen, but they incorporated prominent names and places to use as word-play to give it a meaning in relation to the stories they were telling (not the actual meanings of real people and places they were borrowing e.g. Pharaoh, Syria). Cp: lebaanon, leibaanon. (Deut.11)

Gerizim; gĕrizîm; جِرز هم/ام ، جيرز هم/ام 'plenty/loads-them/the' 'shudder and skin crawl-them/the' 'gut feeling of intense fear-them/the' 'petrify-them/the', the word means the shudder or skin-crawling a person feels when he/she senses great fear, it is another word of 'petrify' that the fear is so great you cannot move or feel coldness on the inside. It is what is directly implied by 'There shall no man be able to stand before you: for the Lord your God shall lay the fear of you and the dread of you upon all the land that ye shall tread upon, as he hath said unto you'. The reason this negative word is the 'blessing' God promises them is because although it is negative, it is negative towards others and not towards Moses' people i.e. it protects them. Cp: geriz-hum/um, geirizhum/um. (Deut.11:25-29)

Ebal; 'êḇāl; as before it is: عيبآل 'fat sheep' or fat animals 'shaking fat/shaking fat of sheep' 'rolling/shaking like fat sheep'. Although 'Ebal' is a sign of good fortune it is set as the curse against Moses' people should they disobey God. So when God in the story gives them 'a land that floweth milk and honey...thou mayest gather in thy corn, and thy wine, and thine oil...grass in thy fields for thy cattle, that thou mayest eat and be full...' i.e. the fat of the land which will be good fortune to them, if once they have this good fortune they go worship other gods, the curse will be upon them '...and the curse upon mount Ebal.'. Cp: 'eybaal. (Deut.11)

Belial; beliyya'al; بَلِيَّ عَل 'an ailment/curse-on' 'an affliction/illness/suffering-on'. They are called the 'children of Belial' and are described as deceiving people to worship other gods and they are such an affliction that the whole cities' inhabitants will be slaughtered, including animals, and everything will be spoiled and burned with fire, i.e. they are an affliction upon themselves and the inhabitants of the cities they are from. Cp: beliyya-'al. (Deut.12:13-17)

Jeshurun; yĕšurûn; حَشورُن ، حيشورُن 'greedy' in the plural, from the word (maḥshur/ḥshr/حشر/محشور) 'greedy' 'greed'—someone who eats too much and is greedy; it also applies to someone who had nothing to begin with then became greedy when he/she has plenty; and people who have nothing, be it food source or money and are always greedy for what they do not have. The lines refer to Jacob, then describe his descendants (Israel) as 'Jeshurun' and links the word directly to greed, a selfishness especially towards God after he has given them plenty. 'Butter of kine, milk of sheep, with fat of lambs, and lambs of the breed of Bashan, and goats, with the fat of kidneys of wheat; and thou didst drink the pure blood of the grape. But Jeshurun did wax fat, and kicked; thou art waxen fat, thou art grown thick, thou art covered with fatness: then he forsook God which made him, and lightly esteemed the Rock of his salvation.' It reminds the audience of the Rock, directly linking it to God, but in a pagan-like manner—it reminds directly of Jacob using stones as pillows, having a bad dream while God is communicating with him, setting up an altar and naming it Bethel/'bad', reminding the audience Jacob had nothing, but God blessed him and he ended up with flocks and herds, wives—and more importantly, many children. It goes on to emphasise that God will punish them with hunger and their greed will be out of real hunger 'They shall be burnt with hunger, and devoured with burning heat'. Cp: ḥeshooron, ḥeishooron. (Deut.32:9-24)

Hoshea; hôšēa'; هُشيَع 'he became/made ugly' 'he pulled out strands of fibre from clothes/hair/tissue from skin'; هُسيَع 'he wandered aimlessly' 'he wanders around performing debauchery' 'he became debauched/he performed debauchery/promiscuity'; خُشيَع 'breaking/broke to pieces' it means pounding at something with another hard object until it splits open or breaks to pieces. Hoshea can also mean the other meanings under Oshea (see Oshea (Num.13:8,16)); and just like all the other names such as 'Eleazar' when there is killing, ugly destruction of life and brutality as punishment from God, these names are mentioned in the story to enhance its theme; in this instance it is the punishment of Israel and also upon their enemies, and it is after many verses of ugly punishment, blood spilling, terror, vengeance, arrows and swords drinking and devouring blood and flesh—that the name Hoshea is introduced. Like Reuel/Jethro/Raguel Moses' father-in-law whose name changes according to the theme needed in the story—so does Joshua go to Oshea, to Jehoshua and in this line to Hoshea which has the same meanings as Oshea, but with an extra letter (h/هـ) means (he (is/did)). Cp: hosheya', hoseya', khosheya'. (Deut.32:23-44)

Joshua

Rahab; rāḥāḇ; راَحاب 'welcomed' 'spacious' the word is in the plural and suggests intensity or welcoming more than one person; راَكاب 'mounted/rode' 'placed on top of/piled on top of' and can have literal meaning, but also figurative meaning usually used as a vulgar word for a man mounting a woman without wedlock, i.e. illicit sex and this word is also in the plural, the thing/person being mounted is by plural 'mounters/riders'. The character of the same name welcomes the two spies and makes space for them in her house and her profession is a prostitute bringing in the vulgar sexual meaning of 'mounted'. Cp: raaḥaab, raakaab. (Josh.2)

Zaretan; ṣārēṯān; ذاَرِيفاَن ، ذاَرِفاَن 'spilled over' 'flowed over/overflowed' from word (vrf/ذرف) 'overflowed/spilled over': '...(for Jordan overfloweth all his banks all the time of harvest.) That the waters which came down from above stood and rose up upon an heap very far from the city Adam, that is beside Zaretan...' the reason 'Adam' is mentioned here as a city is for one of its meanings 'to last long/keep up' to denote the standing/heaping of the water lasted for as long as the people needed to pass. Cp: vaarefaan, vaareifaan. (Josh.3:15-17)

Gilgal; gilgāl; جِلجاَل 'tossing and rolling motion' 'clear/purify', 'gilgal' means to clear a small amount of grains by making the contents in a circular tray to shift in a tossing, rolling motion, much like waves in the sea roll: it is to clear stones and flakes for preparation of a meal. Using both hands holding the tray, the grain is shaken and regularly tossed, the flakes and impurities are blown off during this motion and the stones gather at the bottom making it easier to separate them from the grain. The removal of impurities with the word which means this action is also from the word (gl/جل) 'clear/purify/make clear' (gil and gal) are the same word in different tense: (gil) جِل 'clear/purify' an order or present continuous, and (gal) جاَل 'is clear/purified' it has been cleared/purified. They are the reason why the motion to toss and roll to remove impurities from grain is 'gilgal' and why the authors used it to denote the people would be purified by circumcision, as it was deemed to be clean and pure—the way God in the story wants people to be physically. 'Make thee sharp knives and circumcise again the children of Israel...all the people that were born in the wilderness by the way as they came forth out of Egypt, them they had not circumcised...And the Lord said unto Joshua, This day have I rolled away the reproach of Egypt from off you. Wherefore the name of the place is called Gilgal unto this day.' Cp: gilgaal. (Josh.5:2-9)

Jericho (Num.22:1) as earlier means 'came-loosened' as the shouting causes the wall to loosen and collapse. 'when they make a long blast with the ram's horn, and when ye hear the sound of the trumpet, all the people shall shout with a great shout; and the wall of the city shall fall down flat...' 'and the people shouted with a great shout...that the wall fell down flat, so that the people went up into the city...and they took the city.' So they come, loosen the wall through shouting so that it collapses and enables them to enter the city to slaughter everyone. (Josh.6)

Achan; 'āḵān; عاَقاَن 'disobedient/disobedience/disobeyed' in the plural and the character of the same name has disobeyed by stealing multiple items from Jericho's spoils, but especially from that which was assigned 'to the treasury of the Lord', and the same negative meaning is transferred to all his family and possessions as they are to be punished along with him. His father's name '**Carmi**' denotes two of its meanings: 'a crumb/eating crumbs' as he has taken a 'wedge of gold', a garment and some money and also because he will 'admit', Josh says to him 'I pray thee...and make confession unto him; and tell me now what thou hast done; hide it not from me.' and Achan admits to everything. Cp: 'aaqaan. (Josh.7)

Zabdi; zaḇdî; زَبدي 'butter' 'cover with ointment' 'a small bowl' as Josh.6:19 mentions gold, silver and bowls of metals are for God's treasury, the wedge of gold was a small bowl of gold or the money was put into a bowl before being buried under his tent; زَبطي 'kicked' and can mean a literal kick, or being beaten in a fight or kicked out which also happens in the story because they have been cursed by Achan's theft; ضَبَطي 'strong' 'tighten' 'publicly discipline' and usually is used when a wife assaults or seriously offends another person and the discipline is publicly disciplining her with a few lashes to the skirt of her dress as a symbol of apology/discipline towards the offended party: in the story not only is Achan publicly executed, but his whole family; شَبطي 'lattice/lattice with rope' 'rope/twine' 'swipe/whip with switch, rope or rope-like object'; شَبَدي 'I will take out/bring out/come out' and it is what happens to the stolen goods, Achan and all his sons, daughters (even his sheep) who are are taken out of the camp and stoned and burned to death. Cp: zabdee, zabṭee, dhabṭee, shabṭee, shabdee.

Ai; ʿay; عَي 'will-he/he will' 'will he?' 'learn and remember(this)' 'be warned' 'beware' 'I dare you, go on' (meant as a warning e.g. I am warning you of punishment if you dare do this), it is also the sound shouted and repeated at goats/sheep when getting them to turn around and come back to the area they are being fed on when one goes or attempts to wander away. It is used as a country name in the story to emphasise and warn of Achan's disobedience, the characters of the story and the audience are to learn a lesson that their defeat was because they are cursed due to a theft of something which belongs to God. Cp: 'ay. (Josh.7:2-12)

Beth-aven; bêṯ 'āwen; بيتئاوَن 'they will moan/groan'; بيتئآذَن 'they will be harmed'; بيتعاوَن 'they will howl' 'they will cooperate/help'. All meanings happen in the story: the people cooperate to attack the inhabitants of Ai; Joshua's people are defeated, killed, and the story narrates their hearts are melting like water out of fear; Joshua moans to God after he rends his clothes over the defeat. Cp: beyt-aawen, beyt-aaven, beyt-'aawen. (Josh.7:2-12)

Shebarim; haššĕḇārîm; هَشّيبآر هم/ام ، هَشَّبآر هم/ام 'I will/look, here-will(make)-them/the pass/go beyond' 'I will-measure by span-them/the': (ha/هـَ) 'I will/look, here' it has other variants but this is what is meant in this instance, (she/ššĕ/شَ،شي) 'will/will make', (bar/ḇār/بار) 'pass/go beyond/beyond', (im/îm/هم،ام) 'them/the'. 'I will-measure by span-them/the': (ha/هـَ) 'I will/look, here', (shebar/ššĕḇār/شّبار،شيبار) measure by finger span, (im/îm/هم،ام) 'them/the'. To measure a person by the finger-span or by the forearm means to lay them on the ground and measure them, a figurative expression which means to beat them physically. And it is what happens in the story: the people are chased 'beyond' or 'past' 'from before the gate even unto Shebarim' and they are defeated, some killed. Cp: hashebaar-hum/um, hasheibaar-hum/um. (Josh.7:5)

Achor; ʿaḵôr; عَفّر 'ruined/spoiled' and also a bad action when done intentionally which is the reason behind giving this word as a name where not only is Achan's crime denoted, but the ugly brutality in how the story has him, all his children, animals and possessions killed by their own people. Cp: 'aqor. (Josh.7:26)

Gibeon; giḇʿôn; جب عون 'bring/fetch/gather-help'; جبئون 'fetched' 'ganged together/gathered many people to help or gang up against something': the people of Gibeon ask Joshua 'make ye a league with us' that is one form of cooperation, but the authors go further to explain the meaning of the word: when they find out they are the inhabitants of the country they had wanted to massacre, bound by the oath they allow them to live but only as slaves: 'but let them be hewers of wood and drawers of water unto all the congregation…and there shall none of you be freed from being bondmen, and hewers of wood and drawers of water…'. Cp: gib-'on, gib-on. (Josh.9)

Chephirah; kĕp̄îrâ; خيفِره/ا ، خَفيره/ا 'musty/mouldy' 'smells musty/mouldy' 'became musty/mouldy'. Named so because to convince Joshua to make league with them, they pretended to come from far away and allowed their bread to become mouldy and musty. Cp: khepheerah(ra), kheipheerah(ra). (Josh.9:3-17)

Kirjath-jearim; qiryaṯ yĕʿārîm; ييعآر هم/ام ، قِريَة/خِرجَة يَعآر هم/ام 'village/came out-lends/disgraces/gloats over-them/the' and is the name of one of the cities. The words denote the narration that they are being disgraced and being gloated over when the people and Joshua decide and tell the Gibeonites that they will forever be their slaves. Cp: qiryat-ye'aar-hum/um, qiryat-yei'aar-hum/um, khirgat-ye'aar-hum/um, khirgat- yei'aar-hum/um. (Josh.9:17-27)

Adoni zedek; 'ăḏōnî ṣeḏeq; نَضوني زَدك 'here I am/here I have done-give more' 'here I am/here I have done-deceive'; نُذوني زَدَك 'they harmed me-gave more/deceived'; (zedek/ ṣeḏeq) could also be: صَدَق 'honestly' 'pounded'; صَدَك 'blocked' 'prevented/absorbed attack'. All these meanings are in the story. Cp: adhoonee zedek, avoonee zedek, adhoonee/avoonee ssedeq, adhoonee/avoonee ssedek. (Josh.10)

Jerusalem; yĕrûšālayîm; يِرسآلي هم/ام 'they see-asked-them/the' 'they see-water flowed/leaked-them/the'; جَرُسآلي هم/ام 'came-saw-asked-them/the' 'came-saw-water flowed/leaked-them/the'; يِرُصآلي هم/ام 'they saw-joined/connected-them/the' 'they saw-reached/arrived/public apology-them/the' 'they see-their/the rocks' 'they see-rocks-them/the'; جَرُصآلي هم/ام 'came-saw-joined/connected-them/the' 'came-saw-reached/arrived/public apology-them/the' 'came-saw-their/the rocks' 'came-saw-rocks-them/the'. The king of Jerusalem sees what Joshua has done to the areas he arrives at and he also sees that Gibeon has made peace (ssalay/arrived/public apology) and joined league with Joshua so the king of Jerusalem goes to kings of other areas and asks them to unite with him to defeat Gibeon; they arrive at Gibeon. Part of the defeat of these kings is God throws down 'great stones' from heaven at the kings and their armies. Cp: yerusaalay-hum/um, gerusaalay-hum/um, yerussaalay-hum/um, gerussaalay-hum/um (Josh.10)

Hoham; hôhām; هُهام 'he is worried' all the five enemy kings are worried by Gibeon being in league with Joshua 'That they feared greatly, because Gibeon was a great city…'. Cp: hohaam. (Josh.10)

Piram; pir'ām; فِرئام 'fled-the' 'so were thrown/killed'; بِرئام 'with the thrown/killed' and all the kings flee from Joshua and are eventually killed. Cp: phiraam, biraam. (Josh.10)

Jarmuth; yarmûṯ; جَرمُت 'pulled-death' 'ran-death' the kings will be brought/led out of the cave; 'pull' has the same meaning as being led out; and as they will be hung to death. Cp: garmut. (Josh.10)

Japhia; yāp̄îa'; جافِيَى 'turned over' as they are put in humiliating positions, probably to crouch on ground or lie prone so the people could put their feet on the necks of the kings. Cp: gaaphee-a.

Lachish; lāḵîs; لآحيس 'licked(plural)'; لآحيش 'vicious/angry/strikes out (verbally/physically)'; لآخيص 'until rotted/went off'. Cp: laaḥees, laaḥeesh, laakheess. (Josh.10)

Eglon; 'eglôn; عَجلُن 'in a rush/panic' 'brash' or 'calf' (bovine); نَجلُن 'clear/clear out/purify' 'a period of time'. Cp: 'eglon, eglon. (Josh.10)

Debir; dĕḇîr; دبيير ، دَبير 'bad fated' 'evil intended'—all the kings meet a terrible ending; ضِبير ، ضيبير 'dhbr tree(s)' as the kings' corpses will be hung from five trees. Cp: debeer, deibeer, dhebeer, dheibeer. (Josh.10)

Beth-horon; bêṯ-ẖôrôn; بيت هُرُن 'they will be chased away' and it comes in the verse '…and chased them along the way that goeth up to Beth-horon…', Cp: beyt-horon. (Josh.10:10)

Azekah; 'ăzēqâ; نَزيقح ، نيزيقح 'sharp hit by a thrown stone' 'sharp hits from stones' also the way dogs send a sharp stream of urine against wall, tree, etc. '…that the Lord cast down great stones from heaven upon them unto Azekah, and they died: they were more which died from hailstones than they whom the children of Israel slew with the sword.' The way hailstones shoot down and hit against surfaces exemplifies the meaning of the word 'Azekah'; عَزيقه/ا ، عيزيقه/ا 'foxes'. Cp: azeyqaḥ, aizeyqaḥ, 'azeyqah(qa), 'aizeyqah(qa). (Josh.10:10-11)

Ajalon; 'ayyālôn; نَجّالُن 'delayed'; عَجّالُن 'hurried/rushed'. It is the first meaning 'delayed meant here as Joshua commands the sun and moon not to move i.e. delayed their setting/rising so the people could take their time killing other people. Cp: aggaalon, 'aggaalon. (Josh.10:12-13)

Jasher; yāšēr, yāšār; عاشار ، عاشير 'pregnant cow' and is the second mention of God being a pregnant cow in the Bible, the first being in Exodus 3.14 (I Am That I Am which is a wrong translation of: 'ehyeh 'ăšer 'ehyeh; نِهيَه عيشَر نِهيَه 'she is-with child/calf-she is' 'she is-pregnant-she is'). In Joshua's story, it is when the sun and moon are ordered to stand still and it is mentioned 'Is it not written in the book of Jasher?' and the following verse states it was God who came down to kill for Israel 'And there was no day like that before it or after it, that the Lord hearkened unto the voice of man: for the Lord fought for Israel.'. Cp: 'aasheyr, 'aashaar. (Josh.10:12-14)

Makkedah; maqqēḏâ; مَكّيده/ا 'covered tightly (with any kind of lid: stone, metal, cloth, etc.)' and the story narrates this exactly: while the kings are hiding in the cave Joshua orders large stones to block the mouth of the cave, and after they are humiliated and killed, they are returned to the same cave and the mouth is covered with stones again. Cp: makkeydah(da). (Josh.10:16-27)

Horam; hōrām; هورآم 'are driven away' 'spoke to angrily/cruelly' 'drive away-the' 'he threw/killed' 'is strewn over distance'; حورآم 'are forbidden' 'are rotten/are stinking rotten' 'are sacred'; خورآم 'are pierced/the pierced' '(are)pierced/burst from the bottom'. Cp: hooraam, ḥooraam, khooraam. (Josh.10:33)

Gezer; gezer; جَزَر 'green pastures' 'harvest' 'cut crops of grass' 'to slaughter or beat up people as if mowing down crops' 'graze animals/let animals graze freely' and is the city of the King that 'Joshua smote him and his people, until he had left him none remaining.'. Cp: gezer. (Josh.10:33)

Jabin; yāḇîn; يآذين 'harmed' 'will harm/will be harmed' the harm is done to or by in plural. Cp: yaaveen. and he is king of Hazor; ḥāṣôr; هاضُر 'I will harm' and is exactly what is done to the king of Hazor and everyone related to him. Cp: haadhor. (Josh.11)

Jobab; yôḇāḇ; as earlier in Genesis, here it means عُباب overflowing water, water rushing like a river, floating in water, something swollen or risen with water. The story places them beside water when they are overcome by Joshua and his men. And he is king of Madon; māḏôn; ماضُن 'are passing on/moving on'; مآذون 'are harmers/are harmed'; مادُن 'bowed/bent over' as in made to bow or bend over 'guilted/made guilty' 'handed/passed/stashed/hid/planted with no one noticing' 'performed underhanded behaviour(done secretly)' 'secreted in/planted' 'hid (something) underneath something hastily' 'put hands on something not his/theirs' 'went over/overstepped/'took liberties". They are chased away from place to place and killed in the narration and also 'Misrephoth-maim' further elaborates why the 'bowed/bent over' has been used as the word-name. Cp: maadhon, maavon, maadon. (Josh.11)

Shimron; šimrôn; شِمرُن 'sleeves/clothes pulled up/unkempt'; سِمرُن 'they stayed up'. Cp: shimron, simron. And he is king of Achshaph; 'akšāp; نَخساف 'chopped pieces' and his word-names reflect Joshua chopping up this king's horses and chariots, the author uses the theme and idea as a real person in such an action would roll up his sleeves, and the horses and chariots would end up in 'chopped pieces' as both the name of king and city reflect. Cp: akhsaaph. (Josh.11)

Dor; dôr, dō'r; دُر ، دوئر 'go/turn around(circle)' 'spin' 'search' 'make with clay/potter' and refers to the part of the story where Joshua goes around killing all the cities and its inhabitants, and takes all the land. Cp: dor, doo-ir. (Josh.11)

Merom; mērôm; مي رُم 'water-thrown/killed' 'water-fouled' 'well/won't he throw down/kill' as the story states they are by water when the first slaughter begins. Cp: mey-rom. (Josh.11)

Zidon; same as **Sidon**.

Misrephoth-maim; miśrĕpôt mayim; مِسرِفُت/مِسريفُت مي ام 'buttocks of water-the': (Misrephot/ miśrĕpôt/مسرِفُت) is 'buttocks of' from (srph/سرف) 'buttocks/bottom', (ma/may/ما/مي) is 'water', (im/im/ ام) 'the' and the compound word means that the bottom is boneless and is the equivalent of 'legs turned to jelly(from fear)'. But it is always said to young children as a joke (which adults find funny too, at the expense of a child) by confusing them by saying to them 'your buttocks are water/sarphitak maayo/may' سرفتَك مايو/مي after they have been startled or scared by something (it distracts the child from what they have been scared by because he/she has to think about how can it be water). Cp: misrephot/misreiphot may-um. (Josh.11:8)

Mizpeh; as earlier **Mizpah** in Genesis but also has meanings of مِسبَح 'body of water/pool of water' as the events between Joshua and the enemy armies takes place near or beside waters: the meanings of مِذبَح 'slaughter' مِصبَه 'pouring place/pouring' as people are slaughtered, and the theme water-related; مِصبَح 'watching with ill-intent' as God is watching and telling Joshua not to fear as they will all be killed. Cp: misbeh, mivbeh, missbeh, missbeh. (Josh.11)

Halak; ḥālāq; حاَلاَق 'to put arms around' 'surrounded/put in a circle' 'circular ring (of any material)' and it refers to Joshua leaving 'nothing undone' but going around every area to kill its inhabitants and possess it so in essence putting his arms around it/circling it. Cp: ḥaalaaq. (Josh.11:15-17)

Baal-gad; ba'al gad; بَعَل جَد 'high/above/higher-found' and reflects how Joshua took over every part of the terrain, from the lowest to the highest, from the plains to the mountain. Cp: ba'al-gad. (Josh.11:16-17)

Anab; 'ănab; عَنَد ، عينَد 'taunted/provoked' and reflects 'There was not a city that made peace with the children of Israel…For it was of the Lord to harden their hearts, that they should come against Israel in battle…'. Cp: 'anad, 'ainad. (Josh.11:19-20)

Geder; geder; جِذِر ، جَذَر 'to remove/cut/strip/harvest by shaking, pulling movement' (it causes more fruit to fall to the ground to be collected, but also leaves some fruit behind on the tree) 'to leave plant/tree(or anything) in tatters or bitten around the edges or all over (e.g. how caterpillars leave plant leaves), 'shuddered/goosepimpled'; جِدِر ، جَدَر 'they caught pox' 'they built wall(s)/walled'; غِدِر ، غَدَر 'they betrayed' 'dark' 'became dark'. Cp: gever, geder, gheder. (Josh.12:13)

Tappuah; tappûaḥ; طَبّوح 'lay on stomach' 'belly uncovered' 'splashed stomach first into water'; تَبّوح 'spread himself/relaxed over large area'; تَفّوَح 'wafted' 'smoked clothes or room with frankincense' 'ate apples'. Cp: ṭabbuaḥ, tabbuaḥ, taphuaḥ. (Josh.12:17)

Aphek; 'ăpēq; عَفيق ، عيفيق 'leaping/leapt' 'kicking and jerking' (usually how a new-born calf behaves); نَفيق ، نيفيق 'part(something)' Cp: 'apheyq, 'aipheyq, a-pheyq, aipheyq. (Josh.12:18)

Lasharon; laššārôn; لاشّآرُن 'will not/may it not be bought' 'will not/may it not be evil'; لاسّآرُن 'will not walk/may it not walk'; لاصّآرُن 'will not be/may it not be/happen' and all three meanings are said in a curse/wish by the 'la' at the beginning. Cp: lashaaron, lassaaron, lassaaron. (Josh.12:18)

Shimron-meron; šimrôn mĕr'ôn; شِمرُن مِرئُن/ميرئُن 'sleeves/clothes pulled up/unkempt-they do not see/ do not listen/are stubborn' 'sleeves/clothes pulled up/unkempt-water-they saw'; شِمرُن مِرعُن/ميرعُن 'sleeves/clothes pulled up/unkempt-evil eyed them'; سِمرُن مِرئُن/ميرئُن 'they stayed up-they do not see/do not listen/are stubborn' 'they stayed up-water they saw'; سِمرُن مِرعُن/ميرعُن 'they stayed up-evil eyed them'. Cp: shimron meron/meiron, shimron mer'on/meir'on, simron meron/meiron, simron mer'on/meir'on. (Josh.12:20)

Taanach; ta'ănāk; تَعَناَق ، تَعيناَق 'with/of throats/necks' an activity involving doing something to necks/throats; دَعَناَك ، دَعيناَك 'we called you' (as in shouted out name, invited/warned, or as in calling God for help); طَعَناَك ، طَعيناَك 'we stabbed you' 'we obeyed you'. Cp: ta'naaq, ta'ainaaq, da'naak, da'ainaak, ṭa'naak, ṭa'ainaak. (Josh.12:21)

Megiddo; mĕgiddô; مَغِدّ ، ميغِدّ 'of swollen glands' which means person has been frustrated or ill to the degree the glands have swollen, 'fed lunch'; مَغِط ، ميغِط 'squeezed/rough-handled to death' when something has been so roughly handled or even petted (such as young kittens/pups) that it results in them dying or physically bent out of shape, 'killed'. Cp: meghiddo, meighiddo, meghiṭṭo, meighiṭṭo. (Josh.12:21)

Jokneam; yoqnĕ'ām; يوقنَع آم ، يوقنيع آم 'convinces-the' 'gives up-the' 'lifts head up-the' 'looks up-the'. Cp: yoqne'-aam, yoqnei'-aam. (Josh.12:22)

Carmel; karmel; قَرم ال 'a crumb/corner-the' 'broke/crumbled(something) from its corners-the' 'answered back-the/retorted (with snarkiness)-the'; قَرمال 'admitted to the' (to what happened); كَرم ال 'try to(or: went ahead)-threw-the' 'generosity/generous-the' 'the hot coal end of log in fire' 'bury in fire/ashes the sharp and burnt end of the log'. Cp: qarm-el, qarmel, karm-el. (Josh.12:22)

Sihor; šîḥôr, šīḥôr, šīḥōr; شيحُر 'desert/dry land' 'became desert' 'dry cough/dry rattle in the chest' 'glared at'; شييحُر،شييحور 'desertification' 'very dry land' 'lots of desert' 'has dry cough or discomfort in chest accompanied by a dry scratchy feeling or sound'. Cp: sheeḥor, shee-eeḥor, shee-eeḥoor. (Josh.13:3)

Mearah; mĕ'ārâ; مَعاَره/ا ، مي عاَره 'a gloating' 'a borrowing/lending' 'borrowed' 'a disgrace' 'water-naked' 'water from his private parts' (sperm/semen is called 'water'). Cp: me'aarah(ra), mei'aarah(ra). (Josh.13:4) It is notable that many of the new word-names introduced are water-related words.

Jahazah; yahṣâ; يَهسه/ا 'he presses down on/packs it' (to make it fit more); يَهزه/ا 'he swings/rocks it'; يَحزه/ا 'he corners/crams it'; جَهزه/ا 'came-rocked it' 'prepared it'; يَخزه/ا 'he insults/swears at him'; يَخذه/ا 'he takes it/him'. Cp: yahsah(sa), yahzah(za), yaḥzah(za), gahzah(za), yakhzah(za), yakhvah(va). (Josh.13:18)

Mephaath; mĕpa'aṯ; مَبَعَط ، مي بَعَط 'is ripped/did not rip' 'water-tore'; مَـ/مي فَعَذ 'did not give protection' 'water-give protection. Cp: meba'aṭ, meiba'aṭ, mepha'av, meipha'av. (Josh.13:18)

Sibmah; śibmâ; صِبمه ، صِبما 'pour water' (directly onto/into something); شِذمه ، شِذما 'I will guilt him/it' 'I will ostracise him/it'. Cp: ssibmah(ma), shivmah(ma). (Josh.13:19)

Zareth-shahar; ṣereṯ haššaḥar; ذَرَف هَشَّحَر 'overflowed-look/I will/this-desert/dry land' 'overflowed this desert/dry land'; ذَرَف هَشَّهَر 'overflowed-look/I will/this-month' 'it overflowed this month'; زَرَة هَشَّحر ، هَشَّهَر 'visited/pilgrimaged/tightened-this-desert' 'visited/pilgrimaged/tightened-this-month'. Cp: vereph-ha-shaḥar, vereph-hashahar, zeret-ha-shaḥar, zeret-hashahar. (Josh.13:19)

Rabbah; rabbâ; رَبّه ، رَبّا 'brought up' 'disciplined' 'mixed and diluted with water' 'his god/master/teacher/head of family/person in charge of matters (family or business, etc.)'; رَبّح 'caused a scene' literally: 'monkeyed' as in made a lot of noise/chatter (arguing/shouting) while throwing things around (literally objects or figuratively accusations and gestures) and is usually used in a pair with 'shammat and rabbaḥ' which means caused an embarrassing scene in front of other people. Cp: rabbah(ba), rabbaḥ. (Josh.13:25)

Ramath-mizpeh; rāmaṯ hammiṣpeh; راَمَت هَمّصبح 'threw around/killed-here/this, ill intentioned' 'saw death-here/this, ill intentioned'; راَمَت هَمّذبَح 'threw around/killed-here/this slaughter' 'saw death-here/this slaughter'; راَمَت هَمّصبه 'threw around/killed-here/this, pouring/poured/pouring vessel'; راَمَت هَمّسبح 'threw around/killed-here/this, body of water/pool'. Cp: raamat hammissbeḥ, raamat hammivbeḥ, raamat hammissbeh, raamat hammisbeḥ (Josh.13:26)

Betonim; bĕṭōnîm; بَطون/بيطون هم/ام 'stomachs-them/the' '(their) underlayer of garment-them/the' 'underlayer of bed (blankets and soft material that make up a mattress (in modern days 'a mattress')-them/the' 'created soft layer/extra layers-them/the'; بَطونهم ، بيطونهم 'stomach illness' consists of stomach ache/upset stomach, diahorrea 'made underlayer (for dress)'. Cp: beṭoon-hum/um, beiṭoon-hum/um, beṭoonhum, beiṭoonhum. (Josh.13:26)

Maaleh-acrabbim; ma'ălē 'aqqrabbîm; مَعيلي نَغَرَبّ هم/ام ، مَ عيلي نَغَرَبّ هم/ام 'rose above/lifted it/him-made them go over/overflow/dip out of sight-them/the' 'what is on him-made them go over/overflow/dip out of sight-them/the' 'nothing on him(not his responsibility/not to worry)-made them go over-them/

the', 'water above-overflow-them/the'. Cp: ma'ailey aghrabb-hum/um, ma-'ailey aghrabb-hum/um. (Josh.15:3)

Adar; 'ădār; نَضَار ، نُيضآر 'the harmed/the harmer' 'the vicious' 'the one with the habit'; نَذآر،نُيذآر 'the sower(of seeds)/the sowed' 'the one with offspring' 'the one who scattered soil(or any powdery substance)'; عَذآر،عِيذآر 'shadows/shadowed' 'excuses/excused'; غَدآر ، غِيدآر 'darkened' (as in night/sky), 'betrayed/ deceived' 'treacherous'. Cp: adhaar, aidhaar, avaar, aivaar, 'avaar, 'aivaar, ghadaar, ghaidaar. (Josh.15:3)

Karkaa; haqqarqaʻ; هَقَّرقَع 'will make bursting noise', onomatopoeic of qarqa', 'will burst'. Cp: haqqarqa'. (Josh.15:3)

Bohan; bōhān; بوهَن 'I can see' 'with vision' a suitable name for 'the son of Reuben' (Reuben: 'saw be-tween'). Cp: boohan. (Josh.15:6)

Adummim; 'ădummîm; نَدومّ/نُيدومّ هم/ام 'I spin-them/the' 'I faint-them/the' 'I make last-them/the' 'I make bleed-them/the' 'is shadowy figure(indistinguishable)-them/the'. Cp: adoomm-hum/um, aidoomm-hum/ um. (Josh.15:7)

En-shemesh; 'ên šemeš; عين شَمَس 'eye/look-possess/touch' 'eye/look-sunbathe'; نُين شَمَس 'where/will-possess' 'where/will-sunbathe'; عين/نُين شَمَش 'eye/will-smell you'. I believe the word (en/eye) does not mean eye as in eyeball, but 'look/see/listen/pay attention'. Cp: 'eyn-shemes, eyn-shemes, 'eyn-shemesh, eyn-shemesh. (Josh.15:7)

En-rogel; 'ên rōgēl; عين روجيل 'look-men' 'look-legs' 'look-breastfed'; نُين روجيل 'where/will be-men' 'where/will be-legs' 'where/will be-breastfed'. Cp: 'eyn-roogeyl, eyn-roogeyl. (Josh.15:7)

Hinnom; hinnōm; هِنّوم 'madly in love' 'we'll sleep(literally or euphemism for sex)', 'insulted' either being insulted or insulting others, 'satisfied/gratified' either being satisfied or satisfying others. Cp: hinnoom. (Josh.15:8)

Nephtoah; neptôaḥ; نَفتَوه 'we crush it/him' 'we pluck it/him'; نَفتَوح 'we open'. Cp: nephtoah, nephtoah. (Josh.15:9)

Baalah; ba'ălâ; بَعَله/ا 'at its top' 'above it' 'on it' 'sold it to him' 'his/her spouse'; بَعيله 'with his sons' 'his spouses' 'with aboveness' 'above him/it'. Cp: ba'alah(la), ba'ailah. (Josh.15:10)

Chesalon; kĕsālôn; حَصالُن ، كِيسالُن 'found/got' 'happened'; كَسالُن ، كيسالُن 'laziness' 'bought them clothes/fabric' 'put/wrapped them in fabric'; غَسالُن ، غيسالُن 'washed'. Cp: ḥessaalon, ḥeissaalon, kesaalon, keisaalon, ghesaalon, gheisaalon. (Josh.15:10)

Ekron; 'eqrôn; عقرُن 'ruined' 'petrified' 'laps'; نَقرُن 'link with wood/rope' 'lead with rope' 'connect' usually used to describe two bulls/cows under one yoke kept moving at the same pace, or tying a rope around a bull/cow's horns or neck to lead them, make them turn around, 'read' 'admit' 'stop moving/fidgeting/ cease'; نَكرُن 'lease to/from'. Cp: 'eqron, eqron, ekron. (Josh.15:11)

Shicron; šikkĕrôn; شِقَّرُن ، شِقِّيرُن 'gaps' 'peeping between gaps or from behind cover' 'will connect/link' 'will tie rope around bull, lead it' 'connect two bulls with one rope/yoke (to make them move as one)' 'will stay put/settle down.'; سِكَّرُن ، سِكِّيرُن 'drunk' 'closed'. Cp: shiqqeron, shiqqeiron, sikkeron, sikkeiron. (Josh.15:11)

Jabneel; yabnĕ'ēl; يَبني نِّل 'builds-the' 'my son/son of-the'; جَبني نِّل 'brought/fetched me-the' 'made cheese-the'; هَبني نِّل 'gave me(away)-the' 'I will build-the'; عَبني نِّل 'packed me-the' 'overflowed me-the' 'floated-the'; حَبني نِّل 'loved me-the' 'kissed me-the'. Cp: yabnei-ill, gabnei-ill, habnei-ill, 'abnei-ill, ḥab-nei-ill. (Josh.15:11)

Achsah; 'aksâ; عَكسه/ا 'reversed it/reverse-him/her/it' 'did opposite' reflected in the story: instead of the groom approaching the family to ask for her hand in marriage, and instead of the bride and the bride's family receiving dowry and gifts, and instead of her family (Caleb) voluntarily giving her a wedding pres-ent, which is the custom, her father has offered her in marriage, and she asks for a specific present con-nected to her marriage; نَخذه/ا 'took it/her' as Caleb offers his daughter for whoever takes a specific area, they repeat 'took it' in that she asks her father for more land which she gets; نَخزه/ا 'embarrassed/insulted' as she embarrasses her groom when she asks him to ask her father for more land so she herself asks for it in-stead. Cp: 'aksah(sa), akhvah(va), akhzah(za). (Josh.15:16–19)

Othniel; 'otnî'ēl; نُوثني نِّل 'idol/idolater-the' 'double-the' and the story narrates Othniel gets double the reward he was promised: Caleb's daughter for smiting a city, and the extra land she asks for. Cp: oophnee-ill. (Josh.15:16–19)

Kabzeel; qab̲ṣĕ'ēl; قَبصي ئِل 'pinch-the' 'repeat part of what someone else said-the(in modern language 'quote'); خَبصي ئِل 'poke fingers into' 'poke finger into anus' (to male or female done as prank over clothing, or naked/sexually), 'dip fingers into' 'make mess/pollute' 'pollute food by dipping fingers into it' كَبسي ئِل 'bury under ashes-the'. Cp: qabssei-ill, khabssei-ill, kabsei-ill. (Josh.15:21)

Jagur; yāgûr; يآجُر 'he/it pulls' 'he/it is dying'; هآجُر 'I will pull' 'abandoned'; عآجُر 'animal fodder'; حآجُر 'stones' 'of stone' 'forbid (as in verbally telling a person and they have to stop what work they are doing in the land until a solution is mediated between them over the dispute of the land)'. Cp: yaagur, haagur, 'aagur, ḥaagur. (Josh.15:21)

Eder; 'ēd̲er; Same **Edar** (Gen.35:21-22).

Kinah; qînâ; قينه/ا 'standing perky' 'estimated pouring liquid/topped up water(liquid)' 'we are, already'. Cp: qeenah(na). (Josh.15:22)

Dimonah; dîmônâ; ديمُنه/ا 'made us bleed' 'our blood' 'make us last/we lasted' 'built a small hut(for cooking)'; ضيمُنه/ا 'they guaranteed' 'he trusted him'. Cp: deemonah(na), dheemonah(na). (Josh.15:22)

Adadah; 'ad̲'ād̲â; عَدعآده 'attempted to uproot/loosen it' (by pushing/pulling or back and forth motion/or using leverage), 'counted it/counted many times' 'returned-became enemy/showed enmity'; عَضعآضه 'gave him sore muscles' 'recompensed him/recompensed him lots' 'bit him/it all over' real or playful bites. Cp: 'ad'aadah, 'adh'aadhah. (Josh.15:22)

Kedesh; qed̲eš; كَدَش 'piled' 'threw on the ground' 'threw on the ground like a heap' the sound of throwing something on the ground 'fell like a heap' 'falls/is thrown to the ground with a loud sound'; قَدَش 'led/was led' 'led/pimped'. Cp: kedesh, qedesh. (Josh.15:23)

Ithnan; yit̲nān; يثنآن 'idols/idol worshippers' (two or more), 'doubled it/did second layer' such as painting wall, henna on skin, the second course of grinding grain. Cp: yifnaan. (Josh.15:23)

Ziph; zîp̄; زيف 'was escorted with procession'; سيف 'carried gently/was carried gently' 'poured gently/pour gentle spurts of water' 'numb/went numb' 'sipped'; صيف 'rocks/stones' 'stacked rocks' 'rock columns' 'columns' 'to flatter' 'to describe someone with insulting comments' 'lice eggs' 'fish oil (fattening product)'. Cp: zeeph, seeph, sseeph. (Josh.15:24)

Telem; t̲elem; تَلَم 'ploughed'. Cp: telem. (Josh.15:24)

Bealoth; bĕ'ālôt̲; بيعآلُف 'with leaves' 'growing leaves'; بيعآلُت 'with rising above' 'placed higher/rose higher' 'with spouses of' 'with family'; بيعآلُط 'it/he strips leaves off stems' (also means to con)' 'eats direct off stem/branch/stalk'; بيغآلُط 'he deceives/shortchanges/cons/lies' 'he makes mistake/does wrong'. Cp: bei'aaloph, bei'aalot, bei'aaloṭ, beighaaloṭ. (Josh.15:24)

Hadattah; ḥăd̲attāh; حيدَتّآه 'they sharpened' 'they bordered/made borders' 'they dared/challenged/stood up to'; حيضَتّآه 'their portion' 'their luck' 'they refused/turned down a good thing'. Cp: ḥaidattaah, ḥaidhattaah. (Josh.15:25)

Kerioth; qĕrîyôt̲; قِريُّت ، قيريُّت 'she/it stood still/settled down' 'she read' 'she admitted'; قِريُّط ، قيريُّط 'cracked/gnashed between teeth' 'grit teeth' 'nipped/nipped between' 'wore earrings'; كِريُّث ، كيريُّث 'ate chives/of chives/grows chives' 'pond' 'pool of naturally collected water' 'takes long draught' 'takes long deep inhalations'. Cp: qereeyot, qeireeyot, qereeyoṭ, qeireeyoṭ, kereeyof, keireeyof. (Josh.15:25)

Amam; 'ămām; نَمآم ، نيمآم 'threaded a needle' 'led people through/led people'. Cp: amaam, aimaam. (Josh.15:26)

Shema; šĕma'; سِمَع 'heard'; سيمَع 'eavesdropped' 'insulted loudly so others could hear (to embarrass/expose person being insulted'. Cp: sema', seima'. (Josh.15:26)

Many of the following word-names are childbirth related:

Moladah; môlād̲â; مُلآده 'having a baby/just given birth' 'speaking nonsense/going around in circles with speech making no sense/not getting to the point'; مُلآذه 'this not for him' 'a fleeing/a place to flee to'; مُلآطه 'flat stones' 'sides stuck together' 'different things stuck together'. Cp: molaadah, molaavah, molaaṭah. (Josh.15:26)

Hazar-gaddah; ḥăṣar gaddâ; '**Hazar**' in all its variants as before (see Hazar): حَذَر/حيذَر 'warned'; حَصَر/حيصَر 'surrounded/blocked' 'great sorrow/despair/regret'; حَسَر/حيسَر 'became thinner-'; followed by: جَدّه 'grandmother' 'his grandfather' 'a thread' 'found him' 'renewed it/him'; غَدّه 'frustrated him' 'made his glands swell' 'fed him lunch'. Cp: (Hazar as before), gaddah, ghaddah. (Josh.15:27)

Heshmon; ḥešmôn; هَشمُن 'belittled' 'crushed bread with broth' (served at new-born celebrations); هَزمُن 'defeated' 'I will time'; حَسمُن 'pity'; حَزمُن 'a bundle/bundled/tied' (as in large bundle of wood); خَشمُن 'bit/ tattered'. Cp: heshmon, hezmon, ḥesmon, ḥezmon, kheshmon. (Josh.15:27)

Beth-pelet; bêṯ peleṭ; بيت فَلَت 'it/he will fall' physically fall down or morally, 'he will become lewd/ immoral' 'a promiscuous girl/daughter'. Cp: beyt-phelet. (Josh.15:27)

Hazar-shual; ḥăṣar šû'āl; حَذَر/حيذَر صُئآل/سُئآل 'warned-reached/arrived/are arriving' 'warned-connected/ are connecting' 'warned-rock/stone/they made layer with stones' 'warned-asked/are asking' 'warned-are flowing water/leaking' 'warned-are entertained/distracted/comforted'; حَصَر/حيصَر صُئآل/سُئآل'surrounded/blocked/sorrow/despair/regret-reached/arrived/are arriving' 'surrounded/blocked/sorrow/despair/ regret-connected/are connecting' 'surrounded/blocked-asked/are asking'; حَسَر/حيسَر صُئآل/سُئآل 'became thinner-reached/arrived/are arriving' 'became thinner-connected/are connecting' 'became thinner-asked/ are asking'. The meanings of 'Hazar' followed by šû'āl: شُعآل 'ablaze', سُعآل 'coughing/a cough'; زُعآل 'upset(plural)'. Cp: ḥavar/ḥaivar ssuaal/suaal, ḥassar/ḥaissar ssuaal/suaal, ḥasar/ḥaisar ssuaal/suaal, ḥavar/ḥaivar/ ḥassar/ḥaissar/ḥasar/ḥaisar shu'aal, su'aal, zu'aal. (Josh.15:28)

Bizjothjah; bizyôṯyâ; بِزيُتهه/ا 'her suckling breast' it means the breast she will be fed from, 'picked her up/ picks her up a lot'; بِذجُتهه/ا 'her baby lamb' and both words are about a female baby born. Note that Bizjothjah of which one wordplay means 'baby lamb' follows Beer-sheba which means 'Good/Piety-Ewes'; in the culture of people who speak the language of the Bible (Arabic), the aunts and uncles of new-born girls gift her a baby lamb or young hen. Cp: bizyot-hah(ha), bivgot-hah(ha). (Josh.15:28)

Azem; 'eṣem; عَزَم 'invited' and these words have been chosen and are still related to the celebration and activities around a new-born. Cp: 'ezem. (Josh.15:29)

Eltolad; 'eltôlaḏ; ئِل تُلَد 'the one who is giving birth' 'is giving birth'. Cp: eltolad. (Josh.15:30)

Chesil; kĕsîl; حَصيل ، حيصيل 'happened' 'found/received/achieved' 'the reality/it is what it is/this is what we got'; كَسيل ، كيسيل 'lazy' 'clothed them(new)' 'wrapped them in fabric'; غَسيل ، غيسيل 'washed' 'ghaseel powder/paste(natural soapy leaves)'. Cp: hesseel, ḥeisseel, keseel, keiseel, gheseel, gheiseel. (Josh.15:30). After a woman gives birth, the ladies around her bring in a wash basin and seat her in it and wash her; the names listed: Eltolad, Chesil, Hormah (woman), show what inspired these names in the author's imagination.

Ziklag; šîqlāg; ضيق لآك 'distress/sufferance for you'; ضيق لآج 'distress/sufferance is coming'; ضيك لآك 'that is for you'; شيخلآق 'it will be born'. Cp: dheeq-laak, dheeq-laag, dheek-laak, sheekhlaaq. (Josh.15:31)

Madmannah; madmannâ; مَضمَنّه/ا 'strongly reassured' 'did not reassure/guarantee' 'passed along/ completed-from him/it/for him', it is also a type of tool used along with the yoke and the action of putting it onto the necks of the bulls which will be ploughing land. Cp: madhmannah(na). (Josh.15:31)

Sansannah; sansannâ; سَنسَنّه/ا 'straightened-straightened it/him' 'direct-in his direction' 'let it go for a year' 'left it for a long time' 'first time done to or by him/it-began custom' directly faced him/it' 'made it straight/made it move in right direction.' it follows Madmannah in this list because Madmannah is a tool used to keep a pair of bulls/cows moving at the same pace together and in a straight line, and also to turn as directed by the men controlling them; صَنصَنّه/ا 'horrible raw odour-horrible raw odour' such as raw eggs, blood. The compound word is made up of repeating the first word because that is how the Arabic emphasises the intensity of the adjective/verb by repeating it. Cp: sansannah(na), ssanssannah(na). (Josh.15:31)

Lebaoth; lĕḇā'ôṯ; لَذآعُت ، ليذآعُت 'she/it gave a whip/whipped' 'it/she bit/stung (e.g. by snake/scorpion)'; لَبآعُث 'may you/it not return/be sent' (curse), 'did not scratch its hoof in the ground' ; ليبآعُث 'why did he send for' 'why did it scratch its hoof in the ground', لَبآعُت ، ليبآعُت 'she/it swiped (sharp swipe/thump)' 'she would have sold' 'may she not sell it (a wish)' 'why did she sell it'. Cp: levaa'ot, leivaa'ot, lebaa'of, leibaa'of, lebaa'ot, leibaa'ot. (Josh.15:32)

Shilhim; šilḥîm; شِلهيم 'take them' 'I will feed well/pamper' 'I will plumpen/fatten(be feeding extra)'; شِلحيم 'I will eat lots of meat' 'I will maul(figuratively)/I will be angry'. Cp: shilheem, shilḥeem. (Josh.15:32)

Eshtaol; 'eštā'ôl; ئَشتآئُل 'pulled more to one side' 'raised from one side/uneven sided' 'moving to one side'. Cp: eshtaa-ul. (Josh.15:33)

Zoreah; ṣor'â; زورئا ، زورئه 'goat stables' 'visit them/it'; ذورئه/ا 'sowed(seed)' 'sorghum/his sorghum' 'his children/offspring' 'was scattered' word use to describe scattering any powdery substance such as soil, flour, etc. Cp: zoor-ah, zoor-a, voor-ah, voor-a. (Josh.15:33)

Ashnah; 'ašnâ; شَسنه/ا 'straightened it/him' 'made him/it face right direction'. Cp: asnah(na). (Josh.15:33)

Zanoah: zānôaḥ; زآنَاه ، زآنوَه 'bastard' 'fornicators/fornicated'; صآنَاه ، صآنوَه 'smelt bad(like blood/raw eggs)'; ذآنَاح ، ذآنوَح 'this/he cried out in distress/loudly'; ذآنَاه ، ذآنوَه 'this/he warned/brought to attention' 'made ears/handles for it'. Cp: zaano-ah, zaanoah, ssaano-ah, ssaanoah, vaano-aḥ, vaanoaḥ, vaanoah, vaano-ah. (Josh.15:34)

En gannim; 'ên gannîm; عين جَنّ هم/ام 'look-demons-them/the' 'look-crazy-them/the'; عين جَنّهم 'look-it drove them insane'; عين غَنّيم 'look-richness' 'look-make rich' 'look-raising goats'; ئين غَنّيم 'it will make them rich' 'we'll raise goats' 'they will make plenty(out of it)' as in they will exploit the situation and make plenty of something (money/resources). Cp: 'eyn-gann-hum/um, 'eyn-gannhum, 'eyn-ghanneem, eyn-ghanneem. (Josh.15:34)

Enam; 'ênām; عين آم 'eye/look-the' 'inspect-the' 'pay attention-the'; غينآم 'richness/plenty' 'making plenty' 'raising goats'; ئين آم 'where is-the' 'will-sleep' the latter literally sleep or euphemism for sex. Cp: 'eyn-aam, gheynaam, eyn-aam, eynaam. (Josh.15:34)

Socoh; śôḵô śôḵōh; سُق 'water(as in give)' 'drive' 'extremely cold'; صُق 'throbbing pain(in teeth/bones)'; شُك 'thread' (such as arrange beads or flowers or jewellery on a string; or to thread/skewer anything on a stick, needle, etc. and also to sew something quickly), when a hen makes a long string of loud clucking noises; شُق 'side' 'his side' 'beside'; شُقوح 'struck sharply' 'sharp pain' 'splinters' 'splinter in skin'; سُقوه 'drive it/him(as in drive animals)' 'water it' 'of market (and means sexually immoral)'; شُكوه 'thread/string it' (as with beads etc.) 'thorns stuck in it' 'remove thorns from it' 'complained about him'. Cp: suqu, ssuqu, shuku, shuqu, shuqooḥ, suqooh, shukooh. (Josh.15:34)

Sharaim; ša'ărayim; شَئيرَيِم 'sickles' (for harvesting/cutting crops and plants); شَئيرَي ام 'evil-the' 'buyer/bought-the' 'will show the' (whether literally show or figuratively 'will beat them up'), 'will penis-the'; شَعرَي ام ، شَعيرَي ام 'I will make naked-the' 'the gold necklace-the/of the' 'I will gloat at-the'. Cp: sh-airayim, sh-airay-um, sh'aray-um, sh'airay-um. (Josh.15:34)

Adithaim; 'ăḏîṯayim; عَديتَي ام ، عيديتَي ام 'you infected-the' 'you gave illness-the' 'you counted-the' 'you made enmity with-the' and all meanings are being said to a female. Cp: 'adeetay-um, 'aideetay-um. (Josh.15:36)

Gederah; gĕḏērâ; جِذيره/ا ، جيذيره/ا 'to remove/cut/strip/harvest by shaking, pulling movement' (it causes more fruit to fall to the ground to be collected, but also leaves some fruit behind on the tree) 'to leave plant/tree(or anything) in tatters or bitten around the edges or all over' (e.g. how caterpillars leave plant leaves), 'shuddered/goosepimpled'; جِديره/ا ، جيديره/ا 'they caught pox' 'they built wall(s)/walled'; غِديره/ا ، غيديره/ا 'they betrayed' 'dark' 'became dark'. Cp: geveyrah(ra), geiveyrah(ra), gedeyrah(ra), geideyrah(ra), ghedeyrah(ra), gheideyrah(ra). (Josh.15:36)

Gederothaim; gĕḏērōṯāyim; جِذيروتآي ام ، جيذيروتآي ام 'removed/cut/stripped/harvested by shaking, pulling movement-the' (causes more fruit to fall to the ground to be collected, but also leaves some fruit behind on the tree) 'left plant/tree(or anything) in tatters, or bitten around the edges/all over (e.g. how caterpillars leave plant leaves)-the', 'shuddered/goosepimpled-the'; جِديروتآي ام ، جيديروتآي ام 'they both caugh pox-the' 'you gave them pox-the' 'they built walls-the'; غِديروتآي ام ، غيديروتآي ام 'she betrayed them both-the' 'they both betrayed-the' and it is female spoken about. Cp: geveyrootaay-um, geiveyrootaay-um, gedeyrootaay-um, geideyrootaay-um, ghedeyrootaay-um, gheideyrootaay-um. (Josh.15:36)

Zenan; ṣĕnân; زِنان ، زينان 'dresses' 'adulterers' 'complainers/naggers'; سِنان ، سينان 'teeth' 'teeth grew(baby)' 'let it go/left it for a while' 'straight' 'direction'; زينهن 'their adornments' 'making/made them pretty'; سينهن 'towards them' 'in front of them' 'in their direction' 'left them for a while' 'let them go'. Cp: zenaan, zeinaan, senaan, seinaan, zeinhn, seinhn. (Josh.15:37)

Hadashah; hăḏāšâ; هَدآشه/ا ، هيدآشه/ا 'a pounding/smashing/battering (with heavy object)' 'cracked open'; هَدآسه/ا ، هيدآسه/ا 'I will/he will-stash it in/sneak it in' 'I will/he will-plant it secretly' 'I will/he will plant it secretly to be found by another' 'I will/he will-plant/whisper bad ideas into another's head/cause enmity by planting bad ideas'. Cp: hadaashah(sha), haidaashah(sha), hadaasah(sa), haidaasah(sa). (Josh.15:37)

Migdal-gad; migdal-gāḏ; مِجدَل جآد 'thrown-found' 'thrown/killed-found' 'had fits/possession by demon-found/new' 'throwing place(means from a high place)-found' 'thrown/killed-new' 'throwing place(means from a high place)-new' 'wooden block/wedge-found/new'; مِغطَل جآد 'killed the-found/new' 'squeezed to death the-new/found'; مِغدَل جآد 'glands swollen-new/found' 'fed lunch-new/found'. Cp: migdal-gaad, mighṭal-gaad, mighdal-gaad. (Josh.15:37)

Dilean; dilĕʿān; دِلعآن ، دِليعآن 'poured heavily (on purpose)' 'gushed out in bursts' 'behaving spoiled/ brattish'. Cp: dile'aan, dilei'aan. (Josh.15:38)

Joktheel; yoqṯĕ'êl; يوقتِئيل ، يوقتي ئيل 'kills' 'gives qat' 'gifts/gives qat-the' 'decorates lower border of wall (with mud)-the' 'decorates hands and feet (with henna, shaavaar or shaavaal)-the'; يوقضِ ئيل ، يوقضي ئيل 'pays back-the'. Cp: yooqte-eyl/ill, yooqtei-eyl/ill, yooqdhe-eyl/ill, yooqdhei-eyl/ill. (Josh.15:38)

Bozkath; boṣqaṯ; بوزقَت 'she passed by' 'she cut up/divided into small units' 'divided into small unit and spread separately' 'take qat'; بوزقَث 'pour water(with short splashes/spurts)'. Cp: boozqat, boozqaf. (Josh.15:39)

Cabbon; kabbôn; كَبُّن 'spilled' 'emptied' 'mouldy(because made wet)'. Cp: kabbon. (Josh.15:40)

Lahmam; laḥmām; لَحمآم 'ate lots of meat' 'ate with greed' 'tore strips of meat off' 'spoke/responded angrily'. Cp: laḥmaam. (Josh.15:40)

Kithlish; kitlîš; قِطليش 'tore tiny pieces off' 'struck fingers/tips' 'snipped off-why' 'snipped off for you'; كِذ ليش 'why like this'. Cp: qiṭleesh, kiv-leesh. (Josh.15:40)

Gederoth; gĕḏērôṯ; ; جِذيرُة ، جيذيرُة 'removed/cut/stripped/harvested by shaking, pulling movement' (causes more fruit to fall to ground to be collected, but also leaves some fruit behind on the tree) 'left plant/ tree(or anything) tattered, or bitten around edges/all over (e.g. how caterpillars leave plant leaves), 'shuddered/goosepimpled'; جِديرُة ، جيديرُة 'caught pox' 'walled/built wall(s)'; غِديرُة ، غيديروت 'the betrayal of' 'darkening'. Cp: geveyrot, geiveyrot, gedeyrot, geideyrot, ghedeyrot, gheideyrot. (Josh.15:41)

Beth-dagon; bêṯ-dāgôn; بيت دآجُن 'he will raise chickens/bring chickens'; بيت تآغُن 'he/it/they will sing/ be made to sing' 'girl/daughter will sing/is singing'; بيت دآقُن 'he will be chinned' 'he will grow a beard' 'he will frown/become grumpy'; بيت دعجُن 'he will steer/drive/corner sheep/goats into specific area'. Cp: beyt-daagon, beyt-taaghon, beyt-daaqon, beyt-d'gon. (Josh.15:41)

Ether; ʿeṯer; عَثَر 'found' 'tripped/slipped'; عَطَر 'twined/twirled/curled' the act of twisting or twirling somethings so it is twine/twirly/curly. Cp: 'efer, 'eṭer. (Josh.15:42)

Ashan; ʿāšān; عآشآن 'they lived' 'for the sake of' 'because'; غآشآن 'covered with membrane' 'they deceived'; ئآشآن I/they want' 'the matter' 'I filter' 'goat/sheep ready to conceive(on heat)'. Cp: 'aashaan, ghaashaan, aashaan. (Josh.15:42)

Jiphtah; yipṯaḥ; يِفتَح 'opens'; يِفضَح 'a scandal/exposes a shame'; يِفدَه 'he sacrifices for him' (a human sacrifice and is used as verbal expression of the preciousness of the person being sacrificed for); يِفذَح 'it's spicy'. Cp: yiphtaḥ, yiphdhaḥ, yiphdah, yiphvaḥ. (Josh.15:43)

Nezib; nĕṣîḇ; نَصيب ، نيصيب 'fate' 'portion' 'we strike/ail' 'stone marker/mark' 'we pour into/onto'; نَصيف ، نيصيف 'half' 'justice' 'flatter' 'speak positively about' 'insult'; نَذيب ، نيذيب 'we melt'. Cp: nesseeb, neisseeb, nesseeph, neisseeph, neveeb, neiveeb. (Josh.15:43)

Keilah; qĕʿîlâ; قَعيله/ا ، قيعيله/ا 'is she/she is related to him' 'my floor for him' 'spasm causing pain' 'caused spasming pain' 'worth to him/her' 'make/happen for him'; قَئيله/ا ، قيئيله/ا 'said to her' 'she said' 'what is (wrong)with her/him' 'he said yes/it is'; قَئيله/ا ، قيئيله/ا 'she is spending time/afternoon' 'a place for spending time with others/a gathering place' 'the gathering/spending time (the event)'; كَعيله/ا ، كيعيله/ا 'testicles' 'struck/strike him in the balls'; كَ عيله/ا ، كي عيله/ا 'like, above him/on him' 'go/try-above/on him/ get higher'. Cp: qe'eelah(la), qei'eelah(la), qe-eelah(la), qei-eelah(la), ke'eelah(la), kei'eelah(la), ke-'eelah(la), kei-'eelah(la). (Josh.15:44)

Achzib; 'akzîḇ; ئَكذيب 'I lie/lie' 'lies'; ئَحزيب 'I adorn myself' 'adorned' the word means when women put on pretty dresses or jewellery. Cp: akveeb, aḥzeeb. (Josh.15:44)

Mareshah; mārēšâ; مآريشه/ا 'wash clothes (quickly)' 'to slip away unnoticed' 'winged'; مآريصه/ا 'slip/ slipped from hands' 'slippery'. Cp: maareyshah(sha), mareyssah(ssa). (Josh.15:44)

Shamir; šāmîr; شآمير 'sleeves/clothes pulled up/unkempt'; سآمير 'stayed up all/late night' 'telling 'staying up/fictional' stories'. Cp: shaameer, saameer. (Josh.15:48)

Jattir; yattîr; يَطّير 'flies away' 'runs away like flying' 'throws out with anger/banishes' (latter used to describe husband sending wife away or son out of house); عَطير 'twisted/entwined/curled' 'perfume/perfumed'. Cp: yaṭṭeer, 'aṭṭeer. (Josh.15:48)

Dannah; dannâ; دَنّه/ا 'a bowing/bending' 'bowed/bent' 'a shame/disgrace'; دَنّح 'head bowed with shame' 'walks with head lowered'. Cp: dannah(na), dannaḥ. (Josh.15:49)

Kirjath-sannah; qiryat-sannâ; قِريَة/خِرجة سنّه/ا 'village-let loose/let go' 'came out/went out/brought out-let loose/let go' 'village/brought out-let go/set straight' 'village/brought out-did first time/made it custom' 'village/came out-treated with senna', the latter 'sanah' plant which causes diahorrea used to treat constipation, malaria, bile and other illnesses (in rural Yemen). قِريَط سنّه/ا 'grit/chewed-senna plant/let loose/set straight'. Cp: qiryat-sannah(na), khirgat-sannah(na), qiryaṭ-sannah(na). (Josh.15:49)

Eshtemoh; 'eštĕmōh; نَشتِموه ، نَشتيموه 'swear at him/insult him'; نَزتِموه ، نَزتيموه 'they have blocked bowels' a painful condition where a person cannot pass water, gas or any bowel movement. Cp: eshtemooh, eshteimooh, eztemooh, ezteimooh. (Josh.15:50)

Anim; 'ānîm; عآن هم/ام 'suffered-them/the' 'directed insults/accusations/words at them/the' 'meant-them/the' when people do not want to talk directly to a person whom they do not like or have problems with, they say what they want to say as if they are just speaking to another person while the person the language is directed at can clearly hear to get the message 'meant for them'; غان هم/ام 'sang/their singer-them/the' 'made/made them make ghn sounds-them/the'; غانيم 'made a lot' (wealth is not only money, but from crops, lands, cattle, etc.) 'took advantage of and made a lot' 'lots of goats' 'raising goats'. Cp: 'aan-hum/um, ghaan-hum/um, ghaaneem. (Josh.15:50)

Holon; ḥōlōn, ḥōlôn; حولون ، حولُن 'they are purified/cleansed/circumcised/made edible/made touchable' 'declared permissible/purified' 'they shed' 'they undressed' 'beaten until skin peeled off/beaten severely' 'they are tricksters/deceivers' 'sweet/sweeteners' 'cock-eyed' spoken about plural, 'go around/in circles' 'circle/surround' 'swapped/changed places or positions/changed' 'babies' cribs' 'they tried' 'they surrounded' 'around them' 'a year'; خولون ، خولُن 'they are empty' 'they emptied' 'they are left behind' 'they left (some)' 'they left behind' 'they allowed'. Cp: ḥooloon, ḥowloon, ḥoolon, khooloon, **khow**loon, khoolon. (Josh.15:51)

Giloh; gilōh; جِلوه 'cleared it' 'made it clear' 'purified it' (the process 'gl/جل' is done by placing a container/vessel onto a pile of hot coals after it has been washed thoroughly; the extreme heat kills germs so the vessel is disinfected for use next time), 'come for him/it' and the meaning indicates 'come and get it/him'. Cp: gilooh. (Josh.15:51)

Arab; 'ărāḇ; عَرآب ، عيرآب 'expressed clearly/spoke clearly' 'he will-god/parent/teacher' 'will he-god/parent/teacher' 'learn and remember(this)-teacher/discipliner/parent/god/the grower/anyone who brings someone up or teaches them/grew fast or well' 'be warned-teacher/discipliner/parent/god/the grower/anyone who brings someone up or teaches them/grew fast or well' 'beware-teacher/discipliner/parent/god/the grower/anyone who brings someone up or teaches them/grew fast or well' 'I dare you, go on-teacher/discipliner/parent/god/the grower/anyone who brings someone up or teaches them/grew fast or well' 'he will/will he-mixed and diluted with water' 'learn and remember/beware/be warned-mixed and diluted with water' 'fucks/fucked' 'fucked a lot' 'got naked with'. From words (A/'ă/عَ/عي) 'will/he will/learn and remember/beware/be warned/I dare you', and (rb/rāḇ/رب/راب) 'teacher/taught/discipliner/disciplined/parent/god/and refers to anyone who has taught, or brought up or grown, children/animals/plants/etc.' 'grew fast and/or well' and in growing 'fast and/or well' can mean well-mannered/good or physically in height or strength, beauty, productivity, etc. 'mixed and diluted with water/soaked'; ('rb/عرب) 'expressing/expressed clearly/speaking/spoke clearly' 'fucked'; and also 'got naked with' (and possibly where the meaning of 'arb/fucked was created) from ('r/عر) 'naked/got naked', (b/ب) 'with'.

Also: نَرآب ، نيرآب 'the mixed and diluted with water' 'mixed and diluted with water' 'is mixed and diluted with water' 'the god/parent/teacher' 'is god/parent/teacher' 'he is-god/parent/teacher' 'is he/which-god/parent/teacher?' 'the teacher/discipliner/parent/god/grower/anyone who brings someone or something up or teaches them/grows them' 'the grown fast and/or well' from (rb/رب) 'mixed and diluted with water/soaked'. Cp: 'araab, 'airaab, a-raab, ai-raab. (Josh.15:52)

Eshean; 'eš'ān; نَش عآن 'what did it/he mean' 'what did he/it suffer'; نَش غآن 'what did he sing' 'what did he moan/gripe about'; نَسعان 'wandering/of wandering' 'seeking/wandering and seeking'. Cp: esh-'aan, esh-ghaan, es'aan. (Josh.15:52)

Janum; yānîm; يآن هم/ام 'yaan-hum/um' is an expression of empathy/pity towards someone or something 'pity/compassion for-them/the'; خآن هم/ام 'soaked-them/the' 'betrayed-them/the' 'brothers/became brothers-them/the; هآنيم 'I will put to sleep' 'I will sleep' 'madly in love'; هآن هم/ام 'satisfied/gave plenty-them/the' 'insulted-them/the'. Cp: yaan-hum/um, khaan-hum/um, haaneem, haan-hum/um. (Josh.15:53)

Beth-tappuah; bêt-tappûah; بيتطَبّوَح 'he/it will lay on stomach' 'he/it will uncover belly' 'he/it will splash stomach first into water' 'he it will be slapped on bald patch'; بيتَبّوَح 'he/it will spread himself/relax over large area'; بيت طَبّوَح 'girl/daughter-lay on stomach' 'girl/daughter-belly uncovered' 'girl/daughter splashed stomach first into water'; بيت تَبّوَح 'girl/daughter- spread herself/relaxed over large area'; بيت تَفّوَح 'it will waft' 'he will smoke clothes or room with frankincense' 'he will eat apples'. Cp: beyttabbuah, beyttabbuah, beyt-tabbuah, beyt-tabbuah, beyttaphuah. (Josh.15:53)

Aphekah; 'ăpēqâ; عَفيقه/ا ، عيفيقه/ا 'leapt' 'kicked and jerked' (usually how a new-born calf behaves). نَفيقه/ا ، نيفيقه/ا 'parted hair' 'hair parting' 'part (something)'. Cp: 'apheeqah(qa), 'aipheeqah(qa), a-pheeqah(qa), aipheeqah(qa). (Josh.15:53)

Humtah; humtâ; حومطه/ا the flakes which come off grain (especially during threshing and winnowing), 'a tickling/persistent cough'. Cp: hoomtah(ta). (Josh.15:54)

Zior; ṣî'ōr; سيعور/شيعور 'will abandon' 'will disgrace'; زيغور/صيغور 'small/little'. Cp: see'oor, shee'oor, zeeghoor, sseeghoor. (Josh.15:54)

Maon; mā'ôn; مآعُن 'a helper/supporter/cooperating' 'not helping/cooperating' 'lewd' 'squishy/jelly texture'. Cp: maa'on. (Josh.15:55)

Juttah; yuttâ; عوطّه/ا 'gave him/it' 'cloyingly sweet'; غوطّه/ا 'covered him/it' 'killed him/it quickly'; حوطه/ا 'placed it/set it down' 'left him/it' 'left him/it behind'. Cp: 'uttah(tta), ghuttah(tta), huttah(tta). (Josh.15:55)

Jezreel; yizrĕ'e'l; جِزري عَ ئل 'grazed-on-the' 'slaughtered-on-the' 'green pastures-on-the/green pastures above the'; يِذري عَ ئل 'scatters-on-the' 'sows seeds-on-the' 'has offspring-on-the'; يِزري عَ ئل 'puts shame/puts grievous disgrace/puts serious insults-on-the'; عِصري عَ ئل 'twists/twisted-on-the' 'twisted muscle-on-the'. Cp: gizrei-'-el, yivrei-'-el, yizrei-'-el, 'issrei-'-el. (Josh.15:56)

Jokdeam; yoqdĕ'ām; يوقطِع آم ، يوقطيع آم 'cuts up-the'; يوخدِع آم ، يوخديع آم 'knives/cuts-the' 'deceives-the'. Cp: yooqte'-aam, yooqtei'-aam, yookhde'-aam, yookhdei'-aam. (Josh.15:56) What you see from the lists in verses Josh.15:55-59 are the initial ideas for the stories and word-names of Gibeah and Jonathan.

Gibeah; gib'â; جِذعه/ا 'broke it into pieces' without separating from main body e.g. causing damage internally; جِبئه/ا 'ganged together' 'came from all over' 'gathered to stand/do something against' 'a group of people' 'brought/fetched'. Cp: giv'ah('a), gibah/gib-ah(-a). (Josh.15:57)

Timnah; timnâ; تِمنه/ا 'concludes/conclusion/finishes' 'wishes' 'gloats/counts and lists'; تِمنح 'gives'. Cp: timnah(na), timnah. (Josh.15:57)

Halhul; halhûl; حَلحُل 'undress quickly' 'of undressing' 'removing bit by bit' 'moving something bit by bit' 'shedding in stages' 'purify/cleanse/circumcise it' 'make it edible/permissible'; هَلهُل 'shedding quickly' 'of shedding' 'small tassle on jewellery' 'something small'. Cp: halhul, halhul. (Josh.15:58)

Beth-zur; bêt-ṣûr; بيتزُر ، بيت زُر 'he/it will be visited/visit/pilgrimage' 'he/it will be squeezed/tightened' 'he/it will swear false oath' 'daughter/girl-visited/visit' 'daughter/girl-squeezed/tightened' 'daughter/girl-swear false oath'. Cp: beytzur, beyt-zur. (Josh.15:58)

Gedor; gĕdôr; جِدُر ، جيدُر 'remove(ed)/cut/stripped/harvested by shaking, pulling movement' (causes more fruit to fall to ground to be collected, but also leaves some fruit behind on the tree) 'left plant/tree(or anything) tattered, or bitten around edges/all over (e.g. how caterpillars leave plant leaves), 'shuddered/goosepimpled'; جِدُر ، جيدُر 'caught pox' 'wall' 'built wall'; غِدُر ، غيدُر 'betrayed' 'became dark/darker'. Cp: gevor, geivor, gedor, geidor, ghedor, gheidor. (Josh.15:58)

Maarath; ma'ărāt; مَعرَآف ، معيرآف 'I don't know/he didn't know/is not aware' 'knowledge' 'well, he knew/found out/knows'; مَعرَآت ، مَعيرآت 'the nakedness of/getting naked' 'the disgrace of/of disgrace/the gloating/of gloating' 'the abandonment or getting lost in wilderness'. Cp: ma'araaph, ma'airaaph, ma'araat, ma'airaat. (Josh.15:59)

Beth-anoth; bêt-'ănôt; بيت نَنُث/نينُث 'he will become effeminate/feminine' as in take on characteristics of females. بيت عَنُد/عينُد 'he will become stubborn/spiteful/provoking'. Cp: beyt-anoph, beyt-ainoph, beyt-'anod, beyt-'ainod. (Josh.15:59)

Eltekon; 'eltĕqôn; نَلتقُن ، نَلتيقُن 'they met' 'they connected'; نَلتَكُن ، نَلتيكُن 'whatever it will be' 'whatever it is' 'she/it is it'. Cp: elteqon, elteiqon, el-tekon, el-teikon. (Josh.15:59)

Beth-arabah; bêṯ-hā'ărāḇâ; بيت هاعَرابه/ا بيت هاعيرابه/ا 'he/they will express clearly/speak clearly' 'he/they will-here/look-learn and remember(this)-brought up/disciplined/diluted and mixed with water/his god/master/teacher/head of family/person in charge of matters (family or business, etc.)/grower/he disciplined them/taught them a lesson/brought them up well/grew them well';

'he/they will-here/look-he will/will he-brought up/disciplined/diluted and mixed with water/his god/master/teacher/head of family/person in charge of matters (family or business, etc.)/grower/he disciplined them/taught them a lesson/brought them up well/grew them well';

'he/they will-here/look-be warned-brought up/disciplined/diluted and mixed with water/his god/master/teacher/head of family/person in charge of matters (family or business, etc.)/grower/he disciplined them/taught them a lesson/brought them up well/grew them well';

'he/they will-here/look-beware-brought up/disciplined/diluted and mixed with water/his god/master/teacher/head of family/person in charge of matters (family or business, etc.)/grower/he disciplined them/taught them a lesson/brought them up well/grew them well';

'he/they will-here/look-I dare you, go on-brought up/disciplined/diluted and mixed with water/his god/master/teacher/head of family/person in charge of matters (family or business, etc.)/grower/he disciplined them/taught them a lesson/brought them up well/grew them well';

'he/they will-here/look-fucked' 'they will fuck/are fucking' 'they will be fucked' 'girl/daughter-I will fuck him/her'. Cp: beyt-haa-'araabah(ba), beyt-haa-'airaabah(ba). (Josh.15:61)

Middin; middîn; مِدّين 'lowered' 'bowed' 'bent' 'reaching out' 'handed' 'laid down' 'guilted'; مِضين 'went past/passing' 'are completing/have completed' 'have signed/marked'. Cp: middeen; midheen. (Josh.15:61)

Secacah; sĕḵāḵâ; سِقاقه/ا ، سيقاقه/ا 'very cold' 'driving (animals)' 'watered/watering' 'of markets(lewd)'; صِقاقه/ا ، صيقاقه/ا 'throbbing' as in bones or teeth or ache. Cp: seqaaqah(qa), seiqaaqah(qa), sseqaaqah(qa), sseiqaaqah(qa). (Josh.15:61)

Nibshan; hanniḇšān; هَنِبصان ، نِبصان 'here is-fallen off cliff/high place' 'here fell off cliff' 'fell off cliff/high place' 'here is the pincher' 'pincher' 'we will-clear cotton' 'clearing cotton': from word (nbss/نبص) 'fall off cliff/high place' 'to remove things by the pinch (crumble by pinching)' (nbssn/نبصن) 'clear cotton of pits/seeds/impurities' and the latter is done in a pinching motion, removing the white fibre from seeds, sticks etc.; هَنِبشان ، نِبشان 'here is/look-digs up' 'the one who/that digs up'. Cp: hannibssaan, nibssaan, hannibshaan, nibshaan. (Josh.15:62)

Salt; melaḥ; مِلح 'salt/salted' 'pretty' 'made pretty' 'good' 'nice' 'done well'. Cp: melaḥ. (Josh.15:62)

En-gedi; 'ên geḏî; عين جدي 'look a kid(goat)' 'look, find it'; ئين جِدي 'where will you end up at' 'end up at' 'where-did he reach/was found' 'you will get to/reach' ئينجِدي 'end up at' 'you end up at' 'save' and is being said to a female. Cp: 'eyn-gedee, eyn-gedee, eyngedee. (Josh.15:62)

Archi; hā'arkî; ها نَركي ، نَركي 'here/I will-lean it against/lean against' 'lean against'; ها نَرخي ، نَرخي 'here/I will-loosen' 'loosen' (it can mean literally loosen or allow to/become immoral/spoiled/bad in manners/character); هاعَرقي ، عَرقي 'here/I will-sweat/vein/take root/' 'my veins/my roots/my sweat'. Cp: haa-arkee, arkee, haa-arkhee, arkhee, haa-'arqee, 'arqee. (Josh.16:2)

Japhleti; yaplēṭî; يَفليتي 'they fall' 'they are immoral/lewd' 'you, immoral (person)'; جَف ليطي 'dried and stuck' 'came who flattens and sticks'; يَفليطي 'he flattens and sticks'; جَفليتي 'came the immoral one'. Cp: yaphleytee, gaph-leyṭee, yaphleyṭee, gaphleytee. (Josh.16:3)

Ataroth-addar; 'ăṭārôṯ 'addār; عَطارُت ، عيطارُت نَضّار 'curled/twirled around-harmed/harmer'; عَطارُت ، عيطارُت نَدّار 'curled/twirled around-the spinner/the spun'; (Ataroth/ 'ăṭārôṯ) could also be نَطارُف ، نَيطارُف 'sides/ends of' 'keep at hand/make ready/prepare' as in getting something to be easily picked up. Cp: 'aṭaarot- adhaar, 'aiṭaarot- adhaar, 'aṭaarot-adaar, 'aiṭaarot-adaar, a-ṭaaroph-adhaar, aiṭaaroph-adhaar, a-ṭaaroph-adaar, aiṭaaroph-adaar. (Josh.16:5)

Michmethah; mikmĕṯāṯ; مِخمَضات ، مِخميضات 'churning of' as in churning milk; مِغمَضات ، مِغميضات 'closing eyes of' 'with closed eyes' 'hide and seek'. Cp: mikhmedhaat, mikhmeidhaat, mighmedhaat, mighmeidhaat. (Josh.15:6)

Taanath-shiloh; ta'ănat šilōh; تَنَنَث/تَنَيْنث شِلوه 'he became feminine/effeminate-take him/carry him'; تَنَنَث/تَنَيْنث سيلوه 'he became feminine/effeminate-ask/question him/asked/questioned him' 'he became feminine/effeminate-of questioning/asking' 'he became feminine/effeminate-flow(ed)/leak(ed)/of flowing' 'he became feminine/effeminate-distract(ed)/entertain(ed)/comfort(ed)'; تَنَنَث/تَنَيْنث صِلوه 'he became feminine/effeminate-reach(ed) it/him' 'he became feminine/effeminate-arrive(d) it/him' 'he became feminine/effeminate-connect(ed) it/him' 'he became feminine/effeminate-publicly apologise(d)-him/to him' 'he became feminine/effeminate-his rock/cover with layer of stones'. Cp: ta-anaf shilooh, ta-ainaf shilooh, ta-anaf silooh, ta-ainaf silooh, ta-anaf ssilooh, ta-ainaf ssilooh. (Josh.16:6)

Janohah; yānôḥâ, yānôaḥ; يآنُحه/ا 'he/they scream out in distress/long like animals'; هآنُهه/ا 'they humiliated her/treated her with degradation' 'they insulted her' 'they gave her plenty/satisfied her'; يآنُهه/ا 'they expressed pity over her/it' 'they said 'yanoh''(an expression of pity and sympathy towards spoken about)' 'yes, they warned' 'oh, you who warn'; يآنوَح 'he cried out in distress/loudly'; يآنوَه 'he warned/brought to attention/reminded' 'he planted stone/seed(of fruit)' 'he intends'. Cp: yaanoḥah(ḥa), haanohah(ha), yaanohah(ha), yaanoaḥ, yaanoah. (Josh.16:6)

Naarath; na'ărātâ, na'ărâ; نَعَرآفه ، نَعيرآفه 'we know' 'we know him/it' 'we will know' 'we will tell/let know' 'we will make him know'; نَعَرآته ، نَعيرآته 'made him sexually excited/gave him erection' 'made stand erect/made stand in front of without speaking or moving' ; نَعَره/ا ، نَعيره/ا 'sexually excited/horny/an erection' (describing two people feeling this way) 'wants sex' 'stood/stood erect/stood in front of without moving nor speaking'; نَيْره/ا ، نَيْيره/ا 'we see him/make him see/we understand/make him understand' 'we show him' 'he penised/insulted with 'penis'/we penis him/we insulted with 'penis'' 'his fire/make fire/we make fire' 'light/make light/we make light/shed light/we shed light'. Cp: na'araaphah, na'airaaphah, na'arah(ra), na'airah(ra), na-arah(ra), na-airah(ra). (Josh.16:7)

Kanah; qānâ; كآنه/ا 'they were' 'it was as if' 'it was'; خآنه/ا 'they/he soaked him/it' 'they/he betrayed him/the'; قآنه 'a channel(water channel)' 'bottle/flask/any transportable drinking vessel/also small water vessel' 'estimating measure of something liquid' (when mixing ingredients), 'topped up (liquid)' 'held head high/body straight posture' 'person or object sitting/place/set upright/erect' 'were perky'. It is same as Elkanah (Exod.6:24). Cp: kaanah(na), khaanah(na), qaanah(na). (Josh.16:8)

Asher Beth-shean; yāšēr, 'āšēr bêt-šĕ'ān; عآشير بيت شَنَآن/شيئآن 'pregnant cow-will be copulated' 'pregnant cow-will be copulated/will copulate/will impregnate' 'pregnant cow-will be on heat/ready to conceive(goats and such animals)' 'a lot of people-will be copulated' 'a lot of people/tribe-will be on heat/ready to conceive'. (Asher) means a gestating cow, or many people (see 'I Am That I Am', see Ashur'); the (shean/šĕ'ān) is the term usually used for goats and sheep and similar animals ready to conceive, on heat, from words (shn/shean/šĕ'ān/شن/شَنَآن/شيئآن) 'fertile animals/sexually excited/ready to conceive/copulated/ready to copulate' which is from the word (nsh/nshy/نش/نشي) which also means the readiness and act of goats copulating (and other such animals), and having been copulated it is the period that follows expecting the goat to conceive from the copulation; (shean/šĕ'ān/ شَنَآن/شيئآن) could also mean 'two things' 'important things' 'wants now' and two people wanting something or two people's matters, but the 'animals on heat' and 'copulating/impregnating' fits in with the word-names in this compound word. Cp: 'aasheyr beyt-she-aan/shei-aan. (Josh.17:11)

Ibleam; yiblĕ'ām; يِضلِع آم ، يِضليع آم 'gets caught in the rib/side-the' 'stitch in the side/ribs-the'; يِبلِغ/يِبليغ آم 'passes message-the' 'informs-the' 'reaches puberty-the'; يِبِل/يِبلي عآم 'afflicts-drank/the one who drank' 'afflicts-blind/the blinded' 'becomes old/worn-the'; يِبِل غآم ، يِبلي غآم 'afflicts-the suffocated/depressed/stifled' 'afflicts-covered face/mouth' 'afflicts-muffled voice'. Cp: yidhle'-aam, yidhlei'-aam, yiblegh-aam, yibleigh-aam, yible-'aam, yiblei-'aam, yible-ghaam, yiblei-ghaam. (Josh.17:11)

En-dor; 'ēn dôr, 'ên dôr; عين/ئين دُر 'see/look/pay attention-spin' 'where-spun/did he spin'; ئيندُر 'send/sent out goats/sheep on their way' (to graze), 'to separate the goats from sheep/or to separate a goat or a sheep from the rest of the flock(for specific purpose such as slaughter/sale); 'ên dō'r; عين/ئين دوئر 'see/look/pay attention-search/look for' 'we will look for/we are looking for' 'where did he search'. Cp: 'eyn dor, eyn-dor, eyndor, 'eyn doo-ir, eyn doo'ir. (Josh.17:11)

Geliloth; gĕlîlôt; جِليلُت ، جيليلُت 'tossed and rolled/cleared grains' 'purified' 'made clear'; جِليلُث ، جيليلُث 'came he who shouted' 'came he who shouted for help' and the latter is the precursor to Goliath's naming. Cp: geleelot, geileelot, geleelof, geileelof. (Josh.18:17)

Keziz; qĕṣîṣ; قَزيز ، قيزيز 'frying' 'frying smells'. Cp: qezeez. qeizeez. (Josh.18:21)

Zemaraim; ṣěmārayim; زِمارَي/زيمارَي ام 'the pipe player(s) of the'; سِمارَي/سيمارَي ام 'told a story-the' 'stayed up late night-the'; ذِمارَي/ذيمارَي ام 'guilted/ostracised-the'. Cp: zemaaray-um, zeimaaray-um, semaaray-um, seimaaray-um, vemaaray-um, veimaaray-um. (Josh.18:22)

Parah; pārâ; فارَه/ا 'they fled' 'they are fleeing'; بارَه/ا 'went past/beyond' 'went past/beyond him/it' 'good/pious' 'were good/pious towards it/him'; بارَح 'pulled up water' 'cleared out/levelled/made tidy'; فارَح 'happiness' 'became happy' 'is happy'. Cp: phaarah(ra), baarah(ra), baaraḥ, phaaraḥ. (Josh.18:23)

Ophrah; ʿoprâ; عوثره/ا 'tripped' 'found' tripped it/him' 'found it/him'; ئوفره/ا 'increased/multiplied/enriched' 'increased him/it'; ئوبرح 'is pulling up water/pulled up water' 'cleared/levelled/tidied'; ئوفرح 'be happy' 'made him happy' 'happiness'; ئوبره/ا '(sewing)needle', a type of rodent, 'furry' 'baby-hair/fuzz'; غوبره/ا 'dusty/cloudy' 'greyish' 'brownish' 'reddish'. Cp: 'oofrah(ra), oophrah(ra), oobraḥ, oophraḥ, oobrah(ra), ghoobrah(ra). (Josh.18:23)

Chephar-haammonai; kěpar hāʿammōnāy; خِفَر/خيفَر هاَعَمّوناَي 'musty-here-they gave me to drink' 'musty-here-they blinded me'; the (ha) can also be 'look/here, take/I will/yes/here I am'. Cp: khephar/kheiphar-haa-'ammoonaay. (Josh.18:24)

Ophni; ʿopnî; عوفني 'went off food/drink' (usually an ill animal when it refuses/cannot eat or drink) 'rotted/stank' 'rotten'; عوفني 'feed me snack/light meal' and is any light meal not at the time of the three main meals and is usually only bread; ئوفني 'said 'ooph'' an expression that something smells bad or expressing frustration with a person or thing. Cp: 'oophnee, **'ow**phnee, oophnee. (Josh.18:24)

Gaba; gebaʿ; جَبَئ 'gathered people against' 'ganged up on' 'brought/fetched' 'came from all over' 'gathered to stand against/do something against' 'a group of people'; جَذع ، جِذع 'broke it into pieces' 'broke without separating from main body' e.g. causing damage internally. Cp: geba/geb-a, geva'. (Josh.18:24)

Ramah; rāmâ; رآمه/ا 'threw around/threw' 'threw/killed' 'strew all over' 'saw water' 'saw what?'. Cp: raamah(ma). (Josh.18:25)

Mozah; mōṣâ; موزه/ا 'banana' 'squeezed'; موزح 'joking/teasing'; موزع 'distributed' 'scalded skin off/scraped skin off'; موصه/ا 'suck it/sucked it'; موسه/ا 'touch(ed) him/it' 'entangled/provoked/fought' 'touched/possessed'. Cp: moozah(za), moozaḥ, mooza', mossah(ssa), moosah(sa). (Josh.18:26)

Irpeel; yirpěʾēl; يربي ئِل 'is god/parent/teacher-the' 'grows/raises-the' 'disciplines-the', it also used when a wound or spot inflames and more pop-up around it, also when someone is ill and the lymph nodes swell and can be seen as a lump (at waist/armpit/neck); عربي ئِل 'expressed clearly/spoke clearly-the' 'he will-god/parent/teacher-the' 'will he-god/parent/teacher-the' 'he will/will he-mixed and diluted with water-the' 'fucked-the' and is in plural action. Cp: yirbei-ill, 'irbei-ill. (Josh.18:27)

Taralah; tar'ălâ; تَرئَله ، تَرئي له 'she sees for him' 'you(fem.) see for him' 'she dreamed for him' 'she waters for him'; تَرئَلا ، تَرئي لا 'she sees to/until' 'you(fem.) see to/until' 'she dreams until' 'she understands/obeys until' 'she waters for/she waters until'; تَرعي له/لا 'you(fem.) shepherd for him' 'you(fem.) shepherd up to/until'. Cp: tara-lah, tar-ai-lah, tara-la, tar-ai-la, tar'ai-lah, tar'ai-la. (Josh.18:27)

Zelah; ṣēlaʿ; سيلَع 'removed peels/peels of skin off' 'ripped limbs off' (usually refers to trees/plants/objects); زيلَع 'ate/killed quickly' 'removed a layer/scalding off a peel of skin (using hot liquid)' 'removing nausea by drinking something hot'; صيلَع 'made bald' 'made bald patches' 'slabs/rounds of'; ضيلَع 'hurt/caught in rib(s)' the action of remedying being 'ribbed' (a stitch in the side or feeling rib is out of place)—a person hangs from his/her hands from top of a door or tree trunk and allows weight of body to pull down so the 'rib/ضلَع' is straightened. Cp: seyla', zeyla', sseyla', dheyla'. (Josh.18:28)

Eleph; 'elep, ha'elep; ئَلَف ، ئِلِف 'gather/pick up' 'wrap' 'get used to' 'made up/exaggerated/fictionalised'; هئَلَف 'I will gather/pick up/wrap' 'I will get used to' 'I will make up stories/statements'; (ha) can also mean: 'look' 'look, here' 'pay attention' 'here' 'here I am' 'take'. Cp: e-leph, eleph, ha-eleph. (Josh.18:28)

Gibeath; gibʿat; جبعَث 'came-searched for(in ground)' 'came-sent' 'came-returned'; جب عَث 'fetched-went around in circles/futilely/a mess' 'answered-went around in circles/futilely/a mess; جِذعَت 'broke (internally)' e.g. if a stem/branch is snapped, but left hanging on to the main body; كِبعَث 'go/try-search'. Cp: gib'af, gib-'af, giv'at, kib'af. (Josh.18:28)

Balah; bālâ; بآله 'ailed him' 'his mind' 'his patience' 'his affliction/afflicted him' 'soaked him/it' 'urinated it/his urine'; بآلح 'dates/ate or gathered dates'. Cp: baalah, baalaḥ. (Josh.19:3)

Beth-marcaboth; bêt hammarkābōt; بيت هَمَّرقآبوت 'it will-here, put on its neck' 'it will-here be necked(as in something will be done related to the neck)' 'pay attention-here, keep eye on/pour water from vessel to vessel'; بيت هَمَّركَابوت 'it will-here, be ridden/mounted' 'girl-will be/here ridden/mounted' and is euphemism for sex. Cp: beyt-hammarqaaboot, beyt-hammarkaaboot. (Josh.19:5)

Hazar-susah; ḥăṣar sûsâ; all the different spellings and meanings of 'hazar' as earlier (see Hazar (Num.34:4)). صُصه 'bad smell like raw eggs/blood' 'be quiet/hush'. Cp: 'hazar' as before, ssussah. (Josh.19:5)

Beth-lebaoth; bêṯ lĕḇā'ôṯ; بيت ليباَعَت 'she/it/they will/girl-she/it swiped (sharp swipe/thump)' 'she/it/they will/girl-she would have sold' 'she/it/they will/girl-may she not sell it (a wish)' 'she/it/they will/girl-why did she sell it' ; بيت ليباَعَث 'it will/girl-may you/it not return/be sent' (curse), 'it will/girl-did not scratch its hoof in the ground' 'it will/girl-why did he send for' 'it will/girl-why did it scratch its hoof in the ground'; بيت ليذاَعَت 'it will/girl-she/it gave a whip/whipped' 'it will/girl-it/she bit/stung (e.g. by snake/scorpion)'. Cp: beyt-leibaa'ot, beyt-leibaa'of, beyt-leivaa'ot.

Sharuhen; šārûḥen; شاَرُحَن 'explained' 'explained until' 'they explained' 'washing basin' 'made it wider' 'opened/ripped it wider' 'a gorge' something wide and gaping whether describing a person's mouth, a wound, a tear in fabric, etc.; شاَرُهَن 'they are evil' 'evil-them' 'they bought them' 'greedy'; ساَرُهَن 'they left/walked/went' 'they are flirtatious/immoral around females' 'I will lease/pawn'; صاَرُهَن 'knotted them' 'bundled them' 'kept secret/kept within/contained'. Cp: shaaruḥen, shaaruhen, saaruhen, ssaaruhen. (Josh.19:6)

Remmon; rimmôn; رِمُّن 'thrown' 'killed' 'rotten/stinking'. Cp: rimmon. (Josh.19:7)

Baalath-beer; ba'ălaṯ bĕ'ēr; بَعيلَت بَئير/بيئير 'I/it on top of/went to top of/spouse of-good/piety' 'I/it made higher-good'; بَعيلَف بَئير/بيئير 'I/it will gather leaves-good' 'I/it will eat leaves-good'; بَغيلَط بَئير/بيئير 'I/it deceives/shortchanges/cons/lies-good/piety' 'I/it makes mistake/does wrong-good/piety'; بَعيلَط بَئير/بيئير 'I/it will stick together-good' 'I/it will strip leaves off-good' (also means to con). Cp: ba'ailat be-eyr/bei-eyr, ba'ailaf be-eyr/bei-eyr, baghailaṭ be-eyr/bei-eyr, ba'ailaṭ be-eyr/bei-eyr. (Josh.19:8)

Ramath; rāmaṯ; راَمَت 'threw around' 'killed' 'saw death'. Cp: raamat. (Josh.19:8)

Maralah; mar'ălâ; مَرعيله/ا 'passed above it/him' 'passed/visited by him/it'; مَرعي له 'a pasture/grazing land for him/it'; مَرئَ/مَرئي له 'look into mirror for him/it' 'dream for him/it' 'a dream for him/it' 'what was seen for him/it?' 'a mirror for him' 'look for him/it' 'water for him/it' 'watering ground for him/it'. Cp: mar-'ailah(la), mar'ai-lah, mar-a/mar-ai-lah. (Josh.19:11)

Dabbasheth; dabbešeṯ; دَبَّشَت ، دَبَّشَت 'mixed/stirred' (a female is doing the action); طَبَّشَت 'splashed around/splashed into'. Cp: dabbeshet, ṭabbeshet. (Josh.19:11)

Sarid; śārîḏ; صاَريد 'coal logs' 'burnt logs' 'burned and buried logs' (for making coal), 'stiffened body/turned away/ignored' 'became like a burnt log/pretended not to hear'. Cp: ssaareed. (Josh.19:12)

Chisloth-tabor; kislôṯ tāḇōr; كِسلُت تاَبور 'she became lazy-ruins reputation/becomes bad'; حِصلُت تاَبور 'she found/got-gets bad reputation/becomes bad/spoiled'; غِسلُت تاَبور 'the washing of/washed-gets bad reputation/spoiled'. Cp: kislot taaboor, ḥislot taaboor, ghislot taaboor. (Josh.19:12)

Daberath; dāḇĕraṯ; داَبيرَت ، داَبِرَت 'brought ill fate upon' 'plotted against' 'discussed a serious matter' 'thought about something hard(usually with bad intentions)' 'backside/anus of' 'made do/sufficed'. Cp: daaberat, daabeirat. (Josh.19:12)

Gittah-hepher; (Gath-hepher); gaṯ haḥēper; قَت هَخيفَر 'qat-look, it is musty'; قَت هَحيفَر 'qat-I will dig'; غَت هَخيفَر 'he dosed off/fell asleep-here, it became musty' 'she deceived/misled(to downfall)-I will make musty'; غَت هَحيفَر 'he dosed off-I will dig' 'he fell into sleep-I will dig' 'she deceived/misled-look, was dug/I will dig'. Cp: qat ha-kheypher, qat ha-ḥeypher, ghat ha-kheypher, ghat ha-ḥeypher. (Josh.19:13)

Ittah-kazin; 'ēt qāṣîn; نيت خاَزين ، يَتخاَزين 'chew(s) qat' 'store qat' and describes the act of chewing qat, storing it in the cheek while spending the afternoon in a social gathering, 'it/she/you-stores' 'it/she/you-insults/swears at' 'came-stores/insults/swears at' 'came-insulted/ashamed'; ئِت/ئيت قاَصين 'came/brought-told stories' 'came/brought-hard/stiffened' 'came/brought-cutting/cut' 'came/brought-hardened hearts/cruel'; ئِت/ئيت قاَشين 'came/brought-burnt remains/litter/fibres' 'came-scraped away/removed in one go' 'came/brought-petrified/scared stiff'; غيت خاَزين 'dosed off/fell asleep-stored' 'dosed off/fell asleep-chewing qat' 'dosed off-insulted/ashamed' 'she misled/deceived(to downfall)-stored' 'she misled/deceived-chewing qat' 'she misled/deceived-insulted/swears at' 'she misled/deceived-insulted/ashamed'; غيت قاَصين 'dosed off/fell asleep-told stories' 'dosed off/fell asleep-hard/stiffened' 'dosed off/fell asleep-cutting/cut' 'dosed off/fell asleep-hardened hearts/cruel' 'she misled/deceived(to downfall)-told stories' 'she misled/deceived-hard/stiffened' 'she misled/deceived-cutting/cut' 'she misled/deceived-hardened hearts/cruel';

غيت قآشين 'dosed off/fell asleep-burnt remains/litter/fibres' 'dosed off/fell asleep-scraped away/removed in one go' 'she misled/deceived(to downfall)-burnt remains/litter/fibres' 'she misled/deceived-scraped away/ removed in one go' 'dosed off/fell asleep-petrified/scared stiff'. Cp: et/eyt-khaazeen, et/eyt-qaasseen, et/ eyt-qaasheen, gheyt-khaazeen, gheyt-qaasseen, gheyt-qaasheen. (Josh.19:13)

Remmon-Methoar; urmvn hmth'aur; وَرمون همثَّور 'throw down/kill-this/him of bulls' 'throw down/ kill-he is boiled'; وَرمون همذعَور 'throw down/kill-this/him the panicked/terrified'. What this list of word-names and the word names beginning from Josh.19:11: Maralah, Dabbasheth, Sarid, Chisloth-tabor, Daberath, Gittah-hepher and Ittah-kazin, show are the themes for Deborah, Jael and Sisera's story in which the latter in fear for his life rushes to Jael's tent where he asks her to keep a lookout for him, but instead she gives him a false sense of security and lulls him to sleep then kills him. Cp: urmoon ha-mf-aor, urmoon ha-mv'oor. (Josh.19:13)

Neah; nē'â; نيعا ، نيعه 'we understand fully and remember' and is linked to the use of qat (Gittah-hepher/ Ittah-kazin) which helps the people who use it think more clearly and have great ideas, understand things better while using it; 'we learn and remember' 'we warn' 'we contain'; نيغا ، نيغه 'we will mislead him to downfall' 'we will deceive/mislead to downfall' and is still related to the Jael/Sisera story. Cp: ney'ah, ney'a, neyghah, neygha. (Josh.19:13)

Hannathon; ḥannāṯôn; خَنّآثّن 'male-male sex making each other female' 'makes males into female(through male-on-male anal sex)' the word is in plural. Cp: khannaafon. (Josh.19:14)

Jiphthah-el; yiptaḥ-'ēl; يِفتَح ئِل 'opens-the'; يِفضَح ئِل 'a scandal-the/exposes a shame-the'; يِفدَه ئِل 'sacrifices for him-the' 'he/it sacrifices for him-the' (a human sacrifice and is used as verbal expression of the preciousness of the person being (verbally) sacrificed for); يِفذَح ئِل 'it's spicy-the'. Cp: yiphtaḥ-ill, yiphdhaḥ-ill, yiphdah-ill, yiphvaḥ-ill. (Josh.19:14)

Kattath; qaṭṭāṯ; قَطّآف 'picks leaves/stems' 'plucks/picks' 'folded and sewed' 'folded' (it is a fold with a hollow space which allows something such as rope/ribbon/twine to be pushed through it); قَطّآت 'of snipping tips off' 'of applying henna to hands/feet' 'of plastering floors/walls'. Cp: qaṭṭaaf, qaṭṭaat. (Josh.19:15)

Nahallal; nahălāl; نَحيلآل 'we circumcise (males)' 'we purify' 'we declare permissible/purified' 'we sweeten' 'we eat sweet' 'we undress' 'we shed' 'we sit in place of/replace'; نَخيلآل 'pick at teeth with toothpick' 'to sift soil/flour' 'hollowed' 'palm trees'. Cp: naḥailaal, nakhailaal. (Josh.19:15)

Idalah; yid'ălâ; يِضئيله ، يِضئي له/ا 'he lights for him' 'he ablutes for him/it/washes up/purifies for him/it' 'he misleads him/leads him down wrong path/do bad'; يِدعي له/ا 'he calls/shouts for him' 'he curses him' 'he claims for him'. Cp: yidhai-lah(la), yidhailah, yid'ai-lah(la). (Josh.19:15)

Chesulloth; kĕsûllōṯ; كيسُلّوت ، كِسُلّوت 'she became lazy' 'she made lazy' as in influenced others to be lazy; حيصُلّوت ، حِصُلّوت 'she found' (plural findings) 'she summed up/totalled'; غيسُلّوت ، غِسُلّوت 'she washed' (many things are being washed). Cp: kesulloot, keisulloot, ḥessulloot, ḥeissulloot, ghesulloot, gheisulloot. (Josh.19:18)

Shunem; šûnēm; سُنيم 'stood/became/made erect' 'was erected/made erect in front of'; صُنيم 'stood before' 'was erected in front of' 'stood still like a statue'. Cp: suneym, ssuneym. (Josh.19:18)

Hapharaim; ḥăpārayim; حيفآرَي ام ، حَفآرَي ام 'they dug up-the' 'holes of-the'; حيفآرَيم ، حَفآرَيم 'they dug up a river/body of water/sea'; خيفآرَي ام ، خَفآرَي ام 'they made musty/damp-the' 'they mustied/ dampened-the'. Cp: ḥaphaaray-um, ḥaiphaaray-um, ḥaphaara-yim, ḥaiphaara-yim, khaphaaray-um, khaiphaaray-um. (Josh.19:19)

Shion; šî'ōn; سيئون 'bad/evil/offense' 'they will supply' 'they will moan/groan(in pain)'; صيئون 'swept/ brushed' 'swept/brushed away'; شيئون 'something' 'important things/matters' 'filtered/filtered impurities out of'. Cp: see-oon/seeoon, ssee-oon/sseeoon, shee-oon/sheeoon. (Josh.19:19)

Anaharath; 'ănāḥărāṯ; ئيناَخيرآت ، ئَنآخَرآت 'the nostrils' 'she snored' 'the riddled with holes' 'the bored with holes/made hollow' 'where is-plenty'; ئيناَحيرآض ، ئَنآحَرآض 'we will incite against' 'where did-incite against'; ئيناَحيرآث ، ئَنآحَرآث 'we will frown' 'where did-frown'; ئيناهيرآث ، ئَنآهَرآث 'we will inherit' 'where will we inherit'. Cp: anaakharaat, ainaakhairaat, anaaḥaraadh, ainaaḥairaadh, anaaḥaraaf, ainaaḥairaaf, anaaharaaf, ainaahairaaf. (Josh.19:19)

Rabbith; rabbîṯ; رَبّيت 'brought up/brought up properly' 'grew/raised' 'grew well' 'disciplined' 'mixed and diluted with water'; رَبّيط 'tied' 'tyings' 'ropes'. Cp: rabbeet, rabbeeṭ. (Josh.19:20)

Kishion; qišyôn; قِشيُن 'paralysed with fear/joy/petrified' 'litter/fibres/burnt remnants' 'scrape away/remove in one go' 'became crispy'; قِصيُن 'hardened' 'cruel' 'cut up' 'told story/news'; كِسيُن 'were clothed(gifted/bought new clothes)' 'covered/wrapped with fabric'. Cp: qishyon, qissyon, kisyon. (Josh.19:20)

Abez; 'eḇeṣ; نَبَز 'I take' 'took' 'lactating breasts(human)' 'breastfeed' 'was breastfed'. Cp: ebez. (Josh.19:20)

Remeth; remeṯ; رَمَت 'threw/she threw' 'killed/she killed' 'saw death'. Cp: remet. (Josh.19:21)

En-haddah; 'ên ḥaddâ; عين حَدّه/ا ، ئين حَدّه/ا 'look/pay attention-it's/his border' 'look/pay attention-sharpened it' 'he/it will-border it' 'he/it will-sharpen it' 'look/pay attention/beware-it's his limits(in patience or literal)' 'where are his/its borders/limits'; عين خَدّه/ا ، ئين خَدّه/ا 'look/pay attention-his cheek' 'look/pay attention-he/it pulled it down/off' 'look/pay attention-removed bread from oven wall' 'he/it will-pull it down/off' 'he/it will-remove bread from oven wall' 'where is his cheek'; عين هَدّه/ا ، ئين هَدّه/ا 'look/pay attention-demolished it' 'look/pay attention-he/it demolished it' 'it will-collapse'. Cp: 'eyn ḥaddah(da), eyn ḥaddah(da), 'eyn khaddah(da), eyn khaddah(da), 'eyn haddah(da), eyn haddah(da). (Josh.19:21)

Beth-pazzez; bêṯ paṣṣēṣ; بيت بَزّيز 'he/it will pick up heavy loads' 'girl/daughter-lactating breasts/breastfeeding'; بيت فَصّيص 'he/it will remove pits/stones(from fruit)' 'he/it will disentangle knots' 'he will disentangle matters/explain clearly' 'he/it will separate' 'he will divorce/separate' 'girl-removing stones (from fruit)' 'girl-disentangle knots'; بيت فَسّيس 'he/it will pass wind' 'he/it will copulate/pass wind into(like cockerel 'passes wind' in hen copulation)' 'girl-passing wind' 'girl- copulate/pass wind into(like cockerel 'passes wind' in hen copulation)'. Cp: beyt-bazzeyz, beyt-phasseyss, beyt-phasseys (Josh.19:21)

Shahazimah; šaḥăṣûmâ; شَحَزُمه ، شَحيزُمه 'I will tie it together/bind it' 'I will bundle it' it is used to describe tying a bundle of firewood together or sheaths of crop for carrying home; شَهَزُمه ، شَهيزُمه 'I will defeat him/it'. Cp: shaḥazumah, shaḥaizumah, shahazumah, shahaizumah. (Josh.19:22)

Beth-shemesh; bêṯ šemeš; بيت شَمَس 'he/it will be possessed/touched' 'he will be entangled/provoked/in fight' 'he/it will sunbathe'; بيت شَمَش 'he/it will smell you'. Cp: beyt-shemes, beyt-shemesh. (Josh.19:22)

Helkath; ḥelqaṯ; حَلقَت 'put arms around' 'hugged' 'shaved' 'circled/encircled' 'a ring/circle'; هَلقَت 'here she found' 'here she threw'; هَلقَط 'here, he picked up' 'I will pick up'; هَلكَت 'she died/perished' 'the perishing of' 'see, she chewed'. Cp: ḥelqat, helqat, helqaṭ, helkat. (Josh.19:25)

Hali; ḥălî; حَلي ، حيلي 'became purified/purified/circumcised/made edible/made clean' 'declared permissible/purified' 'shed' 'undress/undressed' 'sweet/became sweet/sweeten' 'persuade by behaving sweetly' 'tricks/deceit' 'deceive' 'play tricks on' 'replaced'; خَلي ، خيلي 'emptied/empty it' 'left some' 'left it' 'leave some' 'leave it alone' 'allow/allowed' 'imagine' 'daydream' 'hallucinating'. Cp: ḥa-lee, ḥailee, khalee, khailee. (Josh.19:25)

Beten; beṭen; بَطَن ، بِطِن 'stomach' 'got stomach illness' 'underlayer of dress' 'mattress(blankets and other fabrics used as mattress)' 'created layers under'. Cp: beṭen. (Josh.19:25)

Alammelech; 'allammelek; عَلَّمّ لَك 'he showed you' 'he signalled you' 'he left you a mark'; عَلَّمّ عليك 'he told on you' 'he put people up to harm you'; نَلَمّ لَك 'I gather/save for you'; نَلَمّ عليك 'gathered against you/I gather against you'. (Josh.19:26)

Amad; 'am'āḏ; عَم عاد 'uncle/drank/blind-returned' 'uncle/drank/blind-counted' uncle/drank/blind-made enemy(ies)/enmity; عَمئاَد 'stood/positioned itself/himself' 'landed on' 'on purpose/intentionally'. Cp: 'am-'aad, 'am-aad. (Josh.19:26)

Misheal; miš'āl; مِشعال 'walked on/above' 'not on/above/about' 'ablaze'; مِسعال 'of coughing/has cough/coughing'; مِسئال 'questioning' 'did not ask' 'flowed/flowing/leaked/leaking'. Cp: mish'aal, mis'aal, mis-aal. (Josh.19:26)

Shihor libnath; šîḥôr liḇnāṯ; شيحُر لِبنات/لبناد 'became desert-for girls/she added milk' 'became scarce-for building' 'became desert-for closing/closed' (see Sihor(Josh.13:3) for more possible combinations of word 'Shihor'); شيهُر لِبنات/لبناد 'a month/months-for girls/she added milk' 'a month/months-for building' 'a month/months-for closing/closed'. Cp: sheeḥor-libnaat, sheeḥor-libnaad, sheehor-libnaat, sheehor-libnaad. (Josh.19:26)

Bethemek; bêṯ ha'ēmeq; بيت هَغيمَق 'it/he will-look/pay attention-went deeper(below liquid or any substance)' 'daughter/girl-look/pay attention-pushed her deeper(below liquid or any substance)' 'it/he will-look/pay attention-covered face(to hide or conceal identity)' 'daughter/girl-look/pay attention-he covered her face' 'it/he will-look/pay attention-smothered/covered mouth and nose' 'daughter/girl-look/pay attention-he smothered her/covered her mouth and nose' 'it/he will-look/pay attention-dips repeatedly' 'daughter/girl-look/pay attention-he dipped her repeatedly'; بيت هَعيمَك 'he/it will-look/pay attention-give you to drink/blind you' 'daughter/girl-look/pay attention-give you to drink/blind you'; بيت حَنيمَق 'it/he will be foolish/stupid' 'daughter/girl-foolish/made a fool of'. Cp: beyt-ha-gheymeq, beyt-ha-'eymek, beyt-ḥa-eymeq. (Josh.19:27)

Neiel; nĕʻîʼēl; نيعي ئِل 'we understand and remember-the' 'we make understood-the' 'we learn/teach and remember-the' 'we warn-the'; نيغي ئِل 'we mislead/deceive to downfall-the'. Cp: nei'ee-ill, neighee-ill. (Josh.19:27)

Cabal; kāḇûl; كعبُل 'try/go ahead-fill the' 'already-filled the'; قآبُل 'stood/positioned in front of/opposite' 'before' 'accepted' 'good in quality of material, or a person in character, or honest that they meet acceptance/are accepted/desired' 'accepted reluctantly'. Cp: k'bul, qaabul. (Josh.19:27)

Hammon; ḥammôn; حَمّن 'heated' 'they heated' 'made clearing throat sound (ḥmḥm)' 'muttered' 'made 'homhom' noise while speaking' 'eating greedily/quickly with noise'; خَمّن 'guessed' 'spoke nasally' 'spoke unclearly' (words could not be heard properly because spoken nasally or from throat/chest); هَمّن 'they worried' 'a worry'. Cp: ḥammon, khammon, hammon. (Josh.19:28)

Tyre; ṣōr; صور 'made image' 'sculpted image' 'created image/likeness or pattern, etc.' 'left over food' 'left over anything/second-hand(things)' 'aching pain in teeth/bones' 'imagine(ed)' 'it aches' Cp: ssoor. (Josh.19:29)

Hosah; ḥōsâ; حوسه/ا 'crooked footed' 'inward footed' 'feel/touch(it)'; حوزه/ا 'corner/cram/prevent from moving forward'; حوصه/ا 'stuck' 'a problem'. Cp: ḥowsah(sa)/ḥoosah(sa), ḥoozah(za)/ḥowzah(za), ḥoossah(ssa)/ḥowssah(ssa). (Josh.19:29)

Ummah; ʻummâ; عومّه/ا 'drank' 'drink/drink it(said to plural)' 'blind/blinded' 'his uncle' 'aunt'; ئومّه 'his/its mother' 'mother' 'a nation/a lot of people' 'threaded needle' 'led/led people through'. Cp: 'oomah(ma), oomah(ma). (Josh:19:30)

Rehob; rĕḥôḇ, rĕḥōḇ; رَحُب ، ريحُب ، رَحوب ، ريحوب 'welcome/welcomed' 'spacious/made space' 'of spaciousness/of welcoming'; رَكُب ، ريكُب ، رَكوب ، ريكوب 'rid/got on top of' 'of riding/of getting on top of' 'knees'. Cp: reḥob, reiḥob, reḥoob, reiḥoob, rekob, reikob, rekoob, reikoob. (Josh.19:30)

Heleph; ḥēlep; حيلَف 'swore an oath' 'a herb/spice' (called ḥlph); هيلَف 'he will gather' 'he will wrap' 'he will get used to' 'he will develop habit'; خيلَف 'changed' as in clothes or things, to swap something, 'poured water from one vessel to another' (so that the emptied vessel can be used for a chore). Cp: ḥeyleph, heyleph, kheyleph. (Josh.19:33)

Zaanannim; ṣaʻănannîm; زَعَنَّ هم/ام ، زَعينَنّ هم/ام 'was able to force-them/the'; ضَعينَنّ هم/ام 'tired-them/the' 'made tired-them/the'; ذَغينَنّ/شَغينَنّ هم/ام 'this/it/him/I will sing for-them/the' 'this/it/him/I will make sing-them/the' 'it/he/I will no longer need-them/the' 'I will make rich-them/the'; صَنَنّ/صَنئينَنّ هم/ام 'sweeped/swept-them/the' 'put into small bowls-them/the'. Cp: za'anann-hum/um, za'ainann-hum/um, dhaghainann-hum/um, vaghainann-hum/um, shaghainann-hum/um, ssa-anann-hum/um, ssa-ainann-hum/um. (Josh.19:33)

Adami; 'ădāmî; نَدآمي ، نيدآمي 'make last long' 'of blood' 'make bleed' 'upkeep'; عَدآمي ، عيدآمي 'my perishing/my death/may I die' 'of nothing/of scarcity/became nothing' 'my scarcity'; عَضآمي ، عيضآمي 'my bones' 'of bones'. Cp: adaamee, aidaamee, 'adaamee, 'aidaamee, 'adhaamee, 'aidhaamee. (Josh.19:33)

Nekeb; neqeḇ; نَقَب 'dig holes with repeated striking motion' 'sharp repeated pain (in bones or head)'; نَقَف 'chipped at' 'removed by chipping at with a chisel' 'sharp pain in bones/teeth'; نَكَف 'abused and made example of' 'teased/abused in front of others' 'mistreated'; نَكَث 'pour out contents of fire or a vessel where things were burned or used for storing hot coals' 'pour out coal and ashes (anything left behind a fire)' 'pick with stick or tongs between live hot coals or remnants of a fire that has died out' 'revoke/undo(agreement/promise,etc.)'; نَجَث 'fire poker/rod or stick used to poke fire' 'poked fire' 'we dry' 'pounded or poked so hard it hurts' 'struck with rod'; نَكَب 'pour out in one go' non-liquid substances 'pour onto the ground'; نَخَب 'contents burst out of bottom (container/sack/person who soils himself)' 'big pile of something left on ground'. Cp: neqeb, neqeph, nekeph, nekef, negef, nekeb, nekheb. (Josh.19:33)

Lakum; laqqûm; لَقَّم 'hand-fed' 'morsels' 'add ingredients to boiling kettle(through kettle mouth/opening'; لَكّم 'punched' 'for you(plural)'; لَخم 'spitting sputum' 'sputum'. Cp: laqqum, lakkum, lakhum. (Josh.19:33)

Aznoth-tabor; 'aznôṯ tāḇôr; نَزنَت تآبُر 'committed adultery-ruins reputation/becomes bad/gets bad reputation/spoiled'; نَصنَت تآبُر 'eavesdrop(ped)-ruins reputation/becomes bad/gets bad reputation/spoiled'; نَذنَت

تَابَر 'ears/handles of-ruins reputation/becomes bad/gets bad reputation/spoiled' 'announced loudly-ruins reputation/becomes bad/gets bad reputation/spoiled'. Cp: aznot taabor, a<u>ss</u>not taabor, avnot taabor. (Josh.19:34)

Hukkok; ḥûqōq; حُقوق 'rights/belongs to' 'right/truths' 'necklaces' and the necklaces are made of beads of ivory, coral and other natural gems' 'shells(sea shells)'; حُكوك 'itchy/itching/scratching'; حُقوك 'yours/ belong to you' 'your hips'. Cp: ḥuqooq, ḥukook, ḥuqook. (Josh.19:34)

Ziddim; ṣiddîm; زِدّهم/ام 'give more-them/the' 'deceive-them/the'; سِدّهم/ام 'their/the dam' 'settle/resolve-them/the'; صِد هم/ام 'prevent/block-them/the'. Cp: zidd-hum/um, sidd-hum/um, <u>ss</u>idd-hum/um. (Josh.19:35)

Zer; ṣēr; زير 'visit' 'pilgrimage' 'tight/tighten'; سير 'go/leave/walk' 'will see'; صير 'a throbbing pain' (such as in bones or sensitive teeth' 'a whistling-ringing sound' 'knot/bundle/hold within' 'insist'. Cp: zeyr, seyr, <u>ss</u>eyr. (Josh.19:35)

Hammath; ḥammaṯ; حَمَّط 'filled with grain flakes' 'persistent tickle in throat or chest/persistent light cough'; حَمَّض 'soured' and the process of adding one or two drops of churned milk to pure milk to turn it into yoghurt/curds (for churning). Cp: ḥammaṭ, ḥamma<u>dh</u>. (Josh.19:35)

Rakkath; raqqaṯ; رَقَّت 'narrowed/thinned' 'became narrow' 'flowed/poured' 'urinated'; رَكَّت 'she leaned against/she leaned it against' 'became weak'. Cp: raqqat, rakkat. (Josh.19:35)

Adamah; 'ădāmâ; نَدآمه/ا ، نيدآمه/ا 'made it last long' 'of his blood' 'made it/him bleed' 'upkeep'; عَدآمه/ا ، عيدآمه/ا 'his/its perishing/his/its death' 'may he/it die' 'his/its scarcity'; عَضآمه/ا ، عيضآمه/ا 'his/its bones'. Cp: adaamah(ma), aidaamah(ma), 'adaamah(ma), 'aidaamah(ma), 'a<u>dh</u>aamah(ma), 'ai<u>dh</u>aamah(ma). (Josh.19:33)

En-hazor; 'ên ḥāṣôr; عين ، نين 'eye/pay attention/look' 'it/he will/where' followed by the meanings of 'hazor': هاضُر 'I will harm'; حاذُر 'warn(ed)' 'beware of' 'was cautious'; حَاصُر 'surround(ed)' 'great sorrow/despair'; حَاضُر 'prepare(d)' 'ripen(ed)'; حاسُر 'became thin' 'made thin'. Cp: 'eyn/eyn haa<u>dh</u>or, 'eyn/ eyn ḥaavor, 'eyn/eyn ḥaa<u>ss</u>or, 'eyn/eyn ḥaa<u>dh</u>or, 'eyn/eyn ḥaasor. (Josh.19:37)

Iron; yir'ôn; يرئن 'they see' 'they understand' 'they water'; يرعُن 'they shepherd/take care of'. Cp: yir-on, yir'on. (Josh.19:38)

Migdal-el; migdal'ēl; مِجدَل ئِل 'thrown-the' 'the throwing of-the' 'throwing place(means from a high place)-the' 'the fits/possession by demon-the' 'wooden block/wedge-the'; مِغطَل ئِل 'killed/killing of-the' 'squeezed to death-the' 'the squeezing to death of-the'; مِغدَل ئِل 'glands swollen-the' 'fed lunch-the'. Cp: migdal-ill, mi<u>gh</u>ṭal-ill, mi<u>gh</u>dal-ill. (Josh.19:38)

Horem; ḥŏrēm; حوريم ، حويريم 'was forbidden/prevented' 'rotted/stank' 'became sacred' 'women'; هوريم ، هويريم 'driven/chased away from' 'he/they were thrown' 'he threw' 'he killed'; خوريم ، خويريم 'pierced/ was pierced' 'burst from bottom'. Cp: ḥooreym, ḥ<u>oi</u>reym, hooreym, h<u>oi</u>reym, <u>kh</u>ooreym, <u>kh</u>**oi**reym. (Josh.19:38)

Beth-anath; bêṯ-ănaṯ; بيتَنَث/بيتانَث ، بيتينَث 'he will become effeminate/female' as in take on characteristics of females. بيت عَنَد 'he will become stubborn/spiteful/provoking'. Cp: beyt-anaf/beytanaf, beyt-ainaf, beyt-'anad. (Josh.19:38)

Ir-shemesh; 'îr-šemeš; عير شَمَس 'disgrace/gloat-possess/touch' 'disgrace/gloat-entangle/provoke/fight' 'disgrace/gloat-sunbathe'; عير شَمَش 'disgrace/gloat-smell you'. Cp: 'eer-<u>sh</u>emes, 'eer-<u>sh</u>eme<u>sh</u>. (Josh.19:41)

Shaalabbin; ša'albîm; شَعَلب هم/ام 'will plant ilb trees-them/the' 'will feed them on ilb trees'; شَئَلبين 'I will add milk', شَغَلب هم/ام 'I will victor over-them/the' 'I will frustrate-them/the' 'I will make them feel remorse/bitter/envy'. Cp: <u>sh</u>a'alb-hum/um, <u>sh</u>a-albeen, <u>sh</u>a<u>gh</u>alb-hum/um. (Josh.19:42)

Jethlah; yitlâ; يذلح 'he/it is winnowing'; يتله 'he is orating/reading aloud/reciting it'. Cp: yivlaḥ, yitlah. (Josh.19:42)

Thimnathah; timnātâ; ثِمناذه 'the eighth of this' 'the value of this' 'price this'; ضمناذه ، ضمنآته 'guaranteed him/this' 'depended on him/this' 'part of this' 'guaranteed/secured-him/it'; طِمناذه ، طمنآته 'reassured of this' 'reassured him' 'trusted him'. Cp: (Josh.19:43)

Eltekeh; 'eltĕqēh; ئَلتَقيه ، ئَلتيقيه 'meet him' 'connect it' 'snap it shut/make it stick' (like a clip), 'the pious/ the piety'. Cp: elteqeyh, elteiqeyh. (Josh.19:44)

Gibbethon; gibbĕṯôn; جِبِّذُن ، جِبّيذُن 'pulled upwards' 'helped someone upwards' it is the word to describe helping someone up to a higher place by grabbing them by the forearm and pulling them up. Cp: gibbevon, gibbeivon. (Josh.19:44)

Baalath; baʿălāṯ; بَعيلاّت 'I/it on top of/went to top of' 'I/it made higher' 'spouses of'; بَعيلاّف 'I/it will gather leaves' 'I/it will eat leaves'; بَعيلاّط 'I/it will stick together' 'I/it will strip leaves off'; بَغيلاّط 'I/it deceives/ shortchanges/cons/lies' 'I/it makes mistake/does wrong'. Cp: ba'ailaat, ba'ailaaph, ba'ailaaṭ, baghailaaṭ. (Josh.19:44)

Jehud; yĕhûḏ; يَهُد ، ييهُد 'demolishes/collapses', 'Jehud' could also be the meaning of the word 'jew' which I will explain later in the book where there is more evidence from the Bible; عَهُد ، عيهُد 'made a pledge/ promise'; يَحُد ، ييحُد 'he/it sharpens'. Cp: yehud, yeihud, 'ehud, 'eihud, yeḥud, yeiḥud. (Josh.19:45)

Bene-berak; bĕnê-ḇĕraq; بَني/بيني بَرَق/بيرَق 'children/of-moody/sulking' 'in me-moody/sulking' 'became clear/apparent-moody/sulking' and is from the word (brq/برق) which means 'lightning/a lightning stroke', and (bn/بن) 'child' 'in/inside' 'became apparent': it means a person who is moody, easily offended, then refuses to talk with people and especially those he/she is upset by, or only talks reluctantly to show his/her displeasure/upset; the word means his/her personality and mood can change and be offended as quick as a lightning stroke. Cp: beney/beiney beraq/beiraq. (Josh.19:45)

Gath-rimmon; gaṯ rimmôn; قَت رِمُّن 'qat-thrown/was thrown/was killed' 'qat-rotten'; جعث رِمُّن 'sufferance/trouble-thrown/killed' 'sufferance/trouble-rotten'; غت رِمُّن 'misled to downfall/deceived/deceit/ folly-thrown/killed' 'misled to downfall/deceived/deceit/folly-rotten' 'dosed off/fell asleep-thrown/was thrown/killed'. Cp: qat rimmon, g'f rimmon, ghat rimmon. (Josh.19:45)

Me-jarkon; mê hayyarqôn; مي هَيَّرقُن 'water-he/they will-flow/pour' 'he will pass water/urinate' 'water will flow'; مي هَعَّرقُن 'water-he will make sweat' 'well, I will sweat' 'water-veins will pop up' 'water-roots will grow'; مي هَيَّركُن 'water-he will lean it against' 'well, he will/will he-depend on'. Cp: mey-hayyarqon, mey-ha'arqon, mey-hayyarkon. (Josh.19:46)

Rakkon; raqqôn; رَكُّن 'leaned against/leaned it against' 'depended on' 'corner/put in corner' 'weak/became weaker'; رَقُّن 'narrowed/made narrower' 'flowed in narrow stream (of liquid)'. Cp: rakkon, raqqon. (Josh.19:46)

Japho; yāpô; جاَفو ، جاَف 'turned upside down' (so as to dry or allow to trickle out), 'dried'. Cp: gaaphow, gaapho. (Josh.19:46)

Leshem; lešem; لَش ام 'why the'; لَزَم 'held tightly/strong/firmly' 'necessary' 'obligatory' and the story has the children of Dan needing a larger inheritance so they go kill more people to take their land. Cp: lesh-um, lezem. (Josh.19:47)

Timnath-serah; timnaṯ-seraḥ; طِمنَت صَرَح 'the reassurance-spoke openly' and refers to Joshua openly asking for this specific place and getting it. Cp: ṭimnat sseraḥ. (Josh.19:50)

Galilee; gālîl; جاَليل 'came-to' 'came-for' 'came-the/for the' and refers to a person fleeing from manslaughter he has committed and arriving at the suitable named area of 'Galilee'; جاَل يل 'cleared-the' 'made clear-the' as he has to clearly declare what he has committed. Cp: gaaleel, gaal-eel. (Josh.20:7)

Anathoth; 'ănāṯôṯ; ئيناَذُف 'he/it will push off cliff/high place'; نَناَذُف 'pushes off cliff/high place'; ئيناَضُف 'will clean/cleanse'; عيناَدُد 'fierce/stubborn/provocative'; ئيناَثُث ، ئيناَثث 'femininity of' 'became female/ feminine'. Cp: ainaavoph, anaavoph, ainaadhoph, 'ainaadod, ainaafot, ainaafof. (Josh.21:18)

Almon; 'almôn; عَلمُن 'marked' 'showed' 'signalled' 'taught' 'knowledge' 'knew/found out'. Cp: 'almon. (Josh.21:18)

Kibzaim; qiḇṣayim; قِبصَي ام 'pinch-the' 'quote-the'; خِبصَي ام 'poked finger(s) into' 'poked finger into anus' 'dipped fingers into food' 'polluted food by dipping fingers into it' 'made a mess'; كِبسَي ام 'bury with ashes-the'. Cp: qibssay-um, khibssay-um, kibsay-um. (Josh.21:22)

Beesh-tarah; bĕʿeštĕrâ; بيشتيره/ا 'he will purchase it/he purchased it with'; بي نَش تيره/ا 'with what do you/does she see him' 'what do you see him with'; بيعِش تيره/ا 'he will live-you will see him/you will see'. Cp: bei-eshteirah(ra), bei-esh-teirah(ra), bei'esh-teirah(ra). (Josh.21:27)

Kishon; qîšôn; قيشُن 'they/he was petrified' (could be from fear or joy/laughter), 'litter/fibres/burnt remnants' 'burnt stiff/toasted' 'became stiff' 'removed in one go' 'were swept away/scraped away like minute litter'; قيصُن 'told stories/news' 'cut up/cut' 'hard/hardened' 'cruel'; كيسُن 'wrapped/enveloped' 'in wrap/ cased' 'clothed/new clothes' 'covered with fabric'. Cp: qeeshon, qeesson, keeson. (Josh.21:28)

Dabareh; dāḇĕraṯ; دآبيرَت ، دآبِرَت 'brought ill fate upon' 'plotted against' 'discussed a serious matter' 'thought about something hard(usually with bad intentions)' 'the backside/anus of' 'made do(with)/ sufficed'. Cp: daaberat, daabeirat. (Josh.21:28)

Mishal; miš'āl; مِش عآل 'not high' 'not on' 'not about'; مِسئآل 'a questioning' 'did not ask' 'flowed/flowing/ leaking(ed)' 'entertaining/entertainment/distraction/comforting' 'topics/matters'. Cp: mish'aal, mis-aal. (Josh.21:30)

Abdon; 'aḇdôn; عَبدُن 'worshipper' 'servant'; نَبدُن 'bring out/come out' 'never' 'massacre/wipe out'. Cp: 'abdon, abdon. (Josh.21:30)

Hammoth-dor; ḥammōṯ dō'r; حَمّوط دوئر 'flakes(off grains)-all around/spin/search/potter'; هَمّوت دوئر 'she worried-searched/spun/circled/potter'; حَمّوت دوئر 'she heated-searched/spun/circled/potter'. Cp: ḥammooṭ doo-ir, hammoot doo-ir, ḥammoot doo-ir. (Josh.21:32)

Kartan; qārtân; قآرتهن ، قآرتَن 'she read them' 'she admitted to them' 'she told about them' 'she made them stop/stop moving/misbehaving'; قآرطهن ، قآرطَن 'he/it bit them/closed his teeth on them' 'got pinched between'. Cp: qaart-hun, qaartan, qaarṭhun, qaarṭan. (Josh.21:32). Abdon, Kartan and Kartah are initial ideas for the story which evolves into Saul visiting a witch.

Kartah; qartâ; قَرته 'she read it' 'she admitted to it/to him' 'she made him/it stop moving/stop misbehaving'; قَرطه 'a bite/a closing of the teeth/nipping something'. Cp: qartah, qarṭah. (Josh.21:34)

Dimnah; dimnâ; دِمنه 'we lasted' 'we stayed long' 'our blood' 'we bled'. Cp: dimnah. (Josh.21:35)

Ed; 'yd; عيد 'return' 'go back to' 'bring back' 'festival/celebration' and refers to the story which the word 'return' features repeatedly as Joshua repeatedly tells the tribes of Reuben, Gad and the half tribe of Manasseh to return to their allotted places, then after the priests are sent to check on them for disobedience the priests return, it is also bringing in the word 'Ed/عيد' as it features in 'Gilead' as 'festival' (with slaughter and sacrifice) in Genesis and is where the above mentioned tribes have been sent and where the altar is built and named in the same manner as Gilead/Galeed story. Cp: 'yd/'eed. (Josh.22:34)

Gaash; gā'aš; جآئَش 'picked a lot/took too much' 'many people' and the story creators wanted to remind the audience why Joshua was named so at the beginning: because he was asked to pick men to fight the Amaleks, and at the end of his story: 'And Joshua gathered all the tribes of Israel to Shechem, and called for the elders of Israel, and for their heads, and for their judges; and for their officers; and they presented themselves before God.' And he dies after gathering all these people and reminding them of the statutes and they bury him in the suitably named Gaash which has the same meaning as his character name. It could also be جآعَش 'of wild/untamed beard or hair' but it does not fit the story. Cp: gaa-ash, gaa'ash. (Josh.24)

Judges

Bezek; bezeq; بَزَق 'passed by' 'passed in front of' 'pass time' 'divide something into smaller portions' 'scatter/spread small portions of the same thing across various places' and refers to killing of 'ten thousand men' who seem to die as simply as one passes by. Cp: bezeq. (Judg.1:4)

Adoni-bezek; 'ăḏōnî-ḇezeq; نَضوني بَزَق 'here I am/here I have done-divided into small pieces/scattered'; نَذوني بَزَق 'they harmed me-divided into small pieces/scattered'. Both meanings are directly narrated in the story as the king of the same name is subject to parts of his body being cut off in small pieces 'and cut off his thumbs and his great toes.' Cp: a<u>dh</u>oonee-bezeq, avoonee-bezeq. (Judg.1:5-7)

Zephath; ṣĕp̄aṯ; صِفَت ، صيفَت 'became clean/clear' 'cleaned/cleared' 'settled (scores/differences)' 'rocks of/stones of' 'stacked rocks/stones' 'rock columns of' 'made into rows/columns' 'flattered' 'insulted/described negatively'; سِفَت ، سيفَت 'poured gently/poured gentle spurts of water' 'became numb' 'numbed' 'carried gently/with care'; زِفَت ، زيفَت 'escorted by procession/entourage'. Cp: <u>ss</u>e<u>ph</u>at, <u>ss</u>eiphat, se<u>ph</u>at, sei<u>ph</u>at, ze<u>ph</u>at, zei<u>ph</u>at. (Judg.1:17)

Ashkelon; 'ašqĕlôn; نَشقِلُن ، نَشقيلُن 'hang up/hang from ropes/rings' a way to store produce (meat/fish/butter/yoghurt/herbs/vegetables) out of the way of animals/insects and to dry them/cool them (so they do not rot). نَسقِلُن ، نَسقيلُن 'water(water plants/crops) for them'. Cp: a<u>sh</u>qelon, a<u>sh</u>qeilon, asqelon, asqeilon. (Judg.1:18)

Kitron; qiṭrôn; قِطرُن 'drips' 'they drip' 'tar-like substance used for sealing things'; قِظرُن 'they are disgusting' 'disgusting/repulsive' 'they are disgusted by'. Cp: qiṭron, qi<u>dh</u>ron. (Judg.1:30)

Nahalol; nahălōl; نَحَلول ، نَحيلول 'circumcise' 'purify' 'declare permissible/purified' 'sweeten' 'eat sweet' 'undress' 'shed' 'sit in place of' 'replace'; نَخَلُل ، نَخيلول 'leave' 'let/allow' 'pick at teeth with toothpick' 'to sift soil/flour'. Cp: naḥailol, naḥalol, na<u>kh</u>ailol, na<u>kh</u>alol (Judg.1:30)

Accho; 'akkû; عَقّ 'too salty' 'disobedient' 'became disobedient' 'cruel' 'became cruel'; عَكّ 'extremely difficult' 'had great difficulty' 'tried to force/did not know what they were doing'. Cp: 'aqqu, 'akku. (Judg.1:31)

Ahlab; 'aḥlāḇ; نَحلآب 'milking' 'for milking' 'eating fenugreek dip' 'stomach ache(from eating then being exposed to cold weather or wind)'. Cp: aḥlaab. (Judg.1:31)

Helbah; ḥelbâ; حِلبه/ا 'fenugreek' 'fenugreek dip' used as a side dish, its seeds are also toasted and used to flavour leavened and unleavened bread, 'milked it'. Cp: ḥelbah(ba). (Judg.1:31)

Heres; ḥāres; حارَز 'thorny bushes' it is a specific type of bush with long spines of thorns; هارَص 'I will stack/pack'. Cp: ḥaarez, haare<u>ss</u>. (Judg.1:35)

Shaalbim; ša'albîm; شَعَلب هم/ام 'will plant ilb trees-them/the' 'will feed them on ilb trees'; شَنَلبين 'I will add milk'; شَغَلب هم/ام 'I will victor over them/the' 'I will frustrate them/the' 'I will make them feel remorse/bitter/envy'; سَئَل ذيم 'asked-the ostracised/guilted'. Cp: <u>sh</u>a'alb-hum/um, <u>sh</u>a-albeen, <u>sh</u>a<u>gh</u>alb-hum/um, sa-al-veem. (Judg.31)

Aijalon; 'ayyālôn; نَجّآلُن 'delayed'; عَجّآلُن 'hurried/rushed' 'calf'. Cp: aggaalon, 'aggaalon. (Judg.1:)

Bochim; bōḵîm; بوك هم/ام 'went out/went/took them to/go/leave/left-them/the' and is exactly what God is saying through the angel (bringing them out of Egypt, driving the native inhabitants out of the land) and why the word-name created is 'Bochim'. A later editor who possibly did not understand the meaning of the word 'boch/leave/go' or did but wanted to add more wordplay added the 'and wept' giving the meaning 'made weep-them/the'. Cp: book-hum/um. (Judg.2:1-5)

Timnath-heres; timnaṯ-ḥeres ; طِمنَت حَرَز 'the reassurance-thorny bushes'; طِمنَت هَرَص 'the reassurance-I will stack/pack' and refers to Joshua's inheritance which in the last chapter of Joshua was 'Timnath-serah' (the reassurance-spoke openly) has now been changed to suit the narration of '…they shall be as thorns in your sides, and their gods shall be a snare to you.' and that he has been packed into his grave. Cp: ṭimnat ḥerez, ṭimnat here<u>ss</u>. (Judg.2:9)

Baalim; bĕʿālîm; بَعلهم ، بَعل هم/ام ، بيعلهم ، بيعل هم/ام 'their higher places' 'upon-them/the' 'higher/above-them/the' 'with/at their higher places' 'their spouses' 'spouse-them/the'. Cp: be'lhum, be'l-hum/um, bei'lhum, bei'l-hum/um. (Judg.2:11)

Ashtaroth; ʿaštārôṯ; عَشتآرُت ‘raised its/her tail’ describes a cow lifting her tail to be copulated or to excrete; نَشطآرُط/نَشتآرُط ‘teared/split’ ‘put conditions on’. What is interesting is that in all pagan worship, and similarly in monotheistic worship, there is always ‘conditions’ for receiving something in return. E.g. when one asks for fertility, health, blessings (in pagan worship) a condition is made to bring the worshipped deity/object a specific amount of produce in return if the wish is granted; the same when a ‘Nazer’ is made in monotheistic worship asking for help with something and tithes or offers, or even obedience, are made in return; the same applies to fasting, sacrificing in return for blessings, forgiveness etc. to a divine God—blessings, good fortune, heaven/hell are all on condition for specific behaviour. In Judges 2, the narration relays the people did not stick to the conditions which God set, so this God does not keep his end of the bargain, but does keep the negative part of the condition (allowing native inhabitants to remain in the land alongside the incoming settlers) to punish the people for not sticking to the set conditions. Cp: ’ashtaarot, ashṭaaroṭ, ashtaaroṭ. (Judg.2)

Chushan-rishthaim; kûšan rišʿāṯayim; قُصَن رِشئآتَيهم/ام ‘cut their feathers’ ‘cut feathers of-the’ and is an adage which has the same meaning as ‘cut them down to size/put them in their place’, and is what happens in the story when the people continued to disobey God, where God enslaves them to the suitably named ‘Chusan-rishthaim’ and this word-naming also suits as punishment in reverse against the same-named king when God changes his mind and frees the people and has revenge on the king. As is the method of the Biblical authors, even the land this character is made king of in the story is to serve the narration ‘Mesopotamia’; ʿaram nahărāyim; made up of two words one (nahărāyim) used at v.8, and the other (ʿaram) used at v.10 relay with each other and the story being told and both have been translated as ‘Mesopotamia’; عَرَم نَهيرآي ام ‘abandoned-we drove away with cruelty-the’ (abandoned/ ʿaram) (we(did)/na) (drive away with cruelty/hărāy) (the/them/im); also it is wordplay on ‘abandoned-bullied-the’ as (nahărāy) means ‘bullied/ spoke harshly’. Later translators/interpreters would make it into ‘Mesopotamia’ and consider it the actual areas in reality of the real ancient world, but in the Biblical story the words are used as a place-name to serve the narration of the fictional story being told. Cp: qussan rish-aatay-hum/um, ’aram nahairaay-im. (Judg.3:7-10)

Ehud; ’ēhûḏ; نَيحُد ‘he will sharpen’ and is exactly what the character of the same name does as he creates a doubled-edged dagger which he stabs Eglon with (**Eglon** meaning ‘brash’ as he does send all his guards and servants away) so the character is created and named with the purpose of making and using a sharp dagger to kill an enemy king. He is son of **Gera** ‘ran’ as after he leaves, he escapes i.e. ‘ran’ ‘And Ehud escaped while they tarried, and passed beyond the quarries, and escaped unto Seirath’. Cp: eyḥud. (Judg.3:15-26)

Seirath; śĕʿîrâ; سَئيره/ا، سيئيره/ا ‘send him off’ ‘go/walk/travel with him/it’ ‘go along with it (as in agree with speech or actions)’ ‘he will penis him/penetrate him with penis’. Ehud is sent and travels to deliver a gift but intends to deceive Eglon; Eglon goes along with Ehud’s request of being alone with him; the servants go along with it, believing Eglon wants to be alone; سيعيره/ا‘will gloat over him/at him’ ‘will lend/ borrow him’; gloated because Ehud kills Eglon for enslaving the people; شَيغيره/ا ، شيغيره/ا ‘he will save him’ Ehud saves the people from Eglon, and also from the Moabites. Cp: se-eerah(ra), sei-eerah(ra), se’eerah(ra), sei’eerah(ra), shegheerah(ra), sheigheerah(ra). (Judg.3:26)

Shamgar; šamgar; شَمغر ‘I will pulp/pierce/burst’ ‘I will disembowel’ ‘disembowelled’ from the word (mghr/مغر) from word (ghr/غر) which has more than one meaning: ‘funnel’ ‘funnels downwards(as water that goes below ground)’ ‘to pierce holes into something so the contents spill out onto ground’; when used as in fighting, it means to twist, punch, pinch and leave the opponent on the ground motionless; it is the word used to describe when a bull repeatedly rams a person or other animal and disembowels them, or rubs them against the ground or a rock, pierces them with its horns or causes internal injuries from butting. The essence of the word is something being spilt and disappearing underground, bursting and becoming lifeless. It seems the later editors of the story no longer knew what the word meant or were unsure if it was about killing and spilling so they added ‘…and he also delivered Israel.’ so the word could become ‘I will save’; from word (ghr/غر) ‘save’ (it has other meanings depending on how it is used such as ‘argued’) e.g. (mghaara/مغارا) ‘a saving/incident where people were saved’. Again, the essence of the word for when a person is saved, is people swooping/rushing down to save them, much like water rushes downwards quickly or a bull pushes down with its head against a person it is ramming, the etymology of the words different meanings is the same. He is the son of Anath; ʿănāṯ; عَناد ، عيناد ‘stubborn/fierce’ ‘stubbornness/fierceness’, it can also mean نَنآث ، نيناث ‘female(s)/feminine/became feminine’ but that is definitely not intended in this part of the story as the character is described as a fierce person who kills six hundred men ‘with an ox goad’. Cp: shamghar, ’anaad, ’ainaad, anaaf, ainaaf. (Judg.3.31)

Sisera; sîsĕrā'; سيسيراء ، سِيسَرآء 'hangs around women' 'talks a lot with women/flirts' 'spends too much time with women' and although it means a man who prefers to spend time with women than with men, as well as a 'womanizer' in the story it is used because it is women who bring his end: Deborah by planning and Jael by killing. It is also wordplay on 'will walk/leave' as the story emphasizes this meaning '...Sisera lighted off his chariot, and fled away on his feet...Howbeit Sisera fled away on his feet.'. Cp: seeseraa, seeseiraa. (Judg.4)

Harosheth; ḥărōšeṯ; حيرُشَت ، حَرُشَت 'she caused trouble between/she came between' 'she created enmity between' it is the land where the character Sisera lives and the word means a woman caused problems between people and directly refers to Deborah causing problems between the peoples of Sisera's land and Naphtali and Zebulun. From the word (ḥrsh/حرش) which means to cause problems/create enmity between people whether by telling lies, spreading rumours or delivering conversations that actually were said; the word is in the feminine describing a woman is who is causing the problems. Cp: ḥaroshet, ḥairoshet.

Although the word has been translated/interpreted into Gentiles, the compound word actually means 'I will deceive them/the': Gentiles; Hagoiim; haggôyim; هَغّي هم/ام 'I will deceive them/the' 'I will mislead them to downfall-them/the'. and the captain is **Sisera** 'hangs around women' who lives in **Haroshet** of the **Gentiles** 'she created enmity between' 'I will deceive them/the' and that is the theme of the story: people will be harmed, a woman will create enmity between people and she will deceive the people into warring, then another woman will deceive the lead antagonist character and kill him. Cp: haghoy-hum/um. (Judg.4)

Deborah; dĕḇôrâ; ديبُره/ا ، دَبُره/ا 'evil intended/fated' 'brings evil upon' and is in the form of feminine adjective; it also has a similar meaning to 'unlucky' but with a stronger and more malicious meaning as in 'evil intent' 'evil fate' and the person described as being 'deboor/mdbir' brings evil upon those he/she is around. It is Deborah who forces Barak to war against Sisera, and the killing of many people ensues. It has more meanings (negative and neutral) such as 'plot' again to plot with evil/bad intentions towards others; it means 'with a frowning face' 'with a brooding face' meaning the person described as such has a negative temperament, is frowning, sour-faced; there is a simile when a person is in such a mood that 'his/her face is like the backside/anus (dbr/دبر) of a donkey'. It also means 'to make lazy/convince not to do (something that should be done)'. It can also mean to 'discuss and think about'. Her character is to be the catalyst which causes the war, defeat and death of Sisera and all his men. In language use, when a person suffers from the plotting/scheming of another they say '(she) dabbarat on him' دَبَّرَت عليه '(he)dabbar on him' دَبَّر عليه '(they)dabbaroo on her' دَبَّرو عليها . Cp: deborah(ra), deiborah(ra). (Judg.4)

Lapidoth; lappîḏōṯ; لَفّيضُت 'dared speak against' 'spoke falsely against' 'put words in his/her mouth' and is when a person insults another or speaks about another whether 'putting words in their mouth' or creating absolute lies about the person. The whole chapter is about women who lie and deceive, even if the outcome is 'victory' to the fictional warring party, the theme and events are about women who lie and deceive to get their objectives. Cp: laph͟eedh͟ot. (Judg.4)

Barak; bārāq; بآرآق 'in a strop' 'sulking' 'moody' 'upset and sulking' 'upset and refusing to cooperate' and is from the word (brq/برق) which although can mean 'lightning' in this specific Biblical story it means 'upset and not talking' or 'upset and talking reluctantly'. It is from word (ybrq/tbrq/يبرق/تبرق) 'he/she gets upset quickly/easily' and itself is from the word 'lightning' because the person whose personality 'braaq/ybrq' gets offended or upset by anything and quickly, i.e. goes from a good mood to a bad mood as quick as lightning branches and disappears or strikes, and the person described as 'baariq' also stops talking, cooperating, interacting with others and when he/she has to, does so reluctantly. This kind of personality and behaviour are narrated in the story of Barak, even in the dialogue the authors give him show his reluctancy to do what he is supposed to do: 'If thou wilt go with me, then I will go: but if thou wilt not go with me, *then* I will not go.' He is being moody/stroppy. Cp: baaraaq. (Judg.4).

His father Abinoam; 'ăḇînō'am; نَبي/نَيبي نوعَم 'refused/rejected-blessings' 'refused to receive gifts/money/food' and refers to Barak's reluctance to take on the mission and also to Deborah telling him directly, after he reluctantly agrees to go with her, that the mission will not be an honour for him to claim; it is also wordplay on: عَبي نوعَم 'fill with blessings/food/money/gifts/necessities/health' 'fill-make smoother/easier' and Jael fills Sisera with dairy products causing him to feel comfortable and fall asleep which makes it easier for her to kill him; عَبي نونَم 'fill with sleep' 'fill-make sleep' 'fill-he fell asleep' and is what happens to Sisera when Jael fills him with milk or such dairy product and puts him in such comfort that he falls asleep so that she can kill him in his sleep; نَبي/نَيبي نوغَم 'refused/rejected-we stifle/feel stifled' 'refused/

rejected-we suffocate/feel suffocated' 'refused/rejected-we cover/we are covered' 'refused/rejected-we muffle/are muffled' 'refused/rejected-we depress/feel depressed' this refers to Barak's reluctance to war against Sisera and Barak's disgrace for being reluctant, and also to how Jael covers Sisera before she ends his life, and Sisera was both in fear, depressed and disgraced by losing the battle before being killed by a person he trusts causes him more disgrace; عَبي/عيبي نوغم 'fill-we stifle/feel stifled' 'fill/of disgrace/my shame-we suffocate/feel suffocated' 'of disgrace/my shame/fill-we cover/we are covered' 'of disgrace/fill-we muffle/are muffled' 'of disgrace/fill-we depress/feel depressed' for the same aforementioned reasons. The meanings of Barak's surname may also imply that the original story had Barak kill Sisera, or it may be because after Jael filled Sisera with milk, put him to sleep she then shows him to Barak already killed. Cp: abee/aibee-noo'am, 'abee-noo-am, abee/aibee-noogham, 'abee/'aibee-noogham. (Judg.4)

Jael; yā'ēl; جآئيل 'came the' as Sisera comes to her and she encourages him to 'Turn in, turn in to me; fear not...' and he enters her tent and he asks her not to allow any man (enemy) to enter the tent; she meets Barak and asks him to come into her tent so she can show him the killed Sisera; حآئيل 'trickster/deceiver' and she deceives Sisera by making him feel safe, giving him cover, drink and a false sense of safety before she kills him in his sleep; the same word is also related to 'place' 'stay in place' as she stakes him to the ground in his sleep, and these words are related to the word 'tent' 'undressing' 'place' 'place to undress', it mentions twice that Jael 'covered him with a mantle' 'and covered him'. But the emphasis is on 'deceived' as it is her major role in the story. Cp: gaa-ill/eyl, ḥaaill/ḥaaeyl. She is the wife of **Heber** which as earlier in Genesis one of its meanings is 'news' and she brings news to Barak that Sisera has been slain. Cp: kheber.

The themes meant by the words of place names used here can be seen clearly: **Haroshet** of the **Gentiles** 'she created enmity between' 'I will deceive them/the' because **Deborah** creates enmity between the soon-to-be warring parties and deceives them into engaging in this war, and it is mentioned Sisera returning again to Haroshet of the Gentiles where he is deceived by **Jael** although there is no enmity between him and them.

Hobab mentioned for some of its meanings: 'loved' as there is peace between Jabin (which means 'harmed' 'will harm/will be harmed') and Jael's husband who is 'one of the children of Hobab' and its other meaning 'refuses/rejects a good thing' because it mentions he severed himself from the Kennites which allows the story to have his tent pitched in **Zaanaim**: 'was able to force-them/the' because Sisera is forced to flee towards this specific tent and 'tired-them/the' 'made tired-them/the' because Sisera arrives already tired and thirsty from battle and Jael also gives him milk to make him feel more tired/sleepy and **Kedesh** is mentioned next to Zaanaim where the tent is pitched because as already explained earlier when people are tired they 'kadesh' themselves onto the ground, bed, etc., as well as Sisera being 'led' to his own slaughter. Also, **Zaanaim** meaning of 'this/it/him/I will sing for-them/the' 'this/it/him/I will make sing-them/the' because the chapter to follow will be a song.

Naphtali because Sisera and Canaan will be 'crushed' defeated, and **Zebulun** 'stayed' 'misled' because they will stay while Sisera's men will be wiped out and Sisera will be misled he is safe then killed by the person giving him false safety; **Kedesh** 'piles/piled' because that is the sound of people and objects falling, it is how people fall to/pile on the ground and many will be killed in battle, and they have been led to this demise.

Kishon because that is where Sisera and his men will be 'petrified' 'were swept away/scraped away like minute litter'.

Bethel 'evil/bad' because what Deborah is doing and what will ensue in the story is evil/bad just as are the stories' events where Bethel is placed in the narration. **Ramah** 'thrown/killed' because not only will Sisera be thrown down and destroyed, but according to the story so will the king Jabin and all of Canaan.

The story begins and ends with '**Jabin** king of **Canaan**' 'harmed/will harm/will be harmed' king of 'given up any hope/resolved to fate or what will happen' and is what happens to Sisera and his host, as well as the king of the same name. (Judg.4)

Meroz; mērôz; ميرُض 'became ill' 'is not content' 'refused to/did not agree/did not do' and in the story is a curse on people because 'they came not to the help of the Lord'. Cp: meyrodh. (Judg.5:23)

Joash; yô'āš; جُئاش 'grain husks' it is the black shells which hold the grain, the grain is removed from the pod/panicle and husks by threshing then winnowing. The story narrates the angel sits under an oak while Joash and his son are threshing—hence the name of the husks. During intense famine these inedible husks have been used to create bread to prevent death. Cp: go-aash. He is an Abiezrite; 'ăḇî'ezer; ئَبي عَزَر 're-fused/rejected-became ugly' 'father-became ugly' it could be 'rejected' or 'father', or عَبي 'pack/fill' followed by 'visited/tightened' نَزَرْ, or 'shadowed/excused' عَذَر, or نَذَر 'seeds'; but is most likely عبي نَذَر 'pack/fill the seeds' as the character is secretly threshing grain and also 'father/rejected-became ugly' as the people want to put his son to death for demolishing the Baal altar. Cp: abee-'ezer, 'abee-'ezer, abee-ezer, 'abee-ezer, abee-'ever, 'abee-'ever, abee-ever, 'abee-ever. (Judg.6:11) **Ophrah** is used in its meaning of 'increase/multiplication' contrasting how God changed this to scarcity as punishment.

Gideon; gid̲ĕʿôn; جِدِعُن ، جِديعُن 'they uprooted' 'of uprooting' to remove something by pulling it up/out, 'they snapped off the top or a piece off' 'find-help/support'; جِذعون ، جِذيعُن 'they broke' 'of breaking' it is to break something by folding it or breaking it without it separating from the main body (whether object or plant). Both meanings of the word and how they are used describe uprooting, breaking off, and ruining which Gideon does to the altars of other gods, and also 'find-help' because God promises to be with him and he gets help from his men to perform his tasks. Cp: gide'on, gidei'on, give'on, givei'on. (Judg.6)

Jehovah-shalom; YHWH šālôm; يحوه سالَم 'he stayed-survived/safe/intact' 'he stayed him survived/safe' 'he stayed him-asked the' and both are narrated: first Gideon asks the angel 'Depart not hence, I pray thee, until I come unto thee…' so he could present his gift and the angel stays as asked; then when Gideon believes he will die and God tells him he will stay alive and be safe: 'And the Lord said unto him, Peace be unto thee; fear not: thou shalt not die. Then Gideon built an altar there unto the Lord, and called it Jehovah-shalom'. Cp: yḥwh-saalom. (Judg.6:17-24)

Jerubbaal; yĕrubbaʿal; جِروببَعَل ، جيروببَعَل 'they pulled down the 'high above/high'' (**Baal** means above/high place/from high) and is exactly what Gideon and his men do: they pull down the Baal altar and is emphasised why this name was given '…he called him Jerubbaal, saying, Let Baal plead against him, because he hath thrown down his altar.'. (Jeru/yĕru/جِرو) 'pulled/pulled down', (b/b/بـ) denotes to what/who the action is being done, (baal/baʿal/بَعَل) 'the high/the high place/above(Baal)'. Whether the same authors of this story or later editors, it was decided to add an extra meaning to 'Jerubbaal' compound word: يِروبَّ عَل ، ييروبَّ عَل ، جِروبَّ عَل ، جيروبَّ عَل 'he wets on/makes wet/damp on' 'came wet/water/damp on' and means to make something wet or damp; in this story it is the wool fleece and the authors wanted this meaning to be clear to the audience so they not only narrate that first Gideon asks God to make the wool fleece wet while the ground around it is dry but again asks to make the water/moistness on all the ground and leave the fleece dry and each time the water/wetness is on what Gideon has asked it to be on. Cp: ge-ru-b-ba'al, geiru-b-ba'al, yerubba-'al, yeirubba-'al, ge-roobba-'al, gei-roobba-'al. (Judg.6:25-40)

Harod; ḥărōḍ; حَرود ، حيرود 'bent his neck(physically)' 'of bent neck' 'became stubborn' 'incite(d)' 'incites against others/causes problems between others' 'of malicious intent'; حَروض ، حيروض 'incited/incited against' 'got worked up/works up' 'folds(ed)/coils(ed) into itself ready to strike' such as a snake when preparing to defend itself or bite and figuratively used as person getting worked up. All meanings are used in the story: God/Gideon works up the people and incites fear into the people so the men decrease in numbers (as is God's wish in the story); those who bend down on their knees to drink, meaning their necks would also be bent down, are also sent away from the battle. Cp: ḥarood, ḥairood, ḥaroo<u>dh</u>, ḥairoo<u>dh</u>. (Judg.7:1-7)

Moreh holds one of the meanings as earlier in Genesis: 'a dream' 'saw him/it' and refers to the Midianites discussing a dream about Gideon, which is why the narrators set '…the host of the Midianites were on the north side of them, by the hill of Moreh, in the valley' and this enhances the Midianite speaking about his dream 'And thou shalt hear what they say…*there was* a man that told a dream unto his fellow and said, Behold, I dreamed a dream…And his fellow said, This is nothing else save the sword of Gideon…And it was *so* when Gideon heard the telling of the dream…'. (Judg.7:1,13-15)

Phura; purâ; ذوره/ا 'sorghum' 'sorghum bread' or بوره/ا 'barley' 'barley bread' and refers to the cake of bread in the dream which both Phura and Gideon overhear the Midianites talking about. Phura serves no other purpose in the story than to enhance the cake of bread and elucidate its meaning in the story. '…go thou with Phurah…Then went he down with Phurah his servant unto the outside of the armed men that *were* in the host…and, lo, a cake of barley bread tumbled into the host of Midian, and came unto a tent, and smote it that it fell, and overturned it…'. Cp: vurah(ra), burah(ra) (Judg.7:10-13)

Beth Shitta; bêt̲ haššiṭṭâ; بيت هَشِتَّه/ا 'he/it will-I will leaven it' 'he/it will-I will scatter/confuse it' and the 'leaven' is still referring to the cake of bread: when God decreases the numbers of Gideon's men, he 'leavens' them so although they are few he increases their abilities; 'scatter/disperse/confuse': the trumpeting, breaking of pitchers, lights all confuse the enemy and the enemy turn their swords against each other before they 'scatter' fleeing to various places. It could also be بيت هَشِطّه/ا 'he/it will-I will tear it' as in hold something between fingers and tear it quickly: Gideon and his men just say 'the sword of the Lord, and of

Gideon' and the enemy turns its sword against its own before fleeing. Cp: beyt-hashittah(ta), beyt-hashiṭṭah(ṭa). (Judg.7:22)

Zererath; ṣĕrērâ; ذِريره/ا ، ذيريره/ا 'lots of sorghum(grains)/seeds/grains' 'ants' 'crawling/boiling with ants' and holds both meanings: the narration is still linking to the dream of the cake of bread, and the people are scattering like grains of spilled sorghum, running all over the place like an ant infestation or ant colony with ants going in every direction. Cp: vereyrah(ra), veireyrah(ra). (Judg.7:22)

Abel-meholah; 'āḇēl mĕḥôlâ; عآبيل مِحلِه/ميحلِه 'shook fat-in his place/stationary/in one spot' 'shook fat-his undressing' and both refer to the punishment given to two enemy princes suggesting they were tortured (raped) and humiliated before execution. Cp: 'aabeyl-meḥolah, 'aabeyl-meiḥolah. (Judg.7:22)

Tabbath; ṭabbāṯ; طَبّاث 'dipped into' 'dipped fingers into'; طَبّات 'ball shape/spheres' 'patted/patting' 'willies(penis)'. Cp: ṭabbaaf, ṭabbaat. (Judg.7:22)

Beth-barah; bêṯ bārâ; بيت بآره/ا 'he/they/it will-be passed/be surpassed/pass/surpass/go beyond/get ahead of him/it' because they will cut off the Midianites who are trying to return home(**Jordan** 'return home'), 'he/they/it-will be good to it/him' 'he will be innocent of/disown responsibility from'; بيت بآرح 'he/it will be-pulled up(bailing water)' 'he/it will be-cleared out'; the 'bailing water' meaning because Gideon's men are ordered to take the waters before the Midianites to Beth-barah and Jordan, and the latter meaning (cleared-out) because the Midianites will be cleared out of the land. Cp: beyt-baarah(ra), beyt-baarḥ. (Judg.7:23)

Oreb; 'ōrēḇ, 'ôrēḇ; عوريب ، عُريب 'was fucked' 'has been fucked' and the word is in the form that it was done many times. The narrators give both the character and the rock he was slaughtered on the same name, it is the use of derogatory words assigned to the antagonists in the stories. As he is a Midianite, an enemy he is given an insulting name and death. Cp: 'ooreyb, 'oreyb. (Judg.7:25)

Zeeb; zĕ'ēḇ; زِئيب ، زيئيب 'was/has been penised' and again means penetrated with a penis and the word is in the form that it happened many times. Oreb and Zeeb have been paired to leave no uncertainty what is meant by these words. The same as Oreb, both Zeeb the character and the place he was slaughtered have been given the same derogatory word as a name as he is the enemy of the protagonists in the story. Cp: ze-eeb, zei-eeb. (Judg.7:25)

Zebah; zeḇaḥ; ذِبَح 'slaughtered' and is what he does to the enemy king of the same name, and also the people who refuse to provide his men with food and drink while they were pursuing Zebah. Cp: vebaḥ. (Judg.8:5-21)

Zalmunna; ṣalmunnā'; ظَلّمونّاء 'caused us injustice' 'our injustice' and refers to the men of Succoth causing Gideon injustice because they refuse to provide him with food and drink while he is pursuing Zalmunna of the same name who killed relatives of Gideon and therefore caused injustice. Cp: dhalmunnaa-a. (Judg.8:5-21)

Succoth from earlier in Genesis is being used for: سوقُّط 'immoral/fallen' and refers to the people refusing to feed Gideon's men and Gideon threatens them with punishment—whipping similar (though violent as the Bible stories narrate an exaggerated form) to children being spanked by a parent '...then I will tear your flesh with the thorns of the wilderness and with briers...And he took the elders of the city, and thorns of the wilderness, and with them he taught the men of Succoth.' 'taught' as in 'disciplined' which is one way Arabic language speakers say 'discipline' (rabbi, rabbeyt, 'alam, 'alamt). Cp: suqqoṭ. (Judg.8:4-16)

Penuel also takes on an additional meaning to that given it by the original authors of Genesis: pĕnû'ēl; بَنو/بين ئيل 'children of-the' 'show/become apparent-the' now also means 'built-the' and this word-name is chosen so Gideon can give them a threat and fulfil it which is to 'break down this tower' 'And he beat down the tower of Penuel, and slew the men of the city' i.e. something they had built. Cp: benu/beinu-ill. (Judg.8:8-17)

Karkor; qarqōr; قَرقور the sound of 'qarqoor' such as when a stomach rumbles or water glugging out of a vessel, or similar sound, 'stayed in same place/settled down' the latter as that is where they stayed; كَركور 'drove away violently'; خَرخور 'drove away' (with physical action) 'falling to ground/falling/collapsing'. The last two meanings because it is described as 'for there fell an hundred and twenty thousand men that drew sword'. Cp: qarqoor, karkoor, kharkhoor. (Judg.8:10)

Nobah 'harmed' and **Jogbehah** 'ganged/gathered people around' as it describes the surrounding and killing 'and smote the host: for the host was secure.' (Judge.8:11)

Tabor; tāḇôr; تآبُر 'ruins reputation/becomes bad/gets bad reputation/spoiled' when something (bor/ بور/بُر) it has 'become bad' gone from a good state/reputation to a lesser/bad state/reputation. This theme is used when questioning Zebah and Zalmunna that had they not killed Gideon's relatives they may have been spared, but because they did kill them, they have lost their reputation/status '...if ye had saved them alive, I would not slay you.'. Cp: taabor. (Judg.8:18)

Jether; yeṯer; عِذِر ، عَذَر 'excused/excuse' as he was unable to kill the men because he was young and the kings ask his father to kill them instead, 'shadowed/shadow'; could also be wordplay on جِذِر ، جَذَر 'shuddered' and also 'to cut up randomly' 'cut off tips or at different levels' 'to shear off unevenly' as it is a word similar to Gideon's meanings. Cp: 'ever, gever. (Judg.8:20)

Ishmaelites and earrings because the word **Ishmael** is related to hearing and being heard so the earring is used as a reminder for the meaning of the word 'that ye would give me every man the earrings of his prey. (For they had golden earrings, because they *were* Ishmaelites.)'. (Judg.8:24)

Baal-berith; ba'al bĕrîṯ; بَعَل بيريث 'the high-will inherit'; بَعَل بيريض 'the high-will bury in ground/soil/ he creates soil/does with soil'. Both refer to Gideon's death: Gideon will be buried, and the story has the 'Baal' 'high place/above' is worshipped after Gideon's death so it is 'Baal' that inherits Gideon. Also, his son Abimelech will seek to inherit him alone in the following chapter. Cp: ba'al-beireef, ba'al-beireedh. (Judg.8:33)

Abimelech has been used for the meaning 'filled-well/nicely' as the men of Shechem give him a lot. **Shechem** is used for its meanings of 'abdominal ache' and 'screams/cries out loud' as the story narrates Abimelech hires people to slaughter his brothers from the fortune given him by Shechem; his surviving brother, Jotham, will shout a curse/parable against Shechem and his brother. (Judg.8:31; 9)

Jotham; yôṯām; جُذآم 'leper/lepers/leprosy' 'tips/appendages fall/cut off' 'came-guilted' 'came-blamed' 'came-ostracised'; يُذآم 'is ostracised' 'he ostracises' 'is guilted' 'he guilts' 'is blamed' 'he blames' and this character guilts and blames Abimelech and the people of Shechem for what they have done to his family, he then flees to safety. **Beer** is used as to where he fled 'good/piety' as he is the good character in the story and he goes somewhere safe/good for him. Cp: govaam, yovaam. (Judg.9:7-21)

Millo; millô', millō'; مِلّءٌ ، مِلّوْ ، مِلوء 'filled' 'fetched water' 'filled water' 'covered/filled/soiled' 'a small, narrow rod applicator for kohl'. Cp: millo, milloo. (Judg.9:6,20)

Gaal; ga'al; جَعَل 'created' 'did' 'made' 'put' 'influenced' 'bait/baited' 'came-above/rose above'. It refers to the character of the same name mocking Abimelech and 'making' the latter seem unworthy of being king, questioning how Abimelech rose to a higher status and as a king he is above them. Also refers to the character of the same name being baited so as not to notice Abimelech approaching. Cp: ga'al. He is son of Ebed; 'eḇeḏ; عِبِد 'worshipper' 'worshipped' 'servant' 'served' and is the second part of how he insults Abimelech as a servant of others and questions why they should serve him; تَبَد 'never' 'forever' 'wipe out/ kill all' and this too is reflected in Gaal the son of Ebed saying they should stop serving and should never have served Abimelech, and should 'remove Abimelech'—kill him is to remove him forever. Cp: 'ebed, ebed. (Judg.9:26-40)

Zebul; zĕḇul; شَضول ، شيضول 'I will stay' 'he will stay' as Zebul shows Abimelech will remain as leader, he also deceives Gaal not to move forward while Abimelech is approaching to attack; 'I will mislead' 'he will mislead' 'I will shade' 'he will shade' as he misleads Gaal that the approaching army are just shadows; ذَبول ، ذيبول 'wicks' 'withered' and Zebul's dialogue shows a 'withering' of Gaal as he accuses him of boasting and of not being man enough to fight against Abimelech 'Where *is* now thy mouth...go out, I pray now, and fight with them.' and shown in Gaal's defeat. Cp: shedhul, sheidhul, vebul, veibul. (Judg.9:30-41)

Meonenim; mĕ'ônĕnîm; ميعْنين هم/ام 'water-clouded them/the' 'overdiluted in water/became floppy/ watery-them/the' 'lost in immorality-them/the' 'did not help-them/the'. Zebul does the opposite of assist Gaal, he deceives him by convincing him that he does not see the oncoming army, and then does not help him. Cp: mei'onein-hum/um. (Judg.9:37)

Arumah; 'ărûmâ; عَرُمه/ا ، عيرُمه/ا 'abandoned in wilderness' 'lost in wilderness' as Gaal is thrown out of Shechem, 'arum(ah) tree' a specific kind of tree good for firewood and the story that follows involves cutting down trees to make a fire; نُرُمه/ا ، نيرُمه/ا 'they/he threw him/it' 'he/they killed him/it' 'they/he did throw it/him' as 'And Abimelech dwelt at Arumah: and Zebul thrust out Gaal and his brethren, that they should not dwell in Shechem. Cp: 'arumah(ma), 'airumah(ma), arumah(ma), airumah(ma). (Judg.9:41)

Berith; bĕrîṯ; بيريض 'will bury in ground/soil/he creates soil/does with soil'. As earlier, one of the meanings of Berith is to do something to/with soil and in this instance Abimelech 'sowed the land with salt.'. Cp: beiree<u>dh</u>. (Judg.9:45-46)

Zalmon; ṣalmôn; ضَلَمُن 'injustice' and people in the story are burnt alive; the whole story is also about injustice caused to Gideon's murdered sons; then the perpetrators suffer injustice when they turn against each other. Cp: <u>dh</u>almon. (Judg.9:48-49)

Thebez; tēḇēṣ; ثيبيز 'thumped' 'struck with something heavy' and is what a woman does to Abimelech by throwing a piece of a millstone upon his head causing his death; تيبيز 'she carries/she carries something heavy' 'she breastfeeds' referring to her being a woman (important in the story as it disgraces Abimelech to be killed by a woman) and 'she picks up/takes' her actions: she takes a piece of millstone. Cp: feybeyz, teybeyz. (Judg.9:50-54)

Dodo; dôḏô; تُدّ 'says no' 'no'; تُضُ 'shines/glows' 'ablutes/washes'; تُذّ 'harms/is harmed'; ضُدُ 'against'. Cp: todo, to<u>dh</u>o, tovo, <u>dh</u>odo. (Judg.10:1)

Camon; qāmôn; قَامُن 'got up/they got up' 'awoke/they awoke' 'a man's length/height'. Cp: qaamon. (Judg.10:5)

Jephthah; is the same as **Jiphtah** (Josh.15:43); yiptaḥ; يِفتَح 'opens'; يِفضَح 'a scandal/exposes a shame'; يِفدَه 'sacrifices for him' 'he sacrifices for him' (a human sacrifice and is used as verbal expression of the preciousness of the person being sacrificed for); يِفذَح 'it's spicy'. As soon as he is introduced the explanation is given 'he was the son of an harlot…thou art the son of a strange woman' his brothers throw him out and disown him because he 'exposes a shame/a scandal' as the son of a prostitute. It is also 'sacrifices for him' as he offers his daughter to God as a human sacrifice. Cp: yi<u>ph</u>taḥ, yi<u>ph</u>**dh**aḥ, yi<u>ph</u>dah, yi<u>ph</u>vaḥ. (Judg.11)

Tob; tôḇ; تُب 'repent' 'stop bad behaviour', the word is usually used telling the wrongdoer to repent and to change one's ways. It is the place where Jephthah is staying when his people come to ask him to fight for/defend them against the Ammonites: they are remorseful and repenting and will change their ways toward him if they want to receive his help 'Therefore we turn again to thee now…'. Cp: tob. (Judg.11:5-11)

Minnith; minnîṯ; مِنّيت 'listed and told what had been given' 'hoped for/wished for' 'gave/granted' and is related to Jephthah wishing for victory and he will give God a gift/offering and he details how he will offer it: a burnt offering. Cp: minneet. (Judg.11:33)

Shibboleth; šibbōleṯ; سِبّولَت 'hung/drooped low' 'tails of sheep' 'tail of sheep grew' 'tail of sheep lolled' 'hung down like tail of sheep' 'panicle of grain'. Cp: sibboolet. Sibboleth; sîbbōleṯ; شيبّولت 'she wet it' 'she urinated'. Cp: <u>sh</u>eebboolet. It is a pun on **'Ephraim'** as one of its meanings is 'with gap between teeth' and people with a new gap or too many gaps between their teeth have trouble pronouncing the 's/س' as it is pronounced by accident as 'sh/ش', the same with 'ss/ص' is pronounced 'f/ث'. In real life, when someone loses a tooth, both adults and children enjoy teasing them by asking the person with a new gap between his/her teeth to say things like 'onion' 'smooth' and laugh when either the 's' or '<u>ss</u>' is pronounced as '<u>sh</u>' or 'f'. (Judg.12:5)

Ibzan; 'iḇṣān; ئِبزآن 'they take' 'of breast/milking breasts' and all is meant as he has thirty girls who marry abroad and he brings in thirty daughters-in-law for his sons so there are many families being made and lactating breasts, 'they take' meaning because he 'took in thirty daughters from abroad for his sons'. Cp: ibzaan. (Judg.12:9)

Hillel; hillēl; هِلّيل 'cried out loud/praised/chanted' 'cried out word or name repeatedly' 'a hullaballoo' 'loud chaos' 'crescent/crescent moon/slither of moon' 'of tassels/tiny ornaments on ends of jewellery' 'it shed/dropped off(such as skin/leaves); حِليل 'undressed' 'purified/cleansed/circumcised/made edible/made touchable' 'declared permissible/purified' 'shed off' 'beat severely/until skin peeled off' 'made sweet' 'replaced' 'took place of/instead of'. Cp: hilleyl, ḥilleyl. (Judg.12:13)

Pirathon; pir'āṯôn; بِرعآتُن 'galloped' 'a galloping' 'two galloped(female)' 'ran off/ran like scared animals'; فِرعآتَن 'two lightning strikes/thunderclaps' 'a separation/division' 'a separating of a fight/argument' 'two branching(ways/ideas/parties/etc.). Cp: bir'aaton, <u>ph</u>ir'aaton. (Judg.12:13-15)

Zorah; ṣor'â; صورعه/ا 'thrown to ground' 'has epileptic fit' 'is/are knotted'; سورعه/ا 'fast' 'be quick' 'hurry'; ذورئه/ا 'sorghum' 'his sorghum' 'seed/seeded it/him' 'his seed' 'offspring/his/its offspring'; زورعه/ا 'planted it' 'planted' and it refers to Manoah's wife being barren which is why the authors place Manoah from Zorah. The word implies she is 'knotted' barren (just like Sarah) and is 'planted' and as she will conceive, they will have offspring, 'seed' (it is on purpose that whenever a barren woman is visited by God or an angel of god appearing as a man that the said woman becomes pregnant). The introduction of the unnamed wife before the named husband-character is because he is the word-name for her role in the story. Cp: ssoor'ah('a), soor'ah('a), voor-ah(-a), zoor'ah('a) (Judg.13)

Manoah; mānôaḥ; مآنوَه 'has been warned/made aware' 'did not warn/make aware' 'did not/has no-stone/seed' 'has not been seeded/stoned' and the angel of God makes Manoah's wife aware that she will conceive after he emphasises to her that she is barren, he also warns/makes her aware of what not to consume while pregnant, i.e. not put inside her. She in turn makes Manoah aware of the same. The 'seed/stone' is that of a fruit (see Noah, (Gen.)) and although the stories keep pointing out it is the wife unable to become pregnant, the story shows it is the man who is sterile, i.e. his 'seed' does not work, by having God or an angel in the appearance of a man or otherwise 'visit' the barren couple and especially the wife and she becomes pregnant. Cp: maanoah. (Judg.13:1-14)

Samson; šimšôn; شِمسُن 'I will possess' 'I will entangle/cause problems/provoke problems or fighting'. The 'I will possess' as in possessed by a demon or devil, but in the Biblical stories and in this case Samson, possessed by 'the Spirit of the Lord': (sa/ši/شِ) 'I will' and in this story it is God, (mson/mšôn/مسُن) 'possess him or them/possession' 'touch/fight/provoke' all from (ms/مس). Whenever Samson is possessed, he attacks people or causes problems, he is also constantly provoked (unintentionally sometimes) by others which leads him to violence. The story narrates that at some point when Samson has grown, he begins to be possessed: 'And the Spirit of the Lord began to move him' 'And the Spirit of the Lord came mightily upon him' and he tears a lion apart with his bare hands; 'And the Spirit of the Lord came upon him' and he kills thirty men; 'and the Spirit of the Lord came mightily upon him' and the rope which binds him is removed by fire—remember fire is what God uses to kill people with when he is angry, then Samson goes on to kill a thousand men. Once his hair is shaved, which the story tells us is in seven locks, just like the mystical number seven, God's spirit is no longer in him (no longer possesses/comes upon him) 'And he wist not that the Lord was departed from him.'. All his violent and crazy behaviour happens when God's spirit possesses him. Even in current times in areas which have remained remote and unaffected by city-life, modernisation, people believe a person with mental illness and is violent or behaves in an erratic way is possessed by devils/demons 'mimsoos' ممسوس. They do not apply this belief to everyone with mental illness as there is a completely different word for 'crazy/insane/mentally unwell', and it is believed it is not the afflicted person's speech and actions, but the demons' which control the possessed person. All the described behaviours of the character Samson depict a mad person prone to violent outbursts which the authors and audience of the stories of those times would call 'possessed'. Cp: shimson. (Judg.13:25; 14;15;16)

Etam; 'êṭām; عيضآم 'bones' as he slays them 'hip and thigh' and he will also use a jawbone of a donkey to kill many more. Cp: 'eydhaam. (Judg.15:8, 15-16)

Lehi; leḥî; لِهي 'for her' 'for her sake' and in this chapter Samson slaughters people in revenge for murdering his wife. What is interesting is the use of a donkey's jawbone as the murder weapon in connection to Samson's behaviour: to this day, the people who speak Arabic, which is what the Biblical language is, call young men who are brash whether they are violent or just behave foolishly or impulsively 'donkey, chin of a donkey' and that is what is being symbolised in this story with the 'jawbone of an ass', that Samson is behaving as they would categorise him had he been a real person. Cp: lehee. (Judg.15:14-)

Ramath-lehi; rāmaṯ lĕḥî; رآمَت لِهي/ليهي 'thrown around/killed-for her' relayed in when he throws away the jawbone which he used as a weapon to murder a thousand men for his wife's sake and the story has Samson quenched with vengeance for his wife 'And it came to pass, when he had made an end to speaking, that he cast away the jawbone out of his hand, and called that place Ramath-lehi.'. Cp: raamat-lehee/leihee. (Judg.15:17)

En-hakkore; 'ên haqqôrē'; عين/ئين هَقّريع 'look/pay attention-my head will be uncovered' 'where-my head will be uncovered' and Samson's dialogue is asking God not to shame him in front of the Philistines (**Philistine**; 'between coasts/between two (or more) coasts' i.e. the people who live between two great bodies of water and whose mention in the Biblical stories is tied to water and coasts), by dying from thirst after having exacted such great revenge. This needs some explaining to be understood: the 'look/where-my head will be uncovered' attitude in culture is linked to a man's dignity, respect, pride, etc. is shown by men from a certain age in the headwear they don such as a circular cap, head-shawl turbaned around the head, or both (though it is not disgraceful at all for a man to be without, it is a symbol of manhood, position, social status) and there is offence taken if it is purposely knocked off in an altercation. In Samson's story it is the essence of this culture/attitude made into Samson's head-covering which is his hair and tied to his strength: his success and fall are based on never cutting his hair, and when it is cut i.e. his head uncovered—he suffers torture, humiliation then death—so the uncovering of his head is the shameful 'will my head be uncovered'. Cp: 'eyn/eyn haqqorey'. (Judg.16:18-19)

Gaza is mentioned because of its meaning to shear grass/harvest crops and Samson's head will be shaved after this place is mentioned and he will be returned to Gaza directly after it is shaved. Cp: gazza (Judg.16)

Sorek; śōrēq; سوريك 'tell you secret' and the word is in the form of being said to a female; صوريق 'snuck in' 'walked stealthily' 'thieves'. It is exactly as narrated in the story as this part revolves around Delilah trying to get Samson to tell her his secret, and he eventually tells her his secret; there are always antagonists hiding in wait in Delilah's chamber. Cp: sooreyk, ssooreyq. (Judg.15:4-20)

Delilah; dĕlîlâ; دليله/ا ، ديليله/ا 'entice him' 'enticing/enticed' 'pamper him' 'pampered/pampering' 'push yourself/pedal yourself/dangle in front of-for him' and the latter means to go and pedal yourself all over the place even if you are unwanted. All the above meanings are played in the narration as Delilah entices, pampers and pushes herself onto Samson to make him tell her his secret right up to enticing him and pampering him to sleep on her knees so his hair can be shaved off. It is also wordplay on 'guided/showed' as she asks him to tell her where his power is and how it can be destroyed and the story is lengthened by Samson misleading her three out of four times before eventually showing/telling her how he can be defeated. Cp: deleelah(la), deileelah(la). (Judg.16:4-20)

Dagon is used here for one of its earlier meanings (see Beth-dagon (Josh.15:41)); dāgộn; داجُن 'raised/has chickens' 'brings/sells chickens'; تاغن 'is singing/made to sing' 'make 'ghn' sounds'; داقن 'was/is chinned' 'grew a beard' 'frowned/became grumpy'; دعجُن 'steered/drove/cornered sheep/goats into specific area'. The latter meaning of 'steered/drove/cornered sheep/goats into specific area' as Samson is taken to prison then made to perform for his captor's entertainment, he is taken in and out of prison to perform just like goats/sheep are steered into a stable and taken out for shepherding, sale or slaughter. Cp: daagon, taaghon, daaqon, d'gon. (Judg.16:23-27)

Micah; mîḵâ; ميقه/ا ، ميكه/ا 'What is wrong?' 'What is there?' 'What is the situation/problem?' 'What did he say?' 'What happened?'; ميحه/ا 'runny (like egg yolk)' 'cowardly'. ميقه/ا can also mean 'flirting' 'immoral behaviour' 'male behaving feminine' 'coquettish behaviour'. The story of Micah begins with an issue, that of the money Micah stole from his mother; the expressions 'micah/ميقه/ا ، ميكه/ا' are used when there is a problem or trouble and someone is asking basically 'what's happening/what's up?'. It is denoted in the questions the Danites ask the Levite 'Who brought thee hither? and what makest thou in this place? and what hast thou here?' the conversation is a lot of 'Micah'; also, when they ask him about the future—they want to know what awaits them. When Micah catches up with the Danites the narration also exemplifies the meaning of Micah: 'And they cried unto the children of Dan. And they turned their faces and said unto Micah, What aileth thee, that thou comest with such a company? And he said, Ye have taken away my gods which I made, and the priest, and ye are gone away: and what have I more? and what is this that ye say unto me, What aileth thee?'. The 'cowardly' denotation is in the verses that upon seeing they are too many/strong, he simply returns home without an additional word. Cp: meeqah(qa), meekah(ka), meeḥah(ḥa). (Judg.17, 18)

Bethlehemjudah; this name has been combined from 'Bethlehem' and 'Judah' now to be 'a house for them-called' as the man from the village of the same name is looking 'to sojourn where I may find a place.' and he is made a priest by Micah so his work will be calling on/shouting to God. (Judg.17:7-13)

Laish; layiš; لَيش 'why?' and the authors have kept it in theme with 'Micah', when the Danites decide they will invade Laish they also steal Micah's idol, ephod and teraphim which prompts the Levite's dialogue which is a 'Laish/why' question: 'What do ye?'; the way the people of Laish living in prosperity and peace is described and the narration all show how 'Why?' is the name of the city as there is no reason why they killed them: 'and came unto Laish, unto a people *that were* at quiet and secure: and they smote them with the edge of the sword, and burnt the city with fire. And *there was* no deliverer…'. The reason Dan and Danites are chosen as the characters to do this, is because **Dan**, as explained where the word appears in Genesis means 'guilty' (along with bowed, etc.) and in this part of the story they are guilty of stealing Micah's sacred possessions and of attacking a peaceable people and taking their city. Cp: layish. (Judg.18)

Zidonians; ṣîdōnî, ṣîdōnîm; زيدوني 'give me extra' 'of extra' 'of excess' 'deceived me' 'of deceiving'; زيدون هم/ام 'give extra-them/the' 'have excess-them/the' 'deceived-them/the' and the meanings of excess and extra are directly reflected in the story which causes the people of Laish to become a target for the Danites envy and attack. The word can also mean صيدوني ، صيدون هم/ام 'fishermen' 'of fishing' 'fishing-them/

the' 'blocked me/prevented me' but has not been used in this story. Cp: zeedoonee, zeedoon-hum/um, sseedoonee, sseedoon-hum/um. (Judg.18:7-12)

Mahaneh-dan; maḥănēh-dān; مَحنَيه/مَحينيه دآن 'we troubled/put them through a lot-guilty' as they will attack, kill and take the city Laish, they plot for it and are guilty of the attack and crimes; مَهَنيه/مَهينيه دآن 'satisfied/gave enough to them-guilty' as Laish way of life is described repeatedly 'how they dwelt careless, after the manner of the Zidonians, quiet and secure…Arise, that we may go up against them: for we have seen the land, and behold, it is very good…When ye go, ye shall come unto a people secure, and to a large land: for God hath given it into your hands; a place where *there is* no want of anything that *is* in the earth.' And after they set off for the invasion of Laish they camp at Kirjath-jearim, but the authors decide to change the name to Mahaneh-dan to mirror the current story. Cp: maḥaneyh-daan, maḥaineyh-daan, mahaneyh-daan, mahaineyh-daan. (Judg.18:12)

Jonathan; to be explained later when role of same word-name becomes more prominent. (Judg.18:30)

Jebus the same as **Jebusite** (Gen.10:16); yĕḇûs; يَبُس ، ييبُس 'dry/dried' 'stiff/stiffened'; جَبُس ، جيبُس 'stiffens when dry/thick and cloying' is used in both meanings that after being pliable and staying every time he is urged to by his father-in-law, the Levite eventually 'stiffens' his resolve and leaves which is why 'Jebus' is mentioned immediately after he refuses to stay overnight and leaves, the same reason 'Jebus' is mentioned when his servant suggests they stay over in 'this city of the Jebusites' but again the Levite refuses (it is likening him to being 'stiff-necked); خَبُص ، خيبُص the sexual meanings of 'poked finger into' 'poked finger into anus' 'poked into' (e.g. when a man pokes his finger into another man's anus (above clothing) as a joke/prank) but in this story it is used to mean anal sex between men as the men of Gibeah are described of doing and wanting to do even to others who do not agree to it. Cp: yebus, yeibus, gebus, geibus, khebuss, kheibuss. (Judg.19:10-12)

Gibeah; is still: giḇ'â; جِذعه/ا 'broke it into pieces' without separating from main body e.g. causing damage internally and is exactly narrated after the Levite gives his wife to the men of Gibeah who wanted to rape him, they 'abused her all the night until the morning' and she dies at the doorstep i.e. she dies of her internal injuries, but her body is still a whole; جِبئه/ا 'ganged together' 'came from all over' 'gathered to stand/do something against' 'a group of people' 'brought/fetched' because the men of Gibeah 'beset the house round about' and demand the Levite be brought out so they can rape him, and also because the rest of the tribes of Israel will gather against Gibeah. Cp: giv'ah('a), gibah/gib-ah(-a). (Judg.19)

Belial; still has the same meanings as in Deuteronomy: beliyya'al; بِلِيَّ عَل 'an ailment/curse-on' 'an affliction/illness/suffering-on' not only because they kill the Levite's wife (which he too has a hand in as he brought her out to them) but they will bring the consequences upon all of Gibeah and the tribe of Benjamin. Cp: beliyya-'al. (Judg.19)

Bethlehemjudah now is used in a different way. It still retains the essence of the first meaning of Bethlehem in Genesis: 'house-chewed out/tore off strips of meat/ate plenty of meat' 'he will be-chewed out/tear off strips of meat/eat plenty of meat' 'he will be-chewed out' 'girl/daughter-chewed out' as in shouted at/told off angrily; 'he will be-I will chew out' 'girl/daughter-I will chew out', 'he will be-I will chew him out' 'girl/daughter-I will chew out'. As (leḥim/lehimat) 'he/she chewed out…/bit the head off…' and the word is from لَحَم،لِحِم of how a predator tears off meat from its prey and also a human when pulling strips of meat off to eat. So now it denotes the woman being cut up to pieces by her husband which is why she is said to be from Bethlehemjudah and not the husband. It now means literally 'girl/daughter-he tore strips of meat/ate meat-called' 'will-I will tear strips of meat/eat meat-called' as the Levite processes his murdered wife as would a butcher process meat. The 'judah' 'called' part of the name is because when he sends out these meat parcels to the twelve tribes, he is calling them to take revenge for what has happened. (Judg.19)

The way words/compound words are used for character/place names as themes denoting the story can always be seen: In Micah and the Gibeah story '**Ephraim**' (increase/enrich) is used as where Micah came from because he will get money from returning what he has stolen, then he will pay a Levite an annual salary; in Gibeah the old man who assists the Levite also comes from Ephraim (they make a point that he is not from Gibeah but Ephraim) as he either refuses or allows the Levite to use his own food sources for feeding animals and people while they stay in his house—so one of them is still better in wealth—and being fed and making merry is emphasised in this man's house. '**Levite**' is used as the man who comes and becomes a priest for Micah because he answers positively and agrees to becoming Micah's priest, then the same to the Danites; the second Levite because he agrees and stays at his in-law's repeatedly and then his call to the tribes is answered, they too assist and gather for him. (Judg.18,19)

Benjamin has been used as the greater attribute to the Gibeah men because one of 'benjamin' meanings is 'son/child-whose?'; where it was meant to evoke pity for the orphaned-at-birth Benjamin in Genesis, in this part of the story it denotes blame even on a dead/missing mother, implying the children are not brought up properly by their mothers which is why they are perverted/abominations (according to the Bible).

There is a definite blame laid on females in the culture of the Biblical authors: Eve for Adam eating from the forbidden fruit; Dinah being the reason why Jacob becomes Israel: 'El-elohe-Israel'twisted muscle-the'; Rebekah is behind Jacob deceiving both Esau and Isaac; Rachel is blamed for Laban pursuing them over theft of his idols when the whole story narrates Jacob has stolen and taken-off with a lot more to cause Laban to pursue them (you can see the later editors going back in and assigning blame with additions); Tamar for the deaths of Judah's sons; and now the Levite's concubine because 'she played the whore' which caused some upset which led her to stay at her father's home, and although it is the men of Gibeah blamed for her death, it was actually the old man from Ephraim who was offering to give his daughter and his guest's concubine for the men to abuse and it is the Levite who brings her out to them, the same is when Lot offers his daughters in Genesis, and throughout the Bible marrying 'strange women' leads to disobedience followed by catastrophe.

Even the heroines of stories such as Deborah and Jael have negative words for names. Benjamin is because there was no mother to bring him up properly therefore suitable to use as the wider attribute to why the peoples who are his descendants are so wicked. One editor of the Bible has chosen to make it explicitly clearly that the word 'benjamin' has nothing to do with 'right hand/right side' by adding: 'Among all this people *there were* seven hundred chosen men lefthanded; everyone could sling stones at an hair *breadth*, and not miss.' (Judg.19)

Beer-sheba, **Gilead**, **Dan**, for their meanings of pacts, piety, witnessing, oaths, guilt as mentioned before. **Mizpeh** because there will be great slaughter to follow the already slaughtered woman in the story. Gilead and Mizpeh also have a significant meaning which will be explained towards the end of this book. (Judg.20:1)

Baal-tamar; baʿal tāmār; بَعَل دآمآر 'height/above/from higher-destruction'; بَعَل ضآمآر 'height/above/from higher-kept inside/in heart' 'height/above/from higher-hid thoughts/intentions' 'height/above/from higher-hid in soul/head/heart' and means to know, think or feel something but hide the true intentions, meanings or feelings from others, and refers to the ambush prepared and baiting Benjamin to come upwards so they will be encircled and great death and destruction follows. Cp: ba'al daamaar, ba'al dhaamaar. (Judg.20:29-48)

Rimmon; rimmôn; رِمٌّن 'thrown' 'killed' 'rotten/stinking' as earlier but now has direct role in the story, the heaps of corpses are rotten or stinking, as would blood from killing, 'thrown/killed' because the great numbers that are killed and in Arabic 'fell' is another word like 'thrown' which means died or flung to the ground. Cp: rimmon. (Judg.20:45-47)

Gidom; giḏʿōm; جِدعوم 'uprooted them' 'put head down and pushed forward' both describe what was done to Benjamites and how they fled towards Rimmon and through Gidom; also 'came-(special)wall on grave' (gi/ج) 'came' (dom/ḏʿōm/دعوم) plural or its singular du'ama/دُعاما a wall structure built out of stone on top or next to grave of people believed to have special powers/connections to God (a candle is lit in the window left in the wall). In this story it implies the many-killed of Benjamin and how the small number still alive taking refuge in Rimmon are on the verge of extinction. جِدعون 'broke them into pieces' without separating from main body and in this instance although the story has the Benjaminites killed by the tens of thousands, they allow a part of Benjamin tribe to survive and to also remain part of the twelve tribes of Israel, the name uprooted/broke to pieces that they pursue them through and to Rimmon enhances the name/action method of the Biblical stories. Cp: gid'oom, giv'oon. (Judg.20:45-46)

Jabesh-gilead; yāḇêš gilʿāḏ; غآبيش جِلعآد 'absent from rock', and 'absent' followed by all meanings previously mentioned in Genesis for 'Gilead': جِل عآب ، قِل عآب 'coming/saying-to shame'; قِل عآض ، جِل عآض'said recompense/replenish' 'came/coming the-recompense/replenish' 'said-teaching lesson/lecturing' 'came/coming the-teaching lesson/lecturing'; قِلعآذ 'say(ing) protection'; قِلآد ، قِلئآد 'placing responsibility'; قِلعآب ، قِلعآد 'tumbling/rolling stone(s)'. And the authors make sure all the meanings of 'gilead' are covered because the people absent are absent from: the tumbled/rolled rock (Mizpeh); the people who have come are speaking how shameful it is for the group to be absent; they decide it is from these people of the absent tribe that Benjamin's line will be replenished from; they are placing responsibility on those absent as it was an oath to attend; they are also discussing, in between mentioning there is a group missing from attending Mizpeh, that Benjamin's line has to be protected and they 'repent' for Benjamin. Mizpeh is a rock, the tribe missing from attending Mizpeh (a rock) is suitably named 'absent from rock' so it is decided they will be massacred and only young virgins kept to give Benjamin as wives to reproduce from. Cp: g͟haabeysh   gil'aad/gil-'aab/qil-'aab/gil'aad͟h/qil'aad͟h/qil-'aav/qilaad/qil-aad/qil'aab/qil'aad. (Judg.21)

Shiloh; is still 'take it/took it' 'his rock' as they kidnap the young girls who are still virgins from Jabesh-gilead and take them to 'Shiloh'; and again, the girls and women of Shiloh are taken against their will from the festival and taken to Benjamin as wives for the tribe; the decision is made at Mizpeh which is rock-related, the first batch of women to be kidnapped and given to Benjamin are from rock-named tribes/areas (Jabesh-Gilead and Shiloh). Cp: s͟hilooh. (Judg.21:10-23)

Lebonah; lĕb͟ônâ; لبُنه ، ليبُنه 'for his sons' 'for rebuilding' and refers to the girls and women being kidnapped for the sons of Benjamin to repopulate with, and also to them rebuilding their cities. Cp: lebonah, leibonah. (Judg.21:19)

Ruth

Elimelech; ’ĕlîmeleḵ; نِلي/نيلي مَلِح ‘he who/the one who-well/good/pretty’ and is probably ‘good’ which means tastes good as his sons have names which mean ‘sweet’ and Naomi compares her life after his death to bitterness; نِلي/نيلي مَلك ‘he who/the one who-what is wrong with you’ as he dies and so do his sons. Cp: illee/eilee-meleḥ, illee/eilee-melek. (Ruth:1)

Mahlon; maḥlôn; مَحلُن ‘is sweet’ ‘in their/its place’ ‘purified/cleansed/circumcised/made edible/made touchable’ ‘declared purified/permissible’ ‘undressed’ ‘shed’ ‘replaced’. Cp: maḥlon. (Ruth.1)

Chilion; kilyôn; حِلْيُن ‘became sweet(er)’ ‘became pure/cleansed/circumcised/edible/touchable’ ‘undress them’ ‘shed them’; خِلْيُن ‘leave them/leave them behind’ ‘let them/allow them’. Cp: ḥilyon, khilyon. Both names are from ‘purify/sweet’ and they come from Ephratah/Ephrath/Ephratha so both sons are given the ‘sweetness/purified’ meaning from the place name they originate from. The second meanings denote how Naomi wants to leave her daughters-in-law behind so they can continue with their lives, it also denotes Ruth insisting to be allowed to stay with Naomi. (Ruth.1)

Naomi; no‘ŏmî; نوئومي ، نوئويمي ‘put to bed/put to sleep’ ‘make bed/sleep’ and is euphemism for having sex, and in this story she convinces Ruth to sleep with Boaz; نوعومي ، نوعويمي ‘make soft’ ‘make easier/restful’ ‘my blessings/of blessings’ ‘give blessings/fortunes’ ‘receive food/money/anything given by another’ and refers to Naomi’s plan of getting Boaz to have sex with Ruth so that Ruth can have an easier life as his wife and at the same time not lose her husband’s (Naomi’s) inheritance. Cp: noo-oomee, noo-oimee, noo’oomee, noo’oimee. (Ruth)

Mara; mārā’; مآرآء ‘bitter’ as when people ask ‘*Is* this Naomi’ she snaps back ‘Call me not Naomi, call me Mara: for the Almighty hath dealt very bitterly with me…’ and she is comparing the deaths of her husband and sons whose names mean ‘sweet, good, well’ and contrasting it to her life becoming bitterness after their deaths. Also ‘severely/intensely’ as the word ‘mara’ means and is also used as ‘mara/ (Or) mara waahid’ ‘intensely all at once/all at once’ meaning whatever is being spoken about happened ‘all in one go’ or was very intense or extremely harsh and the dialogue reflects this ‘I went out full, and the Lord hath brought me home again empty: why *then* call ye me Naomi…’ showing the contrast between two meanings of her name ‘make easier/restful’ ‘blessings’ and her current situation. Note **Bethlehem** is used here in the sense ‘he will be chewed him out’ as she answers angrily at the people who ask ‘Is this Naomi’. Cp: maaraa. (Ruth.1:19-21)

Orpah; ‘orpâ; عوربه/ا is a vulgar word ‘a fuck/a shag’. Cp: ’oorbah(ba). (Ruth.1)

Ruth; rûṯ; رُث/رُف ، رُفث means the same act as ‘Orpah’ but in a civilised word ‘sexual intercourse/had sex’. Cp: ruf, ruph, ruphf. Both Orpah and Ruth have been given names which mean the same thing, but Orpah crudely because although she does nothing wrong and is devoted to her mother-in-law and deceased husband, she eventually leaves and returns to her Moab family (enemies of Naomi’s people) and will return to their gods. Whereas Ruth refuses to part with Naomi and converts completely to Naomi’s religions and traditions—hence she is given a more ‘decorum’ version of the word than her sister-in-law’s.

Ruth’s meaning is expressed throughout the story: Naomi tells both Ruth and Orpah to return to their own people so they can still marry which will lead to offspring—the product of each of their names; she does not want them to suffer by remaining with her as her late sons’ widows—for she wants what is best for them and gives them an example that she is no longer having sex to produce children and even if she were to marry and conceive that very night what use would it be to the women to wait. At the end of the story using sex to entice Boaz, Ruth marries and bears a child—the whole point of sex in the story. (Ruth.1:8-18; 4:13).

Naomi’s instructions to Ruth are actions to entice Boaz to make love to her without marriage then to marry her. She tells Ruth to make herself attractive, to wash, to anoint (which means to use fragrant smelling substances after washing—women do this with more particularity using perfumes, perfumed oils, waxes, incense when the night nears, for their husbands or lovers, and it is meant to increase pleasure before, during and after sex); Naomi tells Ruth to lie where Boaz sleeps, to uncover his feet, which is just another euphemism where ‘foot/feet’ mean the penis. (Ruth.3:1-5). Ruth does as told, and goes further: she tells Boaz ‘I am Ruth thine handmaid: spread therefore thy skirt over thine handmaid; for thou art a near kinsman.' Its meaning is direct and has been used in earlier stories of the Torah/Bible where the lifting of a man's skirt means to have illicit sex (sex outside marriage) with another man's wife, daughter, etc. So Ruth, like her name, is not asking him to marry her but to make love to her. (Ruth.3:6-18)

Boaz; bōʿaz; بوعَز 'of pride' 'of high standing' 'of dignity/cherishing' and he is introduced as 'a mighty man of wealth'; he shows concern for Ruth's dignity and tells her he will do as she asks 'for all the city of my people doth know that thou art a virtuous woman', he shows concern for his own reputation/dignity when he asks her to sneak out of the threshing floor after spending the night with him as it is important to him 'And he said, let it not be known that a woman came into the threshing floor.'; بوعَص 'slips from/through' such as from hand or through fingers: immediately after he is introduced, Ruth takes permission from Naomi to go pick up corn that falls while the men work Boaz' fields, he orders the men to intentionally allow grain panicles to fall so Ruth can collect them without feeling she is being pitied so even while allowing more grain 'slip from' he is also keeping her 'dignity'; دوعَس 'stepped on' 'feet' and mention of his feet feature greatly in the story as euphemism for the penis 'and uncover his feet, and lay thee down' 'and she came softly, and uncovered his feet, and laid her down.' 'and, behold, a woman lay at his feet.' 'And she lay at his feet until the morning' also the 'a man plucked off his shoe, and gave it to his neighbour...So he drew off his shoe.' Footwear is called 'foot/stepped on' when it is accidentally placed on somebody or when insulting someone (joking or serious). Cp: boo'az, boo'a<u>ss</u>, doo'as. (Ruth.2, 3, 4)

Obed; ʿôb̲ēd̲; عُبيد 'servant' 'of service' 'worshipper' 'of worship', but it is not the last two meanings of worship but 'servant' because the whole narration before he is introduced is about Naomi who was to live out her old age alone and without assistance finally has a kinsman in Boaz and offspring through Ruth to serve her in her old age. Children and grandchildren start to help out with chores when they reach a certain age and by the time a grandparent/parent is old, adult children including daughters/sons-in-law also help out then take over completely the chores so the grandparent can rest in old age and that is what Naomi has been blessed with. 'And Naomi took the child and laid it in her bosom, and became nurse to it' is symbolising breastfeeding as when a mother breastfeeds someone else's child that child becomes equal to being biologically hers too and as a sibling to all her children—that is what is symbolised in the narration although Naomi would not have any breastmilk to nurse it. Cp: 'obeyd. (Ruth.4:11-17)

Salmon; śalmôn; صَلمُن 'arrived-who' 'arrived-from' 'reached-who/from' 'connected-who/from' 'public apology arrived'; سَلمُن 'asked' 'asked who' 'of questions' 'leaked/flowed from' 'intact/whole' 'survived' 'comforted/entertained/distracted-who' and he has been included as an ancestor of Jesse and David (the latter two names will be explained when their roles become more prominent later in the book). He is a precursor to the character that will eventually be named Solomon as Jesse and David's descendant/son and not an ancestor as here in Ruth. The word-name Salmon is also connected to the character Saul, and may be an indication of how later editors/authors changed a more prominent role from 'Saul' to the new and preferred 'Solomon' as both words are connected. Cp: salmon, <u>ss</u>almon (Ruth.4:20-21)

The names and 'lineage' chosen for Obed are solely for the meaning of the words as themes and if understood (as they would be when the Biblical stories originally circulated) they would read as a summarisation of the story of Naomi/Ruth: **Pharez** as he was the baby that 'split through/broke through/emerged' from the **Tamar** 'destruction/hidden intentions' brought upon **Judah** 'called': these themes are invoked because after purchasing Naomi's inheritance, Boaz calls it out and announces it to all the people and the people cry out a blessing for them which is about Pharez/Obed being a blessing that comes after Tamar's and Naomi/Ruth's hidden intentions following the destruction they suffered in the respective stories. **Hezron** 'thinness' 'great despair and sorrow' from the grief, hunger and poverty Naomi and Ruth go through when their husband/sons are **Ram** 'thrown' i.e. die and they grieve **Amminadab** 'uncle/the one who-wails loudly/mourns' over their loss and it is from **Nahshon** 'bad luck/bad omen' but when Ruth **Salmon** 'asked' to stay with Naomi it led to meeting Boaz and then Ruth 'asked' Boaz to have sex with her which led to their marriage and **Boaz** 'dignity/high-standing' will also be Naomi and Ruth's and the result is **Obed** 'servant' who will bring all the good and cherished aspects of having offspring to both mother and grandmother. (Ruth.4:12-22)

1 Samuel

Elkanah's home and lineage are made to suit the story: **Ramathaim-zophim**; rāmāṯayim ṣôpîm; رآماَتي هم/ام زُفهم/ام 'threw around/threw (action by two people)/killed-them/the-send away in a procession-them/the' and it refers to Elkanah having two wives for whom he will present sacrifices on behalf of (throw/kill) and as they are a large family because of Peninnah they are like a procession while travelling. Cp: raamaatay-hum/um zoph-hum/um.

Ephraim 'increase/multiply-them/the', he has plenty of children, two wives and also has a lot of flocks/cattle and he is able to make many offerings to God; the story will also multiply and increase him with Hannah having Samuel. **Elkanah** 'meet us' 'find us' 'the thrown' as during the ritual offering of sacrifices Hannah will meet Eli the priest who gives her a blessing. 'the one with head held high/body straight posture/erect' 'the person or object sitting/place/set upright' 'were perky' and 'the channel(water channel)' 'the bottle/flask/any transportable drink vessel/also small water vessel' 'the topping up(of liquid)' 'the estimating measure of something liquid' (when mixing ingredients) 'the one carrying a bottle/small pot/small drink vessel' and the latter word is a female carrying this bottle/pot—and this meaning of Elkanah reflects on Hannah who is standing praying to God, and who Eli thinks is drinking and tells her to put away the wine, it reflects God will grant her wish and Elkanah's semen (semen/sperm is called 'water') will impregnate her although she is barren.

Jeroham; yĕrōḥām; يِروحاَم ، ييروحام 'he has mercy on' 'of wombs/concerning wombs' as Eli and God have mercy for Hannah and her problem is 'the Lord had shut up her womb'; يِروهاَم ، ييروهام 'he sees-worried' as Eli sees Hannah who is worried by her infertility; جِروح ام ، جيروح ام 'wounded/hurt-the' as Peninnah hurts Hannah over her infertility. Cp: yeroohaam, yeiroohaam, yeroohaam, yeiroohaam, geroohaam, geiroohaam.

Elihu; 'ĕlîhû; ئِلي/ئيلي هو 'he who/the one who' 'yes, it is the one/yes, it is him' and refers to the priest Eli whose character name is similar and who will help Hannah. Cp: illee/eilee-hu.

Tohu; tōhû; توهْ 'lost/misled' as Eli wrongly believes she is drunk; دوهْ 'no' 'it is not' as Hannah responds that she is not drunk and it is the antonym of one meaning of 'Eli', and also 'senile/behaving slightly senile' 'forgetting/misunderstanding/confusing'. Cp: toohu, doohu.

Zuph; ṣûp; زُف 'was led in procession' and refers to one person being escorted by an entourage and this refers to Samuel who will be escorted by Hannah specifically to give him to God as fulfilment of her vow. Cp: zuph. (1Sam.1:1)

Ephrathite for its meanings: 'partings' 'crossings' as eventually Hannah will part with Samuel while he is still a child, when she leaves him at Shiloh; 'cleanser of guts' the verb of pushing/squeezing impurities out of slaughtered animals intestines (in preparation for cooking the cleaned intestines) as the story is set around the annual offerings of sacrifices and vows at Shiloh, and processing the meat to be eaten includes this action.

Hannah; ḥannâ; هَنّه/ا 'he satisfied/gave fill/plenty of' 'satisfaction/gave satisfaction' and the story emphasises although he gives his other wife and children lots of portions, he gives Hannah plenty of meat 'But unto Hannah he gave a worthy portion'. The word in its different forms/tenses is used in daily language about being full, having enough to eat and wishing a person a hearty/fulfilling meal or (not food-related) to be satisfied emotionally and/or physically. Elkanah also satisfies Hannah's emotional needs 'for he loved Hannah' and it presented as loving her more because it is said he gives her a better portion of food because he loved her. She will be satisfied when God gives her a child although she is barren. She will offer God a satisfying number of offerings in return for giving her Samuel 'three bullocks, one ephah of flour, and a bottle of wine' and the whole story shows Elkanah always offers plenty annually. Cp: hannah(na). (1Sam.1)

Peninnah; pĕninnâ; بِنِنّه/ا ، بينِنّه/ا 'has many children' 'has children' 'is bringing up children' which is exactly how she is described in contrast to Hannah 'and the name of the other was Peninnah: and Peninnah had children, but Hannah had no children.'. Cp: beninnah(na), beininnah(na). (1Sam.1:2,4,6)

Eli; 'ēlî; عيلي 'higher above/rose above' 'above me' 'my boys' (as in sons). He is set in a position where he is above Hannah when he observes her actions 'So Hannah rose up…Now Eli the priest sat upon a seat by a post at the temple…'; 'my sons' as his sons also have major roles in the story; ئِلي 'he who/the one who' 'the one/the one that' 'it is/yes, it is' 'for me' and denotes when Eli believes and states Hannah is drunk. Cp: 'eylee, illee/eylee. (1Sam.1)

Samuel; šěmû'ēl; صِمُ ئِل ، صيمُ ئِل 'block(ed)-the' 'plug-the' 'shut up-the'. Hannah is infertile, the authors repeat this by comparing her to fertile Peninnah 'but Hannah had no children; and repeating she is 'blocked-the': 'but the Lord had shut up her womb' she is taunted by her step-wife 'because the Lord had shut up her womb'; she blocks up with fret and cannot eat because she is taunted about being infertile. When Eli mistakes her as being drunk he tells her to 'put away thy wine from thee' which would involve closing/plugging/shutting the wine vessel. The emphasis on her 'blocked/shut up' issue is elucidated in her response which says she does not need to put away wine as she has a great problem and the only thing pouring out is her sorrow over this problem. When she is unblocked by God, she names her son 'block(ed)-the' (Samuel); when the first annual sacrifice since he was born comes up, Hannah does not go because she wants to present him only after Samuel is 'weaned' i.e. her breast shuts-up from feeding him (milk stops producing in the breast when it is no longer sucked out and remains blocked full of accumulating milk for three or more days, then milk production stops) and is also denotation of the meaning of 'samuel'. The only reason 'and called his name Samuel, saying, Because I have asked him of the Lord' would be later editors of this story did not know the meaning of 'Samuel' and could only guess, or wanted to give it a better meaning and likening the name to 'Ishmael' where there was a listening and hearing in the story between God and Hagar, but there is nothing in this word-name which reflects 'asking God' and plenty of examples of her womb being shut-up and he is the result of a blocked womb then blocked breasts; of course part of her prayer to become pregnant does involve the opening of her blocked womb, but the word-name Samuel does not mean 'asking God'. Cp: ssemu-ill, sseimu-ill. (1Sam.1)

The place name for where Elkanah came has gone from Ramathaim-zophim at the beginning of the chapter to Ramah within the same chapter as it is a fictional story with fictional place and character names created to enhance the story. **Ramah** is now used for: rāmâ; رآمه/ا which still retains 'threw around/threw/killed' for sacrifice and offerings, also 'saw water' as semen is called 'water', and Hannah because she conceives from it this time has 'seen water' and it is narrated 'and came to their house to Ramah: and Elkanah knew Hannah his wife; and the Lord remembered her…after Hannah had conceived, that she bare a son…'. Cp: raamah(ma). (1Sam.1:19-20)

Shiloh has been chosen again for its meaning 'take it/took it' 'his rock', the people take their families, their offerings to this place where a special rock is worshipped which Hannah will praise later in the story, Hannah will take and leave Samuel there, Phinehas and Hophni will sin by taking meat they are not supposed to take in Shiloh.

Hophni; ḥopnî; هوفني 'puffed at me/treated me badly' 'treated me badly and drove me away' as the word means to speak angrily or with harsh words and drive the spoken-to away, 'I will eradicate/finish off'. All meanings are used: God sends a messenger to Eli with a 'hophni' message full of anger and severity and promises to bring Eli's line to extinction. Both Phinehas and Hophni characters have been linked with negative words for names, bad behaviour, God's curse and their deaths. Cp: hoophnee. (1Sam.1:3; 2; 3; 4)

As in Exodus and Numbers, **Phinehas** is still: pîněḥās; بينَحآس ، بينيحآس 'will bring bad luck' and is in the form to bring bad luck to himself and/or others; بينَهآس ، بينيهآس 'will breathe'; بينَخآش ، بينيخآش 'will create holes/crumble' 'poke holes at and crumble'; بينَهآش ، بينيهآش 'will maul/take chunks out of'. In this story he brings bad luck because of his sins of stealing from the sacrifices and having illicit sex; he will bring bad luck on all his family and people; he takes meat portions which were not meant for him, God sends a messenger 'Wherefore kick ye at my sacrifice and at mine offering…and honourest thy sons above me, to make yourselves fat with the chiefest of all the offerings…'. Cp: beeneḥaas, beeneiḥaas, beenehaas, beeneihaas, beenekhaash, beeneikhaash, beenehaash, beeneihaash. (1Sam.1,2,3)

Dan has been chosen for 'guilt' of Eli's children which God has spoken to Samuel about. **Beer-sheba**/ beeyr-shewha has been chosen because (as explained in Genesis) it means 'Good/Piety-Ewes'; the word 'ewe/shewha/شوها ' with the same spelling and pronunciation it also can mean 'chat or conversation/shewha/شوها' so it is now used for and means 'Good/Piety-conversation' because in this chapter the emphasis from the beginning is '…the word of the Lord was precious in those days; there was no open vision' and revolves around God chatting/conversing with Samuel, Samuel conversing with Eli, and the subject of the conversation is about Eli and his sons' guilt and their demise (Dan/guilty), and the goodness/piety and the rising of Samuel's status is spoken about 'And all Israel from Dan even unto Beer-sheba knew that Samuel *was* established *to be* a prophet of the Lord.' And to make sure everyone knows the word-pun in the story is 'a chat/conversation' the author ends it with 'And the Lord appeared again in Shiloh: for the Lord revealed himself to Samuel in Shiloh by the word of the Lord.'.

Eben-ezer; 'eb̲en haʿezer; يِذَن هَعَزَر 'so/well-I will make ugly' 'so/well-here/look-became ugly' and suggests terrible death or great slaughter will follow as always when the word 'ezer' is used as a place or person name and 'Israel was smitten before the Philistines: and they slew of the army in the field about four thousand men' 'and there was a very great slaughter; for there fell of Israel thirty thousand footmen' 'And the ark of God was taken; and the two sons of Eli, Hophni and Phinehas, were slain'; Eli and his daughter will also die on hearing the news. You will see earlier in Genesis 'ezer' makes up part of a name where great punishment and death is mentioned, the same in Numbers 25: both Phinehas and Eliezer are given as 'son and patronym' where mention of killing people follows. Here it is Phinehas, his brother, father, wife and tens of thousands of people who will die following this place-name. يِبَن هَعَزَر 'son-I will ugly' 'became apparent/clearly see-I will ugly'. Cp: e-ven ha'ezer, e-ben ha'ezer. (1Sam.4:1)

Aphek for its earlier meanings of 'leaping' 'kicking and jerking' (usually how a new born calf behaves) as both sides (Philistines/Israel) will hesitate then fight; also, for 'part(something)' 'parted hair' as Israel's side will be scattered with men running into their tents. **Shiloh** keeps on being mentioned for 'take it/take' and now the ark of the covenant will be taken from Shiloh to the battleground and then it will be taken by the Philistines. (1Sam.4)

I-cha-bod; 'îk̲āb̲ôd̲; ئيكَابَد 'choked/it chokes' 'chocked-full/it chocks-full' 'stifled/it stifles' and not only 'choke' as in gets caught in the throat and chokes, but also means a great pain in the chest, a heavy painful feeling in the chest of bursting, breaking—especially from grief, shock or distress. It is also the word used for the feeling of eating too quick and feeling a pain in the chest where the morsels jam/congest before going down. It describes the distress and heartbreak Phinehas' wife felt when she heard about the deaths and the ark which causes her labour to come early and '…she named the child I-cha-bod saying, The glory is departed from Israel: because the ark of God was taken, and because of her father in law and her husband.' It also describes Eli's death, although he broke his neck upon falling, it was the distress of hearing of his sons' deaths and the loss of the ark that causes him to fall off his seat. It is an often-used expression about being stifled by not chewing properly or eating something too dry than to go down the throat or oesophagus smoothly, and also it is said '(iktbd/اكتبد) his chest/heart burst/choked/chocked and he died' اكتبد ومات. Also, if someone has done or said something upsetting to another, the affected person will say كبدني ، كبدتني (kbdnee - he stifled/choked/chocked me) (kbdtnee—she stifled/choked/chocked me). (kobd/كُبد) means a feeling of suffocation, tearing, bursting, a knotting, congestion etc., all at the same time (in the chest and soul). Cp: eekaabod. (1Sam.4:12-22)

Ashdod; 'ašdôd̲; نَشدُد 'emigrate/leave' (said to male) and refers to the ark of God leaving Shiloh and staying at Ashdod and then leaving again to be left at another place; 'become more severe/brace yourself' 'become stronger' 'tie strongly' 'strengthen and persevere' denotes how the Philistines are punished in the story and how the punishment increases 'But the hand of the Lord was heavy upon them of Ashdod…'. Cp: as̲h̲dod. (1Sam.5:1-8)

Gath here is; gat̲; جعث 'great sufferance' physical sufferance 'troubling/inconvenience' or even just putting a person to too much trouble or bothering; غت 'misled to downfall/deceived/deceit/folly' and the story narrates the inhabitants of Gath suffered great destruction and physical ailments from God and this was caused because the Philistines took away God's ark, and wherever they send it and set it up at a sequence of Philistine villages, it causes the recipients' downfall and sufferance which the last inconvenienced village is aware will happen, so they are 'misleading to downfall' the people they pass it on to. Cp: g'f, g̲h̲at. (1Sam.5:8-9)

Ekron here holds some of its earlier meanings in Josh., 'ruined' and 'petrified' as the inhabitants of Ekron are in great fear that they will be killed when the ark of God is sent to their city after seeing what happened when it was stored at previous places. (1Sam.5:10-12)

Beth-shemesh is used here as 'he/it will be possessed/touched' 'he/it will possess/touch': every time God's spirit possesses one of the prophets/leaders in the Biblical stories he conducts what is evil, such as Moses trying to kill his own son, or Joshua, Jiphtah, Samson killing great scores of people so here it denotes the evil and destruction caused by taking God's ark and they narrate this exactly: if it goes to Beth-shemesh 'then he hath done us this great evil…' i.e. he 'touched us' as in caused evil (the word is the same as explained in Massah (Exod)). And even when it arrives among the correct people they are touched by evil and destruction for looking into it/touching it. (1Sam.6:9-20)

Joshua here is used again as 'picked a lot' 'many people' as the ark arrives at a field owned by Joshua where there are many people reaping, and they make the sacrificial offerings to God so there is plenty picked up and offered; but also God 'smote of the people fifty thousand and threescore and ten men…' the authors want to make sure the audience does not miss the pun of the meaning of 'joshua/many people' and reiterates in the same verse 'because the Lord had smitten many of the people with a great slaughter.'. (1Sam.6:14-19)

Kirjath-jearim 'village/came out-lends/gloats over-them/the' for its meaning 'came out-lends' as the ark of God will be taken out of Beth-shemesh and will stay at Kirjath-jearim, but the latter is only temporary as it is supposed to return to Shiloh so it is being 'lent'. (1Sam.6:20-21; 7:1-2)

Abinadab; 'ăb̲înādāb̲; نَبي/نُيبي نَآداب 'father-wailed/mourned loudly' 'rejected-wailed/mourned loudly' 'father/rejected-has scars'; نُبي نَاضَاب 'father-has protruding teeth/jaw' 'rejected-has protruding teeth/jaw'. In this part of the story it refers to 'wailing/mourning' as 'all the house of Israel lamented after the Lord.' and the ark is in Abinadab's house; his son Eleazar has the same meanings of 'ugliness' related to destruction in all the stories where this word is used as a character name. Cp: abee/aibee-naadaab, abee/aibee-naadhaab. (1Sam.7:1-2)

Although **Mizpeh** still means slaughter, at 1Sam.7 it is still also used the same way as at Josh.11 for 'body of water/pool of water' مِسبَح and مِصبَه 'pouring place/pouring/pouring vessel' Cp: misbaḥ, missbah, and this is because they want the battle where the Philistines whose name means 'between two(or more) coasts/between coasts' to happen between two bodies of water i.e. between two coasts. It is why the authors narrate that if they want to defeat the Philistines they need to meet some conditions: 'And they gathered together to Mizpeh, and drew water, and poured *it* out before the Lord…' and to create another body of water for Philistines name and role to aptly take place in 'And as Samuel was offering up the burnt offering, the Philistines drew near to battle against Israel: but the Lord thundered with a great thunder on that day upon the Philistines, and discomfited them; and they were smitten before Israel.' So the poured water at Mizpeh and the raining have the Philistines between two bodies of water just as their name suggests, and is why it was chosen for this part of the story. And whether the same authors or later editors, they always want to make sure that 'Philistine' is understood as 'between two coasts' so they add 'So the Philistines were subdued, and they came no more into the coast of Israel.' '…and the coasts thereof did Israel deliver out of the hands of the Philistines'. (1Sam.7)

Beth-car; bêt̲-kār; بيت قآر 'he/it will stop' 'he/it will settle(down)' and it is mentioned in the story to denote this session of warring with Philistines stops. Cp: beyt-qaar. (1Sam.7:11-13)

This also shows how the word-names created are used as themes: **Eben-ezer** 'so/well-I will ugly' 'so/well-here/look-became ugly' is used as earlier to denote terrible death or great slaughter, but now it is in a completely different place than where mentioned in the same story, but with the same name and same meaning because this time defeat/slaughter will happen but in reverse—the first time Eben-ezer was used the Philistines defeat Israel, this time it will be the Philistine's defeat/slaughter. (1Sam.7:12-14)

Shen; šēn; شَين 'filtered' 'he filtered' to filter impurities out of a liquid. It refers to the ritual Samuel has people do earlier in the story at Mizpeh 'And they gathered together to Mizpeh, and drew water, and poured it out before the Lord' and currently 'Then Samuel took a stone and set it between Mizpeh and Shen…' it denotes the Philistines will be completely removed from the coasts just like impurities (fibres of rope, sticks, stones) are filtered out of water. Cp: sheyn. (1Sam.7:12-14)

Joel; yôʻēl; عُئيل ، عُ ئِل 'boys/sons' 'howling/howling-the' 'will they-the' 'they will-the' 'be warned/beware-the' 'learn and remember-the' because the people complain and want a king because of the bad ways of Samuel's sons, and because they want this king they are warned they will end up howling/crying out because of how he will bereave them of everything they have including their sons and daughters '…thy sons walk not in thy ways: now make us a king to judge us…And ye shall cry out in that day because of your king…and the Lord will not hear you in that day.'; حُئيل ، حُ ئِل 'deceiver/trickster' 'undressed' 'stayed-the' 'stayed in place-the' and his character deceives 'took bribes, and perverted judgement.'; جُئيل 'came-the' 'wandered' and his character and brother 'walked not in his ways, but turned aside' as they stray from Samuel's ways. Cp: 'oeyl/'o-ill, ḥo-ill/eyl, go-ill/eyl. (1Sam.8:1-5)

Abiah; 'ăb̲îyâ; نَبييه ، نُيبييه 'they rejected him/it' 'his father'; نُبييا 'they refused' 'my father'. He and his brother refuse to follow their father's ways (Samuel) and reject the right path; the people reject both of Samuel's sons and they will reject Samuel's advice. Cp: abee-yah/abeeyah, aibee-yah/aibeeyah, abeeya. (1Sam.8) **Beer-sheba** is used again here as 'good/piety-chat/conversation' as the people speak about Joel and Abiah's bad behaviour and talk about having a king like other nations; Samuel tries to talk them out of it by telling them to be pious to God and informing them that what they want is not good; Samuel and God have a conversation about the same conversation.

There is a slight difference in the introduction method of 1.Samuel 9, the lineage of Saul's father has more to do with the chapter that precedes it than that which follows, it seems chapter 8 was written/created after chapter 9 by an editor who wanted to make Saul a 'bad' or lesser status character than the original stories, which is why when you read about Saul you get the sense he was meant as one of the greater heroes, yet there are passages which make him bad. Kish; qîš; قيش 'a tiny bit of litter' 'scrape away leave nothing behind' 'toasty/burnt too much' 'to wipe out(remove completely) in one move'; قيص 'hardened' 'cruel' and both meanings refer to Samuel's sons as they are the catalysts for bringing in a king, which lessens the status of Judges, and their behaviour in disobeying God and not walking in Samuel's way would be described as 'cruel/hardened' (can also mean 'cut/cut up' 'told stories/news'; كيس 'enveloped' 'wrapped/encased' 'wrapped/covered with fabric'). Cp: qeesh, qeess, kees. (1Sam.9:1)

Abiel; 'ăḇî'ēl; نَبي ئِل 'rejected/refused-the' 'father-the' and is still referring to Samuel's sons refusing to be obedient to God and their father, and the people refusing to listen to God and Samuel telling them not to ask for a king. Cp: abee-ill. (1Sam.9:1)

Zeror; ṣĕrôr; سيرُر ، سَرُر 'walked' 'continued' 'walked around' 'behaved immorally/chasing women' and although it could also denote Saul walking around searching for the donkeys, it also refers to Samuel's sons not following their father's path; ضيرُر ، ضَرُر 'harm/harmed' and is Samuel's warning to the people that the king they want will harm them. It could be زيرُر ، زَرُر 'tightened' 'buttoned/zipped/closed' but has no meaning in the story. Cp: seror, seiror, dheror, dheiror, zeror, zeiror. (1Sam.9:1)

Bechorath; bĕḵôraṯ; بيكُرَت ، بِكُرَت 'first/firstborn' 'prime' whether animal, person or crop and it denotes all the sons, daughters, crops which Samuel warns the people that the king they want will take the best of all they have from offspring to harvests. بيحُرَت ، بَحُرَت 'good riddance' 'don't care(about what has happened or thing lost/gone)' and is in the dialogue God says to Samuel 'But the thing displeased Samuel...for they have not rejected thee, but they have rejected me, that I should not reign over them.' Cp: bekorat, beikorat, beḥorat, beiḥorat. (1Sam.9:1)

Aphiah; 'ăpîaḥ; عيفيَه/ا ، عَفيَه/ا 'good health' 'wholesome' 'went off food' the latter such as when animals are ill and do not eat/drink, 'boil(ed)'. It still refers to taking the best and most wholesome of their children and crops and in the negative sense how they are rejecting Samuel and God. Cp: 'apheeah(a), 'aipheeah(a). (1Sam.9:1)

Saul; šā'ûl; صاؤل 'reached/reaching' 'arrived/arriving' 'arrived/public apology' and also 'finding' as the word (ssl/صل) makes up the base of the word 'find' (حصل/ḥssl), 'stone/rock' 'made layer with stones': (ssala/صلى) is a large rock, (ssalal/صلل) are flattish five-inch stones used as a layer in the building process of the roof, they fully cover the roof and laid so as to connect each other and fill up gaps); ساؤل 'asked/asking' 'leaked/flowed' 'leaking/flowing' 'entertained/comforted/distracted'. His character and role embody all these meanings: referring to his height, he is taller than all people so he 'reaches' higher (when someone is taller than average they say 'he reaches (yissaul/yissaal) the ceiling' يصل/يصال للقصاع); it also denotes his role in reaching the 'high place' and arriving from place to place, reaching different destinations in his search for the donkeys; his searching but not finding the donkeys as his mission is to 'find' the donkeys; his finding the seer/Samuel 'ye shall straightway find him', and again he has to 'meet/find/reach' 'high place' and Samuel also sends him to reach different destinations and to find and meet various people. For no reason other than to point out Saul means 'find' and 'reaches' the narration has Saul hiding between 'stuff' so that he can be 'found' and how his height 'reaches' higher than others.

The meanings 'asking/asked'. Saul is given as the king because the people asked for a king against God and Samuel's wishes; God tells Samuel to give the people what they are asking for; Saul and his companion want to ask the seer/Samuel about the whereabouts of the donkeys; they ask about Samuel's location; they ask Samuel about the donkeys; they ask each other about what they can offer him so that he can 'enquire [ask] of God'; Samuel asks Saul to eat with him; God reminds Samuel the people have asked for a king and this person is to be met 'to morrow'; Saul asks Samuel about the seer's house; Samuel tells Saul he will be Israel's saviour in the form of questions 'And on whom *is* all the desire of Israel? *is it* not thee and on all thine father's house?'. Saul responds to the questions with questions 'And Saul answered and said, Am not I a Benjamite, of the smallest tribes of Israel? and my family the least of all the families in the tribe of Benjamin? Wherefore then speakest thou so to me?'; when it is known Saul prophesies it raises questions, and even the answers are questions 'the people said one to another, What is this that come unto the son of

Kish? Is Saul also among the prophets? And one of the same place answered and said, But who is their father? Therefore it became a proverb. Is Saul also among the prophets?'; Saul's uncle asks questions as soon as Saul arrives. Samuel reminds the people they asked God for a king; because they cannot find Saul the people ask 'Therefore they enquired of the Lord further, if the man should yet come thither, And the Lord answered…' and when Saul is brought forward, Samuel shows him off with another question 'See ye him whom the Lord hath chosen, that *there is* none like him among all the people?' and the chapter ends with a question in the last line 'But the children of Belial said, How shall this man save us?'. When Saul is overcome by an 'evil spirit' he needs to be entertained and distracted and finds comfort when a harp/music is played. Cp: ssaa-ul, saa-ul. (1Sam.8;9;10)

Shalisha; šālišâ; شالِسه/ا 'chain' 'smooth/fine' 'flowing hair' 'wanted what or who was offensive' and describes Saul and his companion moving from place to place like a chain and the warning is that he will be bad for the people by taking their dearest things yet they still want a king; شالِشه/ا 'took what was wanted/what he wanted' 'took what is/was important' and refers to the earlier chapter where Samuel warns the king will take whatever he wants from the people and that he will take the best of their children and harvests which is why **'Ephraim'** is mentioned 'multiply/increase' as the king will take the best of their fortune. Cp: shaalisah(sa), shaalishah(sha). (1Sam.9:4)

Shalim; šaʿălîm; سَئَل هم/ام ، سَئيل هم/ام 'asked-them/the' and refer to Saul as he goes around from place to place searching for his donkeys that it is presumed he will ask people if they have seen them, but it also refers to his role in the story as a product of the people asking God for a king, his name and the events in the story about questions being asked. (It can also mean 'flowed/leaked-them/the' 'entertained/distracted/comforted-them/the' 'their comfort/distraction/entertainment'.); شَئَل هم/ام ، شَئيل هم/ام 'took-them/the' as it is a warning that the new king will take from the people the things dearest to them. Cp: sa-al-hum/um, sa-ail-hum/um, sh-al-hum/um, sha-ail-hum/um. (1Sam.9:4)

Zuph is mentioned for the distance and procession Saul goes on searching for the donkeys, then for Samuel, then on Samuel's instructions. **Benjamin**, used as negative 'whose son?' as in the questions people raise is to the effect 'who is he that he should prophesy/become king?' and Saul asks the same question 'I am nobody so why do you tell me I'm going to rule Israel?' and also as the negativity of not being brought up properly by two parents (meaning of Benjamin) as eventually Saul will be vilified in the stories. **Gibeah** is not only used as its literal meaning as 'gang/group of people' 'ganging/gathering together against' as it comes in the same line where it says: 'And Saul also went home to Gibeah; and there went with him a band of men, whose hearts God had touched' that is a story editor who wants Saul positive, but it will be used later by other editor(s) in the negative 'Gibeah' theme as it was earlier in the Biblical stories. (1Sam.9;10)

Zelzah; ṣelṣaḥ; زَلزَح ، زِلزَح 'fretted a lot' 'scattered all over' 'poured all over' and refers to either scattering/pouring something all over the place (figuratively or literally) and also to a person vocalising their fret/worry and walking around a room or place speaking out loudly over their worry. It is usually used in a phrase pair 'zelzaḥ and belbaḥ' 'fretted and talked a lot/chattered'. It is what Saul's father is described as doing '…and, lo, thy father hath left the care of the asses, and sorroweth for you, saying, What shall I do for my son?'; it also refers to Samuel pouring the oil on Saul's head. Cp: zelzaḥ. (1Sam.10:1-2)

Tabor 'ruins reputation/becomes bad/gets bad reputation/spoiled' and **Bethel** 'bad/evil' is used here because Saul will begin to 'prophesy' which involves being possessed by God and although in the story it seems to be a good thing to prophesy, it is actually culturally negative; note the people who have 'Spirit of the Lord come upon' them are being possessed and engage in crazy or violent behaviour in these stories. In this story the people have musical instruments—and in real life, this kind of people in the land where this language is spoken, travel from area to area with musical instruments, when they approach people they play their instruments and the group members who have 'spirits' in this group begin to dance, jerk and shake (they are called mgvoob/مجذوب and means 'being pulled' (and the way they move and the meaning of the word can be better understood as in how you see actors in comedy films shaking and jerking when they are electrocuted) while they say things only God, seers, witches etc. and only the normal person concerned would know. They do things such as plunge knives and other objects into their eyes without being hurt and other such tricks, and although people gather around them out of curiosity and for entertainment, this kind of people who 'prophesy' are actually looked down at as a bad thing or lower people because of what they do is 'bad', and this cultural perception is shown in the Biblical stories although presented as a good aspect in the story itself. **Gilgal** is also used for its meaning of 'clearing' i.e. purifying, but also because the way grains are shaken and roll on the tray to clear so the impurities can be removed, is also how persons described in the Biblical story here 'prophesying' and also in the real-life people mentioned above whose bodies shake and jerk when they are being 'spiritually' moved.

Matri; maṭrî; مَطري 'rained' 'fresh/supple' but that is not the meaning of the word here; مَتري 'can't see him' 'what can you see?' because Saul cannot be seen/found as he is hiding; مَدري 'I don't know' 'who knows?' 'maybe, maybe not' as people ask if he will still be presented when he cannot be found. The last two meanings were given as Saul's clan name although this clan was not mentioned at his father's introduction because the Biblical author/editor wanted to make an extra pun in the story. Cp: maṭree, matree, madree. (1Sam.10:21-22)

Nahash; nāḥāš; ناَهاَش 'mauled' 'took chunks out of'; ناَخاَش 'crumbled' 'made holes in' (by poking at something using stick, claw or instrument); ناَحاس 'brought bad luck upon'. The meaning of created holes by poking is what is meant here as this character requests to 'thrust out all your right eyes…' of Jabesh Gilead, and he has the suitable area of Ammonite; 'ammônîm; عَمَّن هم/ام 'blind(ed) them/the' which is what he wants to do. Cp: naahaash, naakhaash, naaḥaas; 'ammon-hum/um. (1Sam.11:1-2)

Jabesh; yāḇêš; عاَبيش 'flawed you' 'shamed/disgraced you' as this is given as the name of the people who Nahash wants to maim and shame; غاَبيش 'absent' (as earlier in part of Jabesh-gilead name and meaning) used in this sense when Saul's dialogue states 'Whoseover cometh not forth after Saul and after Samuel, so shall it be done unto his oxen' so it is a threat to those who think of not attending. Cp: 'aabeysh, ghaabeysh. (1Sam.11:1-7)

Bezek; in its earlier meaning of 'divide something into smaller portions' 'scatter/spread small portions of the same thing across various places' and refers to Saul 'took a yoke of oxen and hewed them in pieces, and sent them throughout all the coasts of Israel by the hands of messengers…'. Cp: bezeq. (1Sam.11:7-8)

Bedan; bĕḏān; بِداَن ، بيداَن 'will guilt' 'will bow/bend down' 'will make bow/bend down/lower' because the story reflects all earlier stories of being saved then doing things which make them guilty and ashamed. It is similar in meaning as Jotham ('is ostracised' 'he ostracises' 'is guilted' 'he guilts' 'is blamed' 'he blames'); could also mean 'came out' 'took out' Cp: bedaan, beidaan. (1Sam.12:11)

Michmash; mikmāš; مِخماَش 'a jumbling' 'a mixing together of different things or one thing into each other'; مِغماس 'to dip into something liquid/push something under liquid' 'to dip quickly under/hide' and it is what is being described of Israelites hiding in/behind rocks, caves, bushes, peaks and pits. مِقماش 'homosexuality' 'sexual acts of homosexuality' ; مِخماَص 'a blocking/plugging' 'plugged/blocked'.

In this instance it means 'jumbling/mixing together' as people will be running and hiding, but it also reflects the mixing of Israel and Philistines 'in abomination': 'and that Israel was also had in abomination with the Philistines.' and this mixing/jumbling can be seen again when it is mentioned that Philistines did not allow Israel to have blacksmiths or sharpening tools, and although they deprive them this necessity the Philistines still allow Israelites to come and sharpen tools other than a sword or spear followed by a verse which states the Israelites had files for this use, and the naming is reminiscent to the open wink of one Bible editor to another about the story as was seen in Genesis where one editor removed Enoch, then another returned him with a brief note that he just no longer existed followed by another editor naming Enoch's son 'Well what happened?': 'Now there was no smith found throughout all the land of Israel: for the Philistines said, Lest the Hebrews make them swords or spears: But all the Israelites when down to the Philistines, to sharpen every man his share, and his coulter, and his axe, and his mattock. Yet they had a file for the mattocks, and for the coulters, and for the forks, and for the axes, and to sharpen the goads.'.

Also 'blocked/plugged' the word is synonym for word 'samuel' and is denoted in Samuel not arriving there leading Saul to present an offering to God, but because he did not wait for Samuel, God's help/favour will now be blocked from Saul and his rule will be 'stopped' as in it will not continue after him; the 'blocking' effect extends to the access of sharpening tools and blacksmiths. Cp: mikhmaash, mighmaas, miqmaash, mikhmaass. (1Sam.13)

Shual; šû'āl; صُئاَل 'they reached/arrived/are arriving' 'they are arriving/public apology' 'they connected/are connecting' 'stone/rock' 'they made layer with stones' (ssalal are flattish five-inch stones); سُئاَل 'asked/are asking' 'are flowing/leaking' 'are entertained/distracted/comforted'; زُعاَل 'they are upset'. All these meanings are shown in the story: Samuel does not arrive on time; the Philistines arrive for battle; Saul asks for sacrificial animals/produce to be brought to him so he can offer to God, one of which is a burnt offering and shows the meaning of 'Shual' شُعاَل 'ablaze'; Samuel arrives and questions why Saul made offerings and expresses another meaning of 'Shual' زُعاَل 'upset' as Samuel is upset but also informs Saul that God is upset with him. It can also mean سُعال 'coughing/a cough' but I cannot find its meaning in the story. Cp: ssuaal, suaal, shu'aal, su'aal, zu'aal. (1Sam.13)

Migron; migrôn; مجرُن part of the yard used for threshing grain and also an underground grain storage room, 'sun with halo around it'. مِغرُن 'pulped/burst' 'funnel' 'funnelled' 'pierced holes into and spilt to ground' 'beat to pulp' 'saved' the second meanings because Jonathan will take off from here and defeat the Philistines. Cp: migron, mighron. (1Sam.14)

Ahiah; 'ăḥîyâ; نَهييه/ا ، نيهييه/ا 'let's go' 'she is/here she is' 'it is her/yes, it is her' and refers to Jonathan and his companion leaving without being noticed but eventually it will be known where they are; نَحييه/ا ، نيحييه/ا 'became better/healed' 'came back to life' and refers to the curse that all Eli and his children's off-spring will die and never be priests in their bloodline, but the story has allowed them to survive and be priests; it also means 'wait/stay/stay still' which also refers to Saul and the other men 'tarried in the utter-most part of Gibeah'; it is also نَخييه/ا ، نيخييه/ا 'his brother' as it mentions he is Ichabod's brother. Cp: a-heeyah(ya), aiheeyah(ya), aḥeeyah(ya), aiḥeeyah(ya), a-kheeyah(ya), aikheeyah(ya). (1Sam.14)

Ahitub; 'ăḥîṭûḇ; نَهي تُب ، نيهي تُب 'here is-repent' 'she is/here she is-repent' and indicates the story allows some kind of repentance to have happened for the same reasons above as allows Eli's seed to survive and be priests; نَخي تُب ، نيخي تُب 'my brother-repent'; نَهي طب ، نيخي طب 'here is/she is-nice/pleasant' 'here is-well, good/all right' 'here is-willy' 'my brother-willy' and refers to the wearer of the ephod and his penis. There is a reason why the ephod with the names of son and patronym are mentioned, this can be better understood when the ephod is understood as a skirt worn by men and not the misinterpreted ideas of what the ephod is in western culture. Cp: a-hee-tub, aihee-tub, akhee-tub, aikhee-tub, ahee-ṭub, aikhee-ṭub. (1Sam.14)

Bozez; bôṣēṣ; بُزيز 'breasts' 'suckling/lactating breasts' and refers to the sharp/pointy shape of the rock named for being so 'there was a sharp rock on the one side, and sharp rock on the other side: and the name of the one was Bozez…'; it also means 'carries/picks up heavy things' and refers to Jonathan's companion 'the young man that bare his armour'. Cp: bozeyz. (1Sam.14)

Seneh; senneh; سِنَّه 'a tooth' 'his tooth' and refers to the second sharp rock named 'tooth' for being so; also means 'in the direction of' 'put it in direction of' and again refers to the verse 'The forefront of one was situate northward over against Michmash, and the other southward over against Gibeah.' and is also referring to the direction Jonathan and his companion will take. Cp: senneh. (1Sam.14)

Zobah; ṣôḇâ, ṣôḇā'; زُبه/ا ، زُباء 'fiercely drove away' 'unrelentingly drove away' 'scary looking'. Cp: zobah(ba), zobaa. (1Sam.14:47)

Ishui as mentioned earlier. (1Sam.14:49)

Melchi-shua; malḵîšûa'; مَلكي شوَع 'why are you freakishly mutated/ugly' 'why are you bleating like a goat'; مَلخيشوَع 'what is this pounding'. Cp: malkee-shua', malkheeshua'. (1Sam.14:49)

Merab; mērāḇ; ميرآض 'did not agree/refused' 'not/is not content' 'ill/disease'; ميرآد 'returned' 'brought back' 'did not want' and both meanings are because there is a refusal to marry David and she marries someone else. Cp: meyraadh, meyraad. (1Sam.14:49)

Michal; mîḵāl; ميقآل 'observing/watching/ogling' 'look at closely/inspect thoroughly(with eyes)' 'what did he say'; ميخآل 'imagined/hallucinated' and is denoted when she 'took an image, and laid it in the bed, and put a pillow of goats' hair for his bolster, and covered it with a cloth.' which she uses to deceive Saul's men into believing it is David. 'observing/watching' as in 2Sam.6 she watches David through a window and it is implied because of what he is wearing and because he is dancing he has uncovered his genitals to the crowds; the meaning of her name is said over and over again 'Michal…looked through the window, and saw king David…who uncovered himself to day in the eyes of the handmaids of his servants…will be base in mine own sight…'. Cp: meeqaal, meekhaal. (1Sam.14:49)

Ahinoam; 'ăḥînō'am; نَهي/نيهي نوعَم 'here she is-softness' 'she is-softness' 'she is/here she is-blessings/money/food source/gifts/anything given to another/health/anything physical that can be received or given' 'she is-blessings/makes life easier/smoother'; نَهي/نيهي نونَم 'she is/here she is-put to sleep' 'she is-put to sleep' and is euphemism for sex. نَخي نوعَم 'my brother-softness' 'my brother-blessings' ; نيخي نونَم 'my brother-put to sleep'. It could also have the above-mentioned meanings of ('ăḥî/نيهي/نيخي) followed by any of the meanings of the second compound word: نوغَم '-we stifle/feel stifled' '-we suffocate/feel suffocated' '-we cover/we are covered' '-we muffle/are muffled' '-we depress/feel depressed' Cp: a-hee-noo'am, aihee-noo'am, a-hee-nooam, aihee-nooam,a-khee/aikhee-noo'am, akhee/aikhee-nooum, a-hee/aihee-noogham, akhee/aikhee-nogham. (1Sam.14:50)

Ahimaaz; 'ăḥîma'aṣ; نَهي/نُيهي مَعَز 'here she is/she is-dignity/dignified/appreciated' 'here she is/she is-condolences' 'here she is/she is-goats'; نَهي/نُيهي مَعَص 'here she is/she is-disobedience/cruel'; نَخي مَعَز 'my brother-dignity/dignified/appreciated' 'my brother-condolences' 'my brother-goats'; نُيخي مَعَص 'my brother-disobedience/cruel'. Cp: a-hee-ma'az, aihee-ma'az, a-hee-ma'ass, aihee-ma'ass, a-khee- ma'az, ai-khee- ma'ass.

Abner; 'ăḇnēr; نَبنير/نُيبنير 'son of penis' may imply he will have bad role; نَذنير / نُيذنير 'if he lights the way/if he shows the way' 'if he makes fire'. Cp: aibneyr, avneyr. (1Sam.14:50)

Ner; nēr; نير 'of penis/use penis on/will penis' 'light' 'show the way/guide' 'fire' and is the father of the person called 'Abner' 'son of Ner'. Cp: neyr. (1Sam.14:50). **Abiel** is the same as earlier 'rejected/refused-the' 'father-the' and also indicates that this character will have a negative role. (1Sam.14:51)

Telaim; tĕlā'îm; طَلآءهم/ام ، طيلآء هم/ام 'took long-them/the' 'longest-them/the' 'completely cover/paint/coat' 'beat-them/the' 'covered them with beatings' from the word طلاء which means to cover something completely not leaving an inch not covered by whatever substance e.g. from whitewash, henna, mud, etc. but is also used to say a person thoroughly or severely beat someone. In the story this is exactly what is requested by God and Samuel of Saul—to thoroughly kill all people be they male or female and he is reminded not to leave even an infant or baby alive, to kill all the animals. Cp: ṭelaa-hum/um, ṭeilaa-hum/um. (1Sam.15:4)

Agag; 'ăgag; عَجعَج ، عيجَج 'made suffer a lot/prolonged suffering' it is to cause both physical and mental/emotional suffering over a long period of time, 'crying and gasping' and means to sob intensely to the degree of gasping and being out of breath, 'overcrowded' 'over spilled(with fortune/good)/field filled with crops whose panicles seem packed and over spilling' 'made crooked/twisted/were not forthright'. Agag goes through both types of suffering: after relief from being spared by Saul, he is now psychologically tormented and suffering from Samuel's open intentions, and this torment is expressed in the narration by Agag's 'delicacy' and in his dialogue 'Then said Samuel, Bring ye hither to me Agag the King of Amalekites. And Agag came unto him delicately' i.e. gingerly from fear 'And Agag said, Surely the bitterness of death is past' so he is mentally tormented by being spared and now back in fear for his life, and Samuel gives a cruel response, then 'Samuel hewed Agag in pieces before the Lord.' So not only is he psychologically tormented, but his death in the story is horrifically painful. 'overcrowded/over spilled with fortune or like a field filled with panicled crops' is shown in the great numbers of people Saul gathers to fight against the Amalek, and then in numbers both killed and spared, and in the quality of the cattle/food produce which Saul and his army spare and keep after destroying everything else. The 'crooked/not forthright' meanings are shown in Saul and his army not following Samuel/God's instructions to kill every living thing (man, woman, child, baby or beast) and in Saul being found not forthright enough/crooked for this reason and being abandoned by Samuel and God for this 'crooked/not forthright'. Cp: 'ag'ag, 'aigag. (1Sam.15:8-9,32-33)

Bethlehem is now used as 'will-I will tear strips of meat/eat meat' and 'he will be well fed/pampered/plumpened' 'house-well fed/pampered/plumpened' as Samuel uses sacrificing at Bethlehem as an excuse to visit and takes with him a cow for sacrificing to God; he calls the people, including Jesse, to come and sacrifice offerings and to join in the eating which will take place. (1Sam.16)

Jesse; yišay, 'îšay; عِسَي ، عيسَي 'my bread/my cold bread' and it means cold bread as in bread prepared earlier in the day or the previous day. Whenever Jesse is mentioned his role involves bread: when Jesse sends David to Saul, the donkey is 'laden with bread' (1Sam.16:20); when his role includes an action he is mentioned sending bread and bread accompaniments: 'And Jesse said unto David his son, Take now for thy brethren an ephah of this parched corn, and these ten loaves…' although he does send 'ten cheeses' cheese is eaten accompanied with bread, the parched corn would be made into bread for another day. Cp: 'isay, 'eesay. (1Sam.16:17:17)

Eliab in this part of the story holds some of the earlier meanings: 'he who/the one who-rejects/refuses/returns' 'he who/the one who-has flaws/fault' because God rejects him in the story. **Abinadab** also has the earlier meaning of 'rejected-has protruding teeth/jaw'. Shammah also has some of the negative meanings of earlier: 'smelled him/it' or a powdered tobacco (similar to snuff) 'named him/it' 'poisoned him/it' 'blocked him/it'. The story has God rejecting all three of them, and although the narration is that God is not judging them based on their appearance but upon the contents of their heart/soul/character—it is a joke in the story because they are being judged on their appearance reflected in the word-names given which include features deemed ugly and also rejection. The joke is further reinforced because the only thing different about David in this part of the story is his appealing looks which cause God to immediately choose him: 'Now he *was* ruddy, *and* withal of a beautiful countenance, and goodly to look to. And the Lord said, Arise, anoint him: for this *is* he.' (1Sam.16)

Shocoh now holds two of the earlier meanings from Josh. (Socoh (Josh.15:34)): شُقّ 'side' 'his side' 'beside' as both the Philistines and Saul's men pitch on either side of the valley; شُقّوح 'struck sharply' 'sharp pain' 'splinters' 'splinter in skin' and describes the pain felt by a sharp hit which is how this battle ends—with a sharp throw of a stone. The narrators reinforce this meaning by mentioning **Azekah**: 'sharp hit with a thrown stone' 'sharp hits from stones' both describe the contact/strike a stone makes against body/surface/object. That is why the fictional place in the story has been named to be suitable for this fictional event as the battle is resolved with the strike of a thrown stone (by David). (1Sam.17)

Ephes-dammim; 'epes dammîm; نَفَص دَمّهم 'separated/I separate-their blood' 'I disentangle their blood'; عَفَص دَمّهم 'twisted out their blood/twisted and crumpled their blood'; نَفَز دَمّهم 'provoked their blood'. All meanings are used because the story has both sides/armies separated on different hills, a clear and defined separation; the narration details the description of Goliath, and gives Goliath a very clear message which states words to the effect 'there is no need for both armies to entangle, when we can untie this 'entanglement/battle' and avoid spilling too much blood with a one-on-one battle which determines which side wins'; the intention is to kill the enemy (squeeze/twist/crumple their blood), but because instead of fighting there is a lot of shouting and insults by Goliath, and his words provoke Saul's men and also provoke David; when David arrives he manages to provoke the anger of his brother Eliab. Cp: e-phess damm-hum, 'ephess damm-hum, e-phez damm-hum. (1Sam.17)

Elah as earlier in Genesis still means عيلاه 'above it/him' 'against it/him' 'above/against/on' 'on it/him' as both Saul and the Philistines who are ready to fight against each other and are rivals, are arrayed on both sides of opposite mountains 'above' the valley of Elah. 'and pitched by the valley of Elah…And the Philistines stood on a mountain on the one side, and Israel stood on a mountain on the other side: and *there was* a valley between them.'. (1Sam.17)

Goliath; golyat; جوليَث 'came/come-he shouted' from the word (lyf/lwf/ليث/لوث) which means 'shout/cries out loud' when a person does 'layaf/lowaf' it is meant to be heard by as many people and as far as possible and is a cry to be saved if the person shouting is facing a threat whether from a man or an animal he/she cannot defend himself/herself against—then the people who hear run to the person's aid. Goliath in the context of the Biblical story is 'shouting loudly' to be heard by Saul's army from across the valley and he is shouting at them to come, he is challenging them to embarrass them because they do not dare to take him on, so like all the names in the Bible it serves a purpose in the story representing what the character is doing, will do or what will be done to them or other characters in the related story. 'And there went out a champion out of the camp of the Philistines, named Goliath…And he stood and cried out unto the armies of Israel, and said unto them, Why are ye come out to set *your* battle in array? am not I a Philistine, and ye servants to Saul? choose you a man for you, and let him come down to me. If he be able to fight with me, and to kill me, then will we be your servants: but if I prevail against him, and kill him, then shall ye be our servants and serve us…And the Philistine said, I defy the armies of Israel this day; give me a man that we might fight together'.

His bold words distress and scare Saul and his army, and all he does is shout out words: day in-day out for forty days Goliath is shouting at Saul's army, daring them to a one-on-one challenge to settle the whole battle 'And the Philistine drew near morning and evening, and presented himself forty days'. He is not described in any part of his story in any fight/combat—all he is doing is coming and shouting, just like his name says he will do '…behold, there came up the champion, the Philistine of Gath, Goliath by name, and spake according to the same words: and David heard *them*.'

David is angered by Goliath's words and audacity shaming Saul's army; it is disgraceful by merely shouting out a challenge day after day, announcing in front of both sides he is prepared to fight to death any one of Saul's men, but because no one dares to take up the challenge, he continues to humiliate them by shouting out to them and presenting himself to them to fight him so David refers to Goliath's shaming tactics '…for who is this uncircumcised Philistine, that he should defy the armies of the living God?'. Even when David approaches Goliath to fight to the death, the story does not allow Goliath to go beyond his 'name limits', all he does is talk and curse and it can be read from the Biblical text that it was shouted for all to hear 'And the Philistine said unto David, *Am* I a dog that thou comest to me with staves? And the Philistine cursed David by his Gods. And the Philistine said to David, Come to me and I will give thy flesh unto the fowls of the air, and to the beasts of the field.' Goliath does not get a chance to fight and does nothing more than shout for challengers to come to him in the story. Cp goolyaf. (1Sam.17)

David; dawîd̲; دَويد ، دَوِد 'the stone rolling pin of grinding stone'; ذَويد ، ذَوِد 'this is/he is stone rolling pin of grinding stone' 'repeat/try again/keep at it' 'repeating the same revolving or to and fro motion' 'hesitates/goes and comes/recoils/revolves' and describes an animal when it hesitates, going back and forth, turning its head or the front part of its body to walk away, but returning to its original position or even walking away then quickly returning to its original location (e.g. when you see an animal hesitating to move away from the corpse of a dead family member, or when in danger and partially turns away or towards a specific direction, but resumes its original position ready to fight or flee) the same is used to describe a person hesitating about an action repeating the same movements out of hesitation or even going back and forth in hesitation or repeatedly returning, from the word (vwd/ذود) 'repeat/hesitate/revolve/try again/to and fro/going in circles'.

The 'rolling pin of grinding stone' meaning from the word (wd/ود) which is the rolling pin part of the stone grinder used to grind grain. It is similar to the manos part of the metate and manos of the Aztecs/Mayans and the grinder comes in various sizes. (da/دَ) and (va/ذَ) 'the/this is/he is' attributes it/the character to (vd/wd̲/ود) 'stone rolling pin of grinder' in this instance—a character. Anyone who has lived among people where shepherding is part of life knows that they use throwing stones to stop their goats/sheep from wandering off or going into other people's land, it makes the animal turn or twist around and stay within the right land, and this action and the material of the rolling pin is what has inspired this character creation and his name.

Shepherding and the use of stones, as well as repeating, hesitating, trying over and over again, going and returning, turning something or someone around, is focused on when introducing David in 1 Samuel and also when he will meet Goliath. Jesse tells Samuel 'There remaineth yet the youngest, and, behold, he keepeth the sheep…' 'But David went and returned from Saul to feed his father's sheep at Bethlehem.'. It is David's repeat motions on a musical instrument which causes the evil spirit to leave Saul, but the spirit itself keeps returning to Saul, and it is connected to David as David becomes the focus of Saul both positively and negatively because of the evil spirit. 'And David rose up early in the morning, and left the sheep with a keeper…' '…and with whom hast thou left those few sheep in the wilderness?'; when Saul tells David he is too young and inexperienced than to fight against a seasoned warrior, David reminds him that he is a shepherd, and what the narration of the story is denoting is that David is good at throwing stones, but also creates the image of a lion and bear moving in the way animals do when in danger or attacking as per the meaning of David. The meanings of hesitation, coming back and forth or going in circles, stand your ground, are all portrayed by David witnessing Israel's army hesitating, then fleeing in fear, in Goliath coming and going repeating his actions, statements, since the beginning of the chapter; in David repeating his speech to the soldiers and it being repeated to Saul; in David removing the armour and sword after having put them on. When the relationship between David and Saul sours, wherever the narration focuses on Saul's hatred or actions against David, the author(s) shows Saul hesitates in what he does, he does not outright attempt to kill David, but gives him opportunity after opportunity to escape, repent, change—the author's way of showing one of the meanings of 'David'.

Instead of using weapons he is not familiar with, or has not 'broken in', David 'chose him five smooth stones out of the brook, and put them in a shepherd's bag which he had, even in a scrip; and his sling was in his hand…'. There is a reason why the author(s) has David choose five specific stones and did not have him pick up any five stones: again, if you watch shepherds, or people whose daily life is partly shepherding sheep/goats—when an animal is running off, or nibbling at crop intended for human or bovine consumption the person shepherding will throw a stone to move the animal onto parts of the land it can graze on, or to make it turn back and return instead of running off. You will see the child or adult reach to the ground to pick up a stone(s) and without looking, just by touch, they will let go of certain stones and pick certain stones because depending on the distance between the person and the goat/sheep, and depending on what the animal is doing and where the animal is, and whether the shepherd wants the goat to fall back in line slightly or to return from over a distance, the velocity of the throw, whether gentle or harsh, whether it is meant to land in front, behind, next to or in the goat's body—directs the animal into the correct direction/behaviour. To get the correct distance and velocity in the throw determines which stones are chosen, their size, weight, texture—which is why the authors of this story have David select stones and not just pick random stones.

His name, 'David', which is an object made of stone used in grinding grain has been created for this character because stone grinders are made from a specific kind of rock/stone, it is extremely dense and weighs more than you expect it to according to its size; it lasts for decades even with daily use (which is hours of grinding on an almost daily basis). When a stone grinder is delivered and new, it is smooth just as the stones are described which David picks (but the rectangular static part of the grinder is chipped at with a sharp stone to create grooves in it to assist the grinding of grain into dough, and with use wears out back into smooth surface). The properties of the (vd/wd̲/ودـ) rolling pin which the character David is named for is that it is heavier than other stones and makes its more suitable to be used as a weapon against Goliath: take e.g. a tennis ball and a golf ball, throwing a tennis ball at a specific velocity at someone may hurt them, but would not kill them, the weight, density of the tennis ball would bounce off the person's head after striking them. If a golf ball though smaller in size, but denser, is thrown at someone with the equal velocity of the above example of a tennis ball, it could kill a person if it lands on the head due to the ball's density. Similarly, the stone which the rolling pin/David is made of is much heavier than other types of stone, even if it were smaller in size, making it the perfect choice for David to use against Goliath and for the author of the story to create the character named after the stone rolling pin.

When Goliath questions David's use of staves as if Goliath were a dog, and disdains such as young man/boy be sent against him it shows hesitation as he sees him an unworthy opponent.

'And David put his hand in his bag, and took thence a stone, and slang *it*, and smote the Philistine in his forehead, that the stone sunk into his forehead; and he fell upon his face to the earth.'. It is interesting that the stone rolling pin David is named for, is obelisk, or cylindrical in shape, its thick middle tapers narrower towards both its ends leaving blunt narrower ends to hold onto while grinding. It would resemble the narrower tip of a bullet/missile. You can see the Biblical author's logic and imagination how something with a sharper end, denser, its weight allowing the correct velocity and its shape to sink into Goliath's head. David's name and his occupation as a shepherd allow his role to enhance the story to be the cause of Goliath's death with a stone.

The word-names of Jesse and David have no connection to Ruth and Boaz as words other than the characters are related to bread-making in the stories: Boaz and Ruth first made love on the threshing floor where Boaz had been threshing. Jesse means cold bread and David is the stone rolling pin used to grind grain into dough. It seems whichever later editor added Jesse and David as descendants of Ruth and Boaz only did so for the relation of the word-names and characters to grain and bread long after the original Ruth story.

There is also another play on why the author(s) gave David as the word-name for this character. When women grind grain, whether they do it in a kneeling position on the ground (which most women avoid because it is bad for the hips) or standing up with the stone grinder on a raised platform, the motion of pushing the rolling pin rapidly back and forth causes the backside and whole body to move back and forth no matter how rigid she keeps her back, it resembles the motion of the male body copulating; the 'repeat/going back and forth' meanings also portray a sexual connotation in how it is used in David's story. Cp: daweed, dawid, vaweed, vawid. (1Sam.16:11;17)

Jonathan; yĕhônāṯān, yônāṯān; خُنَاثَان ، يَخُنَاثَان the literal meaning 'males making each other female by having sex with each other' 'male on male anal sex making each other female' 'he/they soaked each other' 'soaked the second one' 'he/they betray the other' 'betray the second one' and it is in the form of two people doing this act. The form of the word-name is definitely saying the character is engaged in a homosexual relationship and specifically anal sex, the story narrates he is in a homosexual relationship that is both romantic and physical. His name is in the verb of two males engaged in the said activity. Many passages over several chapters make it clear Jonathan is to be understood as a man who has sex with men; the Bible tells us his partner is David, that they both love each other and the Bible makes it crystal clear the basis of Saul's anger at David is his physical and romantic relationship with Jonathan.

Jonathan is introduced as being with one thousand men (army) at Gibeah, Benjamin—the point is in the place: Gibeah, Benjamin where in Judges 19:1-30 a Levite with his wife stop at, where an old man warns the Levite he cannot stay on the street at night, and the story focuses that neither the Levite nor the old man are from Gibeah, Benjamin, but travellers—the Bible does this to point out that the men of Gibeah, Benjamin are homosexual and the story has all the men of Gibeah gang around the old man's house demanding to be allowed to rape the visiting Levite—they are not interested in sex with women. The Bible story makes it abundantly clear the men of Gibeah are conducting homosexual intercourse (a bad thing back then) and that they are violently criminal because even if a man does not have sex willingly, they will 'know him' by force. So the author(s) is making a statement by first introducing Jonathan at Gibeah, Benjamin (1Sam.13:2) along with his direct name, it indicates his role later in the story.

Even before Jonathan and David meet, the authors focus on David's beauty: although the narration has God/Samuel's words to the effect 'it's not the looks of the individual that matter and determine which of Jesse's sons will be chosen, but the contents of his heart' all Jesse's sons who have ugly features or deformities according to their word-names are rejected, but the story emphasises on David's (the chosen one) beauty 'Now he was ruddy, and withal of a beautiful countenance, and goodly to look to.' '...Behold, I have seen a son of Jesse the Bethlehemite, that is cunning in playing, and a mighty valiant man, and a man of war, and prudent in matters, and a comely person...' seeing that David was still a boy or at least a young man and the later chapters show he had never been involved in war, the statements about him being 'man of war, and prudent in matters' was probably added by later editors, while earlier authors/editors only had him looking pretty. So his good looks, nature, his personality, all have traits which are attractive to women, and men—making it easy for the story to have Jonathan fall in love with him. Jonathan's whole character is about being a male in love with a male and having a full relationship with that male, and his word-name literally means anal sex between men which causes them to become female.

There is abundant proof in the Biblical text that Jonathan's relationship with David is a romantic relationship. 'And it came to pass, when he had made an end of speaking unto Saul, that the soul of Jonathan was knit with the soul of David, and Jonathan loved him as his own soul.' Yes, a man can love another man in a platonic/brotherly deep love, but in the Bible the word-name given always has a direct reason, it stands for something and is directly reflected in the story—in this case a homosexual relationship, and also a method of the Biblical stories is the more important a character is in the story the more the authors emphasise and show the meaning intended. It is emphasised how deeply Jonathan loves David, it is repeated to drive the message through that it was not just about having sex, but love too 'Then Jonathan and David made a covenant, because he loved him as his own soul.' (1Sam.18:1) this is not the covenant that David succeed Saul instead of Jonathan, which is made later on, but this is a covenant of their love for each other: 'the soul of Jonathan was knit with the soul of David' repeating 'he loved him as his own soul'. When do two people's souls feel as one's own soul—when you are deeply, deeply in love with the other; when do two souls 'knit' together i.e. become one, mingle and weave into each other—when in emotional love and especially when a person makes love to the person he/she loves. (1Sam.18:1,3)

'And Jonathan stripped himself of the robe that *was* upon him, and gave it to David, and his garments, even to his sword, and to his bow, and to his girdle.' It could be seen as a sign of generosity, but the Bible hardly ever says something for no reason at all, and especially when repeating on the thing they want understood, but it does use euphemisms for sex in the stories between characters. In this instance it focuses the reader on Jonathan not giving David clothes from his bag, trunk, even as a fictional king's son he would obviously own lots of clothes, but the author is telling the reader Jonathan removed every piece of clothing he wore, he stripped off everything in David's presence, he left nothing on—not even 'to his girdle' and becoming naked in the story is euphemism for having illicit sex. (1Sam.18:4)

'But Jonathan Saul's son delighted much in David...' and warns him to hide himself (1Sam.19:2); Jonathan loves him and cares for his life.

When David flees from Saul, he is still able to meet with Jonathan—just like lovers secretly meet against their parents' will. Jonathan does not want David to mention being killed, he cannot bear to hear the words from David's mouth—again, lovers cannot bear to hear the mention or thought of their partner's death. Jonathan replies 'And he said unto him, God forbid; thou shalt not die: behold my father will do nothing either great or small, but that he will shew it me: and why should my father hide this thing from me? it *is* not *so*.'. David knowing Saul has noticed their relationship or at least Jonathan's love for David, and he knows Saul disapproves of it insists 'And David sware moreover and said, Thy father certainly knoweth that I have found grace in thine eyes...' meaning and words to the effect of 'your father knows about us'. And David goes on to express this '...and he saith, Let not Jonathan know this, lest he be grieved: but truly as the Lord liveth, there is but a step between me and death.' The story is narrating David as saying words to the effect 'Your father knows about us, he knows how much you love me, so he doesn't want you to know of his plans until he's killed me'. The authors would not have Saul go to these extremes of attempting to assassinate David unless the relationship was physical and romantic which becomes clearer in the story. 'Then said Jonathan unto David, Whatsoever thy soul desireth, I will even do it for thee.' This is a concrete declaration of absolute affection, protection and love between two lovers. (1Sam.20:2-4)

The dialogue of David asking Jonathan to find out if Saul has 'forgiven' him or if he still wants to harm him is David playing on Jonathan's heartstrings, seeking confirmation of Jonathan's love and devotion, which Jonathan earnestly confirms: 'If he say this, It is well; thy servant shall have peace: but if he be very wroth, then be sure that evil is determined by him. Therefore thou shalt deal kindly with thy servant; for thou hast brought thy servant into a covenant of the Lord with thee; notwithstanding, if there be iniquity in me, slay me thyself: for why wouldest thou bring me to thy father?' i.e. 'If you love me, be kind to me, we made a pact by God—you brought me into this love pact, but now if you feel ashamed of our love, of me, if you see me as a sin—I would rather die at your hands, the man I love. Why would you do such a cruel thing as to let your father who now hates me because we love each other hurt me, and if you hand me over to him, he will kill me.' To which Jonathan responds 'Far be it from thee: for if I knew certainly that evil were determined by my father to come upon thee, then would I not tell it thee?' The conversation is of deep affection 'God forbid I should let anything happen to you. Don't you know how much I love you? If I were aware of something was going to hurt you, do you think I wouldn't tell you?'. (1Sam.20:7-9)

Over and over again, the narration has Jonathan demonstrate his devotion and passion for David (1Sam.20:11-16) swearing another oath/covenant—where if he deceives David, he wishes the same evil upon himself; if he does good towards David, he wants their love to last forever with God as a witness. Although it is being expressed as a covenant between the house of Jonathan and David at verse 16, it is an absolute demonstration of Jonathan's love towards David (prompted by David's girlish/female-like demands) followed by the emphasis on the depth of their love at verse 17 'And Jonathan caused David to swear again, because he loved him: for he loved him as he loved his own soul.' The reason this sentence is repeated by the author, is to make it clear these two people are madly in love. They make each other swear oaths declaring it, they pluck at each other's heartstrings seeking reassurances of the other's love or protection, they love each other as one soul. 'And *as touching* the matter which thou and I have spoken of, behold, the Lord *be* between thee and me forever.' Verse 23 is Jonathan reminding David that even if he has to leave him, his love is everlasting and with God as witness per their covenant/promises to each other.

Jonathan and David's relationship is also physical, the story has them have sexual intercourse and Saul has witnessed it, or been told, expressed clearly in Saul's anger at Jonathan's remark about David's absence: Saul says '...do not I know that thou hast chosen the son of Jesse to thine own confusion, and unto the confusion of thy mother's nakedness?' (1Sam.19:30) Saul's expression is from the use in the Bible of 'nakedness' to represent prohibited sex or the genitals of someone you are not supposed to see. He is telling Jonathan 'I know you're confused and having sex with David' he is shifting Jonathan's 'confusion' (homosexuality) onto David being the reason behind it; he says 'and unto the confusion of thy mother's nakedness?' This means two things: the authors want to say Saul finds Jonathan having sex with David is as abominable as David having sex with Jonathan's mother; and there is also the added confusion because when a man has illicit sex with a woman who is daughter/wife to someone—the person transgressing is 'lifting the skirt' of the woman's male guardian (nakedness again) but by having sex with David it has become confused: as both Jonathan and David are male, so is David lifting Saul's skirt or Jonathan's mother's skirt? that is another confusion Saul speaks of. He is also blaming Jonathan's love for David 'chosen the son of Jesse' to have led him to a more reprehensible (to the author's and Saul's character) physical relationship with a man (David) presented euphemistically 'and unto the confusion of your own mother's nakedness'

Although it is evident from Saul's words and actions that he is aware of the full extent of Jonathan's relationship with David, Jonathan still wants to pretend and plead David's innocence 'And Jonathan answered Saul his father, and said unto him, Wherefore shall he be slain? What hath he done?' The response is a javelin hurtling in Jonathan's direction, which he escapes (1Sam.20:32-33). The lovers meet in a heart-wrenching farewell as they will no longer be able to live together, or enjoy each other's company as lovers under one roof: 'And as soon as the lad was gone, David arose out of the place toward the south, and fell on his face to the ground, and bowed himself three times: and they kissed one another, and wept one with another, until David exceeded.' And they part with Jonathan reminding David of their oath. They hold each other, kiss each other and weep together—it is the heart-breaking scene of lovers torn apart by someone else's intentions. (1Sam.20:41-42)

Although they have parted, they still meet at least one more time: 'And Jonathan Saul's son arose, and went to David into the wood, and strengthened his hand in God. And he said unto him, Fear not: for the hand of Saul my father shall not find thee; and thou shalt be king of Israel, and I shall be next unto thee; and that also my father knoweth.' Jonathan still declares his love for David, he gives up his turn to ascend to the throne after his father so that David can have it and he does not care about it because his love for

David is overwhelming. And as soon as this declaration is made the two of them 'made a covenant before the Lord'—they seem to make a covenant every single time they meet in secret; what is this covenant, this oath? Is it 'sacred' and a synonym to 'Hormah' which means 'sacred' and also 'woman' 'forbidden' and sex is 'sacred' and illicit sex is 'forbidden'—in the Bible when something is repeated regularly it stands for something. Look at David's conversation with the priest in Nob, where David deceives the priest into giving him weapons and bread, claiming the king ordered him to do secret business: 'Now therefore what is under thine hand? give me five loaves of bread in mine hand, or what there is present. And the priest answered David and said, There is no common bread under mine hand, but there is hallowed bread; if the young men have kept themselves at least from women. And David answered the priest and said unto him, Of a truth women *have been* kept away from us about these three days, since I came out, and the vessels of the young men are holy, and *the bread is* in a manner common, yea, thou it were sanctified this day in the vessel. So the priest gave him hallowed bread.' The priest has no idea what David's double-meanings are, but David through the authors, as well as the listening audience of these stories in their times, is/are enjoying David's private joke through wordplay. Look at the words: the priest says they can have hallowed bread if they have not had sex with women, David's response is 'haven't had sex with women, but men's bodies are holy' he is playing on the word 'sacred', holy, 'hormah' (as an oath can be called hormah) and in ancient times sex was considered a sacred act, and women were considered holy vessels, David's speech is wordplay on his name which is how bread is made and Jonathan's name which means male anally penetrating male, and the word 'vessel' as David's name is linked directly to making bread. David is saying he has had sex with a man (Jonathan) and the priest takes it as being 'clean' from any sexual contact with women.

David and Jonathan continue to make an oath/covenant every time they meet in secret, the last time being 'And the two made a covenant before the Lord: and David abode in the wood, and Jonathan went to his house.' (1Sam.23:18). This visit in the wood is followed by verse 19 where the story narrates Saul is told the woods where David is hiding in (where Jonathan had just met with David) is called Hachilah; ḥăḵîlâ; هَحيله ، هيحيله 'I will undress him/take his clothes off' 'he will undress him', in the Bible nakedness and removing of clothes means having illicit sex; هَخيله ، هيخيله 'I will let/allow him' 'he will let him' and it means 'I/he will let him have sex with me/him' when the word 'hachilah' is not followed by a verb such as e.g. 'I will let him go' 'I will let him stay' 'I will let him know' when it is just 'I will let him' it takes on the meaning 'I will let him have sex with me'. Cp: haḥeelah, haiḥeelah, hakheelah, haikheelah. So, in reading the Biblical text correctly it becomes abundantly clear that David and Jonathan are lovers in a romantic and physical relationship. (1Sam.21;23). The reader is reminded of this great love and relationship in David's lamentation over Jonathan's death: 'I am distressed for thee my brother Jonathan: very pleasant hast though been unto me: thy love to me was wonderful, passing the love of women.' (2Sam.1:26)

Saul makes several attempts to kill David, and although there is mention of Saul hating, fearing David because 'the Lord' departed from Saul and was 'with David' and because the people love/praise David more than Saul, but the real reasons as intended by the authors in the original stories still clearly stand out in the text. It is over Jonathan, Jonathan's infatuation and relationship with David. Long before Jonathan notices David, Saul is pleased with David, the latter plays music to soothe Saul, Saul keeps David in his presence, at his court, but allows him free movement, so David comes and goes and still tends to his father's sheep. 'And David came to Saul, and stood before him: and he loved him greatly; and he became his armourbearer. And Saul sent to Jesse, saying, Let David, I pray thee, stand before me; for he hath found favour in my sight. And it came to pass, when the *evil* spirit from God was upon Saul, that David took an harp, and played with his hands: so Saul was refreshed, and was well, and the evil spirit was departed from him.' (1Sam.16:21-23) 'But David went and returned from Saul to feed his father's sheep at Bethlehem.' (1Sam.17:15).

While David comes and goes from Saul, the latter is still fond of David. But things change after David slays Goliath, although Saul's love for him increases to begin with, he no longer allows him to return to his father's home, not by force or negatively, but as an honour, a privilege, a sign of extreme favour. David does Saul's business wherever he sends him, then Saul puts him in charge of an army (although he is young), and with the king's esteem, David's position, status and regard is raised among the public and among Saul's servants (1Sam.18:2-5)

After this extreme regard and honest respect and love from Saul to David, Saul's attitude drastically changes towards David, and although verse 7 states it is due to Saul hearing women praise David in a song that 'Saul eyed David from that day and forward' even in the story itself how likely would that cause him to try and impale him against the wall when it is Saul himself who has set up and raised David to be successful and popular? (1Sam.18:7-11). The opening verses of Chapter 18 do give a more credible reason as to why Saul's feelings changed so drastically towards David, and it also explains the nature and degree of Saul's behaviour/actions. The opening verses of Chapter 18 tell us Jonathan was smitten by David when he heard him speak; it emphasises 'Jonathan loved him as his own soul.'; it narrates Jonathan took off his robe to give to David, but goes on to clearly state Jonathan stripped naked in front of David—a Biblical euphemism for illicit sex. The sentence 'Saul eyed David from that day forward' tells Saul noticed something and is keeping an eye on David's actions. What would cause Saul to suddenly hurl a spear at David whom he loves and favours: a song praising David? Or 'God' being with David which Saul cannot see, but maybe feel? Or Saul, a father and a king, who sees his son enter a prohibited physical and emotional relationship with David? The son of a king named for this purpose in the story 'Jonathan' which means two men engaged in sexual activity with one another (both Jonathan and David) and the act causing them to become 'female', and the lover (David) whose name indicates in a vulgar way the action of copulation between them. Saul does not want to hurt his own son so he takes it out on David, he sees the latter as the cause of his son's 'confusion' ('deviation').

Saul's anger can be understood as being overcome by strong emotions of betrayal and disgust at David when he throws the javelin towards him the first time, which is when he is struggling with what has happened: his son head-over-heels in love with David; David whom he trusted, brought into his house, elevated him in position, power and popularity across the kingdom. The story itself shows despite all the animosity created from the relationship with Jonathan that Saul still cares for David: he does not kill him, does not throw him out (yet), but tries to correct the situation by sending David out with the army: an attempt to: a) create a physical distance between David and Jonathan in hope that whatever caught alight would die out, and things return to normal; b) David among and in charge of a thousand men might take to a different lover, and leave Jonathan alone.

Saul's affection for David and his want to 'correct' the situation between his son and David without hurting David is seen again when he offers his daughter Merab to David as a wife—Saul is trying to 'straighten' David, to keep him away, turn him off Jonathan. He does not try with Jonathan because he does not want to acknowledge his son is sexually oriented towards men, but shifts the blame onto David. Eventually, Saul cannot bring himself to give his daughter to David when he knows the latter has had a sexual relationship with her brother, so he gives his daughter away in marriage to someone else. But the point is: although he is upset with Jonathan/David's relationship, Saul still tries to remedy the situation without harming David. (1Sam.18:7-19) 'And David went out withersoever Saul sent him, *and* behaved himself wisely: and Saul set him over the men of war, and he was accepted in the sight of all the people, and also in the sight of Saul's servants...And Saul eyed David from that day and forward...And it came to pass on the morrow, that the evil spirit from God came upon Saul,' The evil spirit could be suspicions, the whisperings the mind cannot stop because Saul has noticed or seen something and cannot stop thinking and worrying about it '...and David played with his hand, as at other times: and *there was* a javelin in Saul's hand. And Saul cast the javelin; for he said, I will smite David even to the wall *with it.* And David avoided out of his presence twice...Therefore Saul removed him from him, and made him his captain over a thousand; and he went out and came in before the people...And Saul said to David, Behold my elder daughter Merab, her I will give thee to wife...But it came to pass at the time when Merab Saul's daughter should have been given to David, that she was given unto Adriel the Meholathite to wife.'

Saul's second daughter, Michal, loves David. Although it is narrated Saul uses her to snare David into being killed by the Philistines, it is again Saul attempting to remedy Jonathan's situation by cutting off David as a lover. And although Saul could not bring himself to give his eldest daughter to David when the time came, in Michal's case she already loves David and this makes it easier for Saul to allow the marriage to conclude. Had he wanted David dead, or hated him to that degree, Saul could have demoted him, cast him out completely, or he could have ordered his assassination (which he will do later), but until now in the story he still has hope and love for David; therefore, he seeks non-violent methods to solve the issue of David and Jonathan's relationship. (1Sam.18:20-30)

Though it 'pleased' (put at ease) Saul to learn Michal loves David, he continues to observe David, notices nothing has changed between David and Jonathan, so his fears continue 'And Saul saw and knew that the Lord was with David, and that Michal Saul's daughter loved him. And Saul was yet more afraid of David; and Saul became David's enemy continually.' Saul's hope was Michal's love for David would bring the latter's love with Jonathan to an end, but it has not, and now David is part of the family—Saul's distress increases and his hatred of David begins.

The story shows although Saul seems to indicate the only way to end the problem is to kill David, he does not go around getting it done secretly: he tells everyone his intentions (remember the story has David popular and loved even among Saul's servants) including Jonathan who is madly in love with David. He knows Jonathan will warn David so Saul's actions in this part of the story are Saul openly warning David 'Keep away from my son—or else' and this allows Jonathan and David to reconcile with Saul, telling him how David is loyal and assuring Saul that David has done nothing wrong—it seems Saul only has suspicions about Jonathan and David, or knows it for certain but is willing to be convinced that nothing is going on if they will cease the relationship. Jonathan only speaks of the wonderful deeds David has performed for Saul, emphasising David has done nothing sinful; Saul listens and is convinced by Jonathan's words, he at least believes his death threats to David has ended the debacle and Saul swears by God not to kill David and things return to how they were with David being esteemed by Saul.

The reconciliation does not last long, the story mentions David's victory over the Philistines being the cause of Saul's return to hating David, but David is the head of Saul's army so his victory is Saul's victory. Common sense in the story itself dictates with David back in the house, he and Jonathan have resumed their relationship—and this is behind Saul's anger and hatred towards David whom Saul obviously loves and gives chance after chance to reconcile and attempts to keep a good relationship with—not because he needs to, but because he genuinely likes and loves David: 'And Saul spake to Jonathan his son, and to all his servants, that they should kill David. But Jonathan Saul's son delighted much in David: and Jonathan told David, saying, Saul my father seeketh to kill thee...And Jonathan spake good of David unto Saul his father, and said unto him, Let not the king sin against his servant, against David, because he hath not sinned against thee, and because his works *have been* to theeward very good: For he did put his life in his hand and slew the Philistine, and the Lord wrought a great salvation for all of Israel: thou sawest *it* and didst rejoice: wherefore now then will thou sin against innocent blood, to slay David without a cause? And Saul hearkened unto the voice of Jonathan: and Saul sware, *As* the Lord liveth, he shall not be slain. And Jonathan called David, and Jonathan shewed him all those things. And Jonathan brought David to Saul, and he was in his present as in times past.' (1Sam.19:1-7).

Saul is troubled and torn, imagine him sitting, watching David play music, thinking of all the good he has done for David, all his warnings and chances to prevent David from harm, yet David is still Jonathan's lover. The word 'jonathan' خنأثان which means when male and male are having sex, they are making each other female, is on Saul's mind—the act itself is bothering him as others know about it, he then throws a javelin at David out of frustration, but if he had wanted to kill him, he would not have missed. This is what the authors are capturing in the story that Saul is not trying to kill David but to end the relationship with Jonathan. 'And the evil spirit from the Lord was upon Saul, as he sat in his house with his javelin in his hand: and David played with his hand. And Saul sought to smite David even to the wall with the javelin; but he slipped away out of Saul's presence, and he smote the javelin into the wall: and David fled, and escaped that night.' (1Sam.19:9-10)

Saul contemplating David, his suspicions, knowledge, all the thoughts about David (both good and bad) brewing in his mind—he cannot get over David and Jonathan's behaviour after all the warnings and forgiveness that they have not ended their relationship. And when he throws the javelin which always misses David, it is a warning, a cry of disappointment and betrayal he is expressing to David. In rural areas, when a father is greatly upset by a son's actions or words, and they are in the same place or in a room full of people, the father reaches for any object that will not do any damage and throws it in the direction of the disobedient or rude son; the way it is thrown is with a sharpness to express anger/displeasure, but never actually lands on the son, the son is given indication while the father searches for an object to throw and it is thrown so that the son can easily pull away or duck out of the trajectory and flees away from the home until he has apologised, corrected his transgression or simply waits in hiding near the house for a while until the father's anger dissipates and he returns home where everything goes back to normal. This is what is being described (in a more dramatic way to enhance the fictional story) by the authors of the Biblical story, though with a more dramatic action/reaction/reason behind the conflict, but it is undoubtedly actions of a filial-paternal nature, of great hopes put in, then disappointment and betrayal emerging from, the person loved: David.

(1Sam.19:11-17) Saul's actions become more aggressive towards David, he no longer forewarns him as before, but secretly orders his messengers to kill David—he no longer believes threatening or expressing displeasure will work: 'Saul also sent messengers to David's house to watch him, and to slay him in the morning.' But he has not given up completely: just as earlier in the story he lets Jonathan know of his assassination plans so the latter could warn David, the story has him do this again: he has told Michal of his plans, he knows she loves David so she can warn him to avoid being killed, Saul does it in a way which makes David feel he is more serious this time, while still allowing him to flee through Michal's warning '...and Michal David's wife told him, saying, If thou save not thy life tonight, to morrow thou shalt be slain.'

Although the narration has Saul sending assassins to kill David, David does not seem to be bothered to the degree he fears for his life, he does say words to the effect 'your father wants to kill me' it is just an expression meaning 'your father is really angry/upset with me' especially when you read the following verses: 'And David said unto Jonathan, Behold, to morrow is the new moon, and I should not fail to sit with the king at meat, but let me go that I may hide myself in the field unto the third day at even. If thy father at all miss me, then say, David earnestly asked leave of me that he might run to Bethlehem his city, for there is a yearly sacrifice there for all his family. If he say thus, It is well; thy servant shall have peace: but if he be very wroth, then be sure that evil is determined by him.' And before David makes this strange suggestion for someone who is meant to have just survived an assassination attempt by Saul, he says 'And David sware moreover and said, thy father certainly knoweth that I have found grace in thine eyes...' so it has dawned on David, Saul knows of his relationship with Jonathan, but he is not worried of actually being killed because he is not sure if Saul knows of their sexual activities, therefore he would still like to attend the king's feast; but he is wary, he is certain Saul is aware of their love, but he needs to test how much Saul knows and suggests Jonathan find out more, and from Saul's reaction he will know if Saul knows everything and therefore he would be in much bigger trouble with the king, or if it is just a suspicion and they can reconcile again. But one thing for sure in the text of the story, David is certain of his place in Saul's heart and does not feel in fear of his life and would like to return to Saul's side and be in his presence. This is also where later editors have fiddled around with the story, where Saul is made the 'bad' character and David elevated to the 'hero' character; they do not remove completely the original storyline, as they need to keep what is in popular circulation, but the contradictions show the original story is about Saul's anger at his son and David's homosexual relationship where Saul does not intend to kill David and where David is not in fear of his life from Saul.

'Then said David to Jonathan, Who shall tell me? or what if thy father answer thee roughly?' until now both David and Jonathan have hope things will return to normal (1Sam.20:1-10). David was hoping Saul knew nothing about the physical part of their relationship and that a reconciliation would bring David back into Saul's house where he could continue to be close to his love, Jonathan. But all David's hopes of returning to Saul's favour, to continue being able to see Jonathan are crushed by Saul's response which leaves no doubt Saul knows everything, and David cannot return to Jonathan's side, and they are left weeping in each other's arms (1Sam.20:41-42) at having to part.

Saul's dialogue in Chapter 20 leaves no shadow of doubt that the issue with David is over the latter's emotional and physical relationship with his son Jonathan. If Jonathan is known to be homosexual (which is too modern a word—the correct term with regards to the Biblical story is 'become female') who will follow him or accept him as king, who will give their daughter in marriage to Jonathan—therefore Saul's 'seed' is in jeopardy because Jonathan has fallen in love with David, and although Saul and his people may 'look the other way' had it been merely a physical relationship that would not jeopardise Jonathan's ascension to the throne, nor his progeny, but Jonathan is infatuated with David, their souls are 'knit', he loves David as his own soul, but Jonathan has also waived away his right to the throne to allow David to take it—something the story tells us Saul is aware of when Jonathan informs David of his father's awareness of this covenant. But it is implied in the story (as it would be in the real life culture where this story emerged) that the people around Saul and the people of those times would have a problem with Jonathan engaging in homosexual acts because the word 'jonathan' itself meaning both men having sex with each other is from the word (khnf/خنث) 'male on male anal sex making each other female' which is from the word (enf/ أنث) 'female', so 'jonathan' is a physical sexual act making both men/boys involved into females, but not as a female who is normal and wholesome, but as a mutated/perverted being into something feminine but they are neither wholly male nor wholesomely female (in the Biblical story and meaning of the word)—it has a negative, shameful meaning and stigma attached to it: the 'Jonathan' man is not a 'proper' man, somehow feminine or deviated, a mutation, a wrong—therefore cannot be a king of a nation, nor a husband. This stigma, belief, idea is what troubles Saul in the story, and although his son is as much guilty/ responsible for his own behaviour and the author's depict Saul as any parent (even if it was a disapproved of boy-girl relationship) disapproving of a relationship he is laying the blame on David, the other person—not his son. He can get rid of David, but he does not want to get rid of his son, but he wants his son free of David.

In Saul's eyes, removing David from Jonathan's presence is the solution. But what Saul clearly expresses is that it is Jonathan's homosexuality and his relationship and love of David which troubles and angers him, and is the problem between Saul and David. He does not hate David completely, he wonders why he has not attended the feast; maybe he misses him—his seat is empty; but even the genuine feeling of 'David is not in his place' becomes a whisper, a worry, and causes Saul to turn the matter over and over in his mind 'why isn't David here' and the only real problem (real in the story) between David and Saul comes to the forefront of Saul's thinking that David is not clean i.e. has had homosexual sex with Jonathan: 'And the king sat upon his seat, as at other times, *even* upon a seat by the wall: and Jonathan arose, and Abner sat by Saul's side, and David's place was empty. Nevertheless, Saul spake not anything that day: for he thought, Something hath befallen him, he *is* not clean; surely he *is* not clean.' Notice how it is repeated that 'he *is* not clean', when a person has sex with his wife both are considered 'unclean' by the Biblical stories, and in such a culture illicit sex definitely makes its participants unclean which views homosexual sex as an 'abomination' for if husband and wife become unclean from sex, so do illicit lovers—and this is what is eating at Saul's mind, that even now after all the threats and warnings, David and Jonathan are still having sex with each other.

'And it came to pass on the morrow *which was* the second *day* of the month, that David's place was empty: and Saul said unto Jonathan his son, Wherefore cometh not the son of Jesse to meat, neither yesterday, nor today?' It is not Saul concerned for David's whereabouts, but it is Saul very similar to a consumed jealous husband (in this instance a father jealous over his son's reputation/orientation/activities) or wife wanting to know/glean any details about what his/her unfaithful partner and lover have been up to, trying to detect a reassuring response, while at the same time any response only heightens the jealousy, the anger, making a suspicion seem a fact. So when Jonathan gives the response David has instructed him to say that David has gone to Bethlehem to attend an annual family sacrifice and had previously asked for leave, Saul explodes and tells Jonathan exactly what is on his mind: 'Then Saul's anger was kindled against Jonathan, and he said unto him, Thou son of the perverse and rebellious woman,' (mothers are often blamed for their sons not turning out right, insulting the mother is actually a direct insult to the son, meaning 'because your mother is no good, she didn't bring you up properly that is why you turned out bad/something wrong with you.') 'do not I know that thou hast chosen the son of Jesse to thine own confusion, and unto the confusion of thy mother's nakedness?' In other words, what he is saying is 'I know you're in a relationship with David and having sex with him.' 'I know you're homosexual and David's your lover; you're confused and what you are doing is wrong.'. Saul is telling him his lusting after David has made him enter sexual intercourse as abominable as having sex with his own mother—therefore insulting his father gravely. Earlier in Leviticus it is described in euphemism 'uncovering the nakedness' of a woman who 'belongs' to someone else (husband, father, neighbour, etc.) is also uncovering her father's/husband's nakedness; 'nakedness' representing illicit sex and offending those related to the woman who has been copulated. As both David and Jonathan are male, not only has Jonathan confused himself with same-sex love and prohibited sex, but he has also 'confused' his 'mother's nakedness'—because had David had sex with one of Saul's daughters without marriage he would have 'uncovered Saul's nakedness' but because both David and Jonathan are male there is 'confusion' because it is supposed to be Saul who is violated too, but somehow because it is in reverse with David penetrating Jonathan it is Jonathan's mother's nakedness which means Saul's nakedness, dignity, reputation are being transgressed against twice-over—and Saul can see the whole confusion resulting out of it: the same-sex David and Jonathan are having has made offense against Saul as he is the father, but Jonathan has also become a female-male as both dominant and recipient in male sexual intercourse and so it is both Saul's nakedness and Jonathan's mother's nakedness which has been violated. You need to read Leviticus where it shows how having illicit sex is as 'uncovering the nakedness' offending those related to the female being 'had'—in this case it is both Saul and his wife through Jonathan.

Saul explicitly ties and makes certain David and Jonathan's relationship is the real danger to Jonathan, preventing/jeopardising him as a man, a future king and the surety of his kingdom. 'For as long as the son Jesse liveth upon the ground, thou shalt not be established, nor thy kingdom. Wherefor now send and fetch him unto me, for he shall surely die.' Saul is incensed by Jonathan's willingness and complicity to lie on behalf of and for David. When Jonathan (after being told directly and in no uncertain terms that Saul, his father, knows exactly what they are doing, Saul explicitly tells him what they are up to and that it cannot continue) responds 'And Jonathan answered Saul his father, and said unto him, Wherefor shall he be slain, what hath he done?' Jonathan pretending he did not hear or understand his father's crystal-clear statement continues to argue David's innocence (but Jonathan has understood as can be seen in verse 34) which despairs Saul and provokes him to send the ever-missing paternal javelin hurtling towards Jonathan 'And Saul cast a javelin at him to smite him.' (1Sam.20:25-34)

In the most telling part in the story about the reasons behind the Saul/David conflict—the authors do not have Saul say 'David is loved by the people' or 'David has been chosen by God. God departed with me to be with David.' Nor does he say 'David wants to be king, therefore I have to kill him so your ascension to the throne is guaranteed' but what Saul says to Jonathan is 'Your fault, you, your 'confusion', your love of men, your love and sexual acts with David have shamed us—and as long as David's alive you'll continue to be his lover and never be man enough or accepted as king of our people—and that's why David must die.'

The action of the object 'David' (the rolling pin of stone grinder) and its user cause a motion just like that of the male body having sex, and this too is used to enhance the story and make clear that the relationship between Jonathan and David is a sexual one too, even the connection made between David and Jesse to Ruth and Boaz is their stories are related to bread-making and illicit love-making: Boaz and Ruth first made love on the threshing floor where Boaz had been threshing. Jesse means 'my cold bread' and David is the stone rolling pin used to grind grain into dough and this is used to highlight the physical relationship between David and Jonathan.

Jonathan and David's story is a great love story where Jonathan was willing to give up his throne, and defy his father for the sake of the man he loved, even if the authors only created this story as all the other Biblical stories which are for entertainment and are meant to be dramatic, lewd and funny.

Adriel; 'ad̲rî'ēl; عَذري يِل 'excuse-the' 'my excuse is-the' 'shadow-the' 'my shadow-the', it is 'excuse/my excuse-the' because instead of marrying Merab to David, Merab is excused from marrying David and marries Adriel instead. Cp: 'avree-ill. He is a Meholathite; mĕḥōlāt̲î; مَحولآتي ، ميحولآتي 'of taking place/of instead of' 'instead of me' 'taking my place' and refers to Adriel becoming Merab's husband instead of David. The same way as (Gen.28:8-9) Mahalath was given to the character who replaced Esau's wives which his parents disapproved of, her name: Mahalath 'in place of/instead of'. Cp: meḥoolaatee, meiḥoolaatee. (1Sam.18:17,19)

Naioth; nāyôt̲; نآيَة 'went far away' 'far away' 'at a far distance' and the story points out David fled here from Saul, then all the messengers and also Saul will reach this faraway place; نآجُت 'spoke quietly to' 'secret conversation with' 'was saved' and as soon as the story narrates David told Samuel 'all that Saul had done to him.' Naioth is mentioned; also, when Naioth is mentioned all the messengers and Saul are possessed by God and prophesy—when a person prophesies not only are they speaking directly to the people listening, but they are also 'conversing' with 'God' and this part the people around them cannot hear what God says even if they hear what the person speaking with God is saying. Cp: naayot, naagot. (1Sam.19:18-24)

Sechu; śek̲û; سَقُ 'watered' and Ṣaul 'came to a great well', 'drove/steered' and Saul is chasing David so he is driving him, 'extremely cold'; صَقُ 'reach(by extending or stretching arm/body)/can reach' because Saul first causes David to flee to Naioth then sends after him three groups of messengers at different times before Saul himself arrives there. Cp: sequ, s̲s̲equ. (1Sam.19:22)

Ezel; hā'āzel; هآئآزَل 'here/look/pay attention/I will-go/disappear/be removed forever/wiped out' as the message Jonathan will give David and even the words he will say to his servant are 'Go, find out the arrows' and '...go thy way: for the Lord hath sent thee away.' And also describes where the arrows have gone to. From the word (zl/زل) and its meanings are explained under Zilpah (see Zilpah (Gen.29:24; 30:9-10)). It can also mean to be removed completely and this also fits this story as David has to part with Jonathan. 'here/look/pay attention/I will-forever' as the vows and promises Jonathan and David make to each other, and Jonathan asks for David's kindness forever, and 'the Lord be between thee and me for ever.' And when they part knowing they will no longer live together the parting words again reflect both meanings of 'go/disappear' and 'forever' 'Go in peace, for asmuch as we have sworn both of us in the name of the Lord, saying, The Lord be between me and thee, and between my seed and thy see forever. And he arose and departed...'. Cp: haa-aazel. (1Sam.20:14-42)

Ahimelech; 'ăḥîmelek̲; نَخي مَلَك 'brother-what is wrong/what is with you' as this priest fears meeting David and also poses questions to David which reflect the character's name 'Why *art* thou alone, and no man with thee?' Cp: a<u>kh</u>eemelek. And he is in Nob; nōb̲; نوذ 'was harmed' 'we harm(ed)' as he and all priests will be slaughtered for him providing David, unwittingly (David deceives him), with assistance (bread and weapons) but so will everyone in the city of Nob be killed. Cp: noov. (1Sam.21; 22)

Doeg; dō'ēg; دوعيج '(of) steering (or steered) and cornering(ed) sheep into specific area' from word (d'g/ دعج); the form of the word gives the attribute to what is being named that this person performs this action, and Doeg is first described as being 'detained before the Lord' and being in charge of the best/most of Saul's herds; ذوعيج 'he/they/this-were tortured/suffered prolonged torture' 'he/they/this-were overcrowded' 'he/they/this-were over spilling(with fortune/good)/field filled with crops whose panicles seem packed and over spilling' 'he/they/this-are crooked/twisted/not forthright'. In this instance it is Doeg who will be the reason why Ahimelech and other priests are brought to one place in Gibeah then slaughtered by Doeg and his character shows he is in charge of many herds (good fortune) but also the priests will be brought in great numbers as in 'crowds' and suffer great pain in slaughter; the great fortune ('over spilling') is mentioned in Saul's dialogue of how much he has given his servants, but also in how great numbers of people who hold high/privileged positions—the priests—are slaughtered; Doeg is also described as '...his name *was* Doeg...the chiefest of the herdmen...'; the 'crookedness/not forthright' is relayed in how David speaks with the priest of Nob which Doeg witnesses, in Doeg's actions as he misleads Saul to believe the priest conspired against him 'Then answered Doeg...I saw the son of Jesse coming to Nob, to Ahimelech...And he enquired of the Lord for him, and gave him victuals, and gave him the sword of Goliath...Then the king sent to call Ahimelech the priest...and all his father's house, the priests that *were* in Nob: and they came all of them to the king.' 'And Doeg...slew on that day fourscore and five persons that did wear a linen ephod.' Cp: doo'eyg, voo'eyg. (1Sam.21-22)

Achish; 'āḵîš; ئاخيش 'I fear' 'your brother' 'made scratchy/rough' the authors/editors narrate David fled to Achish in fear of Saul, then '...was sore afraid of Achish...'. It may be that a letter was lost in translation and copying over long periods of time that it could have also been the meaning 'scratched/scrammed' (phaakheesh from word phkhsh/فخش) because they describe David scratching at the doors and the story creators mostly use wordplay for multiple meanings with the name. But even as it is, transliterated, the word 'āḵîš shows a result of scratching 'made scratchy/rough'. Cp: aakheesh. He is the king of **Gath** with the meaning of 'troubling/inconvenience' or even just putting a person to too much trouble—and not wanting to be inconvenienced by a madman is what the dialogue has the king of Gath say. (1Sam.21:10-15)

Adullam; 'ădullām; نيظُلّ آم ، نَظولّام 'do injustice to' 'injustice' from word ظلم ; 'darkness' from word ظلام 'dark/darkness'; also 'to mislead-the' from word ظل . It still holds the same meanings as in Gen.38. In this story it means David was caused injustice, forced to flee for his life, as are the men who join him in this cave are either suffering injustice or cause injustice 'And every one *that was* in distress, and every one that *was* in debt, and every one *that was* discontented, gathered themselves unto him...'. A cave would be dark. Cp: adhullaam, adhull-aam. (1Sam.22:1-2)

Gad here holds one of its earlier meanings in Genesis: قعد 'seated/relaxed/waited (while crouching or sitting low)' as the prophet of this name is telling David not to do the meaning of Gad's name 'Abide not in the hold; depart...'. (1Sam.22:5)

Hareth; churth; حورث ، حُرث 'scowled/frowned' 'scowled at' and is reflected in the narration that Gad warns David he is in danger and reflected in that Saul has bad intentions towards David, and the same towards the priests. Cp: ḥurf, hoorf. (1Sam.22:5)

Abiathar; 'eḇyāṯār; نَبي آطار 'father/refused-fled/flew/banished/was banished' 'father/refused-was chased away/sent flying/fleeing/banished' and this priest flees Doeg's slaughter; نَذ عاطار 'harm/if/so/did-twirls'; نَذ عاذار 'harm/if/so/did-shadowed' 'harm/if/so/did-excused' as he is the only one from the family that gets away from the slaughter; نَذ جاذار 'harm/if/so/did-shudder' 'harm/if/so/did-cut up randomly/cut off tips/sheared off unevenly' for the same reason of getting away with his life while everyone else has been slaughtered which is done using sharp weapons; نَبي أضار 'father/refused-harmed/was harmed' as David is saying it is because of him that Abiathar's father and family have been killed, also the same as Abiathar flees and therefore 'refused-harmed' escaped harm. Cp: eby-aaṭaar, ev-'aaṭaar, ev-'aavaar, ev-gaavaar, eby-aadhaar. (1Sam.22:20-23)

Keilah in this part of the Biblical stories has some of the meanings translated under Josh.15:34; qĕ'îlâ; ق نيله/ا 'he said yes/it is' as David 'enquired of the Lord' and God responded with words to the effect that 'yes, he should go against the Philistines'; قَئيله/ا ، قيئيله 'a place for spending time with others/a gathering place' 'the gathering/spending time (the event)' and after killing the Philistines, David stays at Keilah until he 'enquires' of God again; كَعيله/ا ، كيعيله/ا 'testicles' 'struck/strike him in the balls' this is related to the ephod, priests, speaking with God, divining, and it is why the authors of the Bible wanted to make this clear by adding not only was Abiathar wearing an ephod (as a priest) when he arrived at Adullam, but he also carried an extra ephod which he will give to David to divine with (the use of ephod in its true meanings will be discussed elsewhere in this book); كي عيله/ا ، ك عيله/ا 'like, above him/on him' 'go/try-above/on him/get higher' as it describes Saul coming from a higher place 'down' to Keilah to capture or kill David (David's use of the ephod is narrated in a way to show the 'repeat/try again/keep at it/repeating the same revolving or to and fro motion' 'hesitates/goes and comes/recoils/revolves' meanings of the word 'David'). (1Sam.23:1-13)

Sela-hammahlekoth; sela'/sl'y-hmchlqvth; صَلاً/صلئي همهلكُت ، صَلاً/صلئي هم مهلكُت'rock-worried-the death of/perish of' 'rock-here-the death/perish of': (sela/صَلاً/صلئي) 'rock'; (hm(ham)/هَم) 'worried' (h(ha)/هـ) 'here'; (mahlekoth/مَهلَكُت) 'the death of/the perish of' and reflects that David was worried he would die as he was surrounded by Saul and his men while on/in that specific rock; صَلاً/صلئي هم محلقت ، صَلاً/صلئي همحلقت 'rock-worried-the surrounded/circled' 'rock-here-the surrounded' and still describes David worried because he has been circled by Saul and his men while he is on a rock. Cp: ssela/ssl-y hm mhlkot, ssela/ssl'y hmhlkot, ssela/ssl-y hm mḥlqot, ssela/ssl'y hmḥlqot. (1Sam.23:25-29)

En-gedi is still used here for its earlier meaning of 'where will you end up at' 'end up at' 'where-did he reach/was found' and refers to David fleeing and 'ending up at' 'the strong holds at En-gedi.' (1Sam.23: 29)

Nabal; nāḇāl; نآبآل 'we afflict' 'we soak' 'noble/great' and he is described '...and the man was very great' and it describes the thousands of sheep and goats he owns with all the riches that brings, he shows he is proud and understands his rights when David and his men attempt to threaten and force him to give them of his fortune, he refuses and informs them how he has worked hard for his fortune and he needs the food produce for his own workers which causes David to decide to attack him; his 'greatness' and stance bring-on David wanting to attack him and the other afflictions Nabal suffers in the story; نآذآل 'we humiliate/bring down' and it is what David and his men seek to do before Abigail intervenes. After his wife secretly meets with David, Nabal conveniently dies so that David can marry her and all Nabal's fortune.

There is a similarity between Jacob and David's stories that they are both bad people even in storyland, they steal and kill, they lie and deceive. The only difference is the authors of Jacob's stories do not hide his bad behaviour—even though he does evil to almost everyone around him the authors leave it at that, as he is still the hero in the story, but in David's case the later editors do add parts that were probably not in the original story and even when read in English it can be detected where the style and flow of writing differs and it is in the parts justifying David's actions against Nabal, where one of Nabal's men speaks to Abigail and the whole speech is justifying David's threat and want to take what belongs to Nabal, while speaking badly of Nabal (who in the unchanged original story parts takes care of his men and feeds them with feasts like a king's). It seems the later editors of these stories were more aware and sensitive to how the hero of the story is portrayed and made their own revisions to make him look better. Cp: naabaal, naavaal. He is from **Carmel**: 'answered back-the/retorted (with snarkiness)-the' as he snubs David's threats and responds with a rejoinder; 'generosity/generous-the' as he is generous to his family and everyone who works for him. (1Sam.25)

Abigail; 'ăḇîgayil, 'ăḇîgal; تَـ/ئبيغل ، تَـ/ئبيغيل 'the-donkeys' and refers to the great amounts of food produce she loads onto 'asses' and delivers to David, she too 'rode on the ass...' when she meets David the first time 'And it was so as she rode on the ass...David and his men came against her...''...she hasted and lighted off the ass...' and when she meets him again to be his wife 'And Abigail hasted, and arose, and rode upon an ass, with five damsels of hers that went after her...'. Abigail: 'the donkeys' is direct reference to the donkeys which save the day—David did not stop slaughtering Nabal and his men because Abigail asked him to do so but because she '...took two hundred loaves, and two bottles of wine, and five sheep ready dressed, and five measures of parched *corn*, and an hundred clusters of raisins, and two hundred cakes of figs, and laid *them* on asses.' She gave him the goods which David had attempted to coerce Nabal into giving.

Abigail is also: نَبي/ئبيي غيل/غل 'father/refused/rejected-hated intensely/despised' 'father/refused/rejected-dug deep/stabbed deep' (both meanings indicate action/revenge will occur out of the hatred/feelings), 'father/refused/rejected-exploited/took advantage of' 'father/refused/rejected-made more expensive' 'father/refused/rejected-made up laws/rules/made up severe laws/rules' and relays with the hatred David feels and the revenge he wants to commit because Nabal refused to comply with paying David's demands; in the narration that Nabal refuses to be taken advantage of, and in the same narration it depicts Nabal and his men have taken advantage of 'protection' provided by David and his men and then met this action with rejection instead of gratitude which causes David's response which shows despise, revenge and that it will be extreme; it is in a deep stab/betrayal Nabal feels when Abigail informs him of what she gave

David which causes Nabal to die; it is in that David feels Nabal's death is revenge for him conducted by God, and following his death David exploits the situation and Nabal's wealth by marrying Abigail; عبي/عيبي 'fill/pack' 'shame/my shame/disgrace' followed by the meanings of gayil/gal mentioned above: the story is about the wealth of plentiful produce owned by Nabal which David wants to receive from, but Nabal insults by refusing to give, then Abigail packing donkey-loads, and expressing she/and others are ashamed of and refusing Nabal's behaviour and personality. Cp: a-beeghayil, aibeeghayil, a-beeghal, ai-beeghal, abee/aibee ghayil/ghal, 'abee/'aibee ghayil/ghal. (1Sam.25)

The authors do not want the audience to miss the importance of 'Abigail' 'the donkeys' is what is brought of Nabal's fortune from meat, grain, wine etc. so they immediately add another wife to her as soon as she becomes David's wife, the second wife with the same name as Saul's wife: **Ahinoam**; for the meaning 'here she is-blessings/gives food/money/health/(anything physical that can be received or given)' 'she is-blessings' and it is again a direct reference to the goods Abigail brings with her, this is supported by the earlier Ahinoam's father's name: **Ahimaaz** with one of its meanings being 'here she is/she is-goats' even though this Ahinoam (which is not the same character as Saul's wife, but the same character-name used as a theme) is from **Jezreel** one meaning of which is 'grazed-on-the'—so Nabal's wife provides David with Nabal's herds and food produce, and the character of a second wife is created solely so the word-name to accompany 'Abigail' to explain the importance of the food produce she brings. (1Sam.25:43)

Phalti; palṭî; بَلطي 'sticks to/stick to'; فَلتي 'falls/fallen' (both physically to fall or figuratively as become immoral especially sexually) and this is what is meant here because Saul has given Michal, David's wife, to this character. Cp: balṭee, phaltee. He is son of **Laish**; with the same meaning 'why?' as the city earlier in Judges 18. It is an objection as to why she was given away to another man, and will also be an objection as to why she is being taken away from Phalti to be 'given' to David. Gallim; gallîm; غلّ هم/ام 'despised them/the' 'deep hatred-them/the' 'stabbed deep/dug deep into-them/the' and the word (ghl/غل) usually carries an indication that revenge/action will be taken against those hated with such intensity and this occurs in 2Sam.3:13-16 where David and Ish-bosheth take her by force to be 'returned' to David, and Phalti (Phalti-el(Paltiel) in 2Sam) follows his wife, weeping over her. Cp: ghall-hum/um. (1Sam.25:44)

Abishai; 'ăḇîšay; نَبي سَي 'refused-evil/bad'; نَبي شَي 'refused-something'; عَبي سي/شَي 'fill/pack-evil' 'fill/pack-something'; نَذي سَي 'harm-evil' 'to harm is evil'; نَذي شَي 'harm-something' 'to harm a little'. Although they go down to kill Saul (do evil), they end up with David refusing to do this evil and do a lesser harm by stealing his spear and water pot. Cp: abee-say, abee-shay, 'abee-say, 'abee-shay, avee-say, avee-shay. (1Sam.26)

Zeruiah; ṣĕrûyâ; شَرُيه ، شيرُيه 'bought it/him' 'evil-it/him' as Abishai the son of Zeruiah is more insistent to kill Saul than David; ضَرُيه ، ضيرُيه 'became vicious' 'he/it became vicious' 'vicious-it/he/him' 'he/it got used to (specific habit or way)/developed habit' for the same reason as first meaning; سَرُيه ، سيرُيه 'left early in the dark' as they go at night or early pre-dawn while it is still dark and everyone is asleep to kill the sleeping Saul. Cp: sheruyah, sheiruyah, dheruyah, dheiruyah, seruyah, seiruyah. (1Sam.26)

Joab; yô'āḇ; يُعاَب 'is disgraced' 'he disgraces/he is disgraced' 'disgraces (others)'; يُئاَذ 'harms' 'he harms' 'he is harmed'; جوئاَب 'a response' 'responds' 'of responses' 'a letter'; جوئاَذ 'came and harmed'. Although the word-name is only mentioned as the brother of Abishai, it is used as a theme: they want to kill/harm Saul; David feels it would be a disgrace and guilt to kill Saul; David predicts that others will harm/kill Saul so that he himself does not need to; instead, David and Abishai shame/disgrace Abner for not doing his job right in not noticing they were right there next to Saul and took his possessions and could have easily killed him; Saul and David enter the same question and answer conversation: '…*Is* this thy voice my son David? And David said, *It is* my voice…'; David shames Saul for wanting to kill him 'for no reason at all' and Saul feels disgraced/guilty of sinning and repents; Saul states he will no longer harm David and feels a 'fool' i.e. ashamed for doing so; David proves he came in close proximity to Saul and did not harm him although he could. Cp: yo'aab, yo-aav, go-aab, go-aav. (1Sam.26)

Maoch; mā'ôḵ; ماَعُك 'with you' and is the added name given as father to the earlier Achish king of Gath, and now denotes David being/living with Achish and fighting for him. Cp: maa'ok. (1Sam.27)

Ziklag holds the meaning as earlier in Joshua: 'that is for you' as he is given a town to live in and rule; also 'distress for you'; 'distress is coming' as he begins to massacre all the people/cities/towns nearby 'And David smote the land, and left neither man nor woman alive, and took away the sheep, and the oxen, and the asses, and the camels, and the apparel…'. (1Sam.27:5-12)

Jerahmeel; yĕraḥmĕ'ēl; بيرَحميئيل ، يرَحميئيل 'he sees-takes/carries'; جيرَحميئيل ، جِرَحميئيل 'came-saw-takes/carries' 'ran-takes/carries' and refers to someone coming, seeing and taking something or someone; بيرَحمي ئِل ، يِرَحمي ئِل 'he has mercy on the'; جيرَحمي ئِل ، جِرَحمي ئِل 'came-has/had mercy on the'. It denotes David has gone and massacred peoples of Geshur, Gezer and Amalek and carried away their possessions, and shows no mercy towards them, but towards himself, saving himself by leaving no one alive just in case they tell on him. Cp: yera-ḥmeiill, yeira-ḥmeiill, ge-ra-ḥmeiill, gei-ra-ḥmeiill, yeraḥmei-ill, yeiraḥmei-ill, ge-raḥmei-ill, gei-raḥmei-ill, (1Sam.27:8-12)

Gilboa; har haggilbōa'; هَرهَجّلبوَء ، هَرهَج جِلبوَء 'chased/drove away-deserted-fetched' 'chased/drove away-I will fetch'. (hr/هر) 'chased away' as the army will be defeat, as well as mention of all the sorcerers which Saul has either executed or banished; (hg/هج) 'to desert/abandon' as God has abandoned Saul and no longer responds to him; (glb/جلب) 'fetch/bring' refers to the gathering of the army or all the people of Israel in the place of the same name, and also denotes Saul asking his men to find him a witch. Cp: har hag gilbooa, har haggilbooa. (1Sam.28:4-7)

Endor, as in Josh.17, still means: 'ên dôr; نَيندُر 'set goats or sheep on their way' 'to separate the goats from sheep or to separate a goat or a sheep from the rest of the flock(for specific purpose such as slaughter) and it reflects in the story that Saul has 'cut off' and killed all people who deal with sorcery, and the woman fears she is being singled-out or set-up to be killed; it also reflects that Saul has been told he and his sons will die the next day in battle, how the woman tells him she will feed him before she sends him on his way is the same way as separating and sending animals for slaughter; 'ên dō'r; عين دوئر 'see/look/pay attention-seek/look for' نَين دوئر 'we will look for/we are looking for' as Saul has sent messengers to look for a witch and they find her in the suitably-named area of Endor; the woman also looks for Samuel, and Samuel looks for answers for Saul. (1Sam.28:7-25)

Besor; bĕśôr; بِصُر ، بيصُر 'with leftovers' 'with cannot hear/pretending not to hear/pretending to be deaf/ignoring' and refers to the men left behind by David at the brook because they were tired, and leftovers of food or anything is a negative thing to give to anybody and usually refused. '...and came to the brook Besor, where those that were left behind stayed...for two hundred abode behind, which were so faint that they could not go over the brook Besor.' And though the word besor/sor means leftovers of food and things, in the story it refers to the men left behind, but also shown in the narration that David and his men recovered all the women and children, all the 'spoil' which the enemy had taken i.e. it was not 'besor' but in whole returned without being used 'And David recovered all that the Amelkites had carried away: and David rescued his two wives.' His two wives Abigail and Ahinoam are always mentioned as a pair because they symbolise goats, sheep, grain, wine—all kinds of food source 'And there was nothing lacking to them, neither small nor great, neither sons nor daughters, neither spoil, nor any *thing* that they had taken to them: David recovered all.'. Also, he will not give the men 'leftovers/besor' who stayed at the brook Besor, but will give them a fair share from the spoils of war although some 'wicked' men wanted to just return to them their wives and children and send them off i.e. they wanted to give them 'leftovers' things (people in this case) that are neither wanted nor needed. Cp: be<u>ss</u>or, bei<u>ss</u>or. (1Sam.30)

Siphmoth; śipmôṯ; صِف مُت 'describe/flatter/insult-died' 'rock-died' 'stacked rocks-died' 'columns/rows-died'; سِف مُط 'went numb-stretch' 'sipped-stretch(ed)' 'poured water gently-stretched' 'carried gently-stretched; شِف مُت 'saw-died/death'. Cp: <u>ss</u>i<u>ph</u>mot, si<u>ph</u>moṭ, <u>sh</u>i<u>ph</u>mot. (1Sam.30:28)

Eshtemoa; 'eštĕmôa'; يِستيموَع ، يِستِموَع 'eavesdropped/listened' 'insulted loudly made other people hear' (latter is when a person accuses another of things and says them loudly so that not only the person feels embarrassed but further embarrassed by other people hearing these insults about him/her). Cp: estemoa', esteimoa'. (1Sam.30:28)

Rachal; rāḵāl; راَحاَل 'went' 'travelled/departed' 'rested-the' 'appeased/contented/relieved-the'. Cp: raaḥaal. (1Sam.30:29)

Chorashan; kôr'āšān; خُرئاَشاَن 'untied/came loose'; حُرئاَشاَن 'caused problems between' 'communicated gossip/statements'; قُرئاَشاَن 'won/scored' (in games) 'won/took by force' as in war/reality 'scrape and peel away'; خُرئاَصاَن 'collapse/drive and sweep away' (with physical violence); كُرئاَشاَن 'with large bellies' 'intestines' the latter is the stomach of a slaughtered animal, cleaned and cooked with meat (small amounts are eaten raw as a delicacy). Cp: <u>kh</u>or-aa<u>sh</u>aan, ḥor-aa<u>sh</u>aan, qor-aa<u>sh</u>aan, <u>kh</u>or-aa<u>ss</u>aan, koraa<u>sh</u>aan. (1Sam.30:30)

Athach; 'ăṯāḵ; عَطآك ، عيطآك 'gave you'; غَثآك غيثآك 'nourished you' 'nauseated you' 'troubled you or nagged you to the degree of nausea'; تَتآك ، تيتآك 'go quickly' 'hurry' 'came to you'; عَطآق ، عيطآق 'saved' 'liberated/freed'. Cp: 'aṭaak, 'aiṭaak, ghafaak, ghaifaak, a-taak, aitaak, 'aṭaaq, 'aiṭaaq. (1Sam.30:30)

Beth-shan; bêṯ-šan; بيت شَن 'he/it will be-fertile/sexually excited/ready to conceive' 'he/it will be copulated' the meaning relates to animals on heat ready for copulation such as goats, 'he/it will be filtered' 'he/it will be poured or flowed out of/into' 'he/it will be filtered/filtered of impurities' 'he it will filter out' 'it will be important matter/significance'. The narration that Saul's armour was placed in **Ashtaroth** and his body fastened 'to the wall of Beth-shean' symbolises that Saul suffered the same humiliation and torture other fallen kings and princes suffer in the Biblical stories and this is why these word names have been chosen. To understand further see the meanings of Ashtaroth (Judg.2) and Asher Beth-shean (Josh.17:11). Cp: beyt-shan. (1Sam.31:10)

2 Samuel

Helkath-hazzurim; ḥelqaṯ haṣṣūrîm; حَلقَة هَضّورهم 'circle/surround-I will harm them'; هَلكَة هَضّورهم 'the death of-I will harm them'. Both meanings refer to the young men who were supposed to play in a wrestling match, but instead some killed others and it refers to them being linked when they fall and die. Not only do the wrestling men die, but fighting and killing pursues from this match. Cp: ḥelqat ha<u>dh</u>ur-hum, helkat ha<u>dh</u>ur-hum. (2Sam.2:14-17)

Asahel; 'ăśâ'ēl; عَصه/عَصا ئِل ، عيصه/عيصا ئِل 'disobeyed/went against-the' 'disobeyed him/went against him-the' 'became askew/crooked-the' 'a stick-the' 'a stick, him-the' and means straight and unbending like a stick, sticking to what he is doing. The latter meaning can be seen in Asahel '...and in not going he turned not to the right hand nor to the left hand from following Abner.' When Abner attempts to persuade him to stop and take someone's armour the narrators want to show Asahel's 'stick/unbending' meaning by narrating Abner says 'Turn thee aside to thy right hand or to thy left, and lay thee hold...and take thee his armour. But Asahel would not turn aside from following of him...And Abner said again to Asahel, Turn thee aside from following me...Howbeit he refused to turn aside.' Cp: 'a<u>ss</u>ah-ill, 'a<u>ss</u>a-ill,'ai<u>ss</u>ah-ill, 'ai<u>ss</u>a-ill. (2Sam.2:18-23)

Ammah; 'ammâ; عَمّه 'made him blind' 'gave him to drink' 'drank it' 'his uncle' 'aunty'; ئَمّه 'mother/mum' 'his mother' 'led/led through' 'thread a needle'. It is wordplay on the sun going down and people not seeing properly 'made him blind' and the same blindness from anger (refer to the word Giah to see the connection) which misleads to evil; uncle, aunt, mother are all invoked because the dialogue will have Abner point out that they are killing their own brethren. Cp: 'ammah, ammah. (2Sam.2:24-32)

Giah; gîaḥ; جيَه 'they are coming' 'they come' and refers to Joab and Abishai coming to the place; غيَه 'great deceit' 'misleading into evil or wrongdoing or downfall' 'his deceit/misleading to evil' and it is what is mentioned in Abner's words to Joab. Cp: geeah, <u>gh</u>eeah. (2Sam.2:24-32)

Bithron; bitrôn; بِذرُن 'march like ants' because of the walk Abner and his men make, 'leave them'; بِطرُن 'turned down/rejected a good thing' 'became flippant over something good/important'. Cp: bivron, biṭron. (2Sam.2:29)

Note below in the choosing of David's son's character-names they are like the lists which serve as themes and ideas outlining what the story will be. In this case it tells the story of David's sons and what will ensue. Similar names or words with similar meanings in the sequence below can be found in the Deuteronomy list lumped together, from which the current story was inspired and created.

Amnon; 'amnôn, 'amnōn; ئَمنُن ، ئَمنون 'made feel safe/made safe' 'deceive by making feel safe' 'false sense of safety' 'listed all good things given or done to another' (like gloating). Cp: amnon, amnoon. (2Sam.3:2)

Chileab; kil'āḇ; قِل عآب 'say/said a disgrace' 'a tumbling rock' 'a tumbling sound'; حِل عآب 'undressed-disgraced'; حلئآب 'milks/of milking/plenty to milk' 'undress(ed)-refused/rejected'; كِلئآب 'they all refused' 'dogs' 'chased after like dogs' 'chased away like dogs'; قِل ئآذ 'said-harmed'; كل ئآذ 'all were harmed'. Cp: qil'aab, ḥil-'aab, ḥil-aab, kil-aab, qil-aav, kil-aav. (2Sam.3:3)

Absalom; aḇšālōm; عَب سآلوم 'asked for something disgraceful/a disgraceful demand' 'of disgraceful demands/questions' 'disgrace/packed-asked them' 'disgrace/packed-flowed/leaked' 'disgrace/packed-distracted/entertained/comforted' 'disgrace/packed-survived/intact/whole' 'disgrace/packed-received/delivered' 'disgrace/packed-greeted' 'disgrace/packed-of peaceful nature'; عبشآلوم 'fur/hair looking bigger because standing on end(e.g. like cats' fur when scared)' 'disgraceful-took/to take' 'disgrace-I will blame'; اذسآلوم 'harm-asked them' 'harm-survived' 'if he asked' 'then-I will blame' (It can be 'harm/av' followed by any meanings of 'salom' above). Cp: 'absaaloom, 'ab<u>sh</u>aaloom, avsaaloom. (2Sam.3:3)

Maacah; ma'ăḵâ; مَع خا ، مَع خه ، مَعي خا ، مَعي خه 'with his brother' 'I have a brother/with a brother' 'with his brother/I have his brother'; مَعَكا، مَعكه ، مَعيكا ، مَعيكه 'with you' 'it is with you'. Cp: ma' a<u>kh</u>a, ma' a<u>kh</u>ah, ma'ai <u>kh</u>a, ma'ai <u>kh</u>ah, ma'aka, ma'akah, ma'aika, ma'aikah. **Talmai**; talmay; تَلمَي 'carried water by hand' which would be unusual and more strenuous to carry it as a basket, people usually carry it on the head or shoulder because if its weight, could also mean 'tilled me(ploughed)/my lines of land'. **Geshur**; gěšûr; جَشَر ، جيشَر 'bares his teeth/bore his teeth' 'takes/takes a lot/takes everything' and is in the form of a characteristic. حيشُر ، حَشُر 'greedy' 'made hungry/greedy'. Cp: geshur, geishur, ḥeshur, ḥeishur. (2Sam.3:3)

Adonijah; 'ădōnîyâ; نَضوني جه/ا 'here I am coming' 'here I have done-coming'; نَذوني يه/ا 'harmed me-he/them' 'they harmed me'. Cp: adhoonee gah(ga), avoonee yah(ya); Haggith; ḥaggîṯ; هَجّيت 'deserted forever/left forever' 'learned to pronounce correctly'; حجّيت 'covered (with hand or blanket, etc.)' 'sheltered (from something e.g. sun/wind)' 'stood where could not be seen'. Cp: haggeet, ḥaggeet. (2Sam.3:4)

Shephatiah; šĕpaṭyâ, šĕpaṭyāhû; شِفَت يه/ياة ، شيفَت يه/ياة 'saw him' 'saw-he/him' 'she saw him' 'she cured him' 'she gloated at him' 'a gloating/serves you right'; صِفَت يه/ياة ، صيفَت يه/ياة 'cleaned/cleared/purified-he/him' 'stacked rocks-he/him' 'flattered him/described him positively' 'insulted him'; صِفَط يه/ياة ، صيفَط يه/ياة 'teased/joked-he/him' 'got used to/habit-he/him'; صِبَط يه/ياة ، صيبَط يه/ياة 'stuck(to)-he/him'. Cp: shephat-yah/yaahu, sheiphat-yah/yaahu, ssephat-yah/yaahu, sseiphat-yah/yaahu, ssephaṭ-yah/yaahu, sseiphaṭ-yah/yaahu, ssebaṭ-yah/yaahu, sseibaṭ-yah/yaahu. Abital; 'ăḇîṭāl; ئبيطال ، ئبيطال 'heroes/champions' 'is bad/evil' 'wrong/wrongdoing' 'cancel/cease' 'incapacitated/debilitated (permanently or temporarily)' such as an arm or leg that cannot move permanently or temporarily and just hangs there. Cp: a-beeṭaal, aibeeṭaal. (2Sam.3:4)

Ithream; yiṯrĕ'ām; عِطري عام 'pressing/pressed-drank/blind'; يِضريع آم 'breasts/grows breasts-the'; يِضري عام 'gets used to/becomes vicious/develops habit-drank/blind'; يِذري عام 'seeds/sows-drank/blind' 'scatters-drank/blind'; يِذريع آم 'measures by forearm-the' (literal measuring or figurative for beating up). Cp: 'iṭrei-'aam, yidhrei'-aam, yidhrei-'aam, yivrei-'aam, yivrei'-aam. Eglah; 'eglâ; عِجلا ، عِجله 'calf' 'rushed' 'brash' 'went/acted too soon'. Cp: 'eglah, 'egla. (2Sam.3:5)

Rizpah; riṣpâ; رِصفه 'a stack' (of stones usually, or any objects, crops, etc.) 'stack it'; رِزبه 'press on her/it' 'come down severely on her/it' and is used here as euphemism for sexual intercourse: Ish-bosheth accuses Abner of sleeping with her 'And Saul had a concubine whose name *was* Rizpah…Wherefore has thou gone in to my father's concubine?'. Cp: rissphah, rizbah. And she is daughter of Aiah; 'ayyâ; عَجّه 'overcrowded (him/it)' 'over spilling(with fortune/good)/field filled with crops whose panicles seem packed and over spilling (him/it)' 'stirred/shook(him/it)' 'suffered/tortured/prolonged his suffering and torture(him/it)' 'is crooked/twisted/not forthright' 'made crooked/twisted(him/it)' 'crying intensely/crying and gasping' ; عَيّه 'will-he/he will' 'will he?' 'learn and remember-him/it' 'be warned-(of) him' 'beware-him' 'I dare you, go on-him'. It is her father's name to serve the purpose that Ish-bosheth should be wary of Abner, it relays that Abner has designs on and is not forthright with Ish-bosheth who finds him 'crooked' and suspects him, but also the narration shows Abner finds Ish-bosheth's accusations are 'crooked' and his dialogue shows meanings of both 'he will/will he?' and 'he is/is he?' regarding what he has or has not done, the 'overcrowded/over spilled with panicles/crops' meanings match with the 'stack' meanings of her first name, and she is introduced following the mention of David's many sons and David becoming stronger as well as Abner making himself stronger for 'the house of Saul'; ئيّه 'is-he/he is' 'is he?' 'which(e.g. one)' and it is also an expression to show one's displeasure at what has been said/done to him—had these fictional characters been real such as the conversation on each of their parts they would have said 'aiah' at the beginning or end of their dialogue. The close equivalents in English is saying 'really?!' 'Well!'—it is an objection. Cp: 'aggah, 'ayyah, aiyyah. (2Sam.3:7-10)

Ish-bosheth; 'îš-bōšeṯ; ئيص بوشِت 'hush(ed)-he was gobsmacked' (ish/ 'îš/ئيص) from word (ss/assah/assa/ssa/ص/اص/اصه/ص) 'sh/hush/quiet!'; ئيش بوشِت 'how he was gobsmacked' (Ish/ 'îš/ايش) 'how', (bosheth/ bšt/بشت) 'unable to speak/gobsmacked', (boshet/بوشِت) 'he was gobsmacked/unable to speak' and 'gobsmacked' is in the form of describing a male in this state, it also describes when a person sees someone beautiful and is unable to speak, just stare. After Abner's angry response to Ish-bosheth's accusations, the latter is silenced and left unable to speak 'And he could not answer Abner a word again, because he feared him.' Cp: eess-booshet, eesh-booshet. (2Sam.3:7-11)

Bahurim; baḥûrîm; بَهُر هم/ام 'will chase them/the away(using words)'; بَحُر هم/ام 'good riddance of them/the'; بَحُريم 'I will deprive/forbid'. All three meanings are used in the story where this word is used as a place name: David separates and deprives Phalti/Phaltiel and Michal from each other; Abner sends away and gets rid of Phaltiel at Bahurim by using only an order 'Then said Abner unto him, Go return. And he returned.'. 'Michal' 'observing/watching/ogling' is used because David is telling Abner he cannot see his face (i.e. talk with him directly and be taken seriously) until he brings Michal whose name means 'ogling/seeing/inspecting'. Cp: bahur-hum/um, baḥur-hum/um, baḥureem. (2Sam.3:13-16)

Sirah; bôr hassirâ; بُر هَسِّرح 'good/piety/went or go beyond-see/he is gone' and refers to Joab learning that Abner was there and had 'gone in peace' i.e. there was good relations between Abner and David which allowed him to leave unharmed, and that Abner had already left by the time Joab got there; بُر هَصِّرَح 'good/piety/went beyond-I will openly speak' and David announces he is free of guilt of Abner's murder, he speaks openly and makes quite a show of how 'good' Abner was—it is really a show of how 'good' and 'pious' David is; بُر هَصِّرَخ 'good/piety-I will shout' and again is how David makes a scene over Abner's murder (i.e. how the authors make David look better and innocent of the slaying of all his adversaries who first get rid of his enemies for him) as he shouts and mourns and does all the things as described not only in these fictional Biblical stories but also how people of this culture wail and mourn loudly and express grief over a death of a loved-one, '...Rend your clothes, and gird you with sackcloth, and mourn before Abner...' 'And the king lifted up his voice and wept at the grave of Abner...'. (bôr is not 'well/cistern' but 'good/piety'). Cp: bor hassiraḥ, bor hassiraḥ, bor hassirakh. (2Sam.3:22-39)

Baanah; baʿănâ; بَعينه 'by/with his eye' 'watching' and also is a threat/warning which 'by my eye' means 'I'll get you' and he and his brother watch and murder Ish-bosheth as soon as they find an opportunity, this word-name also enhances his brother's word-name; also means 'they sold him' as they have switched their allegiance from Ish-bosheth to David, Ish-bosheth's 'sale' is murder. Cp: ba'ainah. (2Sam.4)

Rechab; rēḵāḇ; ريقآب 'keep eye on' 'pour carefully from one vessel to another' (usually used as word when watching carefully how water is poured from one vessel's opening into another to avoid spilling even a drop of water) here it is used to observe Ish-bosheth and kill him as soon as opportunity is available which is while the latter was laying or sleeping in his bed; 'necks' as they cut off Ish-bosheth's head, and they too will be killed; could also be: ريكآب 'mounted/rid on' 'placed on top of/piled on top of' 'knees' and the 'mounted/rid' meaning can be literal as in 'rode' or 'got on top of' as well as slang/vulgar for having sex with a woman, it indicates they got on top of him and/or knelt on top of him to kill him while he lay on the bed. Cp: reyqaab, reykaab. (2Sam.4)

Rimmon used as their patronym for the word's earlier meanings of 'thrown' as in being killed/dying and 'rotten/stinking' because their corpses or body limbs are left hanging to rot. Their father is from **Beeroth** because of its meanings: 'he gives inheritance to' as David will benefit following this event and inherit becoming the king of Israel; and 'he buries in ground/soil' 'he creates soil/does with soil' as Ish-bosheth who both Baanah and Rechab killed will be given a proper burial, whereas their corpses will be severed to pieces and hung above a pool in Hebron.

Hebron used for: 'told them news/information' 'they told/informed/brought news' 'of news/information/of telling' as Baanah and Rechab bring Ish-bosheth's head to David and inform him they have killed Ish-bosheth as revenge for, and loyalty towards, David, and David's dialogue also relays 'told them/informed/etc.)' as he informs them that they are in the wrong; 'they are doing good' 'will do good/piety towards' 'he/they will be innocent of/do what is right' 'they/he will pass/go beyond' as Baanah and Rechab believe they are doing good towards David; David in turn shows he is innocent of what they have done and punishes them for killing Ish-bosheth; the offenders are hung up in Hebron so people who pass by see what has been done to them, and their victim (Ish-bosheth) is also put to rest in a sepulchre at Hebron and this shows David is being pious/good towards him, but as it is **Abner**'s sepulchre ('son of penis') that he is put in there is a pun of a disgrace against Ish-bosheth, and maybe also showing David and his actions are not innocent.

Gittaim; gittāyim; غِتّآيِم ، غِتّآي ام 'they dosed off/fell asleep' 'dosed off/fell asleep-the' 'they deceived/misled to downfall' 'they were misled/deceived to their downfall' 'they misled/deceived to downfall-the'; جِتّآيِم 'they cut/snipped off the tips, limbs or edges off something' 'they nibbled edges and corners off' 'they cut short'; جِذّآيِم'came-guilted/insulted/blamed/humiliated/ostracised' 'have leprosy-like disease' 'with tips/ends fallen/cut off' 'lepers' 'geckos' the latter is believed to cause leprosy, and its tail severs off so it can get away from danger. The word 'Gittaim' was used as the place name where we are told the Beerothites flee to although this fleeing of the Beerothites is unrelated to what will happen in the story of the murder of Ish-bosheth, but it serves to denote how the two brothers will behead Ish-bosheth then the two brothers will be dismembered 'And David commanded his young men, and they slew them, and cut off their hands and their feet...'. Cp: ghittaayim, ghittaay-um, gittaayim, givvaayim. (2Sam.4)

The first few chapters have David moving to and staying in **Hebron** for its meanings which will be the theme for David's part in the stories: 'told them news/information' 'they told/informed/brought news' 'of news/information/of telling' 'they/he will pass/go beyond' as he and his people will go from Ziklag to Hebron; but mainly for 'he/they are doing good' 'he is doing good' 'he/they will be innocent of' 'he/they do what is right', and in the first few chapters no matter what news of death and murders of everyone who was an obstacle to David becoming king of Israel or to his life, and the events of which serve his interest, the story has David doing good and washing his hands of any guilt, or at least saying good things towards and about those who have been killed (although he does evil towards the murderers even if they were doing it for his sake or bringing him news). (2Sam.1-4)

Mephibosheth; mĕp̄îḇōšeṯ; مَفي/ميفي بوشِت 'there was no/is no-gobsmacked/unable to speak'; and he is created and inserted in an odd place while telling the assassination of Ish-bosheth's story (to show that he had a nephew of a suitable similar name without creating confusion between the two characters). As his name indicates, he is the exact opposite of Ish-bosheth ('how he was unable to speak'), he has no problem in talking (2Sam.9:1-13); where he communicates through Ziba (2Sam.16:1-3); and he speaks more no matter how upset David is with him later in the story. Cp: mephee/meiphee-booshet. (2Sam.19:24-30)

Zion; ṣîyôn; صيُين 'sweep/brush' 'swept/brushed away' and refers to sweeping indoors or outdoors using a brush from palm tree leaves called (msswna/مصونا); سيُين 'bad/offensive/offense'. The word-name given as a city which David entered in Jerusalem, for the story has him confronted by the Jebusites demanding all the blind and the lame be sent away as they cannot enter the city, believing this will prevent David from entering Zion as he will not abandon part of his own people. Instead, David immediately orders the massacre of not only the Jebusites but also 'the lame, and the blind…' (with a promise of great reward for whoever participates in the deed). Therefore Zion is a play on the main word 'sweep' because all the Jebusites will be swept out of the city (i.e. killed) like unwanted refuse, and so will the disabled people because they are the play on the second meaning 'bad' as that is how the authors of the story have David see them and give him a deep hatred towards them '…the Jebusites, the inhabitants of the land: which spake unto David, saying, Except thou take away the blind and the lame, thou shalt not come in hither: thinking, David cannot come in hither. Nevertheless David took the stronghold of Zion: the same is the city of David. And David said on that day, Whosoever getteth up to the gutter, and smiteth the Jebusites, and the lame, and the blind, that are hated of David's soul, he shall be chief and captain. Wherefore they said, The blind and the lame shall not come into the house. Cp: sseeyon, seeyon. (2Sam.5:6-8)

Jebusites are used as the people of Jerusalem for its meanings of: 'dry/dried' 'stiff/stiffened' 'stiffens when dry/thick and cloying' as they are being difficult and believe they can prevent David from entering the city; 'poked finger into' 'poked into' 'poked finger into anus' for its sexual meanings and indications of a man poking his finger into another man's anus (can also mean non-sexually poked such as to unhygienically stick fingers into food making it bad/polluted) and was used in Judg.19:10-12 to reflect anal sex between men of Gibeah in that story and in this current story too, by having David (who the Biblical stories have love Jonathan and engage in sex with) 'hate' and destroy everyone that is related to 'poked/Jebus' or reminds of the story linked to Jebusites as Jebus was the place where no anal sex nor rape would have happened had the Levite listened to his servant and stayed there instead of going to Gibeah where men wanted to rape him (the authors are showing David hates the people who disdain male-on-male sex, i.e. they hate Jonathan and people like David and Jonathan), and by having David hate and destroy people who are blind and lame as disabilities make their eyes/bodies 'polluted' due to the disability (according to the Bible). (2Sam.5:6-8)

Hiram; ḥîrām; خيرآم 'the good/fortune-the' 'the best of-the' 'piercing holes/piercing holes into metal' 'tearing something through to the end that was already a hole/piercing/slit' 'piercing from the bottom', and refers to all the precious resources and skilled labour he sends to David 'And Hiram king of Tyre sent messengers to David, and cedar trees, and carpenters, and masons: and they built David an house.' And is followed by David knowing the greatness of his place and people. It can also mean; حيرآم 'sacred' 'women' 'forbidden/the forbidden' 'the rotten/the stinking rotten'; هيرآم 'the driven away' 'drive away-the' 'he threw' 'is strewn over distance'. Cp: kheer-aam, heeraam, heeraam. (2Sam.5:11-12)

Shobab; šôḇāḇ; شُبآب 'young men' 'young adult'; صُبآب 'pouring into/onto'; سُبآب 'swearing/insulting' 'they swear at' 'they leave' 'have been left behind'. Cp: shobaab, ssobaab, sobaab. (2Sam.5:14)

Nathan; nāṯān; نآثآن 'we double/fold' 'we female/feminine' (means to do something with females, or something feminine); نآدآن 'we guilt'; نآظآن 'we think/suspect'; نآطآن 'we clang' make a tinning or clanging noise'. Cp: naafaan, naadaan, naadhaan, naaṭaan. (2Sam.5:14)

Solomon; šĕlōmōh; سَلوموه ، سيلوموه 'ask him/asks him-what' 'asked him-what' 'of many questions/of questions-what' 'leaked/flowed water' 'they allowed him to survive' 'intact/whole-him/it' 'of surviving' 'delivered/received-him/it' 'distracted/entertained-water/his water' 'comforted-water/his water' 'greeted/greeted him' 'of mild/peaceful nature' 'became mild/peaceful'; صَلوموه ، صيلوموه 'reached/arrived at-water/his water' 'connected-water/his water' 'delivered-water/his water' 'rock-his water' 'publicly apologised/arrived-water/his water/what'. Cp: seloomooh, seiloomooh, sseloomooh, sseiloomooh. (2Sam.5:14)

Ibhar; yibḥār; يِبهاَر 'he becomes dazzled' and means stares and does not speak out of bedazzlement; يِبحاَر 'goes to sea' 'good riddance/says good riddance'. Cp: yibhaar, yibḥaar. (2Sam.5:15)

Elishua; 'ĕlîšûa'; نِلي/نيلي شوَع 'he who/the one who is freakishly ugly/mutated' 'he who/the one who cries out' (similar to animal bleating like a goat e.g.). Cp: illee/eilee-shua'. (2Sam.5:15)

Eliada; 'ĕlyāḏā'; نِلعاَداَء 'the enmity/feud' 'the returned' (two people or more), 'the counted'; نِلياَداَع 'the farewell/parting' 'the one who deposits/leaves in the care of' 'the one who calls' 'the one who claims/makes false claim'; نِلياَضاَع 'the-lost' 'the-misguided' 'the-set/placed'. Cp: el'aadaa, elyaadaa', elyaadhaa'. (2Sam.5:16)

Eliphalet; 'ĕlîpeleṭ; نِلي/نيلي فَلَت 'he who/the one who fell' 'he who/the one who became immoral/lewd'; نِلي/نيلي بَلَط 'he who/the one who-I will squeeze together' 'he who/the one who-I will press against' 'he who/the one who-I will make sag from too much squeezing' 'he who/the one who-I will stuck/get stuck to the side'. Cp: illee/eilee-phelet, illee/eilee-beleṭ. (2Sam.5:16)

Baal-perazim; ba'al pĕrāṣîm; بَعَل فَراَص/فيراَص هم/ام 'the height/high above-broke through them/the' the same way both words have been used in earlier stories: 'Baal' 'high/higher/high place/above', 'perez/pharez' 'split open/push out/emerge by pushing up or out/ divide by breaking or splitting'. David has to 'go up' the battle is set in a higher place than his area of abode. The story narrates the enemy is defeated like splitting open, breaking through 'And David came to Baal-perazim, and David smote them there, and said, The Lord hath broken forth upon mine enemies before me, as the breach of waters. Therefore he called the name of that place Baal-perazim.' Cp: ba'al pheraass/pheiraass-hum/um. (2Sam.5:20)

Geba; geḇa'; جبا/جبَى 'ganged together/ganged up on' 'came from all over' 'brought' 'gathered to stand/do something against' 'a group of people' as the story has God instruct David to surround the enemy by 'fetch a compass behind them, and come upon them over against the mulberry trees'; جذع ، جَذَع 'broke it into pieces' 'broke without separating from main body' e.g. causing damage internally, as the signal for David to move on the enemy is the sound of snapping branches and similar sounds '...when thou hearest the sound of a going in the tops of the mulberry trees, that then thou shalt bestir thyself...and smote the Philistines from Geba until thou come to Gazer.' Cp: geba, geva'. (2Sam.5:23-25)

Gazer; gāzer; جاَزَر 'harvest' 'cut crops of grass' 'to slaughter or beat up people as if mowing down crops' 'graze animals/let animals graze freely' and is used for its meaning of 'slaughter'. Cp: gaazer. (2Sam.5:25)

Baale of Judah; ba'ălê yûḏâ; بَعيلي/بَعَلي يُدع 'will raise (it) above-called' as David will gather people to go with him and 'bring up from thence the ark of God, whose name is called by the name of the Lord of hosts that dwelleth *between* the cherubims.' And just like the word 'Judah' itself does not mean any of the erroneous meanings given it by Biblical scholars, this passage too explains and reminds the true meanings of 'judah' 'he is called'—this is the only reason 'Judah' has been used as a theme name to enhance the story and this can be seen in how what is usually called 'Baal' and is used to mean 'high place/above/higher' has now been used for the same meanings but in the form which means 'will raise (it) above' as that is the narration of the story, David and his group want to bring up the ark of God which is an object where God lives and where his name is called. Cp: ba'ailey yud'a. (2Sam.6:2)

Nachon; nāḵôn; ناَخُن 'kneeled/rested on the ground' and refers to camels and other animals when they stop and rest; ناَحُن 'lowered their heads' 'bellowed' and describes bovine bellowing long. It is used here as the name of the place where the oxen shook the ark of God causing Uzzah to steady it with his hand. Though the story does not narrate the animal carrying the ark knelt down or stooped down to rest, the gist of the story is they did some kind of movement which would cause the ark to move so much that Uzzah feared it would fall or be damaged. Cp: naakhon, naaḥon. (2Sam.6:6)

Uzzah; 'uzzā', 'uzzâ; نوزّح 'shifted/moved to one side' 'removed/eliminated'; نوذّاَء ، نوذّه/ا 'harmed/were harmed' 'harmed him/it'; and all these actions happen in the story of the character of the same name and the story related to him '...Uzzah put forth *his hand* to the ark of God, and took hold of it; for the oxen shook *it*. And the anger of the Lord was kindled against Uzzah; and God smote him there for *his* error; and there he died by the ark of God.' So the name denotes the ark shifting around and Uzzah preventing it from falling or at least steadying it from shifting around, but his piety and care are rewarded with the greatest harm and punishment. Cp: uzzḥ, uvvaa, uvvah, uvva. (2Sam.6:6-7) The use of word-names as themes: in this story Uzzah is the son of **Abinadab** one meaning of which is 'father-mourns loudly/wails' as his son is killed in this story. Similarly, in Leviticus 10, Aaron's sons of one whose name is **Nadab** 'wailing/mourning loudly are also killed by God for presenting 'strange fire', their corpses are picked up by two sons of **Uzziel** whose name means 'removed/be removed/wiped out/be wiped out'. (2Sam.6:3-7)

Perez-uzzah; pereṣ ʿuzzāʿ, pereṣ ʿuzzâ; فَرَص نُوزّح ، فَرَص نُوذّاء ، نُوذّه/ا 'split open/divided by breaking or splitting-shifted/moved to one side/removed/eliminated' 'split open/divided by breaking or splitting-harmed/were harmed/harmed him' and it denotes the action in the story—the character and place names are enhancers of the action happening. Cp: p̲h̲eres̲s̲-uzzḥ, p̲h̲eres̲s̲- uvvaa/uvvah/uvva. (2Sam.6:8)

Ahio; 'aḥyô; نَحيُ 'healed' 'survived/lived' 'stayed/stilled' and contrasts him against his brother Uzzah who dies on the same trip due to a moving action and attempting to keep the ark still. Cp: aḥyo. (2Sam.6:3)

Obed-edom; ʿōḇēḏ-'ĕḏôm; عوبيد نُيدُم 'servant/worshipper/served-I last/make last/lasts long' 'edom' here remains with the same pronunciation and spelling, but where in the renaming of Esau it meant 'I spin/faint' here it means to make last: the story narrates David feared for his life from the ark of God so he leaves it at Obed-edom's house, so the ark is 'lasting long' i.e. staying there, but also the story continues to narrate that Obed-edom's fortune (crop, animals, whatever is related to him) were blessed i.e. increased 'lasted longer' as there is more from God's blessing because they are serving God 'Obed-edom, and all his household…and all that *pertaineth* unto him…'. Cp: oobeyd-eidom. (2Sam.6:10-12)

Gittite; gittîm; غِتّ هم/ام 'deceived-them/the' 'mislead to their downfall-them/the'; جِتّام/جِتّم 'cut/snipped off the tips, limbs or edges off' 'they are snipped' 'nibbled edges and corners off' 'cut short/they are cut short' as the only reason David has left the ark at Obed-edom the Gittite's house is because he fears he will be killed for bringing it to his own house after the death of Uzzah, which the way language is used when you say 'cut them off' as in 'gittim' it means killed them; قِطّ هم/ام and has the exact same meaning as the first but in the word 'cut off/snipped off-them/the' 'cut/snipped them off' and also is used as an expression to mean killed them. These meanings are also expressed in the regular slaughter (which would include the cutting up of) animals every six paces before the ark. Gittite and Gataim (the latter in 2Sam.4:3) are from the same word and used for the same meanings. Cp: g̲h̲itt-hum/um, gittum, gittim, qiṭṭ-hum/um. (2Sam.6:10-13)

Metheg-ammah; meṯeg ha'ammâ; مَتَغ هَئَمّه ، مَتَق هَئَمّه 'plucked its mother' 'snatched its mother' and it is an expression that means the subject being spoken about which has been plucked/snatched off, has been removed or taken completely. From the words (mtq/مَتَق) 'to pull and stretch until it snaps off or comes away in the hand' 'to snatch', and (mtg̲h̲/مَتَغ) 'to pluck off from its roots/to pull off/pluck or snatch off completely'. It is a much-used expression made up of two words (meteg) 'snatched/plucked' and (ammah) 'its mother': to pull hard or quick, snatch, uproot e.g. a stalk out of the ground, a twig off a branch, something out of someone else's hand or arms etc. (ammah) 'his/its mother' adds to the finality and absolute strength of the snatching/plucking/taking clean or completely away; 'his mother' 'your mother' is often used to add severity, drama or humour to the expression/statement being made. This is exactly what is being expressed in the story 'David took Metheg-ammah out of the hand of the Philistines', and though Biblical scholars are confused as they search for a non-existent area/city and are confused by not knowing its meaning and would prefer to rewrite and revise and give it attributes it does not hold—for the people who spoke the language and understood these stories back then, just as they do to this day, it would have been hilarious and clearly understood as it was and still is a daily-used language. Cp: meteq-ammah, meteg̲h̲-ammah, meteq-ha-ammah, metegh-ha-ammah. (2Sam.8:1)

Hadadezer; hăḏaḏʿezer; is the combination of both words used elsewhere in the Biblical stories. (ḥaidad/haidad) 'determined borders' 'sharpened' 'threatened' as David does threaten all those nations around him and they pose a threat to him, it is specifically mentioned 'as he went to recover his border at the river Euphrates.' and the taking of other cities and areas creates new borders. (ezer) 'ugly/makes things ugly' is a word used many times over in the Biblical stories when the ugliness of massacres, death and other bad activities such as the needless chopping up of almost a thousand horses are mentioned, here it is again used in the midst of a story about slaughter all over and around different areas. Cp: ḥaidad'ezer, haidad'ezer. (2Sam.8:1-8)

Betah; beṭaḥ; بَطَح 'lay on his stomach/prone' and is the name of one city David plunders materials from: as the king has been killed his city is 'laying on its stomach' an expression meaning others can do what they want to the person (in this case a city) laying prone. Cp: beṭaḥ. (2Sam.8:8)

Berothai; bērôṯay; بيرُضَي 'from/with the soil' because David takes away a lot of brass which is mined out of the ground, 'with my consent/with consent' although he had to kill thousands of people in the end he has consent (probably his own) to take away materials from the city; بيرُثي 'will inherit' because in a sense by taking whatever resources he wants from Hadadezer's cities, David has inherited these resources and takes and uses them at whim. Cp: beyrod̲h̲ay; beyrofay. (2Sam.8:8)

Toi; tōʿî; طوئي 'fold/roll' 'folded/rolled'; توعي 'vessels(pots/pans/bowls)' 'can fit/carry/contain (in bowl or other vessel)' 'things(household things)/gives things'. Both these meanings are a reference to what he will send with his son to David; طوعي 'is/was obedient/compliant' and this king is obedient to David and supplies him without David asking. Cp: too-ee, too'ee, ṭoo'ee. (2Sam.8:9-10)

Joram; yôrām; I believe this is a misspelling of the first letter of this word which happened over time, which should be the equivalent of 'b' and the word is بُرآم 'pots' 'rolled up' as the character of this name brings all kinds of vessels of gold, silver and brass to David and he is sent by his father Toi 'fold/folded/roll/rolled' and the way pots look and how they are made includes folds/folding/rolls/rolling/coils/coiling. If it is not Boram and 'J' and Joram are correct then it would be: حُرآم 'forbidden' 'sacred' 'rotten/off'; خُرآم 'pierced/torn/slit' 'burst from bottom'; غُرآم 'abandoned/lost in wilderness' 'type of tree'; يُرآم 'throws around/spreads over wide space/kills' 'spread/covers distant locations' 'far apart' 'swollen/swells'; جُرآم 'crimes/bad deeds' 'came threw' 'came from distant location' 'came and covered vast areas'; هُرآم 'he threw/killed' 'he is from far away' 'he spread (things/or self) over far and wide area/distance' 'falling apart' 'shout and belittle/speak unkindly to people in need'; and none of their meanings have any relevance in the story for the character name, which would go against the Biblical authors' method displayed in the whole Bible—which all have names which denote exactly what is narrated in the story. Cp: boraam, ḥoraam, khoraam, 'oraam, yoraam, goraam, horaam. (2Sam.8:9-11)

Jehoshaphat; yĕhôšāpāṭ; يَهْ شآفآت 'he who/he was-saw/cured/was cured' 'which one-saw/cured/was cured' 'he who/he was-cured or satisfied in another's bad luck/revenge/gloating/recompense out of hatred or wrong' 'which one-cured or satisfied in another's bad luck/revenge/gloating/recompense out of hatred or wrong' (and this kind of gloating/revenge is when a person who has been done wrong by another takes satisfaction in the offending person's harm or bad luck), 'he who-makes 'shafoot'' (shaphoot is a dish made by soaking leavened pancakes in churned milk); the first part of this word (jeho) can also be جَهْ 'came he/came to him'; and he is the son of Ahilud; 'ăḥîlûḏ; نَخيلَد 'immortalise/remember forever' 'forever/make forever' 'roast in the sun' 'beat up severely'; نَحيلَد 'reap loads of(fruit/leaves/crop/grain, etc.)'. The first name and surname of the person tasked to record things 'He who saw-remember forever'. There is obviously an intention to make a story (or one existed) where his name is related to food and food sources 'He who-makes shaphoot' and his father's name 'roast in the sun' or 'reap loads of'. Cp: yehoshaaphaat, gehoshaaphaat, akheelud, aḥeelud. (2Sam.8:16-17)

Zadok; ṣāḏôq; صآدُق 'honest/friend' honest because he is priest, but could also have meanings: زآدُك 'gave you extra' as priests get extra food with less work 'extra/remains' 'deceived you'; صآدُك 'blocked you/prevented you' 'fished you/your fish'. Cp: ssaadoq, zaadok, ssaadok. (2Sam.8:17)

Seraiah; śĕrāyâ; سِرآيه 'told secrets-him/he' 'left early in the dark-him/he'. It refers to the scribe whose job allows him to see/know matters not everyone has access to. صِرآيه 'bundled them/it-he him' possibly refers to written documents kept rolled or folded, and refers to the secrecy of his work. Cp: seraayah, sseraayah. (2Sam.8:17)

Benaiah; bĕnāyâ; بعنآيه 'by my eyes' (a threat) 'with care/precision' 'sold-him/he' as he is put in charge of 'Cherethites and Pelethites'; بِنآيه 'built-he' 'with intentions' 'his children/my children'. Cp: b'naayah, benaayah. (2Sam.8:18)

Jehoiada; yĕhôyādāʿ; يَهْ يآدآع 'he who-he is calling/he calls' 'he who-he is claiming/makes false claims' 'he who-leaving/saying farewell' 'he who-depositing/leaving something in the care of' 'which one-is calling/making claims' 'which one-leaving/saying farewell'; جَهْ يآدآع 'came he/came to him-calling/he calls/is claiming/making false claims' 'came he/came to him-leaving/saying farewell' 'came he/came to him-depositing/leaving something in the care of'; يَهْ عآدآء 'he who-returned/returns' 'he who-enemies/created enmity/transgressed against' 'he who-infected' 'he who-counted'; جَهْ عآدآء 'came he/came to him-returned/returns' 'came he/came to him-enemies/created enmity/transgressed against' 'came he/came to him-infected' 'came he/came to him-counted'; يَهْ يآضآع 'he who/which one-is placed/he places/sets' and this latter meaning is because Benaiah son of Jehoiada was set over the Cherethites/Pelethites, 'he who/which one-misguided/misleads' 'he who/which one-loses/he loses'; جَهْ يآضآع 'came he/came to him-is placed/he places/sets' 'came he/came to him-misguided/misleads' 'came he/came to him-loses/he loses'. Cp: yehoyaadaa', gehoyaadaa', yeho'aadaa, geho'aadaa, yehoyaadhaa', gehoyaadhaa'. (2Sam.8:18)

Cherethites; kĕrēṯî, kĕrēṯîm; كِريثي 'ponds/pools' (naturally accumulated bodies of water) 'of taking long deep drink of water or deep inhalation of something' 'growing/selling chives'; كِريتي 'leased/hired' 'drove/chased away/of driving/chasing away'; كِريث هم/ام 'the/their pond' 'the/their chives' 'deep drink/

inhalation-them/the'; كِريت هم/ام 'I leased/hired-them/the' 'drove/chased away-them/the'. Cp: kereyfee, kereytee, kereyf-hum/um, keereyt-hum/um. (2Sam.8:18)

Pelethites; pĕlēṯî; فِليتي 'keeps falling/falling' 'immoral/lewd/bad character'; بِليتي 'ailed/afflicted' 'soaked' 'worn/faded'. Cp: pheleytee, beleytee. (2Sam.8:18)

Ziba; ṣîḇā'; صيباء 'boys' and he has fifteen sons, 'poured onto/into' 'struck/hit target' 'struck with ailment and curse' 'struck with catastrophe' it is when somebody or something has a devastating impact on a person physically, psychologically and/or materially. It is also used to mean 'demons' from the expression 'om assibyaan' ام الصبيان a particularly frightful demon that spawns many young and negatively impacts people that come across it. In this story it denotes both Ziba's many sons and the disability of Mephibosheth, and also the latter's betrayal of David which will bring more negative impact to Mephibosheth when David will give away all Mephibosheth's property to Ziba. Cp: sseebaa. (2Sam.9;16:1-4)

Lo-debar; lô ḏĕḇār, lō' dĕḇār; لُدبيار ، لوءديبار 'if he plots' 'if he figures it out' 'if he discusses/thinks about' 'if he makes lazy/delays' 'he did not plot' 'he did not figure/sort it out' 'he did not think about it' 'he did not make lazy/delay'. It is from the same root word as the word 'Deborah' but this time in the masculine, and the negative/evil meanings are not intended in this part of the story. It refers to Mephibosheth unable to take care of land matters which David sorts out for him when he restores the land to him, and later Mephibosheth will plot against David by hoping Saul's kingdom will be restored following Absalom's acts against his father. Cp: lo deibaar, loo-deibaar. (2Sam.9)

Hanun; hānûn; هآنُن 'humiliated/disgraced' and denotes what Hanun does to the messengers David sends, shaving off half of their beards and cutting off pieces of their clothes to humiliate them and the story narrates how embarrassed this left them '...the men were greatly ashamed...' and David tells them to stay at Jericho until their beards grow back so as to avoid further embarrassment; خآنُن 'betrayed' 'soaked in'. Cp: haanun, khaanun. (2Sam.10)

Beth-rehob; bêṯ rĕḥôḇ; بيت ريكُب/رِكُب '(he/it) will be ridden/mounted' 'will be placed on top of/piled on top of'; بيت ريحُب/رِحُب 'he/it will be made space for' and the latter denotes what will happen in the battle: at the beginning the men of Beth-rehob along with Ish-tob and Maacah are left somewhere spacious '*were* by themselves in the field' while the men of Ammon spread 'at the entering of the gate'. Cp: beyt reikob, beyt rekob, beyt reiḥob, beyt reḥob. (2Sam.10)

Zoba as earlier in 1Sam.14 means 'fiercely drove away' 'unrelentingly drove away', 'scary looking' and the Syrians flee upon Joab and his army arriving. (2Sam.10)

Isḥ-tob; 'îš ṭôb; نيش طُب 'well/how/what-suddenly appeared' 'well/how/what-is good/nice/palatable'; نيش تُب 'well-repent/stop bad behaviour' as with all other cities David smites, the peoples of these cities become David/Israel's 'servants' and obey him. Cp: eesh-ṭob, eesh-tob. (2Sam.10)

Maacah as in 2Sam.3:3 still means 'with his brother', 'with you'. As Joab tells his brother to come and assist him if need be. Also, the different Syrian peoples are being sent to stand together against David. (2Sam.10)

Hadarezer; حَدَر عَزَر 'came down-ugly' or: hăḏaḏ'ezer; حَدَد/حيدَد عَزَر is the combination of both words used elsewhere in the stories (Hadadezer 2Sam.8:1-8). (ḥaidad/haidad) 'determined borders' 'sharpened' 'threatened' 'demolished' combined with (ezer) 'ugly/makes things ugly' as they will be defeated in battle with great slaughter happening all around. This is another case of where the name of a character changes mid-story: although Biblical scholars state this character is king of Zoba due to the similarity of his name in 2Sam.8:3, it is actually an intentional name-change by the Biblical authors so that he can suit the story, he is Hanun king of Ammon at the beginning of this chapter and at verse 16 he is changed to Hadarezer so his name can better reflect the way he and his people 'go down' and be slaughtered with ugly slaughter before they become David's servants. (2Sam.10)

Helam; ḥêlām; هيلآم 'he will gather' and it is what Hadarezer does '...sent, and brought the Syrians that *were* beyond the river...'. Cp: heylaam. (2Sam.10)

Shobach; šôḇaḵ; شُبَخ 'obstruct the way' 'brave' 'thuggish/muscular', the armies which Shobach leads do obstruct an area in that they '...set themselves in array against David...' and to be leader he would be brave; سُبَق 'in front/raced ahead/beat them(as in arrived before)' and he is described '...*went* before them.'. Cp: shobaḥ, sobaq. (2Sam.10)

Joab, Ammon, Rabbah and Jerusalem are used as themes to outline the story to be told: **Joab** for its meanings 'he disgraces' 'is disgraced' 'disgraces others' for what will happen between David, Bath-sheba and Uriah. **Ammon** 'drank/blinded' as David will seek to intoxicate Uriah to cover-up his own misdeed. **Rab-**

bah for 'caused a scene' as he wreaks havoc with the lives of Uriah and Bath-sheba, and 'disciplined' when Nathan will teach David a lesson through a parable. **Jerusalem** for 'they see-asked-them/the' 'they see-water flowed/leaked-them/the' 'came-saw-asked-them/the' 'came-saw-water flowed/leaked-them/the' because: David sees Bath-sheba bathing; he makes enquiries about her; he asks she be brought to him; he has sex with her so 'water(semen)' flows between them and she becomes pregnant from it. (2Sam.11)

Bath-sheba; bat̲-šeb̲a'; بَت شَبأ/شَبَى 'young girl/young woman' and usually refers to when a girl has become a young woman and is therefore ready for marriage, 'it will swell/become rigid' and refers to David's sexual excitement at the sight of Bath-sheba bathing, then having sex with her. Cp: bat sheba. (2Sam.11)

Eliam; 'ĕlî'ām; نِلي/نئيلي عآم 'the one who-drinks/drank/blinded' and it is followed by 'the wife of Uriah the Hittite' because Uriah will be 'blinded' (intoxicated) with alcohol to get him to go home so he can have sex with his wife and think he has impregnated her. Cp: illee/eilee-'aam. (2Sam.11)

Uriah; 'ûrîyâ; غُربيه ، غُربيا 'he was made naked/stripped naked' 'made naked/stripped naked-he/him' as in someone else made him become naked. The husband of Bath-sheba with whom David commits adultery. Again, the name reflects what is happening in the story—David has transgressed against Uriah by sleeping with his wife, according to Leviticus to sleep with another man's wife is to uncover 'his' nakedness (Uriah). The name is in the form that he is not naked out of his own will or action, but denuded by another person. His name stands for the violation/action David has committed against him. Cp: 'ureeyah, 'ureeya. (2Sam.11)

Hittite; as at (Gen.26:34); حطّي 'leave some' 'left (it/him/her) /left behind' 'put it down' 'put load down' 'land it (on ground)' 'hit/struck/land in (where the target hits a person/object)'. Specifically used here because it means: how David wants Uriah to go down to his own house, but Uriah leaves his wife alone in the house and does not go down to her, he sets himself down and sleeps with David's servants; Uriah responds to David that he cannot relax and enjoy his home and wife while he has left the ark and the rest of the men fighting the battle; even when David manages to intoxicate him, Uriah still leaves his wife alone at home and again sets himself/lies down and sleeps with the servants; then David orders Joab to first place/set Uriah in the most dangerous position in the battlefield, and he orders that Joab and the men leave Uriah alone in a vulnerable position so that he can be killed by the enemy i.e. be successfully struck by the enemy (which is also being killed by David who instructed it); comparing him to Abimelech who died at Thebez by a woman throwing a grinding stone on him i.e. it landed on Abimelech and killed him and it refers to a target landing on and killing Uriah with his suitable surname. Cp: ḥiṭṭee (2Sam.11)

Jerrubesheth; yĕrubbešet̲; جي روبَّشَت ، جِ روبِّشِت 'came-caused chaos/panic/confusion/fluster' and refers to the woman that killed Abimelech by Abimelech standing beneath the tower which caused his death. Although in Judges 8 and 9 he is the son of Gideon/Jerubbaal, the story has made him now 'Abimelech the son of Jerubbeshet' to suit the story being told so his surname denotes the confusion surrounding how he stood below the tower and instead of a warrior killing him, it is pandemonium and a disgrace because a woman has killed him. ييروبَّشَت ، يروبِّشِت 'they saw-he was gobsmacked/unable to speak' and this refers to David being taken by Bath-sheba's beauty when he sees her bathing. There is also a double-meaning in Joab's message to David that because he (David) watched Bath-sheba (catalyst of Uriah's murder) from the roof (wall) this has caused the death of Uriah while at the same time making it seem he is speaking about Uriah and Abimelech. Cp: gei-rubbeshet, ge-rubbeshet, yeiru-bbeshet, yeru-bbeshet. (2Sam.11)

Nathan the priest has the same word-meaning as Nathan one of David's sons: 'we guilt' 'we think/suspect' as Nathan makes David suspect the man in the parable is guilty, before he clarifies it is David himself. The guilt, although exempted from David, is laid on his soon-to-be-born son who dies as a result. (2Sam.12:1-18)

Jedidiah; yĕd̲îd̲ĕyâ; ييديديعه ، يِديِدعه 'he puts him to sleep in his arms' 'he lets him nap in his arms' 'he rocks/lulls him to sleep in his arms' 'my hands/hands-he calls him'; ييديدي يه ، ييديدييه 'his hands/in his hands-he/him' 'teaches him to walk by holding him up by his hands' 'holds his hand to help walk'. Exactly as the story narrates that Solomon is 'called' by this name by Nathan because how much Solomon is loved and the word is the exact meaning of what people do for their babies and toddlers, and mentions hands to denote this 'And he sent by the hand of Nathan the prophet; and he called his name Jedidiah, because of the Lord.'. Cp: yeideedei'ah, yedeede'ah, yeideedei-yah, yeideedeiyah. (2Sam.12:24-25)

Tamar is used again to mean 'destruction' 'kept inside/in heart' 'hid thoughts/intentions' 'hid in soul/head/heart' and means to know, think or feel something but not say it out loud, to hide the true intentions, meanings or feelings from others: although Tamar is the victim of her brother's hidden intentions and the major destruction is done to her, what happens to her in the story is also the cause of upheaval between David's sons and eventually destruction for David too which Absalom causes with his plots against Amnon and David. (2Sam.13)

Jonadab; yônāḏāḇ; يُنآدآب 'he brings wailing/mourning' 'he is wailing/mourning'. This character causes Tamar grief by helping Amnon rape her; he causes David to mourn over Amnon's death and fear of all his sons' deaths; his sly ways will bring around Absalom's betrayal in usurping his father David, which ensue after Tamar's rape; Amnon himself will regret raping his sister. The authors emphasise this is the meaning of his name, although he is the plotter of Tamar's rape, the authors insert him again when David is mourning his son's death, and the emphasis is Jonadab speaking and telling the king not to grieve and as soon as he is given another sentence it is followed by the meaning of his name 'the king's sons came, and lifted up their voice and wept: and the king also and all his servants wept very sore.' Cp: yonaadaab. (2Sam.13). He is son of Shimeah; šim'â, šim'â; سِمْهُ 'poisoned him/it' 'made him sick/ill' as he further poisons Amnon's mind by encouraging and plotting for him to rape Tamar, and he encourages Amnon to feign sickness to lure her; سِمعه 'heard him/listened to him/obeyed him' 'reputation' as Amnon listens to Jonadab's scheming and this leads to the ruining of Tamar's reputation, the latter emphasised in the narration of her dialogue and description of her virginal apparel and in tearing her clothes and covering herself in ash. Cp: sim-ah, sim'ah. (2Sam.13)

Amnon; 'amnôn, 'amnōn; نَمَنُن ، نَمنون 'made feel safe/made safe' 'deceive by making feel safe' 'false sense of safety' 'listed all good things given or done to another' (like gloating). He gives Tamar and David a false sense of safety as he is lying about being ill, not that they feared him, but that is how the authors have narrated the sense of the word. Cp: amnon, amnoon. (2Sam.3:2)

Absalom; aḇšālōm; عَب سآلوم 'asked for something disgraceful/a disgraceful demand' 'of disgraceful demands/questions' 'disgrace/packed-asked them' 'disgrace/packed-flowed/leaked' 'disgrace/packed-distracted/entertained/comforted' 'disgrace/packed-survived/intact/whole' 'disgrace/packed-received/delivered' 'disgrace/packed-greeted' 'disgrace/packed-of peaceful nature'; عبشآلوم 'fur/hair looking bigger because standing on end(e.g. like cats' fur when scared)' 'disgraceful-took/to take' 'disgrace-I will blame'; اذسآلوم 'harm-asked them' 'harm-survived' 'if he asked' 'then-I will blame' (it can be 'harm/av' followed by any meanings of 'salom' above.). It is relayed in Amnon has asked Tamar something disgraceful and harmed her by raping her and taking away her virginity; and Absalom's first question to Tamar is asking her if her brother raped her so the questions he poses is about a disgraceful matter and harm; Absalom will ask all his brothers to attend an event where he intends to harm Amnon; the event includes flowing of wine to distract everyone; he demands of his servants to kill Amnon, the narration shows they are reluctant as Amnon is also the king's son; Absalom asks Joab to come to him, but the latter ignores the requests so Absalom harms Joab by burning his fields; Absalom asks to be made ruler over the people so he answers and rules over their disputes, in this he harms David; although Absalom has sought to usurp David, the latter asks that Absalom not be harmed; the volume and beauty of his hair is repeatedly mentioned and ends up being the cause of his death when he gets caught between branches showing meaning of 'fur/hair looking bigger because standing on end(e.g. like cats' fur when scared)'. (2Sam.3:3; 13;14;15;18;19)

Tekoah; tĕqôa'; تيقوَء 'piety' 'sympathy and fear for what is right/wrong'; تيقوَع 'mouth hanging open' as physically stared with mouth open (means slow to understand from stupidity or did not understand), 'crying squeaky(like new-borns)'. The woman from the place name teaches David to have sympathy for his son while the same story shows David's piety, it also shows David did not immediately understand that he was being spoken about. Cp: teiqoa, teiqoa'. (2Sam.14)

Ahitophel; 'ăḥîṯōpel; ئَخي ذوفَل 'my brother-he/him-said (negative thing) and it happened/bad omen' 'my brother was humiliated/shouted at' 'my brother was rejected/thrown out'; ئَهي ذوفَل 'she is/here she is/her-he/him-said (negative thing) and it happened/bad omen' 'she is/here she is/her-humiliated/shouted at/rejected; ئَخي/ئَهي توفَل 'brother/her/she is/here she is-saying bad omen and it happened' 'brother/here she is/she is/her-spit on/spat on/leap on/leapt on' and is reflected in Ahitophel advising Absalom to have sex with his father's wives so that all the people know the hatred and abhorrence between David and Absalom by defiling David's wives (which Absalom does) and is what has been 'spat on' and 'humiliated/thrown out/rejected'. It is also shown in Ahitophel's plans of attacking David are rejected after counselling Hushai because not only is it rejected but compared to be bad in comparison to Hushai's deceptive advice and because his name means 'spat on' he feels this humiliation of being 'spat on' and commits suicide, but only after **Bahurim** is mentioned in the lines proceeding to mean 'good riddance'. Cp: akhee-voophel, ahee-voophel, akhee/ahee-toophel. (2Sam.15:12; 16:21-23; 17:1-23)

Gilonite; gîlōnî; جيلوني 'on a side(as in supporting someone)' as Ahitophel is on Absalom's side against David. Cp: geeloonee. (2Sam.15:12)

Giloh still means 'come for him/it' 'come and get it/him' as Ahitophel is sent for by Absalom. (2Sam.15:12)

Ittai; 'ittay, 'iṯay; نِتَّي ، نِتي 'he came' and refers to Ittai going along with David although he does not need to, before David tells him to stay where he is and the narrators focus the meaning of 'he came' by narrating 'Whereas thou camest *but* yesterday' and mention David does not want to bother him with coming and going. Cp: ittay, itay. **Gittite** still means 'cut them/the off' as the story has David tell him that he does not need to leave as 'thou art a stranger, and also an exile.'. (2Sam.15:19-22)

Olivet; hazzêtîm, zêtîm; هَزّيت هم/ام ، زيت هم/ام ، زيتهم ، زيتام 'I will go/pass quickly' 'I will quickly slice/cut/split open-them/the' 'I will kill quickly-them/the' 'I will flit/flick into/quickly hide-them/the', 'suddenly split open-them/the—suddenly cut them/the open—suddenly sliced them/the open' 'flicked/quickly hid something throwing it into narrow space-them/the'. It is from the word (zt/زت) which means 'a quick cut' 'slicing something with a quick motion' e.g. a sharp slice with a knife, or a rope around someone's hand causing a cut if pulled suddenly with force; it is used to describe someone popping over quickly somewhere or going unnoticed; it can also mean to kill quickly (usually implies cutting of throat, but can also mean other forms of murder). Both meanings of 'to kill quickly' and to 'flit/flick/hide quickly' are meant by this word as David and everyone with him have suddenly fled to hide from Absalom whom they believed was in a rush to kill them.

It can also mean hazzêtîm; هَزّيت هم/ام 'shook/swung-them/the' 'made shake/made swing back and forth-them/the' 'snatched/tugged at/snagged-them/the' but although David's character seems to be shaken by his son's actions (head covered, barefoot and weeping) there is not enough text to support the meaning of 'shook/swung/made shake/made swing back and forth-them/the' in the story; Absalom has 'snatched' the kingship from David.

There is nothing in the word that makes it seem 'olives/Olivet' as although the noun of the olive fruit is 'zeytoon' only half ('zêt') the whole word of 'olive/zeytoon' is in the word 'hazzêtîm, zêtîm'; there is nothing in the story to support it was meant as a mountain 'of olives/where olives grew', and the naming of places with compound words is part of the Biblical authors' method, and they always make sure the names used in the events of the story relay the meaning between the compound word-names used and the events. There is no 'olive/zeytoon' word in this part of the story as its other half 'oon' is missing and without the complete word 'zeytoon' it cannot mean 'olive', whereas the whole of the words meaning to 'quickly cut/split open' and 'flit/flick/hide quickly' is supported by both the word-name itself is the meaning of these words, and the events of the story reflect these meanings too. Cp: hazzeyt-hum/um, zeyt-hum/um, zey-ṯhum, zeytum. (2Sam.15:30)

Hushai; ḥûšay; حُشَي 'to stuff/stuffed' 'be pushed into' and this is the meaning used in this part of the story as he is asked to enter Absalom's service but as a spy and agent for David, 'cut grass'; هشي 'he is something/important matter' 'shoo away' (such as hens or insects); خُشَي 'crumble/of crumbling texture' 'feared'. His surname 'the **Archite**' for its meanings of 'roots' as he will be rooted in 'the king's house' (Absalom) and 'veins' as he will pass on the secrets/plans through a network of priests David has planted into Absalom's service. Cp: ḥushay, hushay, khushay. (2Sam.15:32-37)

Shimei; šim'î; سِمعي 'my hearing' 'to spoil reputation of another by insulting them in the hearing of others' 'to talk badly/insult a person in front of others' and is from the word (sm'/سمع) which means 'to hear/make hear' (samma'/samma'at (be)) (بي) سمّع / سمّعت 'he made hear/she made hear (of me)'. It means to make an example of someone in front of others, when a person says things about another, whether they are true or not, that are bad and swear and curses at them so everybody that hears, hears of the insulted person's 'bad reputation/deeds'—which is what Shimei is doing to David as soon as he is introduced into the story and he reminds the people that David ruined Saul through acts of homosexuality (with Jonathan) which is why the story has Simei call David 'thou man of Belial' (David will use a similar slur describing Simei as 'this Benjamite'). He is son of **Gera** some meanings of which are 'ran' 'insurmountable suffering/pain' 'gave sips/fed in small sips/sipped/forced to sip' as he will come out to meet David and follow him with insults and to throw stones and dust over him as he lists David's crimes which David has to suffer i.e. swallow/sip without retaliation. Cp: sim'ee. (2Sam.16:5-13) The place this occurs is **Bahurim**, used again in the same way as 2Sam.3:13-16, for its meanings 'will chase them away(using words)' 'good riddance of them/the' as that is what Simei's role in the story is doing and saying; 'I will deprive/forbid' David mentions in an example that if his own son wants to deprive David of his life, that it is not his place to deprive Shimei of saying what he wants.

Mahanaim is used for its meanings of 'put them through a lot/bothered-the/them'; 'gave enough/ satisfied-the/them' as it was used in Genesis to denote the events of great bother to the characters in the story and the great abundance and satisfaction of food produce and eating. David and the people are weary, running for their lives in fear of Absalom, at this point they are provided with great amounts and variety of food produce (beds, basins, cooking vessels, wheat, barley, flour, corn, beans, lentils, honey, butter, sheep, cheese) 'for they said, The people is hungry, and weary, and thirsty, in the wilderness.' (2Sam.17:24-29)

Amasa; 'ămāśā'; عَم/عيم عشآء 'drank and fed supper' 'uncle-fed supper' and refers to the food produce Barzillai and others will provide David with in the following verse; عم عصاء 'uncle/drank-disobeyed' 'uncle/drank became askew/crooked' as he is part of Absalom's men who disobey by rising against David; ئـَ/ئيمعزآء 'the goats' and is the coupling of the earlier meaning of Abigail with Ahinoam daughter of Ahimaaz (to be explained below); ئيمآساء 'touched' 'possessed(by demons/spirit)' 'tested/provoked/ entangled' which Amasa will do to Joab, first by being his replacement as the military leader, then by being late for three days and for wearing a garment which belongs to Joab, which provokes Joab so much he kills him in a brutal way. Cp: 'am/'aim '<u>sh</u>aa, 'am '<u>ss</u>aa, am'zaa, aimaasaa.

He is son of Ithra; yiṯrā'; يِذرآء 'he sows (seeds)' 'he makes offspring'; it refers to all the different grains/ lentils David will receive from Barzillai, and also refers to Abigail (to be explained below); عِذرآء 'shadow/ shadowed' 'excuse/excused' as Amasa will replace Joab (Joab is excused from the position) and also not do a good job, and 'shadowed' also refers to Abigail; يِضرآء 'becomes vicious/violent' 'gets used to(habit)' as things in the story will become violent. Cp: yivraa, 'ivraa, yi<u>dh</u>raa.

Nahash for its meanings of 'mauled' 'took chunks out of' 'crumbled' 'poked/made holes in' 'brought bad luck upon' and refers to the eating of food in the end of this chapter, but also to the slaughter and bad fate in following chapters. Nahash is not Zeruiah's sister, but the father of Abigail, Abigail is sister to Zeruiah (latter for meanings of 'evil-it/him' 'became vicious' 'he/it became vicious' 'he/it got used to (specific habit or way)': the authors want Amasa and Joab to be cousins so they can share the theme word-names in this verse as both men will share all the meanings and fate meant by these word-names in their own and shared stories.

Abigail is used because she still denotes all the food source and fortune the character of the same name brought to David at 1Sam.25, and she is included in the introduction of Amasa because of the same meanings in his name as that of **Ahinoam daughter of Ahimaaz** in the earlier stories where these word-names were used. There is also the negative attribute in Amasa 'uncle/drank-disobeyed' added to Abigail's character in this part of the story in addition to the 'Abigail' negative meanings: 'father/refused/rejected-hated intensely/despised' 'father/refused/rejected-dug deep/stabbed deep' (both meanings indicate action/revenge will occur out of the hatred/feelings), 'father/refused/rejected-exploited/took advantage of' 'father/refused/ rejected-made more expensive' 'father/refused/rejected-made up laws/rules/made up severe laws/rules' 'fill/ pack-hated intensely/despised/dug deep/stabbed deep' 'shame/my shame/disgrace-hated intensely/despised/ dug deep/stabbed deep' (see Abigail (1Sam.25)) —she could be a different character altogether than David/ Nabal's wife because the Biblical authors do not care about getting genealogy right for fictional characters when the only use is for the word-meaning, but the way the names and the story narration makes it about abundance of food source indicates the authors wanted this Abigail (mother to Amasa) to be the same as David/Nabal's wife: the story does not narrate 'wife of Ithra' or that Ithra's wife was Abigail, but it says Ithra is a man 'that went in to Abigail the daughter of Nahash' i.e. he had illicit sex with her ('Ithra' 'shadow/shadowed' is also euphemism for sex with the male body above the female engaged in sexual intercourse euphemised as creating a shadow over her; see Edar, Reuben and Bilhah (Gen.35:21-22)) so Amasa (like Jiphtah) is a 'bad product/shame/disgrace' of illicit sex and therefore doomed in the story because everything that is happening in this part of the story is the punishment from God which Nathan tells David earlier about that although God gave David 'thy master's house, and thy master's wives into thy bosom...' and that after this he transgressed and slept and impregnated another man's wife, then had the husband killed '...I will raise up evil against thee out of thine own house, and I will take thy wives before thine eyes, and give them unto thy neighbour, and he shall lie with thy wives in the sight of this sun.' this refers to Ithra sleeping with Abigail and not Absalom sleeping with David's concubines—Absalom is his son, not his neighbour, but Ithra ('sowing seeds' 'making offspring') is an Israelite neighbour to David who is sowing seeds in David's wife. This is why it is told as 'went in to Abigail', 'went in to' and/or 'lay with' is used in the Biblical stories when the woman being slept with is not a wife, nor a full wife (e.g. Bilhah because Rachel insisted upon Jacob to bed her and they enhance this by 'defiling' her with Reuben in Genesis, and David with Bath-sheba in 2Sam.11) instead of 'knew her' which is used as euphemism for sex with wife.

The negativity in this character and his word-meanings is not only towards David, but also in what the characters Amasa and Joab show towards each other in their shared story. (2Sam.17:25; 1Sam.14:50; 25:40-43; Gen.30:4; 35:22; 2Sam.11:4)

Shobi; šōḇî; شوبي 'was swollen/enlarged/rigid' e.g. wood swelling from water, refers to David and his people being strengthened with food sustenance. Cp: shoobee. He is son of **Nahash** for its meanings of 'mauled' 'took chunks out of' as the people will eat after hunger, and also 'brought bad luck upon' as they are going through a troubling event and time. **Rabbah** for its meanings of 'caused a scene' as this is an embarrassing and humiliating time for David as it is his son doing this to him, also for 'God' and 'disciplined' as it is mentioned in the story as a punishment from God; **Ammon** for its meanings of 'blinded/to blind' 'drank' not only because the character is giving them food supplies (they will be able to drink milk) but it is still referring to the crime/sin David committed against Uriah part of which was getting him so drunk and intoxicated he would go home and unknowingly cover-up David's affair with Bath-sheba—when this did not work he had Uriah killed and was promised punishment from God for this matter exactly. (2Sam.17:27-29)

Machir for its meanings of 'of good fortune' for the food supplies Machir provides David with, but it is still a state 'not of good fortune' as mentioned above, they are in fear for their lives, hungry and thirsty and without a place to stay/shelter; **Ammiel** for its meanings of 'drink-the' blind-the' because the character provides food and drink for David and co., and for the same reasons to do with the crime/sin against Uriah using drinking and intoxication mentioned under Shobi/Ammon; **Lo-debar** for meanings of 'if he plots' and refers to David plotting against Uriah then God against David, 'If he figures it out' as they are all trying to sort the mess out. (2Sam.17:27-29)

Barzillai; barzillay; بَرزّلي 'good/pious-go/went towards me/towards me' as he is one of the characters who bring utensils and food supply to assist David and the people. Cp: barzillay. He is a **Gilead**ite for its meanings of 'came-festival' and 'replenished/recompensed' as the event has slaughter of meat, a variety and abundance of food which the character brings with him including sheep and other animal related products to replenish the hungry and tired people; Rogelim; rōgĕlîm; روجل/روجيل هم 'breastfed them' as the character provides them with food sustenance when they are starving and tired, with this name David and his crowd are likened to vulnerable, helpless babies and the food and drink provided is the same as a mother sustaining a baby through breastfeeding; it also means 'walked them' as he will escort David to the river. It is not in the form to mean 'their men/men them' or 'their legs/legs-them' plus there is no context in the story to support these latter meanings. Cp: roogel-hum, roogeil-hum. (2Sam.17:27-29)

Ephraim is used here for its meaning of 'gap between teeth/gap' as Absalom's head gets caught between the boughs. **Absalom** 'fur/hair looking bigger because standing on end(e.g. like cats' fur when scared)', denotes the character's hair which is described as heavy (long, thick), this makes the story interesting for the audience that Absalom's thick hair gets stuck in boughs of the tree of a forest called 'Ephraim/gaps'. (2Sam:18:6-9)

Cushi; kûšî; قُشي 'scrape away' 'kill in one go/one movement' 'remove in one movement' 'left over burnt pieces/toast until crispy or burnt/burnt in fire or from too much heat'; the root word is used as a curse (said in humour or seriousness to express anger or disapproval) 'may God cush you' الله يقَشّك meaning 'may God blow/scrape you away like litter' and is the name given to the character who will deliver the news of Absalom's death to David and as soon as Cushi delivers the news David begins to wail and wish he had been killed instead of his son 'would God I had died for thee.' (the latter narration of David wailing over Absalom until everyone around him starts to doubt him, and/or feel sorrow instead of victory, also shows the meanings of 'repeat/try again/keep at it/repeating the same revolving or to and fro motion' 'hesitates/goes and comes/recoils/revolves' of David's word-name as he has been left like an animal that cannot bring itself to leave the dead body of a family member); قصي 'cut' 'tell a/the story' 'became hardened/heart hardened' 'cruel/was cruel'.

There is nothing to indicate that the character was either Ethiopian or a slave, the word as in '**Cush**' earlier in Genesis has a meaning in the language used in the Bible, and it is unrelated to assumptions made by Biblical scholars of 'Ethiopia(n)'. There is an indication that the original story may have had Cushi be killed after delivering the news about Absalom's slaughter because it follows the same pattern as the messenger who was eager to inform David of Saul and Jonathan's slaughter and was rewarded by David ordering his immediate murder, and for this reason the original story has Joab prevent Ahimaaz son of Zadok from being the first to deliver the bad news and instead sends Cushi to be killed after delivering the news, but editors seem to have changed it as the last several chapters only paint David in an idealised positive light, and have him severely grieved over his son with none of the usual violence his character enjoys against innocent characters in the earlier stories. Cp: qushee, qussee. (2Sam.18:19-33)

Chimham; kimhām; هِمهآم the sound made to imitate a person eating quickly, or to encourage a baby/toddler to eat.The conversation is about Barzillai providing sustenance to David and his people during distressing times, and David now wanting to recompensate Barzillai with a similar show of kindness 'And the King said unto Barzillai, Come thou over with me, and I will feed thee with me in Jerusalem.' When Barzillai declines it is because he is old and his taste buds will not enjoy food to its fullest, but suggests his son be given this reward and his son's name is the sound of a person eating quickly/heartily '...can thy servant taste what I eat or what I drink?...But behold thy servant Chimham; let him go over with my lord the king; and do to him what shall seem good unto thee.' Cp: himhaam. (2Sam.19:31-40)

Sheba for one of its earlier meanings 'will harm' as he leads other people not to accept David as king of Israel and is described 'And David said to Abishai, Now shall Sheba the son of Bichri do us more harm than *did* Absalom...'. Cp: shevaa. He is the son of Bichri; bikrî; بِخري 'will chase out (with physical violence)' 'will shit himself/myself' and this character with this surname is pursued and chased into hiding until he is killed. Cp: bikhree. (2Sam.20)

Beth-maachah; bêt-ma'ăkâ; بيت مَعيكا/مَعَكه 'daughter/girl-with you' 'will-be with you'; بيت مَعَ خه/مَعي خا 'daughter/girl-with his brother'. It is the first meaning as the woman in the city of this name where Sheba Bichri is hiding expresses loyalty to Judah, Israel and the king, and agrees and implements the beheading of Sheba. Cp: beyt ma'aka(kah)/ma'aika(kah), beyt ma'a/ma'ai khah(kha). (2Sam.20:14-22)

Adoram; 'ădōrām; ئَبورآم - ئيبورآم 'the pots' 'the rolled/folded/the roller' 'rolled/I roll'; ئضورآم 'I harm-the'. Cp: abooraam, aibooraam, adhooraam. (2Sam.20:24)

Sheva; šĕwā'; سِوآء ، سيوآء 'made right' 'did' 'made equal/levelled' 'corrected/fixed' and he is the scribe that records everything, so he would need to record it correctly. Cp: sewaa, seiwaa. (2Sam.20:25)

Ira; 'îrā'; عيرآء 'naked' 'made naked'; ئيرآء 'sees' 'penis/penises' and is reference to (or could be a jibe by a later editor) at David's earlier role/character in the Biblical stories as they have him 'chief ruler about David' but also making him a Jairite reinforces this: Jairite; yā'irî; يآئِري 'you, my penis/you, belong to my penis' 'he penises/penetrates with penis' indicates that David sexually belongs to Ira, this phrase is an insult whether said in seriousness or humour and usually as 'ibn ā'irî/ibn airee/son of my dick' as an insult to someone not your son, or to embarrass your son when said in humour. But read as it would side by side 'Ira Jairite' is 'penises-he penises'. Cp: 'eeraa, eeraa, e-yraa; yaa-i-ree. (2Sam.20:26)

Although Adriel is married to Merab at 1Sam.18:19, the current story has him married to Michal: **Adriel** for its meanings 'excuse-the' 'my excuse is-the' as his sons are offered as an apology in the form of a human sacrifice, it is as an apology to the Gibeonites and to God; **Michal** for its meanings 'observing/watching/ogling' because when Adriel and Michal's sons are handed over to the Gibeonites they 'hanged them in the hill before the Lord' so God can see the offering to end the famine; not only does God see them, but because they are not buried their corpses continue to be seen by the public. Although there is no mention of Adriel being son to **Barzillai** at 1Sam.18 where he and Merab are married, this name is also used for its meaning 'good/pious-went towards me/towards me' as this is an act of 'piety' by David towards the Gibeonites and presumably God just as it had the same meaning in Barzillai supplying David and his crowd with food supplies. (2Sam.21)

Armoni; 'armōnî; ئَرموني 'throw me' 'threw me/killed me' and means 'killed me'. In the Biblical stories there is a link between sacrificing and 'throwing' which is showed in place names. In this instance it refers to Saul's son who will be killed to end the famine along with six others. Cp: armoonee.

There appears again editing where there is no earlier mention of Saul having a son named Mephibosheth, but he does have Ish-bosheth who is murdered so David can become king. **Mephibosheth** (2Sam.9:3) appears as Jonathan's son who David swears to protect and be good to. It seems the original story has David go back on his oath and present Mephibosheth among the seven for the Gibeonites to slay, but this did not sit well with the later editors who only want good to be said about David so they add that Mephibosheth was spared by David (2Sam.21:7) and insert it just before verse 8 where they edit the Mephibosheth who is killed in a human sacrifice into Saul's son. (2Sam.21:7-8)

Rizpah; riṣpâ; رصفه still means 'a stack' (of stones usually, or any objects, crops, etc.) 'stack it' but here it denotes that she covers the corpses of her sons who have been murdered, the sackcloth she spreads is not a token of mourning, but she is covering her sons' corpses out of love and respect, she stays and keeps away animals of carrion from eating her sons' bodies. Cp: ri<u>ss</u>**ph**ah. **Aiah**; 'ayyâ; is still عَجّه'overcrowded (him/it)' 'over spilling(with fortune/good)/field filled with crops whose panicles seem packed and over spilling (him/it)' 'stirred/shook(him/it)' 'suffered/tortured/prolonged his suffering and torture(him/it)' 'crying intensely/crying and gasping' 'is crooked/twisted/not forthright' 'made crooked/twisted(him/it)' and her patronym meaning (as well as Rizpah 'a stack') serves the purpose of these human sacrifices were killed so that there would be crops instead of famine and done in the first days of harvest, and this shows the 'over spilling/field full of panicles' meaning as well as 'suffered/tortured/prolonged his suffering and torture(him/it)' that these men and their mother have been tortured (physically and psychologically) by execution then leaving their corpses without burial, it also shows that the actions and conduct of both Saul and David are 'crooked'; عَيّه still means 'will-he/he will' 'will he?' 'learn and remember-him/it' 'be warned-(of) him' 'beware-him' 'I dare you, go on-him' that David should show respect to Saul, Jonathan and their sons after death, whereas he has allowed their corpses to be displayed and exposed to both the elements and for humiliation even after death; نَيّه 'is-he/he is' 'is he?' 'which(e.g. one)' and an expression to show one's displeasure at what has been said/done—Rizpah daughter of Aiah is objecting to the death and disrespect shown towards her relatives by not burying them. Cp: 'aggah, 'ayyah, aiyyah. (2Sam.21:8-14)

Ishbi-benob; yišbî b̲ĕnōb̲; يِشبي ذَنوب/ذينوب 'swells-tail/tails' 'enlarges/stands on end-tail/tails' such as when cats enlarge their tails to scare the danger away by appearing larger in size. The story has Ishbi-benob a giant such as Goliath. (Ishbi يِشبي) 'swells/enlarges/stands on end', (benob/ذَنوب/ذينوب) 'tail(s)'. Either this was intended that the men are large or seem larger than average men that they likened them to a cat's tail enlarging, or maybe the original story had these giants have six tails, but later editors decided this was too far-fetched so stuck with giving them larger bodies and weapons and six fingers and toes on each hand and foot for at least one of these men. It could also be denoting David's character is now physically weaker/less adept at fighting with age so David standing in front of a giant and almost getting killed is David 'swells-tail(s)' as he is smaller and weaker in size and is almost killed by Ishbi-benob. Cp: yi<u>sh</u>bee venoob/veinoob. (2Sam21:16-22)

Gob; gôb̲; جُذ 'abruptly or harshly cut off/to remove from the bottom' 'to remove completely' it is to violently/harshly remove something e.g. a plant, and leave not much of it behind, as if uprooted from the soil, but without actually removing its roots, just so much of it and so forcefully that not much is left of it. It is similar to (gz/جز) which in the Bible 'Gazza' is made from and means to cut crop from the bottom of its stalks (near the soil) but to 'gob/gv' is without a cutting instrument. Cp: gov. (2Sam.21:18-22)

Sibbechai; sibbĕk̲ay; صِبّيحي ، صِبَّحي 'of provoking/causing problems/arguing intensely' and watching and wanting to cause problems or i<u>ll</u>-will, and is used during the day. He is the person who will slay one giant. He is a Hushathite; ḥûšāṯî; حُشاتي 'person who cuts grass' 'of cutting grass' and he kills the giant in the suitably named area where they fight and kill giants 'Gob' which means 'to remove from the bottom' 'to remove completely' it is to violently/harshly remove something e.g. a plant, and leave not much of it behind and is similar in meaning to cut crops. Cp: <u>ss</u>ibbeḥay, <u>ss</u>ibeiḥay; ḥu<u>sh</u>aatee. (2Sam.21:18-19)

Saph; sap̄; صَف 'a row/column' 'stack rocks' 'column of rocks' and is the name of one giant in a line of giants mentioned in this part of the story. Cp: <u>ssaph</u>. (2Sam.21:18)

Elhanan; 'elḥānān; ئِلهانان 'the humiliated/ashamed/insulted(ing)' 'the sufficed/satisfied'; ئِلخانان 'the betrayed/betrayers' 'the soaked'; ئِلحانان 'the affection/affectionate' 'it is time' 'the dyed with henna' 'the dyed dark with henna'; and it is referring to two individuals, and is the name of one person who slays the brother of Goliath. Cp: elhaanaan, el<u>kh</u>aanaan, elḥanaan. Again, there seems to be either a direct indication of the original story referring to David and Jonathan's homosexual relationship, or it was added by a later editor to remind the audience of this relationship between David and Jonathan. The name indicates two men involved in something that humiliates/disgraces them; the setting of the story and the events are the same as David and Goliath which is where David and Jonathan's love-story begins: David was from Bethlehem, so is Elhanan; David slew Goliath, Elhanan slays Goliath's brother who is a Gittite which has some of the same meanings to Gath which is where Goliath is from. The patronym Elhanan is given further supports this: Jaare-oregim; ya'ărê ōrĕgîm; يَئيري وريغيم ، يَئيري وريغ هم/ام 'he penises/penetrates with penis/you, my penis/you belong to my penis-forced/was forced' 'he penises/penetrates with penis/you, my penis/you belong to my penis-were burst internally' 'he penises/penetrates with penis/you, my penis/you belong to my penis-burst internally-them/the'; يَعيري وريغيم ، يَعيري وريغ هم/ام'he makes/made naked-forced/was forced' 'makes/made naked-were burst internally' 'makes/made naked-burst internally-them/the'. Cp: ya<u>ai</u>rey ooreig<u>h</u>eem, ya<u>ai</u>rey ooreig<u>h</u>-hum/um, ya'<u>ai</u>rey ooreig<u>h</u>eem, ya'<u>ai</u>rey ooreig<u>h</u>-hum/um. (2Sam21:19)

Jonathan son of Shimea; **Jonathan** for its earlier meaning 'males making each other female by having sex with each other' 'male on male anal sex making each other female' and it is in the form of two people doing this act and this further supports the current Biblical story wanted to remind the readers David and Jonathan were fully fledged lovers. Shimea; šim'ā'; سِمعآء 'they heard/heard' 'made an example of/ruined reputation of' and means to ruin someone's reputation by letting people hear of their bad deeds (whether true or false). This seems to indicate that David and Jonathan ruined each other's reputation by having an illicit physical and emotional relationship. They have placed this character and reminder directly after the line where the character 'Elhanan' represents David and they link this story by having this giant related to Goliath too. Although 1Sam.16 does mention Jesse has other sons, no mention is made that David has a brother named Jonathan until this story in 2Sam.21—the name is used as a direct reference to Saul's son Jonathan. Cp: sim'aa. (2Sam21:20-21)

Tachmonite; taḥkĕmōnî; تَحكِموني ، تَحكيموني 'you rule me' 'you control/boss me' 'you choose me to rule/judge/arbitrate' the latter meaning as the person has been chosen to rule over a matter or settle a dispute. Cp: taḥkemoonee, taḥkeimoonee. Adino; 'ădīnô; عَدين ، عيدين 'returned'; نَدين ، نيدين 'find guilty' 'bow/bend'. Cp: 'adeeno, 'aideeno, adeeno, aideeno. Eznite; ha'eṣî; هَعِزي 'here/look/here is/will-pride/my pride'; هَعصي 'here/look/here is/will-disobey/become stiff' 'here/look/here is/will-become askew/crooked/stuck'; ha'eṣniw, 'ēṣen; هَنْزِنو ، نيزن 'I will fornicate' 'look, they fornicate' 'look the fornicator' 'he will fornicate' 'fornicator(s)'. Cp: ha-'ezee, ha-'essee, ha-ezniw, eyzen. (2Sam.23:8)

Eleazar as earlier for 'the ugliness/make ugly'; **Dodo** as earlier for the meanings of 'harms/is harmed'; ضُدُ 'against'; Ahohite; 'ăḥôḥî; نُحُحي ، نيحُحي 'of 'ahhing'/making say 'ahh" and is the equivalent of 'ouch/oww', 'of staying/stilling'. Cp: aḥoḥee, aiḥoḥee. (2Sam.23:9)

Shammah as earlier 'smelled him/it' or a powdered tobacco (similar to snuff'; 'named him/it' 'poisoned him/it', 'blocked him/it'. Agee; 'āgē'; نآجيء 'come/will come/I will come'. Cp: a-aagee. Hararite; hahărārî; هَهيرآري 'here is/look/I will-drive/chase away (with words)' 'here is/look-has cats/of cats'; هَحيرآري 'here is/look/I will-make fire' 'here is/look/I will-plough/of ploughing. hā'rārî; هآئرآري 'my cats/many cats' 'always drives people away' 'here-reflect/mirror/dream/see'; حآئرآري 'of ploughing' 'always ploughs'. Cp: haahai-raaree, haaḥai-raaree, haa-raaree, ḥaa-raaree. (2Sam.23:11)

Elika; 'ĕlîqā'; نِليكآء ، نيليكآء 'to you/towards you/is for you'; عَليكآء ، عيليكآء 'against you/upon you/on you/above you/about you'; نِليقآء ، نيليقآء 'he met' 'he found' 'he connected/tied together' 'throw to the ground/he threw to the ground'. Cp: illeekaa, eileekaa, 'eleekaa, 'eileekaa, illeeqaa, eileeqaa. Harodite; hărōdî; حَرودي ، حيرودي and its meanings are as in Judges: 'bent his neck(physically)' 'of bent neck' 'became stubborn' 'incite' 'incites against others/causes problems between others' 'of malicious intent' and حَروضي ، حيروضي 'incited/incited against' 'got worked up/works up' 'folds(ed)/coils(ed) into itself ready to strike' such as a snake when preparing to defend itself or bite and figuratively used as person getting worked up. From the first name given to this character the authors definitely meant 'incites against others/causes problems between others'. Cp: ḥaroodee, ḥairoodee, ḥaroodhee, ḥairoodhee. (2Sam.23:25)

Helez; ḥeleṣ; حَلَس 'pockmark' 'smoothed over'; حَلَص a vine plant whose leaves are boiled and eaten, has a senna-like effect if too much consumed; حَلَز 'a scar' 'healed over/closed up'; خَلَص 'undressed/took clothes off' 'finished'. Cp: ḥeles, ḥeless, ḥelez, kheless. Paltite; happalṭî; هَبَّلتي 'here is-soaked/wets' 'look, you-soaked/wet' 'look, you afflicted' 'made stupid/foolish' (said to female) or 'of stupidity/foolishness' masc. or fem.; هَفَّلتي 'you/here is-picked lice out' 'you/here/here, you-inspect or go thoroughly through (something)"you insulted greatly' as in caused a scene/scandal by shouting and/or insulting a lot and the word is in the form of feminine or 'of grave insults/scene/scandal' masc. or fem, 'here is-of immoral/lewdness'. Cp: habbaltee, haphaltee. (2Sam.23:26)

Ira as earlier 'penis/penises' 'naked' 'made naked'; Ikkesh; 'iqqēš; عِقّيش 'got caught in'; عِقّبص 'stitched' 'thread pulled' 'plaited'; عِكّيش 'of nests/nesting' 'nest/warren/hole' place where animals live/sleep, or something stuffed into a hole/nook/crag. Cp: 'iqqeysh, 'iqqeyss, 'ikkeysh. Tekoite; tĕqô'î; تيقّئي 'of piety'; تيقعي 'with open mouth' as in a person who physically has his mouth open such as daydreaming or as in slow/stupid, 'stinks' Cp: teiqo-ee, teiqo'ee. (2Sam.23:26)

Anethothite; 'antōtî; نَنذوفي 'he/it is of pushing off cliff/high place'; نَنضوفي 'of cleaning/cleansing'; نَنثوتي 'of femininity' 'of becoming female/feminine'. Cp: anvoophee, andhoophee, anfootee Cp: (2Sam.23:27)

Mebunnai; mĕbunnay; مَبونَّي ، ميبونَّي 'my son's water' 'what is wrong with my son?' 'of building' 'did not build'. Cp: meibunnay, mebunnay. **Hushathite** as earlier: 'person who cuts grass' 'of cutting grass'. (2Sam.23:27)

Maharai; mahăray; مَهيرَي 'does chores' 'is falling apart'; مَحيرَي 'keeps fire going' 'makes fire'. Cp: mahairay, maḥairay. Netophathite; nĕṭōpāṭî; نَتوفاتي ، نيتوفاتي 'plucks pubic hair' 'of plucking pubic hair' 'plucks/of plucking' 'leaps' 'of leaping' 'we spit on' 'of spitting on' latter two meanings as a gesture of disrespect or hatred towards what is being spat at/towards; نَطوفاتي ، نيطوفاتي 'of dripping' 'is dripping'; نَظوفاتي ، نيظوفاتي 'cleans' 'of cleaning' 'completely'. Cp: netoophaatee, neitoophaatee, neṭoophaatee, neiṭoophaatee, nedhoophaatee, neidhoophaatee. (2Sam.23:28)

Heleb; ḥēleb; حيلَب 'milked' 'ill with stomach ache' (from eating then being exposed to wind or cold); خيلَب 'became muddy/involved with mud'. Cp: ḥeyleb, kheyleb. (2Sam.23:29)

Ribai; rîbay; ريبَي 'became god' 'my god' 'grew' 'grew well' 'developed swollen lymph nodes' 'mix and dilute with water' 'became damp'. Cp: reebay. (2Sam.23:29)

Hiddai; hidday; هِدَّي 'demolish' 'sing wedding song'. Cp: hidday. (2Sam.23:30)

Abi-albon; 'ăbî-'ălĕbôn; نَبي ئيليبُن 'my father/rejected-the rejected/the refusers'; نَبي عيل/عَل يبُن 'my father/rejected-on the rejected/on the refusers'; عَبي ئيليبُن ، عَبي عيل/عَل يبُن 'pack/fill-the rejected/the refusers' 'pack/fill-on the rejected/on the refusers'; نَبي غيليبُن 'father/refused-those who couldn't' 'father/refused-victoried over them/won/frustrated them'. Cp: abee-aileibon, abee-'ail/'al-eibon, 'abee- aileibon, 'abee-'ail/'al-eibon, abee-ghaileibon. Arbathite; hā'arbāṯî; هاعَرباتي 'here is/look-the expressing clearly/speaking clearly' 'here is/look-the fucker/person who fucks a lot'; could also have other 'Arab' meanings (see Arab (Josh.15:52)). Cp: haa-'arbaatee. (2Sam.23:31)

Azmaveth; 'azmāweṯ; عَزماوت 'cherished to death' 'pride to death' 'invited to meals a lot' 'invited over/intended-stayed'; عَذماوت 'protected to death'; نَذماوت 'if he killed' 'harmed-killed'; نَب ماوت 'father/refused-of death' 'father of killing'. Cp: 'azmaawet, 'avmaawet, avmaawet, abmaawet. Barhumite; barḥumî; بَرحومي 'of clearing/tidying' 'of pulling up water' 'of mercy'. Cp: barḥumee. (2Sam.23:31)

Eliahba; 'elyaḥbā'; نَلي احباء 'he who/the one who-crawls'; نَلي اهباء 'he who/the one who-gave/gives'. Cp: elly-aḥbaa, elly-ahbaa. Shaalbonite; ša'alĕbōn; شَئَليبون 'wanted-those who rejected/refused'; شَغَليبون 'I will defeat/be victorious' 'I will distress/frustrate them'. Cp: sha-aleiboon, sha-ghaleiboon. (2Sam.23:32)

Jashen; yāšēn; ياسين 'you/he-straight/in my direction'; يازين 'you/he-adorned' 'you/he-adulterer/fornicator'; جازين 'rewarded' 'retribution' 'what he/they deserve' 'what they rewarded/retributed'; ياشين 'you/he-filtered impurities out of liquid/filter impurities from liquid' 'you/he-flow/flowed out of/into' 'you/he-ready for copulation/ready to conceive(goats and similar animals)/on heat' 'you/he-copulate/sexually excited/ready to copulate/copulated'. Cp: yaaseyn, yaazeyn, gaazeyn, yaasheyn. (2Sam.23:32)

Ahiam; 'ăḥî'ām; نَحي نام 'say 'ahh' to the' (warning by saying 'ahh'), 'keep still-the' 'make stay-the'; نَخي/نَهي نام 'my brother-the' 'she is/here she is-the'. Cp: a-ḥee-aam, a-khee-aam, a-hee-aam. Sharar; šārār; شارار 'of evil' 'indicated/gestured' 'bought/bought a lot'; سارار 'has indigestion' 'lewd/womaniser'; زارار 'tightened/constricted' 'buttoned/closed' 'visited a lot'. Cp: shaaraar, saaraar, zaaraar. (2Sam.23:33)

Ahasbai; 'ăḥasbay; نَحَسبَي ، نيحَسبَي 'I feel/touch with' 'I reckon with/make accountable' 'I settle my accounts/payments'; نَحَزبَي 'adorn yourself/myself' 'carry large straw basket' 'crammed me' 'made me move over'; نَخَزبَي 'embarrassed/humiliated me' 'made me the talk of people'. Cp: aḥasbay, aiḥasbay, aḥazbay, akhazbay. (2Sam.23:34)

Hezrai; eḥṣray; اِحزرَي 'guess'; اِهزرَي 'pull down at'; اِحذري 'be wary of'; اِحصرَي 'make out of straw/rush/palm fibres' 'surround' 'feel great despair, sorrow, regret'; اِحسرَي 'become thinner'. Cp: eḥzray, ehzray, eḥvray, eḥssray, eḥsray. (2Sam.23:35)

Paarai; pa'ăray; بَعيرَي 'I will make naked/take clothes off(another person)' 'my donkeys/camels'. Cp: ba'airay. Arbite; hā'arbî; هاعَربي 'here is/look-I will express/speak clearly' 'here is/look/I will fuck'; could also have other 'Arab' meanings (see Arab (Josh.15:52)). Cp: haa-'arbee. (2Sam.23:35)

Bani; bānî; باني 'built/builder' 'has offspring' 'children of' 'show/appear' 'show true face/truth'. Cp: baanee. (2Sam.23:36)

Zelek; ṣeleq; زَلَق 'slipped' 'slipped through' 'slipped through unnoticed'; صَلَق 'scalded away' 'stomach peeled away(how extreme stomach ache or diahorrea is described)' 'boiled it off'. Cp: zeleq, sseleq. (2Sam.23:37)

Naharai; naḥăray; نَحيرَي 'we build fires' 'of building fires' 'we slaughter' 'of slaughter'; نَهيرَي 'bullied/spoke harshly' 'we drove away with cruelty' 'we wear out/make it worn/fall apart' 'of wearing out/falling apart' 'rivered' 'my rivers' 'stomach rivered (as in severe diahorrea' 'we river'; نَخيَري 'my nostrils' 'of nostrils' 'of snoring' 'we shit/fear' 'we make shit/fear'. Cp: naḥairay, nahairay, nakhairay. (2Sam.23:37)

Gareb; gārēḇ; جاَريب 'try/attempt' 'skin condition like psoriasis'; غاَريب 'stranger' 'went over' 'dipped down' 'boiled over' a place/ascent in a mountain where a hill goes down and its other side or people who pass over it cannot be seen from the speaker's/viewer's location. Cp: gaareeb, ghaareeb. Ithrite; yiṯrî; يِذري 'sows' 'procreates' 'covers(like crawling ants)'; عِذري 'shadows/my shadow' 'excuse/excuses'; يِضري 'becomes vicious/violent' 'gets used to(specific way)/develops habit'. Cp: yivree, 'ivree, yidhree. (2Sam.23:38)

Tahtim-hodshi; taḥtîm ḥodšî; تَحت هم/ام هودشي 'beneath them/the-smashed/pounded'; تَحطيم هودشي 'smashing/destruction-smashed/pounded'; تَحت هم/ام خودشي 'beneath them/the- bashed'; تَحطيم خودشي 'smashing/destruction-bashed. Cp: taḥt-hum/um-hoodshee, taḥṭeem-hoodshee, taḥt-hum/um-khoodshee, taḥṭeem-khoodshee. (2Sam.24:6)

Dan-jaan; dān yaʿan; داَن يَعَن 'guilted/guilty-he/it suffers/moans' and refers to the sufferance which God makes David choose from then the people suffer from because of David's ordered census. Cp: daan ya'an. Cp: (2Sam.24:6)

Araunah; 'ărawnâ; نُرَونه ، نيرَونه 'we let him see' 'we showed him' 'saw him/it' and it depicts that David 'saw the angel that smote' and it is narrated following mention that the angel is 'by the threshing-place of Araunah the Jebusite'; عيرَونه/ا 'lend/lent us' 'gloat over us' and both are relayed in the story: Araunah tells David he can borrow/use the threshing floor to present sacrifices, and he will also allow David to take whatever materials/resources he needs to be used at the threshing floor for offering sacrifices to God—this is 'lends us', but David refuses and insists on buying it and the way the dialogue is written it shows a person who does not want anyone's charity, money, materials out of pride so no one can say 'I gave this and this to so and so(e.g.)' and this shows 'gloat over us'; **Jebusite** for its earlier meanings of being stubborn/stiff because Araunah does not agree immediately to selling the threshing floor but offers its use, but also because David becomes stubborn and insists on purchasing the threshing floor and purchasing and offering sacrifices from his own gain and not charity/gifts from others as he does not want to pollute his offerings, they must be purely from his own money and offering and this shows the other meaning of 'Jebusite' when something, such as food, is polluted by poking fingers into it. Cp: a-rownah, airownah, 'airownah(na). (2Sam.24:6)

Kings

Abishag; 'ăḇîšag; نَفيشَج 'splay/spread legs wide', women hear it all the time when husbands/lovers ask them to spread their legs wider during sex; it is also used to describe a person who walks strangely with legs splaying outwards as if flared from the hips; it is what girls and young women are chastised for when they sit with their legs splayed as it is against etiquette which is both seen as unseemly when done unintentionally and an invitation for sex when intentional. From word (phshg/فشج) 'legs splayed' and in the story denotes she was there to 'warm him' as in sex, she was meant to lie in David's 'bosom' so that he could 'get heat'. Cp: apheeshag. Shunnamite; šûnammîṯ; سُنَمّيت ، صُنَمّيت 'she stood/became/made erect' 'she stood before' 'she was erected in front of/she made erect in front of' 'she stood still like a statue' and is used when a person just stands there doing nothing and 'Abishag the Shunnamite' character in the story is meant to do that: stand in front of the king, to splay her legs in bed to excite him, but it does not work and 'the king knew her not.' so she is created to show David's weakness in old age as a king through sexual impotence. It is the same word as Shunem (Josh.19:18) but 'Shunammite' is in the feminine. Cp: sunammeet, ssunammeet. (1Kgs.1:1-4)

Rei; rē'î; ريعي 'spilling with water' 'soaked and overflowing' 'of spilling(liquid)' 'of oversaturated texture' 'of shepherding'; ريئي 'seeing/of seeing' 'dreaming/of dreaming' 'watering'. Cp: rey'ee, rey-ee. (1Kgs.1:8)

Zoheleth; zōḥelet; ذوحَلَف 'he/they/she swore/made an oath'; ذوحَلَت 'he/she/they/this-took its place' 'he/she/they undressed'; ذوهَلَت 'this/she has shed' (such as leaves, skin, hair), 'she is in shock' ('helet' can also have other 'ḥl/حل' meanings). Cp: vooḥeleph, vooḥelet, voohelet. Cp: (1Kgs.1:9)

Gihon has been chosen as the place name to anoint Solomon as king for its meaning in Genesis 'come/came here' as Solomon has to be brought there to make a show of his ascension so the news can reach the people and Adonijah, because all the people see Adonijah as king because David did not object to it. (1Kgs.1:33-49)

Solomon; šĕlōmōh ; سَلومِوه ، سيلومِوه 'ask him/asks him-what' 'asked him-what' 'of many questions/of questions-what' 'leaked/flowed water' 'they allowed him to survive' 'intact/whole-him/it' 'of surviving' 'delivered/received-him/it' 'distracted/entertained-water/his water' 'comforted-water/his water' 'greeted/greeted him' 'of mild/peaceful nature' 'became mild/peaceful'; صَلومِوه ، صيلومِوه 'reached/arrived at-water/his water' 'connected-water/his water' 'delivered-water/his water' 'rock-his water' 'publicly apologised/arrived-water/his water/what'. The meanings (survived/peaceful/comforted) and (water/leaked/flowed) is how he is introduced in the story at 2Sam.12:24, Solomon is a result of David **comforting** Bath-sheba after the death of their first son which was punishment against David, so Solomon is a product of David's **water flowing** and he is spared and **survives** what his older sibling did not and his parents are given **peace/pacified** by God after he punishes them with killing their first child, but then soothing them with the aptly named baby Solomon.

The meanings of 'reached him' 'arrived at' 'connected him/it' 'publicly apologised/arrived' are related to how his mother and Nathan helped him arrive at the throne when his brother Adonijah had already assumed the throne with no objection from David: the way Nathan plants gossip or an idea into Bath-sheba's mind by **delivering** her the news of Adonijah's ascension to rule is called (wssl/وصل) '(he)delivered/connected' from the root word (ssl/صل) which makes up one of the meanings of 'Solomon'; he instructs her how to do the same meaning of 'solomon/delivered/connected' into David's head, and the authors make it clear that David is so old he can no longer tell what are his own thoughts than those being suggested to him; the story goes on with Nathan, Bath-sheba and David discussing how he will make Solomon **reach** being king and David details how he will make Solomon **arrive** at the position, and this includes physically **reaching** and **arriving** at a place called 'Gihon/came/come here'; it also includes the news of Solomon's anointment **reaching** Adonijah and all the people; the people are **entertained** and merry at Solomon's anointment; Adonijah grabbing the horns of the altar in fear until Solomon guarantees his **safety** and Adonijah bowing to Solomon is a **public apology** called 'arriving'; when Solomon enacts revenge it **reaches** Joab even though the latter by clinging to the altar believes he will be safe there; Shimei who is put under house-arrest is killed for going to another area (reaching/arriving) and he does this to find his runaway servants and after news of their whereabouts **reach** him, the news is **delivered** to him which causes his demise; the meanings of 'reached him' 'arrived at' 'connected him/it' 'publicly apologised/arrived' continue to be relayed in the narration of Solomon's stories, especially with the visitors he receives and things he is sent and receives.

The meanings 'asks him' as when he becomes king the story shows how he becomes renown for his wisdom as judge—therefore he **asks questions** of the people whose cases/issues he will be hearing. Also, God will say to him 'Ask what I shall give thee' before God gives him wisdom, honour and riches, the latter two because Solomon did not **ask** for any selfish blessings and Solomon's dialogue is also in the form of **questions**; 'And the speech pleased the Lord, that Solomon had asked this thing.' and the author(s) go on to repeat emphasising the 'ask' in his name 'And God said unto him, Because thou hast asked for this thing, and hast not asked for thyself for long life; neither hast asked riches for thyself, nor hast asked the life of thine enemies; but hast asked for thyself understanding to discern judgment.' 'And I have also given thee thou which hast not asked.' He takes action against his brother when Adonijah **asks** to marry Abishag, who was David's wife; even this request is conveyed through his mother Bath-sheba and much is made of the 'asking' aspect by the author(s) in the story.

It is notable how the word-names Saul and Solomon are closely connected and one could easily replace the other without disrupting the stories' narration. This is another indication that Solomon was a character created to replace Saul by later editors/authors (i.e. it may have been Saul made the greatest king of Israel in original stories, but edited later by authors who wanted David and David's line to be the best kings) when they decided to portray Saul negatively so they could increase the positive description of David, and proof of this is in a message within the story of Solomon's anointment: the author(s) put emphasis on the part of the anointment which is riding on the king's donkey, this was not done with David, but the mule is a symbol which refers to Saul whose introduction in his own story was searching for his father's donkeys when he was made king, and whose word-name is all the same meanings of asking, arriving, reaching, etc. as Solomon's. The 'king's mule' which Solomon rides on is a message and symbol the Biblical authors use that David has fully usurped Saul and removed Saul's line from being king (by riding on Jonathan and dislodging both Jonathan and Saul from reigning over Israel, thereby dislodging all of Saul's bloodline from reigning). '...and cause Solomon my son to ride upon mine own mule, and bring him down to Gihon: And let Zadok the priest and Nathan the prophet anoint him there king over Israel...and caused Solomon to ride upon king David's mule...:And Jonathan answered and said to Adonijah, Verily our lord King David hath made Solomon king. And the king hath sent with him Zadok the priest, and Nathan the prophet...and they have caused him to ride upon the king's mule...'.

The names at 1Kgs.1:45 mentioned around the mule also reinforce and relay a message about the mule symbolising how David usurped and got rid of Saul and Jonathan so he could become king: **Zadok** ('honest/friend' 'deceived you' 'blocked you/prevented you') as David befriended Saul, found favour in his eyes before entering a relationship with Jonathan which he used to deceive Jonathan and Saul out of their kingship and then does everything he can to block their descendants from rising to the throne. **Nathan** ('we double/fold' 'we female/feminine') and this indicates how David caused Jonathan to lose his rule by having a sexual relationship with him which caused Saul's actions against David which ultimately led to Saul's downfall. **Benaiah** ('by my eyes' (a threat) 'with care/precision' 'sold-him/he' 'with intentions' 'his children/my children') and Saul described David as a threat to Jonathan's ascension to the throne; it denotes David's intentions towards Saul and Jonathan, and how David ensures none of Saul/Jonathan's children/grandchildren ever ascend the throne as he has them killed in a human sacrifice, as well as others he causes the deaths of before washing his hands of any guilt. **Jehoiada** ('came he/came to him-depositing/leaving something in the care of' 'he who/which one-is placed/he places/sets' 'came he/came to him-misguided/misleads' 'he who/which one-loses/he loses') both Saul and Jonathan put their trust in David—Saul sets him up in powerful positions to succeed and rise in status, Jonathan willingly waivered his right to the throne for David to take his place; David caused Saul and Jonathan and all related progeny to lose claim and chance to the throne; David set his own children as future kings and specifically Solomon in the current story. **Cherethites** ('drove/chased away/of driving/chasing away') David was the catalyst in the fall of both Saul and Jonathan from being kings and brought around the deaths of their children in different stories. **Pelethites** ('keeps falling/falling' 'immoral/lewd/bad character') reminds that Saul and Jonathan have physically fallen (death), and indicates David, using immoral acts, caused their falling from the throne, as well as a falling in their reputation; it also indicates that within the story they have been displaced by other authors/editors who wanted and have increased and flattered David's role at the expense of diminishing and vilifying Saul's role. Cp: seloomooh, seiloomooh, <u>ss</u>eloomooh, <u>ss</u>eiloomooh. (1Kgs.1-11)

Azariah; 'ăzaryâ; عيزَريه 'made ugly-him/he'; عيذَريه 'shadowed-him/he' 'excused-him/he' 'beware/remember/listen and remember-filled with much/crawled with ants/left behind' 'on/upon- filled with much/crawled with ants/left behind'. Cp: 'aizaryah, 'aivaryah. (1Kgs.4:2)

Elihoreph; 'ĕlîḥōrep; نِلي/ئيلي حورِف 'the one who/he who-lettered' 'the one who-changed letters' and he is the secretary/scribe for Solomon. Cp: illee/eilee-ḥoore<u>ph</u>. **Ahiah** for its earlier meaning of 'his brother' in 1Sam.14 where a character with the same first word-name is chosen for this meaning too. In this instance Ahiah is Elihoreph's brother. They are both sons of Shisha; šîšā'; شيشاء 'things, important things' 'things, many things' 'things, amazing/wonderful things/puzzling things' and this phrase is based on the word (<u>sh</u>ee/شيئ/شي) 'thing/matter/important/want' and how it is used when doubled such as '<u>sh</u>ee wa <u>sh</u>aan' شي و شان '<u>sh</u>ow-<u>sh</u>aan' شوشان 'shee wa ashyaa' شي و اشياء and there are many different variations, but they all carry some and sometimes all the meanings that a matter or what is being referred to is important, or amazing, or in great amounts/abundance, richness, greatness, etc. In this part of the story it refers to the importance of the work as secretaries to the king which is why they have been made sons of 'Shisha'. Cp: <u>sh</u>ee<u>sh</u>aa. (1Kgs.4:3)

Zabud; zāḇûḏ; ضآبُط 'strong' 'tight' 'secure' and is also used to describe good friendship. In this instance it describes the character as being a 'principal officer' and as being 'the king's friend.'; شآبُط 'tied tightly with rope' 'latticed with roped' 'whipped/striped' and still refers to a close/tight friendship with the king and a severe/strong position/personality as leader of officers. Cp: <u>dh</u>aaboṭ, <u>sh</u>aaboṭ. (1Kgs.4:5)

Ahishar; 'ăḥîšār; ئَحيشآر 'gather excessively' 'run after and corner' 'be greedy' 'pit between people/create enmity between' the latter by delivering gossip or news to cause differences between people; ئَخيصآر 'eat as side to food' (e.g. a dip with bread, or salad, cheese eaten along with main dish), 'my brother created/sculpted/drew'. Cp: aḥee<u>sh</u>aar, a<u>kh</u>ee<u>ss</u>aar. (1Kgs.4:6)

Adoniram; 'ăḏōnîrām; ئَضوني رآم 'here I am thrown/throwing/killed/killing' 'here I have thrown'; ئَذوني رآم 'they harmed me-thrown/throwing'. Cp: a<u>dh</u>oonee-raam, avoonee-raam. Abda; 'aḇda'; عَبدَء 'worshipper' 'servant'; ئَبدَء 'took out/brought out'; ئَبدَع 'start/begin/began'. Cp: 'abda, abda, abda'. (1Kgs.4:6)

Dekar; deqer, ben-deqer; دَجَر 'gathered or made lentils' (specific kind of lentils); بَن دَجَر 'we will eat/gather lentils' 'child of lentils/gathering lentils'. He is one of the officers in charge of providing food supplies to the king. Cp: deger, ben-deger. (1Kgs.4:9)

Makaz; māqaṣ; مآقَز 'a frying' 'what is frying' 'what is making burning smell'. The word means frying scents, fried foods, the action of frying food. A suitable name-place for area to provide food for the king. Cp: maaqaz. (1Kgs.4:9)

Shaalbim as earlier, one of its meanings is 'I will add milk'. (1Kgs.4:9)

Elon-beth-hanan; 'êlôn bêṯ ḥānān; ئيلُن/عيلُن بيت هآنآن 'until they will be humiliated' 'upon/boys-will be-humiliated' 'above/higher-will be-humiliated/satisfied/given plenty' 'in public will be humiliated' 'until they will be satisfied/given plenty' 'upon/boys-will be-satisfied/given plenty'; ئيلُن/عيلُن بيت خآنآن 'until they will be/are soaked' 'upon/boys-will be/are soaked' 'until-they will be-betrayed' 'upon/boys-will be-betrayed'; ئيلُن/عيلُن بيت حآنآن 'until it is time' 'until they will be affectionate' 'upon/boys-it will be time' 'upon/boys-they will feel affection'. Cp: eylon beyt haanaan,'eylon beyt haanaan, eylon beyt <u>kh</u>aanaan,'eylon beyt <u>kh</u>aanaan, eylon beyt ḥaanaan,'eylon beyt ḥaanaan. (1Kgs.4:9)

Hesed; ben-ḥeseḏ; بَن/بِن حَسَد 'will be/we will be-envied' 'child of envy'; بَن/بِن حَصَد 'will-harvest/reap' 'child of harvest'. Cp: ben-ḥesed, ben-ḥe<u>ss</u>ed. (1Kgs.4:10)

Aruboth; 'ărubbôṯ; ئَروبُّت ، ئيروبُّت 'she mixed and diluted dough with water' 'she mixed and diluted with water' (such as dough, henna, etc.); ئَروبُّط ، ئيروبُّط 'tied/tie' 'I tie/tied'. Cp: arubbot, airubbot, arubboṭ, airubboṭ. (1Kgs.4:10)

Taphath; ṭāpaṯ; طآفَت 'circled around' 'overflowed'; تآفَت 'she is crushing bread/making <u>ph</u>attah (crushed bread dish)' 'she is crushing' 'she leapt'. Cp: ṭaa<u>ph</u>at, taa<u>ph</u>at. (1Kgs.4:11)

Baana; ba'ănā'; بَعَنآء ، بَعينآء 'with particularity/choosiness/care' 'with close inspection' 'by his eye(a threat)' 'sold us/we sold'. Cp: ba'anaa, ba'ainaa. (1Kgs.4:12)

Zartanah; ṣārĕṯanâ; ذآريفَنه 'overflowing' 'it is overflowing' 'he filled us(with insults or dirt'; زآريطَنه 'a swallowing' 'she swallowed it' 'she/it swallowed us' 'we swallowed it'. Cp: vaarei<u>ph</u>anah, zaareiṭanah. (1Kgs.4:12)

Geber; geber; غَبَر 'dust' 'became dusty'; جَبَر 'spoke to' 'comforted' 'mended/fixed' 'forced'. Cp: gheber, geber. (1Kgs.4:13)

Ramoth-gilead; rāmôt gil'ād; is a combination of earlier meanings of 'Ramot' and 'Gilead' which I will not repeat all here (see Ramoth and Gilead to see the different possible combinations). By the name of the character which proceeds it 'Geber/dusty/became dusty' 'forced', Ramoth-gilead is probably: رامُت قِلعاب 'threw/killed-rolling stones' 'saw death-rolling stones'; رامُت قِلاّد ، قِلئاد 'threw/killed-garlanding/placing on or around neck' 'saw death-garlanding/placing on or around neck' as there is a culture in the region of sacrificing or setting free garlanded animals. 1Kgs.4:12-13 refer to sacrifices made and the names (including Taanach, Megiddo, Zartanah, Jezreel, Beth-shean, Abel-meholah) indicate human sacrifice involving throwing from high places, cutting of throats and sexual acts performed on the human offerings and by those making the offerings. Cp: raamot-qil'aab, raamot- qil-aad. (1Kgs.4:13)

Ahinadab; 'ăḥînādab; نَهي نادَب 'here she is/she is-wailing/mourning loudly/scarred'; نَهي ناضَب 'here she is/she is-protruding jaw/teeth'; نَخي نادَب 'my brother-wailing/mourning loudly/scarred'; نَخي ناضَب 'my brother-protruding teeth/jaw'. Cp: ahee-naadab, ahee naadhab, akhee-naadab, akhee-naadhab. (1Kgs.4:14)

Iddo; 'iddô, 'iddō; عِدّ ، عِدّوء 'count' 'prepare' 'enmity/transgression' 'transgress against' 'infect/catch or spread illness'; غِدّ ، غِدّوء 'feed lunch' 'cause lymph nodes/glands to swell' 'frustrate'; غِط ، غِطّوء 'cover' 'put lid on'. Cp: 'iddo, 'iddoo, ghiddo, ghiddoo, ghiṭṭo, ghiṭṭoo. (1Kgs.4:14)

Basmath; bāsĕmat, bośmat; بآصيمَت ، بوصمَت 'she closed her mouth/lips' 'closed lips of'. Cp: baasseimat, boossmat. (1Kgs.4:15)

Aloth; 'alôt; عَلَف 'leaves'; عَلُط 'stripped leaves off stems' (also means to con); غَلُط 'wrong' 'a mistake' 'he deceived/shortchanged'. Cp: 'aloph,'aloṭ, ghaloṭ. (1Kgs.4:16)

Paruah; pārûaḥ; فآرُعه 'lightning strike/thunderclap' 'tall crops/growing stalks of crops' 'split between people fighting' 'divided' '(to)branch', '(to)divide' 'to separate'; فآروه 'fled from him/it'. It is the same as 'Pharaoh'. Cp: phaaru'h, phaaruah. (1Kgs.4:17)

Tiphsah; tipsaḥ; طِبشَه 'splashed in' 'splashed over' and is mentioned in connection to a river; تِفسَح 'allows/gives permission' (to go somewhere/leave), 'makes space/moved over to allow to pass or sit'. Cp: ṭibshah, tiphsaḥ. (1Kgs.4:24)

Azzah; 'azzâ; غَزّه ، غَزّا 'a blunt, deep pain/squeezing pain' 'he felt a deep blunt/squeezing pain' 'a deep resonating sound'; عَزّه ، عَزّا 'cherished him/it' 'pride/proud'. Cp: ghazzah(za), 'azzah(za). (1Kgs.4:24)

Ethan; 'êtān; نيطآن 'a ringing/clanging noise' 'is/he is clanging or making ringing noise; نيظآن 'suspects/he suspects' 'also' 'here is'; نيذآن 'ears/eared/made handles' 'loudly called out an announcement/called out people to assemble' (the same idea as the Islamic call to prayer-a loud announcement); نيثآن 'again/twice' 'doubled/folded' 'idols/idol worshippers'. Cp: eyṭaan, eydhaan, eyvaan, eyfaan. Ezrahite; 'ezrāḥî; يُضراحي 'hang on washing line/dry on rock' 'of hanging clothes to dry'; نَصراحي 'honestly/said clearly/said openly' 'of saying openly'; نَصراخي 'shouting/saying too loud' 'the/of shouting'; يَذراهي 'sow her/it' 'of sowing' 'procreate with her'. Cp: edhraaḥee, essraaḥee, essraakhee, evraahee. (1Kgs.4:31)

Heman; hêmān; هيمآن 'worried' 'worries' 'two worries' 'to govern/hegemonize/rule overbearingly' 'sing quietly/hum'. Cp: heymaan. (1Kgs.4:31)

Chalcol; kalkōl; قَلقول 'talks a lot' 'says a saying' 'rattles on with speech' 'of talking a lot' 'of spreading gossip' 'rattle' 'rattling noise'; خَلخول 'ankle bracelet' usually has bells, 'tinkling noise'; حَلقول 'of throat' (meaning speaks loudly or has booming voice); كَلكول 'eats a lot' 'takes everything' 'gathered everything up and took it away' 'like everybody' Cp: qalqool, khalkhool, ḥalqool, kalkool. (1Kgs.4:31)

Darda; darda'; دَرْدَع 'made loud thumping noise' 'poured all over the place' 'knew-called/claimed', دَردَء 'toothless' 'knew-disease/problem' 'made known' 'knows/of knowledge'. Cp: darda', darda. (1Kgs.4:31)

Mahol; māḥôl; ماحُل 'place' 'instead of/in its place' 'undressing place' 'circumcised/purified/cleansed/made edible/made touchable' 'sweetened' 'shed/of shedding'; ماهُل 'slowly/at your pace/slow down' 'gave another chance/short period(to get something done)' 'what is there/wrong?' 'a shedding (leaves/hair/fur/scales etc.)' 'did not shed (leaves, etc.)'. Cp: maaḥol, maahol. (1Kgs.4:31)

Zif; ziw; سِو 'made/fixed' 'made/make level' 'did' 'bad/offense/offensive'; زِو 'forced and driven'; زِف 'went in procession/escorted'. Cp: sew, zew, zif. (1Kgs.6:1)

Bul; bûl; بُل 'wet' 'soaked' 'urine/urinate' 'with' 'afflicted'. Cp: bul. (1Kgs.6:38)

Jachin; yākîn; يَاقِين 'certainty' 'perky/head held up high, back straight' 'measures/estimates liquid/water' 'tops up water'; يَاخِين 'he soaks' 'he betrays' 'he becomes brotherly'. Cp: yaaqeen, yaakheen. Boaz; bōʿaz as in Ruth could mean: بوعَز 'of pride' 'of high standing' 'of dignity/cherishing', بوعَص 'slips from/through' such as from hand or through fingers, دوعَس 'stepped on' 'feet'. The author(s)/narration does not explain why these word-names were created although there is a definite intention for creating and mentioning such pillars for the story being told. It seems the authors did not get around to elaborating on the story or that later editors removed the stories surrounding the pillars. It seems they were meant to be similar to Ebal and Gerizim where Ebal has an altar for sacrifice built on it, according to the story these two places had opposite functions: one to cause a blessing, the other a curse. This can be seen in the names of Jachin and Boaz: 'certainty' against 'slips from/through', 'head held up high' against 'stepped on' 'feet'. It is possible it is similar to the places of sacrifice or judgement. The name suggests there was a method to how chosen sacrifices were either spared/exempted through 'Jachin' or were sacrificed through 'Boaz' (slipped through/ stepped on), or could be in reverse with 'Jachin' the negative indicator as 'betrays' against a positive 'Boaz' 'of dignity/cherishing/pride'. Cp: boo'az, boo'ass, doo'as. (1Kgs.7:15-22)

Zarthan; ṣārĕṭān; ذَارفآن ، ذَآريفآن 'overflowing/they are overflowing' describes two or plural. Cp: vaare-faan, vaareifaan. (1Kgs.7:46)

Jerusalem (Josh.10); yĕrûšālayim; يِرُسآلَي هم/ام 'they see-asked-them/the' 'they see-water flowed/leaked-them/the'; جَرُسآلَي هم/ام 'came-saw-asked-them/the' 'came-saw-water flowed/leaked-them/the'; يِرُصآلَي هم/ام 'they saw-joined/connected-them/the' 'they saw-reached/arrived/public apology-them/the' 'they see-their/the rocks' 'they see-rocks-them/the'; جَرُصآلَي هم/ام 'came-saw-joined/connected-them/the' 'came-saw-reached/arrived/public apology-them/the' 'came-saw-their/the rocks' 'came-saw-rocks-them/the'. 'Jerusalem' is wordplay on the action(s) which happens in the story, it is also further wordplay on the word-name of the central character of this story, Solomon which also means 'asked-what' 'asked questions-what' 'arrived/reached-water/his water' and what this character does more and requests in this part of the story. It is meant by the authors of the story to be 'came, saw, asked/arrived/reached-them/the':

(Jeru/yĕrû/يِرو) 'they see', (sal/šālay/سآلَي) 'asked', (em/im/ام—هم) 'them or the'.

(Je/yĕ/جَ) 'came', (ru/rû/رو)'saw', (sal/šālay/سآلَي) 'asked', (em/im/ام—هم) 'them or the'.

(Jeru/yĕrû/يِرو) 'they see', (sal/šālay/صآلَي) 'arrived/reached', (em/im/ام—هم) 'them or the'.

(Je/yĕ/جَ) 'came', (ru/rû/رو)'saw', (sal/šālay/صآلَي) 'arrived/reached', (em/im/ام—هم) 'them or the'.

The middle word of Jerusalem (sal/šālay) is the same root word as the first part of the compound word 'Solomon' and with the some of the same meanings, but 'Jerusalem' and this particular story is an even better fit for 'Saul' which ancient Biblical editors probably edited out and replaced with Solomon. Solomon's character was created to fit this part of the story although they could not make his name fit as perfectly as 'Saul' does with 'Jerusalem', the place name Jerusalem was created and used to enhance the story (which may have originally had Saul as its central character). The above-mentioned meanings of 'Jerusalem' fit perfectly with the story being told and the Biblical text supports this as it is denoted throughout 1Kings.8, the meaning is repeated throughout this chapter. You can also see the different meanings of 'Solomon' and 'Saul' (see Solomon, see Saul) featuring greatly in the narration of **asking** people, **asking** God, people **arriving, reaching, delivering**, Solomon asking people to be spared/**left intact**, Solomon asking people be spared if the people **arrive** at Jerusalem or repent in a **public apology** to God, asking God to **deliver** on his promises. The following shows the meanings of both 'Jerusalem' and 'Solomon':

Solomon **asks** the elders of Israel to **come**; they **come** and assemble in a congregation and **watch** him. He **asks** them to bring the ark from Zion to Jerusalem. They **come** and see/watch Solomon. The congregation **watches** Solomon before the altar, they **watch** him spread his hands to heaven **asking** God to keep his promise for David's children; **asking** God to verify his word to David. Solomon is **asking** if God will dwell on earth, **questioning** how Solomon's humble house could fit the Lord; **asking** God to answer his prayer; Solomon is **asking** God to answer his **prayer**; **asking** God to listen to the prayer which is a re-**quest** (an ask) Solomon is making this day; **asking** God to hear and respond to Solomon and the people's **request/supplication** here at Jerusalem—a name with the meaning 'came, saw, asked the/them'—even if he (God) is in heaven.

These verses are followed by a number of **requests** Solomon **asks** regarding if his people sin and repent to God, looking towards the house of Jerusalem, asking for forgiveness, for God to hear, forgive and help them; **asking** if they sin and God sends drought, they **ask** for forgiveness and repent, that God hear them and forgive. He **asks** if there is an affliction of famine or any other problem, that if the people spread their hands 'toward this house' (Jerusalem) **asking** for forgiveness/help—that God answer them.

'Moreover concerning the stranger, that *is* not of thy people Israel, but cometh out of a far country for thy name's sake...when he shall come and pray towards this house; Hear thou in heaven thy dwelling place, and do according to all that the stranger calleth thee for...' So throughout the story there are people: Solomon, people of Israel, strangers **coming** to Jerusalem, they are facing 'this house' i.e. **looking towards/watching/seeing** towards it, and are **asking** God: be it forgiveness, ease of ailment/affliction, victory, etc.: **je**/came-**ru**/saw-**sal**/asked-**em**/the or them. 'If thy people go out to battle against their enemy, withersoever thou shalt send them, and shall pray unto the Lord toward the city which thou hast chosen, and *toward* the house that I have built for thy name: Then hear thou in heaven their prayer and their supplication, and maintain their cause.'

Therefore 'asking' is used constantly as part of the name which makes up 'Jerusalem'. As the congregation **watches**, after the long supplication to God Solomon gets up—it mentions he was kneeling with his hands spread to heaven i.e. he was **asking** God. Cp: yerusaalay-hum/um, gerusaalay-hum/um, yeru<u>ss</u>aalay-hum/um, geru<u>ss</u>aalay-hum/um. (1Kgs.8)

Although 'Jerusalem' is a fictional name which never existed, as most of the place/character names in the Bible are fictional and never existed, the creation of 'Jerusalem' and a house for God are inspired by places which have existed since ancient times long before the Biblical stories were created—and they still exist today. The authors who created the story about Jerusalem, a house for God, and Solomon, did not have Palestine in mind nor the city which the people call in English 'Jerusalem' which the proper name and pronunciation of the physical land and city is al-Quds in Arabic and has no relation to 'Jerusalem' the word nor the 'Jerusalem' of the Biblical story which is also an Arabic word. The real Palestinian city al-Quds is not where the Biblical stories were inspired from and Palestine is not where these stories are set, but elsewhere in the region. This 'house of God' physically exists, but not in Palestine. This will be discussed in detail later in this book.

Ethanim; 'ēṯānîm; نيذآن هم/ام 'called to assemble-them/the' 'called loudly with announcement-them/the' and is what happens in the story: Solomon assembles all the people, requiring they bring the ark of God and assemble at Jerusalem. Cp: eyvaan-hum/um. (1Kgs.8:1-5)

Cabul for its meanings in Josh.19:27 (Cabal): Cabal; kāḇûl; كعبَل 'try/go ahead-fill the' 'already-filled the' as it mentions the great quantities of precious materials Hiram king of Tyre gives Solomon to build the houses and their furnishings; قابَل 'stood/positioned in front of/opposite' 'accepted' 'good in quality of material, or a person in character, or honest that they meet acceptance/are accepted/desired' 'accepted reluctantly'. Cp: k'bul, qaabul. In this part of the story they emphasise 'accepted' 'reluctantly accepted'. When someone does not want to accept an offered gift (e.g. because they do not like the person or the gift is 'beneath them' or they believe accepting the gift deprives its giver of something he/she needs) but at the same time does not want to offend them they say (mqbool mrgoo'/مقبول مرجوع) 'accepted and returned' which means the person is saying 'I've accepted and appreciate your gift and give it back to you'—this avoids upset from refusing to accept it outright (although the present is never physically taken/accepted) or from accepting it and then returning it as it has been figuratively accepted and returned. The story narrates Hiram, who has done and given a lot to both David and Solomon, does not like the cities gifted to him by Solomon, the dialogue has him say it outright 'And Hiram came out from Tyre to see the cities which Solomon had given him; and they pleased him not. And he said, What *are* these cities which thou hast given me, my brother? And he called them the land of Cabul unto this day.' Hiram is disappointed, but reluctantly accepts them to maintain good relations and avoid offending Solomon, although he neither likes nor wants these cities. (1Kgs.9:12-13)

Tadmor; taḏmōr; تضمور 'internal intentions/hides intentions' 'thoughts/keeps thoughts to self' 'shrivels' 'shrinks' 'dries and shrinks' and is used to describe this happening to living things, fruit, vegetables, wounds, boils, this is the probable meaning as it has been paired with Baalath of which some of the meanings are 'will gather leaves-good' 'will eat leaves-good' 'will strip leaves off-good'; تَدمور 'destroys'. Cp: ta<u>dh</u>moor, tadmoor. (1Kgs.9:18)

Eloth; 'êlôṯ; نَيلُث 'will shout/shout loud for help/assistance' and the cities in this verse are described as stores, chariots and horsemen showing they are there for assistance at need or to control; نَيلَف 'gather together' and it is denoted in the story that Solomon creates a navy i.e. gathers ships near this place. Cp: eylof, eylo<u>ph</u>. (1Kgs.9:26)

Ophir is mentioned here and in the following chapter with the Queen of Sheba story for its meaning of نُوبير 'from beyond' 'I go beyond/pass' as they have to go beyond their borders to acquire the needed material, and also Queen of Sheba brings with her precious resources the likes and abundance of which none were ever seen again according to the story. (1Kgs.9:28; 10). Both words (Ophir/Sheba) were used in Genesis as character names in Gen.10:28, and Gen.10:29 where these words are used in consecutive verses. The word as character-name was used for descendants of Noah and other characters in later books.

Sheba; šĕḇā'; شَبآء 'young woman' and this is the character name given to the Queen of Sheba in the Bible. Saba existed as a Yemeni civilisation and left behind plenty of archaeological evidence of its existence. 'Queen of Sheba/Saba' has only been mentioned in the Bible and Quran and in folklore, which is a form of oral history. It is also wordplay on: سَبآء ، سيبآء 'captured' as she is taken by the wealth, wisdom, beauty of house, servants, clothing, food 'there was no more spirit in her'; شَبآء ، شيبآء 'old' 'to swell/become rigid' (with water like wood) and; شَبآع ، شيبآع 'have full stomach(plural)' 'satisfied(plural)'—as in having plenty of food, money or other resources to satisfy basic needs, as Queen of Sheba fills Solomon's stores not only with precious and rare resources, but in great quantities; also there is the same description of copious amounts of gold, almug trees and precious stones coming from Ophir, and the same is indicated by the plenty and wealth she sees Solomon own. She also leaves with great amounts of whatever she desired from Solomon in addition to '*that* which Solomon gave her of his royal bounty.'. Cp: shebaa, sheibaa, sebaa, seibaa, shebaa', sheibaa'. (1Kgs.10:1-13)

Tharshish is used for its meanings as in Genesis 10:4: تَرشيش 'light spraying' or 'a lot of light spray', طَرشيش 'intentionally splashing a little liquid over someone/something' 'deaf' 'scared into stupor/unable to respond, hear, speak' 'pretending not to hear/pretending to be deaf'. Both words indicate the relation to water and being at sea. (1Kgs.10:22)

Ashtoreth; 'aštōreṯ; عَشتورَت 'raised its/her tail' describes a cow lifting her tail to be copulated or to excrete; نَشطورَط/نَشتورَط 'was split/torn' 'put conditions on'. Cp: 'ashtooret, ashṭooreṭ, ashtooreṭ. (1Kgs.11:5)

Milcom; milkōm; مِلقوم 'fed through the mouth' 'added through the mouth(of a vessel)' 'hand-fed' 'given morsels' 'thrown down' 'threw down the/them'. It means when something such as an ingredient is added to a kettle, pot, etc., especially if the kettle/pot is boiling, when something has been added e.g. tea or sugar or any ingredient from the opening at the top of the vessel/kettle (after removing its lid) it is called (milqom/mlqm/ملقم) as using your hand to feed anything (human, animal or object) to its mouth is from the root word (lqm/لقم) 'adding/feeding to/through mouth' 'morsel'. This word can also be broken down further: the act of adding something through an opening or mouth, or even the word of 'morsel/lqm', is based on 'throwing down' or feeding into an orifice/mouth something, i.e. it is being thrown down (lq/لق); it becomes something which is/has been thrown down or into (mlq/ملق) or (lqm/لقم); and the end of the word (om/m/م/وم) creates the word in the intended form/tense/use as meaning singular or plural or even denoting 'them/the'. When deities are mentioned in the Bible, there is always mention of sacrifice to follow. Cp: milqoom. (1Kgs.11:5)

Hadad has been used for its meaning 'threatened' as he threatens Solomon's reign. (1Kgs.11:14-22)

Tahpenes; taḥpĕnês; تَحبي نيس 'loves people/loved people'; تَخبي نيس 'hides people'. Both refer to Pharaoh loving Hadad so much he gives him a house, land and resources to live from, and furthermore gives his sister-in-law as a wife with the name that reflects this love of Pharaoh for this character, and also that the people or Hadad has found refuge/a hiding place of safety. Cp: taḥbei neys, takhbei neys. (1Kgs.11:18-22)

Genubath; gĕnuḇaṯ; جَنوبَت ، جينوبَت 'set aside' 'going to one side' 'avoided' and refers to Hadad choosing to return to his country which Pharaoh takes as a slight and the latter asks why Hadad wants to leave. Cp: genubat, geinubat. (1Kgs.11:20-22)

Rezon; rĕzôn; رَزُن ، ريزُن 'became heavier' 'became stronger' 'slammed hard'. Cp: rezon, reizon. He is the son of **Eliadah** the same name and meaning as David's son (Solomon's brother) in 2Sam.5:16, for its meanings: 'the enmity/feud' 'the returned' (two people or more). (1Kgs.11:23-25)

Jeroboam; yārōḇ'ām; يآروبع آم 'you quarter of-the' 'you quarter/you lock/secure-the' and refers to Solomon being left with only a fraction of the kingdom, while the larger fraction goes to Jeroboam, and that God will secure/lock/ensure Jeroboam's and his descendant's reign, 'he gallops-the' and refers to Jeroboam fleeing Solomon; هآروب نآم 'fled-the' as he flees Solomon, 'here's your gods' which is exactly what he says when he makes gold calves for the people to worship. Cp: yaaroob'-aam, haaroob-aam. Nebat; nĕḇāṭ; نِبعط ، نيبعط 'we tear/rip' and denotes Ahijah ripping the clothing into twelve pieces when he informs Jeroboam that he will be ruler of most of the kingdom; نبَاط ، نيباط 'plucked/plucked out/off' as these areas will be taken away from Solomon and given to Jeroboam. Cp: neb'ṭ, neib'ṭ, nebaaṭ, neibaaṭ. Zereda; ṣĕrēḏâ; صَريده ، صيريده 'became-in his hands/in his hands' as the pieces of garment and the kingdom will be in Jeroboam's hands, while one tribe will be under Solomon's hand; شَريده ، شيريده 'evil at his hands' 'made him homeless/displaced him' and denotes Jeroboam will either do or suffer evil, both which happen in the story; it reflects Solomon did wrong which is why this is happening; it relays that Solomon has chased Jeroboam out of his land and made him a refugee. Cp: ssereydah, sseireydah, shereydah, sheireydah. Zeruah; ṣĕrû'â; شَرُعه ، شيرُعه 'legitimised' Jeroboam's kingship is legitimised by God, 'does according to law' and Ahijah informs Jeroboam the legitimacy of his kingship is to follow God's rules, statutes, commandments and ways. Cp: sheru'ah, sheiru'ah. (1Kgs.11:26-40)

Ahijah; 'ăḥîyâ; نَحييه/ا 'cure-him/he' 'healed him/he' as he is asked to cure Jeroboam's son; نَهييه/ا 'here she is' and denotes the wife of Jeroboam who disguises herself, but God tells Ahijah that she is coming disguised so he is expecting her and the narration shows them saying 'here she is'. Cp: aḥeeyah(ya), aheeyah(ya). Shilonite; šîlōnî, šîlônî; شيلوني ، شيلني 'of taking/carrying' 'take/took/carry/carried me' 'take/took/carry/carried me away' 'of taking/carrying away' as Ahijah is informing Jeroboam most of the kingdom will be taken away from Solomon, and he is asking Jeroboam to take ten pieces of the garment, also Jeroboam's son will be taken away by death. Cp: sheeloonee, sheelonee. (1Kgs.11:29-39; 14:1-18)

Rehoboam; rĕḥaḇ'ām; ريحَب نأم 'welcomed-the' 'made space-the' as the people oppressed by Solomon welcome his son's ascension to the throne and see it as an opportunity that Rehoboam will be fairer towards them, the old men advise him with words to the effect to 'welcome' the people's requests and to make life fairer for them and the people will willingly serve him as they have offered to do; ريحَ بنأم 'went-with the' and the latter meaning is used when a person makes a wrong decision, or listens to bad advice and bad consequences ensue from it and in the story Rehoboam goes with/takes the bad advice and suffers the consequence of losing most of the kingdom and having to flee for his life; ريحَب غآم 'welcomed-stifled/muffled/suffocated' 'made space-stifled/muffled/suffocated' and it relays with the narration that the people were expecting Rehoboam to be less oppressive than Solomon, but due to bad advice he expressed he would oppress them even more than his father; ريكَب نأم 'mounted/rode-the' and refers to Rehoboam getting onto a chariot to escape. Cp: reiḥab-aam, reiḥa-b-aam, reiḥab-ghaam reikab-aam. (1Kgs.11:43; 12:1-24)

Shemaiah; šĕma'yâ; سِمَع يه ، سيمَع يه 'listened-he/him' 'made listen-he/him' and is the name of the character who hears '...the word of God' and is told to inform Rehoboam and all the people who in turn listen to what is conveyed through Shemaiah '...They hearkened therefore to the word of the Lord...'. Cp: sema'yah, seima'yah. (1Kgs.12:22-24)

Bethel is used for the specific meaning along with all the 'evil/bad' meanings which is associated when this place name is mentioned: 'droop/become useless/immobile/hang uselessly/can't move/go dead/numb' and describes when you lose ability to physically move an arm or a leg (temporarily or permanently) which is what happens to Jeroboam's hand 'And his hand, which he put forth against him, dried up, so that he could not pull it in again.' The author(s) decided to use the word-name Bethel as the place instead of giving the nameless 'man of God' an appropriate name for the action as they had already decided Bethel 'bad/gone dead/numb' was enough to denote the story revolving around the evil and bad that will happen along with Jeroboam's withered (then restored) hand. The authors are not satisfied with this and add to the story of the 'man of God' from Judah and have him needlessly killed by God for being deceived into returning to Bethel and having a meal—note: someone always dies for no reason when Bethel is mentioned, the story emphasises that the man of God has done something bad and ceased to do as God orders and so will be punished with something bad, then he is killed by a lion and his corpse left exposed. Although the man of God was deceived, his role in the story is to show 'disobedience' is bad and evil will come to those who disobey. (1Kgs.13)

Samaria; Heb. šōmrôn; Aram. šāmĕrāyin; Gk. Śamáreia; سومرُن ، سآميرآين ، سَمآريا these three are all Arabic words and they all translate and mean 'storytellers' 'they stayed up/staying up late or all night' and the stories they tell are stories told in the evenings to help people stay awake or at least be entertained while awake, which all the Biblical stories are (to be explained in detail later in the book). It is the place name now given as the events foretold in the story shall come to be. Cp: soomron, saameiraayin, samaareia. (1Kgs.13:32)

Abijah Abiah; 'ăḇîyâ; ئَ-/ئبييه ، ئـَ/ئبييا has the same meanings as in 1Sam.8:2-3 'they rejected him/it' 'his father' 'they refused' 'my father', and both also mean 'my father/his father' and it is the name given as Jeroboam's son which both God and his prophet refuse to help and allow to die because of his father; it also refers to Ahijah reminding Jeroboam (through telling his wife) of how Jeroboam rejected God's ways and rejected God and how God now rejects Jeroboam and everyone related to him. abee-yah, aibee-yah, abeeya, aibeeya. (1Kgs.14:1-18)

Naamah has taken on another meaning than (Gen.4.22) 'a blessing', anything physical that can be received or given, something received, e.g. money, food supply, health anything which is received from another and has the same connotations as a 'blessing' whether seen as a gift or the action of blessing the recipient; the person who receives the physical gift whether an external receipt of something or even health in his/her own body—that person is 'blessed' the person or God who has giving it has 'blessed' the recipient, and the thing given is 'a blessing'—which it still does hold these meanings in this part of the story shown in that Rehoboam allows worship of other deities and this gives away from the correct God's house which is from God's blessings, but also as punishment the king of Egypt will come and take all the treasures, which are blessings, from the 'house of the Lord' and the king's house. But it also has a different meaning as in this part of the story they attach her name and emphasise on her being 'an Ammonitess' 'of blindness/blinded' and 'Naamah' now also means 'we are blinded' and denotes 'Judah did evil in the sight of the Lord, and they provoked him to jealousy…' as acts of disobedience are described as being blind to the truth or what is right. Rehobaom's actions in this chapter are framed between 'And his mother's name was Naamah an Ammonitess' authors still attributing wrong-doing to the mother, the female. (1Kgs.14:21,31)

Shishak; šîšaq; شيشَق 'important (matters)-broke through/made way/difficult' first introduced at 1Kgs.11:40 where Jeroboam flees and stays under his protection, then when Shishak himself cuts a path through Jerusalem and takes away 'treasures of the king's house…' so the character is given a role where his importance as a king of Egypt and the significance of what he does and takes away are mentioned. Cp: sheeshaq. (1Kgs.11:40; 14:25-26)

Abijam; 'ăb̲îyām; نُيبيي آم 'they rejected/refused-the' 'my father-the' 'father of the' and refers to 'And he walked in all the sins of his father…and his heart was not perfect with the Lord his God…'. Cp: aibeeyaam. (1Kgs.15:1-3)

Asa; 'āsā'; عآزآء 'cherished'; عآصآء 'disobeyed'. And he does 'right in the eyes of the Lord…' and although he is a good king, blame is still laid on the 'mother' for the bad things in the kingdom—all the mothers seem to be introduced for is to share blame of bringing up impious, immoral children. Even though Asa is 'perfect', his mother is not; and not only does she have the same name as his grandmother but she is also the daughter of Abishalom just like his grandmother (Abijam's mother), they reuse the character-name because it is not real people they write about but invented names and characters to enhance the story. Although some Biblical scholars state Maachah daughter of Abishalom is Asa's grandmother, the Biblical story makes it clear she is his mother and a character with the same names/father is his father's mother too—the Biblical authors are not concerned with the inconsistencies because they and their early audiences knew they were telling fictional stories and what matters is to enhance the story with names which mean exactly what will happen in the story. Cp: 'aazaa, 'aassaa. (1Kgs.15:1-15)

Maachah for its earlier meaning of 'with you' as she is with king Asa; she is daughter of Abishalom; 'ăb̲îšālôm; نُيبي/عيبي شآلم 'refused-took/took away' 'disgrace-took away' and denotes her son Asa refusing to have his mother around and removing her from being queen because of the disgrace of idolatry, and refusing to allow her idols to remain, so he gets rid of them by destroying them. It is clear these ideas were taken from the word-themes used as names for David's children in 2Sam.—these are fictional characters that never existed except as stories: in 2Sam., Absalom's mother is Maachah, in 1Kgs Maachah is daughter to Abishalom, a slight variant of the word 'Absalom', and these word-names are used twice as mother of two kings who are father and son and they have allowed them to have the exact same mother. Cp: aibeeshaalom, 'aibeeshaalom. (1Kgs.15:2,10-14)

Baasha; ba'šā'; بَغشآء 'will overcome/overpower'; بَعصآء 'by force' (literally 'by stick' which means by force') 'with disobedience' 'they slipped through' (such as slipped from hand, through fingers, etc.) 'with twisted/askew/crooked'. The character of the same name does overpower and slaughter Jeroboam's house and uses force to take over, then falls out of favour with God when he disobeys his ways and is overcome by God's punishment which extends to all the family. Cp: baghshaa, ba'ssaa. (1Kgs.15:16-33; 16)

Ben-hadad; ben-hăd̲ad̲; بَن هَدَد 'will be threatened/we will be threatened/threaten'; بَن حَدَد 'will determine borders' 'will sharpen'. Both meanings of 'will threaten/determine borders' is used in this story as his assistance is sought to threaten Baasha of Israel by attacking his borders in Tabrimon, the blockade Baasha enforced against Asa of Judah. Furthermore, Ben-hadad will change the borders of his own country by taking over several cities of Israel. Cp: ben-hadad, ben-ḥadad. He is son of Tabrimon; ṭabrimmōn; تَبرمّون 'you (plural)roll/fold' 'you agree to a contract' and the 'rolling/folding' (as explained under Abram) is what is done to a written contract/deed/title—it equates 'sealing the deal' and the character and Asa make an agreement to break the agreement between Baasha and Ben-Hadad in exchange for gold, silver and treasures. Cp: tabrimoon. Hezion; ḥezyôn; جزيُن 'they were cornered/crammed' and Asa who is asking for 'Ben-hadad, the son of Tabrimon, the son of Hezion' is cornered and blockaded by Baasha and the story narrates Asa wants Ben-hadad's assistance to break the blockade. Cp: ḥezyon. **Damascus** is used as in (Gen.14:14-15) for its meanings: تَمَّزَق 'tore/ripped up' and also 'spat/spat a lot' as Asa asks Ben-hadad to 'come and break thy league with Baasha king of Israel…So Ben-hadad hearkened…' as 'tearing up' and 'spitting on' are terms used when a person turns against something agreed upon. Cp: tammazaq. (1Kgs.15:18-20)

Ijon; ʿiyôn; غِيُن 'deceived to downfall' 'misled to downfall' 'deceit/folly' and is what Ben-hadad does when he assists Asa by breaking the agreement he had with Basha, then attacking and distracting Baasha away from his war with Asa; يُجُن 'they came' and Ben-hadad comes and takes over the cities. Cp: g͟hiyon, i-gon. (1Kgs.15:20)

Cinneroth; kinĕrôṯ; كِنيرُث 'as if we inherit' and refers to one of the cities Ben-hadad takes over. Cp: kineirof. (1Kgs.15:20)

Jehu; yēhô'; جيهُى 'came him/he' 'came to him' 'uncovered'; ييهُى 'who is?' 'which one?' and denotes the word of God coming to him so he can deliver it to Baasha. Cp: gey-(w)ho, yey-(w)ho. Hanani; hănānî; هَنعني ، هينعني 'we will direct words/speech at' and it describes when a person is hinting at with a message/warning/insult directed at someone in particular within hearing range, even at close proximity, while actually talking directly to someone else—it is hinting/delivering the message indirectly. So this character's name 'Jehu Hanani' means 'came to him/came him-we'll direct words at' and his words are directed at and against Baasha and Elah (1Kgs.16:1-7). Cp: han'nee, hain'nee. (1Kgs.16)

Elah for its meaning 'against it/him' 'on/about it/him' 'he is responsible(for)/his responsibility/accountability', although it is Baasha's 'wrongdoing' the curse affects his son Elah and Zimri conspires 'Elah/against it/him'. **Zimri** for its meaning 'of guilt/of insult/of blame/humiliated/ostracised/diseased' as he conspires and kills Elah and massacres all the males of Baasha's family. (1Kgs.16:6-10)

Arza; 'arṣā'; نَرزاع 'throw heavily around/sit by throwing oneself down' 'slam' 'press, thump or shake something to get it to fit more'; نَرصاء 'pack/pile/stack'; نَرصاع 'overpack/pack to brim' when a person presses and packs more into something and overfills it. It refers here to 'throwing heavily around' or seating oneself by throwing down as it describes Elah as extremely drunk 'drinking himself drunk' which left him defenceless against Zimri. Cp: arzaa', arssaa, arssaa'. (1Kgs.16:9)

Omri; ʿomrî; عومري 'of building' 'builder' 'prepare smoking cup for kooz' (by placing fresh koobab mix topped with embers), 'my age'. 'builder/of building' as he builds a city in Shemer/Samaria Cp: 'oomree. (1Kgs.16:16-28)

Tibni; tiḇnî; تِبني 'you build/are you building' 'she is building' and it reflects the author's ideas that either character Omri or Tibni will 'build' something as both have been given 'construction' word-names. Cp: tibnee. Ginath; gînaṯ; جينَت 'she reaped/brought upon herself' and fits because Tibni loses his life by competing for the throne. Cp: geenat. (1Kgs.16:21-22)

Shemer; šemer; سَمَر 'told night stories' 'stayed up (late or all night)'. Cp: semer. **Samaria** is still 'storytellers' of night stories, 'they stayed/staying up late or all night'. (1Kgs.16:24)

Ahab; 'aḥ'āḇ; نَهئاب ، نَه ئاب 'I give' as he builds altars and gives sacrifices/offerings in worship to other Gods, 'he/him-refuses/rejects' as by following other worship he is rejecting the protagonist God's ways. Cp: a-haab, ah-aab. (1Kgs.16:28-33; 17)

Jezebel; 'îzeḇel; قيصَ بال/بَل 'tell a story' 'tell a story of the/with the'; قيصَب ال 'piped-the' and it is taken from the phrase 'she piped/played music for him' (qssbt lh/قصبة له) and is used when talking about a wife (or woman of any relation) who leads her husband into doing bad things, gets her way, getting him to implement her plotting by cunningly making him believe they are doing right; the 'pipe/piping' being music which can put people in a good mood, a trance, leads them to dance to the tune, etc. 'But there was none like unto Ahab, which did sell himself to work wickedness in the sight of the Lord, whom Jezebel his wife stirred up.'.

The 'tell a story/tell a story of the/with the' meaning is also about misleading through lies and these lies are likened to 'telling stories' in her name and this is supported by having Ahab make altars for Baal 'in the house of Baal, which he had built in Samaria', as Baal is used here as 'spouse' to refer to his wife who is blamed for making Ahab evil, and they have him build these altars for his wife indicated by 'Baal' and in Samaria/'tell night time stories/night time stories' again reflecting she is misleading him. Both meanings (piping/telling story) are further supported later in 1Kgs.: when she writes letters she has written a story/script to be acted out against an unwitting Naboth, the story is sent to the elders and nobles and it stresses these men 'that were in his city, dwelling with Naboth' i.e. in Samaria 'fictional night time story', and the narration emphasises the elders and nobles are acting-out the story which Jezebel has written for them to follow 'And the men of his city, *even* the elders and the nobles who were the inhabitants in his city, did as Jezebel had sent unto them, *and* as it *was* written in the letters which she had sent unto them.'; and also supported where the narration has God order Elijah to tell Ahab a story/prediction of what will happen to both he and Jezebel (it is narrated as telling a story which distresses Ahab) (1Kgs.21:18-29). Jezebel is introduced after her husband, just like the mothers of the wicked kings were mentioned after their sons in the earlier chapters. Cp: qe<u>ss</u>e-bel, qee<u>ss</u>eb-el.

She is the daughter of Ethbaal; 'eṯba'al; نِطبَ ئَل ، نِطبَئَل 'tolerate/eat/palate/taste-the' 'could eat/could swallow/not revolted by-the' and the phrase implies something unsavoury about the food/drink/person spoken about and indicates a bad taste or unhygiene; 'beat the drums' 'drum/play music with drum' and is the male equivalent of the phrase used as Jezebel's first name. When a man misleads, encourages, deceives another man to do wrong they say 'he drummed for him' (ṭbl lh/طبل له) as in played music to get him to implement what he is plotting. The 'tolerate/eat/not revolted by-the' meanings are shown in that dogs and carrion birds will eat their bodies/lick up their blood because they are so revolting, they will not be buried. Cp: eṭba-al, eṭbaal. Her father, and therefore name, is king of Zidonians for **Zidon** meaning 'deceived'. (1Kgs.16:31-33; 21)

Hiel; ḥî'ēl; حيئِل ، حي ئِل 'purified/cleansed/circumcised/made edible/made touchable' 'declared purified/permissible' 'shed' 'undressed' 'beat until skin peeled off/severely' 'trickster/deceivers' 'sweet/sweeteners' 'deceit' 'deceives-the' 'stay/stayed/stilled-the' 'cured/healed-the'; هي ئِل 'she is the'. Cp: ḥee-ill, hee-ill.

Bethelite; bêt ha'ĕlî; is not 'Bethel' and cannot mean 'is bad' 'is of evil' 'did bad deed/evil' in this word and spelling. 'Bethelite' is: bêt ha'ĕlî; بيت هَعيلي 'house-I will raise/construct' 'it will/he will-raise/construct' as the narration is also about constructing. Cp: beyt-ha-'eilee. It seems to be unrelated to 'Beth-el' and interpreting it into 'Bethelite' as 'from Bethel' may be the result that later authors/editors of these stories did not understand the Old Arabic of the Bible, e.g. they may have been from Arab countries outside the Arabian Peninsula, or possibly they intentionally wanted it to mean 'Bethel/from Bethel'. But as it stands, the word means either 'house-I will raise/construct' or 'it will/he will-raise/construct' as the story is building-related. The word 'Bethelite' is connected to the word 'Hiel' which in the context of the story and out of all the possible meanings has been used for 'purified/cleansed/made edible/made permissible' and the act of sacrifice, blood shed and purification is related to the building process in the culture of those who created the Biblical stories and whose descendants to this day perform (animal) sacrifices at the beginning and completion of house/structure building. bêt ha'ĕlî could also be: بيت حَئيلي 'house/he will/it will-purify/cleanse/make edible/touchable/shed' 'he/it will-stay/remain still for me'; بيت هَئيلي 'house-she is the/she is the one that' 'it will/he will-she is the/she is the one that'; and then 'Hiel the Bethelite' would correctly read 'purified-he will cleanse' or 'purified-house-he will cleanse/make touchable' 'purified-he/it will stay/remain still for me', and so forth. The sons' names also further support this meaning as they are compound words to show they were sacrificed in the process of the building.

There is a connection in the story of Hiel sacrificing his sons with his name-meanings ḥî'ēl bêt ha'ĕlî both containing the same root words and meanings 'stay/stayed/stilled-the' 'she is the' which makes up the name of the protagonist god 'Jehovah' and the same protagonist god being called a female 'I Am That I Am' ('ehyeh 'ăšer 'ehyeh 'she is-with child/calf-she is') and a female El-elohe-Israel ('ēl 'ĕlōhê yiśrā'ēl 'the-yes it is her/yes she did-twisted muscle the'), and the story of Abraham sacrificing Isaac but being prevented by God offering a ram which he makes stay and the place being called 'Jehovah-jireh' 'he stayed/stilled it-he sees it'. Where in Abraham/Isaac's story of sacrifice the 'Jehovah/stay' is a good thing in the story, in Hiel and his sons' sacrifices it is a bad thing connected to a female in the story. Cp: beyt-ḥa-eilee, beyt-ha-eilee.

If one submits and accepts that 'Bethelite' to correctly or possibly be 'Bethel', and of course wherever Bethel is mentioned someone's death happens and in this case two children of Hiel: **Abiram** which still means 'father/refused-(was)thrown/killed' as he dies because his father builds Jericho and the narration suggests he was sacrificed by his father at the beginning of the rebuilding and his youngest son at the end—which people of the culture/region continue to do even nowadays but with the slaughter of animals when they begin to build a new house and when it is complete. In both cases, whether the story meant the sons of Hiel were sacrificed or simply died, the deaths and the word-names given are what the author(s) intended for the story. Segub; śĕgûb̲; شَغُب ، شيغُب 'screamed' 'screaming' 'will become thirsty' and refers to a painful, terrifying death where this son was screaming. Cp: sheghub, sheighub.

Although the story mentions Hiel, his sons and Jericho, the word-names are themes denoting Jezebel's role in the story (Hiel) 'she is' and eventually her blood will be shed and the country purified of her sins, (Bethelite) 'house-I will raise/construct' 'house/he will/it will-purify/cleanse/make edible/touchable/shed' 'house-she is the/she is the one that' 'it will/he will-she is the/she is the one that' as she will be thrown from above (a window) and she will die (her blood shed) and suffer an unusual death which includes being (Abiram) 'rejected and thrown' and (Segub)'screaming'. (1Kgs.16:34)

Elijah; 'ēlîyāhû; ئيلي ياَهُ 'he who/the one who-is him'; ئيلي حاَهُ 'he who/the one who-made him alive/cured him' 'he who/the one who-made him stay'. It denotes what happens to Elijah of staying, sustaining i.e. keeping alive, and also curing and/or bringing back to life: after warning Ahab, Elijah is told to hide (to avoid death) and stay in areas where he cannot sustain himself, but each time 'God' commands animals and people to sustain Elijah. In Arabic, the word to sustain also means 'to cure/get better' to 'keep alive' احييه. '...and I have commanded the ravens to feed thee there.' And ravens bring him 'bread and flesh' morning and evening; the widow who feeds him in Zarephath, 'I have commanded a widow woman there to sustain thee.' And the meaning of his name is in his role/action when the widow's son dies from illness and Elijah performs a ritual and a prayer and the boy comes to life again, so he has 'cured' him and 'brought back to life'. He kills two groups of fifty men with their respective captains then allows to live a third group. It is also in God telling Elijah he has to face Ahab and only then will God 'send rain upon the earth'; when it rains the earth comes alive and it is described with the same word as Elijah's name. Cp: eylee-yaahu, eylee-ḥaahu. Tishbite; hattišbî; هَتِّشبي 'will swell with/become rigid with' and means such as wood swelling from water, a head feeling swollen from cold, a penis with blood; هَتِّزبي 'will penis' and means will use penis either insulting or penetrating sexually; هَطِّشبي 'will splash over with/will splash water over with'. It denotes Elijah becoming stronger, the strange ritual of laying over the dead boy and stretching over him (Tishbite/will penis), the water he has poured several times over the meat offerings and wood (Tishbite/will splash water over with) to prove whose god is real. Cp: hattishbee, hattizbee, haṭṭishbee. (1Kgs.17; 18).

Elijah's 'ability' to make food increase, birds and humans serve him for no reason, just command (the woman from Zarephath, Elisha who stops what he is doing and runs after Elijah when all he does is throw his mantle at him), the ability to bring people back to life, people slaying prophets at his orders is an intentional depiction by the author(s) that Elijah not only hears/executes the word of God in prophesy, but he is depicted as 'God' or at least embodies God in the stories. The character's first name is what people of faith believe only God can do: 'he who/the one who-made him alive/cured him' and also bringing rain which people say brings the land to life.; part of his name 'stay' is the same as 'Jehovah' After he brings the boy back to life the woman describes him 'thou *art* a man of God, *and* that the word of the Lord in thy mouth is truth.' Though it can be argued that her words mean he is delivering God's message, it is again God possessing i.e. being inside the selected prophet of the story, be it Moses, Joshua, Samuel, Samson, Jephitah, Elijah. And although it follows the similar method of the earlier Biblical stories of Moses, Joshua, etc., there is a slight change beginning from Ahijah. Where in Moses, Joshua and Samuel, God's spirit possesses them for brief periods where they behave either with massacring abilities or madmen (Moses and Zibborah, Samuel and his brutal killing and torture of others, Samson and his manic violence) the 'Spirit of the Lord' 'departs' and they resume to normal men. But with Ahijah and Elijah, e.g., they behave like madmen continuously, there is no preamble of a visit from God in a dream or mountain, it is part of them—they hear him like a whisper in the head; the author(s) make this abundantly clear in 1Kgs.19:4-13) that God is not in the wind, not in the earthquake, and not even in the fire which was previously the authors' preferred entrance for God, but he is in a small voice i.e. a voice inside Elijah's head. In this latter part of the story the clash between different 'editors' can be seen—the original has Elijah as God, a later editor does not agree with this (maybe it did not fit into his religious beliefs) so the sentence 'and the Lord passed by' is added, but another editor does not want the original story changed so he puts in that God was not in wind, earthquake or fire (it could be the original story already said God was not in these things, but the later editor who wanted God as a separate entity that could not be embodied by man added 'the Lord passed by') and this clash of editors ideas/beliefs also explains the contradiction of Elijah having already being approached by 'the word of the Lord' in verse 9, it is repeated with the same exact question as if for the first time at verse 13. Again, there is the real-life culture of men who behave insane are seen as close to God, and this is what is used in the stories. Obadiah tells Elijah that 'the Spirit of the Lord' which controls Elijah 'shall carry thee whither I know not…' (1Kgs.18). Even the 'showing' of Elijah to Ahab is a likening to God appearing to Moses and his people during the wanderings; the miracles Elijah performs use fire and water, rain and famine, just like the Moses story, but where Moses was meek, Elijah is forward. His sudden superhuman strength when 'the hand of the Lord was on Elijah' and he manages to outrun a chariot and beat Ahab to Jezreel. Elijah kills the captains and their units using fire, just like God, and when his story ends, he is taken away on chariots and horses of fire. Even the use of whirlwind is similar to where God made the earth alive by sending a wind on it in Genesis, and in many parts of the story wind and breath are used to bring to life unliving things.

There is a sexual aspect to Elijah's miracles, and it is connected through the male genital being of God-like powers, and the author(s) never fail in these parts of the stories to point out that these stories are 'samaarias' (night time stories for staying up and entertainment) by setting them in or around 'Samaria'. In the earlier stories of Genesis and following books, there are many barren women who become pregnant when visited by God. In the 'crazy prophets' of 1 and 2 Kings, there is always an erratic prophet who stays with a widowed woman where in the culture that would have been unacceptable and deemed a lover, and this features as a regular part of the entertainment in such stories/samaarias; even in the curing narrative, the character takes a 'dead' child into a private room and lies upon him, stretches and the child is revived. The sexual surname of Tishbite 'will penis' is also emphasised in 2 Kings.1 where the deity is named Baal-zebub and people seeking its helps are confronted by Elijah the Tishbite who delivers a message '*Is it* not because *there is* not a God in Israel, *that* ye go to enquire of Baal-zebub the god of Ekron?' i.e. 'You don't need a Baal-zebub (spouse of penises), you have a Tishbite (will penis) right here doing God's work'.

Baalim here still means 'their higher places' 'upon-them-the' 'higher/above-them/the' 'their spouses' 'spouse-them/the', meaning people are sinning because they are listening/following their wives. Throughout the OT, prophets and people are warned not to marry 'foreign' women because they will 'corrupt' the husband and have them 'follow their ways' and 'follow/worship' their gods. In Ahab's story it is made clear again: he married a foreigner and she is telling Ahab what to do, leading him to worship her god(s), leading him to evil. So Elijah's dialogue 'and thou hast followed Baalim' is a play on 'baal' the high place where the higher being is worshipped, but also on 'baal' the spouse. (1Kgs.18:18)

Cherith; kĕrîṯ; كِريث ، كيريث 'ate chives/of chives/grows chives' 'pond' 'pool of naturally collected water' 'takes long draught' 'takes long deep inhalations'; قِريت ، قيريت 'you/it/she stood still/settled down' 'read' 'admitted'; كِريت ، كيريت 'leased/hired' 'drove/chased away' and in this part of the story it means 'pond/brook' 'settled/stopped moving' 'drove/chased away' 'hired' as this is the place name and where Elijah flees to and stays as ordered by God and is 'by the brook of Cherith'; animals and people serve him by God's command, the same as being hired. Cp: kereef, keireef, qereet, qeireet, kereet, keireet. (1Kgs.17)

Zarephath; ṣārĕpaṯ; ذآريفَت ، ذآرفَت 'overflowed' 'she/it overflowed' because the widow ordered to take care of Elijah (feed him) tells him there is scarcely enough to feed herself and her son, but he informs her 'The barrel of meal shall not waste, neither shall the cruse of oil fail…' and when she obeys '…and she, and he, and her house, did eat *many* days…'. Therefore, the almost empty barrel of meal and cruse of oil never finish and there is a constant flow (overflow)/availability of food to sustain them all. Cp: vaareiphat, vaarephat. (1Kgs.17:9-16)

Obadiah; ʿōḇaḏyâ; عوبَديه 'servant-him/he' 'worshipper-him/he' 'served him/worshipped him' and he is described as both a worshipper of God and a servant to Ahab; ئوبَديه 'forever-he/him' 'kill all/wipe out-him/he' and he saves one hundred prophets from being killed; he is sent an errand to avoid the wiping out of the horses and donkeys, and when he is requested to inform Ahab that Elijah wants to see him, he fears his own demise and this part is repeat to emphasise this too is meant by his name. All the 'bad' prophets will be massacred by Elijah's orders in the same chapter. Cp: 'oobadyah, oobadyah. (1Kgs.18)

Hazael; ḥăzā'ēl; حَزآ ئِل ، حيزآ ئِل 'crammed/cornered-the' 'blocked/held in-the'; خَزآئِل ، خيزآئِل 'insulted/swore at-the' 'disgrace/embarrassment-the'; خَذآئِل ، خيذآئِل 'took-the'; هَزآئِل ، هيزآئِل 'here is the removed/killed/killer' 'here is the to-be-removed' 'he will remove/kill'. Cp: ḥazaa-ill, ḥaizaa-ill, khazaa-ill, khaizaa-ill, khavaa-ill, khaivaa-ill, ha-zaa-ill, haizaa-ill. (1Kgs.19:15)

Jehu still means 'came him/he' 'came to him' 'uncovered' 'who is?' 'which one?', but this character is the son of Nimshi; nimšî; نِمشي 'we walk/we leave'; نِمسي 'we spend the evening' 'we cause/provoke problems/arguments/fights'. Cp: nimshee, nimsee. (1Kgs.19:16)

Elisha; 'ĕlîšā'; نيلي شآء 'he who/the one who-wants' and whatever Elisha wants to happen—happens in his stories; نِلي سآع 'he who/the one who-wanders' and his character wanders around from place to place performing miracles. Cp: eillee-shaa, illee-saa'. **Shaphat**, as in Num.13:5 and 2Sam.8:17, still means 'saw/cured/was cured' and his role heals other characters with afflictions. (Note: Shaphat in Numbers, Jehushaphat in 2Sam.8:17 were the idea for the characters/themes Jehu Hanani, Jehu Nimshi, Elijah, Elisha—but the names have been split and changed in 1Kings to suit the story-telling.) **Abelmeholah** is used for its meanings: 'shook fat-in his place/stationary/in one spot' 'shook fat-his undressing' and refers to fat of animals, as well as punishment of adversaries, and suggests sexual acts which Elisha's stories will include. From the beginning, Elisha slaughters bulls he was ploughing with and feeds people upon meeting Elijah—denoting Abelmeholah 'shook fat-in his place/stationary/in one spot' as bovine reared to plough are not slaughtered for food and slaughtering for food is not done in the field, but at home. It also denotes Elisha will be doing 'God's' work instead of Elijah as God has said in the story. (1Kgs.19:16-21)

Ben-hadad appears as repeated word-name but different person in the stories, not because there were actually a sequence of Ben-hadads in real life, but for the meaning of this created character for its word-name which is to threaten and take/change borders along with the threats this reincarnated character poses to the other king characters in the stories. (1Kgs.)

The stories are set in **Samaria** for its meanings of night-stories and the events in the stories follow the popular folklore of this kind of story (to be explained later in the book). (1Kgs.)

Naboth; nāḇôṯ; نآبُت 'grows/sprouts' 'young plants' 'plants growing' and the story revolves around his vineyard and Ahab wanting it so he can grow herbs. **Jezreelite** and **Jezreel** are used for the meanings 'grazed-on-the' 'slaughtered-on-the' as it is a fertile piece of land and Naboth will be killed for it. Cp: naabot. (1Kgs.21)

Micaiah; mîḵāyâ; ميقآيه 'what is there with him?/what is wrong with him now?' 'what did he say?' and is a suitable name for someone whose profession/gift is to say what has been said by God. Ahab and Zedekiah's dialogue states there is something wrong with Micaiah, Zedekiah slaps him and says 'Which way went the spirit of the Lord from me to speak unto thee?'. Imlah; yimlâ, yimlā'; يِملَه/ا ، يِملآء 'dictates/spells out/told what to say' 'instructed/instructs' and is a fitting surname as he will only say what God wants him to say; also, because the 'messenger' asks him to say what he has been instructed, but Micaiah Imlah makes it clear only God will instruct him what to say; 'fills/fills it/him' 'fetches/is fetching water-him' '. Equivalent to Gamaliel (Num.1:10). Cp: meeqaayah, yimlah(la), yimlaa. (1Kgs.22:8-28)

Zedekiah; ṣiḏqîyâ; زِدكي يه 'deceived you-him/he' and refers to the character of the same name deceiving Ahab to go to war under false prophesy that he will be victorious, the author(s) or at least later editors of the story save the inconsistency of how God's prophets can lie and deceive by having a 'lying spirit in the mouth of all his prophets' to deceive them. 'zedeq' can also have meanings of 'gave more-he/him' and 'honest/was honest-he/him' 'blocked-he/him' 'prevented-he/him' 'absorbed attack-he/him', but in this story the word intended is 'deceit'. Cp: zidkeeyah. Chenaanah; kĕna'ănâ; قنَعنه ، قينَعينه 'we convinced him' and is suitable for a surname for a person who has convinced the king with a false prophesy. The word can also mean 'made him give up/lose hope/surrender to his fate' and 'lift his neck/head up/look up' but 'we convinced him' is what is meant in this part of the story. Cp: qena'anah, qeina'ainah. (1Kgs.22:11-28)

Amon; 'āmôn; نآمُن 'secured/made safe' 'gave false sense of safety' 'believed/belief' 'followed' 'followed/lead' 'followed through/led through'; عآمُن 'drinking/giving to drink' and is the name of the character who is 'governor of the city' and he is meant to give Micaiah 'water of affliction' to drink while the latter is imprisoned. Cp: aamon, 'aamon. His son is **Joash** and it still has the earlier meanings in Jud.6:11: 'grain husks' it is the black shells which hold the grain, the grain is removed from the pod/panicle and husks by threshing then winnowing. During intense famine these inedible husks have been used to create bread to prevent death, but the people who ate this almost inedible bread all remember its bitter taste and difficult texture to swallow. And the only reason why Joash his son is mentioned along with Amon is for the suitable word-name of Joash to enhance the story to make the audience understand what is happening 'and feed him with the bread of affliction'. This bread is only eaten under dire circumstances during times of intense famine. (1Kgs.22:26-27)

Jehoshaphat has been used in this chapter for its meaning 'He who/he was-saw' 'came he/came to him-saw' as the character is now a king of Judah and 'he came down to the king of Israel' and he also insists on seeing what God has to say (through the prophets). It is also the same meaning implied when Ahab disguises himself and asks Jehoshaphat to pretend he is the king of Israel by putting on Ahab's clothes so that the enemy soldiers see Jehoshaphat and think he is Ahab; when the enemy soldiers and Jehoshaphat are engaged closer in battle, they see he is not Ahab and stop chasing him. (1Kgs.22)

Azubah; ʿăzûḇâ; عَزُبه ، عيزُبه 'young woman ready for marriage' 'single woman'; عَصُبه ، عيصُبه 'disobeyed with/by her' 'a twinged muscle/nerve' 'a bundle/sheath/bundle it' 'a bad mood/of bad mood' 'made askew with it/her' ; عَذبه ، عيذبه 'sweet' 'tortured/bothered' and it denotes although Jehoshaphat did right by God, he still allowed the offering of incense and worship of other Gods which is a negative thing in the Biblical stories. Cp: 'azubah, 'aizubah, 'assubah, 'aissubah, 'avubah, 'aivubah. Shilhi; šilḥî; شِلهي 'took her' 'of taking'; صِلحي 'of reconciling/making peace' 'of fixing'. Cp: shilhee, ssilḥee. The fact they introduced his mother into the story meant the authors intended the relationship between Jehoshaphat and God to sour (as do most of the 'good' kings in these stories) more than just offering incense at high places, or at least his mother be depicted in a bad light as was Asa's mother (Maachah Abishalom), the similarities of the last names of both mothers 'Abishalom' 'disgraceful-took away' and Azubah Shilhi 'tortured/bothered' 'took her' 'of taking' meant they also wanted her to be deposed of her position and place as well as the idols which remained in the land, but either the authors never got around to it or later editors removed it to leave Jehoshapat in a better light. Her name reflects that Jehoshaphat made peace with Israel. (1Kgs.22)

Ahaziah; 'ăḥazyâ; نَخَذيه ، نيخَذيه 'took-he/him'; نَخَزيه ، نيخَزيه 'swore/insulted-he/him' 'a disgrace-him/he' 'an embarrassment-he/him'. He is a disgrace because he worships Baal. Cp: akhavyah, aikhavyah, akhazyah, aikhazyah. (1Kgs.22:40-53)

Baal-zebub; baʿal zĕḇûḇ; بَعَل زِبُب/زيبُب 'spouse of/high/higher/high place/above-penises/penised'; بَئَل زِبُب/زيبُب 'with the/by the-penises/penised'. Cp: ba'al-zebub, ba'al zeibub, ba-al-zebub, ba-al-zeibub. As earlier, **Ekron** still means 'ruined' 'petrified' 'laps': 'ruined' because Ahaziah will suffer and be destroyed, and 'laps' because the deity the authors have chosen to name 'Baal-zebub/with the/by the penises' is situated in a place called 'laps' referring to the penis being in the area of the lap/crotch. But there is a more specific meaning to this story and its use of Baal-Zebub and Israel: **Israel** is 'twisted muscle-the' and its backstory is that Dinah through an illicit relationship has withered Jacob/Israel's 'muscle' (penis), and Dinah does this act only after God as a man wrestles all day in a specific position with Jacob, and when God touches Jacob's muscle it withers—there is a sexual theme and aspect to God and Jacob's wrestling and the withering away of Jacob's muscle that he becomes 'Israel'. This story about Ahaziah, Elijah and Baal-zebub is regarding the God/Jacob/Israel wrestling/copulating incident: whenever the author through Elijah repeats '*Is it* not because *there is* not a God in Israel, *that* ye go to enquire of Baal-zebub the god of Ekron?' which reads as 'There is God inside 'twisted muscle-the' so why are you going to 'with the penises' the god of 'laps'?'—the original audience would have found that entertaining. (2Kgs.1:2)

Jehoram; yĕhôrām; يَهُ رآم ، يَهُرآم 'he who-threw/thrown/killed' 'which one-thrown/killed' 'is pulled down and out' 'is told off like insides being pulled out' 'pulled out' (the latter e.g. a thread in fabric being tugged and undone or being unstrung) 'is angry/snappy/grumpy'; جَهُ رآم 'came who-threw/thrown/killed' came to him-threw/thrown'; يِخُرآم 'he is pierced/ pierces' 'he pierced/burst from the bottom'; يِحُرآم 'he is deprived of/forbidden' 'he deprives/forbids'. Jehoram's first problem is he is deprived of hundreds of thousands of sheep usually submit by the king of Moab. Cp: yehoraam, gehoraam, yekhoraam, yeḥoraam. (2Kgs.1:17)

Elisha remains 'he who/the one who-wants' and 'he who/the one who-wanders' as his character continues to wander around the storyscape, and this meaning and role does not change after Elijah, except that he not only inherits Elijah's God-like powers but he too is depicted as God. His word-name, as all names and the very Bible, cannot be separated from the people who created these stories, the people to this day use the phrase 'If God wills/Insha Allah/إنشاء الله) meaning God wants/allows/makes/grants things to happen. 'What he wants' is denoted throughout Elisha's role as whatever he requests/wants to happen does occur. At his request he: heals water and land of barrenness; forty-two little children are savagely killed by bears for mocking him; they say of Elisha 'the word of the Lord is with him' so what God says—happens; makes water for Israel's army; oil wells up to pay for debt; he makes a barren woman have a child, and his character being God-like is emphasised in that the earlier Biblical stories usually have messengers bring news of God granting a barren couple a child before 'God visits' the woman and she conceives, but in this particular story it is Elisha who has a room in the woman's house, he informs her of his own accord without there being narration in the story or dialogue that God has said it will be, and she becomes pregnant (which is supposed to be a joke in the story as it is Elisha who impregnates her); brings a dead child back to life; makes poisonous food harmless; makes a small amount of food enough to feed many. When the king of Syria sends Naaman to the king of Israel requesting he cure him of leprosy, the king of Israel's response is words to the effect 'Do you think I'm God? Only God can make people die or live and only God can cure lepers.' These acts are what Elisha is capable of doing: killing people by requesting it, making the dead come back to life, and he goes on to cure Naaman of leprosy. The authors could not make it clearer that Elisha is God, and his stories embody this.

It is also clear that Elisha's character was the inspiration of the Jesus stories, not only are the miracles they conduct similar if not the same, but even both characters' personality is the same: petulant, snappy, retorting, wander around the land, become short and rude with some people seeking their help. (2Kgs.2;3;4;5;6;7;8)

Mesha, as in Genesis 10, still means to 'shepherd/take care of sheep/goats' 'walk/depart(ed)'. The king of the same name 'was a sheepmaster' who provided the king of Israel with 'an hundred thousand lambs, and an hundred thousand rams, with the wool.'; his role in the story revolves around depriving the king of Israel, whose name 'Jehoram' means 'deprived', of these animals. (2Kgs.3)

Kir-hareseth; qîr ḥăreśe̱t; قير هَرِصِت/هيرَصَت 'settle down/stop-stacked'; كير هَرِصِت/هيرَصَت 'clumps of soil/stones or clumps of dry mud-stacked' and refers to ruining the land and blocking the wells by stacking it with stones as well as stoning everything, 'stones' as this is what is used, 'settle down/stop' as this brings the Moabites efforts to an end. Cp: qeer-haresset, qeer-hairesset, keer-haresset, keer-hairesset. (2Kgs.3:20-27)

Shunem is still: 'stood/became/made erect' 'was erected/made erect in front of' 'stood before' 'stood still like a statue' and just as in Abishag and David's story, Abishag the Shunnamite was supposed to stand before David to arouse his sexual desire, this story also plays on the euphemism that the woman 'stands before' Elisha, she 'constrains' him to stay and eat and even convinces her husband to make a special room in the house for him and Elisha visits her regularly—this too is an element of the samaaria/evening stories where wives have affairs with the protagonist of the story, usually under the nose and sometimes openly in front of the husband. The author(s) make a point that Shunem is understood 'And he said to Gehazi his servant, Call this Shunammite. And when he had called her, she stood before him.' 'And he said, Call her. And when he had called her, she stood in the door.'. In Elijah's bringing a child back from death there is a sexual act performed and it is denoted in Elijah's surname 'Tishbite', but in Elisha it is the woman's character name (the woman herself is not named because she is not important, but it is important to the author/story that she be given a label which allows the story to proceed) 'stood before/erected/stood like a statue' which gives the sexual denotation as it is invoking a sexual erection, the author(s) make this clear that Elisha's first gesture is to have his 'staff' placed on the child's face, the staff euphemising Elisha' penis, which leads the story to elaborate in an Elijah-fashion revival of a child in a closed room, on a bed, but Elisha's story gives more detail to allow the audience to understand the ritual is an act of sex. (2kgs.4:8-37)

Gehazi; gêḥăzî; جيهَزي ، جيهيزي 'prepare for me' 'get ready for me' 'came-snatched/tugged at/snagged' and is the name of Elisha's servant whom he sends on errands, and as a servant he would prepare everything for Elisha; he also 'snatches' what he can of gifts from Naaman secretly from Elisha; جي هَذي ، جي هيذي 'came-she/this one' as his character is initially introduced and most of his role in the story is to call the Shunammite to come to Elisha, and then his second action is to go meet her when she comes to see Elisha; in chapter 8 as Gehazi speaks with the king of Israel, the same woman comes and corroborates Gehazi's information; جي خَزي ، جي خيزي 'he came-disgraced/an embarrassment' and جي خَذي ، جي خيذي 'came/he came-took' as Gehazi deceives Naaman into believing Elisha wants to receive some of the gifts Elisha refused which he does in secrecy from Elisha, and part of his disgrace is that he and all his descendants will be marked as lepers. Cp: geyhazee, geyhaizee, gey-havee, gey-haivee, gey-khazee, gey-khaizee, gey-khavee, gey-khaivee. (2Kgs.4:12-36; 5:20-27; 8:4-5)

Baal-shalisha; baʿal šālîšâ; بَعَل شآليشه/ا 'height/above-took what was wanted' 'height/above-took what is/was important'; بَتَل شآليشه/ا 'with-took what was wanted' 'with-took what is/was important'. Both meanings refer to the man bringing Elisha the most important, or at least considered the best, of all fruit: 'bread of the firstfruits'. This further proves Elisha is meant to be God in the original stories as in the earlier books the 'firstfruits' of harvest are reserved for God and brought to God, but here they are being brought to Elisha. The word-name 'Shalisha' still holds the same meanings as it had in 1Sam.9:4, but here has been used because it also plays on the word-name Elisha which the root word and intention of the authors of 'wants/

wills/grants/makes' can be used to enhance the story. Cp: ba'al shaaleeshah(sha), ba-al shaaleeshah(sha). (2Kgs.4:42-44)

Naaman as earlier in Genesis still means 'blessings' 'two blessings' 'of/has blessings' 'soft/smooth' 'receiving something physical e.g. money, food, clothes, etc. any kind of gift/necessity, even health' 'received blessings' 'gave blessings/two blessings' 'made smooth/easy(ier)' 'we stifle/feel stifled' 'we suffocate/feel suffocated' 'we cover/we are covered' 'we muffle/are muffled' 'we depress/feel depressed': Elisha blesses Naaman with a cure, and it heals the ailment which caused problems in his skin and the story has it restored with a child's skin i.e. soft/smooth. It is in the form of two blessings or more and refers to the cure from the illness and also Naaman accepting the faith of Elisha and taking soil from Israel to worship upon. It is two blessings in Elisha curing Naaman and Naaman wanting to give Elisha of his own blessings (his fortune). When Naaman dips into the river seven times it relays the meanings of 'we suffocate/feel suffocated' as the Arabic word (ghm/غم) 'stifle/suffocate/cover/muffle/depress' which is the root word of one meaning of 'Naaman/نَغمَآن/نغيمآن ' is used when water (whether poured over a person or a person submerged into it) causes a person to feel he/she is suffocating and gasp for breath. The story revolves around giving and receiving something physical just as the meaning of Noam/Namaan mean: he offers silver and gold, clothes; he wants and receives physical health; Elisha refuses to receive the gifts; Naaman asks for the gift of soil from the land and receives it; Gehazi asks and receives silver and clothing in secret from Gehazi which turns into Elisha giving and Gehazi receiving leprosy i.e. the opposite of a blessing or the reverse of a blessing which is a curse and reflects the meanings of 'we cover/stifle/depress'. (2Kgs.5)

Abana; 'ăḇānâ; نَبآنه/ا ، نيبآنه/ا 'rejected us' 'our father'; عَبآنه/ا ، عيبآنه/ا 'packed/filled us' 'rude/shamed us'. It is relayed in that Naaman feels Elisha has rejected to actually help him, and in turn Naaman initially rejects Elisha's cure; Elisha rejects the offer of gifts; Naaman asks for two donkey's-load of soil be packed to carry back home; Gehazi causes an embarrassment when he falsely asks for a gift from Naaman in the name of Elisha. Cp: abaanah(na), aibaanah(na), 'abaanah(na), 'aibaanah(na). (2kgs.5:11-23)

Pharphar; parpar; بَربَر 'talked nonsense' 'made unintelligible sounds' 'talked too much' 'talked incoherently'; 'talked nonsense' is meant in this story as Naaman feels instead of performing miraculous gestures such as striking the diseased skin while calling to God that instead Elisha has spoken nonsense when he tells him to wash in the Jordan. The word itself is how a person is mimicked if his/her language is not understood, it is onomatopoeia of what speaking in a foreign language sounds like to the locals, and if a person speaks incoherently or too much. Cp: barbar. (2kgs.5:11-13)

Hazael is used here for the same meanings intended for it in 1Kgs.19:15: حَزآ ئِل ، حيزآ ئِل 'crammed/cornered-the' 'blocked/held in-the' 'crammed/cornered-the' and the meaning 'blocked/held in' which Hazael does to Ben-hadad's breath by suffocating him; خَزآئِل ، خيزآئِل 'insulted/swore at-the' 'disgrace/embarrassment-the'; خَذآئِل ، خيذآئِل 'took-the' he will take kingship from Ben-hadad and he will destroy the children of Israel; هَزآئِل ، هيزآئِل 'here is the removed/killed/killer' 'here is the to-be-removed' 'he will remove/kill' as he will kill/remove the king of Syria and destroy the children of Israel and Elisha sets out the things that will perish at Hazael's hands; Hazael goes on to murder Ben-hadad; the narration has him go on to remove many kings from their dominions, as well as take away their wealth through tributes. (1Kgs.19:15; 2Kgs.7-15)

Joram is still 'pots' as at (2Sam.8:9-11). The reasons why 'Jehoram' has been changed to 'Joram' needs to be explained. It is not a contraction of the word-name 'Jehoram', but for the same reasons as Reuel can become Jethro then Raguel so the same character can be used with a different name and meaning as suits the story-needs. Joram is a completely different word than Jehoram. The problem is Biblical scholars want to treat a completely fictional story (set of stories) as real-life historical accounts which leads to another problem: in the same book and even within the same chapter not only does the same character undergo a name-change with no explanation, but so do the times they 'reigned' as kings of Judah or Israel. Some kings are brought back to life after when another king was meant to have begun to reign only after their death. The reason behind this, the author(s) (unlike today's and earlier Biblical scholars) were not dealing with reality nor pretending to deal with reality, but creating fictional stories which entertained people, even when these oral stories were first put into text the concern was entertaining long before it would be used as a religious book. So, when the authors created these stories it meant nothing to change a character's name to enhance and give new life to the story. Later editors may have attempted to change a name to add what they wanted, what was important to them to be mentioned in the stories, but were reluctant to change it completely as people already knew these stories and would not accept them completely altered, but subtle additions while keeping the original storyline was more acceptable.

Such contradictions can be seen in consecutive chapters (2Kgs.1:17 and 2Kgs.3:11) where Jehoram Ahab begins his reign in the second year of the reign of Jehoram Jehoshaphat (in this part of the story Jehoshaphat has been dead for the last two years), but by 2Kgs.3:11 Jehoram Ahab begins his rule in the eighteenth year of Jehoshaphat's rule. Seeing this is a completely fictional story the creators did not bind themselves with being 'realistic' as would today's authors be expected to show in their writing, but Jehoshaphat was needed by the author for the meaning of his name to have the same role as its meaning did in 1Kgs.22:7 i.e. 'he who/he was-saw' 'came he/came to him-saw' as the character insists on seeing what God has to say through the prophets 'Is there not a prophet of the Lord that we may enquire of him?', and the verses in 2Kgs.3 concerning Jehoshaphat are a repeat of 1Kgs.22 (regarding Jehoshaphat wanting to see what prophets have to say), which Jehoram's name meaning could not serve. And although it did not concern the original authors of the Biblical stories, it has and does concern and poses a problem to those scholars who attempt to create/prove genealogies based on the Biblical stories, genealogies which never existed.

The later editors did not want both parallel kings (of Israel and Judah) to have the same names but because original authors had already given them same names and even when they changed the names to the same single changed-name and because the method of the Biblical stories depends on the character/place name to have an exact meaning(s) reflected in the story, later editors were curbed in how much they could change. More modern Biblical scholars show some etymological gymnastics, or rather they replace gymnastics with pole-vaulting, as they insist that a very clear word with different spelling, pronunciation and meaning "should be read" as a totally different word with all its irrelevancy to the text while the original texts show these glaring inconsistencies, which were intentional, as part of these stories because they are not mistakes.

What becomes obvious from changing both characters' names 'Jehoram king of Israel' and 'Jehoram King of Judah' both to 'Joram/pots' although they have different fathers, kingdoms, ages, is because the authors want to bring in a story about pots and vessels in the kings' possession and reused the character name 'Joram'. It may have been the later editors who reshuffled the 'reign' times of the kings of Israel and Judah to make it a bit more acceptable to the audience: Jehoshaphat is brought back as if he had never died and this was the 'reign record' from the beginning of the story and his son Jehoram is given a later 'reign beginning time'. Jehoram son of Ahab gets a name-change and is also given a different 'reign-time' to allow him alongside Jehoshaphat without too much disruption to the story.

Jehoram/Joram king of Judah is married to Ahab's daughter (Ahab is son of Omri) 2Kgs.8:18, but within the same chapter at verse 26, after Jehoram/Joram's death, his son Ahaziah is made king, but his mother who was supposed to be Ahab's daughter, is now Omri's daughter, i.e. Ahab's sister. Again, the original stories are not concerned with getting it right, they just want to use the words which have been made into fictional names to serve the storyline. It could be by creating two characters in the same story first named as Jehoram then both named Joram caused the later editors some confusion, but the fact is even the name Ahaziah has been recycled in the same story as it is a suitable compound word to be used in the story so it becomes the name of Jehoram/Joram's son when he goes to visit the Jehoram/Joram of Israel.

Zair; ṣā'îr; شآعير 'will disgrace' 'will gloat over/at'; زآغير 'small' 'young'; سآعير 'price/pricing'; زآئير 'visiting' 'visitor' 'pilgrim' 'pilgriming'. Cp: shaa'eer, zaa'eer, saa'eer, zaa-eer. (2Kgs.8:21)

Athaliah; 'ătalyâ; عَضَليه ، عيضَليه 'mice' 'had sore muscles-he/it'; غفَليه ، غيفَليه 'distracted him/it'; نَضَليه ، نيضَليه 'strayed/strays-he/it' 'misleads/has been misled-he' and the female character of this name is depicted as the cause of her husband Jehoram and his son Ahaziah doing 'evil in the sight of the Lord' wherever her name is introduced following their mention; نَذَليه ، نيذَليه 'was humiliated/humiliates-he' and this is depicted in how she is murdered in the horse stables. Cp: 'adhalyah, 'aidhalyah, ghaphalyah, ghaiphalyah, adhalyah, aidhalyah; avalyah, aivalyah. She is first presented as the daughter of **Ahab** 'I give' for its meanings that Ahab gave sacrifices and offerings to other Gods, and as a woman she is the reason behind his misdeeds. She is then changed to the daughter of **Omri** 'my age'. 'builder/of building' as this too represents what is wanted in her stories as 'Omri' refers to the building of altars and the offerings to other gods, as well as the ages (young ages) of the royal descendants she has slaughtered so she can become queen. (2Kgs.8:18,26-27)

The elasticity with which the Biblical authors changed names, lineage etc, to suit the story can be seen again in **Jehu** ('came him/he' 'came to him' 'uncovered' 'who is?' 'which one?'), who was first introduced in 1Kgs.19:16 as 'Jehu the son of Nimshi', but now in 2Kgs.9 has become 'Jehu the son of Jehoshaphat the son of Nimshi' as the authors want to bring the meaning of '**Jehoshaphat**' into his story: 'he who/he was-saw' 'came he/came to him-saw' 'he who/he was-saw/cured/was cured' 'which one-saw/cured/was cured' 'he who/he was-cured or satisfied in another's bad luck/revenge/gloating/recompense out of hatred or wrong' as Jehu will attack Joram while he is healing, and the 'seeing' has to do with the prophets gifts of seeing, whereas earlier introducing Elisha as 'the son of Shaphat' was enough. **Nimshi** still means 'we walk/we leave' 'we spend the evening' 'we cause/provoke problems/arguments/fights'.

The first part of his story has to do with the '**Jehoshaphat**' as he is made king by the prophets delivering to him the message which leads him to massacre Joram/Jehoram and Ahaziah. The meaning of Nimshi 'we cause/provoke problems/arguments/fights' is throughout the story in the battles and massacres.

The meanings of the three compound words that make-up his name are put into the storyline: he and his men go to Jezreel (jehu) to kill Joram who is healing from wounds (jehoshaphat); Jehu and his men leave (nimshi) for Jezreel; Jehu is seen (jehoshaphat) by Joram's men; Ahaziah has also come to see (jehu/jehoshaphat) the healing Joram; Joram and Ahaziah come out to meet (jehu) Jehu in battle; Joram flees (nimshi); Jehu mentions coming with Ahab and seeing (jehoshaphat) the murder of Nabot; Ahaziah flees (nimshi); Jehu shouts out and asks Jezebel's servants 'who is on my side' (jehu); the authors make a point to mention Jehu 'was come in' (jehu) and they have him ask the servants to go see (jehoshaphat) Jezebel and the meaning as in seeing/vision/prophesy is used by mentioning Elijah's prophesy; he sends a threat to Ahab's servants that he is coming (jehu) to slaughter them while they defend Ahab's sons; the following verses in the chapter all emphasise that Jehu will come, letters come (jehu) threatening he will come; instead the severed heads of Ahab's children come to Jehu, Jehu comes out to see them (jehoshaphat), they are placed at the side of the entrance so everyone that comes and goes sees them (jehu/jehoshpahat); he asks Ahaziah's remaining relatives 'who are ye?' (jehu); the themes 'who are you?' and 'come-him/he' are throughout chapter 10.

Bidkar; bid̲qar; بِضقَر 'fling/cast aside/throw out' the name of the character Jehu tells to cast Jehoram's corpse out of the chariot. Cp: bi<u>dh</u>qar. (2Kgs.9:25)

Gur; gûr; جَر 'pull' 'pull up' 'dying' 'on deathbed' and both meanings are used here as Ahaziah dies while the chariot is 'going up to Gur' so it is pulling up the ascent, and Ahaziah is dying; the word 'pull' is used to describe a person dying/on death bed. Cp: gur. (2Kgs.9:27)

Jeho̱naḏab; yĕhônāḏāḇ; جَهُ نآدآب ، جيهُ نآدآب 'came he/came to him-wailing/mourning loudly'; يَهُ نآدآب ، ييهُ نآدآب 'who is/which one-wailing/mourning loudly'. Both refer to the character introduced in the midst of massacres and as the first part of his name suggests, he comes and meets Jehu. Cp: geho-naadaab, geiho-naadaab, yeho-naadaab, yeiho-naadaab. He is the son of **Rechab** which still holds the earlier meanings of 'keep eye on' and 'necks' as he will take part in the massacre of many people, but it is also a play on ريكاب 'ride/mount' 'knees' as he pulls Jehu into the chariot with him. Cp: reyqaab, reykaab. (2Kgs.10:15)

Jehosheba; yĕhôšeḇa'; جَهُ/جيهُ شَبَء 'came he/came to him-young woman' 'came he-grows into young man'; يَهُ/ييهُ شَبَء 'who is/which one-young woman' 'who is/which one-grows into young man' and it is a young woman who saves Joash from Athaliah and allows him to grow into manhood; جَهُ/جيهُ شَبَع 'came he-fed full/full stomach/satisfied'; يَهُ/ييهُ شَبَع 'who is/which one-fed full/full stomach/satisfied'. Cp: geho/geiho-<u>sh</u>eba, yeho/yeiho-<u>sh</u>eba, geho/geiho-<u>sh</u>eba', yeho/yeiho-<u>sh</u>eba'. (2Kgs.11:1-2)

Joash; yô'āš; differs from Judges 6 where it is 'grain husks' and the difference and support for it is dictated by the context of the story: يُعآش 'he is made to live/allowed to live'; هُعآش 'he lives/lived'; جُعآش 'came-lived' and they refer to Joash surviving Athaliah's massacre of his siblings, by Jehosheba saving him; هُئاش 'to strike around blindly/make a mess/not know what to do' 'a small fight/conflict'. Cp: yo'aa<u>sh</u>, ho'aa<u>sh</u>, go'aa<u>sh</u>, ho-aa<u>sh</u>. (2Kgs.11)

Jehoiada, as in 2Sam.8:18, is still: يَهُ يآدآع 'he who-he is calling/he calls' 'he who-he is claiming/makes false claims' 'he who-leaving/saying farewell' 'he who-depositing/leaving something in the care of' 'which one-is calling' 'which one-is calling/making claims' 'which one-leaving/saying farewell'; جَهُ يآدآع 'came he/came to him-calling/he calls/is claiming/making false claims/leaving/saying farewell' 'came he/came to him-depositing/leaving something in the care of'; يَهُ عآدآء 'he who-returned/returns' 'he who-enemies/created enmity/transgressed against' 'he who-infected' 'he who-counted'; جَهُ عآدآء 'came he/came to him-returned/returns' 'came he/came to him-enemies/created enmity/transgressed against' 'came he/came to him-infected' 'came he/came to him-counted'; يَهُ يآضآع 'he who/which one-is placed/he places/sets' 'he who/which one-misguided/misleads' 'he who/which one-loses/he loses'; جَهُ يآضآع 'came he/came to him-is placed/he places/sets' 'came he/came to him-misguided/misleads' 'came he/came to him-loses/he loses'. His role includes calling all rulers and military men, and they come to him; he tells them what to do to make the coup successful i.e. he sets the plan and decides who is placed king and who loses the reign; he calls them to kill the queen who has made a false claim on the kingdom; he determines Athaliah is the enemy; he returns Ahazia's son (Joash) to the throne; when he makes a covenant between him, God and the people he is calling to God, and orders who become priests. (2Kgs.11)

Sur; sûr; سُر 'a secret/keep secret/tell a secret' and refers to Jehoiada and all the people involved in keeping Joash's survival a secret, and also his coronation as king is kept secret until the last moment. It may also have the meanings of 'Shur' (Gen.16:7-16;20) شُر 'discuss' it means talking and also listening, taking into consideration what others have to say before making a decision—the military and religious leaders all follow Jehoiada's instructions and take part in the coup. Cp: sur, shur. (2Kgs.11:6)

Mattan; mattān; مَتّان 'two deaths'; مثّان 'doubled' 'folded' 'wiped away urine/sperm' and may indicate Athaliah and her supporters were raped/humiliated during execution which is what the Biblical authors have done to all enemy/antagonist kings and princes; مَطّان 'stretched' (by two people or to plural things) and is also used to describe when a person is beaten severely 'beaten until he was stretched' and refers to the murder of Athaliah and also Mattan the priest. It is possible that other words from the root word (dan/dn) and (medan/mdn) were also intended in addition to those provided above, such as 'bowed/lowered/bent' 'extended/reached for/reached into/put hands into', 'guilted', 'did not suspect' (see Mattanah). Cp: mattaan, maffaan, maṭṭaan. (2Kgs.11:18)

Jehoash; yĕhô'āš; يه عاش ، ييه عاش 'he who/which one-lived'; جَه عاش ، جيه عاش 'came who-lived' 'came to him-lived'; يَهُئاش ، ييهُئاش 'he struggles/fights/argues with'; جَهُئاش ، جي هُئاش 'came-struggles/fights/conflicts with'. Just as Abram's name changed to Abraham to suit the story and show the change, Joash to Jehoash serves the same purpose. Though in Joash/Jehoash both names are similar in meaning, 'Joash' is more in the present form as 'he lives' according to the current-ness of events as narrated in the story, but 'Jehoash' 'he who lived' 'came who lived' refers to his survival from a past murder attempt, and its second meaning (struggles fights argues) as well as the first part of the compound word 'came he/came to him' allows the word-name to reflect its connection to other characters/actions which become the centre of this character's story. It denotes the current events where he will be in conflict with the priests over the funding of repairs. The (hoash/hô'āš/هُئاش/هوَش) 'struggle/conflict' can be seen in Joash requires them to use money received towards any and all repairs while it is mentioned by the twenty-third year of his reign the priests have still made no repairs at all. As a consequence, Jehoiada and other priests are summoned by Joash who reprimands them and orders they no longer have control over the donated money, and therefore his new name is allowed to reflect the struggle/difference over money with the priests. Cp: yeho-'aa<u>sh</u>, yeiho-'aa<u>sh</u>, geho-'aa<u>sh</u>, geiho-'aa<u>sh</u>, yehoaa<u>sh</u>, yeihoaa<u>sh</u>, ge-hoaa<u>sh</u>, gei-hoaa<u>sh</u>. (2Kgs.12:1-16)

Zibiah; ṣibyâ; زِبيه 'penis-he' 'his penis' 'penetrate with penis-he/him' and is given as Joash's mother's name so the story can make the usual dual claim that although he does 'right in the sight of the Lord' i.e. 'pious and good' (which is also reflected in the Beer-sheba of his mother's identification), he can still be blamed for allowing worship of other gods to continue; صبيه 'poured into/onto-him/he' 'afflicted-him/he' 'injured/struck-him/he' 'a catastrophe'; ذبيح 'was slaughtered' and by the end of this chapter Joash is slaughtered by his own servants, but also: most kings mentioned in the books are introduced as being good, but their 'evil' is in they do not remove the high places, or they continue to burn incense at the high places (forms of worship) to other gods, but in the case of Jehoash the son of Zibiah it is mentioned specifically his ailment occurs when he gives away all of God's and the king's accumulated hallowed things, because the author/editor does not want people to miss this part of the meaning of his name. Cp: zibyah, <u>ss</u>ibyah, vibyaḥ. (2Kgs.12)

Silla; sillā'; سِلّاء 'flowing river' and means a temporary river which only runs when heavy rain occurs, 'flowed/leaked' and denotes Joash's blood flowing when he is murdered. It is mentioned in connection to Millo (which means 'filled' 'fetched water' 'filled water' 'filled/covered/soiled' 'a small, narrow rod applicator for kohl') as they are likening his spilled blood to a gushing strong river, i.e. there was lots of blood. It also relays and ties in with the meanings of his mother's name 'Zibiah' and specifically the meanings of 'penetrate with penis-he/him' 'poured into/onto' to connect to the water and flowing meanings of Silla and Millo. The narrators give Joash a brutal ending because in the story he has given Hazael what was dedicated to God. Cp: sillaa. (2Kgs.12:18-20)

Jozachar; yôzāḵār; يُذاكار 'he is reminded/mentioned' 'he reminds/mentions' and refers to what this character and his accomplice names are reminding the audience of; يُزاقار 'is/he topped up(water/liquid)/he was topped up with water or liquid' and this also ties into the 'water/leaking/flowing' related meanings and is an indication not only of Jehoash's blood flowing, but being raped during his assassination. It is also

يُزآحار 'he groans/pushes a lot' and can also be paired with one of the meanings of his accomplice's name, Jehozabad, which will be explained below. Cp: yovaakaar, yozaaqaar, yozaaḥaar. Shimeath; šimʿā̱t; سِمعات 'listen to' 'reputation' and the 'listen to' is telling the audience to pay attention to what is important to remember; شِمئات 'a disgrace/a scandal' 'a scandal exposed in public' 'a gloating' 'a mess' and this relays the message that Jehoash's reputation and ending were terrible and this too is tied in to the sin he committed which is to give away God's things. Cp: sim'aat, shim-aat. (2Kgs.12:18-21)

Jehozabad; yĕhôzā̱bā̱d; يَهُ/جَهُ بيهُ/جيهُ زآباد 'he who/which one-of bowls/drinking vessels' 'came he/came to him-bowls/drinking vessels' and this is a reference to some of the 'hallowed things' Joash gave to Hazael and is killed for as a consequence (the Bible makes clear the vessels used in worship are important); يَهُ/جَهُ بيهُ/جيهُ زآباط 'he who-kicked a lot' 'came who-kicked a lot' and this is referring to how Joash died, his legs kicking like a slaughtered animal. For the same reason a son called 'Amaziah' of which one meaning is 'the goats' is introduced in the same verse. Cp: yeho-zaabaad, yeiho-zaabaad, geho-zaabaad, geiho-zaabaad, yeho-zaabaaṭ, yeiho-zaabaaṭ, geho-zaabaaṭ, geiho-zaabaaṭ. Shomer; šōmēr; سوميِر 'told a night story/staying awake story' 'stayed awake'. And this is what the author(s) are reminding the audience, that these stories are fictional and made for entertainment as well as teaching what is important; شوميِر 'rolled up sleeves' and is what people do before they slaughter an animal. Cp: soomeyr, shoomeyr (2Kgs.12:18-21)

Jozachar Shimeath and Jehozabad Shomer have been created and coupled in the action to remind the audience of: the things meant for God should not be taken lightly, should be protected at all costs; disobeying protecting God's important things leads to a terrible end. They read as 'remember' 'listen' 'reputation' 'drinking vessels(i.e. God's property)' 'a stay-awake story'. They have also been grouped to remind the audience that this is not a real story, but a fictional tale created to keep people entertained, and that in the entertainment lessons can be taught through these stories.

Amaziah; 'ămaṣyâ; نَمعزيه ، نيمعزيه 'the goats' 'is goats' 'treated him like goat(s)'; نَمعصيه ، نيمعصيه 'the disobedience' 'the difficulty/hardness' 'the askew/crooked'. He is introduced alongside his father's murderers to enhance Jehoash was slaughtered like a goat. From the beginning of his reign he is set in the way of introducing the wicked kings '*that which was* evil in the sight of the Lord' and the story immediately reflects the compound word chosen as his name. Cp: am'zyah, aim'zyah, am'ssyah, aim'ssyah. (2kgs.12:21; 13)

Jehoahaz; yĕhô'ā̱ḥāz; يَهُ/بيهُ جَهُ/جيهُ ئاخاذ 'he who/which one-took(a lot)' 'came he/came to him-took (a lot)'; يَهُ/بيهُ جَهُ/جيهُ ئاخاز 'he who/which one-swore at/insulted/embarrassed/disgraced' 'came he/came to him-swore/insulted/embarrassed/disgraced'. All the meanings are shown in the related story as all of this king and country's fortune, freedom and even the soldiers and servants are taken from him by both Hazael and Ben-hadad whose names and characters are used continuously to invoke the 'removing/wiping out' the 'threatening/taking borders' wherever these word-names are needed in the story. Cp: yeho-aakhaav, yeiho-aakhaav, geho-aakhaav, geiho-aakhaav, yeho-aakhaaz, yeiho-aakhaaz, geho-aakhaaz, geiho aakhaaz. (2Kgs.13:1-9)

The word-name Joash and Jehoash have been revived again, but instead of a king of Judah, as a king of Israel. It is used as in 'survived/saved' as before. The 'reign-times' of the kings of Judah and Israel in the following chapters of 2Kings.13 onwards, are as convoluted and contradictory as the earlier chapters, but again this is only of consequence to people who wish to use the Bible as a historical document, but was of no consequence to the authors who created the stories and the audience listening to these stories being told, as the importance is the word-name given to the characters and places in relation to the story to make it more interesting, funny.

The word-name Ahaz and its variants such as Ahaziah, Jehoahaz, etc. are repeated and created to show how people, possessions, borders, dominion is **taken**, how things which should be given/offered to 'God' but instead are **taken** and offered to different Gods or given as payment to foreign kings to avoid destruction, as it happens frequently in these stories.

Jehoaddan; yĕhô' addān; يَهُ/جَهُ بيهُ/جيهُ عَدآن 'he who/which one-two enemies/transgressed against' 'came he/came to him-two enemies/transgressed against' 'he who/which one-counted' 'came he/came to him-counted'; and not only uses the mother as a negative to explain why king Amaziah still allows prohibited worship, but also denotes the two men who killed his father (Jozachar and Jehozabad) who Amaziah will murder in revenge, but that Amaziah will make unnecessary enemies following this bloodshed. **Jerusalem** is where his mother comes from because the other half of Amaziah's wrongdoings will be based on calling the king of Israel (Judah means 'he is called') and asking him to come and see him face-to-face and the meaning of Jerusalem is 'they see-asked-them/the' 'came-saw-asked-them/the' and the result of this 'looked one another in the face' brings disaster upon Judah and the king, and is why his mother (the female blamed in this instance for her son's 'evil') is attributed to this place-name; it relays in that they are attacked; the numbers of people killed in Edom are counted. Cp: yeho-'addaan, yeiho-'addaan, geho-'addaan, geiho-'addaan. (2Kgs.14:1-15)

Selah; selaʻ; صِلَى ، صِلاء 'arrived' 'connected' and the same word is used when a person who has wronged another arrives at the latter's home, with gifts (qat, confectionaries, other foodstuff) which includes a calf, lamb or ram for slaughter to have lunch and apologise so as to put the issue to rest; the act of 'arriving' is itself a public apology for all to witness. It is used here to show that Amaziah ('disobedience' 'the goats') has slaughtered his father's murderers but will forgive their children as they had no hand in his murder: **Amaziah** 'the goats' name reflects the two servants represent the animal for slaughter in the 'Selah/apology' and this is enough to repay the wrong which is why Selah has been renamed **Joktheel** which as in Josh. has the meanings: 'kills' 'gives qat' 'gifts/gives qat-the', 'pays back-the' i.e. in killing the two servants he has been repaid/avenged for his father's death, although it is told as in the killing of ten thousand Edomites. Cp: ssela. (2Kgs.14:1-7)

Beth-shemesh is used here to denote 'he/it will be provoked/cause problems/fights' and is what happens between the two kings/cities and especially Judah faces greater problems because of Amaziah's actions. (2Kgs.14:8-14)

Jeroboam is used as earlier (1Kgs.11:26-40), for its meanings: 'you quarter of the' 'fraction of', and 'he gallops-the' 'fled-the' and refers to Jehoash of Israel taking away most of Amaziah and Judah's fortunes and taking them hostages, leaving behind a fraction. It also refers to Amaziah fleeing to Lachish. **Lachish** is used for its negative meanings of 'licked(plural)' 'vicious/angry/strikes out (verbally/physically)' 'until rotted/went off' which all imply being completely beaten/destroyed. (2Kgs.14:13-19)

Azariah; ʻăzaryâ; عَزَّريه ، عيزَّريه 'he made him ugly' 'he made ugly/he made become ugly' as he is disfigured by God with leprosy because he does not follow God's rules; عذريه ، عيذريه 'he made a shadow for him' 'he shadowed over him' 'he excused him'. (It is also a precursor to Jonah's story where there is a plant which provides shadow for Jonah as well as Jonah being excused for his disobedience of God and the people being excused from punishment, as a character named Jonah is introduced at verse 25 in connection to the parallel king of Israel); نَذَريه ، نيذَريه 'the sowing of seeds/offspring' as he is immediately linked to the building of **Elath** one of the meanings which is 'leaved/ate leaves'; **Elath** is also used for its meanings نَيلَط 'will get stuck together' as part of the disease he is given has these symptoms; نَيلَف 'will get used to it/habit' 'will gather' as his son is left to gather the people and govern them while his father is still king; عيلَت 'got above' he is punished with leprosy because he did not get rid of the 'high places' where other gods are worshipped; ' غيلَط deceived/shortchanged/conned/lied' 'made mistake/did wrong' and his wrong is not removing the high places but also when people make offerings to other gods they are 'short-changing' the protagonist God of the story. Cp: 'azaryah, 'aizaryah, 'avaryah, 'aivaryah, avaryah, aivaryah. (2Kgs.14)

Jonah; yônâ; يُنه 'oh, pity' and is an expression made when a person feels pity towards the spoken about, whether it is a human or animal. This pity meant by 'jonah' is narrated as God having pity over the sufferance of the people of Israel mentioned in this part of the story. He is the son of Amittai; 'ămittay; نَمدّي ، نَمطي 'reach hand out/extend/touch' 'stretch out/reach/extend' and both can mean to extend the hand to reach/receive something, and in this instance it is used to show the people will receive God's pity through Jonah Amittai who acts as God's hand which is God's kindness out of pity 'He restored the coast of Israel from...according to the word of the Lord God of Israel, which he spake by the hand of his servant Jonah, the son of Amittai...For the Lord saw the affliction of Israel...for there was not any shut up, nor any left, nor any helper for Israel. And the Lord said not that he would blot out the name of Israel from under heaven: but he saved them by the hand of Jeroboam...'.

But Jonah's place-name **Gath-hepher** is chosen for its meaning of: 'qat-look, it is musty' 'qat-I will dig' so the author could enhance the meaning of Israel's bitterness from distress. It narrates that Jeroboam was able to restore some areas of Israel because God had pity on them so he does it through 'Jonah Amittai of Gath-hepher' and this likens it to the bitter taste of qat (although some qat has sweetness in its taste, the most and underlayer is a bitter taste) 'He restored the coast of Israel from...according to the Lord God of Israel, which he spake by the hand of his servant Jonah, the son of Amittai, the prophet, which *was* of Gath-hepher. For the Lord saw the affliction of Israel, *that it was* very bitter...'. Along with the inspiration and idea from Azariah's part of the story, this too was the inspiration for creating Jonah's story (Book of Jonah). (2Kgs.14:25-27)

Zachariah; zĕḵaryâ; ذَكَريه ، ذيكَريه 'reminded-him/he' 'mentioned-he/him' 'remembered-him/he'; زيقَريه 'topped with water or liquid/filled to brim with water/liquid-he/him'; شيقَريه 'peeped at/took quick glances' 'filled with gaps-he/him' 'made slits/gaps-he/him'. Cp: vekaryah, veikaryah, zeqaryah, zeiqaryah, sheqaryah, sheiqaryah. (2Kgs.14:29)

Jecholiah; yĕḵolyāhû, yĕḵolyâ; يِخوليآهُ/يه ، ييخوليآهُ/يه 'he allows him' 'he authorises him' 'he leaves him'. It refers to his wrong of leaving the 'high places', and Azariah allowing/leaving his son to deal with governing. **Jerusalem** is also chosen to denote the people come asking Azariah's son to judge their issues. Cp: yekhoolyaahu/yah, yeikhoolyaahu/yah. (2Kgs.15:2)

Jotham as earlier in Judges means: 'leper/lepers/leprosy' 'tips/appendages fall/cut off' 'came-guilted' 'came-blamed' 'came-ostracised' 'is ostracised' 'he ostracises' 'is guilted' 'he guilts' 'is blamed' 'he blames'. In this part of the story it means 'leper' and refers to Jotham's father having leprosy and Jotham finding the people he judges guilty or not. (2Kgs.15:5,7)

Shallum; šallûm, šallūm; شَلُّم ، شَلّوم 'took' 'of taking' 'small waterfall' 'I will gather' 'of gathering' as he conspires i.e. gathers others support and takes over the kingdom; سَلَم ، سَلوم 'greeted' 'peace/greeted with 'peace'' (Arabic equivalent of 'Hello/Hi) 'of peaceful or mild nature/character' 'left unharmed/intact/survived' 'small river/temporary river after rain' 'leaked/flowed-the' 'of entertaining/distracting/comforting' 'entertained/comforted/distracted' 'delivered/received' 'asked them'. As he 'conspires' he is asking for others to assist him in usurping the throne. Cp: shallum, shalloom, sallum, salloom. He is son of **Jabesh**: 'absent' 'flawed-you' 'disgraced-you' as he makes Zachariah disappear and what he does is shameful. (2Kgs.15:13)

Uzziah; 'uzzîyâ; نوذّييه 'was harmed-he' 'he harmed' and refers to the harm this king will do and suffer (latter from leprosy); نوزّييح 'was removed' 'was wiped out' 'was shifted'. This is a name change for king Azariah to suit the storyline. Cp: uvvee-yah, uzzeeyaḥ. (2Kgs.15:13)

Menahem; mĕnaḥēm; مِنَهيم ، مينَهيم 'winded/struck until wind forced out' 'punctured and wind escaping' 'sighing loudly' the latter refers to a person forcing a sigh to be noticed by others i.e. not a natural sigh, but a pretentious sigh/huff/puff to get attention. The 'winded' meaning is when a person is struck in the abdomen so hard the wind is forced out of them and they find it difficult to breathe—this meaning is used here as the story narrates he rips pregnant women's' bellies open and/or rips out unborn children. Cp: menaheym, meinaheym. He is son of Gadi; gāḏî; جادي 'found/sought and found' 'new/renewed/of renewing' as he exacts vengeance of the people who resist against him; he exacts money from the people to pay the king of Assyria; he pays the king of Assyria to 'confirm the kingdom in his hand' i.e. to renew his reign; غادي 'inflames glands/frustrates extremely' as his actions are brutal and distress the recipients. Cp: gaadee, ghaadee. (2Kgs.15:14-22)

Tiphsah is used for its meaning 'allows/gives permission' 'makes space to allow to pass' as the inhabitants of the place-name do not allow him immediate access and **Tirzah** for its meaning of 'his inheritance' as he will take it by force: '…because they opened not *to him*, therefore he smote *it*…' (2Kgs.15:16)

Pul; pûl; بُل 'wet/soak' 'afflict/ail' 'with'. 'with' is meant as the king of Assyria with this character name will be 'with' i.e. supports Menahem to become king '…and Menahem gave Pul a thousand talents of silver, that his hand might be with him to confirm the kingdom in his hand.' Cp: bul. (2Kgs.15:19)

Pekahiah; pĕqaḥyâ; بِقَه يه ، بيقَه يه 'stayed-he/him' 'stayed it-he/him' 'remained-he/him' 'was left-he/him' and refers to both allowing the 'evil' ways to continue and staying for two years in reign. Cp: beqah-yah, beiqah-yah. (2Kgs.15:22-26

Pekah; peqaḥ; بِقَه ، بيقه 'stayed' 'remained' 'he/it stayed' 'he/it remained' and refers to this character killing Pekahiah and taking his place. Cp: beqah, beiqah. He is the son of Remaliah; rĕmalyāhû; رِمَليآهُ ، ريمَليآهُ 'threw the/killed the-he/him' and refers to Pekah killing Pekahiah and in turn Pekah being assassinated by Hoshea. Cp: remalyaahu, reimalyaahu. (2Kgs.15:27-30)

Argob as in Deutronomy still means: 'observe/keep eye on' 'pour water from one vessel to another' 'flow stream of liquid' and he is one of the assassins of Pekahiah; Arieh; 'aryēh; ئَرييه 'see him' 'watch him' 'show him' the latter can be literal or a threat, 'water him/quench him', and he too is a character who kills Pekahiah for Pekah. Cp: aryeyh. (2Kgs.15:25)

The Pekah/Pekahiah verses are a retelling of the Ish-bosheth and Abner story (2Sam.3-4) with a slight variation of names and parallel characters. Where 'Ish-bosheth' was replaced in the storyline with a different character of the same word-name 'Mephibosheth', in 2Kgs. Pekahiah (Ish-bosheth) is replaced in rule by his assassin 'Pekah' (Abner). Even the assassins have been given the similar word-names with exact same meanings to show their role: **Argob** and **Arieh**, as above, are parallel to **Rechab** 'keep eye on' and **Baanah** 'by/with his eye' 'watching' and also is a threat/warning which 'by my eye' means 'I'll get you'. They also kill Pekahiah in his house just as Ish-bosheth was murdered in his house. Pekah has been given the surname **Remaliah**, and in 2Sam. Baanah and Rechab were from **Rimmon**—both these surname/place name based on 'throw' are used for the conspirators in both stories to indicate violent action against the target.

Tiglath-pileser; tiglat pilʿeser; تِغلَط بِل عِسِر 'make mistake with the difficult/hard' 'make mistake by/during time of difficulty' 'make mistake, by force' and refers to this character (another Assyrian king) who takes by force several areas; تِغلط بِل يُسِر 'make mistake by/with the captured/captives' as this king takes by force captives; تِجلَث بِل عِسِر 'takes all by hardship/force' 'takes all with difficulty/force' and refers to all the areas taken over; تِجلَث بِل يُسِر 'takes all by captive/imprisonment' as he takes the people captive. Cp: tighlaṭ bil'eser, tighlaṭ bil eser, tiglaf bil'eser, tiglaf bil eser. (2Kgs.15:29)

Hoshea; hôšēaʿ; as in (Deut.32:23-44): هُشَيَع 'he became/made ugly' 'he pulled out strands of fibre from clothes/hair/tissue from skin' and just like all the other names such as 'Eleazar' when there is killing, ugly destruction of life and brutality; هُسيَع 'he wandered aimlessly' 'he wanders around performing debauchery' 'he became debauched/he performed debauchery/promiscuity'; خُشيَع 'breaking/broke to pieces' it means pounding at something with another hard object until it breaks to pieces. The first meaning 'made ugly' as he conspires against Pekah and kills him and he is son of **Elah** for one of its meanings 'above it/him' 'against it/him' 'about it/him' 'above/against/on' 'on it/him': 'on it/him' because in language 'against' the same word in Arabic as 'on/upon' and is used where in English it would be the word 'against', and the text narrates 'Hoshea the son of Elah made a conspiracy against Pekah'. Elah is also reflected in Hoshea becoming Shalmaneser's servant so the latter is 'above/on' Hoshea. (2Kgs.15:30)

Jerusha; yĕrûšāʾ; حَرُشآء ، حيرُشاء 'pitted/pits people against each other' 'causes quarrels/problems between people' and is the word used when a person uses gossip, lies, or even conveys something that has been said by one party about another so as to cause enmity or cuts ties between people who were previously on good terms, or causes problems between them. The word-name is in the form of a verb or an adjective attributing this characteristic to the spoken about. This mother character has been given this name because she symbolises the wrong her son is doing. عَرُشآء ، عيرُشاء 'built an upper room' 'built a cow stable (with a high roof)' 'constructed something high' 'rose high' and either the original authors wanted this to be part of a story where Jotham builds a high place in addition to it already referring to the mistake most kings in the Biblical stories are guilty of and that is not removing the worship of other gods in high places, or the later editors did not understand the meaning of 'pitting people against each other' and added the line 'He built the higher gate of the house of the Lord' to make it عَرُشآء. She is daughter of **Zadok** which, as earlier, could mean: 'honest' 'friend' 'gave you extra' 'deceived you'; 'blocked you/prevented you' 'fished you/your fish'. It is most likely 'deceived you' as it matches the first name meaning of deceiving people into quarrels and/or enmity. Cp: ḥerushaa, ḥeirushaa, 'erushaa, 'eirushaa. (2Kgs.15:33-35)

As earlier in similar names, **Ahaz**, 'ăḥāz; نَخآذ ، نيخآذ 'took/took or takes a lot'; نَخآز ، نيخآز 'swore/insulted/swore insulted a lot' 'a disgrace/disgraced a lot' 'an embarrassment/a great embarrassment'. This time a son of Jotham, but still means 'took/took away' and in this story it is emphasised the character of the same name takes from what should be given/offered to 'God' but instead is offering it to other gods 'in the high places, and on the hills, and under every green tree.' He also takes silver and gold from 'the house of the Lord' and 'the king's house' and sends it as payment to Tiglath-pileser in exchange for his protection and alliance. As a result, Tiglath-pileser takes control of Damascus and takes away the inhabitants to Kir. Ahaz takes 'the brasen altar' and places it near his new altar, and orders the taking from the sources which are meant as offerings to the 'correct god' and has them offered on the newly built altar; he goes on to take away the materials which make up different parts of the house and sends them to Tiglath-pileser. His whole character was created to represent his word-name 'took/took away'. Cp: akhaav, aikhaav, akhaaz, aikhaaz. (2Kgs.15:38; 16)

Rezin; rĕṣîn; رَزين ، ريزين 'heavy' 'strong/potent' 'slammed hard' and represents this king of Syria and Pekah king of Israel being strong and attacking Ahaz, but Ahaz too is strong and they cannot overcome him, but are a strong enough threat for Ahaz to request assistance from the king of Assyria; رَصين ،

ريصين 'stacked' describing when something such as rocks is stacked vertically or side by side, or anything that is stacked side-by-side. In this instance it refers to the alliance made with Pekah of Israel, but also reflects Ahaz taking from the treasures of the king's and the Lord's house and giving it in plenteous amounts to Tiglath-pileser. Cp: rezeen, reizeen, resseen, reisseen. (2Kgs.16)

Kir; qîr; قير 'settle/stop/stop moving' 'cease' and denotes Tiglath-pileser did as asked and stopped Rezin and Pekah from warring against him, and denotes the people of Damascus were made to settle (by force) in 'kir'. It also can mean كير as earlier 'stones/clumps of dry mud' but not in this part of the story. Cp: qeer, keer. (2Kgs.16:7-9)

Urijah; 'ûrîyâ; نُري يه 'showed/show him' 'taught/teach him' and is what the Biblical passage supports '...and king Ahaz sent to Urijah the fashion of the altar,' the altar which Ahaz saw 'and the pattern of it, according to all the workmanship thereof. And Urijah the priest built an altar according to all that the king Ahaz had sent from Damascus: so Urijah the priest made it against king Ahaz came from Damascus. And when the king was come from Damascus, the king saw the altar...' So Ahaz 'showed' Urijah exactly what the altar should look like, pattern and all: from the word (r/ر) 'see/show'. Ahaz tells Urijah exactly how to make the altar and also how and what rituals to perform on it—in the language of the Bible, which is Arabic, telling/teaching a person how to do something is the same as showing them how to do it and the word 'show' is used to mean 'teach how to do it' even if only words are used to explain how. Cp: ureeyah. (2Kgs.16:10-16)

Shalmaneser; šalman'eser; شَل مَن يِسِر 'took who he captivated/imprisoned' and not only is Hoshea imprisoned, but all of Israel is taken away captive into Assyria. (the authors/editors remind the audience this is a 'samaaria/fictional entertainment story' being told by mentioning Samaria). Cp: shal man eser. (2Kgs.17)

So; sô'; سؤ ، سُئ 'bad/evil/bothersome/offensive'. There is no role/activity for this character described as 'So king of Egypt', the authors have sufficed the meaning of his name as more than enough to denote Hoshea's 'bad' in not sending the annual present 'And the king of Assyria found conspiracy in Hoshea; for he had sent messengers to So king of Egypt...'. There is no real king So just as there are not any of the Biblical characters, but he is only a created character in the Biblical stories. Cp: sue. (2Kgs.17:4)

Halah; ḥălaḥ; هَلَه ، هيلَه 'shed/shed off' 'is here' 'there/over there', the word is used when telling a person where to set/put something and/or telling them where someone is; حَلَه ، حيلَه 'shed it' 'undressed it/him/her' 'put in its place' and it can have other 'ḥl/حل' meanings but they are not relevant to this part of the story. It refers to what Shalmaneser does to the prisoners in the story '...and placed them in Halah.'. Cp: halah, hailah, ḥalah, ḥailah. (2Kgs.17)

Habor; ḥāḇôr; هاَبُر 'I will lose reputation/ruin reputation' 'I will spoil/become bad' 'I will pass/go beyond' and again refers to the prisoners being taken from their residence to captivity in a different area, and it also refers to the people going from worshipping God to disobeying him and worshipping others as well as conducting prohibited acts; خاَبُر 'told news/informed' 'news' and refers to this punishment which although they had been told and forewarned about it 'Yet the Lord testified against Israel...by all the prophets, and by all the seers, Saying...'. Cp: haabor, khaabor. (2Kgs.17)

Gozan; gôzān; جوزآن ، جُزآن 'permissible/is allowed' 'rewarded' and it means negatively, whether a person did good or bad but received a punishment/negativity in recompense for the good/bad he/she did, 'served them right', and the word 'Gozan' is in the form of being said about plural and refers to all of Israel being rewarded negatively, i.e. 'serves them right' as they are being rewarded punishment for disobeying God '...has sinned against...God...they would not hear...And they rejected his statutes...and worshipped all the host of heaven...Therefore the Lord was very angry with Israel, and removed them out of his sight...'. The verses which follow the places where Shalmaneser 'carried Israel away' all denote the punishment and why they are being punished, and correspond to the meaning of the place-names where they are taken to. Cp: gozaan. (2Kgs.17:6)

Medes; mādāy; مآداي 'reached' 'hand to/offer' 'hand/pass/stash/hide/plant with no one noticing' 'to put hands on something not yours' 'touch/reach into' 'to overstep boundaries/'take liberties'/have confidence to do something that should result in punishment' 'lying down' 'handed/passed with no one else noticing' 'hidden secretly/planted to be found by someone else' 'underhanded behaviour(done secretly)' 'has been secreted in/planted' 'has been hidden underneath something hastily'. In this instance it refers both to captives planted in a foreign area against their will, and also to the same people secretly committing sins against God 'And the children of Israel did secretly those things that were not right against the Lord their god...'. Cp: maadaay. (2Kgs.17:6)

Just like the names of the cities which the punished-by-God Israelites are sent to are given names which reflect the actions in the story, the cities which the people forced from other areas to come and live in Samaria also reflect the same literal actions/role in the story:

Babylon is still Babel: 'swapped' 'changed' as God has punished Israel by sending them to foreign areas while foreigners are made to move into Israel. (2Kgs.17:24)

Cuthah; kûṯâ; كُضه 'away' 'over there' and is usually said in anger or seriousness to make a person place something far away or take it away from presence if the object is unpleasant, or if it is directed at a person to make the person go away or get out of the way, it is an unkind or at the very least an angry expression, but usually is when the object/person is unpleasant, also 'stifled/stifling'. It is used in this way as God has sent away the children of Israel as they have become unwanted by God because of their sins and people from 'Cuthah' have been forced to live in Samaria's cities. Cp: kudhah. (2Kgs.17:24)

Ava; 'awwā; عَفّآ 'went off them' and is when an animal goes off food and does not eat because illness has made food unpleasant to the animal—this refers to God going off the children of Israel for their sins and other people being forced to go live in their cities; ثَوّآ 'made them stay' and again the people from this city are made to stay in Samaria in the story; it is also an exclamation of dismay 'awaa'; عَوّآ 'howled'. Cp: 'aphaa, awwaa, 'awwaa. (2Kgs.17:24)

Hamath for its earlier meaning of 'flakes that come off grain', as these flakes are blown by the wind and get everywhere, when grain is winnowed it is done so that the direction of the wind takes these flakes away from the grain to clear it. The same word derived from this noun is used to describe a persistent and irritant tickling cough. Not only are the people who were taken away from Samaria sent away like winnowed husks, but so are the people made to come to take their place. (2Kgs.17:24)

Sepharvaim; sĕparwayim; سيفَروَيهم ، سِفَروَيهم 'made them travel' 'travelled, and all of them/and them too' and is what happens to the inhabitants of the city of the same name made to leave their areas and travel to live in Samaria. It is worth reminding that most of the cities/countries/characters mentioned in the Bible have never existed except as a fictional character/place in the Biblical stories, but some real place and real person names were used by the Biblical authors but not as real people nor were the events as described in the Bible, but where the names lend themselves in pronunciation to become the meaning required by the fictional story and its fictional events. Cp: sephharwayhum, seipharwayhum. (2Kgs.17:24)

Samaritans; hachssōmĕrōnîm; حَق سّوميرون هم/ام 'belongs to storytellers-them/the' and is a direct referral that the new imported inhabitants are living in the fictional cities the storytellers have created; هقصّ سوميرونهم 'I will tell their night/stay awake stories'. Cp: ḥaq-ssoomeiroon-hum/um, haqss soomeiroonhum. (2Kgs.17:29)

Succoth-benoth; sukkôṯ bĕnôṯ; سوقّف بِنَط/بينَط 'roof-will leap' (dance); سوقّف بِنَت/بينَت 'roofs-built'; سوقّط بِنَت 'dropped/fell-girls' 'became immoral-girls' 'dropped/fell-built'; each name used is directly reflected: so the people of 'Babylon/swapped' have 'swapped' سوقّف بِنَت/بينَت 'roofs-built' into سوقّف بِنَث/بينَث 'roofs-made female/will female/to females' (male becoming female). Cp: suqqoph benoṭ/beinoṭ, suqqoph benot/beinot, suqqoṭ benot/beinot, suqqoph benof/beinof. (2Kgs.17:30)

Cuth; kûṯ; كُظ 'crowded' 'stifled' and Cuthah has been slightly changed by the author/editor to suit Nergal; nērgal; نيرجَل 'fire-cleanse/purify/make clear' 'we breastfeed'. Cp: kudh, neyrgal. (2Kgs.17:30)

Hamath 'flakes that come off grain' create Ashima; 'ăšîmā'; نَشيماء ، ئيشيماء it is an intentional mispronunciation and misspelling of 'crushed bread dish (with broth not milk)' and the pun is: flakes cannot be made into bread as the grain is missing, the authors have left out the first letter of 'ashima' to mean 'crushed bread dish' which is 'hashima' هَشيماء to match the name given to the city. Cp: asheemaa, aisheemaa. (2Kgs.17:30)

Ava which means going off food (especially animals) makes: Nibhaz; nibḥaz; نِبحَذ 'scratch the ground' which animals usually do with their claws or hooves when searching for food, also before settling down to rest in a spot—this suits two of Ava's meanings 'went off food' and 'made them stay' and still fits with 'howled'; نبهَز 'we scare out of breath/we hit out of breath' and is from the word (bhz/بهز) when a person is either startled or struck and becomes breathless out of fear or pain. Cp: nibhav, nibhaz. (2Kgs.17:31)

Tartak; tartāq; تَرطاق/تَرتاق 'snapped shut' 'clipped on' 'sealed/blocked'; طَرطاق 'trampled' 'pound/hammer' and is used in a saying ('alaik ṭurk tiṭruqak/'may paths/feet trample you') عليك طرق تطرقك when someone is being rude, bad, etc. it is said in frustration like a curse meaning 'may you be stepped all over like a path' and still fits with the animal meanings of Ava and Nibhaz. Cp: tarṭaaq, tartaaq, ṭarṭaaq. (2Kgs.17:31)

The Sepharvaim 'made them travel' burn their children for: Adrammelech; 'ad̲rammelek̲; نَضرَم مَلَق 'set ablaze-thrown/cast' and matches the narration that the children were burnt for this god, as well as 'thrown' in different words such as ram/رم means 'killed' throughout the Bible and in Arabic. It is not different than the previous verses of the first chapter where the 'children of Israel...' '...caused their sons and their daughters to pass through the fire...'; نَضر ام مَلَق 'harm/I harm-the thrown/cast' and means a harm done to a possibly sacrificed person/animal i.e. some kind of physical harm (torture) was done before the killing or causing the death. Cp: ad̲h̲ram meleq, ad̲h̲r am meleq. (2Kgs.17:31)

Anammelech; 'ănammelek̲; عين ام مَلَق 'eye-of the-thrown/cast' 'see/look (to/at)-the thrown/cast' and refers to divination as in this name the word 'eye' does not mean a physical eyeball, but the ability to see what others cannot for which people go to witches, sorcerers, seers, prophets, etc. this too can be seen when speaking about the children of Israel 'and used divination and enchantments...' following mention that they made their children walk through fire, and the Sepharvaim (a different people in the story) do the same thing they burn their children for this 'see/look-thrown' deity. Cp: 'ain am meleq. (2Kgs.17:31)

Although this part of the story separates 'the children of Israel' from other people, specifically those who are transferred from outside Samaria to live in it, and although the story explains that these people brought the strange worship of other gods in high places, the burning of children in fire, divination and other forms of worship expressed in the word-names given to these new idols in the story—these forms of worship are what the people of 'Israel' are being punished for and why they have been removed from their homes; the story itself narrates the children of Israel conduct these different forms of worship long before they are 'displaced/replaced' by foreigners.

A possible reason behind these inconsistencies in the stories, and most of the time within a single story itself, is due to earlier stories just carrying the folklore of the people, but much later, when people become more religious or have new religious beliefs, religious leaders attempt to counter what the general population sees and knows that they are one people and these gods have been worshipped, these rituals have been followed and there are diverse customs, deities followed by different groups among the one same people since antiquity. The later editors change the known stories and add to them that the 'children of Israel' are separate from others, they attempt to explain and justify the presence of other forms of worship as being introduced by 'foreigners' (usually 'strange wives', foreign women, and foreign 'daughters of the land') as a way to not only dissuade people from worship of other gods and persuade them to follow the 'correct god' (e.g. Yahweh) but also to disown and sever themselves as a people from ever having worshipped other gods, to distance themselves from their pagan culture and history which they are now ashamed of.

Hezekiah; ḥizqîyâ; حِزكي يه 'squeezed/cornered/crammed-he/him' as this character is put in a tight situation where he is squeezed by Sennacherib surrounding his kingdom and threatening with war and destruction; هِضقي يه 'make suffer/distress-he/him' 'I will force to taste/swallow/eat-he/him' the first is literally saying to cause distress, and the second is a figurative saying that means to make a person suffer or put them through trouble and the phrase to make a person feel pain/sufferance is usually described as making them 'taste/swallow/eat (pain, bitter, sufferance, etc.)' as something unpleasant. This meaning is directly reflected in Hezekiah being put in a distressing situation but the authors want to emphasise this specific meaning by narrating a literal meaning of the word '...to the men which sit on the wall, that they may eat their own dung, and drink their own piss with you?' when Rab-shakeh threatens/warns them of doom; هِزكي يه 'I will flatter/praise-he/him' 'I will predict if he is going to hell or heaven-he/him' 'I will predict if person is good or bad-he/him'; هِسقي يه 'I will water-he/him' and this meaning is used in wordplay by the authors adding at the end of Chapter 20 that Hezekiah created a conduit and pool and brought water into the city. Cp: ḥizkee-yah, hid̲h̲qee-yah, hizkee-yah, hisqee-yah. Abi; 'ăb̲î; نَبي/نَيبي 'refused/rejected'; عَبي/عيبي 'packed/filled' 'my shame/disgrace' and he refuses all forms of wrong worship; he initially refuses to submit to Sennacherib; he sends lots of silver and gold to Sennacherib; he eventually refuses to do what is right by showing his fortunes to Babylonian visitors. Cp: abee, aibee, 'abee, 'aibee.

Zachariah is used not only just as zĕk̲aryâ; ذكَريه ، ذيكَريه 'reminded he/reminded him' 'mentioned he/mentioned him' as a positive but also as a negative; زيقَريه 'topped with water or liquid/filled to brim with water/liquid-he/him' and related to the water-related meaning in 'Hezekiah'; شيقَريه 'peeped at/took quick glances' 'filled with gaps-he/him' 'made slits/gaps-he/him' as he allows visitors to look at all his treasures/fortune; ضَك اريه ، ضيك اريه 'he showed them' 'those/that he showed them' as his descendants' demise is punishment because he showed the Babylonian visitors all his treasures/fortune. Cp: vekaryah, veikaryah, zeqaryah, zeiqaryah, sheqaryah, sheiqaryah, dhekaryah, dheikaryah. (2Kgs.18-20)

Nehushtan; nĕḥuštān; نيهوشتآن ، نَهوشتآن 'bites chunks out of' 'mauls'; نيخوشتآن ، نَخوشتآن 'makes/pokes holes in' 'crumbles'. Both the meanings of 'took chunks out of' and 'makes holes in' applies to what happened to the people in the wanderings stories (Num.21:6-9) as they are bitten by serpents (holes/chunks) which is the inspiration for the author's naming of this idol. Cp: nehushtaan, neihushtaan, nekhushtaan, neikhushtaan. (2Kgs.18:4)

Sennacherib; sanĕḥērîḇ; شَنيحيريب ، شَنحيريب 'we will war(a lot)' which he does against all nations including Hezekiah's; سَني خيريب ، سَنِ خيريب 'years-destruction' and refers to the years which God says will be a sign, from what people should eat, which is linked to the mention of destruction of cities, implying Senacherib's demise. Cp: shaneḥeyreeb, shaneiḥeyreeb, sanekheyreeb, saneikheyreeb. (2Kgs.18:13; 19:20-37)

The three men Sennacherib sends are said to come from **Lachish** for its meanings 'vicious/angry/strikes out (verbally/physically)' as are the events including at least two of the three characters. **Jerusalem** because of its meanings 'came-saw-asked'.

Tartan; tartan; دَردَن 'knew-guilted' 'made aware/became aware-guilted/lowered' 'intentionally pour water like a waterfall' waste is implied in the use of this word; this word and other water-flow related words are used to describe speech and laughter when it is strong, long or merry (or all three). All three men sent by Sennacherib are set by the 'conduit of the upper pool' and their names are water related. They shout out for the king to come out, which implies there was threat or conceit in shouting for him to come out to them; although Tartan and Rab-saris are not given dialogue by the author(s), Rab-shakeh's speech flows for long and strong, it centres around making people aware of the options they have and warns them of the punishment/destruction in following Hezekiah as he will bring them low. Cp: dardan. (2Kgs.18:17-36)

Rabsaris; rab-ṣārîs; رَب ذاريش 'god/parent/teacher-sprayed' 'diluted with water/disciplined-sprayed' 'god/parent/teacher-slipped away/slipped out of' 'diluted with water/disciplined-slipped away/slipped out of' and refers to the characters standing by the pool and of them delivering a castigating message to Hezekiah and the people. (saris/ ṣārîs/ذاريش) has the meaning of 'spray' and also to 'slip away/slip out of' and the advice and warning is not to allow the opportunity of a peaceful and prosperous life slip away should they believe Hezekiah; they are also using this word-name to show that they will not slip out of Sennacherib's hand if he wars upon them just as other nations have not slipped out of his hands. Cp: rab-vaareesh. (2Kgs.18:17-36)

Rab-shakeh; rab-šāqēh; رَب ساَقيه 'god/master/parent/grower-water/drove him/it' 'diluted and mixed with water-water him/it' 'chastised/disciplined-water him/it' 'disciplined-drove him/it' and refers to them standing next to the pool; his words are chastising Hezekiah; there is also mention of delivering horses, mention of horsemen and chariots, and 'drive/drove' means the same thing as bringing horses; the message is to the people from Rab-shakeh's master and not only to Eliakim's master (Hezekiah); رَب شاَقيه 'master/discipline-be rough with him' 'master/discipline-work the land/his labourers' and they are being tough on king Hezekiah in their words and intentions, the word (shakeh/ šāqēh/شاقيه) means 'labourers' and also 'labouring' as in working in your own land and this too is meant as during his castigation of Hezekiah, Rab-shakeh tells the civilians if they do as told they can continue to work and live off their own land, but only temporarily until they are sent to a different land where they will live off its fortune in the same way as the word 'labour in your own land' means. Cp: rab-saaqeyh, rab-shaaqeyh. (2Kgs.18:17-36)

Eliakim; 'elyāqîm; ئَلياَقيم 'the one who stands/the one who stands instead of' 'the one who erects/has an erection/erections', and the 'one who stands/stands instead of' name meanings represent Hezekiah's men as they come out instead of the king because Sennacherib's men were calling for the king to come out; there is no use of the 'erect' meaning in the story; ئَلياَجيم 'the gagger/gag' and means to gag an animal with a physical object such as a mouth muzzle or strap to prevent it from stopping to eat while driving it somewhere specific or travelling. The latter meaning is shown when Eliakim asks Rab-shakeh to stop speaking 'in the Jews' language' to prevent the locals hearing his threats and insults towards Hezekiah. Cp: elyaaqeem, elyaageem. He is the son of Hilkiah; ḥilqîyâ; هِلقي يه 'I will find it/him' 'here/look-found-it/he/him' and refers to Hezekiah's men coming out to meet Sennacherib's men and they find the message is a threat delivered; 'I will throw/cast it/him' 'here/look-threw it/him'. Cp: hilqeeyah. (2Kgs.18:18,26-27,37)

Shebna; šeb̲nā', šeb̲nâ; شِفنه ، شِفناء 'we saw' 'we saw it/him' and refers to Shebna being a scribe who writes down what he sees, but also because he is one of the three who come out and see Sennacherib's men and message. Cp: shephnaa, shephnah. (2Kgs.18:18,26-27,37)

Joah; yô'āḥ; هُئاه 'it is him' 'aired it'; جُئاح ، جوئاح 'echoes/made an echo' and he is introduced as 'the recorder', it reflects he and his fellow characters receiving Rab-shakeh's loud and serious message and relaying it to Hezekiah. Cp: hoaah, goaaḥ He is the son of Asaph; 'āsāp̄; ئاسآف 'sorry/sorrow/remorse'; عاصآف 'twisted/twisted and broken' and the three men return to Hezekiah 'with their clothes rent' as is the way Biblical characters display a calamity/grief, they show their sorrow and fear of a disaster and the insult when they return in such a state to Hezekiah. For other 'Asaph' meanings see 'Abiasaph' (Exod.6:24). Cp: aasaaph, 'aassaaph. (2Kgs.18:18,26-27,37)

Arpad; 'arpād̲; عَربآد 'conducted sexual debauchery' 'debauched'; ئَربآط 'ropes' 'sheathes' 'tied'. Cp: 'arbaad, arbaaṭ. (2Kgs.18:34)

Hena; hēnaʿ; هيناء 'here' and has replaced 'Cuthah/'away' 'over there'. Cp: heyna. (2Kgs.18:34)

Ivah; ʿiwwâ; عِفّه 'went off it/him'; يُوّه 'made him/it stay'; عِوّه 'made him/it howl'. A variant of Ava mentioned earlier. Cp: 'iphah, iwaah, 'iwwah. (2Kgs.18:34)

Isaiah; yĕšaʿyāhû, yĕšaʿyâ; يِسَع ياَهُ ، ييسَع ياَهُ ، يِسَع يه ، ييسَع يه 'he wanders/goes/travels-he/him' 'it fits-him/he'; جِسَع ياَهُ/يه ، جيسَع ياَهُ/يه 'came-wandering/went to/travelled-he/him' 'came-fitted-him/he'; هِسَع ياَهُ/يه ، هيسَع ياَهُ/يه 'will come wandering/going to/travelling-he/him' 'he will come wandering/going to/travelling-he/him' 'will fit him/it will fit him'; يِصَنَياَحُ ، ييصَنَياَحُ ، يِصَنَيح ، ييصَنَيح 'he shouts/they shout' 'they argue'. Cp: yesa'yaahu, yeisa'yaahu, yesa'yah, yeisa'yah, gesa'yaahu, gesa'yah, geisa'yaahu, geisa'yah, hesa'yaahu, hesa'yah, heisa'yaahu, heisa'yah, yessa-yaaḥu, yeissa-yaaḥu, yessa-yaḥ, yeissa-yaḥ. He is son of Amoz; 'āmôz; ئامُز 'I squeeze/wring'; ئامُص 'I suck'; ئامُس 'I touch/possess/provoke fights or arguments'; غامُز 'I squeeze/massage' usually done for an ill or old person, 'winking/facial gesture'.

In the story of Isaiah and Hezekiah, 'amoz' holds the 'massaged/squeezed' meaning as Isaiah always assuages Hezekiah's worries, troubles and physical illness. Cp: aamoz, aamoss, aamos, ghaamoz. 'Isaiah' meaning is reflected throughout the stories related to him: people are sent by Hezekiah seeking information from Isaiah; Isaiah sends a message through Hezekiah's men and the message is about Rab-shakeh sent to 'reproach the living God' and the response is 'I will send a blast upon him…and shall return to his own land' So Sennacherib receives a message sent (by God) and will travel back home. After Hezekiah receives another message from Sennacherib and prays to God, Isaiah sends another message and uses phrase 'By the messengers thou hast reproached the Lord…' also warning Sennacherib God will punish them wherever they may be 'travelling/seeking' ; God will lead Sennacherib by the nose to travel back to his own country; Sennecherib is foretold he will not travel into their city; Sennacherib 'departed, and went and returned' the very definition of 'Isaiah' 'wanders/travels-he/him'. Just like his name, Isaiah goes to Hezekiah then leaves Hezekiah and is turned back to return to Hezekiah just as his name implies, and he always has a message from God to deliver so his coming and going have an objective; even the sign from God is about a shadow travelling/going backwards; Hezekiah receives letters and a present from the king of Babylon which displeases Isaiah because of the actions which follow, but his displeasure is brought by people who have travelled with a mission/objective; Isaiah comes to Hezekiah again, the conversation between them is about the messages and its messengers, about from where these messengers have travelled and it is emphasised they have come from far away. This leads Isaiah to a negative message for Hezekiah and even this punishment is about people being taken away i.e. more travelling, walking, wandering. (2Kgs.19-20)

Tirhakah; tirhāqâ; تِرهاَقه 'drains/fatigues/tires/spills-him/it' and is the name given to the character who Rab-shakeh hears a rumour about that causes Sennacherib's men to be distracted from warring on Hezekiah; طِر هاَقه 'send away/banish/fly/go quickly-peep/quick look' and refers to people noticing Sennacherib's men are away from their usual location and so they begin to attack their areas which causes Sennacherib's men and attention to be diverted from Hezekiah. Cp: tirhaaqah, ṭir-haaqah. (2Kgs.19:9)

Rezeph; reṣep; رَصَف 'stacked' (side by side or vertically) and refers to cities destroyed by Sennacherib, likening them to ruins of stacked stones. Cp: resseph. (2Kgs.19:12)

Eden; (same as Gen.2) ʿēd̲en; ئيدِن 'will guilt' 'will bow/bend/face ground/lower head' and implies the destruction brought upon them as one of the cities which Sennacherib destroys the nations of; عيدَن 'return/returned' 'listen and understand-guilted/bowed/bent' 'remember/be warned-guilted/bowed/bent' 'sticks'. Cp: eyden, 'eyden. (2Kgs.19:12)

Thelasar; tĕla'śśār, tĕlaśśār; ذِل عسّار 'humiliate/belittle-makes difficult/of hardship'; ذِل عصّار 'humiliate/belittle-twisted muscle/twister of muscle' and both these meanings reflect the destruction as narrated in the story to this city; ذِل نسّار 'humiliate/humiliation-the imprisoned/the imprisoner' and denotes how the people will become captives and sent to live in other areas as narrated to the inhabitants of the cities mentioned now and earlier; ذِل عصّار 'humiliate/humiliation-twisted muscle/twister of muscle' and is a reference to how a person with a 'twisted muscle' in the Biblical stories means they were humiliated/withered—something negative has been done to them just like the original naming and meaning of 'Israel'. Cp: vela 'ssaar, vela 'ssaar, vel-assaar, vel-'ssaar. (2Kgs.19:12)

Nisroch; nisrōḵ; نِصروخ 'we shout' and is befitting an assassination event where Sennacherib is murdered. Cp: nissrookh. **Nineveh** has been used for its meanings of 'we bring to your attention/point out' 'we warn you/wake you up/point out' as Sennacherib's demise was forewarned. (2Kgs.19:36)

His assassins are his sons, the authors have re-used a name given in the same story to a Sepharvite god: **Adrammelech** for its meaning of 'harm/I harm-the thrown' (the thrown being the killed as mentioned earlier) now one of Sennacherib's sons who murders him. What is notable is Adrammelech was paired with **Anammelech** 'eye/see/look to-the thrown' in 2Kgs.17:31 and suggests that this may have been the original name of Sennacherib's second son because earlier stories where a king is murdered by two assassins, they usually have word-names and come from place-names which reflect harming, watching and throwing, but for whatever reasons the original authors gave the second assassin character the name of Sharezer instead.

Sharezer; śar'eṣer; شَر عَزر 'will see-made ugly' 'evil-made ugly' and refers to the character observing the victim then killing him; صَر عَزر 'insisted-made ugly'; شَرئزر 'will see-tightened' 'evil-tightened'; صَرئزر 'insisted-tightened' 'knotted-tightened'. Cp: shar'ezer, ssar'ezer, shar-ezer, ssar-ezer. (2Kgs.19:37)

Armenia; 'ărārāṭ; عيرآرآت stuck/abandoned in the wilderness' 'stuck/stranded in a difficult location(such as precipice)' 'abandoned' (see Ararat). Cp: 'airaaraat. (2Kgs.19:37)

Esarhaddon; 'ēsar-ḥaddôn; يُيسَر حَدّن 'imprisoned (them)-bordered/sharpened'; ئيسر هَدّن 'imprisoned-demolished/will make them bow'; عيسَر حَدّن 'difficult/made difficult-bordered/sharpened'; عيسَر هَدّن 'made difficult-demolished/will make them bow'. Cp: eysar-ḥaddon, eysar-haddon, 'eysar-ḥaddon, 'eysar-haddon. (2Kgs.19:37)

Berodach-Baladan; mĕrōḏāḵ bal'ăḏān; ميروضاك بَل ئيدان 'nursed you-with both hands' 'your illness-with both hands' 'nursed you/your illness-but-you are guilty' and all are meant here: Isaiah whose surname is 'Amoz/massage' (which is done for ill people) heals Hezekiah; Hezekiah's illness and cure of it also bring his guilt which will bring punishment (because he shows the Babylonians all his things when they visit him with a present because he is ill); ميرودآك بَلئي دآن 'you will be returned to-ailment-guilt'; ميرودآك بَلئيدآن 'you will be returned to two (or more)countries' and refers to his descendants and people being taken away and out of the country as punishment for Hezekiah's wrong. (mrdk/مردك) is a word used as in 'your return/reward' 'you will be reduced to' 'your just deserts' as in you will be forced to return or suffer for what you did. All these meanings were meant in this wordplay as reflected by the stories. If the correct transliteration is: bĕrō'dak bal'ăḏān; بيرودآك بَل ئيدآن 'I will return you with both hands/by both hands' and refers to the shadow going backwards although the dial does not. Cp: meiroodhaak bal aidaan, meiroodaak balai daan, meiroodak balaidaan, beiroodaak bal aidaan. (2Kgs.20:12)

Manasseh is still 'made him forget' as in distracted him to forget as it was in Genesis. It denotes how Manasseh by restoring worship of other gods has caused all the people to forget God's ways/commandments and to follow other gods. (2Kgs.20:21; 21)

Hephzi-bah; ḥepṣî-ḇāh; هَفسي باه 'I will make her/them pass wind' 'I will pass wind-with her' and means to intensely scare to the degree they lose control of bowels, but also 'copulate-her' which is the term used to describe a rooster copulating a hen: the rooster roughly forces the hen, biting her by her neck and forces her to the ground, the reason it is called 'breaking wind-her' is because the movement and anatomy of a hen looks as if he is copulating her through the anus as if the rooster is passing wind into her; هَفزي باه 'I will provoke with him/her'. Both meanings of Manasseh's mother, denoting the evil Manasseh does which provokes God's anger that God will punish the people with such severity unheard of before. Cp: hephsee-baah, hephzee-baah. (2Kgs.21:1)

Uzza; ʿuzzā'; ئوذّاء 'harmful' 'were harmed' and denotes Manasseh's harm in misleading the people and the harm brought upon them, and also the harm his son Amon will do and receive when he is murdered and they are both buried in this garden with the name 'harmful/were harmed'. Cp: oovvaa. (2Kgs.21:18,26)

Amon (1Kgs.22:26-27) is still 'secured/made safe' 'gave false sense of safety' 'believed/belief' 'followed' 'followed/lead' 'followed through/led through' 'drinking/giving to drink' as in 1Kgs.22:26 but can also mean 'blind/blinded' as he follows his father's 'evil' ways and so do the people under him follow his lead. At 1Kgs.22:26 the character was given the word-name of 'Amon' to denote he was tasked with giving the imprisoned Micaiah 'water of affliction' to drink as punishment. This character naming implies having a false sense of safety and is blind or blinded as he is assassinated by his own servants in his own home; the people are still loyal and follow through with revenge against his assassins. (2Kgs.21:18-26)

Meshullemeth; mĕšullemet̲; مَسولِّمت ، ميسولّمَت 'did not survive' 'provoked the one who died' and refer to her son Manasseh not surviving and being killed, 'well-ask the one who died' 'did not ask the one who died'. Cp: mesullemet, meisullemet. Haruz; ḥārûṣ; حآرُز 'thorny bush' also a condition when splotches of circular spots (like dots) appear on the skin it denotes the punishment will be like the spines of this kind of thorny bush sticking into the skin. Cp: ḥaaruz. Jotbah; yoṭb̲â; يوطبه 'not disgusted by it/him' 'can eat/drink/palate/touch it' and implies something disgusting about the spoken about that the person is not disgusted by or can eat. It reflects the unsavoury meanings given to the mothers to denote outright evil kings or good kings who while being good still do bad, in this case Amon is wholly bad. Cp: yooṭbah. (2Kgs.21:19)

Josiah; yō'šîyāhû; يوئسيياحُ 'they go wandering and seeking'; جوءسيياحُ 'they came seeking' from the word (sḥ/سح) 'wander and seek/seek' and the word, as does how it is used as a character name, implies a person is seeking something in particular and is not wandering around with no specific purpose such as the word (s'/سع) which makes up Isaiah's name and meaning. But 'josiah/ yō'šîyāhû/يوئسيياحُ' 'they go wandering and seeking' ('seeking' for short) means they are trying to find/find out something in particular. Where Josiah's story is mentioned he is sending people to seek something. He sends men to find out the total of collected money and to action the repairs and the dialogue is telling people to go somewhere and do something in particular. He then sends them to seek answers regarding the 'found book' as the answers he seeks are of great importance to him and his people. He does not only go out himself or sends just one individual, he also sends groups of people to find the information or action which explains why his name is in the plural 'they go seeking':

'...that the king sent Shaphan the son of Azaliah...Go up to Hilkiah...that he may sum up the silver...And let them deliver it...' 'And the king commanded Hilkiah the priest, and Ahikam the son of Shaphan, and Achbor the son of Michaiah, and Shaphan the scribe, and Asahiah a servant of the king's, saying, Go ye enquire of the Lord...' the response from the prophetess they seek answers from emphasises the meaning of Josiah's name '...Thus saith the Lord God of Israel, Tell the man that sent you to me,' 'But to the king of Judah which sent you to enquire of the Lord...' 'And the king sent, and they gathered unto him all the elders...' 'Then he said, What title *is* that that I see? And the men of the city told him.' So Josiah is seeking answers, the truth, he is sending others to find out, he goes out himself seeking out all the forms, places and people which are used in worshipping 'other gods' to destroy them; he seeks answers regarding a translation of an inscription of the title on a sepulchre. Therefore Josiah's 'seeking' is for the truth about God, religion and his people's safety and future. Cp: yooseeyaaḥu, goo-seeyaaḥu (2Kgs.22-23)

In 2 Chronicles Josiah's name is made clearer with his actions/intentions being described as seeking after God, maybe the editor/author who wrote this book wanted to ensure the meaning of Josiah's name was understood not only as the original authors as 'sent them seeking' but specifically as seeking God: 'For in the eighth year of his reign, while he was yet young, he began to seek after the God of David his father...' (2Chr.34:1-3)

Jedida; yĕd̲îd̲â; يَديده ، ييديده 'hands reaching' 'his/her hands' 'of hands reaching' 'he teaches baby to walk/he holds by hand to help walk'; جيديده 'came-hands reaching' 'came-held by hand to help walk' 'new/renewed' and although Josiah is depicted as a wholly good king, his mother's name still reflects negativity which is the punishment promised by God because of his grandfather's wickedness and Josiah is reminded of it. Cp: yedeedah, yeideedah, g-eideedah. Adaiah; 'ăd̲āyâ, 'ăd̲āyāhû; عَدآيه ، عيدآيه ، عَدآياهُ ، عيدآياهُ 'became enemy-he/him' 'went against him' 'counted-he/him' 'transgressed-he/him' and still refers to the punishment stated by God to Manasseh and mentioned to Josiah; 'counted-he/him' because he will ask the collected money for repairs be counted. Cp: 'adaayah, 'aidaayah, 'adaayaahu, 'aidaayaahu. Boscath; boṣqat̲; بوزقَت 'divided into small portions and scattered' 'quickly passed by' and means the same one thing that is divided and scattered and still refers to the punishment threatened by God because of Manasseh. Cp: boozqat.

The sins and its punishment narrated during Manasseh's story and reminded that it will happen to the people even if Josiah himself is spared during his lifetime follows the themes of Josiah's mother's name: because Manasseh caused the people to sin with his hands/their hands (Jedida) rebuilding demolished 'high places' idols and altars and practising everything prohibited (Adaiah), 'and Manasseh seduced them to do more evil' he led them from one way of worship of one god, to many different forms of worship and deities (Boscath). The punishment is God will wipe Jerusalem as a person cleans a dish and turns it over which entails using hands (Jedida); he will deliver them into the hand (Jedida) of the enemy (Adaiah); they will become prey and spoil (Boscath) to all their enemies (Adaiah); they have provoked God (Adaiah) since they came out of Egypt and never stopped provoking him by transgressing (Adaiah); Manasseh 'shed innocent blood very much, till he had filled Jerusalem from one end to another' (Adaiah/Boscath). (2Kgs.21; 22:1, 15-20)

Shaphan; šāpān; شآفان 'they saw' two or more people saw, 'they were healed' 'they cured'. It denotes the character being a scribe so he writes down what he sees as part of his work, and also denotes the character is sent to see that Hilkiah totals the money and then to oversee the funds are delivered to each specific group for the work to be done; Shaphan 'they saw' also shows Josiah the book Hilkiah found; he is one of the group sent to ask the prophetess to see what God has to say. He is the son of Azaliah; 'ăṣalyâ, 'ăṣalyāhû; نَصَل يه ، نُيصَل يه ، نَصَل يآهْ ، نُيصَل يآهْ 'reaches-he/him' 'delivers him/it' 'deliver-he/him' and he is the first person sent on a task(s) to find Hilkiah and make sure the money is paid to the workers; the 'found book' reaches Josiah through Shaphan son of Azaliah as he brings it from Hilkiah to Josiah; and because he reaches the prophetess when sent by Josiah. Cp: assalyah, aissalyah, assalyaahu, aissalyaahu.

He is the grandson of Meshullam; mĕšullām; مَسو لّآم 'well ask them' 'what is/has been delivered/received' as Shaphan is tasked with asking Hilkiah to add up the funds, and to pay the wages and to get the labourers to work repairs; he is asked to go 'enquire of the Lord' so they ask the prophetess ; 'well, he survived' as the answer to the questions Josiah sends them to ask ends with him being spared the punishment which will afflict others because of his grandfather's behaviour; مَشو لآم 'what did he/they take/what was taken' 'they did not take'. You will see more than one word-name used in a variation of a recent character either because they wanted to use the same name for its meaning because they could not use the same previous character, but re-use the same word-name with or without a variation. Cp: mesullaam, meshullaam. (2Kgs.22:3-15)

Hilkiah as earlier in 2Kings still means 'I will find it/him' 'here/look-found-he/him' as in this part of the story this word-name is used for the character who finds a book 'And Hilkiah the high priest said unto Shaphan the scribe, I have found the book of the law in the house of the Lord.' It also reflects that he finds out how much money has been collected for the repairs; he is one of the men with suitable names who is sent to find out from the prophetess what God wants. (2Kgs.22:4-14)

Ahikam; 'ăḥîqām; نَخي قآم 'my brother stood' and could be literal as 'stood up' or mean 'protected/stood up for' or 'got up' and did what was being asked to be done. نَحيكآم 'wisdom' 'sayings' 'law/knowledge of law' 'rule'; and the 'found book' is described as 'the book of the law' and this character is one of a group sent to discover answers about this book. Cp: akhee-qaam, aḥeekaam. He is son of **Shaphan** 'they saw' and this is a reused character name from within the same chapter for its meanings, as Ahikam is asked to go see a prophetess so she can see what God says. (2Kgs.22:12)

Achbor; 'akbôr; as in Genesis it still means نَخبُر 'tell/tell the news'. He is son of **Michaiah**(Micaiah) for one of its meanings in 1Kgs.22: 'what is there with him?/what is wrong with him now?' 'what did he say?' as they are asked to find out what the prophetess says which is also finding out what God says. (2Kgs.22:12-15)

Asahiah; 'ăśāyâ; عصآيه/عيصآيه 'disobeyed him/he' 'my disobedience' and it reflects the disobedience of their ancestors which Josiah fears will incur God's wrath and punishment against the current people, followed by the prophetess confirming that the people will be punished for the disobedience of their fathers, except for Josiah as he did not disobey. It is the name given to the servant sent to discover the news from the prophetess. Their names as grouped together by the authors indicate they have been sent to find out if the prophetess can tell them something from God. Cp: 'assaayah, 'aissaayah. (2Kgs.22:12-15)

Huldah; ḥuldâ; حولده 'stripped' 'reaped' 'stripped plenty/loads' 'loads' and is usually used to refer to stripping/harvesting a tree of all its fruits or leaves if the leaf is edible or can be used such as in henna, qat, senna, etc. and this refers to the punishment and warning of desolation that will befall the people i.e. they will be stripped of their prosperity, freedom, wellness; حول ده 'undress him' 'strip it' and refers to her husband being 'keeper of the wardrobe'. خولده 'skin peeled off(from heat or beating)' 'sun/heat roasted' 'severely beat up' 'mole(s)/a mole' 'remembered forever' 'lived forever' and is also a reference to the 'desolation' and 'all the evil' which God says 'I will bring upon this place.' but also refers to Josiah being spared from seeing the evil punishment because he remembered God, and that anything he did in ignorance was because the book had not been found, i.e. he had been blind like a mole because the truth was hidden from him. Cp: ḥuldah, ḥul-vah, khuldah. (2Kgs.22:14-20)

Shallum as in 2Kgs.15:13 still means: شَلُّوم ، شَلَّم'took' 'of taking' 'small waterfall' 'I will gather' 'of gathering' as Huldah's husband is responsible for keeping the wardrobe; سَلُّوم ، سَلَّم 'asked them' as Josiah's men have come to ask her to ask God, 'small river/temporary river after rain' 'leaked the' 'greeted' 'of peaceful/mild nature'. It also relays that the prophetess informs Josiah that he will 'survive/be intact' he will not be punished by God. They show all three meanings in Huldah's husband's name: She is being asked and is asking, she tells Josiah he will be safe and unharmed by punishments, her husband collects a specific person's clothes, Josiah will die peacefully and be gathered with his ancestors '...I will gather thee unto thy fathers, and thou shalt be gathered into thy grave in peace...'. (2Kgs.22:14-20)

Tikvah; tiqwâ; تِقوه 'piety' 'fear of God' and denotes Josiah's fear of God and empathy for feeling fear and despair over his people. Cp: tiqwah. (2Kgs.22:14-20)

Harhas; ḥarḥas; حَرحَص 'moved-despaired' and denotes Josiah's feeling of despair and frustration over the punishment meant for his people: when he finds out, he rips his clothes and he is moved to find out what he should do or what lies ahead. When a person is said to (iḥtr/احتر) it means 'he was moved to take action' out of protectiveness, care, etc. over what he/she is being moved by, from the word (ḥr/حر) one meaning relevant here is 'warm/hot blooded' 'moved to action' 'free'. '(ḥss/حص) is 'deep sorrow'. The words have been combined to show how Josiah's character not only feels this deep despair but is moved to take action by 'enquiring' of God. Cp: ḥarḥass. (2Kgs.22:14-20)

Hilkiah is used for its meaning of 'I will throw it/him' 'here/look-threw it/him' as he is tasked with throwing out and getting rid of all the things related to other gods. 'And the king commanded Hilkiah the high priest...to bring forth out of the temple...and he burned them without Jerusalem in the fields of Kidron...' (2Kgs.23:4)

Kidron; qiḏrôn; قِضرُن 'they are disgusting/unclean/revolting/filthy' and in the Biblical stories this name has been given to a field, valley and river whenever the things crossing it or being destroyed in it are deemed 'unclean/disgusting' and when they talk about vessels and other equipment used to serve 'other gods' it is meant as intrinsically unclean, i.e. they cannot be cleaned as they are unclean to the core. This is why when they are destroyed the place they are scrapped at is called 'kidron', whether it denotes that Absalom did something dirty by betraying his father or that David's filthy deeds have caught up with him as the story narrates he is accused of being bad towards Saul and Jonathan, in both cases whoever the dirty deeds belonged to—David had to pass over the river 'Kidron' to enhance the story and affirm its meaning. It is where Asa destroys and burns his mother's idol. It becomes 'fields of Kidron' where Josiah has all the accoutrements of other gods from the 'temple of the Lord' destroyed. It becomes 'the brook of Kidron' in the same chapter when he has all the things related to other god worship destroyed that were 'the grove out of the house of the Lord'. There is no real river nor fields with this name, nor did these things actually happen, but it enhances the stories being told that whenever something 'unclean' is destroyed, it is disposed of in a field or river which has the name 'they are unclean'.

Bethel is mentioned to show how bad/evil these things and their worship are and slaughter or at least death will follow the mention of the word 'bethel'. Cp: qidhron. To further emphasise how revolting and hated these 'unclean' things should be viewed as, the story has the powdered remnants of the 'unclean' vessels scattered over the graves of dead people who worshipped these gods—making them unclean in their deaths—it is bigoted, but it is what the story creators wanted to emphasise. Homosexual men, women who make weavings for the groves, and priests who service/worship the gods are all equated to 'unclean', they are put out of their occupation, residence and places of worship and their buildings and equipment destroyed. (2Kgs.23:4-24)

Topheth; tōpeṯ; توفَت 'spat at/on' and is also a gesture or expression where a person says 'tooph' at something or someone meaning they have done something bad, 'leapt' 'are being/will be crushed/she crushed/she was crushed' and refers to how the 'unclean' things will be crumbled, broken, reduced to dust. In this part of the story it denotes how Josiah 'defiled' Topheth which belongs to the children of **Hinnom** which at Josh.15:8 means 'madly in love' 'we'll sleep(literally or euphemistically as 'sex')', 'insulted' either being insulted or insulting others, 'satisfied/gratified'. As it follows Sodomites, women that weave for groves and priests of strange gods, it too is deemed unclean. Cp: toophet. (2Kgs.23:10)

Nathan-melech; nĕṯan-meleḵ; the word 'Nathan' has at least two of the earlier meanings in use here: نَدَن/نيدَن مَلح 'we guilt-good/well' 'we bow/lower/make bow-good/well'; نَظَن/نيظَن مَلح 'we think/suspect-good/well' and means they find the actions guilty, but will render it right by bringing them down/removing them, and also that when they offered these horses to the sun-god they thought they were doing good. Cp: nedan-meleḥ, neidan-meleḥ, nedhan-meleḥ, neidhan-meleḥ (2Kgs.23:12)

Pharaoh-nechoh; par'ō, par'ōh nĕḵōh nĕḵô; Pharaoh still holds meanings of فَرعو ، فَرعوه '(to) separate' as between people arguing or fighting; '(to)branch', '(to)divide' 'to separate'; and فَرئو ، فَرئوه 'they fled/they fled him/fled from him'. Nechoh: نَكوه ، نيكوه ، نَكُ ، نيكُ 'wounded him' 'wound' and can mean a physical wound or wounds as in slight/insult, in this instance it means the physical wounding, 'fucked him/fuck him/had sex with him' and this is the usual punishment in the Biblical stories of enemy kings/princes or their sons after being captured in a battle. Cp: phar'oo, phar'ooh, phar-oo, phar-ooh; nekooh, neikooh, neko, neiko. (2Kgs.23:29-30) This is the character whom Josiah tries to prevent passing forward, but is killed by. **Megiddo** is used for its meaning of 'killed' 'squeezed/rough-handled to death' as in Josh.12. (2Kgs.23:29-30)

Jehoahaz; yĕhô'āḥāz; is a different character but with the exact same name, with the same meanings as used earlier in 2Kgs.13:1-9: يَهُ/ييهُ جَه/جيهُ ئآخاذ 'he who/which one-took(a lot)' 'came he/came to him-took (a lot)'; يَهُ/ييهُ جَه/جيهُ ئآخاز 'he who/which one-swore at/insulted/embarrassed/disgraced' 'came he/came to him-swore/insulted/embarrassed/disgraced'. (2Kgs.23:30-32)

His mother is Hamutal; ḥămûṭal; هَمُتَل ، هيمُتَل 'here is-the carried by hand' 'here is the basket' 'here is-died the' 'he will die the' and refers to Jehoahaz being put in bands and carried away to Egypt where he dies. Cp: hamutal, haimutal. She is the daughter of Jeremiah; yirmĕyâ; yirmĕyāhû; يِرمي يه ، يِرمي ياهُ 'he throws-he/him' 'they throw him'; يِرمييه ، يِرمياهُ 'throws it/he throws it' (can also mean 'he kills-he/him' 'he/they kill him'). It refers to the demise of Jehoahaz who is thrown down from his throne as king and taken away to die in Egypt. Cp: yirmei-yah, yirmei-yaahu, yirmeiyah, yirmeiyaahu. Her father is from **Libnah** which still means 'for his son' as it is the mother given the names which depict the bad done by her son. (2Kgs.23:31)

Riblah still means 'return to it/him' and can have a negative meaning as in a wrong or bad a person has done will be returned on him by someone else (the same as 'comeuppance') 'come home to it/him' as it was in Numbers 34. It denotes both his 'just deserts' for being evil, and 'come home' as he is taken to Pharaoh's homeland. (2Kgs.23:33)

Eliakim's name is changed by the author and a character in the story from meaning 'the one who stands/the one who stands instead of' to Jehoiakim; yĕhôyāqîm; يَهُ/ييهُ ياقيم ، جَهُ/جيهُ ياقيم 'he who/which one-stands/the one who stands instead of' 'he who/which one-erects/with an erection/with erections' 'came who/came to him-stands/the one who stands instead of' 'came who/came to him-erects/with an erection/with erections'. It still has the same denotation as in 2Kgs.18:18 where Eliakim and others stood instead of the king Hezekiah answering Sennacherib's men, here it is Eliakim (a different character than 2Kgs.18:18) taking over his brother's place as king. He is approached and appointed by Pharaoh-nechoh to fulfil 'came who-the one who stands instead of'. Cp: yeho/yeiho yaaqeem, geho/geiho yaaqeem. (2Kgs.23:34)

Zebudah; zĕḇîḏâ; زَبيده ، زيبيده 'small clay bowl for drinking' 'buttered/covered/perfumed with ointment' and refers to her son taxing the people greatly so he can stay on good terms with Pharaoh; زَبيطه ، زيبيطه 'kicked him/it' and refers to going against god's ways and following the evil of his ancestors. Cp: zebeedah, zeibeedah, zebeeṭah, zeibeeṭah. She is daughter of Pedaiah; pĕḏāyâ, pĕḏāyāhû; بِدآيه ، بيدآيه ، بِدآياهُ ، بيدآياهُ 'took out-he/him' and refers to both Jehoahaz being taken away and Jehoiakim forwarded as king, it is also wordplay on 'with/by his payment (instead of imprisonment/death)' to avoid sharing the same fate as his brother which he collects by taxing the people; فِدآيه ، فيدآيه ، فِدآياهُ ، فيدآياهُ 'sacrifice-he/him' 'sacrificed for he/him' and refers to one brother taken away and so another could take his place. Cp: bedaa-yah, beidaa-yah, bedaa-yaahu, beidaa-yaahu, phedaa-yah, pheidaa-yah, phedaa-yaahu, pheidaa-yaahu. She is from Rumah; rûmâ; رُمه 'thrown' 'killed' 'rotten' 'saw water' 'strewn around' and is the word used to show how things will be thrown/demolished or character (usually the son) who will be killed or dies. Cp: rumah. (2Kgs.23:36)

Nebuchadnezzar; nĕḇûḵaḏne'ṣṣar; نَبُ قَد نِذَّر 'prophet/news-had already-warned' 'prophet/news-had already-vowed/set aside' and although the narration in this part of the story has it as Manasseh's fault, it was prophesied in Hezekiah's story by Isaiah (2Kgs.20) and was promised as punishment from god because Hezekiah showed the Babylonian visitors all his treasures and possessions, for which God promised punishment of everything he possesses, including his children will be carried away as captives into Babylon. Cp: nebu-qad-nevvar. (2Kgs.24)

Jehoiachin; yĕhôyākîn; جِهُ/جيهُ ياَقين 'came him/to him-what was certain/what was prophesied as certain'; يَهُ/ييهُ ياَقين 'he who/which one-what was certain/what was prophesied as certain' and he and everyone related from family to the people suffer the consequence of what was prophesied when the Babylonian king arrives and they are taken away as servants to the Babylonian king. The word can also mean 'came him/ came to him/he who/which one-sits/stands perky/straight' and other meanings, but only the first meaning is meant and used in this part of the story. Cp: gehoyaaqeen, geihoyaaqeen, yehoyaaqeen, yeihoyaaqeen. (2Kgs.24:6-16)

Nehushta; nĕḥuštā'; نَهوشتآء ، نيهوشتآء 'bite/bit chunks out of' 'mauls/mauled'; نَخوشتآء ، نيخوشتآء 'makes/made holes in' 'crumbles/crumbled/poked holes in'; نَحوستآء ، نيحوستآء 'brought/brings bad luck upon' and the character has been named this word as her son will receive the consequences of his ancestors' sins which includes being dispossessed of all they own. Cp: nehushtaa, neihushtaa, nekhushtaa, neikhushtaa, neḥustaa, neiḥustaa. Elnathan; 'elnāṯān; ئَلناثآن 'the doubled/folded' 'the femaled'; ئَلنادآن 'the guilted' 'the bowed/lowered/bent' 'the called/the two calling out' (refers to two people); ئَلناضآن 'the suspected/the assumed' (and refers to two people); ئَلناطآن 'the-clangers/making clanging or tinning noise'. This also reflects the ancestors' guilt of which punishment is enacted upon Jehoiachin and everyone around him; 'the femaled' relays and reminds that it was prophesied by Isaiah to Hezekiah that their sons will become eunuchs when taken away; it is 'the doubled' because he and the people are paying for Hezekiah and Manasseh's sins. Cp: elnaafaan, elnaadaan, elnaadhaan, elnaaṭaan. (2Kgs.24:6-16)

Mattaniah; mattanyâ; مَتَّن يه 'died twice he/him'; مَثّنيه 'what twice/why twice' and again is a wink between authors or later editors and a pun as they see the repeat story of the recent characters of Eliakim/ Jehoiakim who a foreign king puts in the place of his deposed brother Jehoahaz and leads away into captivity abroad, but this time by making the Mattaniah/Zedekiah character the brother of Jehoahaz whose stories are similar so they give them the same mother and make them brothers. It may very well be the original authors just gave this character the same mother-name (Hamutal Jeremiah from Libnah) as Jehoahaz's for its meanings while making him the brother of the deposed Jehoiachin, and later editors corrected this contradiction by making him brother to Jehoahaz, i.e. Jehoiachin's uncle. It is interesting that what is used as the name the foreign king changes is 'Zedekiah/'deceived you-him/he' because this character-name was introduced earlier as a prophet who misleads, and if the story of 1Kgs.22:11-28 is correctly read you can see that either the original authors or later editors saved an inconsistency which the original story shows that God's prophets can prophesy wrong or outright lie, the author/editor saves this by introducing a 'lying spirit' and a priest/prophet is named Zedekiah/'deceived you-him/he'. The stories are no longer in their original forms, but editors at later times attempting to correct the inconsistencies. Cp: mattanyah, maffanyah. (2Kgs.24:17-20)

Nebusar-adan; Heb. nĕḇûzar'ăḏān; نَبُ زَر ئيضآن 'prophesy/prophesied news-visited also' and refers to the second warning prophesied as punishment during Manasseh's story. Note: the first wave of punishment of kings and their children being taken away was the first punishment prophesied by Isaiah in Hezekiah's story, and it is enacted in Jehoahaz being taken away into captivity to Egypt, then Jehoiachin and his mother, wives and all the people being taken away into captivity in Babylon. The second wave of punishment which was prophesied 'And the Lord spake by his servants the prophets, saying…' (2kgs.21) for Manasseh's sins was total destruction, a complete wiping out of Jerusalem and Judah, and this is enacted by introducing the character Nebusar-adan who destroys even the houses, not just God's and the king's, but every notable house and takes away the rest of the people as the authors of the earlier part of the story have Nebuchadnezzar only take away the 'elite' while making a point in the narration 'none remained, save the poorest sort of people of the land.' Which is remedied by a lower sort of enemy subordinate to the king Nebuchadnezzar picking them up later and again only leaving behind words to the effect 'the poorest sort of people'. There is a reason they have this character do such a thorough job, and it is the same reason of most of the stories of 2 Kings which will be explained later in this book. Cp: nebu-zar-aidhaan. (2Kgs.25)

Seraiah; śĕrāyâ; still holds its earlier meanings of 'told secrets-him/he' 'left early in the dark-him/he' 'bundled them/it-he him'; Zephaniah; ṣĕpanyâ, ṣĕpanyāhû; زَفَن يه ، زيفَن يه ، زَفَن ياَهُ ، زيفَن ياَهُ 'escorted-him/he' 'led in a procession-him/he'; صَفَن يه ، صيفَن يه ، صَفَن ياَهُ ، صيفَن ياَهُ 'cleaned/cleared/purified-him/he' and both these characters have been given names denoting how they were escorted/led away in a procession to Babylon then killed, the way the earlier stories have 'predicted' how everyone will be cleared out of the land as punishment, their escorting and killing reflects the word used to name them. Cp: zephanyah, zeiphanyah, zephanyaahu, zeiphanyaahu, ssephanyah, sseiphanyah, ssephanyaahu, sseiphanyaahu. (2Kgs.25:18-21)

Gedaliah; gĕḏalyâ, gĕḏalyāhû; جَدَل يه ، جيدَل يه ، جَدَل ياَهُ ، جيدَل ياَهُ 'threw/killed-him/he' and refers to him being assassinated. Cp: gedalyah, geidalyah, gedalyaahu, geidalyaahu. He is the son of **Ahikam** which still means 'my brother stood' as in 'stood up' or mean 'protected/stood up for' or 'got up' and did what was being asked to be done, 'wisdom' 'sayings' 'law/knowledge of law' 'rule' as he is made 'ruler' over the remaining people. He too is son of **Shaphan** which still means 'they saw'. Note that earlier in 2Kings.22 the words Ahikam and Shaphan are used for more than one character where there is a role in the story involving people and the characters of the same names seeing something and also something involved with ruling and law. (2Kgs.25:22-25)

Mizpah is used for its meaning of 'slaughter' and Gedaliah's assassination follows. (2Kgs.25:23-25)

Ishmael still means 'he/she listens to-the' as they arrive when they 'heard that the king of Babylon had made Gedaliah governor…'. He is son of Nethaniah; nĕṯanyâ, nĕṯanyāhû; ; نَثَن يه ، نَيثَن يه ، نَثَن ياَهُ ، نيثَن ياَهُ 'we double/fold-he/him' 'we female/feminise-he/him'; نَدَن يه ، نَيدَن يه ، نَدَن ياَهُ ، نيدَن ياَهُ 'we guilt-he/him' 'we lower/bow/bend-he/him'; نَظَن يه ، نَيضَن يه ، نَضَن ياَهُ ، نيظَن ياَهُ 'we think/suspect-he/him'; نَطَن يه ، نَيطَن يه ، نَطَن ياَهُ ، نيطَن ياَهُ 'we clang-he/him' 'make a tinning or clanging noise-he/him'. Used for its meaning of 'finding him guilty' and refers to both Gedaliah being guilty serving a Babylonian king, and Ishmael and his colleagues guilty for assassinating Gedaliah. Cp: nefan-yah, neifan-yah, nefan-yaahu, neifan-yaahu, nedan-yah, neidan-yah, nedan-yaahu, neidan-yaahu, nedhan-yah, neidhan-yah, nedhan-yaahu, neidhan-yaahu, neṭan-yah, neiṭan-yah, neṭan-yaahu, neiṭan-yaahu. (2Kgs.25:23-25)

Johanan; yôḥānān; يُهاَناَن 'they are humiliating/they are being humiliated' 'they are being satisfied/given (or giving) plenty'; جُهاَناَن 'came-both humiliated' 'came-both satisfied/given (or giving) plenty'; يُخاَناَن ، جُخاَناَن 'they are being soaked/are soaked' 'they are being betrayed' 'came-both betrayed/treasonous'. The meanings as in two or more people are being humiliated or are treasonous or will be betrayed. This character is involved in the story where Gedaliah will be killed and people have to flee for their lives and live in exile. It refers to Gedaliah's treason serving under a Babylonian king, and Ishmael and others betrayal of Gedaliah in killing him. Cp: yohaanaan, gohaanaan, yokhaanaan, gokhaanaan. He is the son of Careah; qārēaḥ; كاَريَه 'hated him' 'hired him'; قاَريَه 'read him' 'made him stay/be still/cease' 'confessed to him' and it may be that he confesses to Gedaliah of the assassination plans against him. Cp: kaareyah, qaareyah. (2Kgs.25:23)

Seraiah for its meanings of 'told secrets-him/he' 'left early in the dark-him/he' as they come to Gedaliah and a secret is kept about the assassination. Tanhumeth; tanḥumeṯ; تَنهومَت 'sighed loudly/puffed/a sighing/puffing' to show something is bothering the person, 'winded/struck and winded' 'punctured and wind escaping' 'you warned-died' and may refer to a story where this character was supposed to warn Gedaliah but he still dies. Cp: tanhumet. He is a **Netophathite** which still means 'plucks pubic hair' 'of plucking pubic hair' 'leaps' 'of leaping' 'we spit on' 'of spitting on' latter two meanings as a gesture of disrespect or hatred towards what is being spat at/towards; 'of dripping' 'is dripping'; 'cleans' 'of cleaning' 'completely' as in 2Sam.23—for its meanings they show disrespect towards Gedaliah for his role, which leads to his death. (2Kgs.25:23)

Jaazaniah; ya'ăzanyâ; ya'ăzanyāhû; يَئزَن يه ، يَئيزَن يه ، يَئزَن ياَهُ ، يَئيزَن ياَهُ 'you the fornicator-he/him'; جَئزَن يه ، جَئيزَن يه ، جَئزَن ياَهُ ، جَئيزَن ياَهُ 'came the fornicator-he/him' 'gave him his just deserts/rewarded-he/him' and refers to the character Gedaliah, or another character such as Gedaliah, being a bad character and receiving retribution, 'gave reward-he/him'; يَئذَن يه ، يَئيذَن يه ، يَئذَن ياَهُ ، يَئيذَن ياَهُ 'calls out to gather/assemble/pray-he/him' 'agrees/allows-he/him' Cp: ya-azan-yah, ya-aizan-yah, ya-azan-yaahu, ya-aizan-yaahu, ga-azan-yah, ga-aizan-yah, ga-azan-yaahu, ga-aizan-yaahu; ya-avan-yah, ya-aivan-yah, ya-avan-yaahu, ya-aivan-yaahu. And he is son of a **Maachathite** which still means 'with you is her/she is with you' 'I have one like her/it'. (2Kgs.25:23)

Ishmael 'he/she listens to-the' son of **Elishama** and still means 'he who/the one who-heard' 'he who/the one who-made other hear' and what it means in this form is he exposed or insulted another person and allowed other people to hear (so the recipient of the accusations/insults feels more ashamed) and refers to both Gedaliah and the character(s) who kill him. Although they have the same forename and surname, this Ishmael is meant to be a different character than the Ishmael son of Nethaniah in verse 23. The reason this character has been 'doubled' is reflected in the name in verse 23 and again in verse 25 for the meaning 'Nethaniah' as in 'doubled' and his name is reflected in the first character came because he 'heard' Gedaliah became governor and his surname reflected because they make two different characters with the same first and surname arrive at different times to the same place, and also the second character name is doubled in the meaning of 'hearing' in both forename and surname (Ishmael and Elishama). (2Kgs.25:25)

Evil-merodach; 'ĕwîl mĕrōd̲ak̲; ئَويل/ئيويل ميروضَك 'first-nursed you' 'gave accommodation the/stayed the-nursed you'; ئَويل/ئيويَل ميرودَك 'first-returned you/won't return you' as in will not allow him to return to his country, or will not return him to prison, 'first-returned you/won't return you' 'first-return/reward/retribution' as in you will be forced to suffer for what you did (just deserts), 'stayed the/accommodated the-returned you/won't return you'. All meanings are in play: after a long imprisonment Jehoiachin is first treated well by this character, he sets him up a throne and has him seated at the king's meals. And although he treats him well, he is still a captive. Cp: e-weel/eiweel-meiroodhak, e-weel/eiweel-meiroodak. (2Kgs.25:27-30)

Chronicles

Most of the names in 1 Chronicles are lists of themes which have already been mentioned in Genesis, Numbers, Deuteronomy, Joshua and Judges. The author/editors attempt to do two things: to sort out and streamline the genealogy of characters (unsuccessfully); and to use place-names given to areas in the stories, which are now given to characters so the story can reflect the place was named after a person. Occasionally, they have used as names in Chronicles words which have a similar meaning to that which it had in the earlier books or variants of the words which also have same/similar meanings.

Enosh (1Chr.1:1) is Enos (Gen.)

Kenan; qênān; could be كَينآن 'gathering cain/eating cain' 'sheltered from rain'; قَينآن 'sat up straight/positioned standing/sitting up or straight up' 'made perky' 'topped up (with water/drink)' 'estimated measurements/eyeballed measurements'. Equivalent to Cainan (Gen.5:9). Cp: keynaan, qeynaan. (1Chr.1:2)

Henoch (1Chr.1:3) is Enoch (Gen)

Alian; ʿalyān; عَليآن 'he is above/higher' 'went higher' 'built/building another level(in house)' 'rose in status' 'became stronger, better, etc.'. It is the corresponding and similar name to Alvan 'higher/made higher' (Gen.36:23). Cp: 'alyaan (1Chr.1:40)

Shephi; šěpî; شيفي ، شِفي 'he healed' 'of seeing' 'of gloating'; سيفي ، سِفي 'went numb' 'sipped' 'of sipping' 'of pouring gently/pouring gentle spurts of water' 'carried gently'. Corresponds to Shepho (Gen.36:23). Cp: shephee, sheiphee, sephee, seiphee. (1Chr.1:40)

Jakan; yaʿăqān; يَعقآن/يَعيقآن 'disobedient/he is disobedient' 'hardened heart/he has hardened heart' 'is too salty' 'braying like donkeys' 'delayed/he is delaying' and corresponds to Akan (Gen.36:27) and Bene-jaakan (Num.33.31) with the same meanings in different forms. Cp: ya'aqaan, ya'aiqaan. (1Chr.1:42)

Calcol is the same as Chalcol in (1Kgs.4:31). In 1 Kings.4:31, Chalcol (Calcol), Heman and Darda are sons of Mahol, and Ethan is an Ezrahite; in 1 Chronicles this has been rearranged to make Ethan, Calcol, Heman and Dara (Darda) brothers as the sons of Zerah (Zarah), grandchildren to Judah. (1Chr.2:6)

Dara; dāraʿ; دارء ، دآرء 'he knows' 'he made known' 'went around/circled/spun' and corresponds to Darda 'made known' 'knows/of knowledge' in (1Kgs.4:31). Cp: daara. (1Chr.2:6)

Achar 'he ruined/spoiled' is the same meaning as Achor 'ruined/spoiled' the name given to the place where the character named Achan (Josh.7) who ruins the people's fate and position with God is killed for his transgression. The variant (Achar) of the place-name (Achor) (Josh.7:26) has been used to replace the original character name Achan. Cp: 'aqar. (1Chr.2:7)

Jerahmeel 'he sees-takes/carries' 'came-saw-takes/carries' 'ran-takes/carries' and refers to someone coming, seeing and taking something or someone; 'he has mercy on the' 'came-has mercy on the'. And both meanings were present when this word-name first appeared as a place name in 1Sam.27:8-10, where it reflected David carrying away the possessions of people he had massacred, and showed no mercy towards them, but towards himself, saving himself by leaving no one alive just in case they tell on him. In 1 Chronicles it becomes a person's name. (1Chr.2:9)

Chelubai; kělûḇāy; كيلُبآي ، كِلُبآي 'chased like dogs' (as in hounded); غيلُبآي ، غِلُبآي 'was/were unable to' 'gave up' (as in was unable to open or do something or was frustrated and stopped trying)' 'felt frustration' 'was/were frustrated' 'was/were defeated'. It is a variant of the name Caleb, but Caleb from (Num.13:6,30) is the son of Jephunneh whereas Chelubai and Caleb (1Chr.2:18) are different characters as sons of Hezron; خيلُباي ، خَلُباي 'mud' 'covered in mud/activities involving mud'. Cp: kelubaay, keilubaay, ghelubaay, gheilubaay, khelubaay, kheilubaay. (1Chr.2:9)

Salma; śalmāʾ; سَلماء 'asked what?' 'of questions' 'water leaked/flowed' 'survived' 'entertained/distracted/comforted' 'survived' 'whole/intact' 'greeted' 'mild and peaceful nature'; صَلماء 'arrived/reached-water' 'connected-what' 'apologised-what/who'. It is a variant of the word Salmon 'asked' 'of questions' in Ruth.4:20-21. Both words are variants of the compound words Solomon/Saul. (1Kgs.3:5-13; 8). Cp: salmaa, ssalmaa. (1Chr.2:11)

Shimma is the same word and character as **Shammah** in (Gen.36:13; 1Sam.16) with the same meanings of 'smelled him/it' or a powdered tobacco (similar to snuff) 'named him/it' 'poisoned him/it' 'blocked him/it'. (1Chr.2:13)

Raddai; radday; رَدَّي 'rejected/returned him/her/it' '(he/she) responded' 'return visit(where newly-wed couple visit bride's parents)', also a response in a song or poem said/sung by a second person. This word has been given as a character name here for David's brother to keep in line with the story in 1Sam.16 that all David's brothers were rejected by God, except for David. Cp: radday. (1Chr.2:14)

Ozem; 'ōṣem; نُوزِم 'had a crisis/big problem' 'condition of unable to urinate, defecate or pass wind'; نُوصِم 'was blocked' 'was deaf' 'made to fast'; عوزِم 'was invited for a meal'; عوصِم 'hands were tied (around wrists)' 'was protected' 'defied them'. Cp: oozem, oo<u>ss</u>em, 'oozem, 'oo<u>ss</u>em. (1Chr.2:15)

Jerioth; yĕrî'ôṯ; جِريعُت ، جيريعُت 'she sipped' 'she was made to sip' and is a name of a male character who fathered children brought up as Caleb's children, i.e. the man who Azubah, Caleb's wife, had an affair and children with while married to Caleb. **Azubah** means: 'young woman ready for marriage' 'single woman', 'disobeyed with/by her' 'a twinged muscle/nerve' 'a bundle/bundle it' 'a bad mood/of bad mood' 'made askew with it/her', and 'sweet' 'tortured/bothered' (note: where a female relative has an illicit relationship a similar meaning for 'Israel/twisted muscle-the' is used to denote the wrong). Jerioth 'she sipped' refers to the bitter water test narrated in Num.5:12-31, and explained earlier in this book, where a woman is made to sip from water with dirt in it, and if her stomach swells and thigh 'rots' she is found guilty of adultery, which is why the Caleb in this story is son of **Hezron** (not Jephunneh) which means 'they are thinned/ skinny' and refers to the woman's 'thigh rotting' if she is guilty when she drinks the bitter water. Which is why the character who fathered some of Azubah and Caleb's children is named 'she sipped' and this Caleb character is son of 'they are thinned'. It is also why instead of the usual narration of a male character 'begat' sons with or without mention of the mother they issued from, it is instead narrated as 'And Caleb the son of Hezron begat *children* of Azubah *his* wife, and of Jerioth:' and the sons are attributed to Azubah instead of Caleb 'her sons *are* these: Jesher, and Shobab, and Ardon.' And usually the Biblical authors state male characters marry multiple wives without explaining if it is during or after the first-wife's life or death, but in this story they make a point showing Azubah was killed for her sin, the word-name given to her lover and patronym to her husband indicate she failed the bitter water test 'And when Azubah was dead, Caleb took unto him Ephrath, which bare him Hur.' It is possible that this was an original idea set down as a theme (as most names in lists are made into stories later in the Bible) which was meant to be elaborated upon later, whether such a story existed in more detail—we will never know, but this story has been made clear by the authors and in the method of the original Biblical authors' style. Cp: geree'ot, geiree'ot. (1Chr.2:18-19)

Jesher; yēšer, yešer; حَشَر ، حيشَر 'starved' 'made greedy' 'crowded/crammed/steered into corner'; it is interesting because when Absalom had sex with David's wives, they were crammed into their rooms and never allowed to leave until death; عَشَر ، عيشَر 'pregnant cow/with calf' 'lived among'; حَسَر ، حيسَر 'made thin/skinny' (as in body). Cp: ḥey<u>sh</u>er, ḥe<u>sh</u>er, 'ey<u>sh</u>er, 'e<u>sh</u>er, ḥeyser, ḥeser. (1Chr.2:18)

Ardon; 'ardôn; نَردُن 'come home' 'I come home' 'reduced to/caused great injustice, trouble or harm to'; عَردُن 'wobble head' 'bend neck' 'disgrace-bow with shame'. Cp: ardon, 'ardon. (1Chr.2:18)

Caleb-ephratah combines both words meanings and can have many combinations, I will use just a few combinations as an example: 'to overcome/be victor-tears(as in rips)' 'partings-the sweet/the sweet water' 'flips/turns-over- cleanser of guts (noun of occupation of man who cleans slaughtered animals intestines)' and any other combination, but it would depend on what the author intended to have the story as (see Caleb, Ephratah). (1Chr.2:24)

Bunah; bûnâ; بُنه 'his children' 'brought up children' 'building' 'his building' 'coffee-bean' (the latter used to describe a pretty daughter). Cp: bunah. (1Chr.2:25)

Oren; 'ōren; عورِن 'hurt/wounded' 'insulted' 'made naked' 'exposed his private parts'; نُورِن 'was showed' 'showed them' (literal as 'see' or as threat/punishment) 'taught them'; غورِن 'went underground(water)' 'funnelled down' 'saved/came to help' 'argued/told off'. Cp: 'ooren, ooren, <u>gh</u>ooren. (1Chr.2:25)

Atarah; 'ăṭārâ; عَطآره ، عيطآره 'they twist(ed)/press(ed) out' 'they are perfumed' 'they perfume'; نَطآره ، نيطآره 'he will/he has sent him/her/it away' 'he will/he has banished (him/her/it)' it means not only to throw out but in such a fashion the subject is 'flying or been sent flying' and not to come back, it is equivalent to the phrase 'sent them packing'. Cp: 'aṭaarah, 'aiṭaarah, aṭaarah, aiṭaarah. (1Chr.2:26)

Maaz; maʿaṣ; مَعَز 'goats' 'cherished'; مَعَص 'disobedience/stubbornness/transgressions' 'is stuck/askew/crookedness' 'with sticks'. Cp: ma'az, ma'ass. (1Chr.2:27)

Eker; ʿēqer; عيقَر 'ruined/spoiled a lot' 'laps/in lap' and is similar to Achor/Achar. Cp: 'eyqer. (1Chr.2:27)

Shammai; šammay; شَمَّي 'my scent' 'smell'; سَمَّي 'named/name' 'tell samaaya(naming) story/riddle' 'eye of needle' 'poisoned/poison'. Cp: shammay, sammay. (1Chr.2:28)

Jada; yāḏāʿ; ياداع 'he is calling' 'you, who is calling' 'he is cursing (a negative prayer)' 'he claims' 'he makes false claim' 'he leaves behind' 'he puts away' 'he deposits'; عاداء 'returned/returns' 'enemies/created enmity/transgressed against' 'infected' 'counted'; ياضاع 'he misleads' 'you, who is misguided' 'he gets lost/misplaces' 'he is lost' 'you who is lost' 'he sets/places'; ياداء 'with his hands' 'his hands'; جاداع 'came-called/cursed/claimed' 'broke off/snapped off/uprooted'. Cp: yaadaa', 'aadaa, yaadhaa', yaadaa, gaadaa'. (1Chr.2:28)

Abishur; 'ăḇîšûr; نَبي/نيبي شُر 'rejected-discussion/advice' 'father-discussion/advice' 'rejected/refused-evil' 'father-evil'; نَبيشُر 'omen of good news' 'first to deliver good news' 'expect good news'; عَبي/عيبي شُر 'fill/pack-discussion/advice' 'fill/pack-evil' 'shame/disgrace-discussion/advice' 'shame/disgrace-evil'. Cp: abee/aibee-shur, abeeshur, 'abee/'aibee-shur. (1Chr.2:29)

Ahban; 'aḥbān; نَحبان 'crawling' (e.g. when a baby learns to crawl before walking) 'loved' 'love each other'; نَخبان 'hidden' 'two (or more) hid' 'became damp and mouldy' 'smells musty/mouldy'; نَهبان 'gave/I gave' 'they gave' 'they were given'. Cp: aḥbaan, akhbaan, ahbaan. (1Chr.2:29)

Molid; môlîḏ; مُليد 'born' 'new-born'; مُليط 'flat stones' 'flattened' 'sides stuck together' 'stuck together/against each other' 'squeezed together/sagged/pressed and sagged'. Cp: moleed, moleeṭ. (1Chr.2:29)

Seled; seleḏ; سَلِد/شَلِد 'will give birth'; صَلِد 'mud-packed land (barren)' because too much rain has packed the soil into mud like a slab, 'barren land' because so much drought the land becomes like a hard slab. All meanings are related to fertility or lack of it and he is described as dying without having children. Cp: seled, sheled, sseled. (1Chr.2:30)

Appaim; 'appayim; نَبَّي هم/ام 'refused-them/the' 'their father-them/the'; عَفّي هم/ام 'boiled-them/the' 'went off-them/the' (such as animal going off food); عَبَّي هم/ام 'pack/fill-them/the'. Cp: abbay-hum/um, 'aphay-hum/um, 'abbay-hum/um. (1Chr.2:30)

Ishi; yišʿî; يِشئي 'he wants'; هِشئي 'crawls' 'crawls like insects' (also when the skin feels as if an insect is crawling over it (but it is not)); جِشئي 'picked up handfuls/too much' 'made a stink'; عِشئي 'fed supper' 'ate supper' 'took animals to graze in afternoon' 'went blind in the evening' (the latter happens to some pregnant women who go blind from the afternoon until morning during pregnancy); حِشئي 'cut grass' 'stuffed' 'hid something by stuffing it quickly somewhere'. Cp: yish-ee, hish-ee, gish-ee, 'ish-ee, ḥish-ee. (1Chr.2:31)

Sheshan; šēšān; شيشان 'something important' 'things and important things' 'many things and wonderful things' 'puzzling/serious matters'; شيسان 'wanted something-done' 'something-bad/offensive' 'something did(did something)'; سيشان 'bad/offensive matter/thing' 'did-a matter'; سيسان 'bad/offensive-bad/offense' 'did something bad/offensive' 'did something'. Cp: sheyshaan, sheysaan, seyshaan, seysaan. It has many variants in the Biblical stories preceding its mention in this instance. (1Chr.2:31)

Ahlai; 'aḥlay; نَهلَي 'my family' 'she is here/is she here' 'sheds(hair/fur/leaves)'; نَحلَي 'circumcise' 'purify/cleanse/make edible/make touchable' 'declare purified/permissible' 'shed' 'undress' 'become sweeter' 'prettier' 'replace'; نَخلَي 'empty/pour out' 'allow' 'leave/part' 'leave(some)' 'brother to me/brother for me'. Cp: ahlay, aḥlay, akhlay. (1Chr.2:31)

Zaza; zāzāʾ; ذاذاع 'announced all over' 'spoke everywhere'; زازاء 'sent away in droves' 'fiercely drove away'; صاصاع 'immoral person who goes everywhere' 'goes spreading immorality'; ساساع 'wandered (aimlessly) all over/everywhere'. Cp: vaavaa', zaazaa, ssaassaa', saasaa'. (1Chr.2:33)

Jarha; yarḥāʿ; يَرخاء 'becomes loose' 'loosens' 'lenient' 'becomes lenient' and can be neutral but also negative as in 'loose' not bringing up children properly or becoming immoral; يَرحاء 'makes restful/indulgent' 'rests' 'becomes aired/fans'; يَركاع 'he bows'; جَرحاء 'wounded' 'insulted' 'they wounded/insulted'. Cp: yarkhaa, yarḥaa, yarkaa', garḥaa. (1Chr.2:34)

Attai; ʿattay; عَطّي 'gave'; and he is the son resulting from Sheshan giving his daughter to his slave Jarha. Cp: 'aṭṭay. (1Chr.2:36)

Zabad; zābāḏ; زآباد 'clay bowls/drinking vessels' 'buttered/covered' 'perfumed with ointment'; زآباط 'kicked (a lot)'; شآباط 'latticed/latticed with rope' 'rope/twine' 'swiped/whipped with rope (or with rope-like object)'; ضآباط 'strong/became strong' 'tightened' 'publicly disciplined'; شآباد 'I will take out/bring out/come out'. Cp: zaabaad, zaabaaṭ, shaabaaṭ, dhaabaaṭ, shaabaad. (1Chr.2:36)

Ephlal; 'eplāl; بِبلآل 'soaked/soak' 'with the nights/of the nights/in the nights'; بِفلآل 'jasmines' 'wearing jasmines' 'picking nits' 'going through thoroughly/picking through'. Cp: ephlaal, eblaal. (1Chr.2:37)

Eleasah; 'el'āśâ; بِلعآصه/ا 'the stick' 'the disobedience/disobedient' 'the person disobedient' 'the difficult' 'the askew/crooked' 'the stuck'; بِلعآشه/ا 'the supper' 'the person eating/feeding supper' 'the evening/night' 'the blind/partially blind' 'the lived/survived'. Cp: el'aassah(ssa), el'aashah(sha). (1Chr.2:39)

Sisamai; sismāy; صِصمآي 'blocked/block' 'cover your mouth(shut up)' 'cover your nose(from bad smell or smoke)'. Cp: ssissmaay. (1Chr.2:40)

Jekamiah; yĕqamyâ; يِقَميه ، ييقَميه 'stands-he/him' 'gives him an erection' 'stinks so bad it suffocates' (and usually when something like this happens people say 'block your nose' 'samai' and he is son of Sisamai/blocked), 'he gets up/stands-he/him'; يِغميه ، ييغميه 'it suffocates' 'he suffocates-him/he' and is a word related to 'sisamai/blocked'; جِقميه ، جيقميه 'came-got up/stood-he/him' 'came-gave him an erection' 'came stank so bad it caused suffocation'; جِغميه ، جيغميه 'came-it suffocated' 'came-he suffocated-him/he'; حِكَم يه ، حيكَم يه 'ruled-he/him' 'knowledge-he/him' 'set as arbitrator-he/him'. Cp: yeqamyah, yeiqamyah, yeghamyah, yeighamyah; geqamyah, geiqamyah, geghamyah, geighamyah, hekamyah, heikamyah. (1Chr.2:41)

Raham; raḥam; رَحَم 'had mercy on/for' 'womb'; رَكَم 'piled on top of'. Cp: raḥam, rakam. (1Chr.2:44)

Jorkoam; yorqĕ'ām; يوركيئ آم 'props/leans against-the'; يورخيئ آم 'loosens-the' 'is lenient-the'; يورغيئ آم 'foams-the/makes foam-the'; يوركيع آم 'prostrates/bows-the'; يورجيع آم 'comes back-the' 'returns-the'; يورجيئآم 'they stone' 'they wait-the' 'they shake-the'. Cp: yoorkei-aam, yoorkhei-aam, yoorghei-aam, yoorkei'-aam, yoorgei'-aam, yoorgeiaam. (1Chr.2:44)

Moza; môṣā'; مُزآء 'squeezed' 'squeeze out of'; مُصآء 'suck'; مُشآء 'walking' 'goats/sheep' 'shepherding'; مُسآء 'evening' 'touched' 'possessed' 'caused/provoked problems' 'fought'. Cp: mozaa, mossaa, moshaa, mosaa. (1Chr.2:46)

Gazez; gāzēz; جآزيز 'green pastures' 'cut crops' 'reaping of stalks/crops'; قآزيز 'frying' 'frying scents' 'burning in pan smell'. Cp: gaazeyz, qaazeyz. (1Chr.2:46)

Jahdai; yāhdāy; يآهدآي 'he gives presents' 'he guides' 'they sing wedding song'; جآهدآي 'my utmost effort/my all' 'do your best effort' 'fatigued/tired/worked hard'. Cp: yaahdaay, gaahdaay. (1Chr.2:47)

Regem; regem; رَغَم 'forced' 'despite'; رَجَم 'stoned' 'piled stones upon/buried under stones'. Cp: reghem, regem. (1Chr.2:47)

Geshan; gêšān; جيشآن 'he took a lot/too many' 'they scooped up handfuls' 'two large groups of people' 'came-filtered impurities' 'came-flowed into/out of' 'came-fertile/sexually excited/ready to conceive' 'came-copulated' (latter two regarding goats and similar animals), 'came-important matter/significance'. Equivalent of 'Joshua' and 'Bashan'. Cp: geyshaan. (1Chr.2:47)

Pelet; peleṭ; فَلَت 'fell' (literally or morally) 'lewd/immoral'. Cp: phelet. (1Chr.2:47)

Shaaph; ša'ap̄; شَغَف 'type of small dry bush' (a small bush used as kindle), 'distracted'; شَئَف 'saw' 'toasted/dried' (on fire or in pan). Cp: shaghaph, sha-aph. (1Chr.2:47)

Sheber; šeḇer; شَبَر 'measure by span of fingers' (literally or figuratively to beat someone up); سَبَر 'fixed/made' 'settled(differences)' 'made it right'. Cp: sheber, seber. (1Chr.2:48)

Tirhanah; tirḥănâ; تِرهَنه ، تِرهينه 'leases it out/pawns it'; طِرحَنه/ا ، طِرحينه/ا 'laid it down' 'put it down' 'fed crop to cow in stable' 'collapsed' 'laid up ill in bed'; تِرخَنه ، تِرخينه 'she loosens it' 'you(fem) loosen it'. Cp: tirhanah, tirhainah, ṭirḥanah(na), ṭirḥainah(na), tirkhanah, tirkhainah. (1Chr.2:48)

Machbenah; makbēnâ; مَخبينه/ا 'our hiding place' 'hiding it/him/her' 'what did we hide' and is equivalent to Macphelah, 'it is damp/mouldy/musty'; مَقبينه/ا 'what is wrong with us now?/what is wrong now?' 'what is there in(side) it?'. Cp: makhbeynah(na), maqbeynah(na). (1Chr.2:49)

Hareph; ḥārēp; حآريف 'on the edge/ridge' 'rim/edge' 'lettered' 'changed letters'; حآريث 'frowning' 'frowning at'; خآريف 'demented/senile' 'making up events(from dementia); هآريث 'I will inherit'. Cp: ḥaareyph, ḥaareyf, khaareyph, haareyf. (1Chr.2:51)

Beth-gader; bêt-gāḏēr; بيت غادير 'it will become dark' 'he will be betrayed'; بيت قادير 'he will be able to do it' 'girl/daughter-can'; بيت جادير 'he will catch pox' 'he will wall'; بيت كادير 'it will sour/leaven'. Cp: beyt-ghaadeyr, beyt qaadeyr, beyt-gaadeyr, beyt kaadeyr. (1Chr.2:51)

Haroeh; hārō'eh; هاروئه 'drove away/chased away-it/him/her/them' 'handle of an axe (or any other tool)' 'wooden staff/rod', 'here is-sees/dreams' 'here/look-saw/dreamed' 'here-saw him/it' 'here-told story(ies)/dreamt' 'here-watered/quenched'; حاروئه 'making fire(s)/hot coals' 'moved to action-it/him/her/them'. Cp: haaroo-eh, ḥaaroo-eh. (1Chr.2:52)

Manahethites; mānaḥtî; مانحتي 'did not saw/file' 'we did not saw/file' 'you gave/granted'; مانهتي 'she did not prevent/prohibit/warn' 'we did not prevent/prohibit/warn'; مانحطي 'we do not rest/put down our loads' 'we do not leave any/we do not leave behind'. It is equivalent to Manahath in Gen.36:23. Cp: maanaḥtee, maanahtee, maanaḥṭee. (1Chr.2:54)

Puhites; pûṯî; بتي 'my daughter' 'cut it off(by pulling/tearing at it sharply)/tear' 'decide'. Cp: butee. (1Chr.2:53)

Shumathites; šumāṯî; شوماطي 'of whipping/hitting with a swiping motion' 'throwing with a swiping motion' 'elongated/elastic' 'of stretched shape/texture'; شوماتي 'of in a terrible state/mess' 'of gloating' 'of creating a scene/scandal'; صوماطي 'of wearing fabric/shawl on head' (a specific kind of shawl or way of wearing a head-shawl where it lies flat over the forehead); صوماتي 'of fasting' 'of blocking(things)'. Cp: shoomaaṭee, shoomaatee, ssoomaaṭee, ssoomaatee. (1Chr.2:53)

Mishraites; mišrā'î; مِشراعي 'of legal activities/understanding law' 'not a shepherd' 'does not show care towards'; مِسراعي 'very quick/of quickness/being fast'; مِصراعي 'of fits/convulsions' 'of wrestling' 'of throwing on the ground' 'wrestler'; مِزراعي 'of crops/stalks' 'pasture lands'. Cp: mishraa'ee, misraa'ee, missraa'ee, mizraa'ee. (1Chr.2:53)

Zareathites; ṣṣārĕ'āṯî; صّاريعاتي 'of fits(epilepsy)' 'of throwing onto ground' 'she threw him onto ground' 'she was thrown to ground'. Cp: ssaarei'aatee. (1Chr.2:53)

Eshtaulites; 'eštā'ulî; ئشتائولي 'cock-eyed' has defect where eyes are fixed permanently upwards or to one side, 'asymmetrical' 'tugged/pulled/longer at one side'. Cp: eshtaa-ulee. (1Chr.2:53)

Zorites; haṣṣor'î, ṣor'î; هَصُّرعي ، هَصّورعي ، صورعي 'here is the one with fits' 'here is the one that throws onto ground' 'of fits/is having fit' 'thrown to the ground', the word used for a person who has epileptic fits is the same word as being thrown down (gdl) and also thrown on the ground (ssr') due to the nature of the fits and how the affected person's body moves. Cp: hassor'ee, hassoor'ee, ssoor'ee. (1Chr.2:54)

Jabez; ya'bēṣ; يَعبيص 'jerks around/jumps around like an animal' (usually nervous) 'he removes dirt clumps from sheep' as ('bss/عبص) is the dirt balls which accumulate on sheep wool; يَعبيس 'he is frowning' 'he becomes grumpy' 'he looks grumpy'; خَبيص 'poked finger into anus' 'messed everything up by poking into everything' 'polluted by dipping fingers into'; جَبيس 'thick, cloying and drying' 'thick and dry'; يَبيس 'dried' 'stiffened'. Cp: ya'beyss, ya'beys, kha-beyss, ga-beys, ya-beys. (1Chr.2:55)

Tirathites; tir'āṯîm; ترئات هم/ام 'saw-them/the' 'dreamt-them/the' 'told the story/told them a story'; درعات هم/ام 'defended-them/the' 'fended them/the away' 'slut/loose woman-them/the'. Cp: tir-aat-hum/um, dir'aat-hum/um. (1Chr.2:55)

Shimeathites; šim'āṯîm; سِمعات هم/ام 'heard-them/the' 'listened to-them/the' 'obeyed-them/the' 'their/the reputation'; شِمئات هم/ام 'gloated over them/the' 'disgraced-them/the' 'mess/terrible/nasty-them/the' 'their/the scandal'; سِمئات هم/ام 'named-them/the' 'ill-them/the/their illness' 'poisoned-them/the'. Cp: sim'aat-hum/um, shim-aat-hum/um, sim-aat-hum/um. (1Chr.2:55)

Suchathites; śûkāṯîm; صُخاط هم/ام 'scratched a line-them/the' 'made lines/scrammed-them/the' (as in with a quick movement); شُخاط هم/ام 'scribbled-them/the' 'drew lines-them/the'; سُقاط هم/ام 'fallen-them/the' (literally or morally) 'sluts/immoral/lewd-them/the'; شُكات هم/ام 'they/the-are complainers' 'she complained against them/the' 'thorns-them/the' 'pricked by thorns-them/the'; سُكات هم/ام 'silent-them/the' 'silenced them/the'. Cp: ssukhaaṭ-hum/um, shukhaaṭ-hum/um, suqaaṭ-hum/um, shukaat-hum/um, sukaat-hum/um. (1Chr.2:55)

Daniel; dāni'ēl, dānîy'ēl'; دآن ئِل ، دآنيي ئِل 'bowed-the' 'he is bowed-is the' 'lowered/low-the' 'he is lowered/low-is the' 'facing the ground-the' 'he is facing the ground-is the' 'with face on ground-the' 'his face on ground-with the' 'guilted-the' 'he is guilted-is the' 'is lowly-the'. This is another example of Biblical authors, or later editors, changing the same character into a different word-name as suits whatever was in the author/editor's mind: he is presented here as the second son of David born in Hebron and mothered by 'Abigail the Carmelitess' whereas in 2Sam.3:3 the second son of David born to Abigail is 'Chileab' (only its meanings: 'say a disgrace' 'a tumbling rock' 'a tumbling sound' have a very loose connection to 'Daniel' in meaning). This change in name indicates the author/editor had a specific story in mind to make about 'Daniel' word-meaning or one existed which did not make it into the Biblical texts. Cp: daani-ill, daaneey-ill. (1Chr.3:1)

Nogah; nōgah; نوجَه 'survived/they survived' 'they are speaking/chatting' 'discussing privately/secretly/quietly' and is used to describe a baby making vocal sounds pre-dawn as if in a conversation (folklore has it they are chatting with angels). 'Elishua' (2Sam.5:15) is missing from this list of David's sons although they include 'Elishama' and 'Eliphelet' twice in the same consecutive verses as different sons. 'Elishua' meaning of 'he who/the one who cries out' is similar to the meaning in the context that 'Nogah' is the sound a baby makes when playing and kicking on a bed pre-dawn while people are sleeping, which the whole family can hear. Cp: noogah. (1Chr.3:7)

Abia; 'ăḇîyâ; نَبييه ، نُيبييه 'they rejected him/it' 'his father'; نُبييا 'they refused' 'my father' and is the same name given to Samuel's son and also to Jeroboam's son as it is directly related to the events they represent in their different stories. In 1Chr.3:10 it is given as the name of Rehoboam's son and Asa's father—which is either a mistake as his name in 1Kgs.14;15 was Abijam 'ăḇîyām; نُبيي آم 'rejected/refused-the' 'my father-the/father of the', and although it has similar meaning to 'Abia(h)' it is a different spelling and pronunciation, and it was also a completely different character in the same chapter as 'Abiah/Abia' was Jeroboam's son while Abijam was Rehoboam's. The Biblical authors/later editors do not seem that concerned, as in the end, they want to give fictional characters fictional names and to them (and also to the story) there is no big difference between the meaning of 'Abiah/Abia' and 'Abijam'—it would only pose an issue if it was intended as a historical document, which it is not. Cp: abee-yah/abeeyah, aibee-yah/aibeeyah, abeeya. (1Chr.3:10)

Jeconiah; yĕḵonyâ, yĕḵonyāhû; يَقون يه ، يَقون ياَهُ ، جَقون يه/ياَهُ 'he was certain-he/him' 'came-certain-he/him' 'head held up high/perky posture-he/him' 'estimated/topped up liquid-he/him' and is what the authors/editors decided to change 'Jehoiachin' to (which has the same meanings (2Kgs.24:6-16)). It allows more meanings to be attributed to it for different stories to be made out of the name. It could now be (in addition to the first meaning) يكون يه/ياَهُ 'he makes into peaked piles-he/him'; يَخون يه/ياَهُ 'he deceives-him/he' 'he soaks-him/he' 'he betrays-him/he' 'he becomes brother-him/he'; جَخون يه/ياَهُ 'came-betrayed-him/he' 'horrible/terrible-he/him' 'came soaked-him/he' 'came brother-him/he'. Cp: yeqoon-yah/yaahu, ge-qoon-yah/yaahu, yekoon-yah/yaahu, yekhoon-yah/yaahu, ge-khoon-yah/yaahu.

It is also an example of later editors misunderstanding or wanting to straighten out the earlier story where they seem to doubt whether 'Mattaniah/Zedekiah' was Jehoiachin's uncle or brother, so they make two characters of the same name (Zedekiah) for the list in 1Chr.3:15-16 where Zedekiah is a son of Josiah and also son of Jehoiakim and brother to Jeconiah/Jehoiachin (at 2Kgs.24:17, the author/editor makes it clear Mattaniah/Zedekiah is Jehoiachin's uncle). This is probably due to an original story had existed where Zedekiah was the brother of Jehoiachin/Jeconiah while still sharing the same mother/mother's word-names (Hamutal Jeremiah Libnah) to relay what happens in the stories: both Jehoahaz and Jehoiachin rule for only three months while their respective replacements (Jehoiakim/Eliakim and Zedekiah) both rule for eleven years; both their respective replacements get a name-change by the antagonist character king. More than anything it shows later editors going back into the stories to make changes and/or corrections. (1Chr.3:16)

Note: even in the completely different name given to Jehoahaz (Josiah's firstborn son (1Chr.3:15)) '**Johanan**' one of the meanings of which is 'they are humiliating/they are being humiliated' 'came-both humiliated' has at least one of '**Jehoahaz**' meanings 'he who/which one-swore at/insulted/embarrassed/disgraced' 'came he/came to him-swore/insulted/embarrassed/disgraced' as the similarity in the choice of words given as Johanan instead of Jehoahaz shows this author/editor had a story in mind where Johanan/Jehoahaz main feature was to be insulted or to insult others. (1Chr.3:15)

Salathiel; Salathiĕl, šĕ'altî'ēl, šaltî'ēl; سيئَلتي ئِل ، سَلتي ئِل 'questioned/asked-the' 'leaked-the' 'made flow-the' 'comforted/entertained/distracted-the'; شيئَلتي ئِل ، شَلتي ئِل 'took-the' 'carried-the'; صيئَلتي ئِل ، صَلتي ئِل 'arrived at-the' 'connected-the' 'you arrived at-the' 'you publicly apologised to-the'. It is equivalent/similar to one meaning of **Salchah** 'he reached/arrived you' literally as in arrived or reached, but also means to arrive with apology and show of respect (Deut.3:10), and **Selah** 'arrived' 'connected' (2Kgs.14:1-7). Cp: seialtee-ill, saltee-ill, sheialtee-ill, shaltee-ill, sseialtee-ill, ssaltee-ill. (1Chr.3:17)

Malchiram; malkîrām; مَلقي رآم 'thrown down-thrown/killed'; مَلقيرآم 'what is the snubbing/shortness'; مَلخي رآم 'covered in slimy substance-thrown/killed'; مَل خيرآم 'what is the good/fortune?' 'what is the torn holes/piercings?'; مَل كيرآم 'what is the generous/generosity?' 'well, bury the log in ashes'. Cp: malqee-raam, malqeeraam, mal<u>kh</u>ee-raam, mal-<u>kh</u>eeraam, mal-keeraam. (1Chr.3:18)

Shenazar; šen'assar; شَننَذَّر 'we will warn' 'we will vow/set aside'; شَننَسَّر 'we will-captivate' 'we will be captivated'; شَننَزَّر 'we will/I will tighten/be tightened/be put in tight position' 'we will/I will be visit/ pilgrimage'; شَنعَزَّر 'we will/I will make ugly/become ugly'. Cp: <u>sh</u>en-avvar, <u>sh</u>en-assar, <u>sh</u>en-azzar, <u>sh</u>en'azzar. (1Chr.3:18)

Jecamiah; same as Jekamiah above.

Hoshama; hôšāmā'; حُسآماء 'pitiful' 'they are pitiful' 'sad/they are sad'; حُشآماء 'they are modest/chaste'; خُشآماء 'they bit/are bitten/taken chunks out'; هُسآماع 'he heard' 'he eavesdropped' 'he let other people hear (as in insulted a person loudly so others could hear)'. Cp: ḥosaamaa, ḥo<u>sh</u>aamaa, <u>kh</u>o<u>sh</u>aamaa, hosaa-maa'. (1Chr.3:18)

Nedabiah; nĕdabyâ; نَدَب يه ، نيدَب يه 'wailed/mourned loudly-him/he' 'scarred-him/he'; نَضَب يه ، نيضَب يه 'protruding jaw/teeth-him/he'. Cp: nedabyah, neidabyah, ne<u>dh</u>abyah, nei<u>dh</u>abyah. (1Chr.3:18)

Zerubbabel; zĕrubbābel; ذَروبباَدِل ، ذيرو ببآدِل 'they procreated-in swapped/changed' 'they sowed-in swapped/changed' 'they left-in swapped' 'leave-I will swap/change'; زَرو ببآدِل ، زيرو ببآدِل 'they visited/ pilgrimaged-in swapped/changed' 'they tightened-in swapped/changed' 'they caused great disgrace/insult-in swapped/changed'. Cp: veru-b-baadel, veiru-b-baadel, zeru-b-baadel, zeiru-b-baadel. (1Chr.3:19)

Hananiah; ḥănanyâ, ḥănanyāhû; هَنعنيه/ياَهْ ، هينعنيه/ياَهْ 'we will direct words/speech at him' and it describes when a person is hinting at with a message/warning/insult directed at someone in particular within hearing range, even at close proximity, while actually talking directly to someone else—it is hinting/ delivering the message indirectly, 'we mean him' 'we will eye/inspect/look at him'; هَنغنيه/ياَهْ ، هينغنيه/ياَهْ 'we will make he/him independent/rich' 'we will make him no longer need(someone else's help/ dependence)' 'see, look/he-sang/hummed/made '<u>gh</u>n' noise(used in singing or reading religious books)-he/him'; حَنَن يه/ياَهْ ، حينَن يه/ياَهْ 'hums/humming sound-he/him' 'wears/applies henna-he/him' 'felt affection-he/him'; خَنَن يه/ياَهْ ، خينَن يه/ياَهْ 'betrays-he/him' 'soaks/soaks in-he/him' 'became brotherly-he/him'; هَنَن يه/ياَهْ ، هينَن يه/ياَهْ 'satisfaction to/satisfied-him/he' 'give plenty-he/him'. Similar to Hanani (1Kgs.16:1-7). Cp: han'nyah/yaahu, hain'nyah/yaahu, han<u>gh</u>nyah/yaahu, hain<u>gh</u>nyah/yaahu, ḥananyah/ yaahu, ḥainanyah/yaahu, <u>kh</u>ananyah/yaahu, <u>kh</u>ainanyah/yaahu, hananyah/yaahu, hainanyah/yaahu. (1Chr.3:19)

Hashubah; ḥăšubâ; حاَشوبه 'they got him/her/it involved' 'they stuffed him/her/it in' and indicates the person was brought into a problem for no reason at all 'is carrying on waist' 'tucked around the waist'; خاَشوبه 'timber/lumber/a wooden beam' 'they feared him/her/it' 'they created fear from him/her/it'; هشوبه 'they shooed him/her/it away' 'they swatted him/her/it away'. Cp: ḥaa<u>sh</u>ubah, <u>kh</u>aa<u>sh</u>ubah, haa<u>sh</u>ubah. (1Chr.3:20)

Ohel; 'ōhel; نُوهِل 'family' 'is he/it here' 'is there any' 'shed/fell off'; نُوحِل 'undressed' 'shed off' 'stayed in place' 'sweetened' 'purified/cleansed/declared purified/declared permissible' 'circumcised' 'replaced' 'beat until skin peeled off' 'deceived' 'deceiver/trickster'. Cp: oohel, ooḥel. (1Chr.3:20)

Berechiah; berekyâ, berekyāhû; بَرَك يه/ياَهْ 'knelt-he/him' 'made him kneel-he/him' 'made last/blessed-he/ him' 'underground water cisterns-he/him'; بَرَكيه/ياَهْ 'I will prop/lean it/him against'; بَرَخيه/ياَهْ 'I will let him/it loose' 'I will loosen him/it' 'I will let it go'; بَرق يه/ياَهْ 'is in a mood/sulking-him/he' 'was struck by lightning-he/him'. Cp: berek-yah/yaahu, berekyah/yaahu, bere<u>kh</u>yah/yaahu, beraq-yah/yaahu. (1Chr.3:20)

Hasadiah; ḥăsadyâ; حَسَد يه ، حيسَد يه 'envy-he/him' 'he envied' 'envy'; حَصَد يه ، حيصَد يه 'reaps/reaped-he/him'; هَصَديه 'I will block/prevent him' 'I will make it stuck'; هيصَديه 'he will block/prevent it/him' 'he will closed door(without locking it)' 'he will make it stuck' ; هَشَديه 'I will make emigrate/leave-him/he' 'I will tighten/wrap it around tight' 'I will make it/him severe' 'I will brace it/him'; هيشَديه 'he will make emigrate/leave-him/he' 'he will tighten/wrap it around tight' 'he will make it/him severe'. Cp: ḥasad-yah, ḥaisad-yah, ḥa<u>ss</u>ad-yah, ḥai<u>ss</u>ad-yah, ha-<u>ss</u>adyah, hai-<u>ss</u>adyah, ha-<u>sh</u>adyah, hai-<u>sh</u>adyah. (1Chr.3:20)

Jushab-hesed; yûšab ḥesed; يُصَب حَسَد 'he is struck by envy'(suffers from an envious personality, 'he is ailed by envy(as someone envying him and causing him illness or bad luck'; يُصَب حَصَد 'he pours into/ onto-harvests/reaps'; عُصَب حَسَد 'nerves-envy' 'sheaths/bundles of envy'; عُصَب حَصَد 'sheaths/bundles-harvest'; خُشَب حَصَد 'timber/logs-reaped/harvested';يُشَب حَسَد 'grows up to be envious man' 'swells/becomes rigid-envy; يُشَب حَصَد 'grows up-reaps/harvests' 'swells/becomes rigid-reaps/harvests'. Cp: yussab ḥesed, yussab ḥessed, 'ussab ḥesed, 'ussab ḥessed, khushab ḥessed, yushab ḥesed, yushab ḥessed. (1Chr.3:20)

Pelatiah; pĕlāṭyâ, pĕlāṭyāhû; فيلآت يه/ياة 'fell-he/him' 'immoral/lewd-he/him'. Cp: pheilaat-yah/yaahu. (1Chr.3:21)

Jesaiah; yĕšaʿyâ, yĕšaʿyāhû; exactly the same word as **'Isaiah'**:يِسَع يه ، ييسَع يه ، يِسَع ياَة ، ييسَع ياَة 'he wanders/goes/travels-he/him' 'it fits him/it' 'there is enough space for him/it'; جِسَع ياَة/يه ، جيسَع ياَة/يه 'came wandering/went to/travelled-he/him'; هِسَع ياَة/يه ، هيسَع ياَة/يه 'will come wandering/going to/travelling-he/him' 'he will come wandering/going to/travelling-he/him'. Cp: yesa'yah, yeisa'yah, yesa'yaahu, yeisa'yaahu, gesa'yaahu/yah, geisa'yaahu/yah, yesa'yaahu/yah, yeisa'yaahu/yah. (1Chr.3:21)

Rephaiah; rĕpāyâ; رِبآيه ، ريبآيه 'his god(s)/parent(s)/teacher(s)' 'mix and dilute it with water' 'discipline him' 'bring him up properly' 'swollen lymph nodes during illness' 'inflamed sores/wound'; رِفآيه ، ريفآيه 'eyelid-twitch-he' which is considered a bad omen; رِفع يه ، ريفع يه 'lifted/raised-he/him' 'picked up and put away/tidied-he/him'. Cp: rebaayah, reibaayah, rebaa-yah, reibaa-yah, rephaa-yah, reiphaa-yah, reph'-yah, reiph'-yah. (1Chr.3:21)

Arnan; 'arnān; نَرنآن 'both saw' 'showed both(people)'; عَرنآن 'made both naked'. Cp: arnaan, 'arnaan. (1Chr.3:21)

Shechaniah; šĕkanyāhû; شيكَن ياَة 'they complained about him' 'a complainer-he/him' 'behaved pretentiously/fancy-he/him'; شيخَن ياَة 'he will deceive-him/he' 'he/it will soak-he/him'; سيكَن ياَة 'settled/calmed down-him/he'. Cp: sheikan-yaahu, sheikhan-yaahu, seikan-yaahu. (1Chr.3:21)

Hattush; ḥaṭṭûš; حَطّش 'placed/set it/you' 'left you/it' 'left some' 'of leaving some/of departing/of setting/placing'; خَطّش 'scribbled/wrote' 'drew lines/scribbles'. Cp: ḥaṭṭush, khaṭṭush. (1Chr.3:22)

Igeal; yig'ol, yig'āl; يِجعول ، يِجعُل ، يِجعآل 'he/it creates/creating' 'lays eggs/bait' (usually used to describe a chicken laying an egg; also, the name of the egg placed where a chicken usually lays her eggs so it does not go off and lay its eggs somewhere else.). Cp: yig'ool, yig'ol, yig'aal. The same as Igal (Num.13:7). (1Chr.3:22)

Bariah; bārîaḥ; بآريَح 'bailed up water' 'cleared out/cleared/tidied' 'level open space' 'with the wind' 'I will relax'; بآريَه 'went passed him' 'good/pious-him/he' 'good to him' 'I will see him/it' 'I will show him/it' 'I will teach him/it' 'I will dream' 'I will give animals to drink'. Cp: baareeaḥ, baareeah. (1Chr.3:22)

Neariah; nĕʿaryâ; نِعَريه ، نيعَريه 'sexually excited-he' 'has/had an erection-he/him' 'we strip him naked' 'stood without moving or speaking'; نِئَريه ، نيئَريه 'we see him' 'we make him see' 'we penis/penetrate with penis/insult with penis-he/him' 'we make fire(s)-him/he'. Cp: ne'aryah, nei'aryah, ne-aryah, nei-aryah. (1Chr.3:22)

Elioenai; 'elyôʿênay; ئَليُعينَي 'the one who hints' 'the one who directs message indirectly' 'the one who watches/inspects/looks at' 'the one who directs confrontation' 'the one who suffers/makes suffer'; ئَليُغينَي 'the one who sings' 'the one who makes throaty sound(a sound like ghnn/ghain)' 'the one who no longer needs/no longer wants/no longer dependent on' 'the one who enriches'. Cp: elyo'eynay, elyogheynay. (1Chr.3:23)

Azrikam; 'azrîqām; عَذري قآم 'my shadow stood' 'my excuse-stood/did'; عَزري قآم 'my ugliness-stood/took place' 'my ugliness-had an erection'; نَزريق آم 'quickly/go quickly-the' 'dash to-the'; نَسريق آم 'steal/I steal-the' 'sneak/I sneak into-the'. Cp: 'avree-qaam, 'azree-qaam, azreeq-aam, asreeq-aam. (1Chr.3:23)

Hodaiah; hôdawyâ, hôdawyāhû; هُدَويه/ياَة 'they guided-him/he' 'they sang wedding song-him/he' 'they demolished-him/he' 'gifted-he/him'; هُدَبيه/ياَة 'it/he is a squash/a hollow squash/a churning vessel' 'gifted it/him'; حُدَب يه/ياَة 'is slouching/hunchbacked-he/him'. Cp: hodaw-yah/yaahu, hodabyah/yaahu, ḥodab-yah/yaahu. (1Chr.3:24)

Eliashib; 'elyāšîb; ئَلياَصيب 'the afflicted/injured/hit' 'the bringer of affliction/problems' 'the one who pours onto/into'; ئَلياَشيب 'the aging/aged' the one who becomes young man' 'the one who/which swells/becomes rigid'; ئَلياَسيب 'the one who leaves/lets go/cuts off relations, activities, actions'. Cp: elyaasseeb, elyaasheeb, elyaaseeb. (1Chr.3:24)

Pelaiah; pĕlāyâ; بِل آيه ، بيل آيه ، بِلآيه ، بيلآيه 'with/by the verse/line/sign' 'by…(making sound of displeasure or objection)'ayyah'' 'afflicted-he/him' 'my affliction' 'soaked him/it' 'without him/it' 'faded/worn/

old-he/him/it'; فيلآيه ، فِلآيه ، فيل آيه ، فِل آيه 'in the verse/line/sign' 'saying bad omen/saying and something negative happening' 'pick out nits' 'picking/going through thoroughly' 'wearing jasmines-he/him' 'picking at-he/him'. Cp: bel-aayah, beil-aayah, belaayah, beilaayah, phel-aayah, pheil-aayah, phelaayah, pheilaayah. (1Chr.3:24)

Akkub; 'aqqûḇ; عقّب 'after' (e.g. comes after, says after, etc.) 'babysitter/housesitter' (someone who looks after a child(ren) or house while someone else goes somewhere); عكّب 'forcing open' 'usurping' 'with deformed/debilitated hands'. This word is the equivalent of 'Jacob'. Cp: 'aqqub, 'akkub. (1Chr.3:24)

Dalaiah; dĕlāyâ, dĕlāyāhû; دِل/ديل آيه/آياهْ ، 'show/prove-verse/line/sign' 'show/prove-verses/lines/signs'; دِلاّ/ديلاّ يه/ياهْ 'show/prove/guide-him/he' 'lower/dangle-him/he' 'push/drive(towards)-him/he' 'push(ed)/pedal(ed) from place to place (things or oneself)-him/he'; دِلآيه/ياهْ ، ديلآيه/ياهْ 'slow down/gently-he/him/you' 'my/his bailing pouch/pouches'; ضِل/ضيل آيه/آياهْ 'mislead-line/verse/sign' 'mislead-he/him'; ضِلاّ/ضيلاّ يه/ياهْ 'mislead him' 'shade him'. Cp: del-aayah, del-aayaahu, deil-aayah, deil-aayaahu, delaa-yah/yaahu, deilaa-yah/yaahu, delaayah/yaahu, deilaayah/yaahu, dhel-aayaah/aayaahu, dheil-aayaah/aayaahu, dhelaa-yah/yaahu, dheilaa-yah/yaahu. (1Chr.3:24)

Anani; 'ănānî; عَنآني ، عينآني 'he meant me/hinted at me' 'he is instigating problems with me' 'of hinting/directing indirect messages' 'of confronting' 'of inspecting/watching/looking at'. Cp: 'anaanee, 'ainaanee. (1Chr.3:24)

Reaiah; rĕ'āyâ; ريئ آيه 'saw a sign/line/verse'; ريئا يه 'saw-him/he' 'dreamt-him/he' 'showed-him/he' 'water-him/it'; ريعايه 'shepherded-he/him' 'looked after-he/him' 'shepherds' 'soaked/flooded with urine/water' 'well watered/succulent/overwatered'. Cp: rei-aayah, reiaa-yah, rei'aayah. (1Chr.4:2)

Jahath; yaḥaṯ; جَحَت 'dragged'; جَحَث 'bailing pouch (during drought)' (made of dried baby-squash); يَحَث 'he encourages/insists/pushes(figuratively)' 'he creates fringes'; يَحَت 'he creates borders' (on walls with mud plaster or whitewash; on hands/feet with henna and other decorative substances; on clothes using textiles/embroidery); يَحَط 'he places/sets down on ground/unloads' 'he leaves behind'. Cp: gaḥat, gaḥaf, yaḥaf, yaḥat, yaḥaṭ. (1Chr.4:2)

Ahumai; 'ăḥûmay; نَخُمي 'soak and make mess' 'I soak and make mess' 'soak and cover' 'I soak and cover' 'my mother's brother' 'I speak nasally' 'speak nasally' 'of making 'kh' sounds'; نَحُمي 'heat' 'I heat' 'I hover/go in circles around' 'hovers/go in circles around' 'of making 'ḥ' sounds'; نَهُمي 'I worry' 'I make worry' 'you should worry(said to fem.)'; نَهُ مَي 'here's the water'. Cp: akhumay, aḥumay, ahumay, ahu-may. (1Chr.4:2)

Lahad; lahaḏ; لَحَد 'no one' 'to the border/boundary/line/mark'; لَهَد 'did not demolish' 'will/may he not demolish'; لَحَظ 'noticed' 'fire blazed stronger'. Cp: laḥad, lahad, laḥadh. (1Chr.4:2)

Ishma; yišmā'; يِسماء 'he is named'; يِزماء 'he is/gets blocked(bowels)'; يِسماع 'he hears/listens'. Cp: yismaa, yizmaa, yismaa'. (1Chr.4:3)

Idbash; yiḏbāš; يِدباش 'he/it mixes/stirs'; هِدباش 'I will mix/stir'; يطباش 'he/it splashes into water/splashes water'. Cp: yidbaash, hidbaash, yiṭbaash. (1Chr.4:3)

Hazelelponi; haṣṣĕlelpônî; حَصّيل البُني 'find the child'; حَصّيل الثُني 'find the second/the double/the stitch'; هَزّيلل بُني 'this naughty one is my child' 'this naughty child' 'I will make disappear/remove/go away my (or) the child(ren)'; هَزّيلل ثُني 'I will go off again' 'I will join it/connect it again'; هَزّيل الثُني 'I will connect/join the second' 'I will connect/join the stitch/fold' 'I will make disappear/remove the second/other'; هَصّيلل ثُني 'I will lay second layer of stones/I will lay layer of stones again' and refers to part of the roofing process where a layer of flat 5inch stones are spread over the whole roof on top of the sticks that seal the ceiling/roof; هَصّيل البُني 'I will deliver/take home the child' 'I will reach the child'; هَصّيل الثُني 'I will reach/arrive at the second'. Cp: ḥasseil-elbonee, ḥasseil-elfonee, hazzeilel-bonee, hazzeilel-fonee, hazzeil-elfonee, hasseilel-fonee, hasseil-elbonee, hasseil-elfonee. (1Chr.4:3)

Hushah; ḥûšâ; حُشه 'cutting grass' 'to stuff/stuffed (it)' 'be pushed into'; خُشه 'crumble (it)/of crumbling texture' 'feared'; هُشه 'he is something/important matter' 'he wanted/wants' 'shoo it away'. Cp: ḥushah, khushah, hushah. (1Chr.4:4)

Helah; ḥel'â; حَلئه 'undressed it/him' 'circumcised him' 'shed it/him' 'purified/cleansed/made edible or touchable-him/it' 'declare it/him purified/permissible' 'took his/its place' beat him/it until skin peeled off' 'sweeten(ed) him/it'; هَلئه 'she/he/it is here' 'shed it'. Cp: ḥel-ah, hel-ah. (1Chr.4:5)

Naarah; na'ărâ; نعيره ، نَعَرَه 'they/he are horny/sexually excited/have erection' 'they/he stood/stood erect/stood in front of without moving nor speaking' 'we strip him naked'; نَيره ، نَنَرَه 'we see him/make him see/we understand/make him understand' 'we show him' 'he penised/insulted with 'penis'/we penis him/we insulted with 'penis'' 'his fire/make fire/we make fire' 'light/make light/we make light/shed light/we shed light'. Cp: na'arah, na'airah, na-arah, na-airah. (1Chr.4:5)

Ahuzam; 'ăḥuzzām; نيحوزآم ، نَحوزّآم 'I bundled into faggots' 'I tie together' 'I cram/corner the' 'I block/keep in the'; نَخوذآم 'brother of the leper/guilted/ostracised' 'takes the/I take the'; نيخوزآم ، نَخوزّآم 'swears at the' 'I insult the/insults the' 'shames-the'. Cp: aḥuzzaam, aiḥuzzaam, akhuzzaam, aikhuzzaam, akhu-vvaam, aikhuvvaam. (1Chr.4:6)

Temeni; têmĕnî; طيميني ، طيمِني 'reassure(yourself/her/him/them)' 'of reassuring/is reassured'; ظيمِني ، ظيميني 'guarantee/secure' 'of guaranteeing/is guaranteed/secured'. Cp: ṭeymenee, ṭeymeinee, dheymenee, dheymeinee. (1Chr.4:6)

Haahashtari; ha'ăḥaštārî; هَئيه اشتآري ، هَئيهَشتآري 'here/look, I will buy' 'here she is/here it is-buy' 'here she is-become curious/check in on/look into'. Cp: ha-ai-hashtaaree, ha-aih-ashtaaree. (1Chr.4:6)

Zereth; ṣeret; ذَرَف 'overflowed'; زَرَت 'visited/pilgrimaged' 'tightened'; زَرَط 'swallowed'. Cp: vereph, zeret, zereṭ. (1Chr.4:7)

Jezoar; yĕṣōḥar; ييزوحَر ، يِزوحَر 'he growls and pushes' (as in contraction or bowel movement); جيزوحَر 'came-growled and pushed'; ييزوهَر ، يِزوهَر 'it flowers'. Cp: yezooḥar, yeizooḥar, geizooḥar, yezoohar, yeizoohar. (1Chr.4:7)

Ethnan; 'etnān; ثِنآن 'two' 'doubled/folded' 'idols' 'idol worshippers' 'dissuaded'. Cp: efnaan. (1Chr.4:7)

Coz; qôṣ; قُص 'tell story' 'cut' 'hard' 'cruel'; قُز 'fry' 'burnt/burning smell' 'make heart burn/nausea' 'kill(figuratively)' 'large boulder'; كُز 'smoking vessel(similar to sheesha)'. Cp: qoss, qoz, koz. (1Chr.4:8)

Anub; 'ānûb; عآنُد 'stubborn/provoking/taunting/spiteful'; عآنُب 'grapes'; عآنُز 'female goat(s)'. Cp: 'aanud, 'aanub, 'aanuz. (1Chr.4:8)

Zobebah; ṣōbēbâ; صوبييه 'pouring into/onto' 'they are pouring' 'pouring vessel'; زوبييه 'penises' 'they are penising(penetrating with)'; ضوبييه 'a burning smell' 'smoke from burning a dry/empty pan/pot'; سوبييه 'swearing' 'they are swearing' 'leaving/they are leaving' 'leaving behind'; ذوبييه 'flies' 'melt it/him' 'melt with it'. Cp: ssoobeybah, zoobeybah, dhoobeybah, soobeybah, voobeybah. (1Chr.4:8)

Aharhel; 'ăḥarḥēl; نَخَر/نيخرهيل 'last to shed/last shedding' 'she is the last one' 'last one-here'; نَخَر/نيخَر حيل 'last trick/deceit' 'last one-stayed the' 'last to shed/last shedding' 'last one to circumcise/purify/cleanse/make edible/make touchable'; نَخَر/نيخَر خيل 'the last horse' 'the last hallucination/imagined'. Cp: akhar-heyl, aikhar-heyl, akhar-ḥeyl, aikhar-ḥeyl, akhar-kheyl, aikhar-kheyl. (1Chr.4:8)

Harum; hārūm; هآروم 'here is/look-thrown/the thrown/killed' 'I will throw' 'spoke to cruelly/belittled'; حآروم 'prohibited' as in 'what you are doing is forbidden, have pity on…' or just forbidden, 'forbade/deprived' 'rotten/stinking/horrible/bad'; خآروم 'with piercings' 'torn/with holes in it' 'burst from bottom. Cp: haaroom, ḥaaroom, khaaroom. (1Chr.4:8)

Chelub; kĕlûb; كيلُب ، كَلُب 'dog' 'chased after like a dog/chased away like a dog; غيلُب ، غَلُب 'was unable to' 'gave up' (as in was unable to open or do something or was frustrated and stopped trying)' 'felt frustration' 'frustrated', 'victoried/was victorious' 'defeat/was defeated'; خيلُب ، خَلُب 'mud' 'used mud/activity involving mud'. Cp: kelub, keilub, ghelub, gheilub, khelub, kheilub. (1Chr.4:11)

Shuah; šûḥâ; شُهه 'ewe' 'a conversation/chat'; شُحه 'dry/became dry' 'became scarce/scanty'. Cp: shuhah, shuḥah. (1Chr.4:11)

Mehir; mĕḥîr; ميهير ، مَهير 'works hard' 'has many chores' 'chores'; ميخير ، مَخير 'is last' 'was made last' 'no good/no good fortune' 'water-good/good fortune/blessing'. Cp: meheer, meiheer, mekheer, meikheer. (1Chr.4:11)

Eshton; 'eštôn; نَشتُن 'I want' 'important things'; نَشطُن 'become devilish/bad'; نَسطُن 'chief builder/supervisor over building house, etc.' 'medium' 'connector/connecting/joining'; نَصطُن 'swooped down and clung to/clung onto' 'laid hands on'; عِشتُن 'you lived'. Cp: eshton, eshṭon, esṭon, essṭon, 'eshton. (1Chr.4:11)

Beth-rapha; bêt rāpā'; بيت رآفآع 'it will be raised' 'it will be tidied/put in its place'; بيت رآبآع 'it will gallop' 'it will gallop away' 'it will be chased and scattered' 'it/he will run on all fours' and describes an animal galloping but also a person if he/she makes a lot of noise or movements, it is also used to describe when someone, or a group of people, or animals are chased away and run in fear like animals galloping away and being dispersed, 'it will be locked'; بيت رآفاء 'it will twitch/flutter'; بيت رآباء 'it will/he will-be god/ become his god/parent/teacher' 'it will grow' 'his lymph nodes will swell' 'the open sore/wound will inflame (and create sores around it)' 'he/it will be disciplined' 'he/it will be brought up/will grow up' 'he/it will be taught'. Cp: beyt raaphaa', beyt raabaa', beyt raaphaa, beyt raabaa. (1Chr.4:12)

Paseah; pāsēaḥ; فآسيَح 'made spacious' 'made space/moved over to allow to sit or pass' 'gives/gave permission/is loose in giving permission' 'so he wandered/sought' 'so wander/seek'; فآسيَخ 'spoiled/off' 'undid purity' 'broke off engagement'; فآصيَه 'untangled' 'separated/divorced wife' 'explained in detail' 'stone of fruit' 'gems used to decorate jewellery and clothes'; فآصيَح 'eloquent' 'so shout/scream' 'so he shouted/ screamed'. Cp: phaaseyah, phaaseyakh, phaasseyah, phaasseyaḥ. (1Chr.4:12)

Tehinnah; tĕḥinnâ; تَهِنّه ، تيهِنّه 'took/takes satisfaction' 'ate a lot' 'received/gave a lot' 'insulted/humiliated him'; تَحِنّه ، تيحِنّه 'wore henna/put on henna' 'feels/felt affection/yearning' 'hummed/purred'; تَخِنّه ، تيخِنّه 'soaks it/him' 'betrays it/him'. Cp: tehinnah, teihinnah, teḥinnah, teiḥinnah, tekhinnah, teikhinnah. (1Chr.4:12)

Irnahash; 'îr nāḥāš; عير نآحآس 'disgrace/gloat-brought bad luck upon'; عير نآهآش 'disgrace/gloat-mauled' 'disgrace/gloat-took chunks out of'; عير نآخآش 'disgrace/gloat-crumbled' 'disgrace/gloat-made/ poked holes in' (by poking at something using stick, claw or instrument). And again, the purpose of 1Chronicles is a list of theme ideas for stories, as well as an attempt to give every place-name mentioned in earlier stories a person with the same name so as to explain the naming of the place. Cp: 'eer naaḥaas, 'eer naahaash, 'eer naakhaash. (1Chr.4:12)

Rechah; rēḵâ; ريخه 'luxury/plenty' 'loose/loosened' and can be literal or mean loose in morals/behaviour. 'These are the men of Rechah.' means these men were either rich or immoral, or even both, this is also reflected in Eshton and his sons' names: important things, wanting, bad/devilish, raising buildings, spacious buildings, allowing, taking satisfaction, eating to satisfaction/receiving a lot, disgracing and bringing bad luck, mauling. The meaning of 'rechah' can be neutral, but it can also be negative. Cp: reykhah. (1Chr.4:12)

Hathath; ḥăṯaṯ; حَتَت ، حيتَت 'made a line/border' whether with henna on hands/feet or on wall with mud-plaster, whitewash, etc.; حَثَث ، حيثَث 'made fringes/pushed fringe up'; حَطَط ، حيطَط 'placed down/ unloaded' 'left' 'left behind'. Cp: ḥatat, ḥaitat, ḥafaf, ḥaifaf, ḥaṭaṭ, ḥaiṭaṭ. (1Chr.4:13)

Meonothai; mĕ'ônōṯay; مي ئُنوثَي 'will not become/is not female/feminine' 'water-became female/ feminine'; مي عُنودَي 'is not stubborn/provocative/spiteful' 'water-stubborn/provocative/spiteful'; ميعُنوتَي 'of assistance/supportive' 'did not support/will not support'. Cp: mei-onoofay, mei-'onooday, mei'onootay. (1Chr.4:14)

Charashim; ḥărāšîm; خيرآش هم/ام 'untied-them/the'; حيرآش هم/ام 'made problems between-them/the' 'pitted them against each other-them/the'. Cp: khairaash-hum/um, ḥairaash-hum/um. (1Chr.4:14)

Iru; 'îrû; عيرُ 'disgrace' 'gloat' 'lend' and the word is being said to plural people; ئيرُ 'penis' 'penetrate with penis'. Cp: 'eeru, eeru. (1Chr.4:15)

Naam; na'am; نَعَم 'yes' 'blessing(s)' 'blessed' 'gave/received something physical (which can include health)' 'we drink/drank' 'we become blind'; نَغَم 'we stifle/feel stifled' 'we suffocate/feel suffocated' 'we cover/we are covered' 'we muffle/are muffled' 'we depress/feel depressed'. Cp: na'am, nagham. (1Chr.4:15)

Jehaleleel; yĕhallel'ēl; يِهَلِّل ئِل ، ييهَلِّل ئِل 'he cries out loud/chanted-the' and it is to cry out a word or name repeatedly usually as praise, or in song/poem, or prayer, 'makes ornamental tassels or dangles on jewellery' 'he sheds-the'; جَهَلِّل ئِل ، جيهَلِّل ئِل 'came-cried out loud/chanted the' 'the children of the' 'ignorance of the' 'came created tassels or dangles on jewellery'; يِحَلِّل ئِل ، ييحَلِّل ئِل 'he circumcises-the' 'he sheds blood-the' 'he purifies/cleanses-the' 'he declares permissible-the' 'he makes edible/touchable-the' 'he undresses-the' 'he sheds-the' 'he takes place of/replaces-the'; جَحَلِّل ئِل ، جيحَلِّل ئِل 'came circumcised-the' 'came purified/cleansed-the' 'came declared permissible-the' 'came made edible/touchable-the' 'came undressed-the' 'came shed-the' 'came took place of/replaced-the'. Cp: yehallel-ill, yeihallel-ill, gehallel-ill, geihallel-ill, yeḥallel-ill, yeiḥallel-ill, geḥallel-ill, geiḥallel-ill. (1Chr.4:16)

Ziphah; zîpâ; زيفه 'a wedding procession' 'were escorted in a procession' and matches the meaning of Jehaleleel (to cry out word/name in praise/song/poem); صيفه 'described' 'insulted' 'his/its rock(s)' 'stacked rocks' 'rock column' 'row/column/stack' 'lice eggs' 'fish oil product(for fattening)'. Cp: zeephah, sseephah. (1Chr.4:16)

Tiria; tîryā'; تيرياء 'dreamt' 'he dreamt' 'he saw' 'see/show/teach' 'he watered/quenched' 'he narrated/told story or news'; طيرياء 'fresh/soft' 'became soft/pliant' 'fly(as in go quickly)' 'threw out/chased away/banished' 'fled in haste' 'spilled'. Cp: teeryaa, ṭeeryaa. (1Chr.4:16)

Asareel; 'ăśar'ēl; عَصَر نِل ، عيصَر نِل 'twisted muscle-the' 'twisted-the' and is the same as 'Israel'. Cp: 'as-sar-ill, 'aissar-ill. (1Chr.4:16)

Ezra; ʿezrā'; عِزراء 'made ugly/became ugly'; عِذراء 'shadowed' 'excused'; يُزراع 'grow/plant'; يُسراء 'left very early/in the dark' 'captives'; يُسراع 'be fast/he was fast'; يُذراء 'sow' 'create offspring' 'scattered(powdery substance such as flour, soil, ash, etc.)'; يُذراع 'measure by the forearm' 'beat'; يُزراء 'insult deeply/a lot' 'a great disgrace'. Cp: 'ezraa, 'evraa, ezraa', esraa, esraa', evraa, evraa', ezraa. (1Chr.4:17)

Mered; mered; مَرَد 'return' 'returned to' 'reward/recompense' 'reduced to' 'what did he reply/did not reply'; مَرَض 'illness' 'did not agree' 'was not pleased'. Cp: mered, meredh. (1Chr.4:17)

Jalon; yālôn; يالُن 'he/they/it changed colour' (e.g. if it was about someone's face changing colour, means became upset or angry, or attitude became negative towards specific person or about specific matter'; جالُن 'they walked around' 'they ate from another's side(from dish)' 'they made sides' 'purified/made clear' 'tossed and rolled'; عالُن 'high' 'made higher' 'arrogant'. Cp: yaalon, gaalon, 'aalon. (1Chr.4:17)

Ishbah; yišbāḥ; يِشباه 'he resembles' 'he/it makes it swell/rigid' 'swells/becomes rigid'; يِشباح 'stretches legs over' 'jumps to other side' 'becomes strong/brave' 'enlarges with bravery/in size'. Cp: yishbaah, yishbaaḥ. (1Chr.4:17)

Jehudijah; hayhudiyyâ, yĕhudiyyâ; هَيخُدِجَه ، ييخُدِجَه 'he will/he/they/it-miscarried' 'he will/he/it-ripped out/made it drop out'; جَيخُدِجَه 'came-miscarried' 'came-ripped out/made it drop out'; هَيخُدِيّه ، ييخُدِيّه 'he will/he/they/it-removed bread from oven wall' 'he will/he/it-pulled or ripped off something stuck on wall'; جَيخُدِيّه 'came-removed bread from oven wall' 'came-pulled or ripped off something stuck on wall'; هَيهُ/ييهُ دِعّه ، جَيهُ دِعّه 'here is who/who is/which one-called he/him' 'came he/came to him-called he/him'; هَيهُدِيّه ، ييهُدِي يه ، جَيهُدِيّه 'he will sing/he sings wedding song', could also be meaning of the word 'jew'—to be explained later in this book, 'came-sang wedding song' 'he will demolish' 'demolishes-he' 'came-demolished-he' 'made effort-he/him' 'tiring work/fatigued-he/him'; هَيهُ دِيّه ، ييهُ دِيّه ، جَيهُ دِيّه 'here is-money for life/penalty' 'who is/which one-money for life/penalty/ransom' 'came he/came to him-money for life/penalty/ransom'. Cp: haykhudiggah, yeikhudiggah, geikhudiggah, haykhudiyyah, yeikhudiyyah, geikhudiyyah, hayhudi'h, yeihudi'h, geihudi'h, hayhudiy-yah, yeihudiy-yah, geihudiy-yah, hayhu/yeihu-diyyah, geihu-diyyah. (1Chr.4:18)

Socho; śôkô; سُقُ 'water' 'drive/steer' 'extremely cold'; صُقُ 'extend/reach/are able to reach(by extending hand/arm/etc.)' 'throbbing pain(in teeth/bones)'; شُكُ 'thread' (such as arrange beads or flowers or jewellery on a string; or to thread anything on a stick, needle, etc. and also to sew something quickly), when a hen makes a long string of loud clucking noises; شُقُ 'side' 'his side' 'beside'. It is the equivalent of Soco/Socoh. Cp: suqu, ssuqu, shuku, shuqu. (1Chr.4:18)

Jekuthiel; yĕqûṯî'ēl; يِقُتي نيل ، ييقُتينيل 'he brings/sells/gifts qat-the' 'he applies henna(or any decorative substance) to hands/feet-the' 'decorates bottom of wall(with plaster or whitewash' 'gives/gifts qat-the' 'he/it kills'; ييقضي نيل 'pays back-the'; ييقطي نيل 'he snips-the'. Cp: yequtee-ill/eyl, yeiquteeeyl, yeiqudhee-ill/eyl, yeiquṭee-ill/eyl. (1Chr.4:18)

Bithiah; biṯyâ; بِت يه ، بِتيه 'his girl/daughter' 'girl/daughter-he/him' 'tear it/him' 'make decision-him'; بِضيه 'white' 'laid egg(s)' 'abluted/washed' 'with light/shone light'. Cp: bit-yah, bityah, bidhyah. (1Chr.4:18)

Hodiah; hôḏîyâ; هُدي يه ، هُدييه 'was guided-he/him' 'he was guided/brought to sense' 'sang wedding song-he/him' 'was given as present-he/him' 'demolished-he/him' 'demolish him'; خُطي يه ، خُطييه 'wrote/drew a line/letter-he/him' 'stepped-he/him' 'he was made to step over'. Cp: hodeeyah, hodee-yah, khoṭee-yah, khoṭeeyah. (1Chr.4:19)

Naham; naḥam; نَهَم 'sighing/sighed' 'struck and winded' and means sighing or puffing meant to attract attention or being hit/punched in stomach until breath is forced out of you. It is equivalent to Menahem (2Kgs.15:14-22) and Tanhumeth (2Kgs.25:23). Cp: naham. (1Chr.4:19)

Garmite; garmî; جَرمي 'pulled water' 'a crime/an evil/sin'; غَرمي 'boiled over' 'submerged under water flowing over it/him/her' 'my opponent/adversary' 'a deceiver/conner'. Cp: garmee, gharmee. (1Chr.4:19)

Shimon; šîmôn; سيمُن 'clarified butter' 'fat' 'gained weight'(not necessarily meaning 'fat') 'ill' 'poisoned them' 'poison them' 'named' 'name them'; زيمُن 'a long time ago' 'timed'. Cp: seemon, zeemon. (1Chr.4:20)

Rinnah; rinnâ; رِنّه 'a ringing/tinkling noise'; رِنّح 'throwing oneself around' 'branches bent or swaying violently from wind'. Cp: rinnah, rinnaḥ. (1Chr.4:20)

Ben-hanan; ben-ḥānān; بَن هاَناَن 'children-humiliated' 'we will be humiliated' 'children/child-satisfied/given plenty' 'we will be satisfied/given plenty'; بَن خاَناَن 'child(ren)-betrayed' 'we will be betrayed' 'children-soaked' 'we will be soaked' 'children-brothers/became brothers' 'we will become brothers'; بَن حاَناَن 'children-affection' 'we will feel affection' 'children-hennaed' 'children-time is now' 'we will be hennaed' 'our time will be now'. Cp: ben-haanaan, ben-khaanaan, ben-ḥaanaan. (1Chr.4:20)

Tilon; tîlôn; تيلُن 'carry by hand' 'become pliable/soft' 'was coloured/coloured' 'changed colour'; طيلُن 'very early' 'tall' 'long' (time or length). Cp: teelon, ṭeelon. (1Chr.4:20)

Zoheth; zôḥēṯ; ذُحيث 'this/he is instead of'; زُحيت 'became hard(er)' 'became firm' 'was scratched'; صُحيت 'stopped raining/became sunny/became clear' 'woke up'; شُخيط 'wrote/scribbled' 'scratched lines into'; ضُحيت 'dried' 'hung to dry/spread out to dry' (clothes or grain). Cp: vo-ḥeyf, zoḥeyt, ssoḥeyt, shokheyṭ, dhoḥeyt. (1Chr.4:20)

Ben-zoheth; ben-zôḥēṯ; بَن ذُحيث 'children/child-was instead of' 'we will be-instead of'; بَن زُحيت 'child/children-hard(er)' 'child/children-became firm' 'we will/until-become hard(er)' 'we will/until-become firm'; بَن صُحيت 'child/children-stopped raining/became sunny/became clear' 'until-stopped raining/became sunny/became clear' 'child/children-woke up' 'until-woke up'; بَن شُخيط 'child/children-wrote/scribbled' 'we will be-wrote/scribbled on' 'child/children-scratched lines into' 'we will be-scratched'; بَن ضُحيت 'child/children-dried' 'we will be/until-dried' 'child/children-hung to dry/spread out to dry' (clothes or grain). Cp: ben-vo-ḥeyf, ben-zoḥeyt, ben-ssoḥeyt, ben-shokheyṭ, ben-dhoḥeyt. (1Chr.4:20)

Lecah; lēḵâ; ليكه 'for you' 'chewed' 'spoke a lot' 'talks too much' 'goes around in circles/makes no sense/jumps from subject to subject' 'incoherent/nonsense'; ليقه 'met/found him/it' 'connected it/surrounded it/him' 'threw it down'; ليحه 'made pancakes' 'with beards/has beard/grew beard'. Cp: leykah, leyqah, leyḥah. (1Chr.4:21)

Laadah; laʿdâ; لاعده 'may he not come back' 'may he not bring back' 'may he not count' 'may he not be enemy to' and is the form of a curse/insult or prayer. Cp: la'adah. Note: verse 21 mentions 'Shelah' and 'Er' whose stories in Gen.38 showed that they and other brothers were meant to be for (lecah/for you) Tamar and to impregnate her, but they all did things which prevented the marriage from being consummated and 'slipped away' (maresha) from her (Onan ejaculated on the ground instead of inside her which also reminds of the meaning of 'maresha' (Maresha Josh.15:44). (1Chr.4:21)

Ashbea; 'ašbēaʿ; نَشبيَ 'swell and become rigid' e.g. like wood swells from water, head from cold, penis with blood. And it is included in the names of Judah's sons to remind of the story where Judah's sons refused to consummate/impregnate Tamar, so Tamar sexually excited Judah (posing as a prostitute) to have sex with and impregnate her; نَشبيَع 'was sufficed/full/satisfied' 'what was sold'. Cp: ashbeya, ashbeya'. (1Chr.4:21)

Jokim; yôqîm; يُقيم 'gets up/stands up/wakes up' 'stands instead of/represents' 'makes stand upright' 'has an erection'; يُغيم 'becomes cloudy/dark' 'muffles/stifles'. Cp: yoqeem, yogheem. (1Chr.4:22)

Chozeba, kōzēḇā'; كوذيباَء 'they lied' 'they accused of lying' 'they were accused of lying'. And is still related to the Tamar/Judah story as it was mentioned Shelah was born at Chezib. It is equivalent to Chezib (Gen.38:5) and Achzib (Josh.15:44) as well as Cozbi. Cp: kooveybaa.

Saraph; śārāp; ساَراَف 'buttocks' 'wasteful/a waste'; صاَراَف 'got rid of/sent away/made leave' 'changed'; صاَراَب 'sticks used as sealing material' 'sealing with sticks the ceiling' (process in roofing), 'made with sticks'; ساَراَب 'leaked'. Cp: saaraaph, ssaaraaph, ssaaraab, saaraab. (1Chr.4:22)

Jashubi-lehem; yāšuḇî leḥem; ياَشوبي لَحَم 'he returns/goes in circles-eats meat/tears off strips of meat/mauls/responds angrily' 'he swells/becomes rigid-eats meat/tears off strips of meat/mauls/responds angrily'; ياَشوبي لَهَم 'he returns/goes in circles-well fed/plumpened' 'he returns/goes in circles-for them' 'he swells/becomes rigid-well fed/plumpened' 'he swells/becomes rigid-for them'; حاَشوبي لَحَم 'they pushed me/

stuffed me in-ate meat/tore off strips of meat/mauled/responded angrily' 'he carries on waist-ate meat/tore off strips of meat/mauled/responded angrily' 'with clothes folded up and tucked into his waist-ate meat/tore off strips of meat/mauled/responded angrily'; حَاشوبي لَهَم 'they pushed me/stuffed me in-well fed/plumpened/for them' 'he carries on waist-well fed/plumpened/for them' 'with clothes folded up and tucked into waist-well fed/plumpened/for them'; خَاشوبي لَحَم 'of wood-responded angrily/ate meat/mauled/tore off strips of meat' 'wooden yoke-responded angrily/mauled, etc.'; خَاشوبي لَهَم 'of wood-for them/well fed/plumpened' 'wooden yoke-for them/well fed/plumpened'; عَاشوبي لَحَم 'they had supper with me-meat' 'of plants-ate meat/mauled/responded angrily'; عَاشوبي لَهَم 'they had supper with me-well fed/plumpened/for them' 'of plants-well fed/plumpened/for them'. Cp: yaashubee-leḥem, yaashubee-lehem, ḥaashubee-leḥem, ḥaashubee-lehem, khaashubee-leḥem, khaashubee-lehem, 'aashubee-leḥem, 'aashubee-lehem. (1Chr.4:22)

Nemuel; nĕmû'ēl; نَمُ ئِل ، نيمُ ئِل 'slept-the' 'had sex-the'; نعمُ ئِل 'we drink-the' 'we blind-the'. Cp: nemu-ill, neimu-ill, n'mu-ill. (1Chr.4:24)

Jarib; yārîḇ; يآريب 'he mixes and dilutes with water' 'you/he is-god/parent/teacher'; هآريب 'he/it is-god/parent/teacher' 'ran away/is a runaway' 'sent his wife away' (the latter to her parents' home when there is a big problem between husband and wife); جآريب 'came-mixed and diluted with water' 'came-god/parent/teacher' 'try' 'an oasis' (the latter in an enclave dipping down between mountains)', 'has skin condition (similar to chronic eczema or other condition where skin becomes rough, cracked, sore)'; عآريب 'expressed clearly/spoke clearly' 'will-god/parent/teacher' 'will-dilute and mix with water' 'fucked' 'a fucker'; غآريب 'goes over hill/ascent' 'overflows' 'a hill/terrain which dips downwards on other side (you can't see people when they go over it)' 'goes abroad' 'a stranger/foreigner' 'strange'; خآريب 'ruins (as in destroys or makes bad/worse' 'ruins(as in remnants of structure/building' 'destruction' 'it is ruined' 'a destroyer/ruiner'; حآريب 'warring' 'fighting with(as in antagonising, not a war)'. Cp: yaareeb, haareeb, gaareeb, 'aareeb, ghaareeb, khaareeb, ḥaareeb. (1Chr.4:24)

Hamuel; ḥammû'ēl; حَمُّ ئِل 'heat-the'; حَمُّئِل 'carry many loads' 'load' (as in assist another by placing a load on her head/his shoulder); هَمُّ ئِل 'they worried the' 'they were worried by the'. Cp: ḥammu-ill, hammu-ill. (1Chr.4:26)

Zacchur; zakkûr; ذَكُّرٍ 'remember/mention'; شَقُّر 'peep between gaps' 'take quick glances (between hiding behind cover)'; زَقُّر 'top-up/fill with water/liquid/fill gap(s)'. Cp: vakkur, shaqqur, zaqqur. It is the equivalent of Zakariah, Zacur, Jozachar. Note in this part of the story Zacchur, which does not differ from the similar names it is related to in meaning, the character is the son of **Mishma** 'listening' or 'does not hear'; in Num.13:4, **Zaccur** (with exact same meanings as Zacchur) is the father of **Shammua** 'listened (without people's knowledge)' 'eavesdropped'; at 2Kgs.12:18-21, **Jozachar** is the son of **Shimeath** 'listen to' 'reputation'. Even in 2Sam16:5-13, **Shimei** 'my hearing' 'to spoil reputation of another by insulting them in the hearing of others' 'to talk badly/insult a person in front of others' role is to remind David and the audience of David's wrong towards Saul and Jonathan. This shows how words are created to create fictional characters for specific meanings as related to the story being told, and the authors followed a method linking father and son characters with word-meanings to enhance the story. (1Chr.4:26)

Ezem; 'eṣem; عَزَم 'invited' and is the same as Azem (Josh.15:29). Cp: 'ezem. (1Chr.4:29)

Tolad; tôlaḏ; تَلَّد 'is having a baby/childbirth' and is equivalent to Eltolad (Josh.15:30). Cp: tolad. (1Chr.4:29)

Hazar-susim; 'hazar' with all its different meanings as before combined with: susim; sûsîm; صُصهم 'bad smell like raw eggs/blood' and is equivalent to Hazar-susah (Josh.19:5) and Sansannah (Josh.15:31). Cp: ḥasar/ḥaysar-ssuss-hum. (1Chr.4:31)

Beth-birei; bêṯ-bir'î; بيت بِرئي 'he/it will-pass by/be passed by/get ahead of/be surpassed' 'daughter/girl-pass by/be passed by/get ahead of/be surpassed' 'he/it will be good/pious'. Cp: beyt-bir-ee. (1Chr.4:31)

Tochen; tōḵen; ثوخِن 'became thicker/denser'; طوحن 'was ground'. Cp: fookhen, ṭooḥen. (1Chr.4:32)

Meshobab; mĕšôḇāḇ; مي شوبآب 'water-young men' 'not young men' 'water-they are swollen/rigid'; مي صُبآب 'water-pouring onto/into' 'water-flowing heavily'. Cp: mei-shobaab, mei-ssobaab. (1Chr.4:34)

Jamlech; yamlēḵ; يَمليح 'he salts' (food or cows), '(hey)you, pretty/nice'; يَمليك 'he owns' 'river for you'; يَم ليق 'river/sea-found' 'river/sea-thrown down'; عَم ليق 'drank/blind/blinded-thrown down' 'drank/blind/blinded-found'. The (ja/ya) could also be ج/came or هـ/I will/look, followed by the rest of the meanings of (mlech/mlēḵ) which would still hold the same meanings with slight variations. Cp: yamleyḥ, yamleyk, yamleyq, 'amleyq. (1Chr.4:34)

Joshah; yôšâ; يُشه 'he wants' 'he wants him' 'his ewes'; يُسح 'he wanders and seeks' 'he drags on his bottom' (some babies crawl on all fours, others move by leaning forward on arms and pulling bottom against ground'; يُشح 'cries out like a goat/sheep' 'makes a noise like an animal'; جُشه 'pick/take a lot' 'eating roasted corn' 'bad suffocating smell' 'came-ewes'; عَشه 'supper' 'having supper' 'partially blind' 'evening'; حُشه 'stuffed' 'hidden quickly' 'cutting grass'; هُشه 'he is (like) a ewe' 'shoo away/swat away'. Cp: yoshah, yosh, yoshh, goshah, 'oshah, hoshah. (1Chr.4:34)

Josibiah; yôšibyâ; يُصِب يه 'he is afflicted-he/him' 'is ailed/injured/struck-he' 'is attacked-he/him' 'he strikes/attacks him' 'he pours onto/into-he/him'. Cp: yossib-yah. If taken into account with the names included in this verse, it can be seen they are borrowed from Deborah/Sisera story: Joel is both **Jael** and **Deborah**'s deceit in Jud.4; Jehu refers to **Barak** being approached by Deborah and **Sisera** fleeing to **Jael**'s husband's area; Josibiah refers to how **Sisera** will be attacked and defeated in battle and how he will be injured and killed by Jael; Seraiah (leave early in dark morning) represents one meaning of **Sisera** (to walk from place to place); Asiel (disobedience/questions/asking) refers to the disobedience shown in **Barak** not wanting to actually engage in battle, then **Sisera**'s wrong and also Barak asking Deborah to go with him to war, and Sisera asking Jael to do things for him. Without the context of being surrounded by words which indicate Deborah's story, the word 'Joshibia' can also be several other words with different meanings and pronunciations than the one mentioned above as was the method of the Biblical authors, and could only be determined if such a story still existed which would match the meaning of the word and the event/description in the story. (1Chr.4:35)

Asiel; 'ăśî'ēl; عَصي ئِل ، عيصي ئِل 'disobeyed-the' 'became askew/crooked-the' 'became stiff-the'; نَسيئِل ، نيسيئِل 'I question/ask' 'questioned/asked' 'I leaked/flowed' 'leaked/flowed' 'comforted/calmed/distracted/entertained'; نَسي ئِل ، نيسي ئِل 'bad towards-the'. Cp: 'assee-ill, 'aissee-ill, a-see-ill, aisee-ill, asee-ill, aisee-ill. (1Chr.4:35)

Jaakobah; ya'ăqōbâ; يَعقوبه ، يَعيقوبه 'he/they come after/follow-him/it' 'he/they look after/take care of-him/it' (babysit child(ren) or house or both); يَعَكوبه ، يَعيكوبه 'he/they force open-him/it' 'he/they dislocate-him/it' 'he/they force open and take-him/it' 'he/they usurp'. It is the equivalent of 'Jacob' Cp: ya'aqoobah, ya'aiqoobah, ya'akoobah, ya'aikoobah. (1Chr.4:36)

Jeshohaiah; yĕšôḥāyâ; عِشُ/عيشُ خايه 'had supper/fed supper-his brother'; عِشُ/عيشُ حايه 'had supper/fed supper-he healed' 'had supper/fed supper-made him stay/still/contained'; عِشُ/عيشُ هايه 'feed him supper/eat supper- come on/quick' 'had supper/feed supper-she/her'; عِشُه/عيشُه آيه 'his supper is a sign/line/verse' 'feed him supper-a sign/line/verse'. It is notable that putting Jaakobah and Jeshohaiah in one verse was intentional as a reminder or further themes of the story of Jacob and Esau in Genesis. Cp: 'esho-khaayah, 'eisho-khaayah, 'esho-ḥaayah, 'eisho-ḥaayah, 'esho-haayah, 'eisho-haayah, 'eshoh-aayah, 'eishoh-aayah. (1Chr.4:36)

Asaiah; 'ăśāyâ; عَصايه ، عيصايه 'disobedient' 'were disobedient' 'disobeyed-he/him' 'my stick' 'became/made askew/crooked-he/him' 'became difficult/stuck-he/it'. This is also connected to Esau's story. Cp: 'assaayah, 'aissaayah. (1Chr.4:36)

Adiel; 'ădî'ēl; عَدي ئِل ، عيدي ئِل 'be enemy-the' 'count-the'; غَدي ئِل ، غيدي ئِل 'feed lunch-the' 'inflame glands/frustrate-the'. Cp: 'adee-ill, 'aidee-ill, ghadee-ill, ghaidee-ill. (1Chr.4:36)

Jesimiel; yĕśîmi'ēl; يَصيمِ ئِل ، ييصيمِ ئِل 'he fasts-the' 'he blocks-the'; يَسيمِ ئِل ، ييسيمِ ئِل 'he names-the' 'he poisons-the'; هصيمِ ئِل 'I will fast-the' 'I will block-the'; هيصيمِ ئِل 'he will fast-the' 'he will block-the'; جَصيمِ ئِل ، جيصيمِ ئِل 'came fasted-the' 'came blocked-the'; هَسيمِ ئِل 'I will name-the' 'I will poison-the'; هيسيمِ ئِل 'he will name-the' 'he will poison-the'; عَصيمِ ئِل ، عيصيمِ ئِل 'intends to-the'. Cp: yesseemi-ill, yeisseemi-ill, yeseemi-ill, yeiseemi-ill, hesseemi-ill, heisseemi-ill, gesseemi-ill, geisseemi-ill, heseemi-ill, heiseemi-ill, 'esseemi-ill, 'eisseemi-ill. (1Chr.4:36)

Ziza; zîzā'; ذيذاع 'announced all over' 'spoke everywhere'; زيزاء 'sent away in droves' 'fiercely drove away'; صيصاع 'immoral person who goes everywhere' 'goes spreading immorality'; سيساع 'wandered (aimlessly) all over/everywhere'. It is equivalent to Zaza. Cp: veevaa', zeezaa, sseessaa', seesaa'. (1Chr.4:37)

Shiphi; šip'î; شِفعي 'defended/stood up for'; سِبعي 'the seventh/my seventh' 'a week' 'a rest'; شِبعي 'is full/satisfied' 'my fill/satisfaction'. Cp: shiph'ee, sib'ee, shib'ee. (1Chr.4:37)

Allon; 'allôn; عَلّن 'over them' 'in public/in front of everybody'; تَلّن 'until' 'changed colour'. Cp: 'allon, a-llon. (1Chr.4:37)

Jedaiah; yĕda'yâ, yĕdāyâ; ييدع يه ، يِدَع يه 'they/he call him' 'they/he leave him' 'he deposits/leaves in the care of-he/him' 'say farewell-he/him' 'they/he say a prayer for him/call curse on him' 'he/they make a claim/make a false claim-he/him'; ييضع يه ، يِضَع يه 'they place/set-he/him' 'he/they mislead/misguide-he/them' 'they get lost/lose-he/him'; خيدع يه ، خِدَع يه 'knifed-him/he' 'his knife' 'deceived-him/he'; ييدَئيه ، ييدايه 'his hands' 'my hands' 'peeks at/appears and disappears'; ييضَئيه ، ييضايه 'he/they shines/lights-he/him' shines/lights on him' 'he/they ablute-him/he' 'ablutes'; هيدَئيه ، هيدايه 'a guidance/bringing to the right way' 'gifts' 'guided him' 'wedding songs' 'sang wedding songs-he/him' 'demolished-he/him' 'demolished it'; جيدَئيه ، جيدايه 'kids (goats)' 'his kid (goat)' 'find him' 'find-he/him'; عيدَئيه ، عيدايه 'enmity towards him' 'enmity-he/him' 'transgressed against him' 'transgressed-he/him' 'infect(ed)-him/he 'count(ed) it' 'count-he/him' 'return(ed)-he/him' 'return him/it' 'return to him/it' 'festival' 'celebrated festival/visited during festival'; حيدَئيه ، حيدايه 'placenta(s)' 'sharpening/sharpened/sharp' 'sharpen-he/him'. خيدَئيه ، خيدآيه 'miscarried/miscarriage(pregnancy)' 'remove by pulling off' 'pulled off bread from oven wall' 'with palms/hands on cheeks'; غِدَئيه ، غيدايه 'lunch/fed lunch-him/he' 'my frustration/swelling of glands' 'frustrate-him/he'. Cp: yeda'yah, yeid'yah, yedha'yah, yeidh'yah, kheda'yah, kheid'yah, yeida-yah, yeidaayah, yeidha-yah, yeidhaayah, heida-yah, heidaayah, geida-yah, geidaayah, 'eida-yah, 'eidaayah, ḥeida-yah, ḥeidaayah, kheida-yah, kheidaayah, gheida-yah, gheidaayah. (1Chr.4:37)

Shimri; šimrî; شِمري 'will glisten/glitter/shine' 'with sleeves/clothes rolled up or tucked up' the latter to avoid soiling clothes while working; سِمري 'storyteller' 'telling night story' 'staying awake all night/late night' the latter for entertainment or guarding purposes. Cp: shimree, simree. (1Chr.4:37)

Gog; gôg; جُج ، جوج 'overcrowded' 'too many people than can fit in one area/room' 'over spilling with people/things'. Cp: gog, goog. (1Chr.5:4)

Reaia the same as Reaiah (1Chr.4:2). (1Chr.5:5)

Beerah; bĕ'ērâ; بِئيره/ا ، بيئيره/ا 'by his penis' 'will be penised' 'will insult with 'penis'' 'will show him'. It may indicate what earlier authors mentioned that the kings' sons who are taken away by foreign kings will become eunuchs in captivity. Cp: be-eyrah, be-eyra, bei-eyrah, bei-eyra. (1Chr.5:6)

Tilgath-pilneser; tillĕglaṯ piln'eser; تِلّي غلَط بِلنعِصِر ، تِلّي غلَط بِلنِسِر 'carry away-in the wrong way-with the ones we twist their muscles' 'carry away-in the wrong way-with the ones we made prisoners' and is a direct referral to all of 'Israel' being taken away into captivity: (til/tillĕ/تِلّي) 'carry away/carry by hand'; (gath/glaṯ/غلَط) means 'mistake' but also 'in a wrong way' such as causes damage to what is being handled in the wrong way, and in the story refers to the people being warred upon then taken away as prisoners; (pil/بِل) 'with the', (n/ن) 'we' and the spoken about is in plural (n'eser/نعصِر) 'we twist their muscle'; (eser/'eser/عِصِر) 'twisted/twisted muscle' and is the name given to Jacob then the people as 'Israel' which came from twisting/withering a muscle; (eser/'eser/نِسِر) 'was/were imprisoned'. It is a variant on the earlier word-name Tiglath-pileser. Cp: tillei-ghlaṭ-biln'esser, tillei-ghlaṭ-biln-eser. (1Chr.5:6)

Compared to Genesis and other books, there is slight change in accent to how words are pronounced/spelled in some parts of 1Chronicles, the same applies to some parts of Genesis and earlier stories where editing can be detected, but it is more discernible in 1Chronicles. It could be a result of the time span between the authors of the earlier stories and the editors and creators of the 'newer' stories which attempt to fill in the gaps such as 1Chronicles, but it could also be that these stories began in one area of the region with the language accent of the earlier books, and by the time these stories were popular and edited as in Chronicles they had already reached elsewhere in the region from their original point of origin. It is not a different dialect, but accent. Another possibility is that over the millennia and more recent centuries that people involved in translating, interpreting, transliterating have different accents and so read and translate the names as they would pronounce them which is slightly different from the accent/pronunciation of the original authors and audience of the original stories.

Jeiel; yĕ'ê'ēl; يَعي ئِل ، ييعي ئِل 'he understands-the' 'he makes understood-the' 'he contains-the' 'vessels of-the'; جَعي ئِل ، جيعي ئِل 'came and understood-the' 'hungry-the'; جِعيئِل ، جيعيئِل 'created' 'made' 'placed as bait' 'placed egg as bait' (for hen to lay eggs next to); حَئي ئِل ، حيئي ئِل 'healed-the' 'stayed-the' 'stilled/made stay-the'; حَئيئِل ، حيئيئِل 'deceit/trickery' 'is stationary-the' 'purified/purify/circumcise(ed)' 'sweet(ened)' 'shed/undress'. Cp: ye'ey-ill, yei'ey-ill, ge'ey-ill, gei'ey-ill, ge'eyill, gei'eyill, ḥe-ey-ill, ḥei-ey-ill, ḥeeyill, ḥeieyill. (1Chr.5:7)

Zechariah; zĕkaryâ; ذَكَريه ، ذيكَريه 'reminded he/reminded him' 'mentioned he/mentioned him'; زيقَريه 'topped with water or liquid/filled to brim with water/liquid-he/him'; شيقَريه 'peeped at/took quick glances' 'filled with gaps-he/him' 'made slits/gaps-he/him'. The exact same as Zachariah (2Kgs.14:29). Cp: vekaryah, veikaryah zeqaryah, zeiqaryah, sheqaryah, sheiqaryah. (1Chr.5:7)

Azaz; 'āzāz; عازاز 'comforted/gave condolences' 'fortified' 'cherished'; عاذاذ 'said a protection for'; عاباب 'floated/overflowed' 'rotted and stank' 'made feel ashamed' 'disgraced'. Cp: 'aazaaz, 'aavaav, 'aabaab. (1Chr.5:7)

Shapham; šāpām; شاف آم 'saw-the' 'healed-the'. Cp: shaaph-aam. (1Chr.5:12)

Jaanai; ya'nay; يَعنَي 'he/it means' 'he hints'; هَعنَي 'I will mean' 'I will hint'; يَغنَي 'he no longer needs' 'he makes no longer need' 'enriches'. Cp: ya'nay, ha'nay, yaghnay. (1Chr.5:12)

Jorai; yôray; يُرَي 'he sees' 'he shows' 'he teaches' 'he dreams' 'he waters'; عُرَي 'stripped naked'; هُرَي 'he saw' 'chase away(with words)' 'a cat/my cat' 'wooden handle of axe'; جُرَي 'ran' 'happened' 'came and saw' 'pull'; حُرَي 'find out/investigate' 'plough' 'was moved(to act)'. Cp: yoray, 'oray, horay, goray, ḥoray. (1Chr.5:13)

Jachan; ya'kān; يَعقآن 'disobedient' 'have hardened hearts' 'too salty' 'braying like donkeys' and the word is describing two people or more with this action/attribute. Cp: ya'qaan. (1Chr.5:13)

Zia; zîa'; زيَع 'they could/were able' 'fat/plump' and suits them being placed in Bashan ('verdant'). Cp: zeea'. (1Chr.5:13)

Huri; ḥûrî; حُري 'ploughed' 'perplexed' 'checking/looking into'; خُري 'run away or fall in haste/fear' 'collapsed'. The same as Hori in Gen.36:22. Cp: ḥoree, khoree. (1Chr.5:13)

Jaroah; yārôaḥ; يآروَح 'he comes home' 'oh my soul' 'he fans/makes breeze by fanning' 'windy'. Cp: yaaroaḥ. (1Chr.5:14)

Jeshishai; yěšîšay; جَشيشَي ، جيشيشَي 'of picking a lot/taking too much' 'a lot of people'; حَشيشَي ، حيشيشَي 'of grass' 'of cutting grass' 'stuffed something' 'quickly hid something'; هَشيشَي ، هيشيشَي 'crawls with (or like) insects' 'feels around blindly' 'shoos/swats away'; يَشيشَي ، ييشيشَي 'he wants something'; عَشيشَي ، عيشيشَي 'partially blind' 'moving around unable to see properly' 'feed him something for supper'; غَشيشَي ، غيشيشَي 'blurry/not clear/fuzzy' 'deceiving/of deceiving'. Cp: gesheeshay, geisheeshay, ḥesheeshay, ḥeisheeshay, hesheeshay, heisheeshay, yesheeshay, yeisheeshay, 'esheeshay, 'eisheeshay, ghesheeshay, gheisheeshay. (1Chr.5:14)

Jahdo; yaḥdô; يَهدُ 'sings wedding song' 'gives gift(s)' 'demolishes' 'guides to right way (religiously, morally or physically showing the way/route needed)'; جَهدُ 'effort/made effort' 'tiring work/struggle' 'worked hard' 'fatigued'; عهدُ 'a promise/oath'; جَحتُ 'dragged'. Cp: yahdo, gahdo, 'ahdo, gaḥto. (1Chr.5:14)

Ahi; 'āḥî; نَحي ، نيحي 'stay still' 'stay' 'I make stay still' 'I make stay'; نَخي ، نيخي 'my brother'; نَهي ، نيهي 'her/she' 'it is her' 'here she is'. Cp: aḥee, aiḥee, akhee, aikhee, ahee, aihee. (1Chr.5:15)

Abdiel; 'abdî'ēl; عَبدي ئِل 'my servant-the' 'servant-the' 'serve-the' 'my worshipper-the' 'worshipper-the' 'worship-the'; ئَبدي ئِل 'take/bring out/come out-the'. Cp: 'abdee-ill, abdee-ill. (1Chr.5:15)

Sharon; šārôn; شآرُن 'bought' 'they bought' 'evil'; سآرُن 'they walked' 'they walked along'; صآرُن 'happened' 'knotted' 'bundled' 'aches'. Cp: shaaron, saaron, ssaaron. (1Chr.5:16)

Nodab; nôdāb; نُدآب 'they are mourning loudly/wailing' 'scars/scarred'; نُضآب 'they have protruding teeth/jaws'. Cp: nodaab, nodhaab. (1Chr.5:19)

Baal-hermon; ba'al ḥermôn; بَعَل حَرمُن ، هَرمُن ، خَرمُن It could be any combination of baal meanings: 'high/higher/high place/above' 'upon them' 'with upon them' 'spouse'; with the meanings of Hermon: حَرمُن 'deprived(of)' 'forbidden' 'a group of women', 'rotten/stinking'; هَرمُن 'will throw/kill' 'drove/chased away from' 'grumpy' 'spoke to cruelly'; خَرمُن 'fled/chased away from' 'collapsed from' 'pierced' 'burst from bottom'. Cp: ba'al ḥermon, ba'al hermon, ba'al khermon. (1Chr.5:23)

Senir; the same as Shenir (Deut.3:9). (1Chr.5:23)

Eliel; 'ĕlî'ēl; ئِلي ئِل ، ئيلي ئِل 'the one who/he who-the'; عيلي ئِل 'on/upon/above-the' 'rose higher/above-the'. Cp: illee-ill, eilee-ill, 'eilee-ill. (1Chr.5:24)

Azriel; 'azrî'ēl; عَزري ئِل 'make ugly-the'; عَذري ئِل 'shadow/shade-the' 'excuse-the'; ئَذري ئِل 'sow-the' 'make offspring-the' 'scatter(soil/flour/etc.)-the' 'fill/cover with insults-the' 'soil/cover (with dirty substance)-the'; ئَزري ئِل 'greatly insult-the'. Cp: 'azree-ill, 'avree-ill, avree-ill, azree-ill. (1Chr.5:24)

Hodaviah; hôd̲awyâ, hôd̲awyāhû; حُدَب ياَهُ ، حُدَب يه'slouched/hunchbacked-he/him'; حُدَبياَهُ ، حُدَبيه 'is hunchbacked/of hunchbacks'; هُدَبياَهُ ، هُدَبيه 'he/it is a pumpkin/squash' 'he/it is a churning vessel'; هُدَويه ، هُدَوياَهُ 'they guided-him/he' 'they sang wedding song-him/he' 'they demolished-him/he' 'gifted-he/him'. Cp: ḥodab-yah/yaahu, ḥodabyah, ḥodabyaahu, hodabyah, hodabyaahu, ḥodawyah, ḥodawyaahu. (1Chr.5:24)

Jahdiel; yaḥdî'ēl; يَهدي ئِل 'guides-the' 'gives gift-the' 'sings wedding song-the'; جَهدي ئِل 'made work hard-the' 'tired-the' 'effort/made effort-the'; جَحتي ئِل 'drags-the'. Cp: yahdee-ill, gahdee-ill, gaḥtee-ill. (1Chr.5:24)

Hara; hārā'; هاَراَء 'I will see/I will see him' 'well, what is he doing' 'adding wooden handle to tool'; حاَراَء 'built a fire'. Cp: haaraa, ḥaaraa. (1Chr.5:26)

Abishua; 'ăb̲îšûa'; ئَبي شوَع 'my father-freakishly ugly/mutated' 'rejected-freakishly ugly/mutated' 'rejected/father-cried out like an animal'; عَبي شوَع 'fill/pack-freakishly ugly/mutated' 'fill/pack-cried out like an animal'. Cp: abee-shua', 'abee-shua'. (1Chr.6:4)

Uzzi; 'uzzî; عوزّي 'honour' 'a want/need' 'support/provide for'; عوصّي 'disobeyed' 'became askew/crooked' 'became wooden/stiff'; عوضّي 'got stiffened/sore muscles' 'recompensed'; عوذي 'say a protection for/protect'; ئوذي 'harmed/was harmed'. Cp: 'uzzee, 'ussee, 'udhee, 'uvvee, u-vvee. (1Chr.6:5)

Zerahiah; zĕraḥyâ; سَرَح يه ، سيرَح يه 'went/left-he/him' 'made leave-he/him'; صَرَح/صيرَح يه 'said openly-he/him' 'spoke honestly-he/him' 'built worshipping structure/shrine-he/him'; صَرَخ/صيرَخ يه 'shouted-he/him'; زَرَه/زيرَه يه 'squeezed/tightened-he/him' 'visited/pilgrimaged-he/him' 'insulted greatly-he/him'; ذَرَه/ذيرَه يه 'sowed-he/him' 'procreated-he/him' 'scattered-he/him' 'left it-he/him' 'completely soiled-he/him' 'filled with insults-he/him'. seraḥ-yah, seiraḥ-yah, sseraḥ-yah, sseiraḥ-yah, sserakh-yah, sseirakh-yah, zerah-yah, zeirah-yah, verah-yah, veirah-yah. (1Chr.6:6)

Meraioth; mĕrāyôt̲; ميراَيُت '(the/his/her/etc.) dream' 'a dream' 'the mirror of' 'the reflection of' 'what you see/what did you see' 'she/he did not dream' 'he/she did not see'; ميراَيُث 'twitching eyelid' and is considered a bad omen (as in something bad will happen to the person whose eyelid is twitching or someone related to them), 'have had sex' 'did not have sex'. Cp: meiraayot, meiraayof. (1Chr.6:6)

Amariah; 'ămaryâ; ئَمَريه ، ئيمَريه 'a tiny hint/clue' 'a trace/barely visible trace' 'ordered-he/him' 'I show him mirror' 'I make him look into mirror'; عَمَريه ، عيمَريه 'built-he/him' 'built/topped kooz cup(cold coal, tobacco mix, hot coals)-he/him' 'lived long-he/him'. Cp: amaryah/amar-yah, aimaryah,'amar-yah, 'aimar-yah. (1Chr.6:7)

Jehozadak; yĕhôṣād̲āq; يَهُ/ييهُ ، جَهُ/جيهُ صاَداَق 'he who/who is-honest/friendly' 'came who-honest/friendly'; يَهُ/ييهُ ، جَهُ/جيهُ زاَداَك 'he who/who is-gave you more' 'he who/who is-deceived you' 'came who-gave you more' 'came who-deceived you'; يَهُ/ييهُ ، جَهُ/جيهُ صاَداَك 'he who/who is-blocked you/prevented you' 'he who/who is-fished you/your fish' 'came who- blocked you/prevented you' 'came who-fished you/your fish'. Cp: yeho/yeihoo-ssaadaaq, geho/geihoo-ssaadaaq, yeho/yeihoo-zaadaak, geho/geihoo-zaadaak, yeho/yeihoo-ssaadaak, geho/geihoo-ssaadaak. (1Chr.6:14)

Mahli the same as Mahali (Exod.6:19). (1Chr.6:19)

Zimmah; zimmâ; ذِمّه 'conscience' 'responsibility' 'ostracise/guilt-him'. Cp: vimmah. (1Chr.6:20)

Jeaterai; yĕ'atray; يِنفَري/ييِنفَري 'he/it increases'; يِنثَري/ييِنثَري 'he/it influences/harms'; هَنفَري 'I will increase'; هَنثَري 'I will influence'; هينفَري 'he will increase'; هينثَري 'he will influence'; جِنفَري/جينفَرَي 'came-increased' 'shook out of' (when a garment, fabric, or lap is shaken to allow anything to fall out of it (something being looked for or from dust, etc.); جِنثَري/جينثَري 'came-influenced'; يِعتَري 'he has fever/chills'. Cp: ye-phray, yei-aphray, ye-afray, yei-afray, he-aphray, he-afray, hei-aphray, hei-afray, ge-aphray/geaphray, gei-aphray/geiaphray, ge-afray, gei-afray, ye'atray. (1Chr.6:21)

Uriel; 'ûrî'ēl; ئُري ئِل 'show-the' 'showed-the' ('show-the' can mean literally to show something or as a threat) 'saw-the' 'dreamt-the' 'water/quench-the' 'teach/taught-the' (as 'seeing' and 'showing' is the same as 'teaching'). Cp: uree-ill. (1Chr.6:24)

Amasai; 'ămāśay; عَم/عيم عشَي 'drank-had supper' 'drank-was partially blinded'; عَم/عيم عصَي 'uncle-difficult' 'uncle-disobedient' 'drank-disobedient/difficult' 'uncle-became askew/crooked' 'drank-became askew/crooked'; عَماَشَي ، عيماَشَي 'they cannot see' 'partially blind'; ئَماَسَي ، ئيماَسَي 'I possess' 'of being possessed' (as in by demons/spirits) 'I provoke/test/cause arguments or fights' 'I arrive at night/stay at night'. Cp: 'am'shay, 'aim'shay, 'am'ssay, 'aim'ssay, 'amaashay, 'aimaashay, amaasay, aimaasay. (1Chr.6:25)

Ahimoth; 'ăḥîmôṯ; نَخي/نَيخي مُت 'my brother died'; نَهي/نَيهي مُت 'she is dead' 'here she is-dead'; نَحيمُت ، نَيحيمُت 'she heated' 'she is in early pregnancy' 'pathway in front/behind a house' 'she protected'. Cp: ak-hee-mot, ahee-mot, aḥeemot. (1Chr.6:25)

Zophai; ṣôpay; زُفَي 'was escorted by entourage' 'escort with procession'. Cp: zophay. Again, these are fictional names to support fictional stories, though some Biblical scholars would like to claim he is an ancestor of 'Samuel' and an alternate name for 'Zuph' as it appears in 1Sam.1, the truth is all names and characters are fictional and these words are used as names to create the stories which is why Zuph, Zuphai, Ziph and many other variations can be used for different places, different characters and sometimes are changed for the same character as suits the story. But with regards to the claim 'Zophai' being an ancestor to Samuel, even in storyland there is a big contradiction as Ziph is presented as a great grandfather of Elkanah '...Elkanah, the son of Jeroham, the son of Elihu, the son of Tohu, the son of Zuph...' whereas in 1Chr.6:26 'Zophai' is one of Elkanah's sons which at 1Chr.6:35 becomes 'Zuph' so he (Zophai/Zuph) would be a 'brother' to Samuel in the stories. (1Chr.6:26)

Vashni; wašnî; وَزني 'and fornicate' 'my weight' 'weigh'; بَشني 'taking plenty' 'verdant'; بَزني 'will fornicate' 'will take/carry' 'of taking/carrying. These meanings as the character of Samuel's sons appears in 1.Sam as 'Joel' 'deceives/tricks-the' which is now changed to 'Vashni' to reflect his bribe taking character. Cp: waznee, bashnee, baznee. (1Chr.6:28)

Haggiah; ḥaggîyâ; حَجّي يه 'hide him/it' 'cover/shelter (with something .e.g. blanket, hand or take inside)him/it'; هَجّي يه 'learn to pronounce correctly-he/him' 'look, came-he/him 'left forever-he/him'; هَغّي يه 'I will mislead-he/him' 'I will mislead to downfall-he/him'. Cp: ḥaggee-yah, haggee-yah, haghee-yah. (1Chr.6:30)

Shemuel; šĕmû'ēl; سَمُ ئِل ، سيمُ ئِل 'named-the' 'poisoned-the' 'threaded the needle-the'; شَمُ ئِل ، شيمُ ئِل 'smelled-the'; صَمُ ئِل ، صيمُ ئِل 'block(ed)-the' 'by force'. It is similar to Shammah, Shimma, Samuel. Cp: semu-ill, seimu-ill, shemu-ill, sheimu-ill, ssemu-ill, sseimu-ill. (1Chr.6:33). Note: in 1Sam, Joel is the son of Samuel, in this current verse Joel is the son of Shemuel which is a version of the word 'Samuel'. (1Chr.6:33)

Toah; tôaḥ; توَه 'got lost' 'misled' 'confused' 'lost either in speech or physically'; توَح 'was spoken to/narrated to'; طوَه 'pan(s)' 'rolled' 'folded'; دوَه 'no' 'acts of forgetting/senility'; دوَح 'crouched' 'moved in crouching position' 'punctured/pierced/wrecked from bottom'. It is equivalent to Tohu and Toi. Cp: toah, toaḥ, ṭoah, doah, doaḥ. (1Chr.6:34)

Mahath; maḥaṯ; مَحَت 'rubbed out/away'; مَحَث 'has a fringe' 'encouraged'; مَهَط 'scalded' 'cleaned using scalding water'. Cp: mahat, maḥaf, mahaṭ. (1Chr.6:35)

Berachiah; berekyâ, berekyāhû; بَرَك يه/ياَه 'knelt-he/him' 'his underground dam(s)' 'which/whose underground dams?' 'I will lean against-he/him'; بَرخيه/ياَه 'I will loosen him/it'; بِرخ يه/ياَه 'loose-he/him' 'is lenient-he/him' 'is immoral-he/him'. Cp: berek-yah/yaahu, berekhyah(yaahu), berekh-yah/yaahu. (1Chr.6:39)

Baaseiah; ba'ăśēyâ; بَعَصي/بَعيصي يه 'I will disobey-him/he' 'of dropping things/slipping fingers-he/him'; بَعَصيّه ، بَعيصيّه 'with/using sticks' 'with difficulty' 'with/I will make it askew/crooked' 'I will make it stiff/stuck'. Cp: ba'assey-yah, ba'aissey-yah, ba'asseyyah, ba'aisseyyah. (1Chr.6:40)

Malchiah; malkîyâ, malkîyāhû; مَلخي يه/ياَه 'cover with slimy substance-he/him' and can be any clean substance such as henna, etc., or dirty substance such as mud, etc.; مَلخيعه ، مَلخيعاَه 'roll it/him in slimy substance' 'it is slimy/dirty/it is slimy/soiled'; مَلقي يه/ياَه 'throw(n)/cast-he/him' 'did not find him/he' 'what found-him/he'; مَلحي يه/ياَه 'is good-he/him' 'is nice/pretty-he/him' 'has a beard-he/him' 'salted-he/him'; مَلحيَه/ياَه 'well, for his morality/shyness' 'well, he greeted him'. Cp: malkhee-yah/yaahu, malkhee'ah, malkhee'aahu, malqee-yah/yaahu, malḥee-yah/yaahu, malḥeeyah/yaahu. (1Chr.6:40)

Ethni; 'eṯnî; ئَثني 'double/reinforce' 'a double stitching over same part' 'to fold something and sew to make it fit better (length, width or shape)' 'dissuade' 'make leave' 'idol' 'idol worshipper'. Cp: efnee. (1Chr.6:41)

Kishi; qîšî; قيشي 'became paralysed(with joy/fear)' 'became crispy' 'a small piece of litter' 'a fibre' 'scrape away completely/remove in one go'; قيصي 'hardened' 'became too hard' 'became cruel' 'cut/cut off' 'told story'; كيسي 'was given new clothes' 'clothed' 'covered with fabric' 'enveloped'. Cp: qeeshee, qeessee, keesee. (1Chr.6:41)

Abdi; 'aḇdî; عَبدي 'servant' 'my servant' 'serves' 'worship' 'my worshipper' 'worships'; ئَبدي 'come out' 'take out' 'bring out' 'I come out' 'I take out' 'show' 'forever/never'. Cp: 'abdee, abdee. (1Chr.6:44)

Malluch; mallûk; مَلّكْ 'covered you' as in soiled/dirtied, 'what is with you/what is wrong with you' 'filled you' as in physical filled by giving things or as first meaning of 'dirtied'; مّلْق 'thrown down' 'thrown on the ground' 'found what' 'something found'; مَلّخ 'covered in slime/something slimy' 'slimed'; مَلّح 'became nice(er)' 'salty' 'salted'. Cp: malluk, malluq, mallukh, malluḥ. (1Chr.6:44)

Hashabiah; ḥăšabyâ, ḥăšabyāhû; حَشَب يه/ياَهْ ، حيشَب يه/ياَهْ 'carried on his waist-he/him' 'clothes tucked into waist-he/him' 'stuffed-he/him' 'quickly stuffed something somewhere to hide it-he/him'; حَسَب يه/ياَهْ ، حيسَب يه/ياَهْ 'predicted/calculated the future-he/him' 'calculated-he/him' 'thought it was-he/him' 'a sorcerer-he/him' sorcery is called 'calculating' and refers to the man/woman calculating the future and the unknown; هَشَبيه/ياَهْ 'I will make it swell/stiffen/enlarge' 'here is a young man-he/him'; هيشَبيه/ياَهْ 'he will make it swell/stiffen/enlarge' 'he will grow into young man-he/him'; هَسَب يه/ياَهْ 'I will leave/part with-he/him' 'I will swear/insult-he/him'; هيسَب يه/ياَهْ 'he will leave/part with-he/him' 'he will swear/insult-he/him'; خَشَب يه/ياَهْ 'cutting down lumber-he/him' 'bringing lumber' 'his timber'; خيشَب يه/ياَهْ 'setting roof lumber-he/him' the latter خيشَب is the term which describes placing the wooden beams during building process. Cp: ḥashab-yah/yaahu, ḥaishab-yah/yaahu, ḥasab-yah/yaahu, ḥaisab-yah/yaahu, hashab-yah/yaahu, haishab-yah/yaahu, hasab-yah/yaahu, haisab-yah/yaahu, khashab-yah/yaahu, khaishab-yah/yaahu. (1Chr.6:45)

Amzi; 'amṣî; نَمسي 'spend the night' 'evening comes/came' 'touches/I touch' 'get possessed(as in demon/spirit)' 'cause problems/provoke'; نَمزي 'squeeze/squirt'. Cp: amsee, amzee. (1Chr.6:46)

Shamer; šāmer; شاَمِر 'with sleeves/clothes pulled up/unkempt'; ساَمِر 'he is staying up all/late night' 'telling 'staying up' stories'. Cp: shaamer, saamer. The same as Shamir (Josh.15:48). (1Chr.6:46)

Hilen; ḥîlēn; حيلين 'stay here until' said to plural, 'don't move until' 'deceivers/tricksters/conners' 'undressed' 'remove your clothes' and is said to plural, 'purified/cleansed/circumcised/made edible/made touchable' 'declared permissible/purified' 'took place of/replaced'; خيلين 'emptied' 'empty' and is said about/to plural, 'allow/allowed' 'left behind/left some'. Cp: ḥeeleyn, kheeleyn. (1Chr.6:58)

Alemeth; 'ālemeṯ; عاَلّمَت 'showed' 'taught' 'made a sign/mark'. Cp: 'aalemet. (1Chr.6:60)

Jokmeam; yoqmĕ'ām; يوقمي عاَم/نآم 'stinks and suffocates-a year' 'stinks and suffocates-the'; يوغمي عاَم/نآم 'it suffocates-a year' 'it suffocates-the' 'he suffocates-the'; يوغمِغاَم ، يوغميغاَم 'he speaks with muffled voice' 'speaks with mouth covered' 'speaks with face covered'; جوغِم/جوغمي عاَم/نآم 'they/he came-suffocated-year/the' 'they/he came-covered face-year/the'; جوغمِغاَم ، جوغميغاَم 'came-spoke with muffled voice' 'came-spoke with covered mouth/face'; حوغمِغاَم ، حوغميغاَم'stayed/still-speaks with muffled voice' 'stayed/still-speaks with covered face/mouth'; حوغِم/حوغمي عاَم/نآم'stayed/still-suffocated-a year' 'stayed/still-suffocated-the' 'stayed/still-speaks with muffled voice/speaks with covered face/mouth-the' 'stayed/still-speaks with muffled voice/speaks with covered face/mouth-year'; حوكِم/حوكمي عاَم/نآم 'ruled -a year' 'ruled-the' 'wisdom/knowledge-a year' 'wisdom/knowledge-the' 'set as arbitrator-a year' 'set as arbitrator-the'; حوخِم غاَم ، حو خمي غاَم 'makes 'ḥoo' 'khm/khmei' 'ghaam' sounds' 'speech is like clearing throat, nasal sounds and muffled voice/face' 'a person who makes unclear sounds when speaks (as in the sounds'ḥoo' 'khm/khmei' 'ghaam')' 'pronounces 'ḥoo' 'khm/khmei' 'ghaam''. Cp: yooqmei-'aam/aam, yooghmei-'aam/aam, yooghmeghaam, yooghmeighaam, googhme-'aam/aam, googhmei-'aam/aam, googhmeghaam, googhmeighaam, ḥooghmeghaam, ḥooghmeighaam, ḥooghme-'aam/aam, ḥooghmei-'aam/aam, ḥookme-'aam/aam, ḥookmei-'aam/aam, ḥoo-khme-ghaam, ḥoo-khmei-ghaam. (1Chr.6:68)

Bileam; bil'ām; بِلغاَم 'with the-suffocated' 'with the-one with covered mouth/face' 'with the-muffled voice' 'with the one who makes 'ghaam' noises'; بِلعاَم 'with the-drank/drinker/one who drank' 'with the-blind'; بِلعاَن 'on purpose' 'with curses/will curse'. Cp: bilghaam, bil'aam, bil'aan. (1Chr.6:70)

Anem; 'ānēm; غاَنيم 'took advantage made a lot' 'exploited and took a lot' 'made a lot' 'goats/raised goats'. Cp: ghaaneym. It is similar to Enam (Josh.15:34). (1Chr.6:73)

Mashal; māšāl; ماَشاَل 'did not take' 'what did he/it take'; ماَساَل 'matters/important matters' 'what did he ask' 'he did not ask' 'asked a lot' 'did not leak' 'what leaked' 'leaked/leaking/melted'. It is similar to Mishal (Josh.21:30), Mishael (Exod.6:22), Misheal (Josh.19:26). Cp: maashaal, maasaal. (1Chr.6:74)

Hukok the exact same word, pronunciation and meanings as Hukkok (Josh.19:34); ḥûqōq; حُقوق 'rights/belongs to' 'necklaces' and the necklaces are made of beads of ivory, coral and other natural gems' 'shells(sea shells)'; حُكوك 'itchy/itching/scratching'; حُقوك 'yours/belong to you' 'your hips'. Cp: ḥuqooq, ḥukook, ḥuqook. (1Chr.6:75)

Jahzah; yahṣâ; يَحزه 'he corners/crams/keeps it/him in'; جَحزه 'came-crammed/cornered/kept in it/him'; جَهزه 'prepared it/him' 'came-swung it/him' 'came-snatched/tugged at/snagged it/him'; يَهزه 'pulls at it' 'snatches/tugs at it' 'swung it/him'; جَهصه 'with protruding jaws/teeth'. Cp: yaḥzah, gaḥzah, gahzah, yahzah, gahssah.

Jeriel; yĕrî'ēl; يَري ئِل ، ييري ئِل 'he sees-the' 'he shows-the' 'he teaches-the' 'he dreams-the' 'he waters/quenches-the'; جَري ئِل ، جيري ئِل 'ran-the' 'came-saw-the' 'came-showed-the' 'came-watered-the'; هَري ئِل 'I will see-the' 'I will show-the' 'I will teach-the' 'I will water-the' (watering animals); هيري ئِل 'he will see-the' 'he will show-the' 'he will teach-the' 'he will water-the'; عَري ئِل ، عيري ئِل 'was stripped naked-the' 'made strip naked-the' 'lend-the' 'gloat over/at-the' 'my disgrace-the' 'bent head and carried on-the'; حَري ئِل ، حيري ئِل 'made fire-the' 'feels towards/responsibility/cares for/was moved for-the' 'investigated-the'. Cp: yeree-ill, yeiree-ill, geree-ill, geiree-ill, heree-ill, heiree-ill, 'eree-ill, 'eiree-ill, ḥeree-ill, ḥeiree-ill. (1Chr.7:2)

Jahmai; yaḥmay; يَحمَي 'protects/he protects' 'is heating'; هَحمَي 'I will protect' 'look/here-protect' 'I will heat'; جَحمَي 'hot coals'; جَهمَي 'bit and grazed' when something which does not have teeth, or is not sharp, bites/clamps on something, and/or grazes the skin, 'came to him-water'. Cp: yaḥmay, haḥmay, gaḥmay, gahmay. (1Chr.7:2)

Jibsam; yibśām; يِبصاَم 'closes lips' 'stamps/leaves mark'. Cp: yibssaam. (1Chr.7:2)

Izrahiah; yizraḥyâ; يِصرَخ يه 'shouts loud-he/him'; يِصرَح يه 'says openly/honestly-he/him'; يِذرَه يه 'sows it/him-he/him' 'scatters-he/him'; يِزرَه يه 'he fills him with insults-he/him'. Cp: yissrakh-yah, yissraḥ-yah, yivrah-yah, yizrah-yah. (1Chr.7:3)

Ishiah; yiššîyâ, yiššîyāhû; يِسّي يه/ياَهُ 'he does bad/offends-he/him'; يِصّييح ، يِصّيياَحُ 'he shouts' 'they shout'; يِسّييح ، يِسّيياَحُ 'they go walking and seeking' 'melts and leaks'; يِسّييخ ، يِسّيياَخُ 'they/it melts/partially melts' (from heat of day/sun); يِشّي يه/ياَهُ 'he wants-he/him'; هِسّي يه/ياَهُ 'pressed on-he/him'; هِسّييه ، هِسّيياَهُ 'pressed on it/him'; جِسّي يه/ياَهُ 'sit-he/him' 'make it/him sit' 'leave it alone-he/him'; عِسّي يه/ياَهُ 'give cold bread-he/him' 'cold bread-he/him' 'make sounds to make animal come nearer' (e.g. 'tut-tut' to a cat, 'qss' to dog, making a tongue-clicking sound for a cow); عِسّييه ، عِسّيياَهُ 'his cold bread' 'cold bread-he/him'. Cp: yissee-yah/yaahu, yisseeyḥ, yisseeyaaḥu, yisseeyḥ, yisseeyaaḥu, yisseeykh, yisseeyaakhu, yishee-yah/yaahu, hissee-yah/yaahu, hisseeyah, hisseeyaahu, gissee-yah/yaahu, 'issee-yah/yaahu, 'isseeyah, 'isseeyaahu. (1Chr.7:3)

Jediael; yĕḏî'ă'ēl; يَديعَ/ييديعَ ئِل ، يَديعي/ييديعي ئِل 'he calls-the' 'he curses-the' and can be calling out to someone or to God (the latter for help or in prayer), 'he claims-the' 'he makes a false claim-the' 'he leaves/deposits-the'; جَديعَ/جيديعَ ئِل ، جَديعي/جَيديعي ئِل 'came-called/cursed/claimed-the' 'snapped off-the'; هَديعَ/هَديعي ئِل 'I will call-the' 'look/here-call-the'; هيديعَ/هَيديعي ئِل 'he will call-the' 'he will curse-the' 'he will leave/deposit-the' look/here-he will leave/deposit-the'; خَديعَ/خيديعَ ئِل ، خَديعي/خيديعي ئِل 'deceived-the' 'knife of-the' 'knifed-the'. Cp: yedee'a-ill, yeidee'a-ill, yedee'ai-ill, yeidee'ai-ill, gedee'a-ill, geidee'a-ill, gedee'ai-ill, geidee'ai-ill, hedee'a-ill, hedee'ai-ill, heidee'a-ill, heidee'ai-ill, khedee'a-ill, kheidee'a-ill, khedee'ai-ill, kheidee'ai-ill. (1Chr.7:6)

Jerimoth; yĕrîmôṯ; يَريمُت ، ييريمُت 'he sees death' 'he is shown death' ' 'ye/yey'/pay attention-she has thrown/killed'; جَريمُت ، جيريمُت 'came-saw death' 'ran-saw death' 'pulled-saw death' 'crime/evil act'; هَريمُت ، هيريمُت 'look/here-she threw/killed' 'she threw/killed' 'she spoke angrily/was grumpy'; عَريمُت ، عيريمُت 'she was abandoned/stranded in the wilderness' 'she abandoned in the wilderness' 'she/it was stranded'. Cp: yereemot, yeireemot, gereemot, geireemot, hereemot, heireemot, 'ereemot, 'eireemot. (1Chr.7:7)

Iri; 'iri; عيري 'borrow/lend' 'gloat at/over' 'was stripped naked'; ئيري 'show/teach' 'saw/see' 'watered/quenched' 'penis/my penis' 'penised' 'insulted with 'penis''. Cp: 'eeree, eeree. (1Chr.7:7)

Zemira; zĕmîrâ; زَميره ، زيميره 'played pipes'; سَميره ، سيميره 'staying/stayed awake all/late night' 'telling night stories'; ذَميره ، ذيميره 'complaining' 'ostracised/guilty'. Cp: zemeera, zeimeerah, semeerah, seimeerah, vemeerah, veimeerah. (1Chr.7:8)

Zethan; zêṯān; زيتآن 'killed quickly' and refers to two or more people, it could be both being killed or both killing others, 'went/passed quickly' 'flitted/flicked into/quickly hid' 'sharp cuts/slit/slash' any wound involving a quick movement or a sharp object, 'suddenly split open' 'suddenly cut open' 'sliced open' 'flit/flicked/quickly hid something into narrow space'. Cp: zeytaan. (1Chr.7:10)

Ahishahar; 'ăḥîšaḥar; نَخي/نَيخي شَحَر 'my brother-stared angry/scowled with eyes' 'my brother-desert/dry land' 'my brother-dry cough/dry rattle in the chest'; نَخي/نَيخي سَحَر 'my brother-pre-dawn' 'my brother-under spell/magic'; نَخي/نَيخي شَهَر 'my brother-month' 'my brother-moon' 'my brother-exposed/made public example/slander'; نَخي/نَيخي سَهَر 'my brother-stayed awake all night beside'; the word 'brother' can be replaced with نَهي/نَيهي 'she is/here she is' followed by meanings above of 'shahar'. Cp: akhee/aikhee-shaḥar, akhee/aikhee-saḥar, akhee/aikhee-shahar, akhee/aikhee-sahar, ahee/aihee-shaḥar, ahee/aihee-saḥar, ahee/aihee-shahar, ahee/aihee-sahar. (1Chr.7:10)

Ir; 'îr; عير 'disgrace' 'borrow/lend' 'gloat over/at'; نَير 'penis' 'penetrate with penis' 'insult with penis'. It is equivalent to Er (Gen.38:3,6-7), Eri (Gen.46:16), Eri (Num.26:16), Iru (1Chr.4:15), Jeriel (1Chr.7:2). Cp: 'eer, eer. (1Chr.7:12)

Aher; 'aḥēr; نَحير 'puzzled/I puzzle' 'predicament' 'became open infected wound' 'didn't know what to do'; نَخير 'the last' 'delay' 'set back' 'make last'. It is the equivalent of Hirah (Gen.38), Ahira (Num.1:15). Cp: aḥeyr, akheyr. (1Chr.7:12). Note: in Gen.38 when 'Hirah' (Judah's friend) is used for the character who sets the stage in the story for there to be a predicament, 'Er' is used as a character name (for Judah's son) to mean 'disgrace, etc.'. In the 1Chr.7 list, 'Aher' is combined in the same line as 'Ir' which has the same meanings of 'Er'.

Jahziel; yaḥṣî'ēl; يَحزي ئِل 'corners/crams/keeps in-the'; جَحزي ئِل 'came-cornered/blocked-the' يَهزي ئِل 'pulled/snagged-the' 'swung-the'; يَخذي ئِل 'takes-the'; يَخزي ئِل 'swears at/insults/disgraces-the'; جَهزي ئِل 'prepare-the' 'came-pulled/snagged-the' 'came-swung-the'; جَهصي ئِل 'bared his teeth-the' 'with protruding teeth/jaw-the'; يَهسي ئِل 'presses on-the'. Cp: yaḥzee-ill, gaḥzee-ill, yakhvee-ill, yakhzee-ill, yahzee-ill, gahzee-ill, gahssee-ill, yahsee-ill. (1Chr.7:13)

Ashriel; 'aśrî'ēl; عَصري ئِل 'twisted muscle-the' 'twisted-the' and is the same as 'Israel' and 'Asareel' (1Chr.4:16); نَصري ئِل 'knot/bundle-the' and is the same as 'Asriel' (Num.26:31). Cp: 'assree-ill, assree-ill. (1Chr.7:14). Note: the names follow the list in Numbers.

Aramitess; 'ărammî, 'ărammiyyâ; عيرَمّي 'of abandoning or being abandoned in wilderness' 'of wilderness/uninhabited area'; عيرَمّيّه 'of abandoning or being abandoned in wilderness'; عيرَمّي يه 'abandon in wilderness-he/him/it' of abandoning/being abandoned in wilderness-he/him'; نَيرَمّي 'of throwing/of to do with throwing activity' 'killed/of killing' 'from far flung distances/locations' 'yes, saw water' 'he will throw water'; نَيرَمّيّه 'of throwing/of to do with throwing' 'of killing' 'yes, he threw it/yes, throw it' 'yes, saw water/yes, saw water-he/him' 'he will throw water' 'he will throw him/kill him'; نَيرَمّي يه 'of throwing-he/him' 'killed/of killing-he/him' 'yes, throw him/it' 'yes, throw-he/him'. Cp: 'airammee, 'airammiyyah, 'airammiy-yah, airammee, airammiyyah, airammiy-yah. (1Chr.7:14)

Peresh; pereš; فَرَش 'spread out/spread' 'laid it out/explained' 'lay down' 'resting place'. Cp: pheresh. (1Chr.7:16)

Sheresh; šereš; شَرَش 'bought you' 'your evil' 'wrapped garment/fabric around'. Cp: sheresh. (1Chr.7:16)

Ulam; 'ûlām; نُلاّم ، نولاّم 'pain/in pain' 'they are in pain' 'to blame' 'I am blamed'; عُلاّم 'marked' 'taught/have been taught' 'told' 'have been told' 'understood' 'shown' 'have been shown' 'knew/know'. Cp: olaam, oolaam, 'olaam, 'oolaam. (1Chr.7:16)

Rakem; rāqem; راقِم 'tattooed' (with dots) 'dotted/spotted' 'passed urine'; راكِم 'pile on top of each other'; راجِم 'thrown away(because unwanted)' 'stone/throw stones at' 'fill/bury with stones'. Cp: raaqem, raakem, raagem. (1Chr.7:16)

Hammoleketh; hammōleket; هَمّولِحَت ، هَم مولِحَت 'here is the pretty/nice one of' 'here she is salting/salted' 'here is the pancake/pancake pan' 'worried-she made pancake bread'; هَمّولِكَت ، هَم مولِكَت 'here is the one who owns' 'well, she owns' 'worried/worry-the owner of' 'worry/worried-loquacious' 'worry/worried-chewed'; هَمّولِقَت ، هَم مولِقَت 'here is the thrown' 'look-the thrown' 'worried-she found'; هَمّولِقَط هَم مولِقَط ،'here is the picker/gatherer' 'here is the gather of words(means spreads gossip)' 'here is the tongs' 'worry/worried-picked/gathered' 'worry/worried-gathered words(spread gossip)'. Cp: hammoleḥet, ham-mooleḥet, hammooleket, ham-mooleket, hammooleqet, ham-mooleqet, hammooleqeṭ, ham-mooleqeṭ. (1Chr.7:18)

Ishod; 'îšhôd; نَيشُد 'he is emigrating/leaving' 'he is tightening/bracing' 'he is wrapping around'. Cp: eeshod, ee-shod. (1Chr.7:18)

Abiezer; 'ăḇî'ezer; نَبي عَزَر 'rejected/refused-became ugly' 'father-became ugly'; عَبي عَزَر 'pack/fill-became ugly'; نَبي نَزَر 'rejected/refused-tight/tightened' 'father-tight/tightened'; عَبي نَزَر 'pack/fill-tight/

tightened'; نَبي نَذَر 'refused/rejected-sowed/sow/procreated' 'refused/rejected-scattered on ground' 'father-sowed/sow' 'father-scattered on ground'; عَبي نَذَر 'pack/fill-sowed/sow' 'pack/fill-scattered on ground'; نَبي عَذر 'refused/rejected-excuse' 'father-excused'; عَبي عَذر 'pack/fill-excuse/excused'. Cp: abee-'ezer, 'abee-'ezer, abee-ezer, 'abee-ezer, abee-ever, 'abee-ever, abee-'ever, 'abee-'ever. (1Chr.7:18)

Mahalah; maḥlâ; مَحله 'in his/her place' 'instead of' as in physically sitting or standing in the same place instead of another, 'undressing place' 'his/her place' as in building, position etc. 'how sweet (or) pretty she/he/it is' Cp: maḥlah. (1Chr.7:18)

Shemidah the same as Shemida (Num.26:32). (1Chr.7:19)

Ahian; 'aḥyān; نَحيآن 'sometimes' 'they are still/stationary/staying'; نَهيآن 'instigates/provokes' 'they are humiliated'. Cp: aḥyaan, ahyaan. (1Chr.7:19)

Likhi; liqḥî; لِقحي 'pollinates' 'of pollination' 'my pollination' 'has hardened'; لِججي 'goes around in circles' 'turned around' 'looked around' 'searched for'; لِق هي 'found her' 'met her' 'she found' 'she met'; لِك هي 'she is for you'; لِجهي 'it has been uncovered' 'if it is uncovered'. Cp: liqḥee, ligḥee, liq-hee, lik-hee, lig͟hee. (1Chr.7:19)

Aniam; 'ănî'am; نَنيعَم ، نَينيعَم 'blessed' 'blessed with' 'blessings' 'a blessing' 'something given or received: money, food supply, health, gifts anything which is given to or received from another' 'smooth' 'made easier' 'yes, yes/indeed, yes' 'yes, we drink'; نَيني عَم 'where is she-uncle' 'where is she-blind' 'where is-drink'; نَنيغَم ، نَينيغَم 'the depressions/depressed' 'the muffled/stifled' 'we will be depressed/stifled/muffled'; نَيني غَم 'where is she-depressed/stifled/muffled'. Cp: a-nee'am, ainee'am, ainee-'am, a-neeg͟ham, aineeg͟ham, ainee-g͟ham. (1Chr.7:19)

Eladah; 'el'ādâ; نَلعآده 'the usual' 'the norm' 'the counted/the ones who counted' 'the-creating enemies' 'the one who creates enemies' 'the one who transgressed' 'the transgressor' 'the one who infects/was infected' 'the one/those who returned'; نَلغآده 'the lunch' 'the feeds lunch/the fed lunch' 'the one who swells glands/ the swollen glands' 'the one who frustrates/the frustrated'. Cp: el-'aadah, el-g͟haadah. (1Chr.7:20)

Elead; 'el'ād̲; نَلعآد 'the one who returned' 'the returned' 'the counter/counted' 'the enemy' 'the transgressor' 'the normal/usual' 'the normal one' 'the infected' 'the infector'; نَلغآد 'the fed lunch' 'the swollen glands' 'the frustrated'. Cp: el-'aad, el-g͟haad. (1Chr.7:21)

Sherah; še'ĕrâ; سَئيرح 'he went/left'; شَئيره 'bought it/him' 'will penis him'; سَئيره 'they left early/they walked' 'will penis him'. Cp: se-eiraḥ, s͟he-eirah, se-eirah. (1Chr.7:24)

Uzzen-sherah; 'uzzēn še'ĕrâ; نُوذّين سَئيرح 'they were harmed-he went/left' 'they were eared-he went/left' 'they were given permission/he/they gave permission-he went/left' 'he announced/it was announced-he went/left' 'called to assembly/gather-he went/left'; نُوذين شَئيره 'they were harmed-bought him/it' 'they were eared/created handles-bought him/it' 'they were given permission/he/they gave permission-bought him/it' 'he announced/it was announced-bought him/it' 'called to assemble/gather-bought him/it'; نُوذين سَئيره 'they were harmed-left early/they walked' 'they were eared-left early/they walked' 'they were given permission/he/they gave permission-left early/they walked' 'called to assemble/he announced/it was announced-left early/they walked' 'they were harmed-will penis him' 'they were eared-will penis him' 'they were given permission/he/they gave permission-will penis him' 'called to assemble/he announced/it was announced-will penis him'. Cp: uvveyn-se-eiraḥ; uvveyn-s͟he-eirah, uvveyn-se-eirah. (1Chr.7:24)

Rephah; rĕpaḥ; رَبَح ، ريبَح 'monkeyed/caused a scene' (similar to going 'apeshit') 'shouted and threw things around' (literally or figuratively threw things around), 'profited/increased'; رَبَه ، ريبه 'diluted it with water' 'his master/head/god/person who is responsible for him/it' 'disciplined him/it' 'brought him up/it' 'taught him' 'grew him/it'. Equivalent to Meribah (Exod.7), Rabbah (Josh.13). Cp: rebaḥ, reibaḥ, re-bah, reibah. (1Chr.7:25)

Resheph; rešep; رَصَف 'stacks/stacked' (of stones, crops or any objects). It is equivalent to Rezeph (2Kgs.19:12), Rizpah(2Sam.3:7-10). Cp: res̲sep̲h. (1Chr.7:25)

Ṭelah; telaḥ; تَلَح ، تِلَح 'she makes pancakes' 'insists'; تِلَه 'ploughing' 'orating' 'wasting time/distracting'; دِلَه ، دَلَه 'he pushed it/pedalled it' 'his bailing pouch' 'lowered/dangled it' 'went around offering it' (the latter is something no one wants and used in a negative manner), 'slowly/gently'; ذَلَح 'winnowed'. Cp: telaḥ, telah, delah, velaḥ. (1Chr.7:25)

Tahan is the same as in Num.26:35 'ground (grains)'. (1Chr.7:25). Note how the words and at least one of their meanings each in 1Chr.7:25 are food/crop/grain related beginning from Rephah to Tahan.

Laadan; laʿdān; لاعدآن 'may they not return' 'may they not become enemies' 'they did not attack/transgress' 'they did not count'. Cp: la'adaan. (1Chr.7:26)

Non the same as Nun 'baby' 'very young'. (1Chr.7:27)

Naaran; naʿărān; نَعيرآن 'we strip naked/they are naked' 'they/we are lustful/horny/have/had an erection' 'they/we stood/stood erect/stood in front of without moving nor speaking'; نئيرآن 'we see/saw/ make/do see/ they/we understand/make understand' 'we show them' 'they/he penised/insulted with 'penis'/we penis him/we insulted with 'penis'' 'fires/make(s) fire(s)/we make fire' 'light/make light/we/they make light/shed light/we/they shed light'. It is equivalent to Naarath (Josh.16:7), Naarah (1Chr.4:5). Cp: na'airaan, na-airaan. (1Chr.7:28)

Imnah; yimnâ; همنا ، همنه 'our worry/he worries us'; جمنا، جمنه 'small clay jug for storing clarified butter'; يمنا ، يمنه 'to his right/to the right' 'he counts and lists/says he gave and gave' 'grants' 'from him' 'who, from him/from what'; عمنا ، عمنه 'drank/gave to drink/drank it' 'our uncle'. It is equivalent to Jimnah (Gen.46:17). Cp: himnah, himna, gimnah, gimna, yimnah, yimna, 'imna, 'imna. (1Chr.7:30)

Isuah and Ishuai are the same as Ishuah and Isui (Gen.46:17) and Jesui (Num.26:44). (1Chr.7:30)

Birzavith; birzāwiṯ; برزآوط 'good/piety-streaked(to one side or corner)' 'passed-streaked(to one side or corner) 'good/piety-misshaped' 'good/piety-chased after/went after him/antagonised/put him in a corner'. (zavith/zāwiṯ/زآوط) can also be 'rushed like a squirt' 'went rapidly under/behind something or in a specific direction' 'to push out suddenly/to squirt out' 'to fidget or jerk around a lot'; برصآوت 'good/piety-made a sound/called out' 'passed-made a sound/called out'; برسآوت 'good/piety-you did/made' 'good-made peace' 'good/piety-made even/level'; برشآوت 'good/piety-grilled/burnt/burned' 'passed-grilled/burnt/burned' 'good/piety-cried out (like animal)'; برضآوت 'good/piety-shone' 'good/piety-howled/moaned(like animal)' 'good/piety-abluted/washed'; برزآوت 'good/piety-slaughtered quickly/cuts quickly'. (zavith/zāwiṯ/زآوت) from word (zt) زت means 'a quick cut' 'slicing something with a quick motion' e.g. a sharp slice with a knife, or a rope around someone's hand causing a cut if pulled suddenly with force; and it can also mean to kill quickly (usually implies cutting of throat, but can also mean to strangle, etc.) (see Olivet/Zethan). Cp: bir-zaawiṭ, bir-<u>ss</u>aawit, bir-saawit, bir-<u>sh</u>aawit, bir-<u>dh</u>aawit, bir-zaawit. (1Chr.7:31)

Japhlet; yapḻēṯ; يَفليط 'he flattens and sticks'; يَفليت 'he falls' (literally or morally) 'you, immoral'; جَفليت 'came-fell' 'came the immoral(one)' 'foamed at the mouth' 'had a fit and foamed at the mouth'. Equivalent to Japhleti. Cp: ya<u>ph</u>leyṭ, ya<u>ph</u>leyt, ga<u>ph</u>leyt. (1Chr.7:32)

Hotham; ḥôṯām; حُف آم 'make fringes-the' 'have fringes-the' 'encourage-the'; حُت آم 'border/draw a line-the' 'make a rim-the'; حُتآم 'made shorter/tighter' 'sewed or folded to size' 'bordered/cornered/caused stress/in a tight situation/surrounded by difficulty from every side'; حُط آم 'set down/place-the' 'leave-the'; حُطآم 'broken pieces' 'debris of something destroyed'. Cp: ḥof-aam, ḥot-aam, ḥotaam, ḥoṭ-aam, ḥoṭaam. (1Chr.7:32)

Pasach; pāsak; فآسَح 'gave permissions' 'made space/moved over/allowed to pass or sit' 'made wider/baggy'; فآسَخ 'broke off/called off engagement' 'rotted/went off/spoiled'. Cp: <u>ph</u>aasaḥ, <u>ph</u>aasa<u>kh</u>. (1Chr.7:33)

Bimhal; bimhāl; بمهآل 'will allow/give more time' (to get something done/to pay back debt) 'by a slow pace' 'take your time'. Cp: bimhaal. (1Chr.7:33)

Ashvath; ʿašwāṯ; عَشوآت 'suppers' 'fed lots of supper'; غَشوآت 'deceived/conned' 'a conner' 'subtly replaced something good with something inferior or not good' 'membrane/cover'; نَزوآط 'squirt' 'make something go quickly in specific direction' 'misshapen things/people'; نَصوآت 'voices' 'I call out'; نَسوآت 'she made' 'she fixed' 'she levelled' 'she reconciled' 'bad/offense'; نَشوآت 'she grilled/burned' 'she/it cried out (like an animal)'; نَضوآت 'she shone' 'she abluted/washed'; نَزوآت 'quick cuts' 'slices/narrow wounds'. Cp: 'a<u>sh</u>waat, <u>gh</u>a<u>sh</u>waat, azwaaṭ, a<u>ss</u>waat, aswaat, a<u>sh</u>waat, a<u>dh</u>waat, azwaat. (1Chr.7:33)

Rohgah; rohgâ, rôhăgâ; روهيجه ، روهجه 'saw him come' 'loose/baggy' 'slips off' 'wobbles/shakes' 'saw mountainside'; روحيجه ، روحجه 'go, he has come' 'residue at bottom of tea/coffee, etc.' 'shook and mixed' e.g. to blend churned milk with water, 'shook and disturbed/unsettled'. Cp: rooh-gah, roohgah, roh-aigah, rohaigah, rooḥ-gah, rooḥgah, roḥ-aigah, roḥaigah. (1Chr.7:34)

Jehubbah; yĕhubbâ; ييحوبّه ، يَحوبّه 'he loves him/it' 'stays/makes it still-it/him' 'contains-it/him'; يَخوبّه ، ييخوبّه 'he hides him/it'; يَهوبّه ، ييهوبّه 'he sweeps down on' 'wind blows down/scatters' 'he gives it/him'; هَحوبّه 'I will love him/kiss him'; هيحوبّه 'he will kiss him/love him'; هَهوبّه 'I will swoop down/scatter'; هيهوبه 'he will swoop down/scatter'; هَخوبّه 'I will hide him/it'; هيخوبّه 'he will hide him/it'; جَحوبّه ، جيحوبّه 'came-kissed him' 'came-one single unit'; جَخوبّه ، جيخوبّه 'came-hid him/it'; جَهوبّه ، جيهوبّه

'came-swooped down on/scattered' 'came-gave him/it'. Cp: yeḥubbah, yeiḥubbah, yekhubbah, yeikhubbah, yehubbah, yeihubbah, heḥubbah, heiḥubbah, hehubbah, heihubbah, hekhubbah, heikhubbah, geḥubbah, geiḥubbah, gekhubbah, geikhubbah, gehubbah, geihubbah. (1Chr.7:34)

Helem; hēlem; هيلِم 'he will gather/save'. Cp: heylem. (1Chr.7:35)

Zophah; ṣôpaḥ; زُفَه 'was led in a procession' 'led a procession'; زُفَح 'splashed/gushed out heavily' 'flowed heavily'; صَفه 'made in lines/rows' 'stacked' 'stone columns' 'rock/stone' 'cleaned/cleansed/purified/cleared' 'pure/clear'; صُفَح 'flat surfaces or pieces/metal plates'; سُفَه 'vulgar(person)' 'numb' 'poured gently/poured gentle spurts of water' 'carried gently'; سُفَح 'bleeding heavily' 'flowing heavily'. Cp: zophah, zophaḥ, ssophah, ssophaḥ, sophah, sophaḥ. (1Chr.7:35)

Imna; yimnāʿ; يِمناَع 'he/it prevents/prohibits/does not allow'; هِمناَع 'I will prevent/stop'. Cp: yimnaa', himnaa'. (1Chr.7:35)

Shelesh; šēleš; سيلِس 'smooth/fine' 'chains'(metal for prisoners); شيلِس 'smooth/fine' 'necklace' 'chain (gold or metal)'; شيلَش ، شيل اش 'took what?'. Cp: seyles, sheyles, sheylesh, sheyl-esh. (1Chr.7:35)

Amal; ʿāmāl; عامآل 'worked' 'treated'; ئآمآل 'I fill' 'I fetch water'. Cp: 'aamaal, aamaal. (1Chr.7:35)

Suah; sûaḥ; سوَح 'wanderers seeking' 'wandering, seeking'; شوَح 'bleating/crying out like animal sounds'; صوَح 'shouting'. Cp: sooaḥ, shooaḥ, ssooaḥ. (1Chr.7:36)

Harnepher; ḥarnepẹr; خَرنِفَر 'a male and female(in one)-see'; خَر نِفَر 'he chased away violently-we flee' 'he chases-we flee'. Cp: kharnef-er, khar-nepher. (1Chr.7:36)

Beri; bērî; بيري 'by my penis' an insult usually said in humour, serious insult when said in anger. Cp: beyree. (1Chr.7:36)

Imrah; yimrâ; يِمره 'shines/reflects' 'mirrors'; عِمره 'built him/it' 'his/its age' 'building' 'piling tobacco mix and hotcoals on kooz cup' (to smoke); حِمره 'reddened' 'his donkeys' 'he is a donkey' 'he is being foolish/stupid/stubborn/brash'. Cp: yimrah, 'imrah, ḥimrah. (1Chr.7:36)

Hod; hôd; هُد 'demolish' 'was demolished' 'guide' 'was guided'; حُد 'sharpen' 'border' 'draw line'; خُط 'write' 'draw line' 'step' 'step over'. Cp: hod, ḥod, khoṭ. (1Chr.7:37)

Shamma; šammā'; شَمّآء 'tobacco powder' kept between gum and cheek, 'smelled/smelt'; سَمّآء 'named' 'poisoned'; سَمّآع 'listener/obeys/obedient' 'eavesdropper' 'let hear(insult)'. Cp: shammaa, sammaa, sammaa'. (1Chr.7:37)

Shilshah; šilšâ; سِلسَه 'is smooth/fine' 'his/her chains'; شِلسَه 'his/her necklace' 'is smooth/fine'; شِلشه/ا 'took what he wanted/what is important'. It is equivalent to Shalisha (1Sam.9:4) and Shelesh (1Chr.7:35). Cp: silsah, shilsah, shilshah(sha). (1Chr.7:37)

Beera the same as Beerah in (1Chr.5:6). (1Chr.7:37)

Pispah; pispâ; بِزبه/ا ، فِزبه/ا 'will penis/penetrate with penis' 'by penis/by penetrating with penis' 'so penis/penetrate with penis' 'provoke-her/him/it'; بِسفه/ا 'will go numb' 'by/with vulgarity/insults' 'will carry gently' 'will pour water gently/with gentle spurts of water'; فِسفه/ا 'so go numb' 'so carry gently' 'small insect, produces bad smell if touched' 'flatulence' 'passing wind(fart)'; بِصفه/ا 'will become clean/clear' 'will flatter' 'will insult greatly' 'will make in lines/rows' 'with/on rocks'. Cp: bizbah(ba), phizbah(ba), bisphah(pha), phisphah(pha), bis*sph*ah(*pha*). (1Chr.7:38)

Ara; 'ărā'; ئيرآء 'they penised' (physically or insulted by saying the word to another) 'penises' 'see' 'show' 'teach'; عيرآء 'stripped naked' 'naked' 'gloated at/over' 'borrowed/lent'. Cp: airaa, 'airaa. (1Chr.7:38)

Ulla; ʿullā', علّاء 'they are higher/high' 'above/above it' 'made it higher' 'they are delaying/dilly-dallying'; غولّاء 'they are expensive' 'expensive' 'they have ear inflammation' 'ear inflammation' 'river(s)/stream(s)' 'they are hateful/despise' 'they hate/despise' 'intense hatred' 'they stab/dig into-deep/intensely' 'severe/making up things in law/religion'. Cp: 'ullaa, ghullaa. (1Chr.7:39)

Arah; 'ārah; عآرَه 'his private parts' 'his female family/reputation' 'borrowed/lent him' 'disgraced him' 'gloated over/at him'; غآرَه 'quarrelled with him' 'shouted at him' 'funnelled down' 'saved him'. Cp: 'aarah, ghaarah. (1Chr.7:39)

Haniel the same as Hanniel; ḥannî'ēl; هَنّي يِل 'satisfy-the' 'give a lot to-the' and is usually said concerning food or other forms of satisfaction and gratification. It is by giving a lot, or a fair portion, or the best of something to create this satisfaction meant by the word 'hanni'. Cp: hannee-ill. (Num.34:23), and equivalent to Hannah (1Sam.1), Tehinnah (1Chr.4:12) and Mahanaim (Gen.). (1Chr.7:39)

Rezia; riṣyā'; رِصيآئ 'piled on' 'stacked on'; رِصيآع 'overpacked' 'pushed down to pack more in' 'over brimming'; رِضياء 'agreed to' 'became happy' 'happy/content/pleased'. Cp: rissyaa, rissyaa', ridhyaa. (1Chr.7:39)

Aharah; 'aḥĕraḥ; نَحيرَه 'I puzzled him/vexed him' 'I put him in a predicament' 'an open inflamed wound'; نَخيرَه 'the last' 'make him last' 'delay him' 'I defecate'; نَحي رَخ "aḥei' 'rakh" are sounds made to various animals to keep them moving or make them stop; نَخي رَخ 'my brother is loose/lenient' and can be an insult as in loose with his morals or in bringing up his children to be not properly moral, etc. 'my brother-loosened'; نَخي رَه 'my brother saw/saw him/it' 'my brother showed'; نَخي رَح 'my brother went/left'; نَهي رَه 'she-saw/saw him/it' she-showed; نَهي رَح 'she-left/went' 'here she is-left/went'; نَهي رَخ 'she is-loose' 'she is-lenient' 'she-loosened'. Cp: aḥeirah, akheirah, aḥei rakh, akhei-rakh, akhei-rah, akhei-raḥ, ahei-rah, ahei-raḥ, ahei-rakh. (1Chr.8:1)

Noḥah; nôḥâ; نُحه 'they/it screamed out in distress/long like animals'; نُهه 'they warned' 'they were banned; نُخه 'camel knelt' 'made camel kneel'. Cp: noḥah, nohah, nokhah. (1Chr.8:2)

Rapha; rāp̄ā'; رآفاء 'twitched/fluttered' 'they twitched/fluttered'; رآفآع 'lifted up' 'put/tidied away/put things in their place'; رآبآع 'ran on all fours' 'ran/galloped' and describes an animal galloping but also a person if he/she makes a lot of noise or movements, 'put a lock on'; رآباء 'became god(s)/parent(s)/teacher(s)' 'grew' 'grew lots' 'lymph nodes swelled' 'inflamed wound/sore which creates more wounds around it' 'disciplined' 'brought up' 'taught' 'diluted and mixed with water'. It is equivalent to Beth-rapha (1Chr.4:12). Cp: raaphaa, raaphaa', raabaa', raabaa. (1Chr.8:2). Note: the word 'Rapha' has the same meaning as the phrase 'Huppim and Muppim' 'swoop down on them and scatter them' which in Gen.46:21 were used as names of Benjamin's sons. The later editors/authors of 1Chronicles.8 have decided to use a different word but which has the same meaning and replace two characters with one instead: Rapha instead of both Muppim and Huppim. This is just one of thousands of words used as names for fictional characters and places in the Biblical stories. This explains why someone's son can become either father, great great great grandfather, female, brother, uncle or a different character's son or any relative in different parts of the Biblical stories, it only confuses those who wish to use the Bible as a historical document.

Addar; 'addār; نَضّآر 'the harmed/the harmer' 'the vicious' 'the one with the habit'; نَذّآر 'the sower(of seeds)/the sowed' 'the one with offspring' 'the scatterer' 'the leaver'; نَدّآر 'the spinner/the spun' 'the potter'; عَذّآر 'it/he shadows/shadowed' 'he excused/excused'; غَدّآر 'it/he darkened' (as in night/sky or in mood/facial expression), 'a deceiver' 'a treacherous person'. It is equivalent to Adar (Josh.15:3). Cp: adhaar, avvaar, addaar, 'avvaar, ghaddaar. (1Chr.8:3)

Abihud; 'ăḇîhûḏ; نَبي هُد 'refused/rejected-demolish/demolished' 'refused/rejected-guidance/be guided' refused/rejected-gifts' 'father-demolish/demolished' 'father-guidance/was guided'; عَبي هُد 'fill-demolish/demolished' 'fill/pack-guided/guidance' 'fill/pack-gifts'. Cp: abee-hud, 'abee-hud. (1Chr.8:3)

Ahoah; 'ăḥôaḥ; نَحوَه/نَحّاه ، نُيحوَه/نُيحّاه 'stay still/make stay still' 'make him/it stay'; نَهوَه/نَهّاه ، نُيهوَه/نُيهّاه 'it is him' 'here he is'. It is the same as Ehi (Gen.46:21) with slight variation where one of Ehi's meanings is in the feminine while the same meaning in Ahioh is in the masculine (it is him/here he is; her/she is/here she is). Cp: aḥooah, aḥoah, aiḥooah, aiḥoah, ahooah, ahoah, aihooah, aihoah. (1Chr.8:4)

Shephuphan; šĕp̄ûp̄ān; شيفُفآن 'they saw' 'of seeing' 'they dried/toasted' 'they were toasted/dried in pan' 'they gloated at' 'transparent'; شيبُبآن 'put sandals on' 'wore sandals' 'used sandals to hit/chase someone' 'young men/became young men' 'old men/became old'. It is equivalent to Shupham and all its variants which have different meanings and have been given different fathers/sons throughout the Bible in a very contradictory genealogy as the original Biblical authors were not concerned with getting 'genealogy' right for purely fictional characters, but it seems later editors would attempt this. Cp: sheiphuphaan, sheibubaan. (1Chr.8:5)

Huram; ḥûrām; حُرآم 'forbidden' 'they are sacred' 'they are rotten'; خُرآم 'slit/hole/piercing torn completely through' 'piercing holes into metal objects' 'burst from bottom'; هُرآم 'he threw' 'he-thrown' 'chase away(with words)-the' 'speak cruelly to'. It is equivalent to the same character it has replaced: Ahiram (Num.26:35), and also the same or similar to Horam (Josh.10:33), Hiram (2Sam.5:11-12) Malchiram (1Chr.3:18), to name a few. Cp: ḥuraam, khuraam, huraam. (1Chr.8:5)

Shaharaim; šaḥărayim; شَحَرَيم ، شَحيرَيم 'I will prohibit/forbid' 'I will deprive'; شَحَرَي ام ، شَحيرَي ام 'I will make fire-the' 'I will make them care/feel responsible/move them-the' 'I will investigate/find out-the'; شَهَرَيم ، شَهيرَيم 'I will speak unkindly to'; شَهَرَي ام ، شَهيرَي ام 'the moon/moonlight of-the' 'the month of-the' 'make a public scandal/slander-the' 'I will chase away (by speaking cruelly)-the' 'I will make fall apart-the'. Cp: shaḥarayim, shaḥairayim, shaḥaray-um, shaḥairay-um, shaharayim, shahairayim, shaharay-um, shahairay-um. (1Chr.8:8)

Baara; ba'ǎrā'; بَعيرآء 'with disgrace/will disgrace' 'with nakedness/will make naked' 'with gloating/will gloat at'; بَغيرآء 'with another' 'will change' 'with argument/will argue'. Cp: ba'airaa, baghairaa. (1Chr.8:8)

Hodesh; ḥōḏeš; هودِش 'was pounded/cracked'; خودِش 'was hit with heavy object' 'was scratched'; هودِس/هودَس 'he snuck it in and hid it' 'he planted it without anyone noticing' 'he whispered or planted bad ideas/caused enmity/problems(between people)'. Cp: hoodesh, khoodesh, hoodes. (1Chr.8:9)

Malcham; malkām; مَلكآم 'a punching' 'something being processed with punching like motions' 'what is wrong with the sleeves/sleeved' 'what is with the sleeves/what is the sleeves/sleeved'; مَلقآم 'of feeding through mouth by hand' such as a person/animal if sick or adding ingredients to a boiling kettle, etc. through the opening. 'what is wrong/what is with the standing/stood/erect'; مَلخآم 'spitting sputum' 'mucus in chest' 'what is the muttering/unclear/nasal sound' 'what is the musty from covering' 'what is wrong with/what is the speech like clearing throat/nasal sounds' 'what is the muffled sound/speech/voice' 'what is wrong with/what is the muffled voice/speaking with covered face or mouth' 'what is wrong with/what is the person who makes unclear sounds when speaks' 'what is the 'khaam' sounds'; مَلغآم 'what is/well what-the speaking with mouth or face covered' 'what is/well what-the suffocated' 'what is wrong with/what is the covered with face or headveil' 'what is wrong with/what is with the head/face/mouth covered' 'what is wrong with/what is with the head/face veils' 'what is covered/covered with face or head veil' 'what is the 'ghaam' sounds' 'what is muffled/speaking with muffled voice' 'what is wrong with the/what is with the stifled' 'what is stifled'. Cp: malkaam, malqaam, malkhaam, malghaam. (1Chr.8:9)

Jeuz; yĕ'ûṣ; يَعِز ، ييعِز 'he cherishes' 'he needs' 'he supports/provides for'; يَعُص ، ييعُص 'he disobeys' 'he/it becomes hard/stuck' 'he/it becomes askew/bent/crooked-the' 'he uses a stick'; هَعُز 'I will cherish' 'I will need' 'I will support/provide for'; هيعُز 'he will cherish' 'he will need' 'he will support/provide for'; هَعُص 'I will disobey' 'I will/look it-became hard/stuck' 'I will/look it became askew/bent/crooked' 'I will use a stick'; هيعُص 'he will disobey' 'he will/look it-became hard/stuck' 'he will use a stick'; جَعُص ، جيعَص 'lower back/spine' 'backside'; جَعُز ، جيعُز 'rough textured' 'rough fur' 'came and cherished' 'came and needed/asked for assistance'. Cp: ye'uz, yei'uz, ye'uss, yei'uss, he'uz, hei'uz, he'uss, hei'uss, ge'uss, gei'uss, ge'uz, gei'uz. (1Chr.8:10)

Shachiah; śāḵĕyâ; صآخِيه ، صآخي يه 'she is obedient/does as bid' 'obedient/does as told-he/him' 'she would do it' 'would do it-he/him'; سآخيه ، سآخي يه 'she is mild' 'mild-he/him' 'she is generous' 'generous-he/him' 'her heart/conscience would let her' 'heart/conscience would let-he/him'; سآكيه ، سآكي يه 'she is settled/calm' 'calm/settled-he/him' 'she is settled asleep' 'settle asleep-he/him' and usually describes calm waters or anything liquid that separates into layers, grind, silt and liquid above. Cp: ssaakheiyah, ssaakhei-yah, saakheiyah, saakhei-yah, saakeiyah, saakei-yah. (1Chr.8:10)

Mirma; mirmâ; مِرمه 'throwing point/place' 'killing place/point'. Cp: mirmah. (1Chr.8:10)

Abitub; 'ăḇîṭûḇ; نَبي تُب 'refused/rejected-repent' 'father-repent'; عَبي تُب 'pack/fill-repent' 'shame/disgrace-repent'; نَبي طَب 'refused/rejected-willy' 'refused/rejected-good/became good/palatable/tastes nice'; عَبي طَب 'pack/fill-willy' 'pack/fill-good/became good/palatable/tastes nice'. Cp: abee-tub, 'abee-tub, abee-ṭub, 'abee-ṭub. (1Chr.8:11)

Elpaal; 'elpa'al; ئَلفَعَل 'the one who did' 'the action' 'the thing that happened'; ئَلبَعَل 'the spouse(s)' 'the high place/above' 'the one of high place/above' 'the one with high place/above'. Cp: el-pha'al, el-ba'al. (1Chr.8:12)

Misham; miš'ām; مِشغآم 'terrible stomach ache' 'has stomach ache' 'a great shouting/screaming'; مِش غآم 'not suffocated' 'not with mouth/face covered' 'not depressed/stifled'; مِش عآم 'did not drink'; مِش آم 'not-the' 'walked-the'. Cp: mishghaam, mish-ghaam, mish-'aam, mish-aam. (1Chr.8:12)

Shamed; šemeḏ; شَمَط 'swiped (with rope or stalk, etc.)' 'will stretch' 'will stretch towards'; شَمَظ 'tied into small sheaves'; شَمَد 'will extend hand' 'will reach out/into' 'will hand'; سَمَط 'head shawl laid flat on forehead' 'to make something stick flat'; زَمَت 'internally blocked/blocked intestines'; صَمَد 'withstood' 'survived/remained standing or intact' 'became stuck/caught in something sideways'; صَمَت 'is blocked' 'she blocked/stopped' 'is smooth/poreless' 'fasted'. Cp: shemeṭ, shemedh, shemed, semeṭ, zemet, ssemed, ssemet. (1Chr.8:12)

Ono; 'ônô; نُن 'me' 'moan/whine' 'because it is…' 'it is'. Cp: ono. (1Chr.8:12)

Lod; lōḏ; لود 'goes around and around' 'goes in circles in anguish' usually used in a phrase pair (yeḥood wa yelood' يحود ويلود) 'he goes back and forth/in circles' and is used to describe an animal or person in distress/anxious and may be showing signs of anguish; لوض 'crush together' 'burning pain/sensation'; لوت 'crumple/press and crumple'. Cp: lood, loodh, loot. (1Chr.8:12)

Shashak; šāšāq; شآشآق 'wanted a labourer' 'wanted labour/work' 'wanted-difficult' 'wanted-split' 'wanted-pain like splitting' 'cracked/cracked through'; شآشآك 'wanted you' 'important matter-wants you' 'complained a lot'; شآشآغ 'became blurry/unclear/watery' 'blood, water or any liquid rising slowly to surface/oozing'; شآصاق 'I will be able to reach' (as in something high/across, by stretching body or arms) 'I will drive' (as in how people or animals are driven towards a specific direction'. Cp: shaashaaq, shaashaak, shaashaagh, shaassaaq. (1Chr.8:14)

Jeremoth; yĕrēmôṯ; same as Jerimoth (yĕrîmôṯ) (1Chr.7:7). The slight change in spelling does not affect/change the pronunciation and meanings: يَريمُت ، ييريمُت Cp: yereymot, yeireymot parallel to the earlier version: yereemot, yeireemot. (1Chr.8:14)

Zebadiah; zĕḇaḏyâ, zĕḇaḏyāhû; شِبَديه/ياهُ ، شيبَديه/ياهُ 'I will take (or bring) it/him/her out' 'I will turn it/him/her out'; زَبَد يه/ياهُ ، زيبَد يه/ياهُ 'drinking bowls-he/him' 'ointment-he/him' 'massaged/perfumed with ointment-he/him' 'butter-he/him' 'buttered-he/him'; زَبَط يه/ياهُ ، زيبَط يه/ياهُ 'kicked-he/him' 'kicked a lot-he/him'; ضَبَط يه/ياهُ ، ضيبَط يه/ياهُ 'strengthened/tightened/secured-he/him' 'strong-he/him' 'husband publicly disciplining wife-he/him' the latter is when she and other people engage in a quarrel that results in serious insult or assault which the specific wife is proven guilty of; شَبط يه/ياهُ ، شيبَط يه/ياهُ 'tied tightly with rope-he/him' 'latticed with roped-he/him' 'whipped/striped-he/him'. Cp: shebadyah(yaahu), sheibadyah(yaahu), zebad-yah/yaahu, zeibad-yah/yaahu, zebaṭ-yah/yaahu, zeibaṭ-yah/yaahu, dhebaṭ-yah/yaahu, dheibaṭ-yah/yaahu, shebaṭ-yah/yaahu, sheibaṭ-yah/yaahu. (1Chr.8:15)

Ader; ʿāder; غآدَر 'became dark/darker' 'deceived/betrayed'; عآذَر 'shadowed over' 'excused'; ئآضَر 'harmed'. Cp: ghaader, 'aaver, aadher. (1Chr.8:15)

Ispah; yišpâ; يِشبه 'resembles'; يِصبح 'wakes in the morning' 'finds in the morning' 'makes trouble in the morning' 'avoids trouble in the morning'; يِسبه 'is in trance/daydream' 'zones out' 'stares into distance without listening' 'loses track of time or track of conversation'; يِسبح 'swims/floods' 'praises' 'floats in his head(distracted/daydreaming/lapsing)' 'disconnects with reality while conscious/eyes open'; يِشبح 'stretches leg across'. It is equivalent to Ishbah (1Chr.4:17). Cp: yishbah, yissbḥ, yisbah, yisbḥ, yishbḥ. (1Chr.8:16)

Joha; yôḥā'; يُحاء 'is made still/made to stay'; هُحاء 'he/it is still/staying in its place'; جُحاء 'hard and unripe' (usually refers to fruit and vegetables) 'hard' (used to describe fruit, vegetables, or girls/women's breasts), 'came-stayed/stood still'; جُهاء 'uncovered/open' 'came here' 'came, here(take)' 'look/pay attention they have come'. Cp: yoḥaa, hoḥaa, goḥaa, gohaa. (1Chr.18:16)

Hezeki; ḥizqî; حِزكي 'of cornering/being cornered/crammed'; هِسقي 'I will water'; هِزكي 'I will flatter/praise' 'I will predict/say if (person) going to hell or heaven' 'I will predict if (person) good or bad'; هِزقي 'will squirt out of/shoot to'; هِضقي 'will forcibly swallow/suffer'; حِذقي 'clever/of cleverness'; كِزقي 'show me how you squirt' 'try and squirt' 'go ahead, squirt'; حِزقي 'caught in' 'tangled in' 'of getting caught in' (when something thorny or has texture to get caught into fabric); خِزقي 'make holes(in)' 'my hole'. Cp: ḥizkee, hisqee, hizkee, hizqee, hidhqee, ḥivqee, kizqee, ḥizqee, khizqee. (1Chr.8:17)

Ishmerai; yišmĕray; يِسمَري ، يِسميري 'he/they stay awake all/late night' 'he/they tell night stories' 'you, storyteller/you, staying up all night'; يِشمَري ، يِشميري 'he/they roll up/tuck/fold up their sleeves/clothes' (the latter to avoid getting soiled while working) 'you, with the rolled/tucked up clothes'. Cp: yismeray, yismeiray, yishmeray, yishmeiray. (1Chr.8:18)

Jezliah; yizlî'â; هِذليئه 'is shivering'; خِذليئه 'not of sane mind' 'mind is failing' 'take for me'; جِزليئه 'I'm allowed' 'allow me' 'reward for me/retribution on me' 'serves me right'; عِزليئه 'pride/high standing for me' 'cherish for me' 'alone/cut off'; حِزليئه 'corner/move aside for me'; خِزليئه 'swearing at me' 'a disgrace for me'; غِزليئه 'deep ache/low sound for me' 'flirting' 'weaving/spinning or making thread'. Cp: hivlee-ah, khivlee-ah, gizlee-ah, 'izlee-ah, ḥizlee-ah, khizlee-ah, ghizlee-ah. (1Chr.8:18)

Jakim; yāqîm; يآقيم 'he stands' 'he stands instead of/replaces/represents' 'is erect' 'he has an erection'. Cp: yaaqeem. (1Chr.8:19)

Elienai; 'ĕlîʿênay; ئِلي/ئيلي عينَي 'the one who-look' 'the one who-hinted/directed speech' 'the one who-confronted' 'the one who inspected'; ئِلي غينَي 'the one who is rich' 'the one who sang' 'the one who no longer needed/became independent of' 'the one who made throaty sound (ghn/ghain)'. Equivalent to Elioenai (1Chr.3:23). Cp: illee/eilee-'eynay, illee-gheynay. (1Chr.8:20)

Zilthai; ṣillĕṯay; زِلّيتَي ، زِلّتَي 'they went off' talking about two people, 'they disappeared' 'they were removed/wiped out' 'you went off/disappeared/went' the latter said to a female. Cp: zilletay, zilleitay. (1Chr.8:20)

Beraiah; bĕrā'yâ; بيرآى يه ، بِرآى يه 'good/pious-he/him' 'good/pious towards-he/him' 'passed by him' 'passed-he/him' 'innocent-he/him' 'innocent of/disowns-he/him' 'he will dream-he/him' 'in his dream' 'by my penis-him/he' 'he will see him/he will see-he/him' 'he will water him/he will water-he/him'. Cp: beraa-yah, beiraa-yah. (1Chr.8:21)

Shimrath; šimrāṯ; سِمرآت 'night time stories' 'they stayed up'; شِمرآت 'with rolled up/tucked sleeves/clothes'. Cp: simraat, shimraat. (1Chr.8:21)

Shimhi; šim'î; the same as Shimi (Exod.6:17), Shimei (2Sam.16:5). (1Chr.8:21)

Ishphan; yišpān; يِشبآن 'swell and become hard' 'grow into young men/women' 'grow old'; حِشبآن 'carrying on waist'; يسفآن 'become numb' 'carrying gently' 'pouring water gently'; يِصفآن 'become clear/pure' 'become clean' 'settle differences'; يِشفآن 'they are healing'. Cp: yishbaan, ḥishbaan, yisphaan, yissphaan, yishphaan. (1Chr.8:21)

Hanan; ḥānān; هآنآن 'were disgraced' 'insulted/were insulted' two or more people, 'were satisfied/given plenty'; حآنآن 'it is time' 'adorned with henna' 'felt affection'; خآنآن 'soaked' 'betrayed' 'brothers/became brothers'. Cp: haanaan, ḥaanaan, khaanaan. (1Chr.8:23)

Antothijah; 'anĕṯōṯîyâ; نَتيتوفي يه 'pluck it-him/he'; نَتيثوتي يه ، نَتيثوتي يه 'becoming female-he/him'; نَتيذوفي يه 'push him off-he/him'; نَتيضوفي يه 'clean/cleaning-he/him'; عَنيدودي يه 'stubborn/provoking-he/him'. Cp: aneitoophee-yah, aneifoofee-yah, aneifootee-yah, aneivoophee-yah, aneidhoophee-yah, 'aneidoodee-yah. (1Chr.8:24)

Iphedeiah; yipdĕyâ; يِفدِي يه 'he sacrifices/sacrifices for-him/he'; يِبدي يه 'he brings out/takes out-he/him'. It is the equivalent/similar to Pedahel (Num.34:28), Jiphtah (Josh.15:43), Jiphthah-el (Josh.19:14), Jephthah (Judg.11) and Pedaiah (2Kgs.23:36). Cp: yiphdei-yah. (1Chr.8:25)

Shamsherai; šamšĕray; سَمسيرَي 'tell many 'samaria' (late night) stories'; شَمشيرَي 'with rolled up/tucked sleeves/clothes'. Cp: samseiray, shamsheiray. (1Chr.8:26)

Shehariah; šĕḥaryâ; شيهَر يه 'the month of-him/he' 'the moon/moonlight-him/he' 'made public scandal/slander-him/he'; سَيهَر يه 'stayed up all night beside-him/he' 'will drive away (with words)-him/he'; سيحَر يه 'awoke before dawn-him/he' 'had breakfast before dawn-him/he' 'was under a spell/cast a spell-him/he' ; شيحَر يه 'scowled with his eyes-him/he' 'dry land-him/he'. Cp: sheihar-yah, seihar-yah, seiḥar-yah, sheiḥar-yah. (1Chr.8:26)

Jaresiah; ya'ărešyâ; يَغيرِس يه 'he plants-he/him'; هَغيرس يه 'I will plant it' 'look, he planted-he/him'; جَغيرَس يه 'came-planted-he/him'; يَعيرس يه 'he weds-he/him' 'he is newly wed-he/him'; هَعيرِس يه 'I will marry(get him married)-he/him' 'I will be like newly wed'; جَعيرَس يه 'came-wed-he/him'; يَغيرَز يه 'he plaits-he/him' 'he gets stuck in mud/soil/sand-he/him'; هَغيرز يه 'I will plait it/him' 'I will plait-he/him'; جَغيرَز يه 'came-plaited-he/him' 'came-stuck in mud/soil/sand-he/him' and the latter can mean literally or figuratively as in he overstayed his welcome. Cp: yaghaires-yah, haghaires-yah, gaghaires-yah, ya'aires-yah, ha'aires-yah, ga'aires-yah, yaghairez-yah, haghairez-yah, gaghairez-yah. (1Chr.8:27)

Eliah; 'ēliyyâ; ئيلِيّه ، ئيلِي يه 'whichever one it is/whoever it is' 'the one who/he who-him/he' 'it is him' 'for me-him/it'. Cp: eyliyyah, eyliy-yah. (1Chr.8:27)

Zacher; zeker; ذَكير 'remembers/mentions' 'remembered/mentioned', شَقير 'peeped between gaps' 'gaps(between wall)'; زَقير 'top-up/fill gap(s)/fill'. Cp: vekeyr, sheqeyr, zeqeyr. (1Chr.8:31)

Mikloth; miqlôṯ; مِقلَت 'eyeing' 'staring' 'inspecting'; مِقلَد 'with responsibility in his/her neck' 'with garland/responsibility hanging from his/her/its neck' 'copying/mimicking'; مِخلَث 'changed' 'has been changed' 'spoiled/gone off'; مِكلَف 'with/been given responsibility' 'skin condition discolours skin' (starts as dark freckles, when they disappear it leaves the skin discoloured, lighter than rest of the face (people believe it is from too much stress)); مِغلَف 'enveloped in something (skin/fibre/leaves, etc.). Cp: miqlot, miqlod, mikhlof, mikloph, mighloph. (1Chr.8:32)

Esh-baal; 'ešbā'al; نَيص/نَص بآعَل 'hush/quiet-will raise higher'; نَيش/نَش بآعَل 'how/what-will raise higher'. This is another slight name-change for a character. Ish-bosheth 'hush(ed)-gobsmacked'(2Sam.3:7-11) has become a different version, probably intended to suit the story better as the original story in 2Sam. does have the character hushed and gobsmacked by Abner, then after Ish-bosheth is slaughtered his assassins' dismembered bodies are hung up. Cp: e<u>ss</u>-baa'al, e<u>sh</u>-baa'al. (1Chr.8:33)

Merib-baal; mĕrîḇ-bāʿal; this too has been changed from Mephibosheth (2Sam.9:1-13) to make the name suit both places where it was used for two different characters in the story: **Mephibosheth** 'there was no gobsmacked/unable to speak' now becomes ميريض بأعَل 'ill/being nursed due to illness-will raise higher' and this new version of the earlier names suits both characters' stories in (2Sam.3:7-11; 21:7-8)—where first it was introduced as Jonathan's son who talks a lot with the name reflecting this; he has now been given a name to reflect his disability and that he was being taken care of (by David), while at the same time the different character of the same original name (as Saul's son not Jonathan's) has been covered by allowing him to be hung as a human sacrifice for rain (delivered by David to Gibeonites to sacrifice). There is a slight difference in how 'Baal' has been spelled and how it is pronounced to give it a variation from the mostly used 'Baal' in the Biblical stories. Cp: meiree<u>dh</u>-baa'al. (1Chr.8:34)

Pithon; pîṯôn; بيذن 'he will give permission' 'he will announce' 'he will harm/be harmed' 'with ear/handle'; في ذن 'in the ear'; بيتن 'you stay overnight' 'their house'; بيثن 'he will double/fold' 'venomous lizard called 'bethan''; بيضُن 'eggs/lay eggs'; بيظن 'he will think/suspect'; بيطن 'underlayered the garment' 'has stomach ache' 'will clang/tinning noise'; بيدن 'will bow/bend/lower head' 'fair-skinned' 'will guilt' 'brought out'. Cp: beevon, <u>ph</u>ee-von, beeton, beefon, bee<u>dh</u>on, bee<u>dh</u>on, beeṭon, beedon. (1Chr.8:35)

Melech; meleḵ; مِلِح ، مَلَح 'nicely/well/good/pretty' 'salt'; مَلَق 'thrown/cast'; مَلَك 'what is wrong with you/what is with you?' 'owned'. Cp: meleḥ, meleq, melek. (1Chr.8:35)

Tarea; ta'rēaʿ; تَترَيَع 'wet himself' 'passed a lot of urine' 'completely soaked/flooded' but not a flood just lots of water all over whatever it is attributed to. It suits being a son of 'Micah' as one of its meanings is 'cowardly' from the meaning of 'runny/egg yolk' in Judg.17; 18. Note: Whenever a different character is named Micah, the sons always have names which are similar. E.g. Tarea is son of Micah in this verse; Reaiah which also has the meaning 'soaked with urine/water/flooded' is also a son of a different Micah at (1Chr.4:2). The authors/editors have no problem in recycling the names for their word-meanings in the fictional stories as can be seen in their repeated use with or without variations of the word-name. Cp: tareya'. (1Chr.8:35)

Jehoadah; yĕhôʿaddâ; بيهُ عَدّه 'he who/which one-counted' 'he who/which one-transgressed/became or made enemy'; جيهُ عَدّه 'came to him/came he-counted' 'came to him/came he-who made enemy'; بيهُ غَدّه 'he who/which one-fed/ate lunch' 'he who/which one-frustrated/made glands swell'; جيهُ غَدّه 'came to him/came he-ate/fed lunch' 'came to him/came he-frustrated/made glands swell'. Cp: yeiho-'addah, geiho-'addah, yeiho-<u>gh</u>addah, geiho-<u>gh</u>addah. (1Chr.8:36)

Binea; binʿā'; بِنعاء 'we will be warned/understood' 'we will take notice/remember' 'we will contain'. Cp: bin'aa. (1Chr.8:37)

Azel; 'āzēl; نأزيل 'I remove/wipe out' 'leave forever/remove completely' 'I leave/go off/disappear' 'forever'. This too reflects how later editors/authors have attempted to create a character for every place name in an attempt to explain the place-names were named after a person, while the original stories show these fictional place-names were created to enhance the story. Azel (now a character name) is the equivalent of Ezel the name of the stone where David and Jonathan met before David had to leave Saul's palace for good, where they exchanged vows of 'forever' and parted by the suitably named stone(1Sam.20:14-42). Not only is it an equivalent, but the editors have decided to give this word-name, used earlier as a prop/enhancement for the Jonathan/David story, to a descendant of Jonathan's character. Cp: aazeyl. (1Chr.8:38)

Bocheru; bōḵĕrû; بوكيرُ 'firstborn' 'early' 'early tomorrow'; بوخيرُ 'in good health/fine' 'smoked with incense'; بوحيرُ 'good riddance' 'in the sea'; بوقيرُ 'cows/cattle' 'settle or quiet down/stop it/be still' 'ripped open'. Cp: bookeiru, boo<u>kh</u>eiru, booḥeiru, booqeiru. (1Chr.8:38)

Sheariah; šĕʿaryâ; شيعَريه 'he will strip him naked/unclothe him' 'he is a sign'; شيعَر يه 'he will make naked-him/he' 'a sign-he/him' 'he will disgrace-him/he'. This is a reminder of the love story of Jonathan and David. Cp: <u>sh</u>ei'aryah, <u>sh</u>ei'ar-yah. (1Chr.8:38)

Eshek; ʿēšeq; عيشَق ، عيشِق 'has forbidden love affair' 'love affair' 'lover' and refers to a relationship between a man and woman who are not married. In this instance it is still referring to Jonathan and David's full love and sexual relationship; it seems the later editors did not want this to be forgotten nor changed and have added 'descendants' to Jonathan's character in 1Chronicles to record and remind the true meanings of Jonathan and David's story. Cp: 'eysheq. (1Chr.8:39)

Jehush; yĕʿûš; يَعُش ، بيعُش 'grazes/shepherds (in afternoon)' 'lives/he lives'; جَعُش ، جيعُش '(of)furry/long/untamed hair'; جَنَّش ، جينَش 'took lots/picked many/took by the handfuls' 'took too much/many'; يَغُش ، بيغُش 'he deceives/cheats' 'it is not clear/it is blurred'. Cp: ye'ush, yei'ush, ge'ush, gei'ush, ge-ush, gei-ush, yeghush, yeighush. It is the same as Jeush (Gen.36:5). (1Chr.8:39)

Eliphelet; the same as Eliphalet (David's son) in 2Sam.5:16; this is either a pun by the same editor giving Jonathan the same son as David's son (indicating the 'made him female by having sex with him' meaning of Jonathan's name) or is a disdainful editor reminding the audience of his culture or the time's belief that the relationship between David and Jonathan was an immoral one: Eliphelet means ئِلي فَلَت 'he who/the one who fell' 'he who/the one who became immoral/lewd'; ئِلي بَلَط 'he who/the one who-I will squeeze together' 'he who/the one who-I will press against' 'he who/the one who-I will make sag from too much squeezing' 'he who/the one who-I will make stick/get stuck to the side'. Cp: elli-phalet, elli-baleṭ. (1Chr.8:39)

Nethinim; nĕṯînîm; ; نَثين هم/ام ، نَيثين هم/ام 'we double/fold-them/the' 'we female/is feminine-them/the'; نَظين هم/ام ، نيظين هم/ام 'we guilt-them/the' 'we bow/bend/lower-them/the'; نَدين هم/ام ، نيدين هم/ام 'we think/suspect-them/the'; نَطين هم/ام ، نيطين هم/ام 'we clang-them/the' 'make a tinning or clanging noise-them/the'. Cp: nefeen-hum/um, neifeen-hum/um, nedeen-hum/um, neideen-hum/um, nedheen-hum/um, neidheen-hum/um, neṭeen-hum/um, neiṭeen-hum/um. (1Chr.9:2)

Uthai; ʿûṯay; عَتي 'became hard to move/stuck/rusty'; عَذَي 'say a protection/protected' ; عَفي 'gone off food' 'boiled' ; عَضَي 'sore muscles' 'recompense/my recompense' ; عَطي 'was given' 'given/give' ; عَدَي 'come back' 'returned' 'transgressed/became enemy' 'counts' 'my wood/stick' ; غَذي 'was nourished' 'my nourishment' ; غَثي 'was nauseated' 'nausea' 'nagged until nauseated' 'was nourished'; غَضَي 'deep hatred' 'boiling hatred' 'hatred kept under restraint' 'lower eyes' ; غَطي 'cover' 'lid' 'obstructed view' ; غَدَي 'feed lunch' 'visit new mother on the Seventh' 'has/will get swollen glands' 'frustrate/will frustrate'. Cp: 'utay, 'uvay, 'uphay, 'udhay, 'uṭay, 'uday, ghuvay, ghufay, ghudhay, ghuṭay, ghuday. (1Chr.9:4)

Imri; 'imrî; ئِمري 'shine/reflect' 'my business/matters' 'my accountability' 'bossy' 'orders' 'takes orders/instructions obediently'. Cp: imree. (1Chr.9:4)

Jeuel; yĕʿû'ēl; يَعُئيل ، بيعُئيل 'has sons/boys' 'has boys with him' 'howling, screaming and shouting'; يَعْ ئِل ، بيعْ ئِل 'understands-the' 'warns-the' 'learns and remembers-the' 'contains-the'; هَعُئيل 'I will have sons' 'I will have boys helping'; هيعُئيل 'he will have sons' 'he will bring boys (to help)'; جَعُئِل ، جَعُئيل 'created/made' 'made happen' 'laid bait egg'; جَعْ ئِل ، جيعْ ئِل 'came-understood/warned/learned-the' 'hungry/starved-the'. Cp: ye'u-eyl, yei'u-eyl, ye'u-ill, yei'u-ill, he'u-eyl, hei'u-eyl, ge'uill, ge'ueyl, ge'u-ill, gei'u-ill. (1Chr.9:6)

Sallu; sallû', sallu', sallû; صَلّء ، صَلّوء ، صَلّ 'pray' 'reach/arrive' 'connect' 'deliver' 'roast/grill' 'rock/stones'; سَلّء ، سَلّوء ، سَلّ 'comfort' 'entertain' 'distract' 'leak/flow' 'ask/question' 'asks lots of questions'. Cp: ssallu, ssalloo, ssallu, sallu, salloo, sallu. (1Chr.9:7)

Hasenuah; hassĕnu'â, hassĕnû'â; حَسّ نوئه/ نُئه ، حَسي نوئه/ نُئه 'feel his intentions' 'be careful of his intentions' 'feel/beware-warn/remind'; حَسّنوئه ، حَسينوئه ، حَسّنُئه ، حَسينُئه 'make it better' 'pretty' 'good/kind'; حَصّنوئه ، حَصّينوئه ، حَصّنُئه ، حَصّينُئه 'fortified it' 'strengthened it' 'protected it' 'a protection amulet' 'filled with stones/gravel' (the latter part of a building process); خَسّنوئه ، خَسينوئه ، خَسّنُئه ، خَسينُئه 'despicable-he/it'; خَصّنوئه ، خَصينوئه ، خَصّنُئه ، خَصينُئه 'to do with' 'his business/concern' 'we involved him/it' 'castrated him/it'; هَسّنوئه ، هَسينوئه ، هَسّنُئه ، هَسينُئه 'I will straighten/align/make straight' 'here is makes straight/aligns' 'look/here/pay attention-in his direction/make straight' 'pressed on it' 'put weight on it'. Cp: ḥasse noo-ah, ḥasse nu-ah, ḥassei noo-ah, ḥassei nu-ah, ḥassenoo-ah, ḥasseinoo-ah, ḥassenu-ah, ḥasseinu-ah, ḥassenoo-ah, ḥasseinoo-ah, ḥassenu-ah, ḥasseinu-ah, khassenoo-ah, khasseinoo-ah, khassenu-ah, khasseinu-ah, khassenoo-ah, khasseinoo-ah, khassenu-ah, khasseinu-ah, hassenoo-ah, hasseinoo-ah, hassenu-ah, hasseinu-ah. (1Chr.9:7)

Ibneiah; yiḇnĕyâ; يِبنِ يه ، يِبني يه 'son, you' 'son of-he/him' 'builds-he/him'; يِبنِيه ، يِبنييه 'he builds' 'they build'; يِبنِ هه ، يِبني هه 'he builds-look/here/see'; يِبنِهه ، يِبنيهه 'he is building it' 'he impregnates her' 'he brings her up as his own child' يِبنِ جه ، يِبني جه 'he builds-came'. Cp: yibne-yah, yibnei-yah, yibneyah, yibneiyah, yibne-hah, yibnei-hah, yibnehah, yibneihah, yibne-gah, yibnei-gah. (1Chr.9:8)

Michri; mik̲rî; مِخري 'the last' 'the delayed' 'of defecating/faeces'; مِكري 'hired/lent' 'of cunning/deceit/scheming'; مِغري 'of arguing/arguments' 'of funnelling down/disappearing into the ground' 'of tempting/deceiving'. Cp: mikhree, mikree, mighree. (1Chr.9:8)

Shephathiah; the same as Shephatiah (2Sam.3:4). (1Chr.9:8)

Ibnijah is the exact same as **Ibneiah** from the same verse with only a slight difference in spelling and pronunciation which does not change any of its meanings. What is obvious from the names from the beginning of 1Chr.9, is that the authors are listing themes revolving around the intention of a story about building something (**Nethinim, Ammihud, Omri, Imri, Bani, Pharez, Shilonite, Jeuel, Sallu, Meshullam, Hodaviah, Hasenuah, Ibneiah, Elah, Michri, Ibnijah**, to name a few); yib̲nîyâ; يِبني يه 'son, you' 'son of-he/him' 'builds-he/him'; يِبنيه 'he builds' 'they build'; يِبني هه 'he builds-look/here/see'; يِبنيهه 'he is building it' 'he impregnates her' 'he brings her up as his own child;' يِبني جه 'he builds-came'. Cp: yibnee-yah, yibneeyah, yibnee-hah, yibneehah, yibnee-gah. (1Chr.9:8)

Jehoiarib; yĕhôyārîb̲; يَهُ/يِيهُ يآريب 'which one/he who-mixes and dilutes with water' (this too is a process in several steps of building a house/structure); جَهُ/جيهُ يآريب 'came to him/came he-mixing and diluting with water'; هَهُ/هيهُ يآريب 'here he is-mixing and diluting with water'.

The following words could also be meanings of Jehoiarib, but the above-mentioned meanings fit with the drive of the chapter using words as names which are involved in a building of a house process: يَهُ/يِيهُ هآريب 'which one/he who-is running away/fled' 'which one/he who-is god/parent/teacher'; جَهُ/جيهُ هآريب 'came he/came to him-fleeing/the fleeing/the one who ran away' 'came he/came to him-is/here is-god/parent/teacher'; هَهُ/هيهُ هآريب 'here he is-fleeing/running away' 'here he is-is/will-god/parent/teacher'; يَهُ/يِيهُ جآريب 'which one/he who-tried' 'which one/he who-has skin condition (similar to psoriasis)' 'which one/he who-oasis'; جَهُ/جيهُ جآريب 'came he/came to him-attempted' 'came he/came to him-has skin condition (similar to psoriasis)' 'came he/came to him-oasis'; هَهُ/هيهُ جآريب 'here he is-attempted' 'here he is-has skin condition (similar to psoriasis)' 'here he is-oasis'; يَهُ/يِيهُ عآريب 'which one/he who-fucking/fucked' 'which one/he who-expressed/spoke clearly' 'which one/he who-will-become god(s)/parent(s)/teacher(s)' 'which one/he who-taught and brought up well'; جَهُ/جيهُ عآريب 'came he/came to him-fucking/fucked' 'came he/came to him-expressed/spoke clearly' 'came he/came to him-taught and brought up well'; هَهُ/هيهُ عآريب 'here he is-fucking/fucked' 'here he is-expressed/spoke clearly' 'here he is-will-become god(s)/parent(s)/teacher(s)' 'here he is-taught and brought up well'; يَهُ/يِيهُ خآريب 'which one/he who-ruined/ruins/is damaged'; جَهُ/جيهُ خآريب 'came he/came to him-ruined/ruins/is damaged'; هَهُ/هيهُ خآريب 'here he is-ruined/ruins/is damaged'; يَهُ/يِيهُ حآريب 'which one/he who- warring/warred; جَهُ/جيهُ حآريب 'came he/came to him- warring/warred'; هَهُ/هيهُ حآريب 'here he is- warring/warred'. Cp: yeho-yaareeb, yeiho-yaareeb, geho-yaareeb, geiho-yaareeb, heho-yaareeb, heiho-yaareeb, yeho-haareeb, yeiho-haareeb, geho-haareeb, geiho-haareeb, heho-haareeb, heiho-haareeb, yeho-gaareeb, yeiho-gaareeb, geho-gaareeb, geiho-gaareeb, heho-gaareeb, heiho-gaareeb, yeho-'aareeb, yeiho-'aareeb, geho-'aareeb, geiho-'aareeb, heho-'aareeb, heiho-'aareeb, yeho-k̲h̲aareeb, yeiho-k̲h̲aareeb, geho-k̲h̲aareeb, geiho-k̲h̲aareeb, heho-k̲h̲aareeb, heiho-k̲h̲aareeb,yeho-ḥaareeb, yeiho-ḥaareeb, geho-ḥaareeb, geiho-ḥaareeb, heho-ḥaareeb, heiho-ḥaareeb. (1Chr.9:10)

Pashur; pašḥûr; بَشحُر 'I stare at with hatred' ('stares with eyelids slightly lowered and frowning' 'of staring at with hatred'; بَزحُر 'I will push/make abdominal contraction and make sound of pushing' (as when pushing out baby or bowel movement); فشحُر 'then stare at with hatred'; فَزحُر 'then push abdominal and make sound of pushing'; بَشهُر 'by/with months' 'will make known/slander' 'by moonlight' 'eyes will look above'; بَسهُر 'will stay up all night beside/guard' 'by/during pre-dawn'; بَزهُر 'will flower' 'with/will add cloves'; بَصهُر 'will smelt/melt metal' 'will marry into family'; بَس خُر 'stop/enough-drive away violently' 'stop/enough-collapse/fall'; بَصخُر 'will make compliant/make do as bid' 'will stop/plug with small piece of charcoal or small stone'. Cp: bas̲h̲hur, bazḥur, p̲h̲as̲h̲ḥur, p̲h̲azḥur, bas̲h̲hur, bas-hur, bazhur, bas̲s̲hur, bas-k̲h̲ur, bas̲s̲*kh*ur. (1Chr.9:12)

Malchijah; the same as Malchiah (1Chr.6:40). (1Chr.9:12)

Maasiai; maʿăśay; مَعصَي ، مَعيصَي 'disobedience(plural)' 'did not disobey' 'askew/crooked/bent' 'did/did not become stuck/difficult'. Cp: ma'as̲s̲ay, ma'ais̲s̲ay. (1Chr.9:12)

Jahzerah; yaḥzērâ; يَحذيره 'he warns/warns him' 'he is cautious of him'; يَخبيره 'he informs him' 'he gets information/news out of him'; هَحذيره 'I will warn him' 'I will be wary of him'; هَخبيره 'I will inform him' 'I will get news out of him'; يَهزيره 'he tugs/pulls at him' 'he tugs/pulls at him violently'; هَهزيره 'I will pull/

tug at him/tug at him violently'. Cp: yaḥveyrah, yakhbeyrah, haḥveyrah, hakhbeyrah, yahzeyrah, hahzeyrah. (1Chr.9:12)

Meshillemith; mĕšillēmîṯ; ميسِلّيميت 'is of peaceful nature' 'did not survive' 'possessed/provoked the one who died' 'well ask the one who died' 'do not ask the one died'; ميشِلّيميت 'did not take' 'did not take the one who died' 'walked/left the one who died' 'not the one who died'. It is similar to Meshullamet, the only difference is Meshullamet's meaning in 2Kgs.21:19 can be limited to specific meanings supported by the text of the story where it features, but Meshillemith can be any of various meanings (as per the Biblical authors' method of wordplay) which has not yet been defined in this part of the story as it is only listed. Cp: meisilleymeet, meishilleymeet. (1Chr.9:12)

Immer; 'immēr; يِمّير 'of giving orders' 'bossy' 'show a hint/clue' 'a hint' 'a hint or tiny piece of something/a faint trace of something' 'a barely visible trace of something'; عِمّير 'builder' 'of long life/age'. Cp: immeyr, 'immeyr. (1Chr.9:12)

Hasshub; ḥaššûḇ; حَشّب 'carried on his waist' 'folded up (skirt/dress) and tucked it into his waist'; خَشّب 'laid beams for ceiling' 'gathered timber (for building)'; حَسّب '(I/he)thought/believed' 'depends…' 'calculated' 'read/calculated the future' 'sorcerer/seer'. Cp: ḥashub, khashub, ḥassub. (1Chr.9:14)

Bakbakkar; baqbaqqar; بَق بَقّر ، بَقبَقّر 'staying he settled/stopped moving' 'left some-he settled/stopped moving' 'stayed and raised cows' 'ripped open-raised cows' 'ripped open-cows' 'tore/ripped-tore/ripped open'; بَك بَكّر ، بَكبَكّر 'left/went early-early' 'cried/left-awoke in morning/first thing in morning' 'he went early/he visited early' 'left/went early-first/firstborn' 'left/went-heifer'. Cp: baqbaqqar, baq-baqqar, bakbakkar, bak-bakkar. (1Chr.9:15)

Heresh; ḥereš; حَرَش 'caused problems between' (by lying or delivering gossip between two or more people be it truth or not); حَرَز 'thorny bush(es)' 'rashes of spots on skin'; خَرَش 'untied' 'got loose'; خَرَز 'beads'; هَرَش 'scratched'; هَرَس 'made into a smooth or coarse paste' 'name of dish made from hereesa paste'. Cp: ḥeresh, ḥerez, kheresh, kherez, heres. (1Chr.9:15)

Galal; gālāl; جاَلاَل 'made move in rolling-tossing motion' 'cleared' 'purified' 'made clear' 'ate from someone else's side of dish' 'made sides(which belongs to whom)' 'gathered/ate sesame seeds' 'wandered/walked around'; غاَلاَل 'had ear inflammation' 'made flow/made river' 'in river(s)/activity related to rivers or streams' 'carried deep hatred/despised' 'stabbed deep/dug deep into' 'created extreme laws' 'fabricate rules/laws/tenements'. Cp: gaalaal, ghaalaal. (1Chr.9:15)

Jeduthun; yĕḏûṯûn, yĕḏiṯûn; يَدُثُن ، بيدُثُن ، يَديثُن ، بيديثُن 'they play/beat tambourines' 'they pound/beat'; هَدُثُن ، هَديثُن 'I will play tambourines' 'I will pound/beat'; هيدُثُن ، هيديثُن 'he will play tambourines' 'he will pound/beat' 'a playing of tambourines or similar sound'; جَدُثُن ، جيدُثُن ، جَديثُن ، جيديثُن 'severed by hacking with stone(or any object, or by biting with teeth)' 'insulted with a long rant, left in tatters(grievously insulted)'; حَدُثُن ، حيدُثُن 'spoke and explained in detail' 'narrated an old event or story' 'carried in arms/cradled'; حَديثُن ، حيديثُن 'a long explanation in detail' 'an old narration/story'. Cp: yedufun, yeidufun, yedeefun, yeideefun, hedufun, hedeefun, heidufun, heideefun, gedufun, geidufun, gedeefun, geideefun, ḥedufun, ḥeidufun, ḥedeefun, ḥeideefun. (1Chr.9:16)

Talmon; ṯalmōn, ṭalmôn; تَلمون 'ploughed land/ploughed lines of land' 'blame/blamed' 'carried by hand from'; تَلمُن 'a ploughing of land' 'lines of land(within same piece of land)' 'a blaming' 'carried by hand from'; طَلمون 'covered in(any liquid substance)' 'has been beaten all over'; طَل مُن 'appeared from/at' 'came early from'. Cp: talmoon, talmon, ṭalmoon, ṭal-mon. (1Chr.9:17)

Kore; qōrē', qôrē'; قوريئ ، قُريئ 'read' 'read to' 'confessed' 'decided/decides'; قوريع ، قُريع 'tapped/tapping' and can mean musically or just tapping, 'sharp strike/tap' 'uncovered hair/head' 'breakfast/had breakfast'; كوريئ ، كُريئ 'hired' 'leased out' 'chased after/chased away'. Cp: qoorey, qorey, qoorey', qorey', koorey, korey. (1Chr.9:19)

Ebiasaph; 'eḇyāsāp̄; the same as Abiasaph (Exod.6:24). (1Chr.9:19)

Meshelemiah; mĕšelemyâ; mĕšelemyāhû; ميسَلَم يه/ياَه 'is peaceful/of peaceful nature-he/him' 'did not ask them questions-he/him' 'did not survive/was not spared-he/him' 'water passed/leaked/flowed-the-he/him'; ميشَلَم يه/ياَه 'did not take-the-he/him' 'what did he take-the-he/him' 'covered with henna wash-the-he/him' 'walked/left-gathered-he/him'. It is equivalent to Meshillemith (1Chr.9:12), Meshullamet (2Kgs.21:19). Cp: meiselem-yah/yaahu, meishelem-yah/yaahu. (1Chr.9:21)

Mattithiah; mattiṯyâ; mattiṯyāhû; مَطِّط/مَطّيط يه/ياَه 'stretch/stretched-him/he' and this is definitely the meaning for this character as (Mattit/mattit/مَطِط ، مطيط) is a popular Yemeni dish that has existed since antiquity. It is made by boiling flour in a pot while heating it on fire and its cooking includes constantly stretching it which results in the consistency becoming elastic-like, during preparation the texture becomes thick and unyielding and needs strength to stretch it requiring the cook to use effort to stretch it inside the pot by stirring consistently, which is the reason for its name 'mattit/stretching/stretched'. This is supported by the Biblical text 'And Mattithiah…had the set office over the things that were made in the pans.'; where Biblical scholars interpret this as 'baker of cakes' is from ignorance of how bread/cakes are made in ancient and primitive ovens—they are not made in pans like more recent history and modern history, and specifically how western bread and cakes are made, but they are made in ovens and stuck directly onto the oven wall to bake with no pans needed in its creation. The types of bread made in a pan are 'laḥooḥ' a savoury pancake made out of leavened dough and that is made in a frying pan which is not called a 'pan' but 'mllḥh/mallaḥah' from the name of this leavened pancake bread; and fried bread (mlwḫ) made in a frying pan, but neither are meant by 'Mattithiah'. It could also be wordplay on مَتِّت/مَتّيت يه/ياَهُ 'pretended/considered dead-he/him' 'died/killed-he/him'; مَثِت/مَثّيت يه/ياَهُ 'wiped away urine/sperm-he/him'; مَطِّفيه/ياَهُ 'it has gone out' 'what has put it out' such as a fire or lantern; مَطِّف/مَطّيف يه/ياَهُ 'what put it out-he/him' Cp: maṭṭiṭ-yah/yaahu, maṭṭyṭ-yah/yaahu, mattit-yah/yaahu, mattyt-yah/yaahu, maffit-yah/yaahu, maffyt-yah/yaahu, maṭṭiphyah/yaahu, maṭṭiph-yah/yaahu, maṭṭyph-yah/yaahu, (1Chr.9:31)

Jehiel; yĕḥî'ēl; يَحي/ييحي ئِل 'makes stay-the' 'stays/stills-the' 'makes lively-the' (humour, music, presence is liked, brings entertainment and liveliness to a gathering/party); جَحي/جيحي ئِل 'became hard-the' 'came-made still/stay-the' 'came-made lively-the'; هَحي ئِل 'I will make stay/still-the' I will make lively-the'; يَحيئِل ، ييحيئِل 'he removes by nudging/wriggling gently' 'he moves by shifting the position slightly' 'it moves slightly(in small movements)', to make something fit or in the right position by trying to move it slightly/gently or only being able to move it by easing it/wriggling it, 'plays tricks/deceives'; جَحيئِل ، جيحيئِل 'came-removed/nudged gently/small movements' 'came-played tricks/deceit'; هَحيئِل 'I will remove it in small actions' 'I will change its position slightly/gently'; هيحيئِل 'he will remove it in small actions' 'he will change its position slightly/gently'; يَهي/ييهي ئِل 'she is-the' 'which one is the'; هَهي/هيهي ئِل 'here is-the' 'so I see, she is-the'; جَهي/جيهي ئِل 'came-she-the' 'came to her-the' 'uncovered-the' 'uncover-the'. Cp: yeḥee-ill, yeiḥee-ill, geḥee-ill, geiḥee-ill, heḥee-ill, heiḥee-ill, yeḥeeill, yeiḥeeill, geḥeeill, geiḥeeill, heḥeeill, heiḥeeill, yehee-ill, yeihee-ill, hehee-ill, heihee-ill, gehee-ill, geihee-ill. (1Chr.9:35)

Shimeam; šim'ām; سِم ئآم 'name-the' 'poison-the' 'thread-the'; سِمع آم 'heard-the' 'the hearing of-the' 'the reputation of-the'. Cp: sim-aam, sim'aam. (1Chr.9:38)

Tahrea; taḥrēa'; طَح ريَع 'fell/broke-watered/soaked/flooded' 'fell-wet himself/became water' and it usually describes someone in great fear as their stomach 'falling/breaking' or 'wetting' themselves, it is usually described in one way (stomach falling/ 'shitting') or wetting, but the author/editor wants to reinforce this meaning and made this slight variation to what was 'Tarea' a little earlier in the chapter which has the same meaning (one of them). Cp: ṭaḥ-reya'. (1Chr.9:41)

Jarah; ya'râ; يَعره 'makes him naked'; يَعرا 'becomes naked'; هَعره 'I will make him naked' 'look, he is naked'; هَعرا 'I will become naked' 'look he is naked'; جَعره/ا 'cried out (loud or long) like animals' 'goat/sheep dung'; يَغره/ا 'saves him' 'saves' 'has argument with him' 'has arguments'. Cp: ya'rah, ya'ra, ha'rah, ha'ra, ga'rah, ga'ra, yaghrah, yaghra. (1Chr.9:42)

Jashobeam; yāšoḇ'ām; خآشوب ئآم 'set wooden beams on-the' 'the wood/yoke/timber of the'; حآشوب ئآم 'carrying on waist-the' 'clothes uplifted and tucked into waist-the'; عآشوب ئآم'plants/herbs of-the' 'gathering plants/herbs-the'; يآسوب ئآم 'he/it leaves-the' 'he insults-the'; يآشوب ئآم 'swells and stiffens/grows bigger-the' e.g. wood swells from water, 'goes back and forth in circles-the'. It is equivalent and similar to the words: Jashub (Num.26:24), Jashubi-lehem (1Chr.4:22), Hashubah (1Chr.3:20), Hashabiah (1Chr.6:45), Hasshub (1Chr.9:14). Cp: khaashoob-um, ḥaashoob-um, 'aashoob-um, yaasoob-um, yaashoob-um. (1Chr.11:11)

Hachmonite; ben-ḥaḵmônî; بَن حَكمُني 'they/we will-appoint me ruler/arbitrator' 'they will-order me around' 'child-appoint me ruler/arbitrator/order me around'; بَن هَخمُني 'we will-will guess/predict' 'child-will guess/predict'. It is similar to Tachmonite (2Sam.23:8) Cp: ben-ḥakmonee, ben-hakhmonee. (1Chr.11:11)

Shammoth; šammôṯ; شَمُّت 'caused a scene' 'she/it smelled (it)' 'the powdered tobacco'; سَمُّت 'she/it poisoned' 'she named' 'she threaded(needle)' 'she told naming story'; صَمُّت 'she/it blocked' 'she/it blocked mouth'. Cp: shammot, sammot, ssammot. (1Chr.11:27)

Pelonite; pĕlōnî; بَلوني ، بيلوني 'afflicted me' 'of affliction/causing affliction' 'of urinating' 'soaked me' 'of soaking' 'coloured me/will colour/change colour' 'became worn/faded/old'; فَلوني ، فيلوني 'picked nits out' 'went through/over something thoroughly' 'said something and it happened(negative)/said omen and it happened'. It has some of the meanings of **Paltite** (2Sam.23:26), both (pelonite/paltite) have been used as names for 'Helez' surname—the Biblical authors were using the same Arabic word to determine this naming. Biblical scholars usually claim 'errors' on behalf of the ancient authors/editors, erroneously claiming 'The term probably arises from separate errors; Helez is called 'the Paltite' at 2 Sam. 23:26, and Ahijah is called "Eliam son of Ahithophel the Gilonite" at v. 34.' (Freedman, Myers and Beck, 2000: 1025). These wrong assumptions on behalf of Biblical scholars is due to their lack of knowledge of the true language of the Bible, and also their pursuit to understand and translate the Biblical stories through 'Hebrew' which is not a language nor is it the language of the Bible, whereas had they attempted to translate it in Arabic, all the 'mysteries' of the Bible would have been explained and understood in less than a few months from starting date. Cp: beloonee, beiloonee, p͟heloonee, p͟heiloonee. (1Chr.11:27)

Ilai; ʿîlay; عيلَي 'got above/rose above/rose higher' 'above' 'on'; غيلَي 'my river/stream' 'made flow/stream/river' 'despised/great hatred' 'stabbed/dug deep into' 'expensive/became more expensive'. Cp: 'eelay, g͟heelay. (1Chr.11:29)

Heled; ḥēled; حيلَد 'stripped everything/lots off' fruit or leaves from tree/plant; خيلَد 'roasted in heat' as in cooked or suffered from sunstroke, 'severely beat up' 'remembered forever' 'lived forever'. Cp: ḥeyled, k͟heyled. (1Chr.11:30)

Ithai; 'îṯay; ئيتَي 'came' 'he came'. It is the same as Ittai (2Sam.15:19-22). Cp: eetay. (1Chr.11:31)

Hurai; ḥûray; حُرَي 'investigated/looked into' 'ploughed' 'made fire'; خُري 'chased away' 'fell to the ground/collapsed'. It has one of Hiddai's meanings (which it has replaced) (2Sam.23:30) 'demolish' ('fell to the ground'). Cp: ḥuray, k͟huray. (1Chr.11:32)

Hashem; hāšēm; هآشيم 'shooing away' 'crumbling or squashing something' 'a dish made of crumbled bread soaked in broth or churned milk'; هآزيم 'he beats' 'of losing or causing opponent to lose(game/fight/battle)'; حآسيم 'pitiful/compassionate' 'felt-the'; حآزيم 'bundles of wood' 'tied bundle around middle'. Cp: haas͟heym, haazeym, ḥaaseym, ḥaazeym. (1Chr.11:34)

Shage; šāgēh, šāgē'; شآجيه 'I will come to him' 'I will roast him/it' 'he is roasting/roasted it' 'leave it a gap open(of door, e.g.)'; شآجيئ 'I will come' 'I will roast' 'it is roasted' 'I will leave gap open(of door)'; سآجيه 'calm him/it' 'distract him/it' 'make him lapse/forget time/thought'; سآجيئ 'calm' 'in a trance like state distracted' 'lapsed in thought/time'; سآغيه 'swivel/tilt it/him' 'tilt his/its head'; سآغيئ 'tilted/swivelled' 'with head tilted' 'with head tilted attempting to hear/see'. Cp: s͟haageyh, s͟haagey, saageyh, saagey, saag͟heyh, saag͟hey. (1Chr.11:34)

Sacar; śāḵār; صآخآر 'is compliant/does as told' 'made do as told/caused to be compliant' 'made/caused to be mild' 'plugged/stopped with piece of charcoal'; سآخآر 'generous/made generous'; صآقآر 'falcon/eagle' 'behaved/moved like a falcon/eagle' as in emulated the bird of prey movements or swiftness or predatory behaviour. Cp: s͟saak͟haar, saak͟haar, s͟saaqaar. (1Chr.11:35)

Eliphal; 'ĕlîpāl; ئِلي/ئيلي فآل 'the one who-picked nits/went through thoroughly' 'the one who-said and it happened/said bad omen'; ئِلي بآل 'the one who soaked' 'the one who-urinated' 'the one who-is patient/clever'. Cp: illee/eilee-p͟haal, illee-baal. (1Chr.11:35)

Mecherathite; mĕḵērāṯî; ميخيرآثي 'is demented/senile' 'is/of making things up (exaggerating or lying'; ميخيرآطي 'a boaster' 'a liar' 'someone who tends to exaggerate and lie'; ميكيرآثي 'of growing/selling chives'; ميكيرآتي 'of hiring/leasing' 'of chasing away'. Cp: meik͟heyraafee, meik͟heyraaṭee, meikeyraafee, meikeyraatee. (1Chr.11:36)

Hezro; ḥerṣô, eḥṣray; حِرزُ 'amulet with a spell/protection' 'patch of dots on skin' 'an evil spell written'; حِرصُ 'guard/protect/be careful/beware'; خِرصُ 'an earring' 'wearing an earring'; خِرزُ 'beads' 'precious beads'; احزرَي 'guess'; اهزرَي 'tug/pull down at'; احذرَي 'be wary of'; احصرَي 'make out of straw/rush/palm fibres' 'feel great sorrow/despair'. Cp: ḥerzo, ḥers͟so, k͟hers͟so, k͟herzo, eḥzray, ehzray, eḥvray, eḥs͟sray. (1Chr.11:37)

Naarai; naʿăray; نَعيرَي 'we/they make/became naked' 'we/they get naked' 'of sexual excitement/we/they with erection' 'we/they stood/stood erect/stood in front of without moving' 'of standing/standing erect/standing in front of without moving or speaking' 'we/he/they are horny/sexually excited/have erection'; نَئيرَي 'we see him/make see/we understand/make understand' 'of making see/understand' 'we show/of showing' 'we/they/he penised/insulted with 'penis'' 'of penising/insulting with penis' 'of fire(s)/making fire(s)/we make fire(s)' 'light/make light/of making light/shed light/of shedding light'. Cp: na'airay, na-airay. (1Chr.11:37)

Ezbai; 'ezbāy; يِزْبآي 'penetrate with penis'. Note: the editors chose to modify this name but keep its meanings as in the parallel list of 2Sam: the character is Naarai 'we make naked' which also means 'horny(sexually)' and the father, Ezbai, means 'penetrate with penis'. The authors of the parallel account in 2Sam.23:35 give this character the name 'Paarai the Arbite' which as explained earlier translates as and means 'I will make naked/take clothes off(another person)' 'here is/look/I will fuck'. Cp: ezbaay. (1Chr.11:37)

Mibhar; mibḥār; مِبحآر 'a good riddance' 'a matter/person no one cares about' 'sailed' 'in the sea'; مِبخآر 'perfumed with incense smoke' 'incense vessel'; مِبهآر 'a bedazzling sight' 'is bedazzled'. Cp: mibḥaar, mibkhaar, mibhaar. (1Chr.11:38)

Haggeri; hagrî; هَجري 'I will run' 'of abandoning/leaving for good' 'here, pull'; حَجري 'of stone' 'ordered to stop work in land(until dispute is settled)'; هغري 'I will funnel(down)' 'I will seduce/tempt' 'I will save'. Cp: hagree, ḥagree, haghree. (1Chr.11:38)

Adina; 'ădînā'; عَدينآء ، عيدينآء 'returned' (in plural) 'returned to us' 'infected/will infect us' 'our enemies' 'will become our enemy' 'counted/we counted' 'lentils/activity related to lentils'; نَدينآء ، نيدينآء 'guilt' (in plural) 'we guilt/find guilty/blame' 'bowed/bent/lowered' 'make lower(in status)'. Cp: 'adeenaa, 'aideenaa, adeenaa, aideenaa. (1Chr.11:42)

Shiza; šîzā'; شيذآء 'of harming' 'will be harmed'. Cp: sheevaa. (1Chr.11:42)

Joshaphat; yôšāpāṭ; يُشآفآت 'he sees a lot' 'he cures a lot/many' 'he cures or takes satisfaction in another's bad luck/revenge/gloats/is recompensed out of hatred or wrong' 'he gloats at a lot' 'he repeats sentence in high note(to provoke/gloat)' 'he makes dish of 'shaphoot' (savoury pancakes soaked in churned milk); جُشآفآت 'came-saw a lot' 'came-cured or took satisfaction in another's bad luck/revenge/gloats/is recompensed out of hatred or wrong' 'came-repeated in high note(to provoke/gloat)'; يُصآفآط 'he gradually gets used to/he teaches something/someone to gradually get used to(something)' 'he teases/jokes'; يُشآفآط 'he sucks at/sucks out' 'he makes shrivel/wrinkle'; يُزآفآت 'he brings in processions' (escorts/procession moves and stops dividing the length of the procession into shorter journeys(but longer time)). Cp: yoshaaphaat, goshaaphaat, yossaaphaaṭ, yoshaaphaaṭ, yozaaphaat. (1Chr.11:43)

Mithnite; mitnî; مِثني 'doubled over and sewed' 'twice/doubled'. Cp: mifnee. (1Chr.11:43)

Uzzia; 'uzzîyā'; عوزّييآء 'were cherished/rose to great positions'; عوصّييآء 'were disobedient' 'were bent/askew/crooked' 'were stuck/became in fixed position' 'sticks' 'sticks were used(in beating)'; ئوذييآء 'harmed(others)' 'were harmed'; عوذييآء 'they were protected by a spell/prayer'; عوضّييآء 'had sore muscles' 'recompensed/were recompensed'. Cp: 'uzeeyaa, 'usseeyaa, uveeyaa, 'uveeyaa, 'udheeyaa. (1Chr.11:44)

Ashterathite; ha'aštĕrātî; هَعَشتيرآتي 'here is-of raising tail' (from words of ashterath/ashtoreth which means when a cow raises its tail ready to receive copulation (also before it excretes, but word is used in connection when cow wants to conceive)); هَشطيرآطي/هَشَتيرآطي 'here is-of splitting/tearing' 'here is-of setting conditions' 'here are my conditions'. Cp: ha'ashteiraatee, ha-ashṭeiraaṭee, ha-ashteiraaṭee. (1Chr.11:44)

Hothan; the same as Hotham (1Chr.7:32) or ḥôtān; حُفآن 'bare footed' 'they are barefoot'; حُثآن 'they have fringes' 'fringes' 'they encourage'; حُتآن 'bordered/with a line drawn' 'they make rim/border/line/end of something' 'whales' 'border(ed)/corner(ed)/make edges to the sides of something'; حُطآن 'set down/place/unload' 'they set down/placed' 'leave behind/leave some' 'leave it alone'. Cp: ḥophaan, ḥofaan, ḥotaan, ḥoṭaan. (1Chr.11:44)

Tizite; tîṣî; تيسي 'my male goat' 'virile goat' 'a quick poke with the end of something hot'; ديسي 'sneak something in and plant it' 'implant bad thoughts/ill-will between people'; طيزي 'my vagina', and equivalent to: 'who cares/get lost'. Cp: teesee, deesee, ṭeezee. (1Chr.11:45)

Mahavite; hammaḥăwîm; هَمَّحيو هم/ام ، هَمَّحَو هم/ام 'here is who stilled/stayed-them/the'; هَمَّحيو هم ، هَمَّحَو هم 'we will make them stay/be still'. The EDB states about Mahavite/ hammaḥăwîm: 'The term makes little sense as it stands and has been emended to *maḥănî* ("Mahanite") or *maḥănaymî* ("Mahanaimite")' (Freedman, Myers and Beck, 2000: 847). Again, and again, modern Biblical scholars corrupt the text when they cannot understand a meaning of the word and cannot forcibly give it an erroneous translation/interpretation so they choose to change the word which has existed for millennia, while the word itself has a meaning, is a word in use, and is the meaning above. It is from the same root word as Jehovah, Hawaa. Cp: hammaḥaiw-hum/um, hammaḥaw-hum/um, hammaḥaiwhum, hammaḥawhum. (1Chr.11:46)

Jeribai; yĕrîḇay; يِريبَي ، ييريبَي 'lots of/plenty of/loads of' 'he/they mix and dilute with water' 'he is/they are-god/parent/teacher' 'you my god/parent/teacher' 'he/they grow/bring up/discipline/teach' 'he/it has swollen lymph nodes/inflamed sores'; هَريبَي 'move out of the way/stand back' 'here is my god/parent/teacher' 'here, dilute/mix this'; هيريبَي 'he will dilute/mix' 'he will have swollen lymph nodes' 'he will become my god/parent/teacher' 'he will grow(well)/raise lots of/become disciplined'; جَريبَي ، جيريبَي 'came-my god/parent/teacher' 'try/attempt'; عَريبَي ، عيريبَي 'of fucking/fucks a lot' 'he will-god/parent/teacher' 'will he-my god/parent/teacher' 'he will/will he-mix(ed) and dilute(ed) with water' 'of expressing clearly/speaking clearly' 'express(ed)/speak/spoke clearly' 'teach and remember' 'teach and grow/raise/raise well'; حَريبَي ، حيريبَي 'hornets' 'of warring' 'of creating enmity/problems' 'spear(s)'. Cp: yereebay, yeireebay, hereebay, heireebay, gereebay, geireebay, 'ereebay, 'eireebay, ḥereebay, ḥeireebay. (1Chr.11:46)

Joshaviah; yôšawyâ; يُشَويه 'he grills it' 'he wants it/him'; يُصَويه 'it makes sound/squeals like animal/tweets like bird'; عُسَويه 'cold bread-he/him' 'broke/ate bread-he/him'. It is the same as Isui, Ishuah (Gen.46:17), Isuah, Ishuai (1Chr.7:30), Jesui (Num.26:44). Cp: yoshawyah, yossawyah, 'osawyah. (1Chr.11:46)

Elnaam; 'elnaʿam; ئَلنَعَم 'the blessings/gifts/physical things given or received' 'the-yes'; ئَلنَئَم 'the sleeper/sleeping' 'the one who puts to sleep' literally or euphemism for sex; ئَلنَغَم 'the-we depress/stifle/muffle/suffocate'. Cp: elna'am, elna-am, elnagham. (1Chr.11:46)

Ithmah; yiṯmâ; يِثمه 'he/it makes him sinful'. Cp: yifmah. (1Chr.11:46)

Jasiel; yaʿăśî'ēl; يَعيصي ئِل 'he disobeys-the' 'he uses stick-the' 'he bends/warps/twists-the' 'he/it becomes stuck/stubborn-the'; جَعيصي ئِل 'lower spine/lower back-the' e.g. if someone falls and lands on their bottom, they say they hurt the (g'ssee/جعصي) the point between the buttocks and lowest point of the back, 'came-disobeyed-the' 'came-stick-the' 'came-got stuck-the'. Cp: ya'aissee-ill, ga'aissee-ill. (1Chr.11:47)

Mesobaite; hamměṣōḇāyâ; هَمِسوبايه ، هَمّيسوبايه 'here is the one who insults' 'here is the one who leaves/abandons'; هَمِصوبايه ، هَمّيصوبايه 'here is the pourer/pouring place' 'here is the drinking bowl' 'here is the one who causes catastrophes/afflictions'; هَمِزوبايه ، هَمّيزوبايه 'here is the peniser(penetrator with penis)' 'here is the one penetrated with penis'. Cp: hammesoobaayah, hammeisoobaayah, hammessoobaayah, hammeissoobaayah, hammezoobaayah, hammeizoobaayah. (1Chr.11:47)

Sheemah; šěmāʿâ; سِماعه 'heard him' 'listened to him' 'obeyed him'; سيماعه 'made him hear' 'made people hear him being insulted'. Cp: semaa'ah, seimaa'ah. (1Chr.12:3)

Jeziel; yĕzû'ēl, yĕzî'ēl; ييذُ ئِل ، ييذي ئِل 'they harm-the' 'he harms-the' 'harms-the', Cp: yeivu-ill, yeivee-ill. (1Chr.12:3)

Ismaiah; yišmaʿyâ; يِسمَع يه 'he hears-him/he' 'he listens-him/he' 'he obeys-him/he'. Cp: yisma'-yah. (1Chr.12:4)

Berachah; bĕrāḵâ; بيراخه 'he/it will loosen/loosen it' 'he will be lenient/too loose'; بيراحه 'he/they cleared it/levelled it' 'he/they pulled up water' 'take your time/by your own pace' 'with/by restfulness/relaxation'; بيراكه 'he/they/it knelt' 'he/they/it made it kneel' 'underground dam' 'blessed' 'lasted long/sufficed' 'he/they/it leaned (or) leaned it against'; بيراقه 'sulking in a mood' 'refusing to eat/talk because upset' 'lightning stroke'. Cp: beiraakhah, beiraaḥah, beiraakah, beiraaqah. (1Chr.12:3)

Jahaziel; yaḥăzî'ēl; يَحيزي ئِل 'he keeps in-the' 'he corners/crams/blocks-the'; هَحيزي ئِل 'I will keep in/block/corner/cram-the'; جَحيزي ئِل 'came-kept in/cornered/blocked-the'; يَخيذي ئِل 'he takes-the'; هَخيذي ئِل 'I will take-the'; جَخيذي ئِل 'came-took-the'; يَخيزي ئِل 'he swears at-the'; هَخيزي ئِل 'I will swear at-the'; جَخيزي ئِل 'came-swore at-the'; يَهيز ي ئِل 'he rocks/swings-the' 'he tugs at/snags-the'; جَهيزي ئِل 'prepare-the' 'came-swang/rocked-the' 'came-tugged/snagged-the'. Cp: yaḥaizee-ill, haḥaizee-ill, gaḥaizee-ill, yakhaivee-ill, hakhaivee-ill, gakhaivee-ill, yakhaizee-ill, hakhaizee-ill, gakhaizee-ill, yahaizee-ill, gahaizee-ill. (1Chr.12:4)

Josabad; yôzāḇāḏ; يُزآباد 'he butters/spreads' 'he applies/perfumes with ointment' 'he uses drinking bowls'; جوزآباد 'came-buttered/spread' 'came drinking bowls' 'came-perfumed with ointment'; يُزآباط 'he kicks a lot/kicks'; يُضاباط 'he tightens' 'he grows stronger' 'he disciplines his wife' the latter when it is proven she has committed a serious wrong against another person; يُشاباط 'he/it ties/lattices with rope' 'he whips'. Cp: yozaabaad, gozaabaad, yozaabaaṭ, yodhaabaaṭ, yoshaabaaṭ. (1Chr.12:4)

Gederathite; gĕdērāṯî; جِذيرآتي ، جيذيرآتي 'of removing/cutting/stripping/harvesting by shaking, pulling movement' (it causes more fruit to fall to the ground to be collected, but also leaves some fruit behind on the tree) 'of leaving plants/trees(or anything) in tatters/bitten around edges or all over (e.g. how caterpillars leave plant leaves)', 'of shuddering/goosepimples'; جِديرآتي ، جيديرآتي 'have caught pox' 'of building wall(s)/walled' 'my walls'; غِديرآتي ، غيديرآتي 'of betraying' 'became dark'. Cp: geveyraatee, geiveyraatee, gedeyraatee, geideyraatee, ghedeyraatee, gheideyraatee. (1Chr.12:4)

Eluzai; 'elʿûzay; ئَلعُزَي 'the cherished' 'the grieved' 'the guy'; ئَلعُذَي 'the protected' 'the protection chant/spell/prayer'. Cp: el'uzay, el'uvay. (1Chr.12:5)

Bealiah; bĕʿalyâ; بيعَليه 'he/they will build room on higher floor/level' 'his spouses'; بيغَليه 'he will raise its price' 'his donkeys' 'with his river(s)/streams' 'he/they will make it flow/river/stream' 'he/they will despise him' 'he/they will stab deep into' 'he/they will dig deep into'. Cp: bei'alyah, beighalyah. (1Chr.12:5)

Shemariah; šĕmaryâ, šĕmaryāhû; سَمَريه/ياَهُ ، سيمَريه/ياَهُ 'stayed up all/late night-he/him' 'told night stories-he/him'; شَمَريه/ياَهُ ، شيمَريه/ياَهُ 'rolled up/tucked up sleeves/clothes'. Cp: semar-yah/yaahu, seimar-yah/yaahu, shemar-yah/yaahu, sheimar-yah/yaahu. (1Chr.12:5)

Haruphite; ḥărîpî, ḥārûp; حَريفي ، حيريفي 'edge it/set it on the edge/rim' 'of edges' 'on the edge/rim' 'lettered' 'swapped letters/changed letters'; حَرُف ، حيرُف 'edged' 'sat/stood on the edge' 'a letter' 'swapped/changed letters'; حَريثي ، حيريثي 'frowning' 'of frowning'; حَرُث ، حيرُث 'frowned'; خريفي ، خيريفي ، خَرُف ، خيرُف 'demented/senile' 'dementia/senility' 'hallucinating' 'imagining/making up stories or statements'. Cp: ḥareephee, ḥaireephee, ḥaruph, ḥairuph, ḥareefee, ḥaireefee, ḥaruf, ḥairuf, khareephee, khaireephee, kharuph, khairuph. (1Chr.12:5)

Jesiah; the same as Isshiah and Ishiah (1Chr.7:3). (1Chr.12:6)

Azareel; 'ăzar'ēl; عيزَر ئِل 'made ugly-the'; عيذَر ئِل 'shadowed over-the' 'excused-the'; عيصَر ئِل 'twisted-the' 'twisted muscle-the'. Cp: 'aizar-ill, 'aivar-ill, 'aissar-ill. (1Chr.12:6)

Joezer; yôʿezer; يُعَزَر 'he becomes ugly/he makes ugly'; يُعَذَر 'he shadows (over)' 'he excuses'; يُعَصَر 'he twists' 'he twists/turns around'. Cp: yo'ezer, yo'ever, yo'esser. (1Chr.12:6)

Joelah; yôʿē'lâ; يُعيئله 'he treats him like a child/boy' 'he teaches/warns him'; جُعيئله 'came-his children' 'came-raised him' 'came-above him'; يُغيئله 'he makes him like a rushing river' 'he stabs him deeply' 'he digs into him/it deeply' 'he deceives him' 'he despises him/makes him despised'. Cp: yo'ey-lah, go'ey-lah, yoghey-lah. (1Chr.12:7)

Mishmannah; mišmannâ; مِش مَنّه 'not, what is it' 'not from him' 'not from where'; مِسمَنّه 'become strong/fat' 'eating clarified butter'; مِزمنّه 'telling stories of old times' 'has blocked bowel/intestines' 'timed'. Cp: mishmannah, mismannah, mizmannah. (1Chr.12:10)

Elzabad; 'elzāḇāḏ; ئَلزآباَد 'the-butterer/buttered/buttering' 'the-spreader/spread/spreading' 'the-perfumes with ointment/greased' 'the-drinking bowls'; ئَلزآباَط 'the-kicker/kicked/kicking'; ئَلضاَباَط 'the-tightens' 'the-grows stronger' 'the-disciplines his wife' the latter when it is proven she has committed a serious wrong against another person; ئَلشاَباَط 'the-latticing with rope' 'the whipping' 'the twine/rope'. Cp: elzaabaad, elzaabaaṭ, eldhaabaaṭ, elshaabaaṭ. (1Chr.12:12)

Machbanai; maḵbannay; مَخبَنَّي 'our hiding place' 'it is hid' 'hiding it/him/her' and is equivalent to Macphelah and Machbenah, 'it is damp/mouldy'; مَقبَنَّي 'what is wrong with us now?/what is wrong now?' 'what is in(side) it/her now?'. Cp: makhbannay, maqbannay. (1Chr.12:13)

Adnah; ʿaḏnāḥ, ʿaḏnâ; عَدناَه ، عَدنه 'returned him/it' 'brought him/it back' 'counted' 'counted it' 'not yet' 'we have not yet' 'showed enmity towards us/him'. Cp: 'adnaah, 'adnah. (1Chr.12:20)

Jozabad the same as Josabad (1Chr.12:4). (1Chr.12:20)

Hemath; same as Hamath. (1Chr.13:5)

Chidon; kîḏōn; خيدون 'were pulled off/down/away/removed by pulling' and describes pulling bread off oven wall when cooked or pulling down a wall or structure; كيدون 'try/attempt to bow low/become lower' 'go on, lower them/make them bend/bow' 'go on, lower your/their heads' 'a scheming/plot' 'cover tightly (with lid/stone/fabric, etc.)'; قيدون 'lead' whether a person is being led or animals by the reigns/rope, 'tie up/chain' 'record(in writing or otherwise)'. In this instance it has been used to rename the place where Uzzah was killed by God for touching the ark when it was about to fall, although it has changed into a different word, it still holds at least two of the meanings of 'Nachon' of something kneeling or being pulled down, making something or someone bend or bow their heads. This is supported by the narration that the oxen 'stumbled' which means the oxen knelt or bowed their heads low. Cp: kheedoon, keedon, qeedon. (1Chr.13:9)

Beeliada; bĕʿelyāḏāʿ; بِعِل يآدآع ، بيعِل يآدآع 'raise/make higher-he calls/curses/makes claim/makes false claim' 'raise/make higher-he parts/says farewell' the 'raise higher' can mean to physically raise higher or to increase their standing/status, 'spouse(s)-he calls/claims/makes false claim' 'spouse(s)-he deposits/says farewell/parts', 'sell-he calls' 'sell-he parts/says farewell'; بِعِل يآضاع ، بيعِل يآضاع 'raise higher-he misleads/misguides' 'raise higher-he loses' 'raise higher-he sets/places' and same meanings with 'spouse/sell' as first half of compound word. It is only a change to the prefix of the compound word from Eliada in 2Sam. 'he who-calls/etc.' to Beeliada 'raise/sell-he calls'. Cp: be'elyaadaa', bei'elyaadaa', be'elyaadhaa', bei'elyaadhaa'. (1Chr.14:7)

Elizaphan; ʾĕlîṣāp̄ān; ئِلي/ئيلي زآفآن 'he who/the one who-escorted with procession'; ئِلي زآبآن 'he who/the one who-poked loins/below navel to above crotch' 'he who/the one who-penetrated with penis'; ئِلي سآفآن 'he who/the one who-carried gently' 'he who/the one who poured gently/poured gentle spurts of water' 'he who/the one who-sips' 'he who/the one-went numb'; ئِلي صآفآن 'he who/the one who-cleared the air between them' 'he who/the one who-cleaned/cleared/purified' 'he who/the one who-made rock columns/stacked/put in row'. Cp: illee/eilee-zaaphaan, illee-zaabaan, illee-saaphaan, illee-ssaaphaan. (1Chr.15:8)

Kushaiah; qûšāyāhû; قُشآ يآهْ 'went into fit/paralysis-he/him' to say someone 'qsha' means went into some kind of fit out of joy, fright or excitement where the body shakes and stiffens; 'paralysed with fear/joy-he/him' it is used to describe a literal physical state and also figuratively to express great happiness/excitement or fright, 'became crispy-he/him' 'blew away litter/fibres/burnt remnants-he/him' 'removed completely in one swipe/scrape-he/him' 'litter/fibres/burnt remnants-he/him'; قُصآيآهْ 'hardened-he/him' 'told story/news-he/him' 'cut-he/him'; كُسآيآهْ 'were clothed(gifted/bought new clothes)-he/him' 'wrapped/covered with new fabric-he/him' 'made cover of fabric-he/him'. Cp: qushaa-yaahu, qussaa-yaahu, kusaa-yaahu. (1Chr.15:17)

Jaaziel; yaʿăzîʾēl; يَعَزي ئِل ، يَعيزي ئِل 'he cherishes-the' 'he needs-the'; يَغَزي ئِل ، يَغيزي ئِل 'he makes deep squeezing pain-the' 'he makes deep resonating sound-the'. Cp: ya'azee-ill, ya'aizee-ill, yaghazee-ill, yaghaizee-ill. (1Chr.15:18)

Shemiramoth; šĕmîrāmôṯ; زَميرآ/زيميرآ مُت 'played pipes to death' (when saying anything is done 'to death' it means exceedingly whether 'loved to death' 'laughed to death' it means intensity and not actual death); زَميرآ/زيميرآ مُط 'play pipe-stretch' and means to stretch the note; زَميرآ/زيميرآ مُد 'play pipe-extend/reach' and means to extend the note being played; سَميرآ/سيميرآ مُت 'told night stories to death' 'stayed up late/all night to death; سَميرآ/سيميرآ مُط 'tell stories-stretch' and means to extend the scope of the stories to add to them; سَميرآ/سيميرآ مُد 'tell stories-extend/reach out' and means to lengthen the stories by explaining them more. Cp: zemeeraa/zeimeeraa-mot, zemeeraa/zeimeeraa-moṭ, zemeeraa/zeimeeraa-mod, semeeraa/seimeeraa-mot, semeeraa/seimeeraa-moṭ, semeeraa/seimeeraa-mod. (1Chr.15:18)

Unni; ʿunnî; عونّي 'meant' 'on purpose' 'hinted/spoke to indirectly' 'specifically' 'took special care/interest' 'especially for' 'suffered'; غونّي 'sang' 'sing' 'make 'ghn' sounds' 'became rich/enriched'; نُونّي 'moaned/groaned'. Cp: 'unnee, ghunnee, unnee. (1Chr.15:18)

Ben; bēn, ben; بين 'in' 'between' or a prefix to denote something happening, 'became apparent'; بَن 'we will' 'will' denotes something that will happen or be done' 'children'; Biblical scholars also depend on 'Ben' meaning 'son/sons of' because they base it on its more 'modern' Arabic which means 'son', but in the old language and the Bible it means 'child/children' both male and female. Cp: beyn, ben. (1Chr.15:18)

Maaseiah; maʿăśēyâ, maʿăśēyāhû; مَعيصي يه/ياه 'disobedience' 'disobeyed him' 'disobeyed-he/him' 'askew/bent/crooked' 'became askew/crooked-he/him' 'with sticks' 'with sticks-he/him'. Equivalent to Baaseiah (1Chr.6:40), Asaiah (1Chr.4:36). Cp: ma'aisseyyah, ma'aissey-yah, ma'aisseyyaahu, ma'aissey-yaahu. (1Chr.15:18)

Elipheleh; ʾĕlîpĕlēhû; ئِلي فِليهُ ، ئيلي فيليهُ 'he who/the one who-picked out nits/had nits picked out' 'he who/the one who-picked through/went through thoroughly' 'he who/the one who-said and it happened(negative)/said bad omen'; ئِلي بِليهُ ، ئيلي بيليهُ 'he who/the one who-soaked it/became soaked' 'he who/the one who-urinated/his urine' 'he who/the one who-afflicted him' 'he who/the one who-became old/faded' 'he who/the one who-his patience/his intellect'; ئِلي فِليحُ ، ئيلي فيليحُ 'he who/the one who-succeeded/did well' 'he who/the one who-cried out get to work/do well/succeed'. Cp: illee-pheleyhu, eilee-pheileyhu, illee-beleyhu, eilee-beileyhu, illee-pheleyḥu, eilee-pheileyḥu. (1Chr.15:18)

Mikneiah; miqnēyāhû; مِقني ياهُ 'head held up high/sitting or standing perky-him/he'; مِغني ياهُ 'a singer-he/him' 'enriched/does not need-he/him'; مِغنيياهُ 'his song' 'his singing'. Cp: miqney-yaahu, mighney-yaahu, mighneyyaahu. (1Chr.15:18)

Aziel; 'ăzî'ēl; عَزي ئِل ، عيزي ئِل 'cherish-the' 'cherished-the' 'need/needed-the'; غَزي ئِل ، غيزي ئِل 'feel/make deep squeezing pain-the' 'made/felt deep squeezing pain-the' 'make deep resonating sound-the' 'made deep resonating sound-the'. Cp: 'azee-ill, 'aizee-ill, ghazee-ill, ghaizee-ill. (1Chr.15:18)

Alamoth; 'ălāmôt; عَلاّمُت ، عيلاّمُت 'a sign/signal/gesture' 'a mark' 'taught' 'showed' 'knew'. Although most of the Biblical scholars use modern meanings in Arabic to explain ancient Arabic meanings, this one is exemplary in that it shows how it is erroneously used. This well-used word in daily use in Arabic is described by the EDB as 'An obscure term' (Freedman, Myers and Beck, 2000: 40) and goes on to guess that it might be anything from a musical instrument, a melody or a 'cultic procedure'; it goes on to suggest it means singing like a 'young girl' in a high pitch—it bases this misinformation on women (not necessarily young) known as 'almâ (علمه) which is comparatively recent history of the word being used to describe whores in Egypt whose occupation included dancing (but not singing, although some might sing if they wanted to entertain but not related to the word 'Alamoth'), and you can see where this confusion, conflation, arises when the people who are 'experts' do not understand the language they are supposed to be expert in and/or attempt to alter it into a different language that does not exist while depending on the real language (Arabic) but not the correct Arabic meanings which are not in their scope of understanding.

This word in how it is used in the Biblical stories is its direct meaning as intended by Biblical authors and what it means in Arabic: **Alamoth** 'a sign/signal' is used describing the story of bringing the ark back in a procession filled with song and music. For this reason, most of the characters named in 1Chr.15 have at least one meaning (in each character name) of making a musical sound, song or any noise which can be musical or just loud. Alamoth means they play on a signal i.e. like a maestro coordinates an orchestra and most musicians using a signal to begin/stop—the story describes these people with musical names and whose role is to make music and joy in the story, to play according to a signal by an appropriately named person. Cp: 'alaamot, 'ailaamot. (1Chr.15:20)

Azaziah; 'ăzazyāhû; عيزَز ياهُ 'cherished-he/him' 'raised him in status-he/him' 'needed-he/him'; غيزَز ياهُ 'made/felt deep squeezing pain-he/him' 'made deep resonating sound-he/him'. Cp: 'aizaz-yaahu, ghaizaz-yaahu. (1Chr.15:21)

Sheminith; 'al haššĕmînîṯ; عَل هَزّيمِنِت ، هَزّيمينيت 'on timing' 'on, I will time' and again refers to musicians being timed to play properly. ('al/عَل) 'on/upon', (ha/هـ) 'I will/look/pay attention/take/is' here it means 'I will' or 'is', (sheminith/ššĕmînîṯ/زّيمِنِت) 'timed' (it can also mean told stories about the olden days, but here it is used as 'timing') from word (zmn/زمن) 'time/length of time/long ago'. Cp: 'al hazzeimeeneet, 'al hazzeiminit, zeimeeneet, zeiminit. (1Chr.15:21)

Chenaniah; kĕnanyâ, kĕnanyāhû; غينَن يه/ياهُ 'sang a lot-he/him' 'made sing-he/him' 'made 'ghn' sounds-he/him' and this is reflected directly in the lines of the story where he is introduced 'And Chenaniah…was for song: he instructed about the song…'. It could also have other meanings, but not in this part of the story, e.g. قينَن يه/ياهُ 'put something on his head-he/him' 'held head/body perky-he/him' 'estimated/topped up liquid-he/him'; كينَن يه/ياهُ 'gathered/ate 'cain' fruit-he/him' 'sheltered from rain/wind-he/him' the latter means he sheltered people, himself, objects or food sources from the elements (e.g. grain, animal fodder). Cp: gheinan-yah/yaahu, qeinan-yah/yaahu, keinan-yah/yaahu. (1Chr.15:22)

Shebaniah; šĕḇanyâ, šĕḇanyāhû; شيبَن يه/ياهُ 'swelled-he/him' 'stiffened-he/him' 'he will appear-he/him' 'he will explain/make clear-he/him' 'he will show/be exposed-he/him' 'is old-he/him' 'he will become man-he/him'; زيبَن يه/ياهُ 'lower belly-he/him' 'played large tambourine-he/him' 'made music drumming on can/pot-he/him' 'teases/tells jokes-he/him' 'makes merry-he/him'. Cp: sheiban-yah/yaahu, zeiban-yah/yaahu. (1Chr.15:24)

Jehiah; yĕḥîyâ; يِحي يه ، ييحي يه 'makes it stay/still/prevents it from moving-he/him'; يِحييه ، ييحييه 'he/it stays' 'he/it makes he/it stay' 'he makes it lively/entertaining' 'he makes lively/entertains' 'he/it heals/lives' 'he/it makes it heal'. Cp: yeḥee-yah, yeiḥee-yah, yeḥeeyah, yeiḥeeyah. (1Chr.15:24)

Tibhath; ṭiḇḥaṯ; طِبحَت 'lay prone' (it/she), 'had naked belly exposed' 'belly hung out from beneath clothes or clothes were rolled up exposing belly' 'smacked a bald head or exposed belly'. It is equivalent to Tebah (Gen.22:24), Betah (2Sam.8:8). تِبحَث 'scrapes/claws ground with claw searching for food'. Both meanings are reflected in the story as David takes what he wants from this city and he also takes brass which would include getting it out from the ground compared to how a hen scratches at the ground uplifting food. Cp: ṭibḥat, tibḥaf. (1Chr.18:8)

Chun; kûn; كُن 'is' 'piled in peak form' and means literally to pile something which takes on a peak in its piled state e.g. grains, rice if pushed into one pile creates a peak or peaks. In the story it symbolises the great amounts of brass taken from this city. Cp: kun. (1Chr.18:8)

Tou; tōʿû; طوىَ 'folded/rolled'; توعْ 'container/vessel' 'contained/carried/fit in container/vessel'; طوعْ 'obeyed/were compliant'. It is the same word as Toi (2Sam.8:9-10) but in a different tense. It still reflects he will give David 'all manner of vessels…'. Cp: ṭoo-o, too'o, ṭoo'o. (1Chr.18:9)

Hadoram is meant to be the same character of Joram in (2Sam.8:9-11), and just like Joram (pots) and Hadoram (Gen.10:27) it still means 'here is pots' as this is what this Hadoram delivers to David from king Tou; 'here is pots/rolls/folds' 'he will roll/fold' 'I will harm-the' 'he will harm-the' 'here/see, harmed-the'. It is also similar to Adoram (2Sam.20:24) which holds meanings of 'pots' and 'harming'. (1Chr.18:10)

Shavsha; šawšā'; شَوشآء 'made/did things, important things' 'things, many things' 'things, amazing/wonderful things/puzzling things'; سَوساء 'made right' 'did' 'made equal' 'corrected/fixed' 'bad/offense-did bad/offended' 'did something bad/offensive'. It is the same as both Shisha (1Kgs.4:3), Sheva (2Sam.20:25). Cp: shawshaa, sawsaa. (1Chr.18:16)

Medeba (Num.21:30) has been used as where some of the armies gathered for its meanings of 'wailing in mourning' which will happen when they are defeat and 'hair cut short or shaved off completely' because it is part of the humiliating abuse Hanun conducted against David's messengers which causes this battle. (1Chr.19:7)

Shophach; šôpāḵ; this is a slight alteration to Shobach (2Sam.10) to allow an additional wordplay: شُفآك 'saw you' 'served/serves you right'; شُبآح 'obstructing the way' 'are brave' 'are thuggish/muscular'; سُبآق 'are in front/raced ahead/beat them (as in arrived before)'. Note: compare the slight alteration in when Shobach/Shophach are introduced in the parallel accounts and you will see Shophach has been brought forward with a slight alteration to spelling to allow it to reflect the repeated 'and when' Syrians/Ammon 'saw' in the wordplay of the word 'Shophach'. Cp: shophaak, shobaaḥ, sobaaq. (1Chr.19:16)

Sippai; sippay; صِفّي 'make a column/row/line' 'clean/clear/cleanse'. Equivalent to Saph (2Sam.21:18), but in a different tense. Cp: siphay. (1Chr.20:4)

Lahmi; laḥmî; لَحمي 'eats meat/tears off strips of meat/mauls/responds angrily' 'ate meat/tore off strips of meat/mauled/responded angrily' 'meat/my meat'; لَهمي 'well fed/was well fed/feed well' 'pamper(ed)/plumpen(ed)'. It refers to the giant of the same name who will be killed by Elhanan. Note: this is a slight rearrangement of the same story at 2Sam.21:19 where the giant is only referred to as the brother of Goliath, and it is Elhanan said to be a 'Bethlehemite' to allow Elhanan's character to have the name-pun to kill the giant, but in this instance, it is the giant who takes on the name of his role 'Lahmi'. Cp: laḥmee, lahmee. (1Chr.20:5). It is possible, as mentioned earlier in this book, that David was not to have a role other than being Jonathan's lover, but later editors who preferred to make David the star, edited the stories to make Saul and Jonathan 'bad' characters and enlarge and idealise David's role, it may have been Jonathan who killed Goliath in the original stories but later editors changed it to David, later editors who still remember the original stories attempt to reintroduce it, creating more 'Goliaths' 'Jonathans' and 'Davids' (sometimes with the exact same names and sometimes with word-names and puns showing the relation to the name) to be introduced as each later editor tries to fix the story the way he sees it should be. In all cases, the original authors and later editors had no problem in changing names and characters as they deemed fit to tell the story enhanced the way *they* wanted.

Satan; śāṭan; صاطآن 'laid hands on' and it means either two people laid their hands on something/someone they should not have (i.e. harmed them), or have transgressed twice; شآطآن 'two laps/two sides' 'laps/sides' and means went back and forth on the same course/path/way either twice or many times, it is equivalent to going 'back and forth' 'up and down' 'coming and going' and could mean two or more people do this or the action is done twice or several times; صادآن 'fished' 'obstructed' 'of obstructing' 'defended' and means to either block the way or block an action without being provoked or in self-defence.

Although 'Satan' is meant as an individual being, the word is used in its different meanings as a word just as all the word-names in the Bible are merely words used in everyday Arabic language. The meanings above show it is meant as an action, it could also be attributed as an adjective to a person; in common use, when it is meant as the 'devil' the word is used to describe people who stray, provoke, cause problems, act brashly or foolishly as the word 'satan/shayṭaan' is used as a verb/adjective as well as the name of the evil being known as the devil/satan. It seems the authors of the Bible, in this instance, are using it as an individual being/character 'And Satan stood up against Israel, and provoked David to number Israel' (whereas the being which causes David to number the people in Israel at 2Sam.24:1 is God) for one of its abovementioned meanings.

In the same narration there is mention of not falling into the hand of man, and preferring to fall into the hand of God, God smiting, David being given a choice of how he and the people will be punished which all involves punishment against them, when the punishment is put to an end by God there is a clear show in the narration that the punishing angel's hand is doing the punishing and the angel is told 'stay now thine hand' so there is definitely wordplay on the meaning 'laid hands on'. It is similar to Sitnah (Gen.26:21). Cp: shaaṭaan, ssaaṭaan, ssaadaan. (1Chr.21:1-17)

Ornan; 'ornān; ئورنآن 'showed them' 'they saw'; عورنآن 'of lending/borrowing' 'of gloating'. This name-change for the character in 2Sam.24:6 (Araunah) is accompanied by an addition in the story to make clearer the first meaning of the word-name, it seems having David see the angel by the threshing floor in 2Sam.24 was not enough so the later editors add in 2Chr.21 'And Ornan turned back and saw the angel; and his four sons with him hid themselves.' So that Ornan and his children enact the meaning of the word-name. Cp: oornaan, 'oornaan. (1Chr.21:18-21)

Zetham; zēṯām; زيت آم 'kill quickly-the' 'cut/slice with quick movement-the' any wound involving a quick movement of a sharp object, 'went/passed quickly-the' 'flitted/flicked into/quickly hid-the' 'sharp cuts/slit/slash-the' 'suddenly split open-the' 'suddenly cut open-the' 'sliced open-the' 'flit/flicked/quickly hid something into narrow space-the'. Cp: zeyt-aam. (1Chr.23:8)

Haziel; ḥăzî'ēl; حيزي ئِل 'keeps/kept in-the' 'corners(ed)/crams(med)/blocks(ed)-the'; خيزي ئِل 'swears/swore at-the'; خيذي ئِل 'takes-the'; هيزي ئِل 'rocks(ed)/swings/swung-the' 'snags/tugs(ed) at-the'. Cp: ḥaizee-ill, khaizee-ill, khaivee-ill, haizee-ill. (1Chr.23:8)

Zina; zînā'; زينآء 'decorations/adornment' 'dress' (for both sexes), 'fornicator/adulterer'; سينآء 'straight' 'in (specific) direction' 'opposite/facing' 'left for a long time' 'tooth'. Cp: zeenaa, seenaa. (1Chr.23:10)

Zizah; zîzâ; ذيذه 'this and that' 'he is him(the same person)' 'spoke too much' 'turns around and comes back/revolves/repeats'; زيزه 'sent him/her/it away with others' 'fiercely drove him/her/it away'; صيصه 'made squeaky/tweeting animal/bird noises'. Cp: veevah, zeezah, sseessah. (1Chr.23:11)

Shebuel; šĕḇû'ēl; شيبُ ئِل 'swelled/stiffened-the' 'old-the' 'young-the' 'grew into young men/women-the'; شيبُئِل 'put on sandals' 'sandals/footwear'; زيبُ ئِل 'penis-the'; سيبُ ئِل 'let go/leave/leave behind-the' 'leave alone-the' 'captured-the'; سيبُئِل 'sheep tail' 'lolled/flopped (like a sheep tail)' 'walking slowly/ languorous' 'grain panicles'. Cp: sheibu-ill, sheibuill, zeibu-ill, zeibuill, seibu-ill, seibuill. (1Chr.23:16)

Rehabiah; rĕḥaḇyâ, rĕḥaḇyāhû; ريحَب يه/ياَهُ 'welcomed/welcoming-he/him' 'spacious/made space-he/him'; ريكَب يه/ياَهُ 'rid/rode-him/he' 'placed on/piled onto/got on top of-him/he'. Cp: reiḥab-yah/yaahu, reikab-yah/yaahu. (1Chr.23:17)

Jeriah; yĕrîyāhû; يِري ياَهُ ، ييري ياَهُ 'he sees-him/he' 'he shows-him/he' 'he teaches-he/him' 'he waters-him/he' 'he dreams-him/he'; هَري/هيري ياَهُ 'I will/he will see/show-him/he' 'I will/he will water-him/he'. (Je/yĕ/هي /هَـ) can also mean 'here/look/look here, pay attention/here is' followed by meanings of (riah); جِري/جيري ياَهُ 'ran-he/him' 'happened-he/him' 'pulled-he/him' 'dying-he/him' 'came-watered-he/him' 'came-saw/showed-he/him'; عِري/عيري ياَهُ 'lend-him/he' 'gloat at-him/he' 'naked/became naked-him/he' 'disgrace-him/he'; حِري/حيري ياَهُ 'made fire-he/him' 'felt responsible/cared for/moved for-he/him' 'investigated-he/him' 'of ploughing-he/him' 'infected wound-he/him' 'in predicament/puzzled-he/him'; خِري/خيري ياَهُ 'fell to ground-he/him' 'good fortune-he/him' 'chased away violently-he/him' 'defecated-he/him'. Cp: yeree-yaahu, yeiree-yaahu, heree-yaahu, heiree-yaahu, geree-yaahu, geiree-yaahu, 'eree-yaahu, 'eiree-yaahu, ḥeree-yaahu, ḥeiree-yaahu, kheree-yaahu, kheiree-yaahu. (1Chr.23:19)

Jekameam; it is the same as Jokmeam (1Chr.6:68): yĕqam'ām; يِقَم/ييقَم عآم/ئآم 'stinks and suffocates-a year' 'stinks and suffocates-the' 'stands/replaces-the' ; يِغَم/ييغَم عآم/ئآم 'it suffocates/depresses-a year' 'it suffocates/stifles/depresses-the' 'he suffocates-the'; يِغمغآم ، ييغمغآم 'he speaks with muffled voice' 'speaks with mouth covered' 'speaks with face covered'; جِغَم/جيغَم عآم/ئآم 'they/he came-suffocated/stifle/depressed-year/the' 'they/he came-covered face-year/the'; جِغمَغآم ، جيغمَغآم 'came-spoke with muffled voice' 'came-spoke with covered mouth/face'; حِغمَغآم ، حيغمغآم'stayed/still-speaks with muffled voice' 'stayed/still-speaks with covered face/mouth'; حِغَم/حيغَم عآم/ئآم'stayed/still-suffocated-a year' 'stayed/still-suffocated/

stifled/depressed-the' 'stayed/still-speaks with muffled voice/speaks with covered face/mouth-the' 'stayed/still-speaks with muffled voice/speaks with covered face/mouth-year'; حَكَم/حيكَم عام/ئام 'ruled-a year' 'ruled-the' 'wisdom/knowledge-a year' 'wisdom/knowledge-the' 'set as arbitrator-a year' 'set as arbitrator-the'; حَ خم غام ، حي خم غام 'makes 'ḥe/ḥei' 'kham' 'ghaam' sounds' 'speech is like clearing throat, nasal sounds and muffled voice/face' 'a person who makes unclear sounds when speaks (as in the sounds'ḥe/ ḥei' 'kham' 'ghaam')' 'pronounces 'ḥe/ ḥei' 'kham' 'ghaam''. Cp: yeqam-'aam/aam, yeiqam-'aam/aam, yegham-'aam/aam, yeigham-'aam/aam, yeghamghaam, yeighamghaam, gegham-'aam/aam, geigham-'aam/aam, geghamghaam, geighamghaam, ḥeghamghaam, ḥeighamghaam, ḥegham-'aam/aam, ḥeigham-'aam/aam, ḥekam-'aam/aam, ḥeikam-'aam/aam, ḥe-kham-ghaam, ḥei-kham-ghaam. (1Chr.23:19)

Harim; ḥārim; حارِم 'taken a vow never to touch wife again(sexually)' this form is usually a precursor to divorce or a warning to the wife when too many arguments occur between husband and wife or she makes problems with others, 'rotten/rotting/stinking/off' 'sacred/become sacred' 'deprived/forbidden/made forbidden'; خارِم 'punctured' 'a piercing that has been torn/ripped' 'pierced from bottom' 'craving smoke or qat/stimulant'; هارِم 'angry/grumpy' (from age or hunger). Cp: ḥaarim, khaarim, haarim. (1Chr.24:8)

Seorim; śĕʿōrîm; صيغور هم/ام 'small one-them/the' 'made small/smaller-them/the' 'the smallest of them/the'; صيعور هم/ام 'violent-them/the' 'rabid-them/the'; سيعور هم/ام 'priced-them/the' 'will drive hard/quick-them/the' 'will make run away-them/the' 'will hurt/injure-them/the'; شيعور هم/ام 'will drive hard/quick-them/the' 'will make run away-them/the' 'the/their hair' 'the/their poet/poetry' 'will hurt/injure-them/the' 'will gloat over/at them/the' 'sign/a sign-them/the'; صيئور هم/ام 'bundled-them/the' 'knotted-them/the'. Cp: sseighoor-hum/um, ssei'oor-hum/um, sei'oor-hum/um, shei'oor-hum/um, ssei-oor-hum/um. (1Chr.24:8)

Mijamin; mîyāmîn; ميیامين 'right-handed' 'abluted for prayer' 'gone to the right(side)' 'went too far to the right'; مي يامين 'so/well, what is it?' 'so/well, who is it' 'water-of what/of who?'; ميجامين 'who came, who?'; مي جامين 'water from small clay jug'. Cp: meeyaameen, mee-yaameen, meegaameen, mee-gaameen. (1Chr.24:9)

Hakkoz; haqqôṣ; هَقُّز 'I will fry' 'I will reject from disgust' 'I will be revolted'; هَقُّص 'chopped' 'chopping wood' 'look, cut' 'I will tell a story'; هَكَّز 'limped and jerked' 'I will limp and jerk'. Cp: haqqoz, haqqoss, hakkoz. (1Chr.24:10)

Jeshua; yēšûaʿ; جيشوَء 'picked a lot/many/took too much' 'many people'; جيشوَع 'burped' 'greedy' 'came-freakishly ugly/mutated' 'came-cried loudly like animal' 'pulled out by handfuls'. It is the same as **Joshua** (Exod.17:9-14). As it is only listed in this part of the story (unlike Joshua which is anchored to its meaning by the supporting story it is embedded in) Jeshua may also be: خيشوَع 'pounded/pounded until tattered/beaten' 'crumbling (into tears) with piety/affection'; هيشوَء 'shooed/swatted away'; هيشوَع 'he will bleat like a goat/animal' 'he will become freakishly mutated/ugly' 'here is-freakishly mutated/ugly'; حيشوَء 'stuffed quickly/hid quickly by stuffing'. Cp: geyshua, geyshua', kheyshua', heyshua, heyshua', ḥeyshua. (1Chr.24:11)

Shecaniah; šĕkanyāhû; سيكَن ياَهْ 'calmed-he/him' 'settled-he/him'; شيكَن ياَهْ 'complained-he/him' 'of complaining-he/him' 'complained about him' 'acted pretentious-he/him' 'thorn caught in skin-he/him'; شيخَن ياَهْ 'gave orders/resolved problems/told people what to do-he/him' 'he will betray-he/him' 'will leave soak-he/him'; سيحَن ياَهْ 'wandered and sought-he/him' 'sent them wandering-he/him' 'crawled on buttocks-he/him' (dragging lower body on ground using upper body to pull forward), 'will feel affection-he/him'; شيقَن ياَهْ 'a worker/labourer-he/him' 'make work-he/him' 'will hold head/body perky-he/him' 'will estimate/estimate liquid-he/him'. Cp: seykan-yaahu, sheykan-yaahu, sheykhan-yaahu, seyḥan-yaahu. (1Chr.24:11)

Huppah; ḥûppâ; حُبّه 'a kiss' 'love him' 'her/his love' 'a single unit or grain' 'a spot/pimple'; حُفّه 'rim it/make rim, border or edge/don't let it extend over' by using palm of hand; هُبّه 'to throw into air/swoop down on or make plunge up and down', this term is usually said to small children: when parents/relatives play with them by throwing them into air and catching them, they say 'hubbah!' as they throw them up and catch them; 'wind blowing down and scattering things' 'scattering people by chasing them/swoop down on them as if attacking to make them run and scatter' 'a gift' 'gave it/him/her'; هفّه 'to huff/puff' 'to huff/puff away' 'to make scatter through anger or violence'. The word is equivalent to Huppim (Gen.46:21) and Hupham (Num.26:39). Cp: ḥubbah, ḥuphah, hubbah, huphah. (1Chr.24:13)

Jeshebeab; yešeḇ'āḇ; يِشَب ئاب 'he/it swells-rejects/refuses' 'he grows into young man-refuses/rejects' 'swells-returns/back and forth/up and down'; يِشَب عاب 'he/it swells-packs/fills/floats' 'he grows into young man-packs/fills/floats' 'swells-packs/fills/floats' 'he/it swells-disgrace(s)' 'he grows into young man-disgrace(s)' 'swells-disgrace(s)'; 'āb could also be غاب 'thirsty' 'absent' following any of the meanings of (yešeb/يَشب); هَشب ئاب/عاب/غاب; 'I will/here is' (ye/هـ) followed by same previous meanings of the rest of compound word; جَشب ئاب/عاب/غاب 'came' (ye/جَ) followed by same previous meanings of the rest of compound word; عَشب ئاب/عاب/غاب 'plants-refused/rejected' 'plants-packs/fills/floats' 'plants-disgraces' 'plants-thirsty/absent'; خَشب ئاب/عاب/غاب 'lumber-refused/rejected' 'lumber-packed/filled/floated' 'lumber-thirsty/absent'; حَشب ئاب/عاب/غاب 'carried on waist-rejected/refused' 'carried on waist-packs/filled/floats' 'carried on waist-thirsty/absent'. Cp: yesheb-aab, yesheb-'aab, yesheb-ghaab, hesheb-aab, hesheb-'aab, hesheb-ghaab, gesheb-aab, gesheb-'aab, gesheb-ghaab, 'esheb-aab, 'esheb-'aab, 'esheb-ghaab, khesheb-aab, khesheb-'aab, khesheb-ghaab, ḥesheb-aab, ḥesheb-'aab, ḥesheb-ghaab. (1Chr.24:13)

Bilgah; bilgâ; بِلغه 'delivered message to him' 'informed him' 'reached maturity' (latter first menstruation, etc.) 'in proper language' 'by playing around with words' (latter means using wordplay or changing meanings of words, changing letters of words); دِلغه 'a clot' 'a viscous lump/smear'. Cp: bilghah, dilghah. (1Chr.24:14)

Hezir; ḥēzîr; خيضير 'green' 'unripe' 'wet'; حيضير 'ripe/mature' 'attended/present' 'ripen'; حيذير 'is cautious' 'warned'; حيصير 'surrounds' 'of straw/reed' 'grief/great despair/sorrow'; حيسير 'thin/lost weight'; هيزير 'he will tighten/squeeze/insist' 'he tugged'; هيضير 'he/it will harm'; خيصير 'ate with main dish/bit with mouth accompanying bread' 'waist'; خيسير 'lost'. Cp: kheydheer, ḥeydheer, ḥeyveer, ḥeysseer, ḥeyseer, heyzeer, heydheer, kheysseer, kheyseer. (1Chr.24:15)

Aphses; piṣṣēṣ; فِصّيص 'of pitting/removing seed or stones from fruit' 'of untying' 'of separating' 'of disentangling' 'of divorcing/separating from wife' 'small gem like stones used in decorating jewellery or clothes' 'small seeds/stone of fruit'; فِسّيس 'of passing wind' 'of copulating(like chickens)'; فِزّيز 'won/won a lot' 'provoked/provoked a lot'; بِزّيز 'of carrying a lot/doing a lot of carrying' 'carried heavy things'. Cp: phisseyss, phisseys, phizzeyz, bizzeyz. (1Chr.24:15)

Pethahiah; pĕtaḥyâ; بِطَح يه ، بيطَح يه 'lay on stomach-he/him' 'it will break-he/him'; فِطَح يه ، فيطَح يه 'flattened-he/him' 'so it broke-he/him'; فِدَه يه ، فيدَه يه 'sacrificed him/sacrificed for-he/him'; بِدَه يه ، بيدَه يه 'brought/took it/him out-he/him'. Cp: beṭaḥ-yah, beiṭaḥ-yah, pheṭaḥ-yah, pheiṭaḥ-yah, phedah-yah, pheidah-yah, bedah-yah, beidah-yah. (1Chr.24:16)

Jehezekel; yĕḥezqē'l; يِهَزقي ئل ، ييهَزقي ئل 'he is squirting/flitting-the' from word (zq/زق) 'squirted/flitted'; يِهَضقي ئل ، ييهَضقي ئل 'he is tasting/forced to eat/swallowing/suffering-the' 'you, I will make taste/eat by force/swallow/suffer-the' from word (dhq/ضق) 'distress/suffer/taste/forced to swallow' and is used when describing a person who eats something he/she does not like or not want to eat, and is also used figuratively to mean 'suffered/sufferance' 'tasted bitter' 'tasted all the agony' are some ways how sufferance or pain is described as being 'tasted/swallowed/forcibly fed'; يِهَسقي ئل ، ييهَسقي ئل 'you, I will water-the' 'you, who waters-the'; يِحَزكي ئل ، ييحَزكي ئل 'he crams/corners/puts in a tight situation-the'. يِهَزجي ئل ، ييهَزجي ئل 'he tells off-the' 'he snatches/tugs violently at-the'; يِهَزجيئل ، ييهَزجيئل 'sings a work song' 'improvises funny songs while working'. It is the same (with possible additional wordplay due to slight variation of compound word) as Hezekiah (2Kgs.18-20) and Hezeki (1Chr.8:17). Cp: yehezqey-ill, yeihezqey-ill, yehedhqey-ill, yeihedhqey-ill, yehesqey-ill, yeihesqey-ill, yeḥezkey-ill, yeiḥezkey-ill, yehezgey-ill, yeihezgey-ill, yehezgeyill, yeihezgeyill. (1Chr.24:16)

Gamul; gāmûl; جاَمُل 'played nice/pleasantries' 'felt/showed gratitude' 'made nice' 'ingratiated' 'came-fetched water'; غاَمُل 'covered' 'suffocated' 'covered mouth/face' 'muffled voice'. Cp: gaamul, ghaamul. (1Chr.24:17)

Delaiah; the same as Dalaiah (1Chr.3:24). (1Chr.24:18)

Maaziah; ma'azyâ, ma'azyāhû; مَعز يه/ياَهُ 'cherished-he/him' 'goats-he/him; مَعَزيه، مَعَزياَهُ 'gave him condolences'; مَعَص يه/ياَهُ 'cruel/disobedient-he/him'; مَعَصيه ، مَعَصياَهُ 'disobedience' 'his disobedience' 'disobeying him' 'became askew/crooked' 'became askew/crooked-he/him' 'with sticks' 'with his sticks'; مَعَضيه ، مَعَضياَهُ 'she has sore muscles' 'has sore muscles-he/him' 'of recompense/recompense-he/him'. Cp: ma'az-yah/yaahu, ma'azyah, ma'azyaahu, ma'ass-yah/yaahu, ma'assyah, ma'assyaahu, ma'adhyah, ma'adhyaahu. (1Chr.24:18)

Shubael; šûḇā'ēl; شُبآ ئِل 'swelled/stiffened-the' 'young adults/grew into young adults-the' 'old-the'; شُبائِل 'put on sandals' 'sandals/footwear'; زُبآ ئِل 'penis/penised-the'; سُبآ ئِل 'left/leave behind-the' 'left alone-the'; سُبائِل 'sheep tails' 'lolled/flopped (like a sheep tail)' 'walking slowly/ languorous' 'grain panicles'. Cp: shubaa-ill, shubaaill, zubaa-ill, subaa-ill, subaaill. The same as Shebuel (1Chr.23:16). (1Chr.24:20)

Jehdeiah; yeḥdēyāhû; يهدي ياه ، يَهدِياه 'they guide him/it' 'guides-he/him' 'they give him present(s)' 'gifts-he/him' 'they sing wedding song about him' 'sing wedding song-he/him'; يخدي ياه ، يَخدِياه 'they remove bread from oven' 'removes from oven wall-he/him' 'they pull off/pull down' 'they make collapse' 'they beat'. Cp: yehdeyaahu, yehdeiyaahu, yekhdeyaahu, yekhdeiyaahu. (1Chr.24:20)

Isshiah; the same as Ishiah (1Chr.7:3). (1Chr.24:21)

Shelomoth; šĕlōmôṯ; شيلومت ، شَلومُت 'took/take-death/dead'; سيلومت ، سَلومُت 'survived/remained intact' 'asked-death' 'asked to death' 'is of mild/peaceful nature' 'delivered/received'. Cp: sheloomot, sheiloomot, seloomot, seiloomot. (1Chr.24:22)

Jaaziah; ya'ăzîyāhû; يعيزي ياه ، يَعزي ياه 'he cherishes-him/he' 'he raises (in status)-him/he' 'he gives him his condolences'; يغيزي ياه ، يَغزي ياه 'he/it makes deep squeezing pain-him/he' 'he makes deep resonating sound-him/he'; يعيصي ياه ، يَعصي ياه 'he disobeys him/he' 'he becomes stiff/stuck-him/he' 'he becomes askew/bent/crooked-him/he' 'became askew/crooked' 'he uses sticks-him/he'; يعيذي ياه ، يَعذي ياه 'he says a protection prayer for him' 'he says a protection prayer-him/he'. Cp: ya'azee-yaahu, ya'aizee-yaahu, yaghazee-yaahu, yaghaizee-yaahu, ya'assee-yaahu, ya'aissee-yaahu, ya'avee-yaahu, ya'aivee-yaahu. (1Chr.24:26)

Beno; bĕnô; بينُ 'in it/him' 'between' 'appeared/became apparent' also a kind of crop/grain similar to sorghum but its grains are white (not red like sorghum). Cp: beino. (1Chr.24:26)

Shoham; šōham; شوهَم a type of crop/grain similar to sorghum, 'brave and civil'; سوهَم 'portions' 'portion(s) of land'; شوحَم 'animal fat' 'fatty (animals)' any substance that has greasy/waxy texture. Cp: shooham, sooham, shooḥam. (1Chr.24:27)

Ibri; 'iḇrî; عِبري 'of 'ibra" The word 'hebrew' has a meaning in Arabic and is used in daily language which I will explain later in this book where all the evidence is collated to support its meaning. Unlike the earlier mentions of 'Hebrew' which are anchored to its specific meaning by the text, this 'Ibri', like most of word-names which are just listed, has many possibilities so it could also be wordplay on: غِبري 'dusty' 'of dust' 'dust it/clean it'; عِذري 'of shadows/shadowed' 'excused/excuse'; نِبري 'needle/stick needle into' 'thorn or any slim, sharp object sticking into skin, fabric, etc.' 'go beyond/be good or pious towards'. Cp: 'ibree, ghibree, 'ivree, ibree. (1Chr.24:27)

Asarelah; 'ăśar'ēlâ; عيصرئيله ، عَصَرئيله 'twisted for him/for her' 'twisted towards him/her' 'twisted muscle-to him/her/for him-her' 'turned/twisted around towards him-her/for him-her'. Equivalent to Asareel (1Chr.4:16), Ashriel (1Chr.7:14) and Israel. Cp: 'assar-eylah, 'aissar-eylah. (1Chr.25:2)

Zeri; ṣĕrî; زيري 'tighten' 'of tightening' 'visiting/visit/of visiting/pilgriming' 'goat/sheep stable'; صيري 'a whistling/tinning sound' 'a throbbing ache in bones/teeth' 'knotted/bundled' 'knot/bundle/keep in'; شيري 'evil/of evil' 'a tingling noise' 'a tingling in the skin or muscles' 'point/indicate' 'discuss/take advice/opinions' 'bought'. Cp: zeiree, sseiree, sheiree. (1Chr.25:3)

Jeshaiah the same as Jesaiah (1Chr.3:21). (1Chr.25:3)

Bukkiah; buqqîyāhû; بوقّي ياه 'leave it' 'leave some-he/him' 'tear open/burst open-he/him' 'tear/burst it open' 'make a gash in it'; بوكّي ياه 'was made to cry-he/him' 'make him cry' 'cried-he him' 'go/go there-he/him' 'go/go there with him' 'take him there'. Cp: buqqee-yaahu, bukkee-yaahu. It is eqivalent to Bukki (Num.34:22). (1Chr.25:4)

Eliathah; 'ĕlî'āṯâ; ئِلي/ئيلي ئاته 'he who/the one who-came/comes/comes to him' 'he who/the one who-comes or goes quickly sent on errand' 'he who/the one who makes 'ta-ta' noises' 'he who/the one who-stutters'; ئِلي ئاثه 'he who/the one who-huffs/puffs/blows' 'he who/the one who-was disgusted by him' and the blowing/making 'ooph' noises expresses disgust or displeasure towards/about the spoken about; ئِلي ئافه 'he who/the one who-huffs/puffs/blows' 'he who/the one who-was disgusted by him' and the blowing/making 'ooph' noises expresses disgust or displeasure towards/about the spoken about, 'he who/the one who is an abomination/strange creature'. Cp: illee/eilee-aatah, illee-aafah, illee-aaphah. (1Chr.25:4)

Giddalti; giddaltî; جِدّلتي 'you(fem.) threw/threw around' 'you(fem.) had a fit/were possessed(by demon)' 'of throwing around' 'of throwing body to ground' 'of having fits/seizures'. Cp: giddaltee. (1Chr.25:4)

Romamti-ezer; rômamtî 'ezer; رُممتي عَزَر 'the thrown/was thrown/the killed/was killed-made ugly' 'rotted-became ugly', it could denote a ritual where sacrifices are thrown to death or thrown to ground as in killed 'made-ugly'; رُممطي نَزَر 'throw/kill-stretch/extend-tighten/squeeze/visit/pilgrimage' and could refer to making music whether with voice or instrument. Cp: romamtee-'ezer, romamṭee-ezer. (1Chr.25:4)

Joshbekashah; yošbĕqāšâ; يوشبي قآشه 'he stiffens/swells-his reed/reedpipe'; خوشبي قآسه 'lumber/piece of wood-he measured/estimated'; خوشبي قآصه 'lumber/piece of wood-he cut/told story'; يوشبج/يوشبيج عصه 'he thumps/drums with his stick'; يوشبج/يوشبيج آصه 'he thumps-quiet/silence'; يوزبي جعصه 'he penises/penetrates his anus'; يوسبق/يوسبيق آصه 'he quickens-quiet/silence' 'he goes/begins first-quiet'. These are some of the possibilities the word could be, kept within the context that the word-name has been created by the original authors for the role of prophesying which includes musical instruments, music, seizures and sexual acts which is the norm of the culture of 'prophesying' or 'seers' or anyone deemed 'close to God'. Cp: yooshbei-qaashah, khooshbei-qaasah, khooshbei-qaassah, yooshbeg/yooshbeig-'ssah, yooshbeg/yooshbeig-aassah, yoozbei-g'ssah, yoosbeq/yoosbeiq-aassah. (1Chr.25:4)

Mallothi; mallôṯî; مَلّثي 'of shouting/crying out loud'. Cp: mallofee. (1Chr.25:4)

Hothir; hôṯîr; هوثير 'he is passionate/boiling over' 'he is a bull/bulls'; حوذير 'warned' 'was parallel to/made parallel movements' 'made parallel borders/drew parallel lines/drew sides/edges'; حوفير 'dug holes' 'dug/rubbed heels/hoofs into ground'; هوفير 'he boiled (water or something)' 'he ran/fled'. Cp: hofeer, ḥoveer, ḥopheer, hopheer. (1Chr.25:4)

Mahazioth; mahăzî'ôṯ; مَهَزيئُط ، مَهيزيئُط 'the squeaking/creaking noise' 'what is this squeaking/creaking noise'; مَخَضيئُت ، مَخيضيئُت 'churned milk' 'churning/hard shaking'; مَخَزيئُت ، مَخيزيئُت 'the insult of' 'the swearing at' 'the disgrace of'; مَخَزيئُث ، مَخيزيئُث 'flung' 'the flung' 'sound of beating an object with a rope/whip like object'; مَحَزيئُت ، مَحيزيئُت 'the blocking/cramming/keeping in of' 'an intense or long musical note (in an instrument which requires blowing)'. Cp: mahazee-oṭ, mahaizee-oṭ, makhadhee-ot, makhaidhee-ot, makhazee-ot, makhaizee-ot, makhazee-of, makhaizee-of, maḥazee-ot, maḥaizee-ot. (1Chr.25:4)

Jesharelah; yĕśar'ēlâ; عَصَرئيله ، عيصَرئيله 'twisted for him/for her' 'twisted towards him/her' 'twisted muscle-to him/her' 'turned/twisted around towards him-her/for him-her'. Equivalent to Asarelah (1Chr.25:2), Asareel (1Chr.4:16), Ashriel (1Chr.7:14) and Israel. Cp: 'essar-eylah, 'eissar-eylah. (1Chr.25:14)

Jathniel; yaṯnî'ēl; يَثني ئِل 'he doubles-the' 'he stitches double-the' 'he folds-the' 'he makes a second coat of-the' (the latter of whitewash on wall, henna on skin/hair, etc.)' 'he is idolater/idol worshipper-the'; يَدني ئِل 'he guilts-the' 'he makes bow/bend-the' 'he makes lower-the'; يَظني ئِل 'he thinks/suspects-the'; يَطني ئِل 'he clangs-the' makes a tinning or clanging noise'. Equivalent/similar to Nethaneel (Num.1:8) and other 'nathan' word-names Cp: yafnee-ill, yadnee-ill, yadhnee-ill, yaṭnee-ill. (1Chr.26:2)

Jehohanan; yĕhôḥānān; يَهُ/ييهُ هآنآن 'he who/which one-humiliated/disgraced/they disgraced/humiliated/insulted' 'he who/which one-was satisfied/gave satisfactory portions'; جَهُ/جيهُ هآنآن 'came he/came to him-humiliated/disgraced/they disgraced/humiliated/insulted' 'came he/came to him-was satisfied/gave satisfactory portions'; يَهُ/ييهُ خآنآن 'he who/which one-betrayed/they betrayed' 'he who/which one-soaked in' 'he who/which one-became brothers'; جَهُ/جيهُ خآنآن 'came he/came to him-betrayed/they betrayed' 'came he/came to him-soaked/soaked in' 'came he/came to him-brothers/became brothers'; يَهُ/ييهُ حآنآن 'he who/which one-hummed/made humming sound' 'he who/which one-felt affection'; جَهُ/جيهُ حآنآن 'came he/came to him-felt affection/they felt affection'. Cp: yeho/yeiho-haanaan, geho/geiho-haanaan, yeho/yeiho-khaanaan, geho/geiho-khaanaan, yeho/yeiho-ḥaanaan, geho/geiho-ḥaanaan. (1Chr.26:3)

Peulthai; pĕ'ullĕtay; بِعولّفي ، بيعولّيفي 'they gather animal fodder/crops' 'they strip leaves off stalks'; بِغولّفي ، بيغولّيفي 'wrapped/sheathed' 'they wrap' 'they/it has membrane/tissue on/wrapped around it'; فَعولّفي 'so, gather animal fodder/crops' 'so, strip leaves off stalks'; فيعولّيفي 'so they are/will gather animal fodder/crops' 'so they are/will strip leaves off stalks'; فَغولّفي 'so, wrap/envelope it' 'so, the tissue/membrane wrapped around it'; فيغولّيفي 'so they are/will wrap' 'so, they will be wrapped'; بَغولّضَي ، بيغولّيضَي 'with unkindness/strictness/anger/heavy-handed' 'will be unkind/strict/angry/heavy-handed'; فَغولّضَي ، فيغولّيضَي 'so be unkind/strict/angry/heavy-handed' 'so they be unkind/strict/angry/heavy-handed'; فَئولّيتَي ، فيئولّيتَي 'of picking nits/of picking through things/going through things thoroughly' 'of dropping/falling' 'of immorality' 'said and the thing happened (negative)/said bad omen'; فَئول ليفي 'pick through/go through-gather/pick up' 'he said would happen/bad omen-gather/pick up'; بَئولّيتَي ، بيئولّيتَي 'of wetting' 'of urinating a lot' 'of wetting himself' 'of patience/of intelligence' 'worn/faded/old' 'afflicted/of affliction'. Cp: be'ullephay, bei'ulleiphay, beghullephay, beighulleiphay, phe'ullephay, phei'ulleiphay, pheghullephay, pheighulleiphay, beghulledhay, beighulleidhay, pheghulledhay, pheighulleidhay, phe-ulletay, phei-ulleitay, be-ulletay, bei-ulleitay. (1Chr.26:5)

Othni; ʿōṯnî; عوفني 'gave me a light meal/feed me a light meal' and refers to a meal not during regular meal times but in between, 'went off me/turned away from me' 'made me turn away/made me go off food' (this word to go off food is usually used when referring to animals); غوثني 'nauseated me' 'nagged me to nausea/nagged a lot' 'nourished me/nourish me' (the latter when a person is weak or ill and is being fed and taken care of). Cp: 'oophnee, ghoofnee. (1Chr.26:7)

Rephael; rĕpāʾēl; رَفع/ريفع ئِل 'raised/lifted-the' 'put away/tidied-the'; رَفآ/ريفآ ئِل 'twitched/fluttered-the' 'eye twitched-the'; رَبع/ريبع ئِل 'locked-the' 'galloped-the'; رَبآ/ريبآ ئِل 'god/gods-the' 'god/parent/teacher of the' 'grew/brought up/disciplined/taught-the' 'grew up well-the' 'sores increased around-the' 'lymph nodes swelled-the' 'diluted/mixed with water-the'. Cp: reph'-ill, reiph'-ill, rephaa-ill, reiphaa-ill, reb'-ill, reib'-ill, rebaa-ill, reibaa-ill. (1Chr.26:7)

Semachiah; sĕmakyāhû; سَمَخ/سيمَخ ياهُ 'brave and polite-he/him' and the adjective contains all the positive attributes about a good man in one word (smkh/سمخ) (brave, honest, gentle, polite, compassionate, civil, etc.), 'temple(of forehead)-he/him' 'struck/swiped him on forehead'; شَمَخ/شيمخ ياهُ 'flung it far-he/him' 'swiped it far away-he/him' 'nice strong smell lingering in air-he/him'; سَمَح/سيمَح ياهُ 'allowed him' 'he allowed' 'forgave him' 'he forgave' 'kind face-he/him'; شَمَق/شيمَق ياهُ 'made fun-he/him' 'pulled on one side/asymmetrical/untidy/not straight-he/him' 'pulled a face-he/him'; صَمَغ/صيمَغ ياهُ 'glue/glued-he/him'. Cp: semakh/seimakh-yaahu, shemakh/sheimakh-yaahu, semaḥ/seimaḥ-yaahu, shemaq/sheimaq-yaahu, ssemagh/sseimagh-yaahu. (1Chr.26:7)

Simri; the same as Zimri and Shimri. (1Chr.26:10)

Tebaliah; ṭĕbalyāhû; طَبَل/طيبَل ياهُ 'drummed/beat the drums-he/him' and can be a literal beating of drums or means when a man encourages another to do wrong/evil, 'stupid-he/him'. Cp: ṭebal-yaahu, ṭeibal-yaahu. (1Chr.26:11)

Shelemiah; šelemyâ, šelemiyāhû; سَلَم يه ، سَلَم ياهُ 'is peaceful/mild character-he/him' 'survived-he/him' 'intact-he/him' 'asked the-he/him' 'leaked the-he/him'; شَلَم يه ، شَلَم ياهُ 'took the-he/him' 'will gather/collect-he/him'. Cp: selem-yah, selemi-yaahu, shelem-yah, shelemi-yaahu. (1Chr.26:14)

Asuppim; ʾăsuppîm; نَسوبّ هم/ام 'I leave behind-them/the' 'I leave-them/the' 'I insult-them/the' 'I let go-them/the'; نَصوبّ هم/ام 'I pour onto/into-them/the' 'I strike-them/the' 'I bring catastrophe/affliction to them/the'. Both meanings refer to David leaving the ark at Obed-edom (2Sam.6:10-12) when he fears being killed due to what happened to Uzzah. It shows how these lists of word-names remind of the other stories and carry themes for future stories. Cp: asubb-hum/um, assubb-hum/um. (1Chr.26:15)

Shallecheth; šalleket; سَلَّقَت 'climbed' 'crawled upwards'; سَل لَقَت 'asked-found/threw' 'leaked-found/threw' 'entertained/comforted-found/threw'; شَلَّقَت 'stuck/raised in the air' 'hung'; شَل لَقَت 'took/carried-found/threw'; سَلَّكَت 'made use of' 'used(exploited or selfishly)' 'made fine/stringy'; سَل لَكَت 'asked-chewed/was loquacious/crumpled' 'leaked-chewed/was loquacious/crumpled' 'entertained/comforted-chewed/was loquacious/crumpled'; سَلَّخَت 'tore off/apart' 'dismembered'; سَل لَخَت 'asked-for his sister/until his sister' 'leaked-for his sister/until his sister' 'entertained/comforted-for his sister/until his sister'; صَلَّحَت 'she made/she fixed' 'she did do'; صَل لَحَت 'arrived/reached/connected-until decorative border/she made pancakes' 'arrived/reached/connected-she insisted'. Cp: salleqet, sal-leqet, shalleqet, shal-leqet, salleket, sal-leket, sal-lekhet, sal-lekhet, ssalleḥet, ssal-leḥet. (1Chr.26:15)

Jehieli; yĕḥîʾēlî; يَحي/ييحي ئِلي 'cures/heals/makes alive-for me/the one who' 'makes stay-the one who/for me' 'stays stills-the one who/for me' 'makes lively-the one who/for me' (humour, music, presence is liked, brings entertainment and liveliness to a gathering/party); جَحي/جيحي ئِلي 'came-cured/made alive-for me/the one who' 'became hard-the one who/for me' 'came-made still/stay-the one who/for me' 'came-made lively-the one who/for me'; هَحي ئِلي 'I will cure/make alive-the one who/for me' 'I will make stay/still-the one who/for me' 'I will make lively-the one who/for me'; يحيئِلي ، ييحيئِلي 'he removes by nudging/wriggling gently' 'he moves by shifting the position slightly' 'it moves slightly(in small movements)', to make something fit or in the right position by trying to move it slightly/gently or only being able to move it by easing it/wriggling it, 'plays tricks/deceives'; جَحيئِلي ، جيحيئِلي 'came-removed/nudged gently/small movements' 'came-played tricks/deceit'; هَحيئِلي 'I will remove it in small actions' 'I will change its position slightly/gently'; هيحيئِلي 'he will remove it in small actions' 'he will change its position slightly/gently'; يَهي/ييهي ئِلي 'she is-the one who/for me' 'which one is-the one who/for me'; هَهي/هيهي ئِلي 'here she is-the one who/for me' 'so I see, she is-the one who/for me'; جَهي/جيهي ئِلي 'came-she-the one who/for me' 'came to her-the one who/for me' 'uncovered-the one who/for me' 'uncover-the one who/for me'. It can also have (ḥl/حل) meanings. It is equivalent to **Jehiel** (1Chr.9:35). Cp: yeḥee-illee, yeiḥee-illee, geḥeeillee, geiḥee-illee, heḥee-illee, yeḥeeillee, yeiḥeeillee, geḥeeillee, geiḥeeillee, heḥeeillee, heiḥeeillee, yehee-illee, yeihee-illee, hehee-illee, heihee-illee, gehee-illee, geihee-illee. (1Chr.9:35)

Jerijah; yĕriyyâ; يري يه ، ييري يه 'he sees-him/he' 'he shows-him/he' 'he teaches-him/he' 'he waters-him/he' 'he dreams-him/he'; يرييه ، ييرييه 'he dreams'; هَري/هيري يه 'I will see/show/teach-him/he' 'I will water-him/he'. (Je/yĕ/هي /هَـ) can also mean 'here/look/look here, pay attention/here is' followed by meanings of (riah); جِري/جيري يه 'ran-he/him' 'happened-he/him' 'pulled-he/him' 'dying-he/him' 'came-watered-he/him' 'came-saw/showed/taught-he/him'; عِري/عيري يه 'lend-him/he' 'gloat at-him/he' 'naked/became naked/made naked-him/he' 'disgrace-him/he'; حِري/حيري يه 'made fire-he/him' 'felt responsible/cared for/moved for-he/him' 'investigated-he/him' 'of ploughing-he/him' 'infected wound-he/him' 'in predicament/puzzled-he/him'; خِري/خيري يه 'fell to ground-he/him' 'good fortune-he/him' 'chased away violently-he/him' 'defecated-he/him'. It is equivalent to Jeriah (1Chr.23:19). Cp: yeriy-yah, yeiriy-yah, yeriyyah, yeiriyyah, heriy-yah, heiriy-yah, geriy-yah, geiriy-yah, 'eriy-yah, 'eiriy-yah, ḥeriy-yah, ḥeiriy-yah, kheriy-yah, kheiriy-yah. (1Chr.26:31)

Zabdiel; zabdî'ēl; زَبدي ئِل 'butter-the' 'perfume/butter with ointment-the' 'drinking bowls-the'; شَبدي ئِل 'I will take out-the'; زَبطي ئِل 'kick-the' 'of kicking-the' 'sledgehammer-the'; ضَبَطي ئِل 'tighten-the' 'grows stronger-the' 'disciplines his wife-the' the latter when it is proven she has committed a serious wrong against another person; شَبطي ئِل 'lattice with rope-the' 'whipping/striking-the'. Cp: zabdee-ill, shabdee-ill, zabṭee-ill, dhabṭee-ill, shabṭee-ill. (1Chr.27:2)

Dodai; dôday; تُدَي 'says no' 'no'; تُضَي 'shines/glows' 'ablutes/washes'; تُذَي 'harms/is harmed'; ضُدَي 'against me'. It is equivalent to Dodo (Judg.10:1). Cp: today, todhay, tovay, dhoday. (1Chr.27:4)

Ammizabad; 'ammîzābād; عَمّي زَ آبَاد ، نَمّيزآباد 'uncle-buttered(ing)/spread(ing)' 'uncle-perfumed(ing)/butter(ing)/spread(ing) with ointment' 'the one who is buttered(ing)/spread(ing)' 'the one who is perfumed(ing)/spread(ing) with ointment' 'uncle-the drinking bowls' 'the drinking bowls'; عَمّي شآباد ، نَمّيشآباد 'uncle-will take out/bring out' 'the taken out/brought out'; عَمّي زآباط ، نَمّيزآباط 'my uncle-kicked' 'the one who kicks/was kicked' 'the sledgehammer'; عَمّي ضآباط ، نَمّيضآباط 'my uncle-tightened' 'my uncle-grew stronger' 'my uncle-disciplined his wife' the latter when it is proven she has committed a serious wrong against another person, 'the-tightened' 'the-strong/strengthened' 'the one who disciplines his wife'; عَمّي شآباط ، نَمّيشآباط 'uncle-latticed with rope' 'uncle whipped' 'the one that's latticed with rope' 'the one that's been whipped'. Cp: 'amee zaabaad, ameezaabaad, 'amee shaabaad, ameeshaabaad,'amee zaabaaṭ, ameezaabaaṭ, 'amee dhaabaaṭ, ameedhaabaaṭ, 'amee shaabaaṭ, ameeshaabaaṭ. (1Chr.27:6)

Shamhuth; šamhûṯ; شَمحُط 'drag around against his/her will' 'cause problems all over the place or over a prolonged period' 'a slut/prostitute' (but this word is in the masculine where it is usually in the feminine: شَمحوطه/ا ، شَمحُطه/ا) 'a slut/prostitute that drags her lover or adversary all over the place'. When the word is used to describe an immoral woman (slut or prostitute) it means she also drags people all over the place, makes them go through a lot of trouble by making them go from place to place and/or through a lot of problems. When the word is used in the form of a verb to describe a lot of effort/travelling, it is a woman or man who has caused another person to go along with them (willingly or by force) and caused them a lot of physical and/or emotional distress from the effort or problems. شَمهُط 'I will scald' 'I will squash to nothing' and is when boiling water/liquid causes a serious burn or to get feathers off a slaughtered chicken, and when something is completely squashed or beaten up. Cp: shamḥuṭ, shamhuṭ. (1Chr.27:8)

Heldai; ḥelday; حَلدَي 'reaped lots' 'stripped everything/lots off' (fruit or leaves from tree/plant); خَلدَي 'roasted in the sun' 'skin peeled off from sun' 'severely beat up' 'mole(s)/a mole' 'remembered forever' 'lived forever'. Cp: ḥelday, khelday. (1Chr.27:15)

Jaasiel; the same as Jasiel (1Chr.11:47). (1Chr.27:21)

The following passage shows how later editors attempt to correct each other through the Biblical texts. In 2Sam. the story has David order, and Joab conduct, a census of the people, the same story has Joab and the narration cite the 'exact number' of people. But authors/editors of 1Chronicles state 'Joab the son of Zeruiah began to number, but he finished not…neither was the number put in the account of the chronicles of king David.'

The word-names given to characters in the following verses denote their roles in the story: the characters and names were created to suitably match the 'occupation' they were given in the stories to make them entertaining. They drew mostly on the word-names that had already been used in earlier stories, most of the time using them with one of the meanings of its relative compound-word meanings (already explained/translated above) and sometimes using further wordplay to give it new meaning:

Azmaveth 'cherished to death' 'pride to death' 'invited over/intended-stayed' son of **Adiel** 'count-the'. ''Cherished to death/Intended-stayed—Count-the' is in charge of the 'kings treasures' Cp: 'azmaawet, 'adee-ill. (1Chr.27:25)

Jehonathan; yĕhônāṯān; يَخْنَآثَان 'he/they are making each other female by male on male sex' 'he/they soaked each other' 'soaked the second one' 'he/they betray the other' 'betray the second one' and is a version of 'Jonathan' but this meaning is not intended in this part of the story; يَهُ/جَهُ نآثَان 'he who/which one/came he/came to him-we double/fold' 'he who/which one/came he/came to him-we female/is feminine'; يَهُ/جَهُ نآدان 'he who/which one/came he/came to him-we guilt'; يَهُ/جَهُ نآظان 'he who/which one/came he/came to him-we think/suspect'; يَهُ/جَهُ نآطَان 'he who/which one/came he/came to him-we clang/make a tinning or clanging noise' but none of these meanings are used here as it is: يَهْنآتَان ، جَهُنآتَان 'gets full/satisfied/receives satisfying amounts (food)' 'he-gets/gives satisfaction' 'came-gives/gave satisfaction' and this character is made in charge over all storehouses, everywhere'. Son of **Uzziah** which along with one of its meanings 'was shifted' as this is a function of a storeroom where produce is shifted from one place to another for storage before being removed by consumption and distribution, but it has been given a new meaning (which can be found in the similar word-names of Uzziah): عوزّيا 'was cherished/was made higher in status/position' and this has happened to Jehonathan Uzziah as not only been made in charge of specific storehouses, but all those on fields, villages, cities and castles. 'Gets food/full satisfaction—Cherished/Raised in position' is made in charge of all the places where food is stored. Cp: ye<u>kh</u>onaafaan, yehu/gehu-naafaan, yehu/gehu-naadaan, yehu/gehu-naa<u>dh</u>aan, yehu/gehu-naaṭaan, yehonaataan, gehonaataan, uzeeyaḥ, 'oozeeya. (1Chr.27:25)

Ezri; 'ezrî; نَذري ، بِذري 'sow'. Son of **Chelub** 'mud' 'used mud/activity involving mud'. He is in charge of tilling the land 'Sow—Mud/Wet soil'. Cp: evree, <u>kh</u>elub, <u>kh</u>eilub. (Ezri can have other wordplay (words/meanings) but this is specifically what has been used here by the Biblical authors/editors). (1Chr.27:26)

Shimei takes on a new meaning (which is already available in other similar word-names) شِمْئي 'smell(it)' 'smells' 'my smell'. He is from Ramathite; rāmāṯî; رامآتي 'thrown' 'of throwing down' which can mean the authors meant bring down grapes; راماضي 'of sourness/souring' and has to do with checking the condition/suitability of the grapes while ripening as does 'smelling' and his name reads as 'Smells-Sourness/Souring'. When something is extremely sour, they say 'ḥaami<u>dh</u>a raami<u>dh</u>a' حامِضا/ه رامِضا/ه or if it becomes/is becoming or needs to be soured 'ḥami<u>dh</u>ee rami<u>dh</u>ee' حَمّضي رَمّضي. Cp: <u>sh</u>im-ee, raamaatee, raamaa<u>dh</u>ee. (1Chr.27:27)

Zabdi 'drinking bowls' Shiphmite; šipmî; سِفمي 'of going numb' 'of sipping'; صِبمي 'of pouring into/onto'. It is 'of sipping' 'of pouring' intended to be surname for 'Zabdi/drinking bowls' the name of the character who is 'over the increase of the vineyards for the wine cellars'. Cp: za<u>b</u>dee, si<u>ph</u>mee, <u>ss</u>ibmee. (1Chr.27:27)

Baal-hanan 'from high-gave satisfaction/gave plenty to satisfaction'. He is a **Gederite** جِذيري ، جيذيري 'of stripping/harvesting (by shaking, pulling movement that causes more fruit to fall to ground to be collected, but also leaves some fruit behind on the tree). They contrast 'low plains' with the name 'Baal-hanan/from high' and the other half to do with plenty/satisfaction and stripping/harvesting to denote the plentiness of fruit and its harvesting. Cp: ba'al haanaan, geveyree, geiveyree. (1Chr.27:28)

Joash for its meanings 'grain husks' and 'takes plenty/picks a lot/takes palmfuls' so it can denote the plentiness of oil and the fruit pulp which is left behind from oil pressing so he is narrated as 'over the cellars of oil'. Cp: go-a<u>sh</u>. (1Chr.27:28)

Shitrai; šiṭray; شِطرَي 'side of mountain/specific side of land' 'my side of land/mountainside'. Sharonite; šārônî; شآرُني 'of evil/evil' 'bought me' 'bought it' 'of buying'; سآرُني 'walked/went' 'of walking/going'. The name reads as 'My/the side of the land-Bought' and even the narration reflects this is what is meant as it specifies in the story that Shitrai the Sharonite grazed the herds in Sharon while someone else grazes herds in another part of the land. Sharonite's meaning of 'walked' also means moving the flocks to graze while Shitrai represents a specific part of the land he shepherded on. Cp: <u>sh</u>iṭray, <u>sh</u>aaronee, saaronee. (1Chr.27:29)

Shaphat 'seeing/saw'; Adlai; 'a<u>d</u>lay; نَدلَي 'push/drive' 'push/pedal things/oneself'. Shaphat Adlai 'Seeing/Saw-Drives' denotes he is driving the herds to their grazing place and watching over them 'over the herds *that were* in the valleys…'. Cp: <u>sh</u>aa<u>ph</u>aat, adlay. (1Chr.27:29)

Obil; ’ôḇîl; نُبيل ، نُوبيل ‘camels’; the Ishmaelite; yišmĕ‘ē’lîm; يِسمَعي ئل هم/ام ، يِسميعي ئل هم/ام ‘He/She listens to-the-them/the’. The name reads ‘Camels-He listens to/hears them/the’ and denotes he is shepherding camels. Cp: o-beel, yisme’ey-il-hum/um, yismei’ey-il-hum/um. (1Chr.27:30)

Jehdeiah ‘they guide him/it’ ‘they pull off/pull down’; he is Meronothite; mērōnōṯî; ميرونوتي ‘of not seeing’ ‘stubborn’ ‘of stubbornness’ which is how most people depict donkeys even when they call a person a ‘donkey/ass’ (in Arabic) two characteristics (out of many) that could cause a person to be called a donkey is being stubborn and not listening which in Arabic is said also as ‘not seeing’. And this character is in charge ‘over the asses’. Cp: yehdeyaahu, yehdeiyaahu, yekhdeyaahu, yekhdeiyaahu, meyroonootee. (1Chr.27:30)

Jaziz; yāzîz; جآزيز ‘green pastures’ ‘cut crops’ ‘reaping of stalks/crops’ ‘animals grazing’; It is equivalent to Gazez (1Chr.2:46), Gazer (2Sam.5:25), Jazer (Num.32:1-4), Jezer (Num.26:49). He is Hagerite; hagrî; حَجري ‘of stones’ ‘my stones’; هَجري ‘I will run’ ‘pay attention, run’; hagrî’îm; حَجريئ هم/ام ‘stones/throw stones-them/the’ ‘prevent/forbid-them/the’; هَجريئ هم/ام I will make run-them/the’ and both its meanings of throwing stones/chasing/make run as well as Jaziz ‘green pastures/animals grazing’ are to suit the role in the story ‘And over the flocks was Jaziz the Hagerite’. Cp: gaazeez, ḥagree, hagree, ḥagree-hum/um, hagree-hum/um. (1Chr.27:31)

Hachmoni; the same as Hachmonite (1Chr.11:11). (1Chr.27:32)

2 Chronicles

Joppa; yāp̄ô; عآب ‘filled/packed’ ‘full’ ‘floated’. It means both to pack or be filled/full and also when something floats and/or flows, e.g. a specific type of cheese that comes in a bowl filled with its own seeping fluid/water, the cheese floats in the fluid and is called ’owbah/عوبه ; when something ‘floats’ or flows: ya’oob يَعوب ; or flows/rushes quickly (e.g. like rivers) ya’ob يَعُّب ; if it flows strong or heavily or rushes and makes rushing sound ’abeeb عَبيب and if described as intensely bubbling, rushing, roaring, floating the Arabic method of repeating the same word in a phrase to intensify its meaning: ya’ob ’abeeb يَعُّب عَبيب . (It can also have meanings of ‘shamed/disgraced’ ‘rotted and stank’). The story narrates Solomon requesting wood in great quantities ‘Even to prepare me timber in abundance’ to denote the ‘packed’ meaning of Joppa. The narration relays the floating meaning through having lumber floated down the sea/river and naming the place where it will be unloaded as Joppa ‘we will bring it to thee in floats by sea to Joppa…’. The word-name is equivalent to Jobab (Gen.10:29), Abib (Exod.13:4). Cp: ’aabo. (2Chr.2:9,16)

Parvaim; parwāyim; بَرواي ام ‘passed beyond-the’; بَرو آيِم ‘go beyond the sea/river’. The story tells most materials Solomon used to build the house/temple came from abroad. Though both versions of the word seem different in meaning, they still mean the same thing: ‘from/go beyond’. In rural Yemen, especially the region where I lived, anyone or anything considered coming from a different country, especially unknown (abstract to them) is said to come from ‘beyond the sea’ (br al-bḥr/br al-ym/بر البحر/بَر اليم, the word for sea ‘bḥr’ has replaced the word ‘ym’. The people would call me and my brothers ‘the ones who came from beyond the sea’ اللي أجو من بَر البحر (ellee ago min bar el-baḥr), for many years they would call me ‘the girl from beyond the sea’ البنت من بَر البحر (ill-bnt mn br el-bḥr), and sometimes ‘the girl from beyond the sea’ or ‘the girl from the sea’ بنت البحر (bnt el-bḥr), البنت من بَر البحر ، اللي أجَت من البحر (ill-bnt mn br el-bḥr; ellee agat mn el-bḥr).

When telling someone (or talking about someone) they can ‘go away’ or ‘get lost/get lost for all I care’ ‘I don’t care if you go’, to show they do not care where/if he/she goes they say ‘go beyond the sea’ (baree el-bḥr). Cp: barwaay-um, barw aayim. (2Chr.3:6)

There is a direct relation to ‘coming from abroad’ and ‘crossing a sea/river’. Even the word for water overflowing or an ascent in a hill/mountain that dips over and whoever passes over it cannot be seen, is from the word of water overflowing: ‘ghareb’ غَرّب and is the meaning for the sun setting which dips beyond the horizon, and for many people, especially those who speak the language of the Bible and who created its stories would see the sun disappearing into or beyond the sea. This word would become the meaning for ‘west’ ‘sunset’ and also ‘abroad’ a person who has gone abroad to work is said to be in ‘ghurbah’ or has ‘gharrab’ (went over the ascent/flowed over/dipped out of sight), a stranger is (ghareeb). The word is a different than ‘parvaim’ but there is a definite connection to going over waters and being in a foreign land or a foreigner coming from over waters. This is how words come to have meanings which is what I am proving in this book.

Zeredathah; ṣĕrēḏâ, ṣĕrēḏāṯâ; صَريده ، صيريده ‘fire pit’ ‘coal making pit’ (logs are burnt in a particular way then buried in the ground to become good coal), ‘burnt logs’ ‘burnt and blackened’ ‘became like a burnt log' (the latter when a person ignores and does not respond when spoken to, but his/her posture becomes stiff and/or turns away) 'ignores/pretends not to hear/pretends to be deaf'. It is mentioned as where metallic tools were made and they specify 'in the clay ground between Succoth and Zeredathah'. It could also be wordplay on صَربيه ، صيريبه 'sealing roof/ceiling with sticks' 'sticks used as sealing material' it is part of the roofing process in building houses where the space between roof beams are filled with straight sticks (leaving no gaps)). This is possible as they have mentioned Succoth which means 'building the roof'. صَريداته ، صيريداته 'they/it burnt like a log/became like a black log' 'they/it burnt black/hard' 'they are ignoring/turned away'; صَريباته ، صيريباته 'they sealed it (roof/ceiling) with sticks' (it can also mean to reap grain panicles while leaving crops/stalks standing; 'to put something in a large basket' called (mssrb/ مصرب). Cp: ssereydah, sseireydah, ssereybah, sseireybah, ssereydaatah, sseireydaatah, ssereybaatah, sseireybaatah. (2Chr.4:17)

Hamath is used again as 'flakes that come off grain' as during winnowing it comes off in great amounts and gets everywhere. This word has been used in 2Chr.7:8 as word-imagery to describe the feasting people as a crowd which begins in Hamat and ends 'unto the river of Egypt'.

Hamath-zobah; ḥămāṯ ṣôḇâ; حَماض زُبه/ا 'soured-fiercely drove away' 'soured-unrelentingly drove away' 'soured-scary looking'; حَماط زُبه/ا 'flakes that come off grain-fiercely drove away' 'flakes that come off grain-unrelentingly drove away' 'flakes that come off grain-scary looking'; حَماض ذبح 'soured-slaughtered' ; حَماط ذبح 'flakes that come off grain-slaughtered'. Cp: ḥamaadh zobah(ba), ḥamaaṭ, zobah(ba), ḥamaadh vobaḥ, ḥamaaṭ vobaḥ. (2Chr.8:3)

Arabia; 'arbāyē; عَربآيي 'he will-my god/parent/teacher' 'will he-my god/parent/teacher' '(of)learn and remember/beware/be warned-teacher/discipliner/parent/god/master/the grower/anyone who brings someone up or teaches them/grows them (children/animals/plants/etc.)/grew fast and(or) well' it can also be read in the tense 'taught/disciplined/grew well/brought up' 'expressed it clearly' 'he will/will he-mix and dilute with water', 'of getting naked' 'of fucking with' 'fucked a lot with'; تَربآيي 'is mixed and diluted with water' 'the god/parent/teacher' 'is my god/parent/teacher' 'he is-my god/parent/teacher' 'is he/which-my god/parent/teacher?' 'the (or of) mixed and diluted with water' 'mixed and diluted with water' 'the (or of) teacher(ing)/discipliner(ing)/parent/god/grower/anyone who brings someone or something up or teaches them/grows them' 'the grown fast and/or well'. Cp: 'arbaayey, arbaayey. (2Chr.9:14)

Note: The book/prophecy/visions are used for their character names and how it reflects on the story: **Nathan** 'doubled/strengthened' 'we female/is feminine' as Solomon receives great resources and in great quantities and it also refers to queen Sheba arriving and bringing great quantities of rare resources to Solomon; **Ahijah** 'here she is' denoting queen of Sheba and also **Shilonite** 'of taking/carrying' 'of taking/carrying away' as she brings with her great amounts of rare resources and also receives great resources which she carries away with her on her return; **Iddo** is mentioned here for its meaning 'count' as the story narrates the quantities and types of resources Solomon receives. These characters have been cited for their names because the whole chapter 9 is about the resources and the quantities received. (2Chr.9)

Note: in 2 Chronicles there is a slight change in spelling of words, but it still follows the same method of using words as names to denote the event/description in the stories. The change in spelling could be from the original authors/editors (accents) who put these stories into writing, but it could also be from copiers/scribes, later editors or even ancient and modern translators and transliteration interpretation. But the words still hold the same meanings and where there is a story narrated the meanings are clearly supported by the text.

Shamariah; šĕmaryâ; سيمَريه 'staying up all/late night' 'they are staying up all/late night' 'staying up all/late night-he/him' 'telling night stories-he/him' 'they are telling night stories'; شيمَريه 'with rolled up/tucked up sleeves/clothes' 'they are with rolled up sleeves/tucked up clothes' 'rolled/tucked up sleeves/clothes-he/him'. Equivalent to Samaria and Shemariah (1Chr.12:5). Cp: seimaryah, sheimaryah. (2Chr.11:19)

Zaham; zāham; زآهم 'rotting meat'; زآحَم 'crowded/competed'; ذآهَم 'this is a worry' 'this one worried'. Cp: zaaham, zaaḥam, vaaham. (2Chr.11:19)

Note how **Shamariah** 'night time story', **Jeush** (Gen.36:5) 'picked many/took a lot' and **Zaham** 'crowded' are used: these names of Rehoboam's children from first wife are themes telling the audience this is a fictional story and making it funny because what follows the naming of his children from his first wife are themes reflecting these names: he will marry and have children from many wives and concubines 'Jeush' which give him numerous children so 'Jeush' and 'Zaham' are used for 'picked a lot/took many' 'crowded' and are denoted. Whether by the same original author of this story or a later editor, the meanings and how they are used is further enhanced by making them have 'victuals in abundance' and reminding them of the themes by adding the line 'And he desired many wives.' at the end of this passage. (2Chr.11:18-23)

Lubims; lûḇîm; لُب هم/ام 'their/the-pulp/core' 'pulp/core-them/the' 'answer-them/the' 'serve-them/the'. Denoting the enemies entering Israel and taking its cities, taking away its treasure from its midst, but this punishment is also caused because they did not answer and serve God; relayed in when they 'humble' themselves towards God, i.e. will serve him correctly that he will answer their distress by partially saving them; also relayed in that they will serve the enemy as punishment. Cp: lub-hum/um. (2Chr.12:3)

Sukkims; sukkîm; سوّق هم/ام 'drive-them/the' and denotes the chariots in great numbers that will arrive with Shishak, and that the people will be driven to serve Shishak and other countries. Cp: suqq-hum/um. (2Chr.12:3)

Ethiopians; kûšîm; قُش هم/ام 'make crispy/toast them/the' 'scrape/sweep away (like litter/fibres)-them/the' (the latter also a curse said in humour of anger meaning 'May God take you'); قُص هم/ام 'cut/cut up-them/the' 'tell a story-them/the' 'hardened-them/the' 'have hardened hearts/cruel-them/the'. Cp: qush-hum/um, quss-hum/um. (2Chr.12:3)

Shemaiah is used for its meanings of 'listened-he/him' 'made listen-he/him' 'to spoil reputation of another by insulting them in the hearing of others' 'to talk badly/insult a person in front of others' as this character disobeys god and loses his reputation but then listens to god and is 'restored' as a 'good' character in the story. **Iddo** is used again for its meanings of 'count' as the enemies are counted, also the resources which were taken away; but also for 'enmity/transgression' 'transgress against' to denote the wars between Rehoboam/Jeroboam. Iddo's meaning of 'counts' will be used again to reflect the verses about the numbers of cities, wives and children (this time for Abijah) mentioned in the story at 2Chr.13:22. (2Chr.12:15)

Zemaraim used for two of its meanings mentioned before in Josh.18:22, 'told a story-the' 'stayed up late night-the'; 'guilted/ostracised-the'. It is used because Abijah stands on this mountain of the same name to tell Jeroboam and the people of their guilt and to blame them because David's sons are meant to rule and not others. The meaning of storytelling is as used before in its different word versions (samaria/samaritan) to remind the audience that this did not happen but is a fictional story they are being told. (2Chr.13:4)

It is a recycling of the Abimelech and Jotham (latter 'came-guilted' 'came-blamed') story (Judg.9:7-21) where over the same problem of 'king' a character is created named 'Jotham' who stands on a mountain and lays the blame on Abimelech and his supporters; the same is in this story in 2Chr.13 but the character-name of 'guilt/blame' has been given to the mountain which Abijah stands on when he shouts out the blame. Cp: semaaray-um, seimaaray-um, vemaaray-um, veimaaray-um. (2Chr.13:4)

Jeshanah; yěšānâ; يِسآنه ، ييسآنه 'he makes straight' 'makes in his/right direction'; جِسآنه ، جيسآنه 'came-made straight' 'came-in his direction'; يِشآنه ، ييشآنه 'he filters it/him' 'he wants us'; جِشآنه ، جيشآنه 'made us suffocate from bad smell' 'came-filtered it/him' 'picked a lot/many' 'took by the handfuls' 'they took lots from/of it' 'a lot of people' this is one of what is meant in the story as Abijah takes many towns/cities from Jeroboam and through battle; جِزآنه ، جيزآنه 'our/his just deserts' 'we gave him his reward' as the story does narrate this is retribution for worshipping other gods. It is similar to Jashen (2Sam.23:32). Cp: yesaanah, yeisaanah, gesaanah, geisaanah, yeshaanah, yeishaanah, geshaanah, geishaanah, gezaanah, geizaanah. (2Chr.13:19)

Ephrain; ʿeprawin; نِفرَوِن 'multiplied/increased'. Relayed in the story that Abijah/Judah takes many areas from Israel 'Abijah waxed mighty…' and the increase in the number of wives he takes and tens of children he fathers. Equivalent to Ephraim (Gen.41:52) and Ephron (Gen.23). Cp: ephrawin. (2Chr.13:19)

Zerah the Ethipoian; zeraḥ hakkûšî; زَرَه 'squeezed it/tightened it/him' 'squeezed him/it' 'insulted a lot/ disgraced him' 'visited him/pilgrimaged'; صَرَخ 'shouted/he shouted'; سَرَح 'went/he went'; ذَرَه 'sowed it/ seeded it' 'filled him with insults'. It is relayed in thousands of the misnomered 'Ethiopians'; in they will be insulted with great defeat; they will be made to leave fleeing in horror; it is in Asa crying out to God to help them defeat the huge army although they are outnumbered.

'Ethiopian': هَقُشي 'I will scrape away/sweep away (like litter/fibres)' 'I will kill in one go/one movement' 'I will remove in one movement' 'I will leave like left over burnt pieces'; هَقُصي 'I will cut/cut up' 'I will tell a story' 'I will be harden/I will harden' 'I will have hardened heart/I will be cruel'. The narration relays the meanings in how they are devastated with great destruction including their cities being ruined and their livestock plundered. Cp: zerah, sserakh, seraḥ, verah; haqqushee, haqqussee. (2Chr.14:9)

Zephathah; ṣĕpaṯâ; صيفته ، صفته 'cleaned/cleared it' 'settled (scores/differences)' 'flattered him/described him positively' 'insulted him' 'got used to it/him' 'got used to' 'his rock(s)/stone(s)' 'his stacked rocks/ column of rocks' 'his rows/columns'; سيفته ، سِفته 'made it numb' 'carried it/him gently/with care' 'poured gentle spurts of water on it' 'sipped it'; زيفته ، زِفته 'escorted him/it in procession/entourage'. Cp: ssephatah, sseiphatah, sephatah, seiphatah, zephatah, zeiphatah. (2Chr.14:10)

Gerar has been chosen as the place where Zerah and the 'Ethiopians' fled to because of its meanings 'a pulling/drawing' from word (gr/جر) 'pull/draw' and it applies to physically pulling something, but can also be used figuratively, such as 'pulling/drawing' a person into wrongdoing (deceiving/encouraging), or coaxing/knowing how to make a person speak (whether the person is reluctant or just needs prompting), it is also used to describe wayward personalities and their behaviour just as it was used in (Gen.20) and can also mean 'dying' as the person's soul seems to be struggling to pull out of the body. It denotes the 'Ethiopians' drawn on chariots, being drawn into battle, Asa drawing God to help them through conversation/ prayer. (2Chr.14:11-15)

Azariah is used for one of its earlier meanings 'he made him ugly' 'he made ugly/he made become ugly' which is a word often used in the Bible to denote the death and destruction in the stories and this part speaks of destruction of many nations. He is the son of Oded; 'ôḏeḏ; عُدِد 'counted' 'recounted/listed' 'returned' 'attacked/transgressed' and the story speaks of the people straying away from God's ways which results in enmity and wars between all people; the story counts/lists the sins and numbers of sacrifices. Cp: 'oded. (2Chr.15)

Abel-maim; 'abêl-māyim; عَبيل مايِم ، عَبيل ماي ام 'shake sheep fat/shake fat-their water/their river' 'shake fat-water of/water the' and it refers to Israel being defeated and their buildings being destroyed and the other word-names used along with Abel-maim (Ijon, Dan, Naphtali) all describe how Asa and Israel were defeated. Cp: 'abel maayim, 'abel maay-um. (2Chr.16:4)

Benhail; ben-ḥayil; بَن هَيِل 'we will be/between-here's the/she is the' 'we will be/between-cardamom' 'became apparent-here's the' 'became apparent-cardamom'; بَن حَيِل 'we will be/between-stuck in one place/ indecisive/tricks/trickster' to mean stuck to one side or in certain place, 'became apparent -stuck in one place/tricks/trickster' and can also have the other meanings of (ḥl/حل) such as 'we will remove clothes/ undress' 'we will shed (leaves/hair/skin)' 'we will circumcise' 'we will purify/cleanse' 'we will declare purified/permissible' 'we will make edible/touchable' 'we will beat severely/beat until skin peels off' 'we will replace/replaced' 'sweet/sweetened'. It is definitely about declaring what is right and wrong (permissible/ edible/touchable) as the characters are sent to teach the rest of the people, and as the character has obeyed God's ways and God has rewarded him for doing so. Cp: ben-hayil, ben-ḥayil. (2Chr.17:7)

Tobijah; ṭôḇîyāhû; طُبي ياَه 'they could tolerate/eat/palate/taste him/it-he/him' 'they are not revolted-he/ him', the word implies something unsavoury about the food/drink/person and indicates a bad taste or unhygiene: it is from the word (ṭb/طب) which means 'kind/good/pleasant/nice/well(fine)/palatable/could swallow' (and also means the 'penis/willy') but the form of the word in this word-name gives it the unpleasant sense, 'my willy-he/him' 'was willied-he/him'; تُبي ياَه 'repent-he/him' 'make repent-he/him'; ضُبي ياَه 'burning smell-he/him' (this word means a burning smell of a pan/pot or anything metallic on fire with no food in it cooking). It is similar to one meaning of Ethbaal (1Kgs.16:31-33; 21). Cp: ṭobee-yaahu, tobee-yaahu, dhobee-yaahu. (2Chr.17:8)

Tobadonijah; ṭôḇ 'ăḏônîyâ; تُب نَضوني جه/ا 'repent-here I am coming' 'stop bad behaviour-here I am coming' 'repent-here I have done' 'stop bad behaviour-here I have done'; طب نَضوني جه/ا 'well/good/ nice-here I am coming' 'willy-here I am coming' 'well/good/nice-here I have done' 'willy-here I have done' ; تب نَذوني يه/ا 'repent-harmed me-he/them' 'repent-they harmed me' 'stop bad behaviour-harmed me-he/them' 'stop bad behaviour-they harmed me'. Cp: tob-adhoonee gah(ga), ṭob-adhoonee gah(ga), tob-avoonee yah(ya). (2Chr.17:8)

Amasiah; 'ămasyâ; غيمَزيه 'massaged/squeezed-him/it' 'massaged/squeezed-he/him' 'winked-he/him'; غيمَس يه 'dipped him/it into' 'dipped into-he/him'; عيمَش يه 'partially blind-he/him' 'felt around blindly-he/him'; نَيمعزيه 'he will have goats' 'he raises goats-he/him' 'he cherished-he/him' 'the cherished/pride-he/him'; نَيمعشيه 'he will/he is shepherd(ing) flocks in afternoon' 'he will/he is feed(ing) supper'; نَيمعصيه 'he is disobeying/disobedience' 'yes, disobey him' 'yes, it is bent/askew/crooked' 'it is stuck/a tough issue'. Cp: ghaimazyah, ghaimasyah, 'aimash-yah, aim'zyah, aim'z-yah, aim'shyah, aim'ssyah. (2Chr.17:16)

In the story of 2Chr.20, **Jahaziel** (1Chr.12:4) has been used as the one whom God's spirit possesses to prophesy for its meanings of 'corners/crams/blocks-the' 'prepare-the' as he tells Jehoshaphat that they do not need to fight only to prepare themselves because God will fight instead; God blocks/stops the enemies from attacking Jehoshaphat and inflicts destruction against them. Both word-names Jahaziel and **Hazazon-tamar** denote the enemy being blocked from attacking. The destruction is denoted by the theme-name used in the earlier verse of the chapter Hazazon-tamar 'corner/drive-destruction' to corner them (Hazez) then destroy them (tamar). (Gen.14:7). (2Chr.20)

Ziz; ṣîṣ; زيز 'sent away in droves' 'fiercely drove away' as God will use violence to destroy the enemies; ذيذ 'revolve/repeat/turn in circle/go partially forward and back' 'announced loudly' 'spoke for all to hear' as Jehoshaphat instructs the people to sing and praise for all to hear and the story narrates it is when the singing begins that the enemies magically turn against each other. Cp: zeez, veev. (2Chr.20)

Jeruel; yĕrû'ēl; ييرُ ئِل 'they see-the'; جيرُ ئِل 'came-saw-the' and this compound word has been used as this is where Jehoshaphat and his people will find/see the enemies, and it is also reflected in the story that the people do not need to fight the enemy, just see them and watch while God works his magic against them. Cp: yeiru-ill, geiru-ill. (2Chr.20)

Tekoa (2Sam.14) has been used in this story for its meaning of 'piety' 'sympathy and fear for what is right/wrong' as the reason God saves them from the enemies is their piety and show of piety. (2Chr.20)

Berachah (1Chr.12:3) has been used for its meanings of 'he/they cleared it/levelled it' as they spend three to four days stripping and gathering the spoils from the corpses which itself also holds another meaning for Berachah 'lasted long/sufficed' and 'blessed' as apparently, from this story, the soldiers were wearing copious amounts of jewellery and other 'riches' '…they found among them in abundance both riches with the dead bodies, and precious jewels, which they stripped off for themselves, more than they could carry away: and they were three days in gathering of the spoil, it was so much. And on the fourth day they assembled themselves in the valley of Berachah; for there they blessed the Lord: therefore the name of the same place was called, The valley of Berachah, unto this day.'. (1Chr.20:24-26)

Dodavah; dōḏāwāhû; توضاوآحُ 'they broke against rocks' 'stranded on rocks' (the latter is when a person/animal attempts to cross unfamiliar terrain and gets stuck on a difficult mountain face with no way of getting back, 'hung/spread on rocks to dry or to air' (usually clothes or bedding), from word (dhaaḥa/ضاحا) 'rock/dry/hang to dry'; توطاوآحُ 'they broke' 'they broke against' 'lots of breaking', from word (ṭḥ/طح) 'fell/broke/fell and broke'; تو داوآحُ 'thumped until holes appeared' 'they have pierced/cracks from the bottom' 'lots of holes have appeared in it/them', from word (dḥ/دح) 'pierced from bottom/back' 'hole appeared' 'thumped hard until hole appeared/pierced/hurt'. All these words are reflected in the meaning but 'broke against rocks' especially as the story describes ships were broken so that they could not sail. **Eliezer** 'the one who makes ugly' is still used to describe destruction or death and is the name given to the prophet who predicts this destruction, and he is conveniently the 'son of Dodavah' which is how the ships are broken and he is from **Mareshah** 'wash clothes (quickly)' 'to slip away unnoticed' 'slip from hands' 'slippery' and this too denotes the water and slipping in the story. **Tarshish** was the intended destination for its meanings 'light spraying' or 'a lot of light spray' 'intentionally splashing a little liquid over someone/something'. Cp: toodhaawaaḥu, tooṭaawaaḥu, toodaawaaḥu. (2Chr.20:37)

Three of **Jehoram** meanings are reflected in this story: 'is pulled down and out' 'is told off like insides being pulled out' 'pulled out' 'he is pierced/ pierces' 'he pierced/burst from the bottom' as Jehoram will be punished with 'great sickness by disease of thy bowels, until thy bowels fall out by reason of the sickness day by day.'; 'he is deprived of/forbidden' as god will send a plague as punishment on all of Jehoram's wives, children, people and goods before further deprivation when they are taken away as captives. (2Chr.21)

Jehoshabeath; yĕhôšaḇ'aṯ; يَهُ/ييهُ شَبعَت 'he who/which one-she satisfied/fed/filled stomach'; جَهُ/جيهُ شَبعَت 'came he/came to him-she satisfied/fed/filled stomach'; يَهُ/ييهُ شَبئَت 'he who/which one-young woman'; جَهُ/جيهُ شَبَئَت 'came he/came to him-young woman'. The reason why this character name has been changed from **Jehosheba** 'came he-young woman' 'who is/which one-young woman' 'came he-fed full/full stomach/satisfied' in the narration of the same story at 2Kgs.11:1-2, to Jehoshabeath in 2 Chronicles with its meanings of a female feeding/satisfying the hunger of a 'he who/came who', is because later editors may have felt that the audience got the 'young woman' part in 2Kings, but not that the nurse who is hidden with Joash is also meant by this compound word as she is the one who provides Joash with nourishment, satisfies his hunger either as a wet-nurse or someone responsible for feeding him. So the editors change the name where it can still hold the wordplay about 'young woman' denoting the sister that saves Joash, but making the 'full stomach/satisfied' more prominent so that it too can be understood as the entertaining pun in the story of the nurse that was also concealed with him. Cp: yeho-<u>sh</u>ab'at, yeiho-<u>sh</u>ab'at, geho-<u>sh</u>ab'at, geiho-<u>sh</u>ab'at, yeho-shab-at, yeiho-shab-at, geho-shab-at, geiho-shab-at. (2Chr.22:11-12)

Elishaphat; 'ĕlîšāp̄āṭ; ئِلي/ئيلي شآفآت 'he who/the one who-was seen/saw/cured' 'he who/the one-was cured or satisfied in another's bad luck/revenge/gloating/recompense out of hatred or wrong' and this kind of gloating/revenge is when a person who has been done wrong by another takes satisfaction in the offending person's harm or bad luck. The 'shaphat/saw/cured or satisfied in another's bad luck/revenge/gloating/recompense out of hatred or wrong" and 'eli/he/who' can be understood with all their meanings as they have been used previously in the earlier Biblical stories, but when taken in context with this particular narration of the story this compound word is relaying the person doing the seeing is a female, and in the revenge and satisfaction has been taken in doing her harm. It directly refers to Athaliah's part in the story when she sees that Joash is by the pillar and has been made king and in her humiliation and murder. Cp: illee/eilee-<u>sh</u>aa<u>ph</u>aat. (2Chr.23)

All the names mentioned as 'captains of hundreds' (whose names have already been translated in earlier stories) are used as themes for what happens in this chapter: **Azariah** 'makes ugly' as there will be slaughter and deaths which is the focal point of the story resulting from Athaliah having killed all the royal family; he is son of **Jehoram** 'he deprives/forbids' because Athaliah has prevented Joash becoming king, because people fear to let her know he is alive, and also reflected in people are prevented from going into 'the house of the Lord' and anyone who does will be killed; **Ishmael** 'he/she listens to-the' as everyone listens and agrees to Jehioada's plans and Athaliah is unaware of the coup until she 'heard the noise of the people running and praising the king…'; he is son of **Jehohanan** for all its meanings of 'he who/which one-humiliated/satisfied/satisfactory portions/betrayed/humming sound/they felt affection': Athaliah is disgraced not only because she has been betrayed and removed as queen, but in her death it is narrated she is killed at the horse gate; the participants are making music and everyone is fed and satisfied as Jehoiada instructs burnt offerings be made to God; people are rejoicing and described as being happy with the new king. **Azariah** is mentioned twice: the first **Azariah Jehoram** denotes the massacre and deprivation of becoming king caused by Athaliah; the second **Azariah** still means the ugliness of slaughter/death but this time as son of **Obed** 'worshipper/of worship/servant/of service' as the location of all the drama in this story happens in a place of worship 'the house of the Lord' and the main participants in this event are 'Levites' who perform the rituals of worship, and it also denotes that Athaliah is killed following being led out of the place of worship. **Maaseiah** 'disobedience' 'disobeyed him' as Athaliah has been seen as disobeying what is right and she suffers from the disobedience and revolt of her subjects; he is son of **Adaiah** 'became enemy-he/him' 'went against him' reflected in both Athaliah seen as enemy and Jehoiada and others acting against her. (2Chr.23)

The Biblical authors and editors of ancient times still show they have no problem in changing a story completely and contradicting earlier stories, nor do they have a problem with changing the names of characters or adding/removing events and characters of which the difference between the Joash story of 2 Kings and 2 Chronicles is evident.

There is another shift in the Joash stories which later editors have made where the priests' role in ruling the kingdom is strengthened and the king is character-assassinated to allow the priest to have a larger and more important role. This is probably because later editors who controlled the Biblical texts and corrupted them to get the people to obey them, were probably priests, scribes—or held positions religiously related.

A character named **Zechariah** is added for its meanings of 'reminds/mentions-he/him' who castigates Joash and the people and this character is also added to give Joash a crime to commit as he orders the stoning and death of this character, whereas in 2 Kings Joash was a good and pious king, his only mild transgression was giving tribute to King Hazael of Syria from the 'hallowed things' and treasures from God's house to avoid the whole city being attacked. In the earlier story Joash is killed purely by conspiring servants with an indication they killed him because he gave of God's things.

The names of Joash's assassins in 2Kings were **Jozachar** 'he is reminded/mentioned' 'he reminds/mentions' and 'he groans a lot' (son of **Shimeath**), but half the compound word which makes up his name (zachar) and was reflected in the story to remind people of Joash's wrong in giving away of the vessels and treasures dedicated to God, has been given to '**Zechariah**' in 2Chr.24. Instead of **Jozachar Shimeath** he becomes '**Zabad Shimeath**' so he shares the meaning of 'drinking vessels' and 'kicked/kicked a lot' with the character/accomplice in the story **Jehozabad** 'he who/which one-of bowls/drinking vessels' 'he who-kicked a lot'.

The editors alter the new Jehozabad's surname to **Shimrith**; šimrîṯ; سِمريت 'an entertaining night(includes staying up most of the night)/she stayed up all or until late night' 'she told a night time story'; شِمريت 'she rolled up her sleeves' but keep it similar to the earlier name in 2Kgs.12 '**Shomer** 'told a night story/staying awake story'/'rolled up sleeves', and it is still to tell the audience that the story being told is not a real, but fictional story. The surname is attributed to 'mothers' but still **Ammonitess/ Moabitess** is due to the meaning and original stories where Lot's daughters intoxicated their father with wine; in this story it is related to the drinking vessels and the editors not wanting the audience to forget the original story of Joash where he gave away God's things (including vessels).

So the violent death (of Joash) which includes kicking and groaning a lot while being killed is also transferred to '**Zechariah**' who is stoned to death; the compassion, piety and sufferance is taken away from Joash and transplanted to the newly-made character of Zechariah. At the same time the 'goodness' of Joash's character is reversed and he is depicted as ruthless and impious. This is because the editors of these stories wanted to show the kings as less pious than the priests and everyone related to worship service; because of the method of the Biblical stories which uses wordplay this was not difficult for the editors to achieve. The shift can be clearly seen in how authors/editors of this story in 2Chronicles give Jehoiada a larger role and have him buried 'among the kings' while Joash 'they buried him not in the sepulchres of the kings.'. More on the reasons behind this shift of praising kings to diminishing them while praising priests, later in this book.

Jabneh; yaḇneh; يَبنِه 'he builds it' and refers to after breaking down the Philistines walls, Uzziah 'built cities about Ashdod and among the Philistines'. Cp: yabneh. (2Chr.26:6)

Gurbaal; gûr-bāʿal; جُر بآعَل 'pull-from above' 'pull-from high' 'pull-I will raise' and refers to both Uzziah breaking down all those walls, but also the building of towers which is repeated to explain 'Uzziah built towers in Jerusalem at the corner gate, and at the valley gate, and at the turning of the wall…and he built towers in the desert.'. It is equivalent to the word Jerubbaal (Judg.6:25-40). Cp: gur-baa'al. (2Chr.26:6-10)

Mehunim; mĕʿûnî, mĕʿūnîm; مَعْني ، ميعْني ، مَعون/ميعون هم/ام 'means' 'what did he/it mean' 'did not mean' 'helps/supports' 'of helping/supporting' 'did not help' 'helped-them/the' 'did not help-them/the' and the meaning of 'supported' is directly stated in the text 'And God helped him against'. Cp: me'unee, mei'unee, me'oon-hum/um, mei'oon-hum/um. (2Chr.26:7-8)

Just as the names given to 'captains of hundreds' are themes in the 2Chr. Joash narrative, the same is done in the Uzziah narrative. **Jeiel** (1Chr.5:7) 'created' 'made' 'deceit/trickery' to denote the 'engines invented by cunning men'; **Maaseiah** (1Chr.15:18) 'disobedience' 'disobeyed him' for the disobedience Uzziah will show by burning incense for God instead of the priests (which indicates later editors of these stories are priests); **Hananiah** (1Chr.3:19) 'satisfaction to/satisfied-him/he' 'give plenty-he/him' for all the might, power, possessions and success narrated about him, then 'we will direct words/speech at him' when the priests confront and reprimand him for burning incense in the temple.

Also, just as 'Jozachar' which showed a wrong against King Joash was split into a priestly/son of priest character name in 2Chronicles, '**Azariah**' which was King Uzziah's character when first introduced at 2Kings meant 'made ugly' for having leprosy (but in the same story was changed to Uzziah (2Kgs.15:13) to denote he was harmed) in 2 Chronicles it is now given to the character of a priest, this serves two things: first it allows Uzziah, 'was harmed-he' 'he harmed', to be projected more 'evil' in the narration than merely following the original story where he is 'smote' with leprosy by God for not bringing down the 'high places' or preventing worship of other gods, it is now a priest's name who confronts Uzziah in the temple at which point he immediately becomes a leper (Azariah/became ugly). It allows the shift by editors of these stories to make the priestly characters more powerful and more pious than king characters.

Amoz (2Kgs.19-20) is used towards the end of this story for one of its meanings 'I touch/possess/ provoke fights or arguments' as Uzziah has been stricken with an affliction from God for his 'disobedience/transgression'. (2Chr.26)

Ophel; 'ōpel; عوضِل 'muscled/grew muscle' 'infested with mice' 'sore muscles' 'recompense-the'; نوضِل 'rested in shade/created shade/stood or sat in shade' 'I mislead/was misled'; نوفِل 'picked lice' 'picked through/went through thoroughly'. 'muscled/grew muscle' and 'created/rested in shade' is supported by the text as Jotham is described as building many structures whether on high places such as mountains or towers, and winning battles, but further supported by 'So Jotham became mighty…'. Cp: 'oodhel, oodhel, oophel. (2Chr.27:3)

Meshillemoth; mĕšillēmōṯ; ميسِلّيمُت 'is of peaceful nature' 'did not survive' 'possessed/provoked the one who died' 'well ask the one who died' 'do not ask the one died'; ميشِلّيمُت 'did not take' 'did not take the one who died' 'walked/left the one who died' 'not the one who died'. It is the same as Meshillemith (1Chr.9:12). Cp: meisilleymot, meishilleymot. (2Chr.28:12)

Jehizkiah; yĕḥizqîyāhû; يِيهِضقي ياَهْ ، جيهِضقي ياَهْ 'he makes suffer/distress-he/him' 'he forces to taste/swallow/eat-he/him' 'came made suffer/distress-he/him' 'came forced to taste/swallow/eat-he/him' from word (dhq/ضق) 'distress/suffer/taste/forced to swallow' and is used when describing a person who eats something he/she does not like or not want to eat, and is also used figuratively to mean 'suffered/sufferance' 'tasted bitter' 'tasted all the agony' are some ways how sufferance or pain in described as being 'tasted/swallowed/forcibly fed'; يِيهِزقي ياَهْ ، جيهِزقي ياَهْ 'he is squirting/flitting-he/him' 'came squirting/flitting-he/him' from word (zq/زق) 'squirted/flitted'; يِيهِسقي ياَهْ ، جيهِسقي ياَهْ 'you, I will water-it/him' 'you, who waters-it/him' 'came, I will water-it/him'; يِيهِزكي ياَهْ ، جيهِزكي ياَهْ 'he flatters/praises-he/him' 'he predicts going to hell or heaven-he/him' 'he predicts person is good or bad-he/him' 'came flattered/praised-he/him' 'came predicted going to hell or heaven-he/him' 'came predicted person is good or bad-he/him'; يِيحِزكي ياَهْ ، جيحِزكي ياَهْ 'he crams/corners/puts in a tight situation-the' 'came crammed/cornered/put in a tight situation-it/he/him'. يِيهِزجي ياَهْ ، جيهِزجي ياَهْ 'he tells off-he/him' 'came- told off-he/him' 'he tugs/snatches violently at-he/him' 'came-tugged/snatched violently at-he/him' the latter 'tugged/snatched' can also mean when something is snagged by anything else. Cp: yeihidhqee-yaahu, geihidhqee-yaahu, yeihizqee-yaahu, geihizqee-yaahu, yeihisqee-yaahu, geihisqee-yaahu, yeihizkee-yaahu, geihizkee-yaahu, yeiḥizkee-yaahu, geiḥizkee-yaahu, yeihizgee-yaahu, geihizgee-yaahu. (2Chr.28:12)

Hadlai; ḥadlāy; هَدلآي 'I will push/drive' 'I will dangle/lower' 'I will pedal' 'I will go from place to place pedalling/pushing (myself or things)' 'I will throw bailing pouch down'. Cp: hadlaay. (2Chr.28:12)

The grouped 'heads of children of Ephraim' are used as themes: **Azariah** 'made ugly-he/him' depicting the ugliness of massacres and war; **Johanan** 'they are humiliating/they are being humiliated' 'they are being betrayed' to describe the humiliation suffered by the prisoners from Judah taken captive by Israel.

Berechiah 'I will let him/it loose' 'I will let it go' as the discussion is about freeing the captives; **Meshillemoth** 'did not take' 'possessed/provoked the one who died' 'walked/left the one who died' as they are being asked not to take/keep the captives in Samaria, they are discussing releasing them and the captives are those who survived the great slaughters narrated in the stories.

Jehizkiah 'he makes suffer/distress-he/him' 'he forces to taste/swallow/eat-he/him' 'came, I will water-it/him' 'came crammed/cornered/put in a tight situation-it/he/him' 'he tells off-he/him': the captives are already suffering; they have been and still are cornered/crammed and driven to Samaria and are still under forced suffering, and Israel is fearing suffering punishment from God; they will eventually be fed and given to drink; **Shallum** 'took' 'of taking' 'I will gather' 'left unharmed/intact/survived' 'delivered/received' and the people of Judah who survive and are captivated are first taken to Samaria in captivity before they are released, some are physically carried to their freedom.

Amasa 'tested/provoked/entangled' because the returning army will be confronted with words to the effect 'why are you provoking God to harm us? You are causing more sins, transgressions, provocation to bring trouble to us'; 'drank and fed supper' 'uncle/drank-disobeyed' the people of Israel are reminded they have massacred and captivated 'your brethren' which 'uncle' depicts, but the captives will also be given food and drink before they are released. **Hadlai** 'I will push/drive' 'I will pedal' 'I will go from place to place pedalling/pushing (myself or things)' because the captives have been made to go from place to place but so does Israel going to war in Judah then driving the captives to Samaria before returning them to Jericho and then themselves returning to Samaria. **Samaria** is always used to remind the audience these are fictional stories.

Gimzo; gimzô; جِمزُ 'snapped shut on something' 'caught between something which has closed quickly/suddenly'; قِمشُ 'scored' won something or taken/snatched it quickly, it is the verb of a move resulting in winning a token(s)/stone(s) in a game; جِمشُ 'a sheet' the sheets are made of light fabrics used as bedding the same way sheets are used around the world, 'covered with a light sheet' and is supported by the following verse 'for he made Judah naked'; قِمصُ 'put on a dress/robe/shirt' and for the same reason of nakedness being mentioned; غِمزُ 'massaged' 'winked'; غِمسُ 'dipped into' 'dipped something into' and this meaning too is supported by the text as Ahaz taken from 'God's' things and giving to king of Syria, but also to other gods. Cp: gimzo, qimsho, gimsho, qimsso, ghimzo, ghimso. (2Chr.28:18)

If you go back to the meanings, translated in this book, of the compound words given as names to the characters mentioned in 2Chr.29:12-14, these character names have at least one meaning involved in purification/cleansing of 'uncleanness/filth' from a physical area, which is the focal event in this part of the story such as: **Levites**; wrap, gather, sweep up; **Mahath**: scalded, rubbed away; **Amasai**: drank, partially blind, caused provocation, had supper; **Joel**: stayed in place, undressed, deceived/trickster; **Azariah**: made ugly; **Kohathites**: striking motion (how dust is removed from objects, walls, furnishing when there were no vacuum cleaners), brushed/scratched; **Merari**: mirror, shine; **Kish**: fibres/litter, scrape away litter; **Abdi**: take out, remove; **Jehalelel**: cleansed, purified; **Gershonites**: rang or wore bells, plaited; **Joah**: echoed (if many things are removed from a room, it does echo), aired; **Zimmah**: conscience, responsibility, guilt; **Eden**: sticks, guilted, bowing and bending, return, listen and understand.

Note how Azariah is used: **Joel** 'stayed in place' **Azariah** 'made ugly' so Joel's meaning is making the 'ugly' bad thing stay in its place; when used again **Azariah** 'made ugly' is purified by **Jehalelel** 'circumcises/purifies/cleanses' as purifying is also making something 'nice'. The compound words are given as son/father names.

Joah 'aired/echoed' is son of **Zimmah** 'conscience/guilt/ostracised'; then it is **Eden** 'sticks, guilted, bowing and bending, return' son of **Joah** 'aired/echoed'.

This is not a comprehensive list, but the meanings of other names not covered here can be found under their name translations in this book and their meanings cover the music and singing which will be in the other half of the chapter. And of course, the 'unclean' things are thrown into 'the brook of' **Kidron** 'they are disgusting/unclean/revolting/filthy'. (2Chr.29:16)

'And they gathered their brethren, and sanctified themselves, and came, according to the commandment of the king...to cleanse the house of the Lord. And the priests went into the inner part of the house of the Lord, to cleanse *it*, and brought out all the uncleanness that they found in the temple...to carry *it* out abroad into the brook Kidron.'

Azariah for its meanings of 'beware/remember/listen and remember-filled with much/crawled with ants/left behind' 'on/upon-filled with much/crawled with ants/left behind' as the dedicated supplies, tithes, etc. described are in great quantities and amounts; **Zadok** for its meanings of 'gave you extra' 'extra remains' as the story narrates how much is left behind even after the priests eat from it. This is a suitable name for a character who states what his name means 'And Azariah the chief priest of the house of Zadok answered him, and said, Since the people began to bring the offerings into the house of the Lord, we have had enough to eat, and have left plenty...and that which is left is this great store.'. (2Chr.31:1-10)

Cononiah; kônanyāhû; كُنَن يآهْ 'gathered into peaked heaps-he/him' 'sheltered from weather(rain/sun/wind)-he/him' and it is the compound word given to the character made responsible with taking in all these supplies. It is from the word (kwwn/كوِّن) 'make into peaked heaps' and (knnah) كنّه 'a peak/a shelter at the top of a house' 'a peaked structure (usually of animal fodder)' and the word (knn/كنن) 'shelter/take inside/store inside/shelter from the rain'. To understand better the word 'peaked heaps/make into peaked heaps': people who live in rural areas, and live with the lifestyle of ancient times, when food supplies such as grain or panicles are processed or stored the grain/panicles are heaped into peaks to stop them falling about all over the place, it allows easier handling of these grains when transferring from place to place or measuring out into different storage vessels. It is mentioned he is a **Levite** for its meaning 'gather/sweep up' as the action with bare hands or using a bowl/measuring bowl to gather/measure grain produce is (lph(lv)/lphee(lvee)/لفي/لف). Both meanings have been used to make the name of the character who needs to store, shelter and supervise the supplies. 'Then Hezekiah commanded to prepare chambers in the house of the Lord; and they prepared them, And brought in the offerings and the tithes and the dedicated things faithfully: over which Cononiah the Levite was ruler, and Shimei his brother was the next.'. Cp: konanyaahu. (2Chr.31:4-12)

Ismachiah; yismak̲yāhû; يِسمَح يآهْ 'he allows-he/him' 'he forgives-he/him' and he is one of the overseers of the supplies being brought in and out. Cp: yismaḥ-yaahu. (2Chr.31:13)

Kore 'decided/decides' son of **Imnah** 'gives/grants' has been given as name for character who 'was over the freewill offerings of God, to distribute the oblations of the Lord, and the most holy things'. (2Chr.31:14)

Miniamin; minyāmîn; مِن يآمين 'from the right' and is a suitable name for someone who distributes as the custom of the culture of the Biblical authors is to use the right hand when giving/handing something and also to start from the right and move to the left when distributing or greeting people; 'from who?' 'from who says "I gave and gave"/from who counts/lists what he/she gave' and the latter is considered against etiquette for the 'giver' to count and list what was given to another 'who is counting/listing what was given?'. Cp: min-yaameen. (2Chr.31:15)

Joahaz; yô'āḥāz; يُئَآخَاذ 'he takes'; جُئَآخَاذ 'came and took' as his character takes money to the workers to get the repairs done and the narration purposely repeats the 'giving' part in the story. Cp: yo-aakhaav, go-aakhaav. (2Chr.34:8)

Tikvath; toqhaṯ; توقحَث 'strikes' 'sharp striking sound/pinging'; توقحَط 'brushes' 'ground on teeth' 'becomes stiff/hard from heat' it can be literal meaning of 'ground on teeth/stiffened from heat' or it could be in the form of a curse 'will be ground(like on teeth)/will be cooked stiff (because of curse)'. This name change for Huldah's husband's father is to reflect the severity of the curse Huldah prophecies and is directly reflected in the narration. Cp: tooqḥaf, tooqḥaṭ (2Chr.34:22)

Hasrah; ḥasrâ; حَصره 'great despair and sorrow' 'regret, despair and sorrow' 'feel sorry for' and is reflected in the story first by Josiah rending his clothes, fearing the consequences of disobedience, then by Huldah's prophesy of great punishment and mentioning Josiah's sorrow and regret for his people's conduct, and it is reflected in the narration that no matter what—they will be punished even if they do repent; خَصره 'his waist' denoting Shallum's work as keeper of the wardrobe but also خَسره 'a loss' 'sadness over loss' 'what a waste/loss' denoting the prophesied punishment. It still holds a similar meaning to its earlier version Harhas (2Kgs.22:14-20). Cp: ḥassrah, khassrah, khasrah. (2Chr.34:22)

Carchemish; karkĕmîš; قَر قيميص 'be still/stop/don't do it-wore a shirt/dress/hid behind clothes' 'hid behind clothes/disguised' is when a person wears something not his/her usual clothes (e.g. man or woman wearing opposite sex clothes as a disguise) or allows turban/head veil to fall over face to hide it or directly cover on his/her face; and it is denoted exactly as that in the story that Neco warns Josiah that this battle has nothing to do with him so he should not interfere, but Josiah ignores the warning and wears a disguise and goes to battle. Cp: qar-qeimeess. (2Chr.35:20-22)

2 Chronicles, like other stories before it, attempts to explain to the people (the audience of these stories) why there are so many different religions among the one same people, and it attempts to explain why there is no 'house of the king' no 'house of the Lord/temple' no 'Israel' and none of the things mentioned in these stories as the original audiences are well aware of the fictionality of these stories.

Persia; pārāš, pāraš; فآرآش ، فآرَش 'made/prepared resting or sleeping place' 'lay down' 'spread over/lay out' 'mat/bed/resting or sleeping place' 'To fulfil the word of the Lord…until the land had enjoyed her sabbaths [sabbath means sleep/rest]: for as long as she lay desolate she kept sabbath…'. Cp: phaaraash, phaarash.

Also: بآرآز ، بآرَز 'brought forward/pressed on and pushed out' and; فآرآص ، فآرَص 'split open/pushed out/emerged by pushing up or out/ divided by breaking or splitting' denoted in the story as God is making these things happen: the people taken away captives is God's punishment, Jeremiah is speaking God's words not his own (but it's coming out of him), Cyrus is made by God to order and proclaim the building of a house for God; it is also denoted in the story that they will not become free until 'Persia' reigns 'where they were servants to him and his sons until the reign of the kingdom of Persia'. Cp: baaraaz, baaraz, phaaraass, phaarass.

Also: فآرآس ، فآرَس 'divided something into separate units' 'explained/explained in detail/made clear' and is denoted in Jeremiah explaining the word of God, and also in having Cyrus king of Persia state orally and in writing to make it clear what God has 'stirred up' in Cyrus and made him proclaim. Cp: phaaraas, phaaras. (2Chr.36:20-21)

Cyrus; kôreš; قُرِش 'to score/gain' both in real life to gain something physical or in games winning tokens/stones. And it is reflected in the text 'Thus saith Cyrus king of Persia, All the kingdoms of the earth hath the Lord God of heaven given to me…' he is gaining all the kingdoms by a promise/word from God. Cp: qoresh. (2Chr.36:21-23)

This story has been created for the same reasons editing can be seen in other stories of the Bible: to explain why there is no 'house of the Lord'. The reasons for editing are not the same reasons why these stories were created in the first place, I will address the creation of the Biblical stories later in this book.

Ezra

Mithredath; miṯrĕḏāṯ; مِثري ضاَف ، مثري ضعف 'increase/enrich-added' 'increase/enrich-weak' and both meanings are reflected in the story: Cyrus orders, and the people comply, to give the returnees all sorts of riches of precious metals and livestock and particularly mentions 'And all they that were about them strengthened their hands with vessels of silver…'. Cp: mifrei-dhaaph, mifree-dh'ph. (Ezra.1:4-11)

Sheshbazzar; šešbaṣṣar; شِش بَزَّر 'what he wanted-many children/heavy load' 'wonderful/many things/ important things/matters-many children/heavy load/breaking body from heavy load'; this compound word is used to describe all the precious things given to the people sent to build God a house. The description is of 'important' representing the (Shesh) and heavy treasures of vessels of silver and gold, which would be a heavy load and the people are many representing (bazzar) 'litter/many children/broke body from heavy load'. Cp: sheshbazzar. (Ezra.1:6-11)

Nehemiah; nĕḥemyâ; نيهِم يه 'sighing loudly-he him' it means a person forcing a sigh to be noticed by others i.e. not a natural sigh, but a pretentious sigh/huff/puff to get attention, 'winded/struck until wind forced out-he/him' 'punctured and wind escaping-he/him'. It is equivalent to Menahem (2Kgs.15:14-22), Tanhumeth (2Kgs.25:23), Naham (1Chr.4:19). Cp: neihem-yah. (Ezra.2:2)

Reelaiah; rĕʽēlāyâ; ري عيلاَيه 'dreamt about me' 'saw on me/above me'; ريعي لآيه 'shepherded/looked after for me'; ري غيلاَيه 'saw my intense hatred' 'saw-intense hatred-him/he' 'saw-my expensiveness/high price', it can also have other (ghl/غل) meanings. Cp: rei 'eylaayah, rei'ey laayah, rei gheylaayah. (Ezra.2:2)

Mordecai; mordoḵay, mordĕḵay; مورضوخَي ، مورضيخَي 'slather/cover with a substance such as soil/ flour/oil or any substance (clean or not clean)/soil all over'; مورتوكَي ، مورتيكَي 'soil it all over/cover it completely/make dirty all over'; موردوحي ، مورذيحَي 'cover it sparingly all over' 'smear' and refers when there is not enough of the substance to cover generously or when something has been soiled by smearing with whatever substance has been used. All the words are in the form of spoken to a female or giving the spoken about the attribute of the word; موردوكي ، مورديكي 'you will return/be returned to' 'of returning' 'you will be punished for what you do/punishment/retribution will return on you' 'you will end up' 'you will be thrown down/perish/afflicted' 'of being afflicted'. Cp: moordhookhay, moordheikhay, moortookay, moorteikay, moorvookhay, moorveikhay, moordookay, moordeikay. (Ezra.2:2)

Bilshan; bilšān; بِلشاَن 'with the filtering/filter' 'with the flowed out of/into' 'with the ready for copulation/ ready to conceive(goats and similar animals)/on heat' 'with the sexually excited/ready to copulate/ copulated' 'for cheap' 'for free'; بِلساَن 'with tongue' 'told by' 'with tongue out/will poke tongue out' 'with the straight/straightened'. Cp: bilshaan, bilsaan. (Ezra.2:2)

Mispar; mispār; مِسباَر 'made it right/fixed it'; مِصباَر 'aloe vera' 'of patience'; مِصفاَر 'whistle/whistling' 'of whistling' 'yellow/yellowed'. Cp: misbaar, missbaar, missphaar. (Ezra.2:2)

Bigvai; bigway; بِغوَي 'I will deceive/seduce/lead to bad behaviour' 'of deceiving/leading into bad behaviour' 'I will mislead to downfall'; ضِغوَي 'tired/of being tired'; بِقوَي 'left some' 'stayed behind/remained' 'of leaving behind' 'of staying'. Cp: bighway, dhighway, biqway. (Ezra.2:2)

Rehum; rĕḥûm, rĕḥum; ريحُم 'had mercy on' 'felt mercy for'; ريحوم 'of affection/pity/mercy' 'soft-hearted'; ري هُم 'saw-them' 'dreamt of them' 'watered-them'; ري هُم ، ري هوم 'saw-worry' 'saw-worries' 'dreamt-worried' 'watering-worried/worries'; ريهُم 'saw them' 'their watering'; ريكُم ، ريكوم 'saw you(plural)' 'showed you' 'piled/stacked/heaped' (usually stones); ري كُم 'saw how many/much'; ري كوم 'saw heaps'. Cp: reiḥum, reiḥoom, rei hum, rei hoom, reihum, reikum, reikoom, rei kum, rei koom. (Ezra.2:2)

Parosh; parʽōš; بَرعوش 'I will shake'; بَر عوش 'pass by/go by-live' 'live elsewhere' 'good-live' as in live piously/a good life; فَرعوش 'so shake(it)'; فَر عوش 'fled-lived' 'fled to live'. Cp: bar'oosh, bar 'oosh, phar'oosh, phar 'oosh. (Ezra.2:3)

Pahath-moab; paḥaṯ-môʽaḇ; without context there are numerous possibilities what 'Pahath' could be (if included in a later story of the Bible instead of just this list there could be a narrower meaning defined), here are some of them: بَحَث 'scratched the ground and searched'; بَحَت 'medicinal natural crystal' it can also mean the use of this crystal called 'bḥt'; بَحَط 'lost voice' 'causes sore throat' 'I will unload/place down/set' 'I will leave(some)/leave it'; بَخَت 'probably not' 'with his sister/with sister of' 'an insult by saying 'bookh' to someone'; بَهَت 'ill or unable to speak from traumatic experience' 'shocked into fear' 'pale/became pale'; فَحَط 'a persistent light cough' 'a tickle in the throat' 'irritation in the chest/lungs'; فَخَط 'lit' 'lit by scratching surface (similar to how match or flint used to create spark/flame' 'scrammed/scratched' 'a scram/scratch mark'. Moab is still the same meaning even with a slight variation in the spelling/transliteration: مُعَب 'is shame/shamed'; with the possible meanings of pahath being 'sore throat/gobsmacked/tickle in the chest/ persistent cough/lost voice' Moab could also be: مُغب 'is thirsty'. Cp: baḥaf mo'ab/moghab, baḥat mo'ab/ moghab, baḥaṭ mo'ab/moghab, bakhat mo'ab/moghab, bahat mo'ab/moghab, phaḥaṭ mo'ab/moghab, phakhaṭ mo'ab/moghab. (Ezra.2:6)

Zattu; zattû'; زَتّي 'sliced open/split open/cut quickly' 'a narrow cut/wound' 'went quickly/flit/flicked something quickly into tight space/thrown quickly aside'; زعطى 'sent them away/threw them out/told them to leave' it means to send someone away/throw them out in an unfriendly way to make them feel unwelcome in a very clear manner and is usually used when sending away from home unwanted guests and is the word describing when a husband sends his wife away (even if temporarily) from the marital home. It is equivalent to Olivet's proper meaning and Ahuzzath (Gen.26:26-31) Cp: zattu, z'ṭṭu. (Ezra.2:8)

Zaccai; zakkay; سَكّي 'calm it down/let it settle' 'drop it(the matter)/give it a rest/stop thinking or talking about it' 'can you do'; شَكّي 'suspect' 'my suspicions' 'thread things(such as beads, flowers)' 'sew' 'complain/ of complaining' 'continuous clucking(hens make)'; ضَكّي 'there she/it is'; زَقّي 'squirt' 'go quickly/dash there'; صَحّي 'rain stopped/sun came out'; صَقّي 'reach out/reach/stretch and reach/connect'; صَغي 'swivel/ tilt' 'tilt head' 'tilt head and listen or see better'; صَخّي 'make compliant/do as told' 'of obedience/being compliant'. Cp: sakkay, shakkay, dhakkay, zaqqay, ssaḥḥay, ssaqqay, ssaghay, ssakhay. (Ezra.2:9)

Bebai; bēḇay; بيضَي 'lay eggs' 'whiten/brighten' 'it shines/glows' 'ablute/wash'; بيذَي 'with her/this one'. Cp: beydhay, beyvay. (Ezra.2:11)

Azgad; 'azgāḏ; عَزجاَد 'tattered in heavy repetitive motion'; نَزجاَد 'torn off in bird-like pecking motions but heavier'; نَزقاَط 'pecking/is pecking' 'picked up quickly with beak (or hand but quick and sharp motion like a bird peck). Cp: 'azgaad, azgaad, azqaaṭ. (Ezra.2:12)

Adin; 'āḏîn; عاَدين 'they returned/are returning' 'they infected/will infect' 'they are counting/they counted/are counted' 'they are enemies' 'gathering or cooking lentils'; ئاَدين 'I guilt/find guilty/blame' 'was found guilty/blamed' 'I bowed/bent/lowered' 'made to bow/bend/be lower' 'made lower(in status)'. Cp: 'aadeen, aadeen.

Ater; 'āṭēr; ئاَطير 'I am flying' 'I send flying/banish' (the flying is figuratively: 'sent them packing' it means not only to throw out/send away but in such a fashion the subject is 'flying or been sent flying' and not to come back); عاَطير 'twisted/pressed out' 'is twisting/pressing out/squeezing out' 'twirling/twirled' 'perfumed'. It is equivalent to Atarah (1Chr.2:26). Cp: aaṭeyr, 'aaṭeyr. (Ezra.2:16)

Bezai; bēṣay; بيزَي 'with just like' (e.g. just like him) 'take/carry' 'breastfeed/lactating breast(s)'. Cp: beyzay. (Ezra.2:17)

Jorah; yôrâ; يُره 'sees him' 'he/they see him' 'dreamt of him' 'his dream' 'shows him' 'waters him/it; هُره 'he saw it/him' 'he saw' 'he dreamt' 'drove/driven away (with words)' 'speak harshly to him' 'drive him/it away' 'axe handles/wooden handles of tools/batons' 'his cat' 'cat'; جُره 'it happened' 'ran' 'he/they/it ran' 'pull it/ him' 'water vessel'; عُره 'they are naked' 'they stripped him naked' 'forcefully pushing through with head' the latter literally or figuratively carrying on when in the wrong, 'dare him/it' 'abandoned in wilderness/ he/them/it'; حُره 'free(fem.)' 'do as I please' 'plough it' 'made fire' 'moved/moved to action'; خُره 'made collapse' 'drove away with physical violence/actions' 'made defecate' 'made feel great fear(shit them/himself); يُرح 'is windy' 'goes/leaves' 'rests'; جُرح 'wounds' 'wounded' 'insulted/caused upset'. Cp: yorah, horah, gorah, 'orah, ḥorah, khorah, yorah, goraḥ. (Ezra.2:18)

Hashum; ḥāšum; حاَشوم 'modest/chaste' 'stuffed-the' 'got them involved-the'; هاَشوم 'shooed away-the' 'crushed bread(in churned milk/broth)' 'crumbling/squashing something' 'belittled'; هاَزوم 'of beating/ beaten(game/fight/battle)'; حاَزوم 'bundled' (such as firewood), 'tied bundle' 'cornered/crammed/blocked/ prevented from moving-the'; حاَسوم 'feeling pity for/heartbroken' 'felt-the'; هاَسوم 'I will faint'; خاَشوم 'bit/tattered/took chunk(s) out' 'bit/tattered/took chunk(s) out of-the' 'ruined by biting/crumbling/ tattering'. Cp: ḥaashum, ḥaash-um, haash-um, haashum, haazum, ḥaazum, ḥaaz-um, ḥaasum, ḥaas-um, haasum, khaashum, khash-um. (Ezra.2:19)

Gibbar; gibbār; جِبّاَر 'tyrant/bully' 'gangs up on' 'forces' 'mends' 'heals' 'speaks and comforts'. Cp: gibbaar. (Ezra.2:20)

Netophah; nĕṭōpâ; نيتوفه ، نَتوفه 'plucks/plucked pubic hair' 'plucks/plucked' 'leaps/leapt' 'of leaping' 'we leap' 'we spit on' 'of spitting on' latter two meanings as a gesture of disrespect or hatred towards what is being spat at/towards; نيطوفه ، نَطوفه 'of dripping' 'dripped'; نيظوفه ، نَظوفه 'is clean' 'of cleaning' 'cleaned or cleared/removed completely'. Cp: netoophah, neitoophah, neṭoophah, neiṭoophah, nedhoophah, neidhoophah. (Ezra.2:22)

Kirjath-arim; qiryat̲ 'ārim; قِريَت عارِم and although it is similar to Kirjath-jearim (Josh.9:17-27), it is a different word with different meanings used to suit the story of people coming out of captivity and returning: 'village-abandoned/lost in wilderness/stranded'; خِرجَت عارِم 'the coming out-abandoned/lost in wilderness/stranded' 'came out into wilderness' 'came out of abandonment. Cp: qiryat 'aarim, khirgat 'aarim. (Ezra.2:25)

Michmas; the same as Michmash (1Sam.13). The difference of its spelling in the Bible, (mik̲māś at 1Sam.13, mik̲mās at Ezra.2:27) is erroneously described by Biblical scholars as evolution or developments in the 'Hebrew language' as being the reason why there is a difference in spelling. Like most translations of the Biblical names this mistake is made because these scholars have not understood the method of the Biblical authors, nor have they understood the meanings of the words, and this all stems from attempting to translate the Bible from a language that never existed 'Hebrew'. In my translation of the first 'Michmash', you will find it covers all the meanings meant by both spellings of Michmash/Michmas (they are exactly the same) because I am translating it as it is meant in Arabic and I have understood the method of the Biblical authors and how they used language to make the stories, and because I speak Arabic, understand the language of the Bible for what it is: Arabic. (Ezra.2:27)

Magbish; magbîš; مَغبيش 'early murky, dark morning' 'blurry/clouded/murky/not clear' and the term is also used to describe very early in the morning before the sun comes up properly, but not completely dark. Cp: maghbeesh. (Ezra.2:30)

Hadid; ḥādīd; حآديد 'metal' 'sharpened' 'bordered/blocked by a rim/edge'; هآديد 'threats/threatened' 'loud noise from above (similar to thunder but manmade)'; خآديد 'with hand on cheek' (looks sad/worried/ puzzled). Cp: ḥaadeed, haadeed, khaadeed. (Ezra.2:33)

Senaah; sĕnā'â; سينآئه 'in his direction' 'in its direction' 'straight' 'made it straight'; صينآعه 'they created/ made' 'they are upset, looking away, not talking' 'they are upset and frowning'. Cp: seinaa-ah, sseinaa'ah. (Ezra.2:35)

Kadmiel; qad̲mî'ēl; قَدمي ئِل 'put first/let go first-the' 'appeared first-the' 'present/put forward-the' 'offer-the' 'serve(food/drink)-the'; كَضمي ئِل 'suffocate-the' 'cover/muffle-the'. Cp: qadmee-ill, kadhmee-ill. (Ezra.2:40)

Hatita; ḥăṭîṭā'; حيطيطآء 'of unloading' 'placing down loads/putting down objects' 'of leaving behind'; خيطيطآء 'made lines/marks' 'wrote' 'planned' 'they planned'; حيتيتآء 'made borders on bottom of walls' 'made line/border with henna on hands/feet' 'making borders on something'; هيتيتآء 'snapped at angrily(and made recipient cry)'. Cp: ḥaiṭeeṭaa, khaiṭeeṭaa, ḥaiteetaa, haiteetaa. (Ezra.2:42)

Shobai; šōb̲āy; شوبآي 'it/he swelled'. Cp: shoobaay. (Ezra.2:42)

Ziha; ṣîḥā', ṣiḥā'; زيحآء ، زِحآء 'remove' 'shift' 'hardened/stiffened' 'is hardened/stiffened'; زيهآء ، زِهآء 'merriment' 'in good mood'; صيحآء ، صِحآء 'rain stopped/cleared' 'sun come through after rain' 'dried (after rain)' 'shout'; ضيحآء ، ضِحآء 'dried in sun' 'mid-morning' 'large rocks/rock outcrops'; سيحآء ، سِحآء 'moving by dragging on bottom(refers to babies who do not crawl but do this instead)' 'wander, walk, seek'; صيخآء ، صِخآء 'compliant' 'does as bid'; سيخآء ، سِخآء 'are mild' 'are generous' 'his/her heart/ conscience would let him/her' 'brought himself/herself to(be able to)' 'spoiled/melted from heat/sun'. Cp: zeeḥaa, ziḥaa, zeehaa, zihaa, sseeḥaa, ssiḥaa, dheeḥaa, dhiḥaa, seeḥaa, siḥaa, sseekhaa, ssikhaa, seekhaa, sikhaa. (Ezra.2:43)

Hasupha; ḥăśûpā'; خيصُفآء ، خَصُفآء 'fold and broke piece off(bread, sweet, anything which is like a cake/ disc/or single unit)' 'broke chunk off' 'lunar eclipse'; حيصُبآء ، حَصُبآء 'measles' 'caught measles'; حَصُفآء ، حيصُفآء 'blotches/rash(not measles)' 'developed rash/blotches on skin' 'made with rush/twine/straw'. Cp: khassuphaa, khaissuphaa, ḥassubaa, ḥaissubaa, ḥassuphaa, ḥaissuphaa. (Ezra.2:43)

Tabbaoth; ṭabbā'ôt; طَبّآعُت 'disciplined/made behave' and this word is in the feminine doing the action and is usually used when speaking about a child who is rude/misbehaves and is disciplined by his parent(s), 'an action between tapping and patting' 'stamped/made prints(with hands or when henna and other decorative substances accidentally leave print on cheek or clothes)'; تَبّآعُت 'followed' 'followed secretly'; تَبّآعُث

'returned from the dead' 'returned to life from death' 'scratched the ground(with claw/hoof)'. Cp: ṭab-baa'ot, tabbaa'ot, tabbaa'of. (Ezra.2:43)

Keros; qērōs, qêrōs; قيروش 'scored/won token or stone' 'made gains' 'picked at/peeled'; كيروش 'stomach of slaughtered animal eaten cooked(small pieces raw)' 'belly(equivalent to 'beer-belly')'; جيروش 'ground coarsely (just cracked)'; قيروص 'made into circular cakes/pieces' of bread or incense, sweetmeat. Cp: qeeroosh, qeyroosh, keeroosh, keyroosh, geeroosh, geyroosh, qeerooss, qeyrooss. (Ezra.2:44)

Siaha; sî'ăhā'; سيعَهاّء ، سيعيهاء 'wander(ed) after/searching for her' 'wander(ed) seeking it' 'wander(ed) aimlessly' 'wander/wandered around performing debauchery' 'made her become debauched/perform de-bauchery/promiscuous' 'made/make her fit'; شيعَهاّء ، شيعيهاء 'they changed and ruined her/it' 'they devi-ated her/it' 'her mutations' 'they pulled out strands/fibres/hair from her/it'. Cp: see'ahaa, see'aihaa, shee'ahaa, shee'aihaa. (Ezra.2:44)

Padon; pāḏôn; بآدُن 'coming out/went out/bringing out' 'of coming out/bringing out' 'fair-skinned'; فآدُن 'sacrificing for/instead of' (usually means human sacrifice and is said figuratively but may have been literal in the ancient past). Cp: baadon, phaadon. (Ezra.2:44)

Lebanah; lĕḇānâ; ليبآنه 'for his sons/children' 'for rebuilding'; ليفآنه 'wrapped us' 'twisted around us' 'of wrapping/twisting around' 'scooped/swept up'. It is equivalent to Lebonah (Judg.21:19). Cp: leibaanah, leiphaanah. (Ezra.2:45)

Hagabah; ḥăgāḇâ; حيجآبه 'they covered/obscured her/him/it' 'they hid it/her/him' 'they took into the shade it/her/him' 'his/her eyebrows' 'of beautiful eyebrows' 'drew eyebrows(with kohl(for babies)'; هيجآبه 'made him/her leave forever/drove her or him away' 'he will/look, he-brought it/him/her' 'he will bring people/ gang up on' 'he will teach to pronounce-by/with it/him' 'mountain side of land-him/her/it' 'his/her moun-tain side' 'he will answer him'; هيغآبه 'look, they are absent' 'he will become thirsty'. Cp: ḥaigaabah, ḥaigaa-bah, haigaa-bah, hai-gaabah, haigaabah, hai-ghaabah. (Ezra.2:45)

Hagab; ḥăgāḇ; حيجآب 'covered/obscured' 'shaded/covered to protect from sun' 'they hid' 'they took into the shade' 'developed beautiful eyebrows' 'drew eyebrows with kohl(on babies)'; هيج آب 'left forever-refused/returned'; هيجآب 'he will/look-he brought it' 'he will bring people/gang up on' 'he will reply'; هي جآب 'her-he brought' 'her-walked all over the place/walked in circles/repeatedly went and returned'; هيغآب 'look, he is absent' 'he will become thirsty'. Cp: ḥaigaab, haig-aab, haigaab, hai-gaab, hai-ghaab. (Ezra.2:46)

Shalmai; šalmay; شَلمَي 'took water' 'took-not'; سَلمَي 'greet' 'survived/intact' 'mild/peaceful character/ nature' 'asked water' 'leaked/flowed water' 'asked not'. Cp: shal-may, salmay, sal-may. (Ezra.2:46)

Giddel; giddēl; جِدّيل 'of throwing' 'threw' 'of fits(epileptic)/possessed by demons' 'wooden platform(to stand on)'; غِدّيل 'feed lunch-the' 'of feeding lunch' 'frustrate-the' 'glands-the' 'swell glands-the'. Cp: gid-deyl, ghiddeyl. (Ezra.2:47)

Gahar; gaḥar; جَحَر 'drought'; جَهَر 'said openly' 'faced-off' 'came-drove away(with words)'. Cp: gaḥar, gahar. (Ezra.2:47)

Nekoda; neqôḏā'; نَقُضاء 'they/he undid/revoked' 'he/they undid purity' 'unstitched'; نَقُدآء 'poked fire' 're-moved from wall/oven wall by picking or poking at'; نَكُدآء 'a nag' 'nagged' 'covered/we cover open-ing(with lid/fabric/stone)'. Cp: neqodhaa, neqodaa, nekodaa. (Ezra.2:48)

Gazzam; gazzām; جَزّآم 'he dared' 'of daring'; قَزّآم 'turned off food/revolted by' 'of being revolted' (it is equivalent to being a germaphobe and specifically not wanting to drink or eat from same plate/bowl/glass of specific individuals or individual event of being revolted by something/someone); جَذآم 'leper' 'with tips fallen/snipped/chopped off' 'came-ostracised/guilted/unwanted' 'geckos'. Cp: gazzaam, qazzaam, gavvaam. (Ezra.2:48)

Besai; bēsay; بيشَي 'wants/he wants' 'with something' 'there is something/a matter' 'joyful/kind faced' 'plentiful' 'well-bred' 'verdant'. Cp: beyshay. (Ezra.2:49)

Asnah; 'asnâ; نَسنه 'made it straight' 'made it face right direction'; نَزنه 'made him fornicate' 'fornicated' 'adorned him/it' 'bastard'; نَصنه 'hushed us'; عَزنه 'cherished us' 'raised our status'; عَشنه 'we lived' 'fed us supper'. Cp: asnah, aznah, assnah, 'aznah, 'ashnah. (Ezra.2:50)

Nephusim; nĕpîsîm; نيفيس هم/ام 'the same-them/the' 'the same as them' 'the same as the' 'plenty of space-them/the' 'made plenty of space-them/the' 'there is space-them/the' 'passing wind/puncturing-them/the'; نيفيسهم 'by themselves' 'themselves' 'they have plenty of space' 'it is spacious' 'there is space'; نيفيش هم/ام

'scattered-them/the' 'scattered over-them/the' usually used when something light or powdery is being sprayed/scattered over something/someone. Cp: neiphees-hum/um, neipheeshum, neipheesh-hum/um. (Ezra.2:50)

Bakbuk; baqbûq; بَقبُق 'sound of flowing water/glugging' 'talks a lot' 'clucks/clucking' 'clucks like a hen(meaning talks too much)' 'made sound of water flowing out of narrow place' 'water flowing out of a narrow place'; بَكبُك 'went-go' 'of leaving' 'left-leave' 'of lots of going/leaving' 'of going' 'visiting/visiting a lot'. Cp: baqbuq, bakbuk. (Ezra.2:51)

Hakupha; ḥãqûpā'; هيقُفاء 'he/they danced the 'hqpha'' (it is a specific dance done at fire and feast festivals, and at weddings), 'he will turn away/turn his back on' (he is ignoring or won't look at the person), 'he/they will stop'; هي قُفاء 'here is the basket' it is a small basket usually hung up from ceiling to store food or carry food to people working in land. 'turning away/turning back on' and this basket is named after 'back of head' (qphqph/qaphqooph/قفقوف/قفقف) because when a person turns/ignores he/she is showing the back of head, and the basket because its shape is like the back of a head. Cp: haiquphaa, hai-quphaa. (Ezra.2:51)

Harhur; ḥarḥûr; حَرحُر 'tilled/ploughed' 'of hot temper' 'of taking responsibility or caring/being moved to action' 'made a 'ḥarḥûr' or purring sound'; هَرهُر 'drove away/of driving away(with words)' 'falling apart/of falling apart' 'destroying bit by bit'; خَرخُر 'drove away(with physical actions/violence)' 'collapsed/of collapsing' 'is collapsing'; كَركُر 'made a rumbling/'kurkur' noise' 'giggled' 'drove/chased away'. Cp: ḥarḥur, harhur, kharkhur, karkur. (Ezra:2.51)

Bazluth; baṣlûṭ; بَزلُط 'I will make thin' 'I will eat rapidly/in one go'; بَصلُط 'I will oil/add oil' 'I will focus on/antagonise' 'I will make focus on/become zealous' the latter from the meaning of when a person becomes zealous about something or even with causing problems to another person or obsessed about something they use the word (sslṭ/صلط) which means 'oil/oiled' because oil sticks to an object or to skin and is difficult to wash off, its residue remains (the soap used from tree leaves paste or powdered was not as effective as modern soaps and hot/warm water is not always readily available) and this characteristic of oil adhering to skin/material/surface, etc. is what is likened to when a person focuses on something or someone; بَصلُت 'onion'. Cp: bazluṭ, bassluṭ, basslut. (Ezra.2:52)

Mehida; měḥîdā'; ميخيضاء 'shook/churned(milk)'; ميخيداء 'pillow/of pillows' (the latter can be literal or can indicate prostitution), 'concerning cheek(s)/leaning cheek on hand' (the latter can mean looks upset/distressed/worried), 'pulled down/off wall'; ميهيداء 'made smooth' 'made paste' 'a dish' (the latter includes boiling and stirring at the same time to make it a paste); ميكيداء 'an evil plot' 'covered opening with stone/lid/fabric'. Cp: meikheedhaa, meikheedaa, meiheedaa, meikeedaa. (Ezra.2:52)

Harsha; ḥaršā'; حَرشاء 'caused problems between people' 'a rumour with intent to cause problems' 'a tickle in the chest' 'itched/scratched'; خَرشاء 'untied'; هَرساء 'a fine or coarse paste(in cooking)/a dish called 'harsa'' 'a sweetmeat made into fine or coarse paste while boiling(hardens once cooled)'. Cp: ḥarshaa, kharshaa, harsaa. (Ezra.2:52)

Note the word-names in Ezra.2:52 all hold two meanings: one stands for causing problems for people, and the other is food-related.

Barkos; barqôs; بَرقُص 'I will dance' 'with sandals/use sandals on'. Cp: barqoss. (Ezra.2:53)

Thamah; temaḥ; دَمَح 'soot' (on pots, kettles and other metallic objects); طَمَح 'slapped down'. Cp: demaḥ, ṭemaḥ. (Ezra.2:53)

Neziah; nĕṣîaḥ; نيزيَح 'we shift/move'; نيصيه 'forelock/widow's peak'; نيصيَح 'we shout/argue' 'gave advice'. Cp: neizeeaḥ, neisseeah, neisseeaḥ. (Ezra.2:54)

Hatipha; ḥăṭîpā'; هيطيفاء 'drooped/flopped/flapped' also describes when a person walks with droopy posture or drooped arms/head, 'it turned off/put out/went out' 'here/look/pay attention, turn it off/put it out'; هيتيفاء 'plucked out/plucked at/snatched' 'he/they will leap'; حيتيفاء 'bordered/made rims' 'gathered at one end' 'shortened from the sides or every side'; حيطيباء 'gathered firewood' 'firewood'; خيطيباء 'spoke to' 'made a speech' 'got engaged'; خيطيفاء 'kidnapped' 'snatched'. Cp: haiṭeephaa, haiteephaa, ḥaiteephaa, ḥaiṭeebaa, khaiṭeebaa, khaiṭeephaa. (Ezra.2:54)

Sotai; sōṭay, sôṭay; صوطَي ، صُطَي 'stuck to' 'clung to' 'slammed so hard it stuck to' 'swooped down'. Cp: ssooṭay, ssoṭay. (Ezra.2:55)

Sophereth; sôpereṯ; سُفِرِت 'was made to travel' 'became openly vulgar' as in does not hide immorality/sins; سُبِرَت 'was made/made right' 'was fixed' 'she made/fixed/made it right'. Cp: sop<u>h</u>eret, soberet. (Ezra.2:55)

Peruda; pěrûḏā'; بيرُداء 'made cool/cold' 'went cold/felt cold' 'stomach ache(when eating hot then being exposed to cold or wind, causes severe stomach ache)' 'they will return/return it'; فيرُداء 'separated into single units' 'a buttock(half of bottom)' 'so they will return/so they will return it'; ثيرُباء 'made/drank churned milk' 'churned milk'; بيرُباء 'with his god' 'he will bring up/discipline/teach/grow' 'they will be brought up/disciplined/taught/grow' 'they will grow/be brought up well' 'they will mix and dilute with water' 'they will dampen/make damp'; فيرُباء so he will make god' 'in his god/parent/teacher' 'so he will bring up/discipline/teach/grow' 'so they will be brought up/disciplined/taught/grow' 'so they will grow/be brought up well' 'so they will mix and dilute with water' 'so they will become damp'; بيرُضاء 'he will consent/agree' 'with his permission' 'he will be pleased' 'with/in consent'. Cp: beirudaa, <u>ph</u>eirudaa, feirubaa, beirubaa, <u>ph</u>eirubaa, beiru<u>dh</u>aa. (Ezra.2:55)

Jaalah; ya'ălâ; يَعيله 'his sons/boys' 'he/it goes higher/rises'; هَعيله 'I will raise it/him higher' 'here are his boys/sons'; جَعيله 'created/made' 'came-raised it/him' 'came-his boys/sons' 'placed bait/egg'. Cp: ya'ailah, ha'ailah, ga'ailah. (Ezra.2:56)

Darkon; darqôn; دَرقُن 'mood went sour'; تَرقُن 'to pour narrow stream of water'; تَركُن 'depends on/puts trust in' 'left them' 'leaned it in corner' 'became corner'. Cp: darqon, tarqon, tarkon. (Ezra.2:56)

Hattil; ḥaṭṭîl; حَطّ يل 'leave-the' 'leave some of the'; هَطّيل 'light and disparate rain(spitting down)' 'small and irregular drops of water' 'will be early' 'will suddenly appear' 'will be long/take time'. Cp: ḥaṭṭ-eel, haṭṭeel. (Ezra.2:57)

Pochereth; pōḵereṯ; بوخَرَت 'perfumed with incense' and is in the feminine, 'became better/healed'; بوكَرَت 'gave birth to a female calf' 'heifer' 'was early' 'joint(of hand/fingers)' 'tomorrow'; بوحَرَت 'good riddance/said good riddance' 'went into sea'; بوكَرَث 'I will get/eat/grow chives' 'with the pool/pond' 'will inhale/take long drink'; بوكَرَف 'by/with palmful'; بوغَرَف 'will ladel/scoop' 'with rooms'; بوقَرَت 'the cow of' 'tore'; بوقَرَط 'gnashed/nipped'. Cp: boo<u>kh</u>eret, bookeret, booḥeret, bookeref, bookere<u>ph</u>, boo<u>gh</u>ere<u>ph</u>, booqeret, booqereṭ. (Ezra.2.57)

Zebaim; ḥaṣṣěḇāyîm; هَزّيباي هم/ام 'here are penises-them/the' 'I will penis(penetrate)-them/the' 'swing/rock them'; هَصّيباي هم/ام 'I will afflict/strike-them/the' 'I will/here is-pour onto/into-them/the'; هَسّيباي هم/ام 'I will leave alone-them/the' 'I will let go-them/the' 'I will capture-them/the'; هَضّيباي هم/ام 'chop-them/the'; هَذّيباي هم/ام 'you will/I will melt-them/the' 'see, it melted-them/the'; حَزّيباي هم/ام 'adorn with clothes/jewellery-them/the'. Cp: hazzeibaay-hum/um, ha<u>ss</u>eibaay-hum/um, hasseibaay-hum/um, ha<u>dh</u>eibaay-hum/um, havveibaay-hum/um, ḥazzeibaay-hum/um. (Ezra.2:57)

Ami; 'āmî; نَامي 'leading/leading through' 'following through' 'going through narrow opening' 'threading needle'; عَامي 'blinded' 'drank'. Cp: aamee, 'aamee. (Ezra.2:57)

Tel-melah; tēl melaḥ; تيل مِلَح 'carried by hand-salt' 'lifted by hand-salt' 'carried/lifted by hand-nice/well/pretty'. Cp: teyl melaḥ. (Ezra.2:59)

Tel-harsa; tēl ḥaršā'; تيل هَرساء 'carried/lifted by hand-paste/sweetmeat' 'carried/lifted by hand-harsa (Yemeni dish)/grain or flour used to make harsa dish)'; تيل حَرشاء 'carried/lifted by hand-caused problems between people' 'carried/lifted by hand-a rumour with intent to cause problems' 'carried/lifted by hand-a tickle in the chest' 'carried/lifted by hand-itched/scratched'; تيل خَرشاء 'carried/lifted by hand-untied'. As all four word-names in this verse have a food meaning, it is most probably 'carried by hand-paste/sweetmeat/harsa/grain flour of harsa'. Cp: teyl harsaa, teyl ḥar<u>sh</u>aa, teyl <u>kh</u>ar<u>sh</u>aa. (Ezra.2:59)

Cherub; kěrûḇ; كيرُب 'carob' 'eating/gathering carobs' and this is most likely since it is a food like most of the names in this line, 'depression' 'intense distress' 'chased away with'; خيرُب 'destroyed/ruined' 'ruins' 'of chasing away (with violence) with'. Cp: keyrub, <u>kh</u>eyrub. (Ezra.2:59)

Addan; 'addān; نَدّآن 'the guilted' 'the lowered' 'the bowed/bent' 'the lowly'; عَدّآن 'gathering/cooking/eating lentils' 'counted' 'made enemies/transgressed against'. Cp: addaan, 'addaan. (Ezra.2:59)

Verse 59 is filled with names which are food stuff. The name **Immer** is used for its meaning of 'show/show a hint/clue' and the characters who come from these places are said 'could not shew their father's house, and their seed, whether they were of Israel:'. The reason the author used food names to show these people could not prove they belonged could be as simple as that particular author may not like the foods he mentioned, and nothing more—in all cases these character names based on food nouns are linked in narration to being not allowed to eat from food reserved for priests.

Tobiah; ṭôḇîyâ; طُبي يه 'they could tolerate/eat/taste him/it-he/him' 'they are not revolted by-he/him' 'they could palate him/it' the word implies the food/drink/person may taste unpleasant or is unhygienic, 'my willy-he/him' 'was willied-he/him'; تبي يه 'repent-he/him' 'make repent-he/him'; ضُبي يه 'burning smell-he/him' (this word means a burning smell of a pan/pot or anything metallic left on fire with no food in it cooking). It is equivalent to Ethbaal (1Kgs.16:31-33; 21), Tobijah (2Chr.17:8). Cp: ṭobee-yah, tobee-yah, dhobee-yah. (Ezra.2:60)

Habaiah; ḥŏḇayyâ; خوبي يه ، خويبَي يه ، خوبَيّه ، خويبَيّه 'hid/hide-him/he' 'are hidden' 'damp/mouldy-him/he' 'are damp and mouldy' 'are evil/unlucky/bring evil-he/him/it' 'evil/unlucky/bring evil'; خوب/خويب ايّه 'damp/mould-indeed' 'damp/mouldy-a verse/sign' 'hid-a verse/sign' 'evil/unlucky/brings evil-a verse/sign'; هوبَي يه 'blow/scatter-he/him' 'swoop down on and scatter-him/he' 'gives-he/him'; هويبَي يه 'he will reject-him/he' 'he refused-him/he' 'of giving/gave-he/him'; هوب/هويب ايّه 'he refused-a verse/line/sign' 'he gave-a verse/line/sign'. Cp: khoobay yah, khoibay yah, khoobayyah, khoibayyah, khoob/khoib ayah, hoobay yah, hoibay yah, hoob/hoib ayah. (Ezra.2:61)

Koz; qôṣ; قز 'fry' 'frying/burnt/burning smell' 'make heart burn/nausea' 'kill(figuratively)' 'large rock'; كُز 'smoking vessel(similar to sheesha); قص 'tell story' 'cut' 'harden' 'become cruel'. Cp: qoz, koz, qoss. (Ezra.2:61)

The names used in verses 60-61 serve a purpose for the narration: **Delaiah** for its meaning 'show/prove-verse/line/sign' as these characters are asked (and fail) to prove their genealogy. **Barzillai** for 'good/pious-went/towards me' the **Gileadite** 'came-festival' and 'replenished/recompensed' as they are attempting to prove they are from priestly families and failing to excludes them from eating from the 'most holy things'. **Tobiah** 'they could tolerate/eat/palate/taste him/it-he/him' 'they are not revolted by-he/him', **Nekoda** 'he/they undid purity', **Habaiah** 'damp/mouldy-him/he', and **Koz** 'burnt/burning smell' 'make heart burn/nausea', all have meanings which indicate unsavouriness, unhygiene or something that puts a person off anything desirable or appetising, and the story narrates they are rejected for not being able to prove their genealogy and therefore cannot eat from what is reserved for priests. 'These sought their register *among* those that were reckoned by genealogy, but they were not found: therefore were they, as polluted, put from the priesthood.' (Ezra.2:60-63)

Tirshatha; tiršātā'; طِرشآتآء 'vomited/vomited it' 'splashed it'; طِرشآذآء 'vomited this' 'vomited he/it' 'his vomit'; and the narration has this character determine 'that they should not eat of the most holy things...'. Cp: ṭirshaataa, ṭirshaavaa. (Ezra.2:63)

Jozadak; yôṣāḏāq; يُصآدآق ، جُصآدآق 'he is-believed/honest/friendly' 'came-believed/honest/friendly'; يُزآدآك ، جُزآدآك 'he-gives you more/extra' 'he-deceives you' 'came-gave you more' 'came-deceived you'; يُصآدآك ، جُصآدآك 'he-blocks you/prevents you/is opposite you' 'he-fishes you' 'came-blocked you/prevented you/opposite you' 'came-fished you/your fish'. Cp: yossaadaaq, gossaadaaq, yozaadaak, gozaadaak, yossaadaak, gossaadaak. (Ezra.3:2)

Shealtiel; šĕ'altî'ēl, šaltî'ēl; سيئَلتي يِل ، سَلتي يِل 'questioned/asked-the' 'leaked-the' 'made flow-the' 'comforted/entertained/distracted-the'; شيئَلتي يِل ، شَلتي يِل 'took-the' 'carried-the'; صيئَلتي يِل ، صَلتي يِل 'arrived at-the' 'connected-the' 'you arrived at-the' 'you publicly apologised to-the'. The same as Salathiel (1Chr.3:17). Cp: seialtee-ill, saltee-ill, sheialtee-ill, shaltee-ill, sseialtee-ill, ssaltee-ill. (Ezra.3:2)

The names reflect on and relay in the story: **Jeshua**, 'picked many/took too much' many animals are sacrificed to God, many people assist in the building of the altar and much is offered (described as a continual burnt offering every day, morning and evening). Jeshua is the son of 'Jozadak' because people listen to him, believe him, and follow his lead; in the story this is shown through the building and the offerings, and again what is offered to God is in excess/extra.

Zerubbabel 'they procreated in swapped/changed' 'they left in swapped' 'leave-I will swap/change' 'they visited/pilgrimaged in swapped/changed' 'they tightened in swapped/changed' 'they caused great disgrace in swapped/changed'; these meanings are denoted in the story by the people who have lived in exile have left behind that life and will swap it for a more pious life; it is also reflected in their fear 'for fear *was* upon them because of the people of those countries;' which can mean 'tightened' as a feeling of fear. Although in 1Chr.3:19 Zerubbabel is the son of **Pedaiah** 'sacrifice-he/him' 'sacrificed for he/him' 'took out-he/him' and the same Zerubbabel has a son **Meshullam** 'what did he/they take/what was taken', the authors in Ezra want to use these names connected to Zerrubbabel, but with modifications: so Zerubbabel becomes son of **Shealtiel** instead of a son **Meshullam** to denote 'took-the' 'carried-the' and a father **Pedaiah** 'took out-he/him' which is taking offerings and presenting them to God, as well as taking money and food supplies, in exchange these people bring them wood and other resources; and also the second meaning of **Shealtiel** 'you arrived at-the' 'you apologised to-the' which is done by visiting the person you are apologising to and providing a calf, bull or any worthy livestock to be slaughtered for food as a public apology; this surname has replaced **Pedaiah** 'sacrifice-he/him' 'sacrificed for he/him'. The narration shows these events in the building of the altar and the offering of sacrifices.

Kadmiel is used for its meaning 'present/put forward-the' 'offer-the' 'serve(food/drink)-the' shown in the story as 'to set forward the workmen in the house of God:'. (Ezra.3)

Henadad; ḥēnādād; هينعدآد 'he will-force little by little to fall off' 'come on, force little by little to fall off' e.g. the movement/action of using a lever, crowbar or similar tool to remove/break down parts of a wall, 'come on, we will count' 'come on, we will prepare' and refers to assigning the work to numbers of people and also to the activities in building of which laying a foundation is preparation for the building of any house. Cp: heyn'daad, hey-n'daad. (Ezra.3:9)

Esarhaddon has been used for its meanings 'imprisoned (them)-bordered/sharpened' 'imprisoned-demolished/made them bow' 'difficult/made difficult-bordered/sharpened'; 'made difficult-demolished/made them bow'. These meanings are directly reflected in the story where the characters mention they were brought to the area against their will, the authors copy the idea of the story of Sennacherib swapping people from different areas sending them into captivity and exile which is narrated 'we do sacrifice unto him since the days of Esar-haddon…which brought us up hither.' and when their offer of assistance is rejected they make building the house difficult for Zerubbabel and his company 'Then the people of the land weakened the hands of the people of Judah, and troubled them in building,'. (Ezra.4:2-7)

Darius; dārĕyāweš; دآرييآوِس 'educated/studies matters' 'of careful studying' from word (drs/درس) which along with 'education/learning/taught' also means to look into and inspect a matter closely—which this character will do when Zerubbabel's opponents send Darius a letter. دآرييآ وِش 'he/they knew-what/and what' 'he/they found out-what' from words (dr/در) 'know' and (ish/sh/ش/اش) 'what' 'something' 'matter'. And again, Darius' character will find out what is going on. Cp: daareiyaawes, daareiyaa wesh. (Ezra.4:5-24)

Ahasuerus; 'ăḥašwērôš; نَحَشويرُش ، نيحَشويرُش 'they created problems/pitted against others' 'they pitted you against to cause problems' 'they conveyed news/rumours/conversations to cause problems' from the word (ḥrsh/حرش) the word describes when a person(s) delivers news/gossip or even lies to one or more person/party to create problems between both parties or for the spoken about 'And in the reign of Ahasuerus, in the beginning of his reign, wrote they *unto him* an accusation against the inhabitants of Judah and Jerusalem'. Like Darius, the root word has been made into a verb and noun describing both the named character and his actions, as well as the actions, matter of those concerned in the storyline. The name has also been manipulated into a diminutive.

Even if there had been a king/people with such names before or during the Biblical stories were created/written—these names were chosen to be used in the Biblical stories because their names suited the storyline and wordplay used in the Bible for their meanings as pronounced in Arabic—which is the authors' intentions, to give them a role in these stories; if there is physical evidence of such kings as Darius and Ahasuerus existing long after the Biblical stories, it is proof the Bible stories (at least some of them) were edited at a much later date than believed to have been created or at least had become popular enough for people outside of the Arab countries to name themselves after these characters; it seems more likely that these figures never existed, but the stories created for them have confused history with fiction. If historians are using these stories as proof of existence without actual proof there were such kings/officials during pre-biblical times, they are on a folly, and the same goes if they are trying to prove the characters in the stories existed (even those whose real names were borrowed) as they are fictional stories and most of the names are fictional creations—the names are tools used as wordplay to enhance the narration and entertain an audience. Cp: aḥashweyrosh, aiḥashweyrosh. (Ezra.4:6)

Artaxerxes; 'artaḥšastā', Artaxerxēs; نَرتكز استآء 'stood on its head-stood straight/right' 'stood on its head-was offended/bad'; ارتكزاركزيه 'turned on its head-then(stood/set) straight again/set it (or) him straight/right way up'. From words (rkz/ركز) 'stood straight/stood it up/placed it standing/right way up' 'understand matter correctly'; (rtkz/رتكز) 'stood upside down/stood on his/its head' 'misunderstood(matter)'; and (sa/سَ) 'did' 'made right/straight/level' 'offense/offended/wrong/wronged/bad/did bad'. These words mean to physically stand a person or object the right way round/standing up or the wrong way around (upside down), but also to either understand a matter correctly or incorrectly. Note how in both the 'Hebrew' and Greek transliteration there is a slight difference to the second part of the compound word: the Greek version uses the phrase and same root word 'artax' 'stood on its head' then 'erxēs' 'set it straight'. Whereas the 'Hebrew' has the same first half of the compound word 'artaḥš' 'stood on its head' the second half is a different word, but with a similar meaning 'astā'' 'stood/set straight/set right/was level' 'was offended/felt wrong(ed)'.

And the order of the compound word: 'Artax' ارتكز (stood on its head) before 'erxes' اركز 'set it straight/stood right' is because of the role of the character and events in the story first believes the letter of complaint/warning him against allowing the building (Ezra.4:7-24) so 'Artax' 'turns on his head'—turns the whole building project on its head and forces them to cease work (this allows one meaning of the 'Hebrew' second half (astā' (offended/wrong)) to be reflected too). But suddenly in Chapter 6:14, the story narrates Artaxerxes commanded (gave permission and supported) the building of the house—therefore, the second part of the name (erxes/astā'/set or stood right): he stood up straight/turned the situation the right way around (Ezra.6:14) 'And the elders of the Jews builded, and they prospered…' 'And they builded, and they finished *it*, according to the commandment of Cyrus, and Darius, and Artaxerxes king of Persia.' Note how all these names of 'kings of Persia' are used in one story whereas had they been real events it would not be all of them at the same time, but the purpose is to create an entertaining story. In Ezra.7, we are told of Artaxerxes's decree allowing the building, and praising Ezra to show how eventually everything was set right. Cp: artakz-astaa, artakz-erkzeyh. (Ezra.4:7-24; 6:14; 7)

Bishlam; bišlām; بِش لاَم 'with what-blamed' as the letter is a complaint blaming the builders with the intention of sedition; بِسلاَم 'with greetings' 'with/in peace/quiet' 'will deliver/receive' 'will remain intact/whole' 'will survive' and this character is one of the many authors of the letter of complaint which will be both delivered and received. Cp: bi<u>sh</u> laam, bislaam. (Ezra.4:7-24)

Mithredath for its meaning 'increase/enrich-weak' as the convincing point in the letter is that if allowed to build, the Jews will weaken the king's taxes/fortune. (Ezra.1:4-11; 4:7-24)

Tabeel; ṭāḇē'ēl; طاَبي ئِل 'was not disgusted/revolted by-the' 'could eat/palate-the' 'liked the taste of-the' and as the character is a bad one in the narration it implies something unpleasant about him. It is the same as Tobijah (2Chr.17:8) and Tobiah (Ezra.2:60); تعبي ئِل 'fills/packs-the' 'troubled-the' 'tired-the' 'upset-the' 'sad-the'. All these meanings are used as the word 'filled' is used to describe persuading a person to hate or believe negative things about another which the letter does against the Jews; also, they trouble Zerubbabel and his people by causing problems for the building project. It is equivalent to Ethbaal (1Kgs.16:31-33; 21). Cp: ṭaabei-ill, t'bei-ill. (Ezra.4:7-24)

Rehum (Ezra.2:2) has been used for its meanings of 'felt mercy for' 'saw-worries' 'saw how many/much' as the story narrates they are considering and worried by how much will decrease from taxes due to the king if he allows the building to complete; 'piled/stacked/heaped' (usually stones) as that is the image of stones made ready for building which will be left piled which should have been used for the house. (Ezra.4:8-24)

Shimshai; šimšai; سِم سي 'named-bad/wrong/offended' 'poisoned-bad/wrong/offended'; سِم شي 'name-something/an important matter' 'poison-something/an important matter'; صِمصي 'of blocking'; صِم شي 'blocked-something/important matter'. All these meanings are in the story related to this character: he has named the Jews as intending something bad against the king; the king's mind is poisoned against the Jews; the building activities are blocked/stopped; the building project (the house of the Lord) is an important matter to the protagonists and the authors of the story. Cp: sim-sai, sim-<u>sh</u>ai, <u>ss</u>im<u>ss</u>ai, <u>ss</u>im-<u>sh</u>ai. (Ezra.4:8-24)

Dinaites; dînāyē'; ديناَييى 'bowed/bent/lowered' 'lowly' 'sly' 'guilted them/of guilting' the word is in plural or attributing it to the spoken about. The story narrates how the senders of the letter are pitching the Jews as guilty of bad intentions. Cp: deenaayey. (Ezra.4:9-24)

Apharsathchites; 'ăparsĕkāyē'; ئيفرسيخاَييى 'enriching/enriches-it spoiled it/made it split/go off' 'boiled/increase(d)-it spoiled it/made it split/go off' the word is in plural or attributing it to the spoken about. The letter accuses the Jews of intending to spoil the peace and harm the king's income. Cp: ai<u>ph</u>arsei<u>kh</u>aayey. (Ezra.4:9-24)

Tarpelites; ṭarpĕlāyē', ṭarpĕlay; طَربيلاَييى ، طَربيلَي 'play music' 'of playing music' 'play music for me' 'encourage to do a bad thing' the first word is in the plural or attributing it to the spoken about. The letter is urging the king, through presenting it as the senders' concern for the king, to stop the Jews building, he is being encouraged to do something bad to the Jews. It is similar to Jezebel and Ethbaal. Cp: ṭarbeilaayey, ṭarbeilay. (Ezra.4:9-24)

Apharsites; 'ăpārsāyē', 'ăparsay; نيفَرصَي ، نيفآرصاآييئ 'he/they/it split open/push out/emerge by pushing up or out/divide by breaking or splitting' 'of splitting open/pushing out/emerging by pushing up or out/dividing by breaking or splitting'; نيفآرساآييئ ، نيفرسَي 'he/they/it divide something into separate units' 'of dividing something into separate units' 'explain/explain in detail/make clear' 'of explaining/explaining in detail/making clear' the first word is in the plural or attributing it to the spoken about. The letter details what the Jews are doing, what they intend to do, the alleged consequences upon the king; and the senders urge him to take specific action first searching the records then to stop the building project. Cp: aiphaars-saayey, aipharssay, aiphaarsaayey, aipharsay. (Ezra.4:9-24)

Archevites; 'arkĕwāyē', 'arkĕway; نَرخيوآييئ ، نَرخيوَي 'loosen it' 'of loosening/leniency' 'of immorality/looseness'. The letter warns the king not to be lenient i.e. if he allows them to finish building, it will be detrimental to him—so they are telling him not to be lenient. Cp: arkheiwaayey, 'arkheiway. (Ezra.4:9-24)

Babylonians; bābĕlāyē', bablî; بآديلآييئ ، بَدلي 'swap/change' 'of swapping/changing'. The letter talks about a big change that will occur such as sedition, refusal to pay tolls, tribute and custom and damage to the king will ensue, but also that the 'Jews' will become stronger and the 'king' weaker so a change and swap in power and control too. Cp: baadeilaayey, badlee. (Ezra.4:9-24)

Susanchites; šûšankāyĕ', šûšankî; شُشَنكاآييئ ، شُشَنكي 'what/why is it your matter/problem' 'this is your matter/business/this should concern you' 'a matter/matters-yours/your business' 'of matters-yours/your business' it is equivalent to 'what has it got to do with you' and 'this matter is your concern/problem/business'. The senders of the letter make it clear that the king should be interested in the building work as it is a matter that will directly affect him. Cp: shushankaayei, shushankee. (Ezra.4:9-24)

Dehavites; dehāwē', dahăwā'; دَهاَويئ ، دَهيواَء 'tricked into harming himself' 'deceived into trouble' 'of tricking into harming himself/trouble' 'of conning' 'have been conned'. The story narrates that the letter is deceiving and pitting the king into taking action against the Jews, but also that the Jews' actions are deceit and harm to the king. Cp: dehaawey, dahaiwaa. (Ezra.4:9-24)

Elamites; 'ēlĕmāyē', 'almî; عيليماآييئ ، عَلمي 'told/taught/knew/knows/found out/showed' 'of telling/teaching/knowing/finding out/showing' 'he/they told on you' 'he/they put people up to harm you'. The letter both informs the king of what is happening, and teaches him what he should do about it, and instigates against the Jews. Cp: 'eyleimaayey, 'almee. (Ezra.4:9-24)

With the exception of Rehum and Shimshai, the names in Ezra.4:9 have a different accent to them, which could be because the final editor to add to this story was not from the original Biblical authors land therefore had a slightly different accent/pronunciation (although there is no difference in meaning nor method), but it may just be a result of the transliteration.

Asnappar; 'ošnappar, 'ašnapar; عوشنَبَّر ، عَشنَبَر 'we lived good' 'we lived beyond' 'we lived-went beyond' supported by text which states nations were brought to live in the cities by this character. Cp: 'ooshnabbar, 'ashnabar. (Ezra.4:10)

Haggai; ḥaggai; حَجَّي 'cover/shelter'; هَجَّي 'teach to pronounce correctly' 'drove away forever' 'he came/look he is coming/came'. Equivalent to Haggi (Gen.46:16), Haggith (2Sam.3:4), Haggiah (1Chr.6:30). Cp: ḥaggai, haggai. (Ezra.5:1)

Tatnai; tattĕnay; تَتّيني 'of tutting' 'tutted me'; طَطّيني 'squeaked at me' 'of squeaking' and means the person boasts but is ineffective/weak 'mocked/teased me'. Cp: tatteinay, ṭaṭteinay. (Ezra.5)

Shethar-boznai; šĕṯar bôzĕnay; شيطَر بُزيني 'this side of land-of taking' 'he will make leave/banish-of taking' and the character and his companion are described in the narration as 'on this side of the river' (shṭr/شطر) means a person's side of land when talking about land which has more than one owner and also specifics the side/place being spoken about in general, (bz/بز) 'take'. شيتَر بُذيني 'looked in(out of care/curiosity)-with harm for me/of harming' 'looked in/became curious-with ears/with my ears' 'curiosity with my ears' 'looked in/curiosity/checked in-with permission/with my permission/announced' 'looked in/curiosity-harmed me/with harm'; from words (shtr/شتر) 'curiosity/looking into/checking in on', and (vn/ذن) 'ear' 'handle(of object)' 'permission/gave permission/announced', and (av/اذ) 'harm/harmed'. The building activity is what causes Tatnai and Shethar-boznai to become curious and look in on the building project; these two characters ask the builders who gave them permission to build; the request mentioned in Shethar-boznai's letter is that the king become concerned enough to look into the records; mention is made of the people harmed and taken away into captivity and the vessels which were first taken from the house by Nebuchadnezzar then returned and taken back, along with permission to build God's house. Cp: sheiṭar bozeinay, sheitar boveinay. (Ezra.5)

Achmetha; 'aḥmĕtā'; نَغميضاء 'close your eyes' 'they closed their eyes'. Cp: aghmeidhaa. (Ezra.6:1-2)

Medes has been used for the same meanings in (2Kgs.17:6): 'reached' 'hand to/offer' 'hand/pass/stash/hide/plant with no one noticing' 'to put hands on something not yours' 'touch/reach into' 'to overstep boundaries/'take liberties'/have confidence to do something that should result in punishment' 'lying down' 'handed/passed with no one else noticing' 'hidden secretly/planted to be found by someone else'. As most of the Biblical stories this chapter is also laced with puns and humour: it reads, when it was suggested Darius search the 'house of the rolls' the records among 'where the treasures were laid up in Babylon' that this record proving permission to build the house is found at Achmetha 'close your eyes' in the province of Medes 'stash/hide/plant with no one noticing', i.e. the record was planted while no one was looking. Not only that, but Darius goes on to decree even more assistance be given to the returned exiles, even sacrificial animals are to be provided by non-Jews to the exiles, and anyone who defies the ruling will not only be hanged, but hung from the timber removed from the roof of his own house—so the pun becomes bigger with the scale of results in the narration. (Ezra.5-6)

Haggai, **Zechariah** and **Iddo** are used to denote the events in the story, (Zechariah) Darius is 'reminded' of a decree and record allowing the building, and the captives conduct their feasts and rituals; (Haggai) Darius makes a very detailed decree of what will be given to the Jews and a detailed punishment for their antagonists; (Iddo) the types of resources to be provided are listed, and the types and numbers of sacrificial animals are listed in the passage. (Ezra.6)

Adar the month has the same meanings as **Adar** the place name in Josh.15:3; 'ădār; نَضآر ، نيضآر 'the harmed/the harmer' 'the vicious' 'the one with the habit'; نَذآر،نيذآر 'the sower(of seeds)/the sowed' 'the one with offspring' 'the one who scattered soil(or any powdery substance)'; عَذآر،عيذآر 'shadows/shadowed' 'excuses/excused'; غَدآر، غيدآر 'darkened' (as in night/sky), 'betrayed/deceived' 'treacherous'. It is definitely used because it follows the completion of the work after Darius threatens with physical harm anyone who disobeys supplying the Jews with what they need, and following a call for God to destroy people if the building is destroyed. Cp: adhaar, aidhaar, avaar, aivaar, 'avaar, 'aivaar, ghadaar, ghaidaar. (Ezra.6:15)

As in 1Chr.4:17, **Ezra** is still; عِزرآء 'made ugly/became ugly'; عِذرآء 'shadowed' 'excused'; يُزرآع 'grow/plant'; يُسرآء 'left very early/in the dark' 'captives'; يُسرآع 'be fast/he was fast'; يُذرآء 'sow' 'create offspring' 'scattered(powdery substance such as flour, soil, ash, etc.'; يُذرآع 'measure by the forearm' 'beat'; يُزرآء 'insult deeply/a lot' 'a great disgrace'. Most of these meanings are reflected in the story of Ezra.7 onwards.

The titular character is fast to learn the law of Moses; he leaves early from Babylon and arrives early at Jerusalem and this is described due to 'God's hand' being on him (remember Elisha when God's hand was on him so by foot he was able to beat a chariot and arrived at the entrance before the king) so this implies the 'fast' in his name; everything pertaining to Ezra (to be done/announced/implemented/given) is to be done 'speedily' even in previous chapters of Ezra 'and this work goeth fast on' 'I Darius have made a decree; let it be done with speed' 'so they did speedily' 'That though mayest buy speedily with this money bullocks…' that whatsoever Ezra the priest, the scribe of the law of God of heaven, shall require of you, it be done speedily' and for anyone who does not comply 'let judgement be executed speedily upon him' (Ezra.5:8; 6:12-13; 7:6, 9, 17, 21, 26).

Teaching statutes and judgements reflects 'grow/plant' which is how knowledge, religion, morals are described as being 'planted' in the person. Ezra is to teach (plant) and show and encourage (grow/nurture) God's laws among the people (Ezra.7:10,25).

'measure by the forearm' is reflected in Ezra being given the right to purchase as many quantities of food resources for sacrifice/offerings, but also to take out of the king's treasury (Ezra.17, 20).

'made ugly/became ugly' which usually describes death and destruction is what the king wants to avoid 'for why should there be wrath against the realm of the king and his sons?'; making unlawful the taxing of priests and other worship-related offices; and allowing people to be executed if they do not follow both laws 'of thy God, and the law of the king' will be punished at the most extreme with death (Ezra.7:23-26).

'insult deeply/great disgrace' is reflected in those who will not follow both the laws of God and the law of the king, as well as the foreign wives which will be introduced in a later chapter. 'seed/sow/create offspring' the Arabic word 'of seed' means 'offspring/children' to procreate is to 'sow': one of the issues in the

Ezra story is narrated as men marrying 'foreign' women—and the 'corruption issue' they present is the 'corruption' of the 'holy seed'; so he has to resolve this problem of children (seed) born from 'foreign' mothers by forcing the men to 'put away their wives' 'for they have taken of their daughters for themselves, and for their sons so that the holy seed have mingled themselves with the people of those lands.' (Ezra.9-10). Of course all the authors and characters of the Biblical stories and the lands they are set in are Arabic and one people, but the authors' method of creating funny and dramatic stories was through wordplay and also later editors would change it to suit their purposes one of which was they wanted to explain why there were so many different religions being worshipped by the same one people and that these people married from each other without concern. But the people (the original audiences of these stories) who upkept the religion and the stories throughout millennia understood this and were not concerned with the racist narrative as it was meant to be 'funny' and 'entertaining' and not a literal instruction or actual event. It would not be until much later, once these stories had become religious scripture to many, after a span of time and distance across the world that these stories, who are about one people, would be taken as historical fact and attempt to give the Jewish religion a 'race' separate from the Arab population it was one with.

The lineage for Ezra's character is not done for no reason at all, but as is the method I have described of the Biblical authors: **Seraiah** 'left early in the dark-him/he' 'Ezra went up to Babylon'; 'bundled them/it-he him' and refers to written documents kept rolled or folded as this character is presented as a scribe dealing with records 'of the law of Moses'. The story narrates Ezra leaving and arriving early to Jerusalem.

Azariah 'made ugly-him/he' 'the sowing of seeds/offspring' which is related to the feared destruction from God, the punishment of anyone disobeying the laws, and the issue about 'foreign' wives and their offspring. The meaning 'beware/remember/listen and remember-filled with much/crawled with ants/left behind' refers to the law which needs to be taught and remembered and also the issue of children from 'foreign' wives.

Hilkiah for 'I will find it/him' 'here/look-found-he/him' reflected in Ezra being found 'a ready scribe in the law of Moses'; and Ezra is met with the approval, enthusiastic approval, of the king to do and take as he pleases. 'I will throw it/him' 'here/look-threw it/him' refers to the animals which will be slaughtered for sacrifice, but also the disobedient people who will be executed, exiled or imprisoned.

Shallum for 'took' 'of taking' 'I will gather' 'of gathering' as Ezra takes with him a group of exiles, also for all the food materials, treasures, money and other resources he will receive, gather and deliver to Jerusalem; 'said salaam(peace)/greeted' (the Arab greeting equivalent to 'Hello/Hi') 'left unharmed/intact/survived', his letter to Ezra opens with this Arabic greeting; the king hopes he will not suffer the wrath of God.

Zadok for its meaning 'honest/friend' 'gave you extra' as King Artaxerxes deals kindly with Ezra and the other people; Ezra will receive more and more in this part of the story of food stock and treasures, he will also be given more authority than a mere 'scribe'.

Ahitub for 'here is-repent' as the people are being shown God's ways and have a chance to repent once they understand the correct laws; 'here is-nice/pleasant' 'here is-well, good/all right' as Artaxerxes deals pleasantly with Ezra and gives him many good things to use in his mission; the 'goodness' of dealings and physical materials is emphasised also at the end of the chapter at verse 27.

Amariah for 'ordered-he/him' as Ezra is put in charge of many people, many matters and important matters and materials; 'built-he/him' as it is related to the building of the house of God.

Meraioth for 'what you see/what did you see' as Ezra is allowed to do and take as he sees fit. Also '(the/his/her/etc.) dream' 'a dream' 'she/he-did not dream' 'he/she did not see' as Ezra is narrated in the first person and the same narration states he is only a scribe and this denotes that this is a dream of Ezra (just like Samaria is used to remind the audience that the stories being told are fictional) where he is exalted and given authority over people covering various regions and access to the kings treasures to do as he pleases, or a later editor added this name so that it would state 'he did not dream' to present it as an actual event within storyland.

Zerahiah for its meanings 'went/left-he/him' 'visited/pilgrimaged-he/him' as he leaves Babylon for Jerusalem; 'said openly-he/him' 'spoke honestly-he/him' as he is tasked with teaching the laws; 'built worshipping structure/shrine-he/him' as his objective is to build the house of God; 'sowed-he/him' as he is planting laws and teaching the way of God; 'procreated-he/him' 'scattered-he/him' 'left it-he/him' 'completely soiled-he/him' 'filled with insults-he/him' and he is also speaking about the problem of marrying 'foreign' women which (according to the story) pollutes the offspring and he is ordering people to get rid of their wives and children which leads to 'insulted greatly-he/him' 'filled with insults-he/him' as the story narrates the disgrace and shame of marrying these women and the women spoken about are being insulted by the statements.

Uzzi for its meanings 'honour' 'a want/need' as Ezra is lifted in status by being tasked with matter of great importance, and his task creates the needs of physical materials which he receives with support of the king. 'disobeyed' as the people who disobey are mentioned toward the end of the chapter. 'say a protection for/protect' mentioning he was strengthened by 'the hand of God' provides him with not only strength but also protection.

Bukki for its meanings 'leave some/remains' reflected in whatever silver/gold is left after purchasing animals for offerings he can do as he pleases with it. 'go/go there' as he and others have been allowed to go to Jerusalem, but also all over the province of Babylon to collect/purchase what is needed.

Abishua for its meaning 'fill/pack-cried out like an animal' and this is word-imagery reflected in the bullocks, rams, lambs purchased for the offerings which need to be herded towards Jerusalem so it conjures up large flocks with all the bleating and lowing.

Phinehas for its meanings of 'will bring bad luck' 'will create holes/crumble' 'will maul/take chunks out of' as whoever will disobey the laws Ezra brings will face varying punishment.

Eleazar for 'the ugliness' death, confiscation of possessions, exile, imprisonment promised to those who disobey the laws.

Aaron for its meanings 'is-here-see/look' 'see/look/behold' and refers to what Ezra brings with him of change, of laws and the beauty imagined for the house of God; 'drive them away' refers to the 'foreign' wives and being forcefully separated from their husbands in the story.

Pharosh is the same as Parosh (Ezra.2:3). (Ezra.8:3)

Elihoenai; 'elyĕhô'ênay; ئَلَيِيهُ عينَي 'the one who hints' 'the one who directs message indirectly' 'the one who watches/inpsects/looks at' 'the one who directs confrontation'; ئَلَيِيهُ غينَي 'the one who sings' 'the one who makes throaty sound(a sound like ghnn/ghain)' 'the one became rich/independent' 'the one who no longer needs/no longer wants/no longer dependent on'. 'the one who' can also be 'yes/yes it is, the one who'. The same as Elienai (1Chr.8:20), Elioenai (1Chr.3:23) Cp: elyeiho-'eynay, elyeiho-gheynay. (Ezra.8:4)

Hakkatan; haqqāṭān; هَقّاطَان 'pecked' 'they pecked' 'broke/tattered' 'broke/tattered the heart' the latter means heartbroken or feeling great sorrow/empathy towards the spoken about. Note how the author is carrying on with the hen-related actions in Ezra.2 as this is the son of Azgad with the same meaning of 'pecking/is pecking'. Cp: haqqaaṭaan. (Ezra.8:12)

Adonikam; 'ădōnîqām; ئَضوني قآم 'here I am standing' 'here I have an erection' 'here I have done-standing' 'here I have done an erection' 'here I am stood/went and done' 'here I am turned on('horny')' 'with an erection' 'here I have done-stood/went and done' ; ئَذوني قآم 'harmed me-standing' 'harmed me-erection' 'harmed me-stood/went and done' 'stood-went and harmed me'. Cp: adhoonee qaam, avoonee qaam. (Ezra.8:13)

Zabbud; zabbûd; زَبُّد 'buttered/spread' 'perfumed with ointment' 'drinking vessels' 'of drinking vessels'; زَبُّط 'kicked'; ضَبُّط 'tightened' 'strong/became strong' 'disciplined his wife'; شَبُّط 'latticed with rope' 'swiped/whipped with rope or rope-like material'. Cp: zabbud, zabbuṭ, dhabbuṭ, shabbuṭ. (Ezra.8:14)

Ahava; 'ahăwā'; ئَحَوآء ، ئَحيوآء 'stay/be still' 'stay(said to plural)' 'made stay/still' and two are in the form of telling another person to stay or stop moving, and it is exactly what the story narrates they do 'And I gathered them together to the river that runneth to Ahava; and there abode we in tents for three days.'. It is equivalent to Hawwa, Jehova. Cp: aḥawaa, aḥaiwaa. (Ezra.8:15)

Ariel; 'ărî'el; ئيري ئِل 'show-the' (show-the can mean literally to show something or as a threat) 'saw-the' 'dreamt-the' 'teach/taught-the' (as 'seeing' and 'showing' is the same as 'teaching'). It is one of the characters that are 'men of understanding' and Ezra shows/teaches them what to say to Casiphia and they return with 'a man of understanding', it implies people who know what to do and who can teach others what to do. It is equivalent to Uriel (1Chr.6:24). Cp: airee-ill. (Ezra.8:16-18)

Casiphia; kāsipyā'; كآسِفيآء ، كآسِف يآء 'has rejected and hurt' 'has broken his spirit' 'has rejected and broken spirit-he did/is' it is specifically the humiliation or emotion when a person asks for something and is rejected from the word (ksph/كسف) 'broken' 'humiliated/hurt', can also mean 'it has gone numb' 'try to carry it/them gently'; قآصِفيآء ، قآصِف يآء 'rejected and humiliated' 'rejected and made feel ashamed' 'rejected abruptly' 'rejected abruptly-he did/is' and means when a person asks for something or says something but the other person responds with a rude rejection or a retort and embarrasses or offends the first person, 'snapped off-he did/is' 'he is snapping off' 'he is snapped off' and when a person is said to be "casiph' the neck' (mqssooph a-raqaba/مَقصوف الرقبة) 'his neck is snapped short/his neck is short' it means he/she has no shame; from word (qssph/قصف) 'short piece/stub'. Both meanings are reflected in the narration: 'For I was ashamed to require of the king a band of soldiers and horsemen to help us against the enemy in the way:' this shows 'has rejected and broken spirit-he did/is' a humiliation and reluctance to ask; 'because we had spoken unto the king saying: The hand of our God is upon all them that seek him; but his power and his wrath is against all them that forsake him.' showing a fear he might be 'rejected and humiliated' because of what he said about having God's protection. Cp: kaasiphyaa, kaasiph-yaa, qaassiphyaa, qaassiph-yaa. (Ezra.8:17)

Sherebiah; šērēḇyâ; شيريب يه 'drank-he/him' 'will mix and dilute with water-he/him'; شيري بيه 'purchased with' 'purchased with him'; سيريب يه 'is leaking/of leaking-he/him' 'will mix and dilute with water-he/him'; سيري بيه 'walk with him/me' 'leave early in dark with him/me'. It is reflected in being given great amounts of gold, silver and other treasures/resources to carry to the house of the Lord which is why 'Sherebiah/purchased-he/him' and '**Hashabia/** 'carried on his waist-he/him' 'stuffed-he/him'' have been used in this part of the story; the 'offerings' to God is similar to purchasing protecting, fortune, health, life, etc. as is paying 'king's commissions'. Both character names also have meanings 'walk with him' 'leave early in dark with him' (Sherebiah) and 'he will leave/part with-he/him' (Hashabiah) reflected in the narration as parting from the river Ahava. Cp: sheyreyb-yah, sheyrey-byah, seyreyb-yah, seyrey-byah. (Ezra.8:18, 24-36)

Meremoth; mĕrēmôṯ; ميريمُت ، ميري مُت 'the throwing of' 'the killing of' 'saw death' 'dreamt of death' and has to do with sacrificial offerings in great numbers according to the narration; ميري مُد 'saw-handed/extended' 'dreamt-handed/extended' which is supported by the text as all the things being weighed 'by the hand of Meremoth' and the sacrifices being offered to God as well as 'and they further the people, and the house of God.'. Cp: meireymot, meirey-mot, meirey-mod. (Ezra.8:33-36)

Noadiah; nô'aḏyâ; نُعَد يه 'we count-he/him' and is reflected in the things being weighed and counted and recorded 'By number *and* by weight of every one: and all the weight was written at that time.', 'we remove/pull down little by little-he/him' 'we force to fall off by forcing motion(similar how crowbar is used to force something open)-he/him' and means when pieces of a wall or anything is broken/pushed off bit by bit; نُعَديه 'we make enemy him/her/them' 'we transgress against him/her/them' 'we infect' 'we infect him/her/them/it' 'of forcing off'; Equivalent to Henadad (Ezra.3:9). Cp: no'ad-yah, no'adyah. (Ezra.8:33-34)

Binnui; binnûy; بِنُّي 'of/has many children' 'of building' 'I will intend/set my mind on' 'with an intention' 'of intent/I intend'; he is the father of Noadiah so his name reads 'we count-he/him—I intend' and is reflected by the narration that when weighing out the gold, silver, etc. it is for the purpose of making offerings and paying tributes as well as to improve the situation of 'the people, and the house of God.'. Cp: binnuy. (Ezra.8:33-36)

The word-names in Ezra.8:33 are also setting the stage and themes for what will happen in chapter 9 the 'putting away' of the wives and their children.

Meremoth 'the throwing of' 'saw death' 'dreamt of death' as Ezra will be throwing himself to the ground out of despair and the narration is of 'putting away' which could mean 'sending away' the wives and the children, but could also mean killing them (this is a fictional story that never happened, but the reasons behind it will be discussed elsewhere in this book); also the dialogue of God seeing the people in captivity and 'extended mercy unto us in the sight of the kings of Persia'. He is son of **Uriah** 'he was made naked/stripped naked' as Ezra tears his garments, but is also an expression when a wife is separated from her husband under injustice and bad acts of others.

Eleazar the son of **Phinehas**: 'the ugliness' 'will bring bad luck' 'will create holes/crumble' 'will maul/take chunks out of' as the story narrates an ugly and destructive thing to have 'mixed' with 'foreigners' and the actions against these women and the children is ugly and destructive, it tears up families completely (and is impossible as narrated), but also Ezra's dialogue of the ugliness of wars, captivity which the people have suffered.

Jozabad the son of **Jeshua**: these names reflect 'drinking bowls' and 'picked many/took by the handfuls' in relation to Ezra.8 narration of vessels of gold, silver and many things being weighed and carried. In relation to the 'mixed' children and their 'foreign' mothers these names mean: **Jozabad** 'he kicks a lot/kicks' as when someone is asked to leave or rejected the term 'kicked' is used; 'he disciplines his wife' the latter when it is proven she has committed a serious wrong against another person 'he whips' and the narration shows the women are being punished just for existing and being mothers and wives, this is narrated as a transgression against the people and God. **Jeshua**: 'picked a lot/many/took too much' 'many people' because many men will 'put away' their wives and children, and the children will be many, also many men agree to this act of separating from their wives and children. **Jeshua**: 'came-freakishly ugly/mutated' as especially the children are described as something bad as are the mothers/wives; 'came-cried loudly like animal' 'pulled out by handfuls' as Ezra plucks out his hair and beard.

Noadiah the son of **Binnui**: 'we make enemy him/her/them' 'we transgress against him/her/them' 'we infect' 'we infect him/her/them/it' 'of forcing off' 'we remove/pull down little by little-he/him'; Binnui: 'of/has many children' 'with an intention'. As the story is about many children who are the product of 'mixed marriage', and they and their presence are viewed as a sin, an infection/pollution of the 'seed'/bloodline; they are viewed as the enemy, even the men are transgressing against God, but the wives and the children are an embodiment of the transgression. The men have the intention of remedying the situation.

Levites has been used for its meanings of 'answer/respond/do as commanded' 'answered/answer/answer him(or it)' 'served/serve/serve him(or it)' 'answer/respond and assist' as this is what the men will do in this story (and its meanings also apply to Ezra.8 in gathering, collecting etc. the gold, silver, vessels); 'twisted around/entwined' as the story narrates how people have mixed and produced children from these marriages. (Ezra.9-10)

Ezra retires to the chamber of **Johanan** son of **Eliashib** because of his distress over 'mixed marriages' and 'mixed children' which cause both disgrace and transgression against the people and God, and of which the resolution will be to 'put away' the said wives and children. So the compound words of the character name who is only mentioned because his chamber is used, **Johanan**: 'they are humiliating/they are being humiliated' 'came-both humiliated' 'they are being betrayed' 'came-both betrayed/treasonous' and **Eliashib**: 'the afflicted/injured/hit' 'the bringer of affliction/problems' 'the one who leaves/cuts off relations, activities, actions' are all reflected in the story: the great distress, humiliation, despair and the affliction of having such wives and children, then the action to resolve it 'the one who leaves/cuts off relations, activities, actions'. (Ezra.10:6)

All the meanings of names mentioned relay in this story's narration (whether denoting something negative or about listening, complying, supporting), to avoid repetition I will only translate the new ones or those which have an extra specific role supported by the text. Those previously translated can be referred to and the connection made.

Jonathan 'males making each other female by having anal sex with each other' seems to have confused Biblical scholars both ancient and modern, in relation to the Ezra wife-separation story: some believe Jonathan refused or opposed to separate the men from 'strange wives' while some believe he supported Ezra's racist instructions. This is not because of what the text states: the text states 'Only Jonathan the son of Asahel and Jahaziah the son of Tikvah were employed about this matter: and Meshullam and Shabbethai the Levite helped them.' which means they were part of the decision making to enforce the separations. Jonathan was used just like the character Jonathan (David's lover) represented a man who is not a man because of anal sex with another man is not deemed a proper or wholesome man—so too are the wives described as 'foreign/unclean/filth' and their children being a product of an 'unclean foreign wife' (and the uncleanness meant by the authors is not just an external filth but in the skin, bone, marrow, heart and soul) and a 'clean' and 'superior' man: the product (children) are freaks according to the story.

The earlier translators who even if they did not understand the meanings of the word-names, still knew of the negative connotation of the names such as Jonathan, Asahel, etc. and how these word-names are used as themes for the stories, and this creates an idea that if they are unsavoury word-names then they must have opposed Ezra's instructions which the narration is presenting as the 'good' character. **Asahel** still means 'disobeyed/went against-the' 'disobeyed him/went against him-the' and probably refers to the marrying of 'foreign women' being disobedience and going against God, but because of the meaning of Jonathan the translators/scholars split on whether these characters supported or opposed the divorcing of wives and getting rid of children.

Jahaziah; yaḥăzîyâ; يَحيزي يه 'he keeps in-he/him' 'he corners/crams/blocks-he/him'; هَحيزي يه 'I will keep in/block/corner/cram-he/him'; جَحيزي يه 'came-kept in/cornered/blocked-he/him'; يَخيذي يه 'he takes-he/him'; هَخيذي يه 'I will take he/him'; جَخيذي يه 'came-took-he/him'; يَخيزي يه 'he swears at-he/

him'; هَخيزي يه 'I will swear at-he/him'; جَخيزي يه 'came-swore at-he him'; يَهيزي يه 'he rocks/swings-he/him' 'he tugs at-he/him'; جَهيزي يه 'prepare-he/him' 'came-swang/rocked-he/him' 'came-tugged-he/him'. It is equivalent to Jahaz (Num.21:23), Jahazah (Josh.13:18), Jahaziel (1Chr.12:4). Cp: yaḥaizee-yah, haḥaizee-yah, gaḥaizee-yah, yakhaivee-yah, hakhaivee-yah, gakhaivee-yah, yakhaizee-yah, hakhaizee-yah, gakhaizee-yah, yahaizee-yah, gahaizee-yah. (Ezra.10:15)

Jahaziah for the meanings of 'insulting' 'blocking/keeping in' 'a disgrace' denoting meaning the 'strange/foreign' wives and their children and the whole matter which in the narration is a great humiliation and disgrace. He is the son of **Tikvah** for its meaning of 'piety'.

Meshullam 'well ask them' 'what is/has been delivered/received' 'well, he survived' 'he/it did not survive/he/it are not intact' 'what did he/they take/what was taken' 'they did not take': they are examining the matter so things are being asked, women and children are being taken away from their husbands and families and therefore they are no longer 'intact' nor 'spared' some people are found to have 'taken' strange wives while others are not which is stated in the text so some families survive while others do not.

Shabbethai; šabbĕṯay; شَبّيطي 'lattice with rope' 'swipe/whip with rope or rope like object'. The story is about separating women and children from their husbands/fathers. The authors are imagining what it would entail: the separation by force, of which no one would go willingly had it been a real event, they would be swiping and beating at the women and children to leave their husbands and fathers. Take into account the region uses this action to dole out punishment to women when they cause a great offense or physical harm (a stick or rope is used in remote regions by the husband to discipline his wife in front of those she has offended/attacked (and in modern times they do not hurt them but swipe at the skirt of the dress (but it does hurt the woman and her husband emotionally), it is only a gesture of showing who is wrong and bringing around settlement but in ancient times it may have been more aggressive), or in modern Saudi Arabian cities where men and women are publicly and violently flogged for a variety of what Saudi Arabian law and authorities consider as crimes/sins; شَبّيثي 'to cling on to' 'stick to belief/opinion' and means to physically hold onto and not let go, something you do see even in the modern world where parents and children are being forcibly removed from each other, or just holding on to an opinion or stance. Both meanings are used, the women are being forced away from their families, the word-imagery is how a real event would happen if it were enforced. Cp: shabbeiṭay, shabbeifay. (Ezra.10:15)

Some of the characters mentioned for the meanings of their compound word-names: **Maaseiah** for its meaning of 'disobedience' 'disobeyed-he/him'; **Jarib** for its meanings of 'sent his wife away', 'he mixes and dilutes with water' referring to the children being 'mixed', 'goes abroad' 'a stranger/foreigner' 'strange' 'ruins'. (Ezra.10:18-19)

Elasah; 'elʿāśâ; ئَل عاصه 'the disobedient' 'the one who disobeyed him' 'the/the one who askew/crooked/bent/warped' 'the stick'. Cp: el-'aassah. (Ezra.10:22)

Kelaiah; qēlāyâ; قيل آيه 'said a verse/line' 'said 'ayyah'(expression of protest)' 'said don't you(dare)' 'said-he better not'; قيلاً يه 'said-he/him' 'it was said-he/him' 'I was told, him'. Cp: qeyl-aayah, qeylaa-yah. (Ezra.10:23)

Kelita; qĕlîṭā'; قيل يطاء 'said-he made smooth/untangled/straightforward'; غيليطاء 'made a mistake' 'shortchanged/conned'; خيليطاء 'mixed' 'mingled with'. Cp: qeil-eeṭaa, gheileeṭaa, kheileeṭaa. (Ezra.10:23)

Ramiah; ramyâ; رَميه 'a throw/throwing/a killing' 'wounded/struck' 'a wounding/striking' 'saw water' 'rotten/stinking'; رَم يه 'threw/thrown-he/him' 'killed-he/him' 'is rotten/stinking-he/him'. Cp: ramyah, ram-yah. (Ezra.10:25)

Jeziah; yizziyyâ, حِزّيه 'blocked/crammed/prevented him/them/it'; خِزّيه 'was ashamed/disgraced' 'swore at him/them'; هِزّيه 'snatched/tugged at him/it' 'swung him/it'; جِزّيه 'cut it into pieces(usually meat)' 'his reward' 'retribution/his retribution'; عِزّيه 'of pride-he/him' 'cherish/cherished him/her'. Cp: ḥizziyyah, khizziyyah, hizziyyah, gizziyyah, 'izziyyah. (Ezra.10:25)

Miamin; mîyāmîn; ميآمين 'right-handed' 'gone to the right(side)'; مي يآمين 'so/well, what is it?' 'so/well, who is it' 'so/well, gloats/counts and lists/says 'I gave'' 'water-of what/of who?'; ميجامين 'who came, who?'; مي جامين 'water from small clay jug'. The same as Mijamin (1Chr.24:9). Cp: meeyaameen, mee-yaameen, meegaameen, mee-gaameen. (Ezra.10:25)

Aziza; 'ăzîzā'; عيزيزاء 'cherished' 'of pride' 'raised in status'; عيبيباء 'overflowed/floated' 'stank/rotten and stinking'. Cp: 'aizeezaa, 'aibeebaa. (Ezra.10:27)

Zabbai; zabbay; زَبَّي 'penised/penetrated with penis' 'my penis' it can also be an insult if said to a person; صَبَّي 'pour' 'poured onto/into'; شَبَّي 'swelled and became stiff' (such as wood from water/head from cold' 'grew into young men/women'; سَبَّي 'left behind/left' 'let go' 'swore at/insulted' 'captured'. Cp: zabbay, ssabbay, shabbay, sabbay. (Ezra.10:28)

Athlai; 'atlay; عَذلَي 'handicapped'; عَطلَي 'handicapped limb(paralysed or not full use)' 'make stop working/break down' 'broken down'. Cp: 'avlay, 'aṭlay. (Ezra.10:28)

Sheal; šĕ'āl; شيئآل 'of taking/removing' 'taking/removing'; سيئآل 'asking/asked/questions' 'of asking/asked/questions' 'leaking/flowing'; صيئآل 'reaching/arriving' (also reaching in height) 'of reaching/arriving' 'connecting' 'of connecting'; زيئآل 'removing/of removing' 'naughty/of naughtiness' 'of disappearing'. Cp: sheiaal, seiaal, sseiaal, zeiaal. (Ezra.10:29)

Adna; 'adnā'; عَدناء 'we returned him/her/them/it' 'brought him/her/them/it back' 'counted' 'counted it' 'not yet' 'we have not yet' 'made enemy(ies)'. Equivalent to Adnah (1Chr.12:20). Cp: 'adnaa. (Ezra.10:30)

Chelal; kĕlāl; كيلآل 'weighed/measured out' 'gave retribution' 'all of it'; قيلآل 'made little/small amount' 'lessened' 'lessened from importance/severity' 'stayed with/at' 'spent time with/at' 'spent time' 'carries gossip' 'said a lot'; خيل آل 'imaginations of the' 'imagine-the' 'hallucination of the' 'hallucinate-the'; حيلآل 'made clean/pretty' 'made nice' 'circumcised' 'allowed/permissible' 'purified/cleansed' 'shed/shed-the' 'played tricks on/deceived' 'pretended to be sweet(to get something)' 'undressed' 'shed'; حيل آل 'tricks of the' 'tricks-the' 'undressed-the' 'shed-the'. Cp: keilaal, qeilaal, kheil-aal, ḥeilaal, ḥeil-aal. (Ezra.10:30)

Ishijah; yiššiyâ, yiššîyâ; يِشّيعه ، يِشّعه 'pulls thread out of/leaves crumpled or pulled/scarred' 'ruins by pulling strands/strings out of' 'ruins by scarring'; يِشّي يه ، يِشّ يه 'he wants her/him/it'; يِسّعه 'he wanders/wanders around/goes/sees travels' 'it fits him/it'; يِسّيعه 'he wanders aimlessly' 'he wanders around performing debauchery' 'he becomes debauched/he performs debauchery/promiscuity'; يِسّي يه ، يِسّيه 'he/it does bad towards him' 'he makes it smooth/settled/right' 'he does/makes it' 'he does bad-he/him'; يِصّيّح ، يِصّييح 'he shouts'; يِسّيّح ، يِسّييح 'he goes walking and seeking' 'melts and leaks'; هِسّ/هِسّي يه 'press on-he/him/it'; هِسّيّه ، هِسّييه 'pressed on it/him'; جِسّ/جِسّي يه 'sit-he/him' 'leave it alone-he/him'; عِسّ/عِسّي يه/يه 'give cold bread-he/him' 'make sounds to make animal come nearer' (e.g. 'tut-tut' to a cat, 'qss' to a dog, making a tongue-clicking sound for a cow); عِسّيه ، عِسّييه 'his cold bread' 'cold bread-he/him' 'broke/ate bread'. Similar to Ishiah, Ishui, Josiah, Isaiah.Cp: yishi'h, yishee'h, yishi-yah, yishee-yah, yissi'h, yissee'h, yissiyah, yissee-yah, yissiyḥ, yisseeyḥ, yissiyḥ, yisseeyaḥ, hissi-yah, hissee-yah, gissi-yah, gissee-yah, 'issi-yah, 'issee-yah, 'issiyah, 'isseeyah. (Ezra.10:31)

Shimeon the same as Simeon (Gen.29:33). (Ezra.10:31)

Mattenai; mattĕnay; مَتّينَي 'they died' 'of dying'; مَثّينَي 'they wiped away urine/sperm' 'of wiping away urine/sperm'; مَطّينَي 'stretch them/they are stretched' 'stretch/of stretching' 'what is this tinning/clanging noise'; مَدّينَي 'full/inflamed with pus' 'they extended/reached out' 'lay down and stretched out' 'of extending/reaching out' 'what are these lowly/bowed/bent' 'what are these guilted'. Cp: matteinay, maffeinay, maṭṭeinay, maddeinay. (Ezra.10:33)

Mattathah; mattattā; مَتّتّه 'made it die' 'seemed or pretended to die'; مَثّثّه ، مَثّثه 'she wiped away his urine/sperm' 'he/they wiped away urine/sperm' and refers to when urine/sperm is only wiped away instead of also washing genitals; مَدّدّه 'made her/him/it lie down' 'laid it down' 'he lay down' 'extended it' 'reached into/for it' 'pus formed in it' 'inked it'; مَطّطه 'he/she/it/they stretched' 'he stretched it' 'made it over-stretched(by using/touching or stretching too much)'; مَضّضه 'rinsed his/its mouth' 'a type of tree' 'made mark/sign on a document' 'complete/fulfilled it' 'passed on/moved through/left' Cp: mattattah, maffattah, maffaffah, maddaddah, maṭṭaṭṭah, madhadhah. (Ezra.10:33)

Jeremai; yĕrēmay; ييريمَي 'he throws' 'he kills' 'he sees water'; جيريمَي 'came-threw'; هيريمَي 'he will throw around/throw' 'he has thrown' 'angry unkind speech/grumpy' 'told off like pulling guts out'; عيريمَي 'abandoned/stranded in the wilderness' 'of abandoning in the wilderness'; حيريمَي 'prohibited for them/on them' 'deprived them' 'of depriving' 'rotten/stinking/bad' 'became sacred'. Cp: yeireymay, geireymay, heireymay, ḥeireymay. (Ezer.10:33)

Maadai; ma'ăday; مَعيدَي 'of enmity towards' 'of infecting' 'prominent/protuberant'; مَغيدَي 'had lunch/feeding/serving lunch' 'frustrating/of frustration' 'has swollen glands' the latter can be literal or figurative meaning 'frustrated'; مَعيضَي 'with sore muscles' 'recompensed/of recompense'; مَغيضَي 'in a suppressed rage' 'provoking another causing him/her to suppress rage' 'of provoking'. Cp: ma'aiday, maghaiday, ma'aidhay, maghaidhay. (Ezra.10:34)

Uel; 'û'ēl; نُئِل 'and-the' 'oh, the' 'or the' 'wailing/moaning/complaining' 'the first'; عُئِل 'will they-the' 'they will-the' 'teach/learn and remember/be warned-the' 'has boys' 'boys of' 'howling'. Cp: u-ill, 'u-ill. (Ezra.10:34)

Bedeiah; bēḏēyâ; بيدي يه 'brought/took out-he/him' 'with hands-he/him'; بيديه 'by/with my hands' 'went/came out' 'took/brought out'. Cp: beydei-yah, beydeiyah. (Ezra.10:35)

Chelluh; kēlûhî; كيلُهي 'of measuring/weighing' 'so he would be distracted' 'try and distract him/her'; كيلُ هي 'measure/weigh for her' 'measure-she is/her' 'retribution against-she is/her'; كي لُهي 'like that-for her'; قيلُ هي 'they said-her/she is' 'said-she is/her' 'spend time-her/she is'; قيلُهي 'of sanitising/purifying on fire coals/heat' 'of sanitising/purifying'; خيلُهي ، خيلُ هي 'of imagining/hallucinating' 'imagine-her/she is' 'leave her(as in depart)' 'leave her alone/let her be(as in stop bothering)' 'leave-her' 'leave some-her/she is' 'allow her'; حيلُهي ، حيلُ هي 'of undressing' 'undressed-her/she is' 'shed-her/it' 'beat until skin peels off/beat severely-her/she' 'is pretty' 'is pretty-she/she is' 'of sweet nature' 'sweet' 'sweet-she is/her' 'of tricks/deceit' 'of tricks/deceit-she/her' 'of circumcising/circumcised' 'circumcised-her/she is' 'clean and pure/purified/cleansed' 'clean and pure-she is/her'. Cp: keiluhee, keilu-hee, kei-luhee, qeilu-hee, qeiluhee, <u>kh</u>eiluhee, <u>kh</u>eilu-hee, ḥeiluhee, ḥeilu-hee. (Ezra.10:35)

Vaniah; wanyâ; وَنيه 'and me' 'what about me?'; وَن يه 'moaned/groaned/whimpered-he/him'. Cp: wan-yah, wan-yah. (Ezra.10:36)

Jaasau; ya'ăśû; يَعيصُ 'he/they disobey' 'he/they make difficult' 'he/they become askew/bent/crooked' 'he/they use/have sticks'. Cp: ya'ai<u>ss</u>u. (Ezra.10:37)

Machnadebai; ma<u>k</u>na<u>d</u>ēḇay; مَكندَيبَي 'how much/how he/they wailed in grief' 'I/he/they will not/did not wail in grief'; مَقنَديبي 'what is there/what is the matter for wailing in grief?' 'what caused them to wail in grief?' 'how much they wailed in grief'; مَكنَضيبَي 'well, like protruding teeth/jaw'; مَقنَضيبَي 'what is there-protruding teeth/jaw' 'what is the matter-protruding teeth/jaw' 'what has become protruding teeth/jaw'. Cp: maknadeibay, maqnadeibay, makna<u>dh</u>eibay, maqna<u>dh</u>eibay. (Ezra.10:40)

Shashai; šāšāy; شاشاي 'many things and wonderful things' 'many things' 'wonderful things' 'important things' 'many matters, important matters' 'puzzling/serious matters' usually used to imply grandeur and opulence, 'wanted something'; ساساي 'bad did bad' 'evil did evil' 'did great bad' 'bad-bad/bad-evil/evil-evil/offense-offended'; شاساي 'wanted something' 'wanted something done' 'matter-bad/evil/offense/offensive'; ساشاي do/did-something' 'offend/evil/bad-matter/thing' 'bad/offensive-wanted' 'did something'. Cp: <u>sh</u>aa<u>sh</u>aay, saasaay, <u>sh</u>aasaay, saa<u>sh</u>aay. (Ezra.10:40)

Sharai; šārāy; شارآي 'bought' 'of evil'; سارآي 'they left early' 'made them leave early' 'hangs around women' 'flirts/talks a lot with women'. Cp: <u>sh</u>aaraay, saaraay. (Ezra.10:40)

Zebina; zēḇînā'; زيبيناء 'below navel to above crotch' 'they showed their lower bellies'; زي بيناء 'like us/like what happened to us' 'like our children' 'like a building' 'like he built'; ذي بيناء 'she is one of us' 'she has mothered children' 'they/she built'; سيبيناء 'they left us' 'leave us'. Cp: zeibeenaa, zei-beenaa, vei-beenaa, seibeenaa. (Ezra.10:43)

Jadau; yadday, yaddô, yiddō'; يَدّي 'my hand'; يَدُّ 'a hand'; هَدّي ، هَدُّ ، هِدّوء 'sing/sang/are singing wedding song' 'give/gave/are giving present(s)' 'demolish/they demolished/of demolishing' 'serenity/quiet'; جَدّي ، جَدّ 'my grandfather' 'grandfather' 'find' 'new/renew'; جِدّوء 'find'; عَدّي 'count' 'made enemy' 'infected'; عَدّ 'they counted' 'they made enmity' 'they infected'; عِدّوء 'count/of counting' 'enemy' 'makes enemies' 'infects'; حَدّي 'sharp/sharpen it' 'to my point/border' 'my border'; حَدّ 'is sharp' 'they sharpened' 'they drew border/made borders'; حِدّوء 'of sharpness/is sharp' 'of sharpening'; خَدّي 'my cheek(s)'; خَدّ 'a cheek'; خِدّوء 'of cheeks' 'of resting face on cheek(miserable or worried). Cp: yadday, yaddo, hadday, haddo, hiddoo, gadday, gaddo, giddoo, 'adday, 'addo, 'iddoo, ḥadday, ḥaddo, ḥiddoo, <u>kh</u>adday, <u>kh</u>addo, <u>kh</u>iddoo. (Ezra.10:43)

Nehemiah

Nehemia as earlier in (Ezra.2:2) still means 'sighing loudly-he him' it means a person forcing a sigh to be noticed by others i.e. not a natural sigh, but a pretentious sigh/huff/puff to get attention, 'winded/struck until wind forced out-he/him' 'punctured and wind escaping-he/him'. The story narrates that he was sad, especially because he had been mourning and weeping over what he had heard, to the extent this is the first time the king has seen him sad 'And I took up the wine...Now I had not been *beforetime* sad in his presence.' It is stressed the king notices his sadness and that he is not ill, so a sad face, maybe sighing too which is his name 'Wherefore the king said unto me, Why *is* thy countenance sad, seeing thou *art* not sick? this *is* nothing *else* but sorrow of the heart.' When someone is feeling that much sadness, they will sigh 'why should not my countenance be sad.' It also needs to be taken into account that Nehemia makes clear at Neh.1:11, that he intends to make a request of the king, which he is worried about. He goes to the king, but does not want to broach the subject himself so he wears a sad face, but just in case the king does not notice he lets out a sigh every now and then to catch the king's attention which leads to the king probing the matter out of Nehemiah. (Neh.1; 2:1-8)

Hachaliah; ḥăkalyâ; هيخَليه 'he will let him'. His surname reflects the king will allow him to leave the king's service to pursue rebuilding Jerusalem; Nehemia has been allowed by God (when he asked to help him get permission from the king) and allowed by the king to leave. The word is similar to Hachilah (1Sam.21;23), but the context of Nehemiah's story and that of Jonathan/David's story (where Hachaliah/Hachilah comes in) anchors the words to specific meanings according to the different stories. Cp: haikhalyah. (Neh.1:1, 11; 2:6)

Chisleu; kislēw; غِسليو 'they washed' and it refers to Nehemia crying for a long period of time and indicates lots of tears, it also refers to the repent and prayer to God, in effect to 'washing away sins'. '...when I heard these words, that I sat down and wept, and mourned certain days, and fasted, and prayed before the God of heaven.'. Cp: ghisleyw. (Neh.1)

Shushan; šušan; شوشَن 'something important' 'things and important things' 'many things and wonderful things' 'things, important things' 'things, many things' 'things, amazing/wonderful things' 'puzzling matters/serious matters' 'caused a commotion' and this phrase is based on the word (shee/شيئ/شي) 'thing/matter/important/want(ed)' and how it is used when doubled such as 'shee wa shaan' شي وشان, 'showshaan' شوشان, 'shee wa ashyaa' شي واشياء, and there are many different variations, but they all carry some and sometimes all the meanings that a matter or what is being referred to is important, or amazing, or in great amounts/abundance, richness, greatness, etc. Nehemia's story, like Ezra, revolves around an important topic where each one (respectively in the stories) is given the lead role of great importance: leading people to freedom, a rebuilding or magnifying of God's house or Jerusalem, being put in charge of great treasures and a great number of people the lead character has to safely deliver to Jerusalem, bringing order to a chaotic situation, doing it for God and for the people, dealing with matters important in the story. It is equivalent to Shisha (1Kgs.4:3), Sheshan (1Chr.2:31), Shavsha (1Chr.18:16), Shashai Ezra.10:40). Cp: shushan. (Neh.1:1)

Nisan; nîsān; نيسآن 'forgot/forgotten' 'comforted' the latter is when a person is upset or lonely, the verb keeping the person company, comforting and/or distracting them from the situation is called (ns/نس) from the word which means 'people' (ns/نس): it is other people/person who comfort the other by being there, talking, distracting by entertainment or chatting, or just by being there physically, depending on the situation. This month-name has been used for what its meaning can be made in the story: it is the king who comforts Nehemia in his sadness. Although Biblical scholars state it (and other months) as the 'Hebrew calendar' they ignore it is also the Arabic calendar, and specifically an agricultural calendar in rural regions. Cp: neesaan. (Neh.2:1)

Although scholars attempt to use these stories as fact in determining 'timelines' of their occurrence and attempting to tie them into real events/periods and actual civilisations that existed, both Ezra and Nehemia stories contradict each other in events and timeline. They both claim to do the same thing and both stories claim the lead character as the 'person-in-charge' who brings around these events. Ezra claims to arrive with the house already rebuilt, just to 'beautify it' whereas Nehemia's story includes the rebuilding needing timber and other materials. They both use the same characters as leaving with each different lead-character/story, Ezra mentions Nehemia as one of them. There is a reason why these fictional stories were created, but scholars have missed this completely as they tunnel-down attempting to prove a non-existent event and characters to present fictional stories as corroborating calendar dates.

Sanballat; sanballaṭ; سَنبَلّت 'being foolish' 'being droopy/hanging around uselessly' and it comes from the word (sblh/سبله) 'sheep's tail' which also comes from the word (sbl/سبل) 'let down/hangs down/just flops or hangs there'. When someone is walking strangely, his body, e.g. arms drooping or swaying slowly, or if he/she is purposely behaving stupid—they say (sanbal/yitsanbal) if male, or (sanballat/titsanbal) if female. The names of all three characters who oppose Nehemiah is a return to giving insulting names to those who are the antagonists in the story, as well as giving them a foreign 'ethnicity' even if in real life the audience and authors of these stories were of one ethnicity (with different religions). Racism, which is rife in the Bible, was not the intention of the authors in these stories (this is not a justification of the racism in the story, but I am presenting it objectively to understand why such racism was in these stories), but there is a reason why they present it as such; one of the reasons is the names created and the created 'ethnicities' given serve the method and purpose of the Biblical stories which allow the stories to flow with its wordplay and puns, make it funny and enjoyable to its original audiences who are aware of its fictionality and know these names do not address any real people but are fictional characters. There is another important reason which concerned later editors/authors of these stories, but this will be discussed elsewhere in the book.

It is more likey that شَنبَلّت is made up of: the first part of the compound word (san/shan/شَن) is 'fertile animals/sexually excited/ready to conceive/copulated/ready to copulate' followed by the second word (bal-lat/بَلّت) meanings 'she afflicted us/she soaked us' as the marriage from a 'foreigner' is portrayed negatively, as a pollution, in the Biblical stories, and also possibly 'poured or flowed out of/into-she soaked us/afflicted us' 'filter/filter impurities-she soaked us/afflicted us'. 'Sanballat' in all its meanings are describing a female, which makes sense when the narration later in the story has Eliashib, a high priest, has a grandson married to Sanballat's daughter—this allows and explains how he can be both 'foreigner' and be in a place/position which, according to the story, a foreigner would not even be allowed to go anywhere near, and also explains the meanings of his compound-word name. Cp: sanballat, <u>sh</u>anballat.

Sanballat is a Horonite; ḥōrōnî; هوروني 'drove me away/chased me away (with words)' 'of driving away/of chasing away (with words); خوروني 'drove me away/chased me away (with violence)' 'of driving away/chasing away(with violence)' 'of collapsing'. And up until the end of Chapter 2, it is not Sanballat 'driving away' Nehemiah, but Nehemiah reflects this meaning towards Sanballat when he tells them they will not be allowed to participate and have no right to, or in the rebuilding, of Jerusalem '…buy ye have no portion, nor right, nor memorial in Jerusalem.'. Cp: hooroonee, <u>kh</u>ooroonee. (Neh.2:10, 19-20)

Geshem; gešem; جِشِم 'took a hard bite'; قِشِم 'took a small bite' 'bit corner off'; قِسِم 'divided' 'swore an oath' 'fate'; and all meanings indicate these three characters in the story are meant to have wanted to be part of what Nehemia is doing but Nehemia responds he will not let them have any 'portion' or 'right' to it or even 'memorial'. It is equivalent to Gershom (Exod.2:22; 4:24-26), Jeshimon (Num.21:20). He is 'Arabian' for its meanings of: 'he will-my god/parent/teacher' 'will he-my god/parent/teacher' '(of)learn and remember/beware/be warned-teacher/discipliner/parent/god/master/the grower/anyone who brings someone up or teaches them/grows them (children/animals/plants/etc.)/grew fast and(or) well' 'is mixed and diluted with water' 'the god/parent/teacher' 'is my god/parent/teacher' 'he is-my god/parent/teacher' 'is he/which-my god/parent/teacher?' 'the (or of) mixed and diluted with water' 'mixed and diluted with water' 'the (or of) teacher(ing)/discipliner(ing)/parent/god/grower/anyone who brings someone or something up or teaches them/grows them' as the story revolves around making something great and to its best, also about 'mixed races' ('mixed and diluted with water'), and 'Arabian' in this character name also reflects Nehemia will be wary of them. Cp: ge<u>sh</u>em, qe<u>sh</u>em, qesem. (Neh.2:19)

The word-names used in Neh.3 are for at least one of its meanings which is reflected in the work they are portrayed as doing in the story:

Eliashib 'the one who leave/cuts off relations, activities, actions' 'the one who pours onto/into' so Eliashib is the first to stop his usual routine and builds, and his work reaches 'even unto the tower of Meah' Meah; mē'āh, mē'â; ميئاه ، ميئه 'water' 'his water' 'a hundred'. So he is connected by 'pouring' and working to the tower of 'water'. He also works 'unto the tower of Hananeel'. Cp: mey-aah, mey-ah. (Neh.3:1)

Hananeel; ḥănan'ēl; هَنعن ئِل ، هينعن ئِل 'we/I will direct words/speech at the' 'I/we will mean-the' 'he will direct words/speech at the' 'he will mean-the' and it describes when a person is hinting at with a message/warning/insult directed at someone in particular within hearing range, even at close proximity, while actually talking directly to someone else—it is hinting/delivering the message indirectly; حَنَن ئِل ، حينَن ئِل

'hums/humming sound-the' 'wears/applies henna-the' 'felt affection-the'; هَنَن ئِل ، هينَن ئِل 'satisfaction to/satisfied-the' 'give plenty-the'. In this part of the story it is about the rebuilding of the sheep gate and the 'satisfied/gave plenty' in the naming of the towers is because the sheep gate will contain the livestock of which the priests will present as all kinds of offerings and sacrifices, they will also get to eat from too. The passage does not read that the 'tower of Meah' and 'tower of Hananeel' were rebuilt, only the sheep gate in relation to Eliashib is rebuilt and sanctified up to these towers, i.e. the sheep gate is extensive because of the great numbers of animals it will enclose. Cp: han'n-ill, hain'n-ill, ḥanan-ill, ḥainan-ill, hanan-ill hainan-ill. (Neh.3:1)

Jericho: 'came-rested/relaxation/take a break' 'came-loosened' as they are assisting Hananeel and the others. **Zaccur** for: 'peep between gaps' 'take quick glances (between hiding behind cover)' 'top-up/fill/fill gap(s)', any building of walls as in the culture and region includes filling in the gaps after walls are built/doors windows installed which requires placing a stone between the gaps. **Immer** for: 'of giving orders' 'builder' self-explanatory. (Neh.3:2)

Hassenaah; hassĕnā'â; هَسّيناآئه 'we/I will straighten/align/make straight' 'here are the straighteners'; حَصّيناآئه 'fortified it' 'strengthened it' 'protected it'; حَسّيناآئه 'make/made it better'; هَصّيناآعه 'we/I will create it' 'look, they made/created it' 'here are the makers/creators'. In building, things have to be straight/aligned, builders create structures. It emphasises the meaning of 'fortify/protect' by 'who *also* laid the beams thereof, and set up the doors thereof, the locks thereof, and the bars thereof.'. It is equivalent to Hasenuah and Senaah. Cp: hasseinaa-ah, ḥas̲s̲einaa-ah, ḥasseinaa-ah, has̲s̲einaa'ah. (Neh.3:3)

The assistants in this work are **Meremoth** for: 'the throwing of' 'saw-handed/extended'; **Urijah** 'showed him' 'show him' (as in shown what to do/how to work/what to make it like); he is son of **Koz** for: 'large rock' as rocks would be removed and also rocks are broken into building stones, 'cut' as materials will need to be cut to size, 'burnt/burning smell' as there are substances burnt to fend off 'demons/spirits' when building a new house or when entering a long abandoned building/structure. Both Meremoth and Koz which respectively mean 'dreamt-death' 'tell a story' may be reminders to the audience that the narration is fictional.

Meshullam for 'what did he carry/take' and he is son of **Berechiah**: 'knelt-he/him' 'I will prop/lean it/him against' 'I will loosen him/it' and these are actions in building, but also 'underground water cisterns-he/him' which need to be built, but also because they are assisting in the building of 'the fish gate'. He is also the son of Meshezabeel; mĕšêzab̲'ēl; ميشيذب ئِل 'is trimmed-the'; ميشيزَ بئِل 'used large sickle-with the'. Cp: meis̲h̲eyvab-ill, meis̲h̲eyza-bill. **Zadok** for its meaning of 'fished you/your fish' and he is son of **Baana** for: 'with particularity/choosiness' 'with close inspection'. (Neh.3:4)

Tekoites for: 'of piety' as the verse narrates this work is for God, but also because they are repairing the fish gate and the narration tells some of the Tekoites would not work denoting the meanings: 'with open mouth' as in a person who physically has his mouth open such as daydreaming or as in slow/stupid, 'stinks' because they are dealing with a fish gate. (Neh.3:5)

The old gate is being repaired by **Jehoiada** for: 'he who-is calling/he calls' 'he who is-leaving/saying farewell' 'he who is-depositing/leaving something in the care of' and he is the son of **Paseah**: 'made spacious' 'gives permission(to do/go/leave)' both names indicate people would come and go from this gate. **Meshullam** for the same reasons above of Neh.3:4; this character is the son of Besodeiah; bĕsôd̲yâ; بيصُديه ، بيصُد يه 'he/they will close the door' and (s̲s̲d/صد) in relation to a door it means to close it without locking it, 'he/they will block/absorb attack' 'he/they will block/prevent it' 'he/thy will block/prevent-he/him/it' and the latter meanings are supported by mention of bars and locks. It can also mean 'he/they will fish'. Cp: beis̲s̲odyah, beis̲s̲od-yah. (Neh.3:6)

Melatiah; mĕlaṭyâ; ميلَطيه ، ميلَط يه 'flat stones/rocks' 'sides stuck together/squished against each other' 'flat stone-he/him' 'squeezed/stuck sides together-he/him' 'pressed against something firm-he/him' 'became saggy from too much squeezing-he/him' 'made it stick'. It is equivalent to Lot (Gen.11:27; 19:1-10), Lotan (Gen.36:20). It reflects stones used in building and also making sides or materials to stick together/be pressed against each other. He is a **Gibeonite** for its meanings of 'bring/fetch/gather-help' as many people are helping repair this. Cp: meylaṭyah, meylaṭ-yah. (Neh.3:7)

Jadon; yād̲ôn; يآدُن 'a hand/hands' 'he bows/bends/lowers his head' and does suit the '**Meronothite**' given him as it means 'of not seeing' 'stubborn' 'of stubbornness' when this area name was given, it was to someone in charge of donkeys, this reflects a person who carrying heavy rocks/loads on his shoulders (which is normal work for labourers). Cp: yaadon. (Neh.3:7)

Mizpah is used for: 'pouring place/pouring/pouring vessel' 'marker', and is a stone set on a piece of land to demark whose land starts/ends and where, when more than one person partially owns parts of the same piece of land. The narration mentions the work reaching 'unto the throne of the governor on this side of the river.'. (Neh.3:7)

Uzziel for its meanings: 'became wooden/stiff-the' 'fiddle it/shift it/move it in all directions(to make it right or fit)-the' 'removed/be removed/wiped out/be wiped out' and still refers to the repairing of the old gates, mentioning 'goldsmiths' indicates they are meant to be working with items/materials/techniques which are finnicky. He is the son of Harhaiah; ḥarhăyâ; هَرهييه ، هَرهي يه 'it is falling apart' 'falling apart-he/him' and still refers to the repair of the old gate; حَرهييه ، حَرهي يه 'made fire/is hot-come on' 'of making fire/making hot-he/him' which a goldsmith would do. Cp: harhaiyah, harhai-yah, ḥarhaiyah, ḥar-hai-yah. (Neh.3:8)

Hananiah (1Chr.3:19) has been used for its meaning 'satisfaction to/satisfied-him/he' 'give plenty-he/him' as they repair a large part of a wall. (Neh.3:8)

Rephaiah for: 'lifted/raised-he/him' 'picked up and put away/tidied-he/him'. He is son of **Hur** for: 'fall apart' 'fall down/collapse'. (Neh.3:9)

Jedaiah for: 'he deposits/leaves in the care of-he/him' 'they place/set-he/him' 'his hands' 'my hands' 'demolished-he/him' 'demolished it' 'remove by pulling off'. He is son of: Harumaph; ḥārûmap; هيرُمَف ، هيرُمَب 'he/it will be thrown into' 'he/it will be thrown by' 'fell to pieces in it' 'fell to pieces by' ; خيرُمَف ، خيرُمَب 'collapsed into' 'collapsed by' 'lots in' 'lots by' ; كيرُمَب ، كيرُمَف 'heaped by' 'heaped in' 'large gravel by' 'large gravel in' (different kinds of gravel are used for different parts of the building process in real life). Cp: hairumaph, hairumab, khairumaph, khairumab, kairumaph, kairumab. (Neh.3:10)

Hattush for: 'placed/set it/you' 'of leaving some/of departing/of setting/placing' 'scribbled/wrote' 'drew lines/scribbles' and he is son of Hashabniah; ḥăšabněyâ; حيشَبني يه 'carried on waist/carried me on his waist-he/him' 'of carrying on waist-he/him' 'folded and tucked up his clothes into waist-he/him' (which is what men and women do with their clothes when working to avoid being soiled, burnt or tripping), 'of tucking clothes into waist-he/him'; خيشَبني يه 'supplied me with timber-he/him' 'of supplying timber-he/him' 'set ceiling beams-he/him' 'of setting ceiling beams-he/him'; حيسَبني يه 'settled payments with me-he/him' 'settled scores with me-he/him' 'calculated with/for me-he/him' 'he counted me part of it/counted on me-he/him' 'he thought I was him' 'punished me/gave me what I deserved-he/him'. Cp: ḥaishabnei-yah, khaishabnei-yah, ḥaisabnei-yah. (Neh.3:10)

Malchijah for: 'cover with slimy substance-he/him' and can be any clean substance such as henna, etc, or dirty substance such as mud, etc., 'roll it/him in slimy substance' 'it is slimy/dirty and slimy/soiled' and he is son of **Harim**; 'rotten/rotting/stinking/off'. **Hashub**; same as in 1Chr.9:14: حَشُب 'clothes folded and tucked into waist' 'carried on waist'; خَشَب 'timber/wood' 'set beams in ceiling' 'collected/supplied timber'. He is son of **Pahath-moab** which at Ezra.2:6 had many possibilities without a story surrounding it, but in this verse of Neh.3 it has been anchored by its context to mean: 'lit/lit by scratching surface (similar to how match or flint used to create spark/flame)-is thirsty' as they are repairing 'the tower of the furnaces which would include coal, ash and soot, 'lost voice-is thirsty'' 'causes sore throat-is thirsty' for same reason, 'scrammed/scratched/a scram/scratch mark-is thirsty' as the mess would need to be cleaned away, 'with his sister/with sister of-is thirsty' as the verse that follows in Neh.3:12 has 'the daughters' of **Shallum** working with him. Cp: phakhaṭ-moghab, baḥaṭ-moghab, bakhat-moghab. (Neh.3:11)

Shallum for: 'took' 'of taking' 'I will gather'. He is son of Ḥalohesh; hallôḥēš; هَلُّهيش 'she is here' and refers to the daughters there working alongside the men; حَلّ حيش 'they undressed/shed-rolled up their sleeves' and refers to the dirty work of repairing the tower of furnaces; خَلُهيش 'leaver her/it be' 'leave her/it there' 'allow her'. Cp: halloheysh, ḥallo-ḥeysh, khalloheysh. (Neh.3:12)

Hanun for 'humiliated/disgraced' 'soaked in', and he is son of **Zanoah** for: 'bastard' 'smelt bad(like blood/raw eggs)' 'soaked in' it reflects as everything was in disrepair the contents of the dung gate had ended up in the valley so they have been given humiliating character names to reflect what it would be like had it been real. (Neh.3:13)

Malchiah is used again for: 'cover with slimy substance-he/him' and can be any clean substance such as henna, etc, or dirty substance such as mud, etc., 'roll it/him in slimy substance' 'it is slimy/dirty/it is slimy/soiled' and he is son of **Rechab**: 'knees' 'necks' 'keep eye on' 'ride/mount'. It denotes they are responsible for repairing the dung gate which is the verb (Malchiah) of when a person is handling cow dung (cleaning cow stable) especially if fresh or wet, and of handling of any substance of wet/thick/slimy texture which is usually repulsive.

He is ruler of Beth-haccerem; bêṯ-hakkerem; بيت هَخِّر هم/ام 'it will/it will happen-he will make them shit/ he will make shit-the'; 'it will/it will happen-he will chase them away (with violence)'; بيت حَقِّر هم/ام 'he will despise them/the' 'it will(happen)-denigrate-them/the'. It is definitely the meaning of excrement as it is related to the 'dung gate'. Cp: beyt-hakher-hum/um, beyt-ḥaqqer-hum/um. (Neh.3:14)

Shallun; šallûn; شَلُّن 'took' 'small waterfall'; سَلُّن 'leaked' 'small river/temporary river after rain' 'distracted/ entertained/comforted' 'asked'; the same as Shallum. For: 'small waterfall' 'small river/temporary river after rain' 'leaked' because they are dealing with 'the gate of the fountain' and 'the wall of the pool'. For the same reasons the other names in this line are related to water and pool and blocking water from escaping. Cp: shallun, sallun. He is son of Col-hozeh: kol-ḥōzeh; كول حوزه ، قول حوزه 'all of it-block/restrain/ corner/cram it' 'say-restrain/block/corner/cram it' and refers to blocking water or making repairs that allow this water to be blocked to have a fountain and pool; قول حوسِه ، كول حوسه 'say-a well/his well' 'every well' and is still water related. He is made ruler of part of **Mizpah** for: 'body of water/pool of water' 'pouring place/pouring/pouring vessel' (as in 1Sam.7). Cp: kool-ḥoozeh, qool-ḥoozeh, qool-ḥooseh, kool-ḥooseh. (Neh.3:15)

Siloah; šilōaḥ; سِلوَه ، سيلوه 'small flowing river' a diminutive of a temporary river which only runs during and after heavy rain occurs, 'it flowed/leaked'. It is reflected in the repairing of 'the wall of the pool'. It is equivalent to Silla (2Kgs.12:18-20). Cp: silooah, sylooah. **Nehemiah** is used here for its meaning of: 'punctured and wind escaping-he/him' as it implies the fountain, pool and its walls are in disrepair and water is escaping. He is son of Azbuk; 'azbûq; نَذْبُق 'if it made water flowing sound/glugging sound' sound of water passing through a narrow place; نَشْبُق 'pad/place rags to absorb'. Both words are reflected in the story (Nehemia's 'punctured and wind escaping') and Azbuq's 'sound of water glugging out/padding a flow with rags' as this character is repairing a place related to a fountain, pool, waterway. Cp: avbuq, ashbuq. (Neh.3:15)

Bavai; bawway; بَوَّي 'will stay'; بَذّي 'with this(one)/with her'. Cp: bawway, bavvay. (Neh.3:18)

Baruch; bārûḵ; بآرُك 'kneeling' 'blessed' 'lasted long' 'underground water cistern' 'I will prop/lean against'; بآرُخ 'I will loosen/be lenient'; بآرُق 'sulking in a mood' 'struck by lightning'; بآرُح 'I will go/leave' 'pull up water' 'level/clear/tidy'. Cp: baaruk, baarukh, baaruq, baaruḥ. (Neh.3:20)

Ananiah; 'ănanyâ; عينَن يه 'hinted speech at-he/him' 'made suffer-he/him'; غينَن يه 'sang-he/him' 'made 'ghn' noise-he/him' 'was enriched/no longer needed-he/him'. Cp: 'ainan-yah, ghainan-yah. (Neh.3:23)

Palal; pālāl; بآلآل 'wet/soaked' 'became old/faded' 'had mind/patience' 'was afflicted with many afflictions'; فآلآل 'picked lice out of hair' 'went through/over thoroughly' 'shook out of hair/clothes, etc.' 'said something(negative) and it happened/said bad omen'; ضآلآل 'shaded/sat or stood in shade/rested in shade' 'wore a hat(to shade from sun)' 'misled'. Cp: baalaal, phaalaal, dhaalaal. (Neh.3:25)

Uzai; 'ûzay; عُزَي 'cherished' 'grieved' 'guy'; عُذَي 'protected' 'protection chant/spell/prayer'; نُذَي 'was harmed' 'of harming'. Cp: 'uzay, 'uvay, uvay. (Neh.3:25)

Zalaph; ṣālāp; زآلآف 'took long peels/patches off' 'long peels/patches'; صآلآف 'compacted soil' a loose type of sandy/grainy soil; صآلآب 'made compact and smooth' 'slabs/made slabs of' 'mud packed land(from too much rain or drought where soil becomes compact and appears to be one slab)'. Cp: zaalaaph, ssaalaaph, ssaalaab. (Neh.3:30)

Miphkad; mipqād; مِفخاط 'something that ignites by scratching(the way a match does)' 'a scratching alight'; مِفقاد 'small fire between stone structure' 'longing for/missing' 'checking everything is there'. The meanings of igniting and small fire for creating something on is related to character being a goldsmith's son. Cp: miph*kh*aaṭ, miphqaad. (Neh.3:31)

Gashmu; gašmû; جَشْمُ 'took a hard bite' 'a hard bite'; قَشْمُ 'took a small bite' 'a small bite/bit(of something)' 'bit corner off'; قَسْمُ 'divided' 'swore an oath' 'a promise/oath' 'fate'. Cp: gashmu, qashmu, qasmu. (Neh.6:6)

Shemaiah was used to depict 'listened-he/him' 'made listen-he/him' as Nehemiah is made to listen to what this character says as he has visited this character's house. He is son of **Delaiah** for its meanings 'shade him' as the story repeats he is 'shut up' and wants to close all the doors in the temple, 'push/pedal from place to place (things or oneself)-him/he' 'mislead-he/him' as he attempts to convince Nehemiah to go with him to the temple and the story narrates he was trying to deceive Nehemiah to go there. He is son of **Mehetabeel** for its meaning of 'scalded with' 'slouched or hands flapping when walks' 'moving slowly' 'depressed/

behaving depressed' because the character is 'shut up' in his house and is trying to invoke fear into Nehemiah. **Noadiah** is chosen as the prophetess name to depict a negative character who attempts to deceive Nehemiah for its meaning of 'we make enemy him/her/them' 'we transgress against him/her/them'. (Neh.6:10-14)

Elul; 'ĕlûl; نَيْلَل 'made sounds of pain' the word people say when warning a child of something that will hurt them, this is relayed in the story that the enemies are hurt by Nehemiah's success in rebuilding the wall. It is also a month in the Arabic agricultural year; غيلل 'ear inflammation' 'of rushing rivers/streams' 'carried deep hatred' 'hated intensely/despised/dug deep/stabbed deep' (and indicate action/revenge will occur out of the hatred/feelings) and is reflected in the antagonists upset about the wall completion. Cp: eilul, <u>gh</u>eilul. (Neh.6:15)

Judah is used in Neh.6 for its meaning of 'he is called' and not only to call on God, but to shout out or call for anyone like calling out to your mother or friend in another room, 'to make a claim' 'make a false claim or an unproven claim'. It is reflected when Nehemia's adversaries ask him to meet them at a specific place. It is reflected in the sense of 'to make a claim' 'make a false claim or an unproven claim' as claims are being made about what is being said about Nehemia, which Nehemia's dialogue narrates 'there are no such claims being made'. Shemaiah calls him to meet in the temple. In the verse 'they reported his good deeds before me, and uttered my words to him.' it is still making claims about what one is saying about another.

Tobiah 'not repulsed by/they could eat/touch/palate/taste-he/him' is described as the son-in-law of **Shecaniah** 'complained about him' 'make work-he/him' as both Nehemiah and Tobiah have been complaining about each other and about the work Nehemiah is conducting. He is son of **Arah** 'his private parts' 'his female family/reputation' 'disgraced him' as Shecaniah should be disgraced for marrying into Tobiah's family (according to this story). **Johanan** 'they are/they are being humiliated' as they too are being disgraced for marrying to and from Tobiah's family. **Meshullam** 'well ask them' 'what did he/they take/what was taken' as they are bringing and receiving news between Nehemiah and Tobiah. He is the son of **Berechiah** for 'I will loosen him/it' and 'loose' can have meanings of not brought up well morally, as he is presented as immoral or unpleasant; 'I will prop/lean it/him against' as the notables of Judah, and he being Shecaniah's son-in-law, as well as other family ties through marriage are support for Tobiah. (Neh.4:17-19)

Raamiah; raʿamyâ; رَعَميه 'saw a blind person' 'saw-blinded him/he'; رَعَ ميه 'shepherded/grew a hundred' 'took care of water' 'took care of a hundred'. Cp: ra'amyah, ra'a-myah. (Neh.7:7)

Nahamani; naḥămānî; نَهيمآني 'of sighing' 'they winded me' 'of being winded' 'of puncturing allowing air to escape'. Cp: nahaimaanee. (Neh.7:7)

Mispereth; misperet̠; مِسبَرَت 'made it right/fixed it' 'the fixing of'; مِصبَرَت 'aloe vera' 'aloe vera of' 'she did not have patience' 'she was patient over a lot'; مِصفَرَت 'the whistle/whistling of' 'yellow/yellowed' 'has yellow disease/bile'. Cp: misberet, mi<u>ss</u>beret, mi<u>ss</u>*ph*eret. (Neh.7:7)

Nehum; nĕḥûm; نَهُم ، نيهُم 'sighing/sighed' 'of sighing' 'struck and winded' and means sighing or puffing meant to attract attention or being hit/punched in stomach until breath is forced out of you. Cp: nehum, neihum. (Neh.7:7)

Hodevah; hôd̠ĕwâ, hôd̠ĕyâ; هُدييه ، هُدي يه 'was guided-he/him' 'he was guided/brought to sense' 'sang wedding song-he/him' 'was given as present-he/him' 'demolished-he/him' 'demolish him'; خُطيوه 'wrote/drew a line/letter' 'stepped' 'stepped over' 'a step'; هُديوه 'they guided/he was guided' 'of guiding to right thing/path' 'they sang wedding song' 'they demolished'; هُدييه 'it/he is a squash/a hollow squash/a churning vessel' 'he gathered/ate or did something related to squash or vessels made out of squash'; حُدييه 'is slouching/hunchbacked' 'hunchback'. It is equivalent to Hodiah (1Chr.4:19), Hodaiah (1Chr.3:24), Hodaviah (1Chr.5:24). Cp: hodeiyah, hodei-yah, <u>kh</u>oṭeiwah, hodeiwah, hodeibah, ḥodeibah. (Neh.7:43)

Phaseah; the same as Paseah (1Chr.4:12). (Neh.7:51)

Meunim; mĕʿûnîm; ميعُن هم/ام 'help/support-them/the' 'did not help/support-them/the'; ميعُنهم 'inspected them closely' 'they are jelly-like/squishy'; ميغُن هم/ام 'well he sings-them/the' 'what will enrich-them/the' 'what will make not need-them/the' 'well he is making '<u>gh</u>n' sounds'; ميغُنيم 'he has many goats' 'he brings up goats' 'well he is exploiting/taking advantage/making a lot of fortune' 'well he is enriched' 'he is not making a fortune/not taking advantage' 'he is not raising goats'. Cp: mei'un-hum/um, mei<u>gh</u>un-hum/um, mei<u>gh</u>uneem. (Neh.7:52)

Nephishesim; nĕpûšĕšîm, nĕpîšĕšîm; نيفُسيس هم/ام ، نيفيسيس هم/ام 'the same as them/the' 'plenty of space-them/the' 'made plenty of space-them/the' 'there is space-them/the' 'wind passing/puncturing-them/the'; نيفسيسهم ، نيفيسيسهم 'by themselves' 'themselves' 'they have plenty of space' 'it is spacious' 'there is space' 'make them spacious'; نيفُشيش هم/ام ، نيفيشيش هم/ام 'scattered-them/the' 'scattered over-them/the' usually used when something light or powdery is being sprayed/scattered over something/someone. Equivalent to Nephusim (Ezra.2:50). Cp; neiphuseis-hum/um, neipheeseis-hum/um, neiphuseishum, neipheeseishum, neiphusheish-hum/um, neipheesheish-hum/um. (Neh.7:52)

Bazlith; baṣlîṯ; بَزليط 'I will make thin' 'I will eat rapidly/in one go'; بَصليط 'I will oil/add oil' 'with oil' 'I will focus on/antagonise' 'I will become zealous' 'I will make focus on' the latter from the meaning of when a person becomes zealous about something or even with causing problems to another person or obsessed about something; بَصليت 'onion' 'added/ate/gathered onions'. Equivalent to Bazluth (Ezra.2:52). Cp: bazleeṭ, bassleeṭ, bassleet. (Neh.7:54)

Tamah; tāmaḥ; دآمَح 'applied soot to' 'soot'; طآمَح 'slapped down'. Equivalent to Thamah (Ezra.2:53). Cp: daamaḥ, ṭaamaḥ. (Ezra.7:55)

Perida; pĕrîdā'; بيريداء 'made cool/cold' 'felt cold'; فيريداء 'separated into single units' 'a buttock(half of bottom)'; ثيريباء 'churned milk' 'made/drank churned milk' 'of churned milk'; بيريباء 'they will bring up/discipline/teach/grow' 'they will be brought up/disciplined/taught/grow' 'they will grow/be brought up well' 'they will mix and dilute with water'; فيريباء 'so they become god(s)/parent/teacher' 'in their god(s)/parent(s)/teacher(s)' 'so they will bring up/discipline/teach/grow' 'so they will be brought up/disciplined/taught/grow' 'so they will grow/be brought up well' 'so they will mix and dilute with water'; بيريضآء 'he/they will consent/agree' 'with his permission' 'he/they will be pleased'. Equivalent to Peruda (Ezra.2:55). Cp: beireedaa, pheireedaa, feireebaa, beireebaa, pheireebaa, beireedhaa. (Neh.7:57)

Anaiah; 'ănāyâ; عينآيه 'my eyes' 'special care/thoroughly' 'messages/hints to him' 'means-him/he' 'suffered/suffered-he/him'; غينآيه 'songs' 'sang-him/he' 'made 'ghn' sounds-him/he' 'enriched-him/he' 'no longer needed-him/he'. Cp: 'ainaayah, 'ainaa-yah, ghainaayah, ghainaa-yah. (Neh.8:4)

Hashbadana; ḥašbaddānâ; حَش بَذّآنه 'stuffed-with call to gather/pray' 'stuffed-our ears/his ears'; حَز بَذّآنه 'crammed/cornered with his call to gather/pray' 'crammed/cornered-our ears/his ears' 'crammed/cornered-with his permission'; حَز بَدّآنه 'crammed/cornered with bodies/with his body'; حَش بَدّآنه 'stuffed with bodies/with his body'; هَز بَدّآنه 'shook/swayed with bodies/with his body'; هَش بَدّعنه 'shooed away-we began'; هَص بَدّعنه 'be quiet-we have started'; خَشبَ ذآنه 'wood/timber-called out to gather/assemble/pray' it is most likely the latter as they emphasise Ezra stood on a 'pulpit of wood' when he reads the law. Cp: ḥash bavvaanah, ḥaz bavvaanah, ḥaz baddaanah, ḥash baddaanah, haz baddaanah, hash badd'nah, hass badd'nah, khashba vvaanah. (Neh.8:4)

Hodijah; the same as Hodiah (1Chr.4:19). (Neh.8:7)

Zidkijah; ṣidqiyyâ; صِدقِي يه ، صِدقِيّه 'honest/friend-he/him' 'believe-he/him' 'of honesty/friendliness': زِدكِي يه ، زِدكِيّه 'gave you extra-he/him' 'extra remains-he/him' 'deceived you-he/him' 'of giving extra' 'of remaining extra' 'of deceit'; صِدكِي يه ، صِدكِيّه 'blocked you/prevented you-he/him' 'fished you/your fish-he/him' 'of blocking/preventing' 'of fishing'. Cp: ssidqiy-yah, ssidqiyyah, zidkiy-yah, zidkiyyah, ssidkiy-yah, ssidkiyyah. (Neh.10:1)

Ginnethon; ginnĕṯôn; خِنّيثُن 'male having anal sex with male, becoming female' 'they are making him female(with male/male sex)' 'they are having sex (male/male)' the change in either original spelling or its transliteration could indicate the people in charge of these texts no longer wanted to use 'Jonathan' due to its meaning; جِنّيثُن 'came who doubled/folded' 'came who did again/second layer' 'came who femaled/is feminine'; جِنّيدُن 'came the guilted/bowed'; جِنّيضُن 'came who suspected'; جِنّيطُن 'came who clangs/clanged'. Cp: khinneifon, ginneifon, ginneidon, ginneidhon, ginneiṭon. (Neh.10:6)

Bilgai; bilgay; بِلغَي 'delivered/deliver message to' 'tell him/her/them' 'informed/inform him/her/them' 'reached maturity' (latter, first menstruation, etc.) 'in proper language' 'by playing around with words' (latter means using wordplay or changing meanings of words, changing letters of words); دِلغَي 'made/make a clot' 'made/make a viscous lump/smear' 'smear something thickly'. Equivalent to Bilgai (1Chr.24:14). Cp: bilghay, dilghay. (Neh.10:8)

Azaniah; 'ăzanyâ; ئيزَن يه 'the fornicator-he/him'; ئيذَن يه 'called out to gather/assemble/pray-he/him' 'agreed/allowed-he/him' 'ears/eared-he/him' 'made handles-he/him' 'made handles on it' 'then it is he/him'; ئيضَن يه 'him too'. Cp: aizan-yah, aivan-yah, aidhan-yah. (Neh.10:9)

Beninu; bĕnînû; بينيُن 'children' 'lots of children' 'offspring/lots of offspring' 'mothering/having children' 'with baby(ies)' 'bringing up as own child(ren)' 'tiny' 'fingers/doing (something) with finger(s)'. Cp: beineenu. (Neh.10:13)

Hizkijah; hizqiyyâ; حزكِي يه ، حزكِيّه 'squeezed/cornered/crammed-he/him' 'of squeezing/cornering/cramming'; هِزكِي يه ، هِزكِيّه 'I will flatter/praise-he/him' 'I will predict if he is going to hell or heaven-he/him' 'I will predict if person is good or bad-he/him'; هِضقِي يه ، هِضقِيّه 'make suffer/distress-he/him' 'I will force to taste/swallow/eat-he/him' 'of making suffer/distress' 'of forcing/forced to swallow' the first is literally saying to cause distress, and the second is a figurative saying that means to make a person suffer or put them through trouble and the phrase to make a person feel pain/sufferance is usually described as making them swallow something unpleasant; هِسقِي يه ، هِسقِيّه 'I will water-he/him' 'of watering'. Cp: ḥizkiyyah, ḥizkiyyah, hizkiy-yah, hizkiyyah, hidhqiy-yah, hidhqiyyah, hisqiy-yah, hisqiyyah. (Neh.10:17)

Azzur; 'azzur; عَزُّر 'made ugly' 'ugly'; نَزُّر 'the false oath/the lying under oath' 'tighten/the tightening' 'the visiting/pilgrimaging/am visiting'; غَزُر 'became heavy' 'heavy' (rain/blood), 'flowed heavy' 'flowed heavier'. Cp: 'azzur, a-zzur, ghazzur. (Neh.10:17)

Nebai; nêḇāy, nôḇāy; نيبآي ، نُبآي 'messenger' 'prophet' 'predicted news' 'news/information' 'on behalf of' 'taking turns' 'bees' 'canine teeth' 'canine teeth are emerging from gum' 'we refuse' 'we reject'; نيضآي ، نُضآي 'we shine a light' 'we light the way' 'we ablute/wash'. Cp: neybaay, nobaay, neydhaay, nodhaay. (Neh.10:19)

Magpiash; magpî'āš; مَجبي عآش 'whatever he brought/gathered-lived' 'whatever he brought/gathered-nestled' ; مَغثي عآش 'nauseated-lived' 'nauseated-nestled' 'the nauseated-lived'; مَغبي عآش 'thirsty-lived' 'the thirsty-lived' 'thirsty-nestled'; مَغبيئآش 'early murky, dark morning' 'blurry/clouded/murky/not clear' and the term is also used to describe very early in the morning before the sun comes up properly, but not completely dark. It is equivalent to Magbish. (Ezra.2:30). (Neh.10:20)

Pileha; pilḥā'; بِلهآء 'stupid/dumb(fem.)' 'soak' 'afflict it/her' 'with distraction'; فِلهآء 'remove nits from her/it' 'go thoroughly through/inspect it' 'in distraction'; ضِلهآء 'her/its shadow' 'shadow over it/protect her or it with shade' 'misled/mislead her'; بِلحآء 'with beards' 'bearded' 'a promise/word/oath/agreement' the latter because 'with beard' is part of a gesture to show support, agreement, promise or guarantee when a matter is being discussed or something requested. Cp: bilhaa, philhaa, dhilhaa, bilḥaa. (Neh.10:24)

Shobek; šôḇēq; شُبيق 'put leg over leg' 'put/wrapped leg across/over someone else's body/leg' 'pads made of rags' 'padded with rags to absorb(water/blood/any liquid)' (mshbq/مشبق is the noun for rags women fold or sew together and use to absorb menstrual blood the way a sanitary towel is used in cities); سُبيق 'beat/was first'. Cp: shobeyq, sobeyq. (Neh.10:24)

Athaiah; 'ăṯāyâ; غيثآيه ، غيثآ يه 'my nauseation' 'nauseated-he/him' 'my nourishment' 'nourishment-he/him' the word can mean to nourish with food when a person is ill and too ill to make or bring his/her own food; ئيتآيه 'they came/came quickly' 'came/came quickly-he/him' 'they came to me'; غيطآيه ، غيطآ يه 'my cover/lid' 'cover it/put lid on it' 'covered-he/him'; غيدآيه ، غيدآ يه 'my lunch' 'fed lunch-he/him'. Cp: ghaifaayah, ghaifaa-yah, aitaayah, ghaiṭaayah, ghaiṭaa-yah, ghaidaayah, ghaidaa-yah. (Neh.11:4)

Hazaiah; ḥăzāyâ; حيزآيه 'they are being blocked/crammed/kept in/cornered'; حيزآ يه 'block/cram/prevent-him/he' 'they blocked/crammed/prevented him(moving)'; خيذآيه 'took it' 'took-he/him'; خيزآيه 'they are ashamed'; خيزآ يه 'he swore-he/him' 'they swore at him' 'a disgrace/shame-he/him'; حيسآيه 'my wells' 'wells-he/him'. Cp: ḥaizaayah, ḥaizaa-yah, khaivaayah, khaizaayah, khaizaa-yah, ḥaisaayah. (Neh.11:5)

Joiarib; yôyārîḇ; جُيآريب 'came-mixing/diluting with water'; هُيآريب 'he is mixing/diluting with water'. يُهآريب 'he is moving out of the way' 'he is helping to run away'; جُهآريب 'came fleeing' 'came the one who ran away'; هُهآريب 'he is fleeing/running away'; يُجآريب 'he is trying/experiencing' 'he is getting skin condition (similar to psoriasis)' 'he has an oasis'; جُجآريب 'came and attempted' 'came the one with a skin condition (similar to psoriasis)' 'came to an oasis'; هُجآريب 'he has tried/experienced'; يُعآريب 'he is expressing clearly/speaking clearly' 'he is fucking'; جُعآريب 'came expressing/speaking clearly' 'came fucking/fucked'; هُعآريب 'he is of expressing/speaking clearly' 'he is fucked'; يُحآريب 'he is warring/causing problems'; جُحآريب 'came warring'; هُحآريب 'he has warred'. It is equivalent to Jehoiarib (1Chr.9:10) and may have additional 'Arab' meanings. Cp: go-yaareeb, ho-yaareeb, yo-haareeb, go-haareeb, ho-haareeb, yo-gaareeb, go-gaareeb, ho-gaareeb, yo-'aareeb, go-'aareeb, ho-'aareeb, yo-ḥaareeb, go-ḥaareeb, ho-ḥaareeb. (Neh.11:5)

Shiloni; šîlōnî, šîlônî; شيلُني ، شيلوني 'of taking/carrying' 'take/took/carry/carried me' 'take/took/carry/carried me away' 'of taking/carrying away'; سيلني ، سيلوني 'asked me' 'of asking' 'many questions' 'leaked/flowed' 'of leaking/flowing' 'of temporary running river' 'comforted/entertained me' 'of comforting/entertainment'. Cp: sheeloonee, sheelonee, seeloonee, seelonee. (Neh.11:5)

Joed; yô'ēd; يُعيد 'he returns/returns it' 'he does/says it again' 'he celebrates festival' 'he causes a commotion' 'he counts'; جُعيد 'wrinkled'; يُعيض 'he recompenses' 'he bites at/on'. Cp: yo'eyd, go'eyd, yo'eydh. (Neh.11:7)

Ithiel; 'îṯî'ēl; ئيذي ئِل 'if-the/if it is-the' 'harm/harmed-the'; ئيتي ئِل 'came-the' 'brought-the'. Cp: eevee-ill, eetee-ill. (Neh.11:7)

Kolaiah; qôlāyâ; قُلاّيه 'a false statement' 'putting words in someone's mouth' 'a statement' 'it was said' 'sanitised(on heat)'; قُلاّ يه 'say it to him' 'say-him/he' 'say it-him/he' 'they are sanitised' 'they are sanitised-he/him'; كلاّيه 'all of it' 'ate/eat-him/he' (the latter can mean a curse as in 'God eats'), 'my kidneys' 'his kidneys'. Cp: qolaayah, qolaa-yah, kolaayah, kolaa-yah. (Neh.11:7)

Gabbai; gabbay; جَبّي 'gathers' 'gathers many people' 'a gang of people' 'brought' 'of bringing/gathering' 'answering'; غَبّي 'thirsted' 'my thirst' 'they are thirsty'. Cp: gabbay, ghabbay. (Neh.11:8)

Sallai; sallay; سَلّي 'eased/comforted' 'entertained' 'asked questions' 'leaked/flowed' 'of temporary running river'; صَلّي 'pray' 'connect/join' 'grill' 'arrive/reach'. Cp: sallay, ssallay. (Neh.11:8)

Senuah; sĕnu'â, sĕnû'â; سينُئه ، سِنُئه ، سينوئه ، سِنوئه 'straightened/aligned it/him' 'went in his direction' 'went straight' 'opposite/facing him/it' 'spent a year'; صينُعه ، صِنُعه ، صينوعه ، صِنوعه 'they created/made' 'created/made' 'of creating/making' 'upset face' 'frowning and refusing to talk' 'of getting upset quickly and refusing to talk'. It is equivalent to Hasenuah (1Chr.9:7), Senaah (Ezra.2:35), Hassenaah (Neh.3:3). Cp: senooah, seinooah, senuah, seinuah, ssenoo'h, sseinoo'h, ssenu'h, sseinu'h. (Neh.11:9)

Pelaliah; pĕlalyâ; بيلَل يه 'he soaked it' 'soaked-he/him' 'became old/faded' 'became old/faded-he/him' 'had mind/patience-he/him' 'was afflicted with many afflictions-he/him'; فيلَل يه 'picked lice out of hair-he/him/for him' 'wore jasmines-he/him' 'went through/over thoroughly-he/him' 'shook out of hair/clothes, etc.-he/him' 'said a bad omen-he/him'; ضيلَل يه 'shaded/sat or stood in shade/rested in shade-he/him' 'wore a hat(to shade from sun)-he/him' 'misled-he/him' 'he was misled'. Cp: beilal-yah, pheilal-yah, dheilal-yah. (Neh.11:12)

Ahasai; 'aḥzay; نَحزَي 'hold in/gather/cram/corner'; نَهزَي 'swing/rock' 'pull at/tug'; نَخذَي 'take/of taking'; نَخزَي 'swear at' 'embarrass/insult'; نَحسَي 'a well/the well'. Cp: aḥzay, ahzay, akhvay, akhzay aḥsay. (Neh.11:13)

Bakbukiah; baqbuqyâ; بَقبُق يه 'talks a lot-he/him' 'clucks/clucking-he/him' 'clucks like a hen(meaning talks too much)-he/him' 'made sound of water flowing out of narrow place/glugging-he/him' 'passed wind-he/him' 'water flowing out of a narrow place-he/him' 'tore-he/him' 'of tearing-he/him'; بَكبُك يه 'went-go-he/him' 'left-leave-he/him' 'of lots of going/leaving-he/him' 'of going-he/him' 'visiting-he/him'. Cp: baqbuq-yah, bakbuk-yah. (Neh.11:17)

Gispa; gišpā'; جِشباء 'yanked out a lot' (e.g. grass, plants, hair), 'picked a lot with'; جِزفاء 'folded and creased' 'creased' 'broke off by creasing/folding'; قِصفاء 'broke into pieces' 'broke off a piece' 'a short piece' 'a stub' 'humiliated with a retort'. Cp: gishbaa, gizphaa, qissphaa. (Neh.11:21)

Jekabzeel; yĕqaḇṣĕ'ēl; ييقَبصي ئِل 'he pinches-the'; جيقَبصي ئِل 'came pinched-the'; هيقَبصي ئِل 'he will pinch-the'; ييخَبصي ئِل 'he pokes into-the' 'he pokes finger into anus-the' 'he pokes fingers into and pollutes-the' 'he makes a mess-the'; جيخَبصي ئِل 'came-poked into-the' 'came-poked finger into anus-the' 'came-poked fingers into and polluted-the' 'came-made a mess-the'; هيخَبصي ئِل 'he will poke into-the' 'he will poke finger into anus-the' 'he will poke fingers into and pollute-the' 'he will make a mess-the'; ييكَبسي ئِل 'he buries under ashes-the'; جيكَبسي ئِل 'came buried under ashes-the'; هيكَبسي ئِل 'he will bury under ashes-the'. It is equivalent to Kabzeel (Josh.15:21). Cp: yeiqabsei-ill, geiqabsei-ill, heiqabsei-ill, yeikhabsei-ill, geikhabsei-ill, heikhabsei-ill, yeikabsei-ill, geikabsei-ill, heikabsei-ill. (Neh.11:25)

Mekonah; mēḵōnâ; ميكونه 'it will be' 'what will it be/what it will be' 'it will not be' 'will make into peaked heap' 'not a peaked heap' 'water from top room/hut on roof'. Cp: meikoonah. (Neh.11:28)

Aija; 'ayyâ; عَجّه ، عَجّا 'overcrowded/packed (him/it)' 'over spilling(with fortune/good)/field filled with crops whose panicles seem packed and over spilling(him/it)' 'stirred or shook(him/it)' 'made suffer(him/it)' 'prolonged suffering/torture(him/it)' 'crying intensely/crying and gasping' 'is crooked/twisted/not forthright' 'made crooked/twisted(him/it)'; نَجّا ، نَجّه 'he came/he's arriving'; نَيّا ، نَيّه 'is-he/he is' 'is he?' 'which(e.g. one)', an exclamation of displeasure/objection; عَيّا/عَيّه a sound made to stop animals running off and bring them back to the right land/path, 'will-he/he will' 'will he?' 'learn and remember-him/it' 'be warned-(of) him' 'beware-him' 'I dare you, go on-him'. It is equivalent to Ajah (Gen.36:24), Agag (1Sam.15:8-9,32-33), Aiah (2Sam.21:8-14). Cp: 'aggah, 'agga, aggah, agga, ayyah, ayya, 'ayyah, 'ayya. (Neh.11:31)

Neballat; nĕb̲allaṭ; نبلّط 'we tile'; نبيلّت 'the noble(s)/nobility of' 'made noble/great'; نيضلّت 'she shook rigorously' (to make fall out) 'it protruded' 'it came out in the wrong place'. Cp: neiballaṭ, neiballat, nei-dhallat. (Neh.11:34)

Ginnetho; ginnĕṯoy; خِنّيثوي 'he is female because he has anal sex with men' 'he has sex with men, becoming female' 'they are making him female(with male/male sex)' 'they are having sex (male/male)'; جِنّيدوي 'came who causes evil-eye with his statements' 'came who called'; جِنّيضوي 'came to shine a light/light the way' 'came the abluted/came to ablute/wash'; جِنّيطوي 'came to fold'. It is similar to Ginnethon (Neh.10:6) only in relation to its 'Jonathan/male on male sex' meaning. Cp: khinneifooy, ginneidooy, ginneidhooy, ginneiṭooy. (Neh.12:4)

Maadiah; ma'ad̲yâ; مَعَديه 'of enmity towards' 'of infecting' 'counted/of counting' 'raised surface/raised or too lumpy/bumpy' 'there is none left, see/hey'; مَغديه 'she has had lunch' 'she is visiting wedding/Seventh' 'she is feeding/serving lunch' 'she is frustrated/of frustration' 'she has swollen glands' the latter can be literal or figurative meaning 'frustrated'; مَعَضيه 'she/it has sore muscles' 'she is recompensed/recompensing'; مَغضيه 'she is in a suppressed rage' 'she is provoking another causing him/her to suppress rage' 'she is of provoking'. It is equivalent to Maadai (Ezra.10:34). Cp: ma'adyah, maghadyah, ma'adhyah, maghadhyah. (Neh.12:5)

Amok; 'āmôq; غامُق 'deep' 'dipped hands or arms into something(unhygienic)', dipping into something more than once or in a way that causes others to be put off from eating from it, 'covered mouth/part of face/whole face'. Cp: ghaamoq. (Neh.12:7)

Joiada; yôyād̲ā'; جُيادآع 'came-he is calling' 'came calling/cursing' 'came-claiming/making false claim' 'came-leaving/saying farewell' 'came depositing/leaving something in the care of'; يُعادآء 'he/they is/are returning/returns' 'he/they create enmity/transgresses against' 'he infects' 'he counts'; جُعادآء 'came-returning/returned' 'came-enemies/created enmity/transgressing against' 'came-infecting/infected' 'came-counted'; جُياضآع 'came-he is placed/he places/sets' 'came-misguided/misleads/he misleads' 'came-loses/he loses' '. Equivalent to Jehoiada (2Sam.8:18). Cp: goyaadaa', yo'aadaa, go'aadaa, goyaadhaa'. (Neh.12:11)

Meraiah; mĕrāyâ; ميرآيه 'a dream' 'he had a dream' 'a mirror' 'his mirror'. Cp: meiraayah. (Neh.12:12)

Melicu; mallûk̲î; مَلّكي 'filled you/covered you(soiled)' 'what is with you/what is wrong with you' 'filled you' as in physically filled by giving things or as first meaning of 'dirtied'; مَلّقي 'thrown/cast' 'what was found' 'found what' 'something found'; مَلّخي 'cover in slime/something slimy' 'slime'; مَلّحي 'make nice(er)' 'add salt'. Equivalent to Malluch (1Chr.6:44). Cp: mallukee, malluqee, mallukhee, malluḥee. (Neh.12:14)

Helkai; ḥelqāy; حِلقآي 'my throat' 'throats' 'my ring' 'rings' 'hug/embrace' 'shave' 'a circle' 'surround'; هِلقآي 'it will be found' 'I will find' 'is thrown/cast' 'it will be thrown/cast' 'I will throw'. Cp: ḥilqaay, hilqaay. (Neh.12:15)

Piltai; pilṭāy; بِلطآي 'it will stick to' 'I will stick to'; فِلتآي 'fallen' 'immoral/lewd'. Cp: bilṭaay, philtaay. (Neh.12:17)

Kallai; qallay; قَل لَي 'told me' 'less for me'; قَلّي 'lessen' 'sanitise(on heat)'; كَل لي 'all for me' 'eat for me'; كَلّي 'all of it' 'eat'. Cp: qal-lay, qallay, kal-lay, kallay. (Neh.12:20)

Hoshaiah; hôša'yâ; هُسَعيه 'he wandered/wanders/went/goes/travels/travelled-he/him'. Cp: hosa'yah. (Neh.12:32)

Azarael; the same as Azareel (1Chr.12:6). (Neh.12:36)

Milalai; milălay; مِليلَي 'singing a lullaby' 'singing a child to sleep' 'repeating the word 'lail'(night)' which is an element of Arab music culture. Cp: milailay (Neh.12:36)

Gilalai; gilălay; جِليلَي 'came sang lullaby' 'came sang a child to sleep' 'repeating the word 'lail'(night)' an element of Arab music culture, 'came-night' 'my turn for trouble/good has come' 'praised the goodness/magnificence' (chanting praise of God or person), 'cleared/purified' 'clear'. Cp: gilailay. (Neh.12:36)

Maai; mā'ay; مآعَي 'with me' 'repeating 'ai/'ay sound(usually for goats/sheep to fall in line)'. Cp: maa'ay. (Neh.12:36)

Jezrahiah; yizraḥyâ; يِصرَخ يه 'shouts/screams-he/him' 'yells loud-he/him' and the narration 'And the singers sang loud, with Jezrahiah *their* overseer'. Equivalent to Izrahiah (1Chr.7:3). Cp: yi<u>ss</u>ra<u>kh</u>-yah. (Neh.12:42)

Note: Milalai, Gilalai, Maai, Nethaneel all have clear musical meanings. Azarel 'twisted muscle-the' 'twisted the' could also refer to twisting something and making noise/music. Hanani 'humming sound/making humming sound'. Judah 'called/is called' for its meaning of calling out to others or to God, and is used here to indicate a chant or song. (Neh.12:36)

Artaxerxes is used again relating to the Tobiah situation and other matters: it is the wrong way up (Artax) with Tobiah inside the house of God, so with Nehemiah throwing him out and having it cleaned and purified the situation is the corrected (erxes/astā'). The same for how things were and how Nehemiah's character goes around correcting them. (Neh.13)

Eliashib's other meanings come into play at the end of Nehemiah 'the afflicted/injured/hit' 'the bringer of affliction/problems' 'the one who leaves/cuts off relations, activities, actions'. As this word-name is used to depict these meanings as the person who allies himself with Tobiah, and also reflected in the grandson of **Eliashib** the high priest who Nehemiah chases away as he is married into Sanballat the Horonite's family: **Joiada** for 'came calling/cursing' 'he/they create enmity/transgresses against' 'he infects' 'came-enemies/created enmity/transgressing against' as Nehemia describes them as a pollution and sees them as transgressing against priesthood and God. **Sanballat** for: 'fertile animals/sexually excited/ready to conceive/copulated/ready to copulate-she afflicted us' as the stories show that marrying a 'foreigner' 'pollutes' the bloodline; **Horonite** for: 'chased me away/of chasing away (with words)' 'of driving/chasing away (with violence)' as Nehemia chases this character away.

The clear and simple method of the Biblical authors and the Arabic meanings of the words can be clearly seen in every name and story of the Bible.

Esther

Ahasuerus: 'they created problems/pitted against others' 'they pitted you against to cause problems' 'they conveyed news/rumours/conversations to cause problems' has the exact same meaning as it held in Ezra.4:6: the word is from (ḥrsh/حرش) and in the form of (ḥaarashoo/حارشو) 'they caused problems/pitted against others' and is done through one individual/party delivering news, lies, etc. to another, Ahasuerus in this case, to cause between him and another person/party trouble/enmity, etc.

In Ezra, it was the people who wrote a letter against the returned exiles to Ahasuerus to prevent them building. In the Book of Esther, though it is mainly Heman and Mordecai/Esther doing the meaning of 'Ahasuerus' against each other, it is also Memucan who takes advantage of Ahasuerus' anger and upset to drive a wedge between him and Vashti, whom in the story he obviously loves; the king's servants suggest he replace Vashti; Haman carries words and causes problems for Mordecai and the Jews; Mordecai and Esther do the same against Haman; Mordecai does the same, using Esther, to cause the execution of Bigthan and Teresh (regardless if they are guilty or not in the story, the point is everything to do with Ahasuerus is linked to the word-name meaning: driving wedges/causing trouble through communicating news/gossip). And living up to his character name, every time Ahasuerus is fed news/gossip and incited against a certain party—he does so and acts as based on the news fed to him, causing trouble between him and the affected party. (Esther)

Shushan still holds the same meaning as in Neh.1:1 (and all similar words throughout the earlier Biblical stories) 'something important' 'things and important things' 'many things and wonderful things' 'puzzling matters/things' 'things, important things' 'things, many things' 'things, amazing/wonderful things' and the latter is used when describing a matter, or gathering, or event of great magnificence, importance, variety, wealth, social status of those hosting and/or attending, the scale of the event, the things served/presented—all kinds of matters which show great importance, or wealth, splendour, enjoyment of the event, all boiled down to two words in a phrase (compound in the story) 'shay wa sha-n' 'Shushan'. It is exactly described as the event happening in Shushan palace: an important event; the social status of the host and guests; the king's wealth on show; his generosity and hospitality displayed in an event which is held over a long period of time: 'When he showed the riches of his glorious kingdom and the honour of his excellent majesty many days, *even* an hundred and fourscore days.' And extended another seven days beyond. The decorations, the estate, the expanse of kingdoms he rules, the cutlery, the wine served, are all mentioned of great variety, importance and magnificence. And depending on how the word is used, 'Shushan' شّي وشأن can also express wonder and puzzlement over a matter 'but the city Shushan was perplexed.' (Esth.1; 3:15)

Vashti; waštî; وَشْتِي 'and I want' from the word (ashtee/اشتي) 'I want' which is from (sh/ش) 'want'; وَسْتِي 'and offended' 'and did bad' 'and was offended'. She is the king's wife, he wants her to appear before the princes and people as the king wants the people to see how beautiful she is 'When the heart of the king was merry with wine, he commanded…the seven chamberlains…To bring Vashti the queen before the king with the crown royal, to shew the people and the princes her beauty: for she *was* fair to look on.'. So he wanted her brought out, he wanted everyone to see and admire her beauty but she offends him by not complying. Also, Memucan's dialogue of advice can be read as: because she did not do what her husband wanted, women all over the land will not do what their husbands want them to do i.e. she will be an example for other women to do bad towards their husbands; and to keep women obeisant to what husbands' want—Ahasuerus should punish Vashti.

Even after he sends out a decree, Ahasuerus' anger dies down and regrets what has happened, including his decree against her, he loves and still wants her and feels bad about what he has done. This is what his servants notice and therefore suggest he finds another to replace her—to stop his longing for her. In rural Yemen when a man loves a woman, whether in an illicit relationship or for marriage they use the word yshtee-ha/'he wants her' and the same with women expressing they want a certain man. Cp: washtee, wastee. (Esth.1:9-22; 2:1-2, 4)

Memucan; mĕmûķān; مِيمُكَان 'what can be done' 'was not able/was able to/get a grasp on/got to do' 'not a place' 'do not allow/enable' and these meanings are reflected in Memucan's role. The king asks what can be done about Vashti's disobedience and Memucan answers how Vashti's action will enable women to disobey their husbands, and he suggests to enable men to get a hold on women's conduct there has to be punishment for Vashti. The answer also encapsulates there will not be any place where the news of Vashti's disobedience will not reach and cause women to disobey husbands; and part of the solution is to send letters to every country, so that each household hears the decree. The word is made up from (mkn/مكن) 'place' and 'enabled/was able to do'. Cp: meimukaan. (Esth.1:15-21)

Persia (2Chr.36:20-21) and **Media/Medes** (2Kgs.17:6) were used for the specific Biblical author method of enhancing the story with place names which reflect in the events of the story, not as a country/city/village but as an adjective or verb which will feature in the story. Media/Medes; mādāy; مادآي (2Kgs.17:6) for its meanings of 'hand/pass/stash/hide/plant with no one noticing' 'underhanded behaviour(done secretly)' 'has been secreted in/planted' 'to put hands on something not yours' 'to overstep boundaries/'take liberties'/have confidence to do something that should result in punishment' as Vashti takes liberties in refusing the king's request; other characters in the story will also gain power and attempt to hurt innocent people: Haman does not get away with it at the end, but Mordecai and Esther do get away with it as the protagonists in the story.

Persia; pārāš; بآرآز baaraaz: the meaning 'brought forward/pressed on and pushed out' can be seen in Vashti doing what she pleases. Memucan presenting the solution.

Persia; فآرآص phaaraass: the meaning 'split open/pushed out/emerged by pushing up or out/ divided by breaking or splitting' and, فآرآس phaaraas: 'divided something into separate units' 'explained/explained in detail/made clear' is reflected in how Memucan breaks down the problem and shows Ahasuerus how bigger it really is by explaining it in detail.

Persia; فآرآش phaaraash The meaning 'made/prepared resting or sleeping place' 'lay down' 'spread over/lay out' 'mat/bed/resting or sleeping place' is reflected in Memucan's suggestion that Ahasuerus remove Vashti and put another woman in her place, this 'place' can be referred to as a 'sleeping/resting place' which means a relationship, or marital home, or direct female relatives, something that is related to the respective person (the literal use of this word meaning as 'bed/sleeping/resting place' will come into effect again later in the story). (Esth.1)

It is important to understand that by '...the wise men, which knew the times...' does not mean people who are educated or counsel based on facts, but it refers to people who have the ability to read the future, and perform what would be called sorcery. This king, like all the other kings mentioned in the Biblical stories depends on and seeks advice from 'seers/prophets/prophecy/lots/visions' and this will become more evident in the story which is written by a people and culture who believe in sorcery and reading/predicting the future.

Carshena; karšĕnā'; قَر سيناء 'settle/stop before-in direction/face/opposite/towards' 'settle/stop-make straight/right/straighten' and the problem they are being asked to look into is Vashti refusing to appear before the king and all the people and princes; قَرشيناء 'we won a token/stone' 'we made a gain' and there is someone winning and losing whether it is a game or real life when this word is used. In this case Vashti has made a move and the king has 'lost face', but the advice he seeks is so he can 'score'. Cp: qar-seinaa, qarsheinaa. (Esth.1:14)

Shethar; šēṯār; سيتآر 'curtain' 'covered' 'covered a shame' 'protected from harm' and it reflects the problem that Vashti chose to cover herself from people's view, and now the problem is how to protect and cover the king from the embarrassment he felt and harm from this act. Cp: seytaar. (Esth.1:14)

Admatha; 'aḏmāṯā'; نَدمآتآء 'made bleed' 'she made bleed/hurt' such as hurt the feelings or pride of another. When a person regrets doing something or is warned that he/she will regret doing something, in particular, the phrase 'you/he/she will cry the tears blood'. In this story it is both Vashti, for her actions, and Ahasuerus who regrets separating from her. Cp: admaataa. (Esth.1:14)

Tarshish as in (Gen.10:4); taršîš; تَرشِش/تَرشيش 'light spraying' or 'a lot of light spray', طَرشِش/طَرشيش 'a lot of vomiting' or intentionally splashing a little liquid over someone/something, 'deaf' 'scared into stupor/unable to respond, hear, speak' 'pretending not to hear/pretending to be deaf'. It reflects how Vashti's actions will spread across the whole land and region, how women will ignore and disrespect their husbands and not be grateful towards them, this disobedience/lack of respect can be viewed as 'vomit/vomiting' 'pretending not to hear'. Cp: tarsheesh, ṭarsheesh. (Esth.1:14)

Meres; meres; مِرِص ، مَرَص 'slipped/slippery' because of its slippery texture; مِرِش ، مَرَش 'a spraying/spray' 'slipped away/got away unnoticed' 'washed the soiled/stained part of garment' ' a quick rinse/wash (of clothes)' and the meanings are used to depict Vashti has slipped out of favour and lost everything she had as Ahasuerus' wife, but also that this disobedience should not be allowed to pass without punishment, 'a spraying' 'rinsed' and refers again to Vashti's action spreading to other women, and that they need to cleanse the king from the embarrassment. Cp: mere<u>ss</u>, mere<u>sh</u>. (Esth.1:14)

Marsena; marsĕnā'; مَرشيناآء 'our spraying/spray' 'we slipped away/got away unnoticed' 'we washed the soiled/stained part of garment' 'we quickly rinsed/washed(clothes)'; مَر سيناء 'walked/passed along-in the direction' 'walked-straight/straightened/make right' 'walked/passed along-in the face of/opposite/towards' and is still referring to Vashti's refusal to stand before the king and crowd, but also the letters he will send in every direction with the decree of her punishment and that all men should 'bear the rule in his own house...'. It also reflects in that men should make women behave correctly and, in the culture, when speaking about any person (male or female) to make a person 'walk straight' means to correct their behaviour. The corrective actions which are done with haste relay the meanings of quickly washing something soiled or stained. Cp: mar<u>sh</u>einaa, mar-seinaa. (Esth.1:14)

Hege/Hegai; hēgay, hēgē'; هي جَي ، هي جيئ ، هيجَي ، هيجيئ 'she is coming/she has come' 'they will come' 'he will come/is coming' and is reflected in the story as many women will come to this character wanting to be Ahasuerus' 'harim' (which means 'women'). All virgins will be brought to Shushan palace where Hege will be in charge of them. Cp: hey-gay, hey-gey, heygay, heygey. (Esth.2:2)

Mordecai as earlier in (Ezra.2:2) means 'slather/cover with a substance such as soil/flour/oil or any substance clean or not clean/soil all over' 'soil it all over/cover it completely/make dirty all over' 'cover it sparingly all over' 'smear', 'you will return/be returned to' 'of returning' 'you will be punished for what you do/punishment/retribution will return on you' 'you will end up' 'you will be thrown down/perish/afflicted' 'of being afflicted'. These meanings are all reflected in relation to Mordecai's character: Esther ends up in Mordecai's care at her parents' death; Mordecai is always going and returning from 'the court of the women's house' to know what is going on with Esther; it is Mordecai's actions/orders which determine where Esther ends up at. 'Mordecai walked everyday before the court of the women's house to know what Esther did and what should become of her' (mrddha/مردّها) from the same root word of 'Mordecai' in Arabic means 'what would become of her' and is one of the meanings as above.

Mordecai covers himself with ashes—in previous parts of the Bible when people are in distress, they put soil on their head—so the words which mean to 'soil/cover/smear' is reflected in the story: 'When Mordecai perceived all that was done, Mordecai rent his clothes, and put on sackcloth with ashes, and cried with a loud and bitter cry.' 'And in every province, withersoever the king's commandment and his decree came, *there* was great mourning among the Jews, and fasting, and weeping, and wailing; and many lay in sackcloth and ashes.'.

Also, Mordecai 'you will end up' is displayed again in his warning to Esther that just because she is in the king's house, not to think she can escape the fate of her brethren, whether by people or from God—meaning: she will end up harmed. The dialogue also narrates that she has been brought to this kingdom to maybe save the Jews—meaning words to the effect 'you ended up here for a reason' 'Think not with thyself that thou shalt escape in the king's house more than all the Jews...but thou and thy father's house shall be destroyed; and who knoweth whether thou art come to the kingdom for *such* a time as this?'. The 'punishment' and 'perish/retribution' meanings will be relayed in Haman attempting to cause the killing of all Jews then in the killing of Haman, his sons and all the non-Jews. (Esth.2:5, 7, 11; 4:1-3, 13-14)

Mordecai's character has been given the lineage of Jair, Shimei, Kish and Benjamite to depict his character and role in the story. It is obvious from the choice of compound words given as his ancestors and place of origin reflect the author's intention that he is an unsavoury character even if he is the protagonist. The author's intentions to merely entertain with a funny story is very different than in more modern times where Mordecai's role is seen as a 'hero' character, it is the original story which clearly shows he is the protagonist but a 'bad' person as he deceives, lies, he puts Esther into sexual service of the king, and this is why he has been given unsavoury character names and especially 'Benjamite' which in the earlier stories always indicates something wrong, sexually immoral and 'below' the other characters and tribes in the OT stories.

Jair for 'you penis' 'he penises' 'you-disgrace' 'he shames/gloats over' as he places Esther into the harim of king Ahasuerus; 'ruthless' 'intolerable sufferance' as he will cause the execution of several characters who did not deserve punishment (excluding Haman), before causing multiple genocides (in storyland) of innocent people.

Shimei for 'my hearing' 'to spoil reputation of another by insulting them in the hearing of others' 'to talk badly/insult a person in front of others' as he uses eavesdropping but also tarnishing other people's reputations, carrying gossip or fabricated rumours about some of the king's servants. His reputation is sullied because he has put Esther into sexual service of the king. He goes daily to hear what is happening with Esther and to pick up news he can use for his intentions.

Kish for: 'a tiny bit of litter' 'scrape away leave nothing behind' 'toasty/burnt too much' 'to wipe out(remove completely) in one move'. The story narrates he and Esther rise from nothing into very powerful positions; Haman's plot is to wipe out all Jews; Mordecai's plot is to wipe out all non-Jews. 'hardened' 'cruel' as his and Haman's conduct show cruelty in getting innocent people murdered to reach their objectives; when Haman and Mordecai (respectively) convince Ahasuerus to commit genocide against innocent people it is 'hardening' of the heart and outright cruelty.

Benjamite for 'son/child-whose?' as Esther is an orphan, but also because of what 'Benjamin/Benjamite' is presented as in earlier stories of sexual immorality, wrong-doing, lowliness and other aspects which the tribe of Benjamin and any character given the Benjamite attribute is depicted as in the earlier stories. So although Mordecai is the 'hero' his conduct is devious and immoral. Note: most 'heroes' or at least protagonists in the OT are bad in character even if glorified by these stories. (Esth.2:5)

Hadassah; hăd̲āssâ; هيدآسّه ، هَدآسّه 'he will/I will-stash it in/sneak it in' 'he will/I will-plant it secretly' 'he will/I will plant it secretly to be found by another' 'he will/I will-plant/whisper bad ideas into another's head/cause enmity by planting bad ideas' and means to place something somewhere it should not be, without anyone noticing, for it to be either hidden or found as if it had been there naturally/legally or all along. It is from the word (ds/دس) 'surreptitiously stash/hide/plant' 'whisper/plant bad ideas'. It is reflected in the story by Mordecai telling, and Esther complying, to hide her origins i.e. her Jewish religion, and in her convincing Ahasuerus to allow several genocides to occur. He has figuratively 'snuck her in' among the other women to be concubines to the king so as to influence the king's decisions—so she has been planted, brought in with no one knowing who she really is but with a purpose to be 'found' so as to implement Mordecai's intentions of influencing the king: 'And he brought up Hadassah, that *is*, Esther...and when many maidens were gathered together unto Shushan the palace, to the custody of Hegai, that Esther was brought also into the king's house, to the custody of Hegai, keeper of women...Esther had not shewn her people nor her kindred: for Mordecai had charged her that she should not shew *it*.' Also, Mordecai's ways of communicating with Esther is secrecy, supplying her with information and orders to manipulate king Ahasuerus to their advantage. Cp: haidaassah, hadaassah. (Esth.2:7-8, 10-11, 19-22; 4:5-12)

Esther; 'estēr; نَستير ، نِستير 'cover/hide(something)/conceal' 'do not show/expose' and it can also mean 'protect' from harm or embarrassment. It is from the word (str/ستر) 'cover'. Esther's character does both: she hides her true identity from the king and everyone as ordered by Mordecai, she also protects the Jews through her actions (Esth.2:7,10,20). She also hides her request from the king until everything has fallen into place—that is, to save her people from what the evil Haman had planned for them. Cp: esteyr. (Esth.5:3-8; 7:1-10; 8:1-17)

Shaashgaz; šaʿašgaz; شَئَش غَز 'wants/wanted you-deep, squeezing pain/deep resonating sound'. It is the name given to the king's servant in charge of the women in the 'second house of the women' where when the king requests the women he wants to come to him, they are called by name. It is made clear these are sexual wants by the (Shaash/šaʿaš/شَئَش) 'wants you' and (gaz/غَز) 'deep pain/squeezing pain/deep resonating sound' of this character's name and also the process described in how women went in and out servicing the king with their company: 'she returned into the second house of the women, to the custody of Shaashgaz, the king's chamberlain which kept the concubines: she came into the king no more, except the king delighted in her, and that she were called by name.'. Cp: sha-ash-ghaz. (Esth.2:14)

Abihail (Num.3:35) has been given as her surname for its meanings 'father-purified/cleansed/circumcised' 'father-shed/undressed' (as in shed clothes, leaves, hair, skin, etc.) 'father-stuck in one place/indecisive' 'father-deceit/trickster' 'rejected-stuck in one place/indecisive/tricks/trickster' 'packed-purified/cleansed/made edible/touchable' 'packed/father-declared permissible/edible' 'packed-stuck in one place/tricks/trickster' 'packed-she is the' 'rejected-she is the' 'packed-here's the' 'rejected-stuck in one place/tricks/trickster' 'packed-stuck in one place/tricks/trickster'. It reflects Esther and the other women packed in one place; the women going through a purification process to make them pure enough, presentable enough, to be presented to and touched by the king. It reflects Esther is there to deceive the king and other characters for the benefit of her people. It is reflected in Esther doing differently than the other concubines instead of 'whatsoever she desired was given her to go with her out of the house of the women unto the king's house.' So women can take whatever they want and as much as they want of the king's things and servants, but Esther plays it smartly 'she required nothing but what Hegai...appointed.' And in doing so she gains popularity with the king. It is also reflected that she goes from the 'second house of the women' which is packed with concubines, to the king's house where there would be more spacious living quarters. (Esth.2:12-16)

Tebeth; ṭēḇēṯ; طيبيت 'was treated good/good treatment' 'perfumed with ṭēḇ/ṭeeb' which is a powdery or waxed perfumed substance used by women, 'suddenly appeared/came/came unexpected' e.g. when a person suddenly arrives unexpected. It can also mean 'liked its taste' 'could eat it/palatable' which can also be understood and used in a negative sense of 'how could you eat/touch it' (e.g. like Tobiah) but in this instance it is about 'good treatment/nice perfumes'. The women are described as being put through a 'purification' process before they approach the king which involves being covered in different cleansing oils and perfumes, but it is mostly to do with 'Esther obtained favour in the sight of all of them that looked upon her…And the king loved Esther above all women, and she obtained grace and favour in his sight more than all the virgins…and made her queen instead of Vashti.', and with her arriving quickly at the king's house and in his favour. Like all other months mentioned in the Biblical stories, it has been chosen because it lends itself to the wordplay employed in the stories. Cp: ṭeybeyt. (Esth.2:16-18)

Bigthan; bigēṯān, bigēṯāna'; بِغيثآن ، بِغيثآنَى 'will be nauseated' 'I'm nauseated/I'm sick and tired of' 'he makes us nauseated/sick and tired'; بِغيتآن ، بِغيتآنَى 'they were scared' 'we/they were startled/shocked and scared' 'wanted/they wanted/we wanted' 'were misled to their downfall' 'will mislead (them/us) to downfall/of misleading to downfall' 'were immoral/sexually immoral'; Teresh; tereš; طَرَش ، طِرِش 'vomited' 'was immobilised with fear/lost his sanity from fear' 'struck dumb by shock' 'deaf' 'pretended to be deaf'.

Both these characters who share the same role and fate in the story have names related to 'vomiting', to 'surprise/shock', and 'fear' as well as Bigthan meanings being misled towards demise, and Teresh meanings of 'deaf/pretended to be deaf'. The choice and wordplay for these names was chosen to tell more in the story, they are both upset with the king and the story narrates they 'sought to lay hand on the king' but their character-names add that they were complaining about the king just like any person complains about work, or a bad boss—it relays that Mordecai did not really hear them want to hurt the king: 'deaf', but made himself deaf to what they were really saying 'pretended to be deaf'; it also indicates that Mordecai made up that they wanted to 'lay hands on the king' which causes their great shock and immobilising fear and Mordecai uses this misleading and fabricated report to cause their downfall.

Remember, the story has Mordecai had a plan he wanted implemented even before he sent Esther to be a concubine for the king, and before any problems and enmity arose between him and Haman: he loiters in front of the women's house to pick up information about what is happening inside, he is now 'sat in the king's gate' listening (i.e. spying) and waiting to see how he can make a move to serve his intentions. So the narration indicates Bigthan and Teresh are fed up of working for the king and griping about him, but also that Mordecai (take into account the negative meanings the author has given their names/ and Mordecai's lineage which connects to 'Bigthan' meanings of 'making up' and 'immoral') has made up part of the claim of what Bigthan/Teresh said (it is how samaara and samaaya stories are told and the Biblical stories cannot be understood nor 'read' without knowing the intended meanings of the word-names, allowing the audience to engage in wondering and asking about the story e.g. 'what if he did this…' 'what if he lied…' as indicated by the character/place name). Mordecai's actions do not only 'save' the king, but gain him credibility with the king at the expense of these two characters being 'hung from a tree'. Cp: bigheifaan, bigheifaana, bigheitaan, bigheitaana, ṭeresh. (Esth.2:19-23)

Haman; hāmān; هآمآن 'of importance' 'of worries' it can mean more than 'two' but does also mean 'two important matters/individuals' 'two worries' 'two people who are worried'; حآمآن 'heated and angry' 'protected' 'defended'. Haman is 'of importance' as the king promotes him to a position of importance over everybody else; he is accorded reverence by all because the king wants it and has elevated him; the king listens and agrees to everything he says, according it importance; Haman is given free reign of the kingdom, its resources and people '…king Ahasuerus promote Haman the son of Hammedatha the Agagite, and advanced him, and set his seat above all the princes that *were* with him. And all the king's servants that *were* in the king's gate bowed, and reverenced Haman…And the king said unto Haman, The silver *is* given unto thee, the people also, to do with them as seemeth good to thee.'.

Haman is proud of his rise in status, he also mistakes Esther's plot of inviting him to a banquet as a reflection of his importance 'And Haman told them of the glory of his riches, of the multitude of his children, and all *the things* wherein the king had promoted him…Yea, Esther the queen did let no man come in with the king unto the banquet, that she had prepared but myself: and tomorrow am I invited unto her also with the king.'. Haman is so pleased with himself, his importance, when the king asks how he should reward someone he honours (Mordecai), Haman mistakes this person as himself and suggests many honourable and generous actions from gifts to proclaiming to the whole city of the man's respect in the king's eyes.

Haman 'of worries' as he worries and plans how to dispose of Mordecai and his people; he goes home worried, distressed and speaks to his wife and friends of his new worries.

Haman 'heated and angry' is reflected in the story when Mordecai is the man honoured and risen in favour with the king; whenever Mordecai refuses to show respect towards Haman, the latter becomes 'full of wrath' 'but when Haman saw Mordecai in the king's gate, that he stood not up, nor moved for him, he was full of indignation against Mordecai'. Cp: haamaan, ḥaamaan. (Esth.3; 5)

Hammedatha; hammĕd̲āt̲ā'; هَمّيداآثاء ، هَمّيداآفاء 'here is the one covered with a blanket/sheet' and (dp̲h̲/df/ دف، دث) 'to cover/warm' and means to cover or wrap with a blanket, sheet or any fabric/garment in order to warm up, to sleep, or for any reason. When Ahasuerus honours Mordecai, Haman covers his head 'But Haman hasted to his house mourning, and having his head covered.'. The whole Esther story follows the proper Yemeni storytelling of what is called Samaara (night time/staying up stories) and Samaaya (naming stories): humorous, erotic, love triangles, men killing thousands, exaggerated strength, tricks and cleverness where characters and places are named for their role in the story. The decisive point against Haman is when the king returns to the room and finds Haman who has just fallen onto the bed out of fear, but in the story Ahasuerus mistakes it as Haman wanting to make love to Esther.

When read properly and with taking into account the direct meaning of his surname 'covered with blanket/sheet' it shows Haman is distressed and mourning as his life is in danger; it is indicated he may have covered himself or at least his head with a blanket or bed sheet (just as he covered his head when he was in mourning earlier in the story) and to make sure the audience does not miss this pun, the authors have Haman's face covered as soon as the king finishes wondering if Haman was going to rape Esther in front of him. We are told Haman fell upon the bed out of fear, begging for his life—so was the imagery of him clutching at the sheets/blankets, or his head and shoulders covered while he is on Esther's bed begging to be spared? What is definite is that the event in the story is indicated by his father's name 'here is the one covered with a blanket/sheet' which would explain why Ahasuerus character thought Haman was about to rape Esther or making advances. Esther was on the bed, as beds are not only used for sleeping, but for sitting/reclining on during the day.

'Then Haman was afraid before the king and queen. And the king arising from the banquet of wine in his wrath *went* into the palace garden: and Haman stood up to make request for his life to Esther the queen; for he saw that there was evil determined against him by the king. Then the king returned out of the palace garden into the place of the banquet of wine; and Haman was fallen upon the bed where Esther *was*. Then said the king, Will he force the queen also before me in the house? As the word went out of the king's mouth, they covered Haman's face.'. With it being a banquet of wine, the author is indicating both men, Ahasuerus and Haman were slightly drunk and not fully sober. Cp: hammeidaafaa, hammeidaap̲h̲aa. (Esth.)

Agagite; 'ăgagî; عيجَجي 'of suffering a lot/prolonged suffering' it is to cause both physical and psychological/emotional suffering over a long period of time, 'of overcrowding' 'of over spilling(with fortune/good)/ field filled with panicled crops it seems packed and over spilling' 'of stirring/shaking' 'of being/making crooked/twisted/not forthright' 'of crying and gasping' and means to sob intensely to the degree of gasping and being out of breath. It is equivalent to Ajah, Og, Doeg, Aiah, Aija, Agag, but Biblical scholars make the mistake of treating Biblical characters as real people and present wrong and unsubstantiated theories such as Haman being related to 'King Agag' of the Saul/Samuel story, or being connected to the 'Amalekite' people, some even present the story is supposed to link Mordecai (because of 'Benjamite') to Saul because Haman is given the 'Agagite' title and Saul defeated king Agag in the earlier story. This is because Biblical scholars have failed to understand the Biblical authors' method; and this is a consequence of either unintentionally or intentionally not identifying the true language of the Bible which is Arabic.

Haman is given the name of 'Agagite' to mean: he achieves a lot of personal wealth, and the king's power, treasury and authority are placed under his hand; the narration shows Mordecai being 'of being/ making crooked/twisted/not forthright' in his actions towards Haman which provoke the latter, and also both Haman and Mordecai's intentions and actions towards the general populations (of Jews and non-Jews) is crooked; Haman, Mordecai and Esther's actions linked to 'Agagite' meaning and role of Haman causes them to kill many people 'overcrowd/overspill/torture/suffer'; everything related to what Haman will do and receive, and by extension what Mordecai and Esther do and receive is in great numbers and/or quantities 'of over spilling(with fortune/good)/field filled with panicled crops it seems packed and over spilling' as well as what they achieve is done using underhanded tactics, not being direct or forthright 'of being/making crooked/twisted/not forthright' such as Esther's vague request of Ahasuerus until the banquet which also shows 'prolonged suffering', the 'banquet of wine' also shows 'over spilling (with fortune/good)'; Haman intends to make many people suffer a lot physically, but in the end he will suffer a lot both physically and psychologically, which he does first psychologically as soon as Mordecai is honoured, and again when he knows for certain that he will be killed as he is begging for his life, also reflecting 'sobbing and gasping' and his execution. Cp: 'aigagee. (Esth.3; 5)

Nisan is used here for its meaning of 'forgot/forgotten' 'comforted' as Haman's intention is to massacre all the Jews, to wipe them out which is to make them 'forgotten' and as mentioned earlier the word Nisan and its meaning is from the root word which also means 'people', but it shows that during this period of time the Jews are not attacked. The lots are cast for a whole year until the month of Adar. As mentioned earlier, these months are not used as actual dates or spans of time, but for their meaning as employed by Biblical authors. **Adar** is used for one of its meanings already used in Josh.15:3 and Ezra.6:15. In Esther it is used for 'the harmed/the harmer' as Haman seeks to harm all the Jewish people in the country. Which is why the story has him casting lots for a whole year which begins with 'Nisan' people being forgotten or comforted until the month 'Adar' where the word can mean 'harmed' which is Haman's intent. Cp: a<u>dh</u>aar, ai<u>dh</u>aar. (Esth.2:7-13)

Pur will be explained with Purim. (Esth.2:7)

Hatach; hăṯāk; هَتَاك ، هيتَاك 'here, go quickly/make haste' 'here he is coming to you' from word (at/ات) 'go quick/make haste' 'it/he is coming' and is used when asking someone to go do something or somewhere for you on an errand and especially if they want the thing done quick. Both Esther and Mordecai are sending Hatach to communicate secret messages between them; the urgency is because she is told Mordecai is wearing sackcloth and covered in ashes, i.e. he is in distress, and because she worries his appearance will cause him trouble; Mordecai tells her to urgently intervene and prevent the massacre of the people. Even Hatach's given role in the story is to 'attend upon her' do her bidding/errands. 'Then called Esther for Hatach…and gave him commandment to Mordecai…So Hatach went forth to Mordecai unto the street of the city…' Mordecai sends Hatach with a message 'And Hatach came and told Esther the words of Mordecai…Again Esther spake unto Hatach, and gave him commandment unto Mordecai…' and the story continues with Esther and Mordecai sending 'commanded/bade' Hatach with messages between them. Cp: haitaak, hataak. (Esth.3:5-15)

Zeresh; ṣereš; زَرَش 'insulted you greatly/filled you with insults'; ضَرَش 'harms/harmed you'. It is the name of Haman's wife introduced following Haman being insulted by Mordecai's constant refusal to get up and bow to him. It is also reflected in his wife and friends advise him to build gallows to hang Mordecai upon (harm), but as her name suggests the harm he plans for Mordecai has harmed Haman as he will be killed on the same gallows she suggested he build and which her character predicts will happen after Mordecai has been honoured. Cp: zere<u>sh</u>, <u>dh</u>ere<u>sh</u>. (Esth.5:14; 6:9-10)

Harbonah; ḥarĕḇônā', ḥarĕḇônâ; خَرِيبُنَآء ، خَرِيبُنَه 'they have ruined us' 'they have ruined him/it' 'our ruin'; خَرِي بُنَآء ، خَرِي بُنَه 'collapsed-his buildings/structures/his children' 'chased away with violence-his buildings/his children' and these meanings refer to Haman being ruined as the character Harbonah suggests hanging him on the gallows he had built for Mordecai. Later in the story all his children will be executed too. Cp: <u>kh</u>areibonaa, <u>kh</u>areibonah, <u>kh</u>arei-bonaa, <u>kh</u>arei-bonah. (Esth.7:9-10)

Sivan; sîwān; صيوَآن 'sweep away/brush away' 'swept/brushed away' 'sweeping brushes(made of date palm branches or rush)' and it refers to killing everybody and making them leave either by death, destruction or expelling them, the same word was used in the exact same way when David told the people to kill all the Jebusites, the lame and the blind out of Zion at 2Sam.5:6-8 as if they were sweeping away dirt; سيوَآن 'bad/they are bad' 'the same/they are the same' and it refers to the evil that will be done towards the non-Jews, it also reflects on the non-Jews who wanted to harm the Jews, but it is a clear message by the author of the story that both Haman, Mordecai and Esther did 'bad' in harming innocent people. It is equivalent to Zion. Cp: <u>ss</u>eewaan, seewaan. (Esth.8:9)

Adar 'the harmed/the harmer' is used again when the event is the killing and massacre of people, except this time it is against non-Jews as the Jews have been given permission 'to destroy to slay, and to cause to perish, all the power of the people and the province that would assault them, *both* little ones and women, and *to take* the spoil of them for a prey.'. (Esth.8:11-17)

Parshandatha; paršandāṯā'; بَر شَندآثاء 'the good/piety/will go beyond/surpass-we will cover(with blanket/sheet)' and is referring to these characters as Haman's sons were innocent of his deeds/intentions, which is why the second half of the compound word is the same as Haman's surname. Cp: bar-shandaafaa. (Esth.9:7)

Dalphon; dalpôn; تَلْفُن 'a ruin/spoiling' 'ruined them/it' 'destroyed for no reason' 'wrapped around/wrapped' 'deceived/went around in circles' and refers to the needless deaths narrated in the story as the people being killed were innocent of Haman's intentions; but also, these deaths were caused by Mordecai and Esther deceiving Ahasuerus. Cp: talphon. (Esth.9:7)

Aspatha; 'aspāṯā'; نَصبآطاء 'they stuck it on' 'they/it stuck on' and refers to the accusation and injustice being wrongly applied against them when they are murdered because of their father. assbaaṭaa. (Esth.9:7)

Poratha; pôrāṯā'; بُرآتاء 'they are innocent/good' 'they went beyond/surpassed' and refers to Haman's sons and the tens of thousands of innocent people being killed. Cp: boraataa. (Esth.9:8)

Adalia; 'ăḏalyā'; نيضَلْيآء 'they will mislead you/he is misleading you' 'he is leading you on the wrong path'. Refers to the atrocities being described as something good and the people being merry about it is actually misleading (it is the Biblical author pointing this out to the real audience). Cp: aidhalyaa. (Esth.9:8)

Aridatha; 'ărîḏāṯā'; عيريضآتاء 'they objected/stood against'. It refers to the editor/author objecting to the glorification of massacres regardless of a person's religion. Cp: 'aireedhaataa. (Esth.9:8)

Parmashta; parmaštā'; بَر مَستآء 'piety/good-offended/upset' and refers to morals, ethics, religious piety all being offended by massacres of innocent people and is again the authors of the Biblical stories directly addressing their audience that these fictional genocides are bad and nothing to be merry about. Cp: barmastaa. (Esth.9:9)

Arisai; 'ărîsay; عيريسي 'disgrace-bad' 'gloating-is bad' 'wedding/married' 'disgrace/shame-offends/is bad' it is still referring to the abnormal joy in the narration of the story regarding the massacres of tens of thousands of people who did not do anything to bring this upon themselves. Cp: 'aireesay. (Esth.9:9)

Aridai; 'ărîḏay; عيريضَي 'object(ed) to' 'stand against it/speak up against it'. Still refers to objecting to the description of genocide and joy narrated. Cp: 'aireedhay. (Esth.9:9)

Vajezatha; wayzāṯā'; وَيصآطاء 'and he attacks/swoops down on and clings to' 'an attack/swooping down/clinging to'; وَيسآتاء 'and he carries on making things bad' 'and he carries on offending' 'a bad action/an offense(offensive action)'; ويزآتاء 'and they/he kill quickly/slit open/cut open'. And this is at least one Biblical author/editor referring to whoever the original author of the parts of Esther who wrote genocide and glorified it. Cp: wayssaaṭaa, waysaataa, wayzaataa. (Esth.9:9)

The Book of Esther contains many indications that the Biblical authors were wary that people might take literally the delight displayed in massacring people, so the authors are making it clear that the killing of people of the Jewish faith as well as the killing of non-Jews is wrong. It could be the original author of this story, or likely an editor at a later time, went in and redid the story which delights and glorifies the genocide of non-Jews to be more clear that it is fictional and to make it more humane (to avoid stirring up discrimination among the real audience who are one people) and pointing this out with word-names how the description of being merry with genocide is not true and should not be taken literally, but an evil. It also explains why Haman's ten sons can be described as being slaughtered in the first wave of genocide against non-Jews, then brought back to life to be hung from the gallows all in the same part of Chapter 9; it is to bring people's attention to the sons' names and to understand the story is fictional and the glorifying or right to murder other people is not true. This is another prime example of editors going back into the story (maybe at much later dates) and adding their own thoughts and beliefs.

Pur and Purim; pûr; بُر ، بور 'ruin/destroy/lose or ruin reputation/go bad/lose flavour/pour out'. It has many meanings and use, some negative: of something or someone going from one state into a worse state. It can mean to do bad, or to make another person's reputation bad among other people. This word was used to name 'the lots' which Haman used to forecast (or maybe cast a spell) against Mordecai and Jews. Interestingly, there is a connection to the cup of a 'kooz' (hubbly bubbly) which is called a (booree/بوري)—when the flavour of the tobacco mix fades, they pick up the cup/bûrî and pour out the mix along with the hot coals some of which will have gone out. When you think of sorcery or ever seen people who practice sorcery (I do not mean movies but cultures and communities where it is believed and practised), in Arabic countries the sorcerer casting stones, or sticks, or fire, or the 'seer' reading tea leaves/coffee grounds—the cup is also poured out (the excess liquid) and turned upside down before the 'seer' looks into it to read the future/fate, etc. But with the kooz cup/pûrî/booree the old tobacco gone bad/flavourless is poured/tipped out: when a person suffers 'pur/بور' they have been harmed, or done wrong, given a bad reputation, become nothing or bad in other people's eyes, i.e. they too have lost their 'flavour/goodness'.

Purim; pûrîm; بُرهم/بورهم 'ruin/destroy/lose flavour/make bad/pour out-them' 'ruin their reputation' this is used as the word for the celebration because the 'pur/losing of reputation/destroying-them' had been Haman's intention upon Mordecai and Jews, but it backfires and it was Haman and his lot who are destroyed physically and in reputation (as well as tens of thousands of others in this story which seem to be killed for nothing but the joy of it (earlier stories also have unrealistic scope and delight in 'smiting/wiping out/killing women and children' but they attempt to justify it with 'clearing out the land' so they can take their place)). 'They cast Pur, that is, the lot, before Haman, from day to day, and from month to month…' then Haman incites Ahasuerus against Mordecai's people and asks 'they may be destroyed…' 'Because Haman, the son of Hammedatha, the Agagite, the enemy of all the Jews, had devised against the Jews to destroy them, and had cast Pur, that is, the lot, to consume them. And to destroy them; But when *Esther* came before the king, he commanded by letters that his wicked device, which he devised against the Jews, should return upon his own head, and that he and his sons should be hanged on the gallows. Wherefore they called these days Purim, after the name of Pur.'. Cp: bor, boor, borhum, boorhum. (Esth.3:7-15; 9:24-26)

Job

Uz in Job still holds the same meanings as in Gen.10:23: 'to need' (help or something material) 'to need support' 'to support(with help, money, food, clothing(i.e. take care of material needs); 'raise(in status)', 'twisted/bent/not straight'. The word 'Uz/need' means, and is used, when someone needs something or does not need anything; it can denote a person who takes care of his parents', or other relatives, needs (they are dependent on him). As the titular character is described as not needing anything, he has every material need in abundance, the story goes further to have Satan elucidate Job is only pious because God is providing for him and has not made him need for anything; he has many children, cattle, estate and wealth making his life easier—the land is called 'want/need' and Job has everything he could ever want or need. The authors bring in the 'twisted/not straight meaning' by allowing him to make sacrifices just in case his children have done something wrong. This is why the story begins with 'There was a man in the Land of Uz' substituting the usual introduction where the character's 'lineage' is laid out with the themes as names depicting the story to be told. (Job.1:11)

Job; 'iyyôb, yôb; يُيَّب ، يُب 'is/of returning/returns/going to and fro, or up and down' 'returning/returns/going to and fro, or up and down' 'is/of being jerked up and down' 'jerked up and down' 'is/of coming-going and coming-going' 'coming-going and coming-going'; يُجُّب ، جُب 'of/is go(ing) around all over the place' 'go around all over the place' 'is/of answer(ing)/reply(ing)/respond(ing)' 'answer/reply/respond'; يُعُّب ، عُب 'is/of shamed/disgraced' 'shamed/disgraced' 'is/of fill(ing)/filled/pack(ing)/packed' 'fill/filled/pack/packed'. When the word is used as (yb-yb/يبيب) describes when someone or something is physically going to-and-fro, up or down, and also when someone goes back and forth about a matter at hand—having one opinion, then turning against it, then going back to the initial opinion and so forth, it is also the name of the toy known as 'yo-yo' across the world which is (yb-yb in Arabic).

It is exactly what Job's character does in distress over losing everything, especially his family, in regarding how he sees God and God's behaviour. Though he initially sticks to his piety and belief in God's righteousness, Job changes his opinion, questions everything about God, but even during his loss of belief he still returns to make statements acknowledging God's supremacy/higher knowledge then returning to loss in this belief, but eventually going back to God—exemplifying the meaning of the word 'job/returns/goes back and forth(up and down)'. The 'answering' and 'go around all over the place' is in the whole story as Job responds to his friends' statements, and their statements are also called 'responses'; Satan is described as having travelled all over the earth. The 'shame/packed' is because Job begins with being filled with great fortune of every kind from children to material wealth; and in Job's friends' statements to Job, words to the effect that he should be ashamed of himself for saying such things as he does.

Even 'Satan's' actions (the word Satan شآطآن, as described in (1Chr.21:1-17), in its own right means 'two laps/two sides' 'laps/sides' and means went back and forth on the same course/path/way either twice or many times (in the Job story Satan is always going back and forth), it is equivalent to going 'back and forth' 'up and down' 'coming and going' and could mean two or more people do this or the action is done twice or several times) when God asks him where he has been, he replies 'going to and fro' 'walking up and down', this is related to Job to emphasise the meaning of 'Job'. Immediately after Satan's reply God asks Satan 'Hast thou considered my servant Job.'. Also, Job mentions himself as 'to and fro'. It is similar to one of the meanings in Eliab ('he who/the one who-rejects/refuses/returns' (Num.1:9)) and Aholiab ('he's the one who returns' (Exod.31:2-5)) Cp: iyyob, yob, iggob, gob, i'ob, 'ob. (Job.1; 7:4; 13:25; 23:8-9)

In addition to the meaning as described under 'Job', '**Satan**' still holds its meanings as explained under 1Chr.21:1-17. صآدآن 'obstructed' 'of obstructing' 'defended' and means to either block the way or block an action without being provoked or in self-defence, from the word (śd/صد) reflected in the narration 'Hast not thou made a hedge about him, and about his house, and about all that he hath on every side?'; صآطآن from the word (śṭ/صط) meaning 'to harm/strike/take away/swoop down on/attack' 'stick to/cling to' 'slip/fall and stick to the ground (fall hard or painfully)' 'laid hands on' and it means either two people laid their hands on something/someone they should not have (i.e. harmed them), or have transgressed twice.

Satan tells God that Job is only pious as long as God is protecting him and providing him with everything he needs, but if God were to smite, harm or take away from Job—Job would blaspheme 'But put forth thine hand now, and touch all that he hath.'. God gives Satan permission to harm and take away everything from Job, initially with the exception he is not to harm Job physically (not to lay his hands on Job) so Satan goes and harms, takes away, destroys everything and everyone Job has before receiving permission from God to lay his hands on and physically harm Job: 'And the Lord said unto Satan, Behold, all that he have *is* in thy power; only upon himself put not forth thine hand.' Smiting is done with the hand physically but in the Arabic language when someone goes and does something or actions it, whether personally or by instruction it is said to be done by 'the hand'—the language means 'to cause' and this is reflected as Satan's name and role shows this in the events and dialogue of the story '...and still he holdeth fast his integrity, although thou movedst me against him, to destroy him without cause. And Satan answered the Lord and said, Skin for skin, yea, all that a man hath will he give for his life. But put forth thine hand now, and touch his bone and his flesh, and he will curse thee to thy face. And the Lord said unto Satan, Behold, he *is* in thine hands; but save his life. So went Satan forth from the presence of the Lord, and smote Job with sore boils from the sole of his foot to his crown.'

There is a further nuance to the compound word 'Satan' 'smote/harm/etc.' is in the form of twice the (an/ān/ان) in the word, as in the story Satan harms Job twice (first harming everyone and everything Job has, then in Job's body/health), but also because it is both God and Satan who have harmed Job, Satan did not do it without God allowing and wanting to see what the harm would result in, God says 'although thou movedst me against him, to destroy him without cause'. Therefore, he is harmed twice, and harmed by two beings/characters: God and Satan. (Job.1:6-19; 2:1-7)

Sabeans; the same as Seba (Gen.10:7): 'captured/took away/took captives' and the word was chosen because of the word which lent itself to the role given in the story 'And the Sabeans fell upon them, and took them away' telling of all the ox and donkeys being stolen. (Job.1:14-15)

Chaldeans; Chaldíōn, Chaldaí, Chaldaíoi, kaśdîm, kaśdāy; خَلديوي ، خَلدَي ، خَلديون 'sun/heat roasted' 'severely beat up' 'mole(s)/a mole' 'remembered forever' 'lived forever' 'of roasting' 'they are of roasting' 'of roasting in sun or on fire/heat' 'skin peeled off(from heat or beating)', the different variations of the word all hold the same meaning, only nuance is that any of the words can refer to singular or plural, or can attribute the action or be an adjective depending on how it is used; kaśdîm; قَشط ام ، قَشط هم 'make/made crispy-them/the' from word to make bread crispy/toasty; قَشدهم/ام 'boiled-them/the' 'beat/killed-them/the' (the latter can mean figuratively too), which also means to boil on intense heat for a long period of time when clarifying butter. kaśdāy; قَشداي 'clarified the butter/boiled on heat for a long time' the process of which includes removing the impurities and excess fat through intense and prolonged heat, 'killed/caused to suffer in great numbers'. As you can see all the words have the same meaning of something roasting or changing due to excessive heat, all words are Arabic, but Biblical scholars seek to understand them from Greek, 'Hebrew' 'Akkadian' and they still do not understand the meaning of the words as opposed to seeing their direct and only meanings in the Bible all come from Arabic. It relays in the story about the sheep and the servants being 'burned up' by a fire from God, and to the slaying of the servants and theft of the camels, also to all the destruction befalling everyone Job loves and everything he owns. It is equivalent to Chaldees (Gen.11:28). Cp: khaldeeoon, khaldai, khaldaiwee, qashṭ-hum/um, qashd-hum/um, qashdaay. (Job.1:16-17)

Eliphaz for its meaning 'the one who provoke(d)/wins(won)' (Gen.36:4). 'The one who won' as this character's opening response is reminding Job those who are good will win/be saved in the end. Although he is trying to comfort the mourning Job, he manages to provoke him, as his name suggests, even his words/ preaching needle Job. Job's dialogue as a first response expresses this clearly 'To him that is afflicted pity should be shewed from his friend,'. In his second response, his 'answer' is void of any comforting words (void of even reminding that good will win in the end) and is harsher and more provoking to Job, the latter responds 'I have heard many such things: miserable comforters are ye all.'. (Job.16:2)

Bildad; bildad; بِلدَد 'with talking/talked/uttered nonsense' 'talked all over the place' 'with empty talk'; بِلتَت 'talked all over the place/incoherent' 'broke or crumbled things into small pieces all over the place'. It is equivalent to Eldad (Num.11:16-29). Bildad's opening sentence to Job is words to the effect of 'How long will you speak nonsense?': 'How long wilt thou speak these *things*? and *how long shall* the words of thy mouth be like a strong wind?' the very meaning of 'Bildad' talk. Then Bildad himself embarks on speaking nonsense, preaching to Job, presenting many examples of what seems coherent, but to a mourning Job are meaningless examples plucked from all Bildad can think up. Job's first reply is the same as followed to Eliphaz's first dialogue as it is directed to all three friends 'miserable comforters are ye all' but also 'Shall vain words have an end? Or what emboldeneth thee that thou answerest?' this is also directed at all three friends.

Bildad's second reply offers more nonsense, this time warning of wickedness for the wicked, but still his opening line is saying Job is speaking too much and speaking nonsense: 'How long will *it be ere* ye make an end of words? mark, and afterwards we will speak. Wherefore are we counted as beasts, *and* repeated vile in your sight?' And Job expresses his frustration with the amount of nonsense Bildad preaches: 'How long will ye vex my soul, and brake me in pieces with words? These ten times have ye reproached me: ye are not ashamed *that* ye make yourselves strange to me.' And after Bildad's third response, which although it uses big imagery—says nothing at all, Job responds with 'How hast thou helped *him that is* without power? *how* savest thou the arm *that hath* no strength? How hast thou counselled *him that hath* no wisdom? and *how* hast thou plentifully declared the thing as it is?'. In other words: you've spoken a lot, but said nothing, offered no sound or any advice, comfort or wisdom—again, the very meaning of 'bildad'. Cp: bildad, biltat. (Job.)

Zophar; ṣôpar; زُفَر 'forced to leave quickly' 'exhaled' 'a big exhalation'; صُفَر 'whistled/whistling' 'bile' 'malaria' 'yellowed'. 'exhalation' and 'whistled' because Zophar's condemnation and aggressive speech to Job is like the blasting of hot air. Cp: zophar, ssophar. Zophar's opening lines accuse Job of 'empty talk': 'should not the multitude of words be answered? and should a man full of talk be justified?' i.e. you've spoken a lot, but your words are empty of meaning (like hot air). 'Should thy lies make men hold their peace? and when thou mockest, shall no man make thee ashamed?' again: lies, mockery—nonsense. But Zophar is preparing to blast Job, the words زفر ، صفر both apply to making a spectacle of the target, and the character embarks on a very harsh accusation and gloats at Job's misfortune: 'For thou hast said, My doctrine *is* pure, and I am clean in thine eyes. But oh that God would speak, and open his lips against thee; And that he would shew thee the secrets of wisdom, that *they are* double that which is! Know therefore that God exacteth of thee *less* than thine iniquity *deserveth*.'

Job's response is either genuine, or as I believe it to be sarcastic as people in my area (of origins) use the same expression in sarcastic retort 'No doubt but *ye* are the people, and wisdom shall die with you.' Before going on with 'But I have understanding as well as you; I *am* not inferior to you...But ye *are* forgers of lies, ye *are* all physicians of no value.' Directed at all three: they are only provokers, speak nonsense, speak empty words with no real meaning or advice, therefore: 'O that ye would altogether, hold your peace! and it should be your wisdom.'

Job's response to Eliphaz in Chapter 16 is directed at all three friends, but the following is specifically for Zophar 'I could also speak as ye *do*: if your soul was in my soul's stead. I could heap up words against you, and shake mine head at you.' as it is Zophar condemning Job harshly.

The other meaning of Zophar's name 'forced to leave quickly' is in Zophar's final response (Chapter 20), it is full of descriptions of things being forced out, no matter how long they will eventually leave, and quickly: 'triumphing of the wicked is short...joy of the hypocrite but for a moment', no matter how much a person rises 'ye he shall perish like his own dung; they which have seen him will say, Where is he?...He shall fly away as a dream...he shall be chased away as a vision of the night' neither eye nor place will see/hold him 'He hath swallowed down riches, and he shall vomit them up again: God shall cast them out of his belly' and this goes on to the end of the chapter.

In response to Zophar's accusations, or belief, that the wicked are punished, their wealth and health taken away by God as punishment—Job responds by pointing out how even people known to do evil, live and prosper and go through life untroubled. All throughout the dialogue there is a 'back and forth' which also reflects Job's character name. (Job.)

The surnames of Job's friends have also been chosen to suit the role in the story—which is to arrive together to mourn with and comfort Job—at least that is the case when they are introduced: Eliphaz is a Temanite; têmāṇî; طيماني 'reassured/reassure' 'of reassuring/reassurance' 'my reassurance'; Bildad is a Shuhite; šûḥî; شوهي ، شُهي 'chat/talk/conversation' 'of chatting'; Zophar is a Naamathite; na'ămāṯî; نَعيماتي 'blessed/softened/soft/smoothed/smooth'. They are to mourn with and comfort Job in his grief, and their surnames 'reassure/chat/soften' all indicate they arrive and want to ease his pain. Job makes a point of reminding them, this is what they were supposed to do for him when he tells them they are 'miserable comforters'. He points out if he were in their place, he too could reproach and shake his head at them, but instead '...I would strengthen you with my mouth, and the moving of my lips should assuage your grief' and that 'thou hast made desolate all my company.'. Cp: ṭeymaanee, shoohee, shohee, na'aimaatee. (Job.2:11-13)

Elihu for 'he who/the one who' 'yes, it is the one/yes, it is him' and he will be the one who does not engage in a back and forth, to-ing and fro-ing of arguments and opinions, but will state what he believes is the answer, the dialogue states he sees Job and his friends as not answering at all, or presenting the wrong answer.

He is son of Barachel; bāra<u>k</u>'ēl; بآرَك ئِل 'made kneel-the' 'made last long-the' 'blessed-the' shown in the narration that God will restore youth and health to those who show remorse and pray for mercy; بآرَق ئِل 'put into a sulk-the' 'put into a strop/mood-the' 'stopped talking/eating(out of upset)-the' 'struck lightning-the' as he is in a temper and outraged over what has been said and what he believes Job's friends allowed Job to get away with without setting him straight by only blaming him without answering his questions; Elihu is indignant and so are the older men because of Elihu, the older men are described also as 'stopped talking out of upset/temper': 'Then was kindled the wrath of Elihu...wherefore I was afraid and durst not shew you mine opinion...They were amazed, they answered no more: they left off speaking. When I had waited, (for they spake not, but stood still, and answered no more;)'. Either an addition by a later editor, or the original author, has 'Elihu Barachel' 'the one who-lightning strikes-the' to mean and relay '(God) is thunder and lightning', as in literally thunder and lightning are God's voice and the sound of him moving around in the clouds, making noise in his tabernacle (Job.36-37); بآرَخ ئِل 'I will loosen-the' shown in the narration that Elihu allows himself to speak, also that God will be lenient towards those who have someone to speak for them to God or shows regret. Cp. baarak-ill, baaraq-ill, baara<u>kh</u>-ill (Job.32-33)

He is a Buzite; bûzî, bûziy; بُزِي ، بُزي 'take/carry' 'take away' so it can reflect God will kill(take) him if he attempts to flatter the others 'For I know not to give flattering titles; in so doing my maker would soon take me away.'. Cp: buzee, buzey. (Job.32:2, 22)

He is related to Ram; rām; رآم 'thrown/killed' 'throwing/killing' 'has thrown' to reflect how Elihu finds Job throwing around his opinions and accusations to justify himself instead of looking at it as coming from God, supported by repeated narration of Job speaking 'without knowledge', and also because the three friends have thrown accusations and condemnation against Job without addressing anything Job had presented and questioned. Cp: raam. (Job.32)

Mazzaroth; mazzārô<u>t</u>; مَزّآرُت 'made to visit' 'the visit/pilgrimage/the visit of' 'what has visited'; مَسّآرُت 'the path of' (in modern Arabic 'the orbit of'). Both meanings reflect the narration of God asking Job if he has the power to make 'Mazzarot' visit/follow a specific path i.e. is it Job or a higher being that controls and brings these things in their seasons, puts them on a path. Cp: mazzaarot, massaarot. (Job.38:32)

Behemoth; behēmô<u>t</u>; بَهيمَة 'an animal' it can be any animal, and literally means a living creature that cannot speak, understand or think like a person; it is also used to describe/insult a person who behaves brashly, foolishly or is stupid, or simply does not understand what is being said when what is being said is very clear. Both the current and previous chapter speak of animals which cannot speak, or understand; Job at the beginning of chapter 40 states he will put his hand on his mouth, i.e. become dumb like an animal. Cp: beheymot. (Job.40)

Leviathan; liwyā<u>t</u>ān; لِوياآتآن 'twists/two twists' 'they are not forthright/they are dishonest' 'they twisted/entwined/twirled' or two things(living or objects) that twist/twirl/entwine, and the author has twisted the descriptions of more than one animal into the 'Leviathan'; لِبياآثآن 'for the 'bethans' (a venomous reptile)'; لِوياآضآن 'for the luminous millipedes' 'twisted/entwined-shine/shone/glow/abluted/suspects/thinks'. Part of the description is of a crocodile: teeth, shut-up scales, make deep to boil—when going underwater quickly, make path to shine after him, the trail a crocodile leaves on banks coming out of a river; it may also be inspired by an armadillo coat and behaviour (regarding sealed scales); it seems the description has been twisted with that of a 'bethan', a reptile whose poison is more lethal and kills quicker than snake venom: it lives/hides in crags, holes, under rocks—there is no time to save a person from its bite even when cars were available to get to hospitals in modern times. The description is also mixed with that of a luminous millipede called 'wa<u>dh</u>een', in the dark/night you can see the luminous drops of yellow, white or green phosphorous matter that fall from its legs and leave behind it a glowing trail—its phosphorous matter can burn skin. The 'burning lamps, and sparks of fire leap out' are from the luminous millipedes characteristics; 'out of his nostrils goeth smoke, as out of a seething pot or cauldron' could be a crocodile bubbling water as it surfaces—or it could be any land animal that puffs through its nostrils (whether in soil or not) it gives the imagery of smoke; 'he maketh the deep to boil like a pot' as a crocodile or shark when diving. Cp: liwyaataan, libyaafaan, liwyaa<u>dh</u>aan. (Job.41)

Jemima; yĕmîmâ; ييميمه a diminutive of mother 'mummy/mum'; هيميمه 'he will lead him/lead him through' 'cares/is active/energetic'; حيميمه diminutive of pigeon/dove, 'close/intimate/caring'. It refers to

God leading Job back to the right path and among his recompense are beautiful and loving daughters who are also loved. Cp: yeimeemah, heimeemah, ḥeimeemah. (Job.42:14)

Kezia; qĕṣîʿâ; كيذيئه 'fragrant plant(called kaavee)' 'smells like kaavee'; قيصيعه 'good-looking/perfect looking' 'a jar/can' which is what attractive/beautiful girls/women are described as, or when they wear a certain dress that looks good on them; جيزيئه 'rewarded him' 'his reward'. Refers to the unpleasantness of what Job went through and being rewarded with children, relatives and wealth, among them beautiful daughters. Cp: keivee-ah, qeis̲s̲ee'ah, geizee-ah. (Job.42:12)

Keren-happuch; qeren happûḵ; قَرَن حَبُّك 'stay still so we/I can kiss you' 'stay still until I/we kiss you' 'admitted to loving you' 'your horn-loved you' 'settled you-loved you'. It refers to after losing all his loved ones, being shunned by others, Job is now surrounded by a larger family who return to loving him, the 'horn' loving him has to do with the culture (which is Arabic (Yemeni to be specific)) who believe in 'horns' (to be discussed elsewhere in this book) which the narration has Job state 'and defiled my horn in the dust.'. Cp: qeren habbuk. (Job.42:12)

Psalms

It is believed that 'psalms' comes from the Greek word 'psalmoí' which means 'songs of praise'. I disagree. For the Greek to translate the word from the OT and give 'Psalms' the fitting title would necessitate understanding it in its local language and context, from the local people. The word itself 'psalm' is an Arabic word, it is not a far stretch to see the local language from which it was taken (whether you want to call it Arabic or Hebrew) has created a new word in a foreign culture (Greek). In fact, there are many words of Arabic origins which can be seen in the English language today, their roots forgotten over time, I can identify them because Arabic is a language I never stopped using since I learnt it in my childhood. Just as 'Hawaa' was made into 'Eve' to make it simple for the foreign tongue to pronounce it, substituting 'Hawaa' with its synonym allowed it to keep its exact meaning—so has the word 'psalm' been offered to the Greek instead of 'mizmor' with the latter's correct pronunciation being more difficult for the foreigner to articulate, but it also allowed the foreigner translating the 'Arabic/Hebrew' into Greek to understand better what the 'psalm/mizmor' actually is.

Mizmor; mizmôr; مِضمُر 'kept/keep inside oneself' 'hidden thoughts/intentions' 'what is kept inside/in heart' 'kept in heart' 'hide in soul/head/heart' and means to know, think or feel something but not say it out loud, to hide the true intentions/meanings/feelings from others. It is what Psalms are doing, hiding the original stories by removing parts and adding parts to alter the story. The word may have been misunderstood as مِزمُر 'pipe' 'musical horn' which also misleads towards misinterpreting the psalms as being songs/hymns. Cp: mi<u>dh</u>mor.

Psalm; psalmoí; بسَلمُي 'intact' 'whole' 'survived' 'let live(slightly different than 'saved' although it could be understood that way)' 'with/in peace' 'with gentle/mild nature'. In regards to Psalms of the OT, it definitely means 'intact' 'whole' and when the work is read correctly, you can see how and why. The Psalms are not individual complete works (per psalm), but they are parts of the OT stories which were removed, but the editors did not want to dispose of, should they need to return to them to make the edited OT stories 'whole' 'intact' again. Some psalms are new additions which were meant to be inserted in between the original OT stories, but for one reason or another had not been added. In the following, it will become evident how this works and the findings will support this opinion. Cp: bsalmoy.

To begin with, what is being interpreted as 'To the Chief Musician' is an error. There are two possibilities for lamĕnaṣṣēaḥ; لَمينَسّيَه 'why did he forget/why did he make forget' 'for/to make forget' or; لَمينَصّيَح 'when we shout' 'for who/what we advise' 'for/to who advises'. Cp: lameinasseyah, lameina<u>ss</u>eyaḥ.

First, if read correctly 'why did he make forget' 'for/to make forget' and refers to the psalm which is part of the original OT story related to David's stories so e.g.Psalm 4 instead of reading 'To the chief Musician on Neginoth, A Psalm of David' it should read: *Why did he make forget about 'saved us(neginoth)', the whole/hidden (story) for David*; or: *To make forget about 'saved us(neginoth)', the whole/hidden (story) for David*; and the psalm was either an original part of the story removed from the earlier OT story in Sam., etc., or was a newly written addition which a later editor wanted to insert between the old/original story (but never got around to) and with regards to this psalm because it is about being saved (Neginoth) it was taken from or meant to be inserted where David was saved from a particular threat.

If it is 'when we shout' then this part whether it was removed or supposed to be inserted, when these stories were told, this particular part was supposed to be recited loudly or passionately, and/or emphasised on.

In all cases, these are instructions to whoever was responsible for restoring, removing and adding the editions to the Biblical texts once they were compiled as written documents. Which is why some psalms have direct instructions of where to add or where they were removed from: 'A Psalm of[*for*] David when he fled from Absalom' is self-explanatory; '*Shiggaion of David, which he sang unto the Lord, concerning the words of Cush the Benjamite.*' refers to the part of the earlier story where David is informed of his son Absalom's death; the translation of the word 'sang unto the Lord' also indicates a mistranslation/misinterpretation—who sings to God when they hear their beloved child has been killed? But the original story does tell us that exactly at this part David was making passionate statements of grief while crying out and weeping in distress over Absalom.

The psalms without notes were either removed from being used, or had not been looked into, therefore no designation of where they were to be added made. Some notes above the psalms indicate the content of the psalm. It is possible that nothing about the psalms is 'musical' even if, for example, they rhymed in the original language, that does not mean they were songs, but stories of the area, and even religious texts are written in rhyme. But what has caused Biblical psalms to be wrongly seen as songs, is the misinterpretation of laměnaṣṣēaḥ 'why did he forget/make forget' as '*To the Chief Musician*'. Even the psalms about characters involved in musical events, it is still sections removed from, or parts that were to be added, into the original story which just happened to be about making music (e.g. when returning the ark).

Neginoth; něgînâ; نيجينه 'we survived' 'we were saved' 'saved him' and is also the same as Neginah; něgînat; نيجينة 'the saving of'. Both mean 'save/rescue me/us' 'saved us'. In every single Psalm with this note, it is asked of God to: save him, or his people, or mentions having saved him; requests saving from enemies who surround him. In one psalm the request is made subtly and as a negotiation with God, words to the effect 'save me—and we'll bless/praise you.'. Cp: neigeenah, neigeenat. (Ps.4; 6; 54; 55; 61; 67; 76)

Nehiloth; něḥîlâ, něḥîlôt; نيهيله ، نيهيلةُ 'we will cry out loud/praise/chant' 'we will cry out word or name repeatedly' 'we'll praise/glorify him' 'we'll cry his name', 'the praising of/the glorifying of' 'the crying out his name of' from the word (hll-l/hallil/هَلِل) which means to shout out a name in a welcoming (or glorifying) manner, chant, cry out loud, (the name could be a person's or even God's), and throughout the psalm with this note, the text emphasises and repeats crying out to God; praying; praising him; asking to allow them to rejoice, to find joy in his name; but to ignore the praising of his enemies as their praising/crying/worship is just deceit, fake, etc. Cp: neiheelah, neiheelot. (Ps.5)

Shiggaion; šiggāyôn; شِجّآيَن 'passionate/painfully passionate' and the note mentions it is about when Cush delivered the information of Absalom's death (2Sam.18:19-33; 19:4). This supports the possibility that the Psalms were revised rewritings which were supposed to be inserted into the earlier books to replace what was originally written: e.g. in this case (in 2Sam.) David is broken over his son's death, he is crying and screaming 'O my son Absalom, my son, my son Absalom! would God I had died for thee, O Absalom, my son, my son!'. His weeping, grief, are so profound the people, and even his soldiers, are distressed. But this Psalm has rewritten and wants (or was intended) to replace David's mourning and grief with happiness and satisfaction with God destroying his enemies, even gloating over his son being thrown in a ditch. It shows how the Torah/Bible has been distorted by additions/editing and rewritten to suit later authors/editors' beliefs and ideas. Cp: shiggaayon. (Ps.7)

Muthlabben; mûṯ labbēn; مُط لَبّين 'extend/stretch into'; مُطلَب بين 'Requested in/Requested to put into' 'two requests'. If it is 'extend/stretch into' it is an instruction to insert the text; the same for 'requested in'. 'two requests' refers to the nature/content of the text which is asking God for two things: for God to judge the people; and to be a refuge for the oppressed. Cp: muṭ labbeyn, muṭlab beyn. (Ps.9)

Higgaion; higgāyôn; هِجّآيَن 'pronunciation' or 'teach to pronounce/those who teach pronunciation' and is a term used to teach someone how to pronounce properly. It is done beginning with babies and is called 'haggeeh/هَجّيه' 'teach him/her to pronounce', and is where the mother is heard making clear sounds, while smiling, looking down at her baby while making eye contact, and the baby starts to attempt to replicate her sounds (leads to words later on) while still only a few months old. The most used sound/word by mothers in the early stages is (haggoo, hagooh/هَجّو ، هجوه) 'teach to pronounce'. The same word means teaching/learning to pronounce the accentuations correctly of words in Arabic language and also the Quran. The form of the word written as 'higgaion' is an instruction to teach others how to properly pronounce the words, how they should sound. Cp: higgaayon. (Ps.9)

Gittith; gittîṯ, 'alhagittîṯ; غِطّيت ، عَلهَغِطّيت 'covered' 'about there covered'; غِضّيت ، عَلهَغِضّيت 'nourished' 'strengthened' 'about there nourished' 'about there strengthened' and in all psalms with this note, both meanings are present in the text. All speak of covering/crowning with glory, honour; mention 'nourishment': baby suckling turning into strength; mentions making all foods/needs/animals under man's hands/feet: sheep, ox, beasts, birds, fish—all for man's nourishment/nutrition. Nourishing (gittith/غِضّيت) leads to strength; 'Sing aloud unto God our strength' 'open thy mouth wide, and I will fill it'. Narrates getting Joseph and the people out of trouble in Egypt/Merebah so (cover/غِطّيت) means to 'shield/protect'; narrates if they had listened to God 'He should have fed them with the finest of the wheat; and with the honey out of the rock should I have satisfied thee.'. In Ps.84 it is mostly about 'cover'—the tabernacles, a house, a nest, altars, house of God: 'I had rather be a doorkeeper in the house of God, than to dwell in the tents of wickedness' 'for the Lord is a sun and shield'. Cp: ghiṭṭeet, 'alhaghiṭṭeet, ghidheet, 'alhaghidheet. (Ps.8; 81; 84)

Selah; selâ; صَلَه ، صِله 'a connection'. It means connecting a letter to a letter (written or vocally) within a word, or word to another word such as in reading religious text or praying, or even singing. It is still about pronunciation as the words/letters connected are connected in how they are pronounced smoothly without interruption/pause. There are different types of 'selah'. It is an instruction embedded in the text of the psalms giving directions to the reader/copier/scribe, etc. what to connect and how to pronounce the words (connected). Cp: ṣṣelah.

Michtam; miḵtām مِخْتَام 'the end/seal/finish with' but this is not supported by the text. It is more likely: مِكْتَام ، مِغْتَام 'to muffle/suffocate/hide/keep under wraps/covered'. Again, it takes on the appearance of text from the earlier Biblical stories either removed from the original, or meant to replace or be added to the original. When read as miḵtām lĕḏāwiḏ; مِكْتَأم/مِخْتَام it is not 'of David' but 'muffling/hiding/covering *for* David', there is a difference between something being 'of' or 'for'.

Ps.16 is a David confident in God, but who seemingly relies on some kind of sorcery/witchcraft as he mentions 'the lines are fallen unto me in pleasant places,' and 'my reins also instruct me in the night seasons'—but this use of 'lines' and how they fall by David has not been removed from elsewhere in the 2Sam. story. At the same time the psalm shows David as never veering from God's path, which in the earlier stories he has been presented as having gone astray from God's path (in the earlier books of the Bible), but here in psalms it presents him as 'I have set the Lord always before me: because *he* is at my right hand, I shall not be moved.' 'for thou wilt not leave my soul in hell; neither wilt thou suffer thine Holy One to see corruption.'. It is very different than how David is presented in the earlier stories.

In Ps.56 the note above it states 'To the chief Musician upon Jonath-elem-rechokim, Michtam of David, when the Philistines took him in Gath'. It is important to understand sometimes translation/interpretation creates errors. As a speaker of the language of the Bible, I can see the error (not just here, but also in other parts of the Bible where one word is given a different meaning by mistake/misunderstanding) and I can also see how it was mistaken when it is a word similar to 'on/upon' when it actually means 'about'.

So from the note mentioned above this psalm, you can see it is an instruction 'to make forget(not to chief musician)' but should read '*about* Jonath' and not '*upon* Jonath'. 'upon Jonath' would only be correct if it were meant to supersede what was written earlier in that part of the story and replace it with the new written version.

This specific psalm note refers to when Saul is informed by the people of Ziph of David being in Hachilah woods after Jonathan meets him there (note how the author of this note uses the word (jonath/خَنَث) not as a name, but an adverb)—the sentence in the note directs (whoever it is instructing) to this specific part of the earlier story, the sentence 'Jonath-elem-rechokim' reads 'male anal sex-found out-they relieved you':

'**jonath**' '(male and male)had anal sex made each other female' refers to Saul finding out where David is, the latter having met Jonathan for sex there;

'**elem**' Saul knows/found out;

'**rechokim**' 'they relieved you' (Saul knows where to find David to bring an end to it). It is the people who informed Saul and he responds (in the earlier story) 'And Saul said, Blessed be ye of the Lord; for ye have compassion on me,' (1Sam.23)

Not only is 'michtam' an instruction for 'lamĕnaṣṣēaḥ/to make forget/why made forget', but also the text itself is an attempt to 'muffle/hide' how David was originally presented—this psalm presents David as fearless of death and of what man could do to him, in contrast to 1Sam.23 where he is described as being in fear of his life, even the place he hid at (which was surrounded by Saul and his men) was named 'rock-worried-the death of/perish of(Sela-hammahlekoth)'. The psalm text also has David prayed to God 'then shall mine enemies turn back' which in 1Sam.23 does noes not happen, but a messenger informing of a Philistine attack elsewhere causes Saul to turn back, so this text was meant either to replace or be added to that part regarding Saul/David.

Again in (michtam/muffle/hide) Ps.57, it shows David as desperate and fearful while he is in the cave, it seems he does not even trust those who are on his side—the complete opposite of the text in Sam. in how he refuses to kill Saul but is brave/confident enough to cut off the skirt Saul's wearing while he sleeps.

Ps.60 (michtam/muffle/hide) is either a text that has been removed from the original story or was meant to be added or to replace the original text (earlier story). In this Psalm it is a desperate plea to a God that has abandoned David and his people, and they seem to be losing the battle 'scattered us' whereas in the earlier books/stories and in all its events (mentioned in the Psalm 60 instructions) show a strong David defeating the enemies with ease, in contrast to the desperate and reproaching tone in Psalm 60. Cp: mikhtaam, miktaam, mightaam. (Ps.16; 56-60)

If the instructed were meant to change, add, delete (or did so) from the original story—how much of the Bible stories which have been read for centuries were actually corrupted by editing, we will never know. Even without Psalms, upon reading the OT there is obvious corruption to the Biblical stories. What Psalms does is prove my belief stated in many parts of this book where there are obvious changes and contradictions, different writing styles where you can see additions have been made, which I have touched upon earlier in this book.

Aijeleth Shahar; 'ayyelet šaḥar; عَيجَلة شَهَر ، عَيجَلة سَهَر which could mean 'a month-old calf' or 'impatience/haste of the month' 'impatience of staying up (all night)'. Regarding 'month-old calf', the content of the psalm is about a young subject, barely out of his mother's womb, followed by mentioning being surrounded by (human) predators who are compared to bulls 'many bulls have compassed me: strong bulls of Bashan have beset me round. They gaped upon me *with* their mouths *as* a ravening and a roaring lion.' And following this comparison of his weakness/innocence to their strength/predation, the protagonist expresses total (and accurately described) fear and the physical reactions a person in great fear goes through (v.14-15).

'impatience of staying up(all night)', verse 2 'O my God, I cry in the daytime, but thou hearest not; and in the night season, am not silent' expressing both impatience and frustration.

It could be just a note from the author to 'the Musician[a misinterpretation (see Chief Musician)]' expressing this is what could be rushed in a month—or something about a calf. Cp: 'aygelet shahar, 'aygelet sahar. (Ps.22)

Maschil; maskîl; مَسقيل ، مَسق يل 'watering/pouring of the'; مَسخيل ، مَسخ يل 'comparing to/turning into animals-the' 'ruining/mutating-the' or 'corrupting-the' and can mean to physically become disfigured/animal-like (babies born with deformities (sometimes animal-like are called 'mskh') and/or to go from being good to bad/evil. Ps.44 pours out a prayer and praise, describes mutation as being corrupted like sheep, bad things in enemies' eyes. The main themes in the psalms with this title are as follows:

Ps.32 and 42: about both 'watering/pouring' and 'comparing to animals' or 'corrupting'.

Ps.45: pouring prayer and praise to each other and God.

Ps.53: about corrupt people.

Ps.54: pour out soul to God.

Ps.55: a complaint to God about another person's corruption.

Ps.74: pouring out of all wrong, asking God to help, feeling abandoned, seeing corruption/defilement being allowed.

Ps.78: corruption of people throughout.

Ps.88: about being corrupted, pouring out complaint to God (مسقيل 'watering/pouring of the'), afflicted with something mutated and abhorred (مسخيل 'turning into/comparing to animals/ruining/mutating-the' 'corrupting-the') even loved ones will not come near him—disfigured/unwanted. Cp: masqeel, masq-eel, maskheel, maskh-eel. (Ps.32; 42; 44; 52; 53; 54; 74; 78; 88)

Ps.89: begins with outpour of heavy praises but turns to accusing God of corruption/corrupting/ruining David to the end.

Ps. 142: David pouring prayer to God.

Throughout psalms titled or with note of 'Maschil' there is a pouring of a person's soul to God, a verbal outpouring of either praise/prayer or anger/accusation; the same between people. There is also, in most Maschils, the changing/corruption/mutating into evil as the subject matter of the text.

Jeduthun as earlier 'they play/beat tambourines' 'they pound/beat'. Ps.39 'To the chief Musician[not 'chief musician' see Chief Musician correct translation], even to Jeduthun...' Jeduthun mentioned earlier in Chronicles, has the same meaning here of beating on tambourines or such an instrument similar to tambourine.

Sheminith 'timed/timing' to keep on time and refers to (1Chr.15) the groups are playing different musical instruments and one group playing 'with harps on the Sheminith to excel' means they played their instruments on time. (Ps.6; 12)

The names of the Levite/Korahites who attend to the tabernacle, the word-names are all to do with sounds, and many of those named to praise/play before the ark have names regarding musical sounds/instruments, just like Jeduthun 'they beat on tambourines'; **Mikneiah** 'a singer-he/him'; **Chenaniah** 'sang a lot-he/him' 'made sing-he/him'; **Kore** 'tapped/tapping' 'sharp strike/tap' 'read' 'read to', who is a 'descendant' of **Korah** 'striking sound' 'bursting sound' gives Korahite more meaning than just a 'loud noise'. The meanings of Kore 'tapping' 'breakfast' are supported with text that he/they prepare food and are involved in musical rituals.

It further elucidates how word-names are made up. If we return to the names of the Levites charged with taking care of the tabernacle:

(Num.3:25-26) **Gershon** family, 'bells' 'rang/wore bells' 'made ringing sound', are in charge of the tabernacle, the tent, the covering, the hangings of the court and its cords—if you go back to Exodus, most of the hangings/coverings have rings of gold and other metals, tashes of gold for the curtains, and tashes of brass. All these metallic objects would make ringing noises when opened and closed, when being disassembled and carried on journeys—reflecting the characters' naming and how the authors took this into consideration when imagining the story.

(Num.3:27-31) **Kohath** family, 'struck sharply with a throw' 'a sharp striking sound', such as made when hard objects bump together or make abrupt contact. This family is in charge of the ark, the table, the candlestick, the altars, and vessels of the sanctuary—again, these objects are made of solid wood, gold, silver, etc. and will make the 'kohath' sound. The same word is used to describe having a headache 'my head is striking sharply' (raasee yiqḥaf/راسي يقحف)' or 'he struck me with a stone' (qḥfnee biḥagrah/ قحفني بحجره).

(Num.3:33-37) **Merari** 'mirrors' 'made reflections/lots of glinting'. This family is in charge of the boards, bars, pillars, sockets of the tabernacle and all its related vessels, as well as the pillars of the court along with its sockets, pins and cords. All sockets are of silver, the boards are overlaid with gold, the rings and bars are of gold—all vessels used are of precious shiny metals, so everything Merari are taking care of shines, reflects, glints, and the word-imagery shows when they handle objects, or with the movement of the objects, the shine/glinting or reflection increases.

All three names of families/lines reflect what happens when they take care of and carry the items of the tabernacle. They reflect the sounds, movements, visuals of what would happen if these things were being handled and transported.

The city/area Alemeth; 'ălāmôṯ; عَلاّمُت ، عيلاّمُت'a sign/signal/gesture' 'a mark' 'taught' 'showed' 'knew' (same as Alamoth(1Chr.15:20)) is mentioned as being given to the Korahite families, and the '*residue of* the sons of Kohath' were given 'Aijalon [similar to Aijeleth] with her suburbs' (1Chr.6:54-69), maybe the notes at the beginning of the psalms are related to this original story. Also, as translated earlier in this book (see 1Chr.16), when David brings the ark, appoints musicians (1Chr.15:16-28), a group playing cymbals, a group playing 'psalteries on Alamoth' it does not mean a place 'Alamoth' but they play 'on a sign/mark'; a group playing harps on the Sheminith(timing) 'to excel', and Chenaniah 'sings-he' instructing others to sing; another group blowing the trumpet before the ark. It makes sense: a group to sound with the cymbals'; a group 'with psalteries on a signal/Alamoth', and a group 'with harps on the timing/Sheminith to excel', and Chenaniah instructing the whole song—it is a symphony/band playing in-sync (on signal/timing), not just making random noises. In Chronicles most of the 'music'-related names represent the sound made by instrument/role they play previously dictated by the objects they carry. These are the same explanations to some of the notations in Psalms. The text supports these translations and findings. They also show how later editors of the original (and older) stories worked to add/remove i.e. change stories from its original form into what would end up being found and considered by the world as the Bible, the Bible which has been in circulation for centuries.

Ps.46: Alamoth 'a sign/signal/gesture' 'a mark' 'taught'. The note 'To the chief Musician for the sons of Korah, A song upon Alamoth'—note: Alameth is said to have been given (a city/area and its suburbs) to the family of Kohathites. The word Alamoth definitely means 'signal/sign' and it is what this psalm is about: it centres around signs from God; the mountains, earth, sea all shake abnormally, i.e. a 'sign', but not to fear because God will make things happen: signs. Earth melts, wars cease, breaks the bow, splits the spear, burns chariots, makes desolation on earth—all are signs to the good and the wicked. It is also the meaning in 'And Zechariah, and Aziel, and Shemiramoth, and Jehiel, and Unni, and Eliab, and Maaseiah, and Benaiah, with psalteries on Alamoth' so they play when signalled to. (1Chr.15:20)

Amen; 'āmēn; تآمين This word carries more than one meaning all rolled into the expression of this single word: 'I hope it will happen/come to be'; 'followed/lead' 'followed through/led through'; 'I trust it will happen/come to be'; I have faith it will be; I have hope, trust, faith in God and God will make it happen, said following a prayer/request directed to God, or if someone else wishes you good, or says out loud asking for good or something in general—the people who hear the request/statement say 'Amen'; you lead, I follow (faithfully/with faith in leader); we follow (through something/towards something/in something whether physically or figuratively). It does not matter if it is a prayer/request to God, or just an expression wishing another, or the general public, good—people respond with 'Amen'. It is from the word (amn/امن) 'trust/security/believe/safe' 'lead through/follow'– believing it will come true, hoping God will make it true. The person who is called 'Ameen' whether as an adjective of his character or his job title meaning 'trustworthy/integrity' someone you can fully trust, or whose job it is to write/create legal documents, oversee all criteria is met and legitimate, e.g. overseeing marriage/divorce documents, etc. should have the above qualities.

An example of what 'Amen' as a word means and how it is used: a person with bad vision unable to thread a needle asks another to do so for him/her; the thread put through the narrow eye of a needle is being ('Amenned'), the person threading the needle is being the ('Ameen') trusted to get the thread through the needle-eye; the visually-impaired person is the person saying or wishing ('Amen') that the thread will go through the needle. In the same way whether in prayer or wishing something the wish/prayer, and the person announcing it and the person(s) saying 'amen' after it has been pronounced are what is being (amenned/led through), and God/the person who will make it come true/through is the ('amen-er/Ameen'). The 'entrusted' and the 'trusting' in being led through to the correct end, is the amen/trust being put into the (amenner) and wanted for/from what and who is being (amen-ned).

'Amen' following a prayer/request is putting your trust/belief/hope in it (or God mainly) and optimism that it will happen. In Psalm 41, it comes at the end, after the praying to God to protect, heal, strengthen, raise a person out of a bad situation, and to keep the speaker in integrity and in God's face (a privilege hoped for by people with belief)—followed by 'Amen', hoping, believing it will come to be. This psalm also blessed God, and hopes good for him). Ps.72: praying to God much good for the king, and the people, blessing God, wishing his glory fills the earth followed by 'Amen' hoping it comes true.

Ps.89 begins with a good/pleasant atmosphere, but as a 'Maschil' it goes sour and turns to accusing God of negative behaviour towards David, it ends with a grumpy reminder of his love/kindness towards David—which is asking for its return, before blessing God. Still, the 'Amen' is about wishing/trusting/believing good will come/happen (although the protagonist sounds both angry and doubtful).

There are earlier uses of the word 'Amen' wishing/believing good will come following a prayer: following David giving instructions of how to crown Solomon king, he tells them 'for he shall be king in my stead; and I have appointed him ruler over Israel and over Judah. And Benaiah the son of Jehoida answered the king, and said: Amen: the Lord God of my lord the king say so too. As the Lord hath been with my lord the king, even so be he with Solomon, and make his throne greater than the throne of my lord king David.' So Benaiah wishes the words of David to come true by asking/referring it to God, a soft reminder to the king and the audience of the story (through the author) to ask it from God (1Kgs.1:35-37). The same use of 'Amen' follows a request/prayer for salvation in 1Chr.16:35-36). Cp: aameyn.

Asaph mentioned in Psalms 50, 73-83, has more than one meaning and all are used in each psalm mentioned. To begin with the most obvious, as introduced in Chronicles, Ezra and Nehemiah this character/word-name is involved in music, singing, composing songs/music, playing musical instruments so his name Asaph means 'played music', this character is mentioned many times along with other characters who sing/play music during rituals. In Psalms it has the same meaning, but attributing songs to being his compilations (a fictional character) is misinterpretation—the correct meaning of the notes above the psalms is 'for Asaph' (not 'of Asaph'), i.e. to be inserted (or has been removed) where this character is present in the original stories. In 2Chr.30 Hezekiah the king, and other princes, command people to sing 'with the words of David and Asaph the seer' implying David and Asaph are authors of songs, and this could be a later editor's addition and may very well have served as a 'place-holder' for the related psalms to be inserted.

Asaph has three more meanings and they all represent what happens in the text of the psalms where he is mentioned or the word 'Asaph' is included in the notes above each psalm.

Asaph; عازآف 'turned away from/ignored' 'turned away(head or body)/avoided' 'went off food/drink' and is used when a person or God turns away from the other or removes their presence from the other, or person from person, or person from religion; when a person or animal goes off food from illness; going off or turning away from food, habit, etc. usually the reason is an upset, loss of belief, disapproval, anger, etc.

Asaph; عآصاف 'twisted' (such as twist an ankle or twist something until it breaks off) 'twisted/twisted and broken' 'twisted crop'. To break something to pieces, whether by twisting, crumpling, blowing it down like wind does to crop/grass/vegetation, or animals running amok in vegetation.

Asaph نآساف 'sorrow' 'sorry/remorseful'.

All three meanings are present in each psalm: 50, 73-83: people have turned away from God; people turned away from religion. The most prominent feature is God has turned away from people, David, those calling on God—with the reason sometimes presented as due to people having left the right path, followed wrong, and they themselves turned away from God, causing him to turn away from them. The author/narrator, mostly angrily, is reproaching, upbraiding God for turning away from them, from David, while asking God to face them, shine on them, guide them again, i.e. return to be in their presence.

It is also filled with the destruction of 'enemy people', or their own people, the destruction of land and animals. At least once the description is being left as 'stubble' from strong winds—the very meaning of 'asaph', but all the destruction, slaughter implies the same meaning too.

Sorrow is abundantly present in these psalms, mixed with anger and despair. Sorrow over God turning away, over the better past that has gone, over the state of the people, over the state of David, over the desolation, the slaughter, the way things stand. Even the psalms which begin upbeat, praising God for his goodness/blessings, suddenly turn darkly opposite and throw reproach at God.

Al-taschit; 'altašḥēt; has more than one meaning/wordplay used. From the way the psalms are written you get the impression that maybe different people interpreted it differently, adding on what they believed the word to be: of course, it could be intentional as many words are meant to be played on by the authors of the Bible.

Altaschit; 'altašḥēt; ئَلْتَسكيت 'the silencing' which can also mean 'the destruction'; ئَلْتَسخيط 'anger with vengeance/revenge'; and ئَلْتَصحية 'the clearing up/awakening'. Cp: altaskeyt, altas<u>kh</u>eyṭ, altas<u>s</u>ḥeyt.

Psalms 57, 58, 59 are about silencing those who speak ill of David; also, about the silence David must keep until he is safe; the silencing of wicked people verbally and in their physical destruction.

'the awakening': there is the mention of God's glory awakening; of David's musical instruments awakening—to praise God's glory once He has awakened and destroyed/silenced David's enemies.

Anger and vengeance can be felt in the depictions of the enemy/the wicked, and in the violent manner he would like to see them punished. In Ps.75 the meanings 'the silencing/destruction' can be seen in being warned not to raise their horns, nor speak; that their horns will be cut off—in the latter narration 'anger/vengeance' can be seen as well as in 'the wicked' drinking the 'dregs'.

Mahalath; maḥălaṯ; مَحيلَة ، مَحَلَة 'in place of/instead of' (as in Gen.28:8-9); مَخيَلث ، مَخَلَث 'changed/changed towards' 'spoiled/gone bad' it can also mean 'did not change'. In Ps.53 it is presented as the majority of people, if not all, have become bad 'corrupted', 'done abominable iniquity', none do good; 'they are altogether become filthy'. The speaker also wishes for change to happen.

In Ps.58, Mahalath still means 'changed/gone bad' as the narration talks of a change in situation—all loved ones and friends have changed towards him, left him; he is afflicted, something has changed in his body. Cp: maḥalat, maḥailat, ma<u>kh</u>alaf, ma<u>kh</u>ailaf.

Leannoth; lĕʿannôṯ; لَيعَنَّة 'even though/despite'; ليعَنِّد 'why is he being stubborn/not moving(ed)'. In the notes of Ps.88 it represents what the protagonist is saying, in words to the effect 'You've caused so much bad change to me/my situation, but I'm still praying to you'—i.e. even though you have done all this to me, I am still turned towards you. It also shows that God is being stubborn by ignoring his pleas for help. For although God has caused all these negative changes to happen to him, he is still crying out to God, praying to God to change his affliction, to turn it around. After listing everything God has wronged him, he says 'But unto thee have I cried.'. Cp: lei'annot, lei'annod.

Shoshannim; šûšan, šûšanîm; شوشنهم ، شُشَن as in Esther (and elsewhere) it means 'things/matters and of great magnificence/importance' it can also mean 'things/matters and status' 'their things/matters/their matters of importance'. It can be regarding objects, wealth, etc. or depending on what it is regarding and how it is said/used, can also express wonder and puzzlement at the matter in hand:

Ps.45 describes magnificence, beauty, wealth, righteousness, high status, victory.

Ps.69 is about the falling in status, and about the variety and number of the protagonist's enemies; he is puzzled at why he has been allowed to 'sink' when it was for God's sake that he did what he did.

Ps.80 is also about wonder at why God made them so great then caused them to fall so low; mentioning the different families proudly; how God delivered them out of Egypt, gave them possession of different countries—then how he turned away/abandoned them.

Proverbs

The word for 'proverb' itself is yet another example of misinterpretation: mĕšālîm is not 'proverbs/ ميثآل (هم/ام ، ميثآليم) which is the Arabic word for an example/proverb, but it is not the correct translation of the word mĕšālîm in the Biblical 'Proverbs' or its meaning of which the correct word is directly linked to why they chose to attribute it to Solomon—not because they are Solomon's words but as is the Biblical authors' method of enhancing the stories/what is being said with a compound word which reflects the events/ content of the story.

mĕšālîm; ميسآل هم/ام ، ميسآليم 'asks/questions-them/the' 'matters/topics-them/the' 'their matters/topics' 'mild/peaceful conduct/nature' 'friendly/kind/peaceful', and this word is directly linked to Solomon's meaning which is the same: 'ask him/asks him-what' 'asked him-what' 'of many questions/of questions-what' 'they allowed him to survive' 'of surviving' 'of mild/peaceful nature' 'became mild/peaceful'. Solomon's meaning and why this character was created and how the compound word-name reflected in the events of the story can be referred to earlier in this book under 'Solomon'. In brief, the character and word were denoted in being something that pacified and soothed his parents (David/Bath-sheba), as being a character who asks questions and through asking finds/receives wisdom. It is used in the same way here both as 'mĕšālîm (wrongly translated/interpreted as 'proverbs')' and Solomon.

The whole text supports this translation of 'mildness/peace' 'questions/asks' 'matters'. From the beginning of 'Proverbs' the content speaks against, and contrasts sharply against, the earlier stories of the OT of killing people because they are 'different', of taking the 'spoils' from attacked peoples. In Prov.2, 5, it does not describe the 'stranger' woman as a 'foreigner' but as any person who calls towards wrong-doing likening 'evil/sin/crime' to having relations without marriage (the latter is bad in the culture of the authors of the Bible). There is a great difference in narration/instruction between the earlier stories (Genesis through to Esther) of unending massacres and the glorification of gratuitous killing and theft, and between 'Proverbs/Peace' content which calls against killing and other forms of evil. In fact, it calls to be peaceful, kind, merciful—the very meaning of mĕšālîm/'mild/peaceful conduct/nature' 'friendly/kind/peaceful' and the author(s) has ground this peaceful nature/conduct as being attained through wisdom which can only be found by asking the right questions and questioning the morality/intention and nature of those calling/ asking you to do evil such as kill, rob and hate.

It brings together all the correct meanings of mĕšālîm—the 'peaceful nature/conduct' and the 'asking', the 'matters' being inspected. The very content and instruction call to be mĕšālîm/peaceful, to question; and the narration itself uses questions to pose this matter for thought, to clarify it to the audience. Although the examples/proverbs in each line are straightforward, each line is supposed to make the audience stop at it and think about it, just like a question posed needs consideration—the misnomered 'proverb' needs to be inspected before it is understood properly: it (the matter/proverb) is questioning the person's mind/thought process and makes the person question what has been said/read, and when they reach the conclusion (each to his own) they have found 'wisdom' posed by the presented '[proverbs]questions/ matters'.

Proverbs 1-9 are mentioned along with David because the questions and word-imagery posed revolve mainly around a man following evil by having relations with a woman not his wife (Bath-sheba and Uriah). For this reason, they have grouped the examples where an illicit relationship/bad woman equates evil, a good wife equates goodness.

Proverbs 10-24 are introduced about a child either being a good or bad thing for his parents. This group is tied loosely together because they do not differ much than the first batch of proverbs, except they are interspersed with the mention of the introducing proverb that a bad child equates his parents' suffering, a good child their ease/pleasure.

The reason why Prov.25 has 'the men of Hezekiah king of Judah' as copying the 'proverbs' at this point is due to the examples presented reflect on the correct actions, but also the wrong-doing of Hezekiah and other characters in his earlier story: e.g. Rab-Shakeh and his companions shouting and shaming Hezekiah in front of the people; Hezekiah's mistake in showing his visitors all his treasures which incurred punishment but was deferred later onto the people; mentioning of the fig-tender and the loyal servant reminding Isaiah healed Hezekiah with figs, but the latter committed a 'wrong' when he showed his things to the visitors; the mentions of confessing and repenting, 'troubled fountain' and 'broken spring' also invoke Hezekiah's word-name meaning and the events in his story.

Agur; 'āgûr; نَآجُر 'the brute' 'I deal brutally/cause great suffering' 'dealt brutally/caused great suffering' from the word (gowr/جور) and supported by 'The words of Agur.' 'Surely I *am* more brutish than *any* man, and have not the understanding of man.'. Sufferance/distress is also given in the examples, e.g. hunger, theft and punishment, a cruel son which is considered a great sufferance in the culture, the violent who attack the vulnerable. The same word also means 'protect from' and the protagonist asks to be protected from 'vanity and lies'; نَآغُر 'funnels downwards/disappears into the earth/cannot be held or contained' and throughout this chapter which is introduced with this wordplay, there are examples given of things that cannot be held in the hand or understood with the mind (according to the narration): some are: the proof of heaven or the ability to fly, capturing wind in the hand, containing water using a garment (all have the imagery and idea of water running downwards that cannot be accessed, seen nor stopped), even the four examples reflect the meaning of the word-name 'agur/filter down/disappear into the ground' described as not being satisfied and their capacity to envelope/devour more: the grave and the fire are self-explanatory as they devour and do not return what has entered; the soil 'that is not filled with water' 'the barren womb' no matter how much water/semen it receives—nothing returns from it: both do not return or give any fertility whether crop or offspring. The chapter continues with examples of things the narration presents as cannot be withheld by hand or mind, and the examples are of small animals or insects which also reflect the second meaning (to go downwards) and ends with returning it to suffering/distress '...so the forcing of wrath bringeth forth strife.'. Cp: aagur, aag͟hur. (Prov.30)

Agur is the son of Jakeh; yāqeh; حآكَه 'told a story' 'told a story to him' 'spoke with' spoke with him' 'weaved': 'The words of Agur the son of Jakeh, even the prophecy: the man spake unto Ithiel and Ucal.'—he is telling them a story and speaking to them; حآقَه 'give him right/justice' 'keep him in the right' 'say I am right' 'his' 'belongs to him' reflected in asking not to be denied basic food and to be kept on the right path away from 'vanity and lies'; عآقَه 'disobeyed' 'disobeyed him' 'be cruel/hardened heart' 'be cruel/harsh to him' 'delayed him' and is reflected when he asks not to be pushed into sinning whether theft or denying God's blessings on him, it is the same word used to describe adult child(ren) who are cruel or disobedient to their parent(s) and this is mentioned in the chapter. Cp: ḥaakeh, ḥaaqeh, 'aaqeh. (Prov.30)

Ithiel the same as Neh.11:7 for its meanings: 'came-the' 'brought-the' such as enough fortune and food source which leads to the second meaning 'if-the' 'if it is-the' 'harm/harmed-the' to avoid causing him to do harm by stealing, cursing i.e. to avoid harming himself and God. (Prov.30)

Ucal; 'uk̲āl; عوقآل 'mind/wisdom' 'mature/sensible'. Agur is narrated 'I neither learned wisdom' but the narration goes on to show wisdom in his words; نُوكآل 'eat/ate/consumed/cursed(with punishment or death)' as mention of 'feed me with food convenient for me', but also because the examples given are of things that consume but do not get enough (grave, fire, barren land, barren womb), or things that are self-sufficient in feeding themselves (ants, locusts, spiders, lions), many of the other examples mean 'eat' as in killed or cursed with suffering which is how the same word is used in the language; نُوقآل 'made to say' 'had words placed in his mouth' and is reflected in the example of not being made vain or a liar so as not to be forced to deny God or falsely swear by God, also in 'Add thou not unto his words...and thou be found a liar.'. Cp: 'uqaal, ukaal, uqaal. (Prov.30)

Lemuel; lĕmû'ēl; ليمُ ئِل 'to/for-mother/mothered-the' 'blamed-the' 'gathered-the' 'what is it for-the' 'what/why-the'. The whole chapter revolves around the role of a good wife and mother. 'what is it for-the' 'what/why-the' is emphasised in how the mother repeats 'what' in her lessons/questions to her son 'The words of king Lemuel, the prophecy that his mother taught him. What, my son? and what, the son of my womb? and what, the son of my vows?' and in teaching that strength is not to be wasted on women and things to one's own detriment. 'blamed-the' in the lesson blaming people who drink wine (kings or not) to make bad judgements, causing injustice and the downfall of kings. 'gathered-the' is reflected in a 'good wife/mother' whose work gathers food resources, makes food, and food and clothes for the husband, the household and can even turn it into a business, where the 'gathering' is the gathering of fortune. Cp: lei-mu-ill. (Prov.31:1-2)

Ecclesiastes

Qohelet (misinterpreted as 'the preacher') stands for words with different meanings in wordplay as do many word-names created in the Biblical stories. The way Ecclesiastes has been written is to allow the wordplay to express all its intended meanings. I will break them down into sections of some examples to display how wordplay has been used:

Qoheleth; qōhelet; قو هَلَة 'has gone away/has shed away/leaves' 'said, gone away/said, shed away/said, left (e.g. when a tree sheds leaves): 'What profit hath a man of all his labour...' '*One* generation passeth away, and *another* generation cometh:' 'The sun also ariseth, and the sun goeth down...' 'The thing that hath been...and that which is done...' 'There is no remembrance of former things; neither shall there be any remembrance of things that are to come with *those* that shall come after'. Cp: qoohelet.

Qoheleth; qōhelet; قوحَلَة 'to harden/hardened with sufferance' 'to suffer' 'said, hardened' 'said, suffered': '...this sore travail hath God given to the sons of man...' '...all *is* vanity and vexation of spirit'. Cp: qooḥelet.

Qoheleth; qōhelet; قو هَلَف 'has gathered/has already gathered' 'said, gathered' 'said, already gathered': 'I made great works; I builded me houses; I planted me vineyards'. The narrator tells us he gathered or sought to accumulate knowledge/wisdom and gathered great estate. The narration goes on to add gardens, orchards, trees, pools, woods, servants, maidens, possession of cattle, 'I gathered me also silver and gold, and the peculiar treasure of kings and provinces,' he also gathered singers and 'the delights of the sons of men, as musical instruments, and that of all sorts.'. Cp: qooheleph.

After accumulating all these materialistic possessions, he goes back to realising it will all go, he will 'fade away/shed' when he dies, nothing will remain, the foolish and the wise all go the same way—returning to the meaning of Qoheleth قو هَلَة 'has gone away/has shed away/leaves'.

Qoheleth; qōhelet; قو هَلَة 'It is time(for)' 'said, it has come/is here' 'said, it is time': 'To everything there is a season, and a time,' and continues about 'a time to...'.

Also Qoheleth; قوحَلَة 'to harden/hardened with sufferance' 'to suffer': 'What profit hath he that worketh in that he laboureth? I have seen the travail which God hath given to the sons of men to be exercised in it.'

3:15 joins Qoheleth 'it's time for' and 'shed away': 'That which have been is now; and that which is to be hath already been', even man and beast will die, i.e. 'shed away'.

Chapter 4: Qoheleth; قوحَلَة 'to harden/hardened with sufferance' 'to suffer': the narration/protagonist considers the oppressed, and expressed it would have been better to have died or never existed than to see the sufferance in the world.

Qoheleth; qōhelet; قوحَلَث 'has already sworn(by God)' 'said, he swore(by God)': he warns not to be hasty swearing/making a vow to God 'When thou vowest a vow unto God, defer not to pay it,' 'Better *is it* that thou shouldest not vow, than thou shouldest vow and not pay.'. Cp: qooḥelef.

Chapter 5 returns to the rich who gather (قو هَلَف/qooheleph) wealth, their wealth turning into sufferance (قوحَلَة/qooḥelet), and in the end he/they will have nothing and die (قو هَلَة /qoohelet): 'There is a sore evil which I have seen under the sun, *namely,* riches kept for the owners thereof to their hurt. But those riches perish to evil travail; and he begetteh a son, and *there* is nothing in his hand. As he came forth from his mother's womb, naked shall he return to go as he came, and shall take nothing of his labour,'—this brings in Qoheleth/ قوحلَة meaning 'become barren/useless/dried up' which is used to describe land becoming barren from drought and scorching sun 'that in all points as he came, so shall he go: and what profit hath he that hath laboured for the wind?'. The same word and similar also mean when things become extremely dire for a person in circumstances.

Also, qoheleth the sun/sky قوحَلَة الشمس ، قوحَلَة السماء 'the sky/sun has darkened'; also qoheleth; كوهَلَة (Cp: koohelet) means the same 'darkening' and can also mean of sky, sun, face, circumstances: 'All his days also he eateth in darkness, and *he hath* much sorrow and wrath with his sickness'

This method of wordplay on the meanings of 'qoheleth' continues in the remaining chapters to express, repeat and reflect all the meanings intended for 'Qoheleth' in this story: assembling, gathering; a time for/a time to; shedding away, leaving; to swear a vow; to suffer, to become barren, to darken.

It is equivalent to Kehelatha (Num.33:22).

Song of Solomon

This erotic love poem follows the same method of the older Biblical stories in using word-names as themes to reflect and enhance the narration. What stands out, is this work did not have one author, additions stand out in how the narration does not flow as a single piece of work.

Jerusalem has been used for 'they see-asked-them/the' 'came-saw-asked-them/the' and the narration has one lover asking not to be looked at because her skin is black, and that the sun has looked at her (causing her darkened skin). (Cant.1)

Kedar has been used for its meaning of 'pots used on fire', of which the external side is blackened by the fire, used to support how the protagonist is described as black. Cant.1:5-6)

Solomon has been chosen for its meanings of 'ask him/asks him-what' 'asked him-what' 'of many questions/of questions-what' 'comforting' 'leaked/flowed water'. The narration is an erotic love story and one way it is portrayed is through many questions in the narration, and direct references to physical contact and alludes figuratively to physical comforting. The description of his kisses and mouth like ointment being poured with a direct reference it is like his name relays the meaning 'leaked/flowed water'. (Cant.1)

Pharaoh for its meaning to separate between people (arguing/fighting (but not meant in this instance)) and also creating a physical divide of something. Both are reflected where it asks the lover 'for why should I be as one that turneth aside by the flocks of thy companions?' and describing the features of horse and the lover as 'rows' i.e. separating them to detail their beauty. (Cant.1:7-11)

En-gedi 'look a kid(goat)' 'look, find it' 'where will you end up at' 'end up at' 'where-did he reach/was found' 'you will get to/reach' 'save' and is being said to a female. Most of these meanings are available in the narration of the first chapter: After asking where they can meet, it narrates 'If thou know not, O thou fairest among women, go thy way forth by the footsteps of the flock, and feed thy kids beside the shepherd's tents.'. Telling the lover where to go/end up at, tying the location to 'kids'; followed by 'Behold,' then describing her beauty. (Cant.1:8-17)

The mention of beams and rafters of the house as 'cedar' and 'fir' is not a narrative device representing the 'land' as some scholars suggest, but is a normal description of a house that would have beams made of specific wood, the symbolisation reflects lying on a bed (after lovemaking) and staring at the ceiling, it may also mean just as the physical beauty of the lover is superior to others, that the timber used for ceiling beams and rafters is also of superior wood. (Cant.1:16-17)

Sharon for its meanings: 'aches' and the ache symbolises wanting to satisfy the lust with physical contact, told as being a lily among thorns—it wants to pluck it, an apple tree—wanting to be in its shadow and eat of its fruit. The meaning 'they walked' 'they walked along' as the protagonist(s) has the lover searching for his/her love among the men and women, being accompanied to banquets, walking(skipping) over mountains, searching houses by looking through the windows, asking the lover to come away with him/her. (Cant.2)

Bether; beṯer; بَتَر 'snapped/cut off' 'abruptly cut off' 'a stub' 'a stub of rock' 'a smooth rock'. It reflects that they do not stop making love until they are interrupted by daybreak 'Until the day break, and the shadows flee away, my beloved, and be thou like a roe or a young hart upon the mountains of Bether.' It is better understood with the verse that precedes it '...he feedeth among the lilies.' The lover is the lily (as the female lover is described in a previous verse) and his feeding is sexual intercourse. Cp: beter. (Cant.2:16-17)

Israel is mentioned for 'twisted muscle-the' it refers to the penis (muscle) being squeezed/twisted with vagina (muscle) in an illicit relationship (see Israel, Dinah, El-elohe-Israel), and in this part of the Song of Solomon it means to have sex. This is why Israel has been mentioned along with 'bed' and other allusions to sexual intercourse and figurative descriptions of genitalia. (Cant.3)

Lebanon is used for 'for building/builders' as a description of beds and chariots is being made. 'for children/sons' meaning is reflected in that this is for the men and women to find love and sexual satisfaction in. Lebanon is also invoking a superior type of wood or one that makes the 'build' stronger and better, which is why Solomon's chariot made 'of the wood of Lebanon' has been chosen to convey a beautiful, strong body and strength in sexual intercourse. The imagery of chariots, horses, swords upon thighs, pillars of silver are all sexual symbols of virility and descriptions of the phallus. The 'pillars of smoke, perfumed with myrrh and frankincense' symbolises the lust, the fire of passion and when lovers meet (specifically in this culture frankincense is used to heighten the erotic and sexual activity) perfume is also accentuated with incense—the author is invoking the senses not only of beautiful smoke of incense which both married and unmarried lovers use before meeting, but also of the hot coals which burn the incense representing the passion and lust of the lovers. (Cant.3)

Zion for its meaning 'sweep/brush' 'swept/brushed away' and is reflected in the story that she went around the city i.e. swept through it, until the lover was found, sweeps him into her mother's bed 'into the chamber of her that conceived me' and again the word-imagery symbolises the rocking, to and fro motion of making love (like sweeping) which why at both ends of this passage, mothers (of all things) are used to remind of the bed being the place of love-making, reinforced by 'zion's' repetitive sweeping motion. And although when invoking Solomon, they mention his mother crowning him, it is again referring to the first mention of mother symbolising sex (in the mother's bed), saying there is no shame in love-making as it creates such great people as kings. (Cant.3)

Gilead is used for its meaning 'tumbling/rolling stone(s)' (as lover's tumble and roll each other while making love) and 'came-festival' 'came-greeted with merriment'. First, this is invoked by comparing her hair with 'a flock of goats, that appear from mount Gilead.' The sheep/goats on mount Gilead were used in a festival/feast ending the feud between Laban and Jacob with feasting and joy, preceded by a stone-tumbling ritual. What is invoked is the female body of the lover is likened to a mountain (Gilead), her features are rich and beautiful likened to the animals presented and feasted upon on mount Gilead (but with an erotic sense not a literal food sense). This is reinforced by capping it with the repeated sentence of 'Until the day break, and the shadows flee away, I will get me to the mountain of myrrh, and to the hill of frankincense.' the latter half of the sentence referring to her buttocks and venus mound. (Cant.4)

David is used to symbolise her neck for its meaning of 'the stone rolling pin of grinding stone' because of its natural smooth texture, and the slender shape of the 'david/rolling pin' in comparison to the wider grinding-stone slab it grinds against: 'Thy neck is like the tower of David…'. (Cant.4:4)

Amana; 'ămānâ; ئيمانه 'in the trust of' 'the entrusted/trusted with' 'follow him/it' 'the being taken through' (see 'Amen'). These are all meant when the lover is asked to 'Come with me from Lebanon: look from the top of Amana…'. Cp: aimaanah. (Cant.4:8)

Shenir is used for its meanings 'stakes/dowels' as the lover is described as ravishing the partner's heart. (Cant.8-9)

Hermon is used for its meanings 'forbidden' 'a group of women' as this word also means 'sacred', and women are viewed as sacred, as is sex. (Cant.4)

Lebanon is now used for its meaning 'milk/lots of milk' with the lover's taste being described as milk and honey (a popular drink in rural Yemen, and food combination with clarified butter (and is a phrase often used to describe a delicious or sweet taste, and also a phrase used across the Arab world to describe two different people getting along extremely well, or a matter going well)). (Cant.4:8-16)

Jerusalem is used again for its meanings of 'they see-asked-them/the' 'came-saw-asked-them/the', as the lover asks them if they have seen him to let her know; she gives them a description to allow them to 'see' him when the 'daughters of Jerusalem' question what is so special about him and tell her that he is just another ordinary lover, so the narration in great description of his features allows him to be 'seen' and answers their question which they 'ask'. (Cant.5)

Tirzah has been used for its meaning 'his inheritance/heritage': 'I *am* my beloved's, and my beloved *is* mine…'. (Cant.6:3-4)

Amminadib has been used for 'the one who has protruding jaw/teeth' 'the one who is wailing/mourning loudly' as it reflects the story that although the lover is beautiful, it is likened to 'terrible as *an army* with banners?' and also overwhelmingly beautiful 'Turn away thine eyes from me, for they have overcome me…'. (Cant.6)

Shulamite; šûlammîṯ; شُلَمّيت 'carry/take-is dead' and is linked to Amminadib 'the one who is wailing/mourning loudly' as the verse has the lover crying out 'return, return, O Shulamite; return, that we may look upon thee…'. It could also be: سُلَّميت 'greeted' 'delivered/received' 'was intact/survived' 'asked to death (was questioned intensely)'. It is the same as Shelomith (Lev.24). Cp: shulammeet, sulammeet. (Cant.6:13)

Heshbon for its meaning 'to carry on waist/hip' (like a child is carried) and this is reflected in the lover's body likened to a palm tree, then the other lover saying 'I said, I will go up to the palm tree, I will take hold of the boughs thereof…'. Going up a palm tree entails wrapping legs around its trunk and holding on with hands, just like small children wrap their legs around the person when carried on the waist/hip. It is referring to sexual intercourse. (Cant.7)

Beth-rabbim; bat-rabbîm; بَتْ رَبّهم 'will grow well' 'will grow them well' 'grow lots'. It also can have different meanings ('will be mixed and diluted with water' 'will be dampened/become damp' and other 'Arab' meanings), but with regards to the Song of Solomon this is the meaning anchored by the text. It describes the body of the lover like a palm tree, i.e. something that has grown well, her breasts and other body parts are likened to well-grown fruit and plants and they want to spend time together noticing the maturing fruits budding (which could literally mean fruits or figuratively describing the lover's body): '…thy stature is like to a palm tree, and thy breasts to clusters *of grapes…whether* the tender grape appear, *and* the pomegranates bud forth…The mandrakes give a smell, and at our gates *are* all manner of pleasant *fruits*…'. Cp: bat-rabbhum. (Cant.7)

Damascus for its meaning 'sucked/sucked a lot' as the lover's breasts are likened to grapes and vines, her taste/mouth to wine 'now also thy breasts shall be as clusters of the vine…And the roof of thy mouth like the best wine for my beloved, that goeth down sweetly…'. (Cant.7)

Carmel is used for its meanings of 'generosity/generous-the' as her hair and beauty is likened to the generous and rich displayings of a king; 'the hot coal end of log in fire' 'bury in fire/ashes the sharp and burnt end of the log' refers to making love and satisfying the physical burning with intercourse, the reflection comes at the end of the chapter '…there I will give thee my loves.'.

Baal-hamon; ba'al hāmôn; بَعَل هآمون 'upon high/above-wandered' 'upon high-lost/abandoned' 'above-counted and listed' and describes not only passionate love and its intoxicating effects (likening it to vineyards (where the plants grow on walls or structured supports)), but it still describes the physical beauty of the lover, here her body is a well-built wall and her breasts which catch her lover's attention are described as 'towers' in contrast to her sister whose 'wall' needs building and decoration to make her attractive; the narration lists the fruit and payments for Solomon's vineyard before returning to the protagonist's vineyard and also listing what can be found in the lover's vineyard. Cp: ba'al haamon. (Cant.8:8-10)

Solomon is invoked again for its meaning of 'asked/questions' because when people will ask for the less-'endowed' sister's marriage, it raises further questions how they can make her physical form more beautiful/attractive due to her lack of towering breasts. Solomon is also mentioned because the earlier stories give him a ridiculously fictional number of wives and concubines (1Kgs.11:3), both stories bring up images of virile sexual activity.

Although it can be described as a love poem, it is mainly erotic and concerned with physical attraction and the love of a beautiful physical body. It is not about emotional satisfaction and attributes. All the connotations from word-imagery are of a physical nature. It is void of any religious/spiritual content. It is void of any story-telling with regards to 'Israel' and its notable characters, the only mention of Israel, David, Solomon, Jerusalem and other places is to do with connotations of shape, texture and action and unrelated to any of their earlier stories, they are used only as words and not as related major storylines.

Isaiah

Isaiah as in 2Kgs still holds its meanings of 'wanders/goes/travels-he/him' and is used for this purpose in the story. The character is still travelling, sent by God to discover and inform. In 'visions' he is going to and seeing different places, he goes to the prophetess and to other people and places, including God. He is sent on a mission to deliver God's message. He is wandering and travelling to this purpose; even the people the message is sent to, and the remembrance of the people in the message is about being sent/travelling/wandering/being taken and walking away as captives, etc. His surname **Amoz** is still used as 'I squeeze/wring' 'I suck' 'I touch/possess/provoke fights or arguments' 'I squeeze/massage' and are reflected in the story as people filled with wounds, bruises and sores not being tended to which 'I squeeze/massage' means 'they have not been closed, neither bound up, neither mollified with ointment.'; 'I suck' is meant as in breastfeed as God is narrated as saying 'I have nourished and brought up children, and they have rebelled against me.'; the other meanings of Amoz are reflected in the disobedience of the people provoking God to punish them, and the punishment itself. (Isa.1)

Uzziah used for 'was harmed-he' 'he harmed' and the people will be harmed by God and the punishment and people he sends to punish them.

Jotham used for 'leper/lepers/leprosy' 'came-guilted' 'came-blamed' 'came-ostracised' as the people's disobedience is described as an affliction which has caused them to be filled with wounds, bruises, putrefying sores i.e. like leprosy fills and covers the body.

Ahaz used for 'took/took or takes a lot' 'swore/insulted/swore insulted a lot' 'a disgrace/disgraced a lot' 'an embarrassment/a great embarrassment' as the disobedience takes a lot away from God, the punishment God doles out will take a lot away from the people, the disobedience and punishment are disgrace/insult to God and the people.

Hezekiah used for 'squeezed/cornered/crammed him-he/him' as the people will be cornered by punishment and crammed towards a specific direction: captivity. 'make suffer/distress-he/him' 'I will force to taste/swallow/eat-he/him' the distress will be great as a punishment.

Judah used for 'he is called/calls' 'call, or 'curse' 'to make a claim' 'make a false claim or an unproven claim' as Isaiah is calling out the message/prophecy to the people. It is in the narration that God will not hear them when they call to him (as when a person spreads his hand and prays, it is meant he is asking/calling to God).

Zion has been used for 'sweep/brush' 'swept/brushed away' 'bad' the same as it was first introduced into the Biblical stories. Due to the people's bad (zion/siyyon/سيِّين) behaviour the punishment sweeps/brushes everything away; how it is described 'Your country is desolate, your cities are burned with fire…strangers devour it…' are all images and mean the same method of something being swept out (zion/ssiyon/صيِّين)' the same way dirt or anything is cleaned away with the strokes of a 'misswana/مصونا' which is what the word 'Zion' has been made from. It is supported by using **Sodom** ('black soot') and **Gommorah** ('to be buried/submerged under' 'hot coal') as an example regarding both how people and everything has been brushed out but also how people have been left behind (i.e. not thoroughly swept/brushed away)—'soot/hot coals/buried under' is what one chore called 'zion' deals with: to brush and scoop away ashes, soot, charcoal from the oven/fireplace and there is always a 'remnant' left behind. In the story it is used in the same way as brushing away dirt/litter when the narration again uses Zion when describing removing the impurities (in the people/land) 'And I will turn my hand upon thee, and purely purge away thy dross, and take away all thy tin…Zion shall be redeemed with judgement, and her converts with righteousness.' (Isa.1:7-10, 21-28)

Sodom and **Gomorrah** have also been used to picture the desolation of which is '…your countries are burned with fire…'. (Isa.1:7-9)

Jerusalem has been used for 'they see-asked-them/the' 'came-saw-asked-them/the' 'came-saw-reached/arrived/public apology-them/the' 'came-saw-rocks-them/the' 'they saw-reached/arrived/public apology-them/the' 'they see-rocks-them/the' as at the end of times God's mountain will arrive and be seen, and its arrival is not described as being built by man, but coming down from God, i.e. appearing with a whole new mountain not yet available (in the narration) on earth that the 'mountain of the Lord's house shall be established in the top of the mountains…'. Although there is 'house' mentioned it is the whole mountain that is God's house and not a man-made house/structure.

There is an important shift in Isaiah: from the first chapter it speaks against the former stories' insistence on great amounts of sacrifices, burnt offerings, fat and blood, oblations, new moon and sabbath feasts; Isa.1 claims these are not true, are not God's instructions. In the same way it states that the 'house of the Lord' in previous stories is not true either, but that God lives in a mountain or in a rock. This Isaiah narration fits with the narration of earlier stories of Moses where God is in a mountain. Jerusalem 'they see-asked-them/the' 'came-saw-asked-them/the' 'came-saw-rocks-them/the' 'they saw-reached/arrived/public apology-them/the' is reflected that once 'the mountain of the Lord's house shall be established in the top of the mountains, and shall be exalted above the hills…' that '…all nations shall flow unto it.' i.e. visit and see it as opposed to their current visiting-seeing-asking the wrong gods/idols; when people pilgrim to any religious site there is always something asked of God or the site/saint/etc. whether material or spiritual, for this world or for the afterlife. (Isa.2)

Jacob has been used in the same way as in the character's first story: for its meaning of 'he follows/comes after' 'look after/take care of' it means babysitting a child or a house or taking care of household chores or to watch over/take care of anything left in your care while another person usually goes outside the house to fetch wood, water, crops etc.. It is used here as with the emergence of the 'mountain of the Lord's house' not only will it be 'exalted', but God will look after the people by teaching them the right ways, and the people will look after God's ways by taking care to follow his instructions '…for out of Zion[bad/badness] shall go forth the law'.

Jacob's second meaning is also used as it was in the story between Jacob and Esau: 'forces open' 'dislocates' 'forces open and takes/usurps' it describes opening something in a fashion similar to using a crowbar to break a lock/chain and is usually done for theft or when a key is lost, or something is jammed, taking something which belongs to someone else i.e. usurp. Isa.2 shows how worship of idols has usurped/replaced the worship of the 'true' god, but this will be set right when God returns and the description in the story is of these idols being broken down and God taking their place in worship through forceful events: destroying, bringing low everything and everyone that 'stands tall', leaving only God or his mountain standing high.

The meaning of 'bad/**zion**' can be seen again in its use as 'the daughters of Zion' which goes on to describe wrong-doing of females which brings on its meaning of 'sweep/brush' reflected in good things taken away, strong people losing in wars, desolation and other negative consequences (Isa.3:12-26; 4)

Seraphim; śārapîm, śērapûm; سآرَفهم ، سآرَف ام ، سيرَفُم 'their buttocks' 'buttocks-of the' supported by the text that these seraphim have human form as one takes a live coal in his hand, which he picked up using tongs, described as having six wings: one pair cover his face, the other pair cover his feet so whether it actually means covering his feet or euphemism for covering his genitals (if the pair are folded over to cover its feet, the genitals would be covered), the point is: a pair fold forward to cover its face, another pair fold forward to cover the feet, the last pair are used to fly with, the wings (like winged animals) cover part of the back, most of the back would be covered with six pairs, so the only body part which is left uncovered is its buttocks hence the name 'seraphim'. 'Above it stood the seraphims: each one had six wings: with twain he covered his face; and with twain he covered his feet, and with the twain he did fly.' Cp: saar-aphhum, saaraph-um, seyraphum. (Isa.6:1-7)

Shear-jashub; šĕ'ār yāšûḇ; سيئآر خآشُب 'walked/left-lumber/wood' reflected in '…his heart was moved, and the heart of his people, as the trees of the wood are moved with the wind.'.

شيعآر يآشُب 'he will disgrace/be disgraced-goes around in circles' and سيئآر يآشُب 'walked/left-(fire)ignites fast or large/blazes' is reflected as Pekah and Rezin described as wanting to move against Jerusalem and as 'smoking firebrands' that should not be feared as they will be defeated and disgraced.

شيعآر يآشُب 'a sign-goes around in circles' (goes back and forth) and is reflected in the story by Isaiah/Shear-jashub telling Ahaz to ask for a sign from God but when he refuses they respond with words to the effect 'do not waste our and God's time and strength', it is also 'a sign-grows adolescent/becomes young man' as the sign God will send is a boy born to a virgin who by the time he grows old enough to discern right from wrong, both kings will be gone: 'Ask thee a sign of the Lord thy God…But Ahaz said, I will not ask…*Is it* a small thing for you to weary men, but will ye weary my God also?' 'Therefore the Lord himself shall give you a sign…a virgin…shall conceive a son…For before the child shall know to refuse the evil, and choose the good, the land…shall be forsaken of both her kings.'.

The first part of 'Shear-jashub' character name is made up with a word similar to his 'father's'/ Isaiah(travelling/walking) name as (shear/ šĕ'ār/سيئار) means 'walking/he is walking/leaving/he is leaving/ has left' and is reflected at his introduction 'Then said the Lord unto Isaiah, Go forth now to meet Ahaz, thou, and Shear-jashub thy son, at the end of the conduit of the upper pool in the highway of the fuller's field;'. Cp: sei-aar khaashub, shei'aar yaashub, sei-aar yaashub. (Isa.7)

Tabeal; ṭāḇĕ'al; طآبي ئَل 'was not disgusted/revolted by-the' 'could eat/palate-the' 'liked the taste of-the' there is absolutely no difference in meaning between **Tabeel**/Tabeal, ṭāḇĕ'ēl, ṭāḇĕ'al, the slight change in spelling of the second part of the compound word still both mean 'the' and only a slight difference in pronunciation of 'ēl (ill), 'al (al(pronounced like 'ull' from 'dull') and just as in Ezra.4:7-24 because the character is a bad one in the narration it implies something unpleasant about him, the same is employed here in Isa.7, that 'Tabeal' is unsavoury reflected in the antagonists wanting to 'set a king in the midst of it, *even* the son of Tabeal:' i.e. even if most people do not like him/can barely palate him; تعبي ئَل 'fill/pack-the' 'troubled-the' 'tired-the' 'upset-the' 'sad-the' is also reflected as these meanings are used as to describe persuading a person to hate or believe negative things about another resulting in some negative action (in this instance against Ahaz/Judah). Cp: ṭaabei-ill, ṭaabei-al, t'abei-ill, t'abei-al. (Isa.7:5-6)

There is an interruption in the middle of the Isaiah/Shear-jeshub/Ahaz story being told (possibly by a later editor) where a clear message is sent to the audience using the same Biblical method of storytelling. It is connected by using the antagonist king of Syria/Israel word-names: **'Thus saith the Lord God, It shall not stand, neither shall it come to pass.'** a clear reminder to the audience these stories are fictional, they never happened nor will the threatened 'punishment' ever happen, but told in the Biblical method's entertaining way:

The head of Syria; 'ărām; 'wilderness/uninhabited place (where it's easy to get lost)' 'to abandon something or someone in the wild' 'a tree called 'aram/fetched wood of 'aram tree' 'see-the/I see the' 'penis-the/ insult with 'penis-the'' 'to throw/to do with throwing' 'killed/the killed/the killer' 'thrown, strewn or located over a vast distance/over different areas' 'vast/distant/covering wide or many different areas' (see Aram (Gen.10:22)). The story relays many of these meanings: the trees/wood; the conspiracy to kill and destroy; God reassuring the protagonists that the enemies will be killed and scattered 'that it be not a people'. But it is notable that whoever translated the story from the local language wanted to use the meanings of 'Syria' as in 'Asshur/Assyria' ('gestured/to signal'/'visit/the visit' 'squeeze' 'the tight/squeezed' 'the false oath' (see Asshur (Gen.10:11)) [i.e. the story about a 'sign' being 'squeezed/punished/destroyed' is fictional or a lie]

***is* Damascus** ('tore/ripped up' and also 'spat/spat a lot' 'sucked/sucked a lot' 'sucked at his teeth'), [no people will be torn/ripped up/ or sucked and spat out]

and the head of Damascus *is* Rezin ('heavy' 'strong/potent' 'stacked' describing when something such as rocks is stacked vertically or side by side, or anything that is stacked side-by-side.); [heavy as in too heavy to destroy, also means 'wise/measured' and no such brash actions happen]

and within threescore and five years shall Ephraim ('increase/multiply-them/the' 'with gap between teeth' usually describes a person with a gap between big front teeth and also when a front tooth is missing such as removed milk tooth or lost adult tooth) **be broken, that is not a people.** [the real people were not and will not be harmed, but will continue to increase]

And the head of Ephraim *is* Samaria ('storytellers' of night stories, 'they stayed/staying up late or all night'), [this is a fictional story do not take it as fact or seriously]

and the head of Samaria is Remaliah's son ('threw/killed-he' 'threw/killed him'). **If ye will not believe, surely ye shall not be established.** [everything being told about people/nations being thrown/ killed is a fictional story, the last sentence is a pun where the line says 'if you don't believe, you won't be established' it is actually saying this is a big joke, do not take seriously]

It intentionally left out 'Pekah' and emphasises that 'Ephraim *is* Samaria and Samaria *is* Remaliah's son' to highlight the fictionality—remember **Pekah** who is 'Remaliah's son' and means 'stayed' 'remained' is the character who assassinated **Pekahiah** to take his place (the names used in the earlier stories of 2Kgs.15, Pekah and Pekahiah('stayed-he' 'remained-he') hold the same meanings and are fictional to show a literal meaning in the earlier story between word-name and event in story. The author/editor of this part of Isa.7 was worried that the audience of the time would not understand and miss these original truths about the stories, he seems to be worried they would be taken as literal or religious texts instead of fiction. (Isa.7:7-9)

Immanuel; ʿimmānû'ēl; عِمّآنُ ئِل 'drink-the' 'give to drink-the'; ئِمّآنُ ئِل 'either in the' 'belief in the'. Although there is text to support all three meanings, most of the text supports 'drink-the' 'give to drink-the'. From the word (ʿm/عم) 'drink/drank' (see Ben-ammi, Ammon).

First, ئِمّآنُ ئِل 'either in the' 'belief in the': Ahaz is warned 'If ye will not believe, surely ye shall not be established.'. When Ahaz is offered to specify a sign from God in order he believe, he is given a choice 'Ask thee a sign of the Lord thy God: ask it either in the depth, or in the height above.'. Due to Ahaz refusing to request a sign from God, which Isaiah took as indication of Ahaz questioning God's words, the sign is a child who will be named Immanuel 'belief in the' 'either in the'. It is either the original authors of these stories from the get-go intended wordplay, or later editors added a meaning to the already set name by playing on its letters and adding to the story to give its new meanings.

Immanuel 'drink/give to drink-the' and the story narrates this child will eat 'butter and honey'. Combining clarified butter and honey remains popular in food and drink to this day in rural Yemen, not only because it tastes delicious together, but is believed and does have high nutritional value, believed to give strength and good health if eaten regularly. It is poured over hot bread crushed in milk, the butter and honey are poured and mixed together as they are in a liquid state and absorbed by the bread and into the milk, the excess left in the bowl is always mopped up. Butter (clarified) is also taken in liquid form by being heated and added with honey to milk to be drunk as it is believed in this form to be more nourishing, to provide strength and increase a person's weight/fatten with great health benefits. The drinking of butter and honey in milk is what the people of the older generations measure the fortune, fecundity and goodness of the land by, especially when they compare it to modern times when the availability of milk, butter and honey became scarce due to drought which resulted in lesser yield from cows, and scarcity of honey when bee-keeping was no longer common in households in the region (of the rural area I speak of). Drinking butter, honey and milk, as well as drinking pure milk and buttermilk (churned milk), in plentiful amounts was a sign and reality of the good fortune and prosperity of the land. In the story it is used to contrast the 'briers and thorns', barrenness as punishment.

The compound word used as a name 'Immanuel' from the word 'drink/give to drink' and linking it to butter and honey in the story meant good fortune was for the inhabitants of the land: 'Behold, a virgin shall conceive, and bear a son, and shall call his name Immanuel. Butter and honey shall he eat, that he may know to refuse the evil, and choose the good...And it shall come to pass, for the abundance of milk *that* they shall give he shall eat butter: for butter and honey shall everyone eat that is left in the land.' Although the word 'eat' is used for consuming the 'butter and honey' the same word in Arabic language means to consume whether food or drink, just as to smoke a cigarette in Arabic it is to 'drink a cigarette' or any other imbibement of smoke. (Isa.7:9-25)

In this part of the story I will only translate the new words, or words which have a great or new meaning on the current story. The connection of theme/meaning and how it reflects in the story can be made from those words already translated earlier.

Jeberechiah; yĕb̲erek̲yāhû; ; جي/ييبَرَك ياَهُ 'he/which one knelt-he/him' 'came knelt-he/him' 'he/which one made him kneel-he/him' 'came made him kneel-he/him' 'which are his underground water cisterns-he/him' 'came underground water cisterns-he/him'; جيبَرَك ياَهُ 'spoke and comforted with you-he/him' 'fixed you-he/him' 'discussed with you-he/him' 'mended/healed (something broken such as bone, heart)-he/him'; جي/ييبَرَكياَهُ 'he will prop/lean it/him against' 'came leaned/propped it against'; جي/ييبَرَخياَهُ 'he will let him/it loose' 'he will loosen him/it' 'he will let it go' 'came to let him/it loose' 'came to loosen him/it' 'came to let it go'; جي/ييبَرَق ياَهُ 'he gets into mood/sulk-he/him' 'has gone into a mood/sulking-him/he' 'came-went into mood/sulk-he/him'.

I believe Jeberechiah is 'he will/came leaned/propped it against' and 'discussed with you he/him' as he has been used as a witness in the story in addition to **Uriah** (show(ed) him) and **Zechariah** (reminded/mentioned he/him); **Zechariah** for 'topped with water or liquid/filled to brim with water/liquid-he/him' as there is a lot of mention of flowing waters and brimming rivers and also regarding 'And I went unto the prophetess; and she conceived, and bare a son.' and the son is named with meanings of overflowing waters and this relates to semen being called 'water', and ties it with Jeberechiah 'came underground water cisterns-he/him' meanings. Cp: yeiberek-yaahu, geiberek-yaahu, yeiberekyaahu, geiberekyaahu, yeiberek̲h̲yaahu, geiberek̲h̲yaahu, yeibereq-yaahu, geibereq-yaahu.

Maher-shalal-hash-baz; mahēr šālāl ḥāš baz; four verbs/themes which will happen and be reflected in the story and they are used not only in the literal sense but also figuratively to overpower/shalal, to overwork or enslave/maher, to drive away/hash, to captivate or appropriate by force/baz.

Maher; مَهير 'put to work/work for/do chores for' means someone working hard or many chores.

Shalal; شآلآل 'waterfalls/water overflowing' 'made water flow all over' ('overpower/overcome' 'took/took a lot or many times').

Hash; هآش 'drove/shooed away' (treat as animals); to drive or shoo away anything or anyone with your arms, hand, stick or anything else or with gestures.

Baz; بَز 'took/takes' (take by force/captivate).

All the words are reflected in the actions/narration of the story 'Moreover the Lord said unto me, Take thee a great roll, and write in it with a man's pen concerning Maher-shalal-hash-baz' and after a son is born 'Then said the Lord to me, Call his name Maher-shalal-hash-baz.'. The meanings of the four words which make up this name can be seen in the narration of the story how king of Assyria will be defeat, as well as the story of how he was victorious over Israel. I will give some examples of where this can be seen in the storyline, the meaning/theme of the word will be in parenthesis and their related part underlined.

'For as much as this people refuseth the waters of Shiloah [refuse to 'maher'/chores/serve] that go softly, and rejoice in ['maher'/work for]Rezin and Remaliah's sons,' **Shiloah** is the same as **Siloah** 'small flowing river' (Neh.3:15) and **Shiloh** 'take/carry away' (Judg.21:10-23) and all indicate a place where feasting and rituals occur, and rituals include the need of 'chores' as rituals include sacrifice, burning, cooking, cleaning, etc. the refusal of 'the waters of Shiloah…and rejoice in Rezin and Remaliah's sons' means giving up the worship/rituals of Shiloah and working/performing rituals and following the ways of Rezin/Remaliah.

'Now therefore, behold, the Lord bringeth upon them the waters of the river [shalal/water overflows/overpower/overcome], strong and many, *even* the king of Assyria, and all his glory: and he shall come up over all his channels, and go over all his banks: And he shall pass through Judah; he shall overflow and go over, he shall reach even unto the neck;[shalal/overflow/overpower]'

'O Assyrian, the rod of mine anger, and the staff in their hand is my indignation [hash/rod used to shoo/drive away animals, people, etc.]. I will send him against an hypocritical nation, and against the people of my wrath will I give him charge [maher/to serve], to take the spoil, and to take the prey [baz/take/appropriate], and to tread them down like the mire of the streets.'

'For he saith, By the strength of mine hand I have done *it* [maher/done the work], and by my wisdom, for I am prudent: and I have removed the bounds of the people [hash/driven away/shooed], and have robbed their treasures [baz; taken], and have put down the inhabitants like a valiant man [hash/shooed, driven away—maher/did the work]:'

'And my hand hath found as a nest the riches of the people [maher/did the work; hash/shooed away]: and as one gathereth eggs *that are* left, have I gathered all the earth [baz/taken; maher/did the chore/done the work]; and there was none that moved the wing, or opened the mouth, or peeped [hash/no one shooed or drove him away].

'Shall the axe boast itself against [shalal/overpower] him that heweth therewith [maher/does the chore]? *or* shall the saw magnify itself against [shalal/overpower] him that shaketh it [maher/does the chore]? as if the rod should shake itself against [hash/shoo or drive away; shalal/overcome] them that lift it up [maher/did the work], or as if the staff should lift up *itself* [hash/shoo or drive away; maher/do the work], as if it were no wood.'

'…the remnant…shall no more again stay upon him that smote them [maher/serve, do the chores for who: shalal/overpowered/overflowed]; but shall stay upon the Lord [maher/serve].'

'…the consumption decreed shall overflow with righteousness [shalal/overflow/overcome].'

'…he shall smite thee with a rod, and shall lift up his staff against thee…[hash/shoo and drive away; shalal/overpower].'

'And it shall come to pass in that day, that his burden shall be taken away from off thy shoulder, and his yoke from off thy neck…[baz/take away; maher/chores/serve; hash/driving away; shalal/overpowering]'.

Cp: maheyr, shaalaal, haash, baz. (Isa.8:1-4, 6-8; 10: 5-6, 13-15, 20, 22, 24, 27)

Zebulun (Gen.30:20) is used for 'they will stay' 'stayed/lingered' 'shaded' 'misguided/misled' as the people described are doing wrong, have been misguided by their leaders and walk in the dark, but it has also been given a new meaning with wordplay supported by the text: zĕḇûlûn; ذيبُلن 'withered/they withered' 'wicks/made wicks/placed wicks' and is the wick of anything which can be ignited such as candlewick, lantern wick, etc. that produces a lasting flame to shed light or ignite a fire. Along with 'they will stay' it is used here to indicate the people who had stayed in the darkness 'The people that walked in darkness have seen a great light: they that dwell in the land of the shadow of death, upon them hath the light shined.'. Cp: sheidhulun, veibulun. (Isa.9:1-2)

Naphtali (Gen.30:8) has been used for its earlier meaning of 'we crush for me', but this too has also been given a new meaning: naptālî; نَفتَالي 'we entwine/create twine' 'of twining/entwining' and means the action of creating twine from fibres which necessitates making separate fibres twirl against each other rapidly until they become one twine—it has been used here and paired with Zebulun because it is how wicks are made, by twining, so Naphtali here, too, indicates the light which will shine upon people in the 'darkness' and the 'shadow of death' as well as Naphtali 'we crush for me' indicates they have been afflicted as described in verse 1. Cp: naphtaalee. (Isa.9:1-2)

The rest of chapter 9 keeps up the theme of wicks and light, where people 'afflicted' with great punishment are both the fuel and wicks of this fire which keeps up the darkness, i.e. they are the fuel of this fire. What is evident is the contradiction, where anyone reading only verse 2 of Isa.9 is led to believe the 'great light…the light shined' is a message of hope, because it is not, it promises in verse 1 that the people in Zebulun and Naphtali who were only 'lightly afflicted' will be more severely punished and this is what happens throughout the description of the rest of Isa.9, the light is fire and punishment to be delivered from 'beyond Jordan' **Jordan** (Gen.13: 8-11) 'they come/are coming home' and in 'Galilee of the nations' **Galilee** (Josh.20:7) 'came-to' 'came-for' 'cleared-the'—Jordan/Galilee used because this punishment is coming home to the people, and the people will be 'cleared' purged and destroyed as punishment.

The only other way to read this is: if Isa.9:2 was meant as a light of hope—then it must have been added by a later editor and not the original author of Isaiah. But this contradicts the whole chapter in which it is narrated as a punishment.

Midian (Gen.25:2) used for 'passing by/is passing' as the verse speaks about a people likened to a beast of burden no longer being driven forward by its owner/oppressor: the yoke keeps cows/bulls stepping in line together when ploughing/tilling land; the staff because a staff keeps the person going or used to hang heavy loads from when carried over a distance; the 'rod of his oppressor' because a rod or similar object such as a switch is used to keep cattle and flocks moving in the right direction. (Isa.9:4)

David (1Sam.16:11;17) 'the stone rolling pin of grinding stone' is used because it is a durable stone which lasts a very long time which is why he is mentioned to indicate a strong and long-lasting kingdom. (Isa.9:7)

Jacob (Gen.25:26-34; 27) and has been used for 'forces open' 'dislocates' 'forces open and takes/usurps' because in the story the name Jacob was usurped by the name Israel, just like Jacob usurped Esau, and **Israel** (Gen.32:28) 'twisted-the' has been used because things will be twisted, made wrong, because people are twisting things to cause the people to sin. (Isa.9:8)

Ephraim (Gen.41:52) used for 'with gap between teeth/gap(s)' to mean the gaps which will be left by the destroyed houses, and Ephraim is mentioned as the inhabitant of **Samaria** (1Kgs.13:32) 'storytellers' 'night stories' because what the people are doing is lying to themselves when they tell themselves that they will rebuild with stronger materials. (Isa.9:9)

Rezin (2Kgs.16) 'heavy' 'strong/potent' 'slammed hard' 'stacked' as the enemy who will cause the stones of houses to fall and be cut down, who will deliver the severe punishment described from beginning to the end of this chapter. (Isa.9:11)

Syrian for 'to throw/to do with throwing' 'killed/the killed/the killer' as the story is about the punished being thrown down and killed. (Isa.9:12)

Philistines (Gen.10:14) (Exod.15:14) 'between/in two (or more) shores/coasts' 'in the coast-the' 'in two (or more) coasts' 'in their coast' because verse 1 of the chapter narrates the punishment will come 'by way of the sea' and emphasised 'beyond Jordan' and most of the time Jordan is describing a river. So where in other stories the narration has created two coasts or two bodies of water for a battle to take place in, in this story it has done this again with the words and word-imagery. (Isa.9:12)

Israel is used again to show the 'twisted-the' described as the head and tail which will be cut off because they have misled the people to disobey God. (Isa.9:14)

Ephraim 'with gap between teeth' is used again to reflect missing body parts described as self-cannibalisation and **Manasseh** (Gen.41:51) used for 'made him forget', to forget he has eaten and therefore remain unsatisfied, but also to forget he is eating his own arm/killing his own brethren. **Judah** (Gen.29:35) 'he is called/calls' to 'call, or curse' is invoked because they have reached this devastation by not calling on God who is punishing them for their disobedience, and it is God who has brought this punishment on them, and the outstretched arm of God punishing the people is also a reminder to call to God for help/ mercy/etc. (Isa.9:21)

Calno; kalnô; قُلْنَ 'we said'; كَلْنَ 'all of us' 'we ate it'. It is the same as Calneh (Gen.10:10). Cp: qalno, kalno. (Isa.10:9)

Aiath; 'ayyāṯ; عيّآت 'learnt and remembered(this)' 'was warned/careful' 'warned' 'was wary' 'dared to go on' 'made repeated sound at goats/sheep' 'learnt and understood'. Cp: 'ayyaat. (Isa.10:28)

Madmenah; maḏmēnâ; مَضمينه/ا 'strongly reassured' 'did not reassure/guarantee', it is also a type of tool used along with the yoke and the action of putting it onto the necks of the bulls who will be ploughing land. It is used with exactly the meaning of there was no reassurance/guarantee of safety 'Madmenah is removed; the inhabitants of Gebim gather themselves to flee.'. It is the same as Madmannah (Josh.15:31). Cp: ma<u>dh</u>meynah(na). (Isa.10:31)

Gebim; gēḇîm; جيب هم/ام 'gathered/ganged-them/the' and is direct reflection of '...the inhabitants of Gebim gather themselves to flee.'. Cp: geyb-hum/um. (Isa.10:31)

Pathros; paṯrôs; بَفرُص 'I will separate' 'I will split open/push out/pushing up or out/divide by breaking or splitting'. Cp: ba<u>ph</u>ro<u>ss</u>. (Isa.11:11)

Lucifer; hêlēl; هيليل 'cry out loud/praise/chant' 'cry out word or name repeatedly' 'a hullaballoo' 'loud chaos' 'crescent moon' 'new moon' when the moon is only a slither/crescent. When a person or something is described as 'hilal/crescent moon' it means something or someone so beautiful or great that they are followed like a guiding light. As Babylon and its king are described as the most glorious, mightiest of all kingdoms, it is this description of it being like a heavenly body which all eyes follow and are guided by, and in its downfall it compares it to a crescent moon falling out of heaven/sky 'How art thou fallen from heaven, O Lucifer, son of the morning! how art thou cut down to the ground, which didst weaken the nations!'. Cp: heyleyl. (Isa.14.12)

Ar 'a disgrace' 'naked' and is still linked to 'Moab' ('of disgrace') as it was used in (Num.21:15). **Kir** 'settle/ stop/stop moving' 'stones/clumps of dry mud' as in (2Kgs.16:7-9) to show how the nation will be ruined and 'silenced' cease to be. These two words are used to show how 'Moab' an enemy country will be destroyed. (Isa.15:1)

Bajith; bayit; باجِث 'pierce and burst out'; باغِت 'to fear/scare/surprise and scare' 'wanted' 'conducted immoral behaviour' 'prostituted/immoral sexual activities'; باعِت 'sold'; باعِط 'ripped/tore'. The meanings of 'pierced and burst' 'to scare' are in the narration as Moab has been attacked at night, and the people are fleeing and weeping out of fright and bereavement and it ties to the 'immoral' meanings of 'Moab'. Equivalent to Nebajoth (Gen.25:13). Cp: bagif, ba<u>gh</u>it, ba'it, ba'iṭ. (Isa.15:2)

Dibon used for its meaning 'harmed/harm' (Num.21:30); **Nebo** for 'we will harm/ostracise' (Num.32:3); **Medeba** for 'wailing in mourning' 'hair cut short or shaved off completely' (Num.21:30) and employed here exactly how it was used in (1Chr.19:3-7) where it relayed in both the defeat of the army and the humiliation which Hanun caused David's messengers by shaving them. In Isa.15 it shows this exact use where there is much slaughter and wailing, but more so 'Moab shall howl over Nebo, and over Medeba: on all their heads shall be baldness, and every beard cut off...on the tops of their houses, and in their streets, every one shall howl, weeping abundantly.'. (Isa.15:2-3)

Zoar (Gen.14:2-8) has been used for its meanings 'roar/groan' like an animal, 'small' and also 'small' as in humiliated as the fleeing people are screaming, howling, weeping and 'flee to Zoar'—they have emphasised the groaning like an animal by likening the people and Zoar 'an heifer of three years old' which lows non-stop if separated from its mother (in the real world). (Isa.15:5)

Luhith; lûîṯ; لُيث 'loud cry/shouted' 'a loud cry for help' and is exactly what is being described 'for by the mounting up of Luhith with weeping shall they go it up; for in the way of Horonaim they shall raise up a cry of destruction'. It is equivalent to Goliath (1Sam.17). Cp: lueef. (Isa.15:5)

Horonaim; ḥōrōnayim; هورونَيهم 'we drove/chased them away (with words)/with cruel words'; خورونَيهم 'we chased them away with violence' 'we made them collapse'.

Note the way the authors of the Bible use these compound word-names as enhancers to make the story clearer and more entertaining, it is interesting to see the stark contrast in difference compared to how some Biblical scholars wrongly use it as actual 'mapping' or 'proof' of a non-existent land based on an event which never happened: the EDB states under Horonaim: 'In Isaiah's oracle the expression "road to Horonaim" is used parallel to the "ascent of Luhith". This seems to indicate that Horonaim was located along a roadway that led from the Moabite plateau down to the Dead Sea. It may be identified with modern el-ʿIrāq (211055), ca. 15 km. (9 mi.) E of the Dead Sea, SW of Kerak, or with the northern side od Wadi el-Kerak atop ed-Der, SW of Rabbah.' (Freedman, Myers and Beck, 2000: 608).

The story uses the compound words 'Horonaim' along with 'Luhith' as place names to create the imagery of people screaming, weeping, being violently slaughtered and chased away, fleeing towards more danger instead of safety. The whole chapter is about slaughter, weeping, blood, disgrace, defeat, screaming for and seeking safety and not finding it. Cp: hooroonayhum, <u>kh</u>ooroonayhum. (Isa.15:5)

Nimrim; nimrîm; نِم ريم 'nag-rot'; نِمر هم/ام 'bully-them/the' as the land and people will be punished, attacked and driven out of their homes, and made to wither 'For the waters of Nimrim shall be desolate: for the hay is withered away, the grass faileth, there is no green thing.'. Similar to Nimrod (Gen.10:8), Nimrah (Num.32:3). Cp: nim-reem, nimr-hum/um. (Isa.15:6)

Eglaim; 'eglayim; نِجلاي هم/ام 'clear-them/the' 'made clear-them/the' 'purify(on heat)-them/the'; نِجلا يم 'clear-river/sea' 'purify(on heat)-river/sea'. In the context of the story, it is as the meaning of the word cleaning/purifying something bad, unclean, e.g. when a utensil is purified with the same word of 'Eglaim' it is sterilised on heat, when a bowl is washed with the same word of 'Eglaim' it is being scrubbed clean from any residue after being used. Here it is the inhabitants of Moab who are being cleared out with death and destruction. Cp: eglay-hum/um, egla-yim. (Isa.15:8)

Beer-elim; bĕ'ēr 'ēlîm; بيئير ئيلهم 'good for them' 'piety for them' 'good/piety-well fed/plumpen/pamper' and sounds here like gloating at slaughter, as the howling, desolation is what is being described as 'good/piety for them' as well as relaying the 'abundance' the people will carry to the 'brook of willows' i.e. all the sustenance and goods they had stored will be of little comfort to them now; بيئير عيليم 'good/piety-understood' 'good/piety-knew/found out' 'good/piety-was shown' 'good/piety-was shown and understood' 'good/piety-show' and still sounds like gloating in this part of the story; بيئير ئيليم 'good/piety-pained/felt pain/are blamed/will blame' and still reflects a gloating that people are in pain or could be describing the 'good/piety' as innocent people are in pain, 'good/piety-are gathered/will gather' as the people are being driven to gather at a place they flee to. It is similar to **Elim** (Exod.15:26-27; 16:1-12) with a slight difference in its pronunciation and variable to its meanings, but it is used in the same way that Elim was used in the Exodus story to show when God was teaching people how to avoid being punished while they were wandering, and to reflect their pain and suffering. Cp: bei-eyr eylhum, bei-eyr 'eyleem, bei-eyr eyleem. (Isa.15:8)

Dimon; dîmôn; ديمُن 'blood' 'bled' 'they bled' and is described 'For the waters of Dimon shall be full of blood: for I will bring more upon Dimon, lions upon him that escapeth…'. It is equivalent to Dimona (Josh.15:22), Dimnah (Josh.21:35). Cp: deemon. (Isa.15:9)

Sela the same as **Selah** has been used in the same way as at (2Kgs.14:1-7) 'arrived' 'connected' and the same word is used when a person who has wronged another arrives at the latter's home, with gifts (qat, confectionaries, other foodstuff) which includes a calf, lamb or ram for slaughter to have lunch and apologise so as to put the issue to rest; the act of 'arriving' is itself a public apology for all to witness. This is meant in 'Send ye the lamb to the ruler of the land from Sela to the wilderness…'. (Isa.16:1)

Zion 'sweep/brush away' 'bad' is used to reflect 'bad women' and the bad which will befall them 'daughters of Zion' 'daughters of Moab' suggest the 'enemies' females (Moab) will be treated badly and swept away (Zion) likened to a bird pushed out of its nest without safety, without cover, without protection. **Arnon** 'naked/nakedness' 'disgraced' 'abandoned in wilderness' is linked with **Moab** 'of disgrace/disgraced' just as Moab and Arnon were linked for these meanings at (Num.21:13). (Isa.16:1-2)

Noph; nōp; نوف 'ceased to exist/died/wiped out/exiled/negated/denied' and this is exactly what is being described. Equivalent to Nophah (Num.). Cp: noo<u>ph</u>. (Isa19:13)

Canaan has been used for its meaning 'given up on' 'given up any hope' as the story describes the Egyptians having no hope as they are being destroyed by their own 'cruel lord' who will use Egyptians to kill Egyptians, the giving up and despair is meant by 'In that day shall five cities in the land of Egypt speak the language of Canaan…'. (Isa.19:18)

Sargon; sargôn; شَرجُن 'route' 'channel/waterway' it is a route made of stones which turns into a waterway during heavy rain, channelling water to specific land; it is also a path which is well-used to the degree its erosion marks it out as a path in the mountain; 'anus'. This meaning is supported by the text as **Tartan** (a word-name used at 2Kgs.18:17-36) 'intentionally pour water like a waterfall' is sent by Sargon 'route' 'channel/waterway'—when Tartan is used in 2Kgs., it is to stand by the pool/conduit and speak to Hezekiah. It is connected to the verses in the previous chapter 'In that day shall there be a highway out of Egypt to Assyria…' and that is the meaning of Sargon. The meaning of 'anus' is in that Isaiah will walk around naked for three years, and so will the people be taken away naked and emphasis is put on 'even with their buttocks uncovered to the shame of Egypt'. Cp: <u>sh</u>argon. (Isa.19:23; 20:1)

Dumah is the same as in (Gen.25:14) 'last long' 'shadowy figure(or something you can see but not tell what it is' 'spinning/dizziness': 'shadowy figure' and is the word used to describe such when the thing being viewed cannot be clearly seen/identified, and the 'Watchman' is trying to make out what is happening at a distance, in this instance in the dark 'The burden of Dumah. He calleth to me out of Seir, Watchman, what of the night? Watchman, what of the night?'.

The meaning Dumah 'last long' is connected to the word **Arabia** 'grows well/takes care of' (2Chr.9:14) depicted as a forest that provides shelter to those who need help; and Dumah 'last long' and 'spinning/dizziness' with **Tema** 'extremities or skin falls off' 'quenching thirst/dryness' 'giving to drink/watering' (Gen.25:15) are assisting and allowing those people falling apart and fleeing to last a little longer by given them to drink; but **Kedar** 'are able' (Gen.25:13) will not last long i.e. they will not be able to last long as they too will be 'diminished': 'The burden upon Dumah…The burden upon Arabia. In the forest in Arabia shall ye lodge, O ye travelling companies of Dedanim. The inhabitants of the land of Tema brought water to him that was thirsty, they prevented with their bread him that fled…from the grievousness of war…all the glory of Kedar shall fail…shall be diminished.'. (Isa.21:11-17)

Dedanim; dĕdānîm; تيدآن هم/ام 'make/made to bow/bend' 'to guilt them/the' and the story speaks of people carrying a burden and fleeing war. Cp: teidaan-hum/um. (Isa.21:13)

Shebna as in (2Kgs.18:18) still means; šeḇnā', šeḇnâ; شِفنآء ، شِفنه 'we saw' 'we saw it/him' but has been given additional meanings 'will make cease to exist/wipe out/die/kill' as he will be violently tossed out of the kingdom and die in shame, also this character has built some kind of structure which causes God's anger; شِبنآء ، شِبنه 'will build' 'will build it': '…unto Shebna, which is over the house…that thou hast hewed thee out a sepulchre here, *as* he that heweth him out a sepulchre on high, *and* that graveth an habitation for himself in a rock?...the Lord will carry thee away with a mighty captivity…He will surely violently turn and toss thee like a ball into a large country: there thou shalt die…'. and refers to Shebna being a scribe who writes down what he sees, but also because he is one of the three who come out and see Sennacherib's men and message. Cp: <u>sh</u>e<u>ph</u>naa, <u>sh</u>e<u>ph</u>nah, <u>sh</u>ebnaa, <u>sh</u>ebnah. (2Kgs.18:18,26-27,37)

Eliakim still means 'the one who stands/the one who stands instead of' but instead of the character replacing his brother as king, or the other character of the same name standing instead of King Hezekiah along with Shebna to answer Senecharrib's men, this time Eliakim takes the place of Shebna who is now described as a treasurer but seems to have the authority of a king, even this Eliakim seems to have been given more authority than a treasurer.

In Isa.22 there is obviously an intentional combining (or mix-up out of confusion) of the ideas of the story of Eliakim the king's son who takes over Jehoahaz his brother and king's place at 2Kgs.23, and the characters of Eliakim who is in charge over the king's household and Shebna who is a scribe at 2Kgs.18:18. At Isa.22 Eliakim seems to become a king, the displaced Shebna who was earlier a scribe seems to be a ruler more than a treasurer. But this does not matter to the original Biblical authors nor does it affect the storyline, as what is important is the use of the compound words (presented as character names) and what they are telling the audience about the story. (Isa.22:15-25)

Ariel, as earlier in (Ezra.8:16-18), is used for its meanings of 'show-the' ('show-the' can mean literally to show something or as a threat) 'saw-the' 'teach/taught-the' (as 'seeing' and 'showing' is the same as 'teaching'). There is 'show-the' as a threat from God; 'saw-the' 'see-the' 'show-the' as people's inability to see is described; 'dreamt-the' this description is included in the Ariel story of Isaiah; 'show-the' as in 'teach-the' as the people are unable to understand/learn because their vision has been cursed by God, presented as being like uneducated people who cannot read, or those who can but the 'sealed book' does not open for them so they too cannot learn. It is present in the narration '…that seek deep to hide their counsel from the Lord, and their works are in the dark, and they say, Who seeth us? and who knoweth us?'; it is in the description that eventually even the blind will see, deaf will hear, the meek and poor will understand—it is all about seeing/learning/understanding the correct ways (according to the story). From the beginning to its end this chapter repeats the meanings of 'Ariel'. (Isa.29)

Hanes; ḥānēs; هآنيش 'humiliated/insulted you' 'I will copulate' 'look, he/it is copulating' (the 'copulating' meanings are from the word used to describe goats and other similar animals copulating); حآنيش 'snake' 'deals like a snake' (i.e. a deceitful person who will harm you); خآنيش 'betrayed you'. All three meanings (except 'copulation') are in Isa.30. Cp: haaneysh, ḥaaneysh, khaaneysh. (Isa.30)

Idumea; 'ĕḏôm; is the same as **'Edom'** (Gen.25:30) but only its meanings of 'bleeding/bloody/of blood' 'made to bleed' 'made to bleed a lot' 'became bloodied' or 'lasts/lasts long'; and the references to great slaughter of man and animals is mentioned with emphasis on the great quantities of blood and specifically 'The sword of the Lord is filled with blood'. (Isa.34:6)

Jesurun; the same as **Jeshurun** 'greedy' in the plural, still holds the same meaning used and intended at (Deut.32). The greed is an unsatisfied hunger used as a metaphor to show worshipping other gods is unfulfilling: after reassuring the faithful with blessings, quenching their thirst, the text goes on to describe what will happen to those who stray from God's ways: 'O Jacob, my servant; and thou, Jesurun, whom I have chosen. For I will pour water upon him that is thirsty...They that make a graven image are all of them vanity; and their delectable things shall not profit...The smith with the tongs both worketh in the coals, and fashion it with hammers, and worketh it with the strength of his arms: yea he is hungry and his strength faileth: he drinketh no water and is faint...The carpenter stretcheth out his rule...Then shall it be for a man to burn...with part thereof he eateth; he roasteth roast and is satisfied...They have not known nor understood...for he hath shut their eyes that they cannot see; and their hearts that they cannot understand...he feedeth on ashes; a deceived heart has turned him aside, that he cannot deliver his soul, nor say, Is there not a lie in my right hand?' therefore he (his soul) remains hungry as he is not really 'feeding' on truth. (Isa.44)

Sinim; sînîm; سينهم ، سين هم/ام 'in the direction/in their direction' 'put them on right direction' 'set them straight' 'towards them/the' 'For he that hath mercy on them shall lead them, even by the springs of water shall he guide them...And I will make all my mountains away, and my highways shall be exalted...Behold, these shall come from far: and, lo, these from the north and the west; and these from the land of Sinim...yet will I not forget thee. Behold, I have graven thee upon the palms *of my* hands; thy walls *are* continually before me...Lift up thine eyes round about, and behold: all these gather themselves together, *and* come to thee.'. Cp: seenhum, seen-hum/um. (Isa.49:10–18)

Hephzi-bah still has one of the meanings from (2Kgs.21:1): 'I will make her/them pass wind' 'I will pass wind-with her' and means to intensely scare to the degree they lose control of bowels, but also 'copulate-her' 'breaking wind-her' which is the term used to describe a rooster copulating a hen: while copulating, it seems he is passing wind into her. This very meaning and imagery is used by the Biblical author of this part of Isaiah's story: '...but thou shalt be called Hephzi-bah, and thy land Beulah: for the Lord delighteth in thee, and thy land shall be married.' The following part clarifies the Hephzi-bah means copulation, a male bowing over a female during intercourse 'and as the bridegroom rejoiceth over the bride, so shall thy God rejoice over thee.'. (Isa.62:4–5)

Beulah; bĕʽûlâ; بيعْلة 'husbands/spouses' 'above her/it' 'will be above' and it is a literal description of a husband and being on top of the 'bride' while having sexual intercourse. It is in the plural because all the sons of the land are described as marrying land 'but thou shalt be called Hephzi-bah, and thy land Beulah: for the Lord delighteth in thee, and thy land shall be married. For as a young man marrieth a virgin, so shall thy sons marry thee: and as the bridegroom rejoiceth over the bride, so shall thy God rejoice over thee.'. Cp: bei'ulah. (Isa.62:4–5)

What can be seen from the contradictions in the messages of the stories within Isaiah, and the different writing styles, is there is obviously more than one author (and editors) to the Book of Isaiah. None of the story was authored by 'Isaiah' as he is a fictional character whose name and role are used in the Book of Isaiah and earlier OT stories.

Parts of Isaiah are reworkings and recyclings with variations of earlier stories (e.g. Deut.32 where you can see the prototype of Isaiah is **Hoshea** (the latter word-name has the same meanings and is introduced at Deut.32 under the story which the authors of Isaiah borrowed from). There are new ideas and beliefs introduced with focus on 'the Holy One' (the interpretation/translation of what is presented as 'the Holy One' is a mistranslation/misinterpretation in itself). Isa.5 (at least) is in the writing style of the Song of Solomon. Some authors/editors feel the need to emphasise that Jehovah is a male, and imply he was considered female by insisting 'I am he', in all cases the word-name given to the God of the OT is 'Jehovah/ stayed' and this meaning is reflected in Isaiah 'To whom he said, This is the rest wherewith ye may cause the weary to rest; and this is the refreshing: yet they would not hear.' (Isa.28:12)

Isa.42, which the western copiers of the Bible have decided speaks of Christ (the KJV titles the header with 'Office of Christ' and other such titles), does not describe Jesus' character of the NT, but maybe describes either Elias or John of the NT. Due to the fact the story in Isaiah describes this character as mild, kind, meek, not raising his voice; whereas the story in the NT describes Jesus as turning over tables and shouting in anger, being rude to his mother for no obvious reason, preaching to the people and openly accusing those who follow the religion of the 'scribes' 'pharisees' and 'Sadducees' as liars, and it is narrated as being done in a very confrontational manner. It is not about how people see/believe Jesus as in Christianity, I am not discussing that, but I am objectively addressing what the stories and text state, and the special person being prophesied about could not be Jesus of the NT due to the great difference in how both characters are portrayed.

From Isa.46 onwards, the different Biblical authors/editors of Isaiah wrangle with what they present, maybe wrangle with what they believe and/or want people to believe (the wrangling and contradictions are because different authors/editors would add their own ideas/stories (maybe remove others') at later times). There is an obvious change and yo-yoing of contradicting messages from the worship of one God towards three (or at least two) connected deities—there is an 'I from beginning', God, and God's Spirit. There is a wrangling over whether God is an 'I am he' or if he is a she. There is a narrative which will eventually become, or be the basis built on, for the Jesus/NT story, but in primitive state. It is worth mentioning that 'Isaiah' in the Book of Isaiah seems to be one of many original characters which inspired the stories of Jesus/NT. The words used as names themselves are somewhat similar in pronunciation in Arabic between Isaiah of the OT, and 'Jesus' as in the Quran, whereas there is a greater difference between the word pronunciation and meaning between Isaiah (OT) and Jesus of the NT, although the OT/NT Isaiah/ Jesus stories are similar.

There is a struggle to hold onto the 'I Am That I Am' eheyah-'aishar-eheyah 'she is-with child/calf-she is' 'she is-pregnant-she is' of (Exod.3) which is the deity of the earliest OT stories (and people's beliefs) and the transformation can be seen in Isa.45 and 54 where ''Ashera' becomes a prototype of the virgin/Mother Mary albeit the metaphor may be speaking about a land, but it is the seeds of the idea.

At Isa.46:3-5 the narration has God claim to carry Jacob/the people in his 'belly' and deliver it through the womb—even if the narration states 'I am he' it is still a representation of a pregnant female god carrying her worshippers, her offspring. Is it 'Ashera? Is it another female deity in the psyche and culture of author and audience?

Isa.48:16 'Come ye near unto me, hear this: I have not spoken in secret from the beginning; from the time that it was, there am I: and now the Lord God, and his Spirit, hath sent me.' Although Jewish religion is monotheistic, its beginnings were not, and this part of Isaiah shows a third deity next to a God who is already joined by 'his Spirit' which acts as a separate being albeit doing God's will. This third deity is the protagonist and narrator of the story: Isaiah.

Isaiah whose story is much like the Jesus/NT story, is speaking of himself, especially at Isa.61 and previous chapters. The similarity in the word-name of Isaiah and how Jesus is pronounced in the Quran should not be overlooked.

Jeremiah

As in (2Kgs.23:31) **Jeremiah** still means 'he throws-he/him' 'they throw him' 'throws it/he throws it' 'he kills-he/him' 'he/they kill him'. Throughout the chapters, God gives Jeremiah a message to his people telling them he will 'cast' them out of the land, i.e. 'throw them'; he will 'cast' them out of his sight, etc. The potter's vessel Jeremiah breaks would need to be thrown down to break it; the trees will be 'cast' into the fire; Jeremiah is thrown into prison as well as down a hole, or the dungeon was like a hole (Jer.38). He is son of **Hilkiah** for its meaning of 'I will throw it/cast it' 'here/look-threw it/him' (2Kgs.18:18,26-27,37). He is from the area of **Anathoth** for its meaning 'pushes off cliff/high place' 'he/it will push off cliff/high place'; in the land of **Benjamin** 'son/child-calls them mother/makes them mother' 'son/child-whose?' because God chooses him while he is still a foetus, but adult Jeremiah objects that he is too inexperienced or insignificant (the same way Benjamin was used in Saul's story that 'who am I that I should be chosen...' linked to being Benjamite)'for I *am* a child'.

All the character and place names are used to show what is happening in the story: **Josiah** 'they go wandering and seeking' (2Kgs.22-23) as Jeremiah is tasked with a mission 'for thou shalt go to all that I shall send thee'; **Amon** (1Kgs.22:) 'secured/made safe' 'followed/lead' 'followed through/led through' as God reassures him no harm will come to him, and that God will lead him (deliver) through the mission 'be not afraid...for I am with thee to deliver thee...' 'believed/belief' 'followed'. (1Kgs.22); **Jehoiakim** (2Kgs.23:36) 'he who/which one-stands/the one who stands instead of' 'came who/came to him-stands/the one who stands instead of' as by touching his hand at Jeremiah's mouth it is now God who will be speaking while Jeremiah will just be physically standing there i.e. they both represent each other, but also Jeremiah is being asked to stand in front of the people 'I have put my words in thy mouth'; **Judah** (Gen.29:35) 'he is called/calls' to 'call, or curse' 'to make a claim' 'make a false claim or an unproven claim' it is regarding people who call on other gods instead of the correct one, also in that God will 'utter my judgements against them touching their wickedness...and worshipped the works of their own hands.' But also because Jeremiah throughout the book is asked to go stand and deliver i.e. call out God's message in front of/in the middle of the people; **Zedekiah** (1Kgs.22:11-28) 'deceived you-him/he' because the people have deceived themselves with worshipping idols they make, also in God warning Jeremiah to be brave otherwise he will 'confound thee before them', 'gave more-he/him' and 'blocked-he/him' 'prevented/absorbed attack-he/him' as the story narrates God defending Jeremiah and likening his defence and Jeremiah to a fortress; **Jerusalem** 'they see-asked-them/the' came-saw-asked-them/the' the narration has Jeremiah being told he will be sent to the people, he is asked and sent by God, the people will see him (for more meanings which are connected to this story, see Jerusalem). This compound word is expounded on in the narrative: God sees Jeremiah while he is still a foetus, and designates him a prophet, a prophet is sent to the people and asked questions and to prophecy; twice the narrative has God ask Jeremiah what he sees, and Jeremiah answers about what he sees, and God's response to both answers is that something which has been seen is coming.

There is an obvious intention by the author(s) of Jeremiah to make Jeremiah a character who is similar to both Moses and Aaron in this story, where Moses claimed his meekness and God allowed Aaron to be with him so he could speak better. The almond rod is also a symbol of Aaron, whereas the seething pot symbolises both Esau and Jacob, and this symbolisation stands for Aaron = priest = good, Jacob = greed = bad. (Jer.1)

There is a reason why the author of Jer.7 rails against claims of 'the temple'. First, the word translated in the Bible and interpreted as 'temple', is not 'temple' at all, but something else. The author, through Jeremiah's character who in the story is speaking God's words, is saying all the stories about the 'temple[the true meaning of the word not 'temple']' are false and the importance put on it (put on what modern people erroneously believe means 'temple', but the original audiences of these stories knew exactly what it meant so it refers to what the real meaning of the word is (to be explained later in this book, where it is more relevant).

Uphaz; 'ûpāz; نوفآز 'provokes/is provoked' 'succeeds/wins' and both refer to the idol worship provoking God, that the idols being worshipped will not help their worshippers, but God and those who worship him will succeed. Cp: u-phaaz. (Jer.10)

There is a struggle between different authors/editors of Jeremiah with at least one author/editor stating the whole 'The temple of the Lord, The temple of the Lord, The temple of the Lord' is a lie, but other authors/editors are sticking to the older stories where it is a sin to offer things to any other god.

Anathoth has been used again as meaning 'pushes off cliff/high place' 'he/it will push off cliff/high place' as it narrated 'the men of Anathoth' wish to kill Jeremiah. (Jer.11:21)

Moses (Exod.2:1-10) for 'squeeze him/it' as the narration states even if Moses were there to speak i.e. put pressure on God (squeeze) to spare the people. Even if **Samuel** (1Sam.1) 'block(ed)-the' 'plug-the' 'shut up-the' were there to speak for the people, he too would not be able to stop God from punishing the people.

Manasseh (2Kgs.20:21; 21) 'made him forget' is used as it was earlier in the stories where he caused people to follow the wrong ways i.e. forget the way of God, and his (and the people's) punishment is represented both in his father's name **Hezekiah** (2Kgs.18-20) 'squeezed/cornered/crammed him-he/him' 'make suffer/distress-he/him' 'I will force to taste/swallow/eat-he/him' and in the narration of the earlier story and Jeremiah. In Jeremiah, the punished people and their suffering will be overlooked and forgotten; they are being squeezed and cornered from all sides and with all kinds of punishment; there will be no one and God will refuse to block this punishment from afflicting them.

Hinnom (Josh.15:8) 'insulted' either being insulted or insulting others, 'satisfied/gratified' either being satisfied or satisfying others as the people will be disgraced and no longer be satisfied with the fortune of the land, but in reverse—the land, the animals shall feed and fill with their carcasses and the people themselves will resort to cannibalising their own children. **Topheth** (2Kgs.23:10) 'spat at/on' as the people will be tortured, starved, slaughtered, they will be hissed at.

Pashur (1Chr.9:12) 'of staring at with hatred' 'will make known/slander' who in this part is the son of **Immer** (1Chr.9:12) 'of giving orders' 'bossy' 'show' 'show a hint/clue' 'a hint' 'a hint or tiny piece of something/a faint trace of something' is used to show what is happening: Pashur does not believe in Jeremiah's 'prophecy' but his actions state that he hates Jeremiah and believes he is lying, he not only assaults Jeremiah but orders his imprisonment and his public humiliation, but Jeremiah will go on to rename him and in renaming Pashur there is a hint/clue to what will be his demise and the events of the story.

Note how two separate characters from the listed compound words at 1Chr.9:12 are used to create a new character as father and son to suit this story. It continues to prove all the lists in the OT are not 'genealogies' or a 'numbering', but a repository of themes and ideas for the authors to draw from and use in creating the stories and/or expanding them.

Magor-missabib; māḡôr missāḇîḇ; مَاجُر مِسّآبيب 'great sufferance-the cause of' and just as it literally translates to 'the cause of great sufferance' and not only will this character cause his own great sufferance, but also that of the others by mistreating and not believing Jeremiah, as will Jeremiah suffer distress expressed throughout this chapter: 'Then Pashur smote Jeremiah...and put him in the stocks...Then said Jeremiah unto him, The Lord hath not called thy name Pashur, but Magor-missabib...I will make thee a terror to thyself and to all thy friends...and I will give all Judah into the hand of the king of Babylon...'.

(gor/جور) means 'great sufferance/a distressing ordeal'—(gayer/gaa-ir/جايِر/جائر) means 'a brute/tyrant/ruthless/cruel person/person who causes great sufferance'; (ma/mā/ما) here means 'what/such' and as a prefix to 'gor/great sufferance' means '(the/such/what) great sufferance' and also attributes the sufferance to someone. (sbb/سبب) means '(to)cause/the cause/for/(the)reason' and in this story is in the form of 'the cause(er)' and (mi/مِـ) is as before a suffix which creates an article attributing the verb/adjective to who/what is indicated by it—in this case the character Pashur who Jeremiah is telling 'you are the cause of all the great sufferance which will happen to you and the people.'. Cp: maagor missaabeeb. (Jer.20:1-6)

Zedekiah (1Kgs.22:11-28) 'blocked-he/him' 'prevented/absorbed attack-he/him' is reflected in the king of the same name sends his men to ask Jeremiah to request God help them turn away the warring Nebuchadrezzar, but instead the narration shows how God 'deceived you-him/he' 'gave more-he/him' as God will give the king of Babylon more strength and fight with him against Judah and make the men and weapons of Judah weak. (Jer.21)

Pashur (1Chr.9:12) 'eyes will look above' as Zedekiah and the people are seeking reassurance from God, but the story goes on to narrate that God hates them and will punish them for their sins, those who are not slaughtered will be driven out and live a life of fear reflecting the meanings 'I stare at with hatred' 'stop/enough-drive away violently'; **Melchiah (Malchiah)**the meanings of 'throw-he/him' thrown-he/him' 'did not find him/he' 'found-him/he' are reflected in the narration as Zedekiah/Judah find neither mercy nor support from God, but will be 'thrown/cast' i.e. killed, defeated, everything destroyed, 'cover with slimy substance-he/him' (Malchiah. (1Chr.6:40) 'cover with slimy substance-he/him' 'roll it/him in slimy substance' 'it is slimy/dirty/it is slimy/soiled'. (Jer.21)

Zephaniah (2Kgs.25:18-21) 'escorted-him/he' 'led in a procession-him/he' 'cleaned/cleared/purified-him/he' as Zedekiah and his men are asking God to lead the king of Babylon away from them, but God leads him directly to them and the narration has God fighting on the king of Babylon's side against Judah, the people will be taken out of their homes and into captivity. **Maaseiah** 'disobedience' 'disobeyed him' 'disobeyed-he/him' this punishment is for the people's disobedience of God. 'with sticks' 'with sticks-he/him' (1Chr.15:18). (Jer.21)

David is used for its meaning of 'the stone rolling pin of grinding stone' due to the strength and durability of the stone which can withhold being rolled and smacked down during grinding, here it represents the strength of the houses built of stone and the throne 'O house of David' 'that sittest upon the throne of David' will be destroyed if they do not correct their ways. (Jer.21:12-14; 22)

Nebuchadrezzar; nĕb̲ûk̲ad̲re'ṣṣar; نَبّ قَد رِزَّر 'prophet/prophesy-had/already-slapped/slammed down/smacked and pressed down' 'prophet/prophesy-had already-saw/seen-tightened/squeezed/visited/pilgrimaged'. It is reflected in the story as the heavy-handed punishment God sends with this king/army and how the people will be savagely treated and defeated which Jeremiah prophesies before it happens. Cp: nebu-qad-rezzar, nebu-qad-r-ezzar. (Jer.21:7)

Coniah; konyāhû; قون ياهُ 'was certain-he/him' 'sat with head high/perky-he/him; كون ياهُ 'made into peaked piles-he/him' 'was/be-he/him' 'shelter-he/him' (from elements); خون ياهُ 'deceive/deceived-him/he'. All meanings are reflected in the story: narrating it as God's words '*As* I live, saith the Lord' means the punishment is **certain**; in even if he were a diamond set **peaked** on God's hand he would still punish him; that God is **betraying** them as punishment; the punishment will also be that there will be **no shelter to hide from the punishment** of captivity, even the 'seed' his children, relatives, people, will be like **unwanted heaps thrown out all over the region but not at home.** Cp: qoon-yaahu, koon- yaahu, k̲hoon-yaahu. (Jer.22)

Jer.22 also shows different versions of the same stories existing, and later authors/editors going back into these stories and changing them, leaving the only stories available full of inconsistencies, which are today's Bible based on the found texts: Biblical authors and later editors had no problem in changing the names of characters to suit the story they had in mind; Jehoahaz at 2Kgs.23 is changed into 'Johanan' at 1Chr.3:15 who is Josiah's firstborn son (see Johanan (1Chr.3:15)) used as a suitable word-name meaning/theme, which you can see still reflected in the Jer.22 story about the same character but now with a different name of 'Shallum' with the meanings of the latter name also reflected in Jer.22 for its meanings of 'took' 'of taking' as Jeremiah is lamenting over Shallum/Jehoahaz being taken away and dying in captivity far from home: At Jer.22:24-30, Jeconiah undergoes a new name-change of a completely different character to suit the narration.

'Shallum' at Jer.22 is still Jehoahaz, despite the inconsistency that Shallum is described as Josiah's youngest (fourth son) while the author of 2Chr.3:15 who renames Jehoahaz as 'Johanan' makes him Josiah's firstborn while 'Shallum' is a different character altogether and is the youngest. The whole story does not suffer because the Biblical authors were not pretending to narrate true accounts, but were creating completely fictional stories with completely fictional characters, but it seems to have bothered later Biblical editors whose work you can see attempts and fails to correct the inconsistencies of order of birth, name, age, and reign:

- Shallum (who has replaced the word name/character of Jehoahaz and also Johanan) is described as the youngest who, as the same character of Jehoahaz, first becomes king after his father Josiah's death, and begins to rule at 23 years of age (for three months);

- Zedekiah is the third-born (so he is older than Shallum (who is Jehoahaz at Jer.22) according to 1Chr.3:15—but younger than Johanan/Jehoahaz at the same 1Chr.3:15) and he begins to reign at the age of twenty-one years, but only eleven years and three months have passed after the deposition of Jehoahaz/Shallum because the latter was followed by Jehoiakim ruling for eleven years, then Jehoiachin ruling for three months—yet Zedekiah is still younger when he begins to rule at the age of 21 whereas the youngest brother Shallum/Jehoahaz whose rule began first after Josiah's death is already older (23) than his older brother Zedekiah even though Zedekiah the older brother does not become king until eleven years and three months later– the whole thing is convoluted, and is only of importance when scholars attempt to present these kings as actual historical figures and attempt to explain it away as 'birth names' and 'throne names' and tie it into 'history' whereas the truth is they are only used in the Bible as word-names and fictional characters: 1Chr.15 author has removed Jehoahaz and replaced him with Johanan; Jer.22 author has removed Jehoahaz and replaced him with Shallum, and so forth.

- 2Chr.36 also makes it crystal clear what was already apparent as being edited at 1Kgs.24 that in the story, Zedekiah is Jehoiachin/Jeconiah/Coniah's brother.
- Jer.22 also shows how the same character is given different word-names to suit the story being told (see the three different word-names for the same single character 'Jehoiachin', given to accord the respective story the themes of the word-names); and how different authors raise or lessen a character's status within the stories by editing them: e.g. Jehoiakim does not seem to do any wrong at 1Kgs.24 but is punished for 'the sins of Manasseh' who shed 'innocent blood', but still he dies and is buried like a respectable king 'So Jehoiakim slept with his fathers'. But at Jer.22 he is given the same burial as donkeys: dragged and thrown outside the gates of the city with the humiliation of being where donkey carcasses are removed to (2Chr.36 also shows editing where Manasseh's sins are replaced by Jehoiakim's own sins and suggests he was taken away as captive in chains to Babylon or at least threatened to be).
- Again, none of this mattered to the original authors of the Biblical stories, because none of these events happened as can be seen in the word-names of characters and how these word-names match what happens in the story, and how these word-names are changed further to reflect the different versions of the same story to according to what the respective Biblical author wanted to narrate.

Micah (Judg.17, 18) is still 'what is wrong?' 'what is there?' 'what is the situation/problem?' 'what did he say?' 'what happened?' and the narration tells of this Micah speaking a prophesy in the past which itself spoke of trouble, without Micah getting into trouble with the king and people, it is saying look what happened to him and how he was dealt with. He is a Morasthite; môraštî, môrešet; مُرَصتي ، مُرَصَت 'of piling/stacking heaps' 'of heaping' 'piled/stacked/heaped' and it is narrated his prophecy was all about punishment which left Judah in heaps 'Zion shall be plowed like a field, and Jerusalem shall become heaps, and the mountain of the house as the high places of a forest.'. Cp: morasstee, moresset. (Jer.26:18)

Hananiah (1Chr.3:19) has been used as before for its meanings 'we will direct words/speech at him' and it describes when a person is hinting at with a message/warning/insult directed at someone in particular within hearing range, even at close proximity, while actually talking directly to someone else—it is hinting/delivering the message indirectly. First this character directs a message to Jeremiah, but it is indirectly meant to the people to believe in his prophesy. Then God sends a message warning of punishment to Hananiah and this too is meant for all the people who are to suffer if they do not heed the message. It is also 'betrayed/betrays-he/him' because Hananiah is causing the people to believe a lie, a false prophesy, he is betraying the people and God. 'satisfied/gave plenty-he/him' because as punishment God will give plenty of treasures and the people for Nebuchadnezzar to use. (Jer.28)

He is son of **Azur**; the same as Azzur (Neh.10:17): 'the false oath/the lying under oath' 'tighten/the tightening'. Used to show he is speaking in God's name falsely (just as when a person who swears by God that he is telling the truth but lies) and the story narrates exactly that. (Jer.28)

He is from **Gibeon** (Josh.9) for its meanings: 'ganged together/gathered many people to help or gang up against something' 'bring/fetch/gather-help' as Hananiah confronts Jeremiah with an opposing prophesy 'in the presence of the priests and of all the people…' and the prophecy itself speaks of a large group of people being brought out of captivity from Babylon and also the fetching of 'the vessels'. (Jer.28)

Elasah (Ezra.10:22) used for 'the disobedient' 'the one who disobeyed him' as the story revolves around disobeying God. He is son of **Shaphan** (2Kgs.22:3-15) for 'they saw' two or more people saw, 'they were healed' 'they cured' because the warning to the people is not to believe those who claim to see prophecies or see false dreams, it goes on to narrate that they will be returned home, i.e. 'healed' of the suffering. (Jer.29)

Gemariah; gĕmaryâ, gĕmaryāhû; جيمَر يه ، جيمَرياَهُ 'hot coals-he/him' 'hot coal vessel-he/him' and reflects the false prophets whose punishment will be 'roasted in the fire'. He is son of **Hilkiah** (2Kgs.18:18,26–

27,37) for its meanings 'I will find it/him' 'here/look-found-he/him' 'I will throw/cast it' 'here/look-threw it/him'. The story narrates that the people will eventually find God and God will find them, give his mercy/forgiveness. Also, the false prophets will be punished because God finds them guilty of deceit and will punish them with death. Cp: geimar-yah/yaahu. (Jer.29)

Ahab (1Kgs.16:28-33; 17) used for 'I give' as God will 'deliver them into the hand of Nebuchadrezzar'. He is son of **Kolaiah** (Neh.11:7) 'a false statement' 'putting words in someone's mouth' 'a statement' 'it was said' 'sanitised(on heat)' as he has made false prophesies and statements about God, put words in God's mouth; the narration emphasises this, but he will also be executed using heat, the same way vessels are sanitised of germs through heat 'whom the king of Babylon roasted in the fire.'. (Jer.29)

Zedekiah (1Kgs.22:11-28) used for 'deceived you-him/he' as this is what he and other prophets have done in this story. He is son of **Maaseiah** (1Chr.15:18) 'disobedience' 'disobeyed him' 'disobeyed-he/him' because his misleading the people and false statements about God and prophesies are disobedience, which also cause the people to disobey. (Jer.29)

Shemaiah (1Kgs.12:22-24; 2Chr.12:15) is used for 'listened-he/him' 'made listen-he/him' 'to spoil reputation of another by insulting them in the hearing of others' 'to talk badly/insult a person in front of others'; Nehelamite; hanneḥĕlāmî; هَنّخيلامي 'here is/I will-make hollow/poke holes through' 'of-here is/I will-hollow/poke holes through' 'of-sifting through/falling through holes in sift' 'here is/I will-make sifted/go through holes of sieve'; هَنّحي لآمي 'I will/here is-set aside/demote-blamed'; هَنّهي لآمي 'I will prevent-gathering/gathered'. All is being expressed in the narration: this character is attempting to ruin Jeremiah's reputation and have him removed/demoted from being a prophet, and encouraging the priests to claim Jeremiah is mad, to imprison him and put him 'in the stocks.'; he questions the priests as to why they have not blamed Jeremiah for his prophesies and not taken any action against him; this character has had his reputation ruined by God exposing him as a liar; his punishment is that all his male 'seed' will not survive, the word-imagery is of seeds falling through or being caught in a sieve; his family will not be gathered 'among his people' nor will he be able to benefit from the good which God promises the people. Cp: hannekheilaamee, hanneḥeilaamee, hanneheilaamee. (Jer.29:24-32).

Throughout these stories **Zion** is used as 'swept/brushed away' and 'bad' always supported by the text which describes events or characteristics of something being swept out and something that is bad: 'because they called thee an Outcast, *saying*, This *is* Zion, whom no man seeketh after.'. (Jer.30:12-17)

Ramah (Josh.18:25) has been used for its meanings 'threw around/threw' 'saw water' 'saw what?' as the mother 'Rahel' is weeping because her children have been thrown out of their land and the tears reflect 'saw water'. (Jer.31:15)

Rahel; rāḥēl; راَح يل 'left-the' 'went-the'; رآحيل 'has left/departed/journeyed' and the character of the same name is crying over the departure/separation of her children. It is not the same as 'Rachel' and this can be seen by what Rachel's meaning was anchored by in the Genesis story, and what this word is anchored by in its story. Cp: raaḥ-eyl, raaḥeyl. (Jer.31:15-17)

Hananeel (Neh.3:1) is used for 'felt affection-the' 'satisfaction to/satisfied-the' 'give plenty-the' relayed in the story by the forgiveness shown when God will release the people from captivity and they will build and prosper. It will be such great work it will reach **Gareb** (2Sam.23:38) 'went over' 'flow over' a place in a mountain where a hill goes down and its other side or people who pass over it cannot be seen from the speaker's/viewer's location, i.e. it will go extend. It will also come to Goath; gō'â, gō'ātâ; غوئه ، غوئآته 'deceit/deceived him/his deceit' 'deceived him/them' 'his deceit' 'collapse/downfall through deceit' 'brought his/its downfall through deceit' 'his downfall through deceit' 'misled to downfall' and the word means downfall by being led-on or encouraged by another to do something which eventually brings the downfall of the doer (backfires or brings the negative consequences back onto the deceived person and not on the deceiver). Cp: ghoo-ah, ghoo-aatah. (Jer.31:38-39)

Kidron (2Kgs.23:4) has been used for 'they are disgusting/unclean/revolting/filthy' when narrating about an area where dead bodies and ashes are mentioned. The horse gate (which in an earlier story was chosen as the place where queen Athaliah was killed (as further humiliation for the character)), has been used to show it is related to filth, possibly to do with horse dung, which is why it has been mentioned along with **Kidron** 'disgusting/unclean/filthy'.

Hanameel; ḥănam'ēl; هينَم يِل 'satisfied-the' 'hegemonized-the' 'controlled everyone/everything-the'; هينَمئِل ، هينَمئيل 'he will make us incline(to/towards)' 'he/it will turn/slide towards'. This is reflected in how God inclines people to do one thing or another and gives control of one party/thing over another: he inclines Jeremiah to buy his cousin's land which gives Jeremiah control of this land; and the same act symbolises to the people to be inclined to believe they will be free again and have control of their own lands; it reminds of God giving the people the control of a land which was not theirs to have, yet they were inclined to disobey God instead of follow his ways; this causes God to give Babylon/Chaldeans control over the disobedient people; it speaks of everything being under God's hands (control); God will eventually be inclined to forgive the people, but only that he will incline them to obey him and his ways, i.e. they will lose control and by God's will they will fear him and not disobey. Cp: hainam-ill, hainamill/eyl.

He is son of **Shallum** (2Kgs.15:13) for its meanings 'took' 'of taking' 'I will gather' 'of gathering' 'peace/greeted with 'peace'' 'of peaceful or mild nature/character' 'left unharmed/intact/survived' 'delivered/received' and all these meanings are employed in the story: Jeremiah is asked to take the field being offered for sale; in the process Jeremiah/Hanameel deliver/receive payment and documents, Jeremiah takes witnesses then the evidence to register his purchase; God has gathered the people as reminded of the earlier stories; God delivers and the people receive 'this land' (of the earlier stories); God delivers the land and people into the receiving hands of the Babylonians and Chaldeans; it is expressed in God giving teachings towards good which the people refuse to receive; when God's anger reduces, he will gather the people from all over the region to return them to the 'land' where the stories are set; God will allow them to live in peace and safety; in giving them 'one heart and one way' he is replacing their 'stiff-necked' character (which is how the Biblical stories usually describe the people of these stories) with a peaceful/mild nature; God is giving all the good things intact, in full 'with my whole heart and my whole soul'. (Jer.32:6-44)

Baruch (Neh.3:20) has been used for its meanings 'I will go/leave' 'blessed' 'lasted long' 'underground water cistern' as Jeremiah goes to Baruch to submit to him evidence of the purchase, and the narration also states that Jeremiah places the proof of purchase into a clay vessel 'that they may continue many days.' this is to do with underground water-cisterns are meant to last longer than wells even during drought and in normal times so that the owners can make the water last long so they do not need to fetch water from the well (which is usually further away).

He is son of Neriah; nḗrîyâ; نيري يه ، نيرييه 'we show him' 'we show-him/he' and the story narrates exactly that Jeremiah shows and submits proof of purchase and responsibility of its safe-keeping to this character and 'in the sight of Hanameel…and in the presence of the witnesses that subscribed the book of purchase, before all the Jews that sat in the court of the prison.'. Cp: neyreeyah, neyree-yah.

He is son of Maaseiah; maḥsēyâ; مَحصي يه ، مَحصييه 'counted/accounted' 'counted-he/him' 'accounted for-he/him' and is narrated that this character is made responsible for checking the proof of purchase and keeping it safe; مَحسي يه ، مَحسييه 'his wells' 'into a well/put into a well' 'into a well-he/him' and again refers to the documents meant to be kept for a long time and safely. Note the wordplay where '**Maaseiah**/disobeyed him' is the son of **Baruch** at Neh.11:5 and the grandson of **Col-hozeh**/'say-a well/his well' 'every well' (Col-hozeh at Neh.3:15; 11:5) whose great grandfather **Hazaiah**/'my wells' 'wells-he/him' (Neh.11:5) show the ideas of the Biblical authors of what may have been their intentions to expand the stories to make them water/well related, or possibly just a pun or symbolising the documents being hidden/kept safe as water is underground, and the use of names which invoke underground water cisterns and wells which last long for the people's use. Cp: maḥs̱s̱eyyah, maḥs̱s̱ey-yah, maḥseyyah, maḥsey-yah. (Jer.32:12-14)

Jaazaniah (2Kgs.25:23) is used for 'gave him his just deserts-he/him' 'gave reward-he/him' 'calls out to gather/assemble/pray-he/him' 'agrees/allows-he/him' and the story narrates the 'Rechabites' are following their ancestor's command not to drink wine and abstain from other things so as to live long, and as a reward God promises their seed will last forever; it is also reflected in the people who have disobeyed God, God will have retribution on them.

He is son of **Jeremiah** (2Kgs.23:31) 'he throws-he/him' 'they throw him' 'throws it/he throws it' as the 'Rechabites' throw away (another expression to abstain from) and get rid of all the practises their ancestor dictated so as to avoid being wiped out, whereas the people have discarded God's commandments and therefore will perish and be subject to various kinds of 'thrown' punishments.

He is son of Habaziniah; ḥăḇaṣṣinyâ; هيب سّنيه 'gave-in front of them' 'fear and respect towards him' as Jeremiah and God test them by placing lots of wine in front of them, but out of fear and respect towards 'Jonadab the son of Rechab' and his commandments they do not drink the wine, this is contrasted against the people of Judah/Jerusalem breaking all of God's commandments. Cp: haiba-ssinyah. (Jer.35)

Rechabites; rĕkāḇîm; ريقآبهم ، ريقآب هم/ام 'kept an eye on them' 'pour carefully from one vessel to another-them/the', usually used as word when watching carefully how water is poured from one vessel's opening into another to avoid spilling even a drop of water or an order to pour carefully from one vessel to another, 'their necks' 'necks of-them/the'. In this story it refers to Jeremiah pouring the wine into different vessels for them to drink from, then observing to see if they will be tempted and drink; it is also the observing and contrast of the people who commit every wrong (according to the story) which they are warned not to do.

The meanings of 'their necks' is because responsibility and accountability are expressed and believed to be carried in the neck of its doer, the contrast between the Rechabites and the rest of the people is that the former show responsibility whereas the people do not, so their sins will be in their necks.

The meaning ريكآبهم ، ريكآب هم/ام 'rode on them' 'ride/mount-them/the' 'they are riding/rode-them/the' this expression can be literal but also the figurative expression means to make your mind up decidedly, or make a stubborn decision and it is reflected in both the Rechabites having made a decision and sticking to it, and the people and their many decisions in breaking God's commandments and going their own way in what they decide to do. Cp: reyqaabhum, reyqaab-hum/um, reykaabhum, reykaab-hum/um. (Jer.35)

Hanan (1Chr.8:23) for 'were disgraced' two or more people, 'were satisfied/given plenty' 'betrayed' 'it is time' and this is relayed in the story that although Jeremiah pours plenty of wine, the Rechabites have decided to not betray the commandments (of Jonadab) and find satisfaction in living as ordered which results by the end of the chapter in being satisfied with a reward from God; it is reflected in the people who are dissatisfied with God's commandments and betray them.

The meaning 'it is time' because God has found enough time has passed to show the Rechabites appreciation for their devotion towards Jonadab's orders.

He is son of Igdaliah; yigdalyāhû; يِجدَل يآهُ 'he gets thrown-he/him' 'he throws it/him' 'he has fits-he/him' and this is for more than one reason: the Rechabites who are the pivotal example in this story are being tempted in Hanan the son of Igdaliah's chamber to throw away their abstinence from wine and their adherence to Jonadab's commandments, which is why the authors have his chamber above **Maaseiah** (1Chr.15:18) 'disobedience' 'disobeyed him' 'disobeyed-he/him' as they are tempting them to disobey and Maaseiah is son of **Shallum** for 'took' 'of taking' 'small waterfall' 'peace/greeted with 'peace'' 'of peaceful or mild nature/character' 'left unharmed/intact/survived' 'small river/temporary river after rain' 'leaked the' 'delivered/received' 'asked them' because Jeremiah is asking them to drink wine, he is pouring streams of wine into pots and cups, they refuse and therefore remain intact, remaining faithful to their peaceful and simple ways which in turn they receive a reward delivered by God that their 'seed' will remain forever.

Igdaliah is described as 'a man of God' because as his name (and other stories in the text of the Bible) suggests 'he gets thrown-he/him' 'he throws it/him' 'he has fits-he/him' people who suffer from fits/epilepsy are believed to be possessed by demons (in the culture of the real people who created and disseminated both the Biblical stories and the Jewish religion) and in the Bible as well as in the real culture of living people whose culture is described in the story, people who are possessed and have fits are also believed to be close to God. Cp: yigdal-yaahu. (Jer.35:4).

Regarding '**Jonadab**' which means 'he brings wailing/mourning' 'he is wailing/mourning' (2Sam.13) is the author/editor of this particular story using the story and character-role of Jonadab son of Shimea in 2Sam.13 who was the catalyst in causing a lot of grief, wailing and mourning where the greatest grief climaxes at Amnon's assassination by Absalom. It is not the word-name/compound word used here, but the dependence on the audience will recall the story that Absalom used wine to mollify, intoxicate, at the least to distract Amnon so that he could be easily killed for raping Tamar. The author of this 'Rechabite/Jeremiah' story is building on the idea that Jonadab's name is linked to bad things happening when wine is involved, i.e. he encouraged and plotted how Amnon was to rape Tamar, then his character shows regret through his word-name and through trying to calm a distraught and wailing king David that it is only Amnon killed and not all of David's sons.

The point is although 'Jonadab the son of Rechab' is a different character than 'Jonadab the son of Shimea', it builds on the role of his story (which everyone who wrote, told and listened to these stories understood) how these wordplay and compound word-names were used and meant that it would create a connection that 'Jonadab' has had a traumatic and regretful experience through wine consumption which resulted in the wiping out of a particular bloodline, that he warns his descendants to keep away from it.

This helps to reinforce the message of obeying 'God's commandments to the audience, which in the stories the 'people' do not.

In the same way the 'Jonadab the son of Rechab' (Jer.35) is not meant to be the same 'Jehonadab the son Rechab' of (2Kgs.10:15) even if their names are similar. Confusion and conflating these names/characters as this or that 'person' only arises when scholars want to make these fictional characters into real people that existed, and this is due to the Biblical scholars' lack of knowledge of these words and stories meanings and the culture they come from because either accidentally or intentionally they overlook/ignore that these words and stories only make sense when read in Arabic. (Jer.35)

Baruch is still used as 'lasted long' 'I will go/leave' as the words which he hears then writes and reads from/for Jeremiah to cover God's warnings that span the length of time 'from the day I spake unto thee, from the days of Josiah, even unto this day.' And Baruch this time is to go to a designation. It also includes 'I will loosen/be lenient' as God is giving the people another chance to repent and show they will be 'upright'. **Neriah** is as earlier we show him' 'we show-him/he' as first Jeremiah dictating the words to Baruch is 'showing' him what to do, and when Baruch will read these words out in front of the people, he too is showing them the right ways. (Jer.36:1-8)

Shaphan (2Kgs.22:3-15) is used as earlier 'they saw' two or more people saw, and has been used as a surname for two characters because the story lays out that two sets of people have seen Baruch as he reads out of the book: the people who are in the 'chamber of Gemariah the son of Shaphan' and 'Michaiah the son of Gemariah the son of Shaphan'. (Jer.36:10-11)

Elishama (Num.1:10) for 'he who/the one who-heard' 'he who/the one who-made other hear' as he is one who hears the news of the book.

Delaiah (1Chr.3:24) 'show/prove-verse/line/sign' 'slow down/gently-he/him/you' as they are talking about a book that has verses and/or lines with Gods words and warnings, he is also one of the characters who will attempt to slow down the king's rash actions of burning the book. He is the son of **Shemaiah** (1Kgs.12:22-24) 'listened-he/him' 'made listen-he/him' as one of the characters who listens to the news about the book then the words of the book and who in turn repeats these words so the king hears them too.

Elnathan (2Kgs.24:6-16) 'the doubled/folded' 'the guilted' and this refers to first hearing the book from Michaiah then hearing it read by Baruch, and with regards to 'the guilted' it means both Jeremiah and Baruch will be accused of something and whom are advised to hide. He is the son of **Achbor** (Gen.36:38) 'tell/tell the news' because he hears the news from Michaiah, then the words directly from Baruch before being part of the group to inform the king (Note at 2Kgs.22:12-15 'Achbor' is 'the son of Michaiah' when his character is tasked to go find out news from the prophetess Huldah these are just some examples of what is the method of creating names out of compound words and how they are used to tell fictional stories).

Gemariah (Jer.29) 'hot coals-he/him' 'hot coal vessel-he/him' is used to depict the worry the group feels when they realise they have to inform the king, and the consequences it may have, the story narrates the fear, and also a fear for Jeremiah and Baruch's lives; this character will also be used as one of the three who attempt, and fail, to dissuade the king from burning the book. He is the son of **Shaphan** for the same reasons mentioned above for which the word-name was used.

Zedekiah (1Kgs.22:11-28) 'gave more/extra-he/him' and 'believed/honest/was honest-he/him' as Zedekiah along with the others hears the words of the book twice, and from their fear and worry the narration implies they believed the words of the book which is why they fear telling the king, but are compelled to do so. He is the son of **Hananiah** (1Chr.3:19) 'we will direct words/speech at him' it describes when a person is hinting at with a message/warning/insult directed at someone in particular within hearing range, even at close proximity, while actually talking directly to someone else—it is hinting/delivering the message indirectly, 'we mean him' and as the story narrates it is everything which was in the previous chapters of the Book of Jeremiah where the kings and other officials as well as the rest of the people are blamed and criticised, warned of punishment and their humiliation and/or violent deaths predicted—this becomes the reason why the message is directed at the king and also why they fear informing him.

Michaiah (1Kgs.22:8-28) 'what is there with him?/what is wrong with him now?' 'what did he say?' as this character first hears Baruch then informs the group who want to know what the matter is, and want to hear what was said directly from Baruch. (Jer.36:11-20)

Jehudi; yĕhûḏî; جيخُدي ، ييخُدي 'he comes back/returns/goes back and forth' 'came-went back/returned/ went back and forth' from the phrase 'yeḥood wa yelood' which means when a person goes back and forth or in circles whether physically or in speech and usually out of worry. This meaning is reflected in both times he is mentioned as he is sent to retrieve a person or a book 'Therefore all the princes sent Jehudi...unto Baruch, saying, Take in thine hand the roll wherein thou hast read in the ears of the people, and come.' And when the king sends him to get it from Elishama's chamber 'So the king sent Jehudi to fetch the roll...'; جيهودي ، ييهودي and this is the word 'jew' as a verb and an adjective and used in the Bible only as a word for use like all the other words used as names, and not as a name of the Jewish religion. It has specific meanings and use long before it would become the name of a religion, and is supported by an abundance of Biblical text, but needs to be explained and translated later in this book as there is much evidence in the Biblical stories itself and it is the same meaning of the word as a pure word in daily use in Arabic, but it needs a chapter of its own to be explained sufficiently without disrupting the story(ies) where it is used by the Biblical authors. Cp: yeiḥudee, geiḥudee, yeihoodee, geihoodee. (Jer. 36:14-25)

He is son of Nethaniah, son of Shelemiah, son of Cushi, and his surnames all reflect his actions in the story. He is son of **Nethaniah** (2Kgs.25:23-25) 'we double/fold-he/him' 'we guilt-he/him' because he is sent twice to do something, the 'guilt' is about how Jeremiah and Baruch will be viewed by the king. Son of **Shelemiah** (1Chr.26:14) 'took the-he/him' 'will gather/collect-he/him' 'intact-he/him' as he will first bring Baruch to the king's house, then take the roll out of Elishama's room and bring it to the king, the princes in warning Jeremiah and Baruch to hide are attempting to keep them safe; it also reflects that Jehudi brings the roll intact to the king. Son of **Cushi** (2Sam.18:19-33) 'scrape away' 'kill in one go/one movement' 'remove in one movement' 'left over burnt pieces/toast until crispy or burnt/burnt in fire or from too much heat' 'cut' 'tell a/the story' and this character performs all these actions in the story. He brings Baruch and the book in one go; he removes the book from Elishama's chamber; he reads the book i.e. tells the story to the king and everyone; as he reads, he (or the king) cuts out the pages and burns them in the fire. (Jer.36:14-25)

All the names of characters ordered to 'take' Jeremiah and Baruch reflect the events in this part of the story: **Jerahmeel** (1Sam.27:8-12) 'he sees-takes/carries' 'came-saw-takes/carries' 'ran-takes/carries' as they are commanded to capture and take Jeremiah and Baruch; 'he has mercy on the' because God does not allow this to happen 'but the Lord hid them.'. He is son of Hammelech; hammelech; حَمَّلك 'carried you' 'carried hate' 'carried burden' 'loaded on you'; هَمَّلك 'I will soil you/cover you with filth(could be clean substance but because it splatters on person's clothes means it is soiled)' as they are being hated because of the words spoken/written, and they want to carry Jeremiah and Baruch to either imprisonment or death, this includes soiling their reputation. Cp: ḥammelek, hammelek. (Jer.36:26)

Abdeel; 'aḇdĕ'ēl; عَبدي ئِل 'my servant-the' 'servant-the' 'serve-the' 'my worshipper-the' 'worshipper-the' 'worship-the'; ئبدي ئِل 'take/bring out-the' and it is this latter meaning meant in this part of the story. It is the same as Abdiel (1Chr.5:15). Cp: 'abdei-ill, abdei-ill. (Jer.36:26)

Note from the beginning of the Bible stories where **Chaldees** was used as 'roasted/burned/cooked from heat' where 'Haran' died it continues throughout the Bible that wherever **Chaldees/Chaldean** is used, there is fire and burning, death and perishing as can be seen at Jer.37 and other Biblical stories.

Jehucal; yĕhûḵal; ييه قَل ، ييهُقَل 'which one/he-said' 'which one/he-made say'; جيه قَل 'came to him-said' 'came he-said' 'came to him/came he-made say'. He is the character Zedekiah sends to Jeremiah asking the latter to pray to God on their behalf. As Jeremiah does not want to, and refuses, the narration means they are trying to make him say something. It is equivalent to Ucal (Prov.30). Cp: yeihuqal, yeihu-qal, geihu-qal. (Jer.37:3)

Irijah; yir'îyâ; يِر ئي به ، يِر ئيبه 'he sees/saw him' 'saw/sees-him/he' 'he is dreaming' 'dreaming-him/he' and both senses are meant: Irijah sees Jeremiah leaving, but he wrongly believes, i.e. imagines, Jeremiah wanting to join the Chaldeans. He is the son of **Shelemiah** 'took the-he/him' as he takes Jeremiah back to the princes. He is the son of **Hananiah** for 'we will direct words/speech at him' 'betrays/betrayed-him/he' as an accusation of betrayal is levelled at Jeremiah. Cp: yir-eeyah, yir-ee-yah. (Jer.37:11-15)

Many times, you will come across a sentence or phrase which will stand out as erratic amidst the Biblical text as translated in English and as interpreted by scholars. One such example is 'and they should give him daily a piece of bread out of the baker's street'. The odd phrase is 'baker's street'. It is not a baker's guild as some scholars describe it, nor is it a baker's quarter—there is no part of the original word that would translate to 'street' or 'baker's' or one that could be interpreted as 'guild' or 'quarter':

'Baker's street'; ḥûṣ hā'ōpîm; خش هاعوفهم/ام 'yard/courtyard-I will feed them/the light meal'. (ḥûṣ/hush/خش) is the outdoor area directly outside a house and in modern use is the 'yard' in its modern sense. This is supported by the text as Jeremiah complains of difficult/dangerous circumstances inside the prison which is 'the house of Jonathan', and Zedekiah the king orders that he be moved outside 'they should commit Jeremiah into the court of the prison'. The living circumstances are bad, maybe crowded, not enough food, but the narration 'lest I die there' indicates danger, even the naming of the prison 'in the house of Jonathan the scribe' implies sexual activity between males or sexual assault against the prisoners or between them. He is moved from inside the prison to outside the prison, i.e. the yard/courtyard of the prison.

(hā/هآ) 'I will/here/look/pay attention' in this instance is 'I will'. ('ōp/عوف) 'feed/eat/light meal' and means to either feed or eat a meal at a time that is not the regular meal-time, or a light meal—and the light meal is usually a piece of bread. (îm/ام/هم) 'them/the'. This is exactly what the story is narrating 'they should commit Jeremiah into the court of the prison, and that they should give him daily a piece of bread out of the baker's street, until all the bread in the city were spent. Thus Jeremiah remained in the court of the prison.'. Cp: ḥush haa'ooph-hum/um. (Jer.37:15-21)

All the names mentioned as princes who hear Jeremiah, reflect the action they perform or symbolise in the story, what will happen to Jeremiah. **Shephatiah** (2Sam.3:4) 'saw him' 'saw-he/him' the son of **Mattan** (2Kgs.11:18) 'two deaths' 'stretched' 'bowed/lowered/bent' 'extended/reached for/reached into/put hands into' and is reflected in the story: they witnessed Jeremiah's prophecy; his prophecy predicts their deaths/destruction; he is deemed guilty; they had to lower Jeremiah by cords, i.e. they had to extend him on ropes so he could reach the bottom of the hole where they imprisoned him.

Gedaliah (2Kgs.25:22-25) 'threw/killed-him/he' the son of **Pashur** (1Chr.9:12) 'I stare at with hatred' 'will make known/slander' 'stop/enough-drive away violently' 'stop/enough-collapse/fall' because Jeremiah will be thrown into a dungeon because the princes will hate him as they feel his prophecies are slanderous and will cause people to be weak, their soldiers will collapse out of fear instilled by Jeremiah's words if they do not bring an end to Jeremiah's speeches and the solution is to throw him into a hole-like dungeon.

Jucal; yûḵāl; يُقال 'it is said' 'is saying' 'is made to say' and he is the son of **Shelemiah** (1Chr.26:14) 'survived-he/him' 'took the-he/him' and is reflected in the princes believing Jeremiah to be making up these prophecies; in the princes speaking to the king of what Jeremiah says and what they believe; in Jeremiah's words that the only people who will survive or have a chance at survival are those who go to the Chaldeans.

Pashur (for the same meanings as above) is the son of **Malchiah** (1Chr.6:40) 'cover with slimy substance-he/him' 'roll it/him in slimy substance' 'it is slimy/dirty/it is slimy/soiled' 'throw/cast-he/him' thrown-he/him' and Jeremiah is thrown into a hole-like dungeon and the description is that it is swampy, slimy, muddy, and filthy, and as he sinks into it they have effectively 'rolled him in slimy substance'.

The latter explanation of Pashur son of Malchiah is reinforced as the authors seemed to want this not to be lost on the audience, they use the same theme/pun in having the owner of the dungeon named 'Malchiah the son of **Hammelech**' i.e. 'roll him/it in slimy substance'—'I will soil you/cover you with filth'. Hammelech's (Jer.36:26) other meanings of 'carried you' 'carried hate' 'carried burden' 'loaded on you' are all in play too, as Jeremiah is hated and seen as a burden/problem; he is carried and lowered like a load into the dungeon, but more importantly, he is covered in filth. (Jer.38:1-6)

Ebed-melech; 'eḇeḏ meleḵ; عَبَد مَلَك 'worshipper/servant-what is wrong with you' 'worshipper/servant-soiled/covered you' and this character's name and actions both refer to Jeremiah being a servant of God and Zedekiah's treatment of him in throwing him into a dungeon of 'mire' as wrong; the character is criticising Zedekiah's men's actions towards a prophet/servant of God (Jeremiah). عَبَد مَلح 'servant/worshipper-good/well' and still refers to Jeremiah being a good prophet who should not be treated badly and also the actions given to the character Ebed-melech who will treat Jeremiah good, first by interceding to have him spared then taking part in pulling him out of the dungeon. ئَبَد مَلَك 'never-what is wrong with you' 'never-soil/cover you' 'wipe out/kill all-what is wrong with you' as the character points out that this mistreatment of Jeremiah could cause his death.

He is a '**Cushite**' 'scrape away' 'kill in one go/one movement' 'remove in one movement' 'left over burnt pieces/toast until crispy or burnt/burnt in fire or from too much heat' 'to blow away litter/fibres/burnt remnants' 'remove completely in one swipe or scrape' 'litter/fibres/burnt remnants' and this is what is being expressed in tandem with the similar meanings of 'Ebed' and supported by the text and it refers to

Jeremiah being thrown into a filthy dungeon as if he is litter—something that is burnt and unwanted; Jeremiah's enemies seek to wipe him out and his words away; he is helpless like a tiny fibre in the dungeon and Ebed-melech will remove him from there; the authors have thirty men in addition to Ebed-melek pull him out to conjure up the image he was pulled out like a tiny piece of fibre/litter and the meaning of 'cushi' 'scrape away/remove in one movement'. Cp: 'ebed melek, 'ebed meleḥ, ebed melek.

The character Ebed-melek is presented in English with the wrong translation as 'Ethiopian' for 'cushite', and this incorrect translation/interpretation of the word has been used in many places while this word means nothing at all related to 'Ethiopian'—it is a pretty naïve translation and loose interpretation to think just because the word has been used once to describe 'dark skin' that it refers to 'Ethiopians'. Even modern scholars who use it to mean 'slave' or both a 'slave' and 'Ethiopian' are basing it on very racist angles (even if the scholars themselves are not racist) where even if the character is neither described as black nor a slave in the text, because it represents to them (the scholars) someone who has dark skin, then the character must be a slave and Ethiopian.

As translated and explained earlier in this book 'Cush/Kush/Kish/Cushi(ite)' have specific meanings of litter, scraping away litter, something burnt or crispy (see Cushi (2Sam.18:19-33)). Ebed as earlier (see Gaal son of Ebed (Judg.9:26-40)) can mean a servant (which does not necessarily mean a slave) or worshipper and also the meanings 'kill/wipe out/never/forever'. There is nothing in the word 'Cush/Cushite' to indicate a black African. Where the people who wrote this book mention black skin, in these stories being black does not mean with African-black features, just darker skin (which could include African-black), and specifically when you understand this book was written not by people who inhabited where Palestine, Syria, Lebanon, Iraq stands today but was written by Arabs of the Arabian Peninsula—the people being described and who populate these books are anything from white-skinned (not western-white but Arab-white to black-skinned, including African features because of the geographical location and cross-culture pasts with African countries bordering the Red Sea) but the Biblical stories do not state 'Ethiopian' or 'slave' as the English translation and other interpretations wrongly suggest. (Jer.38:7-13)

Nergal-sharezer is a combination of earlier character word-names Nergal (2Kgs.17:30) and Sharezer (2Kgs.19:37). If a real Babylonian person existed with such a name, it was only his name used in the Biblical story because its pronunciation suited the wordplay and meanings in Arabic for the story, and not that the event actually happened.

nērgal šar'eṣer; نيرجَل شَر عَزَر 'fire-cleanse/purify/make clear-will see-made ugly' 'fire-cleanse/purify/make clear-evil-made ugly'; نيرجَل صَر عَزَر 'fire-cleanse/purify/make clear-insisted-made ugly'; نيرجَل شَر نَزَر 'fire-cleanse/purify/make clear-will see-tightened' 'fire-cleanse/purify/make clear-evil-tightened'; نيرجَل صَرنَزَر 'fire-cleanse/purify/make clear-insisted-tightened' 'fire-cleanse/purify/make clear-knotted-tightened'.

All the meanings are in the story: ugly death occurs just as God through Jeremiah had warned he would clear the cities of the people who disobeyed him and purge the cities which came to disgust him (God) by having them completely destroyed; the cities are burnt with fire (which earlier in the Biblical stories means they are cleansed); Zedekiah and the other officials insistence to disbelieve Jeremiah is what caused the prophecy of all the ugly death and destruction to occur; even when they try to escape they are captured and returned to the Babylonian king who will implement severe torture and death. Cp: neyrgal shar-'ezer, neyrgal ssar-'ezer, neyrgal shar-ezer, neyrgal ssar-ezer. (Jer.39)

Samgar-nebo; samgar-nĕḇô; شَمغَر نيذُ 'I will pulp/pierce/burst-we will harm/ostracise' 'I will funnel-we will harm/ostracise' 'I will pierce holes into something (so the contents spill out onto ground)/funnel-we will harm/ostracise'; شَمغر نيبُ 'I will save-prophesied/predicted news or event' 'I will pulp/pierce/burst-prophesied/predicted news or event'.

All these themes happen in the story, the people including kings and princes are harmed, with Zedekiah having to witness his own sons' murders before his eyes are poked out. The punishment was predicted by Jeremiah, and so was Jeremiah being saved by the Babylonians. Nebo (Num.32:3) Shamgar (Judg.3.31). Cp: shamghar-neivo, shamghar-neibo. (Jer.39)

Sarsechim; sarsĕḵîm; شَرشيخ هم/ام 'throw down (or against) and split them/the' 'throw down (or against) and cracked them/the' and is described in the city walls being broken down and the people being murdered; شَرشيح هم 'publicly humiliated/strew them' and means caused great harm and humiliation especially in front of others with Zedekiah witnessing his sons' murders and then he being humiliated and tortured in front of the others before being taken away into captivity. Cp: sharsheikh-hum/um, sharsheiḥ-hum. (Jer.39)

Rabsaris; rab-ṣārîs; رَب ذآريش the same as in (2Kgs.18:17-36) with only a slight difference as the word (rab) here means 'master/lord/person in charge' instead of 'diluted with water': 'person in charge/master/lord-slipped away/slipped out of' and refers to the king and other officials who run away unnoticed at night (eventually caught). Cp: rab-vaareesh. (Jer.39)

Rabmag; rab̲-māg; رَب مآج 'god/lord/master/person in charge-off/spoiled/rotten' and (mag) means when food goes off or when a person is immoral. In this story it is the king of Judah and 'all the men of war' as they abandon defending the people and run away at night. When they are caught, they are physically 'spoiled' i.e. murdered, tortured, eyes poked out. Cp: rab-maag. (Jer.39)

Nebushasban; nĕb̲ûšazbān; نيبُ شَسبآن 'prophecy/predict-will release/let you go/leave you' 'prophecy/predict-will capture/take you prisoner' and the captivity is the Babylonians take king Zedekiah and the others away and the 'release/leave you' is what happens towards the end of this chapter where Jeremiah is released by the Babylonians and the prophecy guarantees Ebed-melech safety ('leave you' means to not trouble you); نيبُ شَزبآن 'prophecy/predict-will penetrate with penis' and indicates captured kings/prince were sexually assaulted. Cp: neibo-shasbaan, neibo-shazbaan. (Jer.39)

Ephai; 'êpay; غيثَي 'nagging' 'nauseating/nauseation' 'nagging until nauseation'. This is reflected in the story that Johanan repeatedly speaks of Ishmael wanting to assassinate Gedaliah, then Johanan offering to secretly murder Ishmael, but Gedaliah not only expresses revulsion and rejection of the idea and Johanan, but he also accuses him of lying. This character was added and is not mentioned in the original story at (2Kgs.25:23-25), but 'Ephai' has been used to show how Gedaliah gets fed up with Johanan's warnings. Cp: gheyfay. (Jer.40:13-16)

Baalis; ba'ălîs; بَغيليش 'by great despise of you' 'with great despise of you' 'by/with stabbing deep in you' 'by/with digging deep into' 'with misleading to your downfall' 'with-misleading to downfall-for you' by/with-making up laws/rules/made up severe laws/rules-for you' and it is relayed in the warning that Gedaliah will be assassinated and also in Gedaliah accusing Johanan of wanting to deceive and mislead him; بَعيليش 'he scattered it all over/made a mess of it' a diminutive of the word (bl'sh/بلعش) 'scattered all over/made mess/untidy' and is reflected in the narration that the king of the same name has ordered Gedaliah's assassination which Johanan warns Gedaliah will cause 'all the Jews which are gathered unto thee should be scattered…'. Cp: baghaileesh ba'aileesh. (Jer.40:14-15)

Tahpanhes; taḥpanḥēs; تَخب نحيس 'hid-bad luck/bad fate'. طَح بَنحيس 'fell/broke-with/the unlucky/bad fated'. Both meanings are present in Jer.43 as the people who escaped the punishment implemented in Judah will face the same punishments and bad fate in the place they sought refuge to hide in; also, Jeremiah is ordered to hide large stones in a clay vessel to represent the people hiding in Tahpanhes will still be broken/destroyed by the person and punishment they had fled and hid from. It is similar to Tahpenes (1Kgs.11:18-22). Cp: takhba nḥeys, ṭaḥ banḥeys. (Jer.43)

Pharaoh-hophra; par'ō ḥopra', par'ōh ḥopra'; on فَرعو هوفرَع ، فَرعوه هوفرَع 'separate(to) separate' 'separate upon separate' 'they separated-he separated' as between people arguing or fighting; '(to)branch upon branch', '(to)divide upon divide' 'to separate upon to separate' as in splitting/separating things/objects; it also means crops stalks growing high in length—a good, strong crop. فَرئو/فَرئوه هوفرَء 'they fled him upon fled him/fled from him upon fled from him'. This is the Arabic way in repeating the same word as to express the greatness, intensity, seriousness, quantity, etc. to exaggerate the word by repeating it (sometimes with (ha/will) before the first or second of the same word if a person is saying 'he/I will…' followed by the word) to emphasise its meaning and concentrate its meaning more by repeating it this way as a superlative. In this instance, it warns the people who are disobeying God that their punishment will be unmatched and great, with an example that the Pharaoh-hophra (one of the meanings of his name means a high and strong-grown stalk) king of Egypt will be executed by the king of Babylon. The narration also mirrors how the people have stated they find the protection/worship of a female goddess more powerful than the usually favoured god of the Biblical stories which Jeremiah under instruction from this god is calling them to leave other gods and worship only him. Cp: phar'oo hoophra', phar'ooh hoophra', phar-oo hoophr-a, phar-ooh hoophr-a. (Jer.44:30)

Misgab; miśgāb; مِشغآب 'screaming/long loud screaming' 'terrified screaming' and this is repeated throughout the whole chapter. Cp: (Jer.48:1)

Merathaim; mĕrāṯayim; ميرآثَي ام 'twitching of eyes of-the' and is a bad omen, 'the inheritance of/the inheritance-the'; ميرآتي ام 'the dream/the dream of-the' 'a dream-the' 'the mirror of-the' 'the reflection of-the' 'what you saw/what did you see-the' 'they/she/he did not dream-the' 'they/he/she did not see-the'; ميرآطي ام 'swallowing whole-the/swallowed whole-the' 'they swallowed/are swallowing whole-the' 'they were swallowed-the/will be swallowed whole-the' and it is reflected in the narration of its complete destruction'. It is equivalent to Meraioth (1Chr.6:6). Cp: meiraafay-um, meraatay-um. meiraaṭay-um. (Jer.50:21)

Pekod; pĕqôḏ; بيقُد 'will sizzle with fire' 'cause emotional/mental distress like sizzling with fire' 'will light a fire' 'will lead with a leash' and is reflected in how the men and women are described as bullocks to the slaughter. Cp: beiqod. (Jer.50:21)

From Jer.46 there is an obvious change in authorship where the stories return to everyone and every nation being killed and everything destroyed. The previous chapters of Jeremiah show Babylon and its king as being favoured by God (and the author(s) of Jeremiah), this too changes into great hate for doing essentially what according to the stories God caused them to do and was happy with. It seems the authors of the later chapters did not agree, or at the very least disliked that the stories narrated the inhabitants of Judah/Jerusalem/Israel were destroyed completely along with every brick in these stories so they levelled it out by having every nation/country destroyed too and with a special vengeance against Babylon in the story (not in real life). It shows the conflicting beliefs and ideas in the stories themselves and how the authors/editors felt about them.

Ezekiel

Chebar; kĕḇār; خيبار 'news' 'informed/told'. The name of the river where God's word comes specifically to Ezekiel, i.e. he informs him of news. Cp: kheibaar. (Ezek.1:1-3)

Ezekiel; yĕḥezq'ēl; is similar to **Jehezekel** (1Chr.24:16), and specifically for one of its meanings: بيهَضق جيهَضق ئِل ، ئِل 'came he/he is-tasting/forced to eat/swallowing/suffering-the' 'you, I will make taste/eat by force/swallow/suffer-the' 'came he/he-tasted/forced to eat/swallowed/suffered-the'; from word (ḏhq/ ضق) 'distress/suffer/taste/forced to swallow' and is used when describing a person who eats something he/ she does not like or not want to eat, and is also used figuratively to mean 'suffered/sufferance' 'tasted bitter' 'tasted all the agony' are some ways how sufferance or pain in described as being 'tasted' 'swallowed' 'forcibly fed'. Cp: yeiheḏhq-ill, geiheḏhq-ill.

This character is made to swallow a roll of book containing lamentations, mourning and woe which are the meanings of the word ('zek'/ḏhq/ضق) 'distress/suffer/taste/forced to swallow' so the author, in one expression, has the character do everything his name means: the physical swallowing and he is swallowing all different kinds of suffering/distress. The word itself carries the meaning 'made to eat' meaning had to suffer/bear this event(s)—and throughout Ezekiel we see him go through many tough tasks, which include eating unpleasant food, to deliver God's message/punishment. His name also reflects what the people, whom God intends for punishment, go through too.

'But thou, son of man, hear what I say unto thee; Be not thou rebellious like that rebellious house: open thy mouth, and eat that I give thee. And when I looked, behold, an hand *was* sent unto me; and, lo, a roll of a book *was* therein; And he spread it before me; and it *was* written within and without: and *there was* written therein lamentations, and mourning, and woe. Moreover he said unto me, Son of man, eat that thou findest; eat this roll, and go speak unto the house of Israel. So I opened my mouth, and he caused me to eat that roll. And he said unto me, Son of man, cause thy belly to eat, and fill thy bowels with this roll that I give thee.'

And although the passage ends describing the taste of the book as sweet as honey, the words of woe, lamentation, mourning, the expression 'and he caused me to eat that roll' express an unpleasant experience which is emphasised in the naming 'Ezekiel' 'forced to swallow/bear/suffer/etc.'

Even how God describes the house of Israel not listening to him, being stubborn, etc. all this is expressed in the compound word 'Ezekiel': they are causing God to bear/suffer/swallow their stubbornness and bad deeds.

Ezekiel being made to go prophesy is also sufferance forced upon him, the narration makes it clear he goes against his will. God tells him to go speak to the people 'Then the spirit took me up...' 'So the spirit lifted me up, and took me away, and I went in bitterness, in the heat of my spirit; but the hand of the Lord was strong upon me...'. (Ezek.1-48)

As is the case of all Biblical names and events, Ezekiel the character and the events in The Book of Ezekiel are all works of fiction, which the proper translation proves. Even without the translation which I present in this book there are still abundant contradictions in the Biblical text itself, and the impossibility and the obvious fictionality of these stories is evident to all who read it. Note how all the names of 'priests' and 'prophets' (and all characters) are fictional compound words reflecting the events in the stories, yet Biblical scholars 'academically' explain them as actual events even if the 'chronology' and logic does not fit these stories. No matter how impossible that these stories be true accounts, scholars attempt to give them an actual place and location in time, history and geography. Take as an example the character 'Ezekiel', Biblical scholars psychoanalyse a figment of an author's imagination as if he were a real person that once existed, describing and debating whether his behaviour (as presented in the Biblical stories) is that of a hopefully passionate believer or that of an emotionally imbalanced individual or that of a person suffering psychosis. All these follies would have been avoided had they read the Bible as it is presented and was intended: in Arabic with very clear meanings.

'Chaldean' once again is used when fire is introduced in the story this time a 'fire infolding itself' from a whirlwind where brightness, light and colours come 'out of the midst of the fire.' 'As for the likeness of the living creatures, their appearance *was* like burning coals of fire, *and* like the appearance of lamps...and the fire was bright, and out of the fire went forth lightning'. There are reasons why fire features in the stories which will be explained with evidence later in this book. (Ezek.1:1-5)

Tel-abib; tēl 'āḇîḇ; similar to **Abib** (Exod.13:4) but with an extra word to suit the current story: تيل عآبيب 'carried by hand(handle)-flowing' 'carried-overflowing' 'carried-swollen with water' 'carried-bubbling or roaring water' 'carried-floating in' 'carried-lots of'. (tl/تل) is to carry/lift by the hand or something by its handle, the story describes Ezekiel being carried away and placed down at 'Tel-abib' a place where people live next to a river (Chebar). 'abib' is the word used to describe the sight and sound of a rushing river with water bubbling, flowing fast and strong (see Abib (Exod.13:4) and Joppa (2Chr.2:9,16)). 'Then I came to them of the captivity at Tel-abib, that dwelt by the river of Chebar.'. Cp: teyl 'aabeeb. (Ezek.3:15)

Diblath; diblâ, diblātâ; ذبله ، ذبلآته 'withered' 'it withered' 'it made it wither' 'wick' 'its wicks' and refers to how God will cause the people to die from pestilence, sword and famine until they are as a desolate wilderness—in other words comparing them to shrivelled, withered plants that die 'and make the land desolate, yea, more desolate than the wilderness towards Diblath, in all their habitations.'. It is similar to **Almon-diblathaim** (Num.33:46). Cp: viblah, viblaatah. (Ezek.6:11-14)

Jaazaniah (2Kgs.25:23) the son of **Shaphan** (2Kgs.22:3-15) is used for: Jaazaniah 'calls out to gather/assemble/pray-he/him' as it describes 'seventy men of the ancients' assembled before a wall of images; 'you the fornicator-he/him' as they are burning incense and worshipping 'other' gods which is described as fornication in the Bible; 'agrees/allows-he/him' as the priests/people have agreed to do these things which the story presents as abominations; 'gave him his just deserts-he/him' 'gave reward-he/him' as the chapter will end with a promise of retribution. Shaphan 'they saw' two or more people saw as both Ezekiel and God see the sins Israel is doing, and both parties (God/Ezekiel and the ancients of Israel) are seeing something: the ancients seeing the images and worshipping them, God/Ezekiel witnessing this; also, the sinning people believe they cannot be seen by God. It also covers all the other sins and things 'seen' to the end of the chapter. (Ezek.8-18)

Tammuz; tammûz; تَمُّز 'is squeezing/she is squeezing' and although this is another month from the Arabic agricultural calendar, here it is used as in squeezing their tears out for a deity named Tammuz 'there sat women weeping for Tammuz.'. Cp: tammuz. (Ezek.8:14)

Jaazaniah 'calls out to gather/assemble/pray-he/him' as it describes 'twenty-five men' assembled at the door of the gate; 'gave him his just deserts-he/him' 'gave reward-he/him' as God will bring retribution against them; 'calls out to gather/assemble/pray-he/him', after Ezekiel's plea, God promises to gather the scattered people and bring them back to assemble in the land, but also into the proper ways of worship. Son of **Azur** for 'the false oath/the lying under oath' as they are described as giving 'wicked counsel in this city'; 'tighten/the tightening' they will be under severe circumstances when God exacts punishment by putting them at the mercy of strangers. (Ezek.11)

Pelatiah (1Chr.3:21) 'fell-he/him' as they cause the slaughter of others which will result in their own falling/slaughter; this character is made to both physically and figuratively 'fall' in that he falls to the ground and dies at the same time and Ezekiel falls to the ground on his face; 'immoral/lewd-he/him' as they cause 'mischief' and lead the people to do wrong. Son of **Benaiah** (2Sam.8:18) for 'by my eyes' (a threat) 'with care/precision' as God knows everything they do even their inner thoughts/intentions, and he will exact precise revenge on them; 'with intentions' as Ezekiel prophecies that 'for I know the things that come into your mind, *every one of* them.'; 'his sons'. (Ezek.11)

Chaldea has been used here differently by focusing on a specific meaning of the word, although its spelling and pronunciation remain the same: the word in the text is 'kaśdîm' 'make/made crispy-them/the' 'scraped/dragged-them/the' 'boiled-them/the' 'beat/killed-them/the' but it plays on its other word used in the Biblical stories and as it appears in the KJV: Chaldíōn, Chaldai, Chaldaioi which have the same and similar meanings of being burnt, killed, cooking on or under intense heat, and this latter word is also the noun in Arabic for a 'mole/خلدي' (the animal); the mole is blind and burrows underground, unseen by the people who only see in the day the mounds of soil left from its activities. The narration has God instruct Ezekiel to conduct the same behaviour of a mole, the comparisons the text makes about people who have eyes 'but see not', they are blind like a mole, but in their disobedience/sins. God orders Ezekiel to dig beginning in one place and to end up in another—like moles do; the narration makes a point in that Ezekiel is ordered to cover his face so he cannot see the ground i.e. he has to use his other faculties to dig through the wall—just like a mole. The example of Chaldea/Chaldeans—mole(s)—carries on with the people being told they will be made to do the same (dig blindly/go through captivity where they will suffer not being able to properly live, likened to blindness). The words used for 'Chaldea' in both the English versions and the 'Hebrew' texts show that at some point 'Chaldíōn, Chaldaí, Chaldaíoi' was replaced with 'kaśdîm', and although both hold very similar meanings, what is obvious from everywhere the latter word is used is that 'Chaldea' meanings were originally meant by the stories and at some point later editors of the Biblical stories changed them to 'kaśdîm', but left the stories intact as the meanings were still similar. It also points to whoever assisted in the earliest translations to a non-local language (the local language being what is called 'Hebrew' which is in fact Arabic) spoke Arabic and were aware of the correct word of the word-name in the story and gave 'Chaldíōn, Chaldaí, Chaldaíoi' instead of 'kaśdîm' and only a person who fluently speaks and understands the original language of the Bible would be able to provide a word with the exact meanings relayed in the story and similar to 'kaśdîm' which appears in the 'Hebrew' texts (and the same goes for changing 'Chaldee' to 'kasdim' in the Hebrew texts), and the fact that everywhere in the Bible 'Chaldíōn, Chaldaí, Chaldaíoi' is mentioned its exact meanings are relayed also show that the original stories were understood with this word and used this word and is why when it needed to be translated into a foreign language someone corrected the replacement word 'kaśdîm' and gave the original word as pronounced 'Chaldíōn, Chaldaí, Chaldaíoi'. (Ezek.11:24; 12:13)

These three characters have been invoked: **Noah** (Gen.5:29-32;6) 'cried out in distress/loudly' describes an animal such as a cow when it bellows for a long time 'warned/brought to attention' 'If I cause noisome beasts to pass through the land…'; **Daniel** (1Chr.3:1) 'bowed-the' 'he is bowed-is the' 'lowered/low-the' 'he is lowered/low-is the' 'facing the ground-the' 'he is facing the ground-is the' 'with face on ground-the' 'his face on ground-with the' 'guilted-the' 'he is guilted-is the' as the people will be found guilty no matter how much they bow and pray, for as long as they do not wholly follow God's ways they will be lowered; the people and land are destroyed because of the people's guilt ; **Job** (Job.1) 'returning/returns/going to and fro, or up and down' 'being jerked up and down' 'coming-going and coming-going' as God will make the land uninhabitable for the people so they cannot return or pass through it. All three word-names also mean they warned guilty people to return to the right ways, and of God's punishment, and went back and forth attempting to convince people to obey, not to sin so as not to be lowered/brought to the ground with punishment—the story first describes it as only their three souls would have been saved, but then narrates that some people will return to obeying God's ways, but it makes it clear that the guilting and lowering/destruction was not done without warning or cause. (Ezek.14)

Bamah; bāmâ; بآمه ، بَمه 'for what?' 'why?' 'what for?' 'with what?' and they express: I brought you/saved you and gave you this land—so for what reason, why, what led you to blaspheme against me (God) and worship idols? The question 'Then I said unto them, What is the high place whereunto you go? And the name thereof is called Bamah unto this day.' does not ask 'where are you going?' as in 'what's the name of the place you go to?', but it is a reproach 'what are you doing?' 'what are you doing this for and why?' as in 'look at all I've done for you, for what reasons are you leaving my worship and forsaking everything?'. Cp: baamah, bamah. (Ezek.20:27-29)

Aholah; 'ohŏlâ; نُوخُله ، نُوحويله 'strip/stripped clothes/stripped naked' 'remove/removed clothes' and it is in the feminine, and literally means stripping a female of her clothes. To commit adultery in the Bible is called being naked, or others seeing the concerned 'nakedness'. It says because this character (representing Samaria 'fictional late-night stories') 'whored' herself, God delivered her 'into the hand of the Assyrians' and 'These discovered her nakedness'. Earlier books euphemistically used the word 'nakedness' for adultery, but the passages concerning Aholah and her sister are explicit and crude in describing Ahola's fornications and then the brutal sexual violence narrated as her punishment—and have given her a name exactly depicting what is said and done in this story. The other meanings of 'ḥl/حل' in 'Aholah' are also intended and relayed in the story: 'declared permissible/purified' 'purified/cleansed/circumcised' 'shed' 'beaten until skin peeled off/beaten severely' 'replaced/took place of' 'sweetened'. Cp: ooḥolah, oo-ḥoilah. (Ezek.23)

Aholibah; 'ohŏlîḇâ; نُوخُليبه ، نُوحويلي به 'take off(fem) the clothes' 'they took off her clothes' 'they stripped her naked'. It is the same meaning as Aholah above, with the variation of (î/ي) showing it is done by more than one person and (bah/ḇâ/به) 'to her/with her' denoting it was done to her by others, i.e. her clothes were stripped off by others. It does not necessarily mean against her will (although it can take that meaning if used in that context). In this story it first means she was undressed by her 'lovers', but in verses 25-27 it is in the context that she was stripped of her clothes and made to stand naked in front of others against her will: 'Then I saw she was defiled…And that she increased her whoredoms…And the Babylonians came to her into the bed of love, and they defiled her with whoredom…So she discovered her whoredoms, and discovered her nakedness…' these verses denote her willingness, but the following shows why the authors used a variant in her name while her sister-city did the same thing 'thus saith the Lord God: I will raise up thy loves against thee…and they shall deal furiously with thee: they shall take away thine nose and thine ears...They shall also strip thee out of thy clothes, and take away thy fair jewels...' while her sister is depicted as only willingly undressing, Aholibah is depicted as both willingly at first then against her will as punishment. The other meanings of 'ḥl/حل' are also in the word 'Aholibah' and relayed in its story (see Aholah). Cp: ooḥolee-bah, oo-ḥoilee-bah. (Ezek.23)

Note how (with exception of 'Babylonian' used as 'changed/swapped' as the sisters/cities status will change for the worse) the assailers who come to sexually attack Aholibah/Jerusalem, under the title of **Chaldean** for its 'heat/fire' related meanings, are all given word-names which are fire-related: **Pekod** as in (Jer.50:21) is still 'will sizzle with fire' 'cause emotional/mental distress like sizzling with fire' 'will light a fire' 'will lead with a leash'. Shoa; šôa'; شوَء 'grilled/roasted'. Koa; qôa'; كوَء 'branded with iron' which is usually a red-hot brand used to cause an infected wound to expel pus, or the same method used to cure of illness by branding the scalp (in humans), or to mark an animal. As the names reflect so does the story narrate her punishment will be '...and thy residue shall be devoured by the fire.'. It also reflects both Aholah/Samaria and Aholibah/Jerusalem '...have also caused their sons, whom they bare unto me, to pass for them through *the fire*, to devour *them*.'. Cp: sho-a, ko-a. (Ezek.23)

Tyre (Josh.19:29) Tyrus; صور for 'made image' 'sculpted image' 'created image or pattern 'imagined' 'created likeness/image' and the story describes the beauty of its appearance but also everything related to it from its ships, people, visitors, merchandise, market activities: '...O Tyrus, thou hast said, I am of perfect beauty...thy builders have perfected thy beauty.'

Senir (Deut.3:9; 1Chr.5:23) used for 'stakes/dowels': 'They have made all thy *ship* boards of fir trees of Senir'

Lebanon (Cant.3) used for 'for building/builders': 'they have taken cedars from Lebanon to make masts for thee.'

Bashan (Num.21:33) for 'fertile/verdant land' (has many trees): '*Of* the oaks of Bashan have they made thine oars;'

Ashurites (Asshur (Gen.10:11) for 'visit/the visit' 'the pilgrimage') Asher (Gen.30:10-13) for 'a lot of people' 'a group of people': 'the company of the Ashurites have made thy benches *of* ivory,'

Chittim (Num.24:24) for 'coast/shore-them/the': 'benches of ivory, *brought* out of the isles of Chittim.'

Egypt/Mizraim (Gen.10:6) for 'put scarf on-them' 'put scarf on-the', or 'knot/bundle-them/the' (the small square head scarf worn by women, folded into a triangle) which the sails are likened to: 'Fine linen with broidered work from Egypt was that which thou spreadest forth to be thy sail;'

Elishah (Gen.10:4) for 'the one who wants' 'whatever he wants' as in chose from the best, and what was wanted (blue and purple are the favoured colours (probably mean textures of specific material too) in the Biblical stories and the culture of the region of its authors): 'blue and purple from the isles of Elishah was that which covered thee.'

Zidon/Sidon (Gen.10:15) for 'fish/to fish' 'give(s) extra' and **Arvad** (Gen.10:18) for 'wobbled' (head or object carried on head) as sailors would know how to fish, the way the sea rolls would have sailors wobbling their heads: 'The inhabitants of Zidon and Arvad were thy mariners;'

Gebal; gĕḇāl; قيبال 'from before' 'from old times' 'experienced' 'facing/in front of' 'meeting' 'accepting' 'so good (in quality of material or a person in character)or honest/ meet acceptance/are accepted/desired'. Cp: qeibaal. 'The ancients of Gebal and the wise *men* thereof were in thee thy calkers; all the ships of the sea with their mariners were in thee to occupy their merchandise.' (Ezek.27:9)

Persia (2Chr.36:20-21) 'split open/pushed out/emerged by pushing up or out/ divided by breaking or splitting'; **Lud.** (Gen.10:22) 'to fold or press together hard' 'crumple/press and crumple'; **Phut** (Gen.10:6) 'crush' (whether a person, food or object) to represent actions of men of war: 'They of Persia and of Lud and of Phut were in thine army, thy men of war...'

Arvad here has been used for 'stood widthways/obstructed'; 'The men of Arvad with thine army *were* upon thy walls round about,'

Gammadims; gammāḏ; غمّاد ، غمّاد هم/ام 'sheathed/sheaths' 'sheathed-them/the' and means anything that can be put into a sheath or is sheathed, here it refers to the soldiers sheathed in the towers and also sheathing the walls with their shields. Cp: g͟hammaad, g͟hammaad-hum/um. 'and the Gammadims were in thy towers: they hanged their shields upon thy walls round about...'. (Ezek.27:11)

Tarshish (Gen.10:4) for 'light spraying' or 'a lot of light spray' as it mentions lots of different goods being traded: 'Tarshish was thy merchant by reason of the multitude of all *kind of* riches…'

Javan (Gen.10:2) 'assisted/helped'; **Tubal** (Gen.10:2) 'a drum/drummed' 'good of' 'is shown' 'is pedalled'; **Meshech** (Gen.10:2) for 'held/caught' 'pull at something until it gives or snaps'. All these meanings are shown as these three are described as cooperating, dealing in the giving and taking, sale and purchase of commodities, the 'held/caught/drummed/pedalled/pull until it snaps or gives' are all descriptions of bartering and negotiating: 'Javan, Tubal, and Meshech, they *were* thy merchants: they traded the persons of men and vessels of brass in thy market.'

Togarmah (Gen.10:3) 'scraped/bruised/battered' 'made loud thumping or knocking sound/noise' 'corners or edges have been battered/broken off' 'made hollow or sharp knocking/tapping noise' and this is the name used to denote the sound and action of horses and horsemen in a crowded market: 'They of the house of Togarmah traded in thy fairs with horses and horsemen and mules.'

Dedan (Gen.10:7) 'made to bow/bend' to conjure up the images of bowing horns, or the hunters who would bend to cut off the horns and the ebony: 'The men of Dedan *were* thy merchants; many isles were the merchandise of thine hand: they brought thee for a present horns of ivory and ebony.'

Syria 'ărām; عَرآم ، عيرآم 'wilderness, uninhabited place where it's easy to get lost' 'to abandon something or someone in the wild.'; نَرآم ، نيرآم 'to throw/to do with throwing' 'thrown, strewn or located over a vast distance/over different areas' 'vast/distant/covering wide or many different areas'. It indicates the wide variety of goods laid as if thrown all over, most of which are collected from wilderness/difficult to get to places such as emeralds, coral and agate. Cp: 'araam, 'airaam, a-raam, airaam. (Ezek.27:16)

Judah (Gen.29:35) 'he is called/calls' and it is used to name what the different grains are called: 'Judah, and the land of Israel, they were thy merchants: they traded in thy market wheat of Minnith, and Pannag…'

Israel (Gen:32:24-32) for 'twisted muscle-the' 'twisted-the' as this is the motion needed to squeeze honey out of its honeycomb, also to get oil out of seeds which is by a man twisting a manual press or donkeys/camels turning the press in circles creating the squeezing/pressing motions, the product of which is being sold, and to get the ingredients out of plants, etc. to make balms: 'Judah, and the land of Israel, they were thy merchants: they traded in thy market wheat of Minnith, and Pannag, and honey, and oil, and balm.'

Damascus (Gen.14:14-15) 'sucked/sucked a lot' 'sucked at his teeth' as a trader in wine; the wine is from Helbon; ḥelbôn; حَلبُن 'milked' 'stripped in copious amounts' the latter could mean a tree being stripped of fruit or leaves or anything that large amounts can be reaped from and here both grapes and sheep are meant. Cp: ḥelbon. It is coupled with Damascus 'sucked a lot' to conjure up word-imagery of plenty of wine for sale. The wine likened to the 'milking of cows' i.e. lots of grape juice flowing to make wine: 'Damascus was thy merchant in the multitude of the wares of thy making, for the multitude of all riches; in the wine of Helbon, and white wool.' (Ezek.27:18)

Dan (Gen.14:14-15) 'bowed, bent, facing the ground, with face on ground, lowered, low' and **Javan** 'assisted/helped' are used as traders or buyers of items such as herbs/plants and iron of which the gathering/extraction or inspection would necessitate bending/kneeling/bowing low and Javan 'helped' indicates a group effort to collect amounts needed for sale and states there is a lot of 'to and fro': 'Dan also and Javan going to and fro occupied in thy fairs; bright iron, cassia, and calamus, were in thy market.'

Arabia (2Chr.9:14) 'grower/anyone who brings someone or something up or teaches them/grows them' and here specifically 'raiser of lambs, rams and goats' it has been coupled with **Kedar** (Gen.25:13) 'pots used on fire' as that is where the mentioned animals will end up being cooked in: 'Arabia, and all the prince of Kedar, they occupied with thee in lambs, and rams, and goats…'

Sheba (Gen.10:7, 28) 'to swell' (like wood from water), 'have full stomach(plural)' 'satisfied(plural)'—as in having plenty of food, money or other resources to satisfy basic needs, and this is indicated in the mentioned goods are in plenty and of rareness. It is coupled with **Raamah** (Gen.10:7) 'saw water' 'threw around' 'at a long distance apart/covering a great distance' as the produce is swollen, i.e. in large amounts or big in size, just as wood swells from water; also the meaning they are 'thrown around/cover large distance' that they occupy a large space which also implies large amounts and lots of variety: 'The merchants of Sheba and Raamah…they occupied in thy fairs with chief of all spices, and with all precious stones, and gold.'

Haran (Gen.11:27) for '(two) wooden batons' (usually handles of tools) which chests would have. Canneh; kannēh; حَنّيه 'make it rich in colour' 'is rich in colour' 'apply henna to it/him'; قَنّيه 'hold it up high/set it straight' 'is perky/standing or sitting straight/head held high'. Both are present in the description of goods as in their colours and textures, as well as in the word-imagery of clothes/fabrics being held up for inspection by buyers or chests and things made of wood being carried away. Cp: ḥanneyh, qanneyh. **Eden** (2Kgs.19:12) 'will bow/bend/face ground/lower head' 'return/returned' and are actions which would occur in buying and selling of the goods described. **Asshur** (Gen.10:11) 'the tight/tightened/squeezed' and refers to the goods being bound with cords as well as the word-imagery of things being wrapped, tied at purchase to take away. Chilmad; kilmad̲; كِلمَض 'wrapped in a garment/fabric' 'threw into a garment or fabric(usually a shawl)' it implies either wrapping things to be carried, but hurriedly or randomly throwing something into a sack or fabric to carry it or hide it, it also means to put different things in the same bundle/garment for carrying away or hiding/storing. In this instance it is used to describe the buying and wrapping of different produce. Cp: kilma<u>dh</u>. (Ezek.27:23): 'Haran, and Canneh, and Eden, the merchants of Sheba, Asshur, *and* Chilmad, *were* thy merchants. These *were* thy merchants in all sorts *of things*, in blue clothes, and broidered work, and in chests of rich apparel, bound with cords, and made of cedar, among thy merchandise.'

Tarshish is used again but this time including its meaning 'a lot of vomiting' as it is expelling/selling all these goods and the merchants leaving, which is the word-imagery by using this word to explain how it is replenished after the markets die down then return, but still for its meanings of 'light spraying' or 'a lot of light spray' 'intentionally splashing a little liquid over someone/something' as it mentions ships again and that Tyrus is surrounded by seas, i.e. it is an island: 'The ships of Tarshish did sing of thee in thy market: and thou wast replenished, and made very glorious in the midst of the seas.'

Syene; sĕwēnēh, sīnīm; سيوينيه 'we levelled it' 'we made it straight' 'we did it'; سيينييم 'straightened them/the' 'they are straight/aligned' 'in the direction of the river/sea' 'in their/the direction' 'directly' 'direct to sea/river'. Most of these meanings are meant in the story: God will level the land, make it a waste, the river is repeatedly mentioned with destruction towards it stated, even the symbolisation of Pharaoh as a dragon in the river will be uprooted and thrown down. It also means the desolation and levelling of the land will go from Egypt straight to 'Ethiopia' but again the word translated as 'Ethiopia' is incorrect as the correct translation means 'scrape away' 'kill in one go/one movement' 'remove in one movement' 'left over burnt pieces/toast until crispy or burnt/burnt in fire or from too much heat' 'to blow away litter/fibres/burnt remnants' 'remove completely in one swipe or scrape' 'litter/fibres/burnt remnants', and is similar to the meaning of Syene 'we levelled it' and is the waste and desolation which the story about destroying Egypt narrates. Note how the author gives them the same wandering for forty years and scattering just as the theme of stories about Moses and his people. Cp: seiweyneyh, seyeyneyeym, seyeyney-eym. (Ezek.29:1-12)

The same way there is mistranslation and misinterpretation of what the word Cush/Cushite is and is wrongly presented as 'Ethiopia' the same applies to Libya and Lydia. Scholars present both words Lubim and Ludim as 'Lybia', even though the Biblical authors use them in the same sentence as two separate words, representing two separate peoples in the story. These words are used to enhance the meaning of what punishment will do in the wars/destruction mentioned in the stories they feature in.

'Ethiopia' is **Cush** 'scrape away' 'kill in one go/one movement' 'remove in one movement' 'left over burnt pieces/toast until crispy or burnt/burnt in fire or from too much heat' 'to blow away litter/fibres/burnt remnants' 'remove completely in one swipe or scrape' 'litter/fibres/burnt remnants'. As explained before.

Lubims (2Chr.12:3) 'their/the-pulp/core' 'pulp/core-them/the' i.e. that the punished people will be cored, their innards ripped out just as the cities and buildings will be gutted.

Ludim (Gen.10:13) 'fold and press-them/the' 'crush them together' 'crush together-the' 'crumple/press and crumple them/the' 'crumpled them/the' 'pressed and crumpled them/the' i.e. the people will be destroyed, the cities and buildings will collapse.

Lydia; Lydía, lûd; لِدييه ، ليدييه ، لُد 'fold and press it/him/he' 'it was folded and pressed' 'fold and press' 'crush it/him together'; لِضييه ، ليضييه ، لُض 'dent it/force both sides to meet-it/him/he' 'dented/both sides crushed against each other' 'burnt' 'burning sensation/pain'; لِتييه ، ليتييه ، لُت 'crumple it/press and crumple it/him/he' 'crumpled' 'pressed and crumpled'—it is the action of washing clothes when a garment or garments are pressed and crumpled against each other to cause the soap substance (in the past it was natural substances used) and the garments to rub against each other, or when mixing substances/ingredients together, etc. It is similar to Lud/Ludim. Cp: lydee-yah, lidee-yah, lud, ly<u>dh</u>ee-yah, li<u>dh</u>ee-yah, lu<u>dh</u>, lytee-yah, litee-yah, lut. (Ezek.30:5)

'...when the slain shall fall in Egypt, and they shall take away her multitude, and her foundations shall be broken down. Ethiopia and Libya, and Lydia, and all the mingled people and Chub, and the men of the land that is in league, shall fall with them by the sword.' (Ezek.30)

This confusion arises from the fact that the scholars do not understand the nuances of the Biblical language, which is Arabic, and how it used, where 'people' 'stranger' 'country' does not necessarily mean a different country or a different people, but can mean the same country just a different village or city or area, or what the author/person views as not his direct 'home-town'. Furthermore, they have not understood these are words in everyday use, used by the Biblical authors as themes and puns to make the storyline flow and enhance it to entertain the audience—the authors did not use them as names of actual countries but as the word in its usage by the people. But because some Biblical scholars want to give fictional stories, characters, places and events a 'reality', they cast around and stick it to real countries, and in doing so corrupt the stories, corrupt history and lead away from ever understanding the true meanings of the Bible and its stories.

You can see all the meanings of the words happening in the events described of breaking, burning, falling, levelling, hiding, etc, (Lud, Lubim, Cush (i), Chub, etc. (Libya/Lydia/Ethiopia)) described throughout the chapter.

Chub; kûb; خُب 'hide/hid' 'damp and musty' 'ominous/brings bad fate upon'; كُب 'dumped/poured out in one go' as their blood will be spilt: 'shall fall with them by the sword'. Cp: kub. (Ezek.30:5)

No; nō'; نوء ، نو 'set apart/far away/stand at distance/distance (oneself)/have nothing to do with it' 'intention/intend' and both meanings are used as the narration is of exile, desolation, removal of people from the land, then judging based on the intentions of who is being judged. Cp: noo', n-o'. (Ezek.30:15-16)

Aven; 'āwen, 'wn; نّاوِن ، نون 'moaned/groaned' 'moan/groan'; نّأذَن ، نذن 'was/were harmed' 'harmed'. It reflects how the people will be harmed, the pain they will suffer. It is equivalent to Beth-aven (Josh.7:2-12). Cp: aawen, a-wn, aaven, a-vn. (Ezek.30:17)

Pi-beseth; pî-ḇeseṯ; فيبَسَط 'so he will/it will stretch(arms or legs) forward' mostly used to describe animals and specifically cats when they lie down but with forelegs stretched ahead of them, and also when a person sits with legs stretched straight ahead, 'so he will take over/spread over' the latter means when a person takes over the rights of a land which he/she believes is legally his/hers even if it is under dispute, the 'spreading over' means they are working the land or living in/on it and therefore have 'taken over' it, and also when something such as plaster or any substance is spread to make a roof or other structure waterproof or smooth. It has other meanings (ḇeseṯ/بسط), but they have not been used in the narration. Cp: phee-beset. (Ezek.30:17)

Tehaphnehes; tĕḥapnĕḥēs; تيخَب نيحيس 'hid/they hid-bad luck/bad fate'; طيح بنيحيس 'fell/broke-with/the unlucky/bad fated'. Both meanings are present as the narration tells of the breaking of the 'yoke' and strength of Egypt; the day darkening, a cloud covering her and her daughters going into captivity are all describing something being concealed. It is equivalent to Tahpenhes (Jer.43). Cp: teikhab neiḥeys, ṭeiḥa bneiḥeys. (Ezek.30:18)

Lebanon (2Kgs.19:12) has been used for 'for building/builders' and **Eden** (2Kgs.19:12) for 'will guilt' 'will bow/bend/face ground/lower head' 'return/returned' 'listen and understand-guilted/bowed/bent' 'remember/be warned-guilted/bowed/bent' 'sticks' to give as a metaphor of Pharaoh and his demise. Note the whole chapter and the word-names used in it also play on the meaning of Pharaoh 'a shooting stalk/ something that has grown strong and high' (which in the Moses/Pharaoh story directly reflected him being cut down like a stalk).

Lebanon is compared to a tall strong cedar and is described as something high and strong which is what the word 'building' means (to raise something up, from the ground upwards). It is compared against the trees of Eden which no matter how majestic, tall, strong they be—compared to Lebanon's cedars they seem like 'sticks' that envy Lebanon's beauty, height and strength. Lebanon ('building/builders') tree is taller, it compares against the 'will bow/bend/face ground/lower head' meaning of Eden.

Eden 'will guilt' 'will bow/bend/face ground/lower head' 'return/returned' 'listen and understand-guilted/bowed/bent' 'remember/be warned-guilted/bowed/bent' is also reflected in the narration of Pharaoh's demise that no matter how high he rose or will rise, he will always return to the ground, fall low. (Ezek.31)

Gog of Magog

Note how these words have been used to depict the events which happen in the story:

Meshech (Gen.10:2) 'held/caught' 'pull at something until it gives or snaps' 'scared silly/frightened extremely'. The armies are described as being pulled like animals both to arrive and how they will leave—as in humiliated. They arrive wanting to scare and slaughter the people, but will end up undergoing a great fear and being slaughtered. It relays how fish, birds and other animals, including man will shake in fear of God's fury.

Tubal (Gen.10:2) 'good of' the best of these peoples are in the armies and get killed. 'gets soaked/wet' as God will rain over the enemy and also rain large hail stones. 'gets humiliated/denigrated' 'is shown' they will suffer a humiliating defeat and be shown God's fury. The introduction depicts Gog from the land of Magog as being forced to come or deceived/encouraged to come, likened to being hooked in the jaw and pulled towards warring against Jerusalem, 'drum/drummed' means to encourage a person to do something which is bad and usually to the detriment of the doer and/or victim—and this is what happens: God has made them come and they end up slaughtered.

Persia (2Chr.36:20-21) 'made/prepared resting or sleeping place' 'lay down' as they intend to attack a people who are vulnerable 'at rest'. 'spread over/lay out' as part of Gog/Magog, while they are alive, they cover a large area of land at arrival, and in death they still cover the surface. 'mat/bed/resting or sleeping place' 'brought forward/pressed on and pushed out' 'split open/pushed out/emerged by pushing up or out/divided by breaking or splitting' 'divided something into separate units' they arrive as not only Gog from Magog but other armies also join it and increase its size and also its strength in being able to break and destroy Israel and the same meanings are shown when they are broken and destroyed instead; walls, mountains and steep places will all be broken down by God's shaking and from fear of his fury. 'explained/explained in detail/made clear' the story narrates in detail the armies and what they have, where they are from.

Ethiopia/Cushi (2Sam.18:19-33) 'scrape away' 'kill in one go/one movement' 'remove in one movement' 'left over burnt pieces/toast until crispy or burnt/burnt in fire or from too much heat' 'remove completely in one swipe or scrape' 'litter/fibres/burnt remnants' 'cut' 'hardened hearts/cruel' as they arrive to wipe away the people but instead they are killed just as the word 'Cushi' means they are scraped away as if fibres, they are left strewn all over the land/mountains and have to be scraped away and burnt as if dealing with refuse. 'tell a/the story' this is a story being told which the audience is reminded so as to never forget it is fictional.

Libya/Lubim (2Chr.12:3) 'their/the-pulp/core' 'pulp/core-them/the' they arrive with the intention of killing and emptying Jerusalem and end up being cored of their lives and their countries cored of its inhabitants as they never return, but also those who never went to war will be slaughtered and punished in their own lands.

Gomer (Gen.10) 'submerged (in water or dirt)' 'upset/envious/spiteful' 'hot coals/hot' 'stifled/were stifled-saw/water/dreamt'. They arrive like a storm cloud ready to release its contents on all the land, but they will end up being buried in the soil, their weapons burnt. God's anger and action is described as a fire. They will be submerged and stifled with 'overflowing rain, great hailstones, fire, and brimstone.'. God speaks of his jealousy and upset over his name which they have offended.

Togarmah (Gen.10:3) 'scraped/bruised/battered' 'made loud thumping or knocking sound/noise' 'corners or edges have been battered/broken off' 'made hollow or sharp knocking/tapping noise'. These words reflect on horses and horsemen, and also on the sounds and images of battle, destruction. It also conjures up the imagery and sounds of being struck with large hailstones and brimstone.

Sheba (Gen.10:7, 28) 'captured' 'to swell' 'will harm' 'have full stomach(plural)' 'satisfied(plural)'—as in having plenty of food, money or other resources to satisfy basic needs. Gog from Magog is already a vast horde in its own right, but the story increases this by swelling its size with other armies and bands that join it. Much is made of the quantities of weapons and clothes. Their destruction is described as being like a feast of which man and beast feast on. Also, at their arrival the narration has Sheba asking Gog about what spoils of cattle and goods they think they will capture.

Dedan (Gen.10:7) 'made to bow/bend' they will be lowered to the ground in humiliation, reputation and physically through death. At their arrival the narration has Dedan asking Gog what spoil of cattle, goods, silver and gold do they expect to carry away, invoking images of bending while picking up and carrying away great treasures.

Tarshish (Gen.10:4) 'light spraying' or 'a lot of light spray' 'a lot of vomiting' or intentionally splashing a little liquid over someone/something. They are likened to a storm cloud ready to release their strength and weapons on the people. There will be rain which comes down on them, but even their death is likened to vomiting, the pestilence will cause them to haemorrhage blood while alive. Before the warring begins, a question is presented which also covers 'a lot of light spray' meaning lots of things—which, in this case, the narration presents as what they thought the many kinds of spoil they would take away.

Bashan (Num.21:33) 'to filter impurities out of liquid' 'fertile/verdant land'. They are the 'unclean/filth' as antagonists in the story, their mass-slaughter is a filtering of the impurities, which fire is used to purify and cleanse. The dead bodies of men are likened to the sheep of fertile lands which is always linked to Bashan to denote their fatness, the goodness and plenty of their blood, meat and fat.

Gog (1Chr.5:4) 'overcrowded' 'too many people than can fit in one area/room' 'over spilling with people/ things' and they are from **Magog** (Gen.10:2) 'moves like a wave' and refers to an area or land filled with people or crop, that its movement looks fluid like a current or wave.

'Gog' 'great crowd/ a huge number of people' is used whether describing a great crowd crammed into a place which is meant/practical for much less people, or hordes of people in an open space. The phrase used to describe hordes or overcrowding is (ya'og 'agoog/يَعُج عجوج) 'it is crowded/over spilling-overcrowded/ it is crowded-crowded'.

Magog 'moves like a wave' is the description of something that moves this way and that, whether fast or slow, and is specifically used to describe something packed such as a field full of crops, or tall grass, being moved by the wind and according to the wind direction—similar to the movement of water current or waves. The same is applied to describe the movement of hordes, or the movement of people or things in an overcrowded space because the movement appears to be fluid due to the vast numbers of the crowd/ packed substance, etc.—just as crops or grass have a fluid movement when wind blows, as well as the movement of waves and how they settle. One phrase used to describe a field full of crop swaying this way and that with the wind, and the same phrase describing the movement of a large crowd (as seen by an observer from afar) is (ya'oog wa yamoog/يعوج ويموج) 'it is over spilling/overcrowded and moves like waves' (see Ajah, Og, Doeg, Aiah, Aija, Agag, Agagite).

So there is no surprise the authors of the Bible used these two words and their meanings, which any person who knows the language can see the imagery conjured by the story, which describe a vast crowd and the movement of anything which is a horde, overcrowded or overfilled, to name the people who arrive in great numbers to war on Jerusalem. The words chosen to name the characters and place name from the noun and adverb is used perfectly to depict and enhance what will and does happen in the story: Gog and Magog arrive in such a great horde of 'multitude' that even when they are defeated, the victorious will spend a great span of time (seven years) burning their weapons (of Gog/Magog) and a great length of time burying their bodies as explained in Hamon-gog. The imagery of the warring armies in such hordes and the name conjures up a field of crop moving like a wave, or an ants' nest boiling with ants.

'Son of man, set thy face against the Gog, the land of Magog...I will bring thy army, horses, and horsemen, all of them clothed with all sorts *of armour*, even a great company *with* bucklers, and shields, all of them handling swords...Thou shalt ascend and come like a storm, thou shalt be like a cloud to cover the land, thou, and all thy bands, and many people with thee...And thou shalt come from thy place out of the north parts, thou and many people with thee, all of them riding upon horses, a great company, and a mighty army...and I will rain upon him, and upon his bands, and upon the many people that *are* with him...Thou shalt fall upon the mountains of Israel, thou and all thy bands, and the people that *is* with thee...'. The weapons of Gog: 'and they shall burn them with fire seven years...and there shall they bury Gog and all his multitude...And seven months shall the house of Israel be burying of them.' (Ezek.38-39)

Hamon-gog; hămôn gôg; هيمُن جُج 'wandered/abandoned/lost-crowds/overcrowded' the first part of the word (hamon) from (hăm/هيم) means to abandon in a far away place/wilderness, get lost in far away place/ wilderness or wander off and get lost, it is used mostly to describe people who abandon unwanted cats/ kittens and when a person is lost in the wilderness by getting lost or being intentionally or unintentionally stranded by others or stuck in a dangerous spot in a mountain where the person or animal cannot come back from, cannot move because it is dangerous and therefore dies either way. The (on/ن) means it is in plural and/or done to them. This is exactly what the story narrates of the 'multitude', first they are brought here by God to die, to have their power and ability to fight taken away so they are brought there to be stranded and die, and even in death their corpses are abandoned on the ground as it will take seven months to bury them all, and it will take seven years of burning to get rid of their weapons and hence giving the place its name: 'and there they shall bury Gog and his multitude: and they shall call *it* The valley of Hamon-gog. And seven months shall the house of Israel be burying of them...And they shall sever out men of continual employment, passing through the land to bury with the passengers those that remain upon the face of the earth'. Cp: haimon gog. (Ezek.38-39)

Hamonah; hămônâ; هيمُنه 'they were abandoned/stranded' a suitable name for a city named after characters who arrive solely for God's (and thc author's) intention to have them killed then their corpses stranded for a period of time. Similar to Hamon-gog above. (Ezek.39:8-20)

En-eglaim; 'ên 'eglayim; ئين ئِجلاي ام ، ئين ئِجلايم 'he/it will cleanse/purify-the' 'he/it will purify/cleanse the river/sea' 'he/it will clear/make clear-the (or) the sea/river' 'he/it will purify(on heat)-the/the sea/river' supported by the text which narrates water being healed and the opposite of 'miry' (**En-gedi** has been used for its meanings of 'where will you end up at' 'end up at' 'where-did he reach/was found' to show how far the waters reach) 'these waters issue out toward...which being brought forth into the sea, the waters shall be healed...that every thing that liveth...withersoever the rivers shall come, shall live...because these waters shall come thither: for they shall be healed; and everything shall live wither the river cometh'. Equivalent to Eglaim (Isa.15:8). Cp: eyn eglay-um, eyn eglayim. (Ezek47:10)

Hethlon; ḥetlōn; حَثلون 'they made borders/fringes' 'made borders/fringes-until/up to' 'they kept within borders' 'they encouraged' 'encourage-until' and the definite meaning here is about borders of land as the story narrates. Equivalent to Heth (Gen.10:15) Cp: ḥefloon. (Ezek.47:15)

Berothah; bērôtāh; بيرُثآه 'they inherit'; بيرُضآه 'with his consent' 'they bury in ground/soil' 'they create soil/do with soil' the word itself does not mean 'land' but soil and the form of the word that something is to be done involving soil, and the verse is about inheriting land. Cp: beyrofaah, beyrodhaah. (Ezek.47:16)

Sibraim; sibrayim; سِبرَي ام/هم ، سِبرَيِم 'fixed/fix-the/them' 'mended/mend relationship/settled differences-the/them' 'fixed/made right-river/sea' and is still related to making borders which is described as going 'from the great sea'. Cp: sibray-im/him, sibra-yim. (Ezek.47:16)

Hazar-hatticon; ḥăṣar hattîkôn; حيصَر خَطّيكُن 'surrounded-your line/border/step' I have eliminated the other meanings of 'Hazar' because it has been anchored to one meaning of 'Hauran/surrounded/around' used here as a name of the coast which is described as being by Hazar-hatticon; حيصَر حَطّيكُن 'surrounded-leave you here/left you behind/allowed you' as they will end up staying there; حيصَر هَتّيكُن 'surrounded-tear it into shreds' 'surrounded-here you will be' and for the same reasons as the land is being divided, and the people who inherit it will set up their lives in that place. Cp: ḥaissar khaṭṭeekon, ḥaissar ḥaṭṭeekon, ḥaissar hatteekon. (Ezek.47:16)

Hauran; ḥawrān; حَورآن 'puzzled/in a predicament' 'cannot understand/figure out' 'attempting' 'surrounded/around'; خَورآن 'craving' 'wants/in need' 'bellowing(like an animal)/lowing' 'collapsed/ran away in fear'. Cp: ḥawraan, khawraan. (Ezek.47:16)

Hazar-enan the same as in (Num.34:9) with only slight difference to spelling and pronunciation of 'aynaan/aynaan being 'aynon/aynon but no difference to the meanings. (Ezek.47:17)

Meaning of 'kadesh' 'qodesh' 'm'kaddesh' 'mekkadesh'

This is a good place to explain what the meaning of the word 'temple' really is in the only language that has explained all the Bible perfectly and made sense of it. But to understand the meaning of the words used and mistranslated and misinterpreted as 'temple', first the meaning of the word 'qodesh' and its variants must be understood.

Not only in Ezekiel, but throughout the OT, the word 'kadesh' 'qodesh' 'm'kaddesh' 'mekkadesh' and all its variants has been incorrectly translated into 'holy' and synonyms of 'holy'. This mistake has been made because since early translations and interpretations whoever translated it from 'Hebrew' (which is not 'Hebrew' but Arabic) depended on the Arabic word: (qds/قدس) which does mean 'holy/sacred'. So they took the meaning of the Arabic word 'holy/qds/qodes' and erroneously applied it to the word 'qodesh' which they believed to be Hebrew. But the word 'qodesh/kodesh/m'kaddesh' is another Arabic word with no relation to the Arabic word 'holy/qds' but has a different meaning which is much used in the Biblical stories. It is a completely different word than 'holy', and its use (qodesh and its variants) has great importance in the Bible due to its correct meaning. Just as all the words I have translated and explained all have their evidence in the Torah/Bible, so does this word, and it has been explained earlier in this book (and in the Bible) when the place name 'Kadesh' is mentioned, it has the same meaning. How it became significant is due to what is done in the Biblical stories, what it means to the authors and the audience, and it is very important to the Biblical stories. First, we need to go back to the meaning of the root word 'kadesh' and how it is used in the OT stories:

Kadesh (Gen.14:7); qāḏēš; كآديش ، كادِش 'falls like a heap' 'falls is thrown to the ground with a loud sound' 'pile/piles' (things on the ground) 'piled'; قآديش ، قادِش 'led/led you/of being led' and refers to an animal being led by a rope/leash and is also used when a person is tied up as in imprisoned or led around as a prisoner, also when a person is the mediator between a woman and a man for an illicit relationship the 'mediator' is called qowaad/qowaada, and is equivalent to the meaning/idea of a 'pimp'—as the woman being led/misled into an affair is being led like an animal that is taken to get copulated to conceive (the animal not the lover). It is from the root word (kdsh/كدش) 'piled/pile(s)' 'to throw something on the ground' 'to fall with a sound or a heavy sound(with the sound of landing on the ground)' 'to pile something high' 'to pile' and 'plenty', and the word was probably created from the sound a load makes when thrown or unloaded onto the ground; and from word (qdsh/قدش) 'led/led by rope' which is how an animal is led to its sacrifice or slaughter. In Gen.14:7 it described what was to happen to the kings who were to be 'smote' and would fall. Cp: kaadeysh, kaadesh, qaadeysh, qaadesh.

In Num.13-14, 'kadesh' is still used as the place name and the theme setting for what was to happen in the story: Moses, Aaron and the children of Israel are in or near Kadesh to reflect 'fall like a heap/a pile/plenty' and the story reflects this when the spies return carrying piles of heavy fruit (a bunch of grapes needed to be carried by two people, figs and pomegranates), i.e. plenty, piles of fruit, and they set it down to show it to the people and they inform them how much abundance there is in the land.

Also wordplay on 'kadesh' 'fall like a heap, etc.' and 'lead': when the people of Israel wail over why the Lord led them here (qadesh/led) and will make them fall by the sword (kadesh/heap); Moses and Aaron falling on their faces to the ground is (kadesh/heap); God threatening to smite all the people for disobedience also displays (kadesh/fall like a heap)—as it is the sound and appearance people and objects make when falling to the ground. The word also means to beat them so they are a 'heap/pile' on the ground 'your carcases shall fall in the wilderness' is 'kadesh'.

Num.20:1-13, 'Kadesh' is where Miriam dies which fits into 'falls like a heap/falling sound'. When Moses strikes the rock instead of speaking to it also reflects the meaning of the word 'kadesh'.

In Jud.4 'Kedesh' is used in the same way to depict its meaning of 'fall like a heap/pile/heaps' for the story is once again set in/near 'Kedesh'—all stories in the Bible are given names to match what is to happen, what or who is described—and as the meaning of the word 'Kedesh' implies, Sisera and his 'tens of thousands' of men and chariots will all fall, and all will be killed/destroyed, so there are heaps of bodies and instruments. The main climatic event in the story is not only emphasised by the place-name for the event 'kadesh/to fall like a heap/pile' but it is also emphasised by giving the same-themed place-name for the area that the character Barak comes from 'And she sent and called Barak the son of Abinoam out of Kedesh-naphtali…' and he will lead the battle against Sisera and his men, and will crush Sisera's men, killing them all. Kedesh has been explained, but look at how two compound word-names have been combined to reflect how Barak will defeat Sisera's men 'Kedesh-naphtali' 'fall like a heap-crush for me'.

Secondly, 'kadesh, m'kaddesh, mekadesh, qodesh' and its variants have been used to emphasise the importance of specific items and ideas. Unfortunately, due to error in giving this word the meanings of 'holy' from the different Arabic word 'holy/qds/قدس', it has distorted and distracted from the true meaning of the word 'qodesh/mekadesh' which is 'heaps' and 'piled high' 'led', etc.

'piles/heap' is the meaning of the word 'kodesh' and in wordplay 'qodesh/lead/leads' and it refer to animals/meat, grain, oil, wine, crops, and all other offerings/gifts which are given to be offered in the rituals. It also describes how Aaron and his ministers get to eat from these piles/heaps of offerings. The place where these offerings are presented gets its importance (its adjective) from the things offered, or to be precise from the description/the amount of the things offered: 'Most Holy Place' is a wrong translation: qodesh haqqodashim/kodesh hakkodashim 'piled high' 'piles upon piles': qōḏeš haqqŏḏāšîm; كودِش هَكّوداآش هم/ام 'piled, I will pile them/it/the'; قودِش هَقّوداآش هم/ام 'lead/led, I will lead them/it/the'. Cp: koodesh hakkodaash-hum/um, qoodesh haqqodaash-hum/um. It is the Arabic language method of emphasising the intensity of what is described, e.g. if something is being struck between two hard objects, and specifically, for example, the action of a pestle and mortar the word is (lkd/لكد), but if it has been thoroughly pounded, or even a person beaten up, the phrase is (lkd likkaad/لَكّد لِكّآد) 'pounded-pounded' 'pounded-pounded a lot/severely' (lkduh likkad/لَكّدُه لِكّآد) 'pounded it/him-pounded/pounded severely' (lkkd-hum likaad/لَكّدهم لِكّآد) 'pounded them-pounded'. If the thing or person will be pounded/beaten up or is being threatened/stating to do so, you would say (halakkiduh likkaad/lkd halakkiduh/لكد هَلَكِّدُه/لكد هَلَكِّدُه), if the spoken about are in plural (lkd halakkid-hum/halakkid-hum likkad/لكد هَلَكِّدهم/هَلَكِّدهم لِكَّاد) 'pound, I will pound them/it' 'I will pound them, pound/pounding' the same word is repeated to show the intensity, and 'ha' is used as a suffix for the first or the repeated word to show 'I will/she will/etc', the intention to do so.

This repeat of the same word to make it a superlative description is used a lot and one of many words used this way is 'kadesh'. When a person is describing she/he has piled a lot of something be it grain, crops, fabric, etc. they will say 'mkdsh kiddaash/مكدش كِدّاش' i.e. 'it is piles upon piles' 'it is piled high'. If intending to continue to gather and pile or accumulate a lot of something 'hakkaddeshhum kiddaash/هَكَّدِّشهم كِدّاش' 'I will pile them-pile(s)', 'hakkaddesh-kiddaash/هَكَّدِّش كِدّاش' 'I will pile piles'.

The importance of the place in the 'tabernacle' of the Bible is not 'most holy place' as the word itself does not mean 'holy', but it gains its importance from the significance of the offerings which are 'piled high/piles upon piles' presented, it is also the only true meaning of the word 'kadesh' 'qodesh' 'm'kaddesh', etc. (even the intended meaning of qodesh/leads/led, the animals which are led to this place end up being piled as meat, fat and blood for the rituals), and this meaning and its direct use by the Biblical authors can be seen consistently throughout the OT.

In Num.18 it is used to describe the meat sacrifices which Aaron and the priests get to eat from and wherever 'most holy' ('holy' and similar words) is used should in fact be read as 'piles upon piles' or 'heaps', and the description in the text is that of all the things which should be piled/given to God—which Aaron and priests get to eat from: 'And the Lord spake unto Aaron, Behold, I also have given thee the charge of mine heave offerings of all the hallowed things of the children of Israel: unto thee have I given them by reason of the anointing, and to thy sons, by an ordinance forever. This shall be thine of the most holy [heaps/piles] things, *reserved* from the fire: every oblation of theirs, and every meat offering of theirs, and every sin offering of theirs, which they shall render unto me, shall be most holy [piled high] for thee and for thy sons.'. The narration goes on to mention the things which shall be heaped or piled as offerings, which Aaron and priests get to eat from and how it will be piled for them to take from: 'In the most holy *place* [piled upon piles/piled high] shalt thou eat it; every male shall eat it: it shall be holy [piled] unto thee. And this is thine; the heave offering of their gift, with all the wave offerings of the children of Israel: I have given them unto thee, and to thy sons and to thy daughters with thee, by a statute forever: every one that is clean in thy house shall eat of it. All the best of the oil, and all the best of the wine, and of the wheat, the firstfruits of them which they shall offer unto the Lord, them have I given thee. And whatsoever is first ripe in the land, which they shall bring unto the Lord, shall be thine; everyone that is clean in thy house shall eat of it. Every thing devoted in Israel shall be thine. Every thing that openeth the matrix in all flesh, which they bring unto the Lord, *whether it be* of men or beasts, shall be thine: nevertheless the firstborn of man shalt thou surely redeem, and the firstling of unclean beasts shalt thou redeem. And those that are to be redeemed from a month old shalt thou redeem, according to thine estimation, for the money of five shekels after the shekel of the sanctuary, which *is* twenty gerahs. But the firstling of a cow, or the firstling of a sheep, or the firstling of a goat, thou shalt not redeem; they *are* holy [piled]: thou shalt sprinkle their blood upon the altar, and shalt burn their fat *for* an offering made by fire, for a sweet savour unto the Lord. And the flesh of them shall be thine, as the wave breast and as the right shoulder are thine. All the heave offerings of the holy [piled] things, which the children of Israel offer unto the Lord, have I given thee, and thy sons and thy daughters with thee, by a statute forever: *it is* a covenant of salt for ever before the Lord unto thee and to thy seed with thee.'

In 1Kgs. and 2Chr. though there is a contradiction in how the 'house of the Lord' was built by Solomon, with 1Kgs. stating olivewood doors separated the 'most holy place' but in 2Chr. it is said he used a 'veil' to separate the 'most holy place', it is important to remember the translation is wrong and what the original authors are talking about covering or separating is actually 'piled upon piles' i.e. food substances, i.e. the 'place' is where the offerings were stored and used.

During those times, and even in current times especially in rural areas, these piles or heaps are precious: grain, meat, oil, wine, etc. and need to be properly stored, not allowed to be soiled, contaminated or spoiled by the elements—which is why imagery of cherubim wings covering them has been used to indicate how precious these heaps/stores of things are, and whether it was olivewood doors or a veil/curtain (the real meaning of the word which has been translated as 'curtain/veil' may be another mistranslation/ misinterpretation of what is actually meant in the original language by the word) the story reflects how practically, as in real life, valuable vital resources such as grain, flour, meat would be protected from unhygienic or spoiling elements as well as using magical, mystical imagery of cherubim wings meeting like a cover symbolising the importance of what is heaped in piles below them.

In Lev.16 the meaning of 'qodesh/kodesh' which is erroneously taken as 'holy' proves it is actually 'piled/piles/heaps'. Aaron is warned not to enter the 'holy place' (which I should point out that not even 'place' is mentioned in that misinterpreted phrase) which should read 'piled on piles' until he is ordered to come in wearing garments—which are special because they allow the slaughter, cutting up, waving, and moving around without exposing the genitals (a sin) so are not 'holy garments' 'holy linen coat' but 'piled/piles garment' 'piled/piles linen coat', i.e. special garments to be worn when performing the rituals which revolve around the piles of meat, grain, flour, etc.—and when bringing in the sacrificial animals which will become piles of meat whether they are eaten or taken away to be burnt far out from the place of process.

Lev.16 also states that in the 'holy place' (the piled piles 'place') is where the heaps of all the sins and transgressions will be placed on a goat's head, i.e. the wrongdoing/sins of the people is piled onto the goat's soul to bear instead of the people—so the authors and text are still speaking about piles and heaps: the scapegoat is first piled with all of Israel's sins, iniquities, transgressions while the goat is still inside the 'piled' place before being sent away—the significance of the place (tabernacle/altar/Lord's house) is not from who is in it, but by *what* is in it, its quality and abundance reflected in how it is stored, and what is done to what is in it, not a 'holy' place, but the piles stored inside.

Levites, Aaron and his sons gain importance, not because they are Aaron and related to Aaron, but because of the exclusive privilege they are allowed by entering and making contact with the heaped piles offered to the Lord, and their services which include coming into contact, gathering, processing, being responsible for accumulating and/or taking care of the heaps of produce to be offered even if they are not allowed into the 'holy[piled] place' as 1Chr.6 states the Levites are in the service of the tabernacle, but only Aaron and his sons work in the 'piled upon piles' or as mistranslated 'place most holy'. 'Their brethren also the Levites *were* appointed unto all manner of service of the tabernacle of the house of God. But Aaron and his sons offered upon the altar of the burnt offering, and on the altar of incense, *and were appointed* for all the work of the *place* most holy, and to make an atonement for Israel, according to all that Moses the servant of God had commanded.'

Also 1Chr.23 '...and Aaron was separated, that he should sanctify the most holy things, he and his sons forever, to burn incense before the Lord, to minister unto him, and to bless in his name forever...These *were* the sons of Levi after the house of their fathers; *even* the chief of the fathers, as they were counted by number of names by their polls, that did the work for the service of the house of the Lord, from the age of twenty years and upward...For by the last words of David the Levites were numbered from twenty years and above: Because their office *was* to wait on the sons of Aaron for the service of the house of the Lord, in the courts, and in the chambers, and in the purifying of all holy things, and the work of the service of the house of God; Both for the shewbread, and for the fine flour for the meat offering, and for the unleavened cakes, and for *that which is baked in* the pan, and for that which is fried, and for all manner of measure and size; And to stand every morning to thank and praise the Lord, and likewise at even; And to offer all burnt sacrifices unto the Lord in the sabbaths, in the new moons, and on the set feasts, by number, according to the order commanded unto them, continually before the Lord: And that they should keep the charge of the tabernacle of the congregation, and the charge of the holy *place*, and the charge of the sons of Aaron their brethren, in the service of the house of the Lord.'. It is because of what is inside/stored/offered which gives importance to both the place and the designated people (Aarons/Levites) working in contact with these stores. It is about piled stores/offerings, piles and heaps of flour, oil, bread, cakes, meat. 'qodesh/mekadesh' does not mean 'holy' but is the importance of piled and heaped food stores.

2Chr.7:7 further proves the word 'qodesh' is 'piled/pile/piles' and it is the piling of sacrificial goods (be it animals or crop) which gives the place its importance and adjective-name. As Solomon hallows the middle of the court outside 'the Lord's house' which was not 'holy'—but it tells us he 'hallowed' it, it became 'hallowed' because Solomon made many offerings which were too much than to fit in the altar Solomon had made—therefore the place where animals/meat/fat was piled and lots of blood spilled became 'hallowed/holy' ('piled/piles') only because offerings were piled there, and again you have to remember all these words translated as 'hallowed' 'sanctify' 'holy' are just one word in the original language in its different tenses, suffixes, prefixes, but it is always the word 'piled/qodesh/كدش', and another word sometimes used in the OT for 'sanctified/consecrated/etc.' is: ml'a; ملئ 'filled' and is the same meaning as piling, stacking, heaping, e.g. Aaron's 'holy/hqdsh garments' are to be his sons to be 'consecrated/ml'a in them'.

Note how the authors of the Biblical stories restrict the sacrificing, sanctifying, slaughter of offerings to the priests—but here it shows again the importance is not who does it, but the significance is in the 'piled' sacrifices and offerings, which is how although Solomon is not a priest, the mere fact the altar was not large enough to handle the abundance of piles of sacrifices, the court outside which was insignificant gained 'hallowed[piled]' status because he had to use it to accommodate the quantity of sacrifices as per the story: 'Moreover Solomon hallowed the middle of the court that *was* before the house of the Lord: for there he offered burnt offerings, and the fat of the peace offerings, because the brasen altar which Solomon had made was not able to receive the burnt offerings, and the meat offerings, and the fat.'

In 2Chr.24 the importance of the Levites in gathering/piling everything needed for the 'house of the Lord' is emphasised again. Their importance is because they are responsible for gathering money in abundance, for preparing vessels and goods in abundance. It also shows the importance of the place is because of what is brought into it, stored in it. It is only after the Levites collect great amounts of money, when vessels are made for use in offerings, and when burnt offerings resume that the 'house of God' is restored to its importance:

'And it came to pass after this, *that* Joash was minded to repair the house of the Lord. And he gathered together the priests and the Levites, and said to them, Go out unto the cities of Judah, and gather of all Israel money to repair the house of your God from year to year, and see that ye hasten the matter. Howbeit the Levites hastened *it* not. And the king called for Jehoiada the chief, and said unto him, Why hast not thou required of the Levites to bring in out of Judah, and out of Jerusalem the collection, *according to the commandment* of Moses servant of the Lord, and of the congregation of Israel, for the tabernacle of witness?...And at the king's commandment they made a chest, and set it without at the gate of the house of the Lord. And they made a proclamation through Judah and Jerusalem, to bring in to the Lord the collection *that* Moses servant of God *laid* upon Israel in the wilderness. And all the princes and all the people rejoiced, and brought in, and cast into the chest, until they had made an end. Now it came to pass, that at what time the chest was brought unto the king's office by the hand of the Levites, and when they saw that *there was* much money, the king's scribe and the priest's high officer came and emptied the chest, and took it, and carried it to his place again. Thus they did day by day, and gathered money in abundance...So the workmen wrought, and the work was perfected by them, and they set the house of God in his state, and strengthened it. And when they finished *it*, they brought the rest of the money before the king and Jehoiada, whereof were made vessels for the house of the Lord, *even* vessels to minister, and to offer *withal*, and spoons, and vessels of gold and silver. And they offered burnt offerings in the house of the Lord continually all the days of Jehoiada.' Therefore, store, the importance of the Levites and even the 'house of the Lord', is when there are piles of money, abundances of offerings, and heaps of vessels.

Also, in 2Chr. when a king begins to sacrifice and present offerings in places other than the 'house of the Lord' he is depicted as a bad king and significance is attached to presenting offerings elsewhere other than the 'house of the Lord' because it lessens the quantity, the abundance which should be presented at the 'house of the Lord'. Remember the importance is in the meaning of and description by the word 'qodesh haqqodashim' ('piled, I will pile them/it/the'), 'qodesh' (pile(s)) and 'led/of being led'), so taking away to offer and sacrifice in other places is shown in the story to leave the 'house of the Lord' neglected, and to deplete or divert away the offerings and tithes from it is a 'sin' and great wrong. This can be seen in 2Chr. especially 2Chr.28 where 'king Ahaz' (whose name means 'took/took or takes a lot') not only commits the same sins as previous kings of Israel of burning incense on high hills and making sacrifices, but he also takes from the stored goods in the 'house of the Lord' to give to another king and to go sacrifice and offer elsewhere—therefore his greatest sin is that he lessened from the 'pile/qodesh' which is central to the importance of the place:

'He sacrificed also and burnt incense in the high places, and on the hills, and under every green tree...For the Lord brought Judah low because of Ahaz king of Israel; for he made Judah naked, and transgressed sore against the Lord...For Ahaz took away a portion *out* of the house of the Lord, and *out* of the house of the king, and of the princes and gave *it* unto the king of Assyria: but he helped him not. And in the time of his distress did he trespass yet more against the Lord: this *is that* king of Ahaz. For he sacrificed unto the gods of Damascus, which smote him: and he said, Because the gods of the kings of Syria help them, *therefore* will I sacrifice to them, that they may help me. But they were the ruin of him, and of all Israel. And Ahaz gathered together the vessels of the house of God, and cut in pieces the vessels of the house of God, and shut up the doors of the house of the Lord, and he made him altars in every corner of Jerusalem. And in every several city of Judah he made high places to burn incense unto other gods, and provoked to anger the Lord God of his fathers.' Therefore, in the Biblical stories depleting from the stores of what is offered to the 'correct' god and offering in places other than the correct place is wrong because the importance lies in the abundance of goods to be offered.

Conversely, following kings who are bad because they deplete and lessen what is piled in the 'house of the Lord', the good kings always do the exact opposite: they accumulate great piles in the 'house' whether an abundance of money, abundance of sacrificial animals and all other goods which go along with presenting offerings such as flour, bread, oil, wine, incense. Significance is restored to the place by piling high the sacrifices, goods, and its utensils—the 'good' of the king is because he is restoring the piles of goods significant and central to the importance of the place and the story.

Following Ahaz destroying the importance of the 'house' by taking from its stored goods, in 2Chr.29 his son Hezekiah does the complete opposite, and again the importance of piles and abundance of everything related to the offerings shows how it is this concept: 'piled high/piles' = qodesh/كدش and is the meaning and significance of the place and story; 'piled' not 'holy/sanctified/consecrated'. 'qodesh haqqodashim' is 'piled high/piled on piles/piles upon piles' 'piled, I will pile them/it/the' not 'most holy/holy of holies'.

Hezekiah denounces the fathers who did not burn incense nor burn offerings 'in the holy place' (which should read 'in the piled high/piled upon piles') and the story goes on to show what makes the 'holy place' (which should be 'piled high') important is piles of sacrifices and other offerings: vessels are piled in front of the altar; to begin with, seven bullocks, seven rams, seven lambs, and seven hegoats all sacrificed and offered in the 'house', followed by hundreds of bullocks, rams, lambs, thousands of oxen and sheep—it is all about abundant piles of food sources offered in the place which takes its name from these substances 'm'kaddesh/piled high'.

A simple way to show how mistranslation and misinterpretation has made the word 'piled' into 'holy/consecrated' can be seen in the following sentence and elsewhere in the Bible where the correct word is more logical:

- And the **consecrated** things were six hundred oxen and three thousand sheep.
- And the **piled** things were six hundred oxen and three thousand sheep.
- And the **hakkadoshim** were six hundred oxen and three thousand sheep.

Throughout the Bible, OT and NT, character and place names are made to reflect and relay with what the character will do and/or what events will unfold in the story. With regards to what has been misnomered as 'the most holy place' and 'holy of holies' and 'holy', it is 'qodesh haqqodashim/kodesh hakkodashim' and the correct meaning is 'piled high/piles upon piles/piled, I will pile them/it/the' 'lead/led, I will lead them/it/the', and it is the heaps and piles and abundance of piled goods reflected in every part of the stories where it is mentioned:

'And said unto them, Hear me, ye Levites, sanctify now yourselves, and sanctify the house of the Lord God of your fathers, and carry forth the filthiness out of the holy *place*. For our fathers have trespassed, and done *that which was* evil in the eyes of the Lord our God, and have forsaken him, and have turned away their faces from the habitation of the Lord, and turned their backs. Also they have shut up the doors of the porch, and put out the lamps, and have not burned incense nor offered burnt offerings in the holy *place* unto the God of Israel.'

'Then they went into Hezekiah the king, and said, We have cleansed all the house of the Lord, and the altar of burnt offering, with all the vessels thereof, and the shewbread table with all the vessels thereof. Moreover all the vessels, which king Ahaz in his reign did cast away in his transgression, have we prepared and sanctified, and, behold, they *are* before the altar of the Lord. Then Hezekiah the king rose early, and gathered the rulers of the city, and went up to the house of the Lord. And they brought seven bullocks, and seven rams, and seven lambs, and seven hegoats, for a sin offering for the kingdom, and for the sanctuary, and for Judah. And he commanded the priests the sons of Aaron to offer *them* on the altar of the Lord. So they killed the bullocks, and the priests received the blood, and sprinkled *it* on the altar: they killed also the lambs, and they sprinkled the blood upon the altar. And they brought forth the hegoats *for* the sin offering before the king and the congregation; and they laid their hands upon them:' Note when they touch the hegoats they are piling their sins (transferring) on to the hegoat which will be sacrificed in their stead—the act is piling on the sins to another from the idea that a person carries his/her sins like a load: 'And the priests killed them, and they made reconciliation with their blood upon the altar, to make an atonement for all of Israel: for the king commanded *that* the burnt offering and the sin offering *should be made* for all Israel...Then Hezekiah answered and said, Now ye have consecrated yourselves unto the Lord, come near and bring sacrifices and thank offerings into the house of the Lord. And the congregation brought in sacrifices and thank offerings; and as many as were of a free heart burnt offerings. And the number of the burnt offerings, which the congregation brought, was threescore and ten bullocks, an hundred rams, *and* two hundred lambs: all these *were* for a burnt offering to the Lord. And the consecrated things *were* six hundred oxen and three hundred sheep.'

In the following verses the Biblical authors show how important the piles and abundance of things are, it not only shows the importance is the piles of sacrifices, but also how the piled things are what give the people a 'specialness' who are allowed to handle these things and perform these rituals and this is displayed by allowing the Levites to assist Aaron and his sons to touch and perform the rituals of sacrificing and offering the piled things when need be: 'But the priests were too few, so that they could not flay all the burnt offerings: wherefore their brethren the Levites did help them, till the work was ended, and until the *other* priests had sanctified themselves: for the Levites *were* more upright in heart to sanctify themselves than the priests. And also the burnt offerings *were* in abundance, with the fat of the peace offerings, and the drink offerings for every burnt offering. So the service of the house of the Lord was set in order. And Hezekiah rejoiced, and all the people, that God had prepared the people: for the thing was *done* suddenly.'

The authors make a point so the audience understands the importance is the abundance of offerings and not the ruler, and this too serves to show the importance of the 'piles/piled on piles'. Although Hezekiah is a good king who gives and makes the people give to the house of God in abundance, in 2Kgs.20 Hezekiah's wrong, and postponed punishment, is because he showed Babylonian visitors all his treasures and stored goods, which would result in a grave punishment, foretold by Isaiah first, of which is everything he and his fathers had 'stored' would be taken away by invading kings. This makes it clear not to let anyone go near stored resources and treasures as much as the things in the 'house of God'.

2Chr.30-31 continue to show the 'holiness' is actually the abundance of piles of produce offered at the house, exemplified by massive feasts, multitudes of people, and thousands of bullocks and sheep, therefore piles of meat, blood, flour, oil, wine—piles offered at the 'piled(place)'. 2Chr.31 stress the theme of the story to show how piles of produce are accumulated in the 'house of the Lord', and how this piling of goods is important to the place by making the characters who give are 'good', people of moral standing. In the earlier explanation and translation of 2Chr.31, the meaning of the character in charge of these heaps of produce is a compound word and wordplay 'Cononiah' which means gather into peaked heaps/pile it into peaked heaps/take inside to shield from weather/elements' (see Cononiah). It is the compound word-name given to the character in charge of the heaps of grain, oil, wine, honey, oxen, sheep, everything brought in and piled—remember 'qodesh' is 'piled heaps' and not 'holy'—into the 'house of the Lord'.

The authors of the Bible use made-up names to emphasise the meaning, themes and events of the stories. The 'm'kadesh' 'qodesh haqqodashim' erroneously translated as 'most holy' is 'piled on piles' and the stories keep on pointing this out, over and over again: what is important is piles of produce for offerings: 'Moreover he commanded the people that dwelt in Jerusalem to give the portion of the priests and the Levites, that they might be encouraged in the law of the Lord. And as soon as the commandment came abroad, the children of Israel brought in abundance the firstfruits of corn, wine, and oil, and honey, and of all the increase of the field; and the tithe of all *things* brought in they abundantly. And *concerning* the children of Israel and Judah, that dwelt in the cities of Judah they also brought in the tithes of oxen and sheep, and the tithes of holy things which were consecrated unto the Lord their God, and laid them by heaps. In the third month they began to lay the foundation of the heaps, and finished *them* in the seventh month. And when Hezekiah and the princes came and saw the heaps, they blessed the Lord, and his people Israel. Then Hezekiah questioned with the priests and the Levites concerning the heaps. And Azariah the chief priest of the house of Zadok answered him, and said, Since *the people* began to bring the offerings into the house of the Lord, we have had enough to eat, and have left plenty: for the Lord hath blessed his people; and that which is left *is* this great store. Then Hezekiah commanded to prepare chambers in the house of the Lord; and they prepared *them*, and brought in the offerings and the tithes and the dedicated *things* faithfully: over which Cononiah the Levite *was* ruler, and Shimei his brother *was* the next.' And the chapter goes on to show how abundance and piling offerings are an act of good people, good kings, and piling heaps of produce in the 'piled upon piles' is in the service of God.

In Lamentations, the desolation and punishment of Israel is in the form of scarcity of food (the opposite of 'm'kadesh/qodesh/piled). Even the punishment in the form of throwing down people and buildings gives imagery of heaps, but more importantly the suffering is portrayed as the opposite of 'piled/

m'kadesh'—there is no longer food and drink; the young and old, the commoner and the priests are all starving. And the reason for this punishment is given: they allowed 'strangers' into the 'house of the Lord' to lay their hands on what was inside—and what was inside: m'kadesh/qodesh things '['holy']piled' things. Therefore allowing strangers access to 'piled' things i.e. food stores resulted in its depletion and the subsequent punishment of the locals: Lam.1:4 'The ways of Zion do mourn, because none come to the solemn feasts: all her gates are desolate: her priests sigh, her virgins are afflicted, and she *is* in bitterness'. There is no longer produce for feasts. Lam.1:6 '...her princes are become like harts *that* find no pasture, and they are gone without strength before the pursuer.' No more piles of produce, they are hungry and weak. 'Jerusalem remembered in the days of her affliction and of her miseries all her pleasant things that she had in the days of old...' Lam.1:7. The pleasant things remembered are the 'piled/qodesh' things as later in the story we are told the pleasant things were what was inside the 'Lord's house'. Lam.1:10 'The adversary hath spread out his hand upon all her pleasant things: for she hath seen that the heathen entered into her sanctuary...' The sanctuary being the 'qodesh/piled' place.

Lam.1:11 'All the people sigh, they seek bread; they have given their pleasant things for meat to relieve the soul...' Lam.1:19 '...mine priest and mine elders gave up the ghost in the city, while they sought their meat to relieve their souls...' Even priests are dying of starvation—the priests who once had first access and the choice pick of qodesh things (piled things). The desolation is because there is no longer 'piled' things.

Lam.2 portrays God punishing the people by throwing down, casting down to the ground, the virgins and daughters are sitting on the ground; palaces, strongholds, places of assembly, gates, all kinds of structures are cast down and destroyed conjuring the word-imagery of heaps of rubble, a negative 'pile/qodesh'. In Lam.2 this is contrasted by the question, narrated by babies and children dizzy with hunger, and by the answer of 'where has the food gone' i.e. where did the piled abundance go: 'They say to their mothers, Where is corn and wine? when they swooned as the wounded in the streets of the city, when their soul was poured out into their mother's bosom.'

In Ezra, the stories of the rebuilding of 'God's house', again much stock is put on the abundance of meat, wheat, wine, etc. emphasising the hundreds of bullocks, rams, lambs, wheat, salt, wine, oil 'for the burnt offerings of the God of heaven...' Ezra.6:9,17, on silver and gold abundantly as free will offerings, Ezra7:15-23; 8:24-30,35—everything related to the house/place is in abundant piles 'And that which they have need of, both young bullocks and rams, and lambs, for the burnt offerings of the God of heaven, wheat, salt, wine, and oil, according to the appointment of the priests which *are* at Jerusalem, let it be given them day by day without fail: That they may offer sacrifices of sweet savour unto the God of heaven...And offered at the dedication of the house of God an hundred bullocks, two hundred rams, four hundred lambs; and for a sin offering for all Israel, twelve hegoats, according to the number of tribes in Israel...And to carry the silver and gold, which the king and his counsellor have freely offered unto the God of Israel...And all the silver and gold that thou canst find in all the provinces of Babylon, with the freewill offering of the people, and of the priests, offering willingly for the house of their God...That thou mayest buy speedily with this money bullocks, rams, lambs, with their meat offerings, and offer them upon the altar of the house of your God...The vessels also that are given thee for the service of the house of thy God, *those* deliver thou before the God of Jerusalem.'

The specialness of the 'house of God' is the piles of goods heaped and given. 'Unto an hundred talents of silver, and to an hundred measures of wheat, and to an hundred baths of wine, and to an hundred baths of oil, and salt without prescribing *how much*. Whatsoever is commanded by the God of heaven, let it be diligently done for the house of the God of heaven: for why should there be wrath against the realm of the king and his sons?...Then I separated twelve of the chief of priests, Sherebiah, Hashabiah, and ten of their brethren with them, And weighed unto them the silver, and the gold, and the vessels, *even* the offering of the house of our God, which the kings, and his counsellors, and his lords, and all Israel *there* present, had offered: I even weighed unto their hand six hundred and fifty talents of silver, and silver vessels an hundred talents, *and* of gold an hundred talents; Also twenty basons of gold, of a thousand drams, and two vessels of fine copper, precious as gold. And I said unto them, Ye *are* holy unto the Lord; the vessels *are* holy also: and the silver and the gold are a freewill offering unto the Lord God of your fathers. Watch ye, and keep them, until ye weigh *them* before the chief of the priests and the Levites, and chief of the fathers of Israel, in Jerusalem, in the chambers of the house of the Lord. So took the priests and the Levites the weight of the silver, and the gold, and the vessels, to bring *them* to Jerusalem unto the house of our God.' Note how the author has given two of the twelve priests tasked with delivering all these piles of gold, silver, copper and vessels compound word-names befitting their roles which also reflect the abundance of 'piled' things: Sherebiah 'bought-he/him', Hashabiah 'carried on waist-he/him' 'stuffed-he/him'.

'Now on the fourth day was the silver and the gold and the vessels weighed in the house of our God...By the number and by the weight of everyone: and all the weight was written at that time. *Also* the children of those that had been carried away, which were come out of the captivity, offered burnt offerings unto the God of Israel, twelve bullocks for all Israel, ninety and six rams, seventy and seven lambs, twelve he goats *for* a sin offering: all *this was* a burnt offering unto the Lord.' Everything 'holy' which should read 'piled' is in piles and great abundance.

Nehemia's Book also directly links an abundance and lots of meat, wine, oil, etc. not only to 'God's house' but also to the piety and 'goodness' of the person. Although Nehemiah asks God to think of him as 'good' for all he has done in rebuilding the house, and for all he has done for the people, the narration precedes with him asking God to think good of him by listing all the abundance of ox, sheep, fowls and wine, the abundance of food, at his own table: Neh.5:18–19 'Now *that* which was prepared *for me* daily *was* one ox and six choice sheep; also fowls were prepared for me, and once in ten days store of all sorts of wine; yet for all this required not I of the bread of the governor, because the bondage was heavy upon this people. Think upon me, my God, for good, *according* to all that I have done for this people.'

Neh.10 continues to show importance of bringing in piles of offerings to the sanctuary (piled upon piles/piled, I will pile them/it/the)/house of God, the importance and exclusivity Levites/Aaron priests have in handling and/or performing the rituals and storage of these piles of offerings: 'Also we made ordinances for us, to charge ourselves yearly with the third part of a shekel for the service of the house of our God; for the shewbread, and for the continual meat offering, and for the continual burnt offering, of the sabbaths, of the new moons, for the set feasts, and for the holy things,' remember 'holy' should read 'piled/qodesh' 'and for the sin offerings to make an atonement for Israel, and for all the work of the house of our God...And to bring the firstfruits of our ground, and the firstfruits of all fruit of all trees, year by year, unto the house of the Lord. Also the firstborn of our sons, and of our cattle, as *it is* written in the law, and the firstlings of our herds and of our flocks, to bring to the house of our God, unto the priests that minister in the house of our God: And *that* we should bring the firstfruits of our dough, and our offerings, and the fruit of all manner of trees, of wine and of oil, unto the priests, to the chambers of the house of our God; and the tithes of our ground unto the Levites, that the same Levites might have the tithes in all the cities of our tillage. And the priest the son of Aaron shall be with the Levites, when the Levites takes tithes: and the Levites shall bring up the tithe of the tithes unto the house of our God, to the chambers, into the treasure house. For the children of Israel and the children of Levi shall bring the offering of the corn, of the new wine, and the oil, unto the chambers, where *are* the vessels of the sanctuary, and the priests that minister, and the porters, and the singers: and we will not forsake the house of our God.' To forsake the 'house of God' is to stop supplying the offerings in abundance.

In the story of Nehemiah's anger at Eliashib the priest over installing his ally Tobiah in one of the chambers in the 'house of God', the anger is not because he opposed Nehemiah, but because he has taken up space in the 'temple' which should be for piling and storing only the qodesh things, 'piled' things, so he is occupying space instead of the food produce for offerings. The meaning of Tobiah's name and how the story narrates his expulsion and the reasons why are also related to the proper meaning of the word mistranslated as 'temple' which will be explained later.

Neh.13:4–9 'And before this, Eliashib the priest, having the oversight of the chamber of the house of our God, *was* allied unto Tobiah: And he had prepared for him a great chamber, where aforetime they laid the meat offerings, the frankincense, and the vessels, and the tithes of the corn, and the new wine, and the oil, which was commanded *to be given* to the Levites, and the singers, and the porters, and the offerings of the priests. But in all this time was not I in Jerusalem: for in the two and thirtieth year of Artaxerxes king of Babylon came I unto the king, and after certain days obtained I leave of the king: And I came to Jerusalem, and understood of the evil that Eliashib did for Tobiah, in preparing him a chamber in the courts of the house of God. And it grieved me sore: therefore I cast forth all the household stuff of Tobiah out of the chamber. Then I commanded and they cleansed the chambers: and thither brought I again the vessels of the house of God, with the meat offering and the frankincense.' The story repeats again Nehemiah asking God to consider him 'good' after he lists an abundance of tithes, corn, wine, oil, he organises to be brought to the Levites and to the house of God: 'Remember me, O my God, concerning this, and wipe out not my good deeds that I have done for the house of my God, and for the offices thereof.' Neh.13:10–14.

Nehemiah's story also highlights the problem with marrying 'strangers', which is the same problem presented in Solomon's marriage of 'strange' women who caused him to sin (although he is presented as the greatest king of Israel): Solomon's sin was he began to burn incense, sacrifice and present offerings at 'high places' i.e. other than the designated 'qodesh haqqodashim/'piled, I will pile them/it/the' place—he was using resources, i.e. animals, crop, fruit, incense, wine, oil, etc. at these different places, therefore decreasing the piles of the 'holy/piled place' of the 'correct god'; and in the same manner marrying strangers who worship different gods or have different places of worship negatively affects the supply of produce to the 'house of the Lord' and the priests. Neh.13:23-20 'Did not Solomon king of Israel sin by these things? yet among many nations there was no king like him, who was beloved of his God, and God made him king over all Israel: nevertheless even him did outlandish women cause him to sin. Shall we then hearken unto you to do this great evil, to transgress against our God in marrying strange wives?'.

In the story, Nehemiah's character is the cause of bringing great quantities of gold, silver, sacrificial animals to the 'house of God'; in the narration he credits himself for the restoration of the services in the 'house of God', for setting things right. But still, every time he asks God to remember him as 'good', for his good deeds, he first mentions specific things and amounts he has piled/accumulated for 'God's house' and its rituals—which is how Nehemiah's book ends: Neh.13:31 'And for the wood offering, at times appointed, and for the firstfruits. Remember me, O my God, for good.'

Ezekiel's story continues to prove the piety and goodness are when the sanctuary/house are piled with offerings the way God (in the story) wants them to be. But when people sin/defile the 'sanctuary', the punishment is starvation and death by various brutal means which the narration plays on the meaning of the word 'kadesh/qodesh' 'falling with a heavy sound like a heap on the ground' and 'piles'.

Ezek.5:11 'Wherefore, as I live, saith the Lord God; Surely, because thou hast defiled my sanctuary with all thy detestable things [this also plays on the meaning of Ezekiel which is made swallow something unpleasant and the things in the sanctuary are food produce], and with all thine abominations, therefore will I also diminish thee: neither shall mine eyes spare, neither will I have any pity. A third part of thee shall die with the pestilence, and with famine shall they be consumed in the midst of thee: and a third part shall fall by the sword round about thee; and I will scatter a third part into all the winds, and I will draw out a sword after them...Moreover I will make thee waste, and a reproach among the nations that *are* round about thee...When I shall send upon them the evil arrows of famine, which shall be for their destruction, and which I will send to destroy you: and I will increase the famine upon you, and will break your staff of bread: So will I send upon you famine and evil beasts, and they shall bereave thee; and pestilence and blood shall pass through thee; and I will bring the sword upon thee. I the Lord hath spoken it.' Goodness, piety and good fortune are when the 'sanctuary' (correctly 'piled upon piles') is filled with offerings. When things are done wrong, or cease to be done, at the 'sanctuary', the punishment is the exact opposite of piles and plenty: famine, destruction, and death, with the greater emphasis put on starvation/famine.

The theme of hunger and starvation as punishment for 'defiling' the place dedicated for 'qodesh/piled' things continues in Ezek.7 allowing robbers to enter and 'defile' it (meaning to steal its resources/stores) because the people made images of idols and therefore were probably sacrificing to them—so again, the sin is depletion of stored produce and objects for the 'correct' god going to others: 'The sword is without, and the pestilence and the famine within: he that *is* in the field will die with the sword; and he that *is* in the city, pestilence and famine will devour him...They shall cast their silver in the streets, and their gold shall be removed: their silver and their gold shall not be able to deliver them in the day of the wrath of the Lord: they shall not satisfy their souls, neither fill their bowels: because it is the stumbling block of their iniquity. As for the beauty of his ornament, he set it in majesty: but they made the images of their abominations *and* of their detestable things therein; therefore have I set it far from them...My face will I also turn from them, *and* they shall pollute my secret place: for the robbers shall enter into it and defile it.'

God's punishment in Ezekiel continues in the house of God and the surrounding environment—even the slain are to be piled in the 'holy[mistranslation]/qodesh/piled' places: Ezek.9 'And to the others he said in mine hearing, Go ye after him through the city, and smite: let not your eye spare, neither have ye pity: Slay utterly old *and* young, both maids, and little children, and women: but come not near upon any man upon whom *is* the mark; and begin at my sanctuary. Then they began at the ancient men which *were* before the house. And he said unto them, Defile the house, and fill the courts with the slain: go ye forth. And they went forth and slew in the city.'

Ezek.11 begins with the mention of Ezekiel arriving at the 'east gate of the Lord's house' remember the Lord's house is the 'qodesh/piled' 'qodesh haqqodashim/'piled, I will pile them/it/the' place, and his arrival at God's house is followed by imagery of heaps of slain people filling the streets: piles/heaps; people falling by the sword: the sound and image of 'qodesh/كَدِش/'falling like a heap with a sound': 'Moreover the spirit lifted me up, and brought me to the east gate of the Lord's house...Ye have multiplied your slain in this city, and ye have filled the streets thereof with the slain. Therefore thus saith the Lord God, Your slain whom ye have laid in the midst of it, they *are* the flesh, and this city *is* the caldron:' and although it ties in with an earlier sign of a boiling/seething pot in the Ezekiel story, it is still the authors using the same punishment for the sin of not providing the food supplies or taking away from the food supplies in a metaphor where the sin was depriving God of 'food offerings' and the punishment is the people are now likened to meat being slaughtered and cooked. 'but I will bring you forth out of the midst of it. Ye have feared the sword; and I will bring a sword upon you, saith the Lord God. And I will bring you out of the midst thereof, and deliver you to the hands of strangers, and will execute judgements among you. Ye shall fall by the sword; I will judge you in the border of Israel; and ye shall know that I *am* the Lord, for ye have not walked in my statutes, neither executed my judgements, but hath done after the manner of the heathen that *are* round about you. And it came to pass when I prophesied Pelatiah the son of Benaiah died.' As before 'pelatiah' means 'fell/he/him' and the event and choice of character was for its link to 'kadesh/qodesh/ falling with a sound', and also Hezekiah throws himself to the ground 'on his face'—all these names and events in this story reinforce the meaning of qodesh/piled/fell like a heap with sound.

The importance of keeping the resources of stored offerings and not to sacrifice to other gods is exemplified in Ezek.16 in an analogy of a 'whorish woman' (Jerusalem) which God nurtured and loved and gave many precious fabrics, jewels and food, all in abundance (qodesh/piles): 'Thus wast thou decked with gold and silver; and thy raiment *was* of fine linen, and silk, and broidered work; thou didst eat fine flour, and honey, and oil, and thou wast exceeding beautiful, and thou didst prosper into a kingdom.' But when all these good things are piled onto her and for her, the narration again focuses on 'piled things' because when the woman/city's fornications are described it is depicted as the sins of earlier stories and other books: she begins to divert the 'piled things' to other gods in high places, to give to foreign lovers of them, all depicted as fornication, i.e. the 'piled things' that are supposed to go to God are given to other gods: 'But thou didst trust in thine own beauty, and played the harlot because of thine renown, and pouredst out thine fornications on every one that passed by; his it was. And of thy garments thou didst take, and deckdst thy high places with divers colours, and playedst the harlot thereupon: *the like things* shall not come, neither shall it be *so*. Thou hast also taken thy fair jewels of my gold and of my silver, which I had given thee, and madest to thyself images of men, and didst commit whoredom with them, And tookedst thy broidered garments and coverdst them: and thou hast set mine oil and mine incense before them, My meat also which I gave thee, fine flour, and oil and honey *wherewith* I fed thee, thou hast even set it before them for a sweet savour and thus it was saith the Lord God.' Note: mine gold, mine silver, mine meat and so forth: the sacrifices meant to be offered to the correct 'god' being offered to idols.

The theme of giving away from god's stores continues with 'his' children being sacrificed to the fire of foreign idols, i.e. they are led to worship other gods with all the offerings which go with it, figuratively heightened in the emphasis as the sacrifice of his children by the 'whorish woman/Jerusalem' to other idols. The example is they are being fed and eaten just like animal sacrifices are made to gods, and so the children too symbolise God's stores of food as they are meant to work the land as adults and provide the food produce to be 'qodesh/piled'. 'Moreover thou hast taken thy sons and thy daughters, whom thou hast borne unto me, and these hast thou sacrificed unto them to be devoured. Is this of thy whoredoms a small matter, That thou hast slain my children, and delivered them to cause them to pass through *the fire* for them?'

Mentioning the 'high places' is because the wrongdoing is using resources which should be piled in the correct 'qodesh' place, as 'high places' is where sacrifices, offerings, incense burning are performed 'And it came to pass after all thy wickedness, (woe, woe, unto thee! Saith the Lord God;) that thou hast built unto thee an eminent place, and hast made thee an high place in every street. Thou hast built thy high place at every head of the way, and hast made thy beauty to be abhorred, and hast opened thy feet to every one that passed by, and multiplied thy whoredoms.' And as punishment for wasting her 'beauty' (her resources), God will first punish by creating a lack of food—which is the prime resource of the piles of offerings: 'Behold, therefore I have stretched out my hand over thee and have diminished thy ordinary food…'.

The author(s) make an important clarification in this story just in case there is any misunderstanding: they make clear that the whoring and fornication is the wasting and diverting of the food resources which are meant to be piled for the qodesh place and rituals, and they do this by pointing out that whores are usually paid for their services, but Jerusalem, symbolised as a prostitute, pays and rewards those who use her body by giving them all the produce and jewels, etc. meant for the rituals to the correct god: 'How weak is thine heart, saith the Lord God, seeing thou doest all these things, the work of an imperious whorish woman; In that thou buildest thine eminent place in the head of every way; and makest thine high place in every street; and hast not been as an harlot, in that thou scornest hire. But as a wife that committeth adultery, which taketh strangers instead of her husband [this is an analogy that God (symbolised also earlier in the story) is the husband who consummated with sex his marriage to Jerusalem: a wife serves food to her husband, the analogy is not about sex, but the fornication is offering the food stuffs to other gods]! They give gifts to all whores, but thou givest thy gifts to all thy lovers, and hirest them that they may come unto thee on every side for thy whoredom. And the contrary is in thee from other women in thy whoredoms; whereas none follow thee to commit whoredoms; and in that thou givest a reward, and no reward is given unto thee, therefore thou art contrary.'

Ezek.20:16-39 continues to show offerings and sacrifices made in different places is wrongdoing: the pollution of statutes and defilement is serving other idols: 'For when I had brought them into the land, for the which I lifted up mine hand to give it to them, then they saw every high hill, and all the thick trees, and they offered there their sacrifices, and there they presented the provocation of their offerings, there also they made their sweet savour, and poured out their drink offerings. Then I said unto them, What *is* the high place where unto ye go? And the name thereof is called Bama to this day.' The pollution/transgression is they have made offerings in other places, to other idols; therefore they are still worshipping the 'correct god' (in the story), but he no longer wants their gifts/offerings if they are dividing them; lessening them in quantity is 'polluting' 'his holy name' remember the correct word is 'qodesh/m'qodesh' (and not 'holy') so they are 'polluting' i.e. lessening the importance which is the quantity of offerings of his 'piled/heaps name': 'As for you, O house of Israel, thus saith the Lord God; Go ye, serve ye every one his idols, and hereafter *also*, if ye will not hearken unto me: but pollute ye my holy name no more with your gifts, and with your idols.' The 'holy name' which correctly is the 'piled name' gets its importance from the great piles dedicated only to it—if they are lessening its importance by diverting produce elsewhere, it wants nothing to do with them.

The point is made clearer in verse 40 that the right thing to do is to offer all offerings 'piled things' (not 'holy things') in the 'piled mountain' (not the 'holy mountain'); elucidating the significance is in piling great amounts of offerings. God is 'sanctified[wrong translation]' 'piled' when they give all offerings solely to him: 'For in mine holy mountain, in the mountain of the height of Israel, saith the Lord God, there shall all the house of Israel, all of them in the land, serve me: there will I accept them, and there will I require your offerings, and the firstfruits of your oblations, with all your holy things. I will accept you with your sweet savour, when I bring you out from the people, and gather you out of the countries wherein ye have been scattered; and I will be sanctified in you before the heathen.' Ezek.20:16-41.

Ezek.21, the 'holy places' correctly the 'piled/piles' is mentioned followed by the indiscriminate slaughter of both good and bad people - so it makes a story of piles of slain people after mentioning the 'holy place/piled/piles': 'Son of man, set thy face towards Jerusalem, and drop *thy word* toward the holy places, and prophecy against the land of Israel, And say to the land of Israel, Thus saith the Lord; Behold, I am against thee, and will draw forth my sword out of his sheath, and will cut out from thee the righteous and the wicked. Seeing then that I will cut off from thee the righteous and the wicked, therefore shall my sword go out of his sheath against all flesh from the south to the north. That all flesh may know that I the Lord hath drawn out my sword out of his sheath: it shall not return anymore.'

The story of Ezek.36:17-38 informs the reader that the children of Israel were punished because they worshipped idols instead of God, and because they 'profaned my holy name' which should read 'profaned my piled name' and this is done by worshipping other gods which definitely includes offerings to them. This is the insult to the 'piled name', lessening the offerings by presenting offerings to others—it is the act of piling things which is important in the story. When God changes his mind about the children of Israel, he tells them he does not do it for their sake, but for his 'holy[piled] name', and it is reflected in how he increases the fortunes and fertility of the land combining the meaning of heaps of produce to his 'holy/piled' name. He will also increase the people, and their description emphasises the importance of 'piled' erroneously described as 'holy' for the men will be a 'holy[piled] flock' filling the cities:

'Son of man, when the house of Israel dwelt in their own land, they defiled it by their own way and by their doings: their way was before me as the uncleanness of a removed woman...And when they entered unto the heathen, whither they went, they profaned my holy name.' meaning when they offered the piles of sacrifices to other gods or at other places, they would have described them as 'holy/piled places' thus insulting the 'holy/piled name'. '...when they said to them, These are the people of the Lord, and are gone forth out of his land. But I had pity for my holy name, which the house of Israel had profaned among the heathen, whither they went. Therefore say unto the house of Israel, Thus saith the Lord God; I do not this for your sakes, O house of Israel, but for mine holy name's sake, which ye have profaned among the heathen whither ye went. And I will sanctify my great name, which was profaned among the heathen, which ye have profaned in the midst of them; and the heathen shall know that I am the Lord, saith the Lord God, when I shall be sanctified in you before their eyes.'

So the significance is made clear: the 'people' are not important but the act of piling of offerings is—his name in this part of the narration is attached to the word 'piled' which is the real matter of importance to the authors of these Biblical stories throughout the OT. It cannot be stressed enough the words 'holy' and 'sanctified' are erroneous translations of the root word (kdsh/qdsh/kodesh/qodesh (with different prefixes and suffixes according to the narration)) which means 'piled' and 'lead' and the animals which are led to be sacrificed end up being 'kadesh/piled'. 'I will also save you from your uncleanness: and I will call for the corn, and will increase it, and lay no famine upon you.' Therefore 'uncleanness' is the opposite of 'qodesh/piled', and that opposite is the scarcity of food/produce: famine.

When God's decision is reversed, the ground will once again give abundant produce, which in turn means an abundance of offerings piled to God 'qodesh/kodesh': 'And I will multiply the fruit of the tree, and the increase of the field, that ye shall receive no more reproach of famine among the heathen. Then ye shall remember your own evil ways, and your doings that *were* not good, and shall lothe yourselves in your own sight for your iniquities and for your abominations. Not for your sakes do I *this*, saith the Lord God, be it known unto you; be ashamed and confounded for your own ways, O house of Israel...Thus said the Lord God; I will yet for this be inquired of by the house of Israel, to do *it* for them: I will increase them with men like a flock. As the holy flock, as the flock of Jerusalem in her holy feasts; so shall the waste cities be filled with flocks of men: and they shall know that I am the Lord.'

Ezek.37:15-28, in the example of piling together the sticks with the names of Judah/children of Israel/Joseph and Ephraim, and then combining the different tribes, the different nations mentioned above into one nation reinforced the importance of 'piling' to the authors of the Bible, and is further reinforced by describing how they will be 'multiplied' and this allows the 'sanctuary[should read piled/piles] to be among them, and that God will 'sanctify[pile]' Israel, i.e. when he combines them as one nation, when he multiplies their population and again linking it to the 'sanctuary[piled/piles]' all these are descriptions of 'piling' and 'heaps' of people, the words 'sanctify/sanctuary' are all 'qodesh/kodesh' meaning piled: 'And I will make them one nation in the land upon the mountains of Israel; and one king shall be king unto them all, and they shall be no more two nations, neither shall they be divided into two kingdoms any more at all...Moreover I will make a covenant of peace with them; it shall be an everlasting covenant with them: and I will place them, and multiply them, and will set my sanctuary in the midst of them forevermore...And the heathen shall know that I the Lord do sanctify Israel, when my sanctuary shall be in the midst of them for evermore.'

Ezek.38 intensifies the meanings of 'qodesh/makkadesh' in its different prefixes and suffixes (as explained at the beginning of 'Meaning of 'kadesh' 'qodesh' 'm'kaddesh' 'mekkadesh')', the name given to the people in the story 'Gog from Magog' means 'great crowds/huge number of people/something crammed full and over spilling/moving like a wave': **Gog** 'overcrowded' 'too many people than can fit in one area/room' 'over spilling with people/things'. **Magog** 'moves like a wave' and refers to an area or land filled with people or crop, that its movement looks like a current or wave. It describes something packed moving this way and that, especially a field full of crop, the same is applied describing huge crowds of people and/or the overcrowded hordes' movement which seems fluid like wind blowing crops this way and that, or the rolling of currents or waves. In the story, it is used to describe how a legendary horde of Gog from Magog came to battle and how their bodies will end up being piled-high needing years to dispose of and bury them all. Also, their significance in name and description is also linked to the events of what will happen to them in the story.

To begin with, their link to the meaning of 'qodesh/piled high' has already begun with their name, its meaning and then the description of their numbers. Secondly, the story tells us they are here to steal cattle, goods, silver and gold as spoils of war—in other words they are here to take what is meant to be piled 'qodesh' as offerings to God. This is such a grave transgression, wanting to take what is meant to be piled to God, that God's wrath will cause such a shaking of the land that even fish in the sea, birds in the sky, beasts in the field, reptiles and insects, and all mankind will feel it; the mountains and steep places and every wall will collapse—so even this is qodesh/kodesh as in 'heaps' and 'falling with a sound to the ground in a heap', so these meanings are in addition to 'heaps/piles' as the importance of the quantity of offered things. In this story even the hordes of Gog from Magog, the piling of their bodies 'sanctify God' which should read 'piling for God' (Ezek.38:16). It also shows the meanings of 'led/qodesh' which end up being 'piled/kodesh' as the story makes it clear God has made them come (led them here) just so that they end up being piled corpses; and God will pour/pile heaps of sufferance over Gog/Magog: pestilence, blood, rain, hailstones, fire, brimstone, and this too 'sanctifies[piles]' God (Ezek.38:22-23) '...when I shall be sanctified in thee, O Gog, before their eyes.' Meaning Gog's corpses will become the 'piled things' for God 'Thus I will magnify myself, and sanctify myself...'

Ezek.39 leaves no doubt that the piles of Gog's corpses, which will need months and years to all be found buried and disposed of because of their great numbers, are a 'piled/qodesh/mkadesh' sacrifice, exactly like piles/qodesh of sacrifices people make to God in the 'holy/piled place', except here it is God performing the ritual sacrifice with humans, and instead of priests and people eating the meat, it will be birds and beasts eating the flesh of the sacrificed Gog and drinking their blood. Note the story uses the same ritual of burnt offerings to dispose of all the weapons of Gog while God performs his own burnt offering ritual by sending fire to kill the people in Magog and other isles so they know he is the 'piled one' (or the 'holy one' as it is mistranslated in the Bible), repeating how he will make his 'holy/piled' name known by presenting the corpses of Gog as sacrifice to be eaten (just like offerings which priests are allowed to eat from) while the people in Magog and the isles are burnt completely (just like some burnt offerings are burnt completely by priests in the holy/piled offerings in the 'most holy place [which should read 'piled, I will pile them/it/the']'; the weapons are burned just like incense is offered and wood offerings in the usual rituals of the stories in the 'holy/piled place'.

It further emphasises the dead people in the fields are a sacrifice by God for fowls and beasts to eat from; the flesh and blood of fallen princes to eat from, even the fat of the corpses is mentioned—fat being an important offering in the 'holy/piled' rituals; the burning of spears and bows is set in the story exactly like a burnt offering, drink offering, meat offering, incense offering, and linked clearly and directly to God's 'holiness' which should read as God's 'piled/heaps'. Note earlier in Ezekiel's story it is all about punishing the children of Israel because they sacrificed to different gods/at different places, but when God forgives them it is when others come to steal from the produce which should be offered to him so he forgives the children of Israel and then 'sanctifies'/piles them and himself by a massive human sacrifice:

'Thou shalt fall upon the mountains of Israel, thou and all thy bands, and the people that is with thee: I will give thee to the ravenous birds of every sort, and to the beasts of the field to be devoured. Thou shalt fall upon the open field, for I have spoken *it*, saith the Lord God. And I will send a fire among Magog, and among them that dwell carelessly in the isles: and they shall know that I am the Lord. So will I make my holy name known in the midst of my people Israel; and I will not let *them* pollute my holy name any more; and the heathen shall know that I am the Lord, the Holy One in Israel. Behold, it is done, and it is done, saith the Lord God, this is the day whereof I have spoken. And they that dwell in the cities of Israel shall go forth, and shall set on fire and burn the weapons, both the shields and the bucklers, the bows and the arrows, and the hand staves and the spears, and they shall burn them with fire seven years.' You can imagine the image conjured up by the story that it takes seven years to burn their weapons of how many bodies are piled as sacrifice so as to show God is the 'Holy One' of which the correct translation is the 'Piled One'.

'So that they should take no wood out of the field, nor cut down *any* out of the forests; for they shall burn the weapons with fire: and they shall spoil them that spoiled them, and rob those that robbed them, saith the Lord God...and there they shall bury Gog and his multitude...And seven months shall the house of Israel be burying of them...Yea, all the people of the land shall bury of them: and it shall be to them a renown the day that I shall be glorified, saith the Lord God...And thou, son of man, thus saith the Lord God: Speak unto every feathered fowl, and to every beast of the field, Assemble yourselves, and come, gather yourselves on every side to my sacrifice that I do sacrifice for you, *even* a great sacrifice upon the mountains of Israel, that ye may eat flesh, and drink blood. Ye shall eat the flesh of the mighty, and drink the blood of the princes of the earth, of rams, of lambs, and of goats, of bullocks, all of them fatlings of Bashan. And ye shall eat fat till ye be full, and drink blood till ye be drunken, of my sacrifice which I have sacrificed for you. Thus ye shall be filled at my table with horses and chariots, with mighty men, with all men of war, saith the Lord God. And I will set my glory among the heathen, and all the heathen shall see my judgement that I have executed, and my hand that I have laid upon them. So the house of Israel shall know that I *am* the Lord their God from that day forward. And the house of Israel went into captivity for their iniquity: because they trespassed against me, therefore hid I my face from them. Therefore thus saith the Lord God; Now will I bring again the captivity of Jacob, and have mercy on the whole house of Israel, and will be jealous for my holy name; After that they have borne their shame, and all their trespasses whereby they have trespassed against me, when they dwelt safely in their land, and none made *them* afraid. When I have brought them again from the people, and gathered them out of their enemies' lands, and am sanctified in them in the sight of many nations.'

So the slaughter of Gog from Magog (aptly named to show excessive abundance) were a sacrifice for a sin offering, and all kinds of offerings. The whole story revolves around the significance of 'qodesh ('holy' in error)/piles' of offerings of animals, crops, gold, silver, fat, blood, wine, incense, wood—and in this specific story human life, human meat, blood, and their weapons serving as wood and incense, but the whole story revolves around 'piled upon piles' 'heaps' of offerings.

It is worth mentioning that the Biblical stories dictate only the best of animals, crops etc. are to be presented to God, and in the same way when, in Ezekiel, God offers a sacrifice to atone for the people, the authors intentionally point out the sacrificed humans which animals get to eat of are princes, the 'mighty' of the people, 'men of war' (remember the authors have at least once described God as being a 'man of war'), they are compared to the favoured sacrifices: bullocks, rams, lambs, goats of which the best quality come from Bashan as is mentioned also in other parts of the Bible.

Ezek.41: 'The most holy place' which should correctly read 'piled upon piles/piled high/'piled, I will pile them/it/the', is followed by a description of how high the ceiling of the building is, or how tall its height. Although there are great contradictions within the Biblical stories of how the 'temple/house of god' is in size, layout and décor, but also between how it is described by scholars and in popular belief, I will use how it is described within the Bible regardless of its contradictions. This imagery is to allow the audience of the story to imagine a building able to accommodate the huge amounts of offerings and its stores, the offerings: 'piled upon piles': 'So he measured the length thereof, twenty cubits; and the breadth twenty cubits, before the temple: and he said unto me; This *is* the most holy *place*.' so this specific part is squared where the correct translation is 'piled upon piles/piled, I will pile them/it/the". 'After he measured the wall of the house, six cubits; and the breadth of *every* side; and the breadth of every side chamber, four cubits, round about the house on every side. And the side chambers *were* three, one over another, and thirty in order; and they entered into the wall which *was* of the house for the side chambers round about, that they might have hold, but they had not hold in the wall of the house. And *there was* an enlarging, and a winding about still upward to the side chambers: for the winding about of the house went still upward round about the house: therefore the breadth of the house *was still* upward, and so increased *from* the lowest *chamber* to the highest by the midst. I saw also the height of the house round about: the foundations of the side chambers *were* a full reed of six great cubits.' The emphasis on how it goes still upwards, i.e. its spaciousness is in its height too, and the contradictions about the side chambers which are connected to the wall of the house, and at the same time the story states they are not connected to the house but surround it, is probably the work of an editor going into the story and making his own additions of how it should be.

Ezek.42 also describes the height of the chambers—they need to be high in the author's description so the audience can imagine them being high enough to contain piled things ('holy' which correctly should be 'piled'), and the text tells us directly why they are 'holy/piled': because it is where the priests eat from the 'piled' things ('holy') and where they will pile them as offerings: 'Then he said unto me, The north chambers *and* the south chambers which *are* before the separate place, they be *holy* chambers, where the priests that approacheth unto the Lord shall eat the most holy things: there shall they lay the most holy things, and the meat offering, and the sin offering, and the trespass offering: for the place *is* holy. When the priests enter therein, then shall they not go out of the holy *place* into the utter court, but there shall they lay their garments wherein they minister: for they *are* holy: and shall put on other garments, and shall approach to *those things* which *are* for the people.'

At Ezek.43, when God mentions his 'holy/piled' name he also reminds not to offer/sacrifice to other idols at other places, as what 'defiles' his 'piled' name is the lessening of offerings when doing so. The altar is first mentioned only following the 'law of the house' being 'most holy[correctly 'piled high]' and the altars mention is followed by heaps of animal offerings.

Ezek.44 gives warning about allowing 'strangers' to enter the sanctuary which should read 'piled high' and not 'sanctuary', but note it is 'my sanctuary', the language is possessive of the things inside: the bread, fat, blood and goes further to accuse the house of Israel of not protecting the 'piled things' which belong to him (god) but have set guards to help themselves just as in Ezek.43 the 'whoredom' and the 'defiling' of God's 'holy[piled]' name is taking offerings to other places/idols, therefore lessening the 'piles' which give importance to the place and God (in the story, but it is also what was important to the authors and editors of these stories too), the same is highlighted in Ezek.44 where the 'polluting' and breaking of the laws is allowing strangers to enter who will take from the piles or stores of offerings for other idols and by the 'locals' who do not guard it (the piles) but help themselves. The wrong is in the lessening in quantity of the piled goods: 'And thou shalt say to the rebellious, *even* to the house of Israel, Thus saith the Lord God: O ye house of Israel, let it suffice you of all your abominations, in that ye have brought *into my sanctuary* strangers, uncircumcised in heart, and uncircumcised in flesh, to be in my sanctuary, to pollute it, *even* my house, when ye offer my bread, the fat and the blood, and they have broken my covenant because of your abominations. And ye have not kept charge of mine holy things: but ye have set keepers of my charge in my sanctuary for yourselves.'

This is further reinforced by the text in verses Ezek.44:10-16 where the Levites are said to have gone astray, it is because they performed sacrifices to other idols and therefore cannot come near the holy (piled) things, nor minister to God, nor come into the 'most holy place' 'piled, I will pile'. What this clearly says is the Levites cannot be trusted near the most precious things the 'piled, I will pile them/it/the' erroneously translated as 'most holy place'—the heaps of offerings because as described earlier they have 'stolen' and depleted its quantity before so they can no longer be trusted around it, whereas those who did not 'go astray' of the Levites and priests are trusted to come into contact with the piles of offerings for God but the importance is still on the 'piled' things. A quick note as to why 'Levites' were chosen because the meaning of the word 'levi' ليوي 'twisted around/entwined' 'twisting words/going around/not being forthright/ dishonest' is used to describe and mean when a person is not trustworthy, is deceitful or at the very least not being forthright and evading answering honestly but twisting words or going round and round verbally without being honest (in addition to Levi's meaning لبيي 'served/serve/serve him(or it)' as they serve God and priests).

What can also be seen throughout the OT is that later editors who wanted to reinstate the better version of 'Levites' would reconstitute a better picture of the Levites by adding to various stories how the 'Levites' were ordained or consecrated to perform rituals and minister. 'And the Levites that are gone away far from me, when Israel went astray, which went astray from me after their idols; they shall even bear their iniquity. Yet they will be ministers in my sanctuary, *having* charge at the gates of the house, and ministering to the house: they shall slay the burnt offering and the sacrifice of the people, and they shall stand before them to minister unto them. Because they ministered unto them before their idols, and caused the house of Israel to fall into iniquity: therefore have I lifted mine hand up against them, saith the Lord God, and they shall bear their iniquity. And they shall not come near unto me, nor to come near any of my holy things, in the most holy *place*; but they shall bear their shame, and their abominations which they have committed…But the priests the Levites, the sons of Zadok, that kept the charge of my sanctuary when the children of Israel went away from me, they shall come near to me to minister unto me, and they shall stand before me to offer unto me the fat and the blood, saith the Lord God: They shall enter into my sanctuary, and they shall come near to my table, to minister unto me, and they shall keep my charge.'. Note how the priests who were loyal and trustworthy around the 'holy/piled' things, being aptly named Zadok for 'honest/believed' and 'gave you more' in contrast to 'Levites' 'dishonest' who will be punished by not being allowed to eat/serve of the most holy things, are allowed near the 'piled' things.

Ezek.44:27-30 further confirms the meanings of 'qodesh/kodesh/etc.' 'piled/piled heaps/etc.'. It explains why the priests do not get any inheritance/possession in Israel is because they have the inheritance of the 'piled things', remember even God's name mistranslated as the 'Holy One' and the 'Most Holy' which actually should read 'piled, I will pile them/it/the'; and the verses clearly state the priests get no inheritance (of land) because God is their inheritance, i.e. the 'piled piles' are their inheritance, and the verse goes on to list again what they can eat from the piles of offerings which are piled for God: 'And in the day that he goeth into the sanctuary, unto the inner court, to minister in the sanctuary, he shall offer his sin offering, saith the Lord God. And it shall be unto them for an inheritance: I *am* their inheritance: and ye shall give them no possession in Israel: I *am* their possession.' So by the verses stating God is their inheritance and their possession followed by how they can eat from the piles of offerings, is saying qodesh/piles is their inheritance and possession to live off, i.e. they do not need land to work and live off as they will receive these piled things from all the land, from all who do the work and present offerings: 'They shall eat the meat offering, and the sin offering, and the trespass offering; and every dedicated thing in Israel shall be theirs. And the first of all the firstfruits of all *things*, and every oblation of all, of every *sort* of your oblations, shall be the priest's: ye shall also give unto the priest the first of your dough, that he may cease the blessing to rest in your house.'

Where 'holy' 'most Holy' is mentioned in Dan.9, it is about piles, great quantities of sins, transgressions, and piles of punishment; and it also states the people have a set time to pile their sins and stop, before 'reconciling', i.e. repenting and performing a ritual to receive forgiveness for their sins which is to 'anoint the most Holy'—which means to purge and perform the 'piles upon piles' 'piled, I will pile them/it/the' toward God. (Dan.9:3-24)

Meaning of 'Temple' 'Hekal'

The Torah/OT stories and text clearly show 'qodesh' in all its variants means 'piles' and refers to piles of produce for sacrifice and offerings. The importance of this topic was probably influenced more, and edited, by the priests (than the original authors) who would have been in charge of religious rituals and what would become religious texts as can be seen in and from these stories.

It is important to understand that in the original language of the Bible there is no 'the holy *one*' or 'holy *place*', the words 'one' and 'place' have been added into English and other translations and interpreted and understood that way of those who use the OT/Torah as a religious book, but in a more intense error by those who believe it is a historical document when it is obviously not.

Both wrong translation and misinterpretation of the word have diverted from the true meaning of qodesh/qodesh haqqodashim and erroneously into the 'most holy place' and the 'Holy One' when it is actually 'piled/piles' 'piled, I will pile them/it/the'; there is no 'place' word, and there is no 'one' word. It is 'piles' 'the piled mountain', etc. and it is always referring to heaps of produce which, in the stories of the Bible were narrated as, should be and were heaped into great piles. Due to mistranslation and misinterpretation, and also 'experts' and religious figures transferring their own beliefs (stemming out of the original mistranslation/misinterpretation of the word) has diverted away from the true meaning of the word and its importance in the Biblical stories, which originates from the importance of its correct term and meaning in the lives of the people of those times, both authors and audience of these stories: it is about availability and abundance of food—the most vital source needed and valued. Exaggerating the amount of sacrifices made to God, meat, bread and drink made available to the characters in the stories exemplifies how important and precious it was to the people who created these stories and were its original audience.

The proof of what the correct meaning and translation of what has been mistranslated as 'temple' and also 'palace' is the original word itself: 'hekal' is neither temple nor palace but means 'he/it will eat': hêḵāl; هيكال 'he/it will eat' 'here, eat'. Cp: heykaal. The proof is in the language and in the Bible itself: everywhere it is mentioned there are feasts or at least food and drink revolving around it in the story, it is linked to the 'piled/piles' and 'piled, I will pile' (wrongly called the 'most holy place') as it is connected: where there are piles of food produce and offerings, there is a place where God/priests/public will eat—an area like a mess hall—whether inside for God and priests, or outside for the masses of people.

In the Biblical stories most of the words which describe making offerings to gods have been given 'spiritual/religious' translations and interpretations which stems out of completely not knowing what the words mean, but I will include what they have been mistranslated and misinterpreted as ('temple/palace') and their correct meanings to avoid confusion.

Every word which describes a place where things are offered to God, mostly food and drink offerings, but also incense smoke, has a meaning related to eating and/or storing food:

'temple' 'palace'; hêḵāl; هيكال 'he/it will eat' 'here, eat' as in the stories it is people and/or God eating at that place. Cp: heykaal.

'house of YHWH'; bêṯ YHWH; بيت يحوه 'it/he will-he/it-stays/stayed/contains/contained' 'it will-he/it-stayed/stilled it/contained it'. the word 'bêṯ' could be 'girl' or 'house' but the way it is used makes it definitely 'it will/he will' and not 'house' (see Bethlehem and other 'bêṯ'- word-names) YHWH/Jehova 'he/it-stays/contains/stayed/contained' and this refers to containing/storing food, i.e. as in it being in the stomach or stored—but more importantly as used in the Biblical stories these foods and offerings are presented to God to 'eat' so that he/she will make the good of the land (food) stay, and protect them in the land (stay them in the land they live on), and that God should stay among them i.e. not abandon them because when God/gods abandon their worshippers the protection, fertility of the land, fortune, health, safety, everything leaves with the displeased God(s). Cp: beyt yḥwh.

'house of God'; bêṯ 'ĕlōhîm; بيت ئيلوحيم ، بيت ئيلوحم 'he/it will-tore strips of meat/ate meat' 'he/it will-tear strips of meat/eat meat' 'he/it will-eat plenty of meat'. The ('ĕlōhîm) part is to eat lots of meat, or to eat it in a fashion like animals who eat prey: tear it off in long strips (see Bethlehem and Bethlehemjudah).

It is also بيت ئيلوهيم ، بيت ئيلوهِم 'he/it will(be)-feed well/fed well' 'he/it will-plumpen with food/with various nice food'. The word ('ĕlōhîm) from (lhm/لهم) which can mean 'feed well/pamper/plumpen' with the intention of fattening/plumpening to make an animal or child grow well, or an adult be healthier; out of wanting to slaughter the animal in the future or out of love for a child or wife and wanting them to be healthy. Cp: beyt eilooḥeem, beyt eilooḥim, beyt eilooheem, beyt eiloohim.

Word used for the 'Jerusalem temple'; bêṯ miqdāš; بيت مِكداَش ، بيت مِقداَش 'he/it will be piled/heaped' 'he/it will-a pile/piling' 'he/it will be led'. And as explained under the meanings of 'kadesh/qodesh' it means to pile anything into piles, but also the things that are 'led' are live animals whose meat, fat and blood will end up being in piles for offerings (see Kadesh, qodesh, qodesh haqqodashim). Cp: beyt mikdaa<u>sh</u>, beyt miqdaa<u>sh</u>.

What is clear, not just from these words and how they are mistranslated then misinterpreted, is that the earliest authors and audiences knew exactly what these words were and meant, but much later translators/interpreters and audiences did not understand these words as Arabic and specifically the Old Arabic of the Arabian Peninsula was not the translators/interpreters' original language. Therefore, you can see how some words are mistranslated by only a superficial understanding of the language (I am addressing only those words where the alternative word is the same pronunciation or spelling, but not those which are just guesswork and bias such as modern-day translations and interpretations). E.g. you can see how the word (bêṯ/بيت) could be mistranslated/misinterpreted as 'house' or ('ĕlōhîm/ايلوهيم) as 'God'—but changing (hêḵāl/هيكال) into 'temple' is forcing it by guesswork and taking the more modern Arabic word (modern compared to its age against the Old Arabic) where (hêḵal/هيكَل) means 'structure/frame' such as the skeleton in Arabic is 'hekal a<u>dh</u>mee' 'frame-bone/bone structure or frame' and apply it to mean a building, but that is not what is happening in the translation of the Biblical (hêḵāl/هيكال) as that is only misunderstanding what is meant by the word and applying it to what the translators/interpreters 'wished' for it to mean as they take into account all the 'building' and descriptions of buildings in the stories, while the true meaning is not understood due to lack of knowing the word's true meaning as intended by the authors.

In 1.Sam.1 the mention of the 'temple' (correctly 'he will eat') revolves around eating, feasts and drink, both the people are fed and so is the God who the offerings are presented and sacrificed for: Hannah's husband and family have offered great sacrifices to God at Shiloh (which means 'take/take it'); though Hannah is not eating because she is distressed, she is still at the feast, the eating place where her husband gives her a bigger portion than his other wife and her children; Eli the priest is sitting at the 'temple[he will eat]' watching her; her character name 'Hannah' means 'he satisfied/gave fill/plenty of' 'satisfaction/gave satisfaction' and is used when talking about a meal, e.g. when a person says 'let him/her eat' (as in peace, or without disturbing, or to eat until full' they say "let him/her et-hannah' (let him/her eat until full, in peace, or without disturbing); 'he will eat' is also reflected in how her husband provides a lot of offerings/sacrifices to God, therefore he and his family are also feasting, also reflected in how he gives her a 'worthy portion'. It is also reflected in how God will give her the son she truly hungers for; it is shown in how her husband continues to provide at Shiloh the 'yearly sacrifice, and his vow' which is food produce and feasting; and in when she gives Samuel to the service of God and along with him a lot of produce 'three bullocks, one ephah of flour, and a bottle of wine…' at 'the house of the Lord in Shiloh'; even the first mention of how Samuel serves God as a child is linked to the priests and how they behaved with taking and eating the meat and fat from people who were presenting offerings to God. The 'house of the Lord' is always where piles of produce are delivered and/or sacrificed and therefore there is always the importance and relevance of a place for eating 'hekal' 'he/it will eat' translated as 'temple' in error.

In 1Sam.2 the story continues to revolve around food, piles of sacrifice, the best of which should be offered to God. When the 'temple[he will eat]' is used in 1Sam.3, the story is still focused on food and eating as God informs Samuel that he will punish/wipe out Eli's seed and not accept from them sacrifices nor offerings because they sinned and Eli did not stop them. Their sins are described in great detail in 1Sam.2: they take the best of all offerings which God is possessive about '…mine offerings…'. As throughout the Bible the mention of places is important in the story as these too are given names made of compound words so the meaning and importance of the story is clear to who listens and/or reads the story: the lights go out at the 'temple[he will eat]' then Samuel is informed by God how Eli's sons who eat God's food will be punished: 'Now the sons of Eli *were* sons of Belial; they knew not the Lord. And the priests' custom *was*; *that*, when any man offered sacrifice, the priest's servant came, while the flesh was seething, with a fleshhook of three teeth in his hand; And he struck *it* into the pan, or kettle, or caldron, or pot; all that the fleshhook brought up the priest took for himself. So they did in Shiloh unto all the Israelites that came thither. Also before they burnt the fat, the priest's servant came, and said to the man that sacrificed, Give flesh to roast for the priest; for he will not have sodden flesh of thee, but raw. And *if* any man said unto him, Let them not fail to burn the fat presently, and *then* take *as much* as thy soul desireth; then he would answer him, Nay; but thou shalt give *it me* now: and if not, I will take *it* by force. Wherefore the sin of the young men was very great before the Lord. For men abhorred the offering of the Lord. (1Sam.2:12-17)

Although the story narrates that Eli's sons commit fornication at the tabernacle's door, when God sends a messenger to Eli this transgression is not mentioned, but a lot is said about the most important thing at the 'temple[he will eat]' in the 'house of the Lord' that they take and eat the best of sacrifices and offerings which are supposed to be for God: 'And there came a man of God unto Eli, and said unto him, Thus saith the Lord, Did I plainly appear to the house of thy father, when they were in Egypt in Pharaoh's house? And did I choose him out of all the tribes of Israel *to be* my priest, to offer upon mine altar, to burn incense, to wear an ephod before me? and did I give unto thy father all the offerings made by fire of the children of Israel? Wherefore kick ye at my sacrifice and at mine offering, which I have commanded *in my* habitation; and honourest thy sons above me, to make yourselves fat with the chiefest of all the offerings of Israel my people?' (1Sam.2;27-29)

It follows with the promise of punishment that will wipe out all men from Eli's house, but those who survive will be so lacking in food resources they will be begging the new priest to allow them to work with the priests just to be able to eat: 'Behold, the days come, that I will cut off thine arm, and the arm of thine father's house, that there should not be an old man in thine house...And it shall come to pass, that every one *that* is left in thine house shall come *and* crouch to him for a piece of silver and a morsel of bread, and shall say, Put me, I pray thee, into one of the priest's offices, that I may eat a piece of bread.' (1Sam.2:31-36)

And when God comes to speak to Samuel the 'temple[he will eat]' is mentioned, and God explains he is going to punish Eli by killing Hophni and Phinehas for eating what was meant for God, and no matter what they present of offerings and sacrifices (food presented to God in a ritual) he will not forgive them: 'And ere the lamp of God went out in the temple of the Lord, where the ark of God *was*, and Samuel was laid down to sleep; That the Lord called Samuel: and he answered, Here am I...And the Lord came, and stood, and called as the other times, Samuel, Samuel. Then Samuel answered, Speak; for thy servant heareth. And the Lord said to Samuel, Behold, I will do a thing in Israel, at which both the ears of every one that heareth it shall tingle. In that day I will perform against Eli all *things* which I have spoken concerning his house: when I begin, I will also make an end. For I have told him that I will judge his house forever for the iniquity which he knoweth; because his sons made themselves vile, and he restrained them not. And therefore I have sworn unto the house of Eli, that the iniquity of Eli's house shall not be purged with sacrifice nor offering for ever.' (1Sam.3)

Even the word 'Ichabod' 'choked/it chokes' 'stifled/it stifles' which is the name given to the baby by the wife of one of Eli's sons before she dies of heartbreak/shock at hearing of the deaths of her husband and in-laws, is related to the sin they committed: they were eating the best of God's offerings which the narration has God upset about—so even the naming of the child uses the word describing the pain/stifling felt when under great distress or shock (like a heart attack), but also the same word describes choking on food and the pain felt when too much food is packed in the oesophagus (see I-cha-bod).

In 2Sam.22:7 the mention of God hearing David's cry from 'out of his temple[he will eat]' is ensconced between David's stories of 1Sam and 2Sam, and followed by a mini-retelling as a 'song' in the parlance of the Bible, which reminds us of what David went through before, and how and what he was saved from. In most of David's stories his character is involved with food/eating: shepherding; bringing bread, cheese, corn and wine to Saul, to his brothers; to insisting on attending a meal at Saul's table although the story narrates/suggests Saul wants to kill him and David is aware of it; David lying to the priest at Nob to obtain bread; to going to Keilah at the threshing floors (grain is the major source of food) and coming away with the cattle to sustain himself and his band of men; demanding he be given meat, water and bread which Nabal refuses, but Nabal's wife Abigail loads donkeys with bread, wine, prepared meat, corn, raisins and fig cakes to prevent David killing her husband and others if he attacks; when Abigail returns she finds Nabal having a great feast and when she tells him in the morning what she gave David from the food stores—Nabal dies so she ends up marrying David and goes with him, so David gets a new wife along with all the food resources which he had wanted which were Nabal's. Everywhere David goes to dwell in, be it Gath, the country of the Philistines and everywhere before them—he kills to take away the food source for himself and his men to eat from and survive: 'And David smote the land; and left neither man nor woman alive, and took away the sheep, and the oxen, and the asses, and the camels, and the apparel, and returned, and came to Achish.'

Even when the story turns to Saul in the chapter that follows, it involves eating: the woman/witch slaughters a fat calf, bakes bread, and they eat. When David and his men return to Ziklag and find their wives and children abducted, the first person they run into who helps them locate the Amalekites, the authors make a point that he is given bread, water, fig cakes and raisins and the story stresses that the man is made to eat; when they find the Amalekites they are eating and drinking from the spoil of other lands, including David's food resources; and when David beats them he takes away what was originally taken from him, but also the others' flocks, herds and 'other cattle'. When the tribes of Israel come to David, they remind him that not only did God say David would be their king but that 'Thou shalt feed my people Israel'. Note the meaning of 'David' 'rolling pin of stone grinder' is reflected throughout his stories as this household object turns the grain into dough which can be made into bread—the staple of the diet of both the fictional characters, but also the authors and audience of these stories.

When the 'ark of God' is brought back, David sacrifices oxen and fatlings at every six paces, and when it arrives he makes burnt offerings and peace offerings 'before the Lord', and at the end of the offerings he distributes 'among all the people, *even* among the whole multitude of Israel, as well to the women as men…' bread, meat and flagons of wine. The story continues with God requesting David build a house for him; and this continues with David who goes on to 'smite'/kill various nations and apparently the authors proceed to make the bill of quantities of materials for the building come out of the various other locals, they have him kill and take: chariots, horsemen, footmen, horses, gifts, shields of gold, 'exceeding much brass'; receives vessels of silver, gold, brass which he dedicates [piles] to God along with all the gold and silver 'of all the nations he subdued'.

Part of the kindness David shows towards Saul's relative is restoring his land to him (a major food source) and allowing him to eat at David's table, and emphasis is put on Mephibosheth eating continually at David's table; when David attempts to cover up the illegitimate pregnancy he fathers with Bath-sheba, he sends Uriah home and gifts 'a mess of meat'—still linking David's stories to food/eating. Uriah responds that he cannot go home to eat, drink and relax while the soldiers are out in the field at war for God's sake, so David has him eat and drink before him even if intoxicating him still does not result in what David wants to happen; even the story Nathan tells David to teach him a lesson of the wrong he has done to Uriah is about a man who nurtures a lamb, who feeds and waters it from his own meals, but the lamb is taken by a richer man and slaughtered and served to a guest to eat.

Also, when Saul wants to contact a dead Samuel he first fasts (stops eating) and after contact with Samuel he eats (even if he had to be coaxed to eat). Similarly to Saul's fasting, David fasts and refuses to eat while his son is sick, but the story puts much focus on that as soon as the child dies David immediately eats which provokes the mystification of his servants who ask him why it is that while the child was alive he refused to eat, but as soon as he dies he ate; David goes to war again and returns with more resources: 'And he brought forth the spoil of the city in great abundance'; even when David's son Amnon rapes David's daughter Tamar, food and feeding is the trick Amnon employs to be able to get her alone; the revenge Absalom uses against Amnon is also using eating/drinking to lull the victim.

When Joab refuses to come see Absalom (as the latter wants Joab to convince David to allow him to be in his presence), Absalom forces Joab to come by burning his field of barley (it is Joab's food source) so Joab arrives and complains about his field of barley being set on fire; the story continues with Absalom going to pay a vow to God, i.e. sacrifices and eating.

Ziba meets David to give him two hundred loaves of bread, a hundred bunches of raisins, a hundred of summer fruits, and a bottle of wine; the woman who saves David's spies hiding in the well, spreads ground corn on the cover to hide them (ground corn—bread); again in the stories people who are good, meet David with abundant food supplies: 'And it came to pass when David came to Mahanaim, that Shobi the son of Nahash…' and several others 'Brought beds, and basons, and earthen vessels, and wheat, and barley, and flour, and parched corn, and beans, and lentiles, and parched pulse, And honey, and butter, and sheep, and cheese of kine, for David, and for the people that *were* with him, to eat: for they said, The people *is* hungry, and weary, and thirsty, in the wilderness.'; on David's return journey, Mephibosheth meets him and mentions eating at David's table, David now divides Mephibosheth's land (food source) between Mephibosheth and Ziba as the latter provided David with food at a time of need whereas Mephibosheth did not; Barzillai feeding David at Mahanaim is mentioned again and his reward will be to eat with David 'Now Barzillai was a very aged man *even* fourscore years old: and he had provided the king with sustenance while he lay at Mahanaim; for he *was* a very great man. And the king said unto Barzillai, Come thou over with me, and I will feed thee in Jerusalem. And Barzillai said unto the king, How long have I to live, that I should go up with the king to Jerusalem? I *am* this day fourscore years old: and can I discern between good and evil? can thy servant taste what I eat and what I drink? can I hear anymore the voice of singing men and singing women? wherefore then should thy servant be yet a burden unto my lord the king?' so he states why should such a reward as eating with the king be wasted on him who would not be able to enjoy it, then he nominates Chimham to receive this reward and David agrees: 'chimham' means the sound made to imitate a person eating quickly, or to encourage a baby/toddler to eat, it also represents someone enjoying food too much that they are making sounds while eating.

When famine strikes, the story narrates a human sacrifice which could have been viewed only as an act of revenge by both the Gibeonites and David against Saul's sons and grandsons (five are Saul's grandsons from his daughter who married another man instead of David) had the authors not tied the murder of the innocent characters to the scarcity of food (famine) then again with the abundance of food after they had been murdered. Even when/where they are killed symbolises human sacrifice: put to death in the first days of the barley harvest—it is all done to remove the famine and return fertility to the land (food source/ eating): 'There was famine in the days of David three years, year after year; and David enquired of the Lord. And the Lord answered, It is for Saul, and for *his* bloody house, because he slew the Gibeonites…Wherefore said David unto the Gibeonites, What shall I do for you? And wherewith shall I make the atonement, that ye may bless the inheritance of the Lord?' The inheritance is the food source from the land. 'And they answered the king, The man that consumed us, and that devised against us *that* we should be destroyed from remaining in any of the coasts of Israel, let seven men of his sons be delivered unto us, and we will hang them up unto the Lord in Gibeah of Saul, *whom* the Lord did choose. And the king said, I will give them…But the king took the two sons of Rispah the daughter of Aiah, whom she bare unto Saul, Armoni and Mephibosheth; and the five sons of Michal [in the earlier story it is Merab who marries Adriel instead of David] the daughter of Saul, whom she brought up for Adriel the son of Barzillai the Mahallathite: And he delivered them into the hands of the Gibeonites, and they hanged them in the hill before the Lord: and they fell *all* seven together, and were put to death in the days of harvest, in the *first days*, in the beginning of the barley harvest.' The narrators mention twice that they hung them 'before the Lord' in return for harvest instead of famine: sacrifice to eat, to eat is important and this story, like all David's stories, is linked to the wrongly presented 'temple' which is correctly 'he will eat'.

Which leads to Chapter 22: 'In my distress I called upon the Lord, and cried unto my God: and he did hear my voice out of his temple[he will eat], and my cry did enter into his ears.'

'Temple' should be 'he will eat', it is directly related to food and eating, but mistranslation and misinterpretation has made it something else and not allowed readers, scholars to understand the stories. David's distress, his being saved from death and danger which was recounted over the books 1Sam and 2Sam are all related to food, its scarcity, its importance and precious value to the authors of the Biblical stories. David's 'victories' were him taking over others' food resources as his own; the 'salvation' is in the men meeting him with food and drink every time there was a lack; the 'reward' is abundance of food and drink—'he will eat: hekal [wrongly presented as 'temple']'.

The relation of 'temple/he will eat' with sources of food continues in Chapter 23, comparing David and good/just people with tender grass springing out of the earth is because good grass can be grazed on by animals which in turn are a food source, whereas the enemies are 'thorns'. Shammah is heroic because although the enemies have gathered in a ground full of lentils, he stands his ground and defeats them i.e. he defended/gained a food source; during harvest time David and his men are blockaded by the enemy troops, despite this he longs and thirsts for water from a particular well, and although it is impossible, his men are able to fight through the Philistine troops and back just to bring him a drink of water which he craves from a well in Bethlehem—and even when they bring him the water to drink, he pours it to the ground as an offering to the Lord: this shows how the word 'Bethlehem' and the wrongly translated as 'house of God' bêṯ 'ĕlōhîm are similar if not the same.

The final chapter of 2Sam clearly shows the importance and the connection of abundance of food, piles of food with 'qodesh/piles' (mistaken as 'holy' and 'sanctuary') and with 'hekal(he will eat)' (wrongly translated as 'temple') and how the authors of the Bible keep clearly making this the theme of the stories, and made it the most important part of the Biblical stories because it was the most important thing to have and to worry about if lacking: David incurs God's anger and punishment by having a census of the people, he is made to choose one of three punishments which will befall his people or directly affect him: seven years of famine, three months of being pursued by his enemies, or three days of pestilence. He does not even consider seven years of famine—it is so terrible it is not on the table for consideration; he considers being pursued by his enemies and comes to the conclusion that God will be more merciful on him than his enemies, so he chooses pestilence.

There is significance in where God forgives David and stops the angel tasked with killing people: the angel is at the threshing place of Araunah—a place where grain in its pods/panicles is heaped to be threshed, then its grains heaped to be stored. In the stories, offerings are made to God of grain, flour, crop, animals fattened on crop and grains, wine from the fruits of the land, and the people who work the land and bring these offerings and sacrifices. In real life, the story's audience is sustained from the same sources just like the characters of the Biblical stories. Also, David is ordered to build an altar there on the threshing place owned by Araunah, which he purchases and offers burnt offerings and peace offerings, and God stops the plague from killing the people: to build an altar where grain is usually piled, so 'qodesh(piled)' things can be offered/sacrificed to God—the authors of the story purposely choose place names which have the exact meaning of events relevant to the story—and later in 1Chr.22:1 and 2Chr.3:1, the authors of these stories will have David/Solomon intend/build the 'house of God' on it (Arauna's threshing place), reinforcing the meaning of qodesh and qodesh haqqodashim is 'piled' and 'piled, I will pile the', and not the mistranslated 'most holy place'.

The authors of Chronicles choose to have Solomon's character build 'God's house' on the site of the threshing place for the same reason the authors of 2Sam. choose to have God order, and David build, an altar to sacrifice and offer to God on the threshing place: because of the meaning of 'piled', because of the imagery of piles of panicles waiting to be threshed, then piles of grain pushed into heaps to be cleared from husks, stones and other impurities before they are piled into sacks, barrels or rooms/granaries for storage, and used for eating and future sowing of the land. Both building the altar and 'God's house' which both have 'qodesh/qodesh haqqodashim' (most holy place/sanctuary) 'piles', and 'hekal' (temple) 'he will eat' as both mean literally and figuratively what happens to the produce piled and offered there—whether at Shiloh or where Araunah's threshing place was located in the story—and the audience of these Biblical stories are constantly reminded of this importance of piled produce and eating this piled produce: the 'hekal/he will eat' (not 'temple') and 'qodesh haqqodashim/piled, I will pile' (not 'most holy place') are wherever food produce is offered and sacrificed to God, and priests and people eat from (and God in the stories). 'he will eat/hekal' is not necessarily a fixed place as can be seen from the stories, at times it is at Bethel, or Shiloh, or Gibeon, or at Araunah's threshing place—as long as it is sacrificed/offered only to the correct God in the Biblical stories (Yahweh) and not other gods (although the high places, shrines where the people make offerings/sacrifices to other deities have the same function of hekal/he/it will eat, and is the reason the Biblical authors give these places the word-name mistranslated as 'high place(s)': bmh, bmwth; بمه ، بموت 'for what?' 'why?' 'what for?' 'with what?' and relays with the stories that the protagonist God is always reprimanding them and upset as to why they divert from his piled resources and sacrifice to other gods at the suitably named 'what with/what for/why'. Cp: bmh, bmwt), which as explained earlier ruins/defiles/pollutes the 'qodesh/piles' by lessening what was piled.

The preciousness of food and its sources are behind the importance of 'qodesh haqqodashim/piled, I will pile' and 'hekal/he will eat' as the central and most significant part in the rituals as described in the Biblical stories. Throughout 1Kgs.6-7 and 2 Chr.3-4 (and emphasised more, later in Book of Ezekiel) the size of the 'house of God' which includes 'piled, I will pile ['most holy place']' and 'he will eat ['temple']', is important to allow the imagery of a large place which not only fits great stores of food and animals for sacrifice and offerings, but also 'designed' to be able to store the mythical amounts and quantities suggested in the stories of these goods, and also able to accommodate the eating and feasting by God, priests, the public—the latter which would be in masses and the area it would need to spread the food for eating such amounts and containing vast numbers of people.

The description of the building decorations on or around the 'temple/he will eat' is that of food: oxen, pomegranates on the pillars—decorated with fruit just as the place is about eating as clearly meant by the compound word 'he will eat/hekal'. Even the utensils, their importance is because they are used in the process of slaughtering sacrifices, washing meat and other produce, carrying blood to be sprinkled, cooking the food and serving it. Whether served to God or the people, the 'vessels' of the temple/most holy place which should read correctly as 'he will eat/piled, I will pile' are important because they are used to serve the most precious resource: food. Magnified in importance because they are used to present copious amounts of food and drink to 'God', and the priests and people also get to eat. This is further emphasised in how everything of the utensils used is made of precious metals: gold, silver, brass for use in the 'temple/he will eat' and 'most holy place/piled, I will pile'—these valued vessels magnified in the story out of gold, silver, brass is because what is processed with and served in them is even more precious than what they are made of: food.

This can also be seen in how the two 'areas' where the food for sacrifice is piled and where it will be eaten (the qodesh haqqodashim/piled, I will pile [most holy place] and the hekal/he will eat [temple]), in 1Kgs. the hinges of the doors to 'most holy place' and 'temple' are made of gold, whereas at 2Chr. the authors emphasise further that the doors to both these places were completely of gold, because the authors of the latter want to reinforce and increase the importance of both places (in the stories) and the importance of the ideas (to the audience) of where and how food is stored, sacrificed and where it is served and eaten.

It is also important to note the proximity of the 'temple' and 'most holy place' makes sense for the practicality of cooking then serving food close to where it has been slaughtered and prepared—just as is done in remote areas which still live the same lifestyle as in ancient times, today; it only differs by the stories exaggeration of the quantity used of animals and other food stuffs, and the size of the place/building of the Biblical stories. 'The most holy place ('piled I will pile)' and the 'temple ('he will eat')' are linked in the story because of the logic, especially when using the correct words and meanings for the mistranslated words.

The abundance of foodstuff and costly building materials is important to the stories of Kings and Chronicles, most of the significance is in the huge amounts of food, not only related to the 'qodesh/piles' and 'hekal/he will eat', but also in stories preceding and following it. There is always mention of the numbers (great numbers) of different kinds of animal slain for sacrifice, and other food produce, or for daily meals: oxen, sheep, fat cattle, wheat, barley, oil, wine—sometimes in a day and daily, or in one day, or daily spanning several days—but always it has significance in the stories because of its abundance and reinforces the most important thing is: food.

Whether kings' feasts, kings offering sacrifices, e.g. before Solomon is blessed with wisdom and solved the baby issue, he has offered 'burnt offerings, and offered peace offerings, and made a feast to all his servants.'; Solomon's importance as king is reflected in the story by how much provisions are given to him, and the scope of how many people provide his dietary needs (1Kgs.4) 'And Solomon had twelve officers over all Israel, which provided victuals for the king and his household…'. His status continues to be measured by how much food produce he receives 'And Solomon's provision for one day was thirty measures of fine flour, and threescore measures of meal, Ten fat oxen, and twenty oxen out of the pasture, and an hundred sheep, besides harts, and roebucks, and fallow deer, and fatted fowl. For he had dominion over all the region on this side of the river…And Solomon had forty thousand stalls of horses for his chariots, and twelve thousand horsemen. And those officers provided victuals for king Solomon, and for all that came unto Solomon's table, every man in his month: they lacked nothing. Barley also, and straw for the horses and dromedaries brought they unto the place where *the officers* were, every man according to his charge. And God gave Solomon wisdom and understanding exceeding much, and largeness of heart, even as the sand that is on the sea shore. And Solomon's wisdom excelled all the wisdom of the children of the east country, and all the wisdom of Egypt…'.

Even Solomon's wisdom is described as 'piles' with the imagery of the number of sand grains on a shore, but even the wisdom is preceded by mention of the great amounts of food sources at his daily access, even his horses get a mention of abundant food supply. Note although the narration has Solomon asking God for wisdom, God grants it, but along with it the material riches he has not asked for will also be granted in great abundance, and the riches described in the story are mostly food. This increases when related to the story of building the 'house of God': in exchange for timber, Solomon gives Hiram great amounts of foodstuff; Hiram does not ask for silver or gold, but for something far more important to the authors and audience of the story: food. 'I will convey them…and thou shalt accomplish my desire, in giving food for my household. So Hiram gave Solomon cedar trees and fir trees *according* to his desire. And Solomon gave Hiram twenty thousand measures of wheat *for* food to his household, and twenty measures of pure oil: thus gave Solomon to Hiram year by year.' (1Kgs.5)

Following the completion of the 'house of God' the sacrifices and feasts are bigger than ever, emphasising what the 'house of God' is all about; to the degree the quantity of animals sacrificed are innumerable 'And king Solomon, and all the congregation of Israel, that were assembled unto him, *were* with him before the ark, sacrificing sheep and oxen, that could not be told nor numbered for multitude.' And after Solomon's prayer to God, more offerings in huge quantities, and also the people seated for feasting span from the 'house of the Lord' and is described as beginning from the entering of Hamath all the way to Egypt's river. Not only is the abundance of food signified as well as the large area used to feed/feast the congregation, but also the number of days this feast lasts has been made two weeks to allow the audience to understand the importance of abundance and piles of food at 'God's house' where the most important parts are the 'qodesh haqqodashim/piled, I will pile ('most holy place')' and the 'hekal/he will eat ('temple')': 'And the king and all Israel with him, offered sacrifice before the Lord, And Solomon offered a sacrifice of peace offerings, which he offered unto the Lord, two and twenty thousand oxen, and an hundred and twenty thousand sheep. So the king and all the children of Israel dedicated to the house of the Lord. The same day did the king hallow the middle of the court that *was* before the house of the Lord: for there he offered burnt offerings, and meat offerings, and the fat of the peace offerings: because the brasen altar that was before the Lord *was* too little to receive the burnt offerings, and the meat offerings, and the fat of the peace offerings. And at that time Solomon held a feast, and all Israel with him, a great congregation, from the entering in of Hamath unto the river of Egypt, before the Lord our God, seven days, and seven days, even fourteen days.' (1Kgs.8)

The narration follows with more sacrifices made at 'God's house' And when Queen Sheba visits, not only does she bring great amounts of precious gifts, she too is astounded by Solomon's show of wealth, she also leaves carrying an abundance of presents from Solomon's riches. The story tells us she is impressed by his wisdom, but the same story itself shows she is impressed by his riches, his food, the decadence she sees, and it is all linked to his wisdom, just as in previous chapters the story links his wisdom directly to the abundance of his food, riches, etc. 'And when the queen of Sheba heard of the fame of Solomon concerning the name of the Lord, she came to prove him with hard questions. And she came to Jerusalem with a very great train, with camels that bare spices, and very much gold, and precious stones: and when she was come to Solomon, she communed with him of all that was in her heart. And Solomon told her all her questions: there was not any thing hid from the king, which he told her not. And when the queen of Sheba had seen all of Solomon's wisdom, and the house that he had built, And the meat of his table, and the sitting of his servants, and the attendance of his ministers, and their apparel, and his cup bearers, and his ascent by which he went up to the house of the Lord, there was no more spirit in her. And she said to the king, It was a true report that I heard in mine own land of thy acts and of thy wisdom. Howbeit I believed not the words, until I came, and mine eyes had seen *it*: and, behold, the half was not told me: thy wisdom and prosperity exceedeth the fame which I heard...And she gave the king an hundred and twenty talents of gold, and of spices very great store, and precious stones: there came no more such abundance of spices as these which the queen of Sheba gave to king Solomon...And king Solomon gave unto the queen of Sheba all her desire, whatsoever she asked, beside *that* which Solomon gave her of his royal bounty...' (1Kgs,10).

And the story continues listing the abundance of riches of Solomon, following linking his wisdom to riches 'So king Solomon exceeded all the kings of the earth for riches and for wisdom.' and the narration continues to show this link by having 'all the earth', everyone who seeks Solomon's wisdom brings him gifts in the form of copious amounts of valuables: 'And all the earth sought to Solomon, to hear his wisdom, which God had put in his heart. And they brought every man his present, vessels of silver, and vessels of gold, and garments, and armour, and spices, horses, and mules, a rate year by year.' and the list goes on.

In Kings, the authors tie the emphasis of abundance of food in the event where Hiram asks in exchange for trees used to build 'God's house' he asks and receives a yearly supply of food for his household; in 1Chronicles the same emphasis of tying the abundance of food which is the point of 'God's house' also by emphasising even the skilled workers sent by Huram to hew the trees will receive a great supply of food, and Huram mentions Solomon's wisdom in connection to this event: 'And behold I will give to thy servants, the hewers that cut timber, twenty thousand measures of beaten wheat, and twenty measures of barley, and twenty thousand baths of wine, and twenty thousand baths of oil.' Huram writes to the king 'Huram said moreover, blessed be the Lord God of Israel, that made heaven and earth, who hath given to David the king a wise son, endowed with prudence and understanding, that might build a house for the Lord, and an house for his kingdom.' (2Chr.2)

2Chr. does not merely retell the same story with the importance of the abundance of food at its heart, but additions have been made to make it clear the 'qodesh haqqodashim' and 'hekal' are for food to be piled/stored and for eating. It has God consume the sacrifices in front of Solomon and the whole congregation; the early creators of these stories knew exactly the things they wanted to signify as important, even later authors/editors who added/changed to the stories still knew exactly what these words meant and how the stories revolved around importance of food and its link to 'hekal/he will eat' and 'qodesh haqqodashim/piled, I will pile': in 1Kgs.8:10, it mentions the priests coming out of the 'holy place' (which should read 'piles' and not 'holy place'), which means God is where the piles are: 'And it came to pass, when the priests were come out of the holy *place*, that the cloud filled the house of the Lord.'. In 2Chr.7 it is made absolutely clear: 'Now when Solomon had made an end of praying, the fire came down from heaven, and consumed the burnt offering and the sacrifices: and the glory of the Lord filled the house. And the priests could not enter into the house of the Lord, because the glory of the Lord had filled the Lord's house. And when all the children of Israel saw how the fire came down, and the glory of the Lord upon the house they bowed themselves with their faces to the ground upon the pavement, and worshipped, and praised the Lord, *saying*, *For he is* good: for his mercy endureth forever. Then the king and all the people offered sacrifices before the Lord.' and the listing of the great amounts of sacrifices already narrated in 1Kgs. is retold.

Something worth noting: when God 'eats' anything (which accepting the sacrifices means he ate them), it is through fire—whether the priests burn them on the altar, or God appears, or licks them up with fire, this is clear in Exodus where there is a cloud when God is at the tabernacle (a cloud can be thick smoke), the cloud is over/at the tabernacle by day and fire by night when God is there; before God arrives, Moses puts bread on the table for God: 'And he put the table in the tent of the congregation, upon the side of the tabernacle northward, without the vail. And he set the bread upon it before the Lord; as the Lord had commanded Moses.' The altar of the burnt offering is put by the door of the tabernacle of the tent of the congregation and 'offer upon it burnt offerings, and meat offering; as the Lord had commanded Moses...Then a cloud covered the tent of the congregation, and the glory of the Lord filled the tabernacle'. The children of Israel cannot journey while the cloud covers the tabernacle—only when it is 'taken up', i.e. when God is eating, he should not be disturbed; more to the point, when God eats—he eats through fire, and fire creates the smoke described in the story as a cloud. The tent/tabernacle and the 'temple' as well as the 'most holy place' are for God to eat at.

In Exodus and Leviticus is shows God accepts/eats offerings through fire. In Lev.9:23-24 God appears to the people after they have piled onto the altar a range of offerings and a fire comes out of God and consumes the burnt offerings and the fat which we are told earlier belongs (i.e. is reserved for) to the Lord: 'And Moses and Aaron went into the tabernacle of the congregation, and came out and blessed the people: and the glory of the Lord appeared unto all the people. And there came a fire out from before the Lord, and consumed upon the altar the burnt offering and the fat: *which* when all the people saw, they shouted, and fell on their faces.'. It is also important to understand although in the English translation 'devoured' 'consumed' are described to what God does to devour/consume what is on the altar, in the original language it is most definitely the word 'eat/ate' and the English translation still means 'eating' as would a person eat, but the use of the word 'devoured/consumed' gives it a mystical sense that the meat and other offerings are just 'burned into thin air' by God's fire, whereas the authors intentions is the word 'eat/ate' and meant that God literally ate what was offered on the altar. In the areas which still speak this purest form of the Biblical language, when cursing or responding in anger against a person who has done one wrong, they say 'God eat you', and means to cause your death as easily as eating a meal, and is interchangeable with 'God burn you' which holds the exact same meaning as 'eat you', but can also mean to cause you the same fiery pain/distress/upset you have caused others, and this latter also means to eat your health/peace/pleasure.

Back to the Bible, as can be seen in Exodus and Leviticus, the tabernacle, tent, are for God to come down and eat at from the sacrifices offered by the people—and when the stories give God a permanent dwelling place as can be seen in Kings and Chronicles, the 'most holy place/piled, I will pile' and the 'temple/he will eat' are still for God to come down and eat at from the offered sacrifices which is why they are aptly named 'qodesh haqqodashim/piled, I will pile' and 'hekal/he will eat'. How the authors enhance and link God's eating place to the importance of providing plenteous offerings is by having him appear at places where there is food: threshing floors, fields, and he eats by sending down his fire to accept/eat the offered food which can be seen throughout the Bible, of which two examples are where God through an angel appears to Gideon at a threshing floor while they threshed wheat by a wine press, and when Gideon presents kid meat, cakes and broth, he is asked to place them/pour it out on a rock, then the angel with a touch of a staff causes fire to come out of the rock and the food is devoured (Jud.6:11-23). Also the same when an angel appears to Manoah and his wife, and Manoah offers to give him meat, but the angel tells him he should make it as a burnt offering to the Lord, and when they offer it on a rock to God a fire goes up to heaven from off the rock, described here as an altar, along with the angel (Jud.13:15-23).

Throughout the Bible the authors could not make it clearer the temple/hekal and qodesh haqqodashim, the altars at Shiloh, at Bethel and elsewhere are where God eats offerings, as well as priests performing rituals and the people giving the offerings also eat.

When the scene is repeat in 2Chr.7, after Solomon's prayer and God's appearance in front of all the people and eats the burnt offerings and the sacrifices, followed by the additional offerings king and people make before the Lord, followed by yet more offerings so abundant the usual places cannot accommodate them—the people cover an area from Hamath to Egypt's river feasting for at least two weeks. After all this, the authors emphasise over and over again what is important in these stories, exemplified in how the house built is where God will eat; and when people sin God will cause lack of food whether from drought, locust or illness of the people (who work the land); if they pray to him, he will hear from heaven and forgive: forgiveness is the land returning to fertility—an abundance of food resources.

The story uses God's eating place, exaggerated descriptions of quantities of food to tell a story (teach a lesson maybe) about the most important thing to the real people who listened to these stories back then: food and its source: land. 'hekal' is where the food is eaten; 'qodesh haqqodashim' is where the produce is stored, processed for eating. 'Then Solomon finished the house of the Lord, and the king's house: and all that came into Solomon's heart to make in the house of the Lord, and in his own house, he prosperously effected. And the Lord appeared to Solomon by night, and said unto him, I have heard thy prayer, and have chosen this place for myself for an house of sacrifice. If I shut up heaven that there be no rain, or if I command the locusts to devour the land, or if I send pestilence among my people: If my people, which are called by my name, shall humble themselves, and pray, and seek my face, and turn from their wicked ways; then will I hear from heaven, and will forgive their sins, and will heal their land.'

The emphasis of the word 'hekal' meaning 'he will eat' can also be seen where it is used but wrongly translated as 'palace', this is clear for when it is mentioned 'hekal' but is mistranslated as 'temple' or 'palace', there is food and drink, feasting or people linked to the service or associated with food produce. One example is 1Kgs.21 where Naboth whose name means 'plant/grows' owns a vineyard near the 'palace', Ahab the king wants to buy the vineyard from Naboth who refuses to part with what he inherited from his fathers. Ahab wants to grow a garden of herbs and is ready to give Naboth a different vineyard or money in exchange. Naboth refuses and is killed over the vineyard. The authors have placed the vineyard near the 'palace' (which should read 'he will eat') to link the vineyard, a food source, to the 'palace/he will eat', a place where people eat food in abundance. One of the meanings of Naboth's surname means 'grazed-on-the' and indicates green pastures. From Naboth's word-name meaning, to the vineyard, to the garden of herbs Ahab wants to grow, to locating it near the erroneously named 'palace' which is 'he will eat', the story is about food source. Naboth holding onto the vineyard citing he will not part with his father's inheritance, tells the importance in the story of the land as a food source. 'And it came to pass after these things, that Naboth the Jezreelite had a vineyard, which was in Jezreel, hard by the palace of Ahab king of Samaria. And Ahab spake unto Naboth, saying, Give me thy vineyard, that I may have it for a garden of herbs, because it is near unto my house: and I will give thee for it a better vineyard than it; or, if it seem good to thee, I will give thee the worth of it in money. And Naboth said unto Ahab, The Lord forbid it me, that I should give the inheritance of my fathers unto thee.'. The importance is holding on to land inherited which passes down from parents to children—the same culture described in the Bible is still very strong in rural areas of Yemen who still live a way of life not different than the ancient times described in the Biblical stories: it is about land as a food source.

2Kgs.18, 'temple' or correctly 'he will eat' is used in the story to signify the importance of food produce linking it to the 'hekal/he will eat'. Hezekiah is a good king in the story following God's laws, but he does sin when he gives away silver and gold, but worse still, he cuts off the gold from the doors and the pillars of the 'temple/he will eat' to give to the enemy king of Assyria. When the Assyrian king's men come to make demands, food and drink is mentioned specifically that it will be lacking, with promises of transferring the people to an equally fertile country. After Hezekiah goes to God's house (God's house is a place of piled food and an eating place), Isaiah's message of warning and destruction to Sennacherib also revolves around food and its sources: the drying up of waters (leads to famine), comparing inhabitants of besieged places to grass, green herb, corn spoiled before it has grown (food resources), even the sign to Hezekiah is about food sources and eating: first and second year they will eat of plants which grow themselves, third year they are to sow and harvest then plant vineyards and eat of their production; the people who escape are compared to trees taking root and bearing fruit; after God cures Hezekiah (even the cure is food in the form of figs used to treat the wound) Hezekiah commits a great wrong again, this time in showing visitors sent by the king of Babylon everything he has stored (in 2Kgs.20) and the punishment is his descendants will become eunuchs in the Babylonian palace: palace is 'hekal' 'he will eat' just as 'temple' is 'hekal/he will eat'—and if you read the Biblical stories, eunuchs in 'palaces' are related to the service of food, in charge of stores (including food) and serving food. The wrong in the story was he allowed 'strangers' access to his stores, just as it was wrong in other stories to allow strangers into the 'house of God' where food is stored. Remember 'house of God' is a wrong translation, the correct translation is 'he/it will-feed well/fed well' 'he/it will-plumpen with food/with various nice food' 'he/it will-tear strips of meat/eat meat'.

2Kings continues with the same pattern: good kings destroy 'high places/bmh, bmwth 'for what?' 'why?' 'what for?' 'with what?" and altars where sacrifices are made to other deities; the idea of the Biblical 'high places' where misguided people offer food sacrifices to other gods, which upsets God as he is upset over what and why they take away from his 'hekal/he will eat'/. Bad kings build and/or offer sacrifices at other places—the wrong is in offering food to other Gods when this food should be reserved for the correct God in the stories—the wrongdoing, the punishment and the piety still revolves around food and eating: much importance is put on the vessels which are from the 'he will eat('temple')' being taken out of it, or used to serve sacrifices (food) to other gods.

Josiah (1Kgs.23) in the 'house of the Lord' (where food is stored and served) orders to remove all vessels used in serving Baal, he also orders the execution of all priests who performed rituals to Baal, the sun, moon, planets and other celestial deities (priests' rituals as described in the Bible are all related to serving food in the form of offerings and sacrifices to gods). A point is made (v.8-9) although priests who served other gods have been removed out of the high places, and the places destroyed, they do not (are not allowed) to approach God's altar in Jerusalem (they cannot be trusted near piles of produce and as they are polluted, God does not want them touching his food or things related to serving him food), but are allowed to eat unleavened bread 'among their brethren'. Josiah slays all the priests who served at high places ('for what?' 'why?' 'what for?' 'with what?'/will eat(places)') then commands the people to keep the passover i.e. a feast will follow. What needed to be cleansed/removed from the 'he will eat('temple')' were vessels used for serving food for Baal—the 'temple/he will eat' is for the correct God to eat at and the priests who serve the correct God, but not for idols/other gods and the priests who serve them. The serving of other gods causes the vessels to become 'polluted' because they took away from God's piles of food, but just as 'Tobiah' in an earlier story represents uncleanness as in 'palatable/germs/repulsion' the same is depicted in how the correct God is repulsed and does not want to eat from vessels which other gods and their 'polluted' priests have touched, and the same goes for the unhygienic and repulsive way (in the story) any food touched/served for and to other gods.

Jehoiachin's sin is that he gave to the king of Babylon all the treasures of both the house of God and king, but worse, as emphasis is put on it, he cuts up and gives away all the gold vessels of the 'temple/he will eat'. As the temple vessels are used for serving God, it leaves God without anything to eat from, this results in Jehoiachin, his whole family, and all of Jerusalem being taken captive. So everything and everyone used to feed God are taken to Babylon and what follows is because the things important to feeding God have been destroyed, and everything taken. God does not want Judah nor Jerusalem to have peace, so God makes Zedekiah (the king appointed by king of Babylon) to rebel against the king of Babylon so that God can exact his anger and punishment that the people be destroyed.

More importantly, the authors have the 'house of God', which is bereaved of its vessels which are used in the 'he will eat/temple', destroyed completely—no wall, no pillar, no ornament and no utensils and vessels are left without being crumbled, burnt, cut to pieces or carried away: God is angry because his vessels which were used to sacrifice, prepare and serve to him food were handed over by Jehoiachin earlier—the authors make it clear: if God cannot be served food in the 'house of God/temple' (both mean a place where he gets to eat) because his vessels have gone to strangers, along with all the stores and Jehoiachin, then there is no need for the house—and the authors of the story allow the complete and utter destruction of the fabled 'house of the Lord' and 'house of the king' along with the vessels (which an earlier chapter in the Bible had already narrated these same vessels had all been chopped up and given to the king of Babylon, but as it is fiction this contradiction does not bother the authors/editors nor does it impede the message). But the authors do want to emphasise that if there are no vessels to serve God, if anything is taken by strangers, it negatively effects the wholeness of the 'house of God'—God wants it all or nothing at all.

The story shows that following Jehoiachin allowing the vessels of the 'temple/he will eat' to go, that a famine follows while Zedekiah is king, and it is God that makes Zedekiah brashly war against Babylon to bring around the complete destruction of the 'temple/he will eat/house of God/etc.' seeing he (God) can no longer eat there, it even brings around the murder of the priests (whose purpose and work is to perform the rituals of serving the offerings to God) as in this part of the story they no longer have any purpose, and this too exemplifies what the story is saying: the temple and house are for God to eat at, if this cannot happen then everything related to it will be destroyed. Even when Gedaliah the appointed ruler over the 'remnant' of Judah promises fairness and peace, the authors make a point this will not be allowed because God does not want the people anymore, as they allowed his things to slip away; so Gedaliah is killed so the rest of the people flee from Judah in fear. Although the previous chapter in the Bible alludes to this being God's word as passed on by his prophets that Judah will be destroyed because of the sins of Manasseh, what unfolds is more true (in the story) to the punishment God promised on Hezekiah's descendants because Hezekiah not only gave the king of Assyria all the silver in the 'house of the Lord', but he also removed all the gold from the doors and pillars of the 'temple/he will eat' and after God had forgiven him all this—he went and showed the Babylonians all the treasures in the stores of everything in his kingdom (which would include the 'house of God') and therefore the punishment was promised that everyone and everything would be taken away into captivity.

But the authors make sure the audience does not lose sight of what is most important in the stories (and real life) that even after all the destruction, they make the whole point of the story about food and eating. In doing so they connect the importance of the vessels of the 'temple/he will eat' with eating and food sources by ending the chapter with Jehoiachin although he is a prisoner that after thirty-seven years his punishment is lessened by finally being given bread to eat, and is allowed a place at the king of Babylon's table (which is also to eat), and receives an allowance for the rest of his life.

It is all about food and how important the vessels used in the temple are because the meaning of 'hekal' is 'he will eat' and not 'temple'. In exactly the same vein, Manasseh's sins were in addition to building altars and 'high places/'for what?' 'why?' 'what for?' 'with what?'/'he will eats', sacrificed to other gods at other locations, i.e. lessened the correct God's 'qodesh/piles'; but he also lessened the 'he will eat' for God by building altars inside the house of God and its courts, directly using from the piles which are supposed to be solely to the correct God of the OT: 'And he did that which was evil in the sight of the Lord...For he built up again the high places which Hezekiah his father had destroyed; and he reared up altars for Baal...And he built altars in the house of the Lord, of which the Lord said, In Jerusalem will I put my name. And he built altars for all the host of heaven in the two courts of the house of the Lord.' (2kgs.20). 'And it came to pass in the seven and thirtieth year of the captivity of Jehoiachin king of Judah...that Evil-merodach king of Babylon...did lift up the head of Jehoiachin king of Judah out of prison...and he did eat bread continually before him all the days of his life...' (2Kgs.24-25)

The story emphasises the importance of food in this way: God demands piles and piles of sacrifices/offerings (food) which is 'qodesh haqqodashim'; he is served copious amounts of offerings at the 'he will eat', the 'hekal'; everything related for service in 'God's house' can only be touched by specific people, and only a special group of people get choice picks (the priests) while the best is reserved for God; people do get to eat from specific offerings. If offerings are diverted i.e. lessened, God sends famine and dearth against the people, but when all his vessels have been given away, his treasures and stock given to other gods or conquerors leaving him, in a sense, with nothing to eat, nor there being clean or special vessels of the 'temple' to serve food to him through and on - meaning he will not eat: not only will there be punishment of famine, but the whole people will be taken away into captivity because if there are no stores of food to feed him, and no vessels to serve him food on, then there is no need of the people whose land will no longer produce food as punishment to them, so they are scattered into captivity and as refugees elsewhere; if there are no food stores to feed him, and no vessels to serve to him on—then there is no need for priests whose purpose is to prepare the food: sacrifices/offerings. Moreover, if there are no stores of food for him, there is no 'qodesh haqqodashim' and therefore no need for a 'he will eat' without his 'piles upon piles'. Therefore the 'house of God' which is all about food and eating (even its correct translation is about eating well) then the whole 'house of God' may as well be destroyed as it is already defunct when deprived of its piles of sacrifices/offerings and the vessels they are served on.

In 2Chronicles, the importance of food source and 'he will eat/temple' continues to be shown in the stories: 2Chr.26 shows Uzziah is a good king, and while considered a good king he is portrayed as a strong and intelligent person, but mainly the story links him to the fertility of food sources and the 'he will eat(temple)'. He is skilled at husbandry, has much cattle and vineyards, but the authors have him fall out of favour with God when he enters the 'he will eat' to burn incense—something reserved only for priests who are anointed before they can start working inside the 'he will eat' and accessing the 'piled, I will pile' (qodesh haqqodashim). He refuses to listen to the priests and becomes a leper and is no longer allowed inside 'God's house'—this part of the story is authored to reinforce the importance of priests being the only ones allowed to access these resources, enter the 'place' and be the only ones allowed to perform the rituals (which although the 'he will eat/temple' did not exist, was an attempt by priests in real life to have authority over the general public and gained them material benefits)—and although the stories narrate it as a 'specialness' of their 'seed', it is a privilege for the fictional priests, and a privilege for priests in the real world that they would want to keep restricted. In all cases, the story revolves around emphasising food source, 'he will eat', priests' privileges, and the protection of the food stores.

In the following chapter, Uzziah's son Jotham does exactly the opposite: he does not enter/trespass into the 'he will eat' or 'God's house' and is not only rewarded with silver, but much more amounts of food: 'And he did that which was right in the sight of the Lord...howbeit he entered not into the temple of the Lord...And the children of Ammon gave him the same year an hundred talents of silver, and ten thousand measures of wheat, and ten thousand of barley. So much did the children of Ammon pay unto him, both the second year and the third. So Jotham became mighty, because he prepared his ways before the Lord, his God.'.

2Chr.29 follows the earlier stories as it links both 'qodesh/piles' inside the 'house of the Lord' and the 'he will eat(erroneously 'temple')' with prosperity and abundance of food. It clearly states they have been punished and taken away to captivity because they have disobeyed God, but the disobedience is clearly stated as: they forsook God, turned their backs to him, and have turned their faces away from 'God's house', i.e. they no longer piled food for him in the qodesh haqqodashim and the hekal ('piled, I will pile' 'he will eat'). The 'holy place' and 'temple' are mentioned (being part of God's house) needing to be cleaned out 'carry forth the filthiness' i.e. remove idols, altars for other gods, but it also states 'sanctify yourselves' 'sanctify the house of the Lord' 'they sanctified the house of the Lord' followed by mention of all the sin offerings, then followed by all the abundant thanks offerings and sacrifices—wherever there is the word 'sanctify/consecrate' it should be 'pile yourselves' 'pile the house of the Lord' 'they piled the house of the Lord' 'Now ye have piled (yourselves) unto the Lord'—because it is the correct translation and meaning of the word as intended by the authors of the Biblical stories.

Chapter 29 mentions their punishment, which is described in detail in the preceding Chapter 28, was because they no longer piled food and other things solely to God then completely stopped offering/piling to him at all; the remedy is to fill God's house with piles of sacrifices, and to 'minister' to God means to serve him food, incense, etc. In the events of Chapter 28 the story shows the transgressions of dividing food source/offerings away from God, to 'foreign' deities, i.e. lessening God's piles (qodesh) of food for his 'he will eat' (hekal) results in punishment; when the offender (in this story, king Ahaz) does not learn but gives even more from 'God's house' to other gods and other rulers, and eventually closes 'God's house'—complete captivity of the people is the result/punishment. The bad thing is always to lessen or cease giving God his piles of food and servicing him at his 'he will eat' which both Ahaz and Hezekiah's characters do in their stories. Although there are variants in the telling of the same stories between 2Kings and 2Chronicles, in 2Chronicles the authors/editors have added/altered to make it crystal-clear to the audience that Ahaz's sins were that he gave away God's food and resources, which are supposed to be solely to God and served to him both at 'piled, I will pile' and the 'he will eat', Ahaz is taking it from God's piles and giving it to other gods and rulers. As mentioned before, even his name is 'takes/takes a lot' so the authors create the story and have the pivotal character and actions depict his wrong doing, which is taking from God's piles and giving it to others.

Where in Kings, Ahaz' sin was that he built an altar similar to the altars of Damascus, here in Chronicles it is elaborated on, and the sin is using offerings/sacrifices which are meant for God. But after all the slaughter and punishment Ahaz still continues, and increases, his wrong—the authors want it clear to the audience that the sin is lessening/taking from God's piles shown in the narration by having Ahaz take from 'God's house' and sending them to Syria's king; and the authors want the audience to understand it is about food, God's food, by showing Ahaz increases his sins by sacrificing to other gods (with God's food). And to leave no doubt, the authors have him do what other bad kings in the stories do: he cuts up and takes away the vessels—which means there is nothing to serve God's food with/on, and closes down 'God's house' meaning there is no more food for God to eat, no vessels to serve/prepare the food, and therefore no place for the 'qodesh haqqodashim/pile, I will pile' and the 'hekal/he will eat'. 'For the Lord brought Judah low because of Ahaz king of Israel; for he made Judah naked,' i.e. stripped her of her resources.

As mentioned earlier, 'Kidron' means 'they are disgusting/unclean/revolting/filthy' so the authors use this word as a name for a valley and a brook (when the house of God and other areas are cleansed) where in several of the Biblical stories the vessels, idols, and images used for other deities, which are viewed (in the Bible) as disgusting defilements and dirty, are thrown into. In 1Kgs.15:11-13 by Asa who removes Sodomites, his father's idols, his mother the queen and her idols, and burns the idols by the brook Kidron. In 2Kgs.23:4-6 Josiah has the priests take all the vessels 'out of the temple[he will eat] of the Lord' which were made for Baal, also those for the grove and the host of heaven, and they burn these 'disgusting' things in the field of 'Kidron/they are disgusting/unclean/revolting/filthy'. The same in 2Chr. Hezekiah has them take out the 'uncleanness' and throw it into a brook called Kidron, as well as in 2Chr.30:14 they take the altars of Jerusalem, and altars for incense and throw them into Kidron brook. Arabic words with Arabic meanings used to show exactly what is meant by the authors of the Bible, every major character/place name has events exactly as the meaning of the compound words given to it.

The way the 'unclean' vessels and things are thrown into a brook called 'they are disgusting/unclean/revolting/filthy', also supports the real meaning of 'hekal' is 'he will eat' and not 'temple': i.e. everything that has put-off/revolted God from his food has to be removed and the area and 'his' vessels cleaned for serving before God 'will eat' from them again. Just like people do not want to be put off or disgusted by unclean, unhygienic or just off-putting things when eating or around food preparation, e.g. not wanting to use a spoon another person has had in his/her mouth, not wanting to drink from the same glass another person has put his/her lips on, the dip that no one will touch once someone has 'double-dipped' into it. Now that the 'dirty/off-putting' things have been thrown out and the 'house' cleansed, it is time for the characters in the story to start preparing God's qodesh/piles so he can eat in his 'he will eat', and as discussed earlier in this book, this is when they begin the slaughter and sacrifice of animals in astounding (and unrealistic) quantities, for sin offerings, burnt offerings, followed by sacrifices of free will and thanks offerings—and as explained before, the authors keep repeating this theme/narration to make clear these offerings were 'piled' in abundance.

Ezra.3 also proves 'hekal' mistranslated as 'temple' actually means 'he will eat': the story has the people build an altar 'of the God of Israel' where they offer burnt offerings morning and evening; the narration stresses that during and after the feast of the tabernacles they continue to make burnt offerings in addition to the offerings required according to the feast of the tabernacles, as well as the new moons, and those who make free will offerings, and also the burnt offerings 'of all the set feasts of the Lord that were consecrated'; note the last sentences should read 'of all the set feasts of the Lord that were piled'. So the people are feasting, and so is God. It goes on further to prove 'hekal', as the word literally implies, does mean 'he will eat': 'From the first day of the seventh month began they to offer burnt offerings unto the Lord. But the foundation of the temple of the Lord was not yet laid.' i.e. they are already feeding God through burnt offerings although the 'hekal/he will eat' does not yet exist, even its foundations have not been laid. The authors are explaining the 'he will eat' is where God should be served offerings and sacrifices; they did not say 'the foundation of God's house is not yet laid' because they are speaking about giving offerings to God which, had the 'hekal/he will eat' been already rebuilt, he would have been served his food in there, because God eats in a very specific and private place.

All these offerings as described in Ezra.3:2-6 are offerings 'unto the Lord', the food is all the 'set feasts of the Lord' showing the importance of food in the stories and pointing out it should be in the 'he will eat'. Ezra's Book puts the 'he will eat(temple)' as the most important part of 'God's house'; in past chapters 'God's house' is mentioned a lot, and the 'temple' which correctly is 'hekal/he will eat' is part of and important to it. But in this story the 'hekal/he will eat' is more important as they mention laying its foundation with more emphasis, it is given priority and venerated before mentioning 'the house of God'. And it can be argued they have written the narrative which shows the misnomered 'temple' 'hekal/he will eat' is the whole of God's house—which is true seeing the alternative names of what is believed to be 'God's house' and 'temple' all mean where food is fed/eaten so the concept is interchangeable. All the stories in different books and the different compound words and phrases used all show that 'God's house' and other related 'places' is for storing, serving and eating food (by God and people), the food sources, supply and consumption.

Ezra.4 also shows 'hekal/he will eat' is about serving God food to eat. When the characters described as 'adversaries of Judah and Benjamin' learn about the temple being built they arrive eager to help and participate in completing 'God's house'—and they claim they have a right to it because they have been sacrificing to God (i.e. feeding God) since a long time ago.

The meaning of 'hekal' as 'he will eat' has not only been wrongly translated as 'temple', but the very same word 'hekal' used in the same way about a place where food is eaten has also been wrongly translated as 'palace'. But the importance of food in the story and the way this word is used around an eating/place or eating event in the stories can still be clearly discerned whether mentioned in the English translation as 'temple' or 'palace'. In the same chapter, after not being allowed to participate in building the 'he will eat('temple')' a group send a complaint to the king and it is mentioned they believe the tithes/tributes paid to the king will lessen due to the rebuilding (of the 'temple' 'he will eat'), and the senders of the complaint feel obliged to send the complaint because they receive 'maintenance from the king's palace['he will eat']' i.e. they eat or receive food supplies from the king's 'hekal/he will eat('palace' wrongly)', they are warning him not to allow its completion, that if God's 'he will eat/hekal' is built, resources will stop flowing and accumulating to the king's 'he will eat' as what goes into the temple is food supplies and money. The authors use the same argument used in the narration of God's displeasure that any sacrifice/offerings being diverted to other gods and/or other places do lessen what is received at the right place and for the correct God, but this time it is God's 'he will eat' which will negatively affect the king's 'he will eat'. (Ezra.4:14)

Isaiah 6, the first verse Lord's presence fills the 'temple/he will eat' and most of the chapter revolves around feeding and sustenance in figurative speech: the seraphim putting a live coal to Isaiah's mouth to purge his sin in a similar way to offerings being burnt, the same way God eats things with fire, and kills 'strange/ unclean' things with fire. The people who cannot understand God's message are likened to those suffering the lethargy of overeating.

Isa.13:22 mentions 'dragons in their pleasant palaces' along with 'wild beasts of the islands shall cry in their desolate houses…' animals will take the people's place, and eat in their houses/palaces 'palaces' being 'hekal/he will eat'.

Isa.44, although 'temple' 'hekal/he will eat' is not mentioned until the last verse, the whole chapter's theme is about eating/nourishing or the lack of it whether literally talking about food or symbolising about something else: Jesurun 'greedy'; quenching thirst and flooding the ground is figuratively saying allowing the land to give (fertility); mentions hunger and lack of drink; rain nourishing trees; baking bread, eating roast till full, likening it to feeding but not gaining satisfaction; 'and to the Temple, thy foundation shall be laid'—in earlier books the foundation of the 'hekal' 'he will eat' is linked to piles of food sacrificed/offered to God, and people feasting.

Isa.66 also mentions 'hekal/he will eat', but begins with the verses of God asking about where his 'place of rest' which alludes to his 'hekal/he will eat'; the examples in verse 3 of people sacrificing/slaughtering/ offering in a wrong way as they either eat it for themselves or sacrifice to other gods which it alludes to again later in the chapter 'They that sanctify [pile] themselves, and purify themselves in the gardens behind one tree in the midst, eating swine's flesh, and the abomination, and the mouse, shall be consumed together, saith the Lord.' (Isa.66:17) The word 'mouse' in this sentence is erratic, probably another mistranslation of what is probably a different word.

In Isa.66:20-24 you can see the work of an original story and the edited part of the story between an earlier author whose idea was to destroy all the 'children of Israel' and a later editor who changed it to have the children of Israel spared. Verse 20 clearly alludes to the story of the human sacrifice of Gog on the mountains, and here in Isaiah it clearly states it will be no different than an offering brought in pureness and sacrificed to God. But what is evident is this specific verse states 'Israel/the children of Israel' will be sacrificed and another foreign people will take their place, and priests will be chosen to be priests to God instead of the sacrificed children of Israel. Verses 18-21 clearly sate all the children of Israel, no matter how far they have been driven or travelled, will all be brought back and be sacrificed (massacred by God) so that none remain, but that God will replace them with foreigners whom he will 'take of them for priests, and for Levites, saith the Lord.' Which shows how 'Levites' is not a family name, but a word used to show characters/events who serve/assist (in this instance as in other stories (while other meanings of the word 'Levi' in wordplay are used in other stories)).

Then the addition of another author/editor has added verse 22 to state the complete opposite: i.e. that God swears an oath that the children of Israel (without naming them because it has been inserted between the verses which state they will be slaughtered as a sacrifice) will be kept safe forever.

The verses 23-24 are definitely part of the original story by an author who wanted the story or a following story to be the children of Israel are all slaughtered then replaced by 'different people', as it carries on in the same vein of promising severe punishment for the disobedient in the form of a human sacrifice. The author who wrote Ezekiel may be the same editor who added verse Isa.66:22, to break-up or confuse who was supposed to be sacrificed. Ezekiel's story may very well have been the same as the Isaiah.66:18-21,23-24, but was edited—the whole Bible is full of obvious and clear contradictions and works that have been changed to suit the later editors of these stories. Whether the sacrifice of Gog from Magog was supposed to afflict the children of Israel in Ezekiel, or whether Ezekiel was written that way by the original author(s), we will never know because even the oldest texts of the Bible are already much edited works put together when they were copied into the texts found and known currently as the oldest texts of the Bible which have survived. In all cases, In Isa.66 the story shows it was the children of Israel meant to be killed-off in a horrific huge human sacrifice, and in Ezekiel it is Gog and the other people who arrive with them who are killed-off in the spectacular and horrific human sacrifice.

Jer.7:4 offers greater proof that the word 'temple' is not the correct translation nor meaning of 'hekal', and it also supports the literal meanings of the word 'hekal' is 'he will eat':

'Trust ye not in lying words, saying, The temple of the Lord, The temple of the Lord, The temple of the Lord, *are* these.'

The above sentence does not make sense translated as 'temple'. It only makes perfect sense when you use the correct word for 'hekal':

'Trust ye not in lying words, saying, he will eat of the Lord, he will eat of the Lord, he will eat of the Lord, *are* these.'

Furthermore, the verse and meaning of word 'hekal/he will eat' is supported by verses 21 and 23: 'Thus saith the Lord of hosts, the God of Israel: Put your burnt offerings unto your sacrifices, and eat flesh. For I spake not unto your fathers, nor commanded them in the day that I brought them out of the land of Egypt, concerning burnt offerings or sacrifices: But this thing commanded I them, saying, Obey my voice and I will be your God, and ye shall be my people: and walk ye in all the ways that I have commanded you, that it may be well with you.'

The author of this part of the Bible has contradicted the authors of all the other stories, as obvious and undeniably clear the author has the text narrate God say words to the effect: 'stop making everything about God will eat, God will eat, God will eat; take your burnt offerings, put them on top of your sacrifices and eat them yourselves. I never told your fathers/ancestors (Moses/Aaron/etc.) anything about feeding me, nor did I command them to make burnt offerings or sacrifices to me: all I ordered them to do was be obedient, do as the law I commanded, and you would all be okay.' And the verses that follow state the people did not listen to God and followed all the wrong ways instead of his way.

Now although it contradicts all the other authors/stories who have made God demand food in great supplies for his 'he will eat/hekal', even this chapter is still based on and revolves around the 'hekal/he will eat' theme of food and its source, as well as nourishment and famine similar to the other stories. It mentions 'God's house' then reminds them of Shiloh (the latter is where feasting and rituals used to be held as mentioned as such in earlier books); it has God speak of family effort of children gathering wood, fathers making fires, and women kneading dough to make cakes, as well as drink offerings to other gods—which upsets this one; the fury to be poured onto the place, man, beast, trees of fields and fruit of grounds, is the punishment of drought and famine; the people themselves will end up as carrion and the land will be barren. (Jer.7)

Jer.24 continues with the food-related theme with two baskets of figs left outside God's 'he will eat'; the good figs representing the captives taken out of Judah (which were taken to Babylon), but the last part of the sentence refers to those who fled from the violence to the Chaldees. The bad figs are Zedekiah who was appointed king instead of Jehoiachin, but because God wanted to destroy Judah, as per the earlier books, he compelled him to rebel against the king of Babylon so God could destroy Judah, Jerusalem, and God's house completely (the earlier story was about 'he will eat/hekal' and food offerings going to other gods and ceasing to be presented to the correct God, especially after the special vessels used to serve him were taken and given away). The author describes Zedekiah and his lot in a simile to figs so bad they cannot be eaten. As expected, famine along with war, slaughter and pestilence will wipe them off the land as punishment.

Jer.50 is about revenge of Assyria and especially against Babylon who have taken the things stored in the 'hekal/he will eat' and the 'house of God/'he/it will-tear strips of meat/eat meat' 'he/it will-eat plenty of meat', including its eventual and complete destruction (it refers to when the kings of Judah took goods and treasures from the 'hekal/he will eat/temple') and when they eventually return to destroy it and leave nothing of it behind. The punishment is slaughter and the destruction of buildings, but for the most part it revolves around making the food source desolate, and also uses metaphors of the events likening people to sheep/goats and other food sources to be slaughtered, and it makes it absolutely clear it is revenge for taking the things precious to the author (God in the narrative) or at least the author's ideas for the stories which is the piled things, the food source, and as we know from the earlier stories over the taking away of the vessels of the 'hekal/he will eat'.

The slaughter of people is terrible in the story, but the focus is on cutting off/destroying the food source in revenge for destroying and taking from God's food source: 'the vengeance of his temple[hekal/he will eat]'. The authors choice of likening both Israel and its enemies as livestock is because it enhances the story that this is what the revenge and story is about. '...let none of her escape...according to all that she hath done, do unto her: for she hath been proud against the Lord, against the Holy One[piled, I will pile] of Israel.' The king of Babylon took from the 'he will eat/hekal' and the house including 'piled, I will pile', the latter sentence of the verse should read 'against the 'piled, I will pile' of Israel'.

'Their Redeemer is strong; the Lord of hosts is his name: he shall thoroughly plead her cause, that he may give rest to the land...' Note in earlier books the people are supposed to offer the firstborn male of every animal and man, but God allowed they be redeemed (the humans) with sacrifices/offering of an animal—here it is with the Babylonian people.

Following the killing of men and women of all ages, and the children—which is horrific enough in any story, but in the Bible it is important to the authors to make it about food sources: 'I will also break in pieces with thee the shepherd and his flock; and with thee I will break in pieces the husbandman and his yoke of oxen...The daughter of Babylon *is* like a threshing floor, *it is* time to thresh her: yet a little while, and the time of her harvest shall come. Nebuchadrezzar the king of Babylon hath devoured me, he hath crushed me, he hath made me an empty vessel, he hath swallowed me up like a dragon, he hath filled his belly with my delicates, he hath cast me out.' The author has made God bitter about his food taken by others.

In Ezek.41-42 mention of the 'temple' (hekal/he will eat) is linked to the proximity of the 'qodesh haqqodashim/piled, I will pile'; the description of the 'layout' is for proximity of where food is stored, processed, served. And the emphasis on size and purpose are the same reasons mentioned earlier in the explanations of 'qodesh/qodesh haqqodashim'. The size is large to accumulate stores and to contain those priests and God eating. What it contains is food for God's 'he will eat'.

Dan.1:4: Daniel and his friends story begins with them in the king's 'palace' which correctly reads 'hekal/he will eat', and the story immediately revolves around eating '...and as much as had ability in them to stand in the king's palace...and the king appointed them a daily provision of the king's meat, and of the wine which he drank: so nourishing them three years, that at the end thereof they may stand before the king...But Daniel purposed in his heart that he would not defile himself with the king's portion of the king's meat, nor with the wine which he drank: therefore he requested of the prince of the eunuchs that he might not defile himself...And the prince of the eunuchs said unto Daniel, I fear my lord the king who hath appointed your meat and your drink: for why should he see your faces worse liking than the children which *are* of your sort? then shall ye make me endanger my head to the king. Then said Daniel to Melzar, whom the prince of the eunuchs had set over Daniel, Hananiah, Mishael, and Azariah, Prove thy servants, I beseech thee, ten days; and let them give us pulse to eat, and water to drink. Then let our countenances be looked on before thee, and the countenance of the children that eat of the portion of the king's meat: and as thou seest, deal with thy servants. So he consented to them in this matter, and proved them ten days. And at the end of ten days their countenances appeared fairer and fatter in flesh than all the children which did eat the portion of the king's meat. Thus Melzar took away the portion of their meat, and the wine that they should drink; and gave them pulse.'

In mistranslation the word 'hekal' is still being transformed to either 'temple' or 'palace' when it is 'he will eat', a place where people or God, or both, eat because wherever 'hekal' is mentioned, the story focuses on food, its source and consumption. In Dan.4 the story links 'hekal/he will eat' ('palace'), food sources and resources to 'qodesh/piles' erroneously described as the 'Holy One' and 'holy ones': the king has a disturbing dream while in the 'palace[he will eat]' about a tree which has fruit which all beasts can feed from, a 'piled['holy']' comes down and orders the tree to be cut down [making the tree a heap on the ground as the word 'qodesh' implies], its fruit and the beasts scattered. The stump is to remain in the grass and share with animals. The story narrates the translation is the king is the tree and will be made to eat grass like an animal. No sooner does the story have the king, after one year, enter the 'palace[he will eat]' and within the hour he is already behaving like an animal and eating grass: 'I Nebuchadnezzar was at rest in mine house, and flourishing in my palace:' note although the author mentions the king is already resting in his house, he still mentions 'hekal/he will eat' as a specific place as is the norm in the Bible to make the place relevant to the events unfolding in the story (if you go to the Ahaz/Naboth story (1Kgs.21) you will also find the authors narrate in the same passage that the garden is near the 'palace/he will eat' and describe the king's residence as his 'house'—making a clear distinction that 'hekal' is an eating place) 'I saw a dream which made me afraid...Thus were the visions in mine head on my bed; I saw, and behold, a tree in the midst of the earth, and the height thereof was great...The leaves thereof *were* fair, and the fruit thereof much, and in it *was* meat for all: the beasts of the field had shadow under it, and the fowls of the heaven dwelt in the boughs thereof, and all flesh was fed of it. I saw in the visions of my head upon my bed, and behold, a watcher and an holy one came down from heaven; He cried aloud and said thus; Hew down the tree and cut off his branches, shake off his leaves and scatter his fruit: let the beasts get away from under it, and the fowls from his branches...and *let* his portion *be* with the beasts in the grass of the earth...This is the interpretation...That they shall drive thee from men, and thy dwelling shall be with the beasts of the field, and they shall make thee to eat as oxen...At the end of twelve months he walked in the palace[he will eat] of the kingdom of Babylon. The king spake, and said, Is not this great Babylon, that I have built for the house of the kingdom by the might of my power, and for the honour of my majesty? While the word *was* in the king's mouth, there fell a voice from heaven...The same hour was the thing fulfilled upon Nebuchadnezzar: and he was driven from men, and did eat grass as oxen...'

Dan.5 continues to link 'temple/palace' which is 'hekal/he will eat' with food, drink, eating. Belshezzar and a thousand others are feasting and drinking, he has the gold and silver vessels which his father took from God's 'he will eat' brought so he and his family can drink from them.

Dan.6 continues to use the eating/food theme wherever the word 'hekal/he will eat' (mistranslated as 'temple' 'palace') is mentioned. As soon as the 'palace[he will eat]' is mentioned, the author makes it clear that although the king is at the 'he will eat' he is not eating, but fasting—not religiously, but unable to eat nor sleep, nor enjoy music because he is upset that he has had to throw Daniel to the lions to eat. He goes early in the morning to the lion's den to find out if they have eaten Daniel, but Daniel tells him God has 'shut up' the lions' mouths, i.e. like the king, they are unable to eat. And when Darius decides to punish the conspirators against Daniel, they are thrown to the lions along with their wives and children, upon whom the lions feast as described in the story.

Ezra.5:14-15: the vessels taken from the 'hekal' of the 'house of God' we are told were taken to the 'hekal' in Babylon—so they are taken from one 'he will eat' where they were used for serving food and drink, to another 'he will eat' where they are used for food and drink (the stories in books such as Daniel tell us these vessels were used at feasts and drinking wine (in the stories)); in this part of the story the vessels are returned to Jerusalem to be delivered back to the 'temple[he will eat]'—they will be needed in the 'house of God'. Ezra.6 follows in the same way, mentioning the vessels which were taken away from the 'temple/he will eat' of the 'house of God' to Babylon should be returned to the 'temple' (in Jerusalem) and placed in the 'house of God', and the rest of the chapter is about the great quantities of food resources supplied for sacrifices and feasting.

Hosea 8 also revolves around metaphors/similes of eating followed by the last two verses of the chapter where it makes abundantly clear when it mentions 'temples' (hekal/he will eats) that God will not eat/accept sacrifices because the people have built 'temples' (he will eats) for other gods (therefore have diverted the food to these other gods) so although the people will eat from the sacrifices—God will not eat from them: '...they have transgressed against my covenant, and trespassed against my law...of their silver and their gold have they made them idols, that they may be cut off...For they have sown the wind, and they shall reap the whirlwind: it hath no stalk: the bud shall yield no meal: if so be it yield, the strangers shall swallow it up. Israel is swallowed up: now shall they be among the Gentiles as a vessel wherein there is no pleasure...Because Ephraim has made many altars to sin, altars shall be unto him to sin. I have written to him the great things of my law, but they were counted as a strange thing. They sacrifice flesh *for* the sacrifices of mine offerings, and eat *it*; *but* the Lord accepteth them not: now will he remember their iniquity, and visit their sins: they shall return to Egypt. For Israel hath forgotten his Maker, and buildeth temples [he will eats]; and Judah hath multiplied fenced cities: but I will send a fire upon his cities, and it shall devour the palaces[he will eats] thereof.'

Joel.3: the similes/metaphors of food and food source continues to be used to express the anger of God because his silver and gold vessels have been taken to other 'temples' (he will eats). The vessels used in God's 'hekal/he will eat' are being used by others at their own 'hekal/he will eat'. The link to 'qodesh/piles' (referring to piles of food but wrongly translated as 'holy') to the 'temple' (correctly 'he will eat) is shown in 'my holy[piled] mountain' 'then shall Jerusalem be holy[piled]' it is followed by the narration of mountains flowing with wine and milk, water to the valley, this invokes rich agriculture (more things to eat in abundance). Note: it should be 'piled mountain/mountain piled' 'then shall Jerusalem be piled'—'qodesh' is about the heaps of produce just as the 'hekal/he will eat' is about eating: '...and sold a girl for wine, that they might drink...swiftly and speedily will I return your recompense upon your own head; Because ye have taken my silver and my gold, and have carried into your temples my goodly pleasant things...Beat your plowshares into swords, and your pruning hooks into spears...Put ye in the sickle, for the harvest is ripe: come, get ye down, for the press is full, the fats overflow; for the wickedness is great...So shall ye know that I *am* the Lord your God dwelling in Zion, my holy mountain: then shall Jerusalem be holy, and there shall no strangers pass through her anymore. And it shall come to pass in that day, that the mountain shall drop new wine, and the hills shall flow with milk, and all the rivers of Judah shall flow with waters, and a fountain shall come forth of the house of the Lord, and shall water the valley of Shittim.'

Jonah's story also uses eating/food along with the mention of the 'temple' (hekal/he will eat): the sailors offer God a sacrifice; the fish swallows Jonah; and it is while Jonah is in the belly of the fish that he cries out to God, i.e. he is being eaten while the narrative speaks of him calling out to God and mentioning he will face God's 'holy temple' which should read God's 'piled he-will-eat'; while he describes that he is dying being digested, the story again narrates God hears him in his 'holy temple/piled he-will-eat'; and when Jonah declares he will sacrifice to God and pay his vow (sacrifices/vows are usually food produce brought to the ritual place to be offered to God (or fasting a set number of days) and this is invoked by the narration) then God allows the fish to vomit Jonah which is also an act related to 'temple/he will eat': spewing out what was eaten.

It continues with the eating theme of 'hekal/he will eat': when Nineveh's people hear God's warning, they fast—even the animals are made to fast. The lesson Jonah is taught is through a worm destroying a plant is also about eating: whether a caterpillar or another living thing is meant by the 'worm', plants are eaten by the caterpillars, other insects, etc. and wither and die because the way these insects eat the plant causes its withering.

The story uses 'eating' as the events in relation to the mention of 'holy temple [piled he-will-eat]': 'Then the men feared the Lord exceedingly, and offered a sacrifice unto the Lord, and made vows. Now the Lord had prepared a great fish to swallow up Jonah. And Jonah was in the belly of the fish for three days and three nights. Then Jonah prayed unto the Lord his God out of the fish's belly, And said, I cried by reason of mine affliction unto the Lord, and he heard me; out of the belly of hell cried I, *and* thou heardest my voice. For thou hadst cast me into the deep, in the midst of the seas; and the floods compassed me about: all thy billows and thy waves passed over me. Then I said, I am cast out of thy sight; yet I will look again toward the holy temple...When my soul fainted within me, I remembered the Lord, and my prayer came in unto thee with the voice of thanksgiving: I will pay *that* that I have vowed. Salvation is of the Lord. And the Lord spake unto the fish, and it vomited Jonah upon the dry *land*...So the people of Nineveh believed God, and proclaimed a fast...by the decree of the king and his nobles, saying, Let neither man nor beast, herd nor flock, taste anything: let them not feed, nor drink water...But God prepared a worm when the morning rose the next day, and it smote the gourd that it withered,'

Book of Micah begins the story with mention of the 'holy temple'. i.e. the 'piled he-will-eat', and the imagery of the text is related to the destruction of food source, related to eating, and piles of food produce; metaphors are acts of harvesting/processing crops, or flocks, all food sources, which when prepared are piles and heaps, and eventually eaten.

'Hear, all ye people, hearken, O earth, and all that therein is: and let the Lord God be witness against you, the Lord from his holy temple...Therefore I will make Samaria as an heap of the field, *and* as plantings of a vineyard: and I will pour down the stones thereof into the valley, and I will discover the foundations thereof. And all the graven images thereof shall be beaten to pieces, and all the hires thereof shall be burned with fire...And they covet fields and take *them* by violence; and houses, and take *them* away: so they oppress a man and his house, even a man and his heritage...and say, we be utterly spoiled: he hath changed the portion of my people, how hath he removed it from me! turning away he hath divided our fields...I will surely gather the remnant of Israel; I will put them together as the sheep of Bozrah, as the flock in the midst of their fold...Who hate the good, and love the evil: who pluck off their skin from off them, and their flesh from off their bones; Who also eat the flesh of my people, and flay their skin from off them; and they break their bones, and chop them in pieces, as for the pot, and as flesh within the caldron...Therefore for your sake shall Zion be plowed *as* a field, and Jerusalem shall become heaps, and the mountain of the house as the high places of the forest...and he shall beat their swords into plowshares, and their spears into pruning hooks: nation shall not lift up a sword against nation, neither shall they learn war anymore. But they shall sit every man under his vine and under his fig tree...And thou, O tower of the flock...Be in pain, and labour to bring forth, O daughter of Zion, like a woman in travail: for now shalt thou go forth out of the city, and thou shalt dwell in the field, and thou shalt go *even* to Babylon: there shalt thou be delivered; there shall the Lord redeem thee from the hand of thine enemies...for he shall gather them as the sheaves into the floor. Arise and thresh, O daughter of Zion: for I will make thine horn iron, and I will make thy hoofs brass: and thou shalt beat in pieces many people: and I will consecrate[pile] their gain unto the Lord, and their substance unto the Lord of the whole earth...And he shall stand and feed in the strength of the Lord, in the majesty of the name of the Lord his God...And the remnant of Jacob shall be among the Gentiles in the midst of many people as a lion among the beasts of the forest, as a young lion among the flocks of sheep: who, if he go through, both treadeth down, and teareth in pieces, and none can deliver...Wherewith shall I come before the Lord *and* bow myself before the high God? shall I come before him with burnt offerings, with calves of a year old? Will the Lord be pleased with thousands of rams, *or* with ten thousand rivers of oil? shall I give my firstborn *for* my transgression, the fruit of my body for the sin of my soul?...Are there yet treasures of wickedness in the house of the wicked, and the scant measure *that is* abominable? Shall I count *them* pure with the wicked balances, and with the bag of deceitful weights?...Therefore will I also make *thee* sick in smiting thee, in making *thee* desolate because of thy sins. Thou shalt eat, but not be satisfied; and thy casting down *shall be* in the midst of thee; and thou shalt take hold, but shalt not deliver; and *that* which thou deliverest will I give up to the sword. Thou shalt sow, but thou shalt not reap; thou shalt tread the olives, but thou shalt not anoint thee with oil; and sweet wine, but thou shalt not drink wine. For the statutes of Omri are kept, and all the works of the house of Ahab, and ye walk in their counsels; that I should make thee a desolation, and the inhabitants thereof an hissing...'.

The earlier books tell the story of Omri sinning by following the ways of Jeroboam who not only sacrificed to other/strange gods, but built golden calves for people to worship and to sacrifice at so as to stop them going to worship, i.e. stop them offering sacrifices, at the 'house of the Lord in Jerusalem'—so he put one calf in Dan, and one calf in Bethel, his sin and the reason it is brought up in this story is that he caused God's 'piles' to decrease, therefore there is a disruption of the food supply chain and lessening at God's 'he will eat'. Ahab also built a grove for offerings and sacrificing, therefore lessening the piles and food at God's 'he will eat' and his 'piled, I will pile', 1Kgs.16:33-34 makes him worse than other bad kings of Israel, attributing that during his reign people performed human sacrifice (Hiel sacrificing his two sons). Both Omri and Ahab are mentioned as sinners who took and diverted food piles away from 'God's house'. They are also used for the meaning of 'omri/ordered' as it talks about statutes' and 'ahab/give/gave' as it narrates giving to the wrong places/gods. 'Woe is me! For I am as when they have gathered the summer fruits, as the grape gleanings of the vintage: *there is* no cluster to eat: my soul desired the firstripe fruit...Notwithstanding the land shall be desolate because of them that dwell therein, for the fruit of their doings. Feed thy people with thy rod, the flock of thine heritage, which dwell solitarily in the wood, in the midst of Carmel: let them feed in Bashan and Gilead as in the days of old.'

Nahum also uses 'palace/hekal/he will eat' in the same manner, and the punishment is total destruction in revenge for emptying God's 'temple', correctly God's 'he will eat'. Their 'palace[he will eat']' will now be destroyed and the narration speaks of plentiful abundance turned into desolation, it mentions place names in the Biblical stories used to represent green pastures and fat livestock, it mentions feasts, animals tearing prey to pieces; figs ready to be shaken and eaten; insects eating up plants/trees to destroy/devour them.

Habbakuk also revolves around eating, sacrifice, God in 'holy temple' which I cannot stress enough is neither 'holy' nor 'temple' but is 'piled he-will-eat'. The similes and metaphors described are about food sources; animals of prey and how they eat; men and how they catch fish, but instead of worshipping the right God, sacrifice to the wrong gods. As in earlier stories wherever there are 'graven images' 'molten images', i.e. idols, offerings and sacrifices are made to them, this angers God because they take from his 'qodesh/piles'. Note how the author of Habbakuk stresses the images are lifeless objects, whereas the correct god of the story (always described as the 'living God') is narrated as actually being in the 'holy temple[piled he-will-eat]'; the story is reminding the audience not to waste food on a lifeless idol which the worshippers had to create with their own hands, but to sacrifice, offer and pile food to the living God who is in his 'piled he-will-eat'—waiting for offerings and sacrifices.

Haggai completely revolves around the 'temple/he will eat' which has not been rebuilt in this story. The narration has God say 'because you have not built my 'he will eat', the house where 'qodesh/piles' should be stored and served, and directly states there is a drought because they have not built it; because they have not provided the place where God can eat his piled piles—they will not eat from the land, and no matter how hard they work, God will not bless it but make it dwindle. Both chapters stress because the people did not build his 'he will eat' (temple), the land will not be fertile.

Even the lesson where Haggai teaches them about uncleanness revolves around food: 'Thus speaketh the Lord of hosts, saying, This people say, The time is not come, the time that the Lord's house should be built. Then came the word of the Lord by the prophet Haggai saying, *Is it,* time for you, O ye, to dwell in your ceiled houses, and this house *lie* waste? Now therefore thus saith the Lord of hosts; Consider your ways. Ye have sown much, and bring in little; ye eat, but ye have not enough; ye drink, but ye are not filled with drink; ye clothe you, but there is none warm; and he that earneth wages earneth wages *to put it* into a bag with holes...Go up to the mountain, and bring wood, and build the house; and I will take pleasure in it, and I will be glorified, saith the Lord. Ye looked for much, and, lo, *it came* to little...Why? saith the Lord of hosts. Because of mine house that *is* waste, and ye run every man unto his own house. Therefore the heaven over you is stayed from dew, and the earth is stayed from her fruit. And I called a drought upon the land, and upon the mountains, and upon the corn, and upon the new wine, and upon the new oil, and upon that which the ground bringeth forth, and upon men, and upon cattle, and upon all labour of the hands...Who is left among you that saw this house in her first glory? and how do you see it now? is it not in your eyes in comparison of it as nothing? ...For thus saith the Lord of the hosts; Yet once, it is a little while, and I will shake the heavens, and the earth, and the sea, and the dry *land*; And I will shake all nations, and the desire of all nations shall come: and I will fill this house with glory saith the Lord of hosts. The silver *is* mine, and the gold *is* mine, saith the Lord of hosts. The glory of this latter house, shall be greater than of the former, saith the Lord of hosts...'.

Note: the shaking of the sea, land, sky—the link of glory filling the house with silver and gold being his, in a possessive manner, meaning the house will be filled with the produce and treasures of the earth. 'Thus saith the Lord of hosts: Ask now the priests *concerning* the law, saying, If one bear holy[piled] flesh in the skirt of his garment, and with his skirt do touch bread, or pottage, or wine, or oil, or any meat, shall it be holy[piled]? And the priests answered and said, No. Then said Haggai, If *one* that *is* unclean, touch any of these, shall it be unclean? And the priests answered and said, It shall be unclean. Then answered Haggai and said, So *is* this people, and so *is* this people before me, saith the Lord; and so *is* every work of their hands; and that which they offer there *is* unclean. And now I pray you, consider from this day and upward, from before a stone was laid upon a stone in the temple[he will eat] of the Lord: Since those days were, when *one* came to an heap of twenty *measures*, there were *but* ten: when *one* came to the pressfat to draw out fifty *vessels* out of the press, there were *but* twenty. I smote you with blasting and with mildew and with hail in all the labours of your hands; yet ye *turned* not to me, saith the Lord. Consider now from this day and upward...even from the day that the foundation of the Lord's temple[he will eat] was laid, consider *it*. Is the seed yet in the barn? yea, as yet the vine, and the fig tree, and the pomegranate, and the olive tree, have not brought forth: from this day I will bless *you*.'

Zechariah: 'Thus saith the Lord of hosts; I am jealous for Jerusalem and for Zion with a great jealousy. And I am very sore displeased with the heathens *that are* at ease: for I was but a little displeased, and they helped forward the affliction. Therefore thus saith the Lord; I am returned to Jerusalem with mercies: my house shall be built in it...My cities through prosperity shall yet be spread abroad...'.

God's displeasure at the 'heathens' 'ease' is their prosperity as it is used in offering and sacrificing to others—which is why he brings good news 'mercies' that his house will be built again: his house where the prosperity of the people and the land is piled for offerings to be consumed at his 'he will eat' in the 'house'.

(Zech.1:14-17) The man measuring Jerusalem's breadth and length, mentioning the largeness of the city is due to the numbers of cattle and people, this is followed by God being a fire around her, and the glory in its middle is the same reason—multitudes of cattle to be used at 'God's house'. This is supported by the imagery of the text of fire and God's glory being in its middle, as it has been made clear in earlier stories that when God consumes food a fire comes out, and when he is in his 'place (tabernacle or tent, temple or house)' his 'glory' fills it (sometimes described as smoke).

Making the high priest wear clean mitre and clothes, telling him to obey his commandments, is because priests serve food to God which arrive as offers and sacrifices.

'...and I will remove the iniquity of that land in one day.' Means he will allow the land to prosper once his (God's) house, his eating place, is in order, especially as the verse that follows was used in the same way in relation to God's 'temple/hekal/he will eat'. 'In that day saith the Lord of hosts, shall ye call every man his neighbour under the vine and under the fig tree.' i.e. when they build God's house and serve in it, the famine/drought is lifted and the land allowed to be fertile, and the people will live in ease and prosperity (Zech.3).

Zech.4 describes the candlestick similar to what Moses made in Exodus, and would light and set over the table when it was time to prepare the burnt and meat offerings for God, and God would come down to eat (Exod.40). The candlestick imagery is supported with mention of Zerubbabel who begins and completes rebuilding the temple—it is still about feeding God.

The narrative in Zech.5 still revolves around earlier stories regarding the 'temple [he will eat]' and all the chambers in 'God's house': 'a flying roll' reminds of the roll Ezekiel was made to eat; although Zech.5:3 explains the 'flying roll' is a curse punishing anyone who steals, the measurements mentioned in the narration 'I see a flying roll; the length thereof is twenty cubits, and the breadth thereof ten cubits' is very similar to the measurements describing the area in front of the chambers of which the chambers are where the priests eat from the 'holy[piled] things' in Ezekiel.42 'Over against the twenty *cubits*, which *were* for the inner court, and over against the pavement which *was* for the utter court, *was* gallery against gallery in three *stories*. And before the chambers *was* a walk of ten cubits breadth inward, a way of one cubit; and their doors toward the north' on the other side 'The chambers *were* in the thickness of the wall of the court toward the east, over against the separate place, and over against the building. And the way before them *was* like the appearance of the chambers which *were* toward the north, as long as they, and as broad as they: and all their goings out *were* both according to their fashions, and according to their doors. And according to the doors of the chambers that *were* toward the south was a door in the head of the way, even the way directly before the wall toward the east, as one entereth into them. Then said he unto me, The north chambers and the south chambers, which are before the separate place, they be holy[piled] chambers, where the priests that approach unto the Lord shall eat the most holy[piled, I will pile] things: there shall they lay the most holy[piled, I will pile] things, and the meat offering, and the sin offering, and the trespass offering; for the place is holy[piled]'.

Before Zech.6, all the preceding chapters invoke imagery of God's tabernacle, tent, the temple—where he ate/was served food during the wanderings, then in God's house; the imagery of a high priest; and reminder of Ezekiel and the measurements taken outside the holy chambers where the holy priests lay the offerings to God, and where they eat; the candlestick set over against the table before meat/sin offerings are set at the tabernacle door. In Zech.6 it mentions the 'hekal/he will eat(temple)' several times; silver and gold are to be 'taken' and made into a crown which is set on the high priest's head, invoking the silver and gold vessels which earlier stories have as the vessels used by priests to serve God in the temple, followed by mention of the building and memorial of the temple, tying all the previous chapters of Zechariah with Chapter 6.

Zech.7 follows with priests; the 'house of God'; fasting, eating and drinking but for themselves instead of God; and because they are disobedient (towards God) the land becomes desolate. Then when God mentions the laying of the foundation of 'God's house', God will allow prosperity of produce and fertility of the land. It is tied to the proper meaning of the 'hekal/he will eat' (erroneously 'temple') and the 'holy mountain' which should be the 'piled mountain' is also mentioned at the beginning of the chapter. Promise of prosperity is followed by the answer regarding fasting and joyful feasting '...and the mountain of the Lord of the hosts the holy[piled] mountain...which *were* in the day *that* the foundation of the house of the Lord of hosts was laid, that the temple[he will eat] might be built. For before these days there was no hire for man, nor was there hire for beast...But now I *will* not *be* unto the residue of this people as in the former days, saith the Lord of hosts. For the seed *shall be* prosperous; the vine shall give her fruit, and the ground shall give her increase, and the heavens shall give their dew; and I will cause the remnant of this people to possess all these *things*.'

Zech.14:20-21 gives undeniable support to 'holy' being about piles, not only do the people who worship the correct God (in the Biblical stories) go to Jerusalem, but so are the heathens forced to do so, and what does going to Jerusalem mean? To go sacrifice and present offerings: 'In that day shall there be upon the bells of the horses, HOLINESS[piled/piles] UNTO THE LORD; and the pots in the Lord's house shall be like the bowls before the altar[i.e. full]. Yea, every pot in Jerusalem and in Judah shall be holiness unto the Lord of hosts: and all they that sacrifice shall come and take of them, and seethe therein: and in that day there shall be no more the Canaanite in the house of the Lord of hosts.' this does not mean literally the Canaanite will not enter the house of God, what it means is Canaanite; kĕnaʿanî; قينَعني ، قينَعاني 'given up on' 'given up any hope' 'resolved to fate or what will happen' 'he/they were convinced/satisfied with answer/situation' 'he/they looked up/craned necks' and means that before, some people were not fed and were looking up at others while they were eating, hoping to be given some food or resolved they would not be fed, but now there will no longer be people hungry and staring up at those eating as all will be fed. Cp: qeina'aanee, qeina'anee.

The whole of Malachi reinforces the centrality of food/eating in offerings/sacrifices are the most important thing for the audience of these stories to understand. Malachi is entirely about serving food to God, and not any kind of food, but only the best. He does not want to share it with other deities; he is offended by those who mock his food; he is angered that the people keep the best animals for themselves and sacrifice to him 'damaged' animals. They will be cursed/punished in their food supplies and in their offspring.

God's 'holiness'—his 'piles' (of food) have been corrupted because people have gone after other gods, offering sacrifices which should be presented to him, narrated in an analogy about marrying 'stranger' women. When the 'temple[he will eat]' is mentioned it is along with a special messenger and again the silver and gold along with Levites/priests are mentioned and this too alludes to the gold and silver vessels used by priests to service God, and it is made clear by mentioning after they are purged like gold and silver i.e. are purged of impurities, the priests can make an offering to God.

The significance of supplying God with food is also reiterated here as in all the Torah/Bible stories; God makes it clear the people have robbed him of his tithes and offerings, and he demands his house be supplied in its stores with all tithes, that there has to be food in 'God's house': it has always been 'hekal/he will eat' reflecting this and also 'qodesh/piles' of food at the heart of the Torah/OT stories. The authors have God offer a deal, if the people supply him with food, he will protect their food sources from others' aggression: a cycle—keep providing food to 'God's house' and you will always have food to survive on in exchange. It ends with the warning the wicked (who do not follow what was commanded) will be burned—no root nor branch will remain alive, i.e. no fruit of the land to live on; whereas those who are righteous (who provide supplies for God) will grow like healthy and well-reared calves, i.e. there will be plenty of nourishment from produce of the land: 'A son honoureth *his* father, and a servant his master: if then I *be* a father, where *is* mine honour? and if I *be* a master, where *is* my fear? saith the Lord of hosts unto you, O priests that despise my name. And ye say, Wherein have we despised thy name? Ye offer polluted bread *upon* mine altar; and ye say, Wherein have we polluted thee? In that ye say, The table of the Lord *is* contemptible. And if ye offer the blind in sacrifice, *is it* not evil? and if ye offer the lame and sick, *is it* not evil? offer it now unto thy governor; will he be pleased with thee, or accept thy person? saith the Lord of hosts...neither do ye kindle fire on mine altar for nought. I have no pleasure in you saith the Lord of hosts, neither will I accept an offering at your hand...But ye have profaned it, in that ye say, The table of the Lord is polluted; and the fruit thereof, *even* his meat, is contemptible...and ye brought that which was torn, and the lame, and the sick; thus ye brought an offering: should I accept this of your hand? saith the Lord...Behold, I will corrupt your seed, and spread dung upon your faces, *even* the dung of your solemn feasts...Behold, I will send my messenger, and he shall prepare the way before me: and the Lord, whom ye seek, shall suddenly come to his temple[he will eat], even the messenger of the covenant, whom ye delight in...for he is like a refiner's fire, and like fullers' soap: And he shall sit as a refiner and purifier of silver, and he shall purify the sons of Levi, and purge them as gold and silver, that they may offer unto the Lord an offering of righteousness. Then shall the offering of Judah and Jerusalem be pleasant unto the Lord...Will a man rob God? yet ye have robbed me. But ye say, Wherein have we robbed thee? In tithes and offerings. Ye *are* cursed with a curse: for ye have robbed me, even this whole nation. Bring ye all the tithes into the storehouse, that there may be meat in mine house, and prove me now herewith, saith the Lord of hosts, if I will not open you the windows of heaven, and pour you out a blessing, that *there shall* not *be room* enough *to receive it.* And I will rebuke the devourer for your sakes, and he shall not destroy the fruits of your ground; neither shall your vine cast her fruit before the time in the field, saith the Lord of hosts...'

Throughout the OT 'qodesh/piles' 'qodesh haqqodashim/piled, I will pile' and 'hekal/he will eat' are all about providing abundant piles of food to be eaten by God; people and priests also get to eat from these piles linked to the 'he will eat/hekal'. Whether the original authors of the stories made it important to bring food supplies to a specific place, linking it to the 'blessing' and fertility of the land, to teach people its importance by making God in the stories have a 'he will eat/hekal' to eat at, and a 'piled, I will pile' dedicated to God which he was very possessive over, to teach the audience of these stories the importance of land as a food source; or if the early and/or later authors really believed God would come down and eat at the 'he will eat/hekal'; or real people who were priests had a more worldly and material interest in having a constant food source supplied to them by the worshippers and general public—whatever the reasons and intentions behind these stories, the text of the OT, its meanings in compound word-names and its plots, themes, all show 'qodesh' is piles of food, and 'hekal' is a place for eating where these piles of food are consumed.

Although all the OT stories are fictional, and their characters and places never existed, and because their events never happened does not mean the authors of the Bible were not describing a partial reality of a culture, of experiences. The real elements of the stories are inspired by the environment and lived life of the authors and the audience (the earliest authors and audiences).

The 'hekal/temple' never existed, there was never a real city called Jerusalem. The 'Jerusalem' of today is not what the original native inhabitants call their city, its real name is al-Quds and not Yerusaalay-hum/um, Gerusaalay-hum/um which is what much later people, not necessarily from the region would call it based on what they believed was the land described in the Bible. The building and location where al-Aqsa mosque stands is not what inspired the Biblical stories neither in the fictional building of God's house/temple or hekal in the stories nor its location.

The real place of rituals and worship which the authors based the fictional stories of a 'house of God/temple in Jerusalem' does exist and survives to this day, but more on this later in the book where who wrote the Biblical stories and why they were written will be presented with proof.

Daniel

The introduction sets the themes of the story: **Jehoiakim** 'he who/which one-stands/the one who stands instead of' 'he who/which one-erects/with an erection/with erections' 'came who/came to him-stands/the one who stands instead of' 'came who/came to him-erects/with an erection/with erections' as the pivotal characters and events have the lead characters standing in front of the king, and the king erects a statue to be worshipped.

Judah 'he is called/calls' as the lead characters' names will be changed and will be called by these new names; Daniel and friends are called to appear before the king; the people including Daniel's friends are asked to worship a statue (worshipping includes calling on who is worshipped for something or in praise).

Nebuchadnezzar for the meanings 'prophet/news had warned' 'prophet/news had vowed would happen/set aside' as he has a dream which troubles him and wants to be told what it is; he warns the wise men if they do not predict/interpret the dream, i.e. give him information of what the future holds, he will punish them. Daniel gives the king the interpretation of the dream which is predicted/prophesied news to become a reality (in the story).

Babylon for its meanings 'swapped' 'changed' as the characters original names are swapped/changed; Daniel and his friend's diet changes; the situation of the kingdom(s) will change according to the interpretation of the king's dream.

Jerusalem for 'they see-asked-them/the' 'they see-water flowed/leaked-them/the' 'came-saw-asked-them/the' 'came-saw-water flowed/leaked-them/the' 'they saw-joined/connected-them/the' 'they saw-reached/arrived/public apology-them/the' 'they see-their/the rocks' 'they see-rocks-them/the' 'came-saw-joined/connected-them/the' 'came-saw-reached/arrived/public apology-them/the' 'came-saw-their/the rocks' 'came-saw-rocks-them/the' and is reflected in several events in the stories: the point of taking great care of the children is so they can be knowledgeable when they come before the king and are asked questions/advice, and Daniel and friends do exactly this; Daniel goes to the prince of eunuchs and Melzar and asks them to change their diet, and only after Melzar observes they are not thinner/unwell but healthy that their request is accepted; the astrologers, magicians and sorcerers (the 'wise men') are asked to come and stand before the king so he can ask them something, they comply and end up asking the king to tell them about the dream; more than once, Daniel ends up coming to the king and asking of him time, before he comes to the king and answers the question of the dream's meaning which leads to Daniel always being in the presence of the king, as well as making a request for his friends which is granted by the king; it is also in the king demanding all the people to come and worship the statue he created, and worshipping usually involves asking things from the thing/being that is being worshipped; it is also in the king, and others, seeing the three friends walking around in the fire, prompting the king to ask those around him if they saw what had happened and what they see now; the king wrongs Daniel's friends and ends up apologising; Daniel and his friends reach high positions (similar to tall height reaching higher, but in status).

Ashpenaz; 'ašpĕnaz; نَسبي نَس 'capture/captives people'; نَشبع نَس 'satisfied people's hunger/fed people' as the story mentions feeding the children he is in charge of; نَسبي نَش ، نَشبع نَش 'capture/captives-copulated(like goats)' 'satisfied/fed-copulated(like goats)' ('naz'/nsh/نَش) means 'goat copulation' and the story does have a sexual nature which will be explained below; عَش بعنَز 'lived with female goats' as the children chosen from the children of Israel, and other children and princes will be corralled in a specific area and reared the same way goats are. Cp: asbei-nas, ashb'-nas, asbei-nash, ashb'-nash, 'ash-b'naz. (Dan 1)

Chaldeans is used for its meaning of 'roasted' 'killed from heat' and other related meanings: 'and whom they might teach the learning and the tongue of the Chaldeans' is a joke as the three of the four children will be thrown into a fire to be killed (although they survive).

Although the story narrates these children are separated to be brought up to serve the king, the naming of the character 'Ashpenaz' and how it is narrated shows these children are in the sexual service of the king. Daniel is a male version of Esther, the latter character was entered with a mass of women into the sexual service of the king character of her story; both Daniel and Esther's stories have eunuchs who provide the women/children with special produce to make sure after a specific period of time they are clean and good enough to approach the king; both Daniel and Esther find favour/special treatment from the eunuchs; the story tells us they are children and although it tells they are 'skilful in all wisdom, cunning in knowledge, and understanding science,' that is contradicted by the fact they are still children, and there are puns created by the names and what the story is actually saying.

They have to be 'Children in whom there *was* no blemish, but well favoured': animals that are sacrificed to God have to be without blemish according to the Biblical stories, and these children are likened to goats as per more than one meaning of the name of the eunuch in charge of them; David also was described as good to look at, as was Esther's character and both stories had them in sexual and romantic relationships with Jonathan/Ahasuerus, respectively. The children are taken care of to make them healthy and good-looking enough to 'stand before the king', not only does the story make them be taken care of like prized animals which are well-fed and given special care as the animals will be slaughtered in the future, but it states these children including Daniel and his friends will be nourished well for three years so they will be good enough to 'stand before the king', just like 'Abishag' who was also created to 'stand before' king David to arouse his sexual desire, and this is relayed with the meanings of **Jehoiakim** 'came who/came to him-erects/with an erection/with erections' and **Jerusalem** 'came-saw-water flowed/leaked-them/the'. Both Esther and Daniel begin in the sexual service of the king, but become wife/'ruler of Babylon' wielding influence over the respective king, and authority over all the kingdom(s).

Daniel is the same as translated at (1Chr.3:1): 'bowed-the' 'he is bowed-is the' 'lowered/low-the' 'he is lowered/low-is the' 'facing the ground-the' 'he is facing the ground-is the' 'with face on ground-the' 'his face on ground-with the' 'guilted-the' 'he is guilted-is the' the first part of the word (dani/dāni/داني/دآنِ) from the word (dn/دن) 'bow(ed)/low(ered)/guilty/guilted'. It is equivalent to Dan.

It could mean lowly or a bad person, or just someone who is standing at a lower geographical point, and the meanings are straightforward in bowed, guilted, etc. In Daniel's Book it means to bow, kneel, to fall on one's face, and also uses the meaning 'lowly/corrupted' because he refuses to make himself 'low' i.e. 'defiled' by eating something against his beliefs. The story is full of text to support the meanings presented above of his compound word-name meanings:

'But Daniel purposed in his heart that he would not defile himself' with unclean food 'he requested of the prince of eunuchs that he might not defile himself.' 'Then the king Nebuchadnezzar fell upon his face, and worshipped Daniel.' 'Now when Daniel knew that the writing was signed, he went into his house; and his windows being open in his chamber toward Jerusalem, he kneeled upon his knees three times a day, and prayed, and gave thanks before his God, as he did aforetime.' 'Then I heard one saint speaking, and another saint said to that certain *saint* which spake, How long *shall be* the vision *concerning* the daily *sacrifice*, and the transgression of desolation, to give both the sanctuary and the Host to be trodden underfoot?' 'So he came near where I stood: and when he came, I was afraid, and fell upon my face,' 'Now as he was speaking with me, I was in a deep sleep on my face toward the ground; but he touched me, and set me upright' 'And I Daniel fainted, and was sick *certain* days; afterward I rose up,' 'Yet heard I the voice of his words: and when I heard the voice of his words, then was I in a deep sleep on my face, and my face toward the ground. And, behold, an hand touched me, which set me upon my knees and upon the palms of my hands. And he said unto me, O Daniel, a man greatly beloved, understand the words that I speak unto thee, and stand upright' 'And when he had spoken such words unto me, I set my face toward the ground, and I became dumb.'. Daniel's character spends a fair amount of time on the ground unconscious or praying, which the authors want to make clear in his naming and the narration of events. (Dan.1:6,8; 2:46; 6:10; 8:13,17,27; 10:9-11,15)

Hananiah (1Chr.3:19) is used for 'satisfaction to/satisfied-him/he' 'give plenty-he/him' as the children are provided for, but when Daniel and his three friends refuse to eat meat and wine, they are still satisfied and nourished with 'pulse to eat, and water to drink'. 'we will direct words/speech at him' 'we mean him' as the king wants to know the meaning of the dream; 'hums/humming sound-he/him' 'wears/applies henna-he/him' as a later character connected to Daniel in the story will be adorned with henna and another adorning product; 'felt affection-he/him' as the king will become fond of Daniel.

Mishael (Exod.6:22) is used for 'walked-the' 'not-the'; 'what is he carrying?' 'what did he take?'; 'what is he asking?' 'what did he ask?' 'lots of questions' 'Not asking' 'Doesn't care'. This character, along with his friends, does not take from the meat and wine, and gets what has been asked for (through Daniel) of dietary needs; he and his friends become wise men of the king.

Azariah (1Kgs.4:2) used for 'beware/remember/listen and remember-filled with much/left behind' 'on/upon-filled with much/left behind' because he and his friends are aware enough not to defile themselves with the king's meat and wine. 'made ugly-him/he' as the statue the kings makes is not uniformly beautiful but made of mis-matching parts; 'shadowed-him/he' 'excused-him/he' after the king sees the three friends unharmed by fire, he excuses them from the decreed punishment.

Belteshazzar; bēlṯĕša'ṣṣar; بيل تيشَئذَّر 'with/done-to who wears 'shavvar'' and its action and role come later in the Book of Daniel—to be explained further with Belshazzar. Cp: beyl-teisha-vvar. (Dan.1)

All three word-names of these three characters (Shadrach, Mesach, Abed-nego) are always mentioned together, never individually, for the reason they reflect what is happening in the same part of the story:

Shadrach; šaḏraḵ; شَدرَك 'I'll catch on/understand/realise' 'I'll catch up with' reflects when the king realises they will not worship his God 'Then Nebuchadnezzar in *his* rage and fury commanded to bring Shadrach, Meshach, and Abed-Nego…Then was Nebuchadnezzar full of fury, and the form of his visage was changed against Shadrach, Meshach, and Abed-nego.'; 'I'll save/save just in time' and also the meaning of 'realises' is reflected when the king realises they are surviving and not dying in the fire 'Then Nebuchadnezzar was astonied, and rose up in haste, *and* spake, and said unto his counsellors, Did we not cast three men bound into the midst of the fire?'. Cp: shadrak. (Dan.1-3)

Meshach; mêšaḵ; ميشَك 'made you walk' 'your walking' 'your ways'; ميسَك 'held/caught'. 'walking/ways' and 'held' reflects the three friends who hold onto their beliefs and walk in God's ways, i.e. worship God and/or obey religion correctly and is reflected in their refusal to worship the gold statue 'Shadrach, Mesach, and Abed-nego answered and said to the king…be it known unto thee, O king, that we will not serve thy gods, nor worship the golden image which thou hast set up.'. 'walking' is also reflected in after being thrown into the fire they can see them walking 'He answered, and said, Lo, I see four men loose, walking in the midst of the fire,'; ميشَق 'to pull at something until it gives or snaps' 'broke/cut loose' 'scared silly/frightened extremely' the meanings of 'snapped/broke/cut loose' and 'frightened' is reflected in how after they have been thrown into the fire the king is surprised to see them walking and emphasis is put on that they were 'bound' before thrown into the fire, so they have loosened and removed whatever was tying them 'I see four men loose…'; ميسَخ 'changed words/actions/appearance/corrupted' 'a freak/mutation/mutated' is reflected in the freak which is the statue Nebuchadnezzar created, and also in the changing of the king's attitude and statements 'and have changed the king's word'. Equivalent to Meshech (Gen.10:2). Cp: meyshaq, meysak, meysakh. (Dan.1-3)

Abed-nego; ʿăḇēḏ nĕgô; عيبيد نيجُ 'servants/worshippers-survived' as the three friends refuse to worship other gods and remain loyal to the worship of their own God and are saved from certain death, as although they are in the fire, they survive 'If it be *so*, our God whom we serve is able to deliver *us* from the burning fiery furnace, and he will deliver us out of thine hand.', it is also shown in Nebuchadnezzar's dialogue where he directly expresses the meaning of the compound word 'Abed-nego': 'Then Nebuchadnezzar spake, and said, Blessed be the God of Shadrach, Meshach, and Abed-nego, who hath sent his angel and delivered his servants who trusted in him.'. Cp: 'aibeyd-neigo. (Dan.1-3)

The final statement encompasses all three word-names: Shadrach, the king realised they knew the truth; Meshach, they walked/stuck to God's ways; and Abed-nego, they were physically saved because they worshipped God. (Dan.3)

Melzar; melṣār; ملضار 'what is the harm?' and reflects the eunuch realising there is no harm to Daniel and his friends nor harm to himself by not feeding them meat, whereas the earlier eunuch character had expressed worry over depriving them of meat would cause them to become thin and sickly and lead to his own execution, but upon seeing no harm came to them (quite the opposite, they became fatter and fairer than the others) Melzar removes meat and wine from their provisions. Cp: meldhaar. (Dan.1:10-16)

Chaldeans as explained above. **Syriack** for its meaning of 'wilderness/uninhabited place (where it's easy to get lost)' 'to abandon something or someone in the wild' 'a tree called 'aram/fetched wood of 'aram tree' 'see-the/I see the' 'penis-the/insult with 'penis-the'' 'to throw/to do with throwing' 'killed/the killed/the killer' 'thrown, strewn or located over a vast distance/over different areas' 'vast/distant/covering wide or many different areas' as the king puts the 'wise men' in an impossible position wanting them to interpret the dream without telling them what happened in the dream; they ask him to tell(tell is the same as 'see/show') them so they can show him what it means but he threatens to cut them to pieces and destroy their houses, but his promises of punishment will be far-reaching and extend to all the wise men of Babylon. **Babylon** for its meaning of 'changed/swapped' because the king has changed how the sorcerers, astrologers, etc. are dealt with by his irrational request, then seeks to change their situation by destroying them, and also because he accuses them of preparing to use 'lying and corrupt words' i.e. 'changed the truth' before he adds the reason of their deceit as directly 'for ye have prepared lying and corrupt words to speak before me, till the time be changed'.

Arioch (Gen.14:1) has been used for 'I'll show you' as in a threat, and 'your dream' as all the wise men are going to be killed because they have not interpreted the dream which the king will not tell them about. Also 'I'll show you' because Daniel will tell the king what the dream means and the authors have this character of the same name/meaning (Arioch) involved in the events. (Dan.2:1-25)

Dura; dûrā'; دُرآء 'they know' 'they understand' and it is the name of the plain/place where Nebuchadnezzar erects a golden statue for worship, at which it is announced whoever does not worship will be burnt alive; the people are aware of the three friends stance regarding this and in turn make the king aware; although they already know they will be sentenced to a horrible death Shadrach, Mesach and Abed-nego refuse to worship this statue because they know the 'true God'. The whole story of this chapter is about these three knowing and because they know the true God, they are saved. Cp: duraa. (Dan.3)

'Son of God' mentioned in this part of the story is interesting. They are talking about a 'burning fiery furnace' and the authors emphasise how intense this heat is that even the 'most mighty men that were in his[king's] army' who threw the restrained three friends into this fire, described as more intense than any other fire in the narration, are killed by its heat although they do not land in it, they just go near to throw the three friends into it. When the king and the people notice Daniel's friends are unharmed and walking around in the fire, a fourth man who has appeared out of nowhere (later in the chapter will be called an 'angel') 'I see four men loose, walking in the midst of the fire, and they have no hurt;' he is described as 'and the form of the fourth is like the Son of God.'. If you recall Job.1-2, Satan is described as one of the sons of God. The culture of the region, which has influenced the three 'divine' religions of the region (Judaism, Christianity and Islam (not to mention different religions of the region where Satan is not an 'evil' being)) has Satan, the Devil, living or punished in hell, made out of fire or thrown into the fire for punishment and such similar stories. There is no removing the culture, stories of the people (Arabs) of the region from the influence and creation of the Biblical stories.

Belshazzar; bēlša'ṣṣar; بيل شَذَّر 'with shevvar' 'he who wears shevvar'. And this character's name has been made to suit the pivotal event of the story being told.

Both the king and Daniel's names, Belshazzar and Belteshazzar, are based on the noun 'shazzar' (shavvar/ شذر) which can also be a verb when implying its application to the person it is adorning or an adverb of the person adorned with it. To understand how the names were created for the story and why these compound words were used, first we need to understand what 'shazzar/shavvar' is.

Since antiquity women have used henna to adorn their bodies, dry powdered or freshly ground henna leaves are made into a paste to decorate the hands and feet with; it is also used as a body mask for purifying, or beautifying product. Up until the near past even men adorned their hands and feet with henna just like women, but this went out of fashion and custom so nowadays men only use it to dye white beards and hair and also for a body mask or purification.

The henna is applied to less than half the palm with a curved 'S' border, up until the near past (into the 1970s) they used to cover three quarters of the palm and the border between the coloured and uncoloured skin was a straight line. The pads on the inside of fingers are also covered with a column of henna, henna is also ringed around the top-third back segments of fingers including the nails. The same is done to the soles of feet and henna also rings the toes with the toenail. When used only as a body wash or dye for white hair, it only becomes a yellow or orange colour. But when it is used to adorn hands and/or feet, it is left on for hours until it becomes a dark red, or brown colour and sometimes black. Women and girls (and men in the past) apply consecutive coats of henna in the same day or following days to achieve the darkest/ richest colour possible as the darker colours are deemed the prettiest.

To achieve a black colour, a different substance is added after the last coat of henna paste has been removed. It is a substance called (shvr/شذر) and comes in a powder or stone form. This shavar is quarried from a certain rock, burnt then finely powdered and/or compacted into a stone like form. After the last coat of henna has been applied and washed off, the shevar powder is applied to the wet hands/feet along with rubbing it against the palms and skin dyed with henna, it creates an intense heat which turns the dyed henna black on the skin—which is the desired result.

The point in explaining this is that this same result I have described of a hand adorned with 'shavar' '(bel/belt)shazzar' is creating the action in the Biblical story. In rural Yemen (at least where no electricity exists) in the evening when inside rooms are lit with lanterns, and outside is either completely dark/unlit with any light source or a little light is shed from inside the house, women whose hands and feet are dyed black or even just dark brown with henna, the henna or shevar (spelled 'shazzar' in the English versions of the Bible) looks completely black. Not only does the hennaed hand or foot look black, but the girls'/women's hands and feet look incomplete, the non-coloured parts of their hands and feet seem to float disembodied from the arm/wrist which is covered by the sleeves of the dress and the legs by the trousers or dress. The tips of fingers coloured black by shavar cannot be seen properly, only the backs of the hands and the uncoloured backs of fingers stand out starkly.

In the Belshazzar story it is a hand writing on the wall which he sees moving alone without a body. The character is named after the substance used and what the person who is having or has had hands and/or feet adorned with shavar, and the action in the story is based on what the appearance of a hand adorned with shavar looks like in the dark.

Daniel's second name Belteshazzar is also connected to the name of the substance and the adverb of the person adorned with it. Furthermore, Belshazzar's name denotes his direct experience with this 'hand' or a 'shevvared-hand', while Belteshazzar's name (Daniel's) denotes his position in the story is connected to the person who experienced this shevvarred-hand, but not directly himself. i.e. Daniel's experience like his second name is 'done to who wears shavvar' 'with who wears shavvar' because Daniel did not see the hand. But Belshazzar did so his name is directly related as reflected in the name 'with shevvar' 'with the one who wears shevvar' and in both names it is the disembodied hand that is adorned with shevvar which both characters have been named for and is the pivotal part in this specific part of the story.

Belshazzar is drinking wine with others when 'In the same hour came forth fingers of a man's hand, and wrote over and against the candlestick upon the plaister of the wall of the king's palace: and the king saw the part of the hand that wrote'. The visual effect hands decorated with henna/shevar have is exactly like a dark stage with a dark background where figures are covered in black material and only the parts of the body or props visible are those not covered by black material and these visible parts seem to be floating, detached from the rest of the unseen body. Belteshazzar (Daniel) says to Belshazzar 'Then was the part of the hand sent from him; and this writing was written.'. Cp: beyl-sha-vvar (Dan.5:1-24)

MENE, MENE; mĕnē', mĕnē'; مينيى مينيى 'from me, from me' 'listing and gloating over what was given(to another)'. It means when a person does the vulgar act of counting and listing what he/she gave to others—be it as gifts or charity—the listing is against etiquette as it embarrasses the recipient/former recipient and is the same as gloating. The story reflects this 'listing/from me, from me' in more than one way: Belshazzar is reminded of his father's sin who was driven insane to behave like an animal after he attributed all his kingdom and achievements to himself instead of God 'Is this not great Babylon, that I have built for the house of the kingdom by the might of my power, and for the honour of my majesty?' (Dan.4:30-37); it is reflected in the narration of Daniel refusing to accept the offered reward (although later in the story he does not mind accepting them) but the point is his refusal is not allowing anyone to have the chance to 'mn/list/from me' on him.

In the culture of the authors of the Bible it is rude to 'mn/mene' upon another person—but at the same time the story has God doing 'mene, mene' on Belshazzar as the latter is reminded that the true God gave both Belshazzar and his father all the power, might, wealth and majesty in their kingdom, furthermore God is 'listing/mene mene' the things which were taken from 'God's house/temple'—the precious vessels, which is why the hand appears to tell him 'from me, from me' when they bring them out and drink from them i.e. these vessels have been taken from me and not the gods you have listed and praised as if they gave you these things. The word is repeated to mimic how a person goes on and on and repeats what he has given another, and in real life when a person is criticised or mimicked, they repeat the word even more than twice to show how uncouth it is to say 'from me, from me, from me'. It is similar to Manna, Minnith, Miniamin, and the latter part of Benjamin. Cp: meiney, meiney. (Dan.5:25-30)

TEKEL; tĕqel; تيقِل 'you lessen' 'you have become less/will become less' and refers to Belshazzar has lessened the vessels which belong to God by drinking from them, both he and his father did things to make their status as kings less because they lessened the respect/credit/thanks which should be displayed towards the correct God of the stories, and the punishment for this wrong is: Nebuchadnezzar was lessened in sanity and as a human to live like an animal, Belshazzar will be killed and his kingdom destroyed. Cp: teiqel. (Dan.5:25-30)

UPHARSIN; ûparsîn; وفَرصين 'break/split through' 'divide'; وفَرسين 'divide into separate units' 'explain in detail/made clear'. In both Belshazzar and his father's stories it is made clear to them that their kingdom will eventually be broken up and divided between different rulers. This was explained to both characters in their respective stories in great detail. After Belshazzar is killed it goes to the suitably named kingdoms of Persia (which has all the same meanings of 'upharsin'), and Medes of which one meaning is reflected in this story 'to put hands on something not yours'. Cp: oo-pharsseen, oo-pharseen. (Dan.5:25-31)

PERES is the same as Perez, Pharez, Persia. It is used for the same reasons as 'upharsin'. (Dan.5:28)

Darius is still being used as earlier for 'educated/studies matters' 'of careful studying/look into' and his role is still reflected as to look into and inspect a matter closely as he sets many princes not only to rule but to communicate things through a reporting chain. It is also reflected in he studies Daniel and finds him to be suitable to 'set over the whole realm' above all other officials. It is also reflected in how Daniel's adversaries are putting a lot of effort into finding a careful and successful way to remove Daniel. (Dan.6)

Ancient of days; ʿattîq yômîn; عطّيق يُمين 'liberator/saviour-from where/from who/from since when' 'liberator-whose' 'liberator-what is it?' 'liberator-who is it' liberator-of what/of who?' 'liberator-he grants/gives/blesses' 'liberator-he lists/counts'. The word which has been mistranslated as 'ancient': ('attîq/عتّيق), is a modern meaning of the word: ('tq/عتق) 'old/falling apart' applied in modernity to antiques and 'ancient', the same original word means something 'stuck, tugging or pulling intensely/sharply at something/someone' but not anything to do with 'ancient' as that is how the word is used in modern Arabic; neither this word nor its modern and original meanings are the word mistranslated as 'Ancient' in the Bible; but it is 'liberator' from ('ṭq/عطق) 'grant/free/release/merciful'. Anyone who frees or puts a living thing out of its misery, or liberates someone in distress, servitude, debt, any kind of trouble is said to 'aṭaq/liberated/freed/saved' the subject of the action.

The second part of the name translated as 'of days' is also incorrect: (yômîn/يُمين) is not in the spelling to mean 'days', and if it were corrected it would mean specifically and only 'two days', but it is not spelt to make it anything to do with 'days'. It is a compound word of which the basis is (mn/من) 'who, what, where, when' with the (yô/يُـ) prefix it becomes 'from who' 'from where' 'from since when' 'from what' 'what is it' who is it' 'he grants/blesses' or negatively 'he lists/gloats/counts'. It is equivalent to Manna, Minnith, Miniamin, 'Mene, mene', and the latter part of the compound word 'Ben**jamin**' and similar words.

All these meanings are available and supported in the narration of the story: 'liberator' is because when he arrives one beast is killed and the others have their 'dominion' deprived, even if they continue to live it is only for a while. Also, when the 'liberator' arrives the story narrates some kind of justice occurs.

Daniel is asking 'what is this' 'who is this', the narration is stating 'since a long time ago' and also that it is about different times playing on the 'when' meaning. The narration purposely creates the ambiguity to make the audience wonder 'who is this/what is this/when are they talking about/since when has this existed/what are they talking about'.

When 'liberator-he grants/blesses/lists' arrives the narration lists how 'thousands and thousands' serve him, how a hundred million stand before him (it purposely keeps ambiguous who or what, it could be believed people are serving and/or standing before him for judgement, but it does not say who or what to make it specific).

'Ancient of days' which is correctly translated as 'liberator/saviour-from where/from who/from since when' 'liberator-whose' 'liberator-what is it?' 'liberator-who is it' liberator-of what/of who?' 'liberator-he grants/gives/blesses' 'liberator-he lists/counts'—his actions are not of someone old/ancient/falling apart but of a 'liberator/saviour' as he arrives while four powerful and frightful beasts are destroying (destroying what has not been made clear either); he kills and completely destroys the body of one beast and takes away the dominions/power of the other beasts. The same is reiterated in the interpretation for Daniel, where he is told four kings/nations will rule the earth, then be liberated by ʿattîq yômîn for the saints. The same is explained again with emphasis on the most horrific beast/worst king whose kingdom will destroy the earth until ʿattîq yômîn arrives to save the world and give the kingdom, and the world, to a 'higher' (maybe better/righteous) ruler. The story is about oppression/oppressors, wars and warmongers and the liberation of the world from these 'kings/beasts' who are oppressors and warmongers. Cp: 'aṭṭeeq yomeen. (Dan.7)

Ullai; 'ûlay; غلّي 'deep hatred/despise/extreme vengeance' 'deep stabbing/deep digging' (and indicates action/revenge will occur out of the hatred/feelings), 'flowed/rushed like river' 'exploited/took advantage of' 'made more expensive' 'made up laws/rules/made up severe laws/rules': and Daniel's vision begins at a river; the ram is exploiting his strength against others unable to 'deliver out of his hand'; the hegoat arrives in a powered fury relaying 'deep hatred/vengeance', and as it attacks the ram it is indicated using his horns so 'deep stabbing' as well as the acts of revenge fuelled by hatred are relayed too; the hegoat becomes stronger and exploits its strength and causes more severe 'deep stabbing/deep digging' and shows 'made up laws/rules/made up severe laws/rules' as it attacks the 'host of heaven' and transgresses against the 'daily sacrifice' and the 'sanctuary'; عُلي 'above me' 'rise above(physical location or in status)' and Daniel is standing by the river Ullai 'above me' when he sees a ram above him; he needed to lift his eyes to see it '...and I was by the river Ullai, Then I lifted up mine eyes, and saw, and, behold, there stood before the river a ram...'. But also the ram's horns are described as 'one *was* higher than the other' and the description of how nothing can defeat it and it becomes great also shows the meaning of the word as in 'high/risen in status', then the narration of what ensues is about one creature/nation rising in status against others. Cp: ghulay, 'ulay. (Dan.8:2-3)

Gabriel; gabrî'ēl; جَبري يَل 'talked with-the' 'fixed/comforted-the' 'forced/made do-the' and is from the word (gbr/جبر) which means 'talk with' and the talking with a person described this way is usually to comfort them, 'comfort' 'heal/fix/mend' 'force'. The first thing Gabriel does is rouse/heal Daniel from his unconsciousness caused by fright (mend/fix/heal-the). Then he talks to Daniel, and the voice above Ullai tells Gabriel to speak with Daniel, to explain to him the vision, therefore Gabriel 'speak with-the'. While Daniel is praying to God, asking him to fix the desolation in Jerusalem, Gabriel arrives again to explain, to teach him skill and understanding, so he is there to speak to Daniel again; and in his speech the mention of fixing/building Jerusalem. 'And I heard a voice between *the banks of* Ullai, which called and said, Gabriel, make this *man* to understand the vision. So he came near where I stood: and when he came, I was afraid, and fell upon my face: but he said unto me, Understand, O son of man, for at the time of the end *shall be* the vision. Now as he was speaking with me, I was in a deep sleep on my face toward the ground; but he touched me, and set me upright. And he said, Behold I will make thee know what shall be in the last end of the indignation...' and Gabriel continues to speak with Daniel, making him understand.

'And while I *was* speaking and praying, and confessing my sin, and the sin of my people Israel, and presenting my supplication before the Lord my God for the holy mountain of my God; Yea, whiles I *was* speaking in prayer, even the man Gabriel, whom I had seen in a vision at the beginning, being caused to fly swiftly, touched me about the time of the evening oblation,' the emphasis is put on Gabriel arriving while Daniel was speaking in prayer, to connect Gabriel's name, so while Daniel is speaking to God, Gabriel arrives, plus it is still Gabriel's job to 'talk with' Daniel. If you go back to the beginning of chapter 8, you will see that even when Gabriel is first introduced there is a conversation going on, first between 'saints' speaking with one another, and then with Daniel and in the middle of this talking between different characters, Gabriel is introduced: 'Then I heard one saint speaking, and another saint said unto that certain *saint*, which spake...And he said unto me...then, behold, there stood before me as the appearance of a man. And I heard a man's voice between the banks of Ullai, which called and said, Gabriel, make this *man* understand the vision.' This last sentence includes the meaning 'forced/made do-the' as it is making Daniel understand.

Gabriel arrives again in the middle of a conversation being narrated, and he will also talk with Daniel 'And he informed me, and talked with me, and said, O Daniel, I am now come forth to give thee skill and understanding, At the beginning of thy supplications the commandment came forth, and I am come to shew thee; for thou art greatly beloved: therefore understand the matter, and consider the vision.' Gabriel continues to speak with Daniel. Cp: gabree-ill. (Dan.8-9)

Messiah; māšîaḥ; ماسَيَح 'rubbed/stroked(with)' similar to when a 'chosen' person in the stories is anointed with oil over the head—here it is mentioned following the line 'and to anoint the most holy' (Dan.24-26); it also means 'wipe/wipe clean/wipe away' and the narration related to the mentioned Messiah is of total destruction and end of time, i.e. just like something that is wiped completely away. 'wanders/walks/searches all over' and means with a mission/objective e.g. for truth or to find something, etc. Cp: maaseeaḥ.

Messiah; māšîaḥ; ماسَيه 'touched' 'touched him/touched-he/him' 'possessed' 'possessed him/possessed-he/him' 'entangled/caused problems/provoked problems or fighting'; the 'touched' means physically and depending on how the word is used and in what context can mean gently (i.e. non-violent) and can be similar to the 'messiah/rubbed/stroked/massaged' including with a substance being rubbed in/over or anointed with; and can also have a violent meaning as being attacked verbally or physically, involved in a fight or argument, or caused trouble; the latter can also mean to be possessed by a spirit/demon—which in the Bible, the characters of the prophets (and sometimes kings) are possessed by God. Cp: maaseeah. (Dan.9:25-27)

Hiddekel (Gen.2.14) 'will-enter' or 'I will enter' is used to reflect no food or drink entered Daniel, and also the people who will hide from fear. **Uphaz** (Jer.10) 'provokes/is provoked' 'succeeds/wins' used because the appearance of the man 'girded with fine gold of Uphaz' is what provokes the fear inside the people although they cannot see him. (Dan.10:5)

Michael (Num.13:13) is used for all its meanings: 'what is said' 'who said' 'who said-the' 'what is there-the' 'what is-the' 'what is the matter-the' as things are said about Michael, and events which happen around him, to Daniel who seems confused and fatigued from worry and lack of nutrition due to a vision which disturbs him, but from the text the name given of 'Michael' is around conversations being spoken, but only describes being touched/helped by a being similar to man, leaving Michael the only name linked to the events. Also, Michael/'spending time at/spending time with' 'stay(ing)/wait(ing)' as throughout chapters 10 and 11 both waiting and staying are mentioned. Also meant by Michael in all three chapters is Michael 'is hallucinating/has hallucinated/imagined' which Daniel's dialogue expresses after he describes being in a bad physical and mental condition, saying 'O my lord, by the vision my sorrows are turned upon me, and I have retained no strength. For how can the servant of this my lord talk with this my lord? for as for me, straightaway there remained no strength in me, neither is there breath left in me.'.

The mention of Michael at the beginning and end of narrating Daniel's fatigue and confusion lends itself to give the meaning 'imagining' 'hallucinating' 'is hallucinating/has hallucinated/imagined' 'hallucination/imagination' especially right at the end of chapter 10, when Daniel is being told to be strong, the speaker/angel says 'But I will shew thee that which is noted in the scripture of truth: and there is none that holdeth with me in these things, but Michael your prince' this could be understood to mean 'nobody is helping me (angel/speaker) in the fight except for Michael', but it is said 'Michael your prince' so it means 'you are ruled/ordered by your imagination/hallucinations' 'no one compares to these visions except you are hallucinating/imagining'. Before it returns in chapter 12 to being about a conversation between two men/angels standing on opposite sides of the river saying things to each other and to Daniel concerning Michael which returns to the meaning of this name 'what is said' 'who said' 'what is-the' 'who said-the' 'what is the matter-the' and 'waiting' as they say it will be for a long time, before returning to the meaning 'hallucination/imagination', i.e. confusion because again Daniel cannot understand, and the response he gets is that most people will not be able to understand. (Dan.10-12)

Grecia; yĕwānî; جيوآني ، هيوآني ، ييوآني 'he is moaning/groaning' 'he is making moan/groan' 'he will moan/groan' he will make moan/groan' 'came-moaning/groaning' 'came-made moan/groan; عيوآني 'of howling'; غيوآني 'of misleading to downfall' 'misled me to my downfall'. Meanings of 'howling' 'moaning/groaning' and 'misleading to downfall' are meant and supported by the narration: the howling/moaning/groaning as he causes many to attack Grecia, but also in attacking Grecia and in this fourth king's peak of might, this will cause his downfall and the collapse of his whole kingdom. It is equivalent to **Gentiles/Hagoiim** (Judg.4) and **Goath** (Jer.31:38-39). Cp: yeiwaanee, heiwaanee, geiwaanee, 'eiwaanee, gheiwaanee. (Dan.11:2)

Minor Prophets

Hosea

In brief, these names are used as follows: **Uzziah** (2Kgs.15:13) 'was harmed-he' 'he harmed' 'was removed' 'was wiped out' 'was shifted'. Narration mentions a harm done between Jezreel and Jehu for which Israel will be harmed; the wife will be shifted from her home and living status to a wilderness, nakedness, hunger and thirst.

Jotham (Judg.9:7-21) 'is ostracised' 'he ostracises' 'is guilted' 'he guilts' 'is blamed' as characters are blamed and they will be ostracised in parts of the story.

Ahaz (2Kgs.15:38; 16) 'took/took or takes a lot' as Hosea is instructed to take a specific kind of wife; 'swore/insulted/swore insulted a lot' 'a disgrace/disgraced a lot' 'an embarrassment/a great embarrassment' as the wife and people do a lot of disgraceful things that cause both the husband and God to be embarrassed. The husband/God will take away clothing, shelter and food from the wife/people.

Hezekiah (2Kgs.18-20) 'squeezed/cornered/crammed him-he/him' 'make suffer/distress-he/him' 'I will force to taste/swallow/eat-he/him' (literally saying to cause distress, and the second is a figurative saying that means to make a person suffer or put them through trouble and the phrase to make a person feel pain/sufferance is usually described as making them 'taste/swallow/eat (pain, bitter, sufferance, etc.)' as something unpleasant), The wife/people are making husband/God swallow unpleasant sufferance because of her/their actions; in turn she/they will be made to suffer. 'I will water-he/him' as the wife/people believe her/their lovers/deities will give them food, water, clothing and drink.

Judah 'he is called/calls' reflected in that God tells Hoseah what to call/name his children.

Jeroboam (1Kgs.11:26-40) 'you quarter of the' their lifestyle of plenty will be much reduced with nakedness, hunger and exposure to the elements; 'fled-the' 'removed/moved aside-the' as the wife/people have been '*departing* from the Lord.'; and because husband/God will move wife/people out of their usual living style and place, and husband/God's mercy and help will be removed.

Joash (Judg.5: 'grain husks'; (2Kgs.11)) 'he is made to live/allowed to live' 'he lives' 'came-lived' as wife/people are allowed to live a good life, but this will be taken away because of their sins; 'to strike around blindly/make a mess/not know what to do' the wife is described as trying to find her lovers and their assistance, and in not finding it wants to return to her husband; 'a small fight/conflict'

Israel (Gen.32:) 'twisted muscle-the' 'twisted-the' and is linked to Jezreel of which one meaning has exactly the same meanings of the compound word 'israel'. The use of Israel here is the same way it was used when its naming for a character and introduction into the Bible was to bring in a female relative's act of sexual immorality (Dinah) which caused her male family's 'muscle' to be twisted which results in withering. In Hosea it is a wife/people who wither her husband/God's muscle—shames them.

Hosea is the same as **Hoshea** (Deut.32:23-44) 'he became/made ugly' 'he wanders around aimlessly' 'he wanders around performing debauchery' 'he became debauched/he performed debauchery/promiscuity'. The protagonist of the same name and almost the whole book describes its characters, places (cities/towns) as debauched, promiscuous people who are whores and whoredoms. Everything they do from promiscuity, to trade, to worship (other gods) is described as whoredom/debauchery—so the narrator has been given a fitting name. It also emphasises the seeking and going a distance or to certain places to conduct the immoral acts. It is the same as/equivalent to **Hoshea** (Deut.32:23-44), **Oshea** and **Jehoshua** (Num.13:8,16). (Hos.)

Beeri (Gen.26:34) 'with/by my prick/penis' which is an oft-used insult denoting how little respect for the person or thing being spoken about, has been given as Hosea's surname/father's name to further emphasise the sentiment in the story that all people spoken of whether individuals or entire cities, are debased. Add to this the meaning of the compound word first name 'Hosea Beeri' reads 'Going around committing debauchery-with my penis'.

Gomer (Gen.10) used for 'hot coals/hot' 'submerged (in water or dirt)' 'covered with face or headveil' 'head/face veils', implies a punishment with fire and also being deprived of the 'cover' which is clothing and shelter formerly provided by the character's husband; name of his wife whom he describes as a whore and accuses of committing immoral sins. And goes further to support this meaning for her name as he threatens 'Lest I strip her naked, and set her as in the day that she was born, and make her as a wilderness, and set her like a dry land, and slay her with thirst'. All this stripping, leaving her outside (in the heat) starving her, depriving her of drink—punishment associated with heat/sun/fire, taking away her clothing leaving her exposed to the elements and shame. 'upset/envious/spiteful' her husband is a jealous husband because of her adultery, and so is God because of the people's worship of others which in this story as well as others is described as fornication.

Diblaim; diḇlāyim; ذِبلآي هم/ام 'wither(ed) them/the' 'wicks/their wicks-them/the' her surname reflects she is left to wither, i.e. left like a plant or a plant in dry land and thirsty as above. It also enhances the original meanings of 'Israel/Jezreel' as a muscle withering because it was twisted/withered in sexual act with a female God then sexual misconduct by the females of the family (Israel/Hosea) in their respective stories. It is similar to Almon-diblathaim, Diblath. Cp: viblaay-hum/um (Hos.1:3; 2:3)

Jezreel (Josh.15:56) used for 'grazed-on-the' 'slaughtered-on-the' 'scatters-on-the' 'sows seeds-on-the' and in Hosea has these meanings as the story tells blood will be avenged; it also speaks of the corn, wine and oil of the earth linking it to green pastures, fertile land; Hosea is told to name his son Jezreel 'for yet a little while, and I will avenge the blood of Jezreel upon the house of Jehu' the violence will happen in a valley called Jezreel 'And the earth shall have here the corn, and the wine, and the oil; and they shall hear Jezreel.'.

'puts shame/puts grievous disgrace/puts serious insults-on-the'; 'twists/twisted-on-the' 'twisted muscle-on-the' and these meanings of Jezreel are reflected in the shame, disgrace caused by the insult of adultery and worship of other Gods and linked to the original meaning of 'Israel' in Genesis 32, the sexual nature is made clear with 'I will break the bow of Israel in the valley of Jezreel.' The bow being the penis, the valley being the vagina which causes Israel's muscle to wither. (Hos.1:4-5; 2:22)

Jehu (1Kgs.16) 'came him/he' 'came to him' 'who is?' 'which one?' as there will be revenge against 'the house of Israel' for spilling the blood of the 'house of Jehu' the way it is narrated you cannot tell who is the wrong party, because it states in the same verse that Israel will be wiped out, then in the same chapter it shows that they, or at least some of them will be spared from slaughter. 'uncovered' husband will uncover his wife's body as punishment.

Lo-ruhamah; lō' rūḥāmâ; لوء رويحآمه 'no mercy' 'have no mercy on them/him' 'may he have no mercy' from (rḥm/رحم) 'mercy/had mercy/womb'. 'Call her name Lo-ruhamah: for I will no more have mercy upon the house of Israel.'. Cp: loo-roiḥaamah. (Hos.1:6)

Lo-ammi; lō' 'ammî; لوء عمّي 'no/not my uncle' uncles and cousins are those biologically related as uncles and cousins, but the words are also used when speaking in general (to outsiders) regarding the people being a person's 'people/community' as in relatives, friends, neighbours, countrymen. The 'lo' makes it a negative, i.e. not my people/countrymen 'Call his name Lo-ammi: for ye are not my people'. Cp: loo-'ammee. (Hos.1:9)

Ammi; 'ammî; عمّي 'uncle/my uncle' and is used as in 'my people' when the story takes on a soft tone when asking them to give warning—as it is trying to reconciliate 'Say ye, unto your brethren, Ammi; and to your sisters, Ru-hamah. Plead with your mother, plead…' and by the end of the chapter the wife/people will be the spouse/people of husband/God again '…and I will say to *them which were* not my people, Thou *art* my people…'. Cp: 'ammee. (Hos.2)

Ru-hamah; ruḥāmâ; روحآمه 'merciful' 'had mercy on them/him' 'he/they have received mercy' and for the same reasons above the husband/God is pleading with children/people to mediate to make wife/people follow the correct way and return to husband/God wholly; if only she/they would do so—they would receive forgiveness and mercy, which by the end of the chapter is given and received. '…and I will have mercy upon her that had not obtained mercy…'. Cp: ruḥaamah. (Hos.2)

Achor (Josh.7:26) 'ruined/spoiled' and also a bad action when done intentionally and the wife's/people's actions are intentional acts of disobedience/sins/betrayal—the story narrates it as the name of the door as a hope she/they can come back through to the right path/ways/conduct. (Hos.2)

Ishi (1Chr.2:31) used for 'he wants' from verse 3:14 the threat/violence ceases in this section and it expresses luring Gomer/Israel (in a feminised allegory) with kind words, making her happy; it goes on to the end of the chapter with a happy consummation where everybody ends up pleased; and at verse 16, after she is happy and singing just like the good old days, she will call him 'Ishi/he wants' i.e. whatever he wants.;

'crawls' 'crawls like insects' because it mentions animals, serpents and insects crawling; 'picked up handfuls/too much' as she/they dress beautifully for, and abundantly serve things, to lovers/other gods, and believes she receives from them abundant resources such as food, clothing, shelter, but husband/God will take them away making her want them back, and he will give them back; 'fed supper' 'ate supper' as being fed is mentioned more than once as being provided, deprived then provided; 'hid something by stuffing it quickly somewhere' as first action husband/God will take away the food, clothing and shelter provided to the wife/people, then husband/God will make her forget the names of her/their lovers/deities. (Hos.2)

Baali; ba'lî, ba'ălî; بَعيلي ، بَعلي 'my husband(s)/spouse(s)' and can be both as 'my' of a singular spouse or 'my' as plural spouses (of the wife/(gods to the people), husband/god no longer wants to be called Baali because this term is too close to the deities worshipped with the same word meaning 'above/higher' 'Baal', which has angered God; nor does her husband because it reminds him of her lovers as the text has tied her meetings to the lovers with worshipping Baal or meeting where they worship and has used clever word-play to describe them as Baalim 'spouses' a pun about their partners in adultery and the name of the god or place they worship—which both God and husband want her to forget completely. Cp: ba'lee, ba'ailee. (Hos.2)

David used for 'repeat/try again/keep at it/repeating the same revolving or to and fro motion' 'hesitates/goes and comes/recoils/revolves' as the chapter is about another wife whom the narrator warns not to return to adultery and so her character is wont to revolve around adultery, as well as the chapter ending on a positive note promising the 'children of Israel' will return to worshipping and fearing God. Although 'David' in the sentence is used as a positive king reminding of glory in the last sentence of the chapter, the word and character is used to remind of his fornication with Jonathan and his adultery with Bath-sheba, although she was beautiful to look at, she and David (a glorious king in the stories) are both adulterers and here symbolise how the people betray God 'Then said the Lord unto me, Go yet, love a woman beloved of her friend, yet an adulteress…'. (Hos.3)

Here **Judah** is used for 'call, or curse' 'to make a claim' 'make a false claim or an unproven claim' as they are asked not to swear by God; **Gilgal** (Josh.5:2-9) 'clear/purify' has been used to state do not come to Gilgal which is pure to defile it with your sins/uncleanness; **Beth-aven** (Josh.7:2-12) used for 'they will moan/groan' they will be harmed' as in keep away so you do not bring harm/bad influence which will result in harm of others that are not debauched: 'Though thou, Israel, play the harlot, *yet* let not Judah offend; and come not ye unto Gilgal, neither go ye up to Beth-aven, nor swear, The Lord liveth.' (Hos.4)

Mizpah (Gen.31:44-55) is used for 'slaughter' 'pouring place/pouring/pouring vessel' 'watching with ill-intent' as it is mentioned 'revolters are profound to make slaughter' but God is preventing them; the pouring of blood, wine, wrath like water are mentioned over the two chapters. **Tabor** (Judg.8:18) is used for 'ruins reputation/becomes bad/gets bad reputation/spoiled' because Israel, Ephraim and others are committing 'whoredoms' ruining the status of their standing with God, and their physical situation. **Ephraim** (Gen.41:52) at Hos.4:17-19 is used for its meaning 'increase/multiply-them/the' as the wine which they increase is bad due to the increase of their worship of idols and the increase of offering sacrifices to the wrong gods; at Hos.5 it is used for 'with gap between teeth' as the story narrates three of the cities will fall; they will not find God, he will be missing as he removes himself from their presence; the rest of the descriptions including Ephraim are all to do with something completely missing, or uprooted, with holes caused by a moth and so forth. (Hos.4-5)

Jareb; yārēḇ; يآريب 'he mixes and dilutes with water' 'he teaches/disciplines/parents/is god/master/grows/brings someone or something up or teaches them/grows them' 'he grows/brings them up fast and/or well' and in this story the meaning seems to be that Ephraim and Judah turned to 'Jareb' an Assyrian king to help them, to cure their wounds which means to support them like a God or master does, to restore them to fullness of health and an intact body; جاريب 'try/attempt' 'skin condition like psoriasis' as Ephraim and Judah are trying to be cured of a sickness, but they cannot be healed just as the skin condition is chronic and never heals completely; غاريب'stranger' 'went over' 'dipped down' 'boiled over' a place in a mountain where a hill/ascent goes down and its other side or people who pass over it cannot be seen from the speaker's/viewer's location—because they are seeking assistance/cure from a stranger instead of God, and God has gone to a location where he cannot be seen/found just as the topography called 'jareb' conceals those who go over it. It has the same meanings as Arab, Arabia, Rabbi, Rabbah, Irpeel, Beth-arabah and other similar words which have the same/similar meanings. Some of the meanings are the same as Gareb (2Sam.23:38). Cp: yaareyb, gaareyb, g͟haareyb. (Hos.5:13-15)

Ephraim is used for 'increase/multiply-them/the' as the baker's actions is exactly what is meant by this word that something small increases in size/quantity, etc. (Hos.7)

Samaria (1Kgs.13:32) 'storytellers' 'they stayed/staying up late or all night' 'night stories for staying up and entertainment' and is still used to state the stories being told are fictional 'When I would have healed Israel, then the iniquity of Ephraim was discovered, and the wickedness of Samaria: for they commit falsehood...' '...yet they have spoken lies against me...yet do they imagine mischief against me...their princes shall fall by the sword for the rage of their tongue...'. (Hos.7)

Memphis; mōp; موف 'wipe urine/sperm using stone/leaves' and means to wipe after urinating/ejaculation the same way toilet paper is used without water. The description is of dry land, or resources drying up, what wine, bread is produced is inferior to before—just as only wiping with a stone or rock after urinating is not as clean as washing it away with water, which is why the story likens the things people will eat as punishment will be inferior in quality and unclean in nature. Cp: moo<u>ph</u>. (Hos.9)

Baal-peor (Num.25) 'high/higher/above/spouse-so he will disgrace/will be disgraced/will push forward blindly/behave brashly' 'high/higher/above/spouse-will be/become naked' 'high/higher/above/spouse-lose reputation/bad reputation/ruin the reputation/spoiled/stale/expired' 'high/higher/above/spouse-untrustworthy' because they have gone from being like the best and freshest of figs to degrading in quality and reputation and linked to sexual immorality in the verses 'as in the days of Gibeah...' 'I saw your fathers as the firstripe in the fig tree at her first time: *but* they went to Baal-peor, and separated themselves unto *that* shame...'. (Hos.9:10)

Shalman; šalman; شَل مَن 'took who/from' 'took what' also meaning he took what he pleased/did what he pleased. The author of this part of Hosea has been inspired by two characters in the Bible to create this word-name: the most obvious because of the choice and use of similar word-phrase is **Shalmaneser** 'took who he captivated/imprisoned' (2Kgs.17). It is interesting to see how this was used in 2Kgs., where the king of Israel is named **Hoshea** and is exactly the same word and meanings as **Hosea** of the Book of Hosea, but in 2Kgs Hoshea is a king of Israel who has behaved badly towards the Assyrian king Shalmaneser; Hoshea's bad was that he sent a gift and requested support from 'So king of Egypt' the latter had no role in the story other than the word 'So' represent the 'bad' that Hoshea committed. Just as the mention of a king of Egypt named So 'bad/evil/bothersome' is linked to a king called Shalmaneser and a king Hoshea in 2Kgs, the use of the word Beth-el/**Bethel** (Gen.28:10-19) which means 'bad' 'evil' 'dreadful' is linked to a 'Shalman' in this story, and as everywhere Bethel is mentioned, death follows in the narration of the story—the same applies here 'So shall Beth-el do unto you because of your great wickedness: in a morning shall the king of Israel utterly be cut off.'

The second character from an earlier story which the author of Hosea has based 'Shalman' on ('took who/from' 'took what/from' meaning he took what he pleased/did what he pleased) is **Joshua** 'picked a lot' 'many people' not only does 'Joshua' mean took lots of things/people, but his character was created and introduced as someone who had to pick a lot of people to go fight with him against the enemy. This is supported by giving as an example the name of an area/city 'Beth-arbel' (see Beth-arbel for its meanings) and linking it to where even women and children were ruthlessly and barbarically massacred by this character: in the Book of Joshua he is ordered to kill every man, woman and child, and in each city/area/country they attack, the narration makes a point in specifying not one person was left alive, all are depicted as being completely killed in a sequence of genocides from area to area. Out of the many areas listed as what Joshua conquered (i.e. would have killed the mothers and their children too as the stories describe killing all the inhabitants and leaving none alive) and then divided between the victorious people, two have similar word-names with the same/similar meanings to Beth-arbel (Hos.10:14): Beth-arabah (Josh.15:61) and Irpeel (Josh.18:27). Cp: <u>sh</u>alman. (Hos.10:14-15)

Beth-arbel; bêṯ 'arb'ēl; بيت تَرب بَل 'it/he will-god/parent/teacher-the' 'it/he will-grow/raise/discipline/teach-the' 'he/it will-dilute and mix with water-the'; بيت عَرب بَل 'it/he will express clearly/speak clearly' 'it will-be clearly expressed' 'it/he will-he will/will he-god/parent/teacher-the' 'it/he will-be warned/look, learn and remember- grow/raise/discipline/teach-the' 'it/he will-be warned/look, learn and remember-dilute and mix-the' 'it/he will-fuck-the' 'it/he will-be fucked-the'. Cp: beyt-arb-ill, beyt-'arb-ill. (Hos.10:14)

Joel

Joel (1Sam.8:1-5) 'howling/howling-the' and chapter 1 is full of howling: 'Awake, ye drunkards, and weep; and howl...Lament like a virgin girded with sackcloth for the husband of her youth...the land mourneth...howl, O ye vindressers...Gird yourselves and lament, ye priests: howl ye ministers of the altar...and cry unto the Lord...How do beasts groan...O Lord to thee I will cry...The beasts of the field also cry unto thee.'; 'beware-the' 'learn and remember-the' 'boys/sons' it is narrated from the first verses as a warning, something to learn from and beware of, and is to be taught to children and coming generations to learn from and be wary of too 'Hear this, ye old men, and give ear, all ye inhabitants of the land. Hath this been in your days, or even in the days of your fathers? Tell ye your children of it, and *let* your children *tell* their children, and their children another generation.'. (Joel)

Pethuel; pĕṯû'ēl; بيذْ ئِل ، بيذْئيل 'it will shrivel/wither/shrink-the' 'it will shrivel/shrink/wither' from the word (vw/ذو) 'shrivelled/shrank'. '...the harvest of the field is perished...The vine is dried up, and the fig tree languisheth; the pomegranate tree, the palm tree also, and the apple tree, even all the trees of the field are withered: because joy is withered away from the sons of men...for the corn is withered...and the flame has burned all the trees of the field...for the rivers of waters are dried up, and the fire hath devoured the pastures of the wilderness.'. The virgin deprived of her husband, the priests and God deprived of drink offerings, the new wine evaporating all describe a withering/shrinking/shrivelling related to water being unavailable, as in drought. Cp: beivu-ill, beivueyl. (Joel.1)

Jehoshaphat (2Sam.8:16-17) has been used for 'he who/he was-saw/cured/was cured' 'came he/came to him- saw/cured/was cured' 'which one-saw/cured/was cured' 'he who/he was-cured or satisfied in another's bad luck/revenge/gloating/recompense out of hatred or wrong' 'which one-cured or satisfied in another's bad luck/revenge/gloating/recompense out of hatred or wrong' 'came/he/he who-makes 'shaphoot'' (shaphoot is a dish made by soaking leavened pancakes in churned milk). It reflects how God will bring 'all nations' to the valley of the same name so people will come and see the judgements and the revenge to be taken for the violations caused against the people. The curing is in the 'recompense' (revenge) when the situation is reversed and the people will do to their oppressors what their oppressors had done to them. The 'shaphoot' dish is reflected when this revenge will happen it is described as something which is a characteristic of the shaphoot dish, as it is soaked in plenty of buttermilk and the spongy nature of the bread becomes full and overflows at the touching '...and come up to the valley of Jehoshaphat: for there will I sit to judge all the heathen round about. Put ye in the sickle, for the harvest is ripe: come, get you down; for the press is full, the fats overflow; for their wickedness is great.' (Joel.3)

Tyre (Josh.19:29) 'left over food' 'left over anything/used and or unwanted things' as the boys and girls are being handed around like left over food that no one wants in exchange for drink, the girls and boys are being used as a commodity and not for how they should be cherished as children. (Joel.3:4)

Zidon/Sidon (Gen.10:15) 'give(s) extra' because the narration describes how the wrongdoing will be avenged quickly with more of the same wrongdoing against the original perpetrators. (Joel.3:4)

Palestine (Exod.15:14) has been used for 'between/in shores/coasts' because the narration has described this, again, as being between shores 'and all the coasts of Palestine'. The reason Palestine has been used in the narration is because it depends on the then audience being familiar with what this represents from the stories of Pharaoh drowning where, again, the meaning of the word 'Palestine' was used and meant between two or more shores/coasts which Pharaoh drowned in. This chapter of Joel and specifically these verses speak of revenge upon those who have wronged the people. (Joel.3:4)

Grecians; yĕwānîm; غيوآن هم 'misled to downfall-them' 'their misleading to their downfall'; عيوآن هم 'howling-them/their howling' as the nations described conducting wrong against the children of Jerusalem and Judah have committed actions which will bring negative consequences back onto the instigators—so they have misled themselves and it will bring their own downfall; in both cases, grievous wrong is being done to children separated from their parents and the word-imagery has wailing/howling in grief for children and the children for their parents. It is the same way as Grecia was used earlier but in different form. Cp: gheiwaan-hum, 'eiwaan-hum. (Joel.3:6)

Gentiles which is the same root word used for 'Grecia/Grecians' has been used again as it was earlier in (Judg.4) as 'I will deceive them/the' 'I will mislead them to downfall-them/the' as they are told to gather and come with their weapons ready to war, so they arrive thinking they are stronger and believing they will massacre God's people 'let the weak say, I am strong.' only to end up as a human sacrifice—it is similar to the Gog from Magog story, but this time the word used is 'Gentiles' for the above-mentioned meaning. (Joel.3)

Amos

Amos; 'āmôs; تأمُس 'I touch' 'I possess' 'I cause fight/problem(s)' and it means to physically touch; or possess as in a devil or spirit possessing a person; when a person provokes or gets involved in verbal or physical conflict with another.

The meaning of 'provoked into physical conflict' is expressed by naming the people/city to be afflicted then giving reasons as to why—meaning the people being punished have provoked the violence by the transgressions of the past. It mentions the things they did wrong against Israel to provoke the punishment.

Placing him among men from **Tekoa** 'piety' 'sympathy and fear for what is right/wrong' as this story attempts to bring piety and fear, or respect, for what is right and wrong to people's attention.

It seems the author of this story wanted to concentrate in compact sentences the link between the words used as names, but why? For better entertainment value, or for showing his cleverness in wordplay? All the compound word-names used are used for their meanings which have a direct relation to the narration being described which the ancient audiences of the time would understand the puns/link immediately, and find entertaining just like all the Biblical stories, except this author's work seems to want the fictionality of these stories to be more prominent and over the top:

Zion is still used as 'bad' and 'sweep/brush' 'swept/brushed away' (as in brushing dirt away using brush of the same name) the word was also used throughout 'Joel'. **Carmel** 'a crumb/corner-the' 'crumbled(something) from its corners-the' because it would need to be 'zion/swept', and the 'hot coal end of log in fire' 'bury in fire/ashes the sharp and burnt end of the log' as what happens to this log as the buried end is buried in ash and hot coals, is it slowly turns into hot coals and its tip breaks off when removed, and the remaining tip is withered and scorched.

Damascus for 'tore/ripped up' as it is described as striking **Gilead** 'tumbling/rolling stone(s)' with iron and also **Gilead**'s meaning of 'placing responsibility' is put on **Damascus** because it 'tore/ripped up' Gilead.

Hazael 'he will remove/kill' will be killed/removed with fire which will also remove the threats and borders of **Ben-hadad** 'will be threatened' 'will determine borders'.

Damascus again for 'tore/ripped up' as now its 'bar' will be broken and the inhabitants will be moaning and groaning from the harm because they are in **Aven** 'moaned/groaned' 'was/were harmed' 'harmed'.

The people from **Eden** 'he will guilt' 'he will bow/bend/face ground/lower head' are guilty and so will be punished too.

The people from **Syria** 'wilderness/uninhabited place (where it's easy to get lost)' 'to abandon something or someone in the wild' 'thrown, strewn or located over a vast distance/over different areas' 'vast/distant/covering wide or many different areas' (see Aram (Gen.10:22)); and the local translator still plays on 'squeeze' 'the tight/squeezed' 'visit/the visit' 'the pilgrimage' 'the false oath' (see Asshur (Gen.10:11)) as the people will be forced to visit a country not theirs because they will be pushed into captivity abroad, but they will stop at **Kir** 'settle/stop/stop moving'.

He will cause pain to **Gaza** 'a blunt or deep pain/squeezing pain' because they delivered the people who were weak and vulnerable as captives to **Edom** 'I am spinning/dizzy' and **Edom** also shows the punishment will also 'I last/make last'.

The most valued things in the stories 'palaces' which should read 'he will eat' as they are places where food is stored/eaten will be destroyed/cut down which is why the author mentions again **Gaza** 'to cut crop/grass' 'cherished him/it' 'pride/proud'.

The punishment is severe and inhabitants will be 'cut off' from **Ashdod** 'emigrate/leave' 'become more severe' 'become stronger' 'tie strongly' 'strengthen and persevere'; and this continues and is linked to the people who 'holdeth the sceptre' in **Ashkelon** 'hang up/hang from ropes/rings' and its other meaning 'water(water plants/crops) for them' is linked to **Philistines** 'between two (or more) coasts' (in 1Sam.7 Samuel performed a ritual at Mizpeh (body of water/pool where water was drawn and poured out implying the defeat was between two bodies of water and to have the battle happen between two bodies of water where they were battling the Philistines—both Mizpeh/pool and Philistines/between two coasts were used as words to enhance this (and in Exodus where Pharaoh dies between two coasts) but this time it is **Ekron** 'ruined', and just like placing **Ekron** between **Ashkelon** and **Philistine** in the story links them, so the 'ruined' meaning of Ekron applied to them.

Tyrus is mentioned again for 'left over food' 'left over anything/second-hand (things) 'aching pain in teeth/bones' as they will be punished and their eating places (hekal/'palaces) destroyed; and **Edom** 'I am spinning/dizzy' 'I last/make last' as the hatred of Edom against Jacob lasted long (according to the author of this story although Genesis shows Edom received Jacob well at his return) and it is used as a reminder of the enmity in the story between Jacob and Edom happened over a dizzy Esau being deceived with food to give up his birth right, and then he lost his father's blessing through Jacob's deceit of Isaac. Due to the importance of food in the stories, the author of Joel repeats the mention of Edom.

Teman 'guaranteed' as it is guaranteed they will be destroyed along with the eating places (palaces) of **Bozra** 'unripe/still green (fruit, vegetables, grain)' as the eating places and what is in it, including people, will be burned/destroyed before they are eaten, but **Bozrah** also for 'a litter' of children as the 'children of' **Ammon** 'blinded/to blind' (as they will be punished) 'drank' as they are connected to the sentence of the destruction of Bozrah's 'he will eats/palaces) are responsible for murdering the women pregnant with 'child of' **Gilead** which means 'placing responsibility' on the children of Ammon; but also **Gilead** for its 'tumbling/rolling stone(s)' because in demarcating land, stones are used as borders/markers and they have killed the women of Gilead 'that they might enlarge their border'.

But the punishment will reach **Rabbah** 'brought up' 'disciplined' as the things they have raised and accumulated whether food for the 'hekal/palaces' or their kings, all will be disciplined with punishment but also **Rabbah** for 'caused a scene' 'monkeyed' as in made a lot of noise/chatter (arguing/shouting) while throwing things around (literally objects or figuratively accusations and gestures) as the destruction will be accompanied 'with shouting in the day of battle, with a tempest in the day of the whirlwind'.

Moab 'Of shame' as their destruction will be accompanied 'with the sound of the trumpet' as if something joyous is happening so there will be gloating over Moab's disgrace and the mention of **Edom** 'I last/make last' has been connected to **Kerioth** 'cracked/gnashed between teeth' 'grit teeth' because Moab has burnt the bones of king of Edom long enough it has turned 'into lime'; **Kerioth** cracked/gnashed between teeth' is connected to the palaces which correctly should read as 'he will eat'.

Judah 'he is called/calls' was called by God to follow 'his commandments' and law, but they made a false way, false claims of commandments/laws of which **Judah** means 'to make a claim' 'make a false claim or an unproven claim' and will be **Judah** 'call, or curse' and this is linked to **Jerusalem** 'they see-asked-them/the' 'came-saw-asked-them/the' as they saw the truth, were asked to follow the truth which in these stories is God's law/commandments, but instead they followed their own ways.

Israel 'twisted muscle-the' 'twisted-the' because the story narrates they have twisted things and made them not how they should be, e.g. 'they sold the righteous for silver, and the poor for a pair of shoes...and turn aside the way of the meek...and they drink the wine of the condemned *in* the house of their god.'. The sexual immorality meaning of 'Israel/twisted muscle-the' is not left out 'and a man and his father will go in unto the *same* maid, to profane my holy name...'

Amorite 'a builder' mentioned because 'the Amorite...whose height was like the height of the cedars, and he was strong as the oaks; yet I destroyed...'.

Egypt/Mizraim for 'put scarf on-them/the' 'knot/bundle-them/the' (people bundle things into scarfs or knot small things/small amounts into scarf or fabric for storage and/or travel) and this is meant in 'Also I brought you up from the land of Egypt, and led you forty years through the wilderness, to possess the land of the' **Amorite** mentioned again for 'a builder' but also for 'an order' as they are given this land that is not theirs to take except for God told them to.

Nazarite 'warned/a warning/is warning' 'a vow' 'been set aside' 'of vows' 'of setting aside' of which can be fasting from food/drink which is expressed in this verse, which is why the author brings in the word **Israel** 'twisted-the' (as above) because the right things have been twisted into the wrong way, and it mentions sending prophets and their job is to warn people—the narrator accuses the people of telling the prophets not to prophesy/warn 'And I raised up of your sons for prophets, and even of your young men for Nazarites, *Is it* not even thus, O ye children of Israel? saith the Lord. Buy ye gave the Nazarites wine to drink; and commanded the prophets, saying, Prophesy not.'

Israel 'twisted muscle-the' 'twisted-the' is mentioned again for its twisting of 'truths' or of the 'right ways/commandments/laws'.

Ashdod 'emigrate/leave', **Egypt/Mizraim** 'knot/bundle-them/the' (people bundle things into scarfs or knot small things/small amounts into scarf or fabric for storage and/or travel) is now used together to indicate the people are packing and carrying their things while emigrating—the author uses this verse intentionally to address the stories of the people who came out of Egypt, i.e. emigrated, carried their things on travel, and states they will gather 'upon the mountains of Samaria', **Samaria** 'late night stories/staying up late stories' and the description of the 'great tumults' and 'oppressed' in the middle of **Samaria** has a clear meaning.

The author is saying the stories of coming out of Egypt, wandering, the stories of massacring people, people being oppressed, are all fictional samarias, as are the stories of amassing great amounts of stores into 'hekal/he will eat' to justify 'who store up violence and robbery in their palaces[he will eat/hekal]'; this is saying two things: the stories about piling produce into the 'he will eat' (in plural) are fictional but also that it is wrong to justify these stories where the massacre and oppression of many different peoples just to access food sources and supply the 'he will eat/hekal/palaces' is also false, but also the idea and essence of the stories is wrong, immoral.

This is further supported by the author continuing to state and remind the audience of these stories that these are fictional stories with no relation to reality nor to what is morally right, by this verse 'Thus saith the Lord; As the shepherd taketh out of the mouth of the lion two legs, or the piece of an ear; so shall the children of Israel be taken out that dwell in Samaria in the corner of a bed, and in Damascus in a couch.':

When people listen to samarias 'late night/staying up late stories' they gather and assemble in one place; they also recline or sit on beds, on cushions, mats on the floor listening to the fictional story being told, and that is what the author of Amos.3 is describing. The verse is saying these 'children of **Israel** 'twisted muscle-the/twisted-the' stories will cause people who forget they are fictional stories (the people who are sitting on beds/cushions, etc. being fed from the mouth of the storytellers) and if they believe the twisted and immoral narration of killing, robbing, deceiving and how it is important to fill the eating places 'he will eat/hekal' (which in this part of the story is called a palace) then they will be '**Damascus**: 'tore/ripped up' as a real people (the audience) if they are used to attack/hate each other.

It mentions **Israel** for the meaning of twisting things/doing wrong, then **Bethel** is used for 'bad/evil' to mean evil will befall those who follow these things which have been twisted and taken out of proper meaning and context.

The beginning of Amos.4 also continues with a message that points out these are fictional stories and their message is an immoral one: 'Hear this word ye kine of Bashan, that are in the mountain of Samaria, which oppress the poor, which crush the needy, which say to their masters, Bring, and let us drink.' **Bashan** 'to filter impurities out of liquid' 'fertile/verdant land' the Biblical stories have the best livestock come from Bashan as its name suggests it is fertile and green where animals become fat and the best for food, the audience of the 'samarias' have been likened to cows because they are fat on the stories being fed/told, the author wants to 'filter impurities' by making them see what is wrong in these stories or wrong in believing these stories:

'The Lord God hath sworn by his holiness, that, lo, the days shall come upon you, that he will take you away with hooks, and your posterity with fishhooks. And ye shall go out at the breaches; every *cow at that which is* before her; and ye shall cast *them* into the palace[hekal/he will eat], saith the Lord.' i.e. if you believe other people can be killed and robbed just to fill the 'hekal/he will eat' then it should be justified that the same is done to you if you can do it to others.

Bethel, as always, is used to show evil/bad 'Come to Bethel, and transgress' even when you come to sacrifice at Bethel, or believe in its stories, you are committing a wrong/sin 'at Gilgal multiply your transgression,' **Gilgal** means 'clear/purify' in a sense similar to one meaning of **Bashan** 'filter impurities' it is saying the audience who believes in offering sacrifices were offered at a place called 'evil/bad/bethel' are themselves increasing their sins/wrongs.

'and bring your sacrifices every morning, *and* your tithes after three years: And offer a sacrifice of thanksgiving with leaven, and proclaim *and* publish the free offerings: for this liketh you, O ye children of Israel, saith the Lord God.' the author is saying through giving God this dialogue that the many sacrifices daily, annually or regularly is something that the people who twist what is right into something else ('(children of) israel/twisted muscle-the/twisted-the) want and not what God wants, i.e. God did not ask for this (supported by the text in Jer.7:4).

There is an intentional stating that the author is making things happen to the people of the stories (the fictional people), and what he is saying is these stories were created by authors like him: 'I have smitten you with blasting and mildew…saith the Lord. I have sent among you the pestilence after the manner of Egypt; your young men have I slain with the sword, and have taken away your horses…saith the Lord. I have overthrown *some* of you, as God overthrew Sodom and Gomorrah, and ye were as a firebrand plucked out of the burning: yet have ye not returned unto me, saith the Lord.'

He has shown this first by writing punishments similar to what has been narrated in other stories, then he goes on to make a pun 'I have overthrown some of you, as God overthrew Sodom and Gomorrah,' i.e. he, the author of Amos, punished and overthrew these people in the stories no different than how God is narrated to have overthrown Sodom and Gomorrah which the author also pokes fun at with 'and ye were as a firebrand plucked out of the burning' as Sodom means 'soot' and Gomorrah means 'hot coals' and 'submerged under' he is making fun that they are one people, not different, that these things never happened or they would not exist as a real people, but also making a joke how the people who survive were plucked out of a pile of hot coal and ashes (Sodom and Gomorrah are what you find in every household in rural areas who use basic ovens of clay and firewood for making bread at least two-three times a day). (Amos.4)

The author continues to show the Biblical stories are false by pointing out the sacrifices during the wanderings, and also the stories about the tabernacle and carrying it are also false: 'Have ye offered unto me sacrifices and offerings in the wilderness forty years, O house of Israel? But ye have borne the tabernacle of your Moloch and Chiun your images, the star of your god, which ye made to yourselves.' This is the author poking holes at the impossibility of wandering forty years, the impossibility of sacrifices and offerings where it would have been impossible to even sustain a small amount of people in the wilderness for forty years. It goes on to point out the idea and stories of the tabernacle and its god worship are no different than the ideas of worshipping Moloch and Chiun, with a direct accusation that these things were fabricated.

This author follows the Biblical authors' methods of using compound word-names, but uses them to show how they are fictional, he uses sarcasm to rage against these stories, it is almost as if he came from a time when the people were a later audience and took them as real instead of the original/earlier audiences who understood them for what they were: fictional stories made for entertainment, or he may have just been morally outraged at the death, destruction, glorification of murdering people, robbing and other negative activities given to the protagonists of these stories. 'Therefore I will cause you to go into captivity beyond Damascus, saith the Lord, whose name is the God of hosts.' is another sarcastic remark that the author will write in his story that the people will go into captivity since they could not have possibly sacrificed to God in their fictional wandering stories, but he also pokes fun at this because the 'God of hosts' correct meaning is eating to full (stomach), getting lots of food to be full and satisfied with; the translation of the word 'hosts' is a mistranslation.(Amos.3-5)

Chiun; kiyyûn; كيّن 'created' 'heaped into peaks' as the author of Amos continues to describe the wandering stories, the carrying of the tabernacle and making sacrifices as fabrications and compares them to being no different than other pagan worship; خيّن 'betrayed/betrayer(s)' as the people the author Amos accuses are deceiving away from the truth, and therefore he himself narrates for them a punishment where they are betrayed by God allowing them to go into captivity for their own betrayals. Cp: kiyyun, <u>kh</u>iyyun. (Amos.5:26)

'Woe to them that are at ease in Zion,' it is not a good thing to trust in 'bad/sweep away/**zion**'; 'and trust in the mountain of Samaria' and who believe the fictional 'late night/staying up stories/**samaria**'; 'which are named chief of the nations, to whom the house of Israel came!' a criticism of the fictional stories which are used as the best cities/nations in these stories although the meanings and actions inspired by the meanings and intentions of these stories and their authors mean '**Zion**/bad - **Samaria**/late night story' and it shows the negative meaning of the compound word '**Israel**/twisted muscle-the/twisted-the' so he is still criticising how stories which have negative meanings, fictional names can glorify the 'bad' things which are abundant in these stories. And he continues to use the Biblical authors' method of compound word-names, but to emphasise how wrong these stories are (in his opinion (which is evident in how he criticises everything in the earlier chapters, but also in this chapter he criticises David's musical instruments, Joseph's troubles, Jacob's stories and he uses the meanings of these word-names to criticise what he is honing in on) and how fictional it is. (Amos.6)

Amos.7 is more akin to stand-up comedy than the usual Biblical stories, it still uses the Biblical method of compound word-names to deliver the pun, but it also parodies other OT stories such as Ezekiel and the man with the flax measuring reed, how bad kings plot to hurt prophets, but even Amos is not a prophet, but a shepherd and also a fruit gatherer—poking fun at more stories of the Bible—who is 'taken' by God to become a prophet who delivers a prophecy which is a succinct and humorous threat of punishment of several stories' plotlines combined into one.

Note the parody about the basket of summer fruit which has no message to it, except an unrelated statement that God will no longer pass by 'my people Israel' intimating the fruit are left to wither and the 'withered' penis of Israel 'twisted muscle-the' story. Then the intentional contradiction to make it a joke of the howling over the dead bodies all over the temple but who are buried or killed silently.

It disparages and criticises the stories of the floods of Noah, the expelling of the children of Israel in Egypt and Pharaoh drowning, and it makes it clear that they are not hearing 'the words of the Lord' because the sin is, they are believing the fictionalities of **Samaria** stories 'They that swear by the sin of Samaria…'.

Amos.9 begins with a parody of the story of the Passover, delivered in reverse of the original story: the people are not allowed to leave and anyone who escapes or tries to escape will be found and killed. Many other Biblical stories are poked at with the author's concise style: the mystical Leviathan is mentioned; then two things that cannot go together have been compared as the same, per statement:

'Ethiopian' a mistranslation which correctly is **Cushi/Cushite** something crispy or a tiny bit of fibre/litter is said to be the same as **Israel** 'twisted muscle-the'—the crispy/burnt thing or fibre has no muscle to be twisted, they are completely different.

Israel 'twisted muscle-the' 'twisted-the' coming out of **Egypt/Mizraim** 'put scarf on-the' 'knot/bundle-them/the' because you cannot wear a scarf on, or bundle inside a scarf and carry, the genitals which are meant by the muscle of the Jacob/Israel story.

You cannot **Caphtor** '(Try) break fast-them/the' (give food to break the fast) with only water as **Philistines** are 'between two(or more) coasts' and most of their stories in the Bible are tied to water and coasts; also the same as an earlier writing of the word **Philistim** which can still mean 'between their/coast(s)' but also 'squash/flatten-them/the' which is different to the meaning of **Caphtor** 'fold-them/the'.

Syrian 'to throw/to do with throwing' 'thrown, strewn or located over a vast distance/over different areas' 'vast/distant/covering wide or many different areas' is the opposite of **Kir** 'settle/stop/stop moving'.

'Are ye not as children of the Ethiopians unto me, O children of Israel? saith the Lord. Have not I brought up Israel out of the land of Egypt? and the Philistines from Caphtor, and the Syrians from Kir?'

It continues with intentional contradictory statements within the same sentence to parody what happens in the other Biblical stories: '…and I will destroy it from off the face of the earth; saving that I will not utterly destroy the house of Jacob, saith the Lord.' no one will be destroyed or wiped off the face of the earth.

'…I will sift the house of Israel among all nations, like as corn is sifted in a sieve, yet shall not the least grain fall upon the earth.' i.e. they will not be scattered anywhere.

'All the sinners of my people shall die by the sword, which say, The evil shall not overtake nor prevent us.' i.e. the good or innocent people are killed in the stories who refuse to allow 'evil' to affect them.

'In that day will I raise up the tabernacle of David that is fallen, and close up the breaches thereof…' as the tabernacle was made during Moses' time and not during David's but this is a joke that the tabernacle (a tent) that was carried around as the people wandered for forty years was made of stone, and the author's opinion of the tabernacle and wandering has already been made clear earlier, but here he adds a joke that it was made of the same heavy stone and the household utensil from which the character David gets his name from.

Amos.9:12-15 seems to be written by a different author than who wrote all the previous chapters and verses including the first parts of chapter 9 because the humour, sarcasm and style disappears and is replaced by the usual Biblical stories style of killing everybody to possess everything they own. Funnily enough, it seems the author of Amos (like his name) provoked a later editor to change the ending to bring it back in line with other Biblical stories of dispossessing so you can possess, and the importance of food.

Obadiah

Obadiah (1Kgs.18) 'servant-him/he' 'worshipper-him/he' and the text speaks of God being angered by Edom supporting others against Jacob, his actions have made him one of the 'heathen'. Most of the text revolves around food and food source which is the basis of the worship rituals in the Biblical stories, and the original name of the character Edom has been brought back because Esau means 'having supper/supper' 'disobeyed/did wrong' with even the same deceit in the story which Jacob employed against Esau being mentioned that the people will do to him '*they that eat* thy bred have laid a wound under thee'.

The last verse states the kingdom will be the Lord's, i.e. people will worship him; 'mount Esau' has been mentioned due to the focal point of the OT revolving around food and 'Esau' means 'they fed supper' 'supper' 'they disobeyed/did wrong', and his story revolved around food, being fed, and disobedience which is why '…saviours shall come up on mount Zion to judge the mount of Esau, and the kingdom shall be the Lord's'.

Sepharad; sēp̄āraḏ; سيفآر عد 'travelled-returned'; سيفآرَط 'he will help pass through/along' 'he will make slip/lose' 'he will cross it' 'he will pass it' 'he will lose/lose chance/be deceived out of opportunity or wealth/money/possessions' 'he will split/tear it'. All the meanings could be possible or even just one of them: the people taken into captivity will return and take over the land; what Esau and the others had will be lost to the captives; it is God who will safely deliver the captives of Israel and Jerusalem back into the land and to possess the land. Cp: seyp̱haar 'd; seyp̱haaraṭ. (Obad.1:20)

Jonah

Jonah (2Kgs.14:25-27) 'oh, pity' son of **Amittai** 'reach hand out/extend/touch' 'stretch out/reach/extend'. As explained under Jonah at 2Kgs., it is an expression of pity over someone or something (including over an animal) expressed as 'yonah/yanah'. Ammitai is because God is reaching out both to Jonah and the people of Nineveh to repent and correct their ways.

The sailors' reaction towards Jonah is that of pity. They know they should throw him overboard, he is in trouble with God, but out of pity they do not and attempt to get to dry land instead of throwing him overboard. Even when it becomes clear they have to, first they beseech God.

Jonah is pitying himself in Chapter 2, from inside the whale his words are that of pity for himself 'I cried by reason of my affliction unto the Lord, and he heard me; out of the belly of hell cried I, *and* thou heardest my voice'. After Jonah's prayer, God has pity on him and orders the fish to vomit him.

The king of Nineveh who repents and leads his whole nation to repent, his final lines of dialogue wonder if God will have pity on them and refrain from punishment—and God does have pity on them. 'Who can tell if God will turn and repent, and turn away from his fierce anger, that we perish not?...And God saw their works, that they turned from their evil way; and God repented of the evil, that he had said he would do unto them; and he did *it* not.'. The animals fasting and wearing sackcloth like people also conjures up a picture of pitying, the authors use how people would feel compassion at a sight that would cause anyone to have compassion: animals girded with sackcloth, a sign of grief, and asking for compassion.

Jonah (whose name is an expression of pity used in daily language, and the word can be further broken down to 'Oh, me/Oh, I' and people pronounce it with emotion, feeling empathy with what is being viewed/spoken about) is angered by God's pity for Ninevah.

God pities Jonah sitting under a shack and grows a plant over him to provide better shade, only to destroy it (to teach Jonah a lesson) and have Jonah feel so much pity for himself (having suffered a heatstroke) he wishes to die—the lesson was to teach Jonah to have pity for others as he has for himself.

The whole story and word of 'Jonah' is about pity. The theme of 'pity' is further emphasised towards the end of the story 'Then said the Lord, thou hadst had pity on the gourd, for which thou hast not laboured, neither madest it grow; which came up in a night, and perished in a night: And should I not spare Nineveh, that great city, wherein are more than sixscore thousand persons that cannot discern between their right hand and their left hand; and *also* much cattle.'

Tarshish (Gen.10:4) 'light spraying' or 'a lot of light spray' 'a lot of vomiting' deaf' 'scared into stupor/unable to respond, hear, speak' 'pretending not to hear/pretending to be deaf' and **Joppa** (2Chr.2:9,16) 'filled/packed' 'full' 'floated' have been used to enhance a story taking place in a ship and in the middle of the sea, so there is lots of water spraying, the ship is floating, the fish that swallows Jonah is in the sea, and eventually vomits him; Jonah does not listen/obey God and instead behaves as one that is deaf or pretends to be deaf by not doing as God has ordered; the sailors are afraid of the storm, but Jonah is so deaf to it and to God's request, and his deafness to the storm which is a warning is shown in that he is asleep and not disturbed by it—so he still does not hear.

Nineveh (Gen.10:11) 'we bring to your attention/point out' 'we warn you/wake you up/point out' and this name has been chosen for the city in the story as its name lends itself to the storyline, a story where Jonah is sent to warn the people of Nineveh about the coming punishment, to point out to them their wrongdoings and to wake them up to stop from the wrong ways.

Micah

Micah (Judg.17, 18) 'What is wrong?' 'What is there?' 'What is the situation/problem?' 'What did he say?' 'What happened?' and the theme of this expression is made in the text when Micah informs the people of God coming down, and punishment coming for the sins of Jacob and Israel—the questions reiterated by the author 'What is the transgression of Jacob?' and 'what are the high places of Judah?' is understood as the people who are being promised to be punished are naturally asking/wondering 'What is there/what is wrong/what have we done?' and relays with the similar meanings of 'high places/'for what?' 'why?' 'what for?' 'with what?"—which the authors include and answer. The same can be seen in 'Now why dost thou cry out aloud?' 'Is there no king in thee? is thy counsellor perished?' O my people what have I done unto thee? and wherein have I wearied thee? testify against me.' All these show the meanings of 'Micah/what is wrong/what is the matter? Etc.' (Mic.1:5; 4:9; 6:3)

Morasthite (Jer.26:18) 'of piling/stacking heaps' 'of heaping' as the punishment described leaves the punished in heaps: '...and will come down, and tread upon the high places of the earth. And the mountains shall be molten under him...Therefore I will make Samariah as an heap of the field...I will pour the stones thereof into the valley...And all the graven images thereof shall be beaten to pieces...'. (Mic.1)

Jotham (Judg.9:7-21) 'leper/lepers/leprosy' 'tips/appendages fall/cut off' 'came-guilted' 'came-blamed' 'came-ostracised' as the description is of buildings and people being cut to pieces or cut off when God comes to punish them. Also, they are blamed for this punishment.

Ahaz (2Kgs.15:38; 16) 'swore/insulted/swore insulted a lot' 'a disgrace/disgraced a lot' 'an embarrassment/a great embarrassment' as they will be disgraced, God is also being disgraced and embarrassed as the metaphor has him stripped naked as he howls through the land.

Hezekiah (2Kgs.18-20) 'make suffer/distress-he/him' as the punishment will make many people suffer greatly; 'I will water-he/him' as some of the imagery of the punishment has mountains melting and valleys melting like wax, 'as the waters that are poured down a steep place.'

Judah (Gen.29:35) 'he is called/calls' 'call, or curse' 'to make a claim' 'make a false claim or an unproven claim' as Micah is calling out to the people telling them of the punishment to come.

The text follows the style and content of Amos: **Jacob** (Gen.25:26-34; 27) is used for 'forces open' 'dislocates' 'forces open and takes/usurps' as it describes the punishment is because of 'the transgressions of Jacob' and it states **Samaria** 'late night/staying up late stories' 'storytellers' are the transgressions which have usurped (Jacob/force open/dislocate) the truth. This usurping of the truth with fictional stories is further elucidated as the stories about 'high places/ 'for what?' 'why?' 'what for?' 'with what?' (a reference to the 'he will eat') of **Judah** 'make a false claim or an unproven claim'. The false claims 'Judah/make a false claim or an unproven claim' are the stories about **Jerusalem** (1Kgs.8) 'came-saw-asked-them/the' 'they see-asked-them/the' 'came-saw-rocks-them/the' and the statement is that Judah and Jerusalem are one and the same, and they are related to rocks and worship.

The story continues that it will destroy the fictional stories **Samaria** 'late night/staying up late stories' by disassembling them piece by piece and it uses the meaning of **Judah** 'he is called/calls' 'call, or curse' combined with the meaning of **Jerusalem** 'came-saw-asked-them/the' to express their meanings with God personified as animals 'wailing/mourning' will come to Judah (the calling is the wailing/howling/mourning of dragons/owls) and Jerusalem 'came-saw-asked-them/the' is reflected in God or his punishment 'is come unto Judah; he is come unto the gate of my people, *even* to Jerusalem.'

The narration of uncovering Samaria's foundations (rocks are the foundations of buildings) 'and I will discover the foundations thereof' is the author's statement of showing the building blocks of these stories are the word-names given to its characters and places, and specifically Judah and Jerusalem are based on rocks and false claims along with Samaria/late night story and Jacob/forces open/dislocates is the action which causes rocks to fall down, be removed '…and what *are* the high places of Judah? *are they* not Jerusalem? Therefore I will make Samaria as an heap of the field, *and* as plantings of a vineyard; and I will pour down the stones thereof into a valley, and I will discover the foundations thereof.'. And the author goes on to show how this is done by using the concise and very lucid style of using word-names to mean exactly what is said in very short sentences, not buried among long passages and chapters as in earlier stories, but in the same sentence (the same as the author of Amos).

Israel 'twisted muscle-the/twisted-the' are also blamed as being the sins/sinners 'and for the sins of the house of Israel.' and it is in the same verse where Jacob and Israel's sins are explained as the fictional Samaria stories' 'what *are* the high places' of **Judah** ('false claim') and **Jerusalem** 'came-saw-asked-them/the', i.e. the stories about Judah, Jerusalem, 'house of the king' 'house of God' 'temple' are all false stories which cause people to do wrong/misleads them away from God (according to the story).

Israel's meaning is still connected to perversion of the truth, twisting of things from right way to wrong way, and sexual immorality, and it reminds the audience the creation of the name 'Israel' 'twisted muscle-the' was because of Dinah's illicit sexual affair without marriage: '…she *is* the beginning of the sin to the daughter of **Zion**['bad']: for the transgressions of Israel were found in thee.' (Mic.1:13).

This meaning is clarified again in the following verses of the same chapter by reminding of Judah having sex with his daughter-in-law Tamar, who he thought was a prostitute, which provided her with offspring, her heirs: 'Yet I will bring an heir unto thee, O inhabitant of Mareshah: he shall come unto Adullam the glory of Israel.' There is less parody in Micah than in Amos, but the style uses word-names directly linked to other stories to point out their fictionality. Here it reminds of Tamar and Judah's illicit sex, and the product of their incest which is the heirs/offspring of that encounter, without actually naming them: it uses word-names with the same meaning: Moresheth-gath and Mareshah 'slipped away' meanings and gath/sufferance remind of Tamar's husbands who are all of Judah's sons slipping away from her by death and/or not having sex with her, one made her suffer by ejaculating on the ground, and his name meant 'groaning/moaning/pain' she was in pain because she wanted to mother a child; **Achzib** is mentioned because one of her potential husbands, Judah's son, was conceived or born in a similar named area. Then **Adullam** is mentioned because it is the name of where Judah's friend came from, Hira the Adullamite was made central to the story about Tamar/Judah's marriage, the legal and illicit sex in the story and therefore linked to the offspring they conceive from their illicit encounter. (Mic.1:13-15)

The work is clever in that it has layers, it invokes the other stories, and at the same time also has specific meanings within the context of the current story (which will be explained below).

The following verse also uses Amos' style of opposites within the same sentence which although are contradictory, emphasise the message the author is sending:

Gath (1Sam.5:8-9) 'great sufferance' 'physical sufferance' 'troubling/inconvenience' and Aphrah; aprâ; افرح 'be happy' are used in contradiction to their meanings and the role they have in the story is that of the other word-name: Gath 'sufferance' is told not to cry at all, while Aphrah 'be happy/happiness' is rolling in the dust which is a sign of great distress or grief 'Declare ye *it* not at Gath, weep ye not at all: in the house of Aphrah roll thyself in the dust. Cp: a<u>ph</u>rḥ. (Mic.1:10)

Saphir; šāpîr; سافير 'travel(ed)' 'sins/immoral acts done openly' 'exposing parts of body in public' 'openly immoral' and the verse is expressing exactly that in telling the inhabitants of Saphir to leave with their shame (described as nakedness) exposed 'Pass ye away, thou inhabitant of Saphir, having thy shame naked:'. Cp: saa<u>ph</u>eer. (Mic.1:11)

Zaanan; ṣa'ănān; زَعينآن 'was able to force'; ضَغينآن 'tired/made tired'; شَغينان 'I will sing' 'I will make sing' 'I will become independent/I will no longer need' 'I will become/make rich'; صَئينآن 'swept' 'put into small bowls'. It indicates the inhabitants were too tired/lazy than to attend the mourning and therefore will no longer be needed. Cp: za'ainaan, <u>dh</u>a<u>gh</u>ainaan, <u>sh</u>a<u>gh</u>ainaan, <u>ss</u>a-ainaan. (Mic.1:11)

Beth-ezel; bêṯ ḥā'ēṣel; بيت هآعيزِل ، بيت هاعيزَل 'it/he will-look/here-paid condolences-the' 'it/he will-look/here-isolated/was isolated'; بيت هائيزَل 'it/he will-see-went off/disappeared/removed' 'it/he will-look/pay attention/here-forever'; بيت خائيذَل 'it/he will be disappointed' 'he will lose his sanity/lose some of his sanity'. All meanings are in the verse regarding Beth-ezel, as the absence from 'the mourning' is likened to not attending a funeral/wake to pay condolences/comfort the bereaved; not attending holds the meaning of 'went off/disappeared' as well as 'isolated'; the sentence is expressing 'disappointment' over Zaanan not coming forth. It is similar to Ezel (1Sam.20:14-42). Cp: beyt-haa'eyzel, beyt-haa-eyzel, beyt <u>kh</u>aa-eyvel. (Mic.1:11)

Maroth; mārôṯ; مآرُث 'eye twitch/flutter(a bad omen)' and in rural Yemen it is considered a sign of something bad/evil to happen to you or those related to you. The same thing is expressed in Micah, the inhabitants whose name means the bad omen of the eye-twitch 'Maroth waited carefully for good: but evil came down from the Lord unto the gate of Jerusalem.'. The word 'Jerusalem/came-saw-asked-them/the' is to enhance that these inhabitants had come and asked/prayed to God and were waiting/expecting to see something good of it (but in the story evil is delivered). Maroth is similar to Riphath (Gen.10:3), Meraioth (1Chr.6:6), Merathaim (Jer.50:21). Cp: maarof. (Mic.1:12)

Lachish (Josh.10) 'licked(plural)' 'vicious/angry/strikes out (verbally/physically)' 'until rotted/went off' all these meanings are used: the 'licked/vicious/strikes out' enhances the idea of the chariot which is bound to the animal to pull it; the meaning of 'until rotted/went off' is again related to the meaning of 'Israel' because when Jacob wrestled with man-God and God touched that part of his body, it withered—the muscle wastes away if twisted out of place for a long time and becomes thinner and/or weaker (sometimes completely useless) compared to unaffected muscles. The story meant the withering of Jacob and all his male relatives' reputation/dignity symbolised in the twisting and withering of the muscle because of what Dinah would do, and as explained above under Mic.1:13-15.

Zion 'bad' as it describes what is done to and by the daughters (Dinah, Tamar, and 'daughters of Zion' in this part of the story) as 'bad'. (Mic.1:13-15)

Moresheth-gath; môrešeṯ gaṯ; مُرَصَت جعث 'a piling of sufferance/troubles' 'slipped/slippery-sufferance/troubles'; مُرَصَت قَت 'a piling/heap of qat' qat is usually offered as presents; مُرَصَت غَت 'a piling of misled/deceived/deceit/folly' 'slipped/slippery-fell asleep/dozed off'. It is definitely suffering and troubles which are being heaped due to misleading and deceit as the other half of the verse indicates it is all lies about 'the kings of Israel' i.e. the stories about the kings of Israel are a heaping of lies and 'twisted-the/Israel' a distortion of the stories. Cp: moresset g'f, moresset qat, moresset ghat. (Mic.1:14)

Achzib (Josh.15:44) 'I lie/lie' 'I adorn myself', as the sentence implies gifts were given, and usually the gifts being described are something women can wear/adorn themselves with (see Jerusalem likened to a woman, Aholah and Aholibah, and the wife of Hosea), but these are all 'lies' as both the word Achzib and its use in this sentence clearly indicates. (Mic.1:14)

Mareshah (Josh.15:44) 'wash clothes (quickly)' 'to slip away unnoticed' 'slip from hands' 'slippery' as although it describes giving an heir to Israel, it is also saying it/the heir/offspring will quickly slip away from the 'parents', described as the children going into captivity in the following verse of the chapter.

Adullam (Gen.38:1, 12,20-26) 'do injustice to' 'injustice' 'to mislead-the', how it invokes Tamar/Judah's story has been mentioned above, but even if the Tamar/Judah story were removed from its context, the sentence itself at Mic.1:15 has a very direct message: it is criticising the injustice which is glorified in the stories as being victories for Israel 'he shall come unto Adullam the glory of Israel'. Everywhere 'Adullam' has been used whether in Tamar and Judah's story or in David fleeing Saul and being in a cave called Adullam with other men, in both stories 'do injustice to' 'injustice' 'to mislead-the' was indicated by the word itself and enacted in the narration: Tamar was being misled, promised offspring from brothers of her first deceased husband; Judah was misled by a disguised Tamar to have sex with his daughter-in-law; David suffered injustice and had to hide in a cave, and the other men with him in the cave were either fleeing from injustice or because they had caused injustice. Both stories are linked to sexual acts of immorality as per the Biblical story standards (Judah with Tamar, David with Jonathan) and this too has been linked by using the word 'Israel/twisted muscle-the' so 'he shall come to Adullam the glory of Israel' is saying 'injustice is the glory of twisted muscle-the' i.e. it is misleading to make the product and protagonists of sexual perversions in stories to be glorified; and it means glorifying what is wrong (killing, robbing, illicit sexual relations, and all kinds of oppression and injustice) is a perversion of the truth, of morality. (Mic.1:15)

From Micah.4 onwards seems to be the work of a different author than the author of Micah.1-3, with the writing style and content returning to killing all neighbouring nations and revolving around food.

Nahum

Nahum; naḥûm; نَهُم 'sighing/sighed' 'struck and winded' and means sighing or puffing meant to attract attention or being hit/punched in stomach until breath is forced out of you. The story revolves around God harshly punishing/destroying the intended people and the people being left breathless from this punishment. It is the same as Naham (1Chr.4:19), Tanhumeth (2Kgs.25:23), Nehum (Neh.7:7). Cp: nahum.

He is given a surname of Elkoshite; 'elqōšî; نَلقوشي 'the blower away litter/fibres/burnt remnants' 'the litter/fibres/burnt remnants' 'the scraper away' 'the scraped away' 'the killer/remover in one go/one movement' 'the killed/removed in one movement' 'the left-over burnt pieces/toast until crispy or burnt/burnt in fire or from too much heat' 'the paralysed with fear/joy/shock; نَلقوصي 'the storyteller/telling of story' 'the cut/cutter' 'the cruel/hardened'.

The story revolves around his surname/area name too, and the narration describes the exact meanings of his word-name happening to the people of the story, as the people are suffering 'harsh destruction' and complete destruction, they are being blown away, burned, 'he will make an utter end of the place thereof' 'they shall be devoured as stubble fully dry' 'he is utterly cut off'.

It is the same as Cush (Gen.10:6), Cushi (2Sam.18:19-33), Cushite (Jer.38:7-13), Kishion (Josh.19:20), Kishon (Josh.21:28), Kishi (1Chr.6:41), Kish (1Sam.9:1), Kushaiah (1Chr.15:17). Cp: el-qoo<u>sh</u>ee, el-qoo<u>ss</u>ee. (Nah.)

Huzzab; huṣṣaḇ; حوزّب 'adorned' and is used as a noun, adjective and verb to describe a woman adorned or dressing-up with jewellery, beautiful clothes, etc. usually done for a special gathering/event or daily for her husband. It is used here to describe the falling of a city as a woman/women called Huzzab 'adorned' being led away to captivity. Cp: huzzab. (Nah.2:7)

Habbakuk

Habbakuk; ḥăbaqqûq; حبيَكُّك 'wreaked havoc' 'wreaked havoc for you' 'weaved' 'weaved you/for you' 'plotted' 'plotted for you' 'caused you turmoil' 'a hullaballoo' 'caused you hullabaloo/tumult' from the word (ḥbk/حبك) 'havoc/cause havoc/weave/plot/cause tumult/turn over/uproot'. All these meanings are reflected in the turmoil, distress, evil intentions/plotting, which Habbakuk complains about and the story describes, the uprooting and devastation God sends against the people; the havoc wreaked by both wicked people and enemy nations, spreading across the country. In the last chapter it describes the havoc wreaked upon the mountains, hills, sea from God's arrival, then God threshing 'the heathen in anger'; the havoc happening in the narrator's body from fear of God, ending in three verses which state words to the effect 'no matter what havoc has been wreaked against us (the crops, agriculture, cattle, flocks all failing to produce or cut off), he will still praise God who will strengthen/save him. It is notable how the Arabic word (ḥbk/حبك) used in this story to reflect its exact meanings sounds like the English word 'havoc'. Cp: ḥaibakkuk. (Hab.)

Shigionoth; šigyōnôṯ; شِجيونت 'became passionate/became painfully passionate' and there is a passionate voice praising God, also afraid but passionately holding on to believing God has come/will come for 'the salvation of thy people'. It can also mean 'became curious'.

This chapter has either been inspired by or taken from Psalms which I explained earlier were the edited works (either new revisions/additions to be added, or removed pieces that the people in charge did not want to discard but maybe reuse at later times as deemed suitable), and specifically this chapter resembles 'A Psalm of[*for*] David when he fled from Absalom'; '*Shiggaion of David, which he sang unto the Lord, concerning the words of Cush the Benjamite.*' Which was a Shiggaion/passionate theme, and also note the inspiration from the 'Cush' in that psalm (who was the character who delivered the bad news of Absalom's murder to David who passionately expressed he would rather have died than Absalom his son (in the original Sam. story)), and how this word has been used to express the same meaning of 'Cush' in Hab.3 under a psalm which is also passionate/Shigionoth and includes the use of the word 'Cush/Cushan' for its meanings. Cp: <u>sh</u>igyoonot.

Cushan; kûšān; قُشآن 'went into fit/paralysis' to say someone 'qu<u>sh</u>a' means out of joy, fright or excitement went into some kind of fit where the body shakes and stiffens; 'paralysed with fear/joy' it is used to describe a literal physical state and also figuratively to express great happiness/excitement or fright, 'became crispy' 'blew away litter/fibres/burnt remnants' 'removed completely in one swipe/scrape' 'litter/fibres/burnt remnants'; قُصآن 'hardened' 'told story/news' 'cut'; كُسآن 'were clothed(gifted/bought new clothes)' 'covered with new fabric' 'made cover of fabric'.

The meanings of paralysed with fear, trembling or fits before being petrified motionless, as well as 'clothed/covered with fabric' are used at the same time to show the 'tents of Cushan' (which are fabric)shaking with fear, also the use of 'the curtains of the land of Midian did tremble' because **Midian** (Gen.25:2) means 'reaches out with hand/stretches hand' 'extends/offers something to another (with hand)' 'reach for/stretch arm to reach for' so the word-imagery is trembling hands holding/touching the curtains in Midian.

The 'hardened/cruel' and 'crispy/removed or scraped away in one movement, etc.' are shown in how the people are affected because 'Before him went the pestilence, and burning coals went forth at his feet.' and other descriptions of similar destruction. The word is similar to Kushaiah (1Chr.15:17) and other Cush/Kush words. Cp: qushaan, qussaan, kusaan. (Hab.3)

Zephaniah

Zephaniah (2Kgs.25:18-21) has been used for 'escorted-him/he' 'led in a procession-him/he' 'cleaned/ cleared/purified-him/he' and it begins with clearing away every living thing on earth (destroying them). It continues at Chapter 3 narrating all the nations will be gathered i.e. escorted/led to a specific place, and it describes how God will purify the country which begins the description with 'woe to her that is filthy and polluted; to the oppressing city!' describing how he purified it 'I have cut off nations...I have made their streets waste...so that there is no man, that there is none inhabitant...' so all God's destruction in the previous chapters is 'purified-he/him/Zephaniah'—and more purification is promised and the story ends with a people from which the 'wicked' have been cleansed/killed, and the purged people remaining are pure, their ways and belief are pure: 'Therefore, wait ye upon me, saith the Lord, until the day that I rise up to the prey: for my determination is to gather the nations, that I may assemble the kingdoms, to pour upon them my indignation,' and remember God's indignation as well as the purification/cleansing rituals in the stories all use burning with fire 'even all my fierce anger: for all the earth shall be devoured with the fire of my jealousy. For then will I turn to the people a pure language, that they may call upon the name of the Lord, to serve him with one consent.' (Zeph.1-2; 3:1-9)

As usual, the Biblical authors use the ancestors of the narrator and the king who reigned (according to the story) and these names are words whose themes will be used in the story being told:

Cushi 'scrape away' 'kill in one go/one movement' 'remove in one movement' 'left over burnt pieces/toast until crispy or burnt/burnt in fire or from too much heat' 'scrape away' 'kill in one go/one movement' 'remove in one movement' 'left over burnt pieces/toast until crispy or burnt/burnt in fire or from too much heat' 'cut' 'tell a/the story' to clear away something leaving nothing behind whether as in hygienic practise or killing, also when something is taken away abruptly or forcefully, and these meanings fill Zephaniah's chapters.

Gedaliah 'threw/killed-him/he' and this also is used as, and carries the same destructive meaning, of something or people being thrown down from a height 'and I will cut off the remnant of Baal from this place' **Baal** meaning 'high/above'.

Amariah 'a tiny hint/clue' 'a trace/barely visible trace' 'ordered-he/him' 'I show him mirror' 'I make him look into mirror' 'built-he/him' 'built/topped kooz cup(cold coal, tobacco mix, hot coals)-he/him' 'lived long-he/him'—the story has buildings being destroyed along with the lives of its inhabitants 'And them that worship the host of heaven upon the housetops...'.

Hizkiah the same as **Hezekiah** for its meaning 'squeezed/cornered/crammed him-he/him' 'make suffer/ distress-he/him' 'I will force to taste/swallow/eat-he/him' 'I will flatter/praise-he/him' 'I will predict if he is going to hell or heaven-he/him' 'I will predict if person is good or bad-he/him' 'I will water-he/him'. The people are cornered by death and destruction, they are suffering great physical pain and stress. Also, the story includes the meanings of people guessing or pretending to know if a person does/did good or bad in his/her life—which is only supposed to be known by God and no person has the right to predict or state as fact about another person. This is shown in God seeking out all those who predicted/said that God would do good or evil. i.e. they are committing 'Hizkiah'. 'And it shall come to pass at that time, that I will search Jerusalem with candles, and punish the men that are settled on their lees: that say in their heart: The Lord will not do good, neither will he do evil.'

Josiah for 'they go wandering and seeking' 'they came seeking' as the people are described left wandering blindly due to punishment 'And I will bring distress upon men, that they shall walk like blind men...'. This verse also covers the meaning of **Amon** 'blind/blinded'.

Amon also means 'drinking/giving to drink' (represented by the Chemarims 'wines'),'followed' 'followed/ lead' 'followed through/led through' 'secured/made safe' 'believed/belief' as even those who follow the correct God, believe in him and those who turn away and do not follow his ways—all of them will not be spared 'and them that worship *and* that swear by the Lord...And them that are turned back from the Lord;

and those that have not sought the Lord, nor inquired for him.' Until the contradiction in the last chapter where the remaining people are promised safety and also narrated as worshipping/believing with one mind-set—that of the correct God's ways.

Judah 'he is called/calls' 'call, or curse' 'make a false claim or an unproven claim' 'to make a claim'. When a person is 'Judah' he/she are either calling out to somebody, or saying a prayer, or calling to God for help—in this story it is denoted in that even if the people call out to God, they will not be saved (he will not respond) and not be spared from the punishment—and over many other books of the Bible you will find the mention of the use of silver and gold vessels in the rituals of worship where God is called upon, Zephaniah uses this imagery to show even if they worship (using gold and silver vessels to serve food, pour drink and blood offerings) and call on God he will not answer their calls 'And I will bring distress upon men, that they shall walk like blind men, because they have sinned against the Lord: and their blood shall be poured out as dust, and their flesh as the dung. Neither their silver nor the gold shall be able to deliver them in the day of the Lord's wrath; but the whole land shall be devoured by the fire of his jealously: for he shall make even speedy riddance of all them that dwell in the land.'. Note how the description mirrors sacrifice and offering rituals which God eats with fire, except here, like in Ezekiel to Gog, it is people treated as the sacrificial animals. (Zep.1)

Jerusalem 'came-saw-asked-them/the' 'they see-asked-them/the' is also linked to the verb of 'Judah' calling on God/gods as the people who are being killed are those who are worshipping other gods, so their arms are stretched out calling for protection, health or fortune, etc. they are calling to their gods, asking, and as some of them are idols they are seeing them while they are asking/praying.

The following three word-names used are all related to religious leaders/offices and they are all described as wearing 'strange apparel', specifically something to do with sleeves, and covering their heads, faces or mouths which results in their speech being 'k͟hm/g͟hm'-like (muffled/unclear/nasal/soaked and musty/stifled), and this has been tied through the word-names to being covered with a head/face veil and also due to intoxication with wine, congestion with sputum and other nasal/chest mucous (the 'k͟hm' meaning is the same as the sound of someone with a congested chest/nose). It is why things which either are disgusting (sputum/snot/mucous) which people naturally dispose of, or deemed disgusting are mentioned and used as word-names because in the story they cause people to behave badly towards God such as the 'wine' and the way the people dress and perform religious rituals in Zeph.1 given as a name of people to be destroyed. These word-names all tie into the name and meanings of the character given as a prophet in the book which means 'purification/clearing' as they will be 'cut off' i.e. get rid of:

Chemarims; kĕmārîm; خيمآر هم/ام 'their wines/wines of-them/the' 'their fermented/ferment of-them/the' 'their veils/head veils/face veils' 'veils/head veils/face veils-them/the'; غيمآر هم/ام 'their head veils/face veils' 'covered with face/headveil-them/the' 'head/face/mouth covered-them/the' 'muffled/were muffled-them/the' 'muffled voice/speaks with face or mouth covered-them/the' 'their covering' 'covered/submerged (in water or dirt)-them/the'; and in the story it is males who cover their heads, faces, mouths or all three while they conduct religious rituals as they are described as priests. Cp: k͟heimaar-hum/um, g͟heimaar-hum/um. (Zep.1)

Malcham (1Chr.8:9) is still: malkām; مَلْكآم 'a punching' 'something being processed with punching like motions' 'what is wrong with the sleeves/sleeved' 'what is with the sleeves/what is the sleeves/sleeved'; مَلْقام 'of feeding through mouth by hand' such as a person/animal if sick or adding ingredients to a boiling kettle, etc. through the opening. 'what is wrong/what is with the standing/stood/erect'; مَلْخام 'spitting sputum' 'mucus in chest' 'what is the muttering/unclear/nasal sound' 'what is the musty from covering' 'what is wrong with/what is the speech like clearing throat/nasal sounds' 'what is the muffled sound/speech/voice' 'what is wrong with/what is the muffled voice/speaking with covered face or mouth' 'what is wrong with/what is the person who makes unclear sounds when speaks' 'what is the 'k͟haam' sounds'; مَلْغام 'what is/well what-the speaking with mouth or face covered' 'what is/well what-the suffocated' 'what is wrong with/what is the covered with face or headveil' 'what is wrong with/what is with the head/face/mouth covered' 'what is wrong with/what is with the head/face veils' 'what is covered/covered with face or head veil' 'what is the 'g͟haam' sounds' 'what is muffled/speaking with muffled voice' 'what is wrong with the/what is with the stifled' 'what is stifled'. The meanings refer to the mentioned religious figures, what they wear, and how they conduct prayers, rituals and/or speech. Cp: malkaam, maalqaam, malk͟haam, malg͟haam. (Zep.1)

Maktesh; maktēš; مَخطيش 'snot/mucous' 'wipe away snot/mucous'; مَغطيش 'covered/put lid on-you' 'covered/put lid on-something/the matter'. Both meanings tie in with 'Chemarim' and 'Malcham' as it also conduces to being covered, muffled, nasal or chesty, and the sound being unclear. It seems either the same original author purposely intended, or a later editor may have added text, to make wordplay on this word to also mean مكديش 'heaped/piled/fell like a heap or with the sound of kadesh' as the text shows the sound and appearance of 'kadesh' as it describes God is preparing a sacrifice, and when it is God in these stories making a sacrifice there are heaps of bodies piled up greater than the heaps of animals usually piled up for him; leaping 'on the threshold' makes the 'kadesh' sound, and filling 'masters' houses with violence and deceit' is piling these vices and their accumulated sins; the visual imagery and sound of 'kadesh' in 'and a great crashing from the hills'; the screaming 'inhabitants of Maktesh, for all the merchant people are cut down; all they that bear silver are cut off' indicates the piled goods the merchants usually buy and sell, also their bodies piling up, the silver being piled. Cp: mekhṯeysh, meghṯeysh, mekdeysh. (Zep.1)

The rest of the chapters continue with word-names already explained earlier in this book, their meanings can be consulted and the link made from their word-names, as they use literal word-meanings to show what is being narrated.

Haggai

Darius (Ezra.4:5-24) has been used for its meaning 'educated/studies matters' 'of careful studying' 'education/learning/taught' also means to look into and inspect a matter closely as God and Haggai teach the people more than one lesson.

Judah 'he is called/calls' as Haggai (and God) are calling the people to do something in particular.

Haggai (Ezra.5:1) 'cover/shelter' 'teach to pronounce correctly' 'drove away forever' 'he came/is coming' and the story reflects all three meanings. 'he came' is not because of the verse 'came the Lord of the word by Haggai,' because most of the 'prophets' stories begin with this or similar introduction, but compounded with the meaning of his name and because it is through Haggai the 'word' has come to Zerubbabel and Joshua 'came the word of the Lord by Haggai the prophet unto Zerubbabel the son of Shealtiel, governor of Judah, and to Joshua the son of Josedech, the high priest saying…' Then it is repeated 'came the word of the Lord by the prophet Haggai'.

Haggai 'teach to pronounce correctly' is denoted in the way he asks things he knows priests know about: rules and religion, he asks—they reply like students being taught, checking they know and remember and can repeat what they learnt from the previous lesson before moving onto the new lesson. The way it is narrated Haggai says something which is basically already the answer, and they reply in one voice what he has just taught them—just like teaching to pronounce.

Haggai 'cover/shelter/hide' is reflected in when he (and God) upbraids them about leaving God without a house while they have the comfort and shelter of their own roofed houses 'This people say, The time is not come, the time that the Lord's house should be built…*Is it* time for you, O ye, to dwell in your ceiled house, and this house *lie* waste?...Go up to the mountain, and bring wood, and build the house, and I will take pleasure in it…Because of mine house that is waste, and ye run every man unto his own house.' The verses 'the heaven over you is stayed from dew, and the earth is stayed from her fruit' have meanings linked to 'cover/shade/hide'.

Zerubbabel 'they procreated in swapped/changed' 'they sowed in swapped/changed' 'they left in swapped' 'leave-I will swap/change' 'they tightened in swapped/changed' 'they caused great disgrace in swapped/changed' as the punishment is no matter how much they work, only little is gained from it, and it is being narrated because they did not build God's house so God has changed the situation where hard work should give big returns, but instead only barely enough is made, and they have made the wordplay suit they are being squeezed by this 'swapping' but also it is likened to sowing a lot but reaping a very poor harvest.

He is the son of **Shealtiel** (Ezra.3:2) 'questioned/asked-the' is because God through Haggai is questioning them over their lack of desire to build him (God) a house, this questioning is through asking them to consider why they are not blessed, to think about the connection between God not having a house and the people not benefitting from harvest and work. The meaning of 'took-the' 'carried-the' is left to the very end, almost as an addition, an afterthought, and is made clear to mean 'taken' 'carried' by singling out Zerubbabel for this message that he will be carried in the hand of God like a ring 'Speak to Zerubbabel, governor of Judah, saying, I will shake the heavens and the earth…In that day, saith the Lord of hosts, I will take thee, O Zerubbabel, my servant the son of Shealtiel, saith the Lord, and will make thee a signet: for I have chosen thee saith the Lord of the hosts.'

Joshua (Exod.17:9-14) has been used for 'picked a lot' 'many people' 'greed/greedy' 'pull out/pluck by the handfuls'. And his name also is enhanced by following Zerubbabel Shealtiel meanings of 'sow/take' where a lot was expected but very little was brought home/gained. 'You looked for much, lo it came to little; and when you brought it home I did blow upon it...' meaning you put a lot into it, but it is still not enough for you (as punishment). Joshua still holds the meaning 'many people' as his name is mentioned after Zerubbabel then followed by mention of 'all the remnant of the people.'

He is son of Josedech/**Jozadak** (Ezra.2:63)/ **Jehozadak** (1Chr.6:14) 'he is-believed/honest/friendly' 'came-believed/honest/friendly' 'he who/who is-honest/friendly' 'came who-honest/friendly' 'he who/who is-gave you more' 'he who/who is-deceived you' 'came who-gave you more' 'came who-deceived you' 'he who/who is-blocked you/prevented you' 'he who/who is-fished you/your fish' 'came who-blocked you/prevented you' 'came who-fished you/your fish'. It reflects every time Haggai tells Joshua, Zerubbabel and the people, they all believe him and obey 'Then Zerubbabel the son of Shealtiel, and Joshua the son of Josedech, the high priest, with all the remnant of the people, obeyed the voice of the Lord their God, and the words of Haggai the prophet...and they came and did the work in the house...'.

Josedech/Jozadak/Jehozadak 'he-blocks you/prevents you/is opposite you' is because they have not built God's house, God is blocking them from having successful harvests, trade, etc.

Josedech/Jozadak 'he-gives you more' as God promises this new house will be filled with more stores/treasures/glory than the previous house; also the people are promised more fruitful gains from their work in harvest, money, etc. as soon as the foundation of the 'Lord's temple[he will eat/hekal]' is laid.

Zechariah

Zechariah (1Chr.5:7) Zachariah (2Kgs.14:29) 'reminded-him/he' 'mentioned-he/him' 'remembered-him/he' 'topped with water or liquid/filled to brim with water/liquid-he/him' 'peeped at/took quick glances' 'filled with gaps-he/him' 'made slits/gaps-he/him'. The narration is of God reminding the people he was upset with their ancestors, their behaviour towards him, he mentions/tells them to remember him (God) and he will remember them. It narrates former prophets all mentioned God (and his warnings/promises) to their ancestors, who chose not to remember God. Now that ancestors are long dead, who remembers them? It narrates 'two olive trees' then 'two olive branches' which empty oil into a bowl; the topping-up/filling with liquid or water is also connected to 'Chisleu'; when God stops his punishment it is by allowing the skies to rain, copulation and pollination to result in offspring/fruit; drinking, water and wine are promised to fill bowls and the altar; Chapter 10 begins with rain causing fertility and ends with its opposite as punishment for the enemies in the seas and rivers; Chapter 13 also begins with a fountain opened to David's house and Jerusalem before it turns to punishment for the antagonists; mention of rivers and 'living waters' connecting to two seas which shows the 'topping-up with liquid/water' meanings, while punishment for adversaries is drought connected to forcing them to make offerings in Jerusalem, and the filled bowls and altar mean both meat and drink will be abundant (blood, too, which is what is on the altar for God). The author uses a man standing 'among the myrtle trees' i.e. he is watching the world through the gaps between the trees/branches.

Zechariah mentions and asks about everything he sees in the night when he is approached by a horseman; the angels remind God how long he has been upset with the people and mention it is a long time; the angels tell Zechariah to mention the good news to the people; when an enquiry is made about weeping in certain months, God's response is 'over the seventy years did you ever fast, or eat, for me' i.e. you did not remember me to fast for me, serve me food—in my remembrance or as piety towards me.

Berechiah (1Chr.3:20) 'knelt-he/him' 'made him kneel-he/him' 'made last/blessed-he/him' 'underground water cisterns-he/him 'I will prop/lean it/him against' 'I will let him/it loose' 'I will loosen him/it' 'I will let it go' 'is in a mood/sulking-him/he'. Chapter 8 speaks of blessing the people with prosperity in offspring, agriculture, and the text of speaking of the blessings is also reminding them of the past (zechariah) so that they learn from it.

Iddo (1Kgs.4:14) 'infect/catch or spread illness' 'feed lunch' 'cause lymph nodes/glands to swell' because God is frustrated with the people; but eventually food and drink will be in plenty and no one will go hungry. 'count' 'prepare' 'enmity/transgression' 'transgress against': the ancestors have disobeyed God's orders; God will give rain, fortune and protection from enemies; the people's enemies will be destroyed.

Sebat; šĕḇāṯ; سيبآت 'a person who leaves things' 'ceased/left it/let it go' and means to stop doing something in particular; سيبعت 'doing weeks' and means stayed somewhere other than the normal residence and means 'holiday' 'rest'; شيباط 'swipe/whip/strike with switch' 'rope(s)/twine' 'thrown/swiped' 'lattice(with rope)'. It is supported by seeing the man and horses 'by night' and the only thing the horseman and horses do is walk through the earth so that it 'sitteth still, and is at rest.'. Both meanings of 'cease' 'rest' are supported by the angels questioning God about the duration of his anger towards the people, they are asking him to cease from it. The man standing by the myrtle tree symbolises the 'switch' from trees used to discipline which is connected to 'swipe/whip/strike with switch'; first it is Jerusalem and Judah being disciplined but then it changes to disciplining their enemies once God has forgiven the former; 'latticed' is relayed in the strengthening of Jerusalem and Judah once God forgives them spurred by his displeasure at the 'heathen'. These are the meanings meant by it in this part of the story although it states it is the month of 'sebat' (<u>sh</u>ebaaṭ) which is also a month in the Arabic agricultural year (and also Islamic year, but the agricultural year has existed before the Islamic, and is used not for counting years, but knowing the seasons for agricultural purposes). It is equivalent to **Sabbath** (Gen.2:2-3; Exod.16), **En-misphat** (Gen.14:7), **Zabdi** (Josh.7) and other '**Zabad/zbd**' words, **Shabbethai** (Ezra.10:15).

It is also wordplay on شيواط 'laps' and 'branch(es) used as switch to swipe at something or drive an animal' and the action of 'swiping with a switch' which is what the horseman and horses do as they 'walk to and fro through the earth' and why they are seen standing 'among the myrtle trees'; it can also mean 'withered/shrivelled/wrinkly'. It is similar to one of **Satan**'s (1Chr.21:1-17) meaning of 'two laps' (from same root word) Cp: seibaat, seib't, <u>sh</u>eibaaṭ, <u>sh</u>eiwaaṭ.

Joshua's (Exod.17:9-14) meaning of 'came-freakishly ugly/mutated' is used here because he is described as being 'clothed with filthy garments' while he stands before the angel...Take away the filthy garments from him...I have caused thine iniquity to pass from thee, and I will clothe thee with change of raiment', the 'ugliness' is his 'iniquity' which has been removed from him, and the dirty and new clothes symbolise the ugliness/filthiness of sin/iniquity and the beauty/pureness of good/obedience, and he is clothed with clean and beautifying clothes. (Zech.3)

Satan (1Chr.21:1-17) here is used for 'obstructed' 'of obstructing' as while he stands on Joshua's right hand he intends 'to resist him.'. (Zech.3:1)

Zerubbabel (1Chr.3:19) meaning of 'they visited in swapped/changed' is anchored here with the narration that once God's spirit is in Zerubbabel when he arrives or looks at a mountain it will change completely into a flat plain. (Zech.4:6-7)

Ephah (Gen.25:4) means 'an abomination(physically mutated or a demon)' and also 'gone off food' (usually describes a sick animal refusing to eat) both of which are meant in the story as the woman in the middle of the 'ephah' is 'wickedness' and she and the lead are cast into its middle before the whole thing is sent away to a place which holds meanings of something unwanted. (Zech.5:5-11)

Shinar (Gen.10:10) 'we will be disgraced' 'to go to a place aside/or cast aside' 'to change direction' (on a journey), and these meanings can be seen as it describes the 'wicked' 'ephah' being carried away by two mutated women who 'had wings like the wings of a stork' and are able to fly. The narration has the wind carry them and their load which is the ephah, to be in the land of Shinar—it is a disgrace and unwanted in this land, so it is sent away, cast into a different area where it can be an abomination out of the reach of the people of this land. (Zech.5:5-11)

Heldai (1Chr.27:15) 'reaped lots' 'stripped everything/lots off' 'roasted in the sun/heat' 'skin peeled off from sun' 'severely beat up' 'mole(s)/a mole' 'remembered forever' 'lived forever', and has been used for a group of people who will arrive 'lots', and lots of silver and gold will be used to make crowns, these metals are usually mined out of the ground imitating the burrowing nature of moles, heat is needed to melt these crowns and then beat them into shape, and these will be a 'memorial in the temple[he will eat/hekal] of the Lord' for the people to remember.

Tobijah (2Chr.17:8) 'they could tolerate/eat/palate/taste him/it-he/him' 'they are not revolted-he/him' 'burning smell-he/him', because it supports the way Joshua was made ugly with filth/sin earlier in the story and how his nature, clothes, and soul were changed into a beautiful and clean purity of obedience—'tobijah' being something some people can swallow while others cannot, here it can be turned into something pleasant/good (just as did **Joshua**/freakishly mutated turn into something good), and like 'Heldai' was used for its first and second meanings, the other meaning of the word-name Tobijah is a 'burning smell' and this kind of burning smell/Tobijah is from burning metal, providing the word-imagery of gold and silver being melted and shaped.

Jedaiah (1Chr.4:37) 'they/he call him' 'he deposits/leaves in the care of-he/him' as the men are called to come from Babylon, and the crowning and 'BRANCH' is announced to the people as a memorial.

Babylon (2Kgs.17:24) 'swap/change' 'of swapping/changing' as silver and metal is being changed into crowns, people's status is swapping from captivity to freedom, disobedience to obedience, filth to cleanliness, ugliness to beauty, no place to eat to a 'he will eat', from 'captivity' to sitting on thrones as priests/ high priest.

Josiah (2Kgs.22-23) 'they came seeking' 'they go wandering and seeking' as the people are coming from Babylon and are asked to go into the 'house of Josiah' with a mission.

Zephaniah (2Kgs.25:18-21) 'escorted-him/he' 'led in a procession-him/he' 'cleaned/cleared/purified-him/ he' as the people are arriving in a group and are being taken as Zechariah has been ordered to bring them there; the story is a process of cleanliness/purification: of sins to obedience, uncleanness to hygiene, silver and gold further purified into a crown.

Helem (1Chr.7:35) 'he will gather/save(accumulate)': the people are being gathered; gold and silver has been gathered; priests have been gathered into one place; and the people who are gathered are to build the 'temple[he will eat] of the Lord' where food produce is gathered.

Hen; ḥēn; حين 'at the time/when' 'hennaed/coloured or purified with henna' as there is a time when this will happen and henna is used as a purification substance.; هين 'satisfied/full' as the abundance of silver and gold is enough to make the crowns; the people are enough to build the 'temple/he will eat', and once the temple is built people, priests and God will be satisfied with food. Cp: ḥeyn, heyn. (Zech.6:9-15)

Chisleu (Neh.1) 'they washed' and can mean 'washing away sins' and is also the word used to mean purification for specific rituals, it is used the same way as in Nehemiah, where he cries a lot and is also about having sins washed away, which Sherezer and Regem-melech's story also uses as thy enquire about a period of weeping as worship as an act of piety. (Zech.7)

Sherezer/**Sharezer** (2Kgs.19:37) 'will see-made ugly' 'evil-made ugly' 'insisted-made ugly' 'will see-tightened' 'evil-tightened' 'insisted-tightened' 'knotted-tightened' and all these meanings are used in Zechariah: God is telling them he does not want this (any kind of 'wrong' worship in the Biblical stories is 'ugly'); they insist on ignoring what God and prophets have told them in the past and what they are telling them now; they insist on carrying on in the wrong/ugly ways; God is warning them not to 'tighten-ugly' nor 'evil-tightened' described as not oppressing the vulnerable. (Zech.7)

Regem-melech; regem meleḵ; رَغم مَلَح 'despite-good' despite the good they think they are doing by weeping and fasting, God is not interested, and despite the good from the prophecy/warning/God's reply—they are still not going to change their ways; رَجَم مَلَح 'stoned-well/good/pretty' and; رَغم مَلَق 'forced-thrown' as they will be forced out of their country likened to be taken by winds and thrown into different areas; رَجَم مَالك 'stoned-what is wrong with you/what is with you?' رَجَم مَلَق 'piled stones upon/ buried under stones-thrown' 'stoned/stopped with-thrown' as despite being shown the good/right way they insist on the wrong way and this ignoring of God's words and being stubborn about their ways is likened to stopping their ears with something (both the people and God), being hardened like stones, of which the consequences will be a whirlwind which will scatter them and cast them into different areas not their own. Cp: reg͟hem meleḥ, reg͟hem meleq, regem meleḥ, regem melek, regem meleq. (Zech.7)

Hadrach; ḥadrāḵ; هدر آك 'speak to/conversation/your conversation/words/way you speak' 'sound of your conversation' 'look, see/pay attention/here/he-realised/I realised/will realise' 'look, see/pay attention/here/ he-understood/I will understand' 'look, see/pay attention/here/he-caught up with/I caught up with/will catch up with' and it means when a person realises/understands something, or catches up with someone/ something already ahead of them or catches up just in time (including saving just in time). It begins with the 'conversation/spoke' meaning: 'The burden of the word of the Lord in the land of Hadrach, and Damascus shall be…' and goes on to show it is about when all of Israel will realise and repent/look towards God and how neighbours/antagonists will suffer punishment catching up with them (note how meanings of **Damascus** 'tore/ripped up' 'spat/spat a lot' 'sucked/sucked a lot' 'sucked at his teeth' relay with the narration as do all the other word-names used as areas in this chapter (see previously translated word-names and meanings and how they relay with story being told in Zeph.9).

Although English interpretations of these chapters believe it is Jesus being described (whose story does mention riding on two donkeys (one a foal)), Zeph.9:9 is describing David who usurped both Saul and Jonathan (see **Solomon** and **mule** to understand how the donkey(s) symbolises David riding both Saul and

Jonathan to reach the throne and to secure the throne for his descendants). Chapters 9 to 14 revolve around antagonists who see Judah/Jerusalem as an easy target, but will come to realise they are protected by God; not only are the two cities protected, but God's punishment will catch up to neighbours and to the antagonists wherever they may be. Once God defends Judah/Jerusalem and pours grace and prayers on the inhabitants, they will realise how much they have wronged God who is described as being wounded (pierced)—and although Western interpretations like to state in the header of Bibles and believe it is a prophecy about Jesus, it is actually about the protagonist God of the OT who was upset with Judah/ Jerusalem and had abandoned/punished them but now in repent has allowed them to see their wrong against him which is further detailed in the rest of Zeph.12. that the people will regret wronging him and be as grievous as mourning being bereaved of a firstborn child. It is equivalent to **Shadrach** (Dan.1-3). Cp: hadraak. (Zech.10-14)

Beauty; nō'am; نوعم 'blessings' 'blessed' 'gave/received blessing' something received, e.g. money, food supply, health anything which is received from or given to another and has the same connotations as a 'blessing' whether seen as a gift or the action of blessing the recipient; the person who receives the physical gift whether an external receipt of something or even health in his/her own body—that person is 'blessed' the person or God who has giving it has 'blessed' the recipient, and the thing given is 'a blessing'; it also means 'smooth' and the meaning of 'blessing' is still connected as a blessing makes things/life smoother and easier; 'blessings/money/food source/gifts/anything given to another/health/anything physical that can be received or given' 'blessings/blessed/made life easier/smoother'; نوغم 'we stifle/feel stifled' 'we suffocate/feel suffocated' 'we cover/we are covered' 'we muffle/are muffled' 'we depress/feel depressed'.

The chapter revolves around blessings such as wood, abundant and healthy animals which are a food and money source, health, safety, and the freedom which God gave the people all being taken away represented by a staff which is broken, misinterpreted as 'Beauty' when the correct word is 'blessings/gave or received blessings' and the 'depressed/stifled' meanings; even the money received is given away 'cast them to the potter'. The people will be stifled from the blessings taken away, the hatred described between God and the shepherds shows they were feeling stifled by each other 'and my soul lothed them, and their soul also abhorred me.'; the stifling and depression is reflected in how all the people even innocent people '*even* you, O poor of the flock.' will be made to suffer all kinds of punishments from being killed, oppressed, a lessening in blessings/fortune/livestock Cp: noo'am, noog̲ham. (Zech.11:7)

Bands; chblym; حبل ام ، حبلهم 'rope of the/rope-the' 'their rope'; هبل ام ، هبلهم 'I will afflict them' 'stupid/ foolish-the/them' 'their fools/idiots' 'fools of the' 'I gave them/the' 'give them'. All the meanings are relayed in the story: the staff mistranslated as 'Bands' which correctly means 'rope' is reflected in the things being cut-off like a rope can be cut, and is a result of the staff being cut: the brotherhood between people, and the pact between God and the people are severed. The 'give' meanings shown in the silver paid upon request; and the people, both good and bad, will be given to a ruthless oppressor. The 'afflict' and 'idiots/fool' meanings are reflected as the people who will suffer these afflictions are described as 'foolish'. Cp: ḥbl-um, ḥblhum, hbl-um, hblhum. (Zech.11:7)

Hadadrimmon; hăd̲ad̲-rimmôn; هيدَد رِمّن 'threatened-thrown/cast/killed'; حيدَد رِمّن 'sharpened/ bordered/made borders-thrown/cast/killed' and 'thrown' here means thrown to their death(s) and seems like a sacrifice in pagan worship, especially that it has been linked to 'a great mourning' and 'in the valley of Megiddon' Megiddon; mĕgiddôn; ميغِدّن'of/with-swollen glands' which means person has been frustrated or ill to the degree the glands have swollen, 'fed lunch/of feeding lunch'; ميغِطّن 'killed/they were killed' 'squeezed/rough-handled to death' 'squeezed/rough handled them to death' e.g. when something has been so roughly handled or even petted (such as young kittens/puppies) that it results in them dying or physically bent out of shape. The story reflects 'killed' 'squeezed/rough-handled to death' 'of-swollen glands' which could be from excessive crying. Cp: haidad-rimmon, ḥaidad-rimmon, meig̲hiddon, meig̲hiṭṭon.

This is not the first time the Biblical stories narrate through word-names the rituals of human sacrifice and in connection to the word-name 'thrown/Rimmon/Ramoth' and 'Megiddon' as well as others (including Taanach, Megiddo, Zartanah, Jezreel, Beth-shean, Abel-meholah (see Ramoth-gilead 1Kgs.4:12-13). This is why it uses the example that the mourning in Jerusalem will be 'as the mourning of Hadadrimmon in the valley of Megiddon.' And before this verse, the previous verse emphasises the sadness and grief which the people in Jerusalem will feel is akin to losing a child '...and they shall mourn, as one mourneth for *his* only *son*, and shall be in bitterness for him, as one that is in bitterness for *his* firstborn.'—firstborns are usually what are sacrificed which although in the Biblical stories have been allowed to be 'redeemed', many parts of the Biblical stories allude to human sacrifice.

Even the way the author has chosen to separate the husbands from the wives for reasons of mourning separately indicates a child should not be conceived during this ritual—even if the people in the story's 'mourning' are only likened to those mourning over a loss of a child in human sacrifice, the example carries on to show word-names of the characters which show a clear separation between what the other half's object/act as a word-name would need to complete its action (the separation of the husband from the wife); David separated from his wife—is the stone grinder rolling pin separated from its other half: the rectangular stone slab it grinds on (it is intentionally sexual reference on the Biblical author's part).

Three of 'Nathan' meanings also cannot be performed if its other half is missing: 'we double' 'we female/is feminine', if husband and wife are separated they cannot double/fold against each other (it is avoiding the comfort of sex to avoid conceiving a child), and it becomes clearer that the meaning 'we female' has sexual meaning as in 'have sex with a woman' which in this part of the story cannot happen when husbands are separated from wives; 'we clang' this cannot happen as Nathan and variants of this word name are used to describe clanging musical instruments—there has to be a striking object (e.g. drum stick) and an object which is struck (drum/tin), if they are separated the 'clanging' cannot be made.

Levi's meanings of 'twisted around/entwined' what is twisting around something cannot happen if the object being entwined is not available; 'answered/answer/answer him(or it)' if only one person is available the other cannot be answered nor assisted.

Shimei's meanings 'my hearing' nothing can be heard (as in hearing another's speech) if a person is alone.

These word-names were not chosen randomly by the Biblical author of these verses in Zech.12. They have been chosen because they were used as characters related to sexual conduct and conception of a child: **David** for his part in impregnating Bath-sheba with an illegitimate child which dies when she is his wife; he comforts her and sex is part of what he comforted her with resulting in immediate conception of Solomon; **Nathan** is related to this story too as he criticised David's murder of Bath-Sheba's husband Uriah which resulted in punishment for both David and his wife that the child they conceived died. **Levi** was named so because Leah believed Jacob would love her romantically and physically and they would be 'entwined/twisted around' physically and emotionally as a result of this further male-child. **Shimei** is mentioned because he publicly insults David when the latter and his men flee Absalom's coup: Shimei's character reminds the audience of David's sexual immorality and of him being the catalyst of Saul and Jonathan's deaths, although it does not mention Uriah's murder due to David impregnating his wife and that child's death, it is also implied—both Absalom and the illegitimately conceived new born die (in their respective stories), leaving David and/or Bath-sheba in mourning. All the use of these stories in Zech.12 following what is possibly a human sacrifice ritual of children, is supported by keeping the wives separated from the husbands during this mourning period to avoid sex and therefore conception which seems to be prohibited during this ritual, and further reinforced by the choice of characters for their word-names and for their backstories. (Zech.12:10-14)

(Mount of) Olives; hazzêtîm, zêtîm; هَزّيت هم/ام ، زيت هم/ام again this word is a mistranslation and its correct meanings are 'fled away/hid quickly(usually in fear for life because running away from being 'zat/zut'). 'sliced open/cut them' 'killed them quickly' 'killed them with quick slit with knife'.

It is still used the same way as when first mentioned when David and the rest were fleeing for their lives at 2Sam.15: 'I will quickly slice/cut/split open-them/the' 'I will kill quickly-them/the' 'I will flit/flick into/quickly hide-them/the', 'suddenly split open-them/the—suddenly cut them/the open—suddenly sliced them/the open' 'flitted/flicked/quickly hid something throwing it into narrow space-them/the' 'shook/swung-them/the' 'made shake-them/the' 'shook/swung/made shake/made swing back and forth-them/the'.

It makes it clear the word is about being sliced/split open 'And his feet shall stand in that day upon the mount of Olives ['I will slice/split open-them/the'], which is before Jerusalem to the east, and the mount of Olives shall cleave in the midst thereof toward the east and toward the west, *and there shall be* a very great valley; and half of the mountain shall remove toward the north, and half of it toward the south.

In this part of the story it is still about people fleeing for their lives 'And ye shall flee...yea, ye shall flee, like as you fled before the earthquake...'. As the narration of this verse, and following verses, suggest an earthquake and maybe also a volcanic eruption, there is definitely هَزّيت هم/ام'shaking/swinging-them/the' implied in the story.

It is similar to words Birzavith (1Chr.7:31), Ashvath (1Chr.7:33), Zetham (1Chr.23:8), Zattu (Ezra.2:8). Cp: hazzeyt-hum/um, zeyt-hum/um. (Zech.14:4)

Azal; 'āṣāl; نآزآل 'he/it removed/wiped out' 'was removed/wiped out 'it/he left/disappeared' 'disappeared/left' 'left forever' 'gone forever' 'forever' 'from a long time ago(similar to ancient times or long period of time)'. It is stating the split which has occurred in the misnomered mount 'Olives' is permanent; نآصال 'I will reach/arrive' 'connected' 'rocks/stones' and it describes people reaching this place as well as the valley which is connected due to what seems to be an earthquake or volcanic eruption which the Biblical author may mean rocks splitting or flying through the air, and God is mentioned (God is mentioned as a rock in many parts of the OT) as arriving at Azal. It is equivalent to Ezel (1Sam.20:14-42), Azel (1Chr.8:38), and similar to Beth-ezel; similar to Shaul/Saul and other similar word-names. Cp: aazaal, aa<u>ss</u>aal. (Zech.14:5).

Uzziah has been used for its meaning 'was removed' 'was wiped out' 'was shifted' as the mountain has been described as splitting and the land shifting, and also an earthquake is being described in this story, so the author has used the word to describe this as the king of the period, there was no king Uzziah, just a word-name used for its enhancement effect for the story. The word also means 'was harmed-he' 'he harmed', but this has not been used here as it was used in (2Kgs.15:13), only 'shifted' 'was removed/wiped out' is present in the use of Uzziah in this verse. It is equivalent to Uzzah (2Sam.6:6-7). (Zech.14:4-5)

Malachi

Malachi; mal'āḵî; مَل نآخي 'what is wrong, brother/my brother?'; مَلنآكي 'what is with you? what is wrong?' 'what is (wrong) with you now?' 'soiled you/covered you completely(with any substance clean or unclean)'. The expressions of 'what is wrong, brother/what is wrong/what is the matter?' is stated in different ways in the narration of Mal.1.

The people are upset and doubt that God loves them. God is complaining about something that is not right and bothering him. The people are asking words to the effect 'What is it? What is the matter? What is wrong? What have we done?'. An example is given that if they had shown the same disrespect towards their governor, he would find a problem in it and them too, and would be displeased. There is such a big 'malachi/what is the matter' in the whole story that God will accept anything the Gentiles and heathens offer and say than from the people who are supposed to be closest to him because something is wrong, there is a problem.

'Soiled you/covered you with something dirty/or not dirty but soiled the person/clothing' begins with a warning and curse to soil them 'Behold, I will corrupt your seed, and spread dung upon your faces, *even* the dung of your solemn feasts; and *one* shall take you away with it.'. The narration has God expressing they have soiled his table because they have presented 'polluted' foods on it. Cp: mal-aa<u>kh</u>ee, mal-aakee.

For the explanation of what the story revolves around see meanings of temple/hekal (Meaning of 'kadesh' 'qodesh' 'm'kaddesh' 'mekkadesh').

The New Testament

The New Testament follows in the same way of the OT, the character and place names are made up of words used in daily language and reflect the character/place name's meaning as it will be the description, theme or event in the related story.

Despite the NT being written in Koine Greek, the word-names are still made up of Arabic words with Arabic meanings, and make perfect sense in the story, just as they do as words used in everyday language uncut since antiquity. This shows the authorship of the New Testament originates from the same people who authored the Old Testament, Arabs, and although scholars and the West claim they are Jewish or Hebrew and mean by this a race/ethnicity and language separate from the Arab, this is because not only have they not understood the language of the Bible, but they also do not know what 'Hebrew' as a word means and what 'Hebrew' was as used by the authors and editors of the Bible. It is because they are Arabs whose religions began as pagans before becoming Jewish, then Christian that the language remains the same Arabic language with its Arabic meanings in the stories of both the OT and the NT, and the lives of the Arabic people who speak it to this day.

There is not much difference in the Biblical authors' methods between the OT and the NT, and even if the oldest original documents of the NT that have been found are in Greek, the authors of these stories spoke Arabic so they circulated and existed as Arabic (what would be called 'Hebrew' in error) in original form. Where the OT would sometimes use real civilisations or names such as Egypt, Pharaoh, Babylon but as in what these words meant as words/compound words pronounced in Arabic, along with completely fabricated fictional names, the same goes with the NT where even if some of the names used were real Greek names, they were used for what they meant as pronounced in Arabic as compound words and the meanings as in Arabic words used in everyday language.

The characters never existed as per the Biblical stories, nor did the events happen as per the Biblical stories as these characters are fictional. The borrowing of real Greek names of people who existed just shows the continuity of the Biblical authors' methods when creating the NT stories. Even if some of the Greek, Roman, Persian and other regional figures existed with those names which were used in the Biblical stories, they are not the same characters of these stories—and not as can be seen in how Biblical scholars and other experts attempt to reconstruct a very shaky and loose corroboration of the Biblical stories as a reality and historical figure/place/event. Who knows how much of written history of the estimated times of what it is believed when these Biblical stories events 'occurred' (as the suggested times are nothing but estimations based on completely fictional stories and therefore never happened, but true events/figures times have been mis-estimated due to tying it into fictional accounts of the Bible) and how that has perverted true history and its estimated times? What becomes undeniably evident when the word-names of characters and places in the NT are correctly translated is that not only is the NT from Arab origins, but so is Greek mythology: the stories of Olympians, Titans, etc. transliterate perfectly pronounced Arabic compound words as names and perfectly translate and shed light on the stories told in these Greek myths no different in method from the Biblical authors' methods in creating stories. An example of this: Pasiphae is بَزِبيَ ، فَزِبيَ (Cp: bazibya, phazibya) 'will penis/being penised' 'so/will be penised' and what does she do in her story? She asks another character to create a fake cow which she hides in to align her vagina with the opening so she can have sex with her father's favourite bulls who mistake the statue for a real cow. The pregnancy results in giving birth to a half man/half bull creature which is named Minotaur; مَنَثور ، من اثور (minafowr/min afowr) 'from the bull'. The proof is undeniable, Arabic has existed for longer than has been estimated; the Arabic people have influenced the most ancient cultures and the Greek civilisation must have begun as an Arabic civilisation which eventually ended up being diluted by foreign cross-culture exposure. The only thing that has remained undiluted is the proof of these stories' and culture's Arab origins which have been kept in pure form by keeping the names of the characters and their stories alive.

Some examples I can give of this are as follows: Biblical scholars, historians use the Biblical stories to assist in estimating the portion of time when these characters are assumed to have lived, when these events took place, and where these events happened as in geographical location; as the Biblical stories show, the Biblical authors have used these word-names for fictional places, characters, and events—so if some of the characters whose names exist in real history that happened, of real figures who existed, then the NT stories were created at a much later date and not the dates/periods where it is estimated they happened as described in the Biblical stories because a fictional event cannot 'happen' and take up a place in time and space, nor can its fictional characters for that matter. The other alternative is that the Biblical stories inspired people and civilisations to name themselves and their places from names in the Bible, and that too would confuse scholars if real people named after popular fictional stories were later in prominent roles—but that can only be true if these 'historical' figures, i.e. figures who are believed to have existed at some point in history, do not have stories attributed to them which match and reflects their compound word-name as that disproves their existence and proves not only was this character mistaken as a historical figure, but so was the story/stories surrounding him/her also fictional.

If some of the fictional characters used in these stories borrowed their names from actual figures who existed and the historians have given the actual figure who existed a time and place according to what has been narrated in the Biblical stories, then this estimation is a wrong one, the real person with physical archaeological/historical evidence will not match the fictional character of the same name because the character of the Bible never existed, his reign/authority/occupation never happened (the character in the Bible) and therefore real history has been corrupted as the Biblical author could have written the story with the character of the same name in mind after or during the real figure's existence, while the person lived or ruled, or long after he died, or at much later dates—therefore the Biblical story does not corroborate measuring real time and history but through misuse corrupts history. It is even worse if a fictional character in the Bible is given a place, time, location in 'documented' history just based on the Biblical story which is not a historical record, but a creation for entertainment and other reasons.

Who knows when the Biblical stories, including the NT, became popular, and how much they influenced the naming of ancient people in the western world close to the Middle East, e.g. you can see this in comparatively recent history in the popularity of naming people in the European world is influenced by both the OT and the NT—has anyone ever wondered why most of the compound words used as names were never used as names among the people of the region (the Arab region, even among those of the Jewish and Christian religions) where these stories were created, where these religions were first practised and spread before these religions spread to the western world? Of course you have to eliminate the naming of Christian Arabs whose Christianity does not originate from its original and organic occurrence in the Arab region, but comes from when it was re-introduced through western missionaries (and of course the advent of Zionism and its effect: Arabs of the Jewish faith who live in modern-Israel have changed their real Arab names, where even the Europeans who came to this area have changed their European names, and replaced them with names from the Bible)—only these countries touched by missionaries will you find people named John, Jonathan, Samuel, Matthew, Peter, Luke, Rebecca, Ruth and other words as pronounced in the 'Europeanised' way, and not as pronounced in the Arabic of the Bible. It becomes further obvious when it is only the Biblical word-names which are made up of compound words that give it an offensive, lewd or negative meaning that are avoided, whereas names which are not offensive are used but they are not that popular.

In all cases, the NT is full of fictional characters, places and events which follow the Arabic Samaara and Samaaya stories, where the naming suggests the theme, and both the name and event relay its meanings within the stories.

Matthew

Esrom; Esrōm; اصروم 'harvest/reap' to harvest the stalks and/or the panicles, also the name of a type of tree. Cp: essroom. (Matt.1:3)

Abiud; Abioúd; نَبي/ابي عود 'rejected/refused-do it again/return' and this is an instruction to the author/editor of this part of the story in Matt.1, to be explained below under 'Matthan'. Cp: abee-'ood. (Matt.1:13)

Azor; Azṓr; عزور ، عازور 'ugly' 'he made ugly/he made become ugly' and is meant by the Biblical author to be instead of Azariah (2Kgs.14:21) and is also the same character as Uzziah (2Kgs.15:13), to be explained below under 'Matthan'. Cp: 'azoor, 'aazoor. (Matt.1:13)

Achim; Achím; اقييم 'stand/replace/stand instead of' 'erection/penis stood' and is the same character as king Eliakim of 2Kgs.23:34, to be explained below under 'Matthan'. Cp: aqeem. (Matt.1:14)

Eliud; Elioúd; الي عود 'he who/the one who-returns/does it again' 'yes-return/do it again' and like Abioud above is an instruction to a Biblical author/editor, to be explained below under 'Matthan'. Cp: ellee-'ood. (Matt.1:14)

Matthan; Matthán; مَتّآن 'two deaths/died twice'; مَثّآن 'what twice/why twice/what is the second one' (can also be 'wiped away urine/sperm'), and is the same character as Mattaniah/Zedekiah (2Kgs.24:17-20). Cp: mattaan, maffaan. (Matt.1:15)

What can be clearly seen in the word-names and characters chosen for the 'lineage' of Joseph son of Jacob (fiancé to Mary mother of Jesus) is that the authors and later editors of Matt.1 are dealing with the confusion of the earlier stories (OT), and it is evident it has confused them enough that they accidentally skipped 'Eliakim/Jehoiakim' who is supposed to be placed between Josiah and Jechoniah. What has happened is Eliakim and a similar word-name has been added twice instead at later stages in the convoluted 'genealogy' of Jesus which does not even lead to Jesus but misses him completely as it is misdirected to the man who was his mother's fiancé/husband in the story. Anyone who reads 2Kgs. can see how the original confusion arises and how attempts were made to remedy the most confusing part by the authors, it is easy to see why this part would confuse them too as they attempt to straighten a disjointed line of ancestry.

The passage of Matt.1 was not a finished nor final work of the editors, they had left words as instructions to return to this passage and to study the earlier stories to find out the correct way to write them up. Abiud 'rejected/refused-do it again/return' Eliud 'he who/the one who-returns/does it again' 'yes-return/do it again' are notes and direct instructions to authors/editors to return to these stories and the stories they need to go back to are those concerning: the character Eliakim who in the event of the story has his name changed to Jehoiakim by Pharaoh at 2Kgs.23:34, and remains Jehoiakim to his death at 2Kgs.24:6. The authors/editors seem confused (first because the original author of Matt.1 has overlooked adding him to the lineage) by this king Eliakim and a character of the same name at (Isa.22:15-25) who is not a king but in charge of the household/treasurer—the confusion arises because this second Eliakim sounds more like a king than a treasurer/in charge of the household and the same confusion can be seen at Isa.22 (already explained earlier in this book), which is why they attempt to differentiate between the two by having one 'Eliakim' and the other 'Achim'—it is a note they can return to clarify and edit (but for whatever reasons this does not happen and they all end up being part of the 'lineage').

The word-names Jehoiachin and Jehoiakim seem only slightly similar in English, but written in Arabic and using the writing which was still not the current Arabic letters, but **scripture** which is currently called 'Hebrew scripture' caused the authors/editors of this part of Matt. confusion as the letters were probably difficult to discern (this will become clearer to the reader, especially when the meaning of the word 'Hebrew' and how this was used is explained later in the book and understood). So due to an author missing 'Jehoiakim', later editors could not tell if it was intentional or oversight so they replace 'Jehoiachin' with 'Jeconiah'—as in the original story at 2Kgs.24:6, 8 it is Jehoiachin and remains so until the end of 2Kgs. where his story ends with him still in captivity, but at 1Chr.3.15-16 Jehoiachin is changed to 'Jeconiah' (it still has similar meanings to Jehoiachin).

Azor 'ugly' 'he made ugly/he made become ugly' has been used to highlight and mark for resolving about the use of Azariah, the Uzziah-character's original name at 2Kgs., and this reminder is to decide whether to use 'Uzziah' or 'Azariah' and to be inserted before 'Jotham' because Zedekiah was the maternal grandfather (of Jotham) mentioned 'Sadoc/Zadok' which has been inserted after Azor so it serves to remind the editor where to make the final changes about Uzziah once decided. Eleazar 'the ugliness' refers to the same character word-name and its original story and is left by a different editor (possibly more than one were working at the same time or a later editor at a different time trying to understand what the previous were trying to do).

Zerubbabel/Zorobabel has also been confused because at 1Chr.3 he is not Shealtiel's son, but Pedaiah's son, so the editors are confused by which 'father' of Zerubbabel to go with.

Sadoc/Zadok is for Zedekiah as this was 'Mattaniah's' changed name by the Babylonian king who made him king instead of Jehoiachin, it is also the name of the mother of Jotham, and this serves as a reminder that Jehoiachin's role ended with him in the story being in exile, and there was a different king: Zedekiah/ Mattaniah (Jehoiachin's uncle at 2Kgs.24. but the same character is his brother at 2Chr.36) who became the last king before the whole kingdom and everything in it was destroyed in the story. Which is why 'Mattan' has been used also as a note/indicator of an issue that needs to be sorted out before finalising the lineage which will lead to a man named Joseph the son of Jacob (which of course plays on the original Joseph son of Jacob from Genesis even if meant as completely different characters, they are meant to be linked in the minds of the audience).

Mattan has been used the same way 'Mattaniah' was used at (2Kgs.24:17-20) which I had believed was a pun and wink between authors and editors, but in light of the unfinished state of Matt.1 lineage for Joseph, it was obviously left as an edit-reminder and message between the Biblical editors but for whatever reasons was not returned to, or they just left it as it was, unable to smooth it out further. Mattan is used as Mattaniah as a note about the issue of repetitiveness of recent characters of Jehoahaz, Eliakim, Jehoiakim, Jehoiachin and Zedekiah whom foreign kings put in the place of the deposed brother/nephew (Jehoahaz/ Jehoiachin) and lead away into captivity abroad so the authors or editors of Matt.1 are still unconvinced with the last version of the Jehoiakim/Jehoiachin/Zedekiah/Mattaniah at 2Kgs.24 (due to the same character, role and story in the OT is for the same 'Zedekiah' but as Jehoiachin(Jeconiah)'s brother at 2Chr.36) and need to sort it out before finalising Matt.1's lineage.

Even the Jacob at Matt.1:15-16 was probably meant as a placeholder and note for the editor and used for its meaning 'look after/usurp' because the names/characters of Eliakim, Jehoiachin, Zorobabel are left as placeholders, their issue arises from the inconsistencies of their original backstories where they usurp each other not only as characters, but the word-names changed by mistake on behalf of original authors or intentionally have caused confusion—and because the editors working on Matt.1 need to sort them out then replace or add to the lineage in the correct order to make it a straight line from Joseph (Mary's fiancé) all the way to Abraham. This is further supported by these obvious reminder/note-names have been inserted where the issues arise and use word-names directly linked to the problem of skipping a father in the lineage line and the confusion of similar word-names originally used—the placeholder names are not related to the names from Abraham to Joram as these are straightforward, but concentrate on 'Eliakim' whose name 'Jehoiakim' has been missed between Josiah and Jeconiah, and also the editor's desire to use either Uzziah or Azariah which is the name of the same character (changed to Uzziah in the original story at an author's want to use this name for the storyline instead of Azariah at 2Kgs.15:13)

These word-names are used as placeholders, the same word altered slightly because the author/editor understands what he has meant by this and will work on it at a later date. Either the work was abandoned by the editors, or corrected versions did not survive which has left only this unfinished version of the reworked Matt.1. We will never know why they were not finished.

Just as **Joseph** (Gen.30:22-24;37) 'of sorrow/feels sorrow/regret' 'pours water gently over/rinses/ cleanses' was used to reflect the sorrow felt by Rachel, and then Joseph himself in Genesis, this Joseph; Iōséph; يوسييف is in sorrow due to his fiancé being pregnant without wedlock, and apparently he is not the father, and he remains 'of sorrow' i.e. upset and does not approach her until after she delivers the baby, showing he remained sorrowful and upset for a long time. It is also a joke about Joseph's water/sperm being what impregnated Mary, or at least another man's sperm did the job while Joseph's name and character cleanses her from disgrace by still being her fiancé then husband. He is also the same as Joseph of the Jacob story because his involvement is that he has dreams just like Joseph's story in Genesis revolved around dreams. Cp: yooseieyph.

Although the long introduction to what seems to be the 'lineage' connecting Jesus to David and through David to Isaac and directly to Abraham, the whole thing is meant as a pun in the fashion of samaara stories: all this lineage which is supposed to connect Jesus to David and Abraham, fails to do so because it is presented as Joseph's ancestors, and not Mary's—therefore just as Jesus is not Joseph's son, only Mary's, he cannot be linked to David and Jesse.

Also, the lewd nature of many samaaras is present: through the lineage passage Mary is likened to four women who are either prostitutes, 'sluts' or adulterers in the Biblical stories: **Tamar** presented herself as a prostitute to commit incest with her father-in-law Judah so as to have his 'seed' which resulted in conceiving Pharez and Zarah. Matt.1 suggests that Boaz' mother was **Rachab/Rahab** who was a prostitute in Josh. **Ruth** seduced Boaz under instruction from her mother-in-law Naomi so that he would marry her and it resulted in conceiving Obed. **Bath-sheba** committed adultery with David and became pregnant from this adultery (the child that died). The mention of Bath-sheba without using her name is intentional to remind she had relations with David while married to another man ('Uriah' 'he was made naked/stripped naked' is a direct reference to an illicit sexual act), this is why her name is not mentioned but her marriage to Uriah is 'and David the king begat Solomon of her that had been the wife of Urias' when they could have just used Bath-sheba's name—but the point of mentioning these women is not 'ancestry' or 'pedigree' but for their immoral sexual relations and the result of these relations. Mary mother of Jesus is linked to these women because she too is pregnant without wedlock.

The word-names of specific fictional male characters are linked to Jesus as purely words. To be discussed later.

Mary; María, Mariám; مَري ، مَريآم 'pass along' 'pass/cross/pass by' 'pass along the river/sea' and is exactly the same word as Miriam (Exod.1:3-7; 15:20-21) and it is used the same way Miriam was used in the OT; 'bitter/made bitter' 'bitter-river/sea' 'bitter/made bitter-the' and in both language use (of real people) and in the NT stories is used to mean 'great sufferance/great sufferance-the'. The major themes relayed by and revolving around Mary/Jesus is water/sea/coast-related, but there is also great bitterness and suffering. Wherever there is a 'Mary' character the story relays great sufferance and 'bitterness': Mary becomes pregnant as a virgin which causes Joseph bitterness/sufferance; she and her family are made to flee from place to place as Jesus' life is in danger; in more than one NT story Jesus mistreats her or at the very least publicly disrespects her showing his bitterness towards her as her name represents and relays 'great sufferance' which he knows he has to eventually suffer; Martha is caused bitterness by her sister Mary; Mary and Martha are caused bitterness due to Lazarus' death and by Jesus not immediately coming to cure him; Jesus is crucified and parts of his story relay he is aware of his future demise and feels remorse about it and suffering mentally from this knowledge; many different Mary-characters are connected to Jesus' bitter crucifixion, mostly by being present and watching him die and/or taking part in his cleansing and burial. Cp: mareea, maryaam.

To begin with the shortened form of this character's name 'Mary' 'pass along' 'pass/cross/pass by' it is reflected in how she has to pass/cross from one place to another protecting Jesus from Herod, first to Egypt, then back intending to go to Judaea, but having to go to Bethlehem then to Nazareth. Even when/if the shortened version of the name Mary 'pass along/pass by' was used, the author of Matt. has kept the full name intact (Mariám 'ran along the river') in a clever and clear way, for where in the OT Miriam enacted the meaning of her name by following the river which took Moses in basket to Pharaoh's daughter—in the NT, Mary's full name meaning is enacted first by Mary 'passing along' from place to place, then completed by her son Jesus' action/role who passes along rivers, waters, seas throughout his stories, and this latter action is given in abundance throughout Matthew to show Jesus' actions complete his mother Mary(am) name meaning: you will note throughout the majority of Matthew, Jesus is passing, walking along, staying in: rivers, waters, sea, ships, coasts, i.e. 'Maryam/Miriam/Mariám'; even some of his biggest miracles involve the sea, and specifically walking on water, catching fish out of the sea to make payment, but he is always travelling along rivers, coasts, and seas:

'Then cometh Jesus from Galilee to Jordan unto John, to be baptised of him.' (the river Jordan).

'And leaving Nazareth, he came and dwelt in Capernaum, which is upon the sea coast, in the borders of Zabulon and Nephtalim: That it might be fulfilled which was spoken by Esaias the prophet saying: The land of Zabalon and the land of Nephtalim, *by* way of the sea, beyond Jordan, Galilee of the Gentiles...'

'And Jesus, walking by the sea of Galilee, saw two brethren, Simon called Peter, and Andrew his brother, casting a net into the sea, for they were fishers.'

'And when he was entered into a ship, his disciples followed him, And, behold, there arose a great tempest in the sea, insomuch that the ship was covered with waves: but he was asleep...Then he arose, and rebuked the winds, and the sea; and there was a great calm. But the men marvelled, saying, What manner is this, that even the winds and the sea obey him!'

'And behold, the whole city came out to meet Jesus: and when they saw him, they besought *him*, that he would not depart out of their coasts.'

'And he entered into a ship, and passed over, and came into his own city.'

The actions of Jesus meant as the second half of Mary(am)'s compound word-name is clearly meant to be understood 'While he yet talked to the people, behold, *his* mother and his brethren stood without, desiring to speak with him. Then one said unto him, Behold, thy mother and thy brethren stand without, desiring to speak with thee. But he answered and said unto him that told him, Who is my mother, and who are my brethren? And he stretched out his hand toward his disciples, Behold my mother, and my brethren! For whosover shall do the will of my father which is in heaven, the same is my brother, and sister, and mother. The same day went Jesus out of the house, and sat by the seaside. And the great multitudes were gathered together unto him, so that he went into a ship, and sat; and the whole multitude stood on the shore…'

'When Jesus heard of *it*, he departed thence by ship into a desert place apart…'

'But the ship was now in the midst of the sea, tossed with waves…Jesus went unto them, walking on the sea. And when the disciples saw him walking on the sea…And Peter answered him and said…bid me come unto thee on the water…And when Peter was come down out of the ship, he walked on water to go to Jesus…and beginning to sink, he cried, saying, Lord, save me…Then they that were in the ship came and worshipped him, saying, Of a truth thou art the Son of God.'

'Then Jesus went thence, and departed into the coasts of Tyre and Sidon. And behold a woman of Canaan came out of the same coasts...'

'And Jesus departed from thence, and came nigh unto the sea of Galilee…'

Then he feeds a huge crowd with little food 'And he sent away the multitude, and took ship, and came into the coasts of Magdala.'

'Notwithstanding, lest we offend them, go thou to the sea, and cast an hook, and taketh the fish that first cometh up…'

'And it came to pass *that* when Jesus had finished these sayings, he departed from Galilee, and came into the coasts of Judaea, beyond Jordan; And great multitudes followed him; and he healed them there.'

So you have Jesus constantly walking alongside rivers, along coasts, shores, on seas, across seas and other bodies of water; you have his disciples walking/passing along the same shores, rivers, seas; finally you have the 'multitudes' of people living in these coasts, and other crowds coming out of the cities towards Jesus, attracted by his speeches, his miracles—all the events enacting the meaning of his mother's full name 'María, Mariám'. Where in the OT the male lineage of characters relays the themes of the stories, in the NT it is Jesus' mother Mary as Jesus has no human father; similarly to how maternal word-names relay negative themes/attributes to male kings in the OT—so do Mary's negative meanings of bitterness/sufferance in the NT on her son. (Matt.2:16; 12:46; 13:1; 3:13; 4:13-15, 18; 8:23-27, 34; 9:1; 12:46-50; 13:1-3; 14:13, 24-33; 15:21-22, 29-30, 39)

An important note related to Mary and the Jesus stories, it has been explained earlier in this book where in the OT there are similar names which were precursors and/or inspiration of the Jesus character, and also characters with completely different or similar names to Jesus whose stories and actions are similar to the Jesus stories. This indicates that the stories which would end up being considered separate from the OT and part of the NT, were in origin (as obvious from the Arabic word-names) no different and part of the stories of what would end up being compiled as the OT stories. All the stories (OT/NT) were popular stories circulated orally and by the one same people of the same culture, there was no difference—it is only when these stories would be compiled into works of text, i.e. gathered in the form of written stories that they would go through processes of editing which included elimination. Elimination of stories and changes to them would be furthered once these stories would become the basis of the Jewish religion, then the same with the emergence of the Christian religion. The people in charge of the Jewish religious texts would end up denying Jesus as a prophet, thus stories directly related to his mention removed. The people in charge of the Christian religious texts would take an extremely negative and discriminatory stance towards the Jewish religion and the people in charge of religious texts, this is blatantly stated in different parts of what make up the NT. But there still remains plenty of evidence within both the OT and NT to prove how they were stories taken from one cultural pool before they were altered and customised to suit who used them, and these give the indications mentioned in the passages below.

Please note, I am not attempting to discredit Jesus as the son of the virgin Mary, I am merely reading and explaining what the words and text is actually saying.

There are a number of reasons why the author(s) of Matthew chose to link Jesus, or at least attempt to, to David. One could be for the simple fact this is a samaara story where dirty jokes are implied and here it is implied Mary has upset Joseph by having sex with another man while claiming to be a pregnant virgin. Another could be a later editor upset by the accusations made against those of who would come to be known as 'Jewish', and as retaliation added the 'lineage' of Jesus as a slur/joke against the whole story, contradicting its body about a child born out of virginity or the son of God.

Proof that these stories were part of older stories (both the OT and the NT) is that although the unsuccessful attempt to link Jesus to David removes both David and Jesus completely from each other—it does prove the stories and word-names used are from one cultural source. Although the 'genealogy' passage in Matt.1 is attributed to Joseph, many of the names mentioned are connected to 'Mary(am)/Miriam' and through the house/family of Amram (in Matt.1 'Aram'); from the list of descendants used in Matt.1 he is obviously the OT character Amram. If you recall from the OT, Amram fathered three children mentioned in Exod.6:20: Moses, Aaron and Miriam (Mariám), and repeat in Num.26:59-60. Those used as Joseph's ancestors (which again does not make sense as even in storyland Joseph is biologically unrelated to Jesus—for the author has chosen to give Joseph this bloodline from David, making it irrelevant to Jesus' ancestry as he can only have ancestors through his mother, the virgin Mary) are connected to a different character with the same name 'Miriam/ Mariám', and Mary/ Mariám is the only character Jesus in the story can have a blood connection through, as he has no human father.

Although I have not taken into consideration anything from the Quran with regards to translating and understanding the OT, there is an important fact between the Mary mother of Jesus of the NT and the Maryam mother of Jesus of the Quran which should not be overlooked as it does throw light on how these stories are from one source—and that source is the culture and stories of the real people who would go on to create or receive these divine books.

In Islam and the Quran, Maryam the mother of Jesus is born to a daughter from the house/family of ' 'Amran', note the similarity to 'Amram' of the OT/NT, her mother (daughter of aal-'amran) makes a vow that the baby she gives birth to will be dedicated to the worship of God (and the baby born is a girl who goes on to be named Maryam and the mother of Jesus), i.e. she will be a Nazer/Naver نذر what is called a 'Nazerite' in the Bible, and in the Bible and Christianity Mary is connected to Nazareth. Also in the Quran, Maryam the mother of Jesus is called 'sister of Aaron'—note the similarity with the OT where Miriam, Aaron and Moses are siblings and their father is Amram. Being called 'sister of Aaron' in Arabic does not necessarily have to mean a sibling, but could also mean from his family or descendants. I am not trying to credit Jesus to David through Mary, or to discredit it for that matter, but it is important to see the connections of these words given as names, and to see where these ideas have come from, understanding the meanings of these words help us to understand why they were used, and that will help us to know who created the Biblical stories and why they were created.

Jesus; Iēsoús; عيسوَا ، عيسوَه 'bread/cold bread' 'broke/ate bread' 'breaking/eating bread' from the word (js/ 's/عس) 'bread/cold bread'. The meaning of bread and/or breaking or eating cold bread is reflected and relayed throughout the Jesus story; his role, the miracles he performs and warnings he makes revolve around bread. The authors or later editors have connected Jesus name, his role in the story to David and Jesse (Jesse 'my bread/my cold bread') because David 'stone rolling pin grinder' grinds the grains which are made into dough for bread. Both Jesse and Jesus are the same word in different forms. Just as the meaning of 'Jesus' is literally bread and breaking/eating bread so do most of his actions and role in the story pivot around bread and breaking bread. Jesus takes a little bread and makes it enough for large crowds (people who understand the language know how bread is broken and passed to another person which is the meaning of the word 'Jesus', and specifically the kind of bread made in simple ovens, its texture and how it is eaten; it is an action done every day throughout the day); bread is constantly mentioned in Jesus' dialogue and the narration of his story.

'The book of the generation of Jesus Christ, the son of David…and Obed begat Jesse; And Jesse begat David the king…'

'Then was Jesus led up of the Spirit into the wilderness to be tempted of the devil. And when he had fasted forty days and forty nights, he was afterward an hungered. And when the tempter came to him, he said, If thou be the Son of God, command that these stones be made bread. But he answered and said, It is written, Man shall not live by bread alone, but be every word that proceedeth out of the mouth of God.'

'Give us this day our daily bread'

'Or what man is there of you, whom if his son ask bread, will he give him a stone?'

'And when Jesus departed thence, two blind men followed him, crying, and saying, Thou son of David, have mercy on us…' i.e. Jesus 'bread' is the son of David 'stone rolling pin of grinding stone'—the child of the grinding stone is dough/bread.

'At that time Jesus went on the sabbath day through the corn; and his disciples were an hungered, and began to pluck the ears of corn, and to eat. But when the Pharisees saw *it*, they said unto him, Behold, thy disciples do what is unlawful to do upon the sabbath day. But he said unto them, Have ye not read what David did, when he was an hungered, and they that were with him; How he entered into the house of God, and did eat the shewbread, which was not lawful for him to eat, neither for them which were with him, but only for the priests?'

'Another parable spake he unto them; The kingdom of heaven is like unto leaven, which a woman took, and hid in three measures of meal, till the whole was leavened.'

'And when it was evening, his disciples came unto him, saying, This is a desert place, and the time is now past; send the multitude away that they may go into the villages, and buy themselves victuals. But Jesus said unto them, They need not depart; give ye them to eat. And they say unto him, We have here, but five loaves and two fishes. He said, Bring them hither to me. And he commanded the multitude to sit down on the grass, and took the five loaves, and the two fishes, and looking up to heaven, he blessed, and brake, and gave the loaves to *his* disciples, and the disciples to the multitude. And they did all eat, and were filled: and they took up of the fragments that remained twelve baskets full. And they that had eaten were about five thousand men, beside women and children.'

'Then came to Jesus scribes and Pharisees, which were of Jerusalem, saying, Why do thy disciples transgress the tradition of the elders? for they not wash their hands when they eat bread.' 'But he answered and said, It is not meet to take the children's bread, and to cast it to dogs.'

'Then Jesus called his disciples *unto him*, and said, I have compassion on the multitude, because they continue with me now three days, and have nothing to eat: and I will not send them away fasting, lest they faint in the way. And his disciples say unto him, Whence should we have so much bread in the wilderness, as to fill so great a multitude? And Jesus saith unto them, How many loaves have ye? And they said, seven, and a few little fishes. And he commanded the multitude to sit on the ground. And he took the seven loaves and the fishes, and he gave thanks, and brake *them*, and gave to his disciples, and the disciples to the multitude. And they did all eat, and were filled: and they took up the broken *meat* that was left seven baskets full.'

'And when his disciples were come to the other side, they had forgotten to take bread. Then Jesus said unto them, Take heed and beware of the leaven of the Pharisees and the Sadducees. And they reasoned among themselves, saying, *It is* because we have taken no bread. *Which* when Jesus perceived, he said unto them, O ye of little faith, why reason ye among yourselves, because ye have brought no bread? Do ye not understand, neither remember the five loaves of the five thousand, and how many baskets ye took up? Neither the seven loaves of the four thousand, and how many baskets ye took up? How is it that ye do not understand that I spake *it* not unto you concerning bread, but of the doctrine of the Pharisees and of the Sadducees. Then understood they how that he bade *them* not beware of the leaven of bread, but of the doctrine of the Pharisees and of the Sadducees.'

The sign of the person who will betray Jesus is while dipping bread into a dip 'And he answered and said, He that dippeth *his* hand with me in the dish, the same shall betray me.'

'And as they were eating, Jesus took bread and blessed *it*, and brake *it*, and gave *it* to the disciples and said, Take, eat; this is my body.'.

There are similar word-names to **Jesus** in the OT: **Ishuah** (Gen.46:17), **Isui** (Gen.46:17), **Jesui** (Num.26:44), **Jesse** (1Sam.16:17:17), **Jesaiah** (1Chr.3:21). There is similarity in word-name to **Isaiah** (2Kgs.19-20), and in the narration and ideas of the stories in the **Book of Isaiah** and especially Isa.42, Isa.46 and Isa.61. There is a similarity in the characters and events in the stories of **Elijah** (1Kgs.17; 18) and

Elisha (1Kgs.19:16-21; 2Kgs.2;3; 4;5; 6;7; 8). Cp: 'eysoowah, 'eysoowa. (Matt.1:1-17; 4:1-4; 6:11; 7:9; 9:27; 12:1-4; 13:33; 14:15-21; 15:1-2, 26, 32-37; 16:5-12; 26:23,26)

Christ; Christós; قرصه ، قرصته 'cake of/circle of' 'cake/circle of bread' 'his cake of' 'his cake/circle of bread' and means a cake or circle of bread, as bread was (and continues to be) made in circular cakes called (qrss/قرص). It can also be applied to a cake/circle of anything such as sweetmeat, incense. It is the Arabic word which has given the Greek translation the naming for Jesus Christ as that is how he is described in the story, it is not 'Anointed' as this is again forcing what scholars, etc. want to believe it means (even if in Greek and other languages it may come to mean this word influenced by misinterpretations of the original word in the Bible), whereas the word for 'anointed' is Messiah (see Messiah for explanation), but 'Christ' just means cake/circle and with regards to the Jesus story it means a cake/circle of bread.

Jesus' name, 'Jesus Christ' would read عيسوَه قرصته 'broke bread-his cake of bread' 'broke/ate his cake of bread'. Just as the word 'Christ' قرص means 'bread' 'cake/circle of bread', 'Christ' reads 'his cake of' and 'bread/circle of bread' 'his circle of bread'. This is evident in how he is sometimes described as 'the Christ' i.e. 'the cake/circle of bread'; 'Jesus the Christ' i.e. 'broke/ate bread-the circle of bread' 'bread-the circle of bread' 'breaking/eating bread-the circle of bread'. And the meaning of a 'circle/cake of bread is supported throughout the story along with the meaning of 'Jesus/bread/breaking and/or eating bread.

'He saith unto them, But who say ye that I am? And Simon Peter answered and said, Thou art the Christ, the Son of the living God.' 'Then charged he his disciples that they should tell no man that he was Jesus Christ.' And just as the word in Arabic is used alone to mean 'a cake of bread, e.g. when someone asks to be given a 'christ' it means a whole circle of bread, there are many instances in Matt. where Jesus is referred to simply as 'Christ/قرص/circle of bread': 'Whom will ye that I release unto you? Barabbas, or Jesus which is called Christ?' 'What shall I do then with Jesus which is called Christ?'—and what he ends up doing to Jesus is 'breaking-circle of bread' i.e. 'jesus-ing Christ' as Jesus is tortured to death through crucifixion i.e. the whole circle of bread '**Christ**' is broken/broke bread/'**Jesus**'. Cp: qrissoh, qrisstoh. (Matt.1:1; 16:15-16, 20; 27:17,22)

Herod; Hērṓdēs; حيروديه 'incited him against' 'bent his neck(physically)' 'of bent neck' 'became stubborn' 'incite' 'incites against others/causes problems between others' 'went to one side (while moving)' 'became stubborn' 'incited/incited against' 'focused on with malicious intent' 'of malicious intent'; حيروضيه 'incited him/incited him against' 'got worked up/works up' 'folds(ed)/coils(ed) into itself ready to strike' (e.g. a snake when preparing to defend itself or bite, or a person getting worked up). These meanings are reflected directly in how Herod is upset upon hearing of Jesus' birth, then plots and sets into action assassination attempts. 'When Herod the king had heard these things, he was troubled, and all Jerusalem with him...behold, the angel of the Lord appeareth to Joseph in a dream, saying, Arise, and take the young child and his mother, and flee into Egypt, and be thou there until I bring thee word: for Herod shall seek the young child to destroy him...and slew all the children that were in Bethlehem, and in all the coasts thereof...according to the time which he had diligently enquired of the wise men. It is the same as Haradah (Num.33:24), Harod (Judg.7:1-7), Harodite (2Sam.23:25). Cp: ḥeyroodeyh, ḥeyroodheyh. (Matt.2:3-8, 12, 16)

The stories still use the already explained meanings of the words, although it must be said the editors of some parts of Matt. seem to have a weaker understanding of the Arabic or at least one of them intentionally just writes what he wants it to be, e.g. **Emmanuel/Immanuel** means 'drink-the' and also could mean 'belief in the' this latter meaning has been stretched to make it 'which being interpreted is, God with us' which it does not mean 'God is with us' but 'belief in the' could mean fortify your belief/trust in God, but not 'God is with us'.

Notwithstanding, the words are still used as usual to set the stage and theme: **Bethlehem** because Herod is trying to kill them; when he is deceived, he will become angry and order the slaughter of all children in Bethlehem of a certain age. Both 'angry' and killing are meanings of 'Bethlehem'.

Judaea/Judah is 'he is called/calls' as he requests all the chief priests and scribes to assemble so they determine where Jesus will be born.

Jerusalem 'came-saw-asked-them/the' 'they see-asked-them/the' they saw-reached/arrived/public apology-them/the' 'came-saw-reached/arrived/public apology-them/the' as both the wise men and Herod want to reach Jesus; the wise men come and ask Herod of Jesus' whereabouts so that they can go see him to worship him; Herod asks the wise men, and also the priests and scribes, to see and tell him where the child can be found. The wise men coming, following the star, coming to see Jesus, and worshipping him (worship can be asking something from what is being worshipped).

Egypt/Mizraim, is used for its meaning of 'put scarf on-the', or 'knot/bundle-them/the' as people bundle things into scarfs or knot small things/small amounts into scarf or fabric for storage and/or travel as Joseph, Mary and Jesus are made to travel to Egypt or from Egypt. (Matt.2)

Israel 'twisted muscle-the' 'twisted-the' still implies the female of the story committed an immoral sexual act which shamed her male relatives—Joseph 'of sorrow' in this story—and also that something is still not set straight which is although God has told them to return, once they are there, they find themselves still in danger and need to change their course of travel. (Matt.2:21)

Archelaus; Archélaos; ارحيلوه 'leave/get or go away/travel' and is said to a plural, which Joseph, Mary and Jesus have to travel elsewhere when they hear the character of the same name is the ruler; ارخيلوه 'loosen for him' and can mean a literal loosening of something and a figurative loosening of morals, and is still speaking about Mary's pregnancy before marriage; when a woman is said to 'loosen her trouser band' it means both the literal and figurative 'loosening' of both the clothes and the dropping of morals to allow the man to have sex with her. Cp: arḥeilowh, ar<u>kh</u>eilowh. (Matt.2:22)

Galilee (Josh.20:7) 'made clear-the' as God has warned Joseph and made clear the threat Archelaus poses. (Matt.2:22)

Nazareth; Nazarét, Nazaréth; نَذَرِت ، نَذَريت 'she/I vowed/set aside/dedicated to God' 'the vow/set aside/dedication to' 'warned' 'she/I warned' and it is used here to indicate Jesus was vowed/dedicated to God, but it also means the prophets who predicted/warned of the coming of a person who would claim to be from God: because the word and passage is in the form of 'warning' 'Nazareth', it is not the same as 'prophesying/naba' which can be good or bad, but the way Nazareth has been used is warning and specifically of a 'false prophet' the 'dreamer of dreams' which the OT stories narrated that if he were to come he should be killed (which this NT story has happen, following the idea of the earlier OT stories). نَصَرِت ، نَصَريت 'she/I helped to succeed/succeeded victors/supporters(ed) of/aides of' 'helpers of/helpers to victory/succeed' is also meaning of Nazareth. Cp: navaret, navareyt, na<u>ss</u>aret, na<u>ss</u>areyt. (Matt.2:23)

Nazarene; Nazarēnós, Nazōraíos; نَذَرينه ، نَذورَيه 'they vowed/dedicated him' 'they set him/it aside' 'they warned of/about him' 'they warned him' 'warned-he/him'; نَصَرينه ، نَصورَيه 'they helped him victor/win' 'they assisted him to victory' 'succeeded/helped to succeed-he/him'. In the same way Samson was 'a Nazerite unto God from the womb' (Jud.13), similarly Mary and Jesus are made to live in Nazareth 'vowed', but Jesus is also *the* 'vow' which will be sacrificed/offered by God at the end of his story just like offerings and sacrifices are made to God throughout the Bible; and Jesus' life in the story is completely calling people to God's ways and to avoid the 'wrong ways', and he is called a 'Nazarene' in the story, his teachings and the narration of his dialogue in Matt. are warnings to his audiences. It is still also reminding of the stories of the OT where the prophets have warned a false prophet and/or 'dreamer of dreams' will arise and should be killed for his lies, and the styling of the sentence has made this clearly the meaning. 'And he came and dwelt in a city called Nazareth: that it might be fulfilled which was spoken by the prophets, He shall be called a Nazarene.'. Cp: navareynoh, navooraioh, na<u>ss</u>areynoh, na<u>ss</u>ooraioh. (Matt.2:23)

John; Iōánnēs; خوآنّيه ، خوَنّيه 'soaked it/him (in)' 'brothers' 'betrayed'; جوآنّيه ، جوَنّيه 'sacks' 'sackcloth' 'put/wrap it/him in sack/sackcloth' from word (gownia(h)/جونيه/جونيا) 'sack' which is made of burlap/burlap-like course material. His character is described as soaking people under/with water, he himself will be soaked with water as he baptises people, especially if he is standing in the river as popularly depicted and reflects 'soaked it/him' meaning of his character name. The form of the word 'John/ Iōánnēs' means to wrap or place something/someone with/in a sack, the colour of which is usually beige/camel, and is exactly what John is described as wearing 'In those days came John the Baptist…And the same John had his raiment of camel's hair, and a leathern girdle about his loins.' Supported by the verses where Jesus comments on people's expectations and what John is wearing (a rough texture) 'And as they departed, Jesus began to say to the multitudes concerning John, What went ye out into the wilderness to see? A reed shaken with the wind? But what went ye out for to see? A man clothed in soft raiment? behold, they that wear soft *clothing* are king's houses. But what went ye out for to see? A prophet? yea, I say unto you, and more than a prophet.'. Cp: <u>kh</u>ooaaneyh, <u>kh</u>ooanneyh gooaaneyh, gooanneyh. (Matt.3:1-3; 11:7-9)

Baptist; baptistēs; بغطِستيه 'will dip/duck you under water' 'of dipping (you/it) under water' from the word (<u>gh</u>ts/غطس) 'go(ing)/pushing under water', (<u>gh</u>tst/غطست) 'went under water'; the (b/ba/بـ) indicates 'by/

with' i.e. done by someone. It is how John the Baptist 'baptises' people—by ducking them under water in the river and this too complements his forename ('John/soaked he/him'): 'Then went out to him Jerusalem, and all Judaea, and all the region round about Jordan, confessing their sins...I indeed baptise you with water unto repentance...And Jesus, when he was baptised, went up straightaway out of the water.'. Cp: bag͟h͟tisteyh. (Matt.3:1-15)

Judah is still used as 'he is called/calls'. Note the authors of the NT sometimes use Judaea instead of Judah (spelt Judas in NT as Greek transliteration from the original language into (Arabic/Hebrew) seems to turn words that end in ('ah'/'a' into 's': Judah/Judas; Hezekiah/Ezekias). 'Judaea' is the same word and meaning of Judah, 'he calls/he calls out', and John is calling out to people to repent.

Isaiah/Esaias (2Kgs.19-20) has been used for its meaning 'he shouts/they shout' and not only for the link to the Isaiah stories: 'For this is he that was spoken of by the prophet Esaias, saying, The voice of one crying in the wilderness...'. Also the way John the Baptists speaks to the people, and specifically to the Pharisees and Sadducees, is as if he is shouting at them.

Jerusalem (1Kgs.8:1-5) 'they see-asked-them/the' 'came-saw-asked-them/the' 'they saw-arrived/public apology-them/the' 'came-saw-arrived/public apology-them/the' as people are coming to see John and what he is doing and what it is all about; the nature of John's role is he is asking them to do something: be baptised, follow God's ways, repent—and the repent is a public apology to God and in the story it is done publicly.

Jordan (Gen.13: 8-11) 'they come/are coming home' as they are all coming to John and he is bringing them to the correct religion/God's ways of the story.

Abraham (Gen.17:5) 'pull up/draw up-the' 'clear-the' as John is addressing the Pharisees and Sadducees who have come to the baptism, the people being baptised are in a sense performing the same action as the word 'Abraham' means—they are being plunged under water then pulled out of it, there is a submersion then an emergence out of the water just like a pouch or any other bailing object used to 'Abrah'. It also implies they will not be pulled out of the fire/punishment, and that if they do not honestly repent being baptised with water 'Abraham' will not help them; also the meaning of 'clearing-the' is used in the same way, that if no real repentance towards God is made, they will be cleared away like bad trees. (Matt.3:7-10)

Galilee (Josh.20:7) 'came-to' 'came-for' 'cleared-the' as Jesus like everyone else is coming to John to be baptised, baptism clears the previous sins away, it purifies. This is reinforced when John states Jesus need not have come to him as he does not need to be 'purified' but John should have come to Jesus to be purified by him.

Sadducees; Saddoukaíoi; زَدّوكَيوي ، زَدّوكَايوي 'of deceit/deceiving' 'they deceived/tricked you' 'of giving extra' 'they gave you extra'; صَدّوكَيوي ، صَدّوكَايوي 'of blocking/denying' 'they blocked/denied you'; صَدّوقَيوي ، صَدّوقَايوي 'believed you/of believing' 'honest-you/of honesty' 'befriended you/of befriending/friendly' as they tell Jesus they will believe him, but only if he shows them specific proof at their request. This word-name is the same as Zadok (2Sam.8:17), Zedekiah (1Kgs.22:11-28) and all similar 'zadok' word-names of the OT. In Matthew, these characters are described to be blocking Jesus from spreading the word/religion, they want to stop him; but they are also described by both John the Baptist and Jesus, and in the story events, as being deceptive, attempting to trick John, God, and Jesus, they are accused of deceiving the people and blocking them from following God's true laws: John the Baptist 'But when he saw many of the Pharisees and Sadducees come to his baptism, he said unto them, O generation of vipers, who hath warned you to flee from the wrath to come? Bring forth therefore fruit meet for repentance: And think not to say within yourselves, We have Abraham to *our* father: for I say unto you, that God is able of these stones to raise up children unto Abraham. And now also the axe is laid to the root of the trees: therefore every tree which bringeth not good fruit is hewn down, and cast into the fire. I indeed baptise you with water unto repentance: but he that cometh after me is mightier than I, whose shoes I am not worthy to bear; he shall baptise you with the Holy Ghost, and *with* fire...'

'The Pharisees also with the Sadducees came, and tempting desired him that he would shew them a sign from heaven...O *ye* hypocrites, ye can discern the face of the sky; but can ye not *discern* the signs of the times? A wicked and adulterous nation seeketh after a sign...'

'Then Jesus said unto them, Take heed and beware of the leaven of the Pharisees and of the Sadducees...Then understood they how that he bade them *not* of the leaven of the bread, but of the doctrine of the Pharisees and of the Sadducees.'

'And when the chief priests and Pharisees had heard his parables, they perceived that he spake of them. But when they sought to lay hands on him, they feared the multitude, because they took him for a prophet.'

'The same day came to him the Sadducees,' the same day as the Pharisees plotted how to trick Jesus through conversation 'which say, that there is no resurrection, and asked him…' and they present him with a theory in order to stump him, but 'Jesus answered and said unto them, Ye do err, not knowing the scriptures, not the power of God…' and he gives a response which silences them 'And when the multitude heard *this* they were astonished at his doctrine. But when the Pharisees had heard that he had put the Sadducees to silence, they were gathered together.'

Cp: zaddookaiwee, zaddookaaaiwee, ssadookaiwee, ssadookaaaiwee, ssadooqaiwee, ssadooqaaaiwee. (Matt.)

Pharisees; Pharisaíoi; فَرِشَيوي ، فَرِشايوي 'of spreading out/over/laying out'; فَرِصَيوي ، فَرِصايوي 'of splitting open/pushing out/emerging by pushing up or out/ dividing by breaking or splitting' 'of taking opportunity/chance' 'broke/split through' 'opportunity/chance' 'broke (things) into pieces'; فَرِسَيوي ، فَرِسايوي 'of dividing something into separate units' 'of explaining/explaining in detail/making clear' 'divided/separated things into units' 'sorted things into separate units' 'explained things in detail/broke things down to explain in detail'; بَرِزَيوي ، بَرِزايوي 'of bringing forward/pressing on and pushing out' 'brought forward/pressed on and pushed out'.

All meanings meant by 'Pharisees' are available in Matthew: they are described as understanding the laws of God, but intentionally distorting them; they are described as trying to break Jesus (whose name itself means break bread/Jesus) as in discredit him and eventually cause his death. They attempt to bring around his murder by using 'explanations and detailing' of laws and theories of God's commandments. They eventually get to 'press and push out' Jesus when they finally get him to state something which they request the explanation of which results in that they beat and push him around before he is taken to trial then execution on the cross.

Although most meanings of these words meant by 'Pharisees' are in Matthew, the overwhelming mention of Pharisees is supported with text depicting these characters as taking advantage of opportunities as they arise, in a negative way; even when they are described as understanding or having the ability to read religious laws/text, this is also depicted negatively, implying they either do not understand it, and/or intentionally distort it to gain from it, i.e. opportunists. The word is the same as Persia (2Chr.36:20-21), Pharez (Gen.38:29), Perez (2Sam.6:8), PERES (Dan.5:28).

Beginning with John the Baptist's interaction with the Pharisees (in the story), noticing their arrival he denigrates them, accuses them of being given a chance to flee punishment but being disingenuous about it, then he admonishes them not to think they have a chance of escape through Abraham.

The story narrates and portrays them as whenever they see or hear Jesus' actions or speech, it provides them with a chance to attack and 'expose' him; the narration has them take every opportunity when this arises to attempt to deceive him; within Jesus' replies, the Pharisees have an opportunity to learn what the truth is, they have a chance to know what is truly right and wrong (according to the story), and in the same response to the Pharisees, he says (Jesus) he has come to give a chance to the sinners to repent. When the Pharisees see the disciples plucking corn and eating on the sabbath, they take the opportunity to point out the wrongdoing to Jesus and hold it against him; 'And they asked him, saying, Is it lawful to heal on the sabbath day? that they might accuse him…' they are seeking a chance (like the name given to them by the Biblical author(s)) to catch him out; 'Then the Pharisees went out, and held a council against him, how they might destroy him…' and Jesus knows it, and decides to withdraw and asks the crowd not to tell i.e. not give the Pharisees an opportunity to destroy him.

When they seek the opportunity of accusing him of dealing with the devil, he retorts and ends it with a warning that those who blaspheme against the 'Holy Ghost' will not be given a chance to repent in this life, nor the hereafter. They go on to request a sign (miracle), giving him a chance to prove to them that he is the prophet/Son of God but his response is that a sign has already been given 'and there shall no sign be given to it, but the sign of the prophet Jonas.' And when you read Jonah, the whole story is about people, including Jonah, being given chances and opportunities to repent and do right. Jesus' last example to the Pharisees in chapter 12, is of chances and opportunities wasted 'When the unclean spirit is gone out of man, he walketh through dry places, seeking rest, and findeth none. Then he saith, I will return into my house from whence I came out; and when he is come, he findeth *it* empty, swept, and garnished. Then goeth he, and taketh with himself seven other spirits more wicked than himself, and they enter in and dwell there: and the last *state* of that man is worse than the first. Even so shall it be unto this wicked generation.'

In Chapter 15 when the Pharisees take the opportunity about the disciples not washing their hands before eating, Jesus responds by pointing out how they profit by transgressing God's commandments, their own rules, when it is opportunistic for them to do so 'But he answered and said unto them, Why do ye also transgress the commandment of God by your tradition? For God commanded, saying, Honour thy father and mother: and, He that curseth his father or mother, let him die the death. But ye say, Whoseover shall say to *his* father or *his* mother, *It is* a gift, by whatsoever thou mightest be profited by me; And honour not his father or his mother, *he shall be free*. Thus have ye made the commandment of God of none effect by your tradition. Ye hypocrites, well did Esaias prophesy of you, saying…'

The interaction and narration are of breaking down matters into details, explaining them, and also of chances and opportunities. And when he warns his disciples of the doctrine of the Pharisees and Sadducees, he is warning against being opportunistic, i.e. distorting religion for personal gain.

Chapter 19, the Pharisees seek opportunities to condemn Jesus by presenting questions and hoping he will explain (detail) and in his response bring condemnation upon himself 'The Pharisees also came unto him, tempting him, and saying unto him, Is it lawful for a man to put away his wife for every cause?...They say unto him, Why did Moses then command to give a writing of divorcement, and to put her away?'

Chapter 21 is still full of the Pharisees attempting to get a chance to hold something against Jesus; his response is parables which explain the loss of chances, which eventually rile the chief of priests and Pharisees to want to physically attack him. Chapter 22 continues with the Pharisees being told parables by Jesus which pivot around lost chances; the Pharisees continue in their effort to find an opportunity to take action against Jesus, to 'entangle' him, but he knows what they are trying to do and confronts them. They leave and return with a lawyer to help them find a reason to get Jesus into trouble. Then it is Jesus who takes the opportunity of the gathered Pharisees to pose a question to them which they should be able to explain/answer, but they are unable to respond 'While the Pharisees were gathered together, Jesus asked them…And no man was able to answer him a word, neither *durst* any man from that day forth ask him any more *questions*.'

Chapter 23 begins with Jesus condemning the Pharisees, describing their deeds, making it clear they take opportunity for their own gain: making others carry heavy loads while they do not lift a finger; how they do things as a show to be seen by others to be esteemed and to gain status; he accuses and warns the Pharisees that they block people's chance of entering heaven and in doing so lose their own chance of entering heaven; he accuses the Pharisees of taking advantage of widows by using religion 'for ye do devour widows' houses and for a pretence make long prayer'; and continues pointing out how they take opportunity using religion as a cover, and ends it bemoaning how they had a chance but lost it by choosing to let it go.

They find opportunity to harm Jesus through Judas approaching them—Judas is seeking an opportunity to betray Jesus, but he also makes money too. And when Jesus refuses to speak they (both the Pharisees and Sadducees) find a way to get him to give them reason to harm him by asking him in the name of God and his response finally gives them the opportunity (through the explanation). The authors have created their names to relay with and reflect that they will physically attack Jesus, and kill Jesus. When Judas repents and returns to the priests, admitting he has betrayed an innocent person, they are no longer interested because they have gained what they previously needed—the opportunity to accuse/condemn Jesus—but the authors still use this event to show the meaning of the Pharisees and Sadducees: when Judas throws the money back at them, they find an opportunity to get the money back, they decide it cannot be put in the treasury so instead they put it to use in purchasing land for a cemetery.

Even when Jesus is dying on the cross, the authors still show the meaning of the word Pharisee (and Sadducees 'believed you/of believing' 'honest-you/of honesty') in how they mock Jesus, as in their mockery there is still the meaning of this is his chance to prove he is the Son of God, and if he can save himself, they will believe in and follow him 'Likewise the chief priests mocking him, with the scribes and elders said, He saved others; himself he cannot save. If he be the king of Israel, let him now come down from the cross, and we will believe him.'

After he dies the story goes on to show they do not want to leave anything to chance by requesting and implementing his burial site be sealed and guarded to make sure no one 'fakes' a resurrection, and when stories of the resurrection spread, they bribe soldiers to claim that Jesus' disciples stole his body. Cp: pharishaiwee, pharishaaaiwee, pharissaiwee, pharissaaaiwee, pharisaiwee, pharisaaaiwee, barizaiwee, barizaaaiwee. (Matt.3:7-12; 9:9-13, 32-34; 12:1-15, 24-37, 38-45; 15:1-14; 16:1-4, 6-12; 19:3-9; 21:23-46; 22:1-22, 34-36, 41-46; 23:1-5, 13-16, 23-32; 26:14-16, 47, 59-68; 27:1-7, 41-43, 62-66; 28:11-15)

Satan (1Chr.21:1-17) has been used for all three of its meanings: 'laid hands on' and it could mean two people laid their hands on something/someone they should not have (i.e. harmed them), or have transgressed twice: the devil tempts Jesus to use his power to turn stones into bread to satisfy his anger, which Jesus makes clear he will not transgress.

Satan 'two laps/two sides' 'laps/sides' and means went back and forth on the same course/path/way either twice or many times, it is equivalent to going 'back and forth' 'up and down' 'coming and going' and could mean two or more people do this or the action is done twice or several times, and as in Job, Satan tries more than twice to tempt Jesus into sinning.

Satan 'obstructed' 'of obstructing' 'defended' and means to either block the way or block an action without being provoked or in self-defence as Jesus meets Satan's attempts with refusal, i.e. he defends himself by blocking both Satan and the sins he tries to cause him to commit.

What is interesting is that Satan is described in the OT as a 'son of God', Jesus in the NT is also described as the 'Son of God' which the authors of Matt. have both Satan, and the Pharisees/Sadducees question and doubt, both groups (Satan and the humans) want to see proof of Jesus' claim to be Son of God—as the Sons of God have special powers as seen in the Job and Daniel stories. The conversation between both 'sons of God' is a conversation between God's favourite thing: food and eating (bread/Jesus), and God's way of eating and punishing (fire/Satan): as this is how things are eaten and Satan is linked to fire through 'the Son of God' walking in and moving around the fire to save Daniel's friends, and also in the culture hell/hellfire is where Satan lives or ends up living as punishment for eternity.

Also there is a connection between 'Satan' 'eating' and 'fire' in the culture that created all the stories of which the OT and NT (as well as Quran) originate from which can be seen in the Bible without the need to turn to other sources: in Genesis it is merely a serpent which deceives Adam and Eve to eat from the forbidden tree, there is no mention of a devil/Satan, just an animal 'beast' punished to slither on its stomach for eternity (a snake); but in culture and religion it is Satan/the devil who tricks Adam and Eve into eating from the tree; in the NT it is Satan attempting to do the same with Jesus by have him turn stones into bread to eat; in the OT fire is how God eats and also how he purifies people, land, food, vessels and materials they are made from, and how he purges sin and wicked people; in the NT it is also how God purifies/purges and punishes people.

Capernaum; Kapharnaoúm, kĕpar naḥum; قَبَرنَووم ، قَبَرنَوْم ، قَبَرنَوهُم ، قيبَر نَهوم 'buried-the asleep' 'buried-sleep' 'we buried them' 'buried-sighing/sighed' 'buried-struck and winded' and the 'nahum' part means sighing or puffing meant to attract attention or being hit/punched in stomach until breath is forced out of you. It means the people who will be saved from death/darkness 'The people which sat in the darkness…and to them which sat in the region and shadow of death…'. The 'sleep' part because the people said to be living in darkness and under the shadow of death is similar to sleep (people of the culture call sleep 'the small death'), and the light and punishment is the same as being awakened from sleep. The sighing part of the word-name suggests the people need and want to be saved/shown the right way to be saved from death/darkness. Cp: qabar-naoum, qabar-na-oum, qabarnao-hum, qeibar nahum. (Matt.4:13)

Matt.4:12-17 has borrowed verses from Isa.9 and made them to suit the current story being told. It is possible the author of Matt.4 added verse.2 of Isa.9, the latter verse stands in contradiction to the rest of Isa.9 (of course it could be because 'light' is deemed as something positive and the way out of darkness, but the original author meant by it the light of a punishing fire—therefore it would only be that the author of Matt.4 borrowed the verses and idea from Isa.9 and made a different (positive) story out of the same verse).

The place-names have been used for the same reasons (see Isa.9) Zabulon/**Zebulun**, Nephthalim(may have additional meaning in this form)/**Naphtali**, **Jordan** and **Galilee**. But Galilee here as well as the 'light' mentioned are positive in that God/Jesus will make clear the right way to God/heaven, and Jesus begins to 'preach'.

Gentiles (Judg.4); ethnōn; يثنون ، اثنون 'he/they do it again/double it/fold it/repeat it' 'he/they dissuade/make leave' 'he/they are idolaters/pagans' 'idols' 'praise/praises' 'idol worshippers' 'idolatry/worshipping idols' has been added and it still carries the meaning of 'I will deceive them/the' (haggoyim in OT) in its meanings of 'he/they dissuade/make leave' of the NT. Also from the meaning of the word in the

OT 'I will mislead them to downfall-them/the' which is what happens to all of Israel, Judah, Ephraim, Manasseh, etc. at Isa.9, but here in Matt.4 it may be a pro-OT editor poking fun at a pro-NT author by editing his work at a later date in which 'Galilee of the Gentiles' reads and means 'came to-I will mislead them to downfall-them/the' and the pun is enhanced because Galilee also means 'cleared-the'—so what is supposed to lead them to clarity instead leads them to downfall, or hell, depending on what the author's beliefs were; Satan repeatedly attempts to dissuade Jesus from God's path; Satan attempts to get Jesus to worship him; with each response to Satan, Jesus' faith is reinforced and finally he makes Satan give up and leave; it plays with 'Galilee of the Gentiles' to mean 'came to-dissuade the idolaters/idol worshippers'. Cp: yfnoon, ifnoon. (Matt.4:15)

Galilee has been used for 'came-to' 'came-for' because as soon as Simon/Peter and Andrew are asked to follow Jesus, they come to him. (Matt.4:18)

Simon; Símon, šim'ôn; سيمون ، سِمْئُن 'ill/sick/weak' as the disciples first task is to take care of the ill; سيمعن ، سِمعُن 'have heard/to hear/heard' 'obeyed/obey' (to listen or hear can also mean to obey) as both Simon Peter and his brother immediately listen to Jesus request to follow him. Cp: seemoon, sim-on, seem'n, sim'on.

Peter; Pétros; بَتروه ، بيتروه ، باتروه 'his/its stub/shortness' 'he has cut him/it short' 'he/it has been snapped short' 'he/it has been abruptly cut off' 'they have snapped him/it/cut him/it short' 'his stub of rock' 'his smooth rock' all the meanings imply 'short/abrupt/quick/a stub/interrupted'. It is from the word (btr/بتر) snapped/stub/broken or chopped off and is used to describe someone or something of short or stubby stature, someone who responds quickly/abruptly, an action which is quick and abrupt, e.g. it is the word used to describe snapping a piece of thread from the spool or from a garment, the action of quickly cutting off anything, including relationships, it is also the name of a viper with a short body (btr/abtar). Along with his brother, Peter is all these things as he abruptly leaves fishing, his livelihood, family, and work at hand in the middle of the work and immediately follows Jesus—this is why he has been given a second name instead of his 'original' name. It is the same as Bether (Cant.2:16-17). The meanings of both his names are reflected as follows:

Jesus arrives at Peter-Simon's house to find his mother-in-law extremely ill ('Simon'). Both Simon/Peter meanings are in Jesus' speech to his disciples when he first assembles them together: a lot of the speech is about healing illnesses (covering the two Simons meanings). There is only short time for 'preach, saying, The kingdom of heaven is at hand'. Peter is always quick to engage/answer/enquire with Jesus: when Jesus walks upon a raging sea, Peter immediately wishes to try it, and just as quickly allows fear to take over and lose his balance; eagerly asks Jesus to explain the parable; quick to give the answer about Jesus Christ, Son of God.

The meaning of shortness in stature is portrayed in how Jesus compares Peter's name with his shortness, and contrasted against how he will be rewarded in heaven—a high place. Peter is quick to interrupt Jesus praying to God that nothing bad of what Jesus mentioned should befall him. Out of the three disciples who witness Jesus' transfiguration, and Moses and Elias speaking with him—it is Peter who interrupts to suggest they make tabernacles for each prophet. Quick to answer that Jesus will pay tribute money, although initially Jesus does not seem pleased about it; and Peter's abruptness in talking/answering is parodied in Jesus' miracle telling Peter (who rushed to say Jesus does pay tribute) to cast a hook, pick up the first fish and he will find a coin upon opening its mouth—to pay the tribute.

Peter suggests a limited number of times when enquiring how many times before no longer forgiving those who sin against him—Jesus responds with endless forgiveness, and this indicates Peter's suggestion seems like he has a short span of patience. Out of all the disciples it is Peter quick to ask what they will be rewarded having let go of everything to follow Jesus.

When Jesus informs them they will be offended by him that very night, Peter is quick to express his affection, love and devotion by saying he would never be offended by Jesus; when Jesus goes further to tell him that he will deny even knowing Jesus—again, Peter is quick to object. Although they have been asked to stay awake with Jesus, they quickly fall asleep 'Peter, What, could ye not watch with me one hour?'; and Jesus sorrowful about his nearing torment is also abrupt in reproaching them 'Watch and pray, that ye enter not into temptation: the spirit indeed *is* willing, but the flesh *is* weak.'. When Jesus is arrested all the disciples take off 'Then all the disciples forsook him, and fled…But Peter followed him afar off unto the high priest's palace, and went in and sat with the servants, to see the end.' So all the disciples initially abandoned him, including Peter, and although Peter inconspicuously hangs around to find out what happens to Jesus—his final actions are true to his name: he quickly denies having anything to do with, or even knowing, Jesus: his name 'Peter' 'his stub/shortness' 'he has cut him short' 'he has been snapped short' 'he has been abruptly cut off' 'they have snapped him/cut him short' as he has cut off any relationship to/with Jesus. 'Now Peter sat without the palace: and a damsel came unto him, saying, Thou also wast with Jesus of Galilee. But he denied before *them* all, saying, I know not what thou sayest. And when he was gone out into the porch, another *maid* saw him, and said unto them that were there, This fellow was also with Jesus of Nazareth. And again he denied with an oath, I do not know the man. And after a while came to him *they* that stood by, and said to Peter, Surely thou art also *one* of them; for thy speech bewrayeth thee. Then began he to curse and to swear, *saying*, I know not the man. And immediately the cock crew. And Peter remembered the word of Jesus, which said unto him, Before the cock crow thou shalt deny me thrice. And he went out and wept bitterly.' Cp: betrooh, beitrooh, baatrooh. (Matt.4:18-20; 8:14; 10:2; 14:28-31; 15:15; 16:16, 23; 17:4, 24, 26; 18:21; 19:27; 26:33-35, 37-41, 58, 69-75)

Andrew; Andréas; اندريَه 'send out/sent him/it out' 'separated/separated him/it' and is mostly used to describe sending off sheep/goats in the right direction towards pastures to graze ('sent him/it out'), and used to describe separating between sheep and goats, whether to sort and separate them to send to different areas, or to separate one or more from the rest of the flock in order to slaughter or sell them ('separated him/it'). The same as En-dor/Endor (Josh.17:11).

Both meanings of 'sent him/it out' and 'separated him/it' are used in Matthew: Andrew and his brother leave their work and follow Jesus, they set off in a specific direction; also Jesus' dialogue to them is that they will be catching men instead of fish (both senses of the word is used here as they will be sending people in the right direction towards God, and in doing so sorting the 'good' from the 'wicked') 'follow me and I will make you fishers of men. And they straightaway left *their* nets, and followed him.'

The meaning of Andrew's word-name is further emphasised by Jesus telling them what their role as his disciples will be 'go rather to the lost sheep'; the action is with a specific group of the 'flock' 'cast out devils'. The disciples are likened to goats/sheep when sent out to graze without a shepherd watching over them 'Behold, I send you out as sheep in the midst of wolves'. Cp: andreyah. (Matt.4:18-20; 10)

James; Iákōbos; يآقوبَس ، يقوبَس 'he/it pinches' which also means to say something from a story or said by someone else (the modern eqivalent would be to 'quote'); يآخوبَص ، يخوبَص 'he pokes finger into' 'he pokes finger into anus' (sexually or as a prank over clothing) 'he pokes fingers into food/he pollutes food by poking fingers into it' 'he makes a mess' The Greek 'I' transliteration equates to the 'Hebrew/Arabic' 'j/y' transliteration, therefore a word that begins with (I/j/y could be: ي ، هـ ، جـ ، عـ ، حـ ، خـ and the most used in the OT represent 'I-he' 'g-came' 'h-I will/he will/look, etc.) so instead of 'he/it pinches' it could also mean 'came-pinched' 'he/I will pinch' 'look, he pinched' as you can see in similar word-names which begin with the above mentioned prefix. I will only use (y/he/it) to avoid repetition as the others do not change the meaning of the word, only its tense, I will only use the other letters where there is definitely a completely different meaning or a specific prefix supported by the text of the story. It is the same as 'Jebus' of the OT.

James has been given the name 'he/it pinches' 'he it pokes' because it is the action fishermen do when they are untying knots, pushing things in and out of holes/narrow places and smoothing out kinks from the fishnet, and also the way they sew/mend the fishnets seems they are poking and pinching at it.

There is an odd and notable difference between the Greek transliteration Iákōbos and its English transliteration 'James'—they are by no means similar to each other; all the other names sound similar as they do when pronounced in the original language they were translated/transliterated from. This difference is probably due to the same reasons 'Hawaa' was made into 'Eve' to make it easier for the English/Latin/foreign speakers/translators, as there is a similarity in what 'James' (the alternative to Iákōbos) means and Iákōbos/he pinches/pokes where 'James' is probably ('āmôz—Amoz—ghamoz—غآمَز) 'massaged' and as they wanted him to have the prefix of 'I/he/J' it would be (ye'āmôz/ je'āmôz/—Yeamoz/Geamoz—yeghamoz— يغآمَز / جغآمَز). You can see the similarity between the words 'pinch' and 'massage' as an action fishermen seem to make with their hands as they smooth out and fix things on the fishing nets.

Another similarity between 'Eve' and 'James' use of words is that you cannot find an actual transliteration for these two words as they stand transliterated into English—dictionaries and databases only provide the transliteration of the original word 'Hawaa' and 'Iákōbos'. This proves again that at least up until the times these two words were translated into English or Latin, there were still local Arabs who understood the Bible was in Arabic and who provided the foreigner with alternative Arabic words and spellings with similar, if not the same, meanings as the word too difficult for the western foreigner to pronounce, transliterate and spell.

Because the transliteration of 'James' which is not the same word as 'Iákōbos', there is a possibility that it had more than one meaning in wordplay which is why the person who gave this word to the foreign translators chose it, and this is supported by the related Biblical story and is also related to fixing nets and dealing with ill people such as the following: James; ye'āmôz, 'āmôz; يِجآمُس ، جآمُس ، يِجآمُز ، جآمُز 'he binds together' 'bound together' 'he/it thickens/sets quickly' 'thickened/set' and the latter refers to a substance that sets with air or time passing such as moulds, casts, mud and other substances used in the household or for simple medical treatment; it means fixing something with usually involves holding parts or a specific part coated with a substance and sometimes using the hand(s) as a mould until it is set, dried or has gone back to normal, and this shows 'James' similar meanings with 'Jebus' and 'Iákōbos'. This fits with 'he massaged' which is an action where a person either holds or massages with the hand the pained part or person until he/she/it is better or feels slight relief. Both meanings of 'James/(ye)Amoz' are similar to 'Iákōbos/he pinches' as they use the same hand movements, they indicate a similar action or the appearance of the same action, and all can be applied to mending nets and taking care of sick people. It is similar to Amoz and Amos.

I do not want to go far with conjecture about what and why 'James' was chosen as an alternative, but there is a strong possibility that the (s) at the end of James is (h) because for whatever reasons the Greek changed words that ended with (h) to end with (s) instead when transliterated from Hebrew/Arabic. This allows one more possibility for the meanings of 'James': ye'āmôs, 'āmôs; يِغامُه ، غامُه 'he suffocates it/him' 'he covers his its face' 'he covers his/its mouth/nose' 'suffocated him/it' 'covered his/its face' 'covered his/its nose or mouth (or both)' and this word is used to describe any kind of suffocation literally or figuratively from smoke, a bad smell or submersion under water, and is used especially to tell a person going under water or having water poured heavily from over the head to cover their mouth/nose, and is also used to describe when a person (especially a small child) is left gasping for air during washing if too much water has been poured and ran heavily or for a long time over the face causing them to almost suffocate. It is from the same root words as Malcham and its meanings can also be seen in the narrative of disciples healing the sick (see Malcham (1Chr.8:9; Zep.1) for all of 'James' possible meanings). It can be seen in the story as fish nets and other fishing tools would be covered for safekeeping, maybe pieces of sackcloth were sewn onto the holes in the fish nets as temporary fixes, and also in treating ill people maybe some were ducked under water or covered with sheets/blankets, or with dry or wet compresses to treat different ailments.

It is also similar to Ibleam (Josh.17:11), Jekamiah (1Chr.2:41), Jokmeam (1Chr.6:68), Bileam (1Chr.6:70), Malcham (1Chr.8:9), Misham (1Chr.8:12), Jekameam (1Chr.23:19), Gamul (1Chr.24:17), Michtam Ps.16. Cp: yaaqoobos, yaqoobos, yaakhooboss, yakhooboss, yeghaamoz, ghaamoz, yegaamos, gaamos, yegaamoz, gaamoz, yeghaamoh, ghaamoh. (Matt.4:21; 10)

John is still 'soaked it/him (in)' 'brothers' 'betrayed' 'sacks' 'sackcloth' 'put/wrap it in sack/sackcloth' and has been used because he, his brother and father are fixing the fish nets when Jesus finds them. As fishermen they are constantly soaked during work; it reflects they are brothers, and also in leaving their father and following Jesus this is a betrayal of their father who they are supposed to work with and for. The reason behind the 'sack/sackcloth' meaning is when people have sacks weaved out of strong fibres (and any other materials where resources are hard to come by) they pick out long pieces of thread from it to store for future use such as to fix other things where fibre stronger than thread is needed to keep the respective object bound together or serving its purpose. This is why he has been given the same name as another character in the same story. (Matt.4:21)

Zebedee; Zebedaíos; شَبَطيه 'tie tightly with rope' 'latticed it' 'latticed-he/him' 'swipe/whip(with a switch or rope)' and it is what anyone making or fixing a fish net would do; ضَبَطيه 'strong-he/him' 'strengthened it' 'strengthened-he/him' 'tight/tightened-he/him/it' 'secure/secured-he/him/it' 'publicly disciplined-he/him'. The words 'lattice' and 'strengthened' is used to described creating a net, girdle, a bed (among other objects) which would need the lattice to hold up the matting/bedding/etc. and the people using it. The reason why this word has been used is because it conjures up the latticing action of mending things with rope, fibres and similar materials, and also because it creates the strong support which is in the weaving and tightening where it begins from one side then moves to the opposite other, e.g. in making a bed or net the rope/fibre/material used would begin from the right frame to the left side and be pulled, tightened to keep it from slacking as the rope is weaved/inserted from right to left, then when the breadth has been latticed, the person doing the work will begin latticing it from the top to the bottom. It creates a strong net/lattice. The word could also be زَبديه 'butter it/spread it' 'butter/spread over him' 'perfume/spread it/him with ointment' 'his drinking bowl'. This too could apply to fixing nets and depending on what was being fixed it may have been spread/covered with some kind of wax (ointment) or butter or any kind of grease product.

The same word شَبَطَيْه can also mean 'swipe/whip(with a switch or rope)' and is relevant as they were exorcizing demons out of ill people in the story as that is an action used when forcing a demon out of the person it has possessed (this is still done in countries who believe in such occurrences of which specifically Yemen and other Arab countries do still practise this kind of exorcism). It is the same/similar to Zabud (1Kgs.4:5), Zebadiah (1Chr.8:15), Josabad (1Chr.12:4), Zabdiel (1Chr.27:2), Ammizabad (1Chr.27:6), Zabbud (Ezra.8:14), Shabbethai (Ezra.10:15). Cp: shebeṭaioh, dhebeṭaioh, zebedaioh. (Matt.41:21; 10)

Syria used for 'thrown/threw' 'injured' as ill people are coming to him to be healed, also 'thrown' as his fame has spread far and wide. (Matt.4:24)

Galilee 'came-to' 'came-for' 'cleared-the' is used as the places he healed because he is going to these places, people are coming to him to be healed, and he is clearing away their ailments.

Decapolis; Dekápolis; تِقَآبولِه ، تِقَآبوليه 'he/she/it meets him' 'he/she/it faces him' 'he/she accept him/it because of good quality (whether material, or a person in character, honesty)' 'he/she accepts him(or it)/ accepts him(or it) reluctantly' (for last meaning see Cabal); تِكعبولِه ، تِكعبوليه 'they packed/filled for him' 'they tried to pack/fill for him'. It is reflected in the story as people coming to see Jesus, and they are coming in 'great multitudes' i.e. they are filling/crowding the area Jesus is at, to see him in order to be cured by him. It is the same as Cabal (Josh.19:27), Cabul (1Kgs.9:12-13). Cp: teqaaboolih, teqaabooleeh, tek'boolih, tek'booleeh. (Matt.4:25)

Jerusalem 'they see-asked-them/the' 'came-saw-asked-them/the', people are coming to see Jesus and to ask him to heal them. (Matt.4:25)

Judaea 'he is called/calls' 'call, or curse' as they are calling to be healed and it is similar to when a person asks God to heal them, and they are suffering from an ailment, and illness is often described as a curse. (Matt.4:25)

Jordan 'they come/are coming home' as the people are coming to Jesus, he is coming to them, once they are healed, they will be comfortable in life, just as a person who comes home after being out; also because he is preaching and teaching them the right ways which will bring them to a better peace. (Matt.4:25)

Raca; rhaká; رَخا 'loosened/loose' and as an insult means not brought up properly or not bring up one's children properly, or immoral and/or allowing his/her children to become immoral; it also means not masculine, not having manly qualities or not behaving manly. Cp: rakhaa. (Matt.5:22)

Mammon; mamōnás, mammōnás; مَمونآه ، مَمّونآه 'security/secured' 'his security/has security' 'is not secured/security' 'does not have security' 'listing of things given' 'listing of wealth/wealth' 'counting and listing of wealth' 'do not count/list/do not 'from me'' and is the same as MENE, MENE ('from me, from me' 'listing and gloating over what was given(to another)'Dan.5:25-30). Mammon has been used to mean believing in the security of wealth, money, goods, etc. that a person owns, and it also means when listing what has been given and done for others. The word has been reflected and its theme repeated throughout Matt.6: people are told they should not make a show of what they do for God or for good, just to be noticed by people that they are fasting, praying, giving charity as this is 'mammon/Mene mene'; people should not try to find security in wealth by saving/hording treasures as it is not the proper thing to worship/be valued as compared to believing in God; the story narrates you cannot love both God and the security of wealth, meaning: if a person devotes himself to securing money and other wealth it becomes his/ her priority and leaves no time, or not enough time, for the worship of God which is the true wealth. The narration further emphasises this in that people should not be concerned about securing an income or thinking about where their food and clothing will come from, they are encouraged to live by the moment and the day like birds and flowers, with no worry nor planning for the security of worldly needs as God will provide them with this (in this world and the hereafter). Cp: mamoonaah, mammoonaah. (Matt.6)

Gentiles; ethnē; يثني ، اثني 'he does it again/twice/doubles it/folds it/repeats it' 'he dissuades/makes leave' 'he is an idolater/pagan' 'idols' 'he praises' 'idol worshippers' 'idolatry/worshipping idols'. Also, from OT meanings of Gentile: 'I will deceive them/the' 'I will mislead them to downfall-them/the'. It is shown in the people who make their expressions sad wanting to be praised for fasting; in Jesus dissuading people from doing the things he warns of and especially from doubling their wealth; the increase of wealth or seeking profit, or even making a living is likened to serving two masters, then likened to worshipping two Gods, and one God (mammon) is an idol; Jesus is dissuading the people of the importance of worldly things; the 'Gentiles' who are idol worshippers are only concerned with these things and this is to their own downfall. This meaning has been used to show that people who run after or seek the security/ mammon of wealth will end up bad/unsecure and it is placed in the sentence to show they are being misled to downfall 'Therefore take no thought, saying, What shall we eat? or, What shall we drink? or, Wherewithal shall we be clothed? (For after all these things do the Gentiles['I will mislead them to downfall-them/the'] seek:) for your heavenly Father knoweth that ye have need of all these things.'. Cp: yfney, ifney. (Matt.6:16-32)

Moses (Exod.4:22-26) 'touched/possessed/was possessed/touched' has been used in connection to the healed leper as when Jesus touches him, he is cured of leprosy then Moses is mentioned. (Matt.8:2-4)

Capernaum (Matt.4:13) 'we buried them' 'buried-sighing/sighed' 'buried-struck and winded' and the 'nahum' part means sighing or puffing meant to attract attention or being hit/punched in stomach until breath is forced out of you. This is reflected in that Jesus gets rid of the illness (buries) the centurion's servant suffers from, but it is Jesus left 'nahum/winded' as he is astonished that the centurion has such faith that Jesus can cure him from a distance without seeing or touching him, but my merely saying it. It is also reflected in one of his disciples asking permission to bury his father to which Jesus refuses with 'Follow me; and let the dead bury their dead' which implies the 'buried' part of the name and the 'winded' as that is what a person would feel or an audience listening to such a response regarding burying a father. (Matt.8)

Abraham 'Pull up/draw up-the' 'clear-the' and **Isaac** (Gen.17:15-19; 18:9-14; 21:1-7) 'he pulls up water little by little' 'swipes/drags water' both which mean bailing up water (Isaac during drought) are invoked to show how 'the children of the kingdom shall be cast out into darkness', just like water is pulled up then poured out into a different vessel, the 'weeping' and 'gnashing of teeth' is denoted by the sufferance and harshness the way bailing is difficult during drought and comes up mostly empty. **Jacob** 'forces open' 'dislocates' 'forces open and takes/usurps' as the people being described as being cast out are being forcibly removed by circumstances, other people, or God. (Matt.8)

Israel 'twisted muscle-the' 'twisted-the' to mean people twisting faith/commandments and is used to contrast this man's blind faith in Jesus' ability to cure just by 'speak the word only, and my servant shall be healed', but also because the meaning of Israel as a word and how people disobey, and disobedience in the stories meant by 'Israel' is contrasted against how the centurion's men obey him 'For I am a man under authority, having soldiers under me: and I say to this *man*, Go, and he goeth; and to another, Come, and he cometh; and to my servant, Do this, and he doeth it. When Jesus heard *it*, he marvelled, and said to them that followed, Verily I say unto you, I have not found so great faith, no, not in Israel.'. (Matt.8:5-10)

Peter's mother-in-law is found ill and cured by Jesus through touch (Moses/touched) which reminds that Peter's original name was **Simon** 'ill/sick/weak'. (Matt.8:14-15)

Gergesenes; Gērasēnoí; جيرَسينوي ، جيرَسينُي 'they ran straight/direct to' 'they ran in my direction' 'came-saw-straight/direct' and the story has the possessed men see and come to Jesus; the demons go out of the men and directly into a herd of pigs; the pigs run straight into the sea; the pig-keepers run direct to the city; the people come straight to see Jesus, and directly tell him to leave. Cp: geyra-seyn<u>oi</u>, geyra-seyn<u>ooi</u> (Matt.8:28-34)

Matthew; Maththaíos; مَضيُّوه ، مَضيُّه 'they passed/left/walked off/gone' 'passed him/walked off-him/he' 'finished/complete it/him/he' 'marked/signed it/him/he' and all meanings are present in the story with emphasis on the 'passed' meanings as Jesus is passing when he sees the character of the same name, and Matthew immediately leaves with Jesus; the beginning of Matt.9 is about getting up and leaving/walking as a paralysed man is cured by Jesus and emphasis is put on 'For whether is easier to say, Thy sins be forgiven thee; or to say, Arise and walk?'. 'finished complete' is about people completing payment and delivery of their taxes of which Matthew is the recipient, and 'marked/signed' is when people submit a payment they owe e.g. debt or if a person is being written a release from any kind of matter there is a signing of a document (receipt or release), and it does not have to be a 'signature' but for illiterate people just making a mark whether by the person being released or paying or the person who is issuing the release document or the receipt. It indicates Matthew recording who or what was paid. It is similar to Midian (Gen.25:2) Cp: ma<u>dh</u>aioh, ma<u>dh</u>aiooh. (Matt.9:1-9)

John 'soaked it/him (in)' 'brothers' 'betrayed' 'sacks' 'sackcloth' 'put/wrap it in sack/sackcloth' used earlier to mean a man soaked/soaking himself or others in water, and wearing clothes made of sack material (John the Baptist), and another **John** (son of Zebedee) used to mean soaked with water as a fisherman, brothers who betray their father Zebedee, and are fixing holes/patching fish nets with fibres or material from sacks.

It is now used here again to show the meaning of 'soaking' 'patching up' but using 'sack' to indicate this as the sacks stronger material/fibres is used to fix many different things which is why it is used here too, by having 'the disciples of John' ask Jesus about fasting (and the use of the wordplay and word-names can be seen as the author could have allowed the Pharisees to ask this, but the point of these stories is to use compound words as names to entertain the audience so characters related to a person-name 'sack/sackcloth' 'soaked it/him (in)' is used) and Jesus' reply is about patching things up or things with holes/gaps in them and about how new wine in old bottles causes them to soak through and burst whereas putting them in new bottles does not: 'Then came to him the disciples of John, saying, Why do we and the Pharisees fast oft, but thy disciples fast not? And Jesus said unto them…No man putteth a piece of new cloth unto an old garment, for that which is put in it to fill it up taketh from the garment, and the rent is made worse…'. (Matt.9:14–17)

'Thou Son of David' is a pun on bread (Jesus) being the child of the 'stone rolling pin of grinding stone' as it makes the dough which will be baked into bread, but also reflects the meanings of 'repeat/try again/keep at it/repeating the same revolving or to and fro motion' 'hesitates/goes and comes/recoils/revolves' as this repetitive motion is how the 'stone rolling pin/David' is used to create the dough, but also because the men are blind their movements are not sure movements, but hesitant and Jesus poses a question to see if they are hesitant in their faith before he heals them. (Matt.9:27)

Note whenever there is a problem which affects the muscle(s) the mention of **Israel** 'twisted muscle-the' is mentioned following the person(s) cure: the centurions servant suffering from palsy followed with 'I have not found so great faith, no, not in Israel.'; the 'dumb man possessed with a devil' when healed he can speak followed with 'It was never so seen in Israel.' (Matt.8:5–10; 9:32–33)

Philip; Phíllipos; فيلّبه ، فيلّبوه 'in its core/pulp', (Phi/Phí/في/'in'), (lip/llip/لب/'middle or core'), (os/ه/its or his); 'pick out/cleanse/remove it' 'so he answers/responds/assists/serves-him' 'he will/should answer/respond/assist/serve-him', (Phílli/فيلِ/pick out or through or remove), (pos/به/ 'it' or 'with/from it'). As one of the disciples he is given power to remove 'unclean spirits' to cleanse lepers and other healing powers. The word 'pick out' is usually used to describe picking out lice, but is also used for picking out, removing, cleansing or meticulously going through a variety of other things. Cp: <u>ph</u>eeliboh, <u>ph</u>eelibooh. (Matt.10)

Bartholomew; Bartholomaíos; بَر ضُلْمَيُه ، بَر ضُلْمَيوه 'good piety/they were caused injustice' and is referring to Jesus telling his disciples that although they do good, for Jesus/God's sake, they will suffer (Jesus and the disciples) and be hated 'Behold, I send you forth as sheep in the midst of wolves: be ye therefore wise as serpents, and harmless as doves. But beware of men for they will deliver you up to the councils, and they will scourge you in their synagogues…And the brother shall deliver up the brother to death, and the father the child; and the children shall rise up against *their* parents, and cause them to be put to death. And ye shall be hated of all *men* for my name's sake: but he that endureth to the end shall be saved.'. It is similar to Adullam and Adullamite (Gen.38:1), Zalmonah (Num.33:), Zalmunna (Judg.8:5–21), Zalmon (Judg.9:48–49). Cp: bar <u>dh</u>olomaioh, bar <u>dh</u>olomaiooh. (Matt.10)

Thomas; Thōmás; ذوماَه ، ذومَه 'lepers/diseased' 'they are lepers' 'conscience' 'their responsibility' 'ostracised/they were ostracised' 'guilty/guilted/blamed' 'they were blamed/guilted' 'insulted/humiliated' 'they were insulted/humiliated'. Like the other disciples his name reflects what their work will be in curing illnesses, but also the hate, injustice, blame, humiliation, accusations, injustice and ostracization they will face due to following Jesus and God's ways and the events as narrated by the story. Similar to Zimran (Gen.25:2), Gatam (Gen.36:11), Zimri; (Num.25), Zemaraim (Josh.18:22), Jotham (Judg.9:7–21), Gittaim (2Sam.4), Zemira (1Chr.7:8), Zimmah (1Chr.6:20). Cp: voomaah, voomah. (Matt.10)

James son of Alphaeus; Iákōbos; يآقوبُس ، يَقوبُس ، يآخوبُص ، يَخوبُص 'he/it pinches' 'he pokes finger into'. Halphaíos; هَلَفَيُه ، هلفيوه 'I will gather/collect it' 'I will pick it up' 'I will wrap it'. The pinching/poking motion is involved with treating the ill and the possessed along with the wrapping motion of wrapping something in cloth or with a cover as ill people would be; حَلَفَيُه ، حَلفيوه 'swore(an oath)-he him' 'they made him swear an oath' along with the 'pinching' the 'swearing' is because they will be put on trial or persecuted for following and helping Jesus as Matt.10 narrates. Cp: yaaqoobos, yaqoobos, yaa<u>kh</u>oobo<u>ss</u>, ya<u>kh</u>oobo<u>ss</u>, hal<u>ph</u>aioh, hal<u>ph</u>aiooh, ḥal<u>ph</u>aioh, ḥal<u>ph</u>aiooh. (Matt.10)

Lebbaeus; Lebbaíos; لِبَّيُه ، لِبّيوه 'his/its core' 'they answered/assisted him' 'served him' 'they are responders/helpful/servants'; لِفّيُه ، لِفّيوه 'wrap it' 'gather/collect it' 'pick it up' 'he goes around in circles-he/him(deceptive not honest)'; لِوَّيُه ، لِوَّيوه 'twisted/twirled it/around it' 'goes around in circles/dishonest/not forthright'. The word meanings show how people's illnesses which are inside their bodies (diseases/wounds/devils) will be treated and removed from their core; the disciples answer and assist Jesus and the ill and vulnerable, also when/if they are persecuted they are told not to think about their responses as it will be God answering instead of them; the actions of wrapping, twirling something around another are also present in the treatment, but also the 'wolves' and the people who will persecute them, even the disciples are asked to be as 'wise as serpents' the serpent being a cunning and deceptive animal (which deceived Adam and Eve into falling out of God's favour). It is similar to Levi (Gen.29:35) (Exod.32:26-29), Libni (Exod.6:17), Libnah (Num.33:20). Cp: lebbaioh, lebbaiooh, lephaioh, lephaiooh, lewwaioh, lewwaiooh. (Matt.10)

Thaddaeus; Thaddaíos; ضَدَّيُه ، ضَدَّيوه 'against him' 'they are against him' and refers to people being against the disciples when persecuting them, people being against each other as described as 'the brother shall deliver up the brother to death, and the father the child: and the children shall rise up against their parents…'; صَدَّيُه ، صَدَّيوه 'blocked/prevented him' 'they blocked/prevented him' and refers to 'whosoever shall not receive you, nor hear your words…'. It is similar to Zedekiah (1Kgs.22:11-28), Besodeiah (Neh.3:6) Cp: dhaddaioh, dhaddaiooh, ssaddaioh, ssaddaiooh. (Matt.10)

Simon the Canaanite; Símon; سِمئُن 'ill/sick/weak' as the disciples will be healing the ill but also the people who do not know Jesus/God's message i.e. they are not aware yet of the right way to worship God; سِمعن 'have heard/to hear/heard' 'obeyed/obey' as they are being asked to obey Jesus/God; Kananaíos; قَنعنَيُه ، قَنعنيوه 'convinced him' 'gave up on him' 'no hope with him' 'raised his/their necks/heads/looked up' 'made him lift his head/crane his neck' and this refers to the people who refuse to listen to Jesus' disciples, they are described as being as hopeless and as doomed as Sodom and Gomorrah, as well as the action the disciples are told to make (dusting off feet) is a gesture showing the respective people in that house/city have no hope, that the disciples give up hope, have been convinced they cannot change them (make them see and turn to God's right ways) and are resolved to have given up on those specific people who will have bad fate because they would not listen/obey, the 'given up' is shown in 'when ye depart out of that house or city, shake off the dust of your feet' which is similar to 'wash your hands of'. It is the exact same word and meaning as Canaan (Gen.9:22-27), Canaanite (Zech.14:20-21). Cp: seem-oon, sim'n, qan'naioh, qan'anaiooh. (Matt.10)

Judas Iscariot; Ioúdas ho Iskariṓtēs; يوُدَه ، يودَه 'his hands' as the disciples are given power to heal through touch like Jesus, also they are told not to take any kind of payment, they are told to salute when they enter houses and greeting includes a handshake or at least a gesture with the hand; but the pivotal part of Judas'/'his hands' role is Jesus identifies Judas as the one who will betray him, emphasised as the one whose hand will reach into the bowl the same time as Jesus which the author of this story has made it unmistakeable in the very naming of Judas 'his hands'. The (ho/هو/him) further reinforces it is Judas, 'him' that did it, that betrayed Jesus as his name reads 'his hands-him'.

Although scholars are confused by his name and by the motives for killing Jesus, the explanation is pretty simple. His name is straightforward as it literally means 'his hands-him'. They also seem confused as to why Judas would betray Jesus, and the problem scholars face is due to the fact they are trying to find real reasons for two fictional characters as if they really existed and therefore need a real and convincing motive(s) for Judas to have betrayed Jesus. The theories presented reach outside the confines of the story such as: Judas would make more sense if he had been an outsider and not part of Jesus' closest disciples; that Judas was more zealous and was displeased with Jesus' ineffective leadership; Judas did this for politico-religious reasons when he saw Jesus not doing what he was supposed to do as a Messiah.

In treating a fictional story as if it were an event in real history and its fictional characters as if they were people who existed, they have ignored the very obvious reason (which would have been clearer if they had read the Biblical name in its correct language (Arabic)) that this was just a story where a character named Judas was supposed to betray and lead to the murder of Jesus. The reasons why he killed him within the story's boundaries are very clear, part of Judas' full name: Judas Iscariot; Iskariṓtēs; اذكَرِعوتيه ، اذكَر عُتيه '(if/when)she poured it heavily/she spilled it' from the word (kr'/كرع) 'spill/spilt' 'pouring/poured heavily' and it indicates the accidental spilling or intentional pouring heavily of any liquid, it also suggests a person is not careful and wasting what is being poured. The word 'Iscariot/cariot' is in the form that a female did the spilling/pouring/wasting. And in the story, it is this action of a woman pouring precious ointment over Jesus' head that caused all his disciples to be upset and point out it is being wasteful; and is the direct cause in the story leading Judas Iscariot (named and created for the very purpose 'his hands-him-(if/when)she spilled/poured heavily') to betray Jesus. Cp: youdah, yoodah hoo iv kari'ooteyh, iv kari'oteyh.

Like all other major and minor characters that have active roles in the Biblical stories, Judas Iscariot has been given the perfect compound word-name describing his role and the events of the story. Neither his name nor role is a mystery with its direct and literal link in the story.

'And as they did eat, he said, Verily I say unto you, that one of you shall betray me. And they were exceeding sorrowful and began every one to say unto him, Is it I? And he answered and said, He that dippeth *his* hand with me in the dish, the same shall betray me...Then Judas, which betrayed him, answered and said, Master, is it I? He said unto him, Thou hast said.'

'...There came unto him a woman having an alabaster box of very precious ointment, and poured it on his head, as he sat at meat. But when his disciples saw *it*, they had indignation, saying, To what purpose is this waste? For this ointment might have been sold for much, and given to the poor. When Jesus understood it, he said unto them, Why trouble ye the woman? for she hath wrought a good work upon me. For ye have the poor always with you; but me ye have not always[he recently told them he will be betrayed and killed]. For in that she hath poured this ointment on my body, she did *it* for my burial. Verily I say unto you wherever this gospel shall be preached in the whole world, *there* shall also this, that this woman hath done, be told for a memorial of her. Then one of the twelve, called Judas Iscariot, went unto the chief priests, And said *unto them*, What will ye give me, and I will deliver him unto you? And they covenanted with him unto thirty pieces of silver. And from that time he sought opportunity to betray him.' So Judas' surname Iscariot 'When she spilled it/poured it heavily' has fulfilled its role.

Even in Judas' repentance the authors still imply his hands and spilling—but this time his hands are guilty of spilling innocent blood: 'Then Judas, which had betrayed him, when he saw that he was condemned, repented himself, and brought again the thirty pieces of silver to the chief priests and the elders. Saying, I have sinned in that I have betrayed innocent blood...And he cast down the pieces of silver in the temple, and departed, and went and hanged himself. And the chief priests took the pieces of silver, and said, It is not lawful for to put them into the treasury, because it is the price of blood. And they took counsel, and bought with them a potter's field, to bury strangers in. Wherefore that field was called, The field of blood, unto this day.'. (Matt.10; 26:1-16; 27:3-8)

When Matt.10 is read, the meaning of the compound word-names of all twelve disciples are represented in the narration of events/descriptions:

Peter 'short/abrupt' 'the kingdom of heaven is at hand'

Both Simons 'to heal all manner of sickness and all manner of disease...heal the sick...nor hear your words...'

Andrew 'go to the lost sheep of Israel...I send you forth as sheep in the midst of wolves...'

James (pinches/pokes) 'Provide neither gold, nor silver, nor brass in your purses' as a person's hand does the motion of pinching/poking around when picking out coins from a purse/bag.

Johns and Zebedee 'Nor scrip for *your* journey, neither two coats, neither shoes...' as sack material can be a scrip and used for garments, and any material soaked (including sackcloth) can be used as a cold press to bring fever down.

Matthew 'These twelve Jesus sent forth...when ye depart out of that house...But when they persecute you in this city, flee ye into another...

Judah Iscariot 'heal the sick, cleanse the lepers, raise the dead, cast out the devils...'

Philip and Lebbaeus 'heal the sick...cast out devils...inquire who in it is worthy...let your peace come upon it...I send you forth as sheep in the midst of wolves...but the Spirit of your Father which speaketh in you...'

Canaanite 'And whosoever shall not receive you, nor hear your words, when ye depart out of that house or city, shake off the dust of your feet...It shall be more tolerable for the land of Sodom and Gomorrah in the day of judgement, than for that city.'

Alphaeus, Bartholomew, Thomas, Thaddaeus 'But beware of men: for they will deliver you up to the councils...And ye shall be brought before governors and kings for my sake, for a testimony against them...and the children shall rise up against *their* parents, and cause them to be put to death...And ye shall be hated of all *men* for my name's sake...but when they persecute you...' (Matt.10)

Sodom and **Gomorrah** were not used only for the meaning of doomed fate/no hope in this part of Matt.10, but they were used for their word-imagery of soot and ashes of which the disciples are likened to wipe/shake off their feet. (Matt.10:14-15)

Gentiles has been used twice in different forms: ethnōn; يثنون ، اثنون 'he/they do it again/double it/fold it/repeat it' 'he/they dissuade/make leave' 'he/they are idolaters/pagans' 'idols' 'praise/praises' 'idol worshippers' 'idolatry/worshipping idols' because Jesus warns them to avoid two areas (the Samaritans and the Gentiles); they are to repeat all the acts of healing, preaching and helping people; they are dissuaded to take or accept any payments in return; if a house is 'praised' i.e. found worthy they are to assist; if the people of the house are not dissuaded and refuse to listen, the disciples are to leave it.

The second form of the word is ethnesin; يثني/اثني سِن/سين '**ethne**': 'he/they do it again/double it/fold it/repeat it-' 'he/they dissuade/make leave-' 'he/they are idolaters/pagans-' 'idols-' 'praise/praises-' 'idol worshippers-' 'idolatry/worshipping idols-'; followed by '**sin**' meanings: 'in the direction of/towards me/in the face of/in front of/straight/straight line/direct/opposite me' and from the OT 'I will deceive them/the' 'I will mislead them to downfall-them/the'. It is reflected in the disciples will be made to face the authorities and they will be oppose them because the disciples have chosen to face God and follow his ways; but it is also a time where the disciples will bear witness of Jesus/God in front of the Gentiles; the Gentiles and other religions are deemed idol worshippers; the disciples are dissuaded from planning their defence and/or speech as God will be speaking direct through them.

It is also used for its OT meaning of 'I will deceive them/the' 'I will mislead them to downfall-them/the', first the disciples are told not to go to them i.e. time is not to be wasted with people who God or the author wants to intentionally mislead and doom, then again in the same manner when the disciples' foretold persecution will be a witness against governors, kings and the people who mislead to downfall 'And ye shall be brought before governors and kings for my sake, for a testimony against them and the Gentiles'. Cp: yfnoon, ifnoon, yfney/ifney-sin/syn. (Matt.10:5- 23)

Samaritans; Samareítēs; سَمَرَيتيه 'told late night story' 'storyteller' 'stayed up late/all night' 'my late-night story' and the warning not to go there has been coupled with not going to the **Gentiles** 'I will mislead them to downfall-them/the'. Samaritans is being used as it has been earlier along with 'Samaria' and other variants of the same word to show the story being told (in this case Matthew) is a fictional story for night entertainment. The authors are plainly telling the audience if you believe these fictional stories it will lead you to your downfall, while making a pun that one fictional story and storytellers—being told in the Gospel of Matthew—cannot be used to heal another fictional story and storytellers 'Samaritan'. Cp: samareiteyh. (Matt.10:5)

Israel has been described as the lost sheep, and in this part of the story it is the people with illnesses, injuries and demonic possessions so it is still representing 'twisted muscle-the' 'twisted-muscle' which often means a physical problem and also disobedience in these stories.

Beelzebub; Beelzeboúl; بيل زِبوال/زِبوَل ، بيل زيبوال/زيبوَل 'with/by-penis/penising-the' and is meant as it was used at (2Kgs.1:2 Baal-zebub). Jesus makes a humorous point the words to the effect 'if this is what they call the Lord ['with/by penising-the'], imagine what they will call his servants'. Cp: beel-zeboo-al/ul, beel-zyboo-al/ul. (Matt.10:25)

Elias; Ēlías; الي يَه/ياه ، ايلي يَه/ياه 'he who/he is' 'yes, it is him' 'which one/which one is he'; الي جَه/جاه ، ايلي جَه/جاه 'he who came/he who came to him' 'he did come/he did come to him' and more than once the narration has Jesus state that Elias who was prophesied to come is John the Baptist, and he states that John the Baptist does not eat nor drink causing the people to believe he is possessed by a devil—if you recall earlier in the OT the 'sons of God' which include Satan in Job, are also described as one and the same in Daniel where the 'son of God' who saves Daniel's friends in the fire is also called an angel; the earlier stories from Genesis onwards whenever an angel appears they do not eat: the angels who Abraham serves a meal to, the angel Manoah serves food to, the angel Gideon serves food to. And now Jesus and the author state not only is John the Baptist the awaited messenger, but that he does not eat and it is presented as proof that he is the prophesied messenger—they do not say he is fasting, the story states he does not eat.

This is further corroborated by a consecutive verse where the narrator makes a point that Jesus is the 'son of Man' and not the 'son of God' because he eats and drinks (which sons of God do not do). Of course, there are other parts of the NT where Jesus is described as the 'Son of God' but are these contradictions that repeat Jesus is the 'son of Man' and the 'son of God' the work of later editors who want Jesus and not John the Baptist to be the son of God, or due to different versions of the same story being compiled in one place (the current NT)? Matt.11 reinforces John the Baptist is the prophesied one to arrive by renaming him 'Elias/he who/he is/yes, it is him/he who came/which one/which one is he/he who came to him/he did come/he did come to him'.

'But what went ye to see? A prophet? yea, I say unto you, and more than a prophet. For this is he, of whom it is written, Behold, I send my messenger before thy face, which shall prepare thy way before thee.' and this is stated following John sending men to check with Jesus if he is the precursor of the one to come and to which Jesus tells them to inform John of all the miracles being performed. So the author is narrating that Jesus was a messenger sent to prepare the way before John the Baptist and goes on to have Jesus say 'For this is he, of whom it is written, Behold I send my messenger before thy face, which shall prepare thy way before thee…And from the days of John the Baptist until now the kingdom of heaven suffereth violence, and the violent take it by force. For all the prophets and the law prophesied until John. And if ye will receive it, this is Elias, which was for to come…'

It goes on with Jesus telling people that they cannot understand this out of child-like ignorance or stupidity and goes on to state that John the Baptist is Elias and is the Son of God 'For John came neither eating nor drinking, and they say, He hath a devil.' Then the narrator points out Jesus is the 'son of Man' 'The Son of man came eating and drinking, and they say, Behold a man gluttoness, and a winebibber, a friend of publicans and sinners…' reminding the audience of the story that Jesus sat to eat with 'publicans and sinners'. It is equivalent to Elijah (1Kgs.17; 18). Cp: illee-yah/yaah, eylee-yah/yaah, illee-gah/gaah, eylee-gah/gaah. (Matt.11:1-19)

Confirming to his disciples that he (Jesus) is not Elias, Jesus asks them 'And they said, Some say that thou art John the Baptist: some Elias; and others, Jeremias, or one of the prophets. He saith to them, But whom say ye that I am?' and Peter responds with Christ, Son of God, but he does not say Elias 'he is/he who' which Jesus has already made clear is John the Baptist.

In Chapter 17, Jesus confirms Elias/Eliah 'he who/he is' 'yes, it is him' 'which one/which one is he' 'he who came/he who came to him' 'he did come/he did come to him' (John the Baptist) has already come—so when the disciples witness the transfiguration: Elias is John the Baptist with Moses speaking to Jesus: 'And his disciples asked him saying, Why then say the scribes that Elias must first come? And Jesus said unto them, Elias shall truly first come, and restore all things. But I say unto you, That Elias is come already, and they knew him not[recall the verses where Jesus points out John's clothing and what the people were expecting to see], but have done unto him whatsoever they listed. Likewise shall also the Son of man suffer of them. Then the disciples understood that he spake unto them of John the Baptist.' Elias/Eliah/'he is/he who' comes before Jesus: 'yes, it is him/he is/Elias' will preach to the people before Jesus; 'he is/Elias' will suffer before Jesus; Jesus is the 'Son of man' who will also suffer; i.e. 'Elias/he is/he who' is John the Baptist who has already come. (Matt.16:13-16; 17:3-13)

Chorazin; Chorazín; خوراصين 'drive away (with violence)/collapse-sweep away' and has been used as its meaning 'collapse-sweep away' fits nicely with what it is compared against: **Tyre** (Josh.19:29) 'imagined' 'left over food' 'left over anything/second-hand (things)' as the city being reprimanded is asked to 'imagine(Tyre)' that if Tyre had seen the miracles seen in Chorazin, Tyre would have repented, and at the same time the meaning of Tyre 'leftovers' can be imagined as being 'swept away' by the meaning of Chorazin which is being warned it will collapse and be swept away for not repenting. It is the same as Chorashan (1Sam.30:30). Cp: <u>kh</u>ora<u>ss</u>een. (Matt.11:21-22)

Bethsaida; Bēthsaïdá; بيت صَيِيدآ ، بيت صَيِيده 'it will/they will be fished/fish' which is being warned that its inhabitants will be punished and contrasted against the matching city-word-name **Sidon** (Gen.10:15) 'fish/to fish' give(s) extra' 'leaves extra/remains' 'deceives' the latter would have caught the fish, i.e. understood and took heed of the miracles and therefore repented, unlike Bethsaida which is being warned with punishment because it is deceiving itself (deceives/Sidon) for not taking the miracles seriously. Cp: beyt-<u>ss</u>ayeedaa, beyt-<u>ss</u>ayeedah. (Matt.11:21-22)

Capernaum 'we buried them' is described as being buried in hell and compared to **Sodom** 'soot' the country that was buried under brimstone and fire. This contrast serves as a warning that even Sodom would have repented had it been given miracles/chances to repent as Capernaum has been given—the latter is being warned it will suffer the same punishment as the former. (Matt.11:23)

The more you read Matthew, the more it becomes evident that the author is having a joke with people who understand the original language with which it was written in (Arabic which is currently believed to be 'Hebrew'); the way the story is narrated and how the sentences are laid out—they are mocking who believe in Jesus and the story being told: 'And in his name shall the **Gentiles** trust' i.e. ethnē; يثني 'he does it again/twice/doubles it/folds it/repeats it' 'he dissuades/makes leave' 'he is an idolater/pagan' 'idols' 'he praises' 'idol worshippers' 'idolatry/worshipping idols'. It relays with Jesus dissuading those he heals not to speak about his miracles; in the Pharisees claiming he worships an idol/devil (Beelzebub) instead of God, in order to dissuade from his ways; It shows Esaias praising the one to come who turns out to be Jesus; 'And in his name shall 'I will lead to their downfall-them/the' trust.' (Matt.12:21)

This is further enhanced with Matt.15:4 'For God commanded, saying, Honour they father and mother: and, He that curseth father or mother, let him die the death.' And this is what happens to Jesus, he is constantly rude to his mother, denies she is his mother, and in the end he dies crucified.

The reference that it is better to insult 'the Son of man' than it is to insult 'the Holy Ghost' then make it clear that both the 'tree' which is the 'Holy Ghost' and the fruit of the tree is 'Son of man' and that they can only be either corrupt or good as one comes out of the other is a direct reference to Jesus' conception. It is saying the jokes about Mary (without mentioning her) are slanderous and blasphemous about God, and these jokes about Mary affect and apply to Jesus who would be a 'bastard[the fruit of the tree]' according to these verses as the 'Holy Ghost' is what impregnated a virgin Mary. This would explain why authors make Jesus so inexplicably rude to Mary, the author is making this evident that Jesus wants nothing to do with her, he is ashamed because she has caused him shame. I do not know if the verses Matt.12:31-32 were added by a later editor who wanted to correct what verses 33, 46-50 clearly show of a Jesus and narration angry at Mary for conceiving him illegitimately, but it is evident there are contradicting ideas and drive between these verses in the same chapter and regarding the same topic. 'Wherefore I say unto you, All manner of sin and blasphemy shall be forgiven unto men: but the blasphemy *against* the *Holy* Ghost shall not be forgiven unto men. And whosoever speaketh a word agains the Son of Man[Jesus], it shall be forgiven him: but whosoever speaketh against the Holy Ghost[God], it shall not be forgiven him, neither in this world, neither in the *world* to come. Either make the tree good, and his fruit good; or else make the tree corrupt, and his fruit corrupt: for the tree is known by *his* fruit.'

'While yet he talked to the people, behold, *his* mother and his brethren stood without, desiring to speak with him. Then one said unto him, Behold, thy mother and thy brethren stand without, desiring to speak with thee. But he answered and said unto him that told him, Who is my mother? and who are my brethren? And he stretched forth his hand toward his disciples, and said, Behold my mother and my brethren! For whosoever shall do the will of my Father which is in heaven, the same is my brother, and sister, and mother.'

It is not unusual of the Biblical authors to blame and/or punish the female character in the stories by the male authors, this has been a theme repeated in Adam and Eve, Deborah and Jael, Jonathan's mother, Jezebel, the 'strange women' kings and commoner marry; and here in Matthew, the Holy Ghost a male God as 'Father' and his male fruit/son is excused while the human female/mother is not. Nothing is mentioned about punishment or forgiveness for those who blaspheme or insult her, but her derogatory treatment by her own son and the author is made very clear.

Mary 'pass along' 'pass/cross/pass by' 'pass along the river/sea' as the story discusses what happens to Jesus when he comes to his own country, but also from the beginning of the chapter Jesus 'went out of the house, and sat by the sea side' and in the rest of the narration either people in his parables are passing somewhere or the audience listening also go somewhere. (Matt.13)

James 'he/it pinches/pokes' the word Iákōbos/يقوبس/يَخبُص 'pinch(es)' also means to say something from a story or said by someone else (the modern equivalent would be to 'quote') and this meaning is used in Matt.13, and 'pokes' means to make a mess or jump from thing to thing causing confusion and this too is reflected: the people are wondering where he is getting this knowledge from i.e. they seem to be puzzled that he is 'educated' as in 'knowledgeable' knows what people who read books/texts know; the same is reflected in his speaking in parables, instead of straightforward speech, he is giving the ideas in short stories, the 'knowledge/understanding' condensed in short snatches of sentences to help the people understand it better; even the content of the parables, sowing as when seed is taken it is similar to a pinching motion, and depending on what is being sowed may not be just scattered into the ground, but planted with care (such as herb seeds are planted individually and not scattered from a standing position). (Matt.13)

Joses; Iōsēs; يوسييح 'he goes wandering and seeking' as this is what Jesus does in most of the NT including Matt.13, but also the people come seeking him, characters in his parables come and seek to do specific things, and the people wonder when he has come across all the 'wisdom'; يوسييه 'he offends it/him' 'it offends/it offends him' and the people are described of being 'offended' by Jesus' 'wisdom' and 'mighty works'—they do not approve of his behaviour. It is the same word as Josiah (2Kgs.22-23). Cp: yooseeyḥ, yooseeyh. (Matt.13)

Simon 'ill/sick/weak' 'have heard/to hear/heard' 'obeyed/obey' have been used as the people of Jesus' country seem to believe he is too insignificant than to have this great knowledge and 'mighty works', and they form this opinion when they hear his speeches/preaching while he teaches in their synagogue. The people come to hear and understand Jesus from the beginning of this chapter, and throughout it the narration speaks of people hearing/not hearing and understanding/not understanding. The parables are about good, strong plants and weak plants and this too is linked to hearing and understanding God's instructions.

Judas here is **Judah** just as in Matt.1:2 Judas means 'Judah son of Jacob'. The way to read if Judas/yudah 'his hands' is meant or if it is Judas/Judah/yud'aa 'he is called' is by taking into account its context (which is the case for all word-names in the Biblical stories) as the narration tells exactly which word is meant of which the Greek transliteration of words ending with an 'a/ا' or 'h/ـه' sound/letter are changed/written into (s).

Judah is used for 'he is called/calls' and 'to make a claim' 'make a false claim or an unproven claim' as Jesus is calling people to the way of God, and when teaching people he is still calling them to God; this is also expressed at his people's displeasure when they mention the names his family members are called by, and the reaction of the people is that he is making 'false claims' which cause them to be offended. (Matt.13)

Herodias; Hērōdiás; حيروديآه 'incited against-he/him' 'bent his neck(physically)-he/him' 'of inciting against' 'became stubborn-he/him' 'of becoming stubborn' 'causes problems between others-he/him' 'went to one side (while moving)-he/him' 'focused on with malicious intent-he/him' 'of malicious intent'; حيروضيآه 'incited against-he/him/she incited against-he/him' 'got worked up/she got worked up-he/him' 'of getting worked up' 'folded/coiled into itself ready to strike' 'of folding/coiling into itself'. It is the same as Herod, but in a slightly different form with 'he/him' or feminised suffix. Both Herod and Herodias' name in this chapter are reflected in their direct role of causing the imprisonment and execution of John the Baptist; the narration in having her daughter bring her John's head further emphasises the meaning of her name and role that she plotted John's demise and in how she used her daughter to get Herod worked up. Cp: ḥeyroodyaah, ḥeyroodhyaah. (Matt.14)

Philip has been used as 'in its core/pulp' as the narration mentions 'mighty works do show themselves in him' and Herod believes the dead John the Baptist has returned to life inside Jesus; 'pick out/cleanse/remove it' 'so he answers/responds/assists/serves-him' 'he will/should answer/respond/assist/serve-him' as John was killed (removed) because John opposed Herod's marriage to his brother Philip's wife; it is further emphasised with Herod fearing the people will assist John and turn against Herod; in Herodias' daughter assisting her mother in securing John's execution, and in Herod promising to give Herodias' daughter whatever she requests, and her request is to be served John's head, but Herod answers her request, i.e. serves her requests. (Matt.14:3)

Gennesaret; Gennēsarét; جنّي سريت ، جنّي صريط 'demon-walked' 'demon-walked in the early dark' 'demon-went/left' 'demon-made path' and it is the name given to the land in the story after Jesus scares the disciples when people see him walking on water towards them and believe it is a demon (spirit) walking on the sea and coming towards them, it is described as if a demon is walking on a path, and when they recognise it is Jesus even Peter wants to try walking on this strange path which is water: 'And when the disciples saw him walking on the sea, they were troubled, saying, It is a spirit; and they cried out in fear...Then they that were in the ship came and worshipped him, saying, Of a truth thou art the Son of God. And when they were gone over, they came into the land of Gennesaret.'.

It is also جن نيصَريت 'came-assisted/helped to succeed' 'came-the helpers to succeed/victors/supporters/aides' (helpers/helped to succeed/victors/supporters(ed)/aides' is also meaning of Nazareth/Nazarene. Cp: neyssareit, and is reflected in the final part of the chapter where the people of this land learn that Jesus and his group have arrived at, send out word and the crowds bring all their ailed and diseased to be cured by Jesus. It is from the word (nēsarét/نيصَريت) from (nssr/نصر) the noun and verb used in Arabic describing the first Christians who assisted Jesus in spreading God's words, the word itself means 'help to succeed/victor' which is what Jesus, his disciples and the people who would end up being called 'Christians' were first called, and it is this word and noun which gives the real city misnomered 'Nazareth', because its name in Palestine and in Arabic is not called 'Nazereth' (which is also an Arabic word but a fictional name in the Bible) but a-Naassira named after the first Christians who were Arabs. Cp: genney sareit, genney sareiṭ, gen neyssareit. (Matt.14:22-36)

The Pharisees in Matt.15 are made to be from **Jerusalem** so 'came-saw-asked-them/the' can be reflected in that they **came** from Jerusalem, they **saw** the disciples not washing their hands before eating, they **see** Jesus and **ask** him about it.

Now watch how the Biblical authors weave words into names and relay the meanings between the word-names and the events in the narration: **Jesus** 'bread' 'broke/ate bread' is called 'Thou Son of David' a pun on 'bread/Jesus' being the child of the '**David**/stone rolling pin of grinding stone' as it makes the dough which will be baked into bread and also for 'David/repeat/try again/keep at it/repeating the same revolving or to and fro motion' 'David/hesitates/goes and comes/recoils/revolves' as Jesus is hesitant to help this woman and the word meanings are used in the same way as already used in Matt.9:27. The bread and crumbs as a result of breaking bread are used in the story in the woman's response which wins Jesus over and removes his hesitation to help her.

Tyre 'left over food' and **Sidon** 'leaves extra/remains' is used because Jesus refuses to give his help (his bread) to the woman and in her answer that even crumbs i.e. the leftovers of food are given to dogs (the Canaan woman).

Canaan 'given up on' 'given up any hope' 'resolved to fate or what will happen' 'look up (crane neck and lift head)' to look up (crane neck and lift head) from a lower position to who or what you are looking at is used because the woman is begging Jesus who refuses to help her and there is no hope because he does not respond at all, she is looking up at him imploring him, and this is further enhanced with her being likened to a dog by Jesus and the narration to which she replies 'Truth, Lord: yet the dogs eat of the crumbs which fall from their masters' table.' And this word-imagery is of a dog looking up at his master waiting for crumbs to fall. (The language does sound racist, but if the meanings of the word are understood correctly it can be seen the original author (of at least these verses) does not have racism in his intentions but only the meanings of the words which make the story funny, but unfortunately later generations and especially the west will take these word-names and consider them actual people/nations)

Israel 'twisted muscle-the' 'twisted-the' and because Jesus says 'I am not sent but unto the lost sheep of Israel' it means although her daughter is suffering from an affliction, it is deemed she is not lost, i.e. Jesus is looking for the people with the most chronic conditions of 'twisted muscle-the' and this does not mean only those with physical ailments, but those who have lost their religious/spiritual ways, or have never known the correct way to God.

'Then Jesus went thence, and departed into the coasts of Tyre and Sidon. And, behold, a woman of Canaan came out of the same coasts, and cried unto him, saying, Have mercy on me, O Lord, *thou* son of David; my daughter is grievously vexed with a devil. But he answered her not a word. And his disciples came and besought him, saying, Send her away; for she crieth after us. But he answered and said, It is not meet to take the children's bread, and to cast *it* to dogs. And she said, Truth, Lord: yet the dogs eat of the crumbs which fall from their masters' table. Then Jesus said unto her, O woman, great *is* thy faith: be it unto thee even as thou wilt. And her daughter was made whole from that very hour.' (Matt.15:21-28)

Magdala; Magdalá; مَجدلا 'a throwing around' 'has fits/having fits/possessed by demons' as people who have fits fall to the ground and convulse on the ground, it is believed by many to be being possessed by a demon(s). In this part of the story it is named because before leaving to this place Jesus healed the possessed (with a devil) daughter of the Canaan woman who had, and also the ill and injured were brought in 'great multitudes…and cast them down at Jesus' feet' whom he healed. The same and similar to Magdiel (Gen.36:43), Migdol (Exod.14:2-3), Migdal-gad (Josh.15:37), Migdal-el (Josh.19:38), Gedaliah (2Kgs.25:22-25), Giddalti (1Chr.25:4), Giddel (Ezra.2:47), Igdaliah (Jer.35:4). Cp: magdalaa. (Matt.15:22,29-39)

Caesarea Philippi; Kaisáreia hē Philíppou; كَيسآريا حي فِليبّو 'broke it-living/alive-in his/its core/middle' as Peter answers and is correct that 'Jesus/break bread' is 'Christ' 'circle/cake of bread' which is inevitably broken and nutrition gained from eating what is its core, linking both names Jesus and Christ to the meaning of Kaisáreia hē Philíppou: 'And Simon Peter answered and said, Thou art Christ, the Son of the living God.'

'Keep secret-living/alive-in his/its core/middle' as the narration explicitly states this that the disciples are asked to keep it a secret that Jesus is 'Jesus the Christ' i.e. 'broke/ate bread-the circle of bread' (and again this is the author of Matt. making a joke that Jesus Christ is telling his disciples who have guessed correctly what he is to keep it a secret because he is a cake of bread meant to be broken): 'Then charged he his disciples that they should tell no man that he was Jesus the Christ.'

'broke it-living/alive-so respond/assist/serve' and means they have to follow Jesus' instructions that **Kaisáreia**/Jesus/broke bread, who will be resurrected **hē**/living/alive, and they have to follow him **Philíppou**/ respond/assist serve: 'Then said Jesus unto his disciples, If any man will come after me, let him deny himself…and follow me. For whosoever will save his life shall lose it: and whosoever will lose his life for my sake shall find it…For the Son of man shall come in the glory of his Father…There be some standing here, which shall not taste of death, till they see the Son of man coming in his kingdom.'

It is also قَيصآريا حي فِليبّو 'short/shortcoming is he-stays/contains-so respond/assist/serve' and is connected directly to Peter whose name means 'short/stubby/abrupt' will be given the 'keys of the kingdom of heaven' which will contain and stay whatever Peter 'looses' or 'binds' in earth. 'That thou art Peter, and upon this rock I will build my church; and the gates of hell shall not prevail against it. And I will give unto thee the keys of the kingdom of heaven: and whatsoever thou shalt bind on earth shall be bound in heaven: and whatsoever thou shalt loose on earth shall be loosed in heaven.' Cp: kaisaareiaa ḥey phileebboo, qaissaareiaa ḥey phileebboo. (Matt.16:13-28)

Simon Bar-jona; Símon; Simon is still 'heard/listened/obeyed' and Bariōnás; بَر عوناَه 'piety/good-helped him' 'innocent of/disowned responsibility of-helped him' 'be passed/be surpassed/pass/surpass/go beyond/ get ahead of-helped him'; and as earlier in Hagar and other stories where there is 'bar/good/piety' mentioned and a person listening—he/she is listening to God, and this is supported by the narration of Jesus giving Peter a new nickname 'Simon Bar-jona' telling Peter Simon that the truth of who/what he (Jesus) is has been revealed (told) to Peter by God; it is reflected that Peter is innocent of receiving any help from man in knowing the correct answer; it is reflected in no matter how 'short/stubby' 'his stub of rock' 'his smooth rock' (meanings of 'Peter' 'And I say also unto thee, That thou art Peter, and upon this rock I will build my church…') Peter is, he will surpass others in the reward in heaven to the degree nothing can go beyond what Peter chooses to bind or release in earth and the same will be mirrored in heaven; and due to this Peter, just like the literal word-meanings of 'Peter', is likened to a rock used in building: 'And Jesus answered and said unto him, Blessed art thou, Simon Bar-jona: for flesh and blood hath not revealed *it* unto thee, but my Father which is in heaven.'. Cp: sim'n bar-'oonaah. (Matt.16:17)

Jericho (Num.22:1) gets an additional wordplay from the NT author(s) of Matt.20 than it had at Numbers: yĕrîḥô; جيريهُ ، بيريهُ 'they see him/it' 'he makes them see' 'came his sight' 'came showed him/made him see' and this directly relays the event of the two blind men who Jesus restores vision for. Cp: yeireeho, geireeho. (Matt.20:29-34)

Jerusalem is used twice in this chapter in the way it is always used: 'they see-asked-them/the' 'came-saw-asked-them/the' 'they saw-arrived/public apology-them/the' 'came-saw-arrived/public apology-them/the' first because if the disciples are seen taking the donkey/colt, they will be asked about it; then when Jesus arrives and the people see him, they ask about him: 'And when they drew nigh unto Jerusalem, and were come to Bethphage…then sent Jesus two disciples…And if any man say ought unto you, ye shall say, The Lord hath need of them…' 'And when he was come into Jerusalem, all the city was moved, saying, Who is this?'. (Matt.21:1-3, 10)

Olives (mount of) is still being mistranslated and still means: 'fled away-them/the' 'flitted/flicked/quickly hid something throwing it into narrow space-them/the' as Jesus is telling his disciples to steal the ass and its colt, and only to provide an explanation if seen and asked, the owner is expected to send them immediately because God has required them. The meaning 'suddenly split open-them/the' and 'made shake-them/ the' as even if riding only the donkey, Jesus' legs would be splayed across it, but since he is riding both at the same time, he will have his legs split further apart which is why the narration has him need his disciples to 'set *him* thereon.'. (Matt.21:1)

Sion/Zion used as 'bad' because a donkey is considered a bad, stubborn animal and when linked to a character in the OT stories it has been to show the bad/wrong/stubbornness of the character (Balaam and his donkey, Samson and the donkey jawbone), but also to ride an animal that is either not strong enough nor normal to ride (such as a sheep or lamb) or is too young/frail to ride (such as a very young donkey) is considered cruel behaviour by people whose lives involve the upbringing and use of such animals. The meaning of 'swept away' is also indicated by branches of trees being cut down and thrown on the ground as tree branches (especially palm tree branches) make the brush called 'misswana' which is the same word from 'Zion/ssion/brush/sweep away'. (Matt.21.5-8)

Hosanna; hōsanná; هوسَنّه ، هوسَنّآ 'he made it straight/aligned it' 'he comes towards us/in our direction' and this is what Jesus does and the people whose direction he is arriving towards are exclaiming 'And the multitudes that went before, and that followed, cried, saying, Hosanna to the Son of David: Blessed *is* he that cometh in the name of the Lord…'; 'son of David' is used for the meanings of 'grinding stone rolling pin/hesitating/returning over and over again/repeating' for its link to bread but to also emphasise that Jesus came straight to the people. It is similar to Hasenuah (1Chr.9:7), Senuah (Neh.11:9). Cp: hosannah, hosannaa. (Matt.21:9)

Bethpage; Bēthphagḗ; بيفشَجه ، بيفشَجي 'he/they will spread his legs wide/will splay his legs' and describes Jesus having to splay his legs wide over two animals, both the ass and the colt. It is the equivalent of Abishag (1Kgs.1:1-4); بيذجه ، بيذجي 'lamb' and is used to describe the offspring of a sheep, but here in Matt. it has been used to refer to the colt, the donkey's young from the word (bvg/بذج) 'lamb', and it is not only used to describe the newly-born lamb, but even a young lamb that has grown and become strong or big enough to slaughter, the word is used to refer to the young of a specific ewe. The word is used in Matt. in the same manner to refer to the foal which Jesus will arrive on and it is made clear that Jesus will arrive riding on both the ass and its foal at the same time—it is possible, as indicated by the word-name choice that the original idea was to have him riding in on a young lamb/or baby donkey, but because the authors saw it unlikely that a small animal could carry a grown man decided to add a mature animal with Jesus splayed over both of them. 'Behold, thy king cometh unto thee, meek, and sitting upon an ass, and a colt the foal of an ass…And brought the ass and the colt, and put on them their clothes, and they set *him* thereon. Cp: beyp͟h*sh*ageh, beyp͟h*sh*agey beyvvageh, beyvvagey. (Matt.21:1-7)

The whole event including compound word-names and symbolisation is linked to what Jesus will do as soon as he arrives, which is enter the 'temple of God', throw things around and clear it out while accusing people of robbery. The **Bethphage**/donkeys taken away and ridden represent the people in the temple whom Jesus throws out; The **Zion**/bad is Jesus' actions, and the conduct of the people whom he throws out (thievery). The **Zion**/sweep away, **Hosanna**/make straight, **Galilee**/'came-to' 'came-for' 'cleared-the' is the buyers and sellers being thrown out of the temple i.e. restoring it for worship only—making it straight; and **Nazareth**/'I warned' the dialogue of Jesus is a warning to them.

Bethany; Bēthanía; بيثانيا 'with the other one' 'did it again'; بيتانيا 'with/of the figs' 'girl/daughter' 'my girl/daughter' 'of girls/girlish' and refers to Jesus entering the temple again and the repeated disturbance/annoyance he causes the scribes and chief priests. 'with the other one' is present in the questions he asks them; in that they fear giving one answer or the other; then they have to answer which son out of two was obedient to his father; the man who owns a vineyard and keeps sending his servants and eventually his son to be killed while requesting their share of the harvest; and ends with Jesus telling the elders and priests that the kingdom will be taken from them and be given to another people; the fig tree Jesus wants to eat from but upon finding no edible fruit curses it and it withers/dies. Cp: beyfaaneeaa, beytaaneeaa. (Matt.21:17-46)

Herodians; Hērōdianoí; حيرودِانوي ، حيروديانوي 'they incited against-he/him' 'of inciting against' 'of bent neck(physically)' 'of becoming stubborn' 'they are stubborn' 'of causing problems between others-he/him' 'of causing problems between others-he/him' 'of going to one side (while moving)' 'they are going to one side(direction)' 'they are focused on with malicious intent' 'of malicious intent'; حيروضِانوي ، حيروضيانوي 'of inciting against' 'they incited' 'they incited against' 'of getting worked up' 'they got worked up/work up' 'they folded/coiled into itself ready to strike'. This is reflected in the narration that when the Pharisees seek 'how they might entangle him in *his* talk.' They choose to send their disciples 'with the Herodians'. Cp: ḥeyroodiaanoi, ḥeyroodeeaanoi, ḥeyroodhiaanoi, ḥeyroodheeaanoi. (Matt.22:15-16)

Caesar; Kaisar; كيسَر 'broke' 'keep/like secret'; قيصَر 'shortened/shortcoming/failed to complete or obey'. Both meanings are used in the story: they are trying to break('caesar/broke') Jesus (whose character name means 'break bread') by getting him in trouble with the authorities which he avoids by responding anything due to Caesar should be paid to Caesar and anything due to God should be paid to God—therefore he cannot be blamed for 'failing to pay and obey/caesar' the taxes to Caesar (which is why this name was chosen for its meaning as pronounced in Arabic wordplay). Cp: kaisar, qaissar. (Matt.22:15-22)

Moses is used for 'entangled/caused problems/provoked problems or fighting' as the Sadducees are attempting to provoke Jesus to cause problems which will lead to his own problems with the authorities, including giving the priests, Sadducees, Pharisees an excuse to physically harm him as the aim is to get Jesus to say something provocative (moses); 'touched/possessed/was possessed/touched' the theory they present to him is about 'touching/possessing' as euphemism and literally about brothers who consecutively die and all marry the same woman, in turn, and therefore have all 'touched(moses)' her sexually and 'possessed(moses)' her as a wife, the problem they present to Jesus is that if there is such a thing as resurrection then which husband in the afterlife will have a claim (possess) to the wife since they were all her husbands during life. (Matt.22:23-31)

Abraham and **Isaac** are used to show how God brings back the dead because of their meanings of 'pulling up/bailing' water (water being the source of life) so God can easily bring up the dead back to life just as people continue with life whether they pull up plenty of water or need to 'swipe/scrape' it up in small amounts. **Jacob** is used because of its meaning 'looks after' (children/house/affairs) as God is looking after living people just like a babysitter takes care of babies and children; the meaning of 'usurp' as he will replace the dead people by bringing them back to life—which forces a thing open to claim it (death is forced open and the life brought back). (Matt.22:29-32)

Moses has been used for 'squeeze him/it' 'suck him/it' 'touched/possessed/was possessed/touched' 'entangled/caused problems/provoked problems or fighting': Jesus is warning people not to do as the 'Pharisees' who 'sit in Moses' seat' as it leads to problems of which is mentioned they mislead people which prevents them entering heaven and cheating them out of their fortunes. They 'squeeze him/it' by burdening people with more than they can handle while the Pharisees do not even touch ('touched/possessed/was possessed/touched') these burdens likened to not lifting a finger to help. They 'suck him/it' is reflected in the scribes and Pharisees exploiting and using up vulnerable and trusting widows' fortunes using religion as the vehicle to take advantage of the vulnerable.

Rabbi; rhabbí; رَبّي 'my god/parent/teacher' 'brought up/brought up properly/bring up/bring up properly' 'grew/grew well/grew or raised many' 'disciplined' 'diluted and mixed with water'. Just as where the word has featured before in the OT, in this verse it also means: teacher, discipliner, parent, god, master, the grower, and anyone who brings someone up or teaches or grows children/animals/plants/etc. Cp: rabbee.

In Matt.23 it is used specifically to mean 'my master/God/father' and also to mean the accumulation/hording of things the people Jesus accuses (scribes and Pharisees) of loving more than religion/God—there is a word also based on the root word (rb/رب) which is (yaarabbah/يارَبّاه/يارَبّه) which is used to mean 'plenty of/loads of(thing spoken about)' (it can also mean 'oh god' 'dilutes' as they are all based on the same word and its meanings). Rabbi is the same and/or similar to: Arbah (Gen.35:22-29), Rabbath (Deut.3:11), Rabbah (Josh.13:25), Arab (Josh.15:52), Beth-arabah (Josh.15:61), Irpeel (Josh.18:27), Rabbith (Josh.19:20), Rephaiah (1Chr.3:21), Beth-rapha (1Chr.4:12), Rephah (1Chr.7:25), Rapha (1Chr.8:2), Jeribai (1Chr.11:46), Rephael (1Chr.26:7), Arabia (2Chr.9:14), Beth-rabbim (Cant.7), Jareb (Hos.5:13-15), Beth-arbel (Hos.10:14).

'...and to be called of men, Rabbi, Rabbi. But be not ye called Rabbi: for one is your master, *even* Christ; and all ye are brethren. And call no man your father upon the earth: for one is your Father, which is in heaven. Neither be ye called masters: for one is your Master, even Christ.' Shows the meaning of teacher, discipliner, parent, god, master.

'But woe unto you, scribes and Pharisees...for ye devour widows' houses...for ye compass sea and land to make one proselyte...which say, Whosoever shall swear by the temple, it is nothing; but whosoever shall swear by the gold of the temple, he is a debtor! *Ye* fools and blind: for whether is greater, the gold or the temple that sanctifieth the gold? And whosoever shall swear by the altar, it is nothing; but whosoever shall swear by the gift that is upon it, he is guilty...' and this shows the meaning of accumulation/hording of things which Jesus accuses scribes and Pharisees of loving more than religion/God.

Note that although the narration is directed against 'scribes and Pharisees' (and also Sadducees in Matt.) this specific narration of Matt.23 does not go against the importance of 'piled things(mistranslated as 'holy/sanctify' in the OT)' which is the essence and most important thing in the OT stories.

In fact, the text of Matt.23 supports the importance and meanings of 'qodesh/piled' 'hekal/he will eat('mistranslated as 'temple')' as it states 'for whether is greater, the gold, or the temple[hekal/he will eat] that sanctifieth the gold?' i.e. the single/individual gold is not more than the 'temple/he will eat' where the gold is 'sanctified[piled/qodesh]' (in Greek, the word will be 'sanctified' but the story is taken from an original Arabic (Hebrew) story where the word is 'qodesh/piled' and mistranslated as 'holy/sanctified/consecrated'). The same in 'for whether *is* greater, the gift, or the altar that sanctifieth the gift?' i.e. what is greater, the individual gift or the altar where gifts are 'sanctified/piled/qodesh'—and remember the whole point in the OT stories is about piling lots and lots of produce for God on the altar.

If Matthew is read correctly and objectively, its narrative does not support the 'Jesus/Christian' story—it mocks it, it rails against it with humour. It would only become the basis of the Christian religion much later when these stories would become popular and re-found in a region and country(ies) not the original country of these stories or their authors and original audience. It is possible that the editing in the NT stories has been done by pro-Christian-belief editors or unbiased editors, but where the rhetoric against people of the Jewish religion becomes prominent—the accusations made against characters and the use of the word 'Jews' is only used as a word-name, a pun with specific meanings of the basic word 'jew' linking it to what is happening in the respective stories no different than how the word 'jew' was used in the OT, and not as 'Jew' as in the person of the Jewish religion. Like most of the OT stories they existed (or at least began) for non-religious purposes (to be explained later), it is possible that Matthew which pokes fun at an opposing and new religion was the first story to inspire the NT stories, which do not differ much from its narrative, but it could also be because Matthew mocks these stories that it was written after an original 'pro-Jesus/Christianity' NT story became more popular: the nature of the editing and the fact of not knowing the true dates these stories were created does not allow a definite conclusion of which came first (except as a non-religious story in its original form) as by the time they were made into text is a much later date than when they probably circulated (this is because most of the region would hear these stories through storytelling(oration)), this is further exacerbated by scholars who have obfuscated the fictional Biblical stories with historical fact, and confused and linked fictional characters with people/figures who may (or may not) have existed in reality which has created a mess of what the history of the region is, and what is correct (in relation to the Bible and the region where the Biblical stories are believed to have 'occurred'). (Matt.23)

Zacharias/**Zachariah** for 'reminded-him/he' 'mentioned-he/him' 'remembered-him/he' for reminding the people of obeying and not disobeying God's laws, and was consequently stoned to death at 2Chr.24:20-21. But in the original story this character is the son of Jehoiada and not the son of Barachias/ Berechiah (Zechariah of the Book of Zechariah is Berechiah's son). But again, this is not important to the Biblical authors because it is not about getting right or proving a genealogy when they are creating fictional characters: the Zechariah that was stoned to death between the house and court of the house of the Lord has been made son of Berechiah in Matthew because the compound word used for his current father 'Berechiah' suits the storyline.

Berechiah (1Chr.3:20) for one of its meanings: 'made last-he/him' because God is making last as witness and punishment against them every drop of blood from the first person innocently killed in the Biblical stories (Abel/Gen.) up until Zechariah (2Chr.24:20-21). The reason **Abel** is used is not only so the span can last (Berechiah) for a long time, but for its meaning of 'will shake fat of sheep' as this too is done at altars, where fat is offered to God and also eaten by people. The blood and fat are also reminders (Zecharias(ah)) of what is served at the altars, and important to the OT stories. (Matt.23:35)

Jerusalem 'came-saw-asked-them/the' 'they see-asked-them/the' 'they saw-arrived/public apology-them/the' 'came-saw-arrived/public apology-them/the' 'they see-rocks-them/the' 'came-saw-rocks-them/ the' is used because of its meanings and the events they are reminded of: prophets coming to them, they seeing the prophets, the prophets asking them to follow God's ways and to see wrong from right, the people stoning the prophets, God asking them to remember what has already been witnessed. (Matt.23:37)

Daniel (1Chr.3:1) is used for 'bowed-the' 'he is bowed-is the' 'lowered/low-the' 'he is lowered/low-is the' 'facing the ground-the' 'he is facing the ground-is the' 'with face on ground-the' 'his face on ground-with the' 'guilted-the' 'he is guilted-is the' and what it means is there will be a statue/image of an animal/beast brought into the place where the qodesh haqqodashim is piled and the meaning of 'Daniel/'bowed-the'/ 'facing the ground-the' means that people will worship statues of animals/beasts/deities instead of God who is supposed to be worshipped, that proper worship of God (as according to the OT stories) will cease and when this ceases the piling/qodesh of produce ceases which brings on God's punishments where even bread will no longer be available (among devastation of other kinds such as wars, plagues, etc.).

Similarly, the use of **Judaea** used in connection with this event 'Then let them which be in Judaea flee into the mountains...' i.e. those 'Judaea/calling out/calling for' protection or food or anything which people who worship ask from God—they are being told to flee because they are calling to/worshipping a statue made by man, but the 'real' God's punishment is coming for them. (Matt.24)

Noe; Nōe; نوي 'warned/brought to attention/reminded' 'the stone/seed(of fruit)' 'intended' 'the intentions/ unspoken thoughts'. This has been used to specifically depict intentions that are not voiced, the person (God in this instance) has already decided and set his mind to punish the people and send the flood, but instead of the story of Genesis where Noah was used earlier to depict warning/bringing of attention of a punishment (in Noah's, the flood/this story's, 'your Lord doth come' i.e. punishment) instead here it is used to show there will be no warning of God's intentions and when he will send punishment or the 'Son of

God' these things remain in his 'Noe' (secret intentions) just like a stone or seed is hidden in the middle of fruit—it has been decided/is there, but no one knows of it or can see it. But the story of Matt.24:37 is still serving as a reminder/warning of not to wait until God's punishment arrives. It is equivalent to Noah (without the called out loud meanings). Cp: <u>kn</u>owee. (Matt.24:37)

Caiaphas; Kaïáphas; كَيّآفَه 'how-he/him' 'they figured out how/thought about it' 'thought how/about-he/him' 'of thinking things/in good mood to think about matters'; قّيّآفَه 'of turning back of head to/turning (his)back towards' 'turned back of his head or his back towards-he/him'. Both meanings are supported in the narration: the elders assemble to figure out how to kill Jesus without getting caught. Assassinating Jesus by surprise, or killing anyone by surprise is the same as what is meant by 'with his back towards/turned': 'Then assembled together the chief priests, and the scribes, and the elders of the people, unto the palace of the high priest, who was called Caiaphas. And consulted that they might take Jesus by subtility, and kill *him*.'. Ç̧p: kayeeaa<u>ph</u>ah, qayeeaa<u>ph</u>ah. (Matt.26:1-5)

Bethany (Matt.21:17-46) 'with the other one' 'did it again' 'with/of the figs' 'girl/daughter' 'my girl/daughter' 'of girls/girlish' has been used again for the same reasons but this time to show: that Jesus is in Bethany again; and this Simon is another Simon other than the two disciples named Simon (Peter and the Canaanite); the woman who pours ointment onto Jesus.

A note on erratic words and phrases which do not seem to fit in with the stories and the way the authors thought and wrote, and possibly their own personal beliefs, is this erratic sentence '...Drink ye all of it; For this is my blood of the new testament, which is shed for many for the remission of sins.'. This sentence jars with the Biblical authors' method to name according to what is described and will happen, and there is nothing in Jesus' word-name that suggests blood, only bread and breaking/eating bread is mentioned which also ties in with the stories because it is important to the authors and to the audience who originally listened to the stories. Having the disciples drink from a cup then narrate it symbolises Jesus' blood is being drunk, whatever the beverage inside it, it stands out and indicates a late editor added it, but not an editor like the editors of the OT and the NT who knew the language and the meanings of the words, and the additions they made worked with wordplay on the same word or what could be made of the same/similar word, this addition seems to be made by someone who does not know the OT/NT language 'Hebrew'/Arabic. Plus, none of the OT stories have people drinking blood, even when humans (Gog and friends) were made as a human sacrifice, it was animals invited to eat from the meat and drink the blood—not humans. In fact, the way animals are slaughtered in the stories on altars or at least a stone, indicates there was a practise of allowing blood to drain out of the slaughtered animal to make the meat purer, good/better, as people of the culture of the region would have done then and still do today, what today would be called 'kosher' and 'ḥalal', and at least one OT story states eating meat along with the undrained blood is a sin.

Gethsemane; Gethsēmaní; جَفسيمَني 'of squatting' 'of sleeping with haunch pushed out or up' it describes when a person sits in an unusual position, not squatting properly but leaning forward with the backside slightly raised or pushed back as if ready to get up, and also if a child is asleep but has turned over and lifted their knees so that the bottom is raised. The text supports this meaning because Jesus is asking his disciples to sit and wait, that he will not be long, and he is surprised to find them asleep; غَت زيمَني 'dosed off-my time' 'he dosed off/fell asleep-my time' 'she deceived/misled(to downfall)-my time' 'misled to downfall/deceived/deceit/folly-my time'; جعث زيمَني 'great sufferance/trouble-my time' 'troubling/inconvenience-my time'; جَذ زيمَني 'abruptly or harshly cut off/remove from the bottom/completely/removed in one cut or pull-my time'; and in his prayers, Jesus' dialogue states both that his time is almost out before he is tortured and killed, he also asks that this being cut off from life and tortured be removed but that he will comply with God's will, and his dialogue expresses he is suffering mentally from fear of the physical suffering to come; the same is relayed in that his disciples cut-off watching and fall asleep quickly. It is also expressed in one of his disciples chopping off an ear of those who arrest Jesus, and Jesus telling him words to the effect that it was time for this to happen and inevitable 'But how then shall the scriptures be fulfilled, that thus it must be?'. It is also expressed in that Jesus' disciples will ostracise him and not only the people who hate him; that he will be guilted, humiliated and blamed; his life will be cut off. It is equivalent to Gob (2Sam.21:18-22), Gittah-hepher (Josh.19:13), Gath-rimmon (Josh.19:45), Gath (1Sam.5:8-9); and similar to Gatam (Gen.36:11), Jotham (Judg.9:7-21), Gittaim (2Sam.4), Gazzam (Ezra.2:48). Cp: ge<u>ph</u>sey-manee, <u>gh</u>et-zeymanee, g'f-zeymanee, gev-zeymanee. (Matt.26:36-75)

Peter has been used for 'his stub/shortness' 'he has cut him short' 'he has been snapped short' 'he has been abruptly cut off' 'they have snapped him/cut him short' all the meanings imply 'short/abrupt/quick/a stub/interrupted' as all things are expressed in this chapter: Jesus actions and prayer to God, express he feels he is being cut off too soon; it is only a short time before the disciples fall asleep; Jesus states it is only a short time before he will be betrayed; in chopping off the ear; in how abruptly his disciples abandon him; in the short period and abruptness in how Peter denies knowing Jesus. (Matt.26:37-75)

Zebedee used for 'tie tightly with rope' 'latticed it' 'latticed-he/him' 'tie tightly with rope' 'swipe/whip(with a switch or rope)' 'strengthened-he/him' 'tight/tightened-he/him/it' 'secure/secured-he/him/it' 'publicly disciplined-he/him': Jesus is asking his disciples to be like a safety net for him, to stay up while he prays, he wants their support with the heavy burden of worry he carries inside him—just like the lattice of a bed strengthens it and carries its burden; although the physical violence does not mention 'whipping', that he is physically pushed, pulled, beat, spat on, all give an image of him being whipped around during the abuse and this is done in public as he is officially arrested. (Matt.26:37-75)

Caiaphas is mentioned again to show: 'of turning back of head to/turning (his)back towards' 'turned back of his head or his back towards-he/him' this time his disciples have turned their backs on Jesus, even Peter following discreetly is to avoid being noticed and associated to him; it is in Peter turning his back further on Jesus every time he denies knowing him. 'how-he/him' 'they figured out how/thought about it' 'thought how/about-he/him' 'of thinking things/in good mood to think about matters' as the 'chief priests, and elders, and all the counsel' are still trying to find a way to find him guilty so they can kill him; then it is in their dialogue when they mock him in asking him to see if he can tell who hit him. (Matt.26:56-75)

Pontius Pilate; Póntios Pilátos; فونتيُه فلاَتُه ، فونتيوه فِلاَتُه 'so you and him/he-are his fall/let him fall' 'so you and him/he-let him loose/go'; بونتيُه فِلاَتُه ، بونتيوه فِلاَتُه 'his girl/daughter-are his fall/let him fall' 'his girl/daughter-let him loose/go' 'you became apparent/the truth has become apparent-let him fall/let him loose/go' 'your intentions have become apparent-let him fall/let him loose/go'. All meanings are reflected in the use of the word and the narration, as 'fall' means to physically fall or to die, it can also mean immoral or to let someone go (letting them go can be also be used figuratively to allow them become lewd/immoral) or to fall in status/reputation/esteem. Póntios/فونتيُه to say 'so you' has been given so it can be said of both a male and female: (p/ف) 'so', (ónti/ونتي) 'you(fem/masc)', Pónti/بونتي 'girl/daughter' 'became apparent/surfaced', (os/هٌ ، وه) 'and him/he'. (Pilát/فِلاَت) 'fall/fell/loosed/let go/immorality/lewdness', the (os/هٌ) or even the (s/هـ) on its own 'he/him/his' as a suffix attributes the 'pilat(o)/falling/girl/apparent' to a 'he/him/it'.

The meanings of 'you' both masculine and feminine and 'let him fall' as in death or disgrace and 'let him go' as in free are available in the first half of this chapter where the word-name used features: Jesus is delivered to Pontius Pilate with the express desire that he be put to death; Judas states he has caused the death of an innocent man and states the elders and chief priests are his accomplices in the 'Pontius Pilate/'so you and him/he-are his fall/let him fall' of Jesus, and because he kills himself the meaning of the word applies to his death too; the chief priests explicitly tell him it has nothing to do with them but entirely on Judas 'Saying, I have sinned in that I have betrayed innocent blood. And they said, What *is that* to us? see thou *to that*.'; it is the people including the elders and chief priests demanding Jesus' execution; when Pilate allows the decision-making about Jesus to fall from his hands, it goes to the elders, chief priests and the people to influence his execution; it is in delivering him to be crucified.

The meaning 'Pontius Pilate/'so you and him/he-let him loose/go' is expressed in the narration that Pilate favours releasing a prisoner of the people's choosing; he offers them choice between freeing Jesus or Barabbas; 'Pontius Pilate/'his girl/daughter-let him loose/go' as Pilate and his wife want to release Jesus; the chief priests and elders persuade the people to choose Barabbas for Pilate's pardon; 'you became apparent/the truth has become apparent-let him fall/let him loose/go' 'your intentions have become apparent-let him fall/let him loose/go' in Pilate noticing the situation is falling out of his hands i.e. getting out of control as the people are riled 'but *that* rather a tumult was made'; Pilate 'washes his hands' of Jesus' murder i.e. he has let the order fall from his hands so that the people, elders, chief priests are in charge of making the decision and implementing the execution of Jesus; it is in Pilate's soldiers torturing and humiliating Jesus.

It is equivalent to Palti (Num.13:9), Peleth (Num.16:1), Beth-pelet (Josh.15:27), Japhleti (Josh.16:3), Phalti (1Sam.25:44), Pelethites (2Sam.8:18), Pelatiah (1Chr.3:21), Japhlet (1Chr.7:32), Piltai (Neh.12:17). Cp: <u>ph</u>oontyoh <u>ph</u>ilaatoh, <u>ph</u>oontyooh <u>ph</u>ilaatoh, boontyoh <u>ph</u>ilaatoh, boontyooh <u>ph</u>ilaatoh. (Matt.27:1-31)

Barabbas; Barabbás; بَرَبّاَه 'with plenty' 'with his god/master/lord/boss/employer', as a compound word it can have other meanings related to the root word 'rabbah', but is anchored to the story to the meaning of 'many' and something/someone 'grown well/risen high'. He is first described when Pilate is considering releasing a prisoner which the authors have coincide with a feast—so the meaning of 'with plenty' is not lost on the audience; just as the word means 'brought up/raised well/grows fast' he is described as a 'notable prisoner'; 'with plenty' is reflected in the elders and the chief priests persuading 'the multitude that they should ask Barabbas' be freed; Barabbas is released to the large crowd of people. Cp: barabbaah. It is equivalent to the words such as Arab, Rabbi, etc. (Matt.27:15-26)

Simon Cyrene; Simon is still 'have heard/to hear/heard/obey' and in this instance means 'listened/obeyed' as he is 'compelled' to bear Jesus' cross. Kyrēnē; كيرييني 'hired them/paid them/rented them' 'drove/chased/forced them with violence' and only the latter fits the story as he has been 'compelled' to carry Jesus' cross but there is no evidence for the 'hired' meaning; قيرييني 'of reading' 'read to me/teach me to read' 'stopped moving/fidgeting' 'stopped what they were doing' 'linked them' 'linked them with wood/rope' and it is what is done to a pair of bulls or cows when working the land to keep them moving at the same pace, also to keep one animal linked to another so that it does not run off. In this instance, what the narration is suggesting is that either Simon forced to carry Jesus' cross is likened to an animal put under a yoke/wood, or that he and Jesus were tied with the same rope/chain, it states that both Simon and Jesus were carrying the cross—still likened to a pair of bulls put under the same yoke/rope as they have to move together. Cp: kyreeeyney qyreeeyney. (Matt.27:32)

Golgotha; Golgothá; خُل/خول غوثآ ، خُل/خول غوثه 'vinegar-nauseated/nausea' 'vinegar-nauseated him/his nausea' and is reflected directly in that he was given 'vinegar mingled with gall' which he refused to drink any more—i.e. it made him nauseated/unwell. It is equivalent to Athach (1Sam.30:30), Uthai (1Chr.9:4), Othni (1Chr.26:7), Magpiash (Neh.10:20), Athaiah (Neh.11:4), Bigthan (Esth.2:19-23), Ephai (Jer.40:13-16). Cp: khol/khool ghufaa, khol/khool ghufah. (Matt.27:33-34)

Eli, Eli, lama sabachthani; ēlí ēlí lemá sabachthání, ēlōí ēlōí lemá sabachthání; ايلي ايلي لِمآ سَبَقتآني ، الي الي لِمآ صَبَحتآني ، الوي/ايلوي الي/ايلي لِمآ سَبَقتآني 'he-who, he-who, why did you come before me'; الوي/أيلوي آلي/أيلي لِمآ صَبَحتآني 'he-who, he-who, why did you cause me problems/sufferance'. 'Eli/he-who' is Jesus referring to two people by the name of Eli as the verb 'sabachthani' is in the form of two people, of which one is 'Elias/Eliah' and the other is probably John the Baptist as he is both Eli and John the Baptist in the NT, but there is a possibility because the author or an editor of Matthew likes to refer to the OT stories that a prophet with the name 'Eli' came before Jesus, of which there are several that could be the two characters meant by the Matt. author/editor: it could be Elijah, or Elisha, as they both had roles and stories similar to Jesus' stories.

If the phrase directly addresses Elias/Eliah who was John the Baptist and whose character (throughout Matthew) Jesus has directly said will and has come before him, the story narrated and confirmed that first Eliah (Elias) comes and only after him can Jesus go through with his mission and eventually suffer and be killed/crucified—so in great pain and distress Jesus cries out and bemoans why Eli had to come before him. It is more likely that the two characters are meant as Eliah/Elias and John the Baptist who seems to be a reincarnation of Eliah/Elias (maybe Elijah who did not die in the OT but was lifted in a whirlwind to heaven then returned in the NT as John the Baptist?) because the narration of the story continues with confirming this, people standing nearby believe he is calling Elias.

The translation in the Bible is wrong, the words have nothing to do with 'God' or 'abandonment/forsaken' 'Eli, Eli, lama sabachthani' does not translate to 'My God, my God, why hast thou forsaken me?'. There are two reasons why the Greek translation would have this big error: the person translating for them from the original story intentionally mistranslated (as there were persons who knew Arabic translating due to the rest of the words being translated correctly so why would translators who can translate the rest of the story perfectly to be written into Greek only get this phrase wrong unless it was intentionally mistranslated), or that the local translator did not speak the Old Arabic and was not familiar with all the meanings of these words and especially those in this phrase. The second possibility is that the Greek translator or person overseeing the translation may have found it 'unfitting' for Jesus the Son of God crying out in such distress to be calling out to another human being (in the story), that whoever was in charge changed it as a desperate and distressed complaint to God. I do not believe a third reason to be possible which would be that the Greek translation does correctly translate 'Eli Eli lema sabachthani' matching the translation that I have provided, but whoever translated it into Latin/English decided it was not suitable for Jesus to cry out to another man and changed it to Jesus crying out to God—but that is impossible as scholars would have found this inconsistency a long time ago and would have corrected it since the Greek language is well-known, so that only leaves the first two possibilities.

So in distress and great pain Jesus wishes that Eli had not come before him, and as the Biblical authors employ wordplay throughout the OT and NT, most words for major characters and place names have more than one meaning and he is complaining that Eliah (Elias) and John the Baptist have entangled him into this problem, for had they not then Jesus himself would not have ended up on the cross, or maybe Jesus was wishing he had come first and had gotten over the pain.

It is important to note whenever there is a word that loses its meaning if translated into a foreign language you can see where the Arabic translators, working with the non-Arabic translators/copiers, insist that it be transliterated so as to be pronounced exactly as meant so that it does not lose its true meanings and the pun will also be lost if translated instead of transliterated—why else would there be phrases intentionally transliterated and not translated as words in the new language where their meanings in the sentence are meant to serve the same way as compound words for character and place names are used. Such phrases as the 'Eli, Eli' phrase, 'mammon'.

Cp: eylee eylee lemaa sabaqtaanee, illee illee lemaa ssabaḥtaanee, illoiee illoiee/eyloiee eyloiee lemaa sabaqtaanee, illoiee illoiee/eyloiee eyloiee lemaa ssabaḥtaanee. (Matt.27:46-49)

Mary Magdalene; Mary is still 'pass along' 'pass/cross/pass by' 'pass along the river/sea' 'bitter/made bitter' 'bitter-river/sea' 'bitter/made bitter-the' used as 'great sufferance/great sufferance-the'. Magdalēnḗ; مَجدَليني 'of being thrown around/to the ground' 'throwing me around' 'thrown down/away' 'having fits/epilepsy/possessed by demons'. In Matt., Mary Magdalene is used for 'pass along/cross/pass by' 'bitter/suffer' as Mary is watching Jesus pass away, then she watches when Joseph from Arimathaea leaves, she and another Mary pass by Jesus' tomb; they are sent to pass on news of Jesus' resurrection to his disciples and on the way, they pass by Jesus. Magdalene has been used to describe throwing down, and in Matt.27 when she throws herself down to hold his feet to worship him; although it is not mentioned in Matt. in other Gospels it is mentioned that she was possessed by devils, and this serves two things: in real life of the culture of the authors and audience, people who have fits, epilepsy are believed to be possessed by demons, but they are also believed to be close to God and have special powers; the NT (as does the OT, see Igdaliah) uses both these meanings by having her close to Jesus, and also formerly possessed by devils. Cp: mareea, maryaam, magdaleyneyei. (Matt.27:56)

Mary the mother of James and Joses. **Mary** has been used as 'pass along' 'bitter/suffer' just like Mary Magdalene'; her sons have been used for the meanings of their names: **James** 'he/it pinches/pokes' and this still can be seen as used for the hand movement, as when Jesus will be prepared for burial there will be washing, the use of spices and ointments do necessitate 'pinching/poking' out of a jar or to release the oils and/or fragrance of many spices, ointments are rubbed between the fingers to prepare them for application, but it still seems to me the alternative meaning of James such as 'massaged' 'he binds together' 'bound together' 'he/it thickens/sets quickly' 'thickened/set' and even 'he suffocates it/him' 'he covers his its face' 'he covers his/its mouth/nose' 'suffocated him/it' 'covered his/its face' 'covered his/its nose or mouth (or both)' were meant as massaging, binding with cloths and the shroud, washing with water, covering the face are all part of cleansing and preparing a body for burial. **Joses** has been used for 'he goes wandering and seeking' as the two Marys and other characters are said to follow Jesus to serve him; the meaning 'he offends it/him' 'it offends/it offends him' is in how Jesus was killed—for offending religious people, but also in Joseph asking for his body to be brought down to be treated with dignity in burial, as humiliation and disgrace are part of the punishments meant through crucifixion even after the death of the tortured person.

As in the OT, here in the NT the authors do not have a problem with using the same characters as different characters for the sake of using the meanings of the word-names and for creating a consistent theme in the story. You can see this in how Mary is mother to Jesus, then she is also mother to James and Joses in addition to Jesus at Matt.13, but here at Matt.27-28 'Mary the mother of James and Joses' is a different Mary and not the same Mary mother of Jesus regardless of other Gospels who make her into the mother of Jesus. In Matt.27-28 she is just another Mary where her sons are mentioned just for the use of their word-name meanings as they have no role in the story other than to indicate the rituals which would be performed prior to a burial. The same can be seen in combining a new Joseph and new Jacob as father and son (fiancé of Mary) in Matt.1 and how the character name appears again as a different character for the meaning of its name at Matt.27. (Matt.27:56)

Mother of Zebedee's children. Again, the point of this character is to represent what the name reflects on the narration of the story: she is left nameless, but referred to as 'the mother of Zebedee's children because the meanings of **Zebedee** and specifically 'tie tightly with rope' 'latticed it' 'latticed-he/him' 'butter it/spread it' 'butter/spread over him' 'perfume/spread it/him with ointment' is used here to create imagery of these women washing, applying cleansing and perfuming ointments and spices to Jesus' body before he is wrapped and tied into a shroud for burial. Why not 'the wife of Zebedee' instead of 'the mother of Zebedee's children'? Because the author wants the audience to also think of the meanings of James (whether it is 'pinching/poking' or 'massaging/covering/binding together') and John for the meaning of 'soaked it/him (in)' 'brothers' 'betrayed' 'sack/sackcloth' and this indicates the material used as Jesus' shroud in the story, but also his preparation being washed or wiped with material soaked in water or other cleansing ointments, and that he was betrayed.

The way these names have been used and concentrated together: **Mary** is repeat to suggest they have passed by water and brought it to wash Jesus' body with, and his great sufferance on the cross; **James** is repeat as the son of the 'other Mary' and as Zebedee's son because there will be a lot of what the word-name meanings being done to Jesus' body, and this too is repeat again with extra provision of ointments and spreading it over in **Zebedee**'s name. The author wanted to show, and did focus, these characters stand for the imagined action of purifying a body before laying it to rest. It seems the author knew the people would understand exactly what was meant and did not explain it further, because it is very obvious to whoever speaks the real language of these word-names, and it could be that authors of the other gospels who explained it further as 'spices and ointments' being used by these women on Jesus may have felt that the more foreign audiences were not understanding it in its original version in Matt. (Matt.27:56)

Arimathaea Joseph; **Joseph** (Gen.30:22-24;37) is still 'of sorrow/feels sorrow/regret' 'pours water gently' 'rinses/cleanses' and in this part of Matthew the meaning of 'rinses/cleanses' can be seen as he also takes part in the burial process. There is no narration of washing, perfuming, covering with ointment because it is represented by the names. The meaning of 'joseph/rinses' has a specific meaning more precise than wash because it means only the action of 'pouring water gently' over someone while someone else does the rubbing/cleansing which is why 'Joseph' was chosen specifically. Arimathaía; أرِمَضَيّ 'saw him pass/pass by' 'saw him leave/walk off/go' 'saw him finish/complete it' and it reflects this Joseph from Arimathaea being there at the end not only when Jesus passed out of life, but completing his life, and role in the story, by laying him in the tomb and sealing it.

The second half of the compound word 'Ari<u>mathaea</u>' is the same as 'Matthew' which nicely ties it in in a reverse chronology: at the beginning of Matt. a lively Jesus passes by Matthew the tax collector who receives completion of tax payments and the latter leaves his work and follows Jesus; at the end of the story, this Joseph from Arimathaea follows a melancholy Jesus' and watches Jesus leave life on earth, then he 'completes' Jesus in burial.

Both characters are based on the same person, maybe originally it was supposed to be Matthew all the way to the end, but because the story had all the disciples abandon Jesus and flee for their lives the author saw an inconsistency that this character would not be able to approach the authorities so he makes a 'clone' of Matthew: their names are essentially the same 'Matthew' 'man from Arimathaea'; Matthew is a tax collector or was receiving payments owed, Joseph from Arimathaea is 'a rich man of Arimathaea'; Matthew was Jesus' disciple, the man from Arimathaea who has no mention earlier in the story appears at the end and he 'also himself was Jesus' disciple'. Cp: yooseiey<u>ph</u>, arima<u>dh</u>aia. (Matt.27:57)

Pilate 'are his fall/let him fall' 'let him loose/go' is used because Joseph from Arimathaea asks for the release of Jesus' body, and for it to be brought down from the cross; also because the chief priests and elders are still describing Jesus as an immoral person who must not be allowed to get away with what they described as 'deceit' and a hoax of a resurrection—they are not letting this 'fall' to happen as the story narrates it would be worse than his actions during life. (Matt.27:58)

Galilee 'came-to' 'came-for' 'cleared-the' 'made clear-the' because the angel is making clear to both Marys where they can find the resurrected Jesus, and the angel tells them they can find Jesus in a place called 'came-to/for' and when he invites them to come into the sepulchre and they find it empty of Jesus i.e. 'cleared-the'; on their way they meet Jesus which is also 'came-to/for' as he tells them to inform the disciples to go see him there; and the story ends on a rather sad note as although the disciples 'came-to' Galilee and can see 'made clear-the/Galilee' Jesus is alive, it seems they cannot recognise him as it narrates 'And when they saw him, they worshipped him: but some doubted.'. And Jesus instructs them to 'make clear-the' commandments of Jesus/God. (Matt.28:7-10, 16)

Amen is as explained under Psalms: 'I hope it will happen/come to be'; 'followed/lead' 'followed through/led through'; I trust it will happen/come to be; I have faith it will be; I have hope, trust, faith in God and God will make it happen, said following a prayer/request directed to God, or if someone else wishes you good, or says out loud asking for good or something in general—the people who hear the request/statement say 'Amen'; you lead, I follow (faithfully/with faith in leader); we follow (through something/towards something/in something whether physically or figuratively). This is how it is used following Jesus' instructions and hopes 'Go ye therefore, teaching all nations, baptizing them…Teaching them to observe all things whatsoever I have commanded you: and, lo, I am with you always, *even* unto the end of the world. Amen.'. (Matt.28:20)

Mark

Gospel; this word is explained as the English translation of the Greek word 'euangélion, euangélia'. The word euangélion is explained to mean '...in its most general sense...refers to the word of salvation made available to the world in and through Jesus Christ' (Freedman, Myers and Beck, 2000: 521). As in Eve/ Hawaa, James/ Iákōbos, there is a difference between 'Gospel' and 'euangélion' and as with Eve and James this difference is the result of the difficulty for a foreigner, foreign to the original language of the OT/NT stories, having difficulty in pronouncing the Arab words as transliterated. The solution, as in Eve and James, is for the Arab speaker to provide an alternative Arab word with a similar or same meaning for the foreign transliterator and his local audience for whom he translates to be able to pronounce without the difficulty of the original word.

Evangel; euangélion; does not mean 'salvation' nor does it mean 'good news'. يوَنجيليون ، اذَنجيليون 'they become clear/clarify' 'they make clear/clarify' 'they purify/sanitise' 'if they make clear/clarify' 'if they become clear/clarify' 'if they purify/sanitise' 'if they are clear/clarified/pure/sanitised' 'if they become pure' and it has a very direct meaning of making clear/clarifying the message, the truth, or any matter which the word refers to, and clarifying/purifying a person/matter.

It is from the same root word as '**Galilee**' of which one meaning is 'cleared-the' 'made clear-the' and the reason why the authors of the Gospels (not the titular characters) have Jesus and his disciples working mostly in Galilee—is to reinforce the message. And the meaning of euangélion as clarification/making clear is done through telling stories: making clear what the message is about. The stories themselves contain the 'sanitising/purification/clearing' of the ill of their diseases, possessed of their devils, hungry of their hunger, the people on the wrong way shown the right (God's) path, the misunderstanding of ambiguity, the deceived of their deceivers, etc. But either 'euangélion' was too difficult for Latin/English speakers to pronounce or 'gospel' was too difficult for Greek speakers to pronounce leading one to be replaced with the other. Cp: euangeileeoon, evangeileeoon.

'Gospel' is قُص بَل 'tell story of the' 'tell story with the' and is the same word of 'Jezebel' with the same meanings as meant in the OT. Every time it is used in Matthew and Mark it is about telling the story, preaching the story. It is used in a specific way 'gospel' قُص بَل 'tell story of the/tell story with the' with a very specific meaning: 'tell story of the...' and it is specified which story to tell, and even in modern use today as the NT, these stories are being told with that meaning (even if the storytellers/preachers do not know the meaning of 'gospel' and the same applies to 'make clear/clarify' 'euangélion, euangélia'). Furthermore, Jesus delivers his message through 'parables' i.e. stories, which his disciples feel need to be clarified more, but Jesus states the people absorb and understand these stories differently than how the disciples understand his teachings which is why he tells them in stories/parables.

The meaning is first exemplified in Matt.4:12-17 where Jesus leaves for Galilee, and the OT verse is reworked into a positive story of people in the dark and under the shadow of death seeing a shining light means 'made clear/became clear' and from this point 'From that time Jesus began to preach, and to say, Repent...'; 'And Jesus went about all Galilee, teaching in their synagogues, and preaching the gospel[tell story of the] of the kingdom, and healing all manner of sickness[clearing/purifying/sanitising] and all manner of disease among the people.' (Matt.4:23); in warning the disciples not to go to engage the 'Gentiles/dissuade/I will lead them to their downfall' because the very naming of their 'kind' are meant not to be able to see/understand the 'clarification', and also to avoid the cities of the 'Samaritans' 'storytellers/late night stories' is also a pun as 'how can you tell a story/gospel/euangélion (make clear) to storytellers/ Samaritans', how can you convince with a fictional story/gospel what is itself a fictional story/Samaritan; the warning about the 'leaven of the Pharisees and Sadducees' which is a warning against believing 'the doctrine of the Pharisees and Sadducees' is the authors' ways of saying do not believe the stories of the Pharisees/Sadducees' and purposely compared against the bread/stories of Jesus because Jesus means 'bread/ eating and/or breaking bread' so just as Jesus' warning against the bread/stories of Pharisees/Sadducees—the author is saying Jesus bread/story is better to be believed, or at the very least making it about one version of stories against another version of stories using the bread metaphor then making it clear it is about stories; 'And this gospel of the kingdom shall be preached in all the world for a witness unto all nations...' (Matt.24:14); regarding his disciples' displeasure over the woman pouring expensive ointments over Jesus

'Verily, I say unto you, Wheresoever this gospel shall be preached [wherever this story will be told] in the whole world, *there* shall also this, that this woman hath done, be told of a memorial of her.' (Matt.26:13). Cp: q<u>o</u>ss bel.

'The beginning of the gospel of Jesus Christ, the Son of God...' the beginning of 'tell story of Jesus Christ. 'And he said unto them, Go ye into all the world, and preach the gospel to every creature...' 'The blind receive their sight, and the lame walk, the lepers are cleansed, and the deaf hear, the dead are raised up,' i.e. all these different ailed people get 'cleared/purified/made clear-the' and 'and the poor have the gospel preached to them.' the poor get stories told to them, that is their 'clarification, purification' they are shown the right way, a hopeful life in this world and the hereafter but through stories told. (Mark.1:1, 14; 8:35; 16:15)

What becomes evident upon reading Mark, is it is a summarisation of Matthew. There are two reasons for this: either the person who originally wrote Mark did not understand the original language of the Biblical story and the Biblical authors' method of creating word-names linked to the narration of events, but then a local author/editor went through Mark and made additions to give it the Biblical method. Or the author of Mark wanted to show his authorial abilities and chose to summarise Matthew and only use the Biblical method of using words and compound words for character/place names differently than Matthew's book so as to show his own imprint on the story. The latter is more probable because the text shows this: the author of Mark is not using the Biblical method where Matthew has already used it, and omits most of Matthew's wordplay, but the author of Mark does change sequence of events and names to show his own wordplay and his own skill at the Biblical authors' method: e.g. you will see he will slightly rearrange a story to show his own specific wordplay where in Matt.13:54-58 where Mary, James, Joses, Simon and Judas (Judah) are used 'Judah' is used to show Jesus is calling/preaching to people and that the people of his own area consider his 'calling/Judah/yud'aa, yud'ah(Gen.29:35)' is a 'false claim/Judah/yud'aa, yud'ah'. But in Mark.6:1-6 the author uses Judas(Judah) as 'his hands/Judah/yoodah(Matt.10; 26:1-16; 27:3-8)'. The author of Mark chooses to change what in Matthew regarding the same event narrates it is about 'calling/false claim' and ends it with 'And he did not many mighty works there because of their unbelief.', to show 'Judah/his hands' by adding to it 'And he could there do no mighty work, save that he laid his hands upon a few sick folk, and healed *them*.'. The same can be seen where a word-name is added in Mark which is not featured in Matthew.

Mark; Márkos; مآرجوه 'did not/they did not wait/stay/become still' and implies the person(s) being in a hurry. From word (rg/رج) 'waited/stayed/still/stationary'. The way Mark has summarised the whole Jesus story as it is in Matthew, causes the events to happen faster, and although they are repeating what is mostly the same story as Matthew and because it does not lengthen the stories dispersed by long narration it does give the effect that when the words 'straightway/immediately' are used as if the characters are not waiting at all and in a hurry, just like the word 'mark' means.

Mark's meaning 'did not/they did not wait/stay/become still' can also be see in Jesus' response to the question about his disciples not fasting while other disciples do: instead of just about not waiting to eat, the narration makes it also an example about the brides (it is plural in the narration) not waiting nor delaying enjoying the bridegroom because when he leaves, they will have to wait for his return as he will not stay. The same meaning is implied in Pilate being surprised that Jesus has already died, i.e. he expected his life to last a little longer as per crucifixions go.

Although 'Mark' as name for a character is not mentioned in the whole gospel of Mark, Mark as a character does make a sneaky appearance: he is the naked young man who drops his clothes and runs off after touching Jesus who is being led away. This character does not wait for Jesus to die but runs off, he does not even wait to grab the linen cloth which had covered part of his nakedness. The author having him naked, and making a point that it is known he is naked under the linen loosely around him, making him touch Jesus, then drop his linen cloth which is more like a shroud than a garment and run away naked in public—is so the audience of the story notices this is 'Mark/they did not wait/stay/become still'.

As most Biblical word-names have more than one meaning and more than one word, it is possible that Mark; Márkos; مآرجوه is also 'did not intensely ask/intreat' and the asking is not the same as begging, nor insisting but something in between, 'did not shake/unsettle it' 'did not drive him insane' as the word (rg/رج) 'shake/shook' is also used to say a person is 'mad/insane' or even slightly mad, the meaning from the mind has been shaken/unsettled; مآرجوه 'plastered it' from word (mrg/مرج) which is plaster made from mixing soil with cow dung and water, used to plaster inside walls, floors and other surfaces inside and outside the house. The only meaning of Mark present in the gospel of Mark is 'did not wait/stay'. Cp: maar-gooh. (Mark)

Levi has replaced **Matthew**, and although it is a completely different word-name with different meanings the word chosen suits the character function: Levi 'gather/collect' as he is 'sitting at the receipt of custom' and 'answer/respond/serve' because he immediately answers Jesus' call to follow him. So a different word-name than Matthew, but a word chosen for its own suitable meanings as has been used before in the OT.

Even Levi's surname has been borrowed from another disciple's character word-name: Alphaeus 'I will gather/collect it' 'I will pick it up' 'I will wrap it' which was the surname of James Alphaeus at Matt.10:3. to relay the meaning in the story. Cp: leyphee, leybee, halphaioh, halphaiooh. (Mark.2:14)

Boanerges; Boanērgés; بوَن يرجيز 'children of-he curses/makes unclean/filthy' 'of when/with when-he curses/makes clean/filthy'; بوَني رجيز 'children of curse(s)/uncleanness/filth'. Cp: boan-eyrgeiz, boaney-rgeiz. (Mark.3:17)

Gadarenes; Gadara; قَدَر 'was able/were able' and it is reflected in the people no matter how they bind the possessed man, he is able to break loose while they are unable to keep him restrained; and it is in Jesus who is able to free him of the devils. Cp: qadara. (Mark.5:1-20)

Legion; legiṓn; لِجيون 'for many demons' 'why/from where are they coming/for those coming' 'comes to/they came to' 'they are coming' i.e. 'refugees' and this is exactly what is happening in the story 'My name is Legion: for we are many.'. The word 'refugees' can be broken down 'legion': (le/لِ) 'for/from/why', (gi/ج) 'come/came/coming' and the (ṓn/ون) makes it 'them/they' i.e. the 'coming' is in plural; and indicates a people coming from elsewhere seeking safety or reassurance, and in this part of the story it is about 'devils/demons' asking not to be sent out of the country, but are sent out of the body they occupy and into the pigs: 'And he besought him much that he would not send them away out of the country...And all the devils besought him, saying, Send us into the swine, that we may enter into them.'. Cp: legyoon. (Mark.5:9-13)

Decapolis is used in the same way as in (Matt.4:25) for 'he/she/it meets him' 'he/she/it faces him' 'he/she accept him/it because of good quality (whether material, or a person in character, honesty)' 'he/she/it accepts him/accepts him reluctantly' 'they packed/filled for him' 'they tried to pack/fill for him'. It is reflected in the story as people coming to see Jesus as in Matt., but this time because the cured man has spread the word about Jesus' abilities and again people meet him, and the narration shows how overcrowded/overpacked the people are coming to see him in vast numbers. But it also shows how it is used to mean 'reluctantly accepts' which in the OT 'Cabul' from the same root word and meaning which was shown that king of Tyre reluctantly accepted the towns gifted to him, but the narration was saying he accepted them nominally but returned them immediately (to avoid causing offense)—and here it is shown that although Jesus does not want the man to accompany him, he does not say it directly, but gently tells him he can be of more use if he returns to his own people and tells them what God has done for him '...he that had been possessed...prayed him that he might be with him. Howbeit Jesus suffered him not, but saith unto him, Go home to thy friends, and tell them how great things the Lord hath done for thee...' (Mark.5:19-21)

Jairus; Iáíros; حايروه 'perplexed him' 'troubled him' 'inflamed/chronic open wound' all meanings are reflected in the story: the daughter is certainly dying implying she has a terminal illness; the woman who is healed when she touches Jesus is suffering from a chronic illness which causes her to bleed for twelve years—women whose bleeding is heavy or continuous are said to have an open sore (ulcer) in the womb—and it goes further to show her doctors are puzzled and unable to cure her predicament; Jesus is perplexed by who touched him and drew out his 'virtue', and the disciples are puzzled he would ask who touched him when he is being pressed by a crowd of people; the people who come from Jairus' house tell him not to trouble Jesus (because his daughter is dead). It is the same as Hirah (Gen.38:1, 12,20-26). Cp: ḥaaeerooh. (Mark.5:22-35)

Peter 'he has been abruptly cut off' 'they have snapped him/cut him short' reflects she is believed to have died; it is reflected in Jesus short response 'Be not afraid, only believe'.

James has been used 'he/it pinches/pokes' as the people who mock Jesus: when a person is mocked, some people (doing the mocking) lightly pinch, poke or squeeze the hand or any part of the person sitting next to them (or wink/or any other facial gesture) to show they are mocking the speaker. It may also have been used for its meaning 'he suffocates it/him' 'he covers his its face' 'he covers his/its mouth/nose' 'suffocated him/it' 'covered his/its face' indicating the girl is no longer breathing which is made clearer by Jesus stating she is not dead, only sleeping.

John 'soaked it/him (in)' 'brothers' 'betrayed' 'sacks' 'sackcloth' 'put/wrap it in sack/sackcloth' as the daughter is ill she would have been covered by a sheet or blanket, soaked fabric used as cold presses, and especially if believed to have passed away she would have been covered with some kind of fabric and eventually wrapped in a fabric shroud, which a sack/sack material indicates. (Mark.5:35-40)

Talitha cumi; talithá koúm; تَلَتا/تَليتا قوم 'took/carried her by the hand-awake/stand' from the word (tl/تل) 'carry by hand/handle', and (qm/قم) 'wake/stand/do'. 'And he took the damsel by the hand, and said unto her, Talitha cumi, which is being interpreted, Damsel, I say unto thee, arise, And straightway the damsel arose, and walked...' There are words in the Biblical stories which are transliterated and not translated and followed in the narration with words to the effect 'which is being interpreted' and go on to give a wrong interpretation and what this shows is the person who put the story into Greek writing and/or translator did not understand the original language of the Biblical story—he may have spoken Arabic but maybe not the pure Arabic of the Arabian Peninsula (e.g. may have been Syrian or Iraqi Arabic and therefore did not understand the words), or did not speak it at all and relied on the translation of another. The first word is the same as all the 'Tel' names: Tel-melah (Ezra.2:59), Tel-harsa (Ezra.2:59), Tel-abib (Ezek.3:15). The second word is similar to: Eliakim (2Kgs.18:18), Jehoiakim (2Kgs.23:34), Jokim (1Chr.4:22), Jakim (1Chr.8:19), Adonikam (Ezra.8:13), Achim (Matt.1:14). Cp: talitaa/talytaa qoom. (Mark.5:41-42)

Corban; Korbán; قوربآن 'presented/served' 'served to' 'sacrificial gift/sacrifice' and takes its meaning from the word (qrb/قرب) 'near/neared/made near' used when serving food or drink, setting down a meal, and when offering sacrifices, tithes to God; as whether it is God or people being served food, the food is being placed near so the person being served/offered can eat from it. The word and its meaning are used exactly this way in Mark. Cp: qoorbaan. (Mark.7:10-13)

An important note on how the word 'Greek' and 'Gentile' are used in the NT. They suffer from the same mistranslation/misinterpretation of the original word as do other words in the whole Bible. There are different words which have been assigned different meanings even when the word does not change. Of course, a word in pronunciation and spelling can have completely different meanings as per the context it is used in, but this is not the case in how 'héllēn' in its various forms, and 'ethnē' in its various forms are used to mean 'Greek' 'Gentile' 'heathen' 'nation' 'people'. To avoid repetition and taking too much space, I will not translate every single time the word 'Gentile', 'Greek', 'heathen', 'nations', and 'people' appear in the NT stories and only mention when there is great significance. Also to avoid repetition the correct meanings of these words and how and why they have been confused to mean all the above will be detailed later in this book, whereas where a translation of the word 'Greek' and 'Gentile' is used I will give its meaning as intended by the original NT author, and the detailed explanation of the words translated as Gentile, Greek, heathen, nation, people, which will be presented later in the book will help clarify this better, and can be used to identify the correct meanings of the words (Greek, Gentile, heathen, nation, people) where they appear in the Bible.

Greek; hellēnís; حيلّينييه ، حَلّينيه 'purified/circumcised/made clean/made edible him/it' 'of purification/edibility/cleanliness/circumcision' 'declared purified/permissible' 'undressed him/her/it' 'of undressing' 'deceived/tricked him/her/it' 'of deceit/tricks' 'beat severely/beat until skin peeled off him/it' 'of beating/being beaten severely' 'shed its skin/hair/leaves/etc. him/it' 'of shedding skin/hair/leaves' 'replaced him/it' 'of replacing' 'sweet/sweetened him/it' 'of sweetness/sweetening'. This reflects that Jesus was only interested in helping, cleansing, converting people who were already physically 'purified' through circumcision, it may also reflect that the woman was partially 'pure' which is why he ended up helping her, but that there was something lacking making her not pure enough to be helped immediately; the rejection Jesus initially shows towards her is replaced with healing her daughter and is come about because she was able to respond in a manner which amused Jesus and made him kinder/sweeter towards her.

The 'Koine Greek'/Arabic meaning and word used to show this woman's 'foreign-ness' is not far from the OT 'Hebrew'/Arabic meaning and word for Greek/Grecian and this is used in connotation within the narration: yěwān; عيوآن 'howling' because the woman and her kind is likened to a dog; غيوآن 'misleading to downfall' because Jesus states it would be wrong to help people he was not sent to help, likened to giving dogs bread to eat (Jesus/cold bread) that was meant for children, but also indicates the woman's daughter is having problems because of the 'devil/demon' inside her (people often act strange and/or engage in dangerous and self-harming or harming others where it is believed they are possessed by demons). Cp: ḥeilleyne͟e͟yh, ḥelleynyh,'eiwaan, g͟heiwaan. (Mark.7:25-30)

Syrophenician; Syrophoiníkissa; صيروفوي نيجسّه/ا 'go away/get rid of/send away the unclean/dirty/impure woman/female' 'go away/send away-impurity/filth/unclean'. From words (ssrph/صرف) 'go/send away/get rid of/change' and it is in the form of being spoken to more than one person (Syrophoi/صيروفوي) and in the Matt. story the disciples are asking Jesus to get rid of her, although they are not mentioned by name, Jesus still wants her to go away and it is implied in the word that more than one person wants her to leave.

The word (ngs/نجس) 'defile/dirty/unclean' can mean something that is only impure temporarily because of an action such as sex, menstruation, contaminated with urine—which can all be cleaned and the person/object returns to 'pureness' (in this sense it does not necessarily mean 'unclean' as in contaminates what is around it or what he/she touches but means is in a state that needs to be cleaned before it can perform or be used in certain rituals such as prayer, e.g.); and the word is in the form of describing a female. Its other sense is that it means intrinsically dirty/unclean/impure and this is used to describe dogs of which the culture does consider them unclean in the fibre of their physical body and when used to describe a very bad person (who does evil or extremely bad things to others) means his/her soul is intrinsically impure/unclean. The second meaning is used because the woman is compared to dogs not only reflected in the narration and in the compound word 'Syrophenician' but the author wanted to show this by coupling it with the word 'Greek' for its meaning 'howling' i.e. when she speaks and asks Jesus for help, she is like a dog howling; the same meaning of 'Greek, Syrophenician' is used to denote the 'unclean spirit' in her daughter which she wants Jesus to 'send out'.

The 'Canaan' woman in Matt.15 is a prime example of how the author of Mark wanted to show his own skills at the Biblical author method of wordplay, as he has taken the same story, but where in Matthew 'Canaan/looking up/with head lifted looking up' woman was used to compare her to an expectant dog looking up and waiting for his master to throw him some food in order to show how hopeless it was of her to seek help Jesus was unwilling to give—in Mark, the author has chosen to use 'Greek/made clean/howling' and 'Syrophenician/send away the filthy woman' in a more discriminatory emphasis that she is no different than a dog that no one should touch. The exercise of writing Mark was to show the author's ability to create his own wordplay and narration of what is essentially the same story. Cp: sseyroophoi neegissa(h). (Mark.7:25-30)

Ephphatha; Ephphatha; افف ذَ 'ooph ooph/phew phew-him/this', the word is onomatopoeic as the word is made of the huff sound people make and/or sound people make when they smell something unpleasant or are fed up with something/someone or disgusted by them. When there is an unpleasant smell they say 'ooph' or 'ooph-ooph' and usually spit after saying it in an attempt to get the smell out of the nose or because they feel nauseated by it. In use, when describing someone is making these sounds of smelling something unpleasant or being fed up they say he/she '(masc.)yit-eph-eph/يتأفأف/(fem.)tit-eph-eph/تتأفأف). Also, the sound people make when they pretend to be spitting figuratively at something/someone is 'tph'.

The narration portrays Jesus is fed up, or has caught scent of something unpleasant, or was just disgusted because he had to poke his fingers into the man's ears and touch his tongue. He is spitting, looking up to heaven and sighing before he says 'Ephphatha'. And again, the text of the Bible shows there is a disparity between what the word means and what is being said in its interpretation, and this betrays that either the translator or the editor did not know the true meaning of the word, or the wrong interpretation was made by a later editor—the word has nothing to do with the phrase 'Be opened' or even the word 'open' there are not the letters nor sequence of letters to make it 'Be opened'.

'And they bring unto him one that was deaf, and had an impediment in his speech…And he took him aside from the multitude, and put his fingers into his ears, and he spit, and touched his tongue; And looking up to heaven, he sighed, and saith unto him, Ephphatha, that is, Be opened. And straightway his ears were opened, and the string of his tongue was loosed, and he spake plain.'. Cp: eph*ph*a va. (Mark.7:32-37)

Dalmanutha; Dalmanouthá; ضَلَّمَنوذه/آ 'caused injustice-him/he/this' 'misled-wished for/what is-this' and is reflected in the Pharisees attempting to get Jesus to show them a sign from heaven; and also in Jesus' disciples misunderstanding what Jesus is talking about, believing him to be actually talking about bread instead of the 'doctrine of the Pharisees and Herod', note how Mark author has replaced 'Sadducees; with 'Herod' 'incite against'. Cp: dhalmanoo va(h). (Mark.8:10-21)

Jericho has been used the same way as in (Matt.20:29-34): 'they see him/it' 'he makes them see' 'came his sight' 'came showed him/made him see' as in this part of the story Jesus will restore a blind character's vision. (Mark.10:46-52)

Bartimaeus; Bartimaíos; بَرذِمَيُه ، برذميوه 'passed by-they ostracised him/he' 'good/piety-they ostracised/guilted/insulted/blamed/humiliated/ostracised/diseased-him/he' and this is the first name of the blind character who is sitting by the highway begging, and although it does not say he has been ostracised—he is sitting at the highway begging, denoting ostracization; also when the people tell him to be quiet, he is being 'shamed/humiliated' and blamed for doing something inappropriate (calling out to Jesus). The authors have the first part of his name created of 'passed by' as Jesus and his group pass him by, and only when he calls out to Jesus do they stop and wait for him; also 'piety/good' because he has been made whole because of his faith/piety. Cp: bar vimaioh, bar vimaiooh. (Mark.10:46-52)

Timaeus; Timaíos; ذِمَيُه ، ذميوه 'guilted/insulted/blamed/humiliated/ostracised/diseased-him/he' and the author has repeated what is one of the two words making up this character's first name, not out of laziness but because he wants to indicate the meaning of 'guilted/blamed/ostracised/etc.' twice: first because he is diseased and has become ostracised due to his illness/blindness and has to beg for a living; and then because the people 'blame/shame' him for crying out to Jesus. Cp: vimaioh, vimaiooh. (Mark.10:46-52)

The author has Bartimaeus cry out 'Jesus of **Nazareth**' instead of 'Jesus Christ', or any other title, for Nazareth's meanings of 'helpers/helped to succeed/victors/supporters(ed)/aides' 'she/I warned' as Bartimaeus is calling out for Jesus to help him, the people warn him to be quiet, Bartimaeus continues to plead for help and Jesus aids him in regaining his vision. (Mark.10:47-52)

Abba; abbá; ابّه ، ابّا 'father' but with a more endearing nuance e.g. a child, whether a young or adult child, would usually say (yabba/يابّا/ يابّه), but when using a more affectionate tone, especially when making a request, asking for something they use (abba/abbah/ابّا/ابّاه); it also means 'rejected/refused/said no' 'refused it/him/rejected him/it'. The exact same meanings are being used here in the narration: Jesus is asking God in an endearing manner to spare him from the pain and suffering already prophesied, but the narration shows that God has not accepted but remained silent about it, i.e. rejected Jesus' requests; Jesus is feeling sad, depressed, anxious, he is sorrowful and asking his father to make something which will affect him go away; he is asking his father to protect him and not allow it to happen—the same worry and anxiety, and the pleas is in Matthew but without the mention of the endearing transliteration of 'Father/Abba'. Jesus knows or has an idea of what is in store for him (just like a pregnant woman knows the excruciating pain waiting for her at the end of her pregnancy, and prays and asks God to make it as painless as possible or to make her not pregnant, but no matter how much she hopes she still knows it is coming, and nearer to the time she will become sorrowful, fearful, tearful), and he pleads with God, his father, and expresses he wishes that it be cancelled, but he does it without being disobedient, but is submitting to it, words to the effect 'you can stop it from happening, father, but I will accept whatever your will be' so he is affectionately imploring God to spare him the sufferance and demise in the fashion predicted. This is shown in the affectionate and sorrowful tone of the narration of his pleas, and how he repeats these requests on the hope God/father will grant them.

It is equivalent to Abiah (1Sam.8), Abijah (1Kgs.14:1-18), Abijam (1Kgs.15:1-3), Abi (2Kgs.18-20). Cp: abbah, abbaa. (Mark.14:30)

Praetorium; aulē; عولي 'upon him' 'above him' 'rose in status' 'arrogant' and is reflected in the soldiers who clothe Jesus like a king with a purple robe on his body and crown of thorns on his head, then mock-worship him as if he is above them like a God; غولي 'deep hatred/despise/extreme vengeance' 'deep stabbing/deep digging' and this is displayed in their abuse towards Jesus. Cp: 'ooley, ghooley. (Mark.15:16-20)

Simon Cyrenian is used just as it was in Matthew, but the author of Mark further enhances the story by giving this character two sons, the character 'Simon/listened/obeyed' 'Cyrene' 'linked them' 'linked them with wood/rope' as he is 'compelled' to carry Jesus' cross, it still suggests Jesus also carried it along with Simon. But the compound words given as sons' names also paint a picture of further abuse:

Alexander; Aléxandros; عليك سَندروه 'on you/upon you-I will send it/him out' 'on you/upon you-I will separate him/it'. And as explained in Andrew (Matt.10) it is mostly used to describe sending off sheep/goats in the right direction towards pastures to graze ('sent him/it out'); and used to describe separating between sheep and goats, whether to sort and separate them to send to different areas, or to separate one or more from the rest of the flock in order to slaughter or sell them ('separated him/it'). This time it means Jesus has been sent out and separated from the flock for slaughter; 'the upon you' refers to both Simon who carries the cross and Jesus for the separation and sending out for slaughter. Similar to Andrew (Matt.10) Cp: 'aleik sandroh. (Mark.15:21)

Rufus; Rhoúphos; روفوه ، رؤفوه 'they had sex with him' and this is also implied in the 'parting of the garments' although the latter may be understood as 'divided his garments between them', it does not fit the narration and it is the same Biblical euphemism as in 'lifting a man's skirt' (which means have sexual intercourse with; when they have illicit sex with a female relative of the respective man it is as if they had sex with the man. See Leviticus). This can be seen and read in Matthew where 'and parted his garments', but it is further confirmed by the word given as a son of 'Simon a Cyrenian' 'Rufus/they had sex with him'. It is also supported by the OT stories where princes and kings are given names which indicate they were raped before being killed, and in Saul asking one of his men to kill him to avoid being humiliated, and when the soldier does not, Saul attempts to kill himself. Jesus is being mocked as a king, and treated as a king would be facing execution.

This is why in both Matthew (20:20-23) and Mark (10:35-40) the narration has Jesus reply to John and James (at their own and their mother's request to be seated beside him in the 'kingdom') with a cryptic response which if read correctly means they will be persecuted 'drink from the cup' and they will be 'baptised' physically suffer, but that although they will be persecuted they cannot want nor handle to drink from the same cup as Jesus—the cup is his torture and suffering and crucifixion; and he also tells them they will not be baptised the way he will be—the baptism here is not about John the Baptist baptising him with water, but it is a direct reference to the sexual abuse and the water is the semen of the men who rape him (semen/sperm is called 'water'); when Jesus tells them they will not be the ones who are at his right and left was not Jesus/the narration denying them a place in heaven but sparing and informing them that the two men (thieves) on his right and left are the two men crucified beside him who undergo the same abuse (and subsequent painful death) as he does before and during crucifixion. (Cp: ro<u>ou</u>phooh. (Mark.15:21; Matt.27:35)

Salome; Salṓmē; شَلويمي 'carried/of carrying' 'carried/took water' and is used to show she helped carry and prepare Jesus' body as well as bring spices for preparing him, and her name completes the meaning for the two Marys the water they need to wash him (according to the meaning of their names María, Mariám 'pass along' 'pass along the river/sea'); سَلويمي 'asked/of asking' 'intact/survived/whole' 'leaked/flowed water' and this is shown in relation to her name where they wonder who will remove the stone for them to access Jesus' body, but are surprised to be told he is alive again i.e. 'survived/intact' or at least back 'whole' and alive, it is also reflected in they are so afraid they say nothing which shows they felt lucky to survive the experience. Cp: <u>sh</u>aloymey, saloymey. (Mark.15:40; 16:1-8)

Luke

Luke; Loukás; لوكاه 'talks(ed) too much/talks too much nonsense' 'rambling/loquacious' 'his nonsense/ramblings' 'chew(ed)' 'for you'. From the word (luk/لوك) which means: rambling, talking too much, talking nonsense, rambling in speech jumping from one thing to another, being annoying because talks or is talking too much, talking either complete nonsense or of unimportant things, can also mean nagging. The word can also mean 'chew' 'for you' 'crumpled/crumpled against each other' but the meanings meant for Luke in the Gospel are of talking too much, etc.

A note on the writing style: at first glance it appears to differ greatly from both Matthew and Mark, even Mark there seems a possibility that it was written by a non-local author whose style differed slightly from the OT method because he summarised the story and did not apply a lot of wordplay by ignoring those already used in Matthew, only to show he was a local by using his own wordplay in different areas of the story. Luke gives the impression that it was written in a foreign manner (foreign to the local authors of the OT, and Matt. and Mark) in both style and tone and even supported by the purpose of the story—but only if not read closely. The possibility of 'Luke' having been written by a non-local is contradicted due to the very nature of the story portraying the meaning of 'Luke' in the narration of the story as per the Biblical authors' method and according to the Arabic meaning of 'Luke' although no mention of 'Luke' as a character is used within the story itself (it was probably referred to as Luke (loquacious) and that is how it ended up being its title). That it could be written by a non-local is also contradicted by the author's intricate understanding of several OT stories and the multiple meanings of individual characters' word-names which have been used in Luke, showing a complete understanding of not only the OT and original stories (which may have existed long before the OT was compiled as documents) and innovating in how the wordplay and relay between compound word-names of characters, but also of the Arabic language of the Bible as presented in the OT and used in the word-names and stories of the NT. The author makes the audience connect the message of the gospel of Luke with references to older stories only by using old and new word-names as current in Luke and delivering the message of the story through use of this relay between the stories of the OT and the NT, but with a message different than the other gospels.

In the following are points which could cause a reader to believe Luke was written by a foreigner (non-Arab). Other gospels place much emphasis on John the Baptist/Elias coming and passing, whereas Luke focuses on Jesus and even this focus on Jesus is to a lesser extent compared to Matthew and Mark. Luke focuses on 'things said' as presented in Luke.

Other gospels retain their local flavour, flare, style even translated as Greek and then into English (the same goes for the OT), but Luke seems foreign, not from or by an Arab locality and author, and this foreign manner/writing style has made the prose less dramatic, events seem mundane, but at the same time using more words making what is essentially the same story even longer giving it the Arabic meaning of 'luke'.

The story portrays Pilate (and his people) as 'just', not wanting to condemn/execute Jesus (although the other gospels portray Pontius Pilate and his soldiers had no problem and no qualms implementing what the 'elders and chief priests' wanted done). The story of Luke shifts Jesus' persecution/humiliation onto Herod (and his people), but reserves the complete blame and accountability onto the chief priests and their people (Jews, or the locals) who are the same as Herod and his people. The story goes at length to present Pontius Pilate being against hurting Jesus; the story, like the text itself (in style), can seem to be written by a non local, a foreigner who seeks to sanitise Pilate—therefore his whole people's culpability in what part they took in Jesus' demise, and this extends from the fictional story to the real audiences of people. But in fact, it is still in line with Matthew where it seems to mock the Jesus and Christian story and when the word 'Gentiles' is used, it is used to mean 'dissuade' 'I will deceive them/the' 'I will mislead them to downfall-them/the' (and other meanings listed under the translations of these words).

The following points show where and how the meaning of 'luke' is used in the Gospel of Luke: More verbiage is used giving it the meaning of 'luke'.

It dwells longer on one action/segment in the story and goes on about it, although the prose is much advanced in style, it can still be termed as 'luke'.

Luke gets events/characters muddled and mixed up; presents the stories in a different order, adds events not mentioned in the other gospels; it uses the stories of other gospels, but jumps from one part of that story and places it in the middle of another event such as using the long line of descendants of Jesus between where John baptises him and the devil tempting him.

It uses the same section of a story, told in Matt/Mark, more than once inserted in different chapters of Luke, telling them in a different setting. Previous stories are chopped up, and used and begin without a proper sequence of events of introduction into what leads up to it.

Although it 'talks' more in words, it is only using more words, it does not reveal anything new if you cannot read and understand the word-names in Arabic and with their wordplay meanings; this makes it seem actions/events added give no additional insight into the stories already told in Matt/Mark. It does not explain or reveal extra meaning to the earlier stories, but are haphazard in presentation and give no added value, but do confuse the events and how things happened—even Jesus' travel/preachings for one area to another lose their streamlined force, lessened in their significance compared to the other gospels. i.e. like its fictional author-name suggests 'Luke' speaks a lot, but does not deliver clarity, nor make sense. But this is intentional as it has placed emphasis on a different element of the gospels which although can be seen in other gospels, in Luke it has become the most important theme/idea.

Chopping up the stories then placing them in a different sequence to teach a certain lesson, e.g. forgiveness or salvation, removes the 'cause and event' sequence from other parts of the story (which in other gospels can clearly be seen as the cause then event in the original stories). E.g. the woman pouring ointment over Jesus being the reason why Judas Iscariot is prompted to betray Jesus; in Luke, the author has chopped it up, moved the ointment incident elsewhere and in doing so removed the cause that Judas betrayed Jesus for; in Luke it has been left at Judas betrayed Jesus and that is it—no reason/cause given.

The actions within the story also represent and reflect 'luke': Simeon talks a lot about Jesus' future; when Jesus is left behind in Jerusalem, while he is in the temple not only is he listening but asking a lot of questions—the people are in 'wonder' at his speech/understanding—meaning he talked a lot; when his mother finds him and tells him how worried they were, even his response leaves her confused—the very meaning of 'luke'. The way an older Jesus' speech is presented is as the meaning of 'luke', he rambles (Luke.4:22-29), and although the first verse mentions his 'gracious' speech, the actual narration and text shows it jumps from one thing to another without a clear message; the narration shows it annoys *all* the people in the synagogue, meaning they cannot have found his speech 'gracious' but so annoying it resulted in them throwing him out of the city and attempting to kill him.

Luke.9:43-45, again Jesus is speaking in the meaning of 'luke', even his disciples do not understand what he means. Luke.11:53-54 the scribes and Pharisees urge him to 'speak of many things' so they can 'entangle' him—indicating Jesus speaks a lot, rambles, which they hope to use to condemn him. Luke.18:2-5, a woman with a case keeps coming and going, she will not cease raising and speaking about her case—the text presents the 'unjust judge' finding her 'luke' and is the only reason he looks into her case, to stop her from coming and speaking of it 'luke/nagging'. Luke.18:34, again the disciples do not understand what Jesus is saying, and although in other gospels the disciples have been portrayed as not understanding what Jesus means in his speech, this has been further heightened and focused on in Luke by making everything else around it in the story 'talks too much/talks too much nonsense' 'rambling' in the style of 'luke'.

Finally, at Luke.24:11 when the women inform the men of the angels, and Jesus' resurrection, the men take their words as 'idle tales' i.e. the meaning of Luke: 'nonsense'. Cp: lookaah. (Luke)

Theophilus; Theóphilos; ضيوفِلوه ، ضيوفِلُه 'add to it/for him' 'guest(s) for him' 'hosted-him/it'. The meaning used in Luke is 'added to it/him' as it aims to add to the Jesus stories and the author claims to have 'perfect understanding', and this knowledge will be added to the fictional character's understanding (to 'Theophilus' which means 'add to it/for him'), as it makes clear the person being spoken to 'Theophilus' has already received information, but the author and narrator want to complete and add to whatever information he already has 'That thou mightest know the certainty of those things, wherein thou hast been instructed.'. Cp: dheoophilooh, dheoophiloh. (Luke.1:1-4)

Zacharias is used for 'remembered-he/him' 'reminded he/reminded him' 'mentioned he/mentioned him' 'he showed them' 'those/that he showed them' 'topped with water or liquid/filled to brim with water/liquid-he/him' as Zacharias sees an angel and the angel shows him that he will have a son although he is old and unable to produce a son, and this son will show people the right way. Zacharias is the son of **Abia**

'they rejected him/it' 'they refused' 'my father' 'his father' as he is being told he will become a father despite his old age, and barrenness of his wife.

The authors have not only borrowed the same and much-used compound word-names of Zechariah and Abia, but they have also borrowed the same character name and use of its meanings from 2Kgs.18-20 where Hezekiah's mother is 'Abi the daughter of Zachariah' but in Luke the word is used for a male 'Abia' who is father to 'Zacharias' because there is something important in the OT story which the author of Luke wants the audience to understand and it is the meaning of 'Hezekiah' 'I will water-he/him'.

The importance of having Zacharias and Abia names in one character without mentioning the word-name 'Hezekiah' but the meaning of 'I will water-he/him' is reinforced with **Zacharias** 'topped with water or liquid/filled to brim with water/liquid-he/him' and with **Mary** 'pass along' being the incomplete name of 'Miriam' 'pass along-river/sea' (see how 'Mary/pass along' is complete by the authors using Jesus to travel and go to coasts, shores, seas, on ships to connect Mary to 'water' and her pregnancy which did not involve the 'water of a man/semen' but the product of this pregnancy through God/Holy Ghost is her son Jesus whose story is mostly set in water-related locations) and in the Luke story Mary and her pregnancy are connected again to the 'Holy Ghost' but this time directly as semen/water. As can be seen in the OT stories, wherever there is a barren and/or old woman and a sterile and/or old husband, a special visit by God or a God-sent angel occurs, and the woman is miraculously impregnated. The same is happening with a virgin Mary and her abstinent fiancé Joseph, and the barren and aged Elisabeth and Zacharias. The story is saying they are being impregnated by God in a sexual act but most importantly by God's water/semen, and the Holy Ghost/God is filling them with his semen and semen/sperm is called 'water' in this language and culture. The naming of the son **John** and using it in Luke.1 is for its meanings 'soaked it/him (in)' 'brothers' 'betrayed' 'put/wrap it in sack/sackcloth' as God through his angel or Holy Ghost/Spirit is covering the female with his body when he fills her womb with semen/water (see when God covers a female Jerusalem with his body and clothes her) but is also soaking her and the child which will be conceived with his water/semen.

'And they had no child, because that Elisabeth was barren, and they both were *now* well stricken in years...But the angel said unto him...thy wife Elisabeth shall bear thee a son, and thou shalt call his name John...and he shall be filled with the Holy Ghost, even from his mother's womb.'. If you recall, John the Baptist actions revolve around dipping/soaking people below water, 'baptising' them—the Holy Ghost has filled his mother's womb, while John is in it, with semen/water, and John has been chosen in this story to be the child/character from holy water because his stories revolve around water and wearing clothes made of sack material (in Matthew), and the characteristic of sack material is that its rough fabric absorbs more water than other materials which is why the author of Luke has chosen to make him another 'holy' child as his name shows how God's water/semen is absorbed as he soaks in it and keeps it, to make it fit with the story that it can make the people who this character baptises 'pure/cleansed' not only in body but also in their ways/religion and from sins.

The 'John' meaning of 'brothers' is because Jesus and John are similar to brothers: God impregnates Mary and when Mary rushes to Elisabeth only then is Elisabeth filled by the Holy Ghost, i.e. John, six-months a foetus, is soaked in the same semen/water from God that Jesus is conceived by so they are similar to brothers. **Israel** is mentioned 'And many of the children of Israel shall he turn to the Lord their God' and this means 'Israel/twisted muscle-the' which was caused by illicit sex will now be set straight by two children who were conceived of 'holy ghost/holy water/semen' (John/Elias and Jesus) i.e. both the twisted muscle as a (deformed) genital and also as the 'conduct/behaviour' of the 'sinning' people will be straightened.

To make sure the audience does not miss understanding that these two women have been impregnated with God's water/sperm, the author makes it more obvious by depicting acts of sex between God/Holy Ghost and Mary, and by extension with Elisabeth through Mary: 'And in the six month the angel Gabriel was sent from God...To a virgin...and the virgin's name *was* Mary...And the angel said...Fear not, Mary: for thou hast found favour with God. And, behold, thou shalt conceive in thy womb, and bring forth a son, and shalt call his name JESUS...Then said Mary unto the angel, How shall this be, seeing I know not a man? And the angel answered and said unto her, the Holy Ghost shall come upon thee, and the power of the Highest shall overshadow thee', the 'overshadow thee' is figurative speech indicating sexual intercourse 'therefore that holy thing which shall be born of thee shall be called the Son of God.' And Gabriel continues to tell her that her cousin Elisabeth has also been given a miracle pregnancy and it is only when Mary (carrying the holy water in her womb) enters the room where Elisabeth awaits her that Elisabeth (her womb) is filled by the same Holy Ghost that filled Mary's womb to which the baby reacts. 'And Mary arose...and went into the hill country with haste...And entered into the house of Zacharias, and saluted Elisabeth. And it came to pass, that, when Elisabeth heard the salutation of Mary, the babe leaped in her womb; and Elisabeth was filled with the Holy Ghost...'. These verses also play on why John would state in Matthew that Jesus does not need to be baptised, but John believes he should be baptised by Jesus because Luke has Jesus and his mother as the recipients of the first 'Holy Ghost' which delivers God's water/sperm, and only after it is inside Mary's womb does she arrive quickly at Elisabeth's and only then is it (Holy Ghost/God's water) transferred to cover and soak an already six-month-old foetus/John (making Jesus the original/stronger); it also shows this is the first baptism in Mary' womb followed by John's baptism in Elisabeth's womb and the baptising is done with God's semen/water. (Luke.1)

Elisabeth; Elisábet; الي زآبَط ، الي زآبيط 'the one who-kicked', 'kicked' is used to describe when a baby moves inside its mother's belly; the story narrates that as soon as Mary enters, the baby moves (leaped) inside Elisabeth. It is also الي زآبَد ، الي زآبيد 'the one who-drinking bowls' as both Elisabeth and Mary are receptacles chosen to receive God's water/semen, and for the baby to grow in, 'the one who-buttered/perfumed with ointment/greased' as women's wombs/cervix are believed to be coated and filled with water/semen and so are baby John at six months in his mother's womb, and Jesus created from this water/semen—this creates a link between 'messiah' of which one of the meanings means to 'rub with something', 'massage into' and the OT stories support every time a king or other important character is appointed he has oil poured over his head (oil is one of the many substances used and massaged into hair and body by the people of the culture (also butter, oil and wax-based perfumes, ointments, etc.)) and the author of Luke is playing on the audiences' understanding of this practise and the language (Arabic). It also links 'messiah' meaning of 'wipe/wipe clean/wipe away' with God's water/semen, and the water of the river which John Baptist ('ducks under water') wipes away the sins of the people he is dipping under the water; الي ضآبَط ، الي ضآبيط 'the one who-tightens' 'the one who-grows stronger/is strong' as Gabriel informs Zacharias his son 'shall be great in the sight of the world' ; الي شآبَط ، الي شآبيط 'the one who-latticed' 'the one who-whipped' 'the one who-entwined'.

'Elisabeth' has been given an additional meaning in wordplay: الي شآبَت ، الي شآبيت 'the one who-grew old/aged' 'the one who-swelled' as in wood swells with water, penis with erection, head with cold, etc. The last two meanings are also indisputably supported by the text as both Elisabeth and Zacharias are described as being very old, and this is supported by making her from the 'daughters of Aaron' and depends on the audience knowing the story of Exodus where Aaron marries Elisheba (Exod.6.23) whose name means 'the one who-young woman' (does not apply to Elisabeth) 'the one who-swells'—this latter meaning applies to Elisabeth. The meaning of 'the one who-swells' is also to indicate her son John swelling with God's water and the water in the river he stands soaking in as it causes the rough and thick fibre of the sack clothing he wears to swell with water, and as 'John' is the soaking and the sack and he is saturated by God's water he too has been swollen (made greater/stronger) by God's water even while he was in his mother's womb 'and he shall be filled with the Holy Ghost even from his mother's womb'; it is also indicated again by mentioning he will cause 'Israel/twisted muscle-the' to be straight again 'And many of the children of Israel shall he turn to the Lord their God' and is intentional; as mentioned before, Israel gets its meaning because God withered Jacob's muscle during a wrestling match which was of a sexual nature, followed by Dinah causing all her male relatives 'withering' by having sex without marriage with her lover prince Shechem, followed by all the OT stories show the 'children of Israel' are twisted in constant disobedience against God, and the penis swelling with blood is intentionally meant here to show how John whose name along with his mother's means swollen sackcloth will make this twisted and withered muscle of Israel/Jacob to be straight again, straight being in the direction of the Lord.

It is the same as Elzabad (1Chr.12:12), and equivalent to Jehozabad (2Kgs.12:18-21), Zebudah (2Kgs.23:36), Zabad (1Chr.2:36), Zebadiah (1Chr.8:15), Josabad (1Chr.12:4), Zabdiel (1Chr.27:2), Ammizabad (1Chr.27:6), Zabbud (Ezra.8:14), Zebedee (Matt.41:21; 10). Cp: elee-zaabeṭ, elee-zaabeyṭ, elee-zaabed, elee-zaabeyd, elee-dhaabeṭ, elee-dhaabeyṭ, elee-shaabeṭ, elee-shaabeyṭ, elee-shaabet, elee-shaabeyt.

Aaron 'is-here-see/look' is used because Zacharias will see an angel, the angel will tell him what he cannot see in the future (conception and birth of John) and his son John making people see the 'right' path of God. 'drive them away' 'make them flee'. (Luke.1)

Herod is used for 'incited him against' 'bent his neck(physically)' 'of bent neck' 'became stubborn' 'incite' 'incites against others/causes problems between others' 'went to one side (while moving)' 'became stubborn' 'incited/incited against' 'focused on with malicious intent' 'of malicious intent' and also **Judah** 'call, or curse' 'to make a claim' 'make a false claim or an unproven claim' to show that the people currently are on the wrong path and disobeying God, but also to remind the audience of the stories about the kings of Judah and Israel and their people who constantly disobeyed God no matter how they were called to follow the right ways (Zachariah is also used to 'remind' the audience), emphasised by stating Elisabeth and Zachariah are righteous and blameless of any disobedience towards God. (Luke.1:5-6)

Elias 'he who/he is' 'yes, it is him' 'which one/which one is he' 'he who came/he who came to him' 'he did come/he did come to him' is used again in this story to confirm what Matthew already has that John the Baptist is the one awaited for, the word (illa/illah/إِلَّه/إِلَّا) means 'yes, it is/it is' and confirms the already stated fact/truth when someone doubts something said, it is used this way in the NT stories.

Gabriel as a compound word and character resumes its role to mean 'talked with-the' 'fixed/comforted-the' 'forced/made do-the' as he appears to speak with Zacharias and then Mary. He forces Zacharias to be unable to speak when the latter doubts God's information; he fixes Elisabeth and Zacharias' barrenness; he speaks of 'many of the children of Israel' who will be straightened towards the right path, i.e. 'fixed/healed'.

Galilee 'came-to' 'came-for' 'cleared-the' 'made clear-the' as Gabriel is sent to Mary to speak to her and make clear what is going to happen. **Nazareth** 'she/I vowed/set aside/dedicated to God' 'the vow/set aside/ dedication to' 'warned' 'she/I warned' is used because she is still a virgin, i.e. she is pure just like the things that are offered to God in sacrifices and offerings, and especially the 'firstfruits'; its meanings of warning are in that she is wary of the angel when it arrives and she issues a kind of warning that she is a chaste woman.

There is clever wordplay used, people of the times and/or who still live the culture and/or lifestyle and speak the language will immediately understand as the words draw an image and give a clear message: water of God is implied again as **Joseph** 'pour water gently on' of the house of **David** 'rolling pin stone grinder' and because it is 'the house of David' and **Mary** 'pass along' 'pass/cross/pass by'. This is how it is understood: water is poured over the rolling pin/David and the grinder as it is washed before and after grain is ground on it; the rolling pin/'David' smacks down on the slab of the grinder, moving to and fro and is also the motion of sexual intercourse; the verse reads 'a man whose name was Joseph, of the house of David' so the water being poured is issuing from the David/rolling pin smacking down going back and forth on the grinding slab—this is sex resulting in ejaculation of 'water/sperm' (specifically God's through the Holy Ghost or Gabriel) and as it finishes the sentence with Mary—she is receiving this action and its results, and the reason why her name has been shortened to Mary is complete with the climax and ejaculation of water represented by the words 'Joseph', 'David', and the message implied. Also, the shape of the David/rolling pin also indicates the penis and helps with this word imagery.

The reason for these explanations is not to be intentionally lurid or graphic, but objectively these are what the words and stories mean, and what was intended by the Biblical authors; to avoid stating clearly what these words mean and why they were used out of 'shyness' or 'conservative' worries would be just as bad as accidentally or intentionally giving the words and stories false or erroneous meanings which has been the case for most of Biblical scholars, historical and contemporary religious interpreters and their guesses which have no relation to the Biblical stories being told and have no relation or factuality with the words being translated/interpreted.

This is further supported by verse Luke.1:32 as the child resulting from this activity is promised that God 'shall give unto him the throne of his father David'. Again, the throne of a David/rolling pin is the rectangular slab it moves on during use and rests on when not in use, but more importantly this 'throne of David' which means the rectangular slab of the grinding stone when in use has heaped on it the ground dough ready for baking into bread, i.e. Jesus before he is baked. 'And, behold, thou shalt conceive in thy womb, and bring forth a son, and shalt call his name JESUS. He shall be great, and shall be called the Son of the Highest: and the Lord God shall give unto him the throne of his father David.' (Luke.1:26-35)

Jacob 'look after/take care of' and used when babysitting children or a house, is used because the son Mary is told about will 'reign over the house of Jacob forever'; it is also used for 'forces open' 'dislocates' 'forces open and takes/usurps' as Mary's next question and her nature in the NT is that she is virgin which no man touches, but in the description that follows in the consecutive verse is that the 'Holy Ghost' will 'come upon thee, and the power of the Highest shall overshadow thee: therefore also that holy thing which shall be born of thee shall be called the Son of God.' so her virginity will be forced open by godly 'spirit' and powers—and like any vagina or virgin intruded upon by the male organ the 'fruit' of that encounter is usually called the son of the male who caused it. (Luke1:33-34)

It is important to remind readers that these Biblical stories did not begin as religious stories, although they did eventually end up being taken as religious stories.

Juda is used for it meaning of calling out to somebody as when Mary arrives and salutes Elisabeth, Elisabeth's baby reacts to her sound, and the author has Elisabeth speaking 'with a loud voice' about the baby reacting because of how Mary did a 'Judah/called out' so this is not missed by the audience. '…and all these sayings were noised abroad throughout all the hill country of Judaea.' (Luke.1:39-44, 65)

Caesar Augustus; Kaisar; كيسَر 'broke' 'keep sęcret/like a secret'; قيصَر 'shortened/shortcoming/failed to complete or obey'. Augoústos; اوغوسطه ، اوغوَسطوه 'dove into/sank them/dipped/pushed them under/buried them under/immersed them under' and can be into or under liquid, dirt or anything including figuratively 'immersing/burying/sinking under', 'lower the flame/lower the intensity/lower the sound' it is reflected in the people being overcome with all the hectic needs of going to their respective places to be taxed; in Mary's unborn son in her belly, then swaddling him in clothes to keep him warm because they are not in a proper warm, draught-free room; in the angels lowering the shepherds' fears; in the 'lowering' state contrasted against the high status that baby Jesus who is described as 'Saviour' and 'Lord' is to be found in a stable/manger; the revealing of something hidden/buried is the angels informing the shepherds of Jesus birth which the shepherds confirm is something secret or unseen; in Mary keeping her thoughts and emotions inside her 'kept all these things, and pondered *them* in her heart.'; اوجوشته ، اوجُشتوه 'picked/took too many/much/I took too many/much' 'took by the handful' and refers to the character of the same name taxing the whole world according to the story and the word is equivalent to Joshua; عوجُشته ، عوجشتوه 'shook it' 'unsettled it' and means to shake a liquid or anything so that the contents unsettle or mix together and this is reflected also in the story that people have to go to their own cities/origins to be taxed causing the unsettlement of travel. In both meanings either Caesar 'broke' or 'shortened' can apply, as the people's whole fortune is broken so that a portion goes to taxes, and there is less of it as it is shortened to go to payment of taxes. Also the 'shortened' along with 'shook' is indicated as Mary being 'shaken' and caused to go into labour maybe before expected when they go to Bethlehem to pay taxes. Cp: kaisar, qaissar, aughosṭoh, aughoosṭooh, augoshtoh, augooshtooh, 'ugoshtoh, 'ugooshtooh. (Luke.2)

Cyrenius Syria; Kyrēniou; كيريينيو ، كيرييِنو 'they (or) of rented/hired/paid for' 'they (or of) forced/drove/chased (with violence)' as the people are being made to pay taxes and they have no choice because it is imposed by the authorities. 'Cyrenius' can have all the meanings under 'Cyrene' (see Simon Cyrene). Syria which in Greek is 'Syrias' is based on its OT word and is used for 'thrown/wide and far/extending over vast and distant locations' which is shown in the 'whole world' being taxed. Cp: kyreyeinyou, kyreyeiniou. (Luke.2:2)

Bethlehem is used for 'he/it will-eat plenty of meat' 'he/it will-feed well/fed well' 'he/it will-plumpen with food/with various nice food' as the stories are still tied to eating bread and having food security which is denoted by using David along with Bethlehem and also having shepherds guarding flocks to be the first to know about Jesus being born and '**Christ**' (cake of bread), **David** (rolling pin which makes the dough for bread) and **Jesus** (bread/broke and or ate bread) are mentioned to signify plenty is coming. (Luke.2)

Jospeh is still used for 'sorrow' as he is unable to secure a proper resting place for Mary and the baby is born in a stable. **Galilee** has been used for 'came-to' 'came-for' cleared-the' 'made clear-the' as they have come to pay taxes in Bethlehem, and also because of the meaning related to 'shook it/Augustus' reflects on Mary being induced into labour (when there is difficulty during childbirth, other women place the pregnant woman on a mat and lift her in the mat and shake her saying 'galgilooha, galgilooha' repeatedly and it means the same thing as clearing stones and impurities from grains where the idea is shaking the birthing mother who is having difficulty birthing will help the baby come out) and also on the connection between Jesus, David and bread. **Nazareth** is used for 'the vow/set aside/dedication to' as the taxes are set aside then delivered to the authorities, but also for (the helpers of/helped to succeed/succeeded/victors/supporters(ed) of/aides of' because the story has Jesus described as a saviour to the people. All the word-names used and narration of even unnamed characters is to symbolise plenty of food promised by God (on condition that people follow God's ways), and the custom which has continued to this day in the culture of the real people is when a baby is born a party is held on the seventh or eighth day (on the fourteenth day if it is delayed) where the baby is circumcised and a 'party/gathering' is held and visitors bring gifts to the new born and his/her mother, and the guests are fed meat and bread. (Luke.2:1-24)

Simeon (Gen.29:33) used for 'have heard/to hear/heard' as when he is possessed by the 'Holy Ghost' and the 'Spirit' (both mean God as it is God in the OT stories who possesses prophets, kings and other characters) he can hear him speaking to him and in this way it is revealed to him that the Lord's Christ (the Lord's cake of bread: Jesus) is born. (Luke.2:25-35)

Anna; Hánna; هآنّا 'satisfied' 'gave plenty/had fill' 'here'; هعنّا 'I saw/eyed' 'look, see-intended/hinted message at' 'I/will-inspect/look at/into' 'look, there he/it is' 'I will make suffer/made suffer' 'I helped/assisted/will help/assist', a sound/word repeated to get cows, sheep or goats back on the right path or back into the correct land; هغنّا 'I will become/make independent/rich/no longer needed' 'see, look-sang/hummed/made 'ghn' noise(used in singing or reading religious books)'.

All these meanings are present in the verses related to Anna: she is given plenty of people around her because she has been attributed to a tribe 'aser' (Asher) which means 'tribe/live with people/many people'; she is giving God plenty of worship in fasting and praying; because she never leaves the temple, and the temple is 'hekal/he will eat', where food is stored and served so she always has plenty to eat; Mary and Joseph bring Jesus during a feasting time which is the annual passover so there is plenty of food and drink; she sees and recognises Jesus and she calls the people to see him as in follow his ways because he is here; Anna is 'here' and so is Jesus; she is suffering because she was widowed early, and Jesus will suffer; as she is speaking of Jesus who in the other stories is likened to a shepherd and the people he wants to save/correct are called sheep/flocks this is symbolised in her name too; she is no longer dependent on her husband as after his death she never leaves the temple worshipping and as a prophetess; as she is a prophetess in the temple she is performing prayers which will include making the 'ghn' sounds in pronunciation and maybe singing songs/chants.

The meanings of her name extend to Jesus in the verses that follow: he is given plenty of health, strength and wisdom; his parents bring him again to the annual feast so there is plenty; he causes his parents to suffer distress as they search for his whereabouts, when they find him he says he is in the place where he is supposed to worship God (here); as he is with doctors, questioning them, this is also meant by 'looked/eyed' as in inspected; the narration shows Jesus is already capable of being independent of his parents. Cp: haanna, h'nna, hghnna. (Luke.2:36-52)

Anna is daughter of Phanuel; Phanouēl; بَنو ئِل/بَئيل 'children of-the' 'became apparent-the' 'build-the' and through her tribe she has many people even if they are not her children, they are her people; it becomes apparent to her that Jesus is a special saviour; the children of Israel are likened to buildings who Jesus' coming will cause to rise or fall. Cp: banoo-ill/eyl. (Luke.2:36-52)

Aser is **Asher** and used for its meanings 'I signal/gesture' as she recognises Jesus as the saviour/sent person; 'a lot of people' 'a group of people' 'lived with people(for a long time)' (and the latter means when a person not originally from the area lives a long time or life with these people), as she is described being the daughter of 'Phanuel' whose meaning indicates lots of offspring; she has lived a long life 'she was of great age'. (Luke.2:36-52)

The character of Anna has been made up based on several other characters/places: Hannah as she has most of her name meanings, but has also been linked by making her the daughter of 'Phanuel' which is based on Peninnah (1Sam.1:2,4,6), Hanna's stepwife who had many children—the many children of Peninna have been replaced by Anna coming from the tribe of 'Asher' (many people). She is also linked because Elkanah would take them all to the annual feast at Shiloh, and although it is Anna always present at the temple it is now Joseph, Mary and Jesus coming to the feast in Jerusalem.

Her character has also been based on the word-name and meanings of Anah (Gen.36:2); along with Pennina, her surname is also based on the word and meanings of Peniel and Penuel (Gen.32:30-32). The author has also paired and contrasted her in the narration to Simeon 'have heard/to hear/heard' as Simeon becomes aware of Jesus through hearing God's words (when he is possessed by God), whereas Anna 'look, see' 'look, there he/it is/there he/it is' sees him.

Tiberius Caesar; Tiberius; Tiberios; تِبَرِيوه ، تِبَرِيْه 'be good/pious towards/to him' 'go past him' 'disowns/states has nothing to do with-him' and Caesar for كيسَر 'broke' 'keep secret/like a secret'; قيصَر 'shortened/shortcoming/failed to complete or obey'. The people are told they should be pious and be obedient towards God before he comes and breaks mountains and levels paths (the latter means to break and/or shorten (Caesar); as the word of God skips two high priests, Annas and Caiaphas, and goes to John Zacharias it has skipped the high priests and the narration depicts God's word going past/ignoring the high priests but being delivered like a secret to John who goes on to preach what only he has heard from God. Cp: tiberyooh, tiberyoh, kaisar, qaissar. (Luke.3:1, 3-18)

Pontius Pilate; Póntios Pilátos; فونتِيه فِلَاّتَه ، فونتيوه فِلَاّتَه 'so you and him/he-are his fall/let him fall' 'so you and him/he-let him loose/go'. The falling is depicted in mountains, hills being levelled, trees falling being cut down; the 'let him loose, let go' meaning is in the narration of John wondering who has told them to attempt to lose their sins and find repentance to avoid punishment 'O generation of vipers, who hath warned you to flee from the wrath to come?'. (Luke.3:1,5,7)

Herod 'incited him against' 'incites against others/causes problems between others' 'focused on with malicious intent' is reflected as John answers the soldiers that they should not harm and make false accusations (false accusations are also 'Judaea') against people 'Do violence to no man, neither accuse any falsely...'; and in Herod imprisoning John. (Luke.3:1,14)

Galilee 'came-to' 'came-for' 'cleared-the' 'made clear-the' as John 'came into all the country,' Judaea 'preaching the...' Galilee 'baptism of repentance for the remission of sins.' (Luke.3)

Jordan 'they come/are coming home' because 'Then said he to the multitude that came forth to be baptised by him...'. (Luke.3:3, 7)

Philip 'in its core/pulp' 'pick out/cleanse/remove it' 'so he answers/responds/assists/serves-him' 'he will/should answer/respond/assist/serve-him' because the people likened to unfruitful trees will be picked and removed (felled) from among the people, the sins will be cleansed/removed by baptism and repentance, and this verse too is tied into the intentions which John accuses people of hiding within them. Also, in the thoughts of people wondering if John is Christ, which John hears although they do not say it out loud. (Luke.3:1, 9, 15)

Ituraea; Itouraía; عطوريبا 'they are twisted/twirled/curled' 'they twisted/twirled/curled' and refers to everything that is crooked or not right will be straightened out whether by punishment or repentance. And it is connected as 'Philip tetrarch of Ituraea' and in the verse it is linked to 'answering/assisting/responding/Philip' as responding to John (as prophesied by Isaiah/Esaias) calling them in the wilderness to leave their sins and follow the right path. It is similar to Ataroth (Num.32:3), Atroth (Num.32:34), Ether (Josh.15:42). Cp: 'ṭouraiya. (Luke.3:1, 4-5)

Trachonitis; Trachōnítis; تَرَكو نيتِه 'left-intentions/his intentions' 'stopped inner thoughts/intentions'; because John warns them not to believe what they think within themselves that Abraham will save them. 'and begin not to say within yourselves, We have Abraham...for I say unto you...'. Cp: trakoo-neetih. (Luke.3:1, 8)

Lysanias; Lysanías; ليسَنيَه 'he will make it straight/right' 'be correct/direct' 'for/in his direction' 'for/in his way(s)' and refers to telling them to follow God's way which is the straight path and that God will straighten the crooked 'Prepare ye the way of the Lord, make his paths straight...and the crooked shall be made straight...'. Cp: lysaneeah. (Luke.3:1, 4-5)

Abilene; Abilēnē; عَبليني 'of moving/shaking fat' 'they are shaken fat' 'of rolls/rolling of fat' (the movement of fat rolling/shaking when fat sheep move). This is used because the people who are being warned when they will 'baptise you with the Holy Ghost and with fire', the cleansing/purging of people is likened to a sacrifice whose fat is offered and burned to God; it also implies sexual abuse as part of the torture as the 'Holy Ghost' represents 'semen/water' and 'Abel' has been used before in the OT to mean rape before execution (See Abel-mehola) as the way sheep fat rolls under the wool is like the shaking of a body being copulated and this is meant here because the author of Luke has made it clear that the original baptism is connected to semen called 'water'. Cp: 'bileyneeei. (Luke.3:1, 9, 16-17)

Annas; Hánnas; هانَّه 'he satisfied/gave fill/plenty of-him/he' 'satisfaction/gave satisfaction-him/he'; هعنّه 'I saw/eyed-he/him' 'look, see-intended/hinted message at-he/him' 'I/will-inspect/look at/into-he/him' 'look, there he/it is-he/him' 'I will make suffer/made suffer-he/him' 'I helped/assisted/will help/assist-he/him', a sound/word repeated to get cows, sheep or goats back on the right path or back into the correct land; هغنّه 'I will become/make independent/rich/no longer needed-he/him' 'see, look-sang/hummed/made 'ghn' noise(used in singing or reading religious books)-he/him'.

'he satisfied/gave fill/plenty of-him/he' 'satisfaction/gave satisfaction-him/he' as the people are being told not to come without true intentions but with real repentance and they are likened to fruit of worthy quality and quantity being served to deserve God's forgiveness 'Bring forth therefore fruits worthy of repentance...'; it is also in the mention of many stones can be made as many children for Abraham to replace those who do not obey 'That God is able of these stones to raise up children unto Abraham.'. It is also in the answers to the people, publicans and soldiers, that just as they are satisfied with food and clothing that they should share it with the less fortunate so they too can have satisfaction, or at least the publicans should be satisfied with what they receive and not demand more; in the soldiers to allow people the content of peace and no harm. '...He that hath two coats, let him impart to him that hath none; and he that hath meat, let him do likewise...And he said unto them, Exact no more than that which is appointed you...and be content with your wages.'

'I saw/eyed-he/him' 'look, see-intended/hinted message at-he/him' 'I/will-inspect/look at/into-he/him' 'look, there he/it is-he/him' 'I will make suffer/made suffer-he/him' 'I helped/assisted/will help/assist-he/him' as John is directing a message to all those who come and listen to him; he is assisting people by baptising them and/or warning them; he speaks of future suffering of those who do not repent before he suffers himself by being thrown into prison; people are watching him and wondering if he is Christ; the people see the Holy Ghost descend on Jesus. The meaning of a sound/word repeated to get cows, sheep or goats back on the right path or back into the correct land is shown as John is attempting to get people back onto the right path. It is the same as Hanna (1Sam.1) and Anna (Luke.2:36-52). Cp: haannah, h'nnah, hghnnah. (Luke.3:2, 8, 10-14)

Caiaphas (Matt.26:1-5) 'how-he/him' 'they figured out how/thought about it' 'thought how/about-he/him' 'of thinking things/in good mood to think about matters' 'of turning back of head to/turning (his)back towards' 'turned back of his head or his back towards-he/him'. The 'how/figure out' meaning is shown in the people asking John what action they should take to avoid punishment. (Luke.3:2, 10-14)

Now the lineage of Jesus (Luke.3:23-38) was created with a very specific purpose. Where in Matt. it was to show how Jesus is related from Joseph all the way to Abraham and the importance was the connection to David, in Luke the importance is connecting it in a paternal lineage which ends with God as the oldest direct father. In Matthew, the author or editor attempted to create as straight a line as possible from Joseph to Abraham, but in Luke there is an intentional obfuscation beginning from after Joseph, and it intentionally repeats the same word-name or almost identical word-name characters to create a wordplay which helps direct the audience that the lineage is not only about a direct line to God, but the importance is on God's 'water' i.e. sperm. Most of the word-names indicate sexual acts or euphemistic indications of gushing water which symbolise semen, or sexual acts which will result in ejaculation.

The author of Luke has created a lineage which goes to Nathan the son of David instead of Solomon, but the Biblical authors have never attempted to create a 'reality' or 'real' story, in all the OT and NT there is an overt nature of the writing which shows it is fictional and these names are meant to represent themes to enhance and support the story being told, and not a genealogy as characters are not real people. For this reason, Solomon and others have been removed, but different word-names which hold the meanings of 'Solomon' have been used even if they are different characters and not Solomon.

The reason different word-names have been used and repeat a lot within the lineage is because the author wants them to reflect and relay with the chapters in Luke which follow Luke.3. All the possible word-name meanings for each word has been provided (by me), even if only the sexual/reproductive word was clearly meant by the Biblical author; this has been done so the reader can see all the possible meanings, then logic will allow the reader to see the common thread between all these names which is definitely the sex/water/semen related meanings.

Joseph 'of sorrow/feels sorrow/regret' 'gently pours water over/rinses/cleanses'

Heli; 'Ēlí; نيلي 'he who/the one who'; عيلي 'over' 'above/rose(physically or in status)'; غيلي 'running river/my running river' 'flowed/rushed like river' 'intense hatred/my intense hatred' (can also have other ghl/غل meanings). Cp eylee, 'eylee, gheylee.

Matthat; Matthát; مَطّاط 'stretched' 'of stretching'; مَطّآت 'she stretched/she stretched it'; مَضّآت 'she passed by' 'she completed' 'she made mark/sign' 'she completed'; مدّاد 'lay down' 'extended with hand/reached for/handed over' 'reached into' 'pus formed' 'inked'; مَثّآت 'she wiped urine/sperm' and means to use a leaf, stone or dry fabric to wipe away from genitals without the use of water; مَثّآث 'of wiping urine/sperm away(without use of water)'; مَضّآض 'rinsed mouth' 'type of tree' 'leaving/left/passing by' 'complete(d)' 'made mark(signed)'. Cp: maṭṭaaṭ; maṭṭaat, madhaat, maddaad, maffaat, maffaaf, madhaadh.

Levi 'twisted around/entwined' 'dishonest/goes around in circles' 'answered/answer/answer him(or it)' 'served/serve/serve him(or it)' 'answer/respond and assist' 'core/middle/pulp'.

Melchi; melchí; مَلخي 'cover with slimy substance'; مَلخع 'roll it/him in slimy substance'; مَلحي 'is good' 'nice/pretty' 'has a beard' 'is salted/salt'; مَلقي 'thrown/cast'; مَلكي 'what is wrong? What is the matter' 'my possession/belongs to me'. Cp: melkhee, melkh', melḥee, melqee.

Janna; Iannaí; يَنّي 'my pity/oh, pity'; جَنّي 'committed crime or bad act' 'demon' 'became insane'; هَنّي 'satisfied/content/filled' 'gave or received plenty'; عَنّي 'meant' 'hinted/directed message indirectly(by saying something to another person within the hearing range of the intended recipient of the message' 'suffered/made suffer a lot' 'for/representing me' 'from me'; حَنّي 'felt/feel affection' 'humming/purring' 'hennaed/applying henna'; خَنّي 'soaked' 'betrayed'. Cp: yannai, gannai, hannai, 'annai, ḥannai, khannai.

Joseph 'of sorrow/feels sorrow/regret' 'gently pours water over/rinses/cleanses'

Mattathias is the same as Mattithiah (1Chr.9:31); Matthathías; مَطّطيَه 'stretched it-he him' 'of stretching-he/him'; مَضّتيَه 'she passed by-him/he' 'she passed time/distracted-him/he' 'she completed-it/him/he' 'she marked/signed-he/him'; مَدّديَه 'lay down-he/him' 'he laid it down' 'extended with hand/reached for/handed over-he/him' 'reached into-he him' 'pus formed in it-he/him' 'inked-it/he/him'; مَتّتيَه 'she wiped urine/sperm-he/him' and means to use a leaf, stone or dry fabric wipe away from genitals without the use of water; مَثّثيَه 'wiped urine/sperm away(without use of water)/of wiping urine or sperm-he him'; مَضّضيَه 'rinsed mouth-he/him' 'gathered (specific type of) tree-he/him' 'passed by/went on/left-he/him' 'completed-he/him' 'made mark(signed)-it/he/him'. Cp: maṭṭaṭyah; madhatyah, maddadyah, maffatyah, maffafyah, madhadhyah.

Amos; Amōs; اموس 'I touch' 'I possess' 'I cause fight/problem(s)'; اموص 'I suck'; ئموز 'I squeeze/wring'; غموز 'I squeeze/massage' 'winking/facial gesture'. Cp: amoos, amooss, amooz, ghmooz.

Naum; Naoúm; نَووم ، نَووِم 'sleeping' 'put to bed/put to sleep' 'make bed/sleep' 'asleep' and all can also be euphemism for sex. It is equivalent to Naomi (Ruth) but where Naomi is a word being said to a female and given to a female character, this version of the same word used as a name is being said to a male and given to a male character. Cp: naoom, na-oum.

Esli; Eslí; اسلي/ئسلي 'comfort' 'distract/entertain' 'ask/ask questions' 'leak/flow'. It is similar to Solomon (2Sam.12:24; 1Kgs.3:5-13), Sallu (1Chr.9:7). Cp: eslee.

Nagge; Naggaí; نَكّي 'poked in wound' 'hurt' 'hurt/insulted' 'fucked'; نَجّي 'survived' 'spoke with quietly/secretly' 'baby making sounds pre-dawn' 'we come'. Both word-name meanings together make up most of the meanings of 'Solomon' (Esli: 'comfort' 'distract/entertain' 'ask/ask questions'; Naggai: 'survived' 'spoke with quietly/secretly'). Cp: nakkai, naggai.

Maath; Máath; مآئط 'stretched' 'stretching'; معط 'became thin/scrawny' 'overhandled until bent it out of shape/killed it'; مآئض 'passed by/passing' 'passed(ing) time/distracted(ing)' 'completed/completing' 'making mark/signing'; معض 'lecturing(ed)/preaching(ed)/giving or gave wisdom' 'has sore muscles' 'recompensing(ed)'; مآئت 'dead/dying'; مآئد 'laid down' 'laying down' 'extending with hand/reaching for/handing over' 'reaching into' 'pus formed/forming' 'inked/inking'; معد 'prepared' 'made enemy of/enmity' 'none left' 'did not return' 'did again/repeated'; مآئث 'wiping/wiped of urine/sperm' and means to use a leaf, stone or dry fabric to wipe away from genitals without the use of water; معذ 'protected(by God)' 'said protection prayer/said protection prayer over'. Cp: maa-aṭ; m'aṭ; maa-adh, m'adh, maa-at, maa-ad, m'ad, maa-af, m'av.

Mattathias; Same as Mattathias above.

Semei; Semeï; سَمَييا 'are ill' 'eye of needle/thread eye of needle' 'named' 'told naming story (samaaya)' 'poisoned'; سَمعييا 'heard' 'made hear' 'insulted in hearing of others' 'obeyed/listened'. Cp: semeyeeaa, sem'yeeaa.

Joseph 'of sorrow/feels sorrow/regret' 'gently pours water over/rinses/cleanses'

Juda 'he is called/calls' 'call, or curse' 'to make a claim' 'make a false claim or an unproven claim'; 'his hands'.

Joanna; Iōánna, Iōanán; يوعنّا 'they help/cooperate' 'they suffer'; جوعنّا 'they came-helped' 'they came-suffered' 'she is hungry' 'they came-directed message'; هوعنّا 'he suffered' 'he assisted' 'he meant/directed message at'; جوانّا 'they put it/him into a sack' 'they wrapped him/it in a sack/sack material'; خوانّا 'they soaked' 'they betrayed' 'they accused of betraying' 'they became brothers' 'they are brothers'; يوَنآن 'they moan/groan'; هوَنآن 'he moaned/groaned' 'he behaved spitefully/provocatively'; جوَنآن 'they put/him in sack' 'they wrapped him/it in sack/sack material'; خوَنآن 'soaked it/them (in)' 'brothers/two brothers' 'they betrayed'; عوَنآن 'they helped/assisted' 'they howled'. As in most lists unsupported by text, there is a number of words/compound words it could be, although its author probably had only one or two or a few specific meanings meant in wordplay, but without text supporting it cannot be anchored, whereas the word-names which only have one possible meaning and the word-names anchored and supported by the text of a narration can be definitively narrowed and determined. 'Joanna' in Luke 3 can be seen in the context of its surrounding word-names and themes as being 'soaked' regarding the process of ejaculation. Cp: yoo'anna, goo'anna, hoo'anna, gooaana, khooaana, yooanaan, hooanaan, gooanaan, khoanaan, 'ooanaan. (Luke.3:27)

Rhesa; Rhēsá; ريصآ 'piled on/they piled' 'stacked on/they stacked'; ريصع 'he/they overpacked' 'he/they pushed down to pack more in' 'over brimming'; ريضآ 'he/they agreed to' 'he/they became happy' 'happiness/contentment'. Equivalent to Rissah (Num.33:21), Rezia (1Chr.7:39). Cp: reyssaa, reyss', reydhaa.

Zorobabel the same as **Zerubbabel**; ذَروببادِل ، ذيرو ببادِل 'they procreated in swapped/changed' 'they sowed in swapped/changed' 'they left in swapped' 'leave-I will swap/change'; زَرو ببادِل ، زيرو ببادِل 'they visited/pilgrimaged in swapped/changed' 'they tightened in swapped/changed' 'they caused great disgrace in swapped/changed'.

Salathiel (1Chr.3:17) سيئَلتي ئِل ، سَلتي ئِل 'questioned/asked-the' 'leaked-the' 'made flow-the' 'comforted/entertained/distracted-the'; شيئَلتي ئِل ، شَلتي ئِل 'took-the' 'carried-the'; صيئَلتي ئِل ، صَلتي ئِل 'arrived at-the' 'connected-the' 'you arrived at-the' 'you publicly apologised to-the'.

Neri; Nērí; نيري 'we see/make see/of seeing/we understand/make understand/of understanding' 'we show/of showing' 'penised/insulted with 'penis'/we penis/we insulted with 'penis'/of insulting with 'penis'' 'fire/make fire/we make fire/of fire/of making fire' 'light/make light/we make light/shed light/we shed light/of light/of making or shedding light'; نعري 'we strip naked/make strip naked/of stripping naked' 'we/he/they are lustful/horny/have/had an erection/of horny/sexual excitement/having erections' 'they/we stood/stood erect/stood in front of without moving nor speaking' 'of standing/of standing erect/of standing in front of motionless without speaking'. It is equivalent to Naarath (Josh.16:7), Naarah (1Chr.4:5), Naaran (1Chr.7:28) Naarai (1Chr.11:37), Neriah (Jer.32:12-14). Cp: neyree, n'ree.

Melchi; same as above: 'cover with slimy substance'; 'roll it/him in slimy substance'; 'is good' 'nice/pretty' 'has a beard' 'is salted/salt'; 'throw/cast'; 'what is wrong? What is the matter' 'my possession/belongs to me'.

Addi; Addí; عدّي 'count' 'make an enemy/create enmity' 'infect' 'prominent/protruding'; غدّي 'feed lunch' 'frustrate' 'swell the glands'. Cp: 'addee, ghaddee.

Cosam; Kōsám; قوسآم 'divided' 'they were divided' 'swore an oath/swore by God'; خوصآم 'adversaries' 'bit directly from cake of bread' 'ate dry bread' (the latter means with no accompanying dip or dish, just bread or biting directly from the cake of bread without breaking it with fingers; قوزآم 'off-putting/off-put'. Cp: qoossaam, khoossaam, qoozaam.

Elmodam; Elmadám; المَدآم 'the bloodied/the of blood' 'the bloodied one/the of blood one' 'the bleeding' 'the lasting/the makes last' 'the makes last-one/the lasting one' 'the spinning/the dizziness'. It is equivalent to the words Adam (Gen.2:7-17) and Edom (Gen.25:30). (Gen.25:30). Cp: el-madaam.

Er (Gen.38:3,6-7) 'a disgrace' 'disgraced/taunted and humiliated' 'penis' 'penetrated with penis' 'insulted with penis(saying it to someone is a slur)'.

Jose; Iōsēch; يوسييح 'he goes wandering and seeking' 'melts and leaks'; it also can be the words and meanings under the names it is the same/similar to as follows: Josiah (2Kgs.22-23), Joses (Matt.13), Ishiah, Ishui (Gen.46:17), Jesui (Num.26:44), Ishiah (1Chr.7:3), Isuah and Ishuai (1Chr.7:30), Ishijah (Ezra.10:31). Cp: yooseeyaḥ.

Eliezer (Gen.15:1-4) 'he who/the one who-is ugly/makes things ugly' 'he who/the one who-squeezes/tightens' 'he who/the one who-visits/pilgrimages'.

Jorim; Iōrím; حوريم 'was forbidden' 'was sacred' 'became rotten/off' 'women'; عوريم 'was abandoned/lost in wilderness' 'type of tree'; خوريم 'pierced/slit/burst' 'burst/pierced from bottom'; يوريم 'throws around/spreads over wide space' 'spread/covered distant locations' 'is far apart' 'swollen/swells'; جوريم 'became criminal/did bad deeds' 'came threw' 'came from distant location' 'came and covered vast area'; هوريم'he threw' 'he killed' 'he is from far away' 'he spread (things/or self) over far and wide area/distance' 'falling apart' 'shouted and belittled/spoke unkindly to people in need' 'grumpy'. It is also meant to be بوريم 'pot/placed in pot' 'was rolled up' 'was rolled and folded' 'of rolls/of rolls and folds'.

The way this word has been used in Luke, and where it has been placed creates a link between 'Joram' (2Sam.8:9-11) which is بُرام 'pots' 'rolled up' and its other meanings which had no relation to the word 'pots/rolled up' in 2Sam.8:9-12, because here it does have a connection between the word 'pots/rolled up' and other meanings such as 'swollen/swells' 'sacred' 'forbidden' as they have been linked to the lineage of Jesus and the other characters in the line of descendancy in Luke. In particular, it is regarding an uncircumcised penis and an erection which is swelling from blood, and eventually will lead to ejaculation of semen. Although in 2Sam.8:9-11 Joram the son of king Toi character has no family relation to Abraham, the use of 'Jorim' (NT) in a lineage which links it to Abraham (attempts to) whose name was Abram (pots/rolled up) creates a character link, but more importantly to the Biblical author of Luke it creates an undisputable word-link between these characters and according to the author's intention. It may also indicate, and does clarify, why 'Joram' of the OT which was a word that obviously started as 'Boram' was changed and that change was most probably intentionally edited by the author of Luke to make the character name usable in the Jesus lineage (see 'Joram'). Cp: ḥooreem, 'ooreem, <u>kh</u>ooreem, yooreem, gooreem, hooreem, booreem.

Matthat; مَطّاط 'stretched' 'of stretching'; مَطّات 'she stretched/she stretched it'; مَضّات 'she stretched' 'she marked' 'she passed by' 'she completed'; مَدّاد 'lay down' 'extended with hand/reached for/handed over' 'reached into' 'pus formed' 'inked'; مَثّات 'she wiped urine/sperm' and means to use a leaf, stone or dry fabric wipe away from genitals without the use of water; مَثّاث 'wiped urine/sperm away(without use of water)'; مَضّاض 'rinsed mouth' 'type of tree' 'made mark(signed)'.

Levi 'twisted around/entwined' 'answered/answer/answer him(or it)' 'served/serve/serve him(or it)' 'answer/respond and assist' 'core/middle/pulp'.

Simeon 'have heard/to hear/heard' 'obey/obeyed'.

Juda 'he is called/calls' 'call, or curse' 'to make a claim' 'make a false claim or an unproven claim'; 'his hands'.

Joseph; 'of sorrow/feels sorrow/regret' 'gently pours water over/rinses/cleanses'.

Jonan; Iōnám; يونآم 'he is put to bed/put to sleep' 'he is made bed/sleep' 'he is sleeping/sleeps' and is euphemism for having sex; 'moans/groans-the'. It is the same as Onam (Gen.36:23), Naomi (Ruth). Cp: yoonaam, yoon-aam.

Eliakim (2Kgs.18:18) 'the one who stands/the one who stands instead of' 'the one who erects/has an erection/erections' 'the gagger/gag'. The word for 'erection' whether erecting a building, object or the stimulated penis is (qm/قم) 'stood/stand' and if saying 'has been turned on' or 'he has an erection' is (qyym/قيّم). Chosen for its meaning which is part of sexual intercourse and producing/delivering sperm.

Melea; Meleá; مَلاَ ، مَليآ 'filled' 'fetched water' 'covered' 'shift/short shirt/undergarment (short shirt/short nightgown)'; مَليع ، مَلع 'hairless and smooth' 'smooth and silky'. The first meaning refers to filling with sperm and the second the smoothness of the phallus. Cp: melyaa, mele-aa, mele', mely'.

Menan; Menná; مِنّآ ، مَنّآ 'from who' 'from what' 'from where' 'listed/counted/gloated over' 'wished', it is also the word which will become 'sperm' in modern Arabic (there is a relation between the Arabic word 'men/menewee(semen)' and what will end up in English 'semen'), 'what is it' 'who is it'. It is the same as Manna, Mene, Minnith, Miniamin, Mammon (Matt.6). Cp: mennaa, minnaa.

Mattatha; Mattathá; the same as Mattathah (Ezra.10:33); مَتّته/آ 'made it die' 'seemed or pretended to die'; مَدّده/آ 'made her/him/it lie down' 'laid it down' 'he lay down' 'extended it' 'reached into/for it' 'pus formed in it' 'inked it'; مَططه/آ 'he/she/it/they stretched' 'he stretched it' 'made it overstretched(by using/touching or stretching too much)'; مَثّته/آ 'she wiped his urine/sperm' and means to use a leaf, stone or dry fabric wipe away from genitals without the use of water; مَثّثه/آ 'wiped his urine/sperm away(without use of water)'; مَضّضه/آ 'rinsed his/its mouth' 'a type of tree' 'made mark/sign on a document' 'passed on/moved through/left' Cp: mattatah, mattataa, maddadah, maddadaa, maṭṭaṭah, maṭṭaṭaa, maffatah, maffataa, maffafah, maffafaa, ma<u>dh</u>a<u>dh</u>ah, ma<u>dh</u>a<u>dh</u>aa.

Nathan (2Sam.5:14); نآثآن 'we double/fold' 'we female/feminine'; نآدآن 'we guilt'; نآظآن 'we think/suspect'; نآطآن 'we clang' make a tinning or clanging noise'.

David 'stone rolling pin of grinding stone' 'this is/he is stone rolling pin of grinding stone' 'repeat/try again/keep at it' 'repeating the same revolving or to and fro motion' 'hesitates/goes and comes/recoils/revolves'.

Jesse 'my bread/my cold bread'.

Obed (Ruth.4:11-17) 'servant' 'of service' 'worshipper' 'of worship'.

Booz is Boaz (Ruth.2, 3, 4) 'of pride' 'of high standing' 'of dignity/cherishing' and 'slips from/through' such as from hand or through fingers: 'stepped on' 'feet'.

Salmon (Ruth.4:20-21); Salmōn; سَلَمُن ، سَلَمون 'asked' 'asked who' 'of questions' 'leaked/flowed from' 'comforted/entertained/distracted-who'.

Naason is **Naashon/Nahshon** (Exod.6:23; Ruth.4:12-22): 'crumble/crumbled' 'poked at and crumbled' 'riddle(d) with holes' 'maul(ed)' 'chunks missing from' 'bad luck' 'bringers of bad luck'.

Aminadab/Amminadab (Exod.6:23, Ruth.4:12-22) 'my uncle has protruding jaw and teeth' 'the one who has protruding jaw/teeth' 'my uncle has scars' 'the one who has scars' 'my uncles is wailing/mourning loudly' 'the one who is wailing/mourning loudly'.

Aram (Gen.10:22) 'wilderness, uninhabited place where it's easy to get lost' 'to abandon something or someone in the wild.' 'penis-the/insult with 'penis-the'' 'to throw/to do with throwing' 'killed/the killed/ the killer' 'thrown, strewn or located over a vast distance/over different areas' 'vast/distant/covering wide or many different areas'. Although 'Ram' was used in Ruth instead of this character to indicate the deaths of all the husbands of the Naomi family, the author of Luke has intentionally used 'Aram' for its 'penetrate with penis' meaning.

Esrom (Matt.1:3) 'harvest/reap' to harvest the stalks and/or the panicles.

Phares/Pharez (Gen.38:29) 'bring forward/press on and push out' 'split open/push out/emerge by pushing up or out/ divide by breaking or splitting' and although in its own story at Gen., it indicated the character's action of splitting through and beating its twin brother out of its mother's vagina, it was also used to indicate the importance of having a child by any means even through incestuous or illicit sex as in Tamar and Ruth's stories. But here in Luke, although the end-result is the same for the theme, the word and story-link is used to show the importance of securing 'water/sperm' as the importance of life, and not any water/sperm but that which is connected to God's.

Juda 'he is called/calls' 'call, or curse' 'to make a claim' 'make a false claim or an unproven claim'; 'his hands'.

Jacob (Gen.25:26-34; 27) 'forces open' 'dislocates' 'forces open and takes/usurps' and is used for meaning of its word as the penis forces open the vagina, the sexual act is of forcing its way into the vagina so that the result is the ejaculation of semen/sperm/'water' into the womb. It also reminds the audience of the importance of 'sperm/water' and how two sisters who wanted to mother children from Jacob were willing to give their handmaids to receive this water to create offspring.

Isaac (Gen.17:15-19; 18:9-14; 21:1-7) 'he pulls up water little by little' 'swipes/drags water' (during drought) and it reminds of the importance of a man's water/semen becoming offspring, but also on the theme that it was only after a special visit by God did Sarah become pregnant.

Abraham (Gen.17) 'pull up/draw up-the' 'clear-the' and although these two meanings were linked first to his role in circumcision, they were also linked to Isaac's conception as both Abraham through his name and also in description where he is described as too old than to be able to father children, and Sarah is compared to a dry well, and both Abraham and Isaac's names are connected to pulling up water in times of plenty (Abraham) and in drought (Isaac), impregnating water/semen happens after God's promise and a special visit to Sarah.

Thara is **Terah** (Gen.11:24); 'set/place down' or 'lay down from tiredness/collapsed' 'sheet(linen)' 'do you see him/it' 'she sees him/it' 'see him/it' and not only continues to attempt to 'link' Jesus to Abraham (which it fails to do) but also links Jesus again to God's water as we are getting closer to God.

Nachor is **Nahor** (Gen.11:22); 'daylight' 'rivered/ran like a river' 'spoke to angrily/with cruelty' 'bored a hole through/hollow' 'snored' 'nostril' and is used for its meaning to 'bore a hole'.

Saruch is **Serug** (Gen.11:21); 'a light' 'sunrise' 'navel/belly button' 'your secret' 'knotted you/bundled you' 'ached you' 'insisted on you' 'blocked you/held within you' and still implies with navel/your secret/knotted you, insisted on you, blocked you as sexual activities, while getting closer to the link to God.

Ragau; rhagaû; Ragau has replaced 'Reu' because although it has the meanings رَئو 'they watered' (and 'they saw') and ريعو 'they watered/soaked/flooded' (and 'they shepherded/took care of'), the author of

Luke wanted a more suitable wordplay for what he was aiming for: ريغَو ، رَغَو 'foamed'; ريجَو ، رَجَو 'they shook' 'they waited' 'they implored'. Similar to Reu (Gen.11:19-21), Reuel (Gen.36:4), Raguel (Num.10:29-33). Cp: ra-ao, ry'ao, raghao, ryghao, ragao, ryghao.

Phalec the same as **Peleg**; Phalek; بَلَغ 'passed on message' 'first ejaculation/menstruation' 'reached puberty'; فَلَق 'split/divided'. Both are linked to sexual activity and reproduction. Cp: balegh, phaleq. (Luke.3:35)

Heber the same as **Eber**; 'shadowed over' 'excused' 'extremely disfigured (for a reason)' 'against nature' 'nature in reverse/nature reversed' 'became dusty' 'became cloudy (with dust)' and the author of Luke has Gabriel explain to a virginal Mary how she will become pregnant and one explanation was in the same way a man shadows over a woman during sex 'And the angel answered and said unto her, the Holy Ghost shall come upon thee, and the power of the Highest shall overshadow thee' (Luke.3:35).

Sala is **Salah** (Gen.10:24); 'happened' 'fixed/was fixed' 'mediated/reconciliated' 'rock/stone' 'his rock/stone' 'reached/connected' 'arrived' 'arrived him/it' 'reached him/it' 'connected it' 'reached him/apologised' 'had diarrhoea/defecated' 'a river from rain' 'leaked/flowed' 'asked/questioned' 'comforted/entertained/distracted'.

Cainan; Kaïnám; كَيين آم 'gathered cain-the/ate cain-the' 'sheltered from rain-the'; قَيين آم 'sat up straight-the/positioned straight-the' 'made perky-the' 'estimated liquid/topped up liquid-the' 'estimated measurements/eyeballed measurements-the'. It is equivalent to Cainan (Gen.5:9), Kenan (1Chr.1:2). CP: kayeen-aam, qayeen-aam.

Arphaxad (Gen.10:22) 'your fucking/copulation has increased' 'he fucked you more' 'your smell/scent has increased/become stronger' 'your reputation/fame/knowledge of you has increased' 'your understanding knowledge has increased'.

Sem the same as **Shem** (Gen.5:32); Sēm; شيم 'a smell' or 'smelled'; سيم ''named' 'told samaaya story/naming story' 'poisoned' 'eye of needle' 'will thread needle' 'will be led through/followed'; eye of needle' 'thread needle' and this indicates two things: how a person loves to smell who he/she is making love to, and also the action of threading a needle is the same as a penis penetrating the vagina. Where in Noah's story it was used to show the difficulty and manoeuvring in trying to get animals of different sizes and dimensions through the doors of the ark, here it is to show how a penis initially has difficulty in penetrating (sometimes missing just like a thread goes above the needle-eye or below it) and then the motion of sexual intercourse (the genitals) which is like sewing. This word-name was also explicitly used for Shemeber 'threaded needle(s)'supported by the kingdom they gave him 'king of Zeboiim' 'they penetrated them with penis'—and you know how he and his kingdom ended (See Shemeber king of Zeboiim (Gen.14:2-8)). Cp: sheym, seym.

Noe as in (Matt.24:37) 'warned/brought to attention/reminded' 'the stone/seed(of fruit)' 'intended' 'the intentions/unspoken thoughts'. And is used in this instance as the 'sperm' because the lineage is to show the direct link and passing on of God's water/semen. When a female character is made into 'Noah' it is also to bring attention specifically about the seed of Zelophehad which has ceased because he had no male son (see Noah daughter of Zelophehad (Num.26:33; 27)), which in turn supports a clearer picture of the Biblical authors' intentions who created Noah and his story: they intended this meaning that Noah, his wife and married children, the animals and people in pairs, are the seed/stone 'Noah' that will plant and repopulate a world that has been wiped-out of animals/humans. Even where the word 'noah' makes up part of another compound word-name e.g. Manoah and his wife, it represents the absence of a fertile seed/sperm and about making this fertile semen/water work by a visit/ promise by God and/or his angel for the barren wife to conceive a child and give birth to it (See Manoah and his wife (Judg.13:1-14))

Lamech (Gen.4:19-23); Lámech; لآمَك 'gathered-you' 'blamed-you' and لآمَح 'hinted' 'stealing glances/looking secretly/looking quickly' 'blinked'. It is using the 'gathered-you' for its suitability in copulation. Cp: laamek, laameḥ.

Mathusala is **Methuselah** (Gen.5:24-27) 'What did he do?' or 'What happened?' 'what distracted/entertained him?' 'What comforted him?' 'What leaked/flowed him? /What made him leak/flow?' and is used for its meanings of 'flowed/leaked' and in the original story, in addition to Lamech who will father Noah (Noah being the 'sperm/seed' of mankind and animals after the flood), has himself 'sons and daughters'.

This is a good place to point out something which cannot be ignored. Anyone reading the Bible can see where editing, additions and maybe deletions have been made, there is a jarring effect on the narration.

One of these is the use of exactly the same character names within the same story (and in other stories) where they were obviously meant to be the same characters. In this instance I refer to the Enochs/Noah, Irad/Jared, Methusael/Methuselah, Lamechs, and with Luke.3 it becomes obvious the author or editors of Luke went back into Genesis and made these changes so that the story of Luke and Genesis.5 would have the meaning of 'water/sperm/seed' which the gospel of Luke has made the main theme above all other themes. Now it makes sense why the edited Genesis story did not use different names that would differentiate the new characters (sons of Seth Adam Gen.5) from the earlier characters (sons of Cain Adam Gen.4) and it also explains why the editors could not edit-out the earlier characters who are the sons of Cain whose son's character's names have been given by the later editor of Luke.3/Gen.5 to the sons of Seth.

Why not simply delete the sons of Cain from the story or change their names, one might ask—the answer is, he could not: the problem is these stories were not popularly *read*, but popularly *orated/narrated* and people will not forget nor accept that these characters no longer survive because you cannot stop people telling stories which have been told since ancient times, but you can add stories with the same/similar character names who are someone else's children (in storyland) and these can also circulate without negating the original characters. The reasons are quite clear why the authors or the author of Luke simply did not have them connected through Cain then to Adam and God—because Cain was rejected by God, Abel has been killed by Cain so there is no 'good/pure' character to link Jesus to God with the only surviving son of Adam being not only a murderer, but someone so unloved and repulsive to God that God does not even accept his offerings even before he becomes a murderer of the person who in action and in name offers God's (in the story) favourite food (Abel/shaking, moving fat(of sheep)). The answer was either to give Adam a third son (Seth) or change the names of Seth's sons into the same as Cain's, but most probably there was no Seth until a need for a bloodline from Jesus to God arose; and this narration-need of a bloodline to God is not in any of the stories which do place importance on being Abraham's and/or any other significant characters' genealogy, but it is in Luke's narrative.

Even in Matthew there is significance placed on tying Jesus to David, and goes further to link him to Abraham, but Luke wanted a direct flow, pardon the unintentional pun, from God's water to the water that conceived Jesus and in turn 'baptised' everyone he and John convinced to follow. They all miss the mark by attributing this long line of descendancy to Joseph, this is due to Mary being a virgin and no human fathering Jesus—which further proves my point that whoever wrote or edited (if the original story had ever been different) the stories categorised as NT stories, were actually writing a mocking account about Jesus, Mary and 'Christians' in general. If these stories were written by pro-Jesus or pro-Christianity authors/editors and no significant satirical changes made to them then it seems to have grated on the nerves of male authors (of the time) that the closest connection to both God and Jesus be through Mary, a female, as the authors/editors have redirected the strength and power in the story through a male connection to God and in the male sperm/water. It seems the editors disapproved of a narrative where God both directly chose and was in direct physical contact with a female with no need of any male between her and God that they chose to risk contradicting the immaculate conception and virginity of Mary, as well as Jesus being the 'Son of God', by trying to forcefully connect him by blood/sperm to God in an uncut male link which is completely disconnected to Jesus. None of the stories have Joseph in any way biologically his father (unless you take into account these stories were entertainment and Joseph is meant to be the father who approached his fiancé before marriage which is not unusual to Samaria/samaara and samaaya stories), but that is beside the point regarding the objective of the authors of these stories and specifically the author or editor of Luke.

Enoch (Gen.4:10-17; 5:24-27) 'upset and not eating or talking' 'I will cry out in distress (or loudly)' 'I will warn/bring to attention/remind' 'I will seed/stone(of fruit)/plant' 'I will intend/decide within me' 'I will warn/bring to attention/remind' and is used for the meanings it implies with 'I will seed/stone' which are what the stones/seeds of fruit are called.

Jared (Gen.5:15) 'wobbles/wobbled head' 'neck bent to one side' 'stubborn' 'bruise/bruised/lump/lumpy' 'stripped leaves off completely'; and is used by Luke to indicate the movement bodies make when copulating.

Maleleel; Maleleẽl; مَلِّي يل 'move rod applicator back and forth inside-the' 'rod applicator of kohl bottle', the rod applicator is called (meel/meeloo/ميل/ميلُ/ميلو) and it is both the lid and rod applicator of kohl bottles whether made from precious metal or glass (eventually plastic too in modernity) and when the bottle is closed the 'meel/millo' part rests inside the kohl pot, when kohl is applied to the eye it is poked in and out of the kohl bottle and then placed on the inside of the eyelid, they eye is closed and the rod is run back and forth to make the kohl coat the internal eyerim; 'fetch water-the' 'fill water-the' and the way water is fetched is by going back and forth between the well and home and filling the vessels which it is transported in and poured into for storage. As vulgar as it may sound, the intention of the authors by using this name is to mean the 'in and out' action of the kohl applicator, but also of the water filling the pots and the action of the men and women who go back and forth, up and down while fetching the water and this means to remind of the same action of sex, and the ejaculation of 'water' which results with the climax of sex.

Again, this word is meant to be the same as in the original Genesis story 'Mahaleel' (Gen.5:12) which means 'fidgets-the/moves around-the' 'fidgets/slightly moves or wiggles something (to make it fit/or right)' with the same ideas behind it being about sex, a man fitting into a woman even if there is difficulty at penetration of a tight orifice; it also means 'instead of-the/in the place of-the' 'instead of-the/in the place of-the' and can have 'circumcise/purify/sweeten' and other ḥl/حل meanings. And this is another word which makes it clear this story was in the local language (Arabic) before it was translated into Greek, but with difficulty of pronouncing 'Mahaleel' by the Greek end of the translation process a local has chosen a word which is not the same word, but gives the same theme/idea of which is the action/movement of male and female sexual organs. Maleleel is equivalent to Millo (Judg.9:6,20). Cp: malely-eel.

Cainan; Kaïnám; كَيين آم 'gathered cain-the/ate cain-the' 'sheltered from rain-the'; قَيين آم 'sat up straight-the/positioned straight-the' 'made perky-the' 'topped up (with water/drink/liquid)-the' 'estimated measurements/eyeballed measurements-the'. It is equivalent to Cainan (Gen.5:9), Kenan (1Chr.1:2). Cp: kayeen-aam, qayeen-aam. (Luke.3:36)

Enos (Gen.4:26) 'wriggled/wriggled around' and still has sexual meanings as intended by the author of Luke, and whoever authored this part of Genesis.

Seth (Gen.4:25) 'to carry gently' 'poured gently/pouring gentle spurts of water' and means to try and not move/shake whatever is being carried—and at Gen.4 it seems to also indicate being gentle with a new born and a son after losing two sons (one a victim of murder, the other exiled because of the murder) and gently washing away the sorrow; but the way it is used in Luke is to depict the water/semen at ejaculation and how to gently approach a woman or girl (remember back then girls were probably married very young) and that is to be gentle, not to shake her—(in the culture when a bridegroom approaches his bride (brides are virgins) he is supposed to be gentle because the first time is always painful for a virgin. This is made clear in how although the author of Luke has created a lot of confusion and back and forth using the same character names in an otherwise unavailable-anywhere-else genealogy in the Bible other than in Luke, he has made sure to construct the lineage that leads to God is a virginal setting and theme: Cainan is the foreplay and romance, the caressing, nibbling and kisses (gathered/ate cain fruit) before Cainan the erection ('sat up straight-the/positioned straight-the' 'made perky-the'); Enos is the bride 'wriggling/squirming' in fear or pain, and the male organ going in and out; Seth ('to carry gently' 'poured gently/pouring gentle spurts of water') is the bridegroom being gentle to cause the least pain and achieve the all-important ejaculation of water/semen. Before it leads to Adam.

Adam (Gen.2:7-17) 'is from blood' 'made bleed' 'is to last long' 'is from nothing'. The 'is from blood/made bleed' is the virgin's first sexual intercourse and the sign of a virgin, this is important because Mary the mother of Jesus is a virgin and it was God's Spirit/Holy Ghost (i.e. God) which impregnated her. 'it is from nothing' and remember God wants everything that is virginal: 'first fruits, firstborns' and when he has a son from a human mother the woman is a virgin too, so there will be blood like any sexual encounter with a virgin. But more importantly, the authors of these Biblical stories are fascinated by 'water' that brings life, and whether rain from the sky/God to bring the earth to life, and water from man or beast to breed life, it seems to come from nowhere—a fountain of life which all begins from miraculous water.

God: 'Adam, which was *the son* of God': it is not just a 'line' of descendancy and genealogy for the author of Luke and the gospel of Luke, but an attempt to prove they come from the same 'water/semen' and that superior 'water' is God's water. Right at the beginning of Genesis 'the earth was without form, and void and the darkness *was* upon the face of the deep;' but this changes when God moves over the waters in the same way as he moved over Mary 'And the Spirit of God moved upon the face of the waters.' (Gen.1:2). Something similar is repeat at Gen.2:5-6, it still implies whether water as in rain or mist it is the same idea as sperm (godly or otherwise) and is what brings man to life, although it has not rained there are already plants growing, but man only comes when God causes mist to mingle with the soil 'And every plant of the field before it was in the earth, and every herb of the field before it grew: for the Lord had not caused it to rain upon the earth, and there was not a man to till the ground. But there went up a mist from the earth, and watered the whole face of the ground, And the Lord God formed man of the dust of the ground, and breathed into his nostrils the breath of life, and man became a living soul.'

I will not go into great detail to avoid lengthening this subject, but 'breath' 'wind' bringing things to life or back to life is also from the idea of sex. Anyone who has sex will know the different breathing, panting, lusting, etc. caused by the physical nature and pleasure of having sex. At the end of this breathing, panting and ejaculation of 'water', life comes from pregnancy (the Biblical text is abounding with proof where breath and specifically breathing onto or wind blowing onto something not alive, brings it to life). In Arabic the word for 'spirit/soul' is (rooḥ/ruḥ/روح) and this word comes from (rḥ/reeḥ/رح/ريح) 'wind'.

So in Luke (whether meant as a jibe against Jesus/Christianity or as support for it), God is the ultimate and origin of 'sperm/water' which first brought man to life, but specifically whose 'water' brought Jesus to life out of a virgin untouched by human sexual intercourse, and God's water/sperm gave John the Baptist and Jesus powers to purify, cleanse and purge from physical illnesses and filth as well as from the filth of disobedience by cleansing souls and washing away sins.

Language is the most significant proof of the meanings of words in the Biblical stories which shows exactly what the words and stories mean, but also who wrote these stories; this language also shows how the word 'God' becomes the word to describe the deity who creates all things: in the original language 'God' is 'rb/rab/رب' or even 'rabbi/ربّي' 'dilute(d) and mix(ed) with water' and 'grew/grew well/grew or raised many', and in the stories just as believed in real life 'God/rb/mix and dilute with water' brings the earth to life with rain mixing and diluting with the soil, and humans and animals through male-water/semen mixing and diluting with a female egg. (Luke.3)

The non-sexual meanings of all the word-names are reflected in the themes of the chapters that follow Luke.3, each chapter contains several actions, narrations which reflect at least several of the 'genealogy' name-themes of which the genealogy themes begin with Jesus and end with God (this has not been included in this book to avoid overburdening an already large body of work).

Sarepta; Sárepta; ذارفت 'overflowed'. The same as Zarephath (1Kgs.17:9-16) and based on that story. Cp: vaare<u>ph</u>ta. (Luke.4:26)

Apostle; apostolous, apostoloi; ابوسطولوه ، ابوسطولوي 'spread for him' 'spread for me' 'of spreading' 'explain for him' 'explain for me' 'of explaining', from the root word (bsṭ/بسط): spread, smooth, explain, detail, spread over, stretch, make happy, make content, simple, take over, lay out, pleasure, joy, contentment, ownership. There are different meanings for this word and how it is used, but all are interconnected and worth understanding as it helps understand why Jesus' disciples and the people they would eventually increase to do God's work were titled as such. In addition to 'spread', as in disseminate, it can also mean to physically spread something such as plaster (in modernity cement) as it covers a whole area and makes it smooth and secure as in watertight and this nuance is also in the 'spreading the word of Jesus' meaning i.e. making it clear; 'detailed' 'simple' as the more a matter or story is explained in detail, the simpler it is to understand and be absorbed by its audiences; 'lay out' as in show everything, bring everything out so it can be viewed, and this too can be physical things/objects or to detail something in separate sections to be better understood; 'spread over/take over' to cover a wide area or surface, the way an animal does when it rests such as a cat, or the legal way when someone takes over disputed land and works it and this gives him/her a claim to ownership, and in the story it is about taking over people's old beliefs/convictions/souls and replacing it with Jesus/God's ways; 'pleased/happy/content' and the story has following Jesus/God's way brings joy in this life and the afterlife.

The meaning of 'apostle' encapsulates all the above meanings rolled into its most dominant meaning as used and intended by the Biblical authors: it is to spread the story of Jesus, the story itself is about spreading the word of God, the ways of God, the belief in God—but through spreading the story. A simple example is when the apostles are arrested and brought to trial 'they set *them* before the council: and the high priest asked them, Saying, Did not we straitly command you that ye should not teach in this name? and, behold, ye have filled Jerusalem with your doctrine…'. When an angel frees them from prison it is so as to spread the story of Jesus 'Go, stand and speak in the temple to the people all the words of this life. And when they heard *that*, they entered into the temple early in the morning, and taught…And they departed from the presence of the council, rejoicing that they were counted worthy to suffer shame for his name. And daily in the temple, and in every house, they ceased not to teach and preach Jesus Christ.' (Acts.5:19-42). Had there been a written copy of these stories in their original language the word 'Apostle' would be 'apostel' like all the other 'el/the' ending word-names, but as transliterated in Greek it ends with (ois/os) making the word end with 'for me/for him' (which is probably how Arabs translated it to the

Greeks). It is equivalent to Pi-beseth (Ezek.30:17). The word is similar in meaning to 'Gospel' and 'Evangelion'. Cp: abosoṭoo-loh, abosoṭoo-loi. (Luke.6:13)

Zelotes; Zēlōtēs; صيلوطيه 'oiled/oil/oiling' 'antagonist/antagonising' 'focused on/obsessed with/acting against viciously or determinedly' and is from the word (sslṭ/صلط) which means 'focused on/authority/oil' and the other meanings of focused/antagonising/acting against all stem from the word 'oil'. E.g. the word is used to describe when someone is verbally, or physically attacking another, or when bothering someone about something or picking on them—the person doing the antagonising is called 'sseloṭeyh'; in reproaching the antagonist who is bothering them, they would say to him/her 'what ssllṭ (focused/oiled) you upon/against me?'. The word has come from the nature of oil to stick to the skin, fabric or surface and it cannot be removed easily, i.e. it sticks onto the person or surface, lots of hot/warm water can remove it from skin and metallic or glazed clay objects but not from floor or fabric, and even regarding skin and metallic utensils the soap of those days could not have been harsh, but made from pulping/powdering leaves from a specific type of tree and although effective on hair, skin and clothes, if anything is too greasy would require hot water and more effort to remove it. It is equivalent to Bazluth (Ezra.2:52).

It could also be wordplay on زيلوتيه 'of removing/wiping out/disappearing/walking off' and means to remove something completely or go away doing something not right, e.g. if a man (zl/زل) with a woman it is believed he is having his way with her. It means the person(s) has mischievous intent behind the disappearing or going somewhere out of sight; someone who likes to get rid of things, or carry away things, someone who is misbehaving or will not let people rest/live in peace. This latter name matches the character's surname in Matt.10 where he is Simon the Canaanite ('convinced him' 'gave up on him' 'no hope with him') as when a person gives up on something or someone, or is satisfied with a response/situation—he/she/they leave. It is the same word as the core of Zilpah (Gen.29:24; 30:9-10) and Ezel (1Sam.20:14-42). Cp: sseylooṭeyh, zeylooteyh. (Luke.6:15)

Nain; Naín; نعين 'mourning/they are mourning' from the word (n'/n'y/نعي/نع) 'grief/mourn/mourning'. It is the name of the city Jesus enters and meets a procession of mourners carrying a dead man, and touches the bier the dead man is carried on—which in Arabic is called a (n'sh/نعش) from the same root word (n'y/نعي). When Jesus tells him to come back to life, the dead man does so and sits up—this shows more than one wordplay was going on: in everyday Arabic when a person is revived or refreshed the word (n'sh/نعش) is used because it also means 'revived/refreshed' and is based on the root word ('sh/'ash/عش/عاش) 'live/lived/survived'. Cp: n'een. (Luke.7:11)

Joanna from the translations at (Luke.3:27) we can see the following in this verse; Iōánna, Iōanán; يوعنّا 'they help/cooperate' 'they suffer'; جوعنا 'they came-helped' 'they came-suffered' 'she is hungry' 'they came-directed message'; هوعنا 'he suffered' 'he assisted'; جوانّا 'they put it/him into a sack' 'they wrapped him/it in a sack/sack material'; خوانّا 'they soaked' 'they betrayed' 'they accused of betraying' 'they became brothers' 'they are brothers'. Joanna is mentioned as ministering to Jesus from her own fortune, and Jesus goes on to tell a parable which has a message for the audience to understand from it at which the end there is crying out, but the disciples still need the message to be explained. As she is part of the group who watch Jesus' crucifixion and death, she watches him suffer; as well as assist in bringing/preparing ointments for his burial. Cp: yoo'anna, goo'anna, hoo'anna, gooaana, khooaana. (Luke.8:3-4)

Chuza; Chouzás; خوزاه 'swore at him/insulted him' 'were insulted' because they are servants of 'Herod' which means to 'incite against/malicious intent' and Herod in other gospels plotted to kill a baby Jesus so Joanna is married to 'insulted' to work for Herod; خوذاه 'take him/it' 'they took' and is because Joanna takes from her own fortune and gives to Jesus, also because of her participation in his burial. It has a third meaning: قوزاه 'boulder' and a boulder seals Jesus' tomb and is found removed the next day. It is equivalent to Ahaz (2Kgs.15:38; 16) and other 'ahaz' compound word-names. It is also equivalent to Koz (Ezra.2:61). Cp: khoozaah, khoovaah, qoozaah. (Luke.8:3)

Susanna; Sousanna; شوشَنّ 'something important' 'things and important things' 'many things and wonderful things' 'things, important things' 'things, many things' 'things, amazing/wonderful things' 'puzzling matters/serious matters' 'caused a commotion'. This character also provides for Jesus and serves him from her personal fortune, she also witnesses his death and burial and brings ointments. Her name is also linked to the parables which are important for Jesus' audience to understand but which his disciples feel are puzzling and need explanation; she is among the group left puzzled when they find the boulder removed from the sepulchre and Jesus missing. It is equivalent to Shushan (Neh.1:1), Susanchites (Ezra.4:9-24) and other similar compound word-names in the OT. Cp: shooshanna. (Luke.8:3; 23:49, 55-56; 24:1-7)

Luke.9:54, further proves that **Boanerges** at Mark.3:17 means 'children of curse(s)/uncleanness/filth' 'children of-he curses/makes unclean/filthy' 'of when/with when-he curses/makes unclean/filthy'. There are two reasons why they have been given this nickname in Mark.

First reason is John and James (Zebedee's sons) and their mother ask to be given the place on the right and left side of Jesus. When Jesus speaks he does not speak directly, but in riddles, but the authors of the gospels make it clear when he tells them they cannot drink from his cup, it means the brothers cannot bear the same torture he will face; he tells them they cannot be baptised the way he will be because the baptism he speaks of is his future rape during crucifixion which is a defilement, it makes him filthy: the original baptism was in his mother Mary's womb with God's 'water' (sperm), then in the river by John who was also soaked/baptised with God's water filling his mother Elisabeth's womb while he was in it so when John baptises the people they are being baptised with God's water—purified; so when Jesus is raped he is being given a negative baptism as it is the water/semen of men; so when the brothers are asking to be promised a place at his left and right side and he informs them this place is reserved (and turns out for two thieves who suffer the same torture and death he faces) he (or the author) is saying even if they do face a similar persecution, it will not be with Jesus, and because he(Jesus) knows his end he is wondering why they would want to be defiled and humiliated so what they think they are wishing for is not a blessing, but a curse 'children of curse(s)/uncleanness/filth' 'of when/with when-he curses/makes unclean/filthy'. This leads to why they are always paired in the Gospels either as the 'sons of Zebedee' or 'James and John': they represent rape and defilement: 'James/he pokes in anus' and 'John' with all its meanings of 'soaking in' and absorbing God's water/sperm as explained under John the Baptist—except this time it refers to Jesus being raped by the soldiers at crucifixion—and this is the reason he denies them a place at his right and left, but also why the authors of the Gospels keep using them to indicate this because their word-names serve this purpose.

The second reason which shows they are not 'sons of thunder' as wrongly interpreted in the Biblical text itself, but 'of curse/filth/uncleanness' is when the Samaritans in Luke.9 refuse to receive Jesus, the Zebedee brothers suggest they bring down a fire to kill all the people in the Samaritan's village just as 'Elias' did (the story the author of Luke refers to is Elijah (2Kgs.1; 2Kgs.2:11-12) where twice he sends fire from the sky to kill two captains and their units of soldiers when they separately come to request he attend to the king). The brothers' request alarms Jesus as he states he has not come to cause wars, sufferance and killing of people but to save people (although this dialogue is contradicted by the narration of this same gospel and other gospels as Jesus states he is coming to burn people with fire as well as divide people against each other). He tells them they do not know their own nature, and this implies killing people is evil and their nature is 'of curse/filth/uncleanness' i.e. they are 'of when/with when-he curses/makes unclean/filthy'. (Luke.9:51-56)

Martha; Mártha; مآرض 'nursed back to health/nursed in illness' 'he did not agree to (to do something in particular)' 'unhappy/not satisfied/discontent' 'did not agree/allow' 'did not agree(to do what was asked)' and the unhappy and 'did not agree' meanings are meant and reflected in the story in how Martha feels about her sister Mary (Mary is still 'passing along' 'bitter' and here she chooses to pass along the chores and sit and listen to Jesus instead of help her sister Martha with the work, causing the latter bitterness (Mary listens and sits at the feet of Jesus who is created from and a carrier of the 'water/semen' which brings to life, and this still completes the full name of Mary/Mariam)) and her name also reflects that Jesus does not agree to tell Mary to stop sitting around and help.

As it is in urban life so it is in rural, in ancient as it is in modern times—when a person does not work or does not help out with chores, those encumbered with work voice their discontent as does Martha's character 'and a certain woman named Martha received him into her house. And she had a sister called Mary, who also sat at Jesus' feet, and heard his word. But Martha was cumbered about much serving, and came to him, and said, Lord, dost thou not care that my sister hath left me to serve alone? bid her therefore that she help me. And Jesus answered and said unto her, Martha, Martha, thou art careful and troubled by many things: But one thing is needful: and Mary hath chosen that good part, which shall not be taken away from her.'. Cp: maar<u>dh</u>a.

It is important to note, the author's intentions with Mary being at the feet of Jesus is symbolisation of sexual intercourse—they do not have it happen explicitly but it is to be understood from symbolisation that even through the words Jesus speaks he can transport God's semen into people (just like sex). In Ruth, Naomi instructed Ruth to uncover Boaz' feet and to lie down on them and in Ruth the authors explicitly narrate she has sex with him and 'feet' stand for male genitals (see Ruth, Saraphim). Of course there is mention of washing of feet in the OT where this means literally guests are given water to wash the dust off their feet when arriving at a destination/host's house—but you can tell the difference from the context of the story; in Martha, Mary again (like the virgin Mary) represents a receptacle of God's water which Jesus and John pass on through baptising in literal water which has the effect of God's sperm/water, but Jesus also has been given the act of sex with others to pass on God's water which is evident from this story with Mary. (Luke.10:38-42)

Lazarus; Lázaros; لاَضَروه ، لاَضَرَه 'will not harm him' 'will harm him/to his harm' 'did not develop habit (or get used to a certain way or things)' 'will get used to things/ways/will develop a habit' 'will become vicious/made him/it vicious' 'will not become vicious', and 'developing the habit/dhr' means a negative thing e.g. a child sucking his thumb, a dog biting for no reason except has become vicious by habit/ training, a person taking advantage of people who give him money, etc.; from the word ('zar'/dhr/ضر) 'harm' or 'used to/developed habit or taste'.

Depending on the context in which the phrase Lazarus/لاَضَرَه is used it can mean 'won't (or) will hurt him/develop habit', in this story it means both and applies to both characters in both ways: in the first life the rich man is not harmed and suffers nothing, but Lazarus is harmed and hurts a lot; in the afterlife Lazarus is not harmed at all, whereas the rich man is suffering in hell; the man was used to living carefree and extravagantly whereas Lazarus was not used to any comfort in life—their situation is also reversed in heaven and hell in the afterlife. Cp: laadharooh, laadharoh. (Luke.16:19-31)

Abraham is used for 'pull up/draw up-the' 'clear-the'. Lazarus is described as being lifted up to Abraham and being in his 'bosom' now remember a bailing pouch comes up full of cool water, when the rich man sees this, he asks that Lazarus be allowed to bring him even a drop of water. (Luke.16:22-25)

Moses 'entangled/caused problems/provoked problems or fighting' is mentioned because the rich man wants his brothers to know how he and his lifestyle provoked his own torment in hell so his brothers can avoid the same fate. (Luke.16:27-31)

Zacchaeus; Zakchaíos; سَخَّيُه ، صَخَّيُه 'he is generous/generous-he/him' 'compliant/obedient-he/him' and the character obeys Jesus inviting himself and this shows both compliancy and generosity; then the character makes a statement which describes him as a generous and compliant person 'And Zacchaeus stood, and said unto the Lord, the half of my goods I give to the poor; and if I have taken anything from any man by false accusation, I restore *him* fourfold.' And because he is found compliant, salvation is promised, followed by Jesus telling a parable of which events include generosity, and obedient servants who make their master's one pound into ten and they in turn are made rulers over ten cities, and so-on where compliancy and generosity come hand in hand. Cp: sakhaioh, ssakhaioh. (Luke.19:1-24)

Calvary; Kraníon; كَرَنيون ، كرينيون 'they (or 'of') hired them/paid them/rented them' 'they (or 'of') drove/chased/forced them away with violence'. It is the same word which makes up 'Cyrene' in Simon of Cyrene's character, and used for the same meanings: Both Cyrene and Kranion relay he has been 'compelled' i.e. forced to carry Jesus' cross; قَرَنيون ، قرينيون 'of reading' 'they read to me/teach me to read' 'they (or 'of') stopped moving/fidgeting' 'they stopped what they were doing' 'they linked them' 'they linked them with wood/rope' and it is what is done to a pair of bulls or cows when working the land to keep them moving at the same pace, also to keep one animal linked to another so that it does not run off i.e. their actions become one. It is relayed in the people following Jesus, and Jesus informing them he and they will be linked by a great suffering to come, respectively; it is in Simon Cyrene having to carry the cross like a bull under a yoke and follow Jesus to his crucifixion place; it is in the two 'malefactors' who are also linked to Jesus in fate, and being led along with Jesus to their place of execution; the two men are linked to Jesus' punishment and execution; they are linked and compared to bulls under a wooden yoke as all three of them will be crucified on wood and the narration describes they are aligned next to each other with Jesus in the middle (these are the places on the right and left of Jesus which James and John request, but Jesus tells them they cannot bear and do not want to have the left and right positions next to him if they knew what it really was).

The 'reading' meaning is shown in the sign written which reads 'This is the king of the Jews'. Cp: kraneeon, kraineeon, qraneeon, qraineeon. (Luke.23:33)

Emmaus; Emmaoûs; عمّوه 'were blinded/they are blinded' 'they blinded him/it' 'they were blind to him/it' and it is the name of the village where Jesus first appears to his disciples after death, but the two men do not recognise him; the text narrates they were made unable to see, i.e. unable to recognise him caused by an imposed blindness on what they can see, or the inability to recognise is the blindness, then when their eyes are 'opened' they do recognise him. Cp: 'mmaouh. (Luke.24:15-31)

Cleopas; Kleopás; قليوباه ، قلوباه 'turned it/him over/turn it/him over' (can mean literally turn something over or think and/or speak about it as in 'go over it/think it through') 'turn it/him upside down' 'their hearts/his hearts' 'they said to him/they said with him' 'they turn against' 'his/its heart/core/on the inside' 'it/he is inside out' 'turned it/him inside out' and all these meanings are in the narration of the story: both men, one which is the character word-name, are turning over the events, going over the matters/events which happened with and to Jesus; when Jesus asks them about their conversation they go over everything with him; Jesus mentions their hearts slow to believe; he goes over everything Moses and the scriptures have said about him i.e. he is opening what is hidden inside the scriptures bringing it out in the open for them to understand; finally, after they recognise him and he disappears they say to each other 'Did not our heart burn within us, while he talked with us by the way, and while he opened to us the scriptures?'. Cp: qlyoobaah, qleoobaah. (Luke.24:13-32)

John

As with Luke, John has been written by a local Arab with not only the complete familiarity of the OT stories and Biblical authors' methods, but also a complete mastery of the Arabic language which is used in the Bible. The narration of John is written for an audience which speaks and fully understands the Arabic language, which is not unusual that the organic people are the first audiences of these stories. But the need to explain the meanings of certain words indicate additions made when it was being translated for a foreign (maybe Greek) audience or for an audience which is Arabic, but does not speak the Arabic of the Arabian Peninsula (I will only use Greek as an example to avoid repetition), and the medium between the Arabic (erroneously called Hebrew) stories and the Greek translation of the stories was faced with the task of getting a Greek copier/translator and his Greek audience to understand the multiple meanings and their multiple wordplays which the local Arab would understand instantaneously and simultaneously upon hearing/reading and connect to the other stories within the culture.

As the Greek translator, and by extension the Greek audience, whom these Biblical stories are being translated for cannot make this complex connection with ease and spontaneity upon hearing the word-names and narration, it would require of the Arab translator/interpreter to give all the multiple meanings of wordplay to the translators which would not only ruin the flow of the narration, but also would make it a gruelling and lengthy work which as a document would be bulky—look at this book which I have endeavoured to write all the explanations which are supported in the Bible itself. Now imagine to save time, reduce length of explanations, reduce the bulk of this book (Revelation: A True Translation of the Bible) that I chose only to translate one single meaning for the compound words used as names in the Bible instead of all their different meanings—this book would be a lot shorter and less in bulk; but it would also be incomplete and the meanings of the compound word-names created by the authors would be lost, and with them the meanings of the stories, the intentions of the authors, and along with that the reasons why the Biblical stories were created would also be lost.

The Arab translator chose to give the foreign audience only one meaning of 'Rabbi' (and other words elsewhere in the NT) to avoid confusion and save time, and reduce bulk because even when you give a literal translation of the phrase/compound word you still need to explain it as it can have several different literal meanings, and figurative meanings especially since the Biblical authors used wordplay throughout the OT and NT. Then the translator would have to show how this is a pun, or a connection but would need to explain the many different ways it is a pun or connection because a foreigner would not be able to make the connection if they do not understand the nuances of the Arabic language, but also do not understand the culture and lifestyle which gives the stories meanings and context.

Bethabara is Beth-barah (Judg.7:23); Bēthabará; بيتَبَرآ/ه ، بيتَ بَرآ/ه 'he/they/it will-be passed/be surpassed/pass/surpass/go beyond/get ahead of him/it', 'he/they/it-will be good to it/him' and it also means 'he will be innocent of/disown responsibility from'; بيتَ بَرح 'he/it will be-pulled up(bailing water)' 'he/it will be-cleared out/levelled'.

In John, it has been used to portray John the Baptist distancing himself ('innocent of/disowning' is the same meaning) from being Christ, it also shows he is saying he is the person meant to be 'crying out in the wilderness' i.e. 'outside'. As he is dealing with baptising people with water this portrays the 'bailing' meaning of Bethabara. The 'beyond/passed' meaning is in John being beyond Jordan, but also that Jesus surpasses him in goodness, purity and piety, power, status, etc.

It cannot be overlooked that John.1 is inspired by the stories of Gideon in Judges (and this extends to other Gospels). There is a well named Harod, and the word is the same in pronunciation and meanings as king 'Herod' of NT, after which the men with Gideon are lessened in numbers in an elimination process, one of the elimination processes is seeing who laps water with his hand or gets on his knees to drink from the water (as both necessitate a person to bend his neck). For the OT authors there is a significance in the water symbol, but to the NT authors the use of water as a symbol is much greater. The significance to the OT authors can be seen in Jud.7 where before the Midianites are killed/defeated the symbolic use of empty pitchers broken by Gideon and his men is narrated which causes the enemy soldiers to turn their swords against each other, but also before they are defeated the story narrates 'and take before them the waters unto Beth-barah and Jordan' (a similar narration of Samuel being at Mizpah (both 'slaughter' and 'pool of water') having water poured out before the Philistines are slaughtered).

The author of Luke is playing on the story of Jud.7 where the Midianite princes are raped before they are slaughtered (see Oreb, Zeeb). It is not a coincidence that the gospels and especially Luke and John use the same themes and symbolisations even if they use it slightly differently, but the OT stories and word-name meanings are the inspirations of the NT stories. Where Beth-barah/Bethabara is used in John as described above, the same 'he/they/it will-be passed/be surpassed/pass/surpass/go beyond/get ahead of him/it' was used in Jud.7 because Gideon will cut off the Midianites who are trying to return home(Jordan(return home)), 'he/they/it-will be good to it/him' 'he will be innocent of/disown responsibility from'.

And where in John, Beth-barah/Bethabara 'he/it will be-pulled up(bailing water)' 'he/it will be-cleared out' is used to mean the baptising (ducking under water) will clear/purify sins, the 'bailing water' in Jud.7 was used for: Gideon's men are ordered to take the waters before the Midianites to Beth-barah and Jordan, and the latter meaning (cleared-out) because the Midianites will be cleared out of the land. (Judg.7:23)

In the same vein, the connection to 'bread/Jesus' 'John/sacks' is also connected to Gideon who was found by an angel threshing grain, and this was on the author's mind when creating the gospel of John. Cp: beyta-baraa(ah), beytabaraa(ah), beyta-barḥ. (John.1)

In Matt.23, **Rabbi** which means 'my god/parent/teacher' 'brought up/brought up properly/bring up/bring up properly' 'grew/grew well/grew or raised many' 'disciplined' 'diluted and mixed with water' was used specifically for 'master/God/father' and also to mean the hording and accumulation of things. In John.1, as interpreted within the narration itself, it is used to mean 'master' but the original author's intentions are that it also means 'diluted and mixed with water' and also 'grew well/brought up/raised' because Jesus was born by God's water (Holy Ghost) impregnating his mother Mary, it also refers to John who was soaked in God's water when it filled his six-month-pregnant mother Elisabeth through a visit from Mary who had just been filled by the Holy Ghost 'For he shall be great in the sight of the Lord.' (Luke.115). As every child is created (and grows just as the meanings of the word 'rabbi' mean) beginning from a man's 'water', the importance of Jesus and John are they have been born from and/or soaked in God's water, respectively.

The meanings of 'rabbi' 'raised/brought up' 'grew well' are explicitly made by having Jesus as 'the Lamb of God' i.e. he is the best lamb raised to be sacrificed—just as OT stories focus on only the best and purest being sacrificed/offered to God for his consumption, Jesus is the 'Lamb of God'; he is not sacrificed by people to God, he is sacrificed by God for the people to be forgiven of their sins (even if it is people in the story who murder him, the authors make it explicit that God could prevent it through having Jesus affectionately, and in great distress, plea to God to prevent this from happening).

Now this is where it becomes evident that either the gospels such as Matthew and Luke were written as a mocking account of Jesus and Christianity, or the original stories were corrupted by editors of anti-Jesus, anti-Christianity beliefs: Jesus is not allowed to remain pure because before the sacrifice he is raped and this is reflected in the 'parting' of his clothes which is the same as the skirt-lifting of the OT. Another possibility, which is the greater probability, is these stories (OT/NT) were not created for religious purposes and that eliminates any 'pro' or 'anti' Jesus/Christianity intentions, and this latter theory does not eliminate later editing by anti-Jesus/pro-Jesus editors. The stories make it clear that because only the purest and best things are sacrificed to God, that although his 'son' which he raised well is created from a higher and purer water and being (God) that because Jesus is being sacrificed for humans/mankind therefore he needs to be defiled just before he is offered up and sacrificed, which is what happens in the Jesus stories. Although the stories have been split into an OT and NT category, they, like their authors, audiences, religions and characters, originate from the same one people, the same one culture of which stories, folklore, religion and beliefs are a part of. It makes sense that in the OT stories only God gets the best, unblemished, unpolluted, pure sacrifices, that when it is in reverse and the sacrifice is for the people that the sacrifice is defiled, made impure.

What is present in more than one gospel, and which the gospels attempt to explain, is the real audience (and authors) had split beliefs as to who was the 'Son of God' as the gospels address the issue that some people believed John was the 'Son of God' and not Jesus. This indicates there were earlier stories which have not survived and were not included in the OT and NT as these were compiled by what survived in written form only, and whoever first compiled them had chosen these stories, but no one will ever know the older and more original stories because they do not exist in written form. But the split beliefs are conveyed in the gospels and in the name 'Elias/Eliah' 'he who/he is' 'yes, it is him' 'which one/which one is he' 'he who came/he who came to him' 'he did come/he did come to him'. (John.1:36-51)

Messias is the same as **Messiah** (in OT) and it is a word with meaning and use in everyday language which the Biblical authors would make into characters' special titles: Messías; مَسّيَح 'rubbed/stroked(with)' and this is reflected in God's 'water' covering Jesus and John; it also means 'wipe/wipe clean/wipe away' and the narration related to the mentioned Messiah in the NT is the wiping away of sins. The 'wanders/walks/searches all over' and means with a mission/objective/for truth, etc. is shown in how John is always located at an external location with crowds seeking and coming to him to baptise them; the same with Jesus whose stories have him wandering all over different areas, preaching and performing miracles, and the crowds also coming to see him with objectives of being cured, or set onto the straight path. Cp: maseeaḥ.

Messiah; Messías; مَسّيَه 'touched' 'touched him/touched-he/him' 'possessed' 'possessed him/possessed-he/him' 'entangled/caused problems/provoked problems or fighting'; the 'touched' means physically and depending on how the word is used and in what context can mean gently (i.e. non-violent) and can be similar to the 'messiah/rubbed/stroked/massaged' including with a substance being rubbed in/over or anointed with; and can also mean violently as being attacked verbally or physically, involved in a fight or argument, or caused trouble; the latter can also mean to be possessed by a spirit/demon—which in the Bible the characters of the prophets (and sometimes kings) are possessed by God. Both John and Jesus cause and are caused trouble then both are eventually killed. Cp: masseeah.

Cephas; Kēphás; جيباه 'answered' 'fetched/brought him' 'cave(s)' 'pocket/his pocket' and has no relation to a stone, and to say that because a cave naturally occurs in the stone face of a mountain/rock would be a stretch. What is evident, again, are things lost in translation. Maybe the translator was attempting to explain all the meanings of the word before telling the translator what the author meant, and when he attempted to explain what a cave is the foreign interpreter/copier misunderstood and finally agreed to 'Cephas, which is by interpretation, A stone'. Proof that the original author's intention and the meaning of the word as explained above is in the Bible itself: the author has used a word which means different things but only had in mind two for wordplay: Andrew fetches Peter Simon and brings him to Jesus 'One of the two which heard John *speak*, and followed him, was Andrew, Simon Peter's brother. He first findeth his own brother Simon…And he brought him to Jesus. And when Jesus beheld him, he said, Thou art Simon the son of Jona: thou shalt be called Cephas…' this is the 'brought him' meaning.

The author chose to use the nickname given him by Jesus in the gospel of Matthew which Peter earned by answering correctly a question posed by Jesus, where Jesus stated that it was God that helped him know the answer and earned him the nickname bar-jona 'good/piety-helped him' so the story depends on the audience knowing this other story to see the pun on a name which reflects both 'fetch/brought him' (from John's gospel) and 'answered him' (from Matthew's gospel) and it is one word 'Cephas/جيباه '. It is equivalent to Gibeon (Josh.9), Gibeah (Josh.15:57). Cp: geybaah. (John.1:40-42)

Nathanael and is the same as **Nethaneel** (Num.1:8); Nathanaḗl; نَثَن نيل 'we double/fold-the' 'we female/feminine-the'; نَدَن نيل 'we guilt-the' 'we bend/bow/lower-the'; نَظَن نيل 'we think/suspect-the'; نَطَن نيل 'we clang-the' 'make a tinning or clanging noise-the'.

'we double-the' because when Nathanael asks Jesus how he knows him, Jesus responds that he has seen Nathanael before, under the fig tree, so this is the second time Jesus has seen him. 'we guilt-the' and 'we suspect-the' because of the way Nathanael speaks about nothing good coming from Nazareth, he has judged and decided about Jesus based on what misgivings he has about Nazareth (the misgivings being the negative meaning of 'warned'). Cp: nathana-ill, nadana-ill, na<u>dh</u>ana-ill, naṭana-ill. (John.1:45-48)

Israel 'twisted muscle-the' 'twisted-the' is still being used for these meanings and that concerning disobedience, deceit i.e. twisting things into the wrong or false way as the author has Jesus say 'Behold an Israelite indeed, in whom is no guile!' and in Nathanael calling Jesus 'the King of Israel' also indicates, like the other gospels, that Jesus' end will be like other kings and princes who are sexually abused before being murdered, and this too is reinforced because 'Israel' is a compound word-name created for the character because of a strange encounter with God (the encounter was a sexual one) which caused Jacob's muscle to wither, followed by Dinah's illicit affair which caused more shame for her male family. (John.1:47-49)

Cana is the same as **Kanah** (Josh.16:8); Kaná; كَنَه ، كَنآ 'they were' and the story makes clear Jesus and his mother were there, it also confirms the water was turned into wine; خَنه ، خَنآ 'they/he soaked him/it' 'they betrayed him/the' and refers to being betrayed and crucified; قَنه ، قَنآ 'a channel(water channel)' 'bottle/flask/any transportable drinking vessel/also small water vessel' 'topped up/estimated measure of something liquid' (when mixing ingredients or topping something up with water), 'held head high/body straight posture' 'person or object sitting/place/set upright/erect' 'were perky'—and the meanings related to water channels, liquid, estimating measurements of liquid are reflected in: the wine being changed into water and the servants transporting these water pots of wine to the governor; the governor stating to the bridegroom that the flow of wine usually starts with the best then the lesser quality is used when everyone is intoxicated, except this time the best wine being poured has been saved for last.

The author clearly makes it about Jesus being betrayed and raped, and the water again is about 'semen/water' so when his mother Mary (whose name means 'pass along' but full name means 'pass along-river/sea', and 'bitter/made bitter' 'bitter-river/sea' 'bitter/made bitter-the') speaks to him about wine running out, his abrupt response 'Woman, what have I to do with thee? mine hour is not yet come.' is Jesus expressing (and the author highlighting) his abuse and death (of which being filled/soaked with men's 'water' is part of his crucifixion) has not yet arrived and directly links it to Mary being filled with God's water which brings Jesus' conception, hence 'Woman, what have I to do with thee? mine hour is not yet come.' is telling her it is not time for him to suffer or be filled with 'water'—and it is a pun and method of other gospels that have used the word 'Mary/pass along' being completed as 'Miriam/pass along-river/sea' by having Jesus completing the water-meaning in her name and the narration, as he is travelling along and across seas, coasts and shores. The use of Canah in the NT is the same use of 'Elkanah' in the Hannah story. It is same as Elkanah (Exod.6:24), Kanah (Josh.16:8). Cp: kanah, kanaa, <u>kh</u>anah, <u>kh</u>anaa, qanah, qanaa. (John.2:1)

Galilee (Josh.20:7) 'came-to' 'came-for' 'cleared-the' 'made clear-the' is used in conjunction with the meanings and word of 'Canah' in: making clear Jesus and his mother were there; Jesus making clear it is not yet his time for him to be filled/soaked with water (through rape) and to suffer and clear the sins of mankind (through crucifixion). His mother Mary makes it clear to servants to do as Jesus orders. (John.2:1-11)

The NT also shows proof that the Arabic/'Hebrew' word 'temple' is a mistranslation/misinterpretation and should be 'hekal/he will eat' (the NT stories were circulated and written in the local language before being translated to Greek, and as the interpretation from the original language (Arabic/Hebrew) throughout the OT is wrong, the same goes for the original word translated from Arabic/Hebrew to Greek). The other gospels have a character lie about Jesus saying he would destroy the temple and rebuild it within three days, but the author of John has Jesus say this just so he can connect the 'he will eat(mistaken as 'temple')' with Jesus' body, i.e. Jesus' body is 'bread' 'break/ate bread': 'Jesus answered and said unto them, Destroy this temple, and in three days I will raise it up…But he spake of the temple[he will eat] of his body.'. (John.2:19-21)

Nicodemus; Nikódēmos; نِقوديموه ، نقوديمُه 'we come to him/we present him/we serve(present/offer)him/we come forward him/we forward him' and it can have the same meaning as the root word of 'Corban' meaning placing something near someone for their easy access of it, and in this story it shows Nicodemus comes to Jesus by night and presents a number of questions wanting to know the truth, he also presents a number of questions, and questions the Pharisees when they wish to condemn Jesus; نِخوديموه ، نِخوديمُه 'we serve him/work for him/do him favour(s)' this character is serving/helping Jesus when he presents questions to the Pharisees as he is defending Jesus from condemnation, he also serves Jesus when he brings 'myrrhs and aloes' for his anointment and takes part in preparing Jesus' body for burial. Cp: niqoodeymooh, niqoodeymoh, ni<u>kh</u>oodeymooh, ni<u>kh</u>oodeymoh. (John.3:23-36)

Aenon; Ainṓn; عينون ، عينيون 'they saw/inspected/looked into' 'looked into closely/studied' 'they meant/hinted' 'they suffered'. Most of these meanings are available in the related passage: because a question about purification arises between the disciples and the Jews; also, Jesus and John have been seen baptising; John mentions they have witnessed what he does and says. 'they suffered' is reflected in 'he that not believeth in the Son shall not see life; but the wrath of God abideth on him.'. Cp: 'ainoon, 'aineoon. (John.3:22-36)

Salim is the same as **Salem**, **Shalem** and **Shalim** (1Sam.9:4); Salím; سَليم 'questioned them/the' 'leaked/flowed-them/the' 'flowed-river/sea' 'intact/survived/whole' 'entertained/distracted/comforted'. The flow/leaked/river meanings are reflected 'was baptising in Aenon near to Salim, because there was much water there: and they came, and were baptized.'. 'questioned them/the' as they come and ask John questions'; the example of the friend and the bridegroom plays on the meaning of baptism/water flowing being semen and the meanings of 'entertained/comforted' as the friend finds joy in hearing the happiness of the bridegroom. 'whole/intact' is reflected in the Father/God gives everything into his son's hand. 'survived' is in 'he that believeth on the Son hath everlasting life'.

It is the same as and/or equivalent to Salem (Gen.14:18-24), Shalem (Gen.33:18-19;34), Mishael (Exod.6:22), Shelumiel (Num.1:6), Misheal (Josh.19:26), Mishal (Josh.21:30), Salmon (Ruth.4:20-21), Saul

(1Sam.8;9;10), Shalim (1Sam.9:4), Jerusalem (1Kings.8), Absalom (2Sam.3:3; 13;14;15;18;19), Solomon (1Kgs.3:5-13) Cp: saleem, sal-ym. (John.3:22-36)

Rabbi is used as earlier 'to dilute and mix with water', and refers to both Jesus and John the Baptist being born/affected from God's water, and by extension the people they baptise in normal water has the same effect on the baptised. (John.3:22-36)

Samaria 'storytellers' 'they stayed/staying up late or all night' 'late night stories/staying up late stories' has been coupled this time with 'Jews' just as it (Samaritan) had been coupled at Matt.10:5 with the 'Gentiles' to remind the audience these are fictional stories, but presented in wordplay and as a pun within the story itself. This time it is saying how can 'Jew' (a word which has meanings to be explained later in this book) want help from 'Samaria' a fictional night time story, and what it is saying is how can an action 'Jew' which is related to the Samaria/Samaritan stories need help from a fictional story, it also implies the word 'Jew' in relation to these stories and to 'Samaria' as they are both the same when boiled down to the essence of their meanings as words.

The story of Jesus and the woman from Samaria proves that the gospels' stories, the Holy Spirit, God, and baptising are all about 'sperm/semen'. The 'water of life' is sperm which creates offspring and this offspring also continues to progenate with its own 'water'. The open lewdness in the story is a characteristic and element of the entertaining late night/staying up stories called 'Samaria'. Jesus begins by asking the woman for a drink of water, before he propositions her and tells her that if only she knew and had given him water to drink, he would have given her God's 'water/semen' in return. The author wanted it understood without doubt that the water Jesus was asking and offering is his water through sex and ejaculation which is why the narration has the Samaria woman point out to Jesus he does not have a bailing pouch to draw water from the well he sits on (the people of the country these stories were created in, carry their bailing pouch which consists of the pouch connected to a long spool of rope to the well and bring it home when they finish fetching water) leaving the only drawing and production of water through sex which the whole text of this story explicitly details.

This is reinforced by the reminder of Jacob's story represented as Jacob's well watered Jacob, his children and animals (see Jabbok, Israel)—where in Genesis after Jacob has a sexual encounter with God near a ford named for its meanings of bubbling water and sexual intercourse, his muscle withers, he is named 'Israel/twisted muscle-the' and this encounter with God leads onto more sexual encounters. Although Jacob becomes weaker following this incident, it allows his progeny to become stronger because the sex was with God (and in Genesis, emphasis is put on Jacob's numerous children and cattle which he drives before him to meet Esau), but because his muscle has withered everything Israel do in the stories ends up with their total destruction.

It is further reinforced by the narration showing the woman has had five husbands implying they have not resulted in impregnating her, but 'and he whom thou hast now is not thy husband' i.e. the man she is having now is Jesus who although is not her husband will pass his water onto her symbolised in the water pot she leaves behind. The mention of Sychar and Joseph will be explained below, but are also connected to water/sperm, sex and offspring. The well of water springing up in whoever Jesus gives his water to is a pun on the sperm created from within a man. When he tells her the worship is in 'spirit' it means panting, breathing which increases with sex (even if, for example, it cannot be seen in the Greek word (but the Greek word for 'spirit' is probably an Arab word meaning wind/breath or breath/wind-related), the Arabic word which will be called 'Hebrew' is probably 'rooḥ/reeḥ/ruaaḥ/reaaḥ' or similar word because this word is 'wind' in Arabic and is also 'soul' in Arabic) and if you go to the story where Mary is impregnated by the Spirit of God and/or the Holy Ghost this implies a lot of breathing/panting was involved. The narration has the Samaritan woman leave her water pot to go inform the people in the city, and this is symbolic euphemism that Jesus filled her water pot. More euphemism comes when Jesus speaks that he will eat of 'meat' that the disciples are not aware of, and his dialogue about the sower and the reaper both rejoicing over the fruit of life is the male sower, the female reaper and the fruit is the child which is the result of their copulation.

The author goes further to show wordplay to entertain the audience, by having the Samaritan woman who convinces the people to believe in Jesus, themselves come to Jesus (the author makes sure the word Samaritan is mentioned) and their dialogue means 'fictional stories' in that first they believed the story she told, but since they are Samaritans and have gone and heard the story direct from Jesus' mouth, they no longer believe because of what she told them, but because they have heard the story themselves. It is a relay of the meaning of 'fictional/night time stories'.

'And he must needs go through Samaria. Then cometh he to a city of Samaria, which is called Sychar, near to the parcel of ground that Jacob gave to his son Joseph. Now Jacob's well was there. Jesus therefore, being wearied with *his* journey, sat thus on the well: *and* it was about the sixth hour. There cometh a woman of Samaria to draw water: Jesus saith unto her, Give me to drink. (For his disciples were gone away unto the city to buy meat.) Then saith the woman of Samaria unto him, How is it that thou, being a Jew, askest drink of me, which am a woman of Samaria? for the Jews have no dealings with the Samaritans. Jesus answered and said unto her, If thou knewest the gift of God, and who it is that saith to thee, Give me to drink; thou wouldest have asked of him, and he would have given thee living water. The woman saith unto him, Sir, thou hast nothing to draw with, and the well is deep: from whence hast thou that living water? Art thou greater than our father Jacob, which gave us the well, and drank thereof himself, and his children, and his cattle? Jesus answered and said unto her, Whosoever drinketh of this water shall thirst again: But whosoever drinketh of the water that I shall give him shall never thirst; but the water that I shall give him shall be in him a well of water springing up into everlasting life. The woman saith unto him, Sir, give me this water, that I thirst not, neither come hither to draw. Jesus saith unto her, Go, call thy husband, and come hither. The woman answered and said, I have no husband. Jesus said unto her, Thou hast well said, I have no husband: For thou hast had five husbands; and he whom thou now hast is not thy husband: in that saidst thou truly. The woman saith unto him, Sir, I perceive that thou art a prophet. Our fathers worshipped in this mountain, and ye say, that in Jerusalem is the place where men ought to worship. Jesus saith unto her, Woman, believe me, the hour cometh, when ye shall neither in this mountain, nor yet at Jerusalem, worship the Father. Ye worship ye know not what: we know what we worship: for salvation is of the Jews. But the hour cometh, and now is, when the true worshippers shall worship the Father in spirit and in truth: for the Father seeketh such to worship him. God *is* a Spirit: and they that worship him must worship *him* in spirit and in truth...And upon this came his disciples, and marvelled that he talked with the woman: yet no man said, What seekest thou? or, Why talkest thou with her? The woman then left her waterpot, and went her way into the city...In the mean while his disciples prayed him, saying, Master, eat. But he said unto them, I have meat to eat that ye know not of. Therefore said the disciples one to another, Hath any man brought him *ought* to eat? Jesus saith unto them, My meat is to do the will of him that sent me, and to finish his work. Say not ye, There are yet four months, and *then* cometh harvest? behold, I say unto you, Lift up your eyes, and look on the fields; for they are white already to harvest. And he that reapeth receiveth wages, and gathereth fruit unto life eternal: that both he that soweth and he that reapeth may rejoice together. And herein is that saying true, One soweth, and another reapeth. I sent you to reap that whereon ye bestowed no labour: other men laboured, and ye are entered into their labours. And many of the Samaritans of that city believed on him for the saying of the woman, which testified, He told me all that ever I did. So when the Samaritans were come unto him, they besought him that he would tarry with them: and he abode there two days. And many more believed because of his own word; And said unto the woman, Now we believe, not because of thy saying: for we have heard *him* ourselves, and know that this is indeed the Christ...' (John.4:4-42)

Sychar is the same as **Issachar** (Gen.30:18); Sychár; صيخآر 'became compliant/obedient' 'put at disposal/service of' and what it means is a person does as bid, is compliant/obedient; the author of John.4 is referring the audience to the story where Leah gives Rachel mandrakes in exchange for Jacob having sex with her instead of Rachel that night, the child is named Issachar because Jacob became compliant and did as bid so the name reflected both on Jacob's actions and the product of having sex with Leah which resulted from Rachel putting Jacob at Leah's disposal, and also the author of Gen.30 has Leah state she has been rewarded for making her handmaid Zilbah compliant to have sex with Jacob.

In John, Sychar is the area-name where the well is set showing Jesus wants the Samaria woman to be compliant to his sexual advances which begins with a demand to give him to drink which she does not readily obey, he promises to put at her disposal his water/semen which is eternal life-giving, and by the end of their encounter she is compliant to his demands and believes everything he says, and she causes and convinces the people in the city who all become compliant to Jesus' teachings.

The reason **Jacob** and **Joseph** have been linked by the author is for their wordplay and meanings: Jesus is trying to get an unwilling and wary woman to allow him to give her his water, he is trying to 'Jacob/force open' both her vagina and uterus to receive his water; the meaning of Jacob is to force open something that is locked by using a lever of some sort (stick/metal rod (in modernity crowbar)). 'Joseph/pours water gently over/rinses/cleanses' because once her vagina is open Jesus can pour his 'living water' into her which will bring around the conception then birth of a child. Sex, sperm/water, offspring, continuation of life of the seed-giver and the seed-receiver are all in the stories of Gen.30 and John 4 which is why it was important to John.4 to make it Jacob's well near to the land he gave Joseph which was suitably named Sychar for the reminder of the Issachar story to further emphasise to the audience that the water of life and giving it to the Samaritan was Jesus wanting to have sex with and impregnate her.

Instead of seeing these stories for what they are, which is abundantly clear even when you read them in English, scholars go off on a tangent trying to prove this 'well' and 'Sychar' are actual geographical areas i.e. they are taking this fictional story and fictional places and events and using them as historical and geographical 'fact' and completely overlook that Issachar and Sychar are the same root word: Issachar has the prefix 'yi/'he'' which makes the same root word 'ssachar/sychar—'becomes/made compliant' become 'he becomes compliant', and they ignore that the Biblical story of John.4 is indicating the story of Issachar's conception at Gen.30 to support the theme of the current story being told. Instead, modern scholars attempt to force it to be related to 'Shechem' by theorising that the Greek translation has mistranslated/misspelled the word from 'Shechem' to 'Sychar' which they loosely tie to Sychar in John.4, loosely tying or attempting to tie it together because it was mentioned in the story that Jacob bought a parcel of land there, even in Biblical storyland the purchase of this parcel of land to erect an altar (El-elohe-Israel) has nothing to do with Joseph nor with wells, nor is it in any way connected to the Issachar story. The other reason they attempt to support and give this fictional story a real geographical place is because there is a well in Palestine called 'bir yaqub' which is not necessarily an ancient artefact, but Arab people name their wells, lands, their geographical areas after stories in their own folklore, religion and culture—Y'qoob is a prophet in Islam too, and this naming of a well after Yaqub probably happened very recently in contemporary history. If scholars want to claim this is the well Jesus sat on in the NT story based on a modern event of Arabs naming a well in their own countries after a religious figure, they may as well declare Bethlehem in Washington DC as the birthplace of Jesus. Cp: ssykhaar. (John.4:4-42)

Bethesda; Bēthesdá; بيتِصطآ 'he/it will swoop down on' 'he/it will cling/stick to' and this part refers to the angel which comes down into the pool and the word-name given the pool gives the impression of water rippling, splashing if something like an angel or even a bird would swoop down and plunge into it; it also refers to the man who has been suffering a disease or disability for thirty-eight years, and the other people with diseases clinging to them while they cling on to hope that they will get a chance to enter the water first after the angel; بيتِسطع 'he/it will be able to' 'he/it will slap/smack' and again this refers to the angel smacking the water when it goes down into the pool, but also the man who explains to Jesus he is not able to make it in time into the water before someone else beats him in and is healed, so Jesus tells him to just get up and walk, and the man is able to not only get up and walk but to carry his bed too.

The rest of the chapter also continues with the main theme of being 'able' to do and Jesus claims he is able to do these things and has the authority to do these things because God has given him the ability and the authority to do like God. The meanings of 'cling/stuck' is reflected in Jesus will continue to do what he is doing because he has God with him, and it is also reflected in the belief or disbelief the opposing groups of believers cling to, and in Jesus' accusations that they are not even sticking to their own beliefs which they have in their scriptures and as told by Moses (Moses is used for 'provoked/entangled' as Jesus states God and Moses will accuse them of disbelief/lying/etc.). It is equivalent to Sitnah (Gen.26:21). Cp: beytesstaa, beytesṭ'. (John.5)

Tiberias; Tiberiás; تِبَرياآه ، تِبرِاآه 'went past it/him' 'she/he/it went past it/him' 'you will go past it/him' 'surpassed/exceeded' 'cleared him of guilt' 'declared/made innocent him' 'be good/pious towards/to him' 'disowns/states has nothing to do with-him' and is the same as Tiberius (Luke.3:1, 3-18); تِبَريعه ، تِبرِعه 'they/he/she-galloped/stampeded' and is how animals are described as galloping, but also a person or people if they make a loud noise or run with great haste, also if they are a large crowd, 'donated/gave voluntarily'. It is reflected in the great crowds following Jesus which conjure up an image of people travelling in haste and large groups like herds stampeding; in Jesus wanting to feed the people and not send them away hungry; it is reflected in Jesus going over the sea of the same name and crowds following him; in the numbers of people that exceed the quantity of bread that is available to feed only a few; in what little bread available is able to exceed the people's needs and then the leftovers by the basketfuls which are left; in Jesus leaving and going to be alone; it is in the people and the narration about Jesus going beyond where the people are at, and the people following crossing over beyond their original location to be where Jesus is; when they arrive Jesus reminds them to have piety towards God; and the second half of the chapter is about believing in God and Jesus, doing God's work. Cp: tiberyaah, tiberiaah, tibery'h, tiberi'h. (John.6)

The majority of John.6 also revolves around **Jesus** being bread, and it matches his name exactly 'bread' 'broke/ate bread' 'breaking/eating bread' from the repeated story of the few loaves of bread feeding many, but emphasised further regarding the sign requested like manna was before. **Manna** has been used for its meanings 'what is it' 'from who' 'from what' 'from where' 'listed/counted/gloated over' 'wished' as the question that is presented to Jesus when asked for a sign like 'mannah' which was like bread for the ancestors, they are asking for proof of who sent him, to prove he was sent from where, and the explanation is not so much about who he is, but what he is—and the answer is bread.

Manna being bread from heaven; it is explained it was God/Jesus' Father who gave them bread from heaven, not Moses; Jesus calls himself 'the bread of life'. (John.6)

John.7 opens with '**Galilee**' 'came-to' 'came-for' 'cleared-the' 'made clear-the' and the whole chapter is about Jesus coming to the people, to the place, of other people coming to him (look at Nicodemus meaning of 'came forward' and how this character is chosen at verse 50 and the connection made by the author narrating 'Nicodemus saying unto them, (he that came to Jesus by night, being one of them,)…'); and the narration focuses on narrating going from one place to another, the dialogue of the characters about Jesus being sent and coming to the people, about his antagonists coming and about them not being able to come where he will be, about his hour (demise) not yet arriving. This is why the narration has such a contradiction, although Jesus and the narration has him working and coming and going in secret, the same narration has him shouting out his message which is why Galilee 'made clear-the' and **Judaea** 'he is called/calls' 'to make a claim' 'make a false claim or an unproven claim' is used (also covers the characters and narration who do not believe or at least doubt him) is making clear he is the one sent from God.

Moses is used for 'squeeze him/it'; as they are dealing with Jesus who comes from water and deals with water and this plays on the word and character Moses who was saved from a basket floating in the river; it mostly uses the meanings 'touched/possessed/was possessed/touched' 'entangled/caused problems/provoked problems or fighting' as Jesus accuses the people of wanting to kill him, and this accusation further provokes them and they claim he must be possessed by a devil to hallucinate and make such accusations; the meanings go on to be shown in his example of how although they outlaw work on the sabbath they touch people in their work during circumcision on the sabbath, whereas they cause him problems because he touched/cured a man on the same day. (John.7:19-23)

Jerusalem 'they see-asked-them/the' 'came-saw-asked-them/the' is depicted as the people from Jerusalem are in the narration of questions being asked about Jesus who came and can be seen and heard, and the narration is in the form of questions 'Then said some of them of Jerusalem, Is not this he, whom they seek to kill? But, lo, he speaketh boldly, and they say nothing unto him. Do the rulers know indeed that he is the very Christ? Howbeit we know this man whence he is: but when Christ cometh, no man knoweth whence he is.' (John.7:25-27)

The misnomered mount of '**Olives**' is used again for its true meaning (see Olivet (2Sam.15:30), (Mount of) Olives (Zech.14:4; Matt.21:1)): 'I will quickly slice/cut/split open-them/the' 'I will kill quickly-them/the' 'I will flit/flick into/quickly hide-them/the', 'suddenly split open-them/the—suddenly cut them/the open—suddenly sliced them/the open' 'flitted/flicked/quickly hid something throwing it into narrow space-them/the'; 'shook/swung-them/the' 'made shake-them/the' 'shook/swung/made shake/made swing back and forth-them/the' 'snatched/tugged at/snagged-them/the'.

It is reflected in the woman brought to be stoned to death: her condemnation is supposed to be quick; having her caught in the act also depicts a sudden action when she is exposed (interestingly, this shows the author's perspective: only the woman is brought as a culprit but her male counterpart is not (see Miriam and Aaron, only Miriam being punished for the same 'wrong'); the 'flitted/flicked quickly/quickly hide' meanings are shown in Jesus stooping down and distracting himself with scratching in the ground; the 'I will kill quickly-them/the' is depicted in that the woman in the story is guilty as soon as she is introduced, there is no doubt in the narration that the consequence of her sin/crime is to be stoned to death; the 'kill quickly' and also 'I will flit/flick into/quickly hide-them/the', 'suddenly split open-them/the' 'made shake-them/the' is in how Jesus causes the men who are eager to stone the woman to death to immediately be shaken in their desire, he shakes them off their 'high-horse' position and their conviction when he tells them the person without a sin should begin with stoning her, and as they all walk off the situation has been resolved and the men who had wanted to persecute the woman have been exposed i.e. 'suddenly split open-them/the'.

The meanings of 'flicking to hide' 'killing quickly' are present in Jesus telling them he will go where they are unable to follow just like the meaning of the word hazzêtîm, zêtîm; it is in them wondering if he will kill himself; the slicing/cutting open and shaken meanings are in the narration about being freed and bondage. (John.8)

Abraham has been used for its meanings 'pull up/draw up-the' 'clear-the': the narration from the mention of Abraham becomes about clearing up the 'facts' and clearing away the confusion, and when Jesus mentioned being drawn up by the people (crucified) some of the Jews believe in him, and those that believe Jesus mention the word Abraham in connection to the question about being freed from bondage which does have relation to being 'pull up/draw up' 'clear-the', especially that the original compound word-name was to clear the people from their physical impurity so they could be 'perfect' for God.

It cannot be ignored that where Abraham has been used in the NT in connection to the people described as being his 'seed' that it is the action of the penis in copulation, pushing in and pulling out is what is being used in wordplay and pun (especially when the places 'Abraham's seed/of the seed of Abraham' is used is where baptism by John/Jesus is mentioned which in itself is related to God's sperm/water). The author makes it clearer that the meanings of Abraham 'pull up/draw up-the' are mostly about copulation/seeding in this chapter: Jesus states his acts which are giving people 'living water' which the story makes come from nowhere just like Jesus' birth is from his Father, i.e. God, a higher being than any man, while the rest of the people can give life but in the way of 'Abraham/pull up/draw up-the': 'I speak that which I have seen with my Father: and ye do that which ye have seen with your father'; and as the people remind Jesus they know their father as they have a physical/legitimate act of copulation between man and wife not only from their direct father but all the way to Abraham and they point out that they have a claim to a paternal God/Father through ancestors all the way to God which displaces Jesus and his claim because he is born out of wedlock, and this points to Jesus being born like an illegitimate child that does not know his father or true father where the story narrates Jesus saying 'Ye do the deeds of your father. Then said they to him, We be not born of fornication; we have one Father, *even* God.' (John.8:28-59)

Note how **Samaritan** is used by the author to point out the story is fictional, but also within the narration the people are accusing Jesus of being a storyteller and a fictional story (as well as being insane as claimed earlier when he accused them of wanting to kill him) 'Then answered the Jews, and said unto him, Say we not well that thou art a Samaritan, and hast a devil?'. (John.8:48)

Siloam is the same as **Salem** (Gen.14:18-24) and **Shalem** (Gen.33:18-19;34); Silōam; سِلوَم ، سِلو ام 'greet/greeted' 'in peace/intact (unhurt/alive)' 'of mild/peaceful nature' 'ask/question-the' 'flow/leak-the' 'flowed/leaked-river/sea' 'entertain/distract-the' 'comfort-the' 'survived/intact/whole-the'.

All these meanings are used in the story: the disciples question Jesus about whose sin that caused the man's blindness; Jesus and God's work is distracted by night, interrupted, as per this story Jesus' 'light' cannot work in darkness; Jesus' saliva is a flow of water/body fluid; he sends him to a pool which is called Siloam showing the meanings of all the above (again the interpretation included in the text is wrong '...which is by interpretation, Sent.)' it does not mean this in any shape or form); the neighbours ask among themselves if he is the same blind beggar, then question him about how he regained his sight; the response is with flowing waters in washing; the Pharisees question the man about his regained vision and about Jesus; the Pharisees are distracted by the division among them where some believe Jesus can perform miracles; the Pharisees question the cured man's parents who in turn tell them to ask the cured man, distracting unwanted persecution away from themselves. Cp: silooam, silo-aam. (John.9)

Moses is still being used for 'squeeze him/it' in conjunction with Jesus being created from God's water which allows him to perform miracles, and in conjunction with the meaning of the compound word Siloam, and the water-related events in the story. It is also used for its meanings 'squeeze him/it' 'touched/possessed/was possessed/touched' 'entangled/caused problems/provoked problems or fighting' as the Pharisees further question the cured man wanting to squeeze something out of him to use against Jesus so they can arrest and harm Jesus, and it is over how Jesus has touched and cured this man with his miracle, but the narration has Jesus provoking even the Pharisees who believe in and follow him. (John.9:24-41)

Jerusalem 'they see-asked-them/the' 'came-saw-asked-them/the' 'they see-their/the rocks' 'they see-rocks-them/the' 'came-saw-their/the rocks' 'came-saw-rocks-them/the' and **Solomon** is used for 'ask him/asks him-what' 'asked him-what' 'of many questions/of questions-what' 'they allowed him to survive' 'intact/whole-him/it' 'of surviving' 'distracted/entertained-water/his water' 'comforted-water/his water' 'greeted/greeted him' 'of mild/peaceful nature' 'became mild/peaceful' 'reached/arrived at-water/his water' 'connected-water/his water' 'delivered-water/his water' 'rock-his water' 'publicly apologised/arrived-water/his water/what': as soon as these compound words are mentioned as 'And it was at Jerusalem...And Jesus walked in the temple in Solomon's porch.' the Jews who surround Jesus ask him questions. The beginning of chapter 10 shows the meaning 'comforted' of mild/peaceful nature' 'became mild/peaceful' as the sheep that follow do so because they find comfort and safety in the familiarity of his voice; it shows 'arriving' meanings as it is about Jesus arriving, allowing people to be set on the right path i.e. saved. 'they allowed him to survive' 'of surviving' is shown in the verses where the people who follow Jesus, likened to sheep following a shepherd, will be saved from demise, but also to live in comfort. In keeping with the shepherd theme (using the 'rock' meanings), instead of trying to throw him off a hill/mountain as in earlier stories, instead they attempt to stone him—which is used because a shepherd throws stones (gently and without harming his sheep) to get them back on the right path or to remain within the borders of the owned land they graze on, but as it is in reverse and a fictional reverse of reality when Jesus tells the Jews they are not his sheep which is why they do not listen/believe him it is they likened to sheep who attempt to stone him to death. (John.10)

Bethany is used again for 'with the other one' 'did it again' 'with/of the figs' 'girl/daughter' 'my girl/daughter' 'of girls/girlish'. The girls/daughters are Martha and Mary, and as the characters Lazarus, Martha, and Mary of earlier stories are now collected into one story to be used again in a new narration where Lazarus is now their brother. It also reflects the two days Jesus stays without going to Martha's—important to the story as it allows Lazarus to die and this reflects the withering and dying of the fig tree in Matt.21. The narration makes it intentional that Jesus wants Lazarus to die so he can bring him back to life again. (John.11)

Martha is still 'nursed back to health/nursed in illness' 'he did not agree to (to do something in particular)' 'unhappy/not satisfied/discontent' 'did not agree/allow' 'did not agree(to do what was asked)': as Lazarus' sister, it is implied she took care of him in illness; Jesus does not agree to come immediately; Martha is upset because Lazarus has died; she initially objects to the grave/sepulchre being opened. (John.11)

Mary is still 'passing along' 'bitter' as the author intentionally makes clear she stayed inside the house and when she comes out of the house to reach the location where Jesus is, the people inside the house follow her. Note how the completion of 'water/sea/river' of the full name 'Miriam' is still being complete in actions by the authors of these stories: Mary passes along the way and reaches Jesus (Jesus a product of God's water, whose miracles/powers are from God's water), and to further show the completion of her full name the authors make a point in the abundance of tears: when she arrives she is weeping, the people are weeping and Jesus weeps (where in the first Martha/Mary story Mary sits at his feet and Jesus being a product of God's water completes her name). (John.11)

Lazarus 'will not harm him' 'will harm him/to his harm' 'did not develop habit (or get used to a certain way or things)' 'will get used to things/ways/will develop a habit' again has both meanings of been harmed: by allowing him to die; and not harmed: by being brought back to life. Jesus wants the people who watch him to see and believe by saying the things out loud and is the very meaning how people get others or animals used to being or doing a certain way or thing i.e. 'lazarus' 'will get used to things/ways/will develop a habit'. But the Pharisees: some believe, i.e. get 'lazarus' to the new way, while others remain on their 'lazarus' habit of not believing. (John.11)

Thomas (Matt.10) is still 'lepers/diseased' 'they are lepers' 'conscience' 'their responsibility' 'ostracised/they were ostracised' 'guilty/guilted/blamed' 'they were blamed/guilted' 'insulted/humiliated' 'they were insulted/humiliated' and is used because the disciples are puzzled why Jesus, having being almost killed because his adversaries believe he is guilty and have blamed him of grievous wrong-doing and have ostracised him and his disciples, would want to go Judaea (**Judaea** is used for 'false claim' as the Jews, Pharisees, etc. blame Jesus of making false claims about being God, God's son, Christ, and false teachings). (John.11:7-16)

Didymus; Dídymos; تيتيموه 'muttered/grumbled-he/him' 'muttered about him' from word (tmtm/تمتم) 'muttered/spoke under breath' and (yitmtm/يتمتم) 'he is muttering/speaking under his breath', and usually indicates a person in a grumpy mood; and this is reflected in how the disciples are puzzled Jesus will go where he knows people want to kill him, so Thomas' reply is an under-the-breath snarky comment, words to the effect 'let's all go with him and be killed too' and the author enhances this by giving him a suitable word-name as a nickname. It is also possible to be wordplay on his first word-name (Thomas) and its meanings of being blamed/guilted and ostracised: ذيذيموه 'they-guilted/blamed/ostracised/humiliated/lepers/diseased-him/he' and refers to both the people who are guilting them and those being blamed, as the disciples believe Jesus is leading them into physical danger. Cp: teetymoh, veevymoh. (John.11:7-16)

Romans; Rhōmaíoi; رومَييوي ، رومَيوي 'of throwing' 'throwing/threw' 'of killing/killed' 'spread over vast distance/various locations' 'of spreading/strewn over vast distance/various locations' 'saw water' 'of seeing water' and exactly these meanings are indicated in the verse they are mentioned: the fear expressed is that the people who believe in Jesus will take over everything, not just the land, but the people/nation and this is tied into Jesus and his miracles being from 'God's water/sperm' as the word-name was chosen because the people who will believe in Jesus are named 'saw/of seeing water(Romans)' and it is Jesus and his God's water that they see and will follow. The authors are not talking about Romans from Rome, but have used the word because of its meanings as pronounced in Arabic and according to the themes of the story of which 'God's water(sperm)' is essential to Jesus' birth and powers, i.e. when people convert to Jesus' religion/ways it is the same as changing from Abraham's seed/sperm and into being from Jesus' water which is God's water/sperm, it is not people coming from somewhere else but the same one local people changing from within in belief and in seed/water/sperm; and it is the Biblical authors' method of creating entertaining stories based on wordplay which is uncut throughout all the stories of the OT and NT. This is further reinforced because the authors have chosen to tie the compound word 'Romans' and the Jews worries of this threat directly to the verse that it is the Jews who came to Mary and had seen Jesus perform the miracles causing them to believe in him (Mary and Jesus represent 'walking along' 'passing along' and the original character who received God's water/sperm (and passed it onto Elisabeth/John the Baptist) of which Jesus is a result) who will change into 'Romans' and take over everything.

'Then many of the Jews which came to Mary, and had seen the things which Jesus did, believed on him. But some of them went their ways to the Pharisees, and told them what things Jesus had done. Then gathered the chief priests and the Pharisees a council, and said, What do we? for this man doeth many miracles. If we let him thus alone, all men will believe on him: and the Romans shall come and take away both our place and nation.'. Cp: roomaiee<u>oi</u>, roomai<u>oi</u>. (John.11:45-48)

Caiaphas (Matt.26:1-5) used for 'how-he/him' 'they figured out how/thought about it' 'thought how/about-he/him' 'of thinking things/in good mood to think about matters' 'of turning back of head to/turning (his)back towards' 'turned back of his head or his back towards-he/him' is used as earlier in Matt. The priests are figuring out how to resolve the problem Jesus poses of causing the people to turn their backs on the old ways/religion (of Caiaphas and the priests) to follow Jesus' ways/religion. Caiaphas, the suitably named character has the perfect solution which will not only get rid of Jesus and prevent the people from turning their backs to the old religion, but something which will also cause the people 'scattered abroad' who have also turned their backs on the land by being abroad, to return (verses 52 and 53 seem to be additions by editor(s) who saw the suitability to add this theme which is from the OT stories regarding the people in Babylon scattered in captivity), but Caiaphas' character, and the author who created this story, intended very directly that Jesus had to be killed in order to silence him and his ways so that a whole nation of people would be saved and turned away from following his new ways. (John.11:47-57)

Ephraim (Gen.41:52) is used for 'increase/multiply-them/the' as it speaks of many people coming out of the country and coming to Jerusalem for the Passover, i.e. with the increase in people, increases the chances to capture Jesus and kill him, as does the threat increase for Jesus. Also used for 'with gap between teeth/gap' as he is notably missing, 'Jesus therefore walked no more openly among the Jews…' and goes into a remote area. The opportunity they seek is to kill him and this is meant by both a gap between teeth or gap in general. (John.11:53-57)

Now watch how the Biblical authors masterfully use wordplay to narrate very specific meanings which relay between the word-names and the narrative what is being said in the story: **Greeks**; hellēnes; حيلْينَه ، حَلينيه 'purified/circumcised/made clean/made edible him/it' 'of purification/edibility/cleanliness/circumcision' 'declared purified/permissible' 'undressed him/her/it' 'of undressing' 'deceived/tricked him/her/it' 'of deceit/tricks' 'beat severely/beat until skin peeled off him/it' 'of beating/being beaten severely' 'shed its skin/hair/leaves/etc. him/it' 'of shedding skin/hair/leaves' 'replaced him/it' 'of replacing' 'sweet/sweetened him/it' 'of sweetness/sweetening': they are being nice and want to see Jesus, i.e. they want to be made clean/purified and as dealing with 'Jesus' which means both 'bread' and 'ate bread' they want to be 'declared edible/permissible' so they can take part in the faith; the meaning of the word 'deceived him/it' still shows that within the story they are being deceived (and is reinforced with **Beithsaida** meaning).

The 'shed skin, etc. also reflects they want to 'eat/believe' Jesus Christ (and this relays with meaning of **Phillip**); 'purified/circumcised/made clean/made edible him/it' reflects that they have been converted, or want to be, and is the same as taking meat and making it 'hellenes' 'edible/purified' and the same as taking something unclean and making it purified and this is supported with the use of '**Andrew**' which means to separate an animal from the flock for slaughter which makes it edible for food.

The OT meanings of Greek: عيوآن 'howling' they are likened to dogs begging for bread because they arrive at the feast and are asking to see Jesus whose name means 'bread/ate or broke bread' (remember how it was used in this same explicit way with the Greek Syrophonecian, and before at her description as the Canaanite woman, as well as wherever Greek has been used; غيوآن 'misleading to downfall' as they are coming to worship, and this worship will lead them to their downfall and is further enhanced by using **Philip** 'in its core/pulp' as they want Jesus who is bread at the core, and 'pick out/cleanse/remove it' as when these people are led to their downfall or even misled it leaves the people the authors narrate are on the 'correct' religion with more resources and power.

Bethsaida (Matt.11:21-22) 'it will/they will be fished/fish' as these people have been caught like fish into following a misleading way to their own downfall (Greek). **Andrew** (Matt.4:18-20; 10) 'sent out/sent him/it out' 'separated/separated him/it' and is mostly used to describe sending off sheep/goats in the right direction towards pastures to graze ('sent him/it out'); and used to describe separating between sheep and goats, whether to sort and separate them to send to different areas, or to separate one or more from the rest of the flock in order to slaughter or sell them, and what is happening to these 'Greek' people in John.12:20 is they are being misled that they are to be purified/declared pure, sent on a folly which again ends either with death or sold into something they are not truly aware of.

The story then narrates about following Jesus and goes on to describe being misled, describes downfall/demise, confusion about what Jesus has just said where people require an explanation as to why he claims he will die and ask for a clarification between what is the 'son of man' and 'Son of God' and 'Christ', and ask which is the truth: will he live forever or will he die, and what is the lifting-up business about; but instead of clearing up the contradiction, Jesus hides from the people; the narration deliberately shows how different people are being misled, and deliberately confuses who is misleading and being misled having both the Pharisees, elders, and those who believe in Jesus all being misled and promised salvation or demise. (John.12:11-50)

John.13 displays and highlights the importance of the theme of God's water/sperm which is what Jesus came from and what his mission, as was John the Baptist's, to pass on to all people for its cleansing, purifying, forgiving, and rectifying effects. When Jesus removes all his clothes and wraps around his waist what is called a 'towel' and proceeds to wash each of the twelve disciples feet and wipe them with a towel, what this symbolises is Jesus having sex with each of the twelve disciples so that they become receptacles of his holy water (just how it happened with the virgin Mary who would pass it on to Elisabeth and foetus John), and then whoever they (the disciples) baptise, convert, procreate with—everything they touch also can be converted, forgiven, healed just as Jesus and to a lesser extent John do with either water in a river, or by touch, and even by word (speaking/preaching). Jesus gets his effectivity from being from God's water/sperm.

The Biblical authors, whether their stories are categorised under the OT and NT (they are just one category of story from one people and stem from one culture and one cultural pool), do not name characters with specific compound words for no reason at all without there being a direct relation between the character/place name and the story unfolding; the same goes for how they have specific actions happen in the story, and removing clothes, i.e. becoming naked, as well as 'lifting skirts' 'parting garments' are not described without a very specific event happening in the story and with a very direct message of what is being said. When clothes are removed it indicates a sexual relationship between the characters concerned with this event/description, e.g. when Jonathan removed his clothes the author deliberately made it clear that not one garment, not even a belt/rope remained around his waist but that he stripped naked and this indicated (along with his very expressive word-name) that he was entering a sexual relationship with David. The same goes for Aholah and Aholibah whose clothes are removed whether willingly or by force to show voluntary illicit sexual relationship and then rape. Before David has an affair with Bath-sheba he first sees her washing on the roof, i.e. she was naked and her husband's name Uriah/'was made naked' completes the picture. Leviticus and other chapters clarify the 'lifting of skirts' is euphemism for sex and they explicitly state that when a man has sex with a woman that is not his wife, it is as if the man has 'lifted the skirt' (had sex) with the male relative, be the male relative her father or husband, etc. And in this method the author of the NT, whether it was an original author or a later editor, has made it explicitly clear that Jesus' removal of clothes in the presence of his disciples indicates sexual intercourse with them followed.

The author of John.11 was perfectly capable of expressing Jesus washing their feet without the need to symbolise he removed all his clothes, without the need to further enhance it about a tiny cloth wrapped around his waist then further reinforce this by narrating he put his clothes back on again once he had finished with the disciples' 'feet'. If it had been his intention that this is what happened in the story, and when the washing of feet happens it is as soon as the characters arrive from travel to remove dust and before food is served, and not after they have been fed. But the author of John.11 chose to follow the Biblical authors' method of having him strip naked, bring attention to what has been translated as 'towel' tied around his waist to bring the attention to his crotch area. The author of John.11 chose to use the euphemism for the male genitals 'feet' and all these elements tie into the character's creation of Jesus who comes from the semen/water of God. It is followed by two chapters whose narration explains how God was in Jesus and now Jesus is in all the disciples, and the chapter about God being the husbandman who created Jesus the 'vine' and how now the disciples are also 'branches' emerging from the 'vine', i.e. first Jesus was seeded/pollinated by God, then Jesus has seeded/pollinated his twelve disciples and they continue with his work which is using everything that his water/semen from God gives the same effect: a healing touch, baptising with water, spreading the 'word'—all these actions seed/pollinate people, cleanse their sins, bring them to the right way and make them what will eventually be called 'Christian'.

When Naomi tells Ruth to uncover Boaz' feet and lie down on them, and Ruth implements, they are not talking about Boaz' feet but his genitals. The same goes for when Mary (Martha's sister) sits at Jesus feet. The 'infection' of the word into Mary is the seeding of God's sperm. Likewise, the author narrates and spends time clarifying in following chapters Luke.14-15. 'And supper being ended, the devil having now put into the heart of Judas Iscariot, Simon's *son*, to betray him: Jesus knowing that the Father had given all things into his hands, and that he was come from God, and went to God; He riseth from supper, and laid aside his garments; and took a towel, and girded himself. After that he poureth water into a bason, and began to wash the disciples' feet, and to wipe them with the towel wherewith he was girded. Then cometh he to Simon Peter: and Peter saith unto him, Lord, dost thou wash my feet? Jesus answered and said unto him, What I do thou knowest not now; but thou shalt know hereafter. Peter saith unto him, Thou shalt never wash my feet. Jesus answered him, If I wash thee not, thou hast no part with me. Simon Peter saith unto him, Lord, not my feet only, but also *my* hands and *my* head. Jesus saith unto him, He that is washed needeth not save to wash *his* feet, but is clean every whit: and ye are clean, but not all. For he knew who should betray him; therefore said he, Ye are not all clean. So after he had washed their feet, and had taken his garments, and was set down again, he said unto them, Know ye what I have done to you? Ye call me Master and Lord: and ye say well; for *so* I am. If I then, you Lord and Master, have washed your feet; ye also ought to wash one another's feet…'. In chapter 13 it is expressed in more than one way that God is in Jesus and Jesus is in his disciples e.g. 'At that day ye shall know that I *am* in my Father, and ye in me, and I in you.' In chapter 14 there are examples of the 'word' (such as Mary sister of Martha listened to) and his water/semen are essentially the same thing as the 'word', and both work in the same way 'Now ye are clean through the word[i.e. they have been washed with God's water] which I have spoken unto you' and this is preceded and followed by verses where God is the husbandman, Jesus the vine and the disciples his branches which will bear fruit, 'If ye abide in me, and my words abide in you, ye shall ask what ye will, and it shall be done unto you.' i.e. they gain Jesus' powers given to him from God through the Holy Ghost filling his mother with water/semen. (John.13-15)

Cedron is the same as **Kidron** (2Kgs.23:4-24); Kedrōn; قِضرون ، قِضرُن 'they are disgusting/unclean/revolting/filthy' and is used just as it was used in the OT for 'unclean/revolting' characters and objects, this time it is Judas who at John.13 was described as 'unclean' and a traitor arrives with a group of men to arrest Jesus at Cedron. (John.18:2)

Malchus; Málchos; مآلهوه 'what is wrong with him/it' and depicts the character who has had his ear chopped off; مآلقوه 'threw him' 'threw/cast-he/him' thrown-he/him' 'did not find him/he/it' 'found-him/he/it' and depicts the character having his ear severed, and also finding Jesus; مآلحوه 'is good-he/him' 'is nice/pretty-he/him' 'has a beard-he/him' 'salted-he/him' and refers to Jesus being resolved to his fate as he tells Peter there was no need for violence as he will drink from his father's cup, i.e. suffer terribly. Cp: maalhooh, maalqooh, maalḥooh. (John.18:2-12)

Note how **Nazareth** is used for 'she/I vowed/set aside/dedicated to God' 'the vow/set aside/dedication to' 'warned' 'she/I warned' as Jesus is being led away to be crucified which in the stories is sacrificed for mankind so he is like a dedicated vow which is led to be slaughtered, and this had been foretold to happen so he and his disciples already knew what was coming. (John.18:5-7)

Note how both meanings of **Simon Peter**'s character name are depicted: 'have heard/to hear/heard' 'short' 'he/it has been abruptly cut off' 'they have snapped him/it/cut him/it short' and he cuts off Malchus' ear. (John.18:10)

Annas (Luke.3:2, 8, 10-14) 'he satisfied/gave fill/plenty of' 'satisfaction/gave satisfaction' at first this is mentioned because Jesus is led to him so he can be satisfied with the result and/or proud of his son-in-law's achievement, but it will also reflect on the rest of the chapter where the crucifixion of Jesus will also satisfy Jesus' adversaries. The other meanings: 'I saw/eyed-he/him' 'look, see-intended/hinted message at-he/him'

'I/will-inspect/look at/into-he/him' 'look, there he/it is-he/him' 'I will make suffer/made suffer-he/him' 'I helped/assisted/will help/assist-he/him', a sound/word repeated to get cows, sheep or goats back on the right path or back into the correct land; 'I will become/make independent/rich/no longer needed-he/him' 'see, look-sang/hummed/made 'ghn' noise(used in singing or reading religious books)-he/him'—are depicted with Jesus being interrogated; Jesus made an example of in front of everybody (including Peter being recognised); Peter denying Jesus is a form of 'I will become/make independent/rich/no longer needed-he/him'; the 'ghn' word used in prayer/preaching is depicted as Jesus states he was openly teaching in the synagogue; Jesus is suffering being hit by the officer; they satisfy themselves with food and drink at the feast while Jesus is bound and put into the 'hall of judgement'; Pilate also inspects the matter against Jesus. (John.18:12-40)

Caiaphas 'how-he/him' 'they figured out how/thought about it' 'thought how/about-he/him' 'of thinking things/in good mood to think about matters' 'of turning back of head to/turning (his)back towards' 'turned back of his head or his back towards-he/him'. Used because his character has found a way to dispose of Jesus; reflects Peter turning his back, denying any connection to Jesus; it is in Jesus' statement he did no preaching/teaching in secret but openly; both Pilate and the Jews attempt to solve how to have Jesus prosecuted, both parties show 'turning back towards/back of head towards' as Pilate wants to shift the prosecution to the Jews as it concerns them, but the Jews want to shift the case to Pilate because they want Jesus executed, but their laws prohibit death (which reflects these characters are just trying to shift responsibility as John, and the OT, all depict putting people to death, e.g. they had wanted to stone the adulterous woman, and throughout the gospels, including John, are depicted as wanting to kill Jesus, whether to stone him to death, beat him to death or throw him off a mountain, or crucify him) so they are all trying to turn their backs on the 'responsibility' so that the other party will do the action. (John.18:12-40)

Pilate is still being used as 'are his fall/let him fall' as the Jews attempt to get Jesus killed through Pilate, and 'let him loose/go' as in this story Pilate is against killing Jesus and wants to release him.

Caesar is used for its meanings 'broke' 'shortened/shortcoming/failed to complete or obey' as when they see Pilate tilting towards releasing Jesus, they accuse Pilate of shortcoming towards Caesar and failing to obey Caesar's laws and Jesus of breaking Caesar's laws.

Gabbatha; Gabbathá; جَبَّذَآ ، جَبَّذَه 'they pulled up/tugged upwards' 'they pulled up-he/him' 'they pulled/tugged at-him/he' and is from the word (gbv/جبذ) 'pulled up/drew/tugged up'. It is used to describe when a person from a lower geographical position is helped/pulled upwards by the hand/forearm by someone positioned higher up, or violently tugged forwards. The name indicates the 'seat of judgement' puts the person judging above the person being judged, in this case Pilates over Jesus; it also reflects Jesus will be crucified and how he will be killed which in a previous chapter of John the narration repeatedly emphasises as his death and is described as being 'lifted up' (John.12:32-50). If you think about crucifixion the way it is portrayed in popular culture, in real life it would entail a group of men using ropes and beams to prop and pull up the cross with the crucified body affixed to it which also reflects the word 'Gabbatha'. Cp: gabbavaa, gabbavah. (John.19:13-18)

Cleophas; Klōpás; قلوبآه 'turned it/him over/turn it/him over' (can mean literally turn something over or think and/or speak about it as in 'go over it/think it through') 'turn it/him upside down' 'they turn against' 'his/its heart/core/on the inside' 'it/he is inside out' 'turned it/him inside out'. Again, there is an intentional grouping of Marys, this time three-Marys: Mary Magdalene, Mary his mother, and a third Mary is made into his mother's sister (the authors do not mind using the same word-name no matter how unrealistic that two sisters would have the same name because it is about getting the author's intended message across), and these concentrated Marys serve a purpose in conjunction with the words 'Cleophas' and 'Magdalene' and the events described: the soldiers crucifying Jesus, Jesus' nature in how he was created as a character in the story. Although scholars seem to believe that 'Mary the *wife* of Cleophas' is a separate character than 'and his mother's sister', I believe they are one and the same as the writing style of the NT uses 'and' to separate different characters when listing them as a group, and in all cases whether the sister of Jesus' mother is the same Mary wife of Cleophas or not—it does not make a difference to the grouping of three-Marys in the story and how they are used.

The concentrated Marys standing at Jesus' cross represent the receptacles of water/semen; the names 'Magdalene' is used for its meanings 'of being thrown around/to the ground' 'throwing me around' 'thrown down/away' (no meaning about 'possessed/fits' is used here) and the word 'Cleophas' 'turned it/him over/turn it/him over' 'his/its heart/core/on the inside' 'it/he is inside out' 'turned it/him inside out' describe Jesus being raped by the soldiers, he is thrown down, turned over and raped 'turned it/him inside out', and these two Marys indicate Jesus is now the receptacle filled with a lesser semen/water and his mother Mary is to remind that he is still filled with God's superior sperm/water also. The soldiers' semen/ water prepares him for sacrifice, but the story also allows him and the mother-Mary to pass on what is Jesus/God's water/sperm even after his death, which will be explained below. They have Cleophas the husband of Mary who is Mary the mother of Jesus' sister because it emphasises two things: Jesus was raped by the soldiers (a reverse of man with woman, by man with man), that is how water/sperm was transferred into him making him a suitable sacrifice for mankind ('upside down/inside-out' as only the purest sacrifices are made to God, but for God to sacrifice for humans, the sacrifice has to be impure even if it is still the best 'sacrificial animal/food'), and it also reminds the audience that his mother was copulated by God or an autonomously moving body sent by God (Spirit/Ghost) to create Jesus out of water/sperm.

There is a turning upside down of Mary and Jesus' role, first it was Mary then came God's water to make Jesus, this is reversed in the narration 'Woman, behold thy son! Then saith he to the disciple, Behold thy mother! And from that hour that disciple took her unto his own home.' What this does in the narration is this: although now Jesus is filled with a lesser water/sperm, it only makes him suitable to be sacrificed for man's sake but it does not negate the superiority of God's sperm/water which Mary first received to conceive Jesus and passed on through a visit to Elisabeth to an unborn John the Baptist. Now, by Mary looking at Jesus it is he who passes the sperm onto her and she again becomes a receptacle of God's water/ sperm which she will pass on to the disciple who becomes her son just by becoming his mother and living with him, i.e. he is 'filled' with this Godly/Jesus sperm/water to baptise, heal, preach and spread the word and continue Jesus' message even after Jesus dies.

The author makes a point by narrating immediately after Jesus transfers God's water/sperm to his mother (and by extension to the 'beloved disciple'), that he immediately feels thirsty—now remember, Jesus contains God's water/sperm and earlier in the story this water/semen quenches a person so that he never thirsts, nor dies—after this has been poured back into Mary the receptacle then to the man who becomes her son and the 'waterer' (a 'mini' or 'clone' Jesus), Jesus not only thirsts, but shrivels up and dies. The author(s) of the different gospels could have narrated the story with only minor changes, but because each was showing his own skill at wordplay, they have used the same story, but added, changed, and made it into their own wordplay, where other stories sufficed with showing Jesus born from God's water through copulation with God and Mary, others show this superior God sperm/water through further sexual acts, and/or transfers from one vessel to another which is capable of pouring God's water/sperm into others. Where Golgotha was enough to indicate nausea from vinegar, the author of John has decided to show his dexterity at making his version of the story about Jesus drying up once God's water has been transferred back to Mary then to another man.

Cleophas is the same word as **Cleopas** (Luke.24:13-32) but a different character and although the action is the same, the role of the word and character are different than how used in Luke. Cp: qloobaah. (John.19:23-27)

Rabboni; rhabbouní; رَبّوني and it has all the meanings under 'Rabbi' and in this form it can also mean 'he/ they disciplined me' 'he/they brought me up' 'my master/teacher/god/parent/raiser/shepherd/grower/ discipliner' 'of mixing and diluting with water' 'dampened me' and here is used to mean 'he/they disciplined me' because earlier stories have Jesus expel from her seven devils which possessed Mary Magdalene (in this chapter when she sees the angels and Jesus it is as if she is possessed/hallucinating) as exorcism involves beating and reproaching; it also plays on the word 'Lord/God' 'father' and 'mixed and diluted with water' which are all present in Jesus' story as a whole, but also in John.20 where he passes on his message when he appears to the disciples and passes on to them the 'Holy Ghost'. Cp: rabboonee. (John.20)

Thomas and **Didymus** are still used as in (Matt.10; John.11:7-16) 'lepers/diseased' 'they are lepers' 'conscience' 'their responsibility' 'ostracised/they were ostracised' 'guilty/guilted/blamed' 'they were blamed/ guilted' 'insulted/humiliated' 'they were insulted/humiliated'; 'muttered/grumbled-he/him' 'muttered about him' 'they-guilted/blamed/ostracised/humiliated/lepers/diseased-him/he'. The author has him not among the gathered disciples to show the use of his word-name in the story to enhance the drama so in a sense he is left out 'ostracised/they were ostracised', and when he is informed he is still muttering and his words show a grumpiness that he will not believe unless he physically touches the piercings in Jesus' resurrected body; it is also used to let the audience know even though they are distant and have not seen these signs/ miracles they should still believe. (John.20:24-31)

Tiberias is used as earlier (see Tiberias (John.6)). 'they/he/she-galloped/stampeded' 'donated/gave voluntarily' 'went past it/him', although Peter dives into the sea it is the same idea that he rushed towards/after

Jesus like a gallop/stampede, that he was eager to get to him as soon as possible; it also is reflected in the fish and food cooked which Jesus has made happen as a voluntary act, and the request Jesus makes of Simon to voluntarily give more to Jesus' sheep; 'she/he/it went past it/him' 'you will go past it/him' 'surpassed/exceeded' 'cleared him of guilt' 'declared/made innocent him' 'be good/pious towards/to him' 'disowns/states has nothing to do with-him' are also reflected in the chapter. (John.21)

Beloved Disciple

There is a lot of debate over who the 'beloved disciple' is in the gospel of John. Modern scholars can only base their estimations on knowing he was one of the twelve disciples as narrated in the story, and that he was loved. This has caused some to err that it was Lazarus just because the narration states that Jesus loved him although within the gospels he has never been described as a disciple, and is not part of the twelve. Some believe it is John the disciple based on John being of the twelve, and because he is depicted in other gospels being with Peter when they go with Jesus to certain places is parallel to the same as an unnamed disciple goes with Peter in the gospel of John. Others have claimed that it is a different John. The problem with modern scholars is they attempt to prove a fictional character that was made up of compound words and from the events of an author's imagination as an actual 'historical' figure, while the language and text of the Bible tells them exactly which character it is, and that he and the events around him are fictional.

The identity of the beloved disciple is not hidden, but presented as a riddle for the audience of the stories to solve, the gospel of John proves these are Yemeni samaaras and samaayas, the latter being a story which the names of characters and places mimic the events which engage the audience to guess the name of a specific character, place or thing. The gospel of John has filled the story with clues leading to the identity of the 'beloved disciple', and it not only uses word-names, but events in the story and references to other stories; the author of John may very well have edited and made additions to other gospels as the clues are available in them too, either the author of John edited the other gospels or he was aware of their stories and used them, bending them to his own ideas.

'John' was not a random title chosen by a Greek compilator, but an informed decision based on an Arabic-speaking translator, just like the other titles of Gospels are not random, even if they were not part of the text as titles of these stories, whoever assisted in compiling/translating depended on assistance of someone who spoke the language of the Bible. John son of Zebedee is the 'beloved disciple'. The proof, as always, is within the Bible.

First a reminder of the meanings of the compound word 'John' 'soaked it/him (in)' 'brothers' 'betrayed' 'sacks' 'sackcloth' 'put/wrap it/him in sack/sackcloth'; and how both 'John' characters are portrayed: John the Baptist is the product of God/Holy Ghost filling his mother's womb with him in it and soaking him in God's sperm/water. John the disciple, along with the other disciples, is given healing powers in Matt. through Jesus; baptism and/or contact with Jesus in the story acts like God's sperm/water clearing away sins and giving disciples Jesus-like powers; by the word-name given to him, John the disciple's character has all the meanings of soaking and sackcloth which makes his relation to Jesus as a word-name and character more intense as by nature of the material just like 'John/sackcloth/soaked' (the Baptist) could absorb and swell with God's water, so can John the disciple from Jesus' water, using 'holy water' (semen), to heal the ailed. Just as John Baptist and Jesus are similar to brothers (through shared sperm of God/Father) John is always depicted as a brother, 'sons of Zebedee' 'James and John'; John's brother James is a word-name 'he pokes' and is often used to mean a man poking another in the anus and this is why they are always paired in mention: first comes 'James/he pokes in the anus' then comes 'John/soaked' and absorbing Jesus' water/sperm. Specifically in the Gospel of John, Jesus has sex with all twelve disciples and passes on his and God's water/sperm to all twelve disciples, but the 'beloved disciple' present at his crucifixion is given a higher power/status and more of God's water/sperm by making him and Mary son and mother instead of Jesus—this makes his connection to Jesus through Jesus/God's water/sperm twicefold and a type of 'brother'.

John the disciple is depicted as in a special relationship with Jesus, although at the Passover feast Jesus makes love to all twelve disciples, one disciple is singled out as being loved above all others, not only is he singled out but at John.13:23 this beloved disciple is depicted as 'leaning on Jesus' bosom' although in western modernity 'bosom buddies' comes to mean very close friends due to misinterpreting the meaning of the Bible, in the Bible itself only a wife lies in her husband's bosom and this means has sex with him.

Even the use of his father's name Zebedee 'strong-he/him' 'strengthened it' 'strengthened-he/him' 'tie tightly with rope' 'latticed it' 'latticed-he/him' 'swipe/whip(with a switch or rope)' 'butter it/spread it' 'butter/spread over him' 'perfume/spread it/him with ointment' 'his drinking bowl' (see Zebedee (Matt.41:21; 10)) reinforces not only John as the 'beloved disciple' and a sexual relationship between Jesus and John, but also reminds of Jonathan and David. When David and Jonathan first meet (1Sam.18:1,3) the authors of 1Sam. make a point to show they are interwoven body and soul by having Jonathan strip naked and give his clothes to David, but also 'And it came to pass, when he had made an end of speaking unto Saul, that the soul of Jonathan was knit with the soul of David, and Jonathan loved him as his own soul.' and in more than one place the story narrates Jonathan strengthens David's ascension and that they strengthen each other. The same is meant by the 'Zebedee' for John, and when talking about the 'beloved disciple' although they do not name him, when they mention 'sons of Zebedee' it is to indicate: John comes second of James; Jonathan and David as a couple; John and Jesus as a couple, and also to remind that Jesus and John are physically and emotionally latticed together just like David and Jonathan are knit together. The 'lattice' meanings as well as the 'buttered/spread over' and especially 'his drinking bowl' (a receptacle of God's semen just like Mary) of 'Zebedee' should not be overlooked as they all play a role in identifying the 'beloved disciple' and the nature of the Jesus and John relationship.

John the disciple as Jesus' beloved, i.e. his lover, is proven over and over again in the riddles which fill the gospel of John and these riddles depend on wordplay, knowing the Arabic language and being familiar with the OT stories. Not only is John son of Zebedee Jesus' lover, but he is described as a replica of Jonathan: John + Nathanael = johnnathanael; i.e. John becomes Jonathan (1Sam.13:2) 'males making each other female by having anal sex with each other-the' 'male on male sex making each other female-the' 'made female(with male on male sex)-the'. I will prove how the Nathanael character was created for use of his word-name to show John as Jesus' lover, and to show the relationship between Jesus and John Zebedee is two men in a complete physical and emotional relationship, the same relationship between David and Jonathan.

The Gospel of John begins and ends with a 'John' (first John the Baptist then John the disciple), and use of both 'Johns' are the same to the author of this gospel because of the meanings of their names. So it begins with a John witnessing Jesus/God, and ends with a John witnessing Jesus and his miracles.

Nathanael is used to complete 'John' (of Zebedee) the same way Mary and Jesus complete each other in the gospels: Mary and Jesus do not show a mother/son relationship, but a vessel/receptacle that receives water (receives the seed/sperm(Mary)), and a vessel which pours water (inseminates the pollinating seed(Jesus)). Although Andrew is used to find his brother Peter to bring him to Jesus, instead of using James to find John the author has **Philip** 'in its core/pulp' 'pick out/cleanse/remove it' 'so he answers/responds/assists/serves-him' 'he will/should answer/respond/assist/serve-him' find Nathanael (who does not appear anywhere in the other gospels). It is combining Philip/(core/cleanse) and Nathanael as through this clue 'Nathanael' John and Jesus will reach each other's core, and because the semen of Jesus is 'God's water' it has cleansing properties.

'Nathanael' is used for 'we double/fold-the' 'we female/feminine-the' as the clues regarding John are in 'twos' and what is happening between the beloved disciple and Jesus is the same sexual act as what happens between a man and woman 'we female/feminine' which makes the recipient 'female': John is always the brother of James; **Bethany** is mentioned for its meanings 'of girls/girlish' and is indicating the meaning of 'Jonathan' which means making a man female through anal sex and indicating that combining John with Nathanael makes the beloved disciple Johnathanael i.e. Jonathan; Bethany also indicates 'with the other one' 'did it again' 'again' and 'twice'.

The narration of being 'born again/twice' indicates being born again is through sexual contact which includes God's water/semen (Holy Ghost) and his 'Spirit/breathing/panting', and it specifically alludes to illicit sex which is curiously used as a 'higher/spiritual' and pious copulation in contradiction to how it was viewed and used in the OT. The conversation between Nicodemus and Jesus is about being filled with God/Jesus' sperm: 'Jesus answered and said unto him...Except a man be born again, he cannot see the kingdom of God. Nicodemus saith unto him, How can a man be born when he is old? can he enter the second time into his mother's womb, and be born? Jesus answered, Verily, verily, I say unto thee, Except a man be born of water and of the Spirit, he cannot enter into the kingdom of God.'; the narration sets apart the sexual intercourse between man and woman/husband and wife and is explicitly talking about sex with God, and God is Jesus: 'That which is born of flesh is flesh; and that which is born of the Spirit is spirit. Marvel not that I said unto thee, Ye must be born again.' (recall how although John the Baptist was already six months in his mother's womb that he was 'born again' by being affected by God's sperm through a visit from Mary to Elisabeth) 'The wind bloweth where it listeth, and thou hearest the sound thereof, but canst not tell whence it cometh, and wither it goeth: so is every one that is born of the Spirit. Nicodemus answered and said unto him, How can these things be? Jesus answered and said unto him, Art thou a master of Israel, and knowest not these things?' i.e. Nicodemus being from Israel should know what it means to be copulated by God; **Israel** 'twisted muscle-the' which means illicit sex and recalls the encounter between God as a man with Jacob which ended up withering Jacob's muscle. It is the Biblical authors' method of making very clear what is being narrated.

The meaning of Nathanael 'we double/fold-the' 'we female/feminine-the' and tying it to the meaning of Israel 'twisted muscle-the' as an act of male-on-male sex between God/Jacob, David/Jonathan, Jesus/John is intentional and clear. Meanings of **Nathanael** shown in: using the duo 'sons of Zebedee' and is also a dual clue to John being Jesus' lover, and also the duality of similarity with Jonathan and David, and the meaning behind pairing James with John. Nathanael's character is also used to link to Bethany as a sign towards another clue which leads to Jonathan, but also elucidates the nature of John and Jesus' relationship, just as with Nicodemus and 'born twice' narration ends with connecting it to the illicit sex/superior sex between God and Jacob, and the withering of Jacob's muscle making him 'Israel/twisted muscle-the', so does Jesus first encounter with Nathanael tie the latter to the meaning of **Israel**, where Jesus informs him this is their second encounter and ties it to the fig tree, this is connected to a fig tree which withers at Jesus' command, and the story itself is connected to **Bethany** with all its meanings which in turn connect to John the disciple as the 'beloved' but also to showing Jesus' relationship with John is the same as David's relationship with Jonathan. But the author makes the point of connecting Nathanael with Israel/twisted muscle-the and with John so that they become 'Johnnathanael'—another form of 'Jonathan'.

'Philip findeth Nathanael, and saith unto him, We have found him, of whom Moses in the law, and the prophets, did write, Jesus of Nazareth, the son of Joseph. And Nathanael said unto him, Can there any good thing come out of Nazareth? Philip say unto him, Come and see. Jesus saw Nathanael coming to him, and saith of him, Behold an Israelite indeed [a twisted muscle-the] in whom is no guile! Nathanael saith unto him, Whence knowest thou me? Jesus answered and said unto him, Before that Philip called thee, when thou wast under the fig tree, I saw thee. Nathanael answered and saith unto him, Rabbi, thou art the Son of God; thou art the king of Israel [like David was king of Israel and 'twisted muscle-the' with Jonathan (John+Nathanael)]. Jesus answered and said unto him, Because I said unto thee, I saw thee under the fig tree, believest thou? thou shalt see greater things than these. And he saith unto him, Verily, verily, I say unto you, Hereafter ye shall see heaven open, and the angels of God ascending and descending upon the Son of man.' And the last verse is a direct reference to when John the Baptist baptised Jesus and the 'heavens opened' and the 'Spirit of God' descending on him in the form of a dove—the whole baptism represents God's sperm/semen, and this connects the name of John the Baptist, which is also the exact same as John the disciple's name with Nathanael making them Johnnathanael 'male on male sex making each other female' but where the OT story made it lessen Jonathan and Saul's status and standing, in the NT it raises the recipients.

At John.21 Nathanael is given more word-names as his character name to further show that John the disciple is the 'beloved disciple' and also that the words are related to water/semen/pouring water into a vessel: a vessel that carries and/or pours water/sperm, erection, and the water it pours has '**Galilee**/clearing' properties by using **Cana** (John.2:1) 'a channel(water channel)' 'bottle/flask/any transportable drinking vessel/also small water vessel' 'estimated measure of something liquid' (when mixing ingredients or topping something up with water), 'held head high/body straight posture' 'person or object sitting/place/set upright/erect' 'were perky' 'they/he soaked him/it' 'they betrayed him/the'; and **Galilee** (Josh.20:7; John.2:1-11) 'came-to' 'came-for' 'cleared-the' 'made clear-the' as the place Nathanael comes from. The naming 'Nathanael in Cana of Galilee' sets out what is to happen in the final chapter of John, more sex between Jesus and his disciples' so as to spread the word and cleanse people of sins.

And in this chapter of John, even Peter is competing against the 'beloved disciple' as shown in the symbolism of the story and his character's actions: being naked, unhesitatingly throwing himself into the sea to reach Jesus, and at the end Jesus asks Peter to follow him, but Peter is surprised that the 'beloved disciple' is also following to join in with the '**Jonah**/bar-jona' 'piety/good-helped him'. The repeat question of Jesus asking Peter to prove how much he loves him and asking him to feed his lambs and sheep is that Peter needs to be strengthened, he needs to be given extra Jesus-water/sperm to nourish the lambs and sheep who are the followers of Jesus' ways. Peter's surprise and the narration display that John/'beloved disciple' will be the one giving Peter the water/semen which causes Peter's alarm '…And when he has spoken this, he saith unto him, Follow me. Then Peter, turning about, seeth the disciple whom Jesus loved following; which also leaned on his breast at supper, and said, Lord, which is he that betrayeth thee? Peter seeing him saith to Jesus, Lord, and what *shall* this man *do*? Jesus saith unto him, If I will that he tarry till I come, what is that to thee? follow thou me.' and it ends with stating that the beloved disciple is the author of the gospel/testimony combining John the Baptist into John the disciple.

But note that Peter was expecting to go alone with Jesus, and the author makes a point that it is understood that it is John son of Zebedee in two ways: first, verse 18 shows the meaning of 'Zebedee' 'tie tightly with rope' 'latticed it' 'latticed-he/him' 'swipe/whip(with a switch or rope)' 'strengthened-he/him' 'tight/tightened-he/him/it' and shows Peter is being told that he will be girded by someone else, the girding being around the waist is more euphemism—recall when Jesus removed his clothes and wore a towel before having sex with the twelve disciples, but it also indicates it is John who will pass on this water to Peter to enable him to better take care of the lambs and sheep/people, as he is the son of Zebedee whose word-name covers all the meanings implied of tying tightly with rope, strengthening, sex, soaking in fluid, and whose name reflects 'betrayed' as the author reminds he was lying on Jesus' breast and asked about who betrayed Jesus. The reason it is John the 'beloved disciple' tasked with empowering Peter is because Jesus now needs people who live on earth to continue with his work, as before he died on the cross, he passed this ability (water/sperm) on to John the disciple.

Nathanael 'doubled/folded-the' continues to be shown: two angels one sitting at head and the other at feet where Jesus' head and feet were laid and again this represents Jesus is partnered with John; Bethany and the Lazarus story are also clues: Bethany for its word-name meaning indicate 'with the other one' (the mention of John is always following the mention of James, as brothers), and Lazarus rising from death and covered with burial shrouds at John.11 also indicates towards when the beloved disciple (John) who will find Jesus has risen from the dead and no longer in the sepulchre and only finds his shrouds without his body, and John enters the sepulchre after Peter to keep him 'Bethany' 'with the other one/second'. 'Bethany' is also the same/similar to 'Nathanael' which also connects John to Nathanael making him 'Jonathanael' no different to Jonathan in meaning, character and role in the story. The author uses the burial shroud which is tied around Lazarus and covers his face, as he rises from death and comes towards Jesus, as a symbol meaning John Zebedee: the graveclothes and linen equate 'John/sack/sackcloth' (John the Baptist is also described as wearing sackcloth in Matt.); 'bound hand and foot...bound about with a napkin...' indicate John's surname 'Zebedee' with its 'tie tightly with rope' meaning.

In Jesus' encounter with the woman from Samaria where she is offered 'living water' i.e. sex with Jesus there is also a clue to who the beloved disciple is 'But whosoever drinketh of the water that I shall give him shall never thirst; but the water that I shall give him shall be in him a well of water springing up into everlasting life.'. Towards the end of John, Jesus describes the 'beloved disciple' as not dying, but waiting for him. The latter 'waiting/not dying' this also indicates it is John, where John is likened to Jonathan and Jesus to David as the original lovers had agreed on everlasting love, and agreed that David would wait at the stone named 'Ezel/forever/leave' where Jonathan would inform him if they could remain under one roof or would have to part ways.

John.7:37-38 repeats what has already been clearly made in the story of the Samaria woman and other passages that the 'living water' is sperm through sex 'Jesus stood and cried, saying, If any man thirst, let him come unto me, and drink. He that believeth on me, as the scripture hath said, out of his belly shall flow rivers of living water.'

Just as lovers can get secrets out of their beloved, the narration has Peter use the 'beloved disciple's' special relationship with Jesus to draw information out when Jesus was unwilling to name who would betray him, and the narration makes a point that this disciple is leaning on Jesus' chest—just like antagonists asked Delilah to use her charms to get Samson's secret out of him, but it indicates that it is John by the meaning of his name 'John/betrayed' and he is prompted to get Jesus to name who will betray him: 'Now there was leaning on Jesus' bosom one of his disciples, whom Jesus loved. Simon Peter therefore beckoned to him, that he should ask who it should be of who he spake. He then lying on Jesus' breast saith unto him, Lord, who is it?'

The conversation which initially baffles the disciples is the author has Jesus explain that a person even after death can still be seen in his offspring which carries the essence of the father (in the Bible a play on the word 'father' and 'God' can be seen in words such as, Father/God, rab/rabbi, abbah, rabbah). 'A little while, and ye shall not see me: and again, a little while, and ye shall see me, because I go to the Father.' It means, as they have been seeded/baptised with Jesus/God's water/sperm—wherever children are born, they can see Jesus and God, the son and father, as the children and the fathers of the children (the more the disciples spread Jesus' seed which is spread by the word, baptism, the more children are born (the more fathers and sons are created in the likeness of Jesus). It is about procreation.

At John.19:25-27, the 'beloved disciple' (John) is among the three-Marys (see three-Marys) because his role is to become like Jesus—a vessel which pours out water/seeds others, but also because John/'beloved disciple' is also a receptacle for Jesus' special water which is given in love through a romantic, sexual relationship with Jesus just like Jonathan and David, he and Jesus receive each other's water/sperm through a higher and closer relationship like husband and wife/male and female lovers.

At John.20 the narration has the 'beloved disciple' outrun Peter and arrive first at the sepulchre, but when he arrives he cannot bring himself to go in out of fear/distress of what he might see: he is faster because he loves Jesus more, and for this he is more distressed than Peter and cannot bring himself to immediately enter in fear he may see the man he loves, Jesus, still dead; and the author intentionally showed this heightened distress and connection between Jesus and this particular disciple. As in the Lazarus story at chapter 11, the empty shroud/linen identifies John/sack/sackcloth as the 'beloved disciple' which is also why the author has him the first to see Jesus' empty burial shroud and this also indicates 'Zebedee/tie tightly with rope' as they were tied around Jesus and is a miracle that they have been untied, especially contrasted that Lazarus needed people to untie him from his burial clothes; the linen shroud also indicates to a clue in a different gospel, the young man that is walking around naked, wrapped loosely in a linen cloth, who holds Jesus before dropping the linen cloth and running off naked to show that 'Mark/did not wait/stay', and these clothes show the character indicated as Mark/the naked young man is John/'put/wrap it/him in sack/sackcloth' the beloved disciple (the nakedness is euphemism for sex) who has had love and sex with Jesus (Mark.14:51-52).

The indication of Zebedee also shows 'Zebedee/latticed' which is created by two pieces of rope weaving against each other and is why the burial clothes are made to be laid in two separate places, and to bring in the clue of 'Nathanael/ we double/fold-the' 'we female/feminine-the' as this also points to John as the beloved disciple but also to him being the same as Jonathan which is both John and Nathanael word-names combined. **Nathanael** goes on to indicate Jesus and John are a pair and that John is the beloved disciple not only by Jesus coming back to life (from the living water/sperm he is created in and shares) but also through having the beloved disciple enter second into the sepulchre; in the two angels sitting where Jesus had lain; in pairing of the word-name **Mary** (Magdalene in this case) meeting with **Jesus** (these two word-names always represent the copulation, watering of semen and carrying of semen which results in bringing to life).

The author uses a specific setting where Jesus appears to the disciples at Tiberias, and using fishing and specifically mentioning casting a fishing net on its right side alludes to John as the 'beloved disciple': when Jesus first meets them (in Matt.) they are fixing fishing nets with their father; as it is implied in John.21 that they have caught nothing by throwing the net on the left side, but on the right side they do, what this does is connect it with the passages of two different gospels where either their mother or James and John themselves ask to be placed on the left side and right side of Jesus—there is nothing caught on their initial attempt (the left side) because Jesus has no special relationship with James (also James/he pokes in anus' the sexual act has to come before soaking in water/semen 'John'), but they catch fish on the right side is because he has a physical and loving relationship with John, and because 'Nathanael' and Bethany always refer to the second/double, it is John always mentioned after James who is indicated as the beloved disciple, but also because he and Jesus have 'soaked' in each other's water/semen and this allows them to recognise each other as in 'after a little while you will not see, and again after a while you will see me' as well as the water/baptism/Spirit being mentioned in other chapters that it allows those who believe in Jesus/Father/God to recognise him, because John has received more of Jesus' water/sperm, and because they are in a devoted loving relationship it is John the beloved disciple who recognises Jesus while the others do not.

Narrating that Peter is completely naked specifically in the same sentence that the 'disciple whom Jesus loved saith unto Peter, It is the Lord,' is alluding to the sexual relationship between John/beloved and Jesus for as soon as the beloved disciple tells Peter that it is Jesus standing at the shore, a naked Peter grabs a garment and hurls himself into the sea—it is a reverse of 'Mark/did not wait/stay' as the naked young man who takes off after he touches Jesus but leaves behind his linen cloth (the author of John.21 is making these obvious connections for the audience to see that Peter will become like John). The same event is taken into context with the connected narration of events which follow and show that Jesus is telling Peter that he has to continue spreading Jesus/God's seed/sperm/word/love and the author intentionally makes it about sex and sperm, and depicts Peter loves Jesus, exasperated at having to prove and compete with the beloved disciple's love, and is willing to do anything for Jesus—it also gives Peter a higher status than the remaining ten disciples (John is already elevated in status through Jesus' love and physical relationship). The reason the author has Jesus repeat and Peter have to prove how intense his love is for Jesus is to differentiate the love John the beloved disciple has, and the same which Peter will receive by the end of the chapter, in contrast against the different, lesser level and lesser kind of love and watering from Jesus than the other disciples.

The story again shows the person Jesus loved most out of his disciples is the one who has received extra of his water/sperm, from a homosexual relationship and from the transference of both Jesus' water and mother Mary at the crucifixion before Jesus dies. This is supported by the many clues in the short passage: he has been given the same name and meanings as John the Baptist who was soaked in God's sperm shared by Mary; like John the Baptist is the witness to the beginning of the 'light' at the beginning of this particular gospel, so is John the disciple given as the witness to its end and they are both witnessing the same thing. The recipients of 'living water' are said to have eternal life, David was to wait for Jonathan at a stone named 'Ezel/forever' to know if they could still live together; the narration purposely blurred what Jesus' meant that the 'beloved disciple' will either live forever or wait a while for Jesus to return—the author makes it a point to make it clear that the relationship between the beloved disciple and Jesus includes emotional and physical satisfaction by mentioning again and again that Jesus loves him and that this disciple leans on Jesus' breast like a man and woman in a physical relationship and just like a man and woman after having sex. But this is not the only reason, the author is also making it clear that John the beloved disciple is Mark as Mark means 'did not wait/stay' with these verses regarding the beloved disciple 'Peter seeing him saith to Jesus, Lord and what *shall* this man *do*? Jesus saith unto him, If I will that he tarry till I come, what *is that* to thee? follow thou me. Then went this saying abroad among the brethren, that the disciple should not die: yet Jesus said not unto him, He shall not die; but, if I will that he tarry till I come, what *is that* to thee?' because it brings the audience to connect to 'Mark/he did not wait/stay' who was naked when he followed and left Jesus at Mark.14, and although the current verses are about him waiting if Jesus' wants him to, he is actually not waiting/staying but following Peter and Jesus.

The meaning of **Boanerges** 'of when/with when-he curses/makes unclean/filthy' (Mark.3:17; Luke.9:54) also supports John son of Zebedee is meant to be John+Nathanael: Jonathanael, as the meaning is about a defilement happening, even sex between a husband and wife brings impurity in the OT and the culture of the region (with different degrees of impurity and purification from it between the stories and real-life culture), so homosexual intercourse between David and Jonathan, and Jesus and John the disciple also causes an impurity without negating the NT's theme that God/Jesus' water/sperm cleans away sins and physical impurities.

Bethany is connected at John.1:48 through narrating Jesus has seen Nathanael while he was under the fig tree, the fig tree featured in Matt.21 which Jesus causes to wither when he cannot find edible fruit in it. The fig tree and Nathanael connect to Bethany and lead to Bethphage and what happened in Bethphage: two unnamed disciples (Nathanael/Bethany) are sent to steal an ass and its foal, only if they are caught are they to say it is God's will that they take it without permission; Jesus ends up riding on both the ass and its young at the same time. This passage mirrors the David, Saul and Jonathan story: Saul is introduced seeking his father's lost donkeys and he is accompanied by a second character (Nathaniel/Bethany); it results in Saul becoming king; David ends up 'riding' both Saul and Jonathan, he rides (takes advantage of (which shows Bethany 'with/of the figs' 'my girl/daughter' 'of girls/girlish')) on Saul and takes over the kingdoms, and he physically and sexually rides on Jonathan and this too removes Saul and his offspring from becoming kings, then David becomes king. Saul is symbolised as the ass (and by extension Zebedee who loses his sons to Jesus), and Jonathan is the young colt (and John in the NT), Jesus is David (through the meanings of their word-names and connections in the narratives of their stories) and this is further enhanced by the verse 'Tell ye the daughter of Sion, Behold, thy King cometh…'. It is further enhanced to show sexual meanings and supported by having the disciples remove their clothes as a saddle for Jesus while he is on the donkeys, and by the people throwing their garments to pave the way for David/Jesus riding Saul/Zebedee and Jonathan/John: the dual meanings indicated and literal word meaning of 'double' of Bethany and Nathanael are present and all lead to John and Nathanael equate Jonathan, and Jesus and John have the same relationship as David and Jonathan.

It seems that John.20 may have been intended as the final chapter because it contains the two by two meanings which all lead to clues and show John as the beloved disciple, therefore in Gospel of John, Jesus' second appearance to the disciples was supposed to be the final appearance in the story and the end of the story (verse 31 reads like an end of the story). Chapter 21 seems to have been added to elevate Peter's character, whether by the original author, or more likely a later editor felt that Peter who is prominent in most of the gospels should have been the 'beloved disciple' so the final chapter serves to give him this special treatment (the same as John the beloved disciple) to give his character the power/status the author/editor believes he deserves in the story. Who knows if this was edited when Christianity was already popular as a religion and these stories taken as religious texts instead of fictional stories created for entertainment; The changes may have been made by popular demand if real-life people felt Peter should have been the strongest and most-loved disciple by Jesus, but due to the relay between word-name meanings and events it seems more likely that these stories were made purely for entertainment.

Acts

Theophilus is being used the same way as it was used in Luke (1:1-4) to add information to the already known Jesus stories; ضِيوفِلوه ، ضيوفِلَه 'add to it/for him' 'guest(s) for him' 'hosted-him/it'.

Acts seems to be a continuation of John's Gospel, this is why the author used 'Theophilus' as a word-name and meaning because he is adding to John's Gospel, it continues the theme regarding what is meant by the Gospel of John. Acts narrates about Jesus 'To whom also he shewed himself alive after his passion by many infallible proofs, being seen of them forty days, and speaking of the things pertaining to the kingdom of God…'. Forty is another special number important to the Biblical authors and the culture they are from. In the culture of the people who created the Biblical stories forty days means forty days of 'impurity' before a person returns to purity. It does not mean that the person(s) undergoing forty days of impurity does not wash, they do wash, wear clean clothes, etc. but remain 'impure' regarding they cannot pray, be made love to. This applies to two actions: one is when a mother gives birth, she remains 'impure' for forty days since giving birth. The second is a couple who have engaged in illicit sex also remain impure for forty days from the act of copulation (fornication or adultery). (Acts.1:3)

David 'the stone rolling pin of grinding stone' has been used for the imagery it conjures up of a 'david/stone rolling pin' grinding grains causing them to crack open and their insides be ground into a paste to describe what happens to Judas who purchases a field (fields are for grains to be harvested from) and then 'falling headlong, he burst asunder in the midst, and all his bowels gushed out.' (Acts.1:15-18)

Aceldama; Akeldamách; اكل دمآك 'ate your blood' 'ate-made you bleed' and refers to Judas accepting money for spilling Jesus' blood and it turning into a curse which eats him up (as displayed in Judas bursting), even if in Matt. Judas returns the money and the chief priests purchase a piece of land for a cemetery and in the same story Judas hangs himself. Although the Biblical text it states 'in their proper tongue, Aceldama, that is to say, The field of blood.' again it seems a shortcut to the easiest explanation given by an Arabic translator of how the word 'eats' means the equivalent of 'comes back to bite you/karma/curse'; or is because the Arab translating between the Arab story and the Greek translator does not speak the full Arab language of the Arabian Peninsula because there is no letter to represent the (h/ḥ/ح) necessary for the first letter of 'field' (ḥql/حقل) which modern scholars attempt to explain that the Greek translation got from Aramian language—when it is just Arabic with a specific meaning like every other word in the OT Bible, and the word-names of the Greek Bible. Cp: akel damaak. (Acts.1:18-19)

Barsabas; Barsabbas; بَر سَبَّه 'good/piety-left him/it' 'good/piety-swore at him' 'good/piety-caused him/because of him'; بَر صَبَّه 'good/piety-poured him/it'. These meanings are available in the related story: the two nominees are being considered for the position of Judas—Judas left piety and died and they are being considered for this position because of Judas' actions; Barsabbas is not chosen for this position which would have made him more good/pious so good/piety/God has left him (not abandoned him completely but regarding the role of apostle); vying for the position of apostle means they will be filled with God's water/sperm whether directly from God or through his disciples, and it does not necessarily mean only through the act of sex as with God/Holy Ghost/Spirit Mary, and Jesus and his disciples, but also similar to what happened between Mary visiting Elisabeth and transferring to John in Elisabeth's belly the Holy/Ghost water/sperm powers, and also the way disciples were able to heal and help the afflicted when appointed by Jesus (through the word, breath, touch, using normal water). Cp: bar-sabbah, bar-s͟sabbah.

Joseph of sorrow/feels sorrow/regret' 'pours water gently over/rinses/cleanses' supports the meanings of Barsabbah, as he will be sad not to be chosen, and again the 'pours water/rinses/cleanses' meanings support those explained under Barsabbah.

Justus; Ioústos; يؤصطوه ، يؤصطه 'he clings/sticks to' 'he swoops down on' 'he lays hands on/harms' 'he quickly sticks to/against' the lots indication will 'stick' to the successful candidate; يؤسطوه ، يؤسطه 'he mediates/makes middle/centres/centred' 'centre of house/makes/builds centre of house' 'mediator/builder/foreman/person-in-charge of building' 'intervenes/witnesses/assists' as both men contending for Judas' vacant position need to witness, be the medium testifying to the people, of Jesus' resurrection. The word is connected to the meaning and noun of the middle of the house, which is the same as the person who acts as both architect and chief builder of a construction, supervising and instructing the workers/builders, (usṭh/wsṭh/وسطه/اسطه) which connects all different rooms (and stairs) to each other, and this is from the word (wsṭ/وسط) 'middle/medium/connected'; the nominees are contending to be this middle position which means they will end up connecting converts to Jesus, as well as instructing them on God/Jesus' ways; God is also the mediator as he is choosing/instructing who gets the position; the lots will choose the successful candidate; يوُشتوه ، يوُشتُه 'he/they wants him/it' and both Barsabbah and Matthias want the position; and want God to want them for the position; 'it rises/leavens/ferments it' and the character, if chosen, will swell with the powers of God's water; it could also be هوُشتوه ، هوُشتُه 'he wants him/it' 'he leavens/makes it/him rise' 'shoos him/it away'; جوُشتوه ، جوُشتُه 'picked/took a lot/many/handfuls' 'came-wanted him/it' 'came-leavened/rose him/it'; حوُشتوه ، حوُشتُه 'stuffed him/it' 'cut down-him/it; عوُشتوه ، عوُشتُه 'lived it/lived-him/it'. With the context of the story it would be any of the 'he/they wants him/it' 'it rises/leavens it' meanings. Cp: yousṣṭooh, yousṣṭoh, yousṭooh, yousṭoh, youshtooh, youshtoh, houshtooh, houshtoh, goushtooh, goushtoh, ḥoushtooh, ḥoushtoh, 'oushtooh, 'oushtoh. (Acts.1:22-26)

Matthias; Maththías; مطّطيَه ، مَطّيَه 'stretched it-he him' 'of stretching-he/him' 'stretch-him/he'; مَضيّه ، مضضيَه 'he passed by' 'passed by him/he' 'passed time/distracted' 'passed time/distracted-him/he' 'completed-it/him/he' 'made mark(signed)-it/he/him' 'rinsed mouth-he/him' 'gathered (specific type of) tree-he/him'; مدديه ، مَدّيَه 'lay down-he/him' 'he laid him/it down' 'extended with hand/reached for/handed over-he/him' 'reached into-he him' 'pus formed in it-he/him/it' 'inked-it/he/him'; مَثثيَه ، مثّيَه 'wiped urine/sperm-he/him' 'of wiping urine/sperm-he him' and means to use a leaf, stone or dry fabric to wipe away from genitals. It is equivalent to Matthew (Matt.9:1-9), Matthat, Mattathias, Maath, Mattatha (Luke.3). Cp: maṭ-ṭyah, maṭṭyah, madhyah, madh-dhyah, mad-d-yah, maddyah, maf-fyah, maffayah.

He was created as the second nominee to become an apostle because of the meanings 'to complete' as he will complete the twelve original disciples who have been incomplete with the death of Judas (but also note that because the authors are not dealing with real events nor real people they have also replaced the name of one of the twelve with 'Judas *the brother* of James' as the author wants to use the word-name of 'Judas'); there is the meaning of wiping away urine or sperm in the word-name and this is connected to the power of the 'Holy Ghost' which he will receive; as lots are cast, things are being extended and the one chosen has essentially been marked. (Acts.1:22-26)

Pentecost; pentēkostēs; فَنطيقو هتيه 'so speak it/pronounce it' 'of speaking/pronouncing it' 'so make him pronounce/speak' and this is exactly what happens: fire in the form of tongues comes down upon each apostle, they begin to pronounce/speak in other tongues—which does not mean they spoke different languages exactly, but indicates they were making sounds (like gibberish or moans) and they are doing this because the 'tongues like as of fire' are filling them with the 'Holy Ghost' i.e. God's water/sperm and his 'Spirit/breathing/panting' gives their words meaning (remember Jesus/God's 'word' has been used the same way to indicate God's water/sperm and with the same effects) and the author elucidates that they are speaking in different languages understood by speakers of those languages: 'And when the day of Pentecost was fully come, they were all of one accord in one place. And suddenly there came a wind from heaven as of a rushing mighty wind, and it filled all the house where they were sitting. And there appeared unto them cloven tongues like as of fire, and it sat upon each of them. And they were all filled with the Holy Ghost, and began to speak with other tongues, as the Spirit gave them utterance…Now when this was noised abroad, the multitude came together, and were confounded, because that every man heard them speak in his own language.' And to make sure the audience understands that the apostles are both sounding gibberish and understood clearly in multiple languages the author reminds the audience 'Others mocking said, These men are full of new wine.'. Cp: phenṭeyqoohteyh. (Acts.2:1-13)

Jerusalem is used to show how the people that heard and saw them are asking questions about how can it be that they speak different languages when they know these apostles only speak one language. (Acts.2:5-8)

Galileans is used for its meaning 'cleared-the' 'made clear-the' as multilingual peoples can understand them in separate languages, the apostles' words are clear and understood. (Acts.2:7)

Parthians; Párthos; بآرثُه 'went beyond him/it' 'surpassed/exceeded' 'was pious towards him/it' and refers to the 'devout men' who could hear and also that not only locals could hear them speak but people from all over were in the area and could hear them too. Cp: baartoh. (Acts.2:9)

Medes; Mēdoi; ميدوي 'extends/reaches' 'touches/puts hands into/on' 'extending/reaching' 'echoes/loud sound' and refers to the languages and speech the apostles begin to speak reaching all corners of the earth. Cp: meeydoi. (Acts.2:9)

Elamites; Elamítēs; علميتيه 'showed him/it' 'of showing' 'made marks/signals him/it' of making marks/signals' 'taught him/it' 'of teaching'; الميتيه 'will blame him/it' 'of blaming' 'in pain' 'of pain' 'blamed'. It refers to the people affected by the Holy Ghost and Spirit able to communicate with others in languages they do not speak; it refers to the pain people will suffer by the signs Peter mentions; in the blame Peter lays on people for killing Jesus. Cp: 'lameeteyh, elameeteyh. (Acts.2:9)

Mesopotamia: Mesopotamía is used for its meaning in the original language: ʿaram nahărāyim; عَرَم نَهيراي ام 'abandoned-we drove away with cruelty-the' 'abandoned-bullied-the' 'abandoned-spoke harshly-the'. It relays with Peter stating God's 'Spirit' will be poured onto many people who will prophesy; in the signs which will pour down from God; in the way Jesus was bullied, treated with cruelty and murdered. (Acts.2:9)

Judaea 'he is called/calls'. (Acts.2:9)

Cappadocia; Kappadokía; كَبَّ دوقي 'poured/spilled-noise/noisy' and is because after the Holy Ghost fills (pours into) them they become noisy, speaking multiples tongues. Cp: kabba dooqeea. (Acts.2:9)

Pontus; Póntos; بونتوه ، بونتُه 'his daughter(s)/his girl(s)/his children' 'made clear/apparent' 'became apparent' 'your intentions have become apparent' as the speech has become clear to all who hear them. Cp: boontooh, boontoh. (Acts.2:9)

Asia; Asía; عصيا ، عصي 'disobeyed/disobedient/went against' 'disobeyed him/went against him' 'became askew/bent/crooked/warped' 'sticks' 'used sticks'; اسيا ، اسي 'sorrow' 'bad/offense/insult' 'bad towards/offense/insult towards'; اشيا ، اشي 'things/matters' 'many/lots of things' 'puzzling matters/things' 'wants' 'he wanted' 'speaking in whispers' 'snitching' and this is relevant as the speech of the apostles can be heard everywhere, while some people believe the apostles are drunk; the apostles are speaking about important matters. Equivalent to Asahel (2Sam.2:18-23), Eleasah (1Chr.2:39), Asiel (1Chr.4:35), Asaiah (1Chr.4:36), and other similar word-names. Cp: 'sseea, aseeaa, asheea. (Acts.2:9)

Phrygia; Phrygía; فريجيه '(so) they waited-he/him' 'so wait-he/him/they' 'they opened up' 'opening(s)/orifice(s)' 'openings/orifices-he/him/them' 'opened up/relieved/released/end of difficult period or experience' 'vaginas/vulvas' 'they watched/saw' 'they stared at/watched' 'they created an opening/release-him/he/they'. It is a direct reference to the male-on-male sex which makes them receptacles and vessels which pour it in and out again, by being filled with Jesus/God's water/sperm, and the twelve disciples are present and especially the two who received more of Jesus' water/sperm who are now opening up the other men in the room who once they have been given this special water their words also affect the people who hear them through the word. Cp: phrygeea (Acts.2:10)

Pamphylia; Pamphylía; بَمثيليه 'with like me' 'with the same as me' 'with proverbs/sayings' 'with acting' 'with wiping away urine/sperm for me' and is still related to the speech of the apostles and what actions happened to give them this ability. Cp: ba-mfyleea. (Acts.2:10)

Egypt; Aígypton; is used for its meaning in the original language: miṣrayim; 'put scarf on-them' 'their scarves' 'put scarf on-the' 'knot/bundle-them/the' 'keep within/withhold' 'insulted-them' 'their disgrace/embarrassment' 'offend-the' as some people believe them to be drunk. (Acts.2:10)

Libya; Libýē; لِبياي 'their/the-pulp/core' 'my pulp/core' 'pulp/core-them/the' 'answer/respond/assist-them/the' 'answer/respond/assist me' 'served/serve/serve him(or it)/me', and is regarding the answers being given. Cp: libyaaey. (Acts.2:10)

Cyrene (Matt.27:32) used now for the meaning 'of reading' 'read to me' 'teach me to read' as the apostles have been given instant ability to speak foreign languages, they are reading out to people what God/Jesus wants them to understand. (Acts.2:10)

Rome; Rhṓmē; رومي 'were thrown' 'threw' 'killed' 'spread/strewn over vast distance/various locations' 'saw water' 'became rotten/went off/bad smelling'. They reflect the languages of far flung and various regions which the apostles can suddenly speak the language of. Also, because it is related to God's water which is what the Holy Ghost and Spirit fill them with. Cp: roomey. (Acts.2:10)

Cretes; Krḗtē; كريبتي 'hired/rented/leased' 'of hiring/renting/leasing' 'drove/chased/forced away/forced with violence'; قريبتي 'my village' 'villager' 'of villages' 'of reading a lot' 'read a lot to me/taught me to read/of teaching to read' 'stopped moving/fidgeting' 'stopped what you were doing'. It is still related to teaching people with their own languages the ways of Jesus/God. Cp: kreeeytee, qreeeytee. (Acts.2:11)

Arabians 'he will-my god/parent/teacher' 'will he-my god/parent/teacher' 'expressing clearly/speaking clearly' '(of)learn and remember/beware/be warned-teacher/discipliner/parent/god/master/the grower/ anyone who brings someone up or teaches them/grows them (children/animals/plants/etc.)/grew fast and(or) well' it can also be read in the tense 'taught/disciplined/grew well/brought up', 'of getting naked' 'of fucking with' 'fucked a lot with' 'is mixed and diluted with water' 'the god/parent/teacher' 'is my god/ parent/teacher' 'he is-my god/parent/teacher' 'is he/which-my god/parent/teacher?' 'the (or of) mixed and diluted with water' 'mixed and diluted with water' 'the (or of) teacher(ing)/discipliner(ing)/parent/god/ grower/anyone who brings someone or something up or teaches them/grows them' 'the grown fast and/or well'. The meanings of expressing /speaking clearly as well as the meanings of 'copulated' and 'diluted and mixed with water' are being used because of the apostles speaking clearly in foreign languages, teaching people about God's message, but also because this has happened to them when they have been filled with the Holy Ghost i.e. water/semen from God. (Acts.2:11)

Joel has been used for 'howling' 'be warned/beware-the' 'learn and remember-the' as Peter has 'lifted up his voice' and is speaking severely to his audience, warning and reminding them of punishment, he is informing them that they will also be prophesying/warning. (Acts.2:16)

Israel 'twisted muscle-the' 'twisted-the' is used to show how they disobeyed and killed Jesus. **Jesus** is used as 'bread' linked to **David** 'rolling pin of stone grinder'. **Nazareth** used for dedicated to God and as 'warned' because he was meant to be sacrificed, and he suffered because he warned the people of the wrong ways and punishment if there was no repent. (Acts.2:22-25)

David is used again to show meaning of 'stone rolling pin of grinder' and **Christ** 'cake/circle of bread' as Jesus is being described as the 'fruit of his loins' and if you see how grains are ground and they occupy the middle part of the grinder and when dough is complete it sits on the slab of the grinding stone, it is a literal indication of Jesus being bread and David the rolling pin. (Acts.2:29-31)

Beautiful; and this is based on the mistranslation of (no'am) as 'Beauty' in the OT at Zech.11, when both the OT and NT stories show it is still 'blessings' the receipt or giving another money, food, clothing, gifts, health anything tangible which is called a 'blessing' and also 'we stifle/feel stifled' 'we suffocate/feel suffocated' 'we cover/we are covered' 'we muffle/are muffled' 'we depress/feel depressed' and both positive and negative meanings are relayed in Acts.3: the disabled man is waiting at the gate mistranslated as 'Beautiful' which should be 'blessing/gave or received money, food, clothes, health, gifts, etc.' as he is waiting to ask anyone who enters to give him charity; he asks Peter and John to give him charity; Peter tells him they cannot give him money, but they do give him health, restoring his body which makes his life easier (the very meanings of 'blessing'). Peter again reminds the people they received the greatest 'blessing' (Jesus) but persecuted and killed him, i.e. they muffled his voice/message, they caused him a lot of distress.

It is possible that the medium/translator between the original local story and the Greek copier/ interpreter added his own wordplay into the story as this is what the text in Greek suggests: the word for 'Beautiful' is given in Greek as 'hōraia, hōraian' and the meanings as pronounced in Arabic relays a lot in the chapter: هورَيْ ، هورَيْن 'he saw' 'he saw them' 'he watered/was watered' 'he watered them' 'chase away/he chased away (with words)' 'he chased them away(with words)'; خورَيْ ، خورَيْن 'he chased away with violence' 'he chased them away with violence' 'collapse/he collapsed/he made collapse' 'he made them/it collapse'. This is reflected in the amount of times the author of the chapter makes the act of 'seeing' happen in the story: 'who seeing Peter and John…And Peter, fastening his eye upon him with John, said, Look on us. And he gave heed unto them…And all the people saw him walking and praising God…And when Peter saw *it*…or why look ye so earnestly on us…' and the healing is from the water/semen powers given to the disciples from Jesus (tied word-wise with the water-related meanings of Solomon, Abraham and Isaac), and then the chapter turns to how they caused the persecution and death of Jesus which shows the 'chased away' and 'collapsed' meanings. Cp: hooraia, hooraian, <u>kh</u>ooraia, <u>kh</u>ooraian. (Acts.3:2)

Note how John and Peter have Jesus' healing powers because they received extra love and physical relationship with Jesus. It may have been the author of Acts who added the last chapter to John (John21) giving Peter the same power as John the beloved disciple. (Acts.3)

Solomon has been used for 'ask him/asks him-what' 'asked him-what' 'of many questions/of questions-what' 'leaked/flowed water' 'they allowed him to survive' 'intact/whole' 'of surviving' 'distracted/ entertained-water/his water' 'comforted-water/his water' 'of mild/peaceful nature' 'became mild/peaceful' 'reached/arrived at-water/his water' 'connected-water/his water' 'delivered-water/his water' 'rock-his water' 'publicly apologised/arrived-water/his water/what' as the people have gathered around them and are asking and wondering, staring at Peter and John regarding the healing of the man; Peter and John can heal like Jesus because Jesus' water/sperm has flowed into them and flows back into people through healing/preaching, touch or the word; they have made the lame man 'whole/intact'; Jesus is described as a peaceful person; speaks about not allowing Jesus to survive, but allowing a murderer (Barabbas) to survive; that God allows Jesus to survive by raising him from the dead also shows 'public apology' as does telling the people to repent. (Acts.3:11-16)

Abraham 'pull up/draw up-the' 'clear-the'; the man's illness has been cleared; Peter is making clear God's message of repentance which leads to the clearing away of sins; the way Jesus and the disciples' powers work, or at least originate from, which is God/Jesus water/sperm through sex which apostles can now deliver through the word/speech and/or touch; Jesus is raised up to God like a bailing pouch is drawn up in the word 'Abraham'; this too is reflected in likening Moses and Jesus to each other as both characters are related to being in water, soaked, and being pulled out of the water, or emerge as in born from the water. (Acts.3)

Isaac 'he pulls up water little by little' (in drought) 'swipes/drags water'; because Jesus is no longer there, but his disciples can still provide his powers of healing and preaching, this in itself is trying to collect the people that can be convinced to the ways of Jesus/God is like the pulling up of water, little by little during drought. Also 'swipes/drags water' is also accumulating, moving what liquid/water there is and also symbolises cleaning away people's sins. (Acts.3)

Jacob for its meaning of 'force open/usurp' as instead of allowing Pilate to free Jesus, they choose Barabbas to be freed instead. (Acts.3)

Pilate (Matt.27:1-31) is used again for its meanings 'let him loose/go' 'are his fall/let him fall' as the narration reminds that the people would not allow Jesus to be released, causing his execution/fall, but instead insisted on letting a murderer be released. (Acts.3)

Jesus is used as 'broke/ate bread' for the meaning of 'breaking' as bread is broken to be eaten, this causes the death/consummation of Jesus who is often described in the Bible as a whole circle of bread (Christ). (Acts.3)

Moses is used for 'squeeze him/it' as his character and character name is based on squeezing water out of, which is why the author of Acts has used him as the same as Jesus who was born out of God's water, then Jesus himself squeezed his own water into the disciples, and the powers of his/God's water into healing and converting people 'For Moses truly said unto the fathers, A prophet shall the Lord your God raise up unto you of your brethren, like unto me...'. It also shows the meanings of 'touched/possessed/was possessed/touched' 'entangled/caused problems/provoked problems or fighting' as Jesus is touched by God, Jesus touches the disciples to give them powers and the people to heal and convert, and destruction/punishment is promised those who do not listen to God's message which he delivers. (Acts.3)

Sadducees have been used the same way as in Matt.: 'of deceit/deceiving' 'they deceived/tricked you' 'of giving extra' 'they gave you extra' as they believe Peter and John to be deceiving people; because it is evening, the apostles are left in prison for an extra day. 'believed you/of believing' 'honest-you/of honesty' 'befriended you/of befriending/friendly' the people still believe Peter and John because they have seen the miracle of the lame man cured. 'of blocking/denying' 'they blocked/denied you' because the Sadducees are trying to prevent Peter and John's preachings, prevent people seeing their miracles, block them by beating them and throwing them in prison and attempting to find ways to prevent them spreading Jesus' word. (Acts.4)

The names mentioned as related to the high priest who oppose John and Peter are all names which reflect what is happening in the story. Note how although 'John' is already available in the character of the apostle, still the author has included the word-name as an opposing character of the same name to emphasise the meanings of the word 'John' happening in the story, to make the audience able to see its meanings as intended by the authors:

Annas (Luke.3:2, 8, 10-14) 'he satisfied/gave fill/plenty of-him/he' 'satisfaction/gave satisfaction-him/he'; 'I saw/eyed-he/him' 'look, see-intended/hinted message at-he/him' 'I/will-inspect/look at/into-he/him' 'look, there he/it is-he/him' 'I will make suffer/made suffer-he/him' 'I helped/assisted/will help/assist-he/him', a sound/word repeated to get cows, sheep or goats back on the right path or back into the correct land; 'I will become/make independent/rich/no longer needed-he/him' 'see, look-sang/hummed/made 'g̲hn' noise(used in singing or reading religious books)-he/him';

Caiaphas (Matt.26:1-5) 'how-he/him' 'they figured out how/thought about it' 'thought how/about-he/him' 'of thinking things/in good mood to think about matters'; 'how-he/him' 'they figured out how/thought about it' 'thought how/about-he/him' 'of thinking things/in good mood to think about matters' 'of turning back of head to/turning (his)back towards' 'turned back of his head or his back towards-he/him'.

The priests are examining and questioning John and Peter; they are asking the apostles to explain how they are able to convince people to convert and follow/believe them, and when people convert they are turning their backs on the religion of the priests; what the apostles are doing with the people is the same as a shepherd causes stray sheep/goats/flocks to return to the correct path, also the antagonists who have opposing beliefs to the apostles are doing the same: attempting to get people straying from religion back onto the correct path.

John (Matt.3:1-3; 11:7-9) 'soaked it/him (in)' 'brothers' 'betrayed' 'sacks' 'sackcloth' 'put/wrap it/him in sack/sackcloth': Peter answers only when he has been filled with the 'Holy Ghost' and that reminds of being filled with Jesus' water/semen; this also makes Peter and John similar to brothers (just as John the Baptist and Jesus were because they shared the same God's water/sperm), and both apostles have been soaked in Jesus' water. **Israel** 'twisted muscle-the/twisted-the' reminds that Jesus and his apostles are meant to swell and straighten Israel's twisted muscle which is the people and their disobedience of God, it also indicates the priests and 'their kindred' are still 'twisted-the' refusing to straighten by following God's ways. It highlights that Jesus was betrayed by the high priests and their 'kindred'.

Alexander (Mark.15:21) 'on you/upon you-I will send it/him out' 'on you/upon you-I will separate him/it'; it is mostly used to describe sending off sheep/goats in the right direction towards pastures to graze ('sent him/it out'); and used to describe separating between sheep and goats, whether to sort and separate them to send to different areas, or to separate one or more from the rest of the flock in order to slaughter or sell them ('separated him/it'). It reflects that Jesus and his apostles are trying to send the people towards a better life and afterlife, to a better and/or correct way of life/beliefs. It also reflects that Jesus was sacrificed like a sacrificial animal by God, and also that his execution was implemented by the people. It also reflects that when unable to find a reason to execute them, the priests release John and Peter.

Jerusalem 'they see-asked-them/the' 'came-saw-asked-them/the' 'came-saw-water flowed/leaked-them/the' as the apostles are brought and 'set them in the midst' and the priests question them, and when this happens Peter is filled with the 'Holy Ghost' i.e. water/semen; 'they saw-joined/connected-them/the' 'they saw-reached/arrived/public apology-them/the' 'they see-their/the rocks' 'they see-rocks-them/the' 'came-saw-joined/connected-them/the' 'came-saw-reached/arrived/public apology-them/the' 'came-saw-their/the rocks' 'came-saw-rocks-them/the' as the antagonists are gathered and joined to prevent Jesus' word from reaching further; also relayed and linked to the rock(s) which is important in both the OT and NT stories which Peter's dialogue mentions 'This is the stone which was set at nought of you builders, which is become the head of the corner.'.

Jesus Christ of Nazareth (Matt.) 'broke bread-his cake of bread' 'broke/ate his cake of bread' 'broke/ate bread-the circle of bread' because Jesus also revolved around the breaking of bread, but as a whole circle of bread is always broken to be eaten and shared; it also denotes how he ends up being killed as well as that he will be returned whole/intact; also that the disabled man has been made 'whole' because of the powers of Jesus which flow through the apostles; **Nazareth** (Matt.2:23) 'she/I vowed/set aside/dedicated to God' 'the vow/set aside/dedication to' 'warned' 'she/I warned' because from his conception he was meant as a sacrifice for the people's sake, and his life was about warning people of the wrong ways and showing them the right ways.

Peter 'his/its stub/shortness' 'he has cut him/it short' 'he/it has been snapped short' 'he/it has been abruptly cut off' 'they have snapped him/it/cut him/it short' 'his stub of rock' 'his smooth rock', and **John** as 'sacks' 'sackcloth' 'put/wrap it/him in sack/sackcloth', these meanings are reflected: in the rock/stone Peter refers to in his dialogue, and links to when Jesus described Peter as a rock (see Simon Bar-jona (Matt.16:16-18), the people are questioning and looking at Peter whose name means 'rock' and specifically a stub of rock and/or smooth rock; reflected in Peter and John's way of speech is uneducated, it is 'stubbiness' and rough like the material of sacks: 'Now when they saw the boldness of Peter and John, and perceived that they were unlearned and ignorant men, they marvelled;' and then **Jesus** 'bread' 'ate/broke bread' is used to show and remind these two men have their powers through having 'eaten' Jesus i.e. not just bread, but absorbed from his body through sex and sperm 'and they took knowledge of them, that they had been with Jesus.' (Acts.4)

David 'the stone rolling pin of grinding stone' is again used to connect grain and grinding stone to Jesus/bread, and also for the meaning of when an animal revolves, hesitates and returns whether being cornered to attack, etc. described as all the kings and rulers of the world standing against the whole 'cake of bread' 'Christ'. The shaking of the place also conjures up the sound and vibrations coming from the grinding of grain to make bread which again is linked to Jesus in the verses Acts.4:25-31, as it is the David/rolling pin which does the action and makes the sounds, and crushes grain into dough.

Pontius Pilate 'so you and him/he-are his fall/let him fall', **Herod** 'incited/incited against', **Gentiles** ethnesin; يثني سِن/سِين **'ethne'**: 'he/they do it again/double it/fold it/repeat it-' 'he/they dissuade/make leave-' 'he/they are idolaters/pagans-' 'idols-' 'praise/praises-' 'idol worshippers-' 'idolatry/worshipping idols-'; followed by **'sin'** meanings: in the direction of/towards me/in the face of/in front of/straight/straight line/direct/opposite me'; and the OT meanings of Gentile: 'I will deceive them/the' 'I will mislead them to downfall-them/the', **Israel** 'twisted muscle-the' 'twisted-the'; these word-names are self-explanatory in how they have been used: 'The kings of the earth stood up, and the rulers were gathered together against the Lord, and against his Christ. For of a truth against thy holy child Jesus, whom thou hast anointed, both Herod, and Pontius Pilate, with the Gentiles, and the people of Israel, were gathered together, For to do whatsoever thy hand and thy counsel determined before to be done. And now, Lord, behold their threatenings…' (Acts.4:26-29)

Joses (Matt.13 and is the same word as Josiah (2Kgs.22-23)) 'he goes wandering and seeking'. Also 'he offends it/him' 'it offends/it offends him'. 'he goes wandering seeking' reflected in that he sells his land and brings the money to the apostles; this is combined with his surname which means 'piety/good towards his prophet'.

Barnabas; Barnabás; بَرنَباَه 'piety/good-prophesied news' 'piety/good-prophecy/predict' 'piety/good-prophet/news' 'passed/beyond/passed beyond-prophesied news' 'passed beyond-prophecy/predict' 'passed beyond-prophet/news' 'piety/good towards his prophet' 'piety/good-warned (him)/woke (him) up/pointed out (to him)'. Cp: bar-nabaah.

He is a **Levite** for its meanings of 'answered/answer/answer him(or it)' 'served/serve/serve him(or it)' as he responds to the apostles' preachings and serves them.

They have made this character from Cyprus; Kýpros; كيآثروه ، كيآثرُه 'a lot/became a lot' 'many/became many/multiplied' as he brings a lot of money for the apostles from land he sells; كيآفروه ، كيآفرُه 'see, increased/multiplied it' 'try to increase/multiply it' 'disbelieved(in God or religion or the person)' 'they became disbelievers' 'disbelieved him'; قيآبروه ، قيآبرُه 'buried it/him' 'many burials/graves' 'his grave(s)'. The meaning of 'became a lot' and 'see, increased/multiplied it' is used here as his character has increased the money arriving at the 'apostles' feet' and he is contrasted against Ananias and Sapphira who in the following chapter sell land but do the opposite by not giving it all to the apostles, and a lot of emphasis and narration revolves around their burials. Cp: kyaafrooh, kyaafroh, kyaa*ph*rooh, kyaa*ph*roh, kyaabrooh, kyaabroh. (Acts.4:36-37)

Ananias; Hananías; هَنعنيَه 'we will direct words/speech at him' 'we mean him' 'we will eye/look/inspect him' and is what Peter does towards Ananias first through indirect questions then the direct accusation of not giving all the money to the apostles for the service of God; هَنغنيَه 'we will make he/him independent/rich' 'we will make him no longer need(someone else's help/dependence)' as the character has decided to keep some money for himself, God shows he does not need anyone to be rich so God and Peter cause Ananias to die; حَنَن يَه 'felt affection-he/him' reflects that Ananias loved the money more than to give it all to the apostles; خَنَن يَه 'betrays-he/him' 'soaks/soaks in-he/him' as Ananias has betrayed the apostles and God by keeping some money for himself; note how the apostles/Peter are now the Holy Ghost/God just like Jesus was both the son and God, because they have been 'filled with the Holy Ghost' in this story, but also because they were filled with the same water direct from Jesus in the Gospel of John; هَنَن يَه 'satisfaction to/satisfied-him/he' 'give plenty-he/him' he has chosen to satisfy himself with part of the money from the sale of the land instead of give it all, i.e. instead of 'Hannah-it/give satisfaction' to the apostles/God. It is the same as **Hananiah** (1Chr.3:19) and how a character of the same name was also used at (Jer.28). Cp: han'nyah, hanghnyah, ḥananyah, khananyah, hananyah. (Acts.5:1-11)

Sapphira; Sápphira; سآفِّرا '(she is)openly immoral' 'exposing parts of body in public' and is used to describe a person who commits sins, crimes or acts of lewdness in front of other people without shame, also means when a woman shows parts of her body which are meant to be kept covered and not seen by other people/men. Her immorality is the shared sin of her husband as they have decided to keep part of the proceeds from the sale of land for themselves and not give it all to the apostles/God, for which she (along with her husband) are punished with instant death. It is the same as Saphir (Mic.1:11). Cp: saaphira. (Acts.5:1-11)

Difference in Jesus Execution Narrative

The gospels narrate Jesus was crucified, they also narrate he was raped before crucifixion. But in Acts the narrative states Jesus was executed by being hung from a tree. This is not a mistake nor is it because it is a version of the Jesus' death story which may have emerged or was written around the same time as the gospels; this cannot be because the way it begins just like John begins, and Acts is the idea of Peter and John (eventually all the apostles), receiving Jesus-like powers because at John.21 Peter is also given 'special' love and sex with Jesus and John, and this shows that Acts was created based on the Gospel of John so after the Gospel of John is circulating as a story.

There is a reason why Acts states Jesus was hung from a tree, and that reason is to make the audience recall the story of Joshua and the five enemy kings who hid in Makkedah before they were humiliated, killed then hung from a tree. The reason the author wants the audience to recall this story is because there is a specific way the kings were humiliated before being killed, just like Jesus. Without taking into context how elsewhere the foot is used as euphemism of the penis and for illicit sex or being raped, reading Josh.10 you would think the placing of feet on the kings' necks by many people at Joshua's orders is just the humiliation of being mistreated in a derogatory manner, but there is a deeper symbolism and meaning of what the author of Josh.10 meant and even the lifting of a leg or heel against someone is considered to have offensive and illicit sex or rape meanings. 'And it came to pass, when they brought out those kings unto Joshua, that Joshua called for all the men of Israel, and said unto the captains of the men of war which went with him, Come near, put your feet upon the necks of these kings. And they came near, and put their feet on the necks of them. And Joshua said unto them, Fear not, nor be dismayed, be strong and of good courage: for thus shall the Lord do to all your enemies against whom ye fight. And afterward Joshua smote them, and slew them, and hanged them on five trees: and they were hanging upon the trees until the evening.' (Josh.10:16-27).

It is again the stories of the NT elucidating that Jesus was raped before he was killed. It is also why it is used in the same passage mentioning 'Israel/twisted muscle-the' which Jesus was sent to straighten out both as a people and the male appendage to make the people straight and moral (obedient, following God's ways), and to straighten Jacob/Israel/twisted muscle-the: the withered muscle. As these stories were created as samaaras/samaayas for entertainment which involves lewd and dirty jokes as part of the story it does not matter to the authors that they are using rape and 'illicit' sex, and it seems the real culture of which the earliest authors and audience were, did not have a problem with male homosexual acts, at least not until the stories would come to be taken as religious texts and by people who did not fully understand the Arabian Peninsula Arabic language of the Bible.

'Then Peter and the *other* apostles answered and said, We ought to obey God rather than men. The God of our fathers raised up Jesus, whom ye slew and hanged on a tree. Him hath God exalted with his right hand *to be* a Prince and a Saviour, for to give repentance to Israel, and forgiveness of sins. And we are his witnesses of these things; and so is also the Holy Ghost, whom God hath given to them that obey him.' (Acts.5:29-32)

Apostles is reflected in the apostles are meant to be spreading God's word, explaining Jesus' ways and they reflect the compound word 'spread for him' 'spread for me' 'of spreading' 'explain for him' 'explain for me' 'of explaining' which is what the angel that frees them from prison instructs them to do, then Gamaliel explains to the audience within the story that they should be allowed to do.

Gamaliel is the same as at (Num.1:10); Gamaliél; جَمَلي نئيل 'came-fetched/fetch water-the' came-instructed-the' 'came-told them what to say-the' 'came wearing frock'. His role is exactly as the word name created for his character: he instructs people to give the apostles space to speak and the 'apostles' are filled with special water/semen; he is described as 'a doctor of the law' i.e. he knows how to speak and convince people, understands the law; his examples are about two men who convinced many people to follow them with their words and they all ended up dead and came to nothing; he tells them that if the apostles are making up what they say and teach then it also will come to nothing, but if it is instructions from God then it is not wise to become an obstacle to it; the Sadducees also instruct the apostles to stop preaching in the name of Jesus; the apostles continue to instruct on the ways of Jesus. It is also equivalent to Imlah (1Kgs.22:8-28). Cp: gamali-ill. (Acts.5:34-42)

Theudas; Theudás; ضوداه 'against him/it' and refers to a person who convinced people to rally around him, but because he was lying, he ended up dead, killed by an opposing party, and those people that believed and followed him also ended up having to face opposing action against them and were dispersed. Cp: dheudaah. (Acts.5:36)

Judas of Galilee used as 'he is called/calls' 'call, or curse' 'to make a claim' 'make a false claim or an unproven claim' as it is narrated he called people to follow him, his claims were false and ended badly with him dying; because he is from **Galilee** 'came-to' 'came-for' 'cleared-the' 'made clear-the' the people who followed him were cleared away after he was killed. (Acts.5:37)

Grecians 'purified/circumcised/made clean/made edible him/it' 'of purification/edibility/cleanliness/circumcision' 'declared purified/permissible' 'undressed him/it' 'of undressing' 'deceived/tricked him/it' 'of deceit/tricks' 'beat severely/beat until skin peeled off him/it' 'of beating/being beaten severely' 'shed its skin/hair/leaves/etc. him/it' 'of shedding skin/hair/leaves' 'replaced him/it' 'of replacing' 'sweet/sweetened him/it' 'of sweetness/sweetening'; and the OT meanings (Joel.3:6); غيوآن هم 'misled to downfall-them' 'their misleading to their downfall'; عيوآن هم 'howling-them/their howling'. It is reflected in a story related to the neglect of widows who have been purified because they have entered the faith; in the purified/special food supply they are meant to receive through/from the apostles; the widows have lost their husbands, 'shed' them; the apostles are seeking replacements so both the widows can be serviced and the word of God served; the word 'howling' is being used again to show wailing and grief, it also shows there is misleading and hurt in the neglect of the widows; the disciples feel they are being misled to activities which will lead to their downfall as opposed to preaching the word of God. (Acts.6:1)

Hebrew will be explained later in this book. (Acts.6:1)

Stephen; Stéphanos; شطيفَنوه ، شطفَنوه 'split him/it open/they split him/it open' 'wash/rinse him/it quickly/they washed/rinsed him/it quickly'. The 'splitting open' verb is when a rock is used to be repeatedly thrown against a log needed to make hot coal out of when it is more practical than to use an axe. The 'rinse/wash quickly' meaning is when clothing is not really dirty and just needs a quick rinse with water and hardly any or no soap, it also describes the final rinse of a garment, hair or body with only water to clear away any remaining soap or other residue from cleansing substances.

His story follows his name: first he is cleansed by being filled with the 'Holy Ghost' and the apostles laying their hands on him which leads him to perform 'great wonders and miracles' like Jesus and everyone who has been filled with Jesus/God's water. Then his story ends with a terrible death where he is stoned to death just like the meaning of his name. Cp: shṭeyphanooh, shṭephanooh. (Acts.6:5-15; 7:55-60)

Philip (Matt.10) 'in its core/pulp' 'pick out/cleanse/remove it' 'so he answers/responds/assists/serves-him' 'he will/should answer/respond/assist/serve-him' as one of the seven men appointed to take care of widows he has been chosen to serve God and people, to assist with the apostles' business; he is chosen because, like the others, his core is filled with honesty and 'Holy Ghost, and wisdom'. (Acts.6:3-5)

Prochorus; Próchoros; بروح وْروه 'with the soul/spirit-they showed him/saw him/watered him' and refers to the chosen men being filled with the Holy Ghost and/or seeing it. Cp: brooḥ-orooh. (Acts.6:5)

Nicanor; Nikánōr; نِقآنور 'picked out/purified/cleansed/chose-light' and still refers to the people chosen for their wisdom, being filled with the Holy Ghost and honesty. It also refers to events in Stephen's story; نِكآنور 'hurt/poked in wound/insulted/offended-light' (Nik/نِك can also mean 'fuck') and the first half of the compound word can be when a person has a wound and accidently touches or pokes it causing it to hurt more, also when a person offends another whether intentionally or unintentionally and this is reflected in the Grecians and widows being offended/hurt by the neglect, and in Stephen upsetting the people of the listed synagogues with his words, and they in turn hurt him because of his perceived offensiveness (the narration paints Stephen as 'guileless' by having even his accusers see him as having 'the face of an angel'. Cp: niqaa-noor, nikaa-noor. (Acts.6:5)

Timon; Tímōn; تيمون 'counts and lists/says I gave/gloats over' and is the same as 'Mene, mene' as it is counting and listing what one person has given another. This character will be serving the widows so it is implied they will be given things. Also, because the narration moves on to show the increase in the word of God, the numbers of disciples will increase as well as priests who become obedient to the faith. Cp: teemoon. (Acts.6:5)

Parmenas; Parmenás; بَر مِناه 'good/piety-from him' 'good/piety-counted and listed/said I gave/gloated over' for the same reasons as 'Timon' but showing that it is the faithful, good, pious who have increased in numbers, but also the good and piety itself has increased too. Cp: bar-menaah. (Acts.6:5)

Nicolas; Nikólaos; نِكولَوه 'we eat/feed him/it' 'we make it all' 'we weigh/serve it/him' 'hurt/offended/poked in wound-him/it' and refers to feeding the widows being taken care of, and also to Stephen being hurt and the offense he causes (Nik/نِك can also mean 'fuck'); نِقولَوه 'we purify/cleanse/sanitise-him/it' 'we say/speak it/him' 'we put words in his mouth' 'we chose for him/it' 'moved him/it' and refers to the seven chosen men being purified by the Holy Ghost and disciples, the 'word' also has the same effect on people in the NT stories; about weighing things out and distributing it to the widows; it is about the Grecians/widows being hurt, and Stephen and his words which cause offense and lead him to be arrested and moved to the council for trial. Cp: nikoola-oh, niqoola-oh. (Acts.6:5)

Antioch; Antiócheia; انتيوهيَ 'was finished/over' and refers to Stephen's life being over as he will be killed; انتيوكيَ 'was hurt/offended/poked in wound' and refers to the widows hurt from neglect and the offense and hurt Stephen causes and receives; انتيوقيَ 'was chosen' 'was picked/purified/cleansed' and refers to the seven chosen men who undergo a cleansing ritual/process; انطيوقيَ 'pronounced/spoke/made speak' as the Grecians have pronounced their criticism/hurt over the widows' neglect, and describes how the disciples/apostles 'purify' the people which although it includes the 'Holy Ghost' is often described as 'the word' and this allows whoever receives this treatment to be able to preach and speak beyond their ability as can be seen in Acts and the Gospels. Cp: antyoohe͟ia, antyooke͟ia, antyooqe͟ia, anṭyooqe͟ia. (Acts.6:5)

Libertines; Libertînōn/Libertînos, Libertinois; لِبَرتينون / لِبَرتينوه ، لِبَرتينويه 'of for piety/good' 'for his piety/good' 'of passing beyond' 'of passing beyond-them/it/him' 'of piety/good towards' 'of piety/good towards them/him/it' 'of surpassing' 'of surpassing them/him/it'. The meanings are reflected in the increase and acceptance of 'God's word', in the increase of piety which increases towards God as the disciples numbers increase and the faith of priests becomes stronger; it is in the opposition Stephen faces while he tries to spread 'piety/goodness' which is towards God; it is in the different synagogues listed as they too are meant to be pious and good towards each other and God. Cp: liberteenoon, liberteenoh, liberteenoih. (Acts.6:9)

Cyrenians; Kyrḗnē; كيرييني 'hired them/paid them/rented them' 'drove/chased/forced them with violence'; قيرييني 'of reading' 'read to me/teach me to read' 'stopped moving/fidgeting' 'stopped what they were doing' 'linked them' 'linked them with wood/rope'. Several synagogues have been linked together not only by name in the same verse but in actions just as the meaning 'linked them with wood/rope' links a pair of bulls/cows to move at the same pace and in the same direction. They are all offended by Stephen's teachings. Cp: kyre͟e͟eyney, qyre͟e͟eyney. (Acts.6:9)

Alexandrians same as **Alexander** (Mark.15:21); Alexandria; عليك سَندرِا ، عليك سَندريَ 'on you/upon you-I will send it/him out' 'on you/upon you-I will separate him/it'. And as explained in Andrew (Matt.10) it is mostly used to describe sending off sheep/goats in the right direction towards pastures to graze ('sent him/it out'); and used to describe separating between sheep and goats, whether to sort and separate them to send to different areas, or to separate one or more from the rest of the flock in order to slaughter or sell them ('separated him/it'). It is used in Acts to reflect Stephen going out to preach which the Gospels have shown is like shepherding sheep, and shepherds send their flock on the right path, and it also shows Stephen is being sent out to be sacrificed in the name of God/Jesus and is made similar to Jesus' purpose. Cp: 'leik sandria, 'leik sandrya. (Acts.6:9)

Cilicia; Kilikía; كِلِكيَ 'ate it/you-him/it' 'fed you-him/it' 'all of it-he/him' 'ate you-he/him/it' and refers to the widows being taken care of and fed, and also Stephen feeding the people with preaching and in the end he will be accused and killed as to 'eat/ate' a person means he has been killed/cursed (whether by God, illness, parents) or has been spoken/responded to with anger (it is similar to the same sense of 'bethlehem'); قِلِقيَ 'worried-him/he/it' and the Grecians are worried about the widows, Stephen causes worry among the synagogues. Cp: kilike͟e͟a, qiliqe͟e͟a.

Asia 'sorrow' 'bad/offense' 'things/matters' 'important things/matters' 'wants' 'speaking in whispers' 'snitching'. The Grecians want the widows to be taken care of, their neglect is a bad thing for the disciples to allow to happen, the disciples think it is a bad thing to serve people when they should be attending to spreading the word of God. Stephen's spreading word of God, turns into the synagogues exchanging ideas to stop him because to them what he is doing is bad; Stephen will end badly. (Acts.6)

Saul/Paul; صَوَلَه 'reached him/it' 'arrived-him/it' 'extended/connected-him/it' 'stone/rock-him/it' 'made layer/connected with stones-it/him' is the same word and use as Saul of the OT (see Saul (1Sam.8;9;10), see also Shaul (Gen.46:10)). In the story about Saul/Paul, how the authors of the original story allow a character to be openly transformed from a 'Saul' to a 'Paul' as per the need and intent of the storyline and author can be clearly seen. The authors did not mind changing the character name to accord his character and storyline the wordplay to serve a fictional story.

When Saul is first introduced at Acts.7:58, a point is made that 'witnesses' who see Stephen being stoned death, take off their clothes and place them at Saul's feet—what this does is connect this 'Saul' character of Acts to several different stories and several different characters, and also indicates the themes. First, he is connected to Saul whose son Jonathan as a word-name and character role was in a homosexual relationship with David—editors of the OT were always trying to connect and indicate Saul to Gibeah because Gibeah's men are not only interested in homosexual sex but are depicted as being perverted because they rape unwilling men. The witnesses removing their clothes and placing them at Saul's feet also connects him to the Jesus story of a 'young man' with only a piece of linen wrapped around him touches Jesus as he is led away for crucifixion before he drops his linen wrap and runs away naked (in the respective gospel it was indicating Jesus was to be raped, but also his relationship with John the disciple who abandoned him with the rest (the naked young man is Mark, and Mark is John the disciple). It also connects Saul/Paul to the themes and events in the gospels, including Acts, where sex (especially male/male sex) results in sperm/Holy Ghost filling the person being cleansed and converted to Jesus' ways, which in itself indicates Saul will also undergo this filling and conversion. The word-name 'Saul/connected' is also used because it connects all these different stories and meanings to the current story and Saul.

Just as the original Saul of the OT was introduced as reaching and arriving as he went from place to place, so is this Saul described as fanatically persecuting Christians, reaching them wherever they may be; even the mention of Christians is about them reaching different places due to persecution which in turn allows what they preach to reach further; when the authors have him make a complete change of character it happens while he is on his way trying to reach a specific place so as to get approval and documentation which will allow his persecution of others to reach farther, and so he can arrive at Damascus to perform it. And even when he converts to Christianity his role-name 'Saul' continues to keep him going/reaching/arriving different areas and countries, this time spreading God's word: Damascus, Jerusalem, Caesarea, Tarsus, Pathos, etc. He is introduced before Stephen dies to indicate Stephen, after death, arrives/reaches God:

'...and the witnesses laid down their clothes at a young man's feet, whose name was Saul. And they stoned Stephen, calling upon *God*, and saying, Lord Jesus, receive my spirit.' 'And Saul was consenting unto his death. And at the same time there was a great persecution against the church which was at Jerusalem; and they were all scattered abroad throughout the regions of Judaea and Samaria [Judaea has been used as both 'calling' but also 'false claims' as it has been coupled with Samaria 'storytellers/late night stories' to remind the audience these are fictional stories]...As for Saul, he made havock of the church, entering into every house, and haling men and women committed *them* to prison. Therefore they that were scattered abroad went everywhere preaching the word.' 'And Saul, yet breathing out threatenings and slaughter against the disciples of the Lord, went unto the high priest, And desired of him letters to Damascus to the synagogues, that if he found any of this way, whether they were men or women, he might bring them bound unto Jerusalem. And as he journeyed, he came near Damascus...'

The third wordplay, and meanings of Saul as in the OT comes into play just before he is changed to Paul: the meaning of سَؤله 'asked him': after he sees a light, he hears a question and then himself asks Jesus a question 'And he fell to the earth, and heard a voice say unto him, Saul, Saul, why persecutest thou me? And he said, Who art thou Lord?'. This Saul سَؤله also has additional meanings found in similar word-names used in the OT: 'leaked/flowed-him/it' 'distracted/entertained-him/it' 'comforted-him/it'.

His name-change also reflects what his role and related events in the story will be: Paul; Paúlos; بَوْلُه 'his mind' 'his patience' 'his affliction/afflicted him' (also 'his urine/piss' the meaning of which is used but the water he is urinating is sperm-water not urine-water, the way this meaning is used throughout Paul's story is so obvious and clear I will not mention it to avoid repetition); فَوْله 'his indication/direction' 'follow his indication/go his direction'. From the word (bl/بل) 'mind' 'patience' and covers intelligence, patience, reason, thoughts, thinking about things deeply; and from now on in the story Saul/Paul's character is completely different to his fanatical, eager-to-commit-violence persona when he was 'against' Jesus' doctrine, and has become someone who is very wise, reasonable, and educated showing the 'mind/deeply thinks about' meanings as the latter can be seen in how his character defends himself when he is accused by Jews in the trial story. The authors have him remain patient no matter what events he goes through: he is persecuted, imprisoned, stoned, beaten, threatened—but takes it all in, patiently, just as his name suggests.

The meanings of 'his indication/direction' 'follow his indication/go his direction' is from the word (phl/فل) 'went/followed/direction/indication' and is used as a negative misleading behaviour or encouragement e.g. if a person leads another or encourages another to do something inappropriate or bad, e.g. a parent who encourages, by not bringing up properly, a child to misbehave they say 'he 'phaul-loh(led him on/gave him direction/indication)' warning against it is 'Do not 'phaul' for him/ do not mislead/give indication for him to follow'; it is also used as a negative omen, e.g. is someone says to another or about another 'he will die/become ill/lose everything/his hand will fall off' etc. another person (usually related or who cares for the spoken about will say 'do not 'phaul/فاوُل' on/over him', i.e. the stating of something negative is taken seriously as having the ability of a negative/omen effect; even if a person is talking about him/herself they say 'Don't 'phaully/فاوُلي' (don't lead on omen/bring bad following)'. The 'Saul' meanings can be seen in the majority chapters of Acts after his character is introduced; the 'Paul' meanings can be seen as soon as this character gets his name changed to Paul. Cp: ssa-ulah, sa-ulah, ba-ulah, pha-ulah.

Samaria 'storytellers' 'staying up all night/late night' 'tell night time stories/night time stories' within Acts (as elsewhere in the OT and NT) is used to remind the audience that the story being told is a fictional story, but is also used to depict a character in the story is lying/telling fictional stories to people who believe him, and this too reminds the real people listening to the stories of Acts to understand these are fictional stories. It is ironic that after time would lapse, and stories be rediscovered they would come to be taken as religious texts by the people of the region, but when these stories would become the religious books of the West, not only would they be taken as real stories, but would corrupt 'history' of the Middle East especially where events and characters in the Biblical stories have been pedalled by scholars as fact and have been woven into 'real history' despite them being completely fictional with no relation to the reality and actual history of the Middle East, as attributed to them by modern western academic organisations and beliefs.

'Samaria/storytellers/fictional night time stories' has been given as the place name of '**Simon**' 'heard/listened/obeyed' as because of his falsity people have believed him, and the author of Acts shows how he is a false preacher as he has not been filled with the 'Holy Ghost', the hands of the apostles have not touched him, as only those touched by the apostles and filled with the Holy Ghost can perform miracles. 'But there was a certain man, called Simon, which beforetime in the same city used sorcery, and bewitched the people of Samaria, giving out that himself was some great one: To whom they all gave heed, from the least to the greatest, saying, This man is the great power of God.'

Acts.8 goes further to emphasise that being baptised with normal water is not enough to make a person properly cleansed/purified to the degree he can have miracle-inducing Jesus-powers, this can only be achieved by the Holy Ghost descending on them the way it did with Mary mother of Jesus, or they need to be touched by apostles who themselves have received Jesus' special physical touch (sex) as Jesus is no longer around to do it himself—hence the need for Peter and John.

'But when they believed Philip preaching the things concerning the kingdom of God, and the name of Jesus Christ, they were baptised, both men and women. Then Simon himself believed also: and when he was baptised, he continued with Philip, and wondered, beholding the miracles and signs which were done. Now when the apostles which were at Jerusalem heard that Samaria had received the word of God, they sent unto them Peter and John: Who, when they were come down, prayed for them, that they might receive the Holy Ghost: (For as yet he was fallen upon none of them: only they were baptised in the name of the Lord Jesus.) Then laid they *their* hands on them, and they received the Holy Ghost. And when Simon saw that through laying on of the apostles' hands the Holy Ghost was given, he offered them money, Saying, Give me also this power, that on whomsoever I lay hands, he may receive the Holy Ghost.' (Acts.8:1-19)

The mention of **Samaritans** 'belongs to storytellers-them/the' 'I will tell their night/stay awake stories' is the same as Samaria to remind this is all storytelling and fictional.

Philip 'in its core/pulp' 'pick out/cleanse/remove it' 'so he answers/responds/assists/serves-him' 'he will/should answer/respond/assist/serve-him' as Philip will get inside the chariot, then he will get inside the eunuch, he will assist the eunuch in his questions and faith, and he will physically cleanse the eunuch of sins. (Acts.8:26-40)

Gaza is the same as in OT; Gáza; غآزَ 'a blunt or deep pain/squeezing pain' 'a deep resonating sound'; جآزَ 'to cut crop/grass'; عآزَ 'cherished him/it' 'pride/proud' and this meaning of 'cherished/proud/raised in status' is what is meant as the eunuch of Candace is described as being in charge of her treasure and of great authority. (Acts.8:26-27)

Ethiopia is still **Cushi/Cush** (2Sam.18:19-33) (Gen.10:6) with the meanings of 'to blow away litter/fibres/burnt remnants' 'remove completely in one swipe or scrape' 'litter/fibres/burnt remnants' 'scrape away' 'kill in one go/one movement' 'remove in one movement' 'left over burnt pieces/toast until crispy or burnt/burnt in fire or from too much heat' 'cut' 'tell a/the story' 'became hardened' 'heart hardened/cruel/was cruel'. There is no relevant Arabic meaning for it in its Greek transliteration/pronunciation 'Aithiopia', this is due to misinterpretation when translating the NT story into Greek just as the modern translations of the OT have turned 'Cushi' into 'Ethiopian', as they have taken it to mean a 'black person' or a person with 'a burnt face' and this stems from not understanding what the Arabic/Hebrew word means, but where in the OT Arabic/Hebrew word 'Cush/Cushi' still show its true meanings and it is only foreign interpretation and modern scholars who misinterpret it and give it meanings of 'black African/Ethiopian/slave', the NT directly gives it the word which sounds 'Ethiopia/ Aithiopia'. What is interesting and curious, does the ancient Greek word 'Aithiopia' actually mean 'burnt face' or is this more western scholars forcing ancient languages into what they want them to be to fit with their other errors and misinterpretations? I cannot say that 'Aithiopia' does or does not mean 'burnt face' in Greek because unlike the Arabic of the Bible which I do speak present in both the OT and NT, I do not speak ancient Greek, or any Greek at all. But what I can say with one hundred per cent certainty is the word in the original story of Acts is based on 'Cush/Cushi' or a similar word, and the ancient translators have interpreted/translated it into 'Aithiopia'.

The meanings 'remove completely in one swipe or scrape' 'litter/fibres/burnt remnants' 'scrape away' 'kill in one go/one movement' 'remove in one movement' is used and reflected in what the eunuch is reading in 'Isaiah/Esaias': 'He was led as a sheep to the slaughter…In his humiliation his judgement was taken away…for his life is taken from the earth.'. (Acts.8:27-28, 32-33

Candace; Kandákē; خَنداآقي 'puddle/small pool of water' 'muddy water' 'of puddles/small pools of water/muddy water' 'dipped hand/fingers into something liquid' 'unhygienically dipped into/polluted by dipping into' 'rolled something/dipped it into something liquid' and the meaning of the word indicates unhygiene either in the liquid being dipped into or the act of dipping hand or anything into the liquid is unhygienic as it has caused its pollution. E.g. muddy water or a puddle is unhygienic to drink from; a bowl of water, or a liquid such as milk if someone sticks their hand, fingers or an unclean object the unclean hand/object (the action of Kandákē/خَنداآقي) is an unhygienic act which also makes the clean water/milk unhygienic.

The water which the eunuch and Philip come across, speak about and then 'baptise/duck under' in, is meant by 'Candace'; also because Philip has been joined/possessed by the 'Spirit/breathing/panting(during sex)' in this part of the story it means Philip has experienced with the eunuch the 'Spirit' which means sexual intercourse as can be seen in the gospels so he has 'dipped hand/fingers into something liquid' 'rolled something/dipped it into something liquid'. There is a reason why although the eunuch is a character given high status in the narration it does not fill him with the 'Holy Ghost'. The Holy Ghost is euphemism for God/Jesus' water/sperm given to the disciples; then whoever the disciples baptise and fill with the 'Holy Ghost' transfers into them the powerful life-giving, healing and miracle-abilities to perform on others. But because this character is a eunuch, i.e. there is nothing to produce semen with, there is no use of the penis to pass it on—the author shows he cannot receive nor give the Holy Ghost, but is left cleansed of sins and converted, which is why the usual narration of the Holy Ghost also filling the person being baptised is not narrated but the usual narration is interrupted and Philip whisked away and the narration leaves the eunuch without being filled with the Holy Ghost: 'the Spirit of the Lord caught away Philip, that the eunuch saw him no more: and he went on his way rejoicing.'.

This also supports and is supported by the other meanings of **Gaza**: 'a blunt or deep pain/squeezing pain' 'a deep resonating sound' because the sexual intercourse between Philip and the eunuch does not result in ejaculation, it uses the way men moan, groan, breathe, as they near climax and ejaculation but Philip is not allowed (by the author) to reach climax and ejaculation/the 'Holy Ghost' because the other person is unable to reproduce sperm. This is further supported by describing Gaza 'which is a desert' as a desert lacks water, which reflects what little water there was to be baptised in is not much and not completely clean, i.e. not suitable for a complete 'baptism', and this too reflects the eunuch who cannot be a vessel to receive and pour God's 'Holy Ghost' water/sperm. Cp: khandaaqey. (Acts.8:26-40)

Jerusalem 'came-saw-asked-them/the' 'they see-asked-them/the' as Philip sees and comes to the eunuch, and asks the Eunuch questions; and the same with the eunuch asking Philip to come into the chariot, asking him to explain the passage he is reading in 'Esaias'.

Esaias is still Isaiah; 'wanders/goes/travels-he/him' 'will come wandering/going to/travelling-he/him' 'he will come wandering/going to/travelling-he/him'. This has been used because both the eunuch and Philip are travelling like the meaning of Isaiah/Esaias when they come across each other.

Azotus; Ázōtus; آزوثه 'I quickly slice/cut/split open-him/it' 'I will kill quickly-him/it' 'I flit/flick into/quickly hide-him/it, 'I suddenly split open-him/it—suddenly cut him/it open—suddenly sliced him/it open' 'I flit/flick/quickly hide something into a narrow space' 'I made/will make flee/hide quickly'. Both the sexual intercourse by Philip with the eunuch, and Philip being suddenly taken away, how the Spirit which 'spirits away' Philip from the situation and location is meant here (in the same way as prophet characters are 'spirited away' by the Spirit in the OT, e.g. Ezekiel is carried away to Tel-abib). It is the same as the true meanings of the misnomered mount 'Olivet/Olives' (2Sam.15:30; Zech.14:4; .8:28-59), Birzavith (1Chr.7:31), Ashvath (1Chr.7:33), Zetham (1Chr.23:8), Zattu (Ezra.2:8). Cp: aazootoh. (Acts.8:26-40)

Caesarea is still كيسآريا 'broke it-he/they' 'broke it' 'keep secret-he/they' 'keep secret'; قيصآريا 'short is he/they' 'shortened/shortcoming/failed to complete or obey-he/they'. All meanings are reflected in the story, it is placed at the end of the chapter to show that Philip's baptism of the eunuch fell short because the eunuch's body is 'broken', his reproductive system cannot produce what the 'Holy Ghost' needs from it to spread because he is a eunuch. It shows the interruption and breaking of the ritual as Philip is suddenly whisked away by the Spirit, i.e. while he is breathing heavily/panting and has not finished, the baptism is shortened and incomplete. This is why the author has coupled Azotus with Caesarea to further clarify what is meant. (Acts.8:40)

Damascus has been used for 'tore/ripped up' 'spat/spat a lot' as Saul hates the disciples and will kill them, to bring around their slaughter is his mission, but he is also spitting out Jesus/God's words which is similar to spitting out the 'Holy Ghost' which is God's water/semen here likened to saliva which Saul with his hatred and slaughter of the male and female converts to Jesus' ways is 'spitting out a lot' (the converts called disciples in this verse are the people who have been filled with the Holy Ghost/water/sperm). The meaning of 'sucked/sucked a lot' 'sucked at his teeth' is reflected in once Saul converts and is filled with the 'Holy Ghost/water/sperm' he will not only absorb it, but his story becomes of a character who 'sucks/feeds' a lot from it. The words used here to explain and translate may seem graphic, but they are an honest, objective and to-the-point translation of the words and interpretation as meant by the original Biblical author of this story—it was not meant as 'pornography', it may be seen as 'graphic', but what must be understood is back then (and still in rural areas today) the lewdness and drama in these stories was an important part of the only and most significant entertainment for ancient (and in modernity rural) people, and making people laugh and entertained was the reason these stories were originally created. (Acts.9)

Ananias is the same word and meanings as it was at (Acts.5:1-11) and you can see in the NT the same Biblical authors method of the OT where the same word-name and character meanings are used as different characters for the use of the meanings of its compound words as these names were not names but created for fictional characters. Just like **Hananiah** (1Chr.3:19) it still means 'we will direct words/speech at him' 'we mean him' 'we will eye/look/inspect him' 'we will make he/him independent/rich' 'we will make him no longer need(someone else's help/dependence)' 'felt affection-he/him' betrays-he/him' 'soaks/soaks in-he/him' 'satisfaction to/satisfied-him/he' 'give plenty-he/him'.

It is used because God has given Saul a message 'vision' that Ananias will come to him. Ananias speaks of what Saul has directed of hate speech (and actions) against the converts, and wonders why such a person who has 'betrayed' God/Jesus' words and ways should be assisted. God explains that Saul is meant to be his messenger. Saul will undergo baptism and being filled with the 'Holy Ghost' and whether water/H2O was used or not, he was definitely 'soaks/soaks in-he/him' in water/semen as he becomes Jesus-like in his preachings and abilities as does the narration of him being opposed and persecuted by the 'Jews' just like Jesus' story. Saul will go from hating Jesus and Jesus' followers to complete love and affection for them as he too converts from his old ways and becomes a follower of Jesus (what would be called religion when these stories become religious texts, and as such he goes from being a Jew to being a Christian, although none of the OT/NT stories describe the people who follow what would come to be called the Jewish religion and then the new way which would come to be called the Christian religion as 'Jews' or 'Christians' respectively, because when these words are used in the Bible they are used as word-meanings relevant to the story being told and not as a religion in the story). Before he goes on to preach after he is cured, he is first given a satisfying meal to make him strong for his new mission. Barnabas will provide plenty of proof and testimony to the suspicious disciples that Saul is now also a disciple. (Acts.9:10-31)

Judas/Judah is used for 'he is called/calls' and 'to make a claim' 'make a false claim or an unproven claim' and 'his hands'. God tells Ananias to go to Judas and: ask about a person called Saul of Tarsus; to put his hands on Saul to restore his vision; Ananias' response that Saul has authority means he has been officially called to persecute converts, and Saul's mission is to accuse them of 'make a false claim or an unproven claim' and then lay his hands on them, i.e. arrest and bring them in for trial and execution; Ananias complies and 'puts his hands on' Saul to return his sight. (Acts.9:11-17)

Straight (street called); is another display of mistranslation due to not understanding the nuances and differences in meanings of the Arabic language. Although 'straight' can be seen in that Saul is straightened out, he is supposed to straighten out the 'misled to downfall/**Gentiles**' 'Gentiles/ethnon; يثنون 'he/they do it again/double it/fold it/repeat it' 'he/they dissuade/make leave' 'he/they are idolaters/pagans' 'idols' 'praise/praises' 'idol worshippers' 'idolatry/worshipping idols"; and the 'twisted muscle-the' of **Israel**—'straight' is not the word used here in the original story because when you take it into context with the narration (which is how the Biblical authors of all the Biblical stories have designed the stories to be) the correct word is 'stood/stand/represent/replace/instead of' 'erection/erected(and means the penis is erect)'.

This is supported by Saul's evil, violent, Jesus-hating character being replaced with a good and Jesus-loving character which will go too much in the opposite direction as the authors make him a Jew-hating character in some parts of his stories as Paul; it is shown in Paul the word-name replacing Saul the word-name of the same character (just as Jehoiakim replaced Eliakim in the OT); it is shown in Ananias 'laying his hands' on Saul and the 'Holy Ghost' filling him because baptising is done through a sexual act, or at least water has to be turned into God/Jesus' semen and those made into disciples with powers are given Jesus' water/sperm directly through a sexual act, and pass miracle-powers on to others in the same manner (not to the people they only cure/convert, but the people they make disciples); it is in the narration that Saul has been chosen to become the vessel of Jesus/God: where Mary, Elisabeth were only receptacle vessels, they could only receive, Jesus, John the Baptist and the men they give the full baptism to are all receiving vessels which can in turn pour into other vessels (unlike the female characters who can do it through conceiving and giving birth to males who pass this on, and Mary mother of Jesus whose presence can pass on God's water). The reason Philip and Candace's eunuch story was created and placed at the end of Acts.8 was to contrast it against how Saul can become a 'receiving and pouring vessel' for God's word, his water, his ways whereas those males who cannot pour out (do not have a penis or functioning penis) cannot receive and give the Holy Ghost.

A 'correct pronunciation' transliteration will not be provided for what I believe is the correct word 'street which is called Straight[stood/stand]' because I cannot, and do not want to, guess in which tense it was presented, nor do I want to guess which prefix or suffix it may have been in the original story in the Arabic/Hebrew language. It is definitely a word based on the root word for stand/stood/erect (qm/قم) and there are plenty of equivalent words used in the OT/NT: Kemuel (Gen.22:21), Ahikam (2Kgs.22:12), Eliakim (2Kgs.18:18,26-27,37), Jehoiakim (2Kgs.23:34), Jekamiah (1Chr.2:41), Azrikam (1Chr.3:23), Adonikam (Ezra.8:13), Achim (Matt.1:14). (Acts.9:11)

Tarsus is the same as Tarshish (Gen.10:4) Tharshish (1Kgs.10:22); Tarsós; تَرشوش 'light spraying' 'was sprayed a lot' 'a lot of light spray', طَرشوش 'a lot of vomiting' 'vomited a lot' or intentionally splashing/splashed a little liquid over someone/something, 'deaf/became deaf' 'went into a stupor' 'scared into stupor/unable to respond, hear, speak' 'pretended not to hear/pretended to be deaf'.

It is reflected in Saul being so scared by the experience of being spoken to by Jesus/God which leaves him blind that he has gone into a kind of stupor, he no longer eats or drinks; his cure is using the Holy Ghost and baptism which includes soaking him with water/semen. It is used the same way Tarshish (Esth.1:14) was used as a character name who was a counsellor to the king of Persia when the latter's wife Vashti would not listen to his orders and it was believed it would cause women to stop hearing/listening/obeying their husbands' orders/wishes. It is also similar to Tiras (Gen.10:2). Cp: tar<u>sh</u>oo<u>sh</u>, ṭar<u>sh</u>oo<u>sh</u>. (Acts.9:3-18)

Gentiles; يثنون 'he/they do it again/double it/fold it/repeat it' 'he/they dissuade/make leave' 'he/they are idolaters/pagans' 'idols' 'praise/praises' 'idol worshippers' 'idolatry/worshipping idols' 'I will deceive them/the' 'I will mislead them to downfall-them/the' again is used to show the people who believe these stories will be led to their downfall and is a pun to the audience about foreigners who take these stories as fact; it is used because Saul who will be found at a street called 'stand/replace/erection' to make these people being misled to their downfall be 'straightened' and the meaning of 'erection' is supported by coupling Gentiles with Israel in that Saul has become the 'chosen vessel…to bear my name before the Gentiles, and kings, and the children of Israel' Israel/twisted muscle-the, i.e. the withered muscle of Jacob.

Although only the compound word 'Barnabas' is mentioned at Acts.9, the author of Acts includes all of the related character-name meanings as mentioned at (Acts.4:36-37) (see Barnabas). First **Barnabas:** 'piety/good-prophesied news' 'piety/good-prophecy/predict' piety/good-prophet/news' 'passed/beyond/passed beyond-prophesied news' 'passed beyond-prophecy/predict' 'passed beyond-prophet/news' 'piety/good towards his prophet' 'piety/good-warned (him)/woke (him) up/pointed out (to him)' reflected in that Saul is doing good, warning people about not converting, and converting people; Saul is warned that there will be an attempt on his life by the Grecians and the Jews, and it indicates that he 'knows' just like God allows prophets to know; Saul will pass and go beyond his 'country'/area to preach to people to make them pious and good; Saul is like a prophet, he sees visions and is likened to Jesus in the plot of the story, and Barnabas is 'good/pious' with and towards him; Barnabas speaks of all the good and piety Saul does, i.e. he brings the suspicious disciples news of what Saul has been doing, and news that while Saul was on his way to Damascus that he met Jesus which has converted him to being pious/good.

Joses 'he goes wandering and seeking'. Also 'he offends it/him' 'it offends/it offends him' as Saul does go from place to place preaching and along the way causes offense which leads to Jews and Grecians wanting to kill him; his offensive past is recalled by the disciples.

Levite 'answered/answer/answer him(or it)' 'served/serve/serve him(or it)' Saul has answered God/Jesus' call and is serving God; Barnabas testifies that Saul is calling people in the name of Jesus and serving to spread God's word.

Cyprus 'see, increased/multiplied it' 'try to increase/multiply it' 'disbelieved(in God or religion or the person)' 'they became disbelievers' 'disbelieved him' 'buried it/him' 'many burials/graves' 'his grave(s)'. Saul's work will increase the numbers of followers and he goes to many places doing God's work whose people in different areas are described as being 'multiplied'; the Jews and Grecians no longer trust nor believe in Saul because he is now calling them to Jesus' ways which they do not believe in; initially, the disciples do not believe in Saul's sincerity and distrust his intentions as he was the cause of the deaths of many people who converted. (Acts.9)

Although in earlier gospels the word '**Grecians**' was used to describe people who believe in Jesus and come to him wanting to be baptised and are believers in his message even if it used to show they are 'howling' like dogs, and are being 'misled to their own downfall' which is used to remind the real audience that whoever believes these stories is being misled as they are fictional—this time the word is used to depict a people who disbelieve in Jesus' message and Saul, they believe he is misleading them and want to cause his downfall (and this does not negate the double-meaning which is also directed at the real audience of these stories reminding them not to be misled by these NT stories). It is done using the word 'Grecians'; hellēnístas; حيليني يسته ، حَلين ييسته 'purified/circumcised/made clean/made edible him/it-offended/did bad' 'deceived/tricked him/her/it-offended/did bad' 'beat severely/beat until skin peeled off him/it-offended/did bad' and the 'purified/made edible' is when an animal is killed the correct way to make its meat pure and edible and this is what is relayed in the offense he causes 'and disputed about the Grecians: and they went about to slay him.'; the second part of the compound word can mean 'did it/levelled/made right/right way up'. It also has other 'ḥl' meanings (see Greek). Cp: ḥeilleynee ysth, ḥelleyn yeeysth. (Acts.9:29)

Caesarea has been used as 'shortcoming' and 'broke' because Saul has to cut short his preaching at **Damascus** 'tore/ripped up' 'spat/spat a lot' 'sucked/sucked a lot' 'sucked at his teeth' as the Jews and Grecians now find his words, actions and character ugly, they want to kill him. He will go on to **Tarsus** 'light spraying' 'was sprayed a lot' 'a lot of light spray' 'a lot of vomiting' 'vomited a lot' or intentionally splashing/splashed a little liquid over someone/something, 'deaf/became deaf' 'went into a stupor' 'scared into stupor/unable to respond, hear, speak' 'pretended not to hear/pretended to be deaf' which is reflected in the Jews and Grecians rejecting him and what he says and his very person as they seek to kill him; the Jews and Grecians cannot really hear him, as not believing God/Jesus' words is the same as being deaf or pretending to be deaf; the people who will listen and obey God/Jesus' ways are soaked through baptism which is why the 'Holy Ghost' is also mentioned.

Judaea 'he is called/calls', **Galilee** 'came-to' 'came-for' 'cleared-the' 'made clear-the', **Samaria** 'storytellers' 'night time stories' are all used as places for Saul to be sent to because the word-names mean: Saul is calling them to Jesus' way; he is coming to them and making clear Jesus' message, and in doing so clearing and cleansing them of sins (supported by mention of the Holy Ghost); he is telling them night time stories which are fictional and so is the author about a fictional character named Saul/Paul and all related events in the narration, in an open pun and reminder to the real audience of the Biblical stories being told. (Acts.9:30-31)

Peter 'his/its stub/shortness' 'he has cut him/it short' 'he/it has been snapped short' 'he/it has been abruptly cut off' is used as the character who heals two people in the last part of Acts.9, and he does it in a very quick way: he just tells them to be better and one can walk immediately after eight years of immobility, and the other comes back to life. It is reflected in how he is interrupted and brought as soon as possible to a dead Tabitha. (Acts.9:32-43)

Lydda; Lýdda; ليآدَّ 'goes/went round and round' 'back and forth' 'folded and pressed together hard' and is reflected in the man who cannot leave his bed and whatever slight movements he could make he was going nowhere but remaining in his place on his bed, it is also reflected in the people turning to the Lord, but also the action of making the bed, whether laying it out or folding up the blankets, sheets, etc. to put away, would include folding; ليآضّ 'dented it/forced both sides to meet' 'dented/both sides crushed against each other' 'burnt' 'felt burning sensation/pain' and still describes the ill man who cannot leave his bed, being paralysed he cannot separate his legs or move around and implies his legs were physically deformed as a result; ليآتّ 'crumpled it/pressed and crumpled it' and again refers both to the man suffering from being paralysed for eight years, and then how he is ordered to make the bed which will include folding things together. It is equivalent to Lud (Gen.10:22), Lot (Gen.11:27), Ludim (Gen.10:13), Lod (1Chr.8:12), Lydia (Ezek.30:5). Cp: lyaadda, lyaa**dh**a, lyaatta. (Acts.9:32-35)

Aeneas; Ainéas; عينيَه 'suffered-he/him' and is the character name of the man who suffered eight years of immobility and could not leave his bed. It can have other meanings, but this is the specific meaning given to it as anchored by the text. Cp: 'aineiah. (Acts.9:33)

Saron; Sarōn; سَرون 'they walked' 'they left' 'they left early/in the dark' and refers to the man who is able to walk after Peter orders him to, but also the people who turn to God because of this miracle. Cp: saroon. (Acts.9:35)

Joppa (2Chr.2:9,16); Ióppé; عوبّي ، عوَبّي 'filled/packed' 'full' 'floated' 'shameful/disgraceful' 'lewd' 'did something shameful/lewd'. It means to pack or be filled/full and also when something floats and/or flows, e.g. a specific type of cheese that comes in a bowl filled with its own seeping fluid/water which it floats in just as in 2Chronicles it was used to display timber being packed to provide Solomon with lots of wood and the same timber was floated down a river, and the woman in Acts.9 is described as being 'full of good works' and reflected in the widows which fill the room weeping over Tabitha, and in all the garments she made being shown to Peter.

There is definitely an intentional inclusion of all these seeping/flowing water images whether it is the widows crying over her (making them widows makes their grief and tears double-fold as a symbol (over lost husbands and now Tabitha)), the use of a word-name which means to float and/or seep water, then have all the people leave the room is indicating a sexual act to bring around the miracle as all miracles Jesus and his disciples perform get their power through God/Jesus' water/semen; and there is an intentional meaning of Joppa which was not used at 2Chr.2:9,16 and that is 'shameful/disgraceful/lewd'. It is also why they have the chapter end with Peter 'that he tarried many days in Joppa with one Simon a tanner'—it reconnects Peter with his original name 'Simon/heard/ill/sick' as he has healed a dead woman, but also reconnects him to and reminds the audience that the disciples and Jesus gained their powers from water/semen through a meeting and/or copulation of pairs (see Gospel of John), as does having two men to ask him to come to Tabitha's house, and it indicates the floating and seeping (Joppa) happened between this Peter and this Simon. (Acts.9:36-43)

Tabitha; Tabithá; طَبِتآ 'she became better' 'she healed' 'is good/nice/kind' 'she could palate it/him' 'willied/penised her'; طَبِثآ 'dipped into/dipped fingers into' and is what happens to the character of the same name as she is brought back to life by Peter, and how her character and deeds are described as she does a lot of good work and gives charity; the word-names and whole narrative state he did an act involving his penis which brought her back to life and made her better. It is equivalent to Tabbath (Judg.7:22), Tobijah (2Chr.17:8), Tobiah (Ezra.2:60),. Cp: ṭabitaa, ṭabifaa. (Acts.9:36-43)

Dorcas; Dorkás; دوركآه ، دُركآه 'caught up with her/it' 'they caught up with her/it' from word (drk/درك) 'catch/caught up with/realise/catch on' as in catch up with a person who has already gone ahead or is beating you towards a specific location or in a race/chase. It is reflected in the story that she has already died, but the people come to fetch Peter in hope that he will be able to catch up with her. Cp: doorkaah, dorkah. (Acts.9:36-43)

Caesarea 'broke it-he/they' 'broke it' 'keep secret-he/they' 'keep secret'; 'short is he/they' 'shortened/shortcoming/failed to complete or obey-he/they' and is chosen as the place where Cornelius the character is and he is sent to shorten the already 'many days' Peter spends with Simon the tanner in the last verse of the preceding chapter. He also 'breaks' the physical connection between Peter and Simon which the last chapter makes clear as does the beginning of chapter 10 that it is a physical union of their bodies by making the 'tanner' a 'Simon' while Peter was already a 'Simon' and Acts.10 reminds us that he too is Simon, what the author does is make the pair into one i.e. joined in sexual intercourse which Cornelius is sent to interrupt, and this too is supported by the author adding they live by the seaside to remind of the water element of their union. (Acts.10:1)

Cornelius; Kornḗlios; قورنيليوه 'of reading to him' 'read to him/taught him to read/understand' 'stopped him moving/fidgeting' 'stopped what he was doing' 'linked to him/linked them to/for him' 'linked them with wood/rope to him/for him' and it is what is done to a pair of bulls or cows when working the land to keep them moving at the same pace, also to keep one animal linked to another so that it does not run off, also used to make the animal turn around when needed; كورنيليوه 'hired/paid/rented them for him' 'drove/chased/forced him away with violence' 'drove/chased/forced away with violence for him'.

It is reflected in that he is leader of an army which drives people away with violence, also a centurion and his band/army are linked in a military discipline and line of command. He offers alms which is paying dues to God.

He is sent to Peter who is still spending many days at Simon the tanner's house, and this suggests they are linked like a pair of bulls, but Cornelius coming from Caesarea is to break up this pairing as he is sent by God to Peter. Cornelius is told by the angel that Peter will tell him what to do. The way bulls are made to turn around during working the land under the term (aqrinooh/اقرنوه) is applied to Cornelius' role, as well as what happens in the story to Peter, and what is meant by what Peter, and disciples/apostles, need to do and what will happen to all the people concerned in the story where the apostles' message is being spread. It is Cornelius who is prompted to make Peter 'turn around' and come to his house—which is a turnaround for Peter as he is not supposed to eat/preach with/to Gentiles. But the situation now changes, as this Gentile is aptly named to explain and show how the disciples changed from trying to convert only locals to now converting non-locals. The 'linked with wood/rope' to make animals move and turn around is also reflected in Cornelius accepting the new faith, and the converting of a wider community to the new faith to not only include the Gentiles in the vicinity, but in the wider area/countries the disciples have reached. Cp: qoorneeeylyooh, koorneeeylyoh. (Acts.10)

Italian; italikēs, italikós; could be ايضاليكيه ، ايضاليكُه 'ablution-for/for you' 'cleanse for/for you' 'he abluted/cleansed for you'; ايتاليكيه ، ايتاليكه 'came for you' 'he came for you' 'brought for you' 'he brought for you'; ايطع ليكيه ، ايطع ليكه 'obeyed/obedient for you' 'will be obedient for you'. Reflected in Cornelius being a faithful worshipper of God, providing alms and praying to God constantly; also, in the unclean animals seen in the vision by Peter which a hungry Peter refuses to eat from because they are 'unclean/common' and the response 'What God hath cleansed, that call not thou common.' And this is repeat three times because the author wants the audience to make the connection with the word-name translated as 'Italian' and means 'ablution/cleansed for me' so the intrinsically 'unclean/impure' foreigners are now to be considered clean and no longer like unclean animals the likes of 'dogs', for example; as they are now considered clean, they can obey God and are suitable for conversion; it is reflected in Cornelius obeying the angel's orders and in choosing a third man to send whose description is to show how he is obedient 'and a devout soldier of them that waited on him continually. They come to Peter. Cp: idhaaleekeyh, idhaaleekoh, itaaleekeyh, itaaleekoh, iṭ'leekeyh, iṭ'leekoh. (Acts.10:1)

Joppa is used again for 'filled/packed' 'full' 'floated' 'cheese seeping and floating in water' as he sees a vision of a vessel/cloth filled with all kinds of animals for him to choose and eat from. The floating is reflected as the vessel is let down gently as if on a great sheet; the floating/seeping because he is next to the sea and his relationship with Simon the tanner, and this is because the author wants to point to the significance of what is happening in this story/chapter which is likened to when Jesus, John the disciple and Peter at the end of John.21 are joined in a sexual act to give them the miracle-inducing Jesus-water, and now this represents the importance of allowing the formerly considered 'unclean/impure' foreigners to also be clean in body and soul. (Acts.10)

Peter and his original name are used because Peter 'his/its stub/shortness' 'he has cut him/it short' 'he/it has been snapped short' 'he/it has been abruptly cut off' 'they have snapped him/it/cut him/it short' is asked to kill and eat the animals he likes (to kill is to cut short); **Simon** 'have heard/to hear/heard/obey(ed)' because he hears a voice speak to him; God orders him to obey regarding the 'unclean' becoming 'clean'; 'ill/sick/weak' because 'unclean' animals are deemed the same way as ill, injured animals in that they are not healthy nor good enough to be eaten as their meat will be polluted. And this is a turning point in the NT stories, as well as the OT stories, where the foreigners 'Gentiles' are now considered abluted and cleansed by God.

This is supported by the narration that after Peter arrives the Holy Ghost also falls on the Gentiles who begin to 'speak with tongues' and worship God (so the same as 'Pentecost/make them speak/pronounce') but the fact that the circumcision plays a role and is important enough to be mentioned that it shocks the circumcised local (clean) people that uncircumcised (i.e. unclean) foreigners can be filled with the Holy Ghost further indicates that the penis is involved in the baptism, miracles, conversion, the word of God, etc. as has been explained earlier. How the male genital ties-in with the whole Bible will be explained later in this book.

There is another matter which the author makes clear in Acts, the meaning of 'Jesus' which is 'break/ate bread' and Christ is a whole 'cake/circle of bread' which Jesus tells his disciples in Matt. (and other gospels) as they break and eat bread, they are eating from his body/flesh is also an allusion to physical acts of sexual intercourse between Jesus and the disciples (or at least the theme and idea of it)—the unclean animals which are not allowed to be eaten just like the 'unclean' people are not meant by Jesus in the gospels because he is only coming to attempt to convert and save the circumcised 'clean' local people who are the same as him (in the story these are Arabs just like the local audience of these stories are Arabs) and is irritated when the odd non-local asks for his help as the authors have him direct all his activities towards local people. It is important to remember that 'local/non-local' 'foreigner' does not necessarily mean someone from a different country in the Biblical stories, but can mean from a different village, area or even just someone who is different (e.g. the circumcised and uncircumcised people). In Acts, this is made abundantly clear that the authors have chosen a new direction and to expand the disciples' healing power (which is God/Jesus' powers and water) to extend to the 'unclean/impure' uncircumcised 'foreigners' too. In Acts.10-11 eating, breaking bread, breaking Jesus Christ, is the same as having sex with the Holy Ghost, transferring water/sperm with Jesus Christ and his super-water/sperm which is from God in the stories. This is symbolised in the sheet-ful of unclean animals God offers an unwilling Peter to eat from, followed by telling him they are now clean enough to be allowed to be eaten/copulated to share food and bodily fluids with; reinforced by the narration in Acts.10 that although Peter does not eat with them, it makes sure they are filled with the Holy Ghost and baptised in the same place so they are interchangeable according to the author of Acts. This is further reinforced by the author who wants to make it clear as he has the circumcised people say to Peter in Acts.11 'Thou wentest in to men uncircumcised, and didst eat with them.' and has Peter reiterate the vision of the unclean animals and the coming down of the Holy Ghost upon all both circumcised local and uncircumcised Gentile with the Holy Ghost coming after the Spirit/breathing/panting has led Peter to them so they could all rejoice in God and Jesus Christ. (Acts.10-11)

Acts.11 begins with the circumcised characters in **Judaea**/'he is called' hear that the **Gentiles**/ethnē; يثني 'he does it again/twice/doubles it/folds it/repeats it' 'he dissuades/makes leave' 'he is an idolater/pagan' 'idols' 'he praises' 'idol worshippers' 'idolatry/worshipping idols', most of the meanings are relayed in 'Gentiles', that are now being called to God and can avoid being punished, but the circumcised characters express to **Peter**/'abrupt/stubby/cut short/snapped', which is a pun about the circumcised penis (although it does not decrease in length due to circumcision but the wordplay plays on it being cut) and the pun on 'Gentile/he folds it' of the uncircumcised penis skinfolds, that he is being led to his downfall because he is interacting with 'uncircumcised' 'he folds it' people who as 'gentiles' means they are being misled to downfall. Note the nuance between Gentiles/ethnē (Acts.11:1) and Gentiles/ethnesin (Acts.11:18) which has all the meanings of (ethne) but with the suffix (sin) which means became straight, towards me, straight direction, faced me, etc. but with it being directed towards someone or a direction, whether God directing calling and repentance towards 'Gentiles', or the 'Gentiles' facing God, becoming right by worshipping him, e.g. a few but not all word-meanings of ethnesin: '**ethne**': 'he/they do it again/double it/fold it/repeat it-' 'he/they dissuade/make leave-' 'he/they are idolaters/pagans-' 'idols-' 'praise/praises-' 'idol worshippers-' 'idolatry/worshipping idols-'; followed by '**sin**' meanings: in the direction of/towards me/in the face of/in front of/straight/straight line/direct/opposite me' and from the OT 'I will deceive them/the' 'I will mislead them to downfall-them/the'.

Which brings the mention of **Stephen** with its meanings of 'split him/it open' (with a rock, and one of Peter's meanings is 'his stub of rock/smooth rock') 'washed/rinsed him/it quickly' and these two together indicate the combining of something being split, cut, spliced (circumcised people) and something which is just washed with 'water' (uncircumcised people) can all be 'cleansed in the same way': the Holy Ghost and Jesus/God-giving water/sperm supersedes Abraham's circumcision and the ideas of the OT authors about what is pure and impure.

But to show the difference, they are still only preaching to Jews, i.e. locals, as can be seen in the word Phenice; Phoiníkēs; فوينيقيه 'so he chooses/selects' 'will choose/select' 'so he picks out impurities/clears/cleans' 'will pick out impurities/clear/clean'; فوينيكيه 'so hurt/poke wound' 'so hurt/offend' 'will hurt/poke wound' 'will hurt/offend' 'so have sex with' 'will have sex with'; فوينيجيه 'so he saves/delivers to safety him/them/it' 'will save him/them/it' 'so he will talk/discuss secretly-he/him/them'. Relayed in: the circumcised people are offended that Peter is mixing and talking with 'Gentiles'; the vision of God cleansing the Gentiles; this makes the 'Gentiles' suitable to convert and as can be seen in all the gospels and stories within Acts, the conversion includes a sexual act, at the very least the pouring of water/semen or its cleansing abilities onto/into those being converted; allowing Gentiles without circumcision to be converted and interacted with causes their rescue from punishment in the afterlife, and a better life in this world.

Antioch 'was chosen' 'was picked/purified/cleansed' to represent they are selecting only a specific kind/group of people to preach to, who happen to be considered 'purified' in body; of which **Cyprus**; 'see, increased/multiplied it' 'try to increase/multiply it' 'disbelieved(in God or religion or the person)' 'they became disbelievers' 'disbelieved him' 'buried it/him' 'many burials/graves' 'his grave(s)' as Acts.11:19 mentions Stephen's persecution which ended with his death, and does not make clear if the Jews believed or not, the use of the word 'Jews' suggests they did not. And what they succeed with in converting or not converting the Jews results in them being either of Antioch's meanings; 'was finished/over' if they do not believe, or 'was hurt/offended/poked in wound' if they disbelieve the apostles, or 'was purified/cleansed' 'pronounced/spoke/made speak' accept the ways of Jesus also known as 'the word'; in all accounts the apostles, converts go around pronouncing and preaching God/Jesus' message attempting to convert others. Cp: p̱hoineeqeyh, p̱hoineekeyh, p̱hoineegeyh. (Acts.11:19)

But once they know they can preach to Gentiles, some of the converts being from **Cyrene**; 'of reading' 'read to me/teach me to read/read to understand' 'stopped moving/fidgeting' 'stopped what they were doing' 'linked them' 'linked them with wood/rope' who are already linked because they are from the same Gentile people can 'teach' them about Jesus' ways and 'Cyprus' now represents them disbelieving in their old beliefs as they convert to the new, which also brings the other meaning of Cyprus that they 'increased/multiplied/became a lot' and is exactly what is narrated. The use of **Antioch** as before, but now the old beliefs are over and the people pronounce and speak the words of Jesus/God, which allows **'Grecians'** who are usually described in the NT as dog-like in their impurity and behaviour as the word means 'howling-them/their howling' 'misled to downfall-them' 'their misleading to their downfall' but also 'purify/purified/circumcise/circumcised/make clean/made clean/make edible/made edible' as they have been purified by entering into the faith. Not only does the use of the word **Antioch**/'pronounced/spoke/made speak' make them able to be human-like again in the story, but also allows them to be 'was chosen' 'was purified/cleansed' saved by the 'correct' religion in these stories being preached to them which during the stories where Jesus was alive, Jesus and the authors of the Jesus stories strongly opposed. (Acts.11:20-21)

Barnabas as 'piety/good-prophesied news' 'piety/good-prophet/news' 'passed/beyond/passed beyond-prophesied news' returns to the story because 'then tidings of these things came unto the ears of the church which was in Jerusalem' and Barnabas is sent to go as far as 'Antioch/pronounced/spoke/made speak' 'was chosen' 'was purified/cleansed' as he has been chosen (and himself will choose Saul to accompany him) to preach to the people and ask them to believe and call on God.

Note how the authors use the meanings of all the word-names (character and place names) in the NT just as the Biblical authors' method of the OT where every single place/character name reflects what is happening in the story, and cannot be a real person/place: When Barnabas needs someone to help him teach others, teaching involving answering questions and matters, the author have him 'seek Saul' for **Saul**'s meanings of 'reached him/it' 'arrived-him/it' 'extended/connected-him/it': as first Barnabas has to find and reach Saul before they both arrive/reach Antioch where they can teach and answer questions about the new faith. And Antioch 'pronounced/spoke/made speak' 'was chosen' 'was purified/cleansed' is because the people of Antioch by accepting and following God's words have become cleansed, and the people of Antioch choose to call the disciples 'Christians' which is Jesus in his wholesome and purest form when he was not yet broken, nor eaten by the adversary soldiers, so in a sense the breaking/eating of bread (doing 'Jesus') meaning brings around an intact 'circle of bread' (Christ which is still Jesus) making the people 'wholesome' in body and spirit, physically and religiously.

Agabus; Ágabos; عَجَبُه 'a wonder' 'his wonder' 'miming/acting/playing/entertaining' 'what a wonder' 'what a puzzling act/action/statement' 'his miming/acting/playing' done to make other people smile or laugh, used especially to make toddlers/babies distracted or entertained. In the first sense 'a wonder' the person or action is making others perplexed or shocked, awed or surprised. The second meaning to say or act (sometimes just be silly) to make someone else smile or laugh and is usually like a mime show. Both meanings are employed: he signs/mimes/enacts something is to happen—which does happen and that is a miracle/wonder that he can predict. And he has been used as a contrast to Antioch/'pronounced/spoke/made speak': 'And in these days came prophets from Jerusalem to Antioch. And there stood up one of them named Agabus, and signified by the spirit that there should be great dearth throughout all the world: which came to pass in the days…'. In daily use, when asking a person to distract/entertain a very young child they say ('aggb-lh/عَجِّب له); when someone sees or hears of something wondrous, or shocking, dismaying, or perplexing, they exclaim (waa-'agabaah!/وا عَجَباه!). From word ('gb/عجب) which means 'wonder(ful)/shocking/puzzling/inexplicable/miming/acting/entertain/act' and also means 'like(s)/fancy(ies)'. Cp: 'gaboh. (Acts.11:27-28)

Claudius Caesar; Klaúdios; قلَوديه 'placed responsibility on him' 'hung it around his neck' 'hung responsibility around his neck' 'garlanded-he/him' 'placed responsibility/accountability on him/it' 'acted/copied him/it' and is reflected in that Agabus is miming or acting what is going to happen of famine in the world, and also reflected in the disciples feeling responsibility in that they send whatever they can to their people in Judaea. Caesar is still: كيسَر 'broke'; قيصَر 'shortened/shortcoming/failed to complete or obey' as the good news has been broken, but there will also be a shortage of food. Cp: qlaudyoh, kaisar, qaissar. (Acts.11:28-30)

Barnabas 'piety/good-prophet/news' 'passed beyond-prophet/news' will travel again to deliver the charity to help people in Judaea from the predicted prophesy by the prophet Agabus. **Saul** 'reached him/it' 'arrived-him/it' 'extended/connected-him/it' will accompany Barnabas to arrive/reach the people in Judaea to bring to them the relief supplies, just as both characters' word-name meanings dictate what they will do in all their stories. (Acts.11:28-30)

Acts.12 is reminding the audience that John is the beloved disciple, although they describe Peter arriving at the house of 'Mary mother of John, whose surname was Mark' and this means John the beloved disciple who is the son of Zebedee (see Beloved Disciple). Mary and John became mother and son at Jesus' crucifixion in the Gospel of John.

Mark is used as its word-meaning 'did not wait' for although Peter is kept waiting at the door while the characters inside the house, out of joy and disbelief, do not open the door as soon as they do open the door, he gives them a quick message (like the abruptness in Peter's meaning) and does not wait as he leaves towards another destination. It is reflected in Herod not hesitating to execute the soldiers he believes allowed Peter to slip away, and in that Herod does not wait/stay but goes from Judaea to Caesarea to stay. When Herod forgets to glorify God, not only is he not allowed to stay alive, but even his body is not allowed to have a physical intactness as he is 'eaten of worms' and dies. All this ensconced between mentions of Mark/they did not wait/stay (which the author intentionally makes 'John Mark' so none of the audience can miss the connection to the stories in the other gospels, and especially that the young man who walked around with only a linen cloth is **John**/'put/wrap it/him in sack/sackcloth' before he 'streaked' away as **Mark**/'they did not wait/stay') and ends the chapter with more not waiting nor staying as Barnabas and Saul take with them 'John, whose surname was Mark.' (Acts.12)

Rhoda; Rhódē; روضي 'was glad/gladness/joy' 'agreed/allowed' 'agreed/was convinced' and is exactly how the character feels when she sees Peter at the gate, and how the other characters refuse to believe Rhoda although she is convinced and insists. Cp: roodhey. (Acts.12:13-16)

Tyre 'made image' 'sculpted image' 'created image or pattern, etc.' 'left over food' 'left over anything/second-hand (things) 'aching pain in teeth/bones' 'imagined' 'created likeness/image' and **Sidon** 'give(s) extra' 'leaves extra/remains' 'deceives'. Both have been used because they rely on Herod's kingdom to receive food and money; although Herod is a person and not a sculpture/painting, the narration assigns to him the same worship that characters in the stories show towards idols; they deceive him with their praise likening him to God, and he deceives himself with believing it, or at least not correcting them and by not directing the praise to God as he should have; his punishment will result in aching in his body as when he is harmed he is eaten from the inside-out by worms. (Acts.12:20-24)

Blastus; Blástos; بلاّصطوه 'with laying hands on/harming him/it' 'without-clinging/holding onto him/it' 'with swooping down on him/it' 'without-swooping down on him/it'. It is reflected in Tyre and Sidon clinging on to Herod as they want peace; in people sticking a false praise onto Herod and Herod holding onto it which he has no claim to as the glory is God's; it is in an angel which is sent down and strikes him leaving Herod unable to cling onto life. It is similar to Sitnah (Gen.26:21), Satan (1Chr.21:1-17), Bethesda (Gen.26:21). Cp: blaassṭooh. (Acts.12:20-23)

Antioch has been used for 'was finished/over' 'was chosen' 'was picked/purified/cleansed' 'pronounced/spoke/made speak' all the work at Antioch is about teaching and preaching God's ways so the people can be 'purified'; Barnabas and Saul's work currently at Antioch has finished as they are chosen and sent by God/the Holy Ghost on a new mission which is also preaching, teaching and cleansing people through conversion. (Acts.13:1-4)

Simeon 'have heard/to hear/heard' 'obey/obeyed' as both Barnabas and Saul hear the Holy Ghost and obey its instructions; Niger; Níger; نيجَر ، نييجِر 'we pull' 'warn/distance/disown-pull' 'we are or cause/of great injustice and suffering' 'distance/set aside/protect-great injustice and suffering' 'we protect/say prayer for protection' 'we protect from harm/evil'; نيغر ، نييغِر 'we funnel/funnel down' 'we save' 'warn/distance/disown-save' 'warn/distance/disown-funnel'. The meanings are present: the teachers and prophets are warning and teaching to save the people; to help people avoid punishment in afterlife; as they are dealing with the Holy Ghost water/semen, or even the 'word' which has the same effect, is being funnelled into the people and specific characters; their work attempts to protect the people from evil and harm; Barnabas and Saul will be sent away; the results of teaching God's ways is distancing the people from the wrong ways, gets them to disown old beliefs and ways; two characters are being sent a distance to spread all these other meanings. Cp: neeger, neeyger, neegher, neeygher. (Acts.13:1)

Lucius Cyrene; Loúkios; لوكيه ، لوُك يه 'talks too much-he/him' 'talks too much nonsense-he/him' 'rambling/loquacious-he/him' 'his nonsense/ramblings' 'chew it-he/him' 'him/he for you' and has all the meanings of 'Luke' of the Gospel of Luke regarding rambling, talking too much, talking nonsense, rambling in speech jumping from one thing to another, being annoying because talks or is talking too much, talking either complete nonsense or of unimportant things, can also mean nagging; and this is meant to apply to Saul because he becomes Paul, and from this chapter onwards Paul does go on and irritates others with his long speeches and the content of his speeches. Although in the western world everything in the NT stories about Saul/Paul will come to be considered intellectual, philosophical, and instead of these stories which are written by an author and 'Saul/Paul' is a figment of these authors' imagination—the west will consider him a real 'historical' figure and they will attribute and accredit 'Paul's' activities and attempt to trace a 'real' line for his journeys whereas in reality he is just a fictional character whose only activities are restricted to the pages of the Biblical stories.

This misunderstanding, like all the others, has distorted history although the Bible makes it clear these are fictional stories filled with fictional events and characters. When they would become part of the new religions, people of the local region would accept them knowing they are fictional, but when these stories spread further to non-local regions where the audiences have no way of knowing the meanings of the words and word-names and were circulated, these stories would eventually be taken as 'actually happened'; the latter has been further compounded by contemporary Biblical scholars who have gone out of their way to force fictional characters, fictional events as real people and real travels, and the fictional stories as 'history'. To say that people from ancient and, more recently, medieval times would not be drawn to religion had it not been real and had the stories and the characters of these stories not been real, then they are misunderstanding or underestimating how all religions begin from superstition and/or fictional stories, and over time a culture's collective superstitions and folklore become firm beliefs and religion.

Maybe modern scholars are not being realistic enough to understand that during times when science was primarily non-existent, most of the people of different nations uneducated, and even being 'educated' may have meant the ability to read or write, and even having an education just meant being able to think deeply, philosophise, maybe write or orate at length, and not an erudite education as in modern terms—and how this lack of scientific knowledge, lack of education or education as known today, does allow people to believe in all kinds of stories which are accepted as religions (look at every single ancient civilisation and see the mythologies of specific Gods/deities and how these stories came to be basis of religions). Notwithstanding, there are always people who see that these stories are fictional throughout ancient, medieval and modern times, which is why even in documented history there are always people pointing out how fictional the stories which are deemed 'religious' texts are and how impossible it is that they are real—which is why there is always a struggle and emergence of new religions which explain away and usurp the old, why they all claim to be the only true religion, condemning every other religion and its followers to falsity and/or punishment whether in this world or the hereafter. The point being made here, is the original authors of Acts and other NT stories never intended that their fictional characters be believed as historical figures, their intentions were solely based on creating entertaining stories for local audiences, but language barriers, custom barriers, cultural differences would cause these stories to be viewed as 'divine' when they reached the western world, and more modern scholars in contemporary times would imbue these stories and their characters with a 'historicity' which simply does not exist. The language of the Bible is the proof of what the Biblical stories are and what they are not, and it is a physical and tangible proof.

Instead of seeing how these fictional stories and their popularity (coupled with nations' 'mentality' (everything from state of education, pagan beliefs (every single nation that ever lived has created and believed in pagan religions stemming out of superstitions and stories) according to the times when these religions were introduced) among western nations when first introduced to them, is what influenced the spread of Christianity—instead the scholars will believe and entrench in academia that a fictional character (such as Saul/Paul) travelled and 'he', a person that never existed except as a character in a story, went from country to country becoming the most influential person ('after Jesus') to spread Christianity. Whereas the truth is it is the *stories* about Jesus and the *stories* about Paul which spread Christianity and influenced western countries to convert to Christianity from their former pagan religions and beliefs. A story circulated by oration, and later by text, can reach farther and faster than any one single person, especially when that person is a figment of an author's imagination.

Cyrene for 'hired them/paid them/rented them' 'of reading' 'read to me/teach me to read' 'stopped what they were doing' 'linked them' 'linked them with wood/rope' as although no mention of them being paid is made, but they are employed and tasked to do a certain job: preach/teach; their work is about teaching others the ways of God; they are all linked by the same work, the same objective just like bulls are linked to keep pace together to get one job done, and the people are being turned around to the right way just like real bulls are made to turn in the correct direction when a rope is tied around their neck or horns during tilling/ploughing land.

Manaen; Manaén; مَنعيين 'well I have eyed/inspected/seen/watched' 'what/who have I eyed/inspected/watched' 'who/what I have assisted/made cooperate' and it reflects that these teachers and prophets are co-operating to teach God/Jesus' ways, and in doing they are helping people to be saved by getting them on the right path; it also indicates that Barnabas and Saul have been chosen and assigned a specific and new task. Cp: man'<u>ee</u>yn. (Acts.13:1-4)

Herod has been used for 'bent his neck(physically)' 'of bent neck' 'went to one side (while moving)' as the people are praying, and there is a bent neck in all kinds of prayer whether in the bowing of the head or the craning of the neck; and Barnabas and Saul are being sent in a specific direction to preach, teach and convert new followers in new regions; and the converted people are being sent on a specific 'direction' figuratively when they follow a new religion (in this case Christianity). There are none of the negative meanings of 'Herod/incitement, etc.' in this passage. (Acts.13:1-4)

Seleucia; Seleúkia, Seleúkeia; سَلوكي ، سَلوكَي 'they leaked/flowed to' 'they leaked/flowed to-him/it' 'they followed a line/way' 'they made their way/path' 'they are smooth/fine' "make-do' with it/him/he' and the meanings refer to the two men travelling first to Seleucia then all their travels; it refers to sailing; it refers to the Holy Ghost which has been given them only by touch through those who have been filled with the Holy Ghost (note Barnabas and Saul have not been filled with the Holy Ghost and/or Spirit so they cannot perform miracles the way apostles and those who have received God/Jesus' water/sperm). Their objective is to make the path smooth for converts to follow the 'correct' religion/way. Cp: seleukya, seleukeya. (Acts.13:1-4)

Cyprus for 'many/became many/multiplied' 'try to increase/multiply it' 'disbelieved(in God or religion or the person)' 'they became disbelievers' 'disbelieved him' as they are being sent to many places and their mission is to speak to and convert many non-believers at multiple locations and to increase the number of followers. (Acts.13)

Salamis; Salamís; سَلَميه 'leaked/flowed water' 'survived/were intact' 'greeted' 'delivered/received' 'were peaceful' 'asked' and means they arrived travelling over waters, but also their preaching spreads God/Jesus' word which is God/Jesus 'water/semen' and this is further elucidated by mentioning that John is now their companion too and present—it gives all the meanings of the word-name 'John' associated to God's water/sperm soaking it, etc. and making people brothers through it, as well as the meaning of the character and his backstory (as his word-name also holds the meanings to) that he was a receptacle for God/Jesus' water instead of Mary and also a vessel which can pour out onto and into others instead of Jesus (like other disciples). John gives his effective powers to the Barnabas-Paul stories. Cp: salameeh. (Acts.13:5)

Paphos; Páphos; بآثُه ، بآثوه 'burst out/went forth/emerged (from)/went forward' 'came out of/emerged from' 'imbued/imbued it with' 'blew it out/scattered from' 'filled it with air' 'broadcast it' and is exactly how this word-name is used: the travellers 'go through the isle unto Pathos' they emerge from the isle and arrive at 'Pathos'; but also they find a 'false prophet' i.e. someone who imbues himself and his words/claims with something unreal/not available; Saul now becomes 'Paul' and he himself is filled with the 'Holy Ghost' but again it is because John is present with him extending and imbuing to Saul/Paul's character the ability to deal with the false prophet (Bar-jesus). Cp: baafoh, baafooh. (Acts.13:12)

Bar-jesus; Bariēsoús; بَر عيسوَه ، عيسوَا 'be good/pious towards-cold bread/broke/ate bread/breaking/eating bread' 'distance from/be innocent of/disown responsibility from-cold bread/broke/ate bread/breaking/eating bread' 'be passed/be surpassed/pass/surpass/go beyond/get ahead of-bread/broke/ate bread/breaking/eating bread'. It is reflected in that this character is described as being a 'false prophet' i.e. he is pretending to know Jesus/God's ways and preaching/teaching falsely in the name of Jesus; it is also reflected in that another character (Sergius Paulus) wants to hear the true 'word of God' from Barnabas and Saul (Barnabas meanings also contrast against the meanings of Bar-jesus). The name shows that Jesus and Jesus' ways are innocent of anything the false prophet claims, the true apostles/preachers of Jesus distance themselves from Bar-Jesus' falsities and they disown him. The narration which connects what Bar-jesus means to what Sergius Paulus wants is also indicated because the latter character wants the truth, he is good/pious towards Jesus and his ways. Cp: bar-'eysoowah/'eysoowa. (Acts.13:7)

Sergius Paulus; Sérgios Paúlos; سيرجِوه ، سيرجيوه 'he will implore him' 'he will make him wait/stay/be still' 'he shook/unsettled him' 'he will shake/unsettle him' and is from the root word (rg/رج) 'wait(ed)/stay(ed)/still/ stationary' 'shook/unsettled' (it is the same root word and use of 'Mark' in Gospel of Mark). It is reflected in the narration as the character of the same name asks/desires Barnabas and Saul to come to him and to speak to him 'the word of God'; it is reflected in the false prophet Bar-jesus or the sorcerer Elymas attempting to keep Sergius in his state of current beliefs (the story does not make clear if Bar-jesus/Elymas are one and the same character); it is in Sergius Paulus not minding shaking things up about religion to find out the truth then in him being astonished at 'the doctrine of the Lord'; in Saul unsettling Elymas/Bar-jesus and causing him to go blind and in the 'imploring/intreating' meaning in the blinded false prophet/sorcerer 'seeking some to lead him by the hand.' as he can no longer see.

Paulus, which is the surname of Sergius, means: Paúlos; بَؤلُه 'his mind' 'his patience' 'his affliction/afflicted him'; فَؤلَه 'his indication/direction' 'follow his indication/go his direction' and all these meanings are available in the respective passage where he is introduced: he has both the intelligence, mind-set and patience to listen to different preachers, opinions—he is described as prudent, and although the false prophet is his friend/colleague/acquaintance it does not stop Paulus' open-minded character from sending for Barnabas and Saul to hear their version of what God says. The 'follow his indication/go his direction' is reflected in the same narration as he is willing to seek the truth, i.e. he is not convinced and wants to know the truth and will follow the available sources in his vicinity (in storyland) to find out and follow the truth; it is indicated in Elymas trying to turn Paulus from the right direction to follow the wrong direction (faith); it is in the way Saul states something out loud and it happens to Elymas just as the meaning of 'Paul/Paulus' means as a bad omen which is someone saying something negative and then it coming true about the spoken about (see Saul/Paul).

What becomes obvious, and is important as it stands out without a doubt, is that Saul was never meant to get a name-change into 'Paul', but the author of the story liked the idea of 'Sergius Paulus' wordplay and meanings so much that coupled with the versatility of Saul rhyming with Paul, that the author himself did not mind changing Saul to Paul no matter how obvious changing Saul into 'Paul' at this point in the story directly after Sergius Paulus was introduced. The Biblical authors show no qualms at all about changing the names of important characters as can be seen throughout the OT/NT, or giving the same name to multiple characters even if they are in the same story or even directly related in the same story as family or friends, or even enemies.

Cp: seirgiooh, seirgyooh, ba-ulah, p͟ha-ulah. (Acts.13:6-12)

Elymas; Elymais; الـي مَيس 'the one who/he who-was touched/possessed' 'he who/the one who-provoked/ was provoked/entangled/caused problems/caused fight'. Like his name suggests he is accused of being filled with the devil, which is exactly what 'touched' and 'possessed' means; he attempts to cause problems by attempting to pervert the conversion of Sergius Paulus which ends up backfiring as God through Saul is provoked and brings greater problems upon Elymas who ends up being punished with blindness and asking for help to be led around. His word-name also reflects on Saul who is being possessed by the 'Holy Ghost' (just like prophets and kings and other characters before him have been possessed by God or God's spirit to do God's will) so God in a provoked state can enact punishment onto Elymas: 'Then Saul, (who also *is called* Paul,) filled with the Holy Ghost, set his eyes on him, And said, O full of subtilty and all mischief, *thou* child of the devil...And now, behold, the hand of the Lord *is* upon thee, and thou shalt be blind...'. Of course, the author has made this possible while John is in the picture and present in this scene. Cp: illee-mais. (Acts.13:8-11)

Perga; Pérgē; فيرجي 'so he stays/stayed/so stay' 'opened up/opens up/an opening/orifice' 'opened up/relief/ release/end of difficult period or experience' 'vagina/vulva' 'watched/saw'. This is important because it has been linked to John with all the meanings that he is a receptacle and pouring vessel of God/Jesus' water/ sperm (see John), and to **Pamphylia** which means 'with like me' 'with the same as me' 'with proverbs/ sayings' 'with acting' as the authors have decided to have John leave Barnabas and Saul, but the authors want Barnabas and Saul to have the same receptacle/vessel of God/Jesus' water/sperm abilities so the words **Paphos** 'burst out/went forth/emerged (from)/went forward' 'came out of/emerged from' 'imbued/imbued it with' 'blew it out/scattered from' 'filled it with air' 'broadcast it' along with the meanings of John, Pamphylia and Perga are combined to show that John passed on Jesus' sperm/water through a sexual act with Saul and Barnabas making the latter two both receptacles and pouring vessels of the Jesus/God/Holy Ghost effectivity—this allows John to be removed from the story as the author obviously wants to concentrate on enlarging and expanding on Saul/Paul's character. Cp: pheirgey. (Acts.13:13-52)

Antioch for 'was finished/over' 'was hurt/offended/poked in wound' 'was chosen' 'was picked/purified/ cleansed' 'pronounced/spoke/made speak' is combined with the events of Pisidia, as through preaching and teaching i.e. speaking, Saul/Paul is trying to cleanse people of sins which is expressed, and will offend many people. (Acts.13:14-52)

Pisidia is the same as **Besodeiah** (Neh.3:6); Pisidía; بِصِديَ 'he/they will close the door' and (ssd/صد) in relation to a door it means to close it without locking it, 'he/they will block/absorb attack' 'he/they will block/prevent it' 'he/they will block/prevent-he/him/it' as in they rejected or physically stopped and this is contrasted against the meanings of 'Perga' 'so he stays/stayed/so stay' 'opened up/opens up/an opening/ orifice' 'opened up/relief/release/end of difficult period or experience' 'vagina/vulva' 'watched/saw' as although Barnabas and Saul (who from this point is Paul) have come from the meanings of being made into orifices/vessels to pour (and have received) God's 'word'—they will be rejected and face opposition, which Paul's stance and speech towards the people is the same, he is rejecting that they are on the right path and trying to prevent them from following their old religion by the very nature of wanting to convert them to his new religion (and in his speech the meaning of Lucias/loquacious can be seen). Mentioning that the people expelled Barnabas and Paul from their coasts makes it clear they prevented and blocked these two individuals from pouring God/Jesus' water/word over the people: 'But the Jews stirred up the devout and honourable women, and the chief men of the city, and raised up persecution against Paul and Barnabas, and expelled them out of their coasts. But they shook off the dust of their feet against them...'. It is equivalent to all the Zadok/Zedek-based names of the OT (for its blocked/prevented meanings), and Sadducees of the Gospels. Cp: bissideea. (Acts.13:14-52)

Gentiles ethnē; يثني ، اثني 'he does it again/twice/doubles it/folds it/repeats it' 'he dissuades/makes leave' 'he is an idolater/pagan' 'idols' 'he praises' 'idol worshippers' 'idolatry/worshipping idols' and ethnon; يثنون ، اثنون 'he/they do it again/double it/fold it/repeat it' 'he/they dissuade/make leave' 'he/they are idolaters/ pagans' 'idols' 'praise/praises' 'idol worshippers' 'idolatry/worshipping idols' used to show Paul is dissuading them away from idolatry and at the same time it hints he is leading them onto more idolatry but in a different way; Paul is being praised as God's messenger; the Gentiles glorify the word of God; 'I will deceive them/the' 'I will mislead them to downfall-them/the' is used as a multiple pun that the people who follow Paul's teachings will be led to their own downfall, and at the same time it is for the audience to understand that these are still false stories. (Acts.13:42-52)

Iconium; Ikónion; اكونيون ، اكونيُن 'they were' and this emphasises that Barnabas and Paul were 'filled with joy, and with the Holy Ghost.'; اخونيون ، اخونيُن 'they were soaked/soaked him/it' 'they were betrayed' 'they are/became brothers' as although they have been treated badly by the people of Pisidia they are still full of joy, and the joy is because they can fill each other with the Holy Ghost and because the original water/semen (Mary/Jesus) comes from God it makes them all brothers; اقونيون ، اقونيْن 'they are water channels' 'they are bottles/flasks/any transportable drinking vessel or small water vessel' 'they topped up (with water/liquid)/they estimated measure of something liquid' 'they held head high/body straight posture' 'they sat/placed/set upright/erect' 'they were perky'—and all these meanings related to water channels, liquid, estimating measurements of liquid topping-up of any kind of beverage or pure water in a vessel, as these are two disciples and the 'Holy Ghost' has been mentioned as filling them after they are filled with joy, it is water/semen which has filled Barnabas and Paul. Equivalent to Cana (John.2:1), Kanah (Josh.16:8), and other names such as Elkanah (OT). Cp: ikoonyoon, ikoonyon, i<u>kh</u>oonyoon, i<u>kh</u>oonyon, iqoonyoon, iqoonyon. (Acts.13:51-52)

Lysatra; Lýstra; ليآستَر 'so he/may he protect them/him' 'may he not protect them/him' 'so he/may he cover them' 'may he not cover them/him' and is used as to describe a person being kept safe or provided protection, also something being covered e.g. from a scandal being exposed/loss of reputation or depending on how it is said it is a curse/call/prayer for the opposite. From word (str/ستر) 'protection/cover/curtain'; لياسطَر 'may he pour line of water into' 'may he pour water out' 'may he drain water out of it' 'so he pours/will pour/drain/will drain water out of it' 'may he not pour line of water into' 'may he not/he did not pour water out/drain water out of it' 'may he make it/him a straight line' 'may he not make it a straight line'; from word (sṭr/سطر) 'pour/drain/line/align/make row'. In Acts.14 it is used as a place name and to reflect both disciples fled and were provided with protection; the same is reflected in the crippled man as in healing him Paul has provided a cover from the issues he would have been facing and a protection; all Paul's miracles (and the disciples') are linked to the water/semen poured in and out of them; the crippled man is made straight and able to walk. Cp: lyaastra, lyaasṭra. (Acts.14:1-9)

Derbe; Dérbē; ضيربي 'beat/beaten' 'beat me' 'of fighting' 'banged(copulation between bovine)' 'a unit of measurement' 'harmed me' 'harm in me'; ديربي 'was aware of me' 'made me aware' 'around/surrounds me' 'made me spin/dizzy', it is also a structure, part wall, part door (kept open during day, shut at night) outside the house, 'senile/forgetfulness/confusion/dementia' 'lapsed in thought or judgement/forgot'. It has been used to reflect that the Jews and Gentiles had attempted to beat or kill Paul and Barnabas; to reflect the crippled man's problem; then to reflect that the Jews succeeded in stoning Paul and leaving him for dead, but as it turns out he was only severely beaten by the stoning and remained alive. It reflects the apostles being aware of the Gentile/Jew attack; the 'region that lieth round about'; Paul aware of the crippled man's faith; the people mistaking Paul and Barnabas for gods is a type of 'lapse in thought'. Cp: <u>dh</u>eirb<u>ey</u>, <u>dh</u>eir-b<u>ey</u>, deirbey, deir-bey. (Acts.14:5-10, 19-21)

Lycaonia; Lykaonía; ليكَوني 'of loquaciousness/rambling/talking nonsense-he/him' 'of chewing-he/him' 'for you' (said to singular or plural), 'what if it's him/them' 'but why?' and refers to the people believing the disciples are Gods (Jupiter and Mercury) and that this is nonsense as expressed by Paul; it also reflects they are bringing sacrifices which will be made to the disciples so the sacrifices which will be eaten are 'for you' (for Paul and Barnabas) and 'chewing-he/him' (which Paul prevents them from doing), and Paul's shock and objection as to why they are bringing animals and want to sacrifice to them while they are just human like everyone else; ليقَوني 'they found me' 'of finding' 'they threw me/cast me' 'of throwing/casting' 'they met me' 'of meeting' 'they extended/connected to me' 'of extending/connecting' and this can be seen in the disciples running from being stoned to death as any form of being killed/slaughtered is considered 'thrown/cast'; in Paul finding the crippled man to heal; in Paul connecting with the crippled man through seeing him and 'perceiving' he has enough faith to be healed; in the people coming to perform sacrifices. Cp: lykowneea, lyqowneea. (Acts.14:6-14)

Jupiter; Diós, Zeús; ذيوه ، ذِوه 'it is' 'this' 'this is' 'it is her/him' 'here it/she/he is' 'is it this/her/him/this one?' 'it is her/him' 'is it her/him?' 'him/her/them/it'; ضيوه ، ضِوه 'there it is' 'his/its ablution/purification with water' 'his/its light' and this is connected that Jesus/God's water is like light at the beginning of the Gospel of John, and in that water not only is 'the water of life/sperm' which cleanses but also has the same cleansing abilities as normal water; reflected in Paul with his water-induced abilities curing the man. Also reflected in that the Lycaonians believe Barnabas to be Jupiter and Paul, Mercury. Cp: veeooh, veuh, <u>dh</u>eeooh, <u>dh</u>euh. (Acts.14:8-18)

Mercurius; Hermḗs; هَرمييه ، هَرمي يه 'I will throw-him/he/it' 'I will kill-him/he/it' 'here, see/saw his water' 'chased away-water-he/him' 'chased away his water'. The meanings are reflected in they see Paul cure the crippled man, and Paul cures with his water/semen which is now God/Jesus' water/sperm. It is in the people arriving to throw down sacrifices i.e. slaughter and offer sacrifices to the disciples whom they believe to be deities. Cp: herm<u>ei</u>eyh, herm<u>ei</u>-eyh. (Acts.14:8-18)

The **Lystra** meaning of 'drained/poured water out of it' as they believe they have killed Paul, i.e. poured his life out, he is a vessel which carries the 'water of life', and his life has been poured out. **Antioch** has been used for its meaning of 'was finished/over' as they believe they have stoned him to death. **Iconium** has been used for 'they were' 'they were soaked him' 'they are bottles/flasks/any transportable drinking vessel or small water vessel' 'they topped up (with water/liquid)/they estimated measure of something liquid' 'they sat/placed/set upright/erect' as the disciples who are vessels of God/Jesus' water stand around him and although he has been stoned, supposedly to death, they top him up with their water/semen-induced powers and he gets up. **Derbe** is used to indicate the beating and harm Paul has received. **Barnabas** is used to show they are bringing and teaching the news of God, pious news, to different areas.

The return to **Lystra**, **Iconium** and **Antioch** is again to show the pronouncing/preaching is linked to draining/pouring water from the disciples to the people, and it also indicates that when Paul and Barnabas return there is a topping-up of liquids described as 'Confirming the souls of the disciples, and exhorting them to continue in the faith…' i.e. reinforcing their spirit and energy, their will and determination to spread God's word. (Acts.14:19-22)

Attalia; Attáleia; اتّآلَي 'he came to me/for me'; اطّع لَي 'he obeyed me' 'he became obedient for me'. This is reflected in Paul and Barnabas being recommended 'to the grace of God for the work which they fulfilled.' They come to Antioch and part of the speech/news they bring is that God has 'opened the door of faith unto the Gentiles.' which is why the author has them go through Perga again before arriving at Antioch to stay for Perga's meanings of 'so he stays/stayed/so stay' 'opened up/opens up/an opening/orifice'. Cp: attaa-leya, aṭṭ'-leya. (Acts.14:25-28)

Phenice is used again for 'so he chooses/selects' 'will choose/select' 'so he picks out impurities/clears/cleans' 'will pick out impurities/clear/clean'; 'so hurt/poke wound' 'so hurt/offend' 'will hurt/poke wound' 'will hurt/offend'; 'so he saves/delivers to safety him/them/it' 'will save him/them/it'; and for the same reasons as earlier as the matter of circumcision, bodily and spiritual cleanliness, and being saved is raised again. (Acts.15)

Although James was killed with the sword by Herod at Acts.12:2, the author or a later editor has him back alive within the same chapter at verse 17 without resurrection or any story to explain it—he is just back alive. The reason the author or later editor does not mind overlooking he has been dead, is the significance of the word-name for which his character was created 'he pinches/he pokes'. When he is killed at verse 2 it is said 'with a sword' so the association of stabbed through can be made with the meaning of his name; and when he is back in the scene it is to reflect the many holes which will consume the person who killed him, Herod who is eaten by worms creating holes throughout his whole body.

James 'he pinches/he pokes' is returned regarding the circumcision debate. It cannot be ignored the word-name meaning of 'poked' does have a meaning of men poking each other in the anus and the dialogue given to James is about the Gentiles who although are uncircumcised they (and their poking appendage) are suitable to receive and do God's work, and this is reinforced by adding the mention of **David** of which the 'stone rolling pin' symbolises the penis and the character mention reflects on his sexual relationship with Jonathan which was a complete and loving relationship between two men. The conversation is about not troubling the Gentiles with the pain of circumcision (they are talking about grown men) whose member would be pinched and pulled at as part of the circumcising procedure. The meaning of 'poking and polluting' is mentioned as they are told to avoid things that are polluted: fornication (poking); polluted foods which are not slaughtered correctly; the blood which should be let out if slaughtered correctly. (Acts.12:2, 17, 23)

Barsabas is recycled for its meanings 'good/piety-left him' 'good/piety-poured him' 'good/piety-caused him/because of him' and he is now Judas Barsabas whereas he is built on the character Joseph Barsabas of Acts.1:23 who was competing to replace Judas' Iscariot's vacant position, but was not chosen. This character is now chosen and his first 'event' which reflects both Judas meanings of 'his hands' and 'he called/false claim' is to write or at least carry letters explaining the news of the Gentiles having to be circumcised is false; then travelling to spread God's word, preaching, etc. As he is a prophet, he too can pour God's word/water onto/into his audience. (Acts.15:22-33)

Silas; Sílas; سيلَه 'flowed/leaked (it)' 'temporary running river' 'asked/questioned him'; صيلَه 'arrived at/reached him' 'connected him/it' 'apologised publicly' 'delivered it'. The word-name allows Paul to use the

'Saul' meanings as he will now part with Barnabas whose word-name also has 'going/leaving/reaching beyond/surpassing' meanings but is replaced by Silas as a travel companion. It is reflected in he will deliver the letters to the Gentiles; he will deliver news of which part of it is an apology or sorrow over the Gentiles being troubled by false news of needing to be circumcised. The 'flowed/leaked/water' meanings represent the all-important 'water/sperm' of God/Jesus carried and distributed by disciples, apostles, prophets. This too allows the author to have Paul become independent of John the disciple (John Mark) and Peter (by having Silas as his companion) as the author's intention is to have Paul (originally Saul) the major figure of these stories. Cp: seelah, <u>ss</u>eelah. (Acts.15:22-41)

Cilicia is used for 'ate it/you-him/it' 'fed you-him/it' 'all of it-he/him' 'ate you-he/him/it' 'worried-him/he/it' as the letter sent to the Gentiles addresses the upset and concerns raised about needing circumcision; they are told they can leave their genital intact; and are given instructions over what foods to avoid eating. (Acts.15:23)

John Mark is used for its meaning of John/'soaked it/him (in)' 'brothers' 'betrayed'/'sacks' 'sackcloth' 'put/wrap it/him in sack/sackcloth'—Mark/'did not/they did not wait/stay/become still': because Paul does not want John Mark to accompany them because at Pamphylia John Mark left them without completing God's work (as his name implies); John is soaked in Jesus' water/semen and is essential for spreading God's work, but as Paul has by now been filled with the 'Holy Ghost/God's water' John Mark is no longer needed because Paul himself is both an absorbent of Jesus/God's water/sperm and a vessel which can pass it on to others; having **Silas** his own 'temporary river/leaking/flowing' also renders John Mark useless to Paul, and Silas being also 'reached/arrived at/connected/delivered' allows Paul to no longer need (at this point) Barnabas' word-meanings so the divide and upset and the eventual parting of ways reflected by 'Mark' is also made clear: Barnabas and John are useless because Paul is now one of the Jesus/God's water/sperm vessels and he has use of a new partner, Silas, to keep it topped-up and reaching target audiences in other areas. (Acts.15:32-41)

Epistle; epistolḗ; اِبسطوليي It is the exact same as 'Apostle' 'spread for me' 'explain for me' 'of spreading/explaining' and all the nuances meant from the word (bsṭ/بسط) (see Apostle) including 'make happy/content for me' 'of joy/content'. It is used not only as in 'delivered the letter' but they read it out, they tell the story, spread the news 'and when they had gathered the multitude together, they delivered the epistle: *Which* when they had read, they rejoiced for the consolation.'. They have also simplified a complicated matter of mandatory circumcision, rendering it needless. Cp: abisṭoo<u>lei</u>ey. (Acts.15:32-33)

Timotheous; Timótheos; تِموضِوه ، تِموضيوه 'she passes him/walks past him/she makes him go' 'will you pass him/will you make him walk past/go' 'she completes/finishes it/he/him' 'will you complete/finish it/him/he' 'she marks/signs it/him/he' 'will you mark/sign it/him/he/will you make him mark/sign'; تِموثِوه ، تِموثيوه 'she wipes away his urine/sperm(without use of water)' 'will you wipe away his urine/sperm'. The compound word is given a female prefix showing a female does the action of the verb and this is intentional just as the character of the mother has been intentionally created a 'Jew'—Jewish males are circumcised at birth so the irregularity of him being uncircumcised/unclean (Greek father) then circumcised/clean is because of his Jewish mother allows for it therefore the word-name is in the feminine doing an action to the masculine.

Timotheus will **pass along** different places and people when Paul takes him with him; as he becomes Paul's companion and helps him spread God/Jesus' word, his name and the circumcision imply he has had water/sperm (probably by Paul or Silas) poured into him which makes him able to pour it out onto/into others as he spreads God/Jesus' word. The way wordplay and fictional word-names for fictional events is used can be clearly seen in all parts of the Bible, but Acts.16 is a good example: following all the hullabaloo over circumcision in the lives of the inhabitants of the story which it clearly makes unnecessary and not practised against 'Gentiles' over several chapters including Acts.15, the author of Acts.16 decides it is necessary for someone who will accompany Paul and engage in the sexual acts of filling and pouring water, i.e. Paul's companion cannot be 'Gentile' nor uncircumcised which according to the NT stories is innately 'polluted/unclean/impure' so the author uses wordplay and plotline in having Timothy's mother a local and his father a foreigner; note 'Jew' and 'Greek' are not used as nationalities/ethnicities but as word-meanings, and the narration which shows Timotheus meanings and the meanings of other words are interconnected as the mention of his mother being 'Jew' (associated with being pure/clean in body and soul in both OT/NT stories but also what the action of the word 'jew' means associated with what Paul has done in this part of the story), his father being 'Greek' denotes something has to be changed as there is something wrong/unclean in his body (and maybe soul) which needs to be 'purified/circumcised/made good' and this is the meaning of 'Greek' being relayed and used.

Greek; hellēn; حيلّين ، حلّين 'purify/purified/circumcise/circumcised/make clean/made clean/make edible/made edible' 'of purification/edibility/cleanliness/circumcision' 'declare/declared purified/permissible' 'undress/undressed' 'of undressing' 'deceive/deceived/trick/tricked' 'of deceit/tricks' 'beat/beaten severely/beat/beaten until skin peeled off' 'of beating/being beaten severely' 'shed skin/hair/leaves/etc.' 'of shedding skin/hair/leaves' 'replace/replaced' 'of replacing' 'sweet/sweetened' 'of sweetness/sweetening'. And these meanings are what is done to Timotheus in his role and how the word 'Greek' is used. He is purified with circumcision; this makes him 'clean/pure/edible' to be Paul's companion, and receptacle and pouring vessel. Cp: ḥeilleyn, ḥelleyn.

Timotheus is equivalent to Matthew (Matt.9:1-9), Matthat, Mattatha, Maath, Mattathias, Matthat (Luke.3), Matthias (Acts.1:22-26). Cp: timoodheooh, timoodhyooh, timoofeooh, timoofyooh. (Acts.16:1-5)

The story has Timotheus' parents well-known among the inhabitants of Lystra and Iconium because **Lystra** 'so he/may he protect them/him' 'may he not protect them/him' 'so he/may he cover them' 'may he not cover them/him' 'may he pour line of water into' 'may he pour water out' 'may he drain water out of it' 'so he pours/will pour/drain/will drain water out of it' 'may he not pour line of water into' 'may he not/he did not pour water out/drain water out of it' 'may he make it/him a straight line' 'may he not make it a straight line'; and **Iconium** 'they were' 'they were soaked him' 'they were betrayed' 'they are water channels' 'they are bottles/flasks/any transportable drinking vessel or small water vessel' 'they topped up (with water/liquid)/they estimated measure of something liquid' 'they held head high/body straight posture' 'they sat/placed/set upright/erect' 'they were perky'. All these meanings are reflected in the story: it is what will be done to Timotheus so he can do to others in terms of 'water-pouring' as he becomes a vessel which receives and pours water. Also, the state of uncircumcision is presented as an embarrassment which could betray Timotheus and by extension Paul, because he is supposed to be circumcised (note all the protagonists who have positive lead roles in the NT stories are locals so they are circumcised as the norm during first week of life) and Paul has protected Timotheus from this scandal by circumcising him, but also shows he is definitely pure in body and soul just in case the disciples/elders got it wrong about the Gentiles not needing to be circumcised to be accepted by religion and God. (Acts.16:1-5)

Acts.16 begins with Paul arriving and Timotheus being at **Derbe** ('harmed me' 'harm in me' 'was aware of me' 'made me aware' 'around/surrounds me') and **Lystra** because the impure body and soul of Timotheus, due to being uncircumcised, is a harm which can be held against both Timotheus and Paul, and a state which the local people are aware of, but it will be set straight by Paul circumcising him. (Acts.16:1-5)

Phrygia '(so) they stayed-he/him' 'so stay-he/him/they' 'they opened up' 'opening(s)/orifice(s)' 'openings/orifices-he/him/them' 'opened up/relieved/released/end of difficult period or experience' 'vaginas/vulvas' 'they watched/saw' 'they stared at/watched' 'they created an opening/release-him/he/they' and is used to show that Paul and company are making their way performing these works which spread God's word. (Acts.16:6)

Galatia; Galatía; قلتي ، قلتيي ، قل اتي ، قل اتيي 'said/he said-came here/come here' 'sanitised on heat' 'sanitised it/him on heat' 'he said he came/he said he would come' غلطي ، غلطيي 'made mistake/he/they made mistake' 'of making mistakes' 'made mistake-he/him/she/her' 'of making mistakes-he/him/she/her' 'is deceiving/tricking/shortchanging' 'of deceiving/tricking/shortchanging-he/him/she/her' 'is wrong' 'he/she/they is/are wrong'. It refers to Paul and his group wanting to go and preach/spread the word in Asia and Bithynia but being prevented; in that there being something wrong or bad, or mistakes being made in Galatia (something unfavourable) which causes 'the Holy Ghost' to forbid Paul from going to Asia. What is being forbidden is God/Jesus' water/sperm being poured into/onto the people there, there is something wrong with them either in body or soul, or both, which prevents the 'Holy Ghost' transfer from happening, embodied by the 'Holy Ghost' preventing it. This is connected to **Asia**'s meanings (see Asia) as described earlier of 'disobedience/offense' and also about 'become askew/bent/crooked/warped' there is definitely a portrayal of something bad related to the physical status of the inhabitants of Galatia and because spreading the word and Paul's work involves God's water/sperm the 'wrong/warped', the problem the Holy Ghost has with them is related to the penis. Cp: qalateea, qalateeya, qal-ateea, qal-ateeya, ghalaṭeea, ghalaṭeeya. (Acts.16:6)

Mysia; Mysía; معصي ، معصيي 'disobedience/went against' 'disobeyed-he/him' 'went against-he/him/she/her' 'crooked/warped/bent/askew' 'became askew/bent/crooked/warped-he/him/she/her' 'is stuck' 'is stuck-he/him/she/her' 'sticks' 'used/has sticks'; ميسيَ ، ميسييَ 'sorrow' 'sorrow-he/him/she/her' 'bad/offensive/insulting-he/him' 'offends/insults/bad-he/him' 'bad towards/offense/insult towards-he/him'; ميشيَ ، ميشييَ 'water/semen-things/matters' 'lots of water/semen' 'no/not' 'nothing' 'not important' 'wants water/semen' 'does not want' 'left/he/they left' 'walked/he/they walked' 'of speaking in whispers' 'of snitching/telling'. This too is related to the 'Spirit' and the 'Spirit' is the breathing/panting/wind of sexual intercourse and just as the 'Holy Ghost/water/sperm' prevented Paul from going to 'Asia', while in 'Mysia' which does not differ much as a word and in many meanings than 'Asia' the 'Spirit/breathing/panting' prevents Paul from going to Bithynia—and again the word-names and how the story is narrated show something wrong in the physical, and maybe spiritual, characteristics of the 'people' in this land. Equivalent to Asia (Acts.2:9), Maasiai (1Chr.9:12), Maaseiah (1Chr.15:18). Cp: m'sseea, m'sseeya, myseea, myseeyaa, mysheea, mysheeya.

Bithynia; Bithynía; بِثينيَ ، بِثينييَ 'with the other one/second one' 'will do it again/will do it to the other one' 'will fold/double-it/he/him'; بِتينيَ ، بِتينييَ 'girls/girlish' 'of girls' 'his girls/daughters-he/him' 'with figs/of figs' 'is figs'. It indicates there is something too feminine about the people, as it does not elaborate whether the majority or all were female, or if the men were too effeminate, it would be conjecture to determine what was wrong with the people of Bithynia that the 'Spirit' stopped Paul from going; but it is definitely connected to 'female/girl' and to the fig tree at Bethany that could not produce edible fruit and Jesus caused to wither and die, and this too connects it to Nathanael who was a clue to make John into 'Johnathan' (making male into female with anal sex). Equivalent to Bethany (Matt.21:17-46), Nathanael (John.1:47-49). Cp: bifyneea, bifyneeya, bityneea, bityneeya. (Acts.16:7)

Troas; Trōás; تروآه 'watered it/him' 'gave it/him to drink(water)/quenched' 'dreamed it/him' 'dreamed' 'told story' with all these meanings interweaved in the story as Paul is told in a dream to go preach at Macedonia so as to help them, and as explained before, the meaning of spreading God/Jesus' water/semen is the 'word' also, but it also quenches the thirst which 'Troas' as a word means in giving to drink water and watering. Cp: trooaah. (Acts.16:8-11)

Macedonia; Makedonía; مَكِدونييَ ، مَكيدونيَ 'of plotting/deceiving' 'plotting/deceiving-him/he/she/they' 'covered tightly (with any kind of lid: stone, metal, cloth, etc.)/of covering tightly(with lid, etc.)' 'covered me with a lid/fabric/stone/etc.'; مَخِدونييَ ، مَخيدونيَ 'of pillows' 'pillows/with pillows' 'resting on pillows' 'with hand on cheeks' 'of cheeks' 'cheeks' 'pulled off/down/away/removed by pulling' 'pulled bread off oven wall' 'pulled down wall/structure'. All meanings are related to Lydia of Thyatira—she is a prostitute just like Rahab of the OT who allows two strangers to stay at her house, the 'pillows' in the Bible and culture are used to mean a prostitute. The 'plotting/deceiving' is unintentional and a result of them going into her house which provides them with the same sort of 'covered/covered with lid/fabric/stone' meanings (see Makkedeh (Josh.10:16-27)), and the same applies to the damsel whose body is a lid/cover over the 'spirit/demon' inside her, this demon/spirit uncovers Paul's intentions which he apparently wants to keep secret in this part of the story. The story makes more sense now as to why the narration has the 'Holy Ghost' and 'Spirit' prevent Paul from going to 'Asia' and 'Bithynia' and go through 'Mysia', using them as word-names to denote something is wrong in these places and the more you read Acts.16 the more it becomes apparent that what is meant is females who will have an active role in this chapter are problematic, are intrinsically trouble, and just as in the OT are blamed even when the narration is depicting them as protagonists it depicts them with negative atmosphere and word-names (see Deborah, Jael), and in this case the females in the story.

As soon as Paul and company engage in 'baptising' females or attempting to heal a female who is possessed, things go wrong for Paul as a direct result: because of the female character (the possessed damsel) Paul and his group are beaten and imprisoned; but the 'wrong' begins with a sexual baptising of Lydia, and in going to her house. Although the gospels and other stories have Jesus and disciples healing females, it is requested for them by or through an external party (such as the Syrophoenician for her daughter, Jairus for his daughter), but as soon as the story suggests that there is a direct sexual encounter with Lydia where she is baptised (given the same water/sperm treatment as the male characters from those directly imbued by God/Jesus' water) things go wrong. This is intentional as the authors of the NT have the same attitude as the authors of the OT, and that is females are inferior, only cause trouble and are negative even if what they do is positive in the story. So all the meanings of 'disobedience' and something being wrong with the water/semen and the male reproductive organ from the beginning of this chapter reflects that women have no place, or at least an inferior place, in the Biblical stories and the inability or degraded ability to spread God's word which is necessary by spreading God/Jesus' water (and it is not meant as sex between man and woman, but between man and man which keeps it pure and powerful—see the 'genealogy' given to Jesus is completely male and taken away from the one person who could have connected it to Jesus (Mary) because the authors want it to be carried through males only and not pass through Mary because she is female and without a penis). The whole story is tied together with the relay created through the word-names and events of the whole chapter (just like the other stories). Bithynia, with all its meanings—the 'girlish' problem, the 'second one/with the other one' as first Lydia is baptised but it is the 'second/other one' female who makes the big problem when Paul casts a devil out of a girl who was making money for her bosses which brings around his suffering.

Cp: makedooneeya, makydooneea, makhedooneeya, makhydooneea. (Acts.16:9-40)

Samothracia; Samothrákē; سَموت/سَمُت رآكي 'named-your story/storytelling' 'named-saw you' 'named-your watering/quenching' 'told story/riddle(samaaya)-your story/storytelling' 'told story/riddle(samaaya)-saw you' 'told story/riddle-your watering/quenching'; شَموت/شَمُت رآكي 'caused a scene/scandal-saw you' 'caused a scene-your water/quenching' 'caused a scene-your story/storytelling'; سَموت/سَمُت رآخي 'named/told story or riddle-loose/immoral'; شَموت/شَمُت رآخي 'caused a scene/scandal-loose/immoral'.

All meanings are used: the author is reminding the audience these are fictional stories 'samaar-as(Samaria)' and 'samaayas' based on creating word-names and wordplay; the possessed damsel is exposing Paul who is both spreading God's word and pouring his water/semen in converting people, his preaching is storytelling; the damsel, or the devil inside her, can see what and who Paul is and exposes him; Paul in turn sees what the problem in the girl is (the devil), but in curing her inadvertently causes the detriment of her exploitive bosses who were making money out of her predictions—so Paul also has 'seen their fictional stories' and caused them chaos/a scene.

The acts of the women are 'loose/immoral' and can mean a physical looseness too, but here it speaks of an immoral lewdness, Lydia is a prostitute, the damsel under her employers' directions is making 'illegal' gains; Paul and Silas (maybe Timotheus too) although they are protagonists, the acts Jesus/disciples/apostles conduct is a sexual act (see Beelzebub) which would be called 'raca/rakhe/loose/immoral'.

The word-name meanings take a positive turn as soon as Paul and Silas, and the narration, do the same acts but this time to a male character—the 'keeper of the prison'; as soon as they perform their 'storytelling/watering' and he sees their 'storytelling/watering' can tell their 'namings' as meant in the translations of 'Samothracia' above, the story takes a good and positive turn for Paul and Silas: the male prisoners hear Paul and Silas' prayers; they speak to prison-keeper the word of the Lord; he washes their wounds (which he caused) and in turn gets baptised; although the magistrates have already notified them that they are free, the author makes a point that Paul makes it known he is 'Roman' not only because of its water-related word-meaning but because it restores their dignity and erases the wrong-doing through 'naming' something in particular (see Roman, Rome). Note although the females did not actually seek to harm Paul, the narration has them the cause of 'bad/evil', and although the male prison-keeper actively took part in Paul's harm, going the extra mile by putting them 'into the inner prison, and made their feet fast in the stocks.' his role is connected to all-positivity. Cp: samoot-raakey, samot-raakey, shamoot-raakey, shamot-raakey, samoot-raakhey, samot-raakhey, shamoot-raakhey, shamot-raakhey. (Acts.16:11-40)

Neapolis; Neápolis; نِعبولِه ، نيعبوليه 'we shake his/her/its fat/sheep fat'; نِآبولِه ، نيآبولِه ، نيآبوليه 'warned/brought to attention/reminded-soak it/him/her' 'planted the stone/seed(of fruit)-soak it/him/her' 'intended/decided-soak it/him/her' 'the intentions/unspoken thoughts-soak it/him/her'. The 'fat shaking' is a euphemism for a sexual act but in a positive light in this story, but the 'shaking fat(of sheep)' which is shaking is a good thing, a fortune, the best quality of meat or livestock (see Abel (Gen.4:4), Abel-mizraim (Gen.50:6-14), Abelmeholah (1Kgs.19:16-21)) as Paul and Silas are spreading God/Jesus' water/sperm which involved planting the seeds/stones of fruit into others and soaking them in this 'holy water' which comes from God/Jesus, it applies both to the preaching of the 'word' but also the physical aspect of baptism which gets its effectivity from God's water/semen. Cp: ne'boolih, ny'boolyh, neaaboolih, nyaaboolih, nyaaboolyh. (Acts.16:11-40)

Philippi used the same way as at Matt.16:13-28 for 'in his/its core/middle' 'so respond/assist/serve' as in Paul is responding to a call for assistance which he sees come to him in a dream; he is serving both the people he is trying to convert and God at the same time; his work requires reaching the cores/insides of people both as in reaching their souls, changing their minds, but also euphemistically through pouring his water into them, as well as causing a physical change which happens both to the body and soul through these actions. (Acts.16:12-40)

Lydia (Ezek.30:5) is used for 'fold and press it/him/he' 'it was folded and pressed' 'fold and press' 'crush it/him together' 'dent it/force both sides to meet-it/him/he' 'dented/both sides crushed against each other' 'burnt' 'burning sensation/pain' 'crumple it/press and crumple it/him/he' 'crumpled' 'pressed and crumpled' because the woman works as a seller of 'purple' (and how this is related to her character/role will be explained with 'Thyatira'); because the woman is a prostitute as indicated by 'Macedonia', the actions of being pressed, crushed, and because she will be baptised by Paul, show the same meanings of how 'Lot' indicates the backside being pressed, crushed, sagged, a sexual activity is also implied; it is because leaving her house and going to prayer Paul and Silas run into the possessed damsel which brings around a physical assault against them followed by an official flogging ('crushed/dented/burning sensation or pain'). (Acts.16:14-40)

Thyatira; Thyátira; ذيعطِر ، ذعآطِر 'he/they are twisting/wringing' 'squeezing water or liquid out of' 'he/it-twisted/squeezed/wrung water/liquid out of'. This, coupled with the meaning of Lydia (one meaning is the action of washing clothes: the crumpling, lathering, rubbing, crushing garments against each other or itself), enhances the character 'Lydia from Thyatira' who is a 'seller of purple' (indigo? madder?)—again it is important to remember whether the authors used fictionally created word-names that did not exist or if they used real names of real places/people, in these Biblical stories the people and places are not real but used to lend and enhance meaning to the story and storyline. Therefore, the city Lydia comes from, who we are told sells purple fabrics, is named after an important step in the process of creating purple/blue-dyed clothes/fabrics: twisting and squeezing, wringing (yátira/átira) from word ('ṭr/عطر) 'twist/squeeze/wring' (can also mean 'perfume(d)' 'twisted/turned around'). Twisting, squeezing, wringing, is an important step repeated throughout the process of indigo/madder dyeing, it removes excess colour/dye/water.

As the Biblical authors of the NT tend to use multiple meanings to indicate multiple actions and to multiple stories, they are likening it to 'Israel/twisted muscle-the' where after a sexual encounter between God and Jacob another sexual encounter between Dinah and Shechem causes a lot of negativity in the story; the author of Acts.16 indicates the female negativity through the word-names meanings and the narration of preventing Paul from going to these negative word-names before the characters interact with the female characters in the following verses, followed by negative incidents. Cp: vy'ṭira, v-'aaṭira. (Acts.16:14-40)

Romans (John.11:45-48) still means 'of throwing' 'throwing/threw' 'killed' 'spread over vast distance/various locations' 'of spreading/strewn over vast distance/various locations' 'saw water' 'of seeing water' and this is not used as a race, nationality or ethnicity but as a word-meaning no different than how it was used earlier (see Romans (John.11:45-48) as a word-meaning and what was implied by the narration of 'Jews' fearing the new religious followers (not yet called Christians) described as 'saw water/of seeing water' will convert all the people and take over everything through what today would be called 'Christianity' which is converting people through use and spread of water. In Acts.16:37, it is used as Paul and Silas 'of seeing water' who convert people by making them 'see water' have been treated wrongly; 'of throwing/throwing/threw/killed' as they have been thrown into prison, so they want the people in charge who did them wrong 'of throwing/threw' who threw them into prison, convicted and beat them when they were innocent, to come and take them out of the prison, i.e. to see Paul and Silas is for their offenders to 'see water', and it results in the antagonists throwing them out of the area by asking them to leave the city. (Acts.16:37-40)

Amphipolis; Amphípolis; امثي بولِه 'wipe/I wipe away urine/sperm-soaked/his soaked' 'wipe/I wipe away his urine' as Paul is discussing the matter of Jesus Christ and converting people to Christianity which includes both the use of his sperm/water and/or at least water in the telling of Jesus' story and in converting people to Christianity. Cp: amphee-bolih. (Acts.17:1-16)

Apollania; Apollōnía; ابْأّوْنيَ ، ابْلّونيي 'they soaked me' 'of soaking' 'they made me pass water/urinate' 'of passing water/urinating' 'they afflicted me' 'of affliction' for the same reasons as Amphipolis, and it is because many are being converted the 'soaking' and 'wiping' meanings of these two word-names is emphasised; and Paul speaks of the necessity of Jesus being afflicted with sufferings; the locals cause problems for Paul and whoever assisted Paul. Cp: abollooneea, abollooneeya. (Acts.17:1-16)

Thessalonica; Thessaloníkē; ذِسَّلونيكي ، ذيسَّلونيكي 'he/they-asked/questioned-wounded/poked wound/hurt/offended/fucked' 'he/they/it-leaked/flowed-wounded/poked wound/hurt/offended/fucked' 'he/they/it-comforted/entertained/distracted-wounded/poked wound/hurt/offended/fucked'; ذِسَّلونيقي ، ذيسَّلونيقي 'he/they-asked/questioned-picked out impurities/cleared/cleaned/chose/selected' 'he/they/it-leaked/flowed-picked out impurities/cleared/cleaned/chose/selected' 'he/they/it-comforted/entertained/distracted-picked out impurities/cleared/cleaned/chose/selected'; ذِسَّلونيجي ، ذيسَّلونيجي 'he/they-asked/questioned-saved/delivered to safety/talked/discussed secretly' 'he/they/it-leaked/flowed-saved/delivered to safety/talked/discussed secretly' 'he/they/it-comforted/entertained/distracted-saved/delivered to safety/talked/discussed secretly'.

These meanings are available: Paul and the 'Jews' are discussing Jesus; discussing that Jesus was meant to be hurt in order to cleanse the people of their sins; as they are familiar with the story they are familiar with the sexual activities of the stories and conversion; as many convert, Paul is cleansing/purifying and saving them as Jesus did; as many seek to hurt Paul, it indicates they are offended by his claims and seek to hurt him physically; the story makes a point that the people the 'Jews' gather are perverted or corrupt 'took unto them certain lewd fellows of the baser sort' implying immorality; Paul and Silas are saved from being arrested/hurt. Similar to Salathiel (1Chr.3:17), Sallu (1Chr.9:7), Shiloni (Neh.11:5) and other similar words; Pharaoh-nechoh (2Kgs.23:29-30), Nicanor, Nicolas (Acts.6:5), Phenice (Acts.11:19). Cp: ve-ssalooneekey, vy-ssalooneekey, ve-ssalooneeqey, vy-ssalooneeqey, ve-ssalooneegey, vy-ssalooneegey. (Acts.17:1-16)

Jason; Iásōn; يعصون 'they disobey/go against' 'they become difficult' 'they became askew/bent/crooked/warped' and is reflected in the 'Jews' who gather people to go against Paul, but when they cannot find him, take away Jason instead; جعصون 'lower back(spine area)' 'of lower back' 'up the ass(rectum)' 'of up the ass' and both meanings are related to each other: the word means a specific location on/in the body, which is best described as where the spine ends at the lower back, when people fall and feel pain in the lower spine they say 'I fell on (g'ssee/جعصي)' which means 'I fell on my ass' but at the same time means the pain is felt deep in the spine at the lowest point of the back; when a person asked about the whereabouts of an object or another person and the latter responds in anger or sarcasm 'in g'ssee/جعصي' which means 'up my ass' it is actually referring so deep up it reaches the lower back/spinal cord, which although the pain or any feeling can be felt where the lower back is concerned, it cannot be accessed externally through the skin as it is hidden deep in the lower back.

All the meanings of 'disobeying/acting against/etc.' and 'up the ass' are used in Acts.17: the character name (Jason) as the house who hosts Paul, is introduced only after making the people the Jews bring to cause the disobedience and to act against Paul/Jason described as 'lewd fellows of the baser sort', and just in case the audience does not get that the author means either they are the same as the men of Gibeah who gather around the house wanting to sexually assault the Levite man in the OT, or that they are going to give Paul his own treatment (but because Paul is the protagonist his activities carry God's water/sperm and have cleansing abilities whereas these 'lewd' 'base' fellows sexual assaults can only defile and debase); so the author makes it clear that the angry people accused Paul and by extension Jason of turning the world 'upside down', and this refers to Sodom and Gomorrah who were destroyed because of male homosexuality and this is not only in the Bible, but the folklore of the culture itself describes the destruction as completely destroying these two people/areas and by turning them upside down; and the reference in the Acts.17 also implies the 'turning upside down' of a man having sex with woman replaced by a man having sex with a man; the disobedience meaning and the 'up the ass' is also portrayed in that they are attempting to cause 'shortcomings' and 'breaking' the law (meanings of Caesar) by not complying to Caesar's laws in seeking Jesus ways to be followed. Cp: y'ssoon, g'ssoon. (Acts.17:5-9)

Berea; Béroia, Bérroia; بيرويَ ، بيرّويَ 'they passed/went past/surpassed/went beyond' 'they are/were innocent' 'they were/became good/pious towards' 'they disowned/distanced from' 'they watered' 'they told story' and all meanings are used: by telling the story of Jesus many people are converted and the story/preaching of Jesus is the same as spreading his 'water' i.e. watering; the converted people have become pious, as are Paul's activities; it is where Paul and Silas are sent after Jason has been 'secured', but Paul causes the same controversy and is sent away i.e. made to go beyond. It seems the only reason Silas and Timotheus were made to stay at Berea and then immediately sent for to join Paul is to emphasise the meanings of Berea 'went beyond' and the similar meanings of Silas 'arrived at/reached' and Timotheus 'he/they/it passes/walks past/goes' and both their water-related meanings as nothing else happens in between. Cp: beiroya, beirroya. (Acts.17:9-15)

Athens; Athēnai; اثيينَي 'of doubling/twice' 'of folding and sewing/reinforcing' 'idols/statues/sculptures' 'of idolatry/idols/statues' 'of worshipping idols'. It is reflected in Paul being sent away twice; in his requesting both Silas and Timotheus to join him as they reinforce his mission; in the people of 'Athens' worshipping idols. Cp: afeyeinai. (Acts.17:15)

Epicurians; Epikoúreioi; اِبكوَرِيوي 'virgin/virginal/of virginity/first/of first' 'I make/of making a virgin/first/new' 'early/of early' 'innovative/inventive/new creation/new creativity'; اِفكوَرِيوي 'new thought/new idea' 'thinking/of thinking' 'of creating new idea'. The meanings are relayed in the story as the Athenians and all the people around them are described as only being interested in hearing the newest/latest stories/news. Cp: ebikoureioi, ephikoureioi. (Acts.17:18)

Stoicks; Stōikoi; شدوِقوي 'of set jaw/stubborn' 'set in his ways/set in what he says/insists on/talks a lot' 'will/is a nag' 'talks too much/causes too much noise' 'will make bent/twisted/curved' as they find Paul's preaching 'blabbing', they are set in their ways and refuse to believe the new religion he is bringing; it also reflects on Paul who sees them the same way. It could also be the same as Sadducees: زدوِكوي 'of deceit/deceiving' 'they deceived/tricked you' 'of giving extra' 'they gave you extra'; صدوِكوي 'of blocking/denying' 'they blocked/denied you'; صدوِقوي 'believed you/of believing' 'honest-you/of honesty' 'befriended you/of befriending/friendly'—the 'blocking/deceiving' meanings apply in the related verse. Cp: shdooiqoi, zdooikoi, ssdooikoi, ssdooiqoi. (Acts.17:17-18)

Areopagus; Áreios págos; آريوه بآجوه/فآجوه 'saw him/showed him-they brought him' 'saw him-they came' 'saw him-so they came' 'saw him/showed him-so they came/brought him' 'dreamt him-so they came/brought him' 'watered-they brought him/they came/so they came/brought him'; عريوه بآغوه 'stripped him/stripped him naked-they wanted him/it' 'stripped him naked-made him immoral/were immoral' 'stripped him naked-they prostituted/engaged in prostitution/engaged immoral sexual activities'. The 'saw/showed' meanings are reflected in Paul showing them the right way by preaching Jesus; in the people bringing him to the place which is called 'saw him/showed him-they brought him/it/etc.; in Paul's speech that he came and saw them worshipping idols; in if they seek God, they will find him, i.e. if they come to him.

The 'stripped him/stripped him naked-wanted him/it' 'stripped him naked-made him immoral/were immoral/prostituted' meanings are reflected in the narration that the majority mock and doubt him, 'strip' Paul/Paul's claims and credibility and find him immoral; also reflected in they stick to their own 'immoral' ways by not believing in him. Cp: aareioh-baagooh, phaagooh, 'reioh-baaghooh. (Acts/17:19)

Mars the same as **Areopagus.** (Acts.17:22)

Dionysius; Dionysios; دِعنيسيوه ، دِعنيسيُه 'called/called him-forgot' 'called-people/his people'; دِيُنيسيُه ، ديونيسيوه 'they defiled/dirtied/lowered/soiled/shamed-him/it'; both meanings reflect Paul calling the people to the new faith but the majority of 'Athenians' are just interested in new things then get bored and forget about it as they move onto the newer things; it is about them mocking and shaming him, sticking to their own 'impure' ways; it is also wordplay referring the real audience to an OT story (to be explained under 'Damaris'); دِيُن عصيُه/عصِوه 'religion-disobeyed' 'religious disobedience' and they reject the new religion; ذيُن/ضيُن عصيُه/عصِوه 'they-disobeyed' 'they are disobedient/stubborn' 'light-disobeyed' 'light/shone-disobedient/stubborn' 'ablution/purification-disobeyed/disobedience'; ذيُ/ذيو ضيُ/ضيو نعصيُه 'he/it is/here is-we disobey him' 'they/there they-we disobey/we warp/twist him/it' 'he/it/here/they/there-we make it stuck'. It is still about most of the people disobeying by not believing Paul; about being stuck on their old ways while a few 'clave' to Paul and do believe; it is about Jesus' word cleansing those who believe in it/him. Cp: di'nysyoh, di'nysyooh, diyonysyoh, diyoonysyooh, diyon-'ssyoh, diyon-'ssioh, vyon-'ssyoh/'ssioh, dhyon-'ssyoh/'ssioh, vyo/vyoo-n'ssyoh, dhyo/dhyoo-n'ssyoh. (Acts.17:34)

Aeropagite; Áreopágítēs; آريو بآجيتيه/فآجيتيه 'saw him/showed him-will come to him/will bring him' 'saw him-they came to him' 'saw him/showed him-so they will come/will bring him' 'dreamt him-so they will come/bring him' 'watered-they will bring him/they will come/so they came/brought him'—it can also give the meaning 'of' followed by all the different word-meanings attributing them to the spoken about; عريو بآغيتيه 'stripped him/stripped him naked-they wanted him/it' 'stripped him naked-made him immoral/were immoral' 'stripped him naked-they prostituted him/her/them/engaged in prostitution he/her/them him/her/them/engaged immoral sexual activities'. This word-name also refers/reminds the real audience to an OT story which will be explained under 'Damaris'. Cp: aareio-baageeteyh, phaageeteyh, 'reio-baagheeteyh. (Acts.17:34)

Damaris; Dámaris; دآمَره، دآمَريه 'destroyed-him/it' 'his/its destruction' and refers to the people destroying/discrediting Paul and his debate, his calling them to God/Jesus as they reject both the call and the caller; ضآمَره ، ضآمَريه 'kept inside mind/thoughts/heart' 'kept alive inside heart/mind/soul' and means to believe something, or never forget something, but these things are not voiced but kept within the person, it also means 'withered/shrivelled/shrank in size'. This is reflected in the few people in Athens who believed Paul and his message.

There is also a referral of the audience to the OT story of Judah and Tamar not only for the meanings of their word-names, but also for the message of their story: Dionysius is Judah, Damaris is Tamar, and Aeropagite is Tamar disguised as a prostitute and Judah using the services of a prostitute; Tamar would not give up on carrying Judah's seed even though a lot of death and destruction kept reoccurring causing her to lose the opportunity of conceiving from even one of his son's she was meant to conceive from (all were either killed by God or avoided her, all avoided giving her Judah's 'seed'), but seeing she was being deceived, disguised as a prostitute she was able to lure Judah to copulate her and from that one incident conceived Phares and Zerah to continue with Judah's line; the meaning of 'shrivelled' continues with the 'Israel/twisted muscle-the' alluding to illicit/immoral sexual conduct, but also of Tamar first carrying the plot silently within her own mind, before secretly carrying Judah's seed until it was impossible to hide it. Although there was the initial destruction of Judah's seed and reputation of all concerned, it achieved the most important thing: the continuation of Judah's progeny, Tamar was forgiven and deemed 'more righteous' than Judah himself. The author of Acts.17 has played on all these meanings, and messages of the OT story and employed them to give a similar message to the NT story: God's word is a 'seed/water/sperm' and it is also achieved, specifically in Acts.17, by calling people to the religion ('Judah' in essence), and although Paul is mocked and his credibility among the Athenians destroyed (Tamar) it is enough that one man and one woman carry this seed and it will spread among people just the way offspring/progeny and procreation works. There is an intentional and intellectual use of old stories and employing them in the new NT stories to get the message across; the relay between Areopagus/ite, Dionysius, Judah, Damaris, Tamar and all the different wordplay is strong and clear, creating an even stronger message in one single verse (v.34). Cp: taamarih, taamaryh, <u>dh</u>aamarih, <u>dh</u>aamaryh.

Corinth; Kórinthos; خورِنثُه 'both male and female (at the same time)' it applies to a male or female who either has both male and female reproductive organs, and/or behaves like a male when he/she is female or vice-versa. This marks where the author of Acts uses male and female pairing of characters for his stories where the characters embody one event, or role in the story, they are still just word-names like the rest of the Biblical characters as well as other male/female pairings, but he points this out further so that the audience does not miss the message being told by these pairings, and is again to remind the audience these are fictional stories. It seems to be that giving females more active roles seems too 'butch' for the author of Acts, as well as for his audience, which he plays on—he is making it clear these women should not have roles in spreading God's word but by making them like the opposite sex (masculine) allows them and clarifies how they can be given significant roles in the NT stories, and that is why he has used 'Corinths' as the place name here.

It is also: قورِنثُه 'linked to him/linked him' 'linked them/him' 'linked him with wood/rope' and still refers to the pairing of male/female characters who do/embody the same thing just as a pair of bulls or cows when 'linked' with yoke or rope have to move at the same pace while doing the same work; there is also 'his opposite/opposed him' 'his horn/his spirit of strength(or power)' as they are linked as a pair and this is also linked to the 'horn' mentioned a lot in the OT which needs to be discussed elsewhere in this book; 'read to him/taught him' 'stopped him/it moving/fidgeting' 'made him stop what he was doing' and may have other meanings found in 'Cyrene'. Paul is also linked to them as a craftsman specialising in 'tentmaking'; he will stay with them and teach at the synagogue, but as soon as the special meanings of the word-names 'Silas' and 'Timotheus' and their functions and symbols as characters are linked again to Paul as they arrive to reinforce him that 'Paul was pressed in the spirit, and testified to the Jews *that* Jesus *was* Christ.'; it is also in the opposition and objections he faces. Cp: <u>kh</u>oorinfoh, qoorintoh. (Acts.18:1-6)

Aquila; Akýlas; اقيآلَه 'his sayings' 'told him/I told him' 'put words in his mouth' 'stayed/spent time' 'stayed/spent time with him' 'staying/spending time/they are staying spending time' 'gathering place/place people gather at to spend time together' 'of spending time' 'removed him' 'of removing' (the removing part means a physical removal of a person or object and in modernity would come to be the root word used for 'resignation'); عقيآلَه 'his cleverness/intelligence/mind/wisdom' 'made him reasonable/calmed him' 'gave him mind/logic/cleverness' 'calmed him down/made him knowledgeable/patient' 'his mind/patience/knowledge' 'made him rational' 'kept him in a specific place'. All meanings are present as Paul stays with them and they build tents which are places where people stay, spend time and eventually remove and move elsewhere; and Paul spends time at Corinth; they seem to have a calming influence on him as his preaching to the 'Jews' and the 'Greeks' is described as a calm and intellectual discussion 'he reasoned in the synagogue every sabbath, and persuaded the Jews and the Greeks.' which turns into rhetoric and hostility against them when his other less-cranial influences arrive (Silas/Timotheus). Cp: aqyaalah, 'qyaalah. (Acts.18:1-6)

Pontus is still 'his daughter(s)/his girl(s)/his children' 'made clear/apparent' 'became apparent' 'your intentions have become apparent' as there is a female involved; also, the words Paul teaches become clear, his message (which is God's) come across to the intended audience in the story; also reflected in that the Jews/Greeks rejection of his message becomes apparent. (Acts.18:1-6)

Italy; Italía; اضلَي 'ablution/abluted-for me 'cleanse/cleansed for me' 'he abluted/cleansed for me' 'shone for me'; اتلَي 'came for me' 'he came for me'; اطع لي 'obeyed/obedient for me' 'he obeyed/obeys for me'. It is reflected in Paul helping out with the tentmaking and being mollified in his preaching; the cleansing/ablution is reflected in Paul pointing out that he is 'clean/pure' indicating the Jews and Greeks are 'unclean/impure'. Cp: i<u>dh</u>aleea, italeea, iṭ'leea. (Acts.18:2)

Priscilla; Príska, Prískilla; بريشَق 'good/piety-he works/labours' 'go/goes beyond/surpasses/passes-he works/labours' 'innocent/disowns/distances from-he works/labours; بريسكَ 'good/piety-he is able/he can do it' 'go/goes beyond/surpasses/passes-he is able/he can do it' 'innocent/disowns/distances from-he is able/he can do it'; it is reflected in Paul remaining and working as a tentmaker and his ability to make tents while he also preaches God's words; in Paul disowning and distancing himself by blaming the 'Jews' and the 'Greeks' for their disbelief; and eventually for leaving them 'going beyond' to preach to the 'Gentiles' instead of the 'Jews' and Greeks'. It is also بريشقِلا 'good/piety-I/I will tell him' 'good/piety-I/I will remove/move him/it' 'go/goes beyond/surpasses/goes past-I/I will tell him' 'innocent/disowns/distances from-I/I will tell him' 'good/piety-he did work/labour' 'go/goes beyond/surpasses-he did work' 'innocent/disowns/distances from-he did work/labour'; بريسقِلا 'good/piety-I/I will tell him' 'good/piety-I/I will remove/move him/it' 'go/goes beyond/surpasses/goes past-I/I will tell him' 'innocent/disowns/distances from-I/I will tell him' 'good/piety-he did water'; بريسكِلا 'good/piety-yes, he is able/yes, he can do it' 'go/goes beyond/surpasses/passes-yes, he is able/yes, he can do it' 'innocent/disowns/distances from-yes, he is able/yes, he can do it'. These meanings are also reflected: the piety, leaving, working, disowning, telling, the confirmation that he can or is able to perform/do something, all as before but with the addition that it can also mean 'watered' as Paul's work, as was Jesus and the original disciples', is giving people to drink/watering (through preaching) from God's water which cleanses and converts them.

The pairing of Aquila with Priscilla is shown in the story and as what they will do in the story: they explain the 'way of God' better so the 'good' in Priscilla's word-name is about explaining it better, clearer; the 'piety' is the religious matters; the last part of her name is that she is telling him, i.e. explaining. As it is connected to Aquila in character and word meanings 'told/I told him' he too is explaining the matter, i.e. to another person; and the other meanings of his name 'wise/reasonable/understanding' is in he and his wife are explaining to a third person 'God's way' more clearly: the couple/husband and wife/compound word and compound word, have been given the perfect names for their role in the story: 'And a certain Jew named Apollos...an eloquent man, *and* mighty in the scriptures, came to Ephesus. This man was instructed in the way of the Lord; and being fervent in the spirit, he spake and taught diligently the things of the Lord...and he began to speak boldly in the synagogue: whom when Aquila and Priscilla had heard, they took him unto *them*, and expounded unto him the way of God more perfectly.' And to enhance the meanings of their names, Apollos also goes on to be able, thanks to them, to convince Jews with Jesus Christ—making the 'piety/good' in Priscilla's talk and name, and the 'wisdom/understanding' in Aquila's words and name, be more far-reaching in the story itself. Cp: bareey<u>sh</u>qa, bareeyska, bareey<u>sh</u>qilla, bareeysqilla, bareeyskilla. (Acts.18)

Claudius (Acts.11:28-30) is used for 'placed responsibility on him' 'hung it around his neck' 'hung responsibility around his neck' 'garlanded-he/him' 'placed responsibility/accountability on him/it' 'acted/copied him/it' as it is this character who has forced the Jews out of Rome (Rome used for 'were thrown' 'threw' 'spread/strewn over vast distance/various locations' 'saw water' 'became rotten/went off/bad smelling' as the Jews are being thrown out of Rome; because Aquila and Priscilla will be used to spread God's words which covers both the 'spread over distance/locations' and 'water' meanings; and 'off/rotten' because Paul will have a difference with Jews and Greeks).

As Claudius makes it a responsibility that 'Jews' leave Rome; also reflects Paul has been given a work responsibility (tentmaking) by Aquila/Priscilla; Paul removes the responsibility of the 'Jews' and 'Greeks' disbelief from himself and places the consequences and responsibility on them. (Acts.18)

Macedonia (Acts.16:9-40) used for 'of plotting/deceiving' 'plotting/deceiving-him/he/she/they' 'of pillows' 'pillows/with pillows' 'resting on pillows' 'with hand on cheeks' 'of cheeks' 'cheeks' because Paul's relationship with Jews and Greeks is amicable (in this chapter) until Silas and Timotheus arrive and then he becomes openly hostile and derogatory towards them. The relationship and how it works between apostles has been explained and does contain a sexual meaning fundamental to their work, this indicates that when Priscilla and Aquila were Paul's influences he was a nicer person with a good attitude towards others of different faiths/opinions, but as soon as the people (Silas/Timotheus) who by nature of their powers and preaching, strengthen each other, have deceived him to be antagonistic towards people who do not believe in Jesus. (Acts.18)

Justus (Acts.1:22-26) many of its meanings are used again 'he mediates/makes middle/centres/centred' 'centre of house/makes/builds centre of house' 'mediator/builder/person-in-charge of building' are used as the house of Justus is connected to the synagogue showing how the house and synagogue are connected not only as a building but also reinforces the symbolisation that the people in the house follow God's ways, and are connected the same way as the house to the synagogue as it allows the easy access, conversion and mediation of converting the people in the synagogue to Christianity; 'intervenes/witnesses/assists' 'he quickly sticks to/against' as many people believe and are baptised; 'lived it/lived-him/it' as Paul lives with them for a year and a half; 'he clings/sticks to' 'he swoops down on' 'he lays hands on/harms' as God asks Paul to be bolder in his preachings and that God will not allow anyone to harm Paul, but Paul is arrested. (Acts.18)

Crispus; Krispos; قرِص بُه ، قرِصبوه 'partially washed/cleaned' and means when something, e.g. a hem of a dress or specific stain on the skirt of a dress, is folded and only that soiled part washed quickly (whether the person removes it or does not need to remove it to wash the soiled part)—here it means only some people believed and so only some were made 'clean' and only some were cleansed of their sins and impurities by baptism and belief; 'by/with cake/circle of bread' as they are believing in Jesus (ate/broke bread) who is Christ (cake/circle of bread). Cp: qri<u>ss</u>-boh, qri<u>ss</u>booh. (Acts.18)

Corinthians; Korínthiōn; خورينثيون 'both male and female (at the same time)' 'they are both male and female(in one)'and although it means a male and female in one, or behaving/looking like the gender of the opposite sex, here it is about making the people (the Gentiles) in the synagogue into Christians (and maybe it means turning a Jew into a Christian and a Greek into a Christian, but that would be putting modern interpretations onto the Biblical stories whereas 'Jew' 'Greek' and 'Gentile' are used as word-names and meanings and do not necessarily mean Jewish/Jew, or Greek, or Gentile, as we understand it today to mean people who follow the Jewish faith, a person of Greek ethnicity, and a 'foreigner' respectively, because that is not how these words were used nor intended by the Biblical authors). But what it is doing is showing the 'Gentile' ethnē; يثني ، اثني 'he does it again/twice/doubles it/folds it/repeats it' 'he dissuades/ makes leave' 'he is an idolaters/pagan' 'idols' 'he praises' 'idol worshippers' 'idolatry/worshipping idols', and 'I will mislead to their downfall' following God's ways which is against the 'gentiles' nature as according to the Biblical stories and how and why they created this compound word as a name.

The meanings of Corinthian; قورينتيون 'linked to him/linked him' 'linked them/him' 'linked him with wood/rope' as they are linked by Paul having access to a building which links these people together, and those that convert end up being linked by the new religion, and Paul is leading them like a bull is tied with a rope around his horns/neck and led in the right direction; 'read to him/taught him' as Paul achieves this through teaching/preaching the new religion; 'stopped him/it moving/fidgeting' 'made him stop what he was doing' as God makes Paul stop his constant travels and stay for a long time in this place. Cp: <u>kh</u>ooreenfyoon, qooreentyoon. (Acts.18)

Gallio; Gallíōn; جَلّيون ، جَلّييون 'they made clear/clarified/purified' 'they cleared/clarified/purified' 'they are clear' 'they came to' 'they came for'; غَلّيون ، غَلّييون 'of rushing river(s)/stream(s)/of flowing' 'of deep hatred/of despise' 'they are despised/they despise' 'of stabbing/stabbing deep' 'of digging deep into' 'digging deep into' and the 'despise/stabbing/digging deep' carry the meaning of vengeance or action will be taken. All meanings are reflected: the 'Jews' act against Paul and Paul's activities which are about water/semen-related activities, they come for him and bring him to the deputy of 'Achaia'; they make it clear he is disobeying the law; Gallio makes it clear to them that he will not hear the case against Paul, but his dialogue and the narration that he 'drives them' from the 'judgement seat' and does nothing when 'Greeks' attack, this indicates he despises the 'Jews' and the meaning of the word-name 'they cleared' applies here too. It is equivalent to Gilgal (Josh.5:2-9), Galilee (Josh.20:7), Gallim (1Sam.25:44), Galal (1Chr.9:15). Cp: galleeoon, galleeyoon, <u>gh</u>alleeoon, <u>gh</u>alleeyoon. (Acts.18)

Achaia; Achaía; اغَيي 'I mislead him/them to downfall/I will mislead him/them to his/their downfall' 'his misleading to downfall' 'I deceive him/them/I will deceive'; اعَيي 'I make him/them howl' 'I will make him/them howl' 'I warn/teach him/them' 'I will contain him/it'. It is the same meaning as the word 'Greek' as used in the OT and NT, and the same root word used for 'Gentile' in the OT. 'Greek' 'Grecian'

'Greece' 'Achaia' all have great significance in what they tell about the culture of the people who wrote the Bible (OT and NT), it is also a very telling and significant proof to what has happened to what is called 'history'; the meanings and significance will be discussed later in this book.

The meanings are reflected in that Paul is being accused of deceiving and misleading people away from God and the law; Gallio is accusing the 'Jews' of being deceitful and misleading which causes an attack on the 'chief ruler of the synagogue'. Cp: a<u>gh</u>a<u>ee</u>ya, a'a<u>ee</u>ya.

Greek; hellēnes; حيلّينيه 'purified/circumcised/made clean him/her/it' 'of purification/edibility/cleanliness/circumcision' 'declared permissible/edible' 'undressed her/him/it' 'of undressing' 'deceived/tricked him/her/it' 'of deceit/tricks' 'beat severely/beat until skin peeled off him/it' 'of beating/being beaten severely' 'shed its skin/hair/leaves/etc. him/it' 'of shedding skin/hair/leaves' 'replaced him/it' 'of replacing' 'sweet/sweetened him/it' 'of sweetness/sweetening'; it is used to show 'howling' 'misled to downfall' 'allowed' 'undressed/beat until skin peeled off' as the 'Greeks' attack Sosthenes and Gallio allows them to get away with it. (Acts.18:17)

Sosthenes; Sōsthénēs; سوشذينيه ، سوشذانيه ، سوش ذينيه ، سوش ذانيه 'bad/evil/offense-will/did harm him/them' 'bad/evil/offense-called out/called out to gather assembly' 'did/caused/made-will/did harm him/them' 'offense/bad/evil-gave permission' 'did cause/made/bad/evil/offense-gave ear to/heard him/them'; سوشثينيه ، سوشثانيه ، سوش ثينيه ، سوش ثانيه 'bad/evil/offense-again/did it again/twice/the second(one)' 'did/caused/made-again/twice/to the other or second(one)'. All the meanings are reflected: the people have gathered to harm Paul; this is the second time in the chapter where Paul has a big disagreement with the locals; they are calling for him to be tried and punished; they find Paul and his preaching offensive and bad; instead Gallio treats Paul with indifference and channels offense and hatred towards the locals; Gallio refuses to hear any complaint about Paul; Sosthenes is harmed in a physical assault by 'Greeks'; in neither preventing nor condemning the assault against Sosthenes, Gallio has in effect given permission for the assault which his speech directed at the 'Jews' instigates in the first place. Cp: soo<u>sh</u>veineyh, soo<u>sh</u>vaneyh, soo<u>sh</u>-veineyh, soo<u>sh</u>-vaneyh, soo<u>sh</u>feineyh, soo<u>sh</u>faneyh, soo<u>sh</u>-feineyh, soo<u>sh</u>-faneyh. (Acts.18:11-17)

Cenchrea; Kenchreaí; كَن قريعي 'he was (with) bald/shaved/uncovered head/hair' 'he was tapping/making tapping noise' 'he was having/he had breakfast' 'it was my breakfast' 'it was unripe' 'was dates(a specific type of date fruit named 'unripe because they are picked and eaten unripe and can ripen and be eaten after picking)'; قَن قريعي 'held head high/perky-bald/shaved/uncovered head/hair' 'carried perky-breakfast/my breakfast' 'carried dates(fruit)'. It is directly narrated that Paul had shaved his head at this fittingly named place; the word can mean uncovered hair or head (or hat/veil/scarf/turban/shawl) or shaved of its hair. Equivalent to En-hakkore (Judg.16:18-19) Cp: ken-qry'ee, qen-qry'ee. (Acts.18:18)

Ephesus; Éphesos; افيصوه ، افِصُه 'disentangle/untie (him/it)' 'disentangle knots or problems/matters(it/him)' 'separate it/him' 'break down into small and understandable pieces(it/him)' 'explain/break down into detail(it/him)' 'small seeds/stone of fruit' 'pit/remove seed/stones from fruit' 'divorce/separate from wife(him)' 'small gem like stones used in jewellery/clothes'; افيسوه ، افِسُه 'pass wind in him' 'make it/him break wind' can mean literally or to beat up or scare, 'copulate/pass wind into' the latter word is used to describe chicken copulation; عفيصوه ، عِفصُه 'twisted/crumpled it' 'twisted/crumpled-he/him' 'made a mess of it/him'; افيزوه ، افِزُه 'provoked/provoked him/it'. The meanings of 'separating' as distance are shown as Paul separates from Aquila and Priscilla at this place, and then separates from Ephesus, emphasised by the locals asking him to stay but Paul responding he has to leave but will return.

The 'breaking down and explaining in detail' is in the 'reasoned with the Jews'; in Priscilla and Aquila using the meanings of their word-names in explaining God's way to Apollos which allows him in turn to explain it better when he teaches and preaches. The 'messed up/crumpled/twisted' meanings are in that Apollos is 'fervent' (but is made more rational by Aquila and Priscilla word-meanings and characters) and the narration has him only understand through a limited way 'knowing only the baptism of John' but Aquila and Priscilla meanings allow him to become better and more knowledgeable. It is indicated that the way Apollo was teaching/preaching caused Priscilla and Aquilla to fear he would provoke a negative response which causes them to take him in 'and expounded unto him the way of God more perfectly.' Which enables him to be recommended and planted elsewhere to teach in detail and spread the word further. The 'stone/seed of fruit' meanings are in the preaching/teaching of all characters and the conversion of Jews and other locals to Christianity: Paul and Apollos plant seeds/stones of Jesus Christ in people through teaching/preaching, Aquilla and Priscilla do the same with Apollos. Equivalent to Vophsi (Num.13:14), Beth-pazzez (Josh.19:21), Ephes-dammim (1Sam.17), Hephzi-bah (2Kgs.21:1), Aphses

(1Chr.24:15) Cp: ephyssooh, ephyssoh, ephysooh, ephysoh, 'physsooh, 'physsoh, ephyzooh, ephyzoh. (Acts.18:19-28)

Apollos; Apollṓs; ابْلوه ، ابلّوَه 'soak/soaked him/it' 'afflict/afflicted him/it'. He is 'soaked' because before Aquila and Priscilla enlighten him further, all that he knows is from being baptised by John—i.e. ducked under water/soaked with water. Cp: abollooh, abolloah. (Acts.18:24-28)

Alexandria used the same way **Alexandrians** (Acts.6:9) to reflect Stephen going out to preach is like shepherding sheep, and shepherds send their flock on the right path: 'on you/upon you-I will sent it/him out' 'on you/upon you-I will separate him/it' which is mostly used to describe sending off sheep/goats in the right direction towards pastures to graze ('sent him/it out'); and used to describe separating between sheep and goats, whether to sort and separate them to send to different areas, or to separate one or more from the rest of the flock in order to slaughter or sell them. It is used in Acts.18 to show Apollos is shepherding people towards Jesus Christ; that Aquila and Priscilla have shepherded Apollos in a better direction and way of shepherding/preaching/converting people; and Apollos will go on to be a better shepherd of God's flocks. (Acts.18:24-28)

Tyrannus; Týrannos; طيآرَنُّه 'they caused him/it to leave in haste/fly' 'they banished/chased him/it out/away' 'they spilled it'. The meaning of caused to leave is used as when Paul faces opposition he leaves and does not come back, staying two years at the school of a suitably named 'Tyrannus'. Cp: ṭyaarannoh. (Acts.19:8-10)

Sceva; Skeuás; سقِوآه ، سقيوآه 'of markets/pedalling/immoral/lewd' 'exposed as being 'of markets'/lewd' 'watered/given to drink water' 'drove/driven' 'chase/chased'. The seven sons of 'Sceva' are pretending to have Paul's abilities which is derived from pouring Jesus/God's water/semen—'watering'; this results in that they are exposed as immoral imposters and chased away. The 'of markets' is a derogatory term used to insult or describe person(s) as it means people of ill-repute, of immoral character just as the phrases (sooqee/dasooqee/سوقي/دسوقي) 'walks/wanders a lot in markets/pedals a lot at markets' and (bint-sooq/بنت سوق) 'girl/daughter of markets//girl/daughter of pedalling' and although the literal translation means to go a lot to the markets (without need), it actually means they go out a lot, wander around (not necessarily market places) looking for illicit relationships, sex, etc.—the same context has been used for Sceva and his sons in this story. Describing them as exorcists ('drive out' meaning) and also vagabonds implies they wander around and have no fixed place, but the author finds this not enough, so as to emphasise the meaning of 'Sceva/of markets' the story has them leave the house naked and wounded, which is how 'daughters of markets' and 'wanders/walks a lot in markets' are said to be found naked, semi-naked, with skirt lifted, caught in act of illicit sex, their reputations wounded. Cp: sqewaah, sqywaah. (Acts.19:13-16)

Erastus; Érastos; ايرَصتُه ، ييرَصتُه 'yes, stack it/stack/pack' 'he stacked/stacked/packed it' 'made it in a row'; عرَسِتُه ، عيرَستُه 'his bride/his wedding'; غرَستُه ، غيرستُه 'planted it' 'stuck it in mud/fell into/stuck out of mud/soil'; غرَزتُه ، غيرَزتُه 'plaited it' 'got stuck in mud/soil/sand' e.g. the way an animal and/or cart get stuck in deep sand, soil or mud and cannot easily get out (or car in modernity). It reflects the books that were piled and burned but also the 'curious arts' which is connected to these books is sorcery, calculation i.e. witchcraft which uses books and also the plaiting and/or knotting of hair, string and other fibres; the price of the burnt books; the character of the same name is support for Paul and Timotheus so he is their 'stack/row'; that he is Timotheus' new partner; it reflects Paul staying in Asia. Cp: eiyrasstoh, yeiresstoh, 'rastoh, 'eirastoh, ghrastoh, gheirastoh, ghraztoh, gheiraztoh. (Acts.19:17-22)

Demetrius; Dēmḗtrios; ذي ميثَريُه 'she/this is enriching him/it' and refers to Demetrius and silversmiths becoming rich/making profits from selling silver shrines for 'Diana'; تيميذَريُه 'she/they/it leaves him/it' 'she/they/it let it/him go'. Cp: vey-meeyfrioh, vey-meeyvrioh. (Acts.19:23-41)

Diana; Ártemis; آرتمِه ، آرتميه 'was thrown/thrown down' 'threw down headlong' 'was killed/was wounded' 'collapse/collapsed' 'saw water/she showed him water/saw his water' 'quenched/she quenched-water/his water' 'was watered/was quenched-with water/his water'. It is reflected in Demetrius' dialogue that Paul converting people to a different religion will bring around the destruction of 'Diana/artemis' worship, her shrines, her status and reputation, as well as referring to how Paul converts people with water/semen; it is relayed in her image being described as falling down from Jupiter, the latter verse also connects the word-name meaning, the idea behind the story of such a deity to the meanings of Jupiter (see Jupiter (Acts.14:8-18)) and its meanings of 'it is her' 'ablution' and their connection to the word-names and also fictional stories of the NT and Jesus-water/sperm. Cp: aartemih, aartemyh. (Acts.19:24-41)

Gaius; Gáïos; غآيُه ، غآييوه 'his misleading to downfall/his deceit to downfall' 'they misled him to his downfall/they deceived him to his downfall'; عآيُه ، عآييوه 'made him howl' 'make him howl' 'learn and remember him/it' 'warn him/warned/taught him' 'they warned/taught him' 'beware of him/it' 'contained/prevented him/it'. It is reflected in Demetrius warning the people what will happen if Paul continues to convert people; they see Paul as misleading them towards downfall and are warning of his influence; it is in disciples preventing and warning Paul from entering the place of assembly as they know he will only make matters worse because in all his stories although he tries to teach, he manages to provoke; the assembled people are also described as being led around as they do not seem to know what they are doing. Gaius, although a different word-name, is meant to be Timotheus' equivalent as Timotheus and Erastus have been sent to Macedonia, but are symbolised in 'Gaius and Aristarchus' who are now also 'Paul's companions' and 'men from Macedonia'; it is part of the NT authors' intricate wordplay and coded messages that Paul, Demetrius and other characters are misleading people to downfall; there is also the meaning of 'Gaius' contained him/it' as Timotheus becomes a receptacle and vessel of God/Jesus' water through Paul. Equivalent to Aiah (2Sam.3:7-10). Cp: ghaayeeoh, ghaayeeooh, 'aayeeoh, 'aayeeooh. (Acts.19:29-32)

Aristarchus; Arístarchos; اريص تَرخُه ، ارييص تَرخوه 'stack/pack-loosen/immoral-him/it' 'stacked/packed-loosened/are immoral-him/it' 'put in a row-loosen/loosened/immoral/are immoral-him it'; عريس تَرخُه ، عرييس تَرخوه 'bridegroom/his wedding-loosen/immoral' 'married-immoral/loosened-him/it'; غريس تَرخُه ، غرييس تَرخوه 'planted/plant it-immoral/loosened it/him' 'stuck/stick it in mud/fall/fell into/sticking/stuck out of mud/soil-loosened/immoral-it/him'; غريزتَرخُه ، غرييزتَرخوه 'plaited-immoral/loosened-it/him' 'got stuck/stick in mud/soil/sand-loosened/immoral-it/him' (the way animal and/or carts get stuck in deep sand, soil or mud and cannot easily get out (or car in modernity)); اري/اريي شتَرخُه ، اري/اريي شتَرخوه 'see/show/saw/taught-you/it will be loosened/split open/cracked/muscles loosened' 'water/give to drink-you/it will be loosened/split open/cracked/muscles loosened'; اري/اريي شتَرحُه ، اري/اريي شتَرحوه 'see/show/saw/taught-you will rest/be relieved/relaxed' 'see/show/saw/taught-you will make rest/relieve/relax' 'see/show/saw/taught-you will be split wide open/torn with long, wide gash/explain long and in detail'; عري/عريي شتَرخُه ، عري/عريي شتَرخوه 'strip naked/was naked/was stripped naked-you/it will be loosened/split open/cracked/muscles loosened'; عري/عريي شتَرحُه ، عري/عريي شتَرحوه 'strip naked/was naked/was stripped naked-you will rest/be relieved/relaxed' 'strip naked/was naked/was stripped naked-you will make rest/relieve/relax' 'strip naked/was naked/was stripped naked-you will be split wide open/torn with long, wide gash/explain long and in detail'.

The words (Ari/Arí) for 'see, etc./water/strip naked/was naked' is in both singular and plural, as is the second half of the compound word referring to plural (at least two) individuals doing the action or having this action applied to them.

Most meanings are reflected: they are deemed immoral and fallen because of their association to Paul and his activities, plus Aristarchus is the same as 'Erastus' in character as well as in many wordplay meanings as Erastus was Paul's travel companion who along with Timotheus was sent to Macedonia, and Aristarchus symbolises him as the latter is from Macedonia and also Paul's travel companion; he has fallen into a problem, arrested and caught by an angry crowd (fallen/stuck in mud and stacked/packed meanings) accusing him of being part of Paul's offences against the locals; he is morally loose/immoral as per the angry crowds views of Paul and their projection in the stories; he and his friend Gaius are loosed/let go by the intervention of another character; as he is Paul's travelling companion, he is being watered and spreading water, and the sexual activity implications is intentional by the author of Acts as that is how the authors of the Gospels and other NT stories have Jesus/God's water pass between men and especially apostles/disciples. Paul wants to go in to explain, but as he is prevented, and Gaius and Aristarchos are captured instead to be prosecuted and therefore to provide explanations. Cp: areess-tarkhoh, aryeess-tarkhooh, 'rees-tarkhoh, 'ryees-tarkhooh, ghrees-tarkhoh, ghryees-tarkhooh, ghreez-tarkhoh, ghryeez-tarkhooh, aree/areey-shtarkhoh/shtarkhooh, aree/areey-shtarḥoh/shtarḥooh, 'ree/'reey-shtarkhoh/shtarkhooh, 'ree/'reey-shtarḥoh/shtarḥooh. (Acts.19:29-41)

Alexander (Mark.15:21) has been used for 'on you/upon you-I will send it/him out' 'on you/upon you-I will separate him/it' and this is what happens to the character of his name, he is selected and brought forward to explain matters 'And they drew Alexander out of the multitude, the Jews putting him forward...' and as he is prevented from speaking by the crowd, it remains the only reason this compound-word and character was used to show its meaning. But the meanings of his word-name are taken up by an unnamed character (which the author intentionally leaves unnamed so 'Alexander' meanings can apply to it undiluted) of the 'townclerk' who in calming the angry crowd, sets things straight and sends the people away on the right path—just like a shepherd does with his flocks and shown in the 'ander' of 'Alexander/'on you/upon you-I will send it/him out'/'on you/upon you-I will separate him/it''. (Acts.19:33-41)

Sopater of Berea; Sṓpatros; شوبَترُه ، سوبَترُه 'will/I will cut/snap it/him short' 'I will interrupt him/it'; **Berea** 'they passed/went past/surpassed/went beyond' 'they are/were innocent' 'they disowned/distanced from'. This reflects how Paul will cut his travel short to avoid the ambush, and the ambush itself which seeks to cut his life short and how he distances himself from the danger and travels to a different area. Cp: <u>sh</u>oobatroh, soobatroh. (Acts.20:1-12)

Thessalonians (Acts.17:1-16) **Aristarchus** (Acts.19:29-41); both words are reflected in Paul's preaching which purifies converts; the people who receive him are comforted in his presence; Paul offends the Jews with his preaching; he survives the plotted ambush by avoiding it; water is part of preaching; the man who falls is saved from death as Paul brings him back to life and the people are comforted by this too; the people find relief in Paul's message; the split open/muscles loosened meanings are reflected in the breaking of bread (which means has a meal with them) and in the man who falls. (Acts.20:1-12)

Secundus; Sekoúndos; سَقوُن ذُه ، سيقوُن ذوه ، سَقوُنتُه ، سيقوُنتوه 'watered-he/he is' 'they watered-him/it' 'has been driven(away)-he/he is' 'they drove him' 'you water it/him' 'you drove it/him' and is tied to all the meanings of Thessalonians and Aristarchus as water and watering are included in preaching and Paul/disciples' work; سَكوُن ذه ، سيكوُن ذوه ، سَكوُنتُه ، سيكوُنتوه 'calmed-he is' 'calmed/settled him' 'this is his home/residence/where he/it lives' reflected in Eutychus falling asleep lulled by Paul's long speech; the calming of people's stress/grief when he is brought back to life. Cp: seqoun-voh, seiqoun-vooh, seqountoh, seiqountooh, sekoun-voh, seikoun-vooh, sekountoh, seikountooh. (Acts.20:1-12)

Gaius is used for 'learn and remember him/it' 'warn him/warned/taught him' 'beware of him/it' 'contained/prevented him/it' as Paul and the disciples are teaching God's ways; the 'misleading to downfall' meanings are meant because 'Jews' are said to lay in wait to kill him, but also because for the author of Acts it is important to link the word and character 'Gaius' to Macedonia and to Timotheus as the author is pointing out Gaius and Timotheus are one and the same (see Gaius (Acts.19:29-32)); of **Derbe** 'harmed me' 'harm in me'; 'was aware of me' 'made me aware' 'around/surrounds me' 'made me spin/dizzy' as Eutychus falls asleep during Paul's long speech, falls and dies before he is brought back to life; and **Timotheus** for its 'passing/walking/going' 'urine/sperm wiping' meanings as the whole group are passing from area to area, preaching and spreading God's word/water where they go. (Acts.20:1-12)

Asia 'things/matters' 'many/lots of things' 'wants' 'he wanted' 'speaking in whispers' meanings are used as there is a lot of speech and discussion in this story. (Acts.20:1-12)

Tychicus; Tychikós; طيحِخوه ، طيح اخوه 'fell/broke-his brother'; طيحِحوه ، طيح احوه 'fell/broke-healed/cured him' 'fell/broke-made him still/stay' and refers to Eutychus falling and dying from the fall then being brought back to life. Cp: ṭyḥi<u>kh</u>ooh, ṭyḥ-i<u>kh</u>ooh, ṭyḥiḥooh, ṭyḥ-iḥooh. (Acts.20:1-12)

Trophimus; Tróphimos; تروفي مُه 'you see in water' 'quenched in water' 'watered/given to drink water' 'dreamt in water' 'what do you see in it?' 'what do you see' 'what did you dream?' and it still refers to the God/Jesus water/semen powers which cleanse, heal, bring to life. Cp: troo-phi/phy-moh. (Acts.20:1-12)

Eutychus; Eútychos; يوطيحُه 'he breaks it/him' 'he makes it/him fall' 'he drops it/him' and refers to Paul's speech being the reason Eutychus falls and dies and also Paul falling on Eutychus and bringing him back to life. Cp: yuṭyḥoh. (Acts.20:1-12)

Troas for 'watered it/him' 'gave it/him to drink(water)' 'dreamed it/him' 'dreamed' 'told story' as the whole story is about characters who use normal water and God/Jesus' water in their preaching, healing, and miracles. It is combined with **Philippi** 'in his/its core/middle' 'so respond/assist/serve' as these water-based activities reach the core of its recipients and issuers and both the giver and the recipient are 'responding/serving/assisting'. There is another wordplay on these two words which the author has combined with 'unleavened bread': the unleavened bread is related to the old religion which includes and is specifically what would be the Jewish religion, as the NT stories and especially the gospels have Jesus speak against 'the leaven of the Pharisees and Sadducees' where it is made clear the bread is meant to be the story/doctrine/, what the author of Acts is doing is making 'unleavened bread' into 'leavened bread'—bread is leavened by adding something to it which makes it rise or slightly sour, the new religion/Jesus' religion adds something to people and that something is water; when bread is leavened a popular leavened bread is prepared overnight then diluted with water and allowed to rise again and made into savoury pancakes—and the author of Acts is playing on this to show by adding water they have created a different bread/way/religion and because Jesus means 'cold bread/broke bread/ate bread' it is important that the author includes mentioning unleavened bread, water-based word-names, and then 'And upon the first day of the week, when the disciples came together to break bread…' to show how water, bread (the components which make Jesus as a word, character and the events of his story) are included, in a circuit-relay. This also relays with Tychicus and Eutychus. (Acts.20:1-12)

Assos; Ássos; أشّه ، آشّوه 'I/they wanted him/it' 'want/wanted' 'his things/matters' 'chatted/I chat' 'spoke in whispers' as Paul wants them to go ahead of him to Assos and to receive him; although he describes it as being 'bound in the spirit' he wants to go to Jerusalem although he feels something bad may happen to him. (Acts.20:13-38)

Mitylene; Mitylḗnē; مِثيلييني 'they are like me/they are alike' 'they are acting/actors' 'they made example of me' 'the gave examples/sayings'. Reflected in Paul teaching everything and hiding nothing has made all the people (elders of the church/disciples) like him, able to perform what he has done; he warns of people who appear and act like them but will actually teach perverse things, will draw away disciples and teach wrong. Cp: mifyl<u>ei</u>eyney. (Acts.20:13-38)

Chios; Chíos; خيُه ، خيوه 'his brother'; حيُه ، حيوه 'made it/him stay/still/stationary' 'greeted him' 'healed him' 'his modesty'. Reflected in the disciples and people are his brethren; in that he has not differentiated between himself (his own kind), and 'Jews' and 'Greeks'; he stays with them for some time; Paul mentions his own 'humility'. Cp: <u>kh</u>eeoh, <u>kh</u>eeooh, ḥeeoh, ḥeeooh. (Acts.20:13-38)

Samos; Sámos; شاَمُس 'will/I will touch/possess' 'I will entangle with/provoke/cause problems/fights'. It is reflected in that there will be people who will entangle disciples into wrong-doing, false teachings; in the people who wanted to harm Paul in ambushes and the harm he suffered while spreading God's word; Paul speaks of 'I go bound in the spirit to Jerusalem', he feels compelled, controlled to go there; the 'wolves' he knows will harm the converts and/or disciples; the people 'of your own selves' who will harm or cause problems by diverting from the proper ways. Cp: <u>sh</u>aamos. (Acts.20:13-38)

Trogyllium; Trōgýllion; تروجياّليون 'saw/see-they are clearing/cleansing/purifying/making clear' 'saw/see-they are coming to/for' 'saw/see-they are clear/pure/cleansed' 'tell story-they are clearing/cleansing/purifying/making clear' 'tell story-they are coming to/for' 'tell story-they are clear/pure/cleansed' 'watered-they are clearing/cleansing/purifying/making clear' 'watered-they are coming to/for' 'watered-they are clear/pure/cleansed' 'dream/dreamt-they are clearing/cleansing/purifying/making clear' 'dream/dreamt-they are coming to/for' 'dream/dreamt-they are clear/pure/cleansed'. Paul is telling them what has happened to him, and what will happen in the future; he mentions telling the story/gospel of Jesus; he asks them to continue taking care of the flock, cleansing them of impurities and sins; he makes clear all the details: what he has done, what will happen, warning of dangers which will arise, tells them what they should do. Cp: troogyaallyon. (Acts.20:13-38)

Miletus; Mílētos; ميليتُه 'filled it/covered it' 'soiled it/covered it' 'his frock/short shirt' 'you/I filled/covered it' 'filled it with water' 'fetched water'. Reflected in his preaching and converting (as it is the same as fetching water from a well and pouring it into vessels); in his many tears which is covering with water. Cp: meeleytoh. (Acts.20:13-38)

Ephesus 'disentangle/untie (him/it)' 'disentangle knots or problems/matters(it/him)' 'separate it/him' 'break down into small and understandable pieces(it/him)' 'explain/break down into detail(it/him)' 'small seeds/stone of fruit' 'pit/remove seed/stones from fruit' 'divorce/separate from wife(him)' 'small gem like stones used in jewellery/clothes'; 'pass wind in him' 'make it/him break wind' can mean literally or to beat up or scare, 'copulate/pass wind into' the latter word is used to describe chicken copulation; 'twisted/crumpled it' 'twisted/crumpled-he/him' 'made a mess of it/him' 'provoked/provoked him/it' as Paul will detail what he wants to say, and because he will be separated from them and never see them again; because of how he converts people; he speaks of people wanting to harm him. (Acts.20:13 38)

Asia has been used for 'things/matters' 'many/lots of things' 'wants' 'he wanted' 'speaking in whispers' 'snitching' 'disobeyed/disobedient/went against' 'disobeyed him/went against him' 'became askew/bent/crooked/warped' 'sticks' 'used sticks' 'sorrow' 'bad/offense/insult' 'bad towards/offense/insult towards'. He speaks to the people about many important things which includes disobedience; people who will warp things from their correct meanings and ways, who will go against what is God's ways; sorrow between Paul and the people who will not see each other again. (Acts.20:13-38)

Coos is the same as **Cush** (Gen.10:6): Kṓs; قوش ، قوآش 'blow away litter/fibres/burnt remnants' 'remove completely in one swipe or scrape' 'of blowing away litter/removing completely in one swipe/scrape/go' 'litter/fibres/burnt remnants'; قوص ، قوآص 'tell a story' 'cut' 'became hard' 'became hardened/heart hardened' 'cruel/was cruel'. It describes the ships load being removed; the warning that Paul will be harmed if he goes to Jerusalem; Agabus warning of the same but telling it like a story. Cp: qoosh, qoaash, qooss, qoaass. (Acts.21:1)

Rhodes; Rhódos; رودُه 'return him/it' 'reply to him' 'his reply'; روضه 'agreed/with his permission' 'his joy/happiness/content' 'were/was convinced'. More than one character is convinced that Paul should not go to Jerusalem and attempt to get him to go back; they have responses for him, he is not convinced and gives his own replies; there is joy/content when he meets with other disciples and welcoming people who allow him to stay with them. Cp: roodoh, roodhoh. (Acts.21:1-7)

Patara; Pátara; باتَر 'cut (it) short/snapped it' 'made (it) stub/short' 'cut him/it short' 'abruptly cut off' 'snapped /cut short' 'stub of rock/smooth rock' as different characters in the story attempt to cut short Paul's travel and to convince him to return and not go to Jerusalem; Paul's reply cuts their request short. Cp: baatara. (Acts.21:1-14)

Phenicia 'so he saves/delivers to safety him/them/it' has been chosen as a ship has been found to safely transport them; the disciples who deliver a message from 'the Spirit' want Paul to be safe which is why they warn him not to go to Jerusalem, the same for the other characters; also for 'so he chooses/selects' 'will choose/select' 'so he picks out impurities/clears/cleans' 'will pick out impurities/clear/clean' 'will save him/them/it' 'so he will talk/discuss secretly-he/him/them' as the 'Spirit' chooses to relay a message through the other disciples to Paul instead of directly to Paul; 'so hurt/poke wound' 'so hurt/offend' 'will hurt/poke wound' 'will hurt/offend' 'so have sex with' 'will have sex with' as the warnings are Paul will be hurt at Jerusalem; these warnings seem to offend Paul as he is zealous to spread God/Jesus' gospel no matter the threat it poses to him personally. (Acts.21:2-14)

Cyprus 'a lot/became a lot' 'many/became many/multiplied' 'see, increased/multiplied it' 'try to increase/multiply it'. **Cyprus** has been used for 'many/a lot' and refers to the many loads carried by the ship which are unloaded at the suitably-named **Syria** 'to throw/to do with throwing' before what or who is left on the ship also arrives at the suitably-named **Tyre** 'left over food' 'left over anything/second-hand (things); Cyprus is also reflected in the many warnings he receives not to go to Jerusalem; 'disbelieved(in God or religion or the person)' 'they became disbelievers' 'disbelieved him' as the warnings mean people will not believe him or God's message of the gospels; Paul does not believe or is not convinced in their warnings, and even if he believes the threat he does not believe he should not go to Jerusalem. (Acts.21:3-14)

Ptolemais; Ptolemaïs; بطُلِمَييه ، بطلي مَييه 'bad/evil/wrong-his water/of water' 'of bad/evil/wrong' 'stop/cease-his water/of water' 'of ceasing/stopping' 'hero-his water/of water' 'of heroism/fighting (and winning)' 'heroes-one hundred' 'will cover/paint/slather-his water/watery' 'of covering/painting/slathering' 'will beat-one hundred/his water' 'of beating(severely)' 'will be early-he/him' 'of being early' 'suddenly appeared-he/him' 'of suddenly appearing'; بتلِمَييه ، بتُليمَي يه 'will gather/collect-him/it' 'of gathering/collecting' 'will till the ground' 'of tilling(ground)' 'will till the ground-he/him' 'will blame-him/he' 'of blaming' 'will carry water' 'will carry water-him/he' 'of carrying water'. First half of compound word is equivalent to Bethel (OT).

It is used to show there is a gathering of disciples as Paul meets them on the way; in the many disciples, including Paul, who carry God/Jesus' water and message; in the evil/bad disciples; in the Spirit and Agabus warn Paul of what will befall him; in these disciples who carry Jesus' water asking Paul who also carries water to call off going to Jerusalem; there is not 'blame' but a kind of reproach by Paul towards the disciples and other characters for wanting him to stop spreading Jesus' word/water in Jerusalem; Cp: bṭolemayeeh, bṭoly-mayeeh, btolemayeeh, btolymy-eeh. (Acts.21:7-14)

Philip the evangelist: **Philip** still means 'in its core/pulp' 'pick out/cleanse/remove it' and because they are talking about virgin daughters the meaning of 'evangelical/evangelist' (explained earlier under Mark/Evangel) can be seen that as virgins they are clean and pure to their core, allowing them to prophesy: 'evangelist' means 'they become clear/clarify' 'they make clear/clarify' 'they purify/sanitise' 'if they make clear/clarify' 'if they become clear/clarify' 'if they purify/sanitise' 'if they are clear/clarified/pure/sanitised' 'if they become pure'.

It further proves the meaning of 'evangel/evangelical': having Philip the evangelist daughters prophesy means they deliver and make clear the message (from God); the reason we are told they are virgins is to enhance the mean (gl/جل) 'clear/pure/sanitised' with their virginity symbolising purity, cleanliness and clarification. If we look at the words of the same language (Arabic) and how it is related to the Bible, the Arabic word for the Christian/NT Bible is (ingeel/انجيل) 'makes/made clear/clarified' 'if it makes clear/

clarifies'. 'Evangelists' are not what it has come to mean today of zealous or fanatical people who preach the Bible with great zeal (but it is still in what they attempt to do even if they do not know the meaning of the word, and do not interpret the Biblical stories as they are meant by the original authors) but as above means 'becomes clear/they make clear/clarify' and is meant originally people who preach and explain Jesus/ God's way/religion, i.e. stories and people who tell these stories to make the ways, religions, message, its prophets' actions clear to others.

The same can be seen in the word 'angel' which although academics will tell you is a Greek word, is in fact an entirely Arabic word and in origin from the same root word (gl/جل) of Galilee, Gilgal, etc.: ángelos; أنجيله ، أنجِلَه 'made/became clear/pure/cleansed/clarified/they made it clear' from (angel/انجِل) 'became clear'. Angels are believed to be beings whose main purpose in most stories, beliefs and the three divine books (Torah, Christian Bible, Quran) has been to deliver messages to humans, to make clear messages, to make clear what is to happen or why it is to happen. In many instances the stories of angels delivering messages include the angels being asked (by the recipient of the message) for clarifications, which the angel always gives (e.g. see Mary and Gabriel, Daniel and Gabriel, Balaam and the angel) and explains making the message even more clear to the recipient (they sometimes give clear instructions to the human of what to do or what they are supposed to do). The same root word has all these meanings in rural Yemen and e.g. is the verb to sanitise vessels (on heat) used in collecting milk, butter and other dairy products. (Acts.21:8-9)

Agabus is used the same way as (Acts.11:27-28) 'a wonder' 'his wonder' 'miming/acting/playing/ entertaining' 'what a wonder' 'what a puzzling act/action/statement' 'his miming/acting/playing' as this time Agabus enacts and narrates along with the acting what will happen to Paul, and is still a 'wonder' because he precisely predicts it: 'And as we tarried there many days, there came down from Judaea a certain prophet, named Agabus. And when he was come unto us, he took Paul's girdle, and bound his own hands and feet, and said, Thus saith the Holy Ghost, So shall the Jews bind the man that owneth this girdle, and shall deliver *him* into the hands of the Gentiles.'. (Acts.21:10-11)

What Acts also does is recreate a character to take both Jesus and the original twelve disciples' place and status. The author(s) gives Paul the Jesus-like sufferings and powers/miracles, he is both Jesus and the disciples; the author attributes sufferings and persecutions similar to Jesus: he is a local who the other locals want to kill because of his new religion; it is the Jews who want him dead and arrest him, then foreigners who hear his case, and just like with Jesus it is the Jews who want him dead and the foreigners who find him innocent. To avoid a repeat crucifixion, the author has Jews stone Paul to death who comes back to life—so like Jesus he is resurrected. The 'special numbers' attributed to Paul in the storyline of Acts also imbue him with the status and importance of Moses. There is emphasis on how much this character suffers for God and mankind—just as Jesus was made to suffer for the same purpose. Paul goes from place to place, country to country exceeding while mimicking Jesus' travels and preaching. Most of his miracles replicate Jesus' miracles: he tells a crippled man to be healed and it is done; he brings the dead back to life; he does not have to actively heal people, but just like the woman who healed her haemorrhage by merely touching Jesus' clothes, Acts has people being healed by receiving handkerchiefs and garments which have been in contact with Paul's body; he can identify possessed people and expel demons/devils by merely commanding them.

Maybe the author of Acts felt that the Gospels, the Jesus stories, did not end strongly enough; maybe he felt a new character was needed to inject life back into them as the Gospels do end in a lukewarm and loose, almost sad and desperate way so he created Paul to give the Jesus story the vigour it needed to continue. (Acts)

Caesarea is used for 'broke it' 'keep secret' 'short is he/they' 'shortened/shortcoming/failed to complete or obey' reflected in Paul asking them not to break his heart about going to Jerusalem and doing God's will; in the disciples/brethren asking Paul to keep secret the things he states about the Gentiles not needing circumcision which the people/Jews who believe in Moses and Moses' law will find as shortcomings and breaking the law; it is reflected in Paul being asked to purify himself and to shave men (cut their hair short) who have made a vow to show Paul himself is complying with Moses' law and not failing to obey it. (Acts.21:16-26)

Mnason of Cyprus; Mnásōn; مناسون 'made him forget' 'they are forgetful/of forgetting'; من عصون 'from disobedience/difficulty' 'from sticks' 'from stubbornness' 'from warped/bent/askew/curved' 'who did they disobey/who disobeyed' 'listed/counted-disobeyed/disobedience/difficulty' 'who-stuck/became askew/

bent/warped/difficult'; مناصون 'with widow's peak/with forelock(extra tuft of hair top of forehead more prominent than rest of hairline)'.

Chosen as compound words for the disciple who will give lodging for Paul and his companions, so that his word-name meanings can reflect **Cyprus**/'disbelieved(in God or religion or the person)' 'they became disbelievers' 'disbelieved him'. 'see, increased/multiplied it' 'a lot/became a lot' 'buried it/him' 'many burials/graves' 'his grave(s)': it is mentioned Paul has been able to convert many Jews to Christianity; and coupled with the meanings of 'Mnason' it is mentioned his statements and beliefs about circumcision will cause many to find him breaking the laws of God by disbelieving and doing actions which are disobedience which the disciples fear will lead to him being harmed and eventually does cause his life to be endangered; his actions will be found warping religion and beliefs; the way they want to hide/bury Paul's beliefs to avoid him being mobbed is that he shaves the hair of men who made a vow which is why 'forelock' has been used; as the narration will mention '**Israel**/twisted muscle-the' and the issue is over circumcision—disobedience and specifically around the male genital reflects these meanings too; Paul's good deeds and also the difficulties he has raised are listed; in making him take part in purification and also the purification of others, they are trying to make the Jews forget Paul's disobedience/difficulties/stubbornness in what he preaches and believes. Cp: mnaasoon, mn-'ssoon, mnaassoon. (Acts.21:16-29)

James 'he/it pinches' 'he quotes/states' 'he pokes finger into' 'he pokes finger into anus' (sexually or as a prank over clothing) 'he pokes fingers into food/he pollutes food by poking fingers into it' 'he makes a mess(by dipping/poking here and there)' as although the people listen and praise Paul's achievements, they also point out his provocations of the Jews which they prefer to keep quiet (exemplified in they have already sent a letter to the Gentiles that they do not need to be circumcised so there is no need for Paul to broadcast this belief); they do not want a mess from Paul antagonising Jews, but he manages to have already done that through his many and extensive preaching and provocation of people throughout his travels in the areas within storyland. Not only do his antagonists seek to kill him, but the whole city is in a riotous mess over Paul which reaches the 'chief captain of the band' and the mention of Paul bringing in 'Trophimus an Ephesian' into the temple indicates the offended people believe Paul committed sexual acts in the temple which goes against the 'Jewish/old religion' as these homosexual acts are first an 'abomination' according to the OT, but also the temple has been polluted by this act (people have to be purified even from sex with wife in the OT before performing specific rituals), but these same homosexual acts as presented in the NT are seen as 'purification' by the new religion/Christian, and explains why there is such anger towards Paul as intended by the author of Acts. Trophimus: 'you see in water' 'quenched in water' 'watered/given to drink water' 'what do you see in it?' 'what do you see'; and Ephesian: 'pass wind in him' 'make him break wind' can mean literally or to beat up or scare, 'copulate/pass wind into' the latter word is used to describe chicken copulation, and are used because Paul and Trophimus have been seen having sex in the Temple, and 'Ephesus/Ephesian' is how a cockerel is described as copulating a hen as it seems to be through the anus.

The meanings of '**Ptolemais**' (see Ptolemais) are also used here (and the meanings of **Phenice**): a centurion and his soldiers come to calm the uproar which Paul and his water/semen activities have caused; Paul is being beaten and blamed for the evil/bad he has done or is believed to have done inside the temple; the people are preventing Paul from carrying on with this bad activity related to water/semen and from carrying on with his actions inside the temple; the soldiers are the reason the people stop beating Paul; Paul is collected from the temple and the meaning of 'will gather/collect-him/it' 'will carry water-him/he' is emphasised in the soldiers have to carry him in to protect him from the violence he has instigated. (Acts.21:18-36)

Asia (Acts.2:9) is used for all its meanings of 'disobeyed/disobedient/went against' 'disobeyed him/went against him' 'became askew/bent/crooked/warped' 'sticks' 'used sticks' 'sorrow' 'bad/offense/insult' 'bad towards/offense/insult towards' 'things/matters' 'many/lots of things' 'wants' 'he wanted' 'speaking in whispers' 'snitching' as Paul is being assaulted as a result of his offending statements and teachings which are viewed as disobedience of God and Moses' laws and his views on these matters have become known because people who were in 'Asia' have informed the local people of what he has said about these important matters. (Acts.21:27-32)

Tarsus used for 'deaf/became deaf' 'went into a stupor' 'scared into stupor/unable to respond, hear, speak' 'pretended not to hear/pretended to be deaf' as although the narration has the crowds so violent the soldiers can barely protect Paul, once Paul (or the author) mentions 'Tarsus' everybody hushes into 'a great silence', but also because Paul completely ignores the chief captain's question if Paul had just recently caused an uproar when he led 'into the wilderness four thousand murderers'; **Cilicia** used for 'all of it-he/him' 'worried-him/he/it' as the chief captain is worried by Paul's possible disruption wherever he goes; and all the people hush up once Paul gestures with his hand. (Acts.21:37-40)

Gamaliel 'came-fetch water-the' came-instructed-the' 'came-told them what to say-the' 'came wearing frock'. Reflected in that he was brought up by Gamaliel; instructed/educated in the law; when he speaks they are already silent, but the author emphasised they become even more silent so he is telling 'what's-what' and they are listening; 'came wearing frock' reminds the audience (both Paul's audience and the real audience listening to Acts.22) that Paul was introduced as Saul when people who witness (and may have participated) in the killing of converts removed their clothes and laid it at Saul/Paul's feet, and the narration of Acts.22 also reminds as does this reference to the story that Saul/Paul also fanatically persecuted Christians. (Acts.22:1-5)

Ananias (Acts.5:1-11) 'we will direct words/speech at him' 'we mean him' 'we will eye/look/inspect him'; 'we will make he/him independent/rich' 'we will make him no longer need(someone else's help/dependence)'; 'felt affection-he/him'; 'betrays-he/him' 'soaks/soaks in-he/him' 'satisfaction to/satisfied-him/he' 'give plenty-he/him'. Most of the meanings are used as they have been for two other characters of the same name in Acts: as Paul is being examined; Paul directs words at Ananias because he had someone strike him on the mouth; Paul feigns affection for the priest when he learns he is the high priest; just as he turns his back on what he is originally as his character continues to do so throughout Acts: first he is of the Jewish faith, then Christian, then when he is in a bind he claims to be Roman, then when he is in another difficult situation he claims he is a Jew then he claims he is Roman again—the author elucidates that Paul changes his claim of what he is (Jew, Christian, Roman, etc.) according to what he perceives will get him out of trouble by identifying with the people he fears retribution from or who they fear, love or respect.

Paul constantly betrays what he stands for or believes in: at the end of Chapter 21 and beginning of Chapter 22 Paul claims he is a Jew; by the end of Chapter 22 he claims to be a Roman; at the beginning of Chapter 23, when he sees he can find an opening to escape punishment by appealing to the Pharisees' beliefs he claims to be not only a Pharisee, but a Pharisee through-and-through 'But when Paul perceived that the one part were Sadducees, and the other Pharisees, he cried out in the council, Men and brethren, I am a Pharisee, the son of a Pharisee: of the hope and resurrection of the dead I am called in question.' It is important to understand all these word-names used are not intended by the author as 'Jew' a religion, 'Roman' a nationality, but for their word-meanings and then the pun on how it makes people laugh at how swiftly he moves between religion and religion, ethnicity to ethnicity to whichever gets him out of his current pickle. And as both Sadducees and Pharisees argue and hostilities arise between them Paul no longer needs them, he no longer fears them as he is going to be sent to Rome as a result of the tensions he instigated between them. (Acts.23)

Rome 'were thrown' 'threw' 'killed' 'spread/strewn over vast distance/various locations' 'saw water' 'became rotten/went off/bad smelling' as Paul is now proud of his Christianity, being spoken to by God, the author can now show 'became rotten' as the forty 'Jews' place a curse to neither eat nor drink until they have killed Paul; Paul as he is a carrier of God/Jesus' water/sperm is also reflecting 'bad-smelling' because of 'Paul/his urine' meanings combined with other meanings of Rome 'were thrown' 'saw water' 'strewn over vast distances/locations' as the plotters plan to kill him before he is taken there. (Acts.23)

Claudius Lysias; **Claudios** is still 'placed responsibility on him' 'hung it around his neck' 'hung responsibility around his neck' 'garlanded-he/him' 'placed responsibility/accountability on him/it' 'acted/copied him/it' Lysías; ليشييَه ، ليشيَه 'nothing/absolutely nothing/for nothing' 'disintegrated/fell apart' 'why-he/him' 'for what?' 'for what-he/him?' 'for things/matters' 'for many/lots of things' 'he wants something' 'he wanted something for him' 'for speaking in whispers' 'for snitching'; ليسييَه ، ليسيَه 'for offending/insulting' 'for bad towards/offense/insult towards' 'for his bad' 'no bad/did no bad/insult' 'for what he did/made'. Together Claudius Lysias word-name reads 'placed responsibility/accountability around his neck-for nothing/for what he did' and all the meanings above are reflected: the adversaries of Paul plot against him (murder); Paul's nephew is speaking secretly to Paul and the chief captain informing of the plot that the people will pretend they want to ask Paul about a specific matter but intend to kill him; that there is nothing to hold against Paul for any kind of punishment as he just questioned the laws of his adversaries causing them to be offended; the chief captain will not carry responsibility of convicting or punishing an innocent person but will refer it to the governor. Cp: qlaudyoh, ly<u>sh</u>eeyah, ly<u>sh</u>eeah, lyseeyah, lyseeah. (Acts.23:

Felix; Phélix; فييِلقص ، فيآلِقص 'so he will tell a story' 'so tell the story' 'so he will crack pit/stone open' (such as done to a fruit-stone which contains edible seed). The chief captain's letter is telling the story to the governor Felix; referring the case is so Felix can also hear the story, from both sides. Cp: pheyeiliqss, pheyaaliqss. (Acts.23:25-30)

Antipatris; Antipatrís; انتِبَتريه ، انتِبَترييه 'you decide(it)' 'you will see him/it' 'you cut/snap it/him short' 'his/its stub/shortness' 'you abruptly cut off-him/he/it' 'you have snapped him/it/cut him/it short' the meanings still imply 'short/abrupt/quick/a stub/interrupted' as well as 'decide' and decision-making meanings supported by the text. Paul stops at this place on his way to be sent to Felix who will hear and decide on the matter, the journey itself is interrupted as he stops at this place before being sent the next morning to the governor. Cp: anti-batreeh, anti-batreeyh. (Acts.23:31-32)

Tertullus; Tértyllos; تيرتيلُّه ، تَرتيلُّه 'his oration' 'he orated' 'recited off-by-heart' 'spoke clearly in order'. The very name, meaning and role of this character in the story, from word (trtl/ترتل) to speak from memory, clearly and in order, used in narrating loudly poems, stories, songs, lists, genealogy, religious text. As his name indicates, Tertullus speaks clearly and goes on to orate a list of accusations against Paul. Cp: teirtylloh, tertylloh. (Acts.24:1-9)

Felix is used again to show 'so he will tell a story' 'so tell the story' 'so he will crack pit/stone open' as he insists on learning the truth and will wait for Lysias which means 'for what?' 'for what-he/him?' 'for things/matters' to find out more of the truth and is like getting at the core of a stone to access its hidden seeds. After hearing both sides of the story from Paul and his accusers, Felix requests Paul to tell him the story of the Christian faith; he informs Paul that he will call him to hear more stories when it is convenient; the story goes on to narrate that in hope of receiving a bribe, Felix keeps sending for Paul to speak with him i.e. 'hear' him, more stories as the compound word 'Felix' implies. It is further supported by the compound word-name given to Felix' wife: Drusilla. (Acts.24)

Drucilla; Droúsilla; دروسِلَّ ، دروَسِلَّ ، دروس الّا 'lessons-for her/him' 'taught him/her' 'lessons-it is/yes, it is' 'taught-yes, he did/yes, it is' 'studied matters-her/him' 'studied matters-yes, he did/yes, it is' as both Felix and Drusilla are taught about Christ, religion, right and wrong from Paul. Cp: droosilla, drousilla, droosilla. (Acts.24:24-26)

Porcius Festus; Pórkios; بوركيُه 'kneeling/kneeled-he' 'will lean/prop him/it against' as Porcius is first mentioned when he enters a room, and in the same sentence we are informed Felix has left Paul bound.

Phḗsṭos; فييصطُه ، فيآصطُه 'so he will/so he swoops down on/lay hands on/harms/clings to/sticks to-him'; فييسطُه ، فيآسطُه 'so he mediates/connects-him/so he will mediate/connect-him'; فييزتُه ، فيآزتُه 'so he will/so he provokes-him' 'so he will flit/flee/hide quickly-him' 'so he will slice open/cut-him' 'so he will kill him quickly' 'so he will kill him with quick slit with knife' 'so he flitted/flicked/quickly hid something throwing it into narrow space-him'. Most of these meanings are available in the related narration: Festus replaces Felix and becomes the medium between what the Jews want to do to Paul and Paul's freedom/life as he now oversees the case; Festus quickly flits from place to place; the Jews want Festus to send Paul their way so they can harm and kill him; Festus refuses to send Paul in harm's way without a proper trial; Festus attempts to flick Paul to Jerusalem (where he will be killed if guilty) to be tried if Paul will agree; Festus describes Paul being innocent of any punishment-worthy wrong-doing, but finds the Jews case against him is because he has provoked them about their laws; Festus allows more 'mediums' to hear the case; Festus interrupts Paul's defence with a provocative statement that Paul must have lost his mind. Cp: boorkyoh, pheieyssṭoh, pheyaassṭoh, pheieysṭoh, pheyaasṭoh, pheieyztoh, pheyaaztoh. (Acts.24:27; 25; 26:24)

Caesarea 'broke it-he/they' 'broke it' 'keep secret-he/they' 'keep secret' 'short is he/they' and **Caesar** (Luke.2) 'shortened/shortcoming/failed to complete or obey' 'broke' are still being used for these meanings: Festus has broken up the flow of Felix' actions; Festus spends shorts amounts of time at different places, breaking and going elsewhere even if it is about the same matter; the Jews still secretly want to shorten and break Paul's life and preaching; he finds Paul's accusers fail to provide any proof and Paul's shortcomings are because he has questioned their beliefs; Paul shows he has not fallen short of any laws. (Acts.25)

Augustus 'dove into/sank them/pushed them under/buried them under/immersed them under' and can be into or under liquid, dirt or anything including figuratively 'immersing/burying/sinking under', 'lower the flame/lower the intensity/lower the sound' 'picked/took too many/much/I took too many much' 'took by the handful' 'shook it' 'unsettled it' as used in other stories: Paul's accusers want to bury him with accusations they believe he has committed; Paul is accused of many severe crimes; Festus tries to shake things up by having Paul sent to Jerusalem, by allowing other people to look into the case, and the matter is also shaken up/unsettled because Paul appeals to Caesar which causes more unsettling as he would have been freed had he not made this appeal. (Acts.25)

Agrippa; Agríppas; اغريبَّه ‘finds strange’ ‘strangeness/superstitions’ ‘went over/went over ascent’ ‘went abroad’ ‘strangers’ ‘overflowed’ ‘went over rim/edge’ ‘set(such as sun or planet)/went over/under’ ‘seduce/tempt-him/her’ ‘deceive-him/her’ ‘went west’; اغريفه ‘spoon/ladle-it’ ‘take lots/scoop up lots’ ‘wastes/wastes it’ ‘makes loads/makes money or fortune’ ‘be seduced/tempted in it/her’ ‘be deceived in it/her’; اجريبَّه ‘try it/him/her’ ‘run with it/him/her’ ‘run off with it/him/her’ ‘of chronical skin disease (psoriasis?)’ ‘skin removed/rough/raw/sore(from scratching)’ ‘oasis’ ‘pay wages-him/her’ ‘lease for money-it/him/her’ ‘my reward in him/her/it’; اجريفَّه ‘shovel/scrape/rake it/him/her away’ ‘drag away’ ‘run in/for it/him/her’ ‘my reward in it/him/her’ ‘my wages in it/him/her’; اقريبَّه ‘related to him/her’ ‘near it/him/her’ ‘come closer/bring closer/place closer-it/him/her’ ‘present it/him/her’ ‘serve it/him/her’ ‘admit/confess it/him/her’ ‘decide it/him/her’ ‘read it/him/her’ ‘read with it/him/her’ ‘settle/allow to settle with it/him/her’ ‘water/drink flasks’ ‘gifts’ ‘sacrifices’; اقريفه ‘chip it/chipped it’ ‘read in it/him/her’ ‘admit/confess in it/him/her’ ‘settle/stay still/stop moving in it/him/her’; اكريبَّه ‘depression/gloominess’ ‘depress/sadden/upset/stifle it/him/her’ ‘nag him/her’ ‘rent/lease with it/him/her’ ‘lease/hire it/him/her’ ‘violently chase away-it/him/her’ ‘bury with large/coarse gravel-it/him/her’; اكريفه ‘take up by palmfuls’ ‘take deep inhalations/long sips’ ‘smell deeply-it/him/her’ ‘they smell/inhale deeply’ ‘they take long, deep sips/drinks’ ‘pools/ponds’ ‘their/his/her palms’ ‘scoop with palms’ ‘rent/hire in it/him/her’ ‘eat chives/gather chives/of chives’.

In Acts, some of Agrippa’s possible meanings are used: he arrives from elsewhere so he is a stranger or has returned from abroad (abroad does not necessarily mean a completely different country in the language of the Bible and its creators, but to come from a different village/area); Festus explains to Agrippa and Bernice that he finds the accusations against Paul strange (based on superstitions) without any proof or real accusation, but also strange that Paul would claim a man called Jesus who is believed to be dead is still alive; Festus is sending Paul to be heard at different places and by different people; Agrippa finds the case curious and wants to hear himself, too; the case, and Paul, will be presented before Agrippa in hope he might be able to read/find some kind of confession from Paul so that Festus can have something to write to Augustus; Festus expresses it is strange/unreasonable to send a prisoner without having crimes recorded against him; when Paul explains before Agrippa it is about why should the people find it strange that God can resurrect the dead; Pauls speaks when as ‘Saul’ he made people disappear into prison or through death which is a form of ‘setting/going over’ and the gloom/stifled meanings which he caused the converts; ‘compelled *them* to blaspheme’ is Paul admitting he forced Christians to admit things they did not believe and was against their religion; he mentions pursuing them to ‘strange cities’ and is ‘violently chase away-it/him/her’; it is in Paul wanting Agrippas to confess to being a Christian. Cp: a<u>gh</u>reebbah, a<u>gh</u>ree<u>ph</u>ah, agreebbah, agree<u>ph</u>ah, aqreebbah, aqree<u>ph</u>ah, akreebbah, akree<u>ph</u>ah. (Acts.25-26)

Bernice; Berníkē; بَرنيكي ، بَر نييكي ‘good/piety/innocent-poked wound’ ‘good/piety/innocence-insulted/offended/fucked’; بَر نيجي ، بَر نييجي ‘good/piety/innocence-survived/delivered to safety’ ‘good/piety/innocence-discussed quietly/secretly/discussed between them’ ‘good/piety/innocence-we come’; بَرنيقي ، بَر نييقي ‘good/piety/innocence-chooses/selects’ ‘good/piety/innocence-picks out impurities/clears/cleans’. All meanings are reflected: Festus is discussing the case with Agrippa and Bernice; Paul has offended the Jews; this and previous chapters and the naming of ‘Bernice’ as a character also imply that Paul committed a sexual act in the temple causing even greater offense as it pollutes the temple; in Jesus surviving death by being resurrected and the same applies to resurrection of others; in Paul’s choice of appealing to Caesar; Paul speaks of when he harmed Christians when he was still of the old religion; in Festus finds Paul innocent of the accusations levelled against him and that they did not even bring the expected accusations against him; in Paul proclaiming his innocence of the same; in Paul describing his discussion with Jesus on the road to Damascus; in Jesus telling him he (Paul) had been chosen to deliver God’s message and religion and that he would be delivered safely from those who would attempt to harm him; in that all the people can be delivered safely from harm if they convert to Christianity; and in that Agrippas and his group also find Paul innocent of insulting or any crime towards the Jews, but because Paul has chosen to be heard by Caesar he has to remain imprisoned. Cp: ber-neekey, ber-neeykey, ber-neegey, ber-neeygey, ber-neeqey, ber-neeyqey. (Acts.25:13-27; 26)

Italy (Acts.18:2) has been chosen for its meanings ‘ablution-for/for me’ ‘cleanse for/for me’ ‘he abluted/cleansed for me’ ‘shone for me’ ‘came for me’ ‘he came for me’ ‘obeyed/obedient for me’ ‘will be obedient for me’ because they have to obey the person overseeing their transport, Julius; he has come for them, to take them to their designation; Paul who is ‘cleansed’ is the reason they are allowed to survive the perilous journey; when they obey Julius and/or the ship owner’s orders they risk death, but when they obey Paul they survive. (Acts.27)

Julius; Ioúlios; يوَلّيُه 'he makes him his guardian/in charge of him' 'he is in charge of him' 'he becomes loyal to him'; هوَلّيُه 'he is his guardian' 'he is in charge of him' 'he is loyal to him'; جوَلّيُه 'walked him around' 'let him go wandering' 'walked/wandered to the other side' 'made sides' 'ate from another's side (in dish)' 'his side/his turn' 'came and made him in charge'; عوَلّيُه 'raised him' 'rose him/it' 'above him' 'higher than him(physically or in status)' 'his arrogance' 'depended on him/receive allowance from him'; غوَلّيُه 'misled him to his downfall' 'folly to downfall' 'his rivers/streams' 'his running rivers/streams/flowing' 'chained him' 'despised him' 'deep hidden hatred/anger for him' 'dug deep/stabbed deep into it/him' 'exploited/took advantage of him'; حوَلّيُه 'around it/him/surrounds it/him' 'tried/attempted-him' 'cock-eyed him/made his vision go funny'; خوَلّيُه 'allowed him' 'allow him to go' 'gave him authority' 'tasked him' 'left him' 'emptied/empty it/him'. Most of these meanings are present in the related story: Paul is under Julius' custody so Julius is his guardian and therefore 'above' Paul and the other prisoners; he has been tasked with delivering prisoners to Italy; as prisoners being transported they are confined maybe with chains, whether chains or not, they do not have freedom of movement nor escape; they intend to sail around Asia; Julius allows Paul to wander off and visit his friends, he gives him permission to do so; the crew shows loyalty to Julius, and Julius shows loyalty to the captain/owner instead of listening to Paul's advice (initially); they do everything they can to get the ship to safety but fail; the ships loads/goods are thrown out to lighten the ship (emptied). Cp: yo-wlyoh, ho-wlyoh, go-wlyoh, 'o-wlyoh, gho-wlyoh, ḥo-wlyoh, kho-wlyoh. (Acts.27)

Adramyttium; Adramýtteion; اضرَمياآتّيون 'harm/harmed-those/what is on board(ship)' 'ḫarm/harmed-coming/what is coming/is not coming' 'harm/harmed-dead/they are dead/will die'; اضرَم يآتّيون 'set ablaze-they will come'. Reflected in the journey becoming dangerous and Paul warning of harm to goods, vessel, but more importantly to their lives then the actual harm, distress and damage that occurs. Cp: adhra-myaatteioon, adhram-yaateioon. (Acts.27)

Aristarchus (Acts.19:29-41) for at least these meanings: 'see/show/saw-you/it will be loosened/split open/cracked/muscles loosened' 'water/give to drink-you/it will be loosened/split open/cracked/muscles loosened' 'see/show/saw-you will be split wide open/torn with long, wide gash/explain long and in detail' 'strip naked/was naked/was stripped naked-you will be split wide open/torn with long, wide gash/explain long and in detail'.

He is from **Macedonia** for its meanings 'of plotting/deceiving' 'plotting/deceiving-him/he/she/they' 'covered tightly (with any kind of lid: stone, metal, cloth, etc.)/of covering tightly(with lid, etc.)' 'covered me with a lid/fabric/stone/etc. 'pulled off/down/away/removed by pulling' 'pulled bread off oven wall' 'pulled down wall/structure' (Acts.16:9-40) (equivalent to Chidon (1Chr.13:9)) and from **Thessalonica** for its meanings 'he/they/it-leaked/flowed-wounded/poked wound/hurt/offended/fucked' 'he/they/it-leaked/flowed-saved/delivered to safety/talked/discussed secretly'.

All these meanings can be seen in the story: Paul explains and warns of what will happen, but is ignored; the ship and its passengers end up being tossed around and the ship destroyed which would include the breaking off of parts of its structure, water leaking, gashes, etc.; they are in danger of not surviving, but Paul informs them that they will survive and be safely delivered even if the ship does not make it; they cannot see anything due to the storm and are like something/someone covered with a stone/fabric/lid; towards the end of the chapter when the ship runs aground and its half torn up, the soldiers want to kill the prisoners to prevent them escaping, but instead the broken-off pieces of the ships structure is used by some to get safely to land; but the way the ship is destroyed is as meant in 'see/show/saw-you will be split wide open/torn with long, wide gash/explain long and in detail' and they arrive safely at land as in Thessalonica 'he/they/it-leaked/flowed-saved/delivered to safety/talked/discussed secretly'. (Acts.27)

Cyprus (Acts.4:36-37) 'a lot/became a lot' 'many/became many/multiplied' 'see, increased/multiplied it' 'try to increase/multiply it' 'disbelieved(in God or religion or the person)' 'they became disbelievers' 'disbelieved him' 'buried it/him' 'many burials/graves' 'his grave(s)'. There are many passengers on the ship and they all face the possibility of dying at sea and from shipwrecking; the wind overpowers them and they end up travelling many different routes and not what they had planned; Julius does not believe Paul's advice until the end of the chapter. (Acts.27)

Myra; Mýra; ميآر 'he does not see/he does not understand/he does not listen/obey' although it is 'does not see' it is used when a person refuses to see the truth, or to listen/obey and remains stubborn or doing the wrong thing, 'by hand' 'a circular grinding stone'. Julius does not listen to Paul's warnings and remains set on his way until it is too late; when they are run onto the island of Clauda, and the damage done is conjuring word-imagery—if you know the sound of a 'circular grinding stone' which is a heavy manual grinder which needs two women to work it is made up of two large and heavy circular stone slabs, the top slab has a handle which is moved in a whole circle (two women/girls take over moving their respective half side) and it creates a grating, rumbling noise like you would imagine a boat running on rocks/land would make; it is reflected in they cannot see 'sun nor stars' due to the storm. Cp: myaara. (Acts.27)

Lycia; Lykía; ليكيي ، ليكي 'for you' 'dented/crumpled it/them' 'were thrust/pushed against' 'so that/so that we' 'spoke too much/rambled/talked nonsense' 'chewed/chewed it'; ليقيي ، ليقي 'they/he found' 'threw/they threw/cast/they cast' 'they/he met' 'they he extended/connected'; ليحيي ، ليحي 'beard/has beard' 'will live' 'so that we live/survive' 'so still/stay it/him/them' 'make it/he/them stop moving'. They and the ship they are in are tossed around and the ship damaged; and although the author presents Paul as a loquacious rambler, Julius has ignored the advice Paul offered him and instead has listened to the rambling of the owner of the ship; when it gets more dangerous they lighten the ship by throwing off loads; Paul tells them the ship will be damaged, but they will survive; Paul informs them they have to be thrown onto a specific island; the ship ends up destroyed when they are thrust onto ground; some men survive by swimming to land while others float on broken pieces of ship they find; they all survive by finding land and meeting there. Cp: lykeea, lykeeya, lyqeea, lyqeeya, lyḥeea, lyḥeeya. (Acts.27)

Alexandria (Acts.6:9) for 'on you/upon you-I will send it/him out' 'on you/upon you-I will separate him/it' just as it is used before, this time it is a ship on which they are put on and sent out towards a specific location; when the journey becomes dangerous they all lose hope of surviving and believe they will die; in the soldiers cutting away the anchors and the ship once again is adrift, but because Paul through God has been told they are to be thrown onto a specific island they are in fact being 'sent out' to this location just as shepherds do to sheep/goats. (Acts.27)

Cnidus; Knídos; كنيدُه 'like he said in simile as bad omen/like he called out' 'like his simile/bad omen' as Paul warns them of danger and harm but they did not listen, but what he said would happen—happened. The word is from (nd/ند) 'to call out/say something negative/bad omen(through saying something)' and the superstition is saying something in a simile or just saying something out loud which causes something negative to happen, e.g. saying a person's face is like a juicy apple then that specific person's face suffers an injury or illness (it is similar to 'evil-eye' and 'Paul/phaul/bad omen'. Cp: k̲needoh. (Acts.27)

Crete; 'hired/rented/leased' 'of hiring/renting/leasing' 'drove/chased/forced away/forced with violence'; 'my village' 'villager' 'of villages' 'of reading a lot' 'read a lot to me/taught me to read/of teaching to read' 'stopped moving/fidgeting' 'stopped what you were doing'. Reflected in they hire a different ship at Alexandria; are being forced to follow a different course of sea travel due to the wind and are forced to stop at unexpected locations; in the sailors who anchor the ship, stopping it from moving, but Paul informs the soldiers they have to stop the men from fleeing from the ship, i.e. they have to stay on the ship until finally ship-wrecked; they have to stay on the specified island. (Acts.27)

Salmone; Salmṓnē; سَلمونيي ، سَلموني 'asked from me' 'asked who' 'of questions from me/of asking from me' 'leaked/flowed from me' 'comforted/entertained/distracted-me/who' 'survived' 'let me be/left me unharmed' 'of mild, peaceful nature' 'delivered/received-to me'; شَلمونيي ، شَلموني 'they took/carried me' 'what did they take/carry' 'of taking/carrying' 'took from me' 'took supplies'. They are carried away on a different course by the wind; they refuse to listen to Paul who is of Jesus' water; Paul speaks of damage to their loads but that they will remain unharmed as in not die; when things become dire, Paul manages to distract them with food and comfort them by guaranteeing they will arrive safely on land, and by eating they also join in and are comforted; the ship falling apart and being tossed around in the sea shows the 'leaked/flow' meanings. It is possible there are 'Saul/arrived/reached/connected' and other 'Saul' meanings in the word-name which also connect to Paul who is originally 'Saul'. Cp: salmoonee, salmoonyee, s̲h̲almoonee, s̲h̲almoonyee. (Acts.27)

Lasea; Lasaía; لَسَي 'would have done it/made it right/fixed it' 'well, do it/well, make it right/well, fix it' 'would have been bad' 'to his bad/insult/offence' 'for his bad/insult/offence'; لَشَي 'nothing' 'nothing important' 'disintegrated/fell apart' 'will tell/whisper' 'why did you do this' 'for this/for this matter'. It is similar to Lysias (Acts.23). They do not listen to Paul's warnings; it is a bad move on Julius' part; the ship is falling apart; an angel which only Paul can hear has informed him they will be allowed to survive because Paul has to get to Caesar; Julius does not allow the soldiers to kill any prisoners as Paul needs to be delivered to Caesar, but also all the men have to stay together in order to survive as predicted and 'proved'(in the story) by Paul's predictions. Cp: lasaya, las̲h̲aya. (Acts.27)

Euroclydon; Euroklýdōn; يوروح ليآدون 'it goes somewhere wrong/it goes somewhere without' 'it winds/blows somewhere wrong/it winds/blows somewhere without'. Exactly that happens in the story the tempest of the same name drives them off course. Cp: yorooḥlyaadoon. (Acts.27:14)

Clauda; Klaudē, Klaudēn; قلَودي ، قلَودين 'of placing responsibility on' 'they placed responsibility on' 'of hanging around neck(s)' 'they hung it around his/its/their neck(s)' 'of hanging responsibility around neck(s)' 'they hung responsibility around his/its/their neck(s)' 'of garlanding' 'they garlanded him/it/themselves' 'of placing responsibility/accountability on' 'they placed responsibility/accountability on him/it/them' 'of acting/copying' 'they acted/copied him/it/them'. The passengers and crew of the ship have a lot of work and responsibility to do on the boat to avoid shipwrecking/dying; using 'helps' and 'undergirding' the boat is similar to garlanding something around except they did it to reinforce the boat; like accountability and responsibility hang around a person's neck and when it is negative can weigh a person down, the ship is lightened of its responsibility which are its goods and this also shows Paul and the rest have responsibility to stay alive; when hope of surviving is lost, Paul gets up and assumes responsibility of guiding the crew and passengers to safety, but first he puts accountability on his captors and the ship who did not listen to his advice and warning from the beginning. Cp: qlaudey, qlaudeyn. (Acts.27:16)

Adria; Adrías; ادريَه ، ادرييَه 'they knew/made him know' as the closer they get to the island they become aware of how deep the sea is, determining they are in danger of being shipwrecked and so anchor to prevent this; when people want to leave the ship out of fear Paul makes them aware that if anyone leaves the ship they will die. Cp: adreeah, adreeyah. (Acts.27:27-44)

Melita; Melítē; مَليطي 'a flat rock' 'stuck together/clung/stuck to it' and refers to the island being like a rock in the middle of the sea; also in the way the authors have the snake instead of bite Paul and recoil, have it bite him and stick to his hand and the locals can see it hanging from his hand while it remains clasped to him; مَليتي 'filled it' 'fetched water/filled water' 'short dress/shirt' and is reflected in the locals covering the shipwrecked people with kindness and hospitality; and also the rain which has covered and filled the characters which in itself reminds that Paul is filled with special water (God/Jesus' water) which will come in handy not only in that he is not affected by a venomous snake-bite but in healing others on the island which in turn leads them to giving Paul and his company many necessary supplies. Cp: meleeṭey, meleetey. (Acts.28:1-6)

Publius; Poplios; فوبليُه ، فوبليوه 'so soak him/it' 'in him is soaked' 'in him is affliction/ailment' 'afflict him' 'in his affliction/ailment' and is reflected that Publius' father suffers from diseases but Paul is able to cure him, which leads to other locals filled with diseases seeking Paul to cure them. Cp: <u>ph</u>oblyoh, <u>ph</u>obliooh. (Acts.28:7-9)

Alexander is still 'on you/upon you-I will send it/him out' 'on you/upon you-I will separate him/it' as on this ship Paul and the rest will resume travel after winter, and they will leave Melita towards where he is expected to be put on trial then maybe executed. (Acts.28:11)

Castor and **Pollux** is another example of word-names being changed and replaced to accommodate the translation to a foreign translator (and maybe his foreign audience), by an Arab speaking translator between the original story and the foreign translation. Castor and Pollux show as only one word in the Greek text: Dióskouri, Dioskourois; but in the KJV it appears as two separate word-names: Castor and Pollux, and it is not a matter of splitting 'Dioskourois' into two separate words as they do not equate 'Castor and Pollux'. Both 'Dioskourois' and 'Castor and Pollux' have meanings in Arabic and exactly as reflected in the story, although it seems to me 'Dioskouris' was what was originally meant as it fits much better with the story:

Castor and Pollux; Dióskouri, Dioskourois; ذيُصخورِ ، ذيُصخورويه ، ضيُصخورِ ، ضيُصخورويه 'he/it makes compliant/did as bid/puts under your command/puts under your use' 'he/it makes it/him/her compliant(for/to you)' 'there he/it makes compliant/did as bid/puts under your command/puts under your use' 'there he/it makes it/him/her compliant(for/to you)'and what it reflects is that from hereon it is smooth sailing in the ship to their destination. Cp: vyo<u>ss</u>**kh**ouri, vyo<u>ss</u>**kh**ouroih, <u>dh</u>yo<u>ss</u>**kh**ouri, <u>dh</u>yo<u>ss</u>**kh**ouroih (Acts.28:11)

Castor; كَستُر 'try to protect/cover' 'like protecting/covering' and means protecting from harm or covering from shame; كَسطر 'try to pour/drain' 'like pouring/draining' 'try to make lines/write' 'like making lines/writing' 'try a straight line' 'like making a straight line'. It is reflected in the perilous journey now becomes safe; they figuratively make a straight line as in they are not blown off course again; it is the Arab translator having to make up lines and find a replacement for Dioskouris which seems to pose a difficulty in understanding on behalf of a foreign translator copying these stories into his own language. Cp: kastor, kaṣtor. (Acts.28:11)

Pollux; بُلّوقص ، بولُّقص 'by estimation/with estimation' 'by telling story' 'with telling story' 'with cracking open fruit-stone to expose seeds'; بُل/بول لُقص 'mind/intelligence/patience-estimated/will estimate/by estimating/with estimation' 'mind/intelligence/patience-told story/will tell story/by the story/with the story'. Again this along with 'Castor' is directly showing an Arab-speaking translator trying to find an alternative compound word to suffice the meaning of 'Disokourois' and you can see that combining some meanings of Castor 'protect' 'straight line' and some meanings of Pollux 'by estimation/patience-told story' can combine to almost make the meanings of 'making compliant/Diskouris'; it also shows that the overextended and dangerous journey has been overcome by 'patience/intelligence' which is one of the meanings of 'Paul' and Paul can continue to preach the gospel which he does more intensely towards the end of the chapter. Cp: bolluqss, boolluqss, bol-luqss, bool-luqss. (Acts.28:11)

Syracuse; Syrákousai; سيرآقوصَي 'they will see-hardened/become cruel' 'they will leave-hardened/become cruel' 'they will see-cut/told story' 'walk/leave/go-cut' 'walk/leave/go-told story/tell the story'. It is reflected in Paul and his group leave and arrive at other destinations until they arrive at the final destination; Paul tells them first the story of why he has arrived against his will at Rome, then he will tell the story of Jesus Christ and also the story of Esaias/Isaiah; it is reflected in that some people will believe when they hear the story, but most will have hardened hearts and refuse to accept the new religion, and Paul repeats the 'hear/not understand-see/not perceive' which means they are stubborn, too set in their ways, their hearts too hardened than to accept it. Cp: syraa-qoussai.

Rhegium; Rhēgion; ري يجيون 'saw/watered/quenched-they came/come' as they go over water to reach the destinations; ريجيون ، رييجيون 'they waited' 'they implored' as they wait for the wind to arrive so that they can set sail and when they arrive they are entreated to stay for seven days with their brethren; upon arriving in Rome, Paul will be made to stay/wait with a soldier; Paul will wait three days then he will invite the Jews and implore them to understand his predicament but also to convert to Christianity; he will stay there two years preaching. Cp: rei-eygyoon, reigyoon, reieygyoon. (Acts.28:11-31)

Puteoli; Potioloi; بوتيُلي 'stay at his house/in a house' 'will make a final decision' 'a house for me'. Paul has to live with a soldier; he invites the Jews and attempts to convert them, when he fails he makes a decision that they are the intended by the Isaiah-prophesied 'hardened/cannot see/hear/understand' so he makes a decision that he is meant to save/preach/convert the Gentiles; he lives in a house of his own for two years; بوطيُلي 'of lengthening/long/staying or lasting long' 'of bad/evil/wrong' 'ceasing/stopping/giving up' and is reflected in the long time Paul spends discussing, preaching, trying to convince the Jews, but eventually decides they are the 'bad' people who do not want to understand as prophesied in Isaiah/Esaias so he gives up and ceases trying to convert them but spends two years, at least in this house, spreading God/Jesus' word, and the author makes a point that unlike where he lived before—nobody here is making him stop from preaching. Cp: bootyoloi, booṭyoloi. (Acts.28:13-31)

Appii forum; Appious phóron, phorou; عبِّوَه/عبّيوَه فُرون ، فورو 'packed/filled-increased/multiplied'; ابِوَه/ابّيوَه فُرون ، فورو 'refused/rejected/they refused/they rejected-for they saw/so show'. First he is reinforced with courage as he is reinvigorated by the brethren who meet him; then reflected by the Jews whom he informs he has been harassed by other Jews in Jerusalem, and who refuse to believe as they have not heard nor been shown evidence of any such criticism of him or any harm happening against him; Paul spends a lot of time meeting with them and explaining, filling them with the knowledge/beliefs he has, but in the end it is all met with rejection. Paul fills his life with packing/filling people with the word of God. Cp: 'bbiouh/'bbyouh-phoroon, 'bbiouh/'bbyouh-phooroo, abbiouh/abbyouh-phoroon, abbiouh/abbyouh-phooroo. (Acts.28:15-31)

The Epistles

Romans

Paul was chosen by the author of Romans as the narrator for its meanings 'his mind' 'his patience' 'his affliction/afflicted him' 'his indication/direction' 'follow his indication/go his direction': and Epistle to the Romans shows the meanings of intelligence, reasoning, deep-thinking about the matters raised in the stories as well as the recipients of these letters are being asked to do as he tells them, indicates to them; the letters show he says something and wants it to happen.

Jesus Christ, David: this has been explained before, but it is repeat in the NT by different authors because it was important to them that people understand the meanings: **Jesus Christ** 'broke bread-his cake of bread' 'broke/ate his cake of bread' is from the seed/flesh of David. **David** is 'the stone rolling pin of grinding stone'—the rolling pin of a grinding stone grinds the seeds/grain and turns them into dough which becomes 'bread' when baked and is broken to be eaten: 'Concerning his Son Jesus Christ our Lord, which was made of the seed of David, according to the flesh;'. (Rom.1:1-3)

Rome is still used for its meanings 'were thrown' 'threw/killed' 'spread/strewn over vast distance/various locations' 'saw water' 'became rotten/went off/bad smelling' as the story narrates of spreading God's word, God's word is water, the narrator is explaining he is unable to travel (cross the distance) but he will still send and spread God's word, they are called 'God's beloved' as a pun because Jesus was made of God's water/semen so an area named 'saw water/Rome' is used for this story. (Rom.)

Gentiles is still ethnesin; يثني/اثني سِن/سين '**ethne**': 'he/they do it again/double it/fold it/repeat it-' 'he/they dissuade/make leave-' 'he/they are idolaters/pagans-' 'idols-' 'praise/praises-' 'idol worshippers-' 'idolatry/worshipping idols-'; followed by '**sin**' meanings: in the direction of/towards me/in the face of/in front of/straight/straight line/direct/opposite me' and from the OT 'I will deceive them/the' 'I will mislead them to downfall-them/the'.

To the local people who first heard these stories in its original language before it was translated to Greek, this would have been funny as the narrator is poking fun 'Now I would not have you ignorant' that he is preaching and teaching to peoples who he has named 'I will mislead them to downfall'. It is also reflected in how people have misled each other by worshipping their own creations instead of God. The pun is concentrated further as the whole idea and story of Jesus (especially from gospel of John onwards) is about spreading God/Jesus' water/sperm and most effectively through sex between two males (which is why David and Jesus are mentioned at the beginning of the chapter as they both had male lovers and engaged in homosexual sex in the respective OT and NT stories). But at verse 27 it returns to describing homosexual sex as a sin, which may be the work of a conservative editor at a later time, but if it is the original author's work it does not necessarily contradict the stories of the NT, as when read properly and with the understanding of the meanings of the word-names the NT stories always seem to mock the new (Christian) faith—and again these came to be understood as pro-new/Christian faith stories because the new audiences of these stories did not speak the language of the Bible and its authors and therefore (mis)understood them differently than the authors' intentions. (Rom.1:13-32)

Greeks hellēsin; حيلّي سِن/سين ، حِلّي سِن/سين meanings of 'hellē' followed by meanings of '**sin**': 'purify/purified/circumcise/circumcised/make clean/made clean/make edible/made edible-**in the direction of/towards me/in the face of/in front of/straight/straight line/direct/opposite me**' 'of purification/edibility/cleanliness/circumcision-' 'declare/declared purified/permissible-';

'undress/undressed-**in the direction of/towards me/in the face of/in front of/straight/straight line/direct/opposite me**' 'of undressing-' 'deceive/deceived/trick/tricked-' 'of deceit/tricks-';

'beat/beaten severely/beat/beaten until skin peeled off-' 'of beating/being beaten severely-'; 'shed skin/hair/leaves/etc.-' 'of shedding skin/hair/leaves-' 'replace/replaced-'; 'of replacing-' 'sweet/sweetened-' 'of sweetness/sweetening-' and is used to mean 'purified/circumcised/sweetened/cleansed'. In this form of the word 'Greek' it reflects exactly the narration of meanings directed towards the Greek (just as it meant Paul wanted to come in the direction of the Gentiles of which the compound word ends with the same suffix (sin)).

At Rom.1:16 'Greek' is in the form of: hellēni; حَلّيني ، حيلّيني 'purified/circumcised/made clean/made edible him/it' 'of purification/edibility/cleanliness/circumcision' 'declared purified/permissible' 'undressed him/her/it' 'of undressing' 'deceived/tricked him/her/it' 'of deceit/tricks' 'beat severely/beat until skin peeled off him/it' 'of beating/being beaten severely' 'shed its skin/hair/leaves/etc. him/it' 'of shedding skin/hair/leaves' 'replaced him/it' 'of replacing' 'sweet/sweetened him/it' 'of sweetness/sweetening' as it is used in the form of the addressed.

As addressed in earlier stories, the use of this word means purity, sweetening, undressing, shedding, circumcising, cleansing which in the NT stories the 'Gentiles/Greeks' have been allowed to become 'pure/purified' without undergoing physical circumcision—but deemed the same physical and spiritual cleanliness of the circumcised. It is reflected in the impurities of man and animals which people have made images of God as, which leads to the people becoming unclean in body and soul. (Rom.1:14-32)

Barbarians is the same as **Pharphar** (2kgs.5:11-13); Bárbaros; بآربَرُه 'they talked nonsense' 'they made unintelligible sounds' 'they talked too much' 'they talked incoherently' where in 2Kgs. it portrayed Naaman finding Elisha talking nonsense when he told him to wash in the river to cure his leprosy. It does not have the modern meaning of 'barbaric' as in violent or uncivil as this meaning would affix to it later—but in the NT as in the OT and in the Arabic language, it means to make unintelligible sounds whether a foreign language or to speak incoherently. But here it is also used in wordplay to mean 'good/piety-went beyond/surpassed' as God/Jesus' word is being spread further abroad and is the message of the story, but also it is the original author's true intentions of the story and its message that the new faith (Christianity) is nonsense as opposed to the old faith (what would come to be called 'Jewish' faith, but also possibly other pagan faiths of the times). Cp: baarbaroh, baar-baroh. (Rom.1:14-32)

Rom.8:15 still uses '**Abbah**' for 'father'.

Osee; Hōsēé; حوسيي 'crooked footed' 'walks in wrong direction/with crooked steps'. It reflects the disobedient people walking crookedly, even if they walk on God's path they are being crooked on that path, changing things and not as God said/ordered; it shows the same going in the wrong or crooked direction in that God can go off to another people instead of the original chosen people and not the people that he loved; هوسيي 'he made/can make' 'he/it is bad'; هوشيي 'he wants/wanted/wanted it to be' 'he/it important matters/things'. All these meanings relay with each other and the first meaning of 'crooked footed' as God just like a potter can make things good or bad, he can replace what he makes with something better if he finds the original bad; God can do what he wishes even if it is showing important matters to people who should not be receiving these things and in giving love to a people he does not really love. Cp: ḥooseyei, hooseyei, hoo<u>sh</u>eyei. (Rom.9:25)

Sabaoth; sabaōth; شَبعوت 'was filled/ate plenty' 'she is full(stomach)/has had enough' and the latter can mean fill of food or has 'had it/exasperated with', 'well off' ; شَبعوث ، سَبعوث 'I will send' 'I will resurrect' 'I bring back to life after death' and all these meanings are used: God has had enough of the 'bad' characters or those he 'hates' (Esau, Pharaoh, Sodom and Gomorrah); the narration shows it is enough to conceive one child, and these children will either fill the earth with good or make God fed up with them, and the latter is relayed in the narration that God has 'endured with much long suffering the vessels of wrath fitted to destruction.'; the 'elder' who serves the 'younger' and Jacob and Esau have been mentioned because it was over Esau being so hungry he sold his birth right to Jacob, as well as Jacob and Rebekkah using deceit giving Isaac a satisfying meal he thinks is from Esau that he mistakenly blesses Jacob, and Jacob will go on to promise tithes and filling God with offerings (at Bethel); the 'well off' meanings are shown by reminding of the Moses-Pharaoh story as well as narration relaying the meaning of the word; even the criticism of 'Israel' in not following God's faith but following 'works of the law' all relays the 'full stomach/satisfied' meanings as in the stories Israel make great offerings to feed God, and the mention of the 'stumbling stone' refers to making offerings to rocks or a specific rock—and where offerings/sacrifices are made there are people and God eating/feasting; God has sent the message to people other than Israel; the people, according to Paul quoting Esaias, have been brought back to life in contrast to Sodom and Gomorrah who were killed completely with no chance of return to life. Cp: <u>sh</u>ab'oot, sab'oof, <u>sh</u>ab'oof. (Rom.9:29)

Deliverer; Lytrōtēs, Lytrōtēn; ليتروتييه ، ليتروتين 'to water him/it/them' 'to tell story-him/them/it' 'to narrate it' 'to quench him/it/them' 'to see him/it/them' 'for their stories' 'for their watering/quenching' 'for their narration' 'for him/them to see it'. This plays on the stories of the OT and NT: that if Israel listens and accepts the narration of the NT stories they can be saved from their disobedience; the watering process of the NT can deliver Israel and straighten them out and help them to see the truth and correct ways of God (i.e. deliver Israel out of its 'Sion/bad'; it plays on 'Israel/twisted muscle-the' and the way the disciples and Jesus' stories transfer the new religion through water/sperm can straighten Jacob's twisted and withered muscle; as a grafted olive tree is being used as a metaphor, it (and Israel) needs to be watered with Jesus-water to survive and avoid withering and dying; it reminds they are all just stories being narrated. Cp: lytrootei̲e̲ieyh, lytrooteyn. (Rom.11:26)

Illyricum; Illyrikón; الّي ريكون ، الّي رِكون 'the one who/he who-watered you/your watering/quenching' 'the one who/he who-saw you/showed you/your vision/sight' 'the one who/he who-told you stories' 'he who/the one who-depended/made a corner' and refers to Paul being the one who spread God/Jesus' water/sperm and word from **Jerusalem** (used for 'came-saw-asked-them/the' 'they see-asked-them/the' as he has come to them, they have seen him and he has asked them to convert) to 'Illyricum' as converting people with the word and water quenches the thirst as described in the gospels; Paul has showed them, helped them and led them to see and be on the proper God's ways; the narration mentions not building on someone else's foundation and here the narration has Paul specifically separate what Jesus achieved and what he achieved, his (Paul's) being the greater achievement; it describes that through depending on Christ, Paul has been able to build solid corners for Christianity in places where Jesus laid no foundations for it—this too is the author enlarging Paul's role in the Biblical stories. Cp: illy-rykoon, illy-rikoon.

Rom.15:12-33, the author (who is mistakenly presumed to be Paul, which is impossible since Paul is a fictional character) has the narrator Paul remind the 'Gentiles' of Isaiah's prophecy of the root of Jesse to rule over them, earlier having mentioned that he (Paul) is from the same stock/seed; now he tells them he would like to be 'the minister of Jesus Christ to the Gentiles'—in other words, he is telling them he is the Isaiah-prophesied 'seed of Jesse', not Jesus, who will reign over the Gentiles, i.e. lead them to salvation.

In the same chapter the story narrates Paul telling the 'recipients' how he has wanted to come to see them for years but has been hindered, then promises to come to see them and this is repeat in many epistles: promises to arrive/visit, but something or other prevents him—but always someone else arrives instead and is sent to collect money. From verse 16 the narration takes on hinting that money or some material donations have been given by the 'Gentiles' and that these donations become acceptable/holy/sanctified i.e. cleansed and acceptable by going through Paul i.e. Paul receiving these donations (he is a Holy Ghost vessel). The message becomes more direct from verse 23 onwards, where Paul puts a condition that he first be filled with the company of the people the story/letter is directed at then he will come, and that Paul receives donations and uses it in the services of the 'poor saints of Jerusalem'.

Spain; Spanía; زبَنييه 'penised me-he/him' 'my lower belly(area below navel and above crotch)'; زفَنييه 'escorted me-he/him' 'wedding entourage-he/him'; شبَنييه 'I will give him child(ren)/adopt him'; شَفنييه 'saw me-he/him' 'gloated/satisfied in me-he/him'. This is intentional wordplay by the author of Romans: Paul is telling them he wants to fill and be filled by the recipients of this letter: it plays on how God/Jesus' word and water are spread through sexual activity; the lower belly of one or both of a couple, between the navel and crotch, are what rub against each other during foreplay and sexual intercourse; it also plays on the sender of the letter wanting to receive a monetary contribution, to be sent so he can use it to 'minister/serve' the saints in Jerusalem, to satisfy their needs; that when he arrives he will be escorted with an entourage to arrive at the recipient's location but only once they have sent him a contribution so he can give this fruit to satisfy the in-need saints of Jerusalem as the 'fruit/son' of this story is the money contributions which result from it; satisfaction is also meant by the sexual activity. Cp: zbaneeyh, zp̲h̲aneeyh, s̲h̲baneeyh, shp̲h̲aneeyh.

Now watch how the Biblical authors spin wordplay and puns with the narration of the story, these words are meant to show that the 'Gentiles' are being deceived to donate money and gifts; the author does it in a very in-your-face manner that everyone who reads/listens to this story who speaks the original language would see the humour and the links in what is being said, but only non-Arabic speakers would fail to see and understand:

Macedonia (Acts.16:9-40) 'of plotting/deceiving' 'plotting/deceiving-him/he/she/they' 'covered tightly (with any kind of lid: stone, metal, cloth, etc.)/of covering tightly(with lid, etc.)' 'covered me with a lid/fabric/stone/etc.' 'of pillows' 'pillows/with pillows' 'resting on pillows' 'with hand on cheeks' 'of cheeks' 'cheeks' 'pulled off/down/away/removed by pulling' 'pulled bread off oven wall' 'pulled down wall/structure'.

Reflects that the Macedonians have already been deceived in sending donations to a person called 'Paul' on the promise that he will come, but as he never actually arrives, he is like an object under a tight lid, unseen. The pillows suggest the sexual nature of what the story implies to the recipients of the current epistle. At the end of asking them to send contributions so that he can satisfy the saints' needs which will also allow him to visit the recipients of the letter 'I shall come in the fullness of Christ' i.e. 'Christ' a whole circle of bread as that is what the donations are needed for: to feed the 'saints'.

Achaia (Acts.18:17) 'I mislead him/them to downfall/I will mislead him/them to his/their downfall' 'his misleading to downfall' 'I deceive him/them/I will deceive' 'I make him/them howl' 'I will make him/them howl' 'I warn/teach him/them' 'I will contain him/it'.

Reinforces what the word-names already clearly show that the people are being misled to donate to a person (Paul) who they do not know, but which the letter promises will visit them to teach them God/Jesus' ways; the 'howling' reflects the sexual implications of the story.

Jerusalem 'came-saw-asked-them/the' 'they see-asked-them/the'; the story is about a letter which asks the recipients to send donations to support the service of the saints in Jerusalem; it promises that once these donations are sent, Paul will be able to come and see the recipients in their own countries.

Gentiles ethnē; يثني ، اثني 'he does it again/twice/doubles it/folds it/repeats it' 'he dissuades/makes leave' 'he is an idolaters/pagan' 'idols' 'he praises' 'idol worshippers' 'idolatry/worshipping idols', 'I will deceive them/the' 'I will mislead them to downfall-them/the' and this plays on that just like they have misled them about spiritual matters/matters of faith, it is also perfectly sensible that they should be misled in carnal/physical matters: misled to send them money, misled about sexual activities as part of 'cleansing' and spreading God's word.

The message is that once the people have been misled 'Macedonia, Achaia, Gentiles' and the 'fruit' secured i.e. the donated money has been received then Paul 'I will come by you into Spain.' **Spain** again for its meanings of sexual penetration and satisfaction; satisfaction of receiving the 'fruit/child' of the donations which is the result of the letter in the story.

To enhance the story which is presented as a letter to people in 'Spain', **Judaea** 'he/they were called' 'he/they made claim' 'he/they made false/unproven claim' is used to show: the narrator is making a false claim; the people in Judaea do not believe what he is calling them to, but also that the narrator of the story/letter is making a false claim: he claims he cannot bear to live in Judaea/Jerusalem yet remains there, he claims he will come to visit the 'recipients' of the letter yet he never does

Jerusalem 'came-saw-asked-them/the' 'they see-asked-them/the' 'and that my service which I have for Jerusalem may be accepted of the saints' portrays his assignment is to promise to come and see the recipients, based on asking them to send to him (Paul) contributions—not for him, but for the saints, which he has to receive and then based on that he may be able to joyfully visit the recipients of the letter of this story.

Phebe; Phoíbē; فويبي ، فُيبي 'fulfil/complete me/fulfil for me/complete for me/complete with/in me' and means to fulfil promise, payment, conditions, etc. and he is asking whoever the epistle is directed at to fulfil receiving and assisting her, in her activities and needs. The story ends with Phebe carrying the epistle, according to the note. These 'epistle/letters' may very well have begun as samaara/samaaya stories just like all the OT and NT stories, as is obvious from the use of compound words as names and used in word-play exactly as their meanings stand—but that is not how they remained, as they came to be used (and believed) as letters from a 'real' person called Paul despite its obvious fictionality. The key is the people/areas that first believed these to be actual letters and Paul to be a real person instead of a character in the stories are non-local people who do not speak Arabic and therefore would not understand the original use of these stories and took them for fact instead.

Phebe's meaning of 'complete/fulfil-in/with/for me' is not only shown in what the recipients of the 'letter' and Phebe should give and do towards Phebe, but also in the thanks, gratitude and greetings shown towards the long list of compound-word-names which all stand for either completing the meanings of Paul and the other word-names and themes in the story and/or are somehow related to it in other stories which may not have made it into the surviving documents which end up being the Bible as it is currently known. Cp: phooeebey, phoyeebey. (Rom.16)

Cenchrea has been used for some of its meanings: 'he was with bald/shaved/uncovered head/hair' 'he was having/he had breakfast' 'it was my breakfast' 'held head high/perky-bald/shaved/uncovered head/hair' 'carried perky-breakfast/my breakfast'. A person who makes a vow to God or has been vowed to God does not shave his hair during the vow's term, once the vow is complete the hair can be cut/shaved (you can see this influence and how it mutated through time and over distance and cultures becoming the bald-pate monks would have in the middle of their hair)—Phebe, although a female, has been described as a saint and should be received like a saint by the recipients of the letter she carries.

It also delivers the pun that the sender of the letter has sent it to secure money to feed himself (and maybe his associates) from and this is further highlighted (after the thanks he asks to be given to a long list of compound-word-named characters) by warning them of the people who make false claims just to deceive the 'simple-hearted' believers out of their money, as these deceitful people only do it to make gain to feed their own bellies—and again this is the Biblical authors' way of making it absolutely clear that this is intended by these stories and word-names by not only giving them the obvious and made-up 'names' but also reinforcing the meanings in the very narration of the story's text. 'For they that are such serve not our Lord Jesus Christ, but their own belly; and by good words and fair speeches deceive the hearts of the simple.'. The authors deliberately make deceiving people out of their money the theme of the story, then point out that it is deceit and warn against it. (Rom.16)

Priscilla and **Aquila** for all their meanings as in (Acts.18) as this story has Paul thanking and asking others to thank the characters who assisted him in spreading God's word and/or supported him personally, or had a direct/indirect effect on him, but the author of Romans is also showing the local audience the fictionality of the stories within Romans and beyond. (Acts.16)

Epaenetus; Epaínetos; ابَيينَتُه 'made him a girl' 'made him/it apparent/clear/prominent' 'showed/made apparent his true intentions' and he is described as 'wellbeloved' there is a riddle here that the audience is supposed to figure out to be able to identify him and to get to his 'real' character-name, much like the riddle/samaaya created over John the disciple being Jesus' beloved. The author of Romans is still projecting Paul as Jesus-like, imitating a secret-beloved like John but for Paul this time. It is most probably Timotheus for the meanings of his name; because of the context it has been presented followed by Mary who also means to 'pass along' like one of the meanings of Timotheus, but the meaning of Mary as 'pass along the river/sea' coupled with her role in all the stories no matter which 'Mary' character they use which shows passing along but also carrying water/liquid and completing 'Jesus' as her character is a receptacle vessel for God's water—this too is linked to Timotheus as his name also means 'she wipes away his urine/sperm(without use of water)' so Mary and Timotheus complete each other in this context (Mary provides and indicates the water/sperm); Paul has him circumcised so although the story has him rail and exhort against circumcision of 'foreigners' because Timotheus' character from its introduction was meant to have significance as Paul's intimate companion this is why he/the author has him circumcised—not only does the phallus become more 'apparent' like the word-name Epaenetus meanings, but the penis as a member becomes cleaner than an uncircumcised penis having too many folds of skin; supported also by Timotheus being the son of a Greek man, and this Epaenetus being from Achaia which also has the same meanings of 'Greek'. Where in Acts it is Timotheus' mother unnamed and only identified as a 'Jewess' to provide the female indication towards his feminine-prefixed name, in this instance it is Mary who becomes the (Ti/she(did)) prefix of his name and purpose as character role in the riddle. Cp: ebayeenetoh. (Rom.16)

Mary (Matt.) 'pass along' 'pass/cross/pass by' 'pass along the river/sea' as without her there would be no Jesus, no water to spread and she was the original receptacle of God's water which would produce Jesus then be transferred to other disciples through Jesus thus allowing not only Paul to become the latest and most significant carrier of this water, but also so the author could use it as the narrator showing Mary began this thing which allowed the narrator to profit from it. (Acts.16)

Andronicus; Andrónikos; اندرونيكُه ، اندرونيكوه 'sent out/sent him/it out-fucked him/wounded him/poked him in wound' 'separated/separated him/it-fucked him/wounded him/poked him in wound'; اندرونيجُه ، اندرونيجوه 'sent out/sent him/it out-survived/delivered to safety' 'sent out/sent him/it out-discussed quietly/secretly/discussed between them' 'sent out/sent him/it out-we come' 'separated/separated him/it-survived/delivered to safety' 'separated/separated him/it-discussed quietly/secretly/discussed between them' 'separated/separated him/it-we come'; اندرونيقُه ، اندرونيقوه 'sent out/sent him/it out-chooses/selects' 'sent out/sent him/it out-picks out impurities/clears/cleans' 'separated/separated him/it-chooses/selects' 'separated/separated him/it-picks out impurities/clears/cleans'.

He represents Andrew the disciple as he was among the first twelve who believed in Christ; the word name also reflects they and Paul came out of prison safely; they spread the word of God to Jesus' flocks which is the meaning of Andrew as a word to send out flocks on the right path. Cp: androo-neekoh, androo-neekooh, androo-neegoh, androo-neegooh, androo-neeqoh, androo-neeqooh. (Acts.16)

Junia; Iouvía, Iounía; يوويي 'stays/they stay' 'he let them stay over' and is similar to Eve, but although I do not like to change/challenge the spelling of what is in the original text especially that it has proven to be spot-on, but I do strongly believe this is a mistake in transliteration and that it should be (n) not (v) in Iou<u>v</u>ía, Iou<u>n</u>ía as this is supported by the text as well as Junia being transliterated from Greek text as 'Iounia': Andronicus is a play on 'Andrew' and Junia is 'John' the disciples as the story credits them with being apostles and believers in Christ before Paul. But to complete all possible meanings of Junia as Iouvía: هوويَ 'he was with him' 'him and him' 'aired/they aired/fanned' 'they stayed with/they stayed'; جوويَ 'he/they came with him' 'came-him and him'; عوويَ 'they howled'; حوويَ 'they stayed/they were made to stay/they became still/they were made still' 'stayed with him' 'became still them and he'; خوويَ 'brothers/became brothers' 'hollow/became hollow/were hollowed' 'collapsed from frailty/hollowness'. Cp: youweeya, houweeya, gouweeya, 'ouweeya, ḥouweeya, khouweeya.

Junia; Iounía; جونيَ 'a sack' 'wrapped in a sack/placed in a sack' 'sackcloth/of sackcloth'; خونيَ 'soaked in/were soaked in' 'brothers/my brothers' 'betrayed/were betrayed/they betrayed' and this reminds of both John the Baptist and John the beloved disciple, the latter was essential in carrying and transferring/spreading Jesus' water after Jesus died, although the authors of Acts decided to present him in a negative light and negative in Paul's eyes so they could raise Paul's significance without competition of a character who is higher in status in the NT stories because he not only received extra of Jesus/God's water/sperm but was also loved by Jesus above all others in a full physical and emotional relationship, the authors of Rom.16 use him as part of the wordplay; عونيَ 'he/they assisted' 'he/they suffered' 'he they directed speech/meaning at' and these two are mentioned as assisting in spreading God's word, suffering with Paul in prison; يونيَ 'oh, pity/oh, my pity' 'they moan/groan'. Cp: gouneeya, khouneeya, 'ouneeya, youneeya. (Rom.16)

Amplias; Ampliátos; امثلِاَتُه ، امثلياَته 'like him' 'the same as him' 'his proverbs/sayings' 'his acting/acts' 'I wipe away his urine/sperm for him' 'he wipes away urine/sperm for me' and is similar to Pamphylia (Acts.2) and Amphipolis (Acts.17:1-16). It indicates he is 'my beloved in the Lord.' because he likes the same things or behaves the same way as Paul; امبلِاَته ، امبلياَته 'I caused him suffering/problems/afflictions' 'he caused me afflictions' 'I soak/soaked him/it' 'he soaked me/for me' and still refers to what Paul does in God's name. Cp: amfliaatoh, amflyaatoh, ambliaatoh, amblyaatoh. (Rom.16)

Urbane; Ourbanós; وُوربَنُه ، ئُوربَنوه 'is/they are-his god(s)/parent(s)/teacher(s)' 'is he/are they/which one-his god(s)/parent(s)/teacher(s)' 'raised him/it/brought him up' 'is/are-mixed and diluted with water' 'mixed and diluted him/it with water' 'his teacher/discipliner/parent/god/grower/anyone who brought up or taught or grew him(it)' 'they brought him up/grew him fast and/or well'; عوربَنُه ، عوربَنوه 'he will/will he/they will/will they-his god(s)/parent(s)/teacher(s)' 'he will/will he/they will/will they-mix and dilute him(it) with water' 'naked/stripped naked-became apparent/clear' 'naked-built it/constructed it' 'fucked him/fucked him a lot' 'ordered it in advance' 'expressed/spoke clearly' 'his clear expression/speech' 'expressed it clearly' 'learn and remember(this)-taught him/brought him up well/disciplined him' 'be warned-his teacher/his teachings' 'be warned-see his teachings'. It refers to another 'beloved' mentioned in the same sentence (Stachys), but also to the actions of Paul and his companions, the themes of the stories in Romans, and also to the warning in the same chapter of caution from those who teach falsely and mislead simple people. It can also have more meanings such as those found under Arab, Arabian, Rabbi but in the form of a compound word which is 'his/it' (see Arab (Josh.15:52), Arabia (2Chr.9:14), Rabbi (Matt.23)). Cp: o-rbanoh, oorbanooh, 'orbanoh, 'oorbanooh. (Rom.16)

Stachys my beloved; Stáchys; ستاَحيه 'he is shy/his shyness' 'has shame/is embarrassed-he/him' 'she will make him still/stay' 'she will make him shy/embarrassed/ashamed' and is still referring to Paul's beloved who the author is making to be shy which pushes the reader to identify Paul's beloved and again the form of the compound word is a female doing something to a male and this points to Timotheus again for the same reasons mentioned earlier (see Epaenetus). Cp: staaḥyh. (Rom.16)

Apelles; Apellēs; ابلّيَه 'soak it/him' 'soak/soaked him/it' 'afflict him/it' and is the same as Apollos (Acts.18:24-28) who was already well-versed and working hard in preaching Christ and who Priscilla and Aquila made better at it. Cp: abelleyah. (Rom.16)

Aristobulus; Aristóboulos; ارثتوبولُه ، ارثث بولوه 'inherited-his soaked/wetness/urine' 'inherited-his illness/afflictions/problems' 'inherited-gave him problems/afflictions' 'inherited-became in charge/guardian/became loyal' 'inherited-came after him' 'inherited-his mind/patience/intelligence'; ارضث بولُه ، ارضث بولوه 'eased/appeased/convinced-his soaked/wetness/urine' 'eased/appeased/convinced-his illness/afflictions/problems' 'eased/appeased/convinced-gave him problems/afflictions' 'eased/appeased/convinced-became in charge/guardian/became loyal' 'eased/appeased/convinced-came after him' 'eased/appeased/convinced-his mind/patience/intelligence'; 'buried/laid in ground-his soaked/wetness/urine' 'buried/laid in ground-his illness/afflictions/problems' 'buried/laid in ground-gave him problems/afflictions' 'buried/laid in ground-became in charge/guardian/became loyal' 'buried/laid in ground-came after him' 'buried/laid in ground-his mind/patience/intelligence' (the first half of the compound word Aristó/ارِضثْ can also be 'does with soil-' or 'termites or: termites ate/hollowed (as termites can turn anything from plaster/wood that they consume into a soil like mound) followed by any of the meanings of the second half of the compound word boulos/بولَه).

Specifically, in Rom.16 it refers to Apollos who is Apelles in the same verse (16:10) as Aquila and Priscilla are able to convince him to bring down his fervour and be a better orator, but also to understand better the teachings of and how to preach about Jesus Christ and his ways; Aristobulus also refers that all Apollos had before was what he inherited through being baptised (soaked) by John the Baptist until the latter couple were able to distil in him more knowledge and better understanding. Cp: arifto-bouloh, arifto-boulooh, aridhto-bouloh, aridhto-boulooh. (Rom.16)

Herodion; Hērōdíōn; حيروديون 'they incite against' 'of inciting against' 'of bent neck(physically)' 'of becoming stubborn' 'they are stubborn' 'they cause problems between others' 'of causing problems between others' 'of going/they go to one side/direction (while moving)' 'they are focused on with malicious intent' 'of malicious intent'; حيروضييون 'of inciting against' 'they incite against' 'of getting worked up' 'they get worked up/work up' 'they fold/coil into itself ready to strike'. It is referring to at least one of the prophets/teachers mentioned at (Acts.13:1-4) as related to Herod; it could be indicating Barnabas who was a great help and companion to Saul/Paul in Acts and the riddle is although they were 'brethren' and close when they faced a dispute over John Mark, both Paul and Barnabas became 'Herod/bent neck/stubborn' and went their own ways as a result (see Acts.15:36-40). It also reflects the verse where the people are warned about others who will come pretending to teach but will cause 'divisions and offences' between them. Cp: ḥeyroodeeyoon, ḥeyroodheeyoon. (Rom.16)

Narcissus; Nárkissos; نآرجِزُّه ، نآرجيزّوه 'we curse/make unclean/filthy' and confirms that the 'Herodion' meant by the same verse.11 is Barnabas and he has been given this code-name for people to figure out it is Barnabas for the reason mentioned above of Barnabas leaving with John Mark (Mark being John the disciple) because Saul/Paul and Barnabas had a difference over John as Saul/Paul saw him as undevoted to God/Jesus' work because he left them at an earlier point of the story instead of work with them; John (and his brother James) were called Boanerges بوَن يرجيز 'children of-he curses/makes unclean/filthy' 'of when/with when-he curses/makes clean/filthy'; بوَني رجيز 'children of curse(s)/uncleanness/filth' in Mark (see Boanerges (Mark.3:17) and (Luke.9:51-56)). Cp: naargizzoh, naargyzzooh. (Rom.16)

Tryphena; Trýphaína; ترياآفَيينَ ، ترياآبَيينَ 'she was watered-where' 'she was quenched where' 'she was watered in what' 'she was watered/quenched in us/with us' 'they were/will be watered/quenched where/in what' 'they were/will be watered in us/with us' 'she saw/dreamt in us' 'they saw/will see/dreamt/will dream in us' 'she sees clearly/with certainty' 'they will see clearly/with certainty'. This refers to three characters: first to Barsabas (Acts.15:22-33) who was needed to deliver the letter regarding the matter of circumcision of the Gentiles which was looked into thoroughly and decided absolutely that there is no need for circumcision; it also refers to Lydia of Thyatira who was baptised by Paul and Silas and the possessed damsel who could see God/Jesus' holy water in Paul and exposed them (Acts.15-16). Cp: tryaa-phaeeyna, tryaa-baeeyna.

Tryphosa; Tryphṓsa; تري فوَصَ 'she waters/is watered/sees/saw-untangled them/them in detail/they were recommended/sent'; تري فوَسَ 'she waters/is watered/sees/saw-broke wind/copulate(d) anally them/whisper like devils' and this too refers to three different characters: Silas (Acts.15:22-41) because he too was chosen along with Barsabas to deliver the letter which completely resolves that there is no need for circumcision among 'gentiles' and also detailed what they should avoid; it is also about Lydia of Thyatira because the baptism and further acts she receives from Paul and Silas includes anal sex to transfer Jesus-water to her (which goes wrong for both Paul and Silas in the story (the word phṓsa/فوسَ means a silent passage of wind from the anus, and also is the word used to mean how chickens copulate as it seems the cockerel is delivering his semen through the hens' anus); and again the possessed damsel who knows they are bringing the salvation of God because her devil tells her, the devil also tells her the secrets which are considered prophesy to the paying customers and as only she can hear the devil which possesses her it is like whispering which is the meaning of the latter word; Paul disentangles/separates her from the devil which also separates between her employers and their profits (see Acts.15-16). It also reflects the warning about people coming to divide them with false preaching. Cp: trei-phoassa, trei-phoasa. (Rom.16)

Persis; Persís; فَرشييه 'is my bed/resting place-him/he' 'make/prepare resting/sleeping place-he/him' 'lay him down' 'spread him over/lay him out'; برزييه 'brought forward/pressed on and pushed out-he/him'; فرصييه 'split open/push out/emerged by pushing up or out/ divide by breaking or splitting-he/him';

فرسييه'divided into separate units-he/him' 'explained/explain in detail/made clear-he/him'. All these still refer to Timotheus, not only because he is Paul's beloved, but these three word-names have been lumped in one verse: Tryphena, Tryphosa, Persis to show the characters indicated who were with Paul in the earlier stories, and Timotheus was with Silas and Paul: the author is making it clear 'explaining by breaking it into details' for the audience to catch on the explicit and specific meanings of what Timotheus is to Paul, he is Paul's bed/resting place, the author is pushing this up and out, splitting it open and bringing it forward in detail for the audience to understand, and to also see the fictionality of these stories. Cp: phershee-yh, berzeeyh, phersseeyh, pherseeyh. (Rom.16)

Rufus (Mark.15:21) 'they had sex with him' which was used to indicate Jesus was raped in the gospel of Mark and is now used to further emphasise that the NT stories are about having sex, the sex is what converts and cleanses a person to be God's; it refers to both Mary, God and Jesus for Jesus' creation/conception; to Jesus' rape before he is offered as a sacrifice by God for mankind; to Jesus, John and Mary who will continue being receptacles and pouring vessels of God/Jesus' water/sperm; to Paul and Timotheus and the latter's mother who although has only been identified as a Jew was important for Timotheus to be good enough to be chosen by Paul to be his partner, and his mother is still important to this relationship between Paul and Timotheus, and as the verse narrates Rufus(Timotheus) is 'chosen in the Lord'. (Rom.16)

Asyncritus; Asýnkritos; اسيآن كريتُه the first half of the compound word: Asýn/اسيآن means 'went straight to' 'became straight' 'straightened out' 'followed the correct path(morally)' 'faced right direction(positionally)' 'set in right direction/face right direction' 'make straight' 'set straight' 'faced/opposite'. The second half of the compound word kritos/كريتُه 'hired/rented/leased-it/him' 'drove/chased/forced away/forced with violence-it/him'; قريتَه 'his village' 'read it/read to him/taught him to read/taught him' 'made him/it stop moving/fidgeting' 'stopped what he/it was doing'.

A number of meanings can be made by combining the two halves of the compound words which make up the character name. What it refers to is the story where Paul and everyone on the ship were forced to travel to Crete due to strong winds (Acts.27). The riddle is that it is telling people to read the word-names and understand their meanings and the message of the author as intended by the author. Cp: asyaan-krytoh, asyaan-qrytoh. (Rom.16)

Phlegon; Phlégōn; فليجون 'so they will come' 'so they are refugees' 'so they sought safety/came for safety' although it is similar to 'Legion' (Mark.5:9-13) it does not seem to have any meanings of 'for many demons' or any meaning related to demons; فليغون 'so they play with words' 'so they change meanings' 'in the languages' 'in their languages'. It also refers to the story where Paul and company were shipwrecked, but it also points the audience that the authors of the Biblical stories have used wordplay and changed the meanings according to wordplay. Cp: phleigoon, phleighoon. (Rom.16)

Hermas; Hermás; هَرماه 'I will throw-him/he/it' 'I will throw water' 'I will kill-him/he/it' 'here, see/saw his water' 'chased away-water-he/him' 'chased away his water' 'grumpy and bitter'. It is the same as Hermes. It still refers to the Acts.27 voyage, and having to throw off the ships loads and supplies. Cp: hermaah. (Rom.16)

Patrobas; Patrobás; بَتروباه ، بَترُباه 'stubbed/shortened-him' 'were short/abrupt with him' 'snapped/cut him/it short' 'abruptly cut him/it off' 'interrupted him' 'stub of rock/smooth rock-with him' 'with/by soil'. It seems to refer to Peter the disciple and the other original twelve while it still refers to the voyage of Acts.27 which was interrupted by a storm. It refers to Peter/cut short between two similar word-names Hermas and Hermes, and this is to remind the audience of the story regarding circumcision where many were falsely claiming that even the 'Gentiles' had to be circumcised while the decision-makers decided there was no need; Peter was dealt with curtly and with anger because he was the first to mix with the uncircumcised people. It also reflects on warning about false preaching. Cp: batroobaah, batrobaah. (Rom.16)

Hermes (Acts.14:8-18 (Mercurius)) 'I will throw-him/he/it' 'I will kill-him/he/it' 'here, see/saw his water' 'chased away-water-he/him' 'chased away his water'. For the same reasons as Patrobas and Hermas. Cp: hermeeyh, hermee-yh

Philologus; Philólogos; فِلولوجوه ، فيلولوجوه ، فِلولُجه ، فيلولُجه 'in, who sought safety' 'in who sought safety in him/it' 'flee if they come' 'in who if they sought refuge'; فِلولوغوه ، فيلولوغوه ، فِلولُغه ، فيلولُغه 'in playing with words' 'in what they changed meanings' 'in the language' 'in his/their language'. It could be referring to the Pentecost where Peter and the other disciples all spoke different languages which could be understood by speakers of many different languages, which is why it has been put in the same verse where one name refers to Peter and two names refer to 'saw his water' as the Holy Ghost and the Spirit came down and filled the disciples and caused them to speak in tongues (Acts.2). It may also refer to Paul and the ship passengers/crew having to find safety due to the storm. Cp: philooloogooh, phylooloogooh, philoologoh, phyloologoh, philooolooghooh, phylooolooghooh, philoologhoh, phyloologhoh. (Rom.16)

Julia; Ioulía; يوليَ 'he makes him guardian/in charge' 'he is in charge' 'he becomes loyal/is loyal'; هوليَ 'he is the guardian/leader' 'he is in charge' 'he is loyal' 'he is for me'; جوليَ 'walked around' 'wandered' 'walked/wandered to the other side' 'my side/my turn' 'came and made him in charge' 'came-loyal' 'came for me'; عوليَ 'raised him/became higher' 'rose above' 'higher than(physically or in status)' 'arrogance/ became arrogant' 'depended on/receive allowance from/supported' 'howled/howled for me' 'my children/ boys'; غوليَ 'my rivers/streams' 'made flow/rush like river' 'chained/were chained' 'despised' 'deep hidden hatred/anger' 'dug deep/stabbed deep' 'made up rules/laws/made more severe rules' 'exploited/took advantage' 'became more expensive' ; حوليَ 'around it/me/surrounds it/me' 'tried/attempted/they tried' 'cock-eyed/made vision go funny'; خوليَ 'allowed/allowed me' 'allowed to go/do' 'gave authority/gave authority to me' 'tasked/tasked me' 'leave/left it/me' 'emptied/empty it/me'.

It refers to Julius of Acts.27. It is the same as Julius (Acts.27) but because it is not anchored by any specific text/story it can have any meanings shown above which are more than when Julius was anchored to specific narration. Cp: youleeya, houleeya, gouleeya, 'ouleeya, ghouleeya, ḥouleeya, khouleeya. (Rom.16)

Nereus; Nēreús; نيريوه 'we see him/it' 'we show him' 'we teach him' 'we dream him/it' 'we water/quench him/it' 'we penis/penetrate or insult with penis-him/it' 'we narrate him/it' 'we tell the story' 'we shine on it/shine light for him' 'we create fire(s)'. It refers to the stories being told and that these stories are based on the quenching powers of water. Cp: neyryuh. (Rom.16)

Olympas; Olympás; عليم بآه ، علِم بآه 'knew of it/him/her' 'was aware of it/him/her' 'had knowledge of it/ him/her' 'marked it/him/her' 'made signal with it/him/her' 'showed/taught-him/it/her'; اولِم بآه ، اوليم بآه ، وُلم بآه ، وُليم بآه 'was gathered with it/him/her' 'collected with him/her/it' 'was hurt/ached by it/him/her' 'had whole knowledge/awareness of it/him/her' 'was aware/wary of it/him/her' 'was blamed for/by-him/ her'; عليم فآه ، علِم فآه 'knew of in it/him/her' 'was aware in it/him/her' 'showed/taught-in it/him/her' 'had knowledge in it/him/her' 'marked in it/him/her/was marked in it/him/her' 'made signal in it/him/her'; اولِم فآه ، اوليم فآه ، وُلم فآه ، وُليم فآه 'was gathered in it/him/her' 'collected in him/her/it' 'was hurt/pained in it/him/her' 'had whole knowledge/awareness in it/him/her' 'was aware/wary in it/him/her' 'was blamed in it/him/her'. It refers to having knowledge of the teachings of the stories, the meanings of the stories; being cautious of false preachings; it also refers to 'all the saints' and everyone the narrator is addressing. Cp: 'lym-baah, 'lim-baah, oolim-baah, oolym-baah, o-lim-baah, o-lym-baah, 'lym-phaah, 'lim-phaah, oolim-phaah, oolym-phaah, o-lim-phaah, o-lym-phaah. (Rom.16)

Satan is used for 'laid hands on' 'two laps/two sides' and means went back and forth on the same course/ path/way either twice or many times, and the narration promises God will hurt Satan, trample him under the apostles' feet, and this is done by apostles/preachers/teachers going back and forth teaching God's ways and preaching the story of Jesus. (Acts.16)

These four word-names of characters mentioned in verse 21 have been placed in the same sentence to summarise the whole story's themes of ramblings, events, importance of matters to the stories, completion of tasks, fulfilment of promises and donations, disobedience and obedience, the sexual acts which bring about the story's 'purification/conversion'; it also indicates the author is proud to show off his word-play and story-telling skills:

Timotheus (Acts.16:1-5) 'she passes him/walks past him/she makes him go' 'will you pass him/will you make him walk past/go' 'she completes/finishes it/he/him' 'will you complete/finish it/him/he' 'she marks/ signs it/him/he' 'will you mark/sign it/him/he/will you make him mark/sign' 'she wipes away his urine/ sperm(without use of water)' 'will you wipe away his urine/sperm'. It is used to remind the audience of the character's purpose and the stories' theme; to remind the 'recipients' are being asked to fulfil something specific (a contribution). (Rom.16)

Lucius (Acts.13:1-4) 'talks too much-he/him' 'talks too much nonsense-he/him' 'rambling/loquacious-he/him' 'his nonsense/ramblings' 'chew it-he/him' 'him/he for you' and refers to the long list of thanks and salutes, a pun on the author's own loquacity. (Rom.16)

Jason (Acts.17:5-9) 'they disobey/go against' 'they become difficult' 'they became askew/bent/crooked/ warped' 'lower back(spine area)' 'of lower back' 'up the ass(rectum)' 'of up the ass' and reflects the opposition and disobedience the characters of the stories faced. (Rom.16)

Sosipater; Sōsípatros; شوشي بَترُه 'important matters/many matters/wonderous matters-cut/snap it/him short/his stub of rock/his smooth rock' 'many things and important things-cut/snapped/snap short/his stub of rock/his smooth rock' 'wanted to interrupt him/it'; سوشي بَترُه 'did/fixed something/matters-cut/snapped/snap it/him short/his stub of rock/his smooth rock' 'bad matter/thing-cut/snap it short/interrupt him/it/his stub of rock/his smooth rock' and refers to the important matters covered in the stories; it indicates that the author of these stories could go on and have expanded had he wanted to but has chosen to cut it short. Cp: shooshee-batroh, soo-shee-batroh. (Rom.16)

Tertius; Tértios; تيرتيُه ، تيرتيوه ، تَرتيُه ، تَرتيوه 'narrates it/tells it' 'his narration' 'waters/quenches it' 'dreamt/dreams it'. This is the author making clear he, not Paul, wrote this epistle story, and that it is his creation, even the choice of word-name 'narrates/tells it' 'his narration' is the Biblical authors' method of showing these stories are fictional and to be marked as the creation of an author, it is not a letter written by Paul, it is not even a letter written by 'Tertius' it is the author still showing his skill at wordplay and storytelling and making it clear these are fictional stories 'I Tertius, who wrote *this* epistle, salute you in the Lord.'. Cp: teirtyoh, teirtyooh, tertyoh, tertyooh. (Rom.16)

Gaius (Acts.19:29-32) 'his misleading to downfall/his deceit to downfall'; 'made him howl' 'make him howl' 'learn and remember him/it' 'warn him/warned/taught him' 'beware of him/it' 'contained/prevented him/it'. Reflects all the events in the story are about being misled and causing the downfall of characters and anyone who believes these stories, but also refers to Timotheus as it is important for the author to identify Timotheus as significant to Paul (Gaius was a temporary wordplay replacement for Timotheus in an earlier story (see Gaius (Acts.19:29-32)). (Rom.16)

Erastus (Acts.19:17-22) 'yes, stack it/stack/pack' 'he stacked/stacked/packed it' 'made it in a row'; 'his bride/his wedding'; 'planted it' 'stuck it in mud/got stuck in mud/soil' and this is used to reinforce the importance of Timotheus as Paul's beloved because Erastus was paired with Timotheus when Paul sent them to Macedonia, it serves to get the audience to look back at the Timotheus/Paul stories and understand their relationship and the stories' meanings through connecting their word meanings (see Erastus (Acts.19:17-22), Aristarchus (Acts.19:29-41)). (Rom.16)

Quartus; Koúartos; قوَرتُه ، قوَرتوه 'read it aloud/spoke it publicly/in front of everyone' 'confessed/admitted it' 'spoke the truth openly' and refers to the author making everything clear: he is detailing a story, what happened in it and what it means within the story; he is also explaining and making public knowledge the secrets of the wordplay which may have eluded some of the audience so the author has made it clear: the mysteries and secrets have been confessed, made public, read aloud and detailed 'according to the revelation of the mystery, which was kept secret since the world began, But is now made manifest…' ascribes it to prophets writings and God 'made known to all nations for the obedience of faith.'. Cp: qouartoh, qouartooh. (Rom.16)

1Corinthians

Paul was chosen by the author of epistles for the same reason and use of the word-name in the epistle to the Romans for its meanings 'his mind' 'his patience' 'his affliction/afflicted him' 'his indication/direction' 'follow his indication/go his direction': and the story shows these meanings of Paul: intelligence, reasoning, deep-thinking, knowledge about matters raised (both he and the recipients of the letter) as well as the recipients of these letters being asked to do as he tells them, indicates to them; the letters show he says something and wants it to be followed through with its recipients actioning it. (1Cor.)

Sosthenes (Acts.18:11-17) 'bad/evil/offense-will/did harm him/them' 'bad/evil/offense-called out/called out to gather assembly' 'did/caused/made-will/did harm him/them' 'offense/bad/evil-gave permission' 'did cause/made/bad/evil/offense-gave ear to/heard him/them' 'bad/evil/offense-again/did it again/twice/the second(one)' 'did/caused/made-again/twice/to the other or second(one)'. Paul is informing them they have to remain united and assembled in one faith, belief and actions; he wishes/promises that through their belief in Jesus Christ they will not be harmed; he has heard a bad report about the differences, the issues between them; the reason he is calling them to unite is because there is offense and division between them which he has heard about. (1Cor.1)

Chloe; Chlóē; قلوي 'told me' 'all told/all said/all say' 'of gossiping/transporting news/gossip' and it just happens it is 'the house of Chloe' who inform Paul of the problems between the people he is addressing and he requests them to all speak and think the same thing; كلوي 'all/all of you/us' 'everything' 'eat/of eating' and as the word suggests the story narrates of Paul wanting them all to be of one word, one action, one belief, of the same thoughts, he wants them to be united; and what unites them is they believe and eat of 'Jesus/break/ate bread' and are pulled together in eating of the whole cake of bread 'Christ' (which is Jesus intact) 'circle/cake of bread'. Cp: qloey, kloey. (1Cor.1:11)

Corinthians the same as Corinth (Acts.18:1-6): خورِنثه 'both male and female (at the same time)' it applies to a male or female which either has both male and female reproductive organs, and/or behaves like a male when he/she is female or vice-versa: قورِنثه 'linked to him/linked him' 'linked them/him' 'linked him with wood/rope' and still refers to the pairing of male/female characters who do/embody the same thing just as a pair of bulls or cows when 'linked' with yoke or rope have to move at the same pace while doing the same work; there is also 'his opposite/opposed him' 'his horn/his spirit of strength(or power)' 'read to him/taught him' 'stopped him/it moving/fidgeting' 'made him stop what he was doing'; may have other meanings found in 'Cyrene'.

It is reflected in the narration of marrying two opposing parties although they have differences about the same matters much like making one person both male and female or taking on the appearance or behaviour of the opposite sex; linking them like bulls under one command, one pace, they are to obey and believe, think, do the same things as Paul (on behalf of God) instructs them; their 'horn' does not make them powerful or Paul's horn or any others' he mentions (Apollos', Cephas' (Peter)), but God's power is what gives them strength; they are linked by one belief in Christ; the opposed and opposite meanings are shown in that they have differences; they are ordered to cease from their squabbles and divisions and to unite; then narration goes on to merge opposites such as foolishness with wisdom, weakness with strength, the 'base' things being chosen by God who usually wants perfect things and people, people who are knowledgeable and strong are for the perishing while the weak and foolish are for the saving—all these show the 'male/female in one/behaving like the opposite sex' as well as 'opposites' and other meanings of 'Corinthian'. (1Cor.1)

This is how the story reads and how the author of 1Cor. has used the word meanings to reflect on the narration of the story: **Paul** 'his mind' 'his patience' 'his affliction/afflicted him', 'his indication/direction' 'follow his indication/go his direction' i.e. think about what Paul is telling you to do.

Apollos: 'soak/soaked him/it' 'afflict/afflicted him/it' you have been baptised, soaked in God's water.

Cephas: 'answered' 'fetched/brought him' 'cave(s)' 'pocket/his pocket' you need to answer/respond with what 'Paul' is telling you what to do, and why 'Apollos' has converted you through water to be. And that is '**Christ**' 'cake/circle of bread' all of you ('**Chloe**') to be intact in belief and actions in the ways of Jesus/God.

'Is Christ divided' is a pun as 'Christ' is a whole circle of bread before it is 'Jesus' broken from and eaten. (1Cor.1)

Crispus (Acts.18) 'partially washed/cleaned' 'by/with cake/circle of bread' as Paul states to only have baptised these two men in Corinth, and the 'Crispus/partial wash/cleanse' means he did not do a full 'baptism' which would instil in them the Holy Ghost/water, but the normal baptism which allows them to be whole 'Crispus/by with cake/circle of bread' (the 'cris' is the same as 'Christ').

Gaius (Acts.19:29-32) 'his misleading to downfall/his deceit to downfall' 'they misled him to his downfall/they deceived him to his downfall' 'made him howl' 'make him howl' 'learn and remember him/it' 'warn him/warned/taught him' 'beware of him/it' 'contained/prevented him/it'. The narration shows the people who follow God's ways will be saved as they have been warned/made aware; also because the narration has Paul make statements which are contradictory and openly show how these stories mislead who believes them, i.e. those who believe Paul and others are being misled, because Paul's name means 'wisdom/thought/intellect' and all his work in the stories is about preaching and teaching the meanings and ways of God/Christ, but now he states it is not so while he contradicts in the same statement that he was sent to preach the gospel i.e. epistle 'tell the story/explain/spread', but in the same sentence claims the wisdom of words makes the 'cross of Christ should be made of none effect.'—this is not a mistake on the author's part, but again shows these stories were mocking Jesus and Christianity.

The verses continue with double-meanings about wisdom and knowledge being foolishness or saving its believers, and causing those who are wise and prudent to be rendered unwise, without understanding. It goes on to elucidate that people's ability to understand words, meanings and wisdom has ceased and goes further to make it clear that the wordplay in these stories is intentional, but only fools believe it as true stories or as commandments from God: 'Where *is* the wise? where *is* the scribe? where *is* the disputer of this world? hath not God made foolish the wisdom of this world? For after that in the wisdom of God the world by wisdom knew not God, it pleased God by the foolishness of preaching to save them that believe.' and although religious scholars would take this to mean the people who believe without understanding will be saved for their belief, it is the same continuance of puns and wordplay which begin in the OT all the way to the end of the NT—and it is only people who can read the original language (which is preserved in word-names even in the English translations) and understand the wordplay and puns who can see exactly what is meant in these stories and in the names and their puns, its role in the stories. (1Cor.1)

Stephanas; Stephanás; شطفناه 'we split him/it open' 'we washed/rinsed him/it quickly' and it is the same as Stephen (Acts.6:5-15; 7:55-60). It is used the same as Crispus and Gaius that Paul and the 'Crispus/partial wash/cleanse' and 'Stephanas/quick rinse' means although he converted them and baptised them, he did not do anything additional which fully soaks them in God/Jesus' water which allows them to perform more miracles. Cp: shṭephanaah. (1Cor.1)

In using **Paul** and **Apollos** as an example to explain it is God's religion—neither Paul nor Apollos'—the example still uses Paul 'his mind' 'his patience' 'his affliction/afflicted him' 'his indication/direction' 'follow his indication/go his direction' as Paul plants the knowledge/words and Apollos meaning of 'soaked' waters them, which allows them to grow, be nurtured in its recipients: 'Who then is Paul, and who is Apollos...I have planted, Apollos watered; but God gave the increase.'. (1Cor.3:4-6)

1Cor.4, the narrator tells of how apostles who do God's work but suffer, that others are better off, but they (apostles and saints) do it for Christ's sake; he informs how they are without food, clothing or residence—telling the recipients that the only reason he writes about these matters, is not to shame them, but to 'warn' them, before reminding them he has 'got' them through the gospel then beseeches them to be his (Paul's) followers. Mentioning he and apostles are their fathers while comparing their (the recipients of the letter) wealth, security and status to their (the apostles and saints) poverty, weakness and suffering is also a direct message that good sons provide for their fathers. This is immediately followed by informing them this is the reason he has sent Timotheus, to teach them Paul's ways, just as he (Paul) does 'everywhere in every church'.

Just as in the epistle to Romans/Spain, he promises to come to them, from the narration it seems he has promised this before, but he cannot visit them currently but has sent Timotheus (who happens to have written this epistle). The last chapter tells and reminds them to go ahead with collecting donations—and for whatever reasons (obvious reasons if these stories are read correctly) he does not want the money collection to wait until he visits, it is important that they begin to collect donations before he comes and not to wait for him to arrive for this to happen, he encourages them that only when he arrives that he will expect them to send a person of their choosing to bring the donations to Jerusalem: this implies that there is mistrust over the intentions of the letter and Paul, which he mollifies by guaranteeing they do not have to send anything until they actually see him, but the same chapter informs them that Timotheus, now described as his son, which chapter 4 tells us carries this letter and the note at the end of the epistle shows he also took part in authoring the letter, this leads the audience (real audience not the 'recipients' of the letter in the story) to understand Timotheus is sent to collect and deliver the donations as he is just a 'son' like the obedient 'sons' Paul wants the Corinthian recipients of the letter to be towards their impoverished and suffering devout father, Paul. 'Now concerning the collection for saints, as I have given order to the churches of Galatia, even so do ye. Upon the first *day* of the week, let every one of you lay by him in store, as *God* hath prospered him, that there be no gatherings when I come!' He then promises he will come, will winter with them, and if possible, stay with them a while, but ends this promise with that he cannot pass by nor see them now, but does ask them to 'take care' of Timotheus, to allow him to conduct his work in peace—and he reminds them 'for he worketh the work of the Lord, as I also *do*.' He informs them Apollos will not be able to come because currently he does not want to. The narration shows that both Paul and Apollos were meant to visit earlier, but do not—this is significant: the two important figures who convert others to Christianity are never seen, but always promise to come, but the money-collectors who happen to write and carry the epistles, and carry their own recommendation letters (the epistle itself) always do arrive in the stories of the epistles. (1Cor.4; 9:6-15; 15)

The repeated promises of Paul promising to arrive through the epistles he is supposedly the author of (although the carriers of the epistles always have a hand in authoring them) while he never arrives, but encourages money to be collected with urgency and emphasis that they do not wait for his (Paul's) arrival, has the appearance of a scam. This scamming people out of money is the joke in, and theme of, the epistles' stories, and the authors of these epistle stories make no bones about it, it is clearly indicated in the wordplay they use and the narration which makes it obvious that the person who pretends to be Paul writing the letters is deceiving people to part with their money. Now the original audiences of these stories would have found them entertaining, but foreign audiences may have believed these stories to be true, they may have believed these stories were actual letters, and the belief that these letters/epistles were real letters would become part of the foreign audiences'/areas' folklore then in later times, and also modern times, mistaken as history. What may have started as an entertaining story about people being scammed by a pseudo-Paul and the authors/carriers of the letters, the Phoebes and Timotheus, etc., may have remained just that—a story, which became part of the foreign folklore, then mistaken and accredited as 'history' by later scholars; it may be that after the popularity of these stories among foreign audiences who believed it to be true that people who spoke and were from the countries of origin of these letters took advantage of the gullibility of the new foreign audiences, and as the letters do indicate, a scam was going on. If ever an individual claiming to be Paul did arrive at these foreign churches, how would the hosts know who he is claiming to be when there was no way to disprove who he claims to be? But an even more telling detail is the names of these churches are also compound word-names whose meanings reflect exactly what happens in the stories: if such churches in reality were named with these same names it is because these churches were built and named after the fictional churches in the stories of these epistles and that is after these stories became popular in foreign areas.

It is interesting if any (unbiased) expert ever looked into any real proof if 'Paul' or at least someone claiming to be Paul arrived at churches not just those named after the fictional churches of the NT stories, but any churches in the regions of Paul's fictional travels (if such proof ever existed) and if they would find a) he never arrived; b) where it is claimed he arrived (through proof outside the NT stories as the NT stories are purely fictional as are the churches written about) if it overlaps with other people claiming to be Paul arriving in churches at other areas where the distance and time cannot allow this person to be at those dates at the given dates; c) if there is proof that he truly existed, other than letters which are just copies of the NT epistle stories which anyone could reproduce—when did he live, where did he live, what proof is there that he went to these places it is claimed he visited—especially when the epistles have him promising to come, but always sending others to teach and collect donations.

Galatia (Acts.16:6) 'said/he said-came here/come here' 'sanitised on heat' 'sanitised it/him on heat' 'he said he came/he said he would come'; 'made mistake/he/they made mistake' 'of making mistakes' 'made mistake-he/him/she/her' 'of making mistakes-he/him/she/her' 'is deceiving/tricking/shortchanging' 'of deceiving/tricking/shortchanging-he/him/she/her' 'is wrong' 'he/she/they is/are wrong'. This reflects that what is happening is wrong, they are making a mistake by linking the gathering and sending of donations with Paul arriving, so he corrects their understanding by telling them he will come but that they should begin collecting money and not wait for him to come. Of course, it is also the author indicating that the recipients of the letter are being duped out of their money: that the church of 'Galatia' 'shortchanged/deceived-he/she/him/her' has already been asked to donate and implied the sent donations is to make this current church/recipient of the letter to want to do the same or better (in Romans it was the people in Macedonia and Achaia who were happy to have already made donations to induce the recipients of Roman/Spain epistle to also give); it reflects that Timotheus is the one who will come, but also the promises of Paul coming. (1Cor.15)

Timotheus (Acts.16:1-5) 'she passes him/walks past him/she makes him go' 'will you pass him/will you make him walks past/go' 'she completes/finishes it/he/him' 'will you completes/finishes it/him/he' 'she marks/signs it/him/he' 'will you mark/sign it/him/he/will you make him mark/sign'; 'she wipes away his urine/sperm(without use of water)' 'will you wipe away his urine/sperm'. It refers to Timotheus will be the one passing by and he is a completion of Paul's work, able to teach them everything Paul would have had he arrived. The same word-name is made to make clear that he wants them to give him the donations and be allowed to move on to reach Paul without hindrance or delay. (1Cor.15)

Macedonia (Acts.16:9-40) 'of plotting/deceiving' 'plotting/deceiving-him/he/she/they' 'covered tightly (with any kind of lid: stone, metal, cloth, etc.)/of covering tightly(with lid, etc.)' 'covered me with a lid/fabric/stone/etc.; 'of pillows' 'pillows/with pillows' 'resting on pillows' 'with hand on cheeks' 'of cheeks' 'cheeks' 'pulled off/down/away/removed by pulling' 'pulled bread off oven wall' 'pulled down wall/structure'. It is reflected in that no matter how much Paul promises to visit he remains a hidden enigma, someone who is covered out of sight by the distance and remains so; it reflects the scamming people out of the money they gather as donations; the 'pulled down/pulled bread off oven wall' indicates these people are losing their fortunes to deceit and that the person deceiving them and receiving their kind donations is making a living, feeding off their donations. (1Cor.15)

Ephesus (Acts.18:19-28) 'disentangle/untie (him/it)' 'disentangle knots or problems/matters(it/him)' 'separate it/him' 'break down into small and understandable pieces(it/him)' 'explain/break down into detail(it/him)' 'small seeds/stone of fruit' 'pit/remove seed/stones from fruit' 'divorce/separate from wife(him)' 'small gem like stones used in jewellery/clothes'; 'pass wind in him' 'make it/him break wind' can mean literally or to beat up or scare, 'copulate/pass wind into'; 'twisted/crumpled it' 'twisted/crumpled-he/him' 'made a mess of it/him'; 'provoked/provoked him/it'. Reflected in this area Paul will be able to make clear and explain, as well as sow stones/seeds of, the faith through the **Pentecost** (Acts.2:1-13) 'so speak it/pronounce it' which allows him and others to speak to a wider audience. (1Cor.15)

Apollos (Acts.18:24-28) 'soak/soaked him/it' 'afflict/afflicted him/it' and reflects although his name and character have the ability to preach/water faith, he has some kind of problem which he is dealing with and has no intention of visiting them currently. (1Cor.15)

Stephanas (1Cor.1) 'we split him/it open' 'we washed/rinsed him/it quickly' is also used a trick to induce the recipients to give donations as he and others with him are described as giving quickly, and their charity cleanses them, Stephanas' quickness to donate time and physical things is described as an addiction to the service of saints. He is deliberately made to come from **Achaia** (Acts.18:17) 'I mislead him/them to downfall/I will mislead him/them to his/their downfall' 'his misleading to downfall' 'I deceive him/them/I will deceive' 'I make him/them howl' 'I will make him/them howl' 'I warn/teach him/them' 'I will contain him/it' as this further clarifies that these donation requests are acts of deceiving people to part with their money, they are being misled—the way these word-names and sentences are structured show the author of this story was not trying to be subtle at all about the people being deceived by this epistle to give away money. (1Cor.15)

Fortunatus; Phortounátos; فورطوناته 'were split/parted' 'of splitting/parting-he/him/it' 'were deceived out of money/possessions/opportunity/chance' 'of deceiving out of money/possessions/chances-he/him/it' 'were torn' 'of being torn/ripped' 'crossed' 'of crossing' 'helped cross/pass-he/him/it'. This character with the suitable name of deceiving others out of money, etc. is also used to encourage the recipients of the letter to give—and note how although earlier in the chapter the statement is that Paul is not trying to 'shame' them into sending him money, the author does not mind allowing him now to clearly state 'I am glad of the coming of Stephanas and Fortunatus and Achaicus: for that which was lacking on your part they have supplied.' In other words: shame on you! Look, other people are giving and you should give charity too (never mind all the names are about deceiving people and very specific because it is meant to be understood by a local audience). It is equivalent to Euphrates, Ephratah. Cp: p͟hoṛtounaatoh. (1Cor.15)

Achaicus; Achaïkós; اغييكوه 'I mislead you to downfall/I will mislead you your downfall-he/it' 'I mislead you with it' ' 'I deceive you/I will deceive you with it'; اعَييكوه 'I make you howl it' 'I will make you howl with it' 'I warn/teach you' 'I warn/teach you with it' 'I warn you about it/him' 'I teach you about it/him' 'I will contain you/I will contain you with it/him'. It refers that these people are being misled with the preaching, and are being misled and damaged by being scammed out of their money believing they are giving it to the service of God; it reflects that the narrator Paul is telling them he is teaching/warning them not to be selfish and to give, and at the same time it is the author warning about such behaviour and people. It is equivalent to Achaia (Acts.18:17). Cp: ag͟hayeekooh, a'ayeekooh. (1Cor.15)

Asia (Acts.2:9) 'disobeyed/disobedient/went against' 'disobeyed him/went against him' 'became askew/bent/crooked/warped' 'sticks' 'used sticks'; 'sorrow' 'bad/offense/insult' 'bad towards/offense/insult towards'; 'things/matters' 'many/lots of things' 'wants' 'he wanted' 'speaking in whispers' 'snitching'. It reflects that the recipients of the letter have not sent donations and Paul is making them feel disobedient that they are not giving like the characters mentioned who do give; it indicates that he is teaching them about matters, but also wants to receive things, physical things; it shows Paul's disappointment that they have not sent donations; it is also the author showing how it is warped and wrong to deceive people out of what they have. (1Cor.16)

Priscilla (Acts.18) 'good/piety-he works/labours' 'go/goes beyond/surpasses/passes-he works/labours' 'good/piety-I/I will tell him' 'good/piety-I/I will remove/move him/it' 'go/goes beyond/surpasses/goes past-I/I will tell him' 'innocent/disowns/distances from-I/I will tell him' 'good/piety-he did work/labour' 'go/goes beyond/surpasses-he did work' 'good/piety-I/I will remove/move him/it' 'go/goes beyond/surpasses/goes past-I/I will tell him' 'innocent/disowns/distances from-I/I will tell him' 'good/piety-he did water' 'good/piety-yes, he is able/yes, he can do it' 'go/goes beyond/surpasses/passes-yes, he is able/yes, he can do it' 'innocent/disowns/distances from-yes, he is able/yes, he can do it'

Aquila (Acts.18:1-6) 'his sayings' 'told him/I told him' 'put words in his mouth' 'stayed/spent time' 'stayed/spent time with him' 'staying/spending time/they are staying spending time' 'gathering place/place people gather at to spend time together at' 'of spending time' 'removed him' 'of removing' 'his brainy-ness/intelligence/mind/wisdom' 'made him reasonable/gave him clever' 'gave him mind/logic/calmness' 'calmed him down/made him knowledgeable/patient' 'his mind/patience/knowledge' 'made him rational' 'kept him in a specific place'.

This pair have been used here to encourage and push people to donate and do good as they are being asked to give it to the service of God despite the narration making it clear they are being deceived; it shows they are being mentioned in the church of Priscilla and Aquila, and their word-names also means that Paul is trying to get the recipients of the letter to be reasonable, pious and to give the fruits of their work to him. (1Cor.16)

Anathema Maran-atha; anáthema maranathá; انآذِمَ مَرعنَ ذآ ، انآذيمَ مَرعنَ ذآ 'I guilt/ostracise/blame him-he evil eyed us/he evil eyed it' and this reflects more than one thing in the story: anyone who does not love Jesus will be 'evil-eyed' or is an unpleasant person who 'evil-eyes' others because of his/her greed/selfishness. It also reflects that people who are selfish do not give charity because they are greedy, and in this verse are likened to a person called (marraa'/مَرّاع) 'evil-eyer' as some people who see what others have are believed to be able to cause that person or the thing that has been 'eyed' to break, be damaged, catch an illness, be wounded, lost, etc. due to that person seeing it, 'eyeing' it. In the narration of the story the author plays on Paul directing this insult at those who have failed to send donations (the recipients of the epistle), and it is also directed at Paul wanting what others have, what he believes they should send to him as donations. Cp: anaa-vema mar'navaa, anaa-vyma mar'navaa. (1Cor.16)

Philippi has been used as in (Matt.16:13-28) for 'in his/its core/middle' 'so respond/assist/serve' and it means the recipients are expected to give of their money/possessions just as the named Stephanas, Fortunatus, Achaicus have given, all who are mentioned as co-authors of the epistle; it also reflects they are to respond by giving Timotheus, who is also a co-author of the letter, the donations and to assist him as was requested in the chapter and again through the word 'Philippi' in the note of the epistle. (1Cor.16)

2Corinthians

Timothy the same as **Timotheus** 'she passes him/walks past him/she makes him go' 'will you pass him/will you make him walk past/go' 'she completes/finishes it/he/him' 'will you complete/finish it/him/he' 'she marks/signs it/him/he' 'will you mark/sign it/him/he/will you make him mark/sign' 'she wipes away his urine/sperm(without use of water)' 'will you wipe away his urine/sperm'. As Timotheus still serves the same word-meanings and role since he was introduced and that is to pass by from place to place; to be Paul's companion and be as effective as Paul in spreading the word of God/Jesus through an intimate relationship with Paul. (2Cor.1:1)

Achaia 'I mislead him/them to downfall/I will mislead him/them to his/their downfall' 'his misleading to downfall' 'I deceive him/them/I will deceive' 'I make him/them howl' 'I will make him/them howl' 'I warn/teach him/them' 'I will contain him/it'. '...all the saints which are in all Achaia' has been used instead of 'all the saints in Jerusalem' as the author sees this more fitting: the purpose of the letter is to mislead and con the recipients out of money by convincing them what they are doing is piety and for the saints' sake; the story is a warning about deceit while within the story it is done through and made about teaching the recipients of the letter about faith and the correct ways of God. (2Cor.)

2Cor.1:11 is the 'epistles' authors' method of using guilt-tripping, shaming, the recipients of the letter that other people have sent money to Paul while they have not. It is done in this verse by thanking them (Corinthians) for their prayers in Paul and his companions' time of trouble, while it makes clear 'many persons' sent a gift (money).

2Cor.1:13-15, although some may believe it gives the indication that Paul had visited Corinth before (in the story), it is saying he has not and is still promising and yearning to visit them: 'For we write none other thing, unto you, than what ye read or acknowledge; and I trust ye shall acknowledge even to the end; As also ye have acknowledged us in part, that we are your rejoicing, even as ye also *are* ours in the day of the Lord Jesus. And in this confidence I was minded to come unto you before, that ye might have a second benefit; And to pass by you into Macedonia, and to come again out of Macedonia unto you...Moreover I call God for a record upon my soul, that to spare you I came not as yet unto Corinth.' Therefore the 'second benefit' mentioned means the first benefit/contact they have of him is through his epistles—and by promising to come to Corinth they would have the second benefit with him being there to teach and meet them instead of only instruct through the letter(s). It is not detached from the fictional story being told as a letter to Corinth, the use of **Macedonia** 'of plotting/deceiving' 'plotting/deceiving-him/he/she/they' 'covered tightly (with any kind of lid: stone, metal, cloth, etc.)/of covering tightly(with lid, etc.)' 'covered me with a lid/fabric/stone/etc.' 'pulled off/down/away/removed by pulling' 'pulled bread off oven wall' 'pulled down wall/structure' all show the author making it clear to the audience that Paul or someone pretending to be Paul is deceiving the recipients of these letters out of money and that he/she/they are making a living from it, and has never actually appeared he is still hidden from them. For the same latter reasons Macedonia is repeat to emphasise, but also **Judaea** 'he/they were called' 'he/they made claim' 'he/they made false/unproven claim' as Paul is calling people to follow the ways of Jesus, but because the Corinthians are already Christians, according to the letters, it is about Paul calling them to give donations, and it highlights that false claims are being made.

The 'upset' mentioned in Chapter 2 may be over his constant promises to visit then always sending someone else instead. It indicates they have accused him of a scam, of defrauding them as the narration has him state in Chapter 7 'Receive us; we have wronged no man, we have corrupted no man, we have defrauded no man.' and goes on to explain that it is not about condemning them (Corinthians); about him repenting sending a letter; then repenting; briefly explaining the problems he faced in Macedonia (without saying clearly what the problems are (and this too is 'covered with lid' meaning of Macedonia)). After informing them all has been forgiven, the following chapter immediately tells the Corinthians that although the Macedonian churches are in poverty they have been blessed by generously giving and sending him a gift (probably donations), so it is again the purpose of the letter to ask for money, and when like the previous epistle stories where money is asked there is an evasive Paul promising to come, word-names which depict the recipients are being tricked for money, and when the money is asked the recipients are always made to feel or at least depicted as less generous, shortcoming, than the other churches who are said to have given—this serves to make the recipients of the letter feel bad and puts pressure on them to start collecting and sending money to Paul.

Silvanus; Silouanós; سِلوَنوه ، سِلوَنُه 'asked/questioned-him' 'his asking/questions' 'flowed/leaked water-him' 'his flowing/leaking' 'entertained/distracted-him' 'his entertainment/distraction' 'comforted-him/his comfort'. It reflects the recipients of the letter have many questions which they want Paul to answer; Paul is informing the recipients they should and will be comforted in God and Jesus; it also shows the sender is distracting them with these statements. Cp: silwanooh, silwanoh. (2Cor.19-24)

Corinth/Corinthians 'both male and female (at the same time)' 'linked to him/linked him' 'linked them/him' 'linked him with wood/rope' 'his opposite/opposed him' 'his horn/his spirit of strength(or power)' 'read to him/taught him' 'stopped him/it moving/fidgeting' 'made him stop what he was doing'.

The meanings are used the same way as in 1Cor. the recipients are being taught; they are being mollified of any questions that arise; they are being asked to obey and follow teachings and orders just as a pair of bulls linked under one yoke or led around with a rope around the horns; the power 'horn' is God's not the people's; throughout the epistle there is a combining into one of opposing ideas, ways, physical opposites. (2Cor.)

Troas (Acts.16:8-11) 'watered it/him' 'gave it/him to drink(water)' 'dreamed it/him' 'dreamed' 'told story'. Paul is telling them a story of what happened; it is explaining why he was unable to come to them which he buries under tears, sorrow, forgiving them and asking them to forgive him; it is because while he was wanting to preach God's word which is 'watered it/him' he could not find 'Titus' which caused him to go to 'Macedonia' (deceived/hid/covered), and therefore this shows how he avoids being seen by them. (2Cor.2)

Titus; Títos; تيتوه ، تييتوه 'come to him/you come to him' 'bring to him/you bring to him' 'they came/they brought' 'came a lot/brought a lot'; تعطوه 'you give/gave to him'. This reflects that because Paul could not find a person named 'come to him/bring to him' 'you give/gave to him', Paul was unable to come to the Corinthians, i.e. they did not send what they were supposed to send, contributions. It is the same evasiveness used in the narration of the epistles where Paul makes it clear he will not come until something is sent to him, brought by a third party which is a companion of his, and excuses as to why he cannot come to see them (which is why the author has tied 'Titus' to 'Macedonia': they did not send to Paul what he was expecting to be brought to him (contributions which were supposed to be handed to Titus) therefore the result is he goes into Macedonia (which he already is) 'of plotting/deceiving' 'covered tightly (with any kind of lid: stone, metal, cloth, etc.)/of covering tightly(with lid, etc.)').

Titus has come to Corinthians before and brought them letters from Paul before; Titus is also coming to the Corinthians and bringing the epistle, and like the other epistles it includes the sender Paul asking the recipients to take care of him (Titus), and Titus is also the character who wrote the epistle. 2Cor.8 explicitly states Paul's request that the recipients of the letter give generously to Titus, i.e. he will come and they should bring donations to him; Paul asks them to give donations as proof of their love for God; he plays on making them feel inadequate in comparison to the generosity and devotion of the 'churches of Macedonia (deceived)' as the Macedonians gave without being asked to give. The narration of 2Cor.8-9 is done in a way to emphasise how the sender/Paul manipulates, or tries to, the recipients to give money even if they have doubts about the request and the collectors of these donations; the narration employs flattery, warning, shaming, questioning their loyalty and love of God all in relay with word-names which mean they are being deceived (Macedonia/Achaia). Cp: teetooh, teeytooh, t'ṭooh. (2Cor.)

Israel and Moses are used not only for word-name meanings but a message to the recipients: **Israel** 'twisted muscle-the/twisted-the' stand for disobedience, the twisting and corrupting of God's commandments; **Moses** 'squeeze him/it' 'suck him/it' as the narration has Paul want to squeeze money out of the recipients; 'touched/possessed/was possessed/touched' 'entangled/caused problems/provoked problems or fighting' as a problem has arisen between the recipients of the letter and Paul (whether over him not visiting as he promises to do and never fulfils, or over money he requests to be sent).

The recipients are likened to Israel first through flattery: Israel was made the chosen people, circumcised/cleansed/made perfect for God in the flesh of the genital; the recipients/Corinthians have been made cleansed and 'special' through receipt of letters written with ink, but because they have believed through the written word it is the same as receiving a surgical operation in the 'fleshy tables of the heart'.

The accusatory and negative message is the recipients, by questioning and/or accusing Paul, are being like disobedient 'Israel' against the prophet Moses (the authors of NT always have Paul aggrandise himself to Moses, Jesus, the 'one' prophesied by Isaiah/Esaias); they are reminded of an OT story where Moses had to cover his face after meeting face-to-face with God, i.e. the glory/light in Moses' face was so bright it was detrimental for Israel/people to see Moses without a veil covering his face, this is a coded message to the recipients to stop insisting on seeing Paul, stop harassing him to visit and to send the money and when his 'glory' is safe enough for the recipients/Corinthians to receive him, he will visit. (2Cor.3)

Eve (Gen.1) 'stay' is used to reflect the narration: Paul is asking the recipients to bear with him while he explains, i.e. not to lose interest and go, or stop reading; using the serpent which deceived Eve as an example which brings to mind that by being deceived Adam and Eve were no longer allowed to stay in Eden; Paul warns the recipients not to allow the words, the person of those word/preachings, to stay in their hearts and minds—if the recipients believe in the false teachings and false preacher then these false preachings and beliefs will stay in their minds and souls and therefore the true teachings/preaching will not be able to stay with and in them (the recipients). (2Cor.11)

Damascus is used for 'tore/ripped up' and also 'spat/spat a lot' 'sucked/sucked a lot' 'sucked at his teeth'. The meanings of 'sucked at his teeth/sucked a lot/spat a lot' means to show someone who is unpleasant, maybe not clever as Eliezer from Damascus was shown to be when Abraham asks in despair if he (Eliezer of Damascus) is going to be his heir. It is used to enhance Paul's narration that he is a fool, which he states to counteract and moderate the self-aggrandisement which immediately follows when he asks to be considered a fool at verses 16-17. The 'tore/ripped up' meanings enhance the descriptions of the beatings, floggings, stonings and other sufferance he went through to preach God/Jesus' words, and for the sakes of the recipients of the letter. (2Cor.11)

Aretas; Harétas; هريته 'I drove him away/chased him away(verbally)' when a person uses aggressive or unkind language to force a person to leave, 'here, I saw him' 'I saw him' 'I showed him' 'made it/him fall apart' 'here, I watered him' 'I watered him'; خَريته 'I made him flee(with physical violence/action)' 'I made him shit himself(scared him)' 'I made him/it fall down/collapse'. These word-names are brought in at the end of Chapter 11 to enhance all the narration of suffering Paul went through in the whole chapter in order to spread God's word and that it reaches the recipients of the letter as well as everyone Christianity reached. It directly reflects the character Aretas caused Paul to flee for his life. It is similar to Aaron, Hur, Hor. Cp: hareitah, khareitah. (2Cor.11)

Titus is used again in the final chapters of the story for 'come to him/you come to him' 'bring to him/you bring to him' 'they came/they brought' 'came a lot/brought a lot' 'you give/gave to him' as Paul comes to visions of God, or they are brought to him; he comes to paradise; Paul mentions he intends to come a third time, it does not say he came twice and will come a third time, but that this will be his third attempt to try and come to them, it must be read in the context of the whole story; even in this promise of visiting there is a need for him to state that he is not coming to take what is theirs, i.e. their money and possessions (which he has repeatedly asked them to donate) but he will come for them, the people. It is reflected in Titus has already come to them multiple times and will come again. (2Cor.12-13)

The note at the end uses **Philippi** as before, wanting the recipients to 'answer/respond/assist' favourably. **Lucas** 'talks(ed) too much/talks too much nonsense' 'rambling/loquacious' 'his nonsense/ramblings' 'chew(ed)' 'for you' as the letter is long and rambling and it means 'for you' as in the recipients, but also Paul, Titus and whoever wrote, sent and delivered the letter as they hope to make a gain from it. (2Cor. note)

Galatians

Galatia (Acts.16:6) قَلَتيَ ، قَلَتييَ ، قَل اتيَ ، قَل اتييَ 'said/he said-came here/come here' 'sanitised on heat' 'sanitised it/him on heat' 'he said he came/he said he would come' غَلَطيَ ، غَلَطييَ 'made mistake/he/they made mistake' 'of making mistakes' 'made mistake-he/him/she/her' 'of making mistakes-he/him/she/her' 'is deceiving/tricking/shortchanging' 'of deceiving/tricking/shortchanging-he/him/she/her' 'is wrong' 'he/she/they is/are wrong'.

It speaks of the churches of Galatia being in the wrong by following a wrong gospel; it speaks also that the Galatians have suggested or stated that Paul is in the wrong, that he is running after worldly gains; there are others who are deceiving the people by perverting the story of Jesus. (Gal.1)

Jerusalem 'came-saw-asked-them/the' 'they see-asked-them/the' refers to the Galatians being called to Jesus Christ which at verse 6 Pauls states they have left Paul's calling to this, and follow another gospel; it refers to the apostles of Jerusalem who also call to Jesus which he states he did not go to at the point in time he speaks about, and in this point he seems to be addressing concerns that no one knows who he is and that no one save a select few has seen him, and at the same time people who may be claiming he is a false preacher do not actually know him.

Arabia 'expressing clearly/speaking clearly' 'he will-my god/parent/teacher' 'will he-my god/parent/teacher' '(of)learn and remember/beware/be warned-teacher/discipliner/parent/god/master/the grower/anyone who brings someone up or teaches them/grows them (children/animals/plants/etc.)/grew fast and(or) well' it can also be read in the tense 'taught/disciplined/grew well/brought up' 'expressed clearly', 'of getting naked' 'of fucking with' 'fucked a lot with'; 'is mixed and diluted with water' 'the god/parent/teacher' 'is my god/parent/teacher' 'he is-my god/parent/teacher' 'is he/which-my god/parent/teacher?' 'the (or of) mixed and diluted with water' 'mixed and diluted with water' 'the (or of) teacher(ing)/discipliner(ing)/parent/god/grower/anyone who brings someone or something up or teaches them/grows them' 'the grown fast and/or well'.

Most of these meanings are present: the chapter is about people who are preaching and teaching, preachers who are mixing and diluting (negatively) Jesus' story; it reflects that Paul's preaching and expression are clearer than all others as he has received the revelation of the story/teachings direct from Jesus, which is why he does not go to Jerusalem 'but I went to Arabia' as this makes it clear he was in direct contact with God/Jesus, and received a well brought up, well-raised teaching, this enables him to express Jesus' ways and preach better than all others.

Damascus 'tore/ripped up' and also 'spat/spat a lot' 'sucked/sucked a lot' 'sucked at his teeth' this refers again to people who preach falsely but also those who believe it, even the Galatians are meant here as they have followed a different preacher and therefore spat at or spat out Paul's teachings; it refers to how Paul/Saul previously persecuted Christians; it also refers to the indicated rumours about Paul's credibility and identity.

Peter 'his/its stub/shortness' 'he has cut him/it short' 'he/it has been snapped short' 'he/it has been abruptly cut off' 'they have snapped him/it/cut him/it short' 'his stub of rock' 'his smooth rock' all the meanings imply 'short/abrupt/quick/a stub/interrupted'. It reflects the Galatians quickly leaving Paul's ways to follow another; Paul leaving his Jewish faith to follow the Christian faith; Paul visiting Peter and James briefly and being seen by no one else; in his residence being interrupted by travels.

James 'he/it pinches' 'he pokes finger into' 'he pokes finger into anus' (sexually or as a prank over clothing) 'he pokes fingers into food/he pollutes food by poking fingers into it' 'he makes a mess'. Reflected as perversion of preachings and misleading people to follow Jesus in a wrong way; the Galatians following a different and wrong gospel; it reflects the mess which people are making about Paul's intentions, claims and identity.

Syria 'to throw/to do with throwing/killed' 'thrown/wide and far/extending over vast and distant locations' and refers to the accusations being thrown around; the distant and various locations Paul travels to preach God's word.

Cilicia 'ate it/you-him/it' 'fed you-him/it' 'all of it-he/him' 'ate you-he/him/it' 'worried-him/he/it'. It is a form of a curse to be 'eaten' whether by God, illness, etc.; it is Paul worried that the Galatians have been so easily misled away from following him; the curse Paul hopes will befall whoever is misleading people with false teachings.

Judaea 'he is called/calls' 'call, or curse' 'to make a claim' 'make a false claim or an unproven claim'; the story begins about being called to follow God and/or Paul; about following the wrong preachers; it is about curses on misleading preachers; it is about false claims whether misleading gospels or claims about knowing Paul. (Gal.1)

Jerusalem 'came-saw-asked-them/the' 'they see-asked-them/the' as Paul and his companions are come to Jerusalem asking people to convert.

Barnabas 'piety/good-prophesied news' 'piety/good-prophecy/predict' piety/good-prophet/news' 'passed/beyond/passed beyond-prophesied news' 'passed beyond-prophecy/predict' 'passed beyond-prophet/news' 'piety/good towards his prophet' 'piety/good-warned (him)/woke (him) up/pointed out (to him)'. Paul and his companions are bringing the gospel which the narration states is specific to the 'Gentiles' ('**Gentile**' meaning ethnesin; يثني/اثني سِن/سين '**ethne**': 'he/they do it again/double it/fold it/repeat it-' 'he/they dissuade/make leave-' 'he/they are idolaters/pagans-' 'idols-' 'praise/praises-' 'idol worshippers-' 'idolatry/worshipping idols-'; followed by '**sin**' meanings: 'in the direction of/towards me/in the face of/in front of/straight/straight line/direct/opposite me' and from the OT 'I will deceive them/the' 'I will mislead them to downfall-them/the' and 'I will mislead them to their downfall'), so he is teaching them the proper way to worship and leading them to be 'good'/pious; it is reflected in Paul being annoyed that people who could also preach arrived, and the narration has him state that the people with knowledge did not add anything to him, i.e. he found them lesser in knowledge and effectivity than himself.

Titus 'come to him/you come to him' 'bring to him/you bring to him' 'they came/they brought' 'came a lot/brought a lot' 'you give/gave to him'. As Paul and his group are coming to the people in Jerusalem and bringing with them the gospel, God's ways of worship, etc.; in spies wanting to hold something against them to arrest them; the knowledgeable people who arrive and discuss with Paul, but he finds they bring and add nothing to him. (Gal.2)

Peter 'his/its stub/shortness' 'he has cut him/it short' 'he/it has been snapped short' 'he/it has been abruptly cut off' 'they have snapped him/it/cut him/it short' 'his stub of rock' 'his smooth rock' all the meanings imply 'short/abrupt/quick/a stub/interrupted'. Reflected in the circumcision matter is mentioned, which includes the cutting of parts of the penis, the decision that it is not necessary among '**Gentiles**' ethnē; يثني/اثني 'he does it again/twice/doubles it/folds it/repeats it' 'he dissuades/makes leave' 'he is an idolaters/pagan' 'idols' 'he praises' 'idol worshippers' 'idolatry/worshipping idols'. It is also in Paul facing-off with Peter, Paul interrupts and snaps Peter short as he describes Peter being in the wrong. Mentioning Peter, James and John and having them split the target audience of who preaches/converts whom between the first three and Paul serves to make the latter rise in status in the stories by equating him to the original disciples, which is what the author is doing.

James 'he/it pinches' 'he pokes finger into' 'he pokes finger into anus' (sexually or as a prank over clothing) 'he pokes fingers into food/he pollutes food by poking fingers into it' 'he makes a mess'. It is reflected in Paul who finds the people '*to be somewhat* in conference' to not be that knowledgeable but in fact make a mess and confusion of matters; it is reflected in Peter making a mess of preaching the gospel and converting others; it is reflected in the division of preaching/converting that Peter, James and John preach to the circumcised (the clean), and Paul preach to the 'heathen' (the unclean) and the latter means the uncircumcised are polluted or not as clean as the circumcised people.

Cephas 'answered' 'fetched/brought him' 'cave(s)' 'pocket/his pocket'. Reflected in when the three original disciples can see Jesus' work in Paul, this is as being given an answer that he is equal to them in status and preaching/healing ability; also, that Paul has been tasked and can officially be recognised (by three original disciples) as bringing the ways of Jesus to people, i.e. proof of his credibility; it is in Paul answering/confronting Peter (Cephas) when he finds him in the wrong.

John 'soaked it/him (in)' 'brothers' 'betrayed' 'sacks' 'sackcloth' 'put/wrap it/him in sack/sackcloth'. This is portrayed in Paul being tasked by three original disciples all who soaked in Jesus/God's water/sperm direct from Jesus (two with a higher and deeper treatment from Jesus) that now Paul is also soaked in the same piety, knowledge, abilities. It goes further to make Paul even better than Peter because this author paints Paul more pious (supported by the word-name meaning of Barnabas who accompanies him) as the narration shows Peter betraying his calling and faith by fearing men instead of God and Paul calling him out on it.

Peter is still used for meanings 'cut short/interrupted/snapped/quick/abrupt' and **Antioch** for 'was finished/over' 'was hurt/offended/poked in wound' 'was chosen' 'was picked/purified/cleansed' 'pronounced/spoke/made speak': according to Paul, Peter cuts short his dealings with the 'Gentiles' when 'them of the circumcision' arrive; Peter's preaching is over as soon as people who are circumcised arrive; the author through Paul is showing Peter's role as the prominent disciple in all the gospels is over and replaced by Paul; Paul mentions that fearing the law of man and hoping righteousness will come through the laws of man, makes Jesus' sacrifice for nothing, i.e. his preachings and gospels are over if this is how Peter and other preachers will behave.

Paul interrupts Peter, speaks against him and blames him in front of everybody; although this can be seen clearly as an insult to Peter, it is also the author showing Paul is offended by Peter's betrayal or cowardice when it comes to preaching the gospel; it is the author showing how Paul self-aggrandises himself and is showing and pronouncing clearly that he (Paul) is the one person selected by Jesus to preach his ways; Paul is showing his preachings and teachings are the only and best way to become cleansed and purified and that he is the one who should be followed if people want to truly convert to Christianity. It uses the circumcision topic, and the related matter of being innately clean or unclean, to show Peter betraying God/Jesus when he pretends not to deal with the uncircumcised—the author is not concerned that it was Peter directly ordered by God in an earlier NT story who was first to deal with the uncircumcised converts and state that they are pure by conversion with no need of circumcision, and although Peter faced opposition over this he persisted in interacting with the uncircumcised and did as God commanded him in the story. The author of Galatians is not ignorant of this story but just like characters and word-names are repeated and recycled for current/new use, so has this theme: Paul is showing Peter is impure and only Paul is completely pure, only Paul and his teachings can and should be trusted.

It would be a superficial reading to only read Gal.2 as Paul being zealously devoted to Jesus Christ and calling people to Jesus, when in fact it is more about praising Paul and raising his status in the NT stories as the highest authority, the purest and strongest apostle surpassing all original disciples—and the author does this through having Paul self-aggrandise himself to show how Paul of the epistle stories manipulates people, blurs what they know (the recipients of the epistles in storyland and not the real audience of the stories) about Jesus, the disciples, and specifically any concerns they may have over the authenticity of Paul so that when he asks them to collect donations and send them to him that there is no doubt of his intentions; and that no other persons can be trusted, including the original disciples, as he has already tainted their reputations, but also he has created a 'meeting' between himself and the original disciples so that the recipients of the letters feel he and his requests are authentic—and although it is still only Paul of the epistles claiming these meetings and the confrontation with Peter and other disciples, it puts to rest the doubts which are evident in other epistles that nobody seems to know him, and he has never visited (except for the money-collectors he sends). (Gal.2)

Galatians 'said/he said-came here/come here' 'sanitised on heat' 'sanitised it/him on heat' 'he said he came/he said he would come' 'made mistake/he/they made mistake' 'of making mistakes' 'made mistake-he/him/she/her' 'of making mistakes-he/him/she/her' 'is deceiving/tricking/shortchanging' 'of deceiving/tricking/shortchanging-he/him/she/her' 'is wrong' 'he/she/they is/are wrong'. The meanings are emphasised further in Gal.3: their wrong is they have attempted to gain innate purity through bodily cleanliness: circumcision. Paul rails against this not only because his character believes it is unnecessary as purity, both physical and spiritual, can be gained through belief in Jesus and following the ways preached, but because this poses a danger to the Paul of the epistles as it undermines his teachings, renders him less effective. If others do like the people in the churches of Galatia who have circumcised themselves then they become 'clean/pure' in body and soul, they do not need to do more than that, even if they follow preachings and teachings it may embolden them to no longer need to follow all of Paul's specific teachings and this would cause Paul of the epistles to lose income through the donations he constantly requests; even if we set aside his money-making operations, it still causes him to be less significant in what he can do and influence the people through his teachings, it gives him less authority if a people are already intrinsically pure.

Abraham has been used both for what it stands for as a story as he and his children became pure for God through circumcision, but also for its word-name meanings: 'pull up/draw up-the' 'clear-the'. Paul rages about the topic of circumcision because the people of Galatia he is addressing have circumcised themselves. i.e. they have been 'Abrahammed', drawn up like water bailed in a pouch from sins and uncleanness, their sins have been cleared away. This action causes them to no longer need any extra cleansing such as apostles' preachings and the apostles' baptising and cleansing abilities through Jesus' water. Which is why Paul's narration is presented as anger towards the Galatians, he is telling them they cannot become pure through a physical circumcision, although he is contradicted by what other 'Pauls' say about 'Jews' and those 'of circumcision' in other stories; the author of Galatians is aware that Paul also does not believe what he states now in Galatians because as soon as he met a man he liked who was not circumcised (Timotheus), he had him circumcised so that he too could be pure enough to accompany Paul and be a receptacle and pouring vessel of Jesus' water. This has nothing to do with a fictional character having a Jewish mother and Greek father because these are used as wordplay which only when understood can any scholar really understand what these stories are saying and what their characters represent.

You have to remember **Galatia** is used because it means: they are now physically and spiritually wrong because they thought they could circumvent the Christian process or purity through water/baptising/preaching by being circumcised and therefore better cleansed, guaranteed piety, purity and salvation; they have followed gospels and preachings which are wrong and misleading and this has led them to wrong; they have sought to be cleansed like one of their name meanings is to be sanitised on heat, but have been deceived and have made a mistake by getting circumcised and believing this is the way to piety and purity.

The 'of deceiving/tricking/shortchanging-he/him/she/her' 'is wrong' 'he/she/they is/are wrong' meanings of Galatia have been made prominent as Paul continues to mislead the recipients of his letter with what was meant by circumcision and Abraham's seed. He seeks to convince the recipients that only one single 'seed/line' of Abraham was able to be cleansed through circumcision and that seed is through Isaac and connected to Jesus, which even the gospels have been unable to connect to Jesus as he does not have a human father and the stories intentionally give the bloodline/seed/line to David and onwards to Joseph, Mary's fiancé who was not Jesus' father in any shape or form as in all the stories God is Jesus' father. It is not only Abraham and only one of his seed/children (he had many) who become cleansed and 'special' to God although it is the line through Isaac that receives a higher status promise—all the males related to Abraham undergo circumcision and reach purity with Abraham, even those unrelated to him by blood, i.e. all his people even if they are not his relatives. Again, the author of Galatians is aware of this which is why he uses the word 'Galatians' when narrating Paul's claims about Abraham—it is all wordplay, like the whole Bible, understood only when the word-names are understood. (Gal.3)

The author of Galatians subtly slips Paul's requests for donations into his preachings, where it works without being too vulgar a request. When giving Paul credit through Peter, James and John (just before discrediting Peter) Gal.2:10 slips in the mention of giving to the poor (the epistles always claim to be asking so they can provide for the poor saints, or another struggling church) 'Only *they would* that we should remember the poor; the same which I also was forward to do.'; Gal.4:15 following Paul of the epistle telling the Galatians who seem no longer to listen to his preachings, that they once considered him an angel and like Jesus Christ—again this is the author showing how Paul is pressuring them while raising his status by describing himself as 'an angel of God, even as Christ Jesus…' before 'Where is then the blessedness ye spake of? for I bear you record, that, if it has been possible, ye would have plucked out your own eyes, and have given them to me.' and this is the real concern of Paul of the epistles: they are no longer willing to give him money as opposed to before they would have given him everything he asked for. (Gal.3:1-15)

The example of the bondwoman and the freewoman of Abraham have been connected to Sinai and Jerusalem only for the word meanings as wanted by the author of Galatians for Paul to make (i.e. Paul is still deceiving the recipients of the letter), as neither Hagar, Sara, Abraham, or their conceived children had anything to do with mount Sinai or Jerusalem, the mountain and city do not appear in their stories. The use in Gal.4 is for their word meanings: **Sinai** (Exod.16:1) 'in my direction' 'facing me' as Paul would like the recipients to follow him only, face in his direction and follow his teachings only and not any others; and he loosely connects **Jerusalem** 'came-saw-asked-them/the' 'they see-asked-them/the' and Sinai in a negative way which he loosely connects to **Hagar**/Agar (Gen.16;21:10-21) 'to abandon' as the people who he is asking to come and follow him and only believe his preachings have abandoned him and his teachings by following another's directions; and he uses **Jerusalem** in a positive way where he loosely connects it to Sara (without mentioning her name as the author could not do anything with it in wordplay) is asking them, insisting, to only listen to him, only to look for him for instruction to only ask any questions regarding the faith from him and not to go and ask any others.

Arabia (2Chr.9:14) for its meaning '(of)learn and remember/beware/be warned-teacher/discipliner/parent/god/master/the grower/anyone who brings someone up or teaches them/grows them (children/animals/plants/etc.)/grew fast and(or) well' as Paul is speaking to the recipients as if they are his children, but they are also the charges he is responsible for teaching and bringing up to the correct God/faith; he is also warning them to beware of the false gospels, false preachers, the misleading teachings they have listened to. **Isaac** (Gen.17:15-19; 18:9-14; 21:1-7) is used for 'he pulls up water little by little(during drought)' 'swipes/drags water' as he is likening the difficulty he is facing with the recipients of the letter with the same difficulty it is to pull up water during drought which is why Isaac was named 'Isaac' as his parents were old, his mother no longer menstruating and was like a dry well when God allowed her to conceive him. The author has Paul patronise the recipients that they are difficult, they cause him a lot of pain, but in the end, they are 'special' just like Isaac—if only they will listen to him (**Jerusalem**) and follow his directions (**Sinai**). (Gal.4:19-31)

Israel 'twisted muscle-the' 'twisted-the' has been mentioned because it speaks about Israel's twisted and withered muscle which is connected to the male reproductive organ and to acts of sexual immorality, and the author has Paul connect these to circumcision and how it has been used and twisted to pervert Jesus' teachings contrary to Paul's.

The author has the epistle be written from **Rome** (Acts.2), according to the note, for its meanings which are related to Galatians story: 'were thrown' 'threw/killed' 'spread/strewn over vast distance/various locations' 'saw water' 'became rotten/went off/bad smelling': **Galatians** 'wrong' 'mistake' 'deceit' is in they have performed circumcision and this renders Jesus' water through Paul no longer necessary, but Paul is pointing out that they are still not purified and if they do not come back to Paul's ways (being purified with Jesus' word/water) they will rot in spirituality and perish physically.

Ephesians

Ephesians (Acts.18:19-28); Ephésioi; افيصِوي ، افيصيوي 'disentangle/untie' 'of disentangling/untying' 'disentangle knots or problems/matters' 'of disentangling knots or problems/matters' 'separate' 'of separating' 'break down into small and understandable pieces' 'of breaking down into small and understandable pieces' 'explain/break down into detail' 'of explaining/breaking down into detail' 'small seeds/stone of fruit' 'of small seeds/stone of fruit' 'pit/remove seed/stones from fruit' 'of pitting/removing seed/stones from fruit' 'divorce/separate from wife' 'of divorcing/separating from wife' 'small gem like stones used in jewellery/clothes' 'of small gem like stones'; افيسِوي ، افيسيوي 'pass wind in him' 'of passing wind' 'making it/him break wind' 'of making break him/it break wind' can mean literally or to beat up or scare, 'copulating/passing wind into' 'of copulating/passing wind into' used to describe chicken copulation; عفيصِوي ، عفيصيوي 'twisted/crumpled' 'of twisting/crumpling' 'made a mess of' 'of making a mess of'; افيزِوي ، افيزيوي 'provoking' 'of provoking' 'winning' 'of winning'. Cp: epheissioi, epheissyoi, epheisioi, epheisyoi, 'pheissioi, 'pheissyoi, epheizioi, epheizyoi.

The explaining/detailing/separating meanings begin in Chapter 1 where the author makes it clear that the sender/Paul is showing in great detail how they/he are the chosen ones to understand and receive everything related to Jesus Christ and the knowledge thereof; in the faith being planted like a seed into the people who hear the word and believe in it; in Paul wishing the recipients of the letter to further understand by being given knowledge of Jesus Christ.

The disentangle/untying meanings as well as pitting stones from fruit begin in Chapter 2 where although the people were trespassing and sinning, God has untangled, untied and separated them from this twisted crumpled mess (likened to death), and separated them through faith in Christ and his teachings.

The meaning of gem stones is what Jesus is described as, as well as the saints, prophets, and people who will believe in him.

The meanings of 'separated from' 'twisted/crumpled' 'a mess' are shown in that before they were just a mess of sins and physically separate from 'Israel' until God made it unnecessary to be circumcised; and now, they can be straightened and cleaned just like 'Israel' who are already physically clean can be set straight of his/its 'twisted muscle'. In God bringing Jesus into the world and sacrificing him has superseded the old commandments (those which came down on Moses) as the new faith explains and replaces the old.

Before the circumcised and uncircumcised are like a man and wife separated by divorce, but Eph.2 explains this is no longer the case, they are now reunited.

Eph.3 focuses that everything has been explained in detail to Paul, and Paul is now breaking it down and explaining it to the recipients so they too can benefit.

Along with the other meanings of 'Ephesian' such as explaining in detail, etc. the meanings of 'twisting/crumpling/making a mess of/provoking' are also reflected in Chapter 4: in describing before the revelation that the people were being tossed to and fro, being deceived by men and misled; shown in the people who do not believe are still twisted, crumpled, and provoking as they cannot see nor understand God's word or the faith and teachings of Jesus.

Chapter 4 and 5 show the meanings of provocation as the recipients are warned against it; they are urged to remove it and other acts of anger/hate (like pitting stones from fruit) even against those who provoke it. It shows the meanings of 'twisted/crumpled/made a mess' as it warns of being misled by bad people and continues to show this can be done by making understood clearly God's instructions/message, by disentangling themselves from the evil ways and people.

Chapter 6 continues with the themes of breaking down into detail to explain, but also concentrates on not provoking: the children are not to provoke their parents; parents are not to provoke their children; servants are not to provoke their masters; and all in Christ are to obey (not provoke) God. They are warned to beware and fight the provocations of evil, anything that is not in the ways of Jesus and that is not only the devil.

The mention of the 'breastplate of righteousness' (Eph.6.14) is taken from the OT stories of the breastplate worn by Aaron, then any other high priest after him. Although in all cases the misnomered by translation/interpretation 'breastplate' is not a breastplate at all but something else, this does not negate how the author of Ephesians has used it for its meanings of 'gem stones(used in adorning jewellery or garments)' as this 'breastplate' has twelve precious stones. In connection to this 'stone/seeds of fruit' is also meant here by the author in connection to the correct meaning and use of 'breastplate'. (Eph.6)

Tychicus (Acts.20:1-12) 'fell/broke-his brother' 'fell/broke-healed/cured him' 'fell/broke-made him still/stay' and emphasises what the sender warns the recipients of: that there will be many attempting to break their faith, make them fall not physically but in belief; and what will protect them from these attacks and prevent the loss or breaking of faith is 'God's armour', truth, righteousness but more importantly knowledge, knowing and understanding in detail what Paul is teaching of Jesus and God, his ways—these things will heal and protect them against this evil. Tychius is also presented as the author and deliverer of the letter as he is going to explain everything to the recipients, and he will 'comfort your hearts' i.e. heal any worries, doubts.

There are several important things to note about Ephesians. The first, it and the other epistles from Paul do not differ than any other OT/NT story in method and use of wordplay to enhance and relay what is happening in the story. Ephesians differs from the other epistles because it does not request nor require any money or physical gifts be donated by the recipients within the text itself, nor does it accuse or guilt the recipients of the letter of or about anything, contrary to the already discussed epistles where the sender/narrator makes a request for donations to be sent, and shames and guilts the recipients for not doing so like other churches the sender mentions have already done; Ephesians does not accuse them of shortcomings, being selfish, being less loving towards Jesus and Paul (over not sending money) nor does it criticise their actions, their faith—it takes a peaceful and kind tone in urging them to follow God's ways and to reject the misleading evil-doers but without the angry and 'high and mighty' rhetoric of the other Paul epistles.

Another characteristic of Ephesians which differs from the other letter stories is that it does not seek to go over the top with showing how the sender Paul is a fraud, defrauding them of money and misleading them about religion. The other letters go into overkill in making Paul (of the epistles) stand out as scamming the people and misleading them, but the author of Ephesians, although like all Biblical authors does make its fictionality undeniable through use of word-names and narration which relay the same message(s), does not vilify nor caricaturise Paul but keeps it gentle, and 'clean' as there are no lewd puns, it remains about faith and well-wishes for its recipients.

Although scholars believe Paul sent this letter from prison because in Acts he is narrated as being imprisoned, this is a result of believing Paul to have been an actual person who lived and whose stories happened instead of seeing all the epistles are works of authors—not Paul a fictional character, while the word-names of Saul/Paul and the events he is related to as well as all characters related to him within the Biblical stories all show he is a fictional character who never existed. This misunderstanding has led scholars to believe that he sent this letter during and from his spate in prison (in Acts, another fictional set of stories) because of the mention of 'For this cause I Paul, the prisoner of Jesus Christ for you Gentiles' 'I therefore, the prisoner of the Lord, beseech you that ye walk worthy of the vocation wherewith ye are called' '...that I may open my mouth boldly, to make known the mystery of the gospel, For which I am an ambassador in bonds: that therein I may speak boldly, as I ought to speak.' Even within the story of Ephesians itself, these statements do not say that Paul is in an actual prison—it clearly states he is a prisoner enslaved to the word and work of Jesus Christ and God; that he cannot resist but to preach boldly and explain all the mysteries surrounding Jesus which have been revealed to him. It is no different than a figure of speech when a person says he is enslaved to a woman (meaning out of great love for her), i.e. Paul is completely devoted to God/Jesus Christ, and to spreading the knowledge and ways of Jesus/God. (Eph.)

Philippians

Philippi is still 'in his/its core/middle' 'so respond/assist/serve' as they are described as saints, bishops and deacons, as in a fellowship they are all responding, assisting and serving, and as it is in Jesus Christ they do this, it is out of the core of Jesus they do it, and believe in him to their core; also reflected in Paul loves them in his heart. The first half of Phil.1 is about something in its core/middle. The 'responding/assisting/serving' is shown in that God is answering their prayers and the response is or will be in the form of Paul's salvation; in Paul asking them to work in unity.

The bonds spoken of are not necessarily imprisonment, there is no mention that he is imprisoned, but there are circumstances preventing him from going to the places he would like to go: where they are preaching correctly and he loves and would love to be amongst the recipients of the letter, and also where he would like to go to correct or confront the false preachings of brethren who add to his problems.

Timotheus is still used for 'she passes him/walks past him/she makes him go' 'will you pass him/will you make him walk past/go' 'she completes/finishes it/he/him' 'will you complete/finish it/him/he' 'she marks/signs it/him/he' 'will you mark/sign it/him/he/will you make him mark/sign' 'she wipes away his urine/sperm(without use of water)' 'will you wipe away his urine/sperm'. It is reflected that although Paul cannot visit them due to his circumstances which also prevent him and necessitate sending others, that Timotheus will pass by, he will complete the teachings (which they lack knowledge of) not only because he has accompanied Paul but because he has received the further Jesus/God water/sperm properties which his name suggests and the narration of earlier stories makes clear, this allows him to complement Paul's work even in Paul's absence, and of course Paul promises to visit soon but instead sends Epaphroditus.

Epaphroditus; Epaphróditos; عبَ فروضِته ، عب افروضيتُه 'packed/filled-so he was/you were glad/pleased/content/agreed' 'overflowed/floated in/seeped water or liquid-so he was/you were glad/pleased/content/agreed' 'shame/shamed-so he was/you were glad/pleased/content/agreed' 'rotted and stank-so he was/you were glad/pleased/content/agreed'; عبَ فرودِته ، عب افروديته packed/filled-his buttocks/of buttocks' 'overflowed/floated/seeped water/liquid/swelled with water-his buttocks/of buttocks' 'shame/shamed-his buttocks/of buttocks' 'rotted and stank-his buttocks/of buttocks'.

From the above possible combinations of the word-name, several are meant by the author of Philippians: Epaphroditus is mentioned as serving Paul and his needs directly after following the mention of Timotheus and its word-names who is Paul's special companion, these indicate that sexual activities occurred between Paul and Epaphroditus which has allowed him to be able to do Paul's work through the passing of God/Jesus' water between them; this makes him able to minister to the needs of the recipients of the letter. It is reflected in that he provided comfort and joy to Paul and satisfied Paul's needs, and that he will be able to do the same for the recipients of the letter. This character and word-name for him have been created with the meaning of '**Philippian**' 'cored/his middle/his pulp' in mind for its employment in the lewd puns which are at the heart of the NT stories. The 'rotted/stank' meanings are reflected in that he almost died.

Paul has sent the suitably named character to fill the preaching, spiritual and guidance needs of the Philippians, but he points out that they have not fulfilled the service towards Paul i.e. he wants something from the Philippians—it does not state that Epaphroditus is supplying the Philippians with the service they do not receive from Paul because he is unable to get there, but it does clearly state that this man, Epaphroditus, almost died doing the work, serving, assisting, supplying Paul's needs which the Philippians have not fulfilled 'Because for the work of Christ he was nigh unto death, not regarding his life, to supply your lack of service toward me.'. (Phil.2)

Israel 'twisted muscle-the' 'twisted-the' as Paul's statements are contradictory and concern the penis; he warns of people who twist things for evil's sake; **Benjamin** (Gen.35:18) 'son/child-calls them mother/ makes them mother' 'son/child-whose?' 'son/child-counts/lists/reminds' 'son/child-from where' as whenever Paul feels like it, or to be correct whenever the authors of his stories want to show Paul as adopting the ethnicity and/or religion of whichever people he is addressing to get out of a pickle, whether to have them identify with him so as to release him, or to fear him and release him (see the stories where he states and tells the Jews he is Jew, the Romans he is a Roman and so forth, to gain their confidence and to have them believe him); **Hebrew** (to be explained later in the book); **Pharisee** 'of spreading out/over/laying out' 'of splitting open/pushing out/emerging by pushing up or out/ dividing by breaking or splitting' 'of taking opportunity/chance' 'broke/split through' 'opportunity/chance' 'broke (things) into pieces' 'of dividing something into separate units' 'of explaining/explaining in detail/making clear' 'divided/separated things into units' 'sorted things into separate units' 'explained things in detail/broke things down to explain in detail' 'of bringing forward/pressing on and pushing out' 'brought forward/pressed on and pushed out' as he is again explaining things about his conduct and the knowledge of Christ, regarding Jesus coming back to life from death; he explains there are people who preach Christ to make an earthly gain (which the authors are indicating about Paul); his loss of many things are also what have been broken, but he does not mind as he has lost them to bring up and push forward the message of Jesus; he wants to be taken as the foremost example brought forward to be followed as opposed to those who do less or mislead. All the word-names of verse 5 describe the narration and themes of Phil.3. (Phil.3)

Eudios; Euodía; عوديَ 'became enemies'; يودعيَ 'calls/called/he/they call' 'cursed/he/they cursed/put curse on' 'they make a claim' 'they make a false/unproven claim'. It is equivalent to Judah and Judaea. The verse reflects a dispute between the two characters perfectly named to enhance the narration. Then both characters also match what Paul is requesting and the story narrating of calling to God; the gospel is about spreading words in the form of stories, they are mentioned as being in the 'book of life' and both these characters have 'word/speech' meanings in their word-names. Cp: 'oudeeya, youd'eea. (Phil.4)

Syntyche; Syntýchē; شينتياَحي 'exploded in anger' 'of exploding in anger' and means shouted, 'lost it' and voiced great anger and feelings; شينطياَقي 'they will/are/are of speaking/pronouncing/making speak/say'. The meaning to lose it and explode verbally in anger supports and enhances Euodia 'became enemies'. Likewise, 'they will speak/pronounce/etc.' supports the Eudia 'calls/called' meanings as they are both working with Paul in calling to Jesus' faith. Cp: <u>sh</u>yntyaaḥey, <u>sh</u>ynṭyaaqey. (Phil.4)

Clement; Klḗmēs; كلياَميه 'speak to him/her/them' 'his words/statements' 'all of them-water' 'all of them, what?' 'all of them, is it?'; حلياَميه 'all/everything is sweet/sweetened' 'sweetened-water' 'purified/ circumcised/cleansed/shed/undressed-water' 'idealistic/everything is good' 'they are good/of good(ness)'. Clement is being asked to help with reconciliating between the characters in a dispute, and the meaning of 'talk/speak to him/her/them' is clear. It is also reflected in this person is also helping with Paul whose work is spreading the word. They are all from 'water' and 'sweetened water' because they have been baptised to become Christians so they should be able to get along together. The 'all of them water' is also enhanced with 'book of life' because the stories about Jesus are the words, and Jesus was born from, spread, and transferred the water of life to his followers. The 'idealistic' meanings are in verse 7 as everything positive is being described. Cp: klyaameyh, ḥlyaameyh. (Phil.4)

The last half of Phil.4 returns to the theme of the epistle stories where the objective of the letter is requesting contributions and gifts from the recipients. Paul is glad because the recipients of the letter have taken care of him, and **Epaphroditus** meaning 'packed/filled-so he was/you were glad/pleased/content/ agreed' is used again along with the name/character itself to show that Paul is content and joyful in the gift sent to him from the Philippians and the meaning of **Philippian** 'served/responded/assisted' also shows in the same—this further enhances that they have understood he wanted something sent, mentioned at Phil.2:30, and they have responded favourably with a gift. Paul makes a point in letting them know even if he starves and needs things, he has learnt through Christ to be patient (meaning of Paul) and do without, but he does make sure to let them know he would rather have than not have gifts sent to him. **Macedonia** is used again in the epistles to show an unseen and unknown Paul is deceiving the recipients, where in other places he has thanked the Macedonian and other people/churches for sending him contributions to shame the recipients of the respective letters, in this epistle the author chooses to have him point out that since he left Macedonia it is only this church, suitably named Philippian 'assisted/responded/served', who have contacted him about and actually sent contributions.

Thessalonica has been used for 'he/they-asked/questioned-wounded/poked wound/hurt/offended' 'he/they/it-comforted/entertained/distracted-wounded/poked wound/hurt/offended' 'he/they-asked/questioned-picked out impurities/cleared/cleaned/chose/selected' 'he/they-asked/questioned-saved/delivered to safety/talked/discussed secretly' to further emphasise that the responsive and dutiful Philippians have enquired about contributions and dispatched at least one contribution; the word-name also serves to show the audience that the other churches/areas are being asked to send donations to comfort and assist Paul, that in complying they are clearing away their impurities/sins, and the other meanings which can be detected and seen between the narration and the meanings of the compound word Thessalonica.

He makes sure they know he, Paul, does not benefit from these gifts but it is the senders of the gift (the recipients of the epistles) whose reputation and piety increases and gains from donating to Paul. 'Epaphroditus' word-name also reflects that he has carried a gift from the Philippians to Paul and not only is Paul 'full' with it but it pleases him as it is 'a sacrifice acceptable, well-pleasing to God.' and this giving of gifts to Paul will result in God filling all their needs. And the carrier of this epistle is Epaphroditus who also wrote it to show it is a scam.

What cannot be missed is at Phil.2:30 Paul describes the Philippians who have sent him satisfactory gifts of still being lacking in this area, i.e. they could do more, send more, and this is shown in the salutation of the saints from Caesar's household: the donations and gifts Paul asks for in the epistles, he claims are not for him, the author of Philippians purposely made them see he is using them for himself to show that the theme of the epistles is to scam the recipients; the epistles usually show this while Paul makes the requests for donations for the sake of impoverished saints in Jerusalem so 'All the saints salute you, chiefly they that are of Caesar's household' is a sting to the recipients to encourage them to give more, but more importantly a joke for the real audiences of the story who understand **Caesar** 'shortened/shortcoming/failed to complete or obey' 'broke' means 'shortened/shortcoming/failed to complete or obey' on behalf of the recipients for the 'broke' impoverished saints. (Phil.4)

Colossians

Colosse; Kolossaí; خُلْصَّي ، خُلْصِّيي 'finish/finished/emptied/none left' 'the end/cease/bring to end' 'undress' 'strip clothes off' 'loyal/devoted'; جُلْسَّي ، جُلْسِّيي 'sit' 'seat it/him/her' 'set it down/place it' 'position it properly(so it doesn't fall, e.g. or is the right way up)' 'stayed(for a set period of time)/stick to(as in belief or way)'. It speaks of the recipients love and belief which is the meaning of devotion/loyalty; Paul's wishes that their loyalty and devotion to God increases and stays with them/in them; the recipients are found, and hoped to stay/continue 'in the faith grounded and settled, and be not moved away from the hope of the gospel'; he wants them to know and stick to the correct faith; they are urged to place their faith in God, and that this world is only a temporary period of time, while they will spend an eternity with Christ; it mentions Christ being seated beside God, and by extension the recipients will get to be seated in the same vicinity too, if they obey; the end of things whether the 'power of darkness' over the people, Jesus dying and it bringing an end to people's sins like a sacrifice, the wickedness the recipients sometimes fell into has also ended; in informing the recipients their lives are already over, dead, but it is temporary for those who believe in Christ i.e. those who are devout/loyal to the ways; in instructing them to cease from the sins mentioned at Col.3. Cp: kholossay, kholossayee, golossay, golossayee. (Col.)

Epaphras; Epaphrás; عب افرآه 'packed/filled-multiplied/increased it/him' 'overflowed/floated in/seeped water or liquid/swelled with water-increased/multiplied it/him' 'shame/shamed-increased/multiplied it/him' 'rotted and stank-multiplied/increased it/him'. It reflects the increase in knowledge and spirituality the sender hopes the Colossians will achieve; it reflects the compared increase of fruit which is the people's faith. It reflects that Epaphras who is a companion of Paul also transfers the word and water causing this increase to increase further; the 'shame-increased him/it' is in the increasing suffering of Paul who does it willingly for the church's sake; the increase which fills is the Gentiles to follow Christ. Cp: 'b-aphraah. (Col.1)

Laodicea; Laodíkeia; لَوديكِيَ ، لَودييكِيَ 'stitch it/stitching' 'of stitching' 'it is sticky/sticking' 'of stickiness'; لُوضيقِيَ ، لُوضييقِيَ 'threw it away/aside' 'flung it/him/her away/aside' 'of throwing/flinging away/aside' 'will/will not be forced to swallow/suffer/taste it'. The stitching meaning is shown in wanting them to be 'knit together in love'; in the likening of the belief like a body knit together. The 'flung away/aside' meaning is when something is either thrown intentionally aside or flung carelessly aside but results in the thrown object cannot be found easily, it also applies to quickly or ruthlessly throw/send away something/someone unwanted. Both meanings are used here, although there is no indication of Paul being unwanted, the meaning of he cannot be found is clear: neither the Colossian nor Laodiceans have seen Paul 'in the flesh' so he is like something that has been lost or flung away and cannot be found and the way Laodicea has been used in Colossians is the same way 'Macedonia/hidden/deceive' has been used to show Paul has not been seen by the recipients; the meanings of 'sticky' are as when a person gets hand into honey or other sticky substance which sticks to the hand/skin, and means they are being deceived, they have fallen into it and cannot get out of it; it tells them to discard or keep away from 'philosophy' and 'vain deceit'; the people's sins have been thrown/flung away from them as Jesus has taken it away through baptism and also crucifixion 'and took it out of the way nailing it to his cross.'. The 'will/will not suffer/taste/force to swallow' meanings are shown they are told not to accept/believe philosophies and words and specifically those about what they can eat, drink and other matters. Cp: laodeekeia, laodeeykeia, lao<u>dh</u>eeqeia, lao<u>dh</u>eeyqeia. (Col.2)

The word-names used are for their meanings related to not lying as well as: **Greek**; hellēn; 'purify/purified/circumcise/circumcised/make clean/made clean/make edible/made edible' 'of purification/edibility/cleanliness/circumcision' 'declare/declared purified/permissible' 'undress/undressed' 'of undressing' 'deceive/deceived/trick/tricked' 'of deceit/tricks' 'beat/beaten severely/beat/beaten until skin peeled off' 'of beating/being beaten severely' 'shed skin/hair/leaves/etc.' 'of shedding skin/hair/leaves' 'replace/replaced' 'of replacing' 'sweet/sweetened' 'of sweetness/sweetening' 'deceit/misleading' as the narrations speaks of no need of circumcision; **Jew** (to be explained later in book); **Barbarian** 'they talked nonsense' 'they made unintelligible sounds' 'they talked too much' 'they talked incoherently'; Scythian; Skythés; شجيثيه 'set aside/shun/hide/cover/ignore/turn away from/ostracise' 'of setting aside/shunning/hiding/ignoring/turning away from/ostracising' 'shade/mound/hedge/covered or hidden in or beside shade/hedge/mound' 'of being in or hidden beside or behind shade/mounds/hedges'. These word-names are linked to what the people are being told to avoid doing in the chapter and the 'old man' who has been shed or set aside and replaced by the 'new man'; all things and attributes are being set aside. Cp: <u>sh</u>gyfeih (Col.3)

Tychicus 'fell/broke-his brother' 'fell/broke-healed/cured him' 'fell/broke-made him still/stay'. It is used in this instance for the breaking down of news, bringing details of Paul's situation to the recipients, and the recipients' situation to Paul. He stays with both parties: Paul and the recipients. He also happens to be the deliverer and author of the letter and the letter does mention 'charity' as the most perfecting virtue, and although it does not heavily pressure the recipients with requests to give, it cannot be read outside the context that the characters who write and carry the letter in the story are also going to collect and deliver whatever donations the recipients feel they need to give to be perfect in their devotion. (Col.4)

Onesimus; Onḗsimos; عنيي سِمُه 'helps/assists/helped-named him/it/told naming story' 'helps/helped-his illness' 'suffered-named him/it/told naming story' 'suffered-his illness'. The 'help/assist-told story' is reflected in he too is coming to teach the recipients what Paul would have taught them had he visited; Paul's teachings are telling the stories about Christ and like 'Samaria/late night story' 'samaaya/naming story/riddle' is the same kind of fictional story where people and events are connected in the naming of places and characters, so Onesimus will also be telling them stories. Cp: 'nei<u>ey</u>-simoh. (Col.4)

Aristarchus 'water/give to drink-you/it will be loosened/split open/cracked/muscles loosened' 'see/show/saw-you will rest/be relieved/relaxed' 'stack/pack-loosen/immoral-him/it' are three of its meanings which can be seen used in this instance (see Aristarchus (Acts.19:29-41) for more meanings). He is grouped with character word-names which collectively mean bringing news, piety, staying, etc. and this reflects two things: the carriers of the letter are bringing piety and good news to the recipients; and Paul, unable to visit, is the source of the piety (symbolised by the characters and their word-names who remain with him) who will cause the recipients piety and good deeds to increase, to be correct and on the right path as long as they follow his instructions. It is also a pun showing that Paul wants to receive some of the recipients stacked resources, and that they should loosen and give; the same wordplay also shows it is an immoral act that Paul, the deliverers of the letter are trying to achieve. (Col.4)

Marcus the same as **Mark** (Mark); 'did not/they did not wait/stay/become still' 'did not intensely ask/intreat' 'did not shake/unsettle it' 'did not drive him insane'. What is meant is that Paul has not made a direct request for donations, but has made an indirect request for donations by the recipients and it is at Col.3:14 reminding them that charity is the best virtue. It urges the recipients not to wait until they are bluntly asked but to give without Paul or his messengers having to ask or implore them to do so. Note the use of characters whose identity and relation to other characters changes with fluidity: 'John Mark' was from the original twelve disciples, then in Paul's stories he becomes a companion to both Barnabas and Saul/Paul and Mark is unrelated to Barnabas, but now the author likes the idea of the use of Marcus/Mark as a word-name but also wants the character to be the nephew of Barnabas as 'Barnabas' meanings of 'piety' and 'good news' and 'warned/awoke' also enhance the meanings that these people and Paul's letter brings good news, piety, but also is telling them not to wait to do good, donations, they should be warned of not complying with this pious deed.(Col.4)

Barnabas 'piety/good-prophesied news' 'piety/good-prophecy/predict' piety/good-prophet/news' 'passed/beyond/passed beyond-prophesied news' 'passed beyond-prophecy/predict' 'passed beyond-prophet/news' 'piety/good towards his prophet' 'piety/good-warned (him)/woke (him) up/pointed out (to him)'. Covers the good news, piety, the warnings and awakenings to do good which are reinforced in these grouped names; it shows although Paul cannot 'pass beyond' to deliver 'good news' and teach 'piety', his messengers, fellows, (Tychicus and Onesimus) can. (Col.4)

Jesus Justus; **Jesus** 'cold bread' 'broke/ate bread' is reminding the recipients that sharing what they eat from, what they live from, with their fellow brethren (and Paul the sender of the letter and his colleagues are meant here); Paul is already making his contribution: preaching/teaching—the recipients need to make their contribution: donations. **Justus** has been attached to the name Jesus for this character to show that Paul and the people Paul sends are the mediums through which the recipients of the letter will be able to achieve piety, a correct understanding and practise of the ways of Jesus Christ:

Justus meanings 'he mediates/makes middle/centres/centred' 'centre of house/makes/builds centre of house' 'mediator/builder/person-in-charge of building' 'intervenes/witnesses/assists' 'he clings/sticks to' 'he swoops down on' 'he lays hands on/harms' 'he quickly sticks to/against'—is Paul mediating and being the connection which brings the recipients of the letter out of wrongdoing, whether they do wrong out of being misled or just ignorant; by giving Paul what they possess he lays his hands on their donations.

The meaning Justus 'it rises/leavens/ferments it' 'he leavens/makes it/him rise' because they are speaking about bread/Jesus, and bread can be leavened—the author plays on other authors of epistle stories having written Paul speaking about the lump leavening the whole, and what is meant is the people Paul despatches are the lump of '<u>sh</u>twa/شتو' that cause 'Justus/y<u>sh</u>t<u>h</u>/يشته '; and what Paul's leavening of the people with Jesus stories, with piety, makes them increase in faith, piety, understanding, etc.

The meaning Justus 'he/they wants him/it' and also 'picked/took a lot/many/palmfuls' 'came-wanted him/it' 'came-leavened/rose him/it' 'stuffed him/it' all reflect that the recipients want to learn the correct ways of Jesus from Paul, they want to become more pious; Paul wants the same for them, but he also wants to receive generous donations which allow him (according to the epistles) to serve the impoverished saints; he will give them what causes them to gain a lot spiritually, in knowledge, in the afterlife, but he wants to gain what helps the saints survive in this life. The meaning of 'lived it/lived-him/it' is connected to teaching the recipients piety as those who believe and follow Jesus' way as taught by Paul, will live forever; it is also confirmation from Paul to the recipients that Jesus (Christ) did live and was not just a story; but it is also the authors way of delivering a pun that Paul of the epistles is making a living from deceiving the recipients to send him donations. (Col.4)

Epaphras is mentioned again for its meanings of 'packed/filled-multiplied/increased it/him' 'overflowed-increased/multiplied it/him' 'shame/shamed-increased/multiplied it/him' as it is still about filling people with the knowledge and faith in Christ which will bring the increase of their faith, but also is about the gain Paul would like to make which he has tied to the recipients increasing in virtue and faith by the people sending donations. The 'shamed/increase' is also reflected where the author uses the already-used shaming by Paul in the epistles to tell recipients they have not fulfilled sending donations. (Col.4)

Laodicea 'threw it away/aside' 'flung it/him/her away/aside' 'of throwing/flinging away/aside' 'will/will not be forced to swallow/suffer/taste it' 'stitch it/stitching' 'of stitching' 'it is sticky/sticking' 'of stickiness' as Epaphras' love for Laodicea and the recipients sticks to them, is sewn onto them to show great love, but (like Paul) they will not see him currently and only sends his love and greetings. (Col.4)

Hierapolis; Hierápolis; حيِرآبولِه 'they puzzled his mind' 'a predicament/puzzle-his mind/intellect/patience/affliction' 'an open infected wound-his mind/intellect/patience/affliction' 'they warred for him' 'a predicament/puzzle-soaked it/him' 'an open infected wound-soaked it/him'; خير آبوله 'good/fortune his mind/intellect/affliction' 'chose/gave him choice-his mind/intellect/affliction' 'better-his mind/intellect/affliction' 'good/fortune-his affliction/they soaked him/it' 'they destroyed/ruined him' 'they destroyed/ruined for him/it'.

Hierapolis meaning of 'good/fortune-his mind/intellect/affliction' 'good/fortune-his affliction/they soaked him/it' as Paul informs the recipients that Epaphras has great 'zeal' towards the recipients as well as for Laodicea and Hierapolis, meaning he has in mind to do good for them in teaching them, bringing them more faith and piety through knowledge he will impart to them, as well as other good outcomes and good in general as he loves and is devoted to them. It also reflects he is misleading them to their ruin. There is relay between the meaning of 'Paul' and the 'polis' of Hierapolis in play. Cp: ḥyeraa-boolih, ḥyer-aaboo-lih, khyeraa-boolih, khyeraaboo-lih. (Col.4)

Luke 'talks(ed) too much/talks too much nonsense' 'rambling/loquacious' 'his nonsense/ramblings' 'chew(ed)' 'for you' 'chew' 'for you' 'crumpled/crumpled against each other' and reflects that the sender is intentionally confusing the recipients and making a lot of salutations and greetings where there is both positive and negative messages given in wordplay. It reflects how Epaphras talks about and praises the recipients a lot. (Col.4)

Demas; Dēmás; ذيماه 'he/they guilted/blamed/ostracised/humiliated-him/he' 'he/they were guilted/blamed/ostracised/humiliated' 'lepers/diseased' 'they are lepers/diseased' 'have conscience/his/their conscience' 'their/his responsibility' 'he/they are accountable'; تيماه 'muttered' 'he/they muttered about/against him'. Although it does have a positive wordplay that Epaphras mentions them in his prayers, it mostly portrays the pressure Paul's letter puts on the recipients to be good to the carriers of the letter while they stay with them, to show responsibility towards them and what they teach and require of them. It is equivalent to Thomas (Matt.10), Didymus (John.11:7-16). Cp: veymaah, teymaah. (Col.4)

Laodicea 'stitch it/stitching' 'of stitching' 'it is sticky/sticking' 'of stickiness' 'threw it away/aside' 'flung it/him/her away/aside' 'of throwing/flinging away/aside' 'will/will not be forced to swallow/suffer/taste it'. It has sexual and loving meanings of 'stitching' such as their souls and bodies being sewn in love and in sexual intercourse; the meanings of 'sticky/sticking/of stickiness' refers to the water/semen which apostles use to convert and spread the word of God/Jesus and means both a physical sticking of the sperm to its receptacles (the recipients of the letter) but also figuratively in that the faith, knowledge will stick to them. This is enhanced by the context of the meanings of the word-name 'Nymphas', explained below. (Col.4)

Nymphas; Nýmpha; نيآمث 'we wipe away his urine/sperm' 'of wiping away urine/sperm' and the wiping is without use of water; نيآمف 'asleep in/asleep in him' 'they are asleep in/they are asleep in him'; نيآمب 'asleep with/asleep with him' 'they are asleep with/they are asleep in him'. The story reflects what most gospels and NT stories have already covered and portray that the disciples and apostles' abilities and roles are as carriers and distributors of God/Jesus' water/sperm which they pass on to believers to cleanse them in body and spirit. It is why Laodicea is mentioned with Nympha to make clear what they are talking about; the meanings of 'sleep in/sleep with' are both literal and euphemism as it means to have sex with/in and also it is not uncommon to literally sleep with the person who has been made love to. Cp: nyaamfa, nyaam-pha, nyaamba. (Col.4)

Archippus; Árchippos; آرحِبّه ، آرحِبّوه 'welcome it/him' 'make space for it/him'; آركِبّه ، آركِبّوه 'ride it/him' 'mount it/him' and can mean literal ride it, or euphemism or slang for have sex with; آرقِبّه ، آرقِبّوه 'watch/keep eye on it/him' 'pour water into it/him' and the pouring of water in this way means to keep an eye on the stream of water and the narrow opening of the vessel it is being poured into to avoid splashing even one drop. In this story it means to watch and learn from the messenger who carries the letter who will be the recipients' teacher; it also means the sexual activities as well as the water/semen pouring activities the spreading of God/Jesus' word includes; it means to welcome and treat well the messenger/teacher of the epistle. It is equivalent to Rahab (Josh.2), Rechab (2Sam.4; 2Kgs.10:15), Rechabites (Jer.35). Cp: aarḥibbooh, aarḥibboh, aarkibbooh, aarkibboh, aarqibbooh, aarqibboh. (Col.4)

Thessalonians

Paul, as in all the epistles he is mentioned in, is still 'his mind' 'his patience' 'his affliction/afflicted him' 'his indication/direction' 'follow his indication/go his direction' and as in all epistles it reflects the intelligence, deep thinking and writing the authors give Paul; also, his patience over the suffering he goes through and towards others who cause him problems. It reflects he wants people/recipients of the letter to do as he instructs.

Silvanus (2Cor.19-24) 'asked/questioned-him' 'his asking/questions' 'flowed/leaked water-him' 'his flowing/leaking' 'entertained/distracted-him' 'his entertainment/distraction' 'comforted-him/his comfort'. Paul and his two companions are asking God to take care of the Thessalonians (and other things) in their prayers; they are comforted in the faith and actions of the recipients of the letter; in combination with Timotheus, Silvanus (their word-names and characters) along with Paul's character also show that this particular church (the recipients of the letter) have not only found faith and purity from the 'word' only, but have been filled with the 'Holy Ghost' which means they have been filled with God's water/semen either by Paul or one of his messengers/companions.

Timotheus 'she passes him/walks past him/she makes him go' 'will you pass him/will you make him walk past/go' 'she completes/finishes it/he/him' 'will you complete/finish it/him/he' 'she marks/signs it/him/he' 'will you mark/sign it/him/he/will you make him mark/sign' 'she wipes away his urine/sperm(without use of water)' 'will you wipe away his urine/sperm'. It too indicates the 'Holy Ghost' water/sperm filling the recipients which makes them complete in conversion and faith, but also that the Thessalonians in being able to spread God's word have passed into other areas and done this making it unnecessary for Paul and his group to go to those places.

Thessalonians (Acts.17:1-16) ; ذيسَّلونيكي ، ذِسَّلونيكي 'he/they-asked/questioned-wounded/poked wound/hurt/offended/fucked' 'he/they/it-leaked/flowed-wounded/poked wound/hurt/offended/fucked' 'he/they/it-comforted/entertained/distracted-wounded/poked wound/hurt/offended/fucked'; ذِسَّلونيقي ، ذيسَّلونيقي 'he/they-asked/questioned-picked out impurities/cleared/cleaned/chose/selected' 'he/they/it-leaked/flowed-picked out impurities/cleared/cleaned/chose/selected' 'he/they/it-comforted/entertained/distracted-picked out impurities/cleared/cleaned/chose/selected'; ذيسَّلونيجي ، ذِسَّلونيجي 'he/they-asked/questioned-saved/delivered to safety/talked/discussed secretly' 'he/they/it-leaked/flowed-saved/delivered to safety/talked/discussed secretly' 'he/they/it-comforted/entertained/distracted-saved/delivered to safety/talked/discussed secretly'.

All these meanings are available in 1Thes.1, as they have been in receipt of the Holy Ghost's flowing water/sperm, they have been cleansed of impurities and sins, they have been selected and the epistle shows they have received something more completing than the other epistle-story recipients; Paul and his group are comforted and joyous in this completion of conversion and faith which will deliver the recipients of any harm in this life and the afterlife; it also reflects that the Thessalonians have passed the word to other areas/churches/people insomuch that Paul and his group need not go there and preach as it has been achieved by the Thessalonians, and this reinforces that because they have been filled by the Holy Ghost they now have Paul and his special companion's cleansing and converting abilities.

Macedonia 'of plotting/deceiving' 'plotting/deceiving-him/he/she/they' 'covered tightly (with any kind of lid: stone, metal, cloth, etc.)/of covering tightly(with lid, etc.)' 'covered me with a lid/fabric/stone/etc.' 'of pillows' 'pillows/with pillows' 'resting on pillows' 'with hand on cheeks' 'of cheeks' 'cheeks' 'pulled off/down/away/removed by pulling' 'pulled bread off oven wall' 'pulled down wall/structure', and **Achaia** 'I mislead him/them to downfall/I will mislead him/them to his/their downfall' 'his misleading to downfall' 'I deceive him/them/I will deceive' 'I make him/them howl' 'I will make him/them howl' 'I warn/teach him/them' 'I will contain him/it', both show: Paul does not need to appear to people as the Thessalonians can do his work of teaching and warning; they are fully believing in Jesus Christ so they are in effect reaping the bread off the oven wall and eating it (with all its Jesus-word and Jesus-story related meanings); they have been saved from downfall of following the misleading idols. It also carries the meanings that Paul is deceiving and scamming the recipients of the letter; that Paul is still an enigma unseen by recipients of the letters; that Paul and his stories and teachings are misleading the recipients to their downfall. (1Thes.1)

Philippi 'in his/its core/middle' 'so respond/assist/serve' describes Paul and his group's intentions ('in his/its core/middle') arriving to assist and serve the followers of Jesus; it reinforces that they not only 'told stories/gospel' 'So being affectionately desirous of you, we were willing to have imparted unto you, not the gospel of God only, but also our own souls…' and this is pouring out what is the core of them and that is the 'Holy Ghost' God's water/sperm which Paul and these specific two companions carry within them. (1Thes.2)

Chapter 2 indicates that there were accusations and consequences made against Paul and his company of deceit and uncleanness, which probably means sexual immorality. (1Thes.2)

Judaea 'he is called/calls' 'call, or curse' 'to make a claim' 'make a false claim or an unproven claim'. Paul and his companions are calling people to God; they accuse/make claims of mistreatment, and they are also making a claim and accusation against the 'Jews' of Jesus' time mistreating and killing Jesus, and current 'Jews' of persecuting Paul and his followers. (1Thes.2)

Satan is used for 'laid hands on' as he is blamed for being behind obstructing Paul and his friends from reaching the recipients in person. (1Thes.2)

Athens (Acts.17:15) 'of doubling/twice' 'of folding and sewing/reinforcing' 'idols/statues/sculptures' 'of idolatry/idols/statues' is used because Timotheus has been sent to visit them again to reinforce the recipients faith because Paul was unable to visit them due to obstacles he does not make clear; as a 'tempter' and worry that the recipients faith may have been corrupted it also reflects this and that someone is misleading them to follow idolatry or some other corrupted form of Christianity not true, or not as true, to Jesus' ways which the sender/Paul makes clear are Paul's ways. (1Thes.3)

Timotheus is chosen as the character who is sent again to Thessalonica to confirm their level of faith for his word-name meanings 'will you pass him/will you make him walk past/go' 'will you complete/finish it/him/he'. The meanings of 'asked' in **Thessalonica** and its other compound word meanings are also reflected that Timotheus has gone to check, enquire and has found them intact in all ways as per the meanings of the word-name, not only does Timotheus bring back good news, but also charity (donations) and the author does not have to make Paul ask as the name **Thessalonians** already covers the asking element, and this too is reflected in Paul seems to be answering questions they may have sent through Timotheus: Paul asks them to abstain from certain activities, and answers questions about 'concerning them which are asleep' and as Thessalonica covers the word-meaning they are told the 'sleeping' people will also be delivered safely by God; in answer to what seems to be a technical question of 'how' it will be done, Paul (through the author) draws a scene of God and an archangel shouting and/or trumpeting causing those who died and those who are alive and believed in Christ to arise, then be spirited up altogether in the clouds where they will meet 'the Lord' mid-air and get to live there forever, i.e. again the 'safely delivered' meanings of Thessalonians' but also 'Wherefore comfort one another with these words' which is more word-meanings of the compound word-name Thessalonica/ians. (1Thes.3-4)

2Thessalonians begins and emphasises what was missing in 1Thessalonians: the importance of charity towards each other, and although this can be understood as 'kindness' and not the physical contributions of charity—that would be reading it outside its context. Almost all the epistles are about asking for donations, taking care of the requirements and reception of the messenger carrying the epistle. The charity to be given is to the poor in general, but it is about one church/people who teach God's ways giving to another church/people who teach God's ways, the recipient church being the poorer and in-need church and the epistles always make it clear that it is Paul the sender of the epistle who needs to receive it so that he can minister/serve the saints in need.

There is also emphasis on meanings of 'Thessalonians' which regards to offending, wounding, hurting, insulting—and it is reflected in all those who harm or trouble the Thessalonian church(es) will be punished with severe and physical punishment from God. 2Thes. also has other meanings of the word-name reflected (see Thessalonica/Thessalonians (Acts.17:1-16)).

It also reflects the importance of following Paul's instructions and only Paul's instructions. The story clearly shows that other preachers, apostles, are being received or writing to these churches and this concerns Paul as they may direct conflicting instructions, but would also mean lessening the authority Paul has over these recipients/churches and lessening donations he and his group would receive if the other apostles/preachers follow his scheme. These are fictional stories which were written with word-names to show and enhance these meanings, but that does not mean they were not copied and used by scammers who went to non-Arabic speaking areas and took advantage of that people's piety and generosity. (2Thes.)

2.Thes. also is answering a question that the Thessalonians have asked Paul regarding an apostle or some kind of preacher who informed them that 'the day of Christ' i.e. 'Doomsday' or 'Judgement Day' was about to arrive—the author presents it as: it seems to have distressed the Thessalonians and may have disrupted their work, which would also include donations gathering, and Paul is calming them down and reassuring them that it is not near (this in itself contradicts Paul's claims in other epistles that no one knows if it is near or far as no one has knowledge of it except God, but again this does not matter to authors of the epistle stories as they are concerned with the individual story they are telling in the moment), and that they should just resume work as usual. In fact, what the author does in verse 3 of Chapter 2 is clearly state that the story about Jesus returning is all a lie 'That ye be not soon shaken in mind, or be troubled, neither by spirit, nor by word, nor by letter as from us, as that the day of Christ is at hand. Let no man deceive you by any means: for that day shall not come, except there come a falling away first, and that man of sin be revealed…' and although it can be understood as words to the effect that first the 'man of sin' is revealed sitting in the temple of God claiming to be God, and then Jesus will return which is Doomsday, this is not the case—it is actually the author saying through Paul that the worried Thessalonians who have been misinformed and are petrified of the possibility, should calm down as that day will never come. (2Thes.2)

1Timothy

Just as Paul's epistles to churches/areas were just a mode of storytelling with no historical nor any kind of connection to reality, so are the letters sent from a fictional Paul directed to his fictional co-workers. Unfortunately, because scholars have failed to read the word-names as Arabic which would point them towards the fictionality of the stories and characters, and this in turn would lead them to what was behind the writing of such stories, instead scholars have sought to imbue these letters with 'history' with 'realness' and with more religious spirituality than they had—as 'religious text' was never an intention of the authors of these stories.

Paul 'his mind' 'his patience' 'his affliction/afflicted him' 'his indication/direction' 'follow his indication/go his direction' and he is instructing Timothy like a father instructs his son to follow his advice and orders.

Timothy تِموضِوه ، تموضيوه 'she passes him/walks past him/she makes him go' 'will you pass him/will you make him walk past/go' 'she completes/finishes it/he/him' 'will you complete/finish it/him/he' 'she marks/signs it/him/he' 'will you mark/sign it/him/he/will you make him mark/sign'; تِموثِوه ، تموثيوه 'she wipes away his urine/sperm(without use of water)' 'will you wipe away his urine/sperm'.

Timothy is requested to go with Paul from place to place, but here Timothy is asked to remain in Ephesus while Paul goes on to Macedonia. Timothy's work is still based on being filled with the 'Holy Ghost' which 'she wipes away his urine/sperm' was performed through Paul in an earlier NT story; but now it takes on more significance as he is being asked to wipe away the negative effects of false preacher's stories and waterings upon the followers. (1Tim.)

Ephesus ; افيصوه ، افِصّه 'disentangle/untie (him/it)' 'disentangle knots or problems/matters(it/him)' 'separate it/him' 'break down into small and understandable pieces(it/him)' 'explain/break down into detail(it/him)' 'small seeds/stone of fruit' 'pit/remove seed/stones from fruit' 'divorce/separate from wife(him)' 'small gem like stones used in jewellery/clothes'; افيسوه ، افِسّه 'pass wind in him' 'make it/him break wind' can mean literally or to beat up or scare, 'copulate/pass wind into' the latter word is used to describe chicken copulation; عفيصوه ، عفِصّه 'twisted/crumpled it' 'twisted/crumpled-he/him' 'made a mess of it/him'; افيزوه ، افِزّه 'provoked/provoked him/it'.

It is portrayed in Timothy disentangling the false teachings; pitting the stones is removing these false beliefs from among the followers; explaining the correct teachings and separating the followers from the false preacher like a man divorces his wife; as there is a false teacher, he is provoking Paul as he misleads the people; the provoking (and deceiving of Macedonia) is reflected in all the lawbreakers and their crimes listed, the 'explaining/disentangling' in the law being for them; it is also in Paul's description of himself as someone who did great wrong in ignorance but was saved by being chosen by Jesus to become a minister of Christ. (1Tim)

Macedonia 'of plotting/deceiving' 'plotting/deceiving-him/he/she/they' 'covered tightly (with any kind of lid: stone, metal, cloth, etc.)/of covering tightly(with lid, etc.)' 'covered me with a lid/fabric/stone/etc.' 'of pillows' 'pillows/with pillows' 'resting on pillows' 'with hand on cheeks' 'of cheeks' 'cheeks' 'pulled off/down/away/removed by pulling' 'pulled bread off oven wall' 'pulled down wall/structure'.

The activities of the false preacher has caused Paul great concern, but instead of clear it up himself, disentangle the matter, and stay and show the people the right from the wrong, instead Paul disappears to Macedonia which is used in most of the epistles to show he is not in the land of the current epistle's activities, has not been seen; there is a barrier covering him and between him and the concerned followers in almost every epistle.

The false teacher is pulling down or pulling off what Paul created, and what Paul created was Christians who follow the correct ways of Jesus Christ (as per Paul); and by causing them to follow his false teachings the false preacher is basically pulling bread ('christs') off the oven wall and taking them away from Paul. The author intentionally shows these Christians are a source of making money and a living for all preachers, including Paul. Both Ephesus and Macedonia are reflected in Paul's instruction (and the author's message to the audience) that Timothy is to disentangle and disprove, warn against, fictional genealogies and fables, i.e. the OT and the Gospels named after disciples. If this were the work of a real scam artist—then by disputing and rendering the Gospels as nothing but fables and the genealogies nothing but lies, Paul is causing his own teachings and his own authority, the stories about 'Paul', to become more valuable and more authoritative—it does the same even in storyland: they show that Paul does not want the Gospels to be the authoritative sources of Jesus-knowledge, and in the same action he lessens the importance and preachings of the other disciples, especially the notable disciples of the stories. And, of course, the author of this epistle is making the same statement about Paul and the epistles including the current one. (1Tim)

Hymenaeus; Hyménaios; خيمينَيُه ، خيمينَيوه 'estimated/guesswork-he/him' 'his estimations/guesswork' 'estimations/guesswork' 'his unclear/nasal/muffled voice/speech'; هيمينَيُه ، هيمينَيوه 'lorded over/hegemonized' 'lorded over/hegemonized-he/him' 'he will list and count-he/him' 'his listing and counting' 'he will grant wishes/gifts/grants/blesses' 'he will make him wish' 'who is he?/(as in: he is no one)'. The meanings are reflected that this character is not teaching truth, but only making fabrications and guesswork; that this person does not know Jesus nor is he of significance; it is also a dig at the OT and the way people preach (what would come to be called ḥa<u>kh</u>aams) 'his unclear/nasal/muffled voice'; his preachings/teachings i.e. his 'water' is ineffective because it is not true and based on lies and guesswork; by delivering them unto **Satan**/'laid hands on' it is punishment after which they will remember the blessings they were in and learn to count the blessings which Paul and true teachings can bestow on them, as well as a warning to those who follow these preachers that he is leading them to Satan and harming them as Satan will have command/control of them through false teachings; also Timothy will have hegemony over them in a prophesied 'that thou by them mightest war a good warfare'. Cp: <u>kh</u>ymeinaioh, <u>kh</u>ymeinaiooh, hymeinaioh, hymeinaiooh. (1Tim.)

Alexander (Mark.15:21) 'on you/upon you-I will send it/him out' 'on you/upon you-I will separate him/it'. Has been used as explained under Mark, this word usually describes sending off sheep/goats in the right direction towards pastures to graze ('sent him/it out'); and used to describe separating between sheep and goats, whether to sort and separate them to send to different areas to graze, or to separate one or more from the rest of the flock in order to slaughter or sell them ('separated him/it') and the 'on you/upon you' half of the compound word shows it is upon these two characters who Paul has 'delivered unto Satan'; a figurative meaning that he has condemned them for false teachings. (1Tim.)

The themes of the character and place word-names is reflected throughout the epistle: Paul **lists** what he recommends be done; his request for prayers and intercessions also covers kings and other rulers i.e. people who **hegemonize**; the truth for all men is **explaining** as is Paul's preachings and instructions; as opposed to false teachers and their **guesswork** and lies Paul presents himself as a true preacher assigned by Jesus—while the author's pun that Paul is a 'a teacher to the Gentiles in faith and verity' shows he is just another false preacher as **Gentiles** ethnon; يثنون ، اثنون 'he/they do it again/double it/fold it/repeat it' 'he/they dissuade/make leave' 'he/they are idolaters/pagans' 'idols' 'praise/praises' 'idol worshippers' 'idolatry/worshipping idols' and at (Judg.4) means 'I will deceive them/the' 'I will mislead them to downfall-them/the'; the men are asked to humble themselves and not doubt during prayers as doubt is **deceitful** and from confusion of the **mess** false preachers create (**Macedonia/Ephesus**); women are asked to be quiet (**muffled voice/Hymenaios**) and not adorn themselves with gold, pearls and clothes (**Epehsus**/'small gem like stones used in jewellery/clothes'); like elsewhere in the NT women are to be obedient silent followers of men and husbands, i.e. men/husband has hegemony over women/wife (**Hymenaious**/'lorded over/hegemonized-he/him'); compared to men, women are nobody/inferior (**Hymenaious**/'who is he?/(i.e. he is no one)' and Paul **gloats** over women (Eve) being inferior as she/they were born from superior man/Adam; **Adam**/'is to last long' (and men) remained true and did not sin (according to Paul through the author of the epistle) but **Eve**/'stay' (and women) remains in the wrong and her suffering has to continue exemplified in the childbearing pains being her/womankind's punishment which is everlasting for as long as women exist. Her punishment comes for **Macedonia**/deceiving her husband, the punishment delivered through Adam/man through his seed/water (**Ephesus**/'small seeds/stone of fruit') which will cause her to be **Ephesus**/'twisted/crumpled-he/him'. But woman can be saved from her innate 'badness' (**Ephesus**/'disentangle knots or problems/matters(it/him)') if she follows Paul's directions (**Paul**/'follow his indication/go his direction'; both following Paul's instructions and childbearing pains allow her to repent (**Timothy**/'she completes/finishes it/he/him'). (1Tim.2)

Pontius Pilate (Matt.27:1-31) 'so you and him/he-are his fall/let him fall' 'so you and him/he-let him loose/go' it is used for Paul assigning Timothy to do God's work alone, and Paul warning him not to fall into sins and errors. (1Tim.6)

The notes mention the letter is written from word-name places to reflect the following: **Laodicea** 'stitch it/stitching' 'of stitching' 'it is sticky/sticking' 'of stickiness' 'threw it away/aside' 'flung it/him/her away/aside' 'of throwing/flinging away/aside' 'will/will not be forced to swallow/suffer/taste it'; as Paul parting from Timothy is like being flung away; Timothy is being flung into an area of great responsibility and the same for the locals of the area; Paul hopes Timothy will stay strongly connected to his teachings and not get stuck in sins and the same is desired of the inhabitants where Timothy will stay (not Laodicea); Paul hopes Timothy will not suffer false preachers and teachings, as well as not suffer sins and trouble.

Phrygia (Acts.2) for 'so stay-he/him/they' 'they opened up' 'opened up/relieved/released/end of difficult period or experience' as Timothy is asked to stay and lead people back to the right path following false teachings that have corrupted people's faith and understanding.

Pacatiana; Pakatianḗs; بَقَتَيَنيَه 'you/they stayed' 'you/they stayed as you/they are' 'of remaining as is/as you are'; بَهَتَيَنيَه 'they/you are blaspheming/making serious false statements' 'of blaspheming/making false statements'. Both are reflected in that Paul is telling Timothy to stay on the right track and to avoid everything which contradicts his teachings/beliefs; it is also in the 'profane vain babblings, and oppositions of science falsely called so' as it equates blasphemy and is false. Cp: baqatyaneieyh, bahatyaneieyh. (1Tim.note)

2Timothy

Lois; Lōís; لويه ، لوييه 'twist/twirl/entwine around it/him' 'twist/twirl/entwine/go around it/him' 'circle around it/him' 'goes around in circles/twists around/is not forthright-he/him'. It describes the faith as being entwined in his grandmother and coming down into Timothy, i.e. entwined in his fibre; it is also a sexual and romantic reference that Paul and Timothy are entwined in love, and were twirled/twisted around each other physically in sex which Paul reminds he put the faith into Timothy physically with his hands, all the NT stories show this special faith is reached and transferred through sexual intercourse; the 'not forthright' meanings are a pun about what is really being said; Timothy is entwined in Paul's thoughts and prayers. It is the same as Levi, named for Leah hoping her unloving husband would be entwined to her both physically and emotionally in Genesis. Cp: looeeh, looeeyh. (2Tim.1)

Eunice; Euníkē; يونيكي ، يونييكي 'he/they pokes wound' 'he/they insults/offends' 'he/they fuck'; يونيجي ، يونييجي 'he/they survive/deliver to safety' 'he/they discuss quietly/secretly/discuss between them'; يونيقي ، يونييقي 'he/they choose/select' 'he/they pick out impurities/clear/clean'; عونيكي ، عونييكي 'your help' 'they helped you'; عونيجي ، عونييجي 'he/they became emotional/sobbed' it means when the voice breaks up or the person chokes up not wanting to cry, but the sob overtakes them or prevents them from speaking properly; عونيقي ، عونييقي 'of necks/to do with necks' 'they hugged'.

All these meanings are present: whether in a romantic relationship or not, the letter is poking each other's wounds created by their being separated; the sexual intercourse between them (Timothy is created as a partner for Paul like Jesus had John); they are discussing the purpose of Timothy being left in a different area as he is to deliver the people to the correct ways of God and deliver them from the false preachings of others; just like all apostles, Timothy has clearing and cleansing abilities and they have been chosen for this cause, and themselves have been purified; it also reflects that Timothy's mother Eunice and his grandmother are the reason Timothy has this faith i.e. their word-names are an assistance to deliver the meanings of Timothy and enhance the narration as **Timothy**'s meanings are also in play: 'she passes him/walks past him/she makes him go' 'will you pass him/will you make him walks past/go' 'she completes/finishes it/he/him' 'will you complete/finish it/him/he' 'she marks/signs it/him/he' 'will you mark/sign it/him/he/will you make him mark/sign' 'she wipes away his urine/sperm(without use of water)' 'will you wipe away his urine/sperm' as both in Acts where he is introduced and now in 2Tim., the character of his mother serves to enhance his character, word-name and role, first as a nameless 'Jewess' because the word 'Jew' gives Timotheus' role meaning, and now as 'Eunice' where the word-name meanings clarify what the role and relationship in the story between Paul and Timothy are, as well as it delivers the message of the author which is the story. Paul writes that Timothy expresses emotion and tears when thinking about and writing to him; mentioning his memories, remembrance and joy in him is like an embrace to them even if they cannot physically do so because of the distance, the letter and words are like a comforting hug; the comfort is also in the work of God. Cp: yuneekey, yuneeykey, yuneegey, yuneeygey, yuneeqey, yuneeyqey, 'uneekey, 'uneeykey, 'uneegey, 'uneeygey, 'uneeqey, 'uneeyqey. (2Tim.1)

Asia is used for 'disobeyed/disobedient/went against' 'disobeyed him/went against him' 'became askew/bent/crooked/warped' as two characters are named for turning away from Paul, i.e. they have not followed the ways as he has instructed. (2Tim.1)

Phygellus; Phýgelos; فيآغِلوه ، فيآغيلُه 'they make rush/flow like river or stream' 'so make him flow/rush like river' 'they despise/despised him' 'in me is his despise/hatred' 'I despise him' 'in me-stabbed deep/dug deep' 'so they stab deep/dig deep' 'so they are distorting/fabricating/inventing(laws/religion/rules/etc.)' 'so they are becoming strict/heavy handed/severe' 'so they are deepening/increasing his injustice/tyranny' 'so they are increasing/deepening wrong/tyranny/injustice' 'so they are increasing invented strictness/severity(in laws or religion or treatment of others)' 'so they chain/restrain him'; فياجِلوه ، فياجيلَه 'they/so they make it/him clear' 'they/so they make it/him cleared/purified/sanitised' 'they come/so they come for it/him'.

Although it does seem that Paul is speaking about imprisonment, it still seems as imprisoned to the true faith of God and its furthering and not a physical nor legal incarceration. The word-name meanings indicate that these two characters added to, or completely changed, what Paul was teaching; it indicates they made teachings clearer but in their own way; it indicates either that Paul finds their teaching too strict and severe, or that Paul wants it to be more strict/severe; it reflects that even if they are immoral enough to innovate and invent rules, laws, teachings that are unavailable in Jesus/God's ways that Paul remains shackled like a prisoner to the true teachings of Jesus/God, and again the author is presenting that Paul wants no other 'gospel' followed besides his own teachings. Taken into context with the meanings of 'Timothy' the word-name, the message and narration of 1Tim. and 2Tim., and the Gospels, Acts and other NT stories and the word-names and narrative of 2Tim, it does narrate that Paul is found immoral, the 'false preachers' are against homosexual sex which is the only way Jesus/God's word and water can continue to be spread, and this concerns Paul and insults him; it indicates they exposed his true intentions. In both epistles to Timothy, he exhorts Timothy not to be ashamed of what they do and who he is, Paul is narrating that most people are ashamed to be associated with him. Cp: phyaaghelooh, phyaagheeloh, phyaagelooh, phyaageeloh. (2Tim.1)

Hermogenes; Hermogénēs; هَرموغينيه 'chased away(using words)-no longer needed-he/him' 'chased away(with words)-the singer/of making 'ghn' words-he/him' 'chased away(with words)-was enriched-he/him' 'will/he will throw/insult-his enricher/his user/who made him independent' 'will/he will throw-his singer/his songs/who makes 'ghn' sounds'; هَرموجينيه 'chased away(with words)-the spoiler/bad/spoiled/lewd-he/him' 'will/he will throw-who came to him' 'will/he will throw-his demons'. The meanings still reflect that these two unfavourable characters were either sent away or threw someone out; it could be that it describes their turning away and leaving Paul, but the way the word-names are made up and also how Paul describes these two people 'turning away' from him shows they are the ones who initiated the separation/dispute and that makes Paul the 'spoiled/bad/lewd' it may also indicate they believe he exploited the other disciples and gospels until he became independent of these disciples and gospels when he could make up his own and enrich/become independent of them; it may also mean the same but the bad conduct being that of the two named characters (Phygellus and Hermogenes). In all cases there is mention of people who preach indicated by the 'ghn' sounds or singing, who have used someone and then left him when they no longer needed him; Paul has been insulted as he describes others as not being ashamed of him, meaning those who turned away from him are ashamed of him; the 'spoiled/bad' meanings are regarding the distortion of gospels, preachings and God's ways, and Paul's current 'bad/difficult' state. Cp: hermogheineyh, hermo-gheineyh, her-mogeineyh, hermo-geineyh. (2Tim.1)

Onesiphorus; Onēsiphóros; عني سِفورُه ، عني سِفوروه 'helps/assists/helped-made him travel/his travels' 'helps/helped-public immorality/sin' 'helped-exposed private body parts in public' 'suffered-made him travel/his travels' 'suffered-public immorality/sin' 'suffered-exposed private body parts in public; عني سِبورُه ، عني سِبوروه 'helps/assists/helped-made it/him right/fixed it/him' 'helps/helped-his fixer/mender/reconciliator' 'suffered-made it/him right/fixed it/him' 'suffered-his fixer/mender/reconciliator'; عني صِبورُه ، عني صِبوروه 'helps/assists/helped-gave him patience/his patience' 'helps/helped-binded him through/made him last' 'suffered-gave him patience/his patience' 'suffered-binded him through/made him last'.

All are reflected: this character has to travel to reach Paul; as everyone else is ashamed to be associated with Paul, this man suffers and does not mind being viewed as openly immoral by assisting Paul in his troubles; it plays on Paul's activities which include water/semen and/or homosexual sex which are viewed as acts of illicit sex, and on earlier stories where Paul has been accused of committing an openly immoral act in public (it may refer to the sex in the Temple described in Acts.21:26-36); this character gives Paul patience but also provides him with physical service and sustenance; Cp: 'ney-siphooroh, 'ney-siphoorooh, 'ney-sibooroh, 'ney-siboorooh, 'ney-ssibooroh, 'ney-ssiboorooh. (2Tim.1)

Rome 'were thrown' 'threw/killed' 'spread/strewn over vast distance/various locations' 'saw water' 'became rotten/went off/bad smelling'. These meanings are reflected in that Onesiphorus has to travel from a different country/city to find Paul, so he covers vast distances and searches him out until he finds him; Paul is considered as a rotten person, of ill-repute as most people turn away from him; as this man is a fellow Christian, he and Paul 'saw water' in each other and this binds them. What the author(s) of 1Tim., and especially 2Tim., does is refer and remind the audience of Acts.21 where Paul is accused of an act of illicit sex or perversion of sex compounded by the greater crime/sin of doing this in the temple and polluting it, although Tim. does not mention the temple, the mention of chains and all the wordplay which narrates he has fallen out of favour and reputation by acts which involve corruption, water/sperm, and immorality in a public place. (2Tim.1)

Ephesus 'disentangle/untie (him/it)' 'disentangle knots or problems/matters(it/him)' 'separate it/him' 'break down into small and understandable pieces(it/him)' 'explain/break down into detail(it/him)' 'small seeds/stone of fruit' 'pit/remove seed/stones from fruit' 'divorce/separate from wife(him)' 'small gem like stones used in jewellery/clothes'; 'pass wind in him' 'make it/him break wind' can mean literally or to beat up or scare, 'copulate/pass wind into' the latter word is used to describe chicken copulation; 'twisted/crumpled it' 'twisted/crumpled-he/him' 'made a mess of it/him'; 'provoked/provoked him/it'. Onesiphorus assists Paul with his problems; Paul mentions he has already informed Timothy in detail of everything Onesiphorus did for him; in doing good and charity towards Paul, Onesiphorus has planted a stone/seed which will reap him good in the afterlife or 'in that day' which Paul prays and hopes for him. (2Tim.1)

Hymenaeus is used again for 'estimated/guesswork-he/him' 'his estimations/guesswork' 'estimations/guesswork' 'his unclear/nasal/muffled voice/speech' 'lorded over/hegemonized' 'lorded over/hegemonized-he/him' 'he will list and count-he/him' 'his listing and counting' 'he will grant wishes/gifts/grants/blesses' 'he will make him wish' 'who is he?/(as in, he is no one)'. The character is accused of misleading and making mistakes, the babbling is out of lack of knowledge, the message is unclear because it is a wrong message that the preacher does not understand. It reflects that no matter what the hardships Paul and others face, God's word, and his ministers, will rule and stand sure; in telling Timothy all these things. (2Tim.2)

Philetus; Phílētos; فيليتُه ، فييليتوه 'his fall/let him fall/his falling/are his fall/falling' 'so he is/so he has let him fall/is his fall/falling' 'let him loose/go/he is loose/gone' 'so he let him loose/so he is loose/gone' 'immoral/lewd/bad character' 'so he is his immorality/made him immoral/lewd' 'falls/fallen' 'so he iş fallen' 'picked lice out of it/him' 'inspected him/it or went thoroughly through (something)'; بيليته ، بييليتوه 'afflicted him/it' 'made it/him ǫld and worn' 'soaķed/wet it/him' 'so he crumpled it/him' 'so he will/should crumple it/him'; فيليطه ، فييليطوه ، بيليطه ، بييليطوه 'so he will/he will/he flattened/squashed it/him' 'so he will/he will/he squeezed and made it/him sag' 'so he will/he will/so he flattened/squashed/made sag-it/him' 'he will/so he will/so he stuck to it/him' 'so he will press/he pressed/squeezed against (something firm)-it/him'.

These meanings are reflected: at the core, the story is about immoral character but also immoral characters (Hymenaeus, Philates, Paul) and the 'soaking' is the spreading of God's word but also an immoral sexual act; the problems and difficulties Paul is facing and Timothy might face are the 'afflictions' as well as the 'squashing/crumpling'; the sexual acts are the 'squeezing/pressing against and sagging' which is the same root word as 'Lot' whose character and story centred around sodomy—except within Paul's stories and epistles, homosexual sex done to spread God's word/water is a good thing, only presented as immorality by opposing characters; the 'higher' homosexual sex is deemed not made out of lust but out of duty and devotion to God i.e. there is a separation: homosexual sex out of lust is bad, while the same anal sex done to spread God's word is good. Cp: <u>ph</u>eeleytoh, <u>ph</u>eeyleytooh, beeleytoh, beeyleytooh, <u>ph</u>eeleyṭoh, <u>ph</u>eeyleyṭooh, beeleyṭoh, beeyleyṭooh. (2Tim.2)

Jannes; Iánnēs; عانّيه 'meant him/it' 'directed message at him' 'suffered/he suffered'; يانّيه 'oh pity' 'they said 'oh, pity'/they had sympathy for him/it' 'the intention/he is intending(to do)'; هانّيه 'satisfied/gave plenty to him/them/it' 'his intention' 'he/I will intend'; جانّيه 'reaped' 'committed crime/injustice against' 'came with intention'.

It reflects the opposition and suffering Paul and his companions faced or believe they will face, as well as the opposition Moses faced. It enhances the injustice intended and committed by wrong-doers and false preachers. Cp: 'aaneyh, yaaneyh, haaneyh, gaaneyh. (2Tim.3)

Jambres; Iambrḗs; يَمبرياه ، يَمبرييه 'he does not show piety/good towards him/it' 'he does not surpass/go beyond him/it' 'you who do not show piety/good towards him/it' 'you who do not surpass him/it' 'he does not disown/distance from him/it' 'he does not declare/show him innocent' 'you who is pious/good towards him/it' 'you who surpass/went beyond him/it' 'you who distance from/disown him/it' 'you who declare/prove him innocent'; هَمبرياه ، هَمبرييه 'here is/look-does not show piety/good towards him/it' 'here is/look-does not surpass/go beyond him/it' 'here is/look-does not disown/distance from him/it' 'here is/look-does not declare/show him innocent' 'here is/look-who is pious/good towards him/it' 'here is/look-who surpassed/went beyond him/it' 'here is/look-who distanced from/disowned him/it' 'here is/look-who declared/proved him innocent/who will prove him innocent'; جَمبرياه ، جَمبرييه 'came-does not show piety/good towards him/it' 'came-does not surpass/go beyond him/it' 'came-does not disown/distance from him/it' 'came-does not declare/show him innocent' 'came-who is pious/good towards him/it' 'came-who surpassed/went beyond him/it' 'came-who distanced from/disowned him/it' 'came-who declared/proved him innocent/who will prove him innocent'.

It is reflected in all the disobedience, sins, accusations and wrongs committed against Paul and towards God and good people; it is in Paul urging Timothy to stay pious towards God and people no matter what wrong is done towards him or what sins or disobedience he witnesses. Cp: ya-mbreyaah, ya-mbreieyh, ha-mbreyaah, ha-mbreieyh, ga-mbreyaah, ga-mbreieyh. (2Tim.3)

Moses 'squeeze him/it' 'suck him/it' 'touched/possessed/was possessed/touched' 'entangled/caused problems/provoked problems or fighting' and represents the action of the characters who opposed Moses but also the men of the 'last days' whose actions are provocative, crimes and sins. As piety is by cleansing through putting/soaking people in water, Moses 'squeeze/suck' symbolises the removal of water which is in the people's sins, disobedience and unholiness. (2Tim.3)

Antioch, **Iconium** and **Lystra** relay between each other and reflect the narrated story of the current passage: **Antioch** (Acts.6) 'was finished/over' as God has delivered Paul from that persecution; 'was hurt/offended/poked in wound' as he was physically and emotionally hurt by the accusations and persecution; 'was chosen' 'was purified/cleansed' 'pronounced/spoke/made speak' as he was chosen and purified to be the chosen preacher of God's word/water and the major part of his work is preaching.

Iconium (Acts.13:51-52) 'they were' 'they were soaked him' 'they were betrayed' 'they are water channels' 'they are bottles/flasks/any transportable drinking vessel or small water vessel' 'they topped up (with water/liquid)/they estimated measure of something liquid' 'they held head high/body straight posture' 'they sat/placed/set upright/erect' 'they were perky' and it serves to confirm the current message in 2Tim.3 that Paul and his companions are the vessels which carry God's water and cleansing/converting powers; and although they are sent by God and carry the truth and good for men, they were and are still betrayed and persecuted, but they kept their dignity and remained upright carrying God's preachings no matter what they faced.

Lystra (Acts.14:1-9) 'so he/may he protect them/him' 'may he not protect them/him' 'so he/may he cover them' 'may he not cover them/him' 'may he pour line of water into' 'may he pour water out' 'may he drain water out of it' 'so he pours/will pour/drain/will drain water out of it' 'may he not pour line of water into' 'may he not/he did not pour water out/drain water out of it' 'may he make it/him a straight line' 'may he not make it a straight line'. This shows Paul, and maybe his companions, were protected and delivered to safety by God from their persecutors; that they are able to pour God's water into people to convert and cleanse them from sins and teach them the ways of God; it also reflects in the disobedient, sinful and persecuting adversaries of Paul as not receiving the water and its cleansing abilities, and that God is not with these people. (2Tim.3)

Chapter 4 is the author again portraying Paul, or at least have Paul portray and aggrandise himself, as Jesus Christ: informing Timothy that his (Paul's) time is at hand is mirroring Jesus when the latter informed his disciples that his death was coming soon; the persecution is also mirroring Jesus' persecution; Paul describes being ready to be 'offered', likening himself with Jesus being the sacrifice God made for mankind; the mention of people abandoning him (of which at least one has a word-name similar in pronunciation and meaning to one of Jesus' disciples) is mirroring the disciples who abandoned Jesus as soon as he was arrested. (2Tim.4)

Demas 'he/they guilted/blamed/ostracised/humiliated-him/he' 'he/they were guilted/blamed/ostracised/humiliated' 'lepers/diseased' 'they are lepers/diseased' 'have conscience/his/their conscience' 'their/his responsibility' 'he/they are accountable' 'muttered' 'he/they muttered about/against him' and his character abandons and leaves Paul, and Paul blames him for loving worldly things instead of faith and spiritual things.

Demas leaves for **Thessalonica** 'he/they-asked/questioned-wounded/poked wound/hurt/offended/fucked' 'he/they/it-leaked/flowed-wounded/poked wound/hurt/offended/fucked' 'he/they/it-comforted/entertained/distracted-wounded/poked wound/hurt/offended/fucked' 'he/they-asked/questioned-picked out impurities/cleared/cleaned/chose/selected' 'he/they/it-leaked/flowed-picked out impurities/cleared/

cleaned/chose/selected' 'he/they/it-comforted/entertained/distracted-picked out impurities/cleared/cleaned/chose/selected' 'he/they-asked/questioned-saved/delivered to safety/talked/discussed secretly' 'he/they/it-leaked/flowed-saved/delivered to safety/talked/discussed secretly' 'he/they/it-comforted/entertained/distracted-saved/delivered to safety/talked/discussed secretly'. You can see the various wordplay and its relay in the story: he has wounded Paul in doing so; Demas (as Thomas the disciple, or at least his verbal doppelganger) has been distracted from his water-flowing abilities to cleanse and convert people, to spread God's word and instead gone after distractions of this carnal life; Timotheus who is equal to Demas is asked to come quickly to Paul as Timothy can provide Paul with the support and needs as he has the same Jesus-water abilities of Demas; Demas has chosen the safety of worldly things and abandoned Paul and in doing so has gone against spreading God/Jesus' word and in effect has 'spoken/muttered against it'. (2Tim.4)

Crescens; Krḗskēs; قريآشكيه ، قرييشكيه 'read/admitted-is complaining about him' 'settle/cease/stop-complaining about him' 'scored/gained/of scoring/gaining-he/him' and this character too is lumped with Demas as loving this world more than Paul, God, and the service of God which is why Paul is complaining to Timothy about him; the 'scoring/gaining' meanings are shown in him abandoning Paul for worldly gains.

He has gone to **Galatia** 'said/he said-came here/come here' 'sanitised on heat' 'sanitised it/him on heat' 'he said he came/he said he would come' 'made mistake/he/they made mistake' 'of making mistakes' 'made mistake-he/him/she/her' 'of making mistakes-he/him/she/her' 'is deceiving/tricking/shortchanging' 'of deceiving/tricking/shortchanging-he/him/she/her' 'is wrong' 'he/she/they is/are wrong'; because Crescens has abandoned Paul and this is a mistake, he too has been deceived by love of this world/life; also reflects and relays Paul has asked Timothy to come because Paul's group has abandoned him. Cp: qreyaashkeyh, qreyeishkeyh. (2Tim.4)

Titus (2Cor.) 'come to him/you come to him' 'bring to him/you bring to him' 'they came/they brought' 'came a lot/brought a lot' 'you give/gave to him' was used in 2Cor. as a word-name to describe a character who Paul could not find to 'come to him' and this was the reason he could not come to the Corinthians. Titus is still used in this sense, as he has also loved this world instead of Jesus and Paul, and abandoned the latter and gone to Dalmatia instead.

Titus has gone to Dalmatia; Dalmatía; ضَلَمَتيَ ، ضَلَمَتييَ 'darkened/darkness' 'darkened/darkness-he/him' 'caused/was caused/of darkness-he/him' 'injustice' 'unfair/cruel/ overbearing/despotic-he/him' 'caused/was caused/of injustice/cruelty-he/him'. This relays that Titus has caused Paul an injustice, shown cruelty and love of bad things as opposed to Jesus and God's ways. Cp: dhalmateea, dhalmateeya. (2Tim.4)

Luke 'talks(ed) too much/talks too much nonsense' 'rambling/loquacious' 'his nonsense/ramblings' 'chew(ed)' 'for you' 'chew' 'for you' 'crumpled/crumpled against each other'. Demas and the others whose word-names and roles include speaking and watering have departed so Paul needs other characters with word-names and roles who can replace them such as Luke with its 'speaking/too many words' meanings and its meanings of 'for you' as they are staying with, or coming to, Paul; it also reflects Timothy and Mark who Paul has requested to come to him to replace the departed characters as **Timothy** has meanings of 'she passes him/walks past him/she makes him go' 'will you pass him/will you make him walk past/go' 'she completes/finishes it/he/him' 'will you complete/finish it/him/he' 'she marks/signs it/him/he' 'will you mark/sign it/him/he/will you make him mark/sign' 'she wipes away his urine/sperm(without use of water)' 'will you wipe away his urine/sperm' and is a vessel of Jesus' water and he has been asked to come and complete Paul and Paul's work; **Mark** 'did not/they did not wait/stay/become still' 'did not intensely ask/intreat' 'did not shake/unsettle it' and these meanings relay that Luke has already chosen to stay with Paul, and Paul has not had to beg for Timothy and Mark to come, but has merely asked them and they will comply; in Luke, Timothy, and Mark replacing Demas, Crescens, and Titus they have allowed Paul and his efforts to remain settled, unshaken. (2Tim.4)

Tychicus (Acts.20:1-12) 'fell/broke-his brother' 'fell/broke-healed/cured him' 'fell/broke-made him still/stay' and he is sent to **Ephesus** (Acts.18:19-28) 'disentangle/untie (him/it)' 'disentangle knots or problems/matters(it/him)' 'separate it/him' 'break down into small and understandable pieces(it/him)' 'explain/break down into detail(it/him)' 'small seeds/stone of fruit' 'pit/remove seed/stones from fruit' 'divorce/separate from wife(him)' 'small gem like stones used in jewellery/clothes' 'pass wind in him' 'make it/him break wind' can mean literally or to beat up or scare, 'copulate/pass wind into' the latter word is used to describe chicken copulation, 'twisted/crumpled it' 'twisted/crumpled-he/him' 'made a mess of it/him' 'provoked/provoked him/it'. The use of Tychicus and Ephesus meanings still relay the breaking up of Paul's group, the disobedient apostles falling into wrong ways, they are twisted and crumpled, they have made a mess of what they are meant to faithfully do: spread God's word, and love the belief that Jesus will appear, but have fallen from this by abandoning Paul for worldly matters. At the same time it represents the brothers, apostles, who come or are called to come and dispatched elsewhere by Paul to heal the wounds, seal the cracks, to continue with explaining and spreading the word while disentangling any false teachings which are a result of Paul's group splitting not only in geographical directions but also in teachings and beliefs; where the disobedient apostles who abandon their true calling and Paul are the 'pitting stone from fruit', the obedient and incoming brethren are the 'seed/stone of fruits' which will spread God's word and be strength and support for Paul. (2Tim.4)

Troas (Acts.16:8-11) 'watered it/him' 'gave it/him to drink(water)' 'dreamed it/him' 'dreamed' 'told story' used because Paul is requesting his cloak be brought to him, but more importantly he wants his writing tools to be brought from this place as the parchments are what he tells his stories through (especially as these stories are being told as letters) which is the authors way of showing his skill at wordplay and showing these Paul-letters are works of fiction; as Paul (and the real authors) in the stories uses these letters to spread Jesus' word; it is the same as converting people with water so by teaching people through his letters he is converting and preaching just as he would with the use of words and water had he arrived in person.

Carpus; Kárpos; قآربه ، قآربوه 'near it/him' 'bring nearer-it/him' 'serve it/him' 'read with it/him' 'teach with it/him' 'keep still/cease/stop moving-it/him' 'keep still/stop moving/cease with it/him' 'confess/admit it/him' 'confess/admit with it/him' 'offer as sacrifice/gift-it/him'. This is still related to the Troas meanings as Carpus is narrated being in Troas; the 'reading' and 'teaching with' meanings are reflected in the parchments and books which Paul is asking to be brought to him as this is how Paul in the epistles tells his stories through writing letters; the 'offer as sacrifice/gift-it/him' meanings are still likening him to Jesus who was offered as a sacrifice for mankind. Cp: qaarbooh, qaarboh, qaar-booh, qaar-boh. (2Tim.4)

Alexander 'on you/upon you-I will send it/him out' 'on you/upon you-I will separate him/it'. This relays that Paul is asking Timothy to bring his cloak, books and parchment from Carpus in Troas; it relays the likening of Paul being sacrificed/executed the same way as Jesus as Jesus was called a 'lamb of God' and sacrificed to spare mankind and the meanings as explained under Andrew and Alexander mean to send sheep off in a specific direction, and/or to separate specific sheep/goat(s) for slaughter or sale or any other specific use, and this also reflects and enhances that all the people around Paul took off on their own ways and left Paul alone to suffer; it reflects that Paul wants his companions to boycott or at least be wary of Alexander. (2Tim.4)

Prisca (Acts.18) Príska; بريیشَق 'good/piety-he works/labours' 'go/goes beyond/surpasses/passes-he works/labours' 'innocent/disowns/distances from-he works/labours; بريیسَك 'good/piety-he is able/he can do it' 'go/goes beyond/surpasses/passes-he is able/he can do it' 'innocent/disowns/distances from-he is able/he can do it'. This relays the narration which precedes Prisca's mention that God will not only deliver Paul out of harm's way, but will do so because of the good and piety Paul has done; God will continue to support Paul while he does God's work; the importance in the narration of Paul's letter is not that God's work is being done, but that it is through Paul that God's work is being done, and that it is done fully and wholly through Paul—you can see that these stories, once they are mistaken and accepted as real letters from a real person, are what gave Paul, a fictional character and fictional events, the ability to influence and seem to have influenced Christianity almost as much as Jesus—just as Paul in the stories was trying to exceed Jesus' role. (2Tim.4)

Aquila (Acts.18:1-6) for 'his sayings' 'told him/I told him' 'put words in his mouth' 'stayed/spent time' 'stayed/spent time with him' 'staying/spending time/they are staying spending time' 'gathering place/place people gather at to spend time together at' 'of spending time' 'removed him' 'of removing' (the removing part means a physical removal of a person or object and in modernity would come to be the word used for 'resignation') 'his brainy-ness/intelligence/mind/wisdom' 'made him reasonable/gave him clever' 'gave him mind/logic/calmness' 'calmed him down/made him knowledgeable/patient' 'his mind/patience/knowledge' 'made him rational' 'kept him in a specific place'. Most of these meanings can be seen relayed in 2Tim.4. (2Tim.4)

Onesiphorus (2Tim.1) 'helps/assists/helped-made him travel/his travels' 'helps/helped-public immorality/sin' 'helped-exposed private body parts in public' 'suffered-made him travel/his travels' 'suffered-public immorality/sin' 'suffered-exposed private body parts in public' 'helps/assists/helped-made it/him right/fixed it/him' 'helps/helped-his fixer/mender/reconciliator' 'suffered-made it/him right/fixed it/him' 'suffered-his fixer/mender/reconciliator' 'helps/assists/helped-gave him patience/his patience' 'helps/helped-binded him through/made him last' 'suffered-gave him patience/his patience' 'suffered-binded him through/made him last' as God and Timothy, and others, are assisting Paul to get through difficult times, to preach God's word and to hopefully live forever in God's kingdom. (2Tim.4)

Erastus, Corinth, Trophimus and Miletum are used to relay a message: **Erastus** 'yes, stack it/stack/pack' 'he stacked/stacked/packed it' 'made it in a row' 'his bride/his wedding' 'planted it' 'stuck it in mud/fell into/stuck out of mud/soil' 'plaited it' 'got stuck in mud/soil/sand' who has stayed at **Corinth** 'both male and female (at the same time)' it applies to a male or female which either has both male and female reproductive organs, and/or behaves like a male when he/she is female or vice-versa; 'linked to him/linked him' 'linked them/him' 'linked him with wood/rope'; 'his opposite/opposed him' 'his horn/his spirit of strength(or power)' 'read to him/taught him' 'stopped him/it moving/fidgeting' 'made him stop what he was doing' reflects again what all the NT authors are saying: there is male-on-male sex happening (Corinth is similar to Jonathan where the latter means male and male having sex making each other female, while the former means both a male and female in one or behaving like the opposite sex) and is part and parcel to all conversions and teachings, and especially those with apostle abilities; Erastus has been paired/married/linked to Trophimus in the sentence but also in the actions and roles they play and represent so that all the meanings of 'Erastus' and 'Corinth' apply to 'Trophimus' and 'Miletus' and vice-versa.

Trophimus 'you see in water' 'quenched in water' 'watered/given to drink water' 'dreamt in water' 'what do you see in it?' 'what do you see' 'what did you dream?' is left unwell at **Miletum** 'filled it/covered it' 'his frock/short shirt' 'you/I filled/covered it' 'filled it with water' 'fetched water'. The meanings of quenching in water, covering and especially the 'short shirt/frock' is similar to the Biblical 'lifting of skirt' and the water covering has already been dealt with extensively. They all represent and relay what Paul and his group are doing when they preach and teach. (2Tim.4)

Eubulus; Eúboulos; يوبولوه ، يوبولُه 'he soaks him/it' 'he urinates him/it/on him/it' 'he gives/makes him patient' 'he afflicts him' 'he makes him clever'; عوبولوه ، عوبولُه 'shook his fat' 'shook sheep fat' 'their fat shook/moved' 'moving/shaking fat' 'moved/shook fat/his fat/sheep fat'. It is wordplay indicating Paul is meant by all the word-names and their characters actions and meanings; it refers to the soaking and transferring of God/Jesus' water/sperm and the sexual intercourse which causes the body to shake like rolls of fat shake on sheep when they move; it also refers to Paul being 'fat of sheep' a favoured sacrifice by God in the Biblical stories. Cp: yuboulooh, yubouloh, 'uboulooh, 'ubouloh. (2Tim.4)

Pudens; Poúdēs; بوديه ، بوَديه 'I will take him/bring him along' 'in/along his valley(s)/way(s)'; فوديه ، فوَديه 'a sacrifice/his sacrifice' 'make him/it a sacrifice' and means like an animal or human sacrifice 'so take him/so bring him along' 'in his valleys(s)/way(s)'. This reflects that it is Paul's ways; he is asking them to come along or bring things or others along; that Paul is being likened to a human sacrifice as Jesus was made a sacrifice by God for mankind. Cp: poudeyh, pouadeyh, phoudeyh, phouadeyh. (2Tim.4)

Linus; Línos; لينوه/لينُه ، ليينوه/لييِنُه 'made it/him pliable/soft(er)/moister' and this is done physically by kneading something, adding a little liquid to it, or both; in meaning making a person more pliable it can be through any number of actions such as making them happy, laugh or various actions such as reconciliating, kindness, bribery, lying, etc. In this instance it indicates sexual encounters between Paul and the rest of the apostles, preachers who work with him and the others they convert and give preaching abilities to. Cp: leenooh, leenoh, leeynooh, leeynoh.

Claudia; Klaudía; قَلوديَ ، قَلوديِيَ 'they placed responsibility' 'placed/burdened with responsibility' 'they hung it around neck' 'they hung responsibility around neck' 'they garlanded' 'they placed responsibility/accountability on' 'they acted/copied'. This too reflects that Paul and all the characters associated with his preaching, teaching, ways all conduct the same actions, behaviour; they are all accountable and responsible for spreading God's word, but also all responsible and accountable for the negative things and accusations, responsibility of the consequences stemming out of their conduct. Cp: qlaudeea, qlaudeeya. (2Tim.4)

Rome is still used for 'were thrown' 'threw' 'killed' 'spread/strewn over vast distance/various locations' 'saw water' 'became rotten/went off/bad smelling' for its reminder and meaning that Paul conducted acts including sex with males which gave him a bad reputation and entangled him with the law or local community because his preaching and work always include transferring God/Jesus' water/sperm of which he is a vessel and carrier of.

Nero; Nero, Nérōni; نيرو ، نيرُ 'fire/make fire' 'of fire(s)/making fire(s)/we/they make fire(s)' 'light/make light/of making light/shed light/of shedding light' 'we/they make/shed light/of light' 'make light/shine/shed light' 'see/we/they see/make see/of seeing' 'show/we/they show' 'understand/we/they understand/

make understand/of understanding' 'we/they penis him' 'we/they penised him' 'we/they insult him with 'penis"; نعرو ، نعرُ 'we/they make/become naked' 'we/they get naked' 'of nakedness/getting naked' 'of sexual excitement/we/they horny/sexually excited/have erection' 'we/they stood/stood erect/stood in front of without moving' 'of standing/standing erect/standing in front of without moving or speaking'.

Nérōni; نيرونِ ، نيروني 'fires/makes fire/fiery' 'of fire(s)/making fire(s)/we/they make fire(s)' 'light/makes light/of making light/sheds light/of shedding light' 'we/they make/shed light/of light' 'make light/shine/shed light' 'sees/we/they see/makes see/of seeing' 'they made me see' 'shows/we/they show' 'they showed me' 'understands/we/they understand/makes understand/of understanding' 'they made me understand' 'we/they penis him' 'we/they penised him' 'we/they insult him with 'penis' 'they penised me/insulted me with penis'; نعروني ، نعرونِ 'we/they make/become naked' 'we/they get naked' 'of nakedness/getting naked' 'they made me naked' 'of sexual excitement/we/they horny/sexually excited/have erection' 'they sexually excited me/gave me an erection' 'we/they stood/stood erect/stood in front of without moving' 'of standing/standing erect/standing in front of without moving or speaking' 'they made me stand erect/stand in front of without moving or speaking.'.

It reflects the activities of Paul and the apostles, and the themes of the epistles including this current epistle which does include sexual intercourse as a highly spiritual and cleansing activity, especially the closer connected it is to Jesus, which is what disciples and apostles are; Paul and the apostles work also sheds light on the 'mysteries' i.e. the true stories of Jesus Christ, and teaches the people to the correct way as Jesus and Jesus' word, his inception and life have also been called 'light' (see gospel of John); Paul's activities teaches people to understand the stories, ways and faith of Jesus Christ; the author of the epistle is teaching people to understand these stories are fictional. It is equivalent to Naarath (Josh.16:7), Naarah (1Chr.4:5), Naaran (1Chr.7:28) Naarai (1Chr.11:37), Neriah (Jer.32:12-14), Neri (Luke.3). Cp: neyro, n-eyro, neyroo, n'roo, n'ro, neiroonee, neirooni, n'roonee, n'rooni. (2Tim.4)

Titus

The meanings of **Titus** 'come to him/you come to him' 'bring to him/you bring to him' 'they came/they brought' 'came a lot/brought a lot' 'you give/gave to him' begins with the introduction of the epistle story: as God is the one who cannot lie and has promised to give eternal life, this promise has to come true. (Tit.1)

Crete; كريبتي 'hired/rented/leased' 'of hiring/renting/leasing' 'drove/chased/forced away/forced with violence'; قريبتي 'my village' 'villager' 'of villages' 'of reading a lot' 'read a lot to me/taught me to read/of teaching to read' 'stopped moving/fidgeting' 'stopped what you were doing'. Titus is described as being left in Crete so as to appoint elders—the appointment is similar to hiring, to set things in order so that preachings and teachings are effective; the bishop is supposed to be someone who does not have a bad character or violent temper which would drive people away from the faith and church as his job is to teach people so that the stay and believe in the teachings, but he must not be attached to a dishonest or unethical 'hire/lease' called 'filthy lucre'; the meaning of 'stopped what you were doing' is shown in the instructions of what should be avoided. The people 'of circumcision' (meaning people of other faiths and may specifically mean, but not limited to, those of the Jewish faith) who are described as being able to communicate and convince well, which indicates they are well-read and good at teaching, should be made to cease from being able to persuade people from following their teachings; they are described as doing this for profit which shows the 'hire/lease' meanings. The meanings 'stopped moving/fidgeting' 'stopped what you were doing' are reflected in describing the Cretians as 'slow bellies'; to drive them away meaning is in the instruction to speak to them harshly.

The meanings of Titus and Crete are throughout Chapter 2-3.

Artemas; Artemás; ارتَمآه 'was thrown/thrown down' 'threw down headlong' 'was killed' 'was wounded' 'collapse/collapsed' 'saw water/she showed him water/saw his water' 'quenched/she quenched-water/his water' 'was watered/was quenched-with water/his water'. This character and meanings reflect that Titus is about to see Paul's water again; that they are to have sexual intercourse; that Titus is wounded/hurt by this and may have been finding excuses not to come to Paul to avoid copulating with him, but this wounds Paul and Paul sends a temporary replacement so that Titus cannot escape the meeting and its requirements. Cp: artemaah.

Tychicus 'fell/broke-his brother' 'fell/broke-healed/cured him' 'fell/broke-made him still/stay' is used for the same reasons to show that there is a breach which needs to be healed/sealed and that is done by copulating with Paul. (Tit.3)

Nicopolis; Nikópolis; نيقوبوله 'we meet him' 'we face him' 'we accept him/it because of good quality (whether material, or a person in character, honesty)' 'we accept him/accept him reluctantly' 'purified/cleansed/cleared-his mind/intellect/patience/affliction' 'purified/cleansed/cleared-his urine' 'cleared/picked out impurities-his mind/intellect/patience/affliction/urine' 'picked out impurities/cleared/cleaned-his mind/intellect/patience/affliction/urine';

نيقوفوله 'we close/shut it/him' 'purified/cleansed/cleared-his instruction/indication/direction' 'cleared/picked out- his instruction/indication/direction';

نيكوبوله 'we/they fucked-his mind/intellect/patience' 'we/they offended- his mind/intellect/patience' 'we/they wounded/poked in wound-his mind/intellect/patience' 'we/they fucked-his affliction/soaked/urinated/his urine' 'we/they offended-his affliction/soaked/urinated/his urine' 'we/they wounded/poked in wound-his affliction/soaked/urinated/his urine;

نيكوفوله 'we/they fucked-his instructions/his directions/his indication' 'we/they wounded/poked in wound-his instructions/directions/indications';

نيجوبوله 'we respond/answer him' 'we come-his mind/intellect/patience/affliction' 'we come-urinated/his urine' 'survived/they survived/delivered to safety/they delivered to safety-his mind/intellect/patience/affliction' 'survived/they survived/delivered to safety/they delivered to safety-urinated/his urine' 'discussed quietly/secretly/discussed between them/they discussed quietly/they discussed secretly/they discussed between them-his mind/intellect/patience/affliction' 'discussed quietly/secretly/discussed between them/they discussed quietly/they discussed secretly/they discussed between them-urinated/his urine';

نيجوفوله 'survived/they survived/delivered to safety/they delivered to safety-his instructions/his directions/his indication' 'discussed quietly/secretly/discussed between them/they discussed quietly/they discussed secretly/they discussed between them-his instructions/his directions/his indication'.

They are following Paul's instructions and they are to follow his directions of where to go; they are instructed to go to places; Titus is to meet him at Nicopolis; they are to respond to him; they are expected to follow his instructions because he has intelligence and wisdom; they are not to offend or hurt anybody; they are to speak and conduct with humility and meekness; Titus whose name means 'bring/come to' 'you give/gave to him' is to come to Paul and it is indicated by the context of the letter and how the stories are narrated and in context with the other names in the chapter that he and Paul are to have sexual intercourse to cleanse and purify each other, to strengthen and increase their 'Jesus-water' as the selected and already purified apostles; Paul's tone to Titus to begin his journey as soon as the person arrives to relieve him of his position indicates that Titus may be reluctant to go meet Paul, but as the compound words of all their names suggest he is to follow his instructions; Cp: nyqooboolih, nyqoophoolih, nykooboolih, nykoophoolih, nygooboolih, nygoophoolih. (Tit.3)

Zenas; Zēnáh; زيناه 'adulterers/fornicators' 'adorned/his/its adornments' 'his dresses'; ذيناه 'these two/them' 'his ears/their ears/handles' 'gave them permission' 'called/summoned them/called them to assemble'. Titus whose name means 'come to him/you come to him' 'bring to him/you bring to him' 'they came/they brought' 'came a lot/brought a lot' 'you give/gave to him' is to also bring with him Zenas and Apollos to Paul as they are also in need of being strengthened so that their abilities to preach, teach and heal can be at its best. As the name suggests, they are being summoned to come with Titus even if they are on travels, they have permission to come to Paul, they will engage in the sexual activities which gives them more of Jesus' water/sperm which allows them to conduct their apostle/preacher activities; the meaning of 'dresses' also suggests the sexual activity and that this is a privilege and something to be honoured by as the 'zenah' dress (which until recently was a robe/dress warn by both men and women) is being dressed-up for a special occasion. Cp: zeynaah, veynaah. (Tit3)

Apollos 'soak/soaked him/it' 'afflict/afflicted him/it' who Titus is also instructed to bring with him to Paul, and this enhances what the other word-names and characters already have that Paul has summoned Titus and the rest to be copulated so they can soak in God/Jesus' water; because the narration shows Titus is reluctant to do so and is avoiding travelling to Paul until Paul has found a solution which leaves Titus with no excuse—it shows that Titus sees this as an affliction (Apollos/Paul) he would rather avoid. (Tit.3)

Macedonia 'of plotting/deceiving' 'plotting/deceiving-him/he/she/they' 'covered tightly (with any kind of lid: stone, metal, cloth, etc.)/of covering tightly(with lid, etc.)' 'covered me with a lid/fabric/stone/etc.' 'of pillows' 'pillows/with pillows' 'resting on pillows' 'with hand on cheeks' 'of cheeks' 'cheeks' 'pulled off/ down/away/removed by pulling' 'pulled bread off oven wall' 'pulled down wall/structure'. This relays that Titus is attempting to avoid the sexual activities with Paul, and Titus is using plots and deceit, at the same time it is as if Titus is creating a barrier between him and Paul, i.e. covering himself securely with a lid; as Paul wants sexual activities the 'of pillows' meanings of prostitution/illicit or immoral sex are used again (as with Lydia of Thyatira) and Titus is the one 'with hand on cheek' as this means someone who is so upset or worried he/she is leaning with hand on cheek; the 'pulled off oven wall' and 'pulled down wall/ structure' reflects that Titus does not enjoy this physically, maybe means he is hurt physically by this activity, and this is reinforced by the use of Tychicus (see its meanings above) as a character and word-name who may arrive as it is either Artemas or Tychicus who Paul will send so that Titus can come to him—and these two names have been used to also show that **Tychicus**/fell/broke-his brother / fell/broke-made him stay/still, is Titus being hurt by Paul's sexual activities, reluctant to comply but will be made to **Artemas** 'was thrown/thrown down' 'threw down headlong' 'was killed' 'was wounded' 'collapse/collapsed' 'saw water/she showed him water/saw his water' 'quenched/she quenched-water/his water' 'was watered/was quenched-with water/his water' whether he likes it or not. The deceit and misleading meanings of **Macedonia** are also the author's way of showing that these stories are fictional and not to be believed as fact. (Tit.3)

Philemon

Philemon; Philḗmōn; فِليآمون ، بِليآمون 'so he/with/by-counts and lists/counting and listing' 'so he/with/ by-lists and gloats/listing and gloating' 'so he/with/by-grants/blesses/gives/granting/blessing/giving' 'so in/ by-from where/from who/from since when' 'so/by-whose' 'so-what is it?' 'so-who is it' 'so/by/with-of what/of who?' 'so in/by-giving security'. Most of these meanings are present in Phil.: Paul is listing and counting all the many things physical, spiritual, and of service which Philemon has done for them and God, which includes providing something physical to feed the saints; it is in Paul asking that anything Onesimus has wronged Philemon or is in debt to him, to forgive and to settle it for Paul's sake and if a debt to record it against Paul's account—but goes further as Paul takes it as an opportunity to 'count/list/ gloat' over Philemon that Philemon owes his whole self to Paul which the narration is a perfect example of the meaning 'counts and lists/gloats'.

The whole story is about something done, and about someone who is for someone or something else: Philemon conducts and has love and faith towards God, Paul and the saints; Paul beseeches Philemon for Onesimus' sake; Onesimus once meant, and maybe still does, mean nothing or very little to Philemon, but according to Paul he must now mean a lot, or more, to and for Philemon; Paul has sent Onesimus back for Philemon, but also for the service of God if Philemon will accept; Paul expresses he would have kept Onesimus for himself but chose to send him back for Philemon's sake; Paul suggests that Onesimus may have left Philemon for a reason; Paul suggests that Onesimus not return as a servant to Philemon, but as his brother and equal; Paul asks Philemon to forgive Onesimus for Paul's sake; Paul asks Philemon to prepare a room for Paul when he visits. Cp: phileyaamoon, bileyaamoon. (Phil.)

Apphia; Apphía; عب فيَ ، عب فييَ 'packed/filled in me' 'overflowed/floated in/seeped water or liquid-in me' 'shame/shamed-in me' 'rotted and stank-in me'. The meanings of packed/filled and also overflowed are available in the narration as Philemon has given much and filled the saints and Paul in their stomachs and with joy, among giving them other blessings in the service of God; the 'shamed-in me' is available as Paul is subtly making Philemon ashamed of the way he treats Onesimus; the 'overflowed' meanings are in that he served Paul and part of the service is the transference of Jesus' water between them. Cp: 'b pheea, 'ab pheeya. (Phil.)

Archippus 'welcome it/him' 'make space for it/him' 'ride it/him' 'mount it/him' and can mean literal ride it, or euphemism or slang for have sex with 'watch/keep eye on it/him' 'pour water into it/him' and the pouring of water in this way means to keep an eye on the stream of water and the narrow opening of the vessel it is being poured into to avoid splashing even one drop. All these meanings are used again as Paul is asking Philemon to welcome back Onesimus as there may be bad-blood due to his absence while serving Paul; the 'mounting' is in he has become one of Paul's inner circle and assistants which includes having sex to transfer God/Jesus' water, and this also covers the 'pouring water into it/him' meanings; Paul is asking Philemon to make space and prepare a place of stay for him as he promises to visit Philemon. (Phil.)

Onesimus 'helps/assists/helped-named him/it/told story' 'helps/helped-his illness' 'suffered-named him/it/told story' 'suffered-his illness' and this is reflected in that he has assisted Paul in times of need when he was suffering, and Paul now wants Philemon not to consider Onesimus useless, but useful and to make use of the assistance he can provide; in Paul would have preferred to keep Onesimus as Onesimus had filled him physically, and food and/or water/sperm is meant here; Paul is assisting Onesimus in getting him out of trouble with Philemon, and the whole of Philemon is a story being told about the named character's conduct and his own backstory. Note that the epistle is both written and carried by Onesimus himself and this is done as a joke that the real authors of the epistles alleging to be written by Paul are actually letters written by the carriers of the letters to the recipients, and the author and deliverer of these letters is always carrying a self-recommendation letter, it becomes more pointed because Onesimus has written the letter which gets him out of trouble with his employer/master. (Phil.)

Paul 'his mind' 'his patience' 'his affliction/afflicted him' 'his indication/direction' 'follow his indication/go his direction' as although Paul wants Philemon to do as he directs/indicates in the letter, he would rather Philemon do it out of his own mind, his own decision, but this in itself is Paul's 'direction/indication'.

Epaphras 'packed/filled-multiplied/increased it/him' 'overflowed/floated in/seeped water or liquid/swelled with water-increased/multiplied it/him' 'shame/shamed-increased/multiplied it/him' 'rotted and stank-multiplied/increased it/him' and these meanings repeat and relay the whole theme of the story and meanings in the other similar word-names mentioned above and also reflected that by forgiving Onesimus, Philemon will increase his own piety.

Marcus 'did not/they did not wait/stay/become still' 'did not intensely ask/intreat' 'did not shake/unsettle it' 'did not drive him insane' 'plastered it'; Paul is gently asking that Philemon forgive and accept Onesimus back for Paul's sake; the problem is over Onesimus not staying in the service or company of Philemon and going to serve Paul instead; Paul is trying to 'plaster it' i.e. smooth it over between Philemon and Onesimus which is what the action of 'marcus/plaster it' means, making something rough and/or full of gaps—smooth. (Phil.)

Aristarchus for some of its meanings such as: 'stack/pack-loosen/immoral-him/it' 'stacked/packed-loosened/are immoral-him/it' 'put in a row-loosen/loosened/immoral/are immoral-him it'; 'planted/plant it-immoral/loosened it/him' 'stuck/stick it in mud/fall/fell into/sticking/stuck out of mud/soil-loosened/immoral-it/him'; 'plaited-immoral/loosened-it/him' 'got stuck/stick in mud/soil/sand-loosened/immoral-it/him' (the way animal and/or carts get stuck in deep sand, soil or mud and can't easily get out (or car in modernity)); 'see/show/saw-you/it will be loosened/split open/cracked/muscles loosened' 'water/give to drink-you/it will be loosened/split open/cracked/muscles loosened'; 'see/show/saw-you will rest/be relieved/relaxed' 'see/show/saw-you will make rest/relieve/relax'.

Most of these meanings can be seen: both Philemon and Onesimus have stacked/packed Paul or the saints with physical and spiritual good deeds and supplies; both have done something immoral (Onesimus leaving his master's employment without permission and Philemon maybe for mistreating Onesimus, but definitely for being angry or seeking to punish Onesimus for his absence); both have faith planted in them and this will get them out of the problem they are stuck in; through faith and good deeds as instructed by Paul, as well as faith which is the 'word and water', will get them out of this immoral issue between them and this will give them relief from these worldly issues. (Phil.)

Demas 'he/they guilted/blamed/ostracised/humiliated-him/he' 'he/they were guilted/blamed/ostracised/humiliated' 'lepers/diseased' 'they are lepers/diseased' 'have conscience/his/their conscience' 'their/his responsibility' 'he/they are accountable'; 'muttered' 'he/they muttered about/against him'. The going away and also a sense that Onesimus may no longer be welcome and ostracised, or at least found guilty of doing something wrong is narrated in Paul asking Philemon to receive Onesimus after a parting, and asking him to forgive Onesimus for Paul's sake; Paul is holding Philemon accountable for mistreating or having a derogatory view of Onesimus; Paul is acknowledging Onesimus may be accountable for wrong-doing and/or debt towards Philemon, but Paul would like to take the responsibility of blame and debt on Onesimus' behalf. (Phil.)

Lucas 'talks(ed) too much/talks too much nonsense' 'rambling/loquacious' 'his nonsense/ramblings' 'chew(ed)' 'for you'. Paul is dedicating the whole letter about one subject: Onesimus; he is making it clear that not only can Onesimus be of great service to Paul, but that he can be of greater service to Philemon as an equal 'for you'. (Phil.)

Rome 'were thrown' 'threw' 'killed' 'spread/strewn over vast distance/various locations' 'saw water' 'became rotten/went off/bad smelling'. These meanings are reflected in the epistle: Paul seems to be mediating a grave difference between Philemon and Onesimus stemming from the latter travelling far away and for a long time (when he served Paul in Rome), and this has resulted in Onesimus falling out of favour and being in trouble with Philemon as his reputation and his relationship with his employer or master has soured; Paul is stating because Onesimus has entered the faith he is as capable of doing the same work they do but also that he has become a brother to Onesimus, and this is reached through use of water in conversion and believing. (Phil.)

Hebrews

The word 'Hebrew' will be explained later in the book, but like all the titles given to stories in the NT, 'Hebrews' was not randomly chosen based on speculation, but for its meanings; this shows even when at a later date a title was affixed to this epistle story, it was given to it based on the word's meaning and the understanding of the local translator. The theme of 'hebrew', a word in use of the language of the Bible, is relayed throughout the whole Epistle to the Hebrews. Just like all word-names, titles and characters in the Biblical stories, both OT and NT, it does not mean any ethnic group, whether race or religion, nor does it mean a language but an Arabic word with specific meanings as used in the stories everywhere it appears.

Moses is used for its meanings of 'touched/possessed/was possessed/touched' 'entangled/caused problems/provoked problems or fighting' as the mention of the OT stories where the people constantly provoke God and Moses is used as an example; also for its meanings of 'squeeze him/it' (as in squeeze water out of him) 'suck him/it' as his character is compared against Jesus: Moses is portrayed lesser than Jesus in status because of the meaning of his name, and events surrounding him in his OT stories. At birth he is taken out of water, water is squeezed out of him (because he was taken out of the river), he has to be breastfed in order to live; his miracles and tribulations connected to water are mostly negative and need a higher God to bring them around whether crossing the sea or causing water to spring out of a rock, and all are connected to death as the people flee death through the drying/parting of a path through the sea, or they are dying of thirst; when Moses is ordered to stretch his hand over any body of water it brings death in wholesale to adversaries and the opponent's people.

Whereas Jesus' conception comes from water and specifically God's water; it begins with the giving of life and is the 'water of life'; Jesus being of God's water can heal by word and touch, anyone related to God's water (John the Baptist) can cleanse people's sins, souls and bodies with water as can those given the ability through Jesus (disciples, then apostles and so forth); even when Jesus has to be raped and crucified to make him a suitable sacrifice for humankind this negative event and defilement is transcended because he is created from God's water (son of God) and he returns to life because God's water is everlasting life.

The author of Hebrews uses these meanings and stories through wordplay to deploy this message. The message of this story, like all the Biblical stories, could only be understood by an audience who spoke the language of the Bible, all other meanings and explanations are a result of transferring one's own readings, misinterpretations, mistranslations and misunderstandings which are a result of not knowing the true language of the Bible and the method its authors used. (Heb.3)

David is used for its word meaning 'the stone rolling pin of grinding stone' and for its connotations of hardness being made of durable stone; whoever uses it needs to rest as it is a tough and exhausting job to grind grains for bread (Jesus/bread). It is also used for its meanings of 'repeat/try again/keep at it/repeating the same revolving or to and fro motion' 'hesitates/goes and comes/recoils/revolves' to reflect no matter how many times God through Moses and other prophets attempted to guide the people to obedience and the correct ways of God, that the people hesitated in their belief and kept revolving around the same repetitive actions of disobedience, unfaith and everything else these characters have been accused of going back to in a cycle of repeating; it also warns the current audience of the epistle (the fictional audience/recipients within the story, not the real audience of the story) not to hesitate in their belief and not to repeat the mistakes made by other people which prevents them from entering into 'rest'. (Heb.4)

Aaron 'is-here-see/look' 'drive them away' and is reflected in that a priest can see and recognise sins, but is also appointed to drive these sins away by the ritual of offerings; it is reflected in that Melchisedec saw and heard God's words and obeyed, seeing and/or hearing means to understand and/or obey; they are warned about not hearing (listening/seeing as in understanding); the recipients are described as dull of hearing and that means they cannot hear/see i.e. they cannot understand; it is important in the narration because people who cannot see/hear cannot drive away evil as they cannot identify it. (Heb.5)

Melchisedec/**Melchizedek** (Gen.14:18) was chosen as a compound word for a word-name for the versatility in its wordplay which allows it to relay and enhance Heb.5. Not all the word-name combinations (below) nor their meanings are used but many can be seen in the passage. It is exactly the same word and meanings of Melchizedek (Gen.14:18-24) the slight difference of spelling and pronunciation is just the difference of transliteration and has neither altered words nor meanings between Melchisedec of NT and Melchizedek of OT: Melchisédek;

مَلكي صيدَق'what is wrong/what is the matter-believed/honest/friend' 'my possession/belongs to me/I own-believed/honest/friend'. The priest is honest and shows kindness when he tells the truth and/or performs rituals to cleanse the people from sins, he is good for them; he and the people offer from their possessions to appease God.

مَلكي زيدَك 'what is wrong/what is the matter-gave you extra' 'what is wrong/what is the matter-your extra/your remains/leftovers' 'what is wrong/what is the matter-deceived you' 'my possession/belongs to me/I own-gave you extra' 'my possession/belongs to me/I own-your extra/your remains/leftovers' 'my possession/belongs to me/I own-deceived you'. The ignorant people are deceiving themselves; the story always implies that the recipients are being deceived in the epistles both by the sender of the epistle and in the new faith being described; in the OT people are urged to give more of what they own to God, to deliver it to the priests as the priests are the only ones who can perform the rituals of sacrifice and specific offerings; the people in the epistle-stories of the NT are being urged to give more of what they own in charity; the epistle stories indicate the recipients of the letters are either trusting or sceptical of the sender of the letter and are being deceived by him; the people in the OT trust their priests as the only ones who can offer to God.

مَلكي صيدَك 'what is wrong/what is the matter-blocked you/prevented you' 'what is wrong/what is the matter-fished you/your fish' 'my possession/belongs to me/I own-blocked you/prevented you' 'my possession/belongs to me/I own-fished you/your fish'; the recipients are being told their dullness of hearing, their inability to understand, is preventing them from entering the faith and finding salvation/rest; fish/sheep are ways in which the NT stories describe converting people to the new faith and there is something preventing the people from entering the faith, also those who enter the new faith become the possession of Paul, Jesus and God.

مَلقي صيدَق 'throw(n)/cast-believed/honest/friend' 'met/connected-believed/honest/friend' 'did not meet/did not find/did not connect-believed/honest/friend'; reflected in the sacrifices which are killed and offered to God in the OT, Jesus as a sacrifice in the NT, and these show that its followers have believed and are being honest towards God. It also reflects the people who do not connect with the faith and God and do not believe in him or his true message and messengers.

مَلقي زيدَك 'throw(n)/cast-gave you extra' 'met/connected-gave you extra' 'did not meet/did not find/did not connect-gave you extra' 'thrown(n)/cast-your extra/your remains/leftovers' 'met/connected-your extra/your remains/leftovers' 'did not meet/did not find/did not connect-your extra/your remains/leftovers' 'throw(n)/cast-deceived you' 'met/connected-deceived you' 'did not meet/did not find/did not connect-deceived you'. This still refers to sacrifices, trusting or not believing the messengers and the message; it is the sender stating that the recipients who do not believe are being deceived, while the author of the epistle is telling the audience that the recipients are being deceived by the sender.

مَلقي صيدَك 'throw(n)/cast-blocked you/prevented you' 'met/connected-blocked you/prevented you' 'did not meet/did not find/did not connect-blocked you/prevented you' 'throw(n)/cast-fished you/your fish' 'met/connected-fished you/your fish' 'did not meet/did not find/did not connect-fished you/your fish'. This reflects the people who do not believe are being blocked, the passage itself states it is their inability to hear/understand which blocks them.

مَلحي صيدَق 'is good-believed/honest/friend' 'nice/pretty-believed/honest/friend' 'has a beard-believed/honest/friend' 'is salted/salt-believed/honest/friend'.

مَلحي زيدَك 'is good-gave you extra' 'nice/pretty-gave you extra' 'has a beard-gave you extra' 'is salted/salt-gave you extra' 'is good-your extra/your remains/leftovers' 'nice/pretty-your extra/your remains/leftovers' 'has a beard-your extra/your remains/leftovers' 'is salted/salt-your extra/your remains/leftovers' 'is good-deceived you' 'nice/pretty-deceived you' 'has a beard-deceived you' 'is salted/salt-deceived you'.

مَلحي صيدَك 'is good-blocked you/prevented you' 'nice/pretty-blocked you/prevented you' 'has a beard-blocked you/prevented you' 'is salted/salt-blocked you/prevented you' 'is good-fished you/your fish' 'nice/pretty-fished you/your fish' 'has a beard-fished you/your fish' 'is salted/salt-fished you/your fish'.

These three word-plays and their multiple meanings reflect what is being said and relay that there is someone who is good for the people, who honestly leads them to the correct ways of God, hence to salvation (Jesus), and someone whose ways if followed will block and prevent them from God's ways and salvation (Moses). Although it is Moses indicated as the lesser prophet/chosen one, it is referring to the religion of Moses or at least the people who follow any number of faiths based on Moses' laws which is why there is 'salted' and 'meat' and 'milk' mentioned as anything unsalted would not be pleasant to eat. The example of anyone who drinks milk is unskilled in righteousness is another knock at Moses who in Chapter 3 although acknowledged as being 'living in the house' i.e. sent by God and follows his commandments, is inferior to someone who 'is the house' i.e. created from God's own fibre, and specifically water making him intrinsically superior and, in chapter 5, innately righteous—which is Jesus. The milk because Moses needed to be taken out of water then found nurses to breastfeed him, while Jesus' conception resulted from God's water poured into his mother Mary.

Both the following wordplay and their similar meanings reflect the same things: مَلخع صيدَق 'roll it/him in slimy substance-believed/honest/friend'; مَلخع زيدَك 'roll it/him in slimy substance-gave you extra' 'roll it/him in slimy substance-your extra/your remains/leftovers' 'roll it/him in slimy substance-deceived you'; مَلخع صيدَك 'roll it/him in slimy substance-blocked you/prevented you' 'roll it/him in slimy substance-fished you/your fish'.

مَلخي صيدَق 'cover with slimy substance-believed/honest/friend'; مَلخي زيدَك "cover with slimy substance-gave you extra' 'cover with slimy substance-your extra/your remains/leftovers' 'cover with slimy substance-deceived you'; مَلخي صيدَك 'cover with slimy substance-blocked you/prevented you' 'cover with slimy substance-fished you/your fish'.

The birth of Jesus and belief of the followers of the new religion stems from being covered in and growing out of a slimy substance (Jesus born from, and John the Baptist covered and soaked in, God's water); the whole belief being a result of deceit and fictional stories is shown through the word 'deceived'. It is again showing Jesus' superiority over Moses, and Christianity being 'better' and 'truer' than any of the Jewish religions/beliefs (according to the story) and again this is connected to Moses being taken out of water to survive, being given human milk to nourish him, whereas Jesus and John the Baptist sprouted out of God's water, and their message and faith was spread by covering people in this special water whether the average person ducked in H20 or Jesus and disciples giving special water/semen treatments to those meant to do more and be more influential in the stories.

Cp: melkee-sseideq, melkee-zeidek, melkee-sseidek, melqee-sseideq, melqee-zeidek, melqee-sseidek, melḥee-sseideq, melḥee-zeidek, melḥee-sseidek, melkh'-sseideq, melkh'-zeidek, melkh'-sseidek, melkhee-sseideq, melkhee-zeidek, melkhee-sseidek. (Heb.5)

There is significance as to why the author of Hebrews has chosen to use and repeat the importance of identifying Jesus as no different than the priest Melchisedec and of his order. First, a reminder Abraham means 'pull up/draw up-the' 'clear-the' this is used in Hebrews to mean the drawing up of water, and because it is about Jesus it is about the water of life, which is semen, and the mentioned promise from God to Abraham which the latter had to suffer and wait long for is 'Isaac'.

Melchisedec (explained above) and **Salem** (Gen.14:18-24) meanings of 'greet/greeting' 'in peace/intact (unhurt/alive)' 'of mild/peaceful nature' 'ask the' 'flow/leak-the' 'flowed/leaked-river/sea' 'entertain/distract-the' 'comfort-the' 'survived/intact/whole-the' are used to enhance the meanings of the NT stories that Jesus' word and water is transferred through male sexual intercourse and becoming receptacles for Jesus' water/sperm. It is not only the word-name used here, but the OT story specific and connected to Melchisedec and Salem is also employed to clarify this current NT story. Not only does the OT story enhance Heb.6-7, but the latter also clarifies more meanings in the OT story: the king of Sodom was originally killed and fell in a slime pit, usually there is innuendo, euphemism or direct reference through a vulgar word-name given to the character(s) in the OT stories that defeated adversary kings and princes are sexually abused before being killed—the slime pits have served this purpose. Although king of Sodom, who died in the vale of Siddim, is brought back to life in the same chapter (Gen.14), he is brought back to life so as to allow his people and Lot whose sodomy and preference of male same-sex intercourse would be the cause of their destruction as punishment from God. This is why the people are more important than the goods which the authors have the king of Sodom request, although all other OT stories put a greater value and importance on goods, resources and land than on life. The OT story makes Melchisedek not only a king of Salem but also a high priest, and the NT connects him to Jesus i.e. they practise the same religious rituals: male anal sex. Just like the David and Jonathan story, the Melchizedek of the OT and NT show there was a culture and religion where sexual intercourse (deemed illicit by parts of the OT and by the culture of its real people (the authors and audience)) within the stories and within the culture of the real people that same-sex was not that big an issue (at some point) and that maybe there were religions where sexual intercourse whether between unmarried heterosexual couples or homosexual sex was deemed a highly spiritual ritual, part and parcel with the religion which original Christianity as portrayed in the NT stories was one of (Christianity began as fictional stories, but pagan religions and culture of sexual intercourse as spirituality and rites have existed long before Christianity would become a religion and survives today in many different religions including some mutated forms of Islam where sexual orgies are religious/spiritual rituals). The NT 'Hebrews' is narrating that Melchisedec is a high priest where male homosexuality was the highest form of spirituality, just as it is in Jesus' story beginning with all the gospels and continuing in the epistle stories. (Heb.)

Levi is mentioned to connect its meanings to Melchisedec and Jesus for the meanings of 'twisted/twirled/entwined around' which Leah wanted an unloving Jacob to be physically and emotionally towards her; and for 'its/my middle/core/pulp' 'pulp/core/middle' as the worshippers reach into each other's cores physically and spiritually. As there is intentional multiple-meanings in most of the NT on behalf of the authors, its meanings of 'not forthright/dishonest/goes around in circles' and 'answered/answer/answer him(or it)' 'served/serve/serve him(or it)' 'answer/respond and assist' suggest that the sender is misleading the recipient(s) of the letter in what he is and has instructed them to do.

Heb.7 goes on to mention **Juda**/'he is called/calls' 'call, or curse' 'to make a claim' 'make a false claim or an unproven claim' also serves with these double and opposing meanings: the sender of the letter is calling the people to the correct worship of God, the correct ways and faith—the author is saying it is a false claim. The story of the seed of Judah is also why it is mentioned with double-meanings as intended by the author: although it is meant to magnify and raise Jesus in status by being from the seed of Judah, it is also a reminder that the story of Judah's seed is about illicit sex (just as Jesus/disciples/apostles' work is the same), incest between Judah and his daughter-in-law Tamar, which is compounded by Judah going for sex with a prostitute who turned out to be a disguised Tamar. It points to the fictionality of the stories, but also to these stories being lewd late-night stories popular among the culture who created these stories.

The whole 'why was Levi/Levites' made a line of priests if Judah who was not mentioned by Moses as being a line of priests but who eventually produced Jesus—is just more wordplay and entertainment for the original audiences of these stories: Moses has been established by the author of Hebrews to be inferior to Jesus because he is not made of God's water which is carried and transferred through male-on-male sex; Moses is the opposite, his story has him rely on female characters to save him and get him out of water, then save him from starvation by breastfeeding him: first his mother by throwing him into the river, Pharaoh's daughter and maids fishing him out of the river and drying him then seeking to find a lactating woman to feed him, and finally his sister who followed the basket along the river (similar in conception to Mary and Jesus' characters are related to water) who served not only to find any wet-nurse for Moses, but spoke to Pharaoh's daughter and caused his real mother to be reunited with him so he could breastfeed and survive on his real mother's milk.

What the author has the sender of the letter communicate is: the priests ordained by Moses or Moses' God are of lesser powers, spirituality than Melchisedec who precedes Moses and Moses' religion and commandments by generations in the stories, and tying him to Jesus makes it clear it is the male sperm, the water of life, that makes Melchisedec, Jesus and Jesus faith superior in teachings, truthfulness, purification and spirituality and power with immortality and immortality-giving powers. By extension it makes the sender of the letter 'Paul' and all the disciples/apostles (and whoever they transfer the water of life to) into priests who are '...holy, harmless, undefiled, separate from sinners[even if what they do is considered a sin by, and when done by others], and made higher than the heavens...' and this is contrasted against the 'inferiority' of those high priests who follow Moses' laws who continually offer sacrifices for themselves and others to gain purity and forgiveness because Jesus was sacrificed once and it was enough.

By using that Moses did not mention Judah or his children being destined for priesthood—the sender of the letter is stating Moses could not be right, did not have foresight to be able to see this because he is dried of water, escaped from water, had to have women pull him out and save him, while Melchisedec and his connection to Sodom and Jesus through the Gospel and NT stories have their superior powers derived from a superior male water/sperm which became fortified with male homosexual intercourse. The author of Hebrews uses contradictions and errors which are a result of earlier and later authors and editors changing the Biblical stories to suit their own ideas which have left Enoch disappeared without dying, without a role (in Genesis he is merely superseded and replaced by Noah), and Melchizedek appearing without a backstory to explain his presence between king of Sodom and Abram in Genesis—the author of Hebrews has spun these inconsistencies into proof of immortality and loosely tied them both to Jesus. **Enoch** meanings of 'he warns/notifies/etc.' are also used as the author is pointing out there must be true faith to be truly of the faith.

Just as the majority of epistles in the NT are written about religion, calling to Christianity, or teaching its ways, but in the end they are always a letter of recommendation about someone (apostle/minister/etc.) arriving or to arrive at the recipient's location, and the person being recommended to be received well is always the person who wrote and carries the letter—this letter is written and carried by **Timothy** for its meanings of 'she passes him/walks past him/she makes him go' 'will you pass him/will you make him walk past/go' 'she completes/finishes it/he/him' 'will you complete/finish it/him/he' 'she marks/signs it/him/he' 'will you mark/sign it/him/he/will you make him mark/sign' 'she wipes away his urine/sperm(without use of water)' 'will you wipe away his urine/sperm' as the story revolves around the benefits and superiority of transferring God/Jesus' water for the faithful and preachers; it is Timothy who is coming from Italy to the recipients and the letter he carries completes the recipient's understanding and faith if they follow his instructions. (Heb.13)

It is from **Italy** for 'ablution-for/for me' 'cleanse for/for me' 'he abluted/cleansed for me' 'shone for me' 'came for me' 'he came for me' 'obeyed/obedient for me' 'will be obedient for me' as the letter is informing them of the necessity and benefits of continuing using God/Jesus' water to cleanse and make themselves and followers more faithful and pure; the letter is coming with Timothy for their sake and benefit; the letter wants them to obey the sender's instructions and in the end the obedience will do them good. (Heb.13)

Later in this book it will be explained why it is directed at recipients called Hebrews. (Heb.)

James Epistle

James for 'he/it pinches' which also means to say something from a story or said by someone else (the modern equivalent would be to 'quote') 'he pokes finger into' 'he pokes finger into anus' (sexually or as a prank over clothing), 'he pokes fingers into food/he pollutes food by poking fingers into it' 'he makes a mess'.

He makes a mess of preaching from the beginning of the story when he tells the recipients to be joyful for falling for divers temptations; the trap of falling into divers temptations is poking into something and making a mess of it in itself. Of being in great mess is reflected in the example of being in doubt being like a wave which has no control over itself and is tossed and driven as the wind directs it. Unstable men are messed up in every way; it is reflected in everything perishing quickly no matter how fresh, beautiful, high or low and the fleeting of time and life which also reflects 'a pinch' which is a quick motion and/or doing/taking something with a quick motion; a person's sin is a result of the mess he makes himself; being frugal in speech as a virtue reflects the meaning of pinch as in 'quote/short sentence'. The epistle continues with examples of how one can make a mess of faith when dealing with others or within themselves.

Abraham and **Isaac** are mentioned because the word meanings is throwing down a pouch into a hole and pulling it up; **Rahab** mentioned because as a prostitute men were poking into her by nature of her profession, and the thrusting in and out of the penis is the same as 'Abraham' and 'Isaac' actions of throwing in and pulling up a bailing pouch at the end of which results water from a well (Abraham/Isaac), and sperm from ejaculation (Rahab is a prostitute).

The bit in a horse's mouth, the ship controlled from within a small helm, the tongue in a mouth are all about something small inside an orifice poking around it or into it. The fire which the tongue can kindle is a big mess by poking the tongue into wrong matters or misusing it. The pollution of body and/or faith is mentioned.

The corruption of riches is a 'mess/pollution' made; moth-eaten garments are full of holes; ruined silver and gold are filled with holes; the rich men who have made a mess of people's lives and consequentially their own.

Sabaoth is still 'was filled/ate plenty' 'she is full(stomach)/has had enough' and the latter can mean fill of food or has 'had it/exasperated with', 'well off' 'I will send' 'I will resurrect' 'I bring back to life after death' as the narration is about rich people who have plenty but whose plentiful riches/resources will be negative upon them; the narration uses analogies of food resources, slaughter and eating full, but is about sin and a punishment to arrive; Job is used because his story was about a man who is well off (the very meaning of

'Sabaoth') in all riches but especially food resources and children but who is punished as an experiment; and Job's story shows he has 'had enough/exasperated' by both God's punishments but also his friends' criticisms before his story restores to him wealth and family. God warns the unjust rich men, and the disobedient people, that he will send punishment and the consequences of their actions upon them; the cries and calls sent out to God by the harmed people reaches God; the promised coming of the Lord is also about sending, but specifically resurrection as Jesus is to be brought back to life and be sent to earth again. (Jam.5:4)

Job for 'returning/returns/going to and fro, or up and down' 'being jerked up and down' 'coming-going and coming-going' reflected in the farmer waiting for the returning rains and the ripening of fruits which come and go in seasons; in that God's mercy always arrives no matter how long it departs and a person suffers; in Elias causing the rain to cease then causing it to return through prayer.

Elias is still used as 'he who/he is' to reflect 'it is' 'fact' 'being' 'happened' as when he wishes rain to cease it stops raining, and when he wished it to return it resumed.

Peter I

Language and the text of the Bible has proved all the characters in its stories are compound words made up to suit the story being told. Language and the very text of the NT stories has shown Paul is a compound word that went from 'Saul' to 'Paul' as needed by the author and the storyline needs; the Pauline letters are works of fiction written by authors no different than the authors and stories of the OT albeit their themes and heroes are different. Just like Paul has been mistaken by non-Arabic speakers as a real person who wrote real letters and the credit for 'spreading Christianity' has been given to a fictional character who could not even spread the stories he features in, when it should be accredited to the unnamed and unknown authors who wrote these stories, which when by later and more foreign audiences would be mistaken as religious script, were the cause of spreading Christianity.

Peter, like Paul, is a fictional character as can be seen in his compound word-name and events he is related to from where he first appears and everywhere he appears in the Biblical stories. Like Paul, Peter has been imbued with 'reality' and 'historicity' by historic and modern scholars, he has been given an estimated time of life and an estimated time of death, based on other estimations which all rely on fictional stories for 'fact'. This is the problem: hard and undisputable fact (the language, the compound word-names, the fictional events which reflect the compound-word-named characters and places) which shows the fictionality of these stories and everything within these stories is confused and obfuscated (probably in honest error more than due to bias) and considered by academic organisations and scholars ('experts') as historical fact, no matter how loosely and unfounded and shaky this 'historical fact' is presented. The unfortunate consequence is this obfuscation, the inability to see things as they are, leads to distortion not only of history, but it also obstructs scholars and the general public from seeing and understanding these Biblical stories for what they are; from what their authors intended them to be. This also diverts away from truly understanding why they were created in the first place; it prevents from understanding why some or most of the stories were edited whether by deletions, additions, alterations by later authors/editors; and it prevents contemporary audiences whether academic, religious or simply interested, from understanding what the authors are saying and showing through these stories. Like the Pauline letters which could not, and have not, been written by a fictional character called Paul, so are the Petrine letters not written by a fictional Peter.

Peter 'his/its stub/shortness' 'he has cut him/it short' 'he/it has been snapped short' 'he/it has been abruptly cut off' 'they have snapped him/it/cut him/it short' 'his stub of rock' his smooth rock' all the meanings imply 'short/abrupt/quick/a stub/interrupted'

Pontus 'his daughter(s)/his girl(s)/his children' 'made clear/apparent' 'became apparent'

Galatia 'said/he said-came here/come here' 'sanitised on heat' 'sanitised it/him on heat' 'he said he came/he said he would come' 'made mistake/he/they made mistake' 'of making mistakes' 'made mistake-he/him/she/her' 'of making mistakes-he/him/she/her' 'is deceiving/tricking/shortchanging' 'of deceiving/tricking/shortchanging-he/him/she/her' 'is wrong' 'he/she/they is/are wrong'

Cappadocia 'poured/spilled-noise/noisy'

Asia 'disobeyed/disobedient/went against' 'disobeyed him/went against him' 'became askew/bent/crooked/warped' 'sticks' 'used sticks'; 'sorrow' 'bad/offense/insult' 'bad towards/offense/insult towards'; 'things/matters' 'many/lots of things' 'wants' 'he wanted' 'speaking in whispers' 'snitching'

Bithynia 'with the other one/second one' 'will do it again/will do it to the other one' 'will fold/double-it/he/him'; 'girls/girlish' 'of girls' 'his girls/daughters-he/him' 'with figs/of figs' 'is figs'

Most of the above meanings per word-name are relayed in the narration as follows: the elect according to knowledge of God (Pontus/made clear/apparent); Jesus blood being spilled so they can be redeemed and also preach and spread God's word (Cappadocia/poured/spilled-noise/noisy); resurrection and born again (Bithynia/will do it again); uncorruptible (Galatia/sanitised on heat); does not disappear or leave i.e. is not Peter (Peter/he has cut it short/abrupt); ready to be revealed in the last time is (Pontus/became apparent and Bithynia/with the second one/again); temptations and heaviness (Galatia/is deceiving/making mistakes and Asia 'became askew/warped/bad towards/offense'); likened to purged gold, being found honourable at the coming of Jesus (Galatia/sanitised on heat/he said-came here and Bithynia/will fold/double it); rejoicing in love and faith of Jesus is (Cappadocia/poured/spilled-noise/noisy).

The prophesying of salvation which is to come to the people (Pontus/became apparent; Galatia/he said he would come; Asia/matters); Jesus' sufferings and the subsequent glory (Galatia/is wrong; Asia/sorrow/'bad towards/offense/insult towards); only to specific things were matters revealed and the angels wanting to look into things (Pontus/made clear/apparent/became apparent; Asia/speaking in whispers/things/matters/wants/he wanted); the people who reported the gospel have (Cappadocia/poured/spilled-noise/noisy); to tighten their resolve/loins/sobriety (Bithynia/will fold/double-it/he/him); the revelation of Jesus and to be obedient children, but not childish with ignorance (Pontus/made clear/apparent/became apparent/his daughter(s)/his girl(s)/his children; Bithynia/his girls/daughters-he/him /girls/girlish/will do it again/will do it to the other one), the ignorance (Asia/became askew/bent/crooked/warped).

To be holy in all conversations (Cappadocia/poured/spilled-noise/noisy; Asia/things/matters); passing the time in fear (Peter/abrupt/snapped short); the children's father's false beliefs of redeeming with corruptible gold and silver (Pontus/his children; Galatia/is wrong/made mistake/he/they made mistake/became askew/bent/crooked/warped; Asia/disobeyed/disobedient/went against); a purer sacrifice was made as Jesus blood was poured as a sacrifice (Cappadocia/poured/spilled-noise/noisy; Galatia/sanitised on heat; Peter/he has cut him/it short); Jesus manifest for the people (Bithynia/will do it again/will do it to the other one; Pontus/made clear/apparent/became apparent); people having faith in God because of believing in proof of Jesus (Pontus/made clear/apparent/became apparent); the purification of souls (Galatia/sanitised on heat); being born again through God's word (Bithynia/with the other one/second one/will do it again/will do it to the other one/will fold/double-it/he/him; Asia/speaking in whispers); the grass and flower which live short or are picked and cut short (Peter/'he has cut him/it short' 'he/it has been snapped short' 'he/it has been abruptly cut off' 'they have snapped him/it/cut him/it short'); the endurance of God's word and the preaching of the gospel (Pontus/made clear/apparent/became apparent; Cappadocia/poured/spilled-noise/noisy).

The same relay and method continue throughout 1Peter. (1Pet.)

Sion/**Zion** (2Sam.5:6-8) 'sweep/brush' 'swept/brushed away' 'bad'. All the meanings of Zion as used in the OT are used in the same way in 1Pet.: the recipients are asked to remove/lay aside all bad things: malice, guile, hypocrisy, envy and all kinds of evil, which is the same as sweeping, brushing away dust, dirt, stones, impurities, litter. The precious stone which is used as proof of faith for those truly faithful but a stumbling block for the disobedient also relays the sweeping away of bad impurities as only the 'good' will remain while stones and other impurities are swept away—the stone is to enhance what is usually swept away in 'Zion' but here made a positive thing as it will sort out who is good and remains and who is bad and will be removed. The 'stone' and 'rock' are also mentioned in the same way as 'rocks' used in the OT, either as a correctly worshipped rock or wrongly worshipped rocks. (1Pet.2)

Gentiles ethnesin; يثني/اثني سِن/سين '**ethne**': 'he/they do it again/double it/fold it/repeat it-' 'he/they dissuade/make leave-' 'he/they are idolaters/pagans-' 'idols-' 'praise/praises-' 'idol worshippers-' 'idolatry/worshipping idols-'; followed by '**sin**' meanings: in the direction of/towards me/in the face of/in front of/straight/straight line/direct/opposite me' and from the OT 'I will deceive them/the' 'I will mislead them to downfall-them/the'; ethnon; يثنون ، اثنون 'he/they do it again/double it/fold it/repeat it' 'he/they dissuade/make leave' 'he/they are idolaters/pagans' 'idols' 'praise/praises' 'idol worshippers' 'idolatry/worshipping idols' (Judg.4) 'I will deceive them/the' 'I will mislead them to downfall-them/the'. 'Gentiles' is used as always and is self-explanatory. (1Peter.2; 4)

Silvanus (2Cor.19-24) 'asked/questioned-him' 'his asking/questions' 'flowed/leaked water-him' 'his flowing/leaking' 'entertained/distracted-him' 'his entertainment/distraction' 'comforted-him/his comfort'. The passage speaks of comfort whether glory, care of God, being made perfect or strengthened and settled which will come after suffering in the name of and for Jesus Christ. It is distracting the faithful sufferers from ordeals or hardships with stories, asking and answering questions within the letter-story itself, and the perfection and foundation is based on the flowing of God/Jesus' water which brings faith and purity. The narration states the epistle is written by Silvanus (for its meanings) and/or carried by Silvanus who is bringing God/Jesus' water flowing by carrying and/or writing the letter, but the author of 1Pet. makes sure to include a pun that Silvanus is pretending to be Peter in writing the letter as 'Peter' has meanings of being 'short/abrupt/quick/a stub/interrupted' and the story narrates 'By Silvanus, a faithful brother unto you, as I suppose, I have written briefly…'. (1Pet.5)

Babylon; Babylőn; بَديلون 'swap/change' 'swapped/changed' 'they swapped/changed' and is the same in word and meaning as Babel, Babylon in the OT. These meanings are shown in asking the recipients to do things in exchange for a later reward; but also there is instruction of how they are to do it and that is replace bad or worldly intentions with more virtuous intentions: the people who preach are asked not to force people into religion but entice them to come willingly; to do it not for worldly and impure reasons but with clean and clear minds; to not act as superiors but one of the people they are leading; young are to listen to old; pride is to be swapped for humility, and so forth. Cp: badyloon. (1Pet.5)

Marcus 'did not/they did not wait/stay/become still' 'did not intensely ask/intreat' 'did not shake/unsettle it' 'did not drive him insane'. They are told not to wait and expect things to happen, but to be active in preaching and leading the people towards faith as they have a strong and vicious opponent, the devil likened to a roaring and predatory lion; the letter is not strict, nor does it put pressure on the recipients as its 'exhortation' is done in a gentle manner with a light touch, it asks the recipients to do the same towards those it wishes to convert. (1Pet.5)

Peter II

Simon (Peter) 'ill/sick/weak'; 'have heard/to hear/heard' 'obey/obeyed'.

Peter 'his/its stub/shortness' 'he has cut him/it short' 'he/it has been snapped short' 'he/it has been abruptly cut off' 'they have snapped him/it/cut him/it short' 'his stub of rock' 'his smooth rock' all the meanings imply 'short/abrupt/quick/a stub/interrupted'.

Both words multiple meanings are in play: the weakness and illness (Simon) is the corruption in running after worldly things which is likened to illness and physical weakness such as being blind or barren. The 'have heard/listened/obeyed' (Simon) is listening to the preaching and following these teachings, in the strengthening of faith, and this faith, knowledge, etc. is reached by listening to those calling them to the faith, preaching the ways; it is in the sender informing them he will always remind them about these things they should adhere to and the things they should avoid, so they will always 'hear' from Simon Peter. It is in Jesus hearing God's voice; in Peter stating he and the other disciples heard God's voice when God spoke to Jesus. It is in people listening to false prophets and false teachers which leads to obeying them. (2Pet.)

The meanings 'his/its stub/shortness' 'he has cut him/it short' 'he/it has been snapped short' 'he/it has been abruptly cut off' 'they have snapped him/it/cut him/it short' (Peter) is in Peter informing them he does not have much time left; that he will be dead soon; in his abruptness in telling them what is what, especially directly addressing and refuting statements that the Jesus stories and epistles are 'devised fables'; in the shortness of the epistle's length. The shortness and abruptness are in that condemnation and consequence of false preachers will come soon and as an example Noah, Sodom and Gomorrah stories are given to support and show the abruptness of when punishment comes. (2Pet.)

Noah has been used for its meanings 'cried out in distress/loudly' which others can hear loudly (and supports **Simon**'s meanings of 'heard'); 'warned/brought to attention/reminded' 'the stone/seed(of fruit)' 'the/his intentions/unspoken thoughts' as Simon Peter in the epistle is warning the recipients of punishment and planting in them the seeds of 'righteousness' which causes them to be obedient (the meanings of **Simon** 'heard' as in obeyed). (2Pet.2)

Sodom 'black soot' and **Gomorrah** 'to be buried/submerged under' 'hot coal' as the recipients are being warned to avoid ending up in hell like a certain or specific angel(s), hell being a place of fire has soot and hot coals burying the people just like the punishment of Sodom and Gomorrah. (2Pet.2)

Lot 'squeeze(d) together' 'squeezed/pressed against and sagged' as Lot is described in the epistle of being vexed and tried in his soul by sinners and their conduct, and serves to warn the recipients to be patient against being persecuted and against being tempted to sin. (2Pet.2)

Balaam son of Bosor. The author of 2Pet. has given the character **Balaam son of Beor** (Num.22;23;24) a slight name change as he obviously wanted to use 'Balaam' and the donkey as an example of someone who does not listen/obey, but wanted a more suitable word than 'Beor' so he replaces 'Beor' with the word '**Bosor**'; Bosór; بُصور ، بوصور 'with leftovers' 'with/by cannot hear/pretending not to hear/pretending to be deaf/ignoring' 'insisting/with insisting'. It is equivalent to Besor (1Sam.30). Cp: bossoor, boossoor. (2Pet.2:15)

Balaam (Num.22;23;24) 'with/of curses' 'has received message' 'with/of blame' as Peter blames those who preach falsely and also those who commit sins of being unable to receive the message from God through the truthful preachings; he blames them of being unable to hear which is why Balaam son of Beor has to become the more suitably named son of **Bosor** for 'with leftovers' 'with/by cannot hear/pretending not to hear/pretending to be deaf/ignoring' 'insisting/with insisting' as they cannot 'hear' and do not 'hear/obey' (meaning of Simon) because like the word-name suggests they are either intrinsically deaf or wilfully ignore and pretend to be deaf; they are stubborn both like Balaam and the donkey he rode upon in the OT story, and they insist on remaining in their sinful ways and heading for punishment like a stubborn donkey or as Peter describes them 'as natural brute beasts'; and they also insist on misleading other more righteous people towards sin and being deaf and those who had accepted the faith and obeyed who then go against it or back into the sinful ways are more Besor 'insisting/pretending not to hear' and Balaam 'of blame' than those who never heard or obeyed. (2Pet.2)

What the author of 2Peter does, which seems to be the reason for creating this epistle-story, is what the author of 1Peter failed to do: mention and praise Paul. This 2Peter epistle provides the epistle-stories where Paul is the sender, support that at least Peter knows Paul, which one of the Pauline letters used as a theme that nobody seemed to know Paul and maybe rumours were that he was not an apostle, but this letter is part of the set of stories about Paul, where Paul in the epistles is a vague and suspect writer and sender of the letters dealing with concerns about who he really is. (2Pet.3)

John I

John 'soaked it/him (in)' 'brothers' 'betrayed' 'sacks' 'sackcloth' 'put/wrap it/him in sack/sackcloth' and these themes are the only themes relayed throughout the short letter-story: it is about brothers whether real or through faith; it is about betrayal of the faith and betrayal of a brother and brethren; it is about faith being absorbed and contained within its believers.

'John' is also used for its connotations with the stories of John the Baptist baptising people with water and John the disciple receiving a special baptism from Jesus who also cleansed peoples bodies and souls; and for the word meanings of 'betrayed' 'soaked him' 'brothers' as the story narrates what actions or claims cause a person to be deceptive such as claiming to have no sin and therefore not needing to be purified—which goes against the need for 'John'.

The gospel of John is also invoked because the author of 1John. intentionally copies the way the Gospel of John began, and this too invokes both John the Baptist and John the disciple. The meaning of 'brothers' is reflected in that the sender describes the recipients as his 'little children' making them brothers to each other, in calling them 'fathers' 'children' they are also all brothers in the faith, 'brothers' towards each other when describing how they behave towards each other (whether positive or negative behaviour is described).

The 'antichrist' being the opposite of 'Christ' also shows 'betrayed'. The antichrists who are described as being apostles/disciples who have betrayed and gone against or at least perverted teachings about Christ and faith are also described of being from the disciples/apostles' side, as the author has made John the disciple the sender of the epistle, and what it is saying is that the antichrist has emerged from their cloth, showing the meaning of 'sack/sackcloth', but they have shown their true selves and therefore considered not from the cloth.

In describing the faith remaining in the truly faithful and the true believers is also playing on the meaning and role of all 'Johns' in the gospels where their characters by nature of their word-name were able to absorb God and Jesus' water (water is the word and the light and vice-versa) and to spread it to others because they are sackcloth, a highly absorbent and thick material, so this is used to describe how the truly faithful's faith remains inside them and does not leave them.

Cain and his story of killing his brother has been mentioned as it reflects the **John** meaning of 'brothers' and 'betrayed'; all are called brothers and all murderers have betrayed their brothers.

John II and the Elect Lady

John still represents both John the Baptist and John the disciple with the sender of the letter as John the disciple; the word-name itself still represents 'brothers' representing both Jesus and John were brothers from the same God's water/Holy Ghost filling their mothers, as John the disciple also received extra of Jesus/God's water as well as Mary becomes his mother, he too becomes a brother to both Jesus and John the Baptist, and by extension everyone who enters the faith become brethren; 'betrayed' as the letter warns of deceivers and antichrist; 'sack/sackcloth' 'soak/soaked' as this characteristic marked both Johns, and is also used in 1John to symbolise how faithful people absorb God's word, light, faith and it cannot leave them once, and if, absorbed.

The 'elect lady' is Mary mother of Jesus who was first to receive the Holy Ghost and gave birth to Jesus; she was there from the beginning and knows and witnessed everything from the beginning which the narration has the sender state she was, and knows the first commandment was to love one another—it also relays when Jesus was on the cross and made Mary and John the beloved disciple, mother and son to replace Jesus' vacant spot as he was about to die and therefore have the loving bond of mother and son even though they are strangers.

The 'elect sister' is Elisabeth the mother of John the Baptist, and Mary is the 'elect lady' not only because she was the first to receive the Holy Ghost direct and conceive from it, but by visiting her cousin Elisabeth who was already six months pregnant she was the first and only lady in the NT stories to have miraculously poured/transferred God's water from her body into another's (Elisabeth) without touch, by just being there and Elisabeth was filled with the Holy Ghost and John the Baptist soaked in it—making him Jesus' brother. As the virgin Mary first conceived Jesus then Jesus went on to pass God's water to mankind, and because Jesus and the author of John made a point of the beloved disciple and Mary continue this bond which meant to continue to spread God/Jesus' water and faith—all the people who accept the faith are her children because they become of the faith and brethren only from Jesus' water which they can only get from the disciples, apostles, or from Mary herself and so forth.

When the sender warns the 'elect lady' not to receive those who deny that Jesus 'is come in the flesh' it is to avoid her transferring any more 'Holy Ghost' abilities into them which is why she is being told not to allow them into her house as her mere presence can transfer the Holy Ghost into others—which is why the author reinforces it with mention of the 'elect sister' towards the end (to remind how Mary arriving in the same room filled Elisabeth with the Holy Ghost). The meaning of 'betrayed' is also in what **John** warns mother Mary, that even inadvertently assisting those who are guilty of betraying Jesus, is the same as intentional betrayal.

It is possible that 'elect lady' 'elect sister' are mistranslations/misinterpretations of what the original language called them. The Greek transliteration still shows the clear Arabic words and meanings: there is a very strong possibility which is evident that it is: eklektḗ kyría; اخلقتيَ/اخلقتيآ خيريَي 'you/you both created/gave birth-good/goodness/my good/my goodness/the best'; اغلقتيَ/اغلقتيآ خيريَي 'you/you both closed-good/goodness/my good/my goodness/the best'.

This is supported by both the elect lady and elect sister (virgin Mary and Elisabeth) gave birth to sons who brought good to the world through God's water and these sons are depicted in the Gospels and other NT stories of being the best of mankind ever to be sent, i.e. born (Jesus and John the Baptist); John the disciple having been appointed Mary's son by Jesus himself, and having extra love and water from Jesus becomes exchangeable as a son; the 'good/goodness' is in general for all mankind, but the 'my goodness' is the specialness which John the Baptist and Jesus had being born from God's water, and subsequently John the disciple by receiving from Jesus this water and again through the special bond when Jesus commands him and Mary to become mother and son. The 'closing' of the goodness meanings is meant to enhance that John is asking Mary to close access to this special gift by not allowing the deceivers into her presence. Cp: ekhleqteya khyreeya, ekhleqteyaa khyreeya, eghleqteya khyreeya, eghleqteyaa khyreeya. (2John.)

John III

Gaius 'his misleading to downfall/his deceit to downfall' 'they misled him to his downfall/they deceived him to his downfall' 'made him howl' 'make him howl' 'learn and remember him/it' 'warn him/warned/taught him' 'beware of him/it' 'contained/prevented him/it'.

All these meanings are present in 3John: Gaius is teaching and his converts/followers are learning and following God/Jesus' ways; the deceiving and misleading meanings both reflect within the story on the 'bad' character, Diotrephes, but also speak to the real audience to be wary of these stories as they are fictional and misleading if anyone takes them as truth. The 'contained it/him' meaning is in Gaius assisting the followers and preachers on their journey or between their travels. (3John)

Gentiles ethnon; اثنون ، يثنون 'he/they do it again/double it/fold it/repeat it' 'he/they dissuade/make leave' 'he/they are idolaters/pagans' 'idols' 'praise/praises' 'idol worshippers' 'idolatry/worshipping idols' 'I will deceive them/the' 'I will mislead them to downfall-them/the' reflects on Diotrephes the antagonist in this story, but like Gaius there is the double-meaning which the author of the story is relaying to the real audience that these stories are fictional and people who believe in them are being misled to their own detriment. (3John)

Diotrephes; Diotréphēs; ذيو/ذيُ طري فيه 'he/it/this is-threw out/chased away/banished/fled/disappeared/evaporated-in him/it'; ذيو/ذيُ تري فيه 'he/it/this is-see/you see/dream-in him/it' 'he/it/this is-watered/quenched-in him/it'; ضيو/ضيُ طري فيه 'his/its ablution-threw out/chased away/banished/fled/disappeared/evaporated-in him/it' 'his/its light-threw out/chased away/banished/fled/disappeared evaporated-in him/it'; ضيو/ضيُ تري فيه 'his/its ablution-see/you see/dream-in him/it' 'his/its light-watered/quenched-in him/it'.

Most of these meanings can be seen in the related verses: whatever good instilled in Diotrephes through baptism and faith has disappeared, evaporated from inside him as he is being cruel towards fellow Christians; his cruelty is that he turns them away and refuses to host them or even meet them. His actions are symbolised in the word-name: God's light and water which a convert and the faithful accept and carry within them, after being baptised and covered in water, makes them cleansed; this state of purification is shown in good deeds as commanded by the teachers/preachers, but since Diotrephes is behaving in an unchristian fashion that means the water and light which once filled him have evaporated and left him, and his actions are of turning away and throwing out the faithful. It is related in that he wants to be the most notable person in the congregation, i.e. he wants his light to shine brighter so when others who could dim his light due to their own luminosity arrive, he chooses to turn them away to keep the light inside him shining, showing him as the most prominent. The connection between water, light and good as well as darkness and evil has been made in previous epistles and 1John begins with a reminder of this light which also connects to 'water' and 'word' in all Jesus and John stories, and since this light and water or at least the cleansing properties of water have left Diotrophes both he and his actions are evil. Cp: veoo/veo-ṭrei-pheyh, veoo/veo-trei-pheyh, dheoo/veo-ṭrei-pheyh, dheoo/veo-trei-pheyh. (3John)

Demetrius (Acts.19:23-41) 'she/this is enriching him/it' 'she/they/it leaves him/it' 'she/they/it let it/him go' as the sender of the epistle is wishing Gaius prosperity in every physical way as much as his soul is already prospering; it refers to the preachers who travel without taking anything from the 'Gentiles'; it reflects in Diotrephes letting people go without offering them any support or hospitality, in his making people in his own church leave when they opt to help out their brethren; it also reflects that he has let his goodness, his light, his ablution, his purity and faith go by being cruel. It is in the sender advising the recipient to leave all evil and follow good. It is in the character Demetrius enriching the report/reputation of the recipients by praising and positively reporting what they do. (3John.)

Jude

Jude; Ioúdas; يودَه ، يوُدَه 'his hands'; يودعه ، يودعى 'he is called/calls' 'call, or curse' 'to make a claim' 'make a false claim or an unproven claim' like all 'Judas' characters used in (Matt.10; Matt.13:54-58; Acts.1:22-26). Just as the authors used 'Judas' to have the meanings of the word-name of Judas Iscariot 'his hands' and how the same word-name was used interchangeably to mean the same as Judah of the OT (son of Jacob) 'calling' (whether to God or a person) 'to make a claim/false claim' as it suited the author and the story he was telling, the author of Jude is using both (see Matt.13:54-58; Acts.1:22-26 to see how Judas was used as the word-name 'his hands' and as 'he called/claimed' when he appears as Jesus' brother, then as James' brother) 'his hands' to mean laid hands on or touched or with his hands; and 'call/claim' to show calling to God, people, making false claims. Like John's epistles, Jude focuses mainly on the meaning of the words for wordplay throughout the story. Cp: youdah, yoodah, yood'a, yood'h.

Of course, no real 'Jude' wrote this epistle, but all the word-names and events in it are fictional and reflect what the word-names mean as per the Biblical authors' method from the beginning of the OT through to the end of the NT to entertain with wordplay.

Jude begins and ends with Jude calling to God, what would be called a wish or a prayer. v.1-2 are calling God to have mercy, peace and love on the recipients; v.24-25 is the sender calling God to prevent the recipients from falling into sin and to be in the service of God. (Jude.1-2, 24-25)

Jude 'his hands' as he expressly states he is writing a letter; then tells the recipients they have to physically contend to achieve faith. (Jude.3)

Jude 'his hands' and 'making false claim' describes the deceitful people who have infiltrated into the faith/church as making false claims about the religion. What becomes clear is the author is describing what can also be detected in other epistles: that the higher and spiritual male-on-male sex performed to transfer and strengthen God/Jesus' water in disciples, apostles and other preachers, making them more effective in God's work, has been abused by these 'deceivers': the latter have either used this ritual for worldly sexual gratification or have accused the apostles and their followers of engaging in illicit sex for the sole purpose of sexual gratification and perversion—which the sender of the letter is arguing against. (Jude.4)

Jude 'his hands' to show laying hands on: God saved and delivered the people out of Egypt then destroyed them for disbelief. (Jude.5)

Jude 'his hands' as in physically laid hands on, and 'called/claimed': the angels who have disobeyed are in chains; they will remain in chains until they are called to the day of Judgement where claims and disputes, sins and good deeds are called up to be settled. (Jude.6)

Jude 'his hands' and 'called/claimed/false claim': Sodom and Gomorrah's punishment and its reasons are because they physically touched each other in an illicit way. (Jude.7)

Jude 'his hands' and 'false claim': the defilement of flesh is by touching it inappropriately; the false claims as the 'dreamers' as described in the OT are false prophets making false prophesies, and in this verse they also make false claims against 'dignities' and this too refers to accusing the disciples, apostles, Christian preachers of homosexual acts for the sake of lust/sexual gratification, and the author has placed this verse after the example of Sodom and Gomorrah because there is a double-entendre: one within the narration that these are false claims made by evil people within the story being told; and the other message externally to the original local audience of the time that Christian preachers are sexual perverts. (Jude.8)

Jude 'false claim' is used to show false accusations are not to be lightly made (and in context that true accusations are made in seriousness) that even the archangel Michael, guarding Moses' corpse did not dare to make a false accusation against the devil. (Jude.9)

Jude 'false claim' 'his hands': the antagonists make false accusations and claims about the sender and recipients; the sender is making a claim about the antagonists that they engage in beastly conduct by their nature and what is meant here is bestiality and anal sex between men, the latter accusations also cover the physical 'his hands' touching. (Jude.10)

Jude 'he called' and 'his hands': Cain is a fruit which needs to be picked berry by berry from the ground, this fruit and character in Gen. called on God to accept his offering, but God refused it; Balaam was hired by Balaak to lay a curse on Moses and his people; Core; Koré; كوره 'a lot/loads/a heap/heap it' 'hated/hateful' 'in one go'; كورح 'striking sound' (from striking one object with another); قوره 'they read/read it/are educated' 'they teach/read to' 'they stopped moving/ceased what they were doing' 'they admitted'; قورح 'sores/ulcers' 'burst/exploded' 'bursting sound' and it refers to Korah (Num.16) who along with his whole family were killed for punishment for his rebellion against and what he claimed about Moses and Aaron. Cp: koorh, koorḥ, qoorh, qoorḥ. (Jude.11)

Jude 'his hands' and 'he called' is in calling the antagonists 'spots in your feasts' and other negative descriptions; they are also described as making false claims as appearing to be what they are not (pious/good) e.g. clouds without water, trees without fruit and roots. This also reflects the **James** meaning of polluting food by dipping fingers into or unclean fingers into. (Jude.12)

Jude 'he called' 'making a claim' 'false claim' is the continuation of verse 11: the raging waves of sea, foaming out their own shame is the impurities they spew at the sender and recipients of the letter, is like the sea which brings impurities onto a clean beach, i.e. the accusations of evil, filth that the antagonists are making against Jude and the others is their own filth which they vomit through false claims onto others. (Jude.13)

Jude 'called' 'claimed/false claim' as **Enoch** whose meanings are 'warned/bellowed in distress/etc.' has already prophesied i.e. made an unproven claim about these people coming and it extends to the following verse where it elaborates that Enoch will call them up and confront them and show them all their false claims and a specific false claim they made against him. (Jude.14-15)

Jude 'false claims': relayed in all their actions are murmurs, complaints, and speaking empty words. (Jude.16)

Jude 'false claims' and 'making a claim' as well as 'he called': as Jude is calling the recipients to remember they have already been warned of the coming of these people whose mockery and actions are false in claim and nature. (Jude.17-18)

Jude 'his hands' 'he called' 'made claim' 'made false claim': the antagonists actions are false and because they do not have the 'Spirit' this reduces their sexual rituals into only a physical and perverted activity; whereas because the sender and the recipients have both the 'Holy Ghost' and the 'Spirit' their same actions/rituals by virtue of being filled with God's water and breath/panting are cleansing, true and pious. (Jude.19-20)

Jude 'he called': as Jude is calling the recipients to stick to God's love and to do so in hope of receiving eternal life as promised by Jesus, and the eternal life is connected to the sexual rituals of living water which is the point and product of verses 19-20 when done in the name of God/Jesus. (Jude.21)

Jude 'he called' and 'his hands': as the sender tells the recipients to make a difference in various forms of teaching: some are to be called, while others must be allowed to fall into the fire and be burnt before they are physically pulled out and called again into the proper and whole faith. (Jude.22-23)

James 'he/it pinches' which also means to say something from a story or said by someone else (the modern equivalent would be to 'quote') 'he pokes finger into' 'he pokes finger into anus' (sexually or as a prank over clothing) 'he pokes fingers into food/he pollutes food by poking fingers into it' 'he makes a mess' is used because the author has the sender/Jude quote direct from other stories of OT and NT: the creeping in of deceitful preachers and using Sodom and Gomorrah as an example is quoting from Peter and John's epistles; Michael the archangel guarding Moses' corpse from the devil is from Daniel.

The meanings of James/'he pokes finger into' 'he pokes finger into anus' (sexually or as a prank over clothing) 'he pokes fingers into food/he pollutes food by poking fingers into it' 'he makes a mess' because the epistle-story is mainly addressing accusations of illicit sex by the disciples, apostles, preachers. The author is using the meaning to be refuted by the sender of the letter, while at the same time the author is mocking the Christians and the new faith.

Egypt used for its meanings of 'put scarf on-them/the' 'knot/bundle-them/the' 'insult-them' 'offend-the' as the people are the children of Israel who were made to travel from Egypt to wander for forty years with their belongings carried in bundles; but because they have offended God by not following his orders they are offended with punishment and death. (Jude.5)

Sodom 'black soot' and **Gomorrah** 'hot coal' 'to be buried/submerged under' as it describes and reminds of the story where the punishment was fire and brimstone raining down on these cities which were buried under it.

Michael 'what is there-the' 'what is-the' 'what is the matter-the' 'what is said?' 'what is said' 'who said' 'who said-the' 'spending time at/spending time with' 'stay(ing)/wait(ing)' 'imagining' 'hallucinating' 'is hallucinating/has hallucinated/imagined' 'hallucination/imagination'. All these meanings are used: the verse is narrating who said what to whom; it shows that Michael was waiting beside Moses' corpse protecting it; he cannot make an unproven claim(Judah/Judas) as that would be the same as imagining. The meanings of Michael extend to the verse which precedes it and that which follows it: the people are speaking imaginations, they are 'dreamers' i.e. speak lies, fabrications. (Jude.8-10)

Moses for its meanings of 'touched/possessed/was possessed/touched' 'entangled/caused problems/provoked problems or fighting' and this plays on the OT stories where Moses is possessed by God which is no different in method than being possessed by the devil, but now the archangel Michael is fighting to not allow the devil to possess Moses' body. (Jude.9)

Cain 'the fruit called 'cain'/to gather the berries called 'cain'' as usually lots of this fruit are produced and people gather it in heaps, sacks and eat it in plenty, but it is connected as the word-meanings and its connotations along with the abundance of blame meant by **Balaam** which means 'with/of curses' 'with/of blame' 'on purpose' as Cain intentionally plotted and implemented the murder of his brother. (Jude.11)

Enoch 'upset and not eating or talking' (when a person is upset and goes away, or stops eating and/or talking with others, or turns his back towards others because he/she is upset with them over something) 'I will cry out in distress (or loudly)' 'I will warn/bring to attention/remind' 'I will seed/stone(of fruit)/plant' 'I will intend/decide within me'. Most of these meanings are available in the related verses: it shows he is upset because of something spoken against him; he is linked to immortality although he just disappears from the story due to editorial preferences in Genesis, but he is linked by adding his mention to **Adam** and its word-meaning of 'is to last long' and this is reflected in tens of thousands of his saints which are to come with Enoch for a very long judgement; he is calling out to people and making claims about them, or he will do, and he is calling them out because of false claims they have made. (Jude.14-15)

Adam 'is from blood' 'made bleed', 'is to last long' 'is from nothing' as they are being judged and accusations have already been exchanged in these verses; both sides are bleeding (hurt) from false accusations; the judgement is to last long, tens of thousands of Enoch's saints are needed to sort out the mess of claims and false claims in the judgement proceedings; it is a pun on 'is to last long' as Enoch did not last long in the Genesis story although giving him immortality allows him to last long. (Jude.14-15)

Revelation

Apocalypse; apokálypsis; ابوقآلي بشيه ‘trumpeted/announced to me a matter/something(important)’ ‘I will trumpet/announce something/matter (important)’; ابوحآلي بشيه ‘told me a secret/important news/confided in me something/matter(important)’ ‘I will tell/convey/confide a matter/something(important); This is the first meaning for ‘apocalypse/revelation’ and its use from the beginning of Rev. as John is being told about an important matter which will happen in the future and he is being told by an angel, which he then conveys to others;

ابوقآليب سيه ، ابوقآليبسِيه ‘his father has turned over the bad/offense’ ‘they refused-turned over/upturned/turned inside out-the offense/bad’ ‘father of-upturning things/overturning things/turning things inside out’ ‘refused-overturned things/upturned things/turned things inside out’ ‘of overturning/upturning things/turning things inside out’;

ابوقآليب شيه ، ابوقآليبشِيه ‘his father-turned over/upturned/turned inside out-things/matters/many things/important things’ ‘refused-turned over/upturned/turned inside out-things/matters/many things/important things’ ‘father of-turning over/upturning/turned inside out-things/matters/many things/important things’ ‘of turning over/upturning/turned inside out-things/matters/many things/important things’;

ابوغآليب سيه ، ابوغآليبسِيه ‘his father victored over/overcame the bad/offense’ ‘they refused-victored/overcame/made feel remorse/made feel bitterness-over the/his bad/offense’ ‘his father/they rejected-they could not/they gave up/they were frustrated/they frustrated-his bad/offense’ ‘father of-victoring/overcoming’ ‘of victoring/overcoming-bad/offense’ ‘father of-frustrating/being frustrated/being unable to do/giving up/feeling distress’ ‘of frustrating/being frustrated/giving up/unable to do/feeling distress’ ‘father of/of-distressing/victoring/overcoming/frustrating/frustration’;

ابوغآليب شيه ، ابوغآليبشِيه ‘his father-victored over/overcame-things/matters/many things/important things’ ‘father-wanted/wanted him to victor/overcome’ ‘refused-victored/overcome-things/matters/many things/important things’ ‘his father-made feel remorse/frustrated/made feel bitterness-things/matters/many things/important things’ ‘father-wanted/wanted to feel remorse/frustrate/make feel bitterness’ ‘refused-made feel remorse/made feel bitterness-things/matters/many things/important things’ ‘refused-frustrated/felt frustration/gave up-things/matters/many things/important things’ ‘of frustrating/making feel frustrated/giving up/making give up-things/matters/many things/important things’.

All these meanings can be seen in the whole of Revelation: the confiding in John of important and negative matters to happen in the future; the punishment of the disobedient along with innocent people, and the great physical and mental distress the people in Revelation will suffer; the victoring of God/Jesus and eventually pious people because the people have frustrated God; God frustrating people in life with dire punishments, making them feel so bitter they would rather die than live and feel the sufferance; the lives of people and the physical environment/land upturned, inside-out, flipped by God to punish the people; the use of trumpets and announcements before delivering punishment or ending it. God/Jesus and the pious victorious over a now frustrated, remorseful and bitter disobedient masses of people who refused to obey, refused to follow the new faith or were simply not part of the ‘sealed’ and marked people, who formerly frustrated prophets and most importantly frustrated God and Jesus the son of God and eventually offended by killing Jesus the son of God, and refused to accept and listen/obey to the important matters and news they were delivering and warning of; so now God who in the NT is described as Jesus’ father is exacting revenge in the form of the word-names of the compound word ‘apocalypse’.

Cp: abooqaaly-bshyh, abooḥaaly-bshyh, aboo-qaalyb-syh, aboo-qaalybsyh, aboo-qaalyb-shyh, aboo-qaalybshyh, aboo-ghaalyb-syh, aboo-ghaalybsyh, aboo-ghaalyb-shyh, aboo-ghaalybshyh. (Rev.1:1)

John ‘soaked it/him (in)’ ‘brothers’ ‘betrayed’; ‘sacks’ ‘sackcloth’ ‘put/wrap it/him in sack/sackcloth’. John is used for its meanings of ‘sackcloth’ ‘put/wrap it/him in sack/sackcloth’ and ‘soaked it/him (in)’ and is reflected in the recipients/audience need to know, believe and never forget the events narrated in the letter, i.e. it still plays on sackcloth being absorbent and keeping the word/water of Jesus, as it is Jesus given this information by God who then passes it on to John to pass on to the rest of the world, just like Jesus/God’s water/sperm passed from Jesus to John (with more intensity compared to the other disciples) and to the rest of the world. It still plays on the connection and connotation to John the Baptist and the meaning of brothers which God's water makes everyone his children, and therefore 'brothers' in faith too. (Rev.1:1-3)

Asia; 'disobeyed/disobedient/went against' 'disobeyed him/went against him' 'became askew/bent/crooked/warped' 'sticks' 'used sticks'; 'sorrow' 'bad/offense/insult' 'bad towards/offense/insult towards'; 'things/matters' 'many/lots of things' 'wants' 'he wanted' 'speaking in whispers' 'snitching'. It begins with the meaning of 'things/matters' as John is informing the recipients of an important matter; there is ominous warning and the wailing by all the earth following mention of those who 'pierced' Jesus reflects disobedience of the people as well as the 'bad/insult/offense' which did include the use of sticks against Jesus during his arrest, torture; and the sorrow of his death; as important matters are being revealed from God to Jesus then John, and it is in the form of something only John is seeing/experiencing 'speaking in whispers' is shown. (Rev.1:11)

Alpha; α, ālphā; آلفا 'I gather up/collect' 'I wrap' 'I go around/turn around/come from around/behind' 'created/fabricated/fictional creations/fictional stories/fictional fabrications' 'lying/imagining/making up'. Cp: aalphaa. (Rev.1)

Omega; ω, ō mĕgā; وُميجا ، اوميجا ، وُميجع ، اوميجع 'spit out of mouth' 'spit suddenly out of mouth' means to spit food, drink or any substance out of mouth whether chewed or unchewed; اوميجا ، وُميجا 'spoil/went off/ruined/stale' 'bad/rotten food or drink' 'immoral people/person'. With 'Alpha/I gather up/collect' and 'Omega/'spit out of mouth' combined with 'I am the beginning and the ending' shows just like God gathered everything and created the whole world and everything in it, he will also destroy it, and he is destroying it because it is rotten, bad and unwanted; وُميجا ، اوميجا can also mean 'the-came/the one who came' 'or came/who came'. Cp: oomeyg', oo-meyg', oomeygaa, oo-meygaa.

The idea and meanings which have inspired Revelation are the OT stories of God using the people for his service and specifically for feeding him food and drink (it also borrows from the storylines of Ezekiel and Daniel), and this links the ideas of the author of Revelation to those of the OT, especially the stories of complete destruction of Israel when they polluted or failed to supply, or diverted the food source supplies and vessels from the 'hekal/he will eat' which caused God to no longer need the 'temple/hekal/he will eat', the land and the people which the stories have him utterly destroy. Revelation runs on the same themes of disobedience and punishment, cruelty and offense towards and from God through Jesus Christ who is also a food product and the action of eating that food product so the themes of 'spitting out' the people for the offense they cause to Jesus, who in the NT stories is God's son, is still linked to the OT stories and the complete destruction and great suffering which is narrated in such apocalyptic stories.

Alpha 'created/fabricated/fictional story creations/fictional story fabrications/lying/imagining', Omega 'the-came/the one who came' are also reflected in 'I am...the beginning and the ending...which is and which was, and which is to come...' and this portrays: the character God is who created the world and life and who will end it; creating fictional stories and imaginations or outright lies, and this is the author showing these stories are fictional creations of the author and because he borrows a lot from Daniel and Ezekiel visions, prophecy stories he is showing these are fictional too, and as the author of the fictional story he is who begins it and ends it, and as Alpha he has made it 'which is, and which was'; in Alpha he has made the beginning of the stories, but has also gathered all the elements to make the story—with Omega he is spitting them out, ending them in the same 'fabricated fiction' fashion as it is linked to Alpha; and also through Omega he is saying he has come to end these stories and also bringing the end of characters within the Rev. story itself.

Another way 'Alpha and Omega' are used is as letters pronounced together they make the word and sound 'oh, oh/aoo, aoo/aou, aou/oww, oww' and this is the word which is repeated as an expression to warn a person(s) about or from something, no different than 'woe, woe', to express sorrow, warning of something bad to come (usually as a consequence), and it is what people repeat when wailing. The author repeats it twice in the narration just like people use it as an expression, or where people who are crying and wailing create this sound repeatedly and unintentionally out of distress, physical pain and/or fear. (Rev.1)

Patmos; Pátmos, pátmō; فآدموه ، فآدمو 'so they made him bleed' 'make him bleed' 'sacrificed him' 'so they made him last/last long' 'make him last/last long'; فعدموه ، فعدمو 'from nothing' 'so they made nothing' 'so they executed/killed him' 'so it/he became scarce'. All these meanings are relayed in the verses: Jesus was killed and his blood spilled; he was a sacrifice for mankind to have a clean slate and chance of repentance; brought back to life he is now to live forever; John in particular has shown patience and has been working and suffering long, furthering the stories of Jesus Christ; Jesus was created with no human father like Adam so he came from nothing; the description of the 'first and the last' means he came before everything when there was nothing and he will be the last to witness the deaths of everyone and a return to nothing. There is an intentional link in the word-name 'Patmos' with the word-name 'Adam' (see Adam(Gen.)) and the relay in the narration's description. Cp: phaadmooh, phaadmoo, ph'dmooh, ph'dmoo. (Rev.1:9)

As is the method of the Biblical authors, the names used as churches will directly portray what is to happen within the narrative of the respective story. A note on the narrative: the message of warning or promise is being conveyed to and directed at the seven angels (before, by extension, to the people of the churches), each angel is responsible overseeing these seven named churches. What becomes apparent is these angels are being appraised in their work, successes and failures, obedience and disobedience. The story makes clear these angels are fallen angels who have been reduced in power and status due to some unnarrated wrong (which probably exists in other stories which have not been included in the OT or NT).

This can also be understood in the use of seven stars as being part of the arsenal in the hand of the 'Son of man' and also the seven stars representing the seven angels, and when taken into context with the authors and audiences' culture where folklore and some religions have fallen angels reduced to be devils, the Devil (Satan), or angels who live among people and have wisdom or knowledge more than people but are sent to live with men as a test for mankind, or punishment for a wrong the angels committed in heaven, or are punished on earth for a wrong they have committed on earth. In the culture, both in folklore and religion, stars are used to track devils/demons who eavesdrop on angel's commandments from God, i.e. what is to happen in the future so they can pass this on to sorcerers to predict the future. The punishment of those eavesdropping devils is a shooting star which kills them—so if you take into account these seven angels are fallen angels, or at least lower angels, who live on earth; that they are being warned, appraised and given a chance to repent, this makes it clear these seven stars are weapons which can kill the seven angels if they deserve it through disobedience; the power to end the lives of these angels is in the hand of the 'Son of man' represented by stars which in the sky are seen to shoot then fade, and in folklore and religion explode and reduce to nothing the target and the star. (Rev.)

Ephesus 'disentangle/untie (him/it)' 'disentangle knots or problems/matters(it/him)' 'separate it/him' 'break down into small and understandable pieces(it/him)' 'explain/break down into detail(it/him)' 'small seeds/ stone of fruit' 'pit/remove seed/stones from fruit' 'divorce/separate from wife(him)' 'small gem like stones used in jewellery/clothes'; 'pass wind in him' 'make it/him break wind' can mean literally or to beat up or scare, 'copulate/pass wind into'; 'twisted/crumpled it' 'twisted/crumpled-he/him' 'made a mess of it/him'; 'provoked/provoked him/it'.

The message to this church is explaining what the 'Son of man' has conveyed to them; it refers to the provocation of false apostles; the church has 'disentangled' and 'pitted the stone out of fruit' in testing and identifying the false apostles; nevertheless, they too have provoked the Son of man and they have done this by leaving their 'first love' which is the same as 'separating/divorcing from wife'; if the Ephesians do not repent, the son of Man will come to punish them and remove the light from their church, i.e. 'separate/ divorce' and this is because they have 'made a mess of it/him' and 'provoked him' with their disobedience'; the promise to eat from the tree of life, its fruit which give immortality, not only refers to the story of Adam and Eve but is also linked to the 'stone of fruit' meaning of Ephesus which the fruit-stone plants a seed which gives life and this is being used here and also reminds that Adam and Eve had to 'divorce/separate from wife' but from Eden/paradise not each other. (Rev.1:11; 2:1-7)

Smyrna; Smýrna; سمآرَن 'we stayed up all/late night' 'he kept us awake all night' 'we told night time stories' 'he told us night time stories'. The word (smr/سمر) which means to stay up all night or until late at night is always for a purpose: either guarding or keeping watch over something, whether land, over a sick person, for defence in case of an attack, or for entertainment; in all cases, stories called 'samaara' are told to help keep the individuals awake and/or entertained. In Rev.2 it is used to show how this church is told God is watching and knows everything they are suffering from; aware of their good deeds and tells them to hold onto their faith, it is asking them to stay awake i.e. be alert so as not to lose faith no matter what troubles befall them; it intentionally emphasises that the Smyrna church receives the message the same way as being told a story; the latter point is reinforced as the reminder of Adam and Eve story is mentioned again, but this time only mentioning Satan who has caused some of the Smyrna church to be thrown into prison and this likens and reminds how the devil/serpent deceived Adam and Eve and caused them to be thrown out of paradise and into the prison of world where physical pain and suffering could be felt—and it reminds of the tree of life which gives immortality. Cp: smyaarna. (Rev.1:11; 2:8-11)

Pergamos; Pérgamos, Pérgamon; بيآرجَمُه ، بيآرجَموه ، بيآرجَمُن ، بيآرجَمون 'they will stone him' 'they will stone' 'they will bury him/it under rocks' 'they will bury under rocks' 'they will accuse him/throw accusations against him' 'they will accuse/they will throw accusations' and the accusation meaning of this word is an unsubstantiated or false accusation.

The narration of 'I know where you are' gives the impression that they, or some of them, are trying to hide, and this applies especially to the location of 'Satan's seat' and this reflects being buried under stone or hidden/contained under some kind of stone structure; **Satan** is used for 'laid hands on' as the character Antipas is said to have been killed (Pergamos meanings are also related to Antipas meanings, see Antipas below) and the impression it gives is that Antipas was either stoned, or killed in relation to or using stone/rocks and this ties it with Satan's seat being hidden under rocks or a stone structure as it narrates Antipas died where Satan lives.

Balaam ('with/of curses' 'has received message' 'with/of blame') and **Balac/Balaak** ('pass/send on greetings or information through messengers' 'ailed you/afflicted you') are used and relay exactly the narration that the churches are being delivered a message from God and have received it, and that these two are an example of creating problems for people past and present; mentioning **Israel** is to make clear sexual immorality is part of the problem being addressed which in the OT is punished with stoning; the worship of idols is related to rocks as most idols are carved out of stone, and rocks are worshipped as can be seen in the OT; and although Balaam is blamed for causing Balac to trip-up the children of Israel in Rev.2:14, the author and his local audience would know that the original story is Balaam refused to comply with Balak's request and kept responding to him that he could not curse people innocent of any accusations and wrongdoing, the same OT story also reminds the audience that Balak built seven altars to slaughter sacrifices at for Balam to curse and accuse Moses and his people from—this too ties into the stone/rock and throw accusations meanings of Pergamos as altars are built of stone. The white stone which contains an unknown name also reflects the 'stone/rock' meanings of 'Pergamos'. The sword which is in the mouth is the tongue, and the weapon of the tongue is word, so preaching but specifically throwing accusations against the disobedient is meant here. Cp: peyaargamoh, peyaargamooh, peyaargamon, peyaargamoon. (Rev.1:11)

Thyatira; 'he/they are twisting/wringing' 'squeezing water or liquid out of' 'he/it-twisted/squeezed/wrung water/liquid out of' sexual immorality is meant again—in the OT stories Jezebel was tied to 'Israel' with sexual immorality and idol worship; Thyatira was used in Acts, for Lydia who is a prostitute and she inadvertently brought upon Paul and his group bad luck, as twisting and crumpling and squeezing water out of them (baptism and conversion) resulted in their subsequent imprisonment. In Rev.2 'Thyatira' tied to **Jezebel** 'tell a story of the/with the' 'pipe the' whose meanings mean both to tell stories and to encourage into wrongdoing is linked to fornication and idol worship; according to this new narration, Jezebel was given a chance to repent; sexual immorality is further emphasised by throwing her into a bed followed by her adulterers and into great problems, and this relays the 'he/they are twisting/wringing' and 'squeezing water or liquid out of' meanings of Thyatira and reminds of the story of what happened to Paul after he baptised Lydia of Thyatira. The squeezing/wringing meanings of Thyatira will be able to squeeze out and keep away all evil and be rulers over the unfaithful, as well as Jezebel's 'tell a story' meanings are shown in that whoever listens/obeys what the 'Spirit/breathing/panting' is telling the churches so it is a story for everyone and not only the recipient churches. (Rev.1:11; 2:18–29)

Sardis; Sárdeis; سآرديه 'I will kill him' 'I will cause him great grief/trouble' 'I will set him back/bring him down/pile problems or accusations on him' 'I will reduce him to nothing/make him less' 'spoke/told at length/told story at length/narrated'; صآرديه 'burn to blackness' 'burn into coal' 'a log burnt black' 'make him like a burnt log' 'became like a burnt log/ignore and turn away from him/bridled and turned away' 'ignoring/pretending not to hear' 'a fire pit' 'a coal making pit'.

All these dark meanings are relayed in the message to Sardis. They are already dead, and dead in the negative way (not in the positive way of being dead in Christ which means live forever); they are accused that everything they do or have done is riddled with imperfections (sin/disobedience); they are reminded to hold onto what they have already been taught/heard; the darkness/blackness of coal and/or burnt logs is relayed in they will not see punishment when it comes, as it will come as a thief in the darkness of the night; only a few people in Sardis have not been blackened, polluted by sin (they remain in clean clothes and will walk in purity of white clothes as opposed to all the black and polluted meanings of coal pits and burnt logs for charcoal); the obedient and faithful will be included in the book of names where they will be narrated before God and the angels, and the narration meanings applies to all the churches who are told to listen to what is being told. Cp: saardeih, ssaardeih. (Rev.1:11; 3:1-6)

Philadelphia; Philadélphia; فِلعديل فيَ ، فيل عدَل فيَ ، فِلعدَل فيَ 'in me-poured intensely-into me' 'in me-glugged into me' 'so-poured/pour intensely-into me' 'so-glugged/glug into me' 'so he/they will not pour/pour intensely into me' 'may he/they not pour/pour intensely into me' 'so he/they will not glug into me' and the pouring from the word ('dl/عدل) means to pour heavily a lot of water, e.g. in a rush or when the opening of the vessels or one of them is wide enough to be able to pour water in a wider stream without needing to pour gently, 'in me-justice-into me' 'so be just/fair to me' 'he did not do me justice/he was not fair towards me' 'so he/it shifted his/its weight in me' 'so he/it caused me to lose balance and sway/swerve/veer to one side' 'may he not shift his weight inside me' 'may he not cause me to lose balance/sway/swerve/veer' e.g. if weight is not distributed evenly and the load or the person carrying it shifts to one side causing the whole load or person to swerve or move to one side/lose balance, also used when a water vessel which needs to be full to distribute weight evenly is partially empty and shifts/slides/swerves because its weight moves and/or causes the person carrying it to lose balance and/or swerve; (adél/عدل) 'justice/fair' 'shift weight/cause imbalance/swerve'.

The following words and combinations are also a possibility without really changing the meaning of the words above and their combinations as only the suffix-compound-word (phia/فيَ) 'in me/into me/towards me' becomes (bia/بيَ) 'with me/to me', also the prefix of the compound word (Phi/فِـ/في) 'in me/so/will' becomes (bi/بِـ/بي) 'with/with me/to me'. Either both these words can be changed or only the prefix or only suffix part of the compound word, to avoid repetition I will only include a few examples but it applies to all: فِلعديل بيَ ، بيل عدل فيَ ، بِلعدل بيَ 'in me-poured intensely-to me/with me', 'with justice-into/to me' 'by shifting his weight inside me' 'by (he/it) causing me to lose balance/sway/swerve'.

The meanings of shifted weight and imbalance is portrayed in that there is a key which no man can open or shut, i.e. the weight is against the desired action (opening and closing in this example). The people of this church have remained just towards God/Jesus and therefore he has remained just towards them in fairness: the door will be left open for them, they will not be punished with all the punishment and sufferance which the rest of the people will have to go through; the imbalance and shifting of weight is shown by having the 'Jews' bow/prostrate/worship at the feet of the church and this shows how power/control has shifted and a physical and figurative shifting in that they are made/compelled to worship/bow. The church's weakness in comparison to the strength of the disobedience it was being tempted/persecuted with shows the physical imbalance and the shifting of weight, and here it is swerving towards the right direction. The punishment and testing which the rest will go through but Philadelphia will be spared from, all portray the meanings of 'Philadelphia': the temptation is a number of earthquakes, floods, attacks from celestial and demonic creatures; all these apocalyptic events, shaking of earth, crumbling/falling of mountains, people besieged by stronger forces, all have the meaning of 'veer/shift or lose balance/imbalance, etc.'.

The meanings 'in me-poured intensely-into me' 'in me-glugged into me' 'so-poured/pour intensely-into me' 'so-glugged/glug into me' 'so he/they will not pour/pour intensely into me' 'may he/they not pour/pour intensely into me' 'so he/they will not glug into me' reflect what all the other stories of recipient churches have shown: there is a competition between at least two religions which both have an importance in sexual activities, ejaculation of sperm as cleansing, spiritual, etc. and that is why the word-name has been arranged so that it can confirm water has been poured into the spoken about, and at the same time can also mean water has not been poured into the spoken about, i.e. Philadelphia has only accepted the Christian version of this religion and rejected the other religion (Nicolaitans religion); the 'disobedient/hated' Nicolaitans have rejected the Christian-based faith and accepted and follow a different sex-based religion.

David is used here because it is a strong tool made of solid stone that can take a lot of rough-handling; and the people of Philadelphia, no matter how weak they were, resisted all disobedience and persecution which has entitled them to the fair reward which they will receive. It also plays on the connotation that 'David/stone rolling pin of stone grinder' cracks open grain to make into dough which creates 'Jesus Christ/cold bread-the cake/circle of bread' which can then be 'Jesus/broke/ate bread' who returns or will return whole (Christ circle/cake of bread'—the basis of the faith in these stories as this church has wholly accepted Jesus Christ and his stories). The meanings of David 'repeat/hesitate/revolve/try again/to and fro/in circles' also reminds of the actions in creating the dough for bread, but also that no matter how sinners revolved around this church, the church did not hesitate and stuck to the correct faith of the stories.

Satan is used for 'two laps/two sides', 'laps/sides' (means went back and forth on the same course/path/way either twice or many times) which reinforces what the 'David/rolling pin' does to produce the dough which is made into bread/Jesus; it also shows there are two sides, a good/right/just side and a bad/wrong/unjust side—the Philadelphians are on the correct side. The meanings 'obstructed' 'of obstructing' 'defended' no matter what troubles were attempting to obstruct the Philadelphians from the faith, they defended the faith by sticking to it.

Jerusalem 'came-saw-asked-them/the' 'they see-asked-them/the' 'they see-their/the rocks' 'they see-rocks-them/the' 'came-saw-their/the rocks' 'came-saw-rocks-them/the' and is used to show that this 'new Jerusalem' replaces the old, for where in the stories people come to Jerusalem to ask from God who is often described as a rock, where the city got its compound word-name by the authors having the people come to see Solomon and see him ask God for things and the use of 'David' and 'stone' 'pillar' relays the 'rocks' meanings in 'Jerusalem' as they are all made out of rocks/stone, and where it is narrated that people who continue to come, see and ask will be answered—this has now been replaced with a new story and a new meaning or perception according to the story (with no actual change to its meaning) that whoever comes in no longer leaves but remains like a pillar inside, and this is symbolism that the faith of Christianity will be set like stone inside believers and they will remain Christian forever. This is also directed at the churches and everyone who hears that this applies to them, to come, see and listen to the story as it answers all their questions and that they should never part with their new faith: Christianity. Cp: phil'adeil-phya, phyl-'adeil-phya, phil'adeil-phya, phil'adeil-bya, byl-'adeil-phya, bil'adeil-bya. (Rev.1:11; 3:7-13)

Laodicea 'stitch it/stitching' 'of stitching' 'it is sticky/sticking' 'of stickiness'; 'threw it away/aside' 'flung it/him/her away/aside' 'of throwing/flinging away/aside' 'will/will not be forced to swallow/suffer/taste it'. Just as in Colossians where it was first introduced and used to show 'to throw/swipe away', it still has the same meanings and use as when someone throws something carelessly aside then cannot find it, or intentionally throws aside something unwanted. In this instance it refers to the people/church of Laodicea themselves as God or the 'Son of man' finds their faith/actions not passionate or strong enough; as a consequence he informs them he will throw them away like the spitting out of an unpleasant lukewarm beverage and its other meaning 'will/will not be forced to swallow/suffer/taste it' as figuratively he has already put it into his mouth but refuses to swallow it and spits it out. The unpleasant texture or sense of the lukewarm beverage/people is relayed with the 'palatable' meaning and is also portrayed similar to something sticky which most people prefer to remove from skin or objects. Although the church/people believe they are well-clothed, rich and faithful, the message to them is they are naked, poor, weak and unfaithful.

The church can remedy its situation by 'stitching' itself to and with the correct faith and actions and is also being given a chance to become palatable instead of lukewarm because the meaning of Laodicea 'will taste it' is used in the positive as if they repent and be zealous towards God/Jesus/Son of man, they will dine together. (Rev.1:11; 3:22)

Nicolaitans; Nikolaḯtēs; نِقولَييآتيه 'transport/move from place to place-him/it' 'of transporting/moving' 'spread rumours/conversations/news-him/it' 'of spreading rumours/conversation/news' 'of cleansing/choosing/picking out impurities'; نِكولَييآتيه 'fucked-crumpled him/it/them' 'of fucking with him/them' 'offended-crumpled him/them/it' 'of offending' 'wounded/poked in wound-crumpled him/it/them' 'of wounding/poking in wound'; نِجولَييآتيه 'survived/they survived/were delivered to safety-crumpled him/it/them' 'survived/they survived being crumpled' 'they were delivered to safety from being crumpled' 'discussed quietly/secretly/discussed between them-who crumpled/crushed together'.

In addressing Ephesus, 'Nicolaitans' is used to show that the message is they both hate people who spread rumours, and this also means the false apostles; it also relays that John is relaying the message from the 'Son of man' to the church; the 'poking in wound' and 'of fucking with him/them' meanings refers to the false apostles, as other stories have also made it clear that when true apostles and preachers have sex with men it has a cleansing and spiritual effect due to it being a religious ritual done in faith, whereas the false apostles (Nicolaitans) have homosexual sex with the faithful only for carnal purposes and lust; the 'discussing' and 'delivering to safety' is in the church being told of the message, and also because they and the vision/message-sender hate the Nicolaitans; the Ephesus church will be saved and spared from further punishment.

In addressing Pergamos, 'Nicolaitans' the meanings of 'transporting and moving from place to place' relays with the Balaam/Balak story where Balak moved Balam from altar to altar, position to position, to get a better view and to convince him to curse Moses and his people. The sexual activities meanings of 'Nicolaitans' relays the '**Israel**/twisted muscle-the' meaning of sexual immorality and this becomes clearer as the 'doctrine of the Nicolaitans' is meant to be a sexual-activity-based religion—now remember, even according to all the NT stories included in the NT Bible show that Christianity is also a religion based on sexual intercourse, but one that is between male and male, even if it does include females the power and effectiveness is upkept by male homosexual acts of the apostles, preachers, anyone who is in an official position to convert, cleanse and guide the followers of the faith—but any other religions where sexual rites are part of the faith and rituals has to be condemned as it creates competition and confusion of the faithful, especially if they are similar in what lifts a person to a higher level of spirituality, understanding and purity. The meanings of 'survived/delivered to safety' as the message warns them to repent before they are punished so they are given a chance to survive. The meanings of 'spread news' are shown in addressing all the churches to listen in order to survive. Cp: niqoolayeeaateyh, nikoolayeeaateyh, nigoolayeeaateyh. (Rev.2:6-7, 15-17)

Antipas; Antipás; انتِبآص 'he fell off cliff/high place/mountain' and this means dying by smashing against rocks or falling from a height. This character was included under 'Pergamos' of which one meaning is to 'stone to death' 'throw' and this suits a character being killed either stoned or thrown from over a cliff or high place; انتِفاه 'pluck it/him' 'pluck it/him/kill it him' and can mean to literally pluck things off such as hair, feathers, grass, plants, thread, etc. or is used as a curse wishing someone to be killed quickly or describing someone who died suddenly or was killed, or an object that was suddenly removed or destroyed. Cp: antibaass, antiphaah. (Rev.2:13)

David 'this is/he is stone rolling pin of grinding stone' 'repeat/try again/keep at it/repeating the same revolving or to and fro motion' 'hesitates/goes and comes/recoils/revolves' and describes an animal when it hesitates, going back and forth, turning its head or the front part of its body to walk away, but returning to its original position or even walking away then quickly returning to its original location (e.g. when you see an animal hesitating to move away from the corpse of a dead family member, or when in danger and partially turns away or towards a specific direction, but resumes its original position ready to fight or flee) the same is used to describe a person hesitating about an action repeating the same movements out of hesitation or even going back and forth in hesitation or repeatedly returning.

Juda/Judah is used for 'he called' as an angel in the vision calls out asking who can open a sealed book which no one is able to open. David is used for 'hesitates/revolves/recoils/repeats' because no man is able to open it, and in **John** ('soaked' with tears) feeling hesitant about the matter; also David for 'this is/he is stone rolling pin of grinding stone' as just like he can crack grain open and make bread—it is his 'descendant' **Jesus** (called 'Lamb' in this story and elsewhere in the OT) the 'Lamb' who although is in a state of a slaughtered lamb to remind he has been crucified and sacrificed, is able to open the book. This still plays on 'David/rolling pin' cracks open grain to create and bring around 'Jesus/bread/break/ate bread' and this all relays into his descendant Jesus and its word-meanings are able to break open the book. The songs sung about Jesus/Lamb taking over the book through being sacrificed for mankind is stating the Jesus stories (some of the stories which would end up becoming the NT) have replaced the older stories (some of these stories which would end up being the OT), and like the replacement of Jerusalem with 'new Jerusalem' means that the new faith/stories (Christianity/NT) have superseded and replaced the old faith/stories (older pagan and Jewish religions/OT). (Rev.5)

Wormwood; ápsinthos, Artemisia; عب سِنتُه 'packed/filled-straight/in his direction/made him/it straight/aligned/made it(first time)' 'overflowed/floated in/seeped water or liquid-straight/in his direction/made him/it straight/aligned/made it(first time)' 'shame/shamed- straight/in his direction/made him/it straight/aligned/made it(first time)' 'rotted and stank- straight/in his direction/made him/it straight/aligned/made it(first time)'. It definitely plays on 'water/overflowing' as the star falls into rivers and water fountains, and on 'rotted and stank' first half of the compound word, and that it came 'in the direction' of the water sources which is the second half of the compound word meaning: it comes in the direction of the waters; it causes them to turn bitter which when water tastes bad 'rotted/stank' applies to it; both meanings of 'Wormwood' (ápsinthos, Artemisia) relay in the events of verses 7-13, as there is punishment being thrown down from the sky and sent in the direction of living things on earth, and mainly waters, which causes pure and natural things to rot/spoil.

It is interesting that even the scientific name **Artemisia** is also an Arab compound word; ارتيمي/ارتَمي سي 'was thrown/thrown down-bad/offensive/insult/sorrow/bad towards/insult towards' 'was killed-bad/offensive/insult/sorrow/bad towards/insult towards' 'threw down headlong-bad/offensive/insult/sorrow/bad towards/insult towards' 'was wounded-bad/offensive/insult/sorrow/bad towards/insult towards' 'collapse/collapsed-bad/offensive/insult/sorrow/bad towards/insult towards' 'saw water/she showed him water/

saw his water-bad/offensive/insult/sorrow/bad towards/insult towards' 'quenched/she quenched-water/his water-bad/offensive/insult/sorrow/bad towards/insult towards' 'was watered/was quenched-with water/his water-bad/offensive/insult/sorrow/bad towards/insult towards'.

This Arabic compound word also covers all the related meanings as narrated in the story: the star is thrown down; it lands in waters and turns the waters bitter; not only is it bad because it has made the water bitter but has also caused the water to kill many people who drink from it; it causes sorrow because people cannot drink bitter water and due to the deaths. Cp: 'b-sintoh, arteimy-sah, artemy-sah. (Rev.8:7-13)

Abaddon; Abaddṓn; ابدّون ، ابَدّوَن 'brought out' 'wiped out/massacred' 'forever' 'never'; عبدّون ، عبَدّوَن 'worshipper/worshipped' 'servants/served'; اذدّون ، اذَدّوَن 'harmed-except/without/not' 'harmed-not them'; عذدّون ، عذَدّوَن 'protected/said protection for-except/without/not' 'protected/said protection-not them'. All the meanings are present: Abaddon and his army of hideous locusts are servants performing a task required by God; they are brought out to cause great physical agony and mental anguish as people will wish for death but not achieve it; the selected worshippers of the correct faith are protected with a seal and will not be harmed, while the unmarked people will not be protected and will be harmed. Cp: abaddoon, abaddooan, 'baddoon, 'baddooan, avaddoon, avaddooan, 'vaddoon, 'vaddooan. (Rev.9:1-11)

Apollyon; Apollýōn; ابولّيآون ، ابولّيَون 'soak/I soak them' 'afflict/I afflict them' 'were soaked' 'were afflicted'. The meaning of afflicting people is relayed as this character and his army of locusts cause great physical and mental pain to the people it afflicts. Both word-names Abaddon and Apollyon complete each other in relaying and enhancing the narration of the respective verses. Cp: abollyaaoon, abollyaoon. (Rev.9:1-11)

Euphrates (Gen.2:14) 'split/tear/tore/divide(ed) it' 'lose/lost/lose chance/be deceived out of opportunity or wealth/money/possessions'. The four angels are let loose, they come out of the river Euphrates; the people are being killed and it is mentioned that they had a chance to repent of sins, but refused to do so. (Rev.9:14-21)

Sodom 'black soot' and **Egypt/Mizraim** 'put scarf on-them' 'put scarf on-the' 'knot/bundle-them/the' 'insult-them' 'offend-the'. All the meanings are relayed: the monster coming out of the pit to kill the two witnesses conjures up the image of black soot; as they are clothed in sackcloth and not normal garments it is like being covered with a small scarf, the sackcloth also emphasises the meaning of 'black soot' as people in grief and distress in the OT stories put on sackcloth and cover themselves with ashes or soil; the insult is towards the witnesses as instead of being buried with respect, they are left in the streets while the people happily party over their deaths; the meaning of 'put a scarf on-the' is usually done to show modesty, this is relayed in after many people are killed the survivors show humility out of fear and praise God. (Rev.11:1-13)

Michael is used for 'what is there-the' 'what is-the' 'what is the matter-the' 'what is said?' 'what is said' 'who said' 'who said-the' 'spending time at/spending time with' 'stay(ing)/wait(ing)' 'imagining' 'hallucinating' 'is hallucinating/has hallucinated/imagined' 'hallucination/imagination'. All the meanings are reflected in the narration: the woman and the dragon are 'wonders' i.e. 'what is there-the' 'what is-the'; the dragon is waiting for the woman to give birth i.e. 'stay(ing)/wait(ing)'; the woman is to spend a specified and long period of time in the place God prepared for her in the wilderness: 'spending time at/spending time with'; the woman and her descendants are being persecuted because of what they say regarding witnessing and speaking about the testimony of Jesus; John, just like Daniel in the OT, hears voices say things but nothing he sees nor hears is clear or makes sense and is more like a dream, a hallucination, and the author is making it clear it is from the imagination and shows the meanings: 'what is the matter-the' 'what is said?' 'what is said' 'who said' 'who said-the' 'hallucinating' 'is hallucinating/has hallucinated/imagined' 'hallucination/imagination'. (Rev.12)

Sion/**Zion** 'sweep/brush' 'swept/brushed away' 'bad'. The men which accompany the Lamb are clean, i.e. any impurities are swept away from them: as the NT stories keep repeating that copulation with women by disciples/apostles is a polluting act which brings negative consequences as opposed to the cleansing and spiritual characteristics of male-on-male copulation, Rev.14 keeps up this theme: the men are not bad or impure in any way because they are virgins which 'were not defiled by women' i.e. there is neither bad nor impurities in them—they are like a room or ground which has been swept clean and immaculate. This makes them fit to follow Jesus/the Lamb around just like the disciples who followed Jesus around in the first life. (Rev.14:1-5)

Babylon 'swap/change' 'swapped/changed' 'they swapped/changed' and reflects the changed/swapped state of things: Babylon once great is now fallen; anyone who follows the 'beast' will also suffer a negative change in circumstance; the people who follow the correct state are promised rest from suffering and labour. (Rev.14:8-13)

Moses is used for its meanings of 'touched/possessed/was possessed/touched' 'entangled/caused problems/provoked problems or fighting' as the angels are filled with the wrath of God, and because their job is to pour out the seven plagues onto earth it is due to people who have provoked/entangled God; the punishment physically touches and harms people in such a way they cannot get away from it nor bring its end. (Rev.15)

Armageddon; Harmagedṓn; هَر مَغِطون 'chased away/made flee/fled-they/they were killed/squeezed to death/manhandled to death'; the second half of the compound word is the same as **Megiddo** (Josh.12:21)and the death this way is either direct murder or from overhandling something like a child which thinks it is gently stroking or hugging a small pet but actually causing it internal injuries, strangling it, a slow and painful death—which is how the people being tortured by the seven plagues is described. هَر مَغِدون 'chased away/made flee/fled-they/they were frustrated/glands swelled with frustration' still 'Megiddo'and it usually describes someone who is caused/causing so much distress or frustration he/she feels their glands swelling or expresses such a statement to show the degree of frustration/distress. خَر مَجِدون 'collapsed/fled away/made flee-were not found' 'collapsed/fled away/made flee-were mighty/glorified/great'. (mgd/مجد) 'glory/glorify/mighty/great/praised'; and (m/م) 'not/negative' (gd/جد) 'find/found' and the (on/ṓn/"ون") makes the word in the plural. The same is described in the story.

The first part of the compound word (Ar/Har/هَر/خَر) the same as **Hur** (Exod.17:9-12) to chase away, make flee, or to flee, to collapse or make collapse.

In the chapter all these meanings are relayed. People are slaughtered through punishment and there are those who are immediately killed, but there are many who are made to suffer great physical and mental torment from sores, drinking blood, injured or squashed to death by giant hailstones. The hate and anger towards God which wells up out of frustration from the physical and psychological pain they are made to suffer, causing them pain and distress to the degree they gnaw at their tongues. The people are trying to flee but cannot escape the punishment; it is reflected in the islands and mountains fleeing God's punishment and cannot be found; the city and nations who were once great are now fallen, collapsed and physically divided (Babylon chosen for its meaning of swapped/changed to show the reverse in the situation from greatness to destruction). Cp: har-magheṭoon, har-maghedoon, <u>kh</u>ar-magedoon. (Rev.16)

Euphrates is used for 'crosses it' 'passes it' as the angel pours a vial which dries up the river so that kings who arrive from the east can pass/cross it. (Rev.16:12)

Babylon is used again for 'swapped/changed' as Babylon symbolised as a whore is blamed for causing many nations to go from a state of obedience to a state of disobedience—everything she is accused of polluting was once in a purer state; there is the 'swapping' in the narration about the beast which simultaneously 'was, and is not, yet is'; it is shown in the woman/Babylon and those who follow her lead will be destroyed—as a woman dressed in scarlet (richness, royalty, beauty) will end up being stripped naked, her body/flesh torn and eaten alive, then burnt alive. (Rev.17)

Alleluia; halĕlû-yāh; هَليلُ/هَليلو ياه ، هَليلُ/هَليلو جاه'cry out loud/chant-you/him' 'chant his name' 'chant for him' 'praise-he/him' 'cry out loud/chant-came he/came to him' 'praise-came he/came to him' and it is to repeatedly cry out a word or name done usually as praise, or in song/poem, or prayer; حَليلُ/حَليلو ياه ، حَليلُ/حَليلو جاه 'purify/cleanse-you/him' 'circumcise-he/him' 'make legitimate/edible/permissible-you/he/him' 'declare permissible/edible/legitimate-he/him' 'purify/cleanse-came he/came to him' 'circumcise-came he/came to him' 'make legitimate/permissible/edible-came he/came him' 'declare permissible/edible/legitimate-came he/came him' 'sweeten/make sweet-you/he/him' 'sweeten/make sweet-came he/came him/came to him' (it may have other 'ḥl' meanings). It is equivalent to Hillel (Judg.12:13), Jehaleleel (1Chr.4:16). Cp: haleilu/haleiloo-yaah, haleilu/haleiloo-gaah, ḥaleilu/ḥaleiloo-yaah, ḥaleilu/ḥaleiloo-gaah.

The word in most of its possible meanings is used in Rev.19: words are being shouted and God praised; what is being cried out is that the whore has been brought to judgement; words and praise are cried out and loudly. This praise and shouting are over the judgement of the whore, which is Babylon's blood spilled and all this is tied to the second meanings of Hallelujah of: 'purity' 'circumcision' 'legitimisation' 'sweetening' and it is connected to the 'Lamb' which is Jesus, and his 'wife/bride' who is Mary mother of Jesus. This is how it works: Jesus was created without a father; the gospel stories mock Mary mother of Jesus and list her with whores and other promiscuous women from the OT stories, and show Jesus is bitter towards her over it; the authors of the gospels insinuate Jesus is Joseph's son out of wedlock and therefore she is promiscuous while they show she was copulated by God while still a virgin; in both cases Jesus is an illegitimate child, a bastard, marked with impurity which causes bitterness for both Mary and Jesus.

Jesus is God's son, the semen/water represented in the stories as the 'Holy Ghost' and/or 'Spirit' is what filled Mary and created Jesus, and through this godly water/sperm and the authors' narrations—Jesus is God: Mary is his mother, God is his father, but Jesus is also God interchangeable with the 'Son of God', but still God: when after the day of judgement all wrongs have been righted, and blood of Babylon spilled in sacrifice there is only one impurity and wrong left to purify, and that is Jesus' illegitimate conception, birth and being; Jesus/the Lamb marries his Mother Mary and because Jesus is God when he marries Mary it makes Jesus a legitimate child—what bitterness there was is now sweetened, what was wrong is corrected, made purified and declared permissible which is why 'Hallelujah' has been tied with the avenging of the saints' blood from the whore of Babylon; the whore of Babylon and her demise is a contrast to Mary who will be honoured and her story rectified, and the Lamb's bride dressed in white symbolises she was a virgin when she conceived and gave birth to Jesus, and that she was still pure when she marries him, and the saints' blood is her virginity/hymen blood-token; as the 'Lamb/Jesus' has been described as being in a state of slaughter (that is he was showing signs of blood, throat cut) this also symbolises what happens before the bride and groom in weddings in the culture of the real people/audience, and this has been a custom since before Judaism, Christianity and Islam, that a sacrificial lamb is slaughtered before the bride and groom (separately, and again when they are together at the same place).

The woman clothed with the sun who gives birth to a child who will rule mankind from Rev.12 and after giving birth goes into hiding in a place prepared by God for a specified and limited amount of time also symbolises the virgin Mary, if not meant to be Mary herself. This also indicates she was to marry Jesus because in the real lives of people of the culture who created the Biblical stories, before a woman marries she undergoes a custom called 'shading/covering' where she is no longer seen outside the house and is relieved of any usual house-chores and is pampered more than usual so she can prepare herself for the wedding day to look her best, this is also tied with the verse 'and his wife hath made herself ready' Rev.19:7. (Rev.19)

Gog 'great crowd/ a huge number of people' 'overcrowded' and **Magog** 'moves like a wave' which was used in the OT to show great hordes of people so packed and overcrowded their movement seemed like a wave and were used as a human sacrifice, are now used again to show great hordes of people who gather to attack the saints; and the great hordes of people resurrected to be judged, and then great hordes of people either being allowed to live in heaven or cast into 'the lake of fire'.

John for 'soaked' as now the thirsty people will be given to drink and quenched from God's fountain with no conditions set as all wrong/evil has been wiped out and everything is new. That there is no need for water from other individuals as it is available direct from God is symbolised in there is no longer sea on earth. Also 'brothers' as the angel informs him they and the prophets are brethren. 'betrayed' as the people who are disobedient will still be punished and are meant for punishment.

Alpha and **Omega** are used again for: Alpha'I gather up/collect' 'I wrap' 'I go around/turn around/come from around/behind' 'created/fabricated/fictional creations/fictional fabrications'; Omega 'spit out of mouth' 'spit suddenly out of mouth' 'spoil/went off/ruined/stale' 'the-came/the one who came', and for its coded message 'oh, oh (woe,woe)' as it is still reminding and warning all the people whether obedient or disobedient about promise and punishment.

God (and the author of Rev.) has turned everything around, he has wrapped up and put away all negative things; God has created a new world instead of the old he destroyed; the old world is what was spoiled and was spat out by God; there is still a story being told within the story as God tells John to write the truth so it can be conveyed as a warning and teaching to others back in John's world (he is currently in a vision-world), and the author of Rev. is reminding his audience that this is a fictional story which he has fabricated; an angel comes to show John the bride of the Lamb which earlier was Mary, and still is but now the bride of the Lamb represents Jerusalem. Even the meanings of **Jerusalem** 'came-saw-asked-them/the' 'they see-asked-them/the' 'came-saw-their/the rocks' 'came-saw-rocks-them/the' 'came-saw-water flowed/leaked-them/the' 'they saw-joined/connected-them/the' and **Mary** 'pass along' 'pass/cross/pass by' who when completed with God and/or Jesus becomes **Maryam/Miriam** 'pass along the river/sea' and this is how the bride of the Lamb/Jesus is shown in Rev.21 that she is Jerusalem with God and Jesus inside and part of it/her: Jerusalem 'came-saw-asked' reflects on Mary/Maryam 'pass along/pass along river/sea' because when God first sent an angel to Mary: the angel came to her, they both saw each other, she asked him how it was possible that she would become pregnant as she was chaste and he informed her, and then she was filled with God's water to conceive Jesus, now both God and Jesus are inside her as 'Jerusalem' linking the meanings of seeing, asking, coming, joining, rocks, and 'water' flowing.

There is no longer need of the misnomered 'temple' which should read 'hekal/he will eat' because Jesus who is the Son of God and his name means 'bread/ate/broke bread' and his creation and existence was out of God's water (living water), who is also now symbolised as a slaughtered lamb is now bread, water and meat along with God (God is a rock) in the 'temple' 'hekal/he will eat' and God no longer needs to be served sacrifices and food as was done in the OT stories because it has been superseded and replaced by a single character/person who is both food and water of life: Jesus. (Rev.21)

Greek, Grecian and Gentile, Greece and Achaia

The meanings of the words Achaia, Grecian, Greece, Greek, Gentile and how they were used has been discussed earlier in this book, but needs more detail important in connection to its use in the Bible.

These words, like all the word-names in the Biblical stories, are not used to mean the country of Greece, or Greek and Gentile 'people' or ethnicity. They are used as an adjective or verb which depicts a description of the character or theme they are connected to in the story or the events to happen/happening in the story. The word-names used in Koine Greek of the NT are related to the word-names in Arabic ('Hebrew') of the OT. Both the translations into English have suffered mistranslations as the 'Hebrew'/Arabic word does not mean a people or ethnicity, but used as their word-meanings to depict, enhance and relay what is happening in the story.

To begin with, we need to differentiate between what these words have been translated as in the Bible before we move on to their correct meanings which have already been included earlier in this book to see how they were meant to be used as intended by the Biblical authors. The following shows how they have been translated/mistranslated:

The word (**Gentile/ethne**) in the NT has been translated to mean 'Gentile/foreigner' 'nation(s)' 'people' 'heathen'. In the OT the word (**Gentile/goy**) has been translated to mean 'Gentile/foreigner' 'nation' 'heathen'.

The word (**Greek/hellen**) in the NT has been translated to mean 'Greeks/foreigner' 'Gentile/foreigner'. In the OT '**Greece/yavan**' has been used to mean 'Greece/foreigner/ethnicity of Greece'. In the NT (**Achaia**) has been translated to depict an area or people from 'Achaia' which scholars have interpreted to mean 'Greece'.

To avoid too much repetition, I will try to use the most basic meanings without the multiple different tenses, forms (due to suffixes/prefixes) and without alternate ways and combinations within the single one compound word-name being translated (but these can be found under their earlier translations). What these words really translate and mean are as follows:

NT **Gentile**; ethnē; يثني ، اثني 'he/they do it again/double it/fold it/repeat it' 'he/they dissuade/make leave' 'he/they are idolaters/pagans' 'idols' 'praise/praises' 'idol worshippers' 'idolatry/worshipping idols'.

OT **Gentile**; gôwy, haggoyim; غُوي ، هَغّوي هم 'deceit/folly/seduction' 'I will deceive them/the' 'I will mislead them to downfall-them/the'.

NT **Achaia**; achaïas; اغَيي ، اغييه 'I mislead him/them to downfall/I will mislead him/them to his/their downfall' 'his misleading to downfall' 'I deceive him/them/I will deceive'; اعَيي ، اعييه 'I make him/them howl' 'I will make him/them howl' 'I warn/teach him/them' 'I will contain him/it'.

OT **Greece/Grecian**; yāwān, yĕwān; عاوآن ، عيوآن 'howling' 'assisted/helped' 'howled' 'taught/learned and remembered/warned'; غاوان ، غيوآن 'misleading to downfall' 'misled/misled to downfall'.

NT **Greece/Greek**; Hellás, Helláda, hellēn; حَلّاه ، حِلّاتَ/حِلّاذَ ، حَلّين 'purified/circumcised/made clean/made edible him/it' 'declared purified/permissible' 'of undressing' 'of deceit/tricks' 'beat severely/beat until skin peeled off him/it' 'of beating/being beaten severely' 'shed its skin/hair/leaves/etc. him/it' 'replaced him/it' 'of replacing' 'sweet/sweetened him/it'.

Most of these words which seem different due to translation into English are actually from one root word: the OT 'Gentile', OT 'Greece/Grecian' and NT 'Achaia' are all the same root word (g͟hy/غي) 'deceit/folly/mislead/deceive' and ('y/عي) 'howl/teach and remember/warn/contain'.

All the five words (NT Gentile, OT Gentile, OT Greece/Greek, NT Greece/Greek, NT Achaia) have the meaning of deceiving, misleading, downfall, folly and similar meanings. And this is mostly what they have been used for in the OT and NT, but of course they also reflect their individual meanings where you can see it in relation to the story being told in addition to the meaning of being misled/deceived. The NT Greece/Greek (hellenes) has mostly been used to depict something or someone undergoing, or needing, or no longer needing a purification process to become clean, but also its other meanings (where relevant) can be seen when read in its context.

When you look at how these words have been translated to a foreign translator and audience (as well as how modern scholars continue with this mistranslation into misinterpretations) you can see where in ancient history issues or difficulties of making a foreign translator understand the nuances of the original language 'Hebrew'/Arabic have led to the same single word being used to mean specific different things, e.g. look at the NT '**Gentile**' (ethne) which has been translated to mean 'Gentile/foreigner' 'nation(s)' 'people' 'heathen'; and OT '**Gentile**' (goy/gowy) which has been translated to mean 'Gentile/foreigner' 'nation(s)' 'heathen'. Also NT '**Greek**' which has been translated to mean 'Greek' 'Gentile/foreigner'. If read correctly with the correct translations provided in this book, you can see it was not meant as 'Greece/Greek', 'people/nations' but a pun that these people/characters are being misled, being led on a folly to their own downfall, that these characters (possibly both protagonists and antagonists, or maybe the 'gentile/greek' by the protagonist depending on the narration) are being described as nothing but idol worshippers being misled and deceived and it is a pun and enhancement to the relevant story being told respectively. It has nothing to do with what prefix/suffix and form the compound word is presented in to give it different meanings as the same form of the word (whether in a specific tense or with prefix/suffix) have all been used and mistranslated as 'Gentile' 'Greek' 'nation' 'people' 'heathen' so it is not a matter of the form the word is presented in gives it those mistranslated meanings.

And these words all being Arabic, shows the whole language of the Bible, its stories in origin, are Arabic. The OT is in Arabic. The NT stories were not originally in Koine Greek. You can see the strong Arabic root words have influenced the language of the Greek people and what is called Koine Greek in the Bible as the names are Arabic compound words just like the OT. This is further supported by the fact that what the Romans would call the Greek 'graeci' is also an Arabic word with the same meanings as those used above, and scholars seem to be baffled by the origins of the word (graeci/graekoi) whereas it is an Arabic word used in daily life: graeci, graekoi; غرَيكي ، غرَيكوي 'deceived you/seduced/tempted you' 'of deceiving/deceit' 'of tempting/temptation/of seducing/seduction' 'tricked/misled you' 'tricked/misled you to downfall' 'of tricking/misleading' 'of misleading/tricking to downfall'; عرَيكي ، عرَيكوي 'stripped you naked' 'of stripping naked' 'exposed you' 'of exposing you'. Just like the meanings of Greece/Greek; Hellás, Helláda, hellēn (see Greece/Greek), and with similar meanings to the other words mentioned above and used for NT and OT 'Gentile', NT 'Achaia', OT 'Greece/Grecian'. This shows how far back the Arabic language has influenced the naming of civilisations, and the language of those civilisations.

Also important, although the words of 'Greek/Grecian/Gentile' (yāwān, yĕwān, gôwy) as in the OT which mean deceiving, misleading, howling, etc. (see above) have not been used as words in the NT i.e. they are not transliterated into the OT-used words in the NT text, it does seem these were originally used and are at least still implied which would be understood and connected by a local audience of these stories, but dropped when translated into a foreign language; their meanings are always present wherever the alternative words with the same/similar meanings as above appear in the NT.

To avoid repetition, some further examples of 'Greek/Gentile' will be used and explained when showing examples of the meanings and use of the word 'jew', after its explanation under the chapter 'Jew'. Below is a list of some examples where these five words appear in the NT, along with their transliterations and wrong translations/misinterpretations. The list of the word ('goy' and its variants) 'Gentile/heathen' in the OT is only a few examples.

ethnōn—of the Gentiles (Matt.4:15; 10:5; 20:25; Luke.21:24, 25; Acts.14:5; 15:3; 21:11; Rom.3:29; 11:12, 13, 25; 15:16; 16:4; 1Tim.2:7; 2Tim.1:11; 1Pet.4:3);

ethnōn—Gentiles/the Gentiles (Mark.10:42; Luke.2:32; 21:24; Acts.7:45, 9:15; 13:47; 14:2; 15:14, 19, 23; 21:25; 26:17; Rom.9:24; 15:12, 18; Gal.2:12, 15; Eph.3:1; 3John.1:7);

ethnōn—of nations (Luke.21:25)

ethnōn—the heathen (2Cor.11:26)

ethnē—Gentiles (Matt.6:32; Acts.10:45; 11:1; 13:42, 46, 48; Acts.15:7, 17; 18:6; 21:21; Rom.15:9, 11, 16, 27; 1Cor.10:20; 12:2; Gal.2:8, 14; 3:14; Eph.2:11; 3:6; 4:17; 1Thes.4:5; 2Tim.4:17)

ethnē—the Gentiles (Matt.12:21; Acts.22:21; Rom.2:14; 9:30; 15:12)

ethnē—ye Gentiles (Rom.15:10)

ethnē—nations/nation (Luke.21:24; Gal.3:8)

ethnē—the heathen/heathen (Acts.4:25; Gal.2:9; 3:8)

ethnesin—Gentiles/to Gentiles (Matt.10:18; 12:18; Rom.2:24; 11:13; Gal.2:2; Col.1:27);
ethnesin—the Gentiles (Acts.4:27; Rom.15:9; 1Tim.3:16)
ethnesin—<u>to</u> the <u>Gentiles</u> (Matt.20:19; Mark.10:33; Acts.11:18; 26:20, 23; 1Thes.2:16);
ethnesin—<u>unto</u> the <u>Gentiles</u> (Luke.18:32; Acts.14:27; 28:28; Rom.11:11; Rev.11:2)
ethnesin—(among?) Gentiles (Acts.15:12; 21:19; Rom.1:13; 1Cor.5:1; Eph.3:8; 1Pet.2:12)
ethnesin—the heathen (Gal.1:16)

ethnikōs—after the manner of the Gentiles (Gal.2:14)
ethnei—to a nation (Matt.21:43); in Revelations most of the variations of ethne—of nations
ethnos—people (Acts.8:9)

hellás, helláda—Greece (Acts.20:2)

hellēnís—was a Greek (Mark.7:26)
hellēnistí—Greek (John.19:20; Acts.21:37)
hellēnistōn—Grecians (Acts.6:1)
hellēnistas—Grecians (Acts.11:20)
hellēnikóis—of Greek (Luke.23:38)
hellēnikē—Greek tongue (Rev.9:11)
hellēnidōn—were Greeks (Acts.17:12)

hellēnōn—Gentile (John.7:35)
hellēnōn—Greeks (Acts.17:4)
hellēnón—of the Greeks (Acts.14:1)
hellēnas—Gentile (John.7:35; Rom.3:9)
hellēnas—Greeks (Acts.18:4; 19:10; 21:28)

hellēnes—Greeks/Greek (John.12:20; Acts.18:17; 1Cor.1:22)
hellēnes—Gentiles (1Cor.12:13)
hellēn—a Greek/Greek (Acts.16:3; Gal.2:3; 3:28; Col.3:11)

hellēni—to the Greek (Rom.1:16)
hellēni—Gentile (Rom.2:10)
hellēnos—Gentile (Rom.2:9)
hellēnos—the Greek (Acts.16:1; Rom.10:12)

hellēsin—Greeks (Acts.19:17; 1Cor.1:23, 24)
hellēsin—to the Greeks (Acts.20:21; Rom.1:14)
hellēsin—Gentile (1Cor.10:32)

achaΐas—of Achaia (Acts.18:12; Rom.16:5; 1Cor.16:15; 2Cor.11:10)
achaΐan—Achaia (Acts.18:27; 19:21)
achaΐa—Achaia (Rom.15:26; 2Cor.1:1; 9:2; 1Thes.1:7, 8)

haggoyim—of the Gentiles (Gen.10:5)
bēgôyēhem—in their nations (Gen.10:32)
haggôyîm—were the nations (Gen.10:32)

haggôyîm—of the Gentiles (Judge.4:16)

baggôyîm—among the heathen (Deut.4:27)

haggôyîm—the heathen (Lev.25:44)

baggôyîm—among the Gentiles (Mal.1:11)

baggôyîm—among the heathen (Mal.1:11)

All these Arabic words used in wordplay in the Biblical stories and in real life to name the countries such as Greece, Rome, etc. show that Arabic people and culture have influenced the West in ancient history, in language, in religion, in folklore, among other influences. Unfortunately, western bias or genuine misunderstanding and mistakes has made the west believe 'Hellás' 'graeci, graekoi', which are pure Arabic words, to be from the West even if the West have no idea what these words mean i.e. these words have no origin and beginning and no original meaning in the western languages because they did not originate from the West, and the misunderstanding leads to a corruption of history where it is believed the west influenced the Mediterranean when it is the Arab civilisations who have influenced the west with everything ascribed to 'Hellas' and 'Graekoi'.

This does not negate that the Mediterranean, due to its geographical location, has been influenced by both Arab and Western civilisations, that is how the world works. But in a one-world which has been hypothetically divided by the West into a 'West' and 'East' or more contentiously by civilisations based on religions, the West wants to take everything good and great and claim it as its influence, which the language of the Bible, and even the language and naming of these countries which are geographically part of Europe in modernity, proves they began as Arab civilisations, and/or were heavily influenced and populated by Arab civilisations (look at the Greek people physical features, their culture, their cuisine, their language, and their mythology which is based on Arab words and the same wordplay method of the Biblical authors).

It is the Arabic language which has given Greece its name, and other areas—not the West. Despite ancient and modern foreign occupation, large parts of Yemen were always isolated from outside contact, and the more rural areas remained that way into modernity and into the 2000s; the more it was left isolated, untouched and uninfluenced by foreign contact and conquest, its ancestral language and ways would remain purer; the remote mountains of Yemen would remain that way into recent history. It is this ancestral Arabic language unchanged and continuously spoken to this day by Yemenis (and in general the Arabic language all over the Middle East) whose vocabulary is the language, the words and their meanings as they stand, of the fictional stories of the Bible, Greek mythology, and what the West has misunderstood as parts of 'history' (e.g. Alexander the Great, Cleopatra, Julius Caesar, to name a few which are actually fictional characters in stories and folklore which language proves).

Anyone can refer to the translations provided in this book which are the correct meanings and use of these words, and compare to where their English translations are in the Bible and see how many suitable meanings are actually meant by the correct translations provided, and how these words are connected together by the narration of the respective story and per the intentions of the Biblical authors who were masters of wordplay.

Jew

Misinformation, genuine error, or desperation for modern political/religious agendas to be fulfilled have led to explanations of the word 'Jew', used to describe those of the Jewish faith, as stemming from the 'kingdom of Judah'. Another factor which leads to the misinterpretations about the word 'Jew' is based on another misinterpretation of the word and meaning of 'Hebrew', and the language of the Bible described as 'Hebrew' when it is an Arabic word with meanings, and the language of the Bible being Arabic and not a separate language but Arabic still used by the region and countries it originated from and especially in unadulterated form by the specific region whose ways of life and language have remained unchanged due to their remoteness from urban life and resistance/stubbornness towards change and modernisation (along with other factors affecting the specific country as a whole). This misdirection and mistakes have left those who are from the western world interpreting what is believed to be 'Hebrew' according to what Classical Arabic and Modern Arabic meanings hold for these words (which may differ in entirety or many meanings from the Old Arabic of the region, with Old Arabic being the language of the Bible, both OT and NT); and where Classical/Modern Arabic do not provide meaning, scholars and interpreters get the meanings terribly wrong or leave them as of 'unknown origin'.

As earlier in this book 'Judah' has been proven not to be 'yehuda/Jew' but (yud'aa/yud'ah يُدعى/ يُدعه) 'he is called/calls' (see Judah (Gen.29:35) for more of its meanings) and specifically meant in Gen.29:35 to praise/call God as all Jacob's sons were given a story to their conception and birth connecting the name directly to the narration, and Judah's was Leah saying 'Now will I praise the Lord: therefore she called his name Judah' (Gen.29:35).

So where did the word 'Jew' come from and how did it become a noun describing the people of the Jewish faith? The answer—it is an Arab word which has very specific meanings and used in daily language of which the proof is within the Bible itself. It is due to scholars and earlier interpreters of the Bible not being familiar with this Arabic word and its meaning, who have attempted to force 'Jew' onto the word and meaning of 'Judah' which has absolutely nothing to do with the word 'Jew' or 'Jewish' as in meaning of the word, and has nothing to do with why it was applied to those of the Jewish faith.

The true meanings of the word 'Jew' also hold the key as to why such an unfair negative attribute was attached to it and the followers of the Jewish religion. This negative attribute was not used as discrimination by the Arabs who applied it to themselves and the religion, and were Jews themselves. But when the Jewish religion along with the Arab people who practised it would cross the world, and live in greater numbers among the white western world, there had to have been its meanings, or the spirit/gist of the meaning of the word, innocently and honestly communicated to the white western world (through the Bible translation, interpretations, teachings, studies, co-existence), and coupled with the western world's feelings of white and western superiority, i.e. racism, the meaning (which was just a word applied to the religion because of its word-meaning and as emphasised in the Biblical stories) and the fictional conduct of the characters in the Bible would be used in antisemitic attributes against the people who practised the Jewish religion, and antisemitic tropes (along with the already existing antisemitism which burgeoned in the western world) arose towards Jews who were Arabs by race and Jewish in religion and who had lived for centuries in Europe, and eventually this antisemitism would also be directed at the white western Jews who were natives of Europe and whose ancestors had always lived in Europe but had converted to the Jewish religion which the Arab Jews had brought to the continent. It must be stressed that the meaning of the word 'jew' and the Biblical stories are not the reason behind antisemitism, discrimination already existed towards non-white people whether they had lived for centuries in Europe or eventually towards the local people in their respective native countries where European colonialism reached, but the generalised discriminatory attributes against Jews known as antisemitism (e.g. greed, deceit, dishonesty, fuelled by the meanings of the word 'jew' and the Biblical stories) became part of the racism which unfortunately exists and would have existed even without the essence of the Biblical stories and without knowing its use of the word-meaning 'jew'.

Jew; yĕhûḏî, yĕhûḏâ; يَهودي ، ييهودي ، يَهودا/يَهوده ، ييهودا/ييهوده 'he/they disfigures/distorts/makes ugly/changes for or to the worse' 'of disfiguring/distorting/making ugly/changing for or to the worse' 'spiteful/provoking/stubborn/not forthright' 'made/became ugly' 'is asymmetrical/sides or shape uneven' and is from the word (hwd/هود). Cp: yehoodee, yeihoodee, yehooda, yehoodah, yeihooda, yeihoodah. It is used to describe physically disfiguring the appearance of a person, a building, disfiguring anything. It is applied to distorting words, statements, facts, events. It is used to describe ruining things, situations, or people, i.e. taking them from a certain (better) state/situation and rendering them/it worse. It implies intentionally or unintentionally distorting, disfiguring, becoming or making something worse.

Some examples of its use in everyday language: if someone is ugly, they will say 'so and so is hweeda/هويدا/ugly/disfigured'; if a person was handsome/beautiful as a child then grew up and looked physically not as good as expected (according to the commentator's opinion), they say 'thwwd/تهوّد' 'he has been disfigured/became ugly'. If someone gives a child (or adult) a bad haircut, they will say 'hwwdt bh/هوّدت به' 'you ruined/disfigured him'. When makeup was unknown in my region (and deemed sinful according to older women) and I made-up my sister-in-law, her mother became angry and reproached her for allowing me to 'howwdteeha/هَوّدتِّيها/you made her ugly/disfigured' and she told her 'hwwdt bk/هوّدت بك/she disfigured you/made you ugly'. If someone or something's appearance takes on a bizarre or unkempt look, or is physically asymmetrical in proportions, they say 'mahaawad/مَهاود/is disfigured/of asymmetrical proportions'. When someone is twisting his or her words, or 'beating around the bush', or being deviously dishonest they say 'yihaawid(masculine)/tihaawid(feminine)' which means they are playing with words, statements; not being honest; are changing words and statements and/or taking them out of context; the same if purposely being provocative, spiteful, 'digging heels in' or stubborn.

This is the meaning of the word 'jew' in its original use by people unaffected by religion (and specifically unaffected by the newer religions: Jewish religion, Christianity and Islam) who use the word among themselves; they are not in any way aware of its connection to Jews, Islam; to them it is just a mundane word and its meanings as they use it in daily life with no ethnic, racial, religious, nor racist attributes or connotations, just as all the words in their Arabic language which have been used in the Biblical stories.

In a wider regional context the noun 'Jew/يهودي/Jews/يهود' is still the same Arabic word and was applied to describing those of a certain faith, who everyone including those of the same (Jewish) faith believed were distorting facts, events, religion—and this was not, and is not, 'antisemitism'; it is better to remain objective and understand this word and term as how it was used millennia ago as an ordinary word like every other word in language, and to understand the people who were first called Jews were no different in ethnicity and race than those of different faiths such as paganism (and eventually Christianity and Islam when these religions would emerge) in its different forms; and it was used among those of the same faith itself to describe what they saw of parts of the community or even just priests changing and distorting God's commandments which came down on Moses to suit either what they wanted the religion to be, or for personal gain (take for example the Sicarri story/events and why the Sicarri were angry with the priests' religious beliefs and conduct). The Old Testament and New Testament itself bears testimony to the meaning of this word and shows why this noun was eventually applied to 'Jews'. The word 'jew' is a verb, adjective, adverb whose correct meanings is used throughout the OT and NT and is evident in the actions and storylines, and shows how this word ended up as a noun used/applied to certain individuals, and eventually to a certain faith.

It is important to note that Moses and Abraham's religion was never described as 'Jewish', and these two characters, as well as other major Biblical characters, were not described as 'Jews' in their stories. Throughout the majority of the OT it was never used to describe their religion or people, in fact, the earliest regular mention of the word 'Jew' begins with Ezra.4 and appears before that at 2Kgs.16:6 and 2Kgs.18 where it was used as a word-name for its meaning to depict/relay the events happening in the story being told which were a distortion/ruining of the norm/life happening or threatening to happen to the characters. Also important to note, when the narration at Ezra.4 introduces a group of people as being Jews, it is done through having their enemies describe them as Jews: 'Now when the adversaries of Benjamin and Judah heard…Shimshai the scribe wrote a letter…Be it known unto the king, that the Jews which came up from thee to us are come unto Jerusalem…' and the letter goes on to describe how the Jews will ruin and go against the king's laws and interests, reflecting the meanings of 'disfigures/distorts/makes ugly/changes for the worse' and the story goes on to depict that it is confirmed that it is true they do cause and have caused in the past 'insurrection against kings, and rebellion and sedition have been made therein.'.

Throughout the OT the stories reflect the meanings of the word 'jew' 'he/they disfigures/distorts/makes ugly/ruins/changes for or to the worse' 'of provoking' and its other meanings as mentioned above, and although the religion and its prophets and kings (and other characters) are not called 'Jews/Jewish' the word is reflected and relayed in their actions, and in the narration of the people in the story who are the protagonists and antagonist characters in the story. The Bible makes it abundantly clear the followers of Moses all the way through to the arrival of Jesus and after his death, commit acts of the word 'jew/jewish' 'he/they disfigures/distorts/makes ugly/changes for or to the worse' 'spiteful/provoking/stubborn/not forthright' as in the meaning of the word in Old Arabic (but this meaning should be disassociated in the modern use of the word when describing the people of the Jewish faith in current times, as now it simply represents people of the Jewish faith even though it is still the meaning of the word which came to be the name of the religion and its followers in antiquity).

The meaning of the word 'jew/jewish' is present and reflected in the Biblical stories from the creation of the earth and introducing man who does nothing but make things worse for himself, for God and for others; from Adam and Eve ruining their immortality and pain-free life in Eden to be punished with life on earth; God finding Cain's offering unpleasant; Cain disfiguring life by killing Abel; wars and death between different kings and nations; disobeying Moses; disobeying God; perverting/straying out of religion; introducing things not part of God's commandments; changing the meanings of God's commandments/religion to make personal gains; ruining God's plan/promises of a much better state he had planned for them resulting in punishing them with a worse state of being and affairs; God changing his promise to the people.

Staying within the region and the people who created the Biblical stories and among whom the Jewish religion first emerged: prior to Islam (as can be seen in the OT texts) and in Islam, both the OT and Quran and other religious texts claim the Torah/OT and later on the Christian Bible/NT did exist in an original and unaltered form, but that after Moses' death the priests and maybe other important figures in charge of religious texts first became possessive of these written texts not allowing access to all then they changed the OT and the NT by adding and removing parts, and continued to do so until the Torah, NT and other holy scriptures, believed to be sent down by God, no longer existed in their original forms—and these completely altered forms are those of the Bible (OT and NT) which exist today. This is supported by modern academic conclusions (which have existed for decades and continue to this day) that the Biblical stories (both OT and NT) have been subject to revisions, redactions. Therefore, the OT and NT have many authors from different times working on the same one piece of the Bible that the original Bible version no longer exists due to the changes made by different authors who removed, added, changed the Bible to suit whatever reasons they had back then for making these changes—and this is the meaning of the word 'jew/يهو د/distorts/ruins/changes to worse'.

Whether the people of the region got it right—as they have since they are the one and same people who produced the OT and the NT stories and carried these religions within their countries and outwards to the rest of the world—and their beliefs which have been recorded as history and in religion that the Bible has been corrupted and changed completely as supported by modern findings, or whether they only got it partially right: e.g. if they are wrong about the Torah and the Christian Bible(Ingeel) originally being God's words e.g. if they are wrong because it did not come from God and these stories were written as fictional accounts from the beginning (which my translations show as the greatest possibility), they are still right in their claims that these stories have been corrupted and edited out of recognition from their original and unaltered state into what they are today.

If we look at the content of the Bible/OT, i.e. the stories it contains, these stories also tell the same meaning of the word 'jew'. Not only do all stories tell of some kind of 'he/they disfigures/distorts/makes ugly/ruins/changes for or to the worse' 'spiteful/provoking/stubborn/not forthright', but it is also the characters of the generalised 'children of Israel' en masse or named individual characters who (in the story) disobey God, change religion to suit their personal wants, 'but ye have not obeyed my voice, why have ye done this?' 'And the children of Israel again did evil in the sight of the Lord,' are just a few examples of sentences repeated throughout the Torah/Bible, and these authors who are originally writing, and/or rewriting, redacting, changing the OT, they are all of one Arab race as are the characters whom they write about, as are the inhabitants and compatriots of the whole Arab region. Although the majority of the authors attempt to make people (the real audience of the stories) of that group feel hope, feel less despair by casting them in the stories as a different people/ethnicity—as *special*, to lift morale—they too depict the characters/ancestors as people who disobey, ruin and pervert religion and laws. Not only are the mass of 'children of Israel' presented as so, but even the heroes, the greatest/most important prophets and king characters keep disobeying, distorting and changing things to suit such as David, Solomon, and Saul and the list is very long (see Kings and Chronicles). The meaning of the word 'jew' has been used and can be seen as the theme in most stories of the OT and NT.

In Exodus, the story tells how the children of Israel are provoking God and his prophets by complaining and wishing they had stayed in Egypt because life was better in Egypt; they go against God's instructions and go out looking for manna on the Sabbath and God asks outright how long they will continue to break his laws; they continue to complain and cause trouble for Moses. They corrupt and distort God's religion and laws, and they are constantly provoking, stubborn and set on mischief: they demand Aaron create a god for them to worship and they engage in idol worship; Aaron has distorted because he went along with creating the gold statue; after Moses witnesses the corruption of the children of Israel he destroys the molten calf they worshipped: God tells Moses 'Go, get thee down; for thy people which thou broughtest out of the land of Egypt, have corrupted themselves'. Moses says to Aaron '...that thou hast brought so great a sin upon them? And Aaron said, Let not the anger of my Lord wax hot: thou knowest the people, that they *are set* on mischief.'.

They are repeatedly called by God and Moses 'a stiffnecked people' they refuse to enter the land which God instructs them to and he decides he has to ruin them with punishment (again—this is not the first time, and in the stories, they are repeatedly disfigured with punishment, mostly horrific punishment). When they complain about the food they used to eat in Egypt, and wish they were still in Egypt as life was better there with a variety of good food which they list, although the story mentions they were enslaved, they would prefer to be in Egypt than eat manna from heaven in freedom, i.e. the people would prefer to live in a worse situation—from the story, Moses and God's point of view. When God complies with their request for meat, it is done spitefully and in a way which makes them unwell, the descriptions of greediness and how God finds the way they eat disgusting and this is because they have 'despised the Lord' and wished to be back in Egypt which causes God to kill many people, and all this also reflects the meanings of the word 'jew'. (see Exod.16; 17; 32-34; Num.11)

The people wish again that they had died in Egypt, that they had died in the wilderness despite God promising them a better life in a different land; they believe Moses and God have misled them to be killed in battle, and that they ruined the life people had back in Egypt and decide to return to Egypt. So they continue to be stubborn and provoke God, his commandments and prophets—God answers their demands, more often than not he punishes them with gruesome deaths and still they go back to provoking and digging in their heels—again the meaning of the word 'jew' to provoke, be stubborn, disobedient, play with words to go around about a subject, and to make things from a good state to a bad or lesser state. When Joshua and Caleb attempt to convince them to do as ordered, the congregation's reaction is to call everyone to stone those two to death. God engages in a repeated and frustrated conversation with Moses about the people's disobedience and asks how long will it be before they believe him as he has already provided them with signs/miracles which should cause them to be obedient, and God has reached a degree he now wants to punish them and disown them which both the punishments show 'distortion/corruption' and changing something to the worse 'I will smite them with the pestilence, and disinherit them, and will make of thee a greater nation and mightier than they.'

Although God forgives them, he has had enough to the degree he will distort his promise due to the corruption and distortion, the ruining of what God had in mind for them, so the promise he makes is also changed for the worse 'And the Lord said, I have pardoned according to thy word: But *as* truly *as* I live, all the earth shall be filled with the glory of the Lord. Because all those men which have seen my glory, and my miracles, which I did in Egypt and in the wilderness, and have tempted me now these ten times, and have not hearkened to my voice; Surely they shall not see the land which I sware unto their fathers, neither shall any of them that provoked me see it.'

'And the Lord spake unto Moses and unto Aaron saying, How long *shall I bear with* this evil congregation, which murmur against me!' and the story goes on to detail God's punishment to the children of Israel for provoking him, being disobedient and that he will ruin them with a difficult wandering life and death in the wilderness. The people who are sent to spy on the land they intend to invade return and scare the people from entering into the land instead of encouraging them to invade it, and the people who bring the bad report about the new land are killed with the plague for punishment. Instead of learning to obey God, they insist to go up and into the land to battle with the other people when they are told not do so, but Moses tells them they are continuing to disobey God and that they should not go up there now as God is not with them, but they ignore his warnings, and follow disobedience with more disobedience and are killed.

When Korah and others challenge that Moses and Aaron (and Aaron's sons) alone should minister to God, while everybody (according to their dialogue in the story) is equally holy and entitled to be priests and to serve God, it is presented as more disobedience (instead of love and devotion to serve God) against Moses and God; they refuse to obey Moses, and although the rebellious people are against Moses and Aaron, they are enthusiastic about serving God, but because (according to the story) their disobedience is perverting God's commandments not only will they be killed, but in a spectacular way. The story emphasises on Moses making a point that their deaths will be in a very ugly and bad fashion for the corruption they have engaged in and it shows this is to teach the other people in the congregation not to pervert God's commandments. The story narrates all the families related to Korah, along with houses and goods are buried alive—and just in case this disfiguration of life is not ugly and severe enough, the story also has the two-hundred-fifty men which Moses suggested should offer incense to God, be burned from a fire that comes out of God.

So although the majority of the Torah/OT does not refer to the people of the stories as 'Jews' it is easy to see how and why the word 'jew' came to be used to describe those of the faith who believed these stories to be religious text—of which all the stories hold the meaning of the word 'jew/يهود/yehud/yehowid(yhwd)' from disobedience, stubbornness, provocation, changing or corruption of laws and religion (God's commandments), making situations worse, making things disfigured/wrong. Add to this that the real people of the times (the times these stories were popular in their original form and when these stories were being changed to suit the editors/authors) know these stories are being changed and rewritten and retold with differences, and much later when these stories would be considered religious texts the people would know that the texts and religious laws were being changed at the hands of the priests and people in charge of these texts.

It is not only Moses' antagonists who show disobedience and corruption of ways which mean the word 'jew/yehud/yhwd/يهود', but Moses too. When he strikes the rock instead of speaking to it in front of the congregation as God had instructed him to, the story shows this is perverting God's instruction which God points out to Moses and this causes Moses (or God) to ruin his own and Aaron's situation where they would have entered and lived in the land but are now forbidden from doing so and will die without entering it.

The people continue to show the perversion and corruption, ruining a situation, receiving ugly punishment for their provocations: complaining about food and water, claiming to have been deceived and wishing to be back in Egypt, the 'fiery serpents' which fatally bite them, mixing with the women in Moab, worshipping other gods, being ordered to kill the people and make the dead face the sun, the punishment of wandering in the wilderness for forty years instead of entering a land that flows milk and honey. (Num.11; 14:1-12, 20-23, 26-37, 39-44; 16; 17:10; 20:1-13; 21:5-7; 25:1-5; 32:7-11, 13-15).

In the other stories which are organised before Numbers in the English Bible, these books tell many stories of characters who conduct themselves, business and relationships all with the meaning of the word 'jew/yehud/yhwd/يهود' and the audience of those times (whether hearing the stories told orally which is how they were disseminated originally, or in later times read) the audiences would have applied the word 'jew/yehud/yhwd' ('disfigures/distorts/makes ugly/changes for the worse/unkempt/deceitful/dishonest/plays with words/takes things out of context/provoking/stubborn/playing with words and statements') to the actions of the characters of these stories: e.g. both Laban and Jacob are dishonest with each other although they are family and work together: Laban tricks Jacob into marrying Leah, making him work extra years to marry Rachel. Jacob uses deceitful actions and wordplay to deceive Laban out of most of his livestock and out of the best of his livestock. Rebekah and Jacob deceive both Isaac and Esau in order Jacob receive Esau's birth right and blessing. Sara forces Abraham to abandon Hagar and Ishmael in the wilderness. Rachel steals her father's idols, then lies about menstruating to prevent him searching underneath her for the idols. Jacob's sons use deceit to trick Shechem the prince of the country they arrive to live in, and are welcomed in, just so that they can kill him and all the males, although according to the story itself the host country treated them well and with honesty. Joseph's brothers use deceit and corrupt the truth in the respective story; Potiphar's wife uses corruption of the truth and deceit to have Joseph imprisoned.

Any local audience of these stories would see the open narration of dishonesty and deceit in how the characters behave (both the antagonists and protagonists) and deal with each other—these audiences who are the same ethnicity even if their religions differed (which they most probably did) would see this deceit, the corruption, actions and characteristics of the characters in the stories which would lead to the word 'jew' being used to describe the behaviour in the stories, and this was long before these stories would become a religion called 'Jewish'.

'Now therefore hearken, O Israel, unto the statutes and unto the judgements, which I teach you...Ye shall not add unto the word which I command you, neither shall ye diminish ought from it, that ye may keep the commandments of the Lord your God which I commanded you.' But in Matthew and Mark, the authors have Jesus claim they have strayed from God's commandments and ways, creating laws and rules to suit the priests' benefit (and those in charge); the same is mentioned in Jer.7 that the priests and authors of Biblical texts have added lies about the temple (which should read 'hekal/he will eat' and is not a temple at all) and about sacrificing and piling food to God and the narration makes it clear that God did not mention a 'temple/hekal/he will eat' nor did he ask Moses and the ancestors to perform sacrifices and offer food to him (God). (Deut.1; 3:23-26; 4:1-2, 23-27; 9:12-14, 22-24; Matt.; Mark)

'And the children of Israel did evil in the sight of the Lord' is a sentence repeat in many chapters of Judges appearing at the very beginning or first few lines of the chapters. Similar phrases are used in Kings and Chronicles.

Although he is the best king of Israel, according to the stories, even Solomon strays from and corrupts God's ways when he introduces and adds pagan worship to his own God's worship. He builds 'high places' for other gods and burns incense, makes sacrifices and offerings to them. Most of the kings who follow in 1 and 2 Kings are described as walking in the sins of their fathers (corrupt), or doing evil; some worship God, but still do evil and pervert his ways. The few who do follow the way of God, do not get rid of pagan worship in the land and therefore are punished for it. From after David, the kings are described as being completely sinful, corrupt or even pious but corrupted in other varying and similar ways. David himself was a character who was a master in corrupting, in playing with words and deceiving, ruining a good situation for others for his own benefit, sometimes leading to his own detriment; he did not mind disfiguring people with death even if they were his own soldiers, nor did he mind perverting and corrupting God's ways if he could get something out of it.

How the word 'jew' itself is used as a word and wordplay to denote what happens in the related stories is like all the other compound word-names used in the Biblical stories and the evidence is abundant.

When the word 'jew' is used at 2Kgs.16:6 '...Rezin king of Syria...drave the Jews from Elath...' it relays with the narration which shows a ruining and deterioration of the people's situation who are being forced to move, and it is placed in between the acts of King Ahaz who distorts God's religion. Ahaz also corrupts and disfigures the design of God's house and its things by having a new altar designed, by moving things around and although he offers and makes sacrifices to God this is still wrong and corrupting God's instructions which is why the authors have his first acts of distortion of great severity in that he makes his children 'walk through the fire'; he continues to make ugly the things in or outside God's house by cutting them up, rearranging their location, not to mention taking the silver and gold from God's house and sending it as a gift to the Assyrian king.

When the word 'jew' is mentioned at 2Kgs.18 it is when Rab-shakeh is asked not to speak 'in the Jews' language' but he continues to do so. The word is reflected in that the protagonists feel Rab-shakeh's words will distort trust in the king and in God as they can understand what he is saying because he speaks in their language; when the protagonists ask him not to speak in the language 'jew' is relayed in the narration as Rab-shakeh makes it clear he has come to make the people understand that if they do not obey the Ayssrian king that their lives and situation will be ruined, he warns that trusting Hezekiah and Hezekiah's God will cause their ruination; Rab-shakeh lists the countries the Assyrians have ruined and whose people they have destroyed.

As mentioned before, the first regular use of the word 'Jew' in the OT stories begins in Ezra, and by characters termed as the enemies of Judah and Benjamin—and it is notable that these enemy characters worship the same God and are of the same faith of the returned exiles, i.e. they follow the same religion/God's commandments and want to participate in the rebuilding project and the authors have them state they have always sacrificed and worshipped God (the correct God of the stories). What this OT story shows is that long before 'Jew' became the noun of the religion, it may have been used first as a 'nickname' by people living in the same area (same race/ethnicity) whether these people were of the same religion of those they called 'Jews' and of other religions; they chose to describe the people they felt were changing and corrupting religion with the word which is a literal meaning of these actions. When these stories were created and first circulated, there was no Jewish religion, but when the religion emerged—the people of the Jewish faith were not called 'Jews'.

The word 'jew' with its negative meanings is highly unlikely to have been used by those who were being called 'jews' to describe themselves or their religion, and may at first have been used to describe the actions of disobedience in the content of the stories, the rewriting/distorting religious texts (e.g.), and then to describe groups of people or specific individuals who conducted these activities. Through suitability of its word-meaning and popularity of its use (the word 'jew') and the popularity and content of the fictional stories which were known to be corrupted and changed now considered as religious texts by those who followed the religion, it would eventually define the name of the religion—but it is very clear throughout the strongest and majority of the OT and the lengthy periods it claims to have covered, the people following the religion of Abraham, Isaac, Jacob, Moses and David were never called 'Jews', nor the religion 'Jewish' or even 'Judaism' ('Judaism' being a completely different word and meaning than 'Jew(ish)'and only applied by wishful thinking and errors of mistranslation and misinterpretation).

The letter written by the 'adversaries of Judah and Benjamin', the whole passage beginning with enemies of those describing the people returning from exiles as 'jews/yehud/yhwd/يهود' and these people described as 'Jews' have had attributed to them that they are provoking, rebellious, disobedient, that they will ruin the king's revenue, that they will change things to the worse—all these actions are said 'will' happen because these very people have done it before and these negative actions recorded in the king's records. As the story goes, the king finds these acts are registered against Judah and Benjamin therefore the description is accurate (within the fictional story), making the adjective and verb 'Jews' which is the word for 'disfigures/distorts/changes things to the worse/provokes/etc.' reflected in their actions in the story.

And as explained earlier under the meaning of the word 'jew', it also means to twist ones words, beat around the bush, be mystic/opaque, dishonest, purposely provoking and/or stubborn, saying things without giving a real or clear answer; and this is also reflected in the story and can be seen in the actions given to the characters called 'Jews' in the story (no different than all the compound word-names which reflect the role/part in the stories): when others try to prevent the returned exiles from building, they do it by sending a letter, this time to Darius, 'Then said we unto them after this manner, What are the names of the men that make this building? But the eye of their God was upon the elders of the Jews, that they could not cause them to cease, till the matter came to Darius: Then asked we those elders, and said unto them thus, Who commanded you to build this house, and to make up these walls? We asked their names also, to certify thee, that we might write the names of the men that *were* the chief of them. And thus they returned us answer, saying, We are the servants of the God of heaven and earth, and build the house that was builded many years ago, which a great king of Israel builded and set up.' So they respond but without giving their names—another reflection of the word meaning 'jew/yehod/yhwd/يهود' as mentioned previously.

After listing all the miracles and mercy God helped the children of Israel with, saving them from affliction in Egypt, from Pharaoh, parting the sea, giving them the 'commandments, precepts, statutes and laws', satisfying their hunger with bread from heaven, quenching their thirst by providing water out of rocks—it goes on to narrate the children of Israel returned all God's kindnesses with: 'But they and our fathers dealt proudly, and hardened their necks, and hearkened not to thy commandments, And refused to obey, neither were mindful of thy wonders that thou didst among them; but hardened their necks, and in their rebellion appointed a captain to return their bondage…' God forgives them, then: 'Yea, when they had made them a molten calf and said, This *is* thy God that brought thee up out of Egypt, and had wrought great provocations.' It goes on to narrate God forgave them again and continued to give them food and drink in the wilderness, then gave them the land to live where they found plenty, but: 'Nevertheless they were disobedient, and rebelled against thee, and cast thy laws behind their backs, and slew thy prophets which testified against them to turn them to thee, and they wrought great provocations. Therefore thou deliveredst them into the hand of their enemies…' and the narrator goes on to tell that God had mercy and saved them again, 'But after they had rest, they did evil again before thee: therefore leftest thou them in the hand of their enemies, so that they had the dominion over them…' God has mercy and saves them again 'And testified against them, that thou mightest bring them again unto thy law: yet they dealt proudly, and hearkened not unto thy commandments, but sinned against thy judgements, (which if a man do, he shall live in them) and withdrew the shoulder, and hardened their neck, and would not hear. Yet many years didst thou forbear them, and testified against them by the spirit in thy prophets: yet they would not give ear: therefore gavest thou them into the hand of the people of the lands…Neither have our kings, our princes, our priests, nor our fathers, kept they law, nor hearkened unto thy commandments, and thy testimonies, wherewith thou didst testify against them. For they have not served thee in their kingdom, and in the great goodness that thou gavest them, and in the large and fat land which though gavest before them, neither turned they from their wicked works.'

This passage from Nehemiah also shows all the meanings of the word 'jew/yehud/yhwd' as portrayed and emphasised in the story being told, it emphasises no matter how forgiving God was, no matter how much he made and gave for their situation to be better (the children of Israel) they always returned to distorting religion, straying, disobedience, making a situation (whether it was good or difficult) worse, being provocative, stubborn and so forth. (Neh.9)

Although the narration about 'mixed' children is extremely racist as it portrays the children are a disfigurement/corruption of a 'pure seed'/pure offspring due to mixed marriages, it is important to focus on the story being told through Nehemiah's character and how it shows the meanings of 'jew': the authors are focusing on how (in the story) the children of Israel are distorting, changing the religion (according to the story), making a good thing bad, ruining a situation thus being disobedient per the word 'jew/yehud/yhwd/يهود'. The disobedience, distortion and ruination of a good thing here is the warning and commandment not to mix with the Moabites and Ammonites, to observe the Sabbath, to provide tithes to the priests—which the children of Israel pervert/distort by mixing with other 'peoples', not paying tithes, working on the Sabbath. The whole story relays the word 'jew' and its clear meanings can be seen in Neh.13.

In Esther, although the word 'jew' is introduced and linked to Mordecai (because of his actions and then the actions of other characters around him) the meaning of the word is first portrayed in Vashti's action of disobeying the king and the first chapter has the theme of 'jew' meanings: Vashti provokes when she refuses to satisfy the king's request, but by seeking his counsellors' advice, things become worse between Vashti and the king which the author of Esther makes clear by having Ahasuerus still thinking about her at the beginning of Chapter 2. and regrets the decree issued against her ('changing to the worse'). Despite Mordecai's problem begins with Haman when Mordecai refuses to obey the king's commandment to bow and show reverence to Haman, the meaning of the word 'jew' which is used to describe Mordecai is because he is perverting morals by putting his cousin Esther into the sexual service of king Ahasuerus. Mordecai's names/genealogy (Jair, Shimei, Kish and Benjamite) also support that what he is doing is distorting the norms and suggest sexual and moral perversion, the perversion and distortion of his own religious and social morals. It is indicated within the story that Mordecai twisted or lied about what he heard Bigthan and Teresh say and caused their execution so he could curry favour with the king; their alleged intentions to 'lay hands on the king' are also disobedience.

Although all the other servants bow to Haman as ordered by the king, Mordecai refuses even when people around him advise him to do so, this shows he is intentionally provoking and being stubborn the meaning of the word 'jew'. The story shows there was no antagonism between the character Haman and the generalised characters called 'Jews' in Ahasuerus' kingdoms, but this is spoiled by Mordecai's intentional provocation and disobedience and open show of disrespect towards Haman which ruins the peaceful situation and puts the lives of the Jews in a terrible situation with Haman plotting and having approval to commit genocide against them, and genocide means a very ugly disfiguration of life and also reflects the meanings of the word 'jew'. So although Mordecai and Esther are the heroes of the story, note how the authors make clear the wordplay and meanings of 'jew' as a word—Haman's displeasure and evil plots against Mordecai and all Jews are attributed as stemming from Mordecai not following the accepted custom of the court, being disobedient, disrespectful and provoking; Haman's hatred does not originally stem out of Mordecai being Jewish in the sense of a person of the Jewish faith, but from the latter's actions towards him which depict the meanings of the word 'jew'.

The intentions of Haman, and Ahasuerus' support for, to kill all the Jews shows the meaning of the word 'jew' 'he/they disfigures/distorts/makes ugly/changes for or to the worse'; then when the tables are turned and non-jews are subject to several genocides by Mordecai's plotting also shows the same 'he/they disfigures/distorts/makes ugly/changes for or to the worse' as well as its meaning of 'provokes' as Haman and his plans have provoked this reaction. Haman (his wife and friends), Mordecai and Ahasuerus all plot and/or implement a great disfiguration of life (within the story), especially that in both cases when the Jews are the intended targets and the non-Jews end up being the victims, the barbaric slaughter planned and implemented is always against innocent people. Haman being the only one who was killed and deserved to be killed was not punished for plotting against the Jews, but for Ahasuerus mistaking Haman as wanting to have sex with Esther while he was begging for his life to be spared, which shows Ahasuerus' misunderstanding in itself is 'distortion'. While Haman gets what he deserves, Mordecai who is successful in causing many genocides is raised in status and glorified, and Esther expresses delight in being allowed to order more genocides which is the author of Esther's way of showing the meanings of 'he/they disfigures/distorts/makes ugly/changes for or to the worse/provokes'.

The meaning 'disfigures/makes ugly' is shown in Mordecai tearing his clothes and soiling himself with ashes and sackcloth which disfigures his appearance and hygiene in doing so (it causes Esther worry and to send him clean clothes), and this meaning of the word 'jew' is also shown in the same action done by Jews over many other provinces in the story as a sign of distress over what Haman plans to do to them. This is also expressed in Neh.9:1-2 as it is also in other books where those bereaved or in great distress, rend their clothes, put soil on the head or pull out facial hair—all acts of disfigurement (to show grief and/or distress).

Besides 'disobedience/provoking/stubbornness' being used in the storyline to enhance the meanings of the word 'jew/yehud/yhwd', so are the meanings to 'play with words/'beat around the bush'/be unclear' as does Esther's role in the story portray. First in concealing her true identity as in name and her being a Jew, and then in her ambiguous requests of Ahasuerus. The same meanings of misunderstanding, not clear or forthright when talking and also 'changing for the worse' is portrayed in Haman misunderstanding Ahasuerus wanting to reward Mordecai, believing that the king is talking about him (Haman); and this leads to Haman ruining his own situation as he suggests the best reward which elevates Mordecai above all to the king, and once this happens not only does Haman's situation become depressed but his wife mentions that this will be his downfall and all these meanings are connected to the use of the word 'jew' in wordplay.

The meaning of the word 'Pur/Purim' to ruin someone's reputation or something to go bad (see Pur/ Purim (Esth.)) also reflects the meaning of the word 'jew/yehud' because Haman used the 'Pur' to ruin the reputation of and harm not only Mordecai, but all Jews; and when the plot backfires against Haman it is his reputation and harm which occurs, as well as a good situation becoming worse for generalised masses when the genocide of the people begins. (Esther)

In Isaiah, speaking of the children of Israel in Judah and Jerusalem, although the word 'jew' is not used in this part, but the meaning of the word 'jew' is used abundantly to describe the people of Judah and Jerusalem, i.e. 'children of Israel'. It details the meaning of the word 'jew/yehud/yhwd/يهود' of disobedience, disfigurement, stubbornness, changing things from good to worse, corrupting, distorting religion/God's ways for their own personal gain and/or desires, including making up stories about sacrifices demanded and desired by God:

'The vision of Isaiah the son of Amoz, which he saw concerning Judah and Jerusalem...Hear, O heavens, and give eat, O earth: for the Lord hath spoken, I have nourished and brought up children, and they have rebelled against me. The ox knoweth his owner, and the ass his master's crib: *but* Israel doth not know, my people doth not consider. Ah sinful nation, a people laden with iniquity, a seed of evildoers, children that are corruptors: they have forsaken the Lord, they have provoked the Holy One of Israel unto anger, they are gone away backward. Why should ye be stricken anymore? ye will revolt more and more: the whole head is sick, and the whole heart faint. From the sole of the foot even unto the head *there* is no soundness in it; *but* wounds, and bruises, and putrefying sores: they have not been closed, neither bound up, neither mollified with ointment. Your country *is* desolate, your cities *are* burned with fire: your land, strangers devour it in your presence, and *it is* desolate, as overthrown by strangers...Except the Lord of hosts had left unto us a very small remnant, we should have been as Sodom, *and* we should have been like unto Gomorrah. Hear the word of the Lord, ye rulers of Sodom; give ear unto the law of our God, ye people of Gomorrah. To what purpose *is* the multitude of your sacrifices unto me? saith the Lord: I am full of burnt offerings of rams, and the fat of fed beasts; and I delight not in the blood of bullocks, or of lambs, or of he goats. When ye come to appear before me, who hath required this of your hand, to tread my courts? Bring no more vain oblations; incense is an abomination unto me; the new moons and sabbaths, the calling of assemblies, I cannot away with; *it is* iniquity, even the solemn meeting. Your new moons and your appointed feasts my soul hateth: they are a trouble unto me; I am weary to bear *them*. And when ye spread forth your hands, I will hide mine eyes from you: yea, when ye make many prayers, I will not hear: your hands are full of blood. Wash you, make you clean; put away the evil of your doings from before mine eyes; cease to do evil; learn to do well; seek judgement, relieve the oppressed, judge the fatherless, plead for the widow. Come now, and let us reason together, saith the Lord: though your sins be as scarlet, they shall be as white as snow; though they be red like crimson, they shall be as wool. If ye be willing and be obedient, ye shall eat of the good of the land: But if ye refuse and rebel, ye shall be devoured with the sword: for the mouth of the Lord hath spoken *it*. How is the faithful city become an harlot! it was full of judgement; righteousness lodged within it; but now murderers. Thy silver is become dross, thy wine mixed with water: Thy princes *are* rebellious, and companions of thieves: every one loveth gifts, and followeth after rewards: they judge not the fatherless, neither doth the cause of the widow come unto them.'

Both the author of Isaiah and the fictional narrator of the story of Isaiah, as well as all the stories of the Bible/OT all describe the characters as the meaning of the word 'jew/yehud/yhwd'. In reality, the people who are of one ethnicity would describe the actions of those in charge of that faith as 'jew/yehud/yhwd' regarding how they rewrote and kept changing religious stories, laws and practises, and it is how the word 'jew' would become the name of the religion (later on) originating from the meaning of the word 'jew'. (Isa.1)

Jeremiah also reflects the meaning of the word 'jew': '...I have this day set thee over the nations and over the kingdoms, to root out, and to pull down, and to destroy, and to throw down, to build and to plant...Out of the north an evil shall break forth upon all the inhabitants of the land. For lo, I will call all the families of the kingdoms of the north, saith the Lord; and they shall come, and they shall set every one his throne at the entering of the gates of Jerusalem, and against all the walls thereof roundabout, and against all the cities of Judah. And I will utter my judgements against them touching all their wickedness, who have forsaken me, and burned incense unto other gods, and worshipped the works of their own hands...For, behold, I have made thee this day a defenced city, and an iron pillar, and brasen walls against the whole land, against the kings of Judah, against the princes thereof, against the priests thereof, and against the people of the land.' The verb of 'jew' is the corruption/distortion of religion/God's laws, the worshipping of other gods, performing offerings to other gods; and 'the works of their own hands' are the idols they sculpted and stories they made up to replace or add to God's religion/ways. It is also in the punishment and the changing of the situation to a worse situation for Jerusalem and Judah and all its inhabitants. (Jer.1)

The way the word 'jew' is positioned within the story to show its relay and reflection on the whole story of the chapter is notable: Jer.32 places the purchase of land by Jeremiah from his cousin which the author uses to place word 'jew' at verse 12 as people who see (along with other witnesses) the sale of land transaction, but they are presented as 'before all the Jews that sat in the court of the prison' because it reminds the audience that Jeremiah is in prison as a corruption of justice on king Zedekiah's part; King Zedekiah believes Jeremiah is distorting prophesies and fabricating them in which he (Zedekiah) is prophesied to undergo a terrible worsening of situation; immediately after the mention of completing the recording and witnessing of the land transaction which happens in front of the Jews in prison—the author has Jeremiah immediately dive into how God saved and gave Israel only for them to corrupt and disobey causing the worsening of their situation and the theme continues throughout the chapter. (Jer.32)

The meanings of 'making worse' and not telling the truth are present in Jer.38 and linked and relayed in the mention of the word 'jew' at verse 19 'I am afraid of the Jews that are fallen to the Chaldeans, lest they deliver me into their hand, and they mock me.' the king of Judah is using the word 'jew' to describe some and not all his people and specifically people who will do something which spoils, deteriorates or corrupts a situation, person or thing. But it also reflects and relays with the narration of the whole chapter which revolves around antagonist characters who believe Jeremiah is purposely corrupting and fabricating prophesies to deter the men from fighting and to desert and join the Chaldeans; the punishment they want for him is a deterioration of Jeremiah's state and environment as not only will he be put into prison, but an extremely filthy and unpleasant part of prison; it is reflected in Zedekiah requesting and Jeremiah complying with Zedekiah's request that Jeremiah be dishonest and not tell the truth of what he has conveyed to Zedekiah which also shows the meaning of the word 'jew' of 'not forthright'. (Jer.38)

The meaning of 'he/they disfigures/distorts/makes ugly/changes for or to the worse' and twisting words, being deviously dishonest is reflected and used by having at least one of the characters be accused of dishonesty and warning of dishonesty from another character but only following the author makes a point to use 'jew' for those who return when they hear Gedaliah has been made governor, as the character attempting to corrupt a situation, wanting to cause the death of another. And although the subsequent chapters make Johanan's warnings true—in the current chapter the author is using 'jew' as wordplay to show Gedaliah finds Johanan false and corruptive, but to also show there is a distortion in Gedaliah and the people serving the antagonist Chaldeans, and also in Johanan warning Gedaliah of the bad intentions of Ishmael son of Nethaniah. (Jer.40:11-16)

The meanings of the word 'jew' of changing something into something else, and something worse is also used and relayed in the actions and themes of Jer.41. It is evident here, as it is all over the Bible, that the word 'Jews/jew' was not used by the authors as a name for the religion, but a word-name reflecting the actions and themes of the story (this itself shows that the word 'jew' was not originally the name of the religion which would eventually take on this naming): 'Jews' is used to describe the people whom Ishmael

Nethaniah kills, and he kills them for serving the Chaldeans so the meanings of 'jew' are reflected in both Ishmael's actions of killing his own people and in the murdered people's actions of serving the Chaldeans; the meaning of 'he/they disfigures/makes ugly/changes for the worse' as these people who are also from the same people as both the protagonists and antagonists in this chapter have intentionally disfigured themselves with shaving, self-cutting and tearing their clothes; it is in Ishmael Nethaniah disfiguring them further by murdering them. It is important to understand that when the word 'jew' is applied within this chapter, within the story the author has Ishmael Nethaniah view the corrupted people as 'jew' and not all the people are meant by it—there is a distinction made; there is a point the author makes that Ishmael Nethaniah slew the people because they were corrupted by Gedaliah 'Now the pit wherein Ishmael had cast all the dead bodies of the men, whom he had slain because of Gedaliah…'. (Jer.41)

When the narration is God through Jeremiah addressing the people, they are called 'all the Jews…' living in different areas, but they are called 'jews' because it reflects what they did of disobedience and corruption which God lists and all these show the meanings of the word 'jew' as God's punishment making it worse for the people; the people's disobedience of God's commandments and his prophets which he sent; people corrupting by burning incense to multiple gods. The narration itself shows that there was no single religion called 'Jewism(Judaism by misnomer)' to begin with, but the word 'jew' applied to groups of people who distorted, disobeyed, changed religious practise and this term was not applied to all people not even within the Biblical stories of the same people, or who were supposed to be following the same religion—but to those who corrupted and disobeyed or were viewed by other characters within the story as disobeying and distorting. (Jer.44)

This can also be seen in Daniel and Ezekiel. Ezek.11 shows the meaning of the word 'jew' without using the word in the text. It describes everything the 'princes of the people' do is corrupt and causes the deterioration of people's lives with misleading them and causing them to kill each other; it is the author of Ezek.11 criticising the stories which glorify slaughter. Ezek.22 shows how people and people of authority have distorted the correct way of things to increase power even at the expense of shedding blood, oppressing and exploiting strangers and vulnerable parts of society; corrupted religious/sacred rituals and possessions; it directly refers to fictional stories being spread and used to cause massacres 'and in thee are men that carry tales to shed blood'; it lists everything which has been corrupted, made worse by the actions of deceit on part of people in power which in turn causes the punishment which is also a worsening of a specific situation.

Dan.3:8 the word 'jew' is used to show characters accused of disobeying the king's commandments, but it also reflects on the king's commandments to worship a statue which he has made, as in creating an additional statue and creating new and forced religious ritual of bowing and worshipping the statue by Nebuchadnezzar's command is also a distortion of the norm; it relays with the three friends refusal to obey the worship of the statue and any other god other than the protagonist God of all the Biblical stories as worshipping other gods/idols is also distortion; it is in the king's relationship with the three friends deteriorating.

It must be said that although the word 'jew' is not used, from Dan.1 the theme of the meanings of the word is used in this chapter: there is the changing to worse of kings and people of Israel/Judah being carried away into captivity; there is the distortion of four of the character's names from their original names to the names given them by the prince of the eunuchs; it is in Daniel and his friends refusing to be distorted or made worse which would happen if they eat and drink things not part of their permissible religious diet; it is in the eunuch worrying that the four friends' health and appearance will deteriorate due to not eating meat. At Dan.5 when the king asks Daniel if he is 'whom the king my father brought out of Jewry' it means by removing Daniel from his natural environment and religion that this is 'distortion/changing things for worse' because Belshazzar's father is who caused the destruction of the cities and took the people into captivity (which was caused by the people's own distortions of religion and disobedience towards God and prophets); it reflects the corruption in the use of what are meant to be the protagonist God's eating and drinking vessels being used by Belteshazzar; the distortion of a hand which can work even if seemingly severed of its body; the change to worse in the king's merriment to distress; it is the summarised story of the king's father's situation and kingdom deteriorating because he felt too much pride and ended up living like an animal and among animals; it is the message and Daniel's interpretation of it that this king's situation and kingdom will be ruined.

Jer.52 relays and reflects the meanings of the word 'jew' of slaughter, destruction, kings and royal families becoming captives, people being taken away from their country and it is connected by the earlier chapters that this is happening because the people themselves, and especially kings and princes, disobeyed God's commandments, his warnings, they distorted what he ordered and changed to the worse/harmed the prophets (Jeremiah) who had been sent to warn them, and distorted the message from being followed.

There are more descriptions of the ways of the children of Israel as distorting religion, disfiguring, provoking, disobeying: 'Woe be unto the pastors that destroy and scatter the sheep of my pasture! saith the Lord. Therefore thus saith the Lord God of Israel against the pastors that feed my people' the pastors who feed God's sheep/people which results in the scattering of the flock is meant the pastors are distorting religion, religious writings, religious teachings, commands, and rituals which result in the religion being corrupted and its followers being led astray from the correct commandments of God 'Ye have scattered my flock, and driven them away, and have not visited them: behold, I will visit upon you the evil of your doings, saith the Lord.' It also likens and links the disfigurement of the land to the distortion of religion and for disobedience: 'For the land is full of adulterers: for because of swearing the land mourneth; the pleasant places of the wilderness are dried up, and their cause is evil, and their force *is* not right. For both prophet and priest are profane; yea, in my house have I found their wickednesss, saith the Lord. Wherefore their way shall be unto them as slippery *ways* in the darkness: they shall be driven on, and fall therein: for I will bring evil upon them, *even* the year of their visitation, saith the Lord. And I have seen folly in the prophets of Samaria; they prophesied in Baal, and caused my people Israel to err. I have also seen in the prophets of Jerusalem an horrible thing: they commit adultery, and walk in lies: they strengthen the hands also of evildoers, that none doth return from his wickedness: they are all unto me as Sodom, and the inhabitants thereof as Gomorrah.' There is a very clear reason why the authors keep describing the 'children of Israel[twisted muscle-the]' who have distorted religion, become wicked, disfigured the land out of wickedness, etc. with Sodom and Gomorrah; the latter two were destroyed because of sexual perversion which was deemed an abomination, i.e. a distortion/corruption of nature, a corruption of the natural state of being (according to the OT). It is linked in two ways: 'Israel/twisted muscle-the' symbolises illicit and/or sexual perversion like Sodom and Gomorrah; when Sodom and Gomorrah were punished the people were all killed and the land completely disfigured by brimstone and fire—which links with how Israel is described as causing the distortion/corruption/perversion of the people and disfigurement of the land, and this is further proof of the origins of the word 'jew/yehud/yhwd' 'distort/disfigure/makes worse/ugly/etc.'. (Jer.23)

The link between the word 'jew/yehud/yhwd' 'he/they disfigures/distorts/makes ugly/changes for or to the worse' and the 'children of Israel' and to 'Sodom and Gomorrah' is that they pervert, corrupt, make worse/ugly and their punishment is disfigurement of life and land. This can be seen in Deuteronomy where Moses reminds and reproaches the people of the 'disfigurement/made worse' God brought upon Pharaoh and Egypt because of Pharaoh's corruptions and yet the people God saved are still showing their own corruption and disobedience 'Yet the Lord hath not given you a heart to perceive, and eyes to see, and ears to hear, unto this day.'. Moses warns the people of the distortions and corruptions of other people i.e. other people doing 'jew/yehud/yhwd/يهود': 'And ye have seen their abominations, and their idols, wood and stone, silver and gold, which were among them.' which Moses warns even those who are corrupt secretly in their heart their situation will be made worse by curses which will affect them in life and land, and again the land and punishment is likened to Sodom and Gomorrah '...shall say, when they see the plagues of that land, and the sickness which the Lord laid upon it; And that the whole land thereof *is* brimstone and salt, *and* burning, that it is not sown, nor beareth, nor any grass growth therein, like the overthrow of Sodom and Gomorrah, Admah and Zeboim...' and goes on to narrate the people who pass by and wonder what caused this punishment and what the anger shown towards it means, the response is that although God saved the people from Egypt 'they went and served other gods' instead of the correct one. And again, all descriptions of distorting religion, comparing them to sexually perverse and ruined by punishment Sodom and Gomorrah, the warnings that if they pervert/distort God's commandments they will be punished, and not only will their situation go from good to bad and worse, but to a degree that even the landscape (in addition to life) will be disfigured as punishment for the distortion—and all these descriptions are reflected in one word 'jew/yehud/yhwd/يهود'. (Deut.29)

And just as earlier generations (within storyland) in Deuteronomy were warned by Moses of what would become of them, in Jeremiah it has already happened and Jeremiah is pointing out how priests, prophets, princes and people have distorted and corrupted God's religion/commandments—with emphasis on the priests and prophets—which has led to the worsening of people's lives and the disfigurement of the environment they live in, and this description and action is described with one word 'jew/yehud/yhwd' by the original language of both the Bible and the people who still speak the language of the Bible: 'Therefore thus saith the Lord of hosts concerning the prophets: Behold, I will feed them with wormwood, and make them drink the water of gall: for from the prophets of Jerusalem is profaness gone into all the land. Thus saith the Lord of hosts, Hearken not unto the words of prophets that prophesy unto you: they make you vain: they speak a vision of their own heart, *and* not of the mouth of the Lord. They say still unto them that despise me, The Lord hath said, Ye shall have peace; and they say to everyone that walketh after the imagination of his own heart, No evil shall come upon you. For who hath stood in the counsel of the Lord, and hath perceived and heard his word? who hath marked his word and heard it?'. There could not be clearer words and narration accusing priests and prophets of distorting religion—which is where and how the word 'jew' came to describe the Jewish religion because of the content of the OT/Bible stories as well as the conduct of real priests and persons in charge of religion/religious texts and how people perceived them of changing the OT stories and distorting the religion from its original state. (Jer.23)

'Behold, a whirlwind of the Lord is gone forth in fury, even a grievous whirlwind: it shall fall grievously upon the head of the wicked. The anger of the Lord shall not return until he have executed, and till he have performed the thoughts of his heart: in the latter days ye shall consider it perfectly. I have not sent these prophets, yet they ran: I have not spoken to them, yet they prophesied. But if they had stood in my counsel, and had caused my people to hear my words, then they should have turned them from their evil way, and from the evil of their doings...I have heard what the prophets said, that prophesy lies in my name, saying, I have dreamed, I have dreamed. How long shall *this* be in the hearts of the prophets that prophesy lies? yea, *they are* prophets of the deceit of their own heart: Which think to cause my people to forget my name by their dreams which they tell every man to his neighbour...Therefore, behold, I *am* against the prophets, saith the Lord, that steal my words every one from his neighbour. Behold, I *am* against the prophets, saith the Lord, that use their tongues, and say, He saith. Behold, I *am* against them that prophesy false dreams, saith the Lord, and do tell them, and cause my people to err by their lies, and by their lightness; yet I sent them not, nor commanded them...' and goes on to detail about priests and prophets who distort religion and mislead others, ending the chapter with 'And I will bring an everlasting reproach upon you, and a perpetual shame, which shall not be forgotten.'. (Jer.23)

There is more of the people, princes and priests distorting God's religion and commandments, here described as 'polluting', and the meanings of both distortion and making a situation become bad/worse as is the meanings of the word 'jew/yehud/yhwd/يهود':

'*This is* the word that came unto Jeremiah from the Lord, after the king Zedekiah had made a covenant with all the people which *were* at Jerusalem, to proclaim liberty unto them; That every man should let his man servant, and every man his maid servant, *being* an Hebrew or Hebrewess, go free; that none should serve himself of them, *to wit*, of a Jew his brother. Now when all the princes and all the people, which had entered into the covenant, heard that every one should let his manservant, and every one his maidservant, go free, that none should serve themselves of them anymore, then they obeyed, and let *them* go. But afterward they turned, and caused the servants and the handmaids, whom they had let go free, to return, and brought them into subjection for servants and for handmaids. Therefore the word of the Lord came to Jeremiah from the Lord, saying, Thus saith the Lord God of Israel; I made a covenant with your fathers the day I brought them forth out of Egypt, out of the house of bondmen, saying, At the end of seven years let ye go every man his brother an Hebrew, which hath been sold unto thee; and when he hath served thee six years, thou shalt let him go free from thee: but your fathers hearkened not unto me, neither inclined their ear. And ye were now turned, and had done right in my sight, in proclaiming liberty every man to his neighbour; and ye had made a covenant before me in the house which is called by my name: But ye turned and polluted my name, and caused every man his servant, and every man his handmaid, who ye had set at liberty at their pleasure, to return, and brought them into subjection, to be unto you for servants and for handmaids. Therefore thus saith the Lord, Ye have not hearkened unto me, in proclaiming liberty, every one to his brother, and every man to his neighbour: behold, I proclaim a liberty for you, saith the Lord, to the sword, to the pestilence, and to the famine; and I will make you to be removed unto all the kingdoms of the earth. And I will give the men that have transgressed my covenant, which have not performed the words of the covenant which they had made before me, when they cut the calf in twain, and passed between the parts thereof, The princes of Judah, and the princes of Jerusalem, the eunuchs, and the priests, and all the people of the land, which passed between the parts of the calf: I will even give them into the hand of their enemies, and into the hand of them that seek their life: and their dead bodies shall be for meat unto the fowls of the heaven, and to the beasts of the earth. And Zedekiah king of Judah and his princes will I give into the hand of their enemies, and into the hand of them that seek their life, and into the hand of the king of Babylon's army, which are gone up from you. Behold, I will command, saith the

Lord, and cause them to return to this city; and they shall fight against it, and take it, and burn it with fire: and I will make the cities of Judah a desolation without an inhabitant.'

The distortion, perversion of religion, the corruption and disobedience in breaking the covenant with God, the disobedience it led to, the twisting and dishonesty of words in telling servants/slaves that they were free then returning them into servitude, the consequence of all this corruption is punishment making all their lives worse: being attacked and defeated by enemies then taken away as servants, the disfigurement of the environment, a city without inhabitants—all this is described and encapsulated in one Arabic word 'jew/yehud/yhwd/yehowid/يهود/يهَوِّد'. (Jer.34:8-22)

Earlier in this book, the interpretation and translation of 'Jehudi' (Jer. 36:14-25), a character in the Book of Jeremiah, was mentioned as having two word-names (as most word-names have more than one meaning in the Bible as the authors used wordplay in the stories), and the first was Jehudi; ييحُدي ، جيحُدي yeiḥudee, yeiḥoodee, geiḥoodee 'he comes back/returns/goes back and forth' 'came-went back/returned/went back and forth' as his character was sent on errands to return with a person, then later sent to bring back a scroll/book. The other meaning is ييهودي ، جيهودي yeihudee, yeihoodee, geihoodee 'he/they disfigures/distorts/makes ugly/changes for or to the worse' 'he is of disfiguring/distorting/making ugly/changing for or to the worse' 'came and disfigured/distorted/made ugly/changed for or to the worse' and it can also have all the other meanings of, and explained, under 'jew' (see jew/jewish).

As explained earlier, the priests and people in charge of the religious documents have been accused in the OT stories of changing, distorting the religious writings, instructions and God's commandments (religion), and in real life people of the same religion as these priests/people-in-charge and also from other religions (all of the same ethnicity as those accused of distorting) have accused the priests and people in charge of religious teachings and documents of rewriting, destroying or hiding parts of the original texts, adding parts they write themselves, i.e. fabricating/forging and adding to the Bible to change and distort religion to what these priests/scribes wanted the religion and story to be for their own personal religious, political and corrupt agendas. Not only is this an accusation which was made and believed millennia ago, i.e. when the people who wrote/rewrote the Biblical stories and their peers lived and knew what was going on, but it is also supported by the stories of the Bible (both the OT and NT) which clearly state this is exactly what priests, scribes, chiefs and prophets have done. It is an undeniable fact that the Biblical stories underwent revisions and redactions by many different authors/parties, at different periods of time—all rewriting to suit their beliefs and/or personal wants and what we have now of the Bible is not the first, unadulterated version of the Biblical stories in their original form, but an end product of erasures and editions of many differing authors. All these different actions and descriptions have one word to describe them all in the original language of the Bible: 'jew/yehud/yhwd/يهود'.

In Jer.36 the character 'Jehudi/yehudee/يهودي' 'he/they disfigures/distorts/makes ugly/changes for or to the worse' 'he is of disfiguring/distorting/making ugly/changing for or to the worse' 'came and disfigured/distorted/made ugly/changed for or to the worse' reflects what is happening in the story where he is linked by name, action and theme in the story. The first meaning of 'he comes back/returns/etc.' has already been discussed earlier in this book. The second meaning is reflected in his role too: he is involved in destroying God's words which Jeremiah has had written in a scroll and preached to people, i.e. he has distorted God's commandments/religion by destroying the scroll; the physical destruction of the scroll (cutting and burning it) is also 'disfiguring'. It does not matter if it was king Jehoiakim or Jehudi who actually cut and threw the pages into the fire every time Jehudi finished reading 3-4 pages because it is the word-name 'Jehudi' with its meanings and the connection to the action relayed in the story and linked to his involvement in fetching the scroll, reading it to the king, then either he or the king cutting and burning the scroll bit by bit. The extra disfiguration of Jehoikam even after death of his body to be exposed to the elements day and night instead of the dignity of burial is also 'disfigurement' 'making things worse': 'And they went in to the king into the court, but they laid up the roll in the chamber of Elishama the scribe, and told all the words in the ears of the king. So they sent Jehudi to fetch the roll: and he took it out of Elishama the scribe's chamber. And Jehudi read it in the ears of the king, and in the ears of all the princes which stood beside the king. Now the king sat in the winter house in the ninth month: and *there was a fire* on the hearth burning before him. And it came to pass, *that* when Jehudi had read three or four leaves, he cut it with the pen knife, and cast *it* into the fire that *was* on the hearth.'

Not only does the king who along with Jehudi destroys the scroll and attempts to distort God's words, but the story goes on to describe the king wanting to permanently destroy God's words by attempting to have Jeremiah, who the words came through, and Baruch, who wrote them down and read it out to people, killed.

The content of the scroll itself is also about 'corrupting/distorting/making worse' as Jeremiah was asked to record everything God had said against Judah, Israel and all the other nations which means recording not only their corruptive behaviour, how they made things worse, but also what they will suffer from in punishment which does make a situation worse for the punished. It is also a chance for the mentioned people to see their wrong ways and repent, but instead they engage in more distortion and cement making things worse for themselves and everybody by ensuring the promised punishment. (Jer.36)

Malachi also provides proof of the meaning of the word 'jew/yehud/yhwd' and why it eventually was applied to people of a certain religion which started out as being applied only to some groups/individuals of the religion—even by those of the same religion, due to priests/people in charge distorting and disfiguring God's commandments/laws/religion. Here it directly accuses priests of this conduct (and also shows the meaning of making physically ugly): 'And now, O ye priests, this commandment *is* for you. If ye will not hear, and if ye will not lay *it* to heart, to give glory unto my name, saith the Lord of hosts, I will even send a curse upon you, and I will curse your blessings: yea, I have cursed them already, because ye do not lay *it* to heart. Behold, I will corrupt your seed, and spread dung upon your faces, even the dung of your solemn feasts; and one shall take you away with it. And ye shall know that I have sent this commandment unto you, that my covenant might be with Levi, saith the Lord of hosts. My covenant was with him of life and peace; and I gave them to him for the fear wherewith he feared me, and was afraid before my name.' In this passage the text compares Levi's truth/honesty to the accused priests' distortion/corruption of religion: 'The law of truth was in his mouth, and iniquity was not found in his lips: he walked with me in peace and equity, and did turn many away from iniquity. For the priests' lips should keep knowledge, and they should seek the law at his mouth: for he *is* the messenger of the Lord of hosts. Therefore have I also made you contemptible and base before all the people, according as ye have not kept my ways, but have been partial in the law.'

Although the passage seems to be very straightforward that the priests are corrupt and corruptors while Levi (all the Levites) are straight and honest, it is actually more wordplay as the meaning of Levi 'twisted/entwined/goes around in circles/not forthright' also has meanings of dishonesty and the Levites have been described in other OT stories as being thieves who stole from God's 'piled upon piles/qodesh haqoddashim' food sources and were only allowed to assist the Aaronite priests and not serve God directly because they were found untrustworthy. It is the author of Malachi's way of saying all the priests are corrupt, they all distort stories, religion for their own personal gain. (Mal.2:1-9)

In the New Testament the meaning of the word 'jew/yehud/yhwd/يهود' 'he/they disfigures/distorts/makes ugly/changes for or to the worse' 'of disfiguring/distorting/making ugly/changing for or to the worse' is abundantly supported. It is important to point out again that I am addressing and proving the meaning of the word 'jew' as used in its original language, and I am not discussing/proving/indicating in any way or form that this is a characteristic of the 'Jew' as in the Jewish person of the Jewish faith (the attribute of the meanings of the word 'Jew' as a negative characteristic of Jewish people (antisemitism) burgeoned in the European world and was directed at the Arabs who lived in Europe and who were brown/darker skinned and stood out 'different' than the white western people, before antisemitism would also be applied against all Jews including white European Jews who were no different than their white European Christian compatriots except in religion). What is being addressed here in this book is the word 'jew' meanings, why and how it came to be applied as a noun later onto the Jewish religion as the word depicted and used in the Bible.

Part of how antisemitism was spread and found support for, was due to misunderstanding the Bible, the NT, instead of seeing it as stories where groups of people are described as 'Jews' for the wordplay reflecting what happens in the story just as the words 'Gentiles' 'Greeks' 'Corinthians' were used for their word meanings and how they tell, enhance and relay the story not as 'Jewish people' 'Greek people' but a verb or adjective which delivers the wordplay and puns of the Biblical authors' method. Instead, the western world has taken it as meaning 'the Jews' 'the Greeks' 'the Romans'.

The use in the NT is the same as in the OT, that the word 'jew' showed the meanings of 'he/they disfigures/distorts/makes ugly/changes for or to the worse' 'of disfiguring/distorting/making ugly/changing for or to the worse' 'provoking/opaque/not forthright' and sometimes it was reflecting the action of the characters called 'Jews' but it also reflected the actions of the protagonists, Paul for example, or the event happening.

In the NT stories, the author narrates through dialogue of John the Baptist and Jesus the belief within the stories about and towards Pharisees, scribes, rabbis, and Sadducees expressing anger, directly blaming them of distorting religion, whether Moses or God's commandments; they accuse this group of characters of saying things they do not really mean while they harbour in their hearts the opposite intent; changing religion to stroke their own egos or raising their own status in society—much like the accusations made against priests and other disobedient people in the OT. (You can see how these Biblical stories when they arrived in the western world how they have been taken literally as descriptions of Jews.)

When Pharisees and Sadducees arrive at the baptism, John the Baptist accuses them of having false intentions, believing they will be saved in their hearts due to a connection to Abraham i.e. they are being false. Jesus states 'or have ye not read in the law, how that on the sabbath days the priests in the temple profane the sabbath, and are blameless?'; in trying to 'accuse' Jesus for healing a man on the sabbath he responds that they themselves work on the sabbath if it is related to their own property and benefit; it is reflected in how they constantly try to entangle Jesus with his own words by asking him questions designed to trip him up; Jesus responds to a group of characters 'Why do ye also transgress the commandment of God by your tradition?...Thus have ye made the commandment of God of none effect by your tradition. *Ye* hypocrites, well did Esaias prophesy of you, saying, This people draweth nigh unto me with their mouth, and honoureth me with *their* lips; but their heart is far from me. But in vain they do worship me, teaching *for* doctrines the commandments of men.'; it is reflected in '...they be blind leaders of the blind. And if the blind lead the blind, both shall fall into the ditch.'.

Matt.22 storyline continues with describing and narrating actions of Pharisees and Sadducees as 'jew/yehud/yhwd/يهود'—calling them hypocrites for going against God's original commandments; where they seek to 'entangle' Jesus in his talk; in Jesus answering their questions with his own questions and understanding of religious stories/scriptures and pointing out to them their contradictions and distortions 'But Jesus perceived their wickedness, and said, Why tempt me, *ye* hypocrites?' 'Jesus answered and said unto them, Ye do err, not knowing the scriptures, nor the power of God.' 'While the Pharisees were gathered together, Jesus asked them, What think ye of Christ? whose son is he? They say unto him, *The son* of David. He saith unto them, How then doth David in spirit call him Lord, saying, The Lord said unto my Lord...If David then call him Lord, how is he his son? And no man was able to answer a word, neither durst any *man* from that day forth ask him any more *questions*.'

In Matt.23 the story has Jesus continue to preach that the scribes and Pharisees are distorting religion, making up laws/commandments to suit themselves and not as God originally commanded 'Then spake Jesus to the multitude, and to his disciples, saying, The Scribes and the Pharisees sit in Moses seat: All therefore whatsoever they bid you observe, *that* observe and do; but do not ye after their works: For they say, and do not. For they bind heavy burdens, and grievous to be borne, and lay *them* on men's shoulders; but they *themselves* will not move them with one of their fingers. But all their works they do for to be seen of men: they make broad their phylacteries, and enlarge the borders of their garments. And love the uppermost room at feasts, and the chief seats in the synagogue, And greetings in the markets, and to be called of men, Rabbi, Rabbi. But be not ye called Rabbi: for one is your master...But woe unto you, scribes and Pharisees, hypocrites! for ye shut up the kingdom of heaven against men: for ye neither go in *yourselves*, neither suffer ye them that are entering to go in. Woe unto you, scribes and Pharisees, hypocrites! for ye devour widows' houses, and for a pretence make long prayer...' and the passage goes on relaying the meaning of the word 'jew' 'because you build the tombs of prophets, and garnish the sepulchres of the righteous, And say, If we had been in the days of our fathers, we would not have been partakers with them in the blood of the prophets. Wherefore ye be witnesses unto yourselves, that ye are the children of them which killed the prophets...Wherefore, behold, I send unto you prophets, and wise men, and scribes: and *some* of them ye shall kill and crucify; and *some* of them ye shall scourge in your synagogues, and persecute *them* from city to city...'; 'Then assembled the chief priests, and the scribes, and the elders of the people, unto the palace of the high priest, who was called Caiaphas, And consulted that they might take Jesus by subtilty, and kill him. But they said, Not on the feast *day*, lest there be uproar among the people.'

Along with the detailed ways the action and meanings of the word 'jew/yehud' is done to the religion (that is distortion, disobedience, disfigurement, making things/situations worse) one of the biggest sins is to murder, and to murder/abuse prophets—which the antagonists in the stories are said to do throughout the OT and NT. Killing a prophet is one of the biggest disfigurements of God's commandments/religion—or even killing/abusing the miracles he sends down (including prophets), and the story of Jesus culminates with the antagonists described by narration of the story (and later by word 'jew') who Jesus accuses of distortion/disfigurement—they abuse and kill Jesus who is not only a miracle and a prophet, but also the Son of God. The description of the antagonists with the meanings of the word 'jew' does not end at Jesus' death within the same story—but the author has them commit more distortion/perversion/corruption, by bribing soldiers to falsely claim the disciples stole Jesus' body at night—so they can deny and create doubt over the resurrection '...and this saying is commonly reported among the Jews until this day.'. (see Matt.3:7-9; 12:1-14, 33-34, 38-45; 15:1-20; 22; 23; 26:3-5, 47-68; 27:1-50; 28:11-15)

In Mark, the Pharisees and 'certain of the scribes' are accused of the same as it is the same story being re-told with slight variations, but the lines which accuse Jesus' antagonists of distorting/changing God's commandments are mentioned and it is the same action/description of the word 'jew/yehud' of God's laws/religion and is the same accusation against the 'children of Israel' who committed the same thing in the OT books 'Howbeit in vain they worship me, teaching *for* doctrines the commandments of men. For laying aside the commandment of God, ye hold the tradition of men...And he said unto them, Full well ye reject the commandment of God, that ye may keep your own tradition.' This is just another example of the meanings of the word 'jew/yehud' which describes how priests/scribes replaced the 'commandments of God' with fabricated 'doctrines the commandments of men' distorting/disfiguring the original religion/commandment/story into a man-made doctrine; and it is these stories and these meanings which led to the word 'jew/yehud/yhwd/يهود' being applied to the religion and its followers.

When Jesus goes into the temple, throws out people conducting trade and tips over their goods, he preaches 'And he taught, saying unto them, Is it not written, My house shall be called of all nations the house of prayer? but ye have made it a den of thieves'. This describes and holds both meanings of distortion of the religion/commandments and misuse of the misnomered 'temple' and the disfigurement of the house of God from a place of worship with specific worship functions, to a place of trade and profit. Also, the meaning of the word 'jew/yehud/yhwd' is reflected in how the priests and scribes plot to kill Jesus: 'And the scribes, and the chief priests *heard it*, and sought how they might destroy him: for they feared him, because all the people were astonished at his doctrine.'.

The meaning equivalent to 'beating around the bush', and meanings of 'being provoking/stubborn/not forthright' or even 'spiteful' of the word 'jew/yehud/yhwd' is shown in both his antagonists and Jesus' actions when the chief priests, elders and scribes ask him by what authority he conducts his preaching and actions—he answers that only if they can answer a question he presents to them will he inform them where he gets his authority from, as they cannot answer his question he tells them neither can he answer their question about his authority: the intentionally being obscure meanings of the word 'jew/yehud/yhwd'.

The parable Jesus tells regarding the owner of a vineyard creating the vineyard/winepress and the husbandmen not obeying the agreement between them who go on to commit sins of abuse, stoning, theft and murder—all tell a story of distortion of religion, of God's commandments which God perfected and gave to the people, only for the people to change the laws to suit themselves. The stoning and murdering of God's prophets and the vineyard owner's son represents how the antagonists in the Jesus story will murder Jesus, this reflects the disfigurement of religion at the hands of those in charge. The story describes how religion has been corrupted, changed for personal gain and desires; how this disobedience will make the situation worse for the violators.

In the story of Jesus and his disciples passing through the corn, when Pharisees reproach Jesus about his disciples' unlawful corn-plucking on the sabbath, Jesus replies with an example of David lying to get and eat the priest's shewbread and concludes with 'And he said unto them, The sabbath was made for man, and not man for the sabbath: Therefore the son of man is Lord also of the sabbath.' Again clearly stating priests/chiefs/etc. distorted God's commandments from its original form. It is important to highlight a fact of these NT stories, the meaning of the word 'jew/yehud/yhwd' although primarily and mostly emphasised against the antagonists—it is also in Jesus and his disciples' actions as they too are described as going against the norms of religion and community, and are doing things which are disruptive, distortive. It is in Jesus' parables being so opaque that his own disciples need him to explain further.

More text within the Bible which show the meaning of 'jew/yehud/yhwd' is in the description of the characters' actions of distortion of laws, scriptures, being dishonest in what is being said/asked in order to achieve a secret agenda (which is to accuse or catch out and disprove Jesus' claims). When the Pharisees ask about the legality of divorcing a wife, Jesus asks them to refer to Moses' instruction and when the Pharisees reply Moses allowed divorce Jesus states Moses only did so because they forced him to change the true law 'And they said, Moses suffered to write a bill of divorcement, and to put *her* away. And Jesus answered unto them, For the hardness of your heart he wrote you this precept.'

The author is displaying the dishonesty, the breaking of religious rules by the antagonists 'After two days was *the feast of* the passover, and of unleavened bread: and the chief priests and the scribes, sought how they might take him by craft, and put *him* to death. But they said, Not on the feast *day*, lest there be an uproar of the people.' So the disfigurement of God's commandments can also be seen in this story as the priests and scribes are not worried or remorseful about plotting to commit the biggest of sins, murder, nor are they worried to commit it on the day of a holy festival, their only concern is because it is a holy day that the people would be enraged against them. The intention and sin are not the characters' concern and this is done intentionally as they are meant to be pious people and understand God's laws so their action of 'jew/yehud/yhwd' 'disfigurement/ruining' is being displayed and this is how it eventually became the name of the religion and its followers (from the origin of the meaning of the word as a word). (Mark.7:1-13; 11:15-18, 27-33; 12:1-12; 2:23-28; 10:2-5; 14:1-2)

As mentioned at the beginning of this chapter, the word 'jew' means: disfigures, distorts, makes ugly, changes for the worse, ruins, looks ugly, looks bizarre, unkempt, twisting words, beating around the bush, being dishonest, purposely taking things out of context, purposely provoking, being stubborn, disobedience, and is a word used frequently in rural Yemen applied to describe many different situations, actions, appearances, people, animals, objects—a word used abundantly and part of the Arabic language. It is the meanings of this word as used in the Arabic language which is used as meaning and in the actions of the characters of the OT and NT, and to describe what changes, additions, fabrications were added to the religion which caused the people of the same area, ethnicity and even the same (Jewish) religion to apply this word to those they believed and saw as distorting/ruining/changing the religion and its practise and laws, its holy books/scriptures into something different and worse, ruining it. With the passing of time this word would come to be the noun of the religion and its followers.

In Acts, the meaning of this word and how it came to be used as the name of the religion can be seen: 'And when Peter saw *it*, he answered unto the people, Ye men of Israel, why marvel ye at this? or why ye look so earnestly on us, as by our own power or holiness we had made this man to walk? The God of Abraham, and of Isaac, and of Jacob, the God of our fathers, hath glorified his son Jesus; whom ye delivered up, and denied him in the presence of Pilate, when he was determined to let *him* go. But ye denied the Holy One and the Just, and desired a murderer to be granted unto you…' i.e. preferring the worse, causing disfigurement of death of not only an innocent person but one sent by God, disobedience: 'And killed the Prince of life, whom God hath raised from the dead; where of we are witnesses.'

In Acts, just as in the OT, the children of Israel, priests, Sadducees and chiefs are still portrayed as in the meanings of the word 'jew/yehud/yhwd': the antagonists beat the apostles and put them in prison; they discuss in secrecy that the miracle the disciples caused is undeniable yet they are planning on how to discredit it among the people; they choose to threaten the disciples/apostles, to gag them from preaching in Jesus' name any further; although they would like to implement a severer punishment on the apostles, they fear the reaction of the people who witnessed the miracle and so they release the apostles; the antagonists do not change their tactics but attempt to corrupt the truth by persecuting and interrogating the cured man's parents then the cured man himself, eventually accusing him of dishonesty and breaking of laws; the antagonists are accusing the disciples of the same corruption and meanings of 'jew/yehud/yhwd' 'ye have filled Jerusalem with your doctrine' So not only are the antagonists still being portrayed as disobedient, distorting religion, disfiguring religion by killing God's prophets, but this part of the story shows they are attempting through violence and threats to get Peter and the apostles to distort religion by shutting them up and shutting them down, not allowing them to speak and spread God's message.

Distortion, perversion of events, dishonesty, disfigurement in killing people who preach God's message, and many meanings of the word 'jew' is seen in what the antagonists do to Stephen the apostle's character: he performs great miracles and work in converting people; the antagonists described as being from several synagogues cause people to falsely testify against Stephen that he blasphemed against God and Moses; they incite people leading to Stephen's capture and persecution; they cause more people to falsely testify against Stephen, this time against the temple and their laws; Stephen's character gives a speech which summarises Moses' story, and reminds of all the disobedience, distortion, provocation and corruption (all 'jew/yehud/yhwd' meanings) which happened during Moses' time (as according to both OT/NT); and the story ends with Stephen being stoned to death.

In Acts, the word 'jew/yehud/yhwd' with all its meanings of distortion, corruption, disfigurement, etc. is still used as a prompt to show the actions happening in the story. And although the word 'jew' is now being used more directly to describe antagonist characters who seek to corrupt and prevent God's word being preached, it is still used as wordplay relaying with the events of the story just as do all word-names; the antagonists distort what is said, they ruin what is happening for the apostles (Paul/Barnabas) and for the people who are being converted; they are accused of being stubborn and not believing even if they know what the apostles are preaching is true; they speak against what the apostles are preaching and this too is distortion.

But the word 'jew' also reflects on what Paul and the apostles are doing, as they are also viewed as corrupting and ruining the old religion and ways; the meanings of the word 'jew' are used as pun when linked to the Jews refusing to listen so Paul and Barnabas announce they will go preach and convert the 'Gentiles' with the latter having at least one meaning of 'mislead to downfall': it is a pun that Paul and Barnabas are unable to mislead/corrupt the 'Jews' so they turn to a group of people whose word-name is designed to mean they will be misled. The antagonist 'Jews' show the meanings of the word as they incite people to persecute Paul and Barnabas; the pun that 'jew/yehud/yhwd' 'distortion/corruption' as the conduct of both opposing parties is relayed in part of the people in Iconium believe the Jews, while another part believe the apostles which results in the plotting for attacks and stoning; the same occurs and the same meanings depicted when 'Jews' 'moved with envy, took unto them certain lewd fellows of the baser sort, and gathered a company, and set all the city on an uproar, and assaulted the house of Jason…' and the accusation is that the apostles are inciting people to break the law and act against Caesar which ends with Paul and Barnabas being expelled from the city.

The meaning of the word is reflected in the whole of Matt.2 where the wise men ask king Herod 'Where is he that is born king of the Jews? for we have seen his star in the east, and are come to worship him.' and this concerns Herod because a king of 'Jews' threatens his rule as king, poses a change which will ruin Herod's situation; it reflects a change in religion which would be considered by adherents of earlier religions (within the Biblical story) to see it as distortion/ruination; it is in Herod's dishonesty as he pretends to want to know where Jesus is for benign reasons but his intent is to kill him; it is in Herod causing the deaths of many young children and babies; it is in the situation for Joseph and Mary becoming worse as they have to flee for their lives and Jesus'; it is in Joseph and Mary instead of returning home having to change course because Herod's son in now king.

The word 'jew' is used in Matt.27 and its meanings are reflected in the events of the chapter: the governor asks Jesus 'Art thou the king of the Jews?' and the meanings are shown in the elders and chief priests already determining he be put to death before the governor questions him; it is in Judas' situation deteriorating and climaxing in suicide connected to his betrayal of Jesus; it is in the chief priests who employed Judas in betraying Jesus who now wash their hands of any wrong-doing and lay blame squarely on Judas; it is in the narration of Pilate knowing there are no legal or true reasons other than envy in the accusations made against Jesus; it is in Pilate washing his hands of Jesus' execution and laying its responsibility against the people, elders, chief priests, and it applies to Pilate too because he knows Jesus is innocent of any guilt/crime yet he will allow and implement an innocent person's execution; it is in the abuse Jesus receives from the soldiers which includes dressing him up as a 'king' in royal colours and mocking him 'Hail, King of the Jews!'; it is the distortion of life, the ugly spectacle and torture of crucifixion and the author keeps using the word-name 'jew' to show this in the phrase 'king of Jews' and now as a label above the mutilated body of Jesus on the cross 'this is jesus the king of the jews' and the author narrates this is the accusation levelled against him as the story already shows that he is innocent of the accusations made against him which brought around his execution, but it also relays what is apparent in the story: even as the protagonist, Jesus sought to distort the old religion and convert people to a new religion which is what the struggle between both sides in the story is about as the antagonists see his ways and preaching as a corruption of laws and is why the sign placed above his head is described as an accusation: 'And set up over his head his accusation written, this is jesus the king of jews.' and here it is used exactly as the word meaning 'jew' 'corrupted/distorted' and that is what Jesus has been accused of doing.

It is also important to understand that although Jesus' antagonists in the NT are most often described as 'Jews' to show the meaning of the word 'jew' not only reflected in their actions, but also the actions of pro-Jesus characters in later NT stories, but also Jesus himself is 'distorting' the norms of religion and custom (the meaning of the word 'jew') by preaching and teaching the new religion, in his and his disciples' actions, and his antagonists see his actions as 'jew' which the authors allow to be applied to him to enhance the meaning and drama of the stories. The meanings are also reflected in the 'veil of the temple was rent in twain' and the cracking apart of rocks and earthquakes; in the graves opening up; in saints rising from their graves and coming back to life and entering the city. All these events carry the many related meanings of the word 'jew' and it is applied in wordplay as all word-names in the Biblical stories are used.

Paul himself is described as a 'Jew' because he goes from believing in the old religion to being 'corrupted' and believing the new religion; it is shown in his distortion of statements from claiming he is a Jew when he needs to get out of trouble being persecuted by Jews, then claims to be specifically a Pharisee when he sees a lifeline if he can get the sympathy of Pharisees, and claiming he is a Roman to get out of trouble when he believed the locals will fear the Romans and also when he is appealing to a Roman character in authority when he is under Roman custody. (see Acts.3:12-15; 4:1-3, 15-23; 5:16-18, 24-33; 6:8-15; 7:37-42, 51-60; 13:24-28, 41-50; 14:1-5; 17:1-8)

How the Biblical authors used word-names in wordplay and specifically here the word 'jew' can be seen in how they create and connect it with other word-names 'Greek' 'Gentile' and the meanings of these words when paired with 'Jew' further enhance in relay the message of the respective story: e.g. in Acts.14:1 Paul and Barnabas are able to convert and make believe many Jews and Greeks: here 'jew' is Paul has been able to distort the Greek and Jews' old beliefs into believing in Christianity instead, and the word 'Greek' here means 'purified/made clean/clear'. Then in the following verse 'But the unbelieving Jews stirred up the Gentiles, and made their minds evil affected against the brethren', here 'jew' is still 'distort' but also 'make worse/change to the worse', and this is in connection and relay with 'gentile' which here means 'he/they dissuade/make leave' as they are turning people against the teachings of Christianity and with negative intentions towards followers of Christianity.

With regards to the narration of Timotheus' parents being a Jew and a Greek, this is how the meanings of 'Jew' were used in relay with the meanings of 'Greek'. There was a lot of emphasis put on there being no need of circumcising the Gentiles, the Greeks, any non-locals, due to their 'purification' in body and spirit is reached by baptism/conversion to Christianity to replace the need for the people as per the OT stories to be physically cleansed with circumcision; God has granted that the Gentiles and the Greeks do not need to be physically **circumcised** to reach physical and spiritual **cleanliness** which are two of the meanings of the word '**greek**'. Due to the needs of the story, the authors wanted to show the importance of the relationship and its function between Timotheus and Paul and the narration has Paul circumcise Timotheus so he can join him in his travels and convert others and be of assistance to Paul. The meanings of 'Greek' as used to portray Timotheus' father reflects on what will happen to Timotheus as 'Greek' is 'purify/purified/circumcise/circumcised/make clean/made clean/make edible/made edible' the people in the story who no longer need circumcision but Paul performs the circumcision of Timotheus to make him pure and clean in body and soul. For more meanings of 'Greek' and 'Timotheus' and how they were used in wordplay to show the meanings of the story being told, see Acts.16:1-5.

His mother was described as a 'Jewess' to mean 'distort/made ugly' because an uncircumcised penis is deemed aesthetically ugly by the culture of the people who created the Biblical stories; but it is also being used to show there is a distortion, more than one, happening: by Timotheus not being circumcised that is going against, and a distortion of, his mother's culture; when 'Jew' and 'Greek' are mentioned again about the same subject it is used in the narration as the people who are 'Jews' know that Timotheus' father is a Greek and it is reflected as the meanings of 'distortion' and 'not forthright' by Paul circumcising him as Paul is going against, i.e. corrupting what God, all the elders and disciples have already made clear is no longer necessary; it reflects the dishonesty and hidden intentions Paul has for Timotheus and which the story carries as a pun, and through this circumcision Timotheus has not been made 'purified/cleansed' by the word of God alone, but by Paul's physical intervention of circumcising him showing the meaning 'purify(ied)/circumcise(ed)/make(made) clean/make(made) edible' of 'Greek'. (Acts.16:1-5).

In Revelation the tone becomes harsher towards 'Jews' and in the story the word 'Jews' does not apply to the sense of 'Jews' which means to be of the Jewish faith but applies to characters in the story who have corrupted/distorted/disobeyed/etc. and also to the acts of punishment which are also 'distortion/corruption', and the point being discussed is the word 'jew/yehud/yhwd' and its meanings, how and why it was used in these Biblical stories, and how it became the name of a specific religion; and its description which is a word encompassing a variety of negative meanings and how these were used in the narrative of the stories to describe the disobedient and disobedience/distortions of the children of Israel beginning from the earliest stories in the OT all the way through to the end of the NT:

'I know thy works, and tribulation, and poverty, (but thou art rich) and I know the blasphemy of them which say they are Jews, and are not, but are the synagogue of Satan.' 'Behold, I will make them of the synagogue of Satan, which say they are Jews, and are not, but do lie; behold, I will make them to come and worship before thy feet, and to know that I have loved thee.'. The actions in Rev.16 are a depiction and relay of the word 'jew/yehud/yhwd' as the punishments all disfigure, corrupt, make a situation worse, spoil and ruin, and are the reason (along with for being 'spiteful/provoking/stubborn/not forthright') and punishments for the disobedience (punishment is against all people and not just 'Jews' as in the religious Jewish sense, as all the people being punished are 'jews' i.e. guilty of performing disobedience, corruption, etc.). The first viol creates painful sores on those marked for punishment; the second viol turns the seas into clotted blood and sea-life and any human life in it die; the third viol also causes rivers and waters to become blood; in verse 6 it is directly linked to the 'children of Israel' as in the OT, the stories narrate the children of Israel kill, abuse, disobey their prophets sent by God and verses 5-6 narrate 'And I heard the angel of the waters say, Thou art righteous, O Lord, which art, and wast, and shalt be, because thou hast judged thus. For they have shed the blood of saints and prophets, and thou hast given them blood to drink; for they are worthy.' So it is one act of 'jew/yehud/yhwd' (the punishments in the story) in return for other acts of 'jew/yehud' (the sins in the story). The fourth angel uses the sun to scorch people with fire; and still the story shows those punished for disobedience, distortion, disfigurement continue with disobedience, being stubborn, provoking, and blaspheming against God. The fifth punishment causes a darkness so distressing the people are gnawing 'their tongues for pain' and continue in their disfigured and worse state to make things worse by blaspheming more. The sixth viol dries up the river Euphrates and this is making something worse, especially that it clears the way for invading enemy kings to pass through. The seventh viol causes lightning, thunder, earthquakes and hailstones so large they squash the punished people—all this is distortion of the natural way things are in nature and it is done because of a distortion of religion, laws, commandments, disfigurations caused by the people—even topography is distorted and ruined, it is so distressful that islands and mountains have disappeared in fear. (Rev.2:9; 3:9; 16)

Hebrew

The meaning of 'Hebrew' is similar to the meaning of 'jew'. Hebrew; ʿib̲rî; عِبري 'extremely disfigured/against nature/nature reversed' 'of extremely disfiguring/disfigurement/extreme reversal of natural looks(or state)' 'so disfigured there must be a reason' 'so against nature there must be a reason' and when the word is used it means there must be a reason this person has been so disfigured; it is from the word ('ibra/عبرى/عبر) 'extremely disfigured'—and this is the meaning and use of the word by the people (a living people) who still speak the language of the Bible, which is Arabic and which scholars have misidentified as 'Hebrew'. The only time and way this word is used is to describe someone who (in the speaker's opinion) is extremely ugly or has been disfigured (physically). They say 'his appearance/he looks 'ibra/extremely disfigured' 'شكله عبرى', and this is used to emphasise how ugly the person is, or the person speaking believes he/she is.

In Classical Arabic and Modern Standard Arabic where a form of this word (based on the original Old Arabic word and meaning) is used as ('ibra/عبره/عبرى) it means 'a lesson/parable/message/wisdom or point of the message'; and you can see the meaning of the word in the later forms of Arabic (Classical and Modern Standard) originates from the meaning of 'extremely ugly/nature reversed there must be a reason behind his/her disfigurement' i.e. there must be a reason, or a message, or a lesson why this person has been so disfigured. The rural people who used the word 'hebrew/ʿib̲rî/عِبري' have no other use for this word other than it means 'extremely disfigured/nature reversed' 'of extremely disfiguring/disfigurement'. Cp: 'ibree.

The way it is used in the Bible depicts physical disfigurement of person, beast—and also disfigurement of the way of life, or the environment, objects, and just like the word 'jew' in the Bible 'hebrew' is also used to portray a situation becoming wrong; or has become worse; to show something happening in reverse of what it originally began or was expected to happen; to show wrong, i.e. disfigurement of what is right, normal or should be. In the OT and NT, the word 'hebrew' comes amidst text where the person, environment, situation being described is ugly, or polluted, corrupted (or to be so), undergoing some kind of change, where a person's well-being/state has gone through physical sufferance, mutilation or disfigurement, or the character has done wrong—i.e. disfigured religion/law (e.g.).

The first mention in the OT comes in Genesis referring to Abram before he becomes Abraham: 'And there came one that had escaped and told Abram the Hebrew;' and it is in the middle of Abram's extended family being attacked and taken away as captives which Abram will reverse, turning the tables on the victors who are defeated and freeing everyone and everything that is taken away and in the process of doing this people are killed/disfigured. Now remember 'Abram' means 'rolled up' and refers to Abram being uncircumcised, God wants Abram to be physically perfect 'the Lord appeared to Abram, and said unto him, I am the almighty God, walk before me and be thou perfect.' And the covenant/agreement is that Abram and all his people be circumcised so it plays both ways: Abram's uncircumcised penis is extremely disfigured/ugly, but also when he and others will conduct circumcision, they are reversing what nature has created. Also note this is written by authors in an environment and culture where an uncircumcised penis is deemed aesthetically ugly, so the wordplay by the author of the Bible reads 'Abram the Hebrew' 'rolled up(uncircumcised)-the extremely disfigured/nature reversed' (Gen.14:13)

In Joseph's story, Joseph is in a good position with his master, Potiphar, but the situation changes when Potiphar's wife unsuccessfully attempts to seduce Joseph—and after (in the narration) she describes him as 'an Hebrew' 'the Hebrew servant [she accuses him of trying to dishonour her and his master i.e. disfigure/ruin her reputation]'. When the narration mentions he is a Hebrew he is put into prison. Also when Joseph entreats his cellmate to remember him if he can help free him from prison, Joseph mentions he was wronged while in the land of Hebrews, as well as being done wrong here by being put in prison for no fault: the use of 'hebrew' reflects his normal way of life, his right, was 'disfigured' both there (at home) and here (in captivity), i.e. his situation has gone wrong and become worse by disfigurement of justice 'But think of me when it shall be well for thee…and make mention of me unto Pharaoh, and bring me out of this house: for indeed I was stolen away out of the land of the Hebrews: and here also have I done nothing that they should put me into the dungeon.'

Joseph's next mention as 'an Hebrew' is in the middle of the narration where Pharaoh is 'troubled' by a dream, and the chief butler (previously imprisoned with Joseph) remembering a bad time when Pharaoh was angry with his servants and imprisoned them, leading to the mention of meeting 'a young man, an Hebrew' who can interpret dreams—for the chief butler the situation improved, he was freed, but for the baker his situation worsened, he was hanged and his body to be eaten by birds, i.e. physical disfigurement, but also situations reversing from good to bad, bad to good, or bad to worse.

When Joseph invites his brothers to a meal, Joseph and the Egyptians sit apart from Joseph's brothers and it is narrated 'because the Egyptians might not eat bread with the Hebrews; for that *is* an abomination unto the Egyptians.' i.e. abomination: disfigurement, something extremely ugly/unseemly and for a reason as the meaning of the word. (Gen.39:14-17; 40:14-15; 41:8-13; 43:32)

The Hebrew midwives, women and children are mentioned directly with orders to kill all male Hebrew babies—a disfigurement of life and the natural right to life, of the mothers' natural happiness and feelings following the birth of a new born, and the reverse of nature where the beginning of life with birth has been made its death/end; but there is also the reversal meanings as the midwives disobey Pharaoh's orders which also shows they disfigure/go against his orders by saving the babies. The midwives excuse, which they respond to Pharaoh with, is that by the time they arrive, the babies are already born—giving a reason for it: the 'Hebrew women' being different than the Egyptian women 'for they are lively', and although it is a positive term, the differentiation between how Hebrew and Egyptian women give birth implies an aberration to the norm in the former. Before, during and after the word 'Hebrew' is used, death/murder of baby boys is the prominent feature of the passage, again murder is disfigurement of life. (Exod.1:15-22)

Even when Moses in a basket is thrown into the river his life is still in danger: first from drowning, then from dying of starvation; and in both times the situation is reversed and he is saved with the mention of the word 'hebrew': from drowning by Pharaoh's daughter who says 'This *is one* of the Hebrew children.'; from hunger which Moses' sister saves him from by saying 'Shall I go call to thee a nurse of the Hebrew women, that she may nurse the child for thee?'. Note the use of the word 'hebrew' is to show the abnormality of a baby taken away from mother, and also the threat of losing his life, and the reversal of both which happens in the story. (Exod.2:6-7)

When Moses witnesses what is happening to his own kind, he is seeing the injustice, the abnormality of their situation, focused and heightened by the scene of an Egyptian beating a Hebrew man: more disfigurement of justice, which leads Moses to murder the Egyptian: again, disfigurement of life. When he sees two Hebrews fighting and he attempts to intervene between them, one Hebrew (the one he saved the other day) exposes Moses as a murderer and his crime against the Egyptian which leads to Moses life being not only endangered, but disfigured as he is forced to leave the luxury of living not only as an Egyptian but also in Pharaoh's house. There is an intentional creation of 'reverse' when 'hebrew' is narrated: first Moses reverses the situation between the Hebrew being beaten and the Egyptian beating him, then the Hebrew man Moses saved reverses Moses' situation, but also in itself is a reverse as the Moses did the man a favour, and the Hebrew man in return caused Moses harm. (Exod.2:11-15)

The word 'hebrew' is mentioned in connection to Moses demanding Pharaoh free the people, it not only names them as 'Hebrews' but also reflects what will happen in the story passages that follow the mention 'Hebrews': 'And they said, The God of the Hebrews hath met with us: let us go…' and is followed by Moses saying he fears if they do not sacrifice to God that God would 'fall upon us with pestilence, or the sword'—and disfigurement of situation and death. The mention of the word is also followed by Pharaoh making life and work more difficult for the people, resulting in the worsening of their living/working situation; and the people instead of being grateful Moses is trying to free them, blame the deterioration of their situation and the relationship between them and the Egyptians on Moses and Aaron. (Exod.5:3-23)

'And thou shalt say unto him, The Lord God of the Hebrews hath sent unto thee, saying, Let my people go,' and is followed by the meanings of 'hebrew' 'against nature/nature reversed' shown in how animals and environment become unnatural and detrimental to the antagonists and this reversal of nature is because of Pharaoh's actions: rivers, pools, ponds, even vessels containing water turn into blood; a great stink from the death of fish; then frogs, lice and flies to pollute, corrupt and disfigure every aspect of Egyptian life, and it is done for a reason: Pharaoh has refused to let the people go. The disfigurement is both seen and felt: Egyptian cattle die; boils appear on man and animals; hail and fire kill people and cattle; even the landscape is disfigured with hail stripping/destroying vegetation and crops. 'Thus saith the Lord God of Hebrews, How long wilt thou refuse to humble thyself before me?' and the warning and punishment is locusts disfiguring what remained of vegetation and crops, the landscape; then darkness for three days; finally the firstborn male of every man and beast is killed—disfigurement of natural life and family life. There are many reversal meanings shown in this story: the wealth and leisure of Egyptians is tormented; the enslavement of the people is ended and they are freed; the weakness of Moses is reinforced by Aaron and by God; the strength, power and status of Pharaoh is weakened; Pharaoh's refusal to let the people go is reversed and he gives them permission to leave. (Exod.7-12)

Regarding the law pertaining to 'an Hebrew servant' there is the disfigurement in the terms of servitude/freedom in they differ than to a non-Hebrew as the narration emphasises this new law applies only to Hebrew servants. There is a disfigurement of family life and going against nature within this 'freeing' law because if the man has married a woman by being given this woman by his master, even if he has children from this marriage he is only allowed to go free and has to leave his wife and children as they 'belong' to his master—which is the narration showing why a man is not really being offered freedom, but coerced to stay in servitude. There is also a physical disfigurement along with the disfigurement of choosing enslavement instead of freedom, and it is involved in marking a servant who chooses to 'willingly' remain in servitude: 'And if the servant shall plainly say, I love my master, my wife and my children; I will not go out free: Then his master shall bring him unto the judges; he shall also bring him to the door, or unto the door post; and his master shall bore his ear through with an aul; and he shall serve him forever.' (Exod.21:2, 5-6)

There is another mention of special terms of enslavement for 'Hebrew man, or Hebrew woman be sold unto thee,' but are reminded that they too once lived as slaves, i.e. an injustice which is disfigurement of naturally being free—and this too shows the reversal meanings which more often than not are associated with the word 'hebrew': they were all once slaves; they were freed; some remain free while some have been returned to slavery but this time by masters who were once slaves themselves. It is relayed in the mutilation of the ear of the Hebrew servant who chooses to remain. This is followed by mentioning what can and cannot be sacrificed to God, and what cannot be sacrificed are physically disfigured animals: 'And if there be any blemish therein, as if it be lame, or blind, or have any ill blemish, thou shalt not sacrifice it unto the Lord thy God.'. (Deut.15:12-21)

The mention of the word 'Hebrews' is made in the middle of the text where 'children of Israel' are being slaughtered/beaten by their enemies, then mention of the plagues 'that smote the Egyptian'—the plagues/punishments which disfigured Egyptian life in the story; followed by the 'children of Israel's' situation becoming worse as they suffer more defeat in battle. The last verses in the passage tell the story of one of them arriving at Shiloh with his clothes rent, earth on his head which is intentional disfigurement to the person's physical appearance to express distress/grief over death or catastrophe 'And there ran a man of Benjamin out of the army, and came to Shiloh the same day with his clothes rent, and with earth upon his head' and the bad things happening extend to those he brings news to: Eli drops dead, and his daughter-in-law also dies (a reverse is shown in that the son she gives birth to immediately before dying, lives). Every time 'hebrew' is mentioned it is either followed by, preceded with (and sometimes both) a disfigurement, situations getting worse or going into reverse in a variety of forms, but all for reasons and all reflect its meanings—just like all the names in the Biblical stories reflect what is happening where they are introduced and used in the story being told. (1Sam.4)

Even when the story narrates of Saul and his army winning, it all changes for the worse and/or goes into reverse when in the story the word 'Hebrews' is mentioned, beginning with the 'Philistines' gathering in great numbers and the 'men of Israel' losing their nerve and fleeing and hiding from battle whereas immediately before they were celebrating Jonathan's success against the Philistines: 'And Saul blew the trumpet throughout all the land, saying, Let the Hebrews hear…And the Philistines gathered themselves together to fight with Israel…and people as the sand which is on the sea shore in multitude…When the men of Israel saw that they were in a strait, (for the people were distressed) then the people did hide themselves in caves, and in thickets, and in rocks, and in high places, and in pits. And some of the Hebrews went over Jordan to the land of Gad and Gilead. As for Saul, he was yet in Gilgal, and all the people followed him trembling.'. This is followed by Saul being accused of disobeying/disfiguring God/Samuel's commandments for sacrificing to God instead of waiting for the prophet/priest Samuel to arrive—which leads to Saul's situation/status with God deteriorating 'And Samuel said to Saul, Thou hast done foolishly: thou hast not kept the commandment of the Lord thy God; which he commanded thee: for now would the Lord have established thy kingdom upon Israel forever. But now thy kingdom shall not continue.' (1Sam.13).

In the same story, as soon as the word 'Hebrew' is mentioned by the Philistines who are winning the battle, their situation reverses and changes for the worse: '…and the Philistines said, Behold, the Hebrews come forth out of the holes where they had hid themselves…' and despite being in numbers like sand on the sea shore and facing only Jonathan and his armour bearer—they are slaughtered '...and they fell before Jonathan; and his armour bearer slew after him.'. When the narration mentions 'Hebrews' again—not only do Saul's men who fled/deserted in fear (when the same word was first mentioned in the story) return, but even soldiers of the Philistines begin to inexplicably fight against and kill each other, including 'Hebrews' that are not Israelites as they are with the Philistine side and fighting with the Philistines against Israel, but when the word 'Hebrew' is mentioned again (this time introducing these Hebrews who are with the Philistine army) they too reverse their role, they turn against the Philistines to be with Saul and Jonathan and so do the 'men of Israel which had hid themselves in mount Ephraim' return and chase after the fleeing Philistines: 'And Saul and all the people that *were* with him assembled themselves, and they came to the battle: and, behold, every man's sword was against his fellow, *and there was* a very great discomfiture. Moreover the Hebrews that were with the Philistines before that time, which went up with them into the camp *from the country* round about, even they also *turned* to be with the Israelites that *were* with Saul and Jonathan.' (1Sam.14:9-23)

Just as in the other storylines, the central character(s)'s situation changes for the worse when the word 'Hebrew' is mentioned by a character or in the narration, which happens to David too in Chapter 29. Before the mention of the word, he has joined king Achish and lives in the land of the Philistines as one of them; he is accepted, welcomed and loved by Achish. David is treated so well by Achish that he behaves with absolute loyalty towards his host, and even goes further—killing all the people in the areas he attacks and makes a point of sparing absolutely no one as he fears the news of his loyalty to king Achish of the Philistines will be reported to Saul, his own people:

'And David saved no man nor woman alive, to bring *tidings* to Gath, saying, Lest they should tell on us, saying, So did David, and so *will be* his manner all the while he dwelleth in the country of the Philistines. And Achish believed David, saying, He hath made his people Israel utterly abhor him; therefore he shall be my servant forever...And it came to pass in those days, that the Philistines gathered their armies together for warfare, to fight with Israel. And Achish said unto David, Know thou assuredly, that thou shalt go out with me to battle. And David said to Achish, Surely thou shalt know what thy servant can do. And Achish said to David, Therefore will I make thee keeper of mine head forever.' So there is absolute loyalty from David, and trust in him from Achish, even love between them—but when the word 'Hebrews' is introduced into the story, everything changes for David:

'Now the Philistines gathered together all their armies to Aphek: and the Israelites pitched by a fountain which is Jezreel. And the Lords of the Philistines passed on by hundreds and by thousands: but David and his men passed on the rearward with Achish. Then said the princes of the Philistines, What *do* these Hebrews *here*? And Achish said unto the princes of the Philistines, *Is* this not David, the servant of Saul the king of Israel, which have been with me these days, or these years, and I have found no fault in him since he fell *unto me* unto this day? And the princes of the Philistines were wroth with him; and the princes of the Philistines said unto him, Make this fellow return, that he may go again to his place which thou hast appointed him, and let him not go down with us to battle, lest in battle he be an adversary to us: for wherewith should he reconcile himself unto his master? *should it* not *be* with the heads of these men...Then Achish called David, and said unto him, Surely, as the Lord liveth, thou hast been upright, and thy going out and thy coming in with me in the host *is* good in my sight: for I have not found evil in thee since the day of thy coming unto me unto this day: nevertheless the lords favour thee not. Wherefore now return, and go in peace, that thou displease not the lords of the Philistines. And David said unto Achish, But what have I done? and what hast thou found in thy servant so long as I have been with thee unto this day, that I may not go fight against the enemies of my lord the king? And Achish answered and said unto David, I know that thou *art* good in my sight, as an angel of God: notwithstanding the princes of the Philistines have said, He shall not go up with us to the battle. Wherefore now rise up early in the morning with thy master's servants that are come with thee: and as soon as ye be up early in the morning, and have light, depart.'

So no matter what loyalty David showed before, and currently, in his willingness to kill and fight against his own people and Saul which the narration makes crystal clear David is willing to do for Achish (the 'against nature/nature reversed' meanings), because the word 'Hebrew' has been mentioned David is no longer trusted by the Philistines, and although Achish's trust in David remains total, it becomes ineffective as he has to comply with the wishes of the princes who do not trust David in this battle although he has fought and killed for Achish and Philistines in many other battles. But the reverse effect of the word 'hebrew' does not end there for David, as upon his return he finds his village destroyed by enemies and all his wives and children, and all his men's wives, children and possessions, taken away captive—and this is done to reflect the worsening and reverse of a situation meant by 'hebrew', as well as the disfigurement of the landscape/city/environment. (1Sam.27; 28:1-2; 29)

In Jeremiah the word 'Hebrew' is mentioned after king Zedekiah has freed the servants 'after that the king Zedakiah had made a covenant with all the people which *were* at Jerusalem, to proclaim liberty unto them;' and it mentions in the same passage 'That every man should let his manservant, and every man his maid-servant, *being* an Hebrew or Hebrewess, go free;' which they do—only to immediately turn against it and return them into slavery, i.e. disfiguring what God commanded, his laws and a reversal in actions: 'But ye turned and polluted my name, and caused every man his servant…whom ye had set at liberty…to return, and brought them into subjection.' And the punishment for this is disfigurement of life: death, and disfigurement of cities: burnt with fire and made desolate. (Jer.)

In Jonah's story the changing of weather greatly disturbs the captain and sailors, they feel there is something abnormal about this specific storm and that there is a reason behind it; they see it as life-threatening (which is normal) but their actions and the narrative emphasise it being a phenomenon i.e. a disfigurement of the norm. They pray each to his own god, according to respective religion—they wake Jonah, they are so desperate out of fear they want to reach out to every god that could possibly save them. The storm does not abate—they see it more as an aberrance—they call it an 'evil' which must have been caused by a reason which is why they use lots to determine who is responsible for it, and when the lots point at Jonah and they want to know why it is happening and what he has done to cause such an evil, what his occupation is, etc., his first answer is 'I'm a Hebrew': 'Then said they unto him, Tell us, we pray thee, for whose cause this evil *is* upon us; What *is* thine occupation? and whence comest thou? what *is* thy country? and of what people *art* thou? And he said to them I *am* an Hebrew; and I fear the Lord, the God of heaven, which hath made the sea and the dry *land*. Then were the men exceedingly afraid, and said unto him, Why hast thou done this?'

Although they do not want to throw him overboard, the sea does not go back to normal until they do so, the meaning is shown this time by having the person called a Hebrew thrown into the sea: so the meanings of 'hebrew' is shown when they behave in the opposite manner of what the lots has indicated and what Jonah has told them they should do, but as soon as they comply and throw him into the sea, the storm stops; the sea and sky behave abnormally because Jonah the Hebrew is on board, then the weather reverses and goes back to normal as soon as he is thrown overboard.

But note in their questions to Jonah about what he does for a living, who is he, where is he from and what he has done to cause the abnormal state of the storm at sea, the author makes clear the reason through Jonah's answer: 'I *am* an Hebrew', the questions and his answers display the meaning of 'hebrew' which is 'so disfigured/nature reversed there must be a reason'; if you read the text of the OT correctly the text tells you 'Hebrew' is not an ethnicity but a description denoting something different about or in the persons called Hebrew (they are almost like omens and the word in the story is employed as an omen which causes things to change) and it reflects on the events within the stories; it is applied to only some people within the same group of people in the story who are the same ethnicity but not to all of them so 'Hebrew' is not their ethnicity; it is also applied to some people considered foreigners or enemies of the protagonists such as the Hebrews fighting with the Philistines against Israel; it is used by characters to describe themselves or others but it is a word which holds a negative description and every time it is used in the stories something goes wrong, something very ugly is happening, or something goes in reverse to what it originally was. (Jon.1)

In John when 'hebrew' is mentioned as a 'tongue' (language) to interpret the name of a pool, it turns out the pool is surrounded by people whom suffer physical disfigurements and ailments and are waiting to get into the pool to be healed—note the use of word 'hebrew' followed by characters who are disfigured, but also the first to go in after the angel (into the pool with a 'Hebrew' name) is immediately healed of his illness/disfigurement i.e. his situation is reversed. (John.5:2-4)

In Acts when Paul addresses the people in 'Hebrew' his story begins with explaining how he disfigured other people's lives, persecuting them because they were Christians. He speaks of binding and imprisoning them which is an injustice and makes their situation worse—both what he did and how he feels about it show the meaning of the word 'hebrew'; he speaks of persecuting them to death which is the greatest disfigurement of life. He goes on to narrate how while he was in the middle of his mission of ruining the lives of others, that he was blinded following being spoken to by Jesus/God—a physical disfigurement. When he mentions the 'Hebrew tongue' again it is Jesus reproaching him for persecuting him(Jesus)/ Christians—i.e. disfiguring their lives, ruining God's work. (Acts.21:40; 22:1-13; 26:14)

Also in Acts, where 'hebrew' is mentioned it is to reflect the worsening of a situation as well as a disfigurement for specific characters 'And in those days, when the number of the disciples was multiplied, there arose a murmuring of the Grecians against the Hebrews, because their widows were neglected in the daily ministration.' So the situation has worsened for the widows because they are being neglected, but they have also been disfigured by death, as widows their husbands who would have provided for them have died. (Acts.6:1)

In 2Cor. the mention of 'Hebrew' is preceded and followed by mention of false apostles disfiguring Christ's message; Satan transformed into an angel—Paul reproaching how others prefer those which treat them badly (a worse situation); goes on to mention the sender's own sufferance and physical pain at hands of 'Jews', being whipped, beaten and stoned—always the word 'Hebrew' connected to deterioration or disfigurement of physical, environmental state or situation, the author also deploys opposites to show the reverse of what is being said: 'For such are false apostles, deceitful workers, transforming themselves into the apostles of Christ. And no marvel; for Satan himself is transformed into an angel of light. Therefore *it is* no great thing if his ministers also be transformed as the ministers of righteousness; whose end shall be according to their works. I say again, Let no man think me a fool; if otherwise, yet as a fool receive me, that I may boast myself a little. That which I speak, I speak *it* not after the Lord, but as it were foolishly, in this confidence of boasting. Seeing that many glory after the flesh, I will glory also. For ye suffer fools gladly, seeing *ye yourselves* are wise. For ye suffer if a man bring you into bondage, if a man devour *you*, if a man take *of you*, if a man exalt himself, if a man smite you on the face. I speak as concerning reproach, as though we had been weak. Howbeit whereinsoever any is bold, (I speak foolishly) I am bold also. Are they Hebrews? so *am* I. Are they Israelites? so *am* I. Are they seed of Abraham? so *am* I. Are they ministers of Christ? (I speak as a fool) I *am* more; in labours more abundant, in stripes above measure, in prison more frequent, in deaths oft. Of the Jews five times I received forty *stripes* save one. Thrice I was beaten with rods, once I was stoned, thrice I suffered shipwreck, a night and a day I have been in the deep; In journeying often, in perils of waters, in perils of robbers, in perils by mine own countrymen, in perils by the heathen, in perils in the city, in perils in the wilderness, in perils in the sea, in perils among false brethren. In weariness and painfulness, in watchings often, in hunger and thirst, in fastings often, in cold and nakedness.' (2Cor.11:13-27)

In Epistle to the Hebrews, the meaning of the word is reflected in: mention Jesus' death as purging, his death was an ugly disfiguration of life but also a lesson for others to learn from; in replacing and changing angels' status; in the ageing, wearing out of people, the changing of their form; to take heed and not to let things slip; the suffering of Jesus who is a higher person disfigured by death and suffering for the sake of lesser persons and to bring around change in other people; the devil corrupts and kills, death is used to show disfigurement especially that other NT stories have personified death and made it an individual which can be killed, and death itself as an action becomes ineffective to those 'already dead in Christ' i.e. opposite to nature - they cannot die and therefore death's effectivity and its disfigurement itself is corrupted; Jesus choosing to avoid taking on the form of angels, but of man as in 'the seed of Abraham' shows also instead of something beautiful something less beautiful and therefore disfigured; Jesus choice of being more like man/seed of Abraham so he could resist being corrupted by the devil—then when he is sacrificed could clean away the disfigurement and corruption of those who fall for temptation; Moses' people and their disobedience, as well as God in punishment depriving them of what was a good promise of rest also relays the meaning of 'hebrew'; the 'unbelief' of Moses' people as well as an ugly death of perishing like carcasses in the wilderness; it is in the disfigurement of sacrificing to God animals which are offered for the disfigurement of conduct: sin; it is in being born of God's water/sperm is better than needing human procreation and breastmilk; the ugliness of those who once believed and witnessed Jesus Christ and God's word then go against it or invent in it and preach differently, are likened to committing twicefold the ugliness of Jesus' death and suffering at the hands of people who disfigured him, and the beauty of his sacrifice by God and the word of God are likened to good and beautiful plants growing while those who preach differently are thorns and brambles—the bad/deceitful preaching's end is to be burned with fire, i.e. disfigured.

Epistle to the Hebrews concentrates on homosexual sex being the most purifying form of worship—and although this was the author's intentions it plays on the culture where even if it was not 'sinful' it would be something to be ashamed of, not broadcast, and these male-on-male sex stories show the 'mutilated/mutated/freakishly ugly' meanings; the author of Hebrews has the sender of the letter state that Melchisedec and Jesus are better than Moses, that Melchisedec (who was a high priest close to God long before Moses, according to the story) and Jesus ways are the correct way to worship God and this diminishes Moses and the laws and his stories—in effect it mutilates the OT stories and in doing so is a 'freak' in itself, and as the word means something so 'freakishly ugly there must be a reason behind/for it', the double-entendres are that the audience needs to look closer and question the OT stories and see them as fictionality and this too causes the same towards the NT/Jesus stories. The author of Hebrews is saying: what is the point of the priestly line mentioned in the OT, look at these stories and see them for what they are: fiction. The latter point is reinforced by pointing out Jesus who was created without a father is not the first as Melchisedec is without mother, father, child, too, even more than Jesus who has a mother, and this elucidates that the authors, their imaginations are creating characters who live forever and do not die, who can perform miracles and are miracles in themselves but that it should not be forgotten that these are figments of imagination; and as everything that goes against nature is ugly or mutated or a freak—being born without a mother, father or not having offspring, this too reflects the word-meaning.

It is reflected in the sender attempting to convince the recipients that the old ways, including the priests and their work/service/sacrifices are superseded, they are superseded because they are ineffectual; and in superseding this religion which in the stories comes before the new religion this itself is a mutilation, it is a freakishly ugly thing to do to people and their way of life and worship, but behind this ugliness is a meaning, a lesson to be understood and this meaning of the word Hebrew is also shown within the story. The mention of Abel's murder by Cain is against nature and ugly, a mutilation of life and its physical body; Enoch is mentioned because he disappeared from the story to be replaced by Noah at an author's whim, with only an open wink between authors and editors who left him disappeared, until the author of Hebrews has employed this contradiction which is just a mistake by authors who could not bring themselves to remove a popular character from a story, but the author of Hebrews has recycled Enoch the same way he has recycled Melchisedec/Melchizedek to make him immortal and connect him to Jesus.

There is also the reflection of the meanings of the word Hebrew not only in the actions of the protagonists of the OT stories but also in the narration of Heb.11. where it changes what happened in the stories to suit the purpose of the Heb.11 narration and theme. It is based on a semi-retelling of the OT stories where Abraham, Jacob, Isaac, Sara, etc. actions, roles and characters are used as examples of complete and blind faith; whereas if you read the OT, these characters and their roles most times did not trust nor did they have blind faith in what God told them, but Heb.11 creates a reversal of this. In the OT Sara did not believe she would become pregnant and have offspring; Jacob resorted to deceit to obtain Isaac's blessing which was meant for Esau—hardly faith and so on; and re-telling the stories with a reversal of what was in the OT was done intentionally by the author of Hebrews to show the meaning of the word Hebrew as it was his chosen theme for the story he created (epistle to the Hebrews). The only way to believe these characters were depending on faith in God is to solely go with the popular and superficial (and accepted) narrative by religious and biblical scholarly studies—but this can only be done by disregarding what is written and are the actual stories of the Bible.

The retelling of Moses story, presenting his character as being completely faithful from the beginning is in contradiction to the OT: Heb.11 presents Moses as: refusing to be called the son of Pharaoh's daughter, refusing to enjoy the comforts of Pharaonic life but instead choosing to suffer with his own kind, leaving Egypt with all its comfortable life and leaving without the fear of Pharaoh the tyrant king's threat. The original OT story tells us that Moses was brought up and living the life of a Pharaon until he saw two men fighting, one an Egyptian, the other his own kind, and in trying to help his kinsman he strikes the Egyptian thus killing him; after this he continues to live as one of the Pharaons until the very man he saved exposes him for murder—then Moses flees for his life in fear of being punished for murder. Even during his wandering phase with the rest of his people, every time Moses is presented with complaints from the suffering people, his faith wobbles and he questions what God has made them do (more than once). Even when he is tasked to reveal God's message and commandment to Pharaoh to let the people go, Moses does not believe enough even when God reassures him and tells him not to worry, to just go to Pharaoh and God will protect and guide him in what to say and do—Moses still refuses, he is so unsure and hesitant he does not accept until God appoints Aaron as his co-prophet and as the vociferous prophet.

According to the OT stories the children of Israel had no faith in Moses nor God; they continually harassed Moses as they believed he had led them into more sufferance and often wished to return to Egypt where they claim life was better; they make demands on Moses to exact from God; they refused to believe and had no faith in Moses their leader nor in God that either knew what he was doing—which resulted in recurring parts of the story with God punishing them because they had no faith and were 'stiffnecked' and disobedient, with the punishment taking on the form of many horrific methods.

The characters mentioned 'Gedeon, Barak, Samson, David, Samuel' are described as 'righteous' in Heb.11, but if you read their roles in the OT stories (even if they are the heroes/protagonists in the stories) they are depicted of committing crimes and sins against innocents whether of their own kind or not of their own kind, and their actions are very far from 'righteousness'. They did not 'quench the violence of fire' unless quenching it is by instigating murders, wars, etc., as described in the OT. The chapter also claims these characters made 'aliens' flee and intentionally contradicts the point made in the OT stories that the nations/peoples being killed in the OT stories were always the native and rightful inhabitants of their lands and that everyone meant and pertaining to the 'children of Israel' are the aliens, the outsiders without a connection to the land who came from somewhere else to commit genocide (according to the Bible and its stories) against the natives of the specific countries/areas because they felt entitled to the land, needed the land, God had promised them land, and the Biblical stories repeatedly state that God promised and gave them a land that did not belong to them (children of Israel) but rightfully belonged to others.

Heb.12 describes Esau as a 'fornicator' 'profane' for selling his birth right in exchange for a meal—whereas the OT clearly states he sold part of his birth right for a meal, but it was Rebekah and Jacob who diligently deceived both Esau and Isaac, taking advantage of the latter's blindness, and the hunger of the former, to steal both his birth right and blessing from him. In all cases of the examples used in Hebrew 11-12, the twisting and changing of the stories, its events and characters is done to enhance the meaning of 'Hebrew'.

Abraham and Sara both barren and so aged it was impossible to conceive then being pregnant is also a freak/mutation—being barren is the original mutilation; Abraham as Abram had to correct his imperfect body with circumcision which is double-meaning as surgically changing it from how it was naturally is a mutilation; Jacob usurping Esau in everything is a mutilation of the firstborn's birth rights including the blessing from Isaac; Esau is mentioned because he was described as so freakishly hairy his blind father could mistake Jacob wearing goats' fur on his arm as being Esau, and Esau himself going against nature and selling his birth right for food; Isaac as his conception was against nature; Abraham who was going to sacrifice Isaac his son is a show of mutilation and mutation, even God in offering up Jesus is the same as Abraham/Isaac, except Jesus had to go through more mutilations and suffering to make him a suitable sacrifice for mankind as Jesus being God's son had to be brought down a notch to suit mankind—and behind all these examples the author uses as the sender's examples of 'Hebrew**Error! Reference source not found.**' there is always a lesson to be learnt from or behind it. It continues in Jacob insisting on mutilating and reversing the firstborn's birth right by blessing Ephraim before Manasseh, Joseph's sons; in Joseph requesting his bones be dug up and transferred elsewhere is an ugly mutilation of a grave/the dead. Mentioned Moses was hid because he was a proper child not only reminds of the ugliness of killing which Pharaoh caused all the male babies, but that there was something different about him than other children; Moses refusing to be called Pharaoh's daughter's son is because it is unnatural to carry a name not your own or pretend to be something you are not; Hebrews continues with examples from the OT of things going in reverse of what should happen or be, of death, destruction, prostitution, going against one's own grain/character/being to show the meanings of 'mutilated/freakishly ugly/mutated/there must be a reason he is so freakishly ugly/mutated'.

It is shown in the women (Chapter 11) who are tortured in the name of faith and believing in God who end up either severely mutilated, the description is of freakish mutilation of their bodies, or those who do not die are made to live an abnormal wandering and hiding existence but instead of receiving God's promise, the author has the sender state these women will not be saved (in the afterlife) because they did not receive the promise and were not made 'perfect' by the sender of the letter (be it Paul, disciples or apostles), and this in itself is a reversal of the direction that the story and these persecuted women were going. The crucifixion of Jesus is mutilation of both life and body. (Heb.)

In both cases where 'Hebrew' is used in Revelation, it is in the middle of describing great disfigurement of the world, a reverse of nature and the characteristics of natural things, its topography, the landscape, the physics of matter, the physical and psychological state of humans; it describes disfigured beasts which have mixed human, animal and insect features; it describes an already bad situation and state of being and promises/warns to only get worse—more disfigurement. (Rev.9:11; 16:16)

Beginning with Genesis all through to Revelation whenever the word 'hebrew/'ibree/عبري' is introduced (which means extremely ugly/disfigured or nature reversed) it is exactly what happens in the story being told—a disfigurement be it physical to man or environment, or deterioration to the worse of a situation, or a reverse of how things stand/are.

The word 'hebrew/عبره/عبرى/عبري' 'extremely disfigured/nature reversed' in its application as a noun/adjective to the language of the Bible known as 'Hebrew', and also when later it would be claimed that Hebrew is an ethnicity—and how it came to be named 'Hebrew' is self-explanatory, but I will detail it. With regards to being applied to the language 'hebrew' still means 'extremely disfigured' and something in reverse or opposite to its nature, and in being applied to people/groups of people it is still for the same reasons and with the same meanings, and it will be explained in the following paragraphs.

The language of the Bible is Arabic—it is how I have been able to give the true meanings of the people and place names in the Bible, and the literal translation of these Arabic word-names make perfect sense in relation to the story being told, while the world has for centuries been unable to explain, unable to translate these meanings and have only ever presented wrong meanings based on guesswork and desire. Had the Biblical stories not originally been and remained the Arabic language, I would not have been able to translate them and they would make no sense, but as you can see they have a structure and that structure is based on the Arabic language which supports itself (the compound word-names and the stories) which has dumbfounded scholars (religious and academic) who have tried to give meaning using 'Hebrew' (which these scholars have never seen nor heard as in 'Biblical Hebrew'), Aramaic, and Canaanite, when in fact they only get it correct or close and also completely wrong when they use Arabic words' meanings (from the wrong version of Arabic such as Classical or colloquial) and then claim it be Aramaic, possibly based on the scholar's racial/political-driven biases. My exposure to and use of the ancient Old Arabic (which has never stopped being in use) in daily life has allowed me to be able to correctly translate these meanings—and they are precise and logical and supported by the Biblical texts.

Going back to the meaning of the word 'hebrew/'ibree/عبري' from the word ('ibra/عبرا/عبرى) 'extremely disfigured', and looking at the proof available: the Bible, archaeological proof, and living history (of the Arab region), even contemporary history—all prove this is the meaning of the word and why it was applied to some people of the Jewish faith and to what some groups within followers of the Jewish faith were doing to the language, while ethnically/racially and in the language they spoke and wrote, they were no different than their fellow Arab compatriots of other faiths: Hebrew is not a language. Hebrew is Arabic with some letters swapped around in an attempt to create a code which only specific people within specific Jewish groups were meant to be able to understand (a few examples: 'sh' 's' 'ss' 'z' could be swapped/replace each other'; 'h' 'ḥ' 'kh' could replace each other; 'y' 'g' (') 'gh' 'h' 'ḥ' 'kh' could replace each other and be swapped around), but because these stories were created, told, and written first in Arabic, and because the code depended on Arabic to keep its meanings as the original language of these original stories/religious scriptures, it limited how much the language could be changed—which was only swapping Arabic letters around. 'Hebrew' in its true and purest meaning when applied to what was done to the language means the disfiguration of Arabic, the same applies to people, first only those engaged in attempting to swap the Arabic letters around and write in a reverse Arabic before later on in time when things were forgotten and ended up being mistaken as a language and people. It also came to be applied to language/people the same way 'Jew/yehud' came to be applied to the religion because at the beginnings of this conduct the people around them (including people of the Jewish faith) would have described this is what is being done by these people to the language when they coded it (and of course the groups within the Jewish community who changed the texts and made a code out of the Arabic language did it for a reason which will be discussed later in this book).

Look at the word Arab/Arabic and Hebrew/Hebraic, the letters 'r/ر' and 'b/ب' have been swapped to create 'Hebrew':

Arab	Hebrew
عربي	عبري
عـ ر بـ ي	عـ بـ ر ي
'rbi	'bri

There are three reasons how 'Hebrew' was created and came to be mistaken as a language; two are possible reasons why certain groups within the Jewish faith disfigured the language in an attempt to encode it and make it 'their' own. The first is a fact, the latter two are possible reasons: the first reason has nothing to do with disfiguring the Arabic language in order to restrict information nor a group of people wanting to be seen as different, but because one of the amazing organic characteristics of the Arabic language is that it facilitates the swapping of letters around e.g. to become a diminutive of a word, and also to become the opposite of the same word; it is also a tool used in the Arabic language that one letter can be written as a specific letter, but can also stand and be read as another letter in wordplay—so there was already a tool in the Arabic language (known as muwaaraba) which allows one word to become a completely different word by having even just one letter possibly standing for two or more letters which allow it to be read differently, and this also facilitated how 'Hebrew' as a code (not a language) was created.

The second reason, is a group of people wanted to be different, or seen as different to fit in with the stories of a special, chosen people while faced with the reality and general awareness of the fact they were all just one people.

The third reason, which is the more probable reason: historically it has always been claimed that the priests, scribes (people in charge of religious texts, laws, guidance, rituals, etc.) changed, distorted, added, eliminated things from the original Torah/OT, to suit their personal and/or religious agendas. This is an accusation supported by the stories of the OT and NT itself; it is a fact that revisions and redactions have been made to the Bible by many authors and over different times, possibly over a long history of time.

The fact the words 'jew' 'distorted/disfigured/made ugly/disobedience/ruined/etc.' and 'hebrew' 'extremely disfigured/reverse of nature' and these words come to be nouns describing the religion and groups within the religion although these words have negative attributes, indicate it was applied to those deemed as distorting/disfiguring/changing the religion, language, maybe even their physical appearance, by the people around them (of the same Arab ethnicity) and even by those of the same Jewish religion (before it was called Jewish), and was not chosen by the people/priests distorting the religion but applied to them: so the Arab/'rbi/عربي becomes Hebrew/'bri/عبري an Arab who has distorted Arabic to distort customs, language, religion. This word describes exactly what has been done to the Arabic language of the Biblical stories (whether they were first considered just fictional stories and later on as religious texts).

Wanting to be different, wanting to manipulate religion into something else and separate from other religions can be seen in the attempts to:

- Encrypt the Biblical stories in an attempt to create a code understood by only those within specific groups of the Jewish faith;
- Attempt to manipulate the people and especially those of the Jewish religion by creating hierarchy for priests and priestly family to keep the secrets, code, and the true understanding of the real words in Arabic within specific and limited families to hegemonize the control over the religion and what the religion instructs its followers to do within a limited group (knowledge is power).

All this would lead to the word 'hebrew' with its meanings of disfiguring, reversing things, going in the opposite direction.

The disfiguration of Arabic to make an encrypted language (Hebrew) did not last nor succeed in spreading because it could not be changed a lot—even when letters were swapped around it was still evidently Arabic and that is why 'Hebrew' was never a first language nor a dominant language even among Jewish faith communities in its region of creation—the Middle East. It did not survive, did not continue because it was an attempt not at creating a new language, but for specifically coding the Biblical stories which at some point would be deemed religious texts; an attempt to differentiate themselves but also to limit control of religious knowledge to a small group within the Jewish faith. But because they could not create a completely different language as it was meant to be only understood by a priestly hierarchy, also because the people of that faith (Jewish) were all Arabs and Arabic-speakers and daily life was in Arabic and the majority of the people following the Jewish faith did not accept it as the language to be used when reading the religious texts—especially because it was an incomplete code and too similar to Arabic which they already spoke so it was discontinued while Arabic, the original and only language continues to this day.

Of course, one might argue that the scripture of the Biblical texts (OT) is not Arabic, it is what is called 'Hebrew', the answer to that is all the scriptures of the Arabs did not begin with the Arabic scripture of today: ا ، ب ، ج ، د, (abgd) e.g. look at inscriptions on millennia-old Yemeni temples and artefacts, they do not resemble the Arabic scripture, but they do pronounce as Arabic words and make the sounds of Arabic letters (abgd). The fact is, the oldest Biblical texts which have been found and are written in 'Hebrew' scripture are from a much later date and found in a completely different area than when and where the original stories were created and circulated, it is a compilation of the popular stories which were most probably compiled by persons who copied the stories into texts and do not necessarily reflect the original scripture they were written in and originated from, but as the language has been kept intact it is clearly the Arabic language of the Arabian Peninsula in pronunciation and meaning. Language is first spoken, then written letters are invented, they go through evolvement before resting on a modern 'perfected' form, they are basically symbols or patterns which people can understand (read) and replicate the sound and pronunciations of the spoken language; and like most things which begin, language also evolves as does its written form and varies from area to area. The Bible has shown Arabic is a language which has remained close to what it was in ancient times, with modernity making it more fluid in urbanised areas, but in Yemen many areas still pronounce it in its most ancestral and rawest form. The attempt to code it into 'Hebrew' did not succeed as 'Hebrew' was never completed as a language and does not have all the letters and phonemes to pronounce as a language due to it being created only as a code and not as a language, and remained and relied on Arabic to give it its meanings as Arabic had always been its original form.

'Hebrew' is Arabic, not a separate ethnicity, but a word in everyday use, and used as description of people and things (any people, and people unrelated to the Jewish faith) deemed to be 'extremely disfigured' or doing things in reverse whether in appearance such as physically disfigured, or dressing differently, or behaving contrary to the norm (whatever the 'norm' may be as per the opinion of the beholder): Even in the OT 'hebrew' is an adjective/verb/adverb, not an ethnicity, it was a word used by Biblical authors and applied by the 'children of Israel' within the story to describe people deemed not 'children of Israel'. e.g. the authors described certain parts of the Philistine army as Hebrews (who were fighting against the 'children of Israel' in 1Sam.14:20-21. Also in the OT, people from the same 'tribe/people' would call some individuals within the same group 'Hebrew', also one group of people would call another group of people 'Hebrew', following the Biblical authors' method of inventing names for characters and places based on word-play to match the event/theme of the story.

Factually, all archaeological and historical studies have proven there is no such thing as 'Israel' or 'Israelite' as a separate ethnicity or as a separate culture—all archaeological finds prove it is only Canaanite civilisation and culture to have ever existed on what is Palestine and the Palestine which has been renamed by European Zionists as 'Israel' which I call modern-Israel to avoid confusion with the Biblical Israel. All archaeological finds and studies have failed to turn up even one piece of evidence to prove anything called 'Israel' or its existence, and anything even remotely related to the Biblical stories—and that should not be surprising not only because the Bible is a fictional group of stories, but even these fictional stories were not created and were not written in Palestine, Iraq, Syria, Lebanon, Egypt and they are not of these countries cultures; the Biblical stories are not set in Palestine, Iraq, Syria, Lebanon, Egypt but in the landscape of the original authors' homeland which is elsewhere in the Arab region. All the artefacts modern-Israel displays as 'Israelite' are actually Canaanite. All archaeological and other studies and proof show there was no 'Exodus' out of Egypt or from anywhere; Egyptians whose Pharaonic history has been meticulously recorded since millennia ago never mentioned, not even once, 'Israel' or 'children of Israel' 'Israelite' ever existing and do not mention any of the Biblical characters, nor does Egyptian/Pharaonic history ever mention coming into contact with such a civilisation or people—there is absolutely no mention of 'Israel/Israelite' whatsoever, and the Pharaons recorded everything including battles won and lost, practises, details, and they mention all other civilisations they came into contact with. The Hyksos, Assyrians, Akkadian, Nabaetans, Babylonians, etc. their archaeological proof survives and none mention 'Israel' 'children of Israel' etc., although they record and prove their own existence. With all these historically rich and recorded civilisations—none of which mention 'Israel/children of Israel' or 'Hebrew'—along with archaeological excavations, all prove Israel never existed as per the Biblical stories. Then there is what the OT and NT tells us 'hebrew' means, 'extremely disfigured', reversing the nature of the way things are (which is the meaning of the word in rural Yemen and Arabian Peninsula Arabic whose language explains perfectly the true meanings of names and words in the Bible) which also proves what 'hebrew' means and that 'hebrew' is used for the disfigurement of the word 'Arab/Arabic'.

As there is no 'Hebrew' people or race/ethnicity—only Arabs of whom a small portion wanted to feel special, who wanted to have more power over those of the Jewish faith and so used the Arabic language in a short-lived attempt to create a code for the stories, the fact they did not want to deny their Arab origins (nor could they) but only desired to make the Biblical stories understood fully by a select few by encoding these stories, even they held onto the true origin-language, and only swapped letters around to avoid being unable to use the OT whose original language survives in the names and its link to the story being told, and in the language of the text of the OT. Over time, and by crossing into Arab countries not familiar with the Old Arabic of the Arabian Peninsula, this fact would be lost in antiquity, but also in modern times and contemporary history when attention would re-emerge in the Biblical texts, religious and political agendas and biases would get in the way and obstruct admitting, revealing, knowing the true Arabic origins of these words and its authors.

But it remains due to the only language (which existed at the time when these Biblical stories were told/written in the country of origin) was Arabic spoken first before it was written in different scriptures and available throughout the Middle East region (long before the scripture would evolve into the Arabic of today)—when those groups/individuals decided to rewrite, revise, redact and disfigure the stories by copying it in code known as 'hebrew', how much they could change the words of the text was limited due to its availability and popularity in the region as stories told for millennia. How much they could change the words was also limited out of fear of losing the meanings of the words because these stories depend on wordplay to make sense, which is the Biblical authors' method of creating character names made out of compound words directly connected to the events in the story as what they mean happens in the story—but with spans of time, what they feared of the words being forgotten and therefore the stories losing their meanings did happen, especially where the stories ended up at in the Levant (who do not speak the pure Old Arabic of the Arabian Peninsula but a mixed form of Arabic in that specific region, or maybe they spoke the language in antiquity but by the time the Jewish religion spread into the Levant their dialects had already evolved and so they had already forgotten most of the Old Arabic and spoke a more modern or colloquial form of Arabic).

The original authors and audiences of the Biblical stories had no idea how millennia later people would erroneously believe it to be a separate ethnicity and language. Much confusion, especially caused by historic and contemporary religious ideas and progression, and how people identify themselves as well as how language is used, have confused the fact that being Jewish did not mean race/ethnicity but meant the person's faith—this is due to how in the Arabic language (both historically and even in modernity) 'people/nation' does not mean a separate race but used to describe people who may be from a different family, village or area, or a part of society that had different belief systems or the same religion but practised it in a different way, or people who came from a different tribe or any other make-up of social unit is how people identify themselves—and especially when many different religions**Error! Reference source not found.** were not only emerging but spreading and competing to control trade, religious sites, land, civilian and religious authority, influence on the different components of the population and way of life, all on the same piece of geographical land. These facts cause people to identify themselves whether using: village, area, religion, family, tribe, class/cast, etc. but none of these self-identifications or 'classifications' negates they are from the same race/ethnicity and especially true regarding 'Jewish' and the first Jews who were Arabs, and the language of people of the Jewish faith was Arabic. Take for example how prior, during and following the emergence of Islam, Arabs of the Arabian Peninsula (whether they were polytheists, Jews or Muslims) would call some Arabs from the same Arabian Peninsula 'Arabs'—they did not mean a different race, but identified them as 'Arabs from the 'so and so' family' or 'Arabs from the 'so and so' tribe/village/area' and so forth as that is how these units identified/named themselves while the same Arabs from the same areas did not use 'Arab' as part of the identifying noun although they were the same Arabs. But with the competition increasing between polytheists, Jews and Muslims over the same geographical land, the same religious sites, the same trade routes and commercial dominance (what in modernity would be called market share) and especially the competition over people's hearts and minds, i.e. religious beliefs—the identification as 'Jew' 'Muslim' and 'polytheists' (the latter of different kinds) would become more pointed, but it never negated they were Arabs until in more recent history e.g. with the dominance of Islam as the religion of the region, it would become a point to differentiate using religion as an identifier especially because allegiances were being made between different factions of the Arabian Peninsula Arabs who were Jewish, polytheists, and new-Muslims, and this only becomes confused with 'race' the more it progresses into modernity and the further away the identification spreads in geographical space, but early on it was never a doubt that they were all one Arab race with different religious, tribal, societal, allegiance, area and other forms of belonging and connections, identifications and community systems—and despite all these different sub-identifications, Arabic was their only language, they all had a shared history, culture, language, and land.

Although it is a primarily western idea and belief that 'Jew' and 'Hebrew' means a different race/ethnicity with a different language, the modern Arab countries are influenced by western academic beliefs as despite the Arab-Islamic world in the past had progressed and innovated in all sciences and whose work made advances and were the foundation blocks of the western world's advances in science, when the Arab civilisations and the Islamic empire would disintegrate and its nations fall back into ignorance, poverty, etc. (due to many factors not a subject of this book) the West has progressed and are now the leading academic, scientific, industrial leaders—and the west dictates what history 'is'; in the same way what was once known and obvious (and still is among Arab nations), the Arab intellectuals of whom many are schooled in western universities or adopt western schools of thought take influence from what the west is telling them their history is with regards to the Bible and everything related to the Bible—which is wrong as the hundreds of millions of Arabs are aware of the truth that the first Jews, the first Christians, the first Muslims are all originally Arabs who spoke Arabic, and that pagan, Jew, Christian, Muslim are faiths one can convert to at any time without it changing their native Arab ethnicity, and the books which are believed to be divine (Torah, NT, Quran) are part of their culture and heritage. Of course, modern conflicts and specifically the Israeli-Palestinian conflict has further driven the misuse of the word 'Jew/Jewish' as a race/ethnicity, whereas the Palestinians use it as a noun for the Europeans who have militarily occupied Palestine because 'Jew' is the label/noun the Zionist Europeans from multiple European countries chose to collectively call themselves instead of have to list the tens of multiple European countries of their nativities before they named themselves 'Israel'. All documented archaeological proof shows there is no difference in ethnicity of the people who lived in this region (the natives, both ancestors and descendants) and who have always been Arabs and their ancestors—Palestine, e.g., has only ever been inhabited by Palestinians who are the natural and organic descendants of their ancient ancestors, and this too brings us to a more important point: the Bible was not written by Palestinians—or any ancestors of Palestine—nor did the stories and the religions described in the Bible (paganism, Jewish, Christianity) emerge from Palestine, but some of these religions were brought to Palestine by people much later on when these stories were already well-known and the religion practised by another Arab civilisation and people.

This leads to the question of why were stories created about 'children of Israel', a special people? The answer can only be found, and is abundantly clear, when you know who wrote the Bible and all the Torah-related scripts—the original and early versions—and once you know who wrote it then you can understand why, and everything becomes clear just as when I translated the true and correct meanings of the names of characters and places in the Bible, how it becomes clear what is meant by these names in relation to the story being told, as well as understanding why these stories were written (but of course, along with revisions/redactions over different periods of time, the reasons behind the differing authors' actions also differ).

Facts Needed for Clarity

There are facts which need to be understood: Middle East religions were open to all—whether divine, monotheistic (Judaism(a misnomer which correctly should be Jewish), Christianity, Islam) or polytheistic, paganistic. The people and area where these religions originated from are all Middle Eastern and specifically Arabic. Through inward and outward travel these religions spread within the Middle East and further across; the same goes for how these Arab religions spread to the West, especially during foreign conquests and empire building. Just like all religions, when the Jewish religion emerged not everyone converted to it (the same goes for Christianity and Islam), but those who did and do convert do not get an ethnicity/race change—they remain their original ethnicity, and no one is born carrying a religion but is either brought up as an adherent to the specific religion or converts to the specific religion. E.g. if a Japanese man or an English man converted to Judaism or Christianity (or even Islam) they do not become 'Hebrew'/Arabic it is only their religious beliefs (and maybe conduct) which change, not their DNA; and the same goes for all adherents of the Jewish religion whose Jewish faith can change, cease or begin, but not their organic origins which remain constant and is separate from being of the Jewish faith.

When a new religion emerges, or arrives, and spreads—the people of older religions are not scattered around the world: e.g. when Christianity or Islam spread in the Middle East, those who practised the Jewish faith did not all leave the separate countries which they were natives of, and neither did the pagans for that matter with the advent of the Jewish and other religions. It is later generations and especially the West which wants to believe the Biblical stories as 'history', and instead of understanding that the presence of Arabs of the Jewish faith in Europe is due to the natural crossing, ebb and flow of cultures such as travel for better life opportunities or to live a new life in a new place, as well as displacement from conflict being sometimes the cause —instead, western belief takes it as proof of what was described in the Bible as a prophesy would happen, and this erroneous belief is compounded with another erroneous belief that these Jewish people living in Europe are a race separate from those living in the Arab countries although they know that these Jewish people came from the heart of the Arab lands.

The problem is the western world wants to believe the Arab Jews who arrived and chose to live in Europe are a mirror of what happened in the Biblical stories, because the OT spoke of exiling the 'children of Israel' to Babylon, to Assyria, to all the corners of the world—then that must be why these Jewish Arabs are in Europe. It only becomes conflated further when native-European converts to Judaism, who have absolutely no organic connection to any Arab country, claim they all originated from Palestine although they are just converts and not of the original Arab-ethnicity of Jewish-faith people in Europe (the original Arab Jews in Europe whose descendants, along with millions of the European Jews of European nativity, were tragically massacred during the Jewish Holocaust by Nazi Germany).

It is the misunderstanding then the misuse of Biblical stories about 'children of Israel' being completely driven out of their 'land' (in storyland) as punishment by God which the west twists into being how brown Arabs of the Jewish faith ended up all over Europe, and also to explain how white European natives of multiple and distinctly different European countries converted to Judaism which would lead to the horrific 'othering' of both the brown Arab Jew who had lived for centuries in Europe and the 'othering' of the white native European Jew who had only ever lived and whose ancestors had only ever lived in Europe of their native European countries (German Jews native Germans, Polish Jews native Poles, Ukrainian Jews native Ukrainian, and so forth) which would culminate into the horrific Jewish Holocaust although the persecutors who were German Nazis and other European Nazis who joined in the persecution of European Jews were themselves converts to another Arab-borne religion: Christianity.

But do Europeans of the Christian faith (including white Americans) believe they have become organic natives of the Arab country where this Christian faith first emerged, and therefore have the right to massacre the natives of these Arab countries and colonise their lands? Of course not—they know they are not organically connected in any shape or form to the country of Christianity's origin, which they believe to be Palestine. Notwithstanding, the western world has constantly shown it does believe it has the right to lay hold onto what it believes are Biblical lands and non-Biblical lands and everything contained in them, which has been evident since the Christian Crusades to colonialism, where the European Christian invader slaughtered Jews and Muslims alike, and showed a special vengeance towards the Jews, and also showed the first signs of misunderstanding the Bible in its entirety as it implemented the occupation of what they believed to be, and called, Jerusalem (which is not even the correct Jerusalem of the Bible); and in modernity when the Jewish religion would become a white-European religion it would lead Europeans to the genocide of the Palestinian nation although Palestine is not the origins nor the settings of the Biblical stories nor is it the origins of the Jewish religion. It is important to briefly address these issues as they show how misunderstanding the Bible has led to even more misunderstandings and prevents the truth from surfacing about the Bible, its stories, its authors, the origins of Judaism and of Christianity, which is a shame because it is such a book rich with mysteries only because they are ignoring the very language and culture it was written in and is from, and by which answers all the questions about the Bible and its mysteries.

The Bible itself proves it is a fictional collection of stories. In reality, Palestine, which has been mistaken for the land of the Biblical stories and undergone a process of fiction-forced-into-reality by brute force on its land and people in modernity at the hands of Europeans, like all other Arab countries had its multiple faiths even if they were one people; there is nothing to suggest the Arab Jews who ended up in Europe were from Palestine. The descriptions of Jews in novels of the times (when Europeans were addressing people of the Jewish faith as a 'question/issue') as well as painted and photographic portraits show they are from Yemen and what is now modern Saudi Arabia. It does not mean a small minority of Jews never went to live in Palestine, for that is how all the religions spread from the Arab country of origin of these stories and religions and into the Levant including into Palestine, but the Arab Jews from different Arab countries (not necessarily from and probably not from Palestine) who ended up living in Europe and bringing to it the Jewish faith, they were not driven out of their native countries by God, nor did the entire Arab population of the Jewish faith leave their native countries to settle elsewhere in the world—no, that did not happen. Take for example Palestine, the majority of the people who made up the population of Palestine and in faith were pagans, Christians and eventually Muslims—they remained in Palestine, they are the descendants of the Canaanites and other related civilisations who have always dwelt there, uncut: it is very telling that Palestinians were Muslims, Christians, Druse but not Jews as this religion did not seem to flourish in Palestine's history (with only 'Samaritans' who were distinctly other Arabs from outside Palestine arriving briefly and in small numbers prior to Zionist arrival). The people who lived on ancient Palestine were Arabs and were not driven out by punishment from God but have remained in their country until the conflict of 1948 would massacre and forcefully expel many from their land. The Arab Jews who arrived in Europe (from elsewhere than Palestine) centuries ago did not metamorphose into native Polish, Ukrainian, British, Russian and all the other white European ethnicities whose ancestors converted to Judaism in their native European countries, the latter (Europeans) only arrived in Palestine in the 1920s in small numbers then from 1948 onwards in greater numbers in a European colonisation fulfilled by military force, facilitated and implemented in very recent and modern times. All the religions of the region, paganistic, Jewish, Christian and Islamic originated from one place: the Arabian Peninsula before spreading towards the wider

Middle East region then further abroad, including the West, through normal travel, encounters and cross-culture between the Middle East and the West (including conquest and empire) and the religions spread, in the same fashion that news and stories spread.

Not 'one people' of one faith and/or ethnicity appear and disappear from one area to another according to the religion (that only happens in the fictional story-telling of the Bible) because originally, they were all Arabs of differing countries all over the Middle East and North Africa. But history over the millennia and alive even today shows Jewism, Christianity, Islam, and along with paganism which preceded them all, have spread, co-existed and are and have been present in almost all Arab countries; and when the citizens/people adopt a different religion their ethnicities, residence, nativity do not change: Yemeni pagans, Yemeni Jews, Yemeni Christians, Yemeni Muslims—changed their religious ritual practise according to the religion they chose to follow, but they did not suddenly become a different ethnicity, nor move/uproot completely to a different part of the country, region or world (any movements of people would be normal migration, or displacement from war, for economical reasons, etc. but never a complete movement of all people of the one religion. Of course, what local and regional politics, influences and powers including European Zionism did to the majority of Yemeni Jews in the 1950s is a man-made and man-designed forced immigration to Palestine/modern-Israel and is not part of this point being discussed. This is about natural movement of people and religion). And the same goes for civilisations, countries and their native ethnicities of the West influenced by and converted to Jewism, Christianity, Islam. Whether western/European people converted to Judaism or Christianity in the Middle East and brought back these religions to Europe, or were influenced to convert by groups of Arab Jews, Arab Christians (mistakenly believed to be 'Hebrew/Jew') immigrating to European countries—they too brought these Arab religions to the western parts of the world. This is the normal way and the only way how religions spread in the past from Arab countries to convert Europeans to 'Judaism'/Jewism, many to Christianity—but it does not mean the European Jews are 'Hebrew' or 'Jew' in race/ethnicity (as even the very first Arab Jews (and all Jews) are not 'Jew' in race/ethnicity but in their faith), and it does not matter how far back their ancestors converted to Judaism or Christianity, it did not and will never give them an organic connection to the Arab race/ethnicity which is the only and original ethnicity of the first Jews, the first Christians, of the authors of the Bible, the ethnicity/race of its characters, and the Arabs are the only natives of their Arab countries no matter what the name of the country was in antiquity and what the country's name is now in modernity.

To clarify this point further, look at the different ethnicities within the Arab race/region, they are all Arabs, but have unique nativities/ethnicity even if within the same Arab race: just like a Syrian Christian has no ethnical identity to a Yemeni Christian (as Arabs are made up of unique countries with their own (and sometimes shared) cultures, and the uniqueness of distinct Arabic dialects); the Yemeni Jew is not of the same ethnicity/nativity as the Moroccan Jew. The Iraqi Jew, Iraqi Christian, Iraqi Muslim are completely different in ethnicity and nativity than the Yemeni Jew, Yemeni Christian, Yemeni Muslim. Whereas the Iraqi Jew shares the same ethnicity and nativity of the Iraqi Christian and Muslim, but has no ethnic ties to the Yemeni Jew even if they do believe in and share the same religion and share the same Arab race (they may share what all Arabs share: race, language and culture, but also have their unique ethnic cultures and histories, dialects and accents—it does not give the Iraqi and Yemeni Jew a shared ethnicity/nativity. This needs to be understood to avoid falling into the pit where ethnicity/race/religion have been blurred and hijacked for political reasons, and failing to remove politically and religiously charged biases and misinformation (whether by intention or genuine mistake) will prevent from understanding the Bible and its stories which were written long before modern biases and conflicts.

The point of this book is to show the Bible's true meanings as a language and what it shows are its truths, all contained within the Bible. We must face an obvious fact that anyone can have a religion, but it does not change or give a different ethnicity/nativity to its followers. By removing politically motivated assertions about 'Jew' and 'Hebrew' we can objectively view what 'Jew' and 'Hebrew' mean solely as words and how they became nouns of a religion. 'Hebrew' means 'extremely disfigured/nature in reverse' in the language of the OT/NT; within the Bible it is applied to various different people—not only to those of the Jewish faith; it is a verb, a noun, an adjective; outside the Biblical stories, it describes how a group of people attempted to change the language of the Bible through code, 'hebrew', to have more knowledge than others with all the gain and objectives that would entail. In copying the Biblical stories from its original Arabic language and writing it in code they based the make-up and meaning of the word 'Hebrew' a disfigurement of Arabic (an anagram) on swapping certain letters, but still they pronounce and can be understood as Arabic—if they had changed the names of the Biblical characters to something completely different it would have left the stories without the meaning intended by its original authors, so they could not change the names and is why they remain perfectly explainable in Arabic and fit perfectly into the story being told when explained in Arabic using the names as they are in the OT. It cannot be denied that the word 'hebrew' 'extremely disfigured' also reflects the language was purposely disfigured by those in charge (priests/scribes) when interpreting/copying the Bible so it became 'Hebrew' disfiguring its original Arabic language, although it must be said, not enough disfiguring could be done to it and it still reads perfectly in Arabic. In addition to this, it is how it was used within the content of the Bible, this is how and where the words 'hebrew/extremely disfigured' and 'jew/distorted/corrupted/etc.' came to describe first those in charge who distorted the language/religion/religious texts and scriptures, then to describe the followers of the religion and the religion itself.

In disfiguring the language with a malleable encoding to create what is now called 'Hebrew' (Biblical Hebrew), the people who designed this left letters intentionally obscure so as to be able to give more than one meaning to the words depending on which letter was believed to be the correct one. It also served to allow adding when additions were written, sections rewritten, into the original stories. This language device can be seen in Classical Arabic too, where poets and story-tellers use a device called 'muwaaraba' which means to allow a specific letter to be ambiguous enough it can be a different letter and hold two different meanings to allow the pun or the 'swap' in meaning to happen so it can first mean one thing and then mean another depending on how it is read and how the author wants to deliver the pun.

The people of those times knew this 'disfigurement' of Arabic into its anagram 'Hebrew' (عربي/عبري)—it did not need to be explained; the people/priests distorting the religion and language to separate themselves and make them powerful through exclusive knowledge came to be known as 'jew/yehud/distorts/disfigures/makes worse' and 'hebrew/'ibree/extremely disfigured/nature reversed', but it never became a language because it was not even designed to have all the letters and sounds needed to pronounce words in a full language and specifically the language of its authors/audience because it was supposed to be a code, and not a language understood by all, and this explains why it never became the first language, nor the dominant language among Jewish communities and Jewish intellectuals whose first language which they used in everyday life and in the copious amounts of literature they produced and spoke was Arabic. This is why even when these Jewish intellectuals wrote in 'Hebrew' letters they needed to use Arabic to complete the words written in 'Hebrew' as it was never independent of the Arabic language it was created from; and without using Arabic, the 'Hebrew' text could not be used, could not be made into complete words and could not be made into an independent communicative language because that is not what it was designed for. It was designed to obfuscate, not clarify.

Who Wrote the Bible/Torah

As mentioned previously, knowing who wrote the Bible will lead to explain why these stories were written and why the stories focus on certain points. The answer as to who created the Bible, the original version, lies in the stories, the text itself—the Bible tells us who its authors are. The original authors of the Bible are Yemenis from Yemen then Saudi Arabians from ancient-Saudi Arabia. The expression in the narration and how it is presented is rural Yemeni, even after it has been translated into English, due to early foreign translations translating it as close as possible to the literal in the language it was found. Mistaken as 'Hebrew' which is Arabic, it still held on to its Yemeni flavour through how the story is told; the way its characters speak is exactly how Yemenis in remote rural areas (and most of its cities) speak to this day, and many of the words still exist in the vocabulary spoken by Saudi Arabians to this day. Not only is the style of narration and expression exactly how Yemenis speak and express, but also the sayings, proverbs, are rural Yemeni used to this day, and although I use the phrase 'rural Yemeni' or 'remote Yemeni' because in these regions the language is still how they speak to this day, but of course the whole of Yemen once spoke this language as did the whole of the Arabian Peninsula.

Furthermore, actions and customs which may seem peculiar to the western reader such as Laban and Jacob putting between them a stone as witness against them is a custom which has existed in Yemen since pagan times, long before the Biblical stories were created—forgotten and erased from memory in the cities (with the exception of the phrase 'Gilead you, God' still in use by city people), but still alive and practised in remote and rural areas of Yemen. It must be noted that these communities are Muslim and not Jewish—they have no knowledge of the Bible (OT and NT) or its contents as known to the modern world, even the Quran although they know of it—up until the 1990s it was still something relatively new to the Muslim communities who were pagan well into the 21st Century before Islam would be brought back with people who had gone to Saudi Arabia to make a living. The language, customs, rituals described in a dramatized fashion in the Bible are Yemeni customs and language which have been part of everyday life for generations since antiquity. While I was in rural Yemen for most of the 90s, even Islam and Muslim practice was relatively an intruder, 'new', the religious practise and its rules neither known nor followed completely because the region railed against and kept out 'strangers' 'foreigners' and any kind of practise and beliefs, any attempts at introduction to ways of life coming from abroad (such as Saudi Arabia) and even local Yemeni cities were deemed as 'strangers' and 'foreign' as much as anyone and anything coming from outside Yemen.

Of course, the remoteness and inaccessibility to the outside world kept foreigners (including Yemeni locals from outside the region) and change away from this region, but also when relative accessibility allowed locals from the remote region itself to travel to local cities when need be, as well as some to go work in Saudi Arabia, it was the communities' strict adherence to their own way of life, rejecting any modernisation in ways of living, thought, tradition, custom, beliefs to the degree when there was opportunity on more than one occasion that the government was willing, or it was possible to get the government to electrify the region (or at least some parts of it), the whole community, headed by its older generations flatly rejected it, claiming it was a ploy by the government with the real intention of the government of stealing the people's land, which they truly believed. But the inaccessibility due to distance and the harsh terrain, coupled with the communities' rejection towards change, their protection of tradition and the general way of life kept these communities living as people had lived in ancient times—in language, tradition, culture, values and beliefs, well into the 2000s.

My first encounter which taught me Arabic was in this Yemeni region. My use of this language as the only language for the first eight years of living in remote Yemen allowed me to instantly understand what the names in the Bible really mean; because I spoke and speak this language, and it is Arabic still in its purest form in the remote areas of Yemen which allowed me to see how classical Arabic, Modern Standard Arabic and other Arab countries' Arabic are the natural evolvement and modern mutations out of the vernacular of the remote regions' Arabic which remained in its purest form due to its remoteness. Rural Yemenis can understand the dialect of the modern forms, dialects, accents of Arabic in the cities, while the city folk struggle understanding the pure pronunciations of the rural people until their ears get acquainted with hearing the words which are the same Arabic essentially; the rural Yemenis' language covers many meanings given in modernity to different words, but the city people's language whether classical, modern, or colloquial Arabic have forgotten the original meanings of many words in the Old Arabic.

Not only is the prose and narrative of how the Bible is expressed, and the proverbs, absolutely Yemeni, but so are the customs described in the Bible (which will be addressed later in this book), and the actions attributed to the characters and in the stories exactly how people behave, talk, do in rural Yemen; from expression, proverbs, customs, superstitions (positive and negative), terms of description used, the 'wanderings' of Moses and his people, clothing, use of substances in adornment, food ingredients and dishes, the importance put on specific matters, the rituals and customs which become festivals or significant events in the Biblical stories, the way of life as depicted in the Bible—all are uniquely Yemeni (rural), to the degree when I read the Bible it describes exactly what I lived (with exception of killing everybody and miracles) and how daily life is, how people around me spoke, thought, expressed, lived. It was as if the people who wrote the Bible were describing my people and my people's way of life.

Then there is the undisputable fact of the language—the names of people and places are Arabic compound words made up from words used in remote Yemen in everyday life even today; the fact that these words were made into names in the Bible for characters and places and whose actions and/or place of event enacts the very meanings of these words is further proof the authors are Yemeni from ancient times. Not only are the names given in the Bible Arabic words, but although the stories being told are believed to be set in modern Palestine and its neighbouring region—many of the names given as areas in the long lists are areas unique to both Yemen and Saudi Arabia (to be discussed later).

What is obvious and clear from the Biblical text itself is that these Biblical stories and the Jewish religion did not originate from modern Palestine/ancient Canaan, but these stories which would eventually end up as religions were carried by Yemenis and ancient-Saudis to the rest of the Middle East. I use 'Saudi Arabia' but what I am addressing is the ancient inhabitants of the Arabian Peninsula whose country and descendants would become and be named in modernity 'Saudi Arabia'. What is obvious is the authors of the Bible did not want to forget their origins. The stories of the Bible testify to the earliest authors being from Yemen, the Bible itself tells us it is Yemeni/Saudi Arabian.

The strongest possibility is that these stories were created and set in the land of the Arabian Peninsula, both Yemen and ancient Saudi Arabia; this area of land and its inhabitants are the origin of these stories and the origin of the Jewish and Christian religions. The stories, and eventually the religion, was first circulated and popular among the Arabian Peninsula Arabs before it travelled towards the Levant (Palestine, Syria, Lebanon, Iraq, Jordan). Both the stories and religions became so popular among the Levant that they named their villages, towns, cities which they inhabited after the names in the stories.

Language

First, the language as it is shown throughout the OT and NT is rural Yemen Arabic—the continuity in the stories of Arabic for the names of people and places is abundant; the authors created these stories based on their exact meanings as words used in Yemeni Arabic, and followed what I call the 'Biblical authors' method' which is the use of compound words as word-names, and wordplay. Also, the expression, the way the Bible is narrated by the authors is how Yemenis in remote areas speak and express, as is the dialogue ascribed to the Bible's characters; the sayings are uniquely Yemeni. Here are some examples of Bible expressions which are based on Yemeni expressions and phrases:

More than once, the now banal saying of 'you won't hurt a hair on his head' is expressed exactly how it is said in Yemeni villages and by Yemeni people regardless of where they live: 1Sam.14:45 'God forbid, as the Lord liveth, there shall not one hair of his head fall to the ground.', an expression used frequently in rural Yemen 'By God not one hair shall fall from his head' (والله ولاشعرى هتفلت من راسه) .

'There is but a step between me and death' said once by David's character—again although it may be in use now all over the world, the wording and its frequency of use in rural Yemen are distinctively Yemeni in origin. 'There is nothing between me and death but a step' (ما بيني وبين الموت إلّا خطوا).

Describing oneself or everyone around as a stranger and foreigner when identifying non-locals in the Bible is the Yemeni way and expression not necessarily describing someone from a different country, but even someone from outside the respective village of the speaker.

It is a rural Yemeni saying 2Sam.14:14 '...as water spilt on the ground, which cannot be gathered again.'. 'What has been spilt cannot be gathered' (مكترع لايلتف).

Another frequently used phrase, regarding those who do others wrong is 'The evil/wickedness will return in/on your head' (الشر هيرجع في راسك); this is exactly expressed in Kgs.2:44 through Solomon to Shimei (for cursing/insulting his father) '…the Lord shall return thy wickedness upon thine own head'.

'Turn their reproach on their own head' Neh.4:4-5, is used in much the same way as 'return thy wickedness upon thine own head' but here it refers to returning bad behaviour against its provocateurs referring to Sanballat and Tobia mocking the returned exiles building, and the prayer 'turn their reproach upon their own head is based on the Yemeni expression 'What you do/say will return upon you' (اللي تصلحه/تقوله هيرجع عليك/عليكم).

Another rural Yemeni expression showing how little or absolutely no respect/regard the speaker has toward the spoken about is 'I wouldn't look toward him' (ولا هلفت عليه/سناه), and also 'I don't see him' (ولا أثراه) as in he does not exist, cannot be seen as far as the speaker is concerned. It is expressed in exactly the same way at 2Kgs.3:14 by Elisha's expression towards Jehoram, that if it were not for Elisha's regard for Jehoshaphat 'I would not look toward thee, nor see thee…'.

Parvaim (2Chr.3:6); بَرواي ام 'passed beyond-the'; بَرو آيِم 'go beyond the sea/river'. This expression is used a lot in Yemeni regions whose language and traditions has remained unchanged since ancient times, and is used in the form of (br al-bḥr/بر البحر) the word for sea 'bḥr' has replaced the word 'ym' (see Parvaim). The expression is used to describe countries unknown, unfamiliar and/or far away. Both versions of the phrase are exactly the same and mean 'from or go beyond'. In remote Yemen, anyone or anything considered coming from a country relatively unknown or far away is said to come from 'beyond the sea', which is 'Parvaim'. The phrase is also used when telling someone, or talking about someone in particular, that they can 'go away' 'get lost for all I care' to show they do not care where he/she goes which is said as 'go beyond the sea'. The way it was used in Chronicles was to show the distance and importance of from how far away Solomon sourced most of the materials to build the house and misnomered 'temple'; also, how where the gold came from has been given extra emphasis most probably because it is a country special to the authors.

The Bible uses the phrase 'Cover not their iniquity' and this is an overused expression in Yemen where I lived, and it is used in swearing or cursing (both in seriousness and friendly humour) 'Expose them do not cover them' 'He/May He expose them, not cover them' (يكشفهم لا سترهم). The literal meaning is that an adulterous/fornicating couple be caught naked in the act/red-handed, but how it is used, whether seriously or in humour, is usually to point to the spoken to/about that he/she/they are being silly or wrong and it is said to children and adults as an expression pointing out what the concerned person is doing is either wrong or ridiculous, etc. and sometimes said with the literal meaning of exposing adulterers.

Job in distress (Job.3) praying and cursing the day he was born, wishing God had never allowed him to be born 'Let the day perish wherein I was born…Let that day be darkness: let God not regard it from above, neither let the light shine upon it…Let it not be joined…' and all those similar phrases in the chapter are Yemeni expressions based on and summed up in the expressions 'Let God not have fated it/If God had not created it' 'If God hadn't made it' 'If God did not say/had not said it' 'May God not say/May God not fate' (لا قدَّر الله/ لا قال الله); meaning they wish God had not said it, had not made it happen regarding something that has already happened or believed to have happened and when hoping something bad will not happen.

Job's expression after God reproaches him 'Then Job answered the Lord, and said, Behold, I am vile; what shall I answer thee? I will lay mine hand upon my mouth. Once have I spoken; but I will not answer: yea, twice; but I will proceed no further.' (Job.40:1-5). The expression 'I will lay mine hand upon my mouth' is the same expression based on 'I will cover/block my mouth' (هصمّي على لقفي) and means 'I will place my hand on my mouth(and shut up/not speak anymore)'. The same phrase is used to tell someone to shut up 'cover/block your mouth' (صمّي على لقفك). When wanting silence e.g. when in danger or wanting to hear something if a child is bawling, they will say to someone related to the child 'cover/block his mouth' (صمّي على لقفه); when someone has been rebutted for saying something, the upset rebutted person who has been contradicted or told off often says 'I will cover/block my mouth and speak no more' (هصمّي على لقفي ماعدههدر).

Also in Job's narrative when he proclaims his innocence, or denies guilt and wrongdoing, the method and style is uniquely Yemeni which in emphasising innocence/piety uses a prayer-curse which goes 'If I have done [negative action] then may God do to me [negative action]' as follows in Job: 'If my step hath turned out of the way, and mine heart walked after mine eyes, and if any blot hath cleaved to mine hands; *Then* let me sow, and let another eat; yea, let my offspring be rooted out.' 'If mine heart have been deceived by a woman, of if I have laid wait at my neighbour's door; *Then* let my wife grind unto another, and let others bow down upon her.' 'If I have withheld the poor from *their* desire, or have caused the eyes of the widow to fail; Or have eaten my morsel myself alone, and the fatherless hath not eaten thereof...If I have seen any perish for want of clothing, or any poor without covering; If his loins have not blessed me, and *if* he were *not* warmed by the fleece of my sheep; If I have lifted up my hand against the fatherless, when I saw my help in the gate: *Then* let mine arm fall from my shoulder blade, and mine arm be broken from the bone.' 'If I have made my gold my hope, or have said to fine gold, *Thou art* my confidence; If I rejoiced because my wealth was great, and because mine hand had gotten much...And my heart hath been secretly enticed, or my mouth hath kissed mine hand: This also *were* an iniquity *to be pursued by* the judge: for I should have denied God *that is* above.' 'If I rejoiced at the destruction of him that hated me, or lifted up myself when evil had found him...If I covered my transgressions as Adam, by hiding my iniquity in my bosom...Oh that one would hear me! behold, my desire *is*, that the Almighty would answer me, and *that* mine adversary had written a book.' 'If my land cry against me, or that the furrows likewise thereof complain; If I have eaten the fruits thereof without money, or have caused the owners thereof to lose their life: Let thistles grow instead of wheat, and cockle instead of barley.' (Job.31). The words, style, the mode of punishment in this kind of expression is exactly the speech of Yemenis—unadulterated by modernisation and external influence.

One way of expressing a person has felt another's attitude has changed towards him/her is by saying 'his/her face/look isn't like it was towards me before' (وجهه/نظرته ماعاده مثل من قبل تجاهي), and that is what is being expressed in the story between Laban and Jacob when things sour between them: 'And Jacob beheld the countenance of Laban, and, behold, it *was* not towards him as before.' 'And Jacob sent and called Rachel and Leah to the field unto his flock, And said unto them, I see your father's countenance, that it *is* not toward me as before.' (Gen.31:2-5), and he takes off with Laban's flocks, along with his own, without allowing Laban and his daughters and grandchildren to have a farewell. Similarly, when a person is upset or angry with another and it is visibly clear on the person's facial expression, it is said 'his/her face changed' (تغيّر وجهه), and that is the expression used as narrated in Dan.3:19 when Daniel's three friends refuse to worship the king's idol and preach to the king: 'Then was Nebuchadnezzar full of fury, and the form of his visage was changed against Shadrach, Meshach, and Abed-nego: *therefore* he spake, and commanded that they should heat the furnace one seven times more than it was wont to be heated.'.

Another Yemeni expression/ditty used in the Bible narrative is one used when someone sees another bump his head, or himself bumps his head, into something, or forgets something, or has a headache and it is 'Oh my head, My basket of bread' (ياراسي يامتّل اعواسي), this is what the authors based a small part of the Jesus story on: Jesus is 'cold bread' 'ate/broke bread' and he asks his disciples if they have forgotten they have 'the five loaves of the five thousand, and how many baskets ye took up.' (Matt.16:9-10)

In remote Yemen, a person who has a speech impediment caused by a physical issue with the tongue which does not cause them to be dumb, but difficulty pronouncing some letters/words (e.g. r/ر)—the pronunciation being difficult or wrong, they say 'his/her tongue is knotted' (لسانه معقوده) and they show it by making the person/child open his mouth and they point under his/her tongue where the tissue connects the tongue to the tissue beneath it and they explain there is too much 'string/thread' (خيط) which is 'knotting' the tongue by keeping it attached to the bottom of the mouth, i.e. not as flexible to pronounce properly—and in most cases you can see the tongue is restricted by extra tight tissue (more than usual) restricting the movement of the tongue. The exact same idea and expression is made in Mark where Jesus cures a man with a speech impediment: 'And they bring unto him one that was deaf, and had an impediment in his speech; and they beseech him to put his hand upon him.' and Jesus performs a miracle 'And straightway his ears were opened, and the string of his tongue was loosed, and he spake plain.' Note: 'loosing a string' is untying a knot. (Mark.7:32-35).

Also in Mark, the expression 'Ephphatha' which means he made an expression and gesture made in remote Yemen to show displeasure at a bad odour, being disgusted or are fed up with something/someone (see Ephphatha). Jesus' behaviour in those verses (Mark.7:34), looking up to heaven and sighing after poking into the man's ears and poking his tongue, means he was doing the Ephphatha gestures.

In Jacob and Dinah's story, where Simeon and Levi kill all the males including the king and prince of Shechem because the prince and Dinah were having a relationship, within the text itself there is a mistranslation and misinterpretation of the word which has been translated as 'stink'; the original word has a different meaning altogether unrelated to 'stink', but it does seem the translators were having difficulty in getting the copier/translator to understand the true meaning of the word in the text so they used the meaning of another word 'shammat' which means 'caused a scene/scandal/made a spectacle/embarrassed in front of/let people laugh and gloat at me' but this too was mistranslated because of its similarity to 'shm/smell' and that ended up being given as the meaning of the word.

The word in the Biblical text is: bā'aš, lĕhab'îšēniy; بآغَش ، ليهَبغيشيِني 'deceived/forged/not original or pure (a knock-off)' 'why did you deceive/con me' 'for her/distracted-they deceived/conned' and the middle compound word (bghsh/means) when something is pretending to be something it is not such as mixing sugar with honey and selling it as pure honey, or deceiving a person such as when Jacob's sons made a pact with Shechem, deceived him to be circumcised and then killed him and all the people while they were injured, it may also have other meanings in compound word configurations of 'for her/distracted-wanted her/prostituted/sexually immoral behaviour-copulated/filtered impurities' (**lĕha**/for her/distracted-b'î/prostitution/immoral sexual behaviour/wanted-**šēniy**/copulated(like goats)/filtered impurities/flowed) and fits the narration; بآئَش ، ليهَبئيشيِني 'strike randomly/strike all over' 'search randomly/search frantically all over' 'why did you strike randomly/all over' 'for her/distracted-struck all over/searched frantically all over' and the word means to either attack randomly or with striking all over the place, or searching for something but in a frantic manner from place to place and that everything is thrown around with no clear method or goal. These are the meanings of the word and these actions are relayed in the narration of the relevant story. 'And Jacob said to Simeon and Levi, Ye have troubled me to make me stink among the inhabitants of the land, among the Canaanites and the Perizzites…' (Gen.34:30).

Jacob is referring to the embarrassment and disgrace he is feeling due to his sons attacking the people and rulers of a country who welcomed and accepted them into their land. His sons who attacked, murdered and spoiled the people and the city, and stole the inhabitant's property have caused Jacob to be a spectacle in front of other people, he is feeling embarrassed and disgraced and fears retribution; Jacob is feeling disgraced and embarrassed because the inhabitants of the land and its rulers had good relationships with Jacob and his family and had prepared to convert to Jacob's customs and to marry from his family. The misinterpretation of the word is easy to see and identify by anyone who speaks the real language of the Bible, Arabic, where first the original word as it stands has not been translated at all, but a replacement word has been interpreted and has also been misinterpreted into 'stink'.

The original and correct word is directly related to Simeon and Levi's actions as narrated in the story. Both the original word and the replacement word which suffered further mistranslation (shmmt/شمّت) 'caused a scene/scandal/disgraced/embarrassed/made a spectacle of/allowed others to gloat' are used in Yemen. If a person is complaining about another who provoked an argument, shouted, insulted him/her—the person complaining will say (shammat be/شَمَّت بي) 'he made a spectacle of me' 'he disgraced me'; If a man or woman's children have done something very bad (e.g. insulted/stole/anything embarrassing or vulgar) part of the upbraiding by the parent will be (shammatu be/شَمَّتو بي) 'You have disgraced, embarrassed and made a spectacle of me'; if something has turned very bad/wrong or unseemly they say (shamaat/شَمات) 'terrible/a mess' or 'a disgrace'. And this very Yemeni (and Arabic) expression is what is expressed (albeit with a mistake) in Jacob's dialogue 'Ye have made me to stink among the inhabitants'—and always in the real-life expressions of people it is 'You have embarrassed/disgraced/made a spectacle of me among/in front of the people' (شَمَّتّو بي بين الناس/ شمّتّو بي قُدّام الناس).

Another Yemeni proverb 'The day is long/the days are long and vision fails' has been used in Ezekiel, in the latter 'vision' meaning prophecies of the future not coming true, not realising. 'Son of man, what is that proverb that ye have in the land of Israel, saying 'The days are prolonged, and every vision faileth?' (Ezek.12:22). Whereas the original saying which still exists in local Yemeni proverb it just means as people get older, or the days longer, sight becomes weaker, and it is always older people who say it when vision becomes difficult from age, or out of tiredness which they are feeling when they say 'The day becomes long and vision/sight fails' (اليوم يطول والوهان يزول/اليوم يطول والبصر يزول).

'Abba' an endearing term for 'father' (see Abba) is still used to this day in rural Yemen in the same way. In the Bible it is used in Jesus' prayer to his father, God, where he is feeling afraid, sad, he is beseeching his father to spare him the foreseen sufferance. In rural Yemen children (young and adult) call their father 'Yabba(h)', but when using a more affectionate tone it is 'Abba(h)' and this use of Yemeni language is used in the Bible showing the difference of tone when Jesus is anxious, depressed, sorrowful and asking his father for protection, safety and help. (Mark.14:33-39)

Zelotes and refers to a person acting against, antagonising or focused on another with viciousness, determination or constantly. The word is used to describe when someone is attacking or verbally nagging, or physically troubling another person or is obsessed with a topic or specific object or action. E.g. it is used to describe a person's attention, focus on something in particular, e.g. if a man becomes obsessed with removing a tree trunk which is proving problematic to remove, they say he has/is (<u>ss</u>lṭ/t<u>ss</u>lṭ on the tree/ صلّط/تصلّط على الشجرَ) 'he has focused on/become obsessed with the tree(trunk)'. If a person focuses excessively on a certain matter they say (تصّلّط للموضوع) 'he has become [oiled]extremely focused on the matter' (note: the word is literally 'oiled', see Zelọte); if a person is complaining about another who has been or is causing him problems, it is said (تصّلّط لي) 'he has become [oiled] focused hard on me'. The Greek word 'Zelotes' is from the Arabic word 'oil' and refers to once oil is applied to the body, clothes or surface it is not easily removed, i.e. it aggressively sticks to it. How the word 'zealots/Zelotes' is used is a Yemeni expression which reflects how oil sticks to something/someone and does not 'let up'—just like the meanings of fanatical zealots and zealousy has come to mean based on this Arab word. In the Bible this word and expression was used to describe some of Jesus' zealous disciples.

Sceva 'of markets/pedalling/immoral/lewd' and comes from the derogatory term 'children of markets/ pedalling' 'girl/daughter of markets//girl/daughter of pedalling' and similar phrases and is used to describe or insult people of ill repute or immoral character. Though it literally means people who go wandering around markets (not to shop) it is a figurative expression and means wandering around anywhere and everywhere, seeking illicit relationships and sex. In Acts.19:13-16 it is used in the same derogatory context to describe and denigrate Jewish exorcists whom in addition to being named 'Sceva' 'of markets' are made in the story to run out of the house naked and wounded—which is what the Yemeni term 'children/ daughters of markets' conveys as these immoral people are often found naked/compromised in the act of the sex and their reputations wounded. It is just one of many Yemeni phrases used in the Bible.

Anathema Maran-atha 'I guilt/ostracise/blame him-he evil eyed us/he evil eyed it' is a Yemeni phrase and superstition to describe the 'evil' which befalls the victim emanating out of the eye of the person who hates or is jealous of the victim. It is also used when someone who does not hate and is not jealous of the victim, but a person (whether a loved one, relative, well-liked person or a complete stranger) says something in a particular way believed to be able to cause an evil-eye and they say 'Marana-vaa' 'He evil-eyed us/me' and is said in both seriousness and jest also.

Huz and Buz mentioned in Genesis: Huz '(to) hold in/gather/corner/cram' 'to swing back and forth/rock'; Buz 'take/pick up/carry'. They are a phrase used in pairs 'yahuz wayabuz' 'he ḥuz and he buz' يحُز ويبُز 'he corners and takes'; يهُز ويبُز 'he rocks and takes' regarding someone taking things not necessarily theirs, or even if they have the right to take it means they are creating a fuss, a flurry, a commotion; whether taking, cornering, as well as plundering, blundering here and there are involved or not as it can mean someone causing a kerfuffle, a lot of flurry, a lot of noise or talk about something, and in both Genesis and Job where Huz and Buz are mentioned together then in Job where only 'Buzite' (of Buz) is mentioned, you can see the meanings of the expression in use.

In Genesis the first meaning of 'Huz and Buz' reflects how Abraham took and bound Isaac ready to sacrifice him to God, then the same in the ram getting caught in the thicket (Huz) 'crammed/cornered' and 'Buz' when Abraham takes it to sacrifice instead of Isaac and immediately after this event Abraham is notified his brother has children, the first two named 'Huz' and 'Buz'. In Job the same meaning is referred to, although it only mentions Elihu being a Buzite, i.e. from Buz, his actions and character have the exact meaning of 'Huz and Buz' as causing a commotion, making a fuss over something, a lot of noise made over something, making a big deal out of something, a flurry, etc. This is shown that Elihu Barachel the Buzite expresses that due to his young age he may not have the right to speak, but he is going to—and not only is his part in the story just to give a speech, but his manner of speech is grandiose, full of flurry and he is making a bid deal out of Job's three friends choosing silence when they cannot change Job's mind; the three friends react with 'amazement' (stunned/shocked) by his speech, and Elihu goes on and on, making a 'noise/fuss' until God intervenes. Some examples from this story:

'So these three men ceased to answer Job, because he *was* righteous in his own eyes. Then was kindled the wrath of Elihu the son of Barachel, the Buzite, of the kindred of Ram [Note this verse proves the 'Huz and Buz' meaning is implied where Abraham was to sacrifice Isaac then gets a ram to sacrifice instead ('Ram' meaning 'throw/kill') then 'Huz and Buz' are named as his brother's sons]:against Job was his wrath kindled, because he justified himself against God. Also against his three friends was his wrath kindled, because they had found no answer…Now Elihu had waited until Job had spoken, because they *were* elder than he…And Elihu the son of Barachel the Buzite answered, and said, I *am* young, and *ye are* very old; wherefore I was afraid, and durst not shew you mine opinion…Great men are not always wise: neither do the aged understand judgement. Therefore I said, hearken to me; I also will shew mine opinion. Behold, I waited for your words; I gave ear to your reasons, while ye searched out what to say. Yea, I attended unto you, and, behold, *there was* none of you that convinced Job, *or* that answered his words: Lest ye should say, We have found out wisdom; God thrusteth him down, not man. Now he hath not directed *his* words against me: neither will I answer him with your speeches. They were amazed, they answered no more: they left off speaking, When I had waited (for they spake not, but stood still, *and* answered no more;) *I said*, I will answer also my part, I also will show mine opinion. For I am full of matter, the spirit within me constraineth me. Behold, my belly *is* as wine *which* hath no vent; it is ready to burst like new bottles. I will speak, that I may be refreshed: I will open my lips and answer.'—all this 'ado' and he has not given his opinion, just making a fuss and flurry over saying he will speak, which is much the meaning of 'Huz and Buz'. In verse 2 of Job.32 the author makes a pun at the meaning of 'Huz and Buz' as it was meant by the earlier author of its mention in Genesis 'Elihu the son of Barachel the Buzite, of the kindred of Ram...' which further proves the people who authored Genesis and those who authored Job are all Yemeni as they have used Yemeni words and Yemeni expressions to reflect what is happening in the story—in Job it was evidently meant as humour.

Eldad and Medad 'talking nonsense-lying down' 'talking nonsense-spreading/extending/touching' based on the Yemeni expression and meaning of 'eldad meldad' 'lies and tricks/nonsense/he goes back and forth with words/speaks nonsense/talks confusingly and incoherently' and is a phrase used to describe a person who twists his words and 'beats around the bush', goes around in circles, purposely obfuscates and speaks nonsense so as to trick and deceive. Eldad and Medad (Num.) are said to prophesy but Joshua does not like what he hears or sees and asks that they be forbidden showing the meaning of this Yemeni phrase.

Ichabod; although it can mean to choke on a morsel or the pain felt when too many morsels stack up or do not go down easy while eating, can also mean to feel pain in the chest/heart and bursting or breaking especially from grief, shock or distress. When Phinehas' wife cries out 'The glory is departed from Israel...' names her son Ichabod then dies and the narration tells us it is over the news of her husband and father-in-law's deaths, and also Eli dies due to the shock he hears is the meaning of this Yemeni word and phrase and how it is used by Yemenis. It is a pure Yemeni expression, just as all modes of expression, style of narrative and speech in the Bible and NT are Yemeni words and in Yemeni mode, style, flavour and essence.

Rituals and Custom

Weddings

There are many Yemeni rituals featuring in the Biblical stories which are pagan and pre-Islamic rituals, which have been practised since pagan times and never stopped, not even when Islam (comparatively recent to arrive/be accepted to all corners of remote and rural Yemeni areas), and these Yemeni pagan rituals are not only used in the Biblical stories, but some have become part of the religious practise, rituals and festivals in the Jewish religion. In Yemen, where the authors of the Bible obviously originated from, the parts of the country which remained remote and did not change their ways, the people still perform these rituals, traditions, and they have no association to the Jewish religion, but practise and hold these beliefs since ancient times, and even Islam could not stop them from the obviously paganistic practises. Some rituals are not related to paganism, e.g. some wedding rituals that are part of a superstitious tradition with its beginnings in antiquity. The same applies to the current Muslim Saudi Arabian inhabitants of southern parts of Saudi Arabia whose traditions, beliefs and rituals cause the wonder and shock of the urbanised Saudis whom have lived city-life from childhood.

It is a tradition (for the women it is considered a right she has to claim) on the wedding day during the wedding procession from when the bride is given away at her parents' home, the bridegroom takes her by the hand and they walk and/or travel to her new home, her marital home. Along the way, and at many intervals, the bride will release the bridegroom's hand and sit on the side of a path or wherever she can sit and does not get up to continue the journey until the bridegroom pays her lots of money, and at every 'sitting/جلسه' and it is called 'for/right of sittings/حق جلساته'; it is meant to show the groom and his family really want her and must persuade her to come and arrive at his house (it signifies she is not desperate to come to the groom, but he really wants her).

It is also a custom that the bride's family arrive the next day and this custom is called 'following her/ يتبعوها' (and the second day is also a wedding day) to celebrate, and they are to bring presents with them. In the past, the gift would be a small piece of land, but when this became no longer viable or fell out of practise, the bride's family's wedding present would still contain a trunk full of new clothes, fabrics, perfumes along with a piece of gold jewellery with the latter substituting the land; a lamb or two goats are also led up as part of 'following her' ritual, to be slaughtered for a feast along with the animal the groom's family provide. But the gold and clothes (as well as money) have replaced giving the bride a piece of land during her wedding.

In the Bible, the author has made use of both customs—the 'sittings' and the 'following her', to show how land was given to Caleb's daughter: 'And Caleb said, He that smiteth Kirjath-sepher, and taketh it, to him will I give Achsah my daughter to wife. And Othniel the son of Kenaz, the brother of Caleb, took it: and he gave him Achsah his daughter to wife. And it came to pass, as she came *unto him*, that she moved him to ask of her father a field: and she lighted off *her* ass; and Caleb said unto her, What wouldest thou? Who answered, Give me a blessing; for thou hast given me a south land; give me also springs of water. And he gave her the upper springs, and the nether springs.' So the author used this Yemeni custom and made her stop the marriage procession just like Yemeni brides stop to sit, and her father negotiated what she wanted—just like the groom and his relatives do with Yemeni brides at their 'sittings'; then Caleb gives her land just like fathers of Yemeni brides used to gift land then substituted with presents during the 'following her' tradition. The author of that particular Biblical story made the 'sittings' and 'following her' custom into one action to suit the story being told.

Token of Virginity

The 'tokens of virginity' mentioned in Deuteronomy as being brought forth as proof of a bride's virginity when it is being contested by an unhappy husband is also based on Yemeni custom (the virginity token and not the request of proof at a later date). On the wedding night a pure white garment is laid on the marriage bed; during consummation of the marriage the hymen blood marks the white cloth, and it is custom the next morning when the bride's family arrive for the second day of the wedding, both the bride and groom meet them below or near the house and the bride carries with her the white garment which is called 'morning/صبحيا' and she presents it to her mother and aunts when she meets them on the path, then later when guests arrive this white cloth is passed around to the female guests as proof of the bride's virginity on her wedding night.

It is still important to societies such as remote Yemeni societies as it was for the people and audience who authored Deuteronomy, although in Deuteronomy the proof of virginity is narrated as a legal matter and of grave consequences—the husband is chastised, made to pay a fine and has to keep her as wife for life if she shows her 'token of virginity', while if unable to prove she was a virgin on her wedding night the girl/bride is stoned to death—whereas in Yemen villages it is more a matter of reputation, pride, shame, with the worst scenario being the bride is returned to her parents' home and divorced, but in most cases where the bride is found not a virgin the bridegroom eventually forgives and they continue life as normal without shaming her in front of her family and community. But to the point, the Biblical author is describing a Yemeni custom which is still alive today and has been uncut since ancient civilisations. Deuteronomy points out the parents of the 'damsel' take her tokens of virginity i.e. it is in their possession as she hands them over to them after the wedding night, which means she would hand it over but not only just to show them as nowadays, but for her parents' to keep as proof and pride (at least in the Biblical story):

'If any man take a wife, and go in unto her, and hate her, And give occasions of speech against her, and say, I took this woman, and when I came to her, I found her not a maid: Then shall the father of the damsel, and her mother, take and bring forth *the tokens of* the damsel's virginity, unto the elder of the city in the gate: And the damsel's father shall say unto the elders, I gave my daughter unto this man to wife, and he hateth her; And, lo, he hath given occasions of speech *against her*, saying, I found not thy daughter a maid; and yet these *are the tokens* of my daughter's virginity. And they shall spread the cloth before the elders of the city. And the elders of the city shall take that man and chastise him; And they shall amerce him in an hundred shekels of silver, and give *them* unto the father of the damsel, because he hath brought an evil name upon a virgin of Israel: and she shall be his wife; he may not part her away all his days. But if this thing be true, *and the tokens of* virginity be not found for the damsel: Then they shall bring out the damsel to the door of her father's house, and the men of her city shall stone her with stones that she die.'. The 'cloth/tokens of virginity' is another custom, albeit dramatized and modified to use in the Bible, but its authors are Yemeni.

Gold, Frankincense and Myrrh

When a mother births a child, one of the substances brought to her by relatives and neighbours (in addition to what she purchases herself) is frankincense. In the NT it is dramatized as a special gift brought by the wise men for Jesus. It does have a practical use, mothers use it to perfume a baby's clothes and garments with its naturally perfumed smoke: the people in antiquity did not have diapers, nor did they have modern soaps; at least up until the 2000s in remote regions in Yemen diapers were not used, and although washing the garments (whether using modern soap where it is available or the natural foam made from tree leaves) does clean the soiled garments, but neither modern soap nor natural soap removes the unpleasant aftermath smell of baby-poop from the clothes although the garment is clean (it does not smell at all like excrement nor is it dirty or stained—just a strange smell). Women use frankincense to remove the strange smell left on baby's clothes and its natural perfumed smoke does remove the smell, whereas using the processed and heavily perfumed incense which women usually use to perfume their clothes and bodies does not remove the smell which is why all new mothers are given frankincense for their baby's clothes.

Myrrh is administered to the mother to help alleviate the abdominal aches after childbirth. It has medicinal use used in other conditions too.

Gold has been replaced with money, while some new fathers and fathers-in-law still gift a small piece of jewellery to the new mother, but it has been mostly replaced by money as a gift as well as baskets of food produce. Women who arrive at the party held on the seventh day from a child's birth, place the money in the new-born's hand or tuck it under his/her clothes (the mother immediately removes it and stores it elsewhere).

These practical gifts given to new mothers have been dramatized as gifts coming from far away in the story of Jesus' birth in the NT. All three gifts are what mothers use and need when a child is born.

Rock Worship and the Importance of Stones

In rural Yemen, people from all over the area make pilgrimage and present sacrifices and gifts in front of a rock/stone believed to be sacred, holy, special because in the past someone felt a strange feeling or had an incident connected to that specific rock. Gifts and tithes are presented, and people would pray and ask for a variety of blessings (e.g. good fortune, health, offspring, a male heir, etc.) at and of this rock. This is a pagan practise, and the same pagan practise and belief can be seen where it is used and incorporated into Jacob's story where he uses rocks as pillows, has a bad dream, feels superstitious about the rocks, piles and anoints them, calls them 'Bethel' 'bad', and not only does Jacob set up these rocks as a pillar, but makes a vow that if God will protect him and provide for him, he will return and give a tenth of whatever he has to this stone, i.e. a gift, tithes, sacrifice—exactly like pagans have been doing in Yemen long before Judaism, Christianity and Islam, and continued to be practised long after Islam was introduced to the area. Later in the story, Jacob builds an altar there where worship rituals are practised. It is one simple example, a very clear example, of how the author(s) of the Bible had lived in Yemen (or in ancient-Saudi Arabia) and were familiar with its pagan practises, beliefs and ways of life which continued until very recently. There is no difference between the Yemeni villages' pagan practise of pilgrimage towards a rock, presenting and gifting to the rock tithes (which is practised by a living rural people untouched by and who have never encountered the Bible and whose ways have remained unchanged) and between the actions of Jacob in the story at Bethel, the latter written by authors; the similarities of the uncut Yemeni practise and use of it in the Bible cannot be denied. (Gen.28:11-22; 35:1-7).

In rural Yemen when two people (or two parties) are talking about a matter of importance which concerns both sides, while talking, especially when covering a critical part of the issue, the speaker will reach to the ground and pick up a stone and place it between him/her and the other person saying 'here, shahada/witness between me and you/شهادا بين وبينك' or 'bears witness/yshhd between me and you/ يشهد بيني وبينك' and refers to the stone placed between them will bear witness between them. I have witnessed many times, if a stone is not in easy reach, they will use a glass teacup, a piece of hay, any clean object, sometimes a woman will even snap off a fibre/thread from her dress and place it between her and the person she is hashing it out with and state 'witness between me and you'.

This use of a stone (the stone is the preferred object in these cases) is due to the use and belief of objects bearing witness and having sacred powers—and this Yemeni belief and ritual can be seen in Genesis where exactly the same thing is narrated between Jacob and Laban who are reproaching each other over their differences and conduct: stones are piled up and these stones are used as witnesses to what they say, the author(s) name it 'Jegar-sahadutha' the exact meaning and literally 'stones have witnessed this' (Abram does the same using seven ewes as witness between him and Abimelech when making a covenant between them). While hashing it out Laban says 'Now therefore come thou, let us make a covenant, I and thou; and let it be for a witness between me and thee. And Jacob took a stone and set it up *for* a pillar. And Jacob said unto his brethren, Gather stones; and they took stones and made an heap: and they did eat there upon the heap. And Laban called it Jegar-sahadutha: but Jacob called it Galeed, And Laban said, This heap *is* an witness between me and thee this day...' (Gen.31:26-48)

Also, in exactly the same Yemeni method of using stones as witnesses (not to forget stones are also holy or superstitious objects that are worshipped) comes the Yemeni phrase and expression 'Galeed/Gilead you' 'قلّدك', 'Galeed/Gilead you-God' 'قلّدك الله' which means 'God will hold you responsible' (See Galeed/Gilead for breakdown of meanings in detail). Galeed is the 'tumbled/rolled stone' which is used as a witness between people; 'Gilead' is the garlanding/placing of responsibility on a person, it means 'it/this will be witness against you, if you are lying or transgress—you will bear the responsibility' the phrase 'Gilead you-God/God gileaded you' is used when someone is saying something (usually when there is a disagreement over something or doubt over what has been said) and someone doubts the truth/person; even if no stones are used nowadays in cities, it is where the phrase 'Gilead/قلّد' and its use has originated from). This is exactly what the author(s) has used in the Bible depicting what happens between Laban and Jacob and what they are saying to each other is basically '...will be witness against you if you are lying, and you will bear the responsibility of your actions'; the mountain where this is to happen has been suitably named 'mount Gilead'. The authors remind the audience of the story three times that this event is happening in Gilead, and further explain the practise to deliver the pun in the story and to make it crystal clear what Jegar-sahadutha, Gilead and Galeed mean. These beliefs, customs and rituals are taken from Yemeni culture. (Gen.31:21-48)

Mizpah 'marker' 'portion/share' is the Yemeni practice of placing a stone set on a piece of land to mark whose land starts/ends and where, demarcating where one's land boundaries are from another person's when more than one person owns parts of the same piece of land so each party knows he/she cannot pass into the other's land to plough, harvest, graze or take ownership of. And this Yemeni term and practise is exactly how it has been used in the Biblical story showing it is Yemeni authorship. The author(s) does not suffice at using three other Yemeni practises and expression (Gilead, Galeed, Jegar-sahadutha) but goes on with a forth 'Mizpah'. Of course, the whole OT is in Arabic, as are the word-names of the NT, but these are some examples of custom, practise and rituals distinctly Yemeni and of the Arabian Peninsula. This Yemeni practise is used to prevent from intentionally and unintentionally harming another's rights, here used in the Bible by Laban to draw boundaries not only about land but also about Jacob not mistreating Laban's daughters by marrying over them, demarcating not to cross boundaries to harm each other.

Fire Worship

These above examples are not the only Biblical use of Yemeni words, phrases and pagan practise of Yemeni origin used in the Bible which would eventually become Jewish religious practise. Another undeniable and abundant example is the word used for 'priest' in the Bible: kōhēn; كوهين 'fire worshipper' 'estimator/sorcerer' 'created smoke' 'guesser/guessed' in remote Yemen where the language has remained its purest and intact, this word as a noun only has one meaning with all its verb meanings rolled into it and related to it, and that is 'fire worshipper/sorcerer/estimator' and the actions fire worshippers do in prophesying (to tell the future by using fire and other methods) is called (ytkhn/yitkohen/يتكهن/يِتكَهَن) and is a pagan religion and paganistic rituals where fire is worshipped, sacrificed to, and uses fire in many of its rituals. The older generations of the people I lived with in the 90s in rural Yemen could not mention 'fire worshipper/kohen' and could not hear the word 'Cohen/Kohen' without a gasp and mutterance of invocation of repent and protection. The pagan ritual and worship of fire of ancient Yemeni origin is abundant in the Bible, it is the basis of the Jewish religion.

The OT noun for priests is 'kohen/cohen' and a large part of religious rituals described in the Bible are that of fire worshippers—burning sacrifices, whether wholly or partially; burning incense; flames being an important part of the religious ritual. Albeit in the Biblical stories that the religion and other practises later on call this worship to the one God—sacrifices are made to stones and altars, and although edited revisions drive and direct the religion ultimately to the 'one God' belief, and criticise how other pagan religions burn sacrifices and incense at 'high places' and use fire as part of their rituals, nonetheless so does the preferred and protagonist religion of the OT: Abraham goes up to Mount Moriah to offer Isaac as a burnt offering; then burns the ram instead on the mountain; Jacob offers a sacrifice on mount Gilead; whenever Bethel is mentioned it is 'go up to Bethel' i.e. a high place and Bethel is where Jacob builds an altar where sacrifice and tithes are presented to God.

In the OT, 'kohen/priest' which the original and correct meaning is 'fire worshipper/sorcerer' most of the religious ritual as described in the Bible is based on pagan fireworship: the burning of sacrifices, keeping fire/flames alight, burning incense. Another element of kohen/fire worshippers is using fire, smoke, sticks and other materials to read the future, to predict innocence or guilt, to predict good or bad to come and that is exactly what kohens in the Bible do—whether casting lots, using Urim and Thummim, etc. Another element which real life people go to these kohen/sorcerers for, is to be healed of physical ailments and what the kohen does is not physically heal with 'physician-like' methods, but more sorcery and this continues to be used to this day although it is dwindling.

Not only are acts of fire worship included in religious practise of those following the protagonist God in the OT stories, but it also plays a large part in Yemeni festivals which have nothing to do with the Jewish religion, and the Jewish religion has never been the remote Yemeni communities' lives or religious practise, nor do these fire-based festivals have anything to do with Islamic religion as they actually contradict its teachings. One example is Eid Wuzoo 'Festival of Light a Fire' where after weeks of gathering large amounts of wood and kindling for bonfires, the firewood is set up on peaks across the region, and at home on every house small dry bushes are planted in mud balls on the walls of the roof and perimeters of walls. Women prepare and buy sweets, cakes, biscuits and set aside money. On the tenth of a certain month the celebration begins after darkness has fallen, with boys in groups (each group in different areas divided between them) going from house to house chanting about Taassu' and 'Aashuur (deities, see Festival of Light a Fire); they go from house to house, village to village, chanting and calling at each house to ask the women and girls what they (the boys) will be given if they pray and the women's wishes comes true—where the women respond by telling them, listing exactly what she/they will give in return if her wish comes true and the promised goodies will be given a year from the same date. The woman/girl stands on the threshold of the front door and as she closes her eyes and makes a silent wish, the boys shout 'Amen' as loud as they can; the women, young girls, take turns standing at the door being asked, making a wish and being 'Amenned', then the women whose previous year's wish has come true give the boys last year's promised rewards (they give goodies even if the wish did not realise just to make the boys happy, but they let them know the wish has not yet come true and remind them to pray harder). The boys pack their collections into a sack (to be divided between them later) and they go off into the night chanting the same chant about Taassu' and 'Aashuur then all the girls at home set alight the bushes on the walls and roofs; it is a magical scene—the houses look like beautiful rock castles ornate with flaming bushes at regular intervals, in the night they look dazzling, and everywhere you look, the houses at different levels and peaks are adorned with blazing flames, all over the villages. When the boys reach the peaks where the wood has been gathered, they too light their bonfires and it adds to the scene, where there are beacons of light all over the mountains, near and far and the boys chant and dance, and goof around the fire before the confectionaries and money are divided between them.

There are a few points to note about this festival: it is pagan; it is related to fire worship; it is related to gods called 'Aashuur which means 'pregnant cow' and Taassu' which means a virile male goat used for impregnating goats for its pedigree, and both words are connected to the period of gestation of livestock and humans (10 months/9 months); it has nothing to do with Islam as the deities they call on are pagan gods (by 2017 this festival and chant would be banned by 'religious' people introduced to my area, a downside of easier access when roads have been made connecting the city and giving access to outsiders to this remote region which had kept its beautiful and ancient ways of life and beliefs well into the 2000s); all wishes women and girls make are related to offspring, fertility and marriage; it is a merry festival which has been conducted since pagan times for generations; the power of this spiritual and festive night is put on burning fires, fire in every house, huge fires on as many peaks as possible. This is a region and people where the fire worshippers are called 'kohen/sorcerer' as that is the literal meaning of the word, and whose language in its purest form of Arabic explains all the meanings of names (people and places) in the Bible (both OT and NT), and their pagan rituals which have survived are exactly how priests are conducting religious rituals in the Biblical stories.

Look at the Festival of Light a Fire 'Eid Wuzoo': burning bushes and large fires are set on high places and one of the deities' names chanted is 'Aashuur 'pregnant cow'; then look at the stories of the burning bush which Moses sees on Sinai, where God speaks to him, and the OT states God is 'she is-with child/calf-she is' ('ehyeh 'ăšer 'ehyeh mistranslated as 'I Am That I Am'); God comes down in a burning fire; in the story, the 'children of Israel' are guided by a pillar of fire during the night; when the disobedient children of Israel are punished, fire is the most used method in the story; when they rebel against Aaron's priesthood, God uses fire to kill two-hundred-fifty men; God uses fire to punish the people when they complain at Taberah; Nadab and Abihu (Aaron's sons) are punished with death for presenting 'strange fire' to God in their excitement to meet God, and God kills them with fire coming out of him; not only are some sacrifices burnt to God, but when he accepts them they are devoured 'licked up' in fire/flames, such as in the stories of Elijah, Manoah; Manoah's wife is told to make a burnt offering, the offering is accepted from the altar and the angel also goes up to heaven with the flame off the altar. Fire worship is part of Yemeni pagan culture which has also been incorporated into the Biblical stories, into the religious practise of the Biblical stories because its authors are Yemeni; and the same goes for rock worship where stones/rocks have special, superstitious attributes and are part of Yemeni culture existing since pagan times with its belief and importance still expressed in people's expressions and actions to this day.

Another ritual taken from Yemeni culture is the ritual, custom and festivals which has been conducted since ancient times and has been used by the authors of the Bible in the Biblical stories as the feasts and dancing at Shiloh, where girls/daughters of Shiloh who would dance would be kidnapped and given as wives to the men of Benjamin, the latter whose continuity had been jeopardised as according to the story the majority of men, women, boys (apparently all women and girls) were killed because of a crime committed by some Benjamites at Gibeah against a Levite. The Shiloh women are needed for fertility and continuation purposes. A point is made these women/girls be taken during a yearly feast which includes dancing; also, they make a point only the women who dance will be snatched.

The authors of this specific Biblical story are aware of the annual Yemeni festival where men and women congregate at a specific place, there are great fires made surpassing the need of cooking meat, the fires are important to the festival and at this festival there is a special dance called the 'haqfa/هقفا', males and females are paired and dance. The feasting and dancing are a merry atmosphere, and couples disappear for sex before returning (these couples are neither married nor engaged). The dance itself represents copulation and/or virility: both male and female partners stand facing each other; lunge down in a quick squat and jump back up, the lunging and jumping back up begins with one slightly lagging behind the other, before they rhythmically synchronise; at a point the man holds his arm out with his hand hovering above the female's shoulder; they eventually hold each other's hands when squatting and jumping.

This feast and dance continued to be practised well into the 80s, but with more men from the region going to work in Saudi Arabia and Islamic religious knowledge and practise being brought back along with the fortunes and precious materials, it began to be looked down at and gradually turned away from before being banned completely, but women of a certain generation would continue to keep the dance alive at weddings in female dancing pairs. There is/was a generation of elderly and middle-aged people all who still spoke of it fondly as they had grown up attending this festival and shared their memories and show the dance to the much younger generations (the latter younger generations affected by the new introduced Islamic teachings of modesty, etc. would express they find the dance 'obscene'). When the women from older generations recall in great detail the feasts, the fires, the dancing, who danced with whom, who disappeared with whom, and when they talk about it and describe it is not from ancient memory but what they did until recently in their way of life, their eyes light up, they smile and laugh recalling how enjoyable but also how important it was to attend this annual feast and dance, and they believe the lack of rain, the lessening in amounts and quality of milk, honey, meat, grain is due to abandoning this proper (to them) form of worship and way of life. They also yearn for the freedom, fun, and traditions and compare its prohibition and how everything has become verbally 'forbidden/prohibited' today because of people becoming more religious in the new ways, and especially those returning from Saudi Arabia. They note how men and women were not segregated in any activities whether feasts, festivals or weddings as they are now (they were talking about the 90s while I was there), and how some things such as the annual dancing feast that was fun, normal and had existed forever had been slowly turned away from by shaming of a few 'strict' individuals with new (Islamic) ideas. It must be pointed out that they hold nothing against Islam or praying, and consider themselves Muslim even if they did not know most of the religion of Islam (many did not know how to pray at all and were being taught by their children from school books) but they were upset by the few men who had decided to look down on, shame and embarrass people to turn them away from long-standing culture and customs, and ways of life by using religion as an excuse.

Back to the point, this feast where fire, dance and copulation were important elements of, has been used by the author of this part of the Biblical story regarding Benjamin/Shiloh, to use as the saving storyline which allows the continuation of Benjamin's offspring. The similarities of how a real-life people's culture and Yemenis lived and the fictionalised and dramatized use of this culture in the story is too strong than to deny. 'Then the elders of the congregation said, How shall we do for wives for them that remain, seeing the women are destroyed out of Benjamin? And they said, *There must be* an inheritance for them that be escaped out of Benjamin, that a tribe not be destroyed out of Israel. Howbeit we may not give them wives of our daughters: for the children of Israel have sworn, saying, Cursed *be* he that giveth a wife to Benjamin. Then they said, Behold, *there* is a feast of the Lord in Shiloh yearly *in a place* which is on the north side of Bethel, on the east side of the highway that goeth up from Bethel to Shecem, and on the south of Lebonah. Therefore they commanded the children of Benjamin, saying, Go and lie in wait in the vineyards; And see, and behold, if the daughters of Shiloh come out to dance in the dances, then come ye out of the vineyards, and catch you every man his wife of the daughters of Shiloh, and go to the land of Benjamin. And it shall be, when their fathers or their brethren come unto us to complain, that we will say unto them, Be favourable unto them for our sakes: because we reserved not to each man his wife in the war: for ye did not give unto them at this time, *that* ye should be guilty. And the children of Benjamin did so, and took *them* wives, according to their number, of them that danced, whom they caught: and they went and returned unto their inheritance, and repaired their cities, and dwelt in them.' (Jud.21:16-23).

So the author of the Bible used a real annual feast of Yemen to fix a problem in the storyline where an author (the Bible has many authors) created a problem by destroying one of the twelve tribes of Israel which other authors wanted to continue.

It is worth pointing out this culture of dancing and feasting of Yemeni pagan origin is related to fertility and offspring, but it is also connected to more beliefs and customs in the real-life Yemeni culture which has also been used in the fictional story regarding the Benjamin tribe and also in other Biblical stories. Discussed previously are the use of stones, rocks and fire relating to religious practises as presented in the Biblical stories which are taken from Yemeni culture as practised in real life—fire in worship; fire related to fertility. If you look at the use and belief in stones as sacred objects in Yemeni culture where people present and promise more gifts if given offspring, health, etc. you cannot miss how sacred stones are used exactly the same way in the Biblical story with regards to fertility and offspring—the authors of the Bible have been inspired by Yemeni beliefs, rituals and practise and made it central to the stories. The authors of the Biblical stories have intentionally used Yemeni pagan practise, Yemeni superstitions and spiritual associations to fire and rocks not only to enhance the Biblical stories, but have based these Biblical stories on this Yemeni culture. If you look at the Yemeni practice of worshipping rocks, bringing gifts of cattle, sheep, goats, grain, honey, butter, crop, etc. to the rocks, in a pilgrimage where they ask these rocks for health, fertility, fortune, where specific vows are made 'If you grant me [this or this], I will bring to you a gift of [this/they specify what]', and it is exactly what the authors of the Bible have used in scenes where Jacob, e.g., tells the rock/God which he has piled and anointed words to the effect 'If you give me safety and fortune, I'll return and give you a tenth of my fortune'.

Focusing now specifically on Yemen pagan worship requesting offspring from rocks, fire, and fertility gods—you can see it reflected in how the authors of the Bible have used rocks and fertility in their stories:

Rachel's character is one of the important mothers in the Biblical stories. Before Rachel (which means 'leaning against-the' 'propped against-the' 'make lean/prop against-the') is introduced a point is made about a 'great stone' that is 'upon the mouth of the well' linking the stone to Rachel: the stone is on the well's mouth, and Rachel's meanings of 'lean against-the', and it needs great effort to remove the stone from the well's mouth to the degree although three groups of flocks and its shepherds are already waiting to water their flocks, they tell Jacob they cannot roll away the stone then return it until all the flocks of the people are gathered. Jacob decides not to keep Rachel waiting in the sun so he himself rolls away the stone and uncovers the well. This is linked to the sacredness of rocks and their link to fertility as Rachel will become his wife and provide him with offspring (and so will her sister Leah) but only after great difficulty—just like removing and returning the large stone on the well: after fourteen years of service to Laban, being deceived into marrying Leah, and not before giving him Bilhah her handmaid to bed and provide children does Rachel eventually conceive two of her own children and the second causes her death. The point is Rachel whose name means 'leaning against-the' is introduced and her name and character linked to the great stone leaning on the well's mouth, the rock and Rachel are a story about fertility—Jacob's sons who will become the twelve tribes of Israel. (Gen.29)

Even before Rachel is introduced, rocks/stones and the pagan belief that they can cause good or harm, as well as make wishes/needs be granted, such as offspring, is made visibly clear earlier in Genesis. When Jacob uses rocks as pillows and has a bad and frightful dream where God speaks to him, Jacob uses the stones to set up a pillar and makes a vow to it to provide a tenth of his fortune in return for a granted good—just like Yemeni pilgrim rituals to specific stones and idols. The link of rocks to fertility is also evident as God's speech to Jacob in this place where stones have been given sacred and superstitious power and attributes, the speech focuses on offspring:

'And, behold, the Lord stood above it, and said, I am the Lord God of Abraham thy father, and the God of Isaac: the land wherein thou liest, to thee will I give it, and to thy seed; And thy seed shall be as the dust of the earth, and thou shalt spread abroad to the west, and to the east, and to the north, and to the south: and in thee and in thy seed shall all the families of the earth be blessed...And Jacob rose up early in the morning, and took the stone he had put *for* his pillows, and set it up *for* a pillar, and poured oil upon the top of it...And Jacob vowed a vow, saying, If God will be with me, and will keep me in this way that I go, and will give me bread to eat, and raiment to put on, So that I come again to my father's house in peace; then shall the Lord be my God: And this stone, which I have set for pillows shall be God's house: and of all that thou shalt give me I will surely give the tenth unto thee.' (Gen.28) Note how the rock is God's house, not a building but a rock, and God in this stone is being fed or will be fed with the offered tithes, i.e. rock worship.

The whole story which is set around Gilead, Galeed, Jegar-sahadutha and Mizpah—all Yemeni Arabic words and the stories based on Yemeni custom (emanating out of paganism) of using stones as witnesses against what is being said, actions, and as observers of agreements not to cause each other harm—which has survived in the gesture and expression into this modern day—the big issue between Laban and Jacob is not just about the flocks Jacob has taken off with, although taking the flocks would endanger the survival of Laban's son's offspring, but the greatest disagreement is about Laban's daughters and their offspring (Jacob's wives and sons), the 'do no harm' Mizpah is about Laban telling Jacob 'do not marry other women over my daughters' (in remote Yemen (as probably elsewhere) marrying another wife endangers the first wife and her children's stability and fortune). Gilead, Galeed, Jegar-sahadutha, all related to stones, pivot around Jacob taking off with Rachel, Leah and their children without allowing Laban to properly say goodbye, and Laban's reproach is words to the effect of 'your offspring are my offspring; your wives are my daughters—and even all this cattle belongs to me, but who is it for, if not also for my daughters and grandchildren?'. Jacob's excuse before Laban makes this statement is that he was worried Laban would have sent him away without his children and wives, as well as without cattle to sustain them. And the whole continuation of offspring and fertility is directly linked to stones and rocks (Gilead, Galeed, Mizpah) which will feature later on in the Biblical stories also linked to fertility and offspring.

'...and Laban with his brethren pitched in the mount of Gilead. And Laban said to Jacob, What has thou done, that thou hast stolen away unawares to me, and carried away my daughters as captives *taken* with the sword? Wherefore didst thou flee away secretly, and steal away from me; and didst not tell me, that I might have sent thee away with mirth, and with songs, with tabret, and with harp? And hast not suffered me to kiss my sons and my daughters? thou hast now done foolishly in *so* doing. It is in the power of my hand to do you hurt: but the God of your father spake unto me yesternight, saying, Take thou heed that thou speak not to Jacob either good or bad,' Jacob says 'Except the God of my father, the God of Abraham, and the fear of Isaac, had been with me, surely thou hadst sent me away now empty.' 'And Laban answered and said unto Jacob, *These* daughters *are* my daughters, and *these* children *are* my children, and *these* cattle *are* my cattle, and all that thou seest *is* mine: and what can I do this day unto these my daughters, or unto their children which they have born? Now therefore come thou, let us make a covenant, I and thou; and let it be for a witness between me and thee. And Jacob took a stone and set it up *for* a pillar. And Jacob said unto his brethren, Gather stones; and they took stones, and made an heap: and they did eat there upon the heap. And Laban called it Jegar-sahadutha: but Jacob called it Galeed. And Laban said, This heap *is* a witness between me and thee this day. Therefore was the name of it called Galeed; And Mizpah; for he said, The Lord watch between me and thee, when we are absent one from another. If thou shalt afflict my daughters, or if thou shalt take *other* wives beside my daughters, no man *is* with us; see God is witness betwixt me and thee [note again it is the stone between them that is God]. And Laban said to Jacob, Behold this heap, and behold *this* pillar, which I have cast betwixt me and thee; This heap *be* witness, and *this* pillar be witness, that I will not pass over this heap to thee, and thou shalt not pass over this heap and this pillar unto me, for harm. The God of Abraham, and the God of Nahor, the God of their father, judge betwixt us. And Jacob swear by the fear of his father Isaac.' (Gen.31). So the issue and the covenant, all linked to rocks, is about offspring and not harming each other's offspring.

The Yemeni custom and ancient religion of sacredness of stones related to good fortune and specifically granting fertility and offspring is further emphasised, it was important for the authors of the OT to engrain in the stories and to keep re-introducing the sacredness of rocks (a pagan ritual) in relation to fertility and granting of offspring, this is the idea and belief which the stories keep reinforcing. After Jacob and his family are settled in Shecem/Canaan, God orders him to specifically return to the spot where stones were erected as a pillar when Jacob had the bad dream and was told by God he would multiply his seed in an earlier part of the story, at Bethel. He is now told to go back there and make a better altar for worship, and when Jacob and family build the altar (a stone(s)) the narration of God's dialogue with Jacob is again about fertility and offspring, its continuation and increase, and the story has insisted again on linking it directly with the stone and place of the stones (where Jacob had become superstitious) following the building of the altar, and God telling Jacob he will increase his offspring, Jacob sets up more stones and makes offerings there—just like Yemenis do at sacred rocks. 'And God said unto Jacob, Arise, Go up to Bethel, and dwell there: and make there an altar unto God, that appeared unto thee when thou fleddest from the face of Esau thy brother...So Jacob came to Luz, which *is* in the land of Canaan, that *is*, Bethel, he and all the people that *were* with him. And he built there an altar, and called the place El-Beth-el: because there God appeared unto him...And God said unto him, I *am* God Almighty: be fruitful and multiply; a nation and a company of nations shall be of thee, and kings shall come out of thy loins...And God went up from him in the place where he talked with him. And Jacob set up a pillar in the place where he talked with him, even a pillar of stone: and he poured a drink offering thereon, and he poured oil thereon. And Jacob called the name of the place where God spake with him, Bethel.' (Gen.35:1-15)

The Yemeni pagan ritual of worshipping rocks, asking them for fortune and fertility continues in the First Book of Samuel, as does the Yemeni ritual of an annual fertility/copulation feast discussed earlier, also related to offspring and fire worship. Elkanah's barren wife, Hannah, will become pregnant when she makes a vow to God, and not only does her character conceive and give birth to a child resulting from the feasts at Shiloh, but the authors make it clear not only associating the granting of offspring to a rock, but also making God a rock. It is not as modern opinions have it as the 'rock' meaning a strong foundation, but the authors are stating clearly the exact custom of rock worship, i.e. the rock is a god-like being able to grant offspring, fortune, health, etc. Yes, today 'you are my rock' 'God is my rock' means God is the strength, or the person is the strength which helps the speaker, keeps him/her safe or stable but this modern twist is based on the ancient and Biblical 'God is my rock' and this ancient and Biblical meaning is literal and refers to rock worship where God is a literal rock. If early and contemporary scholars unintentionally misunderstand this meaning, it is due to their disregard or lack of knowledge of its origins which are pagan and Yemeni of which these rituals and beliefs of a pagan religion which existed long before any 'divine' religions (Jewish/Christian/Islamic) and survived in them.

The modern (mis)understanding, with its modern, western attributes 'you are my strength, my anchor, etc.' has been put on Hannah's dialogue (and that of other Biblical characters) '*There is* none holy as the Lord: for *there is* none beside thee: neither *is there* any rock like our God.' whereas the true meaning of the Arab people who authored the Bible, who are the characters of the Biblical stories and whose culture is reflected, albeit dramatized and fictionalised, in the Bible, shows even the text itself states that rocks are worshipped, sacrificed to, asked to grant needs and wishes. The Biblical author's intention through Hannah's statement is this rock in Shiloh is the true God which grants and gives offspring and other blessings; the text is saying this one rock in Shiloh is one rock apart from other rocks worshipped (for example there is another rock worshipped in Bethel). The story is based on the Yemeni pagan ritual and belief of fire worship, rock worship, copulation feasts used by the authors of the Bible in the Hannah barren-wife of Elkanah becoming pregnant following her prayer/wish at the annual feast held at Shiloh and then praising the rock as the God who granted her the son:

'...and Peninnah had children, but Hannah had no children. And this man went up out of his city yearly to worship and to sacrifice unto the Lord of the hosts in Shiloh...But unto Hannah he gave a worthy portion; for he loved Hannah: but the Lord had shut up her womb. And her adversary also provoked her sore, for to make her fret, because the Lord had shut up her womb...And she was in bitterness of soul, and prayed unto the Lord and wept sore. And she vowed a vow, and said, O Lord of hosts, if thou indeed will look on the affliction of thine handmaid, and remember me, and not forget thine handmaid, but wilt give unto thine handmaid a man child, then I will give him unto the Lord all the days of his life, and there shall no razor come upon his head...And they rose up in the morning early, and worshipped before the Lord, and returned, and came to their house in Ramah: and Elkanah knew Hannah his wife: and the Lord remembered her. Wherefore it came to pass, when the time was come about after Hannah had conceived, that she bare a son...And when she had weaned him, she took him up with her, with three bullocks, and one ephah of flour, and a bottle of wine, and brought him unto the house of the Lord in Shiloh...And they slew a bullock, and brought the child to Eli. And she said, Oh my lord, *as* thy soul liveth, my lord, I *am* the woman that stood by thee here, praying unto the Lord. For this child I prayed: and the Lord hath given me my petition which I asked of him...And Hannah prayed, and said, My heart rejoiceth in the Lord, mine horn is exalted in the Lord: mine mouth is enlarged over mine enemies; because I rejoice in thy salvation. *There is* none holy as the Lord: for *there is* none beside thee: neither *is there* any rock like our God.'.

When modern scholars, academics, experts, impute modern meanings onto these texts, while these texts have the simple and straightforward meanings of the people and culture who since millennia ago worshipped rocks and is the clear and obvious meaning—this rock which she and her family offer and sacrifice to granted her a son, they worship it as do pagan religions—what these modern imputations do is move people (professionals and laymen) away from understanding the true meanings of the words, it moves away from understanding the text of the Bible (OT and NT), as well as it makes it impossible to understand who wrote the Bible and why they wrote it—and it is very clear in the Biblical text itself it was created by a people whose pagan beliefs, customs and culture have been the basis of the Torah and NT.

It is not only Hannah in the story whose individual role links pagan rock worship, annual fertility feasts to receiving offspring and good fortune, but even her 'adversary' (stepwife) Peninnah whose name itself means 'has many children' which the text as the Biblical authors' method relays that she does have children, and their husband Elkanah who in the story is rich and blessed: Peninnah in her many children, and Elkanah he has the wealth (cattle, wine, finances) to be able to worship and sacrifice annually at Shiloh—his fortune (children as well as wealth) linked to worshipping, sacrificing at Shiloh, at the rock in Shiloh: 'And the man Elkanah, and all his house, went up to offer unto the Lord of hosts in Shiloh…And the man Elkanah, and all his house, went up to offer unto the Lord the yearly sacrifice and his vow.'. When Hannah brings her vow and sacrifices, her gift displays Elkanah's wealth and good fortune because he annually pilgrims and worships, presents sacrifice, makes vows and completes them, delivers his part of the deal of the vow at Shiloh '…three bullocks, and one ephah of flour, and a bottle of wine.' as well as her son is left in the service of God. Shiloh and rocks are used together in other stories of the Bible regarding offspring, fertility and continuation of progeny. (1Sam1; 2:1-8).

The story of taking women who were dancing at the annual feasts at Shiloh being about fertility and continuation through offspring, and how this fictional story is based on the real Yemeni annual feasts where fire, dancing then copulation are the main theme, has been discussed earlier in this book. This Yemeni pagan ritual has been used by the authors of the Bible in giving the Benjamin tribe whose chance of continuation had been destroyed through a genocidal war by its brother-tribes, then given a chance to survive by kidnapping the dancing women at the annual feast of Shiloh. In the very same chapter, in the same story before the final provision of fertile girls and women for the Benjamites are taken from Shiloh, it is preceded by forcefully taking females from a different area, and when these females are not enough to distribute to all the men of Benjamin then the story goes towards the dancing women of Shiloh (Shiloh means 'take it/took it/carry it' and 'his rock').

The story which precedes the kidnapping for fertility at Shiloh is also created around rocks/stones and specifically Mizpeh and Gilead (discussed before). Again, and again, the authors of the OT use pagan rock worship beliefs to be an influence on fertility, barrenness, the continuation of offspring, of people or its discontinuation and destruction. In Judges, when the other tribes of Israel learn of Gibeah men's atrocity against the Levite, they gather to discuss it at Mizpeh—the sacred stone already linked to fertility and offspring in Genesis through the Laban/Jacob story; the eleven tribes of Israel decide, while gathered at Mizpeh, to destroy the 'men, children of Gibeah' that is, to kill them all so no 'perverted' offspring or lineage continue from them and the idea is to kill all the people so no evil offspring continues to be produced, but because all of Benjamin refuses to render the men of Gibeah the remaining eleven tribes decide to destroy all of Benjamin—complete genocide. The point is: the rocks Mizpeh and Gilead linked to fertility and offspring or its opposite is where the people decide to kill the specific line of 'evil' Gibeah Benjaminites: 'Then all the children of Israel went out, and the congregation was gathered together as one man, from Dan even to Beer-sheba, with the land of Gilead, unto the Lord of Mizpeh…But now this *shall be* the thing which we will do to Gibeah; *we will* go up by lot against it…So all the men of Israel were gathered against the city, Knit together as one man. And the tribes of Israel sent men through all the tribes of Benjamin, saying, What wickedness *is* this that is done among you? Now therefore deliver *us* the men, the children of Belial, which *are* in Gibeah, that we may put them to death, and put away evil from Israel.'

But when the Benjamites refuse, both sides engage in battle. The Benjamin tribe is stronger and defeats the rest of the tribes—this story allows authors to bring in another Yemeni pagan ritual also related to worship and fertility/offspring: fire. When the tribes are beaten over and over again by Benjamin, the children of Israel fast and offer burnt offerings, then in the middle of the battle as narrated, it turns out a plan had been made and it is fire (used in pagan worship and also in worship of fertility gods) which will not only turn the battle against the Benjaminites who were up until now victors, but with the ascension of fire and smoke in the story their continuance as a people with offspring to continue their line is put to an end (temporarily):

'And Benjamin went forth against them out of Gibeah the second day, and destroyed down to the ground of the children of Israel again eighteen thousand men; all these drew the sword. Then all the children of Israel, and all the people, went up, and came to the house of God, and wept, and at there before the Lord, and fasted that day until even, and offered burnt offerings and peace offerings before the Lord...And there came against Gibeah ten thousand chosen men out of all Israel, and the battle was sore: but they knew not that evil was near them. And the Lord smote Benjamin before Israel: and the children of Israel destroyed of the Benjamites that day twenty and five thousand and an hundred men: all these drew the sword. So the children of Benjamin saw that they were smitten: for the men of Israel gave place to the Benjamites, because they trusted unto the liers in wait which they had set beside Gibeah. And the liers in wait hasted, and rushed upon Gibeah; and the liers in wait drew *themselves* along, and smote all the city with the edge of the sword. Now there was an appointed sign between the men of Israel and the liers in wait, that they should make a great flame with smoke rise up out of the city. And when the men of Israel retired in the battle, Benjamin began to smite *and* kill of the men of Israel about thirty persons: for they said, Surely they are smitten down before us, as *in* the first battle. But when the flame began to arise up out of the city with a pillar of smoke, the Benjamites looked behind them, and, behold, the flame of the city ascended up to heaven. And when the men of Israel turned again, the men of Benjamin were amazed: for they saw that evil was upon them. Therefore they turned *their backs* before the men of Israel unto the way of the wilderness; but the battle overtook them; and them which *came* out of the cities they destroyed in the midst of them. *Thus* they inclosed the Benjamites round about, *and* chased them, *and* trode them down with ease over against Gibeah toward the sun rising. And there fell of Benjamin eighteen thousand men; all these *were* men of valour.'

So by a sacred rock, Mizpeh, it is determined the Gibeah Benjamite's line will be put to death, and through burnt offerings then by a giant fire the whole of Benjamin's line is put to near extinction. Note now where the fleeing men of Benjamin attempt to escape to, and will become the thread allowing the story to give the Benjamites protection, then the hope that their line will be allowed to continue: they flee to a rock, a rock which even in the Bible, just like in the real-life pagan practise of Yemeni origin, is worshipped, sacrificed and pilgrimaged towards and is directly linked to giving fertility, offspring and continuation of lineage: 'And they turned and fled toward the wilderness unto the rock of Rimmon: and they gleaned of them in the highways five thousand men; and pursued hard after them unto Gidom, and slew two thousand men of them. So that all which fell that day of Benjamin were twenty and five thousand men that drew the sword; all these *were* men of valour. But six hundred men turned and fled to the wilderness unto the rock of Rimmon, and abode in the rock Rimmon four months. And the men of Israel turned again upon the children of Benjamin, and smote them with the edge of the sword, as well the men of *every* city, as the beast, and all that came to hand: also they set on fire all the cities that they came to.' (Gen.20)

At this point it is worth reminding of the meaning of 'Gilead' and how it is used in its original Yemeni meaning which is how it has been used by the Biblical authors to create and assist the storyline in more than one part of the Biblical stories: from the use of stones as witnesses, as well as the superstitious beliefs and sacredness of stones; for its use and meanings, words to the effect of 'this will be witness against you, if you are lying or transgress you will bear the responsibilities' and in Arabic this is said and summed up in one or two words 'Gilead-you/قلدّك' 'Gilead-you God/قلدّك الله', and is usually used when there is a disagreement or hashing-out of things, or an important matter is being discussed, and especially when someone says something which the other side does not believe or has doubts about. Gilead and Galeed are from 'tumbling/rolling stone' and in the Bible first features with these intended meanings between Laban and Jacob where the stones are used as witnesses between them, and the story related to offspring, a covenant of not harming each other's offspring and rights. We see this Yemeni pagan belief, ritual and expression used in the Biblical storyline again: the author(s) of the OT have brought one of the twelve tribes of Israel to certain extinction; this is not desired because either earlier authors or later editors have already written/added that all twelve tribes will survive and multiply forever so the story which drives Benjamin to extinction has to have a 'twist' to allow their lineage to revive and survive.

Just as earlier fertility, fortune, offspring, continuance of 'seed' is expressed through associating and ascribing it to pagan rock worship and also fire worship, it is used here too at this important part of the story which explains how Benjamin's line was saved from extinction (the story itself indicates that maybe in its original form the tribe of Benjamin was meant to be wiped out completely and no longer feature in later stories), and not only is it through the sacred and powerful attributes of the rock, but also 'Gilead' which is an agreement based on the sacredness of the rock. In the final chapter the remaining tribes of Israel are mourning and poring over the near extinction of the Benjamin tribe, it is mentioned they have made an agreement and sworn not to give any of their daughters in marriage to any Benjamite. The discussion to revive Benjamin's seed/line is taking place at Mizpeh, a sacred stone used in the Bible regarding offspring—and in the same chapter it comes to light that they have killed all the wives/girls of Benjamin, coupled with swearing never to marry their daughters to a Benjamite which seals Benjamin's extinction. After building an altar at Mizpeh, offering burnt and peace offerings, they find a solution: whoever had not attended at Mizpeh, described as being the place of the Lord (note wherever there is a sacred rock it is associated with special powers, sacredness and assigned to a God or God is in/at the rock) the absent part will be punished. The authors of the Biblical story conveniently and tellingly name the whole tribe which has now been earmarked to become the channel through which Benjamin's seed and tribe will be allowed to continue 'Jabesh-gilead', literally 'absent from rock' 'absent-tumbling/rolling stone' 'absent-placing responsibility'; and by killing all the men, women and children of Jabesh-gilead they leave only the virgin girls to be given to the surviving men of Benjamin to reproduce from.

So Mizpeh and Gilead, sacred rocks and the meaning of a phrase where stone is invoked, as well as 'Jabesh-gilead' literally meaning they were absent from the discussion which took place at this sacred rock of fertility and continuance of seed are all reflected and relayed in the story being told: the whole of Jabesh-gilead's tribe, the men, children and any woman who has had sexual intercourse, are wiped out because as the name suggests and the story clearly narrates they were absent from the rock/Mizpeh discussions and the related rituals of fertility etc. and there is a responsibility and consequence 'Gilead'; the beneficiaries from the Mizpeh and Gilead and the extermination of Jabesh-gilead, are the surviving men of Benjamin whose survival and reconstitution of the Benjamin line is also tied into the sacredness or rocks/stones in Yemen pagan culture—this time a rock in Rimmon. And when the virgins of Jabesh-gilead are not enough for the numbers of surviving Benjamin men the authors of the Bible reach out and use another Yemeni pagan ritual and custom which survived well into the 1980s—the annual feast of fire, dance and copulation used in the Bible and called 'an annual feast at Shiloh where there are dances' (Shiloh 'his rock') where in the story the fertility and the sacred power of rocks to grant things are linked to annual fertility festival and in so doing emphasising the use of Yemeni culture, religion and rituals in the stories of the OT:

'Now the men of Israel had sworn in Mizpeh, saying, There shall not any of us give his daughter unto Benjamin to wife. And the people came to the house of God, and abode there till even, before God, and lifted up their voices and wept sore; and said, O Lord God of Israel, why is this come to pass in Israel, that there should be today one tribe lacking in Israel? And it came to pass on the morrow, that the people rose early, and built there an altar, and offered burnt offerings and peace offerings. And the children of Israel said, Who *is there* among all the tribes of Israel that came not up with the congregation unto the Lord? For they had made a great oath concerning him that came not up to the Lord to Mizpeh, saying, He shall surely be put to death. And the children of Israel repented them for Benjamin their brother, and said, There is one tribe cut off from Israel this day. How shall we do for wives for them that remain, seeing we have sworn by the Lord that we will not give them of our daughters to wives? And they said, What one *is there* of the tribes of Israel that come not up to Mizpeh to the Lord? And, behold, there came none to the camp from Jabesh-gilead to the assembly. For the people were numbered, and, behold, *there were* none of the inhabitants of Jabesh-gilead there. And the congregation sent thither twelve thousand men of the valiantest, and commanded them, saying, Go and smite the inhabitants of Jabesh-gilead with edge of the sword, with the women and the children. And this *is* the thing which ye shall do, Ye shall utterly destroy every male, and every woman that have lain by man. And they found among the inhabitants of Jabesh-gilead four hundred young virgins, that had known no man by lying with any male: and they brought them unto the camp to Shiloh, which *is* in the land of Canaan. And the whole congregation sent *some* to speak to the children of Benjamin that *were* in the rock Rimmon, and to call peaceably unto them. And Benjamin came again and at that time; and they gave them wives which they had saved alive of the women of Jabesh-gilead: and yet they sufficed them not. And the people repented them for Benjamin, because that the Lord had made a breach in the tribes of Israel. Then the elders of the congregation said, How shall we do for wives for them that remain, seeing the women are destroyed out of Benjamin? And they said, *There must be* an inheritance for them that be escaped of Benjamin, that a tribe be not destroyed out of Israel. Howbeit we may not give them wives of our daughters: for the children of Israel have sworn, saying, Cursed *be* he that giveth a wife to Benjamin. Then they said, Behold, *there is* a feast of the Lord in Shiloh yearly *in a place* which is...' and the kidnapping of the dancing women at Shiloh follows to ensure Benjamin has enough women to procreate with. (Gen.21)

Regarding the Yemeni practise of rock worship, the belief in rock sacredness, and the effects it has on giving, increasing, or taking away and decreasing be it fortune, offspring, health, wealth, etc. just like a god does, can be seen in the Biblical stories. In 1Samuel in both Hannah and David's stories you can see the rock's power and associating it with God giving or taking away continuity. In Hannah when she compares her rock, her God, being unlike any other rock, she shows how he/it gives/takes, increases/decreases or ends. The rock named 'Ezel' which can mean 'here/look/pay attention/I will-forever' 'here/look/pay attention/I will-go/disappear/remove' is used in the David/Jonathan story where David is to wait by this stone called Ezel to find out if his life with Jonathan will continue or end. 'And Hannah prayed, and said, My heart rejoiceth in the Lord, mine horn is exalted in the Lord: my mouth is enlarged over mine enemies; because I rejoice in thy salvation. *There is* none holy as the Lord: for *there is* none beside thee: neither *is there* any rock like our God. Talk no more so exceeding proudly; let *not* arrogancy come out of your mouth: for the Lord *is* a God of knowledge, and by him actions are weighed. The bows of the mighty men *are* broken, and they that stumbled are girded with strength. *They that were* full have hired out themselves for bread; and *they that were* hungry ceased: so that the barren hath born seven; and she that hath many children is waxed feeble. The Lord killeth, and maketh alive: he bringeth down to the grave, and bringeth up. The Lord maketh poor, and maketh rich: he bringeth low, and lifteth up. He raiseth up the poor out of the dust, *and* lifteth up the beggar from the dunghill, to set *them* among princes, and to make them inherit the throne of glory: for the pillars of the earth *are* the Lord's, and he hath set the world upon them.' Note the pillars of the earth are rocks, made of stone. (1Sam.2:1-8)

Jonathan instructs David '...and shalt remain by the stone Ezel. And I will shoot three arrows on the side *thereof*, as though I shot at a mark. And, behold, I will send a lad, *saying*, Go find out the arrows. If I expressly say unto the lad, Behold, the arrows *are* on this side of thee, take them; then come thou: for *there is* peace to thee, and no hurt; as the Lord liveth. But if I say thus unto the young man, Behold, the arrows *are* beyond thee; go thy way: for the Lord hath sent thee away. And *as touching* the matter which thou and I have spoken of, behold, the Lord *be* between thee and me forever.' And this is the author referring to the 'forever' meanings of the Ezel physically between them and linking again that God is the rock. (1Sam.20:18-23).

Also the Yemeni pagan custom of worshipping rocks as they give fortune, health, offspring, etc. can be seen in Deuteronomy where the 'rock' is not only exchangeable with the word 'God', but also other 'rocks' are mentioned in comparison to the correct 'rock' (in the stories narrative), and not with the modern meaning and interpretation of 'God gives strength, stability, etc.' but as in the meaning and practise that the rocks deemed sacred because something superstitious happened around them to a person and were therefore worshipped and believed to grant good fortune, children, etc. if worshipped, presented with sacrifices and gifts, vows made to them—and if this was not performed towards the rock then bad and misfortune would befall the shortcoming person(s). In Deuteronomy where the rock which has become sacred and Moses is reminding the children of Israel, it reminds the reader of Jacob's interaction with the rock at Bethel and how it went from a normal stone he put under his head as a pillow, to becoming a sacred rock representing God, worshipped and believed to give/bring fortune, sustenance and protection for Jacob, just like in Yemen where a superstition leads to rock worship:

'Because I will publish the name of the Lord: ascribe ye greatness unto our God. He *is* the Rock, his is perfect...For the Lord's portion *is* his people; Jacob *is* the lot of his inheritance. He found him in a desert land, and in the waste howling wilderness; he led him about, he instructed him, he kept him as the apple of his eye...So the Lord alone did lead him, and there was no strange god with him. He made him ride on the high places of the earth, that he might eat the increase of the fields; and he made him to suck honey out of the rock, and oil out of the flinty rock...' and it goes on to mention all the good God gave them, but when they became well-off 'then he forsook God which made him, and lightly esteemed the Rock of his salvation...Of the Rock that begat thee thou art unmindful, and hast forgotten God that formed thee.' So both Rock and God are one and the same, the creator upset because Jacob/the people have begun to worship different rocks/gods: 'They provoked him to jealousy with strange *gods*, with abominations provoked they him to anger. They sacrificed unto devils, not to God; to gods whom they knew not, to new *gods that* came newly up, whom your fathers feared not.' And following this comes verse 18 mentioned above, telling them they have forgotten the Rock that created them—again god, power, sacredness is a rock. And following the worship of other rocks, this rock/God will cause them to starve, to feel physical punishment, he will destroy them. And the deity of the narration goes on to tell them they are worshipping the wrong rock, which is why they are being punished—or at least why these wrong rocks cannot give them good fortune or good fate; it emphasises the practise of rock worship among the authors and audience of the Bible, or at least an awareness of it: 'For they are a nation void of counsel, neither *is there any* understanding in them. O that they were wise, *that* they understood this, *that* they would consider their latter end! How should one chase a thousand, and two put ten thousand to flight, except their Rock had sold them, and the Lord had shut them up? for their rock *is* not as our Rock, even our enemies themselves being judges.' It goes on to make comparisons of the negativity of 'their rock', then 'And he shall say, Where are their gods, their rock in whom they trusted, Which did eat the fat of their sacrifices, and drank the wine of their drink offerings? let them rise up and help you, and be your protection.' (Deut.32:1-38)

The sacredness of a rock which becomes exchangeable with 'gods' continues, and again the sacred rock is usually one which becomes sacred after the character in the story has a negative incident around it, superstitiously connecting it with the bad and good of the incident—and in real-life Yemen pagan rituals the idol/sacred object can be a living or dead person, or a rock—and gifts are presented to it (usually food stuff), vows are made in its presence, or elsewhere then the promise kept towards it, and pilgrimage made to it. How the rock through a negative incident becomes sacred to its worshippers, like Jacob and Bethel, Jacob and Mizpeh, is shown again in detail with David and Sela-hammahlekoth 'rock-here-the death/perish of' 'rock-here-the surrounded' and is the name given to the rock where David hid, and was surrounded by Saul and his men, and as the name and the story reflect and relay, David thought he was to be killed, so when he is saved by a message which distracts Saul away, the rock takes on this superstitious aura and becomes associated with powers of protection and considered a god.

This superstitious belief in the rock becoming sacred and god-like, exchangeable with 'god', can be seen elsewhere in David's story where it clearly details its 'powers' and holiness tied to the negative incident of being surrounded by certain death; elsewhere where it is mentioned as 'rock/god' in Psalms it is in one psalm repeating verbatim what has already come in the earlier David story with the note above the psalm indicating it is directly regarding David when he was surrounded by, then saved from, Saul: 'Saul and his men also went to seek *him*. And they told David: wherefore he came down into a rock, and abode in the wilderness Maon. And when Saul heard *that*, he pursued after David in the wilderness of Maon. And Saul went on this side of the mountain, and David and his men on that side of the mountain: and David made haste to get away for fear of Saul; for Saul and his men compassed David and his men round about to take them. But there came a messenger unto Saul, saying, Haste thee, and come; for the Philistines have invaded the land. Wherefore Saul returned from pursuing after David, and went against the Philistines: therefore they called that place Sela-hammahlekoth.' (1Sam.23:25-28). 'And David spake unto the Lord the words of this song in the day that the Lord had delivered him out of the hand of all his enemies, and out of the hand of Saul. And he said, the Lord is my rock, and my fortress, and my deliverer; The God of my rock; in him will I trust: *he* is my shield, and the horn of my salvation, my high tower, and my refuge, my saviour; thou savest me from violence. I will call on the Lord, *who is* worthy to be praised: so shall I be saved from mine enemies. When the waves of death compassed me, the floods of ungodly men made me afraid; The sorrows of hell compassed me about; the snares of death prevented me; In my distress I called upon the Lord, and cried to my God: and he did hear my voice out of his temple, and my cry *did enter* into his ears...For who is God, save the Lord? and who *is* a rock, save our God? God *is* my strength *and* power...Thou hast also given me the shield of thy salvation...The Lord liveth; and blessed *be* my rock; and exalted be the God of the rock of my salvation...Now these *be* the last words of David. David the son of Jesse said, and the man *who was* raised upon high, the anointed of the God of Jacob, and the sweet psalmist of Israel, said, the Spirit of the Lord spake by me, and his word *was* in my tongue. The God of Israel said, The Rock of Israel spake to me, He that ruleth over men *must be* just, ruling in the fear of God.' (2Sam.22; 23:1-3). The same in Psalm 18.

In Psalm 61, 62: 'Hear my cry, O God; attend unto my prayer. From the end of the earth will I cry unto thee, when my heart is overwhelmed: lead me to the rock *that* is higher than I. For thou hast been a shelter for me, *and* a strong tower from the enemy.' 'Truly my soul waiteth upon God: from him cometh my salvation. He only *is* my rock and my salvation: *he is* my defence; I shall not be greatly moved...My soul, wait thou only upon God; for my expectation *is* from him. He only *is* my rock and my salvation: *he* is my defence; I shall not be moved. In God is my salvation and my glory: the rock of my strength, *and* my refuge, *is* in God. Trust in him at all times; ye people pour out your heart before him: God *is* a refuge for us.'

'In thee, O Lord, do I put my trust: let me never be put to confusion. Deliver me in thy righteousness, and cause me to escape: incline thine ear unto me, and save me. Be thou my strong habitation, whereunto I may continually resort: thou hast given commandment to save me; for thou *art* my rock and my fortress. Deliver me, O my God, out of the hand of the wicked, out of the hand of the unrighteous and cruel man.' (Psalm 71)

'I have found David my servant; with my holy oil have I anointed him. With whom my hand shall be established; mine arm shall also strengthen him: The enemy shall not exact upon him; nor the son of wickedness afflict him. And I will beat down his foes before his face, and plague them that hate him. But my faithfulness and mercy *shall be* with him: and in my name shall his horn be exalted. I will set his hand also in the sea, and his right hand in the rivers. He shall cry unto me, Thou *art* my father, my God, and the rock of my salvation.' (Psalm 89:20-26).

Anointing with Oil

Also, a way of life in rural Yemen which has become a religious ritual in the OT is the use of oil poured over the head, and the use of butter as hair cream. In the Bible, it is to anoint a person as leader, king, prophet, etc. whereas since ancient times and to this day Yemenis use sesame oil to harden the fontanelle of babies, it is believed to help harden the soft spot on a baby's head faster and the oils healthy nutrients absorbed into the head. It is also used to massage a baby's body while the mother sunbathes the baby in her lap, in the morning before the sun becomes harsh; the oil with the sunlight is believed to strengthen the baby's body, make it healthy and help it to grow. Pure butter was used as hair cream, especially by women, the older generations of women I lived with claim it made hair better, stronger, longer and that it held onto the perfumed smoke in their hair (b<u>kh</u>oor) better (whereas the younger generations of women would make jokes about how it must have stank as they discontinued its use). It must be noted that although the Biblical authors based their anointing with oil in the stories on both the real-life use of sesame oil and butter, the actual word used in the OT is neither oil nor butter, but 'clarified butter' (smn/سمن) which is butter that has been clarified through boiling it long on heat while impurities are absorbed by cracked sorghum in the bottom of the container leaving only the clarified butter which is poured into a separate vessel/bottle once pure—it becomes solid at room temperature and is heated to become liquid and used to pour over food, believed to be highly nutritious and is one of the most prized food products.

The massaging with oil and pouring oil onto a baby's head is the origin of a Yemeni saying which also proves the use of anointing a special character in the Bible comes from Yemeni authors and origins: 'My despair over the oil[used], if only I had licked it.' ياقهرا على الصليط ، ياريتَني لحسته and to break down and explain what it means: instead of wasting, pouring oil on your head when you were a baby thinking you would turn out good and/or useful, I should not have wasted it pouring it onto your head (because you turned out bad/stupid/useless/disobedient/etc.), if I had known you would be like this I wish I had used the oil in food and eaten it instead of wasting it pouring it onto your head as it has done you no good—all in very much shorter expression which is said most times in humour, sometimes in exasperation. It is just another custom of Yemen life which Yemeni people used in the Bible to show the importance and hope put into a character by other characters pouring oil onto his head, the use of it in the stories invoke the protection from God, which is the same as a real parent protecting the softest part of a baby's body around the most important part (head/brain) and the care showing how special a baby is to its parent.

Purification with Blood

Other anointing rituals which are Yemeni since pagan times, and lived on into modern days, which the authors of the Bible have incorporated into their stories which in turn have been adopted as religious practise, is the use of blood to anoint and/or purify its subjects whether human or object, as well as the subjects touching or being put into contact with the sacrificial animal before it is slaughtered.

Wedding Purification and Sacrifice

In rural Yemen, at the beginning of the wedding day the bride is taken for a ritual called 'washing/purification' and this is not a washing with water. After the bride has already washed her whole body she is seated outside and a goat or lamb is brought before her. The animal is slaughtered in front of her, a man (usually an uncle) takes the blood and dots a smear of it on her forehead and feet—the blood of the sacrificed animal touching her skin 'purifies' her. Not only does it purify her soul, but it also protects her from envious onlookers' sins (the same is done for the bridegroom).

The exact same purification is used in the Bible to consecrate Aaron and the priests where the sacrificed animals' blood is placed on Aaron and his sons; these characters also wash directly before the blood purification ritual, just like Yemeni brides do.

Another Yemeni ritual is when the bride and groom arrive outside the marital home on the wedding day, a ram or lamb is brought in front of them; the groom's father brings the sacrificial animal in front of the couple, the couple are to touch its head and neck by stroking it three strokes—first the bridegroom then the bride—and then the couple go inside and the animal is slaughtered. This serves to take away negative spirits, negative envy and to protect the couple to ensure a happy and pure start to marital life. You can see this pagan custom of Yemeni origin used in the Bible when consecrating Aaron and his sons as priests. The similarities are too strong than to deny: washing the body as part of the ritual before purification with blood; the bride and groom, in the story Aaron and sons, touching the animal in the same manner and for the same purpose: the touch makes a connection and transference between the person and the animal so when the animal is sacrificed, its spilt blood is for the sake of the person who touched it. In both the real life of Yemenis and in the fictional characters of the Biblical stories the blood of the sacrificial animal is linked first by the people/objects it is being sacrificed by touching the live animal, and then it is used to purify/consecrate the person/object by the sacrificed animals blood touching the skin/surface of the object—making a full circle of connection and protection.

The fact the ritual includes the person(s) has to touch it before it is sacrificed so when its blood is spilled in sacrifice it symbolises or is believed to physically be sacrificed instead of a human—which also indicates an older pagan ritual and worship where maybe human sacrifice was once conducted. The blood is also used to purify and protect the building: in real life it is the marital home, in the Bible it is the tabernacle, but the reason is the same—to remove impurities and evil. Where in the Bible it is understood to 'make holy' (which in itself is a mistake as the word means to make 'piled/heap') the character or place, in the real-life Yemeni ritual it is to remove demons, evil spirits, evil eyes, impurities, etc., for good luck, to remove bad luck because this ritual of both the Yemeni people which ended up being used in the Bible emanates from pagan times long before any monotheistic religions.

These purification rituals all show the same culture: washing the body with water; purification of body and soul by touching the animal which is then sacrificed, then taking its blood and smearing or sprinkling it on the person(s) being purified; the same way using the same blood to purify them or a building concerned—all three purification steps have been used in Aaron's consecration story: 'And this *is* the thing that thou shalt do unto them to hallow them, to minister unto me in the priest's office: Take one young bullock and two rams without blemish, And unleavened bread and cakes unleavened tempered with oil, and wafers unleavened anointed with oil: *of* wheaten flour shalt thou make them. And thou shalt put them into one basket, and bring them in the basket, with the bullock and the two rams. And Aaron and his sons thou shalt bring unto the door of the tabernacle of the congregation, and shalt wash them with water. And thou shalt take the garments and put upon Aaron the coat, and the robe of the ephod, and the breastplate, and gird him with the curious girdle of the ephod: And thou shalt put the mitre upon his head, and put the holy crown upon the mitre. Then shalt thou take the anointing oil, and pour *it* upon his head, and anoint him. And thou shalt bring his sons and put coats upon them. And thou shalt gird them with girdles, Aaron and his sons, and put bonnets on them: and the priests office shall be theirs for a perpetual statute: and thou shalt consecrate Aaron and his sons. And thou shall cause a bullock to be brought before the tabernacle of the congregation: and Aaron and his sons shall put their hands on the head of the bullock. And thou shalt kill the bullock before the Lord, *by* the Lord of the tabernacle of the congregation. And thou shalt take of the blood of the bullock, and put *it* upon the horns of the altar with thy finger, and pour all the blood beside the bottom of the altar. And thou shalt take all the fat that covereth the inwards, and the caul *that is* above the liver, and the two kidneys, and the fat that *is* upon them, and burn *them* upon the altar. But the flesh of the bullock, and his skin, and his dung, shalt thou burn with fire without the camp: it *is* a sin offering. Thou shalt also take one ram; and Aaron and his sons shall put their hands upon the head of the ram. And thou shalt slay the ram, and thou shalt take his blood, and sprinkle *it* round about upon the altar. And thou shalt cut the ram in pieces, and wash the inwards of him, and his legs, and put them unto his pieces, and unto his head. And thou shalt burn the whole ram upon the altar: it *is* a burnt offering unto the Lord: it *is* a sweet savour, an offering made by fire unto the Lord. And thou shalt take the other ram; and Aaron and his sons shall put their hands upon the head of the ram. Then shalt thou kill the ram, and take of his blood, and put *it* upon the tip of the right ear of Aaron, and upon the tip of the right ear of his sons, and upon the thumb of their right hand, and upon the great toe of their right foot, and sprinkle the blood upon the altar round about. And thou shalt take of the blood that *is* upon the altar, and of the anointing oil, and sprinkle *it* upon Aaron, and upon his garments, and upon his sons, and upon the garments of his sons with him: and he shall be hallowed, and his garments, and his sons, and his sons' garments with him. And thou shalt take of the ram the fat and the rump, and the fat that covereth the inwards, and the caul *above* the liver, and the two kidneys, and the fat that *is* upon them, and the right shoulder; for it *is* a ram of consecration: And one loaf of bread, and one cake of oiled bread, and one wafer of the basket of unleavened bread that *is* before the Lord: And thou shalt put all in the hands of Aaron, and in the hands of his sons; and shalt wave them *for* a wave offering before the Lord.' (Exod.29:1-25).

So the same ritual in both real Yemeni life and the story of the Bible and done for similar reasons, except in the Bible the offerings are burned to God, but in real life the meat is cooked and served to the family and guests with unleavened bread. Note, these Yemeni people who perform these rituals continue a pagan past, it has nothing to do with Islam (nor with Jewish religion for that matter), the people's knowledge of the Islamic religion remained superficial and although they consider themselves Sunni Muslims, all their rituals and customs remained pagan in origin and conduct, and outrightly contrary to Islamic teachings and rules yet the people remained believing and performing the pagan rituals with firm belief and firmness of attitude that this is how things are and have always been. A people who went from pagan rituals and beliefs to a nominal and slight change by nominally incorporating a very late-to-be-introduced Islam, and a people in the region who have no connection, nor ever were Jewish (I refer to specific remote Yemenis and not the whole of Yemen, as parts of Yemen did become Jewish (then Christian and Muslim) much later on when the Jewish religion would first emerge in the Arabian Peninsula, its birthplace). And even when they adopted Islamic statements and were learning to conduct Muslim prayer, the overwhelming and fastidious conduct, beliefs, and attitudes are absolutely paganistic and idolatry in nature. The people kept their pagan rituals intact and Islamic understanding was minimal, superficial and entwined into an overwhelmingly pagan culture up until I left in 1998, I believe the culture remained that way for over a decade at least after I left before circumstances and changes to roads and access would bring change which would coerce large numbers of the stubborn and unwilling-to-change inhabitants to move to cities and back, bringing a better understanding of Islam, but also a shaming of the locals by outsiders, and this unfortunately brought the banning of some pagan rituals, which is a tragedy in itself that urbanised Yemenis and their modern beliefs about religion, ways of life, speech would see themselves 'above' and 'better' than the locals whose language and ways is a time capsule of how things were in ancient times.

New House Sacrifice

It is practise in rural Yemen to sacrifice an animal on the site where a house is about to be built, then again once the building has been complete. The same ritual is shown in the Hiel the Bethelite story (1Kgs.16:34), albeit dramatized as a human sacrifice of his sons.

As mentioned earlier, the Yemeni authors of the Biblical stories often combined one or more ancient Yemeni pagan rituals into the stories or event in the story which became religious festivals or rituals in the Bible/OT. When a new house is built in remote Yemen regions, as soon as it is complete and before the owners move in, they make the second sacrifice as mentioned above (the first is just before building commences) of an animal called 'sacrifice to demons' where a goat/lamb is slaughtered (not in the name of God and without invoking the name of God) on the doorstep of the house. The sacrificed animal's blood is splashed and smeared on the threshold, the lintel and the side-posts of the door. All the meat is left inside the house for the 'demons' to eat. They do this to get the demons to pass over somewhere else other than this house, to leave—so that they (the demons) do not kill, harm or possess the family who will inhabit the house. When a demon is believed to have killed a child or adult, they say it 'took him/أخذه/شاله'.

This sacrifice is believed to protect the inhabitants of the house by getting the demons, through offering them a sacrifice, to note the blood marking the house protects the people who will live inside; the meat 'eaten' by the demons as an offering appeases them to move on and leave the house. The meat is not eaten by the people as it is for demon and not human consumption; if the meat is still inside the house the next day, it is thrown away (by logic if the meat is no longer there or most of it devoured, it has of course been eaten by a wild animal) and it is thrown away far from the house.

Land Sacrifice

Another similar Yemeni ritual: where demons are believed to live, be found or seen near rocks in land, before ploughing/tilling the land a meal is made of crushed bread, milk and clarified butter (the dish is phtah, the word used to create the compound word-name 'Naphtali') which is a breakfast dish for people, but in this instance it is made especially for the 'demons' of that specific rock/area, and it is called 'phatat al-ginn/ فتة الجن' 'demons' crushed bread'. A day before the ploughing/tilling commences, the prepared dish is taken to and left at the specific rock where they are believed to be, to ensure they cause no trouble for the people working the land. It is similar, but on a smaller scale, to the 'demon sacrifice' of the new house, based on the same idea or belief to present an offering to protect the people from the harm of a supernatural being.

Horns and the Sacrifice for Firstborns

An ancient Yemeni ritual practised even into current modern times by people who never changed their way of life since ancient times can be found regarding a very real problem: what in modern times and cities is scientifically known to be caused by biological circumstances, Rhesus disease which causes the firstborn to survive but all following siblings to die, in the region of Yemen I speak about where up until very recently science, medical knowledge and treatments did not exist, but superstition and pagan rituals have persisted, they believe the cause of all the following siblings' deaths to be based on 'horns' and 'demons'. The belief is every person is born with a (qareen/قرين) literally a 'horn' which is a devil, demon or at least a spirit which can afflict its human owner and/or the people related and in contact with that specific person. Everybody has a 'horn'. When the people talk about the 'qareen/horn' they indicate with their hand over and in front of the temple of the head, which is where they believe it to be—externally at the forefront of the human counterpart i.e. it is not part of the human physical body, but is linked to the human and goes around with him/her. The naming of this spirit which is to one side at the forefront of a person's head either comes from its position is like the position of an animal's (or devil's) horns, or because of the meaning 'linked' as it is linked to its human and is always there even though it is a separate being.

It is believed that if this 'horn' is too powerful, or is non-compatible with another person's 'horn' it causes harm. E.g. if a husband and wife are having arguments or there is discord between them, it is deemed that their 'horns' are incompatible. They will attempt to remedy this problem by changing the wife's name, and the name is changed and chosen using sorcery and calculations done by a sorcerer to identify the cause, and changing her name 'softens' i.e. makes compatible, her 'horn' and resolves the problem.

With regards to the condition when the offspring following a firstborn all die (Rhesus disease)—they believe the firstborn's 'horn/qareen' is stronger than (non-compatible) his parents' 'horns'. The following ritual is done to 'remedy' the situation: a sacrifice such as a bull, goat or lamb is made specifically to demons and the sacrifice is offered and done by an un-related third party; while a man is performing the slaughter to the demons, a woman (unrelated to the concerned parents/child) says 'I have purchased him from you.', and they pierce the firstborn child's ear and place an earring into it indicating he will always belong to the woman who purchased the child from his 'horn'. The floor inside the house is dug up and the meat of the sacrifice (which is for the demons) is buried underneath either the child's or his biological mother's bed. Both blood and meat are a sacrifice and offering to the demons—this meat is not for human consumption. As it goes: because the third party (the unrelated woman) has 'purchased' the child from both his 'horn' and from his biological parents (although he never leaves the family, nor family home, and never physically goes to the 'purchaser') the incompatibility, the excess power/strength of his 'horn' is remedied as he (and it) no longer has anything to do with his parents' 'horns'—and the offspring conceived after this ritual survive. It is a purchase and sacrifice which 'redeems' and ensures the survival of children. Of course I do not have an explanation of how for some families the children conceived after this ritual survive when the condition is a real physical condition which in cities needs medical treatment to allow the conceived children of the incompatible blood-type of parents to survive, but I have witnessed the ritual and know some families who have performed these rituals (my opinion is that the children died from other causes (not Rhesus disease) and those which survived would have survived even without the redeeming ritual).

In both these Yemeni rituals and beliefs of pagan origin, the sacrifice to the demons of a new house with blood put on the threshold, side-posts and lintel; the 'redeeming' of a child through sacrifice to demons and ear-piercing, where blood and meat are also used in the redemption and protection of offspring, you can see how these actual practices have been used and combined in the Biblical stories to inspire and base on the killing of the firstborn as the last plague against Pharaoh/Egypt, and how using sacrifice and marking the doorposts and lintel with blood of the sacrificed animal, how the event is upkept in the story as the children of Israel 'redeeming' their children with sacrifice and offerings—the foundation is the same: it is a purchase in exchange for protection. The plague and the children of Israel's protection, as well as the Passover event and festival, the 'redeeming' through offerings and sacrifice, as well as the stories where a slave who chooses to remain in servitude to his master having his ear pierced and remains the property of the owner forever—these stories are based on and inspired from the ancient Yemeni rituals mentioned above:

'And the Lord said unto Moses, Yet will I bring one plague *more* upon Pharaoh, and upon Egypt…And Moses said, Thus saith the Lord, About midnight will I go out into the midst of Egypt: And all the firstborn in the land of Egypt shall die, from the firstborn of Pharaoh that sitteth upon his throne, even unto the firstborn of the maidservant that *is* behind the mill; and all the firstborn of beasts. And there shall be a great cry throughout all the land of Egypt, such as there was none like it, nor shall be like it anymore. But against any of the children of Israel shall not a dog move his tongue, against man or beast: that ye may know that the Lord doth put a difference between the Egyptians and Israel…' 'And the Lord spake unto

Moses and Aaron in the land of Egypt, saying, This month *shall be* unto you the beginning of months: it *shall be* the first month of the year to you. Speak ye unto all the congregation of Israel, saying, in the tenth *day* of this month they shall take to them every man a lamb, according to the house of *their* fathers, a lamb for an house: And if the house be too little for the lamb, let him and his neighbour next unto his house take *it* according to the number of the souls; every man according to his eating shall make your count for the lamb. Your lamb shall be without blemish, a male of the first year: ye shall take it out from the sheep, or from the goats: And ye shall keep it until the fourteenth day of the same month: and the whole assembly of the congregation of Israel shall kill it in the evening. And they shall take of the blood, and strike *it* on the two side posts and on the upper door post of the houses, wherein they shall eat it. And they shall eat the flesh in that night, roast with fire, and unleavened bread; *and* with bitter *herbs* they shall eat it. Eat not of it raw, nor sodden at all with water, but roast *with* fire; his head with his legs, and with the purtenance thereof. And ye shall let none of it remain until the morning; and that which remaineth of it until the morning ye shall burn with fire. And thus shall ye eat it: with your loins girded, your shoes on your feet, and your staff in your hand; and ye shall eat it in haste: it *is* the Lord's passover. For I will pass through the land of Egypt this night, and will smite all the firstborn of the land of Egypt, both man and beast; and against all the gods of Egypt I will execute judgement: I *am* the Lord. And the blood shall be to you for a token upon the houses where ye *are*: and when I see the blood, I will pass over you, and the plague shall not be upon you to destroy *you*, when I smite the land of Egypt. And this day shall be unto you for a memorial; and ye shall keep it a feast to the Lord throughout your generations; ye shall keep it a feast by an ordinance forever...Then Moses called for all the elders of Israel, and said unto them, Draw out and take unto you a lamb according to your families, and kill the passover. And ye shall take a bunch of hyssop, and dip *it* in the blood that *is* in the bason; and strike the lintel and the two side posts with the blood that *is* in the bason; and none of you shall go out at the door of his house until the morning. For the Lord will pass through to smite the Egyptians; and when he seeth the blood upon the lintel, and upon the two side posts, the Lord will pass over the door, and will not suffer the destroyer to come into your houses to smite *you*. And you will observe this thing for an ordinance to thee and to thy sons for ever.'

'And the Lord spake unto Moses, saying, Sanctify unto me all the firstborn, whatsoever openeth the womb among the children of Israel, *both* of man and beast: it *is* mine. And Moses said unto the people, Remember this day, in which ye came out from Egypt, out of the house of bondage...This day came ye out on the month of Abib...that thou shalt keep this service in this month...And thou shalt shew thy son in that day, saying, *This is done* because of that *which* the Lord did unto me when I came forth out of Egypt. And it shall be for a sign unto thee upon thine hand, and for a memorial between thine eyes, that the Lord's law may be in thy mouth...Thou shalt therefore keep this ordinance in his season from year to year. And it shall be when the Lord shall bring thee into the land of the Canaanites, as he swear unto thee and to thy fathers, and shall give it to thee. That thou shalt set apart unto the Lord all that openeth the matrix, and every firstling that cometh of a beast which thou hast; the males *shall be* the Lord's. And every firstling of an ass thou shalt redeem with a lamb; and if thou wilt not redeem it, then thou shalt break his neck: and all the firstborn of man among they children shalt thou redeem. And it shall be when thy son asketh thee in time to come, saying, What is this? that thou shalt say unto him, By strength of hand the Lord brought us out from Egypt, from the house of bondage: And it came to pass, when Pharaoh would hardly let us go, that the Lord slew all the firstborn in the land of Egypt, both the firstborn of man, and the firstborn of beast: therefore I sacrifice to the Lord all that openeth the matrix, being males; but all the firstborn of children I redeem.'

'Now these *are* the judgements which thou shalt set before them. If thou buy an Hebrew servant, six years he shall serve: and in the seventh he shall go out free for nothing...And if the servant shall plainly say, I love my master, my wife, and my children: I will not go out free: Then his master shall bring him unto the judges; he shall also bring him to the door, or unto the door post; and his master shall bore his ear through with an aul; and he shall serve him for ever.'

'All that openeth the matrix *is* mine; and every firstling among the cattle, *whether* ox or sheep, *that is male*. But the firstling of an ass thou shalt redeem with a lamb and if thou redeem *him* not, then shalt thou break his neck. All the firstborn of thy sons thou shalt redeem. And none shall appear before me empty...And thou shalt observe the feast of weeks, of the firstfruits of wheat harvest, and the feast of ingathering at the year's end. Thrice in the year shall all your men children appear before the Lord God, God of Israel...Thou shalt not offer the blood of my sacrifice with leaven; neither shall the sacrifice of the feast of the passover be left unto the morning. The first of the firstfruits of thy land thou shalt bring unto the house of the Lord thy God...'

'And if thy brother, an Hebrew man, or an Hebrew woman, be sold unto thee, and serve thee six years; then in the seventh year thou shalt let him go free from thee...And it shall be, if he say unto thee, I will not go away from thee; because he loveth thee and thine house, because he is well with thee; Then thou shalt take an aul, and thrust it through his ear unto the door, and he shall be thy servant forever. And also unto thy maidservant thou shalt do likewise.' (Exod.11; 12:1-14, 21-24; 13:1-15; 21:1-6; 34:19-26; Deut.15:12-17).

Sorcery, Fireworship

Therefore, already discussed the expressions, the sayings, the style of narrative, expressions of narrative and its characters are Yemeni, uniquely Yemeni in nature and origin. Also discussed, it is Yemeni pagan rituals, customs and practise lived as they have for millennia right into current times unchanged which have been used by the authors of the Bible to base major events on, to base religious rituals on (as per the OT stories show) whereas in rural Yemen they are beliefs and routine way of life practised and believed in daily life in their original form—not dramatic and fictionalised events as in the Biblical stories which the original Yemeni culture has obviously inspired its authors to incorporate into the Biblical stories.

Take for example the 'bitter water test' in the Bible which a jealous husband suspicious his wife has cheated on him makes her undertake: it includes the bringing of the woman before the priest (and God), uncovering her hair, making her hold an offering which being burnt will help indicate her innocence or guilt; dirt is put into water, curses and oaths are made, the curses are written in the book and blotted out with the 'bitter water' which the woman is then made to drink, all the while she is holding the 'jealousy offering' which after her first dose of the 'bitter water' is taken out of her hand, waved around, then some of it burned before she is made to drink the rest of the 'bitter water'. She is guilty if her belly swells (which it might do having drunk water contaminated with dust/dirt from the floor) and 'thigh rot' and she is condemned. If she remains well, she is found innocent.

What this story has done is combine a number of Yemeni rituals, customs, expressions and way of life into a dramatized telling of a story/law. In rural Yemen when a husband causes his wife (whether in her opinion or other people's opinions) hardship, they say 'he made her sip bitter/bitterness' 'he made her sip from the cup of bitterness', and what this means is the husband is not a good husband and has made her suffer in any number of ways where the community feel sorry for her, as it is not the norm, e.g. he may cause her emotional hurt by being a womaniser/cheat; being cruel to her; not perform his duties as a husband, e.g. not properly providing for her (and their children), or not satisfying her in bed, or in any way causing her continuous emotional distress; it can also mean he is either or both physically and mentally abusive; it could also mean he intentionally made her live a hard life (more difficult than the normal hardships of life). It is said to show a specific woman is suffering or suffered because of her husband's actions.

The expression 'he made her sip bitter/bitterness' 'he made her sip from the cup of bitterness' has nothing to do with putting dirt in water which causes a curse, but is more straightforward: 'bitter' which in Arabic is 'myrrh' is used for medicinal purposes and is so bitter it is difficult to swallow, most people cannot gulp it down no matter how hard they try, with many people vomiting due to its terrible, bitter taste which is what inspired the saying, i.e. the wife whom they sympathise with has been made to live a bitter life just like the drinking medicinal bitter/myrrh—and that is where both the saying comes from and the idea taken by the authors of the Bible who made it into their own version for dramatic storytelling purposes and maybe for ideological purposes too.

The author of this specific Biblical story has not only used the saying about 'bitter' in the 'bitter water test' story, but he has also used other Yemeni ways of life and beliefs and particularly sorcery, witchcraft. In times and areas where no doctors existed for the local population, sorcerers are frequently turned to cure disease, bad luck and problems. They are used for things as benign as finding a cure for an ailing cow and for things as dark as causing a woman to fall in love with a man she does not love, or causing hatred and divorce between a loving couple. Regardless of modern and religious beliefs that we all know as a fact which tell us it is a load of 'hocus-pocus' superstition with nothing related to reality and unable to cause or change anything—these are the beliefs and way of life of people who have always believed and practised pagan rituals, who believe in and practise it daily and it includes sorcerers and their services (but note, not all people turn to sorcerers for evil purposes, but for benign things such as changing of names of wife or children if 'horns' are too strong; for calculating according to sorcery related to astrology when it is a good time/date for marriage, etc. of finding out what is wrong with your ailing cow).

Part of what sorcerers do, and is very well-known in these areas, is the use of writing spells or curses in books then blotting them out with water which is then given to the concerned person or animal to drink (where evil is concerned such as causing love or hatred in unsuspecting parties, the spell is given to the 'customer' of the sorcerer who in turn has to either secretly dissolve it into water and get the unsuspecting person(s) to drink it or burn it or stick it into the wall of the victim's house) which at Num.5:21-22 is what the priest does exactly by writing the curses in the book, then blotting them out with the bitter water which he then gives the accused woman to drink. Remember 'priest' is a misnomer of translation of the word wrongly translated as 'priest'; 'kohen' is 'sorcerer/fire worshipper' supported by the fact that all the word-names in the Bible have meaning in Arabic.

Another Yemeni practise and pagan way of life which was also religious custom and can be seen employed in the same 'bitter water test' story is fireworship, already discussed in an earlier passage of this book. Burning sacrifices was part of fire worship in Yemen, a large part of the fire worship religion and culture was sorcery and sorcerers which included burning things. Note how the accused woman is made to hold the 'jealousy offering' while the 'priest' (which should read 'sorcerer/fire worshipper') reads out the curse, writes it in a book, blots it out with water mixed with dirt, makes her drink it, takes the offering from her hand, waves it around and then burns some of the 'jealousy offering', then makes her drink the rest of the 'bitter water'— these are acts of a sorcerer and not 'priest' as misnomered nor with the meanings of 'priest' in a traditional or divine-religious sense and these pagan practises long precede the arrival of any of the three Abrahamic religions which are all based on pagan religions and rituals:

'And the Lord spake unto Moses, saying, Speak unto the children of Israel, and say unto them, If any man's wife go aside, and commit a trespass against him, And a man lie with her carnally, and it be hid from the eyes of her husband, and kept close, and she be defiled, and *there be* no witness against her, neither she be taken *with the manner*; And the spirit of jealousy come upon him, and he be jealous of his wife, and she be not defiled: Then shall the man bring his wife unto the priest, and he shall bring her offering for her, the tenth *part* of an ephah of barley meal; he shall pour no oil upon it, nor put frankincense thereon; for *it is* an offering of jealousy, an offering of memorial, bringing iniquity to remembrance. And the priest shall bring her near, and set her before the Lord: And the priest shall take holy water in an earthen vessel; and of the dust that is in the floor of the tabernacle the priest shall take, and put *it* into the water: And the priest shall set the woman before the Lord, and uncover the woman's head, and put the offering of the memorial in her hands, which *is* the jealousy offering: and the priest shall have in his hand the bitter water that causeth the curse: And the priest shall charge her by an oath, and say unto the woman, If no man have lain with thee, and if thou hast not gone aside to uncleanness *with another* instead of thy husband, be thou free from this bitter water that causeth the curse: But if thou hast gone aside *to another* instead of thy husband, and if thou be defiled, and some man have lain with thee beside thine husband: Then the priest shall charge the woman with an oath of cursing, and the priest shall say unto the woman, The Lord make thee a curse and an oath among thy people, when the Lord doth make thy thigh to rot, and thy belly to swell; And this water that causeth shall go into thy bowels, to make *thy* belly to swell, and *thy* thigh to rot: And the woman shall say, Amen, amen. And the priest shall write these curses in a book, and he shall blot *them* out with the bitter water: And he shall cause the woman to drink the bitter water that causeth the curse: and the water that causeth the curse shall enter into her, *and become* bitter. Then the priest shall take the jealousy offering out of the woman's hand, and shall wave the offering before the Lord, and offer it upon the altar: And the priest shall take an handful of the offering, *even* the memorial thereof, and burn *it* upon the altar, and afterward shall cause the woman to drink the water. And when he hath made her to drink the water, then it shall come to pass, *that*, if she be defiled, and have done trespass against her husband, that the water that causeth the curse shall enter into her, *and become* bitter, and her belly shall swell, and her thigh shall rot: and the woman shall be a curse among her people. And if the woman be not defiled, but be clean; then she shall be free, and shall conceive seed.' (Num.5:11-28)

Grief Customs

Also, part of rural Yemeni custom when someone dies or catastrophe strikes is to wail and rent and tear clothes off one's own body, tear out hair from head. The rending of clothes, plucking out hair at someone's death or a catastrophe is abundant in the OT stories.

Vows

A vow in rural Yemen is called a 'nvr' (see Nazerite), the root word for 'Nazerite' and 'Nazarene'. The vows are adhered to strictly as they are made towards God which is usually a rock or dead 'special person' known as 'Wali'. E.g. if a woman vows/'naveret' ('Nazerite') to give the produce of clarified butter of the first ten days production of a cow when it first calves—in exchange/on condition for a request she has made to the deity be granted, when the cow calves the butter collected from the first ten days will not be eaten by the woman or her family, not one drop, but collected and prepared no matter how many bottles/vessels it equates to, the butter production of the first ten days is reserved for when she pilgrims to whichever sacred rock or sepulchre, deity she made her vow to. In the OT exactly the same is narrated, e.g. Jacob promising a tenth of his fortune to be offered at Bethel (a sacred rock) to God if God protects and provides for him; the same in Hannah making a vow at Shiloh where she asks for a child in return, a vow which she completes once her wish is granted. It is important to understand the meaning of the word 'vow/nvr' is not only the act of saying/promising it, but the word 'nvr' means the product be it an object or living thing which has been dedicated to God, i.e. it is left for the rock/God i.e. not consumed but set aside then offered to the rock, pagan deity or God as promised.

In real-life Yemen, vows can also be fasting a set number of days, vowing to do something repeatedly or abstain from doing it a specific number of days or until the wish is granted; it can be to vow animals to be sacrificed at the sacred rock or sepulchres, as well as offering crops, fabrics, all sorts of food harvests. Vows are always made in exchange that the sacred rock or deity grant something in particular which the person requests. Not fulfilling a vow which has been granted, i.e. it has been answered, e.g. asking for a child and getting one, or asking for good fortune and realising it then not fulfilling the bringing of the vowed offering, sacrifice or gift, it is believed to bring disastrous punishment upon the defaulting person and his/her family, household, fortune, estate, etc. so these vows are always kept. This custom and belief appears in Jacob's stories and elsewhere in the OT: Hannah asks for a child (Samuel) and will give him as a gift to God; Jephtah makes an 'open' vow that whatever first comes out of his house will be sacrificed to God in exchange for victory, his daughter is the first to come out of his house and she is sacrificed to God.

All tithes in their different versions and the ways they are offered to God in the OT are how Yemeni pagan worship 'Nazer/Nazerite' both mean 'vow(ed)/set aside' is done in real life. In Judges and 1Samuel as well as in Num.6, the people involved in the stories become the vow and the word 'Nazerite' which is the action of the vow is used to describe whom vow themselves to God, or are vowed by others such as Hannah and Manoah's wife who vow the child they wish to be granted to God, Samuel and Samson respectively, and the people whom 'separate themselves, to a vow, a vow of a Nazerite, to separate themselves unto the Lord…' in Num.6 are all called Nazerites. Also part of this culture is fasting from food as per the person specifies in the number of days in exchange something is granted/realised; this too has been incorporated into the Biblical stories, such as Manoah's wife not eating and drinking certain foods; the same for the character 'Nazerite' as well as not cutting their hair, or at least not cutting his/her hair until a specific number of days or specific rituals have been achieved. The latter can be seen in Muslim pilgrims once they intend and embark on the Hajj to 'God's House' (al-K'ba(Ka'ba)) they no longer cut their hair or shave, they do not perfume, and the action or state the pilgrim has begun is called 'yḥrm' which can be understood as 'sacred/becomes sacred' but that really is not what the word means or gets its meaning from in this instance as it also means 'forbidden/forbade' 'becomes rotten' or 'becomes rotten and stinks' as the pilgrim forbids himself/herself from and refrains from combing, shaving and refrains from sex, refrains from other specific activities until he has completed the vow of pilgriming and its rites; they shave their hair and wash and perfume after they have complete the Hajj rituals around the K'bba in Mecca and this too is related to the Yemeni pagan custom of vows.

The latter can be seen in the NT too, where in separate stories Jesus is described as a 'Nazerite' 'Nazarene', and although the NT uses the word-name to name the city as Nazareth to explain this is why he is called a Nazarene, the actual text and story clearly states he has been dedicated to God and by God, from the womb, i.e. like Samson and Samuel, Jesus is a Nazerite, he has been vowed, promised, dedicated to God and Jesus is twicefold a vow/Navr/Nazer because not only is he dedicated to God, but God also serves him as a sacrifice for humankind i.e. Jesus is the vow. In Luke: 'And the angel said unto her, fear not, Mary: for thou hast found favour with God. And, behold, thou shalt conceive in thy womb, and bring forth a son, and shalt call his name Jesus. He shall be great, and shall be called the Son of the Highest…'; in Matt.1:23 it explains the prophets had prophesied Jesus would be a vow 'Nazarene': 'And he came and dwelled in a city called Nazareth: that it might be fulfilled which was spoken by the prophets, He shall be called a Nazarene.'. The vow culture and creation of Nazareth-related word-names arise from the Yemeni pagan custom of vows and vowing practised towards sacred rocks which are considered to have deity-like powers, and 'Walis' which can equate to the western word 'saints' as they serve the same purpose. In the New Testament this custom continues to be employed in the stories related to Saul/Paul where he shaves his head in connection to a vow; and in the narration that the Jews have vowed a fast not to be broken until they are able to kill Paul in Acts.

All these stories of major events and religious ritual described in the OT and NT have originated from Yemeni pagan culture, custom and practise. The authors of the Bible are Yemeni.

Superstition

In ancient times as well as in remote areas in current times where there is no or hardly any education, in regions where attitude and culture has remained unchanged for millennia, superstition is part of life, believed in and unquestioned. In superstitions specifically related to a specific region in Yemen, these superstitions are still part of life, and you can see how the authors of the Bible have used these Yemeni superstitions to base the stories and events in the Bible on, and the creators of these stories have used them a lot.

To begin with: the number seven in rural Yemen has a special meaning attached to it, it is used both positively and negatively. Superstitiously, the number seven is attached to a person being released from some kind of physical pain—and this is where the authors of the Bible/OT have used number seven to be when slaves are released from servitude, seven being a day of rest and so forth. It exists in Yemen, or is used to warn children to keep away from being hurt, e.g. when they see a child or children provoking a specific kind of lizard which has the ability to bite back and shows its defence by opening its mouth and charging at them, and although it is used as a light or off-hand warning to children as they are not in serious danger, it stems from a belief that it is true since generations past, the phrase incorporated into the warning is if the lizard bites you '...it won't let go for seven years, or until a donkey brays seven times'—whichever comes first. Also where the number seven is related to release from pain: a game, or prank, since ancient times is an adult will grab a person by his/her pinkie finger, folding it at its natural joints but compressing it with great pressure (you can feel the bones of your finger wanting to burst at the joints) causing great pain, and the person holding your finger demands you tell him the name of seven old men from the area and he will increase the pressure and pain on your finger to prompt you start naming and the person does not let go until you give him the names of seven old men.

When expressing displeasure at someone is taking too long, or will take too long at getting something done or arriving, the comment or response is an aggravated 'He/she will take seven years', and another version of this expressed displeasure at someone being late, or taking too long at arriving or getting something done is 'He/she will take a year and *seven months*' and stress is put on the 'seven months' indicating those seven months are much and unbearably longer than the year.

In rural Yemeni culture, special attribute is associated with the number seven, and most of the time the release or relief only comes after 'seven [so and so]'. You can see how this special meaning of the number seven has been used in the Bible, both OT and NT, from the beginning to its end the number seven means something special and superstitious, as relief/release is mostly what comes after 'seven years' 'seven times' 'seven days'—and in some cases destruction (with seven being the last, therefore an end/relief from something bad after it ends). Here are some examples of how the real-life Yemeni belief in the special and superstitious effects of the number seven has been used and incorporated into the Biblical stories:

God creates the heavens and earth in six days and rests on the seventh day: 'And on the seventh day God ended his work which he had made; and he rested on the seventh day from all his work which he had made.' (Gen.2:1-3)

Abraham uses seven ewes as witnesses between him and Abimelech: 'And Abraham set seven ewe lambs of the flock by themselves. And Abimelech said unto Abraham, What *mean* these seven ewe lambs which thou hast set by themselves? And he said, For these seven ewe lambs shalt thou take of my hand, that they may be a witness unto me, that I have digged this well.' (Gen.21:22-32)

Jacob works for Laban seven years before he is given Leah to marry, then he serves Laban another seven years before he is given Rachel to marry. (Gen.29:18-30)

The Pharaoh's dream of seven thin and seven fat cows; seven good ears of corn and seven thin ears of corn; as well as the seven years of plenty followed by the seven years of famine interpretation of the dream, and the advice to store up harvests during the seven good years to see them through the seven years of famine. (Gen.41:1-36)

The cured leper becomes healed, then to be purified is sprayed/sprinkled seven times, and becomes 'clean' on the seventh day of the ritual. (Lev.14:1-9)

The man who ejaculates and the woman who menstruates remain 'unclean' and become clean on the seventh day. (Lev.15:1-19)

Animal sacrifices/offerings are to remain seven days 'under the dam' and after the seventh day are fit to be a fire offering. (Lev.22:27)

Concerning sacrifices, fire offerings, etc. many are connected by the number seven: having to be done on the seventh day, or performed for seven days, some have to be seven in quantity, the event is in the seventh month, etc. (Leviticus/Lev.23)

The seventh day of the week, Sabbath, becomes a holy day—rest is compulsory, work prohibited and punishable by death. The land is to be worked and harvested six years, but the seventh year the land is to rest. (Lev.25:1-9)

When Balaam is asked by Balak to curse Moses and his people, Balaam requests the building of seven altars as well as seven bulls and seven rams to be offered at the altars as sacrifices—at the end of these 'sevens' Balaam blesses Moses and his people. (Num.23-24)

Joshua is ordered to go around Jericho for six days, then on the seventh day they are to circulate Jericho seven times, while seven priests carrying seven trumpets wait on the seventh circulation and then blow their trumpets: the people shout and Jericho and its inhabitants are defeat—just like that, with the power of seven. (Josh.6:1-21)

Hannah in her prayer or praise to God, thanking him for blessing her with Samuel mentions 'so that the barren hath born seven' whereas up to this point in the story she has only given birth to one child, but seven is the special number in the culture of the authors' being repeatedly expressed. (1Sam:2:5)

Elisha the prophet tells Namaan to wash in the Jordan seven times to be cured from leprosy, and when he dips seven times into the Jordan, he is cured. (2Kgs.5:1-14)

When the Levites are able to bring the ark back to the city with no one being hurt or killed, they offer seven bullocks and seven rams. (1Chr.15:26)

King Ahasuerus holds a feast spanning a long period of time, at the end he gives an extra seven-day feast at Shushan and on the seventh day Vashti refuses his command that she appear before everybody. (Esth.1:1-12)

Esther is given seven maidens by Hegai. (Esth.2:9)

Job has seven sons (along with three daughters) and all die. (Job.1)

Job's friends mourn seven days and nights with him before anyone speaks and the lecturing and reproaching begins from the eighth day. (Job.2:11-13)

When God upbraids Job's friends for being in the wrong, he tells them to take seven bullocks and seven rams for a burnt offering, and when these are sacrificed and Job prays for his friends, only then will God forgive them, i.e. not punish them. (Job.42:8)

God's words are purity compared to silver that has been purified seven times, i.e. the silver does not become rid of its impurities until the seventh time.

All the mentions of Hebrew servants become free at the end of six years' service, to be freed in the seventh year.

Every time the number seven is mentioned it emphasises the specialness, or the release/relief from physical stress such as rest, end of or victory in battle; receiving blessings or forgiveness; the end of or fighting famine with seven years' worth of harvest; the cure of illness or purification from uncleanness; sacrifices/offerings made in quantities of seven, or on the seventh day, or in the seventh month, or spanning a period of time in the measurement of seven, or relieving the person offering/sacrificing of their sins or giving them blessings. The quantity of seven giving Abraham a special witness when making a do-no-harm agreement. These different situations and events used in the Biblical stories all used in the context of Yemeni culture where 'seven' marks relief, end, arrival, end of wait or pain.

In the New Testament the special meaning of number seven and its relation to ending/relieving pain or sin continues: The seven churches; seven spirits; seven golden candlesticks; and seven stars are all related to informing the churches that their patience and suffering will be rewarded, but also at the same time telling them they must stop their sinning, their wrong conduct so it represents the end of suffering and the end of sinning which will prevent further punishment. (Rev.1:4, 12-13, 16, 20; 2:1; 3:1)

It goes on to become more ominous in Revelation with the seven lamps, the seven spirits of God, the seven seals of a book which eventually lead to terrible sufferance on earth, but conversely marks the end of mortal life and therefore the end of suffering for all 'good' people (although the NT is very selective about whom the 'good' people are) on earth who will be in heaven/God's kingdom. In the same sense, the seven angels with the seven trumpets unleashing terrible punishment for people to repent, those who do not continue in physical sufferance or die. The seventh angel is to bring the end of it all with earth as normal becoming the kingdom of God. The beast with seven heads and seven crowns brings a terrible end (in sin) to those who follow it or have been deceived by it—there end is not good, but still the number seven used in the sense of the end of something particular. Again, seven plagues, seven angels, seven vials mark a violent end to people, life and earth, but at the same time this is meant to be the end of toil on earth as the replacement with heaven or the kingdom of God being a place of rest, peace and immortality—so the end of ending. The New Testament is influenced by the Old Testament use of the number seven, and the Old Testament is influenced by the Yemeni culture and its use of number seven being the release/end of pain.

Superstitions Around Horns

Discussed in an earlier part of this book was how Yemeni pagan rituals and beliefs have been used by authors of the Bible as events and religious ritual, one of which is the 'horn' 'qareen' a spirit or demon-like spirit attached to each person from birth. Part of the superstition regarding the 'horn' is it can affect the person himself/herself, the people around him or in contact with him, as well as give strength, power or luck or its opposites.

In the Old Testament this superstition/belief is clearly expressed in the stories, some examples are as follows: when Hannah praises God and proclaims her 'horn is exalted in the Lord' and her mouth has become stronger than her enemies, this is what has been previously mentioned that the 'horn' of each individual differs, it can be stronger or weaker, compatible or incompatible with others and compared to other people's 'horns'. What Hannah's dialogue is saying is her 'horn' (a spirit attached to her) has been strengthened, found favour by God—which has allowed her 'horn' to overpower, be better or victor over her enemies' 'horns', i.e. their 'horns' have become weaker. Note how she compares herself, her 'horn' to those whom she deems as her adversaries: '...mine mouth is enlarged over mine enemies...The bows of mighty men are broken, and they that stumbled are girded with strength...They that were full have hired themselves out for bread; and they that were hungry ceased...So that the barren hath born seven; and she that hath many children has waxed feeble.' And although she attributes this to God, he has made her 'horn' exalted and allowed her horn to lead her to become stronger, the situation changes to her favour while her enemies become weaker, are diminished—remember in 1Sam. Peninnah her stepwife has many children and the narration calls her Hannah's 'adversary'. What the text in Chapter 2 is describing is exactly how Yemeni culture/superstitions believe 'horns' function as—the more powerful causing damage to the people with less powerful 'horns'. (1Sam.1; 2:1-10). After comparing some more situations becoming positive/negative, her dialogue ends with 'The adversaries of the Lord shall be broken to pieces; out of heaven shall he thunder upon them: the Lord shall judge the ends of the earth; and he shall give strength unto his king, and exalt the horn of his anointed.' So the strength and exaltation are given to the person, but through his 'horn' spirit.

In David's story of being saved from certain death when Saul and his men circled him, when it is retold 2Sam.22 attributes God saving David by being 'horn of my salvation' showing again that 'horns' which are spiritual beings are believed to change/affect the outcome and actions of other people. David's dialogue also goes on to compare how vulnerable he was, and his enemies being stronger, yet God being the 'horn' of his salvation is what saved him from certain death. And although you can see these stories being and originating from purely pagan rituals and beliefs, you can also see as a result of revisions, rewritings where authors of later times pushing towards monotheism, but for whatever reasons have left the original and older stories by not erasing them completely and this is where you can see Hannah, David, in the stories giving credit and praise to a 'rock' (a pagan religion) and also to a 'horn' a spiritual being believed to exist by pagan community and the community's descendants who believe in the superstitions revolving around this 'horn'. Look at verse 17 of Psalm 89 'For thou *art* the glory of their strength; and in thy favour our horn shall be exalted.' Praising God, but it is the 'horn' which will become stronger, causing the defeat of enemies in battle, causing plagues upon them, and protecting David and his people from them 'And I will beat down his foes before his face, and plague them that hate him. But my faithfulness and mercy *shall be* with him; and in my name shall his horn be exalted.'

Sunset

Another superstition which is part of daily life in remote Yemen, existing since ancient times, is related to sunset. At sunset certain activities are to be avoided. People (adult and children) are not supposed to be out anywhere during sunset, that is they should be at home or on its premises or at anyone else's home or on its premises; it is alright to be outside the house, just not far away from it, i.e. they should not be 'on the road', on a path or in the land, but at human dwellings. To be outside or engaged in certain activities at sunset is deemed ominous and will bring negative consequences upon the person, his/her family or others present. This ominous action at sunset and the consequences it could bring are both called 'kheiba/ خيبا/خيبه'. Examples of 'kheiba' are: sweeping the house/yard at sunset—it may cause the destruction or the sweeping out of the fortune of the family; being far away from human dwelling, i.e. in land working at sunset or chasing after animals during sunset and especially cats both of which are believed to be able to cause a human to come into contact with and/or be harmed by demons (such as be attacked, paralysed, driven mad or possessed). The word 'kheiba' the ominous act and its serious consequences is also applied to other activities, believed to be ominous, during any time of the day such as when sitting on a bed, or any high place, and swinging your leg(s) back and forth—people present will always tell the person to stop because it is 'kheiba' i.e. something bad will happen because of it; the same regarding to blowing/puffing out your cheeks in frustration. But what is being addressed in this passage is the specific superstition of 'kheiba' during sunset and how this has featured (like many other Yemeni beliefs, customs, religion, expressions and ways of life) in the Bible.

In Joshua, the lead character has no problem in killing people, humiliating them before killing them, then disrespecting their corpses by hanging them on trees. He shows no fear and no remorse for these actions, but it is at sunset he suddenly orders they be taken down from the trees and thrown into the cave. What you see in the narration is the author's knowledge of the superstition related to sunset, and the bodies swinging from the trees—both are 'kheiba' and can bring evil to the people who are conducting this activity during sunset: the evil and 'kheiba' is not in the killing nor in the hanging them from trees, but the swinging and activity during sunset and what evil it could bring upon those present: 'And it came to pass, when they brought out those kings unto Joshua, that Joshua called for all the men of Israel, and said unto the captains of the men of war which went with him, Come near, put your feet upon the necks of these kings. And they came near and put their feet on the necks of them. And Joshua said unto them, Fear not, nor be dismayed, be strong and of good courage: for thus shall the Lord do to all your enemies against whom ye fight. And afterward Joshua smote them, and slew them, and hanged them on five trees: and they were hanging upon the trees until evening. And it came to pass at the time of the going down of the sun, *that* Joshua commanded, and they took them down off the trees, and cast them into the cave wherein they had been hid, and laid great stones in the cave's mouth, *which remain* until this very day.' (Josh.10:24-27).

Also in Joshua, the same thing happens showing the Biblical author's knowledge of the sunset superstition, this time with the body of king Ai whom they kill then hang from a tree but take down at sunset: 'And the king of Ai he hanged on a tree until eventide: and as soon as the sun was down, Joshua commanded that they should take his carcase down from the tree…' (Josh.8:29).

Also showing the Yemeni authorship and the use of Yemeni way of life and superstitions regarding the ominous activities and aura associated with the sun setting is the Yemeni superstition of people having to be either at home or at any human dwelling place, but not outside engaged in any activity at sunset which is deemed and believed to be 'kheiba'. In the heat of battle between Israel and Syria the story narrative causes the sunset and avoiding activity during sunset to interrupt the battle: 'And the battle increased that day: and the king was stayed up in his chariot against the Syrians, and died at even: and the blood ran out of the wound into the midst of the chariot. And there went a proclamation throughout the host about the going down of the sun, saying, Every man to his city, and every man to his own country.' (1Kgs.22:35-36).

Wind

Another superstition which has long existed in Yemen and become an ironic proverb in modernity is the belief that the wind can impregnate women. According to elderly and middle-aged women (during the

1990s in remote Yemen), it was long believed a woman could become pregnant from the blowing wind and a well-used saying regarding a woman who has become pregnant while her husband has been long abroad, or an unmarried woman becoming pregnant is 'She became pregnant from the wind' meant sarcastically and also put in a rhetorical question 'Did she become pregnant from the wind' (جِبِلت من الريح/ ماهي جِبِلت من الريح؟). Also, when people ask about a recently-married woman and if she is pregnant (which they ask a lot), if it happens her husband has left to work in a city/abroad and she is not pregnant, the person responding will say 'How will she get pregnant—from the wind? Her husband is abroad.'. And although it used to be believed a female could be impregnated by blowing wind, the sarcasm in how the statements are made, as well as people pondering on the subject of being impregnated by wind means the majority of people no longer believe it to be true; the still-in-use expression is due to the long-standing belief that it could happen, e.g. in the 1990s girls and unmarried women who travel far away to shepherd or gather wood were still warned to avoid using stones to wipe clean after urinating just in case a man/boy had wiped semen on the stone at a previous time—and they advise the females to use leaves instead to avoid the unfortunate case of becoming pregnant by using a stone which has come into contact with men's 'water' (which of course there is no chance of being impregnated from the wind or a stone, but out of lack of scientific knowledge these beliefs which have been handed down since ancient times persisted).

It has been mentioned earlier that Islam was new and superficial to the region I speak of in Yemen, and everything done and believed was paganistic in origin, nor did these people have any contact with the OT or NT stories' texts or religion. The majority were illiterate, the minority of men and boys that could read and write was solely for reading/writing letters to relatives abroad or reading deeds for land. In days when Maryam mother of Jesus (Mary in the NT) ever came up in discussion, I would be puzzled by the belief they held regarding the matter because the youngest and oldest would always say that Maryam conceived Jesus by the wind blowing into her. Every time it was mentioned or discussed they do not say 'God blew the spirit into her' but they do say 'God blew the wind into her' and she conceived Jesus this way. At the beginning I thought they must have misheard/misunderstood the Quranic verse because the word for 'soul/spirit' (rooḥ/ruḥ/روح) is from the same root word as 'wind' (rḥ/reeḥ/رح/ريح) pronounced slightly differently between 'soul/rooḥ' and 'wind/reeḥ'. Now these women (young and old) and girls none of them had ever read or written, nor do they read the Quran, so I expected they would understand and be convinced when I would read to them the verse direct from the Quran that it states that the 'spirit' was blown into Mary, but they would shake their heads and be adamant that it was the wind blown into Mary just like long ago (according to the women) that wind could impregnate a woman without a male having any sex with her. And over the years whenever it was brought up, they made it clear that it does not matter what the Quran states (and the locals have a very strong sense of their civilisation and way of life existing longer than any new beliefs and ways of life) because since forever it has been the wind capable of impregnating women—so when they say it is the wind that impregnated Mary/Maryam with Jesus, they understand fully what they mean and say due to coming from a past and existence where it was believed that a girl or woman could become pregnant from the wind (which is a cover by the concerned girl and her family to avoid exposing her for illicit sex, but at the times it was accepted as fact) and where women ('virgins' and otherwise) used the wind and also wiping urine away with a sperm-contaminated stone as a cover-up for an illicit affair which would otherwise cause her great shame, but it was accepted in general that it could happen. This is what they kept making clear to me no matter how hard I explained the meaning of 'spirit/soul'.

To my surprise, decades later when I would read the Bible, I see their version of beliefs being narrated and used in the Biblical stories—the 'Spirit' used by God to impregnate Mary mother of Jesus is based on 'breath' and 'wind' (see (Luke.3 regarding 'wind' 'breath' and 'spirit' under the genealogy list for Jesus). This strong belief of wind creating life is based on breathing and its intensity/quickening during sexual intercourse, and can be seen as part of Yemeni culture from ancient times, and you can see it used in both the OT and NT, as it is used from the very beginning of the Bible. When I read the Bible, not only did I find the names of its characters and places to be made-up from Arabic words, but I also saw my people's pagan culture, beliefs and way of life as I had lived it with them used in the Biblical stories, and I was able to connect with these stories deeply and see exactly what the Biblical authors were doing and saying, I could understand it and where the ideas came from. What the Biblical authors have used to base their stories on is taken from Yemeni culture, and one of these ancient Yemeni beliefs is the wind's ability to impregnate women and is a pun on women's excuses for illegitimate pregnancies and the communities which go along with it to avoid them further embarrassment. The authors of the Biblical stories who are obviously Yemeni are aware of the culture, customs, tradition, superstitions, expressions and speak the language of the Yemeni people (which is the language of all Arabs), and they used this rich culture in the Biblical stories.

The OT and NT have used wind and breath which is a form of wind blown into or upon a non-living object or even dead person(s) to bring them back to life or to create life in them before it existed (which is exactly the belief of a woman becoming pregnant from wind blowing into/onto her means). In the OT, wind and breath are used in the story to bring life to a non-living land/object and to also bring the dead back to life—in one story of the OT a metaphor of wind blowing is used to indicate copulating/pollinating and bringing the fruit of a loved-one to fruition and strikes the image of impregnating and bearing fruit. In the NT although there is no 'blowing of wind' mentioned with Mary's conception, there is a mention of a 'Holy Ghost' i.e. Spirit coming upon her, which is based on 'rooḥ/soul/spirit' and it comes from 'reeḥ/wind'. The Greek word used for 'spirit' and 'ghost' in the NT is also a word related to wind/breath and is Arabic too, and specifically a word based on the root word of 'Nahum/Nehemiah' 'sighing/sighing loudly' 'winded/struck until wind forced out' 'punctured and wind escaping': pneûma, pneumatos, pneumatic; بِنِهمه/ا ، بِنِهمَتَه ، بِنِهمَتي 'with/by sighing/huffing/puffing/panting' 'with/by his sighs/huffs/puffs/pants' 'of sighing/huffing/puffing/panting' 'of/by/with my sighing/huffing/puffing/panting' and all the same suffixes/prefixes around 'winded/struck until wind forced out/punctured and wind escaping'. In other stories of the NT, unrelated to Mary as a character, when there is wind—the Spirit comes upon the specified characters of that particular story, and in one instance Jesus' describes life being created by the 'Spirit' is like wind blowing. In all cases of the OT and NT, the Biblical authors have again used pagan Yemeni beliefs and superstitions to create the stories of the Bible: 'for the Lord God had not caused it to rain upon the earth, and *there was* not a man to till the ground. But there went up a mist from the earth, and watered the whole face of the ground. And the Lord God formed a man *of* the dust of the ground, and breathed into his nostrils the breath of life; and man became a living soul.' (Gen.2:5-7)

In the story about Elisha and a dead child, although it does not narrate that Elisha breathed on the dead child, he does put his mouth onto the child's and this does imply breathing into him, and when the child's body gets warm, Elisha waits then repeats the actions and the child sneezes seven times; sneezing, like breath, is a form of wind: 'And he went up, and lay upon the child, and put his mouth upon his mouth, and his eyes upon his eyes, and his hands upon his hands: and he stretched himself upon the child; and the flesh of the child waxed warm. Then he returned, and walked in the house to and fro; and went up, and stretched himself upon him: and the child sneezed seven times, and the child opened his eyes.' (2Kgs.34-35).

In the Song of Solomon, which is an erotic love poem narrating lovers' feelings and actions, the body is described in simile and metaphor and so is sex: the wind is the male and the act of making love, the garden is the female lover who the 'beloved' male enters through the wind allowing waters to flow and his/her fruits to be eaten. The 'wind' used again to bring life by 'blowing' on the female 'garden'—the fruits and the running waters/spices is life created and sexual pleasure enhanced: 'Thy lips, O *my* spouse, drop *as* the honeycomb: honey and milk *are* under thy tongue; and the smell of thy garments *is* like the smell of Lebanon. A garden inclosed *is* my sister, *my* spouse; a spring shut up, a fountain sealed. Thy plants *are* an orchard of pomegranates, with pleasant fruits; camphire, with spikenard. Spikenard and saffron; calamus and cinnamon, with all trees of frankincense; myrrh and aloes, with all the chief spices: A fountain of gardens, a well of living waters, and streams from Lebanon. Awake, O north wind; and come, thou south; blow upon my garden, *that* the spices thereof may flow out. Let my beloved come into his garden, and eat his pleasant fruits.' (Cant.4:11-16).

At John.3 in discussing and explaining how God brings things to life or back to life, Jesus' dialogue likens the Spirit giving life to how wind blows: 'Nicodemus said unto him, How can a man be born when he is old? Can he enter a second time into his mother's womb, and be born? Jesus answered, Verily, verily, I say unto thee, Except a man be born of water and *of* Spirit, he cannot enter into the kingdom of God. That which is born of flesh, is flesh; and that which is born of Spirit is spirit. Marvel not that I said unto thee, Ye must be born again. The wind bloweth where it listeth, and thou hearest the sound thereof, but canst not tell whence it cometh, and wither it goeth: so is every one that is born of the Spirit.' (John.3:4-8)

And again, breathing on others causes the 'Holy Ghost' to enter them: 'Then said Jesus to them again, Peace *be* unto you: as *my* Father hath sent me, even so I send you. And when he had said this, he breathed on *them*, and saith unto them, Receive ye the Holy Ghost…' (John.20:21-22)

In the OT, Ezekiel's story uses both breath and wind to bring life to the scattered skeletal remains of the dead, and it is wind that gives breath to the dead and non-existent: 'The hand of the Lord was upon me, and carried me out in the spirit of the Lord, and set me down in the midst of the valley which *was* full of bones, And caused me to pass by them round about: and, behold, *there were* very many in the open valley; and, lo, *they were* very dry. And he said unto me, Son of man, can these bones live? And I answered, O Lord God, thou knowest. Again he said unto me, Prophesy upon these bones, and say unto them, O ye dry bones, hear the word of the Lord. Thus saith the Lord unto these bones; Behold, I will cause breath to enter into you, and ye shall live: And I will lay sinews upon you, and will bring up flesh upon you, and cover you with skin, and put breath in you, and ye shall live; and ye shall know that I *am* the Lord. So I prophesied as I was commanded: and as I prophesied there was a noise, and behold a shaking, and the bones came together, bone to his bone. And when I beheld, lo, the sinews and the flesh came upon them, and the skin covered them above: but there was no breath in them. Then said he unto me, Prophesy unto the wind, prophesy, son of man, and say to the wind, Thus saith the Lord God; Come from the four winds, O breath, and breathe upon the slain, that they may live. So I prophesied as he commanded me, and the breath came into them, and they lived, and stood upon their feet, an exceeding great army.' (Ezek.37:1-10)

Eye Related Superstitions

A very much believed superstition in Yemeni culture (and in wider Arab region) is the power of the a person who is envious or just someone who says something about another (even if flippantly) where he/she similes a person to something else, e.g. saying about a woman 'she has become a plump fragrance caterpillar' (meaning beautiful and full) can cause the person spoken about illness, injury, sores, carbuncles, breaking, to fall or trip, to become weaker, lesser, etc. The negative action can affect whatever or whomever is spoken about be it a person, animal or object. The action and affect is called (mr'/مرع/mr'nee/مرعني/mr'anaa/مرعنا) 'evil eye/he evil-eyed me/he evil-eyed me/us' (see Anathema Maran-atha).

The superstition is the harm caused by the person seeing/eyeing something he/she likes or envies, and although it is believed anyone person can say/feel something to cause the evil-eye/mar'naa, there are specific individuals believed to be a regular marraa'/مَرّاع because of the frequency of them causing others harm through the evil-eye—and they are not considered bad or evil, they do not 'attack' with the evil-eye, but it is because they inadvertently cause the harm because their eye and soul have this ability which stems from envy. It stems from the superstitious feeling a person develops about another when it coincides with the latter saying something about a person, animal or object then something bad happening to the spoken about. And although I call it a superstition, to the people who believe it, it is a 'tangible' part of life and not superstition. This superstition can be seen in the NT, in Paul's dialogue 'If any man love not the Lord Jesus Christ, let him be Anathema Maran-atha' which means 'I guilt/ostracise/blame him-he evil eyed us/he evil eyed it' and in the story it is about wanting people to donate from what they have. (1Cor.16:22).

Another uniquely Yemeni superstition believed as fact by the culture, is the eyelid twitch called (mrf/mrph/مرف/مرث) and is considered an omen of something evil or bad to happen to the person who feels his/her eyelid twitch, or to their loved ones. The Yemeni authors have used this Yemeni belief as a place name for people narrated as expecting to receive good, but instead something bad happens to them, and this is just one example out of many Yemeni words and its meanings, as well as its beliefs in the culture of the authors and original audience of the Biblical stories used as place names reflecting and relaying what happens in the story and its themes with exactly the same meanings and use as in Arabic and Yemeni real-life. The exact word and its meaning have been used in Micah: 'For the inhabitant of Maroth waited carefully for good: but evil came down from the Lord unto the gate of Jerusalem.' (Mic.1:12)

Now I will be discussing how normal and practical way of life in Yemen, of which some areas have not changed in practise for millennia, has been used by the earliest authors of the Bible in the writing of Biblical stories, as well as these Yemeni Arabic meanings, customs and words being very well understood, showing the Yemeni origins of the authors of the Bible.

Bill of Divorce

When a woman gets divorced or is expected to be divorced in the rural Yemeni region, they do not always use the word 'divorce' but use a phrase 'he gave her, her bill/paper' 'he will/is going to give her, her bill/paper' 'هب لها ورقتها' 'هيهب لها ورقتها', although there is never an actual 'bill/paper' issued as it is enough that he has verbally announced and decided her divorce (although by the 1990s there was a man who was able to issue official marriage contracts, bills of divorce, etc., no one ever cares to get the divorce deeds although they always get the marriage contract done, but when the marriage is over, it is over), and both the male and female divorced couple move on with their separate lives and go on to marry other people. The same expression meaning 'divorce' which is 'gave her paper/bill' is used in Deuteronomy: 'When a man hath taken a wife, and married her, and it come to pass that she find no favour in his eyes, because he have found some uncleanness in her: then let him write her a bill of divorcement, and give it in her hand, and send her out of his house.' 'And if the latter husband hate her, and write her a bill of divorcement, and give it in her hand, and sendeth her out of his house…'. (Deut.24:1-3)

Perfuming

In Ruth, Naomi's instructions to her daughter-in-law Ruth to wash herself, anoint herself, to put on a clean dress after she returns from a day's work is no different than the way of life of rural Yemeni women. The hard work and chores are usually complete by noon; from morning there is fetching water, wood, preparing breakfast, grinding grain for both breakfast and lunch, cleaning and then ending with preparing lunch and washing the dishes; once this has been complete women wash, perfume, put on a clean dress and their jewellery and anoint themselves with frankincense, to be pretty and desirable for their husbands (also to be seen at their best by everyone else). Special emphasis is put on perfuming and anointing with incense smoke, rubbing fragrant oils and waxes onto the skin and hair on the night when a husband who has been away is to return, and the increased use of perfume and frankincense smoke is used almost every night. Although washing is daily and perfuming as well as anointing body with perfumed smoke, etc. is done even if the husband is always at home, when a husband returning from travel is expected the night of arrival is made more seductive between the couple using perfumed products. And although married and unmarried women perfume and anoint with perfumed smoke, much fuss is made over an adulterous woman who perfumes and uses incense in preparation for meeting a lover.

Slaughter of Animal

When slaughtering a bull, sheep, goat, etc. in remote Yemen, they do it on a rock, or in an area where the rock is part of the outer corridor, passage or steps—slaughtering the animal on a raised stone surface allows the blood to properly drain away from the slaughtered animal/meat and prevents it from getting soil and dirt on it before it is washed and cooked. The same practical practise has been used to add drama to the story of Saul's fasting soldiers being so hungry they slaughtered animals on the ground and ate the meat along with its prohibited blood, to which Saul instructs them to roll a stone towards him to slaughter the animals upon: 'And the people flew upon the spoil, and took sheep, and oxen, and calves, and slew *them* on the ground: and the people did eat *them* with the blood. Then they told Saul, saying, Behold, the people sin against the Lord, in that they eat with the blood. And he said, Ye have transgressed: roll a great stone unto me this day. And Saul said, Disperse yourselves among the people, and say unto them, Bring me hither every man his ox, and every man his sheep, and slay *them* here, and eat; and sin not against the Lord in eating with the blood. And all the people brought every man his ox, and slew *them* there.' (1Sam.14:32-34).

Marriage Designs

When a mother in Yemeni villages wants a certain young man to marry her daughter, one way she nudges him/his family towards asking for her daughter's hand in marriage without appearing 'in the picture' or directly asking for it to avoid seeming desperate, and to avoid making it seem the daughter's family and the concerned daughter are pedalling their daughter and lowering her status in doing so (as it is the man and his family who will go back and forth trying to convince the daughter and her family to accept their son—again it is about pride and status in one's society), one method the mothers employ (if need be) is visiting friends and neighbours and either directly or indirectly getting them to speak to the young man or his parents suggesting the concerned daughter is a perfect match, or the best person a man could wish for, and suggesting he come forward and ask for the concerned daughter's hand in marriage, they speak of the concerned female's virtues (beautiful, chaste, well brought up, a hard worker, her goodness and kindness), and also mentioning what kind comments, love and respect the mother has spoken of in the past about the man's mother and/or family. It is done in a way that the man and his family feel the neighbour or friend has made this suggestion without the concerned mother's knowledge.

The above-mentioned method is used in the storyline in Saul using his servants to prompt David to ask for or accept Michal's (Saul's daughter) marriage: 'And Michal Saul's daughter loved David: and they told Saul, and the thing pleased him. And Saul said, I will give him her, that she may be a snare unto him, and that the hand of the Philistines may be against him. Wherefore Saul said to David, Thou shalt be this day my son in law in *the one of* the twain. And Saul commanded his servants, saying, Commune with David secretly, and say, Behold, the king hath delight in thee, and all his servants love thee, now therefore be the king's son in law. And Saul's servants spake those words in the ears of David. And David said, Seemeth it to you *a light thing* to be the king's son in law, seeing that I *am* a poor man, and lightly esteemed? And the servants of Saul told him, saying, On this manner spake David. And Saul said, Thus shall ye say to David, The king desireth not any dowry…' (1Sam.18:20-25)

Tents, Booths and Roofs

Another part of the way of life in Yemen since ancient times is when there is an event where many people will gather (more than a person's house could accommodate or at a location where no houses exist) such as a wedding or at a pilgrimage to a sacred rock or sepulchre where there are no houses, and tithes are presented and feasting occurs, feasting also at weddings—the people would prepare 'tents' or 'booths' called 'mkhdra/مخدره' which are made by people fetching branches and wood from all sorts of trees available and building temporary roofed structures for the guests to sit in and stay at shaded from the heat of sun and other elements. Whether for a wedding or during pilgrimage at the offering site to present tithes, vows, offerings—animals are slaughtered for feasts, people dance, fires are made specially for cooking, burning incense and for smoking the 'kooz' while other fires are made for pagan rituals and for light. The building of temporary roofed structures are for necessity, to accommodate a large number of people for the event, many which would have travelled far distances to reach the place. This way of life in reality of Yemenis has been used by Biblical authors to mark places in the stories as well as to create major events in the stories.

In Genesis this has been used to mark the place where Jacob builds roofed buildings for his family and animals, we are first told the name of the place is 'Succoth' which means 'roofed/built a roof(s)' and in Yemen 'Succoth' is the word to describe the specific phase of installing/building the roof part of a house or structure, and is exactly why the authors have named the place 'Succoth' (see Succoth for its other meanings in wordplay): 'And Jacob journeyed to Succoth, and built him an house, and made booths for his cattle: therefore the name of the place is called Succoth.' (Gen.33:17).

In Leviticus you can see how the authors have combined the Yemeni way of life with the pagan Yemeni rituals of fire worship, sacrifice and offerings of tithes along with the practical and normal way of Yemeni life of building booths out of wood and branches for the excess guests at weddings and at pilgrim sites—which the Biblical authors have dramatized into a major feast and religious event throughout the Bible, and not just Leviticus, which has been interpreted as 'feast of the tabernacles' 'feast of booths' which in turn have become real-life religious events in the Jewish religion when these stories have been take as religious text although they have been originally taken from both Yemeni practicality of building booths for events, and from pagan Yemeni practise. In Leviticus it describes the details of the feasts (Lev.23) of which I will only partially quote here:

'And the Lord spake unto Moses, saying, Speak unto the children of Israel, and say unto them, *Concerning* the feasts of the Lord, which ye shall proclaim *to be* holy convocations, *even* these *are* my feasts…ye shall do no servile work therein, But ye shall offer an offering made by fire unto the Lord seven days…and say unto them, When ye be come into the land which I give unto you, and shall reap the harvest thereof, then ye shall bring a sheaf of the harvest of your firstfruits unto the priest: And he shall wave the sheaf before the Lord, to be accepted for you…And ye shall offer that day when ye wave the sheaf an he lamb without blemish of the first year for a burnt offering unto the Lord…The fifteenth day of the seventh month *shall be* the feast of tabernacles *for* seven days unto the Lord. On the first day shall be an holy convocation unto you; and ye shall offer an offering made by fire unto the Lord…These *are* the feasts of the Lord, which ye shall proclaim to be holy convocations, to offer an offering made by fire unto the Lord, a burnt offering, and a meat offering, a sacrifice, and drink offerings, everything upon his day: Beside the sabbaths of the Lord, and beside your gifts, and beside all your vows, and beside all your freewill offerings, which ye give unto the Lord. Also in the fifteenth day of the seventh month, when ye have gathered in the fruit of the land, ye shall keep a feast unto the Lord seven days: on the first day *shall be* a sabbath, and on the eighth day *shall be* a sabbath. And ye shall take you on the first day the boughs of goodly trees, branches of palm trees, and the boughs of thick trees, and willows of the brook; and ye shall rejoice before the Lord your God seven days. And ye shall keep it a feast unto the Lord seven days in the year. *It shall be* a statute forever in your generations: ye shall celebrate it in the seventh month. Ye shall dwell in booths seven days; all that are Israelites born shall dwell in booths: That your generations may know that I made the children of

Israel to dwell in booths, when I brought them out of the land of Egypt: I *am* the Lord your God. And Moses declared unto the children of Israel the feasts of the Lord.' (Lev.23). This is the authors taking what their Yemeni culture is and does out of practicality, necessity as well as their pagan rituals, to make it into a symbolic event and/or ritual in the Biblical story.

The same use of this Yemeni practical practise (of building roofed structures for guests and pilgrims) as being a religious practise is also used by the authors of the Bible to describe how the 'children of Israel' are like 'the heathen' as they too build roofed structures for religious rituals (just like the feasts and booths commanded by Moses), except because it is not to the correct God it is portrayed as wrong, but still they use the same concept taken from building roofed structures, albeit they make it 'buildings in high places' to perform religious rituals. The Biblical authors use the same word-name 'Succoth' as 'Succoth-benoth' which means 'roofs-built' literally meaning they built structures with roofs—just like the feast of booths, the feasts of tabernacles, but in this part of the story it is portrayed negatively even if it is similar to the 'right' kind: 'For so it was, that the children of Israel had sinned against the Lord their God, which had brought them out of the land of Egypt...And walked in the statutes of the heathen, whom the Lord cast out from before the children Israel, and of the kings of Israel, which they had made. And the children of Israel did secretly *those* things that *were* not right against the Lord their God, and they built them high places in all their cities...And there they burnt incense in all the high places, as *did* the heathen whom the Lord carried away before them; and wrought wicked things to provoke the Lord to anger: for they served idols...Then one of the priests whom they had carried away from Samaria came and dwelt in Bethel, and taught them how they should fear the Lord. Howbeit every nation made gods of their own, and put *them* in the houses of the high places which the Samaritans had made, every nation in their cities wherein they dwelt. And the men of Babylon made Succoth-benoth...'. Succoth-benoth 'built roofs' no different than Jacob building roofed houses/structures and the word-name given to the place 'Succoth' 'roofed', and no different in building roofed structures whether for feast of firstfruits, booths, tabernacles or for 'heathen' worship and rituals—except what is narrated as right or wrong by the Biblical authors, but in all cases is taken from the Yemeni practise of building temporary roofed structures with branches and wood from available trees and other flora during weddings and pilgrim worship rituals.

The use of this Yemeni practicality-induced way of life is described again in the Bible: 'And they found written in the law which the law had commanded Moses, that the children of Israel should dwell in booths in the feast of the seventh month: And that they should publish and proclaim in all their cities, and in Jerusalem, saying, Go forth unto the mount, and fetch olive branches, and pine branches, and myrtle branches, and palm branches, and branches of thick trees, to make booths, as *it is* written. So the people went forth and brought *them*, and made themselves booths, every one upon the roof of his house, and in their courts, and in the courts of the house of God, and in the street of the water gate, and in the street of the gate of Ephraim. And all the congregation of them that were come again out of the captivity made booths, and sat under booths: for since the days of Jeshua the son of Nun unto that day had not the children of Israel done so. And there was great gladness.' (Neh.8:14-17)

Conduct

Although adultery and fornication are disdained with severity in the remote Yemeni regions, when you live there you come to find out this 'strictness', the shame of it, and its avoidance is more 'said' than 'done'. As in normal life anywhere in the world, in remote Yemen the things that happen show people engage in adultery; whether relayed about affairs in the past, recently or in the present (at that time) which is not just gossip, but witnessed events of when people are in love, or lust, or both, that nothing will stop them engaging in adultery. Women have found ways to bring in their lovers right underneath the noses of their fathers-in-law and/or mothers-in-law, and one way popular among women which is described in great detail is that they use their head veils twisted and tied together to make a rope which is thrown down to the male lover(s) and help pull the lover up through the window, then lower him down out of the window to avoid the parents-in-law hearing the opening and closing of doors (to avoid being caught). This has been a popular way women and men conduct their affairs in the female's marital home if they cannot meet outside during the day, or when daytime meetings are not enough and they cannot keep away from each other. It has become an expression when referring to women who have done this, or speaking about a particular woman's affairs or inability to control their lust 'They pull them up with the headveils' 'يجبذوهم من المقارم/يشدّوهم من المقارم', and this means the lust has made them so brazen they will pull men up through the windows to satisfy their needs.

Exactly the same observation of this way has been used by Biblical authors in describing Rahab and the men who were staying at her house, and whom when under danger she hid then using a rope lowered them through the window so they could escape. Note how the author of this Biblical story is aware that scandalous or immoral women use this method to give their lovers a safe and secret entrance and exit, before he intentionally creates Rahab's character as a prostitute. The author could have made Rahab any kind of woman without attaching immorality to her character especially because she is helping the 'heroes', the good side, in the story and she is spared death by those she helped—in fact, there was no need to make her character a prostitute, except that these stories are fictional and for entertainment, using wordplay in the names and events of the story and that the author used his knowledge of this conduct that women lower men out of their windows and is aware that these women are adulterers, fornicators, immoral people, and the acts of pulling up and lowering down men through the window at night is for an immoral act, by an immoral woman, therefore Rahab is made a prostitute to suit the action and relay the pun which is recognised as an act of immorality by the original audience of the story and would have entertained them: 'And Joshua the son of Nun sent out of Shittim two men to spy secretly, saying, Go view the land, even Jericho. And they went, and came into an harlot's house, named Rahab, and lodged there. And it was told the king of Jericho, saying, Behold, there came in men hither tonight of the children of Israel to search out the country. And the king of Jericho sent unto Rahab, saying, Bring forth the men that are come to thee, which are entered into thine house: for they be come to search out all the country. And the woman took the two men, and hid them, and said thus, There came men unto me, but I wist not whence they *were*: And it came to pass *about the time* of shutting the gate, when it was dark, that the men went out: whither the men went I wot not: pursue after them quickly; for ye shall overtake them. But she had brought them up to the roof of the house, and hid them with the stalks of flax, which she had laid in order upon the roof...Then she let them down by a cord through the window: for her house was upon the town wall, and she dwelt upon the wall.' (Josh.2:1-15).

So you have living people in Yemen where adulterous women, or women in love, help their lovers enter and exit through windows to facilitate the meeting and leave without being caught, and see how this practical behaviour has been used to depict a fictional story of how spies escaped their pursuers. Even the character's name and occupation support the immorality of the conduct connected to pulling up and lowering men out of windows. The author is inspired by the Yemeni way of life, all the stories show the Biblical authors have an intimate knowledge of both the Arabic language and Yemeni life and culture.

Important Things in Life

Land

Another element of Yemeni way of life unchanged and alive since antiquity is the importance of land. It is vital for the survival of its owners and their families, everyone owns land and everyone wants more land, and will go to great lengths (not always moral) no matter how long it takes to purchase or inherit more land; get the best land; to defend their land with great attention paid to its borders, location, water rights, etc. Also, remote rural Yemenis love the land no matter how hard to upkeep and work it, it is something they are proud of as well as its vitality for the family of 'now' and those to come. Owning land allows the ownership of cattle, flocks, which also sustain and enrich the family and its offspring. The inhabitants of remote rural Yemen region will get into lengthy and complicated legal disputes at times of inheritance, especially when there are a lot of extended family members, with each party/individual trying to get as much land as he/she can inherit and also trying to get the most fertile land. This importance and necessity of land, which if you do not have neither you or your children will survive (which is why it is believed in these remote areas that if you do not have land then you are nothing (not meaning insignificant, but will cease to exist or will exist in a very harsh, impoverished, starved life for you and your children)).

This very real, big and important part of Yemeni life has been used and reflected and relayed extensively in the Bible, where the authors' obsession with land has not only been used, but exaggerated to the degree of excusing genocide, the killing of innocent men, women, children, babies, sometimes being explicitly horrific and brutal in the description to take what the Biblical stories clearly narrate is the murdered people's rightful land. The stories of excusing the wiping out of different 'peoples'/nations just so the 'heroes' of the story can take the land which is not theirs (within the Bible it is full of statements such as 'giving you a land not yours' 'giving you towns and cities you did not build' and always mentioning the land belonged to someone else) is to emphasise the importance of land to the authors and audience of the Bible.

Children

Children, and having many children, are important to Yemeni life where modernisation, external influence has not changed the people's way of life because first, external influences were not able to arrive at these remote regions, then secondly because the inhabitants of these regions were strict and refuted and rejected any change to be allowed to enter into their way of life. Children are the pride of their parents and grandparents. A question often asked about others they do not know or only hear news about is 'How many children does she/he have?' even if the conversation has nothing to do with the spoken-about's children; the more children a person has, the prouder he/she can be. The average family has seven to ten children, and this is between a monogamous couple i.e. from the same husband and wife. Although the local people express surprise, it is not considered abnormal or bizarre in these regions when a couple has seventeen children (from the same mother who gives birth naturally with no medical assistance, no doctors, nurses and no trained mid-wife, and no medication and the only available midwife is an untrained midwife who only receives the baby and cuts the umbilical cord), and any wonder is at the mother's health and ability to have so many pregnancies and still be a healthy functioning person.

Children and offspring are considered the pride and adornment of parents. Apart from a mother/father instinctively loving their children, naturally desiring children, the love comes naturally with the birth of a child, there are cultural and practical reasons why progeny is wanted and in great numbers. Culturally, children are a symbol of a man's virility and a woman's fertility (very important attributes/qualities in these regions). Practically, from a certain age, children will begin to help and bear responsibility with chores. In these regions everything is a hard chore whether preparing a meal, to fetching wood, water, grazing the cattle, shepherding flocks, working in the land, to name just a few; the more the members of the family increase as teenagers and adults, the distribution of the burden of work becomes lighter and more effective. This is not a planned intention of procreating to meet work demands, which unfortunately is a false stereotype, but when a couple make love without the use of contraceptives (contraceptives were unheard of, and unavailable in modernity even if heard of) the result from a husband and wife copulating with no contraception is many children, coupled with the fact that life is hard work and when children reach a certain age they can help out with work is a natural way of life and not children being created for and used as 'beasts of burden' which is a false and derogatory claim made by too many.

If you ever live in the region among the people and as one of them like I have, you discover this obsession for children is in everybody's heart and on everybody's tongue, and I do not mean they are obsessed with their own creation and production of progeny, but everybody seems to be obsessed and interested with everyone else's procreation in all stages of becoming pregnant, giving birth, knowing how many children they have, praying and asking God to give and bless others with children or with more children than they already have. E.g. if a woman has already given birth to a son the women and men will, at any point in time, comment to the woman 'Now you need a daughter' or 'Now you need to give him a brother/sister' or 'now you need more', if it is a girl 'Now you need to give her a brother to care for and protect her when they are adults' 'now you need more children to help you out', and the reasons they come up with while commentating to the respective parent(s) they are speaking to, whom they believe need more children, are various and endless, but always the more—the better.

The obsession with children is connected with the obsession for land: the more land you have, the more children you can have (they will be sustained by it and its fortunes); the more children you have, the more members of the family there will be to help work the land and all its chores related to working it: taking care of the animals that necessitates land too, and helping with chores at home linked directly to keep the family going. The more children, the more definite your progeny will survive, continue to own, work and live off the land—and thrive. In the same vein, the more children you have, and the progeny these children will eventually have—the more land you will need. It is important to point out although offspring will eventually help in work, they are loved—both mothers and fathers are affectionate and loving, protective and caring towards their children (whether they are still young or adults); it is not 'progeny for labour', human life and the way people live is more complicated than that and it is unfair to label or simplify it as such, having to work hard (every member of the family works including children from a certain age when their bodies can handle specific work) is a necessity because of the geography, location and circumstances which dictate the way of life in such areas, but it does not make the parents any less loving of their children than the 'city inhabitants' or 'modern countries'. With that said, there is a link between the obsession to have many children, and the obsession to have much land, but it would be similar to the argument of which came first, the egg or the chicken. But from living with the people you see they love their children like any parent from around the world loves his/her child.

This long existing Yemeni obsession to have children, or even many children, is dramatically displayed by the authors in the stories of the OT, where even one single child granted to a major character is promised, and will end up having, innumerable progeny: 'As for me, behold, my covenant is with thee, and thou shalt be a father of many nations.' '...and will multiply thee exceedingly' God tells Abraham, and the importance of having children is highlighted by making it difficult for the major characters to be able to have children, it emphasises how much of a blessing and important it is to have *a* child, and more so *many* children. A 'nation' will come out of Ishmael, as well as a 'nation' from Isaac, both Abraham's seed. 'I will bless thee, and in multiplying I will multiply thy seed as the stars of heaven, and as the sand which *is* upon the sea shore...'. Even though Abraham is already promised a great multiplication of his progeny through Ishmael and Isaac, it still mattered to the Biblical authors to give Abraham a third wife and from her six children, and to list Abraham's children from Keturah's side. The listing of progeny runs through the Bible, not as an account of genealogy, but within the story as a testament to how great they have multiplied as a 'seed'/family, a people and at the same time serving as a list of themes used or to be used in other Biblical stories by the authors. The importance to have many children is reflected in the 'race' between Leah and Rachel, including using their handmaids as wives for Jacob to procreate from.

The dispute between Laban and Jacob over flocks and over leaving with the former's daughters and grandchildren is over offspring, and over the resources needed to sustain each side's progeny: 'And it came to pass, whensoever the stronger cattle did conceive, that Jacob laid the rods before the eyes of the cattle in the gutters, that they might conceive among the rods. But when the cattle were feeble, he put *them* not in: so the feebler were Laban's, and the stronger Jacob's. And the man increased exceedingly, and had much cattle, and maidservants, and menservants, and camels, and asses. And he heard the words of Laban's sons, saying, Jacob hath taken away all that *was* our father's; and of *that* which *was* our father's hath he gotten all his glory.'

When Laban catches up with Jacob at Gilead 'And Laban said to Jacob, What hast thou done, that thou hast stolen away unawares to me, and carried my daughters, as captives taken with the sword...' and Jacob responds that he feared Laban would take away his wives and he lists how long he worked to gain his wives and cattle and he believes if it was not for God's protection 'surely thou hadst sent me away now empty...'. The conversation continues about Jacob's wives and children being Laban's children, and Jacob's cattle and the land he uses are all Laban's land, and that no person could hurt his own children; the conversation ends with an agreement of not trespassing not only a physical land marker but also not trespassing against each other and not harming each other's offspring. (Gen.30).

The importance of having at least one child to create many progenies is shown and the importance of offspring and continuation of offspring is made in the OT by always comparing a major character's barrenness or lack of offspring before giving them at least one child who will eventually fill the land with descendants. Such contrast and point made can be seen between Milcah and Iscah compared against Sarah; Leah compared to Rachel; Peninnah compared to Hannah; and even in Naomi whose sons die without children, but she is recompensed by her daughter-in-law Ruth and a distant relative or a tribesman Boaz procreating Obed whom in the story becomes Naomi's son, and ancestor to an important character, David. As everything else in the OT is taken from Yemeni origins, so is this obsession with children, offspring, continuation which has always been and still is an overwhelming part of Yemeni life, and it has been used by the authors of the Bible as a dominating theme in the Biblical stories because they are Yemenis in origin.

Walking/Travelling

Part and parcel in rural Yemeni life is having to travel a lot by foot in mountainous terrain where walking empty-handed is difficult and strenuous, but because this is the way of life for its inhabitants, their bodies and mindsets are adapted as this has been the only way of life since birth and since their ancestors, they walk with ease up and down steep inclinations while a person coming from the city needs assistance and needs to climb up. They walk with just as much sure-footedness carrying extremely heavy loads on their heads or shoulders as if they were empty-handed; they pass swiftly across mountain face without thinking twice where there is barely a lip of ledge to place the foot on and pass, where city people would turn around and return instead of carrying on, or an adventurer would attempt to pass if he dared with safety harnesses and ropes. The locals do get tired, they are only human, but only after extremely long distances or carrying heavy loads across extremely long distances, but they have the ability to walk without hesitation across difficult and dangerous terrain nigh on impossible for non-locals to pass, and they can cut distances and at a speed city-people would find impossible to do. To what the average city person would be considered a strenuous hike, or even mountain climbing—to the local is a simple and daily walk.

Part of this life in rural Yemen is having to carry heavy loads of goods for miles, carried on their heads (by women) or shoulders (by men), to barter at weekly and monthly markets in distance areas; when faced with drought and/or famine to walk further than usual to find water and where possible anything that can be used as food; and although they all have land in the mountains, many also have land in a different area where the terrain and climate is different (the terrain is level with hills and minor mountains) and according to the season and need they travel by foot over great distances to check on and help with their land (which is left leased or in the trust of others) and stay there for short or long periods of time before they return. E.g. some people who are beekeepers or own bees, when the season becomes cold, they will travel carrying their bees to leave them in the care of others in a different, warmer area before they return back home. It takes days of walking to reach these lower, warmer areas.

Daily walking and travelling distances are a large part of rural Yemeni life, not wandering as nomads or bedouins, not like that at all, but having to travel a lot by foot for days, sometimes weeks before returning back home aside from the daily distance and hikes of daily life which to them is not a hike, nor strenuous at all. But where famine and drought are concerned, the people do collectively wander until they find a water source or food source, but will always return home and make the strenuous and time-consuming travel daily/regularly until the drought/famine is over. One has to live among them and see the distances and terrain they cut, the loads they carry (usually enormous and heavy) to witness the adaptability and strength humans endure out of necessity of environment and circumstances, but when this is the only way of life how the endurance and ability is all in their stride. It is this harsh way of life which inspired the Biblical stories of Moses and the children of Israel 'wanderings' based on its Yemeni authors' experience of way of life.

Famine

The remote Yemeni regions have suffered famine in the past where long drought caused cessation of crops and outlasted all stored grain consumption. It got to the point adults would tie a flat stone against their bellies, and when the pangs of hunger increased tightening the stone against the stomach slightly helped in controlling the pain. During such famine, people who still had grain were able to purchase good land from desperate people in exchange for some handfuls of grain—in some cases taken off the grinding stone still whole because the purchasing family was about to grind it for a meal, but were able to make a hasty exchange for good land—the seller being desperate to provide a meal for his starving family. Not everyone could, nor wanted, to sell any of their land, and everybody suffering reverted to eating what they could of plants (inedible non-poisonous plants), sometimes using unusable parts of vegetation to make into bread.

There are two types of inedible vegetation or parts of vegetation which were used when nothing else was left: one was the black cusp/shell that would hold the grain such as the cusps you see on sorghum panicles (called gowsh/جوش), not the white flake-like chaff, but the hard, sharp black shell which threshing knocks the edible grain out of. Usually this is discarded, even before grinding grain when grain is soaked in water the remnants of these black shells which have escaped the winnowing process are skimmed off the top of the water and thrown into the cow's drinking bucket, but during famine people reverted to grinding this inedible part of the crop and making a bitter and rough-textured bread which only starvation and looming death could make forcibly swallowable. Again, if you have ever eaten normal bread of this region where this black shell has slipped through the sifting process and into the dough, and I am talking about one single tiny shell which has ended up in the dough by accident, it is so sharp and hard (even after going through the grinding process with the grain and being baked) it can lodge into your gums—yet the people of my grandparents' generation and my parents' generation all had to eat it, or die of starvation, and one thing they all say and remember is 'الجوش اللي لايَنطَحِن ولايئتَكِل ، طَحَنّاه وأكلناه من الجوع' 'The (gowsh) shells which cannot be ground and cannot be eaten, we ground and we ate out of hunger.'

The second, and usually inedible, source they turned to was a tree called 'Dhbr/ضبر' (dhibira/ضِبِره in singular), a tree whose fruit are small with no flesh, but a red outer shell which when rubbed peels off and becomes slimy which the people removed to get to a stone like a peach or apricot's stone, which when cracked open with a rock has inside it small seeds. These seeds are collected and pound or ground into a dough then baked into bread—of course, there is never enough of the seed to make a lot or enough bread, nor does it taste good, as the people have to consider everyone needs access to some of these stone/seeds so they share and there is barely enough for families to eat, but enough not to die of starvation. This is a living Yemeni people showing us what hunger and famine made them turn to in order to survive, and the grandparents' generations learned this survival technique of what inedible plants to turn to, to make something similar to bread from their grandparents and earlier generations who went through famine. Earlier generations had more of this kind of tree to take from than the later generations as the later generations' environment had been deforested to make more land and for firewood, but the knowledge was still passed down from generation to generation because famine was a real experience passing on them all, and no matter how long it was only a matter of time before a generation would experience it, and when it happened they knew what tree to seek out.

I believe this is what inspired the Biblical authors to create 'manna' for the stories, but of course with a dramatized twist that it came from God and was abundant. It is also what has been mistranslated as 'oracle' inside the misnomered 'temple' which correctly the 'temple' should read 'hekal/he will eat'. The word mistranslated as 'Oracle' which is 'dabar' is actually 'dhabar' (dhbr)and means this tree and its fruit which the authors and audience of the Biblical stories are aware of saving them during famines which is why in the fictional story a jar of 'manna' is stored and also there is 'dhabar' inside the temple/tabernacle, possibly meaning some branches of the Dhibir tree both remind the audience and the fictional characters of the stories about what saved them. It is easy to define how a word which is the name of a tree, and its wood/branches, and berries were mistranslated and misinterpreted into an 'oracle', the latter which does not fit in with any of the Biblical stories: the people interpreting do not know the meaning of the word in Arabic and do not understand the wordplay which is part of the Biblical author's method; the translators both historical and modern are confusing it with the word 'dabar' which can mean to 'discuss something' usually with bad intent, and also is the same word and meanings of the word Deborah (see Deborah)—so the similarity of the words 'dabar' and 'dhabar' make it easy to mistake if the first word of 'Dhabar' is misinterpreted as 'd', and if the translators/interpreters are not familiar with the Arabian Peninsula Arabic with which the Bible is written; plus there is always projecting what other mythologies and folklore such as Greek folklore and ancient religions include oracles as part of their worship and belief systems and this is wrongly imputed onto the very straightforward beliefs and stories of the Bible.

Also in the remote region of Yemen when someone is feeling famished, when they eat a piece of bread, no matter how dry it is they say 'hunger makes it [taste like] honey/الجوع خلاه عسل', and also telling a person who is being picky 'when you are really hungry it will taste like honey', which are very expressive, and which I understand completely as when I would be unable to eat bread and it was the only food available as I was not yet used to it and found it heavy and dense causing me a jaw-ache and being unable to swallow it because of its taste, and I would go for days and weeks unable to eat and swallow, when my body and hunger could no longer handle extreme hunger—the hunger made it not only edible but tasty; and when you are hungry (I am not talking about being picky, but in there being no food available for periods of time) the things available to eat do become tasty or at least more palatable to eat, hence the people's expression likening a piece of dry bread to honey when a person is hungry enough.

In the Biblical stories, when the people are starving God sends them 'manna' which can be used to make bread just like real-life Yemenis turned to the shells of grains and also to a tree whose stones provided tiny seeds—and both sources which are considered inedible were made into bread by necessity due to famine. In the Biblical stories although it is God who makes manna appear, the people still have to go out to gather it, just like the real-life Yemeni people had to go out and gather what they could find: 'And the whole congregation of the children of Israel murmured against Moses and Aaron in the wilderness: And the children of Israel said unto them, Would to God we had died by the hand of the Lord in the land of Egypt, when we sat by the flesh pots, *and* we did eat bread to the full; for ye have brought us forth into this wilderness, to kill this whole assembly with hunger. Then said the Lord unto Moses, Behold, I will rain bread from heaven for you; and the people shall go out and cover a certain rate every day, that I may prove them whether they walk in my law, or no…' 'And it came to pass that at even, the quails came up, and covered the camp: and in the morning the dew lay round about the host. And when the due that lay was gone up, behold, upon the face of the wilderness *there lay* a small round thing, as small as the hoar frost on the ground. And when the children of Israel saw *it*, they said one to another, It *is* manna, for they wist not what it *was*. And Moses said unto them, This *is* the bread which the Lord hath given you to eat. This is the thing which the Lord hath commanded, Gather of it every man to his eating, an omer for every manner, *according to* the number of your persons; take ye every man for *them* which *are* in his tents. And the children of Israel did so, and gathered, some more, some less. And when they did mete it with an omer, he that gathered much had nothing over, and he that gathered little had no lack; they gathered every man according to his eating. And Moses said, Let no man leave of it till morning. Notwithstanding they hearkened not unto Moses; but some of them left of it till the morning, and it bred worms, and stank: and Moses was wroth with them. And they gathered it every morning, every man according to his eating: and when the sun waxed hot, it melted...' 'And he said unto them, This *is that* which the Lord hath said, To morrow is the rest of the holy sabbath unto the Lord: bake *that* which ye will bake *today*, and seethe that ye will seethe; and that which remaineth over layup for you to be kept until the morning. And they laid it up till the morning: as Moses bade: and it did not stink, neither was there any worm therein...' 'And the house of Israel called the name thereof Manna: and it *was* like coriander seed, white; and the taste of it *was* like wafers *made* with honey...' (Exod.16); 'And the mixt multitude that was among them fell alusting: and the children of Israel also wept again, and said, Who shall give us flesh to eat? We remember the fish that we did eat in Egypt freely; the cucumbers, and the melons, and the leeks, and the onions, and the garlick: But now our soul *is* dried away: there *is* nothing at all, beside this manna, *before* our eyes. And the manna *was* as coriander seed, and the colour thereof as the colour of bdellium. And the people went about, and gathered *it*, and ground *it* in mills, or beat *it* in a mortar, and baked *it* in pans, and made cakes of it: and the taste of it was as the taste of fresh oil. And when the dew fell upon the camp in the night, the manna fell upon it.' (Num.11:1-9); 'And they did eat of the old corn of the land on the morrow after the passover, unleavened cakes, and parched corn in the selfsame day. And the manna ceased on the morrow after they had eaten of the old corn of the land; neither had the children of Israel manna anymore; but they did eat of the fruit of the land of Canaan that year.' (Josh.5:11-12).

In the above passages the Biblical authors are describing famine, even the way the storyline gives orders that they gather only 'a certain rate', it is like real people in famine rationing whatever food source is available, e.g. the Yemeni people with the black shells and also the dhibira tree seeds; in the Bible: the children of Israel with the manna; the authors of the Bible make clear how important rationing is during famine by narrating that even if a person gathers more than what God ordained, or less than his ration: those who gathered more, do not get more, and those who gathered less still receive enough, i.e. rationing is miraculously enforced. The importance of rationing, avoiding wasting too much at one time instead of keeping it as a source for everyone to frugally survive on is again emphasised in the Biblical story by Moses warning not to leave any until the next day, and when people do leave some manna over for the next day, they find it spoiled and stinking (although on the sabbath it miraculously does not rot because God has allowed it). It is worth pointing out the expression 'it bred worms and stank' is a uniquely rural Yemeni expression, when something smells very bad from spoiling, they say it is 'full of worms' not meaning there are literally worms/maggots, but the word 'of worms/became worms' 'mdwd/adwad/مدود/ادود' means 'it stinks' 'it is rotten and stinking'. Also, how the authors of the Bible have used the experience of famine and connected it to the importance of the land can be seen in the narration that as soon as they enter the land of Canaan they eat the land of Canaan's corn, and the manna, which they had to eat and were sick of, ceases: land=survival, but also it reflects how people in real famines such as in Yemen remote areas would cease to need to eat the unpalatable husks and Dhibira seed bread (which was never in enough quantities to satisfy hunger) as soon as it rained and the land was harvested, and also the people who did have corn or sorghum (from previous year(s)) would share with the people who were without once it rained and they knew crops would be fruitful therefore they could afford to give from what remained of their stores.

I believe 'manna' was inspired by Yemeni authors' knowledge of survival methods of Yemeni people during famine: they were describing how people went out gathering tiny seeds, but as it is a story it can (and needed to be) dramatized so unlike real-life Yemeni practise where people had to go to the Dhibira trees and pick, gather and bring home the berries with the slimy red exterior, before cracking it open to access the seeds inside, the Biblical authors made manna appear along with dew at night to be found in the morning like a miracle, whereas it still kept the realistic side of people having to gather it, grind or pound it, then boil or bake it for consumption. In real-life the seed which becomes the survival source for people does not carpet the ground to be collected, but is part of the vegetation whose fruit remain on the tree unless they are manually picked, or when the tree naturally sheds its fruit/seeds.

But the Biblical story needs to be dramatic and for this reason too the authors turned to something which is also part of Yemeni flora for inspiration: the description of manna 'like coriander seed, white' and how it covers all over the ground, what they are describing is a plant called in remote Yemen 'rain/رين' and it grows tall, its stems are covered in white round seeds which are spherical and when they ripen naturally on the plant become dry, soft and furry-like, and if left untouched on the plant they overripen and fall off covering the ground with its small white round seeds; because they are very small and light the wind blows them around and they do seem to carpet the ground, rocks—they have the annoying characteristic of crumbled Styrofoam spheres, sticking and clinging to surfaces and fabrics, blown around easily by a breeze, let alone wind. The colour of these spheres of 'rain' are initially pure white, but during collection and when they shed to the ground, they eventually become an off-white colour, almost stained-yellow white due to mingling with soil, dust, dry leaves, etc. (it may be the same or similar to plant called desert-cotton). This is what the Biblical authors have used as a description for the manna to show how abundant it is. I have never heard of this plant or its spheres being eaten, but what they have been used for since ancient times and into current times is as filling for pillows and cushions as the seeds/spheres are soft and spongy to the touch. And another characteristic of 'rain' which the Biblical stories support being the inspiration behind 'manna' is if a pillow or cushion becomes soaked with the 'rain' confined inside it, it stinks and the women would say 'it will stink/idwid' i.e. the meaning for it stinks but is literally 'becomes worms'—the Biblical authors chose to describe it with a similar expression that if it was stored/laid up it stinks and breeds worms, while in reality the word 'stinks' or even 'rotted and stinks/stank' is based on expressing it has 'become worms'. The authors of the Bible are Yemeni, even with regards to the manna story it is inspired by Yemeni experience of famine, and it is the Biblical authors' knowledge and familiarity with their local Yemeni environment and flora and its uses whether during famine or otherwise that have inspired and provided descriptions and characteristics in the story for the 'manna'.

Lamb of the Bedpost

When a lamb or goat is needed for a special event in remote Yemen, a lamb or goat is picked out for being the best, and it is separated from the rest of the flock. It is no longer sent out to graze, nor is it put into the sheep/goats stable anymore, but is kept for a few weeks tethered to a bed-leg/post (beds are used for sitting on outside) or to a tree. Instead of being sent to graze in the land with the rest of the flock, it is served grass, crops and is watered while tethered to the bedpost, it is also handfed lumps of dough; it is given special attention to its nutritional needs so as to plumpen it before slaughter—and is where the proverb 'lamb of the bedpost/كبش القوقعه' comes from, which is applied to the 'favourite child' of a parent because of the favouritism shown to him/her than the other siblings. And it is this selection and separation process (in order to fatten the lamb) which you can see incorporated into the Passover story in Exodus, where Moses tells the people to select, separate and keep the lamb weeks before its slaughter for the Passover—it is how Yemenis have been doing this fattening-separation-special attention process because it is how things are done to make the animal healthier, fatter and better tasting before it is slaughtered: 'Your lamb shall be without blemish, a male of the first year: ye shall take *it* out from the sheep, or from the goats: And ye shall keep it up until the fourteenth day of the same month: and the whole assembly of the congregation of Israel shall kill it in the evening.' (Exod.12:1-6).

Butter and Honey

Butter and honey are a popular food combination in rural Yemen, the butter is clarified (called smn/سمن). Both butter and honey, individually, are considered healthy foods which not only give health, but also help grow and give strength to whoever eats it. The popularity of butter and honey eaten together is because they make a delicious combination, and when available are poured over a dish made of hot bread and milk crushed together (phta/origin of 'Naphtali'), and many people like to drink clarified butter and honey mixed in milk. When times are prosperous, that is when rain and grass are plentiful, the land is green and animals thrive, including bees; milk, butter and honey production become abundant and are signs of good times. The tasty combination of butter and honey has become a proverb 'like butter and honey' meaning a perfect match and people getting along very well, a proverb used not only in Yemen, but across many Arab countries. In rural Yemen, drinking butter and honey in milk is believed to be more nourishing in this form as it is believed to go direct to the bones and muscles, providing the person with health and strength as well as fattening them. The abundance of butter and honey was/is a marker of the fortune and fecundity of the land.

This very Yemeni diet and the belief of its nutritional benefits and its marker as a sign of fortune and fertility of land has been used as a sign by the Biblical authors of when times will be good in the land where the story is set; even the name of the child to be born of a virgin 'Immanuel' which means 'drink-the' 'give to drink-the', his name and the events in his story are connected to him eating butter and honey, and furthermore his character role and name are directly connected to the abundance of milk and butter, honey and butter for everyone to eat of, i.e. the good fortune and fertility of the land resulting in abundant produce of milk, butter, honey, so much everyone will eat butter and honey (see Isa.7:14-15, 21-22). It is undoubtedly Yemeni way of life being described in the Biblical stories and shows how the authors of the Bible drew on Yemeni ways of life throughout the OT stories.

Female Fertility

Another topic of significance in the life of rural Yemenis is a woman's ability to bear children, or her inability to do so. Just as it is a greatly admired and desired attribute that a woman be able to produce children, on the opposite side it is a great shame, a peculiarity to be unable to bear any children at all. A woman who does not become pregnant quickly is hounded by curious neighbours, relatives, locals—all wanting to know if she is pregnant, and if not—then why not. If with time it becomes seemingly evident that she is barren, she is viewed as abnormal, deficient, something is wrong with her that she cannot become a mother and produce children; and the lack of offspring is always placed on the wife (which is sometimes true that she cannot bear children, but sometimes it turns out it is a husband who is infertile, e.g. when the wife is divorced and she marries another and becomes pregnant; or if she remains his wife or is divorced and he takes on a new wife, and the new wife also does not conceive a child) not on the husband. The wife, whether she actually has a medical condition that does not allow her to have offspring, or whether it is just a matter of time before she does become pregnant, not only does she suffer her own self-induced stress and yearning to be a mother, but she also has the added stress which can cause depression from relatives and neighbour's constant questions, curiosity and their suggestions of how to 'remedy' her 'abnormality'; and if many years pass without a pregnancy the people begin to gossip that she will be divorced or married over, and all this adds to the stress burning her heart and soul.

This reality of way of life and interaction between different parts of community, along with the importance of a wife being fertile, and if she is not then her husband either divorcing her or marrying over her has been used by the Biblical authors for the same matters being important in the Biblical stories: fertility, offspring, continuation, and even major characters have been made 'barren' like Sarah and Hannah just to show the importance of how even having one child can be of great importance and/or this single child can create many progenies to continue the family line, the 'seed'. The importance in the stories is stressed by making the characters barren before being given the miracle of conception by God, a child despite being barren and/or after old age. The attitude towards Sarah, Hannah and Rachel is from Yemeni culture: Sarah is 'despised' (according to Sarah's character) by Hagar once the latter conceives; Jacob responds angrily that it is not his fault Rachel cannot conceive when the latter expresses her desperation to be a mother and have a child; Peninnah (of many children) is described as provoking barren Hannah, causing the latter more fret and sadness. The importance a woman be fertile, and the view of deficiency if she is barren, is also focused on by contrasting the barren characters against their fertile peers: barren Sarah is compared against fertile Milcah (pollination) and Iscah (shooting young crops); Rachel's barrenness is contrasted against fertile Leah who produces child after child; Hannah's barrenness contrasted against Peninnah whose name and narration describes and states she has many children:

'And Abram and Nahor took them wives: the name of Abram's wife *was Sarai*; and the name of Nahor's wife, Milcah, the daughter of Haran, the father of Milcah, and the father of Iscah. But Sarai was barren; she had no child.' 'And he went in unto Hagar, and she conceived: and when she saw that she had conceived, her mistress was despised in her eyes. And Sarai said unto Abram, My wrong *be* upon thee: I have given my maid into thy bosom; and when she saw that she had conceived, I was despised in her eyes: the Lord judge between me and thee.' (Gen.11:29-30; 16:4-5).

'And when the Lord saw that Leah *was* hated, he opened her womb: but Rachel was barren.' 'And when Rachel saw that she bare Jacob no children, Rachel envied her sister; and said unto Jacob, Give me children, or else I die. And Jacob's anger was kindled against Rachel: and he said, *Am* I in God's stead, who hath withheld from thee the fruit of the womb?' (Gen.29:31; 30.1-2).

'And he had two wives; the name of the one *was* Hannah, and the name of the other Peninnah: and Peninnah had children, but Hannah had no children...And her adversary also provoked her sore, for to make her fret, because the Lord had shut up her womb.' (1Sam.1:2,6).

Fertility, barrenness, the respect and stigma towards both respectively and how they are expressed in the Bible are uniquely Yemeni in attitude, expression, and the importance placed on the topics and have always been in rural Yemeni life.

Stepwives

In the Biblical stories where a character has two wives, what you see portrayed in the dynamics between the stepwives of the story is exactly how the dynamics and atmosphere are between stepwives in real life whether in rural Yemen or its cities and probably elsewhere across the region where polygamy exists. The Biblical authors have observed (maybe through personal experience) how real women behave and what usually happens to both wives, their husband and their children. The concerns over issues, the petty or sly behaviour and its consequences, have been used by the authors to portray stepwives; and where they are used in the Bible, the realistic attitudes and actions have been dramatized along with miraculous outcomes for its characters. Sarah and Hagar's relationship has been discussed earlier in this book, but it is worth mentioning with the added proof from the narrated attitudes and actions of other stepwife characters in the Biblical stories (Rachel/Leah, Hannah/Peninnah) and how they realistically mirror life between real stepwives in times past and current (albeit without any miracles of divine intervention).

What the OT depicts is no different than the stressful relationship between modern women who share a husband. Usually the husband finds an excuse to marry over the first-wife, whether it be lack of child, or no male heir (although the wife cannot determine the gender her child is born, she is blamed as an 'inability' to produce a son), and sometimes there is no 'excuse' other than he has fallen in love or wants to marry. In rural Yemen, marrying more than one wife is the exception and not the norm in the villages and remote areas, even if no children or no son is produced. The usual reaction from the first-wife and her family when the husband makes it known he wishes to marry over her, is to acutely oppose it; when everything she and her family do fails to prevent the marriage, the hostility turns towards the 'new' wife—note in Genesis where Laban warns Jacob with a solemn oath never to harm his daughters (Jacob's wives) by marrying another woman over them. Even in cases when the first-wife allows or agrees to her husband marrying another woman, the good-will never lasts long with either wife beginning an antagonistic relationship towards the other.

In communities where it is neither illegal nor immoral to marry more than one wife, it is still viewed as an injustice towards the first-wife, i.e. they do view it as immoral. The women concerned (and her whole family) still oppose it, feel insult, outrage and betrayal and do everything they can to prevent it happening (which does sometimes work), but once a husband has made up his mind—it will happen. Just as any woman around the world would feel betrayed, insulted, embarrassed, angered, ashamed, frustrated if her husband was having a secret affair with another woman, so does the woman whose husband is to marry over her and marries another woman openly. More so, as the new wife will be brought home, they will share the residence as well as the husband so she has to suffer the burn of betrayal daily, watching her husband love the other woman in front of her eyes.

Most first-wives embark on an all-out hostile relationship towards the new-wife, even the first-wives who encourage or are complacent about their husband marrying over them, live to regret it whether the new-wife is cordial, rude or hostile towards the former just as Sarai regretted in Genesis making Abram marry Hagar 'My wrong be upon thee…'. There are cases where both wives are extremely good-natured and get along, but the overwhelming majority of stepwives who are usually good and moral people, human emotions and the stressful nature and dynamic of the relationship coupled with factors of human psychology does make it a hostile relationship ranging from pettiness, bickering and provocation, to much more serious hostilities and plots.

Factors which enflame an already stressful relationship between stepwives can be: one becomes pregnant and not the other; one provides a male heir and not the other; when one wife feels her husband's love for her has lessened, or he has shown an increase of affection towards the other. Although some stepwives do provoke, or are blamed of provoking the other stepwife, even in cases where they are getting along as harmoniously as butter and honey, all it takes is one of the wives to see or feel one of the aforementioned enflaming factors to sour the relationship. When this kind of living situation is forced upon at least one of the wives (the stepwife situation) it is a stressful relationship because of its nature, but when one senses or sees a difference in treatment, whether negatively towards her or positively towards the stepwife—even innocent actions from the other can be misunderstood or distorted as provocation; and these factors, causes, emotions, reactions from real-life relationships which can still be witnessed today in rural Yemen are exactly portrayed and narrated in the Biblical stories. The same can be seen in Rachel and Leah's stepwife relationship (and they are sisters in the story), Rachel is consumed with envy because Leah is giving birth to many children for Jacob while Rachel is not, and her dialogue reiterates her stress. Hannah and Peninnah's relationship is also shown to be hostile, and although Peninnah's character is not given any dialogue, the narration states she provokes her stepwife as well as her word-name meaning she has many children while Hannah is 'closed up' and the story blames Peninnah for adding to Hannah's sadness and stress: Hannah's problem and Peninnah's guilt is that the latter has children while Hannah has not.

All these Biblical stories are based on how women all over the world would behave under similar circumstances, the things that happen when a man brings another wife into the family (with the exception of cults/cult-families as the step-wife relationship and their mentality displays very differently among multiple-wives of cult members influenced by cult-mentality). A number of things threaten stepwives: loss or lessening of a husband's love; the jealousy, distress and hurt stepwives feel because of each other's presence; taking and/or sharing the husband's love and affection; women who want to be mothers but cannot conceive already feel hurt and yearning, this emotion is worsened by a culture where a barren/childless wife is made to feel abnormal or incomplete as a woman—these feelings become a greater stress when a new-wife is married to provide the children, and the stress increases if the stepwife becomes pregnant; both the 'old' and the 'new' wife represent a threat to each other, and either both or one stepwife may feel the other is undermining her—and/or is actually doing so.

The threat felt between stepwives from each other is that the other will cause her status within the family to degrade, status as a wife, financial harm, or cause her children harm—as one could be the reason the other is divorced. Pregnancy, any offspring, one with a male child are reasons believed to give more control over the husband and this could determine the other's fate: whether she gets more or less food, money, clothing, or is even divorced. This puts them into a constant struggle which differs only in its potency if only one is hostile, or both are hostile towards the other. When only one is hostile causing the other (docile) wife problems by using stubbornness, tricks, deceit, usually behind the husband's back, which includes complaining/lying to the husband about the stepwife—in such cases the docile stepwife suffers from her peer's torment, but in many cases suffers further when the husband falls for the hostile stepwife's tricks or succumbs to her complaints. The docile wife can suffer from arguments between herself and the husband caused by the hostile stepwife; she is often 'turned out' of the marital house and sent to her family until issues are resolved between them. The worst case is when the hostile wife convinces the husband to divorce the other.

When both stepwives are hostile or strong-willed they can make life very difficult for each other and the husband when things get out of hand. But what you usually see is one wife dominates the husband more than the other—and the other wife suffers as a consequence. Having a male child usually, but not necessarily, strengthens the mother/wife's position in the family. Although the husband may be infatuated or more loving towards the new-wife, it is usually the wife's character which determines which stepwife will dominate the marriage and family life—there are many 'old' and 'new' wives either being in control or suffering in their respective marriage. One stepwife's hostility usually extends to the other's children; the children of a docile stepwife are usually mistreated and hated by the hostile stepwife, and unfortunately in some cases where the husband is weak or is completely 'under the thumb' of the hostile wife's whim, he also gives preferential treatment to her biological children at the expense of being unfair (with all its negative consequences) towards the docile wife's children.

The Biblical stories reflect these tensions and behaviours between stepwives, but as a fictional story it makes the protagonist wife 'loved' more and discriminates in portrayal which wife and her children get better treatment while the other wife and her offspring get worse or less favourable treatment; but still the stories reflect reasons behind the tension of stepwife characters as in real life: Rachel and Hannah are the preferred and most loved by their respective husbands; both stories show their angst, worry and grief is due to the other wife, Leah/Peninnah, having children; it shows the real behaviour of one wife being provoked by the other whether the other instigates provocation or just for being pregnant/having children. The same tensions and the dominance of the husband by one wife can be seen in the Sarai/Hagar story where although no real reason or action shows Hagar of doing anything wrong, but Sarah's dominance of Abraham causes him to succumb to her wishes: although it grieves him, he sends away and abandons Hagar and his child Ishmael at Sarah's insistence.

These stories were written by authors familiar with the dynamics/behaviour of wives in polygamous marriages who behave exactly as do the women and husbands in rural Yemen societies; the stories are no different than those you see happen in remote Yemen areas and witness yourself if you live there, albeit they do not abandon wife and children in the wilderness (as Abraham does) at the hostile wife's insistence but they do send the docile wife and her children to her family home awaiting either a resolution of issues or a divorce by the husband. Even how the dominant wife, the more loved wife, and how she and her children are treated as opposed to the less loved wife, are straight from Yemeni way of life and its social dynamics.

In the story of Sarah and Hagar, with Sarah the dominant wife, Sarah causes Hagar and her child to suffer—after insisting Abraham marry Hagar for offspring, the authors then give Sarah a very realistic human reaction (a bad one) as soon as Hagar is pregnant: Sarah becomes jealous and suspicious of Hagar, and not only does Sarah beat and abuse Hagar, but she causes Abraham to abandon both Hagar and his child in the wilderness; although Ishmael and Isaac are both young children, still Sarah does not want Ishmael anywhere near her son and accuses him of mocking Isaac then insisting and getting her way forcing Abraham to abandon his wife and child. This antagonistic behaviour towards a stepchild by the stepwife is exactly what you see happening in real Yemeni polygamous families, but they do not abandon the children in wilderness or elsewhere: they send the suffering wife to her marital home and the wife usually takes her children with her if they are young, but if for whatever reasons the children are sent back to the husband's home, they may be abused (treated harshly, unkindly) by the stepwife without the husband/father's knowledge—as the stepwife bears towards them the same hostility and intentions dramatized and represented in Sarah's character towards Ishmael. The real-life antagonism from stepwife relationships which extends to the other stepwife's children is probably the origins of the 'evil stepmother' in fairy tales; even how the children of the docile wife whether she is present, divorced or dead, are treated: given less food, made to work more, given less new clothes, and mistreated in general are like the Cinderella fairy tale (but without the magic or over-the-top happy ending). But in the OT they depict the less loved wife (the docile wife in real life) as receiving the less favourable, and downright unfair treatment e.g. take Hagar and how she is abused, then she and Ishmael abandoned in the wilderness; also, in Jacob's story it is made perfectly clear that he loves Rachel and that he has no love for Leah, and shows the preferential treatment of the children of the wife he loves and in the less love towards Leah is exemplified in how he treats/views both she and her children; the story also shows an even less regard for the handmaids and the children he has fathered from them (of course this story and narration are inspired by the Biblical author's experience, culture and observation of dynamics of real people) shown in the following paragraph.

Jacob loves Rachel; when he will meet again with his brother Esau, Jacob only has Joseph from Rachel. Jacob does not love Leah, but she is still related to him the same way as Rachel (they are his cousins and wives) and he has fathered from her many children. The handmaids Bilhah and Zilpah are mere vessels who gave both Rachel and Leah children from and for Jacob, but he has no love for the handmaids and the narration does not credit them for the offspring but initially dedicates them to Leah and Rachel; these children being the handmaids' children have even less love/status than Leah and Rachel's biological children.

Now in this part of the Genesis story you can see how different authors at later times rewrote, added or removed from the Biblical stories to suit what they wanted these stories to be: although many of Leah's and the handmaids' children in later stories of the OT are given importance such as Judah and Levi, in Genesis 32 and 33 the narrator/author show Jacob does not really care for their safety and survival as much as he does for Rachel and her only biological son up to that point in the story. When Jacob is to meet once again with Esau his brother, whom he deceived out of birth right and blessing resulting in Jacob fleeing for his life, when they are to meet again after many years of separation Jacob is still convinced Esau will harm him—only this time he worries it will be through harming his children and wives.

The story makes it crystal-clear Jacob is certain his children and wives will be killed by Esau so he decides to divide them into groups so even if some are killed, another group will survive—the author uses the dynamics and attitude of a polygamous family's real-life preferential treatment and mistreatment according to the dominance/love of the preferred stepwife. The author shows in the narration that none of Leah's children, nor the handmaids' children have any significance to the author and by design they have no significance to the character Jacob at this part of the Biblical story—the author shows that only Rachel's biological child, Joseph, matters and only he is supposed to have importance in the narrative of Jacob's children, shown through Jacob only caring for Rachel and Joseph's safety and survival while doing the complete opposite towards Leah and her children, and the handmaids and their children.

This is shown by Jacob's character dividing the whole family into groups of wife and her biological children: Rachel and Joseph, Leah and her biological children, each handmaid with her biological children. The story makes it absolutely clear of Jacob's certainty and fear that Esau will kill the mothers and their children so to avoid total loss, he does not divide one mother/wife with an equal number of all his offspring, but he divides and provides them with either safety or presents them to danger according to the wife he loves and her biological child(ren) and according to the degree he loves or dislikes her: so you have the handmaids and their children from Jacob at the forefront and presented and exposed to Esau's suspected and expected violence first; then Leah whom he did not want to marry, and her children next to be exposed to Esau's possible murderous intentions as perceived and expected by Jacob; with Rachel and her son Joseph the farthest behind, ensuring if Esau is peaceful, all the other wives and their children have already passed the expected danger like guinea pigs in a test, or bait to provoke a reaction—and if Esau had begun to murder them it would have ensured Rachel and Joseph would escape by being the most distant with the other groups of wives and children between them and Esau.

In all polygamous marriage examples from the Biblical stories, the characters and the events are dramatized, exaggerated but follow the same dynamics of real-life stories of women, wives, mothers and their children in polygamous marriages as they occur in Yemen, and the consequences and effects upon the children growing and living amidst this atmosphere and polygamous way of life. (See Gen.16; 21:2-21; 29:30-35; 30:1-25; 32:7-11; 33:1-7; 1Sam.1; 2:1-5).

Monkey and Meribah

Another way of life in remote Yemen are actions of human behaviour no different than anywhere else in the world, but the importance of mentioning them here is their unique Yemeni 'expression/term' and where this Yemeni term originates from within Yemeni way of life—and how this exact Yemeni expression for its exact meaning has been used as context and meaning in the OT. The Yemeni expression is 'Meribah' and means to cause a great argument, quarrel, sharp reproach without calming nor backing down, and means creating an incident of such argument to the degree of turning or flipping things over, and/or throwing things around (physically or figuratively). The person who does this is said to have 'Meribah' 'monkeyed' (see Meribah Exod.17:1-7); the actioner and the description of the event is described (regarding one person) (shammat wa rabbaḥ/شَمَّت ورَبّاح) 'he caused a scene/disgrace and monkeyed' (s͟hammat which means to 'cause a scene/scandal and disgrace' so when used as 's͟hammat and meribah' means 'caused a great scene of argument where people gloated at our disgrace' and 'turned everything over' and the person/party being argued with/shouted at are blamed for something(s). The word 'Meribah' and (rabbaḥ/رَبَّح) mean 'monkeyed' (which is from the word (rbḥ/ربح) 'monkey'), and this use of the word originates from the actions of monkeys when they get into land and wreak havoc—pulling out stalks of crop, smashing, flattening growing crop, picking off the fruit eating it or throwing it around—and to put it in a nutshell it is the description of when monkeys go berserk whether out of excitement or hostility and tear things up, pull them out, or throw them around, jump around making a lot of noise and chaos. Monkeys have always been part of life in remote Yemen causing a lot of damage to crops and harvests; this animal behaviour is the origins of the word in remote Yemen and its use in the Biblical 'Meribah', and it is in this context the word 'Meribah' has been used with its Yemeni meaning in the Exodus story (Exod.17:1-7) where the people argue with Moses and speak against him to the degree he declares to God that they are aggressive and ready to stone him.

Illicit Sex

In the passage regarding the Yemeni expression 'Cover not their iniquity' under 'Language/Expressions', I have showed the link between the Biblical expression and its Yemeni origins and how it is used in the Bible with the exact same meaning. But this Yemeni 'Cover not their iniquity' expression is also used elsewhere in the Bible with a coded message. The expression itself means that an adulterous or fornicating couple be caught in the act and not provided cover of their shame by God; whether naked or not is not important because the act of illicit sex is the uncovering of a person's nakedness, and does not mean only the two involved in the illicit act, but also means they have (and the accusation is directed at the male fornicator) exposed the nakedness of another man's wife, niece, daughter, etc. therefore it is her male relative/guardian's nakedness and reputation which has been exposed and violated, too. This Yemeni way of seeing things has been used mostly in Leviticus to define what illicit sex is, and again in the David/Bath-sheba story where the wronged husband is named 'Uriah' 'he was made naked/stripped naked' is a symbol of the wrong of adultery; also used in the Saul/David/Jonathan story where Saul is angry at Jonathan for having a romantic and sexual relationship with David and Saul's dialogue is 'do not I know that thou hast chosen the son of Jesse to thine own confusion, and unto the confusion of thy mother's nakedness?'—in all mentions of 'uncovering nakedness' whether in Leviticus, the David/Bath-sheba/Uriah, or the Saul/David/Jonathan stories, it always represents illicit sex, prohibited relationships, and originates from its Yemeni origin meanings.

Filial Throws

In rural Yemeni life, when a son upsets or disappoints his father, or is cheeky with him or anyone present, the father grabs a stone or whatever non-sharp object his hand can reach and throws it in the direction of the disobedient or 'smart-mouthing' son. But the throwing of the stone/object is done in a way that it does not land in the son, or if it does strike the son it does not cause any hurt or pain—it is thrown by the father to express anger, disappointment or displeasure at the son's actions or comments; and the son always has time to pull or dive away from the stone/object's trajectory, and flees if what misbehaviour he has done is serious, but if what he has done is neither offensive nor serious he will simply avoid the missile but remain in his father's presence. If what he has done is of a serious nature, or offensive, or great disobedience—the son will flee from his father's presence and hide and wait near the home, e.g. behind rocks or behind the stables until his father's anger dissipates and he returns home.

This throwing of an object towards an offensive, disappointing or disobedient son is a paternal expression of anger and disappointment, and an act of warning and discipline. The OT authors have used this rural Yemeni paternal way of expressing disappointment and warning towards sons in the Saul/David/Jonathan story—of course, because it is a fictional story the stone/small object has been replaced by a javelin (this has also been done to emphasise the graveness of what David and Jonathan have done and the seriousness of endangering the kingdom), but the expression as disappointment and warning has been left intact. Even if the story narrates that Saul wants David dead, had this been the intention of the narrative in the story, a seasoned warrior like Saul would not have missed his mark while his target is in an enclosed space playing a musical instrument—but the point of using this Yemeni gesture is made by having every time Saul hurls a javelin towards David, that it misses. Further proof the Biblical author(s) meant this to be understood is shown after twice or thrice hurling a javelin towards David and missing (with David fleeing before re-turning, or wanting to return to Saul's presence/company) is the story has Saul hurling a javelin at his own son Jonathan (whom he is also disappointed in and angry at), Saul clearly does not want to kill Jonathan—he is concerned with Jonathan being prevented from becoming king, but the expression and warning is the same as towards David 'stop what you're doing, it is wrong; I'm angry and disappointed in you. This is a warning' which is what the ever-missing paternal-javelin also indicates just as it does between fathers and sons of Yemeni life which this gesture has been taken from.

'And it came to pass on the morrow, that the evil spirit from God came upon Saul, and he prophesied in the midst of the house: and David played with his hand, as at other times: and *there was* a javelin in Saul's hand. And Saul cast the javelin for he said, I will smite David even unto the wall *with it.* And David avoided out of his presence twice.' 'And the evil spirit from the Lord was upon Saul, as he sat in his house with his javelin in his hand: and David played with *his* hand, And Saul sought to smite David even to the wall with the javelin; but he slipped away out of Saul's presence, and he smote the javelin into the wall: and David fled, and escaped that night.' 'For as long as the son of Jesse liveth upon the ground, thou shalt not be established, nor thy kingdom. Wherefore now send and fetch him unto me, for he shall surely die. And Jonathan answered Saul his father, and said unto him, Wherefore shall he be slain? what hath he done? And Saul cast a javelin at him to smite him: whereby Jonathan knew that it was determined of his father to slay David. So Jonathan arose from the table in fierce anger, and did eat no meat the second day of the month: for he was grieved for David, because his father had done him shame.'. Note that Saul throwing the javelin towards Jonathan does not cause the latter to flee—he knows (as per the author wants it to be) it is a gesture of disappointment and warning—the text has Jonathan remaining seated, he only gets up and leaves, refusing to eat, because he is angry and ashamed because of his father's response and stance towards David. (1Sam.18:10-11; 19:9-10; 20:31-34).

Emergency Call

In remote Yemeni life, the way of life has not changed much since antiquity. Part of this way of life is encountering dangerous predators, animals which a person alone cannot save himself/herself from, as well as the dangers from the evil side of human nature. There was no police, and no telephones to dial '999' to call in an emergency when in danger—there still is not in these areas, but a way of life since antiquity and still used today is a call made as loud as one can scream/shout when in danger the words 'wa lwf/(or)wa lyf' over and over again to be heard from all around, and as far as possible, and everyone who hears the call to be saved drops what they are doing and races towards the point the person is shouting from. It does and has saved lives from being murdered or beaten up by another person, it saves them from being killed by an animal if there are people close enough to save the victim as well as catch the culprit accused of attacking or attempting to murder.

The word (lyf/lwf/ليث/لوث) means 'shout/cries out loud', and the person who is 'lyf'-ing/'lwf'-ing is 'shouting loud' to be saved. When someone feels another is getting too excited and raising his/her voice too loud, they will indicate to him/her to lower their voice by saying 'why are you lwf-ing/lyf-ing [shouting for help] at me?'. This 'lwf/lyf' way of hollering for help in Yemeni culture has been used by the authors of the Bible to give 'Goliath' his name which means 'came-shouted', and as his name suggests all he does from when he is introduced is shout loudly: he shouts challenges at Saul's army every day for forty days, and although he is described as being a giant, a champion. i.e. a seasoned expert warrior/soldier—yet all he does is shout out challenges/speeches and is killed without any fighting on his part in the Biblical story.

Pouring Pur

Other aspects from Yemeni way of life existing for as long as can be remembered and remaining alive into current times, which has also been used in the Bible to create dramatic events and in turn become festivals first in storyland then in real life when the Biblical stories have become religious text to some, is the use of what is a mundane action of a noun/adjective/verb/adverb in daily life and used in sorcery by sorcerers in remote Yemen, and making it the plot and event(s) in the Biblical story. 'Pur' 'ruin/destroy/go bad/pour out' 'lose taste/flavour/reputation/spoil/become stale'; it has many neutral and negative meanings with different applications, but they all mean going from one particular state to a worse state. It can mean to do bad, to cause your own or another's reputation to be bad; it can mean to go stale, to lose flavour. It is the name of a funnel-like clay cup placed on the top of a kooz (hubbly-bubbly-waterpipe) which is filled with a tobacco mix called 'koobab' and topped with red-hot coals; this cup is called '(Puri)/booree/بوري' and when the flavour is lost/fades through smoking, the adjective to describe its loss of flavour or its taste gone bad is 'baayer/باير' which is out of the same root word of 'Pur/Bur/بور'. When it loses flavour the 'booree' cup is taken outside and tipped on the ground, the person pokes around in the used tobacco mix and coals of which some will have gone out while others are still hot to locate a cold piece of charcoal used at the bottom of the bottleneck of the booree to put back in its place (as it is a stopper not allowing the tobacco mix to fall into the pipe body of the kooz—it allows only the smoke to pass through). After putting the 'stopper' (<u>ss</u>**kh**ree/صخري/rock) in its place, fresh tobacco is crumbled into the booree/puri and the live coals picked out of the mess of coal, ashes and stale tobacco mix.

Here it is important to point out how pagan 'seers' and 'sorcerers', at least in remote Yemen, perform some parts of their sorcery: it resembles the mundane action of tipping out and re-picking useable elements when re-topping the Pur/booree cup. The sorcerers (kohen) read the future, or tell their customers what action to take, by throwing things such as incense, as well as other less pleasant things into a bowl of hot coals or other cup made of the same pottery as the 'booree' cups, and then tipping them out onto the ground or into a wide metal pan, and either using a finger or a stick to poke around in the hot coals, ashes, sticks and whatever else that particular sorcerer/seer used (the sorcerer asks the customer questions regarding his/her desire/question/issue while he (the sorcerer/kohen) is throwing in the elements of his craft into the fire bowl of hot coal which will be tipped according to the ritual's timing) to tell the customer his/her future, or to cast a spell which is usually to harm another person. This is where the Biblical authors being familiar with these Yemeni ways of life, and the meanings of the word in Arabic from the meaning of the word 'Pur', to the name of the cup 'Puri/booree' whose stale contents are tipped out, poked around then picked out during smoking, to the methods used in sorcery which resemble to a great extent the action of pouring/tipping and topping of a Puri cup with stale and fresh tobacco and hot coals. Think also of sorcerers/seers who use reading tea leaves and coffee residue for people—the excess liquid is drunk or tipped out, the cup overturned before the tea leaves/coffee grounds are read to tell the person's future. Then look at the word Pur/Purim as explained earlier can mean to ruin, destroy, go bad, lose taste, lose flavour, lose reputation; Purim means the same except it describes giving the negative meaning to a group of people, and is always used when someone or something has caused a group of people (whether rightfully or wrongfully) to lose their reputation, lose face, have a bad thing exposed about them.

In Esther, the authors have used the Yemeni meaning and actions of Pur and Purim as well as the actions of sorcerers, showing the authors' Yemeni origins and their familiarity with the Yemeni way of life which fills the pages and stories of the Bible. They have used this Yemeni way of life in Esther as both the way in which Haman had intended to kill the innocent Jews, and then the same when the tables are turned and the Jews use it to ruin, kill, destroy those whom had intended to harm them as well as to kill those whom had nothing to do with Haman and his plans—but they show exactly how the inspiration and word-names are chosen from Yemeni ways of life: 'And he thought scorn to lay hands on Mordecai alone; for they had shewed him the people of Mordecai: wherefore Haman sought to destroy all the Jews that *were* throughout the whole kingdom of Ahasuerus, *even* the people of Mordecai. In the first month, that *is*, the month Nisan, in the twelfth year of Ahasuerus, they cast Pur, that *is*, the lot, before Haman from day to day, and from month to month, *to* the twelfth *month*, that *is*, the month of Adar. And Haman said unto king Ahasuerus, There is a certain people scattered abroad and dispersed among the people in all the provinces of thy kingdom; and their laws *are* diverse from all people; neither keep they the king's laws: therefore it *is* not for the king's profit to suffer them.'. Note here how Pur is expressed and connected to how sorcery/seers 'lots' are cast, and also in connection to how Haman is destroying another party's (the Jews) reputation, convincing the king that the Jews are ruining the king, as well as Haman seeking to destroy them physically.

'If it please the king, let it be written that they may be destroyed: and I will pay ten thousand talents of silver to the hands of those that have the charge of the business, to bring *it* into the king's treasuries. And the king took his ring from his hand, and gave it unto Haman the son of Hammedatha the Agagite, the Jew's enemy. And the king said unto Haman, The silver is given unto thee, the people also, to do with them as it seemeth good to thee. Then were the king's scribes called on the thirteenth day of the first month, and there was written according to all that Haman had commanded unto the king's lieutenants, and to the governors that *were* over every province, and to the rulers of every people of every province according to the writing thereof, and *to* every people after their language; in the name of king Ahasuerus was it written, and sealed with the king's ring. And the letters were sent by posts into all the kings provinces, to destroy, to kill, and to cause to perish, all Jews, both young and old, little children and women, in one day, *even* upon the thirteenth *day* of the twelfth month, which is the month Adar, and *to take* the spoil of them for a prey. The copy of the writing for a commandment to be given in every province was published unto all the people, that they should be ready against that day.'.

After Esther and Mordecai succeed in convincing Ahasuerus to change his mind, it is Haman and his people whose reputation is destroyed, their lives taken away, and all the other 'peoples' whom are slain by the Jews—so 'Pur' and 'Purim' applies to Haman and his side in this latter part of the story: 'So they hanged Haman on the gallows that he had prepared for Mordecai. Then was the king's wrath pacified.' 'Wherein the king granted the Jews which *were* in every city to gather themselves together, and to stand for their life, to destroy, to slay, and to cause to perish, all the power of the people and province that would assault them, *both* little ones and women, and to take the spoil of them for a prey.' 'Thus the Jews destroyed all their enemies with the stroke of the sword, and slaughter, and destruction, and did what they would unto those that hated them.' 'On that day the number of those that were slain in Shushan the palace was brought before the king. And the king said unto Esther the queen, The Jews have slain and destroyed five hundred men in Shushan the palace, and the ten sons of Haman; what have they done in the rest of the king's provinces? now what is thy petition? and it shall be granted thee: or what is thy request further? and it shall be done. Then said Esther, If it please the king, let it be granted to the Jews which *are* in Shushan to do to morrow also according unto today's decree, and let Haman's ten sons be hanged upon the gallows. And the king commanded it so to be done: and the decree was given at Shushan; and they hanged Haman's ten sons. For the Jews that *were* in Shushan gathered themselves together, and stood for their lives, and had rest from their enemies, and slew of their foes seventy and five thousand…' 'and on the fourteenth day of the same rested they, and made it a day of feasting and gladness.' 'And Mordecai wrote these things, and sent letters to all the Jews that *were* in all the provinces of the king Ahasuerus, *both* nigh and far. To stablish *this* among them, that they should keep the fourteenth day of the month Adar, and the fifteenth day of the same, yearly. As the days wherein the Jews rested from their enemies, and the month which was turned unto them from sorrow to joy, and of sending portions from one to another, and gifts to the poor. And the Jews undertook to do as they had begun, and as Mordecai had written unto them: Because Haman the son of Hammedatha, the Agagite, the enemy of all the Jews, had devised against all the Jews to destroy them, and had cast Pur, that *is*, the lot, to consume them, and to destroy them; But when *Esther* came before the king, he commanded by letters that his wicked device, which he devised against the Jews, should return upon his own head, and that he and his sons should be hanged upon the gallows. Wherefore they called these days Purim after the name of Pur. Therefore for all the words of this letter, and *of that* which had seen concerning this matter, and which had come unto them, The Jews ordained and took upon them, and upon their seed, and upon all such as joined themselves unto them, so as it should not fail, that they would keep these two days according to their writing, and according to their *appointed* time every year; And that these days *should be* remembered and kept throughout every generation, every family, every province, and every city; and *that* these days of Purim should not fail from among the Jews, nor the memorial of them perish from their seed. Then Esther the queen, the daughter of Abihail, and Mordecai the Jew, wrote with all authority, to confirm this second letter of Purim. And he sent letters unto all the Jews, to the hundred twenty and seven provinces of the kingdom of Ahasuerus, *with* words of peace and truth. To confirm these days of Purim in *their* times appointed, according as Mordecai the Jew, and Esther the queen had enjoined them, and as they had decreed for themselves and for their seed, the matters of their fastings and their cry. And the decree of Esther confirmed these matters of Purim; and it was written in the book.'.

The destruction of Haman and his people's reputation, then the destruction and slaughter of people's lives by the 'Jews' (according to the story) in many different provinces coordinated all on the same day, the authors of the story bringing back the mention of Pur and Purim which means all the above actions and also reminding the audience of the story that these actions resulted out of sorcery/casting lots—and it shows how the authors used the Yemeni meanings of Pur/Purim in its negative application, and also in its mundane action in smoking and its use tied to the same action in sorcery, all to create dramatic events in the story, to be the storyline, then to be the basis of a feast and celebration which in the future would be adopted as a celebration in the real world. (Esther.3:6-14; 7:10; 8:11; 9:5, 11-32).

Epilepsy and Possession

In rural Yemen, people who suffer from fits (epilepsy) are called 'Migdol/مجدول' 'thrown/been thrown' 'of fits/suffers epilepsy/possessed by demons' (word 'migdol' also can mean 'killed' 'wooden block/wedge'). They are said to 'yigdal/يجدل' 'he gets thrown' 'he throws' 'he gets fits' 'he gets possessed by demons', or they have 'gadal/جدل' 'throw/throwing/fits'—the meanings of all these words is 'thrown' (to throw a stone, object, person, anything) because when a person gets these fits they involuntary throw themselves down to the ground and their limbs are thrown about as they convulse. Many people know and do consider it a disease, but still many believe it is a disease caused by being possessed by demons. It is also believed that a person who suffers fits and seizures is close to God, deities and can see the future and/or know things he/she could not possibly know (such as things done secretly or privately, or far away by other people). This belief has existed since ancient times in remote Yemen and continues to be believed, and the disease is called 'gadal/جدل' 'throw/throwing/fits' of which the words 'migdol' and 'yigdal' stem from.

The use of this Arabic word and its Yemeni use to describe people who have fits and are believed to be possessed by demons, and/or can see the future and the unknown has been used in the OT to describe people close to God such as 'Igdaliah', and has been used in the NT to create and describe Mary Magdalene her surname meaning 'of being thrown around/to the ground' 'throwing me around' 'thrown down/away' 'having fits/epilepsy/possessed by demons' and in the story she has been possessed by seven devils and is a direct reference of the disease she suffered and was cured from. Also, the resurrected Jesus appears to her first showing her closeness to God (Jesus being God in the story) i.e. exactly what the word has always meant and the condition believed to be in Yemen: 'Now when *Jesus* was risen early the first day of the week, he appeared first to Mary Magdalene, out of whom he had cast seven devils.' (Mark.16:9).

Although in the NT the authors' narration/expression is advanced (compared to the narration of the OT), they still use the Arabic language with specific Yemeni and Arabian Peninsula word-meanings for all the people and place names featuring in the stories, and they still use Yemeni expressions, and ways of Yemeni life which still exists as lived and spoken to this day.

Chores

Another 'part and parcel' of Yemeni life which has not changed over the millennia is the hard work and many chores needing to be done every single day, which are hard and time-consuming due to living at a time (in the Biblical authors' time) and place (both in the past and present of remote Yemen, and possibly all of Yemen in the ancient past before modernisation) where preparing a meal involves a lot of hard work such as grinding the grain, bringing the firewood to the oven's area—both are extremely strenuous chores which cause pain and fatigue, to make bread; the baking of bread in an ancient oven is gruelling in itself as the woman/girl baking has to remain in front of the oven to heat it by feeding more wood into it, then to apply the dough into it which involves her arm reaching into extremely high temperatures of the oven's body, as well as her face, head and upper torso being blasted by the heat—and this is not to mention other chores which are needed to be done to prepare the same meal. Also fetching water is a hard and time-consuming task.

Due to this being the way of life, with it being difficult and time-consuming the whole family does his/her chores in order to survive—and anyone that does not perform their chores, does not help out, is complained about if not directly lambasted. These are difficult, tiring and time-taking things to do even if it is the daily grind for a family alone, but when there are guests or labourers to feed, the individual chores increase in size, in time taken to complete, and the number of times it needs to be done or fetched so as to suffice the increase in persons needed to be fed and provided for. Naturally, the fatigue felt by the person(s) conducting these chores increases, as does the anger and upset with those whom are lazy and do not help at all, or do not help as much as they should. This reality in the way of life in rural Yemen where the terrain and circumstances are harsh is portrayed in Luke, where both Martha's role and even her name 'unhappy/not satisfied/discontent' express this in the story where Jesus and disciples are her guests, and she is overwhelmed by the burden of the chores and expresses her displeasure over her sister, Mary, just sitting around and not helping out 'and a certain woman named Martha received him into her house. And she had a sister called Mary, who also sat at Jesus' feet, and heard his word. But Martha was cumbered about much serving, and came to him, and said, Lord, dost thou not care that my sister hath left me to serve alone? Bid her therefore that she help me.' just like mothers, sisters, brothers, mothers-in-law say in rural Yemen about those who do not help out (Luke.10:38-42).

Grains and Crop Storage

Most of life in rural Yemen is around chores, actions and work related to agriculture, preparing food, fetching resources needed on a daily basis and taking care of those resources. One such activity is how crops and grain are taken care of. Once grain has been threshed it is piled into heaps, the action is called (kwwn/كَوِّن) 'make into peaked heaps' 'pile up/heap up'; after winnowing to get rid of the chaff, the grain is stored in barrels, sacks and cans for future use (up until the 1980s people used to heap it/kwwn in underground rooms/granaries. Storing crops used as animal fodder into peaked ricks is also called (kwwn/كَوِّن) and the rick itself called (knnah/كَنَّه) 'a peak/a shelter at the top of a house/a peaked structure (usually of animal fodder)'; making it into a peaked formation protects it from wind and rain.

Another part of life in rural Yemen in taking care of resources is protecting them from the elements, this includes firewood needed within the week (not the firewood stored outside for the months ahead) which if it is soaked with rain will not ignite and they will not be able to prepare food. If it starts raining or looks like it is going to rain, people begin to pick out of the wood storage area a few days' worth of firewood and carry it inside the house—this activity/action is called 'konan' and the word (knn/كَنّن) 'shelter/take inside/store inside/shelter from the rain'. To 'konan/knn' is applied to other resources such as grain, flour, and even to people who shelter from the rain; and resources are not only sheltered from the rain, but also from the sun, wind and any other elements which can spoil human or animal food.

These very Yemeni words with their exact meanings and ways of everyday life have been used by the Biblical author(s) in Chronicles and for the exact same use in the story as in real life: to pile up/heap, and shelter/store inside food produce—and as throughout the Bible it has given the character concerned with this activity the name of the activity, in Chronicles it is Cononiah 'gathered into peaked heaps-he/him' 'sheltered from weather(rain/sun/wind)-he/him' created for a story about heaps and piles of food from tithes which are to be brought inside and stored (2Chr.31:5-12). The adverb of Yemeni origin from Yemeni way of life is given to the character in the Bible put in charge of heaps of produce, stored inside, just like it was meant to be understood from the word-name given by the author.

Entertainment

Part of rural Yemeni life is that most of its entertainment is telling stories which have been told from generation to generation. They are called 'samaara/سمآره' 'nightime story/fictional story/staying up late night story' and are usually told at night because they are told during nights when people stay awake for fun, and also when people are guarding something at night and need to stay awake, hence the name 'samaara' from the word (smr/samar/سمر) 'stayed awake/stayed up all (or late) night/telling nightime story'. It is this word which has given the fictional 'Samaria' its meaning as the Biblical authors have used it to indicate the story they are narrating is fictional. There is another form which is more like a riddle told in a story with the audience having to guess the name of characters or figure out what will happen according to the word-name of the character and these stories are called 'samaaya/سمآيه' 'naming/named/naming story'.

There are many different stories all told in dramatic narrative, and they all have themes, humour, drama, erotic, horror, and sometimes with a moral message embedded, while some are just meant to be funny and amusing, and the funny stories are always laced with an erotic nature. Two examples of such samaara stories in the OT are Samson which is a prime example, it follows the same themes and structure of samaara stories; and Esther is another example no different than the samaara tales told to entertain. All the stories in the Bible are Samaaras and Samaayas which rely on fictional word-names to create character and place names as well as to indicate and relay the events in the story. What has happened to the Bible is due to authors from later times wanting to make their religious beliefs accepted and promoted, they added religious additions to these stories, but they remain the same as tales told to entertain which have been passed down since antiquity in rural Yemen. Elija and Elisha are also a type of samaara tale: the characters of these stories either have superhuman strength, or are exceedingly clever—and always succeed against great odds stacked against them, sexual innuendo as well as openly erotic themes and actions happen within the stories; look at Samson's actions, look at Esther and Mordecai and how they expose or frame two of the king's servants whom are executed, and then Esther and Mordecai use this event to remind the king so they can shore themselves and their people. Note how Elijah and Elisha just make things happen and deliver sarcastic punchlines in their stories.

Another major element in Yemeni samaaras is many contain a character who either does or claims to 'slaughter a thousand, take captive a thousand, and sets free a thousand', someone is always coming out on top while another is either humiliated or defeat; how the major characters meet their demise or end up is done like slap-stick comedy: look at all the Biblical stories where thousands, or tens of thousands are killed per area or 'peoples' completely wiped out only to pop-up again later in the story in their great numbers only to be wiped out again by the tens of thousands. Look at how Samson ends up captured—by a woman using her 'charms' to 'vex his soul unto death' which leads to him telling her his secret. Take the scene between Esther, Haman and the king—remember also how names in the Bible always reflect something about the character or to happen in the story—Haman's surname is Hammedatha 'here is the one covered with a blanket/sheet' and how does he meet his demise? Both he and the king have been drinking wine, the king steps out while Haman Hammedatha is begging Esther to spare his life, he accidentally falls onto the bed—his surname 'covered with blanket/sheet' reflects this will happen—the king steps back inside and mistakes Haman (who has fallen onto the bed and is begging for his life) as wanting to have sex with Esther. And Haman is immediately executed. Samson uses a donkey jawbone to kill those he is angry with—it is a Yemeni expression to call someone who is stubborn, stupid or brash a 'donkey's chin' or 'donkey, chin of a donkey'.

Language

The greatest and most used way of Yemeni life by the authors of the Bible is the Arabian Peninsula Arabic language. From the beginning at Genesis and throughout the OT, the authors who could only have been Yemeni and Arabian Peninsula Arabs (Saudi Arabian) have used compound words of the Arabic language to make names for the Bible's characters and places, and these names in their Arabic meanings reflect exactly what happens in the Biblical stories where they are mentioned—if they were not Arabic, and had no meaning in Arabic, they would not have the correct meanings as displayed in the Bible and exactly as the Biblical authors meant them to have. Even in the NT, although the use of what seems to be Greek names has increased (and who knows how early the Biblical stories circulated in ancient Greece and influenced the naming of people as how they are used in the Bible shows they are Arabic compound words) they still pronounce as Arabic words and reflect Arabic words and its meanings as they are in rural Yemen and how it is meant to be in the story by its authors—the Biblical text proves the relation to the word-name and the event(s) in the respective story. As discussed before, either the Biblical authors chose Greek names of people and places for the NT stories because of how they pronounce in Arabic and can be understood just like all the authors' wordplay, or these word-names did not exist in ancient Greece and Rome until the popularity of the Biblical stories spread to them, and people named their children after these stories, and in all cases all the names in the NT are Arabic compound words which reflect what happens in the story.

Clothing

In this part I will be discussing the use of uniquely Yemeni apparel as well as substances used in adornment and when and how they have been incorporated into the Biblical stories and made into objects/articles of major importance in the Bible, its stories, and therefore into religion.

Ephod

To begin with, a wrap-around skirt is a very popular Yemeni garment worn by men and boys; it comes in the form sewn at where both ends meet, or just an open rectangular garment (both ends not sewn together)—and both forms need to be wrapped around the waist or loins and are wrapped in an artful manner which not only makes its wearer look smart, but is also very important to be done correctly, by keeping the garment taut while wrapping it around the waist, folding its top end and securing its sides so that it does not suddenly unwrap or fall off while a person is walking, running, seated, working, etc. (although simply adding a belt to the process under the top folds can secure it because there were no belts in the past, and up until recently modern belts were not used as part of wearing the 'ephod' which means 'wrap-around skirt', most men and boys do not use a belt and wear it without a belt as is the old way and the norm. The nature of this wrap-around skirt (ephod), plus the fact that underwear was non-existent in the past in this region, and even in the 1990s underwear was only worn by men who returned from working in Saudi Arabia (and was viewed as a strange and unnecessary garment) due to this, young boys often accidentally expose themselves when sitting or squatting, and men and older boys follow a decorum when sitting/squatting which ensures they do not expose their genitals. The garment is always made of beautiful fabric with comfortable textures and beautiful patterns, and is used not only as clothing but is also used to contain precious things which are wrapped inside it for safekeeping; it is also used to contain the most precious thing: a baby: two ends of an ephod are tied to one side of a mother's bed as a rocking cradle for babies, as well as one or two of an expecting father's ephods are cut up into rectangular pieces by expecting mothers to swaddle babies in from birth. This garment is called (photạh/ephoṭ/فوطه/ايفوط/ئيفوط) singular, (phwaṭ/phoṭaat /فواط/فوطآت) plural, the act of putting it on is (ephoṭ/phwwṭ/فوّط/ئيفوط ، ايفوط) 'place skirt around/dress with skirt/wrap around' 'put on a skirt', and this Yemeni clothing has been used as the main garment for Aaron as high priest, and other priests throughout the Bible. It has also been used as a source of divination, and directly linked to holy rituals (which are paganistic in nature) and other items/practises of divination.

Before beginning with where, how and why it was used in the Bible as divination and other holy rituals, first I will prove the ephod/ئيفوط ، ايفوط is a wrap-around skirt although it has been erroneously interpreted by people as a kind of tunic which is from erroneous reading, misunderstanding and misinterpretation of the OT, as well as unfamiliarity with the true culture of the authors, audience and stories of the OT, which has led people to believe the 'ephod' of Aaron and high priests and the other garments these characters wear in the Biblical stories to be as popularly believed to be in western culture. If the Bible is understood and read correctly it shows the ephod is a skirt and the 'breastplate' is not a breastplate at all, but a pouch worn on top of the ephod directly around the waist. First, the OT interpretation as it stands in English is full of mistakes, mostly because the words are from a language which everyone claims no longer exists, 'Hebrew', which is partially true because 'Hebrew' was never a language as I have already shown, but was a code made out of Arabic with some letters swapped around in an attempt to keep knowledge limited to those in charge of Biblical texts. These same errors in misinterpreting the words have been made in translating and understanding what has become 'shoulder-pieces' in the making of Aaron's high priest garments—and the same goes for 'breastplate'. First there is a need to go through the names of these garments and what they mean in the Yemeni Arabic vernacular which perfectly explains the meanings of all the names (people/places) in the OT because Arabic is the original language of the original Bible. To know the meaning of the garments' nouns will show what they are.

Ephod: ئيفوط ، ايفوط 'wrap-around skirt' 'place skirt around/dress with skirt' 'put on a skirt'. In more than one example the Biblical text shows people in their usual garb can expose themselves (their genitals), considered disgraceful, embarrassing and a sin, which can happen in mere movements such as: walking up steps; think of how a person needs to bend and squat when slaughtering an animal then cleaning and cutting up its meat for sacrifice; think of the movements made when a person has his hands full and needs to pour incense and other things onto hot coals; the movement needed to bring in firewood, water, etc.; twice it is mentioned that God does not want those ministering at his altars exposing their genitals—which means the type of clothing they wore are prone to cause this wardrobe malfunction and is why specific instructions are given on how to make the ephod, by making it a front and back piece sewed together at the top corners only, which allows better movement imagined for the 'priest/sorcerer/kohen' in the Biblical stories and why 'breeches' are still needed to be made to ensure no genitals are exposed. Once in Exod.20 God tells Moses the altars should not have steps to avoid exposing their genitals; in the second instance it is after instructing Moses how Aaron and the priests' clothes should be made and the first load of clothes includes: ephod, robe, breastplate, coat, mitre, and girdle—if all these cannot cover a person's modesty it is because of the nature and length of these garments which supports the ephod being a wrap-around skirt and is why the Biblical story has God instruct the making of more garments and specifically underwear, 'breeches', to cover the private parts as otherwise with only the ephod and the nature of this garment and the nature of the priests' work—genital exposure while performing all the rituals and their tasks is certain. In 2Sam. because David is dancing while wearing an ephod, he exposes his private parts to everybody present which upsets his wife Michal:

'And if thou wilt make me an altar of stone, thou shalt not build it out of hewn stone: for if thou lift up thy tool upon it, thou hast polluted it. Neither shalt thou go up by steps unto mine altar, that thy nakedness be not discovered thereon.' 'And thou shalt make them linen breeches to cover their nakedness; from the loins even unto the thighs they shall reach: And they shall be upon Aaron, and upon his sons, when they come in unto the tabernacle of the congregation, or when they come near unto the altar to minister in the holy *place*; that they bare not iniquity, and die: *it shall be* a statute for ever unto him and his seed after him.'; 'And David danced before the Lord with all his might; and David *was* girded with a linen ephod...Michal Saul's daughter looked through a window, and saw David leaping and dancing before the Lord... And Michal the daughter of Saul came out to meet David, and said, How glorious was the king of Israel today, who uncovered himself today in the eyes of the handmaids of his servants, as one of the vain fellows shamelessly uncovereth himself! And David said unto Michal, *It was* before the Lord, which chose me before thy father, and before all his house, to appoint me over all the people of the Lord, over Israel: therefore I will play before the Lord. And I will yet be more vile than thus, and will be base in mine own sight: and of the maidservants which thou has spoken of, of them shall I be had in honour.' (Exod.20:25-26; 28:42-43; 2Sam.6:14-22).

Although earlier in the Bible the accidental exposure of private parts is narrated as a fatal sin, at 1Sam. the ephod is used to indicate Samuel's accidental exposure is not a sin as he is a child, innocent, compared to the intentional sins of the priest adults around him, the sons of Eli; and the way the mention of the ephod (just like in David's story) explains how they (David/Samuel) exposed themselves is further proof the ephod is a wrap-around skirt: 'Now the sons of Eli *were* sons of Belial: they knew not the Lord.', it explains their guilt and sins then compares them to and points out Samuel's innocence: 'Wherefore the sin of the young men was very great before the Lord: for men abhorred the offering of the Lord. But Samuel ministered before the Lord, *being* a child, girded with a linen ephod.' (1Sam.2:12-18).

Now, how the ephod is described as, and as per the instructions of the making of the garments in the Biblical stories, show it is a wrap-around skirt. To begin with, the names of each garment:

- Ephod; 'ēpōḏ; ايفوط ، ئيفوط 'wrap-around skirt' (similar to kilt, but longer) 'place skirt around/dress with skirt' 'put on a skirt'

- Breastplate; is correctly: choshen, hosen; خُصَن ، حوصَن 'protection' 'protection amulet'; and can mean a protective anything, but in regions where attitudes and life, beliefs and practises have remained unchanged since antiquity a 'choshen/hosen' 'protection/protection amulet' is a pouch or amulet worn on the body which could be around the neck like a necklace, on the arm, waist, ankle, or tucked in a crease or fold of the clothing. This pouch/amulet contains either a piece of paper with a protective spell or prayer inside it, or it contains a substance be it herbs, seeds, anything which the sorcerer determined as protective for the customer. The names and nature of the other garments and the 'breastplate' itself as described in the Biblical text prove it is worn around the waist and not a 'breastplate' at all. Cp: ḥos̲s̲en, ḥoos̲s̲en.

- Robe; me'il; مَع ال 'with the' and also مَئِل ، مَئيل 'short dress' (slightly longer than the length of a modern shirt). By the time I lived in the mountains of Yemen it was no longer worn by men and only women used it underneath a dress if the chest opening had been accidentally been cut too large during tailoring, also worn as a nightie. It is described as 'the robe of the ephod' supporting it as an accessory with the ephod such as a 'short dress/shirt' would complete the outfit by covering the upper torso while the ephod is a lower body garment. Cp: ma'-il, ma-il, ma-eyl.

- Coat; ketonet; كَتونَت 'coat/coated/covered' and can be like a long coat or short in length like a jacket. The garment is open at the front and does not close up, it is worn above the other clothes and leaves them visible from the front opening. Cp: ketoonet.

- Girdle; chesheb; حيشَب ، حَشَب 'clinging on/to/around the waist' 'carrying on the waist' from the word (ḥs̲h̲b/حشب) 'carried on/around the waist', and the phrase (carry/aḥs̲h̲b/احشب) (he is carrying/yḥshb/يحشب) (carry him/it(an order)/aḥshubeeh/احشُبيه) are in different forms and all mean 'to carry on the waist'; its most used application is to tell or describe someone to pick up a child and carry him/her on the waist. In the priestly garments it is a type of rope/fabric which goes around the waist. Cp: ḥesheb, ḥeysheb.

The instructions in the Bible of how to make Aaron's garments are the clearest part which shows the ephod and the misnomered 'breastplate' which correctly is an amulet/pouch, are both garments worn around the waist and on the lower body, beginning from the waist and reach below. 'And they shall take gold, and blue, and purple, and scarlet, and fine linen. And they shall make the ephod *of* gold, *of* blue, and *of* scarlet, and fine twined lined, with cunning work. It shall have the two shoulderpieces thereof joined at the two edges thereof; and *so* it shall be joined together.'. And the mistake in interpretation is made in the word for 'shoulderpieces' when it should correctly read 'sides' as the same word is used to describe the sides of the tabernacle, the sides of the courtgate, to describe how a border reaches the side of the sea, to describe when given the location of which side is which on whose border, in giving directions of many locations—all use the same word to mean 'side' which has been misinterpreted in Aaron's garment-making story as 'shoulderpieces'.

But you can see how human error can cause the misinterpretation: because whoever first misinterpreted the word was thinking of clothing the human body, easy to inject his own idea (by mistake) that what is meant is 'shoulder'(ketepot, kitpot; كَتِفت ، كَتَفت 'shoulder of' 'shouldered' 'carried on shoulder(s)')—and that is why the same word has been interpreted as both 'the shoulders' and 'the shoulderpieces' where at other places in the Bible it is interpreted as 'sides', and how this imputation can have the exact same word with no difference in the original text to be interpreted as both 'the shoulders' and 'the shoulderpieces'. Furthermore where this wrong interpretation is made is due to the Biblical authors' use of wordplay and encrypting the language: the word ketepot, kitpot can very well mean; كَتِفت ، كَتَفت 'shoulder of' in parts of the Bible, but in context with what is being described in the creation of priestly clothes it is: ketepot, kitpot; قِطَفت ، قَطّفت 'fold side/edge and sew' and are words used to describe a certain step in sewing, and has many meanings related to sewing and tailoring such as 'make it tighter' 'folds the hem'(by sewing the edge/fold) 'makes a channel' (by folding some of the fabric in the garment to leave a tubular gap which string, twine or a ribbon can be pushed through to be used as a drawstring). But the error is whoever were first to re-interpret the meanings of these words were not familiar with the true meanings, and it is very easy to see how a person's imagination or misunderstanding of the garment-making passages thought they had 'shoulderpieces' i.e. garments/pieces worn on the shoulder instead of its true meaning 'sides'.

'And the curious girdle of the ephod, which *is* upon it, shall be of the same, according to the work thereof; *even of* gold, *of* blue, and scarlet, and fine twined linen.' Although in popular western belief the girdle is believed to be a separate garment/piece placed onto/around the ephod/priest, the verses actually state it is part of the ephod, i.e. it is a drawstring, which even until modernity women in remote Yemen have always used to keep the female version of an ephod which is a large petticoat called 'wzra/gwgra' in its place: the female skirt is a long petticoat worn underneath the dress, the 'girdle/chesheb' also called 'mḥshb' is a string or ribbon tied around the waist, and the skirt's top part is pulled underneath it all around then folded over the ribbon to keep the petticoat in place, or the skirt itself has a ketepot, kitpot; قِطَفت ، قَطّفت sewn in which is a few centimetres of the fabric at the top all around the skirt is folded and is sewn into place leaving an open part right in the middle at the front where the two ends of drawstring pushed through the channel made will emerge, and it allows the channel resulting from the 'ketepot' to keep the drawstring in place which in itself keeps the skirt/petticoat in place on the waist. This is what is meant by the verse that the 'girdle of the ephod, which is upon it, shall be of the same,' it is incorporated into the garment of the ephod—not only just made of the same fibres. So the girdle is at the top part of the ephod, around the waist, making the ephod clearly a garment of which the top part begins at the waist (although its name 'ephod' is clear enough to identify it as a wrap-around skirt).

The misinterpretation of the meaning of the word being 'shoulders' and 'shoulderpieces' continues—whereas it should read 'sides': 'And thou shalt take two onyx stones, and grave on them the names of the children of Israel: Six of their names on one stone, and *the other* six names of the rest on the other stone, according to their birth. With the work of an engraver in stone, *like* the engravings of a signet, shalt thou engrave the two stones with the names of the children of Israel: thou shalt make them to be set in ouches of gold. And thou shalt put the two stones upon the shoulders of the ephod *for* stones of memorial unto the children of Israel: and Aaron shall bear their names before the Lord upon his two shoulders for a memorial.'—again, only error, misunderstanding and misinterpretation has made the 'sides of the ephod' into the 'shoulders of the ephod' therefore erroneously placing the two stones of memorial on the 'shoulderpieces' of a skirt which does not have shoulders. Regarding Aaron bearing the names, it should read 'Aaron shall bear their names before the Lord upon his two sides for a memorial' because in the culture of the people who the language of the Bible originates from, the person's 'side' is indicated and used in speech to indicate a person's responsibility. Even if we were to accept that in verse Exod.28:12 and specifically the last half 'upon his two shoulders' as the correct word (but different than that used for the sides of the ephod) being a form of the word 'shoulder' regarding Aaron but definitely not this word regarding the ephod—i.e. figuratively speaking it would still mean Aaron bears the responsibility of these people on his shoulders, it does not mean it literally that the two stones are on his shoulders, but it is a fact that the verse specifically reads 'thou shalt put the two stone upon the **sides** of the ephod for stones of memorial…' but misinterpretation of this chapter has turned it into 'upon the shoulders of the ephod' which is impossible as the ephod is a garment worn around the waist and without shoulders. In its original meanings the 'stones of memorial' would be on each side of the front of the ephod/skirt.

The noun 'breastplate' is also a misinterpretation taking the original word 'choshen/hosen', 'protection/protection amulet' out of context based on the erroneous belief that the ephod has 'shoulderpieces'. The real meaning of the word choshen/hosen is 'protection/protection amulet', also wherever it says 'shoulderpieces' in Aaron's priestly garment story, it should read 'sides' and means the two sides at the front of the ephod (left and right) situated around the waist: 'And thou shalt make ouches *of* gold; And two chains *of* pure gold at the ends; *of* wreathen work shalt thou make them, and fasten the wreathen chains to the ouches. And thou shalt make the breastplate[protection/protection amulet] of judgement with cunning work; after the work of the ephod thou shalt make it; *of* gold, *of* blue, and *of* purple, and *of* scarlet, and *of* fine twined linen, shalt thou make it. Foresquare it shall be *being* doubled; a span *shall be* the length thereof, and a span *shall be* the breadth thereof.'.

It goes on to describe four rows by three columns of precious stones with the names to embellish the misnomered 'breastplate' which is actually 'protection/protection amulet' then: 'And thou shalt make upon the breastplate two rings of gold, and shalt put the two rings of gold on the two ends of the breastplate. And thou shalt put the two wreathen *chains* of gold in the two rings *which are* on the ends of the breastplate. And the other two ends of the two wreathen chains thou shalt fasten in the two ouches, and put them on the shoulderpieces [Should read 'sides'] of the ephod before it.' Note in the original language that the exact same word here translated as 'shoulderpieces' has been translated as the 'sides' of the ephod in the same OT. Correctly, the text states the instructions are that the misnomered 'breastplate' (i.e. protection amulet) attached to ouches should be placed on the sides of the ephod.

'And thou shalt make two rings of gold, and thou shalt put them upon the two ends of the breastplate in the border thereof, which is in the side of the ephod inwards.', the two rings are at the ends of the 'breastplate' (correctly 'protection') on its inner side facing the ephod; 'And two *other* rings of gold thou shalt make, and shalt put them on the two sides of the ephod underneath, towards the forepart thereof, over against the *other* coupling thereof, above the curious girdle of the ephod.'. These two rings are to be attached to the inner side of the front part of the ephod and above the girdle—the rings align with the rings on the inner side of the misnomered 'breastplate'. Note again how the same word interpreted as 'shoulder' and 'shoulderpieces' is now interpreted correctly as 'sides'; also note the girdle is part of the ephod so when the rings are placed on the front part of the ephod they are 'above/on' it. 'And they shall bind the breastplate by the rings thereof unto the rings of the ephod with a lace of blue, that *it* may be above the curious girdle of the ephod, and that the breastplate be not loosed from the ephod.' When the misnomered 'breastplate' ('protection/protection amulet') is finally fastened tightly to the ephod, it is meant to be over the girdle of the ephod, the mistakes in translation of above/on/upon are easy to make, but from the description and instructions in the OT Exod.28, once the 'breastplate' is fastened to ephod, it is on and partially covering the girdle on the waist of the ephod. If it was meant to be a chest-piece or on the area of the upper abdomen there would be no need to emphasise that after fastening it should be positioned above/on the girdle—which is how it has been mistakenly perceived as can be seen from the outfits created nowadays as examples of the high priest garments. But the true emphasis in the Bible is the importance of the 'breastplate' ('protection') be situated on the girdle and not be loosened or removed from that particular location on the ephod; there are reasons behind this, important to the authors of the Bible.

'And Aaron shall bear the names of the children of Israel in the breastplate of Judgement upon his heart, when he goeth in unto the holy *place*, for a memorial before the Lord continually.' This verse may have also helped towards the misunderstanding of the 'breastplate' which is not called 'breastplate' but 'protection/protection amulet', which is erroneously believed to be located on the priest's chest just because it mentions Aaron's heart, while what is meant by Aaron bearing the names upon his heart is figuratively speaking, just like wearing the names on his sides, on the ephod's corners and the breastplate/protection all on his waist, it is figuratively speaking (not literally on his chest/heart) that Aaron should always carry them in his heart i.e. they should always be on his mind, not to be forgotten during rituals. 'And thou shalt put in the breastplate of judgement the Urim and the Thummim; and they shall be upon Aaron's heart, when he goeth in before the Lord: and Aaron shall bear the judgement of the children of Israel upon his heart before the Lord continually.' This passage explaining the 'breastplate' more clearly as a pouch—which is clearly made of fabric from the beginning of its introduction in Exod.28, how it came to be called a 'breastplate' is obviously through misunderstanding and misinterpretation. This verse also shows important indications of where the 'breastplate' which is correctly called 'choshen/hosen' 'protection/protection amulet' is worn, as well as it shows again the verses where 'upon Aaron's shoulders/heart' is mentioned they mean his responsibility, always to be remembered and on his mind, not forgotten, etc.

The 'breastplate' which should read 'protection/protection amulet' is a pouch inside which are placed the Urim and Thummim used in casting lots, divining and judging: if this was the reason to make the 'protection/protection amulet' (misnomered 'breastplate' a pouch for storing and keeping handy the Urim and Thummin)—an important part of the priestly duties/activities as per the OT—and as the proper reading of the Bible makes the 'breastplate' worn on the waist, a pouch which carries the Urim and Thummim, with the pouch on the waist the Urim and Thummim can be easily accessed by the priest, whereas if, as popular western belief, the 'breastplate' is located at the chest or upper abdomen (look at all the versions of the 'breastplate' being on the chest with its different sizes)—all show it being ergonomically difficult to access the Urim and Thummim which would be settled at its bottom (pouch) and the priest would need to raise his arm at an awkward angle and rummage around with his hand also at a difficult angle even with only the Urim and Thummim being in the pouch. Logically and ergonomically (not to forget the actual text has the ephod and 'breastplate' as lower body garments) the misnomered 'breastplate' which is not a breastplate at all is attached to the waist of the ephod making the Urim and Thummim easy to access by the high priest wearing his priestly garments. There are also special reasons given throughout the OT making the ephod and misnomered 'breastplate' garments situated beginning from the waist downwards, but these reasons and the Biblical proof will be touched upon later.

The robe (which is a short dress i.e. an ancient shirt/top) and coat are mentioned as 'And thou shalt make the robe of the ephod all *of* blue,' i.e. the robe is an accessory to the ephod, 'And there shall be an hole in the top of it, in the midst thereof; it shall have the binding of the woven work round about the hole...' 'And thou shalt embroider the coat of fine linen...' If the robe and coat were longer than the ephod, as popular belief has shown and projected them to be, there would be no risk of the priests in the stories exposing their genitals—but as the robe is a short shirt worn above the ephod (like a top) they do not cover the genitals hence the need of breeches to be made specifically to cover their 'nakedness' as Exod.28:42-43 clearly highlights.

If you have lived in the areas where wearing ephods and robes (short shirts) are the normal traditional clothing (shirts with ephods in modernity), you would see and understand how the ephod—a wrap-around skirt—behaves according to the movements of the person wearing it, and you see and understand how 'breeches'/underwear are necessary because of the ease and frequency of exposure of the genitals for those who wear ephods. When men wear robes (long white dress) when they need to work, it restricts their movement, gets soiled or gets in the way of what they are doing, which is why from the morning and all the way through to lunchtime which is when most of the physical work is done, men wear ephods because it does not restrict the body's movement, nor gets in the way of the work they are doing; when before or after lunch they wash, they change into long robes or into a fresh ephod and shirt, but most change into robes(long dress).On special occasions such as Eid or weddings the men wear robes from the early morning, then when it is time to slaughter animals for food and/or sacrifice, you see the man hold the hem of his robe and lift it upwards to his waist with the inside facing outwards then he secures both sides of the robe's bottom ends around his waist, wrapping and tightening it just like an ephod so he can perform the slaughter, build the fire, cook the meat and serve without the robe restricting his movements or getting in the way (and this is if he does not have time or cannot be bothered to change into an ephod and shirt to work (no matter how much his wife and adult daughters insist he change so as not to stain or dirty his robe) then back into the robe to receive guests and in between festivities, as the point is to be wearing a clean or new robe on celebration day).

The people who authored the Bible are aware of the chores and the movements entailed by the work needed in slaughtering animals for sacrifice, bringing wood, making fire, cooking, pouring/sprinkling blood, and all the activities given to the priests in the Biblical stories—which are hard, toiling and dirty, requiring a lot of bending down, squatting, lifting up, and many more movements. The same authors of the Bible are also aware of the correct and suitable clothing for such activities, which is an 'ephod' a wrap-around skirt and how it allows a person to go around his work without the hindrance a robe would cause—they are envisioning all the work needed for the priestly characters and how the clothes behave during this work; they are also aware of genital exposure which could result from working in such a garment and therefore included the breeches to cover the private parts of the priest, because you have to remember in the fictional Biblical stories the priests are not slaughtering just one animal in the comfort of their own home which would eliminate or reduce the exposure of their own private parts during work, but the authors have them slaughtering many animals, conducting many activities which would result in an ephod coming undone or parting/lifting up and exposing the priests' private parts.

It is a very Yemeni garment, and also shows the origin of the Biblical authors as it is a very Yemeni way of life. Whether the ephod or the activities of the priests which led the authors to determine in their Biblical stories that the high priest and priests' garments with the main garment being the ephod—the robe is called 'the robe of the ephod', the girdle is called 'the curious girdle of the ephod'; the garments were chosen as according to what real life persons would be wearing while performing the same activities (regardless of the activities religious or non-religious nature) and given more importance, prestige, spirituality to suit the story being told. There is no way the authors of the OT would have the priests wearing long robes or tunics as popular and erroneous belief has them portrayed, this might suit people in more modern times where modernisation, technology, changes in religious ritual allow easier execution of slaughtering animals, cooking, the fetching of heavy and thorny firewood probably removed (with fuel and modern ovens), fetching copious amounts of water also probably removed (with indoor plumbing), other people taking care of cleaning, etc. but the names of the garments, the instructions of how to make them, and why, show the ephod is a wrap-around skirt modified in the story to be 'priestly', a 'breastplate' which is actually a pouch called 'protection/protection amulet' and worn on the waist—all from Yemeni culture and way of life just as are the original authors of the Bible.

Importance of Ephod

Besides the authors of the Bible knowing the practicality of using the ephod/skirt for the priestly activities, stemming from both author's and the garment Yemeni origin, there is also a religious, spiritual or at least superstitious aspect also assigned to the ephod whether Aaron's (and its accessories such as the 'breastplate' and Urim/Thummim) or other ephods mentioned throughout the OT. This belief also stems from Yemeni pagan culture, and possibly they may have been able to blend with other pagan beliefs of the area where the Biblical stories have been set (the Arabian Peninsula and specifically where modern Saudi Arabia stands). There is a direct link to the ephod having powers of divination—whether worn by priests or borrowed by a non-priest major character in the Biblical story.

The priests who divine, prophesy and provide answers to their kings, all wear ephods such as in the story related to Saul; David himself divines (at least twice) when he borrows a priest's ephod. Aaron is obviously meant to divine/judge while wearing an ephod, and the misnomered 'breastplate' is fastened to the ephod. In Gideon's story an ephod is used just as it is in real Yemeni societies to wrap precious possessions in such as jewellery, deeds, saved money and anything precious before the ephod-wrapped things are placed in a trunk—in Gideon's story although the ephod is not mentioned as skirt/garment the story narrates he requests people to break off earrings so that he can create an 'ephod', and the gold jewellery is collected in a garment before Gideon makes it into an ephod, so the collection of the jewellery into a garment, it is the garment which is probably an ephod which gives the created 'ephod' Gideon makes its name and specialness; Goliath's sword is wrapped in a cloth behind the ephod before it is given to David (again the cloth is an ephod which makes the idol or statue-ephod special). In both Gideon and Goliath's sword instances, the idol, sword, object seems to become an ephod i.e. gains its special meaning, its power, from an original garment ephod, and in all stories there is a direct link made between ephods with priests, other characters, and powers of divination, judgement, seeing the future and it is always connected with power of divination to a person in contact with the ephod which brings us back to an already well-established and obvious fact that the majority of religious rituals in the OT stories are taken from pagan origins, and the ephod, its spiritual and mystical powers of divination also stem from pagan rituals, and beliefs which have nothing to do with monotheistic religions but of which the monotheistic religions, ironically, are founded upon.

If you recall in previous chapters how sacrifice such as fire offerings, blood offerings, etc. all stem out of a much older pagan ritual (still carried out today), but adopted as rituals for priests in the Biblical stories, although they are no different than the pagan rituals. Now recall the meaning of the word 'kohen/cohen' in the original Yemeni Arabic language which has translated and translates the meaning of the names in the OT and NT with perfect meanings and proven by the Biblical stories itself—the word 'kohen/cohen' in the same Yemeni Arabic language means 'fire worshipper/sorcerer/estimator' and the activities of sorcery and reading of the future, and fire rituals which is part of their activities; and also the word 'kohen' in the OT is the word mistranslated into 'priest' who burns sacrifices, sprinkles blood and divines, tells the future just like fir worshippers did in Yemen and where people still call fire worshippers and their acts of sorcery which includes reading the future 'kohen'.

Look at what the ephod, the misnomered 'breastplate' and all priestly garments made specially to perform these rituals and what their activities are, then note again the given noun misnomered as 'priest' in the OT in original language is 'kohen' (fire worshipper/sorcerer/estimator). Now go to the story of Saul with the priests at 1Sam.22: Saul accuses the priests, whom the text will mention were wearing ephods, for 'enquiring of God' i.e. divining, seeing the future, providing answers, etc. for David—which the priests deny doing. Nonetheless Saul has them all slaughtered. In a following story after this event it becomes clear how sorcerers, witches, seers and 'priests' (actually called 'kohen' which is sorcerer/fire worshipper in the original language of the OT) are one and the same according to the author(s) of the Bible, and in the storylines of the OT: 1Sam.28 narrates Saul has gotten rid of all 'those that had familiar spirits, and the wizards' i.e. everyone that has the same powers and abilities of the priests/kohen. The story tells us Saul attempts to get divine answers from the Lord through his own use, through Urim and through prophets, but when he gets no response at all—he commands his people to find a sorceress 'a woman that hath a familiar spirit' and requests of her to not only divine for him by the 'familiar spirit' but to also summon up Samuel from the dead so he can speak to him, not to forget Samuel was one of the biggest 'priests/kohen' i.e. 'sorcerer/fire worshipper'—therefore, the priests, wizards, and those 'of familiar spirits' (witches/seers, et al) are one and the same whom Saul ordered to be slaughtered when he believed they were using their occupational abilities to help David with divination.

The ephod is an important part of the divination process, made clear in many chapters of differing stories of the OT. The people who divine are in physical contact with the ephod. And it is the OT stories which tell us clearly why and from where the ephod receives its mystical, supernatural divination powers. Already established is that wearing an ephod in the OT stories allows divination, judgement, etc. Aaron, other high priests and priests wear it; the priests whom Saul accuses of 'enquiring of God' for David are wearing ephods, and it must be noted that the author of this specific story felt it necessary to point out they were wearing ephods, especially as the story would suffer no great difference not to know what they were wearing while accused then killed for suspected treason, but because to the authors it was important to show the ephod as a special garment with special spiritual abilities it is mentioned. The author and therefore the story have the ephod elemental for the storyline as it has significant meaning according to the culture of the people who wrote the Biblical stories. The ephod draws its importance (given to it by the Biblical authors) from something important in the culture and beliefs of the real people among whom the authors of the Bible lived and were a part of.

Just as the ephods they wear are mentioned when Saul had the priests who divine slaughtered, earlier in 1Sam.14 when Jonathan and his armourbearer go to attack the enemy and win against all odds—for no apparent reason the story narrates that Ahia, a priest, is wearing an ephod, this is important and stands for something to the author and the OT story's original audience: the wearer of an ephod is special, and the ephod itself will signify in the story Jonathan's unlikely victory. Also as the ephod is of importance with its special abilities—the story continues with this theme after Saul has the ephod-clad priests killed, in the following chapter Abiathar escapes and flees to David, and it is important to be narrated that 'he came down *with* an ephod in his hand.' which David requests to be brought to him and he himself divines while in contact with it—the story does not tell us if he wore it, held it in his hand, or covered his head with it, but what is certain is priests wear it around their waists while divining as it is how this garment is worn. Again, in Chapter 30 when David is in great distress, he asks Abiathar the priest to give him the ephod and once David has it, he begins to 'enquire of the Lord'—the ephod is the sacred channel to God, wearing it allows for some kind of response to be felt by the diviner (person wearing it).

So where does the ephod get its sacred and spiritual powers in the Biblical stories? The answer is in where the ephod is located on the body when worn, the answer is scattered throughout the OT and is very clear: the ephod is worn around the waist, the 'protection/protection amulet' (erroneously interpreted as 'breastplate') as well as the Urim/Thummim which are inside the 'breastplate' pouch hang from the waist of the ephod, and all three (ephod, 'breastplate, and Urim/Thummim) are in direct contact with the groin i.e. the genitals (male), and this sacredness of genitals is drawn from paganism of which fertility gods were a fact of life in the region where the Bible/OT was written. The authors are from the Arabian Peninsula where 'Ashur the fertility goddess was worshipped, along with gods lesser in importance; 'seed' and offspring (both of man and animal) was a sacred and important part of life and is what most of the Biblical stories revolve around, especially the Five Books of Moses, where 'the seed' and its multiplication is the main idea and objective. The ephod, 'breastplate' which is not a breastplate but 'protection', the Urim and Thummim inside it, all worn on or close to the groin—the 'breastplate' (protection/protection amulet) which is a pouch has the names of the twelve tribes/sons of Jacob to whom the story gives the importance of their 'seed' increasing and not being cut off from the world.

The authors of the Bible, as well as the region where they chose to set their stories, all have paganism a major part of their lives, as displayed in the Biblical stories, and even the pagan worship of penises as mentioned in both the OT and NT, although experts have chosen to overlook this fact or genuinely make erroneous claims to the meaning of 'Baal Zebub' which is mentioned in 2Kgs. (Baal Zebub means 'spouse of/high/higher/high place/above-penises/penised' 'with the/by the-penises'; in the NT in Matt., Mark and Luke mention Beelzebub (Beelzeboúl) which means 'with/by-penis/penising-the') which experts claim is a different word completely (i.e. they change the letters and pronunciation of the word in an attempt to suit what they think it means) turning a word which means 'penises' in the language it was written in to *maybe* mean 'flies' (according to the experts) as in 'Lord of the Flies' which is a completely different word and pronunciation than what 'Baal Zebub' (OT) and 'Beelzebub/Beelzeboul' (NT) is in the Biblical texts. The experts claim what is obviously and correctly 'Baal zebub/Beelzeboul' as being a 'corruption' of 'Be'el dibaba' ('flies' according to the experts) and the experts make this claim based on guessing that back then the people 'corrupted' the name of the god 'ba'al zebul' which the experts connect it through conjecture to Ugarit text which has 'Baal' a storm god—they choose to believe it (Baal Zebub/Beelzebub) is a mistake based on what their belief is a mistake *based* on a mistake, while it has meaning in its own language as it stands in the OT and NT and explicitly means the meaning of the word in its correct language which is 'penis'-related and these meanings are shown and meant in the story told itself. The 'experts' makes this mistake by seeking answers in languages and areas other than that of the actual language of the Bible—Arabic and specifically Arabic of the Arabian Peninsula, which has all the meanings of these words as it is Arabic and still alive in the language of Arabs to this day, as well as past, ancient cultures of fertility god worship are abundant. The Bible text itself—the story told shows the people who lived in the land, in the story it includes 'children of Israel' worshipped fertility gods, 'Ashur was the greatest and most important fertility goddess in the region, in 2Kgs. when Ahaziah injures himself, he sends to 'Baal-zebub' 'Spouse of/With the penises' to ask if he will recover from the disease; all throughout the chapter Elijah's anger and punishment towards Ahaziah the king of Israel revolves around 'why are you seeking help from Baal-zebub?' instead of Elijah's god; by the end of the chapter after Ahaziah dies of his injury and someone completely different (not from his family) becomes king of Israel, the author of the Biblical story tells us exactly why Ahaziah king of Israel worshipped Baal-zebub: he had not produced offspring, not a son at least—which is why he had been sending to Baal-zebub 'Spouse of/With the-penises' in the Biblical story, of which in real-life there were fertility gods worshipped before, during and after the emergence of what would come to be called the Jewish religion.

Even in the New Testament, the Arabic word is meant to be the same. The Greek copy of the original Arabic NT story has kept the names as they are pronounced in the original Arabic stories. So you have in both 2Kgs. of the OT and in the NT the word-names Baal-zebub and Beelzebub both meanings and words based on 'penis' and related to fertility god worship. First it must be understood, in times when Christianity was emerging, pagans and Jews considered Christians 'heathens'; the same goes for Islam's emergence where Christians, Jews and pagans considered Muslims 'heathens' as well as Muslims, Christians and Jews seeing pagans as 'heathens'; in the same way whenever a different set of people are at odds with people of another religion (although they are all from the same race/ethnicity) each believes and claims the 'other' is worshipping devils, demons, Satan, 'works of their own hand'—the other's god(s) become Satan and devils. This, coupled with the region of the Biblical stories worshipping fertility gods, of which the genitals are sacred and idolised, has been used by the authors of the NT, both in accusing Jesus of worshipping 'Beelzebub' and viewing his religion as worshipping devils/Satan—which is the norm when attacking another's religion. The Biblical authors give it a humorous twist with Jesus answering the Jews' accusation of his using/worshipping 'Beelzebub/With the penises' to heal the sick with words to the effect 'If this is what they call the master/Lord ('with/by-penis/penising-the')—imagine what they call his servants!': 'It is enough for the disciple that he be as his master, and the servant as his Lord. If they have called the master of the house Beelzebub, how much more *shall they call* them of his household?' (Matt.10:25).

The wider region has been found, archeologically proven, to be prominently worshipping pagan gods of which 'Ashur the pagan fertility goddess was the dominant religion even when it was wrongly believed by modern scholars that people were all following the Jewish religion—the latter belief has been disproved by archaeologists and historians. The OT itself projects and engrains pagan-inspired fertility sacredness shown in the protagonist god of the OT is originally female 'Ashur, erroneously translated 'I Am That I Am' which is a mistranslation of 'ehyeh 'ăšer 'ehyeh 'she is-with child/calf-she is' 'she is-pregnant-she is' and refers to the deity being a pregnant cow; and the same OT has made the penis a sacred thing which gives powers of divination to ephods, 'breastplate/protection', Urim and Thummim, and those who wear these special garments linked to the groin (genital area), as well as to those who borrow the ephods.

The OT leaves no doubt that the male genital organ is sacred and is what gives the priests and their special garments sacredness and power, it is inspired by the pagan origins and practise of the people who wrote the OT and of the area (Arabian Peninsula) who incorporated all these pagan rituals as well as beliefs of which sacredness and power of the male genital is just one element—but an important one. The proof is always in the Bible, and supported by what is a fact of what and how people have worshipped, performed ritual rites since ancient civilisations and into modernity. To return solely for proof in the OT of the importance of ephod, 'breastplate/protection' and Urim and Thummim worn around the groin area by priests—read what the OT/Torah clearly states after the author(s) decides to create the ephod/skirt and its accessories, and how important it is that Aaron, his seed, his genitals and all priests' genitals not be 'polluted' nor be physically deformed to explain why ephod and breastplate are important in the story.

It was important in the OT to link purity of Aaron, his offspring, priests avoid being 'dirtied' spiritually—nor their genitals be physically mutilated as it would render them the opposite of sacred and pure; the sacredness lies in the completeness of their genitals, the same sacredness in the holiness of genitals because only with sacred and whole, clean genitals would they be suitable for performing 'fire offerings'. The Bible repeats and makes clear that a person with damaged testicles, or damaged penis cannot be sacred, nor can he take part in the burning of the sacrifices or any of its related rituals—showing both the pagan practise of fireworship, pagan worship and pagan belief of fertility gods. Aaron and his sons who are priests are not to 'pollute' their seed with 'dirty' women listed as: prostitutes, profane women, divorced women, widows—he is not to dirty his genitals nor his seed in them.

It makes more than clear in a list of physical deformities which it calls 'blemishes', that even if he is 'of the seed of Aaron', damaged testicles (in Leviticus) and an incomplete or injured penis make him (the injured or physically deformed person) a 'profanity'—not good enough, but also 'dirty'. And they are not holy because their genitals are damaged and therefore cannot touch nor perform 'the offerings of the Lord made by fire', nor will they be allowed to approach/enter 'the vail', nor come near the altar, or any of God's 'sanctuaries' to avoid profaning them. Therefore, a dirty, unholy person is one who has damaged genitalia. A person who is holy and can wear the priestly garments, and perform the priestly rituals has to have a whole and undamaged penis and testicles because it has something to do with divining and performing the rituals which involves wearing an ephod (a skirt), a 'breastplate' which is actually called 'protection' and is pouch that hangs from the waist of the ephod, and carrying the Urim and Thummim inside the pouch. If the man, even if of Aaron's line, has damaged genitalia it renders him unable and unfit to perform a ritual where sacrifices/offerings are burned with fire; it renders him unable and unfit to divine with an ephod, 'protection/amulet' ('breastplate'), Urim and Thummim.

If you look at the details mentioned to be made as part of the sacred clothes of Aaron (high priest and priests), it tells you the importance of this very pagan fertility sacredness represented by genitals is linked to offspring, 'seed'. The names engraved on the two stones of memorial located on both sides of the ephod (left and right) as well as the names engraved on the stones embellishing the misnomered 'breastplate' which too is a pouch hanging fastened to the ephod (in the area of the priest's groin) the names are the twelve sons of Jacob, i.e. his seed, the driver and important part of the OT stories—the twelve tribes of Israel, their 'seed' is put on for holy rituals by a holy priest with holy and whole genitals, and worn over his genitals where the sacredness and holiness exists.

All these rituals incorporated into the OT, all the clothes and especially the ephod, taken from the Biblical authors' Yemeni origins, the stories weaved from and with Yemeni pagan culture, Yemeni pagan worship rituals. The Biblical authors used separate elements of Yemeni culture, clothing, religious practise, superstitious beliefs and the important matters and topics of everyday life to Yemenis to make it into a story about offspring, fertility, continuance revolving around a common Yemeni garment of practicality and fashion, a cultural obsession of having many offspring, and the pagan religions and rituals which have survived well into this day—and have filled the pages of the Bible.

It is easy and immediately evident to a person like me who has lived in a land and area of whom the ancestors most definitely wrote the Bible, when you see and live day-in and day-out with a people who speak, behave, believe and conduct everything the way it has been since pagan times, and whose language, speech, expression is the same as that of the Biblical authors' and their stories—when much later on in life I read the Bible I understood it immediately and can see how and why the Bible connects certain beliefs to certain objects and acts. If you read the Bible objectively without trying to impute onto it scholarly, or political, or even religious views of today—and just read it as it is in the words of its authors and what they meant millennia ago, without trying to complicate it with modern academic theories whether about its structure or prose, and without trying to forcibly connect it to other civilisations to prove the existence of a specific civilisation which never existed, if you just read the Biblical text it tells you exactly what it means and why the ephod, why the priests have to have intact genitals, and it tells you who created the original stories of the Bible: Yemenis.

'And thou shalt make holy garments for Aaron thy brother...And these *are* the garments which they shall make; a breastplate, and an ephod, and a robe, and a broidered coat, a mitre, and a girdle: and they shall make holy garments for Aaron thy brother, and his sons, that he may minister unto me in the priest's office...And thou shalt make them linen breeches to cover their nakedness; from the loins even unto the thighs they shall reach. And they shall be upon Aaron, and upon his sons, when they come in unto the tabernacle of the congregation, or when they come near unto the altar to minister in the holy *place*; that they bear not iniquity, and die: it shall be a statute forever unto him, and his seed after him.' (Exod.28). 'Neither shalt thou go up by steps unto mine altar, that thy nakedness be not discovered thereon' (Exod.20:26). 'And the holy garments of Aaron shall be his sons; after him, to be anointed therein, and to be consecrated in them.' (Exod.29:29).

'But Samuel ministered before the Lord, *being* a child, girded with a linen ephod.' (1Sam.2:18)

'And David danced before the Lord with all *his* might; and David *was* girded with a linen ephod...And Michal the daughter of Saul came out to meet David, and said, How glorious was the king of Israel to day, who uncovered himself in the eyes of the handmaids of his servants, as one of the vain fellows uncovereth himself!' (2Sam.6:14-22)

'And Gideon said unto them, I would desire a request of you, that ye would give me everyman the earrings of his prey.(For they had golden earrings, because they were Ishmaelites.).And they answered, We will willingly give *them*. And they spread a garment, and did cast therein every man the earrings of his prey...And Gideon made an ephod thereof, and out it in his city, *even* in Ophrah: and all Israel went thither a whoring after it: which thing became a snare unto Gideon and to his house.' (Jud.8:24-27)

'Now it came to pass upon a day, that Jonathan the son of Saul said unto the young man that bare his armour, Come, and let us go over to the Philistine's garrison, that *is* on the other side. But he told not his father. And Saul tarried in the uttermost part of Gibeah under a pomegranate tree which *is* in Migron: and the people that *were* with him *were* about six hundred men: And Ahiah, the son of Ahitub, I-chabod's brother, the son of Phinehas, the son of Eli, the Lord's priest in Shiloh, wearing an ephod. And the people knew not that Jonathan was gone.' (1Sam.14:1-3)

'And the priest said, The sword of Goliath the Philistine, whom thou slewest in the valley of Elah, behold, it *is here* wrapped in a cloth behind the ephod: if thou wilt take that, take *it*: for *there is* no other save that here. And David said, There is none like that; give it me.' (1Sam.21:9)

'And it came to pass when Abiathar, the son of Ahimelech fled to David to Keilah, *that* he came down *with* an ephod in his hand...And David knew that Saul secretly practised mischief against him; and he said to Abiathar the Priest, Bring hither the ephod. Then said David, O Lord God of Israel, thy servant hath certainly heard that Saul seeketh to come to Keilah, to destroy the city for my sake. Will the men of Keilah deliver me up into his hand? will Saul come down as thy servant hath heard? O Lord God of Israel, I beseech thee, tell they servant. And the Lord said, He will come down. Then said David, Will the men of Keilah deliver me and my men into the hand of Saul? And the Lord said, They will deliver thee up.' (1Sam.23:6-13)

'So David and his men came to the city, and, behold, *it was* burned with fire; and their wives and their sons, and their daughters were taken captives. Then David and the people that *were* with him lifted up their voice and wept, until they had no more power to weep. And David's two wives were taken captives, Ahinoam the Jezreelitess, and Abigail the wife of Nabal the Carmelite. And David was greatly distressed for the people spake of stoning him; because the soul of all the people was grieved, every man for his sons and for his daughters; but David encouraged himself in the Lord his God. And David said to Abiathar the Priest, Ahimelech's son, I pray thee, bring me hither the ephod. And Abiathar brought thither the ephod to David. And David enquired at the Lord, saying, Shall I pursue after this troop? shall I overtake them? And he answered him, Pursue: for thou shalt overtake *them*, and without fail recover *all*.' (1Sam.30:1-8)

'Then answered Doeg the Edomite, which was set over the servants of Saul, and said, I saw the son of Jesse coming to Nob, to Ahimelech, the son of Ahitub, And he enquired of the Lord for him, and gave him victuals, and gave him the sword of Goliath the Philistine. Then the king sent to call Ahimelech the priest, the son of Ahitub, and all his father's house, the priests that *were* in Nob: and they came all of them to the king. And Saul said, Hear me now, thou son of Ahitub. And he answered, Here I am, my lord. And Saul said unto him, Why have ye conspired against me, ye and the son of Jesse, in that thou hast given him bread, and a sword, and hast enquired of God for him, that he should rise against me, to lie in wait, as at this day? Then Ahimelech answered the king, and said, And who *is so* faithful among all thy servants as David, which is the king's son in law, and goeth at thy bidding, and is honourable in thine house? Did I then begin to enquire of God for him? be it far from me: let not the king impute *any* thing unto his servant, *nor* to all the house of my father: for thy servant knew nothing of all this, less or more. And the king said, Thou shalt surely die, Ahimelech, thou, and all thy father's house. And the king said unto the footmen that stood about him, Turn, and slay the priests of the Lord; because their hand also *is* with David, and because they knew when he fled, and did not shew it to me. But the servants of the kings would not put forth their hand to fall upon the priests of the Lord. And the king said to Doeg, Turn thou, and fall upon the priests of the Lord. And Doeg the Edomite turned, and he fell upon the priests, and slew on that day fourscore and five persons that did wear a linen ephod.' (1Sam.22:9-19)

'Now Samuel was dead, and all Israel had lamented him, and buried him in Ramah, even in his own city. And Saul had put away those that had familiar spirits, and the wizards, out of the land...And when Saul enquired of the Lord, the Lord answered him not, neither by dreams, nor by Urim, nor by prophets. Then said Saul unto his servants, Seek me a woman that hath a familiar spirit, that I may go to her, and enquire of her. And his servants said to him, Behold, *there is* a woman that hath a familiar spirit at Endor...and they came to the woman by night: and he said, I pray thee, divine unto me by the familiar spirit, and bring me *him* up, whom I shall name unto thee. And the woman said unto him, Behold, thou knowest what Saul hath done, how he hath cut off those that have familiar spirits, and the wizards, out of the land: wherefore then layest thou a snare for my life, to cause me to die? And Saul sware to her by the Lord, saying, As the Lord liveth, there shall no punishment happen to thee for this thing. Then said the woman, Whom shall I bring up unto thee? And he said, Bring me up Samuel. And when the woman saw Samuel, she cried with a loud voice: and the woman spake to Saul, saying, Why hast thou deceived me? for thou *art* Saul. And the king said unto her, Be not afraid: for what sawest thou? And the woman said, I saw gods ascending out of the earth. And he said unto her, What form is he of? And she said, An old man cometh up; and he *is* covered with a mantle. And Saul perceived that it *was* Samuel, and he stooped with his face to the ground, and bowed himself. And Samuel said to Saul, Why hast thou disquieted me, to bring me up?' (1Sam.28:3-15)

'And Ahaziah fell down through a lattice in his upper chamber that *was* in Samaria, and was sick: and he sent messengers, and said unto them, Go, enquire of Baal-zebub the god of Ekron whether I shall recover of this disease. But the angel of the Lord said to Elijah the Tishbite, Arise, go up to meet the messengers of the kings of Samaria, and say unto them, *Is it* not because *there is* not a God in Israel, that ye go to enquire of Baal-zebub the god of Ekron? Now therefore thus saith the Lord, Thou shalt not come down from that bed on which thou art gone up, but shalt surely die. And Elijah departed. And when the messengers turned back unto him, he said unto them, Why are ye now turned back? And they said unto him, There came a man up to meet us, and said unto us, Go, turn again unto the king that sent you, and say unto him, Thus saith the Lord, *Is it* not because *there is* not a God in Israel, *that* thou sendest to enquire of Baal-zebub the god of Ekron? therefore thou shalt not come down from that bed on which thou art gone up, but shalt surely die...And the angel of the Lord said unto Elijah, Go down with him: be not afraid of him. And he arose and went down with him unto the king. And he said unto him, Thus saith the Lord, Forasmuch as thou hast sent messengers to enquire of Baal-zebub the god of Ekron, *is it* not because *there is* no God in Israel to enquire of his word? therefore thou shalt not come down off that bed on which thou art gone up, but shalt surely die. So he died according to the word of the Lord which Elijah had spoken. And Jehoram reigned in his stead in the second year of Jehoram the son of Jehoshaphat king of Judah; because he had no son.' (2Kgs.1)

'The disciple is not above *his* master, nor the servant above his lord. It is enough for the disciple that he be as his master, and the servant as his lord. If they have called the master of the house Beelzebub, how much more *shall they call* them of his household?' (Matt.10:16-27)

'Then was one brought to him possessed by a devil, blind, and dumb: and he healed him, insomuch that the blind and dumb both spake and saw. And all the people were amazed, and said, Is this not the son of David? But when the Pharisees heard *it*, they said, This *fellow* doth not cast out devils, but by Beelzebub the prince of devils.' (Matt.12:22-24)

'And the Lord said unto Moses, Speak unto the priests the sons of Aaron, and say unto them, There shall none be defiled from the dead among his people: But for his kin, that is near unto him, *that is*, for his mother, and for his father, and for his son, and for his daughter, and for his brother. And for his sister a virgin, that is nigh unto him, which hath had no husband: for her may he be defiled. *But* he shall not defile himself, *being* a chief man among his people, to profane himself. They shalt not make baldness upon their head, neither shall they shave off the corner of their beard, nor make any cuttings in their flesh. They shall be holy unto their God, and not profane the name of their God: for the offerings of the Lord made by fire, *and* the bread of their God, they do offer: therefore they shall be holy. They shall not take a wife *that is* a whore, or profane; neither shall they take a woman put away by her husband: for he is holy unto his God. Thou shalt sanctify him therefore; for he offereth the bread of thy God: he shall be holy unto thee: for I the Lord, which sanctify you, *am* holy. And the daughter of any priest, if she profane herself by playing the whore, she profaneth her father: she shall be burnt with fire. And *he that is* the high priest among his brethren, upon whose head the anointing oil was poured, and that is consecrated to put on the garments, shall not uncover his head, nor rend his clothes; Neither shall he go into any dead body, nor defile himself for his father, or for his mother; Neither shall he go out of the sanctuary, nor profane the sanctuary of his God, for the crown of the anointing oil of his God *is* upon him: I *am* the Lord. And he shall take a wife in her virginity. A widow, or a divorce woman, or profane, *or* an harlot, these he shall not take: but he shall take a virgin of his own people to wife. Neither shall he profane his seed among his people: for I the Lord do sanctify him. And the Lord spake unto Moses, saying, Speak unto Aaron, saying, Whosoever *he be* of thy seed in their generations that hath *any* blemish, let him not approach to offer the bread of his God. For whatsoever man *he be* that hath a blemish, he shall not approach: a blind man, or a lame, or he that hath a flat nose, or anything superfluous, Or a man that is brokenfooted, or brokenhanded, Or crookbackt, or a dwarf, of that hath a blemish in his eye, or be scurvy, or scabbed, or hath his stones broken; No man that hath a blemish of the seed of Aaron the priests shall come nigh to offer the offerings of the Lord made by fire: he hath a blemish; he shall not come nigh to offer the bread of his God, *both* of the most holy, and of the holy. Only he shall not go in unto the vail, nor come nigh unto the altar, because he hath a blemish; that he profane not my sanctuaries: for I the Lord do sanctify them. And Moses told *it* unto Aaron, and unto his sons, and unto all the children of Israel.' (Lev.21)

'He that is wounded in the stones, of hath his privy member cut off, shall not enter into the congregation of the Lord.' (Deut.23:1)

Indigo

Another popular and traditional Yemeni fabric and substance used in clothing, which features a lot in the Bible, is indigo. The substance used and the fabric it creates is called (sbgh/sbgha/سبغ/سبغا) which means 'dye'; (msboogh/مسبوغ) means 'dyed'. Until very recently it used to be the most valued kind of clothing/fabric in rural Yemen—even when times were hard and a person only had one special change of garment (kept for special occasions) it would be taken once a year to be dyed. In the past, when times were good, both men and women wore only one kind of robe for special occasions which was dyed with indigo. Not only did the people like its look, but it was also believed to be good for the health of the skin and health in general; they believed that it prevented sweating and state that it was 'cool on the skin'; the people recall its purple/blue rub-off adhering to the skin. The change in the availability of this dyed garment (and with it the change in what robes the men and women wore) came around when dyers (whose whole living was based on dyeing other people's clothes and also dyeing fabrics for export nationally and internationally) stopped due to modern fabrics from Yemeni cities and abroad becoming easier to access and becoming popular in the region which in turn made indigo clothes harder to get, especially as the nearest ones ceased to function (and these 'nearest' dyers were considerably distant with difficult terrain to cross to get to).But up until the 1970s it was still popular and some of the ephods men wore were also indigo-dyed. The indigo robe both men and women used to wear is called (zannah/زنّه).

Depending on how long the fabric was left in indigo to soak, and how many times the process of rinsing, airing, pounding, scraping was repeated, determined the colour of the fabric. The fabric could be black (almost completely black), blue-black, deep/dark purple, purple, blue. The most preferred colour for the zannah robe was black-blue or black. The preferred colour for men's' head shawl a shiny purple; the women's headveil—blue-black; ephods—shiny purple.

It is important to point out that in the remote villages which remained living as their ancestors had since antiquity, due to the language not mutating, not evolving with external influences, there are not available in their language words for all the colours of things available, for example, there are nouns for colours such as red, yellow, green, black, yellow, but there is no word for pink, orange, brown, turquoise, scarlet, burgundy, etc. To describe colours which have no adjective or noun in the language is made by using comparisons to things/colours in nature, or comparisons to a colour of clothing another person has been seen wearing, also by using adjectives to describe the colour e.g. red would be called 'red', but pink does not have a word in the language so they would say 'a pale red' or 'faded red' to mean pink; the colour scarlet would need more explanation 'dark, rich red' or 'very, very, very red'; different reds could be described as 'red like dates' (a specific kind of date which is red) 'red like flowing blood'; greens would be described as 'green like a [so and so] plant/tree/leaf'; brown would be described as 'yellow like wood' or 'like coffee', a golden brown 'red like tea'. Orange is called 'red like henna' (which is usually orange in colour), even when girls and women dye their hands and feet with henna, they want it to be a very dark colour, after they wash it off and no matter what degree of orange, or brown if it has darkened a lot: if it is orange they say it is 'yellow', if it becomes a crimson or a dark brown they call it 'red'; if it becomes a very dark burnt brown colour or almost black they call it 'black'; and if describing the colour of a garment that is either orange or brown they say 'red like henna' or 'black like henna' and so on.

The indigo clothing was never called 'indigo' by the people in remote areas, but 'sbgh/sbgha' 'dye/dyed', and colours were not known as 'blue' 'purple' but descriptions made for them. Indigo clothing is something Yemen has historically been known for, and it was an important clothing in all its shades to the people in remote Yemen.

The Biblical authors being Yemenis have used this element of Yemeni life to feature indigo as the most important fabrics to make Aaron's high priest garments because they are highly valued; indigo also features as a special/prized garment and fabric throughout the OT. Indigo is mentioned whenever clothing or fabrics are mentioned as being 'blue' 'purple' 'scarlet' in the OT and it is definitely referring to products of indigo dyed fabrics and fibres.

To understand how 'blue', 'purple' and 'scarlet' in the OT are actually 'indigo products', a fact must be made clear: The original texts which have been translated into the English and other non-'Hebrew'/Arabic versions of the Bible as 'blue' 'purple' 'scarlet', in the original texts which is Arabic, erroneously believed to be Hebrew, these texts do not mention at all 'blue' 'purple' or 'scarlet'—but different words appear, and the only way translators could have arrived at the colours blue, purple, scarlet is by people of the region describing or showing them these colours. But what is important to observe is the words, the actual words in the original texts do not have the word 'blue' nor 'purple' nor 'scarlet' as there was obviously no noun for these colours back then, just like in remote Yemen where language has not been corrupted there are no nouns for all colours.

What you do have in the OT for 'blue' 'purple' 'scarlet' are words which described the three stages of the indigo dyeing process: tĕkēlet; 'argāmān and 'argĕwān; šānî, and tôlā'/tāla. And these words with their meanings do reflect the final stages of the end product of indigo-dyeing which determines the colour. If you recall the colour the fabric comes out as depends on how long it is left in the dye solution (and of course concentration also matters, but it is part of the indigo-dyeing process in Yemen the length of time and number of repeats determine the colour of the fabric) and how many times the steps are repeated, with the less time—a lighter colour; the more time—a deeper/darker colour. And if you translate the words, they give the meaning of the phase/time it took for the fabric to gain colour, and one of the words above is the name of the dyed robe men and women wore when indigo was allowed to make the fabric look black or blue-black. All the words used in the OT for 'blue' 'purple' 'scarlet' are the phase/length of time the fabric was left in the indigo dye to soak, and these words correspond exactly to what the colours would/could be as per the meaning of the word and colour fabric would be at the stage in the process:

- Blue: tĕkēlet; تيقيلت 'lessened': the lesser time produces blue fabric. Cp: teiqeilet.

- Purple: 'argāmān; نَرجاَمان 'leave until' and also the same as word below;

    'argēwān; نَرجيوان 'leave/stay until' from the word (rg/رج) 'waited/stayed' (same as root word used for word-name 'Mark'): when the fabric is left in the dye for a longer period it becomes a purple colour. Note the normal evolution of language: beginning with the Yemeni pure word (rg/'argēwān/'leave/stay until') أرجوان which has become the modern-Arabic word for 'purple' except where the people still speak the old language where there is no word for the colour 'purple' but the word is still a verb. Cp: argaamaan, argeywaan.

- Scarlet: šānî; سآني 'a year' 'let it go' 'leave it' and is what would make the robe spoken about earlier be called 'zannah';

    tôlā'/tāla; طولآء ، طآل 'longest/longer' 'took long/longer': this is the darkest colour achievable through indigo which is black or blue-black achieved by leaving the fabric in indigo dye for the longest period. Both šānî, and tôlā'/tāla 'year' 'leave it' 'longest/took longer' reflect this is the way to achieve the deepest/darkest colour. Cp: saanee, ṭolaa, ṭaala.

Therefore, you have the words describing the final phase, or determining phase, of the indigo-dye product—and its end colour perfectly explained and translated as per the original language of the OT and in accordance with what and how these colours are achieved. Of course, 'scarlet' is actually an almost black or black-blue and maybe is a result of difficulties in translation into English or Latin of what the original Biblical authors intended, but everything is perfectly explained and straightforward using Arabic and Yemeni way of life, Yemeni practise and methods. Indigo—'blue', 'purple', 'scarlet'—is a special and valued Yemeni fabric; the authors of the Bible are Yemeni and their love of, and knowledge of the indigo fabrics, its quality to them as Yemenis is why they chose to make the sacred garments of Aaron as well as God's tabernacle of indigo 'blue', 'purple', and 'scarlet'.

Adornment of Skin

In remote Yemen, women and men use henna and shavaar to adorn their hands and feet, men stopped using henna and shavaar on hands and feet, but women still use it. Henna is used covering half, or less than half the palm, and the inner fingers, as well as ringing around the topmost segments of the fingers including the backs of fingers and nails. In the past it was used to cover more of the palm, about three-quarters or more of the palm. The soles of feet are also coated in henna including ringing around the tops of toes including the nails. It is left on hands and feet for hours to allow it to dye darker—sometimes extra coats of henna are repeat on consecutive days to reach the desired crimson-red, brown, and sometimes almost black colour—which is deemed the prettiest. In addition to the coats of henna, women (and men in the past) use a powdered substance called (shvr/شذر) and comes in a powder or stone form (and comes with another substance called (bayaadha/بياضا) which is its activator). This shavar is quarried from a certain rock, burnt then finely powdered and/or compacted into a stone like form. After the last coat of henna has been washed off, the shevar powder and its activator is applied to the wet hands/feet along with rubbing it against the palms and skin dyed with henna, it creates an intense heat which turns the henna-dyed skin on hands and feet black—which is the desired result.

In rural Yemen where there is no electricity and the only light is from wick lanterns and fires, the corners of the room are dimly lit and outside it is much darker. In this darkness and dimness at night, the hands and feet of girls and women who have applied henna or shavaar seem to meld into the darkness; the person's hands and feet look incomplete, the non-dyed backs of their hands and tops of their feet seem to float in the darkness, it is eerie as you cannot see their feet landing on the ground, the backs of their hands including the backs of the fingers (minus the tips which are black with henna/shavaar) which are not dyed stand out starkly and when they move the hands seem disembodied from the rest of the body and it is due to the black colour of this substance adorning the skin, and the darkness of night, and how a flame(s) does not clearly illuminate (as opposed to electrical-fuelled light). It creates a visual effect such as that used on a dark stage with a black backdrop where only a pair of hands appear starkly against a black background while the rest of the actor's body is covered completely in black or hidden behind a black curtain.

It is the Biblical author's knowledge of this Yemeni adornment, and how the eyes play tricks in the dark when viewing a person whose hands and/or feet are adorned with shavaar which has been used to inspire the storyline and names in Daniel where a disembodied hand appears in the dark and writes a message for 'Belshazzar' whose name means 'with shevvar' 'he who wears shevvar', and the only person who can interpret the writing on the wall is Daniel whose nickname 'Belteshazzar' which means 'with/done-to who wears 'shavvar" (see Dan.5:1-24).

Place Names

Finally, Yemen has many unique place and area names, many have featured in the OT. Not only are locations in Yemen mentioned, but so are areas and tribes unique to Saudi Arabia mentioned in the OT, and it is the Arabian Peninsula where these Biblical stories are set in. These real areas in Yemen and Saudi Arabia are what inspired the naming of some of the fictional places and characters in the Biblical stories. Already explained earlier in this book is how the Biblical authors used compound word-names for characters and places to reflect what is happening or will happen in that specific story, but now this passage will focus on the actual names of real tribes (tribes are named after the areas/villages they originate from), areas, cities, villages and towns which have existed since pre-recorded history and continue to exist to this day in Yemen and in the whole of Saudi Arabia which have been recorded by the Biblical authors in the OT.

This does not mean that the Biblical events or places existed as per the Biblical stories, but it is what the Biblical authors based some of the place names and characters on and especially those featuring in the lists such as in Chronicles, Joshua and elsewhere, and it proves the authorship of the Biblical stories are Arabs of the Arabian Peninsula and specifically Yemen and ancient-Saudi Arabia.

Shebam is **Shibam** in Yemen; Rithmah, the same in Yemen; Gudgodah, the same in Yemen; Bohan is **Bayhaan** in Yemen; Mozah, the same in Yemen; Bene-Berak, the same in Yemen; Cherith, the same in Yemen; Eden is **Aden** in Yemen; Machbenah is **Makbenah** in Yemen; Zebeedee 'from Zebed' and **Zabeed** is in Yemen; Hothan is **Hofan** (حوفان) in Yemen next to Sultanate Oman. Shihor is south of Saudi Arabia; Athach is **Attaq** in Yemen; Jordan (mistaken for river and Jordan of the Levant) is in Yemen (in Shabwa, Yemen); Aram is **Armaa** in Yemen (in Shabwa, Yemen); Helem, the same in Yemen.

Caleb and Chelubai is a name of the **Kulaib** tribe in ancient Saudi Arabia; Canaan is a name of the **Canaanah** tribe in ancient Saudi Arabia; Minnith (Judg.11:33) is **Minna** in Saudi Arabia; Moriah (Gen.22:1-14), Moreh (Gen.12:6) are **al-Marwa** in Saudi Arabia; Hai (Gen.12:8) is **Haa'il** in Saudi Arabia; Sheba is **Sheiba** in Saudi Arabia; Migron is **Najran** in Saudi Arabia (it is actually part of Yemen); Adadah (Josh.15:22) is **Aayidh** (both location and prominent family in Saudi Arabia before the Saud family took place as royals); Tebah, Tappuah (Josh.12:17), Betah (2Sam.8:8) are **al-Abtah** in Saudi Arabia; Ain (Num.34:11) is **Ain** in Saudi Arabia; Gilead (Gen.31), Galeed (Gen.31) are **al-Qaleebah** in Saudi Arabia; Naarath (Josh.16:7), Ashtaroth (Judg.2), Neariah (1Chr.3:22) are **Nu'ayreeyah** in Saudi Arabia; Kishion (Josh.19:20), Kishon (Josh.21:28) are **Qasim** and **al-Qaysuumah** in Saudi Arabia; Kartan (Josh.21:32), Kartah (Josh.21:34) are **Quaryat al-Faw** and **al-Qurayyaat** in Saudi Arabia; Sirion (Deut.3:9), Lasharon (Josh.12:18), Sharaim (Josh.15:34), Sharuhen (Josh.19:6), Beesh-tarah (Josh.21:27), Sharar (2Sam.23:33), Saron (Acts.9:35) are **a-Sharawrah** and **a-Shariya** in Saudi Arabia; Hosah (Josh.19:29) is **Hadjar (al-Hasaa)**; Hapharaim (Josh.19:19) is **Hafar al-Batin**; Hoglah (Num.26:33; 27) is **al-Hajla**; Shaalabbin (Josh.19:42), Ahlab (Judg.1:31), Helbah (Judg.1:31), Heleb (2Sam.23:29) are **Halaban** in Saudi Arabia; Halak (Josh.11:15-17), Helkath (Josh.19:25) is **al-Halaqa** in Saudi Arabia; Haradah (Num.33:24), Harod (Judg.7:1-7), Harodite (2Sam.23:25) are **Haradh**; Arad (Num.21:1-3), Beeroth (Deut.10:6), Berothai (2Sam.8:8), Baal-berith (Judg.8:33), Berith (Judg.9:45-46) are **Riyadh**, **a-Ruwaydhah** and **Harrat al-Uwayrid'** in Saudi Arabia; Reumah, Rimmon-phares (Num.33:19), Ramah (Josh.18:25), Remmon (Josh.19:7), Ramath (Josh.19:8) Arumah (Judg.9:41), Rumah (2Kgs.23:36) are **Wadi a-Rimah** and **Rumaah** in Saudi Arabia; Heres (Judg.1:35), Timnath-heres (Judg.2:9) are **a-Rass** in Saudi Arabia; Hosah (Josh.19:29), Col-hozeh (Neh.3:15) are **Hasa** and **Hassi/Hussi** in Saudi Arabia; Halhul (Josh.15:58), Helah (1Chr.4:5) are **al-Hillah** in Saudi Arabia; Hobah is **Hoban** in Saudi Arabia; Hodaiah (1Chr.3:24) is **Hodaibiah** in Saudi Arabia; city of Adam (Josh.3:16), Adamah (Josh.19:33) are **a-Dawaadimi** in Saudi Arabia; Jashen (2Sam.23:32), Gozan (2Kgs.17:6) are **Jizan** in Saudi Arabia (actually part of Yemen in dispute with Saudi Arabia as Saudia was supposed to return it to Yemen sovereignty but refuses to do so); Ephah, Ava (2Kgs.17:24) is **Afif** in Saudi Arabia; Azzah (Deut.2:23; 1Kgs.4:24) is **Azzah** in Saudi Arabia; Gaza (Gen.10:19) is **al-Aziziyah** in Saudi Arabia; Abbah is **Abha** in Saudi Arabia; El-Paran (Gen.14:6), Paran (Gen.21:12-21) are **al-Anbareeya** in Saudia Arabia; Naarath (Josh.16:7) is **Arafa** in Saudia Arabia; Ararat (Gen.8:4-14), Aroer (Num.32:34), Armenia, ('ărārāṭ) (2Kgs.19:37) are **Ar'ar** in Saudia Arabia; Awwim and Avvim, Avim (Deut.2:23), Ava (2Kgs.17:24) are **Awammiyah** in Saudi Arabia; Succoth is **Areesh** in Saudi Arabia; Seir (Gen.14:6), Assir (Exod.6:24), Seirath (Judg.3:26) are **Assir** in Saudi Arabia; Betonim (Josh.13:26), Beten (Josh.19:25) are **Wadi al-Baateen** in Saudi Arabia; Elealeh (Num.32:3) is **al-**

'Awaalee in Saudi Arabia; Mattanah (Num.21:17-18) is **Sabkhat Mattee** in Saudi Arabia; Hammon (Josh.19:28) is **al-Hamaam**; Kehelatha (Num.33:22), Makheloth (Num.33:25), Heleph (Josh.19:33) is **Wadi Tahlith** in Saudi Arabia; Tophel (Deut.1:1) is **Taif** in Saudi Arabia; Tema (Gen.25:15) is **Taymaa'** and **Tima** in Saudi Arabia; Hadattah (Josh.15:25) is **Uhud** in Saudi Arabia; Sin (Exod.16:1-10), Sinai (Exod.16:1), Sansannah (Josh.15:31) are **Yanbu' al Sinaiyah** in Saudi Arabia; Pison, Ashan (Josh.15:42), Shion (Josh.19:19), Shen (1Sam.7:12-14), Beth-shan (1Sam.31:10) are **Bab a-Shuuna**; Silla (2Kgs.12:18-20) is **Bab as-Seil** in Saudi Arabia; Parah (Josh.18:23), Ophrah (Josh.18:23), Beth-barah (Judg.7:23), Barhumite (2Sam.23:31), Bethabara (John.1:28) are **Barahah** in Saudi Arabia; Beer (Num.21:16) is **al-Bi'r** in Saudi Arabia; Peruda (Ezra.2:55) is **Bureidah** in Saudi Arabia; Chebar (Ezek.1:1-3) is **Chaibar** in Saudi Arabia; Harosheth (Judg.4), Chorashan (1Sam.30:30), Charashim (1Chr.4:14), Chorazin (Matt.11:21-22) are **Chorais** in Saudi Arabia; Dagon (Judg.16:23-27) is **Dahnaa** in Saudi Arabia; Dimonah (Josh.15:22), Dimnah (Josh.21:35), Ephes-dammim (1Sam.17) are **Dammam** in Saudi Arabia; Dumah (Gen.25:14) are **Duumat** in Saudi Arabia; Seir (Gen.32;33) is **Ghawar** in Saudi Arabia; Gerar, Jagur (Josh.15:21) is **Jabal Jar** in Saudia Arabia; Gerar is **Wadi Jareer** in Saudi Arabia; Kabzeel (Josh.15:21), Kibzaim (Josh.21:22) is **(mount) Abu Qubeis** in Saudi Arabia; Ithnan (Josh.15:23) is **(mount) al-Fanna** in Saudi Arabia; Jabneel ('gave me(away)-the') (Josh.15:11) is **(mount) Hindi** in Saudi Arabia; Jokdeam (Josh.15:56) is **(mount) Kadaa** in Saudi Arabia; Makkedah (Josh.10:16-27) is **(mount) Kudaa** in Saudi Arabia; Hamor (Gen.33:19-20;34) is **(mount) Omar** in Saudi Arabia; Amorite (Gen.10:16; 14:7, 13) is **Shi'b 'Aamir** in Saudi Arabia; Beth-aven (Josh.7:2-12) and Jeshurun is **Jaw'an** in Saudi Arabia; Jair (Num.32:41), Havoth-jair (Num.32:41) is **Jiri** in Saudi Arabia; Ebal (Deut.11) is **Jubail** in Saudi Arabia; Gibeah (Josh.15:57), Gaba (Josh.18:24) is **Jubbah** in Saudi Arabia; Eshtemoh (Josh.15:50) is **Khamis Mushayt** in Saudi Arabia; Ramath (Josh.19:8), Remeth (Josh.19:21) are **Umm a-Rimth** in Saudi Arabia; Achor (Josh.7:26), Ekron (Josh.15:11) are **al-Uqayr** in Saudi Arabia; Bahurim (2Sam.3:16) is **Yanba al-Bahr** in Saudi Arabia; Zalmonah (Num.33:41), Zalmon (Judg.9:48-49) is **Zalim** in Saudi Arabia; Kenath (Num.32:42), Beth-anoth (Josh.15:59), Hannathon (Josh.19:14), Beth-anath (Josh.19:38) are **al-Khunfah** in Saudi Arabia; Kinah (Josh.15:22), Kanah (Josh.16:8) is **al-Khunn**; Horam (Josh.10:33), Horem (Josh.19:38) are **Khuraim** in Saudi Arabia; Dilean (Josh.15:38), Cabbon (Josh.15:40) is **Kuba** in Saudi Arabia; Haruphite is **Banee Haaref** in Saudi Arabia; Elealeh (Num.32:3), Baalah (Josh.15:10) are **al-Ma'laa** and **La'laa** in Saudi Arabia; Belial (Deut.12:13-17) is **Layla** in Saudi Arabia; Ullai (Dan.8:2-3) is **al-Ulaa** in Saudi Arabia; Kirjath-huzoth (Num.22:39), Beth-saida (Matt.11:21-22) are **Mahazat a-Sayd** in Saudia Arabia; Sihon (Num.21:23) is **a-Saha** in Saudi Arabia; Socoh (Josh.15:34), Secacah (Josh.15:61), Shocoh (1Sam.17) are **Sakakah** in Saudi Arabia; Cyrus the king of Persia is based on the ancient Saudi tribe and location of **Qureish** in Saudi Arabia; Jabbok (Gen.32:22-23) is **Tabook** in Saudi Arabia; Bakbakkar (1Chr.9:15), Bukkiah (1Chr.25:4), Bakbuk (Ezra.2:51), Bakbukiah (Neh.11:17) are **Buqeiq** in Saudi Arabia; Hebron (Gen.13:18), Habor (2Kgs.17), Chebar (Ezek.1:1-3) are **Khobar** in Saudi Arabia; Massa (Gen.25:14) is **al-Mas'aa** in Saudi Arabia; Middin (Josh.15:61) is **Madina** in Saudi Arabia; Salem/Shalem (Gen.14:18-24) (Gen.33:18-19;34), Mishal (Josh.21:30), Silla (2Kgs.12:18-20), Salim (John.3:22-36), Siloam (John.9) are **al-Misyal**, **Salemmia** and **a-Sulaymaniyah** are in Saudi Arabia; Siloah (Neh.3:15) is **Salwaa** in Saudi Arabia; Shiloh (Gen.49:10) is **a-Sulaayyil** in Saudi Arabia; Abdon (Josh.21:30) is **al-Mu'abda** in Saudi Arabia; Beth-marcaboth (Josh.19:5), Argob (Deut.3:4) are **Mureiqib** in Saudia Arabia; En-gedi (Josh.15:62) is **Najd** in Saudi Arabia; En-rogel (Josh.15:7) is **Rajalil** in Saudia Arabia; Sichem (Gen.12: 6), Shechem (Gen.33:18-19;34) is **al-Quway'eeyah** in Saudi Arabia; Bethel (Gen.12:8) (Gen.28:10-19) is **al-Safaa** in Saudi Arabia. Judah is **Jeddah** in Saudi Arabia; Jerusalem is based on the Saudi **Meccah** which was called **Beccah** before and is also called in the Bible 'the city called by my name' i.e. God's name which is both 'Jehovah' and 'Shaddai' and I will prove later in the following chapter how Mecca is the basis for the fictional Jerusalem.

These are not exhaustive lists of the locations in Yemen and Saudi Arabia which feature in the fictional Biblical stories as the settings of where the stories took place, which coincide with actual place names and tribe/area names in both these countries of the Arabian Peninsula who speak the Arabic language of the Bible. If you look at area and place names in current Saudi Arabia, you will see many more names that exist in Saudi Arabia than I have listed above, and which feature as listed place or character names in the OT, and these real Saudi areas have existed with these names since antiquity.

When I say 'remote' or 'rural' Yemen in this book it is because this is where the Old Arabic of the Bible and the way of life mirrored in the Biblical stories has remained unchanged into modernity; in the past this was once the whole of Yemen's language and also the whole of the Arabian Peninsula's language and ways of life long before modern borders. Yes, Yemen and ancient-Saudi Arabia were different civilisations and 'people' as Yemen has existed as a known and named civilisation exceeding all other countries in the Arabian Peninsula, but the ancient civilisations of the Arabian Peninsula did not follow the same borders of modernity, or the terming of what is a 'people' 'nation' 'country': within the same country and the same race the terminology 'stranger/foreigner/people' could be applied to absolute foreigners but also to someone who has come from a neighbouring village or area but that does not mean they did not share the same language, culture and religions, which they did; 'country' could mean one's village, a neighbouring village or area and not only a completely different country with today's modern sense.

Everything in the Bible is Yemeni and of the ancient lands of current Saudi Arabia. The language is Arabic still spoken in Yemen, Saudi Arabia and other Arab countries. Whether compound words to give names to characters and places—they are Old Arabic of the Arabian Peninsula which is still intact in Yemen, and this Arabic has explained all the meanings of word-names in the Bible. The narrative of the Bible is how Yemenis speak, the way the characters express themselves is exactly how Yemenis do, the proverbs and attitudes are Yemeni. Everything from tradition to pagan ritual sacredness given to rocks, fire, etc., the events and things which become significant in the Biblical stories are all taken from Yemeni way of life. Yemeni customs, superstitions, clothing and adornment have been made into something 'special' and 'sacred' in the OT stories. The matters which have always been of the most importance in remote Yemeni way of life have been made into the most important themes in the Bible. Every single thing in the OT has stemmed from Yemeni and ancient-Saudi Arabian origins, and aspects of Arabian Peninsula way of life. This is because the most original stories in the Bible were created by Yemenis before being added to by ancient-Saudi Arabians.

Reasons Why Biblical Stories were Created

The authors of the OT are Yemeni and ancient-Saudi Arabian, all the stories are inspired and drawn from Yemeni pagan life and ancient-Saudi Arabian life. Now we know who wrote the Bible, we can understand why these stories were created, and why the stories feature a 'chosen people' called 'children of Israel', and why it was important for these Yemeni authors (the original authors of the Bible) to create a 'special' people when all archaeological studies and excavations prove there is no such thing as Israel or Israelite in the whole region of what was Canaan—where only proof is of Canaanite peoples and their cultures ever existed there. With regards to Canaan and other ancient civilisations where the Biblical stories are erroneously believed to be set, the reason nothing 'Israel' or 'Israelite' has ever been found in all the extensive archaeological excavations performed all over Palestine (occupied Palestine and modern-Israel) is because the character Jacob/, the story about Israel and 'children of Israel' are all fictional as the meanings of their word-names and their related stories prove (see Israel).

The second reason is these stories were not set in what was ancestral Palestine, but in the Arabian Peninsula which includes some parts of Yemen and most of Saudi Arabia, the most significant cities in the fictional stories are set in and based on ancient-Saudi areas which still exist today in their modern forms, e.g. the Biblical Canaan is probably based on the ancient-Saudi Canaanah/كنانة which is a tribe, and tribes are named after the area/village they live in and come from. There is no 'Israel' in Yemen as Yemen has also had extensive archaeological excavations and all its ancient civilisations have been identified. The archaeological proof has shown civilisations and proof of their documenting each other's existence (wars, alliances, etc.), and none of these civilisations mention Israel, Israelite or any characters of the Biblical stories. The only place which has not had extensive archaeological excavations, and, in fact, has done the reverse of archaeological excavation and research, is Saudi Arabia. The Kingdom of Saudi Arabia has for decades destroyed pre-Islamic and Islamic-era archaeological sites and artefacts, done in the name of 'religion' and also done in the name of 'modernisation'; it does seem that the Saudi Arabian government (which is the ruling Saud family) are afraid of what their own archaeology turns up, and of their own ancient history.

Luckily enough for the world, artefacts and ruins are not the only evidence of the history of a nation, as the Saudi pre-Islamic and Islamic history, customs, language and folklore and neighbouring countries' history all carry proof of what Saudi Arabia was in ancient history. Although Saudi Arabia seems shy, or terrified, of its own ancient history, it is doubtful because they may have in the past found or are afraid of finding proof of 'Israel' existing in ancient-Saudi Arabia due to the fact that 'Israel' and everything in the Biblical stories are works of fiction. But these works of fiction do reflect parts of reality, which I have shown are Yemeni customs, beliefs and ways of life, and they also mirror and dramatize the culture of the people it encountered, the religious practises and places which it may have originally had in common with, and that is of ancient-Saudi Arabia. Had the Saudis found other forms of Biblical texts and archaeological proof of the Biblical stories being based on ancient-Saudi Arabia and destroyed them out of fear that what happened to Palestine at the hands of European Zionists would happen to them—we will never know. What is definite is any proof of Israel and the Biblical stories being part of Saudi Arabia would also create doubt about the religion of Islam (which may or may not be a real threat as the Quranic stories differ to those of the OT and NT) and the Saudi ruling family would lose its hold on the Saudi people whose lives are being controlled by the government under a strict and invented form of Islam.

First thing to be mentioned is what is obvious, and probably already known: the physical OT as found in what can be called its 'oldest' form is not the oldest form of its existence, and the oldest Biblical texts which have been found are a result of many different authors adding, removing, combining stories and parts of stories as they saw fit and for whatever different reasons over differing spans of time; the Biblical stories began as one thing, but ended up modified.

From the Biblical text itself a number of different reasons emerge as to why these stories were written. Some stories are pure entertainment, and it is obvious that all the stories of the OT and NT began as stories for entertainment (samaaras and samaayas). Some stories were given religious and/or social dimensions; many stories serve agendas of those whom modified/edited the original stories. E.g. different reasons behind the original stories changed over time with different authors and their different reasons: it may be that they were initially created for creativity and entertainment but later on, to inspire people—lift spirit—

things were added; much later, parts of stories were changed, removed, and parts added to suit the 'new authors' (editors) religious and/or personal agendas. Still, there is an abundance of proof in the Biblical text which allows us to understand why the stories were originally created—and also why, much later, they were modified to suit the times and wants of the people authoring the changes.

What is also a fact, the original stories of the OT were first transmitted and kept alive orally, long before scripture was used to record these stories. Ancient civilisations always pass down their customs, ways of life, significant events—all told in interesting dramatic stories, dramatized to make them memorable (myths), told orally and passed down from generation to generation in a natural way where young and adults hear these stories told and absorb them then pass them on through a life-time. We will never know what the original stories looked like, for even if they had been eventually written down in original form they have not survived due to the nature of the materials used and the great span of time—but we do have the original culture they were drawn from, and you can see how the reality of Yemeni rock and fire worship, and their ways of life are all dramatized in the Biblical stories. What we do know is the 'oldest' written scrolls of the Biblical texts are very recent in terms of compared to the original stories which no longer exist as a wholly original and unadulterated form; and what has been found of Biblical texts has already been affected and modified by monotheistic religious beliefs while the basis of the stories are purely pagan, polytheistic, and older than the Abrahamic religions, and are exactly how pagans practised rituals, and believed in supernatural attributes to objects long before monotheistic religions emerged. Fortunately, large regions and communities in Yemen remained closed to the outside world (and the 'outside world' included Yemeni cities) and held onto their ancient way of life, and even when Islam would make its way to them, it was nominally adopted while pagan practise continued uninterrupted well into the 2000s. These communities' language, customs, beliefs—all pagan—have shown us the origins of the Bible and not only explained it as in interpreted words, but also through the way of life of these areas and its people unchanged and uncorrupted by modernisation, and uncorrupted by monotheistic religions (Islam, Judaism, Christianity).

What is striking and most notable in the Biblical stories, is they are obviously written by Yemenis, and incorporated into these stories at maybe a later date is writing by a people far away from their original homeland, who are writing about way of life back home. These Yemenis must have left their own country (and you have to remember 'country' and 'people/nation' does not necessarily mean like today 'abroad/foreign' with today's modern borders, but can also mean another village, another area) either willingly to seek fortune in a different country, or forced by conflict or other environmental and geographical reasons (to be discussed later), but for whatever reasons were unable to go back to Yemen, or decided they could not go back home, e.g. they may have sold all their land and travelled and lost their fortunes and there was no point in returning to Yemen so they decided to remain in ancient-Saudi Arabia and became part of its people (this is supported by the fictional narration of the children of Israel travelling to and taking over Canaan, and 'Canaan' means 'give up hope' 'resolved to fate'), and these ancient-Saudi people may have had a slightly different way of life, but the arriving Yemenis live like them, or perhaps it happened so early whatever cross-culture influence happened between the Yemeni people and the Saudis cannot be detected, but most likely after travelling around the region and losing everything the Yemenis melded into the ancient-Saudi way of life, but held onto the important things in Yemeni life in their hearts and memories which they kept alive in the stories they created. Whatever caused the Yemenis to leave Yemen and live in Saudi Arabia would cause the Yemenis and ancient-Saudi Arabians to move again much later on when things would change in the country, and this would bring the Yemeni/ancient-Saudis into the Levant where they ended up working for locals such as in ancient Lebanon, Iraq, Syria, the numbers of this Arabian Peninsula Arab people is not enough for them to be noticed as in to be significant, but enough to keep and introduce elements of Yemeni culture into these countries, but the numbers of this emigrating Yemeni/Saudi people was probably not in numbers as the exaggerated numbers of the 'children of Israel' exodus/wandering stories which was exaggerated through literary license.

The question is why did the stories not mention 'Yemen' or the ancient kingdoms and areas of Yemen, and the answer is: they did. Although the country at the southernmost end of the Arabian Peninsula has been known as 'Yemen' and we know the names of its ancient civilisations (Saba, Himyar, Hadramawt, Qataban, Ma'in, Awsan), we do not know what it was called before it was known by these names as this is pre-recorded history, but the ancient areas, some of which are listed in the previous chapter of Yemeni locations mentioned in the OT, show how the authors of the Biblical stories did include many names of areas in Yemen from pre-recorded history which exist to this day.

The origins of, and the changes in, the Biblical stories are a reflection of what Yemeni people went through: the most original elements show these stories were created for entertainment only, no different than the samaara and samaaya stories, while still at home in Yemen. Then these stories are given additions to describe their way of life, their customs and beliefs when some people moved to ancient-Saudi Arabia, and because they were of the same language, culture, pagan religions and beliefs these stories mirror both the lives of Yemen and ancient-Saudi Arabia inhabitants i.e. the people of the Arabian Peninsula. Stories of being enslaved, bondage are a result of small numbers of these Arabian Peninsula Arabs (Yemenis and ancient-Saudi Arabians) facing circumstances or opportunities which would lead them to Babylon, Assyria, Lebanon, and possibly Egypt where they may have been mistreated but not enslaved as portrayed in the stories of enslavement in Egypt, Babylon, etc. (more on this later); but everywhere they went, the Arabian Peninsula Arabs carried with them their customs, ways of life, and pagan beliefs which would end up being the basis for all three monotheistic religions. There were obviously feelings of 'othering' between the Arabian Peninsula Arabs: maybe the Yemenis were made to feel they were foreigners by the ancient-Saudi Arabians when they first arrived to live permanently in ancient-Saudi Arabia; the same 'othering' would be shown by the Iraqis, Lebanese, Syrians, and also Egyptians towards the Arabian Peninsula Arabs (Yemenis and ancient-Saudi Arabians) when they would first arrive in the Levant.

After travelling extensively, maybe losing everything they owned, there was no point and probably nohow to returning to their distant lands in Yemen; shame could have been a big part of it, also returning to nothing when they could start from scratch and 'cut losses', so to speak, by remaining in the foreign country; it may very well be that they could not return to their countries/land in Yemen because of a permanent negative change. In all cases the Yemeni immigrants (and later this would include ancient-Saudi Arabians) wanted to make the host country their new home, for this reason the narration and characters in the Biblical stories do not speak of returning to their homeland, but occupying someone else's land and making a home of it and this serves the real and original audiences of the stories by cutting off any hope or painful desire to return home, i.e. removing false hope of returning to Yemen.

At the same time they do not want their people to forget they came from somewhere else so beginning with the Abraham story, 'God' promises him all the land which he has arrived at and travelled through and can see so although he is not from these lands he can have everything his foot and vision lands on; throughout the stories the 'chosen people' as well as the stories' real audience are reminded they came from somewhere else, but they are not reminded where from—the Biblical stories are not a story of returning to one's original home, but all stories are of people making a new home in a foreign country, and are reminded with phrases such as 'the land I promised you', or 'the land I promised your father', and 'These cities and towns I gave you are not cities and towns you built', 'I gave you a land that belongs/belonged to another people'. So the stories remind the audience (initially the intended original audience are Yemeni people) they have come from a different country, but tells them, advises them: make this foreign land your new home and forget about travelling/wandering back, you have to make this your new home.

As mentioned earlier, it is important not to lose sight that it is definite the original stories were made purely for entertainment, and they are similar in structure to entertainment stories still told in remote Yemen. These stories may have been made at times of ease or times of distress, but they were a creative outlet. Then over time other people added to the stories to turn them into more 'religious'-oriented stories which could be used to move people or groups of people into action or religion. But the backbone of most of the stories such as wordplay, lewdness, super strength, deceit, trickery employed by the hero to win in his/her story plot, the use of names which are not names but compound words which mean exactly what the role of the character and/or the events which will happen—are meant as humour and are funny; if you have ever lived among a people untouched by modernisation and education, simple things a 'city person' does not find funny can be hilarious to people who live in the simplicity of antiquity (in no way do I mean that these people are stupid because they are not—what I mean is culture, way of life, exposure or lack of it, and circumstances create different attitudes and perceptions) e.g. a man called 'Abram' 'rolled up/folds' before circumcision and 'Abraham' 'tidy/clear-the' after circumcision would be found funny; Haman Hammedatha whose surname means 'here is the one covered with a blanket/sheet' and is executed because when he falls on a bed begging for his life is mistaken for trying to 'have his way' with the queen, can and would make the people of those times laugh as they understood exactly what the words making up the Biblical names meant and these words conjure up images.

The stories were created to allow, and have allowed, the upkeep of Yemeni pagan rituals, Yemeni way of life, Yemeni traditions. The stories allowed the people to hold onto what was and is important in Yemen culture and life and to incorporate it into their 'new' homeland. Which is why from the beginning of the

OT to its end, everything important, or sacred, and cherished in Yemeni life fills the pages of the Bible: land, offspring, rock worship, fire worship, fertility god worship, all its pagan rituals of fire offerings, tithe offerings, sacrifice and blood on doorsteps of houses for demons to not harm the inhabitants of the house, stepwives, barrenness and fertility, superstitions, popular clothing, popular fabrics, and dramatic humorous stories for entertainment, to name just some of what features. The proof these stories were also meant to upkeep and remind of Yemeni tradition is the fact they have survived throughout those periods, orally then written, even if they were distorted later by deletions and additions made to them to change them towards the 'newer' authors' agendas—they still served the original intention of keeping alive pagan rituals, superstitions, beliefs, traditions, etc. because although later authors tampered with the text, they did not want to remove the elements mentioned earlier, nor could they tamper with the names as it would cause the scriptures to lose meaning—and therefore was preserved.

The fact these authors of the Bible came from Yemen is in how they set their Biblical stories in mountainous and hilly areas, it is because these Yemenis and their stories are from the mountainous regions of Yemen and ancient-Saudi Arabia, they are used to living in mountains and love the terrain of the land they live in regardless whether or not the Yemeni people who would emigrate to live in ancient-Saudi Arabia and later in the Levant would live in hilly or mountainous areas of Saudi Arabia and the Levant or not, these Yemeni authors did describe the Yemeni mountainous terrain in their Biblical stories, although they set the stories mostly in the land of ancient-Saudi Arabia especially its western coast and mid-southern areas (around Mecca). If you read the Biblical stories and look at the land of Palestine, in real life Palestine is not as mountainous as the areas described in the Biblical stories, it is topographically different, but the authors are describing the mountainous terrain of their original home in Yemen (it is important to understand what has been mentioned in the introduction that all the 'hebraised' names currently in Palestine/modern-Israel are due to European Zionists re-naming the Palestinian cities, towns, villages and areas which they took by military force in 1948 with names from the Bible, but they are not the real names of these towns, cities and villages which had different Arab names before the military occupation—this needs to be mentioned to avoid the confusion what a very recent event in history (the creation of modern-Israel which some Israelis themselves call the 'artificial Jewish State') may cause when objectively reading the Bible). The descriptions of cities and towns are the cities and towns of ancient-Saudi Arabia currently called Jeddah which is the fictional Judah, and Mecca which is the fictional Jerusalem (to be explained later in this chapter).

Captivity or Labour, and the Creation of Jehovah

The mountainous people of Yemen are used to repeatedly and daily travelling by foot over great distances in rough mountainous terrain and over dangerous terrain—it is how life was, and still is in remote regions. Also travelling to other countries for trade, exploration, etc. is part of Yemen's ancient history. With regards to the authors of the Bible, whatever reasons led them to leave Yemen be it unliveable circumstances, or trade, seeking a better life/fortune in faraway lands—what becomes evident is when they are in ancient-Saudi Arabia, and the surrounding region, in one way or another they lose or consume their fortune and things go wrong, i.e. they do not succeed in their trade, or attempt at a better life, but end up marginalised, working as labour and maybe even made to feel unwelcome—this can be seen in the Biblical stories they wrote. They probably stood out as foreigners in ancient-Saudi Arabia, then later along with ancient-Saudi Arabians they all stood out as foreigners in the Levant—maybe physical features (this is only guessing) such as skin colour marked them out, and/or their language may have been slightly different than the ancient-Saudi Arabians e.g. a slightly different dialect or accent, and their language/dialect would definitely be different than the languages of Canaan, ancient Iraq, Syria, Lebanon and Egypt; maybe their clothing made them stand out as different. But the bitterness over being treated differently because they were a comparatively different people i.e. they were Arabs but from a different area, is made clear in the stories they told (and an exaggeration of the reality) where in real life reasons led them to initially become labourers, low-paid and overworked, can be seen repeated in the Biblical stories as bondage in Egypt, in Jacob being underpaid/cheated and overworked by Laban, captivity in Babylon and so on.

When reading the Biblical stories, a question arises out of the contradiction in the one same narrative: were they captives in Babylon, or did they go there for work and a better life willingly? The answers to these questions are in the Bible, and these fictional stories of enslavement are exaggerated to reflect what was experienced by the authors of these stories which may have been a lot less than slavery. E.g. if the real authors had been captives in Babylon this experience of forced labour, forced residence, could be what inspired the Egypt-Pharaoh-Children of Israel being enslaved story, but at the same time the fictionality of both the enslavement in Egypt and the exile and enslavement in Babylon stories all show these are stories which were entirely fictional. But they do shine a light that the authors and their people experienced a degradation in way and quality of life when they moved away from their homeland seeking a better future or forced by other circumstances to find a home in foreign lands, and the stories were created and/or modified to give the struggling Yemenis then both struggling Yemenis and ancient-Saudi Arabians overworked and underpaid, hope to lift their morale 'just like we were freed from Egypt—we will be freed from Babylon and return home [to ancient-Saudi Arabia]', the stories of enslavement then freedom gave the Yemenis working in ancient-Saudi Arabia, then the Yemenis/ancient-Saudi Arabians working in the Levant an uplifting story that even people under worse conditions can get better. The Exodus and Egypt enslavement story, and other captivity stories, were created as a myth of hope.

The Biblical stories tell us the authors lived through periods of hard circumstances in foreign land, dramatized in their stories to bondage and captivity. If you look at the Exodus story, the 'children of Israel' are described as being enslaved, treated terribly, and that the Egyptians hate them—but more than once in the same story contradictory statements are made: the Egyptians love them to the degree they give them golden jewellery (enough to make a golden calf out of later in the story) before they leave Egypt, and clothes and livestock to last forty years while they wander. In all stories with major characters as exiled captives in Babylon, although the protagonists are described as 'captives' 'exiles' the characters who are supposed to be their aggressive, oppressive overlords actually care for the protagonists' happiness and do not want to see them sad (according to the self-same Biblical stories) and they send them away with vessels of gold and silver and an abundance of resources and all these treasures the exiles carry away are in unrealistically great amounts. Within the stories of the Babylonian captives/exiles, the protagonist, whether Ezra or Nehemiah, are described more like employees willingly working and do not appear as slaves: they occupy high positions and are close to the kings of the respective story; all they do is say they want to leave and not only are they allowed to leave but they carry away with them most of the Babylonian country's treasures and resources.

What these fictional stories tell us is that some Yemenis originally left their homeland, tried to live in ancient-Saudi Arabia and when this did not work out, they went on to the Levant and ended up working there which may have been specifically in Babylon before returning to ancient-Saudi Arabia again. Whether they only ever went to ancient-Saudi Arabia or ended up going to Babylon and back, and whether they were captives/slaves (unlikely) or were a willing workforce, the collective memory and experience of these Arabian Peninsula Arabs is an unpleasant one; whether they were mistreated, given work they deemed 'beneath them', or overworked—it does seem they suffered from discrimination, and in their stories which would end up being the Bible/OT, the real mistreated people took out their repressed anger in stories of vengeance and destruction of Babylon, Egypt and against other nations in storyland.

One of the ways the Yemenis overcame and uplifted a demoralised Yemeni people who were most probably mistreated and marginalised by the host countries because they came from somewhere else, was that although they had settled in the host countries and lived as one among the original inhabitants of those countries, they created stories to lift morale and encourage their marginalised people to make this foreign land their home—and this is where the legend of a 'special' 'chosen people' is created and arises from, a story where a special people that do not belong to any of the countries of the stories settings which is ancient-Saudi Arabia in both reality and in the stories, but also dramatized to include other areas in the region, with a supernatural deity helping them wander across lands (in an exaggerated tale based on real journeying (but not forty years etc.)) because they have been chosen by God. The mistreatment, discrimination they are being subject to in reality is turned into a positive thing in the story: 'we are not from here' 'we are special' 'we are God's people' 'we are better than every other people' 'we are better than the people who are hurting us'. And the stories make a point (albeit without giving reasons because the original audience knows the reasons which they themselves are suffering from) the Canaanite, the Amorite, Moabite, Ammonite, Edomite—all the peoples of the region in the stories (whether they are real or fictional as the word-names and the stories regarding these mentioned 'nations' are completely fictional) are inferior to the 'chosen people' which the story makes more than clear they are not from Egypt, nor are they from Canaan which in storyland they will settle in.

The story tells the audience not to worry, to be patient, no matter what or how long, they will finally settle in ancient-Saudi Arabia and they will stay and live forever in ancient-Saudi Arabia because God said he would drive out the inhabitants of ancient-Saudi Arabia and all other inhabitants in storyland and give it to the 'chosen people of God' to live in, and to stay in. And this is the most significant proof from the Bible itself: Jehovah/Yahweh/yhwh - يَحويه 'he/it makes him/it stay/still' 'he/it contains him/it' as before at

(Gen.22:13-14) yĕhōwāh, YHWH; يحوه/يحوا ، ييحُوآه /يَحُوآه all mean 'he/it-stays/stayed/contains/contained' and 'he/it-stayed/stilled it/contained it'—is a god that leads them to a foreign land and gives them a land not theirs but will be for them to stay in and live on just like this god's name is 'stays'.

Everywhere this word is used, whether to describe God - Jehovah/Yahweh/yhwh it all means 'stay/stays', and the word also appears in different compound word forms with 'Jehovah' retaining its meaning of 'stay/stays/contains': when God tells Abraham to slaughter Isaac in a human burnt sacrifice, he then sends a ram to replace Isaac as a sacrifice, the place is named Jehovah-jireh; يحوه يرئه 'he stayed/stilled it-he sees it'; yḥwh-yirah; which is what happens in the story with the ram staying because it got caught in the thicket and Abraham seeing it (Gen.22:13-14). It is not coincidental, in fact it is impossible to be coincidental, that the authors of the Bible intentionally chose words to give names to characters and places in the Biblical stories which meant exactly what they were named and what was happening or would happen in the story. So a god named 'he/it-stays/stayed/contains/contained' gives a foreign and wandering people a place/country to stay in forever.

Also, the other name for the same protagonist God is: Shaddai; 'ēl šadday; which, again, misinterpretation and Biblical scholars erroneously state means 'God Almighty' or that it is a word meaning 'breast' or 'mountain', and they rely on Ugarit text which supports their belief that it means 'El of the mountains' based on a Ugaritic description that a deity named 'El' lives on some kind of mountain. In Arabic, the language which has successfully translated every single word-name in the Biblical texts and made sense of the stories being told, this is what the word means: Shaddai; 'ēl šadday; يْل شَدَّي 'the-emigrate/emigrating/leaves forever' 'the-she emigrates/leaves forever' 'is emigrating/leaving forever' i.e. the complete opposite of Jehovah 'stays'. Cp: ill-shadday. The Jehovah compound word is in the masculine, the Shaddai compound word is in the feminine, so not only does it show a transition happening as part of the story of people wandering, and a God named 'emigrating' changing her/his name to a God called 'staying' because the story is now about finding a land for the people to go from a wandering/emigrating state of being to finding a land and settling in it, but also within the same story a female God 'Shaddai' (also called the female 'I Am That I Am' (which is based on 'ashera' as the original name mistranslated 'I Am That I Am' 'ehyeh 'ăšer 'ehyeh actually translates to 'she is-with calf-she is' i.e. pregnant) and a female 'El-Elohe-Israel' in the OT) changes into a male god 'Jehovah'.

You can see how it makes perfect sense for the authors and the audience of these stories that the story narrates God telling Moses that before he (God) used to be called 'the-she emigrates/leaves' but now his name is 'he/it makes him/it stay/still', and this is reflected in the story: first they are people with no land, no home and made to wander from place to place and never settle, except when God decides he will allow them to settle and stay in one country so God's name goes from 'the-emigrate' 'the-she emigrates' to 'he/it makes him/it stay/still': 'And God spake unto Moses, and said unto him, I *am* the Lord: And I appeared unto Abraham, unto Isaac, and unto Jacob, by the name of God Almighty[el-Shaddai/she emigrates], but by my name JEHOVAH[he stays] was I not known to them. And I have established my covenant with them, to give them the land of Canaan, the land of their pilgrimage, wherein they were strangers. And I have also heard the groaning of the children of Israel, whom the Egyptians keep in bondage; and I have remembered my covenant. Wherefore say unto the children of Israel, I *am* the Lord, and I will bring you out from under the burdens of the Egyptians, and I will rid you out of their bondage, and I will redeem you with a stretched out arm, and with great judgements: And I will take you to me for a people, and I will be to you a God: and ye shall know that I *am* the Lord your God, which bringeth you out from under the burdens of the Egyptians. And I will bring you in unto the land, concerning the which I did swear to give it to Abraham, to Isaac, and to Jacob; and I will give it you for an heritage: I *am* the Lord.' (Exod.6:2-8)

The stories were to uplift a part of society of Yemeni origins in ancient-Saudi Arabia because they were made to feel unwelcome, or inferior, so in their stories they aggrandised themselves into a 'chosen' people, a people whom although were outsiders God gave the right to live on the land. If in real-life the situation for these Yemenis was not turning out well, or not as good as they had hoped after long travel from Yemen, and attempts were unsuccessful in ancient-Saudi Arabia and its region—in the stories not only were they to be a 'chosen' people, but a people of unmatchable might, and intelligence, and would always win in the end even if they had to lie and deceive to achieve victory, and nothing displays this more than all the protagonists of the OT stories revert to lies, cheating, deceit, sexually immoral behaviour and other negative behaviour to come out on top against the antagonists, and the stories do not attempt to hide that the hero(es) of the stories engage in unsavoury behaviour: be it Jacob, David, Mordecai, Esther, and what is interesting is the Arab word for 'hero/champion' is (bṭll/ beṭell /بطل/بَطَل) and its origin is from the same word 'Bethel' (bṭll/baṭaal/بَطَل/بَطّال) 'bad' 'evil' 'dreadful' 'wrong' 'cease/stop' which is also used as a place name in the Bible.

This is why it is significant to this topic: if you refer to the interpretation of words regarding, and the Biblical chapters of, Jacob having a bad dream while sleeping with a rock as a pillow, he is promised to be given the land by God in a dream, wakes up, feels scared and claims what a dreadful place this is before making a stone pillar/altar to God and calls it 'Bethel' 'bad'—the word 'hero/champion' 'beṭell' is the same root word 'Bethel/beṭell' 'bad' because winning, coming out on top is to cause another to lose, or to do something negative to another to win, be the champion, e.g. even in benign games or sports: winning a game causes the other to lose, winning a playful wrestling match requires using force and strength to cause another to succumb. Jacob's story keeps on repeating this lesson, as do David's stories, Mordecai and Esther: Jacob cheats Esau his brother out of his birth right and father's blessing causing him to flee where God comes to him in a dream and tells him he will reward him with 'this land you see'—Jacob calls the place 'bad' (Bethel); he immediately goes to live with his uncle Laban and he cheats Laban out of his own and best of flocks, and when he intends to take off with everything without Laban's knowledge Jacob tells his wives it is God of Bethel (Bad) who has told him these cattle are his to take from Laban, while the previous chapter shows Jacob went to great lengths of trickery to cause them to be 'ringstraked' and 'speckled' after an agreement was made with Laban that the ringstraked and speckled would be for Jacob—and he tells his wives that the God of Bethel who is telling him to take these animals as his, is also telling him to leave, so again you have the word 'Bethel' 'bad' associated to bad acts of the hero in the story: the 'bad' becomes 'champion/hero' just like the word in the original language for both meanings is the same word.

Following the episode of 'Bethel/bad' with Laban, God comes down and wrestles with Jacob with the latter winning in the wrestling match, but the narration shows that it is Jacob who has had something bad done to him: his muscle withers and his name is changed to 'Israel/twisted muscle-the' and following this chapter bad things happen to Jacob, but also his character in the stories becomes weaker while his children and all the 'children of Israel' become the protagonists and from this point onwards all the stories of the 'children of Israel' is about the 'chosen people' fighting and winning—most of the stories show the 'chosen people' attack, kill and wipe out whole nations for no other reason than to be able to take that people's land. Furthermore, even characters who are good to the children of Israel such as prince Shechem, his father and people are all slaughtered through Jacob/Israel's sons deceiving them into all being circumcised to disable them then killing them all and destroying their city while they are hurting from circumcision. The characters of the stories change, but it always keeps the theme of the children of Israel attack and win, even if using bad and deceitful behaviour because what matters is coming out on top—and that is the message to the initial and original audience: do what you have to do to survive. (see Gen.28:10-22; 30:27-43; 31; 32:24-32; 33:19; 34:1-30).

This is why no archaeological evidence has ever proved a people called 'Israel' or 'Israelites' or 'children of Israel' ever existed, or the major characters of the Biblical stories: such as Moses, Abraham, David, and the list goes on. Whereas there is abundant archaeological evidence of many other ancient civilisations all over the region, and in these civilisations' many and well-documented and existing archaeological finds none of these civilisations mention an 'Israel/Israelite/children of Israel' or any of its characters. Although the Biblical stories mention great events happening with and within these other real ancient civilisations, none of these civilisations mention, not even once, 'Israel' or any of the Biblical characters, which can only mean this 'chosen people' as per the Biblical stories called 'Israel' never existed. The problem is western scholars and organisations are always trying to use archaeological information of the Middle East to prove everything said in the Bible actually happened, and that everyone mentioned in it existed. Whereas the reality of archaeological information shows it did not exist, and archaeology has proved the Bible not to be a historical document—and the Bible itself shows what it really is: a collection of fictional stories filled with fictional characters and events.

This is a problem when you have Biblical scholars and other organisations attempting to force a story written for other reasons millennia ago into a 'historical reality' which never happened, never was—instead of reading it, understanding it and accepting what actual archaeological finds tell them, and more importantly what the Biblical stories make absolutely clear: it is a made-up story. Due to this attempt and insistence to prove the fictional Biblical stories happened in reality, these experts are distorting and overlooking the real history of the Middle East region, and the experts are missing what the authors of the Biblical stories and their stories are actually saying: the stories are a legend to uplift a real down-trodden people undergoing harsh and hard realities in a foreign land, and urging them to make the land they ended up in a new home, and a permanent home, by creating entertaining stories for a pastime. This is more realistic than trying to prove 'Abram/Abraham' 'rolled up' meaning his uncircumcised penis becoming 'pull up/ draw out/tidy' referring to circumcising his and others' penises because that is the motion done to pull and keep taut the foreskin to be cut off leaving it looking tidy; 'Hagar' 'abandoned' whom he abandons; 'Isaac' which means pulling up water little by little out of a dry well during drought—and it just so happens the story tells us when his mother Sarah conceives him that she is like a dried up well as her menstruation has long ceased 'and it ceased to be with Sarah after the manner of women' yet he is the product of the dried up well; 'Moses' 'squeeze him/it' whom Pharaoh's daughter finds in a river; 'Joshua' 'picked many/took a lot' who is ordered to pick a lot of men and go fight the Amalek; 'David' 'the stone rolling pin of a grinder' which is a dense stone used for grinding grain—and happens to kill his opponent with a stone; Goliath 'came-shouted'—who does nothing but shout out challenges and speeches even until he is killed; Jonathan 'males making each other female by having sex with each other' and his role in the story is a loving and sexual relationship with David, which ends up being the cause of his and his father's (Saul) demise; Jesse 'my bread' and Jesus 'bread' 'broke/ate bread' 'breaking/eating bread' with both these characters in their separate stories revolving around scenes and narration to do with bread. The people of the times knew these were just stories, many different stories, as the language used is the language they spoke and is still spoken to this day: Arabic. The true interpretations of the Biblical character and place names prove how fictional the stories are. But these stories entertained and reassured those who came from Yemen to become a part of the ancient-Saudi Arabian societies, these original authors and their audiences who were not feeling fully integrated, or accepted, but were staying and stayed. The rituals are pagan Yemeni and pagan ancient-Saudi Arabian, the culture, clothing, traditions are uniquely Yemeni in the stories of the Bible, and as time lapsed and went on, the stories would become the basis of monotheistic religions of the region, and spread further across the region, and the stories were altered to suit later times and people.

If read properly, the Biblical stories are hardly religious stories, but stories of revenge, deceit, theft, forceful appropriation, forbidden relationships and a never-ending disobedience towards God. The character who is most deceitful is the hero and gets his way in the end; these major characters which the original stories paint in a bad light (but are still the heroes of the story) do have their images polished further by modifications, even read in the English language you can see where insertions have been made, they either jar with the original text because of the style of prose, or the statement made whether praising one major character or attacking/lessening another character's status. The religious rituals in the Biblical stories are the nature and act of pagan worship and sacrifices offered to rocks, demons and pagan gods—nothing to do with monotheism.

The stories though full of glorified mass murder of innocents (even God himself frequently and extensively kills the 'chosen people' by the hundreds if they question Aaron's priesthood, or even Aaron's two sons for being so excited to meet God with smoking incense they are burnt to death by God, or for asking for water to drink in the desert), they are still full of humour in the responses of its characters, the names and what they mean and how they reflect and relay in the storyline, the way things unfold, and they are or were originally 'samaara' and 'samaaya' tales full of action, humour and erotica, told in the evening. The structure, humour, sexual innuendo just like Yemeni samaaras where characters often 'kill by the thousands' 'capture by the thousands' and 'set thousands of captives free', and the way they mimic and caricaturise real Yemeni life, beliefs and rituals indicate all these stories began solely for entertainment, either modified later to give its audience hope that things would get better, and this land (ancient-Saudi Arabia) would become their home. Even if these stories were modified to lift morale, then much later modified to serve religious/personal agendas—it is very likely these stories were just a pastime, where creative people used their own culture of the Arabian Peninsula to pass it down to younger generations, absorbed while passing time in the only form of entertainment: telling stories.

What the stories all have in common is the people's yearning for a permanent home, a land where they can build homes and families, the stories do not attempt to claim the foreign lands of Canaan and its region as theirs, but emphasise they are the foreigners who will invade and inhabit the land to make their home. In the stories, the country of origin is left out because there is no intent in the stories (and in reality for the audience) of returning home so it is not mentioned, but it is 'Canaan'/give up hope' in the story (ancient-Saudi Arabia in reality) to give these Yemeni immigrants encouragement through fantastical tales to plant themselves among ancient-Saudi Arabians and bear living in a foreign land adopting it as their own where even if they had no roots, time and encouragement would allow them to eventually become one with the people. When did this happen—no one knows, but evidently early enough for no records of archaeology to survive, but due to the similarity of culture (rock and fire worship, fertility gods worship) with ancient-Saudi Arabia and sharing the same Arabic language (the Old Arabic of the Bible) allowed their customs, pagan rituals, superstitions, and beliefs to become an element of ancient-Saudi Arabia; and everything of the culture of these Arabian Peninsula Arabs (the Yemenis and ancient-Saudi Arabians) from pagan rituals, superstitions, expressions, clothing, the very language is the literature contained in the Bible. Early enough to become an element of the ancient-Saudi Arabian civilisation, and evidently the arriving Yemenis were treated with bias to begin with, but with time and generations people forgot the differences and became one with the ancient-Saudi Arabians.

It was also early enough for the stories to have been misinterpreted by later generations as religious texts, moving towards what would first emerge as the western-misnomered 'Judaism' (which should be 'Jewish' or a word from the correct pronunciation and meaning of Jew/Jewish, e.g. Yehudism as the word and character/place word-name 'Judah' and the related story regarding his conception and naming by Leah has absolutely nothing to do with the word 'jew' and the naming of the religion 'Jew(s)/Jewish/Yehudi/ Yehood'), then Christianity, then Islam. These stories and the religion spread out of the Arabian Peninsula and into countries which did not speak the Old Arabic, e.g. the Levant. And with the Jewish religion, like all religions, undergoing change, popularity and fading away, while becoming popular in other regions, the Arabian Peninsula would undergo Christianity becoming its newest emerging religion, besides followers sticking to the Jewish religion, and also followers sticking to the much older pagan religions, before Islam would arrive and most of the Arabian Peninsula inhabitants would turn to Islam and with great spans of time and into modernity (and for a number of reasons mentioned in the Introduction) the inhabitants of the Arabian Peninsula would no longer be concerned with nor connected to any of the Bible (both the OT and NT), despite it being where all three divine religions began before they spread into the other Middle East countries.

From the Bible itself, and the words which would come to describe the people following that certain religion (Yehud/Jew)—and the code they attempted to create out of Arabic (Hebrew)—it is obvious coming from a different Arab country which once made them stand out, no longer did with the lapse of time, they became one with the ancient-Saudi Arabian people. Even if they came from Yemen to live in ancient-Saudi Arabia, they were already one race and when much later in time when the origins and reasons of the Biblical stories were forgotten, and rulers and religious chiefs attempted to use these Biblical stories to serve political and religious agendas and they (the people in charge and who had access to the literature) added to it to give it more religious orientation to convince the people with its message, they sought to take the stories of Israel, Moses, Jacob, etc. to insist the people of that certain religion came from somewhere else - which resulted in the ancient-Saudi Arabian descendants (which the Yemeni immigrants' descendants had long become one with) using the negative or even neutral words 'jew' and 'hebrew' (which means 'distorts/ruins/makes worse' 'extremely disfigured/nature reversed/against nature') to describe the people whom they shared the same race and culture with because they knew these people attempting to claim a 'special' and separate lineage were no different than themselves, Arabian Peninsula Arabs of those times, and the wider public had access to these stories which were disseminated orally, and were aware of the distortion of the Biblical texts/stories, and of the religion, and therefore called them with the verb of the action they were doing: 'Jew' 'Hebrew', and that is how it became the name of a religion (with time) and an adjective for its followers which much later would be mistaken as a separate race by western foreigners, but not by the people of the region. This last point has become obfuscated in modern times with the advent of Zionism and the Israeli-Palestinian conflict, as well as due to Saudi Arabia's misuse of religion to keep not only its own people in check, but Muslims across the region too.

The point is, the numbers of Yemeni immigrants who originally arrived in ancient-Saudi Arabia, did eventually meld into and become one with the ancient-Saudi Arabian people which although they may have been initially discriminated against, they did become one as they are one people in essence to begin with, and they also have the similar culture, the same Old Arabic language, the same pagan worship and beliefs. When for political and/or religious agendas the parts of ancient-Saudi Arabian people wanted a religion to be followed in a certain way, they were not purely Yemeni, or purely the descendants of the Yemeni immigrants to ancient-Saudi Arabia, but were the ancient-Saudi Arabians of which the Yemeni immigrants and their descendants had been absorbed by and diluted into. The only reason we know they were Yemenis is because their stories were so popular and creative, not only did they forever encapsulate Yemeni pagan traditions, Yemeni customs and Yemeni way of life—but these Yemeni pagan rituals, Yemeni stories, all the matters of pagan and practical life important to ancient (and some modern) Yemenis would become the religious rituals, festivals and way of worship of the major religions of the region; even the stories' characters with their Yemeni Arabic compound word-names tailored to suit the events of the story would become the heroes of the monotheistic religions and would come to be erroneously believed to have existed.

With the lapse of time and flux all religions go through, the Jewish religion would survive as a minority in Yemen while Judaism and Christianity disappeared completely from the rest of the Arabian Peninsula due to all its people converting to Islam, and with Judaism and Christianity remaining adopted by minorities further away in Iraq, Syria, Lebanon, Egypt, the real reasons and meanings of the Bible would be forgotten, and this very Yemeni literature would be modified to suit those whom adopted it, used it for other reasons than its initial creation—but the real reasons it was created for still stand out, they are there forever in the text of the Biblical stories: a people of Yemeni origins kept alive Yemeni culture, using it to encourage and uplift its people whom first arrived in ancient-Saudi Arabia, to make roots and a home there through stories set in fictional lands which gave hope to the immigrant people in the new homeland.

A valid question is why was Palestine chosen to set the Biblical stories in? The answer is simple: it was not. All the place-names used in the Biblical stories are word-names which reflect what happens in the stories so if a person or country is called 'Canaan' or 'Canaanite' in the Biblical story, it is for their meanings and roles in the story 'give up hope' 'resolve to fate' 'he/they looked up/craned necks', the same for all other place names created for the Biblical stories. The authors of the stories are obviously aware of neighbouring regions and lands, but no one knows if these popular Biblical stories and their invented place-names are what influenced the future naming of lands, areas and their nations, or if the opposite happened and the countries were already called those names but the Biblical authors used their names because of how their meanings pronounced in Old Arabic could be used as wordplay in the story. E.g. if Canaan (currently modern Palestine) was called Canaan before the Biblical stories then these stories were modified much later than when it was believed to have been created and nothing else changes: they are still of Yemeni origin, written by Yemenis and depict a caricature and dramatization of Yemeni culture and life; they are set in some areas of Yemen, but the stories are mostly set in ancient-Saudi Arabia; the original Yemeni authors are aware of neighbouring countries and civilisations and have included them in the stories for drama and only insofar as the names of these lands and civilisations can be used as word-play to relay and reflect what is happening in the Biblical story being told. It is possible that when the Arabs of the Arabian Peninsula would spread into the Levant which includes Palestine, Iraq, Syria, Lebanon and Jordan, bringing with them not only the Biblical stories but also the Jewish religion, then the Christian and Islamic religions, that the inhabitants which includes the incoming Arabian Peninsula Arabs, and the local Palestinians, Lebanese, Iraqis, Jordanians, Syrians would name some of their areas after the fictional areas of the stories e.g. such as Bethlehem and aNaa<u>ss</u>ira (Nazareth) in current Palestine (it must be noted there were never Jewish peoples/communities living in Palestine, for whatever reasons ancient Palestinians (ancestors) stuck to pagan religions before later on accepting Christianity and Islam but not the Jewish religion). Everything the Biblical stories describe is way of life in the Arabian Peninsula and a dramatized version of culture, conflict and religious rituals of both Yemen and ancient-Saudi Arabia, and these stories are based on things that exist to this day in remote Yemen, but also in modern Saudi Arabia.

Yemenis were a great agricultural people in tune with the land, they could identify where land and environment could be made into suitable living conditions for humans. Since the Bronze Age, Yemeni mountains have been made into fertile man-made stepped terraces flowing with agriculture; the most seemingly uninhabitable, rough, rocky, jagged mountains are inhabited and made into fertile, life-sustaining regions. The people walk, run, skip along and upon the most dangerous and tough terrain and cross the most acute steeps, cliff edges, ridges, at angles and with huge and heavy loads on their heads/shoulders—where someone coming from outside the mountainous region would have great difficulty getting across empty-handed. They build their houses on hilltops and mountain peaks, they love the land—mountain, rock, farmland and all. This is why the Biblical stories set in fictionalised Canaan reflect a more mountainous terrain and land than actual Canaan—because the authors from Yemeni mountains had the land they loved on their minds when creating the stories. Even in the stories they set the 'temples' 'God's house' 'altars' on mountain tops because that is where the real-life authors like to live.

Initially, the stories were created for a limited audience to momentarily escape the reality lived into the lives and events of the stories, while at the same time delivering a message 'this is your new home', 'make this your home'. At some point later in time when more religious ideas emerged, or where pagan religion was formulating towards a monotheistic religion, religious officials would take over the stories (maybe making them into scriptures) and edit them to suit their own religious and personal agendas—attempting to direct the people of the land towards a specific religion. What were separate stories were forced together, parts removed, added, changed—anyone who reads the Bible will notice the jarring, the insertion by a different author, the contradictions in the same story itself. What was once a lamentation of the authors and audience coming from somewhere else (Yemen), and having to make a foreign land home (Saudi Arabia) would be used by the new religious authors, who are more like editors than authors, to drive their ideas as religious instruction.

What is obvious and abundantly available in the text of the Biblical stories is the use of Arabic words to create names of both characters and places. This has already become aboundingly clear in the translations of the Biblical names which I have provided, in the fact that the names created for characters and places were to reflect exactly what the characters would be involved in within their parts of the story being told. The Biblical stories can neither be properly nor fully read, they cannot be understood, without understanding the word-name meanings. Names, especially of characters and places given roles in the respective story, always have a meaning related to the storyline, but not as erroneously linked by Biblical and religious scholars who wrongly attribute names to gods and deities, where they claim names ending with 'el' and 'ah/yah' are connected to a pagan deity 'El' or to 'Jehovah/Yahweh' when actually 'el' and 'ah(yah)' in the word-name is the article or pronoun that connects the character or action to the adjective/adverb/noun part of the compound word-name such as 'ah/yah/yh' the pronoun:

*Hezek***iah** means '*squeezed/cornered/crammed him*-**he/him**';

*Ab***iah** '*they rejected* **him/it**';

*Ur***iah** '**he** *was made naked/stripped naked*' '*made naked/stripped naked*-**he/him**';

In the same way the part of the compound word-name 'el' means 'the/with/who/to/is' and connects the character or action to the adjective/adverb/noun part of the compound word-name:

*Penu***el** '*children of*-**the**' '*in*-**the**' '*in me*-**the**' '*show/become apparent*-**the**';

*Samu***el** '*block(ed)*-**the**' '*plug*-**the**' '*shut up*-**the**';

*Isra***el** '*twisted muscle*-**the**' '*twisted*-**the**';

*Haza***el** '*crammed/cornered*-**the**' '*blocked/held in*-**the**'.

And this is also a remote Yemeni thing done to make others smile or laugh, or to show how clever a person is with words, is to take the name of a person and make a ditty about it, or a joke with a play on the meanings of the word in the name or something the person has said.

Wordplay is also abundant in the use of compound words in the Bible, allowing them to have more than one meaning to suit the story, maybe to suit additions made by later authors (which the code called 'Hebrew' allows with the exchangeability of certain letters). In the exact same way of using words to create fictional names for characters and places, the Biblical authors have done the same thing using the same method but with some names of real civilisations of the region whether Persian, Babylonian, Assyrian, Akkadian, etc. where they could employ the name with its pronunciation and meaning as in Arabic words—therefore using it, too, like the compound word-names the authors created themselves, all to reflect what happens in the story connected to the name. So some names may be real (albeit with how they pronounce and mean in Arabic), but all events and characters are not real—such as 'Hilkiah' which means 'I will find it/him' 'here/look-found-he/him' could not have been given such a name at birth then coincidentally his character 'finds' the book which will cause the dramatic change in the story; 'Ruth' which means 'sexual intercourse' named such because in order to get a husband and provide offspring for her mother-in-law, her mother-in-law instructs (and Ruth obeys), to offer and have illicit sex with a man to entice him into becoming her husband; 'David' 'rolling pin of stone grinder' is named such at birth only to fulfil a coincidental and pivotal event for the ascension of his character which is to kill a giant with a stone; Maryam/Miriam 'pass along the river/sea' who after her baby brother (Moses) is thrown into the river, she follows the river so when the people who find and save him from the river she can suggest to them a wet nurse. Seeing as the same applies to every single character and place name in the Bible, of whom the parents of these characters (had the characters been real living people) could not have possibly foreseen the future to give them the appropriate names beforehand (and the names are not really names but compound words), nor can it be a Bible full of coincidences to match the characters' names, it can only be authors who created the character and the event, the story and the invented word-name to suit what is to happen in the stories. This fact is the reason why no 'Moses' 'Israel' 'children of Israel' or any of the Biblical characters have ever been found mentioned in the archaeology of the whole Middle East region.

This is where Biblical scholars enter a folly, because they do not understand the true and real language of the Bible which is pure and Old Arabic still spoken to this day, due to this they have missed and never known the true meanings of the names given to the characters and places of the Bible—and in doing so have not been able to understand the meanings behind these names, therefore are unable to see who wrote the Bible and the real reasons behind it, from the original and initial reasons to the later reasons. Instead, they go around digging up ancient grounds, and whatever they find they loosely tie, desperately and unconvincingly, as proof of the Biblical events—although none of the archaeological proof mentions, nor is connected to the Bible, but the documentation of rulers, wars, conflicts, events which happened within that specific ancient civilisation and its history which includes all encounters and dealings with other foreign ancient civilisations—and they have never mentioned 'Israel' 'Israelites' 'children of Israel' 'Moses' 'Solomon' 'David' or any other 'kings of Israel', and this all points to the fact that they never existed.

Which leads to the fact that clearly stands out in the Bible: all the events are fictional, the authors took their own travels and tribulations and incorporated them along with their original Yemeni culture into a tale of perseverance and hope told through stories of miraculous escapes, divine assistance; an amalgam of different stories told dramatically, with humour, exaggerated into an exodus of great numbers of people who although have wandered forty years still manage, although they have no bread and no meat at all and anger God with requests for meat to eat, who in following chapters suddenly have enough cattle/flocks to sacrifice many heads per day. They take part of reality—the real life people/Biblical authors travelled long from their homeland, experienced thirst and hunger, rationing would have been a real part of this journey which they chose to end northwards in Saudi Arabia; this real life experience taken and exaggerated in numbers, and how they were sustained and how long they wandered because it is a story told to an audience that wants and needs to be entertained and inspired. Everything they encounter during travel then during residing in ancient-Saudi Arabia, where initially they may have been marginalised, is tempered in the stories by recalling their pagan worship rituals, fertility of the land, the familiar mountainous terrain—everything they cherished back home; and they cool their hearts with stories of revenge, on the original inhabitants of ancient-Saudi Arabia partly by God, and partly by the might and bravery of the 'chosen people' who will make this their home.

The point is, the Biblical stories draw from actual Yemeni life and culture, from custom to clothing, from worries to worship—and in the same manner the authors of the Biblical stories, whether the early Yemeni immigrants or the later authors/editors, looked around them and included the architecture of buildings, palaces, temples, places of worship whether from memory of back home in Yemen, or what they witnessed during their travels and in the land of ancient-Saudi Arabia where they finally settled, and the splendour, temples, and wealth they saw inspired their own creativity and the stories they created. The wars and conflict described in the story may have been conflict they witnessed in other areas including in ancient-Saudi Arabia and its regional neighbours; they may have just heard about these wars, whichever it is, witnessed primarily or through second-hand accounts, these depictions were included in the stories albeit assigned to a fictional people. The conflict could have been witnessed in Yemen where kingdoms warred for reign over each other and over important routes. It is possible that when they initially travelled northwards from Yemen and into ancient-Saudi Arabia, where it may have already been called Becca, they witnessed great hostility in ancient-Saudi Arabia over natural resources such as wells which meant life or death of whole peoples depending if they had a water source or not. Maybe what they witnessed in ancient-Saudi Arabia of tribal warring over wells is what inspired the Biblical authors' stories of hostilities over wells between Abraham and the king, then Isaac, his men and their adversaries. When you think about it, the stories of fighting over wells, taking livestock, and taking away the surviving women and children as slaves—that is exactly how things were in ancient-Saudi Arabia until Islam emerged and put an end to slavery (at least during the prophet's time) and the indiscriminate slaughter of every man, woman and child. The Yemenis would have gone to ancient-Saudi Arabia millennia before Islam, and millennia before the Jewish religion would emerge from the Yemeni pagan worship, Arabian Peninsula pagan worship and the Biblical stories, but they witnessed what fighting over resources and the power of the sword caused among people. No matter what the route they took, what they witnessed of splendour, dearth, wealth, as well as the horrors of human hostilities over vital resources, they included all this in their Biblical stories.

At some later point when monotheism was emerging in the Arabian Peninsula, the OT stories were used and modified by the people now in charge of religious scripts and rituals. The priests/scribes added their ideas, but did not change what had been told and written in the stories regarding the rituals performed such as sacrifices and offerings because these pagan rituals which include rock and fireworship were still the basis of the new religion, Judaism. What is also clear is the new monotheistic (Jewish) religion was based on these pagan religions and rituals—the religious leaders themselves observed these pagan rites, rituals and beliefs wholeheartedly as described in the stories and were not intending to change the core of these rituals, but wanted to strengthen the kohen/'priests' position in the lives of the general public. They did not create a 'new' religion, but held onto the Biblical stories created by pagan Yemenis and pagan ancient-Saudi Arabians, and the priests did the logical and practical step of adding what they wanted to the OT stories, and continued with pagan ritual worship (as it was described in those stories) at its heart, making the process easier to be accepted in changes towards who/what was being worshipped (Jehovah) and whom they were able to convince with their new ideas added to the religion. It was not about 'converting' people to a new religion as they were not really changing the age-old practise of paganism, nor the actual rituals of paganism as in the OT literature and the leading God in these stories 'Jehovah/Yahweh', but convincing them, directing them towards Yahweh being the only one, or the strongest one, or that female Shaddai had turned into male Yahweh, e.g. all the pagan rituals of blood offering, fire offering, drink offering, tithes would still be performed, but made only for Yahweh or the 'one living God'; where there were many sacred rocks—rocks literally worshipped with all the mentioned offerings and sacrifices and gifts made to them—the priests' idea was to shift the sacredness of a number of different sacred rocks, and different sacred deities towards one direction, one God, i.e. one rock.

What was once a story or group of stories created by its original pagan Yemeni immigrants, had lasted for great spans of time, had become the foundation of religions and ritual practise—in the morale-lifting and hope-giving stories the character 'Yahweh/yhwh/hwh' 'stays/stayed' used by the original authors as the deity who provided a wandering people a place to stay, had become the God in real-life ancient-Saudi Arabia for parts of the ancient-Saudi Arabian people who would come to be known as Jews, as he had been the central god created for the stories by the original authors. The priests who were driving towards a 'one god' religion may have done so out of piety, and not disregarding that many priests may have had honest, pious intentions on their agendas and behind this drive, but it cannot be ignored what historical accounts and also the Bible itself tells us—many priests and religious leaders had personal agendas in changing the face and practise of the religion. Be it out of greed for physical things or power, or discriminatory beliefs based on personal experience, it cannot be denied when proof is documented; to deny greed for power or manipulation, or want of materialistic things, and personal assumptions and biases were behind priests altering the religion is to deny human behaviour, human characteristics. It may be a bad or weak side of people, but the priests and others involved in making additions to the religion and to the stories which were the basis of the religion, were only human, prone to everything human be it good or bad.

If you read the Bible you will find the priests are put in charge of the religious life and conduct of the community, they are also in a place of privilege—one can argue that the work they do is hard and dirty work, it is, but they do not need to work for a living: they are provided for by the whole community paying tithes of every kind, making animal sacrifices of burnt, wave offerings, etc.; the priests get the first and choice pick of meat (some kinds reserved exclusively for them, even leftovers cannot be shared with non-priests). They are in charge of the way things are conducted and are the judge upon people—through priestly-pagan 'seeing', Urim and Thummim, etc. people are found innocent or guilty. What priests say has weight. And what is evident from the OT, NT, and from historical accounts of the people of the region, is priests and scribes, those in charge of religious scriptures and the enforcement of religious law began to add, remove and modify scriptures and laws to what suited them and their personal beliefs, agendas, and also for their personal gain. They took religion and religious scriptures out of context and distorted them to give priests and their network (priestly families) more standing, more materialistic profit; it allowed them to manipulate religion so they could prohibit a non-prohibited conduct or matter or make permissible for them a prohibited conduct/matter; it gave them more authority and exclusivity to say who is a religious person or not, to determine what is lawful or unlawful—but often with a double-standard when the same matter applied to them; it gave them more influence over peoples' lives and was used for the priests' benefit (earthly benefit).

If you look outside the Biblical texts you see this complaint reiterated over different spans of history—whether people of the region (Arabs both ancient and modern) claiming this is how priests distorted the Bible into something different than what it was originally so that the priests could personally and materially benefit; you see it again made in the account of the Sicarri rebels, the fanatical rebels' main targets were the priests and their network; the Sicarri are said to have been upset and opposed to how priests and priestly families were taking advantage of the people and their tithes/taxation, to the priests' personal benefit. The Sicarri story may also be a fictional account which exaggerates the reality into a dramatized story, as that is what it seems to be, but that does not mean it did not partially reflect a reality about the priests' misconduct or the tension and opposition the public felt towards it.

Back to the Bible, within the OT itself, some authors have narrated stories where the protagonist or even God himself narrates and states that the 'temple/hekal/he will eat', feasts and sacrifices were not ordained by God at all, and that God had never commanded Moses to conduct sacrifices and feasts, i.e. the narrators of those specific stories are pointing to the additions made to the stories and specifically about priests who would benefit in real life if people increased sacrifices, with the priests the only ones allowed to serve a very private and hidden God. In the New Testament the same accusations are made in no uncertain terms, and we have to remember that it is not a fictional character making the accusation, but the author(s) of the story. The authors narrate Jesus accusing priests, religious lawmakers, Pharisees, scribes, Sadducees of bending and changing the commandments into something different than the original, and for their own and personal gain. Jesus accuses them of changing religious laws so they can benefit materially off the peoples' backs; to avoid having to do hard work while burdening the public; of making a show of giving charity, making a show of praying in front of crowds and loudly—just to be seen, praised and flattered by people, while according to Jesus (or rather the author of the Biblical story), if they followed God's true laws they would give charity without making a show and big deal of it, as well as prayer was meant to be done in private between a person and God, all which states they have distorted God's religious laws for earthly profit. The authors of the NT give Jesus responses to the Pharisees, all which are words to the effect of 'don't you read the scriptures or understand them?' 'you have modified the scriptures to suit your own personal gain and/or to give you power over the people' 'you live by double standards' 'your scriptures as they currently are, are completely fictional'. Most of the accusations and complaint the authors narrate through Jesus' character states the laws the religious people write, the scriptures they have changed, are so altered they are no longer in any resemblance to God's religion and laws because the priests, scribes, Pharisees have changed so much they are actually not God's laws but commandments written by men. The New Testament stories continue with Jesus in most of the narration pointing out and highlighting that the people in charge of religion and religious texts have not only rewritten and distorted God's religion/laws to give the priests material gain at the expense and abuse of the general public, but also points out it is far more serious because in changing the religious laws/texts they have also distorted religion into something not sent down nor decreed by God, and in doing so have led people astray from God's way and prevented themselves and the misled people from entering heaven (according to the story). Of course, as both the OT and NT stories are fictional, the authors of the NT go out of their way to make them stand out as fictional—no one who can read and understand the meaning of the word-names of the characters and places in the NT and see how they directly relay what is happening in the story would then believe they are real stories, as well as the authors of almost every epistle in the NT go out of their way to entertain the audience that the sender of the letter is scamming the recipients of the letter, or attempting to, out of their fortunes i.e. the same accusation continues in both the OT and NT.

Causes of Immigration to Ancient-Saudi Arabia (Biblical 'Canaan')

What could have caused ancient Yemenis to emigrate to ancient-Saudi Arabia? Possibilities of conflict or seeking a better life have already been discussed, but there is a bigger reason which could possibly be what caused Yemenis to migrate to ancient-Saudi Arabia and inspired the Exodus stories: the desertification of the Empty Quarter. There is a traumatic experience carried in the psyche of the Biblical authors and conveyed through their Biblical stories; the desertification of land, causing it to become infertile, wells to dry up, land to become barren, people to starve and thirst, being forced to wander across desert land, people dying in great numbers due to drought and famine which is repeatedly narrated first as an escape from Egypt then as a repeated punishment from God against the protagonists of the stories (and to a lesser extent against adversary nations). As the core of all the stories and what becomes the religious ritual of these stories then of the religions in reality, is pagan Yemeni rock worship and fire worship, this tells us the authors came from Yemen. The stories about Jerusalem, Judah and 'God's house' and 'temple/hekal/he will eat' and the religious rituals and descriptions of religious conduct are those of ancient-Saudi Arabia; and this tells us that the Yemeni authors as part of a group of people left northern Yemen towards ancient-Saudi Arabia and settled specifically in the coasts of Jeddah (Judah in the fictional storytelling) and in Mecca (Jerusalem in the Biblical storytelling).

The Empty Quarter is a desert land mass that covers a large part of southern Saudi Arabia, parts of northern Yemen (and also borders Sultanate Oman and the United Arab Emirates). It is believed that approximately 5000-6000 years ago lakes once existed in the Empty Quarter; who knows what life-sustaining topography the Empty Quarter once contained before 6000 years ago. As remains were found of flora and fauna, it is possible that in pre-recorded history a civilisation lived there; it is possible that no human remains have been found because the people that lived there moved en-masse when the land became unable to sustain human life through farming, and they all left northwards towards ancient-Saudi Arabia. It is unknown if it was human activity or climatic variation that caused the desertification of the Empty Quarter, but science and other recorded desertification occurrences around the world show that human activities and variations in climate can cause the degradation of dry land and fragile ecosystems. Human activities such as deforestation, overgrazing makes the land no longer suitable for farming, it also allows floods to be more probable. If you take into account the Biblical stories repeatedly speak of verdant land becoming barren and desert-like, the stories lament the cattle, the abundance of harvests and the food sources they used to produce—this reflects a real-life situation which we all know can happen and continues to happen in this modern world of drought, famine and climate change. Of course, the desertification/barrenness is narrated as direct punishment from God for the people's disobedience, and the solution or prevention in the narration is to offer God the best and first of all harvests to avoid this happening again.

It does seem the Biblical stories of flooding and desertification, of people forced to leave and wander across the desert before they arrive at the land where they will make a new home (the very meanings of 'Shaddai' and 'Jehovah'), are speaking of the desertification of the life-sustaining land which once covered the area shared between Yemen and ancient-Saudi Arabia, and this fits with how the people felt forced or punished to emigrate northwards into ancient-Saudi Arabia and take up permanent residence in Jeddah (Judah) and Mecca (Jerusalem) where 'God's house' is, and all across ancient-Saudi Arabia, where they were protected from the desertification and the floods. The more northwards they initially travelled from Yemen and into ancient-Saudi Arabia, the Yemenis witnessed the inter-tribal hostilities of ancient-Saudi Arabians fighting over wells or other water sources exacerbated by the drought and climatic changes which caused the desertification of the Empty Quarter, and the immigrants included these inter-tribal wars over vital resources too in their Biblical stories. Whatever the causes and time of desertification, when the land became so barren it could no longer sustain human life, or maybe when repeated floods due to the beginnings of desertification kept threatening the lives of the Yemeni inhabitants of the Empty Quarter and caused them to emigrate northwards into ancient-Saudi Arabia, this has been seared into the minds of the Biblical authors who make all the stories about land fertility, floods, drought and famine, finding new verdant lands where both God and his people have plenty to eat and how to avoid the punishment of drought and famine.

Basis of Biblical Jerusalem, House of God and Temple (hekal)

From the word-name 'Jerusalem' which means 'they see-asked-them/the' 'came-saw-asked-them/the' 'they saw-joined/connected-them/the' 'they saw-arrived/public apology-them/the' 'they see-their/the rocks' 'they see-rocks-them/the' 'came-saw-joined/connected-them/the' 'came-saw-arrived/public apology-them/the' 'came-saw-their/the rocks' 'came-saw-rocks-them/the' and its story at 1Kgs.8, and how the compound word 'Jerusalem' and its meaning is used throughout the Bible—you can see that Jerusalem is a fictional city which had no real existence in any geographical land. But it was based on a real city and based on the significance of a real city in ancient-Saudi Arabia: Mecca(h), which before being changed into 'Mecca' in antiquity had an older name 'Becca'. The meaning of 'Becca(h)' بكّه 'go/went/leave/left' from the word (bk/بك) with the same meanings. Jerusalem is often described as a city called by God's name 'the city which is called by thy name' (Dan.9:18-19), and God's name is 'Shaddai' 'emigrate/leave' i.e. the exact same meaning of 'Becca' which is current-day Mecca's original name. The meaning of the real city which is Becca(Mecca) as well as the activities of real people within ancient-Saudi Arabia and other nations of the region was to go to Beccah, to travel there in order to worship in Beccah and pray towards it, is what inspired the story of Jerusalem 'they see-asked-them/the' 'came-saw-asked-them/the' 'came-saw-arrived/public apology-them/the' 'came-saw-rocks-them/the', etc. because this is where people faced and went and travelled to in order to ask from rocks, statues and other deities that they protect, bless, forgive, grant them their prayers and wishes.

Not only people from within ancient-Saudi Arabia would emigrate and pilgrimage towards Becca, but so would people from Yemen, from ancient Syria, Iraq and other regional civilisations of the Middle East because it is where the greatest place of rock-worship for the peoples of the region had always existed: the-K'ba (el-Ka'ba). The people from within ancient-Saudi Arabia and the ancient peoples of the Middle East who pilgrimaged to worship at the Ka'ba were originally pagans who worshipped rocks; then it was local pagans who worshipped rocks and local Jews who also worshipped in Mecca and at the Ka'ba, and the Jews worshipped many different rocks, but the most significant was specifically the rock in the Ka'ba; then later on it was pagans, Jews, and Muslims who all worshipped at the Ka'ba in Becca/Mecca. It must be mentioned that it is recorded in the history of Arabs and Muslims that there had always been people who were not called Muslims, Jews or Christians but who believed in God and did not worship rocks, and these people who were never pagan but believed in a divine monotheistic God worshipped at the site of al-Aqsa mosque (long before its current mosque structure) in ancestral Palestine in the city of al-Quds, and is why the whole city of al-Quds (misnomered and misidentified by the West as 'Jerusalem' through misinterpretations of the Bible) was and still is important to all Arabs as it has always been, and continues to be, the first worship place and sacred city for Muslims even before the noun 'Islam/Muslim' would be applied to the religion.

If you go back to 1Kgs.8, what the Biblical authors are describing as all people facing the 'house of God' and praying towards it, seeking forgiveness, protection, help, blessings by facing it and praying towards it—what they are describing is el-Ka'ba and how since pre-recorded history and recorded history pagans, Jews, and later on Muslims, have all conducted this ritual towards it. An important distinction must be made between what is meant by 'Jerusalem' of the Bible which is a fictional city based on real-life Mecca/Becca and what through historic and modern peoples' erroneous identification and naming 'Jerusalem' of the Palestinian/Arabic and correctly-named 'al-Quds' which people when translating into English use the word 'Jerusalem' as well as western erroneous belief have made a wrong assumption that the Arabic Quds in Palestine is 'Jerusalem' of the Bible.

This mistake can be explained: first it has to do with the readers of the Biblical stories not understanding the language of the Bible, thus misinterpreting fiction with reality; then it has to do with how al-Quds, the city in Palestine, has always been a holy place to the Arabs and the Arab people who never accepted rock worship, nor polytheism but whose people and civilisations around them would undergo the flux and fading away of all the pagan and the divine religions of the area until Christianity and Islam emerged which fitted in with their beliefs: the Aqsa Mosque and the site it was built upon has never had anything to do with pagan and Jewish worship, although this has been convoluted as time went by and it began to be thought of as where Jews practised religious worship when all history has shown Jews have never had anything to do with the al-Quds city nor with al-Aqsa Mosque (until very recently (from 1948 onwards) when European Zionists would militarily take over al-Quds city (erroneously called 'Jerusalem'). Even post-1948, the European Zionists did not cause the genocide and ethnical cleansing in al-Quds because they wanted it for sacred or Jewish-worship purposes, but only in order to increase the amount of land without Palestinians (i.e. Arabs) which they wanted to create the artificial modern-Israel on (the European Zionists even wanted to keep the whole country's name 'Palestine' and to be called Palestinians as it was named by the organic Palestinians whom they had forcibly expelled out of most of Palestine, but seeing the organic Palestinians would not give up their country and ethnicity the European Zionists decided to find an alternative name to their newly-created state and they agreed on 'Israel'—which has worked to their favour).

Al-Aqsa Mosque was first built in the Higri year 72 (691 CE) by the Calipha Abdulmalik bin Marwan, before that in ancient history it was a religious site which precursors of Muslims called 'Believers' worshipped at, and no other religious group other than Muslims (who were of course Arabs) worshipped at that site. But with great spans of time passing, the original language of the Arabian Peninsula Arabs being distanced from the Biblical stories which they wrote, and with the interference and misleading conclusions which are nothing but guesswork on behalf of historic and also contemporary academics, explorers, travellers, all these would lead to the wrong claim and naming of what is correctly called the 'Quds' in Palestine to the fictional 'Jerusalem' which only westerners and speakers of English use, the Palestinians and all Arabs call the city 'al-Quds' because that has been its name since pre-recorded history (although Arabs and especially Arab politicians do use the misnomered 'Jerusalem' when they speak in English, probably to avoid confusion about what is being spoken about, but al-Quds does not translate into 'Jerusalem' word-wise or in the history and geography of the real land). Logically, and factually, the organic people of these countries which are all Arab countries in antiquity and to this day do know what the names of their cities and areas are called as opposed to what westerners would like to call them. I want to keep this topic completely neutral of the Palestinian-Israeli conflict otherwise it just becomes a tug-of-war between anti and pro-Israel/Palestine with no relation to what the Bible is actually stating, which should be avoided if we want to get to the truth of the Biblical stories and where and what these Biblical stories are based on, and where I do mention places and events related to this modern-day conflict is where I have to address it—otherwise proving the true place of 'Jerusalem' would be incomplete, therefore I am not including in this discussion who is wrong or right in the conflict, but I do have to state the facts which is what today is called 'Jerusalem' is actually al-Quds, and readers have to remember that current day modern-Israel and all its post-1948 namings of what were originally Palestinian Arabic names of areas, towns and cities is a creation of 1948 and are unrelated to the Biblical stories, just as the Palestinian city al-Quds is wrongly called 'Jerusalem' in English and other non-Arabic languages due to both historic and contemporary erroneous beliefs.

If you read 1Kgs.8, and everywhere in the Bible where Jerusalem is depicted as a city named after God and where people come to worship, what you are reading is what has continued in Islam and what the Biblical story is describing in Becca (current day Mecca) and the rituals and rites of how modern Saudi Arabians and Muslims from around the world practise to this day in Mecca. This did not begin from Islam, nor did it begin with the emergence of the Jewish religion, but was preceded by pagan worship where people within ancient-Saudi Arabia, people from Yemen, peoples from the Levant all pilgrimaged and worshipped in Becca/Mecca, and what was worshipped were rocks to begin with, before statues and other idols were added. This practise would continue with the emergence of the Jewish religion with Jews also worshipping in Beccah and the same with Islam and Muslims. The reason Beccah was the place of worship and pilgrimage not only in real life ancient-Saudi Arabia but also in the fictional stories of Jerusalem of the Bible is due to the greatest place of worship being in Becca: the Ka'ba. Not only was the Ka'ba the greatest worship site for pagans (and these pagans did not just follow one pagan god but multitudes of different rocks and idols), but it would also be the greatest place of worship for Jews as Judaism originated from the Arabian Peninsula and was based on rock worship. In the Biblical stories the real-life Beccah 'go/went/leave/left' is depicted as Jerusalem 'they see-their/the rocks' 'they see-rocks-them/the' 'came-saw-their/the rocks' 'came-saw-rocks-them/the', and both in real-life and in the Biblical stories pagans and Jews were arriving to worship the rock in the Ka'ba (later pagans would include more rocks and statues); 'they see-asked-them/the' 'came-saw-asked-them/the', it is also described as 'the city called by thy name' ('Shaddai' 'emigrate/leave') which again is the real city (Mecca) Beccah 'go/went/leave/left'. In the same way, the real-life worship site where people face and pray towards when calling God has been depicted in the fictional re-telling: in the Biblical story it is the misnomered 'temple' which should read 'hekal' and translates to 'he will eat' and in real-life this is the Ka'ba where people slaughter animals and feast and have done so throughout history and beyond recorded history.

There is abundant proof in the Bible and in the history of the Middle East, and specifically the Arabian Peninsula, which shows the fictional Biblical 'Temple/hekal/he will eat' is based on the Ka'ba:

The Ka'ba has always been a place of worship for pagans then followers of the Jewish religion long before Islam, it included praying towards it, sacrificing there, setting garlanded (see Gilead/Galeed) animals free to roam around Becca, the city being a safe-haven for those fleeing danger especially if they had killed someone. The Ka'ba is a rectangular structure (approximately 10mX14mX15m (width, length, height)) made of stone. Originally the stones were not in any way cemented/mortared together, just placed atop each other (which is how remote Yemenis still build their houses with the size and weight of the stones keeping the walls together without cementing them), and the sacred Black Stone (al-Hagar al-Aswad) is built into the eastern wall. It is this stone that was worshipped above all other rocks in the Arabian Peninsula and the neighbouring region which gave the Ka'ba its holiness and importance to pagans, then Jews, then Muslims. The Ka'ba was at some point filled with statues which were pagan deities and rocks, the rocks were worshipped by pagans then by pagans and Jews; although modern-day Muslims, and even the first Muslims, do not worship the Black Stone, its connection to the holiness of el-Ka'ba in Islam which has been worshipped long before any monotheistic religion emerged is undeniable.

It is a wrong and almost juvenile claim and misinterpretation that 'el-Ka'ba' means 'cube/cubed', as the Ka'ba's name does not hold this modern Arabic word-meaning. Ka'ba, el/al-ka'ba; الكعبه 'the-packed/filled' 'is-packed/filled' 'the-try/go ahead-pack/fill it'. It gets its name not only because pagans and Jews packed their sacred rocks and idols into it, but also because it is where sacrifices, offerings, sacrificial animals were led to be sacrificed at that place and were piled before their god(s): the very meaning of Kadesh/Qodesh 'piled/led' and where this latter word used in the Bible gets its naming from (ka'ba and qodesh are the same meaning 'try pack/fill' 'pile/pile heaps'). It is where people lived around and pilgrimaged to and where they ended and fulfilled their vows 'nvr/naveer'. It is the inspiration of the fictional 'hekal/temple' of the Biblical stories as not only is el-Ka'ba where animals and other offerings were sacrificed to a multitude of gods in reality, but the people would also feast on the abundant offerings and sacrifices at this place hence 'hekal' 'he will eat' (misnomered and mistranslated as 'temple' in English and western languages). This spectacle of people coming from all over the region, in addition to the local Arabian Peninsula Arabs, all bringing animals and tithes of all sorts to sacrifice and to offer– these real images and scenes are what inspired the Biblical stories of 'qodesh/qodesh haqqodashim' 'piled high' 'piles upon piles' 'lead/led, I will lead them/it/the' (see Meaning of 'kadesh' 'qodesh' 'm'kaddesh' 'mekkadesh', Meaning of 'Temple' 'Hekal' for detailed explanation).

Arab historians and travellers have richly documented, as well as Arabic and Islamic history has documented, the Ka'ba being *the* place of worship for Jews and pagans and these Jews and pagans were local Arabian Peninsula Arabs, i.e. ancient-Saudi Arabian, as well as it being the most important 'house of God' and place of worship where other pagan peoples would come to sacrifice and worship at from Yemen, Syria, Iraq—but the pagans and Jews around the Ka'ba were local Arabian Peninsula Arabs (what today would be called Saudis). History and historians (including Islamic history) wrote about Arabs of the Arabian Peninsula being a multitude of pagan worshippers and the first followers of the Jewish religion, no different than what all Arab history and Islamic history has always proved. The original authors and fictional 'children of Israel/عِصر آ نئيل' of the Bible are the ancient Saudi Arabians, and if they had been real their only descendants would be the current-day Saudi Arabians, just as in Islam and in the Quran the 'children of Israel/ اسرآئيل' and the Jews around the Ka'ba are ancient Saudi Arabians and their only descendants are current-day Saudi Arabians.

The Ka'ba was destroyed by floods around 1630 CE, it has been destroyed by floods at later dates including those recorded occurring in modern history, it is safe to say that it has probably been destroyed by floods many times in earlier pre-Islamic history. The fact the stones which make up the Ka'ba were not originally bound together made it easier for floods to destroy it. This continuous destruction witnessed by the locals inspired the stories of destruction of the 'temple/hekal' (which is the Ka'ba) in the Biblical stories; these floods are also what inspired the stories of Noah's flood. The same Arabic history also includes the folklore regarding what are versions of the same stories as it is from the same cultural pool, but these probably are earlier than the Biblical versions because of their link to real geographical areas: there are stories about Enoch, Cain, and Noah's flood and they all happen in the Arabian Peninsula and legend has it that Noah's ark finally landed in Jeddah (which is the inspiration of 'Judah' in the Bible) while others have Noah's ark parked somewhere in the mountains of northern Yemen. The real scenes of the wealth and abundance of food produce brought from all over the region and to Becca to be offered at the Ka'ba is what inspired the stories about 'house of God' ('he/it will-tear strips of meat/eat meat' 'he/it will-eat plenty of meat' 'he/it will-feed well/fed well') 'temple/hekal/he will eat' and the huge amounts and quantities of sacrifices made there (qodesh haqqodashim/kodesh hakkodashim), and the repeated destruction of the Ka'ba is what inspired the stories of the destruction of the misnomered 'temple' in the Biblical stories.

'Temple mount' 'Har Habáyit' has no correlation and no connection to al-Aqsa mosque in Palestine which is a purely Muslim place of worship, but 'Har Habáyit' is connected to the Ka'ba in Mecca, Saudi Arabia. It is a shame that many factors have contributed towards modern-day Jews (regardless of their ethnicity being European or otherwise) not knowing their true place of worship and finding a false-alternative for it (the false alternative being al-Aqsa Mosque which Zionists/modern-Israelis have wanted to destroy since 1948) while the place mentioned in the Biblical stories of the OT stands in Mecca and is used as a place of worship by Muslims just as it used to be used by Jews. Some factors have been mentioned as to why people have never understood the Bible, these reasons have also prevented el-Ka'ba and Mecca/Becca from being identified as the place of worship for the first original Jews which lasted until Islam put an end to it. The city in Palestine, al-Quds, which only became a place of interest for Jews since the advent of Zionism is also from western-based misunderstandings, and it is a shame that Muslims and Jews cannot all worship at the true site which has been named as Jerusalem in the Bible and 'hekal/qodash haqoddashim' which is the city of Mecca/Becca and the place of worship el-Ka'ba.

There is neither word for 'mount' nor 'temple' in 'Har Habáyit' mistranslated as 'Temple Mount'. There is a possibility that the Biblical authors were using more than one meaning in wordplay of Har Habáyit and all the meanings reflect and relay things that have happened and happen around the real Har Habáyit which is el-Ka'ba: هر هَبآيت ، خَر هَبايِت 'chased away/collapsed/made collapse-give/they give-came' from words (har/هَر) 'chased away' 'collapsed', (khar/خَر) 'chased away/collapsed/made collapse', (hab/هَبا) 'give/gave/gifted' 'swooped down on', (yit/يِت) 'comes/came'. The people who come to el-Ka'ba and the characters who come to the fictional and misnomered 'Temple/Temple Mount' in the stories give and offer sacrifices and offerings, and they come from their homes whether locally or from the wider region (in both real life and in the Biblical stories). It could also be: هَر هبايِت ، خَر هَبآيت 'chased away/collapsed/made collapse-will/look/this house' 'chased away/collapsed/made collapse-will/look/this-it will', made from words (har/هَر) 'chased away' 'collapsed', (khar/خَر) 'chased away/collapsed/made collapse', (ha/هَـ) 'will/look/this/here', (bayit/بآيت) 'house' 'stayed over/slept the night at' 'it will(happen)/it will…'. It refers to el-Ka'ba which is most definitely called 'God's house' which has collapsed and been completely destroyed more than once in contemporary history by floods, and one recorded time when just before Islam emerged where the prophet Mohammed took part in resolving the issue of which all the tribes wanted to be the ones who lifted the sacred rock, the Black Stone, into its place, by Mohammed mediating a solution where the heads of all tribes participated in lifting the rock.

There is abundant proof in the Biblical stories as well as in Arabic and Islamic history and in the geographical land of Saudi Arabia which proves that el-Ka'ba and Mecca are the 'Jerusalem' and the 'temple/hekal/he will eat' of the Biblical stories:

First, we need to understand what is the rock and its importance in al-Aqsa Mosque in Palestine: it is a rock formation which is also the natural roof of a natural cave beneath it; the rock surface is uneven with dimensions approximately 15 metres in length and 8 metres wide. It cannot be moved and picked up and placed neither in reality nor in a fictional story such as the stone which features in the Biblical story of Jacob using it first as a pillow then picking it up and stacking it with other rocks into a pillar, nor can it be the Biblical 'foundation stone' or 'corner stone'—as the rock in al-Aqsa Mosque under the Dome of the Rock (the Golden Dome) is, as described above, part of a rock formation; it is unmoveable and can in no way be used as a pillow nor can it inspire stories of being used as a pillow. It has never been used as part of a structure of a wall, nor has it ever been a foundation of a building, but as mentioned earlier it serves as a direction which 'Believers' (early Muslims before Islam became name of religion) prayed towards God, with the rock indicating the direction of prayer.

Although it does have great significance in Islam due to belief the prophet Mohammed ascended to heaven from this rock in al-Aqsa Mosque, its significance in Islam precedes the emergence of 'Islam' and precedes the prophet Mohammed by millennia, and this significance as mentioned above is due to Muslims who were called 'Believers' before the emergence of Islam (and Muslims continue to be called 'Believers' throughout Islam and to this day) is because this rock and site have always been sacred to the non-rock worshipping people who believed in a divine God, a one God—the pre-cursors of Muslims. The rock was not worshipped, but it marked an important site towards which Believers prayed, i.e. they prayed in its direction and not to it. The reasons why are not known, they have been lost in antiquity and muddled with the confusion of modern and western studies, as well as local/regional religious stories, but many pre-Islamic stories do exist but nothing have anything to do with the Biblical Jacob or Abraham or any of Abraham's sons.

The rock formation (under Dome of the Rock) in al-Aqsa Mosque was of no interest to the earliest and first Jews who all worshipped at el-Ka'ba and lived around el-Ka'ba in Mecca, Saudi Arabia. This rock formation has no connection to either Isaac or Ismail's slaughter/sacrifice stories because in the Bible Isaac was to be slaughtered 'in the land of Moriah' and in the Quran it is Ismail whom Abraham was ordered to sacrifice to God, but then God saved by providing an animal for slaughter instead of Ismail/Isaac, and the place where Ismail was to be offered as a sacrifice to God by Abraham happens in Minna in ancient-Saudi Arabia, not anywhere in nor near Palestine.

There is a difference between Islamic stories and the Jewish Biblical stories: in the Bible it is Isaac, Abraham's second child who is to be sacrificed to God in 'the land of Moriah', whereas in the Quran it is Ismail (Ishmael), Abraham's firstborn son who is to be slaughtered at Minna which is in Saudi Arabia. These stories are taken from the same one cultural pool, and the Biblical stories have been changed to suit what later editors wanted them to be, we can see that the later editors have changed Ismail (who even in the Bible is Abraham's firstborn) who was supposed to be sacrificed in the original story and has been replaced by Isaac by the editors of the story. According to the whole OT and its Biblical stories, God only ever wants firstborns and firstfruits to be sacrificed to him, and this does include the firstborns of humans which after Abraham shows his devotion in willingness to sacrifice his firstborn son God allows to be redeemed with a sacrificial animal. Isaac, even in the Biblical stories, is not Abraham's firstborn son; Ishmael (Ismail) is his firstborn son, and it cannot be argued that Isaac is Abraham's firstborn son from Sarah because that is not how relationships are viewed in the culture of the region: all children from the same father are considered brothers/sisters, i.e. full siblings and not 'half-brothers' when they come from the father's side so within the same story itself Abraham's firstborn son is Ishmael and not Isaac as Isaac is not the firstborn which God always demands be sacrificed/offered to him. The importance of recognising the Biblical and Quranic stories all come from the same cultural pool no matter what changes have happened to the stories over time, is also that it leads to an important fact about the fictional story, but also about the real land in which these fictional stories and events are set.

Both versions of the story, the Biblical and the Quranic sacrifice of Isaac/Ismail, are set in ancient-Saudi Arabia: Minna in the Quran where Ismail was to be sacrificed by Abraham is still Minna in current Saudi Arabia; the 'land of Moriah' where the Biblical Isaac was to be sacrificed by Abraham is the Marwa of ancient and current Saudi Arabia (where in Islam it is believed Hagar ran back and forth between the Safa and Marwa searching for water for a thirsty Ismail). Minna is where the animals are sacrificed today during Hajj pilgrimage the same way Abraham sacrificed an animal instead of his son. Marwa is the 'Moriah' where Abraham in the Bible was to sacrifice Isaac—Marwa may today be a small hill/promontory but that is because modern-Saudi Arabia had the mountain which connected Mount Marwa to another mountain cut and demolished so as to expand and build leaving only a much smaller part of Mount Marwa (Moriah) as a religious landmark for people to perform the religious rites around. El-Safa which suffered the same demolition by the modern Saudi government was also a mountain and what is interesting is that its name 'Safa/صفا' means 'rock/rocks/flattish rocks' 'stack/row/column' 'stacked column/column of rocks' and this is the inspiration, basis, and location of the Biblical stories of Jacob sleeping and using rocks as pillows underneath his head then building with them a rock pillar/altar which is a column of stacked rocks which he names 'Bethel'. All these within the vicinity of Becca(Mecca) and the Ka'ba.

Another important fact which gives these stories context is the original Muslims before and after being named 'Muslims' did not face el-Ka'ba and did not worship towards the Ka'ba because Jews who worshipped rocks, pagans who worshipped rocks, and pagans/polytheists who worshipped idols all faced el-Ka'ba and worshipped its Black Stone (the 'corner stone' 'foundation stone' of the Bible) and the statues which different kinds of pagans brought into the Ka'ba. Whereas 'Believers' (the pre-cursors to 'Muslims') faced the rock in al-Quds city (Palestine) and worshipped a monotheistic god who was neither a rock nor an idol—the rock formation at the al-Aqsa site is like a compass needle indicating the direction to pray.

When Islam was founded even the first Muslims in the Arabian Peninsula, which included the prophet Mohammed of course, faced towards the Aqsa Mosque to pray and did not face el-Ka'ba which the Jews and pagans did face in the direction of and worshipped at. It is important to understand and to remind that the prophet Mohammed and all the newly converted Muslims of the Arabian Peninsula were previously either Jews or pagans who worshipped and prayed towards el-Ka'ba but when they converted to Islam, they prayed towards the first and original worship site of the Muslim/Believer's god: al-Aqsa. The Quran and Islamic history state that God noticed the prophet Mohammed's fondness of the Ka'ba and his longing to pray and worship God towards it, so that God granted the change of 'Qiblah' from facing al-Aqsa mosque and instead to face and pray towards el-Ka'ba, i.e. to turn and pray towards the same site which Jews worshipped at, which pagans worshipped at, and the house which Jews and rock-worshipping pagans worshipped the Black Stone at which is the 'foundation stone' and holiest place of the Biblical stories.

The fight over el-Ka'ba was long and vicious with the prophet Mohammed and Muslims on one side (and these Muslims are the same Arabs who converted from Judaism and pagan religions with the emergence of Islam) and the Jews of ancient-Saudi Arabia, and the pagans of ancient-Saudi Arabia on the other side. The Muslim side won, all idols and rocks were removed leaving only the Black Stone which is part of the eastern wall of el-Ka'ba which is also called 'God's house'. Both the Ka'ba and the Black Stone, which are one in essence, had a special place in the hearts of the first Muslims of ancient-Saudi Arabia to the degree the prophet Mohammed's fondness and wanting to worship at and towards the Ka'ba caused the 'Qiblah' (which means 'towards' 'in front of' and in the context 'worship/pray towards') to change from towards the Aqsa Mosque and be directed towards Mecca and el-Ka'ba, without lessening the importance of al-Aqsa Mosque and the city of al-Quds being important to Islam and Arabs due to it being the first Qiblah, the first worship site of the Muslims. And again, it is not the Black Stone which is worshipped in Islam, the Black Stone is symbolic—the significance of the Ka'ba to Muslims and the prophet Mohammed is because they as an ancient-Saudi people worshipped it as pagans and as Jews long before Islam. You have all the significant places of worship to original Jews of the Biblical stories all in Mecca, Saudi Arabia.

You have to remember 'God's house' in the Bible starts out not as a house structure, but a rock (before later stories make it into a 'house') '...And this stone, which I have set for pillows, shall be God's house...' (Gen.28) is narrated when Jacob makes the stones he slept on into a pillar/altar and names it Bethel, therefore God is the rock, and is contained/housed in the rock. More than once the Biblical stories state that God's house is a literal 'rock', but so is God a rock in the Bible—so the Black Stone which the first Jews in the world (Arabian Peninsula Arabs/modern-day Saudis) worshipped is God, and God is placed in the wall of 'his house' and this is the Black Stone and the Ka'ba which the Biblical stories are based on. This is the stone which Jacob used as a pillow to sleep on then had a bad dream about God and upon awaking he used it to make it into a pillar, before the Biblical stories expand and make God's house a whole structure in later stories (even if in the Biblical stories God's house is built elsewhere and not where Jacob slept and named it Bethel, i.e. when David/Solomon build a temple they do not build it at Bethel where Jacob slept. But within the Biblical stories and Arabic folklore, the stone which Jacob used as a pillow ended up as part of the wall which built God's house and that stone is the Black Stone in el-Ka'ba, any claims that the Dome of the Rock is where Jacob slept are incorrect as al-Aqsa mosque holds its significance to Arabs and Muslims first because it is where Muslims (called 'Believers') worshipped at and prayed towards then because it is the place where the Prophet Mohammed ascended to heaven from, and nothing to do with Jacob and his stone pillar. The rock under Dome of the Rock in al-Aqsa Mosque is a natural rock formation, whereas the fictional narration of Jacob's stone-pillow which he turns into 'Bethel' by stacking it along with other stones into a pillar is a rock that can be used under the neck and be carried and moved and stacked as part of a pillar, i.e. an individual rock and not physically connected to a naturally solid rock formation—and that is what the Black Stone in el-Ka'ba is: a stone which the Biblical stories which are pagan long before they become the stories of the Jewish religion based these stories on. In fact, you can see how the etymology works and how spans of time change the meanings of words around folklore and religion: it goes from a stone used as a pillow then made part of a sacred pillar which Jacob states is the house of God; then it is named 'Bethel' (bad); the stories end up being about a 'house of God' in the Bible; and the real Arabs in Becca call the Ka'ba 'house of God'; in both real life ancient-Saudi Arabia 'house of God' contains the Black Stone as part of the house, and so do the fictional stories: both the OT and NT narrate the 'stone' which becomes part of the house.

Proof of rock worship as the basis of the religion for the protagonists of the Biblical stories is abounding within the Bible; it also reflects the rock worship of the authors and audience of these stories. Below are some examples how God is described literally as a rock, but also how the different words/synonyms for a literal 'rock' and 'God' are one and the same which shows the original rock worship nature of the stories, its authors and original audience which fits in with the culture and beliefs of the inhabitants of ancient Arabian Peninsula:

ṣûr: 'Behold, I will stand before thee there upon the rock [haṣṣûr] in Horeb…' (Exod.17:6)

'He is the Rock [haṣṣûr], his work is perfect: for all his ways are judgement: a God of truth and without iniquity, just and right is he.' (Deut.32:4)

'Of the Rock [ṣûr] that begat thee thou art unmindful, and hast forgotten God that formed thee.' (Deut.32:18)

'For their rock [kĕṣûrēnû] is not as our Rock [ṣûrām], even our enemies themselves being judges.' (Deut.32:31)

'Come into the mountain of the Lord, the Mighty One [ṣûr] of Israel.' (Isa.30:29)

'Is there a God beside me? yea, no God [ṣûr]; I know not.' (Isa.44:8)

'Who can stand before his indignation? And who can abide in the fierceness of his anger? his fury is poured out like fire, and the rocks [wĕhaṣṣûrîm] are thrown down by him.' (Nah.1:6)

'…and, O Mighty God[wĕṣûr]…' (Hab.1:12)

selaʿ: 'And they turned and fled toward the wilderness unto the rock [selaʿ] Rimmon, and abode in the rock [bĕselaʿ] Rimmon four months.' (Judg.20:45)

'Saul and also his men went to seek him. And they told David: wherefore he came down into a rock [hasselaʿ].' (1Sam.23:25)

'And he said, The Lord is my rock [salʿî], and my fortress, and my deliverer.' (2Sam.22:2)

'I will say unto God my rock[salʿiy], Why has thou forgotten me? Why go I mourning because of the oppression of the enemy?' (Ps.42:9)

'O my dove, that art in the clefts of the rock [hasselaʿ], in the secret places of the stairs, let me see thy countenance, let me hear thy voice…' (Cant.2:14)

In the NT it continues with at least one mention of Jesus being a rock, and what is meant is the rock which is worshipped just like the OT stories. The NT stories also mention a very specific stone, and all references are about the Black Stone in the Ka'ba:

'Jesus saith unto them, Did ye never read in the scriptures, The stone which the builders rejected, the same is become the head of the corner: this is the Lord's doing, and it is marvellous in our eyes.' (Matt.21:42)

'The Stone which the builders rejected is become the head of the corner.' (Mark.13:10)

'This is the stone which was set at nought of you builders, which is become the head of the corner.' (Acts.4:11)

The OT stories which mention idols and images being placed in 'God's house' and worshipped and sacrificed to by the 'children of Israel' causing their punishment by God in Ezek.7 are mimicking and criticising the real-life eventual placement of statues and other images which were idols of pagan/polytheist deities which had been placed in the Ka'ba until Islam put an end to it, leaving only the Black Stone which is a sacred rock to Muslims, but also in the Biblical stories it is a sacred stone for the 'children of Israel' (who in real life would come to be called 'Jews'), and this is why all the people of the Jewish religion (who were all Arabian Peninsula Arabs) worshipped at the Ka'ba and offered sacrifices there: it is where they lived and where they are from.

If you look at one of the Arabic words for 'God' which is 'Allah' and its variant in the form of 'Ilah' which is still 'God', and the Arabic compound word in the Biblical stories and related literature 'bêt 'ĕlōhîm' which means 'he/it will-tore strips of meat/ate meat' 'he/it will-tear strips of meat/eat meat' 'he/it will-eat plenty of meat' and also 'he/it will-feed well/fed well' 'he/it will-plumpen with food/with various nice food' and the latter in the Bible has been misinterpreted as 'God's house'—you can see how it (like all stories in the Bible) mimics the real life 'God's house' of Arabs in the Arabian Peninsula and you can see how it can be misunderstood as being 'God's house' because it has made a wordplay on what the real-life meaning is and the actual activities of providing lots of good food and plenteous meat which both God and the people in the stories get to eat from just like the real-life pagans, then pagans and Jews, then Muslims did, and the latter still do, in Mecca at 'God's house' which is the Ka'ba.

If we ignore the context set by the Biblical stories and how bêt 'ĕlōhîm fits in with the use of this word as intended by the Biblical authors, you can find in it and interpret it into 'house-of their god' which although is similar to 'God's house' it does not fit in with the Biblical stories being told nor with how it was used: e.g. if a Biblical narrator or character states 'bêt 'ĕlōhîm' as in 'house-of their God' he is talking about someone else's god and not the protagonists' god, and the same would apply if a real-life person were to use it as it would still mean talking about someone else's god and not the speaker's god; whereas 'he/it will-eat plenty of meat' and also 'he/it will-feed well/fed well' fits perfectly into the story and makes sense whether it is a Biblical character, narrator, or a person in real-life uses it because they are talking about a place or action where someone or a being (God in the Bible) is being fed well, as well as the people who get to feast on the sacrifices and offerings, and this happened in real life in ancient times and continues to this day at the Ka'ba where pagan gods and Jehovah were once 'fed', and the people too who were making the offering as well as those present, and currently in the Kingdom of Saudi Arabia the people who perform the Hajj pilgrimage sacrifice in the name of God/Allah although they do not offer any food or blood to God, but they do get to eat and feed others from the abundant sacrifices made in God's name at this holy site which has been the worship place of pagans, Jews, and Muslims.

Conclusion

The Yemeni immigrants who went to live in and became part of ancient-Saudi Arabia, taught and reminded their people what were, and still are, the important things in life necessary for both survival and continuation: land and offspring. For without land, back then and today in remote Yemen, you could not survive nor sustain your family; you needed offspring to help you maintain and acquire more land and to work it to meet the needs of a growing family, extended family, community—generations. It is why the stories centred around and made it matter to repeatedly kill nations, whole peoples, so the protagonists could acquire the land—not that they went along and committed genocide in reality to inhabit another people's place, but as an exaggerated, exciting story which stresses and repeats the importance of having land to ensure your offspring will not only survive, but continue for generations to come. To know offspring will survive and generate and carry your name after you are long dead was important back then as it is today in remote Yemen, which also inspired the stories of 'multiplication of seed' to be like sand granules on a beach (in numbers). Watch a beaming Yemeni parent or grandparent's face when his/her young son or daughter recites their name and consecutive grandfathers as far back as the fifteenth great grandfather—nothing says and is hope of continuation of one's life other than children, and the more the better: more chances of survival, more multiplications of seed by the multiplications of your seed.

The origins of the Bible are Yemeni people and their life; the overall story, its reasons and objectives is how to ensure your progeny survives, the name, the line to continue—which was and is important for the remote Yemenis of the past and today, and as the Biblical stories show us, this Yemeni belief became even more important to those who immigrated and whose continuance as a people was imperilled when they ended up far away from home, and initially without land to guarantee the continuance of their seed. 'Seed' another important word used in remote Yemen and used in the Biblical stories based on its importance to Yemenis: vureeyah ذريه 'seed' 'children' from the word (vrh/ذره) which means 'sorghum' 'seed' 'plant/sow', and (ivra/اذر) 'sow seeds', and (yivaaree/يذاري) 'he sows seeds' 'he sows his seed' 'he has children' 'he makes children'; (vaara el-ardh/ذار الارض) 'he sowed the land' 'he filled the land with children' 'he filled the land with offspring'. The Bible is full of God's promise 'your seed will be multiplied'.

The original stories of the Bible were created by Yemeni authors—it is the backbone of the Bible that without there would be nothing left: a story filled with Yemeni customs, Yemeni pagan worship, the Yemeni Arabic (Old Arabic) language, Yemeni expressions, Yemeni way of life, and the matters most important to the Yemenis of the OT just as they still are today to the remote Yemenis who live the same way as in ancient times. They began as stories for entertainment which is part of Yemeni culture, then designed and modified to uplift Yemenis in a strange, foreign land to persevere and integrate into ancient-Saudi Arabia and with the ancient-Saudi Arabian people who maybe had initially marginalised them upon arrival. In reading the OT, you will see these were not stories all made to follow each other in one book, but were individual stories which were told separately. They existed with variations and versions, stories purely for entertainment, some morale-inspiring, all teaching tradition. Whether hope-lifting, funny or lewd, pagan religion was at their heart and making a foreign land bearable was their objective.

When religious ideas would emerge much later after these original stories were already so popular, they were 'set in stone' so to speak—everybody knew and understood these stories—the religious people would begin adding, removing, changing what suited their own agendas. At some point people in charge of religious texts, or maybe just interested in these stories, decided to combine these stories, including all the different versions (and also when the non-Middle Eastern world would become interested in the found religious texts of the Bible, they too would combine more than one version from the different texts into a single Bible) with all its contradictions when these different sources, versions and additions of the same stories were joined together in one story or one book known today as the Bible. Whoever decided to assemble them together with all their contradictory variations and content has allowed us to see what was behind the reasons of creating these stories; all the different reasons behind various modifications during different times. Most importantly, it has preserved the original themes, the foundations of the Torah and therefore the OT and the NT's, it has kept recorded how ancient civilisation in Yemen and Saudi Arabia lived, what they believed in (which lasted into modernity) by making it the core of the Bible.

Although they ended up in ancient-Saudi Arabia, the ancient Yemenis carried in their hearts and engrained in the Biblical stories the way of Yemeni life, and also the way of ancient-Saudi Arabian life in every aspect and belief as you would find it in its most original forms in remote Yemen areas still lived today, those who never left home nor allowed 'foreigners' in. Due to the Bible being purely Arabian-Peninsula Arabic in origin and makeup, you have the people who created the Bible, whose way of life feature in the Bible, not reflecting a mirror-image of each other, but the one and the same people and culture standing and staring at each other through the span of millennia and over the geographical land expanse between them, with the Arabian Peninsula Arabs (descendants of Yemeni immigrants) standing in pre-Biblical times in ancient-Saudi Arabia and their Yemeni compatriots who stayed put at home, then and now, in the mountains of the Southern Arabian Peninsula.

Afterword

Yemen is especially rich in ancient culture and history, with troves of archaeological sites and artefacts, a country with rich ancient civilisations. Yemen is also unique as its ancient history is not only hidden under layers of soil, but is also alive and above the ground; buildings and structures are lived in or around, and are part of everyday Yemeni life and identity. The Yemeni people are living time-capsules of Biblical people and Biblical authors, their language and customs are proof of the origins of the Bible, their culture and beliefs explain the Biblical stories.

Unfortunately, since 2015 the war has destroyed many of Yemen's World Heritage Sites, their 'protected status' did not protect them; some have been severely damaged, others have been completely obliterated, and all were targeted despite there being no military presence in or around them. More distressingly, tens of millions of Yemeni civilians' lives have been put at risk of death from war and its related consequences; tens of thousands of Yemeni civilians have been killed and many more afflicted with life-changing injuries; tens of thousands of Yemeni people have been internally displaced. All these human tragedies from man-made actions also bring negative consequences upon the one people who can help the world understand the Bible through their Arabic language, dialects, and culture. Displacement from war can lead people to adopt 'modern' languages and dialects so as to be understood in the new areas they are displaced to; groups of people moving into a new area also adopt modern customs, traditions and beliefs, including religious beliefs, to be accepted in the new areas. Adopting different dialects often leads to mutations in languages and either the corruption or replacing of the old and purer language; changing belief-systems, customs and rituals also means abandoning ancient ways, and this is not only a loss for the culture and Yemeni people but is also a loss for the whole world interested in the mysteries of the Bible and other ancient civilisations of the region.

Bibliography

1. **Mendel, Yonatan and Ranta, Ronald.** *From the Arab Other to the Israeli Self.* Surrey: Ashgate Publishing Limited, 2016.

2. —. *From the Arab Other to the Israeli Self.* Surrey: Ashgate Publishing Limited, 2016. p. 35.

3. —. *From the Arab Other to the Israeli Self.* Surrey: Ashgate Publishing Limited, 2016. p. 41.

4. —. *From the Arab Other to the Israeli Self.* Surrey: Ashgate Publishing Limited, 2016. p. 42.

5. **Said, Edward W.** *Orientalism.* London: Penguin Books, 2003. pp. xii - xiii.

6. **Pappe, Ilan.** *The Ethnic Cleansing of Palestine.* London: Oneworld Publications Limited, 2007. pp. 163, 226, 233.

7. **Said, Edward W.** *Orientalism.* London: Penguin Books, 2003. p. 21.

8. **Swami, Praveen.** Analysis: Saudi Arabia's War Between God and Archaeology. *Telegraph.* [Online] Telegraph, February 04, 2011. [Cited: January 05, 2019.] <https://www.telegraph.co.uk/news/worldnews/middleeast/saudiarabia/8303974/Analysis-Saudi-Arabias-war-between-god-and-archaeology.html>.

9. **Young, Matt.** Hundreds of Mysterious Ancient Structures Discovered in Saudi Arabia. *news.com.australia.* [Online] November 21, 2017. [Cited: January 05, 2019.] <https://www.news.com.au/technology/science/archaeology/hundreds-of-mysterious-ancient-structures-discovered-in-saudi-arabia/news-story/57c5f0f482351 1af5ac6f4c351963e85.

10. **Shakespeare, Nicholas.** Discovering Saudia Arabia's hidden archaeological treasures. *Independent.* [Online] June 07, 2018. [Cited: January 05, 2019.] <https://www.independent.co.uk/news/long_reads/saudi-arabia-hidden-archaeology-alhijir-petra-charles-doughty-a8373686.html>.

11. **Knell, Yolande.** Missing babies: Israel's Yemenite children affair. *BBC News, Jerusalem.* [Online] June 21, 2017. [Cited: January 06, 2019.] <https://www.bbc.co.uk/news/magazine-40342143>.

12. **Cook, Jonathan.** The shocking story of Israel's disappeared babies: New information has come to light about thousands of mostly Yemeni children believed to have been abducted in the 1950s. *Aljazeera.* [Online] August 05, 2016. [Cited: January 06, 2019.] <https://www.aljazeera.com/news/2016/08/shocking-story-israel-disappeared-babies-160803081117881.html>.

13. **Draper, Robert.** Kings of Controversy. *National Geographic.* [Online] December 2010. [Cited: January 06, 2019.] <https://www.nationalgeographic.com/magazine/2010/12/david-and-solomon/>.

14. **Hasson, Nir.** Is the Bible a true story. *Haaretz.com.* [Online] November 01, 2017. [Cited: January 06, 2019.] <https://www.haaretz.com/archaeology/MAGAZINE-is-the-bible-a-true-story-latest-archaeological-finds-yield-surprises-1.5626647>.

15. **Lori, Aviva.** Grounds for Disbelief. *Haaretz.com.* [Online] May 08, 2003. [Cited: January 06, 2019.] <https://www.haaretz.com/1.4777188>.

16. **Wm. B. Eerdmans Publishing Co.** *Eerdmans Dictionary of the Bible.* [ed.] David Noel Freedman, Allen C. Myers and Astrid B. Beck. Michigan: Wm. B. Eerdmans Publishing Co., 2000. p. 181.

17. **Bowersock, G. W.** Palestine: Ancient History and Modern Politics. [ed.] Edward Said and Christopher Hitchens. *Blaming the Victims: Spurious Scholarship and the Palestinian Question,.* London: Verso, 2001, p. 189.

18. —. Palestine: Ancient History and Modern Politics. [ed.] Edward Said and Christopher Hitchens. *Blaming the Victims: Spurious Scholarship and the Palestinian Question.* London: Verso, 2001, p. 184.

19. —. Palestine: Ancient History and Modern Politics. [ed.] Edward Said and Christopher Hitchens. *Blaming the Victims: Spurious Scholarship and the Palestinian Question.* London: Verso, 2001, p. 182.

20. —. Palestine: Ancient History and Modern Politics. [ed.] Edward Said and Christopher Hitchens. *Blaming the Victims: Spurious Scholarship and the Palestinian Question.* London: Verso, 2001, p. 184.

21. **The Jewish Publication Society of America.** *The Torah.* London: Kuperard, 2004.

22. ***The Holy Bible: King James Version.* Glasgow: Harper Collins Publishers Limited, 1991.**

23. **Messie2Vie. *Messie2Vie.*** [Online] 2013. <https://.messie2vie.fr/>.

24. **King James Bible Online.** King James Bible Online. [Online] 2019. <https://.kingjamesbibleonline.org/>.

25. **Shavit, Ari. *My Promised Land.*** New York: Spiegel & Grau, 2013.

’

A

B

G

H

Hararite, 159
Harbonah, 293
Hareph, 202
Hareth, 139
Harhaiah, 279
Harhas, 194, 257
Harhur, 262
Harim, 241, 279
Harnepher, 223
Harod, 108, 429, 486, 740
Harodite, 159, 429, 740
Haroeh, 203
Haroshet, 106, 107
Harosheth, 106, 741
Harsha, 262
Harum, 208
Harumaph, 279
Haruphite, 236, 741
Haruz, 192
Hasadiah, 205
Hasenuah, 229, 230, 278, 284, 449
hash, 282, 319, 320
Hashabiah, 218, 232, 356
Hashabniah, 279
Hashem, 233
Hashmona, 74
Hashub, 279
Hashubah, 205, 232
Hashum, 259
Hasrah, 257
Hassenaah, 278, 284
Hasshub, 231, 232
Hasupha, 260
Hatach, 293
Hathath, 209
Hatipha, 262
Hatita, 260
Hattil, 263
Hattush, 206, 279
Hauran, 349
Havilah, *1*
Havoth-jair, 73, 741
Hawaa, *2*, *23*, *235*, *301*, *436*, *458*
Hazael, 174, 178, 181, 182, 402, 753
Hazaiah, 283, 332
Hazar-addar, 75
Hazar-enan, 76, 349
Hazar-gaddah, 88
Hazar-hatticon, 349
Hazarmaveth, *10*
Hazar-shual, 89
Hazar-susah, 97, 212
Hazar-susim, 212
Hazazon-tamar, 252
Hazelelponi, 207
Hazerim, 78
Hazeroth, 64
Hazezon-tamar, 15
Haziel, 240
Hazo, 24
Heber, 48, 107, 478
Hebraic, *662*
Hebrew, *233*, *243*, *260*, *301*, *349*, *423*, *516*, *604*, *630*, *654*, *655*, *656*, *657*, *658*, *659*, *660*, *661*, *662*, *663*, *665*, *666*, *668*, *669*, *670*, *699*, *726*, *751*, *753*
Hebron, 13, 43, 65, 146, 741
Hegai, 289, 290, 699
Hege, 289
Helah, 207, 740
Helam, 151
Helbah, 104, 740
Heldai, 246, 416
Heleb, 160, 740
Heled, 233
Helek, 71
Helem, 223, 417, 740
Heleph, 100, 741
Helez, 159, 233
Heli, 473
Helkai, 285
Helkath, 99, 144, 740
Helkath-hazzurim, 144
Helon, 61
Hemam, 41
Heman, 165, 199
Hemath, 236
Hemdan, 41
Hen, 417
Hena, 190
Henadad, 265, 271
Henoch, 199
Hepher, 71
Hephzi-bah, 191, 325, 545
Heres, 104, 740
Heresh, 231
Hermas, 567
Hermogenes, 594
Hermon, 78, 215, 314
Herod, 429, 446, 462, 468, 472, 482, 486, 514, 528, 530
Herodians, 449
Herodias, 446
Herodion, 566
Hesed, 164
Heshbon, 68, 72, 315
Heshmon, 89
Heth, *8*, *25*, *349*
Hethlon, 349
Hezeki, 226, 242
Hezekiah, 188, 190, 195, 242, 309, 316, 324, 328, 354, 355, 374, 397, 408, 412, 467, 753
Hezion, 171
Hezir, 242
Hezrai, 160
Hezro, 233
Hezron, 46, 118, 199
Hiddai, 160, 233
Hiddekel, *1*, *396*
Hiel, 172, 173, 384, 692
Hierapolis, 587
Higgaion, 302
Hilen, 218
Hilkiah, 189, 193, 194, 269, 327, 330
Hillel, 111, 626
Hinnom, 87, 194, 328
Hirah, 44, 220, 460
Hiram, 147, 167, 224, 371
history, *31*, *232*
Hittite, 29, 152
Hivite, *9*
Hizkijah, 283
Hobab, 63, 107
Hobah, 15, 740
Hod, 223
Hodaiah, 206, 281, 740
Hodaviah, 216, 230, 281
Hodesh, 225
Hodevah, 281
Hodiah, 210, 281, 282
Hodijah, 282
Hoglah, 71, 740
Hoham, 84
Holocaust, *667*
Holon, 92
Hophni, 120, 121
Hor, 66, 67, 74, 75
Horam, 84, 224, 741
Horeb, 51, 67
Horem, 101, 741
Hor-hagidgad, 74
Hori, 41, 64, 215
Horite, 14
Hormah, 65, 67, 89, 133
Horonaim, 322, 323
Horonite, 277, 286
Hosah, 100, 740
Hosanna, 448, 449
Hosea, 382, 397, 400, 410
Hoshaiah, 285
Hoshama, 205
Hoshea, 80, 184, 185, 186, 325, 397, 400
Hotham, 222, 234
Hothan, 234, 740
Hothir, 244
house of God', 167, 353, 355, 356, 357, 358, 365, 369, 370, 371, 375, 376, 378, 382, 386, 409, 758, 760, 763
Hukkok, 101, 218
Hukok, 218
Hul, *10*
Huldah, 193, 257, 334
Humtah, 93
Hupham, 72, 241
Huppah, 241
Huppim, 48, 224, 241
Hur, 57, 67, 72, 200, 279, 626
Hurai, 233
Huram, 224, 372
Huri, 215
Hushah, 207
Hushai, 153, 154
Husham, 42
Hushathite, 158, 159
Hushim, 48
Huz, 24, 675
Huzzab, 411
Hymenaeus, 592

I

I Am That I Am, 52, 84, 95, 172, 326, 680, 734, 748
Ibhar, 148
Ibleam, 95, 437
Ibneiah, 229, 230
Ibnijah, 230
Ibri, 243
Ibzan, 111
I-cha-bod, 121, 367
Iconium, 532, 534, 536, 596
Idalah, 98
Idbash, 207
Iddo, 165, 249, 250, 268, 415
Idumea, 325
Igal, 64, 206
Igdaliah, 333, 447, 455, 723
Igeal, 206
Iim, 75
Ije-abarim, 67
Ijon, 171, 251
Ilai, 233
Illyricum, 562
Imlah, 175, 515
Immanuel, 319, 429, 714
Immer, 231, 263, 278, 328
Imna, 223
Imnah, 222, 256
Imrah, 223
Imri, 229, 230
Iphedeiah, 227
Ir, 101, 220
Ira, 157, 159
Irad, *3*, *479*
Iram, 43
Iri, 219
Irijah, 335
Irnahash, 209
Iron, 101

Irpeel, 96, 399, 400, 450
Ir-shemesh, 101
Iru, 209, 220
Isaac, 20, 21, 22, 25, 27, 28, 29, 39, 172, 424, 439, 450, 477, 511, 512, 561, 606, 750, 761
Isaiah, 190, 192, 206, 274, 316, 318, 324, 325, 326, 379, 428, 431, 472, 521, 559
Iscah, *12*, *710*, *715*
Iscariot, 441, 442, 534
Ishbah, 210, 226
Ishbak, 26
Ishbi-benob, 158
Ish-bosheth, 141, 145, 146, 157, 185, 227
Ishi, 201, 398
Ishiah, 219, 236, 243, 274, 475
Ishijah, 274, 475
Ishma, 207
Ishmael, 18, 20, 23, 110, 120, 197, 253, 338, 761
Ishmaelite, 248
Ishmaelites, 110
Ishmerai, 226
Ishod, 220
Ishphan, 227
Ish-tob, 151
Ishuah, 47, 72, 222, 235, 428
Ishuai, 222, 235, 475
Ishui, 72, 126, 274, 475
Islam, *427*, *492*, *607*, *665*, *666*, *670*, *743*, *754*, *758*, *759*, *760*, *761*
Islamic, *165*, *416*, *680*, *684*, *692*, *743*, *752*
Ismachiah, 256
Ismaiah, 235
Ispah, 226
Israel, 32, 35, 36, 37, 52, 67, 70, 71, 115, 124, 125, 142, 172, 174, 176, 187, 191, 200, 210, 214, 220, 243, 244, 313, 315, 320, 321, 340, 344, 362, 363, 379, 397, 398, 403, 404, 405, 406, 409, 410, 430, 439, 440, 443, 447, 467, 468, 469, 488, 490, 492, 503, 511, 513, 514, 515, 522, 523, 539, 542, 552, 561, 576, 584, 621, 623, 711, 714, 744, 746, 749, 751, 753, 760
Israeli, *751*
Issachar, 32, 491, 492
Isshiah, 236, 243
Isuah, 222, 235, 475
Isui, 48, 222, 235, 428
Italian, 525
Italy, 543, 555, 608
Ithai, 233
Ithamar, 54, 60
Ithiel, 284, 310
Ithmah, 235
Ithnan, 88, 741
Ithra, 155
Ithran, 41
Ithream, 145
Ithrite, 161
Ittah-kazin, 97, 98
Ittai, 154, 233
Ituraea, 472
Ivah, 190
Izhar, 53
Izrahiah, 219, 286

J

Jaakobah, 213
Jaalah, 263
Jaalam, 40
Jaanai, 215
Jaare-oregim, 158
Jaasau, 275
Jaasiel, 246
Jaazaniah, 197, 332, 341
Jaazer, 68
Jaaziah, 243
Jaaziel, 237
Jabal, *3*, *741*
Jabbok, 35, 36, 37, 490, 741
Jabesh, 115, 116, 125, 184
Jabesh-gilead, 115, 116, 125, 687
Jabez, 203
Jabin, 84, 107
Jabneel, 87, 741
Jabneh, 254
Jachan, 215
Jachin, 46, 166
Jacob, 20, 25, 27, 28, 29, 30, 32, 33, 34, 35, 36, 37, 38, 39, 43, 46, 49, 71, 80, 140, 176, 207, 213, 214, 317, 321, 327, 408, 410, 424, 439, 450, 468, 469, 477, 488, 490, 491, 503, 512, 523, 539, 561, 674, 678, 679, 688, 698, 761, 762
Jada, 201
Jadau, 275
Jadon, 278
Jael, 98, 106, 107, 115, 213, 537
Jagur, 88, 741
Jahath, 207
Jahaz, 68, 273
Jahazah, 86, 273
Jahaziah, 272, 273
Jahaziel, 235, 251, 273
Jahdai, 202
Jahdiel, 216
Jahdo, 215
Jahleel, 47
Jahmai, 219
Jahzah, 219
Jahzeel, 48
Jahzerah, 230
Jahziel, 220
Jair, 73, 289, 741
Jairite, 157
Jairus, 460, 537
Jakan, 199
Jakeh, 310
Jakim, 226, 461
Jalon, 210
Jambres, 595
James, 32, 436, 437, 440, 442, 445, 455, 456, 458, 460, 464, 483, 484, 501, 502, 503, 504, 505, 509, 534, 552, 577, 578, 608, 615
Jamin, 46
Jamlech, 212
Janna, 474
Jannes, 595
Janohah, 95
Janum, 93
Japheth, *5*
Japhia, 84
Japhlet, 222, 453
Japhleti, 94, 222, 453
Japho, 102
Jarah, 232
Jareb, 399, 450
Jared, *4*, *479*
Jaresiah, 227
Jarha, 201
Jarib, 212, 273
Jarmuth, 84
Jaroah, 215
Jashen, 160, 250, 740
Jasher, 84
Jashobeam, 232
Jashub, 70, 232
Jashubi-lehem, 211, 232
Jasiel, 235, 246
Jason, 540, 568
Jathniel, 244
Jattir, 92
Javan, *6*, *344*
Jazer, 72, 248
Jaziz, 248
Jeaterai, 216
Jeberechiah, 319
Jebus, 114, 147, 436, 437
Jebusite, *8*, *114*, *161*
Jebusites, 147
Jecamiah, 205
Jecholiah, 184
Jeconiah, 204, 329, 330, 423, 424
Jedaiah, 214, 279, 417
Jediael, 219
Jedida, 192
Jedidiah, 152
Jeduthun, 231, 304, 305
Jeezer, 70
Jegar-sahadutha, 33, 678, 683
Jehaleleel, 209, 626
Jehalelel, 256
Jehdeiah, 243, 248
Jehezekel, 242, 340
Jehiah, 238
Jehiel, 232, 245, 306
Jehieli, 245
Jehizkiah, 255
Jehoadah, 228
Jehoaddan, 182
Jehoahaz, 182, 195, 196, 204, 324, 329
Jehoash, 181, 182
Jehohanan, 244, 253
Jehoiachin, 196, 198, 204, 329, 330, 375, 376, 380
Jehoiada, 150, 163, 180, 253, 254, 278, 285, 451
Jehoiakim, 195, 196, 204, 327, 329, 330, 389, 390, 423, 461, 522
Jehoiarib, 230, 283
Jehonadab, 180, 334
Jehonathan, 247
Jehoram, 176, 177, 179, 252, 253
Jehoshabeath, 252
Jehoshaphat, 150, 176, 179, 252, 401
Jehosheba, 180, 252
Jehova, 57, 270, 365
Jehovah, 23, 24, 52, 57, 108, 172, 173, 235, 325, 741, 747, 748, 753, 757, 764
Jehovah-jireh, 23, 24, 172, 748
Jehovah-shalom, 108
Jehozabad, 182, 253, 254, 468
Jehozadak, 216, 415
Jehu, 171, 175, 179, 213, 398
Jehubbah, 222
Jehucal, 335
Jehud, 102
Jehudi, 335, 646
Jehudijah, 210
Jehush, 229
Jeiel, 214, 254
Jekabzeel, 284
Jekameam, 240, 437
Jekamiah, 202, 437, 522
Jekuthiel, 210
Jemima, 299
Jemuel, 46

K

Kartah, 103, 740
Kartan, 103, 740
kaśdāy, 297
kaśdîm, *12*, *297*, *341*
Kattath, 98
Kedar, 26, 313, 324, 344
Kedemah, 27
Kedemoth, 78
Kedesh, 88, 107, 350
Kehelatha, 73, 312, 741
Keilah, 91, 139, 367
Kelaiah, 273
Kelita, 273
Kemuel, 24, 522
Kenan, 199, 478, 480
Kenath, 73, 741
Kenaz, 40
Kenizzites, 17
Kennites, 17, 107
Keren-happuch, 300
Kerioth, 88, 403
Keros, 261
Ketura, 25
Kezia, 300
Keziz, 95
Kibroth-hattavah, 63
Kibzaim, 102, 741
Kidron, 194, 256, 331, 377, 498
Kinah, 88, 741
Kir, 177, 186, 322, 402, 406
Kir-hareseth, 177
Kirjathaim, 73
Kirjath-arba, 25
Kirjath-arim, 260
Kirjath-huzoth, 69, 741
Kirjath-jearim, 83, 114, 122, 260
Kirjath-sannah, 92
Kish, 123, 256, 290, 337, 411
Kishi, 217, 411
Kishion, 99, 411, 740
Kishon, 102, 107, 411, 740
Kithlish, 91
Kitron, 104
Kittim, *6*
Koa, 343
Kohath, 46, 305
Kohathites, 256, 305
Kolaiah, 284, 331
Korah, 40, 66, 305, 615
Kore, 231, 256, 305
Koz, 264, 278, 482
Kushaiah, 237, 411, 412

L

Laadah, 211
Laadan, 222
Laban, 25, 27, 30, 33, 679, 749
Lachish, 84, 183, 189, 410
Lael, 62
Lahad, 207
Lahai-roi, 25
Lahmam, 91
Lahmi, 239
Laish, 113, 114, 141
Lakum, 100
Lamech, *3*, *478*
Laodicea, 585, 587, 623
Lapidoth, 106
Lasea, 557
Lasha, *9*
Lasharon, 85, 740
Lazarus, 425, 484, 495, 501, 504, 505
Leah, 20, 30, 32, 419, 491, 710, 715, 718
Leannoth, 307
Lebanah, 261
Lebanon, *80*, *313*, *314*, *343*, *346*
Lebaoth, 89
Lebbaeus, 440, 442
Lebonah, 116, 261
Lecah, 211
Legion, 460, 567
Lehabim, *8*
Lehi, 112
Lemuel, 310
Leshem, 102
Letushim, 26
Leummim, 26
Levant, *667*, *671*, *740*, *744*, *747*, *751*, *752*
Levi, 30, 58, 419, 441, 460, 473, 476, 607, 673
Leviathan, 299, 406
Levite, 114, 115, 130, 147, 256, 305, 355, 514, 523, 540, 681
Levites, 253, 256, 272, 305, 352, 353, 354, 355, 357, 364, 379, 387, 699
Lewi, 66
Libertines, 517
Libnah, 73, 195, 196, 204, 441
Libni, 52, 441
Libya, 345, 347, 510
Likhi, 221
Linus, 599
Lo-ammi, 398
Lod, 226, 524
Lo-debar, 151, 156
Lois, 593
Lo-ruhamah, 398
Lot, *12*, *15*, *17*, *22*, *115*, *254*, *278*, *524*, *539*, *595*, *606*
Lotan, 40, 278
Lubims, 250, 345
Lucifer, 322
Lucius, 529, 568
Lud, *10*, *343*, *345*, *524*
Ludim, *8*, *345*, *524*
Luhith, 322, 323
Luke, 465, 467, 479, 529, 588
Luz, 29, 38
Lycaonia, 533
Lycia, 557
Lydda, 524
Lydia, 345, 524, 537, 538, 539, 566, 621
Lysanias, 472
Lysatra, 533
Lysias, 553, 554, 557

M

Maacah, 144, 151
Maachah, 25, 170, 176
Maachathi, 79
Maachathite, 197
Maadai, 274, 285
Maadiah, 285
Maai, 286
Maaleh-acrabbim, 86
Maarath, 93
Maaseiah, 237, 253, 254, 273, 306, 329, 331, 332, 333, 537
Maasiai, 230, 537
Maath, 474, 509, 536
Maaz, 201
Maaziah, 242
Macedonia, 537, 539, 543, 547, 556, 562, 563, 572
Machbanai, 236
Machbenah, 202, 236, 740
Machi, 65
Machir, 49, 156
Machnadebai, 275
Machpelah, 25
Madai, *6*
Madmannah, 89, 322
Madmenah, 322
Madon, 84
Magbish, 260, 283
Magdala, 447
Magdalene, 455, 499, 500, 723
Magdiel, 43, 447
Magog, *6*, *346*, *347*, *348*, *361*, *363*, *379*, *402*, *627*
Magor-missabib, 328
Magpiash, 283, 454
Mahalah, 221
Mahalath, 29, 138, 307
Mahaleel, *4*, *480*
Mahali, 53, 216
Mahanaim, 34, 155, 223, 368
Mahaneh-dan, 114
Maharai, 160
Mahath, 217, 256
Mahavite, 234
Mahazioth, 244
Maher, 319, 320
Mahlah, 71
Mahli, 216
Mahlon, 117
Mahol, 165, 199
Makaz, 164
Makheloth, 74, 741
Makkedah, 84, 515, 741
Maktesh, 413
Malachi, 387, 420
Malcham, 225, 413, 437
Malchiah, 217, 230, 279, 328, 336
Malchiel, 48
Malchijah, 230, 279
Malchiram, 205, 224
Malchus, 498
Maleleel, 479, 480
Mallothi, 244
Malluch, 218, 285
Mammon, 438, 476
Mamre, 13, 15
Manaen, 530
Manahath, 41, 203
Manahethites, 203
Manasseh, 45, 49, 191, 192, 321, 328
Manna, 56, 393, 394, 476, 493
Manoah, 111, 112, 373, 478, 680, 697
Maoch, 141
Maon, 93
Mara, 117
Marah, 56
Maralah, 97, 98
Mareshah, 91, 252, 409, 410
Mark, 459, 460, 461, 462, 505, 506, 518, 528, 531, 535, 566, 586
Maroth, 410, 704
Mars, 541
Marsena, 289
Martha, 425, 483, 484, 495, 498, 724
Mary, 326, 423, 424, 425, 426, 427, 430, 445, 455, 467, 469, 478, 479, 480, 483, 489, 490, 495, 497, 498, 499, 500, 501, 502, 505, 506, 519, 522, 528, 533, 538, 564, 626, 702
Maschil, 304, 306
Mash, *10*
Mashal, 218
Masrekah, 43
Massa, 27, 56, 741
Massah, 56, 121

N

O

P

Q

R

S

Shobai, 260
Shobal, 40
Shobek, 283
Shobi, 156, 368
Shocoh, 128, 741
Shoham, 243
Shomer, 182, 254
Shophach, 239
Shophan, 73
Shoshannim, 308
Shuah, 26, 44, 208
Shual, 125
Shubael, 242
Shuhite, 298
Shulamite, 314
Shumathites, 203
Shunem, 98, 162, 177
Shuni, 47
Shunnamite, 162, 177
Shupham, 72, 224
Shuphamites, 72
Shur, 18, 56, 181
Shushan, 276, 287, 482
Shuthelah, 71
Siaha, 261
Sibbechai, 158
Sibboleth, 111
Sibmah, 86
Sibraim, 349
Sichem, *12*, *37*, *741*
Siddim, 14, 17, 606
Sidon, *8*, *9*, *85*, *343*, *401*, *444*, *447*, *528*
Sihon, 68, 741
Sihor, 86, 99
Silas, 534, 535, 538, 540, 542, 543, 567
Silla, 181, 280, 741
Siloah, 280, 320, 741
Siloam, 494, 741
Silvanus, 575, 588, 610
Simeon, 30, 274, 470, 471, 476, 529, 673
Simon, 435, 439, 441, 446, 448, 452, 454, 463, 470, 482, 484, 498, 501, 519, 524, 525
Simri, 245
Sin, 56, 66, 741
Sinai, 56, 680, 741
Sinim, 325
Sinite, *9*
Sion, 79, 448, 561, 610, 625
Siphmoth, 142
Sippai, 239
Sirah, 145
Sirion, 78, 740
Sisamai, 202
Sisera, 98, 106, 107, 213, 350
Sitnah, 28, 240, 492, 529
Sivan, 293
slave, 201
Smyrna, 620
So, 186
Socho, 210
Socoh, 90, 128, 210, 741
Sodi, 64
Sodom, *9*, *13*, *16*, *22*, *316*, *405*, *441*, *443*, *444*, *540*, *561*, *606*, *616*, *625*
Solomon, 118, 147, 152, 162, 163, 166, 167, 168, 169, 309, 313, 315, 325, 352, 357, 371, 417, 419, 473, 474, 490, 494, 511, 524, 623, 703
Sopater, 548
Sophereth, 263
Sorek, 113
Sosipater, 569
Sosthenes, 545, 569
Sotai, 262
Spain, 562, 563
Stachys, 565
Stephanas, 571, 573
Stephen, 516, 517, 518, 527, 546, 571
stepwife, 716, 717, 718
stepwives, 19, 716
Stoicks, 541
Straight (street called), 522
Suah, 223
Succoth, 36, 37, 109, 706, 740
Succoth-benoth, 187
Suchathites, 203
Sukkims, 250
Sur, 181
Susanchites, 267, 482
Susanna, 482
Susi, 64
Sychar, 490, 491, 492
Syene, 345
Syntyche, 584
Syracuse, 559
Syria, *80*, *318*, *344*, *402*, *438*, *470*, *550*, *578*
Syriack, 391
Syrophenician, 462

T

Taanach, 86, 165, 418
Taanath-shiloh, 95
Tabbaoth, 260
Tabbath, 109, 524
Tabeal, 318
Tabeel, 266, 318
Taberah, 63, 680
Tabitha, 524
Tabor, 110, 124, 399
Tabrimon, 170
Tachmonite, 159, 232
Tadmor, 167
Tahan, 71, 221
Tahath, 74
Tahpanhes, 338
Tahpenes, 168, 338
Tahrea, 232
Tahtim-hodshi, 161
Talitha cumi, 461
Talmai, 65, 144
Talmon, 231
Tamah, 282
Tamar, 44, 115, 118, 152, 153, 211, 333, 368, 409, 410, 425, 477, 542
Tammuz, 341
Tanhumeth, 197, 210, 258, 410
Taphath, 164
Tappuah, 85, 740
Tarah, 74
Taralah, 96
Tarea, 228, 232
Tarpelites, 266
Tarshish, *6*, *252*, *288*, *344*, *345*, *348*, *407*, *522*
Tarsus, 522, 523, 552
Tartak, 187
Tartan, 189, 324
Tassu', 52
Tatnai, 267
Tebah, 24, 238, 740
Tebaliah, 245
Tebeth, 291
Tehaphnehes, 346
Tehinnah, 209, 223
TEKEL, 393
Tekoa, 252, 402
Tekoah, 153
Tekoite, 159
Tekoites, 278
Tel-abib, 341, 461, 521
Telah, 221
Telaim, 127
Telem, 88
Tel-harsa, 263, 461
Tel-melah, 263, 461
Tema, 27, 324, 741
Teman, 40, 403
Temani, 42
Temanite, 298
Temeni, 208
temple, 119, 245, 248, 327, 328, 349, 357, 363, 365, 366, 367, 369, 370, 371, 372, 373, 374, 375, 376, 377, 378, 379, 380, 381, 382, 383, 384, 385, 386, 387, 388, 393, 409, 415, 416, 417, 420, 450, 471, 489, 552, 619, 628, 712, 756, 759, 760, 761, 762
Temple mount, 760
Terah, *12*, *477*
Teresh, 287, 291
Tertius, 569
Tertullus, 554
Thaddaeus, 441, 442
Thahash, 24
Thamah, 262, 282
Thara, 477
Tharshish, 168, 522
Thebez, 111, 152
Thelasar, 191
Theophilus, 466, 508
Thessalonica, 539, 556, 585, 596
Theudas, 516
Thimnathah, 101
Thomas, 440, 442, 495, 500, 597
three-Marys, 499, 505
Thummim, 58, 730, 732, 734, 755
Thyatira, 539, 566, 621
Tiberias, 492, 500, 505
Tiberius, 471, 492
Tibhath, 238
Tibni, 171
Tidal, 13
Tiglath-pileser, 185, 214
Tikvah, 194, 273
Tikvath, 257
Tilgath-pilneser, 214
Tilon, 211
Timaeus, 463
Timna, 40
Timnah, 93
Timnath, 45, 102, 104, 740
Timnath-heres, 104, 740
Timnath-serah, 102, 104
Timon, 516
Timotheous, 535
Timotheus, 535, 536, 540, 542, 543, 548, 564, 571, 572
Timothy, 535, 574, 591, 592
Tiphsah, 165, 184
Tiras, *6*, *522*
Tirathites, 203
Tirhakah, 190
Tirhanah, 202
Tiria, 210
Tirshatha, 264
Tirzah, 71, 184, 314
Tishbite, 173, 174, 177
Titus, 575
Tizite, 234
Toah, 217
Tob, 111
Tobadonijah, 251

U

V

W

Y

Z

Printed in Great Britain
by Amazon

13010341R00463